375⁰⁰ oc

THE NEW TESTAMENT

GREEK AND ENGLISH

The Greek Text prepared by the United Bible Societies

Editors

KURT ALAND, MATTHEW BLACK, CARLO M. MARTINI,
BRUCE M. METZGER, AND ALLEN WIKGREN

in cooperation with the

Institute for New Testament Textual Research

and the

Today's English Version

from
"Good News for Modern Man"

●

Second Edition

●

American Bible Society
New York

The Greek Text prepared by the
United Bible Societies

© 1966, 1968

American Bible Society, British and Foreign Bible Society, National
Bible Society of Scotland, Netherlands Bible Society, Württemberg
Bible Society.

U.S. copyright is not claimed for the Preface and Introduction.
No part of this book, except the Prefaces and Introduction, may
be reproduced without written permission from the publisher.

The English Text in Today's English Version

© 1966

American Bible Society

Third Printing, 1970

Greek-English NT AO283TEVDI-56503
ABS-1970-5,000-15,000-K-3

TABLE OF CONTENTS

Page

Introduction............................. v

Preface to the English Translation........ v

Preface to the First Edition of the
Greek Text............................. viii

Preface to the Second Edition of the
Greek Text............................. x

Introduction to the Greek Text.......... xi

  I. The Text........................... xi

  II. The Textual Apparatus............. xii

    1. The Evaluation of Evidence... xii

    2. The Greek Manuscript
       Evidence.................. xiii

    3. The Evidence from Ancient
       Versions.................. xxviii

    4. The Evidence from Church
       Fathers................... xxxii

  III. The Punctuation Apparatus........ xxxvii

  IV. The Cross-Reference System....... xli

  V. Master List of Symbols and
     Abbreviations................. xliii

Bibliography......................... li

Text and Apparatus................... 1—895

  Κατὰ Μαθθαῖον..................... 1
    The Gospel of Matthew

  Κατὰ Μᾶρκον..................... 118
    The Gospel of Mark

  Κατὰ Λουκᾶν..................... 199
    The Gospel of Luke

  Κατὰ Ἰωάννην..................... 320
    The Gospel of John

  Πράξεις Ἀποστόλων................. 416
    The Acts of the Apostles

  Πρὸς Ῥωμαίους..................... 529
    Paul's Letter to the Romans

  Πρὸς Κορινθίους α'................. 578
    Paul's First Letter to the Corinthians

Page

Πρὸς Κορινθίους β'..................... 621
  Paul's Second Letter to the Corinthians

Πρὸς Γαλάτας..................... 648
  Paul's Letter to the Galatians

Πρὸς Ἐφεσίους..................... 664
  Paul's Letter to the Ephesians

Πρὸς Φιλιππησίους..................... 681
  Paul's Letter to the Philippians

Πρὸς Κολοσσαεῖς..................... 692
  Paul's Letter to the Colossians

Πρὸς Θεσσαλονικεῖς α'..................... 704
  Paul's First Letter to the Thessalonians

Πρὸς Θεσσαλονικεῖς β'..................... 714
  Paul's Second Letter to the Thessalonians

Πρὸς Τιμόθεον α'..................... 720
  Paul's First Letter to Timothy

Πρὸς Τιμόθεον β'..................... 731
  Paul's Second Letter to Timothy

Πρὸς Τίτον..................... 739
  Paul's Letter to Titus

Πρὸς Φιλήμονα..................... 744
  Paul's Letter to Philemon

Πρὸς Ἑβραίους..................... 747
  The Letter to the Hebrews

Ἰακώβου..................... 779
  The Letter from James

Πέτρου α'..................... 791
  The First Letter from Peter

Πέτρου β'..................... 805
  The Second Letter from Peter

Ἰωάννου α'..................... 813
  The First Letter of John

Ἰωάννου β'..................... 827
  The Second Letter of John

Ἰωάννου γ'..................... 830
  The Third Letter of John

Ἰούδα..................... 832
  The Letter from Jude

Ἀποκάλυψις Ἰωάννου..................... 836
  The Revelation to John

Index of Quotations..................... 897

Glossary..................... 908

Index of Subjects..................... 915

INTRODUCTION

This Diglot New Testament contains the U. B. S. Greek New Testament (Second Edition, 1968) and the second edition of *Today's English Version* (1967). The purpose of this publication is to combine a new critical edition of the Greek text together with a translation of it which follows special principles in attempting to make the meaning of the text clear and simple to the widest possible range of readers. It is hoped, therefore, that this Diglot will prove valuable to all those, whether students, teachers, pastors, or translators, who wish to know the meaning of the New Testament and to express it clearly and meaningfully to all people today, Christians and non-Christians alike.

PREFACE TO THE ENGLISH TRANSLATION

The purpose of *The New Testament in Today's English Version* is to provide a translation which can be understood by all who read English. It is intended primarily to meet the needs of those who have little if any specialized knowledge of the Christian Scriptures, as well as those for whom English is an acquired language. Therefore, "common" English is used in this translation, by which is meant that form of literary English that is common to all who speak the language, native and non-native speakers, of a high or a low level of education.

In this regard the TEV attempts to follow as much as possible the practice of the authors of the New Testament writings who, for the most part, wrote in the common (*koiné*) Greek used throughout the Roman Empire in the first century A. D. This same kind of translation has already appeared in Spanish, with the publication of the *Versión Popular* in 1966. The Bible Societies are sponsoring similar translations in other major languages such as French, Portuguese, Chinese, Arabic, and Swahili.

PROCEDURES

In answer to the special needs posed by an increasing interest in the Christian Scriptures on the part of non-Christians, as well as the needs of Christians for whom the standard versions offer difficulties in understanding, the American Bible Society decided in 1961 to sponsor a new translation of the New Testament, and appointed Dr. Robert G. Bratcher, of the Translations Department, to prepare it. In 1964 the Society authorized the publication of the Gospel of Mark, under the title *The Right Time*. This was widely distributed, both in the United States and abroad, and elicited many valuable comments and suggestions from readers, which helped in the completion of the task.

In time the Translations Committee of the ABS appointed a Consultative Committee to advise the translator. This committee was composed of the following: the Rev. Howard Beardslee, formerly a missionary in West Africa; the Rev. Dr. Hugo Culpepper, a former missionary in South America and the Philippines, and at that time Professor of Missions in the Southern Baptist Theological Seminary, Louisville, Kentucky; Prof. Howard Kee, of the Theological School of Drew University, Madison, New Jersey, and a member of the Translations Committee; the Rev. Harold K. Moulton, M.A., Deputy Translations Secretary of the British and Foreign Bible Society, who had been cooperating from the very beginning; and Dr. Fred Rex, of the Literature and Literacy Commission of the National Council of Churches. Prof. Kee, as representative of the Translations Committee, read through the draft of the whole New Testament, giving special attention to matters of exegesis; and Miss Dorothy Tyler, a literary critic of Detroit, Michigan, read the whole draft for suggestions on English usage and style. Several members of the Translations Department also made suggestions on various books, as did some members of the Translations Committee.

At its meeting of September 24, 1965, the Translations Committee recommended to the Board of Managers the publication of this New Testament, under the title *Good News for Modern Man: the New Testament in Today's English*. The first edition came off the press on September 15, 1966.

The present text of the TEV is the second edition (1967), which incorporates a number of changes made to bring the translation into closer agreement with the Greek text, and other, more numerous, changes made in the interests of consistency, greater clarity and simplicity of language, and improvement of style.

TEXT

The Greek text from which this translation was made is the U. B. S. Greek New Testament, published in 1966. There are several places in which the TEV departs from this text; some of these are C readings, that is, readings on which there is a considerable degree of doubt; but most of them are D readings, that is, readings on which there is a very high degree of doubt. Most departures from the UBS text were determined by the fact that the TEV, as originally published, did not list any variant readings; it was felt, therefore, that the primary purpose of the TEV demanded that the text make sense to the reader, even though at times this required the adoption of a reading that is manifestly not original. In this Diglot edition there are a number of variant readings and alternative renderings listed in footnotes.

Whenever a secondary addition to the original text, recorded as a variant reading in the UBS text, involved a whole verse or more, this material is included in the TEV in single brackets. As explained in the Preface, this indicates that these verses "are not in the oldest and best manuscripts of the New Testament" (Mt. 17.21, 18.11, 23.14, Mk. 7.16, 9.44, 46, 11.26, 15.28, Lk. 17.36, 22.43–44, 23.17, Jn. 5.3b–4, Ac. 8.37, 15.34, 24.6b–8a, 28.29, Rom. 16.24). In addition, the passages which the UBS text includes within double brackets as "later additions to the text," are also included in the TEV in single brackets (Mt. 21.44; the two endings of Mark; Lk. 22.19b–20; Jn. 7.53—8.11). The TEV does not reproduce the single brackets of the Greek text. In several places the translation departs from the punctuation adopted in the UBS text.

PRINCIPLES OF TRANSLATION

Vocabulary. Since the TEV is intended for the widest possible range of readers, a limited vocabulary has been employed. No artificial limit was set to the number of words used, but most of the vocabulary is included in a list of 3000 common words. Since this is not enough for an adequate translation, a number of words outside that list have been used, most of which are defined in the *Glossary*.

Technical and Cultural Terms. In the interests of historical faithfulness, most of the technical terms for such matters as Jewish and Christian feasts, institutions, and customs have been preserved — such as Sabbath, Passover, Unleavened Bread, Pentecost, Tabernacles, Pharisees, Sadducees, Rabbi, elders, prophet, apostle, synagogue. All of these are defined in the *Glossary*. Such cultural items as weights, measures, and hours of the day are given their modern equivalents. Units of currency offer a particularly difficult problem, since it is virtually impossible to reproduce their purchasing power in modern times, especially since a single modern unit (the American dollar, or the British pound) varies in purchasing power in different places. Where the actual worth of the unit is not relevant, the term is represented by a functional equivalent which does not specify its value (cf. Mt. 17.24, 27; 20.1–16; Lk. 10.35); where the important matter is the relative worth between two or more sums, an identical relation is reproduced in translation, with no strict regard for actual value (cf. Mt. 18.24, 28; 25.14–30; Lk. 7.51; 19.11–27); but where the actual worth, or purchasing power, of the unit is important, then a culturally relevant equivalent is employed. The denarius (and "silver piece") was arbitrarily assigned the value of one dollar (cf. Mk. 6.37; 14.5; Lk. 7.41; Jn. 6.7; 12.5; Ac. 19.19); smaller units are represented by small units of American currency (cf. Mt. 10.29; Mk. 12.42; Lk. 12.6).

Sentences and Clauses. Next in importance to the use of familiar and non-technical language is the length and complexity of sentences, and the relation of clauses and phrases within the sentence. No attempt is made in the TEV to follow the grammatical and syntactical structure of the Greek, Clarity and ease of understanding are considered to be more important than form in meeting the translator's single goal, which is to be faithful in reproducing the meaning of the original. Consequently, clauses are often made coordinate in English, where they are subordinate in Greek; the order of events may be placed in their proper chronological sequence, where an inverse order may be misleading; conditional clauses may often be represented by statements, when the condition is not real but is used for rhetorical effect; negative statements are sometimes represented by their positive counterparts; and rhetorical questions, liable to be misunderstood as requests for information, may be represented by declarative statements.

Word Classes and Forms. Traditional translations into Indo-European languages tend to use the same classes of words used in the original, so that a substantive is represented by a substantive, an adjective by an adjective, a verb by a verb, *et cetera.* This practice often violates the normal· and idiomatic requirements of the receptor language; consequently, a shift in classes is often called for. This is especially true where substantives represent events, and are more faithfully and meaningfully translated by verbs. Word forms must also be often changed: what is expressed in the Greek New Testament by the passive form of the verb, for example, should often be represented in English by the active voice, particularly when the subject of the action may be obscure in translation. This is especially true of passages in which the passive voice in Greek reflects the Semitic tendency of avoiding naming God as the subject. Where it is quite clear that God is referred to, the translation uses the active voice and names God as the subject.

Figures of Speech. Sometimes it was deemed helpful to change metaphors into similes, or else substitute figurative expressions by non-figurative language. Idioms, likewise, are rarely understood if given their literal equivalents in the receptor language. Litotes, or understatement, may sometimes have to be restructured, while abstract qualities must often be represented by persons possessing those qualities or attributes.

Ambiguity and Implicit Information. Since the TEV, as originally published, contained no alternative renderings, it was felt that potentially ambiguous language in the Greek should be translated quite explicitly. This required, of course, that a decision be made as to the meaning intended by the original writer, even where no interpreter can be dogmatic about his choice. At the same time, many passages cannot be understood by today's readers if all information implicit in the original text is left unrepresented in translation. It was not necessary, in the original writing, for the author to make explicit all the information needed to make the text understood, since he and his readers already possessed this information. But the modern reader who does not have this information is placed at a serious disadvantage. In the TEV, therefore, there are many places where supplementary information not textually present in the original is supplied, in an attempt to make the text convey as much information to today's readers as the original text conveyed to the first readers.

SPECIAL FEATURES

The Section Headings have been adapted from the list published for translators by the United Bible Societies. In the Gospels, the parallel passages in other Gospels are indicated immediately underneath the section headings.

The *Glossary* at the end of the volume contains short definitions of 169 persons, places, and subjects; the *Index of Subjects* enables the reader to locate, by references, some 345 different items.

PREFACE TO THE FIRST EDITION
OF THE GREEK TEXT

To meet the growing need for an edition of the Greek New Testament specially adapted to the requirements of Bible translators throughout the world, the American Bible Society, the National Bible Society of Scotland, and the Württemberg Bible Society appointed in 1955 an international and inter-denominational committee of textual scholars to prepare such an edition. The three societies were later joined by the Netherlands Bible Society and the British and Foreign Bible Society.

In keeping with its distinctive purpose, the edition has the following special features: (1) a critical apparatus restricted for the most part to variant readings significant for translators or necessary for the establishing of the text; (2) an indication of the relative degree of certainty for each variant adopted as the text; (3) a full citation of representative evidence for each variant selected; and (4) a second apparatus giving meaningful differences of punctuation. Much new evidence from Greek manuscripts and early versions has been cited. A supplementary volume, providing a summary of the Committee's reasons for adopting one or another variant reading, will also be published.

The Committee carried out its work in four principal stages: (1) on the basis of Westcott and Hort's edition of the Greek New Testament, a comparison was made of the text and apparatus of several other editions, including those of Nestle, Bover, Merk, and Vogels, and to some extent those of Tischendorf and von Soden, in order to determine which of the variant readings warranted further study; (2) data on several thousand sets of variants were gathered, not only from printed editions, commentaries and technical studies, but also from hitherto unused papyri, uncials, minuscules and lectionaries; (3) about six hundred variations in punctuation, which appeared to merit consideration, were selected and compared in editions of the Greek text and in the principal English, German and

French translations; and finally, (4) the Greek text was established, the degree of certainty for the reading adopted in the text was estimated, and decisions were made whether or not to include a set of variants in the apparatus.

This edition has certain calculated limitations: (1) the sets of variants have generally been restricted to readings meaningful for translators; consequently there is an appreciable reduction in the number of variants in the apparatus (but there is fuller attestation for the variants selected). (2) Citations of evidence from the major lettered uncials (see p. xiii) and the Church Fathers have been derived from critical editions of the Greek New Testament, primarily those of Tischendorf and von Soden, but the uncials have been checked where the printed evidence was contradictory or incomplete. (3) As a rule, no attempt has been made to represent the wide range of orthographic variation in the manuscripts; the orthography of Bauer's Lexicon (5th edition; see bibliography) has been followed.[1] (4) The cross-reference system has been limited to the citation of direct quotations (see p. xxxix), definite allusions, and literary and other parallels.

The Editorial Committee which was responsible for preparing this edition consisted of Kurt Aland, Matthew Black, Bruce M. Metzger and Allen Wikgren, with the participation of Arthur Vööbus during the first part of the work. The project was initiated, organized and administered by Eugene A. Nida, who also took part in Committee discussions, especially those relating to major decisions of policy and method. J. Harold Greenlee and Robert P. Markham, as secretaries of the Committee, handled a mass of detail with skill and competence. They were assisted by Karen Munson and the staff of the

---

[1] Exceptions chiefly involve proper names and citations of individual manuscripts within variants. In a few cases the Committee has adopted the spelling proposed for the 6th edition of Bauer (e. g. Μαθθαῖος and Μαθθίας for Ματθαῖος and Ματθίας; τετρααρχέω for τετραρχέω and τετρααρχῆς for τετραρχῆς). Aramaic words are printed without accents and breathing marks.

Institut für neutestamentliche Textforschung at Münster/
Westf., in particular Klaus Junack, Peter Weigandt, Paolo
Ferreira and Barbara Trill.

The Committee also obtained advice by correspondence with
a group of consultants, representative of scholars and churches
in many areas, on questions arising during the course of the
project.

In the collation and evaluation of versional evidence, special
help was provided by Harold K. Moulton and Brynmor F.
Price (Itala and Vulgate), N. Joseph Kikuchi (Syriac), Robert
McL. Wilson (Coptic), J. A. Huisman (Gothic), A. F. J. Klijn
(Armenian), Rochus Zuurmond (Ethiopic, for the Gospel of
Matthew), and T. Amse-de Jong (Georgian). In the assembling
of lectionary evidence, assistance was provided at Chicago by
David Backus. The punctuation apparatus was prepared by
J. Harold Greenlee, Robert P. Markham and Harold K.
Moulton.

Of the members of the Committee, Kurt Aland was responsible for the Greek papyri, numbered uncials, and minuscules;
Allen Wikgren for the lectionary readings. Matthew Black
supervised collations of Syriac data, and Bruce M. Metzger
is preparing the supplementary volume.

Since this edition is intended primarily for translators it is
not to be regarded as in competition with other modern editions,
e. g. the continuing Nestle-Aland editions, which provide a
more restricted selection of data from witnesses on a much
wider range of variant readings. It is the intention of the
Committee from time to time to revise its work in order to
take into account new discoveries and fresh evidence.

August 26, 1965

PREFACE TO THE SECOND EDITION
OF THE GREEK TEXT

This Second Edition of the Greek New Testament incorporates a number of typographical corrections, 45 changes in
evaluation of the evidence (i. e., changes in the ratings of A, B,
C, and D), 11 alterations involving brackets, and five modifications of text or punctuation.

For the second and subsequent editions, the Committee has
been enlarged by the addition of Carlo M. Martini.

KURT ALAND, Münster/Westf.
MATTHEW BLACK, St. Andrews
CARLO M. MARTINI, Rome
BRUCE M. METZGER, Princeton
ALLEN WIKGREN, Chicago

September, 1968

INTRODUCTION TO THE GREEK TEXT

For a better understanding of the special features of this edition, such as the arrangement of materials, the range of evidence and the manner of citation, the following sections describe the text, apparatus and reference system. There are also provided an alphabetical list of symbols and abbreviations, a bibliography and an index of quotations in the New Testament.

The Text

1. The verse divisions are based on the 25th edition of the Nestle-Aland Greek text; these, with a few exceptions, are identical with the verse divisions first introduced by Stephanus in his 1551 edition of the Greek New Testament, and are widely adopted in modern editions. Significant differences are indicated in the punctuation apparatus.

2. The section headings are based upon those published by the United Bible Societies for the use of translators.

3. Cross references to parallel passages are found immediately below the section headings.

4. Superscript numerals in the text refer to the textual apparatus, where, to facilitate reference from apparatus to text; the verse number is also included.

5. Superscript italic letters refer to the punctuation apparatus; multiple use of the same letter indicates that the set of punctuation variants involves more than one position in the text.

6. Bold face type is used to identify direct quotations from the Old Testament. With the exception of an author's adaptation, minor variations are not distinguished typographically.

7. Quoted poetic passages and passages possessing an evidently formal structure are indented, with as many as three degrees of indentation.

xi

8. In matters of punctuation the Committee has paid special attention to the problems and needs of translators. Within paragraphs the following kinds of punctuation "breaks" are used: (a) terminal marks of punctuation, i. e. period (full stop) or question mark, followed by a capital letter; (b) terminal marks followed by a lower-case letter; (c) a colon (raised period), which is always followed by a lower-case letter; (d) a comma. Quotations and direct speech are introduced by a capital letter preceded by a comma. Intraparagraph divisions, indicated in some editions by means of different lengths of space between terminal punctuation marks and following words, have not been used.

9. [ ] Square brackets are used to enclose words which are regarded as having dubious textual validity.

10. ⟦ ⟧ Double square brackets are used to enclose passages which are regarded as later additions to the text, but which are retained because of their evident antiquity and their importance in the textual tradition.

The Textual Apparatus

As has been stated in the Preface, the variant readings cited in the textual apparatus are primarily those which are significant for translators or necessary for establishing the text. A few other variants have been included because they contain important differences in the forms of proper names or because they provide valuable supplementary information.

1. *The Evaluation of Evidence for the Text*

By means of the letters A, B, C, and D, enclosed within "braces" { } at the beginning of each set of textual variants, the Committee has sought to indicate the relative degree of certainty, arrived at on the basis of internal considerations as well as of external evidence, for the reading adopted as the text. The letter A signifies that the text is virtually certain, while B indicates that there is some degree of doubt. The letter C means that there is a considerable degree of doubt whether the text or the apparatus contains the superior reading, while D shows that there is a very high degree of doubt concerning the reading selected for the text.

The apparently large number of C decisions is due to the circumstance that many readings in the A and B classes have had no variants included in the apparatus because they were not important for the purposes of this edition. By far the greatest proportion of the text represents what may be called an A degree of certainty.

2. *The Greek Manuscript Evidence*

The Greek manuscript evidence includes papyri, uncials designated traditionally by capital letters (referred to as "letter uncials"), uncials designated by arabic numbers with an initial 0 (the "numbered uncials"), minuscules (numbered without an initial 0), and lectionaries (numbered with an initial *l*). All manuscripts are cited and identified in accordance with the Gregory-Aland nomenclature found in Kurt Aland, *Kurzgefasste Liste* (see bibliography).

The following papyri have been newly collated and their evidence is cited wherever they provide data for a variant included in the apparatus. Since most of the papyri are fragmentary, their citation is comparatively infrequent.

Number	*Content*[1]	*Location*	*Date*
$\mathfrak{p}^1$	e	Philadelphia	III
$\mathfrak{p}^2$	e	Florence	VI
$\mathfrak{p}^3$	e	Vienna	VI/VII
$\mathfrak{p}^4$	e	Paris	III
$\mathfrak{p}^5$	e	London	III

---

[1] e = Gospels; a = Acts; p = Epistles of Paul; c = Catholic or General Epistles; r = Revelation.

Number	Content	Location	Date
$\mathfrak{p}^6$	e	Strassburg	IV
$\mathfrak{p}^8$	a	Berlin	IV
$\mathfrak{p}^{10}$	p	Cambridge, Mass.	IV
$\mathfrak{p}^{11}$	p	Leningrad	VII
$\mathfrak{p}^{13}$	p	London and Florence	III/IV
$\mathfrak{p}^{15}$	p	Cairo	III
$\mathfrak{p}^{16}$	p	Cairo	III/IV
$\mathfrak{p}^{18}$	r	London	III/IV
$\mathfrak{p}^{19}$	e	Oxford	IV/V
$\mathfrak{p}^{21}$	e	Allentown, Pa.	IV/V
$\mathfrak{p}^{22}$	e	Glasgow	III
$\mathfrak{p}^{23}$	c	Urbana, Ill.	early III
$\mathfrak{p}^{24}$	r	Newton Center, Mass.	IV
$\mathfrak{p}^{25}$	e	Berlin	late IV
$\mathfrak{p}^{26}$	p	Dallas	about 600
$\mathfrak{p}^{27}$	p	Cambridge	III
$\mathfrak{p}^{30}$	p	Ghent	III
$\mathfrak{p}^{33}$	a	Vienna	VI
$\mathfrak{p}^{36}$	e	Florence	VI
$\mathfrak{p}^{37}$	e	Ann Arbor, Mich.	III/IV
$\mathfrak{p}^{38}$	a	Ann Arbor, Mich.	about 300
$\mathfrak{p}^{39}$	e	Chester, Pa.	III
$\mathfrak{p}^{40}$	p	Heidelberg	III
$\mathfrak{p}^{41}$	a	Vienna	VIII
$\mathfrak{p}^{45}$	ea	Dublin: Chester Beatty, and Vienna	III
$\mathfrak{p}^{46}$	p	Dublin: Chester Beatty, and Ann Arbor, Mich.	about 200
$\mathfrak{p}^{47}$	r	Dublin: Chester Beatty	late III
$\mathfrak{p}^{48}$	a	Florence	late III
$\mathfrak{p}^{49}$	p	New Haven, Conn.	late III
$\mathfrak{p}^{50}$	a	New Haven, Conn.	IV/V
$\mathfrak{p}^{51}$	p	P. Oxy. 2157	about 400
$\mathfrak{p}^{58}$	a	Vienna	VI
$\mathfrak{p}^{59}$	e	New York: P. Colt 3	VII

Number	Content	Location	Date
𝔭⁶⁰	e	New York: P. Colt 4	VII
𝔭⁶¹	p	New York: P. Colt 5	about 700
𝔭⁶³	e	Berlin	about 500
𝔭⁶⁴	e	Oxford and Barcelona	about 200
𝔭⁶⁵	p	Florence	III
𝔭⁶⁶	e	Geneva: P. Bodmer II	about 200
𝔭⁶⁷	e	Barcelona	about 200
𝔭⁶⁸	p	Leningrad	VII?
𝔭⁷⁰	e	P. Oxy. 2384	III
𝔭⁷¹	e	P. Oxy. 2385	IV
𝔭⁷²	c	Geneva: P. Bodmer VII, VIII	III/IV
𝔭⁷⁴	ac	Geneva: P. Bodmer XVII	VII
𝔭⁷⁵	e	Geneva: P. Bodmer XIV, XV	early III
𝔭⁷⁶	e	Vienna	VI

The following letter uncials, selected because of their value in determining the text, have been cited from previous editions of the Greek New Testament. They have been checked chiefly where the printed evidence was contradictory or incomplete.

Manuscript		Content[1]	Location	Date
ℵ	01	eapr	London: Sinaiticus	IV
A	02	eapr	London: Alexandrinus	V
B	03	eap	Rome: Vaticanus	IV
C	04	eapr	Paris: Ephraemi Rescriptus	V
D	05	ea	Cambridge: Bezae Cantabrigiensis	VI
D	06	p	Paris: Claromontanus	VI
D^{abs1}		p	*Abschrift* (copy of Claromontanus)	IX
E	07	e	Basel	VIII

---

[1] e = Gospels; a = Acts and Catholic Epistles; p = Epistles of Paul; r = Revelation.

Manuscript		Content	Location	Date
E	08	a	Oxford: Laudianus	VI
F	09	e	Utrecht	IX
F	010	p	Cambridge	IX
G	011	e	London and Cambridge	IX
G	012	p	Dresden: Boernerianus	IX
H	013	e	Hamburg and Cambridge	IX
H	015	p	Athos and elsewhere: Euthalianus	VI
I	016	p	Washington	V
K	017	e	Paris	IX
K	018	ap	Moscow	IX
L	019	e	Paris: Regius	VIII
L	020	ap	Rome	IX
M	021	e	Paris	IX
N	022	e	Leningrad and elsewhere	VI
O	023	e	Paris	VI
P	024	e	Wolfenbüttel	VI
P	025	apr	Leningrad	IX
Q	026	e	Wolfenbüttel	V
S	028	e	Rome	949
T	029	e	Rome	V
U	030	e	Venice	IX
V	031	e	Moscow	IX
W	032	e	Washington: Freer Gospels	V
X	033	e	Munich	X
Y	034	e	Cambridge	IX
Γ	036	e	Leningrad and Oxford	X
Δ	037	e	St. Gall	IX
Θ	038	e	Tiflis: Koridethi	IX
Λ	039	e	Oxford	IX
Ξ	040	e	London: Zacynthius	VI/VIII?
Π	041	e	Leningrad	IX
Σ	042	e	Rossano	VI
Φ	043	e	Athos?	VI
Ψ	044	eap	Athos	VIII/IX

The following numbered uncials have been systematically cited on the basis of fresh collations made by the Institut für neutestamentliche Textforschung, Münster/Westf. In many instances they are fragmentary and therefore their citation is comparatively infrequent:

Number	Content	Date	Number	Content	Date
046	r	X	082	p	VI
047	e	VIII	083	e	VI/VII
048	ap	V	084	e	VI
049	ap	IX	085	e	VI
050	e	IX	086	e	VI
051	r	X	087	e	VI
052	r	X	088	p	V/VI
053	e	IX	090	e	VI
054	e	VIII	092b	e	VI
056	ap	X	093	a	VI
058	e	IV	095	a	VIII
059	e	IV/V	096	a	VII
060	e	VI	097	a	VII
061	p	V	099	e	VII
062	p	V	0100	e	VII
063	e	IX	0102	e	VII
064	e	VI	0105	e	X
065	e	VI	0106	e	VII
066	a	VI	0107	e	VII
067	e	VI	0108	e	VII
068	e	V	0109	e	VII
070	e	VI	0110	e	VI
071	e	V/VI	0111	p	VII
073	e	VI	0112	e	VI/VII
074	e	VI	0113	e	V
076	a	V/VI	0115	e	VIII
078	e	VI	0116	e	VIII
079	e	VI	0117	e	IX
081	p	VI	0119	e	VII

Number	Content	Date	Number	Content	Date
0120	a	IX	0186	p	V/VI
0121a	p	X	0187	e	VI
0121b	p	X	0189	a	IV
0122	p	IX	0190	e	VI
0124	e	VI	0191	e	VI
0125	e	V?	0193	e	VII
0126	e	VIII	0196	e	IX
0128	e	IX	0197	e	IX
0129	p	IX	0201	p	V
0130	e	IX	0202	e	VI
0131	e	IX	0206	a	IV
0132	e	IX	0207	r	IV
0134	e	VIII	0208	p	VI
0136	e	IX	0209	ap	VII
0138	e	IX	0210	e	VII
0141	e	X	0214	e	IV
0142	ap	X	0216	e	V
0143	e	VI	0217	e	V
0146	e	VIII	0220	p	III
0148	e	VIII	0221	p	IV
0155	e	IX	0223	p	VI
0156	a	VIII	0225	p	VI
0159	p	VI	0226	p	V
0162	e	IV	0229	r	VIII
0165	a	V	0230	p	IV
0170	e	V/VI	0232	a	III
0171	e	IV	0234	e	VIII
0172	p	V	0235	e	VI/VII
0175	a	V	0236	a	V
0176	p	IV	0237	e	VI
0177	e	X	0238	e	VIII
0179	e	VI	0242	e	IV
0180	e	VI	0243	p	X
0181	e	IV	0246	a	VI
0182	e	V	0250	e	VIII

The following Greek minuscules, selected after a critical examination of more than one thousand manuscripts, have been cited systematically because they exhibit a significant degree of independence from the so-called Byzantine manuscript tradition. Many of them have not been previously cited in printed editions. They were collated for this edition by the Institut für neutestamentliche Textforschung at Münster/Westf.

Number	Content	Date	Number	Content	Date
1	eap	XII	1195	e	1123
1	r	XII	1216	e	XI
13	e	XIII	1230	e	1124
28	e	XI	1241	eap	XII
33	eap	IX	1242	eap	XIII
81	ap	1044	1253	e	XV
88	apr	XII	1344	e	XII
94	r	XII	1365	e	XII
104	apr	1087	1505	eap	1084
181	ap	XI	1546	e	1263?
326	ap	XII	1611	apr	XII
330	eap	XII	1646	eap	1172
436	ap	XI	1739	ap	X
451	ap	XI	1828	apr	XII
565	e	IX	1854	apr	XI
614	ap	XIII	1859	ar	XIV
629	ap	XIV	1877	ap	XIV
630	ap	XIV	1881	ap	XIV
700	e	XI	1962	p	XI
892	e	IX	1984	p	XIV
945	eap	XI	1985	p	1561
1006	er	XI	2020	r	XV
1009	e	XIII	2042	r	XIV
1010	e	XII	2053	r	XIII
1071	e	XII	2065	r	XV
1079	e	X	2073	r	XIV

Number	Content	Date	Number	Content	Date
2081	r	XI	2344	apr	XI
2127	eap	XII	2412	ap	XII
2138	apr	1072	2432	r	XIV
2148	e	1337	2492	eap	XIII
2174	e	XIV	2495	eapr	XIV/XV

The following minuscules have been cited only when they are of special significance for certain variants. Their evidence has been taken from printed editions of the Greek New Testament and has not been checked.

Number	Content	Date	Number	Content	Date
2	ap	XII	76	eap	XII
4	e	XIII	80	e	XII
4	ap	XV	94	ap	XIII
5	eap	XIV	97	ap	XII
7	p	XI	102	ap	1345
17	e	XV	103	ap	XI
18	eapr	1364	108	e	XI
22	e	XII	110	apr	XII
31	e	XIII	113	e	XI
35	eapr	XI	118	e	XIII
36	a	XII	119	e	XII
37	e	XI	122	eap	XII
38	eap	XIII	124	e	XI
42	apr	XI	127	e	XI
53	e	XIV	130	e	XV
56	e	XV	131	eap	XIV
57	eap	XII	137	e	XI
58	e	XV	138	e	XII
61	eapr	XVI	142	eap	XI
63	e	X	157	e	XII
69	eapr	XV	162	e	1153
71	e	XII	174	e	1052
73	e	XII	179	e	XII

Number	Content	Date	Number	Content	Date
181	r	XV	322	ap	XV
182	e	XIV	323	ap	XI
185	e	XIV	325	apr	XI
205	eapr	XV	327	ap	XIII
206	ap	XIII	328	ap	XIII
209	eap	XIV	336	apr	XV
216	ap	1358	346	e	XII
225	e	1192	348	e	1022
230	e	1013	372	e	XVI
234	eap	1278	378	ap	XII
235	e	1314	397	e	X/XI
237	e	X	407	e	XII
238	e	XI	424	apr	XI
239	e	XI	425	ap	1330
240	e	XII	429	ap	XIV
241	eapr	XI	429	r	XV
242	eapr	XII	431	eap	XI
244	e	XII	435	e	X
245	e	1199	440	eap	XII
248	e	1275	441	ap	XIII
249	e	XIV	460	ap	XIII
253	e	XI	462	ap	XIII
254	apr	XIV	465	ap	XI
255	ap	XII	467	apr	XV
256	apr	XI	468	apr	XIII
259	e	XI	469	apr	XIII
263	eap	XIII	472	e	XIII
273	e	XIII	474	e	XI
274	e	X	482	e	1285
291	e	XIII	483	eap	1295
296	eapr	XVI	489	eap	1316
299	e	X	491	eap	XI
301	e	XI	495	e	XII
307	a	X	517	eapr	XI/XII
309	ap	XIII	522	eapr	1515

Number	Content	Date	Number	Content	Date
543	e	XII	1293	e	XI
544	e	XIII	1311	ap	1090
547	eap	XI	1319	eap	XII
569	e	1161	1321	e	XI
579	e	XIII	1342	e	XIII/XIV
605	ap	X	1396	e	XIV
618	ap	XII	1424	eap	IX/X
623	ap	1037	1443	e	1047
627	apr	X	1445	e	1323
635	ap	XI	1518	ap	XV
692	e	XII	1522	ap	XIV
713	e	XII	1574	e	XIV
788	e	XI	1582	e	949
792	er	XIII	1597	eapr	1289
808	eapr	XII	1626	eapr	XV
826	e	XII	1675	e	XIV
828	e	XII	1689	e	1200
915	ap	XIII	1758	ap	XIII
917	ap	XII	1778	r	XV
927	eap	1133	1835	a	XI
954	e	XV	1836	ap	X
983	e	XII	1837	ap	XI
998	e	XII	1838	ap	XI
1012	e	XI	1873	ap	XII
1047	e	XIII	1898	ap	X
1077	e	X	1906	p	1056
1093	e	1302	1908	p	XI
1110	e	XI	1923	p	XI
1170	e	XI	1925	p	XI
1175	ap	XI	2028	r	1422
1210	e	XI	2029	r	XVI
1215	e	XIII	2030	r	XII
1217	e	1186	2033	r	XVI
1221	e	XI	2038	r	XVI
1224	e	XII	2044	r	1560

Number	Content	Date	Number	Content	Date
2048	r	XI	2074	r	X
2049	r	XVI	2083	r	1560
2050	r	1107	2091	r	XV
2054	r	XV	2193	e	X
2058	r	XIV	2302	r	XV
2067	r	XV	2329	r	X
2068	r	XVI	2351	r	X/XI
2069	r	XV	2386	e	XII
2071	r	1622	2595	r	XV

The following symbols and abbreviations are used in connection with the citation of Greek manuscript evidence:

f^1 "Family 1": manuscripts 1, 118, 131, 209.

f^{13} "Family 13": manuscripts 13, 69, 124, 174, 230 (174 and 230 not used in Mark), 346, 543, 788, 826, 828, 983, 1689.

Byz   the reading of the majority of Byzantine manuscripts.

Byz[pt]   part of the Byzantine manuscript tradition.

[*]   the reading of the original hand of a manuscript.

[c]   corrector of a manuscript.

[o,2,3]   successive correctors of a manuscript; in the case of ℵ, D (Bezae Cantabrigiensis) and D (Claromontanus) the successive correctors are designated traditionally as [a,b,c,d,e].

[mg]   textual evidence contained in the margin of a manuscript.

[gr]   the Greek text of a bilingual manuscript (e. g. D, E, and G) where it differs from the corresponding text in the accompanying language.

[vid]   indicates apparent support for a given reading in a manuscript whose state of preservation makes complete verification impossible.

?   indicates that a witness probably supports a given reading but there is some doubt.

( )   indicate that a witness supports the reading for which it is cited, but deviates from it in minor details.

cj   conjecture

supp   a portion of a manuscript supplied by a later hand where the original is missing.

sic   indicates an abnormality exactly reproduced from the original.

txt   the text of a manuscript when it differs from another reading given in the commentary section which accompanies the text.

comm   the commentary section of a manuscript where the reading differs from the accompanying Greek text.

The following Greek lectionaries, most of them not previously utilized in editions of the Greek New Testament, have been systematically cited in the textual apparatus. Their citation is based upon fresh collations made for this edition at the University of Chicago, or is drawn from the files of the Greek Lectionary project there.

It should be observed that Greek lectionaries have no readings from Revelation and from certain parts of Acts and the Epistles, and that a number give only the Saturday and Sunday lessons instead of the daily ones. This accounts for the absence of citation of lectionary evidence in certain passages. Furthermore, *l* 309, *l* 490, and *l* 1610 are fragmentary.

Number	Content[1]	Date	Number	Content	Date
l 10	e	XIII	*l* 80	e	XII
l 12	e	XIII	*l* 147	a	XII
l 32	e	XI	*l* 150	e	995
l 59	a	XII	*l* 184	e	1319
l 60	ea	1021	*l* 185	e	XI
l 69	e	XII	*l* 211	e	XII
l 70	e	XII	*l* 292	e	IX
l 76	e	XII	*l* 299	e	XIII

----

[1] e = Gospels; a = Acts and Epistles.

Number	Content	Date	Number	Content	Date
l 303	e	XII	*l* 1127	e	XII
l 309	e	X	*l* 1153a	a	XIV
l 313	e	XIV	*l* 1231	e	X
l 333	e	XIII	*l* 1298	a	XI
l 374	e	1070	*l* 1356	a	X
l 381	e	XI	*l* 1364	a	XII
l 490	e	IX	*l* 1365	a	XII
l 547	e	XIII	*l* 1439	a	XII
l 597	a	X	*l* 1441	a	XIII
l 598	a	XI	*l* 1443	a	1053
l 599	a	XI	*l* 1579	e	XIV
l 603	a	XI	*l* 1590	a	XIII
l 680	ea	XIII	*l* 1599	e	IX
l 809	a	XII	*l* 1610	e	XV
l 847	e	967	*l* 1627	e	XI
l 883	a	XI	*l* 1634	e	XII
l 950	e	1289/90	*l* 1642	e	XIII
l 1021	a	XII	*l* 1663	e	XIV

The following Greek lectionaries have been cited from previous editions of the Greek New Testament, where for the most part they are sporadically used. With some exceptions, they have not been checked for this edition.

Number	Content	Date	Number	Content	Date
l 1	e	X	*l* 18	e	XII
l 4	e	XI	*l* 19	e	XIII
l 5	e	X	*l* 20	e	1047
l 6	ea	XIII	*l* 21	e	XII
l 7	e	1204	*l* 24	e	X
l 11	e	XIII	*l* 26	e	XIII
l 13	e	XII	*l* 31	e	XII
l 14	e	XVI	*l* 33	e	XI
l 15	e	XIII	*l* 34	e	IX
l 17	e	IX	*l* 36	e	VIII/IX

Number	Content	Date	Number	Content	Date
l 37	ea	XII	l 305	e	XII
l 38	a	XV	l 331	e	1272
l 44	ea	XII	l 368	a	IX
l 47	e	X	l 372	e	1055
l 48	e	1055	l 574	e	1125
l 49	e	X/XI	l 611	a	XIII
l 51	e	XIV	l 805	e	IX
l 53	ea	XV	l 823	e	X
l 54	ea	1470	l 845	e	IX
l 55	ea	1602	l 850	e	XII
l 57	ea	XV	l 854	e	1167
l 62	a	XII	l 855	e	1175
l 63	e	IX	l 861	e	XII
l 64	e	IX	l 871	e	XII
l 68	e	XII	l 952	e	1148
l 159	e	1061	l 956	e	XV
l 164	a	1172	l 961	e	XII
l 174	ea	XIII	l 983	e	XIII
l 181	e	980	l 997	e	XII
l 183	e	X	l 1014	e	X
l 187	e	XIII	l 1043	e	V
l 191	e	XII	l 1084	e	1292
l 210	e	XII	l 1141	a	1105
l 219	e	XII	l 1291	a	XIV
l 223	ea	XV	l 1294	a	XIV
l 224	e	XIV	l 1300	a	XI
l 225	e	1437	l 1311	a	1116
l 226	e	XIV	l 1345	e	IX
l 227	e	XIV	l 1346	e	X
l 230	e	XIII	l 1348	e	VII
l 241	ea	1199	l 1349	e	IX
l 253	e	1020	l 1350	e	IX
l 260	e	?	l 1353	e	VII
l 276	e	XIII	l 1357	a	XV
l 302	e	XV	l 1440	a	XII

Number	Content	Date	Number	Content	Date
l 1504	a	X	*l* 1613	e	XV
l 1564	e	XII	*l* 1632	e	XIII
l 1578	e	XIV	*l* 1635	e	XIII
l 1602	e	VIII			

The following abbreviations are used in connection with the lectionary evidence:

Lect — the reading of the majority of lectionaries in the Synaxarion (the so-called "movable year" beginning with Easter) and in the Menologion (the "fixed year" beginning September 1), when these agree.

Lect^m — the reading of the majority of lectionaries in the Menologion when it differs from that of the Synaxarion or occurs only in the Menologion.

l^{12,etc.} — an individual lectionary cited by number, following the Gregory-Aland list, when it differs from the majority reading in the Synaxarion passages.

l^{135m,etc.} — an individual lectionary in its Menologion, which differs from the majority of the other lectionaries.

l^{76s,m,etc.} — an individual lectionary in which both the Synaxarion and the Menologion passages are in agreement.

l^{135pt,etc.} — an individual lectionary which contains a passage two or more times, with readings differing from each other, hence listed as supporting a reading in part.

3. *The Evidence from Ancient Versions*

The evidence cited from ancient versions includes the Latin (Itala or Old Latin, and Vulgate), Syriac, Coptic, Gothic, Armenian, Ethiopic, Georgian, and rarely Arabic, Nubian, Old High German, Persian, Provençal and Slavonic. The versional evidence has been derived primarily from printed editions (see bibliography). It must always be employed with caution since the very process of translation frequently obscures its textual basis, and resemblances can be merely accidental, especially if a translation is relatively free. Because of its uncertain character, it is not infrequently cited with a question mark (to indicate that the grammatical structure of the language makes it difficult to cite confidently at this point) or with parenthesis marks (to indicate that there is similarity but not identity of readings).

Itala or Old Latin (Second to Fourth Century)

The following manuscripts have been cited in this edition:

Manuscript[1]	Content	Name		Date	Editor[2]
a	3	e	Vercellensis	IV	Jülicher
a²	16	e	Curiensis	V	Jülicher
ar	61	eapcr	Ardmachanus	IX	Gwynn
aur	15	e	Aureus	VII	Jülicher
b	4	e	Veronensis	V	Jülicher
β	26	e	Carinthianum	VII	Jülicher
c	6	eapcr	Colbertinus	XII/XIII	Jülicher
d	5	eac	Bezae Cantabrigiensis	V	Jülicher

---

[1] Numbers and dates are cited according to the Beuron Catalogue.

[2] See Bibliography.

Manuscript		Content	Name	Date	Editor
d	75	p	Claromontanus	V/VI	Tischendorf
dem	59	apcr	Demidovianus	XIII	Matthaei
div	–	pcr	Divionensis	XIII	Wordsworth-White
e	2	e	Palatinus	V	Jülicher
e	50	a	Laudianus	VI	Tischendorf
e	76	p	Sangermanensis	IX	Tischendorf
f	10	e	Brixianus	VI	Jülicher
f	78	p	Augiensis	IX	Scrivener
ff	66	c	Corbeiensis	X/XI	Wordsworth-White
ff¹	9	eac	Corbeiensis I	X	Jülicher
ff²	8	e	Corbeiensis II	V	Jülicher
g	77	p	Boernerianus	IX	Matthaei
g¹	7	eapcr	Sangermanensis	IX	Jülicher
gig	51	eapcr	Gigas	XIII	Belsheim; Wordsworth-White
gue	79	p	Guelferbytanus	VI	Tischendorf
h	12	e	Claromontanus	V	Jülicher
h	55	acr	Floriacensis	V	Buchanan
haf	–	r	Hafnianus	X	Wordsworth-White
i	17	e	Vindobonensis	V	Jülicher
j	22	e	Sarzanensis	VI	Jülicher
k	1	e	Bobiensis	IV/V	Jülicher
l	11	e	Rhedigeranus	VII/VIII	Jülicher
l	67	eapcr	Legionensis	VII	Fischer
m	–	eapcr	Speculum (or Ps-Augustine)	IV–IX	Jülicher; Wordsworth-White
mon	86	p	Monza	X	Frede
n	16	e	Sangallensis	V	Jülicher
o	16	e	Sangallensis	VII	Jülicher
p	20	e	Sangallensis	VIII	Jülicher
p	54	eapcr	Perpinianensis	XIII	Wordsworth-White

Manuscript		Content	Name	Date	Editor
ph	63	a	Philadelphiensis	XII	Sanders
π	18	e	Stuttgartensis	VII	Jülicher
q	13	e	Monacensis	VII	Jülicher
q	64	c	Monacensis	VII	de Bruyne
r	57	a	Schlettstadtensis	VII/VIII	Morin
r¹	14	e	Usserianus I	VII	Jülicher
r²	28	e	Usserianus II	VIII/IX	Jülicher
r³	64	p	Monacensis	VII	de Bruyne
ρ	24	e	Ambrosianus	VII/VIII	Jülicher
s	21	e	Ambrosianus	V	Jülicher
s	53	ac	Bobiensis	VI	White
t	56	eapcr	Liber Comicus Toletanus	XI	Morin
t	19	e	Bernensis	VI	Jülicher
v	25	e	Vindobonensis	VII	Jülicher
v	81	p	Parisiensis	about 800	Souter
w	83	p	Waldeccensis	XI	Schultze
x	—	p	Bodleianus	IX	Wordsworth-White
z	65	pcr	Harleianus Londiniensis	VIII	Buchanan

Vulgate (Fourth Century)

vg Vulgate, when the Clementine and the Wordsworth-White editions are in agreement.

vg^{cl} the Clementine edition when it differs from Wordsworth-White.

vg^{ww} the Wordsworth-White edition when it differs from the Clementine.

Syriac (Second or Third to Seventh Century)

1. Old Syriac

syr^s Sinaitic (Lewis)

syr^c Curetonian (Burkitt)

2. Peshitta and Later Syriac

syr[p]   Peshitta (Pusey and Gwilliam; B.F.B.S. edition)
syr[pal] Palestinian (Lewis and Gibson, and others)
syr[ph]   Philoxenian (Gwynn)
syr[h]   Harclean (White)
          syr[hmg] a marginal reading.
          syr[hgr] a Greek marginal reading.
          syr[h with *] a reading in the Syriac text, marked by
          asterisks to indicate the existence of a variant.

Coptic (Third to Sixth Century)

cop[sa]   Sahidic (Horner; Kasser; Thompson)
cop[bo]   Bohairic (Horner; Kasser)
cop[fay] Fayyumic (Husselman and others)
cop[ach] Achmimic (Lefort; Thompson)
cop[ach2] Sub-Achmimic (Thompson)

Gothic (Fourth Century)

goth   Gothic (Streitberg)

Armenian (Fourth or Fifth Century)

arm   Armenian (Zohrab)

Ethiopic (Sixth Century)

eth[ro]   Ethiopic (Rome)
eth[pp]   Ethiopic (Pell Platt and Praetorius)
eth[ms]   Ethiopic (Paris Ms. Eth. n. 32, XIII–XIV Century)

Georgian (Fifth Century)

geo   Georgian (Blake, Brière, Garitte)
          geo[1,2] manuscripts representing the two major
          Georgian traditions.
          geo[a,b] manuscripts which form the basis of geo[2].

Nubian (Sixth Century)

nub   Nubian (Griffith)

Other Versions

Occasional citations of the following versions have been derived from printed editions of the Greek New Testament.

arab	Arabic
Old German	Old High German
pers	Persian
Provençal	Provençal or Old French
slav	Old Church Slavonic

4. *The Evidence from Church Fathers*

Evidence for the citation of the Church Fathers has been taken almost wholly from printed editions of the Greek New Testament and has not yet been checked. These data are not always reliable since many of the patristic editions employed by earlier editors of the Greek New Testament are out of date. Moreover, a Church Father not infrequently quotes the same passage in more than one form, often from memory rather than by consulting a manuscript, and may therefore appear in support of differing readings. Furthermore, the manuscripts of the Church Fathers have suffered the usual transcriptional modifications to which all ancient manuscripts were subject; this was especially true for Biblical passages where the tendency of scribes was to accommodate readings to the Byzantine textual tradition.

The following Church Fathers are cited in the apparatus in their presumed chronological sequence, and usually according to the spelling of Altaner. Dates given are generally those accepted for their death; in many cases these are approximate. Because of the considerable difficulties involved in distinguishing traditional abbreviations, and for convenience in use, the names of the Church Fathers are given in full, along with a few other authors and early writings of which the authorship is either unknown or disputed.

Name	Date	Name	Date
Acacius	366	Athenagoras	II
Acts of Pilate	IV	Athanasius	373
Acts of Thomas	III	Augustine	430
Adamantius	300	Basil, the Great	379
Addai (see Teaching of Addai)		Beatus	786
		Bede	735
Africanus	240	Caelestinus, of Rome	IV
Alexander, of Alexandria	328	Caesarius, of Arles	542
Ambrose	397	Caesarius-Nazianzus	369
Ambrosiaster	IV	Carpocrates	II
Ammonius	III	Cassian	435
Ammonius-Alexandria	V	Cassiodorus	580
Amphilochius	394	Chromatius	407
Anastasius-Abbot	VIII?	Chrysostom	407
Anastasius, of Antioch	700	Claudius, of Turin	IX
Andrew, of Caesarea	614	Clement, of Alexandria	215
Andrew-Crete	740	Cosmos	550
Ansbert	VIII	Cyprian	258
Anthony	VIII or XII	Cyril, of Alexandria	444
Antiochus, of St. Saba	614	Cyril-Jerusalem	386
Aphraates	367	de Promissionibus	453
Apollinaris, the Younger	390	Diadochus	468
Apostolic Canons	IV	Diatessaron, of Tatian	II
Apostolic Constitutions	380	Didache	II
Apringius	551	Didascalia	III
Archelaus	278	Didymus, of Alexandria	398
Arethas	914	Diodore	394
Aristides	II	Diognetus	II
Arius	336	Dionysius, the Great; of Alexandria	265
Arnobius	460		
Asterius	341	Docetists	II

Name	*Date*	*Name*	*Date*
Druthmarus	840	Hesychius-Salonitan	418
Ephraem	373	Hieracus	302
Epiphanius	403	Hilary	367
Eugippius	533	Hippolytus	235
Eulogius	607	Ignatius	110
Eusebian Canons	IV	Irenaeus	202
Eusebius, of Caesarea	339	Isidore	435
Eustathius	337	Jacob-Nisibis	338
Euthalius	V	Jerome	420
Eutherius	434	John-Damascus	749
Euthymius	XII	Julian-Eclanum	454
Facundus	569	Julius, I	352
Fastidius	V	Justin	165
Faustinus	380	Juvencus	330
Faustus, of Riez	490	Leo	461
Faustus-Milevis	IV–V	Leontius	VI
Ferrandus	IV	Liberatus	566
Fulgentius	533	Liber Graduum	320
Gaudentius	406	Lucifer, of Cagliari	370
Gelasius-Cyzicus	475	Macarius, Magnes	400
Gennadius, of Marseilles	505	Macrobius	IV
Gennadius-		Manes	277
Constantinople	471	Manicheans	III
Gildas	570	Marcion	II
Gospel of the Ebionites	II	Marcus, Eremita	430
Gospel of the Nazarenes	II	Marius Mercator	V
Gregory-Elvira	392	Maternus	348
Gregory-Nazianzus	390	Maximinus	428
Gregory-Nyssa	394	Maximus, II, of Turin	423
Gregory-Thaumaturgus	270	Maximus-Confessor	662
Haymo	841	Melitius	381
Hegemonius	350	Methodius	III
Hegesippus	180	Naassenes	II/III
Heracleon	II	Nestorius	451
Hesychius, of Jerusalem	450	Niceta	414

Name	Date	Name	Date
Nonnus	431	Ps-Clement	IV
Novatian	III	Ps-Cyprian	?
Oecumenius	VI	Ps-Dionysius	V
Optatus	385	Ps-Hippolytus	?
Origen	254	Ps-Ignatius	V
Orosius	418	Ps-Jerome	V
Orsisius	380	Ps-Justin	IV/V
Pacian	392	Ps-Oecumenius	X
Palladius	431	Ps-Theodulus	VI/VII?
Pamphilus	310	Ps-Titus	?
Papias	II	Ps-Vigilius	?
Papyrus Oxyrhynchus 405	IV	Ptolemy, a Gnostic	II
Paschal Chronicle	630	Rebaptism	
Paulinus-Nola	431	(de Rebaptismate)	III?
Pelagius	412	Rufinus	410
Perateni	III	Rupertus	1135
Peter-Alexandria	311	Salvian	480
Peter-Laodicea	VI	Sedulius-Scotus	IX
Petilianus	V	Serapion	362
Philo-Carpasia	401	Severian	408
Phoebadius	392	Severus	538
Photius	895	Socrates,	
Pierius	309	of Constantinople	439
Polycarp	156	Sozomen	450
Porphyry	III	Sulpicius	420
Possidius	V	Synesius	414
Primasius	552	Tatian (see Diatessaron)	II
Priscillian	385	Teaching of Addai	400
Proclus	446	Tertullian	220
Procopius	538	Theodore, of Mopsuestia	428
Promissionibus, de	453	Theodore-Heraclea	358
Ps-Ambrose	VI	Theodore-Studita	826
Ps-Athanasius	VI	Theodoret	466
Ps-Augustine	?	Theodotus, of Byzantium	II
Ps-Chrysostom	VI	Theodotus-Ancyra	445

Name	Date	Name	Date
Theophilus, Antioch	180	Varimadum	380
Theophylact	1077	Victor-Antioch	V
Theotecnus	III	Victor-Tunis	566
Titus-Bostra	378	Victor-Vita	489
Tyconius	380	Victorinus-Pettau	304
Valentinians	II	Victorinus-Rome, Marius	362
Valentinus	160	Vigilius	484
Valerian	460	Zeno	372

The problem of the Diatessaron of Tatian is particularly complex due to the indirect nature of the evidence, and the resulting diversity of theories and opinions concerning the tradition. When the term Diatessaron is used without superscript designation (see below) it usually refers to the Arabic version, which has been extensively accommodated to the Syriac Peshitta. However, rather than eliminate evidence traditionally cited for the Diatessaron, the Committee has included it, though with this word of caution.

The following abbreviations are frequently used in citing evidence from the Church Fathers:

( )   indicate that a Church Father supports the reading for which he is cited, but deviates from it in minor details.

txt   the lemma, that is, the cited portion of the text of the New Testament, on which the commentary of a Church Father is based, where this differs from the form of text cited in the commentary itself.

comm   the New Testament text cited in the commentary, where the citation differs from the lemma.

ed   published edition(s) of a Church Father.

ms,mss   manuscript(s) of a Church Father when differing from the edited text.

gr   the Greek text of a Church Father as distinct from a version in another language.

lat   the Latin version of a Greek Church Father.

arm   the Armenian version of a Church Father.

slav   the Slavonic version of a Church Father.

acc. to   according to.

1/2, 2/3, 5/7 etc.   the second figure of the fraction indicates the number of times a particular passage is cited by a Church Father, and the first specifies the number of times the passage is cited in the particular form of the variant with which the fraction is placed.

a,b,c   different manuscripts of the writings of Theophylact. The superscripts do not indicate correctors of manuscripts, as is the case with א and D.

a,bav,c,p   different manuscripts of Andrew of Caesarea's Commentary on Revelation.

Special abbreviations used in connection with the Diatessaron include:

a   Arabic

e   quotation by Ephraem

earm   quotation preserved in the Armenian version of Ephraem's commentary.

esyr   quotation preserved in the Syriac text of Ephraem's commentary.

f   Fulda

i   Italian (the agreement of t and v)

l   Liège

n   Old Dutch (the agreement of l and s)

p   Persian

s   Stuttgart

t   Tuscan

v   Venetian

The Punctuation Apparatus

As was noted above, the punctuation apparatus includes some six hundred passages in which difference of punctuation seems to be particularly significant for interpretation of the text. Each successive problem of punctuation is marked by an italic superscript letter in the text, which is repeated at each point where a related set of punctuation alternatives may be employed.

Several acute difficulties are involved in comparing punctuation in different Greek editions and modern-language translations: (1) different editions of the Greek text employ punctuation symbols with different values (one editor, for example, may tend to use colons where another will generally use commas); (2) the value of a mark of punctuation must be analyzed not only in terms of an editor's usual practice, but also in relation to other marks of punctuation within the context; (3) systems of punctuation employed in editions of the Greek New Testament and in modern-language translations do not completely correspond; and (4) translators into modern languages differ even more radically than do editors of the Greek New Testament in the variety of punctuation marks used and the diversity of values associated with them. Accordingly, it has not been possible to set up a system whereby specific punctuation marks can be compared on a purely formal basis. Rather, it has been necessary to evaluate the symbols and to determine their function and "weight" in each set of meaningful variants.

Punctuation marks have therefore been analyzed and evaluated in terms of two major functions: (1) the indication of significant breaks in structure, for example, between paragraphs, between complete sentences, between principal clauses within sentences, and between related phrases, and (2) the identification of the nature of a grammatical construction, e. g. a statement, a question, or a command.

Since, however, the primary function of punctuation marks is to indicate breaks or transition, the different marks of punctuation have been classified as follows: *paragraph*, *major* "break", *minor* "break" and *none*. Other types of breaks are identified by *dashes*, *parentheses*, or dots showing *ellipses*. Terminal punctuation marks, normally indicating some type of major break, serve to indicate differences between *question* (whether indicated by a question mark or an exclamation mark), *statement* and *command*.

Special problems are involved with respect to ὅτι, which

may introduce indirect discourse, direct discourse, a causal construction, a question, or may serve some other function in the sentence. In this edition, when ὅτι introduces indirect discourse no comma precedes, and neither ὅτι nor the word following is capitalized. When ὅτι is used to introduce direct discourse, no mark of punctuation precedes or follows it and the next word begins with a capital letter. When ὅτι introduces a causal construction, a comma may precede; it is always capitalized when it is causal at the beginning of direct discourse.

The major sets of alternatives given in the punctuation apparatus are as follows:

paragraph, major—a paragraph break in contrast with a full sentence break.

major, minor, none—a major break (often equivalent to a period or full stop, a colon, or a semicolon) in contrast with a minor break (usually indicated by a comma), and in further contrast with no punctuation.

question, statement, command—the contrast between question and non-question is usually clearly indicated in Greek texts, but in certain contexts the additional contrast between statement and command may be made explicit only in translation.

exclamation—a category not marked in Greek but often used in translations to render rhetorical questions (which may be marked in Greek as questions) or emphatic statements (which are marked in Greek only by a period or full stop).

dash, parens—dashes and parenthesis marks indicate breaks in structure. A dash is generally employed to indicate a break in the syntax of the sentence, while parenthesis marks are used to enclose explanatory or supplementary material.

ellipsis—words in an incomplete sentence which need to be supplied, indicated by three dots.

direct (or recitative), *indirect, causal, interrogative*—different uses of ὅτι, though in some instances it is difficult to interpret the function of ὅτι since an editor may have preferred to leave it ambiguous (see page xxxvi).

different text—the underlying text is so different that no correspondence can be indicated.

As a rule, alternative forms of punctuation are given only when they are represented by some Greek edition or modern translation, but in a few instances additional possibilities have been noted for which no authority is cited.

The following symbols and abbreviations have also been used with the punctuation apparatus:

?   indicates that citation of a particular edition or translation is doubtful, since the evidence does not clearly support one or another alternative.

( )   parenthesis marks show minor differences of detail in punctuation, while indicating that the authority supports in general the punctuation for which it is cited.

ed   a different edition of a Greek text or a translation which does not agree with other editions at a given point.

mg   a marginal reading in one of the translations.

mg1,mg2   successive alternatives in the margin of a translation.

The following editions of the Greek New Testament and translations into modern languages have been cited in the punctuation apparatus:

TR   Textus Receptus (Oxford, 1873). In cases of differences of verse division, the editions of Stephanus (1551, 1559) and others, were consulted.

WH   Westcott and Hort (1881).

Bov   Bover (4th edition, 1959). In some cases where the type had become illegible, the first edition (1943) was consulted.

Nes   Nestle-Aland (25th edition, 1963).

BF² British and Foreign Bible Society edition of the Nestle Greek text (2nd edition, 1958).

AV Authorized or King James Version. *The New Testament Parallel Edition*, AV and RSV (Nelson, 1961?) and the *New Testament Octapla*, edited by Luther A. Weigle (Nelson, 1962) were used. The Octapla includes the 1873 edition of the AV, edited by F. H. A. Scrivener.

RV Revised or English Revised Version (1881).

ASV American Standard Version (1901).

RSV Revised Standard Version (1946, and subsequent editions).

NEB *The New English Bible, New Testament* (1961).

TT *The New Testament: A Translation for Translators* (1966).

Zür *Die Heilige Schrift* (Zürich, 1942).

Luth *Das Neue Testament*, nach der Übersetzung Martin Luthers, Revidierter Text (1956).

Jer *Le Nouveau Testament* ... de l'École Biblique de Jérusalem (1958).

Seg *Le Nouveau Testament*, Traduction de Louis Segond (Nouvelle Revision, 1962).

The Cross-Reference System

The cross-references, given at the bottom of the page with the principal Greek words involved, include the following categories: (1) quotations from Biblical and non-Biblical books; (2) definite allusions, where it is assumed that the writer had in mind a specific passage of Scripture; and (3) literary and other parallels. References to parallel passages are given immediately below the section headings, rather than in the cross-references. When verse numbers in English editions differ from the Hebrew Old Testament, the numbering of the RSV is followed.

The following abbreviations are used in the reference system:

Gn	Genesis	Sol	Song of Solomon
Ex	Exodus	Is	Isaiah
Lv	Leviticus	Jr	Jeremiah
Nu	Numbers	Lm	Lamentation
Dt	Deuteronomy	Eze	Ezekiel
Jos	Joshua	Dn	Daniel
Jdg	Judges	Ho	Hosea
Ru	Ruth	Jl	Joel
1,2 Sm	1, 2 Samuel	Am	Amos
1,2 Kgs	1, 2 Kings	Ob	Obadiah
1,2 Chr	1, 2 Chronicles	Jon	Jonah
Ezr	Ezra	Mic	Micah
Ne	Nehemiah	Na	Nahum
Est	Esther	Hab	Habakkuk
Job	Job	Zph	Zephaniah
Ps	Psalms	Hg	Haggai
Pr	Proverbs	Zch	Zechariah
Ec	Ecclesiastes	Mal	Malachi

Mt	Matthew	1,2 Th	1, 2 Thessalonians
Mk	Mark	1,2 Tm	1, 2 Timothy
Lk	Luke	Tt	Titus
Jn	John	Phm	Philemon
Ac	Acts	He	Hebrews
Ro	Romans	Jas	James
1,2 Cor	1, 2 Corinthians	1,2 Pe	1, 2 Peter
Ga	Galatians	1,2,3 Jn	1, 2, 3 John
Eph	Ephesians	Jd	Jude
Php	Philippians	Re	Revelation
Col	Colossians		

Bar	Baruch	Ps Sol	Psalms of Solomon
En	Enoch	Sir	Sirach
1,2 Esd	1, 2 Esdras	Sus	Susanna
Jdth	Judith	Tob	Tobit
1,2,3,4 Macc	1, 2, 3, 4 Maccabees	Wsd	Wisdom

Other writings cited:

Aratus	Epimenides
Ascension of Isaiah	Ps-Epimenides
Assumption of Moses	Menander

The following abbreviations are also used in the reference system:

MT   the Masoretic Text, where it differs from the Greek.

LXX   the Septuagint, where it differs from the Hebrew.

Theodotion   Theodotion's text of the Greek Old Testament.

MASTER LIST OF SYMBOLS AND ABBREVIATIONS

{ }   enclose a letter A, B, C, D which indicates the relative degree of certainty for the reading adopted in the text.

[ ]   enclose words which are regarded as having dubious textual validity.

⟦ ⟧   enclose passages which are regarded as later additions to the text, but which are of evident antiquity and importance.

( )   indicate that a witness or edition supports the reading for which it is cited, but with minor differences.

*   the reading of the original hand of the manuscript.

?   indicates that a witness is probably in support of a reading, but that there is some doubt. The question mark is also used when an ancient version, owing to the grammatical structure of the language, is cited as supporting two or more different Greek readings. In the punctuation apparatus it indicates that citation of a particular edition or translation is doubtful, since the evidence does not clearly support one or another alternative.

1/2, 2/3, 5/7 etc.   the second figure of the fraction indicates the number of times a particular passage is cited by a Church Father, and the first specifies the number of times the passage is cited in the particular form of the variant with which the fraction is placed.

2,3,4   superscript numerals used to indicate the successive correctors of a manuscript.

a, b, c, d, e   successive correctors of manuscripts ℵ, D (Bezae Cantabrigiensis) and D (Claromontanus).

a, b, c,   manuscripts of the writings of Theophylact.

a, bav, c, p   manuscripts of the commentary of Andrew of Caesarea on Revelation.

a   indicates that a manuscript in the Gregory-Aland list contains the Acts of the Apostles, and sometimes the Catholic or General Epistles. With lectionaries, a indicates that the manuscript contains lessons from the Acts and the Epistles.

acc. to   according to.

arab   Arabic version.

arm   Armenian version.

ASV   American Standard Version (1901).

AV   Authorized or King James Version (1611).

BF²   Η ΚΑΙΝΗ ΔΙΑΘΗΚΗ (B.F.B.S., 2nd ed., 1958).

Bov   Bover, *Novi Testamenti Biblia Graeca et Latina* (4th ed., 1959).

Byz   the reading of the majority of Byzantine manuscripts.

*Byz*ᵖᵗ   a part of the Byzantine manuscript tradition.

c   indicates that a manuscript contains all or part of the Catholic or General Epistles.

^{c} corrector of a manuscript.

causal   indicates the causal function of ὅτι in a given passage.

cj   conjecture.

^{comm} the commentary section of a manuscript where the reading differs from the accompanying Greek text. Also used to designate the New Testament text cited in the commentary of a Church Father, when the citation differs from the accompanying New Testament text.

cop^{ach} Coptic version, Achmimic dialect.

cop^{ach2} Coptic version, Sub-Achmimic dialect.

cop^{bo} Coptic version, Bohairic dialect.

cop^{fay} Coptic version, Fayyumic dialect.

cop^{sa} Coptic version, Sahidic dialect.

dash   indicates a break in the syntax of a sentence.

Diatessaron$^{a, e, etc.}$ (see pages xxxiv, xxxv).

different text   used in the punctuation apparatus when the text of an edition or version is so different that no correspondence can be indicated with the other editions and versions cited.

direct   indicates that ὅτι introduces direct discourse.

e   indicates that a manuscript in the Gregory-Aland list contains all or part of the Gospels.

^{ed} edition(s) of a Church Father. In the punctuation apparatus it indicates that an edition does not agree with other editions.

ellipsis   words in an incomplete sentence which need to be supplied, indicated by three dots.

eth^{pp} the Pell Platt edition of the Ethiopic version (B.F.B.S. 1826).

eth^{ro} the Rome edition of the Ethiopic version (1548–1549).

exclamation	not marked in Greek texts, but often used in translations to render rhetorical questions (which may be marked in Greek as questions) or emphatic statements (which are marked in Greek only by a period or full stop).
f^1	"Family 1", a group of Greek manuscripts first described by Lake.
f^{13}	"Family 13", a group of Greek manuscripts first described by Ferrar.
geo	Georgian version.
$geo^{1,2}$	manuscripts representing the two major Georgian traditions.
$geo^{A,B}$	manuscripts which form the basis of geo^2.
goth	Gothic version.
^{gr}	the Greek text of a bilingual manuscript (D, E, G) where it differs from the corresponding text in the accompanying language. Also used with Church Fathers to distinguish the Greek text of a Church Father from a version in another language.
indirect	indicates that ὅτι introduces indirect discourse.
interrogative	indicates that ὅτι introduces an interrogative construction.
it	with various superscript letters indicates manuscripts of the Itala or Old Latin (see p. xxvi).
Jer	*Le Nouveau Testament* . . . de l'École Biblique de Jérusalem (1958).
^{lat}	the Latin version of a Greek Church Father.
l	a lectionary, identified by the superscript number following it.
l^m	a lectionary in its Menologion (see p. xxv).
l^s	a lectionary in its Synaxarion (see p. xxv).
l^{pt}	an individual lectionary which contains a passage two or more times with readings differing from each other, hence listed as supporting a reading in "part".

Lect   the reading of the majority of lectionaries in the Synaxarion and in the Menologion, when these agree (see p. xxv).

Lect^m   the Menologion readings when these differ from the Synaxarion or appear only in the Menologion (see p. xxv).

Luth   *Das Neue Testament,* nach der Übersetzung Martin Luthers, Revidierter Text (1956).

LXX   The Septuagint or Greek translation of the Old Testament.

^m   a lectionary in its Menologion (see p. xxv).

major   a major break or transition in the punctuation of a given passage.

minor   a minor break or transition in the punctuation of a given passage.

^{mg}   textual evidence contained in the margin of a manuscript. In the punctuation apparatus, ^{mg} indicates a marginal reading of a modern translation.

^{mg1,2}   successive alternatives in the margin of a translation.

^{ms, mss}   manuscript(s) of an ancient version, or of the writings of a Church Father, when different from the edited text.

NEB   *The New English Bible, New Testament* (1961).

Nes   Nestle-Aland, *Novum Testamentum Graece* (25th ed., 1963).

none   no break or transition in the punctuation of a given passage.

nub   Nubian version.

Old German   Old High German version.

p   indicates that a manuscript in the Gregory-Aland list contains all or part of the Epistles of Paul.

p^{1, etc.}   a papyrus, identified by the superscript number following it.

paragraph	a paragraph break or transition in contrast with a full sentence break.
parens	parenthesis marks are used to enclose explanatory or supplementary material in the Greek text. They are used with manuscripts, ancient versions or modern translations, to indicate similarity but not identity of readings.
pers	Persian version.
Provençal	Provencal version.
r	indicates that a manuscript in the Gregory-Aland list contains all or part of the text of Revelation.
RSV	Revised Standard Version of the New Testament (1946).
RV	Revised or English Revised Version of the New Testament (1881).
^{s}	a lectionary in its Synaxarion (see p. xxv).
Seg	Segond, *Le Nouveau Testament* (1962).
sic	an abnormality exactly reproduced from the original.
slav	Slavonic version.
supp	a portion of a manuscript supplied by a later hand where the original is missing.
syr^c	Curetonian Syriac version.
syr^h	Harclean Syriac version.
syr^{hgr}	a Greek marginal reading in the Harclean Syriac version.
syr^{hmg}	a marginal reading in the Harclean Syriac version.
syr^h with *	asterisks in the Harclean Syriac text indicating a different reading.
syr^p	Peshitta Syriac version.
syr^{pal}	Palestinian Syriac version.
syr^s	Sinaitic Syriac version.
Theodotion	Theodotion's text of the Greek Old Testament.
TR	Textus Receptus (Oxford, 1873).

TT *The New Testament: A Translation for Translators* (1966).

txt the text of a manuscript of the New Testament or of a Church Father when it differs from another reading given in the commentary section which accompanies the text.

vg Vulgate version.

vg^{cl} the Clementine edition of the Vulgate when it differs from the Wordsworth-White edition.

vg^{ww} the Wordsworth-White edition of the Vulgate when it differs from the Clementine edition.

vg^{ww with [ ]} the Wordsworth-White edition prints the word(s) in square brackets to indicate dubious textual validity.

vid indicates apparent support for a given reading in a manuscript whose state of preservation makes complete verification impossible.

WH Westcott and Hort, *The New Testament in the Original Greek* (1881).

Zür *Die Heilige Schrift* (Zürich, 1942).

BIBLIOGRAPHY

Aland, Kurt, *Kurzgefasste Liste der Griechischen Handschriften des Neuen Testaments: I. Gesamtübersicht*. Berlin: Walter de Gruyter und Co., 1963.

Altaner, Berthold, *Patrology*. Translated from the 5th German edition by Hilda C. Graef. Freiburg: Herder; London and Edinburgh: Nelson, 1960.

Bauer, Walter, *Griechisch-Deutsches Wörterbuch zu den Schriften des Neuen Testaments und der übrigen urchristlichen Literatur*. 5th edition. Berlin: Verlag Alfred Töpelmann, 1958. Translated and adapted into English from the 4th German edition by William F. Arndt and F. W. Gingrich. Cambridge University Press and University of Chicago Press, 1957.

Belsheim, Johannes, *Die Apostelgeschichte und die Offenbarung Johannis in einer alten lateinischen Übersetzung aus dem "Gigas librorum" auf der königlichen Bibliothek zu Stockholm*. Christiania, 1879. [it^gig]

———, *Epistulae Paulinae ante Hieronymum Latine translatae ex Codice Sangermanensi*. Christiania, 1885–1887. [E, it^e]

———, *Fragmenta Novi Testamenti in translatione Latina antehieronymiana ex libro qui vocatur Speculum eruit et ordine librorum Novi Testamenti exposuit*. (Skriften udg. af Videnskabsselskabet i Christiania, Hist.-filos. Kl., 1899, nr. ii.) Christiania, 1899. [it^m]

Bensly, R. L., *The Harklean Version of the Epistle to the Hebrews, Chap. XI:28—XIII:25*. Cambridge, 1889. [syr^h]

Beuron, see Vetus Latina.

B.F.B.S., see *The New Testament in Syriac*.

Black, Matthew ed., *A Christian Palestinian Syriac Horologion* (Berlin Ms. Or. Oct. 1019). Cambridge, 1954. [syr^pal]

Blake, Robert P., *The Old Georgian Version of the Gospel of Mark from the Adysh Gospels with the variants of the Opiza and T'bet' Gospels, edited with a Latin translation*. (Patrologia Orientalis, Vol. 20, fasc. 3.) Paris, 1929.

———, *The Old Georgian Version of the Gospel of Matthew from the Adysh Gospels with the variants of the Opiza and the T'bet' Gospels, edited with a Latin translation*. (Patrologia Orientalis, Vol. 24, fasc. 1.) Paris, 1933.

———, and Brière, Maurice, *The Old Georgian Version of the Gospel of*

*John and the Adysh Gospels with the variants of the Opiza and Tbet'
Gospels, edited with a Latin translation.* (Patrologia Orientalis, Vol. 26,
fasc. 4.) Paris, 1950.

Bover, José M., *Novi Testamenti Biblia Graeca et Latina.* 4th edition.
Madrid, 1959.

Brière, Maurice, *La version géorgienne ancienne de l'Évangile de Luc,
d'après les Évangiles d'Adich, avec les variantes des Évangiles d'Opiza et
de Tbet'; éditée avec une traduction latine.* (Patrologia Orientalis,
Vol. 27, fasc. 3.) Paris, 1955.

de Bruyne, Donatien, *Les Fragments de Freising—épîtres de S. Paul et
épîtres catholiques.* (Collectanea Biblica Latina, 5.) Rome, 1921. [it^{r3}]

Buchanan, Edgar S., *The Epistles and Apocalypse from the Codex Harleianus.*
(Sacred Latin Texts, 1.) London, 1912. [it^z]

————, *The Four Gospels from the Codex Corbeiensis, together with fragments
of the Catholic Epistles, of the Acts and of the Apocalypse from the
Fleury Palimpsest.* (Old Latin Biblical Texts, 5.) Oxford, 1907. [it^{ff2,h}]

Burkitt, Francis C., *Evangelion da-Mepharreshê. The Curetonian Version
of the Four Gospels, with the Readings of the Sinai Palimpsest and the
early Syriac Patristic Evidence.* 2 volumes. Cambridge, 1904. [syr^c]

Cureton, William, *Remains of a Very Antient Recension of the Four Gospels
in Syriac.* London, 1858. [syr^c]

The Ethiopic New Testament, edited by Petrus Ethyops *et al.* Rome,
1548–1549. [eth^{ro}]

Fischer, Bonifatius, "Ein neuer Zeuge zum westlichen Text der Apostel-
geschichte," in *Biblical and Patristic Studies in Memory of Robert
Pierce Casey*, edited by J. N. Birdsall and R. W. Thomson (pp. 33–63).
Freiburg: Herder, 1963. [it^1]

Frede, H. J., *Altlateinische Paulus-Handschriften.* Freiburg: Herder, 1964.
[it^{mon}]

Garitte, Gerard, *L'ancienne version géorgienne des Actes des Apôtres;
d'après deux manuscrits de Sinaï.* (Bibl. du Muséon, 38.) Louvain, 1955.

Gregory, C. R., *Prolegomena.* See Tischendorf.

Griffith, Francis L., *The Nubian Texts of the Christian Period.* (Abhand-
lungen der königl. preuss. Akademie der Wissenschaften, phil.-hist.
Classe, 1913, Nr. 8.) Berlin, 1913.

Gwilliam, G. H., *The Palestinian Version of the Holy Scriptures, Five More
Fragments.* (Anecdota Oxoniensia.) Oxford: The Bodleian Library,
1893. [syr^{pal}]

Gwynn, John, *The Apocalypse of St. John in a Syriac Version Hitherto
Unknown.* Dublin and London, 1897. [syr^{ph}]

Gwynn, John, *Liber Ardmachanus: The Book of Armagh*. Dublin, 1913. [it^ar]

————, *Remnants of the Later Syriac Versions of the Bible. The Four Minor Catholic Epistles in the Original Philoxenian Version*. London and Oxford, 1909. [syr^ph]

Harris, J. Rendel, *Biblical Fragments from Mount Sinai*. London, 1890. [syr^pal]

Die Heilige Schrift des Alten und des Neuen Testaments. Zürich: Verlag der Zwingli-Bibel, 1942.

The Holy Bible, Revised Version. Oxford University Press and Cambridge University Press, 1885.

The Holy Bible, American Standard Version. New York: Thomas Nelson and Sons, 1901.

[Horner, George,] *The Coptic Version of the New Testament in the Northern Dialect otherwise called Memphitic and Bohairic*. 4 volumes. Oxford: The Clarendon Press, 1898–1905. [cop^bo]

————, *The Coptic Version of the New Testament in the Southern Dialect otherwise called Sahidic and Thebaic*. 7 volumes. Oxford: The Clarendon Press, 1911–1922. [cop^sa]

Hoskier, H. C., *Concerning the Text of the Apocalypse*. 2 volumes. London: Bernard Quaritch, 1929.

Husselman, Elinor M., *The Gospel of John in Fayumic Coptic*. (The University of Michigan, Kelsey Museum of Archaeology, Studies 2.) Ann Arbor: Kelsey Museum of Archaeology, 1962. [cop^fav]

Jülicher, Adolf; Matzkow, Walter; Aland, Kurt, *Itala: Das Neue Testament in altlateinischer Überlieferung*. 4 volumes [Matthew—John]. Berlin: Walter de Gruyter und Co., 1938–1963.

Η ΚΑΙΝΗ ΔΙΑΘΗΚΗ. 2nd edition with revised critical apparatus. London: British and Foreign Bible Society, 1958.

Kasser, Rodolphe, *Papyrus Bodmer III: Évangile de Jean et Genèse I–IV,2 en bohaïrique*. (Corpus Scriptorum Christianorum Orientalium, Vols. 177, 178. Scriptores Coptici, Tomi 25, 26.) Louvain: Secrétariat du Corpus SCO, 1960. [cop^bo]

————, *Papyrus Bodmer XIX: Évangile de Matthieu XIV,28—XXVIII,20, Épître aux Romains I,1—II,3 en sahidique*. (Bibliotheca Bodmeriana.) Cologny-Genève, 1962. [cop^sa]

Lake, Kirsopp, *Codex 1 of the Gospels and Its Allies*. (Texts and Studies, Vol. VII, No. 3.) Cambridge, 1902. [f^1]

————; Lake, Silva; Geerlings, Jacob, *Family 13 (The Ferrar Group)*. 4 volumes [Matthew—John]. (Studies and Documents, XI, XIX, XX, XXI.) [Mark =] London: Christophers, and University of

Pennsylvania Press, 1941. [Matthew, Luke, and John =] Salt Lake City, Utah: University of Utah Press, 1961–1962. [*f*¹³]

Land, J. P. N., *Anecdota syriaca.* (Lugduni Batavorum, Tomus IV.) Leiden: E. J. Brill, 1875. [syr^{pal}]

Lefort, L. Th., "Fragments bibliques en dialecte akhmîmique," *Le Muséon*, Vol. 66 (1953), pp. 1–30.

———, "Fragments de S. Luc en akhmîmique," *Le Muséon*, Vol. 62 (1949), pp. 199–205.

Legg, S. C. E., *Novum Testamentum Graece secundum Textum Westcotto-Hortianum. Evangelium secundum Marcum.* Oxford: The Clarendon Press, 1935.

———, *Novum Testamentum Graece secundum Textum Westcotto-Hortianum, Evangelium secundum Matthaeum.* Oxford: The Clarendon Press, 1940.

Lewis, Agnes Smith, *Catalogue of the Syriac MSS in the Convent of St. Catharine on Mount Sinai.* (Studia Sinaitica, I.) London, 1894. [syr^{pal}]

———, *Codex Climaci rescriptus:* fragments of sixth century Palestinian Syriac texts of the Gospels, of the Acts of the Apostles and of St. Paul's Epistles. Also fragments of an early Palestinian lectionary of the Old Testament. (Horae Semiticae, 8.) Cambridge, 1909. [syr^{pal}]

———, *The Old Syriac Gospels, or, Evangelion da-Mepharreshê*; being the text of the Sinai or Syro-Antiochene Palimpsest, including the latest additions and emendations, with the variants of the Curetonian text, corroborations from many other MSS., and a list of quotations from ancient authors. London, 1910. [syr^s]

———, and Gibson, Margaret Dunlop, *Palestinian Syriac Texts. From Palimpsest Fragments in the Taylor-Schechter Collection.* London, 1900. [syr^{pal}]

———, and Gibson, Margaret Dunlop, *The Palestinian Syriac Lectionary of the Gospels.* London, 1899. [syr^{pal}]

———; Nestle, Eberhard; Gibson, Margaret Dunlop, *A Palestinian Syriac Lectionary, containing lessons from the Pentateuch, Job, Proverbs, Prophets, Acts and Epistles.* London, 1897. [syr^{pal}]

Luther, Martin, *Das Neue Testament unseres Herrn und Heilandes Jesus Christ.* Revidierter Text. Stuttgart: Württembergische Bibelanstalt, 1956.

Margoliouth, G., *The Liturgy of the Nile.* Reprinted from the *Journal of the Royal Asiatic Society*, 1896, pp. 677–727. London, 1896. [syr^{pal}]

Matthaei, C. F., *Novum Testamentum, XII, tomis distinctum Graece et Latine.* Textum denuo recensuit, varias lectiones nunquam antea vulgatas ex centum codicibus MSS. . . . 12 volumes. Rigae, 1782–1788. [it^{dem}]

Matthaei, C. F., *XIII. Epistolarum Pauli Codex Graecus cum versione Latina veteri vulgo Antehieronymiana olim Boernerianus nunc Bibliothecae Electoralis Dresdensis...* Lipsiae, 1791. [it^g]

Merk, Augustinus, *Novum Testamentum Graece et Latine.* 9th edition. Rome: Pontifical Biblical Institute, 1964.

Morin, Germain, *Études, textes, découvertes.* Contributions à la littérature et à l'histoire des douze premiers siècles. Volume 1. (Anecdota Maredsolana, 2e Série.) Paris: Abbaye de Maredsous, 1913. [it^{rl}]

————, *Liber Comicus sive Lectionarius missae quo Toletana Ecclesia ante annos mille et ducentos utebatur.* (Anecdota Maredsolana, 1.) Maredsoli, 1893. [it^t]

Nestle, Eberhard; Nestle, Erwin; Aland, Kurt, *Novum Testamentum Graece.* 25th edition. Stuttgart: Württembergische Bibelanstalt; New York: American Bible Society, 1963.

Das Neue Testament unseres Herrn und Heilandes Jesus Christ, nach der Deutschen Übersetzung D. Martin Luthers. Revidierter Text. Stuttgart: Württembergische Bibelanstalt, 1956.

The New English Bible New Testament. Oxford University Press and Cambridge University Press, 1961.

The New Testament. Revised Standard Version and King James Version in Parallel Columns. New York: Thomas Nelson and Sons, [1961?].

The New Testament: A Translation for Translators. London: British and Foreign Bible Society, 1966.

The New Testament in Syriac. London: British and Foreign Bible Society, 1905–1920. [syr^p]

Le Nouveau Testament, traduit en français sous la direction de l'École Biblique de Jérusalem Paris: les Éditions du Cerf, 1958.

Perrot, Ch., "Un fragment christo-palestinien découvert à Khirbet Mird, Actes des Apôtres x:28–29; 32–41," *Revue biblique*, 70 (1963), pp. 506–555. [syr^{pal}]

Platt, T. Pell, *The Ethiopic New Testament.* London, 1826. Revised by F. Praetorius. Leipzig, 1899. [eth^{pp}]

Pusey, Philip E., and Gwilliam, G. H., *Tetraevangelium Sanctum juxta simplicem Syrorum versionem ad fidem codicum, Massorae, editionum denue recognitum.* Oxford: The Clarendon Press, 1901. [syr^p]

Rome, see *The Ethiopic New Testament.*

Sanders, H. A., *The Text of Acts in Ms. 146 of the University of Michigan·* (Proceedings of the American Philosophical Society, 77, 1.) Philadelphia, 1937. [it^{ph}]

Schmid, Josef, *Studien zur Geschichte des griechischen Apokalypse-Textes.*

3 volumes. (Münchener Theologische Studien.) München: Karl Zink Verlag, 1955–1956.

Schulthess, Fridericus, *Lexicon Syropalaestinum*. Berlin, 1903. Lists Palestinian Syriac manuscripts and fragments.

Schultze, V., *Codex Waldeccensis*. München, 1904. [it^w]

Scrivener, F. H. [A.], *An Exact Transcript of the Codex Augiensis*. Cambridge and London, 1859. [it^f]

Segond, Louis, *Le Nouveau Testament*. Nouvelle Revision. Paris: Société Biblique Française, 1962.

Soden, Hermann von, *Die Schriften des Neuen Testaments in ihrer ältesten erreichbaren Textgestalt*. 4 volumes. Teil 1, Abteilung 1–3, Berlin: Verlag von Alexander Duncker, 1902–1910; Teil 2, *Text mit Apparat*, Göttingen: Vandenhoeck und Ruprecht, 1913.

Souter, A., *Miscellanea Ehrle 1*. (*Studi e Testi* 137.) Rome, 1924. [it^v]

——, *Nouum Testamentum Graece*, editio altera penitus reformata. Oxonii: E Typographeo Clarendoniano, 1947.

Streitberg, William, *Die gotische Bibel*. 2nd edition, 2 volumes. (Germanische Bibliothek, II, 3.) Heidelberg, 1919; reprinted, 1950.

Thompson, Herbert, *The Coptic Version of the Acts of the Apostles and the Pauline Epistles in the Sahidic Dialect*. Cambridge, 1932. [cop^sa]

——, *The Gospel of St. John According to the Earliest Coptic Manuscript*. London: British School of Archaeology, 1924 [cop^ach, ach2]

Till, W. C., in *Bulletin of the John Rylands Library*, 42 (1959), pp. 220–240. List of cop^fay manuscripts and fragments.

Tischendorf, Constantinus, *Anecdota Sacra et Profana*. Editio repetita, emendata, aucta. Lipsiae, 1861. [it^gue]

——, *Codex Claromontanus*. Lipsiae, 1852. [it^d]

——, *Codex Laudianus, sive Actus apostolorum Graece et Latine*. (Monumenta sacra inedita, nova collectio, vol. 9.) Lipsiae, 1870. [it^e]

——, *Novum Testamentum Graece*. Editio octava critica maior, 2 volumes. Leipzig, 1869–1872. Volume 3, *Prolegomena*, edited by C. R. Gregory. Leipzig, 1894.

Vaschalde, A., in *Revue biblique*, N.S., 16 (1919), pp. 220–43, 513–31; 29 (1920), pp. 91–106, 241–58; 30 (1921), pp. 237–46; 31 (1922), pp. 81–88, 234–58; in *Le Muséon*, 43 (1930), pp. 409–31; 45 (1932), pp. 117–56; 46 (1933), pp. 299–313. Lists of cop^fay manuscripts and fragments.

Vetus Latina: Die Reste der Altlateinischen Bibel, nach Petrus Sabatier neu gesammelt und herausgegeben von der Erzabtei Beuron. 1, *Verzeichnis der Sigel für Handschriften und Kirchenschriftsteller*, Freiburg: Herder, 1949; *Verzeichnis der Sigel für Kirchenschriftsteller*, 2te Aufl., 1963.

24/1, *Epistula ad Ephesios*, 1962–1964. 26, *Epistulae Catholicae, Apocalypsis*; 1–3 Lieferung, Jac—2 Pt., 1956–1960.

Vogels, Henr. J., *Novum Testamentum Graece et Latine*. 4th edition. Freiburg im Breisgau and Barcelona: Herder, 1955.

Westcott, Brooke Foss, and Hort, Fenton John Anthony, *The New Testament in the Original Greek*. Volume 1, *Text*; volume 2, *Introduction [and] Appendix*. Cambridge and London: Macmillan and Company, 1881; 2nd edition of volume 2, 1896.

White, Henry J., *Portions of the Acts of the Apostles, of the Epistles of St. James, and of the First Epistle of St. Peter from the Bobbio Palimpsest*. (Old Latin Biblical Texts, 4.) Oxford: The Clarendon Press, 1897. [it[s]]

White, Joseph, *Actuum Apostolorum et Epistolarum tam catholicarum quam Paulinarum versio Syriaca Philoxeniana*. 2 volumes. Oxford, 1799–1803. [syr[h]]

———, *Sacrorum Evangeliorum versio Syriaca Philoxeniana*. 2 volumes. Oxford, 1778. [syr[h]]

Wordsworth, John, and White, Henry J., *et al.*, *Novum Testamentum Domini Nostri Iesu Christi Latine Secundum Editionem Sancti Hieronymi*. 3 volumes. Oxford: The Clarendon Press, 1889–1954.

Zohrab, J., *The Holy Bible* (Armenian). Venice: Convent of San Lazzaro, 1805.

Zürich, see *Die Heilige Schrift*.

ΚΑΤΑ ΜΑΘΘΑΙΟΝ

The Genealogy of Jesus Christ
(Lk 3.23–38)

1 Βίβλος γενέσεως Ἰησοῦ Χριστοῦ υἱοῦ Δαυὶδ υἱοῦ Ἀβραάμ.

2 Ἀβραὰμ ἐγέννησεν τὸν Ἰσαάκ, Ἰσαὰκ δὲ ἐγέννησεν τὸν Ἰακώβ, Ἰακὼβ δὲ ἐγέννησεν τὸν Ἰούδαν καὶ τοὺς ἀδελφοὺς αὐτοῦ, **3** Ἰούδας δὲ ἐγέννησεν τὸν Φάρες καὶ τὸν Ζάρα ἐκ τῆς Θαμάρ, Φάρες δὲ ἐγέννησεν τὸν Ἐσρώμ, Ἐσρὼμ δὲ ἐγέννησεν τὸν Ἀράμ, **4** Ἀρὰμ δὲ ἐγέννησεν τὸν Ἀμιναδάβ, Ἀμιναδὰβ δὲ ἐγέννησεν τὸν Ναασσών, Ναασσὼν δὲ ἐγέννησεν τὸν Σαλμών, **5** Σαλμὼν δὲ ἐγέννησεν τὸν Βόες ἐκ τῆς Ῥαχάβ, Βόες δὲ ἐγέννησεν τὸν Ἰωβὴδ ἐκ τῆς Ῥούθ, Ἰωβὴδ δὲ ἐγέννησεν τὸν Ἰεσσαί, **6** Ἰεσσαὶ δὲ ἐγέννησεν τὸν Δαυὶδ τὸν βασιλέα.

Δαυὶδ δὲ ἐγέννησεν τὸν Σολομῶνα ἐκ τῆς τοῦ Οὐρίου, **7** Σολομὼν δὲ ἐγέννησεν τὸν Ῥοβοάμ, Ῥοβοὰμ δὲ ἐγέννησεν τὸν Ἀβιά, Ἀβιὰ δὲ ἐγέννησεν τὸν Ἀσάφ,[1] **8** Ἀσὰφ δὲ ἐγέννησεν τὸν Ἰωσαφάτ, Ἰωσαφὰτ δὲ ἐγέννησεν τὸν Ἰωράμ, Ἰωρὰμ δὲ ἐγέννησεν τὸν Ὀζίαν, **9** Ὀζίας δὲ ἐγέννησεν τὸν Ἰωαθάμ, Ἰωαθὰμ δὲ ἐγέννησεν τὸν Ἀχάζ, Ἀχὰζ δὲ ἐγέννησεν τὸν Ἐζεκίαν, **10** Ἐζεκίας δὲ ἐγέννησεν τὸν Μανασσῆ, Μανασσῆς δὲ ἐγέννησεν τὸν Ἀμώς, Ἀμὼς[2] δὲ ἐγέννησεν τὸν Ἰωσίαν, **11** Ἰωσίας δὲ ἐγέννη-

---

[1] **7–8** {B} Ἀσάφ, Ἀσάφ 𝔭[vid] ℵ B C (D[Luke]) *f*[1] *f*[13] 700 1071 *l*[185m pt] it[aur,c,dLuke,g1,k,q] syr[hmg] cop[sa,bo] arm eth geo (Epiphanius) ‖ Ἀσά, Ἀσά K L W Δ Π 28 33 565 892 1009 1010 1079 1195 1216 1230 1241 1242 1365 1546 (2148 Ἀσσά) *Byz Lect*[m] *l*[185m pt] it[a,f,ff1] vg syr[c,s,p,h,pal] Epiphanius Augustine

[2] **10** {B} Ἀμώς, Ἀμώς ℵ B C D[Luke] Δ Θ Π* *f*[1] 33 1071 1079 1546 *l*[1627m] it[c,dLuke,ff1,g1,k,q] cop[sa,bo,fay] arm eth Athanasius Epiphanius ‖ Ἀμών, Ἀμών K L W Π[2] *f*[13] 28 565 (700 892 1195 Ἀμμών, Ἀμμών) 1009 1010 1216

---

1 Βίβλος γενέσεως Gn 5.1 υἱοῦ Δαυίδ 1 Chr 17.11 υἱοῦ Ἀβραάμ Gn 22.18   **2** Gn 21.3 12; 25.26; 29.35; 1 Chr 1.34   **3** Gn 38.29–30; 1 Chr 2.4, 5, 9; Ru 4.12, 18–19   **4–5** Ru 4.13, 17–22; 1 Chr 2.10–12   **6** Ἰεσσαί...βασιλέα Ru 4.17, 22; 1 Chr 2.13–15 Δαυίδ...Οὐρίου 2 Sm 12.24   **7–10** 1 Chr 3.10–14   **11** Ἰωσίας...αὐτοῦ 1 Chr 3.15–16; 1 Esd 1.32 LXX

1

THE GOSPEL OF MATTHEW

The Birth Record of Jesus Christ
(Also Luke 3.23–38)

1 This is the birth record of Jesus Christ, who was a descendant of David, who was a descendant of Abraham.

² Abraham was the father of Isaac; Isaac was the father of Jacob; Jacob was the father of Judah and his brothers; ³ Judah was the father of Perez and Zerah (their mother was Tamar); Perez was the father of Hezron; Hezron was the father of Ram; ⁴ Ram was the father of Amminadab; Amminadab was the father of Nahshon; Nahshon was the father of Salmon; ⁵ Salmon was the father of Boaz (Rahab was his mother); Boaz was the father of Obed (Ruth was his mother); Obed was the father of Jesse; ⁶ Jesse was the father of King David.

David was the father of Solomon (his mother had been Uriah's wife); ⁷ Solomon was the father of Rehoboam; Rehoboam was the father of Abijah; Abijah was the father of Asa; ⁸ Asa was the father of Jehoshaphat; Jehoshaphat was the father of Joram; Joram was the father of Uzziah; ⁹ Uzziah was the father of Jotham; Jotham was the father of Ahaz; Ahaz was the father of Hezekiah; ¹⁰ Hezekiah was the father of Manasseh; Manasseh was the father of Amon; Amon was the father of Josiah; ¹¹ Josiah was

1

the father of Jechoniah and his brothers, at the time when the people of Israel were carried away to Babylon.

12 After the people were carried away to Babylon: Jechoniah was the father of Shealtiel; Shealtiel was the father of Zerubbabel; 13 Zerubbabel was the father of Abiud; Abiud was the father of Eliakim; Eliakim was the father of Azor; 14 Azor was the father of Zadok; Zadok was the father of Achim; Achim was the father of Eliud; 15 Eliud was the father of Eleazar; Eleazar was the father of Matthan; Matthan was the father of Jacob; 16 Jacob was the father of Joseph, the husband of Mary, who was the mother of Jesus, called the Messiah.

17 So then, there were fourteen sets of fathers and sons from Abraham to David, and fourteen from David to the time when the people were carried away to Babylon, and fourteen from then to the birth of the Messiah.

σεν³ τὸν Ἰεχονίαν καὶ τοὺς ἀδελφοὺς αὐτοῦ ἐπὶ τῆς μετοικεσίας Βαβυλῶνος.

12 Μετὰ δὲ τὴν μετοικεσίαν Βαβυλῶνος Ἰεχονίας ἐγέννησεν τὸν Σαλαθιήλ, Σαλαθιὴλ δὲ ἐγέννησεν τὸν Ζοροβαβέλ, 13 Ζοροβαβὲλ δὲ ἐγέννησεν τὸν Ἀβιούδ, Ἀβιοὺδ δὲ ἐγέννησεν τὸν Ἐλιακίμ, Ἐλιακὶμ δὲ ἐγέννησεν τὸν Ἀζώρ, 14 Ἀζὼρ δὲ ἐγέννησεν τὸν Σαδώκ, Σαδὼκ δὲ ἐγέννησεν τὸν Ἀχίμ, Ἀχὶμ δὲ ἐγέννησεν τὸν Ἐλιούδ, 15 Ἐλιοὺδ δὲ ἐγέννησεν τὸν Ἐλεάζαρ, Ἐλεάζαρ δὲ ἐγέννησεν τὸν Ματθάν, Ματθὰν δὲ ἐγέννησεν τὸν Ἰακώβ, 16 Ἰακὼβ δὲ ἐγέννησεν τὸν Ἰωσὴφ τὸν ἄνδρα Μαρίας, ἐξ ἧς ἐγεννήθη Ἰησοῦς ὁ λεγόμενος Χριστός⁴.

17 Πᾶσαι οὖν αἱ γενεαὶ ἀπὸ Ἀβραὰμ ἕως Δαυὶδ γενεαὶ δεκατέσσαρες, καὶ ἀπὸ Δαυὶδ ἕως τῆς μετοικεσίας Βαβυλῶνος γενεαὶ δεκατέσσαρες, καὶ ἀπὸ τῆς μετοικεσίας Βαβυλῶνος ἕως τοῦ Χριστοῦ γενεαὶ δεκατέσσαρες.

1230 1241 1242 1365 1646 2148 *Byz Lect*ᵐ (*l*²¹¹ itᵃᵘʳ,ᶠ Ἀμμών, Ἀμμών) itᵃ vg syrᶜ,ˢ,ᵖ,ʰ,ᵖᵃˡ geo

³ 11 {B} ἐγέννησεν ℵ B C K L W Δ Π *f*¹³ 28 565 700 892 1009 1010 1071 1079 1195 1241 1242 1365 1546 1646 2148 *Byz Lect l*⁷⁰ᵐ,¹⁸⁵ᵐ,³³³ᵐ,⁸⁸³ᵐ itᵃ,ᵃᵘʳ,ᶜ,ᶠ,ff¹,g¹,ᵏ, q vg syrᶜ,ˢ,ᵖ copˢᵃ,ᵇᵒ,ᶠᵃʸ arm eth Eusebius Jerome ‖ ἐγέννησεν τὸν Ἰωακείμ, Ἰωακεὶμ δὲ ἐγέννησεν (Dᴸᵘᵏᵉ itᵈᴸᵘᵏᵉ Ἐλιακείμ, Ἰωακείμ) Θ *f*¹ 33 1216 1230 *l*⁵⁴ syrʰ ʷⁱᵗʰ *,ᵖᵃˡ geo Diatessaron Irenaeusˡᵃᵗ Africanus Eusebius Aphraates Epiphanius

⁴ 16 {B} τὸν ἄνδρα Μαρίας, ἐξ ἧς ἐγεννήθη Ἰησοῦς ὁ λεγόμενος Χριστός 𝔭¹ ℵ B C K L P W (Δ *omit* τόν) Π (*f*¹ *omit* Ἰησοῦς) 28 33 565 700 892 1009 1010 1071 1079 1195 1216 1230 1241 1242 1365 1546 1646 2148 2174 *Byz Lect*ᵐ *l*⁷⁶,²¹¹ itᵃᵘʳ,ᶠ,ff¹ vg syrᵖ,ʰ,ᵖᵃˡ copˢᵃ ethᵐˢ* (ethʳᵒ,ᵖᵖ *the bridegroom of Mary,*) geo Tertullian Augustine ‖ ᾧ μνηστευθεῖσα παρθένος Μαριὰμ ἐγέννησεν Ἰησοῦν τὸν λεγόμενον Χριστόν Θ *f*¹³ *l*⁵⁴⁷ᵐ itᵃ,(ᵇ),ᶜ,ᵈ,ᵍˡ,(ᵏ),q Ambrosiaster ‖ *Joseph to whom was betrothed Mary the virgin, begot Jesus who is called the Christ* syrˢ (Barsalibi) ‖ *to whom was betrothed Mary the virgin, she who bare Jesus the Christ* syrᶜ ‖ *the husband of Mary, who bare Jesus who is called Christ* copᵇᵒ ‖ *the husband of Mary, to whom was betrothed Mary the virgin, from whom was born Jesus who was called Christ* arm

---

11 μετοικεσίας Βαβυλῶνος 2 Kgs 24.12–16; 2 Chr 36.10; Jr 27.20   12 Ἰεχονίας... Ζοροβαβὲλ 1 Chr 3.17, 19; Ezr 3.2   16 Ἰησοῦς...Χριστός Mt 27.17, 22

The Birth of Jesus Christ
(Lk 2.1–7)

18 Τοῦ δὲ Ἰησοῦ Χριστοῦ[5] ἡ γένεσις[6] οὕτως ἦν. μνη-στευθείσης τῆς μητρὸς αὐτοῦ Μαρίας τῷ Ἰωσήφ, πρὶν ἢ συνελθεῖν αὐτοὺς εὑρέθη ἐν γαστρὶ ἔχουσα ἐκ πνεύματος ἁγίου. 19 Ἰωσὴφ δὲ ὁ ἀνὴρ αὐτῆς, δίκαιος ὢν καὶ μὴ θέλων αὐτὴν δειγματίσαι, ἐβουλήθη λάθρᾳ ἀπολῦσαι αὐ-τήν. 20 ταῦτα δὲ αὐτοῦ ἐνθυμηθέντος ἰδοὺ ἄγγελος κυρίου κατ' ὄναρ ἐφάνη αὐτῷ λέγων, Ἰωσὴφ υἱὸς Δαυίδ, μὴ φοβηθῇς παραλαβεῖν Μαριὰμ τὴν γυναῖκά σου, τὸ γὰρ ἐν αὐτῇ γεννηθὲν ἐκ πνεύματός ἐστιν ἁγίου· 21 τέξεται δὲ υἱὸν καὶ καλέσεις τὸ ὄνομα αὐτοῦ Ἰησοῦν, αὐτὸς γὰρ σώσει τὸν λαὸν αὐτοῦ ἀπὸ τῶν ἁμαρτιῶν αὐτῶν. 22 Τοῦτο δὲ ὅλον γέγονεν ἵνα πληρωθῇ τὸ ῥηθὲν ὑπὸ κυρίου διὰ τοῦ προφήτου λέγοντος,

23 Ἰδοὺ ἡ παρθένος ἐν γαστρὶ ἕξει καὶ τέξεται υἱόν,
    καὶ καλέσουσιν τὸ ὄνομα αὐτοῦ Ἐμμανουήλ,

ὅ ἐστιν μεθερμηνευόμενον Μεθ' ἡμῶν ὁ θεός. 24 ἐγερ-θεὶς δὲ [ὁ] Ἰωσὴφ ἀπὸ τοῦ ὕπνου ἐποίησεν ὡς προσέταξεν αὐτῷ ὁ ἄγγελος κυρίου καὶ παρέλαβεν τὴν γυναῖκα αὐτοῦ· 25 καὶ οὐκ ἐγίνωσκεν αὐτὴν ἕως οὗ ἔτεκεν υἱόν[7]· καὶ ἐκάλεσεν τὸ ὄνομα αὐτοῦ Ἰησοῦν.

---

[5] 18 {C} Ἰησοῦ Χριστοῦ 𝔭[1] ℵ C K L P Δ Θ Π f[1] f[13] 28 33 565 700 892 1009 1010 1071 1079 1195 1216 1230 1241 1242 1365 1546 1646 2148 2174 Byz Lect l[185m,333m,883m] syr[p,h,pal] cop[sa,bo] arm eth geo Diatessaron Irenaeus Origen Eusebius Didymus Epiphanius ‖ Χριστοῦ Ἰησοῦ B Origen[gr,lat] Jerome ‖ Ἰησοῦ W Maximus-Confessor ‖ Χριστοῦ it[a,aur,b,c,d,f,ff1,g1,k,q] vg syr[c,s] Theophilus Irenaeus[lat] Theodore Augustine Ps-Athanasius

[6] 18 {B} γένεσις 𝔭[1] ℵ B C P W Δ Θ f[1] syr[h,pal] cop[bo] arm eth? geo (Eusebius) Ps-Athanasius Maximus-Confessor ‖ γέννησις K L Π f[13] 28 33 565 700 892 1009 1010 1071 1079 1195 1216 1230 1241 1242 1365 1546 1646 2148 2174 Byz Lect l[70m,185m,333m,883m] it[a,aur,b,c,d,f,ff1,g1,k,q] vg syr[c,s,p] cop[sa] Diatessaron (Irenaeus) Origen Didymus (Epiphanius) (Augustine)

[7] 25 {A} υἱόν ℵ B 071[vid] f[1] f[13] 33 it[b,c,g1,k] syr[(c),pal mss] (cop[sa,bo]) geo

---

18 μνηστευθείσης...αὐτούς Lk 1.27 ἐν...ἁγίου Lk 1.35 21 τέξεται...Ἰησοῦν Mt 1.25; Lk 1.31; 2.21 αὐτὸς...αὐτῶν Ac 4.12 23 Ἰδοὺ...Ἐμμανουήλ Is 7.14 Μεθ'...θεός Is 8.8, 10 LXX 25 ἐκάλεσεν...Ἰησοῦν Mt 1.21; Lk 1.31; 2.21

The Birth of Jesus Christ
(Also Luke 2.1–7)

[18] This was the way that Jesus Christ was born. His mother Mary was engaged to Joseph, but before they were married she found out that she was going to have a baby by the Holy Spirit. [19] Joseph, to whom she was engaged, was a man who always did what was right; but he did not want to disgrace Mary publicly, so he made plans to break the engagement secretly. [20] While he was thinking about all this, an angel of the Lord appeared to him in a dream and said: "Joseph, descendant of David, do not be afraid to take Mary to be your wife. For it is by the Holy Spirit that she has conceived. [21] She will give birth to a son and you will name him Jesus — for he will save his people from their sins."

[22] Now all this happened in order to make come true what the Lord had said through the prophet: [23] "The virgin will become pregnant and give birth to a son, and he will be called Emmanuel" (which means, "God is with us").

[24] So when Joseph woke up he did what the angel of the Lord had told him to do and married Mary. [25] But he had no sexual relations with her before she gave birth to her son. And Joseph named him Jesus.

Visitors from the East

2 Jesus was born in the town of Bethlehem, in the land of Judea, during the
time when Herod was king. Soon after-
wards some men who studied the stars
came from the east to Jerusalem 2 and
asked: "Where is the baby born to be
the king of the Jews? We saw his star
when it came up in the east, and we have
come to worship him." 3 When King
Herod heard about this he was very
upset, and so was everybody else in
Jerusalem. 4 He called together all the
chief priests and the teachers of the
Law and asked them, "Where will the
Messiah be born?" 5 "In the town of
Bethlehem, in Judea," they answered.
"This is what the prophet wrote:
6 'You, Bethlehem, in the land of
Judah,
Are not by any means the least
among the rulers of Judah;
For from you will come a leader
Who will guide my people Israel.' "
7 So Herod called the visitors from the
east to a secret meeting and found out
from them the exact time the star had
appeared. 8 Then he sent them to Bethlehem with these instructions: "Go and
make a careful search for the child, and
when you find him let me know, so that
I may go and worship him too." 9 With
this they left, and on their way they saw
the star — the same one they had seen
in the east — and it went ahead of them
until it came and stopped over the place
where the child was. 10 How happy they
were, what gladness they felt, when they
saw the star! 11 They went into the house
and saw the child with his mother Mary.

The Visit of the Wise Men

2 *Τοῦ δὲ Ἰησοῦ γεννηθέντος ἐν Βηθλέεμ τῆς Ἰουδαίας*
ἐν ἡμέραις Ἡρῴδου τοῦ βασιλέως, ἰδοὺ μάγοι ἀπὸ ἀνα-
τολῶν παρεγένοντο εἰς Ἱεροσόλυμα 2[a] *λέγοντες,* [a]*Ποῦ*
ἐστιν ὁ τεχθεὶς βασιλεὺς τῶν Ἰουδαίων; εἴδομεν γὰρ αὐτοῦ
τὸν ἀστέρα ἐν τῇ ἀνατολῇ καὶ ἤλθομεν προσκυνῆσαι αὐτῷ.
3 *ἀκούσας δὲ ὁ βασιλεὺς Ἡρῴδης ἐταράχθη καὶ πᾶσα*
Ἱεροσόλυμα μετ' αὐτοῦ, 4 *καὶ συναγαγὼν πάντας τοὺς*
ἀρχιερεῖς καὶ γραμματεῖς τοῦ λαοῦ ἐπυνθάνετο παρ' αὐτῶν
ποῦ ὁ Χριστὸς γεννᾶται. 5 *οἱ δὲ εἶπαν αὐτῷ, Ἐν Βηθλέεμ*
τῆς Ἰουδαίας· οὕτως γὰρ γέγραπται διὰ τοῦ προφήτου·
6 **Καὶ σύ, Βηθλέεμ** *γῆ Ἰούδα,*
οὐδαμῶς **ἐλαχίστη εἶ ἐν τοῖς ἡγεμόσιν Ἰούδα·**
ἐκ σοῦ γὰρ ἐξελεύσεται ἡγούμενος,
ὅστις ποιμανεῖ τὸν λαόν μου τὸν Ἰσραήλ.
7 *Τότε Ἡρῴδης λάθρᾳ καλέσας τοὺς μάγους ἠκρίβωσεν*
παρ' αὐτῶν τὸν χρόνον τοῦ φαινομένου ἀστέρος, 8 *καὶ*
πέμψας αὐτοὺς εἰς Βηθλέεμ εἶπεν, Πορευθέντες ἐξετάσατε
ἀκριβῶς περὶ τοῦ παιδίου· ἐπὰν δὲ εὕρητε ἀπαγγείλατέ
μοι, ὅπως κἀγὼ ἐλθὼν προσκυνήσω αὐτῷ. 9 *οἱ δὲ ἀκού-*
σαντες τοῦ βασιλέως ἐπορεύθησαν, καὶ ἰδοὺ ὁ ἀστὴρ ὃν
εἶδον ἐν τῇ ἀνατολῇ προῆγεν αὐτοὺς ἕως ἐλθὼν ἐστάθη
ἐπάνω οὗ ἦν τὸ παιδίον. 10 *ἰδόντες δὲ τὸν ἀστέρα ἐχά-*
ρησαν χαρὰν μεγάλην σφόδρα. 11 *καὶ ἐλθόντες εἰς τὴν*
οἰκίαν εἶδον τὸ παιδίον μετὰ Μαρίας τῆς μητρὸς αὐτοῦ,

Ambrose // *αὐτῷ υἱόν* syr^{s} // *τὸν υἱὸν αὐτῆς τὸν πρωτότοκον* (*see* Lk 2.7) C D* (D^{c} L *omit* **αὐτῆς**) K W Δ Π 28 565 700 892 1009 1010 1071 1079 1195 1216 1230 1241 1242 1365 (1546 **υἱὸν αὐτοῖς**) 1646 2148 2174 *Byz Lect* $l^{70m,185m,333m,883m}$ it^{aur,f,ff1} (it^{d,q} *omit* **αὐτῆς**) vg syr$^{p,h,pal ms}$ arm eth nub Diatessaron Athanasius Epiphanius Augustine Jerome Ps-Athanasius

[a a] **1–2** *a* number 2, *a* no number: TR^{ed} WH? Bov Nes BF^{2} AV RV NEB TT Zür Jer Seg^{ed} // *a* no number, *a* number 2: TR^{ed} WH? ASV RSV Luth Seg^{ed}

1 Ἰησοῦ...Ἰουδαίας Lk 2.4–7 *ἡμέραις...βασιλέως* Lk 1.5; 3.1 **2** *τὸν ἀστέρα... ἀνατολῇ* Nu 24.17; Mt 2.9 **5** Βηθλέεμ Jn 7.42 **6** Mic 5.2 *ποιμανεῖ...*Ἰσραήλ 2 Sm 5.2; 1 Chr 11.2 **9** *ὁ ἀστὴρ...ἀνατολῇ* Mt 2.2 **11** *ἐλθόντες...αὐτοῦ* Lk 2.16

καὶ πεσόντες προσεκύνησαν αὐτῷ, καὶ ἀνοίξαντες τοὺς
θησαυροὺς αὐτῶν προσήνεγκαν αὐτῷ δῶρα, χρυσὸν καὶ
λίβανον καὶ σμύρναν. **12** καὶ χρηματισθέντες κατ’ ὄναρ
μὴ ἀνακάμψαι πρὸς Ἡρῴδην, δι’ ἄλλης ὁδοῦ ἀνεχώρησαν
εἰς τὴν χώραν αὐτῶν.

The Flight to Egypt

13 Ἀναχωρησάντων δὲ αὐτῶν ἰδοὺ ἄγγελος κυρίου φαίνεται κατ’ ὄναρ τῷ Ἰωσὴφ λέγων, Ἐγερθεὶς παράλαβε
τὸ παιδίον καὶ τὴν μητέρα αὐτοῦ καὶ φεῦγε εἰς Αἴγυπτον,
καὶ ἴσθι ἐκεῖ ἕως ἂν εἴπω σοι· μέλλει γὰρ Ἡρῴδης
ζητεῖν τὸ παιδίον τοῦ ἀπολέσαι αὐτό. **14** ὁ δὲ ἐγερθεὶς
παρέλαβεν τὸ παιδίον καὶ τὴν μητέρα αὐτοῦ νυκτὸς καὶ
ἀνεχώρησεν εἰς Αἴγυπτον, **15** καὶ ἦν ἐκεῖ ἕως τῆς τελευ-
τῆς Ἡρῴδου· ἵνα πληρωθῇ τὸ ῥηθὲν ὑπὸ κυρίου διὰ τοῦ
προφήτου λέγοντος, Ἐξ Αἰγύπτου ἐκάλεσα τὸν υἱόν μου.

The Slaying of the Infants

16 Τότε Ἡρῴδης ἰδὼν ὅτι ἐνεπαίχθη ὑπὸ τῶν μάγων
ἐθυμώθη λίαν, καὶ ἀποστείλας ἀνεῖλεν πάντας τοὺς παῖδας
τοὺς ἐν Βηθλέεμ καὶ ἐν πᾶσι τοῖς ὁρίοις αὐτῆς ἀπὸ διετοῦς
καὶ κατωτέρω, κατὰ τὸν χρόνον ὃν ἠκρίβωσεν παρὰ τῶν
μάγων. **17** τότε ἐπληρώθη τὸ ῥηθὲν διὰ Ἰερεμίου τοῦ
προφήτου λέγοντος,
18   **Φωνὴ ἐν Ῥαμὰ ἠκούσθη,**
      κλαυθμὸς[1] καὶ ὀδυρμὸς πολύς·
   Ῥαχὴλ κλαίουσα τὰ τέκνα αὐτῆς,
      καὶ οὐκ ἤθελεν παρακληθῆναι, ὅτι οὐκ εἰσίν.

---

[1] **18** {C} κλαυθμός ℵ B 0250 *f*[1] it[(a),aur,b,c,f,ff1,g1,k,l,q] vg syr[p,pal] cop[sa,bo]
eth Justin Diatessaron[a,i,n] Hilary Jerome Augustine ∥ θρῆνος καὶ κλαυθμός
(*see* Jr 38.15 LXX; 31.15 MT) C D K L W Δ Π *f*[13] 28 33 565 700 892 1009
1010 1071 1079 1195 1216 1230 1241 1242 1253 1365 1546 1646 2148 2174 *Byz*
Lect *l*[70m,150m,185m,883m] (it[d]) syr[c,s,h] arm geo Origen

11 πεσόντες...σμύρναν Ps 72.10–11, 15; Is 60.6   **12** χρηματισθέντες κατ’ ὄναρ Mt 2.22
13 φαίνεται κατ’ ὄναρ Mt 1.20; 2.19   **15** Ἐξ...μου Ho 11.1   **18** Jr 31.15

They knelt down and worshiped him;
then they opened their bags and offered
him presents: gold, frankincense, and
myrrh.

[12] God warned them in a dream not to
go back to Herod; so they went back
home by another road.

The Escape to Egypt

[13] After they had left, an angel of the
Lord appeared in a dream to Joseph and
said: "Get up, take the child and his
mother and run away to Egypt, and stay
there until I tell you to leave. Herod
will be looking for the child to kill him."
[14] So Joseph got up, took the child and
his mother, and left during the night
for Egypt, [15] where he stayed until
Herod died.

This was done to make come true what
the Lord had said through the prophet,
"I called my Son out of Egypt."

The Killing of the Children

[16] When Herod realized that the visitors
from the east had tricked him, he was
furious. He gave orders to kill all the
boys in Bethlehem and its neighborhood
who were two years old and younger —
in accordance with what he had learned
from the visitors about the time when
the star had appeared.

[17] In this way what the prophet Jeremiah had said came true:

[18] "A sound is heard in Ramah,
   The sound of bitter crying and
      weeping.
Rachel weeps for her children,
She weeps and will not be comforted,
Because they are all dead."

The Return from Egypt

19 After Herod had died, an angel of the Lord appeared in a dream to Joseph, in Egypt, 20 and said: "Get up, take the child and his mother, and go back to the country of Israel, because those who tried to kill the child are dead." 21 So Joseph got up, took the child and his mother, and went back to the country of Israel.

22 When he heard that Archelaus had succeeded his father Herod as king of Judea, Joseph was afraid to settle there. He was given more instructions in a dream, and so went to the province of Galilee 23 and made his home in a town named Nazareth. He did this to make come true what the prophets had said, "He will be called a Nazarene."

The Preaching of John the Baptist
(Also Mark 1.1–8; Luke 3.1–18; John 1.19–28)

3 At that time John the Baptist came and started preaching in the desert of Judea. 2 "Turn away from your sins," he said, "for the Kingdom of heaven is near!" 3 John was the one that the prophet Isaiah was talking about when he said:

"Someone is shouting in the desert:
'Get the Lord's road ready for him,
Make a straight path for him to travel!'"

4 John's clothes were made of camel's hair; he wore a leather belt around his waist, and ate locusts and wild honey. 5 People came to him from Jerusalem, from the whole province of Judea, and from all the country around the Jordan river. 6 They confessed their sins and he baptized them in the Jordan river.

The Return from Egypt

19 Τελευτήσαντος δὲ τοῦ Ἡρῴδου ἰδοὺ ἄγγελος κυρίου φαίνεται κατ' ὄναρ τῷ Ἰωσὴφ ἐν Αἰγύπτῳ 20 λέγων, Ἐγερθεὶς παράλαβε τὸ παιδίον καὶ τὴν μητέρα αὐτοῦ καὶ πορεύου εἰς γῆν Ἰσραήλ, τεθνήκασιν γὰρ οἱ ζητοῦντες τὴν ψυχὴν τοῦ παιδίου. 21 ὁ δὲ ἐγερθεὶς παρέλαβεν τὸ παιδίον καὶ τὴν μητέρα αὐτοῦ καὶ εἰσῆλθεν εἰς γῆν Ἰσραήλ. 22 ἀκούσας δὲ ὅτι Ἀρχέλαος βασιλεύει τῆς Ἰουδαίας ἀντὶ τοῦ πατρὸς αὐτοῦ Ἡρῴδου ἐφοβήθη ἐκεῖ ἀπελθεῖν· χρηματισθεὶς δὲ κατ' ὄναρ ἀνεχώρησεν εἰς τὰ μέρη τῆς Γαλιλαίας, 23 καὶ ἐλθὼν κατῴκησεν εἰς πόλιν λεγομένην Ναζαρέτ, ὅπως πληρωθῇ τὸ ῥηθὲν διὰ τῶν προφητῶν ὅτι Ναζωραῖος κληθήσεται.

The Preaching of John the Baptist
(Mk 1.1–8; Lk 3.1–9, 15–17; Jn 1.19–28)

3 Ἐν δὲ ταῖς ἡμέραις ἐκείναις παραγίνεται Ἰωάννης ὁ βαπτιστὴς κηρύσσων ἐν τῇ ἐρήμῳ τῆς Ἰουδαίας 2 [καὶ] λέγων, Μετανοεῖτε, ἤγγικεν γὰρ ἡ βασιλεία τῶν οὐρανῶν. 3 οὗτος γάρ ἐστιν ὁ ῥηθεὶς διὰ Ἠσαΐου τοῦ προφήτου λέγοντος,

**Φωνὴ βοῶντος ἐν τῇ ἐρήμῳ,
Ἑτοιμάσατε τὴν ὁδὸν κυρίου,
εὐθείας ποιεῖτε τὰς τρίβους** αὐτοῦ.

4 Αὐτὸς δὲ ὁ Ἰωάννης εἶχεν τὸ ἔνδυμα αὐτοῦ ἀπὸ τριχῶν καμήλου καὶ ζώνην δερματίνην περὶ τὴν ὀσφὺν αὐτοῦ, ἡ δὲ τροφὴ ἦν αὐτοῦ ἀκρίδες καὶ μέλι ἄγριον. 5 τότε ἐξεπορεύετο πρὸς αὐτὸν Ἱεροσόλυμα καὶ πᾶσα ἡ Ἰουδαία καὶ πᾶσα ἡ περίχωρος τοῦ Ἰορδάνου, 6 καὶ ἐβαπτίζοντο ἐν τῷ Ἰορδάνῃ ποταμῷ ὑπ' αὐτοῦ ἐξομολογούμενοι τὰς ἁμαρτίας αὐτῶν.

---

19 φαίνεται κατ' ὄναρ Mt 1.20; 2.12   20 τεθνήκασιν...ψυχὴν Ex 4.19   22 χρηματισθεὶς ...ὄναρ Mt 2.12   22–23 τὰ μέρη...Ναζαρέτ Mk 1.9; Lk 1.26; 2.39; Jn 1.45–46   23 Ναζωραῖος κληθήσεται Jdg 13.5, 7; Is 11.1; 53.2
3 2 Μετανοεῖτε...οὐρανῶν Mt 4.17; 10.7; Mk 1.15   3 Φωνὴ...αὐτοῦ Is 40.3   4 τὸ ἔνδυμα...ὀσφὺν αὐτοῦ 2 Kgs 1.8

7 Ἰδὼν δὲ πολλοὺς τῶν Φαρισαίων καὶ Σαδδουκαίων ἐρχομένους ἐπὶ τὸ βάπτισμα αὐτοῦ εἶπεν αὐτοῖς, Γεννήματα ἐχιδνῶν, τίς ὑπέδειξεν ὑμῖν φυγεῖν ἀπὸ τῆς μελλούσης ὀργῆς; 8 ποιήσατε οὖν καρπὸν ἄξιον τῆς μετανοίας· 9 καὶ μὴ δόξητε λέγειν ἐν ἑαυτοῖς, Πατέρα ἔχομεν τὸν Ἀβραάμ, λέγω γὰρ ὑμῖν ὅτι δύναται ὁ θεὸς ἐκ τῶν λίθων τούτων ἐγεῖραι τέκνα τῷ Ἀβραάμ. 10 ἤδη δὲ ἡ ἀξίνη πρὸς τὴν ῥίζαν τῶν δένδρων κεῖται· πᾶν οὖν δένδρον μὴ ποιοῦν καρπὸν καλὸν ἐκκόπτεται καὶ εἰς πῦρ βάλλεται. 11 ἐγὼ μὲν ὑμᾶς βαπτίζω ἐν ὕδατι εἰς μετάνοιαν· ὁ δὲ ὀπίσω μου ἐρχόμενος ἰσχυρότερός μού ἐστιν, οὗ οὐκ εἰμὶ ἱκανὸς τὰ ὑποδήματα βαστάσαι· αὐτὸς ὑμᾶς βαπτίσει ἐν πνεύματι ἁγίῳ καὶ πυρί· 12 οὗ τὸ πτύον ἐν τῇ χειρὶ αὐτοῦ, καὶ διακαθαριεῖ τὴν ἅλωνα αὐτοῦ, καὶ συνάξει τὸν σῖτον αὐτοῦ εἰς τὴν ἀποθήκην [αὐτοῦ][1], τὸ δὲ ἄχυρον κατακαύσει πυρὶ ἀσβέστῳ.

The Baptism of Jesus
(Mk 1.9–11; Lk 3.21–22)

13 Τότε παραγίνεται ὁ Ἰησοῦς ἀπὸ τῆς Γαλιλαίας ἐπὶ τὸν Ἰορδάνην πρὸς τὸν Ἰωάννην τοῦ βαπτισθῆναι ὑπ' αὐτοῦ. 14 ὁ δὲ Ἰωάννης διεκώλυεν αὐτὸν λέγων, Ἐγὼ χρείαν ἔχω ὑπὸ σοῦ βαπτισθῆναι, καὶ σὺ ἔρχῃ πρός με; 15 ἀποκριθεὶς δὲ ὁ Ἰησοῦς εἶπεν πρὸς αὐτόν, Ἄφες ἄρτι, οὕτως γὰρ πρέπον ἐστὶν ἡμῖν πληρῶσαι πᾶσαν δικαιο-

---

[1] 12 {C} αὐτοῦ εἰς τὴν ἀποθήκην αὐτοῦ B W 1071 1216 eth[ro,pp] (eth[ms?] εἰς τὰς ἀποθήκας) geo[B] ‖ εἰς τὴν ἀποθήκην αὐτοῦ (see Lk 3.17) L 892 1195 1253 1546 1646 it[l,ff1,g1] syr[c,s,p,h] arm Irenaeus Ambrose Cyril ‖ αὐτοῦ εἰς τὴν ἀποθήκην ℵ C D[supp] K Δ f[1] 28 33 565 700 1009 1010 1079 1230 1241 1365 2148 2174 Byz it[aur,c,d,f,l] vg cop[sa,bo] Hilary Augustine ‖ εἰς τὴν ἀποθήκην f[13] 1242 it[a,q] geo[1,A] Justin Clement Irenaeus

---

7 Γεννήματα ἐχιδνῶν Mt 12.34; 23.33; Lk 3.7 τίς...ὀργῆς Mt 23.33; Lk 21.23; Ro 1.18; 2.5; 5.9; Eph 5.6; Col 3.6; 1 Th 1.10; Re 6.16–17 9 Πατέρα...Ἀβραάμ Jn 8.33, 37, 39; Ro 4.12 10 πᾶν...βάλλεται Mt 7.19; Lk 13.7, 9; Jn 15.6 11 ἐγὼ...ὕδατι Jn 1.26, 31, 33; Ac 1.5; 11.16 βαπτίζω...μετάνοιαν Ac 13.24; 19.4 ὁ δὲ...ἐρχόμενος Mt 11.3; Jn 1.15 οὗ...βαστάσαι Ac 13.25 αὐτὸς...ἁγίῳ Jn 1.33; Ac 1.5; 11.16 12 συνάξει...ἀποθήκην Mt 13.30

7 When John saw many Pharisees and Sadducees coming to him to be baptized, he said to them: "You snakes — who told you that you could escape from God's wrath that is about to come? 8 Do the things that will show that you have turned from your sins. 9 And do not think you can excuse yourselves by saying, 'Abraham is our ancestor.' I tell you that God can take these rocks and make descendants for Abraham! 10 The ax is ready to cut the trees at the roots; every tree that does not bear good fruit will be cut down and thrown in the fire. 11 I baptize you with water to show that you have repented; but the one who will come after me will baptize you with the Holy Spirit and fire. He is much greater than I am; I am not good enough even to carry his sandals. 12 He has his winnowing-shovel with him, to thresh out all the grain; he will gather his wheat into his barn, but burn the chaff in a fire that never goes out!"

The Baptism of Jesus
(Also Mark 1.9–11; Luke 3.21–22)

13 At that time Jesus went from Galilee to the Jordan, and came to John to be baptized by him. 14 But John tried to make him change his mind. "I ought to be baptized by you," John said, "yet you come to me!" 15 But Jesus answered him, "Let it be this way for now. For in this way we shall do all that God requires." So John agreed.

¹⁶ As soon as Jesus was baptized, he came up out of the water. Then heaven was opened to him, and he saw the Spirit of God coming down like a dove and lighting on him. ¹⁷ And then a voice said from heaven, "This is my own dear Son, with whom I am well pleased."

The Temptation of Jesus
(Also Mark 1.12–13; Luke 4.1–13)

4 Then the Spirit led Jesus into the desert to be tempted by the Devil. ² After spending forty days and nights without food, Jesus was hungry. ³ The Devil came to him and said, "If you are God's Son, order these stones to turn into bread." ⁴ Jesus answered, "The scripture says, 'Man cannot live on bread alone, but on every word that God speaks.'"

⁵ Then the Devil took Jesus to the Holy City, set him on the highest point of the Temple, ⁶ and said to him, "If you are God's Son, throw yourself down to the ground; for the scripture says,

σύνην. τότε ἀφίησιν αὐτόν. 16 βαπτισθεὶς δὲ ὁ Ἰησοῦς εὐθὺς ἀνέβη ἀπὸ τοῦ ὕδατος· καὶ ἰδοὺ ἠνεῴχθησαν [αὐτῷ]² οἱ οὐρανοί, καὶ εἶδεν [τὸ] πνεῦμα [τοῦ] θεοῦ καταβαῖνον ὡσεὶ περιστερὰν [καὶ] ἐρχόμενον³ ἐπ' αὐτόν· 17 καὶ ἰδοὺ φωνὴ ἐκ τῶν οὐρανῶν λέγουσα, Οὗτός ἐστιν ὁ υἱός μουᵃ ὁ ἀγαπητός, ἐν ᾧ εὐδόκησα.

The Temptation of Jesus
(Mk 1.12–13; Lk 4.1–13)

4 Τότε ὁ Ἰησοῦς ἀνήχθη εἰς τὴν ἔρημον ὑπὸ τοῦ πνεύματος, πειρασθῆναι ὑπὸ τοῦ διαβόλου. 2 καὶ νηστεύσας ἡμέρας τεσσαράκοντα καὶ νύκτας τεσσαράκοντα ὕστερον ἐπείνασεν. 3 Καὶ προσελθὼν ὁ πειράζων εἶπεν αὐτῷ, Εἰ υἱὸς εἶ τοῦ θεοῦ, εἰπὲ ἵνα οἱ λίθοι οὗτοι ἄρτοι γένωνται. 4 ὁ δὲ ἀποκριθεὶς εἶπεν, Γέγραπται,

Οὐκ ἐπ' ἄρτῳ μόνῳ ζήσεται ὁ ἄνθρωπος,
ἀλλ' ἐπὶ παντὶ ῥήματι ἐκπορευομένῳ
διὰ στόματος θεοῦ.

5 Τότε παραλαμβάνει αὐτὸν ὁ διάβολος εἰς τὴν ἁγίαν πόλιν, καὶ ἵστησιν αὐτὸν ἐπὶ τὸ πτερύγιον τοῦ ἱεροῦ, 6 καὶ λέγει αὐτῷ, Εἰ υἱὸς εἶ τοῦ θεοῦ, βάλε σεαυτὸν κάτω· γέγραπται γὰρ ὅτι

---

2 16 {C} αὐτῷ ℵᵇ C Dˢᵘᵖᵖ K L P W Δ f¹ f¹³ 28 33 565 700 892 1009 1010 1071 1079 1195 1216 1230 1241 1242 1253 1365 1546 1646 2148 2174 *Byz Lect*ᵐ l76,1579 itᵃ,ᵃᵘʳ,ᵇ,ᶜ,ᵈ,ᶠ,ff¹,g¹,ʰ,ˡ vg syrᵖ·ʰ copᵇᵒ arm ethᵖᵖ (ethʳᵒ,ᵐˢ) geoˡ·ᴬ Irenaeusˡᵃᵗ Hippolytus Eusebius Chrysostom Augustine ∥ *omit* ℵ* B l211ᵐ,1043ᵐ,1627ᵐ syrᶜ·ˢ copˢᵃ geoᴮ Irenaeus Hilary Vigilius

3 16 {C} καὶ ἐρχόμενον ℵᶜ C D K L P W Δ f¹ f¹³ 28 33 565 700 892 1009 1010 1071 1079 (1195 ἐξ οὐρανοῦ καὶ ἐρχόμενον) 1216 1230 1241 1242 1253 1365 1546 1646 2148 2174 *Byz Lect*ᵐ l76,211 itᵈ,ᶠ,ˡ vgᶜˡ syrᶜ·ˢ·ᵖ·ʰ·(ᵖᵃˡ) arm eth geoˡ·ᴬ Irenaeusᵛⁱᵈ (Hippolytus) (Eusebius) Papyrusᵒˣʸ ⁴⁰⁵ ∥ ἐρχόμενον

ᵃ **17** *a* none: TR WH Bov Nes BF² AV RV ASV RSV NEBᵐᵍ TT Zür Luth Jer Seg ∥ *a* minor: WHᵐᵍ RVᵐᵍ ASVᵐᵍ RSVᵐᵍ NEB

---

16 εἶδεν...αὐτόν Jn 1.32   **17** Οὗτός...εὐδόκησα Gn 22.2; Ps 2.7; Is 42.1; Mt 12.18; 17.5; Mk 9.7; Lk 9.35; 2 Pe 1.17
4 1 πειρασθῆναι...διαβόλου He 2.18; 4.15   **2** νηστεύσας...νύκτας τεσσαράκοντα Ex 34.28
3 Εἰ...θεοῦ Mt 4.6; 27.40   **4** Οὐκ...θεοῦ Dt 8.3   **5** τὴν...πόλιν Ne 11.1; Is 52.1; Mt 27.53; Re 11.2; 21.2, 10; 22.19   **6** Εἰ...θεοῦ Mt 4.3; 27.40

Τοῖς ἀγγέλοις αὐτοῦ ἐντελεῖται περὶ σοῦ
καὶ ἐπὶ χειρῶν ἀροῦσίν σε,
μήποτε προσκόψῃς πρὸς λίθον τὸν πόδα σου.
7 ἔφη αὐτῷ ὁ Ἰησοῦς, Πάλιν γέγραπται, **Οὐκ ἐκπειράσεις κύριον τὸν θεόν σου.** 8 Πάλιν παραλαμβάνει αὐτὸν ὁ διάβολος εἰς ὄρος ὑψηλὸν λίαν, καὶ δείκνυσιν αὐτῷ πάσας τὰς βασιλείας τοῦ κόσμου καὶ τὴν δόξαν αὐτῶν, 9 καὶ λέγει αὐτῷ, Ταῦτά σοι πάντα δώσω ἐὰν πεσὼν προσκυνήσῃς μοι. 10 τότε λέγει αὐτῷ ὁ Ἰησοῦς, Ὕπαγε[1], Σατανᾶ· γέγραπται γάρ,

**Κύριον τὸν θεόν σου προσκυνήσεις
καὶ αὐτῷ μόνῳ λατρεύσεις.**
11 Τότε ἀφίησιν αὐτὸν ὁ διάβολος, καὶ ἰδοὺ ἄγγελοι προσῆλθον καὶ διηκόνουν αὐτῷ.

The Beginning of the Galilean Ministry
(Mk 1.14–15; Lk 4.14–15)

12 Ἀκούσας δὲ ὅτι Ἰωάννης παρεδόθη ἀνεχώρησεν εἰς τὴν Γαλιλαίαν. 13 καὶ καταλιπὼν τὴν Ναζαρὰ ἐλθὼν κατῴκησεν εἰς Καφαρναοὺμ τὴν παραθαλασσίαν ἐν ὁρίοις Ζαβουλὼν καὶ Νεφθαλίμ· 14 ἵνα πληρωθῇ τὸ ῥηθὲν διὰ Ἠσαΐου τοῦ προφήτου λέγοντος,

'God will give orders to his angels
about you:
They will hold you up with their
hands,
So that you will not even hurt your
feet on the stones.' "
[7] Jesus answered, "But the scripture also says, 'You must not put the Lord your God to the test.' "
[8] Then the Devil took Jesus to a very high mountain and showed him all the kingdoms of the world, in all their greatness. [9] "All this I will give you," the Devil said, "if you kneel down and worship me." [10] Then Jesus answered, "Go away, Satan! The scripture says, 'Worship the Lord your God and serve only him!' "
[11] So the Devil left him; and angels came and helped Jesus.

Jesus Begins His Work in Galilee
(Also Mark 1.14–15; Luke 4.14–15)

[12] When Jesus heard that John had been put in prison, he went away to Galilee. [13] He did not settle down in Nazareth, but went and lived in Capernaum, a town by Lake Galilee, in the territory of Zebulun and Naphtali. [14] This was done to make come true what the prophet Isaiah had said:

ℵ* B it[a,aur,b,c,ff1,gl],h vg[ww] cop[bo] Irenaeus Hilary Augustine ‖ *omit* cop[sa] geo[B]

[1] **10** {B} ὕπαγε ℵ B C*[vid] K P W Δ f[1] f[13] 565 700 892* 1079 1546 it[f,k] vg syr[p,h,pal] cop[sams,bo] geo[1,A] Ignatius Diatessaron Irenaeus[lat] Tertullian Origen Peter-Alexandria Hilary Ps-Ignatius Jerome ‖ ὕπαγε ὀπίσω μου (*see* Mt 16.23) C[2] D L 28 33 892[vid] 1009 1010 1071 1195 1216 1230 1241 1242 1253 1365 1646 2148 2174 *Byz Lect*[m] l[76] it[b,d,h,l] syr[c,h with *] (syr[s] σου) cop[sa,bo][mss] arm eth geo[B] Justin Liber Graduum Athanasius Ephraem Ambrose Augustine ‖ *vade retro* it[a,aur,c,ff1,gl]

---

6 Τοῖς...πόδα σου Ps 91,11–12   **7** Οὐκ...σου Dt 6.16 (1 Cor 10.9)   **9** πεσὼν προσκυνήσῃς Dn 3.5, 10, 15; Mt 2.11; 18.26; 1 Cor 14.25; Re 4.10; 5.14; 7.11; 11.16; 19.4, 10; 22.8   **10** Κύριον...λατρεύσεις Dt 6.13   **12** Ἰωάννης παρεδόθη Mt 14.3; Mk 6.17; Lk 3.20; Jn 3.24   **13** κατῴκησεν εἰς Καφαρναούμ Jn 2.12

15 "Land of Zebulun, land of Naphtali,
  In the direction of the sea, on the
      other side of Jordan,
  Galilee of the Gentiles!
16 The people who live in darkness
  Will see a great light!
  On those who live in the dark land
      of death
  The light will shine!"

17 From that time Jesus began to preach
his message: "Turn away from your sins!
The Kingdom of heaven is near!"

Jesus Calls Four Fishermen
(Also Mark 1.16–20; Luke 5.1–11)

18 As Jesus walked by Lake Galilee,
he saw two brothers who were fishermen,
Simon (called Peter) and his brother
Andrew, catching fish in the lake with a
net. 19 Jesus said to them, "Come with
me and I will teach you to catch men."
20 At once they left their nets and went
with him.

21 He went on and saw two other
brothers, James and John, the sons of
Zebedee. They were in their boat with
their father Zebedee, getting their nets
ready. Jesus called them; 22 at once they
left the boat and their father, and went
with Jesus.

15 Γῆ Ζαβουλὼν καὶ γῆ Νεφθαλίμ,
    ὁδὸν θαλάσσης, πέραν τοῦ Ἰορδάνου,
    Γαλιλαία τῶν ἐθνῶν,[a]
16 ὁ λαὸς ὁ καθήμενος ἐν σκότει
    φῶς εἶδεν μέγα,
  καὶ τοῖς καθημένοις ἐν χώρᾳ καὶ σκιᾷ θανάτου
    φῶς ἀνέτειλεν αὐτοῖς.

17 Ἀπὸ τότε ἤρξατο ὁ Ἰησοῦς κηρύσσειν καὶ λέγειν,
Μετανοεῖτε, ἤγγικεν γὰρ[2] ἡ βασιλεία τῶν οὐρανῶν.

The Calling of Four Fishermen
(Mk 1.16–20; Lk 5.1–11)

18 Περιπατῶν δὲ παρὰ τὴν θάλασσαν τῆς Γαλιλαίας
εἶδεν δύο ἀδελφούς, Σίμωνα τὸν λεγόμενον Πέτρον καὶ
Ἀνδρέαν τὸν ἀδελφὸν αὐτοῦ, βάλλοντας ἀμφίβληστρον εἰς
τὴν θάλασσαν· ἦσαν γὰρ ἁλιεῖς. 19 καὶ λέγει αὐτοῖς,
Δεῦτε ὀπίσω μου, καὶ ποιήσω ὑμᾶς ἁλιεῖς ἀνθρώπων.
20 οἱ δὲ εὐθέως ἀφέντες τὰ δίκτυα ἠκολούθησαν αὐτῷ.
21 Καὶ προβὰς ἐκεῖθεν εἶδεν ἄλλους δύο ἀδελφούς, Ἰάκωβον τὸν τοῦ Ζεβεδαίου καὶ Ἰωάννην τὸν ἀδελφὸν αὐτοῦ,
ἐν τῷ πλοίῳ μετὰ Ζεβεδαίου τοῦ πατρὸς αὐτῶν καταρτίζοντας τὰ δίκτυα αὐτῶν· καὶ ἐκάλεσεν αὐτούς. 22 οἱ δὲ
εὐθέως ἀφέντες τὸ πλοῖον καὶ τὸν πατέρα αὐτῶν ἠκολούθησαν αὐτῷ.

---

[2] 17 {B} μετανοεῖτε, ἤγγικεν γάρ ℵ B C D K L P W Δ f[1] f[13] 28 33
565 700 892 1009 1010 1071 1079 1195 1216 1230 1241 1242 1253 1365 1546 1646
2148 2174 Byz Lect[m] l[76,211] it[a,aur,b,c,d,f,ff1,g1,h,l] vg syr[p,h,palmss] cop[sa,bo] arm eth
geo ‖ μετανοεῖτε, ἤγγικεν syr[palms] cop[boms] ‖ ἤγγικεν it[k] syr[c,s] Justin
Clement Origen (Eusebius) Victor-Antioch

[a] 15 a minor: TR WH Bov Nes BF² RV ASV TT Zür Luth Seg ‖ a major: AV (NEB) ‖ a dash:
RSV ‖ a exclamation: Jer

15–16 Is 9.1–2   16 Lk 1.79   17 Μετανοεῖτε...οὐρανῶν Mt 3.2; 10.7   18 δύο...
αὐτοῦ Jn 1.40–41

Ministering to a Great Multitude
(Lk 6.17–19)

23 Καὶ περιῆγεν ἐν ὅλῃ τῇ Γαλιλαίᾳ[3], διδάσκων ἐν ταῖς συναγωγαῖς αὐτῶν καὶ κηρύσσων τὸ εὐαγγέλιον τῆς βασιλείας καὶ θεραπεύων πᾶσαν νόσον καὶ πᾶσαν μαλακίαν ἐν τῷ λαῷ. **24** καὶ ἀπῆλθεν ἡ ἀκοὴ αὐτοῦ εἰς ὅλην τὴν Συρίαν· καὶ προσήνεγκαν αὐτῷ πάντας τοὺς κακῶς ἔχοντας ποικίλαις νόσοις καὶ βασάνοις συνεχομένους καὶ δαιμονιζομένους καὶ σεληνιαζομένους καὶ παραλυτικούς, καὶ ἐθεράπευσεν αὐτούς. **25** καὶ ἠκολούθησαν αὐτῷ ὄχλοι πολλοὶ ἀπὸ τῆς Γαλιλαίας καὶ Δεκαπόλεως καὶ Ἱεροσολύμων καὶ Ἰουδαίας καὶ πέραν τοῦ Ἰορδάνου.

The Sermon on the Mount
Matthew 5—7

5 Ἰδὼν δὲ τοὺς ὄχλους ἀνέβη εἰς τὸ ὄρος· καὶ καθίσαντος αὐτοῦ προσῆλθαν αὐτῷ οἱ μαθηταὶ αὐτοῦ· **2** καὶ ἀνοίξας τὸ στόμα αὐτοῦ ἐδίδασκεν αὐτοὺς λέγων,

The Beatitudes
(Lk 6.20–23)

3 Μακάριοι οἱ πτωχοὶ τῷ πνεύματι,
     ὅτι αὐτῶν ἐστιν ἡ βασιλεία τῶν οὐρανῶν.
4[a] μακάριοι οἱ πενθοῦντες,
     ὅτι αὐτοὶ παρακληθήσονται.
5[a] μακάριοι οἱ πραεῖς,
     ὅτι αὐτοὶ κληρονομήσουσιν τὴν γῆν.[1]

---

[3] **23** {C} ἐν ὅλῃ τῇ Γαλιλαίᾳ B *l*[20] (it[k]) syr[c] cop[sa] ∥ ἐν ὅλῃ τῇ Γαλιλαίᾳ ὁ Ἰησοῦς C[3] ∥ ὁ Ἰησοῦς ἐν ὅλῃ τῇ Γαλιλαίᾳ (ℵ* *omit* ὅλη) C* syr[s,p,h,pal] cop[bo] arm eth ∥ ὁ Ἰησοῦς ὅλην τὴν Γαλιλαίαν ℵ[b] D *f*[1] 33 892 2148 *Lect* *l*[883pt,950pt] (*l*[1642] *omit* ὅλην) it[a,aur,b,c,d,f,ff1,g1,h,l] vg geo? Eusebius ∥ ὅλην τὴν Γαλιλαίαν ὁ Ἰησοῦς K W Δ Π *f*[13] 28 565 700 1009 1010 1071 1079 1195 1216 1230 1241 1242 1253 1365 1546 1646 2174 *Byz* *l*[185,211,333,547,883pt,950pt]

[1] **4-5** {B} *4, 5* μακάριοι...παρακληθήσονται.   *5* μακάριοι...τὴν γῆν.

[a a] **4-5** *a* number 4, *a* number 5: TR WH Nes BF[2] AV RV ASV RSV NEB TT Zur Luth Seg ∥ *a* number 5, *a* number 4: Bov Jer

23 Mt 9.35; Mk 1.39   **24** Mk 6.55–56   **25** Mk 3.7–8
5 **4** οἱ πενθοῦντες...παρακληθήσονται Is 61.2–3   **5** οἱ πραεῖς...γῆν Ps 37.11

Jesus Teaches, Preaches, and Heals
(Also Luke 6.17–19)

[23] Jesus went all over Galilee, teaching in their synagogues, preaching the Good News of the Kingdom, and healing people from every kind of disease and sickness. [24] The news about him spread through the whole country of Syria, so that people brought him all those who were sick with all kinds of diseases, and afflicted with all sorts of troubles: people with demons, and epileptics, and paralytics — Jesus healed them all. [25] Great crowds followed him from Galilee and the Ten Towns, from Jerusalem, Judea, and the land on the other side of the Jordan.

The Sermon on the Mount

5 Jesus saw the crowds and went up a hill, where he sat down. His disciples gathered around him, [2] and he began to teach them:

True Happiness
(Also Luke 6.20–23)

[3] "Happy are those who know they are spiritually poor:
     the Kingdom of heaven belongs to them!
[4] "Happy are those who mourn:
     God will comfort them!
[5] "Happy are the meek:
     they will receive what God has promised!

6 "Happy are those whose greatest desire is to do what God requires: God will satisfy them fully!

7 "Happy are those who show mercy to others: God will show mercy to them!

8 "Happy are the pure in heart: they will see God!

9 "Happy are those who work for peace among men: God will call them his sons!

10 "Happy are those who suffer persecution because they do what God requires: the Kingdom of heaven belongs to them!

11 "Happy are you when men insult you and mistreat you and tell all kinds of evil lies against you because you are my followers. 12 Rejoice and be glad, because a great reward is kept for you in heaven. This is how men mistreated the prophets who lived before you."

Salt and Light
(Also Mark 9.50; Luke 14.34–35)

13 "You are like salt for all mankind. But if salt loses its taste, there is no way to make it salty again. It has become worthless; so it is thrown away and people walk on it.

14 "You are like light for the whole

6 μακάριοι οἱ πεινῶντες καὶ διψῶντες τὴν δικαιοσύνην,
 ὅτι αὐτοὶ χορτασθήσονται.

7 μακάριοι οἱ ἐλεήμονες,
 ὅτι αὐτοὶ ἐλεηθήσονται.

8 μακάριοι οἱ καθαροὶ τῇ καρδίᾳ,
 ὅτι αὐτοὶ τὸν θεὸν ὄψονται.

9 μακάριοι οἱ εἰρηνοποιοί,
 ὅτι [αὐτοὶ] υἱοὶ θεοῦ κληθήσονται.

10 μακάριοι οἱ δεδιωγμένοι ἕνεκεν δικαιοσύνης,
 ὅτι αὐτῶν ἐστιν ἡ βασιλεία τῶν οὐρανῶν.

11 μακάριοί ἐστε ὅταν ὀνειδίσωσιν ὑμᾶς καὶ διώξωσιν καὶ εἴπωσιν πᾶν πονηρὸν καθ' ὑμῶν [ψευδόμενοι]² ἕνεκεν ἐμοῦ· 12 χαίρετε καὶ ἀγαλλιᾶσθε, ὅτι ὁ μισθὸς ὑμῶν πολὺς ἐν τοῖς οὐρανοῖς· οὕτως γὰρ ἐδίωξαν τοὺς προφήτας τοὺς πρὸ ὑμῶν.

Salt and Light
(Mk 9.50; Lk 14.34–35)

13 Ὑμεῖς ἐστε τὸ ἅλας τῆς γῆς· ἐὰν δὲ τὸ ἅλας μωρανθῇ, ἐν τίνι ἁλισθήσεται; εἰς οὐδὲν ἰσχύει ἔτι εἰ μὴ βληθῆναι ἔξω καὶ³ καταπατεῖσθαι ὑπὸ τῶν ἀνθρώπων. 14 Ὑμεῖς

ℵ B C K W Δ Θ Π 0196 *f*¹ *f*¹³ 28 565 700 892 1009 1010 1071 1079 1195 1216 1230 1241 1242 1253 1365 1546 1646 2148 2174 *Byz Lect* *l*⁸⁸³ᵐ it^(b,f,q) syr^(s,p,h,pal) cop^(sa,bo) arm eth geo Tertullian Chrysostom Ps-Chrysostom ‖ *5, 4 μακάριοι ...τὴν γῆν. 4 μακάριοι...παρακληθήσονται.* D 33 it^(a,aur,c,d,ff1,g1,h,k,l) vg syr^c Diatessaron^(earm,i,n) Clement Origen Eusebius Aphraates Hilary Ephraem Basil Gregory-Nyssa Jerome Ammonius

² **11** {D} ψευδόμενοι ℵ B C K W Δ Θ Π 0196 *f*¹ *f*¹³ 28 33 565 700 892 1009 1010 1071 1079 1195 1216 1230 1241 1242 1253 1365 1546 1646 (2148 ψευδόμενον) 2174 *Byz Lect* *l*⁸⁸³ᵐ it^(a?aur,f,ff1,l,q) vg syr^(c,p,h,pal) cop^(sa,bo) arm eth Diatessaron Apostolic Constitutions Chrysostom Augustine Cyril Ps-Chrysostom ‖ *omit* D it^(b,c,d,g1,h,k) syr^s geo Diatessaron^v Tertullian Origen Eusebius Hilary Lucifer Augustine

³ **13** {C} βληθῆναι ἔξω καί D K W Δ Θ Π *f*¹³ 28 565 700 1009 1010 1079 1195 1216 1230 1241 1242 1253 1365 1546 1646 2148 2174 *Byz Lect* *l*⁸⁸³ᵐ it^(a,aur,b,c,)

---

7 οἱ ἐλεήμονες...ἐλεηθήσονται Mt 18.33; Jas 2.13   8 Ps 24.3–4   9 εἰρηνοποιοί He 12.14; Jas 3.18   10 μακάριοι...δικαιοσύνης 1 Pe 3.14   11 Mt 10.22; 1 Pe 4.14 12 οὕτως...προφήτας 2 Chr 36.16; Mt 23.30, 37; Ac 7.52; He 11.32–38; Jas 5.10

ἐστε τὸ φῶς τοῦ κόσμου. οὐ δύναται πόλις κρυβῆναι ἐπάνω ὄρους κειμένη· 15 οὐδὲ καίουσιν λύχνον καὶ τιθέασιν αὐτὸν ὑπὸ τὸν μόδιον ἀλλ’ ἐπὶ τὴν λυχνίαν, καὶ λάμπει πᾶσιν τοῖς ἐν τῇ οἰκίᾳ. 16 οὕτως λαμψάτω τὸ φῶς ὑμῶν ἔμπροσθεν τῶν ἀνθρώπων, ὅπως ἴδωσιν ὑμῶν τὰ καλὰ ἔργα καὶ δοξάσωσιν τὸν πατέρα ὑμῶν τὸν ἐν τοῖς οὐρανοῖς.

Teaching about the Law

17 Μὴ νομίσητε ὅτι ἦλθον καταλῦσαι τὸν νόμον ἢ τοὺς προφήτας· οὐκ ἦλθον καταλῦσαι ἀλλὰ πληρῶσαι. 18 ἀμὴν γὰρ λέγω ὑμῖν, ἕως ἂν παρέλθῃ ὁ οὐρανὸς καὶ ἡ γῆ, ἰῶτα ἓν ἢ μία κεραία οὐ μὴ παρέλθῃ ἀπὸ τοῦ νόμου ἕως ἂν πάντα γένηται. 19 ὃς ἐὰν οὖν λύσῃ μίαν τῶν ἐντολῶν τούτων τῶν ἐλαχίστων καὶ διδάξῃ οὕτως τοὺς ἀνθρώπους, ἐλάχιστος κληθήσεται ἐν τῇ βασιλείᾳ τῶν οὐρανῶν· ὃς δ’ ἂν ποιήσῃ καὶ διδάξῃ, οὗτος μέγας κληθήσεται ἐν τῇ βασιλείᾳ τῶν οὐρανῶν. 20 λέγω γὰρ ὑμῖν ὅτι ἐὰν μὴ περισσεύσῃ ὑμῶν ἡ δικαιοσύνη πλεῖον τῶν γραμματέων καὶ Φαρισαίων, οὐ μὴ εἰσέλθητε εἰς τὴν βασιλείαν τῶν οὐρανῶν.

Teaching about Anger

21 Ἠκούσατε ὅτι ἐρρέθη τοῖς ἀρχαίοις, **Οὐ φονεύσεις**· ὃς δ’ ἂν φονεύσῃ, ἔνοχος ἔσται τῇ κρίσει. 22 ἐγὼ δὲ λέγω ὑμῖν ὅτι πᾶς ὁ ὀργιζόμενος τῷ ἀδελφῷ αὐτοῦ[4]

d, f, ff¹, g¹, h, k, l, q vg syr(c,s), p, h, pal arm ethro, pp geo Diatessaron ∥ βληθὲν ἔξω καί 1071 ∥ βληθὲν ἔξω א B C f¹ 33 892 ethms? Origen

[4] **22** {C} αὐτοῦ p⁶⁷ᵛⁱᵈ א* B 2174ᵛⁱᵈ vg eth Gospel of the Nazarenes Ptolemy Justin Irenaeuslat1/3 Tertullianᵛⁱᵈ Origen Eusebius Basil mssacc. to Jerome Augustine Greek mssacc. to Augustine Cassian Ps-Athanasius ∥ αὐτοῦ εἰκῇ אᶜ D K L W Δ Θ Π f¹ f¹³ 28 33 565 700 892 1010 1071 1079 1195 1216 1230 1241 1242 1365 1546 1646 2148 Byz Lect ita, aur, b, c, d, f, ff¹, g¹, h, k, l, q syrc, s, p, h, pal copsa, bo goth arm geo Diatessaron Irenaeusgr, lat2/3 Origen Cyprian Eusebius Lucifer Ps-Justin Chrysostom Cyril

14 τὸ φῶς τοῦ κόσμου Jn 8.12; 9.5; Php 2.15   **15** Mk 4.21; Lk 8.16; 11.33   **16** Eph 5.8-9; 1 Pe 2.12   **17** Mt 3.15; Ro 3.31   **18** ἕως...νόμου Lk 16.17; 21.33   **19** ὃς...ἐλαχίστων Jas 2.10   **21** Οὐ φονεύσεις Ex 20.13; Dt 5.17 (Mt 19.18; Mk 10.19; Lk 18.20; Ro 13.9; Jas 2.11); (Ex 21.12; Lv 24.17)   **22** πᾶς...ἀδελφῷ αὐτοῦ 1 Jn 3.15

world. A city built on a hill cannot be hid. [15] Nobody lights a lamp to put it under a bowl; instead he puts it on the lamp-stand, where it gives light for everyone in the house. [16] In the same way your light must shine before people, so that they will see the good things you do and give praise to your Father in heaven.”

Teaching about the Law

[17] “Do not think that I have come to do away with the Law of Moses and the teaching of the prophets. I have not come to do away with them, but to give them real meaning. [18] Remember this! As long as heaven and earth last, the least point or the smallest detail of the Law will not be done away with — not until the end of all things. [19] Therefore, whoever disobeys even the smallest of the commandments, and teaches others to do the same, will be least in the Kingdom of heaven. On the other hand, whoever obeys the Law, and teaches others to do the same, will be great in the Kingdom of heaven. [20] I tell you, then, that you will be able to enter the Kingdom of heaven only if you are more faithful than the teachers of the Law and the Pharisees in doing what God requires.”

Teaching about Anger

[21] “You have heard that men were told in the past, ‘Do not murder; anyone who commits murder will be brought before the judge.’ [22] But now I tell you: whoever is angry[1] with his brother will

[1] **22** is angry: *some mss. add* without cause

be brought before the judge; whoever calls his brother 'You good-for-nothing!' will be brought before the Council; and whoever calls his brother a worthless fool will be in danger of going to the fire of hell. 23 So if you are about to offer your gift to God at the altar and there you remember that your brother has something against you, 24 leave your gift there in front of the altar and go at once to make peace with your brother; then come back and offer your gift to God.

25 "If a man brings a lawsuit against you and takes you to court, be friendly with him while there is time, before you get to court; once you are there he will turn you over to the judge, who will hand you over to the police, and you will be put in jail. 26 There you will stay, I tell you, until you pay the last penny of your fine."

Teaching about Adultery

27 "You have heard that it was said, 'Do not commit adultery.' 28 But now I tell you: anyone who looks at a woman and wants to possess her is guilty of committing adultery with her in his heart. 29 So if your right eye causes you to sin, take it out and throw it away! It is much better for you to lose a part of your body than to have your whole body thrown into hell. 30 If your right hand causes you to sin, cut it off and throw it away! It is much better for you to lose one of your limbs than to have your whole body go off to hell."

Teaching about Divorce
(Also Matt. 19.9; Mark 10.11–12; Luke 16.18)

31 "It was also said, 'Anyone who divorces his wife must give her a written notice of divorce.' 32 But now I tell you:

ἔνοχος ἔσται τῇ κρίσει· ὃς δ' ἂν εἴπῃ τῷ ἀδελφῷ αὐτοῦ, Ῥακά, ἔνοχος ἔσται τῷ συνεδρίῳ· ὃς δ' ἂν εἴπῃ, Μωρέ, ἔνοχος ἔσται εἰς τὴν γέενναν τοῦ πυρός. 23 ἐὰν οὖν προσφέρῃς τὸ δῶρόν σου ἐπὶ τὸ θυσιαστήριον κἀκεῖ μνησθῇς ὅτι ὁ ἀδελφός σου ἔχει τι κατὰ σοῦ, 24 ἄφες ἐκεῖ τὸ δῶρόν σου ἔμπροσθεν τοῦ θυσιαστηρίου,ᵇ καὶ ὕπαγεᵇ πρῶτον διαλλάγηθι τῷ ἀδελφῷ σου, καὶ τότε ἐλθὼν πρόσφερε τὸ δῶρόν σου. 25 ἴσθι εὐνοῶν τῷ ἀντιδίκῳ σου ταχὺ ἕως ὅτου εἶ μετ' αὐτοῦ ἐν τῇ ὁδῷ, μήποτέ σε παραδῷ ὁ ἀντίδικος τῷ κριτῇ, καὶ ὁ κριτὴς⁵ τῷ ὑπηρέτῃ, καὶ εἰς φυλακὴν βληθήσῃ· 26 ἀμὴν λέγω σοι, οὐ μὴ ἐξέλθῃς ἐκεῖθεν ἕως ἂν ἀποδῷς τὸν ἔσχατον κοδράντην.

Teaching about Adultery

27 Ἠκούσατε ὅτι ἐρρέθη, **Οὐ μοιχεύσεις.** 28 ἐγὼ δὲ λέγω ὑμῖν ὅτι πᾶς ὁ βλέπων γυναῖκα πρὸς τὸ ἐπιθυμῆσαι αὐτὴν ἤδη ἐμοίχευσεν αὐτὴν ἐν τῇ καρδίᾳ αὐτοῦ. 29 εἰ δὲ ὁ ὀφθαλμός σου ὁ δεξιὸς σκανδαλίζει σε, ἔξελε αὐτὸν καὶ βάλε ἀπὸ σοῦ· συμφέρει γάρ σοι ἵνα ἀπόληται ἓν τῶν μελῶν σου καὶ μὴ ὅλον τὸ σῶμά σου βληθῇ εἰς γέενναν. 30 καὶ εἰ ἡ δεξιά σου χεὶρ σκανδαλίζει σε, ἔκκοψον αὐτὴν καὶ βάλε ἀπὸ σοῦ· συμφέρει γάρ σοι ἵνα ἀπόληται ἓν τῶν μελῶν σου καὶ μὴ ὅλον τὸ σῶμά σου εἰς γέενναν ἀπέλθῃ.

Teaching about Divorce
(Mt 19.9; Mk 10.11–12; Lk 16.18)

31 Ἐρρέθη δέ, **Ὃς ἂν ἀπολύσῃ τὴν γυναῖκα αὐτοῦ, δότω αὐτῇ ἀποστάσιον.** 32 ἐγὼ δὲ λέγω ὑμῖν ὅτι πᾶς ὁ

---

⁵ 25 {B} ὁ κριτής 𝔭⁶⁴ᵛⁱᵈ ℵ B f¹ f¹³ 892 1216 1230 itᵏ syrᵖᵃˡ arm eth geoᴮ Carpocrates Irenaeusˡᵃᵗ Clement Hilary Chrysostom Augustine Arnobius ∥ ὁ κριτής σε παραδῷ (see Lk 12.58) (D δώσει) K L W Δ Θ Π 28 33 565 (700 omit σε) 1009 1010 1071 1079 1195 1241 1242 1365 1546 1646 2148 2174 Byz Lect itᵃ, ᵃᵘʳ, ᵇ, ᶜ, ᵈ, ᶠ, ᶠᶠ¹, ᵍ¹, ʰ, ˡ vg syrᶜ, ˢ, ᵖ, ʰ copˢᵃ, ᵇᵒ goth geoˡ, ᴬ Jerome

ᵇ ᵇ 24 b minor, b none: WH Bov Nes BF² (NEB) TT Jer Seg ∥ b none, b major: (AV) RSV ∥ b minor, b minor: TR RV ASV ∥ b none, b none: Zür Luth

25–26 ὁ κριτής...κοδράντην Mt 18.34–35; Lk 12.58–59   27 Οὐ μοιχεύσεις Ex 20.14; Dt 5.18 (Mt 19.18; Mk 10.19; Lk 18.20; Ro 13.9; Jas 2.11)   29–30 Mt 18.8–9; Mk 9.43–47   31 Ὃς...ἀποστάσιον Dt 24.1 (Mt 19.7; Mk 10.4)   32 1 Cor 7.10–11 ἀπολύων τὴν γυναῖκα αὐτοῦ παρεκτὸς λόγου πορνείας ποιεῖ αὐτὴν μοιχευθῆναι, καὶ ὃς ἐὰν ἀπολελυμένην γαμήσῃ μοιχᾶται[6].

Teaching about Oaths

33 Πάλιν ἠκούσατε ὅτι ἐρρέθη τοῖς ἀρχαίοις, **Οὐκ ἐπιορκήσεις, ἀποδώσεις** δὲ **τῷ κυρίῳ τοὺς ὅρκους σου.** 34 ἐγὼ δὲ λέγω ὑμῖν μὴ ὀμόσαι ὅλως· μήτε ἐν **τῷ οὐρανῷ,** ὅτι **θρόνος ἐστὶν τοῦ θεοῦ·** 35 μήτε ἐν **τῇ γῇ,** ὅτι **ὑποπόδιόν ἐστιν τῶν ποδῶν αὐτοῦ·** μήτε εἰς Ἰεροσόλυμα, ὅτι **πόλις ἐστὶν τοῦ μεγάλου βασιλέως·** 36 μήτε ἐν τῇ κεφαλῇ σου ὀμόσῃς, ὅτι οὐ δύνασαι μίαν τρίχα λευκὴν ποιῆσαι ἢ μέλαιναν. 37 ἔστω[7] δὲ ὁ λόγος ὑμῶν ναὶ ναί, οὒ οὔ· τὸ δὲ περισσὸν τούτων ἐκ τοῦ πονηροῦ ἐστιν.

Teaching about Retaliation
(Lk 6.29–30)

38 Ἠκούσατε ὅτι ἐρρέθη, **Ὀφθαλμὸν ἀντὶ ὀφθαλμοῦ** καὶ **ὀδόντα ἀντὶ ὀδόντος.** 39 ἐγὼ δὲ λέγω ὑμῖν μὴ ἀντιστῆναι τῷ πονηρῷ· ἀλλ᾽ ὅστις σε ῥαπίζει εἰς τὴν δεξιὰν σιαγόνα [σου], στρέψον αὐτῷ καὶ τὴν ἄλλην· 40 καὶ τῷ

---

[6] **32** {B} καὶ ὃς ἐὰν ἀπολελυμένην γαμήσῃ μοιχᾶται ℵ K (L γαμήσει) W Δ Θ Π 0250 f[1] (f[13] 700 1009 1071 1230 1242 ἄν) 28 33 565 892 1010 1079 1195 (1216 omit ὅς) 1241 1365 (1546 omit ἐάν and γαμήσῃ) 1646 (2148 ἄν and γαμήσει) 2174 Byz Lect (l[883,950] ἄν) it[h] syr[h] cop[sa,bo] goth arm eth[ro,pp,(ms?)] ǁ καὶ ὁ ἀπολελυμένην γαμήσας μοιχᾶται B (l[184] καὶ ὅς) l[185,1579] geo ǁ καὶ ὃς ἐὰν ἀπολελυμένην γαμήσῃ μοιχᾶται or καὶ ὁ ἀπολελυμένην γαμήσας μοιχᾶται it[aur,c,f,ff1,g1,l] vg syr[c,s,p,pal] ǁ omit D it[a,b,d,k] Greek and Latin mss[acc. to Augustine]

[7] **37** {B} ἔστω ℵ D K L W Δ Θ Π 0250 f[1] f[13] 28 33 565 892 1009 1010 1071 1079 1195 1216 1230 1241 1242 1365 1646 2148 2174 Byz Lect it[a,aur,b,c,d,f,ff1,g1,k,l] vg cop[sa,bo] goth eth geo Justin Irenaeus[lat] Clement[1/2] Tertullian Cyprian ǁ ἔσται B 700 1546 syr[c,s,p,h,pal] Diatessaron Clement[1/2] Eusebius

---

33 Οὐκ...σου Lv 19.12; Nu 30.2; Dt 23.21 **34–35** μήτε...γῇ Jas 5.12 **34** οὐρανῷ...θεοῦ Is 66.1; Mt 23.22; Ac 7.49 **35** γῇ...αὐτοῦ Is 66.1; Ac 7.49; Jas 5.12 πόλις...βασιλέως Ps 48.2 **37** Jas 5.12 ναὶ ναί, οὒ οὔ 2 Cor 1.17 **38** Ὀφθαλμὸν...ὀδόντος Ex 21.24; Lv 24.20; Dt 19.21 **39** ῥαπίζει...σου Jn 18.22 **40** 1 Cor 6.7

---

if a man divorces his wife, and she has not been unfaithful, then he is guilty of making her commit adultery if she marries again; and the man who marries her also commits adultery."

Teaching about Vows

33 "You have also heard that men were told in the past, 'Do not break your promise, but do what you have sworn to do before the Lord.' 34 But now I tell you: do not use any vow when you make a promise; do not swear by heaven, because it is God's throne; 35 nor by earth, because it is the resting place for his feet; nor by Jerusalem, because it is the city of the great King. 36 Do not even swear by your head, because you cannot make a single hair white or black. 37 Just say 'Yes' or 'No' — anything else you have to say comes from the Evil One."

Teaching about Revenge
(Also Luke 6.29–30)

38 "You have heard that it was said, 'An eye for an eye, and a tooth for a tooth.' 39 But now I tell you: do not take revenge on someone who does you wrong. If anyone slaps you on the right cheek, let him slap your left cheek too. 40 And if someone takes you to court to

sue you for your shirt, let him have your coat as well. ⁴¹ And if one of the occupation troops forces you to carry his pack one mile, carry it another mile. ⁴² When someone asks you for something, give it to him; when someone wants to borrow something, lend it to him.''

Love for Enemies
(Also Luke 6,27–28, 32–36)

⁴³ ''You have heard that it was said, 'Love your friends, hate your enemies.' ⁴⁴ But now I tell you: love your enemies, and pray for those who mistreat you, ⁴⁵ so that you will become the sons of your Father in heaven. For he makes his sun to shine on bad and good people alike, and gives rain to those who do right and those who do wrong. ⁴⁶ Why should you expect God to reward you, if you love only the people who love you? Even the tax collectors do that! ⁴⁷ And if you speak only to your friends,

θέλοντί σοι κριθῆναι καὶ τὸν χιτῶνά σου λαβεῖν, ἄφες αὐτῷ καὶ τὸ ἱμάτιον· **41** καὶ ὅστις σε ἀγγαρεύσει μίλιον ἕν, ὕπαγε μετ' αὐτοῦ δύο. **42** τῷ αἰτοῦντί σε δός, καὶ τὸν θέλοντα ἀπὸ σοῦ δανίσασθαι μὴ ἀποστραφῇς.

Love for Enemies
(Lk 6.27–28, 32–36)

43 Ἠκούσατε ὅτι ἐρρέθη, Ἀγαπήσεις τὸν πλησίον σου καὶ μισήσεις τὸν ἐχθρόν σου. **44** ἐγὼ δὲ λέγω ὑμῖν, ἀγαπᾶτε τοὺς ἐχθροὺς ὑμῶν[8] καὶ προσεύχεσθε ὑπὲρ τῶν διωκόντων ὑμᾶς[9], **45** ὅπως γένησθε υἱοὶ τοῦ πατρὸς ὑμῶν τοῦ ἐν οὐρανοῖς, ὅτι τὸν ἥλιον αὐτοῦ ἀνατέλλει ἐπὶ πονηροὺς καὶ ἀγαθοὺς καὶ βρέχει ἐπὶ δικαίους καὶ ἀδίκους. **46** ἐὰν γὰρ ἀγαπήσητε τοὺς ἀγαπῶντας ὑμᾶς, τίνα μισθὸν ἔχετε; οὐχὶ καὶ οἱ τελῶναι τὸ αὐτὸ ποιοῦσιν; **47** καὶ ἐὰν

---

[8] **44** {B} ὑμῶν (see footnote 9) ℵ B f¹ itᵏ syrᶜ·ˢ copˢᵃ·ᵇᵒ Theophilus Irenaeusˡᵃᵗ Origen Cyprian Adamantius mssᵃᶜᶜ· ᵗᵒ ᴾᵉᵗᵉʳ⁻ᴸᵃᵒᵈⁱᶜᵃ ‖ ὑμῶν, εὐλογεῖτε τοὺς καταρωμένους ὑμᾶς 1071 l⁸⁷¹ itᵃ·ᵃᵘʳ·ᵇ·ᶠᶠˡ·ᵍˡ·ˡ vg copᵇᵒᵐˢˢ geo¹ (Athenagoras omit ὑμᾶς) Clement Cassiodorus ‖ ὑμῶν, καλῶς ποιεῖτε τοῖς μισοῦσιν ὑμᾶς 1230 1242* ‖ ὑμῶν, εὐλογεῖτε τοὺς καταρωμένους ὑμᾶς, καλῶς ποιεῖτε τοῖς μισοῦσιν ὑμᾶς (see Lk 6.27–28) Dᶜ (D* ὑμῖν for first ὑμᾶς) K L W Δ Θ Π f¹³ 28 33 565 700 892 1009 1010 1079 1195 1216 1241 1242ᶜ 1365 1546 1646 2148 2174 Byz Lect (l¹⁵⁶⁴ omit second ὑμᾶς) itᶜ·ᵈ·ᶠ·ʰ syrʰ·ᵖᵃˡ (syrᵖ τὸν καταρώμενον) goth arm eth geoᴬ (geoᴮ omit τοῖς μισοῦσιν ὑμᾶς) Aphraates Apostolic Constitutions Chrysostom ‖ ὑμῶν, καὶ εὐλογεῖτε τοὺς καταρωμένους ὑμᾶς καὶ καλῶς ποιεῖτε τοῖς ἐπηρεάζουσιν ὑμᾶς ethᵐˢ

[9] **44** {B} καὶ προσεύχεσθε ὑπὲρ τῶν διωκόντων ὑμᾶς (see footnote 8) ℵ B f¹ itᵏ syrᶜ·ˢ copˢᵃ·ᵇᵒ eth Theophilus (Athenagoras omit καί) Irenaeusˡᵃᵗ Origen Cyprian Adamantius mssᵃᶜᶜ· ᵗᵒ ᴾᵉᵗᵉʳ⁻ᴸᵃᵒᵈⁱᶜᵃ ‖ καὶ προσεύχεσθε ὑπὲρ τῶν ἐπηρεαζόντων ὑμᾶς (1216 omit καί) 1230 1241 l¹⁸⁵ goth (geo¹ Clement ὑμῖν for ὑμᾶς) ‖ καὶ προσεύχεσθε ὑπὲρ τῶν ἐπηρεαζόντων ὑμᾶς καὶ διωκόντων ὑμᾶς (see Lk 6.27–28) Dᶜ (D* omit first ὑμᾶς) K L (W 28 1009 omit first καί) Δ (Θ ἡμᾶς for second ὑμᾶς) Π f¹³ (33 omit second ὑμᾶς) 565 700 892 1010 1071 1079 1195 1242 1365 1546 1646 2148 2174 Byz Lect (l⁷⁶ προσέχετε for προσεύχεσθε, l²¹¹ εὔχεσθε for προσεύχεσθε) itᶜ·ᵈ·ᶠ·ʰ syrᵖ·ʰ·ᵖᵃˡ arm geo Aphraates Apostolic Constitutions Chrysostom ‖ et orate pro persequentibus et calumniantibus vos it⁽ᵃ⁾·ᵃᵘʳ·⁽ᵇ⁾·ᶠᶠˡ·⁽ᵍˡ⁾·ˡ vg Cassiodorus

---

43 Ἀγαπήσεις...σου Lv 19.18 (Mt 19.19; 22.39; Mk 12.31; Lk 10.27; Ro 13.9; Ga 5.14; Jas 2.8) **44** ἀγαπᾶτε...ὑμῶν Ex 23.4–5; Pr 25.21; Ro 12.20 προσεύχεσθε...ὑμᾶς Lk 23.34; Ac 7.60; Ro 12.14; 1 Cor 4.12 **45** ὅπως...οὐρανοῖς Eph 5.1

ἀσπάσησθε τοὺς ἀδελφοὺς ὑμῶν μόνον, τί περισσὸν ποιεῖτε; οὐχὶ καὶ οἱ ἐθνικοί[10] τὸ αὐτὸ ποιοῦσιν; 48 Ἔσεσθε
οὖν ὑμεῖς τέλειοι ὡς ὁ πατὴρ ὑμῶν ὁ οὐράνιος τέλειός
ἐστιν.

Teaching about Almsgiving

6 Προσέχετε [δὲ] τὴν δικαιοσύνην ὑμῶν μὴ ποιεῖν
ἔμπροσθεν τῶν ἀνθρώπων πρὸς τὸ θεαθῆναι αὐτοῖς· εἰ
δὲ μήγε, μισθὸν οὐκ ἔχετε παρὰ τῷ πατρὶ ὑμῶν τῷ ἐν
τοῖς οὐρανοῖς.

2 Ὅταν οὖν ποιῇς ἐλεημοσύνην, μὴ σαλπίσῃς ἔμπροσθέν
σου, ὥσπερ οἱ ὑποκριταὶ ποιοῦσιν ἐν ταῖς συναγωγαῖς καὶ
ἐν ταῖς ῥύμαις, ὅπως δοξασθῶσιν ὑπὸ τῶν ἀνθρώπων·
ἀμὴν λέγω ὑμῖν, ἀπέχουσιν τὸν μισθὸν αὐτῶν. **3** σοῦ δὲ
ποιοῦντος ἐλεημοσύνην μὴ γνώτω ἡ ἀριστερά σου τί
ποιεῖ ἡ δεξιά σου, **4** ὅπως ᾖ σου ἡ ἐλεημοσύνη ἐν τῷ
κρυπτῷ· καὶ ὁ πατήρ σου ὁ βλέπων ἐν τῷ κρυπτῷ [αὐτὸς]
ἀποδώσει σοι[1].

Teaching about Prayer
(Lk 11.2–4)

5 Καὶ ὅταν προσεύχησθε, οὐκ ἔσεσθε ὡς οἱ ὑποκριταί·
ὅτι φιλοῦσιν ἐν ταῖς συναγωγαῖς καὶ ἐν ταῖς γωνίαις τῶν
πλατειῶν ἑστῶτες προσεύχεσθαι, ὅπως φανῶσιν τοῖς
ἀνθρώποις· ἀμὴν λέγω ὑμῖν, ἀπέχουσιν τὸν μισθὸν αὐτῶν.

---

[10] **47** {B} ἐθνικοί ℵ B D *f*[1] 33 892 1071 1216 1230 1241 1365 it[a,aur,b,c,] [(d,f),ff1,(g1),l] vg syr[c,(s,h),pal] cop[sa,bo,fay] eth geo[1] Cyprian (Lucifer) Basil ∥ τελῶναι (*see* 5.46) K L W Δ Θ Π *f*[13] 28 565 700 1009 1010 1079 1195 1242 1546 1646 2148 2174 *Byz Lect* it[h] syr[p] goth geo[2] Diatessaron ∥ τελῶναι καὶ οἱ ἁμαρτωλοί arm

[1] **4** {B} σοι ℵ B D *f*[1] *f*[13] 33 it[aur,d,ff1,k] vg syr[c] cop[sa,bo,fay] (Origen) Cyprian Chromatius Jerome Augustine Greek mss[acc. to Augustine] ∥ σοι ἐν τῷ φανερῷ K L W Δ Θ Π 0250 28 565 (700 σοι αὐτὸς ἐν φανερῷ) 892 1009 1010 1071 1079 1195 1216 1230 1241 1242 1365 1546 1646 2148 2174 *Byz Lect* it[a,b,c,f,g1,h,l,q] syr[s,p,h,pal] goth arm eth geo Diatessaron Apostolic Constitutions Chrysostom Latin mss[acc. to Augustine] Ps-Chrysostom

48 Lv 19.2; Dt 18.13
6 1 μὴ...αὐτοῖς Mt 23.5 **5** ὅπως...ἀνθρώποις Mt 6.16; 23.5

have you done anything out of the ordinary? Even the pagans do that! [48] You must be perfect — just as your Father in heaven is perfect."

Teaching about Charity

6 "Be careful not to perform your religious duties in public so that people will see what you do. If you do these things publicly you will not have any reward from your Father in heaven.

[2] "So when you give something to a needy person, do not make a big show of it, as the show-offs do in the synagogues and on the streets. They do it so that people will praise them. Remember this! They have already been paid in full. [3] But when you help a needy person, do it in such a way that even your closest friend will not know about it, [4] but it will be a private matter. And your Father, who sees what you do in private, will reward you."

Teaching about Prayer
(Also Luke 11.2–4)

[5] "And when you pray, do not be like the show-offs! They love to stand up and pray in the synagogues and on the street corners so that everybody will see them. Remember this! They have already been

paid in full. ⁶ But when you pray, go to your room and close the door, and pray to your Father, who is unseen. And your Father, who sees what you do in private, will reward you.

⁷ "In your prayers do not use a lot of words, as the pagans do, who think that God will hear them because of their long prayers. ⁸ Do not be like them; your Father already knows what you need before you ask him. ⁹ This is the way you should pray:

'Our Father in heaven:
May your name be kept holy,
¹⁰ May your Kingdom come,
May your will be done on earth as it is in heaven.
¹¹ Give us today the food we need;[1]
¹² Forgive us the wrongs that we have done,
As we forgive the wrongs that others have done us;
¹³ Do not bring us to hard testing, but keep us safe from the Evil One.'

---

[1] **11** we need: *or* for today; *or* for tomorrow

---

6 σὺ δὲ ὅταν προσεύχῃ, εἴσελθε εἰς τὸ ταμεῖόν σου καὶ κλείσας τὴν θύραν σου πρόσευξαι τῷ πατρί σου τῷ ἐν τῷ κρυπτῷ· καὶ ὁ πατήρ σου ὁ βλέπων ἐν τῷ κρυπτῷ ἀποδώσει σοι[2]. **7** Προσευχόμενοι δὲ μὴ βατταλογήσητε ὥσπερ οἱ ἐθνικοί, δοκοῦσιν γὰρ ὅτι ἐν τῇ πολυλογίᾳ αὐτῶν εἰσακουσθήσονται. **8** μὴ οὖν ὁμοιωθῆτε αὐτοῖς, οἶδεν γὰρ ὁ πατὴρ ὑμῶν[3] ὧν χρείαν ἔχετε πρὸ τοῦ ὑμᾶς αἰτῆσαι αὐτόν. **9** Οὕτως οὖν προσεύχεσθε ὑμεῖς·

Πάτερ ἡμῶν ὁ ἐν τοῖς οὐρανοῖς,
    ἁγιασθήτω τὸ ὄνομά σου,
10   ἐλθέτω ἡ βασιλεία σου,
    γενηθήτω τὸ θέλημά σου,
        ὡς ἐν οὐρανῷ καὶ ἐπὶ γῆς.
11   Τὸν ἄρτον ἡμῶν τὸν ἐπιούσιον δὸς ἡμῖν
        σήμερον·
12   καὶ ἄφες ἡμῖν τὰ ὀφειλήματα ἡμῶν,
        ὡς καὶ ἡμεῖς ἀφήκαμεν τοῖς ὀφειλέταις
        ἡμῶν·
13   καὶ μὴ εἰσενέγκῃς ἡμᾶς εἰς πειρασμόν,
        ἀλλὰ ῥῦσαι ἡμᾶς ἀπὸ τοῦ πονηροῦ.[4]

---

[2] **6** {B} σοι ℵ B D *f*¹ it^aur,d,ff¹,k vg syr^c,s,pal^ms cop^sa,bo Origen Ps-Clement Eusebius Hilary Ambrose ‖ σοι ἐν τῷ φανερῷ K L W X Δ Θ Π *f*¹³ 28 33 565 700 892 1009 1010 1071 1079 1195 1216 1230 1241 1242 1365 1546 1646 2148 2174 *Byz Lect* it^a,b,c,f,g¹,h,l,q syr^p,h,pal^mss goth arm eth geo Diatessaron

[3] **8** {A} ὁ πατὴρ ὑμῶν ℵ* D K L W Δ Θ Π 0170^vid *f*¹³ 565 700 892^txt 1009 1010 1071 1079 1230 1241 1242 1365 1646 2174 *Byz Lect* it^a,aur,b,c,f,ff¹, g¹,h,k,l,q vg syr^c,s,p,pal cop^bo,fay goth arm geo^1,A ‖ ὁ πατὴρ ἡμῶν *f*¹ 1253 1546 *l*^76,184,1663 ‖ ὁ θεὸς ὁ πατὴρ ὑμῶν ℵ^a B cop^sa Origen ‖ ὁ πατὴρ ὑμῶν ὁ οὐράνιος (*see* 6.9) 28 892^mg 1195 1216 (2148 ἡμῶν ὁ ἐν τοῖς οὐρανοῖς) syr^h eth geo^B (Origen *omit* ὑμῶν)

[4] **13** {A} πονηροῦ. ℵ B D 0170 *f*¹ *l*^547 it^a,aur,b,c,ff¹,h,l vg^ww cop^bo Tertullian Origen Cyprian Hilary Caesarius-Nazianzus Gregory-Nyssa Chromatius Augustine mss^acc. to Peter-Laodicea Maximus-Confessor ‖ πονηροῦ. ἀμήν. 17 vg^cl Cyril-Jerusalem ‖ πονηροῦ, ὅτι σοῦ ἐστιν ἡ βασιλεία καὶ ἡ δύναμις καὶ ἡ δόξα εἰς τοὺς αἰῶνας. ἀμήν. (*see* 1 Chr 29.11-13) K L W Δ Θ Π *f*¹³

---

6 εἴσελθε...θύραν σου Is 26.20   εἴσελθε...πρόσευξαι 2 Kgs 4.33   **8** οἶδεν...ἔχετε Mt 6.32; Lk 12.30   **9** ἁγιασθήτω...σου Eze 36.23   **10** γενηθήτω...σου Mt 26.42; Lk 22.42 **12** Sir 28.2; Mt 18.32-33   **13** μὴ...πειρασμόν Sir 23.1; 33.1; Mt 26.41; Lk 22.40   ῥῦσαι...πονηροῦ Jn 17.15; 2 Th 3.3; 2 Tm 4.18

14 Ἐὰν γὰρ ἀφῆτε τοῖς ἀνθρώποις τὰ παραπτώματα αὐτῶν, ἀφήσει καὶ ὑμῖν ὁ πατὴρ ὑμῶν ὁ οὐράνιος· 15 ἐὰν δὲ μὴ ἀφῆτε τοῖς ἀνθρώποις [τὰ παραπτώματα αὐτῶν]⁵, οὐδὲ ὁ πατὴρ ὑμῶν ἀφήσει τὰ παραπτώματα ὑμῶν.

Teaching about Fasting

16 Ὅταν δὲ νηστεύητε, μὴ γίνεσθε ὡς οἱ ὑποκριταὶ σκυθρωποί, ἀφανίζουσιν γὰρ τὰ πρόσωπα αὐτῶν ὅπως φανῶσιν τοῖς ἀνθρώποις νηστεύοντες· ἀμὴν λέγω ὑμῖν, ἀπέχουσιν τὸν μισθὸν αὐτῶν. 17 σὺ δὲ νηστεύων ἄλειψαί σου τὴν κεφαλὴν καὶ τὸ πρόσωπόν σου νίψαι, 18 ὅπως μὴ φανῇς τοῖς ἀνθρώποις νηστεύων ἀλλὰ τῷ πατρί σου τῷ ἐν τῷ κρυφαίῳ· καὶ ὁ πατήρ σου ὁ βλέπων ἐν τῷ κρυφαίῳ ἀποδώσει σοι⁶.

Treasure in Heaven
(Lk 12.33—34)

19 Μὴ θησαυρίζετε ὑμῖν θησαυροὺς ἐπὶ τῆς γῆς, ὅπου σὴς καὶ βρῶσις ἀφανίζει, καὶ ὅπου κλέπται διορύσσουσιν

28 33 565 700 892 1009 1010 1071 1079 1195 1216 1230 1241 1242 1365 1546 1646 (2148 αἰῶνας τῶν αἰώνων. ἀμήν) 2174 Byz Lect itᶠ·⁽q⁾ (itᵍˡ syrᵖ omit ἀμήν) syrʰ·ᵖᵃˡ copᵇᵒᵐˢˢ goth arm eth geo Diatessaron Apostolic Constitutions Chrysostom ∥ πονηροῦ ὅτι σοῦ ἐστιν ἡ δύναμις εἰς τοὺς αἰῶνας τῶν αἰώνων. itᵏ ∥ πονηροῦ ὅτι σοῦ ἐστιν ἡ δύναμις καὶ ἡ δόξα εἰς τοὺς αἰῶνας. ἀμήν. copˢᵃ·ᶠᵃʸ (Didache omit ἀμήν) ∥ πονηροῦ ὅτι σοῦ ἐστιν ἡ βασιλεία καὶ ἡ δόξα εἰς τοὺς αἰῶνας. ἀμήν. syrᶜ ∥ πονηροῦ ὅτι σοῦ ἐστιν ἡ βασιλεία τοῦ πατρὸς καὶ τοῦ υἱοῦ καὶ τοῦ ἁγίου πνεύματος εἰς τοὺς αἰῶνας. ἀμήν. 1253

⁵ 15 {C} τὰ παραπτώματα αὐτῶν B K L W Δ Θ Π f¹³ 28 33 565 700 892ᵐᵍ 1009 1010 1071 1079 1195 1216 1230 1241 1242 1253 1365 1546 1646 2148 2174 Byz Lect (itᵇ omit αὐτῶν) itᶠ·q syrᶜ·ʰ·ᵖᵃˡ copˢᵃ·ᵇᵒᵐˢˢ goth arm eth geo Ps Chrysostom ∥ omit ℵ D f¹ 892ᵗˣᵗ itᵃ·ᵃᵘʳ·ᶜ·ᶠᶠˡ·ᵍˡ·ʰ·ᵏ·ˡ vg syrᵖ copᵇᵒᵐˢˢ·ᶠᵃʸ Diatessaron Eusebius Augustine

⁶ 18 {A} σοι ℵ B D K L W Θ Π 0250 f¹ f¹³ 28 33 565 700 892 1010 1079 1242 1365 1646 2148 Byzᵖᵗ Lect itᵃᵘʳ·ᶠ·ᶠᶠˡ·ˡ·q vg syrᶜ·ᵖ·ʰ·ᵖᵃˡᵐˢˢ copˢᵃ·ᵇᵒ goth arm Theophilus Ambrose Augustine Euthalius ∥ σοι ἐν τῷ φανερῷ Δ 1009 1071 1195 1216 1230 1241 1253 1546 2174 Byzᵖᵗ l⁵⁴⁷·⁹⁵⁰·¹⁶⁶³ itᵃ·ᵇ·ᶜ·ᵍˡ·ʰ·ᵏ syrᵖᵃˡᵐˢ ethʳᵒ·ᵖᵖ (ethᵐˢˢ ὑμῖν ἐν) geo Ephraem

14 Mk 11.25; Eph 4.32; Col 3.13   15 Mt 18.35   16 Ὅταν...αὐτῶν Is 58.5 ὅπως...ἀνθρώποις Mt 6.5; 23.5   19 Μὴ...ἀφανίζει Jas 5.2—3

Teaching about Fasting

14 For if you forgive others the wrongs they have done you, your Father in heaven will also forgive you. 15 But if you do not forgive the wrongs of others, then your Father in heaven will not forgive the wrongs you have done."

Teaching about Fasting

16 "And when you fast, do not put on a sad face like the show-offs do. They go around with a hungry look so that everybody will be sure to see that they are fasting. Remember this! They have already been paid in full. 17 When you go without food, wash your face and comb your hair, 18 so that others cannot know that you are fasting — only your Father, who is unseen, will know. And your Father, who sees what you do in private, will reward you."

Riches in Heaven
(Also Luke 12.33—34)

19 "Do not save riches here on earth, where moths and rust destroy, and

robbers break in and steal. ²⁰ Instead, save riches in heaven, where moths and rust cannot destroy, and robbers cannot break in and steal. ²¹ For your heart will always be where your riches are.''

The Light of the Body
(Also Luke 11.34–36)

²² "The eyes are like a lamp for the body: if your eyes are clear, your whole body will be full of light; ²³ but if your eyes are bad, your body will be in darkness. So if the light in you turns out to be darkness, how terribly dark it will be!"

God and Possessions
(Also Luke 16.13; 12.22–31)

²⁴ "No one can be a slave to two masters: he will hate one and love the other; he will be loyal to one and despise the other. You cannot serve both God and money.

²⁵ "This is why I tell you: do not be worried about the food and drink you need to stay alive, or about clothes for your body. After all, isn't life worth more than food? and isn't the body worth more than clothes? ²⁶ Look at the birds flying around: they do not plant seeds, gather a harvest, and put

καὶ κλέπτουσιν· **20** θησαυρίζετε δὲ ὑμῖν θησαυροὺς ἐν οὐρανῷ, ὅπου οὔτε σὴς οὔτε βρῶσις ἀφανίζει, καὶ ὅπου κλέπται οὐ διορύσσουσιν οὐδὲ κλέπτουσιν· **21** ὅπου γάρ ἐστιν ὁ θησαυρός σου, ἐκεῖ ἔσται καὶ ἡ καρδία σου.

The Light of the Body
(Lk 11.34–36)

22 Ὁ λύχνος τοῦ σώματός ἐστιν ὁ ὀφθαλμός. ἐὰν οὖν ᾖ ὁ ὀφθαλμός σου ἁπλοῦς, ὅλον τὸ σῶμά σου φωτεινὸν ἔσται· **23** ἐὰν δὲ ὁ ὀφθαλμός σου πονηρὸς ᾖ, ὅλον τὸ σῶμά σου σκοτεινὸν ἔσται. εἰ οὖν τὸ φῶς τὸ ἐν σοὶ σκότος ἐστίν, τὸ σκότος πόσον.

God and Mammon
(Lk 16.13)

24 Οὐδεὶς δύναται δυσὶ κυρίοις δουλεύειν· ἢ γὰρ τὸν ἕνα μισήσει καὶ τὸν ἕτερον ἀγαπήσει, ἢ ἑνὸς ἀνθέξεται καὶ τοῦ ἑτέρου καταφρονήσει· οὐ δύνασθε θεῷ δουλεύειν καὶ μαμωνᾷ.

Care and Anxiety
(Lk 12.22–34)

25 Διὰ τοῦτο λέγω ὑμῖν, μὴ μεριμνᾶτε τῇ ψυχῇ ὑμῶν τί φάγητε [ἢ τί πίητε]⁷, μηδὲ τῷ σώματι ὑμῶν τί ἐνδύσησθε· οὐχὶ ἡ ψυχὴ πλεῖόν ἐστιν τῆς τροφῆς καὶ τὸ σῶμα τοῦ ἐνδύματος; **26** ἐμβλέψατε εἰς τὰ πετεινὰ τοῦ οὐρανοῦ ὅτι οὐ σπείρουσιν οὐδὲ θερίζουσιν οὐδὲ συνάγουσιν εἰς

---

⁷ **25** {C} ἢ τί πίητε B W *f*¹³ 33 1230 it^{aur,c,f,g¹,h,q} cop^{samss,bo} arm eth^{ms?} geo¹ (geo^B *omit* τί) Origen (Eusebius) Athanasius mss^{acc. to Jerome} Marcus Maximus-Confessor ∥ καὶ τί πίητε K L Δ Θ Π (28 1071 πίετε) 565 700 1009 1010 1079 1195 1216 1241 1242 1253 1365 1546 1646 (2148 πίεται [=πίετε]) 2174 *Byz Lect* *l*^{76mg} syr^{p,h} goth eth^{ms?} geo^A Basil ∥ *omit* ℵ *f*¹ 892 it^{a,b,ff¹,k,l} vg syr^{c,pal} cop^{samss} eth^{ro,pp} Justin Clement Origen Adamantius Methodius Hilary Athanasius Basil Epiphanius Chrysostom Augustine (Cyril)

20 θησαυρίζετε...οὐρανῷ Slr 29.11; Mt 19.21; Mk 10.21; Lk 18.22; Col 3.1–2   **23** ἐὰν...ᾖ Mt 20.15; Mk 7.22   **24** μαμωνᾷ Lk 16.9   **25** μὴ μεριμνᾶτε Php 4.6   **26** ἐμβλέψατε... αὐτά Ps Sol 5.9–11 lxx

ἀποθήκας, καὶ ὁ πατὴρ ὑμῶν ὁ οὐράνιος τρέφει αὐτά· οὐχ ὑμεῖς μᾶλλον διαφέρετε αὐτῶν; **27** τίς δὲ ἐξ ὑμῶν μεριμνῶν δύναται προσθεῖναι ἐπὶ τὴν ἡλικίαν αὐτοῦ πῆχυν ἕνα; **28** καὶ περὶ ἐνδύματος τί μεριμνᾶτε; καταμάθετε τὰ κρίνα τοῦ ἀγροῦ πῶς αὐξάνουσιν· οὐ κοπιῶσιν οὐδὲ νήθουσιν[8]· **29** λέγω δὲ ὑμῖν ὅτι οὐδὲ Σολομὼν ἐν πάσῃ τῇ δόξῃ αὐτοῦ περιεβάλετο ὡς ἓν τούτων. **30** εἰ δὲ τὸν χόρτον τοῦ ἀγροῦ σήμερον ὄντα καὶ αὔριον εἰς κλίβανον βαλλόμενον ὁ θεὸς οὕτως ἀμφιέννυσιν, οὐ πολλῷ μᾶλλον ὑμᾶς, ὀλιγόπιστοι; **31** μὴ οὖν μεριμνήσητε λέγοντες, Τί φάγωμεν; ἤ, Τί πίωμεν; ἤ, Τί περιβαλώμεθα; **32** πάντα γὰρ ταῦτα τὰ ἔθνη ἐπιζητοῦσιν· οἶδεν γὰρ ὁ πατὴρ ὑμῶν ὁ οὐράνιος ὅτι χρῄζετε τούτων ἁπάντων. **33** ζητεῖτε δὲ πρῶτον τὴν βασιλείαν καὶ τὴν δικαιοσύνην αὐτοῦ[9], καὶ ταῦτα πάντα προστεθήσεται ὑμῖν. **34** μὴ οὖν μεριμνήσητε εἰς τὴν αὔριον, ἡ γὰρ αὔριον μεριμνήσει αὑτῆς· ἀρκετὸν τῇ ἡμέρᾳ ἡ κακία αὐτῆς.

it in barns; your Father in heaven takes care of them! Aren't you worth much more than birds? [27] Which one of you can live a few years more by worrying about it?

[28] "And why worry about clothes? Look how the wild flowers grow: they do not work or make clothes for themselves. [29] But I tell you that not even Solomon, as rich as he was, had clothes as beautiful as one of these flowers. [30] It is God who clothes the wild grass — grass that is here today, gone tomorrow, burned up in the oven. Will he not be all the more sure to clothe you? How little is your faith! [31] So do not start worrying: 'Where will my food come from? or my drink? or my clothes?' [32] (These are the things the heathen are always after.) Your Father in heaven knows that you need all these things. [33] Instead, give first place to his Kingdom and to what he requires, and he will provide you with all these other things. [34] So do not worry about tomorrow; it will have enough worries of its own. There is no need to add to the troubles each day brings."

---

[8] **28** {B} αὐξάνουσιν· οὐ κοπιῶσιν οὐδὲ νήθουσιν ℵ[a] (Β κοπιοῦσιν) f[1] (33 κοπιοῦσιν and νήφουσιν) (1071 αὐξάνει) it[a,aur,b,c,f,ff1,g1,h,(k),l] vg syr[p,h,pal] cop[sa,bo] eth geo Hilary Athanasius Chrysostom Augustine ∥ οὐ ξένουσιν [=ξαίνουσιν] οὐδὲ νήθουσιν οὐδὲ κοπιῶσιν ℵ[*vid] ∥ αὐξάνει οὐ κοπιᾷ οὐδὲ νήθει (see Lk 12.27) K L W Δ Π f[13] 28 565 700 892 1010 1079 1195 1216 1230 1241 1242 1253 1365 1546 2148 2174 Byz Lect (l[185] νήθη) goth arm Basil ∥ αὐξάνουσιν οὐ νίθουσιν [sic] οὐδὲ κοπιῶσιν Θ syr[c] ∥ αὐξάνει καὶ οὐδὲ νήθει 1646 ∥ αὔξανεν 1009

[9] **33** {C} τὴν βασιλείαν καὶ τὴν δικαιοσύνην αὐτοῦ ℵ (Β τὴν δικαιοσύνην καὶ τὴν βασιλείαν αὐτοῦ) (1646 βασιλείαν αὐτοῦ) (it[k] Cyprian δικαιοσύνην τοῦ θεοῦ it[l] (cop[sa,bo] eth[ro?pp?] Aphraates βασιλείαν αὐτοῦ) Tertullian Eusebius ∥ τὴν βασιλείαν τοῦ θεοῦ καὶ τὴν δικαιοσύνην αὐτοῦ K L W Δ Θ Π f[1] f[13] 28 33 565 700 892 1009 1010 1071 1079 1195 1216 1230 1241 1242 1253 1365 1546 2148 2174 Byz Lect it[a,aur,b,c,f,ff1,g1,h] vg syr[c,p,h,pal] arm eth[ms] geo[l,A] Clement[1/3] Augustine Cyril ∥ τὴν βασιλείαν τῶν οὐρανῶν καὶ τὴν δικαιοσύνην αὐτοῦ 301 (Clement[2/3] omit αὐτοῦ) Chrysostom ∥ τὴν βασιλείαν τοῦ θεοῦ 119 245 482 l[184,187] geo[B] ∥ τὴν βασιλείαν τῶν οὐρανῶν Justin

---

26 οὐχ...αὐτῶν Mt 10.31; Lk 12.7, 24   **29** Σολομὼν...αὐτοῦ 1 Kgs 10; 2 Chr 9
32 οἶδεν...ἁπάντων Mt 6.8; Lk 12.30   **33** Ps 37.4   **34** μὴ...αὐτῆς Ex 16.4

Judging Others
(Also Luke 6.37–38, 41–42)

7 "Do not judge others, so that God will not judge you — ² because God will judge you in the same way you judge others, and he will apply to you the same rules you apply to others. ³ Why, then, do you look at the speck in your brother's eye, and pay no attention to the log in your own eye? ⁴ How dare you say to your brother, 'Please, let me take that speck out of your eye,' when you have a log in your own eye? ⁵ You impostor! Take the log out of your own eye first, and then you will be able to see and take the speck out of your brother's eye.

⁶ "Do not give what is holy to dogs — they will only turn and attack you; do not throw your pearls in front of pigs — they will only trample them underfoot."

Ask, Seek, Knock
(Also Luke 11.9–13)

⁷ "Ask, and you will receive; seek, and you will find; knock, and the door will be opened to you. ⁸ For everyone who asks will receive, and he who seeks will find, and the door will be opened to him who knocks. ⁹ Would any one of you fathers give his son a stone, when he asks you for bread? ¹⁰ Or would you give him a snake, when he asks you for fish? ¹¹ As bad as you are, you know how to give good things to your children. How much more, then, your Father in heaven will give good things to those who ask him!

¹² "Do for others what you want them to do for you: this is the meaning of the Law of Moses and the teaching of the prophets."

Judging Others
(Lk 6.37–38, 41–42)

7 Μὴ κρίνετε, ἵνα μὴ κριθῆτε· **2** ἐν ᾧ γὰρ κρίματι κρίνετε κριθήσεσθε, καὶ ἐν ᾧ μέτρῳ μετρεῖτε μετρηθήσεται ὑμῖν. **3** τί δὲ βλέπεις τὸ κάρφος τὸ ἐν τῷ ὀφθαλμῷ τοῦ ἀδελφοῦ σου, τὴν δὲ ἐν τῷ σῷ ὀφθαλμῷ δοκὸν οὐ κατανοεῖς; **4** ἢ πῶς ἐρεῖς τῷ ἀδελφῷ σου, Ἄφες ἐκβάλω τὸ κάρφος ἐκ τοῦ ὀφθαλμοῦ σου, καὶ ἰδοὺ ἡ δοκὸς ἐν τῷ ὀφθαλμῷ σοῦ; **5** ὑποκριτά, ἔκβαλε πρῶτον τὴν δοκὸν ἐκ τοῦ ὀφθαλμοῦ σου, καὶ τότε διαβλέψεις ἐκβαλεῖν τὸ κάρφος ἐκ τοῦ ὀφθαλμοῦ τοῦ ἀδελφοῦ σου. **6** Μὴ δῶτε τὸ ἅγιον τοῖς κυσίν, μηδὲ βάλητε τοὺς μαργαρίτας ὑμῶν ἔμπροσθεν τῶν χοίρων, μήποτε καταπατήσουσιν αὐτοὺς ἐν τοῖς ποσὶν αὐτῶν καὶ στραφέντες ῥήξωσιν ὑμᾶς.

Ask, Seek, Knock
(Lk 11.9–13)

7 Αἰτεῖτε, καὶ δοθήσεται ὑμῖν· ζητεῖτε, καὶ εὑρήσετε· κρούετε, καὶ ἀνοιγήσεται ὑμῖν. **8** πᾶς γὰρ ὁ αἰτῶν λαμβάνει καὶ ὁ ζητῶν εὑρίσκει καὶ τῷ κρούοντι ἀνοιγήσεται. **9** ἢ τίς ἐστιν ἐξ ὑμῶν ἄνθρωπος, ὃν αἰτήσει ὁ υἱὸς αὐτοῦ ἄρτον — μὴ λίθον ἐπιδώσει αὐτῷ; **10** ἢ καὶ ἰχθὺν αἰτήσει — μὴ ὄφιν ἐπιδώσει αὐτῷ; **11** εἰ οὖν ὑμεῖς πονηροὶ ὄντες οἴδατε δόματα ἀγαθὰ διδόναι τοῖς τέκνοις ὑμῶν, πόσῳ μᾶλλον ὁ πατὴρ ὑμῶν ὁ ἐν τοῖς οὐρανοῖς δώσει ἀγαθὰ τοῖς αἰτοῦσιν αὐτόν.ᵃ **12** Πάντα οὖν ὅσα ἐὰν θέλητε ἵνα ποιῶσιν ὑμῖν οἱ ἄνθρωποι, οὕτως καὶ ὑμεῖς ποιεῖτε αὐτοῖς· οὗτος γάρ ἐστιν ὁ νόμος καὶ οἱ προφῆται.

ᵃ **11** *a* major: WH Bov Nes BF² Luth Seg ∥ *a* question: TR AV RV ASV RSVᵉᵈ ∥ *a* exclamation: RSVᵉᵈ NEB TT Zür Jer

---

1 Μὴ κρίνετε Ro 2.1; 14.4, 10; 1 Cor 5.12; Jas 4.11   **2** ἐν ᾧ μέτρῳ...ὑμῖν Mk 4.24   **7** Αἰτεῖτε, καὶ δοθήσεται ὑμῖν Mk 11.24; Jn 14.13–14: 15.7; 16.23–24; Jas 1.5; 1 Jn 3.22; 5.14–15   **11** ὁ πατὴρ...αὐτόν Jas 1.17   **12** οὗτος...προφῆται Mt 22.40; Ro 13.8–10

The Narrow Gate
(Lk 13.24)

13 Εἰσέλθατε διὰ τῆς στενῆς πύλης· ὅτι πλατεῖα ἡ πύλη[1] καὶ εὐρύχωρος ἡ ὁδὸς ἡ ἀπάγουσα εἰς τὴν ἀπώλειαν, καὶ πολλοί εἰσιν οἱ εἰσερχόμενοι δι' αὐτῆς· **14** τί[2] στενὴ ἡ πύλη[3] καὶ τεθλιμμένη ἡ ὁδὸς ἡ ἀπάγουσα εἰς τὴν ζωήν, καὶ ὀλίγοι εἰσὶν οἱ εὑρίσκοντες αὐτήν.

A Tree Known by Its Fruit
(Lk 6.43–44)

15 Προσέχετε ἀπὸ τῶν ψευδοπροφητῶν, οἵτινες ἔρχονται πρὸς ὑμᾶς ἐν ἐνδύμασιν προβάτων, ἔσωθεν δέ εἰσιν λύκοι ἅρπαγες. **16** ἀπὸ τῶν καρπῶν αὐτῶν ἐπιγνώσεσθε αὐτούς· μήτι συλλέγουσιν ἀπὸ ἀκανθῶν σταφυλὰς ἢ ἀπὸ τριβόλων σῦκα; **17** οὕτως πᾶν δένδρον ἀγαθὸν καρποὺς καλοὺς ποιεῖ, τὸ δὲ σαπρὸν δένδρον καρποὺς πονηροὺς ποιεῖ· **18** οὐ δύναται δένδρον ἀγαθὸν καρποὺς πονηροὺς

[1] **13** {C} ἡ πύλη ℵ[b] B C K L W X Δ Θ Π f[1] f[13] 28 33 565 700 892 1009 1010 1071 1079 1195 1216 1230 1241 1242 1253 1365 1546 2148 2174 *Byz Lect* l[333s, m, 883m] it[aur, f, ff1, g1, l, q] vg syr[c, p, h, pal] cop[sa, bo] goth arm eth geo[l, (2)] Origen[gr, lat1/2] Basil Chrysostom Augustine Fulgentius ‖ *omit* ℵ* 1646 it[a, b, c, h, k] Naassenes Diatessaron Clement Hippolytus Origen[gr, lat1/2] Cyprian Eusebius Lucifer Augustine

[2] **14** {B} τί ℵ[c] (B[3] τί δέ) C K L W X*[vid] Δ Θ Π f[1] f[13] 28 565 700* 892 1009 1079 1195 1216 1230 1241 1242 1253 1365 1646 2174 *Byz Lect* l[12m, 70m, 333s, m, 883m, 1231m, 1599m] it[a, aur, b, c, f, ff1, g1, h, (k), l, q] vg syr[c, p, h, pal] goth eth Cyprian Lucifer Ephraem Faustus ‖ ὅτι ℵ* (B* ὅτι δέ) X[c] 700[c] 1010 1071 1546[vid] l[10, 32, 76, 1043, 1627, 1642] cop[sa, bo] arm geo Naassenes Origen Gaudentius ‖ καί 209 Chrysostom ‖ *omit* 2148

[3] **14** {B} ἡ πύλη ℵ B C K (L *omit* ἡ) W X Δ Θ Π f[1] f[13] 28 565 700 892 1009 1010 1071 1079 1195 1216 1230 1241 1242 1253 1365 1546 1646 (2148 στενὴ δὲ πύλη) 2174 *Byz Lect* l[70m, 333s, m, 883m] it[aur, b, c, f, ff1, g1, l, q] vg syr[c, p, h, pal] cop[sa, bo] goth arm eth geo Origen (Chrysostom) Augustine Ps-Athanasius ‖ *omit* 113 182* 482 544 it[a, h, k] Naassenes Diatessaron[esyr] Clement Tertullian Hippolytus (Origen) Cyprian Ps-Clement Eusebius Aphraates Macarius Ps-Athanasius

14 τεθλιμμένη...ζωήν Ac 14.22 **15** Προσέχετε...ψευδοπροφητῶν Mt 24.11, 24; Lk 6.26; 2 Pe 2.1; 1 Jn 4.1; Re 16.13 λύκοι Eze 22.27; Mt 10.16; Jn 10.12; Ac 20.29 **16–17** Mt 12.33, 35 **16** ἀπὸ...αὐτούς Slr 27.6 μήτι...σῦκα Jas 3.12

The Narrow Gate
(Also Luke 13.24)

[13] "Go in through the narrow gate, for the gate is wide and the road is easy that leads to hell, and there are many who travel it. [14] The gate is narrow and the way is hard that leads to life, and few people find it."

A Tree and Its Fruit
(Also Luke 6.43–44)

[15] "Watch out for false prophets; they come to you looking like sheep on the outside, but they are really like wild wolves on the inside. [16] You will know them by the way they act. Thorn bushes do not bear grapes, and briars do not bear figs. [17] A healthy tree bears good fruit, while a poor tree bears bad fruit. [18] A healthy tree cannot bear bad fruit,

and a poor tree cannot bear good fruit. [19] Any tree that does not bear good fruit is cut down and thrown in the fire. [20] So, then, you will know the false prophets by the way they act."

I Never Knew You
(Also Luke 13.25–27)

[21] "Not every person who calls me 'Lord, Lord,' will enter into the Kingdom of heaven, but only those who do what my Father in heaven wants them to do. [22] When that Day comes, many will say to me, 'Lord, Lord! In your name we told God's message, by your name we drove out many demons and performed many miracles!' [23] Then I will say to them, 'I never knew you. Away from me, you evildoers!'"

The Two House Builders
(Also Luke 6.47–49)

[24] "So, then, everyone who hears these words of mine and obeys them will be like a wise man who built his house on the rock. [25] The rain poured down, the rivers flooded over, and the winds blew hard against that house. But it did not fall, because it had been built on the

ποιεῖν[4], οὐδὲ δένδρον σαπρὸν καρποὺς καλοὺς ποιεῖν[4]. **19** πᾶν δένδρον μὴ ποιοῦν καρπὸν καλὸν ἐκκόπτεται καὶ εἰς πῦρ βάλλεται. **20** ἄρα γε ἀπὸ τῶν καρπῶν αὐτῶν ἐπιγνώσεσθε αὐτούς.

I Never Knew You
(Lk 13.25–27)

21 Οὐ πᾶς ὁ λέγων μοι, Κύριε κύριε, εἰσελεύσεται εἰς τὴν βασιλείαν τῶν οὐρανῶν, ἀλλ' ὁ ποιῶν τὸ θέλημα τοῦ πατρός μου τοῦ ἐν τοῖς οὐρανοῖς. **22** πολλοὶ ἐροῦσίν μοι ἐν ἐκείνῃ τῇ ἡμέρᾳ, Κύριε κύριε, οὐ τῷ σῷ ὀνόματι ἐπροφητεύσαμεν, καὶ τῷ σῷ ὀνόματι δαιμόνια ἐξεβάλομεν, καὶ τῷ σῷ ὀνόματι δυνάμεις πολλὰς ἐποιήσαμεν; **23** καὶ τότε ὁμολογήσω αὐτοῖς ὅτι Οὐδέποτε ἔγνων ὑμᾶς· ἀποχωρεῖτε ἀπ' ἐμοῦ οἱ ἐργαζόμενοι τὴν ἀνομίαν.

The Two Foundations
(Lk 6.47–49)

24 Πᾶς οὖν ὅστις ἀκούει μου τοὺς λόγους τούτους καὶ ποιεῖ αὐτοὺς ὁμοιωθήσεται[5] ἀνδρὶ φρονίμῳ, ὅστις ᾠκοδόμησεν αὐτοῦ τὴν οἰκίαν ἐπὶ τὴν πέτραν. **25** καὶ κατέβη ἡ βροχὴ καὶ ἦλθον οἱ ποταμοὶ καὶ ἔπνευσαν οἱ ἄνεμοι καὶ προσέπεσαν τῇ οἰκίᾳ ἐκείνῃ, καὶ οὐκ ἔπεσεν, τεθεμελίωτο

---

4 18 {B} ποιεῖν...ποιεῖν א[c] C K L W X Δ Θ Π 0250 f[1] f[13] 33 565 700 892 1009 1010 1071 1079 1195 1216 1230 1241 1242 1253 1365 1546 1646 (2148 ποιεῖ...ποιεῖ) 2174 *Byz Lect* l[70m,333s,m] it[a,aur,b,c,f,ff1,g1,h,k,l,q] vg syr[c,p,h] cop[sa,bo] goth arm geo ∥ ἐνεγκεῖν...ποιεῖν B syr[pal] ∥ ἐνεγκεῖν...ἐνεγκεῖν (l[1043] ...ἐνεγκεῖ) Tertullian Origen ∥ ποιεῖν...ἐνεγκεῖν א* syr[pal?] Tertullian Origen

5 24 {C} ὁμοιωθήσεται א B Θ f[1] f[13] 33 700 892 1071 1241 1365 it[a,aur,b,c,ff1,g1,l] vg syr[p,hmg,palmss] cop[sa] arm eth? geo Diatessaron[i] Origen Basil Ambrose Chrysostom Cyril mss[acc. to Euthymius] ∥ ὁμοιώσω αὐτόν C K L W X Δ Π 565 1009 1010 1079 1195 1216 1230 1242 1253 1546 1646 2148 2174 *Byz Lect* (l[211]) it[f,h,k,q] syr[c,h,palms] cop[bo] goth Cyprian Hilary Lucifer Augustine

---

19 Mt 3.10; Lk 3.9; 13.6–9; Jn 15.6 **20** Mt 7.16; 12.33 **21** πᾶς...κύριε Lk 6.46 ὁ ποιῶν...πατρός Mt 21.31; Ro 2.13; Jas 1.22, 25; 1 Jn 2.17 **22** τῷ σῷ ὀνόματι ἐπροφητεύσαμεν Jr 14.14; 27.15 τῷ σῷ ὀνόματι...ἐξεβάλομεν Mk 9.38; Lk 9.49 **23** τότε... ὑμᾶς Mt 10.33; 2 Tm 2.12 ἀποχωρεῖτε...ἀνομίαν Ps 6.8; Mt 13.41–42; 25.41 **24** Πᾶς... αὐτούς Jas 1.22

γὰρ ἐπὶ τὴν πέτραν. **26** καὶ πᾶς ὁ ἀκούων μου τοὺς λόγους τούτους καὶ μὴ ποιῶν αὐτοὺς ὁμοιωθήσεται ἀνδρὶ μωρῷ, ὅστις ᾠκοδόμησεν αὐτοῦ τὴν οἰκίαν ἐπὶ τὴν ἄμμον. **27** καὶ κατέβη ἡ βροχὴ καὶ ἦλθον οἱ ποταμοὶ καὶ ἔπνευσαν οἱ ἄνεμοι καὶ προσέκοψαν τῇ οἰκίᾳ ἐκείνῃ, καὶ ἔπεσεν, καὶ ἦν ἡ πτῶσις αὐτῆς μεγάλη.

28 Καὶ ἐγένετο ὅτε ἐτέλεσεν ὁ Ἰησοῦς τοὺς λόγους τούτους ἐξεπλήσσοντο οἱ ὄχλοι ἐπὶ τῇ διδαχῇ αὐτοῦ· **29** ἦν γὰρ διδάσκων αὐτοὺς ὡς ἐξουσίαν ἔχων καὶ οὐχ ὡς οἱ γραμματεῖς αὐτῶν.

The Cleansing of a Leper
(Mk 1.40–45; Lk 5.12–16)

8 Καταβάντος δὲ αὐτοῦ ἀπὸ τοῦ ὄρους ἠκολούθησαν αὐτῷ ὄχλοι πολλοί. **2** καὶ ἰδοὺ λεπρὸς προσελθὼν προσεκύνει αὐτῷ λέγων, Κύριε, ἐὰν θέλῃς δύνασαί με καθαρίσαι. **3** καὶ ἐκτείνας τὴν χεῖρα ἥψατο αὐτοῦ λέγων, Θέλω, καθαρίσθητι· καὶ εὐθέως ἐκαθαρίσθη αὐτοῦ ἡ λέπρα. **4** καὶ λέγει αὐτῷ ὁ Ἰησοῦς, Ὅρα μηδενὶ εἴπῃς, ἀλλὰ ὕπαγε σεαυτὸν δεῖξον τῷ ἱερεῖ, καὶ προσένεγκον τὸ δῶρον ὃ προσέταξεν Μωϋσῆς,[a] εἰς μαρτύριον αὐτοῖς.

The Healing of a Centurion's Servant
(Lk 7.1–10; Jn 4.43–54)

5 Εἰσελθόντος δὲ αὐτοῦ εἰς Καφαρναοὺμ προσῆλθεν αὐτῷ ἑκατόνταρχος παρακαλῶν αὐτὸν **6** καὶ λέγων, Κύριε, ὁ παῖς μου βέβληται ἐν τῇ οἰκίᾳ παραλυτικός, δεινῶς βασανιζόμενος. **7** καὶ λέγει αὐτῷ, Ἐγὼ ἐλθὼν θεραπεύσω αὐτόν.[b] **8** καὶ ἀποκριθεὶς ὁ ἑκατόνταρχος ἔφη,

---

[a] **4** *a minor:* TR Bov Nes BF² AVᵉᵈ RV ASV RSV NEB TT Zür? Luth? Seg ∥ *a none:* WH AVᵉᵈ Jer

[b] **7** *b statement:* TR WH Bov Nes BF² AV RV ASV RSV NEB TT Zür Luth Jer Seg ∥ *b question:* NEBᵐᵍ

26 πᾶς...αὐτούς Jas 1.23   **27** Eze 13.10–12   **28** ἐγένετο...τούτους Mt 11.1; 13.53; 19.1; 26.1; Lk 7.1   **28–29** ἐξεπλήσσοντο...ἔχων Mk 1.22; Lk 4.32

8 4 Ὅρα...εἴπῃς Mt 9.30; 12.16; Mk 7.36 σεαυτὸν...ἱερεῖ Lv 14.2; Lk 17.14 προσένεγκον ...Μωϋσῆς Lv 14.4–32   **5–7** Jn 4.46–47

---

rock. **26** Everyone who hears these words of mine and does not obey them will be like a foolish man who built his house on the sand. **27** The rain poured down, the rivers flooded over, the winds blew hard against that house, and it fell. What a terrible fall that was!"

The Authority of Jesus

28 Jesus finished saying these things, and the crowds were amazed at the way he taught. **29** He wasn't like their teachers of the Law; instead, he taught with authority.

Jesus Makes a Leper Clean
(Also Mark 1.40–45; Luke 5.12–16)

8 Jesus came down from the hill, and large crowds followed him. **2** Then a leper came to him, knelt down before him, and said, "Sir, if you want to, you can make me clean." **3** Jesus reached out and touched him. "I do want to," he answered. "Be clean!" At once he was clean from his leprosy. **4** Then Jesus said to him: "Listen! Don't tell anyone, but go straight to the priest and let him examine you; then offer the sacrifice that Moses ordered, to prove to everyone that you are now clean."

Jesus Heals a Roman Officer's Servant
(Also Luke 7.1–10)

5 When Jesus entered Capernaum, a Roman officer met him and begged for help: **6** "Sir, my servant is home, sick in bed, unable to move, and suffering terribly." **7** "I will go and make him well," Jesus said. **8** "Oh no, sir," answered the officer. "I do not deserve to have you come into my house. Just give the order and my servant will get well. [9] I, too, am a man with superior officers over me, and I have soldiers under me; so I order this one, 'Go!' and he goes; and I order that one, 'Come!' and he comes; and I order my slave, 'Do this!' and he does it." [10] Jesus was surprised when he heard this, and said to the people who were following him: "I tell you, I have never seen such faith as this in anyone in Israel. [11] Remember this! Many will come from the east and the west and sit down at the table in the Kingdom of heaven with Abraham, Isaac, and Jacob. [12] But those who should be in the Kingdom will be thrown out into the darkness outside, where they will cry and gnash their teeth." [13] And Jesus said to the officer, "Go

Κύριε, οὐκ εἰμὶ ἱκανὸς ἵνα μου ὑπὸ τὴν στέγην εἰσέλθῃς· ἀλλὰ μόνον εἰπὲ λόγῳ, καὶ ἰαθήσεται ὁ παῖς μου[1]. 9 καὶ γὰρ ἐγὼ ἄνθρωπός εἰμι ὑπὸ ἐξουσίαν[2], ἔχων ὑπ' ἐμαυτὸν στρατιώτας, καὶ λέγω τούτῳ, Πορεύθητι, καὶ πορεύεται, καὶ ἄλλῳ, Ἔρχου, καὶ ἔρχεται, καὶ τῷ δούλῳ μου, Ποίησον τοῦτο, καὶ ποιεῖ. 10 ἀκούσας δὲ ὁ Ἰησοῦς ἐθαύμασεν καὶ εἶπεν τοῖς ἀκολουθοῦσιν, Ἀμὴν λέγω ὑμῖν, παρ' οὐδενὶ τοσαύτην πίστιν ἐν τῷ Ἰσραὴλ εὗρον[3]. 11 λέγω δὲ ὑμῖν ὅτι πολλοὶ ἀπὸ ἀνατολῶν καὶ δυσμῶν ἥξουσιν καὶ ἀνακλιθήσονται μετὰ Ἀβραὰμ καὶ Ἰσαὰκ καὶ Ἰακὼβ ἐν τῇ βασιλείᾳ τῶν οὐρανῶν· 12 οἱ δὲ υἱοὶ τῆς βασιλείας ἐκβληθήσονται[4] εἰς τὸ σκότος τὸ ἐξώτερον· ἐκεῖ ἔσται ὁ κλαυθμὸς καὶ ὁ βρυγμὸς τῶν ὀδόντων. 13 καὶ εἶπεν ὁ

---

[1] **8** {C} ὁ παῖς μου (see Lk 7.7) ℵ B C K L W X Δ Θ Π f[13] 33 565 700 892 1009 1010 1071 1079 1195 1216 1230 1241 1242 1253 1365 1546 1646 2148 2174 *Byz Lect* it[aur,c,f,ff1,g1,h,l,q] (it[a,b] *omit μου*) vg syr[c,s,p,h,pal] cop[bo] goth arm eth geo[1] ‖ *my servant* geo[2] ‖ *omit* f[1] it[k] cop[sa,bomss] Origen

[2] **9** {B} ὑπὸ ἐξουσίαν C K L W X Δ Θ Π f[1] f[13] 33 565 700 892 1009 1010 1071 1079 1195 1216 1230 1242 1253 1365 1546 1646 2148 2174 *Byz Lect* l[211c] it[ff1,l] vg[ww] syr[c,(s),p,h] cop[sa] arm (eth) geo Chrysostom ‖ ὑπὸ ἐξουσίαν τασσόμενος (see Lk 7.8) ℵ B l[211*] it[a,aur,b,c,g1,h,k,q] vg[cl] syr[pal] cop[bo?] Diatessaron Hilary Chrysostom Augustine ‖ *omit* 1241

[3] **10** {B} παρ' οὐδενὶ τοσαύτην πίστιν ἐν τῷ Ἰσραὴλ εὗρον B W it[a,k,q] syr[c,hmg,pal] cop[sa,bo] eth[ro,ms?] Diatessaron Augustine ‖ παρ' οὐδενὶ τοσαύτην πίστιν εὗρον ἐν τῷ Ἰσραὴλ 892 ‖ οὐδὲ ἐν τῷ Ἰσραὴλ τοσαύτην πίστιν εὗρον (see Lk 7.9) ℵ C K L X Δ Θ Π 0250 f[13] 33 565 700 1009 1010 1071 1079 1195 1216 1230 (1241 1242 1365 ὅτι οὐδέ) 1253 1546 1646 2148 2174 *Byz Lect* it[aur,b,c,f,ff1,g1,h,l] vg syr[s,p,h] goth arm eth[pp] geo Hilary Augustine ‖ παρ' οὐδενὶ τοσαύτην πίστιν εὗρον f[1]

[4] **12** {C} ἐκβληθήσονται ℵ[a] B C K L W X Δ Θ Π f[1] f[13] 33 565 700 892 1009 1010 1071 1079 1195 1216 1230 (1241 2148 ἐμβληθήσονται) 1242 1253 1365 1546 1646 2174 *Byz Lect* it[aur,f,ff1,l] vg syr[h] cop[sa,bo] goth eth geo[2] Cyprian[1/2] Chrysostom Cosmos ‖ ἐξελεύσονται ℵ* 0250 it[k] syr[s,p,pal] arm Diatessaron[a] Heracleon[acc. to Origen] Irenaeus[gr,lat] Cyprian[1/2] Eusebius Augustine ‖ *ibunt* it[a,b,c,g1,h,q] ‖ *omit* geo[1]

---

10 παρ'...εὗρον Mt 15.28   **11** ἀπὸ...ἥξουσιν Ps 107.3   **11–12** ἀπὸ...ἐξώτερον Lk 13.28-29   **12** ἐκεῖ...ὀδόντων Mt 13.42, 50; 22.13; 24.51; 25.30; Lk 13.28

'Ιησοῦς τῷ ἑκατοντάρχῃ, "Υπαγε, ὡς ἐπίστευσας γενηθήτω σοι. καὶ ἰάθη ὁ παῖς [αὐτοῦ] ἐν τῇ ὥρᾳ ἐκείνῃ[5].

The Healing of Many People
(Mk 1.29–34; Lk 4.38–41)

14 Καὶ ἐλθὼν ὁ 'Ιησοῦς εἰς τὴν οἰκίαν Πέτρου εἶδεν τὴν πενθερὰν αὐτοῦ βεβλημένην καὶ πυρέσσουσαν· 15 καὶ ἥψατο τῆς χειρὸς αὐτῆς, καὶ ἀφῆκεν αὐτὴν ὁ πυρετός· καὶ ἠγέρθη καὶ διηκόνει αὐτῷ. 16 'Οψίας δὲ γενομένης προσήνεγκαν αὐτῷ δαιμονιζομένους πολλούς· καὶ ἐξέβαλεν τὰ πνεύματα λόγῳ, καὶ πάντας τοὺς κακῶς ἔχοντας ἐθεράπευσεν· 17 ὅπως πληρωθῇ τὸ ῥηθὲν διὰ 'Ησαΐου τοῦ προφήτου λέγοντος,

Αὐτὸς τὰς ἀσθενείας ἡμῶν ἔλαβεν
καὶ τὰς νόσους ἐβάστασεν.

The Would-be Followers of Jesus
(Lk 9.57–62)

18 'Ιδὼν δὲ ὁ 'Ιησοῦς ὄχλον[6] περὶ αὐτὸν ἐκέλευσεν ἀπελθεῖν εἰς τὸ πέραν. 19 καὶ προσελθὼν εἷς γραμματεὺς εἶπεν αὐτῷ, Διδάσκαλε, ἀκολουθήσω σοι ὅπου ἐὰν ἀπέρχῃ. 20 καὶ λέγει αὐτῷ ὁ 'Ιησοῦς, Αἱ ἀλώπεκες φωλεοὺς ἔχουσιν καὶ τὰ πετεινὰ τοῦ οὐρανοῦ κατασκηνώσεις, ὁ δὲ

home, and what you believe will be done for you." And the officer's servant was healed that very hour.

Jesus Heals Many People
(Also Mark 1.29–34; Luke 4.38–41)

14 Jesus went to Peter's home, and there he saw Peter's mother-in-law sick in bed with a fever. 15 He touched her hand; the fever left her, and she got up and began to wait on him. 16 When evening came, people brought to Jesus many who had demons in them. Jesus drove out the evil spirits with a word and healed all who were sick. 17 He did this to make come true what the prophet Isaiah had said, "He himself took our illnesses and carried away our diseases."

The Would-be Followers of Jesus
(Also Luke 9.57–62)

18 Jesus noticed the crowd around him and gave orders to go to the other side of the lake. 19 A teacher of the Law came to him. "Teacher," he said, "I am ready to go with you wherever you go." 20 Jesus answered him, "Foxes have holes, and birds have nests, but the Son of

---

[5] 13 {B} ἐν τῇ ὥρᾳ ἐκείνῃ ℵ B K L X Π f[1] f[13] 565 (892 omit ἐν) 1009 1071 1079 1195 1216 1230 1241 1242 1253 1365 1546 1646 2148 2174 Byz Lect (l[211]) it[aur,f,ff1,k,l] vg syr[c,s,p,h] cop[samss,bo] goth eth ∥ ἐν τῇ ἡμέρᾳ ἐκείνῃ W 700 arm geo ∥ ἀπὸ τῆς ὥρας ἐκείνης C Δ Θ 0250 33 1010 l[950,1627] it[a,b,c,g1,h,q] syr[pal] cop[sa,bomss] Eusebius Basil Chrysostom Augustine

[6] 18 {D} ὄχλον B cop[sa] ∥ ὄχλον πολύν W it[c,g1] syr[c,s] cop[samss] eth[ms] geo[2] ∥ πολὺν ὄχλον 1216 geo[1] ∥ ὄχλους ℵ* f[1] (1365 l[184] cop[bo] τοὺς ὄχλους) ∥ πολλούς (1071) 1546* ∥ πολλοὺς ὄχλους ℵ[c] C K L X Δ Θ Π f[13] 33 565 700 892 1009 1010 1079 1195 1230 1242 1253 1546[c] 1646 2148 2174 Byz Lect syr[pal] goth eth[ro] Diatessaron ∥ ὄχλους πολλούς 108 it[a,aur,b,ff1,h,k,l,q] vg syr[p,h] arm eth[pp] Hilary Augustine

---

13 ὡς...ἐκείνῃ Mt 9.29; 15.28; Jn 4.50–51   14 εἰς...αὐτοῦ 1 Cor 9.5   17 Αὐτὸς...ἐβάστασεν Is 53.4   18 ἐκέλευσεν...πέραν Mk 4.35; Lk 8.22   20 ὁ δὲ...κλίνη 2 Cor 8.9

Man has no place to lie down and rest."
21 Another man, who was a disciple, said,
"Sir, first let me go and bury my father."
22 "Follow me," Jesus answered, "and let
the dead bury their own dead."

Jesus Calms a Storm
(Also Mark 4.35–41; Luke 8.22–25)

23 Jesus got into the boat, and his
disciples went with him. 24 Suddenly a
fierce storm hit the lake, so that the
waves covered the boat. But Jesus was
asleep. 25 The disciples went to him and
woke him up. "Save us, Lord!" they
said. "We are about to die!" 26 "Why
are you so frightened?" Jesus answered.
"How little faith you have!" Then he
got up and gave a command to the
winds and to the waves, and there was
a great calm. 27 Everyone was amazed.
"What kind of man is this?" they said.
"Even the winds and the waves obey
him!"

υἱὸς τοῦ ἀνθρώπου οὐκ ἔχει ποῦ τὴν κεφαλὴν κλίνῃ.
21 ἕτερος δὲ τῶν μαθητῶν [αὐτοῦ][7] εἶπεν αὐτῷ, Κύριε,
ἐπίτρεψόν μοι πρῶτον ἀπελθεῖν καὶ θάψαι τὸν πατέρα μου.
22 ὁ δὲ Ἰησοῦς λέγει αὐτῷ, Ἀκολούθει μοι, καὶ ἄφες
τοὺς νεκροὺς θάψαι τοὺς ἑαυτῶν νεκρούς.

The Calming of a Storm
(Mk 4.35–41; Lk 8.22–25)

23 Καὶ ἐμβάντι αὐτῷ εἰς [τὸ] πλοῖον[8] ἠκολούθησαν
αὐτῷ οἱ μαθηταὶ αὐτοῦ. 24 καὶ ἰδοὺ σεισμὸς μέγας ἐγένετο
ἐν τῇ θαλάσσῃ, ὥστε τὸ πλοῖον καλύπτεσθαι ὑπὸ τῶν
κυμάτων· αὐτὸς δὲ ἐκάθευδεν. 25 καὶ προσελθόντες[9] ἤγει-
ραν αὐτὸν λέγοντες, Κύριε, σῶσον[10], ἀπολλύμεθα. 26 καὶ
λέγει αὐτοῖς, Τί δειλοί ἐστε, ὀλιγόπιστοι; τότε ἐγερθεὶς
ἐπετίμησεν τοῖς ἀνέμοις καὶ τῇ θαλάσσῃ, καὶ ἐγένετο
γαλήνη μεγάλη. 27 οἱ δὲ ἄνθρωποι ἐθαύμασαν λέγοντες,
Ποταπός ἐστιν οὗτος ὅτι καὶ οἱ ἄνεμοι καὶ ἡ θάλασσα
αὐτῷ ὑπακούουσιν;

---

[7] **21** {C} τῶν μαθητῶν αὐτοῦ C K L W X Δ Θ Π 0250 f[1] f[13] 565 700
892 1009 1010 1071 1079 1195 1216 1242 (1365 *omit* μαθητῶν) 1546 1646 2174
Byz Lect (*l*[845] ἑαυτοῦ) it[aur,ff1,g1,(k),l] vg syr[c,s,p,h,pal] cop[bo] goth arm eth geo ‖
τῶν μαθητῶν ℵ B 33 2148 *l*[883] it[a,(b,c,h,q)] cop[sa] ‖ τις 1230 1253

[8] **23** {C} τὸ πλοῖον ℵ[*,c] K L W X (Δ τόν) Θ Π 700 1009 1010 1071 1079
1195 1216 1242 1365 1546 2148 2174 *Byz* *l*[185pt,211,333pt,883pt,950pt] cop[sa,bo] arm
Diatessaron Chrysostom ‖ πλοῖον (*see* Lk 8.22) ℵ[b] B C f[1] f[13] 33 565 892
1230 1253 1646 *Lect* *l*[32m,185pt,333pt,547m,883pt,950pt] goth

[9] **25** {C} προσελθόντες ℵ B 33[vid] 892 it[a,aur,c,ff1,k,l] vg[ww] cop[sa,bo] Jerome ‖
προσελθόντες οἱ μαθηταί C[2] K L Δ Π f[13] 565 700 1009 1010 1071 1079 1216
1230 1242 1253 1365 1546 2148 2174 *Byz* *l*[76,150,185,299,547m,883s,m,950,1231m,1579,1599m,]
[1627m,1663m] it[h] arm Eusebius ‖ προσελθόντες οἱ μαθηταὶ αὐτοῦ W X Θ f[1] 1195
1646 *Lect* it[b,g1,q] syr[s,p,h,pal] goth eth Diatessaron ‖ προσελθόντες αὐτῷ
οἱ μαθηταὶ αὐτοῦ C[*vid] vg[cl] geo[1,A] (geo[B] *omit* αὐτοῦ)

[10] **25** {C} σῶσον ℵ B C f[1] f[13] 33 892 *l*[547m] syr[pal] geo[2] ‖ σῶσον ἡμᾶς K L
W X Δ Θ Π 0242[vid] 565 700 1009 1010 1071 1079 1195 1216 1230 1242 1253
1365 1546 1646 2148 2174 *Byz Lect* *l*[883m] it[a,aur,b,c,ff1,g1,h,k,l,q] vg syr[s,p,h] cop[sa?bo?]
goth arm eth geo[1] Diatessaron Eusebius Cyril-Jerusalem Chrysostom

---

21 ἐπίτρεψον...μου 1 Kgs 19.20   **22** Ἰησοῦς...μοι Mt 9.9; Jn 1.43; 21.19   **26** Τί...
ὀλιγόπιστοι Mt 14.31

The Healing of the Gadarene Demoniacs
(Mk 5.1–20; Lk 8.26–39)

28 Καὶ ἐλθόντος αὐτοῦ εἰς τὸ πέραν εἰς τὴν χώραν τῶν Γαδαρηνῶν[11] ὑπήντησαν αὐτῷ δύο δαιμονιζόμενοι ἐκ τῶν μνημείων ἐξερχόμενοι, χαλεποὶ λίαν, ὥστε μὴ ἰσχύειν τινὰ παρελθεῖν διὰ τῆς ὁδοῦ ἐκείνης. **29** καὶ ἰδοὺ ἔκραξαν λέγοντες, Τί ἡμῖν καὶ σοί, υἱὲ τοῦ θεοῦ; ἦλθες ὧδε πρὸ καιροῦ βασανίσαι ἡμᾶς; **30** ἦν δὲ μακρὰν ἀπ' αὐτῶν ἀγέλη χοίρων πολλῶν βοσκομένη. **31** οἱ δὲ δαίμονες παρεκάλουν αὐτὸν λέγοντες, Εἰ ἐκβάλλεις ἡμᾶς, ἀπόστειλον ἡμᾶς εἰς τὴν ἀγέλην τῶν χοίρων. **32** καὶ εἶπεν αὐτοῖς, Ὑπάγετε. οἱ δὲ ἐξελθόντες ἀπῆλθον εἰς τοὺς χοίρους· καὶ ἰδοὺ ὥρμησεν πᾶσα ἡ ἀγέλη κατὰ τοῦ κρημνοῦ εἰς τὴν θάλασσαν, καὶ ἀπέθανον ἐν τοῖς ὕδασιν. **33** οἱ δὲ βόσκοντες ἔφυγον, καὶ ἀπελθόντες εἰς τὴν πόλιν ἀπήγγειλαν πάντα καὶ τὰ τῶν δαιμονιζομένων. **34** καὶ ἰδοὺ πᾶσα ἡ πόλις ἐξῆλθεν εἰς ὑπάντησιν τῷ Ἰησοῦ, καὶ ἰδόντες αὐτὸν παρεκάλεσαν ὅπως μεταβῇ ἀπὸ τῶν ὁρίων αὐτῶν.

The Healing of a Paralytic
(Mk 2.1–12; Lk 5.17–26)

9 Καὶ ἐμβὰς εἰς πλοῖον διεπέρασεν καὶ ἦλθεν εἰς τὴν ἰδίαν πόλιν. **2** καὶ ἰδοὺ προσέφερον αὐτῷ παραλυτικὸν ἐπὶ κλίνης βεβλημένον. καὶ ἰδὼν ὁ Ἰησοῦς τὴν πίστιν αὐτῶν εἶπεν τῷ παραλυτικῷ, Θάρσει, τέκνον· ἀφίενταί σου αἱ ἁμαρτίαι. **3** καὶ ἰδού τινες τῶν γραμματέων εἶπαν

---

[11] **28** {B} Γαδαρηνῶν (see Mk 5.1; Lk 8.26) (ℵ* Γαζαρηνῶν) B C[txt] (Δ) Θ 1010 syr[s,p,h] geo[1] Diatessaron Origen Epiphanius ‖ Γεργεσηνῶν ℵ[c] (C[mg] *at beginning of section*) K L W X Π *f*[1] *f*[13] 565 700 892 1009 1071 1079 1195 1216 1230 1242 1253 1365 1546 1646 2148 2174 *Byz Lect* (*l*[76,547] Γεργεσινῶν, *l*[1663] Γερσινῶν) syr[hmg 1,pal] cop[bo] goth arm eth geo[2] Diatessaron[e] Origen ‖ Γερασηνῶν it[a,aur,b,c,d,f,ff1,g1,h,k,l,q] vg syr[hmg 2] cop[sa] Origen mss[acc.] [to Origen] Hilary

---

29 Τί...θεοῦ 1 Kgs 17.18; Mk 1.24; Lk 4.34
9 **2** παραλυτικὸν...βεβλημένον Mt 8.6; Lk 9.33   ἀφίενταί...ἁμαρτίαι Lk 7.48

---

28 Jesus came to the territory of the Gadarenes, on the other side of the lake, and was met by two men who came out of the burial caves. These men had demons in them and were very fierce, so dangerous that no one dared travel on that road. **29** At once they screamed, "What do you want with us, Son of God? Have you come to punish us before the right time?" **30** Not far away a large herd of pigs was feeding. **31** The demons begged Jesus, "If you are going to drive us out, send us into that herd of pigs." **32** "Go," Jesus told them; so they left and went off into the pigs. The whole herd rushed down the side of the cliff into the lake and were drowned.

33 The men who had been taking care of the pigs ran away and went to the town, where they told the whole story, and what had happened to the men with the demons. **34** So everybody from that town went out to meet Jesus; and when they saw him they begged him to leave their territory.

Jesus Heals a Paralyzed Man
(Also Mark 2.1–12; Luke 5.17–26)

9 Jesus got into the boat, went back across the lake, and came to his own town. **2** Some people brought him a paralyzed man, lying on a bed. Jesus saw how much faith they had, and said to the paralyzed man, "Courage, my son! Your sins are forgiven." **3** Then some teachers of the Law said to them-

selves, "This man is talking against God!"
4 Jesus knew what they were thinking
and said: "Why are you thinking such
evil things? 5 Is it easier to say, 'Your
sins are forgiven,' or to say, 'Get up and
walk'? 6 I will prove to you, then, that
the Son of Man has authority on earth
to forgive sins." So he said to the paralyzed man, "Get up, pick up your bed,
and go home!" 7 The man got up and
went home. 8 When the people saw it,
they were afraid, and praised God for
giving such authority as this to men.

Jesus Calls Matthew
(Also Mark 2.13–17; Luke 5.27–32)

9 Jesus left that place, and as he walked
along he saw a tax collector, named
Matthew, sitting in his office. He said
to him, "Follow me." And Matthew got
up and followed him.

10 While Jesus was having dinner at
his house, many tax collectors and outcasts came and joined him and his disciples at the table. 11 Some Pharisees
saw this and said to his disciples, "Why
does your teacher eat with tax collectors
and outcasts?" 12 Jesus heard them and
answered: "People who are well do not
need a doctor, but only those who are
sick. 13 Go and find out what this scripture means, 'I do not want animal
sacrifices, but kindness.' For I have not
come to call the respectable people, but
the outcasts."

ἐν ἑαυτοῖς, Οὗτος βλασφημεῖ. 4 καὶ εἰδὼς[1] ὁ Ἰησοῦς τὰς
ἐνθυμήσεις αὐτῶν εἶπεν, Ἱνατί ἐνθυμεῖσθε πονηρὰ ἐν ταῖς
καρδίαις ὑμῶν; 5 τί γάρ ἐστιν εὐκοπώτερον, εἰπεῖν,
Ἀφίενταί σου αἱ ἁμαρτίαι, ἢ εἰπεῖν, Ἔγειρε καὶ περιπάτει;
6 ἵνα δὲ εἰδῆτε ὅτι ἐξουσίαν ἔχει ὁ υἱὸς τοῦ ἀνθρώπου ἐπὶ
τῆς γῆς ἀφιέναι ἁμαρτίας — τότε λέγει τῷ παραλυτικῷ,
Ἐγερθεὶς ἆρόν σου τὴν κλίνην καὶ ὕπαγε εἰς τὸν οἶκόν
σου. 7 καὶ ἐγερθεὶς ἀπῆλθεν εἰς τὸν οἶκον αὐτοῦ. 8 ἰδόντες δὲ οἱ ὄχλοι ἐφοβήθησαν[2] καὶ ἐδόξασαν τὸν θεὸν τὸν
δόντα ἐξουσίαν τοιαύτην τοῖς ἀνθρώποις.

The Calling of Matthew
(Mk 2.13–17; Lk 5.27–32)

9 Καὶ παράγων ὁ Ἰησοῦς ἐκεῖθεν εἶδεν ἄνθρωπον
καθήμενον ἐπὶ τὸ τελώνιον, Μαθθαῖον λεγόμενον, καὶ
λέγει αὐτῷ, Ἀκολούθει μοι. καὶ ἀναστὰς ἠκολούθησεν
αὐτῷ. 10 Καὶ ἐγένετο αὐτοῦ ἀνακειμένου ἐν τῇ οἰκίᾳ, καὶ
ἰδοὺ πολλοὶ τελῶναι καὶ ἁμαρτωλοὶ ἐλθόντες συνανέκειντο
τῷ Ἰησοῦ καὶ τοῖς μαθηταῖς αὐτοῦ. 11 καὶ ἰδόντες οἱ
Φαρισαῖοι ἔλεγον τοῖς μαθηταῖς αὐτοῦ, Διὰ τί μετὰ τῶν
τελωνῶν καὶ ἁμαρτωλῶν ἐσθίει ὁ διδάσκαλος ὑμῶν; 12 ὁ
δὲ ἀκούσας εἶπεν, Οὐ χρείαν ἔχουσιν οἱ ἰσχύοντες ἰατροῦ
ἀλλ' οἱ κακῶς ἔχοντες. 13 πορευθέντες δὲ μάθετε τί
ἐστιν, Ἔλεος θέλω καὶ οὐ θυσίαν· οὐ γὰρ ἦλθον καλέσαι
δικαίους ἀλλὰ ἁμαρτωλούς.

---

[1] 4 {C} καὶ εἰδώς B Π[txt] f[1] 565 700 1079 1195 1546 l[184,313,883,1627] (l[76] καὶ
εἰδός, l[547] ἰδώς) syr[h] goth arm? eth[pp,ms] geo[1] ∥ εἰδὼς δέ Θ (syr[p]) cop[sa] arm?
geo[2] ∥ καὶ ἰδὼν ℵ C D K L W X Δ Π[mg] f[13] 33 892 1009 1010 1071 1216 1230
1242 1253 1365 1646 2148 Byz Lect it[aur,b,c,d,f,ff1,g1,k,l,q] vg cop[bo] eth[ro] ∥ ἰδὼν
δέ N Σ 240 244 it[a,h] syr[palmss]

[2] 8 {B} ἐφοβήθησαν ℵ B D W f[1] 33 892 it[a,aur,b,c,d,ff1,g1,h,k,l,q] vg syr[s,p,pal]
cop[sa,bo] Hilary Augustine ∥ ἐθαύμασαν C K L Δ Θ Π f[13] 565 700 1009 1010
1071 1079 1195 1216 1230 1242 1253 1365 1546 1646 2148 Byz Lect syr[h] arm
eth[pp] geo ∥ ἐφοβήθησαν καὶ ἐθαύμασαν (it[f] goth) Diatessaron ∥ they were
afraid and they glorified eth[ro] ∥ they marvelled and they glorified eth[ms] ∥
omit X Irenaeus[lat]

4 εἰδώς...εἶπεν Mt 12.25   6–8 λέγει...ἀνθρώποις Ac 9.33–35   9 λέγει...μοι Mt 8.22;
Jn 1.43; 21.19   10–11 Mt 11.19; Lk 7.34; 15.1–2; 19.7   13 Ἔλεος...θυσίαν Ho 6.6 (Mt 12.7)

The Question about Fasting
(Mk 2.18–22; Lk 5.33–39)

14 Τότε προσέρχονται αὐτῷ οἱ μαθηταὶ Ἰωάννου λέγοντες, Διὰ τί ἡμεῖς καὶ οἱ Φαρισαῖοι νηστεύομεν πολλά[3], οἱ δὲ μαθηταί σου οὐ νηστεύουσιν; **15** καὶ εἶπεν αὐτοῖς ὁ Ἰησοῦς, Μὴ δύνανται οἱ υἱοὶ τοῦ νυμφῶνος πενθεῖν ἐφ᾽ ὅσον μετ᾽ αὐτῶν ἐστιν ὁ νυμφίος; ἐλεύσονται δὲ ἡμέραι ὅταν ἀπαρθῇ ἀπ᾽ αὐτῶν ὁ νυμφίος, καὶ τότε νηστεύσουσιν. **16** οὐδεὶς δὲ ἐπιβάλλει ἐπίβλημα ῥάκους ἀγνάφου ἐπὶ ἱματίῳ παλαιῷ· αἴρει γὰρ τὸ πλήρωμα αὐτοῦ ἀπὸ τοῦ ἱματίου, καὶ χεῖρον σχίσμα γίνεται. **17** οὐδὲ βάλλουσιν οἶνον νέον εἰς ἀσκοὺς παλαιούς· εἰ δὲ μήγε, ῥήγνυνται οἱ ἀσκοί, καὶ ὁ οἶνος ἐκχεῖται καὶ οἱ ἀσκοὶ ἀπόλλυνται· ἀλλὰ βάλλουσιν οἶνον νέον εἰς ἀσκοὺς καινούς, καὶ ἀμφότεροι συντηροῦνται.

The Ruler's Daughter and the Woman Who Touched Jesus' Garment
(Mk 5.21–43; Lk 8.40–56)

18 Ταῦτα αὐτοῦ λαλοῦντος αὐτοῖς ἰδοὺ ἄρχων εἷς ἐλθὼν προσεκύνει αὐτῷ λέγων ὅτι Ἡ θυγάτηρ μου ἄρτι ἐτελεύτησεν· ἀλλὰ ἐλθὼν ἐπίθες τὴν χεῖρά σου ἐπ᾽ αὐτήν, καὶ ζήσεται. **19** καὶ ἐγερθεὶς ὁ Ἰησοῦς ἠκολούθησεν αὐτῷ καὶ οἱ μαθηταὶ αὐτοῦ. **20** Καὶ ἰδοὺ γυνὴ αἱμορροοῦσα δώδεκα ἔτη προσελθοῦσα ὄπισθεν ἥψατο τοῦ κρασπέδου τοῦ ἱματίου αὐτοῦ· **21** ἔλεγεν γὰρ ἐν ἑαυτῇ, Ἐὰν μόνον ἅψωμαι τοῦ ἱματίου αὐτοῦ σωθήσομαι. **22** ὁ δὲ Ἰησοῦς στραφεὶς καὶ ἰδὼν αὐτὴν εἶπεν, Θάρσει, θύγατερ· ἡ πίστις σου σέσωκέν σε. καὶ ἐσώθη ἡ γυνὴ ἀπὸ τῆς ὥρας ἐκείνης.

---

[3] **14** {C} νηστεύομεν πολλά ℵ[b] C D K L W X Δ Θ Π *f*[1] *f*[13] 33 565 700 892 1009 1010 1071 1079 1195 1216 1230 1242 1253 1365 1546 1646 2148 2174 *Byz Lect* it[d,k] syr[p,h,pal] cop[sa,bo] goth arm eth geo[1,A] ‖ νηστεύομεν πυκνά ℵ[a] it[a,aur,b,c,f,ff1,g1,h,l,q] vg syr[s] Hilary ‖ νηστεύομεν ℵ* B cop[sams] geo[B]

14 μαθηταί...νηστεύομεν Mt 11.18; Lk 18.12 **15** Μή...ἐστιν ὁ νυμφίος Jn 3.29 **18** ἐπίθες...αὐτήν Mt 8.3; Mk 6.5; 7.32; 8.23, 25; Lk 13.13 **20** γυνή...ἔτη Lv 15.25 ἥψατο... αὐτοῦ Mt 14.36; Mk 6.56 **22** ἡ πίστις...σε Mk 10.52; Lk 7.50; 17.19; Ac 3.16

The Question about Fasting
(Also Mark 2.18–22; Luke 5.33–39)

[14] Then the followers of John the Baptist came to Jesus, asking, "Why is it that we and the Pharisees fast often, but your disciples don't fast at all?" [15] Jesus answered: "Do you expect the guests at a wedding party to be sad as long as the bridegroom is with them? Of course not! But the time will come when the bridegroom will be taken away from them, and then they will go without food.

[16] "No one patches up an old coat with a piece of new cloth; for such a patch tears off from the coat, making an even bigger hole. [17] Nor does anyone pour new wine into used wineskins. If he does, the skins will burst, and then the wine pours out and the skins will be ruined. Instead, new wine is poured into fresh wineskins, and both will keep in good condition."

The Official's Daughter and the Woman who Touched Jesus' Cloak
(Also Mark 5.21–43; Luke 8.40–56)

[18] While Jesus was saying this to them, a Jewish official came to him, knelt down before him, and said, "My daughter has just died; but come and place your hand on her and she will live." [19] So Jesus got up and followed him, and his disciples went with him.

[20] A certain woman, who had had severe bleeding for twelve years, came up behind Jesus and touched the edge of his cloak. [21] She said to herself, "If only I touch his cloak I will get well." [22] Jesus turned around and saw her, and said, "Courage, my daughter! Your faith has made you well." At that very moment the woman became well.

²³ So Jesus went into the official's house. When he saw the musicians for the funeral, and the people all stirred up, ²⁴ he said, "Get out, everybody! The little girl is not dead — she is just sleeping!" They all started making fun of him. ²⁵ As soon as the people had been put out, Jesus went into the girl's room and took hold of her hand, and she got up. ²⁶ The news about this spread all over that part of the country.

Jesus Heals Two Blind Men

²⁷ Jesus left that place, and as he walked along two blind men started following him. "Have mercy on us, Son of David!" they shouted. ²⁸ When Jesus had gone indoors, the two blind men came to him and he asked them, "Do you believe that I can do this?" "Yes, sir!" they answered. ²⁹ Then Jesus touched their eyes and said, "May it happen, then, just as you believe!" — ³⁰ and their sight was restored. Jesus spoke harshly to them, "Don't tell this to anyone!" ³¹ But they left and spread the news about Jesus all over that part of the country.

Jesus Heals a Dumb Man

³² As the men were leaving, some people brought to Jesus a man who could not talk because he had a demon. ³³ As soon as the demon was driven out, the man started talking. Everybody was amazed.

23 Καὶ ἐλθὼν ὁ Ἰησοῦς εἰς τὴν οἰκίαν τοῦ ἄρχοντος καὶ ἰδὼν τοὺς αὐλητὰς καὶ τὸν ὄχλον θορυβούμενον **24**ᵃ ἔλεγεν, ᵃἈναχωρεῖτε, οὐ γὰρ ἀπέθανεν τὸ κοράσιον ἀλλὰ καθεύδει. καὶ κατεγέλων αὐτοῦ. **25** ὅτε δὲ ἐξεβλήθη ὁ ὄχλος, εἰσελθὼν ἐκράτησεν τῆς χειρὸς αὐτῆς, καὶ ἠγέρθη τὸ κοράσιον. **26** καὶ ἐξῆλθεν ἡ φήμη αὕτη⁴ εἰς ὅλην τὴν γῆν ἐκείνην.

The Healing of Two Blind Men

27 Καὶ παράγοντι ἐκεῖθεν τῷ Ἰησοῦ ἠκολούθησαν [αὐτῷ] δύο τυφλοὶ κράζοντες καὶ λέγοντες, Ἐλέησον ἡμᾶς, υἱὲ Δαυίδ. **28** ἐλθόντι δὲ εἰς τὴν οἰκίαν προσῆλθον αὐτῷ οἱ τυφλοί, καὶ λέγει αὐτοῖς ὁ Ἰησοῦς, Πιστεύετε ὅτι δύναμαι τοῦτο ποιῆσαι; λέγουσιν αὐτῷ, Ναί, κύριε. **29** τότε ἥψατο τῶν ὀφθαλμῶν αὐτῶν λέγων, Κατὰ τὴν πίστιν ὑμῶν γενηθήτω ὑμῖν. **30** καὶ ἠνεῴχθησαν αὐτῶν οἱ ὀφθαλμοί. καὶ ἐνεβριμήθη αὐτοῖς ὁ Ἰησοῦς λέγων, Ὁρᾶτε μηδεὶς γινωσκέτω. **31** οἱ δὲ ἐξελθόντες διεφήμισαν αὐτὸν ἐν ὅλῃ τῇ γῇ ἐκείνῃ.

The Healing of a Dumb Man

32 Αὐτῶν δὲ ἐξερχομένων ἰδοὺ προσήνεγκαν αὐτῷ ἄνθρωπον κωφὸν δαιμονιζόμενον· **33** καὶ ἐκβληθέντος τοῦ δαιμονίου ἐλάλησεν ὁ κωφός. καὶ ἐθαύμασαν οἱ

---

⁴ **26** {B} αὕτη B K L W Δ Π f¹³ 28 565 700 892 1009 1010 1071 1079 1195ᶜ 1216 1230 1242 1253 1365 1546 1646 2148 2174 *Byz Lect* itᵃ,ᵃᵘʳ,ᵇ,ᶜ,ᶠ,ᶠᶠ¹,ᵍ¹, ʰ,ᵏ,ˡ,q vg syrˢ,ᵖ,ʰ goth arm geoᴮ Diatessaron Augustine ∥ αὐτῆς ℵ C Θ f¹ 33 1195* itᵈ⁷ syrᵖᵃˡ copᵇᵒ ethᵐˢ ∥ αὐτοῦ D itᵈ⁷ copˢᵃ,ᵇᵒᵐˢ ethʳᵒ,ᵖᵖ geoᴬ ∥ αὕτη αὐτοῦ geo¹

ᵃ ᵃ **23-24** *a* number 24, *a* no number: TRᵉᵈ WH? Bov Nes BF² AV RV ASV RSV NEB? TT Luth Seg ∥ *a* no number, *a* number 24: TRᵉᵈ WH? NEB? Zür Jer

---

24 οὐ...καθεύδει Jn 11.11   **25** ἐκράτησεν...ἠγέρθη Mk 1.31; 9.27   **27** Mt 20.29-31 **29-30** ἥψατο...ὀφθαλμοί Mt 20.34   **29** Κατὰ...ὑμῖν Mt 8.13; 15.28   **30-31** Ὁρᾶτε... ἐκείνῃ Mk 7.36   **32-33** προσήνεγκαν...κωφός Mt 12.22; Mk 7.32, 35; 9.17, 25; Lk 11.14 **33** ἐθαύμασαν...οὕτως Mk 2.12

ὄχλοι λέγοντες, Οὐδέποτε ἐφάνη οὕτως ἐν τῷ Ἰσραήλ. 34 οἱ δὲ Φαρισαῖοι ἔλεγον, Ἐν τῷ ἄρχοντι τῶν δαιμονίων ἐκβάλλει τὰ δαιμόνια.[5]

The Compassion of Jesus

35 Καὶ περιῆγεν ὁ Ἰησοῦς τὰς πόλεις πάσας καὶ τὰς κώμας, διδάσκων ἐν ταῖς συναγωγαῖς αὐτῶν καὶ κηρύσσων τὸ εὐαγγέλιον τῆς βασιλείας καὶ θεραπεύων πᾶσαν νόσον καὶ πᾶσαν μαλακίαν. 36 Ἰδὼν δὲ τοὺς ὄχλους ἐσπλαγχνίσθη περὶ αὐτῶν ὅτι ἦσαν ἐσκυλμένοι καὶ ἐρριμμένοι ὡσεὶ πρόβατα μὴ ἔχοντα ποιμένα. 37 τότε λέγει τοῖς μαθηταῖς αὐτοῦ, Ὁ μὲν θερισμὸς πολύς, οἱ δὲ ἐργάται ὀλίγοι· 38 δεήθητε οὖν τοῦ κυρίου τοῦ θερισμοῦ ὅπως ἐκβάλῃ ἐργάτας εἰς τὸν θερισμὸν αὐτοῦ.

The Mission of the Twelve
(Mk 3.13–19; Lk 6.12–16)

10 Καὶ προσκαλεσάμενος τοὺς δώδεκα μαθητὰς αὐτοῦ ἔδωκεν αὐτοῖς ἐξουσίαν πνευμάτων ἀκαθάρτων ὥστε ἐκβάλλειν αὐτὰ καὶ θεραπεύειν πᾶσαν νόσον καὶ πᾶσαν μαλακίαν. 2 Τῶν δὲ δώδεκα ἀποστόλων τὰ ὀνόματά ἐστιν ταῦτα· πρῶτος Σίμων ὁ λεγόμενος Πέτρος καὶ Ἀνδρέας ὁ ἀδελφὸς αὐτοῦ, καὶ Ἰάκωβος ὁ τοῦ Ζεβεδαίου καὶ Ἰωάννης ὁ ἀδελφὸς αὐτοῦ, 3 Φίλιππος καὶ Βαρθολομαῖος, Θωμᾶς καὶ Μαθθαῖος ὁ τελώνης, Ἰάκωβος ὁ τοῦ Ἀλφαίου

---

[5] 34 {C} *include verse 34* ℵ B C K L W X Δ Θ Π *f*¹ *f*¹³ 28 33 565 700 892 1009 1010 1071 1079 1195 1216 1230 1242 1253 1344 1365 1516 1646 2148 2174 *Byz Lect* it^aur,b,c,f,ff¹,g¹,h,l,q vg syr^p,h,pal cop^sa,bo goth arm eth geo ‖ *omit verse 34* D it^a,d,k syr^s Diatessaron Juvencus Hilary

---

34 Mt 12.24; Mk 3.22; Lk 11.15   **35** Mt 4.23; Mk 1.39 θεραπεύων...μαλακίαν Mt 10.1; Mk 1.34; Lk 7.21   **36** Ἰδὼν...αὐτῶν Mt 14.14; 15.32; Mk 6.34 ὡσεὶ...ποιμένα Nu 27.17; 1 Kgs 22.17; 2 Chr 18.16; Eze 34.5; Zch 10.2; Jdth 11.19; Mk 6.34   **37** Ὁ μὲν...πολύς Jn 4.35 **37-38** Lk 10.2
10 1 Mk 6.7; Lk 9.1 θεραπεύειν...μαλακίαν Mt 9.35; Mk 1.34; Lk 7.21   **2** Σίμων... Ἀνδρέας ὁ ἀδελφὸς αὐτοῦ Jn 1.40-41   **3** Φίλιππος Jn 1.43

"We never saw the like in Israel!" they exclaimed. 34 But the Pharisees said, "It is the chief of the demons who gives him the power to drive them out."

Jesus Has Pity for the People

35 So Jesus went around visiting all the towns and villages. He taught in their synagogues, preached the Good News of the Kingdom, and healed people from every kind of disease and sickness. 36 As he saw the crowds, his heart was filled with pity for them, because they were worried and helpless, like sheep without a shepherd. 37 So he said to his disciples, "There is a great harvest, but few workers to gather it in. 38 Pray to the owner of the harvest that he will send out more workers to gather in his harvest."

The Twelve Apostles
(Also Mark 3.13–19; Luke 6.12–16)

10 Jesus called his twelve disciples together and gave them authority to drive out the evil spirits and to heal every disease and every sickness. 2 These are the names of the twelve apostles: first, Simon (called Peter) and his brother Andrew; James and his brother John, the sons of Zebedee; 3 Philip and Bartholomew; Thomas and Matthew, the tax collector; James, the son of Alphaeus,

and Thaddaeus; [4] Simon, the patriot,
and Judas Iscariot, who betrayed Jesus.

The Mission of the Twelve
(Also Mark 6.7–13; Luke 9.1–6)

[5] Jesus sent these twelve men out with
the following instructions: "Do not go
to any Gentile territory or any Samaritan
towns. [6] Go, instead, to the lost sheep
of the people of Israel. [7] Go and preach,
'The Kingdom of heaven is near!' [8] Heal
the sick, raise the dead, make the lepers
clean, drive out demons. You have received without paying, so give without
being paid. [9] Do not carry any gold,
silver, or copper money in your pockets;
[10] do not carry a beggar's bag for the
trip, or an extra shirt, or shoes, or a
walking stick. A worker should be given
what he needs.

[11] "When you come to a town or village,
go in and look for someone who is willing
to welcome you, and stay with him until
you leave that place. [12] When you go
into a house say, 'Peace be with you.'
[13] If the people in that house welcome
you, let your greeting of peace remain;
but if they do not welcome you, then

καὶ Θαδδαῖος[1], **4** *Σίμων ὁ Καναναῖος καὶ Ἰούδας ὁ
Ἰσκαριώτης*[2] *ὁ καὶ παραδοὺς αὐτόν.*

The Commissioning of the Twelve
(Mk 6.7–13; Lk 9.1–6)

5 *Τούτους τοὺς δώδεκα ἀπέστειλεν ὁ Ἰησοῦς παραγγείλας αὐτοῖς λέγων, Εἰς ὁδὸν ἐθνῶν μὴ ἀπέλθητε, καὶ
εἰς πόλιν Σαμαριτῶν μὴ εἰσέλθητε·* **6** *πορεύεσθε δὲ
μᾶλλον πρὸς τὰ πρόβατα τὰ ἀπολωλότα οἴκου Ἰσραήλ.*
7 *πορευόμενοι δὲ κηρύσσετε λέγοντες ὅτι*[a] *Ἤγγικεν ἡ
βασιλεία τῶν οὐρανῶν.* **8** *ἀσθενοῦντας θεραπεύετε, νεκροὺς ἐγείρετε, λεπροὺς καθαρίζετε, δαιμόνια ἐκβάλλετε·
δωρεὰν ἐλάβετε, δωρεὰν δότε.* **9** *Μὴ κτήσησθε χρυσὸν
μηδὲ ἄργυρον μηδὲ χαλκὸν εἰς τὰς ζώνας ὑμῶν,* **10** *μὴ
πήραν εἰς ὁδὸν μηδὲ δύο χιτῶνας μηδὲ ὑποδήματα μηδὲ
ῥάβδον· ἄξιος γὰρ ὁ ἐργάτης τῆς τροφῆς αὐτοῦ.* **11** *εἰς
ἣν δ' ἂν πόλιν ἢ κώμην εἰσέλθητε, ἐξετάσατε τίς ἐν αὐτῇ
ἄξιός ἐστιν· κἀκεῖ μείνατε ἕως ἂν ἐξέλθητε.* **12** *εἰσερχόμενοι δὲ εἰς τὴν οἰκίαν ἀσπάσασθε αὐτήν·* **13** *καὶ ἐὰν
μὲν ᾖ ἡ οἰκία ἀξία, ἐλθάτω ἡ εἰρήνη ὑμῶν ἐπ' αὐτήν·
ἐὰν δὲ μὴ ᾖ ἀξία, ἡ εἰρήνη ὑμῶν πρὸς ὑμᾶς ἐπιστραφήτω.*

---

[1] **3** {B} Θαδδαῖος ℵ B f^{13} 892 l^{185} it^{aur,c,ff1,l} vg cop^{sa,bo} // Λεββαῖος D it$^{d,(k)}$ Origen^{lat} mss$^{acc. to Augustine}$ Hesychius // Θαδδαῖος ὁ ἐπικληθεὶς Λεββαῖος 13 346 543 826 828 // Λεββαῖος ὁ ἐπικληθεὶς Θαδδαῖος (C^{*vid} ὁ καὶ Θαδδαῖος) C^2 K L W X Δ Θ Π f^1 28 33 565 700 1009 1010 1071 1079 1195 1216 1230 1242 1253 1344 1365 1546 1646 2148 2174 *Byz Lect* $l^{70m,185m,(211),333s,m}$ it^f syr^{p,h,pal} arm (eth Λεββεδαῖος?) geo // *Judas Zelotes* it^{a,b,g1,h,q} // *add Judas the son of James after* Καναναῖος *in verse 4* syr^s

[2] **4** {B} Ἰσκαριώτης ℵ B K L W X Δ Θ Π f^1 f^{13} 28 33 565 700 892 1009 1010 1071 1079 1195 1216 1230 1242 1253 1344 1365 1546 1646 2148 2174 *Byz Lect* $l^{185s,m,333s,m}$ vg^{cl} syr^h cop^{sa,bo} eth? Chrysostom // Σκαριώτης D it^{d,f,k,l} (it^{a,b,c,ff1,g1,h} *Scarioth*, it^q *Scariota*, it^{aur} *Carioth*) vg^{ww} syr$^{s,p,(pal)}$ arm geo // Ἰσκαριώθ (*see* Mk 3.19; Lk 6.16) C l^{150} // Σίμωνος Ἰσκαριώτου Origen

---

[a] **7** *a* direct: TR WH Bov Nes? BF^2 AV RV ASV RSV NEB TT Zür Luth // *a* indirect: Nes? Jer Seg

---

4 Ἰούδας...αὐτόν Mt 26.25; 27.3; Mk 14.44; Jn 6.64; 12.4; 13.11; 18.2, 5 **6** πρὸς...Ἰσραήλ Jr 50.6; Mt 15.24 **7** Ἤγγικεν...οὐρανῶν Mt 3.2; 4.17; Lk 10.9, 11 **10** μὴ...ὑποδήματα Lk 10.4 ἄξιος...αὐτοῦ Nu 18.31; Lk 10.7; 1 Cor 9.14; 1 Tm 5.18 **12–13** Lk 10.5–6

14 καὶ ὃς ἂν μὴ δέξηται ὑμᾶς μηδὲ ἀκούσῃ τοὺς λόγους ὑμῶν, ἐξερχόμενοι ἔξω τῆς οἰκίας ἢ τῆς πόλεως ἐκείνης ἐκτινάξατε τὸν κονιορτὸν [ἐκ] τῶν ποδῶν ὑμῶν. 15 ἀμὴν λέγω ὑμῖν, ἀνεκτότερον ἔσται γῇ Σοδόμων καὶ Γομόρρων ἐν ἡμέρᾳ κρίσεως ἢ τῇ πόλει ἐκείνῃ.

Coming Persecutions
(Mk 13.9—13; Lk 21.12—17)

16 Ἰδοὺ ἐγὼ ἀποστέλλω ὑμᾶς ὡς πρόβατα ἐν μέσῳ λύκων· γίνεσθε οὖν φρόνιμοι ὡς οἱ ὄφεις καὶ ἀκέραιοι ὡς αἱ περιστεραί. 17 προσέχετε δὲ ἀπὸ τῶν ἀνθρώπων· παραδώσουσιν γὰρ ὑμᾶς εἰς συνέδρια, καὶ ἐν ταῖς συναγωγαῖς αὐτῶν μαστιγώσουσιν ὑμᾶς· 18 καὶ ἐπὶ ἡγεμόνας δὲ καὶ βασιλεῖς ἀχθήσεσθε ἕνεκεν ἐμοῦ εἰς μαρτύριον αὐτοῖς καὶ τοῖς ἔθνεσιν. 19 ὅταν δὲ παραδῶσιν ὑμᾶς, μὴ μεριμνήσητε πῶς ἢ τί λαλήσητε· δοθήσεται γὰρ ὑμῖν ἐν ἐκείνῃ τῇ ὥρᾳ τί λαλήσητε· 20 οὐ γὰρ ὑμεῖς ἐστε οἱ λαλοῦντες ἀλλὰ τὸ πνεῦμα τοῦ πατρὸς ὑμῶν τὸ λαλοῦν ἐν ὑμῖν. 21 παραδώσει δὲ ἀδελφὸς ἀδελφὸν εἰς θάνατον καὶ πατὴρ τέκνον, καὶ ἐπαναστήσονται τέκνα ἐπὶ γονεῖς καὶ θανατώσουσιν αὐτούς. 22 καὶ ἔσεσθε μισούμενοι ὑπὸ πάντων διὰ τὸ ὄνομά μου· ὁ δὲ ὑπομείνας εἰς τέλος οὗτος σωθήσεται. 23 ὅταν δὲ διώκωσιν ὑμᾶς ἐν τῇ πόλει ταύτῃ, φεύγετε εἰς τὴν ἑτέραν³· ἀμὴν γὰρ λέγω ὑμῖν, οὐ

---

³ 23 {C} ἑτέραν ℵ B W 33 892 1253 eth? Origen Peter-Alexandria Athanasius Cyril ∥ ἄλλην C K X Δ Π 28 700 1009 1010 1071 1079 1195 1216 1230 1242 1344 1365 1546 1646 2148 2174 *Byz Lect* l⁷⁰ᵐ,¹⁸⁵ᵐ,³³³ᵐ Clement Origen Apostolic Constituuions ∥ ἑτέραν or ἄλλην itᵃᵘʳ,ᶜ,ᶠ,¹ vg syrᵖ·ʰ copˢᵃ,ᵇᵒ goth geoᴬ Jerome Augustine ∥ ἑτέραν, κἂν ἐκ ταύτης διώκωσιν ὑμᾶς, φεύγετε εἰς τὴν ἄλλην f¹ f¹³ Diatessaronᵉᵃʳᵐ Origen ∥ ἄλλην, κἂν ἐκ ταύτης διώκωσιν ὑμᾶς, φεύγετε εἰς τὴν ἑτέραν (L ἐκδιώξουσιν) Θ (565 εἰς τὴν ἄλλην) ∥ ἄλλην, ἐὰν δὲ ἐν τῇ ἀλλῇ διώκουσιν ὑμᾶς, φεύγετε εἰς τὴν ἄλλην

14—15 Lk 10.10—12   14 ἐκτινάξατε...ὑμῶν Ac 13.51   15 Mt 11.24; Lk 10.12 Σοδόμων καὶ Γομόρρων Gn 18.20—19.28; 2 Pe 2.6; Jd 7   16 Ἰδού...λύκων Lk 10.3 πρόβατα...λύκων Jn 10.12; Ac 20.29 φρόνιμοι...περιστεραί Ro 16.19   17—18 παραδώσουσιν...αὐτοῖς Mk 13.9; Lk 21.12—13 εἰς...ἔθνεσιν Mt 24.14   19—22 Mk 13.11—13; Lk 21.14—19   19—20 Lk 12.11—12   21 ἐπαναστήσονται...γονεῖς Mic 7.6   22 καὶ...μου Mt 24.9 ὁ δὲ...σωθήσεται Mt 24.13

---

take back your greeting. 14 And if some home or town will not welcome you or listen to you, then leave that place and shake the dust off your feet. 15 Remember this! On the Judgment Day God will show more mercy to the people of Sodom and Gomorrah than to the people of that town!"

Coming Persecutions
(Also Mark 13.9—13; Luke 21.12—17)

16 "Listen! I am sending you just like sheep to a pack of wolves. You must be as cautious as snakes and as gentle as doves. 17 Watch out, for there will be men who will arrest you and take you to court, and they will whip you in their synagogues. 18 You will be brought to trial before rulers and kings for my sake, to tell the Good News to them and to the Gentiles. 19 When they bring you to trial, do not worry about what you are going to say or how you will say it; when the time comes, you will be given what you will say. 20 For the words you speak will not be yours; they will come from the Spirit of your Father speaking in you.

21 "Men will hand over their own brothers to be put to death, and fathers will do the same to their children; children will turn against their parents and have them put to death. 22 Everyone will hate you, because of me. But the person who holds out to the end will be saved. 23 And when they persecute you in one town, run away to another one. I tell you, you will not finish your work

in all the towns of Israel before the Son of Man comes.

24 "No pupil is greater than his teacher; no slave is greater than his master. 25 So a pupil should be satisfied to become like his teacher, and a slave like his master. If the head of the family is called Beelzebul, the members of the family will be called by even worse names!"

Whom to Fear
(Also Luke 12.2–7)

26 "Do not be afraid of men, then. Whatever is covered up will be uncovered, and every secret will be made known. 27 What I am telling you in the dark you must repeat in broad daylight, and what you have heard in private you must tell from the housetops. 28 Do not be afraid of those who kill the body but cannot kill the soul; rather be afraid of God, who can destroy both body and soul in hell. 29 You can buy two sparrows for a penny; yet not a single one of them falls to the ground without your Father's consent. 30 As for you, even the hairs of your head have all been counted. 31 So do not be afraid: you are worth much more than sparrows!"

Confessing and Denying Christ
(Also Luke 12.8–9)

32 "Whoever declares publicly that he belongs to me, I will do the same for him before my Father in heaven. 33 But whoever denies publicly that he belongs to me, then I will deny him before my Father in heaven."

μὴ τελέσητε τὰς πόλεις τοῦ Ἰσραὴλ ἕως [ἂν] ἔλθῃ ὁ υἱὸς τοῦ ἀνθρώπου.

24 Οὐκ ἔστιν μαθητὴς ὑπὲρ τὸν διδάσκαλον οὐδὲ δοῦλος ὑπὲρ τὸν κύριον αὐτοῦ. 25 ἀρκετὸν τῷ μαθητῇ ἵνα γένηται ὡς ὁ διδάσκαλος αὐτοῦ, καὶ ὁ δοῦλος ὡς ὁ κύριος αὐτοῦ. εἰ τὸν οἰκοδεσπότην Βεελζεβοὺλ ἐπεκάλεσαν, πόσῳ μᾶλλον τοὺς οἰκιακοὺς αὐτοῦ.

Whom to Fear
(Lk 12.2–7)

26 Μὴ οὖν φοβηθῆτε αὐτούς· οὐδὲν γάρ ἐστιν κεκαλυμμένον ὃ οὐκ ἀποκαλυφθήσεται, καὶ κρυπτὸν ὃ οὐ γνωσθήσεται. 27 ὃ λέγω ὑμῖν ἐν τῇ σκοτίᾳ, εἴπατε ἐν τῷ φωτί· καὶ ὃ εἰς τὸ οὖς ἀκούετε, κηρύξατε ἐπὶ τῶν δωμάτων. 28 καὶ μὴ φοβεῖσθε ἀπὸ τῶν ἀποκτεννόντων τὸ σῶμα, τὴν δὲ ψυχὴν μὴ δυναμένων ἀποκτεῖναι· φοβεῖσθε δὲ μᾶλλον τὸν δυνάμενον καὶ ψυχὴν καὶ σῶμα ἀπολέσαι ἐν γεέννῃ. 29 οὐχὶ δύο στρουθία ἀσσαρίου πωλεῖται; καὶ ἓν ἐξ αὐτῶν οὐ πεσεῖται ἐπὶ τὴν γῆν ἄνευ τοῦ πατρὸς ὑμῶν. 30 ὑμῶν δὲ καὶ αἱ τρίχες τῆς κεφαλῆς πᾶσαι ἠριθμημέναι εἰσίν. 31 μὴ οὖν φοβεῖσθε· πολλῶν στρουθίων διαφέρετε ὑμεῖς.

Confessing Christ before Men
(Lk 12.8–9)

32 Πᾶς οὖν ὅστις ὁμολογήσει ἐν ἐμοὶ ἔμπροσθεν τῶν ἀνθρώπων, ὁμολογήσω κἀγὼ ἐν αὐτῷ ἔμπροσθεν τοῦ πατρός μου τοῦ ἐν [τοῖς] οὐρανοῖς· 33 ὅστις δ' ἂν ἀρνήσηταί με ἔμπροσθεν τῶν ἀνθρώπων, ἀρνήσομαι κἀγὼ αὐτὸν ἔμπροσθεν τοῦ πατρός μου τοῦ ἐν [τοῖς] οὐρανοῖς.

D it[d] ‖ ἑτέραν...ἄλλην or ἄλλην...ἑτέραν or ἄλλην...ἄλλην it[a,b,ff1,g1,(h),(k),q] syr[s] arm geo[1,B] Hilary

23 ἕως...ἀνθρώπου Mt 16.27–28; 24.27, 30, 37, 39, 44; 25.31; 26.64; Mk 13.26; 14.62; Lk 9.26; 17.30; 18.8; 21.27   24 Lk 6.40; Jn 13.16; 15.20   26 οὐδὲν...γνωσθήσεται Mk 4.22; Lk 8.17   28 τὸν δυνάμενον...ἀπολέσαι Jas 4.12   30 1 Sm 14.45; Ac 27.34   31 πολλῶν...ὑμεῖς Mt 6.26; 12.12   32 Re 3.5   33 Mk 8.38; Lk 9.26; 2 Tm 2.12

Not Peace, but a Sword
(Lk 12.51–53; 14.26–27)

34 Μὴ νομίσητε ὅτι ἦλθον βαλεῖν εἰρήνην ἐπὶ τὴν γῆν· οὐκ ἦλθον βαλεῖν εἰρήνην ἀλλὰ μάχαιραν. 35 ἦλθον γὰρ διχάσαι

ἄνθρωπον **κατὰ τοῦ πατρὸς αὐτοῦ**
    καὶ θυγατέρα κατὰ τῆς μητρὸς αὐτῆς
καὶ νύμφην κατὰ τῆς πενθερᾶς αὐτῆς,
36   **καὶ ἐχθροὶ τοῦ ἀνθρώπου οἱ οἰκιακοὶ αὐτοῦ.**
37 Ὁ φιλῶν πατέρα ἢ μητέρα ὑπὲρ ἐμὲ οὐκ ἔστιν μου ἄξιος· καὶ ὁ φιλῶν υἱὸν ἢ θυγατέρα ὑπὲρ ἐμὲ οὐκ ἔστιν μου ἄξιος·[4] 38 καὶ ὃς οὐ λαμβάνει τὸν σταυρὸν αὐτοῦ καὶ ἀκολουθεῖ ὀπίσω μου, οὐκ ἔστιν μου ἄξιος. 39 ὁ εὑρὼν τὴν ψυχὴν αὐτοῦ ἀπολέσει αὐτήν, καὶ ὁ ἀπολέσας τὴν ψυχὴν αὐτοῦ ἕνεκεν ἐμοῦ εὑρήσει αὐτήν.

Rewards
(Mk 9.41)

40 Ὁ δεχόμενος ὑμᾶς ἐμὲ δέχεται, καὶ ὁ ἐμὲ δεχόμενος δέχεται τὸν ἀποστείλαντά με. 41 ὁ δεχόμενος προφήτην εἰς ὄνομα προφήτου μισθὸν προφήτου λήμψεται, καὶ ὁ δεχόμενος δίκαιον εἰς ὄνομα δικαίου μισθὸν δικαίου λήμψεται. 42 καὶ ὃς ἂν ποτίσῃ ἕνα τῶν μικρῶν τούτων ποτήριον ψυχροῦ μόνον[5] εἰς ὄνομα μαθητοῦ, ἀμὴν λέγω ὑμῖν, οὐ μὴ ἀπολέσῃ τὸν μισθὸν αὐτοῦ.

---

[4] **37** {B} καὶ ὁ φιλῶν υἱὸν ἢ θυγατέρα ὑπὲρ ἐμὲ οὐκ ἔστιν μου ἄξιος· ℵ B^mg C K L W X Δ Θ Π f¹ f¹³ 28 33 565 700 892 (1010 *omit* ὑπὲρ ἐμέ) 1071 1079 1195 1216 1230 1242 1253 1344 1365 1546 1646 2148 2174 *Byz Lect* l^70m,(333), 883m it^a,aur,b,c,f,ff¹,g¹,h,k,l,q vg syr^c,s,p,h,pal cop^sa,bo goth arm (eth υἱὸν αὐτοῦ ἢ θυγατέρα αὐτοῦ) geo ‖ *omit* B^txt D 1009 l^871 it^d

[5] **42** {C} ποτήριον ψυχροῦ μόνον p¹⁹ ℵ B C K L P W Δ Θ Π (X 33 1010 1071 1216 1242 1344 2148 l^184,1231,1663 ψυχροῦν) f¹ f¹³ 28 565 700 892 1009 1079 1195 1230 1253 1365 1546 1646 2174 *Byz Lect* l^70m,(211),883m it^k syr^p,h,pal^mss goth? ‖ ποτήριον ψυχροῦ E* geo^B ‖ ποτήριον ὕδατος ψυχροῦ D it^d syr^c,(s)

35-36 ἄνθρωπον...οἰκιακοὶ αὐτοῦ Mic 7.6   **37** Dt 33.9   **38** Mt 16.24; Mk 8.34; Lk 9.23   **39** Mt 16.25; Mk 8.35; Lk 9.24; 17.33; Jn 12.25   **40** Mk 9.37; Lk 10.16; Jn 13.20 Ὁ δεχόμενος...δέχεται Mt 18.5 ὁ ἐμὲ...με Jn 12.44; Ga 4.14   **41** ὁ δεχόμενος προφήτην... προφήτου λήμψεται 1 Kgs 17.9–24; 2 Kgs 4.8–37   **42** Mk 9.41

Not Peace, but a Sword
(Also Luke 12.51–53; 14.26–27)

34 "Do not think that I have come to bring peace to the world; no, I did not come to bring peace, but a sword. 35 I came to set sons against their fathers, daughters against their mothers, daughters-in-law against their mothers-in-law; 36 a man's worst enemies will be the members of his own family.

37 "Whoever loves his father or mother more than me is not worthy of me; whoever loves his son or daughter more than me is not worthy of me. 38 Whoever does not take up his cross and follow in my steps is not worthy of me. 39 Whoever tries to gain his own life will lose it; whoever loses his life for my sake will gain it."

Rewards
(Also Mark 9.41)

40 "Whoever welcomes you, welcomes me; and whoever welcomes me, welcomes the one who sent me. 41 Whoever welcomes God's messenger, because he is God's messenger, will share in his reward; and whoever welcomes a truly good man, because he is that, will share in his reward. 42 And remember this! Whoever gives even a drink of cold water to one of the least of these my followers, because he is my follower, will certainly receive his reward."

The Messengers from John the Baptist
(Also Luke 7.18–35)

11 When Jesus finished giving these instructions to his twelve disciples, he left that place and went on to teach and preach in the towns near there. [2] When John the Baptist heard in prison about Christ's works, he sent some of his disciples to him. [3] "Tell us," they asked Jesus, "are you the one John said was going to come, or should we expect someone else?" [4] Jesus answered: "Go back and tell John what you are hearing and seeing: [5] the blind can see, the lame can walk, the lepers are made clean, the deaf hear, the dead are raised to life, and the Good News is preached to the poor. [6] How happy is he who has no doubts about me!"

[7] While John's disciples were going back, Jesus spoke about John to the crowds. "When you went out to John in the desert, what did you expect to see? A blade of grass bending in the wind? [8] What did you go out to see? A man dressed up in fancy clothes? People who dress like that live in palaces!

11 Καὶ ἐγένετο ὅτε ἐτέλεσεν ὁ Ἰησοῦς διατάσσων τοῖς δώδεκα μαθηταῖς αὐτοῦ, μετέβη ἐκεῖθεν τοῦ διδάσκειν καὶ κηρύσσειν ἐν ταῖς πόλεσιν αὐτῶν.

The Messengers from John the Baptist
(Lk 7.18–35)

[2] Ὁ δὲ Ἰωάννης ἀκούσας ἐν τῷ δεσμωτηρίῳ τὰ ἔργα τοῦ Χριστοῦ[1] πέμψας διὰ τῶν μαθητῶν αὐτοῦ [3] εἶπεν αὐτῷ, Σὺ εἶ ὁ ἐρχόμενος ἢ ἕτερον προσδοκῶμεν; [4] καὶ ἀποκριθεὶς ὁ Ἰησοῦς εἶπεν αὐτοῖς, Πορευθέντες ἀπαγγείλατε Ἰωάννῃ ἃ ἀκούετε καὶ βλέπετε· [5] **τυφλοὶ ἀναβλέπουσιν** καὶ χωλοὶ περιπατοῦσιν, λεπροὶ καθαρίζονται καὶ κωφοὶ ἀκούουσιν, καὶ νεκροὶ ἐγείρονται καὶ **πτωχοὶ εὐαγγελίζονται·** [6] καὶ μακάριός ἐστιν ὃς ἐὰν μὴ σκανδαλισθῇ ἐν ἐμοί. [7] Τούτων δὲ πορευομένων ἤρξατο ὁ Ἰησοῦς λέγειν τοῖς ὄχλοις περὶ Ἰωάννου, Τί ἐξήλθατε εἰς τὴν ἔρημον[a] θεάσασθαι;[a] κάλαμον ὑπὸ ἀνέμου σαλευόμενον; [8] ἀλλὰ τί ἐξήλθατε[b] ἰδεῖν;[b] ἄνθρωπον ἐν μαλακοῖς ἠμφιεσμένον; ἰδοὺ οἱ τὰ μαλακὰ φοροῦντες ἐν τοῖς οἴκοις

---

eth[ro] (Clement) Cyprian Hilary Augustine // ποτήριον ὕδατος ψυχροῦ μόνον it[aur,b,c,f,ff1,g1,h,l,q] vg syr[palms] cop[sa?bo?] goth? arm eth[pp,ms] geo[l,A]

[1] **2** {C} Χριστοῦ 𝔭[19vid] ℵ B C K L P W X Δ Θ Π f[1] f[13] 28 33 565 700 892 1009 1010 1079 1195 1230 1242 1253 1344 1365 1546 1646 2148 2174 Byz l[10,69,76,150,184,211,299,855,883s,m,950,1084,1642] it[a,aur,b,c,f,ff1,g1,h,k,l,q] vg syr[p,h,pal] cop[sa,bo] goth arm eth[pp,ms] geo // Ἰησοῦ D 1071 1216 Lect it[d] syr[c] eth[ro] Origen Chrysostom // κυρίου ἡμῶν syr[s]

---

[a] [a] **7** a none, a question: TR WH Bov Nes BF[2] AV RV ASV RSV NEB TT Luth Jer Seg // a question, a none: Zür

[b] [b] **8** b none, b question: TR WH Bov Nes BF[2] AV RV ASV RSV[mg] NEB TT Luth Jer Seg // b question, b none: RSV Zür

---

1 Καὶ...αὐτοῦ Mt 7.28; 13.53; 19.1; 26.1   **2** Ἰωάννης...δεσμωτηρίῳ Mt 14.3; Jn 3.24   **3** ὁ ἐρχόμενος Mal 3.1; Mt 3.11; Jn 1.15, 27; 6.14; Ac 19.4; He 10.37; Re 1.4, 8   **5** τυφλοὶ...ἀκούουσιν Is 35.5–6; 42.18   πτωχοὶ εὐαγγελίζονται Is 61.1   **6** μακάριος...ἐμοί Mt 13.57; 26.31   **7** περὶ...θεάσασθαι Mt 3.5

τῶν βασιλέων εἰσίν. 9 ἀλλὰ τί ἐξήλθατε[c] ἰδεῖν;[c] προφήτην²;[c] ναί, λέγω ὑμῖν, καὶ περισσότερον προφήτου. 10 οὗτός ἐστιν περὶ οὗ γέγραπται,

Ἰδοὺ ἐγὼ ἀποστέλλω τὸν ἄγγελόν μου πρὸ προσώπου σου,

ὃς κατασκευάσει τὴν ὁδόν σου ἔμπροσθέν σου.

11 ἀμὴν λέγω ὑμῖν, οὐκ ἐγήγερται ἐν γεννητοῖς γυναικῶν μείζων Ἰωάννου τοῦ βαπτιστοῦ· ὁ δὲ μικρότερος ἐν τῇ βασιλείᾳ τῶν οὐρανῶν μείζων αὐτοῦ ἐστιν. 12 ἀπὸ δὲ τῶν ἡμερῶν Ἰωάννου τοῦ βαπτιστοῦ ἕως ἄρτι ἡ βασιλεία τῶν οὐρανῶν βιάζεται, καὶ βιασταὶ ἁρπάζουσιν αὐτήν. 13 πάντες γὰρ οἱ προφῆται καὶ ὁ νόμος ἕως Ἰωάννου ἐπροφήτευσαν· 14 καὶ εἰ θέλετε δέξασθαι, αὐτός ἐστιν Ἠλίας ὁ μέλλων ἔρχεσθαι. 15 ὁ ἔχων ὦτα³ ἀκουέτω.

16 Τίνι δὲ ὁμοιώσω τὴν γενεὰν ταύτην; ὁμοία ἐστὶν παιδίοις καθημένοις ἐν ταῖς ἀγοραῖς ἃ προσφωνοῦντα τοῖς ἑτέροις 17 λέγουσιν,

Ηὐλήσαμεν ὑμῖν καὶ οὐκ ὠρχήσασθε·
ἐθρηνήσαμεν⁴ καὶ οὐκ ἐκόψασθε.

---

[9] Tell me, what did you expect to see? A prophet? Yes, I tell you — you saw much more than a prophet. [10] For John is the one of whom the scripture says: 'Here is my messenger, says God; I will send him ahead of you to open the way for you.' [11] Remember this! John the Baptist is greater than any man who has ever lived. But he who is least in the Kingdom of heaven is greater than he. [12] From the time John preached his message until this very day the Kingdom of heaven has suffered violent attacks,[1] and violent men try to seize it. [13] All the prophets and the Law of Moses, until the time of John, spoke about the Kingdom; [14] and if you are willing to believe their message, John is Elijah, whose coming was predicted. [15] Listen, then, if you have ears!

[16] "Now, to what can I compare the people of this day? They are like children sitting in the market place. One group shouts to the other, [17] 'We played wedding music for you, but you would not dance! We sang funeral songs, but

---

[1] **12** has suffered violent attacks: *or* has been coming violently

---

² 9 {B} ἰδεῖν; προφήτην (see Lk 7.26) ℵ[c] B*[vid] C D K L P X Δ Θ Π f¹ f¹³ 28 33 565 700 1009 1010 1071 1079 1195 1216 1230 1242 1253 1365 1546 1646 2148 2174 *Byz Lect* l[883m] it[a,aur,b,c,d,f,ff1,g1,h,k,l,q] vg syr[c,s,p,h,(pal)] cop[sa] goth arm eth[pp,ms] geo Diatessaron Origen[1/2] Ambrosiaster Hilary Chrysostom Cyril ‖ προφήτην ἰδεῖν ℵ* B[c] W 892 cop[bo] eth[ro] Origen[1/2] Chrysostom

³ 15 {C} ὦτα B D 700 it[d,k] syr[s] ‖ ὦτα ἀκούειν ℵ C K L W X Δ Θ Π f¹ f¹³ 28 33 565 892 1009 1010 1071 1079 1195 1216 1230 1242 1253 1365 1546 1646 2148 2174 *Byz Lect* l[883m] it[a,aur,b,c,f,ff1,g1,h,l,q] vg syr[c,p,h,pal] cop[sa,bo] goth[vid] arm eth geo Docetists Justin Diatessaron Clement Origen[gr,lat]

⁴ 17 {C} ἐθρηνήσαμεν ℵ B D f¹ 892 l[48] it[aur,c,d,f,ff1,g1,k,l] vg cop[sa,bo] goth geo² Clement Chrysostom Augustine ‖ ἐθρηνήσαμεν ὑμῖν C K L W X Δ Θ Π f¹³ 28 33 565 700 1009 1010 1071 1079 1195 1216 1230 1242 1253 1365 1546 1646 2148 2174 *Byz Lect* it[a,b,ff2,h,q] syr[c,s,p,h] arm eth geo¹ Diatessaron Augustine

---

[c c c] **9** c none, c question, c question: TR AV RV[mg] ASV[mg] RSV[mg] ‖ c question, c none, c question (WH Bov Nes BF²) RV ASV RSV NEB TT Zür Luth Jer Seg

---

9 ἰδεῖν...προφήτου Mt 14.5; 21.26; Lk 1.76   **10** Ἰδού...ἔμπροσθέν σου Ex 23.20; Mal 3.1 (Mk 1.2; Lk 1.76; 7.27; Jn 3.28)   **12–13** Lk 16.16   **14** Ἠλίας...ἔρχεσθαι Mal 4.5; Mt 17.10–13; Mk 9.11–13; Lk 1.17; Jn 1.21   **15** Mt 13.9, 43; Mk 4.9, 23; Lk 8.8; 14.35; Re 2.7; 13.9

you would not cry!' ¹⁸ John came, and he fasted and drank no wine, and everyone said, 'He is a madman!' ¹⁹ The Son of Man came, and he ate and drank, and everyone said, 'Look at this man! He is a glutton and wine-drinker, and is a friend of tax collectors and outcasts!' God's wisdom, however, is shown to be true by its results.''

The Unbelieving Towns
(Also Luke 10.13–15)

²⁰ Then Jesus began to reproach the towns where he had performed most of his miracles, because the people had not turned from their sins. ²¹ "How terrible it will be for you, Chorazin! How terrible for you too, Bethsaida! For if the miracles which were performed in you had been performed in Tyre and Sidon, long ago the people there would have put on sackcloth, and sprinkled ashes on themselves to show they had turned from their sins! ²² Remember, then, that on the Judgment Day God will show more mercy to the people of Tyre and Sidon than to you! ²³ And as for you, Capernaum? You wanted to lift yourself up to heaven? You will be thrown down to hell! For if the miracles which were performed in you had been performed

18 ἦλθεν γὰρ Ἰωάννης μήτε ἐσθίων μήτε πίνων, καὶ λέγουσιν, Δαιμόνιον ἔχει· 19 ἦλθεν ὁ υἱὸς τοῦ ἀνθρώπου ἐσθίων καὶ πίνων, καὶ λέγουσιν, Ἰδοὺ ἄνθρωπος φάγος καὶ οἰνοπότης, τελωνῶν φίλος καὶ ἁμαρτωλῶν. καὶ ἐδικαιώθη ἡ σοφία ἀπὸ τῶν ἔργων⁵ αὐτῆς.

Woes to Unrepentant Cities
(Lk 10.13–15)

20 Τότε ἤρξατο ὀνειδίζειν τὰς πόλεις ἐν αἷς ἐγένοντο αἱ πλεῖσται δυνάμεις αὐτοῦ, ὅτι οὐ μετενόησαν· 21 Οὐαί σοι, Χοραζίν· οὐαί σοι, Βηθσαϊδά· ὅτι εἰ ἐν Τύρῳ καὶ Σιδῶνι ἐγένοντο αἱ δυνάμεις αἱ γενόμεναι ἐν ὑμῖν, πάλαι ἂν ἐν σάκκῳ καὶ σποδῷ μετενόησαν. 22 πλὴν λέγω ὑμῖν, Τύρῳ καὶ Σιδῶνι ἀνεκτότερον ἔσται ἐν ἡμέρᾳ κρίσεως ἢ ὑμῖν. 23 καὶ σύ, Καφαρναούμ,
μὴ ἕως οὐρανοῦ ὑψωθήσῃ⁶;
ἕως ᾅδου καταβήσῃ⁷.

---

⁵ 19 {B} ἀπὸ τῶν ἔργων ℵ B* W syrᵖ·ʰ copˢᵃᵐˢ·ᵇᵒ ethʳᵒ mssᵃᶜᶜ· ᵗᵒ ᴶᵉʳᵒᵐᵉ ‖ ἀπὸ τῶν τέκνων (see Lk 7.35) B² C D K L X Δ Θ Π f¹ 28 33 565 700 892 1009 1010 1071 1079 1195 1216 1230 1242 1253 1344 1365 1546 1646 2148 2174 Byz Lect itᵃ·ᵃᵘʳ·ᶜ·ᵈ·ᶠ·ᶠᶠ¹·ᵍ¹·ʰ·ˡ· q vg syrᶜ·ˢ·ʰᵐᵍ copˢᵃ goth arm ethᵖᵖ·ᵐˢ geo Diatessaron Irenaeusˡᵃᵗ Origen Hilary Epiphanius Chrysostom Augustine ‖ ἀπὸ πάντων τῶν τέκνων (see Lk 7.35) itᵏ ‖ ἀπὸ πάντων τῶν ἔργων (see Lk 7.35) f¹³

⁶ 23 {B} μὴ ἕως οὐρανοῦ ὑψωθήσῃ ℵ B* (Bᶜ ἢ ἕως) D W Θ (C f¹ ἕως τοῦ) 1253 itᵃ·ᵃᵘʳ·ᵇ·ᶜ·ᵈ·ᶠᶠ¹·²·(ᵏ) vg (syrᶜ) copˢᵃ·ᵇᵒ arm eth geo Irenaeusˡᵃᵗ Jerome ‖ ἢ ἕως τοῦ οὐρανοῦ ὑψωθεῖσα K (L ὑψοθήσει) X Π* (Δ 33 565 1230 omit τοῦ) 892 1009 1071 1079 1195 1216 1242 1546 1646 Byz Lect itʰ gothᵛⁱᵈ? Caesarius-Nazianzus Chrysostom ‖ ἢ ἕως τοῦ οὐρανοῦ ὑψωθῇς Πᵐᵍ (f¹³ 28 omit τοῦ) 700 1010 1344 1365 (2148 omit ἢ and τοῦ) 2174 itᶠ·(ᵍ¹)·q syrᵖ·ʰ mssᵃᶜᶜ· ᵗᵒ ᴶᵉʳᵒᵐᵉ Chrysostom Maximus-Confessor

⁷ 23 {C} καταβήσῃ (see Is 14.15) B D W itᵃ·ᵃᵘʳ·ᵇ·ᶜ·ᵈ·ᶠ·ᶠᶠ¹·²·ᵍ¹·ʰ·ᵏ·ˡ·q vg syrᶜ·ˢ copˢᵃ goth arm eth geo Irenaeusˡᵃᵗ Caesarius-Nazianzus ‖ καταβιβασθήσῃ (see Lk 10.15) ℵ C K L X Δ Θ Π f¹ f¹³ 28 33 565 700 892 1009 1010 1071 1079 1195 1216 1230 1242 1253 1344 1365 1546 1646 2148 2174 Byz Lect syrᵖ·ʰ copᵇᵒ

---

18 ἦλθεν...πίνων Mt 3.4; 9.14; Lk 18.12   19 ἦλθεν...πίνων Mt 9.14   ἄνθρωπος... ἁμαρτωλῶν Mt 9.11; Lk 15.1-2; 19.7   21–22 Τύρῳ καὶ Σιδῶνι Is 23.1–8; Eze 26—28; Jl 3.4–8; Am 1.9-10; Zch 9.2-4   21 σάκκῳ καὶ σποδῷ Est 4.1; Jon 3.6   23 μὴ...καταβήσῃ Is 14.13, 15

ὅτι εἰ ἐν Σοδόμοις ἐγενήθησαν αἱ δυνάμεις αἱ γενόμεναι ἐν σοί, ἔμεινεν ἂν μέχρι τῆς σήμερον. **24** πλὴν λέγω ὑμῖν ὅτι γῇ Σοδόμων ἀνεκτότερον ἔσται ἐν ἡμέρᾳ κρίσεως ἢ σοί.

Come to Me and Rest
(Lk 10.21–22)

25 Ἐν ἐκείνῳ τῷ καιρῷ ἀποκριθεὶς ὁ Ἰησοῦς εἶπεν, Ἐξομολογοῦμαί σοι, πάτερ, κύριε τοῦ οὐρανοῦ καὶ τῆς γῆς, ὅτι ἔκρυψας ταῦτα ἀπὸ σοφῶν καὶ συνετῶν καὶ ἀπεκάλυψας αὐτὰ νηπίοις· **26** ναί, ὁ πατήρ, ὅτι οὕτως εὐδοκία ἐγένετο ἔμπροσθέν σου. **27** Πάντα μοι παρεδόθη ὑπὸ τοῦ πατρός μου, καὶ οὐδεὶς ἐπιγινώσκει τὸν υἱὸν εἰ μὴ ὁ πατήρ, οὐδὲ τὸν πατέρα τις ἐπιγινώσκει εἰ μὴ ὁ υἱὸς καὶ ᾧ ἐὰν βούληται ὁ υἱὸς ἀποκαλύψαι. **28** Δεῦτε πρός με πάντες οἱ κοπιῶντες καὶ πεφορτισμένοι, κἀγὼ ἀναπαύσω ὑμᾶς. **29** ἄρατε τὸν ζυγόν μου ἐφ' ὑμᾶς καὶ μάθετε ἀπ' ἐμοῦ, ὅτι πραΰς εἰμι καὶ ταπεινὸς τῇ καρδίᾳ, καὶ εὑρήσετε ἀνάπαυσιν ταῖς ψυχαῖς ὑμῶν· **30** ὁ γὰρ ζυγός μου χρηστὸς καὶ τὸ φορτίον μου ἐλαφρόν ἐστιν.

Plucking Grain on the Sabbath
(Mk 2.23–28; Lk 6.1–5)

12 Ἐν ἐκείνῳ τῷ καιρῷ ἐπορεύθη ὁ Ἰησοῦς τοῖς σάββασιν διὰ τῶν σπορίμων· οἱ δὲ μαθηταὶ αὐτοῦ ἐπείνασαν, καὶ ἤρξαντο τίλλειν στάχυας καὶ ἐσθίειν. **2** οἱ δὲ Φαρισαῖοι ἰδόντες εἶπαν αὐτῷ, Ἰδοὺ οἱ μαθηταί σου ποιοῦσιν ὃ οὐκ ἔξεστιν ποιεῖν ἐν σαββάτῳ. **3** ὁ δὲ εἶπεν αὐτοῖς, Οὐκ ἀνέγνωτε τί ἐποίησεν Δαυὶδ[a] ὅτε ἐπείνασεν καὶ οἱ μετ'

---

a a a **3-4** a none, a question, a question: WH Bov BF² TT Jer ‖ a minor, a question, a question: TR Nes Zür Luth ‖ a minor, a major, a question: AV RV ASV RSV Seg ‖ a none, a question, a major: NEB

23 εἰ...σήμερον Gn 19.24–28; 2 Pe 2.6; Jd 7　　**24** Mt 10.15; Lk 10.12　　**25** κύριε...γῆς Tob 7.17 ἔκριψας...νηπίοις 1 Cor 1.26–29　　**27** Πάντα...μου Mt 28.18; Jn 3.35; 13.3; 17.2; Php 2.9 οὐδεὶς...υἱός Jn 1.18; 10.15　　**28** Jr 31.25　　**29** εὑρήσετε...ὑμῶν Jr 6.16 **30** ζυγός...ἐστιν 1 Jn 5.3

12 **1** τίλλειν...ἐσθίειν Dt 23.24–25　　**2** ποιοῦσιν...σαββάτῳ Ex 20.10; Dt 5.14 **3-4** τί...ἔφαγον 1 Sm 21.1–6

---

in Sodom, it would still be in existence today! **24** Remember, then, that on the Judgment Day God will show more mercy to Sodom than to you!"

Come to Me and Rest
(Also Luke 10.21–22)

25 At that time Jesus said: "O Father, Lord of heaven and earth! I thank you because you have shown to the unlearned what you have hidden from the wise and learned. **26** Yes, Father, this was done by your own choice and pleasure.

27 "My Father has given me all things. No one knows the Son except the Father, and no one knows the Father except the Son, and those to whom the Son wants to reveal him.

28 "Come to me, all of you who are tired from carrying your heavy loads, and I will give you rest. **29** Take my yoke and put it on you, and learn from me, for I am gentle and humble in spirit; and you will find rest. **30** The yoke I will give you is easy, and the load I will put on you is light."

The Question about the Sabbath
(Also Mark 2.23–28; Luke 6.1–5)

12 Not long afterward Jesus was walking through the wheat fields on a Sabbath day. His disciples were hungry, so they began to pick heads of wheat and eat the grain. **2** When the Pharisees saw this, they said to Jesus, "Look, it is against our Law for your disciples to do this on the Sabbath!" **3** Jesus answered: "Have you never read what David did that time when he and his men were hungry? [4] He went into the house of God, and he and his men ate the bread offered to God, even though it was against the Law for them to eat that bread — only the priests were allowed to eat it. [5] Or have you not read in the Law of Moses that every Sabbath the priests in the Temple actually break the Sabbath law, yet they are not guilty? [6] There is something here, I tell you, greater than the Temple. [7] If you really knew what this scripture means, 'I do not want animal sacrifices, but kindness,' you would not condemn people who are not guilty. [8] For the Son of Man is Lord of the Sabbath."

The Man with a Crippled Hand
(Also Mark 3.1-6; Luke 6.6-11)

[9] Jesus left that place and went to one of their synagogues. [10] A man was there who had a crippled hand. There were some men present who wanted to accuse Jesus of wrongdoing; so they asked him, "Is it against our Law to cure on the Sabbath?" [11] Jesus answered: "What if one of you has a sheep and it falls into a deep hole on the Sabbath? Will you not take hold of it and lift it out? [12] And a man is worth much more than a sheep! So, then, our Law does allow us to help someone on the Sabbath." [13] Then he said to the man, "Stretch out your hand." He stretched it out, and it became well again, just like the other one. [14] The Pharisees left and made plans against Jesus to kill him.

God's Chosen Servant

[15] When Jesus heard about it, he went away from that place; and many people followed him. He healed all the sick,

αὐτοῦ;[a] 4 πῶς εἰσῆλθεν εἰς τὸν οἶκον τοῦ θεοῦ καὶ τοὺς ἄρτους τῆς προθέσεως ἔφαγον[1], ὃ οὐκ ἐξὸν ἦν αὐτῷ φαγεῖν οὐδὲ τοῖς μετ' αὐτοῦ, εἰ μὴ τοῖς ἱερεῦσιν μόνοις;[a] 5 ἢ οὐκ ἀνέγνωτε ἐν τῷ νόμῳ ὅτι τοῖς σάββασιν οἱ ἱερεῖς ἐν τῷ ἱερῷ τὸ σάββατον βεβηλοῦσιν καὶ ἀναίτιοί εἰσιν; 6 λέγω δὲ ὑμῖν ὅτι τοῦ ἱεροῦ μεῖζόν ἐστιν ὧδε. 7 εἰ δὲ ἐγνώκειτε τί ἐστιν, **Ἔλεος θέλω καὶ οὐ θυσίαν**, οὐκ ἂν κατεδικάσατε τοὺς ἀναιτίους. 8 κύριος γάρ ἐστιν τοῦ σαββάτου ὁ υἱὸς τοῦ ἀνθρώπου.

The Man with a Withered Hand
(Mk 3.1-6; Lk 6.6-11)

9 Καὶ μεταβὰς ἐκεῖθεν ἦλθεν εἰς τὴν συναγωγὴν αὐτῶν· 10 καὶ ἰδοὺ ἄνθρωπος χεῖρα ἔχων ξηράν. καὶ ἐπηρώτησαν αὐτὸν λέγοντες, Εἰ ἔξεστιν τοῖς σάββασιν θεραπεῦσαι; ἵνα κατηγορήσωσιν αὐτοῦ. 11 ὁ δὲ εἶπεν αὐτοῖς, Τίς ἔσται ἐξ ὑμῶν ἄνθρωπος ὃς ἕξει πρόβατον ἕν, καὶ ἐὰν ἐμπέσῃ τοῦτο τοῖς σάββασιν εἰς βόθυνον, οὐχὶ κρατήσει αὐτὸ καὶ ἐγερεῖ; 12 πόσῳ οὖν διαφέρει ἄνθρωπος προβάτου. ὥστε ἔξεστιν τοῖς σάββασιν καλῶς ποιεῖν. 13 τότε λέγει τῷ ἀνθρώπῳ, Ἔκτεινόν σου τὴν χεῖρα. καὶ ἐξέτεινεν, καὶ ἀπεκατεστάθη ὑγιὴς ὡς ἡ ἄλλη. 14 ἐξελθόντες δὲ οἱ Φαρισαῖοι συμβούλιον ἔλαβον κατ' αὐτοῦ ὅπως αὐτὸν ἀπολέσωσιν.

The Chosen Servant

15 Ὁ δὲ Ἰησοῦς γνοὺς ἀνεχώρησεν ἐκεῖθεν. καὶ ἠκολούθησαν αὐτῷ πολλοί[2], καὶ ἐθεράπευσεν αὐτοὺς πάντας,

---

[1] 4 {C} ἔφαγον ℵ B ‖ ἔφαγεν (see Mk 2.26; Lk 6.4) 𝔓[70] C D K L W Δ Θ Π f[1] f[13] 28 33 565 700 892 1009 1010 1071 1079 1195 1216 1230 1242 1253 1344 1365 1546 1646 2148 2174 *Byz Lect* it[a,aur,b,c,d,f,(ff1),g1,h,k,l,q] vg syr[c,s,p,h] cop[sa,bo] arm eth geo Eusebius Chrysostom

[2] 15 {C} πολλοί ℵ B it[a,aur,b,c,ff1,2,g1,k,l] vg (syr[c,s]) eth[ro] Eusebius

4 τοὺς...προθέσεως Lv 24.5-8　δ...μόνοις Lv 24.9　5 τοῖς...εἰσιν Nu 28.9-10　**6** Mt 12.41-42; Lk 11.31-32　7 εἰ...θυσίαν Mt 9.13　Ἔλεος...θυσίαν Ho 6.6　**10** Εἰ...θεραπεῦσαι Lk 14.3　**11** Lk 14.5　**12** πόσῳ...προβάτου Mt 6.26; 10.31; Lk 12.7, 24　ἔξεστιν...ποιεῖν Lk 13.16; Jn 5.9; 7.23; 9.14　**14** Mt 27.1; Mk 11.18; Lk 19.47; Jn 5.16; 18　**15** Mk 3.7-10; Lk 6.17-19

16 καὶ ἐπετίμησεν αὐτοῖς ἵνα μὴ φανερὸν αὐτὸν ποιήσωσιν·
17 ἵνα πληρωθῇ τὸ ῥηθὲν διὰ Ἠσαΐου τοῦ προφήτου λέγοντος,

18   Ἰδοὺ ὁ παῖς μου ὃν ᾑρέτισα,
        ὁ ἀγαπητός μου εἰς ὃν εὐδόκησεν ἡ ψυχή μου·
      θήσω τὸ πνεῦμά μου ἐπ᾽ αὐτόν,
        καὶ κρίσιν τοῖς ἔθνεσιν ἀπαγγελεῖ.
19   οὐκ ἐρίσει οὐδὲ κραυγάσει,
        οὐδὲ ἀκούσει τις ἐν ταῖς πλατείαις τὴν φωνὴν αὐτοῦ.
20   κάλαμον συντετριμμένον οὐ κατεάξει
        καὶ λίνον τυφόμενον οὐ σβέσει,
      ἕως ἂν ἐκβάλῃ εἰς νῖκος τὴν κρίσιν.
21   καὶ τῷ ὀνόματι αὐτοῦ ἔθνη ἐλπιοῦσιν.

Jesus and Beelzebul
(Mk 3.20—30; Lk 11.14—23; 12.10)

22 Τότε προσηνέχθη αὐτῷ δαιμονιζόμενος τυφλὸς καὶ κωφός· καὶ ἐθεράπευσεν αὐτόν, ὥστε τὸν κωφὸν λαλεῖν καὶ βλέπειν. 23 καὶ ἐξίσταντο πάντες οἱ ὄχλοι καὶ ἔλεγον, Μήτι οὗτός ἐστιν ὁ υἱὸς Δαυίδ; 24 οἱ δὲ Φαρισαῖοι ἀκούσαντες εἶπον, Οὗτος οὐκ ἐκβάλλει τὰ δαιμόνια εἰ μὴ ἐν τῷ Βεελζεβοὺλ ἄρχοντι τῶν δαιμονίων. 25 εἰδὼς δὲ[3] τὰς ἐνθυμήσεις αὐτῶν εἶπεν αὐτοῖς, Πᾶσα βασιλεία μερισθεῖσα καθ᾽ ἑαυτῆς ἐρημοῦται, καὶ πᾶσα πόλις ἢ οἰκία μερισθεῖσα

Augustine ‖ ὄχλοι N cop[sa mss] ‖ ὄχλοι πολλοί C D K L W Δ Θ Π f[1] f[13] 28 33 565 700 892 1009 1010 1071 1079 1195 1216 1230 1242 1253 1344 1365 1546 1646 2148 2174 Byz Lect l[12m,32m,70m,150m,185m,883m,1627m,1642m,1663m] it[d,f,h,(q)] syr[p,h] cop[sa ms,bo,fa yv id?] arm geo Diatessaron Origen Eusebius ‖ πολλοὶ ὄχλοι X eth[pp?] Hilary ‖ πολλοὶ ἀπὸ τοῦ λαοῦ eth[ms?]

[3] 25 {C} εἰδὼς δέ N[*,c] B cop[sa] ‖ ἰδὼν δέ 𝔭[21] N[b] D 892* it[d,k] syr[c,s] cop[bo] Chrysostom ‖ εἰδὼς δὲ ὁ Ἰησοῦς C K L W X Δ Θ Π 0106 f[1] f[13] 28 565 700 1009 1010 1071 1079 1195 1216 1230 1242 1253 1344 1365 1546 1646 2148 2174 Byz Lect it[a,aur,b,c,f,ff2,g1,h,l,q] vg syr[p,h] arm eth geo ‖ ἰδὼν δὲ ὁ Ἰησοῦς 33 892[c] (l[70] εἰδών) it[ff1] cop[bo mss]

---

16 Mt 8.4; 9.30; Mk 3.12; 5.43; 7.36   18-21 Is 42.1-4   22-23 Τότε...ἔλεγον Mt 9.32-33
24 Οὗτος...δαιμονίων Mt 9.34

---

16 and gave them orders not to tell others about him, 17 to make come true what the prophet Isaiah had said:
18 "Here is my servant, says God,
      whom I have chosen,
    The one I love, with whom I am
      well pleased.
  I will put my Spirit on him,
    And he will announce my judgment
      to all people.
19 But he will not argue or shout,
    Nor will he make loud speeches in
      the streets;
20 He will not break off a bent reed,
    Nor will he put out a flickering lamp.
  He will persist until he causes justice
    to triumph;
21 And all people will put their hope
    in him."

Jesus and Beelzebul
(Also Mark 3.20—30; Luke 11.14—23)

22 Then some people brought to Jesus a man who was blind and could not talk because he had a demon. Jesus healed the man, so that he was able to talk and see. 23 The crowds were all amazed. "Could he be the Son of David?" they asked. 24 When the Pharisees heard this they replied, "He drives out demons only because their ruler Beelzebul gives him power to do so." 25 Jesus knew what they were thinking and said to them: "Any country that divides itself into groups that fight each other will not last very long. And any town or family that divides itself into groups that fight

each other will fall apart. ²⁶ So if one group is fighting another in Satan's kingdom, this means that it is already divided into groups and will soon fall apart! ²⁷ You say that I drive out demons because Beelzebul gives me the power to do so. Well, then, who gives your followers the power to drive them out? Your own followers prove that you are completely wrong! ²⁸ No, it is God's Spirit who gives me the power to drive out demons, which proves that the Kingdom of God has already come upon you.

²⁹ "No one can break into a strong man's house and take away his belongings unless he ties up the strong man first; then he can plunder his house.

³⁰ "Anyone who is not for me is really against me; anyone who does not help me gather is really scattering. ³¹ For this reason I tell you: men can be forgiven any sin and any evil thing they say;[1] but whoever says evil things against the Holy Spirit will not be forgiven. ³² Anyone who says something against the Son of Man will be forgiven; but whoever says something against the Holy Spirit will not be forgiven — now or ever."

A Tree and Its Fruit
(Also Luke 6.43–45)

³³ "To have good fruit you must have a healthy tree; if you have a poor tree you will have bad fruit. For a tree is known by the kind of fruit it bears.

---

[1] **31** any evil thing they say: *or* any evil thing they say against God

καθ' ἑαυτῆς οὐ σταθήσεται. 26 καὶ εἰ ὁ Σατανᾶς τὸν Σατανᾶν ἐκβάλλει, ἐφ' ἑαυτὸν ἐμερίσθη· πῶς οὖν σταθήσεται ἡ βασιλεία αὐτοῦ; 27 καὶ εἰ ἐγὼ ἐν Βεελζεβοὺλ ἐκβάλλω τὰ δαιμόνια, οἱ υἱοὶ ὑμῶν ἐν τίνι ἐκβάλλουσιν; διὰ τοῦτο αὐτοὶ κριταὶ ἔσονται ὑμῶν. 28 εἰ δὲ ἐν πνεύματι θεοῦ ἐγὼ ἐκβάλλω τὰ δαιμόνια, ἄρα ἔφθασεν ἐφ' ὑμᾶς ἡ βασιλεία τοῦ θεοῦ. 29 ἢ πῶς δύναταί τις εἰσελθεῖν εἰς τὴν οἰκίαν τοῦ ἰσχυροῦ καὶ τὰ σκεύη αὐτοῦ ἁρπάσαι, ἐὰν μὴ πρῶτον δήσῃ τὸν ἰσχυρόν;ᵇ καὶ τότε τὴν οἰκίαν αὐτοῦ διαρπάσει.ᵇ 30 ὁ μὴ ὢν μετ' ἐμοῦ κατ' ἐμοῦ ἐστιν, καὶ ὁ μὴ συνάγων μετ' ἐμοῦ σκορπίζει⁴. 31 Διὰ τοῦτο λέγω ὑμῖν, πᾶσα ἁμαρτία καὶ βλασφημία ἀφεθήσεται τοῖς ἀνθρώποις⁵, ἡ δὲ τοῦ πνεύματος βλασφημία οὐκ ἀφεθήσεται. 32 καὶ ὃς ἐὰν εἴπῃ λόγον κατὰ τοῦ υἱοῦ τοῦ ἀνθρώπου, ἀφεθήσεται αὐτῷ· ὃς δ' ἂν εἴπῃ κατὰ τοῦ πνεύματος τοῦ ἁγίου, οὐκ ἀφεθήσεται αὐτῷ οὔτε ἐν τούτῳ τῷ αἰῶνι οὔτε ἐν τῷ μέλλοντι.

A Tree and Its Fruits
(Lk 6.43–45)

33 Ἢ ποιήσατε τὸ δένδρον καλὸν καὶ τὸν καρπὸν αὐτοῦ καλόν, ἢ ποιήσατε τὸ δένδρον σαπρὸν καὶ τὸν καρπὸν αὐτοῦ σαπρόν· ἐκ γὰρ τοῦ καρποῦ τὸ δένδρον

---

⁴ **30** {A} σκορπίζει B C D K L W X Δ Θ Π f¹ f¹³ 28 565 700 892 1009 1010 1071 1079 1195 1216 1230 1242 1253 1344 1365 1546 1646 2148 2174 *Byz Lect* itᵃ,ᵃᵘʳ,ᵇ,ᶜ,ᵈ,ᶠ,ᶠᶠ¹,²,ᵍˡ,ʰ,ˡ,q vg syrᶜ,ˢ,ᵖ,ʰ,ᵖᵃˡ copˢᵃ arm geo Origen ∥ σκορπίζει με ℵ 33 syrʰᵐᵍ copᵇᵒ eth Chrysostom ∥ διαρπάστω l¹⁸⁵ ∥ *omit* itᵏ

⁵ **31** {B} τοῖς ἀνθρώποις ℵ C D K L W X (Δ *omit* τοῖς) Θ Π f¹ f¹³ 28 33 565 700 892 1009 1010 1071 1079 1195 1216 1230 1242 1253 1344 1365 1546 1646 2148 2174 *Byz Lect* itᵃ,ᵃᵘʳ,ᵇ,ᶜ,ᵈ,ᶠ,ᶠᶠ¹,²,ᵍˡ,ʰ,ᵏ,ˡ,q vg syrᶜ,ˢ,ᵖ,ʰ copᵇᵒ arm ethᵖᵖ,ᵐˢ geo ∥ ὑμῖν τοῖς ἀνθρώποις B syrᵖᵃˡᵐˢˢ copˢᵃ (ethʳᵒ αὐτοῖς τοῖς) Origen Athanasius ∥ *omit* syrᵖᵃˡᵐˢ

ᵇ ᵇ **29** b question, b major: WH Bov Nes AV RV ASV RSV Zür Jer Seg ∥ b minor, b question: TR BF² (NEB) TT (Luth)

---

28 εἰ...δαιμόνια Ac 10.38   **29** πῶς...ἰσχυρόν Is 49.24   **30** ὁ μὴ ὢν...ἐστιν Mk 9.40; Lk 9.50   **31** πᾶσα...ἀνθρώποις 1 Tm 1.13   **33** Mt 7.16-20

γινώσκεται. **34** γεννήματα ἐχιδνῶν, πῶς δύνασθε ἀγαθὰ
λαλεῖν πονηροὶ ὄντες; ἐκ γὰρ τοῦ περισσεύματος τῆς
καρδίας τὸ στόμα λαλεῖ. **35** ὁ ἀγαθὸς ἄνθρωπος ἐκ τοῦ
ἀγαθοῦ θησαυροῦ ἐκβάλλει ἀγαθά, καὶ ὁ πονηρὸς ἄνθρωπος
ἐκ τοῦ πονηροῦ θησαυροῦ ἐκβάλλει πονηρά. **36** λέγω δὲ
ὑμῖν ὅτι πᾶν ῥῆμα ἀργὸν ὃ λαλήσουσιν οἱ ἄνθρωποι
ἀποδώσουσιν περὶ αὐτοῦ λόγον ἐν ἡμέρα κρίσεως· **37** ἐκ
γὰρ τῶν λόγων σου δικαιωθήσῃ, καὶ ἐκ τῶν λόγων σου
καταδικασθήσῃ.

The Demand for a Sign
(Mk 8.11–12; Lk 11.29–32)

38 Τότε ἀπεκρίθησαν αὐτῷ τινες τῶν γραμματέων καὶ
Φαρισαίων λέγοντες, Διδάσκαλε, θέλομεν ἀπὸ σοῦ σημεῖον ἰδεῖν. **39** ὁ δὲ ἀποκριθεὶς εἶπεν αὐτοῖς, Γενεὰ
πονηρὰ καὶ μοιχαλὶς σημεῖον ἐπιζητεῖ, καὶ σημεῖον οὐ
δοθήσεται αὐτῇ εἰ μὴ τὸ σημεῖον Ἰωνᾶ τοῦ προφήτου.
40 ὥσπερ γὰρ **ἦν Ἰωνᾶς ἐν τῇ κοιλίᾳ τοῦ κήτους τρεῖς
ἡμέρας καὶ τρεῖς νύκτας,** οὕτως ἔσται ὁ υἱὸς τοῦ ἀνθρώπου
ἐν τῇ καρδίᾳ τῆς γῆς τρεῖς ἡμέρας καὶ τρεῖς νύκτας.
41 ἄνδρες Νινευῖται ἀναστήσονται ἐν τῇ κρίσει μετὰ τῆς
γενεᾶς ταύτης καὶ κατακρινοῦσιν αὐτήν· ὅτι μετενόησαν
εἰς τὸ κήρυγμα Ἰωνᾶ, καὶ ἰδοὺ πλεῖον Ἰωνᾶ ὧδε. **42** βασίλισσα νότου ἐγερθήσεται ἐν τῇ κρίσει μετὰ τῆς γενεᾶς
ταύτης καὶ κατακρινεῖ αὐτήν· ὅτι ἦλθεν ἐκ τῶν περάτων
τῆς γῆς ἀκοῦσαι τὴν σοφίαν Σολομῶνος, καὶ ἰδοὺ πλεῖον
Σολομῶνος ὧδε.

The Return of the Unclean Spirit
(Lk 11.24–26)

43 Ὅταν δὲ τὸ ἀκάθαρτον πνεῦμα ἐξέλθῃ ἀπὸ τοῦ
ἀνθρώπου, διέρχεται δι' ἀνύδρων τόπων ζητοῦν ἀνάπαυ-

34 γεννήματα ἐχιδνῶν Mt 3.7; 23.33; Lk 3.7   ἐκ...λαλεῖ Mt 15.18; Mk 7.21   38 Mt 16.1;
Mk 8.11; Lk 11.16; Jn 6.30; 1 Cor 1.22   39 Γενεά...Ἰωνᾶ Mt 16.4   40 ἦν...νύκτας Jon 1.17
41 μετενόησαν...Ἰωνᾶ Jon 3.5, 8   πλεῖον...ὧδε Mt 12.6   42 βασίλισσα...Σολομῶνος
1 Kgs 10.1–10; 2 Chr 9.1–12   πλεῖον...ὧδε Mt 12.6

34 You snakes — how can you say good
things when you are evil? For the mouth
speaks what the heart is full of. **35** A good
man brings good things out of his treasure
of good things; a bad man brings bad
things out of his treasure of bad things.
36 "And I tell you this: on the Judgment Day everyone will have to give
account of every useless word he has
ever spoken. **37** For your words will be
used to judge you, either to declare you
innocent or to declare you guilty."

The Demand for a Miracle
(Also Mark 8.11–12; Luke 11.29–32)

38 Then some teachers of the Law and
some Pharisees spoke up. "Teacher,"
they said, "we want to see you perform
a miracle." **39** "How evil and godless
are the people of this day!" Jesus exclaimed. "You ask me for a miracle?
No! The only miracle you will be given
is the miracle of the prophet Jonah.
40 In the same way that Jonah spent
three days and nights in the belly of the
big fish, so will the Son of Man spend
three days and nights in the depths of
the earth. **41** On the Judgment Day the
people of Nineveh will stand up and
accuse you, because they turned from
their sins when they heard Jonah preach;
and there is something here, I tell you,
greater than Jonah! **42** On the Judgment
Day the Queen from the South will
stand up and accuse you, because she
traveled halfway around the world to
listen to Solomon's wise teaching; and
there is something here, I tell you,
greater than Solomon!"

The Return of the Evil Spirit
(Also Luke 11.24–26)

43 "When an evil spirit goes out of a
man, it travels over dry country looking

for a place to rest. If it can't find one, [44] it says to itself, 'I will go back to my house which I left.' So it goes back and finds it empty, clean, and all fixed up. [45] Then it goes out and brings along seven other spirits even worse than itself, and they come and live there. So that man is in worse shape, when it is all over, than he was at the beginning. This is the way it will happen to the evil people of this day.''

Jesus' Mother and Brothers
(Also Mark 3.31–35; Luke 8.19–21)

[46] Jesus was still talking to the people when his mother and brothers arrived. They stood outside, asking to speak with him. [47] So one of the people there said to him, "Look, your mother and brothers are standing outside, and they want to speak with you." [48] Jesus answered, "Who is my mother? Who are my brothers?" [49] Then he pointed to his disciples and said: "Look! Here are my mother and my brothers! [50] For the person who does what my Father in heaven wants him to do is my brother, my sister, my mother.''

The Parable of the Sower
(Also Mark 4.1–9; Luke 8.4–8)

13 That same day Jesus left the house and went to the lakeside, where he sat down to teach. [2] The crowd that gathered around him was so large that he got into a boat and sat in it, while the crowd stood on the shore. [3] He used parables to tell them many things.

σιν,ᶜ καὶ οὐχ εὑρίσκει.ᶜ **44** τότε λέγει, Εἰς τὸν οἶκόν μου ἐπιστρέψω ὅθεν ἐξῆλθον· καὶ ἐλθὸν εὑρίσκει σχολάζοντα σεσαρωμένον καὶ κεκοσμημένον. **45** τότε πορεύεται καὶ παραλαμβάνει μεθ' ἑαυτοῦ ἑπτὰ ἕτερα πνεύματα πονηρότερα ἑαυτοῦ, καὶ εἰσελθόντα κατοικεῖ ἐκεῖ· καὶ γίνεται τὰ ἔσχατα τοῦ ἀνθρώπου ἐκείνου χείρονα τῶν πρώτων. οὕτως ἔσται καὶ τῇ γενεᾷ ταύτῃ τῇ πονηρᾷ.

The Mother and Brothers of Jesus
(Mk 3.31–35; Lk 8.19–21)

46 Ἔτι αὐτοῦ λαλοῦντος τοῖς ὄχλοις ἰδοὺ ἡ μήτηρ καὶ οἱ ἀδελφοὶ αὐτοῦ εἱστήκεισαν ἔξω ζητοῦντες αὐτῷ λαλῆσαι. [**47** εἶπεν δέ τις αὐτῷ, Ἰδοὺ ἡ μήτηρ σου καὶ οἱ ἀδελφοί σου ἔξω ἑστήκασιν ζητοῦντές σοι λαλῆσαι.]⁶ **48** ὁ δὲ ἀποκριθεὶς εἶπεν τῷ λέγοντι αὐτῷ, Τίς ἐστιν ἡ μήτηρ μου, καὶ τίνες εἰσὶν οἱ ἀδελφοί μου; **49** καὶ ἐκτείνας τὴν χεῖρα αὐτοῦ ἐπὶ τοὺς μαθητὰς αὐτοῦ εἶπεν, Ἰδοὺ ἡ μήτηρ μου καὶ οἱ ἀδελφοί μου· **50** ὅστις γὰρ ἂν ποιήσῃ τὸ θέλημα τοῦ πατρός μου τοῦ ἐν οὐρανοῖς αὐτός μου ἀδελφὸς καὶ ἀδελφὴ καὶ μήτηρ ἐστίν.

The Parable of the Sower
(Mk 4.1–9; Lk 8.4–8)

13 Ἐν τῇ ἡμέρᾳ ἐκείνῃ ἐξελθὼν ὁ Ἰησοῦς τῆς οἰκίας ἐκάθητο παρὰ τὴν θάλασσαν· **2** καὶ συνήχθησαν πρὸς αὐτὸν ὄχλοι πολλοί, ὥστε αὐτὸν εἰς πλοῖον ἐμβάντα καθῆσθαι, καὶ πᾶς ὁ ὄχλος ἐπὶ τὸν αἰγιαλὸν εἱστήκει. **3** καὶ

⁶ **47** {C} *include verse 47* ℵᵃ C D K W X Δ Θ Π *f*¹ *f*¹³ 28 33 565 700 892 1010 1071 1079 1195 1216 1230 1242 1253 1344 1365 1546 1646 2148 2174 *Byz Lect* (*l*⁷⁰ *omit* εἶπεν δέ τις αὐτῷ) (*l*³³³) itᵃ,ᵃᵘʳ,ᵇ,ᶜ,ᵈ,f,ff²,g¹,h,l,q vg syrᵖ·ʰ copᵇᵒ arm eth geo Diatessaron Origenˡᵃᵗ Chrysostom ∥ *omit verse 47* ℵ* B L 1009 *l*¹² itff¹,k syrᶜ,ˢ copˢᵃ

ᶜᶜ **43** *c* minor, *c* major: TR WH Bov Nes BF² AV RV ASV RSV (TT) (Zür) (Luth) Jer (Seg) ∥ *c* major, *c* minor: NEB

45 γίνεται...πρώτων 2 Pe 2.20   **46** ἡ μήτηρ...αὐτοῦ Mt 13.55; Mk 6.3; Jn 2.12; Ac 1.14
13 1-2 Lk 5.1, 3

ἐλάλησεν αὐτοῖς πολλὰ ἐν παραβολαῖς λέγων, Ἰδοὺ ἐξῆλθεν ὁ σπείρων τοῦ σπείρειν. 4 καὶ ἐν τῷ σπείρειν αὐτὸν ἃ μὲν ἔπεσεν παρὰ τὴν ὁδόν, καὶ ἐλθόντα τὰ πετεινὰ κατέφαγεν αὐτά. 5 ἄλλα δὲ ἔπεσεν ἐπὶ τὰ πετρώδη ὅπου οὐκ εἶχεν γῆν πολλήν, καὶ εὐθέως ἐξανέτειλεν διὰ τὸ μὴ ἔχειν βάθος γῆς. 6 ἡλίου δὲ ἀνατείλαντος ἐκαυματίσθη καὶ διὰ τὸ μὴ ἔχειν ῥίζαν ἐξηράνθη. 7 ἄλλα δὲ ἔπεσεν ἐπὶ τὰς ἀκάνθας, καὶ ἀνέβησαν αἱ ἄκανθαι καὶ ἔπνιξαν αὐτά. 8 ἄλλα δὲ ἔπεσεν ἐπὶ τὴν γῆν τὴν καλὴν καὶ ἐδίδου καρπόν, ὃ μὲν ἑκατόν, ὃ δὲ ἑξήκοντα, ὃ δὲ τριάκοντα. 9 ὁ ἔχων ὦτα[1] ἀκουέτω.

The Purpose of the Parables
(Mk 4.10–12; Lk 8.9–10)

10 Καὶ προσελθόντες οἱ μαθηταὶ εἶπαν αὐτῷ, Διὰ τί ἐν παραβολαῖς λαλεῖς αὐτοῖς; 11 ὁ δὲ ἀποκριθεὶς εἶπεν [αὐτοῖς] ὅτι[a] Ὑμῖν δέδοται γνῶναι τὰ μυστήρια τῆς βασιλείας τῶν οὐρανῶν, ἐκείνοις δὲ οὐ δέδοται. 12 ὅστις γὰρ ἔχει, δοθήσεται αὐτῷ καὶ περισσευθήσεται· ὅστις δὲ οὐκ ἔχει, καὶ ὃ ἔχει ἀρθήσεται ἀπ' αὐτοῦ. 13 διὰ τοῦτο ἐν παραβολαῖς αὐτοῖς λαλῶ, ὅτι βλέποντες οὐ βλέπουσιν καὶ ἀκούοντες οὐκ ἀκούουσιν οὐδὲ συνίουσιν[2]·

---

[1] 9 {C} ὦτα (see 11.15; 13.43) ℵ* B L itᵃ·ᵉ·ᶠᶠ¹·ᵏ syrˢ Tertullian ‖ ὦτα ἀκούειν (see Mk 4.9; Lk 8.8) ℵᶜ C D K W X Δ Θ Π f¹ f¹³ 28 33 565 700 892 1009 1010 1071 1079 1195 1216 1230 1241 1242 1253 1344 1365 1546 1646 2148 2174 Byz Lect itᵃᵘʳ·ᵇ·ᶜ·ᵈ·ᶠ·ᶠᶠ²·ᵍ¹·ʰ·ˡ·π·q vg syrᶜ·ᵖ·ʰ copˢᵃ·ᵇᵒ arm eth geo Diatessaron Origen Eusebius Ephraem

[2] 13 {B} ὅτι βλέποντες οὐ βλέπουσιν καὶ ἀκούοντες οὐκ ἀκούουσιν οὐδὲ συνίουσιν ℵ B* (Bᶜ συνιῶσι) C K L W X Δ Π 565 700 892 1010 1071 1195 (1216 1253 omit οὐκ ἀκούουσιν and read οὐ for οὐδὲ) 1230 (1241 ἀκούωσιν οὐδὲ συνιῶσιν) 1242 1344 2174 (33 1646 2148 lᵉ²¹¹ συνιῶσιν) (28 1009 1546 l⁷⁶ omit οὐδὲ συνίουσιν) Byz lᵉ¹⁸⁵·⁸⁸³ itᵃᵘʳ·ᶠ·ˡ·π·q vg syrᵖ·ʰ copᵇᵒ arm eth geo ‖ ὅτι βλέποντες μὴ βλέπουσι καὶ ἀκούοντες μὴ ἀκούσωσι μηδὲ συνῶσιν 1365 ‖ ἵνα βλέποντες μὴ βλέπωσιν καὶ ἀκούοντες μὴ ἀκούωσιν

---

[a] 11 a direct: TR? WH Bov BF² RV ASV RSV NEB TT Luth Jer ‖ a causal: TR? Nes AV Zür Seg

---

9 Mt 11.15; 13.43; Mk 4.23; Lk 14.35; Re 2.7; 13.9   11 γνῶναι...οὐρανῶν 1 Cor 4.1; Eph 3.3–4; 6.19; Col 2.2; 4.3   12 Mt 25.29; Mk 4.25; Lk 8.18; 19.26

"There was a man who went out to sow. 4 As he scattered the seed in the field, some of it fell along the path, and the birds came and ate it up. 5 Some of it fell on rocky ground, where there was little soil. The seeds soon sprouted, because the soil wasn't deep. 6 When the sun came up it burned the young plants, and because the roots had not grown deep enough the plants soon dried up. 7 Some of the seed fell among thorns, which grew up and choked the plants. 8 But some seeds fell in good soil, and bore grain: some had one hundred grains, others sixty, and others thirty." 9 And Jesus said, "Listen, then, if you have ears!"

The Purpose of the Parables
(Also Mark 4.10–12; Luke 8.9–10)

10 Then the disciples came to Jesus and asked him, "Why do you use parables when you talk to them?" 11 "The knowledge of the secrets of the Kingdom of heaven has been given to you," Jesus answered, "but not to them. 12 For the man who has something will be given more, so that he will have more than enough; but the man who has nothing will have taken away from him even the little he has. 13 This is the reason that I use parables to talk to them: it is because they look, but do not see, and they listen, but do not hear or under-

stand. ¹⁴ So the prophecy of Isaiah comes true in their case:

'You will listen and listen, but not
    understand;
You will look and look, but not see.
¹⁵ Because this people's mind is dull;
They have stopped up their ears,
And they have closed their eyes.
Otherwise, their eyes might see,
Their ears might hear,
Their minds might understand
And they might turn to me, says God,
And I would heal them.'

¹⁶ As for you, how fortunate you are! Your eyes see and your ears hear. ¹⁷ Remember this! Many prophets and many of God's people wanted very much to see what you see, but they could not, and to hear what you hear, but they did not."

Jesus Explains the Parable of the Sower
(Also Mark 4.13–20; Luke 8.11–15)

¹⁸ "Listen, then, and learn what the parable of the sower means. ¹⁹ Those who hear the message about the Kingdom but do not understand it are like the seed that fell along the path. The Evil One comes and snatches away what was sown in them. ²⁰ The seed that fell on rocky ground stands for those who receive the message gladly as soon as they hear it. ²¹ But it does not sink deep in them, and they don't last long. So when trouble or persecution comes because of the message, they give up at once. ²² The seed that fell among thorns stands for those who hear the message, but the worries about this life and the love for riches choke the message, and they don't

14 καὶ ἀναπληροῦται αὐτοῖς ἡ προφητεία Ἠσαΐου ἡ λέγουσα,

  Ἀκοῇ ἀκούσετε καὶ οὐ μὴ συνῆτε,
    καὶ βλέποντες βλέψετε καὶ οὐ μὴ ἴδητε.
15   ἐπαχύνθη γὰρ ἡ καρδία τοῦ λαοῦ τούτου,
    καὶ τοῖς ὠσὶν βαρέως ἤκουσαν,
      καὶ τοὺς ὀφθαλμοὺς αὐτῶν ἐκάμμυσαν·
      μήποτε ἴδωσιν τοῖς ὀφθαλμοῖς
    καὶ τοῖς ὠσὶν ἀκούσωσιν
  καὶ τῇ καρδίᾳ συνῶσιν καὶ ἐπιστρέψωσιν,
    καὶ ἰάσομαι αὐτούς.
16 ὑμῶν δὲ μακάριοι οἱ ὀφθαλμοὶ ὅτι βλέπουσιν, καὶ τὰ ὦτα ὑμῶν ὅτι ἀκούουσιν. 17 ἀμὴν γὰρ λέγω ὑμῖν ὅτι πολλοὶ προφῆται καὶ δίκαιοι ἐπεθύμησαν ἰδεῖν ἃ βλέπετε καὶ οὐκ εἶδαν, καὶ ἀκοῦσαι ἃ ἀκούετε καὶ οὐκ ἤκουσαν.

The Parable of the Sower Explained
(Mk 4.13–20; Lk 8.11–15)

18 Ὑμεῖς οὖν ἀκούσατε τὴν παραβολὴν τοῦ σπείραντος. 19 παντὸς ἀκούοντος τὸν λόγον τῆς βασιλείας καὶ μὴ συνιέντος, ἔρχεται ὁ πονηρὸς καὶ ἁρπάζει τὸ ἐσπαρμένον ἐν τῇ καρδίᾳ αὐτοῦ· οὗτός ἐστιν ὁ παρὰ τὴν ὁδὸν σπαρείς. 20 ὁ δὲ ἐπὶ τὰ πετρώδη σπαρείς, οὗτός ἐστιν ὁ τὸν λόγον ἀκούων καὶ εὐθὺς μετὰ χαρᾶς λαμβάνων αὐτόν· 21 οὐκ ἔχει δὲ ῥίζαν ἐν ἑαυτῷ ἀλλὰ πρόσκαιρός ἐστιν, γενομένης δὲ θλίψεως ἢ διωγμοῦ διὰ τὸν λόγον εὐθὺς σκανδαλίζεται. 22 ὁ δὲ εἰς τὰς ἀκάνθας σπαρείς, οὗτός ἐστιν ὁ τὸν λόγον ἀκούων καὶ ἡ μέριμνα τοῦ αἰῶνος [τούτου] καὶ ἡ ἀπάτη τοῦ πλούτου συμπνίγει τὸν λόγον, καὶ ἄκαρπος γίνεται.

καὶ μὴ συνιῶσιν μήποτε ἐπιστρέψωσιν (see Mk 4.12) (D συνῶσι) Θ f¹ f¹³ Lect (l¹²,⁷⁰,⁸⁰,²⁹⁹,⁸⁵⁰,¹⁰⁸⁴ συνῶσι) (l¹⁵⁰ οὐ δή for καὶ μή and read συνῶσι, l⁹⁵⁰ μηδὲ for καὶ μή) it(b),c,d,e,(ff2),(g1),(h),k syrᶜ,ˢ (Tertullian) (Eusebius omit καὶ μὴ συνιῶσιν) Cyril-Jerusalem ‖ ἵνα βλέποντες μὴ βλέπωσιν καὶ ἀκούοντες μὴ ἀκούωσιν οὐδὲ συνιῶσιν (l¹⁸⁴ οὐκ ἀκούουσιν) (itᵃ omit οὐδὲ συνιῶσιν) itᶠᶠ¹ copˢᵃ,ᶠᵃʸ

14–15 Ἀκοῇ...αὐτούς Is 6.9–10 (Jn 12.40; Ac 28.26–27)   16–17 Lk 10.23–24   22 ἡ ἀπάτη τοῦ πλούτου Lk 12.16–21; 1 Tm 6.9–10, 17

23 ὁ δὲ ἐπὶ τὴν καλὴν γῆν σπαρείς, οὗτός ἐστιν ὁ τὸν λόγον ἀκούων καὶ συνιείς, ὃς δὴ καρποφορεῖ καὶ ποιεῖ ὃ μὲν ἑκατόν, ὃ δὲ ἑξήκοντα, ὃ δὲ τριάκοντα.

The Parable of the Weeds among the Wheat

24 Ἄλλην παραβολὴν παρέθηκεν αὐτοῖς λέγων, Ὡμοιώθη ἡ βασιλεία τῶν οὐρανῶν ἀνθρώπῳ σπείραντι καλὸν σπέρμα ἐν τῷ ἀγρῷ αὐτοῦ. **25** ἐν δὲ τῷ καθεύδειν τοὺς ἀνθρώπους ἦλθεν αὐτοῦ ὁ ἐχθρὸς καὶ ἐπέσπειρεν ζιζάνια ἀνὰ μέσον τοῦ σίτου καὶ ἀπῆλθεν. **26** ὅτε δὲ ἐβλάστησεν ὁ χόρτος καὶ καρπὸν ἐποίησεν, τότε ἐφάνη καὶ τὰ ζιζάνια. **27** προσελθόντες δὲ οἱ δοῦλοι τοῦ οἰκοδεσπότου εἶπον αὐτῷ, Κύριε, οὐχὶ καλὸν σπέρμα ἔσπειρας ἐν τῷ σῷ ἀγρῷ; πόθεν οὖν ἔχει ζιζάνια; **28** ὁ δὲ ἔφη αὐτοῖς, Ἐχθρὸς ἄνθρωπος τοῦτο ἐποίησεν. οἱ δὲ δοῦλοι λέγουσιν αὐτῷ, Θέλεις οὖν ἀπελθόντες συλλέξωμεν αὐτά; **29** ὁ δέ φησιν, Οὔ, μήποτε συλλέγοντες τὰ ζιζάνια ἐκριζώσητε ἅμα αὐτοῖς τὸν σῖτον. **30** ἄφετε συναυξάνεσθαι ἀμφότερα ἕως τοῦ θερισμοῦ· καὶ ἐν καιρῷ τοῦ θερισμοῦ ἐρῶ τοῖς θερισταῖς, Συλλέξατε πρῶτον τὰ ζιζάνια καὶ δήσατε αὐτὰ εἰς δέσμας πρὸς τὸ κατακαῦσαι αὐτά, τὸν δὲ σῖτον συναγάγετε εἰς τὴν ἀποθήκην μου.

The Parables of the Mustard Seed and the Leaven
(Mk 4.30–32; Lk 13.18–21)

31 Ἄλλην παραβολὴν παρέθηκεν αὐτοῖς λέγων, Ὁμοία ἐστὶν ἡ βασιλεία τῶν οὐρανῶν κόκκῳ σινάπεως, ὃν λαβὼν ἄνθρωπος ἔσπειρεν ἐν τῷ ἀγρῷ αὐτοῦ· **32** ὃ μικρότερον μέν ἐστιν πάντων τῶν σπερμάτων, ὅταν δὲ αὐξηθῇ μεῖζον τῶν λαχάνων ἐστὶν καὶ γίνεται δένδρον, ὥστε ἐλθεῖν τὰ πετεινὰ τοῦ οὐρανοῦ καὶ κατασκηνοῦν ἐν τοῖς κλάδοις αὐτοῦ.

---

30 τὸν...μου Mt 3.12   **31** κόκκῳ σινάπεως Mt 17.20; Lk 17.6   **32** τὰ πετεινὰ...αὐτοῦ Ps 104.12; Eze 17.23; 31.6; Dn 4.12, 21

bear fruit. **23** And the seed sown in the good soil stands for those who hear the message and understand it: they bear fruit, some as much as one hundred, others sixty, and others thirty."

The Parable of the Weeds

24 Jesus told them another parable: "The Kingdom of heaven is like a man who sowed good seed in his field. **25** One night, when everyone was asleep, an enemy came and sowed weeds among the wheat, and went away. **26** When the plants grew and the heads of grain began to form, then the weeds showed up. **27** The man's servants came to him and said, 'Sir, it was good seed you sowed in your field; where did the weeds come from?' **28** 'It was some enemy who did this,' he answered. 'Do you want us to go and pull up the weeds?' they asked him. **29** 'No,' he answered, 'because as you gather the weeds you might pull up some of the wheat along with them. **30** Let the wheat and the weeds both grow together until harvest, and then I will tell the harvest workers: Pull up the weeds first and tie them in bundles to throw in the fire; then gather in the wheat and put it in my barn.' "

The Parable of the Mustard Seed
(Also Mark 4.30–32; Luke 13.18–19)

31 Jesus told them another parable: "The Kingdom of heaven is like a mustard seed, the smallest of all seeds; **32** a man takes it and sows it in his field, and when it grows up it is the biggest of all plants. It becomes a tree, so that the birds come and make their nests in its branches."

The Parable of the Yeast
(Also Luke 13.20–21)

³³ Jesus told them another parable: "The Kingdom of heaven is like yeast. A woman takes it and mixes it with a bushel of flour, until the whole batch of dough rises."

Jesus' Use of Parables
(Also Mark 4.33–34)

³⁴ Jesus used parables to tell all these things to the crowds; he would not say a thing to them without using a parable. ³⁵ He did this to make come true what the prophet had said:
"I will use parables when I speak to them,
I will tell them things unknown since the creation of the world."

Jesus Explains the Parable of the Weeds

³⁶ Then Jesus left the crowd and went indoors. His disciples came to him and said, "Tell us what the parable of the weeds in the field means." ³⁷ Jesus answered: "The man who sowed the good seed is the Son of Man; ³⁸ the field is the world; the good seed is the people who belong to the Kingdom; the weeds are the people who belong to the Evil One; ³⁹ and the enemy who sowed the weeds is the Devil himself. The harvest is the end of the age, and the harvest workers are angels. ⁴⁰ Just as the weeds are gathered up and burned in the fire,

33 Ἄλλην παραβολὴν ἐλάλησεν αὐτοῖς· Ὁμοία ἐστὶν ἡ βασιλεία τῶν οὐρανῶν ζύμῃ, ἣν λαβοῦσα γυνὴ ἐνέκρυψεν εἰς ἀλεύρου σάτα τρία ἕως οὗ ἐζυμώθη ὅλον.

The Use of Parables
(Mk 4.33–34)

34 Ταῦτα πάντα ἐλάλησεν ὁ Ἰησοῦς ἐν παραβολαῖς τοῖς ὄχλοις, καὶ χωρὶς παραβολῆς οὐδὲν ἐλάλει αὐτοῖς· 35 ὅπως πληρωθῇ τὸ ῥηθὲν διὰ³ τοῦ προφήτου λέγοντος,
Ἀνοίξω ἐν παραβολαῖς τὸ στόμα μου,
ἐρεύξομαι κεκρυμμένα ἀπὸ καταβολῆς [κόσμου]⁴.

The Parable of the Weeds Explained

36 Τότε ἀφεὶς τοὺς ὄχλους ἦλθεν εἰς τὴν οἰκίαν. καὶ προσῆλθον αὐτῷ οἱ μαθηταὶ αὐτοῦ λέγοντες, Διασάφησον ἡμῖν τὴν παραβολὴν τῶν ζιζανίων τοῦ ἀγροῦ. 37 ὁ δὲ ἀποκριθεὶς εἶπεν, Ὁ σπείρων τὸ καλὸν σπέρμα ἐστὶν ὁ υἱὸς τοῦ ἀνθρώπου· 38 ὁ δὲ ἀγρός ἐστιν ὁ κόσμος· τὸ δὲ καλὸν σπέρμα, οὗτοί εἰσιν οἱ υἱοὶ τῆς βασιλείας· τὰ δὲ ζιζάνιά εἰσιν οἱ υἱοὶ τοῦ πονηροῦ, 39 ὁ δὲ ἐχθρὸς ὁ σπείρας αὐτά ἐστιν ὁ διάβολος· ὁ δὲ θερισμὸς συντέλεια αἰῶνός ἐστιν, οἱ δὲ θερισταὶ ἄγγελοί εἰσιν. 40 ὥσπερ οὖν συλλέγεται τὰ ζιζάνια καὶ πυρὶ καίεται, οὕτως ἔσται ἐν

---

³ **35** {C} διά א^b B C D K L W X Δ Π 0242 28 565 700 892 1009 1010 1071 1079 1195 1216 1230 1241 1242 1253 1344 1365 1546 1646 2148 2174 *Byz Lect* it^a,aur,b,c,d,(e),f,ff1,2,g1,h,k,l,π,q vg syr^c,s,p,h cop^sa,bo arm eth^ro,pp geo Eusebius mss^acc. to Eusebius Chrysostom Jerome ‖ διὰ Ἠσαΐου א* Θ f¹ f¹³ 33 eth^ms Ps-Clement Porphyry^acc. to Jerome mss^acc. to Eusebius mss^acc. to Jerome ‖ διὰ Ἀσάφ mss^acc. to Jerome

⁴ **35** {C} ἀπὸ καταβολῆς κόσμου (*see* Ps 78.2) א*,c C D K L W X Δ Θ Π f¹³ 28 33 565 700 892 1009 1010 1071 1079 1195 1216 1230 1241 1242 1253 1344 1365 1546 1646 2148 2174 *Byz Lect* it^a,aur,b,c,d,f,ff1,2,g1,h,l,π,q vg syr^(p),h cop^sa,bo,fay arm geo Ps-Clement Hilary Chrysostom ‖ ἀπὸ καταβολῆς א^b B f¹ it^e,k syr^c,s eth Diatessaron¹ Origen

---

33 Lk 13.20–21 ζύμη...ὅλον 1 Cor 5.6; Ga 5.9   **35** Ἀνοίξω...κόσμου Ps 78.2   **36** Διασάφησον...παραβολήν Mt 15.15; Mk 4.10; 7.17; Lk 8.9   **38** οἱ υἱοὶ τοῦ πονηροῦ Jn 8.44; 1 Jn 3.10   **40** συλλέγεται...καίεται Mt 3.10; 7.19; Jn 15.6

τῇ συντελείᾳ τοῦ αἰῶνος[5]·　**41** ἀποστελεῖ ὁ υἱὸς τοῦ ἀνθρώπου τοὺς ἀγγέλους αὐτοῦ, καὶ συλλέξουσιν ἐκ τῆς βασιλείας αὐτοῦ πάντα τὰ σκάνδαλα καὶ τοὺς ποιοῦντας τὴν ἀνομίαν, **42** καὶ βαλοῦσιν αὐτοὺς εἰς τὴν κάμινον τοῦ πυρός· ἐκεῖ ἔσται ὁ κλαυθμὸς καὶ ὁ βρυγμὸς τῶν ὀδόντων. **43** Τότε οἱ δίκαιοι ἐκλάμψουσιν ὡς ὁ ἥλιος ἐν τῇ βασιλείᾳ τοῦ πατρὸς αὐτῶν. ὁ ἔχων ὦτα[6] ἀκουέτω.

Three Parables

44 Ὁμοία ἐστὶν ἡ βασιλεία τῶν οὐρανῶν θησαυρῷ κεκρυμμένῳ ἐν τῷ ἀγρῷ, ὃν εὑρὼν ἄνθρωπος ἔκρυψεν, καὶ ἀπὸ τῆς χαρᾶς αὐτοῦ ὑπάγει καὶ πωλεῖ πάντα ὅσα ἔχει[7] καὶ ἀγοράζει τὸν ἀγρὸν ἐκεῖνον.

45 Πάλιν ὁμοία ἐστὶν ἡ βασιλεία τῶν οὐρανῶν ἀνθρώπῳ ἐμπόρῳ ζητοῦντι καλοὺς μαργαρίτας· **46** εὑρὼν δὲ ἕνα πολύτιμον μαργαρίτην ἀπελθὼν πέπρακεν πάντα ὅσα εἶχεν καὶ ἠγόρασεν αὐτόν.

47 Πάλιν ὁμοία ἐστὶν ἡ βασιλεία τῶν οὐρανῶν σαγήνῃ

---

[5] **40** {C} τοῦ αἰῶνος ℵ B D 892 it[a,aur,b,c,d,e,ff1,2,g1,k,l] vg syr[c,s] cop[sa] arm eth Irenaeus[lat] Origen[lat] Hilary Lucifer Cyril // τοῦ αἰῶνος τούτου C K L P W X Δ Θ Π 0119 0242 0250 f[1] f[13] 28 33 565 700 1009 1010 1071 1079 1195 1216 1230 1241 1242 1253 1344 1365 1546 1646 2148 2174 *Byz Lect* it[f,h,q] syr[p,h] cop[sams,bo,fay] geo Diatessaron Chrysostom

[6] **43** {C} ὦτα (see 11.15; 13.9) ℵ* B Θ 0242 700 it[a,b,e,k] vg[ww] Hilary Augustine // ὦτα ἀκούειν (see Mk 4.9; Lk 8.8) ℵ[c] C D K L P W X Δ Π 0119 0250 f[1] f[13] 28 33 565 892 1009 1010 1071 1079 1195 1216 1230 1241 1242 1253 1344 1365 1546 1646 2148 2174 *Byz Lect* it[aur,c,d,f,ff1,2,g1,h,l,q] vg[cl] syr[c,s,p,h,pal] cop[sa,bo,fay] arm eth geo Diatessaron Origen Eusebius Hilary

[7] **44** {C} πωλεῖ πάντα ὅσα ἔχει ℵ D 0242 f[1] (892 εἶχε) 1009 1079 1546 it[a,aur,b,c,d,(e),(ff1),ff2,g1,(h),k,(l)] vg (syr[c,s,p,pal]) cop[sa,fay] arm eth[pp,ms] geo Origen Chrysostom // πάντα ὅσα ἔχει πωλεῖ C K L P W X Δ Θ Π 0119 0250 f[13] 33 565 700 1010 1071 1195 1230 1241 1242 1344 1365 1646 2148 2174 *Byz Lect* l[185a,m,333m] (it[f,q]) syr[h] eth[ro] Origen // πωλεῖ ὅσα ἔχει B 1216 cop[bo] Origen // ὅσα ἔχει πωλεῖ 28

---

41 ἀποστελεῖ...συλλέξουσιν Mt 24.31; Mk 13.27　συλλέξουσιν...ἀνομίαν Zph 1.3 **42** βαλοῦσιν...πυρός Dn 3.6; Mt 13.50　ἐκεῖ...ὀδόντων Mt 8.12; 13.50; 22.13; 24.51; 25.30; Lk 13.28　**43** οἱ...ἥλιος Dn 12.3　ὁ...ἀκουέτω Mt 11.15; 13.9; Mk 4.23; Lk 14.35; Re 2.7; 13.9 **44** θησαυρῷ κεκρυμμένῳ Pr 2.4

so it will be at the end of the age: [41] the Son of Man will send out his angels and they will gather up out of his Kingdom all who cause people to sin, and all other evildoers, [42] and throw them into the fiery furnace, where they will cry and gnash their teeth. [43] Then God's people will shine like the sun in their Father's Kingdom. Listen, then, if you have ears!"

The Parable of the Hidden Treasure

[44] "The Kingdom of heaven is like a treasure hidden in a field. A man happens to find it, so he covers it up again. He is so happy that he goes and sells everything he has, and then goes back and buys the field."

The Parable of the Pearl

[45] "Also, the Kingdom of heaven is like a buyer looking for fine pearls. [46] When he finds one that is unusually fine, he goes and sells everything he has, and buys the pearl."

The Parable of the Net

[47] "Also, the Kingdom of heaven is like a net thrown out in the lake, which

catches all kinds of fish. [48] When it is full, the fishermen pull it to shore and sit down to divide the fish: the good ones go into their buckets, the worthless ones are thrown away. [49] It will be like this at the end of the age: the angels will go out and gather up the evil people from among the good, [50] and throw them into the fiery furnace. There they will cry and gnash their teeth."

New and Old Truths

[51] "Do you understand these things?" Jesus asked them. "Yes," they answered. [52] So he replied, "This means, then, that every teacher of the Law who becomes a disciple in the Kingdom of heaven is like a homeowner who takes new and old things out of his storage room."

Jesus Rejected at Nazareth
(Also Mark 6.1–6; Luke 4.16–30)

[53] When Jesus finished telling these parables, he left that place [54] and went back to his home town. He taught in their synagogue, and those who heard him were amazed. "Where did he get such wisdom?" they asked. "And what about his miracles? [55] Isn't he the carpenter's son? Isn't Mary his mother, and aren't James, Joseph, Simon, and Judas his brothers? [56] Aren't all his sisters living here? Where did he get all this?" [57] And so they rejected him. Jesus said to them: "A prophet is respected everywhere except in his home town and by his own family." [58] He did not perform

βληθείσῃ εἰς τὴν θάλασσαν καὶ ἐκ παντὸς γένους συναγαγούσῃ· **48** ἣν ὅτε ἐπληρώθη ἀναβιβάσαντες ἐπὶ τὸν αἰγιαλὸν καὶ καθίσαντες συνέλεξαν τὰ καλὰ εἰς ἄγγη, τὰ δὲ σαπρὰ ἔξω ἔβαλον. **49** οὕτως ἔσται ἐν τῇ συντελείᾳ τοῦ αἰῶνος· ἐξελεύσονται οἱ ἄγγελοι καὶ ἀφοριοῦσιν τοὺς πονηροὺς ἐκ μέσου τῶν δικαίων **50** καὶ βαλοῦσιν αὐτοὺς εἰς τὴν κάμινον τοῦ πυρός· ἐκεῖ ἔσται ὁ κλαυθμὸς καὶ ὁ βρυγμὸς τῶν ὀδόντων.

Treasures New and Old

51 Συνήκατε ταῦτα πάντα; λέγουσιν αὐτῷ, Ναί. **52** ὁ δὲ εἶπεν αὐτοῖς, Διὰ τοῦτο πᾶς γραμματεὺς μαθητευθεὶς τῇ βασιλείᾳ τῶν οὐρανῶν ὅμοιός ἐστιν ἀνθρώπῳ οἰκοδεσπότῃ ὅστις ἐκβάλλει ἐκ τοῦ θησαυροῦ αὐτοῦ καινὰ καὶ παλαιά.

The Rejection of Jesus at Nazareth
(Mk 6.1–6; Lk 4.16–30)

53 Καὶ ἐγένετο ὅτε ἐτέλεσεν ὁ Ἰησοῦς τὰς παραβολὰς ταύτας, μετῆρεν ἐκεῖθεν. **54** καὶ ἐλθὼν εἰς τὴν πατρίδα αὐτοῦ ἐδίδασκεν αὐτοὺς ἐν τῇ συναγωγῇ αὐτῶν, ὥστε ἐκπλήσσεσθαι αὐτοὺς καὶ λέγειν, Πόθεν τούτῳ ἡ σοφία αὕτη καὶ αἱ δυνάμεις; **55** οὐχ οὗτός ἐστιν ὁ τοῦ τέκτονος υἱός; οὐχ ἡ μήτηρ αὐτοῦ λέγεται Μαριὰμ καὶ οἱ ἀδελφοὶ αὐτοῦ Ἰάκωβος καὶ Ἰωσὴφ[8] καὶ Σίμων καὶ Ἰούδας; **56** καὶ αἱ ἀδελφαὶ αὐτοῦ οὐχὶ πᾶσαι πρὸς ἡμᾶς εἰσιν; πόθεν οὖν τούτῳ ταῦτα πάντα; **57** καὶ ἐσκανδαλίζοντο ἐν αὐτῷ. ὁ δὲ Ἰησοῦς εἶπεν αὐτοῖς, Οὐκ ἔστιν προφήτης ἄτιμος εἰ μὴ ἐν τῇ πατρίδι καὶ ἐν τῇ οἰκίᾳ αὐτοῦ. **58** καὶ

---

[8] **55** {B} Ἰωσὴφ ℵ[a] B C Θ *f*[1] 33 700[c] 892 *l*[184,997] it[a,aur,b,c,f,ff1,2,g1,h,l,q*] vg syr[c,s,hmg,pal] cop[bomss] eth[pp,ms] geo Origen Eusebius Jerome ‖ Ἰωσῆς K L W Δ Π 0119 *f*[13] 565 1079 1195 1216 1230 1241 1242 1253 1365 1546 1646 2148 2174 *Byz* *l*[12,69,211,303,3338*,m,850,883,1084,1579,1642] it[k,qc] syr[p?h?] cop[sa,bomss,fay] arm eth[ro?] Diatessaron Basil ‖ Ἰωσῆ 700* 1009 1010 1071 *l*[70] syr[p?h?] cop[bomss] eth[ro?] ‖ Ἰωάννης ℵ*vid D X 28 *Lect* it[d] Origen ‖ Ἰωάννης καὶ Ἰωσῆς 1344

50 βαλοῦσιν...πυρός Dn 3.6; Mt 13.42   ἐκεῖ...ὀδόντων Mt 8.12; 13.42; 22.13; 24.51; 25.30; Lk 13.28   **53** Καὶ...ταύτας Mt 7.28; 11.1; 19.1; 26.1; Lk 7.1   **54** ὥστε...αὕτη Jn 7.15 **55** οὐχ οὗτος...υἱός Lk 3.23; Jn 6.42   οὐχ ἡ...Ἰούδας Mt 12.46   **57** καὶ...αὐτῷ Mt 11.6; 26.31 Οὐκ...πατρίδι Jn 4.44

οὐκ ἐποίησεν ἐκεῖ δυνάμεις πολλὰς διὰ τὴν ἀπιστίαν αὐτῶν.

The Death of John the Baptist
(Mk 6.14–29; Lk 9.7–9)

14 Ἐν ἐκείνῳ τῷ καιρῷ ἤκουσεν Ἡρῴδης ὁ τετραάρχης τὴν ἀκοὴν Ἰησοῦ, 2 καὶ εἶπεν τοῖς παισὶν αὐτοῦ, Οὗτός ἐστιν Ἰωάννης ὁ βαπτιστής· αὐτὸς ἠγέρθη ἀπὸ τῶν νεκρῶν, καὶ διὰ τοῦτο αἱ δυνάμεις ἐνεργοῦσιν ἐν αὐτῷ. 3 Ὁ γὰρ Ἡρῴδης[1] κρατήσας τὸν Ἰωάννην ἔδησεν [αὐτὸν] καὶ ἐν φυλακῇ ἀπέθετο διὰ Ἡρῳδιάδα τὴν γυναῖκα Φιλίππου[2] τοῦ ἀδελφοῦ αὐτοῦ· 4 ἔλεγεν γὰρ ὁ Ἰωάννης αὐτῷ, Οὐκ ἔξεστίν σοι ἔχειν αὐτήν. 5 καὶ θέλων αὐτὸν ἀποκτεῖναι ἐφοβήθη τὸν ὄχλον, ὅτι ὡς προφήτην αὐτὸν εἶχον. 6 γενεσίοις δὲ γενομένοις τοῦ Ἡρῴδου ὠρχήσατο ἡ θυγάτηρ τῆς Ἡρῳδιάδος ἐν τῷ μέσῳ καὶ ἤρεσεν τῷ Ἡρῴδῃ, 7 ὅθεν μεθ᾽ ὅρκου ὡμολόγησεν αὐτῇ δοῦναι ὃ ἐὰν αἰτήσηται. 8 ἡ δὲ προβιβασθεῖσα ὑπὸ τῆς μητρὸς αὐτῆς, Δός μοι, φησίν, ὧδε ἐπὶ πίνακι τὴν κεφαλὴν Ἰωάννου τοῦ βαπτιστοῦ. 9 καὶ λυπηθεὶς ὁ βασιλεὺς διὰ[3] τοὺς ὅρκους καὶ τοὺς συνανακειμένους ἐκέλευσεν δοθῆναι, 10 καὶ πέμψας ἀπεκεφάλισεν τὸν Ἰωάννην ἐν τῇ φυλακῇ· 11 καὶ ἠνέχθη ἡ κεφαλὴ αὐτοῦ ἐπὶ πίνακι καὶ ἐδόθη τῷ κορασίῳ, καὶ

---

[1] 3 {C} Ἡρῴδης ℵ C D K L W X Δ Π f[1] 28 33 565 892 1009 1071 1079 1195 1216 1230 1241 1242 1253 1344 1365 1546 1646 2148 2174 *Byz Lect* l[883m] it[a,aur,] b,c,d,f,ff[1,2],g[1],h,(k),l,q vg syr[c,s,p,h] cop[sa,bo,fay] arm eth geo[A] Diatessaron ∥ Ἡρῴδης τότε B Θ f[13] 700 1010 geo[1,B]

[2] 3 {B} Φιλίππου (see Mk 6.17) ℵ B C K L W X Δ Θ Π 0119 f[1] f[13] 28 33 565 700 892 1009 1010 1071 1079 1195 1216 1230 1241 1242 1253 1344 1365 1546 1646 2148 2174 *Byz Lect* l[883m] it[aur,(b),f,(ff2),h,q] syr[c,s,p,h,pal]vid cop[sa,bo,fay] arm eth geo Origen Chrysostom ∥ *omit* (see Lk 3.19) D it[a,c,d,e,ff1,g1,k,l] vg Augustine

[3] 9 {B} λυπηθεὶς ὁ βασιλεὺς διά B D Θ f[1] f[13] 700 it[a,b,d,ff1,2,g1,h] eth? ∥ ἐλυπήθη ὁ βασιλεύς· διὰ δέ ℵ C K (L* *omit* δέ) L[c] W X Δ Π 0106 0136 28 33 565 892 1009 1010 1071 1079 1195 1216 1230 1241 1242 1253 1344 1365 1546 1646 2148 2174 *Byz Lect* l[883m] it[aur,c,f,k,l,q] vg syr[(c),p,h] cop[sa,bo,fay] arm geo

3 Lk 3.19–20 Ἡρῴδης...φυλακῇ Mt 11.2; Jn 3.24 **3–4** Ἡρῳδιάδα...αὐτήν Lv 18.16; 20.21 **5** ὡς...εἶχον Mt 11.9; 21.26; Lk 1.76; 7.26

---

many miracles there because they did not have faith.

The Death of John the Baptist
(Also Mark 6.14–29; Luke 9.7–9)

14 It was at that time that Herod, the ruler of Galilee, heard about Jesus. 2 "He is really John the Baptist who has come back to life," he told his officials. "That is why these powers are at work in him."

3 For Herod had ordered John's arrest, and had him tied up and put in prison. He did this because of Herodias, his brother Philip's wife. 4 John the Baptist kept telling Herod, "It isn't right for you to marry her!" 5 Herod wanted to kill him, but he was afraid of the Jewish people, because they considered John to be a prophet.

6 On Herod's birthday the daughter of Herodias danced in front of the whole group. Herod was so pleased 7 that he promised her: "I swear that I will give you anything you ask for!" 8 At her mother's suggestion she asked him, "Give me right here the head of John the Baptist on a plate!" 9 The king was sad, but because of the vows he had made in front of all his guests he gave orders that her wish be granted. 10 So he had John beheaded in prison. 11 The head was brought in on a plate and given to the girl, who took it to her mother.

¹² John's disciples came, got his body, and buried it; then they went and told Jesus.

Jesus Feeds the Five Thousand
(Also Mark 6.30–44; Luke 9.10–17; John 6.1–14)

¹³ When Jesus heard the news, he left that place in a boat and went to a lonely place by himself. The people heard about it, left their towns, and followed him by land. ¹⁴ Jesus got out of the boat, and when he saw the large crowd his heart was filled with pity for them, and he healed their sick.

¹⁵ That evening his disciples came to him and said, "It is already very late, and this is a lonely place. Send the people away and let them go to the villages and buy food for themselves." ¹⁶ "They don't have to leave," answered Jesus. "You yourselves give them something to eat." ¹⁷ "All we have here are five loaves and two fish," they replied. ¹⁸ "Bring them here to me," Jesus said. ¹⁹ He ordered the people to sit down on the grass; then he took the five loaves and the two fish, looked up to heaven, and gave thanks to God. He broke the loaves and gave them to the disciples, and the disciples gave them to the people. ²⁰ Everyone ate and had enough. Then the disciples took up twelve baskets full of what was left over. ²¹ The number of men who ate was about five thousand, not counting the women and children.

Jesus Walks on the Water
(Also Mark 6.45–52; John 6.15–21)

²² Then Jesus made the disciples get into the boat and go ahead of him to the other side of the lake, while he sent

ἤνεγκεν τῇ μητρὶ αὐτῆς. 12 καὶ προσελθόντες οἱ μαθηταὶ αὐτοῦ ἦραν τὸ πτῶμα καὶ ἔθαψαν αὐτό, καὶ ἐλθόντες ἀπήγγειλαν τῷ Ἰησοῦ.

The Feeding of the Five Thousand
(Mk 6.30–44; Lk 9.10–17; Jn 6.1–14)

13 Ἀκούσας δὲ ὁ Ἰησοῦς ἀνεχώρησεν ἐκεῖθεν ἐν πλοίῳ εἰς ἔρημον τόπον κατ' ἰδίαν· καὶ ἀκούσαντες οἱ ὄχλοι ἠκολούθησαν αὐτῷ πεζῇ ἀπὸ τῶν πόλεων. 14 καὶ ἐξελθὼν εἶδεν πολὺν ὄχλον, καὶ ἐσπλαγχνίσθη ἐπ' αὐτοῖς καὶ ἐθεράπευσεν τοὺς ἀρρώστους αὐτῶν. 15 ὀψίας δὲ γενομένης προσῆλθον αὐτῷ οἱ μαθηταὶ λέγοντες, Ἔρημός ἐστιν ὁ τόπος καὶ ἡ ὥρα ἤδη παρῆλθεν· ἀπόλυσον τοὺς ὄχλους, ἵνα ἀπελθόντες εἰς τὰς κώμας ἀγοράσωσιν ἑαυτοῖς βρώματα. 16 ὁ δὲ [Ἰησοῦς] εἶπεν αὐτοῖς, Οὐ χρείαν ἔχουσιν ἀπελθεῖν· δότε αὐτοῖς ὑμεῖς φαγεῖν. 17 οἱ δὲ λέγουσιν αὐτῷ, Οὐκ ἔχομεν ὧδε εἰ μὴ πέντε ἄρτους καὶ δύο ἰχθύας. 18 ὁ δὲ εἶπεν, Φέρετέ μοι ὧδε αὐτούς. 19 καὶ κελεύσας τοὺς ὄχλους ἀνακλιθῆναι ἐπὶ τοῦ χόρτου, λαβὼν τοὺς πέντε ἄρτους καὶ τοὺς δύο ἰχθύας, ἀναβλέψας εἰς τὸν οὐρανὸν εὐλόγησεν καὶ κλάσας ἔδωκεν τοῖς μαθηταῖς τοὺς ἄρτους οἱ δὲ μαθηταὶ τοῖς ὄχλοις. 20 καὶ ἔφαγον πάντες καὶ ἐχορτάσθησαν, καὶ ἦραν τὸ περισσεῦον τῶν κλασμάτων δώδεκα κοφίνους πλήρεις. 21 οἱ δὲ ἐσθίοντες ἦσαν ἄνδρες ὡσεὶ πεντακισχίλιοι χωρὶς γυναικῶν καὶ παιδίων.

Walking on the Water
(Mk 6.45–52; Jn 6.15–21)

22 Καὶ εὐθέως⁴ ἠνάγκασεν τοὺς μαθητὰς⁵ ἐμβῆναι εἰς τὸ πλοῖον καὶ προάγειν αὐτὸν εἰς τὸ πέραν, ἕως οὗ ἀπο-

---

⁴ 22 {C} εὐθέως (see Mk 6.45) אᵇ B C³ D K L P W X Δ Θ Π 067 0106 f¹ f¹³ 28 33 565 700 892ᵐᵍ 1009 1010 1071 1079 1195 1216 1230 1241 1242 1253 1344 1365 1546 1646 2148 2174 Byz Lect (l²¹¹ καὶ ἠνάγκασεν εὐθέως) itᵃ·ᵃᵘʳ, b,c,d,e,f,ff²,gl,h,l,q vg syrᵖ·ʰ·ᵖᵃˡ copˢᵃ·ᵇᵒ·ᶠᵃʸ arm eth geo Origen ‖ omit א* C* 892ᵗˣᵗ itᶠᶠˡ syrᶜ Diatessaronᵛ Chrysostom

⁵ 22 {B} μαθητάς א C D L W Δ 067 0106 f¹ 28 33 700 1010 1071 1195

---

14 εἶδεν...αὐτοῖς Mt 9.36; 15.32   15 ἀπόλυσον...βρώματα Mt 15.32; Mk 8.3
17 Mt 15.34; Mk 8.5   19–22 Mt 15.35–39; Mk 8.6–10   20 2 Kgs 4.43–44

λύσῃ τοὺς ὄχλους. **23** καὶ ἀπολύσας τοὺς ὄχλους ἀνέβη εἰς τὸ ὄρος κατ᾽ ἰδίαν προσεύξασθαι. ὀψίας δὲ γενομένης μόνος ἦν ἐκεῖ. **24** τὸ δὲ πλοῖον ἤδη σταδίους πολλοὺς ἀπὸ τῆς γῆς ἀπεῖχεν[6], βασανιζόμενον ὑπὸ τῶν κυμάτων, ἦν γὰρ ἐναντίος ὁ ἄνεμος. **25** τετάρτῃ δὲ φυλακῇ τῆς νυκτὸς ἦλθεν πρὸς αὐτοὺς περιπατῶν ἐπὶ τὴν θάλασσαν. **26** οἱ δὲ μαθηταὶ ἰδόντες αὐτὸν ἐπὶ τῆς θαλάσσης περιπατοῦντα ἐταράχθησαν λέγοντες ὅτι Φάντασμά ἐστιν, καὶ ἀπὸ τοῦ φόβου ἔκραξαν. **27** εὐθὺς δὲ ἐλάλησεν [ὁ Ἰησοῦς] αὐτοῖς[7] λέγων, Θαρσεῖτε, ἐγώ εἰμι· μὴ φοβεῖσθε. **28** ἀποκριθεὶς δὲ αὐτῷ ὁ Πέτρος εἶπεν, Κύριε, εἰ σὺ εἶ, κέλευσόν με ἐλθεῖν πρὸς σὲ ἐπὶ τὰ ὕδατα· **29** ὁ δὲ εἶπεν, Ἐλθέ. καὶ καταβὰς ἀπὸ τοῦ πλοίου ὁ Πέτρος περιεπάτησεν ἐπὶ τὰ ὕδατα καὶ ἦλθεν[8] πρὸς τὸν Ἰησοῦν. **30** βλέπων δὲ

the people away. ²³ After sending the people away, he went up a hill by himself to pray. When evening came, Jesus was there alone; ²⁴ by this time the boat was far out in the lake, tossed about by the waves, for the wind was blowing against it. ²⁵ Between three and six o'clock in the morning Jesus came to them, walking on the water. ²⁶ When the disciples saw him walking on the water they were terrified. "It's a ghost!" they said, and screamed with fear. ²⁷ Jesus spoke to them at once. "Courage!" he said. "It is I. Don't be afraid!" ²⁸ Then Peter spoke up. "Lord," he said, "if it is really you, order me to come out on the water to you." ²⁹ "Come!" answered Jesus. So Peter got out of the boat and started walking on the water to Jesus. ³⁰ When he noticed the wind,

---

1216 1230 1241 1253 1646 *Byz*[pt] *l*[32,150,184pt,185pt,299,313,847,1231,1663] it[d,e,f,l] vg arm geo Origen Chrysostom ‖ μαθητὰς αὐτοῦ (*see* Mk 6.45) B K P X Θ Π *f*[13] 565 892 1009 1079 1242 1344 1365 1546 2148 2174 *Byz*[pt] *Lect l*[184pt,185pt] it[a,aur,b,c,ff1,2], g[1,h,q] syr[c,p,h,pal] cop[sa,bo,fay] eth Diatessaron

[6] **24** {D} σταδίους πολλοὺς ἀπὸ τῆς γῆς ἀπεῖχεν B *f*[13] cop[sa?(bo?)] geo Diatessaron ‖ σταδίους πολλοὺς ἀπεῖχεν 983 1689 ‖ σταδίους τῆς γῆς ἀπεῖχεν ἱκανούς 700 ‖ ἀπεῖχεν ἀπὸ τῆς γῆς σταδίους ἱκανούς Θ syr[c,p,pal] arm ‖ μέσον τῆς θαλάσσης ἦν (*see* Mk 6.47) ℵ C K L P W X Δ Π 084 0106 *f*[1] 28 33 565 892 1009 1010 1071 1079 1195 1216 1230 1241 1242 1253 1344 1365 1646 2148 2174 *Byz Lect* (*l*[1663] *omit* ἦν) it[a,aur,b,c,f,ff2,g1,h,l,q] vg syr[h] cop[fay?] eth[ro,pp] (Origen) (Eusebius) Chrysostom ‖ ἦν εἰς μέσον τῆς θαλάσσης (*see* Mk 6.47) D it[d,e,ff1] cop[fay?] eth[ms?] (Eusebius ἐν μέσον) ‖ ἐκινδύνευεν ἤδη μέσον τῆς θαλάσσης 1546

[7] **27** {D} ὁ Ἰησοῦς αὐτοῖς ℵ[a] B 1365 (it[a,aur,b,c,c,ff2,g1,h,l]) (vg) syr[s,p] cop[fay?] ‖ αὐτοῖς ὁ Ἰησοῦς C K L P W X Δ Θ Π 0106 *f*[1] *f*[13] 28 33 565 700 1009 1071 1079 1216 1230 1241 1242 1253 1344 1546 1646 2148 2174 *Byz Lect* it[f,q] syr[h,(pal)] cop[fay?] arm eth? geo ‖ αὐτοῖς (*see* Mk 6.50) ℵ* D 084[vid] 892 1010 it[d,ff1] syr[c] cop[sa,bo] Eusebius ‖ ὁ Ἰησοῦς 1195 *l*[47]

[8] **29** {B} καὶ ἦλθεν B C*[vid] 700 1010 syr[c,s] (cop[sa] *omit* καί) arm geo Chrysostom ‖ καὶ ἐλθεῖν eth[ro] ‖ ἐλθεῖν ℵ[c] C[2] D K L P W X Δ Θ Π 073[vid] 0119 *f*[1] *f*[13] 28 33 565 892 1009 1071 1079 1195 1216 1230 1241 1242 1253 1344

---

23 ἀνέβη…προσεύξασθαι Lk 6.12; 9.28   **26** ἐταράχθησαν…ἐστιν Lk 24.37
29 καταβὰς…Πέτρος Jn 21.7

however, he was afraid, and started to sink down in the water. "Save me, Lord!" he cried. ³¹ At once Jesus reached out and grabbed him and said, "How little faith you have! Why did you doubt?" ³² They both got back into the boat, and the wind died down. ³³ The disciples in the boat worshiped Jesus. "Truly you are the Son of God!" they exclaimed.

Jesus Heals the Sick in Gennesaret
(Also Mark 6.53–56)

³⁴ They crossed the lake and came to land at Gennesaret, ³⁵ where the people recognized Jesus. So they sent for the sick people in all the surrounding country and brought them to Jesus. ³⁶ They begged him to let the sick at least touch the edge of his cloak; and all who touched it were made well.

The Teaching of the Ancestors
(Also Mark 7.1–13)

15 Then some Pharisees and teachers of the Law came to Jesus from Jerusalem and asked him: ² "Why is it that your disciples disobey the teaching handed down by our ancestors? They don't wash their hands in the proper way before they eat!" ³ Jesus answered: "And why do you disobey God's command and follow your own teaching? ⁴ For God said, 'Honor your father and

τὸν ἄνεμον⁹ ἐφοβήθη, καὶ ἀρξάμενος καταποντίζεσθαι ἔκραξεν λέγων, Κύριε, σῶσόν με. 31 εὐθέως δὲ ὁ Ἰησοῦς ἐκτείνας τὴν χεῖρα ἐπελάβετο αὐτοῦ καὶ λέγει αὐτῷ, Ὀλιγόπιστε, εἰς τί ἐδίστασας; 32 καὶ ἀναβάντων αὐτῶν εἰς τὸ πλοῖον ἐκόπασεν ὁ ἄνεμος. 33 οἱ δὲ ἐν τῷ πλοίῳ προσεκύνησαν αὐτῷ λέγοντες, Ἀληθῶς θεοῦ υἱὸς εἶ.

The Healing of the Sick in Gennesaret
(Mk 6.53–56)

34 Καὶ διαπεράσαντες ἦλθον ἐπὶ τὴν γῆν εἰς Γεννησαρέτ. 35 καὶ ἐπιγνόντες αὐτὸν οἱ ἄνδρες τοῦ τόπου ἐκείνου ἀπέστειλαν εἰς ὅλην τὴν περίχωρον ἐκείνην, καὶ προσήνεγκαν αὐτῷ πάντας τοὺς κακῶς ἔχοντας, 36 καὶ παρεκάλουν αὐτὸν ἵνα μόνον ἅψωνται τοῦ κρασπέδου τοῦ ἱματίου αὐτοῦ· καὶ ὅσοι ἥψαντο διεσώθησαν.

The Tradition of the Elders
(Mk 7.1–23)

15 Τότε προσέρχονται τῷ Ἰησοῦ ἀπὸ Ἱεροσολύμων Φαρισαῖοι καὶ γραμματεῖς λέγοντες, 2 Διὰ τί οἱ μαθηταί σου παραβαίνουσιν τὴν παράδοσιν τῶν πρεσβυτέρων; οὐ γὰρ νίπτονται τὰς χεῖρας αὐτῶν ὅταν ἄρτον ἐσθίωσιν. 3 ὁ δὲ ἀποκριθεὶς εἶπεν αὐτοῖς, Διὰ τί καὶ ὑμεῖς παραβαίνετε τὴν ἐντολὴν τοῦ θεοῦ διὰ τὴν παράδοσιν ὑμῶν; 4 ὁ γὰρ

1365 1546 1646 2148 2174 *Byz Lect* it^(a,aur,b,c,d,e,f,ff1,2,g1,h,l,q) vg syr^(p,h,pal) eth^(pp,ms) cop^(bo,fay) Diatessaron^(a,i) ‖ ἐλθεῖν· ἦλθεν οὖν ℵ*

⁹ **30** {C} ἄνεμον ℵ B* 073 33 cop^(sa,bo,fay) ‖ ἄνεμον ἰσχυρόν B² C D K L P X Δ Θ Π 0119 f¹ f¹³ 28 565 700 892 1009 1010 1071 1079 1195 1216 1230 1241 1242 1253 1344 1365 1546 1646 2148 2174 *Byz Lect* it^(a,aur,b,c,d,e,f,ff1,2,g1,h,l,q) vg syr^(c,s,p,h,pal) arm eth geo Origen ‖ ἄνεμον ἰσχυρὸν σφόδρα W

31 Ὀλιγόπιστε...ἐδίστασας Mt 8.26   **32** ἐκόπασεν ὁ ἄνεμος Mk 4.39   **33** Ἀληθῶς ...εἶ Mt 16.16; 26.63; 27.54; Mk 14.61; 15.39; Lk 22.70; Jn 1.49   **36** ἵνα...αὐτοῦ Mt 9.20–21; Mk 5.27–28; Lk 8.44

15 **2** οὐ...ἐσθίωσιν Lk 11.38

θεὸς εἶπεν[1], **Τίμα τὸν πατέρα καὶ τὴν μητέρα,** καί, '**Ο κακολογῶν πατέρα ἢ μητέρα θανάτῳ τελευτάτω**· 5 ὑμεῖς δὲ λέγετε, "Ος ἂν εἴπῃ τῷ πατρὶ ἢ τῇ μητρί, Δῶρον ὃ ἐὰν ἐξ ἐμοῦ ὠφεληθῇς, 6[a] οὐ μὴ τιμήσει τὸν πατέρα αὐτοῦ[2]· [a]καὶ ἠκυρώσατε τὸν λόγον[3] τοῦ θεοῦ διὰ τὴν παράδοσιν ὑμῶν. 7 ὑποκριταί, καλῶς ἐπροφήτευσεν περὶ ὑμῶν 'Ησαΐας λέγων,

8   'Ο λαὸς οὗτος τοῖς χείλεσίν με τιμᾷ,
     ἡ δὲ καρδία αὐτῶν πόρρω ἀπέχει ἀπ' ἐμοῦ·
9   μάτην δὲ σέβονταί με,
     διδάσκοντες διδασκαλίας ἐντάλματα ἀνθρώπων.

10 Καὶ προσκαλεσάμενος τὸν ὄχλον εἶπεν αὐτοῖς, 'Ακούετε καὶ συνίετε· 11 οὐ τὸ εἰσερχόμενον εἰς τὸ στόμα κοινοῖ τὸν ἄνθρωπον, ἀλλὰ τὸ ἐκπορευόμενον ἐκ τοῦ στόματος τοῦτο κοινοῖ τὸν ἄνθρωπον. 12 Τότε προσελθόντες οἱ μαθηταὶ λέγουσιν αὐτῷ, Οἶδας ὅτι οἱ Φαρισαῖοι

---

[1] **4** {C} εἶπεν (see Mk 7.10) ℵ[a] B D Θ 084 f[1] f[13] 700 892 it[a,aur,b,c,d,e,] [ff1,2,g1,l,q] vg syr[c,s,p] cop[sa,bo,fay] arm eth geo Ptolemy Diatessaron[a,esyr] Irenaeus[lat] Jerome Cyril // ἐνετείλατο λέγων ℵ[*,b] C K L W X Δ Π 33 565 1009 1010 1071 1079 1195 1216 1241 1242 1253 1344 1365 1546 1646 2148 2174 *Byz Lect* it[f] syr[h]

[2] **6** {D} τὸν πατέρα αὐτοῦ ℵ B D it[a,d,e] syr[c] cop[sa] geo[1] // τὸν πατέρα ἢ τὴν μητέρα αὐτοῦ Θ f[1] l[184] geo[B] Origen // τὸν πατέρα αὐτοῦ ἢ τὴν μητέρα 084 f[13] 33 700 892 1071 (1216 *omit* αὐτοῦ) (l[883] καὶ τήν) it[ff2,g1,l] vg[ww] Chrysostom Jerome Cyril // τὸν πατέρα αὐτοῦ ἢ τὴν μητέρα αὐτοῦ C K L W X Δ Π 1009 1010 1079 1195 1230 1242 1253 1344 1365 (1546 τῇ μητρί) 1646 2148 2174 *Byz Lect* it[aur,f,ff1] vg[cl] syr[s,p,h] cop[bo?] arm eth Diatessaron[esyr] Origen Cyril // τὸν πατέρα αὐτοῦ καὶ τὴν μητέρα αὐτοῦ 565 1241 it[(b),c,q] cop[bo?] geo[A]

[3] **6** {B} τὸν λόγον (see Mk 7.13) ℵ[a] B D Θ 700 892 1230 it[a,b,d,e,ff1,(ff2)] syr[c,s,p,hmg] cop[sa,bo] arm eth geo[1] Diatessaron Irenaeus[lat] Origen Eusebius Augustine // τὸν νόμον ℵ[*,b] C 084 f[13] 1010 geo[2] Ptolemy Epiphanius // τὴν ἐντολήν (see 15.3) K L W X Δ Π f[1] 33 565 1009 1071 1079 1195 1216 1241 1242 1253 1344 1365 1546 1646 2148 2174 *Byz Lect* it[aur,c,f,g1,l,q] vg syr[h] Origen Cyril

---

[a][a] **5–6** *a* number 6, *a* no number: TR[ed] WH? Bov Nes BF[2] AV RV ASV NEB TT Zür Luth Jer // *a* no number, *a* number 6: TR[ed] WH? RSV Seg

---

4 Τίμα...μητέρα Ex 20.12; Dt 5.16 (Mt 19.19; Mk 10.19; Lk 18.20; Eph 6.2)   'Ο...τελευτάτω Ex 21.17 (Lv 20.9)   **8–9** Is 29.13 LXX   **11** τὸ ἐκπορευόμενον...ἄνθρωπον Mt 12.34

---

mother,' and 'Anyone who says bad things about his father or mother must be put to death.' 5 But you teach that if a person has something he could use to help his father or mother, but says, 'This belongs to God,' 6 he does not need to honor his father. This is how you disregard God's word to follow your own teaching. 7 You hypocrites! How right Isaiah was when he prophesied about you!

8 'These people, says God, honor me
    with their words,
  But their heart is really far away
    from me.
9 It is no use for them to worship me,
  Because they teach man-made commandments as though they were
    God's rules!' "

The Things that Make a Person Unclean
(Also Mark 7.14–23)

10 Then Jesus called the crowd to him and said to them: "Listen, and understand! 11 It is not what goes into a person's mouth that makes him unclean; rather, what comes out of it makes him unclean."

12 Then the disciples came to him and said, "Do you know that the Pharisees

had their feelings hurt by what you said?" [13] "Every plant which my Father in heaven did not plant will be pulled up," answered Jesus. [14] "Don't worry about them! They are blind leaders; and when one blind man leads another, both fall in the ditch." [15] Peter spoke up, "Tell us what this parable means." [16] Jesus said to them: "You are still no more intelligent than the others. [17] Don't you understand? Anything that goes into a person's mouth goes into his stomach and then on out of the body. [18] But the things that come out of the mouth come from the heart; such things make a man unclean. [19] For from his heart come the evil ideas which lead him to kill, commit adultery, and do other immoral things; to rob, lie, and slander others. [20] These are the things that make a man unclean. But to eat without washing your hands as they say you should — this does not make a man unclean."

A Woman's Faith
(Also Mark 7.24–30)

[21] Jesus left that place and went off to the territory near the cities of Tyre and Sidon. [22] A Canaanite woman who lived in that region came to him. "Son of David, sir!" she cried. "Have mercy on me! My daughter has a demon and

ἀκούσαντες τὸν λόγον ἐσκανδαλίσθησαν; **13** ὁ δὲ ἀποκριθεὶς εἶπεν, Πᾶσα φυτεία ἣν οὐκ ἐφύτευσεν ὁ πατήρ μου ὁ οὐράνιος ἐκριζωθήσεται. **14** ἄφετε αὐτούς· τυφλοί εἰσιν ὁδηγοί[4]· τυφλὸς δὲ τυφλὸν ἐὰν ὁδηγῇ, ἀμφότεροι εἰς βόθυνον πεσοῦνται. **15** Ἀποκριθεὶς δὲ ὁ Πέτρος εἶπεν αὐτῷ, Φράσον ἡμῖν τὴν παραβολήν[5]. **16** ὁ δὲ εἶπεν, Ἀκμὴν καὶ ὑμεῖς ἀσύνετοί ἐστε; **17** οὐ νοεῖτε ὅτι πᾶν τὸ εἰσπορευόμενον εἰς τὸ στόμα εἰς τὴν κοιλίαν χωρεῖ καὶ εἰς ἀφεδρῶνα ἐκβάλλεται; **18** τὰ δὲ ἐκπορευόμενα ἐκ τοῦ στόματος ἐκ τῆς καρδίας ἐξέρχεται, κἀκεῖνα κοινοῖ τὸν ἄνθρωπον. **19** ἐκ γὰρ τῆς καρδίας ἐξέρχονται διαλογισμοὶ πονηροί, φόνοι, μοιχεῖαι, πορνεῖαι, κλοπαί, ψευδομαρτυρίαι, βλασφημίαι. **20** ταῦτά ἐστιν τὰ κοινοῦντα τὸν ἄνθρωπον, τὸ δὲ ἀνίπτοις χερσὶν φαγεῖν οὐ κοινοῖ τὸν ἄνθρωπον.

The Canaanite Woman's Faith
(Mk 7.24–30)

21 Καὶ ἐξελθὼν ἐκεῖθεν ὁ Ἰησοῦς ἀνεχώρησεν εἰς τὰ μέρη Τύρου καὶ Σιδῶνος. **22** καὶ ἰδοὺ γυνὴ Χαναναία ἀπὸ τῶν ὁρίων ἐκείνων ἐξελθοῦσα ἔκραζεν λέγουσα, Ἐλέησόν με, κύριε, υἱὸς Δαυίδ· ἡ θυγάτηρ μου κακῶς δαιμονίζεται.

[4] **14** {C} τυφλοί εἰσιν ὁδηγοί B D 0237 it[d] ‖ τυφλοί εἰσιν ὁδηγοὶ τυφλῶν ℵ[a] L Θ f[1] f[13] 33 700 892 1216 1241 it[a,aur,c,e,f,(ff1),ff2,g1,l] vg[(cl),ww] syr[p,h] arm eth[ro,pp?] geo Origen[gr,lat] Cyprian Basil Augustine Cyril ‖ ὁδηγοί εἰσιν τυφλοί ℵ[*,b] (l[12]) cop[sa,bo,fay][vid] ‖ ὁδηγοί εἰσιν τυφλοὶ τυφλῶν C W X Δ Π 565 1009 1010 1071 1079 1195 1230 1242 1253 1344 1365 1546 1646 (2148 omit εἰσιν) 2174 Byz Lect it[q] cop[boms] ‖ ὁδηγοί εἰσιν τυφλῶν K syr[c,s] eth[ms]

[5] **15** {C} τὴν παραβολήν ℵ B f[1] 700 892 cop[sa] geo[B] Origen ‖ τὴν παραβολὴν ταύτην C D K L W X (Δ αὐτήν) Θ Π 0119 33 565 1009 1010 1071 1079 1195 1216 1230 1241 1242 1253 1344 1365 1546 1646 2148 2174 Byz Lect it[a,aur,c,d,e,f,ff1,2,g1,l,q] vg syr[c,s,p,h] cop[sams,bo?] arm eth geo[1,A] Chrysostom ‖ ταύτην τὴν παραβολήν f[13]

13 Πᾶσα...ἐκριζωθήσεται Jn 15.2   **14** τυφλοί...ὁδηγῇ Mt 23.16, 24; Lk 6.39; Ro 2.19 τυφλὸς...πεσοῦνται Lk 6.39   **15** Φράσον...παραβολήν Mt 13.36; Mk 4.10; 7.17; Lk 8.9 **18** τὰ...ἐξέρχεται Mt 12.34   **19** Ro 1.29–31; 1 Cor 5.10–11; 6.9–10; Ga 5.19–21; Eph 5.3–5; Col 3.5, 8; 1 Tm 1.9–10; 2 Tm 3.2–4; 1 Pe 4.3; Re 21.8; 22.15   **22** Ἐλέησον...Δαυίδ Mt 9.27; 20.30, 31; Mk 10.47, 48; Lk 18.38, 39

23 ὁ δὲ οὐκ ἀπεκρίθη αὐτῇ λόγον. καὶ προσελθόντες οἱ μαθηταὶ αὐτοῦ ἠρώτουν αὐτὸν λέγοντες, Ἀπόλυσον αὐτήν, ὅτι κράζει ὄπισθεν ἡμῶν. **24** ὁ δὲ ἀποκριθεὶς εἶπεν, Οὐκ ἀπεστάλην εἰ μὴ εἰς τὰ πρόβατα τὰ ἀπολωλότα οἴκου Ἰσραήλ. **25** ἡ δὲ ἐλθοῦσα προσεκύνει αὐτῷ λέγουσα, Κύριε, βοήθει μοι. **26** ὁ δὲ ἀποκριθεὶς εἶπεν, Οὐκ ἔστιν καλὸν[6] λαβεῖν τὸν ἄρτον τῶν τέκνων καὶ βαλεῖν τοῖς κυναρίοις. **27** ἡ δὲ εἶπεν, Ναί, κύριε, καὶ γὰρ τὰ κυνάρια ἐσθίει ἀπὸ τῶν ψιχίων τῶν πιπτόντων ἀπὸ τῆς τραπέζης τῶν κυρίων αὐτῶν. **28** τότε ἀποκριθεὶς ὁ Ἰησοῦς εἶπεν αὐτῇ, Ὦ γύναι, μεγάλη σου ἡ πίστις· γενηθήτω σοι ὡς θέλεις. καὶ ἰάθη ἡ θυγάτηρ αὐτῆς ἀπὸ τῆς ὥρας ἐκείνης.

The Healing of Many People

29 Καὶ μεταβὰς ἐκεῖθεν ὁ Ἰησοῦς ἦλθεν παρὰ τὴν θάλασσαν τῆς Γαλιλαίας, καὶ ἀναβὰς εἰς τὸ ὄρος ἐκάθητο ἐκεῖ. **30** καὶ προσῆλθον αὐτῷ ὄχλοι πολλοὶ ἔχοντες μεθ' ἑαυτῶν χωλούς, τυφλούς, κυλλούς, κωφούς, καὶ ἑτέρους πολλούς, καὶ ἔρριψαν αὐτοὺς παρὰ τοὺς πόδας αὐτοῦ, καὶ ἐθεράπευσεν αὐτούς· **31** ὥστε τὸν ὄχλον θαυμάσαι βλέποντας κωφοὺς λαλοῦντας, κυλλοὺς ὑγιεῖς[7], καὶ χωλοὺς

---

[6] **26** {C} ἔστιν καλόν (see Mk 7.27) א B C K L W X Δ Θ Π f¹ f¹³ 33 565 700 892 1009 1071 1079 1195 1216 1230 1241 1242 1253 1344 1546 1646 2148 2174 *Byz Lect* it^aur,e,f,k,l,q vg syr^p,h cop^sa,bo arm eth Origen Chrysostom ∥ καλόν ἐστιν 1010 1365 *l*³⁰⁹ geo ∥ ἔστιν 1293 Tertullian Eusebius ∥ ἔξεστιν D it^a,b,c,d,ff1,2,g1,r1 syr^c,s (Diatessaron¹) Origen Ps-Clement Ambrosiaster Hilary Basil Ambrose Jerome

[7] **31** {C} λαλοῦντας, κυλλοὺς ὑγιεῖς C K L P W X Δ Π 1009 1071 1070 1105 1242 1344 1365 1546 1616 2148 2174 *Byz* (*l*¹⁸⁵ κυλλοὺς ὑγιῆς) *l*⁸⁸³,¹²³¹ᵐ it^(d),(t,q) ∥ λαλοῦντας καὶ κυλλοὺς ὑγιεῖς D Θ f¹³ 33 565 1230 1253 *l*ⁱᵇ syr^(p),h ∥ ἀκούοντας, κυλλοὺς ὑγιεῖς B (*l*²¹¹ κυλλοὺς ὑγιῆς) (syr^hmg) ∥ ἀκούοντας, ἀλάλους λαλοῦντας, κυλλοὺς ὑγιεῖς *Lect* ∥ ἀκούοντας καὶ λαλοῦντας κυλλοὺς ὑγιεῖς N O Σ ∥ λαλοῦντας א f¹ 700 892 1010 *l*¹⁸⁴ it^aur,b,c,ff1,2,g1,k,l vg syr^c,s eth^pp geo Origen ∥ ἀκούοντας it^e eth^ro,ms⁷ ∥ *transpose:* χωλοὺς περιπατοῦντας καὶ κωφοὺς λαλοῦντας τυφλοὺς βλέποντας καὶ κυλλοὺς

---

24 εἰς...Ἰσραήλ Mt 10.6   **27** ἐσθίει...τραπέζης Lk 16.21   **28** μεγάλη...πίστις Mt 8.10   γενηθήτω...θέλεις Mt 8.13; 9.29   **29** Καὶ μεταβὰς...Γαλιλαίας Mk 7.31   ἀναβὰς...ἐκεῖ Mt 5.1   **31** ὥστε...τυφλοὺς βλέποντας Mk 7.37

is in a terrible condition." **23** But Jesus did not say a word to her. His disciples came to him and begged him, "Send her away! She is following us and making all this noise!" **24** Then Jesus replied, "I have been sent only to the lost sheep of the people of Israel." **25** At this the woman came and fell at his feet. "Help me, sir!" she said. **26** Jesus answered, "It isn't right to take the children's food and throw it to the dogs." **27** "That is true, sir," she answered; "but even the dogs eat the leftovers that fall from their masters' table." **28** So Jesus answered her: "You are a woman of great faith! What you want will be done for you." And at that very moment her daughter was healed.

Jesus Heals Many People

29 Jesus left that place and went along by Lake Galilee. He climbed a hill and sat down. **30** Large crowds came to him, bringing with them the lame, the blind, the crippled, the dumb, and many other sick people, whom they placed at Jesus' feet; and he healed them. **31** The people were amazed as they saw the dumb speaking, the crippled whole, the lame walking, and the blind seeing; and they praised the God of Israel.

Jesus Feeds the Four Thousand
(Also Mark 8.1–10)

32 Jesus called his disciples to him and said: "I feel sorry for these people, because they have been with me for three days and now have nothing to eat. I don't want to send them away without feeding them, because they might faint on their way home." **33** The disciples asked him, "Where will we find enough food in this desert to feed this crowd?" **34** "How much bread do you have?" Jesus asked. "Seven loaves," they answered, "and a few small fish." **35** So Jesus ordered the crowd to sit down on the ground. **36** Then he took the seven loaves and the fish, gave thanks to God, broke them and gave them to the disciples, and the disciples gave them to the people. **37** They all ate and had enough. The disciples took up seven baskets full of pieces left over. **38** The number of men who ate was four thousand, not counting the women and children.

39 Then Jesus sent the people away, got into a boat, and went to the territory of Magadan.

περιπατοῦντας καὶ τυφλοὺς βλέποντας· καὶ ἐδόξασαν τὸν θεὸν Ἰσραήλ.

The Feeding of the Four Thousand
(Mk 8.1–10)

32 Ὁ δὲ Ἰησοῦς προσκαλεσάμενος τοὺς μαθητὰς αὐτοῦ εἶπεν, Σπλαγχνίζομαι ἐπὶ τὸν ὄχλον, ὅτι ἤδη ἡμέραι τρεῖς προσμένουσίν μοι καὶ οὐκ ἔχουσιν τί φάγωσιν· καὶ ἀπολῦσαι αὐτοὺς νήστεις οὐ θέλω, μήποτε ἐκλυθῶσιν ἐν τῇ ὁδῷ. **33** καὶ λέγουσιν αὐτῷ οἱ μαθηταί, Πόθεν ἡμῖν ἐν ἐρημίᾳ ἄρτοι τοσοῦτοι ὥστε χορτάσαι ὄχλον τοσοῦτον; **34** καὶ λέγει αὐτοῖς ὁ Ἰησοῦς, Πόσους ἄρτους ἔχετε; οἱ δὲ εἶπαν, Ἑπτά, καὶ ὀλίγα ἰχθύδια. **35** καὶ παραγγείλας τῷ ὄχλῳ ἀναπεσεῖν ἐπὶ τὴν γῆν **36** ἔλαβεν τοὺς ἑπτὰ ἄρτους καὶ τοὺς ἰχθύας καὶ εὐχαριστήσας ἔκλασεν καὶ ἐδίδου τοῖς μαθηταῖς⁸, οἱ δὲ μαθηταὶ τοῖς ὄχλοις. **37** καὶ ἔφαγον πάντες καὶ ἐχορτάσθησαν, καὶ τὸ περισσεῦον τῶν κλασμάτων ἦραν, ἑπτὰ σπυρίδας πλήρεις. **38** οἱ δὲ ἐσθίοντες ἦσαν τετρακισχίλιοι ἄνδρες χωρὶς γυναικῶν καὶ παιδίων⁹. **39** Καὶ ἀπολύσας τοὺς ὄχλους ἐνέβη εἰς τὸ πλοῖον, καὶ ἦλθεν εἰς τὰ ὅρια Μαγαδάν¹⁰.

ὑγιεῖς 1216 cop^samss ∥ *transpose:* λαλοῦντας, χωλοὺς περιπατοῦντας, κυλλοὺς ὑγιεῖς τυφλοὺς βλέποντας arm ∥ *transpose: the dumb speaking, the lame walking, the blind seeing, and the deaf hearing* cop^bo (cop^samss *lame, maimed, dumb, blind*)

⁸ **36** {B} μαθηταῖς ℵ B D Θ *f*¹ *f*¹³ 33 700 892^txt 1241 *l*⁵⁴⁷ it^c,d,ff1 syr^pal cop^sams,bo arm geo Chrysostom ∥ μαθηταῖς αὐτοῦ (*see* Mk 8.6) C K L P W X Δ Π 565 892^mg 1009 1010 1071 1079 1195 1216 1230 1242 1253 1344 1365 1546 1646 2148 2174 *Byz Lect* it^a,aur,b,e,f,ff2,g1,l,q vg syr^c,s,p,h cop^sa,boms eth Diatessaron

⁹ **38** {D} γυναικῶν καὶ παιδίων B C K L P W X Δ Π *f*¹³ 33 565 700 892 1009 1010 1071 1079 1195 1216 1230 1241 1242 1253 1344 1365 1546 1646 2148 2174 *Byz Lect* it^f syr^s,p,h,pal arm eth^pp,ms Chrysostom ∥ παιδίων καὶ γυναικῶν ℵ D Θ *f*¹ it^a,aur,b,c,d,e,ff1,2,g1,l,q vg syr^c cop^sa,bo eth^ro geo

¹⁰ **39** {C} Μαγαδάν ℵ* B D it^d (syr^c *Magadon,* syr^pal *Magadin,* syr^p *Magdu*) ∥ Μαγεδάν ℵ^c it^aur,c,f,ff1,g1 (it^a,ff2 *Magedam*) vg syr^s cop^sa eth^ms

---

32 Σπλαγχνίζομαι...ὄχλον Mt 9.36; 14.14; Mk 6.34   **32–33** ἀπολῦσαι...τοσοῦτον Mt 14.15; Mk 6.36; Lk 9.12   **33** Mk 6.37; Jn 6.5   **34–37** Mt 14.17, 19–20; Mk 6.38–43; Lk 9.13–17; Jn 6.9–13   **38** Mt 14.21; Mk 6.44

The Demand for a Sign
(Mk 8 11–13; Lk 12.54–56)

16 Καὶ προσελθόντες οἱ Φαρισαῖοι καὶ Σαδδουκαῖοι πειράζοντες ἐπηρώτησαν αὐτὸν σημεῖον ἐκ τοῦ οὐρανοῦ ἐπιδεῖξαι αὐτοῖς. 2 ὁ δὲ ἀποκριθεὶς εἶπεν αὐτοῖς, ['Οψίας γενομένης λέγετε, Εὐδία, πυρράζει γὰρ ὁ οὐρανός· 3 καὶ πρωΐ, Σήμερον χειμών, πυρράζει γὰρ στυγνάζων ὁ οὐρανός. τὸ μὲν πρόσωπον τοῦ οὐρανοῦ γινώσκετε διακρίνειν, τὰ δὲ σημεῖα τῶν καιρῶν οὐ δύνασθε.[a]][1] 4 Γενεὰ πονηρὰ καὶ μοιχαλὶς σημεῖον ἐπιζητεῖ, καὶ σημεῖον οὐ δοθήσεται αὐτῇ εἰ μὴ τὸ σημεῖον ᾿Ιωνᾶ. καὶ καταλιπὼν αὐτοὺς ἀπῆλθεν.

The Leaven of the Pharisees and Sadducees
(Mk 8.14–21)

5 Καὶ ἐλθόντες οἱ μαθηταὶ[2] εἰς τὸ πέραν ἐπελάθοντο ἄρτους λαβεῖν. 6 ὁ δὲ ᾿Ιησοῦς εἶπεν αὐτοῖς, ῾Ορᾶτε καὶ προσέχετε ἀπὸ τῆς ζύμης τῶν Φαρισαίων καὶ Σαδδου-

---

Eusebius Jerome Augustine ‖ *Magedan or Magedam* it[b,e,l] ‖ Μαγεδάλ eth[pp] ‖ Μαγδαλάν C W 33 565 1079 1195 1546 *l*[5,292] it[q] cop[bo] ‖ Μαγδαλά K L X Δ[gr] Θ Π *f*[1] *f*[13] 700 892 1009 1010 1071 1216 1230 1241 1242 1253 1344 1365 1646 2174 *Byz Lect* syr[h] arm eth[ro] geo Chrysostom

[1] 2–3 {C} ὀψίας γενομένης...οὐ δύνασθε. C D K L W Δ Θ Π *f*[1] 33 565 700 892 1009 1010 1071 1079 1195 1230 1241 1242 1253 1344 1365 1546 1646 2148 2174 *Byz Lect l*[150m] (*l*[185,211,333,950] δύνασθε γνῶναι) it[a,aur,b,c,d,e,f,ff1,2,g1,l,q] vg syr[p,h] cop[boms] eth geo Diatessaron Theophilus Apostolic Canons Juvencus Eusebius Hilary Chrysostom Euthalius ‖ *include* ὀψίας...οὐρανός *with obeli l*[184] ‖ *omit* ℵ B X *f*[13] 1216 syr[c,s] cop[sa,boms] arm Origen mss[acc. to Jerome]

[2] 5 {A} οἱ μαθηταί ℵ B C Θ (D 700 *place after* ἐπελάθοντο) *f*[13] 892 *l*[184] (it[d,e]) cop[sams] arm Hilary ‖ οἱ μαθηταὶ αὐτοῦ K L W X Π *f*[1] 33 565 1009 1010 1071 1079 1195 1216 1230 1241 1242 1253 1344 1365 1546 1646 2148 2174 *Byz Lect* it[(a),aur,(b,e),f,(ff1,2,g1),l,q] vg syr[(c,s),p,h] cop[sa,bo] eth geo Diatessaron (Origen) Hilary ‖ *omit* Δ

---

[a] **2b–3** *a* statement: WH RV ASV RSV Jer Seg ‖ *a* question: TR Bov Nes BF² AV NEB[mg] TT Zür Luth ‖ omit passage: NEB TT[mg]

---

1 Καὶ...πειράζοντες Mt 19.3 ἐπηρώτησαν...αὐτοῖς Mt 12.38; Lk 11.16; Jn 6.30; 1 Cor 1.22 **4** Γενεὰ...᾿Ιωνᾶ Mt 12.39; Lk 11.29 **6** ῾Ορᾶτε...Φαρισαίων Lk 12.1

The Demand for a Miracle
(Also Mark 8.11–13; Luke 12.54–56)

16 Some Pharisees and Sadducees came to Jesus. They wanted to trap him, so they asked him to perform a miracle for them, to show God's approval. ² But Jesus answered:[1] "When the sun is setting you say, 'We are going to have fine weather, because the sky is red.' ³ And early in the morning you say, 'It is going to rain, because the sky is red and dark.' You can predict the weather by looking at the sky; but you cannot interpret the signs concerning these times! ⁴ How evil and godless are the people of this day!" Jesus added. "You ask me for a miracle? No! The only miracle you will be given is the miracle of Jonah." So he left them and went away.

The Yeast of the Pharisees and Sadducees
(Also Mark 8.14–21)

⁵ When the disciples crossed over to the other side of the lake, they forgot to take any bread. ⁶ Jesus said to them, "Look out, and be on your guard against the yeast of the Pharisees and Sad-

---

[1] **2b–3** *Some mss. omit the words in verse 2 after* But Jesus answered, *and all of verse 3.*

ducees." 7 They started discussing among themselves: "He says this because we didn't bring any bread." 8 Jesus knew what they were saying, so he asked them: "Why are you discussing among yourselves about not having any bread? How little faith you have! 9 Don't you understand yet? Don't you remember when I broke the five loaves for the five thousand men? How many baskets did you fill? 10 And what about the seven loaves for the four thousand men? How many baskets did you fill? 11 How is it that you don't understand that I was not talking to you about bread? Guard yourselves from the yeast of the Pharisees and Sadducees!" 12 Then the disciples understood that he was not telling them to guard themselves from the yeast used in bread, but from the teaching of the Pharisees and Sadducees.

Peter's Declaration about Jesus
(Also Mark 8.27–30; Luke 9.18–21)

13 Jesus went to the territory near the town of Caesarea Philippi, where he asked his disciples, "Who do men say the Son of Man is?" 14 "Some say John

καίων. 7 οἱ δὲ διελογίζοντο ἐν ἑαυτοῖς λέγοντες ὅτι[b] "Ἄρτους οὐκ ἐλάβομεν. 8 γνοὺς δὲ ὁ Ἰησοῦς εἶπεν, Τί διαλογίζεσθε ἐν ἑαυτοῖς, ὀλιγόπιστοι, ὅτι ἄρτους οὐκ ἔχετε[3]; 9 οὔπω νοεῖτε, οὐδὲ μνημονεύετε τοὺς πέντε ἄρτους τῶν πεντακισχιλίων καὶ πόσους κοφίνους ἐλάβετε; 10 οὐδὲ τοὺς ἑπτὰ ἄρτους τῶν τετρακισχιλίων καὶ πόσας σπυρίδας ἐλάβετε; 11 πῶς οὐ νοεῖτε ὅτι οὐ περὶ ἄρτων εἶπον ὑμῖν; προσέχετε δὲ ἀπὸ τῆς ζύμης τῶν Φαρισαίων καὶ Σαδδουκαίων. 12 τότε συνῆκαν ὅτι οὐκ εἶπεν προσέχειν ἀπὸ τῆς ζύμης [τῶν ἄρτων][4] ἀλλὰ ἀπὸ τῆς διδαχῆς τῶν Φαρισαίων καὶ Σαδδουκαίων.

Peter's Declaration about Jesus
(Mk 8.27–30; Lk 9.18–21)

13 Ἐλθὼν δὲ ὁ Ἰησοῦς εἰς τὰ μέρη Καισαρείας τῆς Φιλίππου ἠρώτα τοὺς μαθητὰς αὐτοῦ λέγων, Τίνα λέγουσιν οἱ ἄνθρωποι εἶναι[5] τὸν υἱὸν τοῦ ἀνθρώπου; 14 οἱ δὲ

---

[3] 8 {C} ἔχετε (see Mk 8.17) א B D Θ f[13] 700 892 1241 it[a,aur,b,c,d,e,ff1,2,g1,l,q] vg cop[bo] arm geo[2] Diatessaron[a,i] Lucifer ∥ ἐλάβετε C K L W X Δ Π f[1] 33 565 1009 1010 1071 1079 1195 1216 1230 1242 1253 1344 1546 1646 2148 2174 Byz Lect it[f] syr[c,s,p,h] cop[sa] eth? Origen Eusebius Chrysostom ∥ ἐλάβομεν 1365 l[1579] geo[1]

[4] 12 {D} τῶν ἄρτων א[c] B L (f[1] omit τῆς ζύμης) 892 1009 1241 l[48,184,211] it[aur,(e),g1,l] vg cop[sa,bomss] eth? ∥ τοῦ ἄρτου C K W X Δ Π 28 700 1010 1071 1079 1195 1230 1242 1253 1344 1365 1546 1646 2148 2174 Byz Lect it[c,f,q] syr[p,h] cop[sams,bomss] eth? geo[A] Diatessaron ∥ τῶν Φαρισαίων καὶ Σαδδουκαίων א* l[185pt] it[ff1] syr[c] Diatessaron[v] ∥ τῶν Φαρισαίων 33 ∥ omit D Θ f[13] 565 it[a,b,d,ff2] syr[s] arm geo[1,B] Lucifer

[5] 13 {B} τίνα λέγουσιν οἱ ἄνθρωποι εἶναι B l[1353] it[c] vg syr[h,pal] cop[sa,bo] eth[ro,pp] Origen[lat] Ambrose ∥ τίνα λέγουσίν με οἱ ἄνθρωποι εἶναι C W syr[c,(s),p] arm ∥ τίνα με λέγουσιν οἱ ἄνθρωποι εἶναι (see Mk 8.27; Lk 9.18) K L X Δ Θ Π f[13] 28 33 565 892 1009 1010 1071 1079 1195 1216 1230 1241 1242 1253 1344 1365 1546 1646 2148 2174 Byz Lect l[70m,150m,883m] it[aur,d,f,ff2,g1,l] eth[ms]? geo? Irenaeus[lat] Tertullian Origen Adamantius Hilary (Ephraem)

---

[b] 7 b direct: TR? WH Bov Nes? BF[2] RV ASV RSV TT Luth? Jer? Seg ∥ b causal: TR? Nes? AV RV[mg] ASV[mg] NEB Zür Luth? Jer? Seg[mg]

---

9 τοὺς...ἐλάβετε Mt 14.13–21; Mk 6.34–44; Lk 9.11–17; Jn 6.1–13   10 τοὺς...ἐλάβετε Mt 15.32–38; Mk 8.1–9   14 Mk 6.14–15; Lk 9.7–8

εἶπαν, Οἱ μὲν Ἰωάννην τὸν βαπτιστήν, ἄλλοι δὲ Ἠλίαν, ἔτεροι δὲ Ἰερεμίαν ἢ ἕνα τῶν προφητῶν. **15** λέγει αὐτοῖς, Ὑμεῖς δὲ τίνα με λέγετε εἶναι; **16** ἀποκριθεὶς δὲ Σίμων Πέτρος εἶπεν, Σὺ εἶ ὁ Χριστὸς ὁ υἱὸς τοῦ θεοῦ τοῦ ζῶντος. **17** ἀποκριθεὶς δὲ ὁ Ἰησοῦς εἶπεν αὐτῷ, Μακάριος εἶ, Σίμων Βαριωνᾶ, ὅτι σὰρξ καὶ αἷμα οὐκ ἀπεκάλυψέν σοι ἀλλ' ὁ πατήρ μου ὁ ἐν τοῖς οὐρανοῖς. **18** κἀγὼ δέ σοι λέγω ὅτι σὺ εἶ Πέτρος, καὶ ἐπὶ ταύτῃ τῇ πέτρᾳ οἰκοδομήσω μου τὴν ἐκκλησίαν, καὶ πύλαι ᾅδου οὐ κατισχύσουσιν αὐτῆς. **19** δώσω σοι τὰς κλεῖδας τῆς βασιλείας τῶν οὐρανῶν, καὶ ὃ ἐὰν δήσῃς ἐπὶ τῆς γῆς ἔσται δεδεμένον ἐν τοῖς οὐρανοῖς, καὶ ὃ ἐὰν λύσῃς ἐπὶ τῆς γῆς ἔσται λελυμένον ἐν τοῖς οὐρανοῖς. **20** τότε διεστείλατο τοῖς μαθηταῖς ἵνα μηδενὶ εἴπωσιν ὅτι αὐτός ἐστιν ὁ Χριστός.

Jesus Foretells His Death and Resurrection
(Mk 8.31—9.1; Lk 9.22–27)

21 Ἀπὸ τότε ἤρξατο ὁ Ἰησοῦς[6] δεικνύειν τοῖς μαθηταῖς αὐτοῦ ὅτι δεῖ αὐτὸν εἰς Ἱεροσόλυμα ἀπελθεῖν καὶ πολλὰ παθεῖν ἀπὸ τῶν πρεσβυτέρων καὶ ἀρχιερέων καὶ γραμματέων καὶ ἀποκτανθῆναι καὶ τῇ τρίτῃ ἡμέρᾳ ἐγερθῆναι. **22** καὶ προσλαβόμενος αὐτὸν ὁ Πέτρος ἤρξατο ἐπιτιμᾶν αὐτῷ λέγων, Ἵλεώς σοι, κύριε· οὐ μὴ ἔσται σοι τοῦτο. **23** ὁ δὲ στραφεὶς εἶπεν τῷ Πέτρῳ, Ὕπαγε ὀπίσω μου, Σατανᾶ· σκάνδαλον εἶ ἐμοῦ, ὅτι οὐ φρονεῖς τὰ τοῦ θεοῦ

Epiphanius Cyril ‖ τίνα με λέγουσιν εἶναι οἱ ἄνθρωποι f[1] it[ff1] ‖ τίνα με οἱ ἄνθρωποι λέγουσιν εἶναι D[gr] it[a, b, e, q, r1] ‖ τίνα οἱ ἄνθρωποι εἶναι λέγουσιν ℵ* (ℵ[c] λέγουσιν εἶναι) (700 *omit* εἶναι)

[6] **21** {C} ὁ Ἰησοῦς ℵ[b] C (B[3] D *omit* ὁ) K L W X Δ Θ Π f[1] f[13] 28 565 700 1009 1010 1071 1079 1195 1216 1230 1241 1242 1253 1344 1365 1546 1646 2148 2174 *Byz Lect* it[a, aur, b, c, d, (e), f, ff1,2, g1, l, q] vg syr[c, p, h] cop[sams, boms] arm eth geo[1] Origen Augustine ‖ Ἰησοῦς Χριστός ℵ* B* cop[samss, bo] ‖ *omit* ℵ[a] 892 geo[2] Irenaeus[lat] Origen Chrysostom

16 Σὺ...ζῶντος Mt 26.63; Mk 14.61   **17** σὰρξ...οὐρανοῖς Mt 17.5; Ga 1.15–16   **18** σὺ εἶ Πέτρος Jn 1.42   ἐπὶ...ἐκκλησίαν Eph 2.20   πύλαι ᾅδου Job 38.17; Is 38.10; Wsd 16.13   **19** ὃ ἐὰν δήσῃς...λελυμένον ἐν τοῖς οὐρανοῖς Mt 18.18; Jn 20.23   **20** Mt 17.9; Mk 9.9   **23** Ὕπαγε...Σατανᾶ Mt 4.10

the Baptist," they answered. "Others say Elijah, while others say Jeremiah or some other prophet." [15] "What about you?" he asked them. "Who do you say I am?" [16] Simon Peter answered, "You are the Messiah, the Son of the living God." [17] "Simon, son of John, you are happy indeed!" answered Jesus. "For this truth did not come to you from any human being, but it was given to you directly by my Father in heaven. [18] And so I tell you: you are a rock, Peter, and on this rock I will build my church. Not even death will ever be able to overcome it. [19] I will give you the keys of the Kingdom of heaven: what you prohibit on earth will be prohibited in heaven; what you permit on earth will be permitted in heaven." [20] Then Jesus ordered his disciples that they were not to tell anyone that he was the Messiah.

Jesus Speaks about His Suffering and Death
(Also Mark 8.31—9.1; Luke 9.22–27)

[21] From that time on Jesus began to say plainly to his disciples: "I must go to Jerusalem and suffer much from the elders, the chief priests, and the teachers of the Law. I will be put to death, and on the third day I will be raised to life." [22] Peter took him aside and began to rebuke him. "God forbid it, Lord!" he said. "This must never happen to you!" [23] Jesus turned around and said to Peter: "Get away from me, Satan! You are an obstacle in my way, for these thoughts of yours are men's thoughts, not God's!"

²⁴ Then Jesus said to his disciples: "If anyone wants to come with me, he must forget himself, carry his cross, and follow me. ²⁵ For the man who wants to save his own life will lose it; but the man who loses his life for my sake will find it. ²⁶ Will a man gain anything if he wins the whole world but loses his life? Of course not! There is nothing a man can give to regain his life. ²⁷ For the Son of Man is about to come in the glory of his Father with his angels, and then he will repay everyone according to his deeds. ²⁸ Remember this! There are some here who will not die until they have seen the Son of Man come as King."

The Transfiguration
(Also Mark 9.2–13; Luke 9.28–36)

17 Six days later Jesus took with him Peter, and the brothers James and John, and led them up a high mountain by themselves. ² As they looked on, a change came over him: his face became as bright as the sun, and his clothes as white as light. ³ Then the three disciples saw Moses and Elijah talking with Jesus. ⁴ So Peter spoke up and said to Jesus, "Lord, it is a good thing that we are here; if you wish, I will make three tents here, one for you, one for Moses, and one for Elijah." ⁵ While he was talking, a shining cloud came over them and a voice said from the cloud: "This is my own dear Son, with whom I am well pleased — listen to him!" ⁶ When the disciples heard the voice they were so terrified that they threw themselves face down to the ground. ⁷ Jesus came to them and touched them. "Get up,"

ἀλλὰ τὰ τῶν ἀνθρώπων. 24 Τότε ὁ Ἰησοῦς εἶπεν τοῖς μαθηταῖς αὐτοῦ, Εἴ τις θέλει ὀπίσω μου ἐλθεῖν, ἀπαρνησάσθω ἑαυτὸν καὶ ἀράτω τὸν σταυρὸν αὐτοῦ καὶ ἀκολουθείτω μοι. 25 ὃς γὰρ ἐὰν θέλῃ τὴν ψυχὴν αὐτοῦ σῶσαι ἀπολέσει αὐτήν· ὃς δ' ἂν ἀπολέσῃ τὴν ψυχὴν αὐτοῦ ἕνεκεν ἐμοῦ εὑρήσει αὐτήν. 26 τί γὰρ ὠφεληθήσεται ἄνθρωπος ἐὰν τὸν κόσμον ὅλον κερδήσῃ τὴν δὲ ψυχὴν αὐτοῦ ζημιωθῇ; ἢ τί δώσει ἄνθρωπος ἀντάλλαγμα τῆς ψυχῆς αὐτοῦ; 27 μέλλει γὰρ ὁ υἱὸς τοῦ ἀνθρώπου ἔρχεσθαι ἐν τῇ δόξῃ τοῦ πατρὸς αὐτοῦ μετὰ τῶν ἀγγέλων αὐτοῦ, καὶ τότε ἀποδώσει ἑκάστῳ κατὰ τὴν πρᾶξιν αὐτοῦ. 28 ἀμὴν λέγω ὑμῖν ὅτι εἰσίν τινες τῶν ὧδε ἑστώτων οἵτινες οὐ μὴ γεύσωνται θανάτου ἕως ἂν ἴδωσιν τὸν υἱὸν τοῦ ἀνθρώπου ἐρχόμενον ἐν τῇ βασιλείᾳ αὐτοῦ.

The Transfiguration of Jesus
(Mk 9.2–13; Lk 9.28–36)

17 Καὶ μεθ' ἡμέρας ἓξ παραλαμβάνει ὁ Ἰησοῦς τὸν Πέτρον καὶ Ἰάκωβον καὶ Ἰωάννην τὸν ἀδελφὸν αὐτοῦ, καὶ ἀναφέρει αὐτοὺς εἰς ὄρος ὑψηλὸν κατ' ἰδίαν. 2 καὶ μετεμορφώθη ἔμπροσθεν αὐτῶν, καὶ ἔλαμψεν τὸ πρόσωπον αὐτοῦ ὡς ὁ ἥλιος, τὰ δὲ ἱμάτια αὐτοῦ ἐγένετο λευκὰ ὡς τὸ φῶς. 3 καὶ ἰδοὺ ὤφθη αὐτοῖς Μωϋσῆς καὶ Ἡλίας συλλαλοῦντες μετ' αὐτοῦ. 4 ἀποκριθεὶς δὲ ὁ Πέτρος εἶπεν τῷ Ἰησοῦ, Κύριε, καλόν ἐστιν ἡμᾶς ὧδε εἶναι· εἰ θέλεις, ποιήσω ὧδε τρεῖς σκηνάς, σοὶ μίαν καὶ Μωϋσεῖ μίαν καὶ Ἡλίᾳ μίαν. 5 ἔτι αὐτοῦ λαλοῦντος ἰδοὺ νεφέλη φωτεινὴ ἐπεσκίασεν αὐτούς, καὶ ἰδοὺ φωνὴ ἐκ τῆς νεφέλης λέγουσα, Οὗτός ἐστιν ὁ υἱός μου ὁ ἀγαπητός, ἐν ᾧ εὐδόκησα· ἀκούετε αὐτοῦ. 6 καὶ ἀκούσαντες οἱ μαθηταὶ ἔπεσαν ἐπὶ πρόσωπον αὐτῶν καὶ ἐφοβήθησαν σφόδρα. 7 καὶ προσῆλθεν ὁ Ἰησοῦς καὶ ἁψάμενος αὐτῶν εἶπεν, Ἐγέρθητε καὶ

---

24 Εἰ...μοι Mt 10.38; Lk 14.27　　**25** Mt 10.39; Lk 17.33; Jn 12.25　　**26** ἐὰν...κερδήσῃ Mt 4.8–9　　**27** μέλλει...ἀγγέλων Mt 25.31　　ἀποδώσει...αὐτοῦ Ps 28.4; 62.12; Pr 24.12; Sir 35.19; Ro 2.6; Re 22.12　　**28** τὸν...αὐτοῦ Mt 10.23　ἐν...αὐτοῦ Mt 20.21

17 2 2 Pe 1.16–18　　**5** Οὗτος...εὐδόκησα Ps 2.7; Mt 3.17; 12.18; Mk 1.11; Lk 3.22; 2 Pe 1.17　ἀκούετε αὐτοῦ Dt 18.15; Ac 3.22

μὴ φοβεῖσθε. 8 ἐπάραντες δὲ τοὺς ὀφθαλμοὺς αὐτῶν οὐδένα εἶδον εἰ μὴ αὐτὸν Ἰησοῦν μόνον.

9 Καὶ καταβαινόντων αὐτῶν ἐκ τοῦ ὄρους ἐνετείλατο αὐτοῖς ὁ Ἰησοῦς λέγων, Μηδενὶ εἴπητε τὸ ὅραμα ἕως οὗ ὁ υἱὸς τοῦ ἀνθρώπου ἐκ νεκρῶν ἐγερθῇ. 10 καὶ ἐπηρώτησαν αὐτὸν οἱ μαθηταί[1] λέγοντες, Τί οὖν οἱ γραμματεῖς λέγουσιν ὅτι Ἠλίαν δεῖ ἐλθεῖν πρῶτον; 11 ὁ δὲ ἀποκριθεὶς εἶπεν, Ἠλίας μὲν ἔρχεται καὶ ἀποκαταστήσει πάντα· 12 λέγω δὲ ὑμῖν ὅτι Ἠλίας ἤδη ἦλθεν, καὶ οὐκ ἐπέγνωσαν αὐτὸν ἀλλὰ ἐποίησαν ἐν αὐτῷ ὅσα ἠθέλησαν· οὕτως καὶ ὁ υἱὸς τοῦ ἀνθρώπου μέλλει πάσχειν ὑπ' αὐτῶν. 13 τότε συνῆκαν οἱ μαθηταὶ ὅτι περὶ Ἰωάννου τοῦ βαπτιστοῦ εἶπεν αὐτοῖς.

The Healing of a Boy with a Demon
(Mk 9.14–29; Lk 9.37–43a)

14 Καὶ ἐλθόντων πρὸς τὸν ὄχλον προσῆλθεν αὐτῷ ἄνθρωπος γονυπετῶν αὐτὸν 15 καὶ λέγων, Κύριε, ἐλέησόν μου τὸν υἱόν, ὅτι σεληνιάζεται καὶ κακῶς πάσχει[2]· πολλάκις γὰρ πίπτει εἰς τὸ πῦρ καὶ πολλάκις εἰς τὸ ὕδωρ. 16 καὶ προσήνεγκα αὐτὸν τοῖς μαθηταῖς σου, καὶ οὐκ ἠδυνήθησαν αὐτὸν θεραπεῦσαι. 17 ἀποκριθεὶς δὲ ὁ Ἰησοῦς εἶπεν, Ὦ γενεὰ ἄπιστος καὶ διεστραμμένη, ἕως πότε μεθ' ὑμῶν ἔσομαι; ἕως πότε ἀνέξομαι ὑμῶν; φέρετέ μοι αὐτὸν ὧδε. 18 καὶ ἐπετίμησεν αὐτῷ ὁ Ἰησοῦς, καὶ ἐξῆλθεν ἀπ'

he said. "Don't be afraid!" 8 So they looked up and saw no one else except Jesus.

9 As they came down the mountain Jesus ordered them: "Don't tell anyone about this vision you have seen until the Son of Man has been raised from death." 10 Then the disciples asked Jesus, "Why do the teachers of the Law say that Elijah has to come first?" 11 "Elijah does indeed come first," answered Jesus, "and he will get everything ready. 12 But I tell you this: Elijah has already come and people did not recognize him, but treated him just as they pleased. In the same way the Son of Man will also be mistreated by them." 13 Then the disciples understood that he was talking to them about John the Baptist.

Jesus Heals a Boy with a Demon
(Also Mark 9.14–29; Luke 9.37–43a)

14 When they returned to the crowd, a man came to Jesus, knelt before him, 15 and said: "Sir, have mercy on my son! He is epileptic and has such terrible fits that he often falls in the fire or in the water. 16 I brought him to your disciples, but they could not heal him." 17 Jesus answered: "How unbelieving and wrong you people are! How long must I stay with you? How long do I have to put up with you? Bring the boy here to me!" 18 Jesus commanded the demon

---

[1] **10** {C} μαθηταί ℵ L W Θ f[1] 33 700 892 it[a,aur,b,c,d,e,ff1,g1,l] vg syr[pal] cop[ss,bo] arm geo Origen Augustine ‖ μαθηταὶ αὐτοῦ B C D K Δ Π f[13] 28 565 1009 1010 1071 1079 1195 1216 1230 1241 1242 1253 1344 1365 1546 1646 2148 2174 Byz Lect it[f,ff2,q] syr[c,p,h] cop[bomss] eth Diatessaron Chrysostom

[2] **15** {B} πάσχει C D K W X Δ Π f[1] f[13] 28 33 565 700 892 1009 1010 1071 1079 1195 1216 1230 1241 1242 1253 1344 1365 1546 1646 2148 2174 Byz Lect it[a,aur,(b),c,d,e,f,(ff1),ff2,g1,l,q,(r1)] vg syr[c,(s,p),h,pal] arm eth[mss?] geo Chrysostom ‖ ἔχει ℵ B L Θ cop[sa?bo?] Origen Chrysostom

---

9 Μηδενὶ...ἐγερθῇ Mt 16.20   **10-11** Ἠλίαν...πάντα Mal 4.5–6   **12** Ἠλίας ἤδη ἦλθεν Mt 11.14   **13** περὶ...αὐτοῖς Lk 1.17   **17** γενεὰ...διεστραμμένη Dt 32.5, 20

and it went out, so that the boy was healed at that very moment.

¹⁹ Then the disciples came to Jesus in private and asked him, "Why couldn't we drive the demon out?" ²⁰ "It was because you do not have enough faith," answered Jesus. "Remember this! If you have faith as big as a mustard seed, you can say to this hill, 'Go from here to there!' and it will go. You could do anything! [²¹ But only prayer and fasting can drive this kind out; nothing else can.]"

Jesus Speaks again about His Death
(Also Mark 9.30–32; Luke 9.43b–45)

²² When the disciples all came together in Galilee, Jesus said to them: "The Son of Man is about to be handed over to men ²³ who will kill him; but on the third day he will be raised to life." The disciples became very sad.

Payment of the Temple Tax

²⁴ When Jesus and his disciples came to Capernaum, the collectors of the Temple tax came to Peter and asked, "Does your teacher pay the Temple tax?" ²⁵ "Of course," Peter answered.

αὐτοῦ τὸ δαιμόνιον· καὶ ἐθεραπεύθη ὁ παῖς ἀπὸ τῆς ὥρας ἐκείνης. **19** Τότε προσελθόντες οἱ μαθηταὶ τῷ Ἰησοῦ κατ' ἰδίαν εἶπον, Διὰ τί ἡμεῖς οὐκ ἠδυνήθημεν ἐκβαλεῖν αὐτό; **20** ὁ δὲ λέγει αὐτοῖς, Διὰ τὴν ὀλιγοπιστίαν[3] ὑμῶν· ἀμὴν γὰρ λέγω ὑμῖν, ἐὰν ἔχητε πίστιν ὡς κόκκον σινάπεως, ἐρεῖτε τῷ ὄρει τούτῳ, Μετάβα ἔνθεν ἐκεῖ, καὶ μεταβήσεται· καὶ οὐδὲν ἀδυνατήσει ὑμῖν.[4]

Jesus Again Foretells His Death and Resurrection
(Mk 9.30–32; Lk 9.43b–45)

22 Συστρεφομένων[5] δὲ αὐτῶν ἐν τῇ Γαλιλαίᾳ εἶπεν αὐτοῖς ὁ Ἰησοῦς, Μέλλει ὁ υἱὸς τοῦ ἀνθρώπου παραδίδοσθαι εἰς χεῖρας ἀνθρώπων, **23** καὶ ἀποκτενοῦσιν αὐτόν, καὶ τῇ τρίτῃ ἡμέρᾳ ἐγερθήσεται. καὶ ἐλυπήθησαν σφόδρα.

Payment of the Temple Tax

24 Ἐλθόντων δὲ αὐτῶν εἰς Καφαρναοὺμ προσῆλθον οἱ τὰ δίδραχμα λαμβάνοντες τῷ Πέτρῳ καὶ εἶπαν, Ὁ διδάσκαλος ὑμῶν οὐ τελεῖ τὰ δίδραχμα; **25** λέγει, Ναί. καὶ

---

[3] **20** {B} ὀλιγοπιστίαν ℵ B Θ f[1] f[13] 33 700 892 syr[c,pal] cop[sa,bo] arm eth geo Diatessaron[esyr,l] Origen Hilary Chrysostom John-Damascus ∥ ἀπιστίαν C D K L W X Δ Π 28 565 1009 1010 1071 1079 1195 1216 1230 1241 1242 1253 1344 1365 1546 1646 2148 2174 *Byz Lect* it[a,aur,b,c,d,e,f,ff1,2,g1,l,n,q,rl] vg syr[s,p,h] Diatessaron[a] Chrysostom

[4] **20** {B} *omit verse 21* ℵ* B Θ 33 892[txt] it[e,ff1] syr[c,s,pal] cop[sa,bomss] eth[ro,ms] geo Eusebius ∥ *add verse 21* τοῦτο δὲ τὸ γένος οὐκ ἐκπορεύεται εἰ μὴ ἐν προσευχῇ καὶ νηστείᾳ. (see Mk 9.29) (ℵ[b] οὐκ ἐκβάλλεται εἰ) C D K L W X Δ Π f[1] f[13] 28 565 700 892[mg] 1009 1010 1071 1079 (1195 *omit δέ*) 1216 1230 1241 1242 1253 1344 1365 1546 1646 2148 2174 *Byz Lect* it[(a),aur,(b),(c),d,f,ff2,g1,l,(n),q,rl] vg syr[p,(h)] cop[bomss] arm eth[pp] geo[Bmg] Diatessaron Origen Hilary Basil Ambrose Chrysostom Augustine

[5] **22** {C} συστρεφομένων ℵ B f[1] 892 it[a,aur,b,d,f,ff2,g1,l,n,q] vg (syr[pal]) cop[samss] Origen Hilary ∥ ἀναστρεφομένων C (D αὐτῶν δὲ ἀναστρεφομένων) K L W X Δ Θ Π f[13] 28 33 565 700 1009 1010 1071 1079 1195 1216 1230 1241 1242 1253 1344 1365 1546 1646 2148 2174 *Byz Lect* it[c,e,ff1] syr[c,s,p,h] cop[sa,bo] arm eth geo? Chrysostom

---

18 ἐθεραπεύθη…ἐκείνης Mt 8.13; 9.22; 15.28; Jn 4.52–53 **20** ἐὰν…μεταβήσεται Mt 21.21; Mk 11.23; Lk 17.6; 1 Cor 13.2 **23** ἀποκτενοῦσιν…ἐγερθήσεται Mt 16.21 **24** τὰ δίδραχμα Ex 30.13; 38.26

ἐλθόντα εἰς τὴν οἰκίαν προέφθασεν αὐτὸν ὁ Ἰησοῦς λέγων, Τί σοι δοκεῖ, Σίμων; οἱ βασιλεῖς τῆς γῆς ἀπὸ τίνων λαμβάνουσιν τέλη ἢ κῆνσον; ἀπὸ τῶν υἱῶν αὐτῶν ἢ ἀπὸ τῶν ἀλλοτρίων; 26 εἰπόντος δέ[6], Ἀπὸ τῶν ἀλλοτρίων, ἔφη αὐτῷ ὁ Ἰησοῦς, Ἄρα γε ἐλεύθεροί εἰσιν οἱ υἱοί. 27 ἵνα δὲ μὴ σκανδαλίσωμεν αὐτούς, πορευθεὶς εἰς θάλασσαν βάλε ἄγκιστρον καὶ τὸν ἀναβάντα πρῶτον ἰχθὺν ἆρον, καὶ ἀνοίξας τὸ στόμα αὐτοῦ εὑρήσεις στατῆρα· ἐκεῖνον λαβὼν δὸς αὐτοῖς ἀντὶ ἐμοῦ καὶ σοῦ.

The Greatest in the Kingdom
(Mk 9.33–37; Lk 9.46–48)

18 Ἐν ἐκείνῃ τῇ ὥρᾳ προσῆλθον οἱ μαθηταὶ τῷ Ἰησοῦ λέγοντες, Τίς ἄρα μείζων ἐστὶν ἐν τῇ βασιλείᾳ τῶν οὐρανῶν; 2 καὶ προσκαλεσάμενος παιδίον ἔστησεν αὐτὸ ἐν μέσῳ αὐτῶν 3 καὶ εἶπεν, Ἀμὴν λέγω ὑμῖν, ἐὰν μὴ στραφῆτε καὶ γένησθε ὡς τὰ παιδία, οὐ μὴ εἰσέλθητε εἰς τὴν βασιλείαν τῶν οὐρανῶν. 4 ὅστις οὖν ταπεινώσει ἑαυτὸν ὡς τὸ παιδίον τοῦτο, οὗτός ἐστιν ὁ μείζων ἐν τῇ βασιλείᾳ τῶν οὐρανῶν. 5 καὶ ὃς ἐὰν δέξηται ἓν παιδίον τοιοῦτο ἐπὶ τῷ ὀνόματί μου, ἐμὲ δέχεται.

Temptations to Sin
(Mk 9.42–48; Lk 17.1–2)

6 Ὃς δ' ἂν σκανδαλίσῃ ἕνα τῶν μικρῶν τούτων τῶν πιστευόντων εἰς ἐμέ, συμφέρει αὐτῷ ἵνα κρεμασθῇ μύλος ὀνικὸς περὶ τὸν τράχηλον αὐτοῦ καὶ καταποντισθῇ ἐν τῷ

---

6 **26** {C} εἰπόντος δέ B Θ f[1] 700 892[txt] syr[pal vid] cop[sa, bo mss] arm eth[pp] gco[1] Origen Chrysostom Cyril ‖ εἰπόντος δὲ τοῦ Πέτρου 892[mg] (geo[A, B] John-Damascus *omit τοῦ*) ‖ λέγει αὐτῷ ὁ Πέτρος K W X Δ Π f[13] 28 565 1009 1010 1071 1079 1195 1216 (1230 ἔφη αὐτῷ) 1242 1253 1344 1365 1546 1646 2148 2174 *Byz Lect* it[(f), q] syr[(c, p), h] eth[ms] Diatessaron Basil ‖ λέγει αὐτῷ D it[d] cop[bo mss] ‖ *et ille dixit* it[a, aur, b, (c), (e), (ff1), ff2, g1, l, n] vg ‖ ὁ δὲ ἔφη, Ἀπὸ τῶν ἀλλοτρίων. εἰπόντος δὲ ℵ cop[bo mss] eth[ro] ‖ λέγει αὐτῷ ὁ Πέτρος, Ἀπὸ τῶν ἀλλοτρίων. εἰπόντος δὲ αὐτοῦ C (L *omit αὐτοῦ*) 1241 ‖ *omit* syr[s]

1 Lk 22.24   **2-3** Mt 19.14; Mk 10.15; Lk 18.17   **4** Mt 20.26–27; Mk 10.43–44; Lk 22.26   **5** Mt 10.40; Lk 10.16; Jn 13.20

When Peter went into the house, Jesus spoke up first: "Simon, what is your opinion? Who pays duties or taxes to the kings of this world? The citizens of the country or the foreigners?" 26 "The foreigners," answered Peter. "Well, then," replied Jesus, "that means that the citizens don't have to pay. 27 But we don't want to offend these people. So go to the lake and drop in a line; pull up the first fish you hook, and in its mouth you will find a coin worth enough for my Temple tax and yours; take it and pay them our taxes."

Who Is the Greatest?
(Also Mark 9.33–37; Luke 9.46–48)

18 At that moment the disciples came to Jesus, asking, "Who is the greatest in the Kingdom of heaven?" 2 Jesus called a child, had him stand in front of them, 3 and said: "Remember this! Unless you change and become like children, you will never enter the Kingdom of heaven. 4 The greatest in the Kingdom of heaven is the one who humbles himself and becomes like this child. 5 And the person who welcomes in my name one such child as this, welcomes me."

Temptations to Sin
(Also Mark 9.42–48; Luke 17.1–2)

6 "As for these little ones who believe in me — it would be better for a man to have a large millstone tied around his neck and be drowned in the deep sea, than for him to cause one of them to

turn away from me. [7] How terrible for the world that there are things that make people turn away! Such things will always happen — but how terrible for the one who causes them!

[8] "If your hand or your foot makes you turn away, cut it off and throw it away! It is better for you to enter life without a hand or foot than to keep both hands and feet and be thrown into the eternal fire. [9] And if your eye makes you turn away, take it out and throw it away! It is better for you to enter life with only one eye than to keep both eyes and be thrown into the fire of hell."

The Parable of the Lost Sheep
(Also Luke 15.3–7)

[10] "See that you don't despise any of these little ones. Their angels in heaven, I tell you, are always in the presence of my Father in heaven. [[11] For the Son of Man came to save the lost.]

[12] "What do you think? What will a man do who has one hundred sheep and one of them gets lost? He will leave the other ninety-nine grazing on the hillside and go to look for the lost sheep. [13] When he finds it, I tell you, he feels far happier

πελάγει τῆς θαλάσσης. 7 οὐαὶ τῷ κόσμῳ ἀπὸ τῶν σκανδάλων· ἀνάγκη γὰρ ἐλθεῖν τὰ σκάνδαλα, πλὴν οὐαὶ τῷ ἀνθρώπῳ[1] δι' οὗ τὸ σκάνδαλον ἔρχεται. 8 Εἰ δὲ ἡ χείρ σου ἢ ὁ πούς σου σκανδαλίζει σε, ἔκκοψον αὐτὸν καὶ βάλε ἀπὸ σοῦ· καλόν σοί ἐστιν εἰσελθεῖν εἰς τὴν ζωὴν κυλλὸν ἢ χωλόν, ἢ δύο χεῖρας ἢ δύο πόδας ἔχοντα βληθῆναι εἰς τὸ πῦρ τὸ αἰώνιον. 9 καὶ εἰ ὁ ὀφθαλμός σου σκανδαλίζει σε, ἔξελε αὐτὸν καὶ βάλε ἀπὸ σοῦ· καλόν σοί ἐστιν μονόφθαλμον εἰς τὴν ζωὴν εἰσελθεῖν, ἢ δύο ὀφθαλμοὺς ἔχοντα βληθῆναι εἰς τὴν γέενναν τοῦ πυρός.

The Parable of the Lost Sheep
(Lk 15.3–7)

10 Ὁρᾶτε μὴ καταφρονήσητε ἑνὸς τῶν μικρῶν τούτων· λέγω γὰρ ὑμῖν ὅτι οἱ ἄγγελοι αὐτῶν ἐν οὐρανοῖς διὰ παντὸς βλέπουσι τὸ πρόσωπον τοῦ πατρός μου τοῦ ἐν οὐρανοῖς.[2] 12 Τί ὑμῖν δοκεῖ; ἐὰν γένηταί τινι ἀνθρώπῳ ἑκατὸν πρόβατα καὶ πλανηθῇ ἓν ἐξ αὐτῶν, οὐχὶ ἀφήσει τὰ ἐνενήκοντα ἐννέα ἐπὶ τὰ ὄρη καὶ πορευθεὶς ζητεῖ τὸ πλανώμενον; 13 καὶ ἐὰν γένηται εὑρεῖν αὐτό, ἀμὴν λέγω

---

[1] 7 {C} οὐαὶ τῷ ἀνθρώπῳ ℵ D L f¹ 892 l¹⁸⁴ itᵃᵘʳ,ᵈ,ᵍˡ vgʷʷ syrᶜ,ˢ,ᵖ,ʰ copˢᵃᵐˢ,ᵇᵒ (Origen) ‖ οὐαὶ τῷ ἀνθρώπῳ ἐκείνῳ B K X Δ Θ Π f¹³ 28 33 565 700 1009 1010 1071 1079 1195 1216 1230 1241 1242 1253 1344 1365 1546 1646 2148 *Byz Lect* itᵃ,ᵇ,ᶜ,ᵉ,f,ff¹,²,ˡ,ⁿ,q vgᶜˡ copˢᵃ arm eth geo Diatessaron Clement Cyprian Adamantius Lucifer Hilary Basil Augustine Cyril John-Damascus ‖ ἐκείνῳ οὐαὶ τῷ ἀνθρώπῳ W

[2] 10 {B} *omit verse 11* ℵ B L* Θ f¹ f¹³ 33 892ᵗˣᵗ itᵉ,ff¹ syrˢ,ᵖᵃˡ copˢᵃ,ᵇᵒ geoᴬ Origen Apostolic Canons Juvencus Eusebius Hilary Jerome ‖ *add verse 11* ἦλθεν γὰρ ὁ υἱὸς τοῦ ἀνθρώπου σῶσαι τὸ ἀπολωλός. (see 9.13; Lk 19.10) D K W X Δ Π 078 28 565 700 1071 1079 1230 1241 1242 1253 1344 1365 1546 1646 2148 2174 *Byz Lect* l¹⁸⁵ᵖᵗ itᵃ,ᵃᵘʳ,ᵇ,ᵈ,f,ff²,ᵍˡ,ˡ,ⁿ,q,ʳˡ vg syrᶜ,ᵖ arm geoˡ,ᴮ Diatessaron Hilary Chrysostom Augustine ‖ 11 ἦλθεν γὰρ ὁ υἱὸς τοῦ ἀνθρώπου ζητῆσαι καὶ σῶσαι τὸ ἀπολωλός. (see 9.13; Lk 19.10) (Lᶜᵐᵍ *omit* καί) 892ᵐᵍ 1009 1010 1195 1216 (l¹⁰,¹²,⁶⁹,⁷⁰,⁸⁰,¹⁸⁵ᵖᵗ,²¹¹,²⁹⁹,³⁰³,³⁷⁴,¹⁶⁴² καί *for* γάρ) l⁹⁵⁰ itᶜ syrʰ copᵇᵒᵐˢˢ eth

8–9 Mt 5.29–30   10 οἱ...αὐτῶν Ac 12.15; He 1.14

ὑμῖν ὅτι χαίρει ἐπ' αὐτῷ μᾶλλον ἢ ἐπὶ τοῖς ἐνενήκοντα ἐννέα τοῖς μὴ πεπλανημένοις. 14 οὕτως οὐκ ἔστιν θέλημα ἔμπροσθεν τοῦ πατρὸς ὑμῶν[3] τοῦ ἐν οὐρανοῖς ἵνα ἀπόληται ἓν τῶν μικρῶν τούτων.

A Brother Who Sins
(Lk 17.3)

15 Ἐὰν δὲ ἁμαρτήσῃ [εἰς σὲ][4] ὁ ἀδελφός σου, ὕπαγε ἔλεγξον αὐτὸν μεταξὺ σοῦ καὶ αὐτοῦ μόνου. ἐάν σου ἀκούσῃ, ἐκέρδησας τὸν ἀδελφόν σου· 16 ἐὰν δὲ μὴ ἀκούσῃ, παράλαβε μετὰ σοῦ ἔτι ἕνα ἢ δύο, ἵνα **ἐπὶ στόματος δύο μαρτύρων ἢ τριῶν σταθῇ πᾶν ῥῆμα·** 17 ἐὰν δὲ παρακούσῃ αὐτῶν, εἰπὲ τῇ ἐκκλησίᾳ· ἐὰν δὲ καὶ τῆς ἐκκλησίας παρακούσῃ, ἔστω σοι ὥσπερ ὁ ἐθνικὸς καὶ ὁ τελώνης.

18 Ἀμὴν λέγω ὑμῖν, ὅσα ἐὰν δήσητε ἐπὶ τῆς γῆς ἔσται δεδεμένα ἐν οὐρανῷ καὶ ὅσα ἐὰν λύσητε ἐπὶ τῆς γῆς ἔσται λελυμένα ἐν οὐρανῷ. 19 Πάλιν λέγω ὑμῖν ὅτι ἐὰν δύο συμφωνήσωσιν ἐξ ὑμῶν ἐπὶ τῆς γῆς περὶ παντὸς πράγματος οὗ ἐὰν αἰτήσωνται, γενήσεται αὐτοῖς παρὰ τοῦ πατρός μου τοῦ ἐν οὐρανοῖς. 20 οὗ γάρ εἰσιν δύο ἢ τρεῖς συνηγμένοι εἰς τὸ ἐμὸν ὄνομα, ἐκεῖ εἰμι ἐν μέσῳ αὐτῶν.

---

[3] **14** {C} ὑμῶν ℵ Dᶜ K L W X Δ Π *f*[1] 28 565ᵛⁱᵈ 1009 1071 1079 1195 1242 1344 1365 1546 2174 *Byz Lect* itᵃ,ᵃᵘʳ,ᵇ,ᶜ,ᵈ,ᵉ,f,ff1,2,g1,h,l,n,q vg syrᶜ,ᵖ,ʰᵐᵍ Augustine ‖ ἡμῶν Dᵍʳ* 1646 2148 Chrysostom ‖ μου B Θ 078 *f*[13] 33 700 892 1010 1216 1230 1241 1253 *l*184,185,855,997,1084,1627 syrˢ,ʰ copˢᵃ,ᵇᵒ arm eth geo Origen ‖ *omit* syrᵖᵃˡ Diatessaron

[4] **15** {C} ἁμαρτήσῃ εἰς σέ D K L X Δ Θ Π 078 *f*[13] 28 565 700 892 1010 (1071 1195 1344 1546 1646 ἁμαρτήσει) 1079 1216 1230 1241 1242* 1253 1365 2174 *Byz l*32,76,150,184,211,950,1231,1564,1642,1663 itᵃ,ᵃᵘʳ,ᵇ,ᶜ,ᵈ,ᵉ,f,ff1,2,g1,h,l,n,q vg syrᶜ,ˢ,ᵖ,ʰ,ᵖᵃˡ copᵇᵒ arm? eth? geo Cyprian Hilary Lucifer Basil³ᐟ⁶ Chrysostom ‖ ἁμάρτῃ εἰς σέ W 33 1009 1242ᶜ 2148 *Lect* arm? eth? Origen ‖ ἁμαρτήσῃ ℵ B *f*[1] copˢᵃ,ᵇᵒᵐˢˢ Origen Basil³ᐟ⁶ Cyril

---

15 Lv 19.17; Lk 17.3   **16** ἐπὶ...ῥῆμα Dt 19.15; Jn 8.17; 2 Cor 13.1; 1 Tm 5.19   **18** Mt 16.19; Jn 20.23   **19** ἐὰν...οὐρανοῖς Mt 7.7; 21.22; Mk 11.24; Jn 15.7; 16.23; Jas 1.5; 1 Jn 3.22; 5.14–15   **20** ἐκεῖ...αὐτῶν Mt 28.20; Jn 14.23

over this one sheep than over the ninety-nine that did not get lost. [14] In just the same way your Father[1] in heaven does not want any of these little ones to be lost."

A Brother Who Sins

[15] "If your brother sins against you,[2] go to him and show him his fault. But do it privately, just between yourselves. If he listens to you, you have won your brother back. [16] But if he will not listen to you, take one or two other persons with you, so that 'every accusation may be upheld by the testimony of two or three witnesses,' as the scripture says. [17] But if he will not listen to them, then tell the whole thing to the church. And then, if he will not listen to the church, treat him as though he were a foreigner or a tax collector."

Prohibiting and Permitting

[18] "And so I tell all of you: what you prohibit on earth will be prohibited in heaven; what you permit on earth will be permitted in heaven.

[19] "And I tell you more: whenever two of you on earth agree about anything you pray for, it will be done for you by my Father in heaven. [20] For where two or three come together in my name, I am there with them."

---

[1] **14** your Father: *some mss. read* my Father
[2] **15** *Some mss. omit* against you

The Parable of the Unforgiving Servant

²¹ Then Peter came to Jesus and asked, "Lord, how many times can my brother sin against me and I have to forgive him? Seven times?" ²² "No, not seven times," answered Jesus, "but seventy times seven. ²³ Because the Kingdom of heaven is like a king who decided to check on his servants' accounts. ²⁴ He had just begun to do so when one of them was brought in who owed him millions of dollars. ²⁵ He did not have enough to pay his debt, so his master ordered him to be sold as a slave, with his wife and his children and all that he had, in order to pay the debt. ²⁶ The servant fell on his knees before his master. 'Be patient with me,' he begged, 'and I will pay you everything!' ²⁷ The master felt sorry for him, so he forgave him the debt and let him go.

²⁸ "The man went out and met one of his fellow servants who owed him a few dollars. He grabbed him and started choking him. 'Pay back what you owe me!' he said. ²⁹ His fellow servant fell down and begged him, 'Be patient with me and I will pay you back!' ³⁰ But he would not; instead, he had him thrown into jail until he should pay the debt. ³¹ When the other servants saw what had happened, they were very upset, and went to their master and told him everything. ³² So the master called the servant in. 'You worthless slave!' he said. 'I

The Parable of the Unforgiving Servant

21 Τότε προσελθὼν ὁ Πέτρος εἶπεν αὐτῷ[5], Κύριε, ποσάκις ἁμαρτήσει εἰς ἐμὲ ὁ ἀδελφός μου καὶ ἀφήσω αὐτῷ; ἕως ἑπτάκις; **22** λέγει αὐτῷ ὁ Ἰησοῦς, Οὐ λέγω σοι ἕως ἑπτάκις ἀλλὰ ἕως ἑβδομηκοντάκις ἑπτά. **23** Διὰ τοῦτο ὡμοιώθη ἡ βασιλεία τῶν οὐρανῶν ἀνθρώπῳ βασιλεῖ ὃς ἠθέλησεν συνᾶραι λόγον μετὰ τῶν δούλων αὐτοῦ. **24** ἀρξαμένου δὲ αὐτοῦ συναίρειν προσηνέχθη αὐτῷ εἷς ὀφειλέτης μυρίων ταλάντων. **25** μὴ ἔχοντος δὲ αὐτοῦ ἀποδοῦναι ἐκέλευσεν αὐτὸν ὁ κύριος πραθῆναι καὶ τὴν γυναῖκα καὶ τὰ τέκνα καὶ πάντα ὅσα ἔχει, καὶ ἀποδοθῆναι. **26** πεσὼν οὖν ὁ δοῦλος προσεκύνει αὐτῷ λέγων[6], Μακροθύμησον ἐπ᾽ ἐμοί, καὶ πάντα ἀποδώσω σοι. **27** σπλαγχνισθεὶς δὲ ὁ κύριος τοῦ δούλου ἐκείνου ἀπέλυσεν αὐτόν, καὶ τὸ δάνειον ἀφῆκεν αὐτῷ. **28** ἐξελθὼν δὲ ὁ δοῦλος ἐκεῖνος εὗρεν ἕνα τῶν συνδούλων αὐτοῦ ὃς ὤφειλεν αὐτῷ ἑκατὸν δηνάρια, καὶ κρατήσας αὐτὸν ἔπνιγεν λέγων, Ἀπόδος εἴ τι ὀφείλεις. **29** πεσὼν οὖν ὁ σύνδουλος αὐτοῦ παρεκάλει αὐτὸν λέγων, Μακροθύμησον ἐπ᾽ ἐμοί, καὶ ἀποδώσω σοι. **30** ὁ δὲ οὐκ ἤθελεν, ἀλλὰ ἀπελθὼν ἔβαλεν αὐτὸν εἰς φυλακὴν ἕως ἀποδῷ τὸ ὀφειλόμενον. **31** ἰδόντες οὖν οἱ σύνδουλοι αὐτοῦ τὰ γενόμενα ἐλυπήθησαν σφόδρα, καὶ ἐλθόντες διεσάφησαν τῷ κυρίῳ ἑαυτῶν πάντα τὰ γενόμενα. **32** τότε προσκαλεσάμενος αὐτὸν ὁ κύριος αὐτοῦ λέγει

---

[5] **21** {C} ὁ Πέτρος εἶπεν αὐτῷ B (D *omit* ὁ) 892 *Lect* itᵈ (syrᶜ) (geoᴮ εἶπεν τῷ Ἰησοῦ) Origen ∥ αὐτῷ ὁ Πέτρος εἶπεν ℵᶜ K L W X Δ Θ Π f¹ f¹³ 28 33 565 700 1009 1010 1071 1079 1195 1216 1230 1241 1242 1253 1344 1365 1546 1646 2148 2174 *Byz* l⁷⁶,³³³,⁸⁵⁰ itᵃᵘʳ,ᵉ,ˡ,q vg syrᵖ,ʰ arm geo¹,ᴬ Lucifer Chrysostom ∥ αὐτῷ ὁ Πέτρος εἶπεν αὐτῷ itᵃ,ᵇ,ᶜ,f,ff¹,²,g¹,ʰ copˢᵃ,ᵇᵒ eth? ∥ ὁ Πέτρος εἶπεν ℵ* syrˢ John-Damascus

[6] **26** {B} λέγων B D Θ 700 l⁴⁷*,⁷⁶,¹⁸⁴ itᵃ,ᶜ,ᵈ,ᵉ,ff¹,ˡ vg syrᶜ,ˢ arm geo Diatessaronⁱ,ˢ Origen Lucifer Chrysostom ∥ λέγων, Κύριε ℵ K L W Δ Π 058 f¹ f¹³ 28 33 565 892 1009 1010 1071 1079 1195 1216 1230 1241 1242 1253 1344 1365 1546 1646 2148 2174 *Byz Lect* itᵃᵘʳ,(ᵇ),f,ff²,g¹,(ʰ),q,(ʳˡ) syrᵖ,ʰ,ᵖᵃˡ copˢᵃ,ᵇᵒ ethʳᵒ,ᵖᵖ,(ᵐˢ) John-Damascus

---

21-22 ποσάκις...ἑπτά Lk 17.3-4   **27** Lk 7.42

αὐτῷ, Δοῦλε πονηρέ, πᾶσαν τὴν ὀφειλὴν ἐκείνην ἀφῆκά σοι, ἐπεὶ παρεκάλεσάς με· 33 οὐκ ἔδει καὶ σὲ ἐλεῆσαι τὸν σύνδουλόν σου, ὡς κἀγὼ σὲ ἠλέησα; 34 καὶ ὀργισθεὶς ὁ κύριος αὐτοῦ παρέδωκεν αὐτὸν τοῖς βασανισταῖς ἕως οὗ ἀποδῷ πᾶν τὸ ὀφειλόμενον[7]. 35 Οὕτως καὶ ὁ πατήρ μου ὁ οὐράνιος ποιήσει ὑμῖν ἐὰν μὴ ἀφῆτε ἕκαστος τῷ ἀδελφῷ αὐτοῦ ἀπὸ τῶν καρδιῶν ὑμῶν.

Teaching about Divorce
(Mk 10.1–12)

19 Καὶ ἐγένετο ὅτε ἐτέλεσεν ὁ Ἰησοῦς τοὺς λόγους τούτους, μετῆρεν ἀπὸ τῆς Γαλιλαίας καὶ ἦλθεν εἰς τὰ ὅρια τῆς Ἰουδαίας πέραν τοῦ Ἰορδάνου. 2 καὶ ἠκολούθησαν αὐτῷ ὄχλοι πολλοί, καὶ ἐθεράπευσεν αὐτοὺς ἐκεῖ.

3 Καὶ προσῆλθον αὐτῷ Φαρισαῖοι[1] πειράζοντες αὐτὸν καὶ λέγοντες, Εἰ ἔξεστιν ἀνθρώπῳ[2] ἀπολῦσαι τὴν γυναῖκα αὐτοῦ κατὰ πᾶσαν αἰτίαν; 4 ὁ δὲ ἀποκριθεὶς εἶπεν, Οὐκ ἀνέγνωτε ὅτι ὁ κτίσας[3] ἀπ᾽ ἀρχῆς **ἄρσεν καὶ θῆλυ ἐποίησεν**

[7] **34** {C} τὸ ὀφειλόμενον אᵃ B D K Θ f¹³ 700 2148 l⁸⁰⁵ itᵃ·ᵃᵘʳ·ᵇ·ᶜ·ᵈ·ᵉ·ᶠ· ᶠᶠ¹·²·ᵍ¹·ʰ·¹·q vg syrᶜ·ˢ copˢᵃ·ᵇᵒ arm Diatessaronᵃ·ⁱ·¹ ‖ τὸ ὀφειλόμενον αὐτῷ א*·ᵇ C L W Δ Π f¹ 28 33 565 892 1009 1010 1071 1079 1195 1216 1230 1241 1242 1253 1344 1365 1546 1646 2174 *Byz Lect* syrᵖ·ʰ·ᵖᵃˡ eth John-Damascus

[1] **3** {C} Φαρισαῖοι (see Mk 10.2) 𝔓²⁵ᵛⁱᵈ B C L W Δ Θ Π f¹ f¹³ 33 565 700 892 1010 1079 1195* 1546 copˢᵃᵐˢ·ᵇᵒ John-Damascus ‖ οἱ Φαρισαῖοι א D K 28 1009 1071 1195ᶜ 1216 1230 1241 1242 1253 1344 1365 1646 2148 2174 *Byz Lect* copˢᵃ arm Diatessaron Origen Gregory-Nazianzus

[2] **3** {C} ἔξεστιν ἀνθρώπῳ אᶜ C D K W Δ Θ Π 087 f¹ f¹³ 33 (565 *add* τινι) 892 1009 1010 1071 1079 1195 1216 1230 1241 1242 1253 1344 1365 1546 1646 2148 2174 *Byz Lect* (l⁸⁷¹ ethᵐˢ ἄνθρωπον) itᵃ·ᵃᵘʳ·ᵇ·ᶜ·ᵈ·ᵉ·ᶠ·ᶠᶠ¹·²·ᵍ¹·ʰ·¹·q vg syrᶜ·ˢ· ᵖ·ʰ·ᵖᵃˡ copˢᵃ·ᵇᵒ ethᵖᵖ⁷ geo¹·²⁷ Diatessaronᵉˢʸʳ Origen Hilary Gregory-Nazianzus John-Damascus ‖ ἔξεστιν א* B L 28 (700 *add* τινι) ethʳᵒ Clement Augustine ‖ ἔξεστιν ἀνδρί (see Mk 10.2) 4 273 998 1224 ethᵖᵖ⁷ geo²⁷ ‖ ἔξεστίν τινι ἀνδρί arm

[3] **4** {B} κτίσας (see Mk 10.6) B Θ f¹ 700 syrᵖᵃˡ copˢᵃ·⁽ᵇᵒ⁾ arm ethᵖᵖ·ᵐˢ geo Origen Methodius Ps-Clement Athanasius Titus-Bostra ‖ ποιήσας

34 παρέδωκεν...ὀφειλόμενον Mt 5.25–26; Lk 12.58–59   **35** Mt 6.15; Mk 11.25; Eph 4.32; Col 3.13

19 1 Καί...τούτους Mt 7.28; 11.1; 13.53; 26.1   **3** Καί...αὐτόν Mt 16.1   **4** ἄρσεν... αὐτούς Gn 1.27; 5.2

---

forgave you the whole amount you owed me, just because you asked me to. 33 You should have had mercy on your fellow servant, just as I had mercy on you.' 34 The master was very angry, and he sent the servant to jail to be punished until he should pay back the whole amount." 35 And Jesus concluded, "That is how my Father in heaven will treat you if you do not forgive your brother, every one of you, from your heart."

Jesus Teaches about Divorce
(Also Mark 10.1–12)

19 When Jesus finished saying these things, he left Galilee and went back to the territory of Judea, on the other side of the Jordan river. 2 Large crowds followed him, and he healed them there.

3 Some Pharisees came to him and tried to trap him by asking, "Does our Law allow a man to divorce his wife for any and every reason?" 4 Jesus answered: "Haven't you read this scripture? 'In the beginning the Creator made

them male and female, ⁵ and said, "For this reason a man will leave his father and mother and unite with his wife, and the two will become one." ' ⁶ So they are no longer two, but one. Man must not separate, then, what God has joined together." ⁷ The Pharisees asked him, "Why, then, did Moses give the commandment for a man to give his wife a divorce notice and send her away?" ⁸ Jesus answered: "Moses gave you permission to divorce your wives because you are so hard to teach. But it was not this way at the time of creation. ⁹ I tell you, then, that any man who divorces his wife, and she has not been unfaithful, commits adultery if he marries some other woman."

¹⁰ His disciples said to him, "If this is

αὐτούς;ᵃ 5 καὶ εἶπεν, Ἕνεκα τούτου καταλείψει ἄνθρωπος τὸν πατέρα καὶ τὴν μητέρα καὶ κολληθήσεται τῇ γυναικὶ αὐτοῦ, καὶ ἔσονται οἱ δύο εἰς σάρκα μίαν.ᵃ 6 ὥστε οὐκέτι εἰσὶν δύο ἀλλὰ σὰρξ μία. ὃ οὖν ὁ θεὸς συνέζευξεν ἄνθρωπος μὴ χωριζέτω. 7 λέγουσιν αὐτῷ, Τί οὖν Μωϋσῆς ἐνετείλατο **δοῦναι βιβλίον ἀποστασίου καὶ ἀπολῦσαι [αὐτήν]**⁴; 8 λέγει αὐτοῖς ὅτιᵇ Μωϋσῆς πρὸς τὴν σκληροκαρδίαν ὑμῶν ἐπέτρεψεν ὑμῖν ἀπολῦσαι τὰς γυναῖκας ὑμῶν, ἀπ' ἀρχῆς δὲ οὐ γέγονεν οὕτως. 9 λέγω δὲ ὑμῖν ὅτι ὃς ἂν ἀπολύσῃ τὴν γυναῖκα αὐτοῦ μὴ ἐπὶ πορνείᾳ καὶ γαμήσῃ ἄλλην⁵ μοιχᾶται⁶. 10 λέγουσιν αὐτῷ οἱ

א C D K (L *omit* ὁ *and read* ἐποίησας) W Δ Π *f*¹³ 28 565 892 1009 1010 1071 1079 1195 1216 1230 1241 1242 1253 1344 1365 1546 1646 2148 2174 *Byz Lect* itᵃ,ᵃᵘʳ,ᵇ,ᶜ,ᵈ,(ᵉ),f,ff¹,²,g¹,h,l,q vg syrᶜ,ˢ,ᵖ,ʰ Diatessaron Origenˡᵃᵗ Ambrosiaster Apostolic Constitutions Gregory-Nazianzus Chrysostom Augustine John-Damascus ∥ *omit, and add* the Lord *after* αὐτούς ethʳᵒ

⁴ **7** {C} ἀπολῦσαι αὐτήν B C K W Δ Π 078 *f*¹³ 28 33 565 892 1009 1010 1071 1079 1195 1216 1230 1241 1242 1253 1344 1365 1546 1646 2148 2174 *Byz Lect* itf,q syrᵖ,ʰ cop(ˢᵃ),(ᵇᵒ),ᵇᵒᵐˢ ethᵖᵖ,ᵐˢ John-Damascus ∥ ἀπολῦσαι τὴν γυναῖκα *l*⁵ᵐᵍ itᵇ,ᶜ,ff² syrᶜ,ˢ Irenaeusˡᵃᵗ Ambrose ∥ ἀπολῦσαι א D L Θ *f*¹ 700 itᵃ,ᵃᵘʳ, d,e,ff¹,g¹,h,l vg syrᵖᵃˡ arm ethʳᵒ geo Diatessaron Origen Augustine Ps-Chrysostom

⁵ **9** {B} μὴ ἐπὶ πορνείᾳ καὶ γαμήσῃ ἄλλην (*see footnote 6*) א C³ K L (W *omit* καί) Δ Θ Π 078 565 700 892 1010 1071 1079 1195 1230 1241 1242 1253 1344 1365 1546 1646 2174 (28 1009 2148 *l*²²⁶,⁸⁰⁵,⁸⁵⁴,⁸⁷¹ γαμήσει) *Byz Lect* (*l*²²⁶ πορνείας, *l*¹⁶⁶³ πορνείαν) itˡ vg syrˢ,ᵖ,ʰ arm ethᵐˢ? geo ∥ παρεκτὸς λόγου πορνείας ποιεῖ αὐτὴν μοιχευθῆναι (*see* 5.32) 𝔓²⁵ᵛⁱᵈ? B *f*¹ *l*⁵⁴⁷ itff¹ copᵇᵒ Origen Cyril ∥ παρεκτὸς λόγου πορνείας καὶ γαμήσῃ ἄλλην (*see* 5.32) D *f*¹³ 33 itᵃ,ᵃᵘʳ,ᵇ,ᶜ,ᵈ,ᵉ,f,ff²,g¹,h,q,rl syrᶜ copˢᵃ ethʳᵒ?ᵖᵖ? ∥ καὶ γαμήσῃ ἄλλην (*see* Mk 10.11) 1574 ∥ μὴ ἐπὶ πορνείᾳ καὶ γαμήσῃ ἄλλην, ποιεῖ αὐτὴν μοιχευθῆναι C* 1216 ∥ παρεκτὸς λόγου πορνείας καὶ γαμήσῃ ἄλλην, ποιεῖ αὐτὴν μοιχευθῆναι (*see* 5.32) syrᵖᵃˡ

⁶ **9** {B} μοιχᾶται (*see footnote 5*) א C³ D L 1241 1546 *l*³⁰⁵,⁸⁴⁵ itᵃ,ᵇ,ᵈ,ᵉ,ff²,

ᵃ ᵃ **4—5** *a* question, *a* statement: Nes BF² NEB TT ∥ *a* minor, *a* question: TR (WH) (Bov) AV RV ASV RSV (Zür) (Luth) Jer (Seg)

ᵇ **8** *b* direct: TR? WH AV RV ASV RSV NEB Zür Luth Jer ∥ *b* causal: TR? Bov Nes BF² TT Seg?

5 Ἕνεκα...μίαν Gn 2.24 (Eph 5.31)   ἔσονται...μίαν (1 Cor 6.16)   **7** δοῦναι...αὐτήν Dt 24.1; Mt 5.31   **9** Mt 5.32; 1 Cor 7.10—11 μαθηταὶ [αὐτοῦ][7], Εἰ οὕτως ἐστὶν ἡ αἰτία τοῦ ἀνθρώπου μετὰ τῆς γυναικός, οὐ συμφέρει γαμῆσαι. **11** ὁ δὲ εἶπεν αὐτοῖς, Οὐ πάντες χωροῦσιν τὸν λόγον [τοῦτον][8], ἀλλ' οἷς δέδοται. **12** εἰσὶν γὰρ εὐνοῦχοι οἵτινες ἐκ κοιλίας μητρὸς ἐγεννήθησαν οὕτως, καὶ εἰσὶν εὐνοῦχοι οἵτινες εὐνουχίσθησαν ὑπὸ τῶν ἀνθρώπων, καὶ εἰσὶν εὐνοῦχοι οἵτινες εὐνούχισαν ἑαυτοὺς διὰ τὴν βασιλείαν τῶν οὐρανῶν. ὁ δυνάμενος χωρεῖν χωρείτω.

Little Children Blessed
(Mk 10.13–16; Lk 18.15–17)

13 Τότε προσηνέχθησαν αὐτῷ παιδία, ἵνα τὰς χεῖρας ἐπιθῇ αὐτοῖς καὶ προσεύξηται· οἱ δὲ μαθηταὶ ἐπετίμησαν αὐτοῖς. **14** ὁ δὲ Ἰησοῦς εἶπεν, Ἄφετε τὰ παιδία καὶ μὴ κωλύετε αὐτὰ ἐλθεῖν πρός με, τῶν γὰρ τοιούτων ἐστὶν ἡ βασιλεία τῶν οὐρανῶν. **15** καὶ ἐπιθεὶς τὰς χεῖρας αὐτοῖς ἐπορεύθη ἐκεῖθεν.

the way it is between a man and his wife, it is better not to marry." [11] Jesus answered: "This teaching does not apply to everyone, but only to those to whom God has given it. [12] For there are different reasons why men cannot marry: some, because they were born that way; others, because men made them that way; and others do not marry because of the Kingdom of heaven. Let him who can do it accept this teaching."

Jesus Blesses Little Children
(Also Mark 10.13–16; Luke 18.15–17)

[13] Some people brought children to Jesus for him to place his hands on them and pray, but the disciples scolded those people. [14] Jesus said, "Let the children come to me, and do not stop them, because the Kingdom of heaven belongs to such as these." [15] He placed his hands on them and left.

---

g[l,h,l,r] syr[c,s] cop[sa] Origen Chrysostom ‖ μοιχᾶται καὶ ὁ ἀπολελυμένην γαμήσας μοιχᾶται K 28 700 892 1071 1242 1344 1365 1646 2148 2174 *Byz Lect* ‖ μοιχᾶται καὶ ὁ ἀπολελυμένην γαμῶν μοιχᾶται W Δ Θ Π 078 *f*[13] 33 565 1009 1010 1079 1195 1230 1253 *l*[184,547] ‖ μοιχᾶται καὶ ὁ ἀπολελυμένην γαμήσας (or γαμῶν) μοιχᾶται it[aur,c,f,q] vg syr[p,h] arm eth geo ‖ καὶ ὁ ἀπολελυμένην γαμῶν μοιχᾶται (*see* 5.32) (B γαμήσας) C* *f*[1] 1216 syr[pal] cop[bo] ‖ ὡσαύτως καὶ ὁ γαμῶν ἀπολελυμένην μοιχᾶται 𝔭[25]

[7] 10 {C} μαθηταὶ αὐτοῦ 𝔭[25] C D K L W Δ Π 078 *f*[1] *f*[13] 28 33 565 700 892 1009 1010 1071 1079 1195 1216 1230 1241 1242 1253 1344 1365 1546 1646 2148 2174 *Byz Lect* it[a,aur,b,c,d,f,ff2,h,l,q] vg syr[c,s,p,h,pal] cop[sa,bo] arm eth geo Diatessaron ‖ μαθηταί 𝔭[71] ℵ B Θ it[o,ff1,gl] cop[sams] John-Damascus

[8] 11 {C} τὸν λόγον τοῦτον ℵ C D K L W Δ Π 078 *f*[13] 28 33 565 700 892[mg] 1009 1010 1071 1079 1195 1216 1230 1241 1242 1253 1344 1365 1546 1646 2148 2174 *Byz Lect* it[a,aur,b,c,d,f,ff1,2,gl,h,l,q] vg syr[c,s,p,h] cop[sa,bo] arm eth[pp,ms] geo Clement Origen[lat] Ambrose Augustine John-Damascus ‖ τῶν λόγων τούτων Θ ‖ τὸν λόγον B *f*[1] 892[txt] *l*[184] it[e] syr[pal] cop[sams,boms] eth[ro] Origen Cyprian

---

10 οὐ...γαμῆσαι 1 Cor 7.1–2, 7–9   **11** Οὐ...δέδοται 1 Cor 7.7, 9, 17   **14** Ἄφετε... οὐρανῶν Mt 18.2–3

The Rich Young Man
(Also Mark 10.17–31; Luke 18.18–30)

16 Once a man came to Jesus. "Teacher," he asked, "what good thing must I do to receive eternal life?" 17 "Why do you ask me concerning what is good?" answered Jesus. "There is only One who is good. Keep the commandments if you want to enter life." 18 "What commandments?" he asked. Jesus answered: "Do not murder; do not commit adultery; do not steal; do not lie; 19 honor your father and mother; and love your neighbor as yourself." 20 "I have obeyed all these commandments," the young man replied. "What else do I need to do?" 21 Jesus said to him, "If you want to be perfect, go and sell all you have and give the money to the poor, and you will have riches in heaven; then come and follow me." 22 When the young man heard this he went away sad, because he was very rich.

The Rich Young Man
(Mk 10.17–31; Lk 18.18–30)

16 Καὶ ἰδοὺ εἷς προσελθὼν αὐτῷ εἶπεν, Διδάσκαλε[9], τί ἀγαθὸν ποιήσω ἵνα σχῶ ζωὴν αἰώνιον; 17 ὁ δὲ εἶπεν αὐτῷ, Τί με ἐρωτᾷς περὶ τοῦ ἀγαθοῦ; εἷς ἐστιν ὁ ἀγαθός[10]. εἰ δὲ θέλεις εἰς τὴν ζωὴν εἰσελθεῖν, τήρησον τὰς ἐντολάς. 18 λέγει αὐτῷ, Ποίας; ὁ δὲ Ἰησοῦς εἶπεν, Τὸ Οὐ φονεύσεις, Οὐ μοιχεύσεις, Οὐ κλέψεις, Οὐ ψευδομαρτυρήσεις, 19 Τίμα τὸν πατέρα καὶ τὴν μητέρα, καί, Ἀγαπήσεις τὸν πλησίον σου ὡς σεαυτόν. 20 λέγει αὐτῷ ὁ νεανίσκος, Πάντα ταῦτα ἐφύλαξα· τί ἔτι ὑστερῶ; 21 ἔφη αὐτῷ ὁ Ἰησοῦς, Εἰ θέλεις τέλειος εἶναι, ὕπαγε πώλησον σου τὰ ὑπάρχοντα καὶ δὸς τοῖς πτωχοῖς, καὶ ἕξεις θησαυρὸν ἐν οὐρανοῖς, καὶ δεῦρο ἀκολούθει μοι. 22 ἀκούσας δὲ ὁ νεανίσκος τὸν λόγον[11] ἀπῆλθεν λυπούμενος, ἦν γὰρ εχων κτήματα πολλά.

---

[9] **16** {B} διδάσκαλε ℵ B D L f[1] 892[txt] 1010 1365 l[5] it[a,d,e,ff1] cop[bomss] eth[ro,pp] geo[1] Origen Hilary ∥ διδάσκαλε ἀγαθέ (see Mk 10.17; Lk 18.18) C K W Δ Θ f[13] 28 33 565 700 892[mg] 1009 1071 1079 1195 1216 1230 1241 1242 1253 1344 1546 1646 2148 2174 Byz Lect it[aur,b,c,f,ff2,g1,h,l,q,r1] vg syr[c,s,p,h,pal] cop[sa,bomss] arm eth[ms] geo[2] Diatessaron[a,(esyr),i,n] (Irenaeus) Origen Juvencus Basil Cyril-Jerusalem Chrysostom

[10] **17** {B} τί με ἐρωτᾷς περὶ τοῦ ἀγαθοῦ; εἷς ἐστιν ὁ ἀγαθός ℵ (B* omit εἷς) B[2] D L Θ (f[1] 700 omit ὁ) 892[txt] (892[mg] οὐδείς ἐστιν) it[a,d] syr[s,palmss] arm eth[pp] geo Origen ∥ τί με ἐρωτᾷς περὶ τοῦ ἀγαθοῦ; εἷς ἐστιν ὁ ἀγαθός, ὁ θεός it[aur,b,c,(ff1),ff2,l,r1] vg syr[c,palms] cop[bo] geo[Ac] (it[e] Marcion Clement ὁ πατήρ) (Clement Ps-Clement Juvencus ὁ πατήρ μου ὁ ἐν τοῖς οὐρανοῖς) Novatian Jerome ∥ τί με λέγεις ἀγαθόν; οὐδεὶς ἀγαθὸς εἰ μὴ εἷς ὁ θεός (see Mk 10.18; Lk 18.19) C K W Δ f[13] 28 33 565 1009 1010 1071 1079 1195 1216 1230 1241 1242 1253 1344 1365 1546 1646 2148 2174 Byz Lect it[f,q] syr[p,h] cop[sa,boms] eth[ms] Diatessaron[esyr] Irenaeus Origen Hilary Chrysostom ∥ τί με ἐρωτᾷς περὶ τοῦ ἀγαθοῦ; οὐδεὶς ἀγαθὸς εἰ μὴ εἷς ὁ θεός (cf 892[mg] above) it[g1,h] eth[ro] Dionysius Eusebius Antiochus

[11] **22** {C} τὸν λόγον C D K W X Δ Θ f[1] f[13] 28 (33) 565 700 892* 1009

---

16 Διδάσκαλε...αἰώνιον Mt 19.29; Lk 10.25   **17** τήρησον τὰς ἐντολάς Lv 18.5; Lk 10.28   **18-19** Οὐ φονεύσεις...μητέρα Ex 20.12-16; Dt 5.16-20 (Ro 13.9)   **19** Ἀγαπήσεις...σεαυτόν Lv 19.18 (Mt 5.43; 22.39; Lk 10.27; Ro 13.9)   **21** πώλησον...πτωχοῖς Mk 14.5; Lk 12.33; Jn 12.5; Ac 2.45; 4.34-37   ἕξεις...οὐρανοῖς Mt 6.20   **22** ἀπῆλθεν...πολλά Ps 62.10

23 Ὁ δὲ Ἰησοῦς εἶπεν τοῖς μαθηταῖς αὐτοῦ, Ἀμὴν λέγω ὑμῖν ὅτι πλούσιος δυσκόλως εἰσελεύσεται εἰς τὴν βασιλείαν τῶν οὐρανῶν. 24 πάλιν δὲ λέγω ὑμῖν, εὐκοπώτερόν ἐστιν κάμηλον διὰ τρυπήματος ῥαφίδος διελθεῖν ἢ πλούσιον εἰσελθεῖν εἰς τὴν βασιλείαν τοῦ θεοῦ. 25 ἀκούσαντες δὲ οἱ μαθηταί[12] ἐξεπλήσσοντο σφόδρα λέγοντες, Τίς ἄρα δύναται σωθῆναι; 26 ἐμβλέψας δὲ ὁ Ἰησοῦς εἶπεν αὐτοῖς, Παρὰ ἀνθρώποις τοῦτο ἀδύνατόν ἐστιν, παρὰ δὲ θεῷ πάντα δυνατά. 27 Τότε ἀποκριθεὶς ὁ Πέτρος εἶπεν αὐτῷ, Ἰδοὺ ἡμεῖς ἀφήκαμεν πάντα καὶ ἠκολουθήσαμέν σοι· τί ἄρα ἔσται ἡμῖν; 28 ὁ δὲ Ἰησοῦς εἶπεν αὐτοῖς, Ἀμὴν λέγω ὑμῖν ὅτι ὑμεῖς οἱ ἀκολουθήσαντές μοι,[c] ἐν τῇ παλιγγενεσίᾳ, ὅταν καθίσῃ ὁ υἱὸς τοῦ ἀνθρώπου ἐπὶ θρόνου δόξης αὐτοῦ, καθήσεσθε καὶ ὑμεῖς ἐπὶ δώδεκα θρόνους κρίνοντες τὰς δώδεκα φυλὰς τοῦ Ἰσραήλ. 29 καὶ πᾶς ὅστις ἀφῆκεν οἰκίας ἢ ἀδελφοὺς ἢ ἀδελφὰς ἢ πατέρα ἢ μητέρα[13] ἢ τέκνα ἢ ἀγροὺς ἕνεκεν τοῦ ὀνόματός μου ἑκατονταπλασίονα[14] λήμψεται καὶ ζωὴν αἰώνιον κληρονο-

23 Jesus then said to his disciples: "It will be very hard, I tell you, for a rich man to enter the Kingdom of heaven. 24 I tell you something else: it is much harder for a rich man to enter the Kingdom of God than for a camel to go through the eye of a needle." 25 When the disciples heard this they were completely amazed. "Who can be saved, then?" they asked. 26 Jesus looked straight at them and answered, "This is impossible for men; but for God everything is possible."

27 Then Peter spoke up. "Look," he said, "we have left everything and followed you. What will we have?" 28 Jesus said to them: "I tell you this: when the Son of Man sits on his glorious throne in the New Age, then you twelve followers of mine will also sit on thrones, to judge the twelve tribes of Israel. 29 And every one who has left houses or brothers or sisters or father or mother or children or fields for my sake, will receive a hundred times more, and will

be given eternal life. ³⁰ But many who now are first will be last, and many who now are last will be first.''

The Workers in the Vineyard

20 "The Kingdom of heaven is like the owner of a vineyard who went out early in the morning to hire some men to work in his vineyard. ² He agreed to pay them the regular wage, a silver coin a day, and sent them to work in his vineyard. ³ He went out again to the market place at nine o'clock and saw some men standing there doing nothing, ⁴ so he told them, 'You also go to work in the vineyard, and I will pay you a fair wage.' ⁵ So they went. Then at twelve o'clock and again at three o'clock he did the same thing. ⁶ It was nearly five o'clock when he went to the market place and saw some other men still standing there. 'Why are you wasting the whole day here doing nothing?' he asked them. ⁷ 'It is because no one hired us,' they answered. 'Well, then, you also go to work in the vineyard,' he told them.

⁸ "When evening came, the owner told his foreman, 'Call the workers and pay them their wages, starting with those who were hired last, and ending with those who were hired first.' ⁹ The men who had begun to work at five o'clock were paid a silver coin each. ¹⁰ So when the men who were the first to be hired came to be paid, they thought they would get more — but they too were given a silver coin each. ¹¹ They took their money and started grumbling against the employer. ¹² 'These men who were hired last worked only one hour,' they said, 'while we put up with a whole day's work in the hot sun — yet you paid them the same as you paid us!' ¹³ 'Listen, friend,' the owner answered one of them. 'I have not cheated you. After all, you agreed to do a day's work for a silver coin. ¹⁴ Now, take your pay

μήσει. 30 Πολλοὶ δὲ ἔσονται πρῶτοι ἔσχατοι καὶ ἔσχατοι πρῶτοι.

The Workers in the Vineyard

20 Ὁμοία γάρ ἐστιν ἡ βασιλεία τῶν οὐρανῶν ἀνθρώπῳ οἰκοδεσπότῃ ὅστις ἐξῆλθεν ἅμα πρωῒ μισθώσασθαι ἐργάτας εἰς τὸν ἀμπελῶνα αὐτοῦ. 2 συμφωνήσας δὲ μετὰ τῶν ἐργατῶν ἐκ δηναρίου τὴν ἡμέραν ἀπέστειλεν αὐτοὺς εἰς τὸν ἀμπελῶνα αὐτοῦ. 3 καὶ ἐξελθὼν περὶ τρίτην ὥραν εἶδεν ἄλλους ἑστῶτας ἐν τῇ ἀγορᾷ ἀργούς· 4 καὶ ἐκείνοις εἶπεν, Ὑπάγετε καὶ ὑμεῖς εἰς τὸν ἀμπελῶνα, καὶ ὃ ἐὰν ᾖ δίκαιον δώσω ὑμῖν. 5 οἱ δὲ ἀπῆλθον. πάλιν [δὲ] ἐξελθὼν περὶ ἕκτην καὶ ἐνάτην ὥραν ἐποίησεν ὡσαύτως. 6 περὶ δὲ τὴν ἑνδεκάτην ἐξελθὼν εὗρεν ἄλλους ἑστῶτας, καὶ λέγει αὐτοῖς, Τί ὧδε ἑστήκατε ὅλην τὴν ἡμέραν ἀργοί; 7 λέγουσιν αὐτῷ, Ὅτι οὐδεὶς ἡμᾶς ἐμισθώσατο. λέγει αὐτοῖς, Ὑπάγετε καὶ ὑμεῖς εἰς τὸν ἀμπελῶνα. 8 ὀψίας δὲ γενομένης λέγει ὁ κύριος τοῦ ἀμπελῶνος τῷ ἐπιτρόπῳ αὐτοῦ, Κάλεσον τοὺς ἐργάτας καὶ ἀπόδος αὐτοῖς τὸν μισθὸν ἀρξάμενος ἀπὸ τῶν ἐσχάτων ἕως τῶν πρώτων. 9 καὶ ἐλθόντες οἱ περὶ τὴν ἑνδεκάτην ὥραν ἔλαβον ἀνὰ δηνάριον. 10 καὶ ἐλθόντες οἱ πρῶτοι ἐνόμισαν ὅτι πλεῖον λήμψονται· καὶ ἔλαβον [τὸ] ἀνὰ δηνάριον καὶ αὐτοί. 11 λαβόντες δὲ ἐγόγγυζον κατὰ τοῦ οἰκοδεσπότου 12 λέγοντες, Οὗτοι οἱ ἔσχατοι μίαν ὥραν ἐποίησαν, καὶ ἴσους ἡμῖν αὐτοὺς ἐποίησας τοῖς βαστάσασι τὸ βάρος τῆς ἡμέρας καὶ τὸν καύσωνα. 13 ὁ δὲ ἀποκριθεὶς ἑνὶ αὐτῶν εἶπεν, Ἑταῖρε, οὐκ ἀδικῶ σε· οὐχὶ δηναρίου συνεφώνησάς μοι; 14 ἆρον τὸ σὸν καὶ ὕπαγε· θέλω δὲ τούτῳ τῷ ἐσχάτῳ

W X Δ Θ f¹ f¹³ 28 33 565 700 892 1009 1071 1079 1195 1216 1230 1241 1242 1253 1344 1365 1546 1646 2148 2174 *Byz Lect* itᵃ,ᵃᵘʳ,ᵇ,ᶜ,ᵈ,ᵉ,f,ff¹,²,g¹,ʰ,ˡ,ⁿ,q vg syrᶜ,ˢ,ᵖ,ʰ copᵇᵒ arm ethʳᵒ,ᵖᵖ geo Irenaeusˡᵃᵗ Hilary Basil Chrysostom ∥ ἑπταπλασίονα Ephraem ∥ πολλαπλασίονα (*see* Lk 18.30) B L 1010 syrᵖᵃˡ copˢᵃ ethᵐˢ Diatessaron Origen Cyril

30 Mt 20.16; Lk 13.30
20 1 ἀνθρώπῳ...αὐτοῦ Mt 21.28, 33   2 συμφωνήσας...ἡμέραν Tob 5.15   8 ὀψίας... μισθόν Lv 19.13; Dt 24.15

δοῦναι ὡς καὶ σοί. **15** [ἢ]¹ οὐκ ἔξεστίν μοι ὃ θέλω ποιῆσαι ἐν τοῖς ἐμοῖς; ἢ ὁ ὀφθαλμός σου πονηρός ἐστιν ὅτι ἐγὼ ἀγαθός εἰμι; **16** Οὕτως ἔσονται οἱ ἔσχατοι πρῶτοι καὶ οἱ πρῶτοι ἔσχατοι.

A Third Time Jesus Foretells His Death and Resurrection
(Mk 10.32–34; Lk 18.31–34)

17 Καὶ ἀναβαίνων ὁ Ἰησοῦς² εἰς Ἱεροσόλυμα παρέλαβεν τοὺς δώδεκα [μαθητὰς]³ κατ᾽ ἰδίαν, καὶ ἐν τῇ ὁδῷ⁴ εἶπεν αὐτοῖς, **18** Ἰδοὺ ἀναβαίνομεν εἰς Ἱεροσόλυμα, καὶ ὁ υἱὸς τοῦ ἀνθρώπου παραδοθήσεται τοῖς ἀρχιερεῦσιν καὶ γραμματεῦσιν, καὶ κατακρινοῦσιν αὐτὸν θανάτῳ, **19** καὶ παραδώσουσιν αὐτὸν τοῖς ἔθνεσιν εἰς τὸ ἐμπαῖξαι καὶ μαστιγῶσαι καὶ σταυρῶσαι, καὶ τῇ τρίτῃ ἡμέρᾳ ἐγερθήσεται.

---

¹ **15** {C} ἤ ℵ C K W X Δ Π 085 *f*¹ *f*¹³ 28 33 565 892 1009 1010 1071 1079 1195 1216 1230 1241 1242 1253 1344 1365 1546 1646 2148 2174 *Byz Lect* *l*⁸⁸³ᵐ it^a,aur,b,c,e,(f),ff1,2,g1,h,l,n,q,r1 vg syr^p,h,palmss cop^sa,bo arm geo¹ Chrysostom ∥ *omit* B D L Θ 700 it^d syr^c,s,palms eth? geo²

² **17** {C} καὶ ἀναβαίνων ὁ Ἰησοῦς ℵ C D K L W X Δ Θ Π 085 *f*¹³ 28 33 565 700 892 1009 1010 1071 1079 1195 1216 1230 1241 1242 1253 1344 1365 1546 1646 2148 2174 *Byz Lect* (*l*⁷⁶,³³³,⁸⁸³,⁹⁵⁰,¹⁵⁷⁹ *omit* καὶ) it^aur,b,c,d,e,f,ff1,2,g1,h,l,n,q vg syr^c,s,h arm eth geo Origen Chrysostom ∥ καὶ ἀναβαίνων 13 543 826 828 ∥ μέλλων δὲ ἀναβαίνειν Ἰησοῦς B cop^sa?(bo?) ∥ μέλλων δὲ ὁ Ἰησοῦς ἀναβαίνειν *f*¹ syr^p Origen

³ **17** {C} τοὺς δώδεκα μαθητάς B C K W X Δ Π 085 33 565 700 1009 1071 1079 1195 1230 1241 1242 1253 1344 1365 1546 1646 2148 2174 *Byz* *l*⁷⁶,⁸⁸³ it^b,f,ff2,h,l,q vg syr^h cop^samss geo² Chrysostom ∥ τοὺς δώδεκα μαθητὰς αὐτοῦ 13 28 892^mg 1010 1216 *Lect* (*l*¹⁸⁴ αὐτοῦ μαθητάς) it^a,aur,c,e,ff1,g1,n syr^p cop^samss eth^pp,ms ∥ τοὺς δώδεκα (*see* Mk 10.32; Lk 18.31) ℵ D L Θ *f*¹ *f*¹³ 892^txt it^d syr^c,s cop^bo arm eth^ro geo¹ Origen Hilary

⁴ **17** {B} καὶ ἐν τῇ ὁδῷ ℵ B L Θ 085 *f*¹ *f*¹³ 33 700 892 1010 *l*⁴⁸,¹⁸⁵,²¹¹ cop^sa,(bo) arm geo Origen ∥ ἐν τῇ ὁδῷ καί C D K W X Δ Π 28 565 1009 1071 1079 1195 1216 1230 1241 1242 1253 1344 1365 1546 1646 2148 2174 *Byz Lect* it^(a,c),d,e,f,h,(n),q syr^c,s,p,h eth^ms Origen Chrysostom ∥ ἐν τῇ ὁδῷ 346 ∥ καί *l*¹⁰ it^aur,b,ff1,2,g1,l vg Hilary

---

15 ὁ...ἐστιν Mt 6.23; Mk 7.22   **16** Mt 19.30; Mk 10.31; Lk 13.30   **18** Mt 16.21; 17.22–23; Lk 9.22   **19** τῇ...ἐγερθήσεται Mt 16.21; 17.23; Lk 9.22; 24.7, 46; Ac 10.40; 1 Cor 15.4

and go home. I want to give this man who was hired last as much as I have given you. ¹⁵ Don't I have the right to do as I wish with my own money? Or are you jealous simply because I am generous?' " ¹⁶ And Jesus added, "So those who are last will be first, and those who are first will be last."

Jesus Speaks a Third Time about His Death
(Also Mark 10.32–34; Luke 18.31–34)

¹⁷ As Jesus was going up to Jerusalem he took the twelve disciples aside and spoke to them privately, as they walked along. ¹⁸ "Listen," he told them, "we are going up to Jerusalem, where the Son of Man will be handed over to the chief priests and the teachers of the Law. They will condemn him to death ¹⁹ and then hand him over to the Gentiles, who will make fun of him, whip him, and nail him to the cross; and on the third day he will be raised to life."

A Mother's Request
(Also Mark 10.35–45)

²⁰ Then the mother of Zebedee's sons came to Jesus with her sons, bowed before him, and asked him for a favor. ²¹ "What do you want?" Jesus asked her. She answered, "Promise that these two sons of mine will sit at your right and your left when you are King." ²² "You don't know what you are asking for," Jesus answered them. "Can you drink the cup that I am about to drink?" "We can," they answered. ²³ "You will indeed drink from my cup," Jesus told them, "but I do not have the right to choose who will sit at my right and my left. These places belong to those for whom my Father has prepared them."

²⁴ When the other ten disciples heard about this they became angry with the two brothers. ²⁵ So Jesus called them all together to him and said: "You know that the rulers of the people have power over them, and the leaders rule over them. ²⁶ This, however, is not the way it shall be among you. If one of you wants to be great, he must be the servant of the rest; ²⁷ and if one of you wants to be first, he must be your slave — ²⁸ like the Son of Man, who did not come to be served, but to serve and to give his life to redeem many people."

Jesus Heals Two Blind Men
(Also Mark 10.46–52; Luke 18.35–43)

²⁹ As they were leaving Jericho a large crowd followed Jesus. ³⁰ Two blind men who were sitting by the road heard that Jesus was passing by, so they began to

The Request of James and John
(Mk 10.35–45)

20 Τότε προσῆλθεν αὐτῷ ἡ μήτηρ τῶν υἱῶν Ζεβεδαίου μετὰ τῶν υἱῶν αὐτῆς προσκυνοῦσα καὶ αἰτοῦσά τι ἀπ' αὐτοῦ. **21** ὁ δὲ εἶπεν αὐτῇ, Τί θέλεις; λέγει αὐτῷ, Εἰπὲ ἵνα καθίσωσιν οὗτοι οἱ δύο υἱοί μου εἷς ἐκ δεξιῶν σου καὶ εἷς ἐξ εὐωνύμων σου ἐν τῇ βασιλείᾳ σου. **22** ἀποκριθεὶς δὲ ὁ Ἰησοῦς εἶπεν, Οὐκ οἴδατε τί αἰτεῖσθε· δύνασθε πιεῖν τὸ ποτήριον ὃ ἐγὼ μέλλω πίνειν; λέγουσιν αὐτῷ, Δυνάμεθα. **23** λέγει αὐτοῖς, Τὸ μὲν ποτήριόν μου πίεσθε, τὸ δὲ καθίσαι ἐκ δεξιῶν μου καὶ ἐξ εὐωνύμων οὐκ ἔστιν ἐμὸν τοῦτο δοῦναι, ἀλλ' οἷς ἡτοίμασται ὑπὸ τοῦ πατρός μου. **24** Καὶ ἀκούσαντες οἱ δέκα ἠγανάκτησαν περὶ τῶν δύο ἀδελφῶν. **25** ὁ δὲ Ἰησοῦς προσκαλεσάμενος αὐτοὺς εἶπεν, Οἴδατε ὅτι οἱ ἄρχοντες τῶν ἐθνῶν κατακυριεύουσιν αὐτῶν καὶ οἱ μεγάλοι κατεξουσιάζουσιν αὐτῶν. **26** οὐχ οὕτως ἔσται⁵ ἐν ὑμῖν· ἀλλ' ὃς ἐὰν θέλῃ ἐν ὑμῖν μέγας γενέσθαι ἔσται ὑμῶν διάκονος, **27** καὶ ὃς ἂν θέλῃ ἐν ὑμῖν εἶναι πρῶτος ἔσται ὑμῶν δοῦλος· **28** ὥσπερ ὁ υἱὸς τοῦ ἀνθρώπου οὐκ ἦλθεν διακονηθῆναι ἀλλὰ διακονῆσαι καὶ δοῦναι τὴν ψυχὴν αὐτοῦ λύτρον ἀντὶ πολλῶν.

The Healing of Two Blind Men
(Mk 10.46–52; Lk 18.35–43)

29 Καὶ ἐκπορευομένων αὐτῶν ἀπὸ Ἰεριχὼ ἠκολούθησεν αὐτῷ ὄχλος πολύς. **30** καὶ ἰδοὺ δύο τυφλοὶ καθήμενοι παρὰ τὴν ὁδόν, ἀκούσαντες ὅτι Ἰησοῦς παράγει, ἔκραξαν

---

⁵ **26** {C} ἔσται א C K L W X Δ Θ Π 085 0197 *f*¹ *f*¹³ 28 565 700 892 1009 1010 1071 1079 1195 1216 1230 1241 1253 1344 1365 1546 1646 2148 2174 *Byz* (*Lect* δὲ ἔσται) it^{a,aur,b,c,e,f,ff1,2,g1,h,l,n,q} vg syr^{c,p,h} cop^{samss,bo} arm eth^{ro,pp} geo² Origen^{lat} Chrysostom John-Damascus ‖ ἐστίν B D 1242 it^d cop^{sa} eth^{ms?} geo¹ Chrysostom

---

21 καθίσωσιν...βασιλείᾳ σου Mt 19.28; Lk 22.30   **22** τὸ...πίνειν Mt 26.39; Jn 18.11 **25–26** Lk 22.25–26   **26** Mt 23.11; Mk 9.35; Lk 9.48   **28** Lk 22.27 ὁ...διακονῆσαι Php 2.7 δοῦναι...πολλῶν 1 Tm 2.6   **29–30** Mt 9.27

λέγοντες, [Κύριε,] ἐλέησον ἡμᾶς[6], υἱὲ Δαυίδ. **31** ὁ δὲ ὄχλος ἐπετίμησεν αὐτοῖς ἵνα σιωπήσωσιν· οἱ δὲ μεῖζον ἔκραξαν λέγοντες, Κύριε, ἐλέησον ἡμᾶς, υἱὲ Δαυίδ. **32** καὶ στὰς ὁ Ἰησοῦς ἐφώνησεν αὐτοὺς καὶ εἶπεν, Τί θέλετε ποιήσω ὑμῖν; **33** λέγουσιν αὐτῷ, Κύριε, ἵνα ἀνοιγῶσιν οἱ ὀφθαλμοὶ ἡμῶν. **34** σπλαγχνισθεὶς δὲ ὁ Ἰησοῦς ἥψατο τῶν ὀμμάτων αὐτῶν, καὶ εὐθέως ἀνέβλεψαν καὶ ἠκολούθησαν αὐτῷ.

The Triumphal Entry into Jerusalem
(Mk 11.1–11; Lk 19.28–38; Jn 12.12–19)

21 Καὶ ὅτε ἤγγισαν εἰς Ἰεροσόλυμα καὶ ἦλθον εἰς Βηθφαγὴ εἰς τὸ Ὄρος τῶν Ἐλαιῶν, τότε Ἰησοῦς ἀπέστειλεν δύο μαθητὰς **2**[a] λέγων αὐτοῖς, [a]Πορεύεσθε εἰς τὴν κώμην τὴν κατέναντι ὑμῶν, καὶ εὐθέως εὑρήσετε ὄνον δεδεμένην καὶ πῶλον μετ' αὐτῆς· λύσαντες ἀγάγετέ μοι. **3** καὶ ἐάν τις ὑμῖν εἴπῃ τι, ἐρεῖτε ὅτι Ὁ κύριος αὐτῶν χρείαν ἔχει·[b] εὐθὺς δὲ ἀποστελεῖ αὐτούς. **4** Τοῦτο δὲ γέγονεν ἵνα πληρωθῇ τὸ ῥηθὲν διὰ τοῦ προφήτου λέγοντος,

5   Εἴπατε τῇ θυγατρὶ Σιών,
    Ἰδοὺ ὁ βασιλεύς σου ἔρχεταί σοι,
    πραῢς καὶ ἐπιβεβηκὼς ἐπὶ ὄνον,
    καὶ ἐπὶ πῶλον υἱὸν ὑποζυγίου.

shout, "Son of David! Have mercy on us, sir!" [31] The crowd scolded them and told them to be quiet. But they shouted even more loudly, "Son of David! Have mercy on us, sir!" [32] Jesus stopped and called them. "What do you want me to do for you?" he asked them. [33] "Sir," they answered, "we want you to open our eyes!" [34] Jesus had pity on them and touched their eyes; at once they were able to see, and followed him.

The Triumphant Entry into Jerusalem
(Also Mark 11.1–11; Luke 19.28–40; John 12.12–19)

21 As they approached Jerusalem, they came to Bethphage, at the Mount of Olives. There Jesus sent two of the disciples on ahead [2] with these instructions: "Go to the village there ahead of you, and at once you will find a donkey tied up and her colt with her. Untie them and bring them to me. [3] And if anyone says anything, tell him, 'The Master[1] needs them'; and he will let them go at once."

[4] This happened to make come true what the prophet had said:

[5] "Tell the city of Zion:
    Now your king is coming to you,
    He is gentle and rides on a donkey,
    He rides on a colt, the foal of a
       donkey."

---

[1] **3** The Master: *or* Their owner

---

[6] **30** {C} κύριε, ἐλέησον ἡμᾶς B 085 it^(aur,gl,l,rl) vg cop^(sa,boms) eth^ro ∥ ἐλέησον ἡμᾶς, κύριε p^(45vid) C K W X Δ Π f¹ 28 33 1009 1010 1071 1079 1195 1216 1230 1241 1242 1253 (1344 omit ἡμᾶς) 1365 1546 1646 2148 2174 *Byz Lect* it^(f,q) syr^(p,h) cop^(sams) eth^pp geo^Ac Origen Ps-Chrysostom John-Damascus ∥ ἐλέησον ἡμᾶς, Ἰησοῦ (see Mk 10.47; Lk 18.38) ℵ Θ f¹³ 700 *l*⁵⁴⁷ it^(c,e,h,n) syr^palms arm geo ∥ ἐλέησον ἡμᾶς D 565 *l*^(76vid) it^(b,d,ff1,2) syr^c eth^ms ∥ κύριε, ἐλέησον ἡμᾶς, Ἰησοῦ L 892 syr^palmss cop^(samss,bo)

[a a] **1-2** *a* number 2, *a* no number: TR^ed WH? Bov Nes BF² AV RV ASV RSV NEB TT Zür Luth Jer Seg ∥ *a* no number, *a* number 2: TR^ed WH?

[b] **3** *b* major: TR WH Bov Nes BF² AV RV ASV (RSV) NEB TT Zür Luth Seg ∥ *b* none: NEB^mg (Jer)

---

30 ἐλέησον...Δαυίδ Mt 15.22   **34** Ἰησοῦς...ἀνέβλεψαν Mt 9.29–30
21 5 Εἴπατε...Ἰδού Is 62.11   Ἰδού...ὑποζυγίου Zch 9.9

[6] So the disciples went ahead and did what Jesus had told them to do: [7] they brought the donkey and the colt, threw their cloaks over them, and Jesus got on. [8] A great crowd of people spread their cloaks on the road, while others cut branches from the trees and spread them on the road. [9] The crowds walking in front of Jesus and the crowds walking behind began to shout, "Praise to David's Son! God bless him who comes in the name of the Lord! Praise be to God!"

[10] When Jesus entered Jerusalem the whole city was thrown in an uproar. "Who is he?" the people asked. [11] "This is the prophet Jesus, from Nazareth of Galilee," the crowds answered.

Jesus Goes to the Temple
(Also Mark 11.15–19; Luke 19.45–48; John 2.13–22)

[12] Jesus went into the Temple and drove out all those who bought and sold in the Temple; he overturned the tables of the money-changers and the stools of those who sold pigeons, [13] and said to them: "It is written in the Scriptures that God said, 'My house will be called a house of prayer.' But you are making it a hideout for thieves!"

[14] The blind and the crippled came to him in the Temple and he healed them. [15] The chief priests and the teachers of the Law became angry when they saw the wonderful things he was doing, and the children shouting and crying in the Temple, "Praise to David's Son!" [16] So they said to Jesus, "Do you hear what

[6] πορευθέντες δὲ οἱ μαθηταὶ καὶ ποιήσαντες καθὼς συνέταξεν αὐτοῖς ὁ Ἰησοῦς [7] ἤγαγον τὴν ὄνον καὶ τὸν πῶλον, καὶ ἐπέθηκαν ἐπ' αὐτῶν τὰ ἱμάτια, καὶ ἐπεκάθισεν ἐπάνω αὐτῶν. [8] ὁ δὲ πλεῖστος ὄχλος ἔστρωσαν ἑαυτῶν τὰ ἱμάτια ἐν τῇ ὁδῷ, ἄλλοι δὲ ἔκοπτον κλάδους ἀπὸ τῶν δένδρων καὶ ἐστρώννυον ἐν τῇ ὁδῷ. [9] οἱ δὲ ὄχλοι οἱ προάγοντες αὐτὸν καὶ οἱ ἀκολουθοῦντες ἔκραζον λέγοντες,

Ὡσαννὰ τῷ υἱῷ Δαυίδ·

Εὐλογημένος ὁ ἐρχόμενος ἐν ὀνόματι κυρίου·
Ὡσαννὰ ἐν τοῖς ὑψίστοις.

[10] καὶ εἰσελθόντος αὐτοῦ εἰς Ἱεροσόλυμα ἐσείσθη πᾶσα ἡ πόλις λέγουσα, Τίς ἐστιν οὗτος; [11] οἱ δὲ ὄχλοι ἔλεγον, Οὗτός ἐστιν ὁ προφήτης Ἰησοῦς ὁ ἀπὸ Ναζαρὲθ τῆς Γαλιλαίας.

The Cleansing of the Temple
(Mk 11.15–19; Lk 19.45–48; Jn 2.13–22)

[12] Καὶ εἰσῆλθεν Ἰησοῦς εἰς τὸ ἱερόν[1], καὶ ἐξέβαλεν πάντας τοὺς πωλοῦντας καὶ ἀγοράζοντας ἐν τῷ ἱερῷ, καὶ τὰς τραπέζας τῶν κολλυβιστῶν κατέστρεψεν καὶ τὰς καθέδρας τῶν πωλούντων τὰς περιστεράς, [13] καὶ λέγει αὐτοῖς, Γέγραπται,

Ὁ οἶκός μου οἶκος προσευχῆς κληθήσεται,
ὑμεῖς δὲ αὐτὸν ποιεῖτε **σπήλαιον λῃστῶν.**

[14] Καὶ προσῆλθον αὐτῷ τυφλοὶ καὶ χωλοὶ ἐν τῷ ἱερῷ, καὶ ἐθεράπευσεν αὐτούς. [15] ἰδόντες δὲ οἱ ἀρχιερεῖς καὶ οἱ γραμματεῖς τὰ θαυμάσια ἃ ἐποίησεν καὶ τοὺς παῖδας τοὺς κράζοντας ἐν τῷ ἱερῷ καὶ λέγοντας, Ὡσαννὰ τῷ υἱῷ Δαυίδ, ἠγανάκτησαν [16] καὶ εἶπαν αὐτῷ, Ἀκούεις τί

---

[1] **12** {B} ἱερόν (see Mk 11.15; Lk 19.45) ℵ B L Θ f[13] 33 700 892 1009 1010 it[b] syr[pal] cop[sa,bo] arm eth geo[1,B] Diatessaron Origen[2/5] Methodius Hilary Chrysostom ‖ ἱερὸν τοῦ θεοῦ C D K W X Δ Π f[1] 28 565 1071 1079 1195 1216 1230 1241 1242 1253 1344 1365 1546 1646 2148 2174 *Byz Lect* it[a,aur,c,d,e,f, ff1,2,g1,h,l,q] vg syr[c,p,h] geo[A] Origen[3/5] Basil Augustine

9 Ὡσαννὰ...Δαυίδ Mt 21.15   Εὐλογημένος...κυρίου Ps 118.26 (Mt 23.39; Lk 13.35)
13 Ὁ...κληθήσεται Is 56.7; (60.7)   σπήλαιον λῃστῶν Jr 7.11   **15** Ὡσαννὰ...Δαυίδ Mt 21.9

οὗτοι λέγουσιν; ὁ δὲ Ἰησοῦς λέγει αὐτοῖς, Ναί· οὐδέποτε ἀνέγνωτε ὅτι **Ἐκ στόματος νηπίων καὶ θηλαζόντων κατηρτίσω αἶνον**; 17 Καὶ καταλιπὼν αὐτοὺς ἐξῆλθεν ἔξω τῆς πόλεως εἰς Βηθανίαν, καὶ ηὐλίσθη ἐκεῖ.

The Cursing of the Fig Tree
(Mk 11.12–14, 20–24)

18 Πρωῒ δὲ ἐπανάγων εἰς τὴν πόλιν ἐπείνασεν. 19 καὶ ἰδὼν συκῆν μίαν ἐπὶ τῆς ὁδοῦ ἦλθεν ἐπ᾽ αὐτήν, καὶ οὐδὲν εὗρεν ἐν αὐτῇ εἰ μὴ φύλλα μόνον, καὶ λέγει αὐτῇ, Μηκέτι ἐκ σοῦ καρπὸς γένηται εἰς τὸν αἰῶνα. καὶ ἐξηράνθη παραχρῆμα ἡ συκῆ. 20 καὶ ἰδόντες οἱ μαθηταὶ ἐθαύμασαν λέγοντες, Πῶς παραχρῆμα ἐξηράνθη ἡ συκῆ; 21 ἀποκριθεὶς δὲ ὁ Ἰησοῦς εἶπεν αὐτοῖς, Ἀμὴν λέγω ὑμῖν, ἐὰν ἔχητε πίστιν καὶ μὴ διακριθῆτε, οὐ μόνον τὸ τῆς συκῆς ποιήσετε, ἀλλὰ κἂν τῷ ὄρει τούτῳ εἴπητε, Ἄρθητι καὶ βλήθητι εἰς τὴν θάλασσαν, γενήσεται· 22 καὶ πάντα ὅσα ἂν αἰτήσητε ἐν τῇ προσευχῇ πιστεύοντες λήμψεσθε.

The Authority of Jesus Questioned
(Mk 11.27–33; Lk 20.1–8)

23 Καὶ ἐλθόντος αὐτοῦ εἰς τὸ ἱερὸν προσῆλθον αὐτῷ διδάσκοντι οἱ ἀρχιερεῖς καὶ οἱ πρεσβύτεροι τοῦ λαοῦ λέγοντες, Ἐν ποίᾳ ἐξουσίᾳ ταῦτα ποιεῖς;ᶜ καὶ τίς σοι ἔδωκεν τὴν ἐξουσίαν ταύτην;ᶜ 24 ἀποκριθεὶς δὲ ὁ Ἰησοῦς εἶπεν αὐτοῖς, Ἐρωτήσω ὑμᾶς κἀγὼ λόγον ἕνα, ὃν ἐὰν εἴπητέ μοι κἀγὼ ὑμῖν ἐρῶ ἐν ποίᾳ ἐξουσίᾳ ταῦτα ποιῶ· 25 τὸ βάπτισμα τὸ Ἰωάννου πόθεν ἦν; ἐξ οὐρανοῦ ἢ ἐξ ἀνθρώπων; οἱ δὲ διελογίζοντο ἐν ἑαυτοῖς λέγοντες, Ἐὰν εἴπωμεν, Ἐξ οὐρανοῦ, ἐρεῖ ἡμῖν, Διὰ τί οὖν οὐκ ἐπιστεύσατε αὐτῷ; 26 ἐὰν δὲ εἴπωμεν, Ἐξ ἀνθρώπων, φοβούμεθα τὸν ὄχλον· πάντες γὰρ ὡς προφήτην ἔχουσιν τὸν

ᶜ ᶜ 23 c question, c question: TR WH Bov Nes BF² AV RV ASV NEB TT Jer ∥ c minor, c question: RSV Zür Luth Seg

16 Ἐκ...αἶνον Ps 8.3 LXX   **19** ἰδὼν...μόνον Lk 13.6   **21** Mt 17.20; Lk 17.6; 1 Cor 13.2   **22** Mt 7.7-11; 18.19; Jn 14.13-14   **25** τὸ βάπτισμα...ἀνθρώπων Jn 1.6, 33   Διὰ...αὐτῷ Mt 21.32; Lk 7.30   **26** φοβούμεθα...Ἰωάννην Mt 14.5; 21.46

---

they are saying?" "Indeed I do," answered Jesus. "Haven't you ever read the scripture that says, 'You have trained children and babies to offer perfect praise'?" 17 Jesus left them and went out of the city to Bethany, where he spent the night.

Jesus Curses the Fig Tree
(Also Mark 11.12–14, 20–24)

18 On his way back to the city, the next morning, Jesus was hungry. 19 He saw a fig tree by the side of the road and went to it, but found nothing on it except leaves. So he said to the tree, "You will never again bear fruit!" At once the fig tree dried up. 20 The disciples saw this and were astounded. "How did the fig tree dry up so quickly?" they asked. 21 "Remember this!" Jesus answered. "If you believe, and do not doubt, you will be able to do what I have done to this fig tree; not only this, you will even be able to say to this hill, 'Get up and throw yourself in the sea,' and it will. 22 If you believe, you will receive whatever you ask for in prayer."

The Question about Jesus' Authority
(Also Mark 11.27–33; Luke 20.1–8)

23 Jesus came back to the Temple; and as he taught, the chief priests and the Jewish elders came to him and asked, "What right do you have to do these things? Who gave you this right?" 24 Jesus answered them: "I will ask you just one question, and if you give me an answer I will tell you what right I have to do these things. 25 Where did John's right to baptize come from: from God or from man?" They started to argue among themselves: "What shall we say? If we answer, 'From God,' he will say to us, 'Why, then, did you not believe John?' 26 But if we say, 'From man,' we are afraid of what the people might do, because they are all convinced

that John was a prophet." 27 So they
answered Jesus, "We do not know."
And he said to them, "Neither will I
tell you, then, by what right I do these
things."

The Parable of the Two Sons

28 "Now, what do you think? There
was a man who had two sons. He went
to the older one and said, 'Son, go work
in the vineyard today.' 29 'I don't want
to,' he answered, but later he changed
his mind and went to the vineyard.
30 Then the father went to the other
son and said the same thing. 'Yes, sir,'
he answered, but he did not go. 31 Which
one of the two did what his father
wanted?" "The older one," they answered. "And I tell you this," Jesus
said to them. "The tax collectors and
the prostitutes are going into the Kingdom of God ahead of you. 32 For John
the Baptist came to you showing you
the right path to take, and you would
not believe him; but the tax collectors
and the prostitutes believed him. Even
when you saw this you did not change
your minds later on and believe him."

Ἰωάννην. **27** καὶ ἀποκριθέντες τῷ Ἰησοῦ εἶπαν, Οὐκ
οἴδαμεν. ἔφη αὐτοῖς καὶ αὐτός, Οὐδὲ ἐγὼ λέγω ὑμῖν ἐν
ποίᾳ ἐξουσίᾳ ταῦτα ποιῶ.

The Parable of the Two Sons

28 Τί δὲ ὑμῖν δοκεῖ; ἄνθρωπος εἶχεν τέκνα δύο. καὶ
προσελθὼν τῷ πρώτῳ εἶπεν, Τέκνον, ὕπαγε σήμερον
ἐργάζου ἐν τῷ ἀμπελῶνι. **29** ὁ δὲ ἀποκριθεὶς εἶπεν, Οὐ
θέλω, ὕστερον δὲ μεταμεληθεὶς ἀπῆλθεν[2]. **30** προσελθὼν δὲ
τῷ ἑτέρῳ[2] εἶπεν ὡσαύτως. ὁ δὲ ἀποκριθεὶς εἶπεν, Ἐγώ,
κύριε· καὶ οὐκ ἀπῆλθεν[2]. **31** τίς ἐκ τῶν δύο ἐποίησεν τὸ
θέλημα τοῦ πατρός; λέγουσιν, Ὁ πρῶτος[2]. λέγει αὐτοῖς
ὁ Ἰησοῦς, Ἀμὴν λέγω ὑμῖν ὅτι οἱ τελῶναι καὶ αἱ πόρναι
προάγουσιν ὑμᾶς εἰς τὴν βασιλείαν τοῦ θεοῦ. **32** ἦλθεν
γὰρ Ἰωάννης πρὸς ὑμᾶς ἐν ὁδῷ δικαιοσύνης, καὶ οὐκ
ἐπιστεύσατε αὐτῷ· οἱ δὲ τελῶναι καὶ αἱ πόρναι ἐπίστευσαν
αὐτῷ· ὑμεῖς δὲ ἰδόντες οὐδὲ μετεμελήθητε ὕστερον τοῦ
πιστεῦσαι αὐτῷ.

---

[2] **29–31** {C} *οὐ θέλω, ὕστερον δὲ μεταμεληθεὶς ἀπῆλθεν...ἑτέρῳ...ἐγώ, κύριε· καὶ οὐκ ἀπῆλθεν...πρῶτος* (א* *omit δέ*) C* K W X Δ Π 0138 565 1010 1071 1079 1195 (1216 *ὑπάγω κύριε*) 1230 1241 1253 1546 *Byz*^{pt} *l*^{63,76,185,211,883,1642} (*l*^{80} *τίς οὖν*) it^{c,f,q} vg syr^{c,p,h} cop$^{sa^{mss}}$ eth$^{ro?pp?}$ Diatessaron^{a,i,n} Irenaeus Origen Eusebius Hilary Cyril // *οὐ θέλω, ὕστερον δὲ μεταμεληθεὶς ἀπῆλθεν...δευτέρῳ...ἐγώ, κύριε. καὶ οὐκ ἀπῆλθεν...πρῶτος* א^{c} C^{2} L *f*^{1} 28 33 892 1009 1242 1344 1365 1646 2148 2174 *Byz*^{pt} *Lect* (*l*^{1127} *τίς οὖν*) syr$^{pal^{ms}}$ eth$^{ro?pp?}$ Chrysostom // *οὐ θέλω, ὕστερον δὲ μεταμεληθεὶς ἀπῆλθεν...ἑτέρῳ...ἐγώ, κύριε. καὶ οὐκ ἀπῆλθεν...ἔσχατος* D it$^{a,aur,b,d,e,ff^{1,2},g^{1},h,l}$ syr^{s} // *ἐγώ, κύριε· καὶ οὐκ ἀπῆλθεν...δευτέρῳ...οὐ θέλω· ὕστερον μεταμεληθεὶς ἀπῆλθεν...ὕστερος* B (700 *ὑπάγω κύριε...ὕστερον δὲ...ἔσχατος*) syr$^{pal^{mss}}$ (cop^{bo}...*ἔσχατος*) eth^{ms} (geo^{2} *ὑπάγω for ἐγώ and insert "I will not go" before ὕστερον*, geo^{A} *πρῶτος for ὕστερος*) Diatessaron Ephraem Isidore Ps-Athanasius // *ὑπάγω καὶ οὐκ ἀπῆλθεν...ἑτέρῳ...οὐ θέλω· ὕστερον δὲ μεταμεληθεὶς ἀπῆλθεν...ἔσχατος* Θ (*f*^{13} geo^{1} *ὑπάγω κύριε καί*) (*l*^{547}) cop$^{sa?}$ // *ἔρχομαι, κύριε, καὶ οὐκ ἀπῆλθεν...ἄλλῳ...οὐ θέλω, ἀλλὰ ὕστερον μεταμεληθεὶς ἀπῆλθεν ἐν τῷ ἀμπελῶνι...ἔσχατος* arm

---

28 *ἄνθρωπος...δύο* Lk 15.11 *ὕπαγε...ἀμπελῶνι* Mt 20.1 **32** *οὐκ...αὐτῷ* Mt 21.25; Lk 7.30 *τελῶναι...ἐπίστευσαν αὐτῷ* Lk 3.12; 7.29 *ὑμεῖς...αὐτῷ* Lk 7.30

The Parable of the Vineyard and the Tenants
(Mk 12.1–12; Lk 20.9–19)

33 Ἄλλην παραβολὴν ἀκούσατε. Ἄνθρωπος ἦν οἰκοδεσπότης ὅστις **ἐφύτευσεν ἀμπελῶνα καὶ φραγμὸν αὐτῷ περιέθηκεν καὶ ὤρυξεν ἐν αὐτῷ ληνὸν καὶ ᾠκοδόμησεν πύργον,** καὶ ἐξέδοτο αὐτὸν γεωργοῖς, καὶ ἀπεδήμησεν. **34** ὅτε δὲ ἤγγισεν ὁ καιρὸς τῶν καρπῶν, ἀπέστειλεν τοὺς δούλους αὐτοῦ πρὸς τοὺς γεωργοὺς λαβεῖν τοὺς καρποὺς αὐτοῦ. **35** καὶ λαβόντες οἱ γεωργοὶ τοὺς δούλους αὐτοῦ ὃν μὲν ἔδειραν, ὃν δὲ ἀπέκτειναν, ὃν δὲ ἐλιθοβόλησαν. **36** πάλιν ἀπέστειλεν ἄλλους δούλους πλείονας τῶν πρώτων, καὶ ἐποίησαν αὐτοῖς ὡσαύτως. **37** ὕστερον δὲ ἀπέστειλεν πρὸς αὐτοὺς τὸν υἱὸν αὐτοῦ λέγων, Ἐντραπήσονται τὸν υἱόν μου. **38** οἱ δὲ γεωργοὶ ἰδόντες τὸν υἱὸν εἶπον ἐν ἑαυτοῖς, Οὗτός ἐστιν ὁ κληρονόμος· δεῦτε ἀποκτείνωμεν αὐτὸν καὶ σχῶμεν τὴν κληρονομίαν αὐτοῦ. **39** καὶ λαβόντες αὐτὸν ἐξέβαλον ἔξω τοῦ ἀμπελῶνος καὶ ἀπέκτειναν[3]. **40** ὅταν οὖν ἔλθῃ ὁ κύριος τοῦ ἀμπελῶνος, τί ποιήσει τοῖς γεωργοῖς ἐκείνοις; **41** λέγουσιν αὐτῷ, Κακοὺς κακῶς ἀπολέσει αὐτούς, καὶ τὸν ἀμπελῶνα ἐκδώσεται ἄλλοις γεωργοῖς, οἵτινες ἀποδώσουσιν αὐτῷ τοὺς καρποὺς ἐν τοῖς καιροῖς αὐτῶν. **42** λέγει αὐτοῖς ὁ Ἰησοῦς, Οὐδέποτε ἀνέγνωτε ἐν ταῖς γραφαῖς,

Λίθον ὃν ἀπεδοκίμασαν οἱ οἰκοδομοῦντες οὗτος ἐγενήθη εἰς κεφαλὴν γωνίας· παρὰ κυρίου ἐγένετο αὕτη, καὶ ἔστιν θαυμαστὴ ἐν ὀφθαλμοῖς ἡμῶν;

[3] **39** {B} αὐτὸν ἐξέβαλον ἔξω τοῦ ἀμπελῶνος καὶ ἀπέκτειναν (ℵ ἔβαλον) B C K L W X Δ Π 0138 *f*[1] *f*[13] 28 33 565 700 892 1009 1010 1071 1079 1195 1216 1230 1241 1242 1253 1365 1546 1646 2148 2174 *Byz Lect* it[aur, f, ff1, g1, l, q] vg cop[sa?bo?] (arm ἐξέβαλον αὐτόν) Irenaeus[lat] ‖ αὐτὸν ἀπέκτειναν καὶ ἐξέβαλον ἔξω τοῦ ἀμπελῶνος D (Θ ἀπέκτειναν αὐτόν) it[a,b,c,d,e,ff2,h,r1] geo Irenaeus Lucifer Juvencus ‖ αὐτὸν ἐξέβαλον αὐτὸν ἔξω τοῦ ἀμπελῶνος καὶ ἀπέκτειναν αὐτόν syr[c,h,palms] (syr[h with *] *omit second* αὐτόν, syr[s,p,palmss] *omit first* αὐτόν) eth

33 ἐφύτευσεν…πύργον Is 5.1-2   **35** λαβόντες…ἀπέκτειναν Mt 22.6   **39** He 13.12
42 Λίθον…γωνίας Ac 4.11; 1 Pe 2.7   Λίθον…ἡμῶν Ps 118.22-23

The Parable of the Tenants in the Vineyard
(Also Mark 12.1–12; Luke 20.9–19)

[33] "Listen to another parable," Jesus said. "There was a landowner who planted a vineyard, put a fence around it, dug a hole for the winepress, and built a tower. Then he rented the vineyard to tenants and left home on a trip. [34] When the time came to harvest the grapes he sent his slaves to the tenants to receive his share. [35] The tenants grabbed his slaves, beat one, killed another, and stoned another. [36] Again the man sent other slaves, more than the first time, and the tenants treated them the same way. [37] Last of all he sent them his son. 'Surely they will respect my son,' he said. [38] But when the tenants saw the son they said to themselves, 'This is the owner's son. Come on, let us kill him, and we will get his property!' [39] So they grabbed him, threw him out of the vineyard, and killed him.

[40] "Now, when the owner of the vineyard comes, what will he do to those tenants?" Jesus asked. [41] "He will certainly kill those evil men," they answered, "and rent the vineyard out to other tenants, who will give him his share of the harvest at the right time." [42] Jesus said to them, "Haven't you ever read what the Scriptures say?

'The stone which the builders rejected as worthless
Turned out to be the most important stone.
This was done by the Lord,
How wonderful it is!'

43 And so I tell you," added Jesus, "the Kingdom of God will be taken away from you and be given to a people who will produce the proper fruits. [44 Whoever falls on this stone will be broken to pieces; and if the stone falls on someone it will crush him to dust.]"

45 The chief priests and the Pharisees heard Jesus' parables and knew that he was talking about them, 46 so they tried to arrest him. But they were afraid of the crowds, who considered Jesus to be a prophet.

The Parable of the Wedding Feast
(Also Luke 14.15–24)

22 Jesus again used parables in talking to the people. 2 "The Kingdom of heaven is like a king who prepared a wedding feast for his son. 3 He sent his servants to tell the invited guests to come to the feast, but they did not want to come. 4 So he sent other servants with the message: 'Tell the guests, "My feast is ready now; my steers and prize calves have been butchered, and everything is ready. Come to the wedding feast!"' 5 But the invited guests paid no attention and went about their business: one went off to his farm, the other to his store, 6 while others grabbed the servants, beat them, and killed them. 7 The king was very angry, and sent his soldiers, who killed those murderers, and burned down their city. 8 Then he called his servants. 'My wedding feast is ready,' he said, 'but the people I invited did not deserve it. 9 Now go to the main streets and invite to the feast as many people

43 διὰ τοῦτο λέγω ὑμῖν ὅτι ἀρθήσεται ἀφ' ὑμῶν ἡ βασιλεία τοῦ θεοῦ καὶ δοθήσεται ἔθνει ποιοῦντι τοὺς καρποὺς αὐτῆς. ⟦44 Καὶ ὁ πεσὼν ἐπὶ τὸν λίθον τοῦτον συνθλασθήσεται· ἐφ' ὃν δ' ἂν πέσῃ λικμήσει αὐτόν.⟧[4]

45 Καὶ ἀκούσαντες οἱ ἀρχιερεῖς καὶ οἱ Φαρισαῖοι τὰς παραβολὰς αὐτοῦ ἔγνωσαν ὅτι περὶ αὐτῶν λέγει· 46 καὶ ζητοῦντες αὐτὸν κρατῆσαι ἐφοβήθησαν τοὺς ὄχλους, ἐπεὶ εἰς προφήτην αὐτὸν εἶχον.

The Parable of the Marriage Feast
(Lk 14.15–24)

22 Καὶ ἀποκριθεὶς ὁ Ἰησοῦς πάλιν εἶπεν ἐν παραβολαῖς αὐτοῖς λέγων, 2 Ὡμοιώθη ἡ βασιλεία τῶν οὐρανῶν ἀνθρώπῳ βασιλεῖ, ὅστις ἐποίησεν γάμους τῷ υἱῷ αὐτοῦ. 3 καὶ ἀπέστειλεν τοὺς δούλους αὐτοῦ καλέσαι τοὺς κεκλημένους εἰς τοὺς γάμους, καὶ οὐκ ἤθελον ἐλθεῖν. 4 πάλιν ἀπέστειλεν ἄλλους δούλους λέγων, Εἴπατε τοῖς κεκλημένοις, Ἰδοὺ τὸ ἄριστόν μου ἡτοίμακα, οἱ ταῦροί μου καὶ τὰ σιτιστὰ τεθυμένα, καὶ πάντα ἕτοιμα· δεῦτε εἰς τοὺς γάμους. 5 οἱ δὲ ἀμελήσαντες ἀπῆλθον, ὃς μὲν εἰς τὸν ἴδιον ἀγρόν, ὃς δὲ ἐπὶ τὴν ἐμπορίαν αὐτοῦ· 6 οἱ δὲ λοιποὶ κρατήσαντες τοὺς δούλους αὐτοῦ ὕβρισαν καὶ ἀπέκτειναν. 7 ὁ δὲ βασιλεὺς ὠργίσθη, καὶ πέμψας τὰ στρατεύματα αὐτοῦ ἀπώλεσεν τοὺς φονεῖς ἐκείνους καὶ τὴν πόλιν αὐτῶν ἐνέπρησεν. 8 τότε λέγει τοῖς δούλοις αὐτοῦ, Ὁ μὲν γάμος ἕτοιμός ἐστιν, οἱ δὲ κεκλημένοι οὐκ ἦσαν ἄξιοι· 9 πορεύεσθε οὖν ἐπὶ τὰς διεξόδους τῶν ὁδῶν, καὶ ὅσους ἐὰν

---

[4] **44** {C} *omit verse 44* D 33 it[b,d,e,ff1,2,r1] syr[s] Diatessaron[v] Irenaeus[gr,lat] Origen Eusebius ∥ *include verse 44* (*see* Lk 20.18) ℵ B C K L W X Δ Π 0138 (Θ 1079 1546 *omit καί*) f[1] f[13] 28 565 700 892 1009 1010 1071 1195 1216 1230 1241 1242 1253 1344 1365 1646 2148 2174 *Byz Lect* it[aur,c,f,g1,h,l,q] vg syr[c,p,h] cop[sa,bo] arm eth geo Aphraates Ephraem Chrysostom Augustine Ps-Chrysostom

---

44 Dn 2.34–35, 44–45   **46** ἐφοβήθησαν...εἶχον Mt 14.5; 21.26   εἰς...εἶχον Mt 16.14; 21.11; Lk 7.16; 24.19; Jn 4.19; 9.17
22 6 Mt 21.35

εὕρητε καλέσατε εἰς τοὺς γάμους. 10 καὶ ἐξελθόντες οἱ δοῦλοι ἐκεῖνοι εἰς τὰς ὁδοὺς συνήγαγον πάντας οὓς εὗρον, πονηρούς τε καὶ ἀγαθούς· καὶ ἐπλήσθη ὁ γάμος[1] ἀνακειμένων. 11 εἰσελθὼν δὲ ὁ βασιλεὺς θεάσασθαι τοὺς ἀνακειμένους εἶδεν ἐκεῖ ἄνθρωπον οὐκ ἐνδεδυμένον ἔνδυμα γάμου· 12 καὶ λέγει αὐτῷ, Ἑταῖρε, πῶς εἰσῆλθες ὧδε μὴ ἔχων ἔνδυμα γάμου; ὁ δὲ ἐφιμώθη. 13 τότε ὁ βασιλεὺς εἶπεν τοῖς διακόνοις, Δήσαντες αὐτοῦ πόδας καὶ χεῖρας ἐκβάλετε αὐτὸν εἰς τὸ σκότος τὸ ἐξώτερον· ἐκεῖ ἔσται ὁ κλαυθμὸς καὶ ὁ βρυγμὸς τῶν ὀδόντων. 14 πολλοὶ γάρ εἰσιν κλητοὶ ὀλίγοι δὲ ἐκλεκτοί.

Paying Taxes to Caesar
(Mk 12.13–17; Lk 20.20–26)

15 Τότε πορευθέντες οἱ Φαρισαῖοι συμβούλιον ἔλαβον ὅπως αὐτὸν παγιδεύσωσιν ἐν λόγῳ. 16 καὶ ἀποστέλλουσιν αὐτῷ τοὺς μαθητὰς αὐτῶν μετὰ τῶν Ἡρῳδιανῶν λέγοντες, Διδάσκαλε, οἴδαμεν ὅτι ἀληθὴς εἶ καὶ τὴν ὁδὸν τοῦ θεοῦ ἐν ἀληθείᾳ διδάσκεις, καὶ οὐ μέλει σοι περὶ οὐδενός, οὐ γὰρ βλέπεις εἰς πρόσωπον ἀνθρώπων. 17 εἰπὲ οὖν ἡμῖν τί σοι δοκεῖ·[a] ἔξεστιν δοῦναι κῆνσον Καίσαρι ἢ οὔ; 18 γνοὺς δὲ ὁ Ἰησοῦς τὴν πονηρίαν αὐτῶν εἶπεν, Τί με πειράζετε, ὑποκριταί; 19 ἐπιδείξατέ μοι τὸ νόμισμα τοῦ κήνσου. οἱ δὲ προσήνεγκαν αὐτῷ δηνάριον. 20 καὶ λέγει αὐτοῖς, Τίνος ἡ εἰκὼν αὕτη καὶ ἡ ἐπιγραφή; 21 λέγουσιν αὐτῷ, Καίσαρος. τότε λέγει αὐτοῖς, Ἀπόδοτε οὖν τὰ Καίσαρος Καίσαρι καὶ τὰ τοῦ θεοῦ τῷ θεῷ. 22 καὶ ἀκούσαντες ἐθαύμασαν, καὶ ἀφέντες αὐτὸν ἀπῆλθον.

---

[1] 10 {B} ὁ γάμος B^mg D K W X Δ Θ Π 085 ƒ1 ƒ13 28 33 565 700 1009 1071 1079 1195 1216 1230 1241 1242 1253 1344 1365 1546 1646 2148 2174 *Byz Lect* it^a,aur,b,c,d,e,f,ff1.2,g1,h,l,q,r1 vg cop^bo arm geo Origen Chrysostom ‖ ὁ ἄγαμος C ‖ ὁ νυμφών ℵ B* L 0138 892 1010 cop^sa Cyril ‖ ὁ γάμος or ὁ νυμφών syr^c,s,p,h,pal eth

[a] 17 *a statement:* WH RSV NEB Luth Jer Seg ‖ *a question:* TR Bov Nes BF2 AV RV ASV TT Zür

13 ἐκβάλετε...ἐξώτερον Mt 8.12; 25.30   ἐκεῖ...ὀδόντων Mt 8.12; 13.42, 50; 24.51; 25.30; Lk 13.28   15–16 Τότε...Ἡρῳδιανῶν Mk 3.6   21 Ἀπόδοτε...θεῷ Ro 13.7

as you find.' 10 So the servants went out into the streets and gathered all the people they could find, good and bad alike; and the wedding hall was filled with people.

11 "The king went in to look at the guests and he saw a man who was not wearing wedding clothes. 12 'Friend, how did you get in here without wedding clothes?' the king asked him. But the man said nothing. 13 Then the king told the servants, 'Tie him up hand and foot and throw him outside in the dark. There he will cry and gnash his teeth.'" 14 And Jesus concluded, "For many are invited, but few are chosen."

The Question about Paying Taxes
(Also Mark 12.13–17; Luke 20.20–26)

15 The Pharisees went off and made a plan to trap Jesus with questions. 16 Then they sent some of their disciples and some members of Herod's party to Jesus. "Teacher," they said, "we know that you are an honest man: you teach the truth about God's will for man, without worrying about what people think, because you pay no attention to what a man seems to be. 17 Tell us, then, what do you think? Is it against our Law to pay taxes to the Roman Emperor, or not?" 18 Jesus was aware of their evil plan, however, and so he said: "You impostors! Why are you trying to trap me? 19 Show me the coin to pay the tax!" They brought him the coin, 20 and he asked them, "Whose face and name are these?" 21 "The Emperor's," they answered. So Jesus said to them, "Well, then, pay to the Emperor what belongs to him, and pay to God what belongs to God." 22 When they heard this, they were filled with wonder; and they left him and went away.

The Question about Rising from Death
(Also Mark 12.18–27; Luke 20.27–40)

23 That same day some Sadducees came to Jesus. (They are the ones who say that people will not rise from death.) 24 "Teacher," they said, "Moses taught: 'If a man who has no children dies, his brother must marry the widow so they can have children for the dead man.' 25 Now, there were seven brothers who used to live here. The oldest got married, and died without having children, so he left his widow to his brother. 26 The same thing happened to the second brother, to the third, and finally to all seven. 27 Last of all, the woman died. 28 Now, on the day when the dead are raised to life, whose wife will she be? All of them had married her!"

29 Jesus answered them: "How wrong you are! It is because you don't know the Scriptures or God's power. 30 For when the dead are raised to life they will be like the angels in heaven, and men and women will not marry. 31 Now, about the dead being raised: haven't you ever read what God has told you? For he said, 32 'I am the God of Abraham, the God of Isaac, and the God of Jacob.'

The Question about the Resurrection
(Mk 12.18–27; Lk 20.27–40)

23 Ἐν ἐκείνῃ τῇ ἡμέρᾳ προσῆλθον αὐτῷ Σαδδουκαῖοι, λέγοντες[2] μὴ εἶναι ἀνάστασιν, καὶ ἐπηρώτησαν αὐτὸν 24 λέγοντες, Διδάσκαλε, Μωϋσῆς εἶπεν, Ἐάν τις ἀποθάνῃ μὴ ἔχων τέκνα, ἐπιγαμβρεύσει ὁ ἀδελφὸς αὐτοῦ τὴν γυναῖκα αὐτοῦ καὶ ἀναστήσει σπέρμα τῷ ἀδελφῷ αὐτοῦ. 25 ἦσαν δὲ παρ' ἡμῖν ἑπτὰ ἀδελφοί· καὶ ὁ πρῶτος γήμας ἐτελεύτησεν, καὶ μὴ ἔχων σπέρμα ἀφῆκεν τὴν γυναῖκα αὐτοῦ τῷ ἀδελφῷ αὐτοῦ· 26 ὁμοίως καὶ ὁ δεύτερος καὶ ὁ τρίτος, ἕως τῶν ἑπτά. 27 ὕστερον δὲ πάντων ἀπέθανεν ἡ γυνή. 28 ἐν τῇ ἀναστάσει οὖν τίνος τῶν ἑπτὰ ἔσται γυνή; πάντες γὰρ ἔσχον αὐτήν. 29 ἀποκριθεὶς δὲ ὁ Ἰησοῦς εἶπεν αὐτοῖς, Πλανᾶσθε μὴ εἰδότες τὰς γραφὰς μηδὲ τὴν δύναμιν τοῦ θεοῦ· 30 ἐν γὰρ τῇ ἀναστάσει οὔτε γαμοῦσιν οὔτε γαμίζονται, ἀλλ' ὡς ἄγγελοι[3] ἐν τῷ οὐρανῷ εἰσιν. 31 περὶ δὲ τῆς ἀναστάσεως τῶν νεκρῶν οὐκ ἀνέγνωτε τὸ ῥηθὲν ὑμῖν ὑπὸ τοῦ θεοῦ λέγοντος, 32 Ἐγώ εἰμι ὁ θεὸς Ἀβραὰμ καὶ ὁ θεὸς Ἰσαὰκ καὶ ὁ θεὸς Ἰακώβ;

---

2 23 {B} Σαδδουκαῖοι, λέγοντες ℵ* B D W Π* 0138 *f*[1] 28 33 892 1009 1010 1195 1216 1241 1242* 1344 1365 1546 2148 *l*[10,185pt,303,861,950,1642] it[d,(ff1)] (syr[c,s,p]) eth[ro] Origen Methodius (Ephraem) ‖ Σαδδουκαῖοι οἱ λέγοντες (see Mk 12.18; Lk 20.27) ℵ[c] K L Δ Θ Π[2] 0107 565 1071 1079 1230 1242[c] 1646 2174 *Byz Lect* *l*[185pt] it[a,aur,b,c,e,f,ff2,g1,h,l,q,rl] vg syr[h,pal] cop[bo] arm eth[pp?] Hilary ‖ οἱ Σαδδουκαῖοι οἱ λέγοντες *f*[13] (700 1253 *omit second* οἱ) *l*[547] cop[sa] th[pp?] ‖ *Sadducees, who do not believe that the dead will live, and they said unto him, "The dead will not live"* eth[ms] for Σαδδουκαῖοι...αὐτόν

3 30 {C} ἄγγελοι (see Mk 12.25) B D 0197 700 Cosmos[1/3] ‖ οἱ ἄγγελοι Θ *f*[1] cop[sa] Origen ‖ ἄγγελοι *or* οἱ ἄγγελοι it[a,b,c,d,e,f,ff2,h,q,rl] syr[c,s] arm geo Diatessaron[esyr] Ambrose ‖ ἄγγελοι θεοῦ ℵ L *f*[13] 28 33 892 1071 1216 1241 *Lect* *l*[185pt,950pt] Chrysostom Cosmos[2/3] ‖ ἄγγελοι τοῦ θεοῦ K W Δ Π 0138 565 1009 1010 1079 1195 1230 1242 1253 1344 1365 1546 1646 2148 2174 *Byz* *l*[12,76,80,184,185pt,299,303,950pt,997,1127] Methodius Epiphanius ‖ ἄγγελοι θεοῦ *or* ἄγγελοι τοῦ θεοῦ it[aur,ff1,g1,l] vg syr[p,h,pal] cop[bo] eth Diatessaron Origen[lat]

---

23 Σαδδουκαῖοι...ἀνάστασιν Ac 23.8   **24** Ἐάν...γυναῖκα αὐτοῦ Dt 25.5 ἐπιγαμβρεύσει...ἀδελφῷ αὐτοῦ Gn 38.8   **32** 4 Macc 7.19   Ἐγώ...Ἰακώβ Ex 3.6, 15, 16

οὐκ ἔστιν [ὁ] θεὸς[4] νεκρῶν ἀλλὰ ζώντων. **33** καὶ ἀκούσαντες οἱ ὄχλοι ἐξεπλήσσοντο ἐπὶ τῇ διδαχῇ αὐτοῦ.

The Great Commandment
(Mk 12.28–34; Lk 10.25–28)

34 Οἱ δὲ Φαρισαῖοι ἀκούσαντες ὅτι ἐφίμωσεν τοὺς Σαδδουκαίους συνήχθησαν ἐπὶ τὸ αὐτό. **35** καὶ ἐπηρώτησεν εἷς ἐξ αὐτῶν [νομικὸς][5] πειράζων αὐτόν, **36** Διδάσκαλε, ποία ἐντολὴ μεγάλη ἐν τῷ νόμῳ; **37** ὁ δὲ ἔφη αὐτῷ, **Ἀγαπήσεις κύριον τὸν θεόν σου ἐν ὅλῃ τῇ καρδίᾳ σου καὶ ἐν ὅλῃ τῇ ψυχῇ σου** καὶ ἐν ὅλῃ τῇ διανοίᾳ σου· **38** αὕτη ἐστὶν ἡ μεγάλη καὶ πρώτη ἐντολή. **39** δευτέρα δὲ ὁμοία αὐτῇ, **Ἀγαπήσεις τὸν πλησίον σου ὡς σεαυτόν.** **40** ἐν ταύταις ταῖς δυσὶν ἐντολαῖς ὅλος ὁ νόμος κρέμαται καὶ οἱ προφῆται.

The Question about David's Son
(Mk 12.35–37; Lk 20.41–44)

41 Συνηγμένων δὲ τῶν Φαρισαίων ἐπηρώτησεν αὐτοὺς ὁ Ἰησοῦς **42** λέγων, Τί ὑμῖν δοκεῖ περὶ τοῦ Χριστοῦ; τίνος υἱός ἐστιν; λέγουσιν αὐτῷ, Τοῦ Δαυίδ. **43** λέγει αὐτοῖς, Πῶς οὖν Δαυὶδ ἐν πνεύματι καλεῖ αὐτὸν κύριον λέγων,

This means that he is the God of the living, not of the dead.'' [33] When the crowds heard this they were amazed at his teaching.

The Great Commandment
(Also Mark 12.28–34; Luke 10.25–28)

[34] When the Pharisees heard that Jesus had silenced the Sadducees, they came together, [35] and one of them, a teacher of the Law, tried to trap him with a question. [36] "Teacher," he asked, "which is the greatest commandment in the Law?" [37] Jesus answered, " 'You must love the Lord your God with all your heart, and with all your soul, and with all your mind.' [38] This is the greatest and the most important commandment. [39] The second most important commandment is like it: 'You must love your neighbor as yourself.' [40] The whole Law of Moses and the teachings of the prophets depend on these two commandments.''

The Question about the Messiah
(Also Mark 12.35–37; Luke 20.41–44)

[41] When the Pharisees gathered together, Jesus asked them: [42] "What do you think about the Messiah? Whose descendant is he?" "He is David's descendant," they answered. [43] "Why, then," Jesus asked, "did the Spirit inspire David to call him 'Lord'? For David said,

---

[4] **32** {C} ἔστιν ὁ θεός B L Δ *f*[1] 33 1009 *l*[76,184] (*l*[547] ἔστιν δέ) ∥ ἔστιν θεός (*see* Mk 12.27) ℵ D W 28 1242* Irenaeus Origen Eusebius Hilary Chrysostom ∥ ἔστιν θεός or ἔστιν ὁ θεός it[aur,b,c,d,e,f,ff1,2,g1,h,l,q,r1] vg syr[c,s,p,pal] cop[sa,bo] eth? geo[2] (Cyprian) ∥ ἔστιν ὁ θεὸς θεός K Π 0138 (Θ *f*[13] ἔστιν δὲ ὁ) 565 700 892 1010 1071 1079 1195 1216 1230 1241 1242[c] 1253 1344 1365 1646 2148 2174 (1540 *l*[1127] *omit* ὁ) *Byz Lect* syr[h] arm geo[1] Origen Chrysostom

[5] **35** {C} νομικός ℵ B D K L W Δ Θ Π 0138 0197 *f*[13] 28 33 565 700 892 1009 1010 1071 1079 1195 1216 1230 1241 1242 1253 1344 1365 1546 1646 2148 2174 *Byz l*[185pt,211,333] it[a,aur,b,c,d,f,ff1,2,g1,h,l,q,r1] vg syr[c,p,h,hgr,pal] cop[sa,bo] eth ∥ νομικός τις (*see* Lk 10.25) F G H 372 495 713 (*Lect l*[185pt] *beginning of lection*) ∥ *omit* (*see* Mk 12.28) *f*[1] it[e] syr[s] arm geo Origen[gr,lat]

---

33 οἱ...αὐτοῦ Mt 7.28; 13.54; Mk 11.18   **37** Ἀγαπήσεις...διανοίᾳ σου Dt 6.5 (Jos 22.5)
39 Ἀγαπήσεις...σεαυτόν Lv 19.18 (Mt 5.43; 19.19; Ro 13.9; Ga 5.14; Jas 2.8)   **40** Ro 13.10
ὅλος...προφῆται Mt 7.12   **42** Jn 7.42   **43** Δαυὶδ ἐν πνεύματι 2 Sm 23.2

44 'The Lord said to my Lord:
   Sit here at my right side,
   Until I put your enemies under your
      feet.'
45 If, then, David called him 'Lord,' how can the Messiah be David's descendant?"
46 No one was able to answer Jesus a single word, and from that day on no one dared ask him any more questions.

Jesus Warns against the Teachers of the Law and the Pharisees

(Also Mark 12.38–39; Luke 11.43, 46; 20.45–46)

23 Then Jesus spoke to the crowds and to his disciples. 2 "The teachers of the Law and the Pharisees," he said, "are the authorized interpreters of Moses' Law. 3 So you must obey and follow everything they tell you to do; do not, however, imitate their actions, because they do not practice what they preach. 4 They fix up heavy loads and tie them on men's backs, yet they aren't willing even to lift a finger to help them carry those loads. 5 They do everything just so people will see them. See how big are the containers with scripture verses on their foreheads and arms, and notice how long are the hems of their cloaks! 6 They love the best places at feasts and the reserved seats in the synagogues; 7 they love to be greeted with respect in the market places and have people call them 'Teacher.' 8 You must not be called 'Teacher,' for you are all brothers of one another and have only

44 Εἶπεν κύριος τῷ κυρίῳ μου,
   Κάθου ἐκ δεξιῶν μου
      ἕως ἂν θῶ τοὺς ἐχθρούς σου ὑποκάτω τῶν
         ποδῶν σου;
45 εἰ οὖν Δαυὶδ καλεῖ αὐτὸν κύριον, πῶς υἱὸς αὐτοῦ ἐστιν;
46 καὶ οὐδεὶς ἐδύνατο ἀποκριθῆναι αὐτῷ λόγον, οὐδὲ ἐτόλμησέν τις ἀπ' ἐκείνης τῆς ἡμέρας ἐπερωτῆσαι αὐτὸν οὐκέτι.

The Denouncing of the Scribes and Pharisees
(Mk 12.38–40; Lk 11.37–52; 20.45–47)

23 Τότε ὁ Ἰησοῦς ἐλάλησεν τοῖς ὄχλοις καὶ τοῖς μαθηταῖς αὐτοῦ 2 λέγων, Ἐπὶ τῆς Μωϋσέως καθέδρας ἐκάθισαν οἱ γραμματεῖς καὶ οἱ Φαρισαῖοι. 3 πάντα οὖν ὅσα ἐὰν εἴπωσιν ὑμῖν ποιήσατε καὶ τηρεῖτε, κατὰ δὲ τὰ ἔργα αὐτῶν μὴ ποιεῖτε· λέγουσιν γὰρ καὶ οὐ ποιοῦσιν. 4 δεσμεύουσιν δὲ φορτία βαρέα[1] καὶ ἐπιτιθέασιν ἐπὶ τοὺς ὤμους τῶν ἀνθρώπων, αὐτοὶ δὲ τῷ δακτύλῳ αὐτῶν οὐ θέλουσιν κινῆσαι αὐτά. 5 πάντα δὲ τὰ ἔργα αὐτῶν ποιοῦσιν πρὸς τὸ θεαθῆναι τοῖς ἀνθρώποις· πλατύνουσιν γὰρ τὰ φυλακτήρια αὐτῶν καὶ μεγαλύνουσιν τὰ κράσπεδα, 6 φιλοῦσιν δὲ τὴν πρωτοκλισίαν ἐν τοῖς δείπνοις καὶ τὰς πρωτοκαθεδρίας ἐν ταῖς συναγωγαῖς 7 καὶ τοὺς ἀσπασμοὺς ἐν ταῖς ἀγοραῖς καὶ καλεῖσθαι ὑπὸ τῶν ἀνθρώπων, Ῥαββί. 8 ὑμεῖς δὲ μὴ κληθῆτε, Ῥαββί, εἷς γάρ ἐστιν ὑμῶν ὁ διδάσκαλος, πάντες δὲ ὑμεῖς ἀδελφοί ἐστε.

---

[1] 4 {C} βαρέα L Xcomm f1 892 ita, b, e, ff2, h syrc, s, p copbo Diatessarona Irenaeuslat Origenlat ‖ μεγάλα βαρέα ℵ (ethro?pp? μεγάλα καί) ‖ βαρέα καὶ δυσβάστακτα B (D* ἀδυσβάστακτα) Dc K W Δ Θ Π 0107 (0138 δυσβάκτατα) f13 28 33 565 1009 1071 1079 1195 1216 1230 1241 1242 1253 1344 1365 1546 1646 2148 2174 Byz Lect itaur, c, d, f, ff1, g1, l, q vg syrh, pal copsa arm (ethms δισβάστακτα) geo Clement Chrysostom John-Damascus ‖ δυσβάστακτα (see Lk 11.46) Xcomm 700 1010 l847

44 Εἶπεν...ποδῶν σου Ps 110.1 (Ac 2.34-35; 1 Cor 15.25; He 1.13)   46 οὐδὲ...οὐκέτι Mk 12.34; Lk 20.40
   23 3 Mal 2.7-8   5 πάντα...ἀνθρώποις Mt 6.1, 5 πλατύνουσιν...φυλακτήρια Ex 13.9; Dt 6.8   μεγαλύνουσιν τὰ κράσπεδα Nu 15.38-39   6 φιλοῦσιν...δείπνοις Lk 14.7

9 καὶ πατέρα μὴ καλέσητε ὑμῖν ἐπὶ τῆς γῆς, εἷς γάρ
ἐστιν ὑμῶν ὁ πατὴρ ὁ οὐράνιος. 10 μηδὲ κληθῆτε καθη-
γηταί, ὅτι καθηγητὴς ὑμῶν ἐστιν εἷς ὁ Χριστός.ᵃ 11 ὁ δὲ
μείζων ὑμῶν ἔσται ὑμῶν διάκονος.ᵃ 12 ὅστις δὲ ὑψώσει
ἑαυτὸν ταπεινωθήσεται, καὶ ὅστις ταπεινώσει ἑαυτὸν
ὑψωθήσεται.

13ᵇ Οὐαὶ δὲ ὑμῖν, γραμματεῖς καὶ Φαρισαῖοι ὑποκριταί,
ὅτι κλείετε τὴν βασιλείαν τῶν οὐρανῶν ἔμπροσθεν τῶν
ἀνθρώπων· ὑμεῖς γὰρ οὐκ εἰσέρχεσθε, οὐδὲ τοὺς εἰσερχομένους ἀφίετε εἰσελθεῖν.²ᵇ

15 Οὐαὶ ὑμῖν, γραμματεῖς καὶ Φαρισαῖοι ὑποκριταί, ὅτι
περιάγετε τὴν θάλασσαν καὶ τὴν ξηρὰν ποιῆσαι ἕνα
προσήλυτον, καὶ ὅταν γένηται ποιεῖτε αὐτὸν υἱὸν γεέννης
διπλότερον ὑμῶν.

16 Οὐαὶ ὑμῖν, ὁδηγοὶ τυφλοὶ οἱ λέγοντες, Ὃς ἂν ὀμόσῃ
ἐν τῷ ναῷ, οὐδέν ἐστιν· ὃς δ' ἂν ὀμόσῃ ἐν τῷ χρυσῷ τοῦ
ναοῦ ὀφείλει. 17 μωροὶ καὶ τυφλοί, τίς γὰρ μείζων ἐστίν,
ὁ χρυσὸς ἢ ὁ ναὸς ὁ ἁγιάσας τὸν χρυσόν; 18 καί, Ὃς ἂν
ὀμόσῃ ἐν τῷ θυσιαστηρίῳ, οὐδέν ἐστιν· ὃς δ' ἂν ὀμόσῃ ἐν

one Teacher. 9 And you must not call
anyone here on earth 'Father,' for you
have only the one Father in heaven.
10 Nor should you be called 'Leader,'
because your one and only leader is the
Messiah. 11 The greatest one among you
must be your servant. 12 And whoever
makes himself great will be humbled,
and whoever humbles himself will be
made great.''

Jesus Condemns Their Hypocrisy
(Also Mark 12.40; Luke 11.39–42, 44, 52; 20.47)

13 "How terrible for you, teachers of
the Law and Pharisees! Impostors! You
lock the door to the Kingdom of heaven
in men's faces, but you yourselves will
not go in, and neither will you let people
in who are trying to go in!

[14 "How terrible for you, teachers of
the Law and Pharisees! Impostors! You
take advantage of widows and rob them
of their homes, and then make a show
of saying long prayers! Because of this
your punishment will be all the worse!]

15 "How terrible for you, teachers of
the Law and Pharisees! Impostors! You
sail the seas and cross whole countries
to win one convert, and when you
succeed, you make him twice as deserv-
ing of going to hell as you yourselves are!

16 "How terrible for you, blind guides!
You teach, 'If a man swears by the
Temple he isn't bound by his vow; but
if he swears by the gold in the Temple,
he is bound.' 17 Blind fools! Which is
more important, the gold or the Temple
which makes the gold holy? 18 You also
teach, 'If a man swears by the altar he
isn't bound by his vow; but if he swears

---

² 13 {B} Οὐαὶ δὲ ὑμῖν...εἰσελθεῖν. (omit verse 14) ℵ B D L Θ f¹ 33
892ᵗˣᵗ 1344 itᵃ, aur, d, e, ff¹, g¹ vgʷʷ syrˢ, palᵐˢ copˢᵃ, boᵐˢˢ arm geo Origenᵍʳ, lat
Eusebius Jerome Druthmarus // 14, 13 Οὐαὶ δὲ ὑμῖν, γραμματεῖς καὶ
Φαρισαῖοι ὑποκριταί, ὅτι κατεσθίετε τὰς οἰκίας τῶν χηρῶν καὶ προφάσει
μακρὰ προσευχόμενοι· διὰ τοῦτο λήμψεσθε περισσότερον κρίμα. 13 Οὐαὶ
ὑμῖν...εἰσελθεῖν. (see Mk 12.40; Lk 20.47) K W Δᵍʳ Π 0107 0138 28 565
700 892ᵐᵍ (1009 μικρά) 1010 1071 1079 1195 1216 1230 1241 1242 (1253
λήψονται) 1365 1546 1646 2148 2174 Byz Lect (l⁷⁶ μικρά) itᶠ syrᵖ, ʰ copᵇᵒᵐˢˢ
eth Chrysostom Ps-Chrysostom John-Damascus // 13, 14 Οὐαὶ δὲ ὑμῖν...
εἰσελθεῖν. 14 Οὐαὶ δὲ ὑμῖν...κρίμα. (see Mk 12.40; Lk 20.47) f¹³ l⁵⁴⁷ itᵇ, c, ff²,
h, l, r¹ vgᶜˡ syrᶜ, palᵐˢˢ copᵇᵒᵐˢˢ Diatessaronⁿ, ᵗ Origen Hilary Chrysostom

ᵃ ᵃ 10–11 a major, a major: TR Bov Nes BF² AV RV ASV NEB TT Zür Luth Jer Seg // a minor,
a major: WH // a major, a minor: RSV

ᵇ ᵇ 13–14 b verse 13, b omit verse 14: Bov Nes BF² RV ASV RSV NEB TT Zür Jer Seg // b verse
13, b verse 14: TRᵉᵈ AV RVᵐᵍ ASVᵐᵍ RSVᵐᵍ NEBᵐᵍ TTᵐᵍ Zürᵐᵍ [Luth] Jerᵐᵍ Segᵐᵍ // b verse 14,
b verse 13: TRᵉᵈ RVᵐᵍ ASVᵐᵍ RSVᵐᵍ // b verse 13 (numbered as verse 14), b omit verse 14: WH

---

11 Mt 20.26–27; Mk 9.35; 10.43–44; Lk 9.48; 22.26   12 Job 22.29; Pr 29.23; Eze 21.26; Lk 14.11;
18.14   16 ὁδηγοὶ τυφλοί Mt 15.14; 23.24; Ro 2.19

by the gift on the altar, he is bound.'
[19] How blind you are! Which is more
important, the gift or the altar which
makes the gift holy? [20] So then, when
a man swears by the altar he is swearing
by it and by all the gifts on it; [21] and
when a man swears by the Temple he
is swearing by it and by God, the one
who lives there; [22] and when a man
swears by heaven he is swearing by God's
throne and by him who sits on it.

[23] "How terrible for you, teachers of
the Law and Pharisees! Impostors! You
give to God one tenth even of the seasoning herbs, such as mint, dill, and cummin,
but you neglect to obey the really important teachings of the Law, such as
justice and mercy and honesty. These
you should practice, without neglecting
the others. [24] Blind guides! You strain
a fly out of your drink, but swallow a
camel!

[25] "How terrible for you, teachers of
the Law and Pharisees! Impostors! You
clean the outside of your cup and plate,
while the inside is full of things you
have gotten by violence and selfishness.
[26] Blind Pharisee! Clean what is inside
the cup first, and then the outside will
be clean too!

[27] "How terrible for you, teachers of
the Law and Pharisees! Impostors! You
are like whitewashed tombs, which look
fine on the outside, but are full of dead
men's bones and rotten stuff on the

τῷ δώρῳ τῷ ἐπάνω αὐτοῦ ὀφείλει. **19** τυφλοί[3], τί γὰρ
μεῖζον, τὸ δῶρον ἢ τὸ θυσιαστήριον τὸ ἁγιάζον τὸ δῶρον;
20 ὁ οὖν ὀμόσας ἐν τῷ θυσιαστηρίῳ ὀμνύει ἐν αὐτῷ καὶ
ἐν πᾶσι τοῖς ἐπάνω αὐτοῦ· **21** καὶ ὁ ὀμόσας ἐν τῷ ναῷ
ὀμνύει ἐν αὐτῷ καὶ ἐν τῷ κατοικοῦντι αὐτόν· **22** καὶ ὁ
ὀμόσας ἐν τῷ οὐρανῷ ὀμνύει ἐν τῷ θρόνῳ τοῦ θεοῦ καὶ ἐν
τῷ καθημένῳ ἐπάνω αὐτοῦ.

23 Οὐαὶ ὑμῖν, γραμματεῖς καὶ Φαρισαῖοι ὑποκριταί,
ὅτι ἀποδεκατοῦτε τὸ ἡδύοσμον καὶ τὸ ἄνηθον καὶ τὸ
κύμινον, καὶ ἀφήκατε τὰ βαρύτερα τοῦ νόμου, τὴν κρίσιν
καὶ τὸ ἔλεος καὶ τὴν πίστιν· ταῦτα [δὲ] ἔδει ποιῆσαι
κἀκεῖνα μὴ ἀφιέναι. **24** ὁδηγοὶ τυφλοί, οἱ διϋλίζοντες τὸν
κώνωπα τὴν δὲ κάμηλον καταπίνοντες.

25 Οὐαὶ ὑμῖν, γραμματεῖς καὶ Φαρισαῖοι ὑποκριταί,
ὅτι καθαρίζετε τὸ ἔξωθεν τοῦ ποτηρίου καὶ τῆς παροψίδος,
ἔσωθεν δὲ γέμουσιν ἐξ ἁρπαγῆς καὶ ἀκρασίας. **26** Φαρισαῖε τυφλέ, καθάρισον πρῶτον τὸ ἐντὸς τοῦ ποτηρίου[4],
ἵνα γένηται καὶ τὸ ἐκτὸς αὐτοῦ[4] καθαρόν.

27 Οὐαὶ ὑμῖν, γραμματεῖς καὶ Φαρισαῖοι ὑποκριταί,
ὅτι παρομοιάζετε τάφοις κεκονιαμένοις, οἵτινες ἔξωθεν
μὲν φαίνονται ὡραῖοι ἔσωθεν δὲ γέμουσιν ὀστέων νεκρῶν

---

[3] **19** {C} τυφλοί ℵ D L Θ *f*[1] 892 it[a,aur,d,e,ff1,2,g1,h,l] vg syr[c,s] Diatessaron[i,n] ∥ μωροὶ καὶ τυφλοί (*see* 23.17) B C K W Δ Π 0138 *f*[13] 28 33 565
700 1009 1010 1071 1079 1195 1216 1230 1241 1242 1253 1344 1365 1546 1646
2148 2174 *Byz Lect* it[c,f] syr[p,h] with *,pal cop[sa,bo] arm eth geo Origen[lat]

[4] **26** {D} τοῦ ποτηρίου...τὸ ἐκτὸς αὐτοῦ Θ *f*[1] 700 it[a,e] syr[s] geo[1,A] ∥
τοῦ ποτηρίου...τὸ ἐκτός it[ff2,r1] geo[B] Irenaeus[lat] ∥ τοῦ ποτηρίου...τὸ ἔξωθεν
αὐτοῦ D (it[d] Clement *omit* αὐτοῦ) ∥ τοῦ ποτηρίου καὶ τῆς παροψίδος...
τὸ ἐκτὸς αὐτοῦ B* *f*[13] 28 1009 1253 1344 2148 *l*[12,69,70,80,303,333,374,547,850,950pt,1127,1579]
eth Basil[1/2] John-Damascus ∥ τοῦ ποτηρίου καὶ τῆς παροψίδος...τὸ ἐκτὸς
αὐτῶν (ℵ* ἐντὸς) ℵ[c] B[2] C K L W (Δ *omit* τό) Π 0138 33 565 892 1010 1071 1079
1195 1216 1230 1241 1242 1365 1546 1646 2174 *Byz Lect l*[950pt] syr[p,(h),pal] cop[sa,bo]
arm Basil[1/2] ∥ τοῦ ποτηρίου καὶ τῆς παροψίδος...τὸ ἐκτός X it[aur,c,f,ff1,
g1,h,l] vg

---

19 τὸ θυσιαστήριον...δῶρον Ex 29.37   **21** 1 Kgs 8.13; Ps 26.8   **22** Is 66.1; Mt 5.34;
Ac 7.49   **23** ἀποδεκατοῦτε...κύμινον Lv 27.30   τὰ...πίστιν Mic 6.8   **24** ὁδηγοὶ τυφλοί
Mt 15.14; 23.16; Ro 2.19   **25** καθαρίζετε...παροψίδος Mk 7.4   **26** Φαρισαῖε τυφλέ
Jn 9.40   **27** τάφοις κεκονιαμένοις Ac 23.3

καὶ πάσης ἀκαθαρσίας. 28 οὕτως καὶ ὑμεῖς ἔξωθεν μὲν φαίνεσθε τοῖς ἀνθρώποις δίκαιοι, ἔσωθεν δέ ἐστε μεστοὶ ὑποκρίσεως καὶ ἀνομίας.

29 Οὐαὶ ὑμῖν, γραμματεῖς καὶ Φαρισαῖοι ὑποκριταί, ὅτι οἰκοδομεῖτε τοὺς τάφους τῶν προφητῶν καὶ κοσμεῖτε τὰ μνημεῖα τῶν δικαίων, 30 καὶ λέγετε, Εἰ ἤμεθα ἐν ταῖς ἡμέραις τῶν πατέρων ἡμῶν, οὐκ ἂν ἤμεθα αὐτῶν κοινωνοὶ ἐν τῷ αἵματι τῶν προφητῶν. 31 ὥστε μαρτυρεῖτε ἑαυτοῖς ὅτι υἱοί ἐστε τῶν φονευσάντων τοὺς προφήτας. 32 καὶ ὑμεῖς πληρώσατε τὸ μέτρον τῶν πατέρων ὑμῶν. 33 ὄφεις γεννήματα ἐχιδνῶν, πῶς φύγητε ἀπὸ τῆς κρίσεως τῆς γεέννης; 34 διὰ τοῦτο ἰδοὺ ἐγὼ ἀποστέλλω πρὸς ὑμᾶς προφήτας καὶ σοφοὺς καὶ γραμματεῖς· ἐξ αὐτῶν ἀποκτενεῖτε καὶ σταυρώσετε, καὶ ἐξ αὐτῶν μαστιγώσετε ἐν ταῖς συναγωγαῖς ὑμῶν καὶ διώξετε ἀπὸ πόλεως εἰς πόλιν· 35 ὅπως ἔλθῃ ἐφ' ὑμᾶς πᾶν αἷμα δίκαιον ἐκχυννόμενον ἐπὶ τῆς γῆς ἀπὸ τοῦ αἵματος Ἄβελ τοῦ δικαίου ἕως τοῦ αἵματος Ζαχαρίου υἱοῦ Βαραχίου, ὃν ἐφονεύσατε μεταξὺ τοῦ ναοῦ καὶ τοῦ θυσιαστηρίου. 36 ἀμὴν λέγω ὑμῖν, ἥξει ταῦτα πάντα ἐπὶ τὴν γενεὰν ταύτην.

The Lament over Jerusalem
(Lk 13.34–35)

37 Ἰερουσαλὴμ Ἰερουσαλήμ, ἡ ἀποκτείνουσα τοὺς προφήτας καὶ λιθοβολοῦσα τοὺς ἀπεσταλμένους πρὸς αὐτήν, ποσάκις ἠθέλησα ἐπισυναγαγεῖν τὰ τέκνα σου, ὃν τρόπον ὄρνις ἐπισυνάγει τὰ νοσσία αὐτῆς ὑπὸ τὰς πτέρυγας, καὶ οὐκ ἠθελήσατε. ᶜ 38 ἰδοὺ **ἀφίεται ὑμῖν ὁ οἶκος ὑμῶν**

ᶜ 37 c statement: Bov Nes BF² NEB ‖ c question: TR WH AVᵉᵈ ‖ c exclamation: AVᵉᵈ RV ASV RSV TT Zür Luth Jer Seg

---

28 Lk 16.15   **31** υἱοί...προφήτας Ac 7.52   **33** γεννήματα ἐχιδνῶν Mt 3.7; 12.34; Lk 3.7   **34** Ac 7.52; 1 Th 2.15 διώξετε...πόλιν Mt 10.23   **35** τοῦ αἵματος Ἄβελ Gn 4.8; He 11.4 τοῦ αἵματος Ζαχαρίου...θυσιαστηρίου 2 Chr 24.20–21 Ζαχαρίου υἱοῦ Βαραχίου Zch 1.1   **37** λιθοβολοῦσα...αὐτήν Ac 7.59; 1 Th 2.15   **38** 1 Kgs 9.7–8; Jr 12.7; 22.5; Tob 14.4

inside. 28 In the same way, on the outside you appear to everybody as good, but inside you are full of lies and sins."

Jesus Predicts Their Punishment
(Also Luke 11.47–51)

29 "How terrible for you, teachers of the Law and Pharisees! Impostors! You make fine tombs for the prophets, and decorate the monuments of those who lived good lives, 30 and you say, 'If we had lived long ago in the time of our ancestors, we would not have done what they did and killed the prophets.' 31 So you actually admit that you are the descendants of those who murdered the prophets! 32 Go on, then, and finish up what your ancestors started! 33 Snakes, and sons of snakes! How do you expect to escape from being condemned to hell? 34 And so I tell you: I will send you prophets and wise men and teachers; you will kill some of them, nail others to the cross, and whip others in your synagogues, and chase them from town to town. 35 As a result, the punishment for the murder of all innocent men will fall on you, from the murder of innocent Abel to the murder of Zechariah, Barachiah's son, whom you murdered between the Temple and the altar. 36 I tell you indeed: the punishment for all these will fall upon the people of this day!"

Jesus' Love for Jerusalem
(Also Luke 13.34–35)

37 "O Jerusalem, Jerusalem! You kill the prophets and stone the messengers God has sent you! How many times have I wanted to put my arms around all your people, just as a hen gathers her chicks under her wings, but you would not let me! 38 Now your home

will be completely forsaken. [39] From now on you will never see me again, I tell you, until you say, 'God bless him who comes in the name of the Lord.' "

Jesus Speaks of the Destruction of the Temple
(Also Mark 13.1–2; Luke 21.5–6)

24 Jesus left and was going away from the Temple when his disciples came to him to show him the Temple's buildings. [2] "Yes," he said, "you may well look at all these. I tell you this: not a single stone here will be left in its place; every one of them will be thrown down."

Troubles and Persecutions
(Also Mark 13.3–13; Luke 21.7–19)

[3] As Jesus sat on the Mount of Olives, the disciples came to him in private. "Tell us when all this will be," they asked, "and what will happen to show that it is the time for your coming and the end of the age."

[4] Jesus answered: "Watch out, and do not let anyone fool you. [5] Because many men will come in my name, saying, 'I am the Messiah!' and fool many people. [6] You are going to hear the noise of battles close by and the news of battles far away; but, listen, do not be troubled. Such things must happen, but they do

ἔρημος[5]. **39** λέγω γὰρ ὑμῖν, οὐ μή με ἴδητε ἀπ' ἄρτι ἕως ἂν εἴπητε, **Εὐλογημένος ὁ ἐρχόμενος ἐν ὀνόματι κυρίου.**

The Destruction of the Temple Foretold
(Mk 13.1–2; Lk 21.5–6)

24 Καὶ ἐξελθὼν ὁ Ἰησοῦς ἀπὸ τοῦ ἱεροῦ ἐπορεύετο, καὶ προσῆλθον οἱ μαθηταὶ αὐτοῦ ἐπιδεῖξαι αὐτῷ τὰς οἰκοδομὰς τοῦ ἱεροῦ· 2 ὁ δὲ ἀποκριθεὶς εἶπεν αὐτοῖς, Οὐ βλέπετε ταῦτα πάντα; ἀμὴν λέγω ὑμῖν, οὐ μὴ ἀφεθῇ ὧδε λίθος ἐπὶ λίθον ὃς οὐ καταλυθήσεται.

The Beginning of Woes
(Mk 13.3–13; Lk 21.7–19)

3 Καθημένου δὲ αὐτοῦ ἐπὶ τοῦ Ὄρους τῶν Ἐλαιῶν προσῆλθον αὐτῷ οἱ μαθηταὶ κατ' ἰδίαν λέγοντες, Εἰπὲ ἡμῖν[a] πότε ταῦτα ἔσται,[a] καὶ τί τὸ σημεῖον τῆς σῆς παρουσίας καὶ συντελείας τοῦ αἰῶνος.[a] 4 καὶ ἀποκριθεὶς ὁ Ἰησοῦς εἶπεν αὐτοῖς, Βλέπετε μή τις ὑμᾶς πλανήσῃ· 5 πολλοὶ γὰρ ἐλεύσονται ἐπὶ τῷ ὀνόματί μου λέγοντες, Ἐγώ εἰμι ὁ Χριστός, καὶ πολλοὺς πλανήσουσιν. 6 μελλήσετε δὲ ἀκούειν πολέμους καὶ ἀκοὰς πολέμων· ὁρᾶτε, μὴ θροεῖσθε· δεῖ γὰρ γενέσθαι[1], ἀλλ' οὔπω ἐστὶν τὸ τέλος.

---

[5] **38** {B} ὑμῶν ἔρημος (see Jr 22.5) ℵ C D K W X Δ Θ Π 0138 f[1] f[13] (28 ὁ οἶκος ὑμῶν ὑμῖν ἔρημος) 33 565 700 892 1009 1010 1071 1079 1195 1216 1230 1241 1242 1253 1344 1365 1546 1646 2148 2174 *Byz Lect* l[883m] it[a,aur,b,c,d,e,f, ff1,g1,h,l,q,r1] vg syr[p,h,pal] cop[bomss] arm eth geo Irenaeus[lat] Clement Origen Cyprian Eusebius Chrysostom Cyril Cosmos ∥ ὑμῶν B L l[184] it[ff2] syr[s] cop[sa,bomss] Irenaeus[lat] Origen Cyril

[1] **6** {B} γενέσθαι (see Mk 13.7) ℵ B D L Θ f[1] 33 892 it[d] cop[sa,bo] eth[ro,pp] Origen[lat] Cyprian Eusebius Ps-Athanasius ∥ πάντα γενέσθαι C K W Δ Π 0138 f[13] 28 700 1009 1010 1071 1079 1195 1230 1242 1253 1344 1365 1546 1646 2148 2174 *Byz Lect* Chrysostom ∥ ταῦτα γενέσθαι (see Lk 21.9) 565

[a a a] **3** a none, a minor, a major: WH TT Jer ∥ a minor, a minor, a question: Bov Nes BF[2] RSV Zür Seg ∥ a minor, a question, a question: TR AV RV ASV NEB Luth

---

39 Εὐλογημένος...κυρίου Ps 118.26 (Mt 21.9; Mk 11.10; Lk 19.38)
24 2 οὐ μή...καταλυθήσεται Lk 19.44   **3** τί...παρουσίας Mt 24.27, 39   συντελείας τοῦ αἰῶνος Mt 13.39, 40, 49; 28.20   **5** Mt 24.11, 23–24; Jn 5.43; 1 Jn 2.18   **6** δεῖ...γενέσθαι Dn 2.28, 29; 2.45 Theodotion

7 ἐγερθήσεται γὰρ ἔθνος ἐπὶ ἔθνος καὶ βασιλεία ἐπὶ βασιλείαν, καὶ ἔσονται λιμοὶ καὶ σεισμοὶ κατὰ τόπους· 8 πάντα δὲ ταῦτα ἀρχὴ ὠδίνων. 9 τότε παραδώσουσιν ὑμᾶς εἰς θλῖψιν καὶ ἀποκτενοῦσιν ὑμᾶς, καὶ ἔσεσθε μισούμενοι ὑπὸ πάντων τῶν ἐθνῶν διὰ τὸ ὄνομά μου. 10 καὶ τότε σκανδαλισθήσονται πολλοὶ καὶ ἀλλήλους παραδώσουσιν καὶ μισήσουσιν ἀλλήλους· 11 καὶ πολλοὶ ψευδοπροφῆται ἐγερθήσονται καὶ πλανήσουσιν πολλούς· 12 καὶ διὰ τὸ πληθυνθῆναι τὴν ἀνομίαν ψυγήσεται ἡ ἀγάπη τῶν πολλῶν. 13 ὁ δὲ ὑπομείνας εἰς τέλος οὗτος σωθήσεται. 14 καὶ κηρυχθήσεται τοῦτο τὸ εὐαγγέλιον τῆς βασιλείας ἐν ὅλῃ τῇ οἰκουμένῃ εἰς μαρτύριον πᾶσιν τοῖς ἔθνεσιν, καὶ τότε ἥξει τὸ τέλος.

The Great Tribulation
(Mk 13.14–23; Lk 21.20–24)

15 Ὅταν οὖν ἴδητε **τὸ βδέλυγμα τῆς ἐρημώσεως** τὸ ῥηθὲν διὰ Δανιὴλ τοῦ προφήτου ἑστὸς **ἐν τόπῳ ἁγίῳ**, ὁ ἀναγινώσκων νοείτω, 16 τότε οἱ ἐν τῇ Ἰουδαίᾳ φευγέτωσαν εἰς τὰ ὄρη, 17 ὁ ἐπὶ τοῦ δώματος μὴ καταβάτω ἆραι τὰ ἐκ τῆς οἰκίας αὐτοῦ, 18 καὶ ὁ ἐν τῷ ἀγρῷ μὴ ἐπιστρεψάτω ὀπίσω ἆραι τὸ ἱμάτιον αὐτοῦ. 19 οὐαὶ δὲ ταῖς ἐν γαστρὶ ἐχούσαις καὶ ταῖς θηλαζούσαις ἐν ἐκείναις ταῖς ἡμέραις. 20 προσεύχεσθε δὲ ἵνα μὴ γένηται ἡ φυγὴ ὑμῶν χειμῶνος μηδὲ σαββάτῳ· 21 ἔσται γὰρ τότε **θλῖψις** μεγάλη **οἵα οὐ γέγονεν ἀπ᾽ ἀρχῆς κόσμου** ἕως τοῦ **νῦν** οὐδ᾽ οὐ μὴ γένηται. 22 καὶ εἰ μὴ ἐκολοβώθησαν αἱ ἡμέραι ἐκεῖναι, οὐκ ἂν ἐσώθη πᾶσα σάρξ· διὰ δὲ τοὺς ἐκλεκτοὺς κολοβω

l⁴⁷,²¹¹ (itᵃ,ᵇ γενέσθαι ταῦτα) il^aur,c,e,ff¹,?,g¹,h,l,q,,¹ vg eth^ms geo^B Diatessaronᵃ Cyprian ∥ γενέσθαι πάντα Ο Σ 1170 ∥ πάντα ταῦτα γενέσθαι 1216 1241 syr^p,h,pal ∥ ταῦτα πάντα γενέσθαι 544 l^883,950 it^f (arm γενέσθαι ταῦτα πάντα) geo^l,A

7 ἔθνος ἐπὶ ἔθνος 2 Chr 15.6 βασιλεία ἐπὶ βασιλείαν Is 19.2 9 παραδώσουσιν... θλῖψιν Mt 10.17, 23 ἀποκτενοῦσιν ὑμᾶς Jn 16.2 ἔσεσθε...μου Mt 10.22; Jn 15.18 10 σκανδαλισθήσονται πολλοί Dn 11.41 11 Mt 24.5, 24 13 Mt 10.22 14 κηρυχθήσεται...ἔθνεσιν Mt 28.19 εἰς...ἔθνεσιν Mt 10.18 15 τὸ βδέλυγμα...ἁγίῳ Dn 9.27; 11.31; 12.11; 1 Macc 1.54; 6.7 17–18 Lk 17.31 21 Dn 12.1; Jl 2.2 θλῖψις μεγάλη Re 7.14

not mean that the end has come. 7 One country will fight another country, one kingdom will attack another kingdom. There will be famines and earthquakes everywhere. 8 All these things are like the first pains of childbirth.

9 "Then men will arrest you and hand you over to be punished, and you will be put to death. All mankind will hate you because of me. 10 Many will give up their faith at that time; they will betray each other and hate each other. 11 Then many false prophets will appear and fool many people. 12 Such will be the spread of evil that many people's love will grow cold. 13 But the person who holds out to the end will be saved. 14 And this Good News about the Kingdom will be preached through all the world, for a witness to all mankind — and then will come the end."

The Awful Horror
(Also Mark 13.14–23; Luke 21.20–24)

15 "You will see 'The Awful Horror,' of which the prophet Daniel spoke, standing in the holy place." (Note to the reader: understand what this means!) 16 "Then those who are in Judea must run away to the hills. 17 The man who is on the roof of his house must not take the time to go down and get his belongings from the house. 18 The man who is in the field must not go back to get his cloak. 19 How terrible it will be in those days for women who are pregnant, and for mothers who have little babies! 20 Pray to God that you will not have to run away during the winter or on a Sabbath! 21 For the trouble at that time will be far more terrible than any there has ever been, from the beginning of the world to this very day. Nor will there ever be anything like it. 22 But God has already reduced the number of

days; had he not done so, nobody would survive. For the sake of his chosen people, however, God will reduce the days.

²³ "Then, if anyone says to you, 'Look, here is the Messiah!' or 'There he is!' — do not believe him. ²⁴ For false Messiahs and false prophets will appear; they will perform great signs and wonders for the purpose of deceiving God's chosen people, if possible. ²⁵ Listen! I have told you this ahead of time.

²⁶ "Or, if people should tell you, 'Look, he is out in the desert!' — don't go there; or if they say, 'Look, he is hiding here!' — don't believe it. ²⁷ For the Son of Man will come like the lightning which flashes across the whole sky from the east to the west.

²⁸ "Wherever there is a dead body the vultures will gather."

The Coming of the Son of Man
(Also Mark 13.24–27; Luke 21.25–28)

²⁹ "Soon after the trouble of those days the sun will grow dark, the moon will no longer shine, the stars will fall from heaven, and the powers in space will be driven from their course. ³⁰ Then the sign of the Son of Man will appear in the sky; then all the tribes of earth will weep, and they will see the Son of Man coming on the clouds of heaven with power and great glory. ³¹ The great trumpet will sound, and he will send out his angels to the four corners of the earth, and they will gather his chosen people from one end of the world to the other."

θήσονται αἱ ἡμέραι ἐκεῖναι. **23** τότε ἐάν τις ὑμῖν εἴπῃ, Ἰδοὺ ὧδε ὁ Χριστός, ἤ, Ὧδε, μὴ πιστεύσητε· **24** ἐγερθήσονται γὰρ ψευδόχριστοι καὶ ψευδοπροφῆται, καὶ δώσουσιν σημεῖα μεγάλα καὶ τέρατα ὥστε πλανῆσαι, εἰ δυνατόν, καὶ τοὺς ἐκλεκτούς· **25** ἰδοὺ προείρηκα ὑμῖν. **26** ἐὰν οὖν εἴπωσιν ὑμῖν, Ἰδοὺ ἐν τῇ ἐρήμῳ ἐστίν, μὴ ἐξέλθητε· Ἰδοὺ ἐν τοῖς ταμείοις, μὴ πιστεύσητε· **27** ὥσπερ γὰρ ἡ ἀστραπὴ ἐξέρχεται ἀπὸ ἀνατολῶν καὶ φαίνεται ἕως δυσμῶν, οὕτως ἔσται ἡ παρουσία τοῦ υἱοῦ τοῦ ἀνθρώπου. **28** ὅπου ἐὰν ᾖ τὸ πτῶμα, ἐκεῖ συναχθήσονται οἱ ἀετοί.

The Coming of the Son of Man
(Mk 13.24–27; Lk 21.25–28)

29 Εὐθέως δὲ μετὰ τὴν θλῖψιν τῶν ἡμερῶν ἐκείνων,
ὁ ἥλιος σκοτισθήσεται,
　　καὶ ἡ σελήνη οὐ δώσει τὸ φέγγος αὐτῆς,
　　καὶ οἱ ἀστέρες πεσοῦνται ἀπὸ τοῦ οὐρανοῦ,
　　καὶ αἱ δυνάμεις τῶν οὐρανῶν σαλευθήσονται.
30 καὶ τότε φανήσεται τὸ σημεῖον τοῦ υἱοῦ τοῦ ἀνθρώπου ἐν οὐρανῷ, καὶ τότε **κόψονται πᾶσαι αἱ φυλαὶ τῆς γῆς** καὶ ὄψονται **τὸν υἱὸν τοῦ ἀνθρώπου ἐρχόμενον ἐπὶ τῶν νεφελῶν τοῦ οὐρανοῦ** μετὰ δυνάμεως καὶ δόξης πολλῆς· **31** καὶ ἀποστελεῖ τοὺς ἀγγέλους αὐτοῦ μετὰ σάλπιγγος² μεγάλης, καὶ ἐπισυνάξουσιν τοὺς ἐκλεκτοὺς αὐτοῦ ἐκ τῶν τεσσάρων ἀνέμων ἀπ' ἄκρων οὐρανῶν ἕως ἄκρων αὐτῶν.

---

² **31** {B} σάλπιγγος ℵ L W Xᶜᵒᵐᵐ Δ Θ f¹ 700 892ᵗˣᵗ 1195 l¹⁸⁴ itᵉ syrˢ·ᵖ·ʰ copᵇᵒ arm geo Diatessaronᵃ Origenˡᵃᵗ Cyprian Eusebius Cyril-Jerusalem Chrysostom Theodoret ∥ σάλπιγγος φωνῆς B K Xᵗˣᵗ Π f¹³ 28 33 565 892ᵐᵍ 1071 1079 1230 1242 1253 1344 1365 1546 1646 2148 2174 *Byz Lect* ∥ φωνῆς σάλπιγγος syrʰ ʷⁱᵗʰ *·ᵖᵃˡ copˢᵃ eth ∥ μεγάλης φωνῆς copᶠᵃʸ ∥ σάλπιγγος

23–24 Mt 24.5, 11; 1 Jn 2.18　　**24** Dt 13.1–3; 2 Th 2.9–10; Re 13.13–14　　**26–27** Lk 17.23–24 **27** ἡ παρουσία...ἀνθρώπου Mt 24.37, 39; 1 Cor 15.23; 1 Th 2.19; 3.13; 4.15; 5.23; 2 Th 2.1, 8; Jas 5.7, 8; 2 Pe 3.4, 12; 1 Jn 2.28　　**28** Lk 17.37　　**29** ὁ...αὐτῆς Is 13.10; Eze 32.7; Jl 2.10, 31; 3.15; Re 6.12　οἱ...σαλευθήσονται Is 34.4; Hg 2.6, 21; Re 6.13　　**30** κόψονται...γῆς Zch 12.10, 14; Re 1.7　τὸν...πολλῆς Dn 7.13–14; Mt 16.27; 26.64　　**31** ἀποστελεῖ τοὺς ἀγγέλους αὐτοῦ Mt 13.41　μετὰ...μεγάλης Is 27.13; 1 Cor 15.52; 1 Th 4.16　ἐπισυνάξουσιν...αὐτῶν Dt 30.4; Zch 2.6

The Lesson of the Fig Tree
(Mk 13.28–31; Lk 21.29–33)

32 Ἀπὸ δὲ τῆς συκῆς μάθετε τὴν παραβολήν· ὅταν ἤδη ὁ κλάδος αὐτῆς γένηται ἁπαλὸς καὶ τὰ φύλλα ἐκφύῃ, γινώσκετε ὅτι ἐγγὺς τὸ θέρος· **33** οὕτως καὶ ὑμεῖς, ὅταν ἴδητε ταῦτα πάντα, γινώσκετε ὅτι ἐγγύς ἐστιν ἐπὶ θύραις. **34** ἀμὴν λέγω ὑμῖν ὅτι οὐ μὴ παρέλθῃ ἡ γενεὰ αὕτη ἕως ἂν πάντα ταῦτα γένηται. **35** ὁ οὐρανὸς καὶ ἡ γῆ παρελεύσεται, οἱ δὲ λόγοι μου οὐ μὴ παρέλθωσιν.

The Unknown Day and Hour
(Mk 13.32–37; Lk 17.26–30, 34–36)

36 Περὶ δὲ τῆς ἡμέρας ἐκείνης καὶ ὥρας οὐδεὶς οἶδεν, οὐδὲ οἱ ἄγγελοι τῶν οὐρανῶν οὐδὲ ὁ υἱός[3], εἰ μὴ ὁ πατὴρ μόνος. **37** ὥσπερ δὲ αἱ ἡμέραι τοῦ Νῶε, οὕτως ἔσται ἡ παρουσία τοῦ υἱοῦ τοῦ ἀνθρώπου. **38** ὡς γὰρ ἦσαν ἐν ταῖς ἡμέραις ταῖς πρὸ τοῦ κατακλυσμοῦ τρώγοντες καὶ πίνοντες, γαμοῦντες καὶ γαμίζοντες, ἄχρι ἧς ἡμέρας εἰσῆλθεν Νῶε εἰς τὴν κιβωτόν, **39** καὶ οὐκ ἔγνωσαν ἕως ἦλθεν ὁ κατακλυσμὸς καὶ ἦρεν ἅπαντας, οὕτως ἔσται [καὶ] ἡ παρουσία τοῦ υἱοῦ τοῦ ἀνθρώπου. **40** τότε δύο ἔσονται ἐν τῷ ἀγρῷ, εἷς παραλαμβάνεται καὶ εἷς ἀφίεται· **41** δύο ἀλήθουσαι ἐν τῷ μύλῳ, μία παραλαμβάνεται καὶ μία ἀφίεται. **42** γρηγορεῖτε οὖν, ὅτι οὐκ οἴδατε ποίᾳ ἡμέρᾳ ὁ κύριος ὑμῶν

καὶ φωνῆς D 1009 1010 1216 1241 it[a,aur,b,c,d,f,ff1,2,g1,h,l,q,r1] vg Hilary John Damascus

[3] **36** {C} οὐδὲ ὁ υἱός (see Mk 13.32) ℵ[*,b] B D Θ f[13] 28 1195 1230* l[490, 547m,823] it[a,aur,b,c,(e),f,ff1,2,h,l,q,r1] syr[pal] cop[fay] arm eth geo[1,B] Diatessaron Irenaeus[lat] Origen[lat] Hilary Ambrose Chrysostom Latin mss[acc. to Jerome] *||* *omit* ℵ[a] K L W Δ Π f[1] 33 565 700 892 1009 1010 1071 1079 1216 1230[c] 1241 1242 1253 1344 1365 1546 1646 2148 2174 *Byz Lect* it[g1,1] vg syr[s,p,h] cop[sa,bo] geo[A] Origen Greek mss of Adamantius and Pierius[acc. to Jerome] Basil Phoebadius Greek mss[acc. to Ambrose] Didymus Paulinus-Nola Ps-Athanasius John-Damascus Euthymius

34 Mt 16.28 **35** Mt 5.18; Lk 16.17 **36** Ac 1.7; 1 Th 5.1, 2 **37** αἱ...Νῶε Gn 6.9–12 ἡ...ἀνθρώπου Mt 24.27, 39; 1 Cor 15.23; 1 Th 2.19; 3.13; 4.15; 5.23; 2 Th 2.1, 8; Jas 5.7, 8; 2 Pe 3.4, 12; 1 Jn 2.28 **38–39** εἰσῆλθεν...ἅπαντας Gn 6.13–7.24; 2 Pe 3.6 **39** ἡ...ἀνθρώπου Mt 24.27, 37; 1 Cor 15.23; 1 Th 2.19; 3.13; 4.15; 5.23; 2 Th 2.1, 8; Jas 5.7, 8; 2 Pe 3.4, 12; 1 Jn 2.28 **42** Mt 25.13

The Lesson of the Fig Tree
(Also Mark 13.28–31; Luke 21.29–33)

32 "Let the fig tree teach you a lesson. When its branches become green and tender, and it starts putting out leaves, you know that summer is near. **33** In the same way, when you see all these things, you will know that the time is near, ready to begin.[1] **34** Remember this! All these things will happen before the people now living have all died. **35** Heaven and earth will pass away; my words will never pass away."

No One Knows the Day and Hour
(Also Mark 13.32–37; Luke 17.26–30, 34–36)

36 "No one knows, however, when that day and hour will come — neither the angels in heaven, nor the Son;[2] the Father alone knows. **37** The coming of the Son of Man will be like what happened in the time of Noah. **38** Just as in the days before the Flood, people ate and drank, men and women married, up to the very day Noah went into the ark; **39** yet they did not know what was happening until the Flood came and swept them all away. That is how it will be when the Son of Man comes. **40** At that time two men will be working in the field: one will be taken away, the other will be left behind. **41** Two women will be at the mill grinding meal: one will be taken away, the other will be left behind. **42** Watch out, then, because you do not know what day your Lord

---

[1] **33** *the time is near, ready to begin:* or *he is near, ready to come*

[2] **36** *Some mss. omit* nor the Son

will come. 43 Remember this: if the man
of the house knew the time when the
thief would come, he would stay awake
and not let the thief break into his
house. 44 For this reason, then, you also
must be always ready, because the Son
of Man will come at an hour when you
are not expecting him."

The Faithful or the Unfaithful Servant
(Also Luke 12.41–48)

45 "Who, then, is the faithful and wise
servant? He is the one whom his master
has placed in charge of the other servants,
to give them their food at the proper
time. 46 How happy is that servant if
his master finds him doing this when he
comes home! 47 Indeed, I tell you, the
master will put that servant in charge
of all his property. 48 But if he is a bad
servant, he will tell himself, 'My master
will not come back for a long time,'
49 and he will begin to beat his fellow
servants, and eat and drink with drunkards. 50 Then that servant's master will
come back some day when he does not
expect him and at a time he does not
know; 51 the master will cut him to
pieces,[1] and make him share the fate of
the impostors. There he will cry and
gnash his teeth."

The Parable of the Ten Girls

25 "On that day the Kingdom of
heaven will be like ten girls who took
their oil lamps and went out to meet the
bridegroom. 2 Five of them were foolish,
and the other five were wise. 3 The
foolish ones took their lamps but did
not take any extra oil with them, 4 while

[1] **51** cut him to pieces: *or* throw him out

ἔρχεται. **43** *ἐκεῖνο δὲ γινώσκετε ὅτι εἰ ᾔδει ὁ οἰκοδεσπότης
ποίᾳ φυλακῇ ὁ κλέπτης ἔρχεται, ἐγρηγόρησεν ἂν καὶ οὐκ
ἂν εἴασεν διορυχθῆναι τὴν οἰκίαν αὐτοῦ.* **44** *διὰ τοῦτο καὶ
ὑμεῖς γίνεσθε ἕτοιμοι, ὅτι ᾗ οὐ δοκεῖτε ὥρᾳ ὁ υἱὸς τοῦ
ἀνθρώπου ἔρχεται.*

The Faithful or the Unfaithful Servant
(Lk 12.41–48)

45 *Τίς ἄρα ἐστὶν ὁ πιστὸς δοῦλος καὶ φρόνιμος ὃν
κατέστησεν ὁ κύριος ἐπὶ τῆς οἰκετείας αὐτοῦ τοῦ δοῦναι
αὐτοῖς τὴν τροφὴν ἐν καιρῷ;* **46** *μακάριος ὁ δοῦλος ἐκεῖνος
ὃν ἐλθὼν ὁ κύριος αὐτοῦ εὑρήσει οὕτως ποιοῦντα·* **47** *ἀμὴν
λέγω ὑμῖν ὅτι ἐπὶ πᾶσιν τοῖς ὑπάρχουσιν αὐτοῦ καταστήσει αὐτόν.* **48** *ἐὰν δὲ εἴπῃ ὁ κακὸς δοῦλος ἐκεῖνος ἐν τῇ
καρδίᾳ αὐτοῦ, Χρονίζει μου ὁ κύριος,* **49** *καὶ ἄρξηται
τύπτειν τοὺς συνδούλους αὐτοῦ, ἐσθίῃ δὲ καὶ πίνῃ μετὰ
τῶν μεθυόντων,* **50** *ἥξει ὁ κύριος τοῦ δούλου ἐκείνου ἐν
ἡμέρᾳ ᾗ οὐ προσδοκᾷ καὶ ἐν ὥρᾳ ᾗ οὐ γινώσκει,* **51** *καὶ
διχοτομήσει αὐτὸν καὶ τὸ μέρος αὐτοῦ μετὰ τῶν ὑποκριτῶν
θήσει· ἐκεῖ ἔσται ὁ κλαυθμὸς καὶ ὁ βρυγμὸς τῶν ὀδόντων.*

The Parable of the Ten Maidens

25 *Τότε ὁμοιωθήσεται ἡ βασιλεία τῶν οὐρανῶν δέκα
παρθένοις, αἵτινες λαβοῦσαι τὰς λαμπάδας ἑαυτῶν ἐξῆλθον
εἰς ὑπάντησιν τοῦ νυμφίου*[1]. **2** *πέντε δὲ ἐξ αὐτῶν ἦσαν
μωραὶ καὶ πέντε φρόνιμοι.* **3** *αἱ γὰρ μωραὶ λαβοῦσαι τὰς
λαμπάδας αὐτῶν οὐκ ἔλαβον μεθ' ἑαυτῶν ἔλαιον·* **4** *αἱ*

[1] **1** {C} *τοῦ νυμφίου* ℵ B K L W X^{2} Δ Π f^{13} 28 33 565 700 892^{mg} 1009 1010 1071 1079 1195^{c} 1216 1230 1241 1242^{c} 1253 1344 1365 1546 1646 2148 2174 *Byz Lect* l^{883m} syr$^{h, pal}$ cop$^{sa, bo}$ eth geo^{A} Methodius Basil Chrysostom John-Damascus // *τῷ νυμφίῳ* C // *τῶν νυμφίων* 892* // *τοῦ νυμφίου καὶ τῆς νυμφῆς* D X* Θ f^{1} 1195*^{vid} it$^{a, aur, b, c, d, f, ff1,2, g1, h, l, q, r1}$ vg syr$^{s, p, h \text{ with } *, (hmg)}$ arm geo^{1,B} Diatessaron Origen^{lat} Hilary

43 *ποίᾳ...ἔρχεται* 1 Th 5.2; 2 Pe 3.10; Re 3.3; 16.15 **43–44** Lk 12.39–40 **47** *ἐπὶ...αὐτόν* Mt 25.21, 23 **51** *ἐκεῖ...ὀδόντων* Mt 8.12; 13.42, 50; 22.13; 25.30; Lk 13.28
25 **1** *δέκα...νυμφίου* Lk 12.35–36

δὲ φρόνιμοι ἔλαβον ἔλαιον ἐν τοῖς ἀγγείοις μετὰ τῶν λαμπάδων ἑαυτῶν. 5 χρονίζοντος δὲ τοῦ νυμφίου ἐνύσταξαν πᾶσαι καὶ ἐκάθευδον. 6 μέσης δὲ νυκτὸς κραυγὴ γέγονεν, Ἰδοὺ ὁ νυμφίος, ἐξέρχεσθε εἰς ἀπάντησιν αὐτοῦ. 7 τότε ἠγέρθησαν πᾶσαι αἱ παρθένοι ἐκεῖναι καὶ ἐκόσμησαν τὰς λαμπάδας ἑαυτῶν. 8 αἱ δὲ μωραὶ ταῖς φρονίμοις εἶπαν, Δότε ἡμῖν ἐκ τοῦ ἐλαίου ὑμῶν, ὅτι αἱ λαμπάδες ἡμῶν σβέννυνται. 9 ἀπεκρίθησαν δὲ αἱ φρόνιμοι λέγουσαι, Μήποτε οὐκ ἀρκέσῃ ἡμῖν καὶ ὑμῖν· πορεύεσθε μᾶλλον πρὸς τοὺς πωλοῦντας καὶ ἀγοράσατε ἑαυταῖς. 10 ἀπερχομένων δὲ αὐτῶν ἀγοράσαι ἦλθεν ὁ νυμφίος, καὶ αἱ ἕτοιμοι εἰσῆλθον μετ᾽ αὐτοῦ εἰς τοὺς γάμους, καὶ ἐκλείσθη ἡ θύρα. 11 ὕστερον δὲ ἔρχονται καὶ αἱ λοιπαὶ παρθένοι λέγουσαι, Κύριε κύριε, ἄνοιξον ἡμῖν. 12 ὁ δὲ ἀποκριθεὶς εἶπεν, Ἀμὴν λέγω ὑμῖν, οὐκ οἶδα ὑμᾶς. 13 Γρηγορεῖτε οὖν, ὅτι οὐκ οἴδατε τὴν ἡμέραν οὐδὲ τὴν ὥραν.

The Parable of the Talents
(Lk 19.11–27)

14 Ὥσπερ γὰρ ἄνθρωπος ἀποδημῶν ἐκάλεσεν τοὺς ἰδίους δούλους καὶ παρέδωκεν αὐτοῖς τὰ ὑπάρχοντα αὐτοῦ, 15 καὶ ᾧ μὲν ἔδωκεν πέντε τάλαντα, ᾧ δὲ δύο, ᾧ δὲ ἕν, ἑκάστῳ κατὰ τὴν ἰδίαν δύναμιν, καὶ ἀπεδήμησεν. [a]εὐθέως 16[a] πορευθεὶς[2] ὁ τὰ πέντε τάλαντα λαβὼν ἠργάσατο ἐν αὐτοῖς καὶ ἐκέρδησεν ἄλλα πέντε· 17 ὡσαύτως ὁ τὰ δύο

---

[2] 15–16 {C} ἀπεδήμησεν. εὐθέως πορευθεὶς ℵ* B it[b?g1?] arm eth[ms?] geo[1?B?] ‖ ἀπεδήμησεν. εὐθέως δὲ πορευθεὶς Θ f[1] 700 2148 l[26] it[c,f,ff1,2,h,q,r1] syr[palmss] cop[sa] eth[ms?] geo[1?B?] Ps-Chrysostom ‖ ἀπεδήμησεν εὐθέως. πορευθεὶς δὲ ℵ[c] A C D K L W X Δ Π 074 0136 f[13] 28 33 565 892 1009 1010 1071 1079 1195 1216 1230 1241 1242 1253 1344 1365 1546 1646 2174 Byz Lect it[aur,d,l] vg syr[p,h] cop[bo?] eth[pp] geo[A] Diatessaron Origen[lat] Basil ‖ εὐθέως ἀπεδήμησεν. εὐθέως δὲ πορευθεὶς syr[palms] eth[ro]

[aa] 15–16 a no number, a number 16: TR WH? Bov Nes BF[2] AV Zür Jer ‖ a number 16, a no number: WH? RV ASV RSV NEB TT Luth Seg

---

10 ἦλθεν...γάμους Re 19.7, 9   11–12 Lk 13.25, 27   12 Mt 7.23   13 Mt 24.42; Mk 13.35; Lk 12.40   14 Mk 13.34; Lk 19.12–13

---

the wise ones took containers full of oil with their lamps. 5 The bridegroom was late in coming, so the girls began to nod and fall asleep.

6 "It was already midnight when the cry rang out, 'Here is the bridegroom! Come and meet him!' 7 The ten girls woke up and trimmed their lamps. 8 Then the foolish ones said to the wise ones, 'Let us have some of your oil, because our lamps are going out.' 9 'No, indeed,' the wise ones answered back, 'there is not enough for you and us. Go to the store and buy some for yourselves.' 10 So the foolish girls went off to buy some oil, and while they were gone the bridegroom arrived. The five girls who were ready went in with him to the wedding feast, and the door was closed.

11 "Later the other girls arrived. 'Sir, sir! Let us in!' they cried. 12 'But I really don't know you,' the bridegroom answered." 13 And Jesus concluded, "Watch out, then, because you do not know the day or hour."

The Parable of the Three Servants
(Also Luke 19.11–27)

14 "It will be like a man who was about to leave home on a trip: he called his servants and put them in charge of his property. 15 He gave to each one according to his ability: to one he gave five thousand dollars; to the other, two thousand dollars; and to the other, one thousand dollars. Then he left on his trip. 16 The servant who had received five thousand dollars went at once and invested his money and earned another five thousand dollars. 17 In the same way the servant who received two thousand dollars earned another two thousand

dollars. ¹⁸ But the servant who received one thousand dollars went off, dug a hole in the ground, and hid his master's money.

¹⁹ "After a long time the master of those servants came back and settled accounts with them. ²⁰ The servant who had received five thousand dollars came in and handed over the other five thousand dollars. 'You gave me five thousand dollars, sir,' he said. 'Look! Here are another five thousand dollars that I have earned.' ²¹ 'Well done, good and faithful servant!' said his master. 'You have been faithful in managing small amounts, so I will put you in charge of large amounts. Come on in, and share my happiness!' ²² Then the servant who had been given two thousand dollars came in and said, 'You gave me two thousand dollars, sir. Look! Here are another two thousand dollars that I have earned.' ²³ 'Well done, good and faithful servant!' said his master. 'You have been faithful in managing small amounts, so I will put you in charge of large amounts. Come on in and share my happiness!' ²⁴ Then the servant who had received one thousand dollars came in and said: 'Sir, I know you are a hard man: you reap harvests where you did not plant, and gather crops where you did not scatter seed. ²⁵ I was afraid, so I went off and hid your money in the ground. Look! Here is what belongs to you.' ²⁶ 'You bad and lazy servant!' his master said. 'You knew, did you, that I reap harvests where I did not plant, and gather crops where I did not scatter seed? ²⁷ Well, then, you should have deposited my money in the bank, and I would have received it all back with interest when I returned. ²⁸ Now, take the money away from him and give it to the one who has ten thousand dollars. ²⁹ For to every one who has, even more

ἐκέρδησεν³ ἄλλα δύο. **18** ὁ δὲ τὸ ἓν λαβὼν ἀπελθὼν ὤρυξεν γῆν καὶ ἔκρυψεν τὸ ἀργύριον τοῦ κυρίου αὐτοῦ. **19** μετὰ δὲ πολὺν χρόνον ἔρχεται ὁ κύριος τῶν δούλων ἐκείνων καὶ συναίρει λόγον μετ' αὐτῶν. **20** καὶ προσελθὼν ὁ τὰ πέντε τάλαντα λαβὼν προσήνεγκεν ἄλλα πέντε τάλαντα λέγων, Κύριε, πέντε τάλαντά μοι παρέδωκας· ἴδε ἄλλα πέντε τάλαντα ἐκέρδησα. **21** ἔφη αὐτῷ ὁ κύριος αὐτοῦ, Εὖ, δοῦλε ἀγαθὲ καὶ πιστέ, ἐπὶ ὀλίγα ἦς πιστός, ἐπὶ πολλῶν σε καταστήσω· εἴσελθε εἰς τὴν χαρὰν τοῦ κυρίου σου. **22** προσελθὼν δὲ καὶ ὁ τὰ δύο τάλαντα εἶπεν, Κύριε, δύο τάλαντά μοι παρέδωκας· ἴδε ἄλλα δύο τάλαντα ἐκέρδησα. **23** ἔφη αὐτῷ ὁ κύριος αὐτοῦ, Εὖ, δοῦλε ἀγαθὲ καὶ πιστέ, ἐπὶ ὀλίγα ἦς πιστός, ἐπὶ πολλῶν σε καταστήσω· εἴσελθε εἰς τὴν χαρὰν τοῦ κυρίου σου. **24** προσελθὼν δὲ καὶ ὁ τὸ ἓν τάλαντον εἰληφὼς εἶπεν, Κύριε, ἔγνων σε ὅτι σκληρὸς εἶ ἄνθρωπος, θερίζων ὅπου οὐκ ἔσπειρας καὶ συνάγων ὅθεν οὐ διεσκόρπισας· **25** καὶ φοβηθεὶς ἀπελθὼν ἔκρυψα τὸ τάλαντόν σου ἐν τῇ γῇ· ἴδε ἔχεις τὸ σόν. **26** ἀποκριθεὶς δὲ ὁ κύριος αὐτοῦ εἶπεν αὐτῷ, Πονηρὲ δοῦλε καὶ ὀκνηρέ, ᾔδεις ὅτι θερίζω ὅπου οὐκ ἔσπειρα καὶ συνάγω ὅθεν οὐ διεσκόρπισα;^b **27** ἔδει σε οὖν βαλεῖν τὰ ἀργύριά μου τοῖς τραπεζίταις, καὶ ἐλθὼν ἐγὼ ἐκομισάμην ἂν τὸ ἐμὸν σὺν τόκῳ. **28** ἄρατε οὖν ἀπ' αὐτοῦ τὸ τάλαντον καὶ δότε τῷ ἔχοντι τὰ δέκα τάλαντα· **29** τῷ γὰρ ἔχοντι παντὶ δοθήσεται καὶ περισσευθήσεται· τοῦ δὲ μὴ ἔχοντος

---

³ **17** {B} ἐκέρδησεν א B C* L 33 892 1010 1546 it^{aur,g1,l} vg^{(cl),ww} syr^{p,pal} cop^{sa,bo} arm eth? geo Origen^{lat} Basil ‖ καὶ αὐτὸς ἐκέρδησεν D it^d ‖ ἐκέρδησεν καὶ αὐτός A C³ K W X Δ Θ Π 074 *f*¹ *f*¹³ 28 565 700 1009 1071 1079 1195 1216 1230 1241 1242 1253 1344 1365 1646 2174 *Byz Lect* it^h syr^h ‖ *lucratus est et* it^{f,(r1)} ‖ *lucratus est in eis* it^{a,b,c,ff1,2,q}

---

^b **26** *b* question: TR WH Bov Nes BF² RSV NEB TT Zür Jer ‖ *b* statement: AV RV ASV Luth Seg

---

19 ἔρχεται...αὐτῶν Mt 18.23   **21** ἐπὶ ὀλίγα...καταστήσω Mt 25.23; Lk 16.10   ἐπὶ πολλῶν σε καταστήσω Mt 24.47   **23** ἐπὶ ὀλίγα...καταστήσω Mt 25.21; Lk 16.10   ἐπὶ πολλῶν σε καταστήσω Mt 24.47   **24** θερίζων...διεσκόρπισας Jn 4.37   **29** Mt 13.12; Mk 4.25; Lk 8.18

καὶ ὃ ἔχει ἀρθήσεται ἀπ᾽ αὐτοῦ. 30 καὶ τὸν ἀχρεῖον δοῦλον ἐκβάλετε εἰς τὸ σκότος τὸ ἐξώτερον· ἐκεῖ ἔσται ὁ κλαυθμὸς καὶ ὁ βρυγμὸς τῶν ὀδόντων.

The Judgment of the Nations

31 Ὅταν δὲ ἔλθῃ ὁ υἱὸς τοῦ ἀνθρώπου ἐν τῇ δόξῃ αὐτοῦ καὶ πάντες οἱ ἄγγελοι μετ᾽ αὐτοῦ, τότε καθίσει ἐπὶ θρόνου δόξης αὐτοῦ· 32 καὶ συναχθήσονται ἔμπροσθεν αὐτοῦ πάντα τὰ ἔθνη, καὶ ἀφορίσει αὐτοὺς ἀπ᾽ ἀλλήλων, ὥσπερ ὁ ποιμὴν ἀφορίζει τὰ πρόβατα ἀπὸ τῶν ἐρίφων, 33 καὶ στήσει τὰ μὲν πρόβατα ἐκ δεξιῶν αὐτοῦ τὰ δὲ ἐρίφια ἐξ εὐωνύμων. 34 τότε ἐρεῖ ὁ βασιλεὺς τοῖς ἐκ δεξιῶν αὐτοῦ, Δεῦτε, οἱ εὐλογημένοι τοῦ πατρός μου, κληρονομήσατε τὴν ἡτοιμασμένην ὑμῖν βασιλείαν ἀπὸ καταβολῆς κόσμου· 35 ἐπείνασα γὰρ καὶ ἐδώκατέ μοι φαγεῖν, ἐδίψησα καὶ ἐποτίσατέ με, ξένος ἤμην καὶ συνηγάγετέ με, 36 γυμνὸς καὶ περιεβάλετέ με, ἠσθένησα καὶ ἐπεσκέψασθέ με, ἐν φυλακῇ ἤμην καὶ ἤλθατε πρός με. 37 τότε ἀποκριθήσονται αὐτῷ οἱ δίκαιοι λέγοντες, Κύριε, πότε σε εἴδομεν πεινῶντα καὶ ἐθρέψαμεν, ἢ διψῶντα καὶ ἐποτίσαμεν; 38 πότε δέ σε εἴδομεν ξένον καὶ συνηγάγομεν, ἢ γυμνὸν καὶ περιεβάλομεν; 39 πότε δέ σε εἴδομεν ἀσθενοῦντα ἢ ἐν φυλακῇ καὶ ἤλθομεν πρός σε; 40 καὶ ἀποκριθεὶς ὁ βασιλεὺς ἐρεῖ αὐτοῖς, Ἀμὴν λέγω ὑμῖν, ἐφ᾽ ὅσον ἐποιήσατε ἑνὶ τούτων τῶν ἀδελφῶν μου τῶν ἐλαχίστων, ἐμοὶ ἐποιήσατε.

41 Τότε ἐρεῖ καὶ τοῖς ἐξ εὐωνύμων, Πορεύεσθε ἀπ᾽ ἐμοῦ [οἱ] κατηραμένοι εἰς τὸ πῦρ τὸ αἰώνιον τὸ ἡτοιμασμένον[4] τῷ διαβόλῳ καὶ τοῖς ἀγγέλοις αὐτοῦ· 42 ἐπεί-

---

[4] 41 {B} τὸ ἡτοιμασμένον p45 ℵ A B K L W Δ Θ Π 067 074 0128 0136

30 ἐκβάλετε...ὀδόντων Mt 8.12; 22.13   ἐκεῖ...ὀδόντων Mt 13.42, 50; 22.13; 24.51; Lk 13.28   31 Ὅταν...μετ᾽ αὐτοῦ Dt 33.2 LXX; Zch 14.5; Mt 16.27; Jd 14   καθίσει...αὐτοῦ Mt 19.28; Re 3.21; 20.11   32 ὥσπερ...ἐρίφων Eze 34.17   33–34 Lk 12.32   34 κληρονομήσατε...βασιλείαν Lk 22.30   35–36 ἐπείνασα...περιεβάλετέ με Is 58.7   40 ἐφ᾽...ἐμοὶ ἐποιήσατε Pr 19.17; Mt 10.42; 18.5; Mk 9.41   41 Τότε...αἰώνιον Mt 7.23   τὸ πῦρ τὸ αἰώνιον Mk 9.48; Jd 7; Re 20.10

---

will be given, and he will have more than enough; but the one who has nothing, even the little he has will be taken away from him. 30 As for this useless servant — throw him outside in the darkness; there he will cry and gnash his teeth.' "

The Final Judgment

31 "When the Son of Man comes as King, and all the angels with him, he will sit on his royal throne, 32 and all the earth's people will be gathered before him. Then he will divide them into two groups, just as a shepherd separates the sheep from the goats: 33 he will put the sheep at his right and the goats at his left. 34 Then the King will say to the people on his right: 'You who are blessed by my Father: come! Come and receive the kingdom which has been prepared for you ever since the creation of the world. 35 I was hungry and you fed me, thirsty and you gave me drink; I was a stranger and you received me in your homes, 36 naked and you clothed me; I was sick and you took care of me, in prison and you visited me.' 37 The righteous will then answer him: 'When, Lord, did we ever see you hungry and feed you, or thirsty and give you drink? 38 When did we ever see you a stranger and welcome you in our homes, or naked and clothe you? 39 When did we ever see you sick or in prison, and visit you?' 40 The King will answer back, 'I tell you, indeed, whenever you did this for one of the least important of these brothers of mine, you did it for me!'

41 "Then he will say to those on his left: 'Away from me, you who are under God's curse! Away to the eternal fire which has been prepared for the Devil and his angels! 42 I was hungry but you

would not feed me, thirsty but you would
not give me drink; ⁴³ I was a stranger
but you would not welcome me in your
homes, naked but you would not clothe
me; I was sick and in prison but you
would not take care of me.' ⁴⁴ Then they
will answer him: 'When, Lord, did we
ever see you hungry, or thirsty, or a
stranger, or naked, or sick, or in prison,
and we would not help you?' ⁴⁵ The
King will answer them back, 'I tell you,
indeed, whenever you refused to help
one of these least important ones, you
refused to help me.' ⁴⁶ These, then, will
be sent off to eternal punishment; the
righteous will go to eternal life.''

The Plot against Jesus
(Also Mark 14.1–2; Luke 22.1–2; John 11.45–53)

26 When Jesus had finished teaching
all these things, he said to his disciples,
² "In two days, as you know, it will be
the Feast of Passover, and the Son of
Man will be handed over to be nailed
to the cross.''

³ Then the chief priests and the Jewish
elders met together in the palace of
Caiaphas, the High Priest, ⁴ and made
plans to arrest Jesus secretly and put
him to death. ⁵ "We must not do it
during the feast,'' they said, "or the
people will riot.''

Jesus Anointed at Bethany
(Also Mark 14.3–9; John 12.1–8)

⁶ While Jesus was at the house of
Simon the leper, in Bethany, ⁷ a woman
came to him with an alabaster jar filled

νασα γὰρ καὶ οὐκ ἐδώκατέ μοι φαγεῖν, ἐδίψησα καὶ οὐκ
ἐποτίσατέ με, 43 ξένος ἤμην καὶ οὐ συνηγάγετέ με,
γυμνὸς καὶ οὐ περιεβάλετέ με, ἀσθενὴς καὶ ἐν φυλακῇ
καὶ οὐκ ἐπεσκέψασθέ με. 44 τότε ἀποκριθήσονται καὶ
αὐτοὶ λέγοντες, Κύριε, πότε σε εἴδομεν πεινῶντα ἢ
διψῶντα ἢ ξένον ἢ γυμνὸν ἢ ἀσθενῆ ἢ ἐν φυλακῇ καὶ οὐ
διηκονήσαμέν σοι; 45 τότε ἀποκριθήσεται αὐτοῖς λέγων,
Ἀμὴν λέγω ὑμῖν, ἐφ' ὅσον οὐκ ἐποιήσατε ἑνὶ τούτων τῶν
ἐλαχίστων, οὐδὲ ἐμοὶ ἐποιήσατε. 46 καὶ ἀπελεύσονται
οὗτοι εἰς κόλασιν αἰώνιον, οἱ δὲ δίκαιοι εἰς ζωὴν αἰώνιον.

The Plot to Kill Jesus
(Mk 14.1–2; Lk 22.1–2; Jn 11.45–53)

26 Καὶ ἐγένετο ὅτε ἐτέλεσεν ὁ Ἰησοῦς πάντας τοὺς
λόγους τούτους, εἶπεν τοῖς μαθηταῖς αὐτοῦ, 2 Οἴδατε
ὅτι μετὰ δύο ἡμέρας τὸ πάσχα γίνεται, καὶ ὁ υἱὸς τοῦ
ἀνθρώπου παραδίδοται εἰς τὸ σταυρωθῆναι. 3 Τότε συνήχθησαν οἱ ἀρχιερεῖς καὶ οἱ πρεσβύτεροι τοῦ λαοῦ εἰς τὴν
αὐλὴν τοῦ ἀρχιερέως τοῦ λεγομένου Καϊάφα, 4 καὶ συνεβουλεύσαντο ἵνα τὸν Ἰησοῦν δόλῳ κρατήσωσιν καὶ
ἀποκτείνωσιν· 5 ἔλεγον δέ, Μὴ ἐν τῇ ἑορτῇ, ἵνα μὴ
θόρυβος γένηται ἐν τῷ λαῷ.

The Anointing at Bethany
(Mk 14.3–9; Jn 12.1–8)

6 Τοῦ δὲ Ἰησοῦ γενομένου ἐν Βηθανίᾳ ἐν οἰκίᾳ Σίμωνος
τοῦ λεπροῦ, 7 προσῆλθεν αὐτῷ γυνὴ ἔχουσα ἀλάβαστρον

---

f¹³ 28 33ᵛⁱᵈ 565 700 892 1010 1071 1079 1195 1216 1230 1241 1242 1253 1365
1546 1646 2148 2174 *Byz Lect* itᵃᵘʳ,ᶠ,ˡ,q vg syrˢ,ᵖ,ʰ,ᵖᵃˡ copˢᵃ,ᵇᵒ goth arm eth
geo Diatessaron Tertullian¹/² Hippolytus Origenᵍʳ,ˡᵃᵗ Eusebius Hilary
Basil Apostolic Constitutions Didymus Augustine Cyril ∥ τῷ ἡτοι-
μασμένῳ 1009 1344 lᶦ⁶⁶³ ∥ ὃ ἡτοίμασεν ὁ πατήρ μου D f¹ itᵃ,ᵇ,ᶜ,ᵈ,ᶠᶠ¹·²,ᵍˡ,ʰ,ʳˡ
Justin Irenaeusˡᵃᵗ Hippolytus Origenˡᵃᵗ³/⁵ Cyprian Ps-Clement Hilary
Petilianusᵃᶜᶜ·ᵗᵒ ᴬᵘᵍᵘˢᵗⁱⁿᵉ Augustine ∥ ὃ ἡτοίμασεν ὁ κύριος Clement Tertul-
lian¹/² (Origenˡᵃᵗ)

---

46 Dn 12.2; Jn 5.29
26 1 Καὶ...τούτους Mt 7.28; 11.1; 13.53; 19.1   2 τὸ πάσχα Ex 12.1–27 ὁ...σταυρωθῆναι
Mt 20.18–19; 27.26; Mk 15.15; Lk 24.7, 20; Jn 19.16   7 Lk 7.36–38

μύρου βαρυτίμου καὶ κατέχεεν ἐπὶ τῆς κεφαλῆς αὐτοῦ ἀνακειμένου. 8 ἰδόντες δὲ οἱ μαθηταὶ ἠγανάκτησαν λέγοντες, Εἰς τί ἡ ἀπώλεια αὕτη; 9 ἐδύνατο γὰρ τοῦτο πραθῆναι πολλοῦ καὶ δοθῆναι πτωχοῖς. 10 γνοὺς δὲ ὁ Ἰησοῦς εἶπεν αὐτοῖς, Τί κόπους παρέχετε τῇ γυναικί; ἔργον γὰρ καλὸν ἠργάσατο εἰς ἐμέ· 11 πάντοτε γὰρ τοὺς πτωχοὺς ἔχετε μεθ' ἑαυτῶν, ἐμὲ δὲ οὐ πάντοτε ἔχετε· 12 βαλοῦσα γὰρ αὕτη τὸ μύρον τοῦτο ἐπὶ τοῦ σώματός μου πρὸς τὸ ἐνταφιάσαι με ἐποίησεν. 13 ἀμὴν λέγω ὑμῖν, ὅπου ἐὰν κηρυχθῇ τὸ εὐαγγέλιον τοῦτο ἐν ὅλῳ τῷ κόσμῳ, λαληθήσεται καὶ ὃ ἐποίησεν αὕτη εἰς μνημόσυνον αὐτῆς.

Judas' Agreement to Betray Jesus
(Mk 14.10–11; Lk 22.3–6)

14 Τότε πορευθεὶς εἷς τῶν δώδεκα, ὁ λεγόμενος Ἰούδας Ἰσκαριώτης[1], πρὸς τοὺς ἀρχιερεῖς 15 εἶπεν, Τί θέλετέ μοι δοῦναι κἀγὼ ὑμῖν παραδώσω αὐτόν; οἱ δὲ ἔστησαν αὐτῷ τριάκοντα ἀργύρια. 16 καὶ ἀπὸ τότε ἐζήτει εὐκαιρίαν ἵνα αὐτὸν παραδῷ.

The Passover with the Disciples
(Mk 14.12–21; Lk 22.7–14, 21–23; Jn 13.21–30)

17 Τῇ δὲ πρώτῃ τῶν ἀζύμων προσῆλθον οἱ μαθηταὶ τῷ Ἰησοῦ λέγοντες, Ποῦ θέλεις ἑτοιμάσωμέν σοι φαγεῖν τὸ πάσχα; 18 ὁ δὲ εἶπεν, Ὑπάγετε εἰς τὴν πόλιν πρὸς τὸν δεῖνα καὶ εἴπατε αὐτῷ, Ὁ διδάσκαλος λέγει, Ὁ καιρός μου ἐγγύς ἐστιν· πρὸς σὲ ποιῶ τὸ πάσχα μετὰ

---

[1] 14 {B} Ἰσκαριώτης 𝔭⁶⁴ᵛⁱᵈ ℵ A B K L W Δ Θ Π f¹ f¹³ 28 33 565 700 892 1009 1010 1071 1079 1195 1216 1230 1241 1242 1253 1344 1365 1546 1646 2148 2174 Byz Lect vgᶜˡ syrʰ copˢᵃ·ᵇᵒ·ᶠᵃʸ eth Origen Eusebius Chrysostom ∥ Σκαριώτης D itᵈ (itᶠ Scariothes, itᵃ·ᵃᵘʳ·ᵇ·ᶠᶠ²·ᵍ¹·ˡ vgᵂᵂ Scarioth, itᶠᶠ¹ Scariot, itᶜ Scariotha, itᵍ Scariota, itʰ Carioth) syrˢ·ᵖ·ᵖᵃˡ arm geo Diatessaronⁱ·ⁿ (Origenˡᵃᵗ) Augustine

11 πάντοτε γὰρ...ἑαυτῶν Dt 15.11   14-15 πορευθεὶς...αὐτόν Jn 11.57   15 οἱ... ἀργύρια Zch 11.12; (Ex 21.32)   17 Τῇ...ἀζύμων Ex 12.14-20

(Second column — English)

with an expensive perfume, which she poured on Jesus' head as he was eating. [8] The disciples saw this and became angry. "Why all this waste?" they asked. [9] "This perfume could have been sold for a large amount and the money given to the poor!" [10] Jesus was aware of what they were saying and said to them: "Why are you bothering this woman? It is a fine and beautiful thing that she has done for me. [11] You will always have poor people with you, but I will not be with you always. [12] What she did was to pour this perfume on my body to get me ready for burial. [13] Now, remember this! Wherever this gospel is preached, all over the world, what she has done will be told in memory of her."

Judas Agrees to Betray Jesus
(Also Mark 14.10–11; Luke 22.3–6)

[14] Then one of the twelve disciples — the one named Judas Iscariot — went to the chief priests [15] and said, "What will you give me if I hand Jesus over to you?" So they counted out thirty silver coins and gave them to him. [16] From then on Judas was looking for a good chance to betray Jesus.

Jesus Eats the Passover Meal
with His Disciples
(Also Mark 14.12–21; Luke 22.7–14, 21–23; John 13.21–30)

[17] On the first day of the Feast of Unleavened Bread the disciples came to Jesus and asked him, "Where do you want us to get the Passover supper ready for you?" [18] "Go to a certain man in the city," he said to them, "and tell him: 'The Teacher says, My hour has come; my disciples and I will celebrate

the Passover at your house.' " 19 The
disciples did as Jesus had told them and
prepared the Passover supper.
20 When it was evening Jesus and the
twelve disciples sat down to eat. 21 During the meal Jesus said, "I tell you, one
of you will betray me." 22 The disciples
were very upset and began to ask him,
one after the other, "Surely you don't
mean me, Lord?" 23 Jesus answered:
"One who dips his bread in the dish
with me will betray me. 24 The Son of
Man will die as the Scriptures say he
will, but how terrible for that man who
will betray the Son of Man! It would
have been better for that man if he had
never been born!" 25 Judas, the traitor,
spoke up. "Surely you don't mean me,
Teacher?" he asked. Jesus answered,
"So you say."

The Lord's Supper

(Also Mark 14.22–26; Luke 22.15–20;
1 Cor. 11.23–25)

26 While they were eating, Jesus took
the bread, gave a prayer of thanks,
broke it, and gave to his disciples.
"Take and eat it," he said; "this is my
body." 27 Then he took the cup, gave
thanks to God, and gave it to them.
"Drink it, all of you," he said; 28 "for
this is my blood, which seals God's
covenant, my blood poured out for many

τῶν μαθητῶν μου. **19** *καὶ ἐποίησαν οἱ μαθηταὶ ὡς συνέταξεν αὐτοῖς ὁ Ἰησοῦς, καὶ ἡτοίμασαν τὸ πάσχα.* **20** *Ὀψίας
δὲ γενομένης ἀνέκειτο μετὰ τῶν δώδεκα*[2]. **21** *καὶ ἐσθιόντων αὐτῶν εἶπεν, Ἀμὴν λέγω ὑμῖν ὅτι εἷς ἐξ ὑμῶν
παραδώσει με.* **22** *καὶ λυπούμενοι σφόδρα ἤρξαντο λέγειν
αὐτῷ εἷς ἕκαστος, Μήτι ἐγώ εἰμι, κύριε;* **23** *ὁ δὲ ἀποκριθεὶς εἶπεν, Ὁ ἐμβάψας μετ' ἐμοῦ τὴν χεῖρα ἐν τῷ
τρυβλίῳ οὗτός με παραδώσει.* **24** *ὁ μὲν υἱὸς τοῦ ἀνθρώπου
ὑπάγει καθὼς γέγραπται περὶ αὐτοῦ, οὐαὶ δὲ τῷ ἀνθρώπῳ
ἐκείνῳ δι' οὗ ὁ υἱὸς τοῦ ἀνθρώπου παραδίδοται· καλὸν
ἦν αὐτῷ εἰ οὐκ ἐγεννήθη ὁ ἄνθρωπος ἐκεῖνος.* **25** *ἀποκριθεὶς δὲ Ἰούδας ὁ παραδιδοὺς αὐτὸν εἶπεν, Μήτι ἐγώ εἰμι,
ῥαββί; λέγει αὐτῷ, Σὺ εἶπας.*

The Institution of the Lord's Supper

(Mk 14.22–26; Lk 22.15–20; 1 Cor 11.23–25)

26 *Ἐσθιόντων δὲ αὐτῶν λαβὼν ὁ Ἰησοῦς ἄρτον καὶ
εὐλογήσας ἔκλασεν καὶ δοὺς τοῖς μαθηταῖς εἶπεν, Λάβετε
φάγετε, τοῦτό ἐστιν τὸ σῶμά μου.* **27** *καὶ λαβὼν ποτήριον*[3] *καὶ εὐχαριστήσας ἔδωκεν αὐτοῖς λέγων, Πίετε ἐξ
αὐτοῦ πάντες,* **28** *τοῦτο γάρ ἐστιν τὸ αἷμά μου τῆς
διαθήκης*[4] *τὸ περὶ πολλῶν ἐκχυννόμενον εἰς ἄφεσιν ἁμαρ-*

---

[2] **20** {C} *μετὰ τῶν δώδεκα* (*see* Mk 14.17) $\mathfrak{p}^{37vid,45vid}$ B D K *f*^{1} *f*^{13} 28 565 700 1010 1216 1230 1242 1253 1344 1365 1646 2148 2174 *Byz Lect* it^{d} (syr^{s}) geo^{2} Eusebius Chrysostom$^{1/2}$ // *μετὰ τῶν δώδεκα μαθητῶν* ℵ A L W Δ Θ Π 33 892 1009 1071 1079 1195 1241 1546 it^{f,ff1,g1,q,r1} vg^{ww} syr^{h,palmss} cop^{sa,bo} arm eth? geo^{1} Chrysostom$^{1/2}$ Augustine // *μετὰ τῶν δώδεκα μαθητῶν αὐτοῦ* 074 it^{a,aur,b,c,ff2,h} vg^{cl} syr^{p} eth? Origen^{lat} // *μετὰ τῶν μαθητῶν αὐτοῦ* (it^{l} *omit* **αὐτοῦ**) syr^{palms} Origen^{lat}

[3] **27** {C} *ποτήριον* (*see* Mk 14.23) ℵ B L W Δ Θ 074 *f*^{1} 28 33 700 892 *l*^{185,299,547,1634} cop^{sa,bo} arm Diatessaron Chrysostom // *τὸ ποτήριον* (*see* Lk 22.17) $\mathfrak{p}^{37vid,45}$ A C D K Π *f*^{13} 565 1009 1010 1071 1079 1195 1216 1230 1241 1242 1253 1344 1365 1546 1646 2148 2174 *Byz Lect* Justin Diatessaron^{i,n}

[4] **28** {B} *διαθήκης* (*see* Mk 14.24) $\mathfrak{p}^{37,45vid}$ ℵ B L Θ 33 (syr^{palms}) cop$^{bo ms}$

---

23 *Ὁ ἐμβάψας...παραδώσει* Ps 41.9 **24** *ὁ μὲν...αὐτοῦ* Ps 22.7, 8, 16–18; Is 53.9 **26** *λαβὼν...μαθηταῖς* Mt 14.19; 15.36; Mk 6.41; 8.6; Lk 9.16 **26–28** *λαβὼν ὁ Ἰησοῦς...αἷμά μου* 1 Cor 10.16 **28** *τὸ αἷμα...διαθήκης* Ex 24.8; Jr 31.31; Zch 9.11; He 9.20

τιῶν. **29** λέγω δὲ ὑμῖν, οὐ μὴ πίω ἀπ' ἄρτι ἐκ τούτου τοῦ γενήματος τῆς ἀμπέλου ἕως τῆς ἡμέρας ἐκείνης ὅταν αὐτὸ πίνω μεθ' ὑμῶν καινὸν ἐν τῇ βασιλείᾳ τοῦ πατρός μου. **30** Καὶ ὑμνήσαντες ἐξῆλθον εἰς τὸ Ὄρος τῶν Ἐλαιῶν.

Peter's Denial Foretold
(Mk 14.27–31; Lk 22.31–34; Jn 13.36–38)

31 Τότε λέγει αὐτοῖς ὁ Ἰησοῦς, Πάντες ὑμεῖς σκανδαλισθήσεσθε ἐν ἐμοὶ ἐν τῇ νυκτὶ ταύτῃ, γέγραπται γάρ,

Πατάξω τὸν ποιμένα,

καὶ διασκορπισθήσονται τὰ πρόβατα τῆς ποίμνης·
32 μετὰ δὲ τὸ ἐγερθῆναί με προάξω ὑμᾶς εἰς τὴν Γαλιλαίαν. **33** ἀποκριθεὶς δὲ ὁ Πέτρος εἶπεν αὐτῷ, Εἰ πάντες σκανδαλισθήσονται ἐν σοί, ἐγὼ οὐδέποτε σκανδαλισθήσομαι. **34** ἔφη αὐτῷ ὁ Ἰησοῦς, Ἀμὴν λέγω σοι ὅτι ἐν ταύτῃ τῇ νυκτὶ πρὶν ἀλέκτορα φωνῆσαι τρὶς ἀπαρνήσῃ με. **35** λέγει αὐτῷ ὁ Πέτρος, Κἂν δέῃ με σὺν σοὶ ἀποθανεῖν, οὐ μή σε ἀπαρνήσομαι. ὁμοίως καὶ πάντες οἱ μαθηταὶ εἶπαν.

The Prayer in Gethsemane
(Mk 14.32–42; Lk 22.39–46)

36 Τότε ἔρχεται μετ' αὐτῶν ὁ Ἰησοῦς εἰς χωρίον λεγόμενον Γεθσημανί, καὶ λέγει τοῖς μαθηταῖς, Καθίσατε αὐτοῦ ἕως ἂν ἀπελθὼν ἐκεῖ προσεύξωμαι. **37** καὶ παραλαβὼν τὸν Πέτρον καὶ τοὺς δύο υἱοὺς Ζεβεδαίου ἤρξατο

for the forgiveness of sins. [29] I tell you, I will never again drink this wine until the day I drink the new wine with you in my Father's Kingdom." [30] Then they sang a hymn and went out to the Mount of Olives.

Jesus Predicts Peter's Denial
(Also Mark 14.27–31; Luke 22.31–34; John 13.36–38)

[31] Then Jesus said to them: "This very night all of you will run away and leave me, for the scripture says, 'God will kill the shepherd and the sheep of the flock will be scattered.' [32] But after I am raised to life I will go to Galilee ahead of you." [33] Peter spoke up and said to Jesus, "I will never leave you, even though all the rest do!" [34] "Remember this!" Jesus said to Peter. "Before the rooster crows tonight you will say three times that you do not know me." [35] Peter answered, "I will never say I do not know you, even if I have to die with you!" And all the disciples said the same thing.

Jesus Prays in Gethsemane
(Also Mark 14.32–42; Luke 22.39–46)

[36] Then Jesus went with his disciples to a place called Gethsemane, and he said to them, "Sit here while I go over there and pray." [37] He took with him Peter, and Zebedee's two sons. Grief and

---

geo¹ Irenaeus Cyprian Cyril ‖ καινῆς διαθήκης (see Lk 22.20) A C D K W Δ Π 074ᵛⁱᵈ f¹ f¹³ 28 565 700 892 1009 1010 1071 1079 1195 1216 1230 1241 1242 1253 1344 1365 1546 1646 2148 2174 *Byz Lect* itᵃ, ᵃᵘʳ, ᶜ, ᵈ, ᶠ, ᶠᶠˡ·², g¹, ʰ, ˡ, q, rˡ vg syrˢ, ᵖ, ʰ, ᵖᵃˡᵐˢˢ copˢᵃ, ᵇᵒ arm eth geo² Diatessaron Irenaeusˡᵃᵗ Origenᵍʳ, ˡᵃᵗ Cyprian Basil Chrysostom ‖ *novi et aeterni testamenti* itᵇ

30 ὑμνήσαντες Ps 113—118   ἐξῆλθον...Ἐλαιῶν Lk 22.39   **31** Πατάξω...ποίμνης Zch 13.7 (Mt 26.56; Jn 16.32)   **32** Mt 28.7, 16·   **34** ἐν...με Mt 26.69–75; Mk 14.66–72; Lk 22.56–62; Jn 18.25–27   **35** Κἂν...ἀποθανεῖν Jn 11.16   **36** ἔρχεται...Γεθσημανί Jn 18.1
37 παραλαβὼν...Ζεβεδαίου Mt 17.1; Mk 5.37; 14.33; Lk 8.51; 9.28

anguish came over him, ³⁸ and he said to them, "The sorrow in my heart is so great that it almost crushes me. Stay here and watch with me." ³⁹ He went a little farther on, threw himself face down to the ground, and prayed, "My Father, if it is possible, take this cup away from me! But not what I want, but what you want."

⁴⁰ Then he returned to the three disciples and found them asleep; and he said to Peter: "How is it that you three were not able to watch with me for one hour? ⁴¹ Keep watch, and pray, so you will not fall into temptation. The spirit is willing, but the flesh is weak."

⁴² Again a second time Jesus went away and prayed, "My Father, if this cup cannot be taken away unless I drink it, your will be done." ⁴³ He returned once more and found the disciples asleep; they could not keep their eyes open.

⁴⁴ Again Jesus left them, went away, and prayed the third time, saying the same words. ⁴⁵ Then he returned to the disciples and said: "Are you still sleeping and resting? Look! The hour has come for the Son of Man to be handed over to the power of sinful men. ⁴⁶ Rise, let us go. Look, here is the man who is betraying me!"

The Arrest of Jesus
(Also Mark 14.43–50; Luke 22.47–53; John 18.3–12)

⁴⁷ He was still talking when Judas, one of the twelve disciples, arrived. With him was a large crowd carrying swords and clubs, sent by the chief priests and

λυπεῖσθαι καὶ ἀδημονεῖν. 38 τότε λέγει αὐτοῖς, Περίλυπός ἐστιν ἡ ψυχή μου ἕως θανάτου· μείνατε ὧδε καὶ γρηγορεῖτε μετ' ἐμοῦ. 39 καὶ προελθὼν μικρὸν ἔπεσεν ἐπὶ πρόσωπον αὐτοῦ προσευχόμενος καὶ λέγων, Πάτερ μου, εἰ δυνατόν ἐστιν, παρελθάτω ἀπ' ἐμοῦ τὸ ποτήριον τοῦτο· πλὴν οὐχ ὡς ἐγὼ θέλω ἀλλ' ὡς σύ. 40 καὶ ἔρχεται πρὸς τοὺς μαθητὰς καὶ εὑρίσκει αὐτοὺς καθεύδοντας, καὶ λέγει τῷ Πέτρῳ, Οὕτως οὐκ ἰσχύσατε μίαν ὥραν γρηγορῆσαι μετ' ἐμοῦ; 41 γρηγορεῖτεᵃ καὶ προσεύχεσθε,ᵃ ἵνα μὴ εἰσέλθητε εἰς πειρασμόν· τὸ μὲν πνεῦμα πρόθυμον ἡ δὲ σὰρξ ἀσθενής. 42 πάλιν ἐκ δευτέρου ἀπελθὼν προσηύξατο λέγων, Πάτερ μου, εἰ οὐ δύναται τοῦτο παρελθεῖν ἐὰν μὴ αὐτὸ πίω, γενηθήτω τὸ θέλημά σου. 43 καὶ ἐλθὼν πάλιν εὗρεν αὐτοὺς καθεύδοντας, ἦσαν γὰρ αὐτῶν οἱ ὀφθαλμοὶ βεβαρημένοι. 44 καὶ ἀφεὶς αὐτοὺςᵇ πάλινᵇ ἀπελθὼν προσηύξατο ἐκ τρίτου τὸν αὐτὸν λόγον εἰπὼνᶜ πάλιν.ᶜ 45 τότε ἔρχεται πρὸς τοὺς μαθητὰς καὶ λέγει αὐτοῖς, Καθεύδετε τὸ λοιπὸν καὶ ἀναπαύεσθε;ᵈ ἰδοὺ ἤγγικεν ἡ ὥρα καὶ ὁ υἱὸς τοῦ ἀνθρώπου παραδίδοται εἰς χεῖρας ἁμαρτωλῶν. 46 ἐγείρεσθε, ἄγωμεν· ἰδοὺ ἤγγικεν ὁ παραδιδούς με.

The Betrayal and Arrest of Jesus
(Mk 14.43–50; Lk 22.47–53; Jn 18.3–12)

47 Καὶ ἔτι αὐτοῦ λαλοῦντος ἰδοὺ Ἰούδας εἷς τῶν δώδεκα ἦλθεν καὶ μετ' αὐτοῦ ὄχλος πολὺς μετὰ μαχαιρῶν καὶ ξύλων ἀπὸ τῶν ἀρχιερέων καὶ πρεσβυτέρων τοῦ λαοῦ.

ᵃ ᵃ 41 a none, a minor: TR WH Bov Nes BF² AV RV ASV TT Zür Luth Seg ∥ a minor, a none: RVᵐᵍ ASVᵐᵍ NEB ∥ a none, a none: RSV Jer
ᵇ ᵇ 44 b none, b none: WH Bov Nes BF² ∥ b minor, b none: (TR) (AV) (NEB) TT Zür (Luth) (Jer) Seg ∥ b none, b minor: RV ASV RSV
ᶜ ᶜ 44 c none, c major: WH Bov Nes BF² RV ASV NEB TT Zür Jer Seg ∥ c major, c none: WHᵐᵍ ∥ c major, c different text: TR AV RSV Luth
ᵈ 45 d question: ASVᵐᵍ RSV NEB Luth ∥ d statement: Jer? Segᵐᵍ ∥ d command: AV RV ASV TT Zür Seg ∥ d statement or command: TR WH Bov Nes BF²

---

38 Περίλυπος...μου Ps 42.5, 11; 43.5; Jn 12.27   Περίλυπος...θανάτου Jon 4.9
39 He 5.7–8   41 προσεύχεσθε...πειρασμόν Mt 6.13; Lk 11.4   42 γενηθήτω...σου Mt 6.10
44 προσηύξατο ἐκ τρίτου 2 Cor 12.8   45 ἤγγικεν ἡ ὥρα Jn 12.23; 13.1; 17.1   ὁ...
ἁμαρτωλῶν Mt 17.22; Mk 9.31; 10.33; Lk 9.44; 24.7   46 ἐγείρεσθε, ἄγωμεν Jn 14.31

48 ὁ δὲ παραδιδοὺς αὐτὸν ἔδωκεν αὐτοῖς σημεῖον λέγων, "Ὃν ἂν φιλήσω αὐτός ἐστιν· κρατήσατε αὐτόν. **49** καὶ εὐθέως προσελθὼν τῷ Ἰησοῦ εἶπεν, Χαῖρε, ῥαββί· καὶ κατεφίλησεν αὐτόν. **50** ὁ δὲ Ἰησοῦς εἶπεν αὐτῷ, Ἑταῖρε, ἐφ᾽ ὃ πάρει.ᵉ τότε προσελθόντες ἐπέβαλον τὰς χεῖρας ἐπὶ τὸν Ἰησοῦν καὶ ἐκράτησαν αὐτόν. **51** καὶ ἰδοὺ εἷς τῶν μετὰ Ἰησοῦ ἐκτείνας τὴν χεῖρα ἀπέσπασεν τὴν μάχαιραν αὐτοῦ καὶ πατάξας τὸν δοῦλον τοῦ ἀρχιερέως ἀφεῖλεν αὐτοῦ τὸ ὠτίον. **52** τότε λέγει αὐτῷ ὁ Ἰησοῦς, Ἀπόστρεψον τὴν μάχαιράν σου εἰς τὸν τόπον αὐτῆς, πάντες γὰρ οἱ λαβόντες μάχαιραν ἐν μαχαίρῃ ἀπολοῦνται. **53** ἢ δοκεῖς ὅτι οὐ δύναμαι παρακαλέσαι τὸν πατέρα μου, καὶ παραστήσει μοι ἄρτι πλείω δώδεκα λεγιῶνας ἀγγέλων; **54** πῶς οὖν πληρωθῶσιν αἱ γραφαὶ ὅτι οὕτως δεῖ γενέσθαι; **55** Ἐν ἐκείνῃ τῇ ὥρᾳ εἶπεν ὁ Ἰησοῦς τοῖς ὄχλοις, Ὡς ἐπὶ λῃστὴν ἐξήλθατε μετὰ μαχαιρῶν καὶ ξύλων συλλαβεῖν με;ᶠ καθ᾽ ἡμέραν ἐν τῷ ἱερῷ ἐκαθεζόμην διδάσκων καὶ οὐκ ἐκρατήσατέ με. **56** τοῦτο δὲ ὅλον γέγονεν ἵνα πληρωθῶσιν αἱ γραφαὶ τῶν προφητῶν. Τότε οἱ μαθηταὶ πάντες ἀφέντες αὐτὸν ἔφυγον.

Jesus before the Council
(Mk 14.53–65; Lk 22.54–55, 63–71; Jn 18.13–14, 19–24)

57 Οἱ δὲ κρατήσαντες τὸν Ἰησοῦν ἀπήγαγον πρὸς Καϊάφαν τὸν ἀρχιερέα, ὅπου οἱ γραμματεῖς καὶ οἱ πρεσβύτεροι συνήχθησαν. **58** ὁ δὲ Πέτρος ἠκολούθει αὐτῷ ἀπὸ μακρόθεν ἕως τῆς αὐλῆς τοῦ ἀρχιερέως, καὶ εἰσελθὼν ἔσω ἐκάθητο μετὰ τῶν ὑπηρετῶν ἰδεῖν τὸ τέλος. **59** οἱ δὲ ἀρχιερεῖς καὶ τὸ συνέδριον ὅλον ἐζήτουν ψευδομαρτυρίαν κατὰ τοῦ Ἰησοῦ ὅπως αὐτὸν θανατώσωσιν, **60** καὶ οὐχ

ᵉ **50** e command: WH Nes BF² RV ASV RSVᵐᵍ NEB TT Jer Seg ∥ e question. TR Bov AV RSV NEBᵐᵍ Zür Luth

ᶠ **55** f question: TR WH Bov Nes BF² AV RV ASV RSV NEB TT Jer ∥ f statement: Zür Luth Seg

---

51 Jn 18.26   **52** πάντες...ἀπολοῦνται Gn 9.6; Re 13.10   **55** καθ᾽...διδάσκων Lk 19.47; 21.37; Jn 18.20   **56** οἱ...ἔφυγον Zch 13.7; Mt 26.31; Jn 16.32

---

the Jewish elders. **48** The traitor had given the crowd a signal: "The man I kiss is the one you want. Arrest him!" **49** When Judas arrived he went straight to Jesus and said, "Peace be with you, Teacher," and kissed him. **50** Jesus answered, "Be quick about it, friend!"[1] Then they came up, arrested Jesus, and held him tight. **51** One of those who were with Jesus drew his sword and struck at the High Priest's slave, cutting off his ear. **52** Then Jesus said to him: "Put your sword back in its place, for all who take the sword will die by the sword. **53** Don't you know that I could call on my Father for help and at once he would send me more than twelve armies of angels? **54** But in that case, how could the Scriptures come true that say it must happen in this way?"

55 Then Jesus spoke to the crowd: "Did you have to come with swords and clubs to capture me, as though I were an outlaw? Every day I sat down and taught in the Temple, and you did not arrest me. **56** But all this has happened to make come true what the prophets wrote in the Scriptures."

Then all the disciples left him and ran away.

Jesus before the Council
(Also Mark 14.53–65; Luke 22.54–55, 63–71; John 18.13–14, 19–24)

57 Those who had arrested Jesus took him to the house of Caiaphas, the High Priest, where the teachers of the Law and the elders had gathered together. **58** Peter followed him from a distance, as far as the courtyard of the High Priest's house. He went into the courtyard and sat down with the guards, to see how it would all come out. **59** The chief priests and the whole Council tried to find some false evidence against Jesus, to put him to death; **60** but they could

---

[1] **50** Be quick about it, friend! *or* Why are you here, friend?

not find any, even though many came up and told lies about him. Finally two men stepped forward [61] and said, "This man said, 'I am able to tear down God's Temple and three days later build it back up.'"

[62] The High Priest stood up and said to Jesus, "Have you no answer to give to this accusation against you?" [63] But Jesus kept quiet. Again the High Priest spoke to him: "In the name of the living God, I now put you on oath: tell us if you are the Messiah, the Son of God." [64] Jesus answered him: "So you say. But I tell all of you: from this time on you will see the Son of Man sitting at the right side of the Almighty, and coming on the clouds of heaven!" [65] At this the High Priest tore his clothes and said: "Blasphemy! We don't need any more witnesses! Right here you have heard his wicked words! [66] What do you think?" They answered, "He is guilty, and must die."

[67] Then they spat in his face and beat him; and those who slapped him [68] said, "Prophesy for us, Messiah! Tell us who hit you!"

εὗρον πολλῶν προσελθόντων ψευδομαρτύρων. ὕστερον δὲ προσελθόντες δύο **61** εἶπαν, Οὗτος ἔφη, Δύναμαι καταλῦσαι τὸν ναὸν τοῦ θεοῦ καὶ διὰ τριῶν ἡμερῶν οἰκοδομῆσαι[5]. **62** καὶ ἀναστὰς ὁ ἀρχιερεὺς εἶπεν αὐτῷ, Οὐδὲν ἀποκρίνῃ;[g] τί οὗτοί σου καταμαρτυροῦσιν;[g] **63** ὁ δὲ Ἰησοῦς ἐσιώπα. καὶ[6] ὁ ἀρχιερεὺς εἶπεν αὐτῷ, Ἐξορκίζω σε κατὰ τοῦ θεοῦ τοῦ ζῶντος ἵνα ἡμῖν εἴπῃς εἰ σὺ εἶ ὁ Χριστὸς ὁ υἱὸς τοῦ θεοῦ. **64** λέγει αὐτῷ ὁ Ἰησοῦς, Σὺ εἶπας·[h] πλὴν λέγω ὑμῖν,

ἀπ' ἄρτι ὄψεσθε **τὸν υἱὸν τοῦ ἀνθρώπου**
καθήμενον ἐκ δεξιῶν τῆς δυνάμεως
καὶ ἐρχόμενον ἐπὶ τῶν νεφελῶν τοῦ οὐρανοῦ.

65 τότε ὁ ἀρχιερεὺς διέρρηξεν τὰ ἱμάτια αὐτοῦ λέγων, Ἐβλασφήμησεν· τί ἔτι χρείαν ἔχομεν μαρτύρων; ἴδε νῦν ἠκούσατε τὴν βλασφημίαν· **66** τί ὑμῖν δοκεῖ; οἱ δὲ ἀποκριθέντες εἶπαν, Ἔνοχος θανάτου ἐστίν. **67** Τότε ἐνέπτυσαν εἰς τὸ πρόσωπον αὐτοῦ καὶ ἐκολάφισαν αὐτόν, οἱ δὲ ἐράπισαν **68** λέγοντες, Προφήτευσον ἡμῖν, Χριστέ, τίς ἐστιν ὁ παίσας σε;

---

[5] **61** {C} οἰκοδομῆσαι B Θ *f*[1] *f*[13] 700 arm eth[ro] geo Origen ‖ αὐτὸν οἰκοδομῆσαι ℵ C L 090 33 892 it[b,(c),ff2,h,q,rl] cop[sa?bo?] Origen[gr,lat] ‖ οἰκοδομῆσαι αὐτόν A D K W Δ Π 28 565 1009 1010 1071 1079 1195 1216 1230 1241 1344 1365 1646 2174 *Byz Lect* it[a,aur,d,f,ff1,g1,l] vg syr[h] eth[pp,ms] Origen[lat] ‖ οἰκοδομῆσαι αὐτῷ 346 ‖ οἰκοδομήσω αὐτόν 1242 1253 1546 2148 syr[s,p,pal]

[6] **63** {C} καί ℵ[mg] B L Θ *f*[1] *f*[13] 33 892 (1010 ὁ δέ) *l*[547] it[aur,ff1,g1,l] vg syr[pal] cop[(sa),bo] eth geo Diatessaron[a,v] Origen[gr,lat] Cyril ‖ καὶ ἀποκριθείς A C K W Δ Π 090 28 565 700 1009 1071 1079 1195 1216 1230 1241 1242 1253 1365 1546 1646 2148 2174 *Byz Lect* it[a,b,c,f,ff2,h,q,rl] syr[s,p,h] arm Diatessaron ‖ ἀποκριθεὶς οὖν D it[d]

[g,g] **62** *g* question, *g* question: TR WH AV RV ASV RSV Jer Seg ‖ *g* minor, *g* question: Bov Nes BF[2] (NEB) TT Zür Luth Jer[mg] (Seg[mg])

[h] **64** *h* statement: TR WH Bov Nes BF[2] AV RV ASV RSV NEB TT Zür Luth Jer Seg ‖ *h* question: WH[mg]

---

61 Οὗτος...οἰκοδομῆσαι Mt 27.40; Jn 2.19; Ac 6.14   **63** ὁ δὲ...ἐσιώπα Is 53.7; Mt 27.12; 14; Lk 23.9; Jn 19.9   Ἐξορκίζω...υἱὸς τοῦ θεοῦ Mt 16.16–17   **64** τὸν...δεξιῶν Ps 110.1 τὸν...οὐρανοῦ Dn 7.13; Mt 24.30   **65** διέρρηξεν...αὐτοῦ Nu 14.6; 2 Sm 13.19; Ezr 9.3; Job 1.20; 2.12; Jr 36.24; Ac 14.14   **65–66** Ἐβλασφήμησεν...ἐστίν Lv 24.16; Jn 19.7   **67** ἐνέπτυσαν... ἐράπισαν Is 50.6; 53.5

Peter's Denial of Jesus
(Mk 14.66–72; Lk 22.56–62; Jn 18.15–18, 25–27)

69 Ὁ δὲ Πέτρος ἐκάθητο ἔξω ἐν τῇ αὐλῇ· καὶ προσῆλθεν αὐτῷ μία παιδίσκη λέγουσα, Καὶ σὺ ἦσθα μετὰ Ἰησοῦ τοῦ Γαλιλαίου. **70** ὁ δὲ ἠρνήσατο ἔμπροσθεν πάντων λέγων, Οὐκ οἶδα τί λέγεις. **71** ἐξελθόντα δὲ εἰς τὸν πυλῶνα εἶδεν αὐτὸν ἄλλη καὶ λέγει τοῖς ἐκεῖ, Οὗτος[7] ἦν μετὰ Ἰησοῦ τοῦ Ναζωραίου. **72** καὶ πάλιν ἠρνήσατο μετὰ ὅρκου ὅτι Οὐκ οἶδα τὸν ἄνθρωπον. **73** μετὰ μικρὸν δὲ προσελθόντες οἱ ἑστῶτες εἶπον τῷ Πέτρῳ, Ἀληθῶς καὶ σὺ ἐξ αὐτῶν εἶ, καὶ γὰρ ἡ λαλιά σου δῆλόν σε ποιεῖ. **74** τότε ἤρξατο καταθεματίζειν καὶ ὀμνύειν ὅτι Οὐκ οἶδα τὸν ἄνθρωπον. καὶ εὐθέως ἀλέκτωρ ἐφώνησεν. **75** καὶ ἐμνήσθη ὁ Πέτρος τοῦ ῥήματος Ἰησοῦ εἰρηκότος ὅτι Πρὶν ἀλέκτορα φωνῆσαι τρὶς ἀπαρνήσῃ με· καὶ ἐξελθὼν ἔξω ἔκλαυσεν πικρῶς.

Jesus Brought before Pilate
(Mk 15.1; Lk 23.1–2; Jn 18.28–32)

27 Πρωΐας δὲ γενομένης συμβούλιον ἔλαβον πάντες οἱ ἀρχιερεῖς καὶ οἱ πρεσβύτεροι τοῦ λαοῦ κατὰ τοῦ Ἰησοῦ ὥστε θανατῶσαι αὐτόν· **2** καὶ δήσαντες αὐτὸν ἀπήγαγον καὶ παρέδωκαν Πιλάτῳ[1] τῷ ἡγεμόνι.

---

[7] **71** {B} οὗτος (see Mk 14.69) ℵ B D syrˢ copˢᵃ geo¹·ᴮ Diatessaronᵃˌˡ ‖ καὶ οὗτος A C K L W X Δ Θ Π f¹ f¹³ 33 565 700 892 1009 1010 1071 1079 1195 1216 1230 1241 1242 1253 1344 1365 1546 1646 2148 2174 *Byz Lect* itᵃˌᵃᵘʳˌᵇˌᶜˌᶠˌff¹ˌ²ˌᵍˌ¹ˌⁱˌⁿˌqˌʳˡ vg syrᵖˌʰˌᵖᵃˡ (copᵇᵒ) goth arm eth geoᴬ Origenˡᵃᵗ Chrysostom

[1] **2** {C} Πιλάτῳ (see Mk 15.1) ℵ B L 33 syrˢˌᵖˌᵖᵃˡᵐˢ copˢᵃˌᵇᵒ geo Diatessaronᵃ Origen Peter-Alexandria ‖ Ποντίῳ Πιλάτῳ A C K W X Δ Θ Π 0250 f¹ f¹³ 565 700 892 1009 1010 1071 1079 1195 1216 1230 1241 1242 1253 1344 1365 1546 1646 2148 2174 *Byz Lect* itᵃˌᵃᵘʳˌᵇˌᵒˌdˌfˌff¹ˌ²ˌᵍˌʰˌ¹ˌqˌʳˡ vg syrʰˌᵖᵃˡᵐˢˢ goth arm eth Diatessaronⁿˌᵛ Origenˡᵃᵗ Diodore Augustine

---

75 ἐμνήσθη...με Mt 26.34; Mk 14.30; Lk 22.34; Jn 13.38
27 1 Πρωΐας...Ἰησοῦ Lk 22.66   συμβούλιον...αὐτόν Mt 12.14; Mk 3.6

Peter Denies Jesus
(Also Mark 14.66–72; Luke 22.56–62; John 18.15–18, 25–27)

[69] Peter was sitting outside in the courtyard, when one of the High Priest's servant girls came to him and said, "You, too, were with Jesus of Galilee." [70] But he denied it in front of them all. "I don't know what you are talking about," he answered, [71] and went on out to the entrance of the courtyard. Another servant girl saw him and said to the men there, "He was with Jesus of Nazareth." [72] Again Peter denied it, and answered, "I swear that I don't know that man!" [73] After a little while the men standing there came to Peter. "Of course you are one of them," they said. "After all, the way you speak gives you away!" [74] Then Peter made a vow: "May God punish me if I am not telling the truth! I do not know that man!" Just then a rooster crowed, [75] and Peter remembered what Jesus had told him, "Before the rooster crows, you will say three times that you do not know me." He went out and wept bitterly.

Jesus Taken to Pilate
(Also Mark 15.1; Luke 23.1–2; John 18.28–32)

27 Early in the morning all the chief priests and the Jewish elders made their plan against Jesus to put him to death. [2] They put him in chains, took him, and handed him over to Pilate, the Governor.

The Death of Judas
(Also Acts 1.18–19)

³ When Judas, the traitor, saw that Jesus had been condemned, he repented and took back the thirty silver coins to the chief priests and the elders. ⁴ "I have sinned by betraying an innocent man to death!" he said. "What do we care about that?" they answered. "That is your business!" ⁵ Judas threw the money into the sanctuary and left them; then he went off and hanged himself.

⁶ The chief priests picked up the money and said, "This is blood money, and it is against our Law to put it in the Temple treasury." ⁷ After reaching an agreement about it, they used the money to buy Potter's Field, as a cemetery for foreigners. ⁸ That is why that field is called "Field of Blood" to this very day.

⁹ Then what the prophet Jeremiah had said came true: "They took the thirty silver coins (the amount the people of Israel had agreed to pay for him), ¹⁰ and used them to buy the potter's field, as the Lord commanded me."

The Death of Judas
(Ac 1.18–19)

3 Τότε ἰδὼν ᾿Ιούδας ὁ παραδιδοὺς αὐτὸν ὅτι κατεκρίθη μεταμεληθεὶς ἔστρεψεν τὰ τριάκοντα ἀργύρια τοῖς ἀρχιερεῦσιν καὶ πρεσβυτέροις 4 λέγων, ῞Ημαρτον παραδοὺς αἷμα ἀθῷον². οἱ δὲ εἶπαν, Τί πρὸς ἡμᾶς; σὺ ὄψῃ. 5 καὶ ῥίψας τὰ ἀργύρια εἰς τὸν ναὸν³ ἀνεχώρησεν, καὶ ἀπελθὼν ἀπήγξατο. 6 οἱ δὲ ἀρχιερεῖς λαβόντες τὰ ἀργύρια εἶπαν, Οὐκ ἔξεστιν βαλεῖν αὐτὰ εἰς τὸν κορβανᾶν, ἐπεὶ τιμὴ αἵματός ἐστιν. 7 συμβούλιον δὲ λαβόντες ἠγόρασαν ἐξ αὐτῶν τὸν ᾿Αγρὸν τοῦ Κεραμέως εἰς ταφὴν τοῖς ξένοις. 8 διὸ ἐκλήθη ὁ ἀγρὸς ἐκεῖνος ᾿Αγρὸς Αἵματος ἕως τῆς σήμερον. 9 τότε ἐπληρώθη τὸ ῥηθὲν διὰ ᾿Ιερεμίου τοῦ προφήτου λέγοντος, **Καὶ ἔλαβον τὰ τριάκοντα ἀργύρια, τὴν τιμὴν τοῦ τετιμημένου ὃν ἐτιμήσαντο ἀπὸ υἱῶν ᾿Ισραήλ, 10 καὶ ἔδωκαν⁴ αὐτὰ εἰς τὸν ἀγρὸν τοῦ κεραμέως, καθὰ συνέταξέν μοι κύριος.**

---

² 4 {B} ἀθῷον ℵ A B* C K W X Δ Π f¹ f¹³ 33 565 700 892 1009 1010 1071 1079 1195 1216 1230 1241 1242 1253 1344 1365 1546 1646 2148 2174 *Byz Lect* syrᵖ·ʰ·ʰᵍʳ copˢᵃᵐˢ·ᵇᵒᵐˢ goth Origen Eusebius Cyril-Jerusalem Epiphanius Chrysostom ‖ δίκαιον B²ᵐᵍ L Θ itᵃ·ᵃᵘʳ·ᵇ·ᶜ·ᵈ·ᶠ·ᶠᶠ¹·²·ᵍ¹·ʰ·¹·q·ʳ¹ vg syrᵖᵃˡ copˢᵃ·ᵇᵒ arm ethᵖᵖ geo Diatessaronᵉᵃʳᵐ·ⁱ·ˢ Origenᵍʳ·ˡᵃᵗ Cyprian Ambrosiaster Lucifer Augustine ‖ τοῦ δικαίου syrˢ Diatessaron¹ ‖ *innocent blood and that I killed a righteous one* ethʳᵒ·ᵐˢ

³ 5 {D} εἰς τὸν ναόν ℵ B L Θ f¹³ 33 700 ℓ⁵⁴⁷ copˢᵃ·ᵇᵒ goth geo Origen Eusebius Chrysostom ‖ ἐν τῷ ναῷ A C K W X Δ Π f¹ 565 892 1009 1010 1071 1079 1195 1216 1230 1241 1242 1253 1344 1365 1546 1646 2148 2174 *Byz Lect* itᵃ·ᵃᵘʳ·ᵇ·ᶜ·ᵈ·ᶠ·ᶠᶠ¹·²·ᵍ¹·ʰ·¹·q·ʳ¹ vg syrˢ·ᵖ·ʰ·ᵖᵃˡ Origen Lucifer Cyril-Jerusalem

⁴ 10 {C} ἔδωκαν (A*ᵛⁱᵈ ἔδωκεν) Aᶜ B* C K L X Δ Θ Π 064 f¹ f¹³ 33 565 700 892 1009 1010 1071 1079 1195 1216 1230 1241 1242 1253 1344 1365 1546 1646 2148 *Byz Lect* itᵃ·ᵃᵘʳ·ᵇ·ᶜ·ᵈ·ᶠ·ᶠᶠ¹·²·ᵍ¹·ʰ·¹·q·ʳ¹ vg syrᵖᵃˡᵐˢˢ copˢᵃ·ᵇᵒ goth arm eth geo ‖ ἔδωκα ℵ B²ᵛⁱᵈ W 2174 ℓ²⁴·³¹·⁷⁶·¹⁵⁹⁹ syrˢ·ᵖ·ʰ·ᵖᵃˡᵐˢ (Diatessaron) Eusebius ‖ ἔβαλον 69

---

3 ἔστρεψεν...πρεσβυτέροις Mt 26.14–15   4 σὺ ὄψῃ Mt 27.24   **5–10** Ac 1.18–19
9–10 Καὶ ἔλαβον...κύριος Zch 11.12–13; Jr 32.6–9

Jesus Questioned by Pilate
(Mk 15.2–5; Lk 23.3–5; Jn 18.33–38)

11 Ὁ δὲ Ἰησοῦς ἐστάθη ἔμπροσθεν τοῦ ἡγεμόνος· καὶ ἐπηρώτησεν αὐτὸν ὁ ἡγεμὼν λέγων, Σὺ εἶ ὁ βασιλεὺς τῶν Ἰουδαίων; ὁ δὲ Ἰησοῦς ἔφη, Σὺ λέγεις.[a] **12** καὶ ἐν τῷ κατηγορεῖσθαι αὐτὸν ὑπὸ τῶν ἀρχιερέων καὶ πρεσβυτέρων οὐδὲν ἀπεκρίνατο. **13** τότε λέγει αὐτῷ ὁ Πιλᾶτος, Οὐκ ἀκούεις πόσα σου καταμαρτυροῦσιν; **14** καὶ οὐκ ἀπεκρίθη αὐτῷ πρὸς οὐδὲ ἓν ῥῆμα, ὥστε θαυμάζειν τὸν ἡγεμόνα λίαν.

Jesus Sentenced to Die
(Mk 15.6–15; Lk 23.13–25; Jn 18.39—19.16)

15 Κατὰ δὲ ἑορτὴν εἰώθει ὁ ἡγεμὼν ἀπολύειν ἕνα τῷ ὄχλῳ δέσμιον ὃν ἤθελον. **16** εἶχον δὲ τότε δέσμιον ἐπίσημον λεγόμενον [Ἰησοῦν] Βαραββᾶν[5]. **17** συνηγμένων οὖν αὐτῶν εἶπεν αὐτοῖς ὁ Πιλᾶτος, Τίνα θέλετε ἀπολύσω ὑμῖν, [Ἰησοῦν τὸν] Βαραββᾶν[6] ἢ Ἰησοῦν τὸν λεγόμενον Χριστόν; **18** ᾔδει γὰρ ὅτι διὰ φθόνον παρέδωκαν αὐτόν.

---

[5] 16 {C} Ἰησοῦν Βαραββᾶν Θ *f*[1] 700* syr[s, palmss] arm geo[2] Origen mss[acc. to Peter-Laodicea] ∥ Βαραββᾶν ℵ A B D K L W Δ Π 064 0250 *f*[13] 33 565 700[c] 892 1009 1010 1071 1079 1195 1216 1230 1241 1242 1253 1344 1365 1546 1646 2148 2174 *Byz Lect* it[a, aur, b, c, d, f, ff1, 2, g1, h, l, q, r1] vg syr[p, h, palms] cop[sa, bo] goth eth geo[1] Origen[lat]

[6] 17 {C} Ἰησοῦν τὸν Βαραββᾶν (Θ *omit τόν*) *f*[1] 700* syr[s, pal] arm geo[2] Origen[lat] ∥ τὸν Βαραββᾶν B 1010 Origen ∥ Βαραββᾶν ℵ A D K L W Δ Π 064 *f*[13] 565 700[c] 892 1009 1071 1079 1195 1216 1230 1241 1242 1253 1344 1365 1546 1646 2148 2174 *Byz Lect* cop[sa, bo] goth ∥ Βαραββᾶν *or* τὸν Βαραββᾶν it[a, aur, b, c, d, f, ff1, 2, g1, h, l, q, r1] vg syr[p, h] eth geo[1]

---

[a] **11** *a* statement: TR WH Bov Nes BF[2] AV RV ASV RSV NEB TT Zür Luth Jer Seg ∥ *a* question: WH[mg]

---

11 βασιλεὺς τῶν Ἰουδαίων Mt 2.2; 27.29, 37; Mk 15.9, 12, 18, 26; Lk 23.37, 38; Jn 18.39; 19.3, 19, 21   **12** οὐδὲν ἀπεκρίνατο Is 53.7; Mt 26.63; 27.14; Lk 23.9; Jn 19.9   **14** οὐκ...ῥῆμα Is 53.7; Mt 26.63; 27.12; Lk 23.9; Jn 19.9

Pilate Questions Jesus
(Also Mark 15.2–5; Luke 23.3–5; John 18.33–38)

[11] Jesus stood before the Governor, who questioned him. "Are you the king of the Jews?" he asked. "So you say," answered Jesus. [12] He said nothing, however, to the accusations of the chief priests and elders. [13] So Pilate said to him, "Don't you hear all these things they accuse you of?" [14] But Jesus refused to answer a single word, so that the Governor was greatly surprised.

Jesus Sentenced to Death
(Also Mark 15.6–15; Luke 23.13–25; John 18.39—19.16)

[15] At every Passover feast the Governor was in the habit of setting free any prisoner the crowd asked for. [16] At that time there was a well-known prisoner named Jesus Barabbas. [17] So when the crowd gathered, Pilate asked them, "Which one do you want me to set free for you, Jesus Barabbas or Jesus called the Christ?" [18] He knew very well that they had handed Jesus over to him because they were jealous.

19 While Pilate was sitting in the judgment hall, his wife sent him a message: "Have nothing to do with that innocent man, because in a dream last night I suffered much on account of him."

20 The chief priests and the elders persuaded the crowds to ask Pilate to set Barabbas free and have Jesus put to death. 21 But the Governor asked them, "Which one of these two do you want me to set free for you?" "Barabbas!" they answered. 22 "What, then, shall I do with Jesus called the Christ?" Pilate asked them. "Nail him to the cross!" they all answered. 23 But Pilate asked, "What crime has he committed?" Then they started shouting at the top of their voices, "Nail him to the cross!" 24 When Pilate saw it was no use to go on, but that a riot might break out, he took some water, washed his hands in front of the crowd, and said, "I am not responsible for the death of this man! This is your doing!" 25 The whole crowd answered back, "Let the punishment for his death fall on us and on our children!" 26 Then Pilate set Barabbas free for them; he had Jesus whipped and handed him over to be nailed to the cross.

The Soldiers Make Fun of Jesus
(Also Mark 15.16–20; John 19.2–3)

27 Then Pilate's soldiers took Jesus into the Governor's palace, and the whole

19 Καθημένου δὲ αὐτοῦ ἐπὶ τοῦ βήματος ἀπέστειλεν πρὸς αὐτὸν ἡ γυνὴ αὐτοῦ λέγουσα, Μηδὲν σοὶ καὶ τῷ δικαίῳ ἐκείνῳ, πολλὰ γὰρ ἔπαθον σήμερον κατ' ὄναρ δι' αὐτόν. 20 Οἱ δὲ ἀρχιερεῖς καὶ οἱ πρεσβύτεροι ἔπεισαν τοὺς ὄχλους ἵνα αἰτήσωνται τὸν Βαραββᾶν τὸν δὲ Ἰησοῦν ἀπολέσωσιν. 21 ἀποκριθεὶς δὲ ὁ ἡγεμὼν εἶπεν αὐτοῖς, Τίνα θέλετε ἀπὸ τῶν δύο ἀπολύσω ὑμῖν; οἱ δὲ εἶπαν, Τὸν Βαραββᾶν. 22 λέγει αὐτοῖς ὁ Πιλᾶτος, Τί οὖν ποιήσω Ἰησοῦν τὸν λεγόμενον Χριστόν; λέγουσιν πάντες, Σταυρωθήτω. 23 ὁ δὲ ἔφη, Τί γὰρ κακὸν ἐποίησεν; οἱ δὲ περισσῶς ἔκραζον λέγοντες, Σταυρωθήτω. 24 ἰδὼν δὲ ὁ Πιλᾶτος ὅτι οὐδὲν ὠφελεῖ ἀλλὰ μᾶλλον θόρυβος γίνεται, λαβὼν ὕδωρ ἀπενίψατο τὰς χεῖρας ἀπέναντι τοῦ ὄχλου, λέγων, Ἀθῷός εἰμι ἀπὸ τοῦ αἵματος τούτου[7]· ὑμεῖς ὄψεσθε. 25 καὶ ἀποκριθεὶς πᾶς ὁ λαὸς εἶπεν, Τὸ αἷμα αὐτοῦ ἐφ' ἡμᾶς καὶ ἐπὶ τὰ τέκνα ἡμῶν. 26 τότε ἀπέλυσεν αὐτοῖς τὸν Βαραββᾶν, τὸν δὲ Ἰησοῦν φραγελλώσας παρέδωκεν ἵνα σταυρωθῇ.

The Soldiers Mock Jesus
(Mk 15.16–20; Jn 19.2–3)

27 Τότε οἱ στρατιῶται τοῦ ἡγεμόνος παραλαβόντες τὸν Ἰησοῦν εἰς τὸ πραιτώριον συνήγαγον ἐπ' αὐτὸν ὅλην τὴν

---

[7] **24** {B} τούτου B D Θ it[a,b,d,ff2,r1] syr[s] cop[sa,boms] geo[1] Hippolytus Origen[lat] Cyprian Chrysostom Ps-Athanasius ∥ τοῦ δικαίου τούτου ℵ K L W Π f[1] f[13] 33 565 700 892 1009 (1010 *omit* τούτου) 1071 1079 1195 1216 1241 1242 1253 1344 1365 1546 (1646* ἀπὸ τοῦ δικαίου *and omit* τούτου) 1646[c] 2148 2174 *Byz Lect* it[c,ff1,g1,l,q] vg syr[h] cop[samss,bo] arm eth? geo[2?] Apostolic Constitutions Cyril-Jerusalem Theodore Cyril ∥ τούτου τοῦ δικαίου A Δ 064 1230 l[1231] it[aur,f,h] syr[p,pal] eth? geo[2?] Augustine

---

21 Ac 3.14   **22–23** Ac 3.13; 13.28   **24** λαβὼν...τούτου Dt 21.6–9; Ps 26.6   Ἀθῷος ...τούτου Sus 46 Theodotion; Ac 18.6; 20.26 ὑμεῖς ὄψεσθε Mt 27.4   **25** Τὸ...ἡμῶν Eze 33.5; Ac 5.28

σπεῖραν. **28** καὶ ἐκδύσαντες αὐτὸν[8] χλαμύδα κοκκίνην περιέθηκαν αὐτῷ, **29** καὶ πλέξαντες στέφανον ἐξ ἀκανθῶν ἐπέθηκαν ἐπὶ τῆς κεφαλῆς αὐτοῦ καὶ κάλαμον ἐν τῇ δεξιᾷ αὐτοῦ, καὶ γονυπετήσαντες ἔμπροσθεν αὐτοῦ ἐνέπαιξαν[9] αὐτῷ λέγοντες, Χαῖρε, βασιλεῦ τῶν Ἰουδαίων, **30** καὶ ἐμπτύσαντες εἰς αὐτὸν ἔλαβον τὸν κάλαμον καὶ ἔτυπτον εἰς τὴν κεφαλὴν αὐτοῦ. **31** καὶ ὅτε ἐνέπαιξαν αὐτῷ, ἐξέδυσαν αὐτὸν τὴν χλαμύδα καὶ ἐνέδυσαν αὐτὸν τὰ ἱμάτια αὐτοῦ, καὶ ἀπήγαγον αὐτὸν εἰς τὸ σταυρῶσαι.

The Crucifixion of Jesus
(Mk 15.21–32; Lk 23.26–43; Jn 19.17–27)

32 Ἐξερχόμενοι δὲ εὗρον ἄνθρωπον Κυρηναῖον ὀνόματι Σίμωνα· τοῦτον ἠγγάρευσαν ἵνα ἄρῃ τὸν σταυρὸν αὐτοῦ. **33** Καὶ ἐλθόντες εἰς τόπον λεγόμενον Γολγοθᾶ, ὅ ἐστιν Κρανίου Τόπος λεγόμενος, **34** **ἔδωκαν** αὐτῷ **πιεῖν** οἶνον μετὰ **χολῆς** μεμιγμένον· καὶ γευσάμενος οὐκ ἠθέλησεν πιεῖν. **35** σταυρώσαντες δὲ αὐτὸν **διεμερίσαντο τὰ ἱμάτια** αὐτοῦ **βάλλοντες κλῆρον,** **36** καὶ καθήμενοι ἐτήρουν αὐτὸν

---

[8] **28** {B} ἐκδύσαντες αὐτόν ℵ*,b A K L W Δ Θ Π 064 0250 *f*[1] *f*[13] 565 700 892 1009 1010 1071 1079 1216 1230 1241 1242 1253 1344 1365 1546 1646 2148 2174 *Byz Lect* it[aur,ff1,g1,l] vg syr[p,h,palmss] cop[sa,bo] arm geo Origen[lat] Eusebius Chrysostom Augustine ‖ ἐνδύσαντες αὐτόν ℵa B syr[s] eth Origen[lat] ‖ ἐκδύσαντες αὐτὸν τὰ ἱμάτια αὐτοῦ 33 1195 syr[hmg] cop[sams,boms] ‖ ἐνδύσαντες αὐτὸν ἱμάτιον πορφυροῦν καί (see Jn 19.2) D it[a,(b),c,d,(f),ff2,(h),(q)] syr[palms] Origen[lat]

[9] **29** {B} ἐνέπαιξαν ℵ B D L 33 892 1230 it[d] ‖ ἐνέπαιζον A K W Δ Θ Π 064 0250 *f*[1] *f*[13] 565 700 1009 1010 1071 1079 1195 1216 1241 1242 1253 1344 1365 1546 1646 2148 2174 *Byz Lect* it[a,aur,b,c,f,ff1,2,g1,h,l,q] vg syr[s,p,h,pal] arm geo? Eusebius Chrysostom

---

28-30 Lk 23.11   **29** βασιλεῦ τῶν Ἰουδαίων Mt 2.2; 27.11, 37; Mk 15.9, 12, 18, 26; Lk 23.37, 38; Jn 18.39; 19.3, 19, 21   **30** Is 50.6   **34** ἔδωκαν...μεμιγμένον Ps 69.21   **35** διεμερίσαντο...κλῆρον Ps 22.18

company gathered around him. **28** They stripped off his clothes and put a scarlet robe on him. **29** Then they made a crown out of thorny branches and put it on his head, and put a stick in his right hand; then they knelt before him and made fun of him. "Long live the King of the Jews!" they said. **30** They spat on him, and took the stick and hit him over the head. **31** When they finished making fun of him, they took the robe off and put his own clothes back on him, and then led him out to nail him to the cross.

Jesus Nailed to the Cross
(Also Mark 15.21–32; Luke 23.26–43; John 19.17–27)

32 As they were going out they met a man from Cyrene named Simon, and they forced him to carry Jesus' cross. **33** They came to a place called Golgotha, which means "The Place of the Skull." **34** There they offered him wine to drink, mixed with gall; after tasting it, however, he would not drink it.

35 They nailed him to the cross, and then divided his clothes among them by throwing dice. **36** After that they sat there and watched him. ³⁷ Above his head they put the written notice of the accusation against him: "This is Jesus, the King of the Jews." ³⁸ Then they nailed two bandits to crosses with Jesus, one on his right and the other on his left.

³⁹ People passing by shook their heads and threw insults at Jesus: ⁴⁰ "You were going to tear down the Temple and build it up in three days! Save yourself, if you are God's Son! Come on down from the cross!" ⁴¹ In the same way the chief priests and the teachers of the Law and the elders made fun of him: ⁴² "He saved others but he cannot save himself! Isn't he the King of Israel? If he will come down off the cross now, we will believe in him! ⁴³ He trusts in God and says he is God's Son. Well, then, let us see if God wants to save him now!" ⁴⁴ Even the bandits who had been crucified with him insulted him in the same way.

ἐκεῖ. **37** καὶ ἐπέθηκαν ἐπάνω τῆς κεφαλῆς αὐτοῦ τὴν αἰτίαν αὐτοῦ γεγραμμένην· Οὗτός ἐστιν Ἰησοῦς ὁ βασιλεῦς τῶν Ἰουδαίων. **38** Τότε σταυροῦνται σὺν αὐτῷ δύο λῃσταί, εἷς ἐκ δεξιῶν καὶ εἷς ἐξ εὐωνύμων. **39** Οἱ δὲ παραπορευόμενοι ἐβλασφήμουν αὐτὸν **κινοῦντες τὰς κεφαλὰς αὐτῶν 40** καὶ λέγοντες, Ὁ καταλύων τὸν ναὸν καὶ ἐν τρισὶν ἡμέραις οἰκοδομῶν, σῶσον σεαυτόν, εἰ υἱὸς εἶ τοῦ θεοῦ, [καὶ]^{1C} κατάβηθι ἀπὸ τοῦ σταυροῦ. **41** ὁμοίως καὶ οἱ ἀρχιερεῖς ἐμπαίζοντες μετὰ τῶν γραμματέων καὶ πρεσβυτέρων ἔλεγον, **42** Ἄλλους ἔσωσεν, ἑαυτὸν οὐ δύναται σῶσαι·^b βασιλεὺς¹¹ Ἰσραήλ ἐστιν, καταβάτω νῦν ἀπὸ τοῦ σταυροῦ καὶ πιστεύσομεν ἐπ' αὐτόν. **43 πέποιθεν ἐπὶ τὸν θεόν, ῥυσάσθω νῦν¹² εἰ θέλει αὐτόν**· εἶπεν γὰρ ὅτι Θεοῦ εἰμι υἱός. **44** τὸ δ' αὐτὸ καὶ οἱ λῃσταὶ οἱ συσταυρωθέντες σὺν αὐτῷ ὠνείδιζον αὐτόν.

---

¹⁰ **40** {C} καί ℵ* A D it^{a,b,c,d,h} syr^{s,p,pal} Diatessaron Chrysostom Cyril ‖ omit ℵ^c B K L W Δ Θ Π 0250 f¹ f¹³ 33 565 700 892 1009 1010 1071 1079 1195 1216 1230 1241 1242 1253 1344 1365 1546 1646 2148 2174 Byz Lect it^{aur,f,ff1,2,g1,l,q,r1} vg syr^h cop^{sa,bo} arm eth geo Origen^{lat} Eusebius Chrysostom

¹¹ **42** {B} βασιλεύς ℵ B D L 33 892 it^d cop^{sa} ‖ εἰ βασιλεύς A K W Δ Θ Π f¹ f¹³ 565 700 1009 1010 1071 1079 1195 1216 1230 1241 1242 1253 1344 1365 1546 1646 2148 2174 Byz Lect it^{a,aur,b,c,f,ff1,2,g1,h,l,q,r1} vg syr^{s,p,h,pal} cop^{bo} arm eth^{ro,pp} geo Diatessaron Origen^{lat} Eusebius Ps-Athanasius ‖ καὶ εἰ βασιλεύς eth^{ms}

¹² **43** {C} ῥυσάσθω νῦν ℵ B L 33 892 vg^{cl} ‖ ῥυσάσθω νῦν αὐτόν A*^{vid} D K W Δ Θ Π² f¹ f¹³ 700 1071 1195 1216 1230 1241 1242 1253 1344 1365 2148 2174 Byz Lect (l⁵⁴⁷ αὐτῷ) it^{a,aur,b,c,d,f,ff1,g1,h,l,q,r1} vg^{ww} syr^{s,p,h,pal} cop^{sa} goth arm eth geo¹ Diatessaron Eusebius ‖ ῥυσάσθω αὐτόν (see Ps 21.9 LXX) A^c Π* 565 1009 1010 1079 1546 1646 l^{185,883,950,1663} it^{ff2} cop^{bo} geo² Eusebius

---

^b **42** b statement: TR WH Bov Nes BF² AV RV ASV RSV NEB TT Zür Luth Jer Seg ‖ b question: RV^{mg} ASV^{mg}

---

37 ὁ...Ἰουδαίων Mt 2.2; 27.11, 29; Mk 15.9, 12, 18, 26; Lk 23.37, 38; Jn 18.39; 19.3, 19, 21 **38** Is 53.12 **39** κινοῦντες...αὐτῶν Ps 22.7; 109.25; Lm 2.15 **40** Ὁ...οἰκοδομῶν Mt 26.61; Mk 14.58; Jn 2.19–20 εἰ...θεοῦ Mt 4.3, 6; 26.63; Lk 4.3, 9 **42** βασιλεὺς Ἰσραήλ Jn 1.49; 12.13 **43** πέποιθεν...αὐτόν Ps 22.8 ῥυσάσθω...υἱός Wsd 2.18–20 εἶπεν...υἱός Jn 5.18; 10.36; 19.7

The Death of Jesus
(Mk 15.33–41; Lk 23.44–49; Jn 19.28–30)

45 Ἀπὸ δὲ ἕκτης ὥρας σκότος ἐγένετο ἐπὶ πᾶσαν τὴν γῆν ἕως ὥρας ἐνάτης. 46 περὶ δὲ τὴν ἐνάτην ὥραν ἀνεβόησεν ὁ Ἰησοῦς φωνῇ μεγάλῃ λέγων, **Ηλι ηλι λεμα σαβαχθανι;** τοῦτ' ἔστιν, **Θεέ μου θεέ μου, ἱνατί με ἐγκατέλιπες;** 47 τινὲς δὲ τῶν ἐκεῖ ἑστηκότων ἀκούσαντες ἔλεγον ὅτι Ἠλίαν φωνεῖ οὗτος. 48 καὶ εὐθέως δραμὼν εἷς ἐξ αὐτῶν καὶ λαβὼν σπόγγον πλήσας τε **ὄξους** καὶ περιθεὶς καλάμῳ **ἐπότιζεν** αὐτόν. 49 οἱ δὲ λοιποὶ ἔλεγον, Ἄφες ἴδωμεν εἰ ἔρχεται Ἠλίας σώσων αὐτόν.[13] 50 ὁ δὲ Ἰησοῦς πάλιν κράξας φωνῇ μεγάλῃ ἀφῆκεν τὸ πνεῦμα. 51 Καὶ ἰδοὺ τὸ καταπέτασμα τοῦ ναοῦ ἐσχίσθη ἀπ' ἄνωθεν ἕως κάτω εἰς δύο, καὶ ἡ γῆ ἐσείσθη, καὶ αἱ πέτραι ἐσχίσθησαν, 52 καὶ τὰ μνημεῖα ἀνεῴχθησαν καὶ πολλὰ σώματα τῶν κεκοιμημένων ἁγίων ἠγέρθησαν, 53 καὶ ἐξελθόντες ἐκ τῶν μνημείων μετὰ τὴν ἔγερσιν αὐτοῦ εἰσῆλθον εἰς τὴν ἁγίαν πόλιν καὶ ἐνεφανίσθησαν πολλοῖς. 54 Ὁ δὲ ἑκατόνταρχος καὶ οἱ μετ' αὐτοῦ τηροῦντες τὸν Ἰησοῦν ἰδόντες τὸν σεισμὸν καὶ τὰ γενόμενα ἐφοβήθησαν σφόδρα, λέγοντες, Ἀληθῶς θεοῦ υἱὸς ἦν οὗτος. 55 Ἦσαν δὲ ἐκεῖ γυναῖκες πολλαὶ ἀπὸ μακρόθεν θεωροῦσαι, αἵτινες ἠκολούθησαν τῷ Ἰησοῦ ἀπὸ τῆς Γαλιλαίας διακονοῦσαι αὐτῷ· 56 ἐν αἷς ἦν Μαρία ἡ Μαγδαληνὴ καὶ Μαρία ἡ τοῦ Ἰακώβου καὶ Ἰωσὴφ μήτηρ καὶ ἡ μήτηρ τῶν υἱῶν Ζεβεδαίου.

---

[13] **49** {B} αὐτόν. A D K W Δ Θ Π 090 f¹ f¹³ 28 33 565 700 892 1009 1071 1079 1195 1216 1230 1241 1242 1253 1344 1365 1546 1646 2148 2174 *Byz Lect* it^{a,aur,b,c,d,f,ff1,2,g1,h,l,q,r1} vg syr^{s,p,h,palmss} cop^{sa,bo} goth arm eth^{pp,msᵁ} geo Diatessaron Origen^{lat} Apostolic Canons Eusebius Hilary Jerome Augustine ‖ αὐτόν. ἄλλος δὲ λαβὼν λόγχην ἔνυξεν αὐτοῦ τὴν πλευράν, καὶ ἐξῆλθεν ὕδωρ καὶ αἷμα. (see Jn 19.34) ℵ B C L 1010 syr^{palmss} eth^{ro,ms*} Chrysostom^{acc. to Severus}

---

45 Am 8.9   46 Ηλι ηλι...σαβαχθανι Ps 22.1   Θεέ μου θεέ...ἐγκατέλιπες Ps 22.1
48 Ps 69.21   51 τὸ...ναοῦ Ex 26.31–35; He 10.20   52–53 πολλὰ...μνημείων Eze 37.12
53 τὴν ἁγίαν πόλιν Mt 4.5; Re 11.2; 21.2, 10; 22.19   55–56 Lk 8.2–3   56 ἡ μήτηρ... Ζεβεδαίου Mt 20.20

The Death of Jesus
(Also Mark 15.33–41; Luke 23.44–49; John 19.28–30)

45 At noon the whole country was covered with darkness, which lasted for three hours. 46 At about three o'clock Jesus cried out with a loud shout, *Eli, Eli, lema sabachthani?* which means, "My God, my God, why did you abandon me?" 47 Some of the people standing there heard him and said, "He is calling for Elijah!" 48 One of them ran up at once, took a sponge, soaked it in wine, put it on the end of a stick, and tried to make him drink it. 49 But the others said, "Wait, let us see if Elijah is coming to save him!" 50 Jesus again gave a loud cry, and breathed his last.

51 Then the curtain hanging in the Temple was torn in two, from top to bottom. The earth shook, the rocks split apart, 52 the graves broke open, and many of God's people who had died were raised to life. 53 They left the graves; and after Jesus rose from death they went into the Holy City, where many people saw them.

54 When the army officer and the soldiers with him who were watching Jesus saw the earthquake and everything else that happened, they were terrified and said, "He really was the Son of God!" 55 There were many women there, looking on from a distance, who had followed Jesus from Galilee and helped him. 56 Among them were Mary Magdalene, Mary the mother of James and Joseph, and the mother of Zebedee's sons.

The Burial of Jesus
(Also Mark 15.42–47; Luke 23.50–56; John 19.38–42)

[57] When it was evening, a rich man from Arimathea arrived; his name was Joseph, and he also was a disciple of Jesus. [58] He went into the presence of Pilate and asked for the body of Jesus. Pilate gave orders for the body to be given to Joseph. [59] So Joseph took it, wrapped it in a new linen sheet, [60] and placed it in his own grave, which he had just recently dug out of the rock. Then he rolled a large stone across the entrance to the grave and went away. [61] Mary Magdalene and the other Mary were sitting there, facing the grave.

The Guard at the Grave

[62] On the next day — that is, the day following Friday — the chief priests and the Pharisees met with Pilate [63] and said: "Sir, we remember that while that liar was still alive he said, 'I will be raised to life after three days.' [64] Give orders, then, for the grave to be safely guarded until the third day, so that his disciples will not be able to go and steal him, and then tell the people, 'He was raised from death.' This last lie would be even worse than the first one." [65] "Take a guard," Pilate told them; "go and guard the grave as best you can." [66] So they left, and made the grave secure by putting a seal on the stone and leaving the guard on watch.

The Burial of Jesus
(Mk 15.42–47; Lk 23.50–56; Jn 19.38–42)

57 Ὀψίας δὲ γενομένης ἦλθεν ἄνθρωπος πλούσιος ἀπὸ Ἀριμαθαίας, τοὔνομα Ἰωσήφ, ὃς καὶ αὐτὸς ἐμαθητεύθη τῷ Ἰησοῦ· **58** οὗτος προσελθὼν τῷ Πιλάτῳ ᾐτήσατο τὸ σῶμα τοῦ Ἰησοῦ. τότε ὁ Πιλᾶτος ἐκέλευσεν ἀποδοθῆναι. **59** καὶ λαβὼν τὸ σῶμα ὁ Ἰωσὴφ ἐνετύλιξεν αὐτὸ ἐν σινδόνι καθαρᾷ, **60** καὶ ἔθηκεν αὐτὸ ἐν τῷ καινῷ αὐτοῦ μνημείῳ ὃ ἐλατόμησεν ἐν τῇ πέτρᾳ, καὶ προσκυλίσας λίθον μέγαν τῇ θύρᾳ τοῦ μνημείου ἀπῆλθεν. **61** ἦν δὲ ἐκεῖ Μαρία ἡ Μαγδαληνὴ καὶ ἡ ἄλλη Μαρία καθήμεναι ἀπέναντι τοῦ τάφου.

The Guard at the Tomb

62 Τῇ δὲ ἐπαύριον, ἥτις ἐστὶν μετὰ τὴν παρασκευήν, συνήχθησαν οἱ ἀρχιερεῖς καὶ οἱ Φαρισαῖοι πρὸς Πιλᾶτον **63** λέγοντες, Κύριε, ἐμνήσθημεν ὅτι ἐκεῖνος ὁ πλάνος εἶπεν ἔτι ζῶν, Μετὰ τρεῖς ἡμέρας ἐγείρομαι. **64** κέλευσον οὖν ἀσφαλισθῆναι τὸν τάφον ἕως τῆς τρίτης ἡμέρας, μήποτε ἐλθόντες οἱ μαθηταὶ αὐτοῦ κλέψωσιν αὐτὸν[14] καὶ εἴπωσιν τῷ λαῷ, Ἠγέρθη ἀπὸ τῶν νεκρῶν, καὶ ἔσται ἡ ἐσχάτη πλάνη χείρων τῆς πρώτης. **65** ἔφη αὐτοῖς ὁ Πιλᾶτος, Ἔχετε κουστωδίαν· ὑπάγετε ἀσφαλίσασθε ὡς οἴδατε. **66** οἱ δὲ πορευθέντες ἠσφαλίσαντο τὸν τάφον σφραγίσαντες τὸν λίθον μετὰ τῆς κουστωδίας.

---

[14] **64** {A} κλέψωσιν αὐτόν (א κλέψουσιν) A B C* D K W Δ Θ Π f¹ f¹³ 33 1010 1071 1079 1195 1216 1230 1253 1546 1646 l²¹¹ itᵃ,ᵃᵘʳ,ᵇ,ᶜ,ᵈ,ᶠ,ff¹,²,g¹,ʰ,ˡ,ⁿ,q,r¹ vg syrʰ,ᵖᵃˡ copˢᵃ,ᵇᵒ goth geo² Origenˡᵃᵗ Chrysostom John-Damascus ‖ νυκτὸς κλέψωσιν αὐτόν (see 28.13) C³ L 565 700 892 1009 1241 1242 1344 2174 Byz Lect syrˢ arm geo¹ Diatessaron ‖ κλέψωσιν αὐτὸν νυκτός (see 28.13) 28 1365 (2148 κλέψουσιν) syrᵖ eth

---

57-58 Dt 21.22-23   **59-60** λαβὼν...μνημείῳ Mk 6.29; Ac 13.29   **60** προσκυλίσας... μνημείου Mt 28.2; Mk 16.3-4; Lk 24.2; Jn 20.1   **61** Μαρία...Μαρία Mt 27.56; 28.1; Mk 15.40, 47; 16.1; Lk 24.10; Jn 19.25   **63** Μετὰ...ἐγείρομαι Mt 12.40; 16.21; 17.23; 20.19; Mk 8.31; 9.31; 10.34; Lk 9.22; 18.33; 24.7   **64** ἔσται...πρώτης Mt 12.45; Lk 11.26; 2 Pe 2.20

The Resurrection of Jesus
(Mk 16.1–8; Lk 24.1–12; Jn 20.1–10)

28 Ὀψὲ δὲ σαββάτων, τῇ ἐπιφωσκούσῃ εἰς μίαν σαββάτων, ἦλθεν Μαρία ἡ Μαγδαληνὴ καὶ ἡ ἄλλη Μαρία θεωρῆσαι τὸν τάφον. 2 καὶ ἰδοὺ σεισμὸς ἐγένετο μέγας· ἄγγελος γὰρ κυρίου καταβὰς ἐξ οὐρανοῦ καὶ προσελθὼν ἀπεκύλισεν τὸν λίθον καὶ ἐκάθητο ἐπάνω αὐτοῦ. 3 ἦν δὲ ἡ εἰδέα αὐτοῦ ὡς ἀστραπὴ καὶ τὸ ἔνδυμα αὐτοῦ λευκὸν ὡς χιών. 4 ἀπὸ δὲ τοῦ φόβου αὐτοῦ ἐσείσθησαν οἱ τηροῦντες καὶ ἐγενήθησαν ὡς νεκροί. 5 ἀποκριθεὶς δὲ ὁ ἄγγελος εἶπεν ταῖς γυναιξίν, Μὴ φοβεῖσθε ὑμεῖς, οἶδα γὰρ ὅτι Ἰησοῦν τὸν ἐσταυρωμένον ζητεῖτε· 6 οὐκ ἔστιν ὧδε, ἠγέρθη γὰρ καθὼς εἶπεν· δεῦτε ἴδετε τὸν τόπον ὅπου ἔκειτο[1]. 7 καὶ ταχὺ πορευθεῖσαι εἴπατε τοῖς μαθηταῖς αὐτοῦ ὅτι[a] Ἠγέρθη ἀπὸ τῶν νεκρῶν[2],[a] καὶ ἰδοὺ προάγει ὑμᾶς εἰς τὴν Γαλιλαίαν, ἐκεῖ αὐτὸν ὄψεσθε· ἰδοὺ εἶπον ὑμῖν. 8 καὶ ἀπελθοῦσαι ταχὺ ἀπὸ τοῦ μνημείου μετὰ φόβου καὶ χαρᾶς μεγάλης ἔδραμον ἀπαγγεῖλαι τοῖς μαθηταῖς αὐτοῦ. 9 καὶ ἰδοὺ[3] Ἰησοῦς ὑπήντησεν αὐταῖς λέγων,

---

[1] **6** {B} ἔκειτο ℵ B Θ 33 892[txt] it[e] syr[s, palms] cop[sa, bo] arm eth geo[2] Diatessaron[n] Origen[lat] Chrysostom Cyril ∥ ἔκειτο ὁ κύριος A C D K L W Δ Π 0148 f[1] f[13] 28 565 700 892[mg] 1009 1010 1071 1079 1195 1216 1230 1241 1242 1253 1365 1546 1646 2148 2174 Byz Lect it[a, aur, b, c, d, f, ff1,2, g1, h, l, q, r1] vg syr[p, h, palmss] geo[1] Diatessaron Chrysostom ∥ ἔκειτο ὁ Ἰησοῦς Φ ∥ ἔκειτο τὸ σῶμα τοῦ κυρίου 517 954 1424 1574 1675

[2] **7** {C} ἀπὸ τῶν νεκρῶν ℵ A B C K L W Δ Θ Π 0148 f[1] f[13] 28 33 700 892 1009 1010 1071 1079 1195 1216 1230 1241 1242 1253 1344 1365 (1546 ἐκ) 1646 2148 2174 Byz Lect it[aur, c, f, ff2, q] syr[p, h, pal] cop[sa, bo] eth Cyril ∥ omit D 565 it[a, b, d, e, ff1, g1, h, l] vg syr[s] arm geo Diatessaron[a, v] Origen[gr, lat] Cyril-Jerusalem Augustine

[3] **9** {B} καὶ ἰδού ℵ B D K W Θ f[13] 33 700 892 1009 1010 1365 1646

[a a] **7** a direct, a minor: WH Bov Nes[2] BF[2] (NEB) TT Jer ∥ a indirect, a minor: TR RSV ∥ a direct, a major: RV ASV ∥ a indirect, a major: AV (Zür) Luth Seg

---

1 Μαρία ἡ...Μαρία Mt 27.56, 61; Mk 15.40, 47; Jn 19.25   **2** σεισμὸς...μέγας Mt 27.51 ἀπεκύλισεν τὸν λίθον Mt 27.60; Mk 15.46   **3** τὸ...χιών Mt 17.2; Mk 9.3; Lk 9.29; Ac 1.10   **6** ἠγέρθη...εἶπεν Mt 12.40; 16.21; 17.23; 20.19; Mk 8.31; 9.31; 10.34; Lk 9.22; 18.33; 24.7   **7** Ἠγέρθη...Γαλιλαίαν Mt 26.32; Mk 14.28 προάγει...ὄψεσθε Mt 28.10, 16; Jn 21.1–23

The Resurrection
(Also Mark 16.1–10; Luke 24.1–12; John 20.1–10)

28 After the Sabbath, as Sunday morning was dawning, Mary Magdalene and the other Mary went to look at the grave. [2] Suddenly there was a strong earthquake; an angel of the Lord came down from heaven, rolled the stone away, and sat on it. [3] His appearance was like lightning and his clothes were white as snow. [4] The guards were so afraid that they trembled and became like dead men.

[5] The angel spoke to the women. "You must not be afraid," he said. "I know you are looking for Jesus, who was nailed to the cross. [6] He is not here; he has risen, just as he said. Come here and see the place where he lay. [7] Quickly, now, go and tell his disciples: 'He has been raised from death, and now he is going to Galilee ahead of you; there you will see him!' Remember what I have told you." [8] So they left the grave in a hurry, afraid and yet filled with joy, and ran to tell his disciples.

[9] Suddenly Jesus met them and said;

"Peace be with you." They came up to him, took hold of his feet, and worshiped him. [10] "Do not be afraid," Jesus said to them. "Go and tell my brothers to go to Galilee, and there they will see me."

The Report of the Guard

[11] While the women went on their way, some of the soldiers guarding the grave went back to the city and told the chief priests everything that had happened. [12] The chief priests met with the elders and made their plan; they gave a large sum of money to the soldiers [13] and said: "You are to say that his disciples came during the night and stole his body while you were asleep. [14] And if the Governor should hear of this, we will convince him and you will have nothing to worry about." [15] The guards took the money and did what they were told to do. To this very day that is the report spread around by the Jews.

Jesus Appears to His Disciples
(Also Mark 16.14–18; Luke 24.36–49; John 20.19–23; Acts 1.6–8)

[16] The eleven disciples went to the hill in Galilee where Jesus had told them to go. [17] When they saw him they worshiped him, even though some of them doubted. [18] Jesus drew near and said

Χαίρετε. αἱ δὲ προσελθοῦσαι ἐκράτησαν αὐτοῦ τοὺς πόδας καὶ προσεκύνησαν αὐτῷ. 10 τότε λέγει αὐταῖς ὁ Ἰησοῦς, Μὴ φοβεῖσθε· ὑπάγετε ἀπαγγείλατε τοῖς ἀδελφοῖς μου ἵνα ἀπέλθωσιν εἰς τὴν Γαλιλαίαν, κἀκεῖ με ὄψονται.

The Report of the Guard

11 Πορευομένων δὲ αὐτῶν ἰδού τινες τῆς κουστωδίας ἐλθόντες εἰς τὴν πόλιν ἀπήγγειλαν τοῖς ἀρχιερεῦσιν ἅπαντα τὰ γενόμενα. 12 καὶ συναχθέντες μετὰ τῶν πρεσβυτέρων συμβούλιόν τε λαβόντες ἀργύρια ἱκανὰ ἔδωκαν τοῖς στρατιώταις 13 λέγοντες, Εἴπατε ὅτι Οἱ μαθηταὶ αὐτοῦ νυκτὸς ἐλθόντες ἔκλεψαν αὐτὸν ἡμῶν κοιμωμένων. 14 καὶ ἐὰν ἀκουσθῇ τοῦτο ἐπὶ τοῦ ἡγεμόνος, ἡμεῖς πείσομεν αὐτὸν καὶ ὑμᾶς ἀμερίμνους ποιήσομεν. 15 οἱ δὲ λαβόντες τὰ ἀργύρια ἐποίησαν ὡς ἐδιδάχθησαν. Καὶ διεφημίσθη ὁ λόγος οὗτος παρὰ Ἰουδαίοις μέχρι τῆς σήμερον [ἡμέρας].

The Commissioning of the Disciples
(Mk 16.14–18; Lk 24.36–49; Jn 20.19–23; Ac 1.6–8)

16 Οἱ δὲ ἕνδεκα μαθηταὶ ἐπορεύθησαν εἰς τὴν Γαλιλαίαν εἰς τὸ ὄρος οὗ ἐτάξατο αὐτοῖς ὁ Ἰησοῦς, 17 καὶ ἰδόντες αὐτὸν προσεκύνησαν[4], οἱ δὲ ἐδίστασαν. 18 καὶ προσελθὼν

---

l[32,76,184,185pt,211,299,950,1642] it[a,aur,b,c,d,e,ff1,2,g1,h,l,n,r1] vg syr[p,pal] cop[sa,bo] arm eth[pp] geo Origen Eusebius Cyril-Jerusalem Cyril ‖ ὡς δὲ ἐπορεύοντο ἀπαγγεῖλαι τοῖς μαθηταῖς αὐτοῦ καὶ ἰδού (see 28.8) A C K L Δ Π 0148 f1 28 565 1071 (1079 2174 omit καί) 1195 1216 1230 1241 1242 1253 1344 1546 2148 Byz Lect l[185pt] it[f,q] syr[h] eth[ro] (eth[ms] omit καὶ ἰδού) Diatessaron[a,(n,t)]

[4] 17 {C} προσεκύνησαν ℵ B D L 33 it[a,aur,b,c,d,e,f,ff1,2,g1,h,l,n] vg syr[palms] Eusebius Chrysostom ‖ προσεκύνησαν αὐτῷ A K W Δ Θ Π 0148 f1 f13 565 700 892 1010 1071 1079 1195 1216 1242 1344 1546 2148 2174 Byz Lect l[185s,m] cop[sa?bo?] eth Diatessaron Didymus ‖ προσεκύνησαν αὐτόν 074 28 1009 1230 1241 1253 1365 1646 l[32,183,184,303,950,1231,1634] ‖ προσεκύνησαν αὐτοῦ 346 ‖ προσεκύνησαν αὐτῷ (or αὐτόν) it[q] syr[p,h,palmss] arm geo

---

10 ὑπάγετε...μου Jn 20.17
13 Εἴπατε...αὐτόν Mt 27.64

ὑπάγετε...ὄψονται Mt 26.32; 28.7, 16; Mk 14.28; Jn 21.1–23
16 Οἱ...Ἰησοῦς Mt 26.32; 28.7, 10

ὁ Ἰησοῦς ἐλάλησεν αὐτοῖς λέγων, Ἐδόθη μοι πᾶσα ἐξουσία ἐν οὐρανῷ καὶ ἐπὶ γῆς. **19** πορευθέντες οὖν μαθητεύσατε πάντα τὰ ἔθνη, βαπτίζοντες αὐτοὺς εἰς τὸ ὄνομα τοῦ πατρὸς καὶ τοῦ υἱοῦ καὶ τοῦ ἁγίου πνεύματος, **20** διδάσκοντες αὐτοὺς τηρεῖν πάντα ὅσα ἐνετειλάμην ὑμῖν· καὶ ἰδοὺ ἐγὼ μεθ' ὑμῶν εἰμι πάσας τὰς ἡμέρας ἕως τῆς συντελείας τοῦ αἰῶνος.[5]

to them: "I have been given all authority in heaven and on earth. [19] Go, then, to all peoples everywhere and make them my disciples: baptize them in the name of the Father and of the Son and of the Holy Spirit, [20] and teach them to obey everything I have commanded you. And remember! I will be with you always, to the end of the age."

[5] **20** {B} αἰῶνος. א A* B D W 074 f[1] 33 it[aur,d,e,ff1,g1,h,n,q] vg syr[palmss] cop[sa] arm eth[pp,msc] geo[1,B] Origen Chrysostom ∥ αἰῶνος. ἀμήν. A[2] K Δ Θ Π f[13] 28 565 700 892 1009 1010 1071 1079 1195 1216 1230 1241 1242 1253 1344 1365 1546 1646 2148 2174 Byz Lect l[185s,m] it[a,b,c,f,ff2,(l)] syr[p,h,palms] cop[bo] eth[ro,ms*] geo[A]

---

18 Ἐδόθη...γῆς Dn 7.14; Mt 11.27; Jn 3.35; 13.3; 17.2; Eph 1.20–22; Php 2.9–10 **19** πορευθέντες...ἔθνη Ac 1.8   **20** ἐγὼ...εἰμι Hg 1.13; Mt 18.20; Jn 14.23   συντελείας τοῦ αἰῶνος Mt 13.39, 49; 24.3

The Preaching of John the Baptist
(Also Matt. 3.1–12; Luke 3.1–18; John 1.19–28)

1 This is the Good News about Jesus Christ, the Son of God.[1] [2] It began as the prophet Isaiah had written:

" 'Here is my messenger,' says God;
'I will send him ahead of you
To open the way for you.'
[3] Someone is shouting in the desert:
'Get the Lord's road ready for him,
Make a straight path for him
to travel!' "

[4] So John appeared in the desert, baptizing people and preaching[2] his message. "Turn away from your sins and be baptized," he told the people, "and God will forgive your sins." [5] Everybody

---

[1] **1** *Some mss. omit* the Son of God

[2] **4** John appeared . . . baptizing people and preaching: *some mss. read* John the Baptist appeared . . . preaching

---

The Preaching of John the Baptist
(Mt 3.1–12; Lk 3.1–9, 15–17; Jn 1.19–28)

1 Ἀρχὴ τοῦ εὐαγγελίου Ἰησοῦ Χριστοῦ [υἱοῦ θεοῦ][1]. [a]
2 Καθὼς γέγραπται ἐν τῷ Ἠσαΐᾳ τῷ προφήτῃ[2],
   Ἰδοὺ ἀποστέλλω τὸν ἄγγελόν μου πρὸ προσώπου σου,
   ὃς κατασκευάσει τὴν ὁδόν σου·
3   φωνὴ βοῶντος ἐν τῇ ἐρήμῳ,
   Ἑτοιμάσατε τὴν ὁδὸν κυρίου,
   εὐθείας ποιεῖτε τὰς τρίβους αὐτοῦ — [b]
4 ἐγένετο Ἰωάννης βαπτίζων ἐν τῇ ἐρήμῳ καὶ[3] κηρύσσων βάπτισμα μετανοίας εἰς ἄφεσιν ἁμαρτιῶν. 5 καὶ ἐξεπορεύ-

---

[1] **1** {C} Χριστοῦ υἱοῦ θεου ℵ[a] B D L W Diatessaron[p] Irenaeus Severian // Χριστοῦ υἱοῦ τοῦ θεοῦ A K Δ Π f[1] f[13] 33 565 700 892 1009 1010 1071 1079 1195 1216 1230 1242 1253 1344 1365 1546 1646 2148 2174 *Byz Lect*[m] Cyril // Χριστοῦ υἱοῦ θεοῦ or Χριστοῦ υἱοῦ τοῦ θεοῦ it[a, aur, b, c, d, f, ff2, l, q, r1] vg syr[p, h] cop[sa, bo] goth arm eth geo[2] Irenaeus[lat2/3] Origen[lat] Ambrose Jerome Augustine // Χριστοῦ υἱοῦ τοῦ κυρίου 1241 // Χριστοῦ ℵ* Θ 28[c] syr[pal] geo[1] Irenaeus[gr, lat1/3] Origen[gr, lat] Victorinus-Pettau Serapion Titus-Bostra Basil Cyril-Jerusalem Epiphanius Jerome // *omit* 28*

[2] **2** {A} ἐν τῷ Ἠσαΐᾳ τῷ προφήτῃ ℵ B L Δ 33 565 892 1241 Origen Severian // ἐν Ἠσαΐᾳ τῷ προφήτῃ D Θ f[1] 700 1071 2174 Irenaeus[gr, lat] Origen Serapion Titus-Bostra Basil Epiphanius Victor-Antioch // ἐν (or ἐν τῷ) Ἠσαΐᾳ τῷ προφήτῃ it[a, aur, b, c, d, f, ff2, l, q] vg syr[p, hmg, pal] cop[sa, bo] goth geo Porphyry[acc. to Jerome] Victorinus-Pettau Eusebius Ambrosiaster Jerome Augustine // ἐν τοῖς προφήταις A K P W Π f[13] 28 1009 1010 1079 1195 1216 1230 1242 1253 1344 1365 1546 1646 2148 *Byz Lect*[m] syr[h] cop[boms mg] arm eth Irenaeus[lat] Photius Theophylact

[3] **4** {C} βαπτίζων ἐν τῇ ἐρήμῳ καί A K P W Π f[1] f[13] 565 700 1009 1010 1071 1079 1195 1216 1230 1241 1242 1253 1344 1365 1546 1646 2148 2174 *Byz Lect*[m] it[f] syr[h, pal] (cop[sa] *omit* καί) goth arm eth // ὁ βαπτίζων ἐν τῇ ἐρήμῳ καί ℵ L Δ geo[1] cop[bo] // ὁ βαπτίζων ἐν τῇ ἐρήμῳ B 33 892 cop[bomss] // ἐν τῇ ἐρήμῳ βαπτίζων καί D Θ 28 it[a, aur, b, c, d, ff1, l, q, r1, t] vg syr[p] Eusebius Cyril-Jerusalem Augustine // ἐν τῇ ἐρήμῳ καί geo[2]

---

[a] **1** *a* major: WH Bov Nes RV ASV RSV NEB Zür Luth Jer Seg // *a* minor: TR BF[2] AV (TT)

[b] **3** *b* dash: RSV // *b* major: TR WH[mg] BF[2] AV NEB TT Luth Seg // *b* minor: WH Bov Nes RV ASV Zür Jer

---

2 Ἰδοὺ...ὁδόν σου Ex 23.20; Mal 3.1 (Mt 11.10; Lk 1.76; 7.27)   **3** φωνὴ...αὐτοῦ Is 40.3 (Jn 1.23)   **4** ἐγένετο...μετανοίας Ac 13.24; 19.4

ετο πρὸς αὐτὸν πᾶσα ἡ Ἰουδαία χώρα καὶ οἱ Ἱεροσολυ-
μῖται πάντες, καὶ ἐβαπτίζοντο ὑπ' αὐτοῦ ἐν τῷ Ἰορδάνῃ
ποταμῷ ἐξομολογούμενοι τας ἁμαρτίας αὐτῶν. 6 καὶ ἦν
ὁ Ἰωάννης ἐνδεδυμένος τρίχας καμήλου καὶ ζώνην δερματίνην περὶ τὴν ὀσφὺν αὐτοῦ, καὶ ἐσθίων ἀκρίδας καὶ μέλι
ἄγριον. 7 καὶ ἐκήρυσσεν λέγων, Ἔρχεται ὁ ἰσχυρότερός
μου ὀπίσω μου, οὗ οὐκ εἰμὶ ἱκανὸς κύψας λῦσαι τὸν
ἱμάντα τῶν ὑποδημάτων αὐτοῦ· 8 ἐγὼ ἐβάπτισα ὑμᾶς
ὕδατι[4], αὐτὸς δὲ βαπτίσει ὑμᾶς ἐν πνεύματι ἁγίῳ[5].

The Baptism of Jesus
(Mt 3.13–17; Lk 3.21–22)

9 Καὶ ἐγένετο ἐν ἐκείναις ταῖς ἡμέραις ἦλθεν Ἰησοῦς
ἀπὸ Ναζαρὲτ τῆς Γαλιλαίας καὶ ἐβαπτίσθη εἰς τὸν Ἰορδάνην ὑπὸ Ἰωάννου. 10 καὶ εὐθὺς ἀναβαίνων ἐκ τοῦ
ὕδατος εἶδεν σχιζομένους τοὺς οὐρανοὺς καὶ τὸ πνεῦμα
ὡς περιστερὰν καταβαῖνον εἰς αὐτόν· 11 καὶ φωνὴ ἐγένετο
ἐκ τῶν οὐρανῶν[6], Σὺ εἶ ὁ υἱός μου[c] ὁ ἀγαπητός, ἐν σοὶ
εὐδόκησα.

from the region of Judea and the city of Jerusalem went out to hear John. They confessed their sins and he baptized them in the Jordan river.

6 John wore clothes made of camel's hair, with a leather belt around his waist; he ate locusts and wild honey. 7 He announced to the people: "The man who will come after me is much greater than I am; I am not good enough even to bend down and untie his sandals. 8 I baptize you with water, but he will baptize you with the Holy Spirit."

The Baptism and Temptation of Jesus
(Also Matt. 3.13—4.11; Luke 3.21–22; 4.1–13)

9 Not long afterward Jesus came from Nazareth, in the region of Galilee, and John baptized him in the Jordan. 10 As soon as Jesus came up out of the water he saw heaven opening and the Spirit coming down on him like a dove. 11 And a voice came from heaven: "You are my own dear Son. I am well pleased with you."

---

4 8 {B} ὕδατι ℵ B Δ 33 892* 1216 vg arm geo Origen Augustine ‖ ἐν ὕδατι A (D) K L P W (Θ μὲν ὕδατι) Π f¹ f¹³ 28 565 700 892ᵐᵍ 1009 1010 1071 1079 1195 1230 1241 1242 1253 1344 1365 1546 1646 2148 2174 *Byz Lect*ᵐ it⁽ᵃ⁾, aur,b,c,(d),f,(ff²),l,q,(r¹),t copˢᵃ,ᵇᵒ goth eth Hippolytus

5 8 {A} ἐν πνεύματι ἁγίῳ (see Mt 3.12; Lk 3.16) ℵ A D K W Δ Θ Π f¹ f¹³ 28 33 565 700 892 1009 1010 1071 1079 1216 1230 1242 1253 1344 1365 1546 1646 2148 2174 *Byz Lect*ᵐ it⁽ᵃ⁾,c,d,f,ff²,l,q,(r¹) syrᵖ?ʰ?ᵖᵃˡ? copˢᵃ,ᵇᵒ goth eth Hippolytus Origen ‖ πνεύματι ἁγίῳ B L itᵃᵘʳ,ᵇ,ᵗ vg syrᵖ?ʰ?ᵖᵃˡ? arm geo Augustine ‖ ἐν πνεύματι ἁγίῳ καὶ πυρί (see Mt 3.12; Lk 3.16) P 1195 1241 l⁴⁴ᵐ syrʰ with *

6 11 {C} ἐγένετο ἐκ τῶν οὐρανῶν ℵᶜ A B K L P (W ἐκ τοῦ οὐρανοῦ) Δ Π f¹ f¹³ 33 700 892 1009 1010 1071 1079 1195 1216 1230 1241 1242 1253 1344 1365 1546 1646 2148 2174 *Byz Lect* l⁴⁴ᵐ,⁶⁹ᵐ,⁷⁰ᵐ,⁷⁶ˢ.ᵐ,¹⁸⁵ˢ.ᵐ,³³³ˢ.ᵐ,⁵⁴⁷ˢ.ᵐ,⁸⁸³ˢ.ᵐ,¹⁶³⁴ᵐ it⁽ᵃ⁾,aur,(b),c,(f),l vg syrᵖ,ʰ,ᵖᵃˡᵐˢ copˢᵃ,ᵇᵒ goth arm geo²? ‖ ἐκ τῶν οὐρανῶν ἠκούσθη Θ 28 565 geo¹ ‖ ἐκ τῶν οὐρανῶν ℵ* D l¹⁸⁴ itᵈ,ff²,t syrᵖᵃˡᵐˢ Diatessaron

c **11** *c none:* TR WH Bov Nes BF² AV RV ASV RSV NEBᵐᵍ TT Zür Luth Jer Seg ‖ *c minor:* RSVᵐᵍ NEB

---

6 ζώνην...αὐτοῦ 2 Kgs 1.8; Zch 13.4   **7** Ac 13.25   **11** Σὺ εἶ...εὐδόκησα Gn 22.2; Ps 2.7; Is 42.1; Mt 12.18; 17.5; Mk 9.7; Lk 9.35; 2 Pe 1.17

¹² At once the Spirit made him go into the desert. ¹³ He was there forty days, and Satan tempted him. Wild animals were there also, but angels came and helped him.

Jesus Calls Four Fishermen
(Also Matt. 4.12–22; Luke 4.14–15; 5.1–11)

¹⁴ After John had been put in prison, Jesus went to Galilee and preached the Good News from God. ¹⁵ "The right time has come," he said, "and the Kingdom of God is near! Turn away from your sins and believe the Good News!"

¹⁶ As Jesus walked by Lake Galilee, he saw two fishermen, Simon and his brother Andrew, catching fish in the lake with a net. ¹⁷ Jesus said to them, "Come with me and I will teach you to catch men." ¹⁸ At once they left their nets and went with him.

¹⁹ He went a little farther on and saw two other brothers, James and John, the sons of Zebedee. They were in their boat getting their nets ready. ²⁰ As soon as Jesus saw them he called them; so they left their father Zebedee in the boat with the hired men and went with Jesus.

The Temptation of Jesus
(Mt 4.1–11; Lk 4.1–13)

12 Καὶ εὐθὺς τὸ πνεῦμα αὐτὸν ἐκβάλλει εἰς τὴν ἔρημον. **13** καὶ ἦν ἐν τῇ ἐρήμῳ τεσσαράκοντα ἡμέρας πειραζόμενος ὑπὸ τοῦ Σατανᾶ, καὶ ἦν μετὰ τῶν θηρίων, καὶ οἱ ἄγγελοι διηκόνουν αὐτῷ.

The Beginning of the Galilean Ministry
(Mt. 4.12–17; Lk 4.14–15)

14 Μετὰ δὲ τὸ παραδοθῆναι τὸν Ἰωάννην ἦλθεν ὁ Ἰησοῦς εἰς τὴν Γαλιλαίαν κηρύσσων τὸ εὐαγγέλιον[7] τοῦ θεοῦ **15** καὶ λέγων ὅτι Πεπλήρωται ὁ καιρὸς καὶ ἤγγικεν ἡ βασιλεία τοῦ θεοῦ· μετανοεῖτε καὶ πιστεύετε ἐν τῷ εὐαγγελίῳ.

The Calling of Four Fishermen
(Mt 4.18–22; Lk 5.1–11)

16 Καὶ παράγων παρὰ τὴν θάλασσαν τῆς Γαλιλαίας εἶδεν Σίμωνα καὶ Ἀνδρέαν τὸν ἀδελφὸν Σίμωνος ἀμφιβάλλοντας ἐν τῇ θαλάσσῃ· ἦσαν γὰρ ἁλιεῖς. **17** καὶ εἶπεν αὐτοῖς ὁ Ἰησοῦς, Δεῦτε ὀπίσω μου, καὶ ποιήσω ὑμᾶς γενέσθαι ἁλιεῖς ἀνθρώπων. **18** καὶ εὐθὺς ἀφέντες τὰ δίκτυα ἠκολούθησαν αὐτῷ. **19** Καὶ προβὰς ὀλίγον εἶδεν Ἰάκωβον τὸν τοῦ Ζεβεδαίου καὶ Ἰωάννην τὸν ἀδελφὸν αὐτοῦ,[d] καὶ αὐτοὺς ἐν τῷ πλοίῳ καταρτίζοντας τὰ δίκτυα,[e] **20** καὶ εὐθὺς ἐκάλεσεν αὐτούς.[e] καὶ ἀφέντες τὸν πατέρα αὐτῶν Ζεβεδαῖον ἐν τῷ πλοίῳ μετὰ τῶν μισθωτῶν ἀπῆλθον ὀπίσω αὐτοῦ.

---

[7] **14** {A} εὐαγγέλιον ℵ B L Θ *f*[1] *f*[13] 28* 33 565 892 it[b,c,ff2,t] syr[s,h] cop[sa,] [bo mss] arm geo Origen ∥ εὐαγγέλιον τῆς βασιλείας A D K W Δ Π 074 28[mg] 700 1009 1010 1071 1079 1195 1216 1230 1241 1242 1253 1344 1365 1546 1646 2148 2174 *Byz Lect* it[a,(aur),d,f,l,r1] vg syr[p,hmg] cop[bo mss] goth eth Diatessaron[a]

[d] **19** *d minor*: TR WH Bov BF[2] AV RV ASV RSV NEB TT Luth Jer Seg ∥ *d none*: Nes Zür
[e e] **19–20** *e minor, e major*: WH Luth Jer ∥ *e major, e minor*: TR Bov Nes BF[2] AV RV ASV RSV NEB TT Seg ∥ *e major, e minor*: Zür

14 τὸ παραδοθῆναι Mk 6.17–18; Jn 3.24   **15** Πεπλήρωται ὁ καιρός Ga 4.4; Eph 1.10 ἤγγικεν...μετανοεῖτε Mt 3.2   **19** Ἰάκωβον...αὐτοῦ Mt 10.2; Mk 3.17; 10.35; Lk 5.10

The Man with an Unclean Spirit
(Lk 4.31–37)

21 Καὶ εἰσπορεύονται εἰς Καφαρναούμ. καὶ εὐθὺς τοῖς σάββασιν [εἰσελθὼν] εἰς τὴν συναγωγὴν ἐδίδασκεν[8]. 22 καὶ ἐξεπλήσσοντο ἐπὶ τῇ διδαχῇ αὐτοῦ, ἦν γὰρ διδάσκων αὐτοὺς ὡς ἐξουσίαν ἔχων καὶ οὐχ ὡς οἱ γραμματεῖς. 23 καὶ εὐθὺς ἦν ἐν τῇ συναγωγῇ αὐτῶν ἄνθρωπος ἐν πνεύματι ἀκαθάρτῳ, [f]καὶ ἀνέκραξεν 24 [f]λέγων, Τί ἡμῖν καὶ σοί, Ἰησοῦ Ναζαρηνέ; ἦλθες ἀπολέσαι ἡμᾶς;[g] οἶδά σε τίς εἶ, ὁ ἅγιος τοῦ θεοῦ. 25 καὶ ἐπετίμησεν αὐτῷ ὁ Ἰησοῦς λέγων, Φιμώθητι καὶ ἔξελθε ἐξ αὐτοῦ. 26 καὶ σπαράξαν αὐτὸν τὸ πνεῦμα τὸ ἀκάθαρτον καὶ φωνῆσαν φωνῇ μεγάλῃ ἐξῆλθεν ἐξ αὐτοῦ. 27 καὶ ἐθαμβήθησαν ἅπαντες, ὥστε συζητεῖν πρὸς ἑαυτοὺς λέγοντας, Τί ἐστιν τοῦτο; διδαχὴ καινὴ[h] κατ' ἐξουσίαν· [h] καὶ[9] τοῖς πνεύμασι

---

8 21 {C} εἰσελθὼν εἰς τὴν συναγωγὴν ἐδίδασκεν A B K W Π 074 *f*[1] 1009 1010 1071 1079 1195 1216 1230 1241 1242 1253 1344 1365 (1546 συναγωγὴν αὐτῶν) 1646 2148 2174 *Byz* *l*[10,76,80,185,313,1127,1642] it[t] syr[h] cop[boms] ‖ εἰσελθὼν εἰς τὴν συναγωγὴν ἐδίδασκεν αὐτούς D Θ 700 it[(a),aur,b,d,(e),(f),(ff2),l,(q),r1] vg syr[h with *] goth arm eth geo[2] Augustine ‖ εἰσελθὼν ἐδίδασκεν εἰς τὴν συναγωγὴν 33 ‖ ἐδίδασκεν εἰς τὴν συναγωγὴν ℵ (C ἐν τοῖς σάββασιν) L *f*[13] 28 565 syr[(s),pal] (cop[bo]) Origen ‖ ἐδίδασκεν εἰς τὴν συναγωγὴν αὐτῶν Δ 892 (syr[p]) cop[boms] ‖ *in synagogam Capharnaum docebat populum* it[c] ‖ εἰς τὴν συναγωγὴν ἐδίδασκεν Lect (geo[1] συναγωγὴν αὐτῶν)

9 27 {C} τί ἐστιν τοῦτο; διδαχὴ καινὴ κατ' ἐξουσίαν· καὶ ℵ B L 33 (700 καινὴ διδαχὴ ὅτι) (syr[s]) ‖ τί ἐστιν τοῦτο; διδαχὴ καινὴ αὕτη. κατ' ἐξουσίαν καὶ *f*[1] (28* τίς διδαχή) 565* ‖ τί ἐστιν τοῦτο; διδαχὴ καινὴ αὕτη ὅτι κατ' ἐξουσίαν Θ (cop[bo]) geo ‖ τί ἐστιν τοῦτο; τίς ἡ διδαχὴ ἡ καινὴ αὕτη· ὅτι κατ' ἐξουσίαν καὶ C K Δ Π 28[c] 565[c] 892 1009 1010 (1071 εἰ τίς) 1079 1195 1216 1230 1241 1242 1253 1344 1365 1546 1646 2148 2174 *Byz* *l*[80,185,]

f f **23-24** *f* no number, *f* number 24: TR WH? Bov Nes BF[2] AV RV ASV NEB? TT Zür Luth Jer Seg ‖ *f* number 24, *f* no number: WH? RSV NEB?

g **24** *g* question: TR WH Nes BF[2] AV RV ASV RSV NEB TT Zür Jer ‖ *g* statement: Bov NEB[mg] TT[mg] Luth Seg

h h **27** *h* none, *h* major: Bov Nes BF[2] TT Zür ‖ *h* none, *h* exclamation: Luth (Jer) Seg ‖ *h* major, *h* none: WH ‖ *h* exclamation, *h* none: RV ASV RSV ‖ *h* exclamation, *h* major: NEB ‖ different text: TR AV

21 τοῖς...συναγωγὴν Mk 6.2; Lk 4.16; 6.6; 13.10   **22** Mt 7.28–29   **23** ἄνθρωπος...ἀκαθάρτῳ Mk 5.2   **24** Τί...Ναζαρηνέ Mt 8.29; Mk 5.7; Lk 4.34; 8.28   ὁ...θεοῦ Jn 6.69   **26** Mk 9.26

A Man with an Evil Spirit
(Also Luke 4.31–37)

21 They came to the town of Capernaum, and on the next Sabbath day Jesus went into the synagogue and began to teach. 22 The people who heard him were amazed at the way he taught. He wasn't like the teachers of the Law; instead, he taught with authority.

23 Just then a man with an evil spirit in him came into the synagogue and screamed: 24 "What do you want with us, Jesus of Nazareth? Are you here to destroy us? I know who you are: you are God's holy messenger!" 25 Jesus commanded the spirit: "Be quiet, and come out of the man!" 26 The evil spirit shook the man hard, gave a loud scream and came out of him. 27 The people were all so amazed that they started saying to each other, "What is this? Some kind of new teaching? This man

has authority to give orders to the evil spirits, and they obey him!'' ²⁸ And so the news about Jesus spread quickly everywhere in the region of Galilee.

Jesus Heals Many People
(Also Matt. 8.14–17; Luke 4.38–41)

²⁹ They left the synagogue and went straight to the home of Simon and Andrew; and James and John went with them. ³⁰ Simon's mother-in-law was sick in bed with a fever, and as soon as Jesus got there he was told about her. ³¹ He went to her, took her by the hand and helped her up. The fever left her and she began to wait on them.

³² When evening came, after the sun had set, people brought to Jesus all the sick and those who had demons. ³³ All the people of the town gathered in front of the house. ³⁴ Jesus healed many who were sick with all kinds of diseases and drove out many demons. He would not let the demons say anything, because they knew who he was.

τοῖς ἀκαθάρτοις ἐπιτάσσει, καὶ ὑπακούουσιν αὐτῷ. 28 καὶ ἐξῆλθεν ἡ ἀκοὴ αὐτοῦ εὐθὺς πανταχοῦ εἰς ὅλην τὴν περίχωρον τῆς Γαλιλαίας.

The Healing of Many People
(Mt 8.14–17; Lk 4.38–41)

29 Καὶ εὐθὺς ἐκ τῆς συναγωγῆς ἐξελθόντες ἦλθον¹⁰ εἰς τὴν οἰκίαν Σίμωνος καὶ Ἀνδρέου μετὰ Ἰακώβου καὶ Ἰωάννου. 30 ἡ δὲ πενθερὰ Σίμωνος κατέκειτο πυρέσσουσα, καὶ εὐθὺς λέγουσιν αὐτῷ περὶ αὐτῆς. 31 καὶ προσελθὼν ἤγειρεν αὐτὴν κρατήσας τῆς χειρός· καὶ ἀφῆκεν αὐτὴν ὁ πυρετός, καὶ διηκόνει αὐτοῖς. 32 Ὀψίας δὲ γενομένης, ὅτε ἔδυ ὁ ἥλιος, ἔφερον πρὸς αὐτὸν πάντας τοὺς κακῶς ἔχοντας καὶ τοὺς δαιμονιζομένους· 33 καὶ ἦν ὅλη ἡ πόλις ἐπισυνηγμένη πρὸς τὴν θύραν. 34 καὶ ἐθεράπευσεν πολλοὺς κακῶς ἔχοντας ποικίλαις νόσοις, καὶ δαιμόνια πολλὰ ἐξέβαλεν, καὶ οὐκ ἤφιεν λαλεῖν τὰ δαιμόνια, ὅτι ᾔδεισαν αὐτόν¹¹.

---

²⁹⁹,⁸⁸³,⁹⁵⁰,¹¹²⁷,¹⁶⁴² it^{aur, f, l} vg syr^{p, h, pal} goth ‖ τί ἐστιν τοῦτο τίς ἡ καινὴ διδαχὴ αὕτη. ὅτι κατ' ἐξουσίαν καὶ (A αὕτη διδαχή) f¹³ l^{48,76} ‖ τίς ἡ διδαχὴ ἐκείνη ἡ καινὴ αὕτη ἡ ἐξουσία ὅτι καὶ D (it^d) ‖ τίς ἡ διδαχὴ ἡ καινὴ αὕτη ὅτι κατ' ἐξουσίαν καὶ Lect (l²¹¹ κενή [=καινή] and add τοῖς) (arm omit αὕτη) ‖ τίς ἡ διδαχὴ ἡ κενή [=καινή] αὕτη ἡ ἐξουσιαστικὴ αὐτοῦ καὶ ὅτι W (it^q) ‖ quaenam esset doctrina haec? Potestatis et it^{(b,c,d,e,ff2),rl}

10 29 {C} ἐκ τῆς συναγωγῆς ἐξελθόντες ἦλθον ℵ A C K L (Δ εἰσῆλθον) Π 28 33 892 1009 1010 1071 1079 1195 1216 1230 1241 1253 1344 1546 1646 (2174 ἦλθεν) Byz syr^h goth ‖ ἐξελθόντες ἐκ τῆς συναγωγῆς ἦλθον 31 435 vg (syr^{s,p,pal} καὶ ἦλθον) cop^{bomss} geo¹ ‖ ἐκ τῆς συναγωγῆς ἐξελθὼν ἦλθεν B f¹ f¹³ 565 700 1242 1365 2148 (cf 2174 ἐξελθόντες) eth geo²? ‖ ἐξελθὼν ἐκ τῆς συναγωγῆς ἦλθεν D (W ἐξελθὼν δέ) Θ it^{aur,b,c,d,e,f,ff2,(l),q,rl} cop^{bomss} arm

11 34 {A} αὐτόν ℵ* A (D) K Δ Π 090 1010 1071 1079 1230 1253 1344 1546 Byz l^{185,313,1642} it^{a,aur,b,c,d,e,f,ff2,q} vg syr^{s,p,h} goth Ambrosiaster Victor-Antioch ‖ αὐτὸν Χριστὸν εἶναι (see Lk 4.41) B L W Θ f¹ 28 33^{vid} 565 1365 2148 Lect it^l syr^{h with *} arm eth geo Diatessaron^{a,n} ‖ αὐτὸν τὸν Χριστὸν εἶναι (see Lk 4.41) ℵ^c f¹³ 700 1009 1216 1242 1646 2174 cop^{bo} ‖ τὸν Χριστὸν αὐτόν 892 1241 ‖ τὸν Χριστὸν αὐτὸν εἶναι C (1195* τὸν Χριστὸν εἶναι αὐτόν, 1195^c αὐτὸν εἶναι τὸν Χριστόν)

---

28 Mt 4.24   31 ἤγειρεν...χειρός Mt 9.25; Mk 5.41; 9.27; Lk 8.54   32 ἔφερον... δαιμονιζομένους Mt 4.24   34 οὐκ ἤφιεν...αὐτόν Mk 3.12

A Preaching Tour
(Lk 4.42–44)

35 Καὶ πρωῒ ἔννυχα λίαν ἀναστὰς ἐξῆλθεν καὶ ἀπῆλθεν εἰς ἔρημον τόπον κἀκεῖ προσηύχετο. **36** καὶ κατεδίωξεν αὐτὸν Σίμων καὶ οἱ μετ' αὐτοῦ, **37** καὶ εὖρον αὐτὸν καὶ λέγουσιν αὐτῷ ὅτι Πάντες ζητοῦσίν σε. **38** καὶ λέγει αὐτοῖς, Ἄγωμεν ἀλλαχοῦ εἰς τὰς ἐχομένας κωμοπόλεις, ἵνα καὶ ἐκεῖ κηρύξω· εἰς τοῦτο γὰρ ἐξῆλθον. **39** καὶ ἦλθεν[12] κηρύσσων εἰς τὰς συναγωγὰς αὐτῶν[13] εἰς ὅλην τὴν Γαλιλαίαν καὶ τὰ δαιμόνια ἐκβάλλων.

The Cleansing of a Leper
(Mt 8.1–4; Lk 5.12–16)

40 Καὶ ἔρχεται πρὸς αὐτὸν λεπρὸς παρακαλῶν αὐτὸν [καὶ γονυπετῶν][14] καὶ λέγων αὐτῷ ὅτι Ἐὰν θέλῃς δύνασαί με καθαρίσαι. **41** καὶ σπλαγχνισθεὶς[15] ἐκτείνας τὴν χεῖρα αὐτοῦ ἥψατο καὶ λέγει αὐτῷ, Θέλω, καθαρίσθητι· **42** καὶ εὐθὺς ἀπῆλθεν ἀπ' αὐτοῦ ἡ λέπρα, καὶ ἐκαθαρίσθη. **43** καὶ

---

[12] **39** {C} ἦλθεν ℵ B L Θ 892 *l*1632 syrpal copsa,bo eth ‖ ἦν A C D K W Δ Π 090 *f*1 *f*13 28 33 565 700 1009 1010 1071 1079 1195 1216 1230 1241 1242 1253 1344 1365 1546 1646 2148 2174 *Byz Lect* (*l*32) ita,aur,b,c,d,e,f,ff2,l,q,r1 vg syrs,p,h goth arm geo Diatessaron

[13] **39** {B} εἰς τὰς συναγωγὰς αὐτῶν (see Lk 4.44) ℵ A B C D K L W Δ Θ Π 090 *f*1 *f*13 28 565 892 1009 1079 1195 1230 1241 1253 1546 *l*1632 syrpal arm? ‖ ἐν ταῖς συναγωγαῖς αὐτῶν (see Mt 4.23) 700 1010 1071 1216 1242 1344 1365 1646 2148 2174 *Byz Lect* ita,aur,(b),(c),d,f,ff2,l,(q),r1 vg syrh copsa,bo goth arm? geo ‖ *in all the synagogues* ite syrs,(p)

[14] **40** {D} καὶ γονυπετῶν ℵ L Θ *f*1 565 892 1216 1241 1242 1646 2174 ite,f,l,q vg (syrs,p) copbo goth arm geol,A Augustine ‖ καὶ γονυπετῶν αὐτόν A C K Δ Π 090 *f*13 28 33 700 1009 (1010 1071 αὐτῷ) 1079 1195 1344 1546 2148 *Byz Lect* syrh,pal eth geoB Diatessarona ‖ *omit* (see Mt 8.1) B D W 1230 1253 *l*26,211,303,952,956,1627 ita,aur,b,c,d,ff2,r1 copsa

[5] **41** {D} σπλαγχνισθείς ℵ A B C K L W Δ Θ Π 090 *f*1 *f*13 28 33 565 700 892 1009 1010 1071 1079 1195 1216 1230 1241 1242 1253 1344 1365 1546 1646 2148 2174 *Byz Lect* itaur,c,e,f,l,q vg syrs,p,h,pal copsa,bo goth arm geo Diatessarona ‖ ὀργισθείς D ita,d,ff2,r1 Ephraem ‖ *omit* itb

---

35 Mt 14.23; Mk 6.46; Lk 5.16; 6.12   **39** Mt 4.23; 9.35

Jesus Preaches in Galilee
(Also Luke 4.42–44)

[35] Very early the next morning, long before daylight, Jesus got up and left the house. He went out of town to a lonely place where he prayed. [36] But Simon and his companions went out searching for him; [37] when they found him they said, "Everyone is looking for you." [38] But Jesus answered: "We must go on to the other villages around here. I have to preach in them also, because that is why I came." [39] So he traveled all over Galilee, preaching in the synagogues and driving out demons.

Jesus Makes a Leper Clean
(Also Matt. 8.1–4; Luke 5.12–16)

[40] A leper came to Jesus, knelt down, and begged him for help. "If you want to," he said, "you can make me clean." [41] Jesus was filled with pity,[1] and reached out and touched him. "I do want to," he answered. "Be clean!" [42] At once the leprosy left the man and he was clean. [43] Then Jesus spoke harshly with

---

[1] **41** pity: *some mss. read* anger

him and sent him away at once. 44 "Listen," he said, "don't tell this to anyone. But go straight to the priest and let him examine you; then offer the sacrifice that Moses ordered, to prove to everyone that you are now clean." 45 But the man went away and began to spread the news everywhere. Indeed, he talked so much that Jesus could not go into a town publicly. Instead he stayed out in lonely places, and people came to him from everywhere.

Jesus Heals a Paralyzed Man
(Also Matt. 9.1–8; Luke 5.17–26)

2 A few days later Jesus came back to Capernaum, and the news spread that he was at home. 2 So many people came together that there wasn't any room left, not even out in front of the door. Jesus was preaching the message to them 3 when some people came, bringing him a paralyzed man — four of them were carrying him. 4 Because of the crowd, however, they could not get him to Jesus. So they made a hole in the roof right above the place where Jesus was. When they had made an opening, they let the man down, lying on his mat. 5 Jesus saw how much faith they had, and said to the paralyzed man, "My son, your sins are forgiven." 6 Some teachers of the Law who were sitting there thought to themselves: 7 "How

ἐμβριμησάμενος αὐτῷ εὐθὺς ἐξέβαλεν αὐτόν, 44 καὶ λέγει αὐτῷ, "Ὅρα μηδενὶ μηδὲν εἴπῃς, ἀλλὰ ὕπαγε σεαυτὸν δεῖξον τῷ ἱερεῖ καὶ προσένεγκε περὶ τοῦ καθαρισμοῦ σου ἃ προσέταξεν Μωϋσῆς,ⁱ εἰς μαρτύριον αὐτοῖς. 45 ὁ δὲ ἐξελθὼν ἤρξατο κηρύσσειν πολλὰ καὶ διαφημίζειν τὸν λόγον, ὥστε μηκέτι αὐτὸν δύνασθαι φανερῶς εἰς πόλιν εἰσελθεῖν, ἀλλ' ἔξω ἐπ' ἐρήμοις τόποις ἦν· καὶ ἤρχοντο πρὸς αὐτὸν πάντοθεν.

The Healing of a Paralytic
(Mt 9.1–8; Lk 5.17–26)

2 Καὶ εἰσελθὼν πάλιν εἰς Καφαρναοὺμ δι' ἡμερῶν ἠκούσθη ὅτι ἐν οἴκῳ ἐστίν. 2 καὶ συνήχθησαν πολλοὶ ὥστε μηκέτι χωρεῖν μηδὲ τὰ πρὸς τὴν θύραν, καὶ ἐλάλει αὐτοῖς τὸν λόγον. 3 καὶ ἔρχονται φέροντες πρὸς αὐτὸν παραλυτικὸν αἰρόμενον ὑπὸ τεσσάρων. 4 καὶ μὴ δυνάμενοι προσενέγκαι¹ αὐτῷ διὰ τὸν ὄχλον ἀπεστέγασαν τὴν στέγην ὅπου ἦν, καὶ ἐξορύξαντες χαλῶσι τὸν κράβαττον ὅπου ὁ παραλυτικὸς κατέκειτο. 5 καὶ ἰδὼν ὁ Ἰησοῦς τὴν πίστιν αὐτῶν λέγει τῷ παραλυτικῷ, Τέκνον, ἀφίενταί² σου αἱ ἁμαρτίαι. 6 ἦσαν δέ τινες τῶν γραμματέων ἐκεῖ καθήμενοι καὶ διαλογιζόμενοι ἐν ταῖς καρδίαις αὐτῶν, 7 Τί

---

¹ **4** {C} προσενέγκαι ℵ B L Θ (33 προσενέγκειν) 892 *l*⁴⁸ it^aur, f, l vg syr^h, pal cop^sa, bo eth Diatessaron^a Augustine ‖ προσεγγίσαι A C D K Δ Π 090 *f*¹ *f*¹³ 28 565 700 1009 1010 1071 1079 1195 1216 1230 1241 1242 1253 1344 1365 1546 1646 2148 2174 *Byz Lect* (*l*¹¹²⁷) it^a, b, c, d, e, ff², q, r¹ syr^p goth arm geo ‖ προσελθεῖν W

² **5** {B} ἀφίενται (*see* Mt 9.2) B 28 33 565 1241 it^a, aur, c, d, e, ff², l, r¹ vg syr^p, h, pal cop^sa, bo goth geo ‖ ἀφέωνται (*see* Lk 5.20) ℵ A C D K L W (Θ ἀφίωνται) Π 090 *f*¹ *f*¹³ 700 892 1071 1195 1216 1242 1344 1365 1646 2174 *Byz Lect* it^b, f, q arm Diatessaron Clement Basil ‖ ἀφέονται (Δ ἀφίονται) 1009 1010 1079 1230 1253 1546 2148 *l*⁴⁸, ⁷⁰, ¹⁸³, ²¹¹, ²²³, ²²⁴, ²²⁵, ⁵⁴⁷, ⁹⁵⁶, ¹⁵⁷⁸, ¹⁶²⁷, ¹⁶⁴² (*l*⁶⁰ ἀφέοντε, *l*²²⁷ ἀφαίοντα)

ⁱ **44** *i* minor: TR Nes AV RV ASV RSV NEB TT Zür? Luth? Seg ‖ *i* none: WH Bov BF² Jer

---

43–44 ἐμβριμησάμενος...εἴπῃς Mt 9.30   **44** ὕπαγε...Μωϋσῆς Lv 14.2–32
2 5 ἀφίενται...ἁμαρτίαι Lk 7.48

οὗτος οὕτως λαλεῖ; βλασφημεῖ· τίς δύναται ἀφιέναι
ἁμαρτίας εἰ μὴ εἷς ὁ θεός; 8 καὶ εὐθὺς ἐπιγνοὺς ὁ Ἰησοῦς
τῷ πνεύματι αὐτοῦ ὅτι οὕτως διαλογίζονται ἐν ἑαυτοῖς
λέγει αὐτοῖς, Τί ταῦτα διαλογίζεσθε ἐν ταῖς καρδίαις
ὑμῶν; 9 τί ἐστιν εὐκοπώτερον, εἰπεῖν τῷ παραλυτικῷ,
Ἀφίενταί[3] σου αἱ ἁμαρτίαι, ἢ εἰπεῖν, Ἔγειρε καὶ ἆρον
τὸν κράβαττόν σου καὶ περιπάτει; 10 ἵνα δὲ εἰδῆτε ὅτι
ἐξουσίαν ἔχει ὁ υἱὸς τοῦ ἀνθρώπου ἀφιέναι ἁμαρτίας ἐπὶ
τῆς γῆς[4] — λέγει τῷ παραλυτικῷ, 11 Σοὶ λέγω, ἔγειρε
ἆρον τὸν κράβαττόν σου καὶ ὕπαγε εἰς τὸν οἶκόν σου.
12 καὶ ἠγέρθη καὶ εὐθὺς ἄρας τὸν κράβαττον ἐξῆλθεν
ἔμπροσθεν πάντων, ὥστε ἐξίστασθαι πάντας καὶ δοξάζειν
τὸν θεὸν λέγοντας ὅτι Οὕτως οὐδέποτε εἴδομεν.

The Calling of Levi
(Mt 9.9–13; Lk 5.27–32)

13 Καὶ ἐξῆλθεν πάλιν παρὰ τὴν θάλασσαν· καὶ πᾶς ὁ
ὄχλος ἤρχετο πρὸς αὐτόν, καὶ ἐδίδασκεν αὐτούς. 14 καὶ
παράγων εἶδεν Λευὶν[5] τὸν τοῦ Ἁλφαίου καθήμενον ἐπὶ

---

[3] **9** {B} ἀφίενται (see Mt 9.5) ℵ B 28 565 it[a,aur,c,d,e,f,ff2,l,q,rl] vg syr[p,h,pal]
cop[(sa),bo] goth geo ∥ ἀφέωνται (see Lk 5.23) A C (D) K L W Δ Θ Π 090
0130 f[1] f[13] 33 700 892 1010 1079 1195 1216 1241 1242 1344 1365 1646 2148 2174
Byz Lect it[b] arm Diatessaron[a] Clement ∥ ἀφέονται 1009 1071 1230 1253
1546 l[48,224,227,547,956,1627,1635,1642] (l[60] ἀφέοντε, l[70,211] ἀφαίονται)

[4] **10** {B} ἀφιέναι ἁμαρτίας ἐπὶ τῆς γῆς B Θ l[185] eth Marcion ∥ ἀφιέναι
ἐπὶ τῆς γῆς ἁμαρτίας A K Π f[1] f[13] 28 565 1010 1079 1242 1344 1365 1646
2174 Byz[pt] Lect syr[h] Basil ∥ ἐπὶ τῆς γῆς ἀφιέναι ἁμαρτίας (see Mt 9.6;
Lk 5.24) ℵ C D L Δ 090 0130 33 700 892 1009 1071 1230[vid] 1241 1253 1546
2148 Byz[pt] l[60,69,70,76,(150),211,299,303,333,547,883,1127,1663] it[a,aur,c,d,e,f,ff2,l] vg syr[p,pal]
cop[sa,bo] goth arm geo Diatessaron[a] ∥ ἀφιέναι ἁμαρτίας W 1195 1216 it[b,q]

[5] **14** {A} Λευίν C (ℵ[c] B L W Λευείν) f[1] 700 892 1009 1010 1071 1195
1216 1230 1241 1242 1253 1365 2174 Byz Lect (l[60] Λευήν, l[70] Λευείν) it[f] vg[ww]
(Λευί (ℵ* Λευεί) A K Δ Π (28 Λευή) 33 1079 1344 1546 1646 2148 l[225,302,313,]
[956,1642] it[aur,l,q] vg[cl] syr[p,h,pal] (cop[sa] Λευεί) cop[bo] (goth Λευυί) arm geo
Origen) ∥ Ἰάκωβον (see 3.18) D Θ f[13] 565 it[a,b,c,d,e,ff2,rl] Diatessaron[a] Origen
Ephraem Photius

---

7 τίς...θεός Ps 103.3; Is 43.25; 1 Jn 1.9   8 Τί...διαλογίζεσθε...ὑμῶν Mt 16.8
12 Οὕτως...εἴδομεν Mt 9.33

does he dare to talk against God like
this? No man can forgive sins; only
God can!" [8] At once Jesus knew their
secret thoughts, so he said to them:
"Why do you think such things? [9] Is it
easier to say to this paralyzed man,
'Your sins are forgiven,' or to say, 'Get
up, pick up your mat, and walk'? [10] I
will prove to you, then, that the Son
of Man has authority on earth to forgive
sins." So he said to the paralyzed man,
[11] "I tell you, get up, pick up your mat,
and go home!" [12] While they all watched,
the man got up, picked up his mat and
hurried away. They were all completely
amazed and praised God, saying, "We
have never seen anything like this!"

Jesus Calls Levi
(Also Matt. 9.9–13; Luke 5.27–32)

[13] Jesus went back again to the shore
of Lake Galilee. A crowd came to him
and he started teaching them. [14] As he
walked along he saw a tax collector,
Levi the son of Alphaeus, sitting in his

office. Jesus said to him, "Follow me." Levi got up and followed him.

¹⁵ Later on Jesus was having a meal in Levi's house. There were many tax collectors and outcasts who were following Jesus, and some of them joined him and his disciples at the table. ¹⁶ Some teachers of the Law, who were Pharisees, saw that Jesus was eating with these outcasts and tax collectors; so they asked his disciples, "Why does he eat with tax collectors and outcasts?" ¹⁷ Jesus heard them and answered: "People who are well do not need a doctor, but only those who are sick. I have not come to call the respectable people, but the outcasts."

The Question about Fasting
(Also Matt. 9.14–17; Luke 5.33–39)

¹⁸ On one occasion the followers of John the Baptist and the Pharisees were fasting. Some people came to Jesus and asked him, "Why is it that the disciples of John the Baptist and the disciples of

τὸ τελώνιον, καὶ λέγει αὐτῷ, Ἀκολούθει μοι. καὶ ἀναστὰς ἠκολούθησεν αὐτῷ. 15 Καὶ γίνεται κατακεῖσθαι αὐτὸν ἐν τῇ οἰκίᾳ αὐτοῦ, καὶ πολλοὶ τελῶναι καὶ ἁμαρτωλοὶ συνανέκειντο τῷ Ἰησοῦ καὶ τοῖς μαθηταῖς αὐτοῦ· ἦσαν γὰρ πολλοί. καὶ ἠκολούθουν αὐτῷ 16 καὶ οἱ γραμματεῖς τῶν Φαρισαίων, καὶ ἰδόντες⁶ ὅτι ἐσθίει μετὰ τῶν ἁμαρτωλῶν καὶ τελωνῶν ἔλεγον τοῖς μαθηταῖς αὐτοῦ, Ὅτιᵃ μετὰ τῶν τελωνῶν καὶ ἁμαρτωλῶν ἐσθίει⁷;ᵃ 17 καὶ ἀκούσας ὁ Ἰησοῦς λέγει αὐτοῖς [ὅτι] Οὐ χρείαν ἔχουσιν οἱ ἰσχύοντες ἰατροῦ ἀλλ' οἱ κακῶς ἔχοντες· οὐκ ἦλθον καλέσαι δικαίους ἀλλὰ ἁμαρτωλούς.

The Question about Fasting
(Mt 9.14–17; Lk 5.33–39)

18 Καὶ ἦσαν οἱ μαθηταὶ Ἰωάννου καὶ οἱ Φαρισαῖοι νηστεύοντες. καὶ ἔρχονται καὶ λέγουσιν αὐτῷ, Διὰ τί οἱ μαθηταὶ Ἰωάννου καὶ οἱ μαθηταὶ τῶν Φαρισαίων

---

⁶ **15–16** {C} αὐτῷ καὶ οἱ γραμματεῖς τῶν Φαρισαίων, καὶ ἰδόντες ℵ (Δ 0130ᵛⁱᵈ omit καὶ οἱ) (L 33 omit οἱ) (itᵇ) (geo omit first καὶ) ‖ αὐτῷ καὶ οἱ γραμματεῖς τῶν Φαρισαίων ἰδόντες (B omit καί) (W omit ἰδόντες... καὶ τελωνῶν) 28 l⁵⁴⁷ syrᵖᵃˡ ‖ αὐτῷ οἱ γραμματεῖς καὶ οἱ Φαρισαῖοι, καὶ ἰδόντες copᵇᵒ ‖ αὐτῷ. καὶ οἱ γραμματεῖς καὶ οἱ Φαρισαῖοι ἰδόντες A C (D καὶ εἶδαν) K Θ Π f¹ f¹³ 565 892 1009 1010 1071 1079 1195 1216 1230 1241 1242 1253 1344 1365 1546 1646 2148 2174 Byz Lect (l²²⁷) itᵃᵘʳ,(d),f,l,q,(r¹) vg syrᵖ·ʰ (goth omit second οἱ) arm eth Diatessaron ‖ αὐτῷ. οἱ δὲ γραμματεῖς καὶ οἱ Φαρισαῖοι ἰδόντες 700 itᵃ,ᶜ,(ᵉ),(ff²) copˢᵃ

⁷ **16** {B} ἐσθίει (see Mt 9.11) B D W l³⁰² itᵃ,ᵇ,ᵈ,ᵉ,ff²,r¹ ‖ ἐσθίεται Θ ‖ ἐσθίει καὶ πίνει A K Π f¹ 28 33 892 1009 1010 1079 1195 1230 1242 1253 1344 1365 1546 1646 2148 Byz Lect (l⁷⁶ πίννει) itq syrᵖ·ʰ goth ‖ ἐσθίετε καὶ πίνετε (see Lk 5.30) 565 700 1241 l⁵⁴⁷ syrᵖᵃˡ arm geo Diatessaron ‖ ἐσθίει ὁ διδάσκαλος ὑμῶν (see Mt 9.11) ℵ itᵃᵘʳ ‖ ἐσθίει καὶ πίνει ὁ διδάσκαλος ὑμῶν L Δ f¹³ 1071 1216 2174 it(c),f vg copᵇᵒ Augustine ‖ ὁ διδάσκαλος ὑμῶν ἐσθίει καὶ πίνει C it¹ copˢᵃ eth

---

ᵃ ᵃ **16** a interrogative, a question: (TR) WH Bov Nes BF² (AV) RVᵐᵍ ASV RSV TT Zür Jer Seg ‖ a direct, a question: Luth ‖ a direct, a exclamation: NEB ‖ a direct, a statement: RV ASVᵐᵍ

---

14 Ἀκολούθει μοι Mt 8.22; 19.21; Mk 10.21; Lk 9.59; 18.22; Jn 1.43; 21.19, 22 ἀναστὰς... αὐτῷ Mt 4.20, 22 **16** Mt 11.19; Lk 7.34; 15.1-2

νηστεύουσιν, οἱ δὲ σοὶ μαθηταὶ οὐ νηστεύουσιν; **19** καὶ εἶπεν αὐτοῖς ὁ Ἰησοῦς, Μὴ δύνανται οἱ υἱοὶ τοῦ νυμφῶνος ἐν ᾧ ὁ νυμφίος μετ’ αὐτῶν ἐστιν νηστεύειν; ὅσον χρόνον ἔχουσιν τὸν νυμφίον μετ’ αὐτῶν οὐ δύνανται νηστεύειν· **20** ἐλεύσονται δὲ ἡμέραι ὅταν ἀπαρθῇ ἀπ’ αὐτῶν ὁ νυμφίος, καὶ τότε νηστεύσουσιν ἐν ἐκείνῃ τῇ ἡμέρᾳ. **21** οὐδεὶς ἐπίβλημα ῥάκους ἀγνάφου ἐπιράπτει ἐπὶ ἱμάτιον παλαιόν· εἰ δὲ μή, αἴρει τὸ πλήρωμα ἀπ’ αὐτοῦ τὸ καινὸν τοῦ παλαιοῦ, καὶ χεῖρον σχίσμα γίνεται. **22** καὶ οὐδεὶς βάλλει οἶνον νέον εἰς ἀσκοὺς παλαιούς — εἰ δὲ μή, ῥήξει ὁ οἶνος τοὺς ἀσκούς, καὶ ὁ οἶνος ἀπόλλυται καὶ οἱ ἀσκοί[8] — ἀλλὰ οἶνον νέον εἰς ἀσκοὺς καινούς[9].

Plucking Grain on the Sabbath
(Mt 12.1–8; Lk 6.1–5)

23 Καὶ ἐγένετο αὐτὸν ἐν τοῖς σάββασιν παραπορεύεσθαι διὰ τῶν σπορίμων, καὶ οἱ μαθηταὶ αὐτοῦ ἤρξαντο ὁδὸν ποιεῖν τίλλοντες τοὺς στάχυας. **24** καὶ οἱ Φαρισαῖοι ἔλεγον αὐτῷ, Ἴδε τί ποιοῦσιν τοῖς σάββασιν ὃ οὐκ ἔξεστιν; **25** καὶ λέγει αὐτοῖς, Οὐδέποτε ἀνέγνωτε τί ἐποίησεν Δαυίδ,[b] ὅτε χρείαν ἔσχεν καὶ ἐπείνασεν αὐτὸς καὶ οἱ μετ’ αὐτοῦ;[b] **26** πῶς εἰσῆλθεν εἰς τὸν οἶκον τοῦ θεοῦ ἐπὶ

---

[8] **22** {C} ἀπόλλυται καὶ οἱ ἀσκοί B 892 cop^bo ∥ καὶ οἱ ἀσκοὶ ἀπολοῦνται (see footnote 9) D it^a,b,d,e,ff2,i,r1,t ∥ ἐκχεῖται καὶ οἱ ἀσκοὶ L (syr^pal) ∥ ἐκχεῖται καὶ οἱ ἀσκοὶ ἀπολοῦνται (see Mt 9.17; Lk 5.37) ℵ A C K (W ἀπόλλυνται) Δ (Θ ἀπόλλυνται) Π 074 f^1 f^13 28 33 565 700 1009 1010 1071 1079 1195 (1216 ἀπόλλυται) 1230 1241 1242 (1253 ἀπόλονται) 1344 1365 1546 1646 2148 2174 Byz Lect it^aur,c,f,l,q vg^(cl),ww syr^s,(p),h cop^sa goth arm eth geo ∥ ἐκχεῖται l^80

[9] **22** {C} ἀλλὰ οἶνον νέον εἰς ἀσκοὺς καινούς ℵ* B ∥ ἀλλὰ (or ἀλλ’) οἶνον νέον εἰς ἀσκοὺς καινοὺς βλητέον (see Lk 5.38) ℵ^a A C K L Δ^gr Θ Π 074 f^1 f^13 28 33 565 700 892 1009 1010 1071 1079 1195 1216 1230 1241 1242 1253

---

b b b **25–26** b minor, b question, b question: TR (WH) Bov Nes BF^2 AV RV ASV (TT) Zür Luth ∥ b minor, b minor, b question: RSV Jer ∥ b minor, b question, b major: (NEB) Seg

23 ἤρξαντο...στάχυας Dt 23.25   **25–26** τί...οῦσιν 1 Sm 21.1–6   **26** ἐπὶ...ἀρχιερέως 2 Sm 15.35

---

the Pharisees fast, but yours do not?" [19] Jesus answered: "Do you expect the guests at a wedding party to go without food? Of course not! As long as the bridegroom is with them they will not do that. [20] But the time will come when the bridegroom will be taken away from them; when that day comes then they will go without food.

[21] "No one uses a piece of new cloth to patch up an old coat. If he does, the new patch will tear off some of the old cloth, making an even bigger hole. [22] Nor does anyone pour new wine into used wineskins. If he does, the wine will burst the skins, and both the wine and the skins will be ruined. No! Fresh skins for new wine!"

The Question about the Sabbath
(Also Matt. 12.1–8; Luke 6.1–5)

[23] Jesus was walking through some wheat fields on a Sabbath day. As his disciples walked along with him, they began to pick the heads of wheat. [24] So the Pharisees said to Jesus, "Look, it is against our Law for your disciples to do this on the Sabbath!" [25] Jesus answered: "Have you never read what David did that time when he needed something to eat? He and his men were hungry, [26] so he went into the house of God and ate the bread offered to God.

This happened when Abiathar was the High Priest. According to our Law only the priests may eat this bread — but David ate it, and even gave it to his men." 27 And Jesus said, "The Sabbath was made for the good of man; man was not made for the Sabbath. 28 So the Son of Man is Lord even of the Sabbath."

The Man with a Crippled Hand
(Also Matt. 12.9–14; Luke 6.6–11)

3 Then Jesus went back to the synagogue, where there was a man who had a crippled hand. 2 Some people were there who wanted to accuse Jesus of doing wrong; so they watched him very closely, to see whether he would cure anyone on the Sabbath. 3 Jesus said to the man with the crippled hand, "Come up here to the front." 4 Then he asked the people: "What does our Law allow us to do on the Sabbath? To help, or to harm? To save a man's life, or to destroy it?" But they did not say a thing. 5 Jesus was angry as he looked around at them, but at the same time he felt sorry for them, because they were so stubborn and wrong. Then he said to the man, "Stretch out your hand." He stretched it out and it became well again. 6 So the Pharisees left the synagogue and met at once with some members of Herod's party; and they made plans against Jesus to kill him.

A Crowd by the Lake

7 Jesus and his disciples went away to Lake Galilee, and a large crowd followed him. They came from Galilee,

Ἀβιαθὰρ ἀρχιερέως[10] καὶ τοὺς ἄρτους τῆς προθέσεως ἔφαγεν, οὓς οὐκ ἔξεστιν φαγεῖν εἰ μὴ τοὺς ἱερεῖς, καὶ ἔδωκεν καὶ τοῖς σὺν αὐτῷ οὖσιν;[b] 27 καὶ ἔλεγεν αὐτοῖς, Τὸ σάββατον διὰ τὸν ἄνθρωπον ἐγένετο καὶ οὐχ ὁ ἄνθρωπος διὰ τὸ σάββατον· 28 ὥστε κύριός ἐστιν ὁ υἱὸς τοῦ ἀνθρώπου καὶ τοῦ σαββάτου.

The Man with a Withered Hand
(Mt 12.9–14; Lk 6.6–11)

3 Καὶ εἰσῆλθεν πάλιν εἰς τὴν συναγωγήν. καὶ ἦν ἐκεῖ ἄνθρωπος ἐξηραμμένην ἔχων τὴν χεῖρα· 2 καὶ παρετήρουν αὐτὸν εἰ τοῖς σάββασιν θεραπεύσει αὐτόν, ἵνα κατηγορήσωσιν αὐτοῦ. 3 καὶ λέγει τῷ ἀνθρώπῳ τῷ τὴν ξηρὰν χεῖρα ἔχοντι, Ἔγειρε εἰς τὸ μέσον. 4 καὶ λέγει αὐτοῖς, Ἔξεστιν τοῖς σάββασιν ἀγαθὸν ποιῆσαι ἢ κακοποιῆσαι, ψυχὴν σῶσαι ἢ ἀποκτεῖναι; οἱ δὲ ἐσιώπων. 5 καὶ περιβλεψάμενος αὐτοὺς μετ' ὀργῆς, συλλυπούμενος ἐπὶ τῇ πωρώσει τῆς καρδίας αὐτῶν, λέγει τῷ ἀνθρώπῳ, Ἔκτεινον τὴν χεῖρα. καὶ ἐξέτεινεν, καὶ ἀπεκατεστάθη ἡ χεὶρ αὐτοῦ. 6 καὶ ἐξελθόντες οἱ Φαρισαῖοι εὐθὺς μετὰ τῶν Ἡρῳδιανῶν συμβούλιον ἐδίδουν κατ' αὐτοῦ ὅπως αὐτὸν ἀπολέσωσιν.

A Multitude at the Seaside

7 Καὶ ὁ Ἰησοῦς μετὰ τῶν μαθητῶν αὐτοῦ ἀνεχώρησεν πρὸς τὴν θάλασσαν·[a] καὶ πολὺ πλῆθος ἀπὸ τῆς Γαλιλαίας

1344 1365 1546 1646 2148 2174 *Byz Lect* it[aur,c,l,q] vg syr[h,pal] arm ‖ ἀλλὰ οἶνον νέον εἰς ἀσκοὺς καινοὺς βάλλουσιν (*see* Mt 9.17) W it[e,f] syr[s,p] cop[sa,bo] goth eth geo Diatessaron[a] ‖ *omit* D it[a,b,d,ff2,i,r1,t]

10 26 {A} ἐπὶ Ἀβιαθὰρ ἀρχιερέως ℵ B K L 892 1010 1195 1216 1230 1242 1344 1365 1646 2174 *Byz* *l*[69,70,76,80,150,299,883,1127,1634] arm ‖ ἐπὶ Ἀβιαθὰρ

[a a a] **7–8** *a* major, *a* major, *a* minor: (TR) Bov Nes BF² RV ASV ‖ *a* major, *a* minor, *a* minor: WH AV ‖ *a* minor, *a* major, *a* none: RSV (TT) Zür (Luth) (Jer) ‖ *a* major, *a* minor, *a* major: Seg ‖ *a* major, *a* minor, *a* dash: WH[mg] ‖ different text: NEB

---

26 τοὺς...ἱερεῖς Lv 24.5-9   **27** Τὸ...ἐγένετο Ex 20.8-10; Dt 5.12-14
3 4 Lk 14.3   **5** τῇ πωρώσει...αὐτῶν Mk 6.52; 8.17; Jn 12.40; Ro 11.25; Eph 4.18   **6** οἱ ...Ἡρῳδιανῶν Mt 22.15-16; Mk 12.13   **7–8** πολὺ...Ἰορδάνου Mt 4.25

ἠκολούθησεν·[a] καὶ ἀπὸ τῆς Ἰουδαίας 8 καὶ ἀπὸ Ἱεροσολύμων[1] καὶ ἀπὸ τῆς Ἰδουμαίας[2] καὶ πέραν τοῦ Ἰορδάνου
καὶ περὶ Τύρον καὶ Σιδῶνα,[a] πλῆθος πολύ[3], ἀκούοντες ὅσα
ἐποίει ἦλθον πρὸς αὐτόν. 9 καὶ εἶπεν τοῖς μαθηταῖς
αὐτοῦ ἵνα πλοιάριον προσκαρτερῇ αὐτῷ διὰ τὸν ὄχλον ἵνα
μὴ θλίβωσιν αὐτόν·[b] 10 πολλοὺς γὰρ ἐθεράπευσεν, ὥστε
ἐπιπίπτειν αὐτῷ ἵνα αὐτοῦ ἅψωνται ὅσοι εἶχον μάστιγας.[b]
11 καὶ τὰ πνεύματα τὰ ἀκάθαρτα, ὅταν αὐτὸν ἐθεώρουν,
προσέπιπτον αὐτῷ καὶ ἔκραζον λέγοντες ὅτι Σὺ εἶ ὁ

τοῦ ἀρχιερέως A C Θ Π 074 f[1] f[13] 28 33 565 700 1071 1079 1241 1253 1546[c]
2148 Lect cop[sa,bo] ‖ ἐπὶ Ἀβιαθὰρ ἀρχιερέως (or τοῦ ἀρχιερέως) it[aur,c,l,q]
vg syr[(p),h,palmss] geo ‖ ἐπὶ Ἀβιαθὰρ τοῦ ἱερέως Δ it[f] (goth omit τοῦ) ‖
omit (see Mt 12.4; Lk 6.4) D W 1009 1546* it[a,b,d,e,ff2,i,r1,t] syr[s,(palms)]

[1] 7–8 {D} ἠκολούθησεν· καὶ ἀπὸ τῆς Ἰουδαίας καὶ ἀπὸ Ἱεροσολύμων
(see footnote 2) B L 565 ‖ ἠκολούθησαν αὐτῷ καὶ ἀπὸ τῆς Ἰουδαίας
καὶ ἀπὸ Ἱεροσολύμων K[*vid] 1009 1241 1344 1546 Byz[pt] Lect (l[1127] omit second
ἀπό) syr[h] cop[sa?(bomss)] goth arm (eth) Diatessaron[ams] ‖ ἠκολούθησεν αὐτῷ
καὶ ἀπὸ τῆς Ἰουδαίας καὶ ἀπὸ Ἱεροσολύμων A K[2] P Π (700 omit τῆς)
892 1010 1079 1195 1216 1242 1365 1646 2148 2174 Byz[pt] l[185,883,950] syr[p] Diatessaron[ams] Victor-Antioch ‖ ἠκολούθησεν αὐτῷ καὶ ἀπὸ Ἱεροσολύμων καὶ
ἀπὸ τῆς Ἰουδαίας (Θ omit αὐτῷ) f[1] (1230 ἐκ τῆς Ἰουδαίας) 1253 ‖ καὶ
ἀπὸ Ἱεροσολύμων ἠκολούθησαν αὐτῷ καὶ ἀπὸ τῆς Ἰουδαίας 33 ‖ καὶ ἀπὸ
τῆς Ἰουδαίας ἠκολούθησαν αὐτῷ καὶ ἀπὸ Ἱεροσολύμων (Δ αὐτόν) it[aur,f,(l)]
vg ‖ καὶ ἀπὸ τῆς Ἰουδαίας ἠκολούθησαν καὶ ἀπὸ Ἱεροσολύμων ℵ C 1071 ‖
καὶ τῆς Ἰουδαίας καὶ ἀπὸ Ἱεροσολύμων D (f[13] 28 omit τῆς) it[a,(b),c,d,e,]
[ff2,i,(q),r1] (syr[s]) cop[bomss] geo ‖ καὶ τῆς Ἰουδαίας καὶ ἀπὸ Ἱεροσολύμων...
Σιδῶνα ἠκολούθουν αὐτῷ W

[2] 8 {B} καὶ ἀπὸ τῆς Ἰδουμαίας (see footnote 1) ℵ[c] A B C (D[gr]
omit ἀπό) K L P Δ Π f[13] 28 (33 omit ἀπὸ τῆς) 565 700 892 1010 1071 1079
1195 1216 1230 1241 1242 1344 1365 1546 1646 2148 2174 Byz Lect it[a,aur,b,d,e,f,]
[ff2,i,l,q,r1] vg syr[p,h] (cop[bo] geo[1] omit ἀπὸ τῆς) goth ‖ and a great multitude
also from Idumea cop[sa] ‖ omit ℵ* W Θ f[1] 1009 1253 it[c] syr[s] arm geo[2]

[3] 8 {B} πλῆθος πολύ ℵ A B C D K L P Δ Θ Π f[13] 28 33 565 700 892
1009 1010 1071 1079 1195 1216 1230 1241 1242 1253 1344 1365 1546 1646 2148
2174 Byz Lect it[aur,d,e,f,ff2,i,l,q,r1] vg syr[p,h] (cop[bo]) goth arm geo ‖ καὶ πλῆθος
πολύ f[1] ‖ omit W it[a,b,c] syr[s] cop[sa]

[b b] 9–10 b minor, b major: WH Bov Nes BF[2] RV ASV RSV TT ‖ b major, b minor: TR ‖ b major;
b major: AV NEB Zür Luth Jer Seg

---

9 Mk 4.1; Lk 5.3   10 Mt 14.36; Mk 6.56   11–12 Mk 1.34; Lk 4.41

---

from Judea, [8] from Jerusalem, from the
territory of Idumea, from the territory
on the other side of the Jordan, and
from the neighborhood of the cities of
Tyre and Sidon. This large crowd came
to Jesus because they heard of the things
he was doing. [9] The crowd was so large
that Jesus told his disciples to get a
boat ready for him, so the people would
not crush him. [10] He had healed many
people, and all the sick kept pushing
their way to him in order to touch him.
[11] And whenever the people who had
evil spirits in them saw him they would
fall down before him and scream, "You

are the Son of God!'' ¹² Jesus gave a stern command to the evil spirits not to tell who he was.

Jesus Chooses the Twelve Apostles
(Also Matt. 10.1–4; Luke 6.12–16)

¹³ Then Jesus went up a hill and called to himself the men he wanted. They came to him ¹⁴ and he chose twelve, whom he named apostles. "I have chosen you to stay with me," he told them; "I will also send you out to preach, ¹⁵ and you will have authority to drive out demons." ¹⁶ These are the twelve he chose: Simon (Jesus gave him the name Peter); ¹⁷ James and his brother John, the sons of Zebedee (Jesus gave them the name Boanerges, which means "Men of Thunder"); ¹⁸ Andrew, Philip, Bartholomew, Matthew, Thomas, James the son of Alphaeus, Thaddaeus, Simon

υἱὸς τοῦ θεοῦ. **12** καὶ πολλὰ ἐπετίμα αὐτοῖς ἵνα μὴ αὐτὸν φανερὸν ποιήσωσιν.

The Choosing of the Twelve
(Mt 10.1–4; Lk 6.12–16)

13 Καὶ ἀναβαίνει εἰς τὸ ὄρος καὶ προσκαλεῖται οὓς ἤθελεν αὐτός, καὶ ἀπῆλθον πρὸς αὐτόν. **14** καὶ ἐποίησεν δώδεκα, [οὓς καὶ ἀποστόλους ὠνόμασεν,] ἵνα ὦσιν μετ' αὐτοῦ⁴ καὶ ἵνα ἀποστέλλῃ αὐτοὺς κηρύσσειν **15** καὶ ἔχειν ἐξουσίαν ἐκβάλλειν τὰ δαιμόνια· **16** [καὶ ἐποίησεν τοὺς δώδεκα,ᶜ] καὶ⁵ ἐπέθηκεν ὄνομα τῷ Σίμωνιᶜ Πέτρον, **17** καὶ Ἰάκωβον τὸν τοῦ Ζεβεδαίου καὶ Ἰωάννην τὸν ἀδελφὸν τοῦ Ἰακώβου,ᵈ καὶ ἐπέθηκεν αὐτοῖς ὀνόματα Βοανηργές,ᵈ ὅ ἐστιν Υἱοὶ Βροντῆς·ᵈ **18** καὶ Ἀνδρέαν καὶ Φίλιππον καὶ Βαρθολομαῖον καὶ Μαθθαῖον καὶ Θωμᾶν καὶ Ἰάκωβον τὸν τοῦ Ἁλφαίου καὶ Θαδδαῖον⁶ καὶ Σίμωνα

⁴ **14** {C} δώδεκα, οὓς καὶ ἀποστόλους ὠνόμασεν, ἵνα ὦσιν μετ' αὐτοῦ (see Lk 6.13) ℵ B (C*ᵛⁱᵈ *transposes*: ὠνόμασεν δώδεκα, ἵνα) Θ f¹³ (28 περὶ αὐτοῦ) (1195 ὠνόμασεν ἀποστόλους) syrʰᵐᵍ copˢᵃ,ᵇᵒ eth ‖ δώδεκα ἵνα ὦσιν μετ' αὐτοῦ A C² (D *transposes*: ἵνα ὦσιν δώδεκα) K L P Π f¹ 33 565 (700 περὶ αὐτοῦ) 892 1009 1010 1071 1079 1216 1230 1241 1242 1253 1344 1365 1546 1646 2148 2174 *Byz Lect* (l⁷⁶ δέκα) itᵃ,ᵃᵘʳ,ᵇ,ᶜ,ᵈ,ᵉ,f,ff²,ⁱ,l,q,rl,t vg syrˢ,ᵖ,ʰ goth arm geo² Diatessaronᵃ ‖ δώδεκα, ἵνα ὦσιν μετ' αὐτοῦ οὓς καὶ ἀποστόλους ὠνόμασεν W (Δ *transposes*: ἵνα ὦσιν μετ' αὐτοῦ δώδεκα) geo¹

⁵ **16** {C} καὶ ἐποίησεν τοὺς δώδεκα, καὶ ℵ B C* Δ 565 ‖ καὶ A C² D K L P Θ Π 0134 f¹ 28 33 700 892 1009 1010 1071 1079 1195 1216 1230 1241 1242 1253 1344 1365 1546 1646 2148 2174 *Byz Lect* itᵃᵘʳ,ᵇ,ᵈ,f,ff²,ⁱ,l,q,rl,t vg syrˢ,ᵖ,ʰ copᵇᵒ goth arm geo Diatessaronᵖ ‖ πρῶτον Σίμωνα καί f¹³ copˢᵃ ‖ καὶ περιάγοντας κηρύσσειν τὸ εὐαγγέλιον καί W itᵃ,ᶜ,ᵉ

⁶ **18** {A} καὶ Θαδδαῖον ℵ A B C (K Δαδδαῖον) L (Δ* Ταδδαῖον) (Θ *omit* καί) Π 0134 f¹ f¹³ 28 33 565 700 892 1009 1010 1071 1079 1195 1216 1230 1241 1242 1253 1344 1365 1546 1646 2148 2174 *Byz Lect* (l¹⁵⁰,²¹¹ Θαδαῖον) itᵃᵘʳ,ᶜ,f,l vg syrˢ,ᵖ,ʰ copˢᵃ,ᵇᵒ goth arm geo Diatessaronᵖ ‖ καὶ Λεββαῖον D itᵃ,ᵇ,ᵈ,ff²,ⁱ,q,rl ‖ καὶ Λευής mssᵃᶜᶜ· ᵗᵒ Origen ‖ *omit* W itᵉ

ᶜ ᶜ **16** c minor, c none: Bov Nes BF² (NEB) (TT) Zür Luth (Jer) (Seg) ‖ c parens, c parens: WH ‖ different text: TR AV RV ASV RSV

ᵈ ᵈ ᵈ **17** d minor, d minor, d major: (TR) Bov Nes BF² AVᵉᵈ RV ASV RSV NEB Luth (Jer) (Seg) ‖ d parens, d minor, d parens: WH AVᵉᵈ (TT) ‖ d minor, d parens, d parens: Zür

16 Mt 16.17–18; Jn 1.42   **17** Ἰάκωβον...Ἰωάννην Lk 9.54

τὸν Καναναῖον **19** καὶ Ἰούδαν Ἰσκαριώθ[7], ὃς καὶ παρέδωκεν αὐτόν.

Jesus and Beelzebul
(Mt 12.22–32; Lk 11.14–23; 12.10)

20 [e] Καὶ ἔρχεται[8] εἰς οἶκον· [e]καὶ συνέρχεται πάλιν ὄχλος, ὥστε μὴ δύνασθαι αὐτοὺς μηδὲ ἄρτον φαγεῖν. **21** καὶ ἀκούσαντες οἱ παρ' αὐτοῦ[9] ἐξῆλθον κρατῆσαι αὐτόν, ἔλεγον γὰρ ὅτι [f] ἐξέστη. **22** καὶ οἱ γραμματεῖς οἱ ἀπὸ Ἱεροσολύμων καταβάντες ἔλεγον ὅτι Βεελζεβοὺλ ἔχει, καὶ ὅτι ἐν τῷ ἄρχοντι τῶν δαιμονίων ἐκβάλλει τὰ δαιμόνια. **23** καὶ προσκαλεσάμενος αὐτοὺς ἐν παραβολαῖς ἔλεγεν αὐτοῖς, Πῶς δύναται Σατανᾶς Σατανᾶν ἐκβάλλειν; **24** καὶ ἐὰν βασιλεία ἐφ' ἑαυτὴν μερισθῇ, οὐ δύναται σταθῆναι ἡ βασιλεία ἐκείνη· **25** καὶ ἐὰν οἰκία ἐφ' ἑαυτὴν

---

[7] **19** {B} Ἰσκαριώθ ℵ B C L Δ Θ 33 565 892 1241 (l[150] Ἰσκαιώθ) geo[27] ‖ Ἰσκαριώτην A (K Ἰσκαριώτιν) (W Ἰσκαρώτης) Π 0134 f[1] f[13] 28 (700 Ἰσκαριότην) 1009 1010 1071 1079 1195 1216 1230 1242 1253 1344 1365 1546 1646 2148 2174 *Byz Lect* vg[cl] syr[h] cop[sa,bo] goth geo[27] ‖ Σκαριώθ D it[a,aur,b,d,ff2,i,l,q,r1,t] vg[ww] (it[e] *Cariotha*, it[f] *Scariothen*, it[c] syr[s,p] *Scariotha*) arm geo[1] Diatessaron[p]

[8] **20** {C} ἔρχεται ℵ* B W 1241 1646* l[80,211] it[a?b] (it[e,ff2,i,r1] εἰσέρχεται) syr[s] cop[sa,bo] Victor-Antioch ‖ ἔρχονται ℵ[c] A C (D εἰσέρχονται) K L Δ Θ Π 0134 f[1] f[13] 28 33 565 700 892 1009 1010 1071 1079 1195 1216 1230 1242 1253 1344 1365 1546 1646[c] 2148 2174 *Byz Lect* it[aur,d,f,l,q] vg syr[p,h] goth arm geo

[9] **21** {A} ἀκούσαντες οἱ παρ' αὐτοῦ ℵ A B C K L Δ Θ Π 0134 f[1] f[13] 28 33 565 700 892 1009 1010 1071 1079 1195 (1216 2174 περὶ αὐτοῦ) 1230 1241 1242 1253 1344 1365 1546 1646 2148 *Byz Lect* (l[211] ὑπὲρ αὐτοῦ for οἱ παρ' αὐτοῦ) it[aur,l] vg syr[(p,h),hgr] cop[sa,bo] arm eth geo Diatessaron[p] ‖ ἀκούσαντες περὶ αὐτοῦ οἱ γραμματεῖς καὶ οἱ λοιποί W goth ‖ ὅτε ἤκουσαν περὶ αὐτοῦ οἱ γραμματεῖς καὶ οἱ λοιποί D it[(a),(b),(c),d,(e),f,ff2,i,q,r1]

[e] [e] **19–20** e number 20, e no number: TR[ed] WH? Bov Nes BF[2] NEB? TT Zür Luth Jer Seg ‖ e no number, e number 20: TR[ed] WH? AV RV ASV RSV NEB?

[f] **21** f indirect: WH Bov Nes? BF[2] NEB TT ‖ f direct: TR Nes? AV RV ASV RSV NEB[mg] Zür Luth Jer Seg

19 Ἰούδαν...αὐτόν Mt 26.25; 27.3; Jn 18.2, 5   **20** συνέρχεται...φαγεῖν Mk 6.31
21 ἔλεγον...ἐξέστη Jn 10.20   **22** ἐν...δαιμόνια Mt 9.34

---

the patriot, [19] and Judas Iscariot, who became the traitor.

Jesus and Beelzebul
(Also Matt. 12.22–32; Luke 11.14–23; 12.10)

[20] Then Jesus went home. Again such a large crowd gathered that Jesus and his disciples had no time to eat. [21] When his family heard about this they set out to get him, because people were saying, "He's gone mad!"

[22] Some teachers of the Law who had come from Jerusalem were saying, "He has Beelzebul in him!" Others said, "It is the chief of the demons who gives him the power to drive them out." [23] So Jesus called the people to him and told them some parables: "How can Satan drive out Satan? [24] If a country divides itself into groups that fight each other, that country will fall apart. [25] If a family divides itself into groups that

fight each other, that family will fall apart. 26 So if Satan's kingdom divides into groups, it cannot last, but will fall apart and come to an end.

27 "No one can break into a strong man's house and take away his belongings unless he ties up the strong man first; then he can plunder his house.

28 "Remember this! Men can be forgiven all their sins and all the evil things they say,[1] no matter how often they say them. 29 But the person who says evil things against the Holy Spirit can never be forgiven, for he has committed an eternal sin." 30 (Jesus said this because some had said, "He has an evil spirit in him.")

Jesus' Mother and Brothers
(Also Matt. 12.46–50; Luke 8.19–21)

31 Then Jesus' mother and brothers arrived. They stood outside the house and sent in a message, asking for him. 32 A crowd was sitting around Jesus, and they told him, "Look, your mother and brothers are outside, and they want

---

[1] 28 evil things they say: or evil things they say against God

μερισθῇ, οὐ δυνήσεται ἡ οἰκία ἐκείνη σταθῆναι. 26 καὶ εἰ ὁ Σατανᾶς ἀνέστη ἐφ᾽ ἑαυτὸν καὶ ἐμερίσθη, οὐ δύναται στῆναι ἀλλὰ τέλος ἔχει. 27 ἀλλ᾽ οὐ δύναται οὐδεὶς εἰς τὴν οἰκίαν τοῦ ἰσχυροῦ εἰσελθὼν τὰ σκεύη αὐτοῦ διαρπάσαι ἐὰν μὴ πρῶτον τὸν ἰσχυρὸν δήσῃ, καὶ τότε τὴν οἰκίαν αὐτοῦ διαρπάσει. 28 Ἀμὴν λέγω ὑμῖν ὅτι πάντα ἀφεθήσεται τοῖς υἱοῖς τῶν ἀνθρώπων, τὰ ἁμαρτήματα καὶ αἱ βλασφημίαι ὅσα ἐὰν βλασφημήσωσιν· 29 ὃς δ᾽ ἂν βλασφημήσῃ εἰς τὸ πνεῦμα τὸ ἅγιον οὐκ ἔχει ἄφεσιν εἰς τὸν αἰῶνα, ἀλλὰ ἔνοχός ἐστιν[10] αἰωνίου ἁμαρτήματος[11] — 30 ὅτι ἔλεγον, Πνεῦμα ἀκάθαρτον ἔχει.

The Mother and Brothers of Jesus
(Mt 12.46–50; Lk 8.19–21)

31 Καὶ ἔρχεται ἡ μήτηρ αὐτοῦ καὶ οἱ ἀδελφοὶ αὐτοῦ καὶ ἔξω στήκοντες ἀπέστειλαν πρὸς αὐτὸν καλοῦντες αὐτόν. 32 καὶ ἐκάθητο περὶ αὐτὸν ὄχλος, καὶ λέγουσιν αὐτῷ, Ἰδοὺ ἡ μήτηρ σου καὶ οἱ ἀδελφοί σου[12] ἔξω ζητοῦσίν σε.

---

[10] 29 {A} ἐστιν A B C K W Θ Π 074 0134 f[1] f[13] 28 565 700 1009 1010 1071 1079 1195 1216 1230 1242 1253 1344 1365 1546 1646 2148 2174 Byz Lect it[b] syr[p,h] cop[bo] goth geo[2] Diatessaron[p] Cyprian Athanasius ‖ ἔσται ℵ D L Δ 33 892 1241 l[10,48,185] it[a,aur,c,d,e,f,ff2,l,q,r1] vg syr[svid] arm eth[vid] geo[1] Cyprian Augustine Eugippius

[11] 29 {A} ἁμαρτήματος ℵ B L Δ Θ 28 33 565 892[txt] ‖ ἁμαρτίας C*[vid] D W f[13] Athanasius ‖ ἁμαρτήματος or ἁμαρτίας it[a,e] syr[s] goth arm geo[1] Cyprian ‖ κρίσεως 826* 828 ‖ κρίσεως καὶ ἁμαρτίας A C[2] K Π 074 0134 f[1] 700 892[mg] 1009 1010 1071 1079 1195 1230 1241 1242 1253 1344 1365 1546 1646 2148 Byz Lect (l[883] κατακρίσεως) it[f,r1] syr[p,h] cop[bomss] eth geo[2] ‖ κολάσεως 1216 2174 Diatessaron[a,p] ‖ delicti it[aur,b,c,d,ff2,l,q] vg cop[bomss] Augustine Eugippius

[12] 32 {B} σου (see Mt 12.47; Lk 8.20) ℵ B C K L W Δ Θ Π 074 f[1] f[13] 28 33 565 892 1009 1071 1079 1195* 1241 1365 1546 2148 2174 Byz Lect it[aur,e,l,r1] vg syr[s,p,h] cop[sa,bo] arm eth geo Diatessaron[a] Hegemonius Faustus ‖ σου καὶ αἱ ἀδελφαί σου A D 700 1010 1195[c] 1216 1230 1242 1253 1344 1646 l[184,185,883] it[a,b,c,d,f,ff2,q] syr[hmg] goth

---

29 οὐκ...ἁμαρτήματος 1 Jn 5.16   30 ἔλεγον...ἔχει Jn 7.20; 8.48, 52; 10.20   31 ἡ...
ἀδελφοὶ αὐτοῦ Mk 6.3; Jn 2.12; Ac 1.14

33 καὶ ἀποκριθεὶς αὐτοῖς λέγει, Τίς ἐστιν ἡ μήτηρ μου καὶ οἱ ἀδελφοί [μου]; 34 καὶ περιβλεψάμενος τοὺς περὶ αὐτὸν κύκλῳ καθημένους λέγει, Ἴδε ἡ μήτηρ μου καὶ οἱ ἀδελφοί μου. 35 ὃς [γὰρ] ἂν ποιήσῃ τὸ θέλημα τοῦ θεοῦ, οὗτος ἀδελφός μου καὶ ἀδελφὴ καὶ μήτηρ ἐστίν.

The Parable of the Sower
(Mt 13.1–9; Lk 8.4–8)

4 Καὶ πάλιν ἤρξατο διδάσκειν παρὰ τὴν θάλασσαν. καὶ συνάγεται πρὸς αὐτὸν ὄχλος πλεῖστος, ὥστε αὐτὸν εἰς πλοῖον ἐμβάντα καθῆσθαι ἐν τῇ θαλάσσῃ, καὶ πᾶς ὁ ὄχλος πρὸς τὴν θάλασσαν ἐπὶ τῆς γῆς ἦσαν. 2 καὶ ἐδίδασκεν αὐτοὺς ἐν παραβολαῖς πολλά, καὶ ἔλεγεν αὐτοῖς ἐν τῇ διδαχῇ αὐτοῦ, 3 Ἀκούετε. ἰδοὺ ἐξῆλθεν ὁ σπείρων σπεῖραι. 4 καὶ ἐγένετο ἐν τῷ σπείρειν ὃ μὲν ἔπεσεν παρὰ τὴν ὁδόν, καὶ ἦλθεν τὰ πετεινὰ καὶ κατέφαγεν αὐτό. 5 καὶ ἄλλο ἔπεσεν ἐπὶ τὸ πετρῶδες ὅπου οὐκ εἶχεν γῆν πολλήν, καὶ εὐθὺς ἐξανέτειλεν διὰ τὸ μὴ ἔχειν βάθος γῆς· 6 καὶ ὅτε ἀνέτειλεν ὁ ἥλιος ἐκαυματίσθη, καὶ διὰ τὸ μὴ ἔχειν ῥίζαν ἐξηράνθη. 7 καὶ ἄλλο ἔπεσεν εἰς τὰς ἀκάνθας, καὶ ἀνέβησαν αἱ ἄκανθαι καὶ συνέπνιξαν αὐτό, καὶ καρπὸν οὐκ ἔδωκεν. 8 καὶ ἄλλα ἔπεσεν εἰς τὴν γῆν τὴν καλήν, καὶ ἐδίδου καρπὸν ἀναβαίνοντα καὶ αὐξανόμενα[1], καὶ ἔφερεν ἐν[2] τριάκοντα καὶ ἐν[2] ἑξήκοντα καὶ ἐν[2] ἑκατόν. 9 καὶ ἔλεγεν, Ὃς ἔχει ὦτα ἀκούειν ἀκουέτω.

---

[1] 8 {C} καὶ αὐξανόμενα ℵ B 1071 syr^pvid cop^sa geo^27 // καὶ αὐξανόμενον A D L W Δ 892 syr^hvid cop^bo // καὶ αὐξανοντα C K Θ Π f^1 f^13 28 33 700 1009 1010 1079 1195 1216 1230 1241 1242 1253 1344 1365 1546 1646 2148 2171 Byz Lect goth geo^1? // καὶ αὐξανόμενον or καὶ αὐξανοντα it^(a),aur,b,c,d,f,(ff²),i,l,q,rl vg // omit 565 syr^s

[2] 8 {C} ἐν...ἐν...ἐν D (L εἰς...ἐν...ἐν) f^13 1365 1546 Lect it^a,aur,b,(c),d,f,(ff²),i,l,(q),rl vg syr^p cop^sa,bo goth Diatessaron^a // ἐν...ἐν...ἐν (B εἰς...ἐν...ἐν) K Π f^1 33 565 892 1009 1010 1079 1195 1216 1230 1241 1242 1253 1344 1646

---

35 ὃς...θεοῦ Jn 7.17; 9.31
4 1 Mk 3.7–9; Lk 5.1–3   2 ἐδίδασκεν...πολλά Mt 13.34; Mk 4.33–34   9 Ὃς...ἀκουέτω Mt 11.15; 13.43; Mk 4.23; Lk 14.35; Re 2.7, 11, 17, 29; 3.6, 13, 22

you." 33 Jesus answered, "Who is my mother? Who are my brothers?" 34 He looked over the people sitting around him and said, "Look! Here are my mother and my brothers! 35 For the person who does what God wants him to do is my brother, my sister, my mother."

The Parable of the Sower
(Also Matt. 13.1–9; Luke 8.4–8)

4 Again Jesus began to teach by Lake Galilee. The crowd that gathered around him was so large that he got into a boat and sat in it. The boat was out in the water, while the crowd stood on the shore, at the water's edge. 2 He used parables to teach them many things, and in his teaching said to them: 3 "Listen! There was a man who went out to sow. 4 As he scattered the seed in the field, some of it fell along the path, and the birds came and ate it up. 5 Some of it fell on rocky ground, where there was little soil. The seeds soon sprouted, because the soil wasn't deep. 6 Then when the sun came up it burned the young plants, and because the roots had not grown deep enough the plants soon dried up. 7 Some of the seed fell among thorns, which grew up and choked the plants, and they didn't bear grain. 8 But some seeds fell in good soil, and the plants sprouted, grew, and bore grain: some had thirty grains, others sixty, and others one hundred." 9 And Jesus said, "Listen, then, if you have ears to hear with!"

The Purpose of the Parables
(Also Matt. 13.10–17; Luke 8.9–10)

[10] When Jesus was alone, some of those who had heard him came to him with the twelve disciples and asked him to explain the parables. [11] "You have been given the secret of the Kingdom of God," Jesus answered; "but the others, who are on the outside, hear all things by means of parables, [12] so that,

'They may look and look, yet not see,
They may listen and listen, yet not understand,
For if they did, they might turn to God
And he would forgive them.' "

Jesus Explains the Parable of the Sower
(Also Matt. 13.18–23; Luke 8.11–15)

[13] Then Jesus asked them: "Don't you understand this parable? How, then, will you ever understand any parable? [14] The sower sows God's message. [15] Sometimes the message falls along the path; these people hear it, but as soon as they hear it Satan comes and takes away the message sown in them. [16] Other people are like the seeds that fall on rocky ground. As soon as they hear the message they receive it gladly. [17] But it does not sink deep into them, and they don't last long. So when trouble or persecution comes because of the message, they give up at once. [18] Other people are like the

The Purpose of the Parables
(Mt 13.10–17; Lk 8.9–10)

10 Καὶ ὅτε ἐγένετο κατὰ μόνας, ἠρώτων αὐτὸν οἱ περὶ αὐτὸν σὺν τοῖς δώδεκα τὰς παραβολάς. **11** καὶ ἔλεγεν αὐτοῖς, Ὑμῖν τὸ μυστήριον δέδοται τῆς βασιλείας τοῦ θεοῦ· ἐκείνοις δὲ τοῖς ἔξω ἐν παραβολαῖς τὰ πάντα γίνεται, **12** ἵνα

βλέποντες βλέπωσιν καὶ μὴ ἴδωσιν,
καὶ ἀκούοντες ἀκούσωσιν καὶ μὴ συνιῶσιν,
μήποτε ἐπιστρέψωσιν καὶ ἀφεθῇ αὐτοῖς.

The Parable of the Sower Explained
(Mt 13.18–23; Lk 8.11–15)

13 Καὶ λέγει αὐτοῖς, Οὐκ οἴδατε τὴν παραβολὴν ταύτην,[a] καὶ πῶς πάσας τὰς παραβολὰς γνώσεσθε;[a] **14** ὁ σπείρων τὸν λόγον σπείρει. **15** οὗτοι δέ εἰσιν οἱ παρὰ τὴν ὁδὸν ὅπου σπείρεται ὁ λόγος, καὶ ὅταν ἀκούσωσιν εὐθὺς ἔρχεται ὁ Σατανᾶς καὶ αἴρει τὸν λόγον τὸν ἐσπαρμένον εἰς αὐτούς. **16** καὶ οὗτοί εἰσιν[3] οἱ ἐπὶ τὰ πετρώδη σπειρόμενοι, οἳ ὅταν ἀκούσωσιν τὸν λόγον εὐθὺς μετὰ χαρᾶς λαμβάνουσιν αὐτόν, **17** καὶ οὐκ ἔχουσιν ῥίζαν ἐν ἑαυτοῖς ἀλλὰ πρόσκαιροί εἰσιν· εἶτα γενομένης θλίψεως ἢ διωγμοῦ διὰ τὸν λόγον εὐθὺς σκανδαλίζονται. **18** καὶ ἄλλοι εἰσὶν οἱ εἰς

2148 2174 *Byz* *l*[185,211,299,883,950,1127] syr[h?] arm? ‖ εν...εν...εν A C[2vid] (W το εν...το εν...το εν) Θ ‖ ἐν...omit...ἐν 1071 (geo[1] ἐν...omit...omit) ‖ ἐν...ἐν...omit 118 (*l*[76] ἐν...omit...ἐν) (syr[s] ἐν...omit...omit) ‖ εἰς...εἰς...εἰς ℵ C[*vid] Δ 28 700 syr[h?] arm? ‖ omit...omit...omit geo[2]

[3] **16** {B} εἰσιν D W Θ f[1] f[13] 28 565 700 1216 it[a,b,c,d,ff2,i,q,rl] syr[s,p] cop[sa, fay] arm geo Diatessaron Origen ‖ εἰσιν ὁμοίως A B K Π 1009 1010 1079 1195 1230 1242 1253 1344 1365 1546 1646 2148 2174 *Byz* *l*[10,76,185,299,883,1642] it[aur,f,l] vg syr[h] goth ‖ ὁμοίως εἰσίν ℵ C L Δ 33 892 1071 1241 *Lect* cop[bo]

[a a] **13** *a minor, a question:* WH Nes BF[2] Zür Luth Seg ‖ *a question, a question:* TR Bov AV RV ASV RSV NEB TT Jer

10 ἠρώτων...παραβολάς Mt 15.15; Mk 7.17   **12** βλέποντες...αὐτοῖς Is 6.9–10; Jn 12.40; Ac 28.26–27   **17** γενομένης...σκανδαλίζονται Mt 26.31; Mk 14.27

τὰς ἀκάνθας σπειρόμενοι· οὗτοί εἰσιν οἱ τὸν λόγον ἀκούσαντες, **19** καὶ αἱ μέριμναι τοῦ αἰῶνος καὶ ἡ ἀπάτη τοῦ
πλούτου καὶ αἱ περὶ τὰ λοιπὰ ἐπιθυμίαι εἰσπορευόμεναι
συμπνίγουσιν τὸν λόγον, καὶ ἄκαρπος γίνεται. **20** καὶ
ἐκεῖνοί εἰσιν οἱ ἐπὶ τὴν γῆν τὴν καλὴν σπαρέντες, οἵτινες
ἀκούουσιν τὸν λόγον καὶ παραδέχονται καὶ καρποφοροῦσιν
ἐν[4] τριάκοντα καὶ ἐν[4] ἑξήκοντα καὶ ἐν[4] ἑκατόν.

A Light under a Bushel
(Lk 8.16–18)

21 Καὶ ἔλεγεν αὐτοῖς, Μήτι ἔρχεται ὁ λύχνος ἵνα ὑπὸ
τὸν μόδιον τεθῇ ἢ ὑπὸ τὴν κλίνην;[b] οὐχ ἵνα ἐπὶ τὴν
λυχνίαν τεθῇ;[b] **22** οὐ γάρ ἐστιν κρυπτὸν ἐὰν μὴ ἵνα
φανερωθῇ, οὐδὲ ἐγένετο ἀπόκρυφον ἀλλ' ἵνα ἔλθῃ εἰς
φανερόν. **23** εἴ τις ἔχει ὦτα ἀκούειν ἀκουέτω.

24 Καὶ ἔλεγεν αὐτοῖς, Βλέπετε τί ἀκούετε. ἐν ᾧ μέτρῳ
μετρεῖτε μετρηθήσεται ὑμῖν καὶ προστεθήσεται ὑμῖν[5].
25 ὃς γὰρ ἔχει, δοθήσεται αὐτῷ· καὶ ὃς οὐκ ἔχει, καὶ ὃ
ἔχει ἀρθήσεται ἀπ' αὐτοῦ.

---

[4] **20** {B} ἐν...ἐν...ἐν K (L ἐν...ἐν...ἐν) Θ 1009 *Lect* it^aur,(b),c,d,e,f,ff2,i,l,q,r1
vg cop^sa,bo goth geo ‖ ἐν...ἐν...ἐν f1 f13 28 33 565 700 892 1010 1071 1079 1195
1216 1230 1241 1242 1253 1365 1546 1646 2148 2174 *Byz* l^76,185,211,299,333,883,950,1127
syr^p,h arm ‖ εν...εν...εν ℵ A C^2vid D (W το εν...το εν...το εν) Δ Π ‖ εν...
omit...εν C*vid 1344 ‖ εν...*omit*...*omit* B ‖ *some...some...some* cop^fay

[5] **24** {A} καὶ προστεθήσεται ὑμῖν ℵ B C L Δ 700 892 it^aur,c,ff2,i,r1 vg
cop^bo mss arm eth ‖ καὶ προστεθήσεται ὑμῖν τοῖς ἀκούουσιν A K (Θ
περισευθήσεται) Π 0107 f1 f13 (28 προστεθήσεται γὰρ ὑμῖν and *omit* καὶ)
(33 *omit* ὑμῖν) (1009 ἡμῖν) 1010 1071 1079 1195 1216 1230 (1241 *omit* καὶ)
1242 1253 1365 1546 2174 *Byz Lect* it^q syr^p,h cop^sa,bo mss geo Diatessaron^a
et adicietur vobis credentibus it^f goth ‖ τοῖς ἀκούουσιν 1344 1646 2148 l^10,12,
184pt,883,1231m ‖ *omit* (*see* Mt 7.2) D W 565 it^b,d,e,l Cyprian

---

^b b **21** b question, b question: TR Bov Nes BF2 AV NEB TT Zür Jer Seg ‖ b minor, b question:
WH RV ASV RSV ‖ b question, b statement: Luth

---

19 ἀπάτη τοῦ πλούτου Mt 19.23–24; Mk 10.23–24; Lk 12.15–21; 18.24–25   **21** Μήτι...
λυχνίαν τεθῇ Mt 5.15; Lk 11.33   **22** Mt 10.26; Lk 12.2   **23** Mt 11.15; 13.43; Mk 4.9; Lk
14.35; Re 2.7, 11, 17, 29; 3.6, 13, 22   **24** ἐν...μετρηθήσεται ὑμῖν Mt 7.2; Lk 6.38   **25** Mt 13.12;
25.29; Lk 19.26

---

seeds sown among the thorns. These are
the ones who hear the message, [19] but
the worries about this life, the love for
riches, and all other kinds of desires
crowd in and choke the message, and
they don't bear fruit. [20] But other people
are like the seeds sown in good soil.
They hear the message, accept it, and
bear fruit: some thirty, some sixty, and
some one hundred."

A Lamp under a Bowl
(Also Luke 8.16–18)

[21] And Jesus continued: "Does anyone
ever bring in a lamp and put it under a
bowl or under the bed? Doesn't he put
it on the lamp-stand? [22] Whatever is
hidden away will be brought out into the
open, and whatever is covered up will
be uncovered. [23] Listen, then, if you have
ears to hear with!"

[24] He also said to them: "Pay attention
to what you hear! The same rules you
use to judge others will be used by God
to judge you — and with even greater
severity. [25] The man who has something
will be given more; the man who has
nothing will have taken away from him
even the little he has."

The Parable of the Growing Seed

26 Jesus went on to say: "The Kingdom of God is like a man who scatters seed in his field. 27 He sleeps at night, is up and about during the day, and all the while the seeds are sprouting and growing. Yet he does not know how it happens. 28 The soil itself makes the plants grow and bear fruit: first the tender stalk appears, then the head, and finally the head full of grain. 29 When the grain is ripe the man starts working with his sickle, for harvest time has come."

The Parable of the Mustard Seed
(Also Matt. 13.31–32, 34; Luke 13.18–19)

30 "What shall we say the Kingdom of God is like?" asked Jesus. "What parable shall we use to explain it? 31 It is like a mustard seed, the smallest seed in the world. A man takes it and plants it in the ground; 32 after a while it grows up and becomes the biggest of all plants. It puts out such large branches that the birds come and make their nests in its shade."

33 Jesus preached his message to the people, using many other parables like these; he told them as much as they could understand. 34 He would not speak to them without using parables; but when he was alone with his disciples he would explain everything to them.

Jesus Calms a Storm
(Also Matt. 8.23–27; Luke 8.22–25)

35 On the evening of that same day Jesus said to his disciples, "Let us go across to the other side of the lake." 36 So they left the crowd; the disciples got into the boat that Jesus was already in, and took him with them. Other boats

The Parable of the Growing Seed

26 Καὶ ἔλεγεν, Οὕτως ἐστὶν ἡ βασιλεία τοῦ θεοῦ ὡς ἄνθρωπος βάλῃ τὸν σπόρον ἐπὶ τῆς γῆς 27 καὶ καθεύδῃ καὶ ἐγείρηται νύκτα καὶ ἡμέραν, καὶ ὁ σπόρος βλαστᾷ καὶ μηκύνηται ὡς οὐκ οἶδεν αὐτός. 28 αὐτομάτη ἡ γῆ καρποφορεῖ, πρῶτον χόρτον, εἶτεν στάχυν, εἶτεν πλήρη σῖτον ἐν τῷ στάχυϊ. 29 ὅταν δὲ παραδοῖ ὁ καρπός, εὐθὺς ἀποστέλλει τὸ δρέπανον, ὅτι παρέστηκεν ὁ θερισμός.

The Parable of the Mustard Seed
(Mt 13.31–32; Lk 13.18–19)

30 Καὶ ἔλεγεν, Πῶς ὁμοιώσωμεν τὴν βασιλείαν τοῦ θεοῦ, ἢ ἐν τίνι αὐτὴν παραβολῇ θῶμεν; 31 ὡς κόκκῳ σινάπεως, ὃς ὅταν σπαρῇ ἐπὶ τῆς γῆς, μικρότερον ὂν πάντων τῶν σπερμάτων τῶν ἐπὶ τῆς γῆς, 32 καὶ ὅταν σπαρῇ, ἀναβαίνει καὶ γίνεται μεῖζον πάντων τῶν λαχάνων καὶ ποιεῖ κλάδους μεγάλους, ὥστε δύνασθαι ὑπὸ τὴν σκιὰν αὐτοῦ τὰ πετεινὰ τοῦ οὐρανοῦ κατασκηνοῦν.

The Use of Parables
(Mt 13.34–35)

33 Καὶ τοιαύταις παραβολαῖς πολλαῖς ἐλάλει αὐτοῖς τὸν λόγον, καθὼς ἠδύναντο ἀκούειν· 34 χωρὶς δὲ παραβολῆς οὐκ ἐλάλει αὐτοῖς, κατ᾽ ἰδίαν δὲ τοῖς ἰδίοις μαθηταῖς ἐπέλυεν πάντα.

The Calming of a Storm
(Mt 8.23–27; Lk 8.22–25)

35 Καὶ λέγει αὐτοῖς ἐν ἐκείνῃ τῇ ἡμέρᾳ ὀψίας γενομένης, Διέλθωμεν εἰς τὸ πέραν. 36 καὶ ἀφέντες τὸν ὄχλον παραλαμβάνουσιν αὐτὸν ὡς ἦν ἐν τῷ πλοίῳ, καὶ ἄλλα πλοῖα

---

27 Jas 5.7   29 ἀποστέλλει...θερισμός Jl 3.13; Re 14.15   31 ὡς...σινάπεως Mt 17.20; Lk 17.6   32 ὑπὸ...κατασκηνοῦν Eze 17.23; 31.6; Dn 4.12, 21

ἦν μετ᾽ αὐτοῦ. 37 καὶ γίνεται λαῖλαψ μεγάλη ἀνέμου, καὶ τὰ κύματα ἐπέβαλλεν εἰς τὸ πλοῖον, ὥστε ἤδη γεμίζεσθαι τὸ πλοῖον. 38 καὶ αὐτὸς ἦν ἐν τῇ πρύμνῃ ἐπὶ τὸ προσκεφάλαιον καθεύδων· καὶ ἐγείρουσιν αὐτὸν καὶ λέγουσιν αὐτῷ, Διδάσκαλε, οὐ μέλει σοι ὅτι ἀπολλύμεθα; 39 καὶ διεγερθεὶς ἐπετίμησεν τῷ ἀνέμῳ καὶ εἶπεν τῇ θαλάσσῃ, Σιώπα, πεφίμωσο. καὶ ἐκόπασεν ὁ ἄνεμος, καὶ ἐγένετο γαλήνη μεγάλη. 40 καὶ εἶπεν αὐτοῖς, Τί δειλοί ἐστε; οὔπω[6] ἔχετε πίστιν; 41 καὶ ἐφοβήθησαν φόβον μέγαν, καὶ ἔλεγον πρὸς ἀλλήλους, Τίς ἄρα οὗτός ἐστιν ὅτι καὶ ὁ ἄνεμος καὶ ἡ θάλασσα ὑπακούει αὐτῷ;

The Healing of the Gerasene Demoniac
(Mt 8.28–34; Lk 8.26–39)

5 Καὶ ἦλθον εἰς τὸ πέραν τῆς θαλάσσης εἰς τὴν χώραν τῶν Γερασηνῶν[1]. 2 καὶ ἐξελθόντος αὐτοῦ ἐκ τοῦ πλοίου [εὐθὺς] ὑπήντησεν αὐτῷ ἐκ τῶν μνημείων ἄνθρωπος ἐν πνεύματι ἀκαθάρτῳ, 3 ὃς τὴν κατοίκησιν εἶχεν ἐν τοῖς μνήμασιν· καὶ οὐδὲ ἁλύσει οὐκέτι οὐδεὶς ἐδύνατο αὐτὸν δῆσαι, 4 διὰ τὸ αὐτὸν πολλάκις πέδαις καὶ ἁλύσεσιν

---

[6] **40** {A} δειλοί ἐστε; οὔπω ℵ B D L Δ Θ 565 700 892* it[a,aur,b,c,d,ff2,i,l] vg cop[sa,bo] eth geo ‖ δειλοί ἐστε οὕτως W ‖ οὕτως δειλοί οὔπω 28 ‖ δειλοί ἐστε οὕτως πῶς οὐκ A C K Π 33 (892[mg] οὕτως οὔπω) 1009 1010 1071 1079 1195 1216 1230 1241 1242 (1253 *omit* πῶς) 1344 1365 1546 1646 2148 2174 *Byz* (*Lect* οὔτω) (*l*[69,333,883,1127] οὕτως, *l*[211] δηλοί) (it[f]) syr[p,h] goth Diatessaron[a] ‖ οὕτως δειλοί ἐστε οὔπω 𝔭[45vid] f1 f13 arm ‖ *Quid timidi estis?* it[e,q]

[1] **1** {C} Γερασηνῶν (*see* Lk 8.26) ℵ* B D it[aur,b,c,d,e,f,ff2,i,l,q,r1] vg cop[sa] Tertullian Eusebius ‖ Γαδαρηνῶν (*see* Mt 8.28) A C K Π f13 1009 1010 1079 1195 1216 1230 1242 1253 1344 1365 1546 2148 2174 *Byz* *l*[76,185,313,883] syr[p,h] goth Diatessaron[p] ‖ Γεργεσηνῶν ℵ[c] L Δ Θ f1 28 33 565 700 892 1071 1241 1646 *Lect* (*l*[211] Γεργεσινῶν) syr[s,hmg] cop[bo] arm eth geo Origen Epiphanius Theophylact ‖ Γεργυστήνων W

---

2 ἄνθρωπος...ἀκαθάρτῳ Mk 1.23

---

were there too. 37 A very strong wind blew up and the waves began to spill over into the boat, so that it was about to fill with water. 38 Jesus was in the back of the boat, sleeping with his head on a pillow. The disciples woke him up and said, "Teacher, don't you care that we are about to die?" 39 Jesus got up and commanded the wind: "Be quiet!" and said to the waves, "Be still!" The wind died down, and there was a great calm. 40 Then Jesus said to them, "Why are you frightened? Are you still without faith?" 41 But they were terribly afraid, and began to say to each other, "Who is this man? Even the wind and the waves obey him!"

Jesus Heals a Man with Evil Spirits
(Also Matt. 8.28–34; Luke 8.26–39)

5 So they came to the other side of Lake Galilee, to the territory of the Gerasenes. 2 As soon as Jesus got out of the boat he was met by a man who came out of the burial caves. 3 This man had an evil spirit in him and lived among the graves. Nobody could keep him tied with chains any more; 4 many times his feet and hands had been tied, but every time he broke the chains, and smashed the irons on his feet. He was too strong for anyone to stop him! [5] Day and night he wandered among the graves and through the hills, screaming and cutting himself with stones.

[6] He was some distance away when he saw Jesus; so he ran, fell on his knees before him, [7] and screamed in a loud voice, "Jesus, Son of the Most High God! What do you want with me? For God's sake, I beg you, don't punish me!" [8] (He said this because Jesus was saying to him, "Evil spirit, come out of this man!") [9] So Jesus asked him, "What is your name?" The man answered, "My name is 'Mob' — there are so many of us!" [10] And he kept begging Jesus not to send the evil spirits out of that territory.

[11] A large herd of pigs was near by, feeding on the hillside. [12] The spirits begged Jesus, "Send us to the pigs, and let us go into them." [13] So he let them. The evil spirits went out of the man and went into the pigs. The whole herd — about two thousand pigs in all — rushed down the side of the cliff into the lake and were drowned.

[14] The men who had been taking care of the pigs ran away and spread the news in the town and among the farms. The people went out to see what had happened. [15] They came to Jesus and saw the man who used to have the mob of demons in him; he was sitting there, clothed and in his right mind — and they were all afraid. [16] Those who had seen it told the people what had happened to the man with the demons, and about the pigs. [17] So they began to ask Jesus to leave their territory.

[18] As Jesus was getting into the boat, the man who had had the demons begged him, "Let me go with you!" [19] But Jesus would not let him. Instead he told him, "Go back home to your family and tell them how much the Lord has done for you, and how kind he has been to you!" [20] So the man left and went all through the Ten Towns telling what Jesus had done for him; and all who heard it were filled with wonder.

δεδέσθαι καὶ διεσπάσθαι ὑπ' αὐτοῦ τὰς ἁλύσεις καὶ τὰς πέδας συντετρίφθαι, καὶ οὐδεὶς ἴσχυεν αὐτὸν δαμάσαι· 5 καὶ διὰ παντὸς νυκτὸς καὶ ἡμέρας ἐν τοῖς μνήμασιν καὶ ἐν τοῖς ὄρεσιν ἦν κράζων καὶ κατακόπτων ἑαυτὸν λίθοις. 6 καὶ ἰδὼν τὸν Ἰησοῦν ἀπὸ μακρόθεν ἔδραμεν καὶ προσεκύνησεν αὐτῷ, 7 καὶ κράξας φωνῇ μεγάλῃ λέγει, Τί ἐμοὶ καὶ σοί, Ἰησοῦ υἱὲ τοῦ θεοῦ τοῦ ὑψίστου; ὁρκίζω σε τὸν θεόν, μή με βασανίσῃς. 8 ἔλεγεν γὰρ αὐτῷ, Ἔξελθε τὸ πνεῦμα τὸ ἀκάθαρτον ἐκ τοῦ ἀνθρώπου. 9 καὶ ἐπηρώτα αὐτόν, Τί ὄνομά σοι; καὶ λέγει αὐτῷ, Λεγιὼν ὄνομά μοι, ὅτι πολλοί ἐσμεν. 10 καὶ παρεκάλει αὐτὸν πολλὰ ἵνα μὴ αὐτοὺς ἀποστείλῃ ἔξω τῆς χώρας.

11 Ἦν δὲ ἐκεῖ πρὸς τῷ ὄρει ἀγέλη χοίρων μεγάλη βοσκομένη· 12 καὶ παρεκάλεσαν αὐτὸν λέγοντες, Πέμψον ἡμᾶς εἰς τοὺς χοίρους, ἵνα εἰς αὐτοὺς εἰσέλθωμεν. 13 καὶ ἐπέτρεψεν αὐτοῖς. καὶ ἐξελθόντα τὰ πνεύματα τὰ ἀκάθαρτα εἰσῆλθον εἰς τοὺς χοίρους, καὶ ὥρμησεν ἡ ἀγέλη κατὰ τοῦ κρημνοῦ εἰς τὴν θάλασσαν, ὡς δισχίλιοι, καὶ ἐπνίγοντο ἐν τῇ θαλάσσῃ. 14 καὶ οἱ βόσκοντες αὐτοὺς ἔφυγον καὶ ἀπήγγειλαν εἰς τὴν πόλιν καὶ εἰς τοὺς ἀγρούς· καὶ ἦλθον ἰδεῖν τί ἐστιν τὸ γεγονός. 15 καὶ ἔρχονται πρὸς τὸν Ἰησοῦν, καὶ θεωροῦσιν τὸν δαιμονιζόμενον καθήμενον ἱματισμένον καὶ σωφρονοῦντα, τὸν ἐσχηκότα τὸν λεγιῶνα, καὶ ἐφοβήθησαν. 16 καὶ διηγήσαντο αὐτοῖς οἱ ἰδόντες πῶς ἐγένετο τῷ δαιμονιζομένῳ καὶ περὶ τῶν χοίρων. 17 καὶ ἤρξαντο παρακαλεῖν αὐτὸν ἀπελθεῖν ἀπὸ τῶν ὁρίων αὐτῶν. 18 καὶ ἐμβαίνοντος αὐτοῦ εἰς τὸ πλοῖον παρεκάλει αὐτὸν ὁ δαιμονισθεὶς ἵνα μετ' αὐτοῦ ᾖ. 19 καὶ οὐκ ἀφῆκεν αὐτόν, ἀλλὰ λέγει αὐτῷ, Ὕπαγε εἰς τὸν οἶκόν σου πρὸς τοὺς σούς, καὶ ἀπάγγειλον αὐτοῖς ὅσα ὁ κύριός σοι πεποίηκεν καὶ ἠλέησέν σε. 20 καὶ ἀπῆλθεν καὶ ἤρξατο κηρύσσειν ἐν τῇ Δεκαπόλει ὅσα ἐποίησεν αὐτῷ ὁ Ἰησοῦς, καὶ πάντες ἐθαύμαζον.

---

7 Τί...ὑψίστου 1 Kgs 17.18; Mk 1.24; Lk 4.34   υἱὲ...ὑψίστου Lk 1.32; 6.35   ὁρκίζω... θεόν Mt 26.63   19 Ὕπαγε...σου Mt 9.6; Mk 8.26; Lk 5.24; 8.39

Jairus' Daughter and the Woman Who Touched Jesus' Garment
(Mt 9.18–26; Lk 8.40–56)

21 Καὶ διαπεράσαντος τοῦ Ἰησοῦ[2] πάλιν εἰς τὸ πέραν[3] συνήχθη ὄχλος πολὺς ἐπ' αὐτόν, καὶ ἦν παρὰ τὴν θάλασσαν. **22** καὶ ἔρχεται εἷς τῶν ἀρχισυναγώγων, ὀνόματι Ἰάϊρος, καὶ ἰδὼν αὐτὸν πίπτει πρὸς τοὺς πόδας αὐτοῦ **23** καὶ παρακαλεῖ αὐτὸν πολλὰ λέγων ὅτι Τὸ θυγάτριόν μου ἐσχάτως ἔχει, ἵνα ἐλθὼν ἐπιθῇς τὰς χεῖρας αὐτῇ ἵνα σωθῇ καὶ ζήσῃ. **24** καὶ ἀπῆλθεν μετ' αὐτοῦ.

Καὶ ἠκολούθει αὐτῷ ὄχλος πολύς, καὶ συνέθλιβον αὐτόν. **25** καὶ γυνὴ οὖσα ἐν ῥύσει αἵματος δώδεκα ἔτη **26** καὶ πολλὰ παθοῦσα ὑπὸ πολλῶν ἰατρῶν καὶ δαπανήσασα τὰ παρ' αὐτῆς πάντα καὶ μηδὲν ὠφεληθεῖσα ἀλλὰ μᾶλλον εἰς τὸ χεῖρον ἐλθοῦσα, **27** ἀκούσασα περὶ[4] τοῦ Ἰησοῦ, ἐλθοῦσα ἐν τῷ ὄχλῳ ὄπισθεν ἥψατο τοῦ ἱματίου αὐτοῦ· **28** ἔλεγεν γὰρ ὅτι Ἐὰν ἅψωμαι κἂν τῶν ἱματίων αὐτοῦ σωθήσομαι. **29** καὶ εὐθὺς ἐξηράνθη ἡ πηγὴ τοῦ αἵματος αὐτῆς, καὶ ἔγνω τῷ σώματι ὅτι ἴαται ἀπὸ τῆς μάστιγος. **30** καὶ εὐθὺς ὁ Ἰησοῦς ἐπιγνοὺς ἐν ἑαυτῷ τὴν ἐξ αὐτοῦ

[2] **21** {B} τοῦ Ἰησοῦ p[45vid] D Θ f[1] 28 565 700 it[a,b,c,d,e,ff²,i,q,r¹] syr[s] arm geo ‖ τοῦ Ἰησοῦ ἐν τῷ πλοίῳ ℵ A (B omit τῷ) C K L Δ Π 0107[vid] 0132 0134 f[13] 33 892 1009 1010 1071 1079 1195 1216 1230 1241 1242 1253 1344 1365 1546 1646 2148 2174 Byz it[aur,f,l] vg syr[p,h] cop[sa,bo] goth Diatessaron[a] ‖ ἐν τῷ πλοίῳ τοῦ Ἰησοῦ W

[3] **21** {C} πάλιν εἰς τὸ πέραν ℵ[c] A B C K L W Δ Π 0132 0134 0171[vid] f[1] 28 33 892 1009 1010 1071 1079 1195 1216 1241 1242 1344 1365 1546 1646 2148 2174 Byz it[aur,l] vg syr[h] cop[bo] (goth) arm geo Augustine ‖ πάλιν ἦλθεν εἰς τὸ πέραν f[13] (cop[sa] omit πάλιν) ‖ εἰς τὸ πέραν πάλιν ℵ* D 565 700 it[a,b,(c),d,e,(ff²),i,q,r¹] syr[p] cop[bo mss] ‖ εἰς τὸ πέραν Θ 1230 1253 syr[s] Diatessaron[a] ‖ πάλιν p[45vid] it[f]

[4] **27** {C} περὶ ℵ[c] A C[2] D K L W Θ Π 0132[vid] 0134 f[1] f[13] 28 33 565 700 892 1009 1010 1071 1079 1195 1216 1230 1241 1242 1253 1365 1646 2148 2174 Byz Lect syr[p,h,pal] cop[sa?bo?] goth arm eth geo Diatessaron[a] ‖ τὰ περὶ ℵ* B C* Δ 1546 l[33]

23 ἐλθὼν...σωθῇ Mt 8.3; Mk 6.5; 7.32; 8.23, 25; Lk 4.40; 13.13; Ac 9.12, 17; 28.8   **27** ἥψατο ...αὐτοῦ Mt 14.36; Mk 6.56   **30** ὁ Ἰησοῦς...ἐξελθοῦσαν Lk 6.19

Jairus' Daughter and the Woman who Touched Jesus' Cloak
(Also Matt. 9.18–26; Luke 8.40–56)

[21] Jesus went back across to the other side of the lake. There at the lakeside a large crowd gathered around him. [22] Jairus, an official of the local synagogue, came up, and when he saw Jesus he threw himself down at his feet [23] and begged him as hard as he could: "My little daughter is very sick. Please come and place your hands on her, so that she will get well and live!" [24] Then Jesus started off with him. So many people were going along with him that they were crowding him from every side.

[25] There was a woman who had suffered terribly from severe bleeding for twelve years, [26] even though she had been treated by many doctors. She had spent all her money, but instead of getting better she got worse all the time. [27] She had heard about Jesus, so she came in the crowd behind him. [28] "If I touch just his clothes," she said to herself, "I shall get well." [29] She touched his cloak and her bleeding stopped at once; and she had the feeling inside herself that she was cured of her trouble. [30] At once Jesus felt that power had gone out of him. So he turned around in the

crowd and said, "Who touched my clothes?" [31] His disciples answered, "You see that the people are crowding you; why do you ask who touched you?" [32] But Jesus kept looking around to see who had done it. [33] The woman realized what had happened to her; so she came, trembling with fear, and fell at his feet and told him the whole truth. [34] Jesus said to her, "My daughter, your faith has made you well. Go in peace, and be healed from your trouble."

[35] While Jesus was saying this, some messengers came from Jairus' house and told him, "Your daughter has died. Why should you bother the Teacher any longer?" [36] Jesus paid no attention to[1] what they said, but told him, "Don't be afraid, only believe." [37] Then he did not let anyone go on with him except Peter and James and his brother John. [38] They arrived at the official's house, where Jesus saw the confusion and heard all the loud crying and wailing. [39] He went in and said to them, "Why all this confusion? Why are you crying? The child is not dead — she is only sleeping!" [40] They all started making fun of him, so he put them all out, took the child's father and mother, and his three disciples, and went into the room where the child was lying. [41] He took her by the hand and said to her, *Talitha koum,* which means, "Little girl! Get up, I tell you!" [42] She got up at once and started walking around. (She was twelve years old.) When this happened they were completely amazed! [43] But Jesus gave

---

[1] **36** paid no attention to: *or* overheard

δύναμιν ἐξελθοῦσαν ἐπιστραφεὶς ἐν τῷ ὄχλῳ ἔλεγεν, Τίς μου ἥψατο τῶν ἱματίων; 31 καὶ ἔλεγον αὐτῷ οἱ μαθηταὶ αὐτοῦ, Βλέπεις τὸν ὄχλον συνθλίβοντά σε, καὶ λέγεις, Τίς μου ἥψατο; 32 καὶ περιεβλέπετο ἰδεῖν τὴν τοῦτο ποιήσασαν. 33 ἡ δὲ γυνὴ φοβηθεῖσα καὶ τρέμουσα, εἰδυῖα ὃ γέγονεν αὐτῇ, ἦλθεν καὶ προσέπεσεν αὐτῷ καὶ εἶπεν αὐτῷ πᾶσαν τὴν ἀλήθειαν. 34 ὁ δὲ εἶπεν αὐτῇ, Θυγάτηρ, ἡ πίστις σου σέσωκέν σε· ὕπαγε εἰς εἰρήνην, καὶ ἴσθι ὑγιὴς ἀπὸ τῆς μάστιγός σου.

35 Ἔτι αὐτοῦ λαλοῦντος ἔρχονται ἀπὸ τοῦ ἀρχισυναγώγου λέγοντες ὅτι Ἡ θυγάτηρ σου ἀπέθανεν· τί ἔτι σκύλλεις τὸν διδάσκαλον; 36 ὁ δὲ Ἰησοῦς παρακούσας[5] τὸν λόγον λαλούμενον λέγει τῷ ἀρχισυναγώγῳ, Μὴ φοβοῦ, μόνον πίστευε. 37 καὶ οὐκ ἀφῆκεν οὐδένα μετ' αὐτοῦ συνακολουθῆσαι εἰ μὴ τὸν Πέτρον καὶ Ἰάκωβον καὶ Ἰωάννην τὸν ἀδελφὸν Ἰακώβου. 38 καὶ ἔρχονται εἰς τὸν οἶκον τοῦ ἀρχισυναγώγου, καὶ θεωρεῖ θόρυβον καὶ κλαίοντας καὶ ἀλαλάζοντας πολλά, 39 καὶ εἰσελθὼν λέγει αὐτοῖς, Τί θορυβεῖσθε καὶ κλαίετε; τὸ παιδίον οὐκ ἀπέθανεν ἀλλὰ καθεύδει. 40 καὶ κατεγέλων αὐτοῦ. αὐτὸς δὲ ἐκβαλὼν πάντας παραλαμβάνει τὸν πατέρα τοῦ παιδίου καὶ τὴν μητέρα καὶ τοὺς μετ' αὐτοῦ, καὶ εἰσπορεύεται ὅπου ἦν τὸ παιδίον· 41 καὶ κρατήσας τῆς χειρὸς τοῦ παιδίου λέγει αὐτῇ, Ταλιθα κουμ, ὅ ἐστιν μεθερμηνευόμενον Τὸ κοράσιον, σοὶ λέγω, ἔγειρε. 42 καὶ εὐθὺς ἀνέστη τὸ κοράσιον καὶ περιεπάτει, ἦν γὰρ ἐτῶν δώδεκα. καὶ ἐξέστησαν εὐθὺς[6] ἐκστάσει μεγάλῃ. 43 καὶ διεστείλατο αὐτοῖς

---

[5] **36** {B} παρακούσας (א* παρακαούσας) א[b] B L W Δ 892* it[c] ‖ ἀκούσας א[a] A C D K Θ Π 0126 0132 *f*[1] *f*[13] 28 33 565 700 892[c] 1009 1010 1071 1079 1195 1216 1230 1241 1242 1253 1344 1365 1546 1646 2148 2174 *Byz Lect* it[a, aur, b, c, d, f,] ff2,i,l,q vg cop[sa, bo] goth arm eth geo Diatessaron[p]

[6] **42** {D} ἐξέστησαν εὐθύς א B C L Δ 33 892 cop[bo] eth ‖ ἐξέστησαν p[45] A K W Θ Π *f*[1] *f*[13] 28 565 700 1009 1010 1071 1079 1195 1230 1241 1242 1253

---

34 ἡ πίστις...σε Mk 10.52; Lk 7.50; 17.19　　ὕπαγε εἰς εἰρήνην 1 Sm 1.17; 20.42; 2 Sm 15.9; 2 Kgs 5.19; Lk 7.50; Ac 16.36; Jas 2.16　　**37** Πέτρον...Ἰακώβου Mt 10.2; 17.1; Mk 1.29; 3.16–17; 9.2; 13.3; 14.33; Lk 6.14; 9.28; Ac 1.13　　**39** τὸ...καθεύδει Jn 11.11　　**41** σοὶ λέγω, ἔγειρε Lk 7.14　　**43** διεστείλατο...τοῦτο Mk 1.44; 7.36

πολλὰ ἵνα μηδεὶς γνοῖ τοῦτο, καὶ εἶπεν δοθῆναι αὐτῇ φαγεῖν.

The Rejection of Jesus at Nazareth
(Mt 13.53–58; Lk 4.16–30)

6 Καὶ ἐξῆλθεν ἐκεῖθεν, καὶ ἔρχεται εἰς τὴν πατρίδα αὐτοῦ, καὶ ἀκολουθοῦσιν αὐτῷ οἱ μαθηταὶ αὐτοῦ. 2 καὶ γενομένου σαββάτου ἤρξατο διδάσκειν ἐν τῇ συναγωγῇ· καὶ πολλοὶ ἀκούοντες[1] ἐξεπλήσσοντο λέγοντες, Πόθεν τούτῳ ταῦτα, καὶ τίς ἡ σοφία ἡ δοθεῖσα τουτῳ ἵνα καὶ δυνάμεις[2] τοιαῦται διὰ τῶν χειρῶν αὐτοῦ γίνονται; 3 οὐχ οὗτός ἐστιν ὁ τέκτων, ὁ υἱὸς[3] τῆς Μαρίας καὶ ἀδελφὸς Ἰακώβου καὶ Ἰωσῆτος καὶ Ἰούδα καὶ Σίμωνος; καὶ οὐκ εἰσὶν αἱ ἀδελφαὶ αὐτοῦ ὧδε πρὸς ἡμᾶς; καὶ ἐσκανδαλίζοντο ἐν

1344 1365 1546 1646 2148 *Byz Lect* it[a,aur,b,e,l] vg syr[p,h] cop[boms] goth arm geo Diatessaron[p] ‖ ἐξέστησαν πάντες D it[c,d,f,ff2,i,q] cop[sa,boms] ‖ ἐξέστησαν οἱ γονεῖς αὐτῆς (*see* Lk 8.56) 1216 2174 *l*[48]

[1] **2** {A} πολλοὶ ἀκούοντες ℵ A C K W *f*[1] 33 700 1009 1071 1079 1195 1230 1241 1253 1344 1365 1546 1646 2148 *Byz Lect l*[211s,m] goth arm ‖ οἱ πολλοὶ ἀκούοντες B L 28[c] 892 ‖ πολλοὶ (*or* οἱ πολλοί) ἀκούοντες it[aur,d,f,ff2,i,l,q,rl] vg cop[boms] ‖ πολλοὶ ἀκούσαντες D[gr] Δ Θ Π 0126 565 1010 1216 1242 2174 *l*[10,48,184,299,547m,950,1627m,1642] ‖ οἱ πολλοὶ ἀκούσαντες *f*[13] 28* ‖ πολλοὶ (*or* οἱ πολλοί) ἀκούσαντες it[a] syr[p,h,(pal)] cop[sa,bo] geo ‖ *omnes* it[e] ‖ *omit* it[b,c]

[2] **2** {B} ἵνα καὶ δυνάμεις...γίνωνται D K Π 1079 1195 (C* 1365 1546 *l*[7,68,883] γίνονται) it[(b),d,ff2] (syr[p,h]) ‖ ἵνα δυνάμεις...γίνωνται Θ 700 it[i,q,rl] arm ‖ καὶ δυνάμεις...γίνονται A C[2] W *f*[1] (*f*[13] 1071 γίνονται) 28 565 1009 1010 1216 1230 (1241 καὶ αἱ δυνάμεις...γίνωνται) 1253 1344 1646 2148 2174 *Byz Lect l*[211s,m,547m] it[a,aur,c,e,l] vg geo? Theophylact ‖ καὶ αἱ δυνάμεις...γινόμεναι ℵ* (ℵ[c] αἱ δυνάμεις αἱ τοιαῦται αἱ) B (L *omit* αἱ) Δ 33 892 cop[sa,bo] ‖ ὅτι καὶ δυνάμεις...γίνονται 1242 *l*[299] (it[f] goth *omit* καὶ) (syr[pal])

[3] **3** {A} τέκτων, ὁ υἱός ℵ A B C D K L W Δ Θ Π *f*[1] 28 892 1009 1010 1071 1079 1195 1216 1230 1241 1242 1344 1365 (1546 *omit* ὁ) 1646 2174 *Byz Lect* (*l*[211s,m] τέκτον) it[d,f,ff2,l,q] vg syr[p,h] cop[sa,bo] goth geo[1] ‖ τοῦ τέκτονος υἱός (*see* Mt 13.55) (𝔭[45vid] ὁ υἱός) 565 (1253 2148 *omit* τοῦ) (*l*[10] τοῦ τέκτων ὁ υἱός, *l*[547m] ὁ υἱός) it[e] ‖ τοῦ τέκτονος υἱὸς καί (*see* Mt 13.55) *f*[13] 33[vid] 700 *l*[31,48,184,299,1642] it[a,aur,b,c,i,rl] cop[boms] arm geo[2] Origen ‖ ὁ υἱός syr[pal]

2 τίς ἡ σοφία...τούτῳ Jn 7.15   **3** οὐχ...Μαρίας Jn 6.42   ὁ υἱὸς...Σίμωνος Mk 3.31

Jesus Rejected at Nazareth
(Also Matt. 13.53–58; Luke 4.16–30)

them strict orders not to tell anyone, and said, "Give her something to eat."

6 Jesus left that place and went back to his home town, followed by his disciples. [2] On the Sabbath day he began to teach in the synagogue. Many people were there, and when they heard him they were all amazed. "Where did he get all this?" they asked. "What wisdom is this that has been given him? How does he perform miracles? [3] Isn't he the carpenter, the son of Mary, and the brother of James, Joses, Judas, and Simon? Aren't his sisters living here?"

And so they rejected him. 4 Jesus said to them: "A prophet is respected everywhere except in his home town, and by his relatives and his family." 5 He wasn't able to perform any miracles there, except that he placed his hands on a few sick people and healed them. 6 He was greatly surprised, because they did not have faith.

Jesus Sends out the Twelve Disciples
(Also Matt. 10.5–15; Luke 9.1–6)

Then Jesus went to all the villages around there, teaching the people. 7 He called the twelve disciples together and sent them out two by two. He gave them authority over the evil spirits 8 and ordered them: "Don't take anything with you on the trip except a walking stick; no bread, no beggar's bag, no money in your pockets. 9 Wear sandals, but don't wear an extra shirt." 10 He also told them: "When you come to a town, stay with the people who receive you in their home until you leave that place. 11 If you come to a place where people do not welcome you or will not listen to you, leave it and shake the dust off your feet. This will be a warning to them!" 12 So they went out and preached that people should turn away from their sins. 13 They drove out many demons, and poured oil on many sick people and healed them.

The Death of John the Baptist
(Also Matt. 14.1–12; Luke 9.7–9)

14 Now King Herod heard about all this, because Jesus' reputation had spread everywhere. Some people said, "John

αὐτῷ. 4 καὶ ἔλεγεν αὐτοῖς ὁ Ἰησοῦς ὅτι Οὐκ ἔστιν προφήτης ἄτιμος εἰ μὴ ἐν τῇ πατρίδι αὐτοῦ καὶ ἐν τοῖς συγγενεῦσιν αὐτοῦ καὶ ἐν τῇ οἰκίᾳ αὐτοῦ. 5 καὶ οὐκ ἐδύνατο ἐκεῖ ποιῆσαι οὐδεμίαν δύναμιν, εἰ μὴ ὀλίγοις ἀρρώστοις ἐπιθεὶς τὰς χεῖρας ἐθεράπευσεν· 6 καὶ ἐθαύμαζεν διὰ τὴν ἀπιστίαν αὐτῶν.

The Mission of the Twelve
(Mt 10.1, 5–15; Lk 9.1–6)

Καὶ περιῆγεν τὰς κώμας κύκλῳ διδάσκων. 7 καὶ προσκαλεῖται τοὺς δώδεκα, καὶ ἤρξατο αὐτοὺς ἀποστέλλειν δύο δύο, καὶ ἐδίδου αὐτοῖς ἐξουσίαν τῶν πνευμάτων τῶν ἀκαθάρτων· 8 καὶ παρήγγειλεν αὐτοῖς ἵνα μηδὲν ἄρωσιν εἰς ὁδὸν εἰ μὴ ῥάβδον μόνον, μὴ ἄρτον, μὴ πήραν, μὴ εἰς τὴν ζώνην χαλκόν, 9 ἀλλὰ ὑποδεδεμένους σανδάλια καὶ μὴ ἐνδύσασθαι δύο χιτῶνας. 10 καὶ ἔλεγεν αὐτοῖς, Ὅπου ἐὰν εἰσέλθητε εἰς οἰκίαν, ἐκεῖ μένετε ἕως ἂν ἐξέλθητε ἐκεῖθεν. 11 καὶ ὃς ἂν τόπος μὴ δέξηται ὑμᾶς μηδὲ ἀκούσωσιν ὑμῶν, ἐκπορευόμενοι ἐκεῖθεν ἐκτινάξατε τὸν χοῦν τὸν ὑποκάτω τῶν ποδῶν ὑμῶν εἰς μαρτύριον αὐτοῖς. 12 Καὶ ἐξελθόντες ἐκήρυξαν ἵνα μετανοῶσιν, 13 καὶ δαιμόνια πολλὰ ἐξέβαλλον, καὶ ἤλειφον ἐλαίῳ πολλοὺς ἀρρώστους καὶ ἐθεράπευον.

The Death of John the Baptist
(Mt 14.1–12; Lk 9.7–9)

14 Καὶ ἤκουσεν ὁ βασιλεὺς Ἡρῴδης, φανερὸν γὰρ ἐγένετο τὸ ὄνομα αὐτοῦ, καὶ ἔλεγον[4] ὅτι Ἰωάννης ὁ

---

4 **14** {B} καὶ ἔλεγον B W it[a, b, d, ff2] Augustine ∥ καὶ ἔλεγεν ℵ A C K L Δ Θ Π f[1] f[13] 28 33 565 700 892 1009 1010 1071 1079 1195 1216 1230 1241 1242 1253 1344 1365 1546 1646 2148 2174 *Byz Lect*[m] it[aur, c, f, i, l, q, rl] vg syr[s, p, h, pal] cop[sa, bo] goth arm eth geo[1, A] ∥ καὶ ἐλέγοσαν D[gr] ∥ *omit* geo[B]

4 Οὐκ...πατρίδι αὐτοῦ Jn 4.44 **5** ὀλίγοις...ἐθεράπευσεν Mt 14.14; Mk 6.13 ἐπιθεὶς... ἐθεράπευσεν Mt 9.18; Mk 5.23; 7.32; 8.23, 25; Lk 4.40; 13.13; Ac 9.12, 17; 28.8 **7** ἤρξατο...δύο δύο Lk 10.1 **8–9** παρήγγειλεν...σανδάλια Lk 10.4 **10** Ὅπου...ἐκεῖθεν Lk 10.7 **11** ἐκτινάξατε...ὑμῶν Lk 10.11; Ac 13.51 εἰς μαρτύριον αὐτοῖς Mt 8.4; 10.18; Mk 1.44; 13.9; Lk 5.14 **13** ἤλειφον ἐλαίῳ Jas 5.14 πολλοὺς...ἐθεράπευον Mt 14.14; Mk 6.5 **14–15** καὶ ἔλεγον...προφητῶν Mt 16.14; Mk 8.28; Lk 9.19

βαπτίζων ἐγήγερται ἐκ νεκρῶν, καὶ διὰ τοῦτο ἐνεργοῦσιν
αἱ δυνάμεις ἐν αὐτῷ. **15** *ἄλλοι δὲ ἔλεγον ὅτι Ἠλίας*
ἐστίν· ἄλλοι δὲ ἔλεγον ὅτι προφήτης ὡς εἷς τῶν προφητῶν.
16 *ἀκούσας δὲ ὁ Ἡρῴδης ἔλεγεν, Ὃν ἐγὼ ἀπεκεφάλισα*
Ἰωάννην, οὗτος ἠγέρθη. **17** *Αὐτὸς γὰρ ὁ Ἡρῴδης*
ἀποστείλας ἐκράτησεν τὸν Ἰωάννην καὶ ἔδησεν αὐτὸν ἐν
φυλακῇ διὰ Ἡρῳδιάδα τὴν γυναῖκα Φιλίππου τοῦ ἀδελφοῦ
αὐτοῦ, ὅτι αὐτὴν ἐγάμησεν· **18** *ἔλεγεν γὰρ ὁ Ἰωάννης*
τῷ Ἡρῴδῃ ὅτι Οὐκ ἔξεστίν σοι ἔχειν τὴν γυναῖκα τοῦ
ἀδελφοῦ σου. **19** *ἡ δὲ Ἡρῳδιὰς ἐνεῖχεν αὐτῷ καὶ ἤθελεν*
αὐτὸν ἀποκτεῖναι, καὶ οὐκ ἠδύνατο· **20** *ὁ γὰρ Ἡρῴδης*
ἐφοβεῖτο τὸν Ἰωάννην, εἰδὼς αὐτὸν ἄνδρα δίκαιον καὶ
ἅγιον, καὶ συνετήρει αὐτόν, καὶ ἀκούσας αὐτοῦ πολλὰ
ἐποίει, καὶ[5] *ἡδέως αὐτοῦ ἤκουεν.* **21** *Καὶ γενομένης*
ἡμέρας εὐκαίρου ὅτε Ἡρῴδης τοῖς γενεσίοις αὐτοῦ δεῖπνον
ἐποίησεν τοῖς μεγιστᾶσιν αὐτοῦ καὶ τοῖς χιλιάρχοις καὶ
τοῖς πρώτοις τῆς Γαλιλαίας, **22** *καὶ εἰσελθούσης τῆς*
θυγατρὸς αὐτοῦ Ἡρῳδιάδος[6] *καὶ ὀρχησαμένης, ἤρεσεν*
τῷ Ἡρῴδῃ καὶ τοῖς συνανακειμένοις. εἶπεν ὁ βασιλεὺς
τῷ κορασίῳ, Αἴτησόν με ὃ ἐὰν θέλῃς, καὶ δώσω σοι·
23 *καὶ ὤμοσεν αὐτῇ [πολλά]*[7], *Ὅ τι*[8] *ἐάν με αἰτήσῃς*

[5] **20** {C} *ἐποίει, καί* A C D K Π f^{1} f^{13} 28 33 565 700 892 1009 1010 1071 1079 1195 1216 1230 1241 1242 1253 1344 1365 1546 1646 2148 2174 *Byz* $Lect^{m}$ $it^{a,aur,b,c,d,f,ff2,i,l,q,r1}$ vg $syr^{s,p,h,pal\,mss}$ goth arm geo^{B} $Diatessaron^{a}$ // *ἠπόρει, καί* ℵ B L Θ l^{1043} $cop^{sa,bo}$ // *ἠπορεῖτο, καί* W // *omit* Δ $geo^{1,A}$

[6] **22** {D} *θυγατρὸς αὐτοῦ* Ἡρῳδιάδος ℵ B D L Δ 565 // *θυγατρὸς αὐτῆς τῆς* Ἡρῳδιάδος A C K (W *omit τῆς*) Θ Π f^{13} 28 33 700 892 1009 1010 1071 1079 1195 1216 1230 1241 1242 1253 1344 1365 1546 1646 2148 2174 *Byz* $Lect^{m}$ $it^{a,d,ff2,i,l,q,r1}$ vg syr^{h} // *θυγατρὸς τῆς* Ἡρῳδιάδος f^{1} $it^{aur,b,c,f}$ $syr^{s,p,pal}$ $cop^{sa,bo}$ goth arm eth geo $Diatessaron^{a,p}$

[7] **23** {C} *αὐτῇ πολλά* $\mathfrak{p}^{45vid}$ D Θ 565 700 $it^{a,b,d,ff2,i,q}$ arm // *αὐτῇ* ℵ A B C^{vid} K Δ Π f^{1} f^{13} 33 892 1009 1010 1071 1079 1195 1216 1230 1241 1242 1253 1344 1365 1646 2148 2174 *Byz* $Lect^{m}$ $it^{aur,c,f,l}$ vg $syr^{(s),p,h}$ $cop^{sa,bo}$ goth $Diatessaron^{a,p}$ // *πολλά* 28 // *omit* L l^{211m} $cop^{sa\,ms,bo\,ms}$

[8] **23** {C} *ὅ τι or ὅτι* $\mathfrak{p}^{45}$ B Δ 33* 1241 $l^{60m,1127m}$ $syr^{p,h}$ Origen // *ὅτι ὅ* ℵ A K

17–18 Lk 3.19–20 **18** *Οὐκ ἔξεστιν…σου* Lv 18.16 **23** *Ὅ τι…αἰτήσῃς…βασιλείας μου* Est 5.3, 6; 7.2

the Baptist has come back to life! That
is why these powers are at work in him."
15 Others, however, said, "He is Elijah."
Others said, "He is a prophet, like one
of the prophets of long ago."
16 When Herod heard it he said, "He
is John the Baptist! I had his head cut
off, but he has come back to life!"
17 Herod himself had ordered John's
arrest, and had him tied up and put in
prison. Herod did this because of Herodias, whom he had married, even though
she was the wife of his brother Philip.
18 John the Baptist kept telling Herod:
"It isn't right for you to marry your
brother's wife!" 19 So Herodias held a
grudge against John and wanted to kill
him, but she couldn't because of Herod.
20 Herod was afraid of John because he
knew that John was a good and holy
man, and so he kept him safe. He liked
to listen to him, even though he became
greatly disturbed every time he heard
him.
21 Finally Herodias got her chance. It
was on Herod's birthday, when he gave
a feast for all the top government
officials, the military chiefs, and the
leading citizens of Galilee. 22 The daughter of Herodias[1] came in and danced,
and pleased Herod and his guests. So
the king said to the girl, "What would
you like to have? I will give you anything you want." 23 With many vows he
said to her, "I promise that I will give
you anything you ask for, even as much

[1] **22** The daughter of Herodias: *some mss. read* His daughter Herodias

as half my kingdom!" ²⁴ So the girl went out and asked her mother, "What shall I ask for?" "The head of John the Baptist," she answered. ²⁵ The girl hurried back at once to the king and demanded, "I want you to give me right now the head of John the Baptist on a plate!" ²⁶ This made the king very sad; but he could not refuse her, because of the vows he had made in front of all his guests. ²⁷ So he sent off a guard at once with orders to bring John's head. The guard left, went to the prison and cut John's head off; ²⁸ then he brought it on a plate and gave it to the girl, who gave it to her mother. ²⁹ When John's disciples heard about this, they came and got his body and laid it in a grave.

Jesus Feeds the Five Thousand
(Also Matt. 14.13–21; Luke 9.10–17; John 6.1–14)

³⁰ The apostles returned and met with Jesus, and told him all they had done and taught. ³¹ There were so many people coming and going that Jesus and his disciples didn't even have time to eat. So he said to them, "Let us go off by ourselves to some place where we will be alone and you can rest a while." ³² So they started out in the boat by themselves to a lonely place.

³³ Many people, however, saw them leave and knew at once who they were; so they left from all the towns and ran ahead by land and got to the place ahead of Jesus and his disciples. ³⁴ When Jesus

δώσω σοι ἕως ἡμίσους τῆς βασιλείας μου. 24 καὶ ἐξελθοῦσα εἶπεν τῇ μητρὶ αὐτῆς, Τί αἰτήσωμαι; ἡ δὲ εἶπεν, Τὴν κεφαλὴν Ἰωάννου τοῦ βαπτίζοντος. 25 καὶ εἰσελθοῦσα εὐθὺς μετὰ σπουδῆς πρὸς τὸν βασιλέα ᾐτήσατο λέγουσα, Θέλω ἵνα ἐξαυτῆς δῷς μοι ἐπὶ πίνακι τὴν κεφαλὴν Ἰωάννου τοῦ βαπτιστοῦ. 26 καὶ περίλυπος γενόμενος ὁ βασιλεὺς[a] διὰ τοὺς ὅρκους καὶ τοὺς ἀνακειμένους οὐκ ἠθέλησεν ἀθετῆσαι αὐτήν· 27 καὶ εὐθὺς ἀποστείλας ὁ βασιλεὺς σπεκουλάτορα ἐπέταξεν ἐνέγκαι τὴν κεφαλὴν αὐτοῦ. [b]καὶ ἀπελθὼν ἀπεκεφάλισεν αὐτὸν ἐν τῇ φυλακῇ 28[b] καὶ ἤνεγκεν τὴν κεφαλὴν αὐτοῦ ἐπὶ πίνακι καὶ ἔδωκεν αὐτὴν τῷ κορασίῳ, καὶ τὸ κοράσιον ἔδωκεν αὐτὴν τῇ μητρὶ αὐτῆς. 29 καὶ ἀκούσαντες οἱ μαθηταὶ αὐτοῦ ἦλθον καὶ ἦραν τὸ πτῶμα αὐτοῦ καὶ ἔθηκαν αὐτὸ ἐν μνημείῳ.

The Feeding of the Five Thousand
(Mt 14.13–21; Lk 9.10–17; Jn 6.1–14)

30 Καὶ συνάγονται οἱ ἀπόστολοι πρὸς τὸν Ἰησοῦν, καὶ ἀπήγγειλαν αὐτῷ πάντα ὅσα ἐποίησαν καὶ ὅσα ἐδίδαξαν. 31 καὶ λέγει αὐτοῖς, Δεῦτε ὑμεῖς αὐτοὶ κατ᾽ ἰδίαν εἰς ἔρημον τόπον καὶ ἀναπαύσασθε ὀλίγον. ἦσαν γὰρ οἱ ἐρχόμενοι καὶ οἱ ὑπάγοντες πολλοί, καὶ οὐδὲ φαγεῖν εὐκαίρουν. 32 καὶ ἀπῆλθον ἐν τῷ πλοίῳ εἰς ἔρημον τόπον κατ᾽ ἰδίαν. 33 καὶ εἶδον αὐτοὺς ὑπάγοντας καὶ ἐπέγνωσαν πολλοί, καὶ πεζῇ ἀπὸ πασῶν τῶν πόλεων συνέδραμον ἐκεῖ καὶ προῆλθον αὐτούς[9]. 34 καὶ ἐξελθὼν εἶδεν πολὺν

L Θ Π f¹³ 28 33ᶜ 565 700 892 1010 1071 1079 1195 1216 1230 1242 1253 1344 1365 1646 2148 2174 *Byz Lect*ᵐ itᵃ·ᵃᵘʳ·ᵇ·ᶜ·ᵈ·ᶠ·ff²·ⁱ·ˡ·q vg (copˢᵃ·ᵇᵒ) goth arm ∥ ὅ 1009 ∥ εἴ τι Dᵍʳ ∥ *omit* l²¹¹ᵐ·¹⁶³⁴ᵐ syrˢ

⁹ **33** {B} ἐκεῖ καὶ προῆλθον αὐτούς ℵ B (0182ᵛⁱᵈ *omit* ἐκεῖ) 892 l⁴⁹·⁶⁹·⁷⁰·²⁹⁹·³⁰³· ³³³·¹⁵⁷⁹ (l⁹⁵⁰ αὐτοῖς) itᵃᵘʳ·ˡ vg (copˢᵃ·ᵇᵒ) ∥ ἐκεῖ καὶ προσῆλθον αὐτούς L 1241 (Δ Θ

[a] **26** a none: TR WH Bov Nes BF² TT ∥ a minor: AV RV ASV RSV NEB Zür Luth Jer Seg
[b] ᵇ **27-28** b no number, b number 28: TRᵉᵈ WH Bov Nes BF² AV RV ASV RSV NEB TT Zür Luth Jer ∥ b number 28, b no number: TRᵉᵈ Seg

29 ἦραν...μνημείῳ Mt 27.59–60; Lk 23.52–53; Jn 19.38, 41   **30** Lk 10.17   **31** οὐδὲ... εὐκαίρουν Mk 3.20   **34** εἶδεν...ἐπ᾽ αὐτούς Mt 9.36; 15.32; Mk 8.2

ὄχλον, καὶ ἐσπλαγχνίσθη ἐπ᾽ αὐτοὺς ὅτι ἦσαν ὡς πρόβατα μὴ ἔχοντα ποιμένα, καὶ ἤρξατο διδάσκειν αὐτοὺς πολλά. **35** Καὶ ἤδη ὥρας πολλῆς γενομένης προσελθόντες [αὐτῷ] οἱ μαθηταὶ αὐτοῦ ἔλεγον ὅτι Ἔρημός ἐστιν ὁ τόπος, καὶ ἤδη ὥρα πολλή· **36** ἀπόλυσον αὐτούς, ἵνα ἀπελθόντες εἰς τοὺς κύκλῳ ἀγροὺς καὶ κώμας ἀγοράσωσιν ἑαυτοῖς τί φάγωσιν. **37** ὁ δὲ ἀποκριθεὶς εἶπεν αὐτοῖς, Δότε αὐτοῖς ὑμεῖς φαγεῖν. καὶ λέγουσιν αὐτῷ, Ἀπελθόντες ἀγοράσωμεν δηναρίων διακοσίων ἄρτους καὶ δώσωμεν αὐτοῖς φαγεῖν; **38** ὁ δὲ λέγει αὐτοῖς, Πόσους ἄρτους ἔχετε; ὑπάγετε ἴδετε. καὶ γνόντες λέγουσιν, Πέντε, καὶ δύο ἰχθύας. **39** καὶ ἐπέταξεν αὐτοῖς ἀνακλῖναι[10] πάντας συμπόσια συμπόσια ἐπὶ τῷ χλωρῷ χόρτῳ. **40** καὶ ἀνέπεσαν πρασιαὶ πρασιαὶ κατὰ ἑκατὸν καὶ κατὰ πεντήκοντα. **41** καὶ λαβὼν τοὺς πέντε ἄρτους καὶ τοὺς δύο ἰχθύας ἀναβλέψας εἰς τὸν οὐρανὸν εὐλόγησεν καὶ κατέκλασεν τοὺς ἄρτους καὶ ἐδίδου τοῖς μαθηταῖς [αὐτοῦ][11] ἵνα παρατιθῶσιν αὐτοῖς, καὶ τοὺς δύο ἰχθύας ἐμέρισεν πᾶσιν. **42** καὶ ἔφαγον πάντες καὶ ἐχορτάσθησαν· **43** καὶ ἦραν

l[10] αὐτοῖς) *l*[12,80,184,211,1127] arm geo[(1),2] ∥ ἐκεῖ καὶ συνῆλθον αὐτοῦ D[gr] (28 700 αὐτῷ) it[b] ∥ ἐκεῖ καὶ ἦλθον αὐτοῦ 565 it[(a),d,ff2,i,rl] Diatessaron[p] ∥ καὶ ἦλθον ἐκεῖ *f*[1] ∥ προῆλθον αὐτὸν ἐκεῖ syr[p] ∥ πρὸς αὐτοὺς καὶ συνῆλθον πρὸς αὐτὸν 33 ∥ ἐκεῖ καὶ προῆλθον αὐτοὺς καὶ συνῆλθον πρὸς αὐτόν (A συνέδραμον for συνῆλθον) K Π (*f*[13] συνεισῆλθον πρὸς αὐτούς) 1009 1010 1071 1079 1195 1216 1230 1242 (1253 προσῆλθον αὐτοῖς καὶ προσῆλθον πρὸς αὐτόν) (1344 omil ἐκεῖ) 1365 1546 1646 2148 2174 *Byz* *l*[313,883] (*l*[374] ἐξῆλθον for συνῆλθον) (*l*[1642] προσῆλθον αὐτοῖς) it[f,(q)] syr[h] eth ∥ ἐκεῖ W *l*[150] it[c] Euthymius ∥ *and when they came* syr[s]

[10] **39** {B} ἀνακλῖναι A B[2] D K L W Δ Π 33 892* 1009 1010 1079 1195 1216 1230 1241 1365 1540 2148 2174 *Byz Lect* it[f,(ff?),l] vg (syr[p,h]) cop[sa?] geo Origen ∥ ἀνακλιθῆναι (*see* Mt 14.19) א B* Θ 0187 *f*[1] *f*[13] 28 565 700 892[c] 1071 1242 1253 1344 1646 *l*[185] it[a,aur,b,c,d,i,q,rl] (syr[s]) cop[bo] Origen

[11] **41** {C} μαθηταῖς αὐτοῦ 𝔭[45] A D[gr] K W Θ Π *f*[1] *f*[13] 28 565 700 1009 1010 1071 1079 1195 1216 1230 1242 1253 1344 1365 1546 1646 2148 2174 *Byz* *l*[76,184,185, 313,883] it[a,aur,b,c,f,ff2,i,l,q,rl] vg syr[s,p,h] cop[sams] eth geo ∥ μαθηταῖς (*see* Mt 14.19; Lk 9.16) א B L Δ 0187[vid] 33 892 1241 *Lect* it[d] cop[samss,bo] arm

---

34 ἦσαν...ποιμένα Nu 27.17; 1 Kgs 22.17; 2 Chr 18.16; Eze 34.8; Zch 10.2; Jdth 11.19; Mt 9.36 **35–44** Mt 15.32–38; Mk 8.1–9

---

got out of the boat, he saw this large crowd, and his heart was filled with pity for them, because they looked like sheep without a shepherd. So he began to teach them many things. [35] When it was getting late, his disciples came to him and said, "It is already very late, and this is a lonely place. [36] Send the people away, and let them go to the nearby farms and villages and buy themselves something to eat." [37] "You yourselves give them something to eat," Jesus answered. They asked, "Do you want us to go and buy two hundred dollars' worth of bread and feed them?" [38] So Jesus asked them, "How much bread do you have? Go and see." When they found out they told him, "Five loaves, and two fish also."

[39] Jesus then told his disciples to make all the people divide into groups and sit down on the green grass. [40] So the people sat down in rows, in groups of a hundred and groups of fifty. [41] Then Jesus took the five loaves and the two fish, looked up to heaven, and gave thanks to God. He broke the loaves and gave them to his disciples to distribute to the people. He also divided the two fish among them all. [42] Everyone ate and had enough. [43] Then the disciples took up

twelve baskets full of what was left of the bread and of the fish. ⁴⁴ The number of men who ate the bread was five thousand.

Jesus Walks on the Water
(Also Matt. 14.22–33; John 6.15–21)

⁴⁵ At once Jesus made his disciples get into the boat and go ahead of him to Bethsaida, on the other side of the lake, while he sent the crowd away. ⁴⁶ After saying goodbye to the disciples, he went away to a hill to pray. ⁴⁷ When evening came the boat was in the middle of the lake, while Jesus was alone on land. ⁴⁸ He saw that his disciples were having trouble rowing the boat, because the wind was blowing against them; so sometime between three and six o'clock in the morning he came to them, walking on the water. He was going to pass them by.¹ ⁴⁹ But they saw him walking on the water. "It's a ghost!" they thought, and screamed. ⁵⁰ For when they all saw him they were afraid. Jesus spoke to them at once, "Courage!" he said. "It is I. Don't be afraid!" ⁵¹ Then he got into the boat with them, and the wind died down. The disciples were completely

---

² 48 pass them by: *or* join them

κλάσματα δώδεκα κοφίνων πληρώματα καὶ ἀπὸ τῶν ἰχθύων. **44** καὶ ἦσαν οἱ φαγόντες [τοὺς ἄρτους]¹² πεντακισχίλιοι ἄνδρες.

Walking on the Water
(Mt 14.22–33; Jn 6.15–21)

45 Καὶ εὐθὺς ἠνάγκασεν τοὺς μαθητὰς αὐτοῦ ἐμβῆναι εἰς τὸ πλοῖον καὶ προάγειν εἰς τὸ πέραν πρὸς Βηθσαϊδάν, ἕως αὐτὸς ἀπολύει τὸν ὄχλον. **46** καὶ ἀποταξάμενος αὐτοῖς ἀπῆλθεν εἰς τὸ ὄρος προσεύξασθαι. **47** καὶ ὀψίας γενομένης ἦν¹³ τὸ πλοῖον ἐν μέσῳ τῆς θαλάσσης, καὶ αὐτὸς μόνος ἐπὶ τῆς γῆς. **48** καὶ ἰδὼν αὐτοὺς βασανιζομένους ἐν τῷ ἐλαύνειν, ἦν γὰρ ὁ ἄνεμος ἐναντίος αὐτοῖς, περὶ τετάρτην φυλακὴν τῆς νυκτὸς ἔρχεται πρὸς αὐτοὺς περιπατῶν ἐπὶ τῆς θαλάσσης· καὶ ἤθελεν παρελθεῖν αὐτούς. **49** οἱ δὲ ἰδόντες αὐτὸν ἐπὶ τῆς θαλάσσης περιπατοῦντα ἔδοξαν ὅτι φάντασμά ἐστιν, καὶ ἀνέκραξαν· **50** πάντες γὰρ αὐτὸν εἶδον¹⁴ καὶ ἐταράχθησαν. ὁ δὲ εὐθὺς ἐλάλησεν μετ' αὐτῶν, καὶ λέγει αὐτοῖς, Θαρσεῖτε, ἐγώ εἰμι· μὴ φοβεῖσθε. **51** καὶ ἀνέβη πρὸς αὐτοὺς εἰς τὸ πλοῖον, καὶ ἐκόπασεν ὁ ἄνεμος. καὶ λίαν [ἐκ περισσοῦ] ἐν ἑαυτοῖς ἐξίσταντο¹⁵,

---

¹² **44** {C} τοὺς ἄρτους A B K L Δ Π 33 892 1009 1010 1071 1079 1195 1216 1230 1241 1242 1253 1344 1365 1546 1646 2148 2174 *Byz Lect* itᶠ syrᵖ,ʰ copᵇᵒ eth geo ∥ *panes et pisces* itᶜ ∥ *omit* 𝔭⁴⁵ ℵ D W Θ f¹ f¹³ 28 565 700 itᵃ,ᵃᵘʳ,ᵇ,ᵈ,ff²,ⁱ,ˡ,q,r¹ vg (syrˢ) copˢᵃ arm Diatessaronᵃ,ⁿ,ᵖ Theophylact

¹³ **47** {C} ἦν ℵ A B K L W X Θ Π f¹³ 33 565 700 892 1009 1010 1071 1079 1195 1216 1230 1241 1242 1253 1344 1546 1646 2148 2174 *Byz Lect* itᵃᵘʳ,ᶜ,f,ˡ,q vg syrˢ,ᵖ,ʰ copˢᵃ,ᵇᵒ arm geo Diatessaronᵖ ∥ ἦν πάλαι 𝔭⁴⁵ D f¹ 28 1365 itᵃ,ᵇ,ᵈ,ff²,ⁱ ∥ *omit* Δᵍʳ

¹⁴ **50** {B} γὰρ αὐτὸν εἶδον 𝔭⁴⁵ᵛⁱᵈ ℵ A B K L W X Δ Π f¹ f¹³ 28 33 892 1009 1010 (1071 1546 γὰρ εἶδον αὐτόν) 1079 1195 1216 1230 1241 1242 1253 1344 1365 1646 2148 2174 *Byz Lect* (l¹¹²⁷,¹⁵⁷⁹ *omit* γὰρ) itᵃᵘʳ,(f),ˡ vg syr⁽ˢ⁾,ᵖ,ʰ copˢᵃ,ᵇᵒ arm geo ∥ γὰρ αὐτὸν ἰδόντες καί l²¹¹ ∥ *omit* D Θ 565 700 itᵃ,ᵇ,ᶜ,ᵈ,ff²,ⁱ,q

¹⁵ **51** {C} ἐξίσταντο ℵ B L Δ 28 892 itᶜ,ff²,ⁱ,ˡ vg syrˢ copˢᵃ,ᵇᵒ geo ∥ ἐξεπλήσσοντο f¹ ∥ ἐξίσταντο καὶ ἐθαύμαζον (*see* Ac 2.7) A D K W X Θ Π f¹³ 33 565 700 1009 1010 1071 1079 1195 1216 1230 1241 1242 1253 1344 1365

46 ἀπῆλθεν...προσεύξασθαι Mk 1.35; Lk 5.16; 6.12; 9.28 **49** ἔδοξαν...ἐστιν Lk 24.37 **51** ἐκόπασεν ὁ ἄνεμος Mk 4.39

52 οὐ γὰρ συνῆκαν ἐπὶ τοῖς ἄρτοις, ἀλλ' ἦν αὐτῶν ἡ καρδία πεπωρωμένη.

The Healing of the Sick in Gennesaret
(Mt 14.34–36)

53 Καὶ διαπεράσαντες[c] ἐπὶ τὴν γῆν[c] ἦλθον εἰς Γεννησαρὲτ καὶ προσωρμίσθησαν. **54** καὶ ἐξελθόντων αὐτῶν ἐκ τοῦ πλοίου εὐθὺς ἐπιγνόντες αὐτὸν **55** περιέδραμον ὅλην τὴν χώραν ἐκείνην καὶ ἤρξαντο ἐπὶ τοῖς κραβάττοις τοὺς κακῶς ἔχοντας περιφέρειν ὅπου ἤκουον ὅτι ἐστίν. **56** καὶ ὅπου ἂν εἰσεπορεύετο εἰς κώμας ἢ εἰς πόλεις ἢ εἰς ἀγροὺς ἐν ταῖς ἀγοραῖς ἐτίθεσαν τοὺς ἀσθενοῦντας, καὶ παρεκάλουν αὐτὸν ἵνα κἂν τοῦ κρασπέδου τοῦ ἱματίου αὐτοῦ ἅψωνται· καὶ ὅσοι ἂν ἥψαντο αὐτοῦ ἐσῴζοντο.

The Tradition of the Elders
(Mt 15.1–20)

7 Καὶ συνάγονται πρὸς αὐτὸν οἱ Φαρισαῖοι καί τινες τῶν γραμματέων ἐλθόντες ἀπὸ Ἱεροσολύμων[a] **2** καὶ ἰδόντες τινὰς τῶν μαθητῶν αὐτοῦ ὅτι κοιναῖς χερσίν, τοῦτ' ἔστιν ἀνίπτοις, ἐσθίουσιν τοὺς ἄρτους[a] **3** —[b] οἱ γὰρ Φαρισαῖοι καὶ πάντες οἱ Ἰουδαῖοι ἐὰν μὴ πυγμῇ[1] νίψωνται τὰς

1546 1646 2148 2174 *Byz Lect* it[(a),aur,b,d,f,q,rl] syr[h] arm eth Diatessaron[a,p] ‖ ἐθαύμαζον καὶ ἐξίσταντο 517 1424 syr[p]

[1] **3** {A} πυγμῇ A B (D[gr] πυκμῇ) K L X Θ Π 0131 *f*[1] *f*[13] 28 33 565 700 892 1009 1010 1071 1079 1195 1216 1230 1241 1242 1253 1344 1365 1546 1646 2148 2174 *Byz Lect* it[(aur),c,ff2,i,q,rl] (syr[hmg]) Origen Epiphanius ‖ πυκνά ℵ W it[b,f,l] vg syr[p,h] cop[bo] goth arm (eth) geo Diatessaron[a] ‖ *momento* it[a] ‖ *primo* it[d] ‖ *omit* Δ syr[s] cop[sa] Diatessaron[p]

[c c] **53** c none, c none: WH Bov Nes BF[2] ‖ c minor, c none: RV ASV RSV (NEB) Luth Jer ‖ c none, c minor: RV[mg] ASV[mg] (TT) Zür ‖ different text: TR AV Seg

[a a] **1-2** (*see footnote b*) a none, a none ‖ a major, a major: Luth Seg ‖ a minor, a minor: Jer ‖ a major, a minor: Bov Nes BF[2] TT (Zür) ‖ a minor, a major: (WH) RV ASV RSV NEB ‖ different text: TR AV

[b b] **3-4** (*see footnote a*) b dash, b dash: WH Bov Nes BF[2] Zür Jer ‖ b parens, b parens: ASV RSV NEB TT ‖ b no parens or dashes, b major: TR AV RV Luth Seg

---

52 ἦν...πεπωρωμένη Mk 8.17   **56** ἵνα...ἅψωνται Mt 9.20; Mk 5.27; Lk 8.44
7   2 Lk 11.38

---

amazed and utterly confused. **52** They had not understood what the loaves of bread meant; their minds could not grasp it.

Jesus Heals the Sick in Gennesaret
(Also Matt. 14.34–36)

53 They crossed the lake and came to land at Gennesaret, where they tied up the boat. **54** As they left the boat, people recognized Jesus at once. **55** So they ran throughout the whole region and brought the sick lying on their mats to him, wherever they heard he was. **56** And everywhere Jesus went, to villages, towns, or farms, people would take their sick to the market places and beg him to let the sick at least touch the edge of his cloak; and all who touched it were made well.

The Teaching of the Ancestors
(Also Matt. 15.1–9)

7 The Pharisees and some teachers of the Law who had come from Jerusalem gathered around Jesus. **2** They noticed that some of his disciples were eating their food with "unclean" hands — that is, they had not washed them in the way the Pharisees said people should.

3 For the Pharisees, as well as the rest of the Jews, follow the teaching they received from their ancestors: they don't eat unless they wash their hands in the proper way, ⁴ nor do they eat anything that comes from the market unless they wash it first.¹ And they follow many other rules which they have received, such as the proper way to wash cups, pots, copper bowls, and beds.

⁵ So the Pharisees and the teachers of the Law asked Jesus, "Why is it that your disciples do not follow the teaching handed down by our ancestors, but instead eat with unclean hands?" ⁶ Jesus answered them: "How right Isaiah was when he prophesied about you! You are hypocrites, just as he wrote:

'These people, says God, honor me
    with their words,
But their heart is really far away
    from me.

⁷ It is no use for them to worship me,
Because they teach man-made commandments as though they were
    God's rules!' "

⁸ And Jesus said, "You put aside the commandment of God and obey the teachings of men."

⁹ And Jesus continued: "You have a clever way of rejecting God's law in

---

¹ **4** anything that comes from the market unless they wash it first: *or* anything after they come from the market unless they wash themselves first

χεῖρας οὐκ ἐσθίουσιν, κρατοῦντες τὴν παράδοσιν τῶν πρεσβυτέρων, 4 καὶ ἀπ' ἀγορᾶς² ἐὰν μὴ βαπτίσωνται³ οὐκ ἐσθίουσιν, καὶ ἄλλα πολλά ἐστιν ἃ παρέλαβον κρατεῖν, βαπτισμοὺς ποτηρίων καὶ ξεστῶν καὶ χαλκίων [καὶ κλινῶν]⁴ —ᵇ 5 καὶ ἐπερωτῶσιν αὐτὸν οἱ Φαρισαῖοι καὶ οἱ γραμματεῖς, Διὰ τί οὐ περιπατοῦσιν οἱ μαθηταί σου κατὰ τὴν παράδοσιν τῶν πρεσβυτέρων, ἀλλὰ κοιναῖς χερσὶν ἐσθίουσιν τὸν ἄρτον; 6 ὁ δὲ εἶπεν αὐτοῖς, Καλῶς ἐπροφήτευσεν Ἠσαΐας περὶ ὑμῶν τῶν ὑποκριτῶν, ὡς γέγραπται ὅτι

Οὗτος ὁ λαὸς τοῖς χείλεσίν με τιμᾷ⁵,
    ἡ δὲ καρδία αὐτῶν πόρρω ἀπέχει ἀπ' ἐμοῦ·
7   **μάτην δὲ σέβονταί με,**
        διδάσκοντες διδασκαλίας ἐντάλματα ἀνθρώπων.

8 ἀφέντες⁶ τὴν ἐντολὴν τοῦ θεοῦ κρατεῖτε τὴν παράδοσιν τῶν ἀνθρώπων.⁶ 9 Καὶ ἔλεγεν αὐτοῖς, Καλῶς ἀθετεῖτε

---

² 4 {A} ἀγορᾶς 𝔭⁴⁵ᵛⁱᵈ ℵ A B K L X Δ Θ Π f¹ f¹³ 28 33 565 700 892 1010 1071 1079 1195 1216 1230 1241 1242 1253 1344 1365 1546 1646 2148 2174 *Byz Lect* vg syrˢ·ᵖ·ʰ copˢᵃ·ᵇᵒ goth eth Diatessaronᵃ·ᵖ Origen ‖ ἀγορᾶς ὅταν ἔλθωσιν D (W δὲ ὅταν) (1009 ὅταν δὲ εἰσέλθωσιν) itᵃ·ᵃᵘʳ·ᵇ·ᶜ·ᵈ·ᶠ·ff²·ⁱ·ˡ·q·ʳˡ arm geo

³ 4 {A} βαπτίσωνται A D K (L βαπτίζονται) W X (Δ βαπτίζωνται) Θ Π f¹ f¹³ 28 33 565 700 892 1010 1079 1195 1241 1242 1344 1365 1646 (1009 1071 1216 1230 1253 1546 2148 2174 βαπτίσονται) *Byz Lect* (l¹¹²⁷ καταβαπτίσωνται) itᵃ·ᵃᵘʳ·ᵇ·ᶜ·ᵈ·ᶠ·ff²·ⁱ·ˡ·q·ʳˡ vg syrˢ·ᵖ·ʰ copˢᵃ goth arm (eth) Diatessaronᵃ·ᵖ Origen ‖ ῥαντίσωνται ℵ B copˢᵃ geo Euthymius

⁴ 4 {C} καὶ χαλκίων καὶ κλινῶν A D K W X Θ Π f¹ f¹³ 28ᶜ 33 565 700 892 1009 1010 1071 1079 1195 1216 1230 1241 1242 1253 1344 1365 1546 1646 2148 2174 *Byz Lect* (l¹⁰·⁸⁰·³⁰³·³¹³·³³³·³⁷⁴·⁸⁸³·¹¹²⁷ χαλκείων) itᵃ·ᵃᵘʳ·ᵇ·ᶜ·ᵈ·ᶠ·ff²·ⁱ·ˡ·q·(ʳˡ) vg syrᵖ·ʰ copˢᵃ goth arm geo Diatessaronᵃ·ᵖ Origen ‖ καὶ χαλκίων 𝔭⁴⁵ᵛⁱᵈ ℵ B L Δ 28* l⁴⁸ copᵇᵒ ‖ *omit* syrˢ

⁵ 6 {B} τιμᾷ 𝔭⁴⁵ ℵ A B K L X Δ Θ Π f¹ f¹³ 28 33 565 700 892 1009 1010 1071 1079 1195 1216 1230 1241 1242 1253 1344 1365 1546 1646 2148 2174 *Byz Lect* itᵃᵘʳ·ᵈ·ᶠ·ff²·ⁱ·ˡ·q vg syrˢ·ᵖ·ʰ copˢᵃ·ᵇᵒ goth arm ethᵖᵖ·ᵐˢ geo Diatessaronᵖ ‖ ἀγαπᾷ Dᵍʳ W itᵃ·ᵇ·ᶜ Clement²/⁶ Tertullian ‖ τιμᾷ καὶ ἀγαπᾷ ethʳᵒ ‖ φιλοῦσι Clement¹/⁶

⁶ 7–8 {A} ἀνθρώπων. ἀφέντες...ἀνθρώπων. 𝔭⁴⁵ ℵ B L W Δ f¹ 1365 l⁶⁹ᵖᵗ·⁷⁶ᵖᵗ·²¹¹ᵖᵗ·⁸⁸³ᵖᵗ·⁹⁵⁰ᵖᵗ·¹¹²⁷ᵖᵗ copˢᵃ·ᵇᵒ arm geo ‖ ἀνθρώπων. ἀφέντες...ἀνθρώπων.

---

4 βαπτισμοὺς...χαλκίων Mt 23.25; Lk 11.39   6–7 Οὗτος...ἀνθρώπων Is 29.13 ʟxx

τὴν ἐντολὴν τοῦ θεοῦ, ἵνα τὴν παράδοσιν ὑμῶν στήσητε[7]. 10 Μωϋσῆς γὰρ εἶπεν, **Τίμα τὸν πατέρα σου καὶ τὴν μητέρα σου, καί, Ὁ κακολογῶν πατέρα ἢ μητέρα θανάτῳ τελευτάτω·** 11 ὑμεῖς δὲ λέγετε, Ἐὰν εἴπῃ ἄνθρωπος τῷ πατρὶ ἢ τῇ μητρί, Κορβᾶν, ὅ ἐστιν, Δῶρον, ὃ ἐὰν ἐξ ἐμοῦ ὠφεληθῇς, 12 οὐκέτι ἀφίετε αὐτὸν οὐδὲν ποιῆσαι τῷ πατρὶ ἢ τῇ μητρί, 13 ἀκυροῦντες τὸν λόγον τοῦ θεοῦ τῇ παραδόσει ὑμῶν ᾗ παρεδώκατε· καὶ παρόμοια τοιαῦτα πολλὰ ποιεῖτε.

14 Καὶ προσκαλεσάμενος πάλιν τὸν ὄχλον ἔλεγεν αὐτοῖς, Ἀκούσατέ μου πάντες καὶ σύνετε. 15 οὐδέν ἐστιν ἔξωθεν τοῦ ἀνθρώπου εἰσπορευόμενον εἰς αὐτὸν ὃ δύναται κοινῶσαι αὐτόν· ἀλλὰ τὰ ἐκ τοῦ ἀνθρώπου ἐκπορευόμενά ἐστιν τὰ κοινοῦντα τὸν ἄνθρωπον.[8] 17 Καὶ ὅτε εἰσῆλθεν εἰς οἶκον ἀπὸ τοῦ ὄχλου, ἐπηρώτων αὐτὸν οἱ μαθηταὶ αὐτοῦ

___

βαπτισμοὺς ξεστῶν καὶ ποτηρίων καὶ ἄλλα παρόμοια τοιαῦτα πολλὰ ποιεῖτε. (see 7.4) (A omit ἄλλα) K X Π f[13] 33 700 892 1009 1010 1071 (1079 1546 ποιεῖτε πολλά) 1195 1216 1230 (1241 πολλὰ τοιαῦτα) 1242 1253 1646 (2148 omit τοιαῦτα) 2174 Byz Lect l[69pt,76pt,211pt,883pt,950pt,1127pt] (l[303] omit πολλά) it[aur,f,l] vg syr[p,h] cop[boms] goth eth Diatessaron[p] ‖ ἀνθρώπων. βαπτισμοὺς ξεστῶν καὶ ποτηρίων καὶ ἄλλα παρόμοια ἃ ποιεῖται τοιαῦτα πολλὰ ἀφέντες...ἀνθρώπων. (see 7.4) D Θ 0131[vid] (28 παρόμοια τοιαῦτα ποιεῖτε ἀφέντες...) (565 ποτηρίων καὶ ξεστῶν and παρόμοια τοιαῦτα ποιεῖτε ἀφέντες...) it[a,b,c,d,ff2,i,q,r1] Diatessaron[a] ‖ ἀνθρώπων. 9 καλῶς (omit verse 8) syr[s]

[7] 9 {C} στήσητε D[gr] W Θ f[1] 28 565 it[a,b,c,(d),f,ff2,i,q,r1] syr[s,p] arm geo Diatessaron[a,p] Cyprian Zeno Jerome Augustine ‖ τηρήσητε ℵ A K L X Δ Π f[13] 33 700 892 1009 1010 1071 1079 1195 1216 1230 1241 1242 1253 1344 1365 1546 1646 2148 2174 Byz Lect it[aur,l] vg syr[h] cop[sa,bo] goth eth ‖ τήρητε B l[15]

[8] 15 {B} omit verse 16 ℵ B L Δ* 28 Lect l[883pt,950pt,1127pt] cop[boms] geo[1] ‖ include verse 16 εἴ τις ἔχει ὦτα ἀκούειν, ἀκουέτω. (see 4.9, 23) A D K W X Δ[c] Θ Π f[1] f[13] 33 565 700 892 1009 1010 (1071 ὁ ἔχων ὦτα) 1079 1195 1216 1230 1241 1242 1253 1344 1365 1546 1646 2148 2174 Byz l[76,185,313,333pt,950pt,1127pt] it[a,aur,b,c,d,f,ff2,i,l,n,q,r1] vg syr[(s,p),h] cop[ss,homss] goth arm eth geo[2] Diatessaron[a,p] Augustine

___

10 Τίμα...μητέρα σου Ex 20.12; Dt 5.16 (Mk 10.19; Eph 6.2)   Ὁ...τελευτάτω Ex 21.17 Lv 20.9)   17 ἐπηρώτων...παραβολήν Mt 13.36; Mk 4.10; Lk 8.9

___

order to uphold your own teaching! 10 For Moses commanded, 'Honor your father and mother,' and, 'Anyone who says bad things about his father or mother must be put to death.' 11 But you teach that if a person has something he could use to help his father or mother, but says, 'This is Corban' (which means, it belongs to God), 12 he is excused from helping his father or mother. 13 In this way you disregard the word of God with the teaching you pass on to others. And there are many other things of this kind that you do."

The Things that Make a Person Unclean
(Also Matt. 15.10–20)

14 Then Jesus called the crowd to him once more and said to them: "Listen to me, all of you, and understand. 15 There is nothing that goes into a person from the outside which can make him unclean. Rather, it is what comes out of a person that makes him unclean. [16 Listen, then, if you have ears to hear with!]"

17 When he left the crowd and went into the house, his disciples asked him

about this parable. [18] "You are no more intelligent than the others," Jesus said to them. "Don't you understand? Nothing that goes into a person from the outside can really make him unclean, [19] because it does not go into his heart but into his stomach and then goes on out of the body." (In saying this Jesus declared that all foods are fit to be eaten.) [20] And he went on to say: "It is what comes out of a person that makes him unclean. [21] For from the inside, from a man's heart, come the evil ideas which lead him to do immoral things, to rob, kill, [22] commit adultery, covet, and do all sorts of evil things; deceit, indecency, jealousy, slander, pride, and folly — [23] all these evil things come from inside a man and make him unclean."

A Woman's Faith
(Also Matt. 15.21-28)

[24] Then Jesus left and went away to the territory near the city of Tyre. He went into a house, and did not want anyone to know he was there; but he could not stay hidden. [25] A certain woman, whose daughter had an evil spirit in her, heard about Jesus and

τὴν παραβολήν. 18 καὶ λέγει αὐτοῖς, Οὕτως καὶ ὑμεῖς ἀσύνετοί ἐστε; οὐ νοεῖτε ὅτι πᾶν τὸ ἔξωθεν εἰσπορευόμενον εἰς τὸν ἄνθρωπον οὐ δύναται αὐτὸν κοινῶσαι,[c] 19 ὅτι οὐκ εἰσπορεύεται αὐτοῦ εἰς τὴν καρδίαν ἀλλ' εἰς τὴν κοιλίαν, καὶ εἰς τὸν ἀφεδρῶνα ἐκπορεύεται;[c] —[d] καθαρίζων[9] πάντα τὰ βρώματα.[d] 20 ἔλεγεν δὲ ὅτι Τὸ ἐκ τοῦ ἀνθρώπου ἐκπορευόμενον ἐκεῖνο κοινοῖ τὸν ἄνθρωπον· 21 ἔσωθεν γὰρ ἐκ τῆς καρδίας τῶν ἀνθρώπων οἱ διαλογισμοὶ οἱ κακοὶ ἐκπορεύονται, πορνεῖαι, κλοπαί, φόνοι, 22 μοιχεῖαι, πλεονεξίαι, πονηρίαι, δόλος, ἀσέλγεια, ὀφθαλμὸς πονηρός, βλασφημία, ὑπερηφανία, ἀφροσύνη· 23 πάντα ταῦτα τὰ πονηρὰ ἔσωθεν ἐκπορεύεται καὶ κοινοῖ τὸν ἄνθρωπον.

The Syrophoenician Woman's Faith
(Mt 15.21-28)

24 Ἐκεῖθεν δὲ ἀναστὰς ἀπῆλθεν εἰς τὰ ὅρια Τύρου[10]. καὶ εἰσελθὼν εἰς οἰκίαν οὐδένα ἤθελεν γνῶναι, καὶ οὐκ ἠδυνήθη λαθεῖν· 25 ἀλλ' εὐθὺς ἀκούσασα γυνὴ περὶ αὐτοῦ, ἧς εἶχεν τὸ θυγάτριον αὐτῆς πνεῦμα ἀκάθαρτον, ἐλθοῦσα

---

[9] **19** {A} καθαρίζων ℵ A B L W X Δ Θ f¹ f¹³ 28 565 892 1009 1071 1216 1241 1242 1253 1546 1646 Byz^pt l^49,184,211,299,883,950 syr^p,h cop^sa,bo eth Origen Gregory-Nyssa Chrysostom ∥ καθαρίζον Κ Π 33 700 1010 1079 1195 1230 1344 1365 2148 2174 Byz^pt Lect Diatessaron^a ∥ καθαρίζων or καθαρίζον it^a,aur,b,c,d,f,ff²,l,n,q vg ∥ καὶ καθαρίζεται (1047 omit καί) syr^s ∥ καθαρίζων τε l^70 ∥ καὶ καθαρίζει (D l^185 omit καί) it^i,r1 (goth omit καί) arm geo

[10] **24** {A} Τύρου D L W Δ Θ 28 565 it^a,b,d,ff²,i,n,r1 syr^s,pal Origen Ambrosiaster ∥ Τύρου καὶ Σιδῶνος (see Mt 15.21) ℵ A B K X Π f¹ f¹³ 33 700 892 1009 1010 1071 1079 1195 1216 1230 1241 1242 1253 1344 1365 1546 1646 2148 2174 Byz Lect it^aur,c,f,l,q vg syr^p,h cop^sa,bo goth arm eth geo Diatessaron^a,p

---

[c] [c] **18-19** (see footnote d) c minor, c question: WH Bov RV ASV RSV NEB TT (Jer) ∥ c question, c none: TR ∥ c question, c major: Zür Luth Seg ∥ c minor, c minor: Nes BF² AV

[d] [d] **19** (see footnote c) d dash, d major: WH Bov Zür ∥ d none, d major: (TR) RV ASV NEB TT Luth Seg ∥ d none, d question: Nes BF² AV ∥ d parens, d parens: RSV Jer

---

21-22 οἱ διαλογισμοί...ἀφροσύνη Ro 1.29-31; 1 Cor 5.11; 6.9-10; Ga 5.19-21; Eph 5.3-4; Col 3.5; 1 Tm 1.9-10; 2 Tm 3.2-4· 1 Pe 4.3; Re 21.8; 22.15

προσέπεσεν πρὸς τοὺς πόδας αὐτοῦ· 26 ἡ δὲ γυνὴ ἦν
Ἑλληνίς, Συροφοινίκισσα τῷ γένει· καὶ ἠρώτα αὐτὸν ἵνα
τὸ δαιμόνιον ἐκβάλῃ ἐκ τῆς θυγατρὸς αὐτῆς. 27 καὶ ἔλεγεν
αὐτῇ, Ἄφες πρῶτον χορτασθῆναι τὰ τέκνα, οὐ γάρ ἐστιν
καλὸν λαβεῖν τὸν ἄρτον τῶν τέκνων καὶ τοῖς κυναρίοις
βαλεῖν. 28 ἡ δὲ ἀπεκρίθη καὶ λέγει αὐτῷ, Κύριε[11], καὶ
τὰ κυνάρια ὑποκάτω τῆς τραπέζης ἐσθίουσιν ἀπὸ τῶν
ψιχίων τῶν παιδίων. 29 καὶ εἶπεν αὐτῇ, Διὰ τοῦτον τὸν
λόγον ὕπαγε, ἐξελήλυθεν ἐκ τῆς θυγατρός σου τὸ δαιμόνιον. 30 καὶ ἀπελθοῦσα εἰς τὸν οἶκον αὐτῆς εὗρεν τὸ
παιδίον βεβλημένον ἐπὶ τὴν κλίνην καὶ τὸ δαιμόνιον
ἐξεληλυθός.

A Deaf and Dumb Man Healed

31 Καὶ πάλιν ἐξελθὼν ἐκ τῶν ὁρίων Τύρου ἦλθεν διὰ
Σιδῶνος[12] εἰς τὴν θάλασσαν τῆς Γαλιλαίας ἀνὰ μέσον τῶν
ὁρίων Δεκαπόλεως. 32 καὶ φέρουσιν αὐτῷ κωφὸν καὶ
μογιλάλον, καὶ παρακαλοῦσιν αὐτὸν ἵνα ἐπιθῇ αὐτῷ τὴν
χεῖρα. 33 καὶ ἀπολαβόμενος αὐτὸν ἀπὸ τοῦ ὄχλου κατ'
ἰδίαν ἔβαλεν τοὺς δακτύλους αὐτοῦ εἰς τὰ ὦτα αὐτοῦ καὶ
πτύσας ἥψατο τῆς γλώσσης αὐτοῦ, 34 καὶ ἀναβλέψας εἰς
τὸν οὐρανὸν ἐστέναξεν, καὶ λέγει αὐτῷ, Εφφαθα, ὅ
ἐστιν, Διανοίχθητι. 35 καὶ [εὐθέως][13] ἠνοίγησαν αὐτοῦ

came to him at once and fell at his feet.
26 The woman was a foreigner, born in
Phoenicia of Syria. She begged Jesus to
drive the demon out of her daughter.
27 But Jesus answered, "Let us feed the
children first; it isn't right to take the
children's food and throw it to the dogs."
28 "Sir," she answered, "even the dogs
under the table eat the children's leftovers!" 29 So Jesus said to her, "For
such an answer you may go home; the
demon has gone out of your daughter!"
30 So she went back home and there
found her child lying on the bed; the
demon had indeed gone out of her.

Jesus Heals a Deaf and Dumb Man

31 Jesus then left the neighborhood of
Tyre and went on through Sidon to
Lake Galilee, going by way of the territory of the Ten Towns. 32 Some people
brought him a man who was deaf and
could hardly speak, and begged Jesus
to place his hand on him. 33 So Jesus
took him off alone, away from the crowd,
put his fingers in the man's ears, spat,
and touched the man's tongue. 34 Then
Jesus looked up to heaven, gave a deep
groan, and said to the man, *Ephphatha*,
which means, "Open up!" 35 At once
the man's ears were opened, his tongue

---

11 28 {B} κύριε 𝔭45 D W Θ f13 565 700 l185,299 itb,c,d,ff2,i,rl syrs arm geo2 ∥
ναί, κύριε (see Mt 15.27) ℵ A B K L X Δ Π f1 28 33 892 1009 1010 1071 1079
1195 1216 1230 1241 1242 1253 1344 1365 1546 1646 2148 2174 Byz Lect ita,aur,
f,l,n,q vg syrp,h,pal copsa,bo goth geo1

12 31 {A} ἦλθεν διὰ Σιδῶνος ℵ B D L Δ Θ 33 565 700 892 ita,aur,b,c,d,f,
ff2,1,l,n,rl vg syrpal copsamss,bo eth ∥ καὶ Σιδῶνος ἦλθεν 𝔭45 A K W X Π 0131
f1 f13 28 1009 1010 1071 1079 1195 1216 1230 1241 1242 1253 1344 1365 1546
1646 2148 2174 Byz Lect itq syrs,p,h copsa goth arm geo Diatessarona,p

13 35 {C} καὶ εὐθέως 𝔭45 A K W X Θ Π 0131c f1 f13 28 565 700 1009 1010
1071 1079 1195 1216 1230 1241 1242 1253 1344 1365 1546 1646 2148 2174 Byz
Lect itaur,c,f,l vg syrs,p,h,pal copsa goth arm eth geo Diatessarona,p ∥ καὶ
ℵ B D L Δ 0131* 33 892 ita,b,d,ff2,i,q,rl copbo

---

32 παρακαλοῦσιν...χεῖρα Mt 9.18; Mk 5.23; 8.23,25; Lk 4.40; 13.13; Ac 9.12,17; 28.8
33 Mk 8.23   34 ἀναβλέψας...οὐρανόν Mt 14.19; Mk 6.41

was set loose, and he began to talk without any trouble. ³⁶ Then Jesus ordered them all not to speak of it to anyone; but the more he ordered them, the more they told it. ³⁷ And all who heard were completely amazed. "How well he does everything!" they exclaimed. "He even makes the deaf to hear and the dumb to speak!"

Jesus Feeds the Four Thousand
(Also Matt. 15.32–39)

8 Not long afterward, another large crowd came together. When they had nothing left to eat, Jesus called the disciples to him and said: ² "I feel sorry for these people, because they have been with me for three days and now have nothing to eat. ³ If I send them home without feeding them they will faint as they go, because some of them have come a long way." ⁴ His disciples asked him, "Where in this desert can anyone find enough food to feed all these people?" ⁵ "How much bread do you have?" Jesus asked. "Seven loaves," they answered.

⁶ He ordered the crowd to sit down on the ground. Then he took the seven loaves, gave thanks to God, broke them, and gave them to his disciples to distribute to the crowd; and the disciples did so. ⁷ They also had a few small fish. Jesus gave thanks for these and told the disciples to distribute them too. ⁸ Everybody ate and had enough — there

αἱ ἀκοαί, καὶ¹⁴ ἐλύθη ὁ δεσμὸς τῆς γλώσσης αὐτοῦ, καὶ ἐλάλει ὀρθῶς. **36** καὶ διεστείλατο αὐτοῖς ἵνα μηδενὶ λέγωσιν· ὅσον δὲ αὐτοῖς διεστέλλετο, αὐτοὶ μᾶλλον περισσότερον ἐκήρυσσον. **37** καὶ ὑπερπερισσῶς ἐξεπλήσσοντο λέγοντες, Καλῶς πάντα πεποίηκεν· καὶ τοὺς κωφοὺς ποιεῖ ἀκούειν καὶ [τοὺς] ἀλάλους¹⁵ λαλεῖν.

The Feeding of the Four Thousand
(Mt 15.32–39)

8 Ἐν ἐκείναις ταῖς ἡμέραις πάλιν πολλοῦ ὄχλου ὄντος καὶ μὴ ἐχόντων τί φάγωσιν, προσκαλεσάμενος τοὺς μαθητὰς λέγει αὐτοῖς, **2** Σπλαγχνίζομαι ἐπὶ τὸν ὄχλον ὅτι ἤδη ἡμέραι τρεῖς προσμένουσίν μοι καὶ οὐκ ἔχουσιν τί φάγωσιν· **3** καὶ ἐὰν ἀπολύσω αὐτοὺς νήστεις εἰς οἶκον αὐτῶν, ἐκλυθήσονται ἐν τῇ ὁδῷ· καί τινες αὐτῶν ἀπὸ μακρόθεν ἥκασιν. **4** καὶ ἀπεκρίθησαν αὐτῷ οἱ μαθηταὶ αὐτοῦ ὅτι Πόθεν τούτους δυνήσεταί τις ὧδε χορτάσαι ἄρτων ἐπ' ἐρημίας; **5** καὶ ἠρώτα αὐτούς, Πόσους ἔχετε ἄρτους; οἱ δὲ εἶπαν, Ἑπτά. **6** καὶ παραγγέλλει τῷ ὄχλῳ ἀναπεσεῖν ἐπὶ τῆς γῆς· καὶ λαβὼν τοὺς ἑπτὰ ἄρτους εὐχαριστήσας ἔκλασεν καὶ ἐδίδου τοῖς μαθηταῖς αὐτοῦ ἵνα παρατιθῶσιν καὶ παρέθηκαν τῷ ὄχλῳ. **7** καὶ εἶχον ἰχθύδια ὀλίγα· καὶ εὐλογήσας αὐτὰ¹ εἶπεν καὶ ταῦτα παρατιθέναι. **8** καὶ

---

¹⁴ **35** {B} καὶ A B D K W X Θ Π *f*¹ *f*¹³ 28 33 565 700 1009 1010 1071 1079 1195 1216 1230 1241 1242 1253 1344 1365 1546 1646 2148 2174 *Byz Lect* itᵃ,ᵃᵘʳ,ᵇ,ᶜ,ᵈ,ᶠ,ff²,ᵢ,ₗ,q,ʳˡ vg syrˢ,ᵖ,ʰ,ᵖᵃˡᵐˢˢ copˢᵃ,ᵇᵒ goth arm geo ∥ καὶ εὐθύς 𝔭⁴⁵ᵛⁱᵈ ℵ (L εὐθέως) Δ 892 syrᵖᵃˡᵐˢ (eth) ∥ καὶ τοῦ μογγιλάλου 0131

¹⁵ **37** {C} τοὺς ἀλάλους A Dᵍʳ K X Θ Π 0131 *f*¹ *f*¹³ 565 700 1009 1010 1071 1079 1195 1216 1230 1242 1253 1344 1365 1546 1646 2148 2174 *Byz Lect* copˢᵃ,ᵇᵒ ∥ ἀλάλους ℵ B L Δ 33 892 1241 arm ∥ τοὺς ἀλάλους *or* ἀλάλους itᵃ,ᵃᵘʳ,ᵇ,ᶠ,ff²,ᵢ,ₗ,q,ʳˡ vg syrᵖ,ʰ,ᵖᵃˡ goth geo Diatessaronᵃ,ᵖ Augustine ∥ *multis* itᶜ,ᵈ ∥ *omit* W 28 syrˢ

¹ **7** {B} εὐλογήσας αὐτά ℵ B C L Δ Θ 892 1071 1241 copᵇᵒ eth ∥

---

36 διεστείλατο...λέγωσιν Mk 1.44; 5.43   ὅσον...ἐκήρυσσον Mk 1.45   **37** τοὺς κωφοὺς ...λαλεῖν Is 35.5–6
8 1-10 Mt 14.14–21; Mk 6.35–44; Lk 9.12–17; Jn 6.5–13

ἔφαγον καὶ ἐχορτάσθησαν, καὶ ἦραν περισσεύματα κλασμάτων ἑπτὰ σπυρίδας. 9 ἦσαν δὲ ὡς τετρακισχίλιοι. καὶ ἀπέλυσεν αὐτούς. 10 Καὶ εὐθὺς ἐμβὰς εἰς τὸ πλοῖον μετὰ τῶν μαθητῶν αὐτοῦ ἦλθεν εἰς τὰ μέρη Δαλμανουθά².

The Demand for a Sign
(Mt 16.1–4)

11 Καὶ ἐξῆλθον οἱ Φαρισαῖοι καὶ ἤρξαντο συζητεῖν αὐτῷ, ζητοῦντες παρ’ αὐτοῦ σημεῖον ἀπὸ τοῦ οὐρανοῦ, πειράζοντες αὐτόν. 12 καὶ ἀναστενάξας τῷ πνεύματι αὐτοῦ λέγει, Τί ἡ γενεὰ αὕτη ζητεῖ σημεῖον; ἀμὴν λέγω ὑμῖν, εἰ δοθήσεται τῇ γενεᾷ ταύτῃ σημεῖον. 13 καὶ ἀφεὶς αὐτοὺς πάλιν ἐμβὰς³ ἀπῆλθεν εἰς τὸ πέραν.

The Leaven of the Pharisees and of Herod
(Mt 16.5–12)

14 Καὶ ἐπελάθοντο λαβεῖν ἄρτους, καὶ εἰ μὴ ἕνα ἄρτον οὐκ εἶχον μεθ’ ἑαυτῶν ἐν τῷ πλοίῳ. 15 καὶ διεστέλλετο

αὐτὰ εὐλογήσας W 0131 f¹ f¹³ 28 565 1195*? 1216 1230 1253 2174 Lect itᵃ,ᵃᵘʳ, ᵇ,ᶜ,ᶠ,ᶠᶠ²,ⁱ,ˡ,ʳˡ vg syrˢ,ᵖ,ʰ goth arm geo ‖ ταῦτα εὐλογήσας A K Π 1079 1195*? 1546 copˢᵃ ‖ εὐλογήσας Χ 33 700 1010 1195ᶜ 1242 1344 1365 1646 2148 Byz lˡ⁷⁶,³¹³,⁸⁸³,¹⁶⁴² ‖ εὐχαριστήσας D 1009 itᵈ,q

² 10 {B} τὰ μέρη Δαλμανουθά ℵ A (B Δαλμανουνθά) C K L X Δ Π 0131 33 700 892 1009 1010 1079 1195 1216 1230 1242 1253 1344 1365 1546 1646 2148 2174 Byz Lect itˡ,q vg syr⁽ᵖ⁾,ʰ,⁽ʰᵍʳ⁾ copˢᵃ,ᵇᵒ (arm Δαλμανοῦναι) geo¹ ‖ τὰ ὄρη Δαλμανουθά 1071ᶜ ‖ τὸ ὄρος Δαλμοῦναι W (Diatessaronᵖ Δαλμανουθά) ‖ τὰ ὄρια Δαλμανουθά 1241 itᶠ ‖ τὸ ὄρος Μαγεδά 28 (syrˢ Μαγεδάν) ‖ τὰ ὄρια Μελεγαδά Dᵍʳ* (Dʰ Μαγαδά, itᵃᵘʳ Magedan, itᶜ,ᵏ Mageda) ‖ τὰ μέρη Μαγδαλά Θ (565 Μαγεδά) f¹ f¹³ l⁸⁰ (itᵃ,ᵈ Magedan, itᵇ,ᶠᶠ²,ʳˡ Magedam, itⁱ terra Magedam) syrᵖᵃˡ goth geo²

³ 13 {C} πάλιν ἐμβάς ℵ B C L Δ itᵃᵘʳ,ᶠᶠ² vgʷʷ ‖ πάλιν ἐμβὰς εἰς τὸ πλοῖον p⁴⁵ D W (Θ 565 1071 omit τό) f¹³ 28 700 892 itᵃ,ᵈ,ⁱ,q,ʳˡ (syrˢ) arm eth geo ‖ ἐμβὰς πάλιν εἰς τὸ πλοῖον K Π 0131 (A X 33 1010 1242 1365 1646 2148 l¹⁸⁵,³¹³,⁸⁸³,¹⁶⁴² omit τό) f¹ 1009 1079 1195 1216 1230 1253 1344 1546 2174 Byz itᶠ,ˡ vgᶜˡ syrʰ copˢᵃ goth ‖ ἐμβὰς εἰς τὸ πλοῖον l²⁹⁹ itᵇ,ᶜ syrᵖ,ᵖᵃˡ copᵇᵒ ‖ εἰς τὸ πλοῖον ἀπῆλθεν πάλιν Lect (l⁷⁰ εἰσῆλθε) ‖ εἰς τὸ πλοῖον 1241

11 Mt 12.38; 16.1; Lk 11.16; Jn 6.30   12 Τί...ταύτῃ σημεῖον Mt 12.39; Lk 11.29

---

were about four thousand people. 9 Then the disciples took up seven baskets full of pieces left over. Jesus sent the people away, 10 and at once got into the boat with his disciples and went to the district of Dalmanutha.

The Pharisees Ask for a Miracle
(Also Matt. 16.1–4)

11 Some Pharisees came up and started to argue with Jesus. They wanted to trap him, so they asked him to perform a miracle to show God's approval. 12 Jesus gave a deep groan and said: "Why do the people of this day ask for a miracle? No, I tell you! No such proof will be given this people!" 13 He left them, got back into the boat, and started across to the other side of the lake.

The Yeast of the Pharisees and of Herod
(Also Matt. 16.5–12)

14 The disciples had forgotten to bring any extra bread, and had only one loaf with them in the boat. 15 "Look out,"

Jesus warned them, "and be on your guard against the yeast of the Pharisees and the yeast of Herod." 16 They started discussing among themselves: "He says this because we don't have any bread." 17 Jesus knew what they were saying, so he asked them: "Why are you discussing about not having any bread? Don't you know or understand yet? Are your minds so dull? 18 You have eyes — can't you see? You have ears — can't you hear? Don't you remember 19 when I broke the five loaves for the five thou-

αὐτοῖς λέγων, Ὁρᾶτε, βλέπετε[4] ἀπὸ τῆς ζύμης τῶν Φαρισαίων καὶ τῆς ζύμης Ἡρῴδου[5]. 16 καὶ διελογίζοντο πρὸς ἀλλήλους[6] ὅτι[a] "Ἄρτους οὐκ ἔχομεν[7]. 17 καὶ γνοὺς λέγει αὐτοῖς, Τί διαλογίζεσθε ὅτι ἄρτους οὐκ ἔχετε; οὔπω νοεῖτε οὐδὲ συνίετε; πεπωρωμένην ἔχετε τὴν καρδίαν ὑμῶν[8]; 18 **ὀφθαλμοὺς ἔχοντες οὐ βλέπετε καὶ ὦτα ἔχοντες οὐκ ἀκούετε;**[b] καὶ οὐ μνημονεύετε,[b] 19 ὅτε τοὺς πέντε

---

[4] **15** {C} ὁρᾶτε, βλέπετε ℵ A B K L W X Π 33 892 1009 1010 1071 1079 1195 1241 1242 1344 1365 1546 1646 2148 *Byz Lect* vg^ww syr^(p),h cop^bomss Diatessaron^a ‖ ὁρᾶτε καὶ βλέπετε 𝔭^45 C 0131 f^13 28 1216 1230 1253 2174 it^aur,c,f,l vg^cl cop^sa,bo goth Diatessaron ‖ βλέπετε D^gr Θ f^1 565 syr^s arm geo Diatessaron^p ‖ ὁρᾶτε Δ 700 ‖ *videte* it^b,d,ff2,i,q,rl ‖ *cavete* it^a,k

[5] **15** {A} Ἡρῴδου ℵ A B C D K L X Π 0131 33 700 892 1009 1010 1071 1079 1195 1216 1230 1241 1242 1253 1344 1546 1646 2148 2174 *Byz Lect* it^a,aur,b,c,d,f,ff2,l,q,rl vg syr^s,p,h cop^bo goth eth Diatessaron^a,p ‖ τῶν Ἡρῳδιανῶν (see 3.6) 𝔭^45 W Δ Θ f^1 f^13 28 565 1365 it^i,k cop^sa arm geo

[6] **16** {C} πρὸς ἀλλήλους 𝔭^45 ℵ B D W f^1 28 565 700 it^a,b,(c),d,ff2,i,q cop^sa geo ‖ πρὸς ἀλλήλους λέγοντες (see Mt 16.7) A C K L X Δ Θ Π 0131 f^13 33 892 1009 1010 1079 1195 1216 1230 1241 1242 1253 1344 1365 1546 1646 2148 2174 *Byz Lect* it^aur,f,l vg syr^(s,p),h cop^bo goth arm eth ‖ ἐν ἑαυτοῖς λέγοντες (see Mt 16.7) 1071

[7] **16** {C} ἔχομεν ℵ A C L X Δ Θ Π (K 1009 1344 2174 ἔχωμεν) f^13 33 892 1010 1071 1079 1195 1216 1230 1241 1242 1253 1365 1546 1646 2148 *Byz Lect* it^aur,f,l vg syr^s?p,h cop^bomss goth arm eth geo Diatessaron^p,t ‖ ἔχουσιν 𝔭^45 B W f^1 28 565 700 it^k syr^s? cop^sa,bo ‖ εἶχον D it^a,b,c,d,ff2,i,q,rl ‖ ἐλάβομεν (see Mt 16.7) 579 1396 1424

[8] **17** {B} πεπωρωμένην ἔχετε τὴν καρδίαν ὑμῶν 𝔭^45 ℵ B C L W Δ f^1 f^13 (28 ἔχοντες) 33 892* 1009 1195 1241 arm eth geo^2 ‖ πεπωρωμένη ἐστὶν ἡ καρδία ὑμῶν 0143^vid (D* πεπηρωμένη) D^c it^a,(b,c,d,ff2,i) syr^s cop^sa,bo geo^1 ‖ πεπωρωμένη ὑμῶν ἐστιν ἡ καρδία Θ 565 ‖ ἔτι πεπωρωμένην ἔχετε τὴν καρδίαν ὑμῶν A K X Π 700 892^c 1010 1071 1079 1216 (1242 τὴν καρδίαν ὑμῶν ἔχετε) 1344 1365 1546 (1646 *omit* ὑμῶν) 2148 2174 *Byz Lect* (l^70,1579 *omit* ὑμῶν) it^(aur),f,l,(q) vg syr^(p),h ‖ ὅτι πεπωρωμένην ἔχετε τὴν καρδίαν ὑμῶν 047 1230 1253 goth ‖ *omit* 245

---

[a] **16** *a direct:* TR? RV ASV RSV Luth? ‖ *a causal:* TR? AV RV^mg ASV^mg NEB Zür Luth? Seg^mg ‖ *different text:* WH Bov Nes BF² RV^mg ASV^mg TT Jer Seg

[b b] **18** *b question, b minor:* (WH) Bov Nes BF² TT Zür Luth Jer Seg ‖ *b minor, b question:* TR ‖ *b question, b question:* AV RV ASV RSV NEB

---

15 βλέπετε...Φαρισαίων Lk 12.1   **17** Τί διαλογίζεσθε...ὑμῶν Mk 6.52   **18** ὀφθαλμοὺς ...ἀκούετε Jr 5.21; Eze 12.2; Mk 4.12; Ac 28.26   **19** Mt 14.15–21; Mk 6.35–44; Lk 9.12–17; Jn 6.5–13

ἄρτους ἔκλασα εἰς τοὺς πεντακισχιλίους, πόσους κοφίνους κλασμάτων πλήρεις ἤρατε; λέγουσιν αὐτῷ, Δώδεκα. **20** Ὅτε τοὺς ἑπτὰ εἰς τοὺς τετρακισχιλίους, πόσων σπυρίδων πληρώματα κλασμάτων ἤρατε; καὶ λέγουσιν [αὐτῷ], Ἑπτά. **21** καὶ ἔλεγεν αὐτοῖς, Οὔπω συνίετε;

The Healing of a Blind Man at Bethsaida

22 Καὶ ἔρχονται εἰς Βηθσαϊδάν. καὶ φέρουσιν αὐτῷ τυφλὸν καὶ παρακαλοῦσιν αὐτὸν ἵνα αὐτοῦ ἅψηται. **23** καὶ ἐπιλαβόμενος τῆς χειρὸς τοῦ τυφλοῦ ἐξήνεγκεν αὐτὸν ἔξω τῆς κώμης, καὶ πτύσας εἰς τὰ ὄμματα αὐτοῦ, ἐπιθεὶς τὰς χεῖρας αὐτῷ, ἐπηρώτα αὐτόν, Εἴ τι βλέπεις; **24** καὶ ἀναβλέψας ἔλεγεν, Βλέπω τοὺς ἀνθρώπους, ὅτι ὡς δένδρα ὁρῶ περιπατοῦντας. **25** εἶτα πάλιν ἐπέθηκεν τὰς χεῖρας ἐπὶ τοὺς ὀφθαλμοὺς αὐτοῦ, καὶ διέβλεψεν, καὶ ἀπεκατέστη, καὶ ἐνέβλεπεν τηλαυγῶς ἅπαντα. **26** καὶ ἀπέστειλεν αὐτὸν εἰς οἶκον αὐτοῦ λέγων, Μηδὲ εἰς τὴν κώμην εἰσέλθῃς[9].

Peter's Declaration about Jesus
(Mt 16.13–20; Lk 9.18–21)

27 Καὶ ἐξῆλθεν ὁ Ἰησοῦς καὶ οἱ μαθηταὶ αὐτοῦ εἰς τὰς κώμας Καισαρείας τῆς Φιλίππου· καὶ ἐν τῇ ὁδῷ ἐπηρώτα

---

[9] **26** {B} μηδὲ εἰς τὴν κώμην εἰσέλθῃς (ℵ* W μή) ℵᶜ B L f¹ syrˢ copˢᵃ,ᵇᵒ,ᶠᵃʸ geo¹ ‖ μηδενὶ εἴπῃς εἰς τὴν κώμην itᵏ ‖ μηδὲ εἰς τὴν κώμην εἰσέλθῃς μηδὲ εἴπῃς τινὶ ἐν τῇ κώμῃ A C K X Δ Π 33 700 (892 τινὶ τῶν ἐν τῇ κώμῃ) 1009 1010 1071 1079 1195 1230 1241 1242 1253 1344 1365 (1546 ἐν τῇ πόλει) 1646 2148 *Byz Lect* syrᵖ,ʰ copᵇᵒᵐˢˢ goth eth Diatessaronᵃ,⁽ᵖ⁾ ‖ ὕπαγε εἰς τὸν οἶκόν σου καὶ μηδενὶ εἴπῃς εἰς τὴν κώμην (see 2.11; 5.19) D it⁽ᶜ⁾,ᵈ,⁽ᑫ⁾ ‖ ὕπαγε εἰς τὸν οἶκόν σου καὶ ἐὰν εἰς τὴν κώμην εἰσέλθῃς μηδενὶ εἴπῃς μηδὲ ἐν τῇ κώμῃ (Θ *omit* τόν *and* μηδέ) f¹³ (28 *omit* τόν *and read* μηδενὶ μηδὲν εἴπῃς) (565 *omit* μηδέ) (1216 2174 ἐὰν εἰσέλθῃς εἰς τὴν κώμην μηδενὶ μηδὲν εἴπῃς ἐν τῇ κώμῃ) (arm) geoᴬ ‖ ὕπαγε εἰς τὸν οἶκόν σου καὶ ἐὰν εἰς τὴν κώμην εἰσέλθῃς μηδενὶ εἴπῃς it⁽ᵃ⁾,ᵃᵘʳ,ᵇ,ᶠ,⁽ᶠᶠ²⁾,⁽ⁱ⁾,ˡ vg geoᴮ ‖ ὕπαγε εἰς τὸν οἶκόν σου καὶ μηδὲ εἰς τὴν κώμην εἰσέλθῃς μηδὲ εἴπῃς τινὶ ἐν τῇ κώμῃ 124 ‖ καὶ ἐὰν εἰς τὴν κώμην εἰσέλθῃς μηδενὶ εἴπῃς ἐν τῇ κώμῃ syrʰᵐᵍ

20 Mt 15.32–38; Mk 8.1–9   **22–23** φέρουσιν…αὐτῷ Mk 7.32–33   **23** πτύσας…αὐτοῦ Jn 9.6

---

sand people? How many baskets full of leftover pieces did you take up?" "Twelve," they answered. **20** "And when I broke the seven loaves for the four thousand people," asked Jesus, "how many baskets full of leftover pieces did you take up?" "Seven," they answered. **21** "And you still don't understand?" he asked them.

Jesus Heals a Blind Man at Bethsaida

22 They came to Bethsaida, where some people brought a blind man to Jesus and begged him to touch him. **23** Jesus took the blind man by the hand and led him out of the village. After spitting on the man's eyes, Jesus placed his hands on him and asked him, "Can you see anything?" **24** The man looked up and said, "I can see men, but they look like trees walking around." **25** Jesus again placed his hands on the man's eyes. This time the man looked hard, his eyesight came back, and he saw everything clearly. **26** Jesus then sent him home with the order, "Don't go back into the village."

Peter's Declaration about Jesus
(Also Matt. 16.13–20; Luke 9.18–21)

27 Then Jesus and his disciples went away to the villages of Caesarea Philippi.

On the way he asked them, "Tell me, who do people say I am?" 28 "Some say that you are John the Baptist," they answered; "others say that you are Elijah, while others say that you are one of the prophets." 29 "What about you?" he asked them. "Who do you say I am?" Peter answered, "You are the Messiah." 30 Then Jesus ordered them, "Do not tell anyone about me."

Jesus Speaks about His Suffering and Death
(Also Matt. 16.21–28; Luke 9.22–27)

31 Then Jesus began to teach his disciples: "The Son of Man must suffer much, and be rejected by the elders, the chief priests, and the teachers of the Law. He will be put to death, and after three days he will be raised to life." 32 He made this very clear to them. So Peter took him aside and began to rebuke him. 33 But Jesus turned around, looked at his disciples, and rebuked Peter. "Get away from me, Satan," he said. "Your thoughts are men's thoughts, not God's!"

34 Then Jesus called the crowd and his disciples to him. "If anyone wants to come with me," he told them, "he must forget himself, carry his cross, and follow me. 35 For the man who wants to save his own life will lose it; but the man who loses his life for me and for the gospel will save it. 36 Does a man gain anything if he wins the whole world but loses his life? Of course not! 37 There is nothing a man can give to regain life. 38 If, then, a man is ashamed of me and of my teaching in this godless and wicked day, then the Son of Man will be ashamed of him when he comes

τοὺς μαθητὰς αὐτοῦ λέγων αὐτοῖς, Τίνα με λέγουσιν οἱ ἄνθρωποι εἶναι; 28 οἱ δὲ εἶπαν αὐτῷ λέγοντες [ὅτι] Ἰωάννην τὸν βαπτιστήν, καὶ ἄλλοι, Ἠλίαν, ἄλλοι δὲ ὅτι εἷς τῶν προφητῶν. 29 καὶ αὐτὸς ἐπηρώτα αὐτούς, Ὑμεῖς δὲ τίνα με λέγετε εἶναι; ἀποκριθεὶς ὁ Πέτρος λέγει αὐτῷ, Σὺ εἶ ὁ Χριστός. 30 καὶ ἐπετίμησεν αὐτοῖς ἵνα μηδενὶ λέγωσιν περὶ αὐτοῦ.

Jesus Foretells His Death and Resurrection
(Mt 16.21–28; Lk 9.22–27)

31 Καὶ ἤρξατο διδάσκειν αὐτοὺς ὅτι δεῖ τὸν υἱὸν τοῦ ἀνθρώπου πολλὰ παθεῖν καὶ ἀποδοκιμασθῆναι ὑπὸ τῶν πρεσβυτέρων καὶ τῶν ἀρχιερέων καὶ τῶν γραμματέων καὶ ἀποκτανθῆναι καὶ μετὰ τρεῖς ἡμέρας ἀναστῆναι· 32 καὶ παρρησίᾳ τὸν λόγον ἐλάλει. καὶ προσλαβόμενος ὁ Πέτρος αὐτὸν ἤρξατο ἐπιτιμᾶν αὐτῷ. 33 ὁ δὲ ἐπιστραφεὶς καὶ ἰδὼν τοὺς μαθητὰς αὐτοῦ ἐπετίμησεν Πέτρῳ καὶ λέγει, Ὕπαγε ὀπίσω μου, Σατανᾶ, ὅτι οὐ φρονεῖς τὰ τοῦ θεοῦ ἀλλὰ τὰ τῶν ἀνθρώπων. 34 Καὶ προσκαλεσάμενος τὸν ὄχλον σὺν τοῖς μαθηταῖς αὐτοῦ εἶπεν αὐτοῖς, Εἴ τις θέλει ὀπίσω μου ἐλθεῖν, ἀπαρνησάσθω ἑαυτὸν καὶ ἀράτω τὸν σταυρὸν αὐτοῦ καὶ ἀκολουθείτω μοι. 35 ὃς γὰρ ἐὰν θέλῃ τὴν ψυχὴν αὐτοῦ σῶσαι ἀπολέσει αὐτήν· ὃς δ' ἂν ἀπολέσει τὴν ψυχὴν αὐτοῦ ἕνεκεν [ἐμοῦ καὶ][10] τοῦ εὐαγγελίου σώσει αὐτήν. 36 τί γὰρ ὠφελεῖ ἄνθρωπον κερδῆσαι τὸν κόσμον ὅλον καὶ ζημιωθῆναι τὴν ψυχὴν αὐτοῦ; 37 τί γὰρ δοῖ ἄνθρωπος ἀντάλλαγμα τῆς ψυχῆς αὐτοῦ; 38 ὃς γὰρ ἐὰν ἐπαισχυνθῇ με καὶ τοὺς ἐμοὺς λόγους[11] ἐν τῇ

---

[10] 35 {C} ἐμοῦ καί א A B C K L W X (Δ ἐμοῦ ἤ) Θ Π 0214 f¹ f¹³ 565 892 1009 1010 1071 1079 1195 1216 1230 1241 1242 1253 1344 1365 1546 1646 2148 2174 Byz Lect l185ˢ·ᵐ,211ˢ·ᵐ,333ˢ·ᵐ,883ˢ·ᵐ itaur,c,f,l,q vg syrp,h,pal copsa,bo goth geo Diatessarona,p Basil ∥ ἐμοῦ 33 itff² syrˢ copfay ∥ omit 𝔭⁴⁵ D 28 700 ita,b,d,i,(k),n,r¹ arm eth Origen

[11] 38 {B} λόγους (see Lk 9.26) א A B C D K L X Δ Θ Π f¹ f¹³ 28 33 565

28 Mk 6.14–15; Lk 9.7–8   29 Σὺ...Χριστός Jn 6.69 mg   30 Mk 9.9   31 δεῖ... ἀποκτανθῆναι Mt 17.12; Mk 9.12; Lk 17.25   34 Εἴ τις θέλει...μοι Mt 10.38; Lk 14.27   35 Mt 10.39; Lk 17.33; Jn 12.25   38 Mt 10.33; Lk 12.9

8.29   Since this is preceeded by all Mrks miracles, Messiah = Θεῖος ἀνήρ
Peter rebuked not because he call Christ the Θεῖος ἀνήρ Messiah, but because he denied the Suffering Messiah

γενεᾷ ταύτῃ τῇ μοιχαλίδι καὶ ἁμαρτωλῷ, καὶ ὁ υἱὸς τοῦ ἀνθρώπου ἐπαισχυνθήσεται αὐτὸν ὅταν ἔλθῃ ἐν τῇ δόξῃ τοῦ πατρὸς αὐτοῦ μετὰ[12] τῶν ἀγγέλων τῶν ἁγίων. **9** Καὶ ἔλεγεν αὐτοῖς, Ἀμὴν λέγω ὑμῖν ὅτι εἰσίν τινες ὧδε τῶν ἑστηκότων οἵτινες οὐ μὴ γεύσωνται θανάτου ἕως ἂν ἴδωσιν τὴν βασιλείαν τοῦ θεοῦ ἐληλυθυῖαν ἐν δυνάμει.

The Transfiguration of Jesus
(Mt 17.1–13; Lk 9.28–36)

2 Καὶ μετὰ ἡμέρας ἓξ παραλαμβάνει ὁ Ἰησοῦς τὸν Πέτρον καὶ τὸν Ἰάκωβον καὶ τὸν Ἰωάννην, καὶ ἀναφέρει αὐτοὺς εἰς ὄρος ὑψηλὸν κατ' ἰδίαν μόνους. καὶ μετεμορφώθη ἔμπροσθεν αὐτῶν, 3 καὶ τὰ ἱμάτια αὐτοῦ ἐγένετο στίλβοντα λευκὰ λίαν οἷα γναφεὺς ἐπὶ τῆς γῆς οὐ δύναται οὕτως λευκᾶναι. 4 καὶ ὤφθη αὐτοῖς Ἠλίας σὺν Μωϋσεῖ, καὶ ἦσαν συλλαλοῦντες τῷ Ἰησοῦ. 5 καὶ ἀποκριθεὶς ὁ Πέτρος λέγει τῷ Ἰησοῦ, Ῥαββί, καλόν ἐστιν ἡμᾶς ὧδε εἶναι, καὶ ποιήσωμεν τρεῖς σκηνάς, σοὶ μίαν καὶ Μωϋσεῖ μίαν καὶ Ἠλίᾳ μίαν. 6 οὐ γὰρ ᾔδει τί ἀποκριθῇ, ἔκφοβοι γὰρ ἐγένοντο. 7 καὶ ἐγένετο νεφέλη ἐπισκιάζουσα αὐτοῖς, καὶ ἐγένετο φωνὴ ἐκ τῆς νεφέλης, Οὗτός ἐστιν ὁ υἱός μου ὁ ἀγαπητός, ἀκούετε αὐτοῦ. 8 καὶ ἐξάπινα περιβλεψάμενοι οὐκέτι οὐδένα εἶδον ἀλλὰ τὸν Ἰησοῦν μόνον μεθ' ἑαυτῶν.

---

700 892 1009 1010 1071 1079 1195 1216 1230 1241 1242 1253 1344 1365 1546 1646 2148 2174 *Byz Lect* *l*883s, m it^{a,aur,b,c,d,f,ff2,i,l,n,q,r1} vg syr^{s,p,h,pal} cop^{bo,fay} goth arm geo Diatessaron^a Clement Origen Cyril ‖ *omit* 𝔭^{45vid} W it^k cop^{sa} Tertullian

12 38 {B} μετά ℵ A B C D K L X Δ Θ Π *f*¹ *f*¹³ 28 33 565 700 892 1009 1010 1071 1079 1195 1216 1230 1241 1242 1253 1344 1365 1546 1646 2148 2174 *Byz Lect* *l*883s, m it^{a,aur,b,c,d,f,ff2,i,k,l,n,q,r1} vg syr^{p,h,pal} cop^{sa?bo?} goth geo ‖ καί 𝔭⁴⁵ W syr^s cop^{fay} arm

---

1 εἰσίν...ἐληλυθυῖαν Mk 13.30   2–8 2 Pe 1.17–18   2 Πέτρον...Ἰωάννην Mt 10.2; Mk 1.29; 3.16–17; 5.37; 13.3; 14.33; Lk 5.10; 6.14; 8.51; Ac 1.13   7 Οὗτος...ἀγαπητός Ps 2.7; Mt 3.17; 12.18; Mk 1.11; Lk 3.22; 2 Pe 1.17   ἀκούετε αὐτοῦ Dt 18.15; Ac 3.22

9 in the glory of his Father with the holy angels." And he went on to say: "Remember this! There are some here who will not die until they have seen the Kingdom of God come with power."

The Transfiguration
(Also Matt. 17.1–13; Luke 9.28–36)

2 Six days later Jesus took Peter, James, and John with him, and led them up a high mountain by themselves. As they looked on, a change came over him, 3 and his clothes became very shining and white; nobody in the world could clean them as white. 4 Then the three disciples saw Elijah and Moses, who were talking with Jesus. 5 Peter spoke up and said to Jesus: "Teacher, it is a good thing that we are here. We will make three tents, one for you, one for Moses, and one for Elijah." 6 He and the others were so frightened that he did not know what to say. 7 A cloud appeared and covered them with its shadow, and a voice came from the cloud: "This is my own dear Son — listen to him!" 8 They took a quick look around but did not see anybody else; only Jesus was with them.

9 As they came down the mountain Jesus ordered them: "Don't tell anyone what you have seen, until the Son of Man has been raised from death." 10 They obeyed his order, but among themselves they started discussing the matter: "What does this 'rising from death' mean?" 11 And they asked Jesus: "Why do the teachers of the Law say that Elijah has to come first?" 12 His answer was: "Elijah does indeed come first to get everything ready. Yet why do the Scriptures say that the Son of Man will suffer much and be rejected? 13 I tell you, however, that Elijah has already come, and that people did to him all they wanted to, just as the Scriptures say about him."

Jesus Heals a Boy with an Evil Spirit
(Also Matt. 17.14–21; Luke 9.37–43a)

14 When they joined the rest of the disciples, they saw a large crowd there. Some teachers of the Law were arguing with the disciples. 15 As soon as the people saw Jesus, they were greatly surprised and ran to him and greeted him. 16 Jesus asked his disciples, "What are you arguing with them about?" 17 A man in the crowd answered: "Teacher, I brought my son to you, because he has an evil spirit in him and cannot talk. 18 Whenever the spirit attacks him, it throws him to the ground, and he foams at the mouth, grits his teeth, and becomes stiff all over. I asked your disciples to drive the spirit out, but they could not." 19 Jesus said to them: "How unbelieving you people are! How long must I stay with you? How long do I have to put up with you? Bring the boy to me!" 20 And they brought him to Jesus. As soon as the spirit saw Jesus, it threw the boy into a fit, so that he fell on the ground and rolled around, foaming at the mouth. 21 "How long has he

9 Καὶ καταβαινόντων αὐτῶν ἐκ τοῦ ὄρους διεστείλατο αὐτοῖς ἵνα μηδενὶ ἃ εἶδον διηγήσωνται, εἰ μὴ ὅταν ὁ υἱὸς τοῦ ἀνθρώπου ἐκ νεκρῶν ἀναστῇ. 10 καὶ τὸν λόγον ἐκράτησαν[a] πρὸς ἑαυτοὺς[a] συζητοῦντες τί ἐστιν τὸ ἐκ νεκρῶν ἀναστῆναι. 11 καὶ ἐπηρώτων αὐτὸν λέγοντες, Ὅτι[b] λέγουσιν οἱ γραμματεῖς ὅτι Ἠλίαν δεῖ ἐλθεῖν πρῶτον;[b] 12 ὁ δὲ ἔφη αὐτοῖς, Ἠλίας μὲν ἐλθὼν πρῶτον ἀποκαθιστάνει πάντα, καὶ πῶς γέγραπται ἐπὶ τὸν υἱὸν τοῦ ἀνθρώπου ἵνα πολλὰ πάθῃ καὶ ἐξουδενηθῇ; 13 ἀλλὰ λέγω ὑμῖν ὅτι καὶ Ἠλίας ἐλήλυθεν, καὶ ἐποίησαν αὐτῷ ὅσα ἤθελον, καθὼς γέγραπται ἐπ' αὐτόν.

The Healing of a Boy with an Unclean Spirit
(Mt 17.14–20; Lk 9.37–43a)

14 Καὶ ἐλθόντες πρὸς τοὺς μαθητὰς εἶδον ὄχλον πολὺν περὶ αὐτοὺς καὶ γραμματεῖς συζητοῦντας πρὸς αὐτούς. 15 καὶ εὐθὺς πᾶς ὁ ὄχλος ἰδόντες αὐτὸν ἐξεθαμβήθησαν, καὶ προστρέχοντες ἠσπάζοντο αὐτόν. 16 καὶ ἐπηρώτησεν αὐτούς, Τί συζητεῖτε πρὸς αὐτούς; 17 καὶ ἀπεκρίθη αὐτῷ εἷς ἐκ τοῦ ὄχλου, Διδάσκαλε, ἤνεγκα τὸν υἱόν μου πρὸς σέ, ἔχοντα πνεῦμα ἄλαλον· 18 καὶ ὅπου ἐὰν αὐτὸν καταλάβῃ ῥήσσει αὐτόν, καὶ ἀφρίζει καὶ τρίζει τοὺς ὀδόντας καὶ ξηραίνεται· καὶ εἶπα τοῖς μαθηταῖς σου ἵνα αὐτὸ ἐκβάλωσιν, καὶ οὐκ ἴσχυσαν. 19 ὁ δὲ ἀποκριθεὶς αὐτοῖς λέγει, Ὦ γενεὰ ἄπιστος, ἕως πότε πρὸς ὑμᾶς ἔσομαι; ἕως πότε ἀνέξομαι ὑμῶν; φέρετε αὐτὸν πρός με. 20 καὶ ἤνεγκαν αὐτὸν πρὸς αὐτόν. καὶ ἰδὼν αὐτὸν τὸ πνεῦμα εὐθὺς συνεσπάραξεν αὐτόν, καὶ πεσὼν ἐπὶ τῆς γῆς ἐκυλίετο ἀφρίζων. 21 καὶ ἐπηρώτησεν τὸν πατέρα αὐτοῦ, Πόσος χρόνος ἐστὶν ὡς τοῦτο γέγονεν αὐτῷ; ὁ δὲ εἶπεν,

---

    a a **10** *a* none, *a* none: WH Bov Nes BF² ‖ *a* none, *a* minor: TR (AV^ed) RSV ‖ *a* minor, *a* none: (AV^ed) RV ASV NEB TT (Zür) (Luth) Jer Seg

    b b **11** *b* interrogative, *b* question: TR WH Bov Nes BF² AV RV^mg ASV RSV NEB TT Zür Jer Seg ‖ *b* direct, *b* statement: RV ASV^mg Luth

    9 διεστείλατο...διηγήσωνται Mt 12.16; Mk 8.30   **11–12** λέγουσιν...πάντα Mal 4.5–6   **12** γέγραπται...ἐξουδενηθῇ Ps 22.1–18; Is 53.3   **13** Ἠλίας ἐλήλυθεν Mt 11.14

'Εκ παιδιόθεν· 22 καὶ πολλάκις καὶ εἰς πῦρ αὐτὸν ἔβαλεν καὶ εἰς ὕδατα ἵνα ἀπολέσῃ αὐτόν· ἀλλ' εἴ τι δύνῃ, βοήθησον ἡμῖν σπλαγχνισθεὶς ἐφ' ἡμᾶς. 23 ὁ δὲ Ἰησοῦς εἶπεν αὐτῷ, Τὸ Εἰ δύνῃ[1] — πάντα δυνατὰ τῷ πιστεύοντι. 24 εὐθὺς κράξας ὁ πατὴρ τοῦ παιδίου[2] ἔλεγεν, Πιστεύω· βοήθει μου τῇ ἀπιστίᾳ. 25 ἰδὼν δὲ ὁ Ἰησοῦς ὅτι ἐπισυντρέχει ὄχλος ἐπετίμησεν τῷ πνεύματι τῷ ἀκαθάρτῳ λέγων αὐτῷ, Τὸ ἄλαλον καὶ κωφὸν πνεῦμα, ἐγὼ ἐπιτάσσω σοι, ἔξελθε ἐξ αὐτοῦ καὶ μηκέτι εἰσέλθῃς εἰς αὐτόν. 26 καὶ κράξας καὶ πολλὰ σπαράξας ἐξῆλθεν· καὶ ἐγένετο ὡσεὶ νεκρός, ὥστε τοὺς πολλοὺς λέγειν ὅτι ἀπέθανεν. 27 ὁ δὲ Ἰησοῦς κρατήσας τῆς χειρὸς αὐτοῦ ἤγειρεν αὐτόν, καὶ ἀνέστη. 28 καὶ εἰσελθόντος αὐτοῦ εἰς οἶκον οἱ μαθηταὶ αὐτοῦ κατ' ἰδίαν ἐπηρώτων αὐτόν, Ὅτι[c] ἡμεῖς οὐκ ἠδυνήθημεν ἐκβαλεῖν αὐτό;[c] 29 καὶ εἶπεν αὐτοῖς, Τοῦτο τὸ γένος ἐν οὐδενὶ δύναται ἐξελθεῖν εἰ μὴ ἐν προσευχῇ[3].

---

[1] **23** {B} τὸ εἰ δύνῃ (p45 *omit* τό) א* (אc C* L δύνασαι) B (W τοῦτο) Δ f1 892 (itk geo17 *omit* τό) copsa?bo? arm eth geo2 ‖ εἰ δύνασαι πιστεῦσαι Κ Π (D Θ 28 565 δύνῃ) f13 700c 1009 1010 1071 1079 1195* 1216 1253 1546 2174 l60,185,1627 (l547?847? δύνῃ) itaur,b,c,d,f,i,l,q vg syrp,h,pal (Diatessarona) ‖ τὸ εἰ δύνασαι πιστεῦσαι A (C3vid πιστεύσει) Χ Ψ 33 700* 1195c 1230 1241 1242 1344 1365 1646 2148 *Byz Lect* (l70,950 τῷ [sic] εἰ δύνασε πιστεῦσε) goth ‖ *if you believe* syrs ‖ *Quid est, si quid potes? Si potes credere* ita

[2] **24** {A} παιδίου p45 א A* B C* L (W) Δ Ψ 28 700 1216 itk syrs copsa,bo arm eth geo ‖ παιδίου μετὰ δακρύων A2 C3 D K Χ Θ Π (f1 παιδός) f13 33 565 892 1009 1010 1071 1079 1195 1241 1242 (1253 παιδός, *with* μετὰ δακρύων *before* ὁ πατήρ) 1344 1365 1546 1646 2148 (1230 2174 l547 μετὰ δακρύων *before* ὁ πατήρ) *Byz Lect* ita,(aur),c,d,f,l,rl vg syrp,h,pal copbomss goth Diatessarona,p ‖ μετὰ δακρύων (*and omit* τοῦ) l547 itb,i,q

[3] **29** {A} προσευχῇ א* B itk geo1 Clement ‖ προσευχῇ καὶ νηστείᾳ (*see* 1 Cor 7.5 mg) p45vid אb A C D K L W Χ Δ Θ Π Ψ f1 f13 28 33 565 700 892 1009 1010 1071 1079 1195 1216 1230 1241 1242 1253 1344 1365 1546 1646 2148 2174 *Byz Lect* ita,aur,b,c,d,f,ff2,i,l,q,rl vg syrh copsa,bo goth geo

c c **28** c interrogative, c question: TR WH Bov Nes BF2 AV RVmg ASV RSV NEB TT Zür Luth Jer Seg ‖ c direct, c statement: RV ASVmg

23 πάντα...πιστεύοντι Mt 21.21; Mk 11.23-24; Lk 17.6   **24** βοήθει...ἀπιστίᾳ Lk 17.5   **26** κράξας...ἐξῆλθεν Mk 1.26   **27** Mt 9.25; Mk 1.31; 5.41; Lk 8.54; Ac 3.7

been like this?" Jesus asked the father. "Ever since he was a child," he replied. 22 "Many times it has tried to kill him by throwing him in the fire and in the water. Have pity on us and help us, if you possibly can!" 23 "Yes," said Jesus, "if *you* can! Everything is possible for the person who has faith." 24 The father at once cried out, "I do have faith, but not enough. Help me!"

25 Jesus noticed that the crowd was closing in on them, so he gave a command to the evil spirit. "Deaf and dumb spirit," he said, "I order you to come out of the boy and never go into him again!" 26 With a scream the spirit threw the boy into a bad fit and came out. The boy looked like a corpse, so that everybody said, "He is dead!" 27 But Jesus took the boy by the hand and helped him rise, and he stood up.

28 After Jesus had gone indoors, his disciples asked him privately: "Why couldn't we drive the spirit out?" 29 "Only prayer can drive this kind out," answered Jesus; "nothing else can."

Jesus Speaks again about His Death
(Also Matt. 17.22–23; Luke 9.43b–45)

30 They left that place and went on through Galilee. Jesus did not want anyone to know where he was, 31 because he was teaching his disciples: "The Son of Man will be handed over to men who will kill him; three days later, however, he will be raised to life." 32 They did not understand what this teaching meant, but they were afraid to ask him.

Who Is the Greatest?
(Also Matt. 18.1–5; Luke 9.46–48)

33 They came to Capernaum, and after going indoors Jesus asked his disciples: "What were you arguing about on the road?" 34 But they would not answer him, because on the road they had been arguing among themselves about who was the greatest. 35 Jesus sat down, called the twelve disciples and said to them: "Whoever wants to be first must place himself last of all and be the servant of all." 36 He took a child and made him stand in front of them. Then he put his arms around him and said to them, 37 "The person who in my name welcomes one of these children, welcomes me; and whoever welcomes me, welcomes not only me but also the one who sent me."

Who Is not against Us Is for Us
(Also Luke 9.49–50)

38 John said to him, "Teacher, we saw a man who was driving out demons in your name, and we told him to stop,

Jesus Again Foretells His Death and Resurrection
(Mt 17.22–23; Lk 9.43b–45)

30 Κἀκεῖθεν ἐξελθόντες παρεπορεύοντο διὰ τῆς Γαλιλαίας, καὶ οὐκ ἤθελεν ἵνα τις γνοῖ· 31 ἐδίδασκεν γὰρ τοὺς μαθητὰς αὐτοῦ καὶ ἔλεγεν αὐτοῖς ὅτι Ὁ υἱὸς τοῦ ἀνθρώπου παραδίδοται εἰς χεῖρας ἀνθρώπων, καὶ ἀποκτενοῦσιν αὐτόν, καὶ ἀποκτανθεὶς μετὰ τρεῖς ἡμέρας ἀναστήσεται. 32 οἱ δὲ ἠγνόουν τὸ ῥῆμα, καὶ ἐφοβοῦντο αὐτὸν ἐπερωτῆσαι.

Who is the Greatest?
(Mt 18.1–5; Lk 9.46–48)

33 Καὶ ἦλθον εἰς Καφαρναούμ. καὶ ἐν τῇ οἰκίᾳ γενόμενος ἐπηρώτα αὐτούς, Τί ἐν τῇ ὁδῷ διελογίζεσθε; 34 οἱ δὲ ἐσιώπων, πρὸς ἀλλήλους γὰρ διελέχθησαν ἐν τῇ ὁδῷ[4] τίς μείζων. 35 καὶ καθίσας ἐφώνησεν τοὺς δώδεκα καὶ λέγει αὐτοῖς, Εἴ τις θέλει πρῶτος εἶναι ἔσται πάντων ἔσχατος καὶ πάντων διάκονος. 36 καὶ λαβὼν παιδίον ἔστησεν αὐτὸ ἐν μέσῳ αὐτῶν καὶ ἐναγκαλισάμενος αὐτὸ εἶπεν αὐτοῖς, 37 Ὃς ἂν ἓν τῶν τοιούτων παιδίων δέξηται ἐπὶ τῷ ὀνόματί μου, ἐμὲ δέχεται· καὶ ὃς ἂν ἐμὲ δέχηται, οὐκ ἐμὲ δέχεται ἀλλὰ τὸν ἀποστείλαντά με.

He Who is Not against Us is for Us
(Lk 9.49–50)

38 Ἔφη αὐτῷ ὁ Ἰωάννης, Διδάσκαλε, εἴδομέν τινα ἐν τῷ ὀνόματί σου ἐκβάλλοντα δαιμόνια, καὶ ἐκωλύομεν

Diatessaron[a,p] Basil ‖ νηστείᾳ καὶ προσευχῇ (see 1 Cor 7.5 mg) syr[s,p,pal] cop[bo ms] arm eth

[4] 34 {B} ἐν τῇ ὁδῷ ℵ B C K L W X Θ Π Ψ f[1] f[13] 28 565 700 892 1009 1010 1071 1195 1216 1230 1241 1242 1253 1344 1365 1646 2148 2174 Byz Lect it[aur,c,ff2,k,l] vg syr[p,h,pal] cop[sa,bo,fay] arm eth geo[2] Diatessaron[p] Origen ‖ omit A D Δ 1079 1546 it[a,b,d,f,i,q,r1] syr[s] goth geo[1] Diatessaron[a,n,t]

31 Ὁ...ἀναστήσεται Mt 16.21; 20.18–19; Mk 8.31; 10.33–34; Lk 18.32–33; 24.7   34 πρὸς... μείζων Lk 22.24   35 Εἰ...διάκονος Mt 20.26–27; 23.11; Mk 10.43–44; Lk 22.26   37 Ὃς... παιδίων δέξηται...με Mt 10.40; Lk 10.16; Jn 13.20

αὐτόν, ὅτι οὐκ ἠκολούθει ἡμῖν[5]. **39** ὁ δὲ Ἰησοῦς εἶπεν, Μὴ κωλύετε αὐτόν, οὐδεὶς γάρ ἐστιν ὃς ποιήσει δύναμιν ἐπὶ τῷ ὀνόματί μου καὶ δυνήσεται ταχὺ κακολογῆσαί με· **40** ὃς γὰρ οὐκ ἔστιν καθ᾽ ἡμῶν, ὑπὲρ ἡμῶν ἐστιν. **41** Ὃς γὰρ ἂν ποτίσῃ ὑμᾶς ποτήριον ὕδατος ἐν ὀνόματι[6] ὅτι Χριστοῦ ἐστε, ἀμὴν λέγω ὑμῖν ὅτι οὐ μὴ ἀπολέσῃ τὸν μισθὸν αὐτοῦ.

Temptations to Sin
(Mt 18.6–9; Lk 17.1–2)

42 Καὶ ὃς ἂν σκανδαλίσῃ ἕνα τῶν μικρῶν τούτων τῶν πιστευόντων [εἰς ἐμέ][7], καλόν ἐστιν αὐτῷ μᾶλλον εἰ περίκειται μύλος ὀνικὸς περὶ τὸν τράχηλον αὐτοῦ καὶ

because he doesn't belong to our group."
[39] "Do not try to stop him," answered Jesus, "because no one who performs a miracle in my name will be able soon after to say bad things about me. [40] For whoever is not against us is for us. [41] Remember this! Anyone who gives you a drink of water because you belong to Christ will certainly receive his reward."

Temptations to Sin
(Also Matt. 18.6–9; Luke 17.1–2)

[42] "As for these little ones who believe in me — it would be better for a man to have a large millstone tied around his neck and be thrown into the sea, than for him to cause one of them to turn

---

[5] **38** {C} καὶ ἐκωλύομεν αὐτόν, ὅτι οὐκ ἠκολούθει ἡμῖν (see Lk 9.49) ℵ B (L οὐκ ἀκολουθῇ μεθ᾽ ἡμῶν) Δ Θ Ψ (892 ἀκολουθεί) *l*[44m pt] it[aur, f] syr[s, p, pal] eth Diatessaron[a, n, t] ‖ καὶ ἐκωλύσαμεν αὐτὸν ὅτι οὐκ ἀκολουθεῖ ἡμῖν C 1071 (*l*[44m pt] αὐτῷ for αὐτόν) *l*[185] cop[sa, bo, fay] ‖ ὃς οὐκ ἀκολουθεῖ ἡμῖν καὶ ἐκωλύσαμεν αὐτόν (D[gr] ἀκολουθεῖ μεθ᾽ ἡμῶν...ἐκωλύομεν) (W ἠκολούθει) X (*f*[1] ἐκωλύομεν) *f*[13] 28 (565 ἠκολούθει) (700 ἀκολουθεῖ) 1195 1241 1253 1365 it[a, b, c, d, ff2, i, k, l, q, r1] vg syr[h] (arm) geo ‖ ὃς οὐκ ἀκολουθεῖ ἡμῖν καὶ ἐκωλύσαμεν αὐτὸν ὅτι οὐκ ἀκολουθεῖ ἡμῖν A K Π 1010 1079 1216 1344 (1546 ἀκολουθεῖ ὑμῖν...ἀκολουθεῖ ὑμῖν) 1646 2148 2174 *Byz Lect* (*l*[1127] ὑμῖν for first ἡμῖν) syr[h with *] goth ‖ ὃς οὐκ ἀκολουθεῖ ἡμῖν 1009 1230 1242

[6] **41** {A} ἐν ὀνόματι ℵ[c] A B C* K L Π* Ψ *f*[1] 892 (1071 ἐν τῷ) 1079 1241 1546 syr[s, p, h] (arm ἐν τῷ or ἐν τούτῳ) geo[1] ‖ ἐν τῷ ὀνόματί μου D Δ Θ 28 565 700 1009 1216 1242 2174 *l*[10, 32m, 185, 313, 950, 1231m, 1579, 1599m] ‖ ἐν ὀνόματί μου ℵ* C[3] W X Π[2] 1010 1195 1230 1253 1365 1646 2148 *Byz Lect* ‖ ἐν (or ἐν τῷ) ὀνόματί μου it[a, aur, b, c, d, f, ff2, i, k, l, q, r1] vg syr[hmg] cop[sa, bo, fayvid] goth eth geo[A] Origen[lat] ‖ ἐπὶ τῷ ὀνόματί μου *f*[13] 1344 *l*[44m] syr[pal] ‖ ἕνεκεν τοῦ ὀνόματος *l*[1663m] ‖ *omit* geo[R]

[7] **42** {C} πιστευόντων εἰς ἐμέ (see Mt 18.6) A B C[2vid] K L W X Θ Π Ψ *f*[1] *f*[13] 28 565 700 892 1009 1010 1071 1079 1195 1216 1230 1241 1242 1253 1344 1365 1546 1646 2148 2174 *Byz Lect* it[aur, c, f, l, q] vg syr[s, p, h] cop[sa, bo, fay] goth arm eth geo Diatessaron[p] ‖ πιστευόντων ℵ C[*vid] Δ it[b, ff2, i, k] cop[bomss] ‖ πίστιν ἐχόντων D it[a, d]

---

40 Mt 12.30; Lk 11.23

away from me. 43 So if your hand makes
you turn away, cut if off! It is better for
you to enter life without a hand than to
keep both hands and go off to hell, to the
fire that never goes out. [44 There 'their
worms never die, and the fire is never
put out.'] 45 And if your foot makes you
turn away, cut it off! It is better for
you to enter life without a foot than to
keep both feet and be thrown into hell.
[46 There 'their worms never die, and the
fire is never put out.'] 47 And if your eye
makes you turn away, take it out! It is
better for you to enter the Kingdom of
God with only one eye, than to keep both
eyes and be thrown into hell. 48 There
'their worms never die, and the fire is
never put out.'
49 "For everyone will be salted with

βέβληται εἰς τὴν θάλασσαν. **43** *Καὶ ἐὰν σκανδαλίζῃ σε ἡ
χείρ σου, ἀπόκοψον αὐτήν· καλόν ἐστίν σε κυλλὸν εἰσελθεῖν εἰς τὴν ζωὴν ἢ τὰς δύο χεῖρας ἔχοντα ἀπελθεῖν εἰς
τὴν γέενναν, εἰς τὸ πῦρ τὸ ἄσβεστον*[8].[9] **45** *καὶ ἐὰν ὁ πούς
σου σκανδαλίζῃ σε, ἀπόκοψον αὐτόν· καλόν ἐστίν σε
εἰσελθεῖν εἰς τὴν ζωὴν χωλὸν ἢ τοὺς δύο πόδας ἔχοντα
βληθῆναι εἰς τὴν γέενναν*[10].[11] **47** *καὶ ἐὰν ὁ ὀφθαλμός σου
σκανδαλίζῃ σε, ἔκβαλε αὐτόν· καλόν σέ ἐστιν μονόφθαλμον
εἰσελθεῖν εἰς τὴν βασιλείαν τοῦ θεοῦ ἢ δύο ὀφθαλμοὺς
ἔχοντα βληθῆναι εἰς τὴν γέενναν,* **48** *ὅπου* **ὁ σκώληξ
αὐτῶν οὐ τελευτᾷ καὶ τὸ πῦρ οὐ σβέννυται·** **49** *πᾶς γὰρ*

---

[8] **43** {B} *εἰς τὴν γέενναν, εἰς τὸ πῦρ τὸ ἄσβεστον* ℵ^{*,b} A B C K X Θ Π 565 1009 1010 1071 1079 1216 1230 1241 1242 1253 1344 1365 1546 1646 2148 2174 (1195 $l^{69,333,1127}$ *omit τήν*) *Byz Lect* it^{a,aur,f,l} vg (syr^{h}) cop^{bo} goth arm geo^{ms} // *εἰς τὴν γέενναν ὅπου ἐστὶν εἰς τὸ πῦρ τὸ ἄσβεστον* D it$^{b,c,d,ff^2,i,k,r^1}$ // *εἰς τὴν γέενναν* ℵ^{a} L Δ Ψ 700 892 l^{1642} syr^{p} eth // *εἰς τὸ πῦρ τὸ ἄσβεστον* W f^1 f^{13} 28 syr^{s} geo^{1,A} // *εἰς τὴν γέενναν τοῦ πυρός* geo^{B} // *εἰς τὴν γέεναν τοῦ πυρὸς τοῦ ἀσβέστου* (it^{q}) cop$^{sa,bo^{mss}}$

[9] **43** {A} *omit verse 44* ℵ B C L W Δ Ψ f^1 28 565 892 1365 l^{260} it^{k} syr^{s} cop^{sa,bo,fay} arm geo // *include verse 44 ὅπου ὁ σκώληξ αὐτῶν οὐ τελευτᾷ καὶ τὸ πῦρ οὐ σβέννυται.* (*see* Is 66.24) A D K X Θ Π f^{13} 700 1009 1010 1071 1079 (1195 *τὸ πῦρ αὐτῶν*) (1216 *omit ὁ*) 1230 1241 1242 1253 1344 (1546 *σκόλυξ ὁ ἀκύμητος καί*) 1646 2148 2174 *Byz Lect* it$^{a,aur,b,c,d,ff^2,i,l,q,r^1}$ vg syr^{p,h} goth (eth) Diatessaron^{a,p} Irenaeus^{lat} Augustine // *ὅπου ὁ σκώληξ αὐτῶν οὐ τελευτᾷ.* it^{f}

[10] **45** {A} *εἰς τὴν γέενναν* ℵ B C L W Δ Ψ f^1 (28 *omit τήν*) 892 1365 l^{260} it^{b,k} syr^{s,p} cop^{sa,bo,fay} arm geo Diatessaron^{p} // *εἰς τὴν γέενναν τοῦ πυρός* l^{70} (it^{aur,c,l} vg *add τοῦ ἀσβέστου*) // *εἰς τὸ πῦρ τὸ ἄσβεστον* 700 // *εἰς τὴν γέενναν εἰς τὸ πῦρ τὸ ἄσβεστον* A D K (X *omit τήν* Θ Π f^{13} 565 1010 1071 1079 1195 1216 1230 1241 1242 1253 1344 1546 1646 2148 2174 *Byz Lect* (l^{883} *εἰς πῦρ*) it$^{(a),d,f,(ff^2),(i),q,(r^1)}$ syr^{h} goth eth Diatessaron

[11] **45** {A} *omit verse 46* ℵ B C L W Δ Ψ f^1 28 565 892 1365 l^{19} it^{k} syr^{s} cop^{sa,bo,fay} arm Diatessaron^{a} // *include verse 46 ὅπου ὁ σκώληξ αὐτῶν οὐ τελευτᾷ καὶ τὸ πῦρ οὐ σβέννυται.* (*see* Is 66.24) A D K X Θ Π f^{13} 700 1010 1071 1079 1195 1216 1230 (1241 *πῦρ αὐτῶν*) 1242 (1253 *omit αὐτῶν*) 1344 1546 1646 2148 2174 *Byz Lect* it$^{a,aur,b,c,d,f,ff^2,i,l,q,r^1}$ vg syr^{p,h} goth (eth) geo Diatessaron^{p} Augustine

---

43 *ἐὰν...γέενναν* Mt 5.30 **47** Mt 5.29 **48** *ὁ...σβέννυται* Is 66.24

πυρὶ ἁλισθήσεται[12]. 50 Καλὸν τὸ ἅλας· ἐὰν δὲ τὸ ἅλας
ἄναλον γένηται, ἐν τίνι αὐτὸ ἀρτύσετε; [d]ἔχετε ἐν ἑαυτοῖς
ἅλα, καὶ εἰρηνεύετε ἐν ἀλλήλοις.

Teaching about Divorce
(Mt 19.1–12)

10 Καὶ ἐκεῖθεν ἀναστὰς ἔρχεται εἰς τὰ ὅρια τῆς Ἰουδαίας [καὶ] πέραν[1] τοῦ Ἰορδάνου, καὶ συμπορεύονται
πάλιν ὄχλοι πρὸς αὐτόν, καὶ ὡς εἰώθει πάλιν ἐδίδασκεν
αὐτούς. 2 καὶ [προσελθόντες Φαρισαῖοι][2] ἐπηρώτων
αὐτὸν εἰ ἔξεστιν ἀνδρὶ γυναῖκα ἀπολῦσαι, πειράζοντες
αὐτόν. 3 ὁ δὲ ἀποκριθεὶς εἶπεν αὐτοῖς, Τί ὑμῖν ἐνετείλατο

---

[12] **49** {B} *πᾶς γὰρ πυρὶ ἁλισθήσεται* (ℵ *ἐν πυρί*) B L (W *ἁλισγηθήσεται*) Δ f^1 f^{13} 28* 565 700 l^{260} syr^{s} cop$^{sa,(bo)}$ arm geo Diatessaron^{apt} // *πᾶς γὰρ πυρὶ ἁλισθήσεται καὶ πᾶσα θυσία ἁλὶ ἁλισθήσεται* A (C *ἐν πυρί*) K (X *πυρὶ ἁλὶ ἁλισθήσεται*) (Θ *πυρὶ ἀναλωθήσεται*) Π (Ψ *θυσία ἀναλωθήσεται*) 28^{c} 892 1010* 1071 1079 (1195 *ἐν πυρὶ δοκιμασθήσεται*) 1216 1230 1241 1242 1253 1344 1365 1646 2148 2174 (1009 1010^{c} 1546 $l^{303,1127c}$ *omit* ἁλί) *Byz Lect* it^{f,l,q} vg^{cl} (vg^{ww} *omit* ἁλί) syr^{p,h} cop^{bomss} goth eth Diatessaron^{apt,p} // *πᾶσα γὰρ θυσία ἁλὶ ἁλισθήσεται* (*see* Lv 2.13) D it$^{(a),b,d,ff2,i}$ (it^{aur,c} *omit* ἅλί) // *Omnia autem substantia consumitur* it^{k}

[1] **1** {C} *καὶ πέραν* ℵ B C* L Ψ 892 1009 cop^{sa,bo} // *διὰ τοῦ πέραν* A K X Π 700 1010 1079 1195* 1230 1242^{c} 1253 1344 1546 (2148 *εἰς τὸ πέραν*) *Byz* $l^{76,150,185,883}$ syr^{h} // *καὶ διὰ τοῦ πέραν* 1071 // *πέραν* (*see* Mt 19.1) C^{2} D W Δ Θ f^1 f^{13} 28 565 1195^{c} 1216 1241 1242* 1365 1646 2174 *Lect* it^{aur,b,c,d,f,ff2,i,k,l,q} vg syr^{s,p} goth arm geo Diatessaron^{a,p} Augustine

[2] **2** {C} *καὶ προσελθόντες Φαρισαῖοι* A B K L Δ Π Ψ f^{13} 28 700 892 1010 1079 1546 1646 *Byz*^{pt} cop^{bo} goth // *καὶ προσελθόντες οἱ Φαρισαῖοι* ℵ C X (f^1 *οἱ Φαρισαῖοι after αὐτόν*) 1009 1071 1195 1216 1230 1241 1242 1253 1344 1365 2148 2174 *Byz*^{pt} (*Lect omit καί at beginning of lection*) Diatessaron^{a} // *προσελθόντι τῷ Ἰησοῦ οἱ Φαρισαῖοι* l^{185} // *καὶ προσελθόντες οἱ* (*or omit οἱ*) *Φαρισαῖοι* it^{aur,c,f,l,q} vg syr^{p,h} geo // *οἱ δὲ Φαρισαῖοι προσελθόντες* W Θ 565 cop$^{sa,(fay)}$ arm // *et accendentes quidam* it^{ff2} // *καί* D it^{a,b,d,k,r1} syr^{s} Origen

---

[d] **50 (51)** *d* no number: TR WH Bov Nes BF^{2} AV RV ASV RSV NEB TT Zür Luth Jer Seg^{ed} // *d* number 51: Seg^{ed}

---

50 *ἐὰν...ἀρτύσετε* Mt 5.13; Lk 14.34 *ἔχετε...ἅλα* Col 4.6 *εἰρηνεύετε ἐν ἀλλήλοις* Ro 12.18; 1 Th 5.13

fire. 50 Salt is good. But if it loses its
saltness, how can you make it salty
again? Have salt in yourselves, and be
at peace with one another."

Jesus Teaches about Divorce
(Also Matt. 19.1–12; Luke 16.18)

10 Then Jesus left that place, went to the region of Judea, and crossed the Jordan river. Again crowds came flocking to him and he taught them, as he always did.

2 Some Pharisees came to him and
tried to trap him. "Tell us," they asked,
"does our Law allow a man to divorce
his wife?" 3 Jesus answered with a question: "What commandment did Moses

give you?" ⁴ Their answer was, "Moses gave permission for a man to write a divorce notice and send his wife away." ⁵ Jesus said to them: "Moses wrote this commandment for you because you are so hard to teach. ⁶ But in the beginning, at the time of creation, it was said, 'God made them male and female. ⁷ And for this reason a man will leave his father and mother and unite with his wife, ⁸ and the two will become one.' So they are no longer two, but one. ⁹ Man must not separate, then, what God has joined together."

¹⁰ When they went back into the house, the disciples asked Jesus about this matter. ¹¹ He said to them: "The man who divorces his wife and marries another woman commits adultery against his wife; ¹² in the same way, the woman who divorces her husband and marries another man commits adultery."

Jesus Blesses Little Children
(Also Matt. 19.13–15; Luke 18.15–17)

¹³ Some people brought children to Jesus for him to touch them, but the disciples scolded those people. ¹⁴ When Jesus noticed it, he was angry and said

Μωϋσῆς; 4 οἱ δὲ εἶπαν, Ἐπέτρεψεν Μωϋσῆς **βιβλίον ἀποστασίου γράψαι καὶ ἀπολῦσαι.** 5 ὁ δὲ Ἰησοῦς εἶπεν αὐτοῖς, Πρὸς τὴν σκληροκαρδίαν ὑμῶν ἔγραψεν ὑμῖν τὴν ἐντολὴν ταύτην. 6 ἀπὸ δὲ ἀρχῆς κτίσεως **ἄρσεν καὶ θῆλυ ἐποίησεν αὐτούς**³· 7 ἕνεκεν τούτου καταλείψει **ἄνθρωπος τὸν πατέρα αὐτοῦ καὶ τὴν μητέρα [καὶ προσκολληθήσεται πρὸς τὴν γυναῖκα αὐτοῦ]**⁴, 8 **καὶ ἔσονται οἱ δύο εἰς σάρκα μίαν·** ὥστε οὐκέτι εἰσὶν δύο ἀλλὰ μία σάρξ. 9 ὃ οὖν ὁ θεὸς συνέζευξεν ἄνθρωπος μὴ χωριζέτω. 10 Καὶ εἰς τὴν οἰκίαν πάλιν οἱ μαθηταὶ περὶ τούτου ἐπηρώτων αὐτόν. 11 καὶ λέγει αὐτοῖς, Ὃς ἂν ἀπολύσῃ τὴν γυναῖκα αὐτοῦ καὶ γαμήσῃ ἄλλην μοιχᾶται ἐπ᾽ αὐτήν, 12 καὶ ἐὰν αὐτὴ ἀπολύσασα τὸν ἄνδρα αὐτῆς γαμήσῃ ἄλλον μοιχᾶται.

Little Children Blessed
(Mt 19.13–15; Lk 18.15–17)

13 Καὶ προσέφερον αὐτῷ παιδία ἵνα αὐτῶν ἅψηται· οἱ δὲ μαθηταὶ ἐπετίμησαν αὐτοῖς. 14 ἰδὼν δὲ ὁ Ἰησοῦς ἠγανάκτησεν καὶ⁵ εἶπεν αὐτοῖς, Ἄφετε τὰ παιδία ἔρχεσθαι

³ **6** {B} αὐτούς (see Mt 19.4) ℵ B C L Δ 1242 itᶜ copˢᵃ, ᵇᵒ, ᶠᵃʸ geo² Diatessaronᵃ·ᵗ ∥ αὐτοὺς ὁ θεός A K X Θ Π Ψ f¹ f¹³ 28 565 700 892 1009 1010 1071 1079 1195 1216 1230 1241 1253 1344 1365 1546 1646 2148 2174 *Byz Lect* itᵃ, ᵃᵘʳ, ˡ, q vg syrˢ·ᵖ·ʰ arm geo¹ Diatessaronᵖ Augustine ∥ ὁ θεός D W itᵇ·ᵈ·ᶠ· ff²·ᵏ·ʳ¹ goth eth

⁴ **7** {C} καὶ προσκολληθήσεται πρὸς τὴν γυναῖκα αὐτοῦ (see Gn 2.24) D K W X Θ Π f¹³ 28 565 (700* μητέρα for γυναῖκα) 700ᶜ 892ᵐᵍ 1009 1010 1071 1079 1195 1216 1230 1241 1242 1253 1344 1365 1646 2148 2174 *Byz Lect* (l⁷⁰ μητέρα) itᵇ·ᵈ·ff²·ˡ·(q) vg syrᵖ·ʰ copˢᵃ·ᵇᵒ·ᶠᵃʸ arm eth geo Diatessaronᵖ Basil ∥ καὶ προσκολληθήσεται τῇ γυναῖκι αὐτοῦ (see Mt 19.5) A C L Δ f¹ 1546 l¹² itᵃ·ᵃᵘʳ·ᶜ·ᶠ·ʳ¹ ∥ *et inprobitas mulierem* itᵏ ∥ omit ℵ B Ψ 892* l⁴⁸ syrˢ goth

⁵ **14** {C} καί ℵ A B C D K L X Δ Π Ψ 700 892 1009 1010 1071 1079 1195 1216 1230 1241 1242 1253 1344 1365 1546 1646 2148 2174 *Byz Lect* itᵃ·ᵃᵘʳ· ᵇ,ᶜ,ᵈ,ᶠ,ff²,ᵏ,ˡ,q,ʳ¹ vg syrᵖ·ʰ copˢᵃ·ᵇᵒ goth eth Diatessaronᵃ·ᵖ ∥ καὶ ἐπιτιμήσας W Θ f¹ f¹³ 28 565 syrˢ·ʰᵐᵍ arm geo

4 Ἐπέτρεψεν...ἀπολῦσαι Dt 24.1, 3 (Mt 5.31; 19.7)   **6** Gn 1.27; 5.2   **7–8** ἕνεκεν...μίαν Gn 2.24 (Eph 5.31)   **11–12** Ὃς...ἄλλον μοιχᾶται Mt 5.32; Lk 16.18; 1 Cor 7.10–11

πρός με, μὴ κωλύετε αὐτά, τῶν γὰρ τοιούτων ἐστὶν ἡ βασιλεία τοῦ θεοῦ. 15 ἀμὴν λέγω ὑμῖν, ὃς ἂν μὴ δέξηται τὴν βασιλείαν τοῦ θεοῦ ὡς παιδίον, οὐ μὴ εἰσέλθῃ εἰς αὐτήν. 16 καὶ ἐναγκαλισάμενος αὐτὰ κατευλόγει τιθεὶς τὰς χεῖρας ἐπ' αὐτά.

The Rich Man
(Mt 19.16–30; Lk 18.18–30)

17 Καὶ ἐκπορευομένου αὐτοῦ εἰς ὁδὸν προσδραμὼν εἷς καὶ γονυπετήσας αὐτὸν ἐπηρώτα αὐτόν, Διδάσκαλε ἀγαθέ, τί ποιήσω ἵνα ζωὴν αἰώνιον κληρονομήσω; 18 ὁ δὲ Ἰησοῦς εἶπεν αὐτῷ, Τί με λέγεις ἀγαθόν; οὐδεὶς ἀγαθὸς εἰ μὴ εἷς ὁ θεός. 19 τὰς ἐντολὰς οἶδας· **Μὴ φονεύσῃς, Μὴ μοιχεύσῃς, Μὴ κλέψῃς, Μὴ ψευδομαρτυρήσῃς, Μὴ ἀποστερήσῃς**[6], **Τίμα τὸν πατέρα σου καὶ τὴν μητέρα.** 20 ὁ δὲ ἔφη αὐτῷ, Διδάσκαλε, ταῦτα πάντα ἐφυλαξάμην ἐκ νεότητός μου. 21 ὁ δὲ Ἰησοῦς ἐμβλέψας αὐτῷ ἠγάπησεν αὐτὸν καὶ εἶπεν αὐτῷ, Ἕν σε ὑστερεῖ· ὕπαγε ὅσα ἔχεις πώλησον καὶ δὸς [τοῖς] πτωχοῖς, καὶ ἕξεις θησαυρὸν ἐν οὐρανῷ, καὶ δεῦρο ἀκολούθει μοι. 22 ὁ δὲ στυγνάσας ἐπὶ τῷ λόγῳ ἀπῆλθεν λυπούμενος, ἦν γὰρ ἔχων κτήματα πολλά.

23 Καὶ περιβλεψάμενος ὁ Ἰησοῦς λέγει τοῖς μαθηταῖς αὐτοῦ, Πῶς δυσκόλως οἱ τὰ χρήματα ἔχοντες εἰς τὴν βασιλείαν τοῦ θεοῦ εἰσελεύσονται. 24 οἱ δὲ μαθηταὶ ἐθαμβοῦντο ἐπὶ τοῖς λόγοις αὐτοῦ. ὁ δὲ Ἰησοῦς πάλιν ἀπο-

---

[6] 19 {C} μὴ ἀποστερήσῃς ℵ A B² C D X Θ 565 892 1009 1071 1195 1216 1230 1241 1253 1344 1365 1646 2174 *Byz Lect* it^(a, aur, b, c, d, f, ff², k, l, q, r¹) vg syr^(p, h) cop^(sa, bo) goth eth Diatessaron^(a, p) ‖ *omit* (*see* Mt 19.18; Lk 18.20) B* K W Δ Π Ψ f¹ f¹³ 28 700 1010 1079 1242 1546 2148 l^(10, 883, 950, 1642) syr^s arm geo Irenaeus Clement

---

15 Mt 18.3 Dt 24.14; Jas 5.4 Mk 4.19   19 Μὴ φονεύσῃς...μητέρα Ex 20.12-16; Dt 5.16-20   21 θησαυρὸν ἐν οὐρανῷ Mt 6.20; Lk 12.33   Μὴ ἀποστερήσῃς   23 Πῶς...εἰσελεύσονται

---

to his disciples: "Let the children come to me! Do not stop them, because the Kingdom of God belongs to such as these. 15 Remember this! Whoever does not receive the Kingdom of God like a child will never enter it." 16 Then he took the children in his arms, placed his hands on each of them, and blessed them.

The Rich Man
(Also Matt. 19.16–30; Luke 18.18–30)

17 As Jesus was starting again on his way, a man ran up, knelt before him, and asked him: "Good Teacher, what must I do to receive eternal life?" 18 "Why do you call me good?" Jesus asked him. "No one is good except God alone. 19 You know the commandments: 'Do not murder; do not commit adultery; do not steal; do not lie; do not cheat; honor your father and mother.'" 20 "Teacher," the man said, "ever since I was young I have obeyed all these commandments." 21 With love Jesus looked straight at him and said: "You need only one thing. Go and sell all you have and give the money to the poor, and you will have riches in heaven; then come and follow me." 22 When the man heard this, gloom spread over his face and he went away sad, because he was very rich.

23 Jesus looked around at his disciples and said to them, "How hard it will be for rich people to enter the Kingdom of God!" 24 The disciples were shocked at these words, but Jesus went on to say:

"My children, how hard it is to enter the Kingdom of God! 25 It is much harder for a rich man to enter the Kingdom of God than for a camel to go through the eye of a needle." 26 At this the disciples were completely amazed, and asked one another, "Who, then, can be saved?" 27 Jesus looked straight at them and answered: "This is impossible for men, but not for God; everything is possible for God."

28 Then Peter spoke up: "Look, we have left everything and followed you." 29 "Yes," Jesus said to·them, "and I tell you this: anyone who leaves home or brothers or sisters or mother or father or children or fields for me, and for the gospel, 30 will receive much more in this present age. He will receive a hundred times more houses, brothers, sisters, mothers, children, and fields — and persecutions as well; and in the age to come he will receive eternal life. 31 But many who now are first will be last, and many who now are last will be first."

Jesus Speaks a Third Time about His Death
(Also Matt. 20.17–19; Luke 18.31–34)

32 They were now on the road going up to Jerusalem. Jesus was going ahead of the disciples, who were filled with alarm; the people who followed behind were afraid. Once again Jesus took the twelve disciples aside and spoke of the things that were going to happen to him.

κριθεὶς λέγει αὐτοῖς, Τέκνα, πῶς δύσκολόν ἐστιν[7] εἰς τὴν βασιλείαν τοῦ θεοῦ εἰσελθεῖν· 25 εὐκοπώτερόν ἐστιν κάμηλον διὰ τρυμαλιᾶς ῥαφίδος διελθεῖν ἢ πλούσιον εἰς τὴν βασιλείαν τοῦ θεοῦ εἰσελθεῖν. 26 οἱ δὲ περισσῶς ἐξεπλήσσοντο λέγοντες πρὸς ἑαυτούς[8], Καὶ τίς δύναται σωθῆναι; 27 ἐμβλέψας αὐτοῖς ὁ Ἰησοῦς λέγει, Παρὰ ἀνθρώποις ἀδύνατον ἀλλ' οὐ παρὰ θεῷ, πάντα γὰρ δυνατὰ παρὰ τῷ θεῷ. 28 Ἤρξατο λέγειν ὁ Πέτρος αὐτῷ, Ἰδοὺ ἡμεῖς ἀφήκαμεν πάντα καὶ ἠκολουθήκαμέν σοι. 29 ἔφη ὁ Ἰησοῦς, Ἀμὴν λέγω ὑμῖν, οὐδείς ἐστιν ὃς ἀφῆκεν οἰκίαν ἢ ἀδελφοὺς ἢ ἀδελφὰς ἢ μητέρα ἢ πατέρα ἢ τέκνα ἢ ἀγροὺς ἕνεκεν ἐμοῦ καὶ ἕνεκεν τοῦ εὐαγγελίου, 30 ἐὰν μὴ λάβῃ ἑκατονταπλασίονα νῦν ἐν τῷ καιρῷ τούτῳ οἰκίας καὶ ἀδελφοὺς καὶ ἀδελφὰς καὶ μητέρας καὶ τέκνα καὶ ἀγροὺς μετὰ διωγμῶν, καὶ ἐν τῷ αἰῶνι τῷ ἐρχομένῳ ζωὴν αἰώνιον. 31 πολλοὶ δὲ ἔσονται πρῶτοι ἔσχατοι καὶ [οἱ] ἔσχατοι πρῶτοι.

A Third Time Jesus Foretells His Death and Resurrection
(Mt 20.17–19; Lk 18.31–34)

32 Ἦσαν δὲ ἐν τῇ ὁδῷ ἀναβαίνοντες εἰς Ἱεροσόλυμα, καὶ ἦν προάγων αὐτοὺς ὁ Ἰησοῦς, καὶ ἐθαμβοῦντο, οἱ δὲ ἀκολουθοῦντες ἐφοβοῦντο. καὶ παραλαβὼν πάλιν τοὺς δώδεκα ἤρξατο αὐτοῖς λέγειν τὰ μέλλοντα αὐτῷ συμ-

---

[7] **24** {C} ἐστιν ℵ B Δ Ψ it^k cop^(sa,bomss) ‖ ἐστιν τοὺς πεποιθότας ἐπὶ χρήμασιν A C K X Π (D Θ f¹ f¹³ 28 565 1344 ἐπὶ τοῖς) 700 892 1009 1010 1071 1079 1195 1216 1230 1242 1253 1365 (1546 ἐπὶ τὰ χρήματα) 1646 2148 2174 *Byz Lect* it^(a,aur,b,d,f,ff²,l,q) vg syr^(s,p,h) cop^bo goth arm (eth) geo Diatessaron^(a,p) Clement ‖ ἐστιν πλούσιον (W πλούσιον *after* εἰσελθεῖν) it^c ‖ οἱ τὰ χρήματα ἔχοντες 1241

[8] **26** {B} πρὸς ἑαυτούς A D K W X Θ Π f¹ f¹³ 28 565 700 1010 1071 1079 1195 1216 1230 1241 1242 1253 1344 1365 1546 1646 2148 2174 (1009 l^(150,185,883) αὐτούς) *Byz Lect* it^(b,d,f,ff²,l,q) vg syr^(s),h goth arm eth Augustine ‖ πρὸς ἀλλήλους M* it^(a,aur,c),k syr^p geo ‖ πρὸς αὐτόν ℵ B C Δ Ψ 892 cop^(sa,bo) ‖ *omit (see* Mt 19.25; Lk 18.26) 4 179 273 569 (l^950 *beginning of lection*) Clement

27 πάντα...θεῷ Gn 18.14; Job 42.2; Zch 8.6 LXX; Mk 14.36   **31** Mt 20.16; Lk 13.30

βαίνειν, **33** ὅτι Ἰδοὺ ἀναβαίνομεν εἰς Ἱεροσόλυμα, καὶ ὁ υἱὸς τοῦ ἀνθρώπου παραδοθήσεται τοῖς ἀρχιερεῦσιν καὶ τοῖς γραμματεῦσιν, καὶ κατακρινοῦσιν αὐτὸν θανάτῳ καὶ παραδώσουσιν αὐτὸν τοῖς ἔθνεσιν **34** καὶ ἐμπαίξουσιν αὐτῷ καὶ ἐμπτύσουσιν αὐτῷ καὶ μαστιγώσουσιν αὐτὸν καὶ ἀποκτενοῦσιν, καὶ μετὰ τρεῖς ἡμέρας[9] ἀναστήσεται.

The Request of James and John
(Mt 20.20–28)

35 Καὶ προσπορεύονται αὐτῷ Ἰάκωβος καὶ Ἰωάννης οἱ υἱοὶ Ζεβεδαίου λέγοντες αὐτῷ, Διδάσκαλε, θέλομεν ἵνα ὃ ἐὰν αἰτήσωμέν σε ποιήσῃς ἡμῖν. **36** ὁ δὲ εἶπεν αὐτοῖς, Τί θέλετέ [με] ποιήσω ὑμῖν; **37** οἱ δὲ εἶπαν αὐτῷ, Δὸς ἡμῖν ἵνα εἷς σου ἐκ δεξιῶν καὶ εἷς ἐξ ἀριστερῶν καθίσωμεν ἐν τῇ δόξῃ σου. **38** ὁ δὲ Ἰησοῦς εἶπεν αὐτοῖς, Οὐκ οἴδατε τί αἰτεῖσθε. δύνασθε πιεῖν τὸ ποτήριον ὃ ἐγὼ πίνω, ἢ τὸ βάπτισμα ὃ ἐγὼ βαπτίζομαι βαπτισθῆναι; **39** οἱ δὲ εἶπαν αὐτῷ, Δυνάμεθα. ὁ δὲ Ἰησοῦς εἶπεν αὐτοῖς, Τὸ ποτήριον ὃ ἐγὼ πίνω πίεσθε καὶ τὸ βάπτισμα ὃ ἐγὼ βαπτίζομαι βαπτισθήσεσθε, **40** τὸ δὲ καθίσαι ἐκ δεξιῶν μου ἢ ἐξ εὐωνύμων οὐκ ἔστιν ἐμὸν δοῦναι, ἀλλ' οἷς[10] ἡτοίμασται[11].

---

[9] **34** {A} μετὰ τρεῖς ἡμέρας ℵ B C D L Δ Ψ 892 it(a),b,(c),d,ff2,i,k,(q),rl syrhmg copsa,bo ∥ τῇ τρίτῃ ἡμέρᾳ (see Mt 20.19; Lk 18.33) (A*vid omit τῇ) Ac K W X Θ Π f1 f13 28 565 700 1009 1010 1071 1079 1195 1216 1230 1241 1242 1253 1344 1365 1546 1646 2148 2174 Byz Lect (l1613 omit τῇ) itaur,f,l vg syrs,p,h,pal goth arm eth geo Diatessarona,p Origen

[10] **40** {A} ἀλλ' οἷς A B (C* αλλοι) C2 K Θ Π Ψ f1 f13 28 565 700 892 1009 1010 1071 1079 1195 1216 1230 1241 1242 1253 1344 1365 1546 1646 2148 2174 Byz Lect itaur,c,f,i,l,q vg syrp,h,pal copbo goth arm geo ∥ αλλοις ℵ D L W X Δ 0146 ∥ ἄλλοις 225 ita,b,d,ff2,k copsa eth ∥ ἄλλοις δέ syrs

[11] **40** {B} ἡτοίμασται ℵa A B C (D* ἡτοίμαθαι, Dc ἡτοίμασθαι)

33-34 Mt 16.21; 17.22–23; Mk 8.31; 9.31; Lk 24.7   **35** Ἰάκωβος...Ζεβεδαίου Mt 4.21; 10.2; 17.1; Mk 1.19, 29; 3.17; 5.37; 9.2; 10.41; 13.3; 14.33; Lk 5.10; 6.14; 8.51; 9.28, 54; Ac 1.13   **36** Τί θέλετε...ὑμῖν Mt 20.32; Mk 10.51; Lk 18.41   **37** Δὸς...δόξῃ σου Mt 19.28; Lk 22.30   **38** τὸ ποτήριον...πίνω Jn 18.11   τὸ βάπτισμα...βαπτισθῆναι Lk 12.50   **39** Τὸ ποτήριον... βαπτισθήσεσθε Ac 12.2

[33] "Look," Jesus told them, "we are going up to Jerusalem where the Son of Man will be handed over to the chief priests and the teachers of the Law. They will condemn him to death and then hand him over to the Gentiles. [34] These will make fun of him, spit on him, whip him, and kill him. And after three days he will be raised to life."

The Request of James and John
(Also Matt. 20.20–28)

[35] Then James and John, the sons of Zebedee, came to Jesus. "Teacher," they said, "there is something we want you to do for us." [36] "What do you want me to do for you?" Jesus asked them. [37] They answered: "When you sit on your throne in the glorious Kingdom, we want you to let us sit with you, one at your right and one at your left." [38] Jesus said to them: "You don't know what you are asking for. Can you drink the cup that I must drink? Can you be baptized in the way I must be baptized?" [39] "We can," they answered. Jesus said to them: "You will indeed drink the cup I must drink and be baptized in the way I must be baptized. [40] But I do not have the right to choose who will sit at my right and my left. It is God who will give these places to those for whom he has prepared them."

41 When the other ten disciples heard about this they became angry with James and John. **42** So Jesus called them all together to him and said: "You know that the men who are considered rulers of the people have power over them, and the leaders rule over them. **43** This, however, is not the way it is among you. If one of you wants to be great, he must be the servant of the rest; **44** and if one of you wants to be first, he must be the slave of all. **45** For even the Son of Man did not come to be served; he came to serve and to give his life to redeem many people."

Jesus Heals Blind Bartimaeus
(Also Matt. 20.29–34; Luke 18.35–43)

46 They came to Jericho. As Jesus was leaving with his disciples and a large crowd, a blind man named Bartimaeus, the son of Timaeus, was sitting and begging by the road. **47** When he heard that it was Jesus of Nazareth, he began to shout, "Jesus! Son of David! Have

41 Καὶ ἀκούσαντες οἱ δέκα ἤρξαντο ἀγανακτεῖν περὶ Ἰακώβου καὶ Ἰωάννου. **42** καὶ προσκαλεσάμενος αὐτοὺς ὁ Ἰησοῦς λέγει αὐτοῖς, Οἴδατε ὅτι οἱ δοκοῦντες ἄρχειν τῶν ἐθνῶν κατακυριεύουσιν αὐτῶν καὶ οἱ μεγάλοι αὐτῶν κατεξουσιάζουσιν αὐτῶν. **43** οὐχ οὕτως δέ ἐστιν[12] ἐν ὑμῖν· ἀλλ' ὃς ἂν θέλῃ μέγας γενέσθαι ἐν ὑμῖν, ἔσται ὑμῶν διάκονος, **44** καὶ ὃς ἂν θέλῃ ἐν ὑμῖν εἶναι πρῶτος, ἔσται πάντων δοῦλος· **45** καὶ γὰρ ὁ υἱὸς τοῦ ἀνθρώπου οὐκ ἦλθεν διακονηθῆναι ἀλλὰ διακονῆσαι καὶ δοῦναι τὴν ψυχὴν αὐτοῦ λύτρον ἀντὶ πολλῶν.

The Healing of Blind Bartimaeus
(Mt 20.29–34; Lk 18.35–43)

46 Καὶ ἔρχονται εἰς Ἰεριχώ. καὶ ἐκπορευομένου αὐτοῦ ἀπὸ Ἰεριχὼ καὶ τῶν μαθητῶν αὐτοῦ καὶ ὄχλου ἱκανοῦ ὁ υἱὸς Τιμαίου Βαρτιμαῖος τυφλὸς ἐκάθητο παρὰ τὴν ὁδὸν προσαιτῶν[13]. **47** καὶ ἀκούσας ὅτι Ἰησοῦς ὁ Ναζαρηνός[14] ἐστιν ἤρξατο κράζειν καὶ λέγειν, Υἱὲ Δαυὶδ Ἰησοῦ,

K L W X Δ Π Ψ 0146 *f*[13] 28 565 700 892 1009 1010 1079 1195 1216 1230 1242 1253 1344 1646 2148 2174 (1546 *l*[183,547] ἡτοίμασθαι = *l*[1127] ἡτοίμασθε) *Byz Lect* it[aur,b,c,d,f,ff2,i,k,l,q] vg syr[s,p,h,pal] cop[sa,bo] goth arm eth geo ‖ ἡτοίμασται ὑπὸ τοῦ πατρός μου (see Mt 20.23) ℵ[*,b] (Θ 1365 παρά) *f*[1] 1071 1241 (*l*[60] παρά and omit μου) it[a,rl vid] (syr[hmg]) (cop[boms]) Diatessaron

[12] **43** {A} ἐστιν (see Mt 20.26) ℵ B C* D L W Δ Θ Ψ 700 1253 it[a,aur, b,c,d,f,ff2,i,k,l,rl] vg cop[sa,bo] ‖ ἔσται (see 10.43b) A C³ K X Π *f*[1] *f*[13] 28 565 892 1009 1010 1071 1079 1195 1216 1230 1241 1242 1344 1365 1546 1646 2148 2174 *Byz Lect* (*l*[76vid]) it[q] syr[s,p,h,pal] cop[boms] goth arm geo Diatessaron[a]

[13] **46** {C} ἐκάθητο παρὰ τὴν ὁδὸν προσαιτῶν A C² K W X Π *f*[1] *f*[13] 28 700 1009 1010 1071 1079 1195 1216 1230 1241 1242 1253 1344 1365 1546 1646 2148 2174 *Byz Lect* it[a,aur,b,c,d,f,ff2,i,l,q,rl] vg syr[s?p?h?] cop[sa,boms?] goth eth geo Diatessaron ‖ ἐκάθητο παρὰ τὴν ὁδὸν ἐπαιτῶν D Θ 565 syr[s?p?h?] cop[boms?] Origen ‖ προσαίτης ἐκάθητο παρὰ τὴν ὁδόν (ℵ καὶ προσαίτης) B L Δ Ψ (892 ἐκαθέζετο) it[k] cop[bo] arm ‖ ἐκάθητο παρὰ τὴν ὁδόν C* Diatessaron[p]

[14] **47** {A} Ναζαρηνός B (D* Ναζορηνός, D[c] Ναζωρηνός) L W Δ Θ Ψ

42 Lk 22.25   43–44 ὃς ἂν θέλῃ μέγας...δοῦλος Mt 23.11; Mk 9.35; Lk 22.26   45 1 Tm 2.5–6   47 Υἱὲ...με Mt 9.27; 15.22

ἐλέησόν με. **48** καὶ ἐπετίμων αὐτῷ πολλοὶ ἵνα σιωπήσῃ· ὁ δὲ πολλῷ μᾶλλον ἔκραζεν, Υἱὲ Δαυίδ, ἐλέησόν με. **49** καὶ στὰς ὁ Ἰησοῦς εἶπεν, Φωνήσατε αὐτόν. καὶ φωνοῦσιν τὸν τυφλὸν λέγοντες αὐτῷ, Θάρσει, ἔγειρε, φωνεῖ σε. **50** ὁ δὲ ἀποβαλὼν τὸ ἱμάτιον αὐτοῦ ἀναπηδήσας ἦλθεν πρὸς τὸν Ἰησοῦν. **51** καὶ ἀποκριθεὶς αὐτῷ ὁ Ἰησοῦς εἶπεν, Τί σοι θέλεις ποιήσω; ὁ δὲ τυφλὸς εἶπεν αὐτῷ, Ραββουνι, ἵνα ἀναβλέψω. **52** καὶ ὁ Ἰησοῦς εἶπεν αὐτῷ, Ὕπαγε, ἡ πίστις σου σέσωκέν σε. [a] καὶ εὐθὺς ἀνέβλεψεν, καὶ ἠκολούθει αὐτῷ ἐν τῇ ὁδῷ.

The Triumphal Entry into Jerusalem
(Mt 21.1–11; Lk 19.28–40; Jn 12.12–19)

11 Καὶ ὅτε ἐγγίζουσιν εἰς Ἱεροσόλυμα εἰς Βηθφαγὴ καὶ Βηθανίαν πρὸς τὸ Ὄρος τῶν Ἐλαιῶν, ἀποστέλλει δύο τῶν μαθητῶν αὐτοῦ **2** καὶ λέγει αὐτοῖς, Ὑπάγετε εἰς τὴν κώμην τὴν κατέναντι ὑμῶν, καὶ εὐθὺς εἰσπορευόμενοι εἰς αὐτὴν εὑρήσετε πῶλον δεδεμένον ἐφ' ὃν οὐδεὶς οὔπω ἀνθρώπων ἐκάθισεν· λύσατε αὐτὸν καὶ φέρετε. **3** καὶ ἐάν τις ὑμῖν εἴπῃ, Τί ποιεῖτε τοῦτο; εἴπατε, Ὁ κύριος αὐτοῦ χρείαν ἔχει, [a] καὶ εὐθὺς αὐτὸν ἀποστέλλει πάλιν[1] ὧδε.

---

f¹ (28 Ναζωρινός) 892 it^{a,b,f,i,k} (it^{d,l,q^c} *Nazorenus*) vg cop^{sa,bo} geo² Diatessaron^p Origen ∥ Ναζωραῖος (see Lk 18.37) א A C (K* Ναραῖος) K^c X Π f¹³ 565 (700 Ναζοραῖος) 1009 1010 1071 1079 1195 1216 1230 1241 1242 1253 1344 1365 1546 1646 2148 2174 *Byz Lect* it^{ff2,q*} (it^{aur,c} *Nazareus*) syr^{s?p?h?} cop^{bomss} goth arm geo¹

¹ **3** {B} αὐτὸν ἀποστέλλει πάλιν א D^{gr} L 892 1241 *Lect* Origen ∥ αὐτὸν ἀποστελεῖ πάλιν f^{10,1127} it^{(a),d,(q)} cop^{sa} ∥ ἀποστέλλει πάλιν αὐτόν B (it^c) ∥ αὐτὸν πάλιν ἀποστέλλει C^{*vid} ∥ πάλιν ἀποστέλλει αὐτόν Θ ∥ πάλιν ἀποστελεῖ αὐτόν cth ∥ ἀποστέλλει πάλιν Δ Origen ∥ αὐτὸν ἀποστελεῖ W Π Ψ f¹ 700 1079 1195 1546 it^{i,i} vg cop^{bo} ∥ ἀποστελεῖ αὐτόν it^{ff2} arm geo ∥ αὐτὸν ἀποστέλλει A C² K X f¹³ 28 565 1009 1010 1071 1216 1230 1242 1253 1646 2148 2174 *Byz* l^{547,883,950,1642} it^{aur,b,(k)} Origen ∥ ἀποστέλλει αὐτόν 1344 1365 it^l ∥ αὐτὸν ἀποστελεῖ or αὐτὸν ἀποστέλλει syr^{s,p,h} goth

---

^a **52** (53) a no number: TR WH Bov Nes BF² AV RV ASV RSV NEB TT Zür Luth Jer Seg^{ed} ∥ a number 53: Seg^{ed}

^a **3** a minor: TR WH Bov Nes BF² AV RV ASV (RSV) NEB (TT) Zür (Luth) (Jer) ∥ a major: Seg

---

51 Τί...ποιήσω Mk 10.36   **52** ἡ πίστις...σε Mt 9.22; Mk 5.34; Lk 7.50; 8.48; 17.19

---

mercy on me!" ⁴⁸ Many scolded him and told him to be quiet. But he shouted even more loudly, "Son of David, have mercy on me!" ⁴⁹ Jesus stopped and said, "Call him." So they called the blind man. "Cheer up!" they said. "Get up, he is calling you." ⁵⁰ He threw off his cloak, jumped up and came to Jesus. ⁵¹ "What do you want me to do for you?" Jesus asked him. "Teacher," the blind man answered, "I want to see again." ⁵² "Go," Jesus told him, "your faith has made you well." At once he was able to see, and followed Jesus on the road.

The Triumphant Entry into Jerusalem
(Also Matt. 21.1–11; Luke 19.28–40; John 12.12–19)

11 As they came near Jerusalem, at the towns of Bethphage and Bethany they came to the Mount of Olives. Jesus sent two of his disciples on ahead ² with these instructions: "Go to the village there ahead of you. As soon as you get there you will find a colt tied up that has never been ridden. Untie it and bring it here. ³ And if someone asks you, 'Why are you doing that?' tell him,' The Master[1] needs it and will send

---

[1] **3** The Master: *or* Its owner

it back here at once.' " ⁴ So they went and found a colt out in the street, tied to the door of a house. As they were untying it, ⁵ some of the bystanders asked them, "What are you doing, untying that colt?" ⁶ They answered just as Jesus had told them, so the men let them go. ⁷ They brought the colt to Jesus, threw their cloaks over the animal, and Jesus got on. ⁸ Many people spread their cloaks on the road, while others cut branches in the fields and spread them on the road. ⁹ The people who were in front and those who followed behind began to shout, "Praise God! God bless him who comes in the name of the Lord! ¹⁰ God bless the coming kingdom of our father David! Praise be to God!"

¹¹ Jesus entered Jerusalem, went into the Temple, and looked around at everything. But since it was already late in the day, he went out to Bethany with the twelve disciples.

Jesus Curses the Fig Tree
(Also Matt. 21.18–19)

¹² The next day, as they were coming back from Bethany, Jesus was hungry. ¹³ He saw in the distance a fig tree covered with leaves, so he went to it to see if he could find any figs on it; but when he came to it he found only leaves, because it was not the right time for figs. ¹⁴ Jesus said to the fig tree: "No one shall ever eat figs from you again!" And his disciples heard him.

Jesus Goes to the Temple
(Also Matt. 21.12–17; Luke 19.45–48; John 2.13–22)

¹⁵ When they arrived in Jerusalem, Jesus went to the Temple and began to drive out all those who bought and sold

4 καὶ ἀπῆλθον καὶ εὗρον πῶλον δεδεμένον πρὸς θύραν ἔξω ἐπὶ τοῦ ἀμφόδου, καὶ λύουσιν αὐτόν. 5 καί τινες τῶν ἐκεῖ ἑστηκότων ἔλεγον αὐτοῖς, Τί ποιεῖτε λύοντες τὸν πῶλον; 6 οἱ δὲ εἶπαν αὐτοῖς καθὼς εἶπεν ὁ Ἰησοῦς· καὶ ἀφῆκαν αὐτούς. 7 καὶ φέρουσιν τὸν πῶλον πρὸς τὸν Ἰησοῦν, καὶ ἐπιβάλλουσιν αὐτῷ τὰ ἱμάτια αὐτῶν, καὶ ἐκάθισεν ἐπ' αὐτόν. 8 καὶ πολλοὶ τὰ ἱμάτια αὐτῶν ἔστρωσαν εἰς τὴν ὁδόν, ἄλλοι δὲ στιβάδας κόψαντες ἐκ τῶν ἀγρῶν. 9 καὶ οἱ προάγοντες καὶ οἱ ἀκολουθοῦντες ἔκραζον,

Ὡσαννά·

Εὐλογημένος ὁ ἐρχόμενος ἐν ὀνόματι κυρίου·

10   Εὐλογημένη ἡ ἐρχομένη βασιλεία τοῦ πατρὸς ἡμῶν Δαυίδ·

Ὡσαννὰ ἐν τοῖς ὑψίστοις.

11 Καὶ εἰσῆλθεν εἰς Ἱεροσόλυμα εἰς τὸ ἱερόν· καὶ περιβλεψάμενος πάντα, ὀψίας ἤδη οὔσης τῆς ὥρας, ἐξῆλθεν εἰς Βηθανίαν μετὰ τῶν δώδεκα.

The Cursing of the Fig Tree
(Mt 21.18–19)

12 Καὶ τῇ ἐπαύριον ἐξελθόντων αὐτῶν ἀπὸ Βηθανίας ἐπείνασεν. 13 καὶ ἰδὼν συκῆν ἀπὸ μακρόθεν ἔχουσαν φύλλα ἦλθεν εἰ ἄρα τι εὑρήσει ἐν αὐτῇ, καὶ ἐλθὼν ἐπ' αὐτὴν οὐδὲν εὗρεν εἰ μὴ φύλλα· ὁ γὰρ καιρὸς οὐκ ἦν σύκων. 14 καὶ ἀποκριθεὶς εἶπεν αὐτῇ, Μηκέτι εἰς τὸν αἰῶνα ἐκ σοῦ μηδεὶς καρπὸν φάγοι. καὶ ἤκουον οἱ μαθηταὶ αὐτοῦ.

The Cleansing of the Temple
(Mt 21.12–17; Lk 19.45–48; Jn 2.13–22)

15 Καὶ ἔρχονται εἰς Ἱεροσόλυμα. καὶ εἰσελθὼν εἰς τὸ ἱερὸν ἤρξατο ἐκβάλλειν τοὺς πωλοῦντας καὶ τοὺς ἀγοράζοντας ἐν τῷ ἱερῷ, καὶ τὰς τραπέζας τῶν κολλυ-

---

9 Ὡσαννά...κυρίου Ps 118.25–26 (Mt 21.15; 23.39)   10 Εὐλογημένη...Δαυίδ Lk 1.32–33; Ac 2.29   13 ἰδὼν...μὴ φύλλα Lk 13.6   14 Μηκέτι...φάγοι Mk 11.20

βιστῶν καὶ τὰς καθέδρας τῶν πωλούντων τὰς περιστερὰς κατέστρεψεν, 16 καὶ οὐκ ἤφιεν ἵνα τις διενέγκῃ σκεῦος διὰ τοῦ ἱεροῦ. 17 καὶ ἐδίδασκεν καὶ ἔλεγεν αὐτοῖς, Οὐ γέγραπται ὅτι

Ὁ οἶκός μου οἶκος προσευχῆς κληθήσεται πᾶσιν τοῖς ἔθνεσιν;
　　　ὑμεῖς δὲ πεποιήκατε αὐτὸν **σπήλαιον λῃστῶν.**
18 καὶ ἤκουσαν οἱ ἀρχιερεῖς καὶ οἱ γραμματεῖς, καὶ ἐζήτουν πῶς αὐτὸν ἀπολέσωσιν· ἐφοβοῦντο γὰρ αὐτόν, πᾶς γὰρ ὁ ὄχλος ἐξεπλήσσετο ἐπὶ τῇ διδαχῇ αὐτοῦ. 19 Καὶ ὅταν ὀψὲ ἐγένετο, ἐξεπορεύοντο ἔξω τῆς πόλεως².

The Lesson from the Withered Fig Tree
(Mt 21.20–22)

20 Καὶ παραπορευόμενοι πρωῒ εἶδον τὴν συκῆν ἐξηραμμένην ἐκ ῥιζῶν. 21 καὶ ἀναμνησθεὶς ὁ Πέτρος λέγει αὐτῷ, Ῥαββί, ἴδε ἡ συκῆ ἣν κατηράσω ἐξήρανται. 22 καὶ ἀποκριθεὶς ὁ Ἰησοῦς λέγει αὐτοῖς, Εἰ ἔχετε³ πίστιν θεοῦ, 23 ἀμὴν λέγω ὑμῖν ὅτι ὃς ἂν εἴπῃ τῷ ὄρει τούτῳ, Ἄρθητι καὶ βλήθητι εἰς τὴν θάλασσαν, καὶ μὴ διακριθῇ ἐν τῇ καρδίᾳ αὐτοῦ ἀλλὰ πιστεύῃ ὅτι ὃ λαλεῖ γίνεται, ἔσται αὐτῷ. 24 διὰ τοῦτο λέγω ὑμῖν, πάντα ὅσα προσεύχεσθε καὶ αἰτεῖσθε, πιστεύετε ὅτι ἐλάβετε⁴, καὶ ἔσται

---

² **19** {C} ἐξεπορεύοντο ἔξω τῆς πόλεως A B K Δ Π Ψ 565 700 1009 1071 1079 it^{aur,c,d,r1} syr^{p,hmg} geo¹ ‖ ἐξεπορεύετο ἔξω τῆς πόλεως ℵ C (D^{gr}) X Θ f¹³ 33 892 (1010 ἐπορεύετο) 1195 1216 1230 1241 1242 1253 1344 1365 1546 1646 2148 2174 *Byz Lect* it^{a,b,f,ff2,i,k,l,q} vg syr^{s,h,pal} cop^{sa,bo} goth eth geo² ‖ ἔξω τῆς πόλεως ἐξεπορεύετο f¹ ‖ ἔξω τῆς πόλεως ἐξεπορεύοντο W 28 arm ‖ ἔξω τῆς πόλεως L

³ **22** {B} εἰ ἔχετε ℵ D Θ f¹³ 28 33^s 505 700 1071 it^{a,b,d,i,i1} syr^{s,palms} arm geo¹ Ephraem ‖ ἔχετε A B C K L W X Δ Π Ψ f¹ 33* 892 1009 1010 1079 1195 1216 1230 1241 1242 1253 1344 1365 1546 1646 2148 2174 *Byz Lect* it^{aur,c,f,ff2,k,l,q} vg syr^{p,h,palmss} cop^{sa,bo} goth eth geo²

⁴ **24** {A} ἐλάβετε ℵ B C L W Δ Ψ 892 cop^{sams,boms} geo^{1,2?} ‖ λαμβάνετε A K X Π f¹³ 28 33 1009 1010 1071 1079 1195 1216 1230 1241 1242 1253 1344 1365 1546 1646 2148 2174 *Byz Lect* syr^{s,p,h,pal} cop^{sams,bo} goth arm Origen ‖

---

17 Ὁ...ἔθνεσιν Is 56.7　ὑμεῖς...λῃστῶν Jr 7.11　**18** ἤκουσαν...ἀπολέσωσιν Mk 14.1; Lk 20.19; 22.2　**20-21** Mk 11.14　**23** ἀμὴν...αὐτῷ Mt 17.20; Lk 17.6; 1 Cor 13.2

---

in the Temple. He overturned the tables of the money-changers and the stools of those who sold pigeons, 16 and would not let anyone carry anything through the Temple courts. 17 He then taught the people, "It is written in the Scriptures that God said, 'My house will be called a house of prayer for all peoples.' But you have turned it into a hideout for thieves!"

18 The chief priests and the teachers of the Law heard of this, so they began looking for some way to kill Jesus. They were afraid of him, because the whole crowd was amazed at his teaching.

19 When evening came, Jesus and his disciples left the city.

The Lesson from the Fig Tree
(Also Matt. 21.20–22)

20 Early next morning, as they walked along the road, they saw the fig tree. It was dead all the way down to its roots. 21 Peter remembered what had happened and said to Jesus, "Look, Teacher, the fig tree you cursed has died!" 22 Jesus answered them: "Remember this! If you have faith in God, 23 you can say to this hill, 'Get up and throw yourself in the sea.' If you do not doubt in your heart, but believe that what you say will happen, it will be done for you. 24 For this reason I tell you: When you pray and ask for something, believe that you have received it, and everything

will be given you. 25 And when you stand
praying, forgive whatever you have
against anyone, so that your Father in
heaven will forgive your sins. [26 If you
do not forgive others, neither will your
Father in heaven forgive your sins.]"

The Question about Jesus' Authority
(Also Matt. 21.23–27; Luke 20.1–8)

27 So they came back to Jerusalem.
As Jesus was walking in the Temple,
the chief priests, the teachers of the
Law, and the elders came to him 28 and
asked him: "What right do you have to
do these things? Who gave you the
right to do them?" 29 Jesus answered
them: "I will ask you just one question,
and if you give me an answer I will tell
you what right I have to do these things.
30 Tell me, where did John's right to
baptize come from: from God or from
man?" 31 They started to argue among
themselves: "What shall we say? If we
answer, 'From God,' he will say, 'Why,

ὑμῖν. **25** *καὶ ὅταν στήκετε προσευχόμενοι, ἀφίετε εἴ τι*
ἔχετε κατά τινος, ἵνα καὶ ὁ πατὴρ ὑμῶν ὁ ἐν τοῖς οὐρανοῖς
ἀφῇ ὑμῖν τὰ παραπτώματα ὑμῶν.[5]

The Authority of Jesus Questioned
(Mt 21.23–27; Lk 20.1–8)

27 *Καὶ ἔρχονται πάλιν εἰς Ἱεροσόλυμα. καὶ ἐν τῷ*
ἱερῷ περιπατοῦντος αὐτοῦ ἔρχονται πρὸς αὐτὸν οἱ ἀρχι-
ερεῖς καὶ οἱ γραμματεῖς καὶ οἱ πρεσβύτεροι **28** *καὶ ἔλεγον*
αὐτῷ, Ἐν ποίᾳ ἐξουσίᾳ ταῦτα ποιεῖς;[b] *ἢ τίς σοι ἔδωκεν*
τὴν ἐξουσίαν ταύτην ἵνα ταῦτα ποιῇς;[b] **29** *ὁ δὲ Ἰησοῦς*
εἶπεν αὐτοῖς, Ἐπερωτήσω ὑμᾶς ἕνα λόγον, καὶ ἀποκρίθητέ
μοι, καὶ ἐρῶ ὑμῖν ἐν ποίᾳ ἐξουσίᾳ ταῦτα ποιῶ· **30** *τὸ*
βάπτισμα τὸ Ἰωάννου ἐξ οὐρανοῦ ἦν ἢ ἐξ ἀνθρώπων;
ἀποκρίθητέ μοι. **31** *καὶ διελογίζοντο πρὸς ἑαυτοὺς λέγον-*
τες[6]*, Ἐὰν εἴπωμεν, Ἐξ οὐρανοῦ, ἐρεῖ, Διὰ τί [οὖν] οὐκ*

λήμψεσθε (*see* Mt 21.22) D Θ (f^{1} 565 700 λήψεσθε) it$^{a,aur,b,c,d,f,ff^2,i,k,l,q}$ vg cop$^{sa^{mss},bo^{ms}}$ geo$^{2?}$ Origen Cyprian // *omit* ὅτι ἐλάβετε l^{70}

[5] **25** {A} *omit verse 26* א B L W Δ Ψ 565 700 892 1216 it^{k,l} vg^{ms} syr^{s,pal} cop^{sa,bo} arm geo // *include verse 26* εἰ δὲ ὑμεῖς οὐκ ἀφίετε, οὐδὲ ὁ πατὴρ ὑμῶν ὁ ἐν τοῖς οὐρανοῖς ἀφήσει τὰ παραπτώματα ὑμῶν. (*see* Mt 6.15) A (D *omit* τοῖς *and add* ὑμεῖν *after* ἀφήσει) K X Θ Π (C f^{1} 1079 l^{1627m} *omit* τοῖς) (f^{13} ἀφήσει ὑμῖν) 28 (33 *omit* ὁ ἐν τοῖς οὐρανοῖς *and add* ὑμῖν *after* ἀφήσει) (1009 ἀφῇ ὑμῖν) 1010 1071 1195 1230 1241 1242 (1253 *omit* ὁ ἐν τοῖς οὐρανοῖς *and* παραπτώματα) 1344 1365 1546 1646 2148 2174 *Byz Lect* ($l^{10,12pt,32s,m,69,70,80,303,333,374}$ *omit* ὁ ἐν τοῖς οὐρανοῖς) ($l^{313,1579}$ πατὴρ ὑμῖν *and* ἀφέσει) it$^{a,aur,b,c,d,f,ff^2,(i),q,r^1}$ vg syr^{p,h} cop$^{bo^{mss}}$ goth eth Diatessaron (Cyprian) Augustine

[6] **31** {C} λέγοντες (*see* Mt 21.25; Lk 20.5) 𝔭^{45vid} א A B C K L (W *add* ὅτι) X Δ Π Ψ f^{1} 33 892 1009 1010 1071 1079 1195 1216 1230 1241 1242 1253 1344 1365 1546 1646 2148 2174 *Byz Lect* it^{aur,f,l,q} vg syr$^{(s,p),h}$ cop^{sa,bo} goth arm geo // τί εἴπωμεν 69 (it^{c}) // λέγοντες, Τί εἴπωμεν D Θ f^{13} 28 565 700 it$^{a,(b),d,(ff^2),(i),(k),(r^1)}$

---

b b **28** *b* question, *b* question: TR WH Bov Nes BF² AV RV ASV NEB TT Zür Luth Jer // *b* minor, *b* question: RSV Seg

---

25 ἀφίετε...παραπτώματα ὑμῶν Mt 6.14 εἴ τι ἔχετε κατά τινος Mt 5.23; Re 2.4, 14, 20 **27** οἱ ἀρχιερεῖς...πρεσβύτεροι Mt 16.21; 27.41; Mk 8.31; 14.43, 53; 15.1; Lk 9.22; 22.66 **30** τὸ βάπτισμα...ἦν Jn 1.33 **31** Mt 21.32; Lk 7.30

ἐπιστεύσατε αὐτῷ; 32 *ἀλλὰ εἴπωμεν, Ἐξ ἀνθρώπων; —*[c]
ἐφοβοῦντο τὸν ὄχλον, ἅπαντες γὰρ εἶχον[7] *τὸν Ἰωάννην*
ὄντως ὅτι προφήτης ἦν. 33 *καὶ ἀποκριθέντες τῷ Ἰησοῦ*
λέγουσιν, Οὐκ οἴδαμεν. καὶ ὁ Ἰησοῦς λέγει αὐτοῖς, Οὐδὲ
ἐγὼ λέγω ὑμῖν ἐν ποίᾳ ἐξουσίᾳ ταῦτα ποιῶ.

The Parable of the Vineyard and the Tenants
(Mt 21.33–46; Lk 20.9–19)

12 *Καὶ ἤρξατο αὐτοῖς ἐν παραβολαῖς λαλεῖν,* **Ἀμπελῶνα** *ἄνθρωπος* **ἐφύτευσεν, καὶ περιέθηκεν φραγμὸν καὶ
ὤρυξεν ὑπολήνιον καὶ ᾠκοδόμησεν πύργον,** *καὶ ἐξέδετο*
αὐτὸν γεωργοῖς, καὶ ἀπεδήμησεν. 2 *καὶ ἀπέστειλεν πρὸς*
τοὺς γεωργοὺς τῷ καιρῷ δοῦλον, ἵνα παρὰ τῶν γεωργῶν
λάβῃ ἀπὸ τῶν καρπῶν τοῦ ἀμπελῶνος· 3 *καὶ λαβόντες*
αὐτὸν ἔδειραν καὶ ἀπέστειλαν κενόν. 4 *καὶ πάλιν ἀπέστει-*
λεν πρὸς αὐτοὺς ἄλλον δοῦλον· κἀκεῖνον ἐκεφαλίωσαν καὶ
ἠτίμασαν. 5 *καὶ ἄλλον ἀπέστειλεν, κἀκεῖνον ἀπέκτειναν,*
καὶ πολλοὺς ἄλλους, οὓς μὲν δέροντες οὓς δὲ ἀποκτέν-
νοντες. 6 *ἔτι ἕνα εἶχεν,*[a] *υἱὸν ἀγαπητόν· ἀπέστειλεν αὐτὸν*
ἔσχατον πρὸς αὐτοὺς λέγων ὅτι Ἐντραπήσονται τὸν
υἱόν μου. 7 *ἐκεῖνοι δὲ οἱ γεωργοὶ πρὸς ἑαυτοὺς εἶπαν ὅτι*
Οὗτός ἐστιν ὁ κληρονόμος· δεῦτε ἀποκτείνωμεν αὐτόν,
καὶ ἡμῶν ἔσται ἡ κληρονομία. 8 *καὶ λαβόντες ἀπέκτειναν*
αὐτόν, καὶ ἐξέβαλον αὐτὸν ἔξω τοῦ ἀμπελῶνος. 9 *τί*
[οὖν] ποιήσει ὁ κύριος τοῦ ἀμπελῶνος; ἐλεύσεται καὶ
ἀπολέσει τοὺς γεωργούς, καὶ δώσει τὸν ἀμπελῶνα ἄλλοις.

---

[7] **32** {B} *εἶχον* ℵ A B C K L X Δ Π Ψ *f*[1] *f*[13] 33 892 1009 1010 1071 1079 1195 1216 1230 1241 1242 1253 1344 1365 1546 1646 2148 2174 *Byz Lect* it[l] vg syr[s, p, h] cop[sa, bo] goth // *εἴχουσαν* 28 // *ᾔδεισαν* D W Θ 565 it[a, aur, b, c, d, f, ff2, i, k, q, r1] arm geo // *οἴδασι* 700

---

[c] **32** *c* question and dash: WH Bov Nes BF[2] RV[mg] ASV[mg] RSV NEB TT Zür Luth // *c* question: Jer // *c* dash: RV ASV // *c* minor: TR AV // *c* ellipsis: Seg

[a] **6** *a* minor: WH Bov Nes BF[2] RV ASV RSV NEB TT Zür Luth Jer // *a* none: Seg // different text: TR AV

---

32 *ἐφοβοῦντο...ἦν* Mt 14.5; 21.46

12 1 *Ἀμπελῶνα...πύργον* Is 5.1–2   **6** *υἱὸν ἀγαπητόν* Gn 22.2; Mt 3.17; 17.5; Mk 1.11, 9.7; Lk 3.22; 2 Pe 1.17   **8** He 13.12

then, did you not believe John?' 32 But
if we say, 'From man . . .' " (They were
afraid of the people, because everyone
was convinced that John had been a
prophet.) 33 So their answer to Jesus
was, "We don't know." And Jesus said
to them, "Neither will I tell you, then,
by what right I do these things."

The Parable of the Tenants in the Vineyard
(Also Matt. 21.33–46; Luke 20.9–19)

12 Then Jesus spoke to them in parables: "There was a man who planted a
vineyard, put a fence around it, dug a
hole for the winepress, and built a watch-
tower. Then he rented the vineyard to
tenants and left home on a trip. 2 When
the time came for gathering the grapes,
he sent a slave to the tenants to receive
from them his share of the harvest.
3 The tenants grabbed the slave, beat
him and sent him back without a thing.
4 Then the owner sent another slave; the
tenants beat him over the head and
treated him shamefully. 5 The owner
sent another slave, and they killed him;
and they treated many others the same
way, beating some and killing others.
6 The only one left to send was the man's
own dear son. Last of all, then, he sent
his son to the tenants. 'I am sure they
will respect my son,' he said. 7 But those
tenants said to one another, 'This is the
owner's son. Come on, let us kill him, and
the vineyard will be ours!' 8 So they
took the son and killed him, and threw
his body out of the vineyard.
9 "What, then, will the owner of the
vineyard do?" asked Jesus. "He will
come and kill those men and turn over

the vineyard to other tenants. ¹⁰ Surely you have read this scripture?

'The stone which the builders rejected as worthless
Turned out to be the most important stone.
¹¹ This was done by the Lord,
How wonderful it is!' "

¹² The Jewish leaders tried to arrest Jesus, because they knew that he had told this parable against them. They were afraid of the crowd, however, so they left him and went away.

The Question about Paying Taxes
(Also Matt. 22.15–22; Luke 20.20–26)

¹³ Some Pharisees and some members of Herod's party were sent to Jesus to trap him with questions. ¹⁴ They came to him and said: "Teacher, we know that you are an honest man. You don't worry about what people think, because you pay no attention to what a man seems to be, but you teach the truth about God's will for man. Tell us, is it against our Law to pay taxes to the Roman Emperor? Should we pay them, or not?" ¹⁵ But Jesus saw through their trick and answered: "Why are you trying to trap me? Bring a silver coin, and let me see it." ¹⁶ They brought him one and he asked, "Whose face and name are these?" "The Emperor's," they answered. ¹⁷ So Jesus said, "Well, then, pay to the Emperor what belongs to him, and pay to God what belongs to God." And they were filled with wonder at him.

The Question about Rising from Death
(Also Matt. 22.23–33; Luke 20.27–40)

¹⁸ Some Sadducees came to Jesus. (They are the ones who say that people will not be raised from death.) ¹⁹ "Teacher," they said, "Moses wrote this law for us: 'If a man dies and leaves a wife, but no children, that man's brother must marry the widow so they can have children for the dead man.' ²⁰ Once there were seven

10 οὐδὲ τὴν γραφὴν ταύτην ἀνέγνωτε,

**Λίθον ὃν ἀπεδοκίμασαν οἱ οἰκοδομοῦντες,
οὗτος ἐγενήθη εἰς κεφαλὴν γωνίας·**
11 **παρὰ κυρίου ἐγένετο αὕτη,
καὶ ἔστιν θαυμαστὴ ἐν ὀφθαλμοῖς ἡμῶν;**

12 Καὶ ἐζήτουν αὐτὸν κρατῆσαι, καὶ ἐφοβήθησαν τὸν ὄχλον, ἔγνωσαν γὰρ ὅτι πρὸς αὐτοὺς τὴν παραβολὴν εἶπεν. καὶ ἀφέντες αὐτὸν ἀπῆλθον.

Paying Taxes to Caesar
(Mt 22.15–22; Lk 20.20–26)

13 Καὶ ἀποστέλλουσιν πρὸς αὐτόν τινας τῶν Φαρισαίων καὶ τῶν Ἡρῳδιανῶν ἵνα αὐτὸν ἀγρεύσωσιν λόγῳ. 14 καὶ ἐλθόντες λέγουσιν αὐτῷ, Διδάσκαλε, οἴδαμεν ὅτι ἀληθὴς εἶ καὶ οὐ μέλει σοι περὶ οὐδενός, οὐ γὰρ βλέπεις εἰς πρόσωπον ἀνθρώπων, ἀλλ' ἐπ' ἀληθείας τὴν ὁδὸν τοῦ θεοῦ διδάσκεις· ἔξεστιν δοῦναι κῆνσον Καίσαρι ἢ οὔ; ᵇδῶμεν ἢ μὴ δῶμεν; 15ᵇ ὁ δὲ εἰδὼς αὐτῶν τὴν ὑπόκρισιν εἶπεν αὐτοῖς, Τί με πειράζετε; φέρετέ μοι δηνάριον ἵνα ἴδω. 16 οἱ δὲ ἤνεγκαν. καὶ λέγει αὐτοῖς, Τίνος ἡ εἰκὼν αὕτη καὶ ἡ ἐπιγραφή; οἱ δὲ εἶπαν αὐτῷ, Καίσαρος. 17 ὁ δὲ Ἰησοῦς εἶπεν αὐτοῖς, Τὰ Καίσαρος ἀπόδοτε Καίσαρι καὶ τὰ τοῦ θεοῦ τῷ θεῷ. καὶ ἐξεθαύμαζον ἐπ' αὐτῷ.

The Question about the Resurrection
(Mt 22.23–33; Lk 20.27–40)

18 Καὶ ἔρχονται Σαδδουκαῖοι πρὸς αὐτόν, οἵτινες λέγουσιν ἀνάστασιν μὴ εἶναι, καὶ ἐπηρώτων αὐτὸν λέγοντες, 19 Διδάσκαλε, Μωϋσῆς ἔγραψεν ἡμῖν ὅτι ἐάν τινος ἀδελφὸς ἀποθάνῃ καὶ καταλίπῃ γυναῖκα καὶ μὴ ἀφῇ τέκνον, ἵνα λάβῃ ὁ ἀδελφὸς αὐτοῦ τὴν γυναῖκα καὶ ἐξαναστήσῃ σπέρμα τῷ ἀδελφῷ αὐτοῦ. 20 ἑπτὰ ἀδελφοὶ ἦσαν· καὶ

ᵇ **14-15** ᵇ no number, ᵇ number 15: TRᵉᵈ WH Bov Nes BF² NEB? Zür Luth Jer Seg ∥ ᵇ number 15, ᵇ no number: TRᵉᵈ AV RV RSV NEB? TT

10-11 Λίθον...ἡμῶν Ps 118.22–23   **10** Λίθον...γωνίας Ac 4.11; 1 Pe 2.7   **12** ἐζήτουν... ὄχλον Mt 14.5; Lk 22.2   **13** τινας...Ἡρῳδιανῶν Mk 3.6   **17** Τὰ...Καίσαρι Ro 13.7 **18** ἔρχονται...εἶναι Ac 23.8   **19** ἐάν...ἀδελφῷ αὐτοῦ Gn 38.8; Dt 25.5

ὁ πρῶτος ἔλαβεν γυναῖκα, καὶ ἀποθνῄσκων οὐκ ἀφῆκεν
σπέρμα· 21 καὶ ὁ δεύτερος ἔλαβεν αὐτήν, καὶ ἀπέθανεν
μὴ καταλιπὼν σπέρμα· καὶ ὁ τρίτος ὡσαύτως· 22 καὶ οἱ
ἑπτὰ οὐκ ἀφῆκαν σπέρμα. ἔσχατον πάντων καὶ ἡ γυνὴ
ἀπέθανεν. 23 ἐν τῇ ἀναστάσει [, ὅταν ἀναστῶσιν,]¹ τίνος
αὐτῶν ἔσται γυνή; οἱ γὰρ ἑπτὰ ἔσχον αὐτὴν γυναῖκα.
24 ἔφη αὐτοῖς ὁ Ἰησοῦς, Οὐ διὰ τοῦτο πλανᾶσθε μὴ εἰδότες
τὰς γραφὰς μηδὲ τὴν δύναμιν τοῦ θεοῦ; 25 ὅταν γὰρ ἐκ
νεκρῶν ἀναστῶσιν, οὔτε γαμοῦσιν οὔτε γαμίζονται, ἀλλ'
εἰσὶν ὡς ἄγγελοι ἐν τοῖς οὐρανοῖς. 26 περὶ δὲ τῶν νεκρῶν
ὅτι ἐγείρονται οὐκ ἀνέγνωτε ἐν τῇ βίβλῳ Μωϋσέως ἐπὶ
τοῦ βάτου πῶς εἶπεν αὐτῷ ὁ θεὸς λέγων, Ἐγὼ ὁ θεὸς
Ἀβραὰμ καὶ [ὁ] θεὸς Ἰσαὰκ καὶ [ὁ] θεὸς Ἰακώβ; 27 οὐκ
ἔστιν θεὸς νεκρῶν ἀλλὰ ζώντων· πολὺ πλανᾶσθε.

The Great Commandment
(Mt 22.34–40; Lk 10.25–28)

28 Καὶ προσελθὼν εἷς τῶν γραμματέων ἀκούσας αὐτῶν
συζητούντων, ἰδὼν ὅτι καλῶς ἀπεκρίθη αὐτοῖς, ἐπηρώτησεν αὐτόν, Ποία ἐστὶν ἐντολὴ πρώτη πάντων; 29 ἀπεκρίθη
ὁ Ἰησοῦς ὅτι Πρώτη ἐστίν, Ἄκουε, Ἰσραήλ, κύριος ὁ
θεὸς ἡμῶν κύριος εἷς ἐστιν, 30 καὶ ἀγαπήσεις κύριον
τὸν θεόν σου ἐξ ὅλης τῆς καρδίας σου καὶ ἐξ ὅλης τῆς
ψυχῆς σου καὶ ἐξ ὅλης τῆς διανοίας σου καὶ ἐξ ὅλης τῆς
ἰσχύος σου. 31 δευτέρα αὕτη, Ἀγαπήσεις τὸν πλησίον
σου ὡς σεαυτόν. μείζων τούτων ἄλλη ἐντολὴ οὐκ ἔστιν.

---

¹ 23 {D} ἐν τῇ ἀναστάσει, ὅταν ἀναστῶσιν, Χ 1010 1195 1242 (1344 ἀναστωσοισι) 1305 2148 Byzᵖᵗ l⁸⁸³ itᵃ syrʰ goth geo ‖ ἐν τῇ οὖν ἀναστάσει, ὅταν ἀναστῶσιν, Α Κ Π 1009 1079 1216 1230 1241 1546 1646 2174 Byzᵖᵗ Lect arm? ‖ ἐν τῇ ἀναστάσει οὖν ὅταν ἀναστῶσιν, Θ f¹ 28 565 700 1071 itᵃ⁾·ᵃᵘʳ·⁽ᵇ⁾· ff²·⁽ⁱ⁾·ˡ vg syrˢ·ʰ with * arm? ‖ ὅταν οὖν ἀναστῶσιν ἐν τῇ ἀναστάσει, f¹³ ‖ ἐν τῇ ἀναστάσει (see Lk 20.33) א Β C* L Δ Ψ itᵏ copᵇᵒ ‖ ἐν τῇ οὖν ἀναστάσει C² 33 1253 l⁷⁶·²¹¹ ‖ ἐν τῇ ἀναστάσει οὖν (see Mt 22.28) D W 892 itᶜ·ᵈ·ʳ¹ syrᵖ copˢᵃ ‖ ὅταν οὖν ἀναστῶσιν eth

26 ἐν...βάτου Ex 3.2 Ἐγὼ...Ἰακώβ Ex 3.6, 15, 16 29–30 Ἄκουε...ἰσχύος σου Dt 6.4–5; Jos 22.5; Lk 10.27 31 Ἀγαπήσεις...σεαυτόν Lv 19.18 (Ro 13.9; Ga 5.14; Jas 2.8)

brothers; the oldest got married, and died without having children. 21 Then the next one married the widow, and he died without having children. The same thing happened to the third brother, 22 and then to the rest: all seven brothers married the woman and died without having children. Last of all, the woman died. 23 Now, when all the dead are raised to life on the day of resurrection, whose wife will she be? All seven of them had married her!"

24 Jesus answered them: "How wrong you are! And do you know why? It is because you don't know the Scriptures or God's power. 25 For when the dead are raised to life they will be like the angels in heaven, and men and women will not marry. 26 Now, about the dead being raised: haven't you ever read in the book of Moses the passage about the burning bush? For there it is written that God said to Moses, 'I am the God of Abraham, the God of Isaac, and the God of Jacob.' 27 That means that he is the God of the living, not of the dead. You are completely wrong!"

The Great Commandment
(Also Matt. 22.34–40; Luke 10.25–28)

28 A teacher of the Law was there who heard the discussion. He saw that Jesus had given the Sadducees a good answer, so he came to him with a question: "Which commandment is the most important of all?" 29 "This is the most important one," said Jesus. " 'Hear, Israel! The Lord our God is the only Lord. 30 You must love the Lord your God with all your heart, and with all your soul, and with all your mind, and with all your strength.' 31 The second most important commandment is this: 'You must love your neighbor as yourself.' There is no other commandment

more important than these two." **32** The teacher of the Law said to Jesus: "Well done, Teacher! It is true, as you say, that only the Lord is God, and that there is no other god but he. **33** And so man must love God with all his heart, and with all his mind, and with all his strength; and he must love his neighbor as himself. It is much better to obey these two commandments than to bring animals to be burned on the altar and offer other sacrifices to God." **34** Jesus noticed how wise his answer was, and so he told him: "You are not far from the Kingdom of God." After this nobody dared to ask Jesus any more questions.

The Question about the Messiah
(Also Matt. 22.41–46; Luke 20.41–44)

35 As Jesus was teaching in the Temple he asked the question: "How can the teachers of the Law say that the Messiah will be the descendant of David? **36** The Holy Spirit inspired David to say:

'The Lord said to my Lord:
Sit here at my right side,
Until I put your enemies under your feet.'

37 David himself called him 'Lord': how, then, can the Messiah be David's descendant?"

32 καὶ εἶπεν αὐτῷ ὁ γραμματεύς, Καλῶς, διδάσκαλε, ἐπ' ἀληθείας εἶπες ὅτι[c] **εἷς ἐστιν καὶ οὐκ ἔστιν ἄλλος πλὴν αὐτοῦ· 33 καὶ τὸ ἀγαπᾶν αὐτὸν ἐξ ὅλης τῆς καρδίας καὶ ἐξ ὅλης τῆς συνέσεως καὶ ἐξ ὅλης τῆς ἰσχύος καὶ τὸ ἀγαπᾶν τὸν πλησίον ὡς ἑαυτὸν περισσότερόν ἐστιν πάντων τῶν ὁλοκαυτωμάτων καὶ θυσιῶν.** 34 καὶ ὁ Ἰησοῦς ἰδὼν [αὐτὸν] ὅτι νουνεχῶς ἀπεκρίθη εἶπεν αὐτῷ, Οὐ μακρὰν εἶ ἀπὸ τῆς βασιλείας τοῦ θεοῦ. καὶ οὐδεὶς οὐκέτι ἐτόλμα αὐτὸν ἐπερωτῆσαι.

The Question about David's Son
(Mt 22.41–46; Lk 20.41–44)

35 Καὶ ἀποκριθεὶς ὁ Ἰησοῦς ἔλεγεν διδάσκων ἐν τῷ ἱερῷ, Πῶς λέγουσιν οἱ γραμματεῖς ὅτι ὁ Χριστὸς υἱὸς Δαυίδ ἐστιν; 36 αὐτὸς Δαυὶδ εἶπεν ἐν τῷ πνεύματι τῷ ἁγίῳ,

Εἶπεν κύριος τῷ κυρίῳ μου,
Κάθου ἐκ δεξιῶν μου
ἕως ἂν θῶ τοὺς ἐχθρούς σου ὑποκάτω[2] τῶν ποδῶν σου.

37 αὐτὸς Δαυὶδ λέγει αὐτὸν κύριον, καὶ πόθεν αὐτοῦ ἐστιν υἱός; καὶ [ὁ] πολὺς ὄχλος ἤκουεν αὐτοῦ ἡδέως.

The Denouncing of the Scribes
(Mt 23.1–36; Lk 20.45–47)

38 Καὶ ἐν τῇ διδαχῇ αὐτοῦ ἔλεγεν, Βλέπετε ἀπὸ τῶν γραμματέων τῶν θελόντων ἐν στολαῖς περιπατεῖν καὶ ἀσπασμοὺς ἐν ταῖς ἀγοραῖς 39 καὶ πρωτοκαθεδρίας ἐν ταῖς συναγωγαῖς καὶ πρωτοκλισίας ἐν τοῖς δείπνοις·[d] 40 οἱ κατεσθίοντες τὰς οἰκίας τῶν χηρῶν[3] καὶ προφάσει μακρὰ προσευχόμενοι,[d] οὗτοι λήμψονται περισσότερον κρίμα.

The Widow's Offering
(Lk 21.1–4)

41 Καὶ καθίσας κατέναντι τοῦ γαζοφυλακίου[4] ἐθεώρει πῶς ὁ ὄχλος βάλλει χαλκὸν εἰς τὸ γαζοφυλάκιον· καὶ πολλοὶ πλούσιοι ἔβαλλον πολλά· 42 καὶ ἐλθοῦσα μία χήρα πτωχὴ ἔβαλεν λεπτὰ δύο, ὅ ἐστιν κοδράντης. 43 καὶ προσκαλεσάμενος τοὺς μαθητὰς αὐτοῦ εἶπεν αὐτοῖς, Ἀμὴν λέγω ὑμῖν ὅτι ἡ χήρα αὕτη ἡ πτωχὴ πλεῖον πάντων ἔβαλεν τῶν βαλλόντων εἰς τὸ γαζοφυλάκιον· 44 πάντες γὰρ ἐκ τοῦ περισσεύοντος αὐτοῖς ἔβαλον, αὕτη δὲ ἐκ τῆς ὑστερήσεως αὐτῆς πάντα ὅσα εἶχεν ἔβαλεν, ὅλον τὸν βίον αὐτῆς.

---

[3] 40 {A} τῶν χηρῶν (see Mt 23.14 mg; Lk 20.47) ℵ A B K L X Δ Θ Π Ψ f¹ 33 700 892 1009 1010 1071 1079 1195 1216 1230 1241 1242 1253 1344 1365 1546 1646 2148 2174 Byz Lect itaur,e,k,l vg syrs,p,h copsa,bo,fay arm geo ‖ χηρῶν καὶ ὀρφανῶν D W f¹³ 28 565 ita,b,c,d,ff²,i,q,rl syrpal

[4] 41 {B} καθίσας κατέναντι τοῦ γαζοφυλακίου ℵ L Δ 892 1195 ita,k copbo,fay ‖ καθίσας ἀπέναντι τοῦ γαζοφυλακίου B Ψ 2148 ‖ καθίσας ὁ Ἰησοῦς κατέναντι τοῦ γαζοφυλακίου A K X Π 700 1009 1010 1071 1079 1216 1241 1242 1546 1646 2174 Byz l184,299,313,883,950,1579,1642 itaur,b,c,ff²,i,l,rl vg syrp,h copsa eth ‖ καθίσας ὁ Ἰησοῦς ἀπέναντι τοῦ γαζοφυλακίου 33 1230 1253 1344 1365 Lect ‖ κατέναντι τοῦ γαζοφυλακίου καθεζόμενος ὁ Ἰησοῦς D itd,q ‖ ἑστὼς ὁ Ἰησοῦς κατέναντι τοῦ γαζοφυλακίου W Θ f¹ f¹³ 28 565 syrs,hmg,pal arm geo Origen

---

[d d] 39–40 d major, d minor: WHmg Bov Nes BF² RV ASV NEB (TT) Zür ‖ d major, d major: TR AV ‖ d minor, d major: WH RSV Luth Jer Seg

---

41 καθίσας...γαζοφυλακείου Jn 8.20   ἐθεώρει...γαζοφυλακείον 2 Kgs 12.9
43–44 ἡ χήρα...βίον αὐτῆς 2 Cor 8.12

Jesus Warns against the Teachers of the Law
(Also Matt. 23.1–36; Luke 20.45–47)

The large crowd heard Jesus gladly. 38 As he taught them he said: "Watch out for the teachers of the Law, who like to walk around in their long robes and be greeted with respect in the market place; 39 who choose the reserved seats in the synagogues and the best places at feasts. 40 They take advantage of widows and rob them of their homes, then make a show of saying long prayers! Their punishment will be all the worse!"

The Widow's Offering
(Also Luke 21.1–4)

41 As Jesus sat near the Temple treasury he watched the people as they dropped in their money. Many rich men dropped in much money; 42 then a poor widow came along and dropped in two little copper coins, worth about a penny. 43 He called his disciples together and said to them: "I tell you that this poor widow put more in the offering box than all the others. 44 For the others put in what they had to spare of their riches; but she, poor as she is, put in all she had — she gave all she had to live on."

Jesus Speaks of the Destruction
of the Temple
(Also Matt. 24.1–2; Luke 21.5–6)

13 As Jesus was leaving the Temple, one of his disciples said, "Look, Teacher! What wonderful stones and buildings!" [2] Jesus answered: "You see these great buildings? Not a single stone here will be left in its place; every one of them will be thrown down."

Troubles and Persecutions
(Also Matt. 24.3–14; Luke 21.7–19)

[3] Jesus was sitting on the Mount of Olives, across from the Temple, when Peter, James, John, and Andrew came to him in private. [4] "Tell us when this will be," they said; "and tell us what is the sign that will show that it is the time for all these things to happen."

[5] Jesus began to teach them: "Watch out, and don't let anyone fool you. [6] Many men will come in my name, saying, 'I am he!' and fool many people. [7] And don't be troubled when you hear the noise of battles close by and news of battles far away. Such things must happen, but they do not mean that the end has come. [8] One country will fight another country, one kingdom will attack another kingdom. There will be earthquakes everywhere, and there will be famines. These things are like the first pains of childbirth.

[9] "You yourselves must watch out. For men will arrest you and take you to court. You will be beaten in the syna-

The Destruction of the Temple Foretold
(Mt 24.1–2; Lk 21.5–6)

13 Καὶ ἐκπορευομένου αὐτοῦ ἐκ τοῦ ἱεροῦ λέγει αὐτῷ εἷς [ἐκ] τῶν μαθητῶν αὐτοῦ, Διδάσκαλε, ἴδε ποταποὶ λίθοι καὶ ποταπαὶ οἰκοδομαί. 2 καὶ ὁ Ἰησοῦς εἶπεν αὐτῷ, Βλέπεις ταύτας τὰς μεγάλας οἰκοδομάς; οὐ μὴ ἀφεθῇ ὧδε λίθος ἐπὶ λίθον[1] ὃς οὐ μὴ καταλυθῇ.

The Beginning of Woes
(Mt 24.3–14; Lk 21.7–19)

3 Καὶ καθημένου αὐτοῦ εἰς τὸ Ὄρος τῶν Ἐλαιῶν κατέναντι τοῦ ἱεροῦ ἐπηρώτα αὐτὸν κατ᾽ ἰδίαν Πέτρος καὶ Ἰάκωβος καὶ Ἰωάννης καὶ Ἀνδρέας, 4 Εἰπὸν ἡμῖν πότε ταῦτα ἔσται,[a] καὶ τί τὸ σημεῖον ὅταν μέλλῃ ταῦτα συντελεῖσθαι πάντα.[a] 5 ὁ δὲ Ἰησοῦς ἤρξατο λέγειν αὐτοῖς, Βλέπετε μή τις ὑμᾶς πλανήσῃ· 6 πολλοὶ ἐλεύσονται ἐπὶ τῷ ὀνόματί μου λέγοντες ὅτι Ἐγώ εἰμι, καὶ πολλοὺς πλανήσουσιν. 7 ὅταν δὲ ἀκούσητε πολέμους καὶ ἀκοὰς πολέμων, μὴ θροεῖσθε· δεῖ γενέσθαι, ἀλλ᾽ οὔπω τὸ τέλος. 8 ἐγερθήσεται γὰρ ἔθνος ἐπ᾽ ἔθνος καὶ βασιλεία ἐπὶ βασιλείαν, ἔσονται σεισμοὶ κατὰ τόπους, ἔσονται λιμοί[2]. [b]ἀρχὴ ὠδίνων ταῦτα. 9[b] βλέπετε δὲ ὑμεῖς ἑαυτούς·

---

[1] **2** {B} ὧδε λίθος ἐπὶ λίθον (see Mt 24.2) ℵ B L W Δ Θ Ψ f¹ f¹³ 28 33 700 892 1071 *Lect* itᵃ,ᵃᵘʳ,ᵇ,ᵈ,q ‖ ὧδε λίθος ἐπὶ λίθῳ D 565 1195 1344 Cyprian ‖ ὧδε λίθος ἐπὶ λίθῳ (*or* λίθον) syrˢ,ᵖ,ʰ with * copˢᵃ arm geo ‖ λίθος ἐπὶ λίθον ὧδε copᵇᵒ ‖ λίθος ἐπὶ λίθον X Π 1009 1079 1241 1242 1253 1546 itᶠᶠ²,ⁱ,ˡ,ʳˡ vg ‖ λίθος ἐπὶ λίθῳ (see Lk 21.6) A K 1010 1216 1230 1365 (1646 ἐπὶ λίθως) 2148 2174 *Byz* *l*⁷⁶,²⁹⁹,¹⁶⁴² ‖ *in templo* itᵏ ‖ *in isto templo lapis super lapidem* itᶜ,⁽ᵉ⁾

[2] **8** {B} ἔσονται λιμοί (see Mt 24.7) ℵᵇᵐᵍ B L Ψ copˢᵃᵐˢ,ᵇᵒ (eth) ‖

ᵃ ᵃ **4** a minor, a major: WH (Jer) ‖ a minor, a question: TR Bov Nes BF² RSV TT Zür Seg ‖ a question, a question: AV RV ASV NEB Luth

ᵇ ᵇ **8–9** b no number, b number 9: TRᵉᵈ WH Bov Nes BF² AV RV ASV RSV NEB TT Zür Luth Jer Seg ‖ b number 9, b no number: TRᵉᵈ

---

2 οὐ…καταλυθῇ Lk 19.44   **6** Jn 5.43   **8** ἐγερθήσεται…βασιλείαν Is 19.2; 2 Chr 15.6   **9** Mt 10.17–18

παραδώσουσιν ὑμᾶς εἰς συνέδρια^c καὶ εἰς συναγωγὰς^c δαρήσεσθε^c καὶ ἐπὶ ἡγεμόνων καὶ βασιλέων σταθήσεσθε ἕνεκεν ἐμοῦ εἰς μαρτύριον αὐτοῖς.^d 10 καὶ εἰς πάντα τὰ ἔθνη^d πρῶτον δεῖ κηρυχθῆναι τὸ εὐαγγέλιον. 11 καὶ ὅταν ἄγωσιν ὑμᾶς παραδιδόντες, μὴ προμεριμνᾶτε τί λαλήσητε, ἀλλ' ὃ ἐὰν δοθῇ ὑμῖν ἐν ἐκείνῃ τῇ ὥρᾳ τοῦτο λαλεῖτε, οὐ γάρ ἐστε ὑμεῖς οἱ λαλοῦντες ἀλλὰ τὸ πνεῦμα τὸ ἅγιον. 12 καὶ παραδώσει ἀδελφὸς ἀδελφὸν εἰς θάνατον καὶ πατὴρ τέκνον, καὶ ἐπαναστήσονται τέκνα ἐπὶ γονεῖς καὶ θανατώσουσιν αὐτούς· 13 καὶ ἔσεσθε μισούμενοι ὑπὸ πάντων διὰ τὸ ὄνομά μου. ὁ δὲ ὑπομείνας εἰς τέλος οὗτος σωθήσεται.

The Great Tribulation
(Mt 24.15–28; Lk 21.20–24)

14 Ὅταν δὲ ἴδητε **τὸ βδέλυγμα τῆς ἐρημώσεως** ἑστηκότα ὅπου οὐ δεῖ, ὁ ἀναγινώσκων νοείτω, τότε οἱ ἐν τῇ Ἰουδαίᾳ φευγέτωσαν εἰς τὰ ὄρη, 15 ὁ [δὲ] ἐπὶ τοῦ δώματος μὴ καταβάτω μηδὲ εἰσελθάτω ἆραί τι ἐκ τῆς οἰκίας αὐτοῦ, 16 καὶ ὁ εἰς τὸν ἀγρὸν μὴ ἐπιστρεψάτω εἰς τὰ ὀπίσω ἆραι τὸ ἱμάτιον αὐτοῦ. 17 οὐαὶ δὲ ταῖς ἐν γαστρὶ ἐχούσαις καὶ ταῖς θηλαζούσαις ἐν ἐκείναις ταῖς ἡμέραις. 18 προσεύχεσθε δὲ ἵνα μὴ γένηται χειμῶνος·

καὶ λιμοί D it^{a,aur,b,c,d,ff2,i,k,l,n,r1} vg ∥ λιμοὶ ταραχαί W (syr^s cop^{samss} λιμοὶ καί) ∥ καὶ λοιμοὶ καὶ ταραχαί Θ (565 700 geo^B λιμοί) ∥ καὶ ἔσονται λιμοὶ καὶ ταραχαί A K X Δ Π f¹ f¹³ (28 892 omit first καί) 33 1009 1010 1071 1079 1195 1216 1230 1241 1242 1253 1344 1365 1546 1646 2148 2174 Byz Lect it^q syr^{p,h} geo^A Origen^{lat} ∥ καὶ ἔσονται λιμοὶ καὶ λοιμοὶ καὶ ταραχαί (see Mt 24.7 mg; Lk 21.11) Σ 1342 ∥ καὶ ἔσονται σεισμοὶ καὶ λιμοὶ κατὰ τόπους καὶ ταραχαί l⁸⁸³ ∥ λιμοὶ καὶ λοιμοὶ καὶ ταραχαί arm ∥ hunger and thirst geo¹

^{c c c} **9** c none, c none, c none: WH Bov Nes BF² ∥ c minor, c none, c minor: TR AV RV ASV RSV (NEB) TT Zür Luth (Jer) Seg ∥ c none, c minor, c none
^{d d} **9–10** d major, d none: TR WH Bov Nes BF² AV RV ASV RSV NEB TT Zür Luth Jer Seg ∥ d none, d major

11 Mt 10.19–20; Lk 12.11–12   **12** ἐπαναστήσονται...γονεῖς Mic 7.6   **13** Mt 10.22 ἔσεσθε...μου Jn 15.18–21   **14** τὸ...ἐρημώσεως Dn 9.27; 11.31; 12.11; 1 Macc 1.54   **15–16** Lk 17.31   **17** Lk 23.29

gogues; you will stand before rulers and kings for my sake, to tell them the Good News. ¹⁰ The gospel must first be preached to all peoples. ¹¹ And when they arrest you and take you to court, do not worry ahead of time about what you are going to say; when the time comes, say whatever is given to you then. For the words you speak will not be yours; they will come from the Holy Spirit. ¹² Men will hand over their own brothers to be put to death, and fathers will do the same to their children; children will turn against their parents and have them put to death. ¹³ Everyone will hate you because of me. But the person who holds out to the end will be saved."

The Awful Horror
(Also Matt. 24.15–28; Luke 21.20–24)

¹⁴ "You will see 'The Awful Horror' standing in the place where he should not be." (Note to the reader: understand what this means!) "Then those who are in Judea must run away to the hills. ¹⁵ The man who is on the roof of his house must not lose time by going down into the house to get anything to take with him. ¹⁶ The man who is in the field must not go back to the house for his cloak. ¹⁷ How terrible it will be in those days for women who are pregnant, and for mothers who have little babies! ¹⁸ Pray to God that these things will not

happen in wintertime! ¹⁹ For the trouble of those days will be far worse than any the world has ever known, from the very beginning when God created the world until the present time. Nor will there ever again be anything like it. ²⁰ But the Lord has reduced the number of those days; if he had not, nobody would survive. For the sake of his chosen people, however, he has reduced those days.

²¹ "Then, if anyone says to you, 'Look, here is the Messiah!' or, 'Look, there he is!' — do not believe him. ²² For false Messiahs and false prophets will appear. They will perform signs and wonders for the purpose of deceiving God's chosen people, if possible. ²³ Be on your guard! I have told you everything ahead of time."

The Coming of the Son of Man
(Also Matt. 24.29–31; Luke 21.25–28)

²⁴ "In the days after that time of trouble the sun will grow dark, the moon will no longer shine, ²⁵ the stars will fall from heaven, and the powers in space will be driven from their course. ²⁶ Then the Son of Man will appear, coming in the clouds with great power and glory. ²⁷ He will send out the angels to the four corners of the earth and gather God's chosen people from one end of the world to the other."

The Lesson of the Fig Tree
(Also Matt. 24.32–35; Luke 21.29–33)

²⁸ "Let the fig tree teach you a lesson. When its branches become green and tender, and it starts putting out leaves,

19 ἔσονται γὰρ αἱ ἡμέραι ἐκεῖναι **θλῖψις** οἵα οὐ γέγονεν **τοιαύτη ἀπ' ἀρχῆς κτίσεως** ἣν ἔκτισεν ὁ θεὸς **ἕως τοῦ νῦν** καὶ οὐ μὴ γένηται. **20** καὶ εἰ μὴ ἐκολόβωσεν κύριος τὰς ἡμέρας, οὐκ ἂν ἐσώθη πᾶσα σάρξ. ἀλλὰ διὰ τοὺς ἐκλεκτοὺς οὓς ἐξελέξατο ἐκολόβωσεν τὰς ἡμέρας. **21** καὶ τότε ἐάν τις ὑμῖν εἴπῃ, "Ἴδε ὧδε ὁ Χριστός, "Ἴδε ἐκεῖ, μὴ πιστεύετε· **22** ἐγερθήσονται γὰρ ψευδόχριστοι καὶ ψευδοπροφῆται καὶ δώσουσιν³ σημεῖα καὶ τέρατα πρὸς τὸ ἀποπλανᾶν, εἰ δυνατόν, τοὺς ἐκλεκτούς. **23** ὑμεῖς δὲ βλέπετε· προείρηκα ὑμῖν πάντα.

The Coming of the Son of Man
(Mt 24.29–31; Lk 21.25–28)

24 Ἀλλὰ ἐν ἐκείναις ταῖς ἡμέραις μετὰ τὴν θλῖψιν ἐκείνην

ὁ ἥλιος σκοτισθήσεται,
    καὶ ἡ σελήνη οὐ δώσει τὸ φέγγος αὐτῆς,
25 καὶ οἱ ἀστέρες ἔσονται ἐκ τοῦ οὐρανοῦ πίπτοντες,
    καὶ αἱ δυνάμεις αἱ ἐν τοῖς οὐρανοῖς σαλευθήσονται.
26 καὶ τότε ὄψονται **τὸν υἱὸν τοῦ ἀνθρώπου ἐρχόμενον ἐν νεφέλαις** μετὰ δυνάμεως πολλῆς καὶ δόξης. **27** καὶ τότε ἀποστελεῖ τοὺς ἀγγέλους καὶ ἐπισυνάξει τοὺς ἐκλεκτοὺς [αὐτοῦ] ἐκ τῶν τεσσάρων ἀνέμων ἀπ' ἄκρου γῆς ἕως ἄκρου οὐρανοῦ.

The Lesson of the Fig Tree
(Mt 24.32–35; Lk 21.29–33)

28 Ἀπὸ δὲ τῆς συκῆς μάθετε τὴν παραβολήν· ὅταν ἤδη ὁ κλάδος αὐτῆς ἁπαλὸς γένηται καὶ ἐκφύῃ τὰ φύλλα,

---

³ **22** {B} δώσουσιν (see Mt 24.24) ℵ A B C L W X Δ Π Ψ 0235 f¹ 700 892 1009 1010 (1071 δώσωσιν) 1079 1195 1216 1230 1241 1242 1253 1344 1365 1546 1646 2148 2174 *Byz Lect* it^aur,b,c,ff²,i,k,l,q,r1 vg syr^s,p,h cop^sa,bo,fay goth arm geo¹ ‖ ποιήσουσιν D K Θ f¹³ 28 565 it^a,d eth geo² Diatessaron^a (Origen) Victor-Antioch

---

19 ἔσονται...νῦν Dn 12.1; Re 7.14   **22** Dt 13.1–3; Re 13.13   **24–25** ὁ ἥλιος... σαλευθήσονται Is 13.10; 34.4; Eze 32.7–8; Jl 2.10, 31; 3.15; Re 6.12–14; 8.12   **26** τὸν υἱὸν... δόξης Dn 7.13–14; Mk 8.38; Re 1.7   **27** ἐπισυνάξει...οὐρανοῦ Dt 30.4; Zch 2.6, 10   **28** Mt 21.19; Mk 11.13

γινώσκετε ὅτι ἐγγὺς τὸ θέρος ἐστίν. **29** οὕτως καὶ ὑμεῖς, ὅταν ἴδητε ταῦτα γινόμενα, γινώσκετε ὅτι ἐγγύς ἐστιν ἐπὶ θύραις. **30** ἀμὴν λέγω ὑμῖν ὅτι οὐ μὴ παρέλθῃ ἡ γενεὰ αὕτη μέχρις οὗ ταῦτα πάντα γένηται. **31** ὁ οὐρανὸς καὶ ἡ γῆ παρελεύσονται, οἱ δὲ λόγοι μου οὐ μὴ παρελεύσονται.

The Unknown Day and Hour
(Mt 24.36—44)

32 Περὶ δὲ τῆς ἡμέρας ἐκείνης ἢ τῆς ὥρας οὐδεὶς οἶδεν, οὐδὲ οἱ ἄγγελοι ἐν οὐρανῷ οὐδὲ ὁ υἱός, εἰ μὴ ὁ πατήρ. **33** βλέπετε ἀγρυπνεῖτε⁴· οὐκ οἴδατε γὰρ πότε ὁ καιρός ἐστιν. **34** ὡς ἄνθρωπος ἀπόδημος ἀφεὶς τὴν οἰκίαν αὐτοῦ καὶ δοὺς τοῖς δούλοις αὐτοῦ τὴν ἐξουσίαν, ἑκάστῳ τὸ ἔργον αὐτοῦ, καὶ τῷ θυρωρῷ ἐνετείλατο ἵνα γρηγορῇ. **35** γρηγορεῖτε οὖν, οὐκ οἴδατε γὰρ πότε ὁ κύριος τῆς οἰκίας ἔρχεται, ἢ ὀψὲ ἢ μεσονύκτιον ἢ ἀλεκτοροφωνίας ἢ πρωΐ, **36** μὴ ἐλθὼν ἐξαίφνης εὕρῃ ὑμᾶς καθεύδοντας. **37** ὃ δὲ ὑμῖν λέγω, πᾶσιν λέγω, γρηγορεῖτε.

The Plot to Kill Jesus
(Mt 26.1—5; Lk 22.1—2; Jn 11.45—53)

14 Ἦν δὲ τὸ πάσχα καὶ τὰ ἄζυμα μετὰ δύο ἡμέρας. καὶ ἐζήτουν οἱ ἀρχιερεῖς καὶ οἱ γραμματεῖς πῶς αὐτὸν ἐν δόλῳ κρατήσαντες ἀποκτείνωσιν· **2** ἔλεγον γάρ, Μὴ ἐν τῇ ἑορτῇ, μήποτε ἔσται θόρυβος τοῦ λαοῦ.

you know that summer is near. **29** In the same way, when you see these things happening, you will know that the time is near, ready to begin.[1] **30** Remember this! All these things will happen before the people now living have all died. **31** Heaven and earth will pass away; my words will never pass away."

No One Knows the Day or Hour
(Also Matt. 24.36—44)

32 "No one knows, however, when that day or hour will come — neither the angels in heaven, nor the Son; only the Father knows. **33** Be on watch, be alert, for you do not know when the time will be. **34** It will be like a man who goes away from home on a trip and leaves his servants in charge, each one with his own work to do; and he tells the doorkeeper to keep watch. **35** Watch, then, because you do not know when the master of the house is coming — it might be in the evening, or at midnight, or before dawn, or at sunrise. **36** If he comes suddenly, he must not find you asleep! **37** What I say to you, then, I say to all: Watch!"

The Plot against Jesus
(Also Matt. 26.1—5; Luke 22.1—2; John 11.45—53)

14 It was now two days before the Feast of Passover and Unleavened Bread. The chief priests and teachers of the Law were looking for a way to arrest Jesus secretly and put him to death. **2** "We must not do it during the feast," they said, "or the people might riot."

---

⁴ **33** {C} ἀγρυπνεῖτε B D itᵃ·ᶜ·ᵈ·ᵏ copᶠᵃʸ ∥ ἀγρυπνεῖτε· προσεύχεσθε lᵏ⁸³ copᵇᵒᵐˢˢ ∥ ἀγρυπνεῖτε καὶ προσεύχεσθε (see 14.38) ℵ A C K L W X Δ Π Ψ f¹ 700 892 1009 1010 1071 1079 1195 1216 1230 1241 1242 1253 1344 1365 1546 1646 2148 2174 *Byz Lect* l⁷⁰ᵐ·¹⁸⁵ˢ·ᵐ·³³³ˢ·ᵐ itᵃᵘʳ·ᶠ·ᶠᶠ²·ⁱ·ˡ· q·rˡ vg syr⁽ˢ⁾·ᵖ·ʰ copᵇᵒ arm Diatessaron Augustine ∥ καὶ ἀγρυπνεῖτε καὶ προσεύχεσθε Θ f¹³ 28 565 l²¹¹ᵐ copˢᵃ eth geo

---

ᵉ ᵉ ᵉ **34–35** *e* major, *e* minor, *e* minor: WH Bov Nes BF² AV RV ASV TT Luth Jer Seg ∥ *e* minor, *e* minor, *e* minor: TR ∥ *e* major, *e* dash, *e* dash: RSV ∥ *e* major, *e* minor, *e* dash: NEB ∥ *e* dash, *e* exclamation, *e* minor: Zür

---

31 Mt 5.18; Lk 16.17   **32** Ac 1.7   **33** Mt 25.13   **34** Mt 25.14   **35–36** Lk 12.36–38
14 1 ἐζήτουν…ἀποκτείνωσιν Mk 11.18; Lk 19.47

[1] **29** the time is near, ready to begin: *or* he is near, ready to come

Jesus Anointed at Bethany
(Also Matt. 26.6–13, John 12.1–8)

[3] Jesus was in the house of Simon the leper, in Bethany; while he was eating, a woman came in with an alabaster jar full of a very expensive perfume, made of pure nard. She broke the jar and poured the perfume on Jesus' head. [4] Some of the people there became angry, and said to each other, "What was the use of wasting the perfume? [5] It could have been sold for more than three hundred dollars, and the money given to the poor!" And they criticized her harshly. [6] But Jesus said: "Leave her alone! Why are you bothering her? She has done a fine and beautiful thing for me. [7] You will always have poor people with you, and any time you want to you can help them. But I shall not be with you always. [8] She did what she could: she poured perfume on my body to prepare it for burial ahead of time. [9] Now, remember this! Wherever the gospel is preached, all over the world, what she has done will be told in memory of her."

The Anointing at Bethany
(Mt 26.6–13; Jn 12.1–8)

3 Καὶ ὄντος αὐτοῦ ἐν Βηθανίᾳ ἐν τῇ οἰκίᾳ Σίμωνος τοῦ λεπροῦ κατακειμένου αὐτοῦ ἦλθεν γυνὴ ἔχουσα ἀλάβαστρον μύρου νάρδου πιστικῆς πολυτελοῦς·[a] συντρίψασα τὴν ἀλάβαστρον κατέχεεν αὐτοῦ τῆς κεφαλῆς. 4 ἦσαν δέ τινες ἀγανακτοῦντες πρὸς ἑαυτούς[1], Εἰς τί ἡ ἀπώλεια αὕτη τοῦ μύρου γέγονεν; 5 ἠδύνατο γὰρ τοῦτο τὸ μύρον πραθῆναι ἐπάνω[2] δηναρίων τριακοσίων καὶ δοθῆναι τοῖς πτωχοῖς· καὶ ἐνεβριμῶντο αὐτῇ. 6 ὁ δὲ Ἰησοῦς εἶπεν, Ἄφετε αὐτήν· τί αὐτῇ κόπους παρέχετε; καλὸν ἔργον ἠργάσατο ἐν ἐμοί. 7 πάντοτε γὰρ τοὺς πτωχοὺς ἔχετε μεθ' ἑαυτῶν, καὶ ὅταν θέλητε δύνασθε αὐτοῖς εὖ ποιῆσαι, ἐμὲ δὲ οὐ πάντοτε ἔχετε. 8 ὃ ἔσχεν ἐποίησεν· προέλαβεν μυρίσαι τὸ σῶμά μου εἰς τὸν ἐνταφιασμόν. 9 ἀμὴν δὲ λέγω ὑμῖν, ὅπου ἐὰν κηρυχθῇ τὸ εὐαγγέλιον εἰς ὅλον τὸν κόσμον, καὶ ὃ ἐποίησεν αὕτη λαληθήσεται εἰς μνημόσυνον αὐτῆς.

---

[1] 4 {C} ἦσαν δέ τινες ἀγανακτοῦντες πρὸς ἑαυτούς ℵ B C* L Ψ 892* (it^k) cop^bomss ∥ ἦσαν δέ τινες ἀγανακτοῦντες πρὸς ἑαυτοὺς καὶ λέγοντες A C² K X Δ Π (28 omit καί) 700 892^mg (1009 αὐτούς) 1010 1071 1079 1195 (1216 2174 καθ' ἑαυτούς) 1230 1241 1242 1253 1344 1365 1546 1646^c 2148 Byz (Lect cop^sa, bo, fay omit καί) l^10,185,299 it^aur, f, l, q vg syr^(s), h (eth) ∥ ἦσαν δέ τινες ἀγανακτοῦντες πρὸς ἑαυτοὺς καὶ λέγοντες f¹ 1646* geo ∥ ἦσαν δέ τινες τῶν μαθητῶν ἀγανακτοῦντες πρὸς ἑαυτοὺς καὶ λέγοντες W f¹³ l^547 (syr^p) ∥ οἱ δὲ μαθηταὶ αὐτοῦ διεπονοῦντο καὶ ἔλεγον D Θ 565 it^(a), d, (ff²), (i), r¹ (arm omit αὐτοῦ)

[2] 5 {B} ἐπάνω ℵ A B C D K L W X Δ Θ Π Ψ f¹ f¹³ 28 565 700 892 1009 1010 1071 1079 1195 1216 1230 1241 1242 1253 1344 1365 1546 1646 2148 2174 Byz Lect l^70m, 333s, m it^a, aur, d, f, ff², i, l, q, r¹ vg syr^p, h cop^sa, bo goth arm ∥ omit (see Jn 12.5) 517 954 1675 it^c, k syr^s geo Origen

---

[a] 3 a minor: TR WH Bov Nes BF² AV RV ASV RSV Zür Luth Seg ∥ a dash: WH^mg ∥ a major: NEB TT Jer

---

3 κατακειμένου...κεφαλῆς Lk 7.37–38 7 πάντοτε...ἑαυτῶν Dt 15.11 8 προέλαβεν ...ἐνταφιασμόν Jn 19.40

Judas' Agreement to Betray Jesus
(Mt 26.14–16; Lk 22.3–6)

10 Καὶ Ἰούδας Ἰσκαριὼθ³ ὁ εἷς τῶν δώδεκα ἀπῆλθεν πρὸς τοὺς ἀρχιερεῖς ἵνα αὐτὸν παραδοῖ [αὐτοῖς]. **11** οἱ δὲ ἀκούσαντες ἐχάρησαν καὶ ἐπηγγείλαντο αὐτῷ ἀργύριον δοῦναι. καὶ ἐζήτει πῶς αὐτὸν εὐκαίρως παραδοῖ.

The Passover with the Disciples
(Mt 26.17–25; Lk 22.7–14, 21–23; Jn 13.21–30)

12 Καὶ τῇ πρώτῃ ἡμέρᾳ τῶν ἀζύμων, ὅτε τὸ πάσχα ἔθυον, λέγουσιν αὐτῷ οἱ μαθηταὶ αὐτοῦ, Ποῦ θέλεις ἀπελθόντες ἑτοιμάσωμεν ἵνα φάγῃς τὸ πάσχα; **13** καὶ ἀποστέλλει δύο τῶν μαθητῶν αὐτοῦ καὶ λέγει αὐτοῖς, Ὑπάγετε εἰς τὴν πόλιν, καὶ ἀπαντήσει ὑμῖν ἄνθρωπος κεράμιον ὕδατος βαστάζων· ἀκολουθήσατε αὐτῷ, **14** καὶ ὅπου ἐὰν εἰσέλθῃ εἴπατε τῷ οἰκοδεσπότῃ ὅτι Ὁ διδάσκαλος λέγει, Ποῦ ἐστιν τὸ κατάλυμά μου ὅπου τὸ πάσχα μετὰ τῶν μαθητῶν μου φάγω; **15** καὶ αὐτὸς ὑμῖν δείξει ἀνάγαιον μέγα ἐστρωμένον ἕτοιμον· καὶ ἐκεῖ ἑτοιμάσατε ἡμῖν. **16** καὶ ἐξῆλθον οἱ μαθηταὶ καὶ ἦλθον εἰς τὴν πόλιν καὶ εὗρον καθὼς εἶπεν αὐτοῖς, καὶ ἡτοίμασαν τὸ πάσχα. **17** Καὶ ὀψίας γενομένης ἔρχεται μετὰ τῶν δώδεκα. **18** καὶ ἀνακειμένων αὐτῶν καὶ ἐσθιόντων ὁ Ἰησοῦς εἶπεν, Ἀμὴν λέγω ὑμῖν ὅτι εἷς ἐξ ὑμῶν παραδώσει με, **ὁ ἐσθίων μετ' ἐμοῦ.** **19** ἤρξαντο λυπεῖσθαι καὶ λέγειν αὐτῷ εἷς κατὰ εἷς, Μήτι ἐγώ; **20** ὁ δὲ εἶπεν αὐτοῖς, Εἷς [ἐκ] τῶν

---

³ **10** {B} Ἰσκαριὼθ ℵ* B C*ᵛⁱᵈ ‖ ὁ Ἰσκαριὼθ ℵᶜ L Θ Ψ 565 892 ‖ ὁ Ἰσκαριώτης A C² K W X Δ Π f¹ f¹³ 700 1009 1010 1079 1195 1216 1230 1241 1242 1253 1344 1546 2148 2174 (28 1071 1365 1646 *l*²⁹⁹*,⁵⁴⁷ *omit* ὁ) Byz Lect vgᶜˡ copˢᵃ,ᵇᵒ goth (Origen *omit* ὁ) Eusebius ‖ Σκαριώτης D itᵈ,ᵏ,ˡ,q (itᵃ,ᵃᵘʳ,ff²,ⁱ,ʳ¹ *Scarioth*, itᶠ *Schariothe*, itᶜ syrˢ,ᵖ *Scariotha*) vgʷʷ syrʰ arm geo (Augustine *Scarioth*)

---

12 τῇ...ἔθυον Ex 12.6, 14–20 **18** εἷς...παραδώσει...ἐμοῦ Ps 41.9

Judas Agrees to Betray Jesus
(Also Matt. 26.14–16; Luke 22.3–6)

10 Then Judas Iscariot, one of the twelve disciples, went off to the chief priests in order to hand Jesus over to them. **11** They were greatly pleased to hear what he had to say, and promised to give him money. So Judas started looking for a good chance to betray Jesus.

Jesus Eats the Passover Meal with His Disciples
(Also Matt. 26.17–25; Luke 22.7–14, 21–23; John 13.21–30)

12 On the first day of the Feast of Unleavened Bread, the day the lambs for the Passover meal were killed, Jesus' disciples asked him: "Where do you want us to go and get your Passover supper ready?" **13** Then Jesus sent two of them out with these instructions: "Go into the city, and a man carrying a jar of water will meet you. **14** Follow him to the house he enters, and say to the owner of the house: 'The Teacher says, Where is my room where my disciples and I shall eat the Passover supper?' **15** Then he will show you a large upstairs room, fixed up and furnished, where you will get things ready for us." **16** The disciples left, went to the city, and found everything just as Jesus had told them; and they prepared the Passover supper.

17 When it was evening, Jesus came with the twelve disciples. **18** While they were at the table eating, Jesus said: "I tell you this: one of you will betray me — one who is eating with me." **19** The disciples were upset and began to ask him, one after the other, "Surely you don't mean me, do you?" **20** Jesus answered: "It will be one of you twelve, one who dips his bread in the dish with me. ²¹ The Son of Man will die as the Scriptures say he will; but how terrible for that man who will betray the Son of Man! It would have been better for that man if he had never been born!"

The Lord's Supper
(Also Matt. 26.26–30; Luke 22.15–20; 1 Cor. 11.23–25)

²² While they were eating, Jesus took the bread, gave a prayer of thanks, broke it, and gave it to his disciples. "Take it," he said, "this is my body." ²³ Then he took the cup, gave thanks to God, and handed it to them; and they all drank from it. ²⁴ Jesus said: "This is my blood which is poured out for many, my blood which seals God's covenant. ²⁵ I tell you, I will never again drink this wine until the day I drink the new wine in the Kingdom of God." ²⁶ Then they sang a hymn and went out to the Mount of Olives.

δώδεκα, ὁ ἐμβαπτόμενος μετ' ἐμοῦ εἰς τὸ τρύβλιον[4]. **21** ὅτι ὁ μὲν υἱὸς τοῦ ἀνθρώπου ὑπάγει καθὼς γέγραπται περὶ αὐτοῦ, οὐαὶ δὲ τῷ ἀνθρώπῳ ἐκείνῳ δι' οὗ ὁ υἱὸς τοῦ ἀνθρώπου παραδίδοται· καλὸν αὐτῷ εἰ οὐκ ἐγεννήθη ὁ ἄνθρωπος ἐκεῖνος.

The Institution of the Lord's Supper
(Mt 26.26–30; Lk 22.15–20; 1 Cor 11.23–25)

22 *Καὶ ἐσθιόντων αὐτῶν λαβὼν ἄρτον εὐλογήσας ἔκλα-σεν καὶ ἔδωκεν αὐτοῖς καὶ εἶπεν, Λάβετε, τοῦτό ἐστιν τὸ σῶμά μου.* 23 *καὶ λαβὼν ποτήριον εὐχαριστήσας ἔδωκεν αὐτοῖς, καὶ ἔπιον ἐξ αὐτοῦ πάντες.* **24** *καὶ εἶπεν αὐτοῖς, Τοῦτό ἐστιν τὸ αἷμά μου τῆς διαθήκης[5] τὸ ἐκχυννόμενον ὑπὲρ πολλῶν·* 25 *ἀμὴν λέγω ὑμῖν ὅτι οὐκέτι οὐ μὴ πίω[6] ἐκ τοῦ γενήματος τῆς ἀμπέλου ἕως τῆς ἡμέρας ἐκείνης ὅταν αὐτὸ πίνω καινὸν ἐν τῇ βασιλείᾳ τοῦ θεοῦ.* **26** *Καὶ ὑμνήσαντες ἐξῆλθον εἰς τὸ Ὄρος τῶν Ἐλαιῶν.*

---

[4] **20** {B} εἰς τὸ τρύβλιον ℵ A C[2] D K L P W X Δ Π Ψ *f*[1] *f*[13] 28 700 892 1009 1010 1071 1079 1195 1216 1230 1241 1242 1344 1365 1546 1646 2148 2174 *Byz Lect* it[a] cop[sa,bo] arm? geo Origen ∥ εἰς τὸ ἐν τρύβλιον B C* Θ 565 ∥ ἐν τῷ τρυβλίῳ 1253 *l*[10,70,950] it[aur,c,d,f,ff2,i,k,l,q] vg syr[s,p,h] arm? Apostolic Constitutions

[5] **24** {B} τῆς διαθήκης (*see* Mt 26.28) ℵ B C D[b] L Θ Ψ 565 it[k] cop[sams,bo] geo[1] ∥ τὸ τῆς διαθήκης D* W it[d] ∥ τὸ τῆς καινῆς διαθήκης (*see* Mt 26.28 mg; Lk 22.20; 1 Cor 11.25) A K P Δ Π *f*[1] *f*[13] 28 700 892 1009 1010 1071 1079 1195 1216 1230 1241 1253 1365 1546 1646 2148 2174 *Byz Lect* it[b,i,r1] ∥ τῆς καινῆς διαθήκης X 1242 1344 it[a,aur,c,f,l,q] vg syr[s,p,h] cop[sa,bomss] arm eth geo[2] Diatessaron ∥ *omit* it[ff2]

[6] **25** {C} οὐκέτι οὐ μὴ πίω A B K X Δ Π Ψ *f*[1] *f*[13] 28 700 1009 1010 1071 1079 1195 1216 1230 1241 1242 1253 1344 1365 1546 1646 2148 2174 *Byz Lect* it[aur,b,ff2,i,l,q] vg syr[s,p,h] cop[sa] geo ∥ οὐ μὴ πίω (*see* Mt 26.29) ℵ C L W 892 *l*[211,950] it[c,k] cop[bo] eth ∥ οὐ μὴ προσθῶ πεῖν D it[a,d,f] arm ∥ οὐκέτι οὐ προσθῶ πιεῖν 565 ∥ οὐκέτι οὐ μὴ προσθῶμεν πιεῖν Θ

---

22 λαβὼν...αὐτοῖς Mt 14.19; 15.36; Mk 6.41; 8.6; Lk 9.16   **23–24** λαβὼν...μου 1 Cor 10.16 **24** τὸ αἷμα...διαθήκης Ex 24.8; Zch 9.11; He 9.20

Peter's Denial Foretold
(Mt 26.31–35; Lk 22.31–34; Jn 13.36–38)

27 Καὶ λέγει αὐτοῖς ὁ Ἰησοῦς ὅτι Πάντες σκανδαλισθήσεσθε, ὅτι γέγραπται,

Πατάξω τὸν ποιμένα,
   καὶ τὰ πρόβατα διασκορπισθήσονται·
28 ἀλλὰ μετὰ τὸ ἐγερθῆναί με προάξω ὑμᾶς εἰς τὴν
Γαλιλαίαν. 29 ὁ δὲ Πέτρος ἔφη αὐτῷ, Εἰ καὶ πάντες
σκανδαλισθήσονται, ἀλλ' οὐκ ἐγώ. 30 καὶ λέγει αὐτῷ
ὁ Ἰησοῦς, Ἀμὴν λέγω σοι ὅτι σὺ σήμερον⁷ ταύτῃ τῇ
νυκτὶ πρὶν ἢ δὶς ἀλέκτορα φωνῆσαι⁸ τρίς με ἀπαρνήσῃ.
31 ὁ δὲ ἐκπερισσῶς ἐλάλει, Ἐὰν δέῃ με συναποθανεῖν σοι,
οὐ μή σε ἀπαρνήσομαι. ὡσαύτως δὲ καὶ πάντες ἔλεγον.

The Prayer in Gethsemane
(Mt 26.36–46; Lk 22.39–46)

32 Καὶ ἔρχονται εἰς χωρίον οὗ τὸ ὄνομα Γεθσημανί,
καὶ λέγει τοῖς μαθηταῖς αὐτοῦ, Καθίσατε ὧδε ἕως
προσεύξωμαι. 33 καὶ παραλαμβάνει τὸν Πέτρον καὶ
[τὸν] Ἰάκωβον καὶ [τὸν] Ἰωάννην μετ' αὐτοῦ, καὶ
ἤρξατο ἐκθαμβεῖσθαι καὶ ἀδημονεῖν, 34 καὶ λέγει αὐτοῖς,
Περίλυπός ἐστιν ἡ ψυχή μου ἕως θανάτου· μείνατε ὧδε
καὶ γρηγορεῖτε. 35 καὶ προελθὼν μικρὸν ἔπιπτεν ἐπὶ

---

⁷ **30** {B} σήμερον ℵ A B C K L W X Δ Π Ψ 0112 f¹ 28 892 1009 1010
1071 1079 1195 1216 1230 1241 1242 1253 1344 1365 1546 1646 2148 2174 *Byz*
Lect itᵃᵘʳ,ᶜ,ᵏ,⁽ˡ⁾ vg syrˢ,ᵖ,ʰ copˢᵃ,ᵇᵒ geo ‖ omit (see Mt 26.34) D Θ f¹³ 565 700
itᵃ,ᵇ,ᵈ,f,ff²,i,q arm

⁸ **30** {C} ἢ δὶς ἀλέκτορα φωνῆσαι A B K L X Δ Π Ψ 0112 f¹ 28 892
1010 1071 1079 1195 1216 1230 1241 1242 1253 1344 1305 1546 1646 2174 *Byz*
Lect itᵃᵘʳ,f,q vgᵂᵂ syrˢ,ᵖ,ʰ geo ‖ ἢ ἀλέκτορα φωνῆσαι δίς C² copˢᵃ,ᵇᵒ ‖
ἀλέκτορα δὶς φωνῆσαι Θ f¹³ 565 700 1009 itˡ vgᶜˡ ‖ ἢ ἀλέκτορα φωνῆσαι
C* 2148 ‖ ἀλέκτορα φωνῆσαι (see Mt 26.34; Lk 22.34; Jn 13.38) ℵ D W
f⁷⁶,¹⁵⁰,⁹⁵⁰ itᵃ,ᵇ,ᶜ,ᵈ,ff²,i,k arm eth

---

27 Πατάξω διασκορπισθήσονται Zch 13.7; Mt 26.56; Mk 14.50   28 Mk 16.7   31 Ἐὰν
δέῃ με...σοι Jn 11.16   32 ἔρχονται...Γεθσημανί Jn 18.1   33 Πέτρον...Ἰωάννην Mt 17.1;
Mk 5.37; 9.2; 13.3; Lk 5.10; 6.14; 8.51; 9.28; Ac 1.13   34 Περίλυπος...μου Ps 42.5, 11; 43.5;
Jn 12.27   Περίλυπος...θανάτου Jon 4.9

Jesus Predicts Peter's Denial
(Also Matt. 26.31–35; Luke 22.31–34;
John 13.36–38)

27 Jesus said to them: "All of you will
run away and leave me, for the scripture
says, 'God will kill the shepherd and the
sheep will all be scattered.' 28 But after
I am raised to life I will go to Galilee
ahead of you." 29 Peter answered, "I
will never leave you, even though all the
rest do!" 30 "Remember this!" Jesus said
to Peter. "Before the rooster crows two
times tonight, you will say three times
that you do not know me." 31 Peter
answered even more strongly: "I will
never say I do not know you, even if I
have to die with you!" And all the
disciples said the same thing.

Jesus Prays in Gethsemane
(Also Matt. 26.36–46; Luke 22.39–46)

32 They came to a place called Gethsemane, and Jesus said to his disciples,
"Sit here while I pray." 33 Then he
took Peter, James, and John with him.
Distress and anguish came over him,
34 and he said to them: "The sorrow in
my heart is so great that it almost
crushes me. Stay here and watch."
35 He went a little farther on, threw

himself on the ground and prayed that, if possible, he might not have to go through the hour of suffering. ³⁶ "Father!" he prayed, "my Father! All things are possible for you. Take this cup away from me. But not what I want, but what you want."

³⁷ Then he returned and found the three disciples asleep, and said to Peter, "Simon, are you asleep? Weren't you able to stay awake for one hour?" ³⁸ And he said to them, "Keep watch, and pray, so you will not fall into temptation. The spirit is willing, but the flesh is weak."

³⁹ He went away once more and prayed, saying the same words. ⁴⁰ Then he came back to the disciples and found them asleep; they could not keep their eyes open. And they did not know what to say to him.

⁴¹ When he came back the third time, he said to them: "Are you still sleeping and resting? Enough! The hour has come! Look, the Son of Man is now handed over to the power of sinful men. ⁴² Rise, let us go. Look, here is the man who is betraying me!"

The Arrest of Jesus
(Also Matt. 26.47–56; Luke 22.47–53; John 18.3–12)

⁴³ He was still talking when Judas, one of the twelve disciples, arrived. A crowd carrying swords and clubs was

τῆς γῆς, καὶ προσηύχετο ἵνα εἰ δυνατόν ἐστιν παρέλθῃ ἀπ' αὐτοῦ ἡ ὥρα, 36 καὶ ἔλεγεν, Ἀββα ὁ πατήρ, πάντα δυνατά σοι· παρένεγκε τὸ ποτήριον τοῦτο ἀπ' ἐμοῦ· ἀλλ' οὐ τί ἐγὼ θέλω ἀλλὰ τί σύ. 37 καὶ ἔρχεται καὶ εὑρίσκει αὐτοὺς καθεύδοντας, καὶ λέγει τῷ Πέτρῳ, Σίμων, καθεύδεις; οὐκ ἴσχυσας μίαν ὥραν γρηγορῆσαι; 38 γρηγορεῖτε[b] καὶ προσεύχεσθε,[b] ἵνα μὴ ἔλθητε εἰς πειρασμόν· τὸ μὲν πνεῦμα πρόθυμον ἡ δὲ σὰρξ ἀσθενής. 39 καὶ πάλιν ἀπελθὼν προσηύξατο τὸν αὐτὸν λόγον εἰπών⁹. 40 καὶ πάλιν ἐλθὼν εὗρεν αὐτοὺς καθεύδοντας, ἦσαν γὰρ αὐτῶν οἱ ὀφθαλμοὶ καταβαρυνόμενοι, καὶ οὐκ ᾔδεισαν τί ἀποκριθῶσιν αὐτῷ. 41 καὶ ἔρχεται τὸ τρίτον καὶ λέγει αὐτοῖς, Καθεύδετε τὸ λοιπὸν καὶ ἀναπαύεσθε;[c] ἀπέχει·[d] ἦλθεν¹⁰ ἡ ὥρα,[d] ἰδοὺ παραδίδοται ὁ υἱὸς τοῦ ἀνθρώπου εἰς τὰς χεῖρας τῶν ἁμαρτωλῶν. 42 ἐγείρεσθε ἄγωμεν· ἰδοὺ ὁ παραδιδούς με ἤγγικεν.

The Betrayal and Arrest of Jesus
(Mt 26.47–56; Lk 22.47–53; Jn 18.3–12)

43 Καὶ εὐθὺς ἔτι αὐτοῦ λαλοῦντος παραγίνεται Ἰούδας εἷς τῶν δώδεκα καὶ μετ' αὐτοῦ ὄχλος μετὰ μαχαιρῶν καὶ

---

⁹ **39** {A} τὸν αὐτὸν λόγον εἰπών ℵ A B C K L W X Δ Θ Π Ψ 0112 0116^vid f¹ f¹³ 28 565 700 892 1009 1010 1071 1079 1195 1216 1230 1241 1242 1253 1344 1365 1546 1646 2148 2174 *Byz Lect* it^aur, f, l, q vg syr^s, p, h cop^sa, bo arm geo ‖ *omit* D it^a, b, c, d, ff², k

¹⁰ **41** {B} ἀπέχει· ἦλθεν ℵ A B C K L X Δ Π 0112 f¹ 28 700 1010 1079 1195 1230 1241 1242 1253 1344 1546 1646 2148 2174 *Byz Lect* it^aur, l vg cop^sa, boms Augustine ‖ ἀπέχει τὸ τέλος· ἦλθεν (see Lk 22.37) (W τέλος· ἰδοὺ ἦλθεν) (Θ τὸ τό) f¹³ 565 1009 1071 1216 1365 it^(a), b, f, ff², rl syr^(s), p, h arm Diatessaron^a ‖ ἀπέχει τὸ τέλος· καὶ D it^c, d, q (geo *add* ἦλθεν) ‖ ἦλθεν Ψ 892 (it^k) cop^boms

---

^b b **38** b none, b minor: WH Bov Nes BF² AV RV ASV TT Luth Seg ‖ b minor, b none: RV^mg ASV^mg NEB ‖ b minor, b minor: Zür ‖ b none, b none: TR RSV Jer

^c **41** c question: ASV^mg RSV NEB Luth ‖ c statement: Jer? Seg^mg ‖ c command: AV RV ASV TT Zür Seg ‖ c statement or command: TR WH Bov Nes BF²

^d d **41** d major, d minor: WH Bov Nes BF² Zür Jer Seg ‖ d minor, d major: TR AV Luth ‖ d major, d major: RV ASV RSV NEB ‖ d exclamation, d exclamation: TT

---

36 Ἀββα ὁ πατήρ Ro 8.15; Ga 4.6   οὐ τί ἐγὼ θέλω...σύ Jn 5.30; 6.38   **38** προσεύχεσθε ...πειρασμόν Mt 6.13; Lk 11.4

ξύλων παρὰ τῶν ἀρχιερέων καὶ τῶν γραμματέων καὶ τῶν πρεσβυτέρων. **44** δεδώκει δὲ ὁ παραδιδοὺς αὐτὸν σύσσημον αὐτοῖς λέγων, ῞Ον ἂν φιλήσω αὐτός ἐστιν· κρατήσατε αὐτὸν καὶ ἀπάγετε ἀσφαλῶς. **45** καὶ ἐλθὼν εὐθὺς προσελθὼν αὐτῷ λέγει, ῾Ραββί, καὶ κατεφίλησεν αὐτόν. **46** οἱ δὲ ἐπέβαλον τὰς χεῖρας αὐτῷ καὶ ἐκράτησαν αὐτόν. **47** εἷς δέ [τις] τῶν παρεστηκότων σπασάμενος τὴν μάχαιραν ἔπαισεν τὸν δοῦλον τοῦ ἀρχιερέως καὶ ἀφεῖλεν αὐτοῦ τὸ ὠτάριον. **48** καὶ ἀποκριθεὶς ὁ ᾿Ιησοῦς εἶπεν αὐτοῖς, ῾Ως ἐπὶ λῃστὴν ἐξήλθατε μετὰ μαχαιρῶν καὶ ξύλων συλλαβεῖν με;ᵉ **49** καθ᾿ ἡμέραν ἤμην πρὸς ὑμᾶς ἐν τῷ ἱερῷ διδάσκων καὶ οὐκ ἐκρατήσατέ με· ἀλλ᾿ ἵνα πληρωθῶσιν αἱ γραφαί. **50** καὶ ἀφέντες αὐτὸν ἔφυγον πάντες.

The Young Man Who Fled

51 Καὶ νεανίσκος τις συνηκολούθει αὐτῷ περιβεβλημένος σινδόνα ἐπὶ γυμνοῦ, καὶ κρατοῦσιν αὐτόν· **52** ὁ δὲ καταλιπὼν τὴν σινδόνα γυμνὸς ἔφυγεν.[11]

Jesus before the Council
(Mt 26.57–68; Lk 22.54–55, 63–71; Jn 18.13–14, 19–24)

53 Καὶ ἀπήγαγον τὸν ᾿Ιησοῦν πρὸς τὸν ἀρχιερέα, καὶ συνέρχονται πάντες οἱ ἀρχιερεῖς καὶ οἱ πρεσβύτεροι καὶ οἱ γραμματεῖς. **54** καὶ ὁ Πέτρος ἀπὸ μακρόθεν ἠκολούθησεν αὐτῷ ἕως ἔσω εἰς τὴν αὐλὴν τοῦ ἀρχιερέως, καὶ

---

[11] **52** {C} γυμνὸς ἔφυγεν ℵ B C ‖ ἔφυγεν γυμνός L Ψ 892 itᵃᵘʳ,ᶜ,ᵏ syrᵖ copˢᵃ,ᵇᵒ,ᶠᵃʸ eth ‖ γυμνὸς ἔφυγεν ἀπ᾿ αὐτῶν A Dᵍʳ K P W X Θ Π f¹ f¹³ 28 565 700 1009 1010 1079 1195 1216 1230 1241 1242 1253 1344 1365 1546 1646 2148 2174 Byz Lect itᵃ,(ᵇ),ᶠ,ˡ vg syrʰ goth geo¹ ‖ ἔφυγεν γυμνὸς ἀπ᾿ αὐτῶν Δ 1071 ˡ¹⁸⁴ itᵈ,ᶠᶠ² arm geo² ‖ ἔφυγεν ἀπ᾿ αὐτῶν γυμνός 237 itᵠ syrˢ

ᵉ **48** e question: TR WH Nes BF² AV RV ASV RSV NEB TT ‖ e statement: Bov Zür Luth Seg ‖ e exclamation: Jer

43 ἀρχιερέων...πρεσβυτέρων Mt 16.21; 27.41; Mk 8.31; 11.27; 14.53; 15.1; Lk 9.22; 20.1 **49** καθ᾿...διδάσκων Lk 19.47; 21.37; Jn 18.20 **50** Zch 13.7; Mt 26.31; Mk 14.27 **53** ἀρχιερεῖς ...γραμματεῖς Mt 16.21; 27.41; Mk 8.31; 11.27; 14.43; 15.1; Lk 9.22; 20.1

---

with him, sent by the chief priests, the teachers of the Law, and the elders. **44** The traitor had given the crowd a signal: "The man I kiss is the one you want. Arrest him and take him away under guard."

45 As soon as Judas arrived he went up to Jesus and said, "Teacher!" and kissed him. **46** So they arrested Jesus and held him tight. **47** But one of those standing by drew his sword and struck at the High Priest's slave, cutting off his ear. **48** Then Jesus spoke up and said to them: "Did you have to come with swords and clubs to capture me, as though I were an outlaw? **49** Day after day I was with you teaching in the Temple, and you did not arrest me. But the Scriptures must come true." **50** Then all the disciples left him and ran away.

51 A certain young man, dressed only in a linen cloth, was following Jesus. They tried to arrest him, **52** but he ran away naked, leaving the linen cloth behind.

Jesus before the Council
(Also Matt. 26.57–68; Luke 22.54–55, 63–71; John 18.13–14, 19–24)

53 Then they took Jesus to the High Priest's house, where all the chief priests, the elders, and the teachers of the Law were gathering. **54** Peter followed far behind and went into the courtyard of the High Priest's house. There he sat down with the guards, keeping himself warm by the fire. 55 The chief priests and the whole Council tried to find some evidence against Jesus, in order to put him to death, but they could not find any. 56 Many witnesses told lies against Jesus, but their stories did not agree.

57 Then some men stood up and told this lie against Jesus: 58 "We heard him say, 'I will tear down this Temple which men made, and after three days I will build one that is not made by men.'" 59 Not even they, however, could make their stories agree.

60 The High Priest stood up in front of them all and questioned Jesus: "Have you no answer to the accusation they bring against you?" 61 But Jesus kept quiet and would not say a word. Again the High Priest questioned him: "Are you the Messiah, the Son of the Blessed God?" 62 "I am," answered Jesus, "and you will all see the Son of Man seated at the right side of the Almighty, and coming with the clouds of heaven!" 63 The High Priest tore his robes and said, "We don't need any more witnesses! 64 You heard his wicked words. What is your decision?" They all voted against him: he was guilty and should be put to death.

65 Some of them began to spit on Jesus, and they blindfolded him and hit him.

ἦν συγκαθήμενος μετὰ τῶν ὑπηρετῶν καὶ θερμαινόμενος πρὸς τὸ φῶς. 55 οἱ δὲ ἀρχιερεῖς καὶ ὅλον τὸ συνέδριον ἐζήτουν κατὰ τοῦ Ἰησοῦ μαρτυρίαν εἰς τὸ θανατῶσαι αὐτόν, καὶ οὐχ ηὕρισκον· 56 πολλοὶ γὰρ ἐψευδομαρτύρουν κατ' αὐτοῦ, καὶ ἴσαι αἱ μαρτυρίαι οὐκ ἦσαν. 57 καί τινες ἀναστάντες ἐψευδομαρτύρουν κατ' αὐτοῦ λέγοντες 58 ὅτι Ἡμεῖς ἠκούσαμεν αὐτοῦ λέγοντος ὅτι Ἐγὼ καταλύσω τὸν ναὸν τοῦτον τὸν χειροποίητον καὶ διὰ τριῶν ἡμερῶν ἄλλον ἀχειροποίητον οἰκοδομήσω· 59 καὶ οὐδὲ οὕτως ἴση ἦν ἡ μαρτυρία αὐτῶν. 60 καὶ ἀναστὰς ὁ ἀρχιερεὺς εἰς μέσον ἐπηρώτησεν τὸν Ἰησοῦν λέγων, Οὐκ ἀποκρίνῃ οὐδέν·¹ τί¹² οὗτοί σου καταμαρτυροῦσιν;¹ 61 ὁ δὲ ἐσιώπα καὶ οὐκ ἀπεκρίνατο οὐδέν. πάλιν ὁ ἀρχιερεὺς ἐπηρώτα αὐτὸν καὶ λέγει αὐτῷ, Σὺ εἶ ὁ Χριστὸς ὁ υἱὸς τοῦ εὐλογητοῦ; 62 ὁ δὲ Ἰησοῦς εἶπεν, Ἐγώ εἰμι,

καὶ ὄψεσθε τὸν υἱὸν τοῦ ἀνθρώπου
ἐκ δεξιῶν καθήμενον τῆς δυνάμεως
καὶ ἐρχόμενον μετὰ τῶν νεφελῶν τοῦ οὐρανοῦ.

63 ὁ δὲ ἀρχιερεὺς διαρρήξας τοὺς χιτῶνας αὐτοῦ λέγει, Τί ἔτι χρείαν ἔχομεν μαρτύρων; 64 ἠκούσατε τῆς βλασφημίας·ᵍ τί ὑμῖν φαίνεται; οἱ δὲ πάντες κατέκριναν αὐτὸν ἔνοχον εἶναι θανάτου. 65 Καὶ ἤρξαντό τινες ἐμπτύειν αὐτῷ καὶ περικαλύπτειν αὐτοῦ τὸ πρόσωπον καὶ κολαφί-

---

¹² 60 {B} τί (see Mt 26.62) א A C D K L P X Δ Θ Π 067 f¹ f¹³ 28 33 565 700 892 1009 1010 1071 1079 1195 1216 1230 1241 1242 1253 1344 1365 1546 1646 (2148 τοί) 2174 Byz Lect syrˢ·ᵖ·ʰ copˢᵃ·ᶠᵃʸᵛⁱᵈ goth arm geo Origen ∥ ὅτι B W Ψ l¹¹²⁷ (copᵇᵒ)

ƒ ƒ 60 ƒ question, ƒ question: TR WH Bov BF² AV RV ASV RSV TT Jer Seg ∥ ƒ none, ƒ question: Nes NEB (Zür) (Luth) Jerᵐᵍ Segᵐᵍ
ᵍ 64 ᵍ statement: TR Bov Nes BF² AV RV ASV RSV NEB TT Zür Luth Jer Seg ∥ ᵍ question: WH

---

58 Ἐγώ...οἰκοδομήσω Mk 15.29; Jn 2.19   60-61 ἐπηρώτησεν...ἀπεκρίνατο οὐδέν Is 53.7; Mk 15.4-5; Lk 23.9   61 Σὺ...εὐλογητοῦ Mt 16.16; Mk 5.7; Lk 8.28; Jn 11.27; 20.31   62 ἐκ...δυνάμεως Ps 110.1; Mt 22.44; Lk 20.42; Ac 2.34; Eph 1.20; Col 3.1; He 1.3, 13; 10.12; 12.2   ἐρχόμενον...οὐρανοῦ Dn 7.13; Mt 24.30; Mk 13.26; Lk 21.27; Re 1.7; 14.14   63 διαρρήξας...αὐτοῦ Nu 14.6; Ac 14.14   64 Lv 24.16; Jn 19.7

ζειν αὐτὸν καὶ λέγειν αὐτῷ, Προφήτευσον[13], καὶ οἱ
ὑπηρέται ῥαπίσμασιν αὐτὸν ἔλαβον.

Peter's Denial of Jesus
(Mt 26.69–75; Lk 22.56–62; Jn 18.15–18, 25–27)

66 Καὶ ὄντος τοῦ Πέτρου κάτω ἐν τῇ αὐλῇ ἔρχεται μία
τῶν παιδισκῶν τοῦ ἀρχιερέως, **67** καὶ ἰδοῦσα τὸν Πέτρον
θερμαινόμενον ἐμβλέψασα αὐτῷ λέγει, Καὶ σὺ μετὰ τοῦ
Ναζαρηνοῦ ἦσθα τοῦ Ἰησοῦ. **68** ὁ δὲ ἠρνήσατο λέγων,
Οὔτε οἶδα οὔτε ἐπίσταμαι[h] σὺ τί λέγεις.[h] καὶ ἐξῆλθεν ἔξω
εἰς τὸ προαύλιον[· καὶ ἀλέκτωρ ἐφώνησεν][14]. **69** καὶ ἡ
παιδίσκη ἰδοῦσα αὐτὸν ἤρξατο πάλιν λέγειν τοῖς παρεστῶσιν ὅτι Οὗτος ἐξ αὐτῶν ἐστιν. **70** ὁ δὲ πάλιν ἠρνεῖτο.
καὶ μετὰ μικρὸν πάλιν οἱ παρεστῶτες ἔλεγον τῷ Πέτρῳ,
Ἀληθῶς ἐξ αὐτῶν εἶ, καὶ γὰρ Γαλιλαῖος εἶ. **71** ὁ δὲ
ἤρξατο ἀναθεματίζειν καὶ ὀμνύναι ὅτι Οὐκ οἶδα τὸν
ἄνθρωπον τοῦτον ὃν λέγετε. **72** καὶ εὐθὺς ἐκ δευτέρου[15]

[13] **65** {C} προφήτευσον ℵ A B C D K L Π 067 28 1010 1079 1230 1241
1253 1365 1546 1646 *Byz* it[(d),ff2,l,q] vg syr[p] cop[bomss] goth ‖ προφήτευσον
νῦν f[1] ‖ προφήτευσον νῦν ἡμῖν syr[s] ‖ προφήτευσον ἡμῖν Ψ l[14,883] it[c,f,k]
cop[samss] ‖ προφήτευσον ἡμῖν Χριστέ 1242 it[aur] ‖ προφήτευσον νῦν Χριστὲ
τίς ἐστιν ὁ παίσας σε W f[13] (1071 νῦν ἡμῖν) ‖ προφήτευσον ἡμῖν Χριστὲ
τίς ἐστιν ὁ παίσας σε (see Mt 26.68) X (Δ ὁ πέμψας σε) Θ 33 565 700 892
1009 1195 1216 1344 2148 2174 (syr[h] ἡμῖν *with**) cop[samss,(bo)] arm eth geo
Diatessaron (Augustine) ‖ προφήτευσον ἡμῖν τίς ἐστιν ὁ παίσας σε (see
Lk 22.64) *Lect*

[14] **68** {D} καὶ ἀλέκτωρ ἐφώνησεν (see 14.72) A C D K X Δ Θ Π 067
f[1] f[13] 28 33 565 700 1009 1010 1071 1079 1195 1216 1230 1241 1242 1253 1344
1365 1546 1646 2148 2174 *Byz Lect* it[a,aur,d,f,ff2,k,l,q] vg syr[p,h] cop[samss,boms] goth
arm eth geo[2] Eusebius ‖ *omit* (see Mt 26.71; Lk 22.57; Jn 18.25) ℵ B L W
Ψ 892 l[17,76] it[c] syr[s] cop[samss,bo] geo[1] Diatessaron

[15] **72** {C} ἐκ δευτέρου (see 14.68) A B C[2vid] D K W X Δ Θ Π Ψ f[1] f[13]
28 33 565 700 892 1009 1010 1071 1079 1195 (1216 1344 *omit* ἐκ) 1230 1241 1242
1253 1365 1546 1646 2148 2174 *Byz Lect* it[a,aur,d,ff2,k,l,q] vg syr[(s,p),h] cop[sa,bo]
goth arm Eusebius ‖ *the first time* geo ‖ *omit* (see Mt 26.74; Lk 22.60;
Jn 18.27) ℵ C[*vid] L it[c] Diatessaron[i,s]

[h] [h] **68** h none, h statement: TR WH Bov Nes BF[2] AV RV ASV RSV NEB TT (Zür) (Luth) Jer
Seg ‖ h major, h question: WH[mg] RV[mg] ASV[mg]

Peter Denies Jesus
(Also Matt. 26.69–75; Luke 22.56–62;
John 18.15–18, 25–27)

"Guess who hit you!" they said. And
the guards took him and slapped him.

[66] Peter was still down in the courtyard
when one of the High Priest's servant
girls came by. [67] When she saw Peter
warming himself, she looked straight at
him and said, "You, too, were with
Jesus of Nazareth." [68] But he denied it.
"I don't know ... I don't understand
what you are talking about," he answered, and went out into the passage-
way. Just then a rooster crowed. [69] The
servant girl saw him there and began to
repeat to the bystanders, "He is one of
them!" [70] But Peter denied it again.
A little while later the bystanders accused Peter again: "You can't deny that
you are one of them, because you, too,
are from Galilee." [71] Then Peter made
a vow: "May God punish me if I am
not telling the truth! I do not know
the man you are talking about!" [72] Just
then a rooster crowed a second time, and

Peter remembered how Jesus had said to him, "Before the rooster crows two times you will say three times that you do not know me." And he broke down and cried.

Jesus before Pilate
(Also Matt. 27.1–2, 11–14; Luke 23.1–5; John 18.28–38)

15 Early in the morning the chief priests met hurriedly with the elders, the teachers of the Law, and the whole Council, and made their plans. They put Jesus in chains, took him away and handed him over to Pilate. [2] Pilate questioned him: "Are you the king of the Jews?" Jesus answered: "So you say." [3] The chief priests accused Jesus of many

ἀλέκτωρ ἐφώνησεν. καὶ ἀνεμνήσθη ὁ Πέτρος τὸ ῥῆμα ὡς εἶπεν αὐτῷ ὁ Ἰησοῦς ὅτι Πρὶν ἀλέκτορα φωνῆσαι δὶς τρίς με ἀπαρνήσῃ[16]· καὶ ἐπιβαλὼν ἔκλαιεν[17].

Jesus before Pilate
(Mt 27.1–2, 11–14; Lk 23.1–5; Jn 18.28–38)

15 Καὶ εὐθὺς πρωῒ συμβούλιον ποιήσαντες[1] οἱ ἀρχιερεῖς μετὰ τῶν πρεσβυτέρων καὶ γραμματέων καὶ ὅλον τὸ συνέδριον δήσαντες[1] τὸν Ἰησοῦν ἀπήνεγκαν καὶ παρέδωκαν Πιλάτῳ. 2 καὶ ἐπηρώτα αὐτὸν ὁ Πιλᾶτος, Σὺ εἶ ὁ βασιλεὺς τῶν Ἰουδαίων; ὁ δὲ ἀποκριθεὶς αὐτῷ λέγει, Σὺ λέγεις.[a] 3 καὶ κατηγόρουν αὐτοῦ οἱ ἀρχιερεῖς πολλά.

---

16 72 {B} ὅτι πρὶν ἀλέκτορα φωνῆσαι δὶς τρίς με ἀπαρνήσῃ C² L Ψ 892 it^aur vg syr^s,p ‖ ὅτι πρὶν ἀλέκτορα φωνῆσαι δὶς ἀπαρνήσῃ με τρίς A K X^vid Π f¹ f¹³ 28 33 1009 1010 1071 1079 1195 1216 1230 1241 1242 1253 1344 1365 1546 1646 2148 2174 Byz Lect (l⁸⁸³ ὁ πρίν) syr^h cop^sa,bo goth ‖ ὅτι πρὶν ἀλέκτορα δὶς φωνῆσαι ἀπαρνήσῃ με τρίς Θ 565 700 ‖ ὅτι πρὶν ἀλέκτορα δὶς φωνῆσαι τρίς με ἀπαρνήσῃ B it^k ‖ ὅτι πρὶν ἀλέκτορα φωνῆσαι τρίς με ἀπαρνήσῃ (see Mt 26.75; Lk 22.61) ℵ C^vid W Δ it^c,ff²,l,q (arm add τρίς) eth ‖ ὅτι πρὶν ἀλέκτορα φωνῆσαι δὶς ἀπαρνήσῃ με l³⁶ ‖ before the cock crows once you shall deny me three times geo¹ (geo² omit three times) ‖ omit D it^a,d

17 72 {B} καὶ ἐπιβαλὼν ἔκλαιεν ℵ^c A^c B K^vid L (Δ^gr ἐπιλαβών) Π Ψ 0250 (W f¹ omit καί) f¹³ 28 33 700 892 (1009 ἐπιλαβόμενος) 1010 1071 1079 1195 1216 1230 1241 1242 1253 1344 1365 1546 1646 2148 2174 Byz Lect (l⁸⁰ ἐπιβάλλων) ‖ καὶ ἐπιβαλὼν ἔκλαυσεν (see Mt 26.75; Lk 22.62) ℵ* A^vid C cop^bo? ‖ καὶ ἤρξατο κλαίειν D Θ 565 it^a,aur,c,d,ff²,k,l,q vg syr^s,p,h cop^sa arm geo ‖ and he wept eth ‖ omit 37

1 1 {B} ποιήσαντες...δήσαντες A B K W X Δ Π Ψ (0250 ποιήσαντες... καὶ δήσαντες) f¹ f¹³ 28 33 700 1009 1010 1071 1079 1195 1216 1230 1241 1242 1344 1365 1546 1646 2148 2174 Byz Lect^pt l⁶⁹pt,70pt,76pt,211pt,333,547,883pt,1127pt (l¹⁸⁵pt end of lection, l⁹⁵⁰pt beginning of lection) it^l vg goth arm Augustine ‖ ἑτοιμάσαντες...δήσαντες ℵ C L 892 ‖ ἐποίησαν...δήσαντες l¹⁰,12,80,303,333 ‖ ἐποίησαν...καὶ δήσαντες D Θ 565 1253 Lect^pt l⁶⁹pt,70pt,76pt,185pt,211pt,883pt,950pt,1127pt it^a,aur,c,d,ff²,k,q syr^(s),p,h (cop^sa?bo?) eth geo Origen

---

a 2 a statement: TR WH Bov Nes BF² AV RV ASV RSV NEB TT Zür Luth Jer Seg ‖ a question: WH^mg

---

72 Πρὶν...ἀπαρνήσῃ Mt 26.34; Mk 14.30; Lk 22.34; Jn 13.38
15 1 πρωῒ...συνέδριον Lk 22.66 ἀρχιερεῖς...γραμματέων Mt 16.21; 27.41; Mk 8.31; 11.27; 14.43, 53; Lk 9.22; 20.1

4 ὁ δὲ *Πιλᾶτος* πάλιν ἐπηρώτα αὐτὸν λέγων, Οὐκ ἀποκρίνῃ οὐδέν; ἴδε πόσα σου κατηγοροῦσιν.   **5** ὁ δὲ Ἰησοῦς οὐκέτι οὐδὲν ἀπεκρίθη, ὥστε θαυμάζειν τὸν Πιλᾶτον.

Jesus Sentenced to Die
(Mt 27.15–26; Lk 23.13–25; Jn 18.39—19.16)

6 Κατὰ δὲ ἑορτὴν ἀπέλυεν αὐτοῖς ἕνα δέσμιον ὃν παρῃτοῦντο.   **7** ἦν δὲ ὁ λεγόμενος Βαραββᾶς μετὰ τῶν στασιαστῶν δεδεμένος οἵτινες ἐν τῇ στάσει φόνον πεποιήκεισαν.   **8** καὶ ἀναβὰς ὁ ὄχλος[2] ἤρξατο αἰτεῖσθαι καθὼς ἐποίει αὐτοῖς.   **9** ὁ δὲ Πιλᾶτος ἀπεκρίθη αὐτοῖς λέγων, Θέλετε ἀπολύσω ὑμῖν τὸν βασιλέα τῶν Ἰουδαίων;   **10** ἐγίνωσκεν γὰρ ὅτι διὰ φθόνον παραδεδώκεισαν αὐτὸν οἱ ἀρχιερεῖς[3].   **11** οἱ δὲ ἀρχιερεῖς ἀνέσεισαν τὸν ὄχλον ἵνα μᾶλλον τὸν Βαραββᾶν ἀπολύσῃ αὐτοῖς.   **12** ὁ δὲ Πιλᾶτος πάλιν ἀποκριθεὶς ἔλεγεν αὐτοῖς, Τί οὖν [θέλετε] ποιήσω[4] [ὃν λέγετε][5] τὸν βασιλέα τῶν Ἰουδαίων;   **13** οἱ δὲ πάλιν

---

[2] **8** {B} ἀναβὰς ὁ ὄχλος ℵ* B 892 it[aur, c, ff2, l, r1] vg cop[sa, bo] ‖ ἀναβοήσας ὁ ὄχλος ℵ[h] A C K W X Δ Θ Π Ψ *f*[1] *f*[13] 28 33 565 700 1009 1010 1071 1079 1195 1216 1242 1344 1365 1546 2148 2174 *Byz Lect* syr[s, p, h] arm geo Diatessaron ‖ ἀναβὰς ὅλος ὁ ὄχλος D it[a, d] goth ‖ ἀναβοήσας ὅλος ὁ ὄχλος 1230 1241 1253 1646 ‖ ὅλος ὁ ὄχλος it[k]

[3] **10** {B} οἱ ἀρχιερεῖς ℵ A C D K W X Δ Θ Π Ψ 0250 *f*[13] 28 33 565 700 892 1009 1010 1071 1079 1195 1216 1230 1241 1242 1253 1344 1365 1546 1646 2148 2174 *Byz Lect* (*l*[950] οἱ δέ) it[a, aur, c, d, ff2, (k), l, r1] vg syr[p, h] cop[sa] goth arm geo ‖ *omit* (*see* Mt 27.18) B *f*[1] *l*[10,13,47] syr[s] cop[bo] Diatessaron[a, i, n]

[4] **12** {D} θέλετε ποιήσω (*see* Mt 27.21; Lk 23.20) A D K X Θ Π 0250 28 565 700 1009 1010 1071 1079 1195 1216 1230 1241 1242 1253 1344 1365 1546 1646 2174 *Byz Lect* it[a, aur, d, ff2, k, l, r1] vg syr[s, p, h] goth arm eth Diatessaron ‖ θέλετε ἵνα ποιήσω 2148 *l*[15] it[c] ‖ ποιήσω (*see* Mt 27.22) ℵ B C W Δ Ψ *f*[1] *f*[13] 33 892 cop[sa, bo] geo

[5] **12** {C} ὃν λέγετε ℵ C K X Δ Π Ψ 0250 28 33 892 1009 1010 1071 1079 1195 1216 1230 1241 1242 1253 1344 1365 1546 1646 2148 2174 *Byz Lect* syr[p, h] cop[bo] goth eth ‖ λέγετε B ‖ *omit* A D W Θ *f*[1] *f*[13] 565 700 *l*[13] it[a, aur, c, d, ff2, k, l, r1] vg syr[s] cop[sa] arm geo

---

4–5 ἐπηρώτα...ἀπεκρίθη Is 53.7; Mk 14.60–61; Lk 23.9   **11** Ac 3.14   **12–14** Ac 3.13; 13.28

things, **4** so Pilate questioned him again: "Aren't you going to answer? See how many things they accuse you of!" **5** Again Jesus refused to say a word, and Pilate was filled with surprise.

Jesus Sentenced to Death
(Also Matt. 27.15–26; Luke 23.13–25; John 18.39—19.16)

6 At every Passover Feast Pilate would set free any prisoner the people asked for. **7** At that time a man named Barabbas was in prison with the rebels who had committed murder in the riot. **8** When the crowd gathered and began to ask Pilate to do them the usual favor, **9** Pilate asked them: "Do you want me to set free for you the king of the Jews?" **10** He knew very well that the chief priests had handed Jesus over to him because they were jealous. **11** But the chief priests stirred up the crowd to ask, instead, for Pilate to set Barabbas free for them. **12** Pilate spoke again to the crowd: "What, then, do you want me to do with the one you call the king of the Jews?" **13** They shouted back,

"Nail him to the cross!" ¹⁴ "But what crime has he committed?" Pilate asked. They shouted all the louder, "Nail him to the cross!" ¹⁵ Pilate wanted to please the crowd, so he set Barabbas free for them. Then he had Jesus whipped and handed him over to be nailed to the cross.

The Soldiers Make Fun of Jesus
(Also Matt. 27.27–31; John 19.2–3)

¹⁶ The soldiers took Jesus inside the courtyard (that is, of the Governor's palace) and called together the rest of the company. ¹⁷ They put a purple robe on Jesus, made a crown out of thorny branches, and put it on his head. ¹⁸ Then they began to salute him: "Long live the King of the Jews!" ¹⁹ And they beat him over the head with a stick, spat on him, fell on their knees and bowed down to him. ²⁰ When they had finished making fun of him, they took off the purple robe and put his own clothes back on him. Then they led him out to nail him to the cross.

Jesus Nailed to the Cross
(Also Matt. 27.32–44; Luke 23.26–43; John 19.17–27)

²¹ On the way they met a man named Simon, who was coming into the city from the country, and they forced him to carry Jesus' cross. (This was Simon from Cyrene, the father of Alexander and Rufus.) ²² They brought Jesus to a place called Golgotha, which means "The Place of the Skull." ²³ There they tried to give him wine mixed with a drug called myrrh, but Jesus would not drink it. ²⁴ So they nailed him to the cross and divided his clothes among themselves, throwing dice to see who would get which piece of clothing. ²⁵ It was nine o'clock in the morning when they nailed him to the cross. ²⁶ The notice of the accusation

ἔκραξαν, Σταύρωσον αὐτόν. 14 ὁ δὲ Πιλᾶτος ἔλεγεν αὐτοῖς, Τί γὰρ ἐποίησεν κακόν; οἱ δὲ περισσῶς ἔκραξαν, Σταύρωσον αὐτόν. 15 ὁ δὲ Πιλᾶτος βουλόμενος τῷ ὄχλῳ τὸ ἱκανὸν ποιῆσαι ἀπέλυσεν αὐτοῖς τὸν Βαραββᾶν, καὶ παρέδωκεν τὸν Ἰησοῦν φραγελλώσας ἵνα σταυρωθῇ.

The Soldiers Mock Jesus
(Mt 27.27–31; Jn 19.2–3)

16 Οἱ δὲ στρατιῶται ἀπήγαγον αὐτὸν ἔσω τῆς αὐλῆς, ὅ ἐστιν πραιτώριον, καὶ συγκαλοῦσιν ὅλην τὴν σπεῖραν. 17 καὶ ἐνδιδύσκουσιν αὐτὸν πορφύραν καὶ περιτιθέασιν αὐτῷ πλέξαντες ἀκάνθινον στέφανον· 18 καὶ ἤρξαντο ἀσπάζεσθαι αὐτόν, Χαῖρε, βασιλεῦ τῶν Ἰουδαίων· 19 καὶ ἔτυπτον αὐτοῦ τὴν κεφαλὴν καλάμῳ καὶ ἐνέπτυον αὐτῷ, καὶ τιθέντες τὰ γόνατα προσεκύνουν αὐτῷ. 20 καὶ ὅτε ἐνέπαιξαν αὐτῷ, ἐξέδυσαν αὐτὸν τὴν πορφύραν καὶ ἐνέδυσαν αὐτὸν τὰ ἱμάτια τὰ ἴδια. καὶ ἐξάγουσιν αὐτὸν ἵνα σταυρώσουσιν αὐτόν.

The Crucifixion of Jesus
(Mt 27.32–44; Lk 23.26–43; Jn 19.17–27)

21 Καὶ ἀγγαρεύουσιν παράγοντά τινα Σίμωνα Κυρηναῖον ἐρχόμενον ἀπ᾽ ἀγροῦ, τὸν πατέρα Ἀλεξάνδρου καὶ Ῥούφου, ἵνα ἄρῃ τὸν σταυρὸν αὐτοῦ. 22 καὶ φέρουσιν αὐτὸν ἐπὶ τὸν Γολγοθᾶν τόπον, ὅ ἐστιν μεθερμηνευόμενον Κρανίου Τόπος. 23 καὶ ἐδίδουν αὐτῷ ἐσμυρνισμένον οἶνον, ὃς δὲ οὐκ ἔλαβεν. 24 καὶ σταυροῦσιν αὐτὸν
    καὶ **διαμερίζονται τὰ ἱμάτια** αὐτοῦ,
        βάλλοντες κλῆρον ἐπ᾽ αὐτὰ τίς τί ἄρῃ.
25 ἦν δὲ ὥρα τρίτη καὶ ἐσταύρωσαν⁶ αὐτόν. 26 καὶ ἦν

---

⁶ 25 {A} καὶ ἐσταύρωσαν ℵ A B C K L P X Δ Θ Π Ψ f¹ 28 33 565 700 892 1009 1010 1079 1195 1216 1230 1241 1242 1253 1344 1365 1546 1646 2148 2174 Byz Lect itᶜ,ˡ vg syrˢ,ʰ,ᵖᵃˡ copᵇᵒ goth arm geo Augustine ∥ ὅτε ἐσταύρωσαν f¹³ 1071 itᵃᵘʳ syrᵖ copˢᵃᵐˢ,ᶠᵃʸᵛⁱᵈ ∥ ἐφύλασσον (compare Mt 27.36) D itᵈ,ᶠᶠ²,ᵏ,ⁿ,ʳˡ ∥ ἐσταύρωσαν καὶ ἐφύλασσον copˢᵃᵐˢˢ

17–19 Lk 23.11   **23** ἐδίδουν...οἶνον Ps 69.21   **24** διαμερίζονται...αὐτά Ps 22.18

ἡ ἐπιγραφὴ τῆς αἰτίας αὐτοῦ ἐπιγεγραμμένη, Ὁ βασιλεὺς τῶν Ἰουδαίων. 27 Καὶ σὺν αὐτῷ σταυροῦσιν δύο λῃστάς, ἕνα ἐκ δεξιῶν καὶ ἕνα ἐξ εὐωνύμων αὐτοῦ.[7] 29 Καὶ οἱ παραπορευόμενοι ἐβλασφήμουν αὐτὸν **κινοῦντες τὰς κεφαλὰς** αὐτῶν καὶ λέγοντες, Οὐὰ ὁ καταλύων τὸν ναὸν καὶ οἰκοδομῶν ἐν τρισὶν ἡμέραις, 30 σῶσον σεαυτὸν καταβὰς ἀπὸ τοῦ σταυροῦ. 31 ὁμοίως καὶ οἱ ἀρχιερεῖς ἐμπαίζοντες πρὸς ἀλλήλους μετὰ τῶν γραμματέων ἔλεγον, Ἄλλους ἔσωσεν,[b] ἑαυτὸν οὐ δύναται σῶσαι·[b] 32 ὁ Χριστὸς ὁ βασιλεὺς Ἰσραὴλ καταβάτω νῦν ἀπὸ τοῦ σταυροῦ, ἵνα ἴδωμεν καὶ πιστεύσωμεν. καὶ οἱ συνεσταυρωμένοι σὺν αὐτῷ ὠνείδιζον αὐτόν.

The Death of Jesus
(Mt 27.45–56; Lk 23.44–49; Jn 19.28–30)

33 Καὶ γενομένης ὥρας ἕκτης σκότος ἐγένετο ἐφ' ὅλην τὴν γῆν ἕως ὥρας ἐνάτης. 34 καὶ τῇ ἐνάτῃ ὥρᾳ ἐβόησεν ὁ Ἰησοῦς φωνῇ μεγάλῃ, **Ελωι ελωι λεμα σαβαχθανι;** ὅ ἐστιν μεθερμηνευόμενον Ὁ θεός μου ὁ θεός μου, εἰς τί ἐγκατέλιπές με[8]; 35 καί τινες τῶν

---

[7] **27** {A} *omit verse 28* ℵ A B C D X Ψ *Lect* it[d,k] syr[s] cop[sa,bo mss,fay vid] Eusebian Canons[txt] Ammonius ‖ *include verse 28* καὶ ἐπληρώθη ἡ γραφὴ ἡ λέγουσα, Καὶ μετὰ ἀνόμων ἐλογίσθη. (*see* Lk 22.37; Is 53.12) K L P (Δ καὶ ἡ γραφή) Θ Π 0112 0250 f[1] f[13] 28 33 565 700 892 1009 1010 1071 1079 1195 1216 1230 1241 1242 1253 1344 1365 1546 1646 2148 2174 *Byz* l[10,211,883,1642] it[aur,c,ff2,l,n,rl] vg syr[p,h,pal] cop[bo mss] goth arm eth geo Ps-Hippolytus[vid] Origen Eusebian Canons[mss] Vigilius[vid]

[8] **34** {B} ἐγκατέλιπές με (*see* Ps 22.2 MT; 21.2 LXX) ℵ B Ψ 059 0112 (L 565 892 ἐγκατέλειπες) vg syr[s,p] cop[sa,bo,fay] geo? Valentinians[acc. to] Irenaeus[gr and Justin] Eusebius Epiphanius ‖ με ἐγκατέλιπες (*see* Mt 27.46) C P X Δ Θ (A Π* ἐγκατέλειπες) Π[2] f[1] f[13] 28 700 1010 1071 1079 1195 1216 1230 1241 1242 1253 1344 1365 1546 1646 2148 2174 *Byz Lect* it[aur,d,ff2,l,n] goth arm? geo? Irenaeus[lat] ‖ με ἐγκατέλειπας K 1009 (33 ἐγκατέλιπας) (l[70]) arm? ‖ ὠνείδισάς με D[gr] it[c,i] syr[h] Porphyry mss[acc. to Macarius]

b b **31** b minor, b statement: TR WH Bov Nes BF² AV RV ASV RSV NEB TT Zür (Luth) (Jer) Seg ‖ b major, b question: RV[mg] ASV[mg]

27 ἕνα ἐκ δεξιῶν...αὐτοῦ Mt 20.21; Mk 10.37   **29** κινοῦντες τὰς κεφαλάς Ps 22.7; 109.25; Lm 2.15 ὁ καταλύων...ἡμέραις Mk 14.58; Jn 2.19   **33** Am 8.9   **34** Ελωι...με Ps 22.1

---

against him was written, "The King of the Jews." 27 They also nailed two bandits to crosses with Jesus, one on his right and the other on his left. 28 [In this way the scripture came true which says: "He was included with the criminals."]

29 People passing by shook their heads and threw insults at Jesus: "Aha! You were going to tear down the Temple and build it up in three days! 30 Now come down from the cross and save yourself!" 31 In the same way the chief priests and the teachers of the Law made fun of Jesus, saying to each other: "He saved others, but he cannot save himself! 32 Let us see the Messiah, the king of Israel, come down from the cross now, and we will believe in him!" And the two who were crucified with Jesus insulted him also.

The Death of Jesus
(Also Matt. 27.45–56; Luke 23.44–49; John 19.28–30)

33 At noon the whole country was covered with darkness, which lasted for three hours. 34 At three o'clock Jesus cried out with a loud shout, *Eloi, Eloi, lema sabachthani?* which means, "My God, my God, why did you abandon me?" 35 Some of the people who were

there heard him and said, "Listen, he is calling for Elijah!" ³⁶ One of them ran up with a sponge, soaked it in wine, and put it on the end of a stick. Then he held it up to Jesus' lips and said, "Wait! Let us see if Elijah is coming to bring him down from the cross!" ³⁷ With a loud cry Jesus died.

³⁸ The curtain hanging in the Temple was torn in two, from top to bottom. ³⁹ The army officer, who was standing there in front of the cross, saw how Jesus had cried out and died. "This man was really the Son of God!" he said. ⁴⁰ Some women were there, looking on from a distance. Among them were Salome, Mary Magdalene, and Mary the mother of the younger James and of Joses. ⁴¹ They had followed Jesus while he was in Galilee and helped him. Many other women were there also, who had come to Jerusalem with him.

The Burial of Jesus
(Also Matt. 27.57–61; Luke 23.50–56; John 19.38–42)

⁴² It was getting on toward evening when Joseph of Arimathea arrived. ⁴³ He was a respected member of the Council, who looked for the coming of the Kingdom of God. It was Preparation day (that is, the day before the Sabbath); so Joseph went in bravely to the presence of Pilate and asked him for the body of Jesus. ⁴⁴ Pilate was surprised to hear

παρεστώτων ἀκούσαντες ἔλεγον, Ἴδε Ἠλίαν φωνεῖ. 36 δραμὼν δέ τις καὶ γεμίσας σπόγγον **ὄξους** περιθεὶς καλάμῳ **ἐπότιζεν** αὐτόν, λέγων, Ἄφετε ἴδωμεν εἰ ἔρχεται Ἠλίας καθελεῖν αὐτόν. 37 ὁ δὲ Ἰησοῦς ἀφεὶς φωνὴν μεγάλην ἐξέπνευσεν. 38 Καὶ τὸ καταπέτασμα τοῦ ναοῦ ἐσχίσθη εἰς δύο ἀπ' ἄνωθεν ἕως κάτω. 39 Ἰδὼν δὲ ὁ κεντυρίων ὁ παρεστηκὼς ἐξ ἐναντίας αὐτοῦ⁹ ὅτι οὕτως ἐξέπνευσεν¹⁰ εἶπεν, Ἀληθῶς οὗτος ὁ ἄνθρωπος υἱὸς θεοῦ ἦν. 40 Ἦσαν δὲ καὶ γυναῖκες ἀπὸ μακρόθεν θεωροῦσαι, ἐν αἷς καὶ Μαρία ἡ Μαγδαληνὴ καὶ Μαρία ἡ Ἰακώβου τοῦ μικροῦ καὶ Ἰωσῆτος μήτηρ καὶ Σαλώμη, 41 αἳ ὅτε ἦν ἐν τῇ Γαλιλαίᾳ ἠκολούθουν αὐτῷ καὶ διηκόνουν αὐτῷ, καὶ ἄλλαι πολλαὶ αἱ συναναβᾶσαι αὐτῷ εἰς Ἱεροσόλυμα.

The Burial of Jesus
(Mt 27.57–61; Lk 23.50–56; Jn 19.38–42)

42 Καὶ ἤδη ὀψίας γενομένης, ἐπεὶ ἦν παρασκευή, ὅ ἐστιν προσάββατον, 43 ἐλθὼν Ἰωσὴφ [ὁ] ἀπὸ Ἁριμαθαίας εὐσχήμων βουλευτής, ὃς καὶ αὐτὸς ἦν προσδεχόμενος τὴν βασιλείαν τοῦ θεοῦ, τολμήσας εἰσῆλθεν πρὸς τὸν Πιλᾶτον καὶ ᾐτήσατο τὸ σῶμα τοῦ Ἰησοῦ. 44 ὁ δὲ

⁹ **39** {B} ἐξ ἐναντίας αὐτοῦ ℵ A B C K L X Δ Π Ψ 0112 *f*¹³ 28 33 700 892 1009 1010 1071 1079 1195 1216 1230 1241 1242 1253 1344 1365 1546 1646 2148 2174 *Byz Lect* it^{(aur),c,ff2,(k),(l)} (vg) syr^h cop^{sa,bo,fay} goth Augustine ∥ αὐτῷ W *f*¹ syr^{s,p} eth geo ∥ ἐκεῖ D Θ 565 it^{d,i,n,q} arm Origen^{lat}

¹⁰ **39** {C} ὅτι οὕτως ἐξέπνευσεν ℵ B L Ψ 892 (2148 cop^{bo} *omit* οὕτως) cop^{sa,fay} ∥ ὅτι κράξας ἐξέπνευσεν W Θ 565 syr^s arm geo Origen^{lat} ∥ ὅτι οὕτως κράξας ἐξέπνευσεν A C K X Δ Π *f*¹ *f*¹³ 28 33 700 1009 1010 1071 1079 1195 1216 1230 1241 1242 1253 1344 1365 1546 1646 2174 *Byz Lect* it^{aur,c,ff2,(i),l,n,q} vg syr^{p,h} goth eth Augustine ∥ οὕτως αὐτὸν κράξαντα καὶ ἐξέπνευσεν D (it^d) ∥ *quia sic exclamavit* it^k

36 γεμίσας...ἐπότιζεν αὐτόν Ps 69.21; Mt 27.34; Mk 15.23; Lk 23.36   **38** He 10.19–20   **40–41** γυναῖκες...διηκόνουν αὐτῷ Lk 8.2–3

Πιλᾶτος ἐθαύμασεν εἰ ἤδη τέθνηκεν, καὶ προσκαλεσάμενος τὸν κεντυρίωνα ἐπηρώτησεν αὐτὸν εἰ πάλαι[11] ἀπέθανεν· 45 καὶ γνοὺς ἀπὸ τοῦ κεντυρίωνος ἐδωρήσατο τὸ πτῶμα τῷ Ἰωσήφ. 46 καὶ ἀγοράσας σινδόνα καθελὼν αὐτὸν ἐνείλησεν τῇ σινδόνι καὶ ἔθηκεν αὐτὸν ἐν μνημείῳ ὃ ἦν λελατομημένον ἐκ πέτρας, καὶ προσεκύλισεν λίθον ἐπὶ τὴν θύραν τοῦ μνημείου. 47 ἡ δὲ Μαρία ἡ Μαγδαληνὴ καὶ Μαρία ἡ Ἰωσῆτος ἐθεώρουν ποῦ τέθειται.

The Resurrection of Jesus
(Mt 28.1–8; Lk 24.1–12; Jn 20.1–10)

16 Καὶ διαγενομένου τοῦ σαββάτου[1] Μαρία ἡ Μαγδαληνὴ καὶ Μαρία ἡ Ἰακώβου καὶ Σαλώμη[1] ἠγόρασαν ἀρώματα ἵνα ἐλθοῦσαι ἀλείψωσιν αὐτόν. 2 καὶ λίαν πρωῒ τῇ μιᾷ τῶν σαββάτων ἔρχονται ἐπὶ τὸ μνημεῖον ἀνατείλαντος τοῦ ἡλίου. 3 καὶ ἔλεγον πρὸς ἑαυτάς, Τίς ἀποκυλίσει ἡμῖν τὸν λίθον ἐκ τῆς θύρας τοῦ μνημείου; 4 καὶ ἀναβλέψασαι θεωροῦσιν ὅτι ἀποκεκύλισται ὁ λίθος, ἦν γὰρ μέγας σφόδρα. 5 καὶ εἰσελθοῦσαι εἰς τὸ μνημεῖον εἶδον νεανίσκον καθήμενον ἐν τοῖς δεξιοῖς περιβεβλημένον στολὴν λευκήν, καὶ ἐξεθαμβήθησαν. 6 ὁ δὲ λέγει αὐταῖς, Μὴ ἐκθαμβεῖσθε· Ἰησοῦν ζητεῖτε τὸν Ναζαρηνὸν τὸν

---

[11] 44 {C} εἰ πάλαι א A C K L X^vid Π Ψ f¹ f¹³ 28 33 700 892 1010 1071 1079 1195 1216 1230 1241 1242 1253 1344 1365 1546 1646 2148 2174 *Byz Lect* syr^p,h cop^ss (geo¹⁷) Theodoret ‖ εἰ ἤδη B D W Δ Θ 1009 *l*⁶⁰,¹¹²⁷ it^aur,c,d,ff²,k,l,n,q vg syr^pal cop^bo?fay? goth arm geo⁽¹⁷⁾,² Origen^lat Theophylact ‖ εἰ 544 syr^s Diatessaron^n ‖ *and said, "Is he truly already dead?"* arm

[1] 1 {A} διαγενομένου τοῦ σαββάτου...καὶ Σαλώμη א A B C K L W Δ Π Ψ f¹ f¹³ 28 33 565 700 892 1009 1010 1071 1079 1195 1216 1230 1241 1242 1253 1344 1365 1546 1646 2148 2174 *Byz Lect* it^l,q vg syr⁽ˢ⁾,p,h cop^sa,bo^mss (goth) geo ‖ διαγενομένου τοῦ σαββάτου...καὶ Σαλώμη πορευθεῖσαι Θ it^aur,c,ff² syr^pal cop^bo arm ‖ πορευθεῖσαι D it^d,(k),n

46 καθελὼν...μνημείῳ Ac 13.29
16 5 περιβεβλημένον...λευκήν Re 7.9, 13

---

that Jesus was already dead. He called the army officer and asked him if Jesus had been dead a long time. 45 After hearing the officer's report, Pilate told Joseph he could have the body. 46 Joseph bought a linen sheet, took the body down, wrapped it in the sheet and placed it in a grave which had been dug out of rock. Then he rolled a large stone across the entrance to the grave. 47 Mary Magdalene and Mary the mother of Joses were watching, and saw where Jesus was laid.

The Resurrection
(Also Matt. 28.1–8; Luke 24.1–12; John 20.1–10)

16 After the Sabbath day was over, Mary Magdalene, Mary the mother of James, and Salome bought spices to go and anoint the body of Jesus. 2 Very early on Sunday morning, at sunrise, they went to the grave. 3 On the way they said to one another, "Who will roll away the stone from the entrance to the grave for us?" 4 (It was a very large stone.) Then they looked up and saw that the stone had already been rolled back. 5 So they entered the grave, where they saw a young man, sitting at the right, who wore a white robe — and they were filled with alarm. 6 "Don't be alarmed," he said. "You are looking for Jesus of Nazareth, who was nailed to the cross. But he is not here — he has risen! Look, here is the place where they laid him. ⁷ Now go and give this message to his disciples, including Peter: 'He is going to Galilee ahead of you; there you will see him, just as he told you.' " ⁸ So they went out and ran from the grave, because fear and terror were upon them. And they said nothing to anyone, because they were afraid.

AN OLD ENDING TO THE GOSPEL

Jesus Appears to Mary Magdalene
(Also Matt. 28.9–10; John 20.11–18)

[⁹ After Jesus rose from death, early on the first day of the week, he appeared first to Mary Magdalene, from whom he had driven out seven demons. ¹⁰ She went and told it to his companions. They were mourning and crying; ¹¹ and when they heard her say that Jesus was alive and that she had seen him, they did not believe her.

Jesus Appears to Two Disciples
(Also Luke 24.13–35)

¹² After this, Jesus appeared in a different manner to two of them while they were on their way to the country. ¹³ They returned and told it to the others, but they would not believe it.

ἐσταυρωμένον· ἠγέρθη, οὐκ ἔστιν ὧδε· ἴδε ὁ τόπος ὅπου ἔθηκαν αὐτόν. 7 ἀλλὰ ὑπάγετε εἴπατε τοῖς μαθηταῖς αὐτοῦ καὶ τῷ Πέτρῳ ὅτι ᵃ Προάγει ὑμᾶς εἰς τὴν Γαλιλαίαν· ἐκεῖ αὐτὸν ὄψεσθε, καθὼς εἶπεν ὑμῖν. 8 καὶ ἐξελθοῦσαι ἔφυγον ἀπὸ τοῦ μνημείου, εἶχεν γὰρ αὐτὰς τρόμος καὶ ἔκστασις· καὶ οὐδενὶ οὐδὲν εἶπαν, ἐφοβοῦντο γάρ.

THE LONGER ENDING OF MARK

The Appearance to Mary Magdalene
(Mt 28.9–10; Jn 20.11–18)

⟦9² Ἀναστὰς δὲ πρωῒ πρώτῃ σαββάτου ἐφάνη πρῶτον Μαρίᾳ τῇ Μαγδαληνῇ, παρ' ἧς ἐκβεβλήκει ἑπτὰ δαιμόνια. 10 ἐκείνη πορευθεῖσα ἀπήγγειλεν τοῖς μετ' αὐτοῦ γενομένοις πενθοῦσι καὶ κλαίουσιν· 11 κἀκεῖνοι ἀκούσαντες ὅτι ζῇ καὶ ἐθεάθη ὑπ' αὐτῆς ἠπίστησαν.

The Appearance to Two Disciples
(Lk 24.13–35)

12 Μετὰ δὲ ταῦτα δυσὶν ἐξ αὐτῶν περιπατοῦσιν ἐφανερώθη ἐν ἑτέρᾳ μορφῇ πορευομένοις εἰς ἀγρόν· 13 κἀκεῖνοι ἀπελθόντες ἀπήγγειλαν τοῖς λοιποῖς· οὐδὲ ἐκείνοις ἐπίστευσαν.

---

² 9 {A} omit vv 9–20 ℵ B 2386 (Lect? lection ends with verse 8) syrˢ armᵐˢˢ ethᵐˢˢ geo¹·ᴬ Clement Origen Eusebius mssᵃᶜᶜ·ᵗᵒ ᴱᵘˢᵉᵇⁱᵘˢ Jerome mssᵃᶜᶜ·ᵗᵒ ᴶᵉʳᵒᵐᵉ Ammonius ‖ add vv 9–20 with asterisks, obeli or critical note in ms f¹ 137 138 1110 1210 1215 1216 1217 1221 1241ᵛⁱᵈ 1582 ‖ add vv 9–20 A C D K X Δ Θ Π f¹³ 28 33 274ᵗˣᵗ 565 700 892 1009 1010 1071 1079 1195 1230 1242 1253 1344 1365 1546 1646 2148 2174 Byz l⁶⁰,⁶⁹,⁷⁰,¹⁸⁵,⁵⁴⁷,⁸⁸³ itᵃᵘʳ,ᶜ,ᵈˢᵘᵖᵖ,ff²,l,n,o,q vg syrᶜ,ᵖ,ʰ,ᵖᵃˡ copˢᵃ,ᵇᵒ,ᶠᵃʸ (goth ms lacks vv 12–20) armᵐˢˢ geoᴮ Diatessaronᵃ,ⁱ,ⁿ Justin? Irenaeusᵍʳ,ˡᵃᵗ Tertullian Aphraates Apostolic Constitutions Didymus ‖ add short ending (see page 198) only itᵏ ‖ add short ending and vv 9–20 L Ψ 099 0112 579 syrʰᵐᵍ copˢᵃᵐˢˢ,ᵇᵒᵐˢˢ ethᵐˢˢ ‖ add vv 9–20 and short ending 274ᵐᵍ l⁹⁶¹,¹⁶⁰² ‖ add vv 9–14, long addition, 15–20 (see footnote 4) W

ᵃ 7 a direct: WH Bov Nes? BF² RV ASV NEB TT Zür ‖ a indirect: TR Nes? AV RSV Luth Jer Seg

---

7 Προάγει...ὑμῖν Mt 26.32; Mk 14.28   9 Μαρίᾳ...δαιμόνια Lk 8.2

The Commissioning of the Disciples
(Mt 28.16–20; Lk 24.36–49; Jn 20.19–23; Ac 1.6–8)

14 ῞Υστερον [δὲ] ἀνακειμένοις αὐτοῖς τοῖς ἔνδεκα ἐφανερώθη, καὶ ὠνείδισεν τὴν ἀπιστίαν αὐτῶν καὶ σκληροκαρδίαν ὅτι τοῖς θεασαμένοις αὐτὸν ἐγηγερμένον³ οὐκ ἐπίστευσαν. 15 καὶ εἶπεν αὐτοῖς⁴, Πορευθέντες εἰς τὸν κόσμον ἅπαντα κηρύξατε τὸ εὐαγγέλιον πάσῃ τῇ κτίσει. 16 ὁ πιστεύσας καὶ βαπτισθεὶς σωθήσεται, ὁ δὲ ἀπιστήσας κατακριθήσεται. 17 σημεῖα δὲ τοῖς πιστεύσασιν ταῦτα παρακολουθήσει· ἐν τῷ ὀνόματί μου δαιμόνια ἐκβαλοῦσιν, γλώσσαις λαλήσουσιν καιναῖς⁵, 18 [καὶ ἐν ταῖς χερσὶν] ὄφεις⁶ ἀροῦσιν, κἂν θανάσιμόν τι πίωσιν οὐ

---

³ 14 {A} ἐγηγερμένον C³ D K L W Θ Π Ψ 099 700 1009 1010 1079 1242 1344 1365 1646 2148 2174 Byz Lect l¹⁸⁵ᵐ itᵃᵘʳ,ᶜ,ᵈˢᵘᵖᵖ,ff²,l,o,q vg syrᵖ,ᵖᵃˡ copˢᵃ,ᵇᵒᵐˢˢ ethᵇ geoᴮ Diatessaron ‖ ἐκ νεκρῶν X ‖ ἐγηγερμένον ἐκ νεκρῶν A C* Δ f¹ f¹³ 28 33 565 892 (1071 ἐκ τῶν) 1195 1216 1230 1241 1253 1546 l⁵⁴⁷ syrʰ copᵇᵒᵐˢˢ arm

⁴ 14–15 {A} ἐπίστευσαν. καὶ εἶπεν αὐτοῖς A C (D εἶπεν πρὸς αὐτούς) K L X Δ Θ Π Ψ 099 f¹ f¹³ 28 33 565 700 892 1009 1010 1071 1079 1195 1216 1230 1241 1242 1253 1344 1365 1546 1646 2148 2174 Byz Lect l¹⁸⁵ᵐ,⁽⁸⁸³⁾ itᵃᵘʳ,ᶜ,ᵈˢᵘᵖᵖ,ff²,l,o,q vg syrᵖ,ʰ,ᵖᵃˡ copˢᵃ,ᵇᵒ arm geoᴮ ‖ ἐπίστευσαν. κἀκεῖνοι ἀπελογοῦντο λέγοντες ὅτι ὁ αἰὼν οὗτος τῆς ἀνομίας καὶ τῆς ἀπιστίας ὑπὸ τὸν σατανᾶν ἐστιν, ὁ μὴ ἐῶν τὰ ὑπὸ τῶν πνευμάτων ἀκάθαρτα τὴν ἀλήθειαν τοῦ θεοῦ καταλαβέσθαι δύναμιν· διὰ τοῦτο ἀποκάλυψον σου τὴν δικαιοσύνην ἤδη. ἐκεῖνοι ἔλεγον τῷ Χριστῷ, καὶ ὁ Χριστὸς ἐκείνοις προσέλεγεν ὅτι πεπλήρωται ὁ ὅρος τῶν ἐτῶν τῆς ἐξουσίας τοῦ σατανᾶ, ἀλλὰ ἐγγίζει ἄλλα δεινὰ καὶ ὑπὲρ ὧν ἐγὼ ἁμαρτησάντων παρεδόθην εἰς θάνατον ἵνα ὑποστρέψωσιν εἰς τὴν ἀλήθειαν καὶ μηκέτι ἁμαρτήσωσιν· ἵνα τὴν ἐν τῷ οὐρανῷ πνευματικὴν καὶ ἄφθαρτον τῆς δικαιοσύνης δόξαν κληρονομήσωσιν. ἀλλὰ W Greek mssᵃᶜᶜ· ᵗᵒ ᴶᵉʳᵒᵐᵉ

⁵ 17 {B} λαλήσουσιν καιναῖς A C² (Dˢᵘᵖᵖ λαλήσωσιν) K W X Θ Π f¹ f¹³ 28 33 565 700 892 1009 1010 1071 1079 1195 1216 1230 1241 1242 1253 1344 1365 1546 1646 2148 2174 Byz Lect l¹⁸⁵ᵐ itᵃᵘʳ,ᶜ,ᵈˢᵘᵖᵖ,ff²,l,q vg geoᴮ' Ambrose Augustine ‖ καιναῖς λαλήσουσιν itᵒ syrᶜ,ᵖ,ʰ,ᵖᵃˡ geoᴮ' Hippolytus Jacob-Nisibis Apostolic Constitutions ‖ λαλήσουσιν C* L Δ Ψ copˢᵃ,ᵇᵒ arm

⁶ 18 {C} καὶ ἐν ταῖς χερσὶν ὄφεις C L X Δᵍʳ Ψ 099 f¹ 33 565 892 1230

---

16 ὁ πιστεύσας...σωθήσεται Ac 2.38; 16.31, 33   17 ἐν...ἐκβαλοῦσιν Ac 8.7; 16.18
γλώσσαις...καιναῖς Ac 2.4, 11; 10.46; 19.6; 1 Cor 14.2–40   18 ἐν...ἀροῦσιν Lk 10.19;
Ac 28.3–6

Jesus Appears to the Eleven
(Also Matt. 28.16–20; Luke 24.36–49; John 20.19–23; Acts 1.6–8)

14 Last of all, Jesus appeared to the eleven disciples as they were eating. He scolded them, because they did not have faith and because they were too stubborn to believe those who had seen him alive. 15 He said to them: "Go to the whole world and preach the gospel to all mankind. 16 Whoever believes and is baptized will be saved; whoever does not believe will be condemned. 17 Believers will be given these signs of power: they will drive out demons in my name; they will speak in strange tongues; 18 if they pick up snakes or drink any poison,

they will not be harmed; they will place their hands on the sick, and they will get well."

Jesus Is Taken up to Heaven
(Also Luke 24.50–53; Acts 1.9–11)

[19] After the Lord Jesus had talked with them, he was taken up to heaven and sat at the right side of God. [20] The disciples went and preached everywhere, and the Lord worked with them and proved that their preaching was true by giving them the signs of power.]

ANOTHER OLD ENDING

[[9] The women went to Peter and his friends and gave them a brief account of all they had been told. [10] After this, Jesus himself sent out through his disciples, from the east to the west, the sacred and ever-living message of eternal salvation.]

μὴ αὐτοὺς βλάψῃ, ἐπὶ ἀρρώστους χεῖρας ἐπιθήσουσιν καὶ καλῶς ἕξουσιν.

The Ascension of Jesus
(Lk 24.50–53; Ac 1.9–11)

19 Ὁ μὲν οὖν κύριος [Ἰησοῦς][7] μετὰ τὸ λαλῆσαι αὐτοῖς ἀνελήμφθη εἰς τὸν οὐρανὸν καὶ ἐκάθισεν ἐκ δεξιῶν τοῦ θεοῦ. **20** ἐκεῖνοι δὲ ἐξελθόντες ἐκήρυξαν πανταχοῦ, τοῦ κυρίου συνεργοῦντος καὶ τὸν λόγον βεβαιοῦντος διὰ τῶν ἐπακολουθούντων σημείων.[8]]

A SHORTER ENDING OF MARK

[[Πάντα δὲ τὰ παρηγγελμένα τοῖς περὶ τὸν Πέτρον συντόμως ἐξήγγειλαν. Μετὰ δὲ ταῦτα καὶ αὐτὸς ὁ Ἰησοῦς[9] ἀπὸ ἀνατολῆς καὶ ἄχρι δύσεως ἐξαπέστειλεν δι' αὐτῶν τὸ ἱερὸν καὶ ἄφθαρτον κήρυγμα τῆς αἰωνίου σωτηρίας. ἀμήν.[10]]][11]

1253 *l*[6,253] syr[h] with * geo[B] Acts of Pilate[mss] ‖ καὶ ἐν ταῖς χερσὶν αὐτῶν ὄφεις (syr[c]) cop[sa,bo] arm ‖ ὄφεις A D[supp] K W Θ Π *f*[13] 28 700 1009 1010 1071 1079 1195 1216 1241 1242 1344 1365 1546 1646 2148 2174 *Byz Lect l*[185m] it[aur,c,d supp,l,o,q] vg syr[p,pal] Diatessaron Acts of Pilate[txt] Hippolytus

[7] **19** {C} κύριος Ἰησοῦς C* K L Δ *f*[1] *f*[13] 33 565 892[mg] 1071 1079 1230 1241 1546 *l*[174,230,547,983] it[aur,c,ff2,q] vg[cl] syr[c,p,h,pal] cop[sa,bo] arm eth Irenaeus[gr,lat] ‖ κύριος A C[3] D[supp] X Θ Π[supp] Ψ 28 700 892* 1009 1010 1195 1216 1242 1253 1344 1365 1646 2148 2174 *Byz Lect l*[185m] it[d supp,l] vg[ww] geo[B] Irenaeus[latms] ‖ Ἰησοῦς H 474 ‖ κύριος Ἰησοῦς Χριστός W it[o]

[8] **20** {B} σημείων. A C[2] *f*[1] 33 1079 it[aur,ff2,q] vg[cl] syr[c,p,h,pal] cop[sa] arm geo[B] ‖ σημείων. ἀμήν. C*[vid] D[supp] K L W X Δ Θ Π[supp] Ψ *f*[13] 28 565 700 892 1009 1010 1071 1195 1216 1230 1241 1242 1253 1344 1365 1546 1646 2148 2174 *Byz Lect* it[c,d supp,o] vg[ww] cop[bo] eth

[9] Short ending {A} Ἰησοῦς L 0112 579 syr[hmg] eth[mss] ‖ Ἰησοῦς ἐφάνη Ψ 274[mg] it[k] ‖ Ἰησοῦς ἐφάνη αὐτοῖς 099 cop[samss,bomss]

[10] Short ending {C} σωτηρίας. ἀμήν. Ψ 099 0112 274[mg] 579 it[k] syr[hmg] cop[samss,boms] ‖ σωτηρίας. L cop[boms]

[11] Short ending: *see page 196 footnote 2.*

18 ἐπὶ...ἕξουσιν Ac 4.30; 5.16; 8.7; Jas 5.14–15   **19** ἀνελήμφθη...οὐρανόν 2 Kgs 2.11; Ac 1.9–11; 1 Tm 3.16   ἐκάθισεν...θεοῦ Ps 110.1; Mt 22.44; 26.64; Mk 12.36; 14.62; Lk 20.42; 22.69; Ac 2.33, 34; 5.31; 7.55, 56; Ro 8.34; Eph 1.20; Col 3.1; He 1.3, 13; 8.1; 10.12; 12.2; 1 Pe 3.22   **20** Ac 14.3; He 2.3–4

ΚΑΤΑ ΛΟΥΚΑΝ

Dedication to Theophilus

1 Ἐπειδήπερ πολλοὶ ἐπεχείρησαν ἀνατάξασθαι διήγησιν περὶ τῶν πεπληροφορημένων ἐν ἡμῖν πραγμάτων, **2** καθὼς παρέδοσαν ἡμῖν οἱ ἀπ᾽ ἀρχῆς αὐτόπται καὶ ὑπηρέται γενόμενοι τοῦ λόγου, **3** ἔδοξε κἀμοὶ παρηκολουθηκότι ἄνωθεν πᾶσιν ἀκριβῶς καθεξῆς σοι γράψαι, κράτιστε Θεόφιλε, **4** ἵνα ἐπιγνῷς περὶ ὧν κατηχήθης λόγων τὴν ἀσφάλειαν.

The Birth of John the Baptist Foretold

5 Ἐγένετο ἐν ταῖς ἡμέραις Ἡρῴδου βασιλέως τῆς Ἰουδαίας ἱερεύς τις ὀνόματι Ζαχαρίας ἐξ ἐφημερίας Ἀβιά, καὶ γυνὴ αὐτῷ ἐκ τῶν θυγατέρων Ἀαρών, καὶ τὸ ὄνομα αὐτῆς Ἐλισάβετ. **6** ἦσαν δὲ δίκαιοι ἀμφότεροι ἐναντίον τοῦ θεοῦ, πορευόμενοι ἐν πάσαις ταῖς ἐντολαῖς καὶ δικαιώμασιν τοῦ κυρίου ἄμεμπτοι. **7** καὶ οὐκ ἦν αὐτοῖς τέκνον, καθότι ἦν ἡ Ἐλισάβετ στεῖρα, καὶ ἀμφότεροι προβεβηκότες ἐν ταῖς ἡμέραις αὐτῶν ἦσαν. **8** Ἐγένετο δὲ ἐν τῷ ἱερατεύειν αὐτὸν ἐν τῇ τάξει τῆς ἐφημερίας αὐτοῦ ἔναντι τοῦ θεοῦ,[a] **9** κατὰ τὸ ἔθος τῆς ἱερατείας[a] ἔλαχε τοῦ θυμιᾶσαι εἰσελθὼν εἰς τὸν ναὸν τοῦ κυρίου, **10** καὶ πᾶν τὸ πλῆθος ἦν τοῦ λαοῦ προσευχόμενον ἔξω τῇ ὥρᾳ τοῦ θυμιάματος· **11** ὤφθη δὲ αὐτῷ ἄγγελος κυρίου ἑστὼς ἐκ δεξιῶν τοῦ θυσιαστηρίου τοῦ θυμιάματος. **12** καὶ ἐταράχθη Ζαχαρίας ἰδών, καὶ φόβος ἐπέπεσεν ἐπ᾽ αὐτόν. **13** εἶπεν δὲ πρὸς αὐτὸν ὁ ἄγγελος, Μὴ φοβοῦ, Ζαχαρία, διότι εἰσηκούσθη ἡ δέησίς σου, καὶ ἡ γυνή σου Ἐλισάβετ γεννήσει υἱόν σοι, καὶ καλέσεις τὸ ὄνομα

---

^{a a} 8-9 a minor, a none: TR Bov Nes (NEB) Zür Luth (Jer) (Seg) // a none, a minor: BF² TT // a minor, a minor: AV RV ASV RSV // a none, a none: WH

---

2 οἱ...αὐτόπται Jn 15.27   3 Θεόφιλε Ac 1.1   5 ἐφημερίας Ἀβιά 1 Chr 24.10
9 Ex 30.7

THE GOSPEL OF LUKE

Introduction

1 Dear Theophilus:

Many have done their best to write a report of the things that have taken place among us. [2] They wrote what we have been told by those who saw these things from the beginning and proclaimed the message. [3] And so, your Excellency, because I have carefully studied all these matters from their beginning, I thought it good to write an orderly account for you. [4] I do this so that you will know the full truth of all those matters which you have been taught.

The Birth of John the Baptist Announced

[5] During the time when Herod was king of Judea, there was a priest named Zechariah, who belonged to the priestly order of Abiah. His wife's name was Elizabeth; she also belonged to a priestly family. [6] They both lived good lives in God's sight, and obeyed fully all the Lord's commandments and rules. [7] They had no children because Elizabeth could not have any, and she and Zechariah were both very old.

[8] One day Zechariah was doing his work as a priest before God, taking his turn in the daily service. [9] According to the custom followed by the priests, he was chosen by lot to burn the incense on the altar. So he went into the Temple of the Lord, [10] while the crowd of people outside prayed during the hour of burning the incense. [11] An angel of the Lord appeared to him, standing at the right side of the altar where the incense was burned. [12] When Zechariah saw him he was troubled and felt afraid. [13] But the angel said to him: "Don't be afraid, Zechariah! God has heard your prayer, and your wife Elizabeth will bear you a

son. You are to name him John. ¹⁴ How glad and happy you will be, and how happy many others will be when he is born! ¹⁵ For he will be a great man in the Lord's sight. He must not drink any wine or strong drink. From his very birth he will be filled with the Holy Spirit. ¹⁶ He will bring back many of the people of Israel to the Lord their God. ¹⁷ He will go as God's messenger, strong and mighty like the prophet Elijah. He will bring fathers and children together again; he will turn the disobedient people back to the way of thinking of the righteous; he will get the Lord's people ready for him."

¹⁸ Zechariah said to the angel, "How shall I know if this is so? I am an old man and my wife also is old." ¹⁹ "I am Gabriel," the angel answered. "I stand in the presence of God, who sent me to speak to you and tell you this good news. ²⁰ But you have not believed my message, which will come true at the right time. Because you have not believed you will be unable to speak; you will remain silent until the day my promise to you comes true."

²¹ In the meantime the people were waiting for Zechariah, wondering why he was spending such a long time in the Temple. ²² When he came out he could not speak to them — and so they knew that he had seen a vision in the Temple. Unable to say a word, he made signs to them with his hands.

²³ When his period of service in the Temple was over, Zechariah went back home. ²⁴ Some time later his wife Elizabeth became pregnant, and did not leave

αὐτοῦ Ἰωάννην. 14 καὶ ἔσται χαρά σοι καὶ ἀγαλλίασις, καὶ πολλοὶ ἐπὶ τῇ γενέσει αὐτοῦ χαρήσονται· 15 ἔσται γὰρ μέγας ἐνώπιον [τοῦ] κυρίου, καὶ οἶνον καὶ σίκερα οὐ μὴ πίῃ, καὶ πνεύματος ἁγίου πλησθήσεται ἔτι ἐκ κοιλίας μητρὸς αὐτοῦ, 16 καὶ πολλοὺς τῶν υἱῶν Ἰσραὴλ ἐπιστρέψει ἐπὶ κύριον τὸν θεὸν αὐτῶν. 17 καὶ αὐτὸς προελεύσεται¹ ἐνώπιον αὐτοῦ ἐν πνεύματι καὶ δυνάμει Ἠλίου, **ἐπιστρέψαι καρδίας πατέρων ἐπὶ τέκνα** καὶ ἀπειθεῖς ἐν φρονήσει δικαίων, ἑτοιμάσαι κυρίῳ λαὸν κατεσκευασμένον. 18 Καὶ εἶπεν Ζαχαρίας πρὸς τὸν ἄγγελον, Κατὰ τί γνώσομαι τοῦτο; ἐγὼ γάρ εἰμι πρεσβύτης καὶ ἡ γυνή μου προβεβηκυῖα ἐν ταῖς ἡμέραις αὐτῆς. 19 καὶ ἀποκριθεὶς ὁ ἄγγελος εἶπεν αὐτῷ, Ἐγώ εἰμι Γαβριὴλ ὁ παρεστηκὼς ἐνώπιον τοῦ θεοῦ, καὶ ἀπεστάλην λαλῆσαι πρὸς σὲ καὶ εὐαγγελίσασθαί σοι ταῦτα· 20 καὶ ἰδοὺ ἔσῃ σιωπῶν καὶ μὴ δυνάμενος λαλῆσαι ἄχρι ἧς ἡμέρας γένηται ταῦτα, ἀνθ' ὧν οὐκ ἐπίστευσας τοῖς λόγοις μου, οἵτινες πληρωθήσονται εἰς τὸν καιρὸν αὐτῶν.

21 Καὶ ἦν ὁ λαὸς προσδοκῶν τὸν Ζαχαρίαν, καὶ ἐθαύμαζον ἐν τῷ χρονίζειν ἐν τῷ ναῷ αὐτόν. 22 ἐξελθὼν δὲ οὐκ ἐδύνατο λαλῆσαι αὐτοῖς, καὶ ἐπέγνωσαν ὅτι ὀπτασίαν ἑώρακεν ἐν τῷ ναῷ· καὶ αὐτὸς ἦν διανεύων αὐτοῖς, καὶ διέμενεν κωφός. 23 καὶ ἐγένετο ὡς ἐπλήσθησαν αἱ ἡμέραι τῆς λειτουργίας αὐτοῦ ἀπῆλθεν εἰς τὸν οἶκον αὐτοῦ. 24 Μετὰ δὲ ταύτας τὰς ἡμέρας συνέλαβεν Ἐλισάβετ ἡ γυνὴ αὐτοῦ· καὶ περιέκρυβεν ἑαυτὴν μῆνας πέντε,

---

¹ **17** {A} προελεύσεται ℵ A B³ D K W X Δ Θ Π Ψ 053 *f*¹ 28 33 565 700 892 1009 1010 1071ᶜ 1079 1195 1216 1230 1241 1242 1253 1344 1365 1546 1646 2148 2174 *Byz Lect*ᵐ itᵃ·ᵃᵘʳ·ᵇ·ᶜ·ᵈ·ᵉ·ᶠ·ᶠᶠ²·ˡ·𐞥·ʳˡ vg syrᵖ?ʰ?ᵖᵃˡ? copˢᵃ·ᵇᵒ goth arm geo Origen ‖ προσελεύσεται B* C L *f*¹³ 1071* *l*⁴⁷·⁶⁰ᵐ·⁵⁴⁷ᵐ syrᵖ·ʰ?ᵖᵃˡ? ‖ προπορεύσεται 53 57 259 945 *l*³³ᵐ·⁴⁴ᵐ

15 οἶνον...πίῃ Nu 6.3; Jdg 13.4; 1 Sm 1.11 LXX   **17** αὐτὸς...Ἠλίου Mt 17.11–13 ἐπιστρέψαι...τέκνα Mal 4.5–6; Sir 48.10   ἑτοιμάσαι...κατεσκευασμένον Mal 3.1   **18** ἐγὼ ...αὐτῆς Gn 18.11   **19** Γαβριήλ Dn 8.16; 9.21   ἀπεστάλην...ταῦτα He 1.14   **20** οὐκ ἐπίστευσας...αὐτῶν Lk 1.45

λέγουσα　25 ὅτι Οὕτως μοι πεποίηκεν κύριος ἐν ἡμέραις αἷς ἐπεῖδεν ἀφελεῖν ὄνειδός μου ἐν ἀνθρώποις.

The Birth of Jesus Foretold

26 Ἐν δὲ τῷ μηνὶ τῷ ἕκτῳ ἀπεστάλη ὁ ἄγγελος Γαβριὴλ ἀπὸ τοῦ θεοῦ εἰς πόλιν τῆς Γαλιλαίας ᾗ ὄνομα Ναζαρὲθ　27 πρὸς παρθένον ἐμνηστευμένην ἀνδρὶ ᾧ ὄνομα Ἰωσὴφ ἐξ οἴκου Δαυίδ, καὶ τὸ ὄνομα τῆς παρθένου Μαριάμ.　28 καὶ εἰσελθὼν πρὸς αὐτὴν εἶπεν, Χαῖρε, κεχαριτωμένη, ὁ κύριος μετὰ σοῦ.[2]　29 ἡ δὲ ἐπὶ τῷ λόγῳ διεταράχθη καὶ διελογίζετο ποταπὸς εἴη ὁ ἀσπασμὸς οὗτος.　30 καὶ εἶπεν ὁ ἄγγελος αὐτῇ, Μὴ φοβοῦ, Μαριάμ, εὗρες γὰρ χάριν παρὰ τῷ θεῷ·　31 καὶ ἰδοὺ συλλήμψῃ ἐν γαστρὶ καὶ τέξῃ υἱόν, καὶ καλέσεις τὸ ὄνομα αὐτοῦ Ἰησοῦν.　32 οὗτος ἔσται μέγας καὶ υἱὸς ὑψίστου κληθήσεται, καὶ δώσει αὐτῷ κύριος ὁ θεὸς τὸν θρόνον Δαυίδ τοῦ πατρὸς αὐτοῦ,　33 καὶ βασιλεύσει ἐπὶ τὸν οἶκον Ἰακὼβ εἰς τοὺς αἰῶνας, καὶ τῆς βασιλείας αὐτοῦ οὐκ ἔσται τέλος.　34 εἶπεν δὲ Μαριὰμ πρὸς τὸν ἄγγελον, Πῶς ἔσται τοῦτο, ἐπεὶ ἄνδρα οὐ γινώσκω;　35 καὶ ἀποκριθεὶς ὁ ἄγγελος εἶπεν αὐτῇ, Πνεῦμα ἅγιον ἐπελεύσεται ἐπὶ σέ, καὶ δύναμις ὑψίστου ἐπισκιάσει σοι· διὸ καὶ τὸ γεννώμενον[3] ἅγιον κληθήσεται,[b] υἱὸς θεοῦ.　36 καὶ ἰδοὺ Ἐλι-

2 28 {B} σοῦ. ℵ B L W Ψ 0130^vid f¹ 565 700 1241 l^44m syr^pal cop^sa, bo arm geo Peter-Alexandria Ps-Titus de Promissionibus Paschal Chronicle John-Damascus ∥ σοῦ. εὐλογημένη σὺ ἐν γυναιξίν. (see 1.42) A C D K X Δ Θ Π 053 f¹³ 28 33 892 1009 1010 1079 1195 1216 1230 1242 1253 1344 1365 1546 1646 2148 2174 Byz Lect^m it^a,aur,b,c,d,e,f,ff²,l,q,r¹ vg syr^p.h cop^bomss goth eth geo^Ac Diatessaron^a,c arm,i,n Tertullian Africanus Eusebius Ephraem ∥ σοῦ. εὐλογημένη σὺ ἐν γυναιξὶν καὶ εὐλογημένος ὁ καρπὸς τῆς κοιλίας σου. (see 1.42) (1071 σοι for σύ) Andrew-Crete

3 35 {B} γεννώμενον ℵ A B C³ D K L W X Δ Π Ψ 053 (f¹³ 1546 2148

b **35** *b* minor: WH RV ASV^mg RSV NEB^mg TT ∥ *b* none: TR Bov Nes BF² AV RV^mg ASV NEB Zür Luth (Jer) Seg

25 ἀφελεῖν ὄνειδός μου Gn 30.23　**27** Lk 2.5; Mt 1.16, 18　**31** συλλήμψῃ...Ἰησοῦν Gn 16.11; Jdg 13.3; Is 7.14; Mt 1.21–23　**32-33** δώσει...τέλος Is 9.7; 2 Sm 7.12, 13, 16 **33** Mic 4.7; Dn 7.14　**35** Πνεῦμα...σοι Mt 1.20

the house for five months.　25 "Now at last the Lord has helped me in this way," she said. "He has taken away my public disgrace!"

The Birth of Jesus Announced

26 In the sixth month of Elizabeth's pregnancy God sent the angel Gabriel to a town in Galilee named Nazareth. 27 He had a message for a girl promised in marriage to a man named Joseph, who was a descendant of King David. The girl's name was Mary. 28 The angel came to her and said, "Peace be with you! The Lord is with you, and has greatly blessed you!" 29 Mary was deeply troubled by the angel's message, and she wondered what his words meant. 30 The angel said to her: "Don't be afraid, Mary, for God has been gracious to you. 31 You will become pregnant and give birth to a son, and you will name him Jesus. 32 He will be great and will be called the Son of the Most High God. The Lord God will make him a king, as his ancestor David was, 33 and he will be the king of the descendants of Jacob for ever; his kingdom will never end!"

34 Mary said to the angel, "I am a virgin. How, then, can this be?" 35 The angel answered: "The Holy Spirit will come on you, and God's power will rest upon you. For this reason the holy child will be called the Son of God. 36 Remember your relative Elizabeth. It is

said that she cannot have children; but she herself is now six months pregnant, even though she is very old. [37] For there is not a thing that God cannot do."

[38] "I am the Lord's servant," said Mary; "may it happen to me as you have said." And the angel left her.

Mary Visits Elizabeth

[39] Soon afterward Mary got ready and hurried off to the hill country, to a town in Judea. [40] She went into Zechariah's house and greeted Elizabeth. [41] When Elizabeth heard Mary's greeting, the baby moved within her. Elizabeth was filled with the Holy Spirit, [42] and spoke in a loud voice: "Blessed are you among women! Blessed is the child you will bear! [43] Why should this great thing happen to me, that my Lord's mother comes to visit me? [44] For as soon as I heard your greeting, the baby within me jumped with gladness. [45] How happy are you to believe that the Lord's message to you will come true!"

σάβετ ἡ συγγενίς σου καὶ αὐτὴ συνείληφεν υἱὸν ἐν γήρει αὐτῆς, καὶ οὗτος μὴν ἕκτος ἐστὶν αὐτῇ τῇ καλουμένῃ στείρᾳ· **37** ὅτι **οὐκ ἀδυνατήσει παρὰ τοῦ θεοῦ[4] πᾶν ῥῆμα. 38** εἶπεν δὲ Μαριάμ, Ἰδοὺ ἡ δούλη κυρίου· γένοιτό μοι κατὰ τὸ ῥῆμά σου. καὶ ἀπῆλθεν ἀπ' αὐτῆς ὁ ἄγγελος.

Mary Visits Elizabeth

39 Ἀναστᾶσα δὲ Μαριὰμ ἐν ταῖς ἡμέραις ταύταις ἐπορεύθη εἰς τὴν ὀρεινὴν μετὰ σπουδῆς εἰς πόλιν Ἰούδα, **40** καὶ εἰσῆλθεν εἰς τὸν οἶκον Ζαχαρίου καὶ ἠσπάσατο τὴν Ἐλισάβετ. **41** καὶ ἐγένετο ὡς ἤκουσεν τὸν ἀσπασμὸν τῆς Μαρίας ἡ Ἐλισάβετ, ἐσκίρτησεν τὸ βρέφος ἐν τῇ κοιλίᾳ αὐτῆς, καὶ ἐπλήσθη πνεύματος ἁγίου ἡ Ἐλισάβετ, **42** καὶ ἀνεφώνησεν κραυγῇ μεγάλῃ καὶ εἶπεν, Εὐλογημένη σὺ ἐν γυναιξίν, καὶ εὐλογημένος ὁ καρπὸς τῆς κοιλίας σου. **43** καὶ πόθεν μοι τοῦτο ἵνα ἔλθῃ ἡ μήτηρ τοῦ κυρίου μου πρὸς ἐμέ; **44** ἰδοὺ γὰρ ὡς ἐγένετο ἡ φωνὴ τοῦ ἀσπασμοῦ σου εἰς τὰ ὦτά μου, ἐσκίρτησεν ἐν ἀγαλλιάσει τὸ βρέφος ἐν τῇ κοιλίᾳ μου. **45** καὶ μακαρία ἡ πιστεύσασα ὅτι ἔσται τελείωσις τοῖς λελαλημένοις αὐτῇ παρὰ κυρίου.

2174 γεννόμενον) 28 565 700 892 1009 1010 1071 1079 1195 1216 1241 1242 1344 Byz Lect[m] it[aur, b, d, f, ff2, l, q] vg[ww] syr[h, pal mss] cop[sa, bo] goth geo Tertullian[2/3] Origen[lat] Cyprian Peter-Alexandria Eusebius mss[acc. to Ephraem] Cyril-Jerusalem Apollinaris Epiphanius Augustine Cyril Paschal Chronicle John-Damascus ‖ γεννώμενον ἐκ σοῦ C* Θ f[1] 33 1230 (1253 γεννόμενον) 1365 1646 it[a, c, e, (rl)] vg[cl] syr[(p), pal ms] arm eth Marcion Valentinians Diatessaron[a, e arm, i, n] Irenaeus[lat] Tertullian[1/3] Hippolytus Gregory-Thaumaturgus Adamantius Athanasius Ephraem Diodore Amphilochius Ps-Justin Epiphanius Jerome Augustine John-Damascus

[4] **37** {B} παρὰ τοῦ θεοῦ ℵ* B D L W Ξ 565 ‖ παρὰ τῷ θεῷ ℵ[c] A C K Δ Θ Π Ψ 053 (f[1] l[211m] omit τῷ) f[13] 28 33 700 892 1009 1010 1071 1079 1195 1216 1230 1241 1242 1253 1344 1365 1546 1646 2148 2174 Byz Lect[m] Ambrose Paschal Chronicle ‖ παρὰ τοῦ θεοῦ or παρὰ τῷ θεῷ it[(a), aur, d, f, rl] vg syr[h, pal] cop[sa, bo] goth geo Augustine ‖ τῷ θεῷ 788 it[b, c, e, ff2, l, q] syr[p] Ambrose

---

37 Gn 18.14   **41** ἐσκίρτησεν...αὐτῆς Gn 25.22 lxx   ἐσκίρτησεν...Ἐλισάβετ Lk 1.15   **42** Εὐλογημένη...γυναιξίν Jdg 5.24   εὐλογημένος...σου Dt 28.4   **45** μακαρία...κυρίου Lk 1.20

Mary's Song of Praise

46 *Καὶ εἶπεν Μαριάμ*[5],
Μεγαλύνει **ἡ ψυχή μου τὸν κύριον,**
47 *καὶ* **ἠγαλλίασεν** *τὸ πνεῦμά μου* **ἐπὶ τῷ θεῷ τῷ σωτῆρί μου,**
48 *ὅτι* **ἐπέβλεψεν ἐπὶ τὴν ταπείνωσιν τῆς δούλης** *αὐτοῦ.*
ἰδοὺ γὰρ ἀπὸ τοῦ νῦν μακαριοῦσίν με πᾶσαι αἱ γενεαί·
49 *ὅτι ἐποίησέν μοι μεγάλα ὁ δυνατός,*
καὶ ἅγιον τὸ ὄνομα αὐτοῦ,
50 *καὶ τὸ ἔλεος αὐτοῦ εἰς γενεὰς καὶ γενεὰς*
τοῖς φοβουμένοις αὐτόν.
51 *Ἐποίησεν κράτος ἐν βραχίονι αὐτοῦ,*
διεσκόρπισεν ὑπερηφάνους διανοίᾳ καρδίας αὐτῶν·
52 *καθεῖλεν δυνάστας ἀπὸ θρόνων*
καὶ ὕψωσεν ταπεινούς,
53 *πεινῶντας ἐνέπλησεν ἀγαθῶν*
καὶ πλουτοῦντας ἐξαπέστειλεν κενούς.
54 *ἀντελάβετο Ἰσραὴλ παιδὸς αὐτοῦ,*
μνησθῆναι ἐλέους,
55 *καθὼς ἐλάλησεν πρὸς τοὺς πατέρας ἡμῶν,*
τῷ Ἀβραὰμ καὶ τῷ σπέρματι αὐτοῦ εἰς τὸν αἰῶνα.
56 *Ἔμεινεν δὲ Μαριὰμ σὺν αὐτῇ ὡς μῆνας τρεῖς, καὶ*
ὑπέστρεψεν εἰς τὸν οἶκον αὐτῆς.

---

[5] **46** {B} Μαριάμ ℵ A B C^{2} K L W Δ Θ Ξ Π Ψ 053 *f*^{1} *f*^{13} 28 33 565 700 892 1009 1010 1071 1079 1195 1216 1230 1241 1242 1253 1344 1365 1546 1646 2148 2174 *Byz Lect*^{m} syr^{s,p,h,pal} cop^{bo} goth arm eth geo // Μαρία C* D it$^{aur,c,d,e,f,ff^2,q,r^1}$ vg cop$^{sa,bo^{ms}}$ Tertullian Ambrose Augustine // *Elisabet* it^{a,b,l} Irenaeus^{lat} mss$^{acc.\ to\ Origen^{lat}}$ Niceta

---

46–55 1 Sm 2.1–10 **48** *ἐπέβλεψεν...αὐτοῦ* 1 Sm 1.11 **49** *ἅγιον...αὐτοῦ* Ps 111.9 **50** Ps 103.13, 17 **51** Ps 89.10 *διεσκόρπισεν ὑπερηφάνους* 2 Sm 22.28 **52** *καθεῖλεν δυνάστας* Job 12.19 *ὕψωσεν ταπεινούς* Job 5.11 **53** 1 Sm 2.5 *πεινῶντας...ἀγαθῶν* Ps 107.9 **54** Ps 98.3 *Ἰσραὴλ...αὐτοῦ* Is 41.8 **55** Mic 7.20; Gn 17.7; 22.17

Mary's Song of Praise

46 Mary said:
"My heart praises the Lord,
47 My soul is glad because of God my Savior.
48 For he has remembered me, his lowly servant!
And from now on all people will call me blessed,
49 Because of the great things the Mighty God has done for me.
His name is holy;
50 He shows mercy to all who fear him,
From one generation to another.
51 He stretched out his mighty arm
And scattered the proud people with all their plans.
52 He brought down mighty kings from their thrones,
And lifted up the lowly.
53 He filled the hungry with good things,
And sent the rich away with empty hands.
54 He kept the promise he made to our ancestors;
He came to the help of his servant Israel,
55 And remembered to show mercy to Abraham
And to all his descendants for ever!"
56 Mary stayed about three months with Elizabeth, and then went back home.

The Birth of John the Baptist

[57] The time came for Elizabeth to have her baby, and she gave birth to a son. [58] Her neighbors and relatives heard how wonderfully good the Lord had been to her, and they all rejoiced with her. [59] When the baby was a week old they came to circumcise him; they were going to name him Zechariah, his father's name. [60] But his mother said, "No! His name will be John." [61] They said to her, "But you don't have a single relative with that name!" [62] Then they made signs to his father, asking him what name he would like the boy to have. [63] Zechariah asked for a writing pad and wrote, "His name is John." How surprised they all were! [64] At that moment Zechariah was able to speak again, and he started praising God. [65] The neighbors were all filled with fear, and the news about these things spread through all the hill country of Judea. [66] All who heard of it thought about it and asked, "What is this child going to be?" For it was plain that the Lord's power was with him.

Zechariah's Prophecy

[67] His father Zechariah was filled with the Holy Spirit, and he prophesied:
[68] "Let us praise the Lord, the God of Israel!
For he came to the help of his people and set them free.

The Birth of John the Baptist

57 Τῇ δὲ Ἐλισάβετ ἐπλήσθη ὁ χρόνος τοῦ τεκεῖν αὐτήν, καὶ ἐγέννησεν υἱόν. **58** καὶ ἤκουσαν οἱ περίοικοι καὶ οἱ συγγενεῖς αὐτῆς ὅτι ἐμεγάλυνεν κύριος τὸ ἔλεος αὐτοῦ μετ᾽ αὐτῆς, καὶ συνέχαιρον αὐτῇ. **59** Καὶ ἐγένετο ἐν τῇ ἡμέρᾳ τῇ ὀγδόῃ ἦλθον περιτεμεῖν τὸ παιδίον, καὶ ἐκάλουν αὐτὸ ἐπὶ τῷ ὀνόματι τοῦ πατρὸς αὐτοῦ Ζαχαρίαν. **60** καὶ ἀποκριθεῖσα ἡ μήτηρ αὐτοῦ εἶπεν, Οὐχί, ἀλλὰ κληθήσεται Ἰωάννης. **61** καὶ εἶπαν πρὸς αὐτὴν ὅτι Οὐδείς ἐστιν ἐκ τῆς συγγενείας σου ὃς καλεῖται τῷ ὀνόματι τούτῳ. **62** ἐνένευον δὲ τῷ πατρὶ αὐτοῦ τὸ τί ἂν θέλοι καλεῖσθαι αὐτό. **63** καὶ αἰτήσας πινακίδιον ἔγραψεν λέγων, Ἰωάννης ἐστὶν ὄνομα αὐτοῦ. καὶ ἐθαύμασαν πάντες. **64** ἀνεῴχθη δὲ τὸ στόμα αὐτοῦ παραχρῆμα καὶ ἡ γλῶσσα αὐτοῦ, καὶ ἐλάλει εὐλογῶν τὸν θεόν. **65** καὶ ἐγένετο ἐπὶ πάντας φόβος τοὺς περιοικοῦντας αὐτούς, καὶ ἐν ὅλῃ τῇ ὀρεινῇ τῆς Ἰουδαίας διελαλεῖτο πάντα τὰ ῥήματα ταῦτα, **66** καὶ ἔθεντο πάντες οἱ ἀκούσαντες ἐν τῇ καρδίᾳ αὐτῶν, λέγοντες, Τί ἄρα τὸ παιδίον τοῦτο ἔσται; καὶ γὰρ χεὶρ κυρίου ἦν[6] μετ᾽ αὐτοῦ.

The Prophecy of Zechariah

67 Καὶ Ζαχαρίας ὁ πατὴρ αὐτοῦ ἐπλήσθη πνεύματος ἁγίου καὶ ἐπροφήτευσεν λέγων,
68   Εὐλογητὸς κύριος[7] ὁ θεὸς τοῦ Ἰσραήλ,
      ὅτι ἐπεσκέψατο καὶ ἐποίησεν λύτρωσιν τῷ λαῷ αὐτοῦ,

---

[6] **66** {B} χεὶρ κυρίου ἦν 𝔓⁴ᵛⁱᵈ ℵ A B C K L W Δ Θ Π Ψ 053 0130 f¹³ 28 33 565 700 892 1009 1010 1071 1079 1195 1216 1230 1241 1242 1253 1344 1365 1546 1646 2148 2174 *Byz Lect*ᵐ itaᵃ·ᵃᵘʳ,(b),c,e,f vg syrᵖ·ʰ·ᵖᵃˡ copˢᵃ·ᵇᵒ goth arm geo ‖ χεὶρ κυρίου D itᵝ·ᵈ·ᶠᶠ²·ˡ·ᑫ syrˢ ‖ ἦν χεὶρ κυρίου f¹
[7] **68** {B} κύριος (see Ps 40.14 LXX; 105.48 LXX) ℵ A B C D K L Δ Θ Π Ψ

59 Lk 2.21   ἐν...παιδίον Gn 17.12; Lv 12.3   **59–60** ἐκάλουν...Ἰωάννης Lk 1.13
68 Εὐλογητὸς...Ἰσραήλ Ps 41.13; 72.18; 106.48   ἐπεσκέψατο...αὐτοῦ Ps 111.9; Lk 7.16

69 καὶ ἤγειρεν κέρας σωτηρίας ἡμῖν
  ἐν οἴκῳ Δαυὶδ παιδὸς αὐτοῦ,

70 καθὼς ἐλάλησεν διὰ στόματος τῶν ἁγίων ἀπ' αἰῶνος
  προφητῶν αὐτοῦ[8],

71 σωτηρίαν ἐξ ἐχθρῶν ἡμῶν καὶ ἐκ χειρὸς πάντων
  τῶν μισούντων ἡμᾶς·

72 ποιῆσαι ἔλεος μετὰ τῶν πατέρων ἡμῶν
  καὶ μνησθῆναι διαθήκης ἁγίας αὐτοῦ,

73 ὅρκον ὃν ὤμοσεν πρὸς Ἀβραὰμ τὸν πατέρα ἡμῶν,
  τοῦ δοῦναι ἡμῖν 74 ἀφόβως ἐκ χειρὸς ἐχθρῶν[9]
  ῥυσθέντας
  λατρεύειν αὐτῷ 75 ἐν ὁσιότητι καὶ δικαιοσύνῃ
  ἐνώπιον αὐτοῦ πάσαις ταῖς ἡμέραις ἡμῶν.

76 Καὶ σὺ δέ, παιδίον, προφήτης ὑψίστου κληθήσῃ,
  προπορεύσῃ γὰρ **ἐνώπιον κυρίου ἑτοιμάσαι
  ὁδοὺς αὐτοῦ,**

69 He raised up a mighty Savior
  for us,
  One who is a descendant of his
  servant David.

70 This is what he said long ago by
  means of his holy prophets:

71 He promised to save us from our
  enemies,
  And from the power of all those
  who hate us.

72 He said he would show mercy to
  our ancestors,
  And remember his sacred covenant.

73-74 He made a solemn promise to our
  ancestor Abraham,
  And vowed that he would rescue
  us from our enemies,
  And allow us to serve him without
  fear,

75 To be holy and righteous before
  him,
  All the days of our life.

76 You, my child, will be called a
  prophet of the Most High
  God;
  You will go ahead of the Lord
  To prepare his road for him,

---

053 0130 f¹ f¹³ 28 33 565 700 892 1009 1010 1071 1195 1216 1230 1241 1242 1253 1344 1365 1546 1646 2148 2174 *Byz Lect*ᵐ itᵃᵘʳ,ᵈ,ᵉ,ᶠ,𐞥 vg syrᵖ,ʰ,ᵖᵃˡ copᵇᵒ goth arm geo Irenaeusˡᵃᵗ Origenˡᵃᵗ Cyprian Eusebius Augustine Cyril ‖ *omit* 𝔭⁴ W itᵃ,ᵇ,β,ᶜ,ff²,ˡ,ʳˡ syrˢ copˢᵃ Irenaeus Cyprian Eusebius

[8] **70** {B} τῶν ἁγίων ἀπ' αἰῶνος προφητῶν αὐτοῦ 𝔭⁴ B L Δ 0130 f¹³ geo Origen Eusebius ‖ τῶν ἁγίων ἀπ' αἰῶνος αὐτοῦ προφητῶν ℵ W ‖ τῶν ἁγίων τῶν ἀπ' αἰῶνος προφητῶν αὐτοῦ A C K Θ Π Ψ 053 f¹ 28 33 565 700 892 1009 1010 1071 1195 1216 1230 1241 1242 1253 1344 1365 1546 1646 2148 2174 *Byz l*¹³⁴⁵,¹³⁴⁶,¹³⁴⁸,¹³⁴⁹,¹³⁵⁰ vg goth arm Augustine Cyril Paschal Chronicle ‖ ἁγίων προφητῶν αὐτοῦ τῶν ἀπ' αἰῶνος D itᵃ,ᵃᵘʳ,ᵇ,β,ᶜ,ᵈ,ᵉ,ᶠ,ff²,ˡ,𐞥,ʳˡ syrˢ,ᵖ,ʰ,ᵖᵃˡ (copˢᵃ?ᵇᵒ?) Irenaeusˡᵃᵗ

[9] **74** {C} ἐκ χειρὸς ἐχθρῶν ℵ B L W (0130 1546* τῶν ἐχθρῶν) f¹ f¹³ 565 892 itβ,(ᵉ) arm geo Irenaeusᵍʳ,ˡᵃᵗ Origenˡᵃᵗ ‖ ἐκ χειρὸς ἐχθρῶν ἡμῶν D 33 armᵐˢ goth Origen ‖ ἐκ χειρὸς τῶν ἐχθρῶν ἡμῶν A C Δ Θ Π Ψ 053 0177 28 700 1009 1010 1071 1195 1216 1230 1241 1242 1253 1344 1365 1546ᶜ 1646 2148 2174 *Byz* Cyril Paschal Chronicle ‖ ἐκ χειρὸς τῶν (or omit τῶν) ἐχθρῶν ἡμῶν itᵃ,ᵃᵘʳ,ᵇ,ᶜ,ᵈ,ᶠ,ff²,ˡ,𐞥,ʳˡ vg syrˢ,ᵖ,ʰ,ᵖᵃˡ copᵇᵒ eth ‖ ἐκ χειρὸς πάντων τῶν ἐχθρῶν ἡμῶν K ‖ ἐκ τῶν ἐχθρῶν ἡμῶν copˢᵃ,ᵇᵒᵐˢˢ

---

69 κέρας σωτηρίας Ps 18.2   **71** Ps 106.10   **72** Ps 106.45–46   **72–73** μνησθῆναι... Ἀβραάμ Ps 105.8–9; Gn 17.7; Lv 26.42   **73–74** Gn 22.16–17   **75** Tt 2.12   **76** προπορεύσῃ ...αὐτοῦ Is 40.3; Mal 3.1; Mt 3.3

⁷⁷ To tell his people that they will be
      saved,
      By having their sins forgiven.
⁷⁸ For our God is merciful and
      tender;
      He will cause the bright dawn of
      salvation to rise on us,
⁷⁹ And shine from heaven on all those
      who live in the dark shadow
      of death,
      To guide our steps into the path
      of peace.''

⁸⁰ The child grew and developed in
body and spirit; he lived in the desert
until the day when he would appear
publicly to the people of Israel.

The Birth of Jesus
(Also Matt. 1.18–25)

2 At that time Emperor Augustus sent
out an order for all the citizens of the
Empire to register themselves for the
census. ² When this first census took
place, Quirinius was the governor of
Syria. ³ Everyone, then, went to register
himself, each to his own town.

⁴ Joseph went from the town of Nazareth, in Galilee, to Judea, to the town
named Bethlehem, where King David
was born. Joseph went there because
he himself was a descendant of David.
⁵ He went to register himself with Mary,
who was promised in marriage to him.
She was pregnant, ⁶ and while they were
in Bethlehem, the time came for her to
have her baby. ⁷ She gave birth to her

---

77 τοῦ δοῦναι γνῶσιν σωτηρίας τῷ λαῷ αὐτοῦ
      ἐν ἀφέσει ἁμαρτιῶν αὐτῶν,
78 διὰ σπλάγχνα ἐλέους θεοῦ ἡμῶν,
      ἐν οἷς ἐπισκέψεται¹⁰ ἡμᾶς ἀνατολὴ ἐξ ὕψους,
79 ἐπιφᾶναι τοῖς ἐν σκότει καὶ σκιᾷ θανάτου καθημένοις,
      τοῦ κατευθῦναι τοὺς πόδας ἡμῶν εἰς ὁδὸν
      εἰρήνης.

80 Τὸ δὲ παιδίον ηὔξανεν καὶ ἐκραταιοῦτο πνεύματι,
καὶ ἦν ἐν ταῖς ἐρήμοις ἕως ἡμέρας ἀναδείξεως αὐτοῦ πρὸς
τὸν Ἰσραήλ.

The Birth of Jesus
(Mt 1.18–25)

2 Ἐγένετο δὲ ἐν ταῖς ἡμέραις ἐκείναις ἐξῆλθεν δόγμα
παρὰ Καίσαρος Αὐγούστου ἀπογράφεσθαι πᾶσαν τὴν
οἰκουμένην. ᵃ2 αὕτη ἀπογραφὴ πρώτη ἐγένετο ἡγεμονεύοντος τῆς Συρίας Κυρηνίου.ᵃ 3 καὶ ἐπορεύοντο πάντες
ἀπογράφεσθαι, ἕκαστος εἰς τὴν ἑαυτοῦ πόλιν. 4 Ἀνέβη
δὲ καὶ Ἰωσὴφ ἀπὸ τῆς Γαλιλαίας ἐκ πόλεως Ναζαρὲθ
εἰς τὴν Ἰουδαίαν εἰς πόλιν Δαυὶδ ἥτις καλεῖται Βηθλέεμ,
διὰ τὸ εἶναι αὐτὸν ἐξ οἴκου καὶ πατριᾶς Δαυίδ, 5 ἀπο-
γράψασθαι σὺν Μαριὰμ τῇ ἐμνηστευμένῃ αὐτῷ, οὔσῃ
ἐγκύῳ. 6 ἐγένετο δὲ ἐν τῷ εἶναι αὐτοὺς ἐκεῖ ἐπλήσθησαν
αἱ ἡμέραι τοῦ τεκεῖν αὐτήν, 7 καὶ ἔτεκεν τὸν υἱὸν αὐτῆς

---

¹⁰ **78** {C} ἐπισκέψεται ℵ* B (L ἐπικέψεται) W Θ 0177 syrˢ·ᵖ copˢᵃ·ᵇᵒ
goth ∥ ἐπεσκέψατο pⁱˢⁱᵈ ℵᶜ A C D K Δ Ξ Ψ 053 0130 f¹ f¹³ 28 33 565 700 892
1009 1010 1071 1195 1216 1230 1241 1242 1253 1344 1365 1546 1646 2148 2174
Byz itᵃ·ᵃᵘʳ·ᵇ·β·ᶜ·ᵈ·ᵉ·ᶠ·ᶠᶠ²·ˡ· q·ʳ¹ vg syrʰ·ᵖᵃˡ arm eth geo Irenaeusˡᵃᵗ Gregory-
Nyssa Cyril Paschal Chronicle

ᵃ ᵃ **2** *a a* no parens: TR Bov Nes BF² RV ASV RSV NEB TT Zür Luth Jer Seg ∥ *a* parens,
a parens: WH AV

---

78 ἐπισκέψεται...ὕψους Mal 4.2   **78-79** ἐπισκέψεται...καθημένοις Is 9.2; 58.8; 60.1–2;
Mt 4.16   **80** Τὸ...ἐκραταιοῦτο Lk 2.40 ἦν...Ἰσραήλ Mt 3.1
2 5 Μαριὰμ...αὐτῷ Lk 1.27   **7** ἔτεκεν...πρωτότοκον Mt 1.25

τὸν πρωτότοκον· καὶ ἐσπαργάνωσεν αὐτὸν καὶ ἀνέκλινεν αὐτὸν ἐν φάτνῃ, διότι οὐκ ἦν αὐτοῖς τόπος ἐν τῷ καταλύματι.

The Shepherds and the Angels

8 Καὶ ποιμένες ἦσαν ἐν τῇ χώρᾳ τῇ αὐτῇ ἀγραυλοῦντες καὶ φυλάσσοντες φυλακὰς τῆς νυκτὸς ἐπὶ τὴν ποίμνην αὐτῶν. **9** καὶ[1] ἄγγελος κυρίου ἐπέστη αὐτοῖς καὶ δόξα κυρίου περιέλαμψεν αὐτούς, καὶ ἐφοβήθησαν φόβον μέγαν. **10** καὶ εἶπεν αὐτοῖς ὁ ἄγγελος, Μὴ φοβεῖσθε, ἰδοὺ γὰρ εὐαγγελίζομαι ὑμῖν χαρὰν μεγάλην ἥτις ἔσται παντὶ τῷ λαῷ, **11** ὅτι ἐτέχθη ὑμῖν σήμερον σωτὴρ ὅς ἐστιν Χριστὸς κύριος[2] ἐν πόλει Δαυίδ· **12** καὶ τοῦτο ὑμῖν τὸ σημεῖον, εὑρήσετε βρέφος ἐσπαργανωμένον καὶ κείμενον ἐν φάτνῃ. **13** καὶ ἐξαίφνης ἐγένετο σὺν τῷ ἀγγέλῳ πλῆθος στρατιᾶς οὐρανίου αἰνούντων τὸν θεὸν καὶ λεγόντων,

14 Δόξα ἐν ὑψίστοις θεῷ
    καὶ ἐπὶ γῆς εἰρήνη ἐν ἀνθρώποις εὐδοκίας[3].

---

[1] **9** {C} καί ℵ B L W Ξ 565 700 1241 it^e syr^palmss cop^sams goth arm eth geo Eusebius ‖ καὶ ἰδού A D K Δ Θ Ψ 053 f[1] f[13] 28 33 892 1009 1010 1071 1079 1195 1216 1230 1242 1253 1344 1365 1546 1646 2148 2174 *Byz Lect*^m it^a,aur,b,β,c,d,f,ff2,l,q,rl vg syr^p,h,palms cop^bo Diatessaron Paschal Chronicle ‖ *omit* syr^s cop^sa,boms

[2] **11** {A} Χριστὸς κύριος ℵ A B D^gr K L P Δ Θ Ξ Ψ 053 f[1] f[13] 28 565 700 892 1009 1010 1071 1079 1195 1216 1230 1241 1242 1253 1344 (1365 Χριστὸς καί [= Χριστὸς κύριος?]) 1546 1646 2148 2174 *Byz Lect*^m it^a,aur,b,c,f,ff2,l,q vg cop^sa,bo goth arm geo[2] ‖ κύριος Χριστός W syr^s,p ‖ Χριστὸς κυρίου it^β,rl syr^h,pal Diatessaron Ephraem ‖ Χριστὸς Ἰησοῦς it^d Cyprian ‖ Χριστὸς Ἰησοῦς κύριος it^e ‖ Χριστὸς σωτήρ 346 ‖ Χριστός cop^boms geo[1]

[3] **14** {B} ἐν ἀνθρώποις εὐδοκίας ℵ* A B* D W it^d vg^ww cop^sa goth Origen^gr,lat Cyril-Jerusalem ‖ ἀνθρώποις εὐδοκίας 372 it^a,aur,b,β,c,e,f,(ff2), l,q,rl vg^cl Irenaeus^gr,lat Origen Athanasius^lat Augustine Ps-Athanasius ms^acc. to Erasmus ‖ ἐν ἀνθρώποις εὐδοκία ℵ^c B[3] K L P Δ Θ Ξ Ψ 053 f[1] f[13] 28 565 700 892 1009 1010 1071 1079 1195 1216 1230 1241 1242 1253 1344 1365 1546

---

14 Δόξα...εἰρήνη Lk 19.38

first son, wrapped him in cloths and laid him in a manger — there was no room for them to stay in the inn.

The Shepherds and the Angels

8 There were some shepherds in that part of the country who were spending the night in the fields, taking care of their flocks. **9** An angel of the Lord appeared to them, and the glory of the Lord shone over them. They were terribly afraid, **10** but the angel said to them: "Don't be afraid! For I am here with good news for you, which will bring great joy to all the people. **11** This very night in David's town your Savior was born — Christ the Lord! **12** This is what will prove it to you: you will find a baby wrapped in cloths and lying in a manger." **13** Suddenly a great army of heaven's angels appeared with the angel, singing praises to God:

14 "Glory to God in the highest heaven!
    And peace on earth to men with whom he is pleased!"

15 When the angels went away from them back into heaven, the shepherds said to one another, "Let us go to Bethlehem and see this thing that has happened, that the Lord has told us." 16 So they hurried off and found Mary and Joseph, and saw the baby lying in the manger. 17 When the shepherds saw him they told them what the angel had said about this child. 18 All who heard it were filled with wonder at what the shepherds told them. 19 Mary remembered all these things, and thought deeply about them. 20 The shepherds went back, singing praises to God for all they had heard and seen; it had been just as the angel had told them.

Jesus Is Named

21 A week later, when the time came for the baby to be circumcised, he was named Jesus — the name which the angel had given him before he had been conceived.

Jesus Is Presented in the Temple

22 The time came for Joseph and Mary to do what the Law of Moses commanded and perform the ceremony of purification.

15 Καὶ ἐγένετο ὡς ἀπῆλθον ἀπ' αὐτῶν εἰς τὸν οὐρανὸν οἱ ἄγγελοι, οἱ ποιμένες[4] ἐλάλουν πρὸς ἀλλήλους, Διέλθωμεν δὴ ἕως Βηθλέεμ καὶ ἴδωμεν τὸ ῥῆμα τοῦτο τὸ γεγονὸς ὃ ὁ κύριος ἐγνώρισεν ἡμῖν. 16 καὶ ἦλθον σπεύσαντες καὶ ἀνεῦρον τήν τε Μαριὰμ καὶ τὸν Ἰωσὴφ καὶ τὸ βρέφος κείμενον ἐν τῇ φάτνῃ· 17 ἰδόντες δὲ ἐγνώρισαν περὶ τοῦ ῥήματος τοῦ λαληθέντος αὐτοῖς περὶ τοῦ παιδίου τούτου. 18 καὶ πάντες οἱ ἀκούσαντες ἐθαύμασαν περὶ τῶν λαληθέντων ὑπὸ τῶν ποιμένων πρὸς αὐτούς· 19 ἡ δὲ Μαριὰμ πάντα συνετήρει τὰ ῥήματα ταῦτα συμβάλλουσα ἐν τῇ καρδίᾳ αὐτῆς. 20 καὶ ὑπέστρεψαν οἱ ποιμένες δοξάζοντες καὶ αἰνοῦντες τὸν θεὸν ἐπὶ πᾶσιν οἷς ἤκουσαν καὶ εἶδον καθὼς ἐλαλήθη πρὸς αὐτούς.

21 Καὶ ὅτε ἐπλήσθησαν ἡμέραι ὀκτὼ τοῦ περιτεμεῖν αὐτόν, καὶ ἐκλήθη τὸ ὄνομα αὐτοῦ Ἰησοῦς, τὸ κληθὲν ὑπὸ τοῦ ἀγγέλου πρὸ τοῦ συλλημφθῆναι αὐτὸν ἐν τῇ κοιλίᾳ.

The Presentation of Jesus in the Temple

22 Καὶ ὅτε ἐπλήσθησαν αἱ ἡμέραι τοῦ καθαρισμοῦ αὐτῶν[5] κατὰ τὸν νόμον Μωϋσέως, ἀνήγαγον αὐτὸν εἰς

1646 2148 2174 Byz Lect[m] syr[h,(pal)] cop[bo] arm eth geo Origen Gregory-Thaumaturgus Eusebius Jacob-Nisibis Basil Apostolic Constitutions Cyril-Jerusalem Gregory-Nazianzus Didymus Epiphanius Chrysostom Cyril Proclus Theodotus-Ancyra Cosmos ‖ καὶ εὐδοκία ἀνθρώποις syr[s] ‖ καὶ ἐν ἀνθρώποις εὐδοκία syr[h with *] ‖ and good hope to men syr[p] Diatessaron[a,e] arm Aphraates

[4] 15 {D} οἱ ποιμένες ℵ B L W Θ Ξ f[1] 565 700 1071 (1365 καὶ οἱ) l[1043] (l[1663m] οἱ ποιμαίνοντες) it[a,aur,b,β,e,f,ff2,l,r1] vg syr[s,p,pal] cop[sa,bo] arm geo Diatessaron[a,i,n] Origen[lat] Eusebius Augustine ‖ καὶ οἱ ἄνθρωποι οἱ ποιμένες A D K P Δ Ψ 053 f[13] 28 33 892 1009 1010 1079 1195 1216 1230 1241 1242 1253 1344 1546 1646 2148 2174 Byz Lect[m] it[(c),d,q] goth ‖ καὶ οἱ ἄνθρωποι οἱ ποιμένες syr[h]

[5] 22 {C} αὐτῶν ℵ A B K L W X Δ Θ Ξ Π Ψ 053 f[1] f[13] 28 33 565 700 892 1009 1010 1071 1079 1195 1216 1230 1241 1242 1253 1344 1365 1546 1646 2148

17 περὶ...τούτου Lk 2.10–12   19 Lk 2.51   21 ἐπλήσθησαν...περιτεμεῖν αὐτόν Gn 17.12; Lv 12.3   ἐπλήσθησαν...Ἰησοῦς Lk 1.59   ἐκλήθη...κοιλίᾳ Lk 1.31   22 ἐπλήσθησαν...καθαρισμοῦ Lv 12.3, 6

Ἱεροσόλυμα παραστῆσαι τῷ κυρίῳ, ^b23 καθὼς γέγραπται ἐν νόμῳ κυρίου ὅτι **Πᾶν ἄρσεν διανοῖγον μήτραν ἅγιον τῷ κυρίῳ κληθήσεται,**^b 24 καὶ τοῦ δοῦναι θυσίαν κατὰ τὸ εἰρημένον ἐν τῷ νόμῳ κυρίου, **ζεῦγος τρυγόνων ἢ δύο νοσσοὺς περιστερῶν.**

25 Καὶ ἰδοὺ ἄνθρωπος ἦν ἐν Ἰερουσαλὴμ ᾧ ὄνομα Συμεών, καὶ ὁ ἄνθρωπος οὗτος δίκαιος καὶ εὐλαβής, προσδεχόμενος **παράκλησιν τοῦ Ἰσραήλ,** καὶ πνεῦμα ἦν ἅγιον ἐπ' αὐτόν· 26 καὶ ἦν αὐτῷ κεχρηματισμένον ὑπὸ τοῦ πνεύματος τοῦ ἁγίου μὴ ἰδεῖν θάνατον πρὶν [ἢ] ἂν ἴδῃ τὸν Χριστὸν κυρίου. 27 καὶ ἦλθεν ἐν τῷ πνεύματι εἰς τὸ ἱερόν· καὶ ἐν τῷ εἰσαγαγεῖν τοὺς γονεῖς τὸ παιδίον Ἰησοῦν τοῦ ποιῆσαι αὐτοὺς κατὰ τὸ εἰθισμένον τοῦ νόμου περὶ αὐτοῦ 28 καὶ αὐτὸς ἐδέξατο αὐτὸ εἰς τὰς ἀγκάλας καὶ εὐλόγησεν τὸν θεὸν καὶ εἶπεν,

29 Νῦν ἀπολύεις τὸν δοῦλόν σου, δέσποτα,
      κατὰ τὸ ῥῆμά σου ἐν εἰρήνῃ·
30 ὅτι εἶδον οἱ ὀφθαλμοί μου **τὸ σωτήριόν σου**
31   ὃ ἡτοίμασας **κατὰ πρόσωπον πάντων τῶν λαῶν,**
32 **φῶς εἰς ἀποκάλυψιν ἐθνῶν**
      καὶ **δόξαν λαοῦ σου Ἰσραήλ.**

33 καὶ ἦν ὁ πατὴρ αὐτοῦ καὶ ἡ μήτηρ⁶ θαυμάζοντες ἐπὶ

2174^c *Byz* it^q syr^{p, h, pal} cop^{sa, bomss} goth arm eth geo Origen^{lat} Cyril-Jerusalem Augustine Cyril ‖ αὐτοῦ D 2174* syr^s cop^{sams} Paschal Chronicle ‖ αὐτῆς 76 ‖ αὐτοῦ or αὐτῆς it^{a, aur, b, β, c, d, e, f, ff2, l, rl} vg ‖ *Marie* vg^{ms} ‖ omit 435 cop^{bo} Irenaeus^{lat} Amphilochius

⁶ 33 {B} ὁ πατὴρ αὐτοῦ καὶ ἡ μήτηρ ℵ^a B D W *f*¹ 700 1241 it^d vg geo² Origen^{gr, lat} Jerome Augustine ‖ ὁ πατὴρ αὐτοῦ καὶ ἡ μήτηρ αὐτοῦ ℵ* L syr^s cop^{sa?bo?} (arm *omit first* αὐτοῦ) geo¹ Cyril ‖ Ἰωσὴφ καὶ ἡ μήτηρ αὐτοῦ K X Δ Θ (A Π Ψ ὁ Ἰωσήφ) 053 *f*¹³ 28 565 892 1009 1010 1071 1079 1195 1216 1230 1242 1253 1344 1365 1546 1646 2148 2174 *Byz Lect*^m it^{a, aur, b, β, c, e, f, ff2, l, q, (rl)} syr^{p, h, palmss} cop^{bomss} goth Điatessaron^{a, n, t} ‖ Ἰωσὴφ ὁ πατὴρ

---

^{b b} 23 *b b* no dashes or parens: TR WH Bov Nes BF² Luth Jer ‖ *b* parens, *b* parens: AV RV ASV RSV NEB TT ‖ *b* dash, *b* dash: Zür Seg

---

23 Πᾶν...κληθήσεται Ex 13.2, 12, 15   24 ζεῦγος...περιστερῶν Lv 12.8   25 παράκλησιν τοῦ Ἰσραήλ Is 40.1; 49.13   30–31 Is 40.5 LXX; 52.10; Lk 3.6; Tt 2.11   32 φῶς...ἐθνῶν Is 42.6; 49.6 δόξαν...Ἰσραήλ Is 46.13

So they took the child to Jerusalem to present him to the Lord. 23 This is what is written in the law of the Lord: "Every first-born male shall be dedicated to the Lord." 24 They also went to offer a sacrifice as required by the law of the Lord: "A pair of doves or two young pigeons."

25 Now there was a man living in Jerusalem whose name was Simeon. He was a good and God-fearing man, and was waiting for Israel to be saved. The Holy Spirit was with him, 26 and he had been assured by the Holy Spirit that he would not die before he had seen the Lord's promised Messiah. 27 Led by the Spirit, Simeon went into the Temple. When the parents brought the child Jesus into the Temple to do for him what the Law required, 28 Simeon took the child in his arms, and gave thanks to God:

29 "Now, Lord, you have kept your promise,
      And you may let your servant go in peace.
30 For with my own eyes I have seen your salvation,
31 Which you have made ready in the presence of all peoples:
32 A light to reveal your way to the Gentiles,
      And to give glory to your people Israel."

33 The child's father and mother were amazed at the things Simeon said about

him. ³⁴ Simeon blessed them and said to Mary, his mother: "This child is chosen by God for the destruction and the salvation of many in Israel; he will be a sign from God which many people will speak against, ³⁵ and so reveal their secret thoughts. And sorrow, like a sharp sword, will break your own heart."

³⁶ There was a prophetess named Anna, daughter of Phanuel, of the tribe of Asher. She was an old woman who had been married for seven years, ³⁷ and then had been a widow for eighty-four years. She never left the Temple; day and night she worshiped God, fasting and praying. ³⁸ That very same hour she arrived and gave thanks to God, and spoke about the child to all who were waiting for God to redeem Jerusalem.

The Return to Nazareth

³⁹ When they finished doing all that was required by the law of the Lord, they returned to Galilee, to their home town of Nazareth. ⁴⁰ And the child grew and became strong; he was full of wisdom, and God's blessings were with him.

τοῖς λαλουμένοις περὶ αὐτοῦ. **34** καὶ εὐλόγησεν αὐτοὺς Συμεὼν καὶ εἶπεν πρὸς Μαριὰμ τὴν μητέρα αὐτοῦ, Ἰδοὺ οὗτος κεῖται εἰς πτῶσιν καὶ ἀνάστασιν πολλῶν ἐν τῷ Ἰσραὴλ καὶ εἰς σημεῖον ἀντιλεγόμενον **35** (ᶜκαὶ σοῦ [δὲ] αὐτῆς τὴν ψυχὴν διελεύσεται ῥομφαία)ᶜ, ὅπως ἂν ἀποκαλυφθῶσιν ἐκ πολλῶν καρδιῶν διαλογισμοί.

36 Καὶ ἦν Ἄννα προφῆτις, θυγάτηρ Φανουήλ, ἐκ φυλῆς Ἀσήρ·ᵈ αὕτη προβεβηκυῖα ἐν ἡμέραις πολλαῖς, ζήσασα μετὰ ἀνδρὸς ἔτη ἑπτὰ ἀπὸ τῆς παρθενίας αὐτῆς, **37** καὶ αὐτὴ χήρα ἕως ἐτῶν ὀγδοήκοντα τεσσάρων,ᵈ ἣ οὐκ ἀφίστατο τοῦ ἱεροῦ νηστείαις καὶ δεήσεσιν λατρεύουσα νύκτα καὶ ἡμέραν. **38** καὶ αὐτῇ τῇ ὥρᾳ ἐπιστᾶσα ἀνθωμολογεῖτο τῷ θεῷ καὶ ἐλάλει περὶ αὐτοῦ πᾶσιν τοῖς προσδεχομένοις λύτρωσιν Ἰερουσαλήμ⁷.

The Return to Nazareth

39 Καὶ ὡς ἐτέλεσαν πάντα τὰ κατὰ τὸν νόμον κυρίου, ἐπέστρεψαν εἰς τὴν Γαλιλαίαν εἰς πόλιν ἑαυτῶν Ναζαρέθ. **40** Τὸ δὲ παιδίον ηὔξανεν καὶ ἐκραταιοῦτο πληρούμενον σοφίᾳ, καὶ χάρις θεοῦ ἦν ἐπ' αὐτό.

αὐτοῦ καὶ ἡ μήτηρ αὐτοῦ 157 eth ‖ Ἰωσὴφ καὶ ἡ μήτηρ 33 ‖ οἱ γονεῖς αὐτοῦ vg^ms ‖ ὁ πατὴρ αὐτοῦ syr^hmg ‖ Ἰωσήφ syr^palms

⁷ **38** {B} Ἰερουσαλήμ ℵ B W Ξ Π f¹ 565 1079 l²⁵³ it^aur,b,β,c,e,f,ff²,l,q vg^ww syr^s,p cop^sa,bo goth arm eth Diatessaron Irenaeus^lat Augustine ‖ ἐν Ἰερουσαλήμ A D K L X Δ Θ Ψ 053 f¹³ 28 33 700 892 1009 1010 1195 1230 1241 1242 1253 1344 1365 1546 1646 2148 2174 Byz Lect^m it^d syr^h,pal geo^B Amphilochius Ps-Athanasius (Photius) ‖ Ἰσραήλ (1071 ἐν Ἰσραήλ) 1216 it^a,rl vg^cl cop^boms Diatessaron^s,t Tertullian ‖ ἐν τῷ Ἰσραήλ 5 57 130^lat (348) geo^l,A Apostolic Constitutions

---

ᶜᶜ **35** c parens, c parens: TR AV RSV TT ‖ c dash, c dash: Bov Nes BF² Zür Luth Jer ‖ c c no dashes or parens: WH RV ASV NEB Seg

ᵈᵈ **36–37** d major, d minor: Bov Nes BF² AV Jer Seg ‖ d minor, d major: RSV Zür ‖ d parens, d parens: WH RV ASV ‖ d minor, d minor: TR ‖ d major, d major: NEB TT Luth

---

34 πτῶσιν...πολλῶν Is 8.14; 1 Cor 1.23; 1 Pe 2.8   **37** δεήσεσιν...ἡμέραν 1 Tm 5.5 **38** λύτρωσιν Ἰερουσαλήμ Is 52.9   **39** εἰς τὴν...Ναζαρέθ Mt 2.23   **40** Lk 2.52   Τὸ... ἐκραταιοῦτο Lk 1.80

The Boy Jesus in the Temple

41 Καὶ ἐπορεύοντο οἱ γονεῖς αὐτοῦ κατ' ἔτος εἰς Ἰερουσαλὴμ τῇ ἑορτῇ τοῦ πάσχα. **42** καὶ ὅτε ἐγένετο ἐτῶν δώδεκα, ἀναβαινόντων αὐτῶν κατὰ τὸ ἔθος τῆς ἑορτῆς **43** καὶ τελειωσάντων τὰς ἡμέρας, ἐν τῷ ὑποστρέφειν αὐτοὺς ὑπέμεινεν Ἰησοῦς ὁ παῖς ἐν Ἰερουσαλήμ, καὶ οὐκ ἔγνωσαν οἱ γονεῖς αὐτοῦ. **44** νομίσαντες δὲ αὐτὸν εἶναι ἐν τῇ συνοδίᾳ ἦλθον ἡμέρας ὁδὸν καὶ ἀνεζήτουν αὐτὸν ἐν τοῖς συγγενεῦσιν καὶ τοῖς γνωστοῖς, **45** καὶ μὴ εὑρόντες ὑπέστρεψαν εἰς Ἰερουσαλὴμ ἀναζητοῦντες αὐτόν. **46** καὶ ἐγένετο μετὰ ἡμέρας τρεῖς εὗρον αὐτὸν ἐν τῷ ἱερῷ καθεζόμενον ἐν μέσῳ τῶν διδασκάλων καὶ ἀκούοντα αὐτῶν καὶ ἐπερωτῶντα αὐτούς· **47** ἐξίσταντο δὲ πάντες οἱ ἀκούοντες αὐτοῦ ἐπὶ τῇ συνέσει καὶ ταῖς ἀποκρίσεσιν αὐτοῦ. **48** καὶ ἰδόντες αὐτὸν ἐξεπλάγησαν, καὶ εἶπεν πρὸς αὐτὸν ἡ μήτηρ αὐτοῦ, Τέκνον, τί ἐποίησας ἡμῖν οὕτως; ἰδοὺ ὁ πατήρ σου κἀγὼ ὀδυνώμενοι ἐζητοῦμέν σε. **49** καὶ εἶπεν πρὸς αὐτούς, Τί ὅτι ἐζητεῖτέ με; οὐκ ᾔδειτε ὅτι ἐν τοῖς τοῦ πατρός μου δεῖ εἶναί με; **50** καὶ αὐτοὶ οὐ συνῆκαν τὸ ῥῆμα ὃ ἐλάλησεν αὐτοῖς. **51** καὶ κατέβη μετ' αὐτῶν καὶ ἦλθεν εἰς Ναζαρέθ, καὶ ἦν ὑποτασσόμενος αὐτοῖς. καὶ ἡ μήτηρ αὐτοῦ διετήρει πάντα τὰ ῥήματα ἐν τῇ καρδίᾳ αὐτῆς. **52** Καὶ Ἰησοῦς **προέκοπτεν** [ἐν τῇ] σοφίᾳ καὶ ἡλικίᾳ **καὶ χάριτι παρὰ θεῷ καὶ ἀνθρώποις.**

The Preaching of John the Baptist
(Mt 3.1–12; Mk 1.1–8; Jn 1.19–28)

3 Ἐν ἔτει δὲ πεντεκαιδεκάτῳ τῆς ἡγεμονίας Τιβερίου Καίσαρος, ἡγεμονεύοντος Ποντίου Πιλάτου τῆς Ἰουδαίας, καὶ τετρααρχοῦντος τῆς Γαλιλαίας Ἡρῴδου, Φιλίππου δὲ τοῦ ἀδελφοῦ αὐτοῦ τετρααρχοῦντος τῆς Ἰτουραίας καὶ Τραχωνίτιδος χώρας, καὶ Λυσανίου τῆς Ἀβιληνῆς τετρααρ-

41 ἑορτῇ τοῦ πάσχα Ex 12.24-27; Dt 16.1-8   49 τοῖς τοῦ πατρός μου Jn 2.16
51 ἡ μήτηρ...αὐτῆς Lk 2.19   52 προέκοπτεν...ἀνθρώποις 1 Sm 2.26; Pr 3.4; Lk 1.80

The Boy Jesus in the Temple

[41] Every year Jesus' parents went to Jerusalem for the Feast of Passover. [42] When Jesus was twelve years old, they went to the feast as usual. [43] When the days of the feast were over, they started back home, but the boy Jesus stayed in Jerusalem. His parents did not know this; [44] they thought that he was with the group, so they traveled a whole day, and then started looking for him among their relatives and friends. [45] They did not find him, so they went back to Jerusalem looking for him. [46] On the third day they found him in the Temple, sitting with the Jewish teachers, listening to them and asking questions. [47] All who heard him were amazed at his intelligent answers. [48] His parents were amazed when they saw him, and his mother said to him, "Son, why did you do this to us? Your father and I have been terribly worried trying to find you." [49] He answered them, "Why did you have to look for me? Didn't you know that I had to be in my Father's house?" [50] But they did not understand what he said to them.

[51] So Jesus went back with them to Nazareth, where he was obedient to them. His mother treasured all these things in her heart. [52] And Jesus grew up, both in body and in wisdom, gaining favor with God and men.

The Preaching of John the Baptist
(Also Matt. 3.1–12; Mark 1.1–8; John 1.19–28)

3 It was the fifteenth year of the rule of Emperor Tiberius; Pontius Pilate was governor of Judea, Herod was ruler of Galilee, and his brother Philip ruler of the territory of Iturea and Trachonitis;

Lysanias was ruler of Abilene, ² and Annas and Caiaphas were high priests. It was at this time that the word of God came to John, the son of Zechariah, in the desert. ³ So John went throughout the whole territory of the Jordan river. "Turn away from your sins and be baptized," he preached, "and God will forgive your sins." ⁴ As the prophet Isaiah had written in his book:

"Someone is shouting in the desert:
'Get the Lord's road ready for him,
Make a straight path for him to travel!

⁵ All low places must be filled up,
All hills and mountains leveled off;
The winding roads must be made straight,
The rough paths made smooth;

⁶ And all mankind will see God's salvation!'"

⁷ Crowds of people came out to John to be baptized by him. "You snakes!" he said to them. "Who told you that you could escape from God's wrath that is about to come? ⁸ Do the things that will show that you have turned from your sins. And don't start saying among yourselves, 'Abraham is our ancestor.' I tell you that God can take these rocks and make descendants for Abraham! ⁹ The ax is ready to cut the trees down at the roots; every tree that does not bear good fruit will be cut down and thrown in the fire."

¹⁰ The people asked him, "What are we to do, then?" ¹¹ He answered, "Whoever has two shirts must give one to the man who has none, and whoever has food must share it." ¹² Some tax collectors came to be baptized, and they asked him, "Teacher, what are we to do?" ¹³ "Don't collect more than is legal," he

χοῦντος, 2 ἐπὶ ἀρχιερέως Ἅννα καὶ Καϊάφα, ἐγένετο ῥῆμα θεοῦ ἐπὶ Ἰωάννην τὸν Ζαχαρίου υἱὸν ἐν τῇ ἐρήμῳ. 3 καὶ ἦλθεν εἰς πᾶσαν [τὴν] περίχωρον τοῦ Ἰορδάνου κηρύσσων βάπτισμα μετανοίας εἰς ἄφεσιν ἁμαρτιῶν, 4 ὡς γέγραπται ἐν βίβλῳ λόγων Ἠσαΐου τοῦ προφήτου,

Φωνὴ βοῶντος ἐν τῇ ἐρήμῳ,
Ἑτοιμάσατε τὴν ὁδὸν κυρίου,
  εὐθείας ποιεῖτε τὰς τρίβους αὐτοῦ.

5 **πᾶσα φάραγξ πληρωθήσεται**
  καὶ πᾶν ὄρος καὶ βουνὸς ταπεινωθήσεται,
  καὶ ἔσται τὰ σκολιὰ εἰς εὐθείαν
  καὶ αἱ τραχεῖαι εἰς ὁδοὺς λείας·

6 **καὶ ὄψεται πᾶσα σὰρξ τὸ σωτήριον τοῦ θεοῦ.**

7 Ἔλεγεν οὖν τοῖς ἐκπορευομένοις ὄχλοις βαπτισθῆναι ὑπ' αὐτοῦ, Γεννήματα ἐχιδνῶν, τίς ὑπέδειξεν ὑμῖν φυγεῖν ἀπὸ τῆς μελλούσης ὀργῆς; 8 ποιήσατε οὖν καρποὺς ἀξίους τῆς μετανοίας· καὶ μὴ ἄρξησθε λέγειν ἐν ἑαυτοῖς, Πατέρα ἔχομεν τὸν Ἀβραάμ, λέγω γὰρ ὑμῖν ὅτι δύναται ὁ θεὸς ἐκ τῶν λίθων τούτων ἐγεῖραι τέκνα τῷ Ἀβραάμ. 9 ἤδη δὲ καὶ ἡ ἀξίνη πρὸς τὴν ῥίζαν τῶν δένδρων κεῖται· πᾶν οὖν δένδρον μὴ ποιοῦν καρπὸν καλὸν¹ ἐκκόπτεται καὶ εἰς πῦρ βάλλεται. 10 Καὶ ἐπηρώτων αὐτὸν οἱ ὄχλοι λέγοντες, Τί οὖν ποιήσωμεν; 11 ἀποκριθεὶς δὲ ἔλεγεν αὐτοῖς, Ὁ ἔχων δύο χιτῶνας μεταδότω τῷ μὴ ἔχοντι, καὶ ὁ ἔχων βρώματα ὁμοίως ποιείτω. 12 ἦλθον δὲ καὶ τελῶναι βαπτισθῆναι καὶ εἶπαν πρὸς αὐτόν, Διδάσκαλε, τί ποιήσωμεν; 13 ὁ δὲ εἶπεν πρὸς αὐτούς, Μηδὲν πλέον

---

¹ 9 {C} καρπὸν καλόν (see Mt 3.10; 7.19) ℵ A B C K L W X Δ Θ Π Ψ 0155 f¹ f¹³ 28 33 565 700 892 1009 1010 1071 1079 1195 1216 1230 1241 1242 1253 1344 1365 1546 1646 2148 2174 *Byz Lect*ᵐ itᵇ,ᶜ,ᵈ,ᵉ,f,l,q,rl vgᶜl syrʰ copˢᵃ,ᵇᵒ goth arm eth geo Irenaeusˡᵃᵗᵐˢ Origenˡᵃᵗ ∥ καρποὺς καλούς Dᵍʳ syrᶜ,ˢ,ᵖ,ᵖᵃl ∥ καρπόν 𝔭⁴ itᵃ,ᵃᵘʳ,ff² vgʷʷ copᵇᵒᵐˢ Irenaeusˡᵃᵗ Origen

---

2 Ἰωάννην...ἐρήμῳ Lk 1.80 3 βάπτισμα μετανοίας Ac 13.24; 19.4 4–6 Φωνὴ... θεοῦ Is 40.3–5 6 Lk 2.30–31; Ac 28.28; Tt 2.11 7 Γεννήματα ἐχιδνῶν Mt 12.34 Γεννήματα...ὀργῆς Mt 23.33 8 Πατέρα...Ἀβραάμ Jn 8.39 9 πᾶν...βάλλεται Mt 7.19; Jn 15.6 12 ἦλθον...βαπτισθῆναι Lk 7.29

παρὰ τὸ διατεταγμένον ὑμῖν πράσσετε. **14** ἐπηρώτων δὲ αὐτὸν καὶ στρατευόμενοι λέγοντες, Τί ποιήσωμεν καὶ ἡμεῖς; καὶ εἶπεν αὐτοῖς, Μηδένα διασείσητε μηδὲ συκοφαντήσητε, καὶ ἀρκεῖσθε τοῖς ὀψωνίοις ὑμῶν.

15 Προσδοκῶντος δὲ τοῦ λαοῦ καὶ διαλογιζομένων πάντων ἐν ταῖς καρδίαις αὐτῶν περὶ τοῦ Ἰωάννου, μήποτε αὐτὸς εἴη ὁ Χριστός, **16** ἀπεκρίνατο λέγων πᾶσιν ὁ Ἰωάννης, Ἐγὼ μὲν ὕδατι βαπτίζω ὑμᾶς· ἔρχεται δὲ ὁ ἰσχυρότερός μου, οὗ οὐκ εἰμὶ ἱκανὸς λῦσαι τὸν ἱμάντα τῶν ὑποδημάτων αὐτοῦ· αὐτὸς ὑμᾶς βαπτίσει ἐν πνεύματι ἁγίῳ καὶ πυρί· **17** οὗ τὸ πτύον ἐν τῇ χειρὶ αὐτοῦ διακαθᾶραι τὴν ἅλωνα αὐτοῦ καὶ συναγαγεῖν τὸν σῖτον εἰς τὴν ἀποθήκην αὐτοῦ, τὸ δὲ ἄχυρον κατακαύσει πυρὶ ἀσβέστῳ. **18** Πολλὰ μὲν οὖν καὶ ἕτερα παρακαλῶν εὐηγγελίζετο τὸν λαόν· **19** ὁ δὲ Ἡρῴδης ὁ τετραάρχης, ἐλεγχόμενος ὑπ' αὐτοῦ περὶ Ἡρῳδιάδος τῆς γυναικὸς τοῦ ἀδελφοῦ αὐτοῦ καὶ περὶ πάντων ὧν ἐποίησεν πονηρῶν ὁ Ἡρῴδης, **20** προσέθηκεν καὶ τοῦτο ἐπὶ πᾶσιν, κατέκλεισεν τὸν Ἰωάννην ἐν φυλακῇ.

The Baptism of Jesus
(Mt 3.13–17; Mk 1.9–11)

21 Ἐγένετο δὲ ἐν τῷ βαπτισθῆναι ἅπαντα τὸν λαὸν καὶ Ἰησοῦ βαπτισθέντος καὶ προσευχομένου ἀνεῳχθῆναι τὸν οὐρανὸν **22** καὶ καταβῆναι τὸ πνεῦμα τὸ ἅγιον σωματικῷ εἴδει ὡς περιστερὰν ἐπ' αὐτόν, καὶ φωνὴν ἐξ οὐρανοῦ γενέσθαι, Σὺ εἶ ὁ υἱός μου[a] ὁ ἀγαπητός, ἐν σοὶ εὐδόκησα[2].

---

[2] **22** {C} Σὺ εἶ ὁ υἱός μου ὁ ἀγαπητός, ἐν σοὶ εὐδόκησα (*or* ηὐδόκησα *in most later mss*) (*see* Mk 1.11; Lk 9.35) 𝔭⁴ ℵ A B K L W Δ Θ Π Ψ 0124 f¹ f¹³ 28 33 565 (700 *omit* ὁ υἱός μου) 892 1009 1010 1071 1079 1195 1216 1230 1241 1242 1344 1365 1546 1646 2148 *Byz Lect* l⁶⁹ˢ·ᵐ,⁷⁰ˢ·ᵐ,¹⁸⁵ˢ·ᵐ,¹¹²⁷ˢ·ᵐ itᵃᵘʳ,ᵉ,ᑫ

---

[a] **22** *a none:* TR WH Bov Nes BF² AV RV ASV RSV NEBᵐᵍ TT Zür Luth Jer Seg ∥ *a minor:* RSVᵐᵍ NEB

---

16 ἔρχεται...αὐτοῦ Ac 13.25   **19–20** Mt 14.3–4; Mk 6.17–18   **22** καταβῆναι...αὐτόν Jn 1.32   Σὺ εἶ...εὐδόκησα Gn 22.2; Ps 2.7; Is 42.1; Mt 12.18; 17.5; Mk 9.7; Lk 9.35; 2 Pe 1.17

told them. ¹⁴ Some soldiers also asked him, "What about us? What are we to do?" He said to them, "Don't take money from anyone by force or by false charges; be content with your pay."

¹⁵ People's hopes began to rise; and they began to wonder about John, thinking that perhaps he might be the Messiah. ¹⁶ So John said to all of them: "I baptize you with water, but one who is much greater than I is coming. I am not good enough even to untie his sandals. He will baptize you with the Holy Spirit and fire. ¹⁷ He has his winnowing-shovel with him, to thresh out all the grain and gather the wheat into his barn; but he will burn the chaff in a fire that never goes out!"

¹⁸ In many different ways John urged the people as he preached the Good News to them. ¹⁹ But John spoke against Governor Herod, because he had married Herodias, his brother's wife, and had done many other evil things. ²⁰ Then Herod did an even worse thing by putting John in prison.

The Baptism of Jesus
(Also Matt. 3.13–17; Mark 1.9–11)

²¹ After all the people had been baptized, Jesus also was baptized. While he was praying, heaven was opened, ²² and the Holy Spirit came down upon him in bodily form, like a dove. And a voice came from heaven: "You are my own dear Son. I am well pleased with you."

The Genealogy of Jesus
(Also Matt. 1.1–17)

23 When Jesus began his work he was about thirty years old; he was the son, so people thought, of Joseph, who was the son of Heli, 24 the son of Matthat, the son of Levi, the son of Melchi, the son of Jannai, the son of Joseph, 25 the son of Mattathias, the son of Amos, the son of Nahum, the son of Esli, the son of Naggai, 26 the son of Maath, the son of Mattathias, the son of Semein, the son of Josech, the son of Joda, 27 the son of Joanan, the son of Rhesa, the son of Zerubbabel, the son of Shealtiel, the son of Neri, 28 the son of Melchi, the son of Addi, the son of Cosam, the son of Elmadam, the son of Er, 29 the son of Joshua, the son of Eliezer, the son of Jorim, the son of Matthat, the son of Levi, 30 the son of Simeon, the son of Judah, the son of Joseph, the son of Jonam, the son of Eliakim, 31 the son of Melea, the son of Menna, the son of Mattatha, the son of Nathan, the son of David, 32 the son of Jesse, the son of Obed, the son of Boaz, the son of Salmon, the son of Nahshon, 33 the son of Amminadab, the son of Admin, the son of

The Genealogy of Jesus
(Mt 1.1–17)

23 Καὶ αὐτὸς ἦν Ἰησοῦς ἀρχόμενος ὡσεὶ ἐτῶν τριάκοντα, ὢν υἱός, ὡς ἐνομίζετο, Ἰωσὴφ τοῦ Ἠλὶ 24 τοῦ Ματθὰτ τοῦ Λευὶ τοῦ Μελχὶ τοῦ Ἰανναὶ τοῦ Ἰωσὴφ 25 τοῦ Ματταθίου τοῦ Ἀμὼς τοῦ Ναοὺμ τοῦ Ἐσλὶ τοῦ Ναγγαὶ 26 τοῦ Μάαθ τοῦ Ματταθίου τοῦ Σεμεῖν τοῦ Ἰωσὴχ τοῦ Ἰωδὰ 27 τοῦ Ἰωανὰν τοῦ Ῥησὰ τοῦ Ζοροβαβὲλ τοῦ Σαλαθιὴλ τοῦ Νηρὶ 28 τοῦ Μελχὶ τοῦ Ἀδδὶ τοῦ Κωσὰμ τοῦ Ἐλμαδὰμ τοῦ Ἤρ 29 τοῦ Ἰησοῦ τοῦ Ἐλιέζερ τοῦ Ἰωρὶμ τοῦ Ματθὰτ τοῦ Λευὶ 30 τοῦ Συμεὼν τοῦ Ἰούδα τοῦ Ἰωσὴφ τοῦ Ἰωνὰμ τοῦ Ἐλιακὶμ 31 τοῦ Μελεὰ τοῦ Μεννὰ τοῦ Ματταθὰ τοῦ Ναθὰμ τοῦ Δαυὶδ 32 τοῦ Ἰεσσαὶ τοῦ Ἰωβὴδ τοῦ Βόος τοῦ Σαλὰ[3] τοῦ Ναασσὼν 33 τοῦ Ἀμιναδὰβ τοῦ Ἀδμὶν τοῦ Ἀρνὶ[4]

---

vg syr^h cop^{sa, bomss} arm geo ‖ Σὺ εἶ ὁ υἱός μου ὁ ἀγαπητός, ἐν ᾧ εὐδόκησα X 1253 it^f syr^{s, p, pal} cop^{bomss} goth ‖ Οὗτός ἐστιν ὁ υἱός μου ὁ ἀγαπητός, ἐν ᾧ εὐδόκησα (see Mt 3.17) 1574 cop^{boms} Diatessaron Acts of Pilate ‖ υἱός μου εἶ σύ, ἐγὼ σήμερον γεγέννηκά σε (see Ps 2.7) D it^{a, b, c, d, ff2, l, r1} Diognetus Gospel of the Ebionites Justin (Clement) Origen Didascalia Methodius Juvencus (Ambrosiaster) Hilary Apostolic Constitutions Faustinus (Tyconius) Augustine

³ 32 {B} Σαλὰ 𝔭⁴ ℵ* B syr^{s, pal} cop^{sa, bomss} eth ‖ Σαλμών (see Mt 1.4–5) ℵ^c A D^{gr} K L X Δ Θ Π Ψ 0102 28 33 565 700 892 1009 1010 1071 1079 1195 1216 1230 1241 1242 1253 1344 1365 (1546 add τοῦ Σαλαθιήλ) 1646 2148 2174 Byz Lect it^{a, aur, b, c, e, f, ff2, l, q, r1} vg syr^{p, h} cop^{bo} goth geo Diatessaron ‖ Σαλμάν f¹ f¹³ arm Paschal Chronicle ‖ Solomon it^d

⁴ 33 {C} τοῦ Ἀμιναδὰβ τοῦ Ἀδμὶν τοῦ Ἀρνί 𝔭^{vid} ℵ^c L X (f¹³ Ἀρηί for Ἀρνί) cop^{bo} ‖ τοῦ Ἀδὰμ τοῦ Ἀδμὶν τοῦ Ἀρνί ℵ* 1241 cop^{sa} ‖ τοῦ Ἀμιναδὰμ τοῦ Ἀρὰμ τοῦ Ἀλμεὶ τοῦ Ἀρνί f¹ (1365 add τοῦ Ἰωράμ) (l¹¹²⁷ Ἀμιναδάβ for Ἀμιναδάμ and Ἰωρὰμ τοῦ Δονεὶ for Ἀρνί) ‖ τοῦ Ἀμιναδὰβ τοῦ Ἀρὰμ τοῦ Ἀδμὶν τοῦ Ἀρνί Θ arm geo¹ ‖ τοῦ Ἀμιναδὰβ τοῦ Ἀδμὶν τοῦ Ἀράμ 0102 (1216 Ἀμιναδάμ) (1646 2174 add τοῦ Ἰωράμ) ‖ τοῦ Ἀρὰμ τοῦ Ἀμιναδὰβ τοῦ Ἀρμὶν τοῦ Ἀρνίν syr^{palms, (ms)} ‖ τοῦ Ἀμιναδὰμ τοῦ Ἰωρὰμ τοῦ Ἀράμ 1009 ‖ τοῦ Ἀμιναδὰβ τοῦ Ἀρὰμ

---

23 υἱός...Ἰωσήφ Lk 4.22; Jn 6.42   **27** Ζοροβαβὲλ τοῦ Σαλαθιήλ 1 Chr 3.17; Ezr 3.2   **31** Ναθάμ 2 Sm 5.14   **31–32** Δαυὶδ...Ἰεσσαί 1 Sm 16.1, 13   **31–33** Δαυὶδ...Ἰούδα Ru 4.17–22; 1 Chr 2.1–14

τοῦ Ἐσρὼμ τοῦ Φάρες τοῦ Ἰούδα 34 τοῦ Ἰακὼβ τοῦ
Ἰσαὰκ τοῦ Ἀβραὰμ τοῦ Θάρα τοῦ Ναχὼρ 35 τοῦ
Σεροὺχ τοῦ Ῥαγαὺ τοῦ Φάλεκ τοῦ Ἔβερ τοῦ Σαλὰ
36 τοῦ Καϊνὰμ τοῦ Ἀρφαξὰδ τοῦ Σὴμ τοῦ Νῶε τοῦ
Λάμεχ 37 τοῦ Μαθουσαλὰ τοῦ Ἐνὼχ τοῦ Ἰάρετ τοῦ
Μαλελεὴλ τοῦ Καϊνὰμ 38 τοῦ Ἐνὼς τοῦ Σὴθ τοῦ Ἀδὰμ
τοῦ θεοῦ.

The Temptation of Jesus
(Mt 4.1–11; Mk 1.12–13)

4 Ἰησοῦς δὲ πλήρης πνεύματος ἁγίου ὑπέστρεψεν ἀπὸ
τοῦ Ἰορδάνου, καὶ ἤγετο ἐν τῷ πνεύματι ἐν τῇ ἐρήμῳ
2 ἡμέρας τεσσαράκοντα πειραζόμενος ὑπὸ τοῦ διαβόλου.
καὶ οὐκ ἔφαγεν οὐδὲν ἐν ταῖς ἡμέραις ἐκείναις, καὶ συν-
τελεσθεισῶν αὐτῶν ἐπείνασεν. 3 Εἶπεν δὲ αὐτῷ ὁ διάβολος, Εἰ υἱὸς εἶ τοῦ θεοῦ, εἰπὲ τῷ λίθῳ τούτῳ ἵνα
γένηται ἄρτος. 4 καὶ ἀπεκρίθη πρὸς αὐτὸν ὁ Ἰησοῦς,
Γέγραπται ὅτι **Οὐκ ἐπ' ἄρτῳ μόνῳ ζήσεται ὁ ἄνθρωπος**[1].
5 Καὶ ἀναγαγὼν αὐτὸν ἔδειξεν αὐτῷ πάσας τὰς βασιλείας
τῆς οἰκουμένης ἐν στιγμῇ χρόνου· 6 καὶ εἶπεν αὐτῷ ὁ

τοῦ Ἰωράμ Κ Δ Ψ (28 1242 1344 Ἀμιναδάμ) 700 1010 1195 2148 Byz[pt] Lect
it[b,(e)] (syr[h] Ἀμιναδάμ) Paschal Chronicle ∥ τοῦ Ἀμιναδὰβ τοῦ Ἰωράμ τοῦ
Ἀνμεὶ τοῦ Δονεῖ l[70,(185),(950)] ∥ τοῦ Ἀμιναδὰβ τοῦ Ἀράμ (see Mt 1.4) A D Π
33 565 (892 Ἰωράμ) (1071 Ἀμιναδάμ) 1079 1230 1253 Byz[pt] l[184] it[a,aur,c,d,f,]
[ff2,l,q,r1] vg syr[p] goth geo[2] ∥ τοῦ Νηρὶ τοῦ Ἀμιναδὰμ τοῦ Μελχὶ τοῦ Ἀρὰμ
τοῦ Ἀδδὶ 1546 ∥ τοῦ Ἀδμὶν τοῦ Ἀρνί B (syr[s] Ἀδάμ)

[1] 4 {B} ἄνθρωπος ℵ B L W 1241 syr[s] cop[sa,bo] ∥ ἄνθρωπος ἀλλ' ἐπὶ
παντὶ ῥήματι θεοῦ A K Δ Θ Π Ψ 0102 f[1] f[13] 28 33[vid] 565 700 1009 1010 1079
1195 1210 1230 1242 1344 1365 1546 1646 2148 2174 Byz l[996,851,883] syr[p,h] goth
arm geo ∥ ἄνθρωπος ἀλλ' ἐν παντὶ ῥήματι θεοῦ D 892 1253 it[a,aur,b,c,d,]
[e,f,ff2,l,q,r1] vg ∥ ἄνθρωπος ἀλλ' ἐπὶ παντὶ ῥήματι ἐκπορευομένῳ διὰ
στόματος θεοῦ (see Mt 4.4; Dt 8.3) (1071 ῥήματι θεοῦ ἐκπορευομένῳ)
Lect cop[bomss] eth Diatessaron Theophylact

---

33 Ἰούδα Gn 29.35   **34** Ἰακώβ Gn 25.26; 1 Chr 1.34   Ἰσαάκ Gn 21.3; 1 Chr 1.28, 34
34-36 Ἀβραάμ...Σήμ Gn 11.10–26; 1 Chr 1.24–27   **36-38** Σήμ...θεοῦ Gn 4.25—5.32; 1 Chr 1.1–4
4 2 πειραζόμενος He 4.15   **4** Οὐκ...ἄνθρωπος Dt 8.3   **6** εἶπεν...παραδέδοται
Mt 28.18

Arni, the son of Hezron, the son of Perez,
the son of Judah, [34] the son of Jacob,
the son of Isaac, the son of Abraham,
the son of Terah, the son of Nahor,
[35] the son of Serug, the son of Reu, the
son of Peleg, the son of Eber, the son of
Shelah, [36] the son of Cainan, the son
of Arphaxad, the son of Shem, the son of
Noah, the son of Lamech, [37] the son
of Methuselah, the son of Enoch, the
son of Jared, the son of Mahalaleel,
the son of Cainan, [38] the son of Enos,
the son of Seth, the son of Adam, the
son of God.

The Temptation of Jesus
(Also Matt. 4.1–11; Mark 1.12–13)

4 Jesus returned from the Jordan full of
the Holy Spirit, and was led by the
Spirit into the desert, [2] where he was
tempted by the Devil for forty days.
He ate nothing all that time, so that he
was hungry when it was over.

[3] The Devil said to him, "If you are
God's Son, order this stone to turn into
bread." [4] Jesus answered, "The scripture says, 'Man cannot live on bread
alone.' "

[5] Then the Devil took him up and
showed him in a second all the kingdoms
of the world. [6] "I will give you all this

power, and all this wealth," the Devil told him. "It was all handed over to me and I can give it to anyone I choose. [7] All this will be yours, then, if you kneel down before me." [8] Jesus answered, "The scripture says, 'Worship the Lord your God and serve only him!'"

[9] Then the Devil took him to Jerusalem and set him on the highest point of the Temple, and said to him, "If you are God's Son, throw yourself down from here. [10] For the scripture says, 'God will order his angels to take good care of you.' [11] It also says, 'They will hold you up with their hands so that you will not even hurt your feet on the stones.'" [12] Jesus answered him, "The scripture says, 'You must not put the Lord your God to the test.'" [13] When the Devil finished tempting Jesus in every way, he left him for a while.

Jesus Begins His Work in Galilee
(Also Matt. 4.12–17; Mark 1.14–15)

[14] Then Jesus returned to Galilee, and the power of the Holy Spirit was with him. The news about him spread throughout all that territory. [15] He taught in their synagogues and was praised by all.

Jesus Rejected at Nazareth
(Also Matt. 13.53–58; Mark 6.1–6)

[16] Then Jesus went to Nazareth, where he had been brought up, and on the Sabbath day he went as usual to the

διάβολος, Σοὶ δώσω τὴν ἐξουσίαν ταύτην ἅπασαν καὶ τὴν δόξαν αὐτῶν, ὅτι ἐμοὶ παραδέδοται καὶ ᾧ ἐὰν θέλω δίδωμι αὐτήν· 7 σὺ οὖν ἐὰν προσκυνήσῃς ἐνώπιον ἐμοῦ, ἔσται σοῦ πᾶσα. 8 καὶ ἀποκριθεὶς ὁ Ἰησοῦς εἶπεν αὐτῷ, Γέγραπται,

**Κύριον τὸν θεόν σου προσκυνήσεις
καὶ αὐτῷ μόνῳ λατρεύσεις.**

9 Ἤγαγεν δὲ αὐτὸν εἰς Ἰερουσαλὴμ καὶ ἔστησεν ἐπὶ τὸ πτερύγιον τοῦ ἱεροῦ, καὶ εἶπεν αὐτῷ, Εἰ υἱὸς εἶ τοῦ θεοῦ, βάλε σεαυτὸν ἐντεῦθεν κάτω· 10 γέγραπται γὰρ ὅτι

**Τοῖς ἀγγέλοις αὐτοῦ ἐντελεῖται περὶ σοῦ
τοῦ διαφυλάξαι σε,**

11 καὶ ὅτι

**Ἐπὶ χειρῶν ἀροῦσίν σε
μήποτε προσκόψῃς πρὸς λίθον τὸν πόδα σου.**

12 καὶ ἀποκριθεὶς εἶπεν αὐτῷ ὁ Ἰησοῦς ὅτι Εἴρηται, **Οὐκ ἐκπειράσεις κύριον τὸν θεόν σου.** 13 Καὶ συντελέσας πάντα πειρασμὸν ὁ διάβολος ἀπέστη ἀπ᾽ αὐτοῦ ἄχρι καιροῦ.

The Beginning of the Galilean Ministry
(Mt 4.12–17; Mk 1.14–15)

14 Καὶ ὑπέστρεψεν ὁ Ἰησοῦς ἐν τῇ δυνάμει τοῦ πνεύματος εἰς τὴν Γαλιλαίαν. καὶ φήμη ἐξῆλθεν καθ᾽ ὅλης τῆς περιχώρου περὶ αὐτοῦ. 15 καὶ αὐτὸς ἐδίδασκεν ἐν ταῖς συναγωγαῖς αὐτῶν, δοξαζόμενος ὑπὸ πάντων.

The Rejection of Jesus at Nazareth
(Mt 13.53–58; Mk 6.1–6)

16 Καὶ ἦλθεν εἰς Ναζαρά, οὗ ἦν τεθραμμένος, καὶ εἰσῆλθεν κατὰ τὸ εἰωθὸς αὐτῷ ἐν τῇ ἡμέρᾳ τῶν σαββάτων

---

8 Κύριον...λατρεύσεις Dt 6.13–14   10 Τοῖς ἀγγέλοις...σε Ps 91.11   11 Ἐπὶ χειρῶν ...σου Ps 91.12   12 Οὐκ ἐκπειράσεις...σου Dt 6.16; 1 Cor 10.9   13 συντελέσας... πειρασμόν He 4.15

εἰς τὴν συναγωγήν,ᵃ καὶ ἀνέστη ἀναγνῶναι.ᵃ 17 καὶ
ἐπεδόθη αὐτῷ βιβλίον τοῦ προφήτου Ἠσαΐου, καὶ ἀνα-
πτύξας² τὸ βιβλίον εὗρεν τὸν τόπον οὗ ἦν γεγραμμένον,
18 Πνεῦμα κυρίου ἐπ᾽ ἐμέ,
⠀⠀⠀οὗ εἵνεκεν ἔχρισέν μεᵇ
⠀⠀⠀⠀⠀εὐαγγελίσασθαι πτωχοῖς,ᵇ
⠀⠀ἀπέσταλκέν μεᵇ ᶜκηρύξαι αἰχμαλώτοις ἄφεσιν
⠀⠀καὶ τυφλοῖς ἀνάβλεψιν,
⠀⠀⠀⠀⠀ἀποστεῖλαι τεθραυσμένους ἐν ἀφέσει,
19ᶜ κηρύξαι ἐνιαυτὸν κυρίου δεκτόν.
20 καὶ πτύξας τὸ βιβλίον ἀποδοὺς τῷ ὑπηρέτῃ ἐκάθισεν·
καὶ πάντων οἱ ὀφθαλμοὶ ἐν τῇ συναγωγῇ ἦσαν ἀτενίζοντες αὐτῷ. 21 ἤρξατο δὲ λέγειν πρὸς αὐτοὺς ὅτι
Σήμερον πεπλήρωται ἡ γραφὴ αὕτη ἐν τοῖς ὠσὶν ὑμῶν.
22 Καὶ πάντες ἐμαρτύρουν αὐτῷ καὶ ἐθαύμαζον ἐπὶ τοῖς
λόγοις τῆς χάριτος τοῖς ἐκπορευομένοις ἐκ τοῦ στόματος
αὐτοῦ, καὶ ἔλεγον, Οὐχὶ υἱός ἐστιν Ἰωσὴφ οὗτος; 23 καὶ
εἶπεν πρὸς αὐτούς, Πάντως ἐρεῖτέ μοι τὴν παραβολὴν
ταύτην· Ἰατρέ, θεράπευσον σεαυτόν· ὅσα ἠκούσαμεν
γενόμενα εἰς τὴν Καφαρναοὺμ ποίησον καὶ ὧδε ἐν τῇ
πατρίδι σου. 24 εἶπεν δέ, Ἀμὴν λέγω ὑμῖν ὅτι οὐδεὶς
προφήτης δεκτός ἐστιν ἐν τῇ πατρίδι αὐτοῦ. 25 ἐπ᾽
ἀληθείας δὲ λέγω ὑμῖν, πολλαὶ χῆραι ἦσαν ἐν ταῖς

² 17 {C} ἀναπτύξας ℵ (D* ἀπτύξας) Dᶜ K Δ Θ Π Ψ f¹ f¹³ 28 565 700
1009 1010 1071 1079 1216 1230 1242 1253 1344 1546 1646 2148 2174 *Byz Lect*
*l*⁶⁰ᵐ,⁶⁹ˢ·ᵐ,⁷⁰ˢ·ᵐ,¹¹²⁷ˢ·ᵐ itᵃ·ᵃᵘʳ·ᵇ,ᶜ,ᵈ,ₑ,f,ff²,ₗ,q,r¹ vg goth Origenˡᵃᵗ Eusebius ∥
ἀνοίξας A B L W Ξ 33 892 1195 1241 *l*⁵⁴⁷ᵐ syrˢ·ʰ,ᵖᵃˡ copˢᵃ,ᵇᵒ arm eth geo ∥
ἀνοίξας Ἰησοῦς syrᵖ ∥ ἀναπτύξας Ἰησοῦς Diatessaron

⠀ᵃ ᵃ 16 *a* minor, *a* major: TR WH Bov Nes BF² AV RV ASV TT (Zür) (Luth) Jer ∥ *a* major,
a minor: RSV (NEB) Seg
⠀ᵇ ᵇ ᵇ 18 *b* none, *b* minor, *b* none: TR WH BF² AV RV ASV (RSV) TT (Luth) Seg ∥ *b* major,
b none, *b* minor: (Bov) NEB (Zür) Jer ∥ *b* none, *b* minor, *b* minor: Nes
⠀ᶜ ᶜ 18–19 *c* no number, *c* number 19: TRᵉᵈ WH Bov Nes BF² AV RV ASV RSV NEB TT Zür Luth
Jer Seg ∥ *c* number 19, *c* no number: TRᵉᵈ

⠀18–19 Πνεῦμα...δεκτόν Is 61.1–2; 58.6⠀⠀22 Οὐχὶ υἱός...οὗτος Lk 3.23; Jn 6.42⠀⠀23 ὅσα
...Καφαρναούμ Mt 4.13; Jn 2.12⠀⠀24 οὐδεὶς προφήτης...αὐτοῦ Jn 4.44

synagogue. He stood up to read the
Scriptures, ¹⁷ and was handed the book
of the prophet Isaiah. He unrolled the
scroll and found the place where it is
written:
¹⁸ "The Spirit of the Lord is upon me.
⠀He has anointed me to preach the
⠀⠀Good News to the poor,
⠀He has sent me to proclaim liberty
⠀⠀to the captives,
⠀And recovery of sight to the blind,
⠀To set free the oppressed,
¹⁹ To announce the year when the Lord
⠀⠀will save his people!"
²⁰ Jesus rolled up the scroll, gave it
back to the attendant, and sat down.
All the people in the synagogue had their
eyes fixed on him. ²¹ He began speaking
to them: "This passage of scripture has
come true today, as you heard it being
read." ²² They were all well impressed
with him, and marveled at the beautiful
words that he spoke. They said, "Isn't
he the son of Joseph?" ²³ He said to
them: "I am sure that you will quote
the proverb to me, 'Doctor, heal yourself.' You will also say to me, 'Do here
in your own home town the same things
we were told happened in Capernaum.'
²⁴ I tell you this," Jesus added: "A
prophet is never welcomed in his own
home town. ²⁵ Listen to me: it is true
that there were many widows in Israel

during the time of Elijah, when there was no rain for three and a half years and there was a great famine throughout the whole land. [26] Yet Elijah was not sent to a single one of them, but only to a widow of Zarephath, in the territory of Sidon. [27] And there were many lepers in Israel during the time of the prophet Elisha; yet not one of them was made clean, but only Naaman the Syrian.'' [28] All the people in the synagogue were filled with anger when they heard this. [29] They rose up, dragged Jesus out of town, and took him to the top of the hill on which their town was built, to throw him over the cliff. [30] But he walked through the middle of the crowd and went his way.

A Man with an Evil Spirit
(Also Mark 1.21–28)

[31] Then Jesus went to Capernaum, a town in Galilee, where he taught the people on the Sabbath. [32] They were all amazed at the way he taught, for his words had authority. [33] There was a man in the synagogue who had the spirit of an evil demon in him; he screamed out in a loud voice: [34] "Ah! What do you want with us, Jesus of Nazareth? Are you here to destroy us? I know who you are: you are God's holy messenger!" [35] Jesus commanded the spirit: "Be quiet, and come out of the man!" The demon threw the man down in front of them all, and went out of him without doing him any harm. [36] Everyone was amazed, and they said to one another: "What kind of word is this? With authority and power this man gives orders to the evil spirits, and they come out!"

ἡμέραις Ἠλίου ἐν τῷ Ἰσραήλ, ὅτε ἐκλείσθη ὁ οὐρανὸς ἐπὶ ἔτη τρία καὶ μῆνας ἕξ, ὡς ἐγένετο λιμὸς μέγας ἐπὶ πᾶσαν τὴν γῆν, **26** καὶ πρὸς οὐδεμίαν αὐτῶν ἐπέμφθη Ἠλίας εἰ μὴ εἰς Σάρεπτα τῆς Σιδωνίας πρὸς γυναῖκα χήραν. **27** καὶ πολλοὶ λεπροὶ ἦσαν ἐν τῷ Ἰσραὴλ ἐπὶ Ἐλισαίου τοῦ προφήτου, καὶ οὐδεὶς αὐτῶν ἐκαθαρίσθη εἰ μὴ Ναιμὰν ὁ Σύρος. **28** καὶ ἐπλήσθησαν πάντες θυμοῦ ἐν τῇ συναγωγῇ ἀκούοντες ταῦτα, **29** καὶ ἀναστάντες ἐξέβαλον αὐτὸν ἔξω τῆς πόλεως, καὶ ἤγαγον αὐτὸν ἕως ὀφρύος τοῦ ὄρους ἐφ' οὗ ἡ πόλις ᾠκοδόμητο αὐτῶν, ὥστε κατακρημνίσαι αὐτόν· **30** αὐτὸς δὲ διελθὼν διὰ μέσου αὐτῶν ἐπορεύετο.

The Man with an Unclean Spirit
(Mk 1.21–28)

31 Καὶ κατῆλθεν εἰς Καφαρναοὺμ πόλιν τῆς Γαλιλαίας. καὶ ἦν διδάσκων αὐτοὺς ἐν τοῖς σάββασιν· **32** καὶ ἐξεπλήσσοντο ἐπὶ τῇ διδαχῇ αὐτοῦ, ὅτι ἐν ἐξουσίᾳ ἦν ὁ λόγος αὐτοῦ. **33** καὶ ἐν τῇ συναγωγῇ ἦν ἄνθρωπος ἔχων πνεῦμα δαιμονίου ἀκαθάρτου, καὶ ἀνέκραξεν φωνῇ μεγάλῃ, **34** Ἔα, τί ἡμῖν καὶ σοί, Ἰησοῦ Ναζαρηνέ; ἦλθες ἀπολέσαι ἡμᾶς;[d] οἶδά σε τίς εἶ, ὁ ἅγιος τοῦ θεοῦ. **35** καὶ ἐπετίμησεν αὐτῷ ὁ Ἰησοῦς λέγων, Φιμώθητι καὶ ἔξελθε ἀπ' αὐτοῦ. καὶ ῥῖψαν αὐτὸν τὸ δαιμόνιον εἰς τὸ μέσον ἐξῆλθεν ἀπ' αὐτοῦ μηδὲν βλάψαν αὐτόν. **36** καὶ ἐγένετο θάμβος ἐπὶ πάντας, καὶ συνελάλουν πρὸς ἀλλήλους λέγοντες, Τίς ὁ λόγος οὗτος,[e] ὅτι ἐν ἐξουσίᾳ καὶ δυνάμει ἐπιτάσσει τοῖς ἀκαθάρτοις πνεύμασιν, καὶ ἐξέρχονται;[e]

[d] **34** d question: TR WH Bov Nes BF² AV RV ASV RSV NEB TT Zür Jer ‖ d statement: NEBmg Luth Seg

[e] **36** e minor, e question: TR (WH) Bov Nes BF² RVmg ASVmg ‖ e question, e statement: RV ASV RSV NEB TT Zür Luth ‖ e question, e exclamation: Seg ‖ e exclamation, e statement: AV ‖ e exclamation, e exclamation: Jer

25 Ἠλίου...ἕξ Jas 5.17   ἐκλείσθη...γῆν 1 Kgs 17.1, 7; 18.1   **26** Σάρεπτα...χήραν 1 Kgs 17.9   **27** 2 Kgs 5.1–14   **31** κατῆλθεν...Γαλιλαίας Mt 4.13; Jn 2.12 **32** ἐξεπλήσσοντο...λόγος αὐτοῦ Mt 7.28–29; Jn 7.46   **33–34** ἀνέκραξεν...ἡμᾶς Mt 8.29; Mk 1.23–24; 5.7; Lk 8.28   **34** ὁ ἅγιος τοῦ θεοῦ Lk 4.41; Jn 6.69

37 καὶ ἐξεπορεύετο ἦχος περὶ αὐτοῦ εἰς πάντα τόπον τῆς περιχώρου.

The Healing of Many People
(Mt 8.14–17; Mk 1.29–34)

38 Ἀναστὰς δὲ ἀπὸ τῆς συναγωγῆς εἰσῆλθεν εἰς τὴν οἰκίαν Σίμωνος. πενθερὰ δὲ τοῦ Σίμωνος ἦν συνεχομένη πυρετῷ μεγάλῳ, καὶ ἠρώτησαν αὐτὸν περὶ αὐτῆς. 39 καὶ ἐπιστὰς ἐπάνω αὐτῆς ἐπετίμησεν τῷ πυρετῷ, καὶ ἀφῆκεν αὐτήν· παραχρῆμα δὲ ἀναστᾶσα διηκόνει αὐτοῖς. 40 Δύνοντος δὲ τοῦ ἡλίου ἅπαντες ὅσοι εἶχον ἀσθενοῦντας νόσοις ποικίλαις ἤγαγον αὐτοὺς πρὸς αὐτόν· ὁ δὲ ἑνὶ ἑκάστῳ αὐτῶν τὰς χεῖρας ἐπιτιθεὶς ἐθεράπευεν αὐτούς. 41 ἐξήρχετο δὲ καὶ δαιμόνια ἀπὸ πολλῶν, κραυγάζοντα καὶ λέγοντα ὅτι Σὺ εἶ ὁ υἱὸς τοῦ θεοῦ. καὶ ἐπιτιμῶν οὐκ εἴα αὐτὰ λαλεῖν, ὅτι ᾔδεισαν τὸν Χριστὸν αὐτὸν εἶναι.

A Preaching Tour
(Mk 1.35–39)

42 Γενομένης δὲ ἡμέρας ἐξελθὼν ἐπορεύθη εἰς ἔρημον τόπον· καὶ οἱ ὄχλοι ἐπεζήτουν αὐτόν, καὶ ἦλθον ἕως αὐτοῦ, καὶ κατεῖχον αὐτὸν τοῦ μὴ πορεύεσθαι ἀπ᾽ αὐτῶν. 43 ὁ δὲ εἶπεν πρὸς αὐτοὺς ὅτι Καὶ ταῖς ἑτέραις πόλεσιν εὐαγγελίσασθαί με δεῖ τὴν βασιλείαν τοῦ θεοῦ, ὅτι ἐπὶ τοῦτο ἀπεστάλην. 44 καὶ ἦν κηρύσσων εἰς τὰς συναγωγὰς τῆς Ἰουδαίας[3].

---

³ 44 {B} εἰς τὰς συναγωγὰς τῆς Ἰουδαίας 𝔭75 ℵ B Lect syrs,h ‖ ἐν ταῖς συναγωγαῖς τῆς Ἰουδαίας C L f1 892 1241 1365 copsa?bo? ‖ εἰς τὰς συναγωγὰς τῶν Ἰουδαίων W l18 ‖ εἰς τὰς συναγωγὰς τῆς Γαλιλαίας (see Mt 4.23; Mk 1.39) D Ψ f13 arm? ‖ ἐν ταῖς συναγωγαῖς τῆς Γαλιλαίας (see Mk 1.39 mg) A K X Δ Θ Π 28 33 565 700 1009 1010 1071 1079 1195 1210 1230 1242 (1253 αὐτῶν τῆς) 1344 1546 1646 2148 2174 Byz l211,226,299,854,883 ita,aur,b,c,d,e,f,ff2,l,q,rl vg syrp,hmg copbomss goth arm? eth geo ‖ ἐν ταῖς συναγωγαῖς αὐτῶν (see Mt 4.23) l34,48,1231m

41 Σύ...θεοῦ Mt 8.29; Mk 3.11; Lk 4.34 οὐκ εἴα...εἶναι Mk 3.12   43 Καὶ...θεοῦ Lk 8.1 44 ἦν...Ἰουδαίας Mt 4.23

37 And the report about Jesus spread everywhere in that region.

Jesus Heals Many People
(Also Matt. 8.14–17; Mark 1.29–34)

38 Jesus left the synagogue and went to Simon's home. Simon's mother-in-law was sick with a high fever, and they spoke to Jesus about her. 39 He went and stood at her bedside, and gave a command to the fever. The fever left her and she got up at once and began to wait on them. 40 After sunset, all who had friends who were sick with various diseases brought them to Jesus; he placed his hands on every one of them and healed them all. 41 Demons, also, went out from many people, screaming, "You are the Son of God!" Jesus commanded them and would not let them speak, because they knew that he was the Messiah.

Jesus Preaches in Judea
(Also Mark 1.35–39)

42 At daybreak Jesus left the town and went off to a lonely place. The people started looking for him, and when they found him they tried to keep him from leaving. 43 But he said to them, "I must preach the Good News of the Kingdom of God in other towns also, for that is what God sent me to do." 44 So he preached in the synagogues of Judea.

Jesus Calls the First Disciples
(Also Matt. 4.18–22; Mark 1.16–20)

5 One time Jesus was standing on the shore of Lake Gennesaret while the people pushed their way up to him to listen to the word of God. ² He saw two boats pulled up on the beach; the fishermen had left them and gone off to wash the nets. ³ Jesus got into one of the boats — it belonged to Simon — and asked him to push off a little from the shore. Jesus sat in the boat and taught the crowd.

⁴ When he finished speaking, he said to Simon, "Push the boat out further to the deep water, and you and your partners let your nets down for a catch." ⁵ "Master," Simon answered, "we worked hard all night long and caught nothing. But if you say so, I will let down the nets." ⁶ They let the nets down and caught such a large number of fish that the nets were about to break. ⁷ So they motioned to their partners in the other boat to come and help them. They came and filled both boats so full of fish that they were about to sink. ⁸ When Simon Peter saw what had happened, he fell on his knees before Jesus and said, "Go away from me, Lord, for I am a sinful man!" ⁹ He and all the others with him were amazed at the large number of fish they had caught. ¹⁰ The same was true of Simon's partners, James and John, the sons of Zebedee. Jesus said to Simon, "Don't be afraid; from now on you will be catching men." ¹¹ They pulled the boats on the beach, left everything and followed Jesus.

Jesus Makes a Leper Clean
(Also Matt. 8.1–4; Mark 1.40–45)

¹² Once Jesus was in a certain town where there was a man who was covered

The Calling of the First Disciples
(Mt 4.18–22; Mk 1.16–20)

5 Ἐγένετο δὲ ἐν τῷ τὸν ὄχλον ἐπικεῖσθαι αὐτῷ καὶ ἀκούειν τὸν λόγον τοῦ θεοῦ καὶ αὐτὸς ἦν ἑστὼς παρὰ τὴν λίμνην Γεννησαρέτ, 2 καὶ εἶδεν δύο πλοῖα ἑστῶτα παρὰ τὴν λίμνην· οἱ δὲ ἁλιεῖς ἀπ᾽ αὐτῶν ἀποβάντες ἔπλυνον τὰ δίκτυα. 3 ἐμβὰς δὲ εἰς ἓν τῶν πλοίων, ὃ ἦν Σίμωνος, ἠρώτησεν αὐτὸν ἀπὸ τῆς γῆς ἐπαναγαγεῖν ὀλίγον, καθίσας δὲ ἐκ τοῦ πλοίου ἐδίδασκεν τοὺς ὄχλους. 4 ὡς δὲ ἐπαύσατο λαλῶν, εἶπεν πρὸς τὸν Σίμωνα, Ἐπανάγαγε εἰς τὸ βάθος καὶ χαλάσατε τὰ δίκτυα ὑμῶν εἰς ἄγραν. 5 καὶ ἀποκριθεὶς Σίμων εἶπεν, Ἐπιστάτα, δι᾽ ὅλης νυκτὸς κοπιάσαντες οὐδὲν ἐλάβομεν, ἐπὶ δὲ τῷ ῥήματί σου χαλάσω τὰ δίκτυα. 6 καὶ τοῦτο ποιήσαντες συνέκλεισαν πλῆθος ἰχθύων πολύ,ᵃ διερρήσσετο δὲ τὰ δίκτυα αὐτῶν.ᵃ 7 καὶ κατένευσαν τοῖς μετόχοις ἐν τῷ ἑτέρῳ πλοίῳ τοῦ ἐλθόντας συλλαβέσθαι αὐτοῖς· καὶ ἦλθαν, καὶ ἔπλησαν ἀμφότερα τὰ πλοῖα ὥστε βυθίζεσθαι αὐτά. 8 ἰδὼν δὲ Σίμων Πέτρος προσέπεσεν τοῖς γόνασιν Ἰησοῦ λέγων, Ἔξελθε ἀπ᾽ ἐμοῦ, ὅτι ἀνὴρ ἁμαρτωλός εἰμι, κύριε· 9 θάμβος γὰρ περιέσχεν αὐτὸν καὶ πάντας τοὺς σὺν αὐτῷ ἐπὶ τῇ ἄγρᾳ τῶν ἰχθύων ὧν συνέλαβον, 10 ὁμοίως δὲ καὶ Ἰάκωβον καὶ Ἰωάννην υἱοὺς Ζεβεδαίου, οἳ ἦσαν κοινωνοὶ τῷ Σίμωνι. καὶ εἶπεν πρὸς τὸν Σίμωνα ὁ Ἰησοῦς, Μὴ φοβοῦ· ἀπὸ τοῦ νῦν ἀνθρώπους ἔσῃ ζωγρῶν. 11 καὶ καταγαγόντες τὰ πλοῖα ἐπὶ τὴν γῆν ἀφέντες πάντα ἠκολούθησαν αὐτῷ.

The Cleansing of a Leper
(Mt 8.1–4; Mk 1.40–45)

12 Καὶ ἐγένετο ἐν τῷ εἶναι αὐτὸν ἐν μιᾷ τῶν πόλεων καὶ ἰδοὺ ἀνὴρ πλήρης λέπρας· καὶ ἰδὼν τὸν Ἰησοῦν

ᵃ ᵃ **6** a minor, a major: WH Nes BF² AV NEB TT Zür Luth Jer Seg ‖ a major, a minor: TR RSV ‖ a major, a major: Bov ‖ a minor, a minor: RV ASV

1–3 Mt 13.1–2; Mk 3.9–10; 4.1   **4–10** χαλάσατε...Σίμωνι Jn 21.3–8   **11** ἀφέντες... αὐτῷ Mt 19.27

πεσὼν ἐπὶ πρόσωπον ἐδεήθη αὐτοῦ λέγων, Κύριε, ἐὰν θέλῃς δύνασαί με καθαρίσαι. 13 καὶ ἐκτείνας τὴν χεῖρα ἥψατο αὐτοῦ λέγων, Θέλω, καθαρίσθητι· καὶ εὐθέως ἡ λέπρα ἀπῆλθεν ἀπ' αὐτοῦ. 14 καὶ αὐτὸς παρήγγειλεν αὐτῷ μηδενὶ εἰπεῖν, ἀλλὰ ἀπελθὼν δεῖξον σεαυτὸν τῷ ἱερεῖ, καὶ προσένεγκε περὶ τοῦ καθαρισμοῦ σου καθὼς προσέταξεν Μωϋσῆς,[b] εἰς μαρτύριον αὐτοῖς. 15 διήρχετο δὲ μᾶλλον ὁ λόγος περὶ αὐτοῦ, καὶ συνήρχοντο ὄχλοι πολλοὶ ἀκούειν καὶ θεραπεύεσθαι ἀπὸ τῶν ἀσθενειῶν αὐτῶν· 16 αὐτὸς δὲ ἦν ὑποχωρῶν ἐν ταῖς ἐρήμοις καὶ προσευχόμενος.

The Healing of a Paralytic
(Mt 9.1–8; Mk 2.1–12)

17 Καὶ ἐγένετο ἐν μιᾷ τῶν ἡμερῶν καὶ αὐτὸς ἦν διδάσκων, καὶ ἦσαν καθήμενοι Φαρισαῖοι καὶ νομοδιδάσκαλοι οἳ ἦσαν ἐληλυθότες[1] ἐκ πάσης κώμης τῆς Γαλιλαίας καὶ Ἰουδαίας καὶ Ἰερουσαλήμ· καὶ δύναμις κυρίου ἦν εἰς τὸ ἰᾶσθαι αὐτόν[2]. 18 καὶ ἰδοὺ ἄνδρες φέροντες ἐπὶ κλίνης ἄνθρωπον ὃς ἦν παραλελυμένος, καὶ ἐζήτουν αὐτὸν εἰσενεγκεῖν καὶ θεῖναι [αὐτὸν] ἐνώπιον αὐτοῦ. 19 καὶ μὴ εὑρόντες ποίας εἰσενέγκωσιν αὐτὸν διὰ τὸν ὄχλον ἀναβάντες ἐπὶ τὸ δῶμα διὰ τῶν κεράμων καθῆκαν αὐτὸν σὺν τῷ κλινιδίῳ εἰς τὸ μέσον ἔμπροσθεν τοῦ Ἰησοῦ.

---

[1] **17** {C} οἳ ἦσαν ἐληλυθότες ℵ[a] A[2] B C K L W X Δ Θ Ξ Π Ψ 28 565 700 892 1009 1010 1071 1079 1195 1216 1230 1241 1242 1253 1344 1546 1646 2148 2174 *Byz Lect* it[aur,b,c,f,ff2,l,q,r1] vg syr[p,h,pal] cop[sa,bo] geo ‖ οἳ ἦσαν συνεληλυθότες f[1] f[13] 1365 l[49] it[a] goth arm Cyril ‖ ἦσαν ἐληλυθότες ℵ* (33 συνεληλυθότες) ‖ ἦσαν δὲ συνεληλυθότες D it[d, (e)] syr[svid]

[2] **17** {B} αὐτόν ℵ B L W Ξ cop[sa] eth Cyril ‖ αὐτούς A C D X Δ Θ Π Ψ f[1] f[13] 28 33 565 700 892 1009 1010 1071 1079 1195 1216 1230 1242 1253 1344 1365 1546 1646 (2148 τούτους) 2174 *Byz Lect* it[a,aur,b,c,d,e,f,ff2,l,q,r1] vg syr[p,h] eop[bo] goth arm geo Diatessaron ‖ πάντας K Cyril ‖ αὐτοὺς πάντας syr[pal] ‖ τοὺς ἀσθενούντας l[11]

---

[b] **14** *b* minor: TR Bov Nes BF[2] AV RV ASV RSV NEB TT Zür? Luth? Jer Seg ‖ *b* none: WH

---

14 αὐτὸς...εἰπεῖν Mk 7.36; Lk 8.56   δεῖξον...Μωϋσῆς Lv 14.2–32   **16** αὐτὸς... προσευχόμενος Mk 1.35

---

with leprosy. When he saw Jesus, he fell on his face before him and begged, "Sir, if you want to, you can make me clean!" [13] Jesus reached out and touched him. "I do want to," he said. "Be clean!" At once the leprosy left the man. [14] Jesus ordered him, "Don't tell this to anyone, but go straight to the priest and let him examine you; then offer the sacrifice, as Moses ordered, to prove to everyone that you are now clean." [15] But the news about Jesus spread all the more widely, and crowds of people came to hear him and be healed from their diseases. [16] But he would go away to lonely places, where he prayed.

Jesus Heals a Paralyzed Man
(Also Matt. 9.1–8; Mark 2.1–12)

[17] One day when Jesus was teaching, some Pharisees and teachers of the Law were sitting there who had come from every town in Galilee and Judea, and from Jerusalem. The power of the Lord was present for Jesus to heal the sick. [18] Some men came carrying a paralyzed man on a bed, and they tried to take him into the house and lay him before Jesus. [19] Because of the crowd, however, they could find no way to take him in. So they carried him up on the roof, made an opening in the tiles, and let him down on his bed into the middle of

the group in front of Jesus. ²⁰ When Jesus saw how much faith they had, he said to the man, "Your sins are forgiven you, my friend." ²¹ The teachers of the Law and the Pharisees began to say to themselves: "Who is this man who speaks against God in this way? No man can forgive sins; God alone can!" ²² Jesus knew their thoughts and said to them: "Why do you think such things? ²³ Is it easier to say, 'Your sins are forgiven you,' or to say, 'Get up and walk'? ²⁴ I will prove to you, then, that the Son of Man has authority on earth to forgive sins." So he said to the paralyzed man, "I tell you, get up, pick up your bed, and go home!" ²⁵ At once the man got up before them all, took the bed he had been lying on, and went home, praising God. ²⁶ They were all completely amazed! Full of fear, they praised God, saying, "What marvelous things we have seen today!"

Jesus Calls Levi
(Also Matt. 9.9–13; Mark 2.13–17)

²⁷ After this, Jesus went out and saw a tax collector named Levi, sitting in his office. Jesus said to him, "Follow me." ²⁸ Levi got up, left everything and followed him.

²⁹ Then Levi had a big feast in his house for Jesus, and there was a large number of tax collectors and other people sitting with them. ³⁰ Some Pharisees and teachers of the Law who belonged to their group complained to Jesus' disciples. "Why do you eat and drink with tax collectors and outcasts?" they asked. ³¹ Jesus answered them: "People who are well do not need a doctor, but only those who are sick. ³² I have not come to call the respectable people to repent, but the outcasts."

20 καὶ ἰδὼν τὴν πίστιν αὐτῶν εἶπεν, Ἄνθρωπε, ἀφέωνταί σοι αἱ ἁμαρτίαι σου. **21** καὶ ἤρξαντο διαλογίζεσθαι οἱ γραμματεῖς καὶ οἱ Φαρισαῖοι λέγοντες, Τίς ἐστιν οὗτος ὃς λαλεῖ βλασφημίας; τίς δύναται ἁμαρτίας ἀφεῖναι εἰ μὴ μόνος ὁ θεός; **22** ἐπιγνοὺς δὲ ὁ Ἰησοῦς τοὺς διαλογισμοὺς αὐτῶν ἀποκριθεὶς εἶπεν πρὸς αὐτούς, Τί διαλογίζεσθε ἐν ταῖς καρδίαις ὑμῶν; **23** τί ἐστιν εὐκοπώτερον, εἰπεῖν, Ἀφέωνταί σοι αἱ ἁμαρτίαι σου, ἢ εἰπεῖν, Ἔγειρε καὶ περιπάτει; **24** ἵνα δὲ εἰδῆτε ὅτι ὁ υἱὸς τοῦ ἀνθρώπου ἐξουσίαν ἔχει ἐπὶ τῆς γῆς ἀφιέναι ἁμαρτίας — εἶπεν τῷ παραλελυμένῳ, Σοὶ λέγω, ἔγειρε καὶ ἄρας τὸ κλινίδιόν σου πορεύου εἰς τὸν οἶκόν σου. **25** καὶ παραχρῆμα ἀναστὰς ἐνώπιον αὐτῶν, ἄρας ἐφ' ὃ κατέκειτο, ἀπῆλθεν εἰς τὸν οἶκον αὐτοῦ δοξάζων τὸν θεόν. **26** καὶ ἔκστασις ἔλαβεν ἅπαντας καὶ ἐδόξαζον τὸν θεόν, καὶ ἐπλήσθησαν φόβου λέγοντες ὅτι Εἴδομεν παράδοξα σήμερον.

The Calling of Levi
(Mt 9.9–13; Mk 2.13–17)

27 Καὶ μετὰ ταῦτα ἐξῆλθεν καὶ ἐθεάσατο τελώνην ὀνόματι Λευὶν καθήμενον ἐπὶ τὸ τελώνιον, καὶ εἶπεν αὐτῷ, Ἀκολούθει μοι. **28** καὶ καταλιπὼν πάντα ἀναστὰς ἠκολούθει αὐτῷ. **29** Καὶ ἐποίησεν δοχὴν μεγάλην Λευὶς αὐτῷ ἐν τῇ οἰκίᾳ αὐτοῦ· καὶ ἦν ὄχλος πολὺς τελωνῶν καὶ ἄλλων οἳ ἦσαν μετ' αὐτῶν κατακείμενοι. **30** καὶ ἐγόγγυζον οἱ Φαρισαῖοι καὶ οἱ γραμματεῖς αὐτῶν πρὸς τοὺς μαθητὰς αὐτοῦ λέγοντες, Διὰ τί μετὰ τῶν τελωνῶν καὶ ἁμαρτωλῶν ἐσθίετε καὶ πίνετε; **31** καὶ ἀποκριθεὶς ὁ Ἰησοῦς εἶπεν πρὸς αὐτούς, Οὐ χρείαν ἔχουσιν οἱ ὑγιαίνοντες ἰατροῦ ἀλλὰ οἱ κακῶς ἔχοντες· **32** οὐκ ἐλήλυθα καλέσαι δικαίους ἀλλὰ ἁμαρτωλοὺς εἰς μετάνοιαν.

20 ἀφέωνται...σου Lk 7.48   **21** Τίς ἐστιν...θεός Is 43.25; Lk 7.49   **22** ἐπιγνοὺς...αὐτῶν Lk 6.8; 9.47 Τί...ὑμῶν Mt 16.8   **24** ἔγειρε...πορεύου Jn 5.8   **29–30** ὄχλος...πίνετε Lk 15.1–2

The Question about Fasting
(Mt 9.14–17; Mk 2.18–22)

33 Οἱ δὲ εἶπαν πρὸς αὐτόν, Οἱ[3] μαθηταὶ Ἰωάννου νηστεύουσιν πυκνὰ καὶ δεήσεις ποιοῦνται, ὁμοίως καὶ οἱ τῶν Φαρισαίων, οἱ δὲ σοὶ ἐσθίουσιν καὶ πίνουσιν. **34** ὁ δὲ Ἰησοῦς εἶπεν πρὸς αὐτούς, Μὴ δύνασθε τοὺς υἱοὺς τοῦ νυμφῶνος ἐν ᾧ ὁ νυμφίος μετ' αὐτῶν ἐστιν ποιῆσαι νηστεῦσαι; **35** ἐλεύσονται δὲ ἡμέραι, καὶ ὅταν ἀπαρθῇ ἀπ' αὐτῶν ὁ νυμφίος τότε νηστεύσουσιν ἐν ἐκείναις ταῖς ἡμέραις. **36** Ἔλεγεν δὲ καὶ παραβολὴν πρὸς αὐτοὺς ὅτι Οὐδεὶς ἐπίβλημα ἀπὸ ἱματίου καινοῦ σχίσας ἐπιβάλλει ἐπὶ ἱμάτιον παλαιόν· εἰ δὲ μήγε, καὶ τὸ καινὸν σχίσει καὶ τῷ παλαιῷ οὐ συμφωνήσει τὸ ἐπίβλημα τὸ ἀπὸ τοῦ καινοῦ. **37** καὶ οὐδεὶς βάλλει οἶνον νέον εἰς ἀσκοὺς παλαιούς· εἰ δὲ μήγε, ῥήξει ὁ οἶνος ὁ νέος τοὺς ἀσκούς, καὶ αὐτὸς ἐκχυθήσεται καὶ οἱ ἀσκοὶ ἀπολοῦνται· **38** ἀλλὰ οἶνον νέον εἰς ἀσκοὺς καινοὺς βλητέον[4]. **39** [καὶ] οὐδεὶς πιὼν παλαιὸν θέλει νέον· λέγει γάρ, Ὁ παλαιὸς χρηστός[6] ἐστιν.[5]

---

3 33 {C} οἱ 𝔭[4] ℵ[a] B L W Ξ 33 892* 1241 cop[sa,bo] ‖ διὰ τί οἱ (see Mk 2.18) ℵ*·c A C D K X Δ Θ Π Ψ f[1] f[13] 28 565 700 892[c] 1009 1010 1071 1079 1195 1216 1230 1242 1253 1344 1365 1546 1646 2148 2174 *Byz Lect* it[a,aur,b,c,d,e,f,ff2, l,q,r1] vg syr[p,h,pal] cop[bomss] goth arm eth geo Diatessaron

4 38 {B} βλητέον 𝔭[4] ℵ[a] B L f[1] 33 700 1241 syr[pal] ‖ βάλλουσιν ℵ* (cop[sa,bo]) Marcion ‖ βάλληται W ‖ βλητέον καὶ ἀμφότεροι συντηροῦνται (see Mt 9.17) A C K X Δ Θ Π Ψ f[13] 28 565 892 1009 1010 1071 1079 1195 1216 1230 1242 1253 1344 1365 1546 1646 2148 2174 *Byz Lect* vg syr[h] arm geo Adamantius ‖ βάλλουσιν καὶ ἀμφότεροι τηροῦνται (see Mt 9.17) D it[a,d,e,r1] cop[bomss] ‖ βάλλουσιν καὶ ἀμφότεροι συντηροῦνται it[aur,b,c,f,ff2,l,q] syr[p] goth eth

5 39 {B} *include verse 39* 𝔭[4,75] ℵ A B C K L W X Δ Θ Π Ψ f[1] f[13] 28 33 565 700 892 1009 1010 1071 1079 1195 1216 1230 1241 1242 1253 1344 1365 1546 1646 2148 2174 *Byz Lect* it[aur,f,q] vg syr[p,h,pal] cop[sa,bo] goth arm geo ‖ *omit verse 39* (see Mt 9.17; Mk 2.22) D it[a,b,c,d,e,ff2,l,r1] Marcion Irenaeus Eusebius

6 39 {B} χρηστός 𝔭[4,75vid] ℵ B L W 1241 syr[p] cop[sa,bo] ‖ χρηστότερος A C K X Δ Θ Π Ψ f[1] f[13] 28 33[vid] 565 700 892 1009 1010 1071 1079 1195 1216 1230 1242 1253 1344 1365 1546 1646 2148 2174 *Byz Lect* it[aur,f,q] vg syr[h,pal] goth arm geo

34 Μὴ...νηστεῦσαι Jn 3.29

The Question about Fasting
(Also Matt. 9.14–17; Mark 2.18–22)

[33] Some people said to Jesus, "The disciples of John fast frequently and offer up prayers, and the disciples of the Pharisees do the same; but your disciples eat and drink." [34] Jesus answered: "Do you think you can make the guests at a wedding party go without food as long as the bridegroom is with them? Of course not! [35] But the time will come when the bridegroom will be taken away from them, and they will go without food in those days."

[36] Jesus told them this parable also: "No one tears a piece off a new coat to patch up an old coat. If he does, he will have torn the new coat, and the piece of new cloth will not match the old. [37] Nor does anyone pour new wine into used wineskins. If he does, the new wine will burst the skins, the wine will pour out, and the skins will be ruined. [38] No! New wine should be poured into fresh skins! [39] And no one wants new wine after drinking old wine. 'The old is better,' he says."

The Question about the Sabbath
(Also Matt. 12.1–8; Mark 2.23–28)

6 Jesus was walking through some wheat fields on a Sabbath day. His disciples began to pick the heads of wheat, rub them in their hands, and eat the grain. ² Some Pharisees said, "Why are you doing what our Law says you cannot do on the Sabbath?" ³ Jesus answered them: "Haven't you read what David did when he and his men were hungry? ⁴ He went into the house of God, took the bread offered to God, ate it, and gave it also to his men. Yet it is against our Law for anyone to eat it except the

Plucking Grain on the Sabbath
(Mt 12.1–8; Mk 2.23–28)

6 Ἐγένετο δὲ ἐν σαββάτῳ¹ διαπορεύεσθαι αὐτὸν διὰ σπορίμων, καὶ ἔτιλλον οἱ μαθηταὶ αὐτοῦ καὶ ἤσθιον τοὺς στάχυας ψώχοντες ταῖς χερσίν². 2 τινὲς δὲ τῶν Φαρισαίων εἶπαν, Τί ποιεῖτε ὃ οὐκ ἔξεστιν³ τοῖς σάββασιν; 3 καὶ ἀποκριθεὶς πρὸς αὐτοὺς εἶπεν ὁ Ἰησοῦς, Οὐδὲ τοῦτο ἀνέγνωτε ὃ ἐποίησεν Δαυὶδᵃ ὅτε ἐπείνασεν αὐτὸς καὶ οἱ μετ' αὐτοῦ [ὄντες];ᵃ 4 [ὡς] εἰσῆλθεν εἰς τὸν οἶκον τοῦ θεοῦ καὶ τοὺς ἄρτους τῆς προθέσεως λαβὼν ἔφαγεν καὶ ἔδωκεν τοῖς μετ' αὐτοῦ⁴, οὓς οὐκ ἔξεστιν φαγεῖν εἰ μὴ

---

¹ 1 {C} σαββάτῳ (see Mt 12.1; Mk 2.23) 𝔭⁴,⁷⁵ᵛⁱᵈ ℵ B L W ƒ¹ 33 1241 1365 𝑙⁵⁴⁷ itᵇ,ᶜ,ˡ, q,rˡ syrᵖ,ʰᵐᵍ,ᵖᵃˡ copˢᵃ,ᵇᵒ eth Diatessaronᵃ,ⁱ,ⁿ ‖ τοῖς σάββασι 𝑙⁷⁶ copᵇᵒᵐˢˢ ‖ σαββάτῳ δευτεροπρώτῳ Aᶜ C D K X Δ Θ Π Ψ (ƒ¹³ 28 1344* δευτέρῳ πρώτῳ) 565 700 892 1009 1010 1071 1079 1195 1216 1230 1242 (1253 δευτέρῳ πρώτον) 1344ᶜ 1546 1646 2148 2174 Byz itᵃ,ᵃᵘʳ,ᵈ,f,ff² vg syrʰ goth arm geo Caesarius-Nazianzus Gregory-Nazianzus Ambrose Epiphanius Jerome Isidore Paschal Chronicle Theophylact ‖ sabbato mane itᵉ

² 1 {B} καὶ ἤσθιον τοὺς στάχυας ψώχοντες ταῖς χερσίν 𝔭⁴,⁷⁵ᵛⁱᵈ B (C* χερσὶν αὐτῶν) L 700 892 1230 1241 1253 1646 ‖ τοὺς στάχυας καὶ ἤσθιον ψώχοντες ταῖς χερσίν (ℵ omit τοὺς) A C³ K W X Δ Θ Π Ψ ƒ¹ ƒ¹³ 28 33 565 1009 1010 1079 1195 1216 1242 1344 1365 1546 2148 2174 Byz Lect itᵃᵘʳ,ff²,ˡ vg syrʰ goth ‖ τοὺς στάχυας καὶ ἤσθιον ψώχοντες ταῖς χερσὶν αὐτῶν 1071 itᵇ,ᶜ,rˡ Ambrose ‖ τοὺς στάχυας καὶ ψώχοντες ταῖς χερσὶν ἤσθιον D itᵈ,ᵉ,f (syrᵖ,ᵖᵃˡ) arm geo? ‖ τοὺς στάχυας ψώχοντες ταῖς χερσὶν καὶ ἤσθιον itᵃ,⁽q⁾ copˢᵃ,ᵇᵒ geo?

³ 2 {B} ἔξεστιν (see Mk 2.24) 𝔭⁴,⁷⁵ᵛⁱᵈ B (D τοῖς σάββασιν ὃ οὐκ ἔξεστιν) 700 itᵃ,ᵃᵘʳ,ᵇ,ᶜ,ᵈ,ᵉ,f,ff²,ˡ,rˡ vg copˢᵃ,ᵇᵒᵐˢˢ arm geo Diatessaronᵃ,ᵗ ‖ ἔξεστιν ποιεῖν (see Mt 12.2) ℵ A C K (L ἔξεστιν τοῖς σάββασιν ποιεῖν) W X Δ Θ Π Ψ ƒ¹ ƒ¹³ 28 33 565 892 1009 1010 1071 1079 1195 1216 1230 1241 1242 1253 1344 1365 1546 1646 2148 2174 Byz Lect itᵍ syrᵖ,ʰ,ᵖᵃˡ copᵇᵒ goth eth

⁴ 4 {C} καὶ ἔδωκεν τοῖς μετ' αὐτοῦ 𝔭⁴ᵛⁱᵈ B L W Ψ ƒ¹ itᵃ,ᵃᵘʳ,ᵇ,⁽ᶜ⁾,⁽ᵉ⁾,f,ff²,ˡ,q vg syrᵖ,ᵖᵃˡᵐˢ copˢᵃ goth arm eth? geo Irenaeusˡᵃᵗ ‖ καὶ ἔδωκεν καὶ τοῖς μετ' αὐτοῦ (see Mk 2.26) ℵ A D K X Δ Θ Π ƒ¹³ (28 καὶ τοὺς) 33 565 892

ᵃ ᵃ ᵃ **3-4** a none, a question, a question: (TR) WH Bov (Nes) (BF²) (TT) (Zür) (Luth) ‖ a none, a question, a major: NEB ‖ a minor, a major, a question: AV RV ASV (RSV) (Jer) Seg

---

1 διαπορεύεσθαι...χερσίν Dt 23.25   **2** Τί...σάββασιν Jn 5.10   **3-4** Οὐδὲ...τοῖς μετ' αὐτοῦ 1 Sm 21.1–6   **4** οὓς...ἱερεῖς Lv 24.5–9

μόνους τοὺς ἱερεῖς;[a] 5 καὶ ἔλεγεν αὐτοῖς, Κύριός ἐστιν τοῦ σαββάτου ὁ υἱὸς τοῦ ἀνθρώπου[5].

The Man with a Withered Hand
(Mt 12.9–14; Mk 3.1–6)

6 Ἐγένετο δὲ ἐν ἑτέρῳ σαββάτῳ εἰσελθεῖν αὐτὸν εἰς τὴν συναγωγὴν καὶ διδάσκειν· καὶ ἦν ἄνθρωπος ἐκεῖ καὶ ἡ χεὶρ αὐτοῦ ἡ δεξιὰ ἦν ξηρά· 7 παρετηροῦντο δὲ αὐτὸν οἱ γραμματεῖς καὶ οἱ Φαρισαῖοι εἰ ἐν τῷ σαββάτῳ θεραπεύει, ἵνα εὕρωσιν κατηγορεῖν αὐτοῦ. 8 αὐτὸς δὲ ᾔδει τοὺς διαλογισμοὺς αὐτῶν, εἶπεν δὲ τῷ ἀνδρὶ τῷ ξηρὰν ἔχοντι τὴν χεῖρα, Ἔγειρε καὶ στῆθι εἰς τὸ μέσον· καὶ ἀναστὰς ἔστη. 9 εἶπεν δὲ ὁ Ἰησοῦς πρὸς αὐτούς, Ἐπερωτῶ ὑμᾶς, εἰ ἔξεστιν τῷ σαββάτῳ ἀγαθοποιῆσαι ἢ κακοποιῆσαι, ψυχὴν σῶσαι ἢ ἀπολέσαι; 10 καὶ περιβλεψάμενος πάντας αὐτοὺς εἶπεν[6] αὐτῷ, Ἔκτεινον τὴν χεῖρά σου. ὁ δὲ ἐποίησεν, καὶ ἀπεκατεστάθη ἡ χεὶρ αὐτοῦ. 11 αὐτοὶ δὲ ἐπλήσθησαν ἀνοίας, καὶ διελάλουν πρὸς ἀλλήλους τί ἂν ποιήσαιεν τῷ Ἰησοῦ.

The Choosing of the Twelve
(Mt 10.1–4; Mk 3.13–19)

12 Ἐγένετο δὲ ἐν ταῖς ἡμέραις ταύταις ἐξελθεῖν αὐτὸν εἰς τὸ ὄρος προσεύξασθαι, καὶ ἦν διανυκτερεύων

1009 1010 1071 1079 1195 1216 1230 (1241 *add* οὖσι) 1242 1253 1344 1365 1546 1646 2148 2174 *Byz Lect* it[d] syr[h, pal mss] cop[bo] eth? ‖ *omit* 700

[5] 5 {C} τοῦ σαββάτου ὁ υἱὸς τοῦ ἀνθρώπου (*see* Mt 12.8) א B W 1241 syr[p, pal] cop[bo] Diatessaron ‖ καὶ τοῦ σαββάτου ὁ υἱὸς τοῦ ἀνθρώπου cop[sa, bo mss] eth ‖ ὁ υἱὸς τοῦ ἀνθρώπου καὶ τοῦ σαββάτου (*see* Mk 2.28) A (D) K L X Δ Θ Π Ψ *f*[1] *f*[13] 28 33 565 700 892 1009 1010 1071 1079 1195 1216 1230 1242 1253 1344 1365 1546 1646 2148 2174 *Byz Lect* it[a, aur, b, c, (d), e, f, (ff²), l, q, r1] vg syr[h] goth arm geo (Marcion) Epiphanius

[6] 10 {C} εἶπεν 𝔭[4] א A B K L W Δ Π Ψ 28 33 565 700 892 1009 1010 1079 1230 1241 1242[c] 1253 1344 1546 2148 2174 *Byz Lect* it[f] vg syr[p] cop[sa, bo] goth geo ‖ ἐν ὀργῇ εἶπεν (*see* Mk 3.5) X Θ *f*[1] 1071 1195 1216 1242* 1365 1646 it[(a), aur, b, c, (e), ff², l, q, r1] syr[h, pal] arm eth Diatessaron[a] ‖ μετ' ὀργῆς εἶπεν *f*[13] ‖ ἐν ὀργῇ λέγει D it[d]

7 παρετηροῦντο...Φαρισαῖοι Lk 14.1   8 αὐτὸς δὲ ᾔδει...αὐτῶν Lk 5.22; 9.47

---

priests." 5 And Jesus added, "The Son of Man is Lord of the Sabbath."

The Man with a Crippled Hand
(Also Matt. 12.9–14; Mark 3.1–6)

6 On another Sabbath Jesus went into a synagogue and taught. A man was there whose right hand was crippled. 7 Some teachers of the Law and Pharisees wanted some reason to accuse Jesus of doing wrong; so they watched him very closely to see if he would cure anyone on the Sabbath. 8 But Jesus knew their thoughts and said to the man with the crippled hand, "Stand up and come here to the front." The man got up and stood there. 9 Then Jesus said to them: "I ask you: What does our Law allow us to do on the Sabbath? To help or to harm? To save a man's life or destroy it?" 10 He looked around at them all, then said[1] to the man, "Stretch out your hand." He did so, and his hand became well again. 11 But they were filled with rage and began to discuss among themselves what they could do to Jesus.

Jesus Chooses the Twelve Apostles
(Also Matt. 10.1–4; Mark 3.13–19)

12 At that time Jesus went up a hill to pray, and spent the whole night there

---

[1] **10** said: *some mss.* add angrily

praying to God. ¹³ When day came he called his disciples to him and chose twelve of them, whom he named apostles: ¹⁴ Simon (whom he also named Peter) and his brother Andrew; James and John, Philip and Bartholomew, ¹⁵ Matthew and Thomas, James the son of Alphaeus and Simon (who was called the patriot), ¹⁶ Judas the son of James and Judas Iscariot, who became the traitor.

Jesus Teaches and Heals
(Also Matt. 4.23–25)

¹⁷ Coming down from the hill with them, Jesus stood on a level place with a large number of his disciples. A great crowd of people was there from all over Judea, and from Jerusalem, and from the coast cities of Tyre and Sidon; ¹⁸ they came to hear him and to be healed of their diseases. Those who were troubled by evil spirits also came and were healed. ¹⁹ All the people tried to touch him, for power was going out from him and healing them all.

Happiness and Sorrow
(Also Matt. 5.1–12)

²⁰ Jesus looked at his disciples and said: "Happy are you poor: the Kingdom of God is yours!

ἐν τῇ προσευχῇ τοῦ θεοῦ. **13** καὶ ὅτε ἐγένετο ἡμέρα, προσεφώνησεν τοὺς μαθητὰς αὐτοῦ, καὶ ἐκλεξάμενος ἀπ' αὐτῶν δώδεκα, οὓς καὶ ἀποστόλους ὠνόμασεν, **14** Σίμωνα, ὃν καὶ ὠνόμασεν Πέτρον, καὶ Ἀνδρέαν τὸν ἀδελφὸν αὐτοῦ, καὶ Ἰάκωβον καὶ Ἰωάννην καὶ Φίλιππον καὶ Βαρθολομαῖον **15** καὶ Ματθαῖον καὶ Θωμᾶν καὶ Ἰάκωβον Ἁλφαίου καὶ Σίμωνα τὸν καλούμενον Ζηλωτὴν **16** καὶ Ἰούδαν Ἰακώβου καὶ Ἰούδαν Ἰσκαριώθ⁷, ὃς ἐγένετο προδότης.ᵇ

Ministering to a Great Multitude
(Mt 4.23–25)

17 Καὶ καταβὰς μετ' αὐτῶν ἔστη ἐπὶ τόπου πεδινοῦ, καὶ ὄχλος πολὺς μαθητῶν αὐτοῦ, καὶ πλῆθος πολὺ τοῦ λαοῦ ἀπὸ πάσης τῆς Ἰουδαίας καὶ Ἰερουσαλὴμ καὶ τῆς παραλίου Τύρου καὶ Σιδῶνος, **18**ᶜ οἳ ἦλθον ἀκοῦσαι αὐτοῦ καὶ ἰαθῆναι ἀπὸ τῶν νόσων αὐτῶν· ᶜκαὶ οἱ ἐνοχλούμενοι ἀπὸ πνευμάτων ἀκαθάρτων ἐθεραπεύοντο. **19** καὶ πᾶς ὁ ὄχλος ἐζήτουν ἅπτεσθαι αὐτοῦ, ὅτι δύναμις παρ' αὐτοῦ ἐξήρχετο καὶ ἰᾶτο πάντας.

Blessings and Woes
(Mt 5.1–12)

20 Καὶ αὐτὸς ἐπάρας τοὺς ὀφθαλμοὺς αὐτοῦ εἰς τοὺς μαθητὰς αὐτοῦ ἔλεγεν,
    Μακάριοι οἱ πτωχοί,
        ὅτι ὑμετέρα ἐστὶν ἡ βασιλεία τοῦ θεοῦ.

---

⁷ 16 {C} Ἰσκαριώθ 𝔭⁴·⁷⁵ ℵ* B L 33 (itᵈ *Inscarioth*) Marcion ‖ Ἰσκαριώτην ℵᶜ A K W X Δ Θ Π Ψ f¹ f¹³ 28 565 700 892 1009 1010 1071 1079 1195 1216 1230 1241 1242 1253 1344 1365 1546 1646 2148 2174 *Byz Lect* vgᶜˡ syrʰ copˢᵃ·ᵇᵒ goth geo¹ Marcion Basil Epiphanius ‖ Σκαριώθ Dᵍʳ itᵃᵘʳ·⁽ᶜ⁾·ᵉ·ᶠ·ᶠᶠ²·ˡ·q vgʷʷ (syrˢ·ᵖ arm *Scariota*, geo² *Scarioten*) ‖ *omit* itᵃ·ᵇ·ʳˡ

ᵇ **16** *b major:* TR AV RSV NEB TT Zür Luth Jer Seg ‖ *b minor:* WH Bov Nes BF² RV ASV
ᶜᶜ **17-18** *c number 18, c no number:* TRᵉᵈ WH Bov Nes BF² TT Zür Luth Jer ‖ *c no number, c number 18:* TRᵉᵈ AV RV ASV RSV NEB Seg

13 ἐκλεξάμενος...δώδεκα Jn 6.70   **14-15** Σίμωνα...Ἰάκωβον Ac 1.13

21 μακάριοι οἱ πεινῶντες νῦν,
   ὅτι χορτασθήσεσθε.
   μακάριοι οἱ κλαίοντες νῦν,
   ὅτι γελάσετε.

22 μακάριοί ἐστε ὅταν μισήσωσιν ὑμᾶς οἱ ἄνθρωποι, καὶ
ὅταν ἀφορίσωσιν ὑμᾶς καὶ ὀνειδίσωσιν καὶ ἐκβάλωσιν τὸ
ὄνομα ὑμῶν ὡς πονηρὸν ἕνεκα τοῦ υἱοῦ τοῦ ἀνθρώπου·
23 χάρητε ἐν ἐκείνῃ τῇ ἡμέρᾳ καὶ σκιρτήσατε, ἰδοὺ γὰρ
ὁ μισθὸς ὑμῶν πολὺς ἐν τῷ οὐρανῷ· κατὰ τὰ αὐτὰ γὰρ
ἐποίουν τοῖς προφήταις οἱ πατέρες αὐτῶν.

24 Πλὴν οὐαὶ ὑμῖν τοῖς πλουσίοις,
   ὅτι ἀπέχετε τὴν παράκλησιν ὑμῶν.

25 οὐαὶ ὑμῖν, οἱ ἐμπεπλησμένοι νῦν,
   ὅτι πεινάσετε.
   οὐαί, οἱ γελῶντες νῦν,
   ὅτι πενθήσετε καὶ κλαύσετε.

26 οὐαὶ ὅταν ὑμᾶς καλῶς εἴπωσιν πάντες οἱ ἄνθρωποι[8],
κατὰ τὰ αὐτὰ γὰρ ἐποίουν τοῖς ψευδοπροφήταις οἱ
πατέρες αὐτῶν.

Love for Enemies
(Mt 5.38–48; 7.12a)

27 Ἀλλὰ ὑμῖν λέγω τοῖς ἀκούουσιν, ἀγαπᾶτε τοὺς
ἐχθροὺς ὑμῶν, καλῶς ποιεῖτε τοῖς μισοῦσιν ὑμᾶς, 28 εὐλογεῖτε τοὺς καταρωμένους ὑμᾶς, προσεύχεσθε περὶ τῶν
ἐπηρεαζόντων ὑμᾶς. 29 τῷ τύπτοντί σε ἐπὶ τὴν σιαγόνα
πάρεχε καὶ τὴν ἄλλην, καὶ ἀπὸ τοῦ αἴροντός σου τὸ

---

[8] 26 {C} πάντες οἱ ἄνθρωποι 𝔓⁷⁵ A B K P X Θ Ξ Π Ψ f¹ (W f¹³ omit οἱ)
33 565 700 892ᵐᵍ 1009 1071 1079 1195 1230 1241 (1253 πάντα) 1365 1546 1646
Byzᵖᵗ Lect l⁶⁹⁸,ᵐ,¹⁸⁵⁸,ᵐ,¹¹²⁷⁸,ᵐ itᵃ,ᵃᵘʳ,ᵇ,ᶜ,ᵉ,f,ff2,l,q vgww syrʰ copˢᵃ?ᵇᵒ? goth arm
geo Basil Chrysostom ‖ οἱ ἄνθρωποι πάντες ℵ copˢᵃ?ᵇᵒ? Irenaeusˡᵃᵗ ‖ οἱ
ἄνθρωποι D L Δ 28 892* 1010 1216 1242 1344 2174 Byzᵖᵗ l⁷⁶,²²⁶ itᵈ vgᶜˡ syrˢ,ᵖ
eth Marcion Diatessaron Tertullian Macarius

21 οἱ...χορτασθήσεσθε Jr 31.25   οἱ κλαίοντες...γελάσετε Ps 126.5–6; Is 61.3; Re 7.16–17
22 Jn 15.19; 16.2; 1 Pe 4.14   23 κατὰ τὰ αὐτὰ...αὐτῶν 2 Chr 36.16; Mt 23.30–31; Lk 11.47
24 οὐαὶ...πλουσίοις Jas 5.1   26 οὐαὶ...ἄνθρωποι Jas 4.4   27 ἀγαπᾶτε...ὑμῶν Pr 25.21;
Ro 12.20   28 εὐλογεῖτε τοὺς καταρωμένους ὑμᾶς Ro 12.14   29 τῷ τύπτοντι...ἄλλην
Jn 18.22–23; Ac 23.3

---

21 "Happy are you who are hungry
now:
   you will be filled!
"Happy are you who weep now:
   you will laugh!

22 "Happy are you when men hate you,
and reject you, and insult you, and say
that you are evil, because of the Son of
Man! 23 Be happy when that happens,
and dance for joy, for a great reward is
kept for you in heaven. For their ancestors did the very same things to the
prophets.

24 "But how terrible for you who are
rich now:
   you have had your easy life!
25 "How terrible for you who are full
now:
   you will go hungry!
"How terrible for you who laugh now:
   you will mourn and weep!

26 "How terrible when all men speak
well of you; for their ancestors said the
very same things to the false prophets."

Love for Enemies
(Also Matt. 5.38–48; 7.12a)

27 "But I tell you who hear me: Love
your enemies, do good to those who hate
you, 28 bless those who curse you, and
pray for those who mistreat you. 29 If
anyone hits you on the cheek, let him
hit the other one too; if someone takes

your coat, let him have your shirt as well. ³⁰ Give to everyone who asks you for something, and when someone takes what is yours, do not ask for it back. ³¹ Do for others just what you want them to do for you.

³² "If you love only the people who love you, why should you expect a blessing? Even sinners love those who love them! ³³ And if you do good only to those who do good to you, why should you expect a blessing? Even sinners do that! ³⁴ And if you lend only to those from whom you hope to get it back, why should you expect a blessing? Even sinners lend to sinners, to get back the same amount! ³⁵ No! Love your enemies and do good to them; lend and expect nothing back. You will have a great reward, and you will be sons of the Most High God. For he is good to the ungrateful and the wicked. ³⁶ Be merciful, just as your Father is merciful."

Judging Others
(Also Matt. 7.1–5)

³⁷ "Do not judge others, and God will not judge you; do not condemn others, and God will not condemn you; forgive

ἱμάτιον καὶ τὸν χιτῶνα μὴ κωλύσῃς. 30 παντὶ αἰτοῦντί σε δίδου, καὶ ἀπὸ τοῦ αἴροντος τὰ σὰ μὴ ἀπαίτει. 31 καὶ καθὼς θέλετε ἵνα ποιῶσιν ὑμῖν οἱ ἄνθρωποι, ποιεῖτε⁹ αὐτοῖς ὁμοίως. 32 καὶ εἰ ἀγαπᾶτε τοὺς ἀγαπῶντας ὑμᾶς, ποία ὑμῖν χάρις ἐστίν; καὶ γὰρ οἱ ἁμαρτωλοὶ τοὺς ἀγαπῶντας αὐτοὺς ἀγαπῶσιν. 33 καὶ [γὰρ] ἐὰν ἀγαθοποιῆτε τοὺς ἀγαθοποιοῦντας ὑμᾶς, ποία ὑμῖν χάρις ἐστίν; καὶ οἱ ἁμαρτωλοὶ τὸ αὐτὸ ποιοῦσιν. 34 καὶ ἐὰν δανίσητε παρ' ὧν ἐλπίζετε λαβεῖν, ποία ὑμῖν χάρις [ἐστίν]; καὶ ἁμαρτωλοὶ ἁμαρτωλοῖς δανείζουσιν ἵνα ἀπολάβωσιν τὰ ἴσα. 35 πλὴν ἀγαπᾶτε τοὺς ἐχθροὺς ὑμῶν καὶ ἀγαθοποιεῖτε καὶ δανείζετε μηδὲν¹⁰ ἀπελπίζοντες· καὶ ἔσται ὁ μισθὸς ὑμῶν πολύς, καὶ ἔσεσθε υἱοὶ ὑψίστου, ὅτι αὐτὸς χρηστός ἐστιν ἐπὶ τοὺς ἀχαρίστους καὶ πονηρούς. 36 Γίνεσθε οἰκτίρμονες καθὼς [καὶ] ὁ πατὴρ ὑμῶν οἰκτίρμων ἐστίν. ᵈ

Judging Others
(Mt 7.1–5)

37 Καὶ μὴ κρίνετε, καὶ οὐ μὴ κριθῆτε· καὶ μὴ καταδικάζετε, καὶ οὐ μὴ καταδικασθῆτε. ἀπολύετε, καὶ

---

⁹ 31 {C} ποιεῖτε 𝔭⁷⁵ᵛⁱᵈ B 700 1241 itᵃ,ᵃᵘʳ,ff²,l,rl syrᵖ Irenaeusᵍʳ,ˡᵃᵗ Clement ‖ καλῶς ποιεῖτε syrˢ ‖ ὑμεῖς ποιεῖτε 565 itᵉ,q ‖ καὶ ὑμεῖς ποιεῖτε (see Mt 7.12) ℵ A D K L P W X Δ Θ Π Ψ f¹ f¹³ 28 33 (892 ὁμοίως ποιεῖτε) 1009 1010 1071 1079 1195 1216 1230 1242 1253 1344 1365 1546 1646 2148 2174 Byz Lect itᶜ,ᵈ,f vg syrʰ,⁽ᵖᵃˡ⁾ goth geo Marcion Tertullian ‖ ποιεῖτε καὶ ὑμεῖς itᵇ copˢᵃ?ᵇᵒ? arm Clement

¹⁰ 35 {C} μηδέν A B D K L P Xᶜ Δ Θ Π² Ψ f¹ f¹³· 28 33 565 700 892 1009 1010 1195 1216 1230 1241 1242 1253 1344 1365 1646 2148 2174 Byz Lect itᵃ,ᵃᵘʳ, b,(c),d,e,f,ff²,l,q,rl (vg) copˢᵃ,ᵇᵒ goth (arm) geo² Ambrose ‖ μηδένα ℵ W X* Ξ Π* 1071 1079 1546 syrˢ,ᵖ,ʰ,ᵖᵃˡ ‖ omit geo¹

ᵈ 36 d major: TR Bov Nes BF² AV RV ASV RSV NEB TT Luth Jer Seg ‖ d minor: WH ‖ d exclamation: Zür

---

31 Mt 7.12   35 δανείζετε μηδὲν ἀπελπίζοντες Lv 25.35–36   37 ἀπολύετε, καὶ ἀπολυθήσεσθε Mt 6.14

ἀπολυθήσεσθε· **38** δίδοτε, καὶ δοθήσεται ὑμῖν· μέτρον καλὸν πεπιεσμένον σεσαλευμένον ὑπερεκχυννόμενον δώσουσιν εἰς τὸν κόλπον ὑμῶν· ᾧ γὰρ μέτρῳ[11] μετρεῖτε ἀντιμετρηθήσεται ὑμῖν. **39** Εἶπεν δὲ καὶ παραβολὴν αὐτοῖς· Μήτι δύναται τυφλὸς τυφλὸν ὁδηγεῖν; οὐχὶ ἀμφότεροι εἰς βόθυνον ἐμπεσοῦνται; **40** οὐκ ἔστιν μαθητὴς ὑπὲρ τὸν διδάσκαλον, κατηρτισμένος δὲ πᾶς ἔσται ὡς ὁ διδάσκαλος αὐτοῦ. **41** Τί δὲ βλέπεις τὸ κάρφος τὸ ἐν τῷ ὀφθαλμῷ τοῦ ἀδελφοῦ σου, τὴν δὲ δοκὸν τὴν ἐν τῷ ἰδίῳ ὀφθαλμῷ οὐ κατανοεῖς; **42** πῶς[12] δύνασαι λέγειν τῷ ἀδελφῷ σου, Ἀδελφέ, ἄφες ἐκβάλω τὸ κάρφος τὸ ἐν τῷ ὀφθαλμῷ σου, αὐτὸς τὴν ἐν τῷ ὀφθαλμῷ σου δοκὸν οὐ βλέπων; ὑποκριτά, ἔκβαλε πρῶτον τὴν δοκὸν ἐκ τοῦ ὀφθαλμοῦ σου, καὶ τότε διαβλέψεις τὸ κάρφος τὸ ἐν τῷ ὀφθαλμῷ τοῦ ἀδελφοῦ σου ἐκβαλεῖν.

A Tree Known by Its Fruit
(Mt 7.17–20; 12.34b–35)

43 Οὐ γάρ ἐστιν δένδρον καλὸν ποιοῦν καρπὸν σαπρόν, οὐδὲ πάλιν δένδρον σαπρὸν ποιοῦν καρπὸν καλόν. **44** ἕκαστον γὰρ δένδρον ἐκ τοῦ ἰδίου καρποῦ γινώσκεται· οὐ γὰρ ἐξ ἀκανθῶν συλλέγουσιν σῦκα, οὐδὲ ἐκ βάτου σταφυλὴν τρυγῶσιν. **45** ὁ ἀγαθὸς ἄνθρωπος ἐκ τοῦ ἀγαθοῦ θησαυροῦ τῆς καρδίας προφέρει τὸ ἀγαθόν, καὶ

---

[11] **38** {C} ᾧ γὰρ μέτρῳ ℵ B D L W Ξ 33 892 1241 it^{c,d,e} syr^p cop^{sa,bo} (eth) Clement Origen^{gr,lat} Eusebius Augustine ∥ ᾧ μέτρῳ syr^s Hippolytus Origen ∥ ᾧ γὰρ μέτρῳ ᾧ f^1 ∥ τῷ γὰρ μέτρῳ ᾧ X 1216 1230 1253 ∥ τῷ γὰρ αὐτῷ μέτρῳ ᾧ A C K P Δ Π Ψ 28 565 1009 1010 1071 1079 1195 1242 1344 1365 1546 1646 2148 2174 Byz Lect it^f vg syr^h goth Tertullian ∥ τῷ αὐτῷ μέτρῳ ᾧ p^{45vid} Θ f^{13} 700 l^{34} it^{a,aur,b,ff2,l,q,r1} arm Diatessaron Tertullian

[12] **42** {C} πῶς p^{75vid} B it^{e,ff2} syr^s cop^{boms} ∥ ἢ πῶς (see Mt 7.4) A C^{vid} D K L P W X Δ Θ Ξ Π Ψ f^1 f^{13} 28 33 565 700 1009 1010 1071 1079 1195 1216 1230 1241 1242 1253 1344 1546 1646 2148 2174 Byz Lect it^{a,aur,b,c,d,f,l,q,r1} vg^{cl} syr^{p,h} cop^{sa,bo} goth arm geo Diatessaron ∥ πῶς δέ ℵ 892 ∥ καὶ πῶς 1365 vg^{ww} eth

38 ᾧ γὰρ μέτρῳ...ὑμῖν Mk 4.24   **39** Μήτι...ἐμπεσοῦνται Mt 15.14; 23.16, 24
40 Mt 10.24–25; Jn 13.16; 15.20   **44** ἕκαστον...γινώσκεται Mt 12.33

---

others, and God will forgive you. **38** Give to others, and God will give to you: you will receive a full measure, a generous helping, poured into your hands — all that you can hold. The measure you use for others is the one God will use for you.''

39 And Jesus told them this parable: "One blind man cannot lead another one; if he does, both will fall into a ditch. **40** No pupil is greater than his teacher; but every pupil, when he has completed his training, will be like his teacher.

41 "Why do you look at the speck in your brother's eye, but pay no attention to the log in your own eye? **42** How can you say to your brother, 'Please, brother, let me take that speck out of your eye,' yet not even see the log in your own eye? You impostor! Take the log out of your own eye first, and then you will be able to see and take the speck out of your brother's eye."

A Tree and its Fruit
(Also Matt. 7.16–20; 12.33–35)

43 "A healthy tree does not bear bad fruit, nor does a poor tree bear good fruit. **44** Every tree is known by the fruit it bears; you do not pick figs from thorn bushes, or gather grapes from bramble bushes. **45** A good man brings good out of the treasure of good things in his heart; a bad man brings bad out of his treasure of bad things. For a man's mouth speaks what his heart is full of."

The Two House Builders
(Also Matt. 7.24–27)

⁴⁶ "Why do you call me, 'Lord, Lord,' and don't do what I tell you? ⁴⁷ Everyone who comes to me, and listens to my words, and obeys them — I will show you what he is like. ⁴⁸ He is like a man who built a house: he dug deep and laid the foundation on the rock. The river flooded over and hit that house but it could not shake it, because the house had been well built. ⁴⁹ But the one who hears my words and does not obey them is like a man who built a house on the ground without laying a foundation; when the flood hit that house it fell at once — what a terrible crash that was!"

Jesus Heals a Roman Officer's Servant
(Also Matt. 8.5–13)

7 When Jesus had finished saying all these things to the people, he went to Capernaum. ² A Roman officer there had a servant who was very dear to him; the man was sick and about to die. ³ When the officer heard about Jesus, he sent to him some Jewish elders to ask him to come and heal his servant. ⁴ They came to Jesus and begged him

ὁ πονηρὸς ἐκ τοῦ πονηροῦ προφέρει τὸ πονηρόν· ἐκ γὰρ περισσεύματος καρδίας λαλεῖ τὸ στόμα αὐτοῦ.

The Two Foundations
(Mt 7.24–27)

46 Τί δέ με καλεῖτε, Κύριε κύριε, καὶ οὐ ποιεῖτε ἃ λέγω; **47** πᾶς ὁ ἐρχόμενος πρός με καὶ ἀκούων μου τῶν λόγων καὶ ποιῶν αὐτούς, ὑποδείξω ὑμῖν τίνι ἐστὶν ὅμοιος· **48** ὅμοιός ἐστιν ἀνθρώπῳ οἰκοδομοῦντι οἰκίαν ὃς ἔσκαψεν καὶ ἐβάθυνεν καὶ ἔθηκεν θεμέλιον ἐπὶ τὴν πέτραν· πλημμύρης δὲ γενομένης προσέρηξεν ὁ ποταμὸς τῇ οἰκίᾳ ἐκείνῃ, καὶ οὐκ ἴσχυσεν σαλεῦσαι αὐτὴν διὰ τὸ καλῶς οἰκοδομῆσθαι αὐτήν¹³. **49** ὁ δὲ ἀκούσας καὶ μὴ ποιήσας ὅμοιός ἐστιν ἀνθρώπῳ οἰκοδομήσαντι οἰκίαν ἐπὶ τὴν γῆν χωρὶς θεμελίου, ᾗ προσέρηξεν ὁ ποταμός, καὶ εὐθὺς συνέπεσεν, καὶ ἐγένετο τὸ ῥῆγμα τῆς οἰκίας ἐκείνης μέγα.

The Healing of a Centurion's Servant
(Mt 8.5–13; Jn 4.43–54)

7 Ἐπειδὴ ἐπλήρωσεν πάντα τὰ ῥήματα αὐτοῦ εἰς τὰς ἀκοὰς τοῦ λαοῦ, εἰσῆλθεν εἰς Καφαρναούμ. **2** Ἑκατοντάρχου δέ τινος δοῦλος κακῶς ἔχων ἤμελλεν τελευτᾶν, ὃς ἦν αὐτῷ ἔντιμος. **3** ἀκούσας δὲ περὶ τοῦ Ἰησοῦ ἀπέστειλεν πρὸς αὐτὸν πρεσβυτέρους τῶν Ἰουδαίων, ἐρωτῶν αὐτὸν ὅπως ἐλθὼν διασώσῃ τὸν δοῦλον αὐτοῦ. **4** οἱ δὲ παραγενόμενοι πρὸς τὸν Ἰησοῦν παρεκάλουν

---

¹³ **48** {B} διὰ τὸ καλῶς οἰκοδομῆσθαι αὐτήν 𝔭⁷⁵ᵛⁱᵈ ℵ B L W Ξ 33 892 1241 syrʰᵐᵍ copˢᵃ·ᵇᵒ Cyril ∥ τεθεμελίωτο γὰρ ἐπὶ τὴν πέτραν (see Mt 7.25) A C D K X Δ Θ Π Ψ f¹ f¹³ 28 565 1009 1010 1071 1079 1195 1216 1230 1242 1253 1344 1365 1546 1646 2148 2174 *Byz Lect* itᵃ·ᵃᵘʳ·ᵇ·ᶜ·ᵈ·ᵉ·f·ff²·ˡ·q·ʳˡ vg syrᵖ·ʰ copᵇᵒᵐˢˢ goth arm geo Diatessaron Origen ∥ *omit* 𝔭⁴⁵ᵛⁱᵈ 700 syrˢ

46 Mal 1.6; Mt 7.21
7 2 ἤμελλεν τελευτᾶν Jn 4.47

αὐτὸν σπουδαίως, λέγοντες ὅτι ᾿Αξιός ἐστιν ᾧ παρέξῃ τοῦτο, 5 ἀγαπᾷ γὰρ τὸ ἔθνος ἡμῶν καὶ τὴν συναγωγὴν αὐτὸς ᾠκοδόμησεν ἡμῖν. 6 ὁ δὲ ᾿Ιησοῦς ἐπορεύετο σὺν αὐτοῖς. ἤδη δὲ αὐτοῦ οὐ μακρὰν ἀπέχοντος ἀπὸ τῆς οἰκίας ἔπεμψεν φίλους ὁ ἑκατοντάρχης λέγων αὐτῷ, Κύριε, μὴ σκύλλου, οὐ γὰρ ἱκανός εἰμι ἵνα ὑπὸ τὴν στέγην μου εἰσέλθῃς· 7 διὸ οὐδὲ ἐμαυτὸν ἠξίωσα πρὸς σὲ ἐλθεῖν· ἀλλὰ εἰπὲ λόγῳ, καὶ ἰαθήτω[1] ὁ παῖς μου. 8 καὶ γὰρ ἐγὼ ἄνθρωπός εἰμι ὑπὸ ἐξουσίαν τασσόμενος, ἔχων ὑπ᾿ ἐμαυτὸν στρατιώτας, καὶ λέγω τούτῳ, Πορεύθητι, καὶ πορεύεται, καὶ ἄλλῳ, ῎Ερχου, καὶ ἔρχεται, καὶ τῷ δούλῳ μου, Ποίησον τοῦτο, καὶ ποιεῖ. 9 ἀκούσας δὲ ταῦτα ὁ ᾿Ιησοῦς ἐθαύμασεν αὐτόν, καὶ στραφεὶς τῷ ἀκολουθοῦντι αὐτῷ ὄχλῳ εἶπεν, Λέγω ὑμῖν, οὐδὲ ἐν τῷ ᾿Ισραὴλ τοσαύτην πίστιν εὗρον. 10 καὶ ὑποστρέψαντες εἰς τὸν οἶκον οἱ πεμφθέντες εὗρον τὸν δοῦλον[2] ὑγιαίνοντα.

The Raising of the Widow's Son at Nain

11 Καὶ ἐγένετο ἐν τῷ ἑξῆς[3] ἐπορεύθη εἰς πόλιν καλουμένην Ναΐν, καὶ συνεπορεύοντο αὐτῷ οἱ μαθηταὶ αὐτοῦ[4]

---

[1] 7 {C} ἰαθήτω p75 B L 1241 copsa,bomss ‖ ἰαθήσεται (see Mt 8.8) ℵ A C D K W X Δ Θ Π Ψ f1 f13 28 33 565 700 892 1009 1010 1071 1079 1195 1216 1230 1242 1253 1344 1365 1546 1646 2148 2174 Byz Lect ita,aur,b,c,d,e,f,ff2,l,q,r1 vg syrs,p,h copbo goth arm (eth) geo

[2] 10 {C} δοῦλον p75 ℵ B L W f1 700 892* 1241 ita,aur,b,c,e,ff2,l,q,r1 syrs,pal copsa,bo eth? geo Cyril ‖ ἀσθενοῦντα D itd ‖ ἀσθενοῦντα δοῦλον A C K X Δ Θ Π Ψ f13 28 33 565 892mg 1009 1010 1071 1079 1195 1216 1230 1242 1253 1344 1365 1546 1646 2148 2174 Byz Lect itf vg syrp,h goth arm eth? Diatessarona,s,t

[3] 11 {C} τῷ ἑξῆς p75 ℵc A B L X Δ Θ Ψ f13 33 700 1010 1216 1241 1242 1344 1646 2148 2174 ita,aur,b,ff2,l,q,r1 vg syrs,pal copsa geo ‖ τῇ ἑξῆς ℵ* C D K W Π 28 565 892 1009 1071 1079 1195 1230 1253 1365 1546 Byz itc,d,e,f syrp,h copbo goth arm eth ‖ τῷ [sic] and ἐπορεύετο for ἐπορεύθη f1

[4] 11 {C} αὐτοῦ p75 ℵ B D L W Ξ 1241 l60,b47 ita,aur,d,e,f,ff2,l,r1 vg syrs,p,pal copsa,bo arm geo Diatessarona,i,n ‖ ἱκανοί f1 1009 ‖ αὐτοῦ ἱκανοί A C K X Δ Θ Π Ψ f13 28 33 565 700 892 1010 1071 1079 1195 1216 1230 1242 1253 1344 1365 1546 1646 2148 2174 Byz Lect itb,c,q syrh goth

---

earnestly: "This man really deserves your help. [5] He loves our people and he himself built a synagogue for us." [6] So Jesus went with them. He was not far from the house when the officer sent friends to tell him: "Sir, don't trouble yourself. I do not deserve to have you come into my house, [7] neither do I consider myself worthy to come to you in person. Just give the order and my servant will get well. [8] I, too, am a man placed under the authority of superior officers, and I have soldiers under me. I order this one, 'Go!' and he goes; I order that one, 'Come!' and he comes; and I order my slave, 'Do this!' and he does it." [9] Jesus was surprised when he heard this; he turned around and said to the crowd following him, "I have never found such faith as this, I tell you, not even in Israel!" [10] The messengers went back to the officer's house and found his servant well.

Jesus Raises a Widow's Son

[11] Soon afterward Jesus went to a town named Nain; his disciples and a large

crowd went with him. ¹² Just as he arrived at the gate of the town, a funeral procession was coming out. The dead man was the only son of a woman who was a widow, and a large crowd from the city was with her. ¹³ When the Lord saw her his heart was filled with pity for her and he said to her, "Don't cry." ¹⁴ Then he walked over and touched the coffin, and the men carrying it stopped. Jesus said, "Young man! Get up, I tell you!" ¹⁵ The dead man sat up and began to talk, and Jesus gave him back to his mother. ¹⁶ Everyone was filled with fear, and they praised God: "A great prophet has appeared among us!" and, "God has come to save his people!" ¹⁷ This news about Jesus went out through all of Judea and the surrounding territory.

The Messengers from John the Baptist
(Also Matt. 11.2–19)

¹⁸ John's disciples told him about all these things. John called two of them to him ¹⁹ and sent them to the Lord to ask him, "Are you the one John said was going to come, or should we expect someone else?" ²⁰ When they came to Jesus they said, "John the Baptist sent us to ask, 'Are you the one he said was going to come, or should we expect someone else?'" ²¹ At that very time Jesus healed many people from their sicknesses, diseases, and evil spirits, and

καὶ ὄχλος πολύς. **12** ὡς δὲ ἤγγισεν τῇ πύλῃ τῆς πόλεως, καὶ ἰδοὺ ἐξεκομίζετο τεθνηκὼς μονογενὴς υἱὸς τῇ μητρὶ αὐτοῦ, καὶ αὐτὴ ἦν χήρα, καὶ ὄχλος τῆς πόλεως ἱκανὸς ἦν σὺν αὐτῇ. **13** καὶ ἰδὼν αὐτὴν ὁ κύριος ἐσπλαγχνίσθη ἐπ᾿ αὐτῇ καὶ εἶπεν αὐτῇ, Μὴ κλαῖε. **14** καὶ προσελθὼν ἥψατο τῆς σοροῦ, οἱ δὲ βαστάζοντες ἔστησαν, καὶ εἶπεν, Νεανίσκε, σοὶ λέγω, ἐγέρθητι. **15** καὶ ἀνεκάθισεν ὁ νεκρὸς καὶ ἤρξατο λαλεῖν, καὶ ἔδωκεν αὐτὸν τῇ μητρὶ αὐτοῦ. **16** ἔλαβεν δὲ φόβος πάντας, καὶ ἐδόξαζον τὸν θεὸν λέγοντες ὅτι Προφήτης μέγας ἠγέρθη ἐν ἡμῖν, καὶ ὅτι Ἐπεσκέψατο ὁ θεὸς τὸν λαὸν αὐτοῦ. **17** καὶ ἐξῆλθεν ὁ λόγος οὗτος ἐν ὅλῃ τῇ Ἰουδαίᾳ περὶ αὐτοῦ καὶ πάσῃ τῇ περιχώρῳ.

The Messengers from John the Baptist
(Mt 11.2–19)

18 Καὶ ἀπήγγειλαν Ἰωάννῃ οἱ μαθηταὶ αὐτοῦ περὶ πάντων τούτων. ᵃκαὶ προσκαλεσάμενος δύο τινὰς τῶν μαθητῶν αὐτοῦ ὁ Ἰωάννης **19**ᵃ ἔπεμψεν πρὸς τὸν κύριον⁵ λέγων, Σὺ εἶ ὁ ἐρχόμενος ἢ ἄλλον προσδοκῶμεν; **20** παραγενόμενοι δὲ πρὸς αὐτὸν οἱ ἄνδρες εἶπαν, Ἰωάννης ὁ βαπτιστὴς ἀπέστειλεν ἡμᾶς πρὸς σὲ λέγων, Σὺ εἶ ὁ ἐρχόμενος ἢ ἄλλον προσδοκῶμεν; **21** ἐν ἐκείνῃ τῇ ὥρᾳ ἐθεράπευσεν πολλοὺς ἀπὸ νόσων καὶ μαστίγων καὶ πνευμάτων πονηρῶν, καὶ τυφλοῖς πολλοῖς ἐχαρίσατο

⁵ **19** {C} κύριον B L Ξ ƒ¹³ 33 itᵃ,ff² vgʷʷ copˢᵃ,ᵇᵒᵐˢˢ arm (eth) ‖ Ἰησοῦν ℵ A K W X Δ Θ Π Ψ ƒ¹ 28 565 700 892 1009 1010 1071 1079 1195 1216 1230 1241 1242 1253 1344 1365 1546 1646 2148 2174 *Byz Lect* itᵃᵘʳ,ᵇ,ᶜ,ᶠ,ˡ, q,rˡ vgᶜˡ syrˢ,ᵖ,ʰ copᵇᵒ goth geo Diatessaron Cyril ‖ κύριον Ἰησοῦν syrᵖᵃˡ

ᵃ ᵃ **18–19** *a* no number, *a* number 19: TRᵉᵈ WH Bov Nes BF² TT Zür Luth Jer ‖ *a* number 19, *a* no number: TRᵉᵈ AV RV ASV RSV NEB Seg

12 τεθνηκὼς μονογενής 1 Kgs 17.17; Lk 8.42   **13** Μὴ κλαῖε Lk 8.52   **14** Νεανίσκε... ἐγέρθητι Lk 8.54   **15** ἔδωκεν...αὐτοῦ 1 Kgs 17.23; 2 Kgs 4.36   **16** Ἐπεσκέψατο...αὐτοῦ Lk 1.68; 19.44   **19** ὁ ἐρχόμενος Ps 40.7; Mal 3.1; Re 1.4, 8; 4.8

βλέπειν. **22** καὶ ἀποκριθεὶς εἶπεν αὐτοῖς, Πορευθέντες ἀπαγγείλατε Ἰωάννῃ ἃ εἴδετε καὶ ἠκούσατε· **τυφλοὶ ἀναβλέπουσιν**, χωλοὶ περιπατοῦσιν, λεπροὶ καθαρίζονται καὶ κωφοὶ ἀκούουσιν, νεκροὶ ἐγείρονται, **πτωχοὶ εὐαγγελίζονται**· **23** καὶ μακάριός ἐστιν ὃς ἐὰν μὴ σκανδαλισθῇ ἐν ἐμοί. **24** Ἀπελθόντων δὲ τῶν ἀγγέλων Ἰωάννου ἤρξατο λέγειν πρὸς τοὺς ὄχλους περὶ Ἰωάννου, Τί ἐξήλθατε εἰς τὴν ἔρημον[b] θεάσασθαι;[b] κάλαμον ὑπὸ ἀνέμου σαλευόμενον; **25** ἀλλὰ τί ἐξήλθατε[c] ἰδεῖν;[c] ἄνθρωπον ἐν μαλακοῖς ἱματίοις ἠμφιεσμένον; ἰδοὺ οἱ ἐν ἱματισμῷ ἐνδόξῳ καὶ τρυφῇ ὑπάρχοντες ἐν τοῖς βασιλείοις εἰσίν. **26** ἀλλὰ τί ἐξήλθατε[d] ἰδεῖν;[d] προφήτην;[d] ναί, λέγω ὑμῖν, καὶ περισσότερον προφήτου. **27** οὗτός ἐστιν περὶ οὗ γέγραπται,

**Ἰδοὺ ἀποστέλλω τὸν ἄγγελόν μου πρὸ προσώπου σου,
ὃς κατασκευάσει τὴν ὁδόν** σου **ἔμπροσθέν** σου.

28 λέγω[6] ὑμῖν, μείζων ἐν γεννητοῖς γυναικῶν[7] Ἰωάννου οὐδείς ἐστιν· ὁ δὲ μικρότερος ἐν τῇ βασιλείᾳ τοῦ θεοῦ

---

[6] **28** {C} λέγω 𝔭75vid B Ψ 33 700 1241 *Lect* syrs,p copsa,bo geo ∥ ἀμὴν λέγω (*see* Mt 11.11) ℵ L X Ξ 892 *l*1578 syrpal arm eth Diatessarona Cyril ∥ λέγω δέ D W *f*13 *l*211 ita,aur,b,c,d,e,ff2,l,rl ∥ λέγω γάρ A K Δ Θ Π *f*1 28 565 1009 1010 1071 1079 1195 1216 1230 1242 1253 1344 1365 1546 1646 2148 2174 *Byz l*1508,m,184,299,854 itf,q vg syrh goth

[7] **28** {C} γυναικῶν (*see* Mt 11.11) 𝔭75 ℵ B K L W X Ξ Π *f*1 33 565 1079 1242 1365 1546 2174 ita,b,c,e,ff2,l syrhmg,pal copsa,bo eth Diatessarona,esyr,i,n Origen ∥ γυναικῶν προφήτης A (D) Δ Θ Ψ *f*13 28 700 (892 γυναικῶν Ἰωάννου προφήτης) 1009 1010 1071 1195 1216 1230 1241 1253 1344 1646 2148 *Byz Lect* itaur,(d),f,q,rl vg (syrs,p,h) goth arm geo Marcion (Clement) Ambrosiaster Ambrose

---

b b **24** *b* none, *b* question: TR WH Bov Nes BF2 AV RV ASV RSV NEB TT Zür Luth Jer Seg ∥ *b* question, *b* none

c c **25** *c* none, *c* question: TR WH Bov Nes BF2 AV RV ASV RSV NEB TT Zür Luth Jer Seg ∥ *c* question, *c* none

d d d **26** *d* none, *d* question, *d* question: TR WH Nes BF2 AV RV ASV RSV NEB TT Zür Luth Jer Seg ∥ *d* question, *d* none, *d* question: Bov

---

22 τυφλοὶ...εὐαγγελίζονται Is 35.5; 61.1; Lk 4.18 **26** προφήτην...προφήτου Lk 1.76
27 Ἰδοὺ...ἔμπροσθέν σου Mal 3.1; Ex 23.20 **28** μείζων...ἐστιν Lk 1.15

gave sight to many blind people. 22 He answered John's messengers: "Go back and tell John what you have seen and heard: the blind can see, the lame can walk, the lepers are made clean, the deaf can hear, the dead are raised to life, and the Good News is preached to the poor. 23 How happy is he who has no doubts about me!"

24 After John's messengers had left, Jesus began to speak about John to the crowds: "When you went out to John in the desert, what did you expect to see? A blade of grass bending in the wind? 25 What did you go out to see? A man dressed up in fancy clothes? Really, those who dress like that and live in luxury are found in palaces! 26 Tell me, what did you expect to see? A prophet? Yes, I tell you — you saw much more than a prophet. 27 For John is the one of whom the scripture says, 'Here is my messenger, says God; I will send him ahead of you to open the way for you.' 28 I tell you," Jesus added, "John is greater than any man ever born; but he who is least in the Kingdom of God is greater than he."

²⁹ All the people and the tax collectors heard him; they were the ones who had obeyed God's righteous demands and had been baptized by John. ³⁰ But the Pharisees and the teachers of the Law rejected God's purpose for themselves, and refused to be baptized by John.

³¹ "Now, to what can I compare the people of this day? What are they like? ³² They are like children sitting in the market place. One group shouts to the other, 'We played wedding music for you, but you would not dance! We sang funeral songs, but you would not cry!' ³³ John the Baptist came, and he fasted and drank no wine, and you said, 'He is a madman!' ³⁴ The Son of Man came, and he ate and drank, and you said, 'Look at this man! He is a glutton and wine-drinker, and is a friend of tax collectors and outcasts!' ³⁵ God's wisdom, however, is shown to be true by all who accept it."

Jesus at the Home of Simon the Pharisee

³⁶ A Pharisee invited Jesus to have dinner with him. Jesus went to his house and sat down to eat. ³⁷ There was a woman in that town who lived a sinful life. She heard that Jesus was eating in the Pharisee's house, so she brought an alabaster jar full of perfume ³⁸ and stood behind Jesus, by his feet, crying and wetting his feet with her tears. Then she dried his feet with her hair, kissed them, and poured the perfume on them. ³⁹ When the Pharisee who had invited Jesus saw this, he said to himself, "If this man really were a prophet, he would know who this woman is who is touching him; he would know what kind of sinful

μείζων αὐτοῦ ἐστιν. ^e(29 Καὶ πᾶς ὁ λαὸς ἀκούσας καὶ οἱ τελῶναι ἐδικαίωσαν τὸν θεόν, βαπτισθέντες τὸ βάπτισμα Ἰωάννου· 30 οἱ δὲ Φαρισαῖοι καὶ οἱ νομικοὶ τὴν βουλὴν τοῦ θεοῦ ἠθέτησαν εἰς ἑαυτούς, μὴ βαπτισθέντες ὑπ' αὐτοῦ.)^e

31 *Τίνι οὖν ὁμοιώσω τοὺς ἀνθρώπους τῆς γενεᾶς ταύτης, καὶ τίνι εἰσὶν ὅμοιοι;* 32 *ὅμοιοί εἰσιν παιδίοις τοῖς ἐν ἀγορᾷ καθημένοις καὶ προσφωνοῦσιν ἀλλήλοις, ἃ λέγει,*

> *Ηὐλήσαμεν ὑμῖν καὶ οὐκ ὠρχήσασθε·*
> *ἐθρηνήσαμεν καὶ οὐκ ἐκλαύσατε.*

33 *ἐλήλυθεν γὰρ Ἰωάννης ὁ βαπτιστὴς μὴ ἐσθίων ἄρτον μήτε πίνων οἶνον, καὶ λέγετε, Δαιμόνιον ἔχει·* 34 *ἐλήλυθεν ὁ υἱὸς τοῦ ἀνθρώπου ἐσθίων καὶ πίνων, καὶ λέγετε, Ἰδοὺ ἄνθρωπος φάγος καὶ οἰνοπότης, φίλος τελωνῶν καὶ ἁμαρτωλῶν.* 35 *καὶ ἐδικαιώθη ἡ σοφία ἀπὸ πάντων τῶν τέκνων αὐτῆς.*

A Sinful Woman Forgiven

36 Ἠρώτα δέ τις αὐτὸν τῶν Φαρισαίων ἵνα φάγῃ μετ' αὐτοῦ· καὶ εἰσελθὼν εἰς τὸν οἶκον τοῦ Φαρισαίου κατεκλίθη. 37 καὶ ἰδοὺ γυνὴ ἥτις ἦν ἐν τῇ πόλει ἁμαρτωλός, καὶ ἐπιγνοῦσα ὅτι κατάκειται ἐν τῇ οἰκίᾳ τοῦ Φαρισαίου, κομίσασα ἀλάβαστρον μύρου 38 καὶ στᾶσα ὀπίσω παρὰ τοὺς πόδας αὐτοῦ κλαίουσα, τοῖς δάκρυσιν ἤρξατο βρέχειν τοὺς πόδας αὐτοῦ καὶ ταῖς θριξὶν τῆς κεφαλῆς αὐτῆς ἐξέμασσεν, καὶ κατεφίλει τοὺς πόδας αὐτοῦ καὶ ἤλειφεν τῷ μύρῳ. 39 ἰδὼν δὲ ὁ Φαρισαῖος ὁ καλέσας αὐτὸν εἶπεν ἐν ἑαυτῷ λέγων, Οὗτος εἰ ἦν προφήτης⁸, ἐγίνωσκεν ἂν τίς καὶ ποταπὴ ἡ γυνὴ ἥτις

---

⁸ **39** {C} *προφήτης* ℵ A D K L P W X Δ Θ Π Ψ *f*¹ *f*¹³ 28 33 565 700

^e ^e **29–30** *e* parens, *e* parens: RSV ∥ *e* dash, *e* dash: WH ∥ *e e* no dashes or parens: TR Bov Nes BF² AV RV ASV NEB TT Zür Luth Jer Seg

29–30 Lk 3.7, 12; Mt 21.32   **34** *φίλος...ἁμαρτωλῶν* Lk 15.2   **36** *Ἠρώτα...κατεκλίθη* Lk 11.37   **37** *ἀλάβαστρον μύρου* Mt 26.7; Mk 14.3   **37–38** *κομίσασα...μύρῳ* Jn 12.3

ἅπτεται αὐτοῦ, ὅτι ἁμαρτωλός ἐστιν. **40** καὶ ἀποκριθεὶς ὁ Ἰησοῦς εἶπεν πρὸς αὐτόν, Σίμων, ἔχω σοί τι εἰπεῖν. ὁ δέ, Διδάσκαλε, εἰπέ, φησίν. **41** δύο χρεοφειλέται ἦσαν δανειστῇ τινι· ὁ εἷς ὤφειλεν δηνάρια πεντακόσια, ὁ δὲ ἕτερος πεντήκοντα. **42** μὴ ἐχόντων αὐτῶν ἀποδοῦναι ἀμφοτέροις ἐχαρίσατο. τίς οὖν αὐτῶν πλεῖον ἀγαπήσει αὐτόν⁹; **43** ἀποκριθεὶς Σίμων εἶπεν, Ὑπολαμβάνω ὅτι ᾧ τὸ πλεῖον ἐχαρίσατο. ὁ δὲ εἶπεν αὐτῷ, Ὀρθῶς ἔκρινας. **44** καὶ στραφεὶς πρὸς τὴν γυναῖκα τῷ Σίμωνι ἔφη, Βλέπεις ταύτην τὴν γυναῖκα; εἰσῆλθόν σου εἰς τὴν οἰκίαν, ὕδωρ μοι ἐπὶ πόδας οὐκ ἔδωκας· αὐτη δὲ τοῖς δάκρυσιν ἔβρεξέν μου τοὺς πόδας καὶ ταῖς θριξὶν αὐτῆς ἐξέμαξεν. **45** φίλημά μοι οὐκ ἔδωκας· αὐτη δὲ ἀφ' ἧς εἰσῆλθον οὐ διέλιπεν καταφιλοῦσά μου τοὺς πόδας. **16** ἐλαίῳ τὴν κεφαλήν μου οὐκ ἤλειψας· αὐτη δὲ μύρῳ ἤλειψεν τοὺς πόδας μου. **47** οὗ χάριν, λέγω σοι, ἀφέωνται αἱ ἁμαρτίαι αὐτῆς αἱ πολλαί, ὅτι ἠγάπησεν πολύ· ᾧ δὲ ὀλίγον ἀφίεται, ὀλίγον ἀγαπᾷ. **48** εἶπεν δὲ αὐτῇ, Ἀφέωνταί σου αἱ ἁμαρτίαι. **49** καὶ ἤρξαντο οἱ συνανακείμενοι λέγειν ἐν ἑαυτοῖς, Τίς οὗτός ἐστιν ὃς καὶ ἁμαρτίας ἀφίησιν; **50** εἶπεν δὲ πρὸς τὴν γυναῖκα, Ἡ πίστις σου σέσωκέν σε· πορεύου εἰς εἰρήνην.

---

892 1009 1010 1071 1079 1195 1216 1230 1241 1242 1253 1344 1365 1546 1646 2148 2174 *Byz Lect* cop^(sa,bo) goth arm ‖ ὁ προφήτης Β Ξ

⁹ 42 {C} πλεῖον ἀγαπήσει αὐτόν 𝔭^(3,75vid) ℵ B L W Ξ Ψ 892 1241 syr^(c,s,p) cop^(sa?bo?) eth ‖ πλεῖον αὐτὸν ἀγαπήσει f¹ 1242* (1253 αὐτῶν) it^(f,l) cop^(sa?bo?) ‖ αὐτὸν πλεῖον ἀγαπήσει D it^(a,aur,b,c,d,e,ff2,q,r1) vg cop^(sa?bo?) ‖ εἶπε πλεῖον αὐτὸν ἀγαπήσει (A ἐπί *for* εἶπε) K P Θ Π 079 (X 33 ἀγαπήσει αὐτόν) f¹³ 28 565 700 1009 1010 1071 1079 1195 1216 1230 1242^c 1344 1365 (1646^mg 2148 αὐτῶν) 2174 *Byz Lect* (syr^(h,pal)) goth (arm εἶπεν οὖν τίς πλεῖον) geo ‖ εἶπε πλεῖον ἀγαπήσει Δ 1546 1646* *l*⁵⁴

---

44 ὕδωρ...πόδας Gn 18.4   **45** φίλημα...ἔδωκας Ro 16.16; 1 Cor 16.20; 2 Cor 13.12; 1 Th 5.26; 1 Pe 5.14   **46** ἐλαίῳ...ἤλειψας Ps 23.5   **48-49** Lk 5.20-21   **50** Ἡ πίστις... εἰρήνην Lk 8.48; 17.19; 18.42

life she leads!" [40] Jesus spoke up and said to him, "Simon, I have something to tell you." "Yes, Teacher," he said, "tell me." [41] "There were two men who owed money to a moneylender," Jesus began; "one owed him five hundred dollars and the other one fifty dollars. [42] Neither one could pay him back, so he canceled the debts of both. Which one, then, will love him more?" [43] "I suppose," answered Simon, "that it would be the one who was forgiven more." "Your answer is correct," said Jesus. [44] Then he turned to the woman and said to Simon: "Do you see this woman? I came into your home, and you gave me no water for my feet, but she has washed my feet with her tears and dried them with her hair. [45] You did not welcome me with a kiss, but she has not stopped kissing my feet since I came. [46] You provided no oil for my head, but she has covered my feet with perfume. [47] I tell you, then, the great love she has shown proves that her many sins have been forgiven. Whoever has been forgiven little, however, shows only a little love." [48] Then Jesus said to the woman, "Your sins are forgiven." [49] The others sitting at the table began to say to themselves, "Who is this, who even forgives sins?" [50] But Jesus said to the woman, "Your faith has saved you; go in peace."

Women who Accompanied Jesus

8 Some time later Jesus made a trip through towns and villages, preaching the Good News about the Kingdom of God. The twelve disciples went with him, [2] and so did some women who had been healed of evil spirits and diseases: Mary (who was called Magdalene), from whom seven demons had been driven out; [3] Joanna, the wife of Chuza who was an officer in Herod's court; Susanna, and many other women who helped Jesus and his disciples with their belongings.

The Parable of the Sower
(Also Matt. 13.1–9; Mark 4.1–9)

[4] People kept coming to Jesus from one town after another; and when a great crowd gathered, Jesus told this parable:
[5] "A man went out to sow his seed. As he scattered the seed in the field, some of it fell along the path, where it was stepped on, and the birds ate it. [6] Some of it fell on rocky ground, and when the plants sprouted they dried up, because the soil had no moisture. [7] Some of the seed fell among thorns, which grew up with the plants and choked them. [8] And some seeds fell in good soil; the plants grew and bore grain, one hundred grains each." And Jesus added, "Listen, then, if you have ears to hear with!"

Some Women Accompany Jesus

8 Καὶ ἐγένετο ἐν τῷ καθεξῆς καὶ αὐτὸς διώδευεν κατὰ πόλιν καὶ κώμην κηρύσσων καὶ εὐαγγελιζόμενος τὴν βασιλείαν τοῦ θεοῦ, καὶ οἱ δώδεκα σὺν αὐτῷ, **2** καὶ γυναῖκές τινες αἳ ἦσαν τεθεραπευμέναι ἀπὸ πνευμάτων πονηρῶν καὶ ἀσθενειῶν, Μαρία ἡ καλουμένη Μαγδαληνή, ἀφ' ἧς δαιμόνια ἑπτὰ ἐξεληλύθει, **3** καὶ Ἰωάννα γυνὴ Χουζᾶ ἐπιτρόπου Ἡρῴδου καὶ Σουσάννα καὶ ἕτεραι πολλαί, αἵτινες διηκόνουν αὐτοῖς[1] ἐκ τῶν ὑπαρχόντων αὐταῖς.

The Parable of the Sower
(Mt 13.1–9; Mk 4.1–9)

4 Συνιόντος δὲ ὄχλου πολλοῦ καὶ τῶν κατὰ πόλιν ἐπιπορευομένων πρὸς αὐτὸν εἶπεν διὰ παραβολῆς, **5** Ἐξῆλθεν ὁ σπείρων τοῦ σπεῖραι τὸν σπόρον αὐτοῦ. καὶ ἐν τῷ σπείρειν αὐτὸν ὃ μὲν ἔπεσεν παρὰ τὴν ὁδόν, καὶ κατεπατήθη καὶ τὰ πετεινὰ τοῦ οὐρανοῦ[2] κατέφαγεν αὐτό. **6** καὶ ἕτερον κατέπεσεν ἐπὶ τὴν πέτραν, καὶ φυὲν ἐξηράνθη διὰ τὸ μὴ ἔχειν ἰκμάδα. **7** καὶ ἕτερον ἔπεσεν ἐν μέσῳ τῶν ἀκανθῶν, καὶ συμφυεῖσαι αἱ ἄκανθαι ἀπέπνιξαν αὐτό. **8** καὶ ἕτερον ἔπεσεν εἰς τὴν γῆν τὴν ἀγαθήν, καὶ φυὲν ἐποίησεν καρπὸν ἑκατονταπλασίονα. ταῦτα λέγων ἐφώνει, Ὁ ἔχων ὦτα ἀκούειν ἀκουέτω.

---

[1] **3** {B} αὐτοῖς B D K W Δ Θ *f*[13] 28 700 892 1009 (1010 αὐταῖς) 1071 1230 1242 1344 1646 Byz[pt] *l*[76,150,226,299,950,1642] it[c,d,e,f,ff2,rl] vg[ww] syr[c,s,p,h mg,pal mss] goth geo[B] Diatessaron (Origen) Augustine ‖ αὐτῷ ℵ A L X Π Ψ *f*[1] 33 565 1079 1195 1216 1241 1253[vid] 1365 1546 2148 2174 Byz[pt] Lect it[a,aur,b,l,q] vg[cl] syr[h,pal ms] cop[sa,bo] arm eth geo[1,A] Marcion Tertullian Cyprian

[2] **5** {B} τοῦ οὐρανοῦ 𝔓[75] ℵ A B K L X Δ Θ Ξ Π Ψ *f*[1] *f*[13] 28 33 565 700 892 1009 1010 1071 1079 1195 1216 1230 1241 1242 1253 1344 1365 1546 1646 2148 2174 Byz Lect it[aur,c,f,rl] vg syr[h,pal] cop[sa,bo] goth arm eth geo Origen[lat] ‖ omit (see Mt 13.4; Mk 4.4) D W it[a,b,d,e,ff2,l,q] syr[c,s,p]

---

1 αὐτὸς...θεοῦ Lk 4.43   **2–3** Mt 27.55–56; Mk 15.40–41; Lk 23.49   **8** Ὁ ἔχων...ἀκουέτω Mt 11.15; 13.43; Mk 4.23; Lk 14.35

The Purpose of the Parables
(Mt 13.10–17; Mk 4.10–12)

9 Ἐπηρώτων δὲ αὐτὸν οἱ μαθηταὶ αὐτοῦ τίς αὕτη εἴη ἡ παραβολή. **10** ὁ δὲ εἶπεν, Ὑμῖν δέδοται γνῶναι τὰ μυστήρια τῆς βασιλείας τοῦ θεοῦ, τοῖς δὲ λοιποῖς ἐν παραβολαῖς, ἵνα

βλέποντες μὴ βλέπωσιν
καὶ ἀκούοντες μὴ συνιῶσιν.

The Parable of the Sower Explained
(Mt 13.18–23; Mk 4.13–20)

11 Ἔστιν δὲ αὕτη ἡ παραβολή· Ὁ σπόρος ἐστὶν ὁ λόγος τοῦ θεοῦ. **12** οἱ δὲ παρὰ τὴν ὁδόν εἰσιν οἱ ἀκούσαντες, εἶτα ἔρχεται ὁ διάβολος καὶ αἴρει τὸν λόγον ἀπὸ τῆς καρδίας αὐτῶν, ἵνα μὴ πιστεύσαντες σωθῶσιν. **13** οἱ δὲ ἐπὶ τῆς πέτρας οἳ ὅταν ἀκούσωσιν μετὰ χαρᾶς δέχονται τὸν λόγον, καὶ οὗτοι ῥίζαν οὐκ ἔχουσιν, οἳ πρὸς καιρὸν πιστεύουσιν καὶ ἐν καιρῷ πειρασμοῦ ἀφίστανται. **14** τὸ δὲ εἰς τὰς ἀκάνθας πεσόν, οὗτοί εἰσιν οἱ ἀκούσαντες, καὶ ὑπὸ μεριμνῶν καὶ πλούτου καὶ ἡδονῶν τοῦ βίου πορευόμενοι συμπνίγονται καὶ οὐ τελεσφοροῦσιν. **15** τὸ δὲ ἐν τῇ καλῇ γῇ, οὗτοί εἰσιν οἵτινες ἐν καρδίᾳ καλῇ καὶ ἀγαθῇ ἀκούσαντες τὸν λόγον κατέχουσιν καὶ καρποφοροῦσιν ἐν ὑπομονῇ.

A Light under a Vessel
(Mk 4.21 25)

16 Οὐδεὶς δὲ λύχνον ἅψας καλύπτει αὐτὸν σκεύει ἢ ὑποκάτω κλίνης τίθησιν, ἀλλ' ἐπὶ λυχνίας τίθησιν, ἵνα οἱ εἰσπορευόμενοι βλέπωσιν τὸ φῶς. **17** οὐ γάρ ἐστιν κρυπτὸν ὃ οὐ φανερὸν γενήσεται, οὐδὲ ἀπόκρυφον ὃ οὐ μὴ γνωσθῇ καὶ εἰς φανερὸν ἔλθῃ. **18** βλέπετε οὖν πῶς ἀκούετε· ὃς ἂν γὰρ ἔχῃ, δοθήσεται αὐτῷ, καὶ ὃς ἂν μὴ ἔχῃ, καὶ ὃ δοκεῖ ἔχειν ἀρθήσεται ἀπ' αὐτοῦ.

---

10 βλέποντες...συνιῶσιν Is 6.9–10   **11** Ὁ σπόρος...θεοῦ 1 Pe 1.23   **12** πιστεύσαντες σωθῶσιν 1 Cor 1.21   **16** Mt 5.15; Lk 11.33   **17** Mt 10.26; Lk 12.2   **18** ὃς ἂν γὰρ ἔχῃ... αὐτοῦ Mt 25.29; Lk 19.26

The Purpose of the Parables
(Also Matt. 13.10–17; Mark 4.10–12)

[9] His disciples asked Jesus what this parable meant. [10] Jesus answered, "The knowledge of the secrets of the Kingdom of God has been given to you; but to the rest it comes by means of parables, so that they may look but not see, and listen but not understand."

Jesus Explains the Parable of the Sower
(Also Matt. 13.18–23; Mark 4.13–20)

[11] "This is what the parable means: the seed is the word of God. [12] The seed that fell along the path stands for those who hear; but the Devil comes and takes the message away from their hearts to keep them from believing and being saved. [13] The seed that fell on rocky ground stands for those who hear the message and receive it gladly. But it does not sink deep into them; they believe only for a while, and fall away when the time of temptation comes. [14] The seed that fell among thorns stands for those who hear; but the worries and riches and pleasures of this life crowd in and choke them, and their fruit never ripens. [15] The seed that fell in good soil stands for those who hear the message and retain it in a good and obedient heart, and persist until they bear fruit."

A Lamp under a Bowl
(Also Mark 4.21–25)

[16] "No one lights a lamp and covers it with a bowl or puts it under a bed. Instead, he puts it on the lamp-stand, so that people will see the light as they come in. [17] Whatever is hidden away will be brought out into the open, and whatever is covered up will be found and brought to light.
[18] "Be careful, then, how you listen; for whoever has something will be given more, but whoever has nothing will have taken away from him even the little he thinks he has."

Jesus' Mother and Brothers
(Also Matt. 12.46–50; Mark 3.31–35)

[19] Jesus' mother and brothers came to him, but were unable to join him because of the crowd. [20] Someone said to Jesus, "Your mother and brothers are standing outside and want to see you." [21] Jesus said to them all, "My mother and brothers are those who hear the word of God and obey it."

Jesus Calms a Storm
(Also Matt. 8.23–27; Mark 4.35–41)

[22] One day Jesus got into a boat with his disciples and said to them, "Let us go across to the other side of the lake." So they started out. [23] As they were sailing, Jesus went to sleep. A strong wind blew down on the lake, and the boat began to fill with water, putting them all in great danger. [24] The disciples came to Jesus and woke him up, saying, "Master, Master! We are about to die!" Jesus got up and gave a command to the wind and to the stormy water; they quieted down and there was a great calm. [25] Then he said to the disciples, "Where is your faith?" But they were amazed and afraid, and said to one another: "Who is this man? He gives orders to the winds and waves, and they obey him!"

Jesus Heals a Man with Demons
(Also Matt. 8.28–34; Mark 5.1–20)

[26] They sailed on over to the territory of the Gergesenes, which is across the lake from Galilee. [27] As Jesus stepped ashore, he was met by a man from the town who had demons in him. He had gone for a long time without clothes,

The Mother and Brothers of Jesus
(Mt 12.46–50; Mk 3.31–35)

19 Παρεγένετο δὲ πρὸς αὐτὸν ἡ μήτηρ καὶ οἱ ἀδελφοὶ αὐτοῦ, καὶ οὐκ ἠδύναντο συντυχεῖν αὐτῷ διὰ τὸν ὄχλον. **20** ἀπηγγέλη δὲ αὐτῷ, Ἡ μήτηρ σου καὶ οἱ ἀδελφοί σου ἑστήκασιν ἔξω ἰδεῖν θέλοντές σε. **21** ὁ δὲ ἀποκριθεὶς εἶπεν πρὸς αὐτούς, Μήτηρ μου καὶ ἀδελφοί μου οὗτοί εἰσιν οἱ τὸν λόγον τοῦ θεοῦ ἀκούοντες καὶ ποιοῦντες.

The Calming of a Storm
(Mt 8.23–27; Mk 4.35–41)

22 Ἐγένετο δὲ ἐν μιᾷ τῶν ἡμερῶν καὶ αὐτὸς ἐνέβη εἰς πλοῖον καὶ οἱ μαθηταὶ αὐτοῦ, καὶ εἶπεν πρὸς αὐτούς, Διέλθωμεν εἰς τὸ πέραν τῆς λίμνης· καὶ ἀνήχθησαν. **23** πλεόντων δὲ αὐτῶν ἀφύπνωσεν. καὶ κατέβη λαῖλαψ ἀνέμου εἰς τὴν λίμνην, καὶ συνεπληροῦντο καὶ ἐκινδύνευον. **24** προσελθόντες δὲ διήγειραν αὐτὸν λέγοντες, Ἐπιστάτα ἐπιστάτα, ἀπολλύμεθα. ὁ δὲ διεγερθεὶς ἐπετίμησεν τῷ ἀνέμῳ καὶ τῷ κλύδωνι τοῦ ὕδατος· καὶ ἐπαύσαντο, καὶ ἐγένετο γαλήνη. **25** εἶπεν δὲ αὐτοῖς, Ποῦ ἡ πίστις ὑμῶν; φοβηθέντες δὲ ἐθαύμασαν, λέγοντες πρὸς ἀλλήλους, Τίς ἄρα οὗτός ἐστιν ὅτι καὶ τοῖς ἀνέμοις ἐπιτάσσει καὶ τῷ ὕδατι, καὶ ὑπακούουσιν αὐτῷ;

The Healing of the Gergesene Demoniac
(Mt 8.28–34; Mk 5.1–20)

26 Καὶ κατέπλευσαν εἰς τὴν χώραν τῶν Γεργεσηνῶν[3], ἥτις ἐστὶν ἀντιπέρα τῆς Γαλιλαίας. **27** ἐξελθόντι δὲ αὐτῷ ἐπὶ τὴν γῆν ὑπήντησεν ἀνήρ τις ἐκ τῆς πόλεως

---

[3] 26 {D} Γεργεσηνῶν (see 8.37) ℵ L X Θ Ξ f[1] 33 700 (1241* Γεργεσινῶν) 1241[c] 1365 syr[palms] cop[bo] arm eth geo Titus-Bostra Cyril ‖ Γερασηνῶν (see Mk 5.1) 𝔓[75] B D it[a, aur, b, c, d, e, f, ff2, l, q, rl] vg syr[hmg] cop[sa, boms] Tertullian Cyril ‖ Γαδαρηνῶν (see Mt 8.28) A K W Δ[gr] Π Ψ f[13] 28 565 892 1009 1010 1071 1079 1195 1216 1230 1242 1253 1344 1546 1646 2148 2174 *Byz Lect* syr[c, s, p, h] goth Diatessaron[a]

ἔχων δαιμόνια· καὶ χρόνῳ ἱκανῷ[4] οὐκ ἐνεδύσατο ἱμάτιον, καὶ ἐν οἰκίᾳ οὐκ ἔμενεν ἀλλ’ ἐν τοῖς μνήμασιν. 28 ἰδὼν δὲ τὸν Ἰησοῦν ἀνακράξας προσέπεσεν αὐτῷ καὶ φωνῇ μεγάλῃ εἶπεν, Τί ἐμοὶ καὶ σοί, Ἰησοῦ υἱὲ τοῦ θεοῦ τοῦ ὑψίστου; δέομαί σου, μή με βασανίσῃς. [a]29 παρήγγειλεν γὰρ τῷ πνεύματι τῷ ἀκαθάρτῳ ἐξελθεῖν ἀπὸ τοῦ ἀνθρώπου.[a] πολλοῖς γὰρ χρόνοις συνηρπάκει αὐτόν, καὶ ἐδεσμεύετο ἁλύσεσιν καὶ πέδαις φυλασσόμενος, καὶ διαρρήσσων τὰ δεσμὰ ἠλαύνετο ὑπὸ τοῦ δαιμονίου εἰς τὰς ἐρήμους.[a] 30 ἐπηρώτησεν δὲ αὐτὸν ὁ Ἰησοῦς, Τί σοι ὄνομά ἐστιν; ὁ δὲ εἶπεν, Λεγιών, ὅτι εἰσῆλθεν δαιμόνια πολλὰ εἰς αὐτόν. 31 καὶ παρεκάλουν αὐτὸν ἵνα μὴ ἐπιτάξῃ αὐτοῖς εἰς τὴν ἄβυσσον ἀπελθεῖν.

32 ⸆Ἦν δὲ ἐκεῖ ἀγέλη χοίρων ἱκανῶν βοσκομένη ἐν τῷ ὄρει· καὶ παρεκάλεσαν αὐτὸν ἵνα ἐπιτρέψῃ αὐτοῖς εἰς ἐκείνους εἰσελθεῖν· καὶ ἐπέτρεψεν αὐτοῖς. 33 ἐξελθόντα δὲ τὰ δαιμόνια ἀπὸ τοῦ ἀνθρώπου εἰσῆλθον εἰς τοὺς χοίρους, καὶ ὥρμησεν ἡ ἀγέλη κατὰ τοῦ κρημνοῦ εἰς τὴν λίμνην καὶ ἀπεπνίγη. 34 ἰδόντες δὲ οἱ βόσκοντες τὸ γεγονὸς ἔφυγον καὶ ἀπήγγειλαν εἰς τὴν πόλιν καὶ εἰς τοὺς ἀγρούς. 35 ἐξῆλθον δὲ ἰδεῖν τὸ γεγονὸς καὶ ἦλθον πρὸς τὸν Ἰησοῦν, καὶ εὗρον καθήμενον τὸν ἄνθρωπον ἀφ’ οὗ τὰ δαιμόνια ἐξῆλθεν ἱματισμένον καὶ σωφρονοῦντα παρὰ τοὺς πόδας τοῦ Ἰησοῦ, καὶ ἐφοβήθησαν. 36 ἀπήγγειλαν δὲ αὐτοῖς οἱ ἰδόντες πῶς ἐσώθη ὁ δαιμονισθείς. 37 καὶ ἠρώτησεν αὐτὸν ἅπαν τὸ πλῆθος τῆς

and would not stay at home, but spent his time in the burial caves. 28 When he saw Jesus he gave a loud cry, fell down before him and said in a loud voice: "Jesus, Son of the Most High God! What do you want with me? I beg you, don't punish me!" 29 He said this because Jesus had ordered the evil spirit to go out of him. Many times it had seized him, and even though he was kept a prisoner, his hands and feet tied with chains, he would break the chains and be driven by the demon out into the desert. 30 Jesus asked him, "What is your name?" "My name is 'Mob,'" he answered — because many demons had gone into him. 31 The demons begged Jesus not to send them into the abyss.

32 A large herd of pigs was near by, feeding on the hillside. The demons begged Jesus to let them go into the pigs — and he let them. 33 So the demons went out of the man and into the pigs; the whole herd rushed down the side of the cliff into the lake and were drowned.

34 The men who were taking care of the pigs saw what happened, so they ran off and spread the news in the town and among the farms. 35 People went out to see what had happened. They came to Jesus and found the man from whom the demons had gone out sitting at the feet of Jesus, clothed, and in his right mind — and they were all afraid. 36 Those who had seen it told the people how the man had been cured. 37 Then the whole crowd from the territory of

---

[4] **27** {C} καὶ χρόνῳ ἱκανῷ 𝔓⁷⁵ א*,ᵇ B L Ξ 33 1241 syrʰᵐᵍ·ᵖᵃˡ copˢᵃ·ᵇᵒ eth ∥ καὶ χρόνῳ πολλῷ f¹ arm geo ∥ ἐκ χρόνων ἱκανῶν καὶ אᵃ A K W X Δ Θ Π Ψ f¹³ 28 565 700 892 1009 1010 1071 1079 1195 1216 1230 1242 1253 1344 1365 1546 1646 2148 2174 Byz Lect (l¹²⁷ ἐν χρόνων ἱκανῶν [sic]) itᵃ·ᵃᵘʳ·ᵇ·ᶜ·ᵉ·ᶠ·ᶠᶠ²·ˡ· q,(rl) vg syrᶜ·ˢ·ᵖ·ʰ goth (Ps-Athanasius) ∥ ἀπὸ χρόνων ἱκανῶν ὅς D itᵈ

ᵃ ᵃ ᵃ **29** a a a no parens: TR WH Bov Nes BF² RV ASV NEB TT Zür Luth Jer Seg ∥ a parens, a no parens, a parens: AV ∥ a no parens, a parens, a parens: RSV

---

28 ἀνακράξας...σοί Mt 8.29; Mk 1.23–24; 5.7; Lk 4.34

the Gergesenes asked Jesus to go away, for they were all terribly afraid. So Jesus got into the boat and left. **38** The man from whom the demons had gone out begged Jesus, "Let me go with you." But Jesus sent him away, saying, **39** "Go back home and tell what God has done for you." The man went through the whole town telling what Jesus had done for him.

Jairus' Daughter and the Woman who Touched Jesus' Cloak
(Also Matt. 9.18–26; Mark 5.21–43)

40 When Jesus returned to the other side of the lake the crowd welcomed him, for they had all been waiting for him. **41** Then a man named Jairus arrived, an official in the local synagogue. He threw himself down at Jesus' feet and begged him to go to his home, **42** for his only daughter, twelve years old, was dying.

As Jesus went along, the people were crowding him from every side. **43** A certain woman was there who had suffered from severe bleeding for twelve years; she had spent all she had on doctors,[1]

---

[1] **43** *Some mss. omit* she had spent all she had on doctors

περιχώρου τῶν Γεργεσηνῶν[5] ἀπελθεῖν ἀπ' αὐτῶν, ὅτι φόβῳ μεγάλῳ συνείχοντο· αὐτὸς δὲ ἐμβὰς εἰς πλοῖον ὑπέστρεψεν. **38** ἐδεῖτο δὲ αὐτοῦ ὁ ἀνὴρ ἀφ' οὗ ἐξεληλύθει τὰ δαιμόνια εἶναι σὺν αὐτῷ· ἀπέλυσεν δὲ αὐτὸν λέγων, **39** Ὑπόστρεφε εἰς τὸν οἶκόν σου, καὶ διηγοῦ ὅσα σοι ἐποίησεν ὁ θεός. καὶ ἀπῆλθεν καθ' ὅλην τὴν πόλιν κηρύσσων ὅσα ἐποίησεν αὐτῷ ὁ Ἰησοῦς.

Jairus' Daughter and the Woman Who Touched Jesus' Garment
(Mt 9.18–26; Mk 5.21–43)

40 Ἐν δὲ τῷ ὑποστρέφειν τὸν Ἰησοῦν ἀπεδέξατο αὐτὸν ὁ ὄχλος, ἦσαν γὰρ πάντες προσδοκῶντες αὐτόν. **41** καὶ ἰδοὺ ἦλθεν ἀνὴρ ᾧ ὄνομα Ἰάϊρος, καὶ οὗτος ἄρχων τῆς συναγωγῆς ὑπῆρχεν, καὶ πεσὼν παρὰ τοὺς πόδας τοῦ Ἰησοῦ παρεκάλει αὐτὸν εἰσελθεῖν εἰς τὸν οἶκον αὐτοῦ, **42** ὅτι θυγάτηρ μονογενὴς ἦν αὐτῷ ὡς ἐτῶν δώδεκα καὶ αὐτὴ ἀπέθνησκεν.

Ἐν δὲ τῷ ὑπάγειν αὐτὸν οἱ ὄχλοι συνέπνιγον αὐτόν. **43** καὶ γυνὴ οὖσα ἐν ῥύσει αἵματος ἀπὸ ἐτῶν δώδεκα, ἥτις [ἰατροῖς προσαναλώσασα ὅλον τὸν βίον][6] οὐκ ἴσχυ-

---

[5] **37** {D} Γεργεσηνῶν (*see* 8.26) ℵ* (C² Γεργαρσηνῶν) L P X Θ f¹ f¹³ 33 700 1071 1195ᵐᵍ 1241 1365 syrᵖᵃˡ copᵇᵒ arm eth geo Titus-Bostra ‖ Γερασηνῶν (*see* Mk 5.1) 𝔓⁷⁵ B C* D itᵃ,ᵃᵘʳ,ᵇ,ᶜ,ᵈ,ᶠ,ᶠᶠ²,ˡ, q,ʳˡ vg copˢᵃ Cyril ‖ Γαδαρηνῶν (*see* Mt 8.28) ℵᵃ A K W Δᵍʳ Π Ψ 28 565 892 1009 1010 1079 1195* 1216 1230 1242 1253 1344 1546 1646 2148 2174 *Byz* l⁵⁴⁷ syrᶜ,ˢ,ᵖ,ʰ goth Diatessaron Basil

[6] **43** {D} ἥτις ἰατροῖς προσαναλώσασα ὅλον τὸν βίον ℵᶜ A K L P W Δ Θ Ξ Π f¹ f¹³ 28 33 565 (700 ἅπαντα *for* ὅλον) 892 1009 1010 1195 1216 1241 1242 1344 1365 1546 1646 2148 2174 *Byz Lect* itᵃ,ᶠ,ʳˡ ‖ ἥτις ἰατροῖς προσαναλώσασα ὅλον τὸν βίον αὐτῆς (ℵ* ἑαυτῆς καὶ) C X Ψ (1071 ἑαυτῆς) 1079 1230 1253 l⁹⁵⁰ ‖ ἥτις εἰς ἰατροὺς προσαναλώσασα ὅλον τὸν βίον αὐτῆς itᵃᵘʳ,b,c,ff²,l,q vg syrᶜ,ᵖ,ʰ,ᵖᵃˡᵐˢ copᵇᵒ goth eth ‖ ἥτις 𝔓⁷⁵ B (D) (itᵈ) syrˢ,ᵖᵃˡᵐˢˢ copˢᵃ arm geo

---

42 Lk 7.12

σεν ἀπ᾿ οὐδενὸς θεραπευθῆναι, **44** προσελθοῦσα ὄπισθεν ἥψατο τοῦ κρασπέδου[7] τοῦ ἱματίου αὐτοῦ, καὶ παραχρῆμα ἔστη ἡ ῥύσις τοῦ αἵματος αὐτῆς. **45** καὶ εἶπεν ὁ Ἰησοῦς, Τίς ὁ ἁψάμενός μου; ἀρνουμένων δὲ πάντων εἶπεν ὁ Πέτρος[8], Ἐπιστάτα, οἱ ὄχλοι συνέχουσίν σε καὶ ἀποθλίβουσιν[9]. **46** ὁ δὲ Ἰησοῦς εἶπεν, Ἥψατό μού τις, ἐγὼ γὰρ ἔγνων δύναμιν ἐξεληλυθυῖαν ἀπ᾿ ἐμοῦ. **47** ἰδοῦσα δὲ ἡ γυνὴ ὅτι οὐκ ἔλαθεν τρέμουσα ἦλθεν καὶ προσπεσοῦσα αὐτῷ δι᾿ ἣν αἰτίαν ἥψατο αὐτοῦ ἀπήγγειλεν ἐνώπιον παντὸς τοῦ λαοῦ καὶ ὡς ἰάθη παραχρῆμα. **48** ὁ δὲ εἶπεν αὐτῇ, Θυγάτηρ, ἡ πίστις σου σέσωκέν σε· πορεύου εἰς εἰρήνην.

49 Ἔτι αὐτοῦ λαλοῦντος ἔρχεταί τις παρὰ τοῦ ἀρχισυναγώγου λέγων ὅτι Τέθνηκεν ἡ θυγάτηρ σου, μηκέτι[10]

but no one had been able to cure her. [44] She came up in the crowd behind Jesus and touched the edge of his cloak, and her bleeding stopped at once. [45] Jesus asked, "Who touched me?" Everyone denied it, and Peter said, "Master, the people are all around you and crowding in on you." [46] But Jesus said, "Someone touched me, for I knew it when power went out of me.'' [47] The woman saw that she had been found out, so she came, trembling, and threw herself at Jesus' feet. There, in front of everybody, she told him why she had touched him and how she had been healed at once. [48] Jesus said to her, "My daughter, your faith has made you well. Go in peace."

[49] While Jesus was saying this, a messenger came from the official's house. "Your daughter has died," he told Jairus; "don't bother the Teacher any longer."

[7] **44** {C} ὄπισθεν ἥψατο τοῦ κρασπέδου (see Mt 9.20) 𝔭[75] ℵ A B C L P W X Δ Θ Ξ *f*[1] *f*[13] 28 33 565 700 892 1009 1010 1195 1216 1230 1241 1242 1253 1344 1365 1546 1646 2148 2174 *Byz Lect* it[aur,b,c,f,q] vg (syr[c,s,p,h,pal] add αὐτοῦ) cop[sa,bo] goth arm geo ∥ ἥψατο ὄπισθεν τοῦ κρασπέδου K Π 1079 ∥ ὄπισθεν τοῦ Ἰησοῦ ἥψατο τοῦ κρασπέδου 238 (eth) ∥ ὄπισθεν ἥψατο τοῦ ἱματίου τοῦ κρασπέδου αὐτοῦ (see Mt 9.20) *l*[60] ∥ ἥψατο τοῦ κρασπέδου Ψ 1071 ∥ ἥψατο (see Mk 5.27) D it[a,d,ff2,i,r1]

[8] **45** {B} Πέτρος 𝔭[75] B Π 700 1079 1546 syr[c,s,pal] cop[sa] eth geo ∥ Πέτρος καὶ οἱ σὺν αὐτῷ (see Mk 5.31) ℵ A C D L P W Θ Ξ *f*[1] *f*[13] 33 892 1009 1071 1195 1230 1241 1253 *Lect* ∥ Πέτρος καὶ οἱ μετ᾿ αὐτοῦ (see Mk 5.31) K X Δ Ψ 28 565 1010 1216 1242 1344 1365 1646 2148 2174 *Byz* *l*[32,60,76,150,184,299,883,1627,1642,1663] ∥ Πέτρος καὶ οἱ σὺν αὐτῷ (or μετ᾿ αὐτοῦ) it[a,aur,b,c,d,f,ff2,l,q,r1] vg syr[p,h] cop[bo] goth arm

[9] **45** {C} καὶ ἀποθλίβουσιν 𝔭[75] ℵ B L *f*[1] 1241 1365 syr[pal] cop[sa,bo] arm ∥ καὶ λέγεις, Τίς μου ἥψατο (see Mk 5.31) 1071 (*l*[70] τίς ὁ ἁψάμενός μου) it[a,b,ff2,l,q,r1] ∥ καὶ ἀποθλίβουσιν καὶ λέγεις, Τίς ὁ ἁψάμενός μου A (C* τί) C[3] K P W X Δ Θ Ξ Π *f*[13] 33 565 700 892 1009 1010 1079 1195 1216 1230 1242 1253 1344 1546 1646 (2148 θλίβουσιν) 2174 *Byz Lect* syr[c,(s),p,h] cop[boms] goth eth Diatessaron[a] ∥ καὶ ἀποθλίβουσιν καὶ λέγεις, Τίς μου ἥψατο D Ψ 28 it[aur,c,d,f] vg geo?

[10] **49** {C} μηκέτι 𝔭[75] ℵ B D it[d?] syr[h with *,palms] cop[sa] arm eth Diatessaron[f,n,t] ∥ μή A C K L P W X Δ Θ Ξ Π Ψ *f*[1] *f*[13] 28 565 700 892 1009 1010 1071 1079 1195 1216 1230 1241 1242 1253 1344 1365 1546 1646 2148 2174 *Byz Lect* it[a,aur,b,c,e,f,ff2,l,q,r1] vg syr[c,s,p,h,palmss] cop[bo] goth geo John-Damascus

48 ἡ πίστις...εἰρήνην Lk 7.50; 17.19; 18.42

⁵⁰ But Jesus heard it and said to Jairus, "Don't be afraid; only believe, and she will be well." ⁵¹ When he arrived at the house he would not let anyone go in with him except Peter, John, and James, and the child's father and mother. ⁵² Everyone there was crying and mourning for the child. Jesus said, "Don't cry; the child is not dead — she is only sleeping!" ⁵³ They all made fun of him, because they knew that she was dead. ⁵⁴ But Jesus took her by the hand and called out, "Get up, child!" ⁵⁵ Her life returned and she got up at once; and Jesus ordered them to give her something to eat. ⁵⁶ Her parents were astounded, but Jesus commanded them not to tell anyone what had happened.

Jesus Sends out the Twelve Disciples
(Also Matt. 10.5–15; Mark 6.7–13)

9 Jesus called the twelve disciples together and gave them power and authority to drive out all demons and to cure diseases. ² Then he sent them out to preach the Kingdom of God and to heal the sick. ³ He said to them: "Take nothing with you for the trip: no walking

σκύλλε τὸν διδάσκαλον. **50** ὁ δὲ Ἰησοῦς ἀκούσας ἀπεκρίθη αὐτῷ, Μὴ φοβοῦ, μόνον πίστευσον, καὶ σωθήσεται. **51** ἐλθὼν δὲ εἰς τὴν οἰκίαν οὐκ ἀφῆκεν εἰσελθεῖν τινα σὺν αὐτῷ εἰ μὴ Πέτρον καὶ Ἰωάννην καὶ Ἰάκωβον καὶ τὸν πατέρα τῆς παιδὸς καὶ τὴν μητέρα. **52** ἔκλαιον δὲ πάντες καὶ ἐκόπτοντο αὐτήν. ὁ δὲ εἶπεν, Μὴ κλαίετε, οὐ γὰρ ἀπέθανεν ἀλλὰ καθεύδει. **53** καὶ κατεγέλων αὐτοῦ, εἰδότες ὅτι ἀπέθανεν. **54** αὐτὸς δὲ κρατήσας τῆς χειρὸς αὐτῆς ἐφώνησεν λέγων, Ἡ παῖς, ἔγειρε. **55** καὶ ἐπέστρεψεν τὸ πνεῦμα αὐτῆς, καὶ ἀνέστη παραχρῆμα, καὶ διέταξεν αὐτῇ δοθῆναι φαγεῖν. **56** καὶ ἐξέστησαν οἱ γονεῖς αὐτῆς· ὁ δὲ παρήγγειλεν αὐτοῖς μηδενὶ εἰπεῖν τὸ γεγονός.

The Mission of the Twelve
(Mt 10.5–15; Mk 6.7–13)

9 Συγκαλεσάμενος δὲ τοὺς δώδεκα[1] ἔδωκεν αὐτοῖς δύναμιν καὶ ἐξουσίαν ἐπὶ πάντα τὰ δαιμόνια καὶ νόσους θεραπεύειν, **2** καὶ ἀπέστειλεν αὐτοὺς κηρύσσειν τὴν βασιλείαν τοῦ θεοῦ καὶ ἰᾶσθαι [τοὺς ἀσθενεῖς][2], **3** καὶ εἶπεν πρὸς αὐτούς, Μηδὲν αἴρετε εἰς τὴν ὁδόν, μήτε

---

[1] **1** {C} δώδεκα (see Mk 6.7) 𝔓⁷⁵ A B D K W Δ Π f¹ 28 565 700 1009 1079 1230 1253 1365 1546 1646 2148 Byz itᵈ copˢᵃ geo Marcion Adamantius ‖ δώδεκα αὐτοῦ syrᶜ,ˢ,ᵖ ‖ μαθητὰς αὐτοῦ 1242 l¹⁵⁰,¹⁶⁶³ᵐ ‖ δώδεκα μαθητὰς αὐτοῦ (see Mt 10.1) C³ 1010 1216ᵐᵍ 1344 Lect l⁶⁹⁸,ᵐ itᵇ,ff²,l,q,rl Diatessaronᵃ,ⁱ,ⁿ ‖ δώδεκα ἀποστόλους ℵ C* L X Θ Ξ Ψ 0202 f¹³ 33 892 1071 1195 1216ᵗˣᵗ 1241 2174 itᵃ,aur,c,e,f vg syrʰ,ᵖᵃˡ copᵇᵒ goth arm eth ‖ δώδεκα ὁ Ἰησοῦς ἀποστόλους 346

[2] **2** {C} ἰᾶσθαι τοὺς ἀσθενεῖς ℵ A D L Ξ Ψ (0202 ἰάσασθαι) f¹ 33 1071 1241 itᵃ,aur,b,c,d,e,ff²,l,q,rl vg syrᵖ,ʰ,(ᵖᵃˡ) copˢᵃ?ᵇᵒ? arm geo? ‖ ἰᾶσθαι τοὺς ἀσθενοῦντας C K W X Δ Θ Π f¹³ 28 565 700 892 1009 1010 1079 1195 1216 1230 1242 1253 1344 1365 1546 1646 2148 2174ᵛⁱᵈ Byz Lect l⁶⁹⁸,ᵐ,¹⁵⁸ˢ,ᵐ copˢᵃ?ᵇᵒ? geo? ‖ ἰᾶσθαι πάντας τοὺς ἀσθενοῦντας 407 435 itᶠ goth ‖ ἰᾶσθαι B syrᶜ,ˢ Marcion Adamantius

---

52 Μὴ κλαίετε Lk 7.13   **54** Ἡ παῖς, ἔγειρε Lk 7.14   **56** ὁ δὲ παρήγγειλεν... γεγονός Mk 7.36; Lk 5.14

ῥάβδον μήτε πήραν μήτε ἄρτον μήτε ἀργύριον, μήτε [ἀνὰ] δύο³ χιτῶνας ἔχειν. 4 καὶ εἰς ἣν ἂν οἰκίαν εἰσέλθητε, ἐκεῖ μένετε καὶ ἐκεῖθεν ἐξέρχεσθε. 5 καὶ ὅσοι ἂν μὴ δέχωνται ὑμᾶς, ἐξερχόμενοι ἀπὸ τῆς πόλεως ἐκείνης τὸν κονιορτὸν ἀπὸ τῶν ποδῶν ὑμῶν ἀποτινάσσετε εἰς μαρτύριον ἐπ' αὐτούς. 6 ἐξερχόμενοι δὲ διήρχοντο κατὰ τὰς κώμας εὐαγγελιζόμενοι καὶ θεραπεύοντες πανταχοῦ.

Herod's Anxiety
(Mt 14.1–12; Mk 6.14–29)

7 Ἤκουσεν δὲ Ἡρῴδης ὁ τετραάρχης τὰ γινόμενα πάντα, καὶ διηπόρει διὰ τὸ λέγεσθαι ὑπό τινων ὅτι Ἰωάννης ἠγέρθη ἐκ νεκρῶν, 8 ὑπό τινων δὲ ὅτι Ἡλίας ἐφάνη, ἄλλων δὲ ὅτι προφήτης τις τῶν ἀρχαίων ἀνέστη. 9 εἶπεν δὲ Ἡρῴδης, Ἰωάννην ἐγὼ ἀπεκεφάλισα· τίς δέ ἐστιν οὗτος περὶ οὗ ἀκούω τοιαῦτα; καὶ ἐζήτει ἰδεῖν αὐτόν.

The Feeding of the Five Thousand
(Mt 14.13–21; Mk 6.30–44; Jn 6.1–14)

10 Καὶ ὑποστρέψαντες οἱ ἀπόστολοι διηγήσαντο αὐτῷ ὅσα ἐποίησαν. καὶ παραλαβὼν αὐτοὺς ὑπεχώρησεν κατ' ἰδίαν εἰς πόλιν καλουμένην Βηθσαϊδά. 11 οἱ δὲ ὄχλοι γνόντες ἠκολούθησαν αὐτῷ. καὶ ἀποδεξάμενος αὐτοὺς ἐλάλει αὐτοῖς περὶ τῆς βασιλείας τοῦ θεοῦ, καὶ τοὺς χρείαν ἔχοντας θεραπείας ἰᾶτο. 12 Ἡ δὲ ἡμέρα ἤρξατο κλίνειν· προσελθόντες δὲ οἱ δώδεκα εἶπαν αὐτῷ, Ἀπόλυσον τὸν ὄχλον, ἵνα πορευθέντες εἰς τὰς κύκλῳ κώμας καὶ ἀγροὺς καταλύσωσιν καὶ εὕρωσιν ἐπισιτισμόν, ὅτι ὧδε ἐν ἐρήμῳ τόπῳ ἐσμέν. 13 εἶπεν δὲ πρὸς αὐτούς,

---

³ 3 {C} ἀνὰ δύο A C³ D K W X Δ Θ Π Ψ f¹ f¹³ 28 33 565 700 892 1009 1010 1071 1079 1195 1216 1230 1242 1253 1344 1365 1546 1646 2148 2174 Byz Lect it^d syr^h ∥ δύο (see Mk 6.9; Mt 10.10) ℵ B C* L Ξ 0202 1241 l⁴⁸,⁵⁴⁷ cop^sa,bo ∥ δύο, with ἀνὰ not expressed it^{a,aur,b,c,e,f,ff²,l,q,r¹} vg syr^{c,s,p,pal} goth arm geo

4 Lk 10.5–7   5 Lk 10.10–11; Ac 13.51   7–8 τὸ λέγεσθαι...ἀνέστη Mt 16.14; Mk 8.28; Lk 9.19   9 ἐζήτει...αὐτόν Lk 23.8

---

stick, no beggar's bag, no food, no money, not even an extra shirt. 4 Wherever you are welcomed, stay in the same house until you leave that town; 5 wherever people don't welcome you, leave that town and shake the dust off your feet as a warning to them." 6 The disciples left and traveled through all the villages, preaching the Good News and healing people everywhere.

Herod's Confusion
(Also Matt. 14.1–12; Mark 6.14–29)

7 Herod, the ruler of Galilee, heard about all the things that were happening; he was very confused about it because some people said, "John the Baptist has come back to life!" 8 Others said that Elijah had appeared, while others said that one of the prophets of long ago had come back to life. 9 Herod said, "I had John's head cut off; but who is this man I hear these things about?" And he kept trying to see Jesus.

Jesus Feeds the Five Thousand
(Also Matt. 14.13–21; Mark 6.30–44; John 6.1–14)

10 The apostles came back and told Jesus everything they had done. He took them with him and they went off by themselves to a town named Bethsaida. 11 When the crowds heard about it, they followed him. He welcomed them, spoke to them about the Kingdom of God, and healed those who needed it. 12 When the sun had begun to set, the twelve disciples came to him and said, "Send the people away so they can go to the villages and farms around here and find food and lodging; for this is a lonely place." 13 But Jesus said to them,

"You yourselves give them something to eat." They answered, "All we have is five loaves and two fish. Do you want us to go and buy food for this whole crowd?" [14] (There were about five thousand men there.) Jesus said to his disciples, "Make the people sit down in groups of about fifty each." [15] The disciples did so and made them all sit down. [16] Jesus took the five loaves and two fish, looked up to heaven, thanked God for them, broke them, and gave them to the disciples to distribute to the people. [17] They all ate and had enough; and the disciples took up twelve baskets of what the people left over.

Peter's Declaration about Jesus
(Also Matt. 16.13–19; Mark 8.27–29)

[18] One time when Jesus was praying alone, the disciples came to him. "Who do the crowds say I am?" he asked them. [19] "Some say that you are John the Baptist," they answered. "Others say that you are Elijah, while others say that one of the prophets of long ago has come back to life." [20] "What about you?" he asked them. "Who do you say I am?" Peter answered, "You are God's Messiah!"

Jesus Speaks about His Suffering and Death
(Also Matt. 16.20–28; Mark 8.30—9.1)

[21] Then Jesus gave them strict orders not to tell this to anyone, [22] and added: "The Son of Man must suffer much, and be rejected by the elders, the chief priests, and the teachers of the Law. He will be put to death, and be raised to life on the third day." [23] And he said to all: "If anyone wants to come with me, he must forget himself, take up his cross every day, and follow me. [24] For the person who wants to save

Δότε αὐτοῖς ὑμεῖς φαγεῖν. οἱ δὲ εἶπαν, Οὐκ εἰσὶν ἡμῖν πλεῖον ἢ ἄρτοι πέντε καὶ ἰχθύες δύο, εἰ μήτι πορευθέντες ἡμεῖς ἀγοράσωμεν εἰς πάντα τὸν λαὸν τοῦτον βρώματα. **14** ἦσαν γὰρ ὡσεὶ ἄνδρες πεντακισχίλιοι. εἶπεν δὲ πρὸς τοὺς μαθητὰς αὐτοῦ, Κατακλίνατε αὐτοὺς κλισίας [ὡσεὶ] ἀνὰ πεντήκοντα. **15** καὶ ἐποίησαν οὕτως καὶ κατέκλιναν ἅπαντας. **16** λαβὼν δὲ τοὺς πέντε ἄρτους καὶ τοὺς δύο ἰχθύας ἀναβλέψας εἰς τὸν οὐρανὸν εὐλόγησεν αὐτοὺς καὶ κατέκλασεν καὶ ἐδίδου τοῖς μαθηταῖς παραθεῖναι τῷ ὄχλῳ. **17** καὶ ἔφαγον καὶ ἐχορτάσθησαν πάντες, καὶ ἤρθη τὸ περισσεῦσαν αὐτοῖς κλασμάτων κόφινοι δώδεκα.

Peter's Declaration about Jesus
(Mt 16.13–19; Mk 8.27–29)

18 Καὶ ἐγένετο ἐν τῷ εἶναι αὐτὸν προσευχόμενον κατὰ μόνας συνῆσαν αὐτῷ οἱ μαθηταί, καὶ ἐπηρώτησεν αὐτοὺς λέγων, Τίνα με λέγουσιν οἱ ὄχλοι εἶναι; **19** οἱ δὲ ἀποκριθέντες εἶπαν, Ἰωάννην τὸν βαπτιστήν, ἄλλοι δὲ Ἠλίαν, ἄλλοι δὲ ὅτι προφήτης τις τῶν ἀρχαίων ἀνέστη. **20** εἶπεν δὲ αὐτοῖς, Ὑμεῖς δὲ τίνα με λέγετε εἶναι; Πέτρος δὲ ἀποκριθεὶς εἶπεν, Τὸν Χριστὸν τοῦ θεοῦ.

Jesus Foretells His Death and Resurrection
(Mt 16.20–28; Mk 8.30—9.1)

21 Ὁ δὲ ἐπιτιμήσας αὐτοῖς παρήγγειλεν μηδενὶ λέγειν τοῦτο, **22** εἰπὼν ὅτι Δεῖ τὸν υἱὸν τοῦ ἀνθρώπου πολλὰ παθεῖν καὶ ἀποδοκιμασθῆναι ἀπὸ τῶν πρεσβυτέρων καὶ ἀρχιερέων καὶ γραμματέων καὶ ἀποκτανθῆναι καὶ τῇ τρίτῃ ἡμέρᾳ ἐγερθῆναι. **23** Ἔλεγεν δὲ πρὸς πάντας, Εἴ τις θέλει ὀπίσω μου ἔρχεσθαι, ἀρνησάσθω ἑαυτὸν καὶ ἀράτω τὸν σταυρὸν αὐτοῦ καθ' ἡμέραν, καὶ ἀκολουθείτω μοι. **24** ὃς γὰρ ἂν θέλῃ τὴν ψυχὴν αὐτοῦ σῶσαι, ἀπολέσει

---

17 2 Kgs 4.44   **19** Lk 9.7–8   **20** Ὑμεῖς...θεοῦ Jn 6.68–69   **22** Δεῖ...ἐγερθῆναι Mt 16.21; 20.18–19; Mk 8.31; 10.33–34   **23** Εἴ τις θέλει...μοι Mt 10.38; Lk 14.27   **24** Mt 10.39; Lk 17.33; Jn 12.25

αὐτήν· ὃς δ' ἂν ἀπολέσῃ τὴν ψυχὴν αὐτοῦ ἕνεκεν ἐμοῦ, οὗτος σώσει αὐτήν. 25 τί γὰρ ὠφελεῖται ἄνθρωπος κερδήσας τὸν κόσμον ὅλον ἑαυτὸν δὲ ἀπολέσας ἢ ζημιωθείς; 26 ὃς γὰρ ἂν ἐπαισχυνθῇ με καὶ τοὺς ἐμοὺς λόγους[4], τοῦτον ὁ υἱὸς τοῦ ἀνθρώπου ἐπαισχυνθήσεται, ὅταν ἔλθῃ ἐν τῇ δόξῃ αὐτοῦ καὶ τοῦ πατρὸς καὶ τῶν ἁγίων ἀγγέλων. 27 λέγω δὲ ὑμῖν ἀληθῶς, εἰσίν τινες τῶν αὐτοῦ ἑστηκότων οἳ οὐ μὴ γεύσωνται θανάτου ἕως ἂν ἴδωσιν τὴν βασιλείαν τοῦ θεοῦ.

The Transfiguration of Jesus
(Mt 17.1–8; Mk 9.2–8)

28 Ἐγένετο δὲ μετὰ τοὺς λόγους τούτους ὡσεὶ ἡμέραι ὀκτὼ [καὶ] παραλαβὼν Πέτρον καὶ Ἰωάννην καὶ Ἰάκωβον ἀνέβη εἰς τὸ ὄρος προσεύξασθαι. 29 καὶ ἐγένετο ἐν τῷ προσεύχεσθαι αὐτὸν τὸ εἶδος τοῦ προσώπου αὐτοῦ ἕτερον καὶ ὁ ἱματισμὸς αὐτοῦ λευκὸς ἐξαστράπτων. 30 καὶ ἰδοὺ ἄνδρες δύο συνελάλουν αὐτῷ, οἵτινες ἦσαν Μωϋσῆς καὶ Ἡλίας, 31 οἳ ὀφθέντες ἐν δόξῃ ἔλεγον τὴν ἔξοδον αὐτοῦ ἣν ἤμελλεν πληροῦν ἐν Ἰερουσαλήμ. 32 ὁ δὲ Πέτρος καὶ οἱ σὺν αὐτῷ ἦσαν βεβαρημένοι ὕπνῳ· διαγρηγορήσαντες δὲ εἶδον τὴν δόξαν αὐτοῦ καὶ τοὺς δύο ἄνδρας τοὺς συνεστῶτας αὐτῷ. 33 καὶ ἐγένετο ἐν τῷ διαχωρίζεσθαι αὐτοὺς ἀπ' αὐτοῦ εἶπεν ὁ Πέτρος πρὸς τὸν Ἰησοῦν, Ἐπιστάτα, καλόν ἐστιν ἡμᾶς ὧδε εἶναι, καὶ ποιήσωμεν σκηνὰς τρεῖς, μίαν σοὶ καὶ μίαν Μωϋσεῖ καὶ μίαν Ἡλίᾳ, μὴ εἰδὼς ὃ λέγει. 34 ταῦτα δὲ αὐτοῦ λέγοντος ἐγένετο νεφέλη καὶ ἐπεσκίαζεν αὐτούς· ἐφοβήθησαν δὲ ἐν τῷ εἰσελθεῖν αὐτοὺς εἰς τὴν νεφέλην.

---

[4] **26** {B} λόγους (see Mk 8.38) 𝔭[45,75vid] ℵ A B C K L W X Δ Θ Ξ Π Ψ f[1] f[13] 28 33 565 700 892 1009 1010 1071 1079 1195 1216 1230 1241 1242 1253 1344 1365 1546 1646 2148 2174 *Byz Lect* l[547m] it[aur,b,c,f,ff2,q,r1] vg syr[p,h] cop[sa,bo] goth arm eth geo Origen ‖ *omit* D it[a,d,e,l] (syr[c]) Origen

---

26 Mt 10.33; Lk 12.9; 2 Tm 2.12   **31** τὴν...Ἰερουσαλήμ Lk 9.22; 13.33   **32** εἶδον... αὐτοῦ Jn 1.14; 2 Pe 1.16

his own life will lose it; but the one who loses his life for my sake will save it. 25 Will a man gain anything if he wins the whole world but is himself lost or defeated? Of course not! 26 If a man is ashamed of me and of my teaching, then the Son of Man will be ashamed of him when he comes in his glory and the glory of the Father and of the holy angels. 27 Remember this! There are some here, I tell you, who will not die until they have seen the Kingdom of God."

The Transfiguration
(Also Matt. 17.1–8; Mark 9.2–8)

28 About a week after he had said these things, Jesus took Peter, John, and James with him and went up a hill to pray. 29 While he was praying, his face changed its appearance and his clothes became dazzling white. 30 Suddenly two men were there talking with him. They were Moses and Elijah, 31 who appeared in heavenly glory and talked with Jesus about how he would soon fulfil God's purpose by dying in Jerusalem. 32 Peter and his companions were sound asleep, but they awoke and saw Jesus' glory and the two men who were standing with him. 33 As the men were leaving Jesus, Peter said to him: "Master, it is a good thing that we are here. We will make three tents, one for you, one for Moses, and one for Elijah." (He really did not know what he was saying.) 34 While he was still speaking, a cloud appeared and covered them with its shadow, and the disciples were afraid as the cloud came

over them. ³⁵ A voice said from the cloud: "This is my Son, whom I have chosen — listen to him!" ³⁶ When the voice stopped, there was Jesus all alone. The disciples kept quiet about all this, and told no one at that time a single thing they had seen.

Jesus Heals a Boy with an Evil Spirit
(Also Matt. 17.14–18; Mark 9.14–27)

³⁷ The next day they went down from the hill, and a large crowd met Jesus. ³⁸ A man shouted from the crowd: "Teacher! Look, I beg you, at my son — my only son! ³⁹ A spirit attacks him with a sudden shout and throws him into a fit, so that he foams at the mouth; it keeps on hurting him and will hardly let him go! ⁴⁰ I begged your disciples to drive it out, but they could not." ⁴¹ Jesus answered: "How unbelieving and wrong you people are! How long must I stay with you? How long do I have to put up with you?" Then he said to the man, "Bring your son here." ⁴² As the boy was coming, the demon knocked him to the ground and threw him into a fit. Jesus gave a command to the evil spirit, healed the boy, and gave him back to his father. ⁴³ All the people were amazed at the mighty power of God.

35 καὶ φωνὴ ἐγένετο ἐκ τῆς νεφέλης λέγουσα, Οὗτός ἐστιν ὁ υἱός μου ὁ ἐκλελεγμένος⁵, αὐτοῦ ἀκούετε. 36 καὶ ἐν τῷ γενέσθαι τὴν φωνὴν εὑρέθη Ἰησοῦς μόνος. καὶ αὐτοὶ ἐσίγησαν καὶ οὐδενὶ ἀπήγγειλαν ἐν ἐκείναις ταῖς ἡμέραις οὐδὲν ὧν ἑώρακαν.

The Healing of a Boy with an Unclean Spirit
(Mt 17.14–18; Mk 9.14–27)

37 Ἐγένετο δὲ τῇ ἑξῆς ἡμέρᾳ κατελθόντων αὐτῶν ἀπὸ τοῦ ὄρους συνήντησεν αὐτῷ ὄχλος πολύς. 38 καὶ ἰδοὺ ἀνὴρ ἀπὸ τοῦ ὄχλου ἐβόησεν λέγων, Διδάσκαλε, δέομαί σου ἐπιβλέψαι ἐπὶ τὸν υἱόν μου, ὅτι μονογενής μοί ἐστιν, 39 καὶ ἰδοὺ πνεῦμα λαμβάνει αὐτόν, καὶ ἐξαίφνης κράζει, καὶ σπαράσσει αὐτὸν μετὰ ἀφροῦ καὶ μόγις ἀποχωρεῖ ἀπ' αὐτοῦ συντρῖβον αὐτόν· 40 καὶ ἐδεήθην τῶν μαθητῶν σου ἵνα ἐκβάλωσιν αὐτό, καὶ οὐκ ἠδυνήθησαν. 41 ἀποκριθεὶς δὲ ὁ Ἰησοῦς εἶπεν, Ὦ γενεὰ ἄπιστος καὶ διεστραμμένη, ἕως πότε ἔσομαι πρὸς ὑμᾶς καὶ ἀνέξομαι ὑμῶν; προσάγαγε ὧδε τὸν υἱόν σου. 42 ἔτι δὲ προσερχομένου αὐτοῦ ἔρρηξεν αὐτὸν τὸ δαιμόνιον καὶ συνεσπάραξεν· ἐπετίμησεν δὲ ὁ Ἰησοῦς τῷ πνεύματι τῷ ἀκαθάρτῳ, καὶ ἰάσατο τὸν παῖδα καὶ ἀπέδωκεν αὐτὸν τῷ πατρὶ αὐτοῦ. 43 ἐξεπλήσσοντο δὲ πάντες ἐπὶ τῇ μεγαλειότητι τοῦ θεοῦ.

---

⁵ 35 {B} ἐκλελεγμένος 𝔭⁴⁵,⁷⁵ ℵ B L Ξ 892 1241 ‖ ἐκλεκτός Θ *f*¹ 1365 *l*⁵⁴⁷ᵐ ‖ ἐκλελεγμένος *or* ἐκλεκτός itᵃ,ᵃᵘʳ,ff²,¹ syrˢ,ʰᵐᵍ copˢᵃ,ᵇᵒ arm ‖ ἀγαπητός (*see* Mk 9.7; Lk 3.22) A C* K P W X Δ Π *f*¹³ 28 33 565 700 1009 1010 1071 1079 1195 1216 1230 1242 1253 1344 1546 1646 2148 2174 *Byz Lect* itᵇ,ᶜ,ᵉ,f,q vg syrᶜ,ᵖ,ʰ,ᵖᵃˡ goth geo Marcion Diatessaron Clement Tertullian Epiphanius ‖ ἀγαπητὸς ἐν ᾧ εὐδόκησα (*see* Mt 17.5) C³ D Ψ *l*¹²ᵐ,¹⁹,³¹,⁴⁷,⁴⁸,⁴⁹,⁶⁹ᵐ,¹⁸³,¹⁸⁵ᵐ,²¹¹ᵐ,⁹⁵⁰,¹¹²⁷ᵐ,¹⁶⁴²ᵐ,¹⁶⁶³ᵐ itᵈ copᵇᵒᵐˢ

---

35 Οὗτός...ἐκλελεγμένος Ps 2.7; Is 42.1; Mt 3.17; 12.18; Mk 1.11; Lk 3.22; 2 Pe 1.17

Jesus Again Foretells His Death
(Mt 17.22–23; Mk 9.30–32)

Πάντων δὲ θαυμαζόντων ἐπὶ πᾶσιν οἷς ἐποίει εἶπεν πρὸς τοὺς μαθητὰς αὐτοῦ, 44 Θέσθε ὑμεῖς εἰς τὰ ὦτα ὑμῶν τοὺς λόγους τούτους, ὁ γὰρ υἱὸς τοῦ ἀνθρώπου μέλλει παραδίδοσθαι εἰς χεῖρας ἀνθρώπων. 45 οἱ δὲ ἠγνόουν τὸ ῥῆμα τοῦτο, καὶ ἦν παρακεκαλυμμένον ἀπ' αὐτῶν ἵνα μὴ αἴσθωνται αὐτό, καὶ ἐφοβοῦντο ἐρωτῆσαι αὐτὸν περὶ τοῦ ῥήματος τούτου.

Who is the Greatest?
(Mt 18.1–5; Mk 9.33–37)

46 Εἰσῆλθεν δὲ διαλογισμὸς ἐν αὐτοῖς, τὸ τίς ἂν εἴη μείζων αὐτῶν. 47 ὁ δὲ Ἰησοῦς εἰδὼς[6] τὸν διαλογισμὸν τῆς καρδίας αὐτῶν ἐπιλαβόμενος παιδίον ἔστησεν αὐτὸ παρ' ἑαυτῷ, 48 καὶ εἶπεν αὐτοῖς, Ὃς ἂν δέξηται τοῦτο τὸ παιδίον ἐπὶ τῷ ὀνόματί μου ἐμὲ δέχεται, καὶ ὃς ἂν ἐμὲ δέξηται δέχεται τὸν ἀποστείλαντά με· ὁ γὰρ μικρότερος ἐν πᾶσιν ὑμῖν ὑπάρχων οὗτός ἐστιν μέγας.

He Who is Not against You is for You
(Mk 9.38–40)

49 Ἀποκριθεὶς δὲ [ὁ] Ἰωάννης εἶπεν, Ἐπιστάτα, εἴδομέν τινα ἐν τῷ ὀνόματί σου ἐκβάλλοντα δαιμόνια, καὶ ἐκωλύομεν αὐτὸν ὅτι οὐκ ἀκολουθεῖ μεθ' ἡμῶν. 50 εἶπεν δὲ πρὸς αὐτὸν ὁ Ἰησοῦς, Μὴ κωλύετε, ὃς γὰρ οὐκ ἔστιν καθ' ὑμῶν ὑπὲρ ὑμῶν ἐστιν.

---

[6] 47 {C} εἰδώς ‭א‬ B K Π 700 1079 1546 *l*[76] syr[c,s,p,h] cop[sa] arm eth geo // ἰδών A C D L W X Δ Θ Ξ Ψ 0115 *f*[13] 28 33 565 892 1009 1010 1071 1195 1216 1230 1241 1242 1253 1344 1646 2148 2174 *Byz Lect* it[a,aur,b,c,d,e,f,ff2,l,q,r1] vg cop[bo] goth Origen // γνούς *f*[1] 1365

---

44 ὁ γὰρ...ἀνθρώπων Lk 18.32   45 Mk 9.32; Lk 18.34   46 Lk 22.24   48 Ὃς ἂν δέξηται...με Mt 10.40; Lk 10.16; Jn 13.20   50 ὃς γὰρ οὐκ ἔστιν...ἐστιν Lk 11.23

Jesus Speaks again about His Death
(Also Matt. 17.22–23; Mark 9.30–32)

The people were still marveling at everything Jesus was doing, when he said to his disciples: 44 "Don't forget what I am about to tell you! The Son of Man is going to be handed over to the power of men." 45 But they did not know what this meant. It had been hidden from them so that they could not understand it, and they were afraid to ask him about the matter.

Who Is the Greatest?
(Also Matt. 18.1–5; Mark 9.33–37)

46 An argument came up among the disciples as to which one of them was the greatest. 47 Jesus knew what they were thinking, so he took a child, stood him by his side, 48 and said to them: "The person who in my name welcomes this child, welcomes me; and whoever welcomes me, also welcomes the one who sent me. For he who is least among you all is the greatest."

Who Is not against You Is for You
(Also Mark 9.38–40)

49 John spoke up. "Master," he said, "we saw a man driving out demons in your name, and we told him to stop, because he doesn't belong to our group." 50 "Do not try to stop him," Jesus said to him and to the other disciples; "for whoever is not against you is for you."

A Samaritan Village Refuses to Receive Jesus

[51] As the days drew near when Jesus would be taken up to heaven, he made up his mind and set out on his way to Jerusalem. [52] He sent messengers ahead of him, who left and went into a Samaritan village to get everything ready for him. [53] But the people there would not receive him, because it was plain that he was going to Jerusalem. [54] When the disciples James and John saw this they said, "Lord, do you want us to call fire down from heaven and destroy them?"[1] [55] Jesus turned and rebuked them;[2] [56] and they went on to another village.

The Would-be Followers of Jesus
(Also Matt. 8.19–22)

[57] As they went on their way, a certain man said to Jesus, "I will follow you wherever you go." [58] Jesus said to him,

---

[1] **54** destroy them: *some mss. add* as Elijah did
[2] **55** rebuked them: *some mss. add* and said, "You don't know what kind of Spirit you belong to; for the Son of Man did not come to destroy men's lives but to save them."

A Samaritan Village Refuses to Receive Jesus

51 Ἐγένετο δὲ ἐν τῷ συμπληροῦσθαι τὰς ἡμέρας τῆς ἀναλήμψεως αὐτοῦ καὶ αὐτὸς τὸ πρόσωπον ἐστήρισεν τοῦ πορεύεσθαι εἰς Ἰερουσαλήμ, **52** καὶ ἀπέστειλεν ἀγγέλους πρὸ προσώπου αὐτοῦ. καὶ πορευθέντες εἰσῆλθον εἰς κώμην Σαμαριτῶν, ὡς ἑτοιμάσαι αὐτῷ· **53** καὶ οὐκ ἐδέξαντο αὐτόν, ὅτι τὸ πρόσωπον αὐτοῦ ἦν πορευόμενον εἰς Ἰερουσαλήμ. **54** ἰδόντες δὲ οἱ μαθηταὶ Ἰάκωβος καὶ Ἰωάννης εἶπαν, Κύριε, θέλεις εἴπωμεν **πῦρ καταβῆναι ἀπὸ τοῦ οὐρανοῦ καὶ ἀναλῶσαι** αὐτούς[7]; **55** στραφεὶς δὲ ἐπετίμησεν αὐτοῖς.[8] **56**[a] καὶ ἐπορεύθησαν εἰς ἑτέραν κώμην.

The Would-be Followers of Jesus
(Mt 8.19–22)

57 Καὶ πορευομένων αὐτῶν ἐν τῇ ὁδῷ εἶπέν τις πρὸς αὐτόν, Ἀκολουθήσω σοι ὅπου ἐὰν ἀπέρχῃ. **58** καὶ εἶπεν

---

[7] **54** {C} αὐτούς 𝔭⁴⁵,⁷⁵ ℵ B L Ξ 700* 1241 itᵃᵘʳ,ᵉ,¹ vg syrᶜ,ˢ copˢᵃ,ᵇᵒ arm geo Jerome Cyril ‖ αὐτοὺς ὡς καὶ Ἠλίας ἐποίησεν A C D K W X Δ Θ Π Ψ *f*¹ *f*¹³ 28 33 565 700ᵐᵍ (892 *omit* καί) 1009 1010 1071 1079 1195 1216 1230 1242 1253 1344 1365 1546 1646 2148 2174 *Byz Lect l*⁶⁹⁸,ᵐ,¹⁸⁵⁸,ᵐ,¹¹²⁷⁸,ᵐ itᵃ,ᵇ,ᶜ,ᵈ,ᶠ,q,ʳˡ syrᵖ,ʰ,ᵖᵃˡ copᵇᵒᵐˢˢ goth eth Marcion Diatessaronᵃ,ˢ Ambrosiaster Basil Gaudentius Chrysostom Augustine Antiochus

[8] **55–56** {C} αὐτοῖς. 𝔭⁴⁵,⁷⁵ ℵ A B C L W X Δ Ξ 28 33 565 892 1009 1010 1071 (1241 αὐτούς) itˡ *Lect* syrˢ copˢᵃ,ᵇᵒ eth Basil Cyril-Jerusalem Jerome ‖ αὐτοῖς. καὶ εἶπεν, Οὐκ οἴδατε ποίου πνεύματός ἐστε. D (*l*¹¹²⁷ᵐ ἐστε ὑμεῖς) itᵈ geo ‖ αὐτοῖς. καὶ εἶπεν, Οὐκ οἴδατε οἵου πνεύματός ἐστε ὑμεῖς; **56** ὁ γὰρ υἱὸς τοῦ ἀνθρώπου οὐκ ἦλθεν ψυχὰς ἀνθρώπων ἀπολέσαι ἀλλὰ σῶσαι. K Π Ψ 1079 1242 1546 (1365 ποίου) (2148 ποίου and ἔλθων) (*f*¹ *l*⁶⁹ᵐ ποίου and omit γάρ) (Θ *f*¹³ 1195 omit ὑμεῖς and γάρ) (1230 1253 1344 1646 omit ὑμεῖς and γάρ and read ἀποκτεῖναι for ἀπολέσαι) (2174 ποίου...omit ὑμεῖς and γάρ) (700 1216 ποίου...omit ὑμεῖς and γάρ and read ἀποκτεῖναι for ἀπολέσαι) *Byz l*⁷⁶,¹⁸⁵ᵐ,³³¹,⁸⁵⁴,⁸⁸³,⁹⁵⁰,¹⁵⁷⁹,¹⁶⁴² (*l*¹²ᵐ ποίου) itᶠ,q (itᵃ,ᵇ,ʳˡ omit γάρ, itᶜ omit ἀνθρώπων, itᵃᵘʳ,ᵉ vg omit γάρ and ἀνθρώπων) syrᶜ,ᵖ,ʰ copᵇᵒᵐˢˢ (goth omit ὑμεῖς and ἀνθρώπων) arm Marcion Diatessaron Ambrose Epiphanius Antiochus

---

[a] **58** *On location of verse number see footnote 8.*

51 Mk 10.32   **53** Jn 4.9   **54** πῦρ...αὐτούς 2 Kgs 1.10, 12

αὐτῷ ὁ Ἰησοῦς, Αἱ ἀλώπεκες φωλεοὺς ἔχουσιν καὶ τὰ πετεινὰ τοῦ οὐρανοῦ κατασκηνώσεις, ὁ δὲ υἱὸς τοῦ ἀνθρώπου οὐκ ἔχει ποῦ τὴν κεφαλὴν κλίνῃ. 59 Εἶπεν δὲ πρὸς ἕτερον, Ἀκολούθει μοι. ὁ δὲ εἶπεν, [Κύριε,][9] ἐπίτρεψόν μοι ἀπελθόντι πρῶτον θάψαι τὸν πατέρα μου. 60 εἶπεν δὲ αὐτῷ, Ἄφες τοὺς νεκροὺς θάψαι τοὺς ἑαυτῶν νεκρούς, σὺ δὲ ἀπελθὼν διάγγελλε τὴν βασιλείαν τοῦ θεοῦ. 61 Εἶπεν δὲ καὶ ἕτερος, Ἀκολουθήσω σοι, κύριε· πρῶτον δὲ ἐπίτρεψόν μοι ἀποτάξασθαι τοῖς εἰς τὸν οἶκόν μου. 62 εἶπεν δὲ ὁ Ἰησοῦς, Οὐδεὶς ἐπιβαλὼν τὴν χεῖρα ἐπ' ἄροτρον καὶ βλέπων εἰς τὰ ὀπίσω[10] εὔθετός ἐστιν τῇ βασιλείᾳ[11] τοῦ θεοῦ.

"Foxes have holes, and birds have nests, but the Son of Man has no place to lie down and rest." 59 He said to another man, "Follow me." But he said, "Sir, first let me go and bury my father." 60 Jesus answered, "Let the dead bury their own dead. You go and preach the Kingdom of God." 61 Another man said, "I will follow you, sir; but first let me go and say good-bye to my family." 62 Jesus said to him, "Anyone who starts to plow and then keeps looking back is of no use for the Kingdom of God."

---

[9] **59** {C} κύριε, (see Mt 8.21) 𝔭[45,75] ℵ A B[3] C K L W X Δ Θ Ξ Π Ψ 0181 f[1] f[13] 28 33 565 700 892 1010 1071 1079 1195 1216 1230 1241 1242 1253 1344 1365 1546 1646 2174 *Byz Lect* it[a,aur,b,c,e,f,l,q,r1] vg syr[c,p,h] cop[sa,bo] goth arm geo // *omit* B* D 1009 2148 it[d] syr[s] Origen Basil Theodoret

[10] **62** {C} ἐπιβαλὼν τὴν χεῖρα ἐπ' ἄροτρον καὶ βλέπων εἰς τὰ ὀπίσω (𝔭[75] ἐπιβάλλων) B 0181 f[1] arm geo Valentinus[acc. to Irenaeus] Tertullian (Origen) Basil (Cyril) // ἐπιβαλὼν τὴν χεῖρα αὐτοῦ ἐπ' ἄροτρον καὶ βλέπων εἰς τὰ ὀπίσω ℵ C K X Δ Ξ Π Ψ (A L W Θ ἐπιβάλλων) f[13] 28 33 565 700 1009 1010 1071 1079 1195 1216 1230 1241 1242 1253 1344 1365 1546 1646 2148 2174 (892 l[69,70,184,185,1127] στραφείς for βλέπων) *Byz Lect* it[aur,f,r1] vg syr[c,s,p,h] cop[bo] (cop[sa,boms] ἐπιβάλλων) goth eth Origen[lat] Basil (Chrysostom) (Antiochus) (John-Damascus) // εἰς τὰ ὀπίσω βλέπων καὶ ἐπιβάλλων τὴν χεῖρα αὐτοῦ ἐπ' ἄροτρον 𝔭[45vid] D it[a,b,c,d,e,(l),q] Clement Cyprian (Hilary) Zeno de Promissionibus

[11] **62** {C} τῇ βασιλείᾳ ℵ* B L Ξ 0181 f[1] 33 700 892 it[a,aur,b,c,e,f,l,r1] vg syr[s,p,h,pal] cop[boms] arm geo Clement Origen[gr,lat] Cyprian Hilary // ἐν τῇ βασιλείᾳ 𝔭[75] ℵ[c] 1241 it[q] cop[bo] Marcion Valentinians[acc. to Irenaeus] Basil Epiphanius Chrysostom // εἰς τὴν βασιλείαν A C D K W X (Δ *omit* εἰς) Θ Π Ψ f[13] 28 565 1009 1010 1071 1079 1195 1216 1230 1242 1253 1344 1365 1546 1646 2148 2174 *Byz Lect* it[d] cop[sa] goth Basil Cyril Antiochus

---

61 πρῶτον...μου 1 Kgs 19.20

Jesus Sends out the Seventy-two

10 After this the Lord chose another
seventy-two men and sent them out,
two by two, to go ahead of him to every
town and place where he himself was
about to go. 2 He said to them: "There
is a great harvest, but few workers to
gather it in. Pray to the owner of the
harvest that he will send out more workers
to gather in his harvest. 3 Go! I am sending you like lambs among wolves. 4 Don't
take a purse, or a beggar's bag, or shoes;
don't stop to greet anyone on the road.
5 Whenever you go into a house, first
say, 'Peace be with this house.' 6 If a
peace-loving man lives there, let your
greeting of peace remain on him; if not,
take back your greeting of peace. 7 Stay
in that same house, eating and drinking
what they offer you; for a worker should
be given his pay. Don't move around

The Mission of the Seventy-two

10 *Μετὰ δὲ ταῦτα ἀνέδειξεν ὁ κύριος ἑτέρους*[1] *ἑβδομήκοντα [δύο]*[2]*, καὶ ἀπέστειλεν αὐτοὺς ἀνὰ δύο [δύο] πρὸ
προσώπου αὐτοῦ εἰς πᾶσαν πόλιν καὶ τόπον οὗ ἤμελλεν
αὐτὸς ἔρχεσθαι.* **2** *ἔλεγεν δὲ πρὸς αὐτούς, Ὁ μὲν θερισμὸς
πολύς, οἱ δὲ ἐργάται ὀλίγοι· δεήθητε οὖν τοῦ κυρίου τοῦ
θερισμοῦ ὅπως ἐργάτας ἐκβάλῃ εἰς τὸν θερισμὸν αὐτοῦ.*
3 *ὑπάγετε· ἰδοὺ ἀποστέλλω ὑμᾶς ὡς ἄρνας ἐν μέσῳ
λύκων.* **4** *μὴ βαστάζετε βαλλάντιον, μὴ πήραν, μὴ
ὑποδήματα, καὶ μηδένα κατὰ τὴν ὁδὸν ἀσπάσησθε.* **5** *εἰς
ἣν δ' ἂν εἰσέλθητε οἰκίαν,*[a] *πρῶτον*[a] *λέγετε, Εἰρήνη τῷ
οἴκῳ τούτῳ.* **6** *καὶ ἐὰν ἐκεῖ ᾖ υἱὸς εἰρήνης, ἐπαναπαή-
σεται ἐπ' αὐτὸν ἡ εἰρήνη ὑμῶν· εἰ δὲ μήγε, ἐφ' ὑμᾶς
ἀνακάμψει.* **7** *ἐν αὐτῇ δὲ τῇ οἰκίᾳ μένετε, ἐσθίοντες
καὶ πίνοντες τὰ παρ' αὐτῶν, ἄξιος γὰρ ὁ ἐργάτης τοῦ
μισθοῦ αὐτοῦ. μὴ μεταβαίνετε ἐξ οἰκίας εἰς οἰκίαν.*

---

[1] **1** {C} *ἑτέρους* $\mathfrak{p}^{75}$ B L Ξ 0181 892 1071 2174 it^{r1} syr^{s,p} cop^{sa,bo} eth geo Diatessaron (Cyril) // *καὶ ἑτέρους* א A C D K W X Δ Θ Π Ψ f^1 f^{13} 28 33 565 700 1009 1010 1079 1195 1216 1230 1241 1242 1253 1344 1365 1546 1646 2148 *Byz Lect* it^{a,aur,b,c,d,e,f,l,q} vg syr^{c,h} goth arm Marcion Tertullian Eusebius Basil // *καὶ μαθηταί* syr^{palms}

[2] **1** {C} *δύο* (*see* 10.17) $\mathfrak{p}^{75}$ B D 0181 28 33 it^{a,aur,b,c,d,e,l} vg syr^{c,s} cop^{sa,boms} arm geo Diatessaron^{l,p,t,v} Acts of Thomas Didascalia Origen Adamantius Ambrosiaster Ps-Clement Ephraem Teaching of Addai Augustine // *μαθητάς Lect* // *omit* א A C K L W X Δ Θ Ξ Π Ψ f^1 f^{13} 565 700 892 1009 1010 1071 1079 1195 1216 1230 1241 1242 1253 1344 1365 1546 1646 2148 2174 *Byz* $l^{76,276,854,950}$ it$^{f,q,r1?}$ syr^{p,h,pal} cop^{bo} goth eth Irenaeus^{lat} Clement Tertullian Origen Eusebius Titus-Bostra Basil Ambrose Jerome Cyril

---

[a a] **5** *a* minor, *a* none: TR Bov Nes BF^2 AV RV ASV RSV NEB TT Zür Luth Jer Seg // *a* none, *a* minor: RV^{mg} ASV^{mg} // *a* none, *a* none: WH

---

1 *ἀπέστειλεν...δύο* Mk 6.7 **2** Mt 9.37–38 *Ὁ μὲν...πολύς* Jn 4.35 **4–11** Mt 10.7–14 **4** Lk 9.3 *μηδένα...ἀσπάσησθε* 2 Kgs 4.29 **7** Lk 9.4 *ἄξιος...αὐτοῦ* 1 Tm 5.18; 1 Cor 9.6–14

8 καὶ εἰς ἣν ἂν πόλιν εἰσέρχησθε καὶ δέχωνται ὑμᾶς, ἐσθίετε τὰ παρατιθέμενα ὑμῖν, 9 καὶ θεραπεύετε τοὺς ἐν αὐτῇ ἀσθενεῖς, καὶ λέγετε αὐτοῖς, "Ηγγικεν ἐφ' ὑμᾶς ἡ βασιλεία τοῦ θεοῦ. 10 εἰς ἣν δ' ἂν πόλιν εἰσέλθητε καὶ μὴ δέχωνται ὑμᾶς, ἐξελθόντες εἰς τὰς πλατείας αὐτῆς εἴπατε, 11 Καὶ τὸν κονιορτὸν τὸν κολληθέντα ἡμῖν ἐκ τῆς πόλεως ὑμῶν εἰς τοὺς πόδας ἀπομασσόμεθα ὑμῖν· πλὴν τοῦτο γινώσκετε ὅτι ἤγγικεν ἡ βασιλεία τοῦ θεοῦ. 12 λέγω ὑμῖν ὅτι Σοδόμοις ἐν τῇ ἡμέρᾳ ἐκείνῃ ἀνεκτότερον ἔσται ἢ τῇ πόλει ἐκείνῃ.

Woes to Unrepentant Cities
(Mt 11.20–24)

13 Οὐαί σοι, Χοραζίν· οὐαί σοι, Βηθσαϊδά· ὅτι εἰ ἐν Τύρῳ καὶ Σιδῶνι ἐγενήθησαν αἱ δυνάμεις αἱ γενόμεναι ἐν ὑμῖν, πάλαι ἂν ἐν σάκκῳ καὶ σποδῷ καθήμενοι μετενόησαν. 14 πλὴν Τύρῳ καὶ Σιδῶνι ἀνεκτότερον ἔσται ἐν τῇ κρίσει ἢ ὑμῖν. 15 καὶ σύ, Καφαρναούμ,

μὴ ἕως οὐρανοῦ ὑψωθήσῃ;
ἕως τοῦ ᾅδου καταβιβασθήσῃ[3].

16 Ὁ ἀκούων ὑμῶν ἐμοῦ ἀκούει, καὶ ὁ ἀθετῶν ὑμᾶς ἐμὲ ἀθετεῖ· ὁ δὲ ἐμὲ ἀθετῶν ἀθετεῖ τὸν ἀποστείλαντά με.

from one house to another. 8 Whenever you go into a town and are made welcome, eat what is set before you, 9 heal the sick in that town, and say to the people there, 'The Kingdom of God has come near you.' 10 But whenever you go into a town and are not welcomed there, go out in the streets and say, 11 'Even the dust from your town that sticks to our feet we wipe off against you; but remember this, the Kingdom of God has come near you!' 12 I tell you that on the Judgment Day God will show more mercy to Sodom than to that town!"

The Unbelieving Towns
(Also Matt. 11.20–24)

13 "How terrible it will be for you, Chorazin! How terrible for you too, Bethsaida! For if the miracles which were performed in you had been performed in Tyre and Sidon, long ago the people there would have sat down, put on sackcloth, and sprinkled ashes on themselves to show that they had turned from their sins! 14 God will show more mercy on the Judgment Day to Tyre and Sidon than to you. 15 And as for you, Capernaum! You wanted to lift yourself up to heaven? You will be thrown down to hell!"

16 He said to his disciples: "Whoever listens to you, listens to me; whoever rejects you, rejects me; and whoever rejects me, rejects the one who sent me."

---

[3] 15 {D} καταβιβασθήσῃ p⁴⁵ ℵ A C K L W X Δ Θ Ξ Π Ψ 0115 f¹ f¹³ 28 33 565 700 892 (1009 καταδικασθήσει) 1010 1071 1079 1195 1216 1230 1241 1242 1253 1344 1365 1546 1646 (2148 καταβιβασθεῖσα) 2174 Byz Lect itᵃ,ᵃᵘʳ, ᵇ,ᶜ,ᵉ,f,i,l,q,rˡ vg syrᵖ·ʰ copˢᵃ,ᵇᵒ goth ‖ καταβήσῃ (see Mt 11.23; Is 14.15) p⁷⁵ B D itᵈ syrᶜ·ˢ arm eth geo Diatessaronᵗ

8 ἐσθίετε...ὑμῖν 1 Cor 10.27   10–11 Lk 9.5   11 Καὶ τὸν κονιορτόν...ὑμῖν Ac 13.51; 18.6   12 Mt 10.15   λέγω...ἔσται Mt 11.24   Σοδόμοις...ἀνεκτότερον Gn 19.24–25 13–14 Τύρῳ καὶ Σιδῶνι Is 23; Eze 26—28; Jl 3.4–8; Am 1.9–10; Zch 9.2–4   15 ἕως... καταβιβασθήσῃ Is 14.13, 15   16 Mt 10.40; Jn 5.23; 15.23

The Return of the Seventy-two

17 The seventy-two men came back in great joy. "Lord," they said, "even the demons obeyed us when we commanded them in your name!" 18 Jesus answered them: "I saw Satan fall like lightning from heaven. 19 Listen! I have given you authority, so that you can walk on snakes and scorpions, and over all the power of the Enemy, and nothing will hurt you. 20 But don't be glad because the evil spirits obey you; rather be glad because your names are written in heaven."

Jesus Rejoices
(Also Matt. 11.25–27; 13.16–17)

21 At that same time Jesus was filled with joy by the Holy Spirit,[1] and said: "O Father, Lord of heaven and earth! I thank you because you have shown to the unlearned what you have hidden from the wise and learned. Yes, Father, this was done by your own choice and pleasure.

[1] 21 by the Holy Spirit: some mss. read by the Spirit; others read in his spirit

The Return of the Seventy-two

17 Ὑπέστρεψαν δὲ οἱ ἑβδομήκοντα [δύο][4] μετὰ χαρᾶς λέγοντες, Κύριε, καὶ τὰ δαιμόνια ὑποτάσσεται ἡμῖν ἐν τῷ ὀνόματί σου. 18 εἶπεν δὲ αὐτοῖς, Ἐθεώρουν τὸν Σατανᾶν ὡς ἀστραπὴν ἐκ τοῦ οὐρανοῦ πεσόντα. 19 ἰδοὺ δέδωκα ὑμῖν τὴν ἐξουσίαν τοῦ πατεῖν ἐπάνω ὄφεων καὶ σκορπίων, καὶ ἐπὶ πᾶσαν τὴν δύναμιν τοῦ ἐχθροῦ, καὶ οὐδὲν ὑμᾶς οὐ μὴ ἀδικήσῃ. 20 πλὴν ἐν τούτῳ μὴ χαίρετε ὅτι τὰ πνεύματα ὑμῖν ὑποτάσσεται, χαίρετε δὲ ὅτι τὰ ὀνόματα ὑμῶν ἐγγέγραπται ἐν τοῖς οὐρανοῖς.

The Rejoicing of Jesus
(Mt 11.25–27; 13.16–17)

21 Ἐν αὐτῇ τῇ ὥρᾳ ἠγαλλιάσατο [ἐν] τῷ πνεύματι τῷ ἁγίῳ[5] καὶ εἶπεν, Ἐξομολογοῦμαί σοι, πάτερ, κύριε τοῦ οὐρανοῦ καὶ τῆς γῆς, ὅτι ἀπέκρυψας ταῦτα ἀπὸ σοφῶν καὶ συνετῶν, καὶ ἀπεκάλυψας αὐτὰ νηπίοις· ναί, ὁ πατήρ, ὅτι οὕτως εὐδοκία ἐγένετο ἔμπροσθέν σου.

[4] 17 {C} δύο (see 10.1) p75 B D ita,aur,b,c,d,e,l vg syrhmg copsa,boms arm geo Diatessaronl,p,t,v Acts of Thomas Didascalia Origen Adamantius Ambrosiaster Ps-Clement Ephraem Teaching of Addai Augustine ∥ omit p45 ℵ A C K L W X Δ Θ Ξ Π Ψ 0115 f1 f13 28 33 565 700 892 1009 1010 1071 1079 1195 1216 1230 1241 1242 1253 1344 1365 1546 1646 2148 2174 Byz Lect l69m,70m,185m,1127m itf,i,q syr(c,s),p,h,pal copbo goth eth Irenaeuslat Clement Tertullian Origen Eusebius Titus-Bostra Basil Ambrose Jerome Cyril

[5] 21 {C} ἐν τῷ πνεύματι τῷ ἁγίῳ (p75 B omit ἐν) ℵ D Ξ 1241 ita,b,d,i,l (itaur vg omit ἐν) (syrc,s ἐν τῷ (or τῷ) πνεύματι) copsa,bo ∥ ἐν τῷ πνεύματι p45 ∥ ὁ Ἰησοῦς τῷ πνεύματι f13 2148 l547m (syrpalms) (arm add ἁγίῳ) ∥ τῷ πνεύματι ὁ Ἰησοῦς A W Δ Ψ (0115 892 ἐν τῷ) 28 565 700 1009 1010 1195 1216 1242 1344 1365 1546 1646 2174 Byz Lect l69s,m,70s,m,185m,1127s,m itf (ita ἐν τῷ) goth Clement Basil ∥ τῷ πνεύματι τῷ ἁγίῳ ὁ Ἰησοῦς C K Π f1 1079 1230 l547 syrh copbomss ∥ ὁ Ἰησοῦς ἐν τῷ πνεύματι τῷ ἁγίῳ L X 33 (Θ 1071 1253 omit ἐν) itc,e,ff2,rl (syrp,(pal mss)) geo ἐν τῷ (or τῷ) πνεύματι copbomss

18 τὸν...πεσόντα Jn 12.31; Re 12.8–9   ἐκ...πεσόντα Is 14.12   19 τοῦ πατεῖν...ὄφεων Gn 3.15; Ps 91.13; Mk 16.18   οὐδὲν...ἀδικήσῃ Mk 16.18   20 πνεύματα...ὑποτάσσεται Mt 7.22   τὰ ὀνόματα...οὐρανοῖς Ex 32.32; Php 4.3; Re 3.5   21 ἀπέκρυψας...νηπίοις 1 Cor 1.26–28

22 Πάντα[6] μοι παρεδόθη ὑπὸ τοῦ πατρός μου, καὶ οὐδεὶς γινώσκει τίς ἐστιν ὁ υἱὸς εἰ μὴ ὁ πατήρ, καὶ τίς ἐστιν ὁ πατὴρ εἰ μὴ ὁ υἱὸς καὶ ᾧ ἐὰν βούληται ὁ υἱὸς ἀποκαλύψαι. 23 Καὶ στραφεὶς πρὸς τοὺς μαθητὰς κατ᾽ ἰδίαν εἶπεν, Μακάριοι οἱ ὀφθαλμοὶ οἱ βλέποντες ἃ βλέπετε. 24 λέγω γὰρ ὑμῖν ὅτι πολλοὶ προφῆται καὶ βασιλεῖς ἠθέλησαν ἰδεῖν ἃ ὑμεῖς βλέπετε καὶ οὐκ εἶδαν, καὶ ἀκοῦσαι ἃ ἀκούετε καὶ οὐκ ἤκουσαν.

The Good Samaritan

25 Καὶ ἰδοὺ νομικός τις ἀνέστη ἐκπειράζων αὐτὸν λέγων, Διδάσκαλε, τί ποιήσας ζωὴν αἰώνιον κληρονομήσω; 26 ὁ δὲ εἶπεν πρὸς αὐτόν, Ἐν τῷ νόμῳ τί γέγραπται; πῶς ἀναγινώσκεις; 27 ὁ δὲ ἀποκριθεὶς εἶπεν, **Ἀγαπήσεις κύριον τὸν θεόν σου ἐξ ὅλης [τῆς] καρδίας σου καὶ ἐν ὅλῃ τῇ ψυχῇ σου καὶ ἐν ὅλῃ τῇ ἰσχύϊ σου καὶ ἐν ὅλῃ τῇ διανοίᾳ σου, καὶ τὸν πλησίον σου ὡς σεαυτόν.** 28 εἶπεν δὲ αὐτῷ, Ὀρθῶς ἀπεκρίθης· τοῦτο ποίει καὶ ζήσῃ. 29 ὁ δὲ θέλων δικαιῶσαι ἑαυτὸν εἶπεν πρὸς τὸν Ἰησοῦν, Καὶ τίς ἐστίν μου πλησίον; 30 ὑπολαβὼν ὁ Ἰησοῦς εἶπεν, Ἄνθρωπός τις κατέβαινεν ἀπὸ Ἰερουσαλὴμ εἰς Ἰεριχὼ καὶ λῃσταῖς περιέπεσεν, οἳ καὶ ἐκδύσαντες αὐτὸν καὶ πληγὰς ἐπιθέντες ἀπῆλθον ἀφέντες

---

[6] **22** {B} πάντα (see Mt 11.27) p[45,75] ℵ B D L Ξ Π 0124 f[1] f[13] 33 700 892 1079 1216* (1216[mg] εἶπεν ὁ κύριος, Πάντα at beginning of lection) 1241 1546 Lect l[1858.m] it[a,aur,b,d,e,f] vg syr[c,s] cop[sa,bo] arm eth geo Eusebius // καὶ στραφεὶς πρὸς τοὺς μαθητὰς εἶπεν, Πάντα (see 10.23) A C K W X Δ Θ Ψ (0115 στραφεὶς δέ) 28 565 1009 1010 (1071 1646 2174 μαθητὰς αὐτοῦ) 1195 1230 1242 1253 1344 1365 2148 Byz it[ff2,i,l] (it[c,q,r1] μαθητὰς αὐτοῦ) syr[p,h] cop[bomss] goth Diatessaron // ἔλεγε τοῖς ἀκολουθοῦσιν αὐτῷ l[12m]

---

22 Πάντα...μου Jn 3.35 οὐδεὶς...μὴ ὁ υἱός Jn 10.15   **23** Μακάριοι...βλέπετε Mt 13.16   **24** 1 Pe 1.10   **25** νομικός...αὐτόν Mt 22.35   Διδάσκαλε...κληρονομήσω Mt 19.16; Mk 10.17; Lk 18.18   **27** Ἀγαπήσεις...ἰσχύϊ σου Dt 6.5 (10.12; Jos 22.5; Mt 22.37; Mk 12.3) τὸν πλησίον σου ὡς σεαυτόν Lv 19.18 (Mt 19.19; 22.39; Mk 12.31; Ro 13.9; Ga 5.14; Jas 2.8)   **28** τοῦτο...ζήσῃ Lv 18.5; Ro 10.5; Ga 3.12

22 "My Father has given me all things: no one knows who the Son is except the Father, and no one knows who the Father is except the Son and those to whom the Son wants to reveal him."

23 Then Jesus turned to the disciples and said to them privately: "How happy are you, to see the things you see! 24 For many prophets and kings, I tell you, wanted to see what you see, but they could not, and to hear what you hear, but they did not."

The Parable of the Good Samaritan

25 Then a certain teacher of the Law came up and tried to trap Jesus. "Teacher," he asked, "what must I do to receive eternal life?" 26 Jesus answered him, "What do the Scriptures say? How do you interpret them?" 27 The man answered: " 'You must love the Lord your God with all your heart, and with all your soul, and with all your strength, and with all your mind'; and, 'You must love your neighbor as yourself.' " 28 "Your answer is correct," replied Jesus; "do this and you will live."

29 But the teacher of the Law wanted to put himself in the right, so he asked Jesus, "Who is my neighbor?" 30 Jesus answered: "A certain man was going down from Jerusalem to Jericho, when robbers attacked him, stripped him and beat him up, leaving him half dead.

³¹ It so happened that a priest was going down that road; when he saw the man he walked on by, on the other side. ³² In the same way a Levite also came there, went over and looked at the man, and then walked on by, on the other side. ³³ But a certain Samaritan who was traveling that way came upon him, and when he saw the man his heart was filled with pity. ³⁴ He went over to him, poured oil and wine on his wounds and bandaged them; then he put the man on his own animal and took him to an inn, where he took care of him. ³⁵ The next day he took out two silver coins and gave them to the innkeeper. 'Take care of him,' he told the innkeeper, 'and when I come back this way I will pay you back whatever you spend on him.'" ³⁶ And Jesus concluded, "Which one of these three seems to you to have been a neighbor to the man attacked by the robbers?" ³⁷ The teacher of the Law answered, "The one who was kind to him." Jesus replied, "You go, then, and do the same."

Jesus Visits Martha and Mary

³⁸ As Jesus and his disciples went on their way, he came to a certain village where a woman named Martha welcomed him in her home. ³⁹ She had a sister named Mary, who sat down at the feet of the Lord and listened to his teaching. ⁴⁰ Martha was upset over all the work she had to do; so she came and said, "Lord, don't you care that my sister has left me to do all the work by myself? Tell her to come and help me!" ⁴¹ The Lord answered her, "Martha, Martha! You are worried and troubled over so many things, ⁴² but just one is needed. Mary has chosen the right thing, and it will not be taken away from her."

ἡμιθανῆ. **31** κατὰ συγκυρίαν δὲ ἱερεύς τις κατέβαινεν ἐν τῇ ὁδῷ ἐκείνῃ, καὶ ἰδὼν αὐτὸν ἀντιπαρῆλθεν· **32** ὁμοίως δὲ καὶ Λευίτης [γενόμενος] κατὰ τὸν τόπον ἐλθὼν καὶ ἰδὼν ἀντιπαρῆλθεν. **33** Σαμαρίτης δέ τις ὁδεύων ἦλθεν κατ᾽ αὐτὸν καὶ ἰδὼν ἐσπλαγχνίσθη, **34** καὶ προσελθὼν κατέδησεν τὰ τραύματα αὐτοῦ ἐπιχέων ἔλαιον καὶ οἶνον, ἐπιβιβάσας δὲ αὐτὸν ἐπὶ τὸ ἴδιον κτῆνος ἤγαγεν αὐτὸν εἰς πανδοχεῖον καὶ ἐπεμελήθη αὐτοῦ. **35** καὶ ἐπὶ τὴν αὔριον ἐκβαλὼν ἔδωκεν δύο δηνάρια τῷ πανδοχεῖ καὶ εἶπεν, Ἐπιμελήθητι αὐτοῦ, καὶ ὅ τι ἂν προσδαπανήσῃς ἐγὼ ἐν τῷ ἐπανέρχεσθαί με ἀποδώσω σοι. **36** τίς τούτων τῶν τριῶν πλησίον δοκεῖ σοι γεγονέναι τοῦ ἐμπεσόντος εἰς τοὺς λῃστάς; **37** ὁ δὲ εἶπεν, Ὁ ποιήσας τὸ ἔλεος μετ᾽ αὐτοῦ. εἶπεν δὲ αὐτῷ ὁ Ἰησοῦς, Πορεύου καὶ σὺ ποίει ὁμοίως.

Visiting Martha and Mary

38 Ἐν δὲ τῷ πορεύεσθαι αὐτοὺς αὐτὸς εἰσῆλθεν εἰς κώμην τινά· γυνὴ δέ τις ὀνόματι Μάρθα ὑπεδέξατο αὐτόν⁷. **39** καὶ τῇδε ἦν ἀδελφὴ καλουμένη Μαριάμ, [ἣ] καὶ παρακαθεσθεῖσα πρὸς τοὺς πόδας τοῦ κυρίου ἤκουεν τὸν λόγον αὐτοῦ. **40** ἡ δὲ Μάρθα περιεσπᾶτο περὶ πολλὴν διακονίαν· ἐπιστᾶσα δὲ εἶπεν, Κύριε, οὐ μέλει σοι ὅτι ἡ ἀδελφή μου μόνην με κατέλιπεν διακονεῖν; εἰπὲ οὖν αὐτῇ ἵνα μοι συναντιλάβηται. **41** ἀποκριθεὶς δὲ εἶπεν αὐτῇ ὁ κύριος, Μάρθα Μάρθα, μεριμνᾷς καὶ θορυβάζῃ περὶ πολλά, **42** ἑνὸς δέ ἐστιν χρεία⁸· Μαριὰμ γὰρ τὴν ἀγαθὴν μερίδα ἐξελέξατο ἥτις οὐκ ἀφαιρεθήσεται αὐτῆς.

---

⁷ **38** {C} αὐτόν 𝔭⁴⁵,⁷⁵ B copˢᵃ ‖ αὐτὸν εἰς τὴν οἰκίαν 𝔭³ ℵ*·ᶜ C* (ℵᵃ C add αὐτῆς) L Ξ 33 ‖ αὐτὸν εἰς τὸν οἶκον αὐτῆς A D K (P ἑαυτῆς) W Δ (Θ αὐτοῖς for αὐτῆς) Π Ψ 0190 f¹ f¹³ 28 565 700 892 1009 1010 1071 1079 1195 1216 1230 1241 1242 1253 1344 1365 1546 1646 2148 2174 Byz Lect l⁶⁰ᵐ,⁶⁹ᵐ,⁷⁰ᵐ,¹⁸⁵ᵐ,⁵⁴⁷ᵐ, ¹¹²⁷ᵐ,(¹⁶⁶³ᵐ) itᵃ,ᵃᵘʳ,ᵇ,ᶜ,ᵈ,ₑ,ᶠ,ᶠᶠ²,ᵢ,ᵩ,ʳˡ vg syrᶜ,ˢ,ᵖ,ʰ,ᵖᵃˡ copᵇᵒ arm eth geo Basil

⁸ **41–42** {C} μεριμνᾷς καὶ θορυβάζῃ περὶ πολλά, ἑνὸς δέ ἐστιν χρεία

38–39 γυνὴ...Μαριὰμ Jn 11.1; 12.2–3

Teaching about Prayer
(Mt 6.9–15; 7.7–11)

11 Καὶ ἐγένετο ἐν τῷ εἶναι αὐτὸν ἐν τόπῳ τινὶ προσευχόμενον, ὡς ἐπαύσατο, εἶπέν τις τῶν μαθητῶν αὐτοῦ πρὸς αὐτόν, Κύριε, δίδαξον ἡμᾶς προσεύχεσθαι, καθὼς καὶ Ἰωάννης ἐδίδαξεν τοὺς μαθητὰς αὐτοῦ. 2 εἶπεν δὲ αὐτοῖς, Ὅταν προσεύχησθε, λέγετε,

Πάτερ[1], ἁγιασθήτω τὸ ὄνομά σου·
ἐλθέτω ἡ βασιλεία σου[2,3]

𝔭[45,75] C*,3vid W Θ Basil ‖ μεριμνᾷς καὶ τυρβάζῃ περὶ πολλά, ἑνὸς δέ ἐστιν χρεία A K P Δ Π Ψ f[13] 28 565 700 892 1009 1010 1071 1079 1195 1216 1230 1241 1242 1253 1344 1365 1546 1646 2148 2174 *Byz Lect* l[60m,69m,70m,185m,547m,1127m] Clement Basil Macarius Chrysostom Antiochus John-Damascus ‖ μεριμνᾷς καὶ θορυβάζῃ (or τυρβάζῃ) περὶ πολλά, ἑνὸς δέ ἐστιν χρεία it[aur,f,(q)] vg syr[c,p,h] cop[sa] ‖ μεριμνᾷς καὶ θορυβάζῃ περὶ πολλά, ὀλίγων δέ ἐστι χρεία ἢ ἑνός 𝔭[3] (ℵ* *omit* χρεία) ℵc (B χρεία ἐστίν) C[2] L f[1] 33 syr[hmg] cop[bo] eth Origen[1/2] Basil Jerome Cyril ‖ μεριμνᾷς καὶ θορυβάζῃ περὶ πολλά, ὀλίγων δέ ἐστιν χρεία 38 (syr[pal]) cop[boms] arm geo Origen[1/2] ‖ μεριμνᾷς καὶ θορυβάζῃ περὶ πολλά it[c] ‖ θορυβάζῃ περὶ πολλά (Clement) Augustine ‖ θορυβάζῃ D it[d] ‖ *omit* it[a,b,e,ff2,i,l,r1] syr[s] Ambrose Possidius

[1] 2 {A} πάτερ 𝔭[75] ℵ B f[1] 700 it[aur] vg syr[s] Marcion Tertullian Origen Cyril ‖ πάτερ ἡμῶν L arm ‖ πάτερ ἡμῶν ὁ ἐν τοῖς οὐρανοῖς (*see* Mt 6.9) A C D K P W X Δ Θ Π Ψ f[13] 28 565 892 1009 1010 1071 1079 1195 1216 1230 1241 1242 1253 1344 1365 (1546 ὑμῶν) 1646 2148 2174 *Byz Lect* l[69s,m,185s,m,1127s,m] it[(a),b,(c),d,e,f,(ff2,i),l,q,r1?] syr[c,p,h] cop[sa,bo] eth geo Diatessaron Origen

[2] 2 {B} ἐλθέτω ἡ βασιλεία σου (*see* Mt 6.10) A B K L X Θ Π Ψ (𝔭[75vid] ℵ C P W Δ f[13] 1241 ἐλθάτω) f[1] 28 33 (565 1253 *omit* σου) 892 1009 1010 1071 1079 1195 1216 1230 1242 1344 1365 1546 1646 2148 2174 *Byz Lect* l[69s,m,185s,m,1127s,m] it[s,aur,b,c,e,f,ff2,i,l,q,r1] vg syr[c,s,p,h] cop[sa,bo] arm geo[1,B] Origen ‖ ἐλθέτω τὸ πνεῦμά σου τὸ ἅγιον ἐφ᾽ ἡμᾶς καὶ καθαρισάτω ἡμᾶς (162) 700 Marcion Gregory-Nyssa (Maximus *omit* ἐφ᾽ ἡμᾶς) ‖ ἐφ᾽ ἡμᾶς ἐλθέτω σου ἡ βασιλεία D it[d] ‖ *omit* geo[A]

[3] 2 {A} σου· (*see footnote 2*) 𝔭[75] B L f[1] vg syr[c,s] arm Marcion Tertullian Origen Augustine Cyril ‖ σου· γενηθήτω τὸ θέλημά σου, it[a] vg[mss] cop[sa,boms] geo ‖ σου· γενηθήτω τὸ θέλημά σου ὡς ἐν οὐρανῷ καὶ ἐπὶ τῆς γῆς. (*see* Mt 6.10) (ℵ* οὕτω καὶ ἐπὶ γῆς) ℵ[a] K X Π Ψ (ℵc A C D P W Δ Θ 892 1079 1195 l[48] *omit* τῆς) f[13] 28 33 (565 *omit* σου) 700 1009 1010

---

1 προσεύχεσθαι...αὐτοῦ Lk 5.33

Jesus' Teaching on Prayer
(Also Matt. 6.9–13; 7.7–11)

11 One time Jesus was praying in a certain place. When he finished, one of his disciples said to him, "Lord, teach us to pray, just as John taught his disciples." [2] Jesus said to them, "This is what you should pray:

'Father,
May your name be kept holy,
May your Kingdom come.

³ Give us day by day the food we need.
⁴ Forgive us our sins,
For we forgive everyone who has done us wrong.
And do not bring us to hard testing.' "
⁵ And Jesus said to his disciples: "Suppose one of you should go to a friend's house at midnight and tell him, 'Friend, let me borrow three loaves of bread. ⁶ A friend of mine who is on a trip has just come to my house and I don't have a thing to offer him!' ⁷ And suppose your friend should answer from inside, 'Don't bother me! The door is already locked, my children and I are in bed, and I can't get up to give you anything.' ⁸ Well, what then? I tell you, even if he will not get up and give you the bread because he is your friend, yet he will get up and give you everything you need because you are not ashamed to keep on asking. ⁹ And so I say to you: Ask, and you will receive; seek, and you will find; knock, and the door will be opened to you. ¹⁰ For everyone who asks will receive, and he who seeks will find, and the door will be opened to him who knocks. ¹¹ Would any one of you fathers

3 τὸν ἄρτον ἡμῶν τὸν ἐπιούσιον δίδου ἡμῖν τὸ
καθ᾽ ἡμέραν·

4 καὶ ἄφες ἡμῖν τὰς ἁμαρτίας ἡμῶν,
καὶ γὰρ αὐτοὶ ἀφίομεν παντὶ ὀφείλοντι
ἡμῖν·
καὶ μὴ εἰσενέγκῃς ἡμᾶς εἰς πειρασμόν⁴.

5 Καὶ εἶπεν πρὸς αὐτούς, Τίς ἐξ ὑμῶν ἕξει φίλον καὶ πορεύσεται πρὸς αὐτὸν μεσονυκτίου καὶ εἴπῃ αὐτῷ, Φίλε, χρῆσόν μοι τρεῖς ἄρτους, 6 ἐπειδὴ φίλος μου παρεγένετο ἐξ ὁδοῦ πρός με καὶ οὐκ ἔχω ὃ παραθήσω αὐτῷ· 7 κἀκεῖνος ἔσωθεν ἀποκριθεὶς εἴπῃ, Μή μοι κόπους πάρεχε· ἤδη ἡ θύρα κέκλεισται, καὶ τὰ παιδία μου μετ᾽ ἐμοῦ εἰς τὴν κοίτην εἰσίν· οὐ δύναμαι ἀναστὰς δοῦναί σοι. 8 λέγω ὑμῖν, εἰ καὶ οὐ δώσει αὐτῷ ἀναστὰς διὰ τὸ εἶναι φίλον αὐτοῦ, διά γε τὴν ἀναίδειαν αὐτοῦ ἐγερθεὶς δώσει αὐτῷ ὅσων χρῄζει. 9 κἀγὼ ὑμῖν λέγω, αἰτεῖτε, καὶ δοθήσεται ὑμῖν· ζητεῖτε, καὶ εὑρήσετε· κρούετε, καὶ ἀνοιγήσεται ὑμῖν. 10 πᾶς γὰρ ὁ αἰτῶν λαμβάνει, καὶ ὁ ζητῶν εὑρίσκει, καὶ τῷ κρούοντι ἀνοίγεται⁵. 11 τίνα δὲ ἐξ ὑμῶν αἰτήσει τὸν πατέρα ὁ υἱὸς

1071 1216 (1230 *omit σου and* τῆς) 1241 1242 1253 1344 1365 1546 1646 2148 2174 *Byz Lect* *l*⁶⁹ˢ·ᵐ,¹⁸⁵ˢ·ᵐ,¹¹²⁷ˢ·ᵐ (it^aur,b,c,d,e,f,ff²,i,l,q,r1 syr^p,h cop^bo eth ἐπὶ τῆς γῆς *or* ἐπὶ γῆς) Diatessaron Titus-Bostra

⁴ 4 {A} πειρασμόν 𝔭⁷⁵ ℵ*·ᵃ B L *f*¹ 700 vg syrˢ cop^sa,bo arm geo Marcion Tertullian Origen Augustine Cyril ‖ πειρασμὸν ἀλλὰ ῥῦσαι ἡμᾶς ἀπὸ τοῦ πονηροῦ (*see* Mt 6.13) (ℵᶜ) A C D K W X Δ Θ Π Ψ *f*¹³ 28 33 565 892 1009 1010 1071 1079 1195 1216 1230 1241 1242 1253 1344 1365 (1546 ὑμᾶς) 1646 2148 2174 *Byz Lect* *l*⁶⁹ˢ·ᵐ,¹⁸⁵ˢ·ᵐ,¹¹²⁷ˢ·ᵐ it^aur,b,c,d,f,ff²,i,l,q,r1 syr^c,p,h cop^bomss (eth) Diatessaron

⁵ 10 {C} ἀνοίγεται 𝔭⁷⁵ B D^gr syr^c,s,p,h cop^bo ‖ ἀνοιγήσεται (*see* Mt 7.7, 8; Lk 11.9) 𝔭⁴⁵ᵛⁱᵈ ℵ C L X Θ Ψ *f*¹ *f*¹³ 28 33 565 700 892 1009 1071 1079 1195 1230 1241 1242 1253 1546 1646 2148 *l*⁷⁰ᵖᵗ,⁷⁶ᵖᵗ,¹⁸⁴,¹⁸⁵ˢ·ᵐ,²¹¹,⁹⁵⁰ arm geo ‖ ἀνοιχθήσεται A K W Δ Π 1010 1216 1344 1365 2174 *Byz Lect* *l*⁶⁹ˢ·ᵐ,⁷⁰ᵖᵗ,⁷⁶ᵖᵗ,¹¹²⁷ˢ·ᵐ,¹⁵⁹⁹ᵐ ‖ ἀνοιγήσεται *or* ἀνοιχθήσεται it^aur,b,c,d,f,ff²,i,l,q,r1 vg cop^sa

---

7 Μή...πάρεχε Mt 26.10; Lk 18.5; Ga 6.17   8 διά...χρῄζει Lk 18.5

ἰχθύν⁶, καὶ ἀντὶ ἰχθύος⁷ ὄφιν αὐτῷ ἐπιδώσει;ᵃ **12** ἢ καὶ αἰτήσει ᾠόν, ἐπιδώσει⁸ αὐτῷ σκορπίον;ᵃ **13** εἰ οὖν ὑμεῖς πονηροὶ ὑπάρχοντες οἴδατε δόματα ἀγαθὰ διδόναι τοῖς τέκνοις ὑμῶν, πόσῳ μᾶλλον ὁ πατὴρ [ὁ] ἐξ οὐρανοῦ⁹ δώσει πνεῦμα ἅγιον¹⁰ τοῖς αἰτοῦσιν αὐτόν.ᵇ

give his son a snake when he asks for fish? ¹² Or would you give him a scorpion when he asks for an egg? ¹³ As bad as you are, you know how to give good things to your children. How much more, then, the Father in heaven will give the Holy Spirit to those who ask him!''

⁶ **11** {B} ἰχθύν 𝔓⁴⁵ (𝔓⁷⁵ ἰσχύν) B 1241 itᶠᶠ²,ⁱ,ˡ syrˢ copˢᵃ arm Marcion Origen Epiphanius ∥ ἄρτον μὴ λίθον ἐπιδώσει αὐτῷ; ἢ ἰχθύν ℵ L 28 33 700 892 1344 2148 𝑙³¹,¹⁸⁵ itᵃᵘʳ,ᵇ,ᶜ,(ᵈ),ᶠ,ʳˡ vg copᵇᵒ geo ∥ ἄρτον μὴ λίθον ἐπιδώσει αὐτῷ; ἢ καὶ ἰχθύν (see Mt 7.9) A C (Dᵍʳ αὐτῷ ἐπιδώσει) K W X Δ Θ Π Ψ f¹ f¹³ 1009 1010 1071 1079 1195 1216 (1230 1253 καὶ ἐάν) 1365 1546 2174 *Byz Lect* 𝑙⁶⁹ˢ,ᵐ,⁷⁰ᵖᵗ,¹⁸⁵ᵐ,¹¹²⁷ˢ,ᵐ (𝑙⁷⁰ᵖᵗ δώσει) itᵃ syrᵖ,ʰ (syr⁽ᶜ⁾,ʰ with * εἰ *for* ἢ) eth Adamantius ∥ ἄρτον μὴ λίθον ἐπιδώσει αὐτῷ; ἢ καὶ ἐὰν αἰτήσῃ ἰχθύν (see Mt 7.9) 1242

⁷ **11** {C} καὶ ἀντὶ ἰχθύος 𝔓⁴⁵,⁷⁵ B copˢᵃ Marcion Epiphanius ∥ μὴ ἀντὶ ἰχθύος ℵ A C D K L W X Δ Θ Π (Ψ τοῦ ἰχθύος) f¹ f¹³ 28 33 700 892 1009 1010 1071 1079 1195 1216 1230 1241 1242 1253 1365 1546 2148 2174 *Byz Lect* 𝑙⁶⁹ˢ,ᵐ,¹⁸⁵ˢ,ᵐ,¹¹²⁷ˢ,ᵐ itᵃᵘʳ,ᵇ,ᶜ,ᵈ,ᶠ,ᶠᶠ²,ⁱ,ˡ, q,ʳˡ vg syrᶜ,ˢ,ᵖ,ʰ copᵇᵒ arm geo Origen ∥ μὴ καὶ ἀντὶ ἰχθύος Γ 1012 ∥ μή 1344 copᵇᵒᵐˢˢ

⁸ **12** {C} ἐπιδώσει 𝔓⁴⁵,⁷⁵ B L 892 copˢᵃ ∥ μὴ ἐπιδώσει ℵ A C (D) K W X Δ Θ Π Ψ f¹ f¹³ 28 33 565 700 1009 1010 1071 1079 1195 1216 1230 1241 1242 1253 1365 1546 1646 2148 2174 *Byz Lect* 𝑙⁶⁹ˢ,ᵐ,⁷⁰ᵖᵗ,¹⁸⁵ˢ,ᵐ,¹¹²⁷ˢ,ᵐ itᵃ²,ᵃᵘʳ,ᵇ,ᶜ,ᵈ,ᶠ, ᶠᶠ²,ⁱ,ˡ,q,ʳˡ vg copᵇᵒ arm geo

⁹ **13** {D} ὁ ἐξ οὐρανοῦ (see Mt 7.11) A B C D K W Δ Θ Π f¹ f¹³ 28 565 700 1009 1010 1079 1195 1230 1241 1242 1253 1365 1546 1646 2148 2174 *Byz Lect* 𝑙⁶⁹ˢ,ᵐ,¹⁸⁵ᵐ syr⁽ˢ⁾,ʰ Antiochus ∥ ὑμῶν ὁ ἐξ οὐρανοῦ 𝑙¹¹²⁷ᵐ (𝑙¹¹²⁷ *omit* ὁ) itᵃᵘʳ,ᵇ,ᶜ,ᶠᶠ²,q,ʳˡ ∥ ἐξ οὐρανοῦ 𝔓⁷⁵ ℵ L X Ψ 33 892 1071 1216 itᵃ²,ᵈ,ᶠ vg syrᶜ,ᵖ copˢᵃ,ᵇᵒ arm geo ∥ ὁ οὐράνιος 𝔓⁴⁵ 𝑙¹⁸⁵ itˡ (Epiphanius) Cyril ∥ *omit* itⁱ

¹⁰ **13** {B} πνεῦμα ἅγιον 𝔓⁷⁵ ℵ A B C K W X Δ Π Ψ f¹ f¹³ 28 33 565 700 892 1009 1010 1071 1079 1195 1216 1241 1242 1365 1546 2148 2174 *Byz Lect* 𝑙⁶⁹ᵐ,⁷⁰ᵖᵗ,¹⁸⁵ᵐ,¹¹²⁷ᵐ itᶠ,q syrᶜ,ᵖ,ʰ copˢᵃ,ᵇᵒ geo Tertullian Epiphanius ∥ πνεῦμα ἀγαθόν 𝔓⁴⁵ L 1230 1253 1646 𝑙⁴,¹²,¹⁵,¹⁹,⁶⁹,⁷⁰ᵖᵗ,¹⁸⁵,²¹¹,¹¹²⁷ itᵃᵘʳ vg syrʰᵐᵍ Cyril ∥ ἀγαθὸν δόμα D it⁽ᵃ²⁾,ᵇ,ᶜ,ᵈ,ᶠᶠ²,ⁱ,ˡ,ʳˡ Origen Ambrose mssᵃᶜᶜ·ᵗᵒ ᴬᵐᵇʳᵒˢᵉ ∥ δόματα ἀγαθά Θ 𝑙³²ᵐ,¹⁵⁹⁹ᵐ Diatessaronⁱ,ˡ ∥ ἀγαθὸν δόμα πνεύματος ἁγίου eth ∥ ἀγαθά (see Mt 7.11) syrˢ arm

ᵃ ᵃ **11-12** *a question, a question:* TR WH Bov Nes BF² AV RV ASV TT Luth Jer Seg ∥ *a minor, a question:* RSV NEB Zür

ᵇ **13** *b major:* WH Bov Nes BF² Seg ∥ *b question:* TR AV RV ASV RSVᵉᵈ ∥ *b exclamation:* RSVᵉᵈ NEB TT Zür Luth Jer

Jesus and Beelzebul
(Also Matt. 12.22–30; Mark 3.20–27)

[14] Jesus was driving out a demon that could not talk; when the demon went out, the man began to talk. The crowds were amazed, [15] but some of them said, "It is Beelzebul, the chief of the demons, who gives him the power to drive them out." [16] Others wanted to trap him, so they asked him to perform a miracle to show God's approval. [17] But Jesus knew their thoughts and said to them: "Any country that divides itself into groups that fight one another will not last very long; a family divided against itself falls apart. [18] So if Satan's kingdom has groups fighting each other, how can it last? You say that I drive out demons because Beelzebul gives me the power to do so. [19] If this is how I drive them out, how do your followers drive them out? Your own followers prove that you are completely wrong! [20] No, it is rather by means of God's power that I drive out demons, which proves that the Kingdom of God has already come to you.

[21] "When a strong man, with all his weapons ready, guards his own house, all his belongings are safe. [22] But when a stronger man attacks him and defeats him, he carries away all the weapons the owner was depending on and divides up what he stole.

[23] "Anyone who is not for me, is really against me; anyone who does not help me gather, is really scattering."

Jesus and Beelzebul
(Mt 12.22–30; Mk 3.20–27)

14 Καὶ ἦν ἐκβάλλων δαιμόνιον[, καὶ αὐτὸ ἦν][11] κωφόν· ἐγένετο δὲ τοῦ δαιμονίου ἐξελθόντος ἐλάλησεν ὁ κωφός. καὶ ἐθαύμασαν οἱ ὄχλοι· **15** τινὲς δὲ ἐξ αὐτῶν εἶπαν, Ἐν Βεελζεβοὺλ τῷ ἄρχοντι τῶν δαιμονίων ἐκβάλλει τὰ δαιμόνια· **16** ἕτεροι δὲ πειράζοντες σημεῖον ἐξ οὐρανοῦ ἐζήτουν παρ' αὐτοῦ. **17** αὐτὸς δὲ εἰδὼς αὐτῶν τὰ διανοήματα εἶπεν αὐτοῖς, Πᾶσα βασιλεία ἐφ' ἑαυτὴν διαμερισθεῖσα ἐρημοῦται,[c] καὶ οἶκος ἐπὶ οἶκον πίπτει. **18** εἰ δὲ καὶ ὁ Σατανᾶς ἐφ' ἑαυτὸν διεμερίσθη, πῶς σταθήσεται ἡ βασιλεία αὐτοῦ; ὅτι λέγετε ἐν Βεελζεβοὺλ ἐκβάλλειν με τὰ δαιμόνια. **19** εἰ δὲ ἐγὼ ἐν Βεελζεβοὺλ ἐκβάλλω τὰ δαιμόνια, οἱ υἱοὶ ὑμῶν ἐν τίνι ἐκβάλλουσιν; διὰ τοῦτο αὐτοὶ ὑμῶν κριταὶ ἔσονται. **20** εἰ δὲ ἐν δακτύλῳ θεοῦ ἐκβάλλω τὰ δαιμόνια, ἄρα ἔφθασεν ἐφ' ὑμᾶς ἡ βασιλεία τοῦ θεοῦ. **21** ὅταν ὁ ἰσχυρὸς καθωπλισμένος φυλάσσῃ τὴν ἑαυτοῦ αὐλήν, ἐν εἰρήνῃ ἐστὶν τὰ ὑπάρχοντα αὐτοῦ· **22** ἐπὰν δὲ ἰσχυρότερος αὐτοῦ ἐπελθὼν νικήσῃ αὐτόν, τὴν πανοπλίαν αὐτοῦ αἴρει ἐφ' ᾗ ἐπεποίθει, καὶ τὰ σκῦλα αὐτοῦ διαδίδωσιν. **23** ὁ μὴ ὢν μετ' ἐμοῦ κατ' ἐμοῦ ἐστιν, καὶ ὁ μὴ συνάγων μετ' ἐμοῦ σκορπίζει[12].

---

[11] **14** {D}, καὶ αὐτὸ ἦν A^c C K W X Δ Θ Π Ψ f[13] 28 565 (700*^vid αὐτῷ) 700^c 1009 1010 1071 1079 1195 1216 1230 1242 1253 1365 1546 1646 2148 2174 *Byz Lect* it^a2,aur,b,c,f,ff2,i,l,q,rl vg syr^(p),h geo Diatessaron ∥ omit 𝔭45,75 ℵ A* B L f[1] 33 892 1241 (syr^c,s) cop^sa,bo arm eth

[12] **23** {A} σκορπίζει (*see* Mt 12.30) 𝔭45 (𝔭75 σκορπίσει) ℵ^a A B C* D K W X Δ Π f[1] f[13] 28 565 700 1010 1079 1195 1216 1230 1241 1242 1253 1365 1546 1646 2148 2174 *Byz Lect* it^a2,aur,b,c,d,f,ff2,i,l,q,rl vg syr^c,p,h cop^sa,boms arm geo Diatessaron ∥ σκορπίζει με ℵ*,b C² L Θ Ψ 33 892 1009 1071 (syr^s) cop^bo eth

---

[c] **17** c minor: WH Bov Nes BF² RV^mg ASV^mg RSV TT Zür Luth Jer Seg ∥ c major: (TR) AV RV ASV NEB TT^mg

---

15 εἶπαν...δαιμόνια Mt 9.34; 1 Cor 1.22   **20** δακτύλῳ θεοῦ Ex 8.19   **16** πειράζοντες...αὐτοῦ Mt 12.38; 16.1; Mk 8.11;   **21–22** Ps Sol 5.4   **23** ὁ μὴ ὢν μετ' ἐμοῦ...ἐστιν Mk 9.40; Lk 9.50

The Return of the Unclean Spirit
(Mt 12.43–45)

24 Ὅταν τὸ ἀκάθαρτον πνεῦμα ἐξέλθη ἀπὸ τοῦ ἀνθρώπου, διέρχεται δι᾽ ἀνύδρων τόπων ζητοῦν ἀνάπαυσιν,[d] καὶ μὴ εὑρίσκον[d] λέγει[13], Ὑποστρέψω εἰς τὸν οἶκόν μου ὅθεν ἐξῆλθον· **25** καὶ ἐλθὸν εὑρίσκει σεσαρωμένον[14] καὶ κεκοσμημένον. **26** τότε πορεύεται καὶ παραλαμβάνει ἕτερα πνεύματα πονηρότερα ἑαυτοῦ ἑπτά, καὶ εἰσελθόντα κατοικεῖ ἐκεῖ, καὶ γίνεται τὰ ἔσχατα τοῦ ἀνθρώπου ἐκείνου χείρονα τῶν πρώτων.

True Blessedness

27 Ἐγένετο δὲ ἐν τῷ λέγειν αὐτὸν ταῦτα ἐπάρασά τις φωνὴν γυνὴ ἐκ τοῦ ὄχλου εἶπεν αὐτῷ, Μακαρία ἡ κοιλία ἡ βαστάσασά σε καὶ μαστοὶ οὓς ἐθήλασας. **28** αὐτὸς δὲ εἶπεν, Μενοῦν μακάριοι οἱ ἀκούοντες τὸν λόγον τοῦ θεοῦ καὶ φυλάσσοντες.

The Demand for a Sign
(Mt 12.38–42; Mk 8.12)

29 Τῶν δὲ ὄχλων ἐπαθροιζομένων ἤρξατο λέγειν, Ἡ γενεὰ αὕτη γενεὰ πονηρά ἐστιν· σημεῖον ζητεῖ, καὶ σημεῖον οὐ δοθήσεται αὐτῇ εἰ μὴ τὸ σημεῖον Ἰωνᾶ.

---

[13] **24** {C} λέγει 𝔭45 ℵ* A C D K W Δ Π Ψ *f*1 *f*13 28 565 700 1009 1010 1079 1195 1216 1230 1242 1253 1365 1546 1646 2148 2174 *Byz Lect* it^(a2,aur,c,d,f, ff2,i,q,rl) vg syr^(c,s,p) arm geo ∥ τότε λέγει (*see* Mt 12.44) 𝔭75 ℵc B L X Θ Ξ 0124 33 892 1071 1241 *l*48,184 it^(b,l) syr^h cop^(sa,bo) eth Origen^lat

[14] **25** {B} σεσαρωμένον 𝔭75 ℵ* A D K W X Δ Θ Π 0124 28 565 700 1009 1010 1071 1079 1216 1241 1242 1546 1646 2148 *Byz Lect* it^(a2),aur,b,c,(d),e,ff2,i,q,l vg syr^(c,s,p,h) cop^sa arm geo1 ∥ σχολάζοντα 1365 ∥ σχολάζοντα σεσαρωμένον ℵc B C L Ξ Ψ *f*1 *f*13 33 892 1195 1230 2174 it^(f,l,rl) cop^bo eth Origen^lat ∥ σεσαρωμένον σχολάζοντα 69 124 346 geo2 ∥ σχολάζοντα καὶ σεσαρωμένον 1253 syr^(h with *)

---

d d **24** *d* minor, *d* none: (TR) WH Bov Nes BF2 (AV) (RV) (RSV) (NEB) (TT) (Zür) (Jer) (Seg) ∥ *d* none, *d* major: WH^mg Luth ∥ *d* minor, *d* minor: ASV

---

26 γίνεται...πρώτων Jn 5.14   **27** Μακαρία...σε Lk 1.28, 42, 48   **29** Ἡ γενεὰ... Ἰωνᾶ Mt 16.4 σημεῖον ζητεῖ 1 Cor 1.22

The Return of the Evil Spirit
(Also Matt. 12.43–45)

[24] "When an evil spirit goes out of a man, it travels over dry country looking for a place to rest; if it doesn't find one, it says to itself, 'I will go back to my house which I left.' [25] So it goes back and finds the house clean and all fixed up. [26] Then it goes out and brings seven other spirits even worse than itself, and they come and live there. So that man is in worse shape, when it is all over, than he was at the beginning."

True Happiness

[27] When Jesus had said this, a woman spoke up from the crowd and said to him, "How happy is the woman who bore you and nursed you!" [28] But Jesus answered, "Rather, how happy are those who hear the word of God and obey it!"

The Demand for a Miracle
(Also Matt. 12.38–42)

[29] As the people crowded around Jesus he went on to say: "How evil are the people of this day! They ask for a miracle as a sign of God's approval, but none will be given them except the miracle of

Jonah. ³⁰ In the same way that the prophet Jonah was a sign for the people of Nineveh, so the Son of Man will be a sign for the people of this day. ³¹ On the Judgment Day the Queen from the South will stand up and accuse the people of today, because she traveled halfway around the world to listen to Solomon's wise teaching; and there is something here, I tell you, greater than Solomon. ³² On the Judgment Day the people of Nineveh will stand up and accuse you, because they turned from their sins when they heard Jonah preach; and there is something here, I tell you, greater than Jonah!"

The Light of the Body
(Also Matt. 5.15; 6.22–23)

³³ "No one lights a lamp and then hides it or puts it under a bowl; instead, he puts it on the lamp-stand, so that people may see the light as they come in. ³⁴ Your eyes are like a lamp for the body: when your eyes are clear your whole body is full of light; but when your eyes are bad your whole body will be in darkness. ³⁵ Be careful, then, that the light in you is not darkness. ³⁶ If, then, your whole body is full of light, with no part of it in darkness, it will be bright all over, as when a lamp shines on you with its brightness."

Jesus Accuses the Pharisees and the Teachers of the Law
(Also Matt. 23.1–36; Mark 12.38–40)

³⁷ When Jesus finished speaking, a Pharisee invited him to eat with him; so he went in and sat down to eat. ³⁸ The Pharisee was surprised when he noticed that Jesus had not washed before eating. ³⁹ So the Lord said to him:

30 καθὼς γὰρ ἐγένετο Ἰωνᾶς τοῖς Νινευίταις σημεῖον, οὕτως ἔσται καὶ ὁ υἱὸς τοῦ ἀνθρώπου τῇ γενεᾷ ταύτῃ. 31 βασίλισσα νότου ἐγερθήσεται ἐν τῇ κρίσει μετὰ τῶν ἀνδρῶν τῆς γενεᾶς ταύτης καὶ κατακρινεῖ αὐτούς· ὅτι ἦλθεν ἐκ τῶν περάτων τῆς γῆς ἀκοῦσαι τὴν σοφίαν Σολομῶνος, καὶ ἰδοὺ πλεῖον Σολομῶνος ὧδε. 32 ἄνδρες Νινευῖται ἀναστήσονται ἐν τῇ κρίσει μετὰ τῆς γενεᾶς ταύτης καὶ κατακρινοῦσιν αὐτήν· ὅτι μετενόησαν εἰς τὸ κήρυγμα Ἰωνᾶ, καὶ ἰδοὺ πλεῖον Ἰωνᾶ ὧδε.

The Light of the Body
(Mt 5.15; 6.22–23)

33 Οὐδεὶς λύχνον ἅψας εἰς κρύπτην τίθησιν [οὐδὲ ὑπὸ τὸν μόδιον]¹⁵ ἀλλ' ἐπὶ τὴν λυχνίαν, ἵνα οἱ εἰσπορευόμενοι τὸ φῶς βλέπωσιν. 34 ὁ λύχνος τοῦ σώματός ἐστιν ὁ ὀφθαλμός σου. ὅταν ὁ ὀφθαλμός σου ἁπλοῦς ᾖ, καὶ ὅλον τὸ σῶμά σου φωτεινόν ἐστιν· ἐπὰν δὲ πονηρὸς ᾖ, καὶ τὸ σῶμά σου σκοτεινόν. 35 σκόπει οὖν μὴ τὸ φῶς τὸ ἐν σοὶ σκότος ἐστίν. 36 εἰ οὖν τὸ σῶμά σου ὅλον φωτεινόν, μὴ ἔχον μέρος τι σκοτεινόν, ἔσται φωτεινὸν ὅλον ὡς ὅταν ὁ λύχνος τῇ ἀστραπῇ φωτίζῃ σε.

The Denouncing of the Pharisees and Lawyers
(Mt 23.1–36; Mk 12.38–40; Lk 20.45–47)

37 Ἐν δὲ τῷ λαλῆσαι ἐρωτᾷ αὐτὸν Φαρισαῖος ὅπως ἀριστήσῃ παρ' αὐτῷ· εἰσελθὼν δὲ ἀνέπεσεν. 38 ὁ δὲ Φαρισαῖος ἰδὼν ἐθαύμασεν ὅτι οὐ πρῶτον ἐβαπτίσθη πρὸ τοῦ ἀρίστου. 39 εἶπεν δὲ ὁ κύριος πρὸς αὐτόν, Νῦν

---

¹⁵ 33 {D} οὐδὲ ὑπὸ τὸν μόδιον (see Mt 5.15; Mk 4.21) ℵ A B C D K W X Δ Θ Π Ψ f¹³ 28 33 (565 1365 ἤ for οὐδέ) 892 1009 1010 1071 1079 1195 1216 1230 1242 (1253 l²¹¹ ἐπί for ὑπό) 1344 1546 1646 2174 Byz Lect l⁶⁹⁸,ᵐ,¹¹²⁷ˢ,ᵐ itᵃ,ᵃᵘʳ,ᵇ,ᶜ,ᵈ,ᵉ,ᶠ,ff²,ᶦ,q,rl vg syr⁽ᶜ,ᵖ⁾,ʰ,ᵖᵃˡ copᵇᵒ (copᵇᵒᵐˢˢ ἤ for οὐδέ) (Clement) ‖ omit 𝔭⁴⁵,⁷⁵ L Ξ 0124 f¹ 700 1241 (2148 omit also ἀλλ' ἐπὶ τὴν λυχνίαν) syrˢ copˢᵃ arm geo

31 βασίλισσα...Σολομῶνος 1 Kgs 10.1–10; 2 Chr 9.1–12   32 ἄνδρες...Ἰωνᾶ Jon 3.8, 10
33 Mk 4.21; Lk 8.16   37 ἐρωτᾷ...ἀνέπεσεν Lk 7.36; 14.1   38 οὐ...ἀρίστου Mt 15.2

ὑμεῖς οἱ Φαρισαῖοι τὸ ἔξωθεν τοῦ ποτηρίου καὶ τοῦ πίνακος καθαρίζετε, τὸ δὲ ἔσωθεν ὑμῶν γέμει ἁρπαγῆς καὶ πονηρίας. **40** ἄφρονες, οὐχ ὁ ποιήσας τὸ ἔξωθεν καὶ τὸ ἔσωθεν ἐποίησεν; **41** πλὴν τὰ ἐνόντα δότε ἐλεημοσύνην, καὶ ἰδοὺ πάντα καθαρὰ ὑμῖν ἐστιν. **42** ἀλλὰ οὐαὶ ὑμῖν τοῖς Φαρισαίοις, ὅτι ἀποδεκατοῦτε τὸ ἡδύοσμον καὶ τὸ πήγανον καὶ πᾶν λάχανον, καὶ παρέρχεσθε τὴν κρίσιν καὶ τὴν ἀγάπην τοῦ θεοῦ· ταῦτα δὲ ἔδει ποιῆσαι κάκεῖνα μὴ παρεῖναι[16]. **43** οὐαὶ ὑμῖν τοῖς Φαρισαίοις, ὅτι ἀγαπᾶτε τὴν πρωτοκαθεδρίαν ἐν ταῖς συναγωγαῖς καὶ τοὺς ἀσπασμοὺς ἐν ταῖς ἀγοραῖς. **44** οὐαὶ ὑμῖν, ὅτι ἐστὲ ὡς τὰ μνημεῖα τὰ ἄδηλα, καὶ οἱ ἄνθρωποι [οἱ] περιπατοῦντες ἐπάνω οὐκ οἴδασιν.

45 Ἀποκριθεὶς δέ τις τῶν νομικῶν λέγει αὐτῷ, Διδάσκαλε, ταῦτα λέγων καὶ ἡμᾶς ὑβρίζεις. **46** ὁ δὲ εἶπεν, Καὶ ὑμῖν τοῖς νομικοῖς οὐαί, ὅτι φορτίζετε τοὺς ἀνθρώπους φορτία δυσβάστακτα, καὶ αὐτοὶ ἑνὶ τῶν δακτύλων ὑμῶν οὐ προσψαύετε τοῖς φορτίοις. **47** οὐαὶ ὑμῖν, ὅτι οἰκοδομεῖτε τὰ μνημεῖα τῶν προφητῶν, οἱ δὲ πατέρες ὑμῶν ἀπέκτειναν αὐτούς. **48** ἄρα μάρτυρές ἐστε καὶ συνευδοκεῖτε τοῖς ἔργοις τῶν πατέρων ὑμῶν, ὅτι αὐτοὶ μὲν ἀπέκτειναν αὐτούς ὑμεῖς δὲ οἰκοδομεῖτε[17].

---

[16] **42** {B} ταῦτα δὲ ἔδει ποιῆσαι κἀκεῖνα (or καὶ ἐκεῖνα) μὴ παρεῖναι 𝔓75 B L f13 1071 (28 700 *omit* δέ, 1241 *omit* δέ *and* μή) (𝔓45 C K X Δ Θ Π Ψ 0108 33 892 1009 1079 1546 2148 *l*69,70,185,211,950,1127,1579 ἀφιέναι, *see* Mt 23.23) (ℵ* ἀφεῖναι, ℵc W f1 565 1010 1195 1230 1242 1253 1344 1365 1646 *l*184 ἀφιέναι and omit δέ) (1216 ποιεῖν...ἀφιέναι, 2174 ποιεῖν...ἀφιέναι...omit δέ) (A δεῖ...παραφεῖναι...omit δέ) Byz Lect ita,aur,(b),c,e,f,ff2,i,l,q,r1 vg syr(c,s),p,h copsa,bo (copbomss omit δέ) arm geo ∥ omit D itd Marcion

[17] **48** {C} οἰκοδομεῖτε 𝔓75 ℵ B D L 1241 ita,b,d,e,i,l,r1 syrs copsa,bo ∥ οἰκοδομεῖτε αὐτῶν τὰ μνημεῖα A C K W X Δ Θ Π Ψ 28 33 565 700 892 1071 1079 1195 1216 1230 1242 1253 1344 1365 1546 1646 2148 2174 Byz Lect l69s,m,70s,m,1127s,m itaur,c,f,q vg syrp,h copbomss eth Lucifer ∥ οἰκοδομεῖτε τὰ μνημεῖα αὐτῶν 1009 1010 l184 (Chrysostom) ∥ οἰκοδομεῖτε τοὺς τάφους αὐτῶν f1 Lucifer ∥ τοὺς τάφους αὐτῶν οἰκοδομεῖτε f13 arm geo ∥ *you are the sons of those murderers (see* Mt 23.31) syrc

---

42 ἀποδεκατοῦτε...λάχανον Lv 27.30

"Now, then, you Pharisees clean the cup and plate on the outside, but inside you are full of violence and evil. [40] Fools! Did not God, who made the outside, also make the inside? [41] But give what is in your cups and plates to the poor, and everything will be clean for you.

[42] "How terrible for you, Pharisees! You give to God one tenth of the seasoning herbs, such as mint and rue and all the other herbs, but you neglect justice and the love for God. These you should practice, without neglecting the others.

[43] "How terrible for you, Pharisees! You love the reserved seats in the synagogues, and to be greeted with respect in the market places. [44] How terrible for you! You are like unmarked graves which people walk on without knowing it."

[45] One of the teachers of the Law said to him, "Teacher, when you say this you insult us too!" [46] Jesus answered: "How terrible for you, too, teachers of the Law! You put loads on men's backs which are hard to carry, but you yourselves will not stretch out a finger to help them carry those loads. [47] How terrible for you! You make fine tombs for the prophets — the very prophets your ancestors murdered. [48] You yourselves admit, then, that you approve of what your ancestors did; for they murdered the prophets, and you build their tombs.

[49] For this reason the Wisdom of God said: 'I will send them prophets and messengers; they will kill some of them and persecute others.' [50] So the people of this time will be punished for the murder of all the prophets killed since the creation of the world, [51] from the murder of Abel to the murder of Zechariah, who was killed between the altar and the holy place. Yes, I tell you, the people of this time will be punished for them all!

[52] "How terrible for you, teachers of the Law! You have kept the key that opens the door to the house of knowledge; you yourselves will not go in, and you stop those who are trying to go in!"

[53] When Jesus left that place the teachers of the Law and the Pharisees began to criticize him bitterly and ask him questions about many things, [54] trying to lay traps for him and catch him in something wrong he might say.

A Warning against Hypocrisy
(Also Matt. 10.26—27)

12 [1] As thousands of people crowded together, so that they were stepping on each other, Jesus said first to his disciples: "Be on guard against the yeast of the Pharisees — I mean their hypocrisy. [2] Whatever is covered up will be uncovered, and every secret will be made known. [3] So then, whatever you have said in the dark will be heard in broad daylight, and whatever you have whispered in men's ears in a closed room will be shouted from the housetops."

[49] διὰ τοῦτο καὶ ἡ σοφία τοῦ θεοῦ εἶπεν, Ἀποστελῶ εἰς αὐτοὺς προφήτας καὶ ἀποστόλους, καὶ ἐξ αὐτῶν ἀποκτενοῦσιν καὶ διώξουσιν, [50] ἵνα ἐκζητηθῇ τὸ αἷμα πάντων τῶν προφητῶν τὸ ἐκκεχυμένον ἀπὸ καταβολῆς κόσμου ἀπὸ τῆς γενεᾶς ταύτης, [51] ἀπὸ αἵματος Ἄβελ ἕως αἵματος Ζαχαρίου τοῦ ἀπολομένου μεταξὺ τοῦ θυσιαστηρίου καὶ τοῦ οἴκου· ναί, λέγω ὑμῖν, ἐκζητηθή-σεται ἀπὸ τῆς γενεᾶς ταύτης. [52] οὐαὶ ὑμῖν τοῖς νομικοῖς, ὅτι ἤρατε τὴν κλεῖδα τῆς γνώσεως· αὐτοὶ οὐκ εἰσήλθατε καὶ τοὺς εἰσερχομένους ἐκωλύσατε. [53] Κἀκεῖθεν ἐξελ-θόντος αὐτοῦ ἤρξαντο οἱ γραμματεῖς καὶ οἱ Φαρισαῖοι δεινῶς ἐνέχειν καὶ ἀποστοματίζειν αὐτὸν περὶ πλειόνων, [54] ἐνεδρεύοντες αὐτὸν θηρεῦσαί τι ἐκ τοῦ στόματος αὐτοῦ.

A Warning against Hypocrisy

12 [1] Ἐν οἷς ἐπισυναχθεισῶν τῶν μυριάδων τοῦ ὄχλου, ὥστε καταπατεῖν ἀλλήλους, ἤρξατο λέγειν πρὸς τοὺς μαθητὰς αὐτοῦ[a] πρῶτον,[a] Προσέχετε ἑαυτοῖς ἀπὸ τῆς ζύμης, ἥτις ἐστὶν ὑπόκρισις, τῶν Φαρισαίων[1]. [2] οὐδὲν δὲ συγκεκαλυμμένον ἐστὶν ὃ οὐκ ἀποκαλυφθήσεται, καὶ κρυπτὸν ὃ οὐ γνωσθήσεται. [3] ἀνθ' ὧν ὅσα ἐν τῇ σκοτίᾳ εἴπατε ἐν τῷ φωτὶ ἀκουσθήσεται, καὶ ὃ πρὸς τὸ οὖς ἐλαλήσατε ἐν τοῖς ταμείοις κηρυχθήσεται ἐπὶ τῶν δωμάτων.

---

[1] **1** {C} ἥτις ἐστὶν ὑπόκρισις, τῶν Φαρισαίων p75 B L 1241 ite copsa ‖ τῶν Φαρισαίων ἥτις ἐστὶν ὑπόκρισις (see Mt 16.6; Mk 8.15) p45 ℵ A C D K W X Δ Θ Π Ψ f1 f13 (28 ὅτι) 33 565 700 892 1009 1010 1079 1195 1216 1230 1242 1253 1344 1365 1546 1646 2148 2174 Byz Lect ita,aur,b,c,d,f,i,l,q,r1 vg syrc,s,p,h copbo arm eth geo Marcion Diatessaron Tertullian Lucifer Epiphanius ‖ ἥτις ἐστὶν ὑπόκρισις 1071* (1071mg add τῆς ζύμης τῶν Φαρισαίων)

---

[a] [a] **1** a none, a minor: TR WH Bov Nes BF2 AV RV ASV RSV NEB TT Zür Luth Jer Seg ‖ a minor, a none: RVmg ASVmg Jermg Segmg

---

51 αἵματος Ἄβελ Gn 4.8   αἵματος...οἴκου 2 Chr 24.20–21   **54** Lk 20.20
12 1 Προσέχετε...Φαρισαίων Mt 16.6; Mk 8.15   **2** Mt 10.26; Mk 4.22; Lk 8.17

Whom to Fear
(Mt 10.28–31)

4 Λέγω δὲ ὑμῖν τοῖς φίλοις μου, μὴ φοβηθῆτε ἀπὸ τῶν ἀποκτεινόντων τὸ σῶμα καὶ μετὰ ταῦτα μὴ ἐχόντων περισσότερόν τι ποιῆσαι. **5** ὑποδείξω δὲ ὑμῖν τίνα φοβηθῆτε· φοβήθητε τὸν μετὰ τὸ ἀποκτεῖναι ἔχοντα ἐξουσίαν ἐμβαλεῖν εἰς τὴν γέενναν· ναί, λέγω ὑμῖν, τοῦτον φοβήθητε. **6** οὐχὶ πέντε στρουθία πωλοῦνται ἀσσαρίων δύο; καὶ ἓν ἐξ αὐτῶν οὐκ ἔστιν ἐπιλελησμένον ἐνώπιον τοῦ θεοῦ. **7** ἀλλὰ καὶ αἱ τρίχες τῆς κεφαλῆς ὑμῶν πᾶσαι ἠρίθμηνται. μὴ φοβεῖσθε· πολλῶν στρουθίων διαφέρετε.

Confessing Christ before Men
(Mt 10.32–33; 12.32; 10.19–20)

8 Λέγω δὲ ὑμῖν, πᾶς ὃς ἂν ὁμολογήσῃ ἐν ἐμοὶ ἔμπροσθεν τῶν ἀνθρώπων, καὶ ὁ υἱὸς τοῦ ἀνθρώπου ὁμολογήσει ἐν αὐτῷ ἔμπροσθεν τῶν ἀγγέλων τοῦ θεοῦ· **9** ὁ δὲ ἀρνησάμενός με ἐνώπιον τῶν ἀνθρώπων ἀπαρνηθήσεται ἐνώπιον τῶν ἀγγέλων τοῦ θεοῦ. **10** καὶ πᾶς ὃς ἐρεῖ λόγον εἰς τὸν υἱὸν τοῦ ἀνθρώπου, ἀφεθήσεται αὐτῷ· τῷ δὲ εἰς τὸ ἅγιον πνεῦμα βλασφημήσαντι οὐκ ἀφεθήσεται. **11** ὅταν δὲ εἰσφέρωσιν ὑμᾶς ἐπὶ τὰς συναγωγὰς καὶ τὰς ἀρχὰς καὶ τὰς ἐξουσίας, μὴ μεριμνήσητε πῶς [ἢ τί]² ἀπολογήσησθε ἢ τί εἴπητε· **12** τὸ γὰρ ἅγιον πνεῦμα διδάξει ὑμᾶς ἐν αὐτῇ τῇ ὥρᾳ ἃ δεῖ εἰπεῖν.

---

² 11 {C} πῶς ἢ τί p⁴⁵ᵛⁱᵈ,⁷⁵ ℵ A B K L W X Δ Θ Π Ψ 0191 f¹ f¹³ 28 33 565 700 892 1009 1010 1071 1079 1195 1216 1230 1241 1242 1253 1344 1365 1546 1646 2148 2174 *Byz Lect* l⁶⁹⁸·ᵐ,⁷⁰ˢ·ᵐ,²¹¹ˢ·ᵐ,⁵⁴⁷ᵐ,¹¹²⁷ˢ·ᵐ itaᵘʳ,f vg syrʰ·ᵖᵃˡ cop⁽ˢᵃᵐˢˢ⁾,ᵇᵒ arm geo Basil ‖ πῶς D itᵃ·ᵇ·ᶜ·ᵈ·ᵉ·ff²·ⁱ·ˡ·q syrᶜ·ᵖ copˢᵃ eth Clement Origen Cyril-Jerusalem ‖ τί itʳˡ syrˢ

---

7 αἱ…φοβεῖσθε Lk 21.18; Ac 27.34   πολλῶν…διαφέρετε Lk 12.24   **9** Lk 9.26
10 Mk 3.28–29   **11–12** Mk 13.11; Lk 21.12–15

Whom to Fear
(Also Matt. 10.28 31)

4 "I tell you, my friends, do not be afraid of those who kill the body but cannot afterward do anything worse. **5** I will show you whom to fear: fear God who, after killing, has the authority to throw into hell. Yes, I tell you, be afraid of him!

6 "Aren't five sparrows sold for two pennies? Yet not a single one of them is forgotten by God. **7** Even the hairs of your head have all been numbered. So do not be afraid: you are worth much more than many sparrows!"

Confessing and Denying Christ
(Also Matt. 10.32–33; 12.32; 10.19–20)

8 "I tell you: whoever declares publicly that he belongs to me, the Son of Man will do the same for him before the angels of God; **9** but whoever denies publicly that he belongs to me, the Son of Man will also deny him before the angels of God.

10 "Anyone who says a word against the Son of Man will be forgiven; but the one who says evil things against the Holy Spirit will not be forgiven.

11 "When they bring you to be tried in the synagogues, or before governors or rulers, do not be worried about how you will defend yourself or what you will say. **12** For the Holy Spirit will teach you at that time what you should say."

The Parable of the Rich Fool

[13] A man in the crowd said to him, "Teacher, tell my brother to divide with me the property our father left us." [14] Jesus answered him, "Man, who gave me the right to judge, or to divide the property between you two?" [15] And he went on to say to them all: "Watch out, and guard yourselves from all kinds of greed; for a man's true life is not made up of the things he owns, no matter how rich he may be." [16] Then Jesus told them this parable: "A rich man had land which bore good crops. [17] He began to think to himself, 'I don't have a place to keep all my crops. What can I do? [18] This is what I will do,' he told himself; 'I will tear my barns down and build bigger ones, where I will store the grain and all my other goods. [19] Then I will say to myself: Lucky man! You have all the good things you need for many years. Take life easy, eat, drink, and enjoy yourself!' [20] But God said to him, 'You fool! This very night you will have to give up your life; then who will get all these things you have kept for yourself?' " [21] And Jesus concluded, "This is how it is with those who pile up riches for themselves but are not rich in God's sight."

The Parable of the Rich Fool

[13] Εἶπεν δέ τις ἐκ τοῦ ὄχλου αὐτῷ, Διδάσκαλε, εἰπὲ τῷ ἀδελφῷ μου μερίσασθαι μετ' ἐμοῦ τὴν κληρονομίαν. [14] ὁ δὲ εἶπεν αὐτῷ, Ἄνθρωπε, τίς με κατέστησεν κριτὴν ἢ μεριστὴν[3] ἐφ' ὑμᾶς; [15] εἶπεν δὲ πρὸς αὐτούς, Ὁρᾶτε καὶ φυλάσσεσθε ἀπὸ πάσης πλεονεξίας, ὅτι οὐκ ἐν τῷ περισσεύειν τινὶ ἡ ζωὴ αὐτοῦ ἐστιν ἐκ τῶν ὑπαρχόντων αὐτῷ. [16] Εἶπεν δὲ παραβολὴν πρὸς αὐτοὺς λέγων, Ἀνθρώπου τινὸς πλουσίου εὐφόρησεν ἡ χώρα. [17] καὶ διελογίζετο ἐν ἑαυτῷ λέγων, Τί ποιήσω, ὅτι οὐκ ἔχω ποῦ συνάξω τοὺς καρπούς μου; [18] καὶ εἶπεν, Τοῦτο ποιήσω· καθελῶ μου τὰς ἀποθήκας καὶ μείζονας οἰκοδομήσω, καὶ συνάξω ἐκεῖ πάντα τὸν σῖτον καὶ τὰ ἀγαθά μου, [19] καὶ ἐρῶ τῇ ψυχῇ μου, Ψυχή, ἔχεις πολλὰ ἀγαθὰ κείμενα εἰς ἔτη πολλά· ἀναπαύου, φάγε, πίε, εὐφραίνου. [20] εἶπεν δὲ αὐτῷ ὁ θεός, Ἄφρων, ταύτῃ τῇ νυκτὶ τὴν ψυχήν σου ἀπαιτοῦσιν ἀπὸ σοῦ[4]· ἃ δὲ ἡτοίμασας, τίνι ἔσται; [21] οὕτως ὁ θησαυρίζων ἑαυτῷ καὶ μὴ εἰς θεὸν πλουτῶν.[5]

---

[3] **14** {B} κριτὴν ἢ μεριστήν 𝔭[75] ℵ B L 0191 f[1] f[13] 33 700 892 1241 cop[samss] arm geo ‖ δικαστὴν ἢ μεριστήν A K W X Δ Θ Π Ψ 565 1009 1010 1071 1079 1195 1216 1230 1242 1253 1344 1365 1546 1646 2148 2174 *Byz Lect* Basil ‖ μεριστὴν ἢ δικαστήν 472 *l*[1642] eth ‖ κριτὴν ἢ δικαστήν 69 ‖ κριτὴν (*or* δικαστήν) ἢ μεριστήν it[aur,b,e,f,ff2,i,l,q,r1] vg syr[(p),h] cop[bo] ‖ ἄρχοντα καὶ δικαστήν (*see* Ac 7.27, 35) 157 ‖ κριτήν D it[(a),c,d] (syr[c,s]) Marcion Tertullian ‖ δικαστήν 28 ‖ μεριστήν cop[sams]

[4] **20** {D} τὴν ψυχήν σου ἀπαιτοῦσιν ἀπὸ σοῦ ℵ A K W X Δ Θ Π Ψ f[1] f[13] 28 565 700 892 1009 1010 1079 1195 1216 1230 1241 1242 1253 1344 1365 1546 1646 2148 *Byz Lect* it[a,aur,b,e,f,l,q] vg (arm) Marcion Clement (Tertullian) Origen[gr,lat] Cyprian Basil Augustine Antiochus ‖ τὴν ψυχήν σου αἰτοῦσιν ἀπὸ σοῦ 𝔭[75] B L 070[vid] 33 ‖ τὴν ψυχήν σου ἀπαιτοῦσιν (*or* αἰτοῦσιν) ἀπὸ σοῦ syr[c,s,p,h] ‖ ἀπαιτοῦσιν τὴν ψυχήν σου ἀπὸ σοῦ D 1071 *l*[60] it[(c),(d),ff2] cop[sa,bo] eth geo Irenaeus[lat] (Clement) Origen Cyprian ‖ ἀπαιτοῦσιν ἀπὸ σοῦ τὴν ψυχήν σου 69 it[i] Origen[gr,lat] Antiochus

[5] **21** {B} *include verse 21* 𝔭[45,75] ℵ A B K L W X Δ Θ Π Ψ 070 f[1] 28 33

---

14 τίς...κριτὴν...ὑμᾶς Ex 2.14; Ac 7.27   **15** Ὁρᾶτε...πλεονεξίας 1 Tm 6.9–10
19–20 Sir 11.19   **21** Mt 6.20

Care and Anxiety
(Mt 6.25–34, 19–21)

22 Εἶπεν δὲ πρὸς τοὺς μαθητάς⁶, Διὰ τοῦτο λέγω ὑμῖν, μὴ μεριμνᾶτε τῇ ψυχῇ τί φάγητε, μηδὲ τῷ σώματι τί ἐνδύσησθε. **23** ἡ γὰρ ψυχὴ πλεῖόν ἐστιν τῆς τροφῆς καὶ τὸ σῶμα τοῦ ἐνδύματος. **24** κατανοήσατε τοὺς κόρακας ὅτι οὐ σπείρουσιν οὐδὲ θερίζουσιν, οἷς οὐκ ἔστιν ταμεῖον οὐδὲ ἀποθήκη, καὶ ὁ θεὸς τρέφει αὐτούς· πόσῳ μᾶλλον ὑμεῖς διαφέρετε τῶν πετεινῶν. **25** τίς δὲ ἐξ ὑμῶν μεριμνῶν δύναται ἐπὶ τὴν ἡλικίαν αὐτοῦ προσθεῖναι πῆχυν; **26** εἰ οὖν οὐδὲ ἐλάχιστον δύνασθε, τί περὶ τῶν λοιπῶν μεριμνᾶτε; **27** κατανοήσατε τὰ κρίνα πῶς αὐ-ξάνει· οὐ κοπιᾷ οὐδὲ νήθει⁷· λέγω δὲ ὑμῖν, οὐδὲ Σολομὼν ἐν πάσῃ τῇ δόξῃ αὐτοῦ περιεβάλετο ὡς ἓν τούτων. **28** εἰ δὲ ἐν ἀγρῷ τὸν χόρτον ὄντα σήμερον καὶ αὔριον εἰς κλίβανον βαλλόμενον ὁ θεὸς οὕτως ἀμφιάζει, πόσῳ μᾶλλον ὑμᾶς, ὀλιγόπιστοι. **29** καὶ ὑμεῖς μὴ ζητεῖτε τί φάγητε καὶ τί πίητε, καὶ μὴ μετεωρίζεσθε· **30** ταῦτα γὰρ πάντα τὰ ἔθνη τοῦ κόσμου ἐπιζητοῦσιν· ὑμῶν δὲ ὁ πατὴρ οἶδεν ὅτι χρῄζετε τούτων. **31** πλὴν ζητεῖτε τὴν

---

565 700 1009 1010 1079 1195 1230 1241 1242* 1253 1344 1365 1546 *Byz* *l*⁷⁶,¹⁸⁵,⁹⁵⁰ it^(aur,c,e,f,ff²,i,l,q,r¹) vg syr^(c,s,p,h,palmss) cop^(sa,bo) arm geo ‖ *omit verse 21* D it^(a,b,d) ‖ *after verse 21 add* ταῦτα λέγων ἐφώνει, Ὁ ἔχων ὦτα ἀκούειν ἀκουέτω (see Lk 8.8; Mt 11.15) *f*¹³ 892* (892^mg πρὸς ταῦτα) (1071 *omit* ταῦτα . . . ἐφώνει) 1216 1242^mg 1646 2148 *Lect* syr^palms

⁶ **22** {C} μαθητάς 𝔭⁴⁵ᵛⁱᵈ,⁷⁵ B 1241 it^(c,e) ‖ μαθητὰς αὐτοῦ ℵ A D K L W X Δ Θ Π Ψ 070 *f*¹ *f*¹³ 28 33 565 700 892 1009 1010 1071 1079 1195 1216 1230 1242 1253 1344 1365 1546 1646 2148 *Byz* it^(a,aur,b,d,f,ff²,i,l,q,r¹) vg syr^(c,s,p,h) cop^(sa,bo) arm geo

⁷ **27** {D} αὐξάνει· οὐ κοπιᾷ οὐδὲ νήθει (see Mt 6.28) 𝔭⁴⁵,⁷⁵ ℵ A B K L W X Δ Θ Π Ψ 070 *f*¹ *f*¹³ 28 33 565 700 892 1009 1010 1071 1079 1195 1216 1230 1241 1242 1253 1344 1365 1546 1646 2148 2174 *Byz Lect* it^(aur),(e),f,q vg syr^(p,h) cop^(sa,bo) arm eth geo Diatessaron ‖ οὔτε νήθει οὔτε ὑφαίνει D it^d syr^(c,s) Clement Tertullian ‖ οὔτε ὑφαίνει οὔτε νήθει it^a Marcion ‖ αὐξάνει· οὐ κοπιᾷ οὔτε νήθει οὔτε ὑφαίνει it^(b,ff²,i,l,r¹) (it^c *omit* οὐ κοπιᾷ)

---

24 κατανοήσατε...αὐτούς Ps 147.9   πόσῳ...πετεινῶν Lk 12.7   **27** Σολομὼν...αὐτοῦ 1 Kgs 10.4–7; 2 Chr 9.3–6

Trust in God
(Also Matt. 6.25–34)

22 Then Jesus said to the disciples: "This is why I tell you: Do not be worried about the food you need to stay alive, or about the clothes you need for your body. **23** For life is much more important than food, and body much more important than clothes. **24** Look at the crows: they don't plant seeds or gather a harvest; they don't have storage rooms or barns; God feeds them! You are worth so much more than birds! **25** Which one of you can live a few more years by worrying about it? **26** If you can't manage even such a small thing, why worry about the other things? **27** Look how the wild flowers grow: they don't work or make clothes for themselves. But I tell you that not even Solomon, as rich as he was, had clothes as beautiful as one of these flowers. **28** It is God who clothes the wild grass — grass that is here today, gone tomorrow, burned up in the oven. Won't he be all the more sure to clothe you? How little is your faith! **29** So don't be all upset, always looking for what you will eat and drink. **30** (For the heathen of this world are always looking for all these things.) Your Father knows that you need these things. **31** Instead, put his Kingdom first in your life, and he will provide you with these things.''

Riches in Heaven
(Also Matt. 6.19–21)

32 "Do not be afraid, little flock! For your Father is pleased to give you the Kingdom. 33 Sell all your belongings and give the money to the poor. Provide for yourselves purses that don't wear out, and save your riches in heaven, where they will never decrease, for no thief can get to them, no moth can destroy them. 34 For your heart will always be where your riches are.''

Watchful Servants

35 "Be ready for whatever comes, with your clothes fastened tight at the waist and your lamps lit, 36 like servants who are waiting for their master to come back from a wedding feast. When he comes and knocks, they will open the door for him at once. 37 How happy are those servants whose master finds them awake and ready! I tell you, he will fasten his belt, have them sit down, and wait on them. 38 How happy are they if he finds them ready, even if he should come as late as midnight or even later! 39 And remember this! If the man of the house knew the time when the thief would come, he would not let the thief break into his house. 40 And you, too,

βασιλείαν αὐτοῦ[8], καὶ ταῦτα προστεθήσεται ὑμῖν. 32 Μὴ φοβοῦ, τὸ μικρὸν ποίμνιον, ὅτι εὐδόκησεν ὁ πατὴρ ὑμῶν δοῦναι ὑμῖν τὴν βασιλείαν. 33 Πωλήσατε τὰ ὑπάρχοντα ὑμῶν καὶ δότε ἐλεημοσύνην· ποιήσατε ἑαυτοῖς βαλλάντια μὴ παλαιούμενα, θησαυρὸν ἀνέκλειπτον ἐν τοῖς οὐρανοῖς, ὅπου κλέπτης οὐκ ἐγγίζει οὐδὲ σὴς διαφθείρει· 34 ὅπου γάρ ἐστιν ὁ θησαυρὸς ὑμῶν, ἐκεῖ καὶ ἡ καρδία ὑμῶν ἔσται.

Watchful Servants
(Mt 24.45–51)

35 Ἔστωσαν ὑμῶν αἱ ὀσφύες περιεζωσμέναι καὶ οἱ λύχνοι καιόμενοι, 36 καὶ ὑμεῖς ὅμοιοι ἀνθρώποις προσδεχομένοις τὸν κύριον ἑαυτῶν πότε ἀναλύσῃ ἐκ τῶν γάμων, ἵνα ἐλθόντος καὶ κρούσαντος εὐθέως ἀνοίξωσιν αὐτῷ. 37 μακάριοι οἱ δοῦλοι ἐκεῖνοι, οὓς ἐλθὼν ὁ κύριος εὑρήσει γρηγοροῦντας· ἀμὴν λέγω ὑμῖν ὅτι περιζώσεται καὶ ἀνακλινεῖ αὐτοὺς καὶ παρελθὼν διακονήσει αὐτοῖς. 38 κἂν ἐν τῇ δευτέρᾳ κἂν ἐν τῇ τρίτῃ φυλακῇ ἔλθῃ καὶ εὕρῃ οὕτως, μακάριοί εἰσιν ἐκεῖνοι. 39 τοῦτο δὲ γινώσκετε ὅτι εἰ ᾔδει ὁ οἰκοδεσπότης ποίᾳ ὥρᾳ ὁ κλέπτης ἔρχεται, οὐκ[9] ἂν ἀφῆκεν διορυχθῆναι τὸν οἶκον αὐτοῦ. 40 καὶ

[8] 31 {C} αὐτοῦ ℵ B D^gr* L Ψ 892 it^{a,c} cop^{sa,bo} Athanasius ‖ τοῦ θεου 𝔭45 A D^b K W X Δ Θ Π 070 f[1] f[13] 28 33 565 700 1009 1010 1071 1079 1195 1216 1230 1241 1242 1344 1365 1546 1646 2148 2174 Byz Lect it^{aur,b,d,e,f,ff2,i,l,q,r1} vg^{ww} syr^{c,s,p,h} arm geo Marcion Diatessaron Clement[2/4] ‖ τοῦ θεοῦ καὶ τὴν δικαιοσύνην αὐτοῦ (see Mt 6.33) 1253 vg^{cl} ‖ τῶν οὐρανῶν Clement[2/4] ‖ omit 𝔭75

[9] 39 {B} οὐκ 𝔭75 ℵ* (D omit ἀφῆκεν...αὐτοῦ) it^{(d),e,i} syr^{c,s} cop^{sa,ach} arm Marcion Tertullian ‖ ἐγρηγόρησεν ἂν καὶ οὐκ (see Mt 24.43) (ℵ^a omit ἂν) ℵ^c A B K L P W X Δ Θ Π Ψ 070 f[1] f[13] 28 33 565 700 892 1009 1010 1071 1079 1195 1216 1230 1241 1242 (1253 οὖν ἂν) 1344 1365 1546 1646 2148 2174 Byz Lect it^{(aur),b,c,(f),ff2,(l,q),r1} (vg) syr^{p,h} cop^{sams,bo} (cop^{bomss} omit καὶ) eth geo Diatessaron^{a,i,n} Basil John-Damascus

32 εὐδόκησεν...βασιλείαν Lk 22.29; Re 1.6   33 Πωλήσατε...ἐλεημοσύνην Mt 19.21; Mk 10.21; Lk 18.22   35 ὀσφύες περιεζωσμέναι Ex 12.11; 1 Kgs 18.46; 2 Kgs 4.29; 9.1; Job 38.3; 40.7; Pr 31.17; Jr 1.17; Eph 6.14; 1 Pe 1.13   λύχνοι καιόμενοι Mt 25.1, 7   36 ἀνθρώποις...αὐτῷ Mk 13.35-37   πότε...αὐτῷ Mt 25.6   37 περιζώσεται...αὐτοῖς Lk 17.7-8; Jn 13.4   39-40 Mt 24.43-44   39 ποίᾳ...ἔρχεται 1 Th 5.2

ὑμεῖς γίνεσθε ἕτοιμοι, ὅτι ᾗ ὥρᾳ οὐ δοκεῖτε ὁ υἱὸς τοῦ ἀνθρώπου ἔρχεται.

41 Εἶπεν δὲ ὁ Πέτρος, Κύριε, πρὸς ἡμᾶς τὴν παραβολὴν ταύτην λέγεις ἢ καὶ πρὸς πάντας; **42** καὶ εἶπεν ὁ κύριος, Τίς ἄρα ἐστὶν ὁ πιστὸς οἰκονόμος[b] ὁ φρόνιμος, ὃν καταστήσει ὁ κύριος ἐπὶ τῆς θεραπείας αὐτοῦ τοῦ διδόναι ἐν καιρῷ [τὸ] σιτομέτριον; **43** μακάριος ὁ δοῦλος ἐκεῖνος, ὃν ἐλθὼν ὁ κύριος αὐτοῦ εὑρήσει ποιοῦντα οὕτως· **44** ἀληθῶς λέγω ὑμῖν ὅτι ἐπὶ πᾶσιν τοῖς ὑπάρχουσιν αὐτοῦ καταστήσει αὐτόν. **45** ἐὰν δὲ εἴπῃ ὁ δοῦλος ἐκεῖνος ἐν τῇ καρδίᾳ αὐτοῦ, Χρονίζει ὁ κύριός μου ἔρχεσθαι, καὶ ἄρξηται τύπτειν τοὺς παῖδας καὶ τὰς παιδίσκας, ἐσθίειν τε καὶ πίνειν καὶ μεθύσκεσθαι, **46** ἥξει ὁ κύριος τοῦ δούλου ἐκείνου ἐν ἡμέρᾳ ᾗ οὐ προσδοκᾷ καὶ ἐν ὥρᾳ ᾗ οὐ γινώσκει, καὶ διχοτομήσει αὐτὸν καὶ τὸ μέρος αὐτοῦ μετὰ τῶν ἀπίστων θήσει. **47** ἐκεῖνος δὲ ὁ δοῦλος ὁ γνοὺς τὸ θέλημα τοῦ κυρίου αὐτοῦ καὶ μὴ ἑτοιμάσας ἢ ποιήσας πρὸς τὸ θέλημα αὐτοῦ δαρήσεται πολλάς· **48** ὁ δὲ μὴ γνούς, ποιήσας δὲ ἄξια πληγῶν, δαρήσεται ὀλίγας. παντὶ δὲ ᾧ ἐδόθη πολύ, πολὺ ζητηθήσεται παρ' αὐτοῦ, καὶ ᾧ παρέθεντο πολύ, περισσότερον αἰτήσουσιν αὐτόν.

Jesus the Cause of Division
(Mt 10.34–36)

49 Πῦρ ἦλθον βαλεῖν ἐπὶ τὴν γῆν, καὶ τί θέλω[c] εἰ ἤδη ἀνήφθη.[c] **50** βάπτισμα δὲ ἔχω βαπτισθῆναι, καὶ πῶς συνέχομαι ἕως ὅτου τελεσθῇ.[c] **51** δοκεῖτε ὅτι εἰρήνην παρεγενόμην δοῦναι ἐν τῇ γῇ; οὐχί, λέγω ὑμῖν, ἀλλ' ἢ διαμερισμόν. **52** ἔσονται γὰρ ἀπὸ τοῦ νῦν πέντε ἐν ἑνὶ

---

[b] **42** b none: Bov Nes BF² (RV) (ASV) (RSV) (NEB) (TT) (Zür) (Luth) (Jer) (Seg) ∥ b minor: WH RVᵐᵍ ASVᵐᵍ ∥ different text: TR AV

[c c c] **49–50** c none, c major, c major: Bov Nes BF² ∥ c none, c question, c major: WH ∥ c question, c minor, c question: TR ∥ c question, c exclamation, c exclamation: Segᵐᵍ ∥ c none, c exclamation, c exclamation: ASVᵐᵍ RSV NEB TT Zür Luth Jer ∥ c minor, c question, c exclamation: AV RV ASV Seg

44 ἐπὶ πᾶσιν...αὐτόν Mt 25.21, 23 **47** Jas 4.17 **50** βάπτισμα...βαπτισθῆναι Mk 10.38–39 **51** δοκεῖτε...γῇ Lk 2.14

---

be ready, because the Son of Man will come at an hour when you are not expecting him.''

The Faithful or the Unfaithful Servant
(Also Matt. 24.45–51)

41 Peter said, "Lord, are you telling this parable to us, or do you mean it for everybody?" **42** The Lord answered: "Who, then, is the faithful and wise servant? He is the one whom his master will put in charge, to run the household and give the other servants their share of the food at the proper time. **43** How happy is that servant if his master finds him doing this when he comes home! **44** Indeed, I tell you, the master will put that servant in charge of all his property. **45** But if that servant says to himself, 'My master is taking a long time to come back,' and begins to beat the other servants, both men and women, and eats and drinks and gets drunk, **46** then the master will come back some day when the servant does not expect him and at a time he does not know; the master will cut him to pieces,[1] and make him share the fate of the disobedient.

47 "The servant who knows what his master wants him to do, but does not get himself ready and do what his master wants, will be punished with a heavy whipping; **48** but the servant who does not know what his master wants, and does something for which he deserves a whipping, will be punished with a light whipping. The man to whom much is given, of him much is required; the man to whom more is given, of him much more is required."

Jesus the Cause of Division
(Also Matt. 10.34–36)

49 "I came to set the earth on fire, and how I wish it were already kindled! **50** I have a baptism to receive, and how distressed I am until it is over! **51** Do you suppose that I came to bring peace to the world? Not peace, I tell you, but division. **52** From now on a family of

---

[1] **46** *cut him to pieces:* or *throw him out*

five will be divided, three against two, two against three. 53 Fathers will be against their sons, and sons against their fathers; mothers will be against their daughters, and daughters against their mothers; mothers-in-law will be against their daughters-in-law, and daughters-in-law against their mothers-in-law.''

Understanding the Time
(Also Matt. 16.2–3)

54 Jesus said also to the people: "When you see a cloud coming up in the west, at once you say, 'It is going to rain,' and it does. 55 And when you feel the south wind blowing, you say, 'It is going to get hot,' and it does. 56 Impostors! You can look at the earth and the sky and tell what it means; why, then, don't you know the meaning of this present time?''

Settle with Your Opponent
(Also Matt. 5.25–26)

57 "And why do you not judge for yourselves the right thing to do? 58 If a man brings a lawsuit against you and takes you to court, do your best to settle the matter with him while you are on the way, so that he won't drag you before the judge, and the judge hand you over to the police, and the police put you in jail. 59 You will not come out of there, I tell you, until you pay the last penny of your fine.''

οἴκῳ διαμεμερισμένοι, τρεῖς ἐπὶ δυσὶν καὶ δύο ἐπὶ τρισίν,ᵈ
53 διαμερισθήσονταιᵈ πατὴρ ἐπὶ υἱῷ
    καὶ **υἱὸς** ἐπὶ **πατρί**,
μήτηρ ἐπὶ τὴν θυγατέρα
    καὶ **θυγάτηρ** ἐπὶ τὴν **μητέρα**,
πενθερὰ ἐπὶ τὴν νύμφην αὐτῆς
    καὶ **νύμφη** ἐπὶ τὴν **πενθεράν.**

Discerning the Time
(Mt 16.2–3)

54 Ἔλεγεν δὲ καὶ τοῖς ὄχλοις, Ὅταν ἴδητε [τὴν] νεφέλην ἀνατέλλουσαν ἐπὶ δυσμῶν, εὐθέως λέγετε ὅτι Ὄμβρος ἔρχεται, καὶ γίνεται οὕτως· 55 καὶ ὅταν νότον πνέοντα, λέγετε ὅτι Καύσων ἔσται, καὶ γίνεται. 56 ὑποκριταί, τὸ πρόσωπον τῆς γῆς καὶ τοῦ οὐρανοῦ οἴδατε δοκιμάζειν, τὸν καιρὸν δὲ τοῦτον πῶς οὐκ οἴδατε δοκιμάζειν¹⁰;

Settling with Your Accuser
(Mt 5.25–26)

57 Τί δὲ καὶ ἀφ' ἑαυτῶν οὐ κρίνετε τὸ δίκαιον; 58 ὡς γὰρ ὑπάγεις μετὰ τοῦ ἀντιδίκου σου ἐπ' ἄρχοντα,ᵉ ἐν τῇ ὁδῷᵉ δὸς ἐργασίαν ἀπηλλάχθαι ἀπ' αὐτοῦ, μήποτε κατασύρῃ σε πρὸς τὸν κριτήν, καὶ ὁ κριτής σε παραδώσει τῷ πράκτορι, καὶ ὁ πράκτωρ σε βαλεῖ εἰς φυλακήν. 59 λέγω σοι, οὐ μὴ ἐξέλθῃς ἐκεῖθεν ἕως καὶ τὸ ἔσχατον λεπτὸν ἀποδῷς.

---

¹⁰ 56 {C} πῶς οὐκ οἴδατε δοκιμάζειν 𝔭⁷⁵ ℵ B L Θ 33 892 1241 syrʰᵐᵍ copˢᵃ,ᵇᵒ eth Diatessaronᵃ ∥ οὐκ οἴδατε δοκιμάζειν (itᶠᶠ²,¹) (syrˢ) copˢᵃᵐˢ,ᵇᵒᵐˢˢ Marcion ∥ πῶς οὐ δοκιμάζετε 𝔭⁴⁵ A K W Δ Π Ψ f¹ f¹³ 28 565 700 1009 1010 1071 1079 1195 1216 1230 1242 1253 1344 1365 1546 1646 2148 2174 *Byz Lect* itᵃᵘʳ,ᶠ,q vg syrᵖ,ʰ arm geo ∥ πῶς οὐκ οἴδατε δοκιμάζεται [= δοκιμάζετε] 070 ∥ οὐ δοκιμάζετε D itᵇ,ᶜ,ᵈ,ᵉ,ⁱ,ʳˡ syrᶜ

ᵈ ᵈ 52–53 *d* minor, *d* none: WH (Zür) (Luth) ∥ *d* major, *d* minor: RV ASV RSV Jer ∥ *d* none; *d* minor: Bov Nes BF² (NEB) TT (Seg) ∥ different text: TR AV

ᵉ ᵉ 58 *e* minor, *e* none: TR WH Bov Nes BF² RV ASV RSV NEB TT Zür Luth Jer Seg ∥ *e* none, *e* minor ∥ *e* minor, *e* minor: AV

53 Mic 7.6   54–56 Mt 16.2–3

Repent or Perish

13 Παρῆσαν δέ τινες ἐν αὐτῷ τῷ καιρῷ ἀπαγγέλλοντες αὐτῷ περὶ τῶν Γαλιλαίων ὧν τὸ αἷμα Πιλᾶτος ἔμιξεν μετὰ τῶν θυσιῶν αὐτῶν. 2 καὶ ἀποκριθεὶς εἶπεν αὐτοῖς, Δοκεῖτε ὅτι οἱ Γαλιλαῖοι οὗτοι ἁμαρτωλοὶ παρὰ πάντας τοὺς Γαλιλαίους ἐγένοντο, ὅτι ταῦτα πεπόνθασιν; 3 οὐχί, λέγω ὑμῖν, ἀλλ' ἐὰν μὴ μετανοῆτε πάντες ὁμοίως ἀπολεῖσθε. 4 ἢ ἐκεῖνοι οἱ δέκα ὀκτὼ ἐφ' οὓς ἔπεσεν ὁ πύργος ἐν τῷ Σιλωὰμ καὶ ἀπέκτεινεν αὐτούς, δοκεῖτε ὅτι αὐτοὶ ὀφειλέται ἐγένοντο παρὰ πάντας τοὺς ἀνθρώπους τοὺς κατοικοῦντας Ἰερουσαλήμ; 5 οὐχί, λέγω ὑμῖν, ἀλλ' ἐὰν μὴ μετανοῆτε πάντες ὡσαύτως ἀπολεῖσθε.

The Parable of the Barren Fig Tree

6 Ἔλεγεν δὲ ταύτην τὴν παραβολήν· Συκῆν εἶχέν τις πεφυτευμένην ἐν τῷ ἀμπελῶνι αὐτοῦ, καὶ ἦλθεν ζητῶν καρπὸν ἐν αὐτῇ καὶ οὐχ εὗρεν. 7 εἶπεν δὲ πρὸς τὸν ἀμπελουργόν, Ἰδοὺ τρία ἔτη ἀφ' οὗ ἔρχομαι ζητῶν καρπὸν ἐν τῇ συκῇ ταύτῃ καὶ οὐχ εὑρίσκω. ἔκκοψον [οὖν]¹ αὐτήν· ἱνατί καὶ τὴν γῆν καταργεῖ; 8 ὁ δὲ ἀποκριθεὶς λέγει αὐτῷ, Κύριε, ἄφες αὐτὴν καὶ τοῦτο τὸ ἔτος, ἕως ὅτου σκάψω περὶ αὐτὴν καὶ βάλω κόπρια· 9 κἂν μὲν ποιήσῃ καρπὸν εἰς τὸ μέλλον — εἰ δὲ μήγε², ἐκκόψεις αὐτήν.

---

¹ 7 {C} ἔκκοψον οὖν 𝔭⁷⁵ A L X Θ Ψ 070 *f*¹³ 33 892 1009 1071 1195 1230 1253 1646 it^(a,aur,b,c,f,ff²,i,l,q,r¹) vg syr^h (syr^s δέ) cop^(sa,bo) arm eth ‖ ἔκκοψον ℵ B D K W Δ Π *f*¹ 28 565 700 1010 1079 1216 1241 1242 1344 1365 1546 2148 2174 *Byz Lect* it^(d,e) syr^(c,p) geo Diatessaron Origen Peter-Alexandria Basil (Cyril)

² 9 {C} εἰς τὸ μέλλον — εἰ δὲ μήγε 𝔭⁷⁵ ℵ B L (070 μέλλον ἀφήσεις) 33^vid 892 1216 1241 2174 cop^(sa,bo) Cyril ‖ εἰ δὲ μήγε, εἰς τὸ μέλλον 𝔭^(45vid) A D K W X Δ Θ Π Ψ *f*¹ *f*¹³ 28 565 700 1009 1010 1071 1079 1195 1230 1242 1253 1344 1365 1546 1646 2148 *Byz Lect* it^(a,aur,b,c,d,e,f,ff²,i,l,q) vg syr^(c,s,p,h) arm geo Diatessaron^a Peter-Alexandria

1 Γαλιλαίων...αὐτῶν Ac 5.37　　2 Δοκεῖτε...πεπόνθασιν Jn 9.2　　3 ἐὰν... ἀπολεῖσθε Ps 7.12　　5 ἐὰν...ἀπολεῖσθε Ps 7.12　　6 Συκῆν...εὗρεν Hab 3.17; Mt 21.19; Mk 11.13　　8 ἄφες...ἔτος 2 Pe 3.9, 15

Turn from Your Sins or Die

13 At that time some people were there who told Jesus about the Galileans whom Pilate had killed while they were offering sacrifices to God. ² Jesus answered them: "Because these Galileans were killed in that way, do you think it proves that they were worse sinners than all the other Galileans? ³ No! I tell you that if you do not turn from your sins, you will all die as they did. ⁴ What about those eighteen in Siloam who were killed when the tower fell on them? Do you suppose this proves that they were worse than all the other people living in Jerusalem? ⁵ No! I tell you that if you do not turn from your sins, you will all die as they did."

The Parable of the Unfruitful Fig Tree

⁶ Then Jesus told them this parable: "A man had a fig tree growing in his vineyard. He went looking for figs on it but found none. ⁷ So he said to his gardener, 'Look, for three years I have been coming here looking for figs on this fig tree and I haven't found any. Cut it down! Why should it go on using up the soil?' ⁸ But the gardener answered, 'Leave it alone, sir, just this one year; I will dig a trench around it and fill it up with fertilizer. ⁹ Then if the tree bears figs next year, so much the better; if not, then you will have it cut down.' "

Jesus Heals a Crippled Woman
on the Sabbath

¹⁰ One Sabbath day Jesus was teaching in a synagogue. ¹¹ A woman was there who had an evil spirit in her that had kept her sick for eighteen years; she was bent over and could not straighten up at all. ¹² When Jesus saw her he called out to her, "Woman, you are free from your sickness!" ¹³ He placed his hands on her and at once she straightened herself up and praised God. ¹⁴ The official of the synagogue was angry that Jesus had healed on the Sabbath; so he spoke up and said to the people, "There are six days in which we should work; so come during those days and be healed, but not on the Sabbath!" ¹⁵ The Lord answered him by saying: "You impostors! Any one of you would untie his ox or his donkey from the stall and take it out to give it water on the Sabbath. ¹⁶ Now here is this descendant of Abraham whom Satan has kept in bonds for eighteen years; should she not be freed from her bonds on the Sabbath?" ¹⁷ His answer made all his enemies ashamed of themselves, while all the people rejoiced over every wonderful thing that he did.

The Parable of the Mustard Seed
(Also Matt. 13.31–32; Mark 4.30–32)

¹⁸ Jesus said: "What is the Kingdom of God like? What can I compare it with? ¹⁹ It is like a mustard seed, which a man took and planted in his field; the plant grew and became a tree, and the birds made their nests in its branches."

The Healing of a Crippled Woman on the Sabbath

10 Ἦν δὲ διδάσκων ἐν μιᾷ τῶν συναγωγῶν ἐν τοῖς σάββασιν. **11** καὶ ἰδοὺ γυνὴ πνεῦμα ἔχουσα ἀσθενείας ἔτη δέκα ὀκτώ, καὶ ἦν συγκύπτουσα καὶ μὴ δυναμένη ἀνακύψαι εἰς τὸ παντελές. **12** ἰδὼν δὲ αὐτὴν ὁ Ἰησοῦς προσεφώνησεν καὶ εἶπεν αὐτῇ, Γύναι, ἀπολέλυσαι τῆς ἀσθενείας σου, **13** καὶ ἐπέθηκεν αὐτῇ τὰς χεῖρας· καὶ παραχρῆμα ἀνωρθώθη, καὶ ἐδόξαζεν τὸν θεόν. **14** ἀποκριθεὶς δὲ ὁ ἀρχισυνάγωγος, ἀγανακτῶν ὅτι τῷ σαββάτῳ ἐθεράπευσεν ὁ Ἰησοῦς, ἔλεγεν τῷ ὄχλῳ ὅτι Ἓξ ἡμέραι εἰσὶν ἐν αἷς δεῖ ἐργάζεσθαι· ἐν αὐταῖς οὖν ἐρχόμενοι θεραπεύεσθε καὶ μὴ τῇ ἡμέρᾳ τοῦ σαββάτου. **15** ἀπεκρίθη δὲ αὐτῷ ὁ κύριος καὶ εἶπεν, Ὑποκριταί, ἕκαστος ὑμῶν τῷ σαββάτῳ οὐ λύει τὸν βοῦν αὐτοῦ ἢ τὸν ὄνον ἀπὸ τῆς φάτνης καὶ ἀπαγαγὼν ποτίζει; **16** ταύτην δὲ θυγατέρα Ἀβραὰμ οὖσαν, ἣν ἔδησεν ὁ Σατανᾶς ἰδοὺ δέκα καὶ ὀκτὼ ἔτη, οὐκ ἔδει λυθῆναι ἀπὸ τοῦ δεσμοῦ τούτου τῇ ἡμέρᾳ τοῦ σαββάτου; **17** καὶ ταῦτα λέγοντος αὐτοῦ κατῃσχύνοντο πάντες οἱ ἀντικείμενοι αὐτῷ, καὶ πᾶς ὁ ὄχλος ἔχαιρεν ἐπὶ πᾶσιν τοῖς ἐνδόξοις τοῖς γινομένοις ὑπ' αὐτοῦ.

The Parables of the Mustard Seed and the Leaven
(Mt 13.31–33; Mk 4.30–32)

18 Ἔλεγεν οὖν, Τίνι ὁμοία ἐστὶν ἡ βασιλεία τοῦ θεοῦ, καὶ τίνι ὁμοιώσω αὐτήν; **19** ὁμοία ἐστὶν κόκκῳ σινάπεως, ὃν λαβὼν ἄνθρωπος ἔβαλεν εἰς κῆπον ἑαυτοῦ, καὶ ηὔξησεν καὶ ἐγένετο εἰς δένδρον³, καὶ τὰ πετεινὰ τοῦ οὐρανοῦ κατεσκήνωσεν ἐν τοῖς κλάδοις αὐτοῦ.

---

³ **19** {C} εἰς δένδρον 𝔭⁷⁵ ℵ B L 070 1241 itᵉ copᵇᵒ ∥ δένδρον D itᵃ,ᵃ²,ᵇ,ᵈ,ff²,i,l,rl syrᶜ,ˢ,ᵖᵃˡ copˢᵃ arm geo Ambrose ∥ ὡς δένδρον 892 ∥ δένδρον μέγα

14 ἀγανακτῶν...Ἰησοῦς Mt 12.10; Mk 3.2; Lk 6.7; Jn 5.16; 7.23; 9.14, 16   Ἓξ...σαββάτου Ex 20.9–10; Dt 5.13–14   **15** ἕκαστος...ποτίζει Lk 14.5   **16** θυγατέρα Ἀβραάμ Lk 19.9   **19** πετεινὰ...αὐτοῦ Dn 4.12, 21; Eze 17.23; 31.6

20 Καὶ πάλιν εἶπεν, Τίνι ὁμοιώσω τὴν βασιλείαν τοῦ
θεοῦ; 21 ὁμοία ἐστὶν ζύμῃ, ἣν λαβοῦσα γυνὴ ἐνέκρυψεν
εἰς ἀλεύρου σάτα τρία ἕως οὗ ἐζυμώθη ὅλον.

The Narrow Door
(Mt 7.13–14, 21–23)

22 Καὶ διεπορεύετο κατὰ πόλεις καὶ κώμας διδάσκων
καὶ πορείαν ποιούμενος εἰς Ἱεροσόλυμα. 23 εἶπεν δέ
τις αὐτῷ, Κύριε, εἰ ὀλίγοι οἱ σῳζόμενοι; ὁ δὲ εἶπεν
πρὸς αὐτούς, 24 Ἀγωνίζεσθε εἰσελθεῖν διὰ τῆς στενῆς
θύρας, ὅτι πολλοί, λέγω ὑμῖν, ζητήσουσιν εἰσελθεῖν καὶ
οὐκ ἰσχύσουσιν.[a] 25 ἀφʼ οὗ ἂν ἐγερθῇ ὁ οἰκοδεσπότης
καὶ ἀποκλείσῃ τὴν θύραν, καὶ ἄρξησθε ἔξω ἑστάναι καὶ
κρούειν τὴν θύραν λέγοντες, Κύριε, ἄνοιξον ἡμῖν· καὶ
ἀποκριθεὶς ἐρεῖ ὑμῖν, Οὐκ οἶδα ὑμᾶς πόθεν ἐστέ. 26 τότε
ἄρξεσθε λέγειν, Ἐφάγομεν ἐνώπιόν σου καὶ ἐπίομεν,
καὶ ἐν ταῖς πλατείαις ἡμῶν ἐδίδαξας· 27 καὶ ἐρεῖ λέγων
ὑμῖν[4], Οὐκ οἶδα [ὑμᾶς] πόθεν ἐστέ[5]· ἀπόστητε ἀπʼ

---

f[1] it[c,f,q] syr[p] eth // *ὡς δένδρον μέγα* *l*[60] // *εἰς δένδρον μέγα* 𝔭[45] A K W X Δ Θ Π Ψ *f*[13] 28 33 565 700 1009 1010 1071 1079 1195 1216 1230 1242 1253 1344 1365 1546 1646 2148 2174 *Byz Lect* it[aur] vg syr[h] cop[bomss]

[4] **27** {C} *ἐρεῖ λέγων ὑμῖν* 𝔭[75c] B 28 892 1071 1230 (1546 *omit ὑμῖν*) // *ἐρεῖ, Λέγω ὑμῖν* 𝔭[75*] A D K L W X Δ Θ Π Ψ 070 *f*[1] *f*[13] 565 700 1009 1241 1242 1253 1365 1646 2148 2174 *Byz Lect* it[d] syr[h] arm // *ἐρεῖ, Ἀμὴν λέγω ὑμῖν* syr[s,pal] // *ἐρεῖ ὑμῖν* ℵ 1010 1079 1216 it[a,a2,aur,b,c,e,f,ff2,i,l,q,r1] vg syr[c,p] cop[sa,bo] geo Diatessaron[a,i,s] Lucifer // *ἐρεῖ* 1195 cop[bomss]

[5] **27** {C} *οὐκ οἶδα ὑμᾶς πόθεν ἐστέ* ℵ A K W X Δ Θ Π Ψ *f*[1] *f*[13] 28 565 700 892 1009 1010 1071 1079 1195 1216 1230 1242 1253 1365 1546 1646* 2148 2174 *Byz Lect* it[a,a2,aur,c,f,q,r1] vg syr[c,s,p,h,pal] cop[sa,bo] arm eth? geo Diatessaron Origen // *οὐκ οἶδα πόθεν ἐστέ* 𝔭[75] B L 070 1241 it[b,ff2,i,l] Lucifer // *οὐδέποτε εἶδον ὑμᾶς* D it[d,e] // *οὐκ οἶδα ὑμᾶς* 56 61 71 291 692 cop[samss] Cyril

---

[a] **24** *a* major: TR Bov Nes BF[2] AV RV ASV RSV NEB TT Zur Luth Jer Seg // *a* minor: WH RV[mg] ASV[mg]

---

24 *Ἀγωνίζεσθε...θύρας* 1 Tm 6.12; Mk 10.25 **25** *ἀποκλείσῃ...ἐστέ* Mt 25.10–12 **27** *ἀπόστητε...ἀδικίας* Ps 6.8

The Parable of the Yeast
(Also Matt. 13.33)

20 Again Jesus asked: "What shall I
compare the Kingdom of God with?
21 It is like the yeast which a woman
takes and mixes in a bushel of flour,
until the whole batch of dough rises."

The Narrow Door
(Also Matt. 7.13–14, 21–23)

22 Jesus went through towns and villages, teaching and making his way toward Jerusalem. 23 Someone asked him,
"Sir, will just a few people be saved?"
Jesus answered them: 24 "Do your best
to go in through the narrow door; for
many people, I tell you, will try to go
in but will not be able.

25 "The master of the house will get
up and close the door; then when you
stand outside and begin to knock on
the door and say, 'Open the door for us,
sir!' he will answer you, 'I don't know
where you come from!' 26 Then you will
answer back, 'We ate and drank with
you; you taught in our town!' 27 He will
say again, 'I don't know where you come

from. Get away from me, all you evil-doers!' ²⁸ What crying and gnashing of teeth there will be when you see Abraham, Isaac, and Jacob and all the prophets in the Kingdom of God, while you are kept outside! ²⁹ People will come from the east and the west, from the north and the south, and sit at the table in the Kingdom of God. ³⁰ Then those who are now last will be first, and those who are now first will be last.''

Jesus' Love for Jerusalem
(Also Matt. 23.37–39)

³¹ At that same time some Pharisees came to Jesus and said to him, "You must get out of here and go somewhere else, for Herod wants to kill you." ³² Jesus answered them: "Go tell that fox: 'I am driving out demons and performing cures today and tomorrow, and on the third day I shall finish my work.' ³³ Yet I must be on my way today, tomorrow, and the next day; it is not right for a prophet to be killed anywhere except in Jerusalem.

³⁴ "O Jerusalem, Jerusalem! You kill the prophets, you stone the messengers God has sent you! How many times I wanted to put my arms around all your people, just as a hen gathers her chicks under her wings, but you would not let me! ³⁵ Now your home will be completely forsaken. You will not see me, I tell you, until the time comes when you say, 'God bless him who comes in the name of the Lord.' ''

ἐμοῦ, πάντες ἐργάται ἀδικίας. **28** ἐκεῖ ἔσται ὁ κλαυθμὸς καὶ ὁ βρυγμὸς τῶν ὀδόντων, ὅταν ὄψεσθε ᾿Αβραὰμ καὶ ᾿Ισαὰκ καὶ ᾿Ιακὼβ καὶ πάντας τοὺς προφήτας ἐν τῇ βασιλείᾳ τοῦ θεοῦ, ὑμᾶς δὲ ἐκβαλλομένους ἔξω. **29** καὶ ἥξουσιν ἀπὸ ἀνατολῶν καὶ δυσμῶν καὶ ἀπὸ βορρᾶ καὶ νότου καὶ ἀνακλιθήσονται ἐν τῇ βασιλείᾳ τοῦ θεοῦ. **30** καὶ ἰδοὺ εἰσὶν ἔσχατοι οἳ ἔσονται πρῶτοι, καὶ εἰσὶν πρῶτοι οἳ ἔσονται ἔσχατοι.

The Lament over Jerusalem
(Mt 23.37–39)

31 ᾿Εν αὐτῇ τῇ ὥρᾳ προσῆλθάν τινες Φαρισαῖοι λέγοντες αὐτῷ, ῎Εξελθε καὶ πορεύου ἐντεῦθεν, ὅτι ῾Ηρῴδης θέλει σε ἀποκτεῖναι. **32** καὶ εἶπεν αὐτοῖς, Πορευθέντες εἴπατε τῇ ἀλώπεκι ταύτῃ, ᾿Ιδοὺ ἐκβάλλω δαιμόνια καὶ ἰάσεις ἀποτελῶ σήμερον καὶ αὔριον, καὶ τῇ τρίτῃ τελειοῦμαι. **33** πλὴν δεῖ με σήμερον καὶ αὔριον καὶ τῇ ἐχομένῃ πορεύεσθαι, ὅτι οὐκ ἐνδέχεται προφήτην ἀπολέσθαι ἔξω ᾿Ιερουσαλήμ. **34** ᾿Ιερουσαλὴμ ᾿Ιερουσαλήμ, ἡ ἀποκτείνουσα τοὺς προφήτας καὶ λιθοβολοῦσα τοὺς ἀπεσταλμένους πρὸς αὐτήν, ποσάκις ἠθέλησα ἐπισυνάξαι τὰ τέκνα σου ὃν τρόπον ὄρνις τὴν ἑαυτῆς νοσσιὰν ὑπὸ τὰς πτέρυγας, καὶ οὐκ ἠθελήσατε.^b **35** ἰδοὺ **ἀφίεται ὑμῖν ὁ οἶκος ὑμῶν.** λέγω [δὲ] ὑμῖν, οὐ μὴ ἴδητέ με ἕως [ἥξει ὅτε] εἴπητε⁶, **Εὐλογημένος ὁ ἐρχόμενος ἐν ὀνόματι κυρίου.**

---

⁶ **35** {D} ἕως ἥξει ὅτε εἴπητε D ‖ ἕως ἂν ἥξει ὅτε εἴπητε A W 28 1009 1216 1242^{mg} 1253 Byz^{pt} l^{150,184,299,1014,1578,1599m} Marcion ‖ ἕως (or ἕως ἄν) ἥξει ὅτε εἴπητε it^{aur,(c),d,(ff²),l,q,r¹} vg ‖ ἕως ἂν ἥξῃ ὅτε εἴπητε Ψ f¹ 565 700 1195 1230 1344 1365 1646 2174 Byz^{pt} Lect (l²¹¹ ὅτι for ὅτε) syr^{s,h} ‖ ἕως ὅτε εἴπητε Κ Π 1079 1546 ‖ ἕως εἴπητε p⁷⁵ B L 892 1242* ‖ ἕως ἂν εἴπητε p⁴⁵ ℵ X f¹³ 1010

^b **34** b statement: WH Bov Nes BF² NEB ‖ b question: TR AV^{ed} ‖ b exclamation: AV^{ed} RV ASV RSV TT Zür Luth Jer Seg

28–29 Mt 8.11–12 **29** ἥξουσιν...νότου Ps 107.3 ἀνακλιθήσονται...θεοῦ Lk 14.15 **30** Mt 19.30; 20.16; Mk 10.31 **35** Εὐλογημένος...κυρίου Ps 118.26

The Healing of the Man with Dropsy

14 Καὶ ἐγένετο ἐν τῷ ἐλθεῖν αὐτὸν εἰς οἶκόν τινος τῶν ἀρχόντων [τῶν] Φαρισαίων σαββάτῳ φαγεῖν ἄρτον καὶ αὐτοὶ ἦσαν παρατηρούμενοι αὐτόν. 2 καὶ ἰδοὺ ἄνθρωπός τις ἦν ὑδρωπικὸς ἔμπροσθεν αὐτοῦ. 3 καὶ ἀποκριθεὶς ὁ Ἰησοῦς εἶπεν πρὸς τοὺς νομικοὺς καὶ Φαρισαίους λέγων, Ἔξεστιν τῷ σαββάτῳ θεραπεῦσαι ἢ οὔ; 4[a] οἱ δὲ ἡσύχασαν. [a]καὶ ἐπιλαβόμενος ἰάσατο αὐτὸν καὶ ἀπέλυσεν. 5 καὶ πρὸς αὐτοὺς εἶπεν, Τίνος ὑμῶν υἱὸς ἢ βοῦς[1] εἰς φρέαρ πεσεῖται, καὶ οὐκ εὐθέως ἀνασπάσει αὐτὸν ἐν ἡμέρᾳ τοῦ σαββάτου; 6 καὶ οὐκ ἴσχυσαν ἀνταποκριθῆναι πρὸς ταῦτα.

A Lesson to Guests and a Host

7 Ἔλεγεν δὲ πρὸς τοὺς κεκλημένους παραβολήν, ἐπέχων πῶς τὰς πρωτοκλισίας ἐξελέγοντο, λέγων πρὸς αὐτούς, 8 Ὅταν κληθῇς ὑπό τινος εἰς γάμους, μὴ κατακλιθῇς εἰς τὴν πρωτοκλισίαν, μήποτε ἐντιμότερός σου ᾖ κεκλημένος ὑπ’ αὐτοῦ, 9 καὶ ἐλθὼν ὁ σὲ καὶ αὐτὸν καλέσας ἐρεῖ σοι, Δὸς τούτῳ τόπον, καὶ τότε ἄρξῃ μετὰ αἰσχύνης τὸν ἔσχατον τόπον κατέχειν. 10 ἀλλ’

Jesus Heals a Sick Man

14 One Sabbath day Jesus went to eat a meal at the home of one of the leading Pharisees; and people were watching Jesus closely. [2] A man whose legs and arms were swollen came to Jesus, [3] and Jesus spoke up and asked the teachers of the Law and the Pharisees, "Does our Law allow healing on the Sabbath, or not?" [4] But they would not say a thing. Jesus took the man, healed him and sent him away. [5] Then he said to them, "If any one of you had a son or an ox that happened to fall in a well on a Sabbath, would you not pull him out at once on the Sabbath itself?" [6] But they were not able to answer him about this.

Hospitality and Humility

[7] Jesus noticed how some of the guests were choosing the best places, so he told this parable to all of them: [8] "When someone invites you to a wedding feast, do not sit down in the best place. For it could happen that someone more important than you had been invited, [9] and your host, who invited both of you, would come and say to you, 'Let him have this place.' Then you would be ashamed and have to sit in the lowest place. [10] Instead, when you are invited,

---

1071 (2148 ἄχρις) ‖ ἕως (or ἕως ἄν) εἴπητε it[e,i] syr[p] cop[sa,bomss,fay] arm geo ‖ ἀπ’ ἄρτι ἕως ἄν εἴπητε (see Mt 23.39) Θ 1241 cop[samss,bo] ‖ ἀπ’ ἄρτι ἕως ἄν ἥξει ὅτε εἴπητε Δ ‖ ἕως ἥξει ἡ ἡμέρα ὅτε εἴπητε it[a,b,f] syr[c,h with *]

1 5 {B} υἱὸς ἢ βοῦς 𝔭[45,75] A B W Δ 28 565 700 1009 1010 1195 1216 1242 (1344 *l*[184,1579] υἱὸς ὑμῶν) 1365 2148 Byz Lect it[e,f,q] syr[(p),h] cop[sa] geo Diatessaron Cyril ‖ ὄνος ἢ βοῦς ℵ K L X Π Ψ *f*[1] *f*[13] 33 1071 1079 1230 1241 1253 1546 1646 *l*[547] it[a,aur,b,c,ff2,i,l,r1] vg syr[pal] cop[bo,fay] arm ‖ ὄρος [sic] ἢ βοῦς 892 ‖ βοῦς ἢ ὄνος syr[s] (eth?) ‖ ὄνος υἱὸς ἢ βοῦς Θ ‖ υἱὸς ἢ βοῦς ἢ ὄνος 2174 syr[c] ‖ πρόβατον ἢ βοῦς D it[d]

---

[a][a] **3-4** *a* number 4, *a* no number: TR[ed] WH? Bov Nes BF[2] AV RV ASV RSV NEB? TT Zür Luth Jer Seg ‖ *a* no number, *a* number 4: TR[ed] WH? NEB?

---

1 ἐν...ἄρτον Lk 11.37   3 Ἰησοῦς...οὔ Lk 6.9   5 Mt 12.11; Lk 13.15   6 Mt 22.46
7 πρωτοκλισίας ἐξελέγοντο Mt 23.6   8-10 Pr 25.6-7

go and sit in the lowest place, so that your host will come to you and say, 'Ccme on up, my friend, to a better place.' This will bring you honor in the presence of all the other guests. [11] For everyone who makes himself great will be humbled, and whoever humbles himself will be made great."

[12] Then Jesus said to his host: "When you give a lunch or a dinner, do not invite your friends, or your brothers, or your relatives, or your rich neighbors — for they will invite you back and in this way you will be paid for what you did. [13] When you give a feast, invite the poor, the crippled, the lame, and the blind, [14] and you will be blessed; for they are not able to pay you back. You will be paid by God when the good people are raised from death."

The Parable of the Great Feast
(Also Matt. 22.1–10)

[15] One of the men sitting at the table heard this and said to Jesus, "How happy are those who will sit at the table in the Kingdom of God!" [16] Jesus said to him: "There was a man who was giving a great feast, to which he invited many people. [17] At the time for the feast he sent his servant to tell his guests, 'Come, everything is ready!' [18] But they all began, one after another, to make excuses. The first one told the servant, 'I bought a field, and have to go and look at it; please accept my apologies.' [19] Another one said, 'I bought five pairs of oxen and am on my way to try them out; please accept my apologies.' [20] Another one said, 'I have just gotten married, and for this reason I cannot come.'

ὅταν κληθῇς πορευθεὶς ἀνάπεσε εἰς τὸν ἔσχατον τόπον, ἵνα ὅταν ἔλθῃ ὁ κεκληκώς σε ἐρεῖ σοι, Φίλε, προσανάβηθι ἀνώτερον· τότε ἔσται σοι δόξα ἐνώπιον πάντων τῶν συνανακειμένων σοι. **11** ὅτι πᾶς ὁ ὑψῶν ἑαυτὸν ταπεινωθήσεται καὶ ὁ ταπεινῶν ἑαυτὸν ὑψωθήσεται. **12** Ἔλεγεν δὲ καὶ τῷ κεκληκότι αὐτόν, Ὅταν ποιῇς ἄριστον ἢ δεῖπνον, μὴ φώνει τοὺς φίλους σου μηδὲ τοὺς ἀδελφούς σου μηδὲ τοὺς συγγενεῖς σου μηδὲ γείτονας πλουσίους, μήποτε καὶ αὐτοὶ ἀντικαλέσωσίν σε καὶ γένηται ἀνταπόδομά σοι. **13** ἀλλ' ὅταν δοχὴν ποιῇς, κάλει πτωχούς, ἀναπείρους, χωλούς, τυφλούς· **14** καὶ μακάριος ἔσῃ, ὅτι οὐκ ἔχουσιν ἀνταποδοῦναί σοι, ἀνταποδοθήσεται γάρ σοι ἐν τῇ ἀναστάσει τῶν δικαίων.

The Parable of the Great Banquet
(Mt 22.1–10)

15 Ἀκούσας δέ τις τῶν συνανακειμένων ταῦτα εἶπεν αὐτῷ, Μακάριος ὅστις φάγεται ἄρτον ἐν τῇ βασιλείᾳ τοῦ θεοῦ. **16** ὁ δὲ εἶπεν αὐτῷ, Ἄνθρωπός τις ἐποίει δεῖπνον μέγα, καὶ ἐκάλεσεν πολλούς, **17** καὶ ἀπέστειλεν τὸν δοῦλον αὐτοῦ τῇ ὥρᾳ τοῦ δείπνου εἰπεῖν τοῖς κεκλημένοις, Ἔρχεσθε, ὅτι ἤδη ἕτοιμά ἐστιν². **18** καὶ ἤρξαντο ἀπὸ μιᾶς πάντες παραιτεῖσθαι. ὁ πρῶτος εἶπεν αὐτῷ, Ἀγρὸν ἠγόρασα καὶ ἔχω ἀνάγκην ἐξελθὼν ἰδεῖν αὐτόν· ἐρωτῶ σε, ἔχε με παρῃτημένον. **19** καὶ ἕτερος εἶπεν, Ζεύγη βοῶν ἠγόρασα πέντε καὶ πορεύομαι δοκιμάσαι αὐτά· ἐρωτῶ σε, ἔχε με παρῃτημένον. **20** καὶ ἕτερος εἶπεν, Γυναῖκα ἔγημα καὶ διὰ τοῦτο οὐ δύναμαι ἐλθεῖν.

---

2 17 {C} ἕτοιμά ἐστιν 𝔭⁴⁵ᵛⁱᵈ B itᵇ,ᶜ,ff²,ⁱ,ˡ,q ‖ ἕτοιμά εἰσιν 𝔭⁷⁵ ℵ*,ᶜ L Θ ‖ ἕτοιμά ἐστιν πάντα (ℵᵃ εἰσιν) A K P W X Δ Π Ψ f¹ f¹³ 28 565 700 892 1009 1010 1071 1079 1195 1216 1230 1241 1242 1253 1344 1365 1546 1646 2148 2174 *Byz Lect* itᵃᵘʳ,ᵈ,f,rˡ vg syrʰ copˢᵃ?ᵇᵒ? goth arm eth geo Diatessaron Basil ‖ πάντα ἕτοιμά ἐστιν Dᵍʳ itᵃ,ᵉ syrᶜ,ˢ,(ᵖ),ᵖᵃˡ copˢᵃ?ᵇᵒ? (Eusebius)

11 Mt 23.12; Lk 18.14   **14** ἀναστάσει τῶν δικαίων Jn 5.29   **15** φάγεται...θεοῦ Lk 13.29   **20** Γυναῖκα...ἐλθεῖν 1 Cor 7.33

21 καὶ παραγενόμενος ὁ δοῦλος ἀπήγγειλεν τῷ κυρίῳ αὐτοῦ ταῦτα. τότε ὀργισθεὶς ὁ οἰκοδεσπότης εἶπεν τῷ δούλῳ αὐτοῦ, Ἔξελθε ταχέως εἰς τὰς πλατείας καὶ ῥύμας τῆς πόλεως, καὶ τοὺς πτωχοὺς καὶ ἀναπείρους καὶ τυφλοὺς καὶ χωλοὺς εἰσάγαγε ὧδε. 22 καὶ εἶπεν ὁ δοῦλος, Κύριε, γέγονεν ὃ ἐπέταξας, καὶ ἔτι τόπος ἐστίν. 23 καὶ εἶπεν ὁ κύριος πρὸς τὸν δοῦλον, Ἔξελθε εἰς τὰς ὁδοὺς καὶ φραγμοὺς καὶ ἀνάγκασον εἰσελθεῖν, ἵνα γεμισθῇ μου ὁ οἶκος· 24 λέγω γὰρ ὑμῖν ὅτι οὐδεὶς τῶν ἀνδρῶν ἐκείνων τῶν κεκλημένων γεύσεταί μου τοῦ δείπνου.

The Cost of Discipleship
(Mt 10.37–38)

25 Συνεπορεύοντο δὲ αὐτῷ ὄχλοι πολλοί, καὶ στραφεὶς εἶπεν πρὸς αὐτούς, 26 Εἴ τις ἔρχεται πρός με καὶ οὐ μισεῖ τὸν πατέρα ἑαυτοῦ καὶ τὴν μητέρα καὶ τὴν γυναῖκα καὶ τὰ τέκνα καὶ τοὺς ἀδελφοὺς καὶ τὰς ἀδελφάς, ἔτι τε καὶ τὴν ψυχὴν ἑαυτοῦ, οὐ δύναται εἶναί μου μαθητής. 27 ὅστις οὐ βαστάζει τὸν σταυρὸν ἑαυτοῦ καὶ ἔρχεται ὀπίσω μου οὐ δύναται εἶναί μου μαθητής. 28 τίς γὰρ ἐξ ὑμῶν θέλων πύργον οἰκοδομῆσαι οὐχὶ πρῶτον καθίσας ψηφίζει τὴν δαπάνην, εἰ ἔχει εἰς ἀπαρτισμόν; 29 ἵνα μήποτε θέντος αὐτοῦ θεμέλιον καὶ μὴ ἰσχύοντος ἐκτελέσαι πάντες οἱ θεωροῦντες ἄρξωνται αὐτῷ ἐμπαίζειν 30 λέγοντες ὅτι Οὗτος ὁ ἄνθρωπος ἤρξατο οἰκοδομεῖν καὶ οὐκ ἴσχυσεν ἐκτελέσαι. 31 ἢ τίς βασιλεὺς πορευόμενος ἑτέρῳ βασιλεῖ συμβαλεῖν εἰς πόλεμον οὐχὶ καθίσας πρῶτον βουλεύσεται εἰ δυνατός ἐστιν ἐν δέκα χιλιάσιν ὑπαντῆσαι τῷ μετὰ εἴκοσι χιλιάδων ἐρχομένῳ ἐπ' αὐτόν; 32 εἰ δὲ μήγε, ἔτι αὐτοῦ πόρρω ὄντος πρεσβείαν ἀποστείλας ἐρωτᾷ τὰ πρὸς εἰρήνην. 33 οὕτως οὖν πᾶς ἐξ ὑμῶν ὃς οὐκ ἀποτάσσεται πᾶσιν τοῖς ἑαυτοῦ ὑπάρχουσιν οὐ δύναται εἶναί μου μαθητής.

26–27 Mt 10.37–38 26 μισεῖ...ἑαυτοῦ Dt 33.9; Mt 16.24; Mk 8.34; Lk 9.23; 18.29; Jn 12.25
27 Mt 10.38; 16.24; Mk 8.34; Lk 9.23

21 The servant went back and told all this to his master. The master of the house was furious and said to his servant, 'Hurry out to the streets and alleys of the town, and bring back the poor, the crippled, the blind, and the lame.' 22 Soon the servant said, 'Your order has been carried out, sir, but there is room for more.' 23 So the master said to the servant, 'Go out to the country roads and lanes, and make people come in, so that my house will be full. 24 None of those men who were invited, I tell you all, will taste my dinner!' "

The Cost of Being a Disciple
(Also Matt. 10.37–38)

25 Great crowds of people were going along with Jesus. He turned and said to them: 26 "Whoever comes to me cannot be my disciple unless he hates his father and his mother, his wife and his children, his brothers and his sisters, and himself as well. 27 Whoever does not carry his own cross and come after me cannot be my disciple. 28 If one of you is planning to build a tower, he sits down first and figures out what it will cost, to see if he has enough money to finish the job. 29 If he doesn't, he will not be able to finish the tower after laying the foundation; and all who see what happened will make fun of him. 30 'This man began to build but can't finish the job!' they will say. 31 If a king goes out with ten thousand men to fight another king, who comes against him with twenty thousand men, he will sit down first and decide if he is strong enough to face that other king. 32 If he isn't, he will have to send messengers to meet the other king, while he is still a long way off, to ask for terms of peace. 33 In the same way," concluded Jesus, "none of you can be my disciple unless he gives up everything he has."

Worthless Salt
(Also Matt. 5.13; Mark 9.50)

[34] "Salt is good, but if it loses its taste there is no way to make it good again. [35] It is no good for the soil or for the manure pile; it is thrown away. Listen, then, if you have ears!"

The Lost Sheep
(Also Matt. 18.12–14)

15 One time many tax collectors and outcasts came to listen to Jesus. [2] The Pharisees and the teachers of the Law started grumbling, "This man welcomes outcasts and even eats with them!" [3] So Jesus told them this parable:

[4] "Suppose one of you has a hundred sheep and loses one of them — what does he do? He leaves the ninety-nine sheep in the pasture and goes looking for the lost sheep until he finds it. [5] When he finds it, he is so happy that he puts it on his shoulders, [6] carries it back home, and calls his friends and neighbors together. 'Rejoice with me,' he tells them, 'for I have found my lost sheep!' [7] In the same way, I tell you, there will be more joy in heaven over one sinner who repents than over ninety-nine respectable people who do not need to repent."

The Lost Coin

[8] "Or suppose a woman who has ten silver coins loses one of them — what does she do? She lights a lamp, sweeps her house, and looks carefully everywhere until she finds it. [9] When she finds it, she calls her friends and neighbors together. 'Rejoice with me,' she tells them, 'for I have found the coin I lost!' [10] In the same way, I tell you, the angels of God rejoice over one sinner who repents."

Tasteless Salt
(Mt 5.13; Mk 9.50)

34 Καλὸν οὖν τὸ ἅλας· ἐὰν δὲ καὶ τὸ ἅλας μωρανθῇ, ἐν τίνι ἀρτυθήσεται; **35**[b] οὔτε εἰς γῆν οὔτε εἰς κοπρίαν εὔθετόν ἐστιν· ἔξω βάλλουσιν αὐτό. ὁ ἔχων ὦτα ἀκούειν ἀκουέτω.

The Parable of the Lost Sheep
(Mt 18.12–14)

15 Ἦσαν δὲ αὐτῷ ἐγγίζοντες πάντες οἱ τελῶναι καὶ οἱ ἁμαρτωλοὶ ἀκούειν αὐτοῦ. **2** καὶ διεγόγγυζον οἵ τε Φαρισαῖοι καὶ οἱ γραμματεῖς λέγοντες ὅτι Οὗτος ἁμαρτωλοὺς προσδέχεται καὶ συνεσθίει αὐτοῖς. **3** εἶπεν δὲ πρὸς αὐτοὺς τὴν παραβολὴν ταύτην λέγων, **4** Τίς ἄνθρωπος ἐξ ὑμῶν ἔχων ἑκατὸν πρόβατα καὶ ἀπολέσας ἐξ αὐτῶν ἓν οὐ καταλείπει τὰ ἐνενήκοντα ἐννέα ἐν τῇ ἐρήμῳ καὶ πορεύεται ἐπὶ τὸ ἀπολωλὸς ἕως εὕρῃ αὐτό; **5** καὶ εὑρὼν ἐπιτίθησιν ἐπὶ τοὺς ὤμους αὐτοῦ χαίρων, **6** καὶ ἐλθὼν εἰς τὸν οἶκον συγκαλεῖ τοὺς φίλους καὶ τοὺς γείτονας λέγων αὐτοῖς, Συγχάρητέ μοι, ὅτι εὗρον τὸ πρόβατόν μου τὸ ἀπολωλός. **7** λέγω ὑμῖν ὅτι οὕτως χαρὰ ἐν τῷ οὐρανῷ ἔσται ἐπὶ ἑνὶ ἁμαρτωλῷ μετανοοῦντι ἢ ἐπὶ ἐνενήκοντα ἐννέα δικαίοις οἵτινες οὐ χρείαν ἔχουσιν μετανοίας.

The Parable of the Lost Coin

8 Ἢ τίς γυνὴ δραχμὰς ἔχουσα δέκα, ἐὰν ἀπολέσῃ δραχμὴν μίαν, οὐχὶ ἅπτει λύχνον καὶ σαροῖ τὴν οἰκίαν καὶ ζητεῖ ἐπιμελῶς ἕως οὗ εὕρῃ; **9** καὶ εὑροῦσα συγκαλεῖ τὰς φίλας καὶ γείτονας λέγουσα, Συγχάρητέ μοι, ὅτι εὗρον τὴν δραχμὴν ἣν ἀπώλεσα. **10** οὕτως, λέγω ὑμῖν, γίνεται χαρὰ ἐνώπιον τῶν ἀγγέλων τοῦ θεοῦ ἐπὶ ἑνὶ ἁμαρτωλῷ μετανοοῦντι.

---

[b] **34-35** b number 35: TR[ed] WH Bov Nes BF[2] AV RV ASV RSV NEB TT Zür Luth Jer Seg ∥ b no number: TR[ed]

35 ὁ...ἀκουέτω Mt 11.15; 13.9; 13.43; Mk 4.9, 23; Lk 8.8
15 **2** Lk 5.30   **4** πορεύεται...αὐτό Eze 34.11, 16; Lk 19.10

The Parable of the Lost Son

11 Εἶπεν δέ, ᾿Ανθρωπός τις εἶχεν δύο υἱούς. **12** καὶ εἶπεν ὁ νεώτερος αὐτῶν τῷ πατρί, Πάτερ, δός μοι τὸ ἐπιβάλλον μέρος τῆς οὐσίας. ὁ δὲ διεῖλεν αὐτοῖς τὸν βίον. **13** καὶ μετ᾿ οὐ πολλὰς ἡμέρας συναγαγὼν ἅπαντα ὁ νεώτερος υἱὸς ἀπεδήμησεν εἰς χώραν μακράν, καὶ ἐκεῖ διεσκόρπισεν τὴν οὐσίαν αὐτοῦ ζῶν ἀσώτως. **14** δαπανήσαντος δὲ αὐτοῦ πάντα ἐγένετο λιμὸς ἰσχυρὰ κατὰ τὴν χώραν ἐκείνην, καὶ αὐτὸς ἤρξατο ὑστερεῖσθαι. **15** καὶ πορευθεὶς ἐκολλήθη ἑνὶ τῶν πολιτῶν τῆς χώρας ἐκείνης, καὶ ἔπεμψεν αὐτὸν εἰς τοὺς ἀγροὺς αὐτοῦ βόσκειν χοίρους· **16** καὶ ἐπεθύμει χορτασθῆναι ἐκ[1] τῶν κερατίων ὧν ἤσθιον οἱ χοῖροι, καὶ οὐδεὶς ἐδίδου αὐτῷ. **17** εἰς ἑαυτὸν δὲ ἐλθὼν ἔφη, Πόσοι μίσθιοι τοῦ πατρός μου περισσεύονται ἄρτων, ἐγὼ δὲ λιμῷ ὧδε ἀπόλλυμαι. **18** ἀναστὰς πορεύσομαι πρὸς τὸν πατέρα μου καὶ ἐρῶ αὐτῷ, Πάτερ, ἥμαρτον εἰς τὸν οὐρανὸν καὶ ἐνώπιόν σου, **19** οὐκέτι εἰμὶ ἄξιος κληθῆναι υἱός σου· ποίησόν με ὡς ἕνα τῶν μισθίων σου. **20** καὶ ἀναστὰς ἦλθεν πρὸς τὸν πατέρα ἑαυτοῦ. ἔτι δὲ αὐτοῦ μακρὰν ἀπέχοντος εἶδεν αὐτὸν ὁ πατὴρ αὐτοῦ καὶ ἐσπλαγχνίσθη καὶ δραμὼν ἐπέπεσεν ἐπὶ τὸν τράχηλον αὐτοῦ καὶ κατεφίλησεν αὐτόν. **21** εἶπεν δὲ ὁ υἱὸς αὐτῷ, Πάτερ, ἥμαρτον εἰς τὸν οὐρανὸν καὶ ἐνώπιόν σου, οὐκέτι εἰμὶ ἄξιος κληθῆναι υἱός σου.[2]

---

[1] **16** {C} χορτασθῆναι ἐκ 𝔭75 ℵ B D L *f*1 *f*13 (1241 χορτασθῆναι ἀπό) *l*547 it[d,e,f] syr[(c),pal] cop[sa] goth eth ‖ γεμίσαι τὴν κοιλίαν αὐτοῦ ἀπό A K P X Δ Θ Π Ψ 28 565 700 892 1009 1010 1071 1079 1195 1216 1230 1242 1253 1344 1365 1546 1646 2148 2174 *Byz Lect* it[(a),aur,b,c,ff2,i,l,q,r1] vg syr[s,p,h] cop[bo] arm geo Diatessaron Ps-Chrysostom Jerome ‖ γεμίσαι τὴν κοιλίαν καὶ χορτασθῆναι ἀπό W

[2] **21** {B} υἱός σου. 𝔭75 A K L P W Δ Θ Π Ψ *f*1 *f*13 28 565 892 1009 1010 1071 1079 1242 1365 1546 1646 2148 2174 *Byz Lect* it[a,aur,b,c,e,f,ff2,i,l,q,r1] vg syr[c,s,p,pal] cop[sa,bo] goth arm geo Diatessaron Augustine ‖ υἱός σου. ποίησόν με ὡς ἕνα τῶν μισθίων σου. (see 15.19) ℵ B D X 33[vid] 700 1195 1216 1230 1241 1253 1344 *l*[13,15,60,80,185,883,950,1663] it[d] syr[h] eth

---

13 διεσκόρπισεν...ἀσώτως Pr 29.3   **18** ἥμαρτον...σου Ps 51.4   **20** δραμὼν...αὐτοῦ Tob 11.9

The Lost Son

[11] Jesus went on to say: "There was a man who had two sons. [12] The younger one said to his father, 'Father, give me now my share of the property.' So the father divided the property between his two sons. [13] After a few days the younger son sold his part of the property and left home with the money. He went to a country far away, where he wasted his money in reckless living. [14] He spent everything he had. Then a severe famine spread over that country, and he was left without a thing. [15] So he went to work for one of the citizens of that country, who sent him out to his farm to take care of the pigs. [16] He wished he could fill himself with the bean pods the pigs ate, but no one gave him any. [17] At last he came to his senses and said: 'All my father's hired workers have more than they can eat, and here I am, about to starve! [18] I will get up and go to my father and say, "Father, I have sinned against God and against you. [19] I am no longer fit to be called your son; treat me as one of your hired workers." ' [20] So he got up and started back to his father.

"He was still a long way from home when his father saw him; his heart was filled with pity and he ran, threw his arms around his son, and kissed him. [21] 'Father,' the son said, 'I have sinned against God and against you. I am no longer fit to be called your son.' ²² But the father called his servants: 'Hurry!' he said. 'Bring the best robe and put it on him. Put a ring on his finger and shoes on his feet. ²³ Then go get the prize calf and kill it, and let us celebrate with a feast! ²⁴ For this son of mine was dead, but now he is alive; he was lost, but now he has been found.' And so the feasting began.

²⁵ "The older son, in the meantime, was out in the field. On his way back, when he came close to the house, he heard the music and dancing. ²⁶ He called one of the servants and asked him, 'What's going on?' ²⁷ 'Your brother came back home,' the servant answered, 'and your father killed the prize calf, because he got him back safe and sound.' ²⁸ The older brother was so angry that he would not go into the house; so his father came out and begged him to come in. ²⁹ 'Look,' he answered back to his father, 'all these years I have worked like a slave for you, and not once did I disobey an order of yours. What have you given me? Not even a goat for me to have a feast with my friends! ³⁰ But this son of yours wasted all your property on prostitutes, and when he comes back home you kill the prize calf for him!' ³¹ 'My son,' the father answered, 'you are always at home and everything I have is yours. ³² But we had to have a feast and be happy, for your brother was dead, but now he is alive; he was lost, but now he has been found.' "

The Shrewd Manager

16 Jesus said to his disciples: "There was a rich man who had a manager, and he was told that the manager was wasting his master's money. ² He called him in and said, 'What is this I hear about you? Turn in a complete account of your handling of my property, for you cannot be my manager any longer.' ³ 'My master is about to dismiss me from my job,' the man said to himself.

22 εἶπεν δὲ ὁ πατὴρ πρὸς τοὺς δούλους αὐτοῦ, Ταχὺ ἐξενέγκατε στολὴν τὴν πρώτην καὶ ἐνδύσατε αὐτόν, καὶ δότε δακτύλιον εἰς τὴν χεῖρα αὐτοῦ καὶ ὑποδήματα εἰς τοὺς πόδας, 23 καὶ φέρετε τὸν μόσχον τὸν σιτευτόν, θύσατε καὶ φαγόντες εὐφρανθῶμεν, 24 ὅτι οὗτος ὁ υἱός μου νεκρὸς ἦν καὶ ἀνέζησεν, ἦν ἀπολωλὼς καὶ εὑρέθη. καὶ ἤρξαντο εὐφραίνεσθαι.

25 Ἦν δὲ ὁ υἱὸς αὐτοῦ ὁ πρεσβύτερος ἐν ἀγρῷ· καὶ ὡς ἐρχόμενος ἤγγισεν τῇ οἰκίᾳ, ἤκουσεν συμφωνίας καὶ χορῶν, 26 καὶ προσκαλεσάμενος ἕνα τῶν παίδων ἐπυνθάνετο τί ἂν εἴη ταῦτα. 27 ὁ δὲ εἶπεν αὐτῷ ὅτι Ὁ ἀδελφός σου ἥκει, καὶ ἔθυσεν ὁ πατήρ σου τὸν μόσχον τὸν σιτευτόν, ὅτι ὑγιαίνοντα αὐτὸν ἀπέλαβεν. 28 ὠργίσθη δὲ καὶ οὐκ ἤθελεν εἰσελθεῖν. ὁ δὲ πατὴρ αὐτοῦ ἐξελθὼν παρεκάλει αὐτόν. 29 ὁ δὲ ἀποκριθεὶς εἶπεν τῷ πατρὶ αὐτοῦ, Ἰδοὺ τοσαῦτα ἔτη δουλεύω σοι καὶ οὐδέποτε ἐντολήν σου παρῆλθον, καὶ ἐμοὶ οὐδέποτε ἔδωκας ἔριφον ἵνα μετὰ τῶν φίλων μου εὐφρανθῶ· 30 ὅτε δὲ ὁ υἱός σου οὗτος ὁ καταφαγών σου τὸν βίον μετὰ πορνῶν ἦλθεν, ἔθυσας αὐτῷ τὸν σιτευτὸν μόσχον. 31 ὁ δὲ εἶπεν αὐτῷ, Τέκνον, σὺ πάντοτε μετ' ἐμοῦ εἶ, καὶ πάντα τὰ ἐμὰ σά ἐστιν· 32 εὐφρανθῆναι δὲ καὶ χαρῆναι ἔδει, ὅτι ὁ ἀδελφός σου οὗτος νεκρὸς ἦν καὶ ἔζησεν, καὶ ἀπολωλὼς καὶ εὑρέθη.

The Parable of the Dishonest Steward

16 Ἔλεγεν δὲ καὶ πρὸς τοὺς μαθητάς, Ἄνθρωπός τις ἦν πλούσιος ὃς εἶχεν οἰκονόμον, καὶ οὗτος διεβλήθη αὐτῷ ὡς διασκορπίζων τὰ ὑπάρχοντα αὐτοῦ. 2 καὶ φωνήσας αὐτὸν εἶπεν αὐτῷ, Τί τοῦτο ἀκούω περὶ σοῦ; ἀπόδος τὸν λόγον τῆς οἰκονομίας σου, οὐ γὰρ δύνῃ ἔτι οἰκονομεῖν. 3 εἶπεν δὲ ἐν ἑαυτῷ ὁ οἰκονόμος, Τί ποιήσω,ᵃ ὅτι ὁ κύριός μου ἀφαιρεῖται τὴν οἰκονομίαν ἀπ' ἐμοῦ;ᵃ

ᵃ ᵃ 3 *a minor, a question:* TR (WH) Bov Nes BF² RV ASV RSV (NEB) TT Zür Jer Seg ‖ *a question, a major:* AV Luth

24 νεκρὸς...ἀνέζησεν Eph 2.1, 5; 5.14   **31** πάντα τὰ ἐμὰ σά ἐστιν Jn 17.10

σκάπτειν οὐκ ἰσχύω, ἐπαιτεῖν αἰσχύνομαι. 4 ἔγνων τί ποιήσω, ἵνα ὅταν μετασταθῶ ἐκ τῆς οἰκονομίας δέξωνταί με εἰς τοὺς οἴκους ἑαυτῶν. 5 καὶ προσκαλεσάμενος ἕνα ἕκαστον τῶν χρεοφειλετῶν τοῦ κυρίου ἑαυτοῦ ἔλεγεν τῷ πρώτῳ, Πόσον ὀφείλεις τῷ κυρίῳ μου; 6 ὁ δὲ εἶπεν, Ἑκατὸν βάτους ἐλαίου. ὁ δὲ εἶπεν αὐτῷ, Δέξαι σου τὰ γράμματα καὶ καθίσας ταχέως γράψον πεντήκοντα. 7 ἔπειτα ἑτέρῳ εἶπεν, Σὺ δὲ πόσον ὀφείλεις; ὁ δὲ εἶπεν, Ἑκατὸν κόρους σίτου. λέγει αὐτῷ, Δέξαι σου τὰ γράμματα καὶ γράψον ὀγδοήκοντα. 8 καὶ ἐπῄνεσεν ὁ κύριος τὸν οἰκονόμον τῆς ἀδικίας ὅτι[b] φρονίμως ἐποίησεν· ὅτι οἱ υἱοὶ τοῦ αἰῶνος τούτου φρονιμώτεροι ὑπὲρ τοὺς υἱοὺς τοῦ φωτὸς εἰς τὴν γενεὰν τὴν ἑαυτῶν εἰσιν. 9 Καὶ ἐγὼ ὑμῖν λέγω, ἑαυτοῖς ποιήσατε φίλους ἐκ τοῦ μαμωνᾶ τῆς ἀδικίας, ἵνα ὅταν ἐκλίπῃ δέξωνται ὑμᾶς εἰς τὰς αἰωνίους σκηνάς. 10 ὁ πιστὸς ἐν ἐλαχίστῳ καὶ ἐν πολλῷ πιστός ἐστιν, καὶ ὁ ἐν ἐλαχίστῳ ἄδικος καὶ ἐν πολλῷ ἄδικός ἐστιν. 11 εἰ οὖν ἐν τῷ ἀδίκῳ μαμωνᾷ πιστοὶ οὐκ ἐγένεσθε, τὸ ἀληθινὸν τίς ὑμῖν πιστεύσει; 12 καὶ εἰ ἐν τῷ ἀλλοτρίῳ πιστοὶ οὐκ ἐγένεσθε, τὸ ὑμέτερον[1] τίς δώσει ὑμῖν; 13 Οὐδεὶς οἰκέτης δύναται δυσὶ κυρίοις δουλεύειν· ἢ γὰρ τὸν ἕνα μισήσει καὶ τὸν ἕτερον ἀγαπήσει, ἢ ἑνὸς ἀνθέξεται καὶ τοῦ ἑτέρου καταφρονήσει. οὐ δύνασθε θεῷ δουλεύειν καὶ μαμωνᾷ.

---

[1] **12** {B} ὑμέτερον 𝔓⁷⁵ ℵ A D K P W X Δ Θ Π Ψ f¹ f¹³ 28 565 700 892 1009 1010 1071 1079 1195 1230 1241 1242 1344 1365 1546 1646 2148 2174 *Byz Lect* it^(a, aur, c, d, f, ff², q, r¹) vg syr^(s, p, h, pal) cop^(sa, bo) goth arm geo Origen^lat Cyprian Basil Cyril ∥ ἡμέτερον B L 1253^vid l²¹ Origen ∥ ἐμόν 157 it^(e, i, l) Marcion Tertullian ∥ ἀληθινόν 33^vid 1216

---

[b] **8** *b* Indirect: WH? Bov? Nes? BF²? Zür Luth Seg ∥ *b* causal: TR? AV RV ASV RSV NEB TT Jer

---

8 υἱοὺς τοῦ φωτός Eph 5.8; 1 Th 5.5   **9** En 63.10   **10-12** Mt 25.20-30; Lk 19.17-26 **13** Mt 6.24

'What shall I do? I am not strong enough to dig ditches, and I am ashamed to beg. 4 Now I know what I will do! Then when my job is gone I shall have friends who will welcome me in their homes.' 5 So he called in all the people who were in debt to his master. To the first one he said, 'How much do you owe my master?' 6 'One hundred barrels of olive oil,' he answered. 'Here is your account,' the manager told him; 'sit down and write fifty.' 7 To another one he said, 'And you — how much do you owe?' 'A thousand bushels of wheat,' he answered. 'Here is your account,' the manager told him; 'write eight hundred.' 8 The master of this dishonest manager praised him for doing such a shrewd thing; for the people of this world are much more shrewd in handling their affairs than the people who belong to the light.''

9 And Jesus went on to say: "And so I tell you: make friends for yourselves with worldly wealth, so that when it gives out you will be welcomed in the eternal home. 10 Whoever is faithful in small matters will be faithful in large ones; whoever is dishonest in small matters will be dishonest in large ones. 11 If, then, you have not been faithful in handling worldly wealth, how can you be trusted with true wealth? 12 And if you have not been faithful in what belongs to someone else, who will give you what belongs to you?

13 "No servant can be the slave of two masters: he will hate one and love the other; he will be loyal to one and despise the other. You cannot serve both God and money."

Some Sayings of Jesus
(Also Matt. 11.12–13; 5.31–32; Mark 10.11–12)

[14] The Pharisees heard all this, and they made fun of Jesus, because they loved money. [15] Jesus said to them: "You are the ones who make yourselves look right in men's sight, but God knows your hearts. For what men think is of great value is worth nothing in God's sight.

[16] "The Law of Moses and the writings of the prophets were in effect up to the time of John the Baptist; since then the Good News about the Kingdom of God is· being told, and everyone forces his way in. [17] But it is easier for heaven and earth to disappear than for the smallest detail of the Law to be done away with.

[18] "Any man who divorces his wife and marries another woman commits adultery; and the man who marries a divorced woman commits adultery."

The Rich Man and Lazarus

[19] "There was once a rich man who dressed in the most expensive clothes and lived in great luxury every day. [20] There was also a poor man, named Lazarus, full of sores, who used to be brought to the rich man's door, [21] hoping to fill himself with the bits of food that fell from the rich man's table. Even the dogs would

The Law and the Kingdom of God
(Mt 11.12–13)

14 Ἤκουον δὲ ταῦτα πάντα[2] οἱ Φαρισαῖοι φιλάργυροι ὑπάρχοντες, καὶ ἐξεμυκτήριζον αὐτόν. **15** καὶ εἶπεν αὐτοῖς, Ὑμεῖς ἐστε οἱ δικαιοῦντες ἑαυτοὺς ἐνώπιον τῶν ἀνθρώπων, ὁ δὲ θεὸς γινώσκει τὰς καρδίας ὑμῶν· ὅτι τὸ ἐν ἀνθρώποις ὑψηλὸν βδέλυγμα ἐνώπιον τοῦ θεοῦ. **16** Ὁ νόμος καὶ οἱ προφῆται μέχρι Ἰωάννου· ἀπὸ τότε ἡ βασιλεία τοῦ θεοῦ εὐαγγελίζεται καὶ πᾶς εἰς αὐτὴν βιάζεται. **17** Εὐκοπώτερον δέ ἐστιν τὸν οὐρανὸν καὶ τὴν γῆν παρελθεῖν ἢ τοῦ νόμου μίαν κεραίαν πεσεῖν. **18** Πᾶς ὁ ἀπολύων τὴν γυναῖκα αὐτοῦ καὶ γαμῶν ἑτέραν μοιχεύει, καὶ ὁ ἀπολελυμένην ἀπὸ ἀνδρὸς γαμῶν μοιχεύει.

The Rich Man and Lazarus

19 Ἄνθρωπος δέ τις ἦν πλούσιος, καὶ ἐνεδιδύσκετο πορφύραν καὶ βύσσον εὐφραινόμενος καθ' ἡμέραν λαμπρῶς. **20** πτωχὸς δέ τις ὀνόματι Λάζαρος ἐβέβλητο πρὸς τὸν πυλῶνα αὐτοῦ εἱλκωμένος **21** καὶ ἐπιθυμῶν χορτασθῆναι ἀπὸ τῶν πιπτόντων[3] ἀπὸ τῆς τραπέζης τοῦ πλουσίου· ἀλλὰ καὶ οἱ κύνες ἐρχόμενοι ἐπέλειχον τὰ ἕλκη

---

[2] **14** {C} ταῦτα πάντα 𝔭⁷⁵ ℵ B L Ψ 1241 1242* it(a),b,c,e,f,ff2,l,rl syrs,p copsa,bo arm geo Origen Cyprian Jerome ‖ πάντα ταῦτα itaur,q vg ‖ ταῦτα πάντα καί A P W X Δ Θ f1 f13 28 565 700 892 1009 1010 1071 1216 1230 1242c 1253 1344 1365 1546 2174 Byz Lect goth ‖ πάντα ταῦτα καί K Π 1079 1195 1646 syrh ‖ πάντα καί 2148 ‖ ταῦτα D l150 itd,i Origen ‖ omit syrpal

[3] **21** {B} τῶν πιπτόντων 𝔭⁷⁵ ℵ* B L itb,c,e,ff2,i,l,q,rl syrs,pal copsa,bo Clement Adamantius Ambrose Gaudentius ‖ τῶν ψιχίων τῶν πιπτόντων (see Mt 15.27) ℵc A (D ψιχῶν) K P W X Δ Θ Π Ψ 063 f13 28 33 565 700 892 1009 1010 1071 1079 1195 1216 1230 1241 1242 1253 1344 1365 1546 1646 2148 2174 Byz Lect ita,aur,d,f vg syrp,h copsams,bomss goth arm geo Diatessarona,i,n Clement Ephraem Chrysostom ‖ τῶν πιπτόντων ψιχίων f1

15 οἱ...ἀνθρώπων Mt 23.28; Lk 18.9-14   θεὸς...ὑμῶν Pr 24.12 LXX   **16** Mt 11.12-13 **17** Mt 5.18   **18** Mt 5.32; 19.9; Mk 10.11-12; 1 Cor 7.10-11   **21** ἐπιθυμῶν...τραπέζης Mt 15.27; Mk 7.28: Lk 15 16

αὐτοῦ. 22 ἐγένετο δὲ ἀποθανεῖν τὸν πτωχὸν καὶ ἀπενεχθῆναι αὐτὸν ὑπὸ τῶν ἀγγέλων εἰς τὸν κόλπον Ἀβραάμ· ἀπέθανεν δὲ καὶ ὁ πλούσιος καὶ ἐτάφη. 23 καὶ ἐν τῷ ᾅδῃ ἐπάρας τοὺς ὀφθαλμοὺς αὐτοῦ, ὑπάρχων ἐν βασάνοις, ὁρᾷ Ἀβραὰμ ἀπὸ μακρόθεν καὶ Λάζαρον ἐν τοῖς κόλποις αὐτοῦ. 24 καὶ αὐτὸς φωνήσας εἶπεν, Πάτερ Ἀβραάμ, ἐλέησόν με καὶ πέμψον Λάζαρον ἵνα βάψῃ τὸ ἄκρον τοῦ δακτύλου αὐτοῦ ὕδατος καὶ καταψύξῃ τὴν γλῶσσάν μου, ὅτι ὀδυνῶμαι ἐν τῇ φλογὶ ταύτῃ. 25 εἶπεν δὲ Ἀβραάμ, Τέκνον, μνήσθητι ὅτι ἀπέλαβες τὰ ἀγαθά σου ἐν τῇ ζωῇ σου, καὶ Λάζαρος ὁμοίως τὰ κακά· νῦν δὲ ὧδε παρακαλεῖται σὺ δὲ ὀδυνᾶσαι. 26 καὶ ἐν πᾶσι τούτοις μεταξὺ ἡμῶν καὶ ὑμῶν χάσμα μέγα ἐστήρικται, ὅπως οἱ θέλοντες διαβῆναι ἔνθεν πρὸς ὑμᾶς μὴ δύνωνται, μηδὲ ἐκεῖθεν πρὸς ἡμᾶς διαπερῶσιν. 27 εἶπεν δέ, Ἐρωτῶ σε οὖν, πάτερ, ἵνα πέμψῃς αὐτὸν εἰς τὸν οἶκον τοῦ πατρός μου, 28 ἔχω γὰρ πέντε ἀδελφούς, ὅπως διαμαρτύρηται αὐτοῖς, ἵνα μὴ καὶ αὐτοὶ ἔλθωσιν εἰς τὸν τόπον τοῦτον τῆς βασάνου. 29 λέγει δὲ Ἀβραάμ, Ἔχουσι Μωϋσέα καὶ τοὺς προφήτας· ἀκουσάτωσαν αὐτῶν. 30 ὁ δὲ εἶπεν, Οὐχί, πάτερ Ἀβραάμ, ἀλλ' ἐάν τις ἀπὸ νεκρῶν πορευθῇ πρὸς αὐτοὺς μετανοήσουσιν. 31 εἶπεν δὲ αὐτῷ, Εἰ Μωϋσέως καὶ τῶν προφητῶν οὐκ ἀκούουσιν, οὐδ' ἐάν τις ἐκ νεκρῶν ἀναστῇ πεισθήσονται.

Some Sayings of Jesus
(Mt 18 6–7, 21–22; Mk 9 42)

17 Εἶπεν δὲ πρὸς τοὺς μαθητὰς αὐτοῦ, Ἀνένδεκτόν ἐστιν τοῦ τὰ σκάνδαλα μὴ ἐλθεῖν, πλὴν οὐαὶ δι' οὗ ἔρχεται· 2 λυσιτελεῖ αὐτῷ εἰ λίθος μυλικὸς περίκειται περὶ τὸν τράχηλον αὐτοῦ καὶ ἔρριπται εἰς τὴν θάλασσαν ἢ ἵνα σκανδαλίσῃ τῶν μικρῶν τούτων ἕνα. 3 προσέχετε ἑαυτοῖς. ἐὰν ἁμάρτῃ ὁ ἀδελφός σου ἐπιτίμησον αὐτῷ,

---

31 Εἰ...πεισθήσονται Jn 11.44–48
17 3 Mt 18.15

come and lick his sores. 22 The poor man died and was carried by the angels to Abraham's side, at the feast in heaven; the rich man died and was buried. 23 He was in great pain in Hades; and he looked up and saw Abraham, far away, with Lazarus at his side. 24 So he called out, 'Father Abraham! Take pity on me, and send Lazarus to dip his finger in some water and cool off my tongue, for I am in great pain in this fire!' 25 But Abraham said: 'Remember, my son, that in your lifetime you were given all the good things, while Lazarus got all the bad things; but now he is enjoying it here, while you are in pain. 26 Besides all that, there is a deep pit lying between us, so that those who want to cross over from here to you cannot do it, nor can anyone cross over to us from where you are.' 27 The rich man said, 'Well, father, I beg you, send Lazarus to my father's house, 28 where I have five brothers; let him go and warn them so that they, at least, will not come to this place of pain.' 29 Abraham said, 'Your brothers have Moses and the prophets to warn them; let your brothers listen to what they say.' 30 The rich man answered, 'That is not enough, father Abraham! But if someone were to rise from death and go to them, then they would turn from their sins.' 31 But Abraham said, 'If they will not listen to Moses and the prophets, they will not be convinced even if someone were to rise from death.' ''

Sin
(Also Matt. 18.6–7, 21–22; Mark 9.42)

17 Jesus said to his disciples: "Things that make people fall into sin are bound to happen; but how terrible for the one who makes them happen! 2 It would be better for him if a large millstone were tied around his neck and he were thrown into the sea, than for him to cause one of these little ones to sin. 3 Be on your guard!

"If your brother sins, rebuke him, and if he repents, forgive him. [4] If he sins against you seven times in one day, and each time he comes to you saying, 'I repent,' you must forgive him."

Faith

[5] The apostles said to the Lord, "Make our faith greater." [6] The Lord answered: "If you had faith as big as a mustard seed, you could say to this mulberry tree, 'Pull yourself up by the roots and plant yourself in the sea!' and it would obey you."

A Servant's Duty

[7] "Suppose one of you has a servant who is plowing or looking after the sheep. When he comes in from the field, do you say to him, 'Hurry along and eat your meal'? [8] Of course not! Instead, you say to him, 'Get my supper ready, then put on your apron and wait on me while I eat and drink; after that you may eat and drink.' [9] The servant does not deserve thanks for obeying orders, does he? [10] It is the same with you; when you have done all you have been told to do, say, 'We are ordinary servants; we have only done our duty.' "

Jesus Makes Ten Lepers Clean

[11] As Jesus made his way to Jerusalem he went between Samaria and Galilee. [12] He was going into a certain village when he was met by ten lepers. They stood at a distance [13] and shouted, "Jesus! Master! Have pity on us!" [14] Jesus saw them and said to them, "Go and let the priests examine you."

καὶ ἐὰν μετανοήσῃ ἄφες αὐτῷ· 4 καὶ ἐὰν ἑπτάκις τῆς ἡμέρας ἁμαρτήσῃ εἰς σὲ καὶ ἑπτάκις ἐπιστρέψῃ πρὸς σὲ λέγων, Μετανοῶ, ἀφήσεις αὐτῷ.

5 Καὶ εἶπαν οἱ ἀπόστολοι τῷ κυρίῳ, Πρόσθες ἡμῖν πίστιν. 6 εἶπεν δὲ ὁ κύριος, Εἰ ἔχετε πίστιν ὡς κόκκον σινάπεως, ἐλέγετε ἂν τῇ συκαμίνῳ [ταύτῃ], Ἐκριζώθητι καὶ φυτεύθητι ἐν τῇ θαλάσσῃ· καὶ ὑπήκουσεν ἂν ὑμῖν.

7 Τίς δὲ ἐξ ὑμῶν δοῦλον ἔχων ἀροτριῶντα ἢ ποιμαίνοντα, ὃς εἰσελθόντι ἐκ τοῦ ἀγροῦ ἐρεῖ αὐτῷ,[a] Εὐθέως[a] παρελθὼν ἀνάπεσε, 8 ἀλλ' οὐχὶ ἐρεῖ αὐτῷ, Ἑτοίμασον τί δειπνήσω, καὶ περιζωσάμενος διακόνει μοι ἕως φάγω καὶ πίω, καὶ μετὰ ταῦτα φάγεσαι καὶ πίεσαι σύ; 9 μὴ ἔχει χάριν τῷ δούλῳ ὅτι ἐποίησεν τὰ διαταχθέντα;[1] 10 οὕτως καὶ ὑμεῖς, ὅταν ποιήσητε πάντα τὰ διαταχθέντα ὑμῖν, λέγετε ὅτι Δοῦλοι ἀχρεῖοί ἐσμεν, ὃ ὠφείλομεν ποιῆσαι πεποιήκαμεν.

The Cleansing of Ten Lepers

11 Καὶ ἐγένετο ἐν τῷ πορεύεσθαι εἰς Ἰερουσαλὴμ καὶ αὐτὸς διήρχετο διὰ μέσον Σαμαρείας καὶ Γαλιλαίας. 12 καὶ εἰσερχομένου αὐτοῦ εἴς τινα κώμην ἀπήντησαν [αὐτῷ] δέκα λεπροὶ ἄνδρες, οἳ ἔστησαν πόρρωθεν, 13 καὶ αὐτοὶ ἦραν φωνὴν λέγοντες, Ἰησοῦ ἐπιστάτα, ἐλέησον ἡμᾶς. 14 καὶ ἰδὼν εἶπεν αὐτοῖς, Πορευθέντες ἐπιδείξατε

---

[1] 9 {C} διαταχθέντα; 𝔭75 ℵ B L f1 1010 1241 ite syrpal (arm πάντα διαταχθέντα) geo1 ‖ διαταχθέντα αὐτῷ; X ita syrc,s copsa,bo eth Cyprian ‖ διαταχθέντα; οὐ δοκῶ. A K W Δ Θ Π Ψ 063 28 565 700 892 1009 1071 1079 1195 1216 1230 1242 1253 1344 1365 1546 1646 2148 (2174 διατεταγμένα) Byz Lect itc,s syrh goth Antiochus ‖ διαταχθέντα αὐτῷ; οὐ δοκῶ. D f13 l547 itaur,b,d,f,ff2,i,l,q,r1 vg syrp geo2 Diatessarona

[a a] 7 a minor, a none: WH Bov Nes BF2 RV ASV RSV NEB TT Zür Luth Jer Seg ‖ a none, a minor: TR AV

5 Πρόσθες...πίστιν Mk 9.24   6 Mt 17.20; 21.21   11 ἐν...Ἰερουσαλήμ Lk 9.51; 13.22   διήρχετο...Σαμαρείας Lk 9.52; Jn 4.4   12 λεπροί...πόρρωθεν Lv 13.46   13 Ἰησοῦ...ἡμᾶς Mt 9.27; 15.22; Lk 18.38   14 Πορευθέντες...ἱερεῦσιν Lv 14.2–3; Lk 5.14

ἑαυτοὺς τοῖς ἱερεῦσιν. καὶ ἐγένετο ἐν τῷ ὑπάγειν αὐτοὺς ἐκαθαρίσθησαν. **15** εἷς δὲ ἐξ αὐτῶν, ἰδὼν ὅτι ἰάθη, ὑπέστρεψεν μετὰ φωνῆς μεγάλης δοξάζων τὸν θεόν, **16** καὶ ἔπεσεν ἐπὶ πρόσωπον παρὰ τοὺς πόδας αὐτοῦ εὐχαριστῶν αὐτῷ· καὶ αὐτὸς ἦν Σαμαρίτης. **17** ἀποκριθεὶς δὲ ὁ Ἰησοῦς εἶπεν, Οὐχὶ οἱ δέκα ἐκαθαρίσθησαν; οἱ δὲ ἐννέα ποῦ; **18** οὐχ εὑρέθησαν ὑποστρέψαντες δοῦναι δόξαν τῷ θεῷ εἰ μὴ ὁ ἀλλογενὴς οὗτος;[b] **19** καὶ εἶπεν αὐτῷ, Ἀναστὰς πορεύου· ἡ πίστις σου σέσωκέν σε.

The Coming of the Kingdom
(Mt 24.23–28, 37–41)

20 Ἐπερωτηθεὶς δὲ ὑπὸ τῶν Φαρισαίων πότε ἔρχεται ἡ βασιλεία τοῦ θεοῦ ἀπεκρίθη αὐτοῖς καὶ εἶπεν, Οὐκ ἔρχεται ἡ βασιλεία τοῦ θεοῦ μετὰ παρατηρήσεως, **21** οὐδὲ ἐροῦσιν, Ἰδοὺ ὧδε· ἤ, Ἐκεῖ· ἰδοὺ γὰρ ἡ βασιλεία τοῦ θεοῦ ἐντὸς ὑμῶν ἐστιν. **22** Εἶπεν δὲ πρὸς τοὺς μαθητάς, Ἐλεύσονται ἡμέραι ὅτε ἐπιθυμήσετε μίαν τῶν ἡμερῶν τοῦ υἱοῦ τοῦ ἀνθρώπου ἰδεῖν καὶ οὐκ ὄψεσθε. **23** καὶ ἐροῦσιν ὑμῖν, Ἰδοὺ ἐκεῖ· [ἤ,] Ἰδοὺ ὧδε·[2] μὴ ἀπέλθητε μηδὲ διώξητε[3]. **24** ὥσπερ γὰρ ἡ ἀστραπὴ ἀστράπτουσα

[2] **23** {D} ἰδοὺ ἐκεῖ ἤ, ἰδοὺ ὧδε· (see footnote 3) 𝔭[75] (𝕏 καί for ἤ) B (L omit ἤ) (syr[c,s] καί for ἤ) ‖ ἰδοὺ ὧδε ἤ ἰδοὺ ἐκεῖ· A Δ Θ Ψ 565 1009 1010 1071 1230 1241 1242 1253 1646 Byz l[150,299,883,950,1642] it[a,aur,c,d] syr[h] goth eth (Eusebius) ‖ ἰδοὺ ὧδε ἰδοὺ ἐκεῖ· D[gr] W* X 063 28 33 700 892 1195 1344 Lect it[e,q] vg[ww] ‖ ἰδοὺ ὧδε ἤ ἐκεῖ· f[13] 2148 it[l] (cop[sa,bo]) (arm ἐστιν for ὧδε) geo[1] ‖ ἰδοὺ ὧδε καὶ ἰδοὺ ἐκεῖ· it[b,f,ff2,i,l,r1,s] vg[cl] syr[p] geo[2] ‖ ἰδοὺ ὧδε ἰδοὺ ἐκεῖ ὁ Χριστός· K Π W[c] 1079 1216 1365 1546 (2174 ὧδε ἤ) syr[h with *] ‖ ἰδοὺ ὧδε μὴ διώξητε· ἤ ἰδοὺ ἐκεῖ ὁ Χριστός· f[1]

[3] **23** {C} μὴ ἀπέλθητε μηδὲ διώξητε (see footnote 2) 𝕏 A D K W X Θ Π Ψ 063 28 565 700 892 1009 1010 1079 1195 1230 1241 1253 1344 1365 1546 1646 2148 Byz Lect it[a,aur,b,c,d,e,f,ff2,i,l,q,r1,s] vg syr[c,s,h] cop[bo] goth eth

[b] **18** b question: TR WH Bov Nes BF² RV ASV RSV NEB TT Zür Luth Seg ‖ b statement: AV RV[mg] ASV[mg] ‖ b exclamation: Jer

19 Ἀναστὰς...σε Lk 7.50; 18.42   **20** Οὐκ...παρατηρήσεως Jn 3.3; 18.36   **21** Ἰδοὺ... Ἐκεῖ Mk 13.21; Lk 17.23   **23** Ἰδοὺ...ὧδε Mk 13.21; Lk 17.21 μὴ...διώξητε Lk 21.8

On the way they were made clean. **15** One of them, when he saw that he was healed, came back, praising God with a loud voice. **16** He threw himself to the ground at Jesus' feet, thanking him. The man was a Samaritan. **17** Jesus spoke up: "There were ten men made clean; where are the other nine? **18** Why is this foreigner the only one who came back to give thanks to God?" **19** And Jesus said to him, "Get up and go; your faith has made you well."

The Coming of the Kingdom
(Also Matt. 24.23–28, 37–41)

20 Some Pharisees asked Jesus when the Kingdom of God would come. His answer was: "The Kingdom of God does not come in such a way as to be seen. **21** No one will say, 'Look, here it is!' or, 'There it is!'; because the Kingdom of God is within[1] you."

22 Then he said to the disciples: "The time will come when you will wish you could see one of the days of the Son of Man, but you will not see it. **23** There will be those who will say to you, 'Look, over there!' or, 'Look, over here!' But don't go out looking for it. **24** As the lightning flashes across the sky and

[1] **21** within: or among

lights it up from one side to the other, so will the Son of Man be in his day. 25 But first he must suffer much and be rejected by the people of this day. 26 As it was in the time of Noah, so shall it be in the days of the Son of Man. 27 Everybody kept on eating and drinking, men and women married, up to the very day Noah went into the ark and the Flood came and killed them all. 28 It will be as it was in the time of Lot. Everybody kept on eating and drinking, buying and selling, planting and building. 29 On the day Lot left Sodom, fire and sulphur rained down from heaven and killed them all. 30 That is how it will be on the day the Son of Man is revealed.

31 "The man who is on the roof of his house on that day must not go down into his house to get his belongings that are there; in the same way, the man who is out in the field must not go back to the house. 32 Remember Lot's wife! 33 Whoever tries to save his own life will lose

ἐκ τῆς ὑπὸ τὸν οὐρανὸν εἰς τὴν ὑπ' οὐρανὸν λάμπει, οὕτως ἔσται ὁ υἱὸς τοῦ ἀνθρώπου [ἐν τῇ ἡμέρᾳ αὐτοῦ]⁴. 25 πρῶτον δὲ δεῖ αὐτὸν πολλὰ παθεῖν καὶ ἀποδοκιμασθῆναι ἀπὸ τῆς γενεᾶς ταύτης. 26 καὶ καθὼς ἐγένετο ἐν ταῖς ἡμέραις Νῶε, οὕτως ἔσται καὶ ἐν ταῖς ἡμέραις τοῦ υἱοῦ τοῦ ἀνθρώπου· 27 ἤσθιον, ἔπινον, ἐγάμουν, ἐγαμίζοντο, ἄχρι ἧς ἡμέρας εἰσῆλθεν Νῶε εἰς τὴν κιβωτόν, καὶ ἦλθεν ὁ κατακλυσμὸς καὶ ἀπώλεσεν πάντας. 28 ὁμοίως καθὼς ἐγένετο ἐν ταῖς ἡμέραις Λώτ·ᶜ ἤσθιον, ἔπινον, ἠγόραζον, ἐπώλουν, ἐφύτευον, ᾠκοδόμουν· 29 ᾗ δὲ ἡμέρᾳ ἐξῆλθεν Λὼτ ἀπὸ Σοδόμων, ἔβρεξεν πῦρ καὶ θεῖον ἀπ' οὐρανοῦ καὶ ἀπώλεσεν πάντας.ᶜ 30 κατὰ τὰ αὐτὰ ἔσται ᾗ ἡμέρᾳ ὁ υἱὸς τοῦ ἀνθρώπου ἀποκαλύπτεται. 31 ἐν ἐκείνῃ τῇ ἡμέρᾳ ὃς ἔσται ἐπὶ τοῦ δώματος καὶ τὰ σκεύη αὐτοῦ ἐν τῇ οἰκίᾳ, μὴ καταβάτω ἆραι αὐτά, καὶ ὁ ἐν ἀγρῷ ὁμοίως μὴ ἐπιστρεψάτω εἰς τὰ ὀπίσω. 32 μνημονεύετε τῆς γυναικὸς Λώτ. 33 ὃς ἐὰν ζητήσῃ τὴν ψυχὴν αὐτοῦ περιποιήσασθαι⁵ ἀπολέσει αὐτήν, ὃς δ' ἂν

geo² (Eusebius) ‖ μὴ ἀπέλθητε μηδὲ διώξετε L Δ 1071 1216 1242 2174 *l*²²⁶ ‖ μὴ διώξητε B cop^sa geo¹ ‖ μὴ διώξετε 𝔭⁷⁵ *f*¹³ arm ‖ μὴ ἀπέλθητε syr^p ‖ μὴ πιστεύσητε *f*¹

⁴ 24 {C} ὁ υἱὸς τοῦ ἀνθρώπου ἐν τῇ ἡμέρᾳ αὐτοῦ ℵ A K L W X Δ Θ Π Ψ 063 *f*¹ *f*¹³ 28 565 700 892 1009 1010 1071 1079 1195 1216 1230 1241 1242 1253 1344 1365 1546 1646 2148 2174 *Byz Lect* (*l*¹¹²⁷ καὶ ὁ υἱός) it^aur,q,r¹ vg syr^(c,s),p,h cop^bo goth arm geo ‖ ὁ υἱὸς τοῦ ἀνθρώπου 𝔭⁷⁵ B D it^a,b,d,e,i cop^sa ‖ ἡ παρουσία τοῦ υἱοῦ τοῦ ἀνθρώπου (*see* Mt 24.27) it^c,(l),s cop^boms Ambrose ‖ ἡ παρουσία τοῦ υἱοῦ τοῦ ἀνθρώπου ἐν τῇ ἡμέρᾳ αὐτοῦ it^f Vigilius

⁵ 33 {C} ἐὰν ζητήσῃ τὴν ψυχὴν αὐτοῦ περιποιήσασθαι 𝔭⁷⁵ B L (it^b,c,i,q...*liberare*) ‖ ἐὰν ζητήσῃ τὴν ψυχὴν αὐτοῦ σῶσαι ℵ A K W X Δ Θ Π Ψ 063 *f*¹ *f*¹³ 28 565 700 892 1009 1010 1071 1079 1195 1216 1230 1241 (1242* *omit* σῶσαι) 1242ᶜ 1253 1344 1365 1546 1646 2148 2174 *Byz Lect*

ᶜᶜ 28–29 *c* major, *c* major: TR WH Bov Nes BF² AV RV ASV TT Zür Luth Jer Seg ‖ *c* dash, *c* dash: RSV ‖ *c* major, *c* dash: NEB

25 Mt 16.21; 17.22–23; 20.18–19; Mk 8.31; 9.31; 10.33–34; Lk 9.22; 18.32–33   26 ἐν ταῖς ἡμέραις Νῶε Gn 6.5–12   27 εἰσῆλθεν...πάντας Gn 7.6–23   28 ἐν...Λώτ Gn 18.20–21; 19.1–14   29 Gn 19.15–29   31 Mt 24.17–18; Mk 13.15–16   31–32 μὴ ἐπιστρεψάτω...Λώτ Gn 19.17, 26   33 Mt 10.39; 16.25; Mk 8.35; Lk 9.24; Jn 12.25

ἀπολέσῃ ζωογονήσει αὐτήν. 34 λέγω ὑμῖν, ταύτῃ τῇ νυκτὶ ἔσονται δύο ἐπὶ κλίνης μιᾶς, ὁ εἷς παραλημφθήσεται καὶ ὁ ἕτερος ἀφεθήσεται· 35 ἔσονται δύο ἀλήθουσαι ἐπὶ τὸ αὐτό, ἡ μία παραλημφθήσεται ἡ δὲ ἑτέρα ἀφεθήσεται.[6] 37 καὶ ἀποκριθέντες λέγουσιν αὐτῷ, Ποῦ, κύριε; ὁ δὲ εἶπεν αὐτοῖς, Ὅπου τὸ σῶμα, ἐκεῖ καὶ οἱ ἀετοὶ ἐπισυναχθήσονται.

The Parable of the Widow and the Judge

18 Ἔλεγεν δὲ παραβολὴν αὐτοῖς πρὸς τὸ δεῖν πάντοτε προσεύχεσθαι αὐτοὺς καὶ μὴ ἐγκακεῖν, 2 λέγων, Κριτής τις ἦν ἔν τινι πόλει τὸν θεὸν μὴ φοβούμενος καὶ ἄνθρωπον μὴ ἐντρεπόμενος. 3 χήρα δὲ ἦν ἐν τῇ πόλει ἐκείνῃ καὶ ἤρχετο πρὸς αὐτὸν λέγουσα, Ἐκδίκησόν με ἀπὸ τοῦ ἀντιδίκου μου. 4 καὶ οὐκ ἤθελεν ἐπὶ χρόνον, μετὰ δὲ ταῦτα εἶπεν ἐν ἑαυτῷ, Εἰ καὶ τὸν θεὸν οὐ φοβοῦμαι οὐδὲ ἄνθρωπον ἐντρέπομαι, 5 διά γε τὸ παρέχειν μοι κόπον τὴν χήραν ταύτην ἐκδικήσω αὐτήν, ἵνα μὴ εἰς τέλος ἐρχομένη ὑπωπιάζῃ με. 6 Εἶπεν δὲ ὁ κύριος, Ἀκούσατε τί ὁ κριτὴς τῆς ἀδικίας λέγει· 7 ὁ δὲ θεὸς οὐ μὴ ποιήσῃ τὴν ἐκδίκησιν τῶν ἐκλεκτῶν αὐτοῦ τῶν βοώντων αὐτῷ ἡμέρας καὶ νυκτός, καὶ μακροθυμεῖ ἐπ' αὐτοῖς; 8 λέγω

it; whoever loses his life will save it. 34 On that night, I tell you, there will be two men sleeping in one bed: one will be taken away, the other left behind. 35 Two women will be grinding meal together: one will be taken away, the other left behind. [36 Two men will be in the field: one will be taken away, the other left behind.]" 37 The disciples asked him, "Where, Lord?" Jesus answered, "Where there is a dead body the vultures will gather."

The Parable of the Widow and the Judge

18 Then Jesus told them this parable, to teach them that they should always pray and never become discouraged. 2 "There was a judge in a certain town who neither feared God nor respected men. 3 And there was a widow in that same town who kept coming to him and pleading for her rights: 'Help me against my opponent!' 4 For a long time the judge was not willing, but at last he said to himself, 'Even though I don't fear God or respect men, 5 yet because of all the trouble this widow is giving me I will see to it that she gets her rights; or else she will keep on coming and finally wear me out!'" 6 And the Lord continued: "Listen to what that corrupt judge said. 7 Now, will God not judge in favor of his own people who cry to him for help day and night? Will he be slow to help them? 8 I tell you, he will judge

---

it[a,aur,e,f,ff2,l,rl] vg syr[h] cop[bo] goth arm ‖ ἐὰν θελήσῃ τὴν ψυχὴν αὐτοῦ σῶσαι (see 9.24) geo Diatessaron ‖ ἂν θελήσῃ ζωογονῆσαι τὴν ψυχὴν αὐτοῦ D it[d] syr[c,s,p] cop[sa] eth

[6] **35** {B} omit verse 36 𝔭[75] ℵ A B K L W X Δ Θ Π Ψ 063 f[1] 28 33 565 892 1009 1010 1079 1195 1216 1242 1365 Byz l[184,950] cop[sa,bo] goth eth Basil Maximus Ps-Chrysostom ‖ include verse 36 δύο ἐν ἀγρῷ εἷς παραλημφθήσεται καὶ ὁ ἕτερος ἀφεθήσεται. (see Mt 24.40) D 700 1071 1230 1241 2174 (1253 1344 δύο ἔσονται ἐν τῷ ἀγρῷ) (1646 δύο ἔσονται) (2148 δύο ἔσονται ἐν τῷ ἀγρῷ...προσαφηθήσεται) (Lect ἐν τῷ ἀγρῷ) l[185,1579] it[a,aur,b,c,d,(e),f,ff2,i,l,'q,(rl)] vg syr[c,s,p,h] arm geo Diatessaron[a,i,n] Ambrose Augustine ‖ δύο ἔσονται ἐν τῷ ἀγρῷ· εἷς παραλημφθήσεται ἡ δὲ ἑτέρα ἀφεθήσεται. (see Mt 24.40) f[13]

37 Ὅπου...ἐπισυναχθήσονται Job 39.30
18 1 τὸ...προσεύχεσθαι αὐτούς Ro 12.12; Col 4.2; 1 Th 5.17   5 Lk 11.7-8

in their favor, and do it quickly. But will the Son of Man find faith on earth when he comes?''

The Parable of the Pharisee and the Tax Collector

9 Jesus also told this parable to people who were sure of their own goodness and despised everybody else. 10 "Two men went up to the Temple to pray; one was a Pharisee, the other a tax collector. 11 The Pharisee stood apart by himself and prayed:[1] 'I thank you, God, that I am not greedy, dishonest, or immoral, like everybody else; I thank you that I am not like that tax collector. 12 I fast two days every week, and I give you one tenth of all my income.' 13 But the tax collector stood at a distance and would not even raise his face to heaven, but beat on his breast and said, 'O God, have pity on me, a sinner!' 14 I tell you," said Jesus, "this man, and not the other, was in the right with God when he went home. For everyone who makes himself great will be humbled, and everyone who humbles himself will be made great.''

Jesus Blesses Little Children
(Also Matt. 19.13–15; Mark 10.13–16)

15 Some people brought their babies to Jesus to have him place his hands on them. But the disciples saw them and scolded them for doing so. 16 But Jesus called the children to him, and said: "Let the children come to me! Do not stop them, because the Kingdom of God belongs to such as these. 17 Remember

---

[1] 11 stood apart by himself and prayed: *some mss. read* stood up and said this prayer to himself

ὑμῖν ὅτι ποιήσει τὴν ἐκδίκησιν αὐτῶν ἐν τάχει. πλὴν ὁ υἱὸς τοῦ ἀνθρώπου ἐλθὼν ἆρα εὑρήσει τὴν πίστιν ἐπὶ τῆς γῆς;

The Parable of the Pharisee and the Tax Collector

9 Εἶπεν δὲ καὶ πρός τινας τοὺς πεποιθότας ἐφ' ἑαυτοῖς ὅτι εἰσὶν δίκαιοι καὶ ἐξουθενοῦντας τοὺς λοιποὺς τὴν παραβολὴν ταύτην· 10 Ἄνθρωποι δύο ἀνέβησαν εἰς τὸ ἱερὸν προσεύξασθαι, ὁ εἷς Φαρισαῖος καὶ ὁ ἕτερος τελώνης. 11 ὁ Φαρισαῖος σταθεὶς πρὸς ἑαυτὸν ταῦτα[1] προσηύχετο, Ὁ θεός, εὐχαριστῶ σοι ὅτι οὐκ εἰμὶ ὥσπερ οἱ λοιποὶ τῶν ἀνθρώπων, ἅρπαγες, ἄδικοι, μοιχοί, ἢ καὶ ὡς οὗτος ὁ τελώνης· 12 νηστεύω δὶς τοῦ σαββάτου, ἀποδεκατῶ πάντα ὅσα κτῶμαι. 13 ὁ δὲ τελώνης μακρόθεν ἑστὼς οὐκ ἤθελεν οὐδὲ τοὺς ὀφθαλμοὺς ἐπᾶραι εἰς τὸν οὐρανόν, ἀλλ' ἔτυπτεν τὸ στῆθος αὐτοῦ λέγων, Ὁ θεός, ἱλάσθητί μοι τῷ ἁμαρτωλῷ. 14 λέγω ὑμῖν, κατέβη οὗτος δεδικαιωμένος εἰς τὸν οἶκον αὐτοῦ παρ' ἐκεῖνον· ὅτι πᾶς ὁ ὑψῶν ἑαυτὸν ταπεινωθήσεται, ὁ δὲ ταπεινῶν ἑαυτὸν ὑψωθήσεται.

Little Children Blessed
(Mt 19.13–15; Mk 10.13–16)

15 Προσέφερον δὲ αὐτῷ καὶ τὰ βρέφη ἵνα αὐτῶν ἅπτηται· ἰδόντες δὲ οἱ μαθηταὶ ἐπετίμων αὐτοῖς. 16 ὁ δὲ Ἰησοῦς προσεκαλέσατο αὐτὰ λέγων, Ἄφετε τὰ παιδία ἔρχεσθαι πρός με καὶ μὴ κωλύετε αὐτά, τῶν γὰρ τοιούτων ἐστὶν ἡ βασιλεία τοῦ θεοῦ. 17 ἀμὴν λέγω ὑμῖν, ὃς ἂν

---

[1] 11 {D} πρὸς ἑαυτὸν ταῦτα A K W X Δ Π 063 *f*[13] 28 33[vid] 565 700 1009 1010 1079 1195 1216 1230 1242 1253 1344 1365 1546 1646 2148 2174 *Byz Lect* it[a] syr[c,s,p,h] goth Basil Antiochus ‖ ταῦτα πρὸς ἑαυτόν 𝔭[75] ℵ[c] B (L αὐτόν) T Θ Ψ *f*[1] 892 1241 it[aur,e] vg syr[pal] cop[bo] arm Origen Cyprian ‖ καθ' ἑαυτὸν ταῦτα D it[d] geo[2] ‖ ταῦτα ℵ* *l*[883] it[b,c,f,ff2,i,l,q,r1] cop[sa,ach] eth geo[1] Diatessaron[n,t] ‖ omit 1071

---

12 ἀποδεκατῶ...κτῶμαι Gn 14.20; Mt 23.23   13 ἔτυπτεν τὸ στῆθος Lk 23.48   Ὁ θεός ...ἁμαρτωλῷ Ps 51.1   14 πᾶς...ὑψωθήσεται Mt 23.12; Lk 14.11   17 Mt 18.3

μὴ δέξηται τὴν βασιλείαν τοῦ θεοῦ ὡς παιδίον, οὐ μὴ εἰσέλθῃ εἰς αὐτήν.

The Rich Ruler
(Mt 19.16–30; Mk 10.17–31)

18 Καὶ ἐπηρώτησέν τις αὐτὸν ἄρχων λέγων, Διδάσκαλε ἀγαθέ, τί ποιήσας ζωὴν αἰώνιον κληρονομήσω; **19** εἶπεν δὲ αὐτῷ ὁ Ἰησοῦς, Τί με λέγεις ἀγαθόν; οὐδεὶς ἀγαθὸς εἰ μὴ εἷς ὁ θεός. **20** τὰς ἐντολὰς οἶδας· **Μὴ μοιχεύσῃς, Μὴ φονεύσῃς, Μὴ κλέψῃς, Μὴ ψευδομαρτυρήσῃς, Τίμα τὸν πατέρα σου καὶ τὴν μητέρα.** **21** ὁ δὲ εἶπεν, Ταῦτα πάντα ἐφύλαξα ἐκ νεότητος. **22** ἀκούσας δὲ ὁ Ἰησοῦς εἶπεν αὐτῷ, Ἔτι ἕν σοι λείπει· πάντα ὅσα ἔχεις πώλησον καὶ διάδος πτωχοῖς, καὶ ἕξεις θησαυρὸν ἐν [τοῖς] οὐρανοῖς, καὶ δεῦρο ἀκολούθει μοι. **23** ὁ δὲ ἀκούσας ταῦτα περίλυπος ἐγενήθη, ἦν γὰρ πλούσιος σφόδρα.

24 Ἰδὼν δὲ αὐτὸν ὁ Ἰησοῦς [περίλυπον γενόμενον] εἶπεν[2], Πῶς δυσκόλως οἱ τὰ χρήματα ἔχοντες εἰς τὴν βασιλείαν τοῦ θεοῦ εἰσπορεύονται· **25** εὐκοπώτερον γάρ ἐστιν κάμηλον διὰ τρήματος βελόνης διελθεῖν ἢ πλούσιον εἰς τὴν βασιλείαν τοῦ θεοῦ εἰσελθεῖν. **26** εἶπαν δὲ οἱ ἀκούσαντες, Καὶ τίς δύναται σωθῆναι; **27** ὁ δὲ εἶπεν, Τὰ ἀδύνατα παρὰ ἀνθρώποις δυνατὰ παρὰ τῷ θεῷ ἐστιν. **28** Εἶπεν δὲ ὁ Πέτρος, Ἰδοὺ ἡμεῖς ἀφέντες τὰ ἴδια ἠκολουθήσαμέν σοι. **29** ὁ δὲ εἶπεν αὐτοῖς, Ἀμὴν λέγω ὑμῖν ὅτι οὐδείς ἐστιν ὃς ἀφῆκεν οἰκίαν ἢ γυναῖκα ἢ ἀδελφοὺς ἢ γονεῖς ἢ τέκνα ἕνεκεν τῆς βασιλείας τοῦ

---

[2] **24** {D} αὐτὸν ὁ Ἰησοῦς περίλυπον γενόμενον εἶπεν A K P W X Δ Θ Π Ψ 078 *f*[13] 28 33[vid] 565 700 892 1009 1010 1071 1079 1195 1216 1230 1242 1253 1344 1365 1546 1646 2148 2174 *Byz Lect* it[a,aur,(f),q] vg syr[h] goth arm eth Diatessaron[a] ‖ αὐτὸν ὁ Ἰησοῦς εἶπεν ℵ (B *omit* ὁ) L *f*[1] 1241 syr[pal] cop[sa,bo] geo ‖ αὐτὸν περίλυπον γενόμενον εἶπεν ὁ Ἰησοῦς D it[b,c,d,(e),ff2,i,l,r1] ‖ ὁ Ἰησοῦς αὐτὸν περίλυπον γενόμενον εἶπεν syr[c,s,p]

18 Διδάσκαλε...κληρονομήσω Lk 10.25 **20** Μὴ μοιχεύσῃς...ψευδομαρτυρήσῃς Ex 20.13–16 (Dt 5.17–20) Τίμα...μητέρα Ex 20.12 (Dt 5.16) **22** ἕξεις...οὐρανοῖς Mt 6.20; Sir 29.11 **27** Τὰ ἀδύνατα...ἐστιν Mk 14.36

---

this! Whoever does not receive the Kingdom of God like a child will never enter it."

The Rich Man
(Also Matt. 19.16–30; Mark 10.17–31)

[18] A certain Jewish leader asked him: "Good Teacher, what must I do to receive eternal life?" [19] "Why do you call me good?" Jesus asked him. "No one is good except God alone. [20] You know the commandments: 'Do not commit adultery; do not murder; do not steal; do not lie; honor your father and mother.'" [21] The man replied, "Ever since I was young I have obeyed all these commandments." [22] When Jesus heard this, he said to him: "You still need to do one thing. Sell all you have and give the money to the poor, and you will have riches in heaven; then come and follow me." [23] But when the man heard this he became very sad, because he was very rich.

[24] Jesus saw that he was sad and said: "How hard it is for rich people to enter the Kingdom of God! [25] It is much harder for a rich man to enter the Kingdom of God than for a camel to go through the eye of a needle." [26] The people who heard him asked, "Who, then, can be saved?" [27] Jesus answered, "What is impossible for men is possible for God."

[28] Then Peter said, "Look! We have left our homes to follow you." [29] "Yes," Jesus said to them, "and I tell you this: anyone who leaves home or wife or brothers or parents or children for the

sake of the Kingdom of God ³⁰ will receive much more in the present age, and eternal life in the age to come.''

Jesus Speaks a Third Time about His Death
(Also Matt. 20.17–19; Mark 10.32–34)

³¹ Jesus took the twelve disciples aside and said to them: ''Listen! We are going to Jerusalem where everything the prophets wrote about the Son of Man will come true. ³² He will be handed over to the Gentiles, who will make fun of him, insult him, and spit on him. ³³ They will whip him and kill him, but on the third day he will be raised to life.'' ³⁴ The disciples did not understand any of these things; the meaning of the words was hidden from them, and they did not know what Jesus was talking about.

Jesus Heals a Blind Beggar
(Also Matt. 20.29–34; Mark 10.46–52)

³⁵ Jesus was coming near Jericho, and a certain blind man was sitting and begging by the road. ³⁶ When he heard the crowd passing by he asked, ''What is this?'' ³⁷ ''Jesus of Nazareth is passing by,'' they told him. ³⁸ He cried out, ''Jesus! Son of David! Have mercy on me!'' ³⁹ The people in front scolded him and told him to be quiet. But he shouted even more loudly, ''Son of David! Have mercy on me!'' ⁴⁰ So Jesus stopped and ordered that the blind man be brought to him. When he came near, Jesus asked him, ⁴¹ ''What do you want me to do for you?'' ''Sir,'' he answered, ''I want to see again.'' ⁴² Then Jesus said to him, ''See! Your faith has made you well.'' ⁴³ At once he was able to see, and he followed Jesus, giving thanks to God. When the crowd saw it, they all praised God.

θεοῦ, **30** ὃς οὐχὶ μὴ ἀπολάβῃ πολλαπλασίονα ἐν τῷ καιρῷ τούτῳ καὶ ἐν τῷ αἰῶνι τῷ ἐρχομένῳ ζωὴν αἰώνιον.

A Third Time Jesus Foretells His Death and Resurrection
(Mt 20.17–19; Mk 10.32–34)

31 Παραλαβὼν δὲ τοὺς δώδεκα εἶπεν πρὸς αὐτούς, Ἰδοὺ ἀναβαίνομεν εἰς Ἰερουσαλήμ, καὶ τελεσθήσεται πάντα τὰ γεγραμμένα διὰ τῶν προφητῶν τῷ υἱῷ τοῦ ἀνθρώπου· **32** παραδοθήσεται γὰρ τοῖς ἔθνεσιν καὶ ἐμπαιχθήσεται καὶ ὑβρισθήσεται καὶ ἐμπτυσθήσεται, **33** καὶ μαστιγώσαντες ἀποκτενοῦσιν αὐτόν, καὶ τῇ ἡμέρᾳ τῇ τρίτῃ ἀναστήσεται. **34** καὶ αὐτοὶ οὐδὲν τούτων συνῆκαν, καὶ ἦν τὸ ῥῆμα τοῦτο κεκρυμμένον ἀπ᾽ αὐτῶν, καὶ οὐκ ἐγίνωσκον τὰ λεγόμενα.

The Healing of a Blind Beggar near Jericho
(Mt 20.29–34; Mk 10.46–52)

35 Ἐγένετο δὲ ἐν τῷ ἐγγίζειν αὐτὸν εἰς Ἰεριχὼ τυφλός τις ἐκάθητο παρὰ τὴν ὁδὸν ἐπαιτῶν. **36** ἀκούσας δὲ ὄχλου διαπορευομένου ἐπυνθάνετο τί εἴη τοῦτο· **37** ἀπήγγειλαν δὲ αὐτῷ ὅτι Ἰησοῦς ὁ Ναζωραῖος παρέρχεται. **38** καὶ ἐβόησεν λέγων, Ἰησοῦ, υἱὲ Δαυίδ, ἐλέησόν με. **39** καὶ οἱ προάγοντες ἐπετίμων αὐτῷ ἵνα σιγήσῃ· αὐτὸς δὲ πολλῷ μᾶλλον ἔκραζεν, Υἱὲ Δαυίδ, ἐλέησόν με. **40** σταθεὶς δὲ ὁ Ἰησοῦς ἐκέλευσεν αὐτὸν ἀχθῆναι πρὸς αὐτόν. ἐγγίσαντος δὲ αὐτοῦ ἐπηρώτησεν αὐτόν, **41** Τί σοι θέλεις ποιήσω; ὁ δὲ εἶπεν, Κύριε, ἵνα ἀναβλέψω. **42** καὶ ὁ Ἰησοῦς εἶπεν αὐτῷ, Ἀνάβλεψον· ἡ πίστις σου σέσωκέν σε. **43** καὶ παραχρῆμα ἀνέβλεψεν, καὶ ἠκολούθει αὐτῷ δοξάζων τὸν θεόν. καὶ πᾶς ὁ λαὸς ἰδὼν ἔδωκεν αἶνον τῷ θεῷ.

---

31 πάντα...ἀνθρώπου Lk 24.25–27, 44   **32–33** Lk 9.22, 44   **34** Mk 9.32   **38** Ἰησοῦ ...με Mt 9.27; 15.22; Lk 17.13   **41** Τί...ποιήσω Mk 10.36   **42** ἡ πίστις...σε Lk 7.50; 17.19

Jesus and Zacchaeus

19 Καὶ εἰσελθὼν διήρχετο τὴν Ἰεριχώ. 2 καὶ ἰδοὺ ἀνὴρ ὀνόματι καλούμενος Ζακχαῖος, καὶ αὐτὸς ἦν ἀρχιτελώνης καὶ αὐτὸς πλούσιος. 3 καὶ ἐζήτει ἰδεῖν τὸν Ἰησοῦν τίς ἐστιν, καὶ οὐκ ἠδύνατο ἀπὸ τοῦ ὄχλου ὅτι τῇ ἡλικίᾳ μικρὸς ἦν. 4 καὶ προδραμὼν εἰς τὸ ἔμπροσθεν ἀνέβη ἐπὶ συκομορέαν ἵνα ἴδῃ αὐτόν, ὅτι ἐκείνης ἤμελλεν διέρχεσθαι. 5 καὶ ὡς ἦλθεν ἐπὶ τὸν τόπον, ἀναβλέψας ὁ Ἰησοῦς εἶπεν πρὸς αὐτόν, Ζακχαῖε, σπεύσας κατάβηθι, σήμερον γὰρ ἐν τῷ οἴκῳ σου δεῖ με μεῖναι. 6 καὶ σπεύσας κατέβη, καὶ ὑπεδέξατο αὐτὸν χαίρων. 7 καὶ ἰδόντες πάντες διεγόγγυζον λέγοντες ὅτι Παρὰ ἁμαρτωλῷ ἀνδρὶ εἰσῆλθεν καταλῦσαι. 8 σταθεὶς δὲ Ζακχαῖος εἶπεν πρὸς τὸν κύριον, Ἰδοὺ τὰ ἡμίσειά μου τῶν ὑπαρχόντων, κύριε, τοῖς πτωχοῖς δίδωμι, καὶ εἴ τινός τι ἐσυκοφάντησα ἀποδίδωμι τετραπλοῦν. 9 εἶπεν δὲ πρὸς αὐτὸν ὁ Ἰησοῦς ὅτι Σήμερον σωτηρία τῷ οἴκῳ τούτῳ ἐγένετο, καθότι καὶ αὐτὸς υἱὸς Ἀβραάμ ἐστιν· 10 ἦλθεν γὰρ ὁ υἱὸς τοῦ ἀνθρώπου ζητῆσαι καὶ σῶσαι τὸ ἀπολωλός.

The Parable of the Ten Pounds
(Mt 25.14–30)

11 Ἀκουόντων δὲ αὐτῶν ταῦτα προσθεὶς εἶπεν παραβολὴν διὰ τὸ ἐγγὺς εἶναι Ἰερουσαλὴμ αὐτὸν καὶ δοκεῖν αὐτοὺς ὅτι παραχρῆμα μέλλει ἡ βασιλεία τοῦ θεοῦ ἀναφαίνεσθαι. 12 εἶπεν οὖν, Ἄνθρωπός τις εὐγενὴς ἐπορεύθη εἰς χώραν μακρὰν λαβεῖν ἑαυτῷ βασιλείαν καὶ ὑποστρέψαι. 13 καλέσας δὲ δέκα δούλους ἑαυτοῦ ἔδωκεν αὐτοῖς δέκα μνᾶς καὶ εἶπεν πρὸς αὐτούς, Πραγματεύσασθε ἐν ᾧ ἔρχομαι. 14 οἱ δὲ πολῖται αὐτοῦ ἐμίσουν αὐτόν, καὶ ἀπέστειλαν πρεσβείαν ὀπίσω αὐτοῦ λέγοντες,

---

7 Lk 5.30; 15.2　　8 ἀποδίδωμι τετραπλοῦν Ex 22.1　　9 σωτηρία...ἐγένετο Ac 16.31–34　υἱὸς Ἀβραάμ Lk 13.16　　10 ζητῆσαι...ἀπολωλός Eze 34.16; Lk 15.4, 6, 9　　12 Ἄνθρωπος...μακράν Mk 13.34

Jesus and Zacchaeus

19 Jesus went on into Jericho and was passing through. 2 There was a chief tax collector there, named Zacchaeus, who was rich. 3 He was trying to see who Jesus was, but he was a little man and could not see Jesus because of the crowd. 4 So he ran ahead of the crowd and climbed a sycamore tree to see Jesus, who would be going that way. 5 When Jesus came to that place he looked up and said to Zacchaeus, "Hurry down, Zacchaeus, for I must stay in your house today." 6 Zacchaeus hurried down and welcomed him with great joy. 7 All the people who saw it started grumbling, "This man has gone as a guest to the home of a sinner!" 8 Zacchaeus stood up and said to the Lord, "Listen, sir! I will give half my belongings to the poor; and if I have cheated anyone, I will pay him back four times as much." 9 Jesus said to him, "Salvation has come to this house today; this man, also, is a descendant of Abraham. 10 For the Son of Man came to seek and to save the lost."

The Parable of the Gold Coins
(Also Matt. 25.14–30)

11 Then Jesus told a parable to those who heard him say this. He was now almost at Jerusalem, and they supposed that the Kingdom of God was just about to appear. 12 So he said: "There was a nobleman who went to a country far away to be made king and then come back home. 13 Before he left, he called his ten servants and gave them each a gold coin and told them, 'See what you can earn with this while I am gone.' 14 Now, his countrymen hated him, and

so they sent messengers after him to say, 'We don't want this man to be our king.' 15 "The nobleman was made king and came back. At once he ordered his servants, to whom he had given the money, to appear before him in order to find out how much they had earned. 16 The first one came up and said, 'Sir, I have earned ten gold coins with the one you gave me.' 17 'Well done,' he said; 'you are a good servant! Since you were faithful in small matters, I will put you in charge of ten cities.' 18 The second servant came and said, 'Sir, I have earned five gold coins with the one you gave me.' 19 To this one he said, 'You will be in charge of five cities.' 20 Another servant came and said: 'Sir, here is your gold coin; I kept it hidden in a handkerchief. 21 I was afraid of you, because you are a hard man. You take what is not yours, and reap what you did not plant.' 22 He said to him: 'You bad servant! I will use your own words to condemn you! You know that I am a hard man, taking what is not mine and reaping what I have not planted. 23 Well, then, why didn't you put my money in the bank? Then I would have received it back with interest when I returned.' 24 Then he said to those who were standing there, 'Take the gold coin away from him and give it to the servant who has ten coins.' 25 They said to him, 'Sir, he already has ten coins!' 26 'I tell you,' he replied, 'that to every one who has, even more will be given; but the one who does not have, even the little that he has will be taken

Οὐ θέλομεν τοῦτον βασιλεῦσαι ἐφ᾽ ἡμᾶς. 15 Καὶ ἐγένετο ἐν τῷ ἐπανελθεῖν αὐτὸν λαβόντα τὴν βασιλείαν καὶ εἶπεν φωνηθῆναι αὐτῷ τοὺς δούλους τούτους οἷς δεδώκει τὸ ἀργύριον, ἵνα γνοῖ τί διεπραγματεύσαντο[1]. 16 παρεγένετο δὲ ὁ πρῶτος λέγων, Κύριε, ἡ μνᾶ σου δέκα προσηργάσατο μνᾶς. 17 καὶ εἶπεν αὐτῷ, Εὖγε, ἀγαθὲ δοῦλε, ὅτι ἐν ἐλαχίστῳ πιστὸς ἐγένου, ἴσθι ἐξουσίαν ἔχων ἐπάνω δέκα πόλεων. 18 καὶ ἦλθεν ὁ δεύτερος λέγων, Ἡ μνᾶ σου, κύριε, ἐποίησεν πέντε μνᾶς. 19 εἶπεν δὲ καὶ τούτῳ, Καὶ σὺ ἐπάνω γίνου πέντε πόλεων. 20 καὶ ὁ ἕτερος ἦλθεν λέγων, Κύριε, ἰδοὺ ἡ μνᾶ σου ἣν εἶχον ἀποκειμένην ἐν σουδαρίῳ· 21 ἐφοβούμην γάρ σε, ὅτι ἄνθρωπος αὐστηρὸς εἶ, αἴρεις ὃ οὐκ ἔθηκας καὶ θερίζεις ὃ οὐκ ἔσπειρας. 22 λέγει αὐτῷ, Ἐκ τοῦ στόματός σου κρίνω σε, πονηρὲ δοῦλε. ᾔδεις ὅτι ἐγὼ ἄνθρωπος αὐστηρός εἰμι, αἴρων ὃ οὐκ ἔθηκα καὶ θερίζων ὃ οὐκ ἔσπειρα;[a] 23 καὶ διὰ τί οὐκ ἔδωκάς μου τὸ ἀργύριον ἐπὶ τράπεζαν;[b] κἀγὼ ἐλθὼν σὺν τόκῳ ἂν αὐτὸ ἔπραξα.[b] 24 καὶ τοῖς παρεστῶσιν εἶπεν, Ἄρατε ἀπ᾽ αὐτοῦ τὴν μνᾶν καὶ δότε τῷ τὰς δέκα μνᾶς ἔχοντι [25 — καὶ εἶπαν αὐτῷ, Κύριε, ἔχει δέκα μνᾶς].[2] 26 λέγω ὑμῖν ὅτι παντὶ τῷ ἔχοντι δοθήσεται, ἀπὸ δὲ τοῦ μὴ ἔχοντος καὶ ὃ ἔχει ἀρθήσεται.

---

[1] 15 {C} τί διεπραγματεύσαντο ℵ B D L Ψ it[d,e] syr[c,s] cop[sa,bo,fay] eth geo Origen ‖ τί διεπραγματεύσατο 047 ‖ τίς τί διεπραγματεύσατο A K Θ Π 063 f[1] f[13] 28 33 565 700 892 1009 1010 1079 1195 1230 1242 1253 1344 1546 1646 2148 Byz Lect it[a,aur,b,c,f,ff2,i,l,q,s] vg syr[p,h] goth arm Lucifer ‖ τίς τί ἐπραγματεύσατο W (Δ πραγματεύσατο) 1071 1216 (1365[c] ἐπραγμασεύσατο and omit τίς) ‖ τίς διεπραγματεύσατο 1241

[2] 25 {D} include verse 25 ℵ A B K L Δ Θ Π Ψ 063 f[1] f[13] 28 33 700 892 1009 1010 1071 1079 1195 1216 1241 1242 1344 1365 1546 1646 2148 Byz l[76,150,184,185,299,883,950] it[a,aur,c,f,i,l,q,r1,s] vg syr[p,h] cop[sa,boms] goth arm geo ‖ omit verse 25 (see Mt 25.28) D W 565 1230 1253 Lect it[b,d,e,ff2] syr[c,s] cop[bo] Lucifer Cyril

[a] 22 a question: WH Bov Nes BF² RSV NEB TT Zür ‖ a statement: TR AV RV ASV Luth Jer Seg

[b b] 23 b question, b major: WH Bov Nes BF² TT Zür Luth Jer ‖ b minor, b question: TR AV RV ASV RSV NEB Seg

17 ἐν...πόλεων Lk 16.10   26 παντὶ...ἀρθήσεται Mt 13.12; Mk 4.25; Lk 8.18

27 πλὴν τοὺς ἐχθρούς μου τούτους τοὺς μὴ θελήσαντάς με βασιλεῦσαι ἐπ' αὐτοὺς ἀγάγετε ὧδε καὶ κατασφάξατε αὐτοὺς ἔμπροσθέν μου.

The Triumphal Entry into Jerusalem
(Mt 21.1–11; Mk 11.1–11; Jn 12.12–19)

28 Καὶ εἰπὼν ταῦτα ἐπορεύετο ἔμπροσθεν ἀναβαίνων εἰς Ἱεροσόλυμα. **29** Καὶ ἐγένετο ὡς ἤγγισεν εἰς Βηθφαγὴ καὶ Βηθανιὰ πρὸς τὸ ὄρος τὸ καλούμενον Ἐλαιῶν, ἀπέστειλεν δύο τῶν μαθητῶν **30** λέγων, Ὑπάγετε εἰς τὴν κατέναντι κώμην, ἐν ᾗ εἰσπορευόμενοι εὑρήσετε πῶλον δεδεμένον, ἐφ' ὃν οὐδεὶς πώποτε ἀνθρώπων ἐκάθισεν, καὶ λύσαντες αὐτὸν ἀγάγετε. **31** καὶ ἐάν τις ὑμᾶς ἐρωτᾷ, Διὰ τί λύετε; οὕτως ἐρεῖτε ὅτι^c Ὁ κύριος αὐτοῦ χρείαν ἔχει. **32** ἀπελθόντες δὲ οἱ ἀπεσταλμένοι εὗρον καθὼς εἶπεν αὐτοῖς. **33** λυόντων δὲ αὐτῶν τὸν πῶλον εἶπαν οἱ κύριοι αὐτοῦ πρὸς αὐτούς, Τί λύετε τὸν πῶλον; **34** οἱ δὲ εἶπαν ὅτι^d Ὁ κύριος αὐτοῦ χρείαν ἔχει. **35** καὶ ἤγαγον αὐτὸν πρὸς τὸν Ἰησοῦν, καὶ ἐπιρίψαντες αὐτῶν τὰ ἱμάτια ἐπὶ τὸν πῶλον ἐπεβίβασαν τὸν Ἰησοῦν. **36** πορευομένου δὲ αὐτοῦ ὑπεστρώννυον τὰ ἱμάτια αὐτῶν ἐν τῇ ὁδῷ.

37 Ἐγγίζοντος δὲ αὐτοῦ ἤδη πρὸς τῇ καταβάσει τοῦ Ὄρους τῶν Ἐλαιῶν ἤρξαντο ἅπαν τὸ πλῆθος τῶν μαθητῶν χαίροντες αἰνεῖν τὸν θεὸν φωνῇ μεγάλῃ περὶ πασῶν ὧν εἶδον δυνάμεων, **38** λέγοντες,

Εὐλογημένος ὁ ἐρχόμενος
ὁ βασιλεὺς^3 ἐν ὀνόματι κυρίου·

---

^{3} **38** {C} ὁ ἐρχόμενος ὁ βασιλεύς B syr$^{c?s?p?h?}$ geo? ∥ ὁ ἐρχόμενος βασιλεύς א^c A K L Δ Θ Π Ψ f^1 f^{13} 28 565 700 892 1009 1010 1071 1079 1195 1230 1241 1242 1253 1344 1365 1546 1646 2148 2174 *Byz Lect* ($l^{950pt,1127pt}$) it^{aur,f,q} vg syr$^{c?s?p?h?}$ cop^{sa,bo} goth arm geo? ∥ ὁ βασιλεύς א* (063 $l^{950pt,1127pt}$ *omit* ὁ) it^{e,l}

---

^{c} **31** *c direct:* TR? WH BF² RV ASV RSV NEB TT Zür Luth Jer Seg ∥ *c causal:* TR? Bov Nes AV
^{d} **34** *d direct:* WH BF² RV ASV RSV NEB TT Zür Luth Jer Seg ∥ *d causal:* Bov Nes ∥ *different text:* TR AV

---

32 Lk 22.13   **36** ὑπεστρώννυον...ὁδῷ 2 Kgs 9.13   **38** Εὐλογημένος...κυρίου Ps 118.26

---

away from him. **27** Now, as for these enemies of mine who did not want me to be their king: bring them here and kill them before me!' "

The Triumphant Entry into Jerusalem
(Also Matt. 21.1–11; Mark 11.1–11; John 12.12–19)

28 Jesus said this and then went on to Jerusalem ahead of them. **29** As he came near Bethphage and Bethany, at the Mount of Olives, he sent two disciples ahead **30** with these instructions: "Go to the village there ahead of you; as you go in you will find a colt tied up that has never been ridden. Untie it and bring it here. **31** If someone asks you, 'Why are you untying it?' tell him, 'The Master needs it.' " **32** They went on their way and found everything just as Jesus had told them. **33** As they were untying the colt, its owners said to them, "Why are you untying it?" **34** "The Master needs it," they answered, **35** and took the colt to Jesus. Then they threw their cloaks over the animal and helped Jesus get on. **36** As he rode on, they spread their cloaks on the road. **37** When he came near Jerusalem, at the place where the road went down the Mount of Olives, the large crowd of his disciples began to thank God and praise him in loud voices for all the great things that they had seen: **38** "God bless the king who comes in the name of the Lord! Peace in heaven, and glory to God!''

[39] Then some of the Pharisees spoke up from the crowd to Jesus. "Teacher," they said, "command your disciples to be quiet!" [40] Jesus answered, "If they keep quiet, I tell you, the stones themselves will shout."

Jesus Weeps over Jerusalem

[41] He came closer to the city and when he saw it he wept over it, [42] saying: "If you only knew today what is needed for peace! But now you cannot see it! [43] For the days will come upon you when your enemies will surround you with barricades, blockade you, and close in on you from every side. [44] They will completely destroy you and the people within your walls; not a single stone will they leave in its place, because you did not recognize the time when God came to save you!"

ἐν οὐρανῷ εἰρήνη
　　καὶ δόξα ἐν ὑψίστοις.

39 καί τινες τῶν Φαρισαίων ἀπὸ τοῦ ὄχλου εἶπαν πρὸς αὐτόν, Διδάσκαλε, ἐπιτίμησον τοῖς μαθηταῖς σου. **40** καὶ ἀποκριθεὶς εἶπεν, Λέγω ὑμῖν, ἐὰν οὗτοι σιωπήσουσιν, οἱ λίθοι κράξουσιν.

41 Καὶ ὡς ἤγγισεν, ἰδὼν τὴν πόλιν ἔκλαυσεν ἐπ' αὐτήν, **42**e λέγων eὅτι Εἰ ἔγνως ἐν τῇ ἡμέρᾳ ταύτῃ καὶ σύ4 τὰ πρὸς εἰρήνην5 — νῦν δὲ ἐκρύβη ἀπὸ ὀφθαλμῶν σου. **43** ὅτι ἥξουσιν ἡμέραι ἐπὶ σὲ καὶ παρεμβαλοῦσιν οἱ ἐχθροί σου χάρακά σοι καὶ περικυκλώσουσίν σε καὶ συνέξουσίν σε πάντοθεν, **44** καὶ ἐδαφιοῦσίν σε καὶ τὰ τέκνα σου ἐν σοί, καὶ οὐκ ἀφήσουσιν λίθον ἐπὶ λίθον ἐν σοί, ἀνθ' ὧν οὐκ ἔγνως τὸν καιρὸν τῆς ἐπισκοπῆς σου.

Origen ‖ ὁ ἐρχόμενος W 1216 l18,48,76,547 eth Diatessaron Methodius Titus-Bostra Eulogius ‖ transpose: ὁ ἐρχόμενος ἐν ὀνόματι κυρίου εὐλογημένος ὁ βασιλεύς D ita,c,d,ff2,i,rl,s

4 **42** {C} ἐν τῇ ἡμέρᾳ ταύτῃ καὶ σύ ℵ B L 892 (1241 καί γε ἐν) Origen ‖ καὶ σὺ ἐν τῇ ἡμέρᾳ ταύτῃ D Θ itd,(e),f,q,(s) copsa,bo geo Origenlat ‖ καὶ σὺ καί γε ἐν τῇ ἡμέρᾳ ταύτῃ A Ψ f1 565 1009 1230 1253 2148 (l10 omit γε) l184,185 ‖ καὶ σὺ καί γε ἐν τῇ ἡμέρᾳ σου ταύτῃ K W Δ Π 063 f13 28 33vid 700 1010 1071 1079 1195 1216 1242 1344 1365 1546 1646 2174 Byz Lect itaur vg syrp,h goth Diatessaron (Eusebius) (Basil) ‖ σὺ καί γε ἐν τῇ ἡμέρᾳ σου ταύτῃ it(a),b,c,ff2,(i),l,rl (arm) Diatessaronesyr ‖ καί γε ἐν τῇ ἡμέρᾳ ταύτῃ syrc,s

5 **42** {C} εἰρήνην ℵ B L Θ syrpalms copsa,boms Diatessaronesyr Irenaeus Origen ‖ εἰρήνην σου A K W Δ Π Ψ 063 f1 28 565 700 892 1009 1010 1071 1079 1195 1216 1230 1241 1242 1253 1344 1546 1646 2148 2174 Byz Lect ita syrc,s,p,h,palms copbo goth arm eth geo Diatessaron Origen Eusebius Basil Cyril ‖ εἰρήνην σοι D f13 1365 itaur,c,d,e,f,ff2,i,l,q,rl,s vg Origenlat Eusebius

---

ee **41–42** e number 42, e no number: TRed WH? Bov Nes BF2 AV RV ASV RSV NEB TT Zür Luth Jer ‖ e no number, e number 42: TRed WH? Seg

---

38 ἐν οὐρανῷ...ὑψίστοις Lk 2.14　**41** ἔκλαυσεν Jn 11.35　**42** Εἰ ἔγνως...σου Dt 32.29　νῦν δὲ ἐκρύβη...σου Is 6.9–10; Mt 13.14; Mk 4.12; Lk 8.10; Ac 28.26–27; Ro 11.8, 10　**44** ἐδαφιοῦσιν...σου Ps 137.9　οὐκ ἀφήσουσιν...σοί Mt 24.2; Mk 13.2; Lk 21.6　καιρὸν...σου Lk 1.68

The Cleansing of the Temple
(Mt 21.12–17; Mk 11.15–19; Jn 2.13–22)

45 Καὶ εἰσελθὼν εἰς τὸ ἱερὸν ἤρξατο ἐκβάλλειν τοὺς πωλοῦντας, **46** λέγων αὐτοῖς, Γέγραπται,

Καὶ ἔσται ὁ οἶκός μου οἶκος προσευχῆς,
  ὑμεῖς δὲ αὐτὸν ἐποιήσατε **σπήλαιον λῃστῶν.**

47 Καὶ ἦν διδάσκων τὸ καθ' ἡμέραν ἐν τῷ ἱερῷ. οἱ δὲ ἀρχιερεῖς καὶ οἱ γραμματεῖς ἐζήτουν αὐτὸν ἀπολέσαι καὶ οἱ πρῶτοι τοῦ λαοῦ· **48** καὶ οὐχ εὕρισκον τὸ τί ποιήσωσιν, ὁ λαὸς γὰρ ἅπας ἐξεκρέματο αὐτοῦ ἀκούων.

The Authority of Jesus Questioned
(Mt 21.23–27; Mk 11.27–33)

20 Καὶ ἐγένετο ἐν μιᾷ τῶν ἡμερῶν διδάσκοντος αὐτοῦ τὸν λαὸν ἐν τῷ ἱερῷ καὶ εὐαγγελιζομένου ἐπέστησαν οἱ ἀρχιερεῖς καὶ οἱ γραμματεῖς σὺν τοῖς πρεσβυτέροις, **2** καὶ εἶπαν λέγοντες πρὸς αὐτόν, Εἰπὸν ἡμῖν ἐν ποίᾳ ἐξουσίᾳ ταῦτα ποιεῖς,ᵃ ἢ τίς ἐστιν ὁ δούς σοι τὴν ἐξουσίαν ταύτην.ᵃ **3** ἀποκριθεὶς δὲ εἶπεν πρὸς αὐτούς, Ἐρωτήσω ὑμᾶς κἀγὼ λόγον, καὶ εἴπατέ μοι· **4** Τὸ βάπτισμα Ἰωάννου ἐξ οὐρανοῦ ἦν ἢ ἐξ ἀνθρώπων; **5** οἱ δὲ συνελογίσαντο πρὸς ἑαυτοὺς λέγοντες ὅτι Ἐὰν εἴπωμεν, Ἐξ οὐρανοῦ, ἐρεῖ, Διὰ τί οὐκ ἐπιστεύσατε αὐτῷ; **6** ἐὰν δὲ εἴπωμεν, Ἐξ ἀνθρώπων, ὁ λαὸς ἅπας καταλιθάσει ἡμᾶς, πεπεισμένος γάρ ἐστιν Ἰωάννην προφήτην εἶναι. **7** καὶ ἀπεκρίθησαν μὴ εἰδέναι πόθεν. **8** καὶ ὁ Ἰησοῦς εἶπεν αὐτοῖς, Οὐδὲ ἐγὼ λέγω ὑμῖν ἐν ποίᾳ ἐξουσίᾳ ταῦτα ποιῶ.

ᵃ ᵃ **2** a minor, a statement: WH RSV ∥ a minor, a question: TR Bov Nes BF² NEB TT Jer Seg ∥ a question, a question: AV RV ASV Zür Luth

---

46 Καὶ...προσευχῆς Is 56,7 Καὶ...λῃστῶν Jr 7,11   **47** ἦν...ἱερῷ Lk 21.37; 22.53; Jn 18.20 **47-48** οἱ δὲ...ἀκούων Mt 21.46; Mk 12.12; 14.1-2; Lk 20.19; 22.2; Jn 5.18; 7.30 **20 4** βάπτισμα Ἰωάννου Mt 3.6, 11; Mk 1.4, 5, 8; Lk 3.3, 16; Jn 1.25-26; Ac 1.22; 10.37; 13.24; 18.25; 19.3, 4 **5** Διὰ τί οὐκ ἐπιστεύσατε αὐτῷ Mt 21.32

Jesus Goes to the Temple
(Also Matt. 21.12–17; Mark 11.15–19; John 2.13–22)

45 Jesus went into the Temple and began to drive out the merchants, **46** saying to them: "It is written in the Scriptures that God said, 'My house will be called a house of prayer.' But you have turned it into a hideout for thieves!"

47 Jesus taught in the Temple every day. The chief priests, the teachers of the Law, and the leaders of the people wanted to kill him, **48** but they could not find how to do it, because all the people kept listening to him, not wanting to miss a single word.

The Question about Jesus' Authority
(Also Matt. 21.23–27; Mark 11.27–33)

20 One day, when Jesus was in the Temple teaching the people and preaching the Good News, the chief priests and the teachers of the Law, together with the elders, came **2** and said to him, "Tell us, what right do you have to do these things? Who gave you the right to do them?" **3** Jesus answered them: "Now let me ask you a question. Tell me, **4** did John's right to baptize come from God or from man?" **5** They started to argue among themselves: "What shall we say? If we say, 'From God,' he will say, 'Why, then, did you not believe John?' **6** But if we say, 'From man,' this whole crowd here will stone us, because they are convinced that John was a prophet." **7** So they answered, "We don't know where it came from." **8** And Jesus said to them, "Neither will I tell you, then, by what right I do these things."

The Parable of the Tenants in the Vineyard
(Also Matt. 21.33–46; Mark 12.1–12)

⁹ Then Jesus told the people this parable: "A man planted a vineyard, rented it out to tenants, and then left home for a long time. ¹⁰ When the time came for harvesting the grapes, he sent a slave to the tenants to receive from them his share of the harvest. But the tenants beat the slave and sent him back without a thing. ¹¹ So he sent another slave, but the tenants beat him also, treated him shamefully, and sent him back without a thing. ¹² Then he sent a third slave; the tenants hurt him, too, and threw him out. ¹³ Then the owner of the vineyard said, 'What shall I do? I will send my own dear son; surely they will respect him!' ¹⁴ But when the tenants saw him they said to one another, 'This is the owner's son. Let us kill him, and the vineyard will be ours!' ¹⁵ So they threw him out of the vineyard and killed him.

"What, then, will the owner of the vineyard do to the tenants?" Jesus asked. ¹⁶ "He will come and kill those men, and turn over the vineyard to other tenants." When the people heard this they said, "Surely not!" ¹⁷ Jesus looked at them and asked, "What, then, does this scripture mean?

'The stone which the builders rejected
    as worthless
Turned out to be the most important
    stone.'

¹⁸ Everyone who falls on that stone will be cut to pieces; and if the stone falls on someone, it will crush him to dust."

The Question about Paying Taxes
(Also Matt. 22.15–22; Mark 12.13–17)

¹⁹ The teachers of the Law and the chief priests tried to arrest Jesus on the

The Parable of the Vineyard and the Tenants
(Mt 21.33–46; Mk 12.1–12)

9 Ἤρξατο δὲ πρὸς τὸν λαὸν λέγειν τὴν παραβολὴν ταύτην· Ἄνθρωπός [τις] ἐφύτευσεν ἀμπελῶνα¹, καὶ ἐξέδετο αὐτὸν γεωργοῖς, καὶ ἀπεδήμησεν χρόνους ἱκανούς. 10 καὶ καιρῷ ἀπέστειλεν πρὸς τοὺς γεωργοὺς δοῦλον, ἵνα ἀπὸ τοῦ καρποῦ τοῦ ἀμπελῶνος δώσουσιν αὐτῷ· οἱ δὲ γεωργοὶ ἐξαπέστειλαν αὐτὸν δείραντες κενόν. 11 καὶ προσέθετο ἕτερον πέμψαι δοῦλον· οἱ δὲ κἀκεῖνον δείραντες καὶ ἀτιμάσαντες ἐξαπέστειλαν κενόν. 12 καὶ προσέθετο τρίτον πέμψαι· οἱ δὲ καὶ τοῦτον τραυματίσαντες ἐξέβαλον. 13 εἶπεν δὲ ὁ κύριος τοῦ ἀμπελῶνος, Τί ποιήσω; πέμψω τὸν υἱόν μου τὸν ἀγαπητόν· ἴσως τοῦτον ἐντραπήσονται. 14 ἰδόντες δὲ αὐτὸν οἱ γεωργοὶ διελογίζοντο πρὸς ἀλλήλους λέγοντες, Οὗτός ἐστιν ὁ κληρονόμος· ἀποκτείνωμεν αὐτόν, ἵνα ἡμῶν γένηται ἡ κληρονομία. 15 καὶ ἐκβαλόντες αὐτὸν ἔξω τοῦ ἀμπελῶνος ἀπέκτειναν. τί οὖν ποιήσει αὐτοῖς ὁ κύριος τοῦ ἀμπελῶνος; 16 ἐλεύσεται καὶ ἀπολέσει τοὺς γεωργοὺς τούτους, καὶ δώσει τὸν ἀμπελῶνα ἄλλοις. ἀκούσαντες δὲ εἶπαν, Μὴ γένοιτο. 17 ὁ δὲ ἐμβλέψας αὐτοῖς εἶπεν, Τί οὖν ἐστιν τὸ γεγραμμένον τοῦτο·

Λίθον ὃν ἀπεδοκίμασαν οἱ οἰκοδομοῦντες,
οὗτος ἐγενήθη εἰς κεφαλὴν γωνίας;

18 πᾶς ὁ πεσὼν ἐπ᾽ ἐκεῖνον τὸν λίθον συνθλασθήσεται· ἐφ᾽ ὃν δ᾽ ἂν πέσῃ, λικμήσει αὐτόν. 19 Καὶ ἐζήτησαν οἱ γραμματεῖς καὶ οἱ ἀρχιερεῖς ἐπιβαλεῖν ἐπ᾽ αὐτὸν τὰς

---

¹ 9 {C} ἄνθρωπός τις ἐφύτευσεν ἀμπελῶνα A W Θ f¹³ 1071 1195 1241 1344 1365 2148 Lect (itʳ¹) syrᶜ·ˢ·ᵖ·ʰ arm geo ∥ ἄνθρωπος ἐφύτευσεν ἀμπελῶνα ℵ B K L Δ Π Ψ f¹ 28 33 565 700 892 1009 1010 1079 1216 1230 1242 1253 1546 1646 2174 Byz itᵃᵘʳ·ᶠ vg copˢᵃ·ᵇᵒ goth eth Origen ∥ ἀμπελῶνα ἐφύτευσεν ἄνθρωπος D itᵃ·ᶜ·ᵈ·ᵉ·ᶠᶠ²·ⁱ·ˡ· q Ambrose ∥ ἀμπελῶνα ἄνθρωπος ἐφύτευσεν (see Mk 12.1) C

9 Ἄνθρωπος...ἀμπελῶνα Is 5.1   **10–12** 2 Chr 36.15–16   **17** Λίθον...γωνίας Ps 118.22   **19** ἐζήτησαν...λαόν Mt 21.46; Mk 12.12; 14.1–2; Lk 19.47–48; 22.2; Jn 5.18; 7.30

χεῖρας ἐν αὐτῇ τῇ ὥρᾳ, καὶ ἐφοβήθησαν τὸν λαόν· ἔγνωσαν γὰρ ὅτι πρὸς αὐτοὺς εἶπεν τὴν παραβολὴν ταύτην.

Paying Taxes to Caesar
(Mt 22.15–22; Mk 12.13–17)

20 Καὶ παρατηρήσαντες[2] ἀπέστειλαν ἐγκαθέτους ὑπο-
κρινομένους ἑαυτοὺς δικαίους εἶναι, ἵνα ἐπιλάβωνται
αὐτοῦ λόγου, ὥστε παραδοῦναι αὐτὸν τῇ ἀρχῇ καὶ τῇ
ἐξουσίᾳ τοῦ ἡγεμόνος. **21** καὶ ἐπηρώτησαν αὐτὸν λέγοντες,
Διδάσκαλε, οἴδαμεν ὅτι ὀρθῶς λέγεις καὶ διδάσκεις καὶ
οὐ λαμβάνεις πρόσωπον, ἀλλ' ἐπ' ἀληθείας τὴν ὁδὸν τοῦ
θεοῦ διδάσκεις· **22** ἔξεστιν ἡμᾶς Καίσαρι φόρον δοῦναι ἢ
οὔ; **23** κατανοήσας δὲ αὐτῶν τὴν πανουργίαν εἶπεν πρὸς
αὐτούς, **24** Δείξατέ μοι δηνάριον· τίνος ἔχει εἰκόνα καὶ
ἐπιγραφήν; οἱ δὲ εἶπαν, Καίσαρος. **25** ὁ δὲ εἶπεν πρὸς
αὐτούς, Τοίνυν ἀπόδοτε τὰ Καίσαρος Καίσαρι καὶ τὰ
τοῦ θεοῦ τῷ θεῷ. **26** καὶ οὐκ ἴσχυσαν ἐπιλαβέσθαι αὐτοῦ
ῥήματος[3] ἐναντίον τοῦ λαοῦ, καὶ θαυμάσαντες ἐπὶ τῇ
ἀποκρίσει αὐτοῦ ἐσίγησαν.

The Question about the Resurrection
(Mt 22.23–33; Mk 12.18–27)

27 Προσελθόντες δέ τινες τῶν Σαδδουκαίων, οἱ ἀντιλέγοντες[4] ἀνάστασιν μὴ εἶναι, ἐπηρώτησαν αὐτὸν **28** λέ-

---

[2] **20** {C} παρατηρήσαντες ℵ A B C K L Δ Π Ψ 0117 f¹ f¹³ 33 565 700
892 1009 1010 1071 1079 1195 1216 1230 1241 1242 1253 1344 1365 1546 1646
2148 2174 *Byz Lect* it^aur vg syr^h cop^sa,bo geo ∥ ἀποχωρήσαντες D Θ it^a,c,d,
e,f,ff²,i,l,q,r¹ goth eth ∥ ὑποχωρήσαντες W ∥ μετὰ ταῦτα syr^c,s ∥ μετὰ
ταῦτα παρατηρήσαντες arm ∥ *omit* syr^p

[3] **26** {C} ἐπιλαβέσθαι αὐτοῦ ῥήματος A C K P W Δ Π Ψ f¹ f¹³ 33 565
700 1009 1010 1071 1079 1195 1216 1230 1242 1253 1344 1365 1546 1646 2148
2174 *Byz Lect* it^e syr^c,p,h cop^sa?bo? goth (arm αὐτοῦ ἐπιλαβέσθαι ῥημάτων)
(eth) geo? ∥ ἐπιλαβέσθαι τοῦ ῥήματος ℵ B L (Θ *add* αὐτοῦ) 892 1241 ∥
αὐτοῦ ῥῆμα ἐπιλαβέσθαι D it^(a),aur,c,d,f,ff²,i,l,q,r¹ vg syr^s geo?

[4] **27** {C} οἱ ἀντιλέγοντες A K P W Δ Π f¹³ 700 1009 1010 1079 1195

---

20 Lk 11.54   **21** Διδάσκαλε...διδάσκεις Jn 3.2   **22** φόρον δοῦναι Ro 13.6–7
27 Σαδδουκαίων...εἶναι Ac 23.8

---

spot, because they knew that he had told this parable against them; but they were afraid of the people. **20** So they watched for the right time. They bribed some men to pretend they were sincere, and sent them to trap Jesus with questions, so they could hand him over to the authority and power of the Governor. **21** These spies said to Jesus: "Teacher, we know that what you say and teach is right. We know that you pay no attention to what a man seems to be, but teach the truth about God's will for man. **22** Tell us, is it against our Law for us to pay taxes to the Roman Emperor, or not?" **23** But Jesus saw through their trick and said to them, **24** "Show me a silver coin. Whose face and name are these on it?" "The Emperor's," they answered. **25** So Jesus said, "Well, then, pay to the Emperor what belongs to him, and pay to God what belongs to God." **26** They could not catch him in a thing there before the people, so they kept quiet, amazed at his answer.

The Question about Rising from Death
(Also Matt. 22.23–33; Mark 12.18–27)

27 Some Sadducees came to Jesus. (They are the ones who say that people will not rise from death.) They asked him: **28** "Teacher, Moses wrote this law for us: 'If a man dies and leaves a wife, but no children, that man's brother must marry the widow so they can have children for the dead man.' 29 Once there were seven brothers; the oldest got married, and died without having children. 30 Then the second one married the woman, 31 and then the third; the same thing happened to all seven—they died without having children. 32 Last of all, the woman died. 33 Now, on the day when the dead are raised to life, whose wife will she be? All seven of them had married her!"

34 Jesus answered them: "The men and women of this age marry, 35 but the men and women who are worthy to be raised from death and live in the age to come do not marry. 36 They are like angels and cannot die. They are the sons of God, because they have been raised from death. 37 And Moses clearly proves that the dead will be raised to life. In the passage about the burning bush he speaks of the Lord as 'the God of Abraham, the God of Isaac, and the God of Jacob.' 38 This means that he is the God of the living, not of the dead — for all are alive to him." 39 Some of the teachers of the Law spoke up, "A good answer, Teacher!" 40 For they did not dare ask Jesus any more questions.

The Question about the Messiah
(Also Matt. 22.41–46; Mark 12.35–37)

41 Jesus said to them: "How can it be said that the Messiah will be the descendant of David? 42 Because David himself says in the book of Psalms:

'The Lord said to my Lord:
Sit here at my right side,

γοντες, Διδάσκαλε, Μωϋσῆς ἔγραψεν ἡμῖν, ἐάν τινος ἀδελφὸς ἀποθάνῃ ἔχων γυναῖκα, καὶ οὗτος ἄτεκνος ᾖ, ἵνα λάβῃ ὁ ἀδελφὸς αὐτοῦ τὴν γυναῖκα καὶ ἐξαναστήσῃ σπέρμα τῷ ἀδελφῷ αὐτοῦ. 29 ἑπτὰ οὖν ἀδελφοὶ ἦσαν· καὶ ὁ πρῶτος λαβὼν γυναῖκα ἀπέθανεν ἄτεκνος· 30 καὶ ὁ δεύτερος 31 καὶ ὁ τρίτος ἔλαβεν αὐτήν, ὡσαύτως δὲ καὶ οἱ ἑπτὰ οὐ κατέλιπον τέκνα καὶ ἀπέθανον. 32 ὕστερον καὶ ἡ γυνὴ ἀπέθανεν. 33 ἡ γυνὴ οὖν ἐν τῇ ἀναστάσει τίνος αὐτῶν γίνεται γυνή; οἱ γὰρ ἑπτὰ ἔσχον αὐτὴν γυναῖκα. 34 καὶ εἶπεν αὐτοῖς ὁ Ἰησοῦς, Οἱ υἱοὶ τοῦ αἰῶνος τούτου γαμοῦσιν καὶ γαμίσκονται, 35 οἱ δὲ καταξιωθέντες τοῦ αἰῶνος ἐκείνου τυχεῖν καὶ τῆς ἀναστάσεως τῆς ἐκ νεκρῶν οὔτε γαμοῦσιν οὔτε γαμίζονται· 36 οὐδὲ γὰρ ἀποθανεῖν ἔτι δύνανται, ἰσάγγελοι γάρ εἰσιν, καὶ υἱοί εἰσιν θεοῦ, τῆς ἀναστάσεως υἱοὶ ὄντες. 37 ὅτι δὲ ἐγείρονται οἱ νεκροὶ καὶ Μωϋσῆς ἐμήνυσεν ἐπὶ τῆς βάτου, ὡς λέγει **κύριον τὸν θεὸν Ἀβραὰμ καὶ θεὸν Ἰσαὰκ καὶ θεὸν Ἰακώβ·** 38 θεὸς δὲ οὐκ ἔστιν νεκρῶν ἀλλὰ ζώντων, πάντες γὰρ αὐτῷ ζῶσιν. 39 ἀποκριθέντες δέ τινες τῶν γραμματέων εἶπαν, Διδάσκαλε, καλῶς εἶπας· 40 οὐκέτι γὰρ ἐτόλμων ἐπερωτᾶν αὐτὸν οὐδέν.

The Question about David's Son
(Mt 22.41–46; Mk 12.35–37)

41 Εἶπεν δὲ πρὸς αὐτούς, Πῶς λέγουσιν τὸν Χριστὸν εἶναι Δαυὶδ υἱόν; 42 αὐτὸς γὰρ Δαυὶδ λέγει ἐν βίβλῳ ψαλμῶν,

**Εἶπεν κύριος τῷ κυρίῳ μου,
Κάθου ἐκ δεξιῶν μου**

1216 1242 1344 1546 1646 2148 2174 *Byz* it^{a,aur,c,f,ff2,i,l,q} vg syr^h arm geo ∥ οἱ λέγοντες (*see* Mt 22.23) ℵ B C D L Θ *f*¹ 33 565 892 1071 1230 1241 1253 1365 *Lect* it^{d,e,rl} syr^{c,s,p} cop^{sa,bo} goth eth Diatessaron ∥ οἵτινες λέγουσιν (*see* Mk 12.18) Ψ *l*⁴⁸

28 ἐάν...ἀδελφῷ αὐτοῦ Dt 25.5; Gn 38.8   36 υἱοί...θεοῦ Ga 4.5–7   37 ἐπὶ τῆς βάτου Ex 3.2   τὸν...Ἰακώβ Ex 3.6   38 πάντες...ζῶσιν Ro 14.8–9   42–43 Εἶπεν...ποδῶν σου Ps 110.1

43 ἕως ἂν θῶ τοὺς ἐχθρούς σου ὑποπόδιον τῶν
    ποδῶν σου.
44 Δαυὶδ οὖν κύριον αὐτὸν καλεῖ, καὶ πῶς αὐτοῦ υἱός
ἐστιν;

The Denouncing of the Scribes
(Mt 23.1–36; Mk 12.38–40; Lk 11.37–54)

45 Ἀκούοντος δὲ παντὸς τοῦ λαοῦ εἶπεν τοῖς μαθηταῖς
[αὐτοῦ][5], 46 Προσέχετε ἀπὸ τῶν γραμματέων τῶν θελόντων περιπατεῖν ἐν στολαῖς καὶ φιλούντων ἀσπασμοὺς ἐν
ταῖς ἀγοραῖς καὶ πρωτοκαθεδρίας ἐν ταῖς συναγωγαῖς
καὶ πρωτοκλισίας ἐν τοῖς δείπνοις,[b] 47 οἳ κατεσθίουσιν
τὰς οἰκίας τῶν χηρῶν καὶ προφάσει μακρὰ προσεύχονται·[b]
οὗτοι λήμψονται περισσότερον κρίμα.

The Widow's Offering
(Mk 12.41–44)

21 Ἀναβλέψας δὲ εἶδεν τοὺς βάλλοντας εἰς τὸ γαζοφυ-
λάκιον τὰ δῶρα αὐτῶν πλουσίους. 2 εἶδεν δέ τινα χήραν
πενιχρὰν βάλλουσαν ἐκεῖ λεπτὰ δύο, 3 καὶ εἶπεν, Ἀληθῶς λέγω ὑμῖν ὅτι ἡ χήρα αὕτη ἡ πτωχὴ πλεῖον πάντων
ἔβαλεν· 4 πάντες γὰρ οὗτοι ἐκ τοῦ περισσεύοντος αὐτοῖς
ἔβαλον εἰς τὰ δῶρα[1], αὕτη δὲ ἐκ τοῦ ὑστερήματος αὐτῆς
πάντα τὸν βίον ὃν εἶχεν ἔβαλεν.

---

[5] 45 {C} τοῖς μαθηταῖς αὐτοῦ (see Mt 23.1) ℵ A K L P W Δ Θ Π Ψ
063 f[1] f[13] 33 565 700 892 1009 1010 1071 1079 1195 1216 1230 1241 1242 1253
1344 1365 1546 1646 2148 2174 Byz it[a,aur,c,e,f,ff2,i,q,r1] vg syr[c,s,p,h] cop[sa,bo]
goth geo ∥ τοῖς μαθηταῖς B D it[d,1] arm ∥ τοῖς ἑαυτοῦ μαθηταῖς Γ 235
Lect ∥ πρὸς αὐτούς Q

[1] 4 {B} δῶρα ℵ B L X f[1] 1241 l[1579] syr[c,s,pal] cop[sa,bo] geo Cyril ∥ δῶρα
τοῦ θεοῦ A D K W Δ Θ Π Ψ 063 0102[vid] f[13] 33 565 700 892 1009 1010 1071
1079 1195 1216 1230 1242 1253 1344 1365 1546 1646 2148 2174 Byz Lect
it[a,aur,c,d,e,f,ff2,i,l,q,r1,s] vg syr[p,h] arm (eth) Diatessaron Origen Cyprian
Basil ∥ δῶρα αὐτῶν τοῦ θεοῦ l[1663]

[b h] 46–47 b minor, b major: WH Bov Nes BF[2] AV RV ASV RSV TT Zür Luth Jer Seg ∥ b major,
b minor: NEB ∥ b major, b major: TR

3–4 2 Cor 8.12

---

43 Until I put your enemies
    As a footstool under your feet.'
44 David, then, called him 'Lord.' How
can the Messiah be David's descendant?"

Jesus Warns against the
Teachers of the Law
(Also Matt. 23.1–36; Mark 12.38–40)

45 As the whole crowd listened to him,
Jesus said to his disciples: 46 "Watch
out for the teachers of the Law, who
like to walk around in their long robes,
and love to be greeted with respect in
the market place; who choose the reserved seats in the synagogues and the
best places at feasts; 47 who take advantage of widows and rob them of
their homes, then make a show of saying
long prayers! Their punishment will be
all the worse!"

The Widow's Offering
(Also Mark 12.41–44)

21 Jesus looked around and saw rich
men dropping their gifts in the Temple
treasury, 2 and he also saw a very poor
widow dropping in two little copper coins.
3 And he said: "I tell you that this poor
widow has really put in more than all
the others. 4 For the others offered their
gifts from what they had to spare of their
riches; but she, poor as she is, gave all
she had to live on."

Jesus Speaks of the Destruction
of the Temple
(Also Matt. 24.1–2; Mark 13.1–2)

5 Some of them were talking about the Temple, how beautiful it looked with its fine stones and the gifts offered to God. Jesus said, 6 "All this you see — the time will come when not a single stone here will be left in its place; every one will be thrown down."

Troubles and Persecutions
(Also Matt. 24.3–14; Mark 13.3–13)

7 "Teacher," they asked, "when will this be? And what is the sign that will show that the time has come for it to happen?"
8 Jesus said: "Watch out; don't be fooled. For many men will come in my name saying, 'I am he!' and, 'The time has come!' But don't follow them. 9 Don't be afraid when you hear of wars and revolutions; such things must happen first, but they do not mean that the end is near." 10 He went on to say: "One country will fight another country, one kingdom will attack another kingdom; 11 there will be terrible earthquakes, famines, and plagues everywhere; there will be awful things and great signs from the sky.

The Destruction of the Temple Foretold
(Mt 24.1–2; Mk 13.1–2)

5 Καί τινων λεγόντων περὶ τοῦ ἱεροῦ, ὅτι λίθοις καλοῖς καὶ ἀναθήμασιν κεκόσμηται, εἶπεν, 6 Ταῦτα ἃ θεωρεῖτε, ἐλεύσονται ἡμέραι ἐν αἷς οὐκ ἀφεθήσεται λίθος ἐπὶ λίθῳ[2] ὃς οὐ καταλυθήσεται.

Signs and Persecutions
(Mt 24.3–14; Mk 13.3–13)

7 Ἐπηρώτησαν δὲ αὐτὸν λέγοντες, Διδάσκαλε, πότε οὖν ταῦτα ἔσται,[a] καὶ τί τὸ σημεῖον ὅταν μέλλῃ ταῦτα γίνεσθαι;[a] 8 ὁ δὲ εἶπεν, Βλέπετε μὴ πλανηθῆτε· πολλοὶ γὰρ ἐλεύσονται ἐπὶ τῷ ὀνόματί μου λέγοντες, Ἐγώ εἰμι· καί, Ὁ καιρὸς ἤγγικεν· μὴ πορευθῆτε ὀπίσω αὐτῶν. 9 ὅταν δὲ ἀκούσητε πολέμους καὶ ἀκαταστασίας, μὴ πτοηθῆτε· δεῖ γὰρ ταῦτα γενέσθαι πρῶτον, ἀλλ' οὐκ εὐθέως τὸ τέλος. 10 Τότε ἔλεγεν αὐτοῖς, Ἐγερθήσεται ἔθνος ἐπ' ἔθνος καὶ βασιλεία ἐπὶ βασιλείαν, 11 σεισμοί τε μεγάλοι καὶ κατὰ τόπους λιμοὶ καὶ λοιμοὶ ἔσονται, φόβητρά τε καὶ ἀπ' οὐρανοῦ σημεῖα μεγάλα ἔσται[3].

[2] **6** {C} λίθος ἐπὶ λίθῳ A K Δ Θ Π 063 0102 565 700 1010 1195 1216 1230 1242 1253[vid] 1344 1646 2174 *Byz Lect* syr[p?h?] cop[bo ms] geo ∥ λίθος ἐπὶ λίθον (*see* Mk 13.2) W Ψ 1009 1071 1079 1546 2148 it[aur, f] vg syr[p?h?] ∥ λίθος ἐπὶ λίθῳ ὧδε ℵ* B *f*[13] cop[sa?bo?] ∥ λίθος ἐπὶ λίθον ὧδε ℵ[c] L 892 cop[sa?bo?] ∥ ὧδε λίθος ἐπὶ λίθον (*see* Mt 24.2) X *f*[1] 33 1241 (1365 ἐπὶ λίθῳ) *l*[950] it[e] syr[c,(s)] cop[sa?bo?] arm eth ∥ λίθος ἐπὶ λίθῳ ἐν τοίχῳ ὧδε D it[a,c,d,ff2,i,l,q,r1,s]

[3] **11** {D} καὶ ἀπ' οὐρανοῦ σημεῖα μεγάλα ἔσται B *f*[1] cop[sa?bo?] ∥ καὶ σημεῖα ἀπ' οὐρανοῦ μεγάλα ἔσται A K W X Δ Θ Π Ψ 063 0102 (565 ἔσονται) 700 1009 1010 1079 1195 1216 1230 1242 1253 1344 1365 1546 1646 2148 2174[vid] *Byz Lect* syr[h,pal] cop[sa?bo?] Tertullian ∥ καὶ σημεῖα μεγάλα ἀπ' οὐρανοῦ ἔσται ℵ L (*f*[13] ἔσονται) 33 892 1071 1241 cop[sa?bo?] arm ∥ ἀπ' οὐρανοῦ καὶ σημεῖα μεγάλα ἔσται D it[d,e,f] vg geo[2] (geo[1] *omit* καί) ∥ ἀπ' οὐρανοῦ καὶ σημεῖα μεγάλα ἔσται καὶ χειμῶνες 1012 it[(a),aur,c,ff2,i,l,q,r1,s] syr[(c,s,p),hmg] (eth) Diatessaron (Origen[lat])

[a a] **7** *a* minor, a question: WH RSV Zür Jer Seg ∥ a question, a question: TR Bov Nes BF[2] AV RV ASV NEB TT Luth

6 οὐκ...καταλυθήσεται Lk 19.44　　　**8** Ὁ καιρὸς ἤγγικεν Dn 7.22; Php 4.5　　　**9** δεῖ... γενέσθαι Dn 2.28　　　**10** Ἐγερθήσεται...βασιλείαν Is 19.2; 2 Chr 15.6

12 πρὸ δὲ τούτων πάντων ἐπιβαλοῦσιν ἐφ᾽ ὑμᾶς τὰς χεῖρας αὐτῶν καὶ διώξουσιν, παραδιδόντες εἰς τὰς συναγωγὰς καὶ φυλακάς, ἀπαγομένους ἐπὶ βασιλεῖς καὶ ἡγεμόνας ἕνεκεν τοῦ ὀνόματός μου· 13 ἀποβήσεται ὑμῖν εἰς μαρτύριον. 14 θέτε οὖν ἐν ταῖς καρδίαις ὑμῶν μὴ προμελετᾶν ἀπολογηθῆναι, 15 ἐγὼ γὰρ δώσω ὑμῖν στόμα καὶ σοφίαν ᾗ οὐ δυνήσονται ἀντιστῆναι ἢ ἀντειπεῖν ἅπαντες οἱ ἀντικείμενοι ὑμῖν. 16 παραδοθήσεσθε δὲ καὶ ὑπὸ γονέων καὶ ἀδελφῶν καὶ συγγενῶν καὶ φίλων, καὶ θανατώσουσιν ἐξ ὑμῶν, 17 καὶ ἔσεσθε μισούμενοι ὑπὸ πάντων διὰ τὸ ὄνομά μου. 18 καὶ θρὶξ ἐκ τῆς κεφαλῆς ὑμῶν οὐ μὴ ἀπόληται. 19 ἐν τῇ ὑπομονῇ ὑμῶν κτήσασθε[4] τὰς ψυχὰς ὑμῶν.

The Destruction of Jerusalem Foretold
(Mt 24.15–21; Mk 13.14–19)

20 Ὅταν δὲ ἴδητε κυκλουμένην ὑπὸ στρατοπέδων Ἰερουσαλήμ, τότε γνῶτε ὅτι ἤγγικεν ἡ ἐρήμωσις αὐτῆς. 21 τότε οἱ ἐν τῇ Ἰουδαίᾳ φευγέτωσαν εἰς τὰ ὄρη, καὶ οἱ ἐν μέσῳ αὐτῆς ἐκχωρείτωσαν, καὶ οἱ ἐν ταῖς χώραις μὴ εἰσερχέσθωσαν εἰς αὐτήν, 22 ὅτι ἡμέραι ἐκδικήσεως αὐταί εἰσιν τοῦ πλησθῆναι πάντα τὰ γεγραμμένα. 23 οὐαὶ ταῖς ἐν γαστρὶ ἐχούσαις καὶ ταῖς θηλαζούσαις ἐν ἐκείναις ταῖς ἡμέραις· ἔσται γὰρ ἀνάγκη μεγάλη ἐπὶ τῆς γῆς καὶ ὀργὴ τῷ λαῷ τούτῳ, 24 καὶ πεσοῦνται στόματι μαχαίρης καὶ αἰχμαλωτισθήσονται εἰς τὰ ἔθνη πάντα, καὶ Ἰερου-

---

[4] **19** {D} κτήσασθε ℵ D K L W X Δ Π Ψ 063 *f*[1] 565 700 892 1009 1010 1071 1079 1216 1230 1241 1242 1344 1365 1546 1646 2148 2174 *Byz Lect l*[547m] it[d,l] cop[bo mss] Basil Apostolic Constitutions Macarius Cyril ‖ κτήσεσθε A B Θ *f*[13] 33 1195 (1253 κτίσησθε) *l*[150] it[a,c,e,f,ff2,l,q,rl,s] vg syr[c,s,p,h,(pal)] cop[sa,bo mss] arm eth geo Marcion Tertullian Origen Macarius ‖ σώσετε Marcion

---

12 παραδιδόντες...ἡγεμόνας Mt 10.18; Lk 12.11   **14–15** Mt 10.19; Lk 12.11–12   **15** Ac 6.10   **16–18** Mt 10.21–22   **18** 1 Sm 14.45; Lk 12.7   **22** ἡμέραι ἐκδικήσεως Dt 32.35; Ho 9.7; Jr 46.10   **23** ἀνάγκη μεγάλη 1 Cor 7.26   **24** πεσοῦνται...μαχαίρης Jr 21.7; Sir 28.18   πεσοῦνται...πάντα Ezr 9.7   Ἰερουσαλήμ...ὑπὸ ἐθνῶν Zch 12.3 LXX; Ps 79.1; Is 63.18; Dn 9.26; 1 Macc 3.45, 51

---

12 "Before all these things take place, however, you will be arrested and persecuted; you will be handed over to trial in synagogues and be put in prison; you will be brought before kings and rulers for my sake. 13 This will be your chance to tell the Good News. 14 Make up your minds ahead of time not to worry about how you will defend yourselves; 15 for I will give you such words and wisdom that none of your enemies will be able to resist or deny what you say. 16 You will be handed over by your parents, your brothers, your relatives, and your friends; they will put some of you to death. 17 Everyone will hate you because of me. 18 But not a single hair from your heads will be lost. 19 Hold firm, for this is how you will save yourselves."

Jesus Speaks of the Destruction of Jerusalem
(Also Matt. 24.15–21; Mark 13.14–19)

20 "When you see Jerusalem surrounded by armies, then you will know that soon she will be destroyed. 21 Then those who are in Judea must run away to the hills; those who are in the city must leave, and those who are out in the country must not go into the city. 22 For these are 'The Days of Punishment,' to make come true all that the Scriptures say. 23 How terrible it will be in those days for women who are pregnant, and for mothers with little babies! Terrible distress will come upon this land, and God's wrath will be against this people. 24 They will be killed by the sword, and taken as

prisoners to all countries, and the heathen will trample over Jerusalem until their time is up.''

The Coming of the Son of Man
(Also Matt. 24.29–31; Mark 13.24–27)

25 "There will be signs in the sun, the moon, and the stars. On earth, whole countries will be in despair, afraid of the roar of the sea and the raging tides. 26 Men will faint from fear as they wait for what is coming over the whole earth; for the powers in space will be driven from their course. 27 Then the Son of Man will appear, coming in a cloud with great power and glory. 28 When these things begin to happen, stand up and raise your heads, for your salvation is near.''

The Lesson of the Fig Tree
(Also Matt. 24.32–35; Mark 13.28–31)

29 Then Jesus told them this parable: "Remember the fig tree and all the other trees. 30 When you see their leaves beginning to appear you know that summer is near. 31 In the same way, when you see these things happening, you will know that the Kingdom of God is about to come.

32 "Remember this! All these things will take place before the people now living have all died. 33 Heaven and earth will pass away; my words will never pass away.''

The Need to Watch

34 "Watch yourselves! Don't let yourselves become occupied with too much feasting and strong drink, and the worries of this life, or that Day may come on you suddenly. 35 For it will come like a

σαλὴμ ἔσται πατουμένη ὑπὸ ἐθνῶν, ἄχρι οὗ πληρωθῶσιν καιροὶ ἐθνῶν.

The Coming of the Son of Man
(Mt 24.29–31; Mk 13.24–27)

25 Καὶ ἔσονται σημεῖα ἐν ἡλίῳ καὶ σελήνῃ καὶ ἄστροις, καὶ ἐπὶ τῆς γῆς συνοχὴ ἐθνῶν ἐν ἀπορίᾳ ἤχους θαλάσσης καὶ σάλου, 26 ἀποψυχόντων ἀνθρώπων ἀπὸ φόβου καὶ προσδοκίας τῶν ἐπερχομένων τῇ οἰκουμένῃ, **αἱ γὰρ δυνάμεις τῶν οὐρανῶν** σαλευθήσονται. 27 καὶ τότε ὄψονται **τὸν υἱὸν τοῦ ἀνθρώπου ἐρχόμενον ἐν νεφέλῃ** μετὰ δυνάμεως καὶ δόξης πολλῆς. 28 ἀρχομένων δὲ τούτων γίνεσθαι ἀνακύψατε καὶ ἐπάρατε τὰς κεφαλὰς ὑμῶν, διότι ἐγγίζει ἡ ἀπολύτρωσις ὑμῶν.

The Lesson of the Fig Tree
(Mt 24.32–35; Mk 13.28–31)

29 Καὶ εἶπεν παραβολὴν αὐτοῖς· Ἴδετε τὴν συκῆν καὶ πάντα τὰ δένδρα· 30 ὅταν προβάλωσιν ἤδη, βλέποντες ἀφ᾽ ἑαυτῶν γινώσκετε ὅτι ἤδη ἐγγὺς τὸ θέρος ἐστίν· 31 οὕτως καὶ ὑμεῖς, ὅταν ἴδητε ταῦτα γινόμενα, γινώσκετε ὅτι ἐγγύς ἐστιν ἡ βασιλεία τοῦ θεοῦ. 32 ἀμὴν λέγω ὑμῖν ὅτι οὐ μὴ παρέλθῃ ἡ γενεὰ αὕτη ἕως ἂν πάντα γένηται. 33 ὁ οὐρανὸς καὶ ἡ γῆ παρελεύσονται, οἱ δὲ λόγοι μου οὐ μὴ παρελεύσονται.

Exhortation to Watch

34 Προσέχετε δὲ ἑαυτοῖς μήποτε βαρηθῶσιν ὑμῶν αἱ καρδίαι ἐν κραιπάλῃ καὶ μέθῃ καὶ μερίμναις βιωτικαῖς, καὶ ἐπιστῇ ἐφ᾽ ὑμᾶς αἰφνίδιος ἡ ἡμέρα ἐκείνη· 35 ὡς

---

24 ἄχρι...ἐθνῶν Dn 12.7; Tob 14.5; Ro 11.25; Re 11.2   **25** σημεῖα...ἄστροις Is 13.10; Eze 32.7; Jl 2.30–31; Re 6.12–13   συνοχὴ...σάλου Ps 46.2–3; 65.7; Is 24.19 LXX; Wsd 5.22   **26** δυνάμεις...σαλευθήσονται Hg 2.6, 21   **27** τὸν υἱὸν...νεφέλῃ Dn 7.13; Mt 26.64; Re 1.7   **28** ἐγγίζει...ὑμῶν Ro 13.11; En 51.2   **33** Lk 16.17   **34** Mt 24.48–50; Lk 17.27   ἐπιστῇ...ἐκείνη 1 Th 5.3   **35** Is 24.17

παγὶς γὰρ ἐπελεύσεται⁵ ἐπὶ πάντας τοὺς καθημένους ἐπὶ πρόσωπον πάσης τῆς γῆς. 36 ἀγρυπνεῖτε δὲ ἐν παντὶ καιρῷ δεόμενοι ἵνα κατισχύσητε ἐκφυγεῖν ταῦτα πάντα τὰ μέλλοντα γίνεσθαι, καὶ σταθῆναι ἔμπροσθεν τοῦ υἱοῦ τοῦ ἀνθρώπου.

37 ⁵Ἦν δὲ τὰς ἡμέρας ἐν τῷ ἱερῷ διδάσκων, τὰς δὲ νύκτας ἐξερχόμενος ηὐλίζετο εἰς τὸ ὄρος τὸ καλούμενον Ἐλαιῶν· 38 καὶ πᾶς ὁ λαὸς ὤρθριζεν πρὸς αὐτὸν ἐν τῷ ἱερῷ ἀκούειν αὐτοῦ.⁶

The Plot to Kill Jesus
(Mt 26.1–5, 14–16; Mk 14.1–2, 10–11; Jn 11.45–53)

22 Ἤγγιζεν δὲ ἡ ἑορτὴ τῶν ἀζύμων ἡ λεγομένη πάσχα. 2 καὶ ἐζήτουν οἱ ἀρχιερεῖς καὶ οἱ γραμματεῖς τὸ πῶς ἀνέλωσιν αὐτόν, ἐφοβοῦντο γὰρ τὸν λαόν. 3 Εἰσῆλθεν δὲ Σατανᾶς εἰς Ἰούδαν τὸν καλούμενον Ἰσκαριώτην, ὄντα ἐκ τοῦ ἀριθμοῦ τῶν δώδεκα· 4 καὶ ἀπελθὼν συνελάλησεν τοῖς ἀρχιερεῦσιν καὶ στρατηγοῖς τὸ πῶς αὐτοῖς παραδῷ αὐτόν. 5 καὶ ἐχάρησαν καὶ συνέθεντο αὐτῷ ἀργύριον δοῦναι. 6 καὶ ἐξωμολόγησεν, καὶ ἐζήτει εὐκαιρίαν τοῦ παραδοῦναι αὐτὸν ἄτερ ὄχλου αὐτοῖς.

---

⁵ 35 {C} · ὡς παγὶς γὰρ ἐπελεύσεται A C K W X Δ Θ Π Ψ f¹ f¹³ 33 565 700 892 1009 1010 1071 1079 1195 1216 1230 (1241 1242 2148 ἐλεύσεται) 1253 1344 1365 1546 1646 2174 Byz Lect itaur,f,lᶜ,q,rl vg syrᶜ,s,p,h,pal arm (eth) geo Diatessaron Irenaeuslat Eusebius Basil ‖ ὡς παγίς. ἐπεισελεύσεται γὰρ ℵ* (ℵᶜ L ἐπελεύσεται) B D 0179 ita,b,c,d,e,ff²,i,1* copsa,bo Marcion Tertullian Methodius Jerome Cyril

⁶ 38 {A} αὐτοῦ. ℵ A B C (D αὐτοῦ before ἐν τῷ ἱερῷ) K L W X Δ Θ Π Ψ 0179 f¹ 565 700 892 1009 1010 1071 1079 1195 1216 1230 1241 1242 1253 1344 1365 1546 1646 2148 2174 Byz Lect ita,aur,b,c,d,e,f,ff²,i,1,q,rl vg syrᶜ,s,p,h copsa,bo arm geo ‖ αὐτοῦ. plus John 7.53—8.11 f¹³

36 ἀγρυπνεῖτε κπιρῷ Mk 13.33 σταθῆναι ἀνθρώπου Re 6.17   37 ⁵Ἦν διδάσκων Lk 19.47 τὰς δὲ...Ἐλαιῶν Lk 22.39
22 1 ἑορτὴ...πάσχα Ex 12.1–27   2 ἐζήτουν...λαόν Mt 21.46; Mk 12.12; 14.1–2; Lk 19.47–48; 20.19; Jn 5.18; 7.30   3 Ἰούδαν...δώδεκα Ac 1.17

---

36 Be on watch and pray always that you will have the strength to go safely through all these things that will happen, and to stand before the Son of Man." **37** Jesus spent those days teaching in the Temple, and when evening came he would go out and spend the night on the Mount of Olives. **38** All the people would go to the Temple early in the morning to listen to him.

The Plot against Jesus
(Also Matt. 26.1–5; Mark 14.1–2; John 11.45–53)

22 The time was near for the Feast of Unleavened Bread, which is called the Passover. **2** The chief priests and the teachers of the Law were trying to find some way of killing Jesus; for they were afraid of the people.

Judas Agrees to Betray Jesus
(Also Matt. 26.14–16; Mark 14.10–11)

3 Then Satan went into Judas, called Iscariot, who was one of the twelve disciples. **4** So Judas went off and spoke with the chief priests and the officers of the Temple guard about how he could hand Jesus over to them. **5** They were pleased and offered to pay him money. **6** Judas agreed to it and started looking for a good chance to betray Jesus to them without the people knowing about it.

Jesus Prepares to Eat the Passover Meal
(Also Matt. 26.17–25; Mark 14.12–21;
John 13.21–30)

[7] The day came during the Feast of Unleavened Bread when the lambs for the Passover meal had to be killed. [8] Jesus sent Peter and John with these instructions: "Go and get our Passover supper ready for us to eat." [9] "Where do you want us to get it ready?" they asked him. [10] He said: "Listen! As you go into the city a man carrying a jar of water will meet you. Follow him into the house that he enters, [11] and say to the owner of the house: 'The Teacher says to you, Where is the room where my disciples and I will eat the Passover supper?' [12] He will show you a large furnished room upstairs, where you will get everything ready." [13] They went off and found everything just as Jesus had told them, and prepared the Passover supper.

The Lord's Supper
(Also Matt. 26.26–30; Mark 14.22–26;
1 Cor. 11.23–25)

[14] When the hour came, Jesus took his place at the table with the apostles. [15] And he said to them: "I have wanted so much to eat this Passover meal with you before I suffer! [16] For I tell you, I will never eat it until it is given its real meaning in the Kingdom of God." [17] Then Jesus took the cup, gave thanks to God, and said, "Take this and share it among yourselves; [18] for I tell you

The Preparation of the Passover
(Mt 26.17–25; Mk 14.12–21; Jn 13.21–30)

7 Ἦλθεν δὲ ἡ ἡμέρα τῶν ἀζύμων, [ἐν] ᾗ ἔδει θύεσθαι τὸ πάσχα. **8** καὶ ἀπέστειλεν Πέτρον καὶ Ἰωάννην εἰπών, Πορευθέντες ἑτοιμάσατε ἡμῖν τὸ πάσχα ἵνα φάγωμεν. **9** οἱ δὲ εἶπαν αὐτῷ, Ποῦ θέλεις ἑτοιμάσωμεν; **10** ὁ δὲ εἶπεν αὐτοῖς, Ἰδοὺ εἰσελθόντων ὑμῶν εἰς τὴν πόλιν συναντήσει ὑμῖν ἄνθρωπος κεράμιον ὕδατος βαστάζων· ἀκολουθήσατε αὐτῷ εἰς τὴν οἰκίαν εἰς ἣν εἰσπορεύεται. **11** καὶ ἐρεῖτε τῷ οἰκοδεσπότῃ τῆς οἰκίας, Λέγει σοι ὁ διδάσκαλος, Ποῦ ἐστιν τὸ κατάλυμα ὅπου τὸ πάσχα μετὰ τῶν μαθητῶν μου φάγω; **12** κἀκεῖνος ὑμῖν δείξει ἀνάγαιον μέγα ἐστρωμένον· ἐκεῖ ἑτοιμάσατε. **13** ἀπελθόντες δὲ εὗρον καθὼς εἰρήκει αὐτοῖς, καὶ ἡτοίμασαν τὸ πάσχα.

The Institution of the Lord's Supper
(Mt 26.26–30; Mk 14.22–26; 1 Cor 11.23–25)

14 Καὶ ὅτε ἐγένετο ἡ ὥρα, ἀνέπεσεν καὶ οἱ ἀπόστολοι σὺν αὐτῷ. **15** καὶ εἶπεν πρὸς αὐτούς, Ἐπιθυμίᾳ ἐπεθύμησα τοῦτο τὸ πάσχα φαγεῖν μεθ' ὑμῶν πρὸ τοῦ με παθεῖν· **16** λέγω γὰρ ὑμῖν ὅτι οὐ μὴ φάγω[1] αὐτὸ ἕως ὅτου πληρωθῇ ἐν τῇ βασιλείᾳ τοῦ θεοῦ. **17** καὶ δεξάμενος ποτήριον εὐχαριστήσας εἶπεν, Λάβετε τοῦτο καὶ διαμερίσατε εἰς ἑαυτούς·[2] **18** λέγω γὰρ ὑμῖν [ὅτι] οὐ μὴ πίω

---

[1] **16** {C} ὅτι οὐ μὴ φάγω 𝔭⁷⁵ᵛⁱᵈ ℵ A B L Θ ƒ¹ 1241 1253 *l*⁷⁰ᵖᵗ,¹⁸⁵ᵖᵗ,³⁰³,⁹⁵⁰ᵖᵗ,¹²³¹,¹⁶⁶³ itᵃ copˢᵃ,ᵇᵒ ‖ οὐκέτι μὴ φάγομαι Dᵍʳ ‖ οὐκέτι οὐ μὴ φάγω C* X itᵈ,ˡ,ʳˡ geo ‖ ὅτι οὐκέτι οὐ μὴ φάγω (*see* Mk 14.25) C² K P W Δ Π Ψ 063 ƒ¹³ 565 700 892 1009 1010 1071 1079 1195 1216 1230 1242 1344 1365 1546 1646 2148 2174 *Byz Lect* *l*⁷⁰ᵖᵗ,¹⁸⁵ᵖᵗ,⁹⁵⁰ᵖᵗ itᵃᵘʳ,ᵇ,ᶜ,ᵉ,ᶠ,ff²,ⁱ,q vg syrᶜ,ˢ,ᵖ,ʰ,ᵖᵃˡ arm eth Diatessaronᵃ,ⁿ,ᵛ Origenˡᵃᵗ

[2] **17–20** {B} *verses 17, 18, 19a (omitting 19b–20:* τὸ ὑπὲρ ὑμῶν...ἐκχυν-

---

7 ἡ ἡμέρα...πάσχα Ex 12.6, 14, 15   **8** ἑτοιμάσατε...φάγωμεν Ex 12.8–11
13 ἀπελθόντες...αὐτοῖς Lk 19.32   **16** οὐ...θεοῦ Lk 13.29

ἀπὸ τοῦ νῦν ἀπὸ τοῦ γενήματος τῆς ἀμπέλου ἕως οὗ ἡ βασιλεία τοῦ θεοῦ ἔλθῃ.² 19 καὶ λαβὼν ἄρτον εὐχαριστήσας ἔκλασεν καὶ ἔδωκεν αὐτοῖς λέγων, Τοῦτό ἐστιν τὸ σῶμά μου ⟦τὸ ὑπὲρ ὑμῶν διδόμενον· τοῦτο ποιεῖτε εἰς τὴν ἐμὴν ἀνάμνησιν.² 20 καὶ τὸ ποτήριον ὡσαύτως μετὰ τὸ δειπνῆσαι, λέγων, Τοῦτο τὸ ποτήριον ἡ καινὴ διαθήκη ἐν τῷ αἵματί μου, τὸ ὑπὲρ ὑμῶν ἐκχυννόμενον⟧.² 21 πλὴν ἰδοὺ ἡ χεὶρ τοῦ παραδιδόντος με μετ’ ἐμοῦ ἐπὶ τῆς τραπέζης· 22 ὅτι ὁ υἱὸς μὲν τοῦ ἀνθρώπου κατὰ τὸ ὡρισμένον πορεύεται, πλὴν οὐαὶ τῷ ἀνθρώπῳ ἐκείνῳ δι’ οὗ παραδίδοται. 23 καὶ αὐτοὶ ἤρξαντο συζητεῖν πρὸς ἑαυτοὺς τὸ τίς ἄρα εἴη ἐξ αὐτῶν ὁ τοῦτο μέλλων πράσσειν.

The Dispute about Greatness

24 Ἐγένετο δὲ καὶ φιλονεικία ἐν αὐτοῖς, τὸ τίς αὐτῶν δοκεῖ εἶναι μείζων. 25 ὁ δὲ εἶπεν αὐτοῖς, Οἱ βασιλεῖς τῶν ἐθνῶν κυριεύουσιν αὐτῶν καὶ οἱ ἐξουσιάζοντες αὐτῶν εὐεργέται καλοῦνται. 26 ὑμεῖς δὲ οὐχ οὕτως, ἀλλ’ ὁ μείζων ἐν ὑμῖν γινέσθω ὡς ὁ νεώτερος, καὶ ὁ ἡγούμενος ὡς ὁ διακονῶν. 27 τίς γὰρ μείζων, ὁ ἀνακείμενος ἢ ὁ διακονῶν; οὐχὶ ὁ ἀνακείμενος; ἐγὼ δὲ ἐν μέσῳ ὑμῶν εἰμι ὡς ὁ διακονῶν. 28 ὑμεῖς δέ ἐστε οἱ διαμεμενηκότες μετ’ ἐμοῦ ἐν τοῖς πειρασμοῖς μου·

νόμενον) D it[a,d,ff2,i,l] ‖ verses 17, 18, 19, 20 𝔓75 ℵ A B C K L T[vid] W X Δ Θ Π Ψ 063 f¹ f¹³ 565 700 892 1009 1010 1071 1079 1195 1216 1230 1241 1242 1253 1344 1365 1546 1646 2148 2174 Byz Lect it[aur,c,f,q,r1] vg syr[h,pal] cop[sa,bo] arm geo ‖ verses 19a (καὶ λαβὼν...σῶμά μου), 17, 18 it[b,e] ‖ verses 19, 17, 18 syr[c] ‖ verses 19, 20 l³² syr[p] cop[boms] ‖ verses 19, 20a (μετὰ τὸ δειπνῆσαι), 17, 20b (τοῦτό μου τὸ αἷμα ἡ καινὴ διαθήκη), 18 syr[s]

---

19 λαβὼν...αὐτοῖς Lk 24.30; Ac 27.35   20 καινὴ...αἵματι Ex 24.8; Jr 31.31; 32.40; Zch 9.11 21 ἡ χεὶρ...τραπέζης Ps 41.9; Jn 13.21   23 Jn 13.22   24 τὸ...μείζων Mt 18.1; Mk 9.34; Lk 9.46   25-27 Mt 20.25-27; Mk 10.42-44   26 ὁ μείζων...διακονῶν Mt 23.11; Mk 9.35 27 Jn 13.4-16

---

that I will not drink this wine from now on until the Kingdom of God comes.'' [19] Then he took the bread, gave thanks to God, broke it, and gave it to them, saying, "This is my body [which is given for you. Do this in memory of me." [20] In the same way he gave them the cup, after the supper, saying, "This cup is God's new covenant sealed with my blood which is poured out for you].

[21] "But, look! The one who betrays me is here at the table with me! [22] For the Son of Man will die as God has decided it; but how terrible for that man who betrays him!" [23] Then they began to ask among themselves which one of them it could be who was going to do this.

he Argument about Greatness

[24] An argument came up among the disciples as to which one of them should be thought of as the greatest. [25] Jesus said to them: "The kings of this world have power over their people, and the rulers are called 'Friends of the People.' [26] But this is not the way it is with you; rather, the greatest one among you must be like the youngest, and the leader must be like the servant. [27] Who is greater, the one who sits down to eat or the one who serves him? The one who sits down, of course. But I am among you as one who serves.

[28] "You have stayed with me all

through my trials; ²⁹ and just as my Father has given me the right to rule, so I will make the same agreement with you. ³⁰ You will eat and drink at my table in my Kingdom, and you will sit on thrones to judge the twelve tribes of Israel.''

Jesus Predicts Peter's Denial
(Also Matt. 26.31–35; Mark 14.27–31; John 13.36–38)

³¹ "Simon, Simon! Listen! Satan has received permission to test all of you, as a farmer separates the wheat from the chaff. ³² But I have prayed for you, Simon, that your faith will not fail. And when you turn back to me, you must strengthen your brothers.'' ³³ Peter answered, "Lord, I am ready to go to prison with you and to die with you!'' ³⁴ "I tell you, Peter,'' Jesus answered, "the rooster will not crow today until you have said three times that you do not know me.''

Purse, Bag, and Sword

³⁵ Then Jesus said to them, "When I sent you out that time without purse, bag, or shoes, did you lack anything?'' "Not a thing,'' they answered. ³⁶ "But now,'' Jesus said, "whoever has a purse or a bag must take it; and whoever does not have a sword must sell his coat and buy one. ³⁷ For I tell you this: the scripture that says, 'He was included with the criminals,' must come true about me. For that which was written about me is coming true.'' ³⁸ The disciples said, "Look! Here are two swords, Lord!'' "That is enough!'' he answered.

Jesus Prays
(Also Matt. 26.36–46; Mark 14.32–42)

³⁹ Jesus left and went, as he usually did, to the Mount of Olives; and the

29 κἀγὼ διατίθεμαι ὑμῖν^a καθὼς διέθετό μοι ὁ πατήρ μου^a βασιλείαν **30** ἵνα ἔσθητε καὶ πίνητε ἐπὶ τῆς τραπέζης μου ἐν τῇ βασιλείᾳ μου, καὶ καθήσεσθε ἐπὶ θρόνων τὰς δώδεκα φυλὰς κρίνοντες τοῦ Ἰσραήλ.

Peter's Denial Foretold
(Mt 26.31–35; Mk 14.27–31; Jn 13.36–38)

31 Σίμων Σίμων, ἰδοὺ ὁ Σατανᾶς ἐξῃτήσατο ὑμᾶς τοῦ σινιάσαι ὡς τὸν σῖτον· **32** ἐγὼ δὲ ἐδεήθην περὶ σοῦ ἵνα μὴ ἐκλίπῃ ἡ πίστις σου· καὶ σύ ποτε ἐπιστρέψας στήρισον τοὺς ἀδελφούς σου. **33** ὁ δὲ εἶπεν αὐτῷ, Κύριε, μετὰ σοῦ ἕτοιμός εἰμι καὶ εἰς φυλακὴν καὶ εἰς θάνατον πορεύεσθαι. **34** ὁ δὲ εἶπεν, Λέγω σοι, Πέτρε, οὐ φωνήσει σήμερον ἀλέκτωρ ἕως τρίς με ἀπαρνήσῃ εἰδέναι.

Purse, Bag, and Sword

35 Καὶ εἶπεν αὐτοῖς, Ὅτε ἀπέστειλα ὑμᾶς ἄτερ βαλλαντίου καὶ πήρας καὶ ὑποδημάτων, μή τινος ὑστερήσατε; οἱ δὲ εἶπαν, Οὐθενός. **36** εἶπεν δὲ αὐτοῖς, Ἀλλὰ νῦν ὁ ἔχων βαλλάντιον ἀράτω, ὁμοίως καὶ πήραν, καὶ ὁ μὴ ἔχων πωλησάτω τὸ ἱμάτιον αὐτοῦ καὶ ἀγορασάτω μάχαιραν. **37** λέγω γὰρ ὑμῖν ὅτι τοῦτο τὸ γεγραμμένον δεῖ τελεσθῆναι ἐν ἐμοί, τὸ **Καὶ μετὰ ἀνόμων ἐλογίσθη**· καὶ γὰρ τὸ περὶ ἐμοῦ τέλος ἔχει. **38** οἱ δὲ εἶπαν, Κύριε, ἰδοὺ μάχαιραι ὧδε δύο. ὁ δὲ εἶπεν αὐτοῖς, Ἱκανόν ἐστιν.

The Prayer on the Mount of Olives
(Mt 26.36–46; Mk 14.32–42)

39 Καὶ ἐξελθὼν ἐπορεύθη κατὰ τὸ ἔθος εἰς τὸ Ὄρος τῶν Ἐλαιῶν· ἠκολούθησαν δὲ αὐτῷ καὶ οἱ μαθηταί.

$^{a\ a}$ **29** a none, a none: (TR) Bov Nes BF² AV RV ASV NEB? Luth Jer Seg ∥ a minor ,a none: WH RV^{mg} ASV^{mg} RSV TT Zür

---

29 Lk 12.32   **30** καθήσεσθε…Ἰσραήλ Mt 19.28   **31** Σατανᾶς…ὑμᾶς 2 Cor 2.11 σινιάσαι…σῖτον Am 9.9   **33** Κύριε…πορεύεσθαι Lk 22.54   **34** οὐ…εἰδέναι Lk 22.61 **35** Ὅτε…ὑποδημάτων Mt 10.9–10; Mk 6.8–9; Lk 9.3; 10.4   **36** ὁ μή…μάχαιραν Lk 22.49 **37** Καὶ…ἐλογίσθη Is 53.12 (Lk 12.50)   **39** Jn 18.1   ἐξελθὼν…Ἐλαιῶν Lk 21.37

40 γενόμενος δὲ ἐπὶ τοῦ τόπου εἶπεν αὐτοῖς, Προσεύχεσθε
μὴ εἰσελθεῖν εἰς πειρασμόν. 41 καὶ αὐτὸς ἀπεσπάσθη
ἀπ᾽ αὐτῶν ὡσεὶ λίθου βολήν, καὶ θεὶς τὰ γόνατα προσηύχετο 42 λέγων, Πάτερ, εἰ βούλει παρένεγκε τοῦτο τὸ
ποτήριον ἀπ᾽ ἐμοῦ· πλὴν μὴ τὸ θέλημά μου ἀλλὰ τὸ σὸν
γινέσθω.³ 45 καὶ ἀναστὰς ἀπὸ τῆς προσευχῆς ἐλθὼν πρὸς
τοὺς μαθητὰς εὗρεν κοιμωμένους αὐτοὺς ἀπὸ τῆς λύπης,
46 καὶ εἶπεν αὐτοῖς, Τί καθεύδετε; ἀναστάντες προσεύχεσθε,ᵇ ἵνα μὴ εἰσέλθητε εἰς πειρασμόν.

The Betrayal and Arrest of Jesus
(Mt 26.47–56; Mk 14.43–50; Jn 18.3–11)

47 Ἔτι αὐτοῦ λαλοῦντος ἰδοὺ ὄχλος, καὶ ὁ λεγόμενος
Ἰούδας εἷς τῶν δώδεκα προήρχετο αὐτούς, καὶ ἤγγισεν
τῷ Ἰησοῦ φιλῆσαι αὐτόν. 48 Ἰησοῦς δὲ εἶπεν αὐτῷ,
Ἰούδα, φιλήματι τὸν υἱὸν τοῦ ἀνθρώπου παραδίδως;
49 ἰδόντες δὲ οἱ περὶ αὐτὸν τὸ ἐσόμενον εἶπαν, Κύριε,
εἰ πατάξομεν ἐν μαχαίρῃ; 50 καὶ ἐπάταξεν εἷς τις ἐξ
αὐτῶν τοῦ ἀρχιερέως τὸν δοῦλον καὶ ἀφεῖλεν τὸ οὖς

³ 42 {C} *omit verses 43–44* (see Mt 26.39; Mk 14.36) 𝔭⁷⁵ ℵᵃ A B T W
1071* *Lect* *l*⁶⁹ᵖᵗ,⁷⁰ᵖᵗ,²¹¹ᵖᵗ,¹¹²⁷ᵖᵗ itᶠ syrˢ copˢᵃ,ᵇᵒ geo Marcion Clement Origen
mssᵃᶜᶜ·ᵗᵒ ᴴⁱˡᵃʳʸ Athanasius Ambrose mssᵃᶜᶜ·ᵗᵒ ᴱᵖⁱᵖʰᵃⁿⁱᵘˢ mssᵃᶜᶜ·ᵗᵒ ᴶᵉʳᵒᵐᵉ Cyril
John-Damascus ‖ *transpose* Lk 22.43–44 *after* Mt 26.39 *f*¹³ ‖ *transpose* Lk
22.43–45a (καὶ...προσευχῆς) *after* Mt 26.39 *l*⁶⁰,⁶⁹ᵖᵗ,⁷⁰ᵖᵗ,¹¹²⁷ᵖᵗ ‖ *include verses*
43–44 ὤφθη δὲ αὐτῷ ἄγγελος ἀπ᾽ οὐρανοῦ ἐνισχύων αὐτόν. 44 καὶ γενόμενος ἐν ἀγωνίᾳ ἐκτενέστερον προσηύχετο· καὶ ἐγένετο ὁ ἱδρὼς αὐτοῦ ὡσεὶ
θρόμβοι αἵματος καταβαίνοντος ἐπὶ τὴν γῆν (*with minor variations*).
ℵ*,ᵇ D K L X Δ* Θ Π* Ψ *f*¹ 565 700 892* 1009 1010 1071ᵐᵍ 1230 1241 1242
1253 1344 1365 1546 1646 2148 2174 *Byz* *l*¹⁸⁴,²¹¹ᵖᵗ itᵃ,ᵃᵘʳ,ᵇ,ᶜ,ᵈ,ᵉ,ff²,ⁱ,ˡ,q,ʳˡ vg syrᶜ,
ᵖ,ʰ,ᵛᵃˡ arm eth Diatessaronᵃ,ᵉᵃʳᵐ,ⁱ,ⁿ Justin Irenaeus Hippolytus Dionysius
Ariusᵃᶜᶜ·ᵗᵒ ᴱᵖⁱᵖʰᵃⁿⁱᵘˢ Eusebius Hilary Caesarius-Nazianzus Gregory-
Nazianzus Didymus Ps-Dionysius Epiphanius Chrysostom Jerome Augustine Theodoret Leontius Cosmos Facundus ‖ *include verses 43–44*
with asterisks or obeli Δᶜ Πᶜ 892ᶜ ⁱⁿ ᵐᵍ 1079 1195 1216 copᵇᵒᵐˢˢ

ᵇ 46 *b minor:* TR WH Bov Nes BF² AV RV ASV TT Zür? Luth Jer Seg ‖ *b none:* RSV NEB

40 Προσεύχεσθε...πειρασμόν Lk 22.46 42 μὴ...γινέσθω Mt 6.10 46 προσεύχεσθε
...πειρασμόν Lk 22.40 49 πατάξομεν ἐν μαχαίρῃ Lk 22.36 50 Jn 18.26

disciples went with him. 40 When he
came to the place he said to them,
"Pray that you will not fall into temptation." 41 Then he went off from them,
about the distance of a stone's throw,
and knelt down and prayed. 42 "Father,"
he said, "if you will, take this cup away
from me. Not my will, however, but
your will be done." [43 An angel from
heaven appeared to him and strengthened
him. 44 In great anguish he prayed even
more fervently; his sweat was like drops
of blood, falling to the ground.]
45 Rising from his prayer, he went back
to the disciples and found them asleep,
so great was their grief. 46 And he said
to them, "Why are you sleeping? Rise
and pray that you will not fall into
temptation."

The Arrest of Jesus
(Also Matt. 26.47–56; Mark 14.43–50; John 18.3–11)

47 He was still speaking when a crowd
arrived; Judas, one of the twelve disciples, was leading them, and he came
up to Jesus to kiss him. 48 But Jesus
said, "Is it with a kiss, Judas, that you
betray the Son of Man?" 49 When the
disciples who were with Jesus saw what
was going to happen, they said, "Shall
we strike with our swords, Lord?" 50 And
one of them struck the High Priest's

slave and cut off his right ear. [51] But Jesus answered, "Enough of this!" He touched the man's ear and healed him.

[52] Then Jesus said to the chief priests and the officers of the Temple guard and the elders who had come there to get him: "Did you have to come with swords and clubs, as though I were an outlaw? [53] I was with you in the Temple every day, and you did not try to arrest me. But this hour belongs to you and to the power of darkness."

Peter Denies Jesus

(Also Matt. 26.57-58, 69-75; Mark 14.53-54, 66-72; John 18.12-18, 25-27)

[54] They arrested Jesus and took him away into the house of the High Priest; and Peter followed far behind. [55] A fire had been lit in the center of the courtyard, and Peter joined those who were sitting around it. [56] When one of the servant girls saw him sitting there at the fire, she looked straight at him and said, "This man too was with him!" [57] But Peter denied it: "Woman, I don't even know him!" [58] After a little while, a man noticed him and said, "You are one of them, too!" But Peter answered, "Man, I am not!" [59] And about an hour later another man insisted strongly: "There isn't any doubt that this man was with him, because he also is a Galilean!" [60] But Peter answered, "Man, I don't know what you are talking about!" At once, while he was still speaking, a rooster crowed. [61] The Lord turned around and looked straight at Peter, and Peter remembered the Lord's words, how he had said, "Before the rooster crows today, you will say three times

αὐτοῦ τὸ δεξιόν. **51** ἀποκριθεὶς δὲ ὁ Ἰησοῦς εἶπεν, Ἐᾶτε ἕως τούτου· καὶ ἁψάμενος τοῦ ὠτίου ἰάσατο αὐτόν. **52** εἶπεν δὲ Ἰησοῦς[4] πρὸς τοὺς παραγενομένους ἐπ' αὐτὸν ἀρχιερεῖς καὶ στρατηγοὺς τοῦ ἱεροῦ καὶ πρεσβυτέρους, Ὡς ἐπὶ λῃστὴν ἐξήλθατε μετὰ μαχαιρῶν καὶ ξύλων;[c] **53** καθ' ἡμέραν ὄντος μου μεθ' ὑμῶν ἐν τῷ ἱερῷ οὐκ ἐξετείνατε τὰς χεῖρας ἐπ' ἐμέ· ἀλλ' αὕτη ἐστὶν ὑμῶν ἡ ὥρα καὶ ἡ ἐξουσία τοῦ σκότους.

Peter's Denial of Jesus

(Mt 26.57-58, 69-75; Mk 14.53-54, 66-72; Jn 18.12-18, 25-27)

54 Συλλαβόντες δὲ αὐτὸν ἤγαγον καὶ εἰσήγαγον εἰς τὴν οἰκίαν τοῦ ἀρχιερέως· ὁ δὲ Πέτρος ἠκολούθει μακρόθεν. **55** περιαψάντων δὲ πῦρ ἐν μέσῳ τῆς αὐλῆς καὶ συγκαθισάντων ἐκάθητο ὁ Πέτρος μέσος αὐτῶν. **56** ἰδοῦσα δὲ αὐτὸν παιδίσκη τις καθήμενον πρὸς τὸ φῶς καὶ ἀτενίσασα αὐτῷ εἶπεν, Καὶ οὗτος σὺν αὐτῷ ἦν· **57** ὁ δὲ ἠρνήσατο λέγων, Οὐκ οἶδα αὐτόν, γύναι. **58** καὶ μετὰ βραχὺ ἕτερος ἰδὼν αὐτὸν ἔφη, Καὶ σὺ ἐξ αὐτῶν εἶ· ὁ δὲ Πέτρος ἔφη, Ἄνθρωπε, οὐκ εἰμί. **59** καὶ διαστάσης ὡσεὶ ὥρας μιᾶς ἄλλος τις διϊσχυρίζετο λέγων, Ἐπ' ἀληθείας καὶ οὗτος μετ' αὐτοῦ ἦν, καὶ γὰρ Γαλιλαῖός ἐστιν· **60** εἶπεν δὲ ὁ Πέτρος, Ἄνθρωπε, οὐκ οἶδα ὃ λέγεις. καὶ παραχρῆμα ἔτι λαλοῦντος αὐτοῦ ἐφώνησεν ἀλέκτωρ. **61** καὶ στραφεὶς ὁ κύριος ἐνέβλεψεν τῷ Πέτρῳ, καὶ ὑπεμνήσθη ὁ Πέτρος τοῦ ῥήματος τοῦ κυρίου ὡς εἶπεν αὐτῷ ὅτι Πρὶν ἀλέκτορα φωνῆσαι σήμε-

---

[4] **52** {C} Ἰησοῦς 𝔓[75] ℵ A B T Θ ∥ ὁ Ἰησοῦς K L W X Δ Π Ψ *f*[13] 28 565 700 892 1009 1010 1071 1079 1195 1216 1230 1241 1242 1253 1344 1365 1546 1646 2148 2174 *Byz Lect* Origen ∥ Ἰησοῦς *or* ὁ Ἰησοῦς it[a,aur,c,f,ff2,q,r1] vg syr[p,h] cop[sa,bo] geo ∥ *omit* D *f*[1] it[b,d,e,i,l] syr[c,s] arm

[c] **52** *c* question: TR WH Bov Nes BF[2] AV RV ASV RSV NEB TT Jer ∥ *c* statement: Zür Luth Seg

52 Ὡς...ἐξήλθατε Lk 22.37   **53** καθ'...ἱερῷ Lk 19.47; 21.37   οὐκ ἐξετείνατε...ἐμέ Jn 7.30; 8.20   ἡ ἐξουσία τοῦ σκότους Col 1.13   **54** Πέτρος...μακρόθεν Lk 22.33   **61** Πρὶν ...τρίς Lk 22.34

ρον ἀπαρνήσῃ με τρίς· **62** καὶ ἐξελθὼν ἔξω ἔκλαυσεν πικρῶς.[5]

The Mocking and Beating of Jesus
(Mt 26.67–68; Mk 14.65)

63 Καὶ οἱ ἄνδρες οἱ συνέχοντες αὐτὸν ἐνέπαιζον αὐτῷ δέροντες, **64** καὶ περικαλύψαντες αὐτὸν ἐπηρώτων λέγοντες, Προφήτευσον, τίς ἐστιν ὁ παίσας σε; **65** καὶ ἕτερα πολλὰ βλασφημοῦντες ἔλεγον εἰς αὐτόν.

Jesus before the Council
(Mt 26.59–66; Mk 14.55–64; Jn 18.19–24)

66 Καὶ ὡς ἐγένετο ἡμέρα, συνήχθη τὸ πρεσβυτέριον τοῦ λαοῦ, ἀρχιερεῖς τε καὶ γραμματεῖς, καὶ ἀπήγαγον αὐτὸν εἰς τὸ συνέδριον αὐτῶν, **67**[d] λέγοντες, [d]Εἰ σὺ εἶ ὁ Χριστός, εἰπὸν ἡμῖν. [d]εἶπεν δὲ αὐτοῖς, Ἐὰν ὑμῖν εἴπω οὐ μὴ πιστεύσητε· **68** ἐὰν δὲ ἐρωτήσω οὐ μὴ ἀποκριθῆτε[6]. **69** ἀπὸ τοῦ νῦν δὲ ἔσται **ὁ υἱὸς τοῦ ἀνθρώπου καθήμενος ἐκ δεξιῶν τῆς δυνάμεως τοῦ θεοῦ.** **70** εἶπαν δὲ πάντες, Σὺ οὖν εἶ ὁ υἱὸς τοῦ θεοῦ;[e] ὁ δὲ πρὸς αὐτοὺς ἔφη, Ὑμεῖς λέγετε ὅτι[f] ἐγώ εἰμι. **71** οἱ δὲ εἶπαν, Τί ἔτι ἔχομεν μαρτυρίας χρείαν; αὐτοὶ γὰρ ἠκούσαμεν ἀπὸ τοῦ στόματος αὐτοῦ.

---

[5] **62** {C} *include verse 62* (*see* Mt 26.75; Mk 14.72) 𝔭[75] ℵ A B D K L T W X Δ Θ Π Ψ 063 0124 0250 *f*[1] *f*[13] 28 565 700 892 1009 1010 1071 1079 1195 1216 1230 1241 1242 1253 1344 1365 1546 1646 2148 *Byz Lect* it[aur,c,d,f,1c,q] vg syr[c,s,p,h] cop[sa,bo] arm geo ∥ *omit verse 62* 0171[vid] it[a,b,e,ff2,i,1*,r1]

[6] **68** {C} ἀποκριθῆτε 𝔭[75] ℵ B L T 1241 cop[bo] Cyril ∥ ἀποκριθῆτε μοι Θ *f*[1] 1365 cop[sa] Ambrose ∥ ἀποκριθῆτε μοι ἢ ἀπολύσητε A D K W (X ἀπολύσετε) Δ Π Ψ 063 *f*[13] 28 565 700 (892 *omit* μοι) 1009 1010 1071 1079 1195 1216 1230 1242 1253 1344 (1546 *omit* ἢ) 1646 2148 *Byz Lect* it[(a),aur,b,c,d,f,ff2,(i,1),q,r1] vg syr[c,s,p,h] arm geo Diatessaron[a,i,n]

---

d d d **66–67** *d* number 67, *d* no number, *d* no number: TR[ed] WH? Bov Nes BF[2] NEB? TT Zür Luth Jer Seg ∥ *d* no number, *d* number 67, *d* no number: TR[ed] WH? AV RV ASV RSV NEB? ∥ *d* no number, *d* no number, *d* number 67: TR[ed] NEB?

e **70** *e* question: TR WH Bov Nes BF[2] AV RV ASV RSV NEB TT Zür Luth Seg ∥ *e* exclamation: Jer

f **70** *f* indirect: TR? WH? Bov? Nes? BF[2]? AV RV ASV RSV NEB TT Zür Luth? Seg[mg] ∥ *f* causal: RV[mg] ASV[mg] Jer? Seg? ∥ *f* interrogative: WH[mg]

67 Εἰ...Χριστός...ἡμῖν Jn 10.24   Ἐὰν...πιστεύσητε Jn 3.12; 8.45   **69** ὁ υἱὸς...θεοῦ Ps 110.1; Ac 7.56   **70** Σὺ...θεοῦ Mt 4.3, 6; Lk 4.3, 9

---

that you do not know me."   **62** Peter went out and wept bitterly.

Jesus Mocked and Beaten
(Also Matt. 26.67–68; Mark 14.65)

63 The men who were guarding Jesus made fun of him and beat him. **64** They blindfolded him and asked him, "Who hit you? Guess!" **65** And they said many other insulting things to him.

Jesus before the Council
(Also Matt. 26.59–66; Mark 14.55–64; John 18.19–24)

66 When day came, the elders of the Jews, the chief priests, and the teachers of the Law met together, and Jesus was brought to their Council. **67** "Tell us," they said, "are you the Messiah?" He answered: "If I tell you, you will not believe me, **68** and if I ask you a question you will not answer me. **69** But from now on the Son of Man will be seated at the right side of the Almighty God." **70** They all said, "Are you, then, the Son of God?" He answered them, "You say that I am." **71** And they said, "We don't need any witnesses! We ourselves have heard his very own words!"

Jesus before Pilate
(Also Matt. 27.1–2, 11–14; Mark 15.1–5;
John 18.28–38)

23 The whole group rose up and took Jesus before Pilate, ² where they began to accuse him: "We caught this man misleading our people, telling them not to pay taxes to the Emperor and claiming that he himself is Christ, a king." ³ Pilate asked him, "Are you the king of the Jews?" "You say it," answered Jesus. ⁴ Then Pilate said to the chief priests and the crowds, "I find no reason to condemn this man." ⁵ But they insisted even more strongly, "He is starting a riot among the people with his teaching! He began in Galilee, went through all of Judea, and now has come here."

Jesus before Herod

⁶ When Pilate heard this he asked, "Is this man a Galilean?" ⁷ When he learned that Jesus was from the region ruled by Herod, he sent him to Herod, who was also in Jerusalem at that time. ⁸ Herod was very pleased when he saw Jesus, for he had heard about him and had been wanting to see him for a long time; he was hoping to see Jesus perform some miracle. ⁹ So Herod asked „Jesus many questions, but Jesus did not answer a word. ¹⁰ The chief priests and the teachers of the Law stepped forward and made strong accusations against Jesus. ¹¹ Herod and his soldiers made fun of Jesus and treated him with contempt. They put a fine robe on him and sent

Jesus Brought before Pilate
(Mt 27.1–2, 11–14; Mk 15.1–5; Jn 18.28–38)

23 Καὶ ἀναστὰν ἅπαν τὸ πλῆθος αὐτῶν ἤγαγον αὐτὸν ἐπὶ τὸν Πιλᾶτον. 2 ἤρξαντο δὲ κατηγορεῖν αὐτοῦ λέγοντες, Τοῦτον εὕραμεν διαστρέφοντα τὸ ἔθνος ἡμῶν καὶ κωλύοντα φόρους Καίσαρι διδόναι καὶ λέγοντα ἑαυτὸν Χριστὸν βασιλέα εἶναι. 3 ὁ δὲ Πιλᾶτος ἠρώτησεν αὐτὸν λέγων, Σὺ εἶ ὁ βασιλεὺς τῶν Ἰουδαίων; ὁ δὲ ἀποκριθεὶς αὐτῷ ἔφη, Σὺ λέγεις.ᵃ 4 ὁ δὲ Πιλᾶτος εἶπεν πρὸς τοὺς ἀρχιερεῖς καὶ τοὺς ὄχλους, Οὐδὲν εὑρίσκω αἴτιον ἐν τῷ ἀνθρώπῳ τούτῳ. 5 οἱ δὲ ἐπίσχυον λέγοντες ὅτι Ἀνασείει τὸν λαὸν διδάσκων καθ᾽ ὅλης τῆς Ἰουδαίας, καὶ ἀρξάμενος ἀπὸ τῆς Γαλιλαίας ἕως ὧδε.

Jesus before Herod

6 Πιλᾶτος δὲ ἀκούσας ἐπηρώτησεν εἰ ὁ ἄνθρωπος Γαλιλαῖός ἐστιν· 7 καὶ ἐπιγνοὺς ὅτι ἐκ τῆς ἐξουσίας Ἡρῴδου ἐστὶν ἀνέπεμψεν αὐτὸν πρὸς Ἡρῴδην, ὄντα καὶ αὐτὸν ἐν Ἱεροσολύμοις ἐν ταύταις ταῖς ἡμέραις. 8 ὁ δὲ Ἡρῴδης ἰδὼν τὸν Ἰησοῦν ἐχάρη λίαν, ἦν γὰρ ἐξ ἱκανῶν χρόνων θέλων ἰδεῖν αὐτὸν διὰ τὸ ἀκούειν περὶ αὐτοῦ, καὶ ἤλπιζέν τι σημεῖον ἰδεῖν ὑπ᾽ αὐτοῦ γινόμενον. 9 ἐπηρώτα δὲ αὐτὸν ἐν λόγοις ἱκανοῖς· αὐτὸς δὲ οὐδὲν ἀπεκρίνατο αὐτῷ. 10 εἱστήκεισαν δὲ οἱ ἀρχιερεῖς καὶ οἱ γραμματεῖς εὐτόνως κατηγοροῦντες αὐτοῦ. 11 ἐξουθενήσας δὲ αὐτὸν [καὶ] ὁ Ἡρῴδης¹ σὺν τοῖς στρατεύμασιν αὐτοῦ καὶ ἐμπαίξας περιβαλὼν ἐσθῆτα λαμπρὰν

---

¹ 11 {C} καὶ ὁ Ἡρῴδης 𝔭⁷⁵ ℵ L T X Ψ *f*¹³ 1079 1216 *l*⁵⁴⁷ it^{a,d} cop^{bo mss} arm geo¹ ‖ ὁ Ἡρῴδης A B D^{gr} K Δ Θ Π 063 0124 *f*¹ 28 565 700 892 1010 1071 1230 1253 1344 1365ᶜ 1546 1646 2174 *Byz Lect* it^{aur,b,c,e,f,ff²,i,l,q,rl} vg syr^{c,p,h} cop^{sa,bo} geo²? Diatessaron ‖ Ἡρῴδης W 1009 1195 1241 1242 1365* 2148 geo²?

ᵃ 3 *a* statement: TR WH Bov Nes BF² AV RV ASV RSV NEB TT Zür Luth Jer Seg ‖ *a* question: WH^{mg}

2 φόρους Καίσαρι Lk 20.25   3 1 Tm 6.13   7 ἐκ…Ἡρῴδου Lk 3.1   8 ἦν… γινόμενον Lk 9.9

ἀνέπεμψεν αὐτὸν τῷ Πιλάτῳ. 12 ἐγένοντο δὲ φίλοι ὅ τε Ἡρῴδης καὶ ὁ Πιλᾶτος ἐν αὐτῇ τῇ ἡμέρᾳ μετ᾽ ἀλλήλων· προϋπῆρχον γὰρ ἐν ἔχθρᾳ ὄντες πρὸς αὐτούς.

Jesus Sentenced to Die
(Mt 27.15–26; Mk 15.6–15; Jn 18.39—19.16)

13 Πιλᾶτος δὲ συγκαλεσάμενος τοὺς ἀρχιερεῖς καὶ τοὺς ἄρχοντας καὶ τὸν λαὸν 14 εἶπεν πρὸς αὐτούς, Προσηνέγκατέ μοι τὸν ἄνθρωπον τοῦτον ὡς ἀποστρέφοντα τὸν λαόν, καὶ ἰδοὺ ἐγὼ ἐνώπιον ὑμῶν ἀνακρίνας οὐθὲν εὗρον ἐν τῷ ἀνθρώπῳ τούτῳ αἴτιον ὧν κατηγορεῖτε κατ᾽ αὐτοῦ, 15 ἀλλ᾽ οὐδὲ Ἡρῴδης· ἀνέπεμψεν γὰρ αὐτὸν πρὸς ἡμᾶς[2]. καὶ ἰδοὺ οὐδὲν ἄξιον θανάτου ἐστὶν πεπραγμένον αὐτῷ. 16 παιδεύσας οὖν αὐτὸν ἀπολύσω.[3] 18 ἀνέκραγον δὲ παμπληθεὶ λέγοντες, Αἶρε τοῦτον, ἀπόλυσον δὲ ἡμῖν τὸν Βαραββᾶν· 19 ὅστις ἦν διὰ στάσιν τινὰ γενομένην ἐν τῇ πόλει καὶ φόνον βληθεὶς ἐν τῇ φυλακῇ. 20 πάλιν δὲ ὁ Πιλᾶτος προσεφώνησεν αὐτοῖς, θέλων ἀπολῦσαι τὸν Ἰησοῦν· 21 οἱ δὲ ἐπεφώνουν λέγοντες, Σταύρου, σταύρου αὐτόν. 22 ὁ δὲ τρίτον εἶπεν

---

[2] **15** {C} ἀνέπεμψεν γὰρ αὐτὸν πρὸς ἡμᾶς p[75] ℵ B K L T Θ Π (0124 ἀνέπεμψαν) 892 1071 1079 1216 1241 1546 1646 2174 it[aur, f] cop[sa, bo] ‖ ἀνέπεμψεν γὰρ αὐτὸν πρὸς ὑμᾶς f[13] l[185] ‖ ἀνέπεμψα γὰρ ὑμᾶς πρὸς αὐτόν A D W X Δ Ψ 063 f[1] 28 565 700 1009 1010 1195 1230 1242 1344 1365 2148 Byz Lect (l[47] ἀνέπεμψεν, l[547] ἐνέπεμψα and ἡμᾶς) it[a, b, c, d, e, ff2, (l), q, r1] vg syr[h] (eth) Diatessaron[l] ‖ ἀνέπεμψα γὰρ αὐτὸν πρὸς αὐτόν 274 (1253 μεθ᾽ ὑμῶν πρὸς αὐτόν) l[183] syr[c, s, p] arm geo Diatessaron[a, v] ‖ ἀνέπεμψα γὰρ αὐτὸν πρὸς ὑμᾶς 71 248 788 l[299] syr[hmg] ‖ ἀνέπεμψα ὑμᾶς πρὸς αὐτόν 124 174 230 346

[3] **16** {B} *omit verse 17* p[75] A B K L T Π 0124 892* 1079 1241 1546 l[185pt] it[a] cop[sa, bomss] Diatessaron ‖ *include verse 17* ἀνάγκην δὲ εἶχεν ἀπολύειν αὐτοῖς κατὰ ἑορτὴν ἕνα. (*see* Mt 27.15; Mk 15.6) ℵ W X Δ 063 f[1] f[13] 28 565 700 1010 1195 (1216 1230 1253 1646 2174 ἕνα δέσμιον.) 1242 1365 2148 Byz Lect (l[70] *omit* αὐτοῖς) it[aur, b, c, e, f, ff2, l, q, (r1)] vg syr[p, h] cop[bomss] Eusebius ‖ *include verse 17* ἀνάγκην γὰρ ἦχεν κατὰ τὴν ἑορτὴν ἀπολύειν αὐτοῖς ἕνα δεσμιὸν [*sic*] ἤθελον. 1009 ‖ *include verse 17* ἀνάγκην δὲ εἶχεν κατὰ ἑορτὴν ἀπολύειν αὐτοῖς ἕνα. Θ Ψ (892[mg] ἕνα αὐτοῖς) (1071 *omit* αὐτοῖς) 1344 (arm εἶχεν ἕνα...αὐτοῖς.) geo ‖ *include verse 17 after 19* D it[d] syr[c, s] eth

---

him back to Pilate. 12 On that very day Herod and Pilate became friends; they had been enemies before this.

Jesus Sentenced to Death
(Also Matt. 27.15–26; Mark 15.6–15; John 18.39—19.16)

13 Pilate called together the chief priests, the leaders, and the people, 14 and said to them: "You brought this man to me and said that he was misleading the people. Now, I have examined him here in your presence, and I have not found him guilty of any of the bad things you accuse him of. 15 Nor did Herod find him guilty, for he sent him back to us. There is nothing this man has done to deserve death. 16 I will have him whipped, then, and let him go." [17 At each Passover Feast Pilate had to set free one prisoner for them.] 18 The whole crowd cried out, "Kill him! Set Barabbas free for us!" 19 (Barabbas had been put in prison for a riot that had taken place in the city, and for murder.) 20 Pilate wanted to set Jesus free, so he called out to the crowd again. 21 But they shouted back, "To the cross with him! To the cross!" 22 Pilate said to them the third time: "But what crime has he com-

mitted? I cannot find anything he has done to deserve death! I will have him whipped and set him free.'' ²³ But they kept on shouting at the top of their voices that Jesus should be nailed to the cross; and finally their shouting won. ²⁴ So Pilate passed the sentence on Jesus that they were asking for. ²⁵ He set free the man they wanted, the one who had been put in prison for riot and murder, and turned Jesus over to them to do as they wished.

Jesus Nailed to the Cross
(Also Matt. 27.32–44; Mark 15.21–32; John 19.17–27)

²⁶ They took Jesus away. As they went, they met a man named Simon, from Cyrene, who was coming into the city from the country. They seized him, put the cross on him and made him carry it behind Jesus.

²⁷ A large crowd of people followed him; among them were some women who were weeping and wailing for him. ²⁸ Jesus turned to them and said: "Women of Jerusalem! Don't cry for me, but for yourselves and your children. ²⁹ For the days are coming when people will say, 'How lucky are the women who never had children, who never bore babies, who never nursed them!' ³⁰ That will be the time when people will say to the mountains, 'Fall on us!' and to the hills, 'Hide us!' ³¹ For if such things as these are done when the wood is green, what will it be like when it is dry?''

³² They took two others also, both of them criminals, to be put to death with Jesus. ³³ When they came to the place

πρὸς αὐτούς, Τί γὰρ κακὸν ἐποίησεν οὗτος; οὐδὲν αἴτιον θανάτου εὗρον ἐν αὐτῷ· παιδεύσας οὖν αὐτὸν ἀπολύσω. **23** οἱ δὲ ἐπέκειντο φωναῖς μεγάλαις αἰτούμενοι αὐτὸν σταυρωθῆναι, καὶ κατίσχυον αἱ φωναὶ αὐτῶν⁴. **24** καὶ Πιλᾶτος ἐπέκρινεν γενέσθαι τὸ αἴτημα αὐτῶν· **25** ἀπέλυσεν δὲ τὸν διὰ στάσιν καὶ φόνον βεβλημένον εἰς φυλακὴν ὃν ᾐτοῦντο, τὸν δὲ Ἰησοῦν παρέδωκεν τῷ θελήματι αὐτῶν.

The Crucifixion of Jesus
(Mt 27.32–44; Mk 15.21–32; Jn 19.17–27)

26 Καὶ ὡς ἀπήγαγον αὐτόν, ἐπιλαβόμενοι Σίμωνά τινα Κυρηναῖον ἐρχόμενον ἀπ' ἀγροῦ ἐπέθηκαν αὐτῷ τὸν σταυρὸν φέρειν ὄπισθεν τοῦ Ἰησοῦ. **27** Ἠκολούθει δὲ αὐτῷ πολὺ πλῆθος τοῦ λαοῦ καὶ γυναικῶν αἳ ἐκόπτοντο καὶ ἐθρήνουν αὐτόν. **28** στραφεὶς δὲ πρὸς αὐτὰς [ὁ] Ἰησοῦς εἶπεν, Θυγατέρες Ἰερουσαλήμ, μὴ κλαίετε ἐπ' ἐμέ· πλὴν ἐφ' ἑαυτὰς κλαίετε καὶ ἐπὶ τὰ τέκνα ὑμῶν, **29** ὅτι ἰδοὺ ἔρχονται ἡμέραι ἐν αἷς ἐροῦσιν, Μακάριαι αἱ στεῖραι καὶ αἱ κοιλίαι αἳ οὐκ ἐγέννησαν καὶ μαστοὶ οἳ οὐκ ἔθρεψαν.
30 τότε ἄρξονται **λέγειν τοῖς ὄρεσιν,**
    Πέσετε ἐφ' ἡμᾶς,
  καὶ τοῖς βουνοῖς,
    Καλύψατε ἡμᾶς·
31 ὅτι εἰ ἐν τῷ ὑγρῷ ξύλῳ ταῦτα ποιοῦσιν, ἐν τῷ ξηρῷ τί γένηται;
32 Ἤγοντο δὲ καὶ ἕτεροι κακοῦργοι δύο σὺν αὐτῷ ἀναιρεθῆναι. **33** καὶ ὅτε ἦλθον ἐπὶ τὸν τόπον τὸν καλού-

---

⁴ **23** {C} αὐτῶν 𝔭⁷⁵ ℵ B L 0124 1241 *l*²⁴¹ it^(a,aur,b,e,ff²,l) vg cop^(sa,bo) ‖ τῶν ἀρχιερέων eth ‖ αὐτῶν καὶ τῶν ἀρχιερέων A D K P W X Δ Θ Π Ψ 063 0250 *f*¹ *f*¹³ 28 565 700 892 1009 1010 1071 1079 1195 1216 1230 1242 (1253 τῶν ἀρχόντων) 1344 1365 1546 1646 2148 2174 *Byz Lect* it^(c,d,f) syr^(c,s),p,h cop^(boms) arm geo Diatessaron

---

29 Μακάριαι...ἔθρεψαν Lk 21.23   **30** ἄρξονται...Καλύψατε ἡμᾶς Ho 10.8 (Re 6.16)

μενον Κρανίον, ἐκεῖ ἐσταύρωσαν αὐτὸν καὶ τοὺς κακούργους, ὃν μὲν ἐκ δεξιῶν ὃν δὲ ἐξ ἀριστερῶν. 34 [ὁ δὲ Ἰησοῦς ἔλεγεν, Πάτερ, ἄφες αὐτοῖς, οὐ γὰρ οἴδασιν τί ποιοῦσιν.][5] **διαμεριζόμενοι** δὲ **τὰ ἱμάτια αὐτοῦ ἔβαλον κλῆρον.** 35 καὶ εἱστήκει ὁ λαὸς **θεωρῶν.** ἐξεμυκτήριζον δὲ καὶ οἱ ἄρχοντες λέγοντες, Ἄλλους ἔσωσεν, σωσάτω ἑαυτόν, εἰ οὗτός ἐστιν ὁ Χριστὸς[b] τοῦ θεοῦ[b] ὁ ἐκλεκτός. 36 ἐνέπαιξαν δὲ αὐτῷ καὶ οἱ στρατιῶται προσερχόμενοι, **ὄξος** προσφέροντες αὐτῷ 37 καὶ λέγοντες, Εἰ σὺ εἶ ὁ βασιλεὺς τῶν Ἰουδαίων, σῶσον σεαυτόν. 38 ἦν δὲ καὶ ἐπιγραφὴ ἐπ᾽ αὐτῷ[6], Ὁ βασιλεὺς τῶν Ἰουδαίων οὗτος.

[5] **34** {C} ὁ δὲ Ἰησοῦς ἔλεγεν, Πατήρ, ἄφες αὐτοῖς, οὐ γὰρ οἴδασιν τί ποιοῦσιν. ℵ*,c A C D^b (K εἶπεν for ἔλεγεν) L X Δ Π Ψ 0117 0250 f^1 (f^13 omit δέ) 28 33 565 700 892 (1009 ποιῶσιν) 1010 1071 1079 (1195 ἄ for τί) 1216 (1230 1253 Ἰησοῦς ἐσταυρωμένος ἔλεγεν) 1242 1344 1365 1546 1646 2148 2174 Byz Lect it^aur,b,c,e,f,ff2,l,r1 vg syr^(c),p,(h,hmg),pal cop^bomss arm eth geo Hegesippus Marcion Diatessaron^a,earm,i,n Justin Irenaeus^lat Clement Origen^lat Ps-Clement Eusebius Eusebian Canons Ambrosiaster Hilary Basil Apostolic Constitutions Ambrose Chrysostom Jerome Augustine Theodoret John-Damascus // include ὁ δὲ...ποιοῦσιν. with asterisks E // omit p^75 ℵ^vid B D* W Θ 0124 1241 it^a,d syr^s cop^sa,bomss Cyril

[6] **38** {B} ἐπ᾽ αὐτῷ p^75 ℵ^a B L 0124 1241 cop^sa,bo // ἐπ᾽ αὐτῷ γεγραμμένη C* // γεγραμμένη ἐπ᾽ αὐτῷ it^a (syr^c,s) // γεγραμμένη ἐπ᾽ αὐτῷ γράμμασιν ἑλληνικοῖς καὶ ῥωμαϊκοῖς καὶ ἑβραϊκοῖς (see Jn 19.20) C^3 K W Δ Θ Π 0117 0250 f^1 28 565 700 892 1009 1010 1071 1079 1195 1216 (1242* omit ἐπ᾽ αὐτῷ) 1242^c (1253 omit γράμμασιν and first καί) 1344 1365 1546 1646 2148 2174 Byz Lect (l^60 ἐπ᾽ αὐτῶν γράμμασιν ἑβραϊκοῖς, ἑλλινηκοῖς, καὶ ῥωμαϊκοῖς) (l^70 omit καὶ ἑβραϊκοῖς) it^aur,(c),e,f,ff2,l,r1 vg^cl syr^p,h arm eth geo Acts of Pilate Cyril // ἐπιγεγραμμένη ἐπ᾽ αὐτῷ γράμμασιν ἑλληνικοῖς καὶ ῥωμαϊκοῖς καὶ ἑβραϊκοῖς (see Jn 19.20) A (D omit καί and καί) (l^060 omit καὶ ἑβραϊκοῖς) it^b,d,q vg^ww // ἐπ᾽ αὐτῷ γεγραμμένη γράμμασιν ἑλληνικοῖς καὶ ῥωμαϊκοῖς καὶ ἑβραϊκοῖς (see Jn 19.20) X Ψ f^13 33 1230 // ἐπ᾽ αὐτῷ γράμμασιν ἑλληνικοῖς ῥωμαϊκοῖς ἑβραϊκοῖς (see Jn 19.20) ℵ*,b cop^bomss

b b **35** b none, b none: Bov Nes BF² TT Zür Seg // b none, b minor: WH RV ASV RSV NEB Jer // b minor, b none: Luth // different text: TR AV

33 ἐσταύρωσαν...ἀριστερῶν Is 53.12 **34** Πάτερ...ποιοῦσιν Is 53.12; Mt 5.44; Ac 7.60 διαμεριζόμενοι...κλῆρον Ps 22.18 **35-36** εἱστήκει...στρατιῶται Ps 22.7-8 **36** ὄξος... αὐτῷ Ps 69.21

called "The Skull," they nailed Jesus to the cross there, and the two criminals, one on his right and one on his left. 34 Jesus said, "Forgive them, Father! They don't know what they are doing."[1] They divided his clothes among themselves by throwing dice. 35 The people stood there watching, while the Jewish leaders made fun of him: "He saved others; let him save himself, if he is the Messiah whom God has chosen!" 36 The soldiers also made fun of him; they came up to him and offered him wine, 37 and said, "Save yourself, if you are the king of the Jews!" 38 These words were written above him: "This is the King of the Jews."

[1] **34** *Some mss. omit* Jesus said . . . they are doing."

39 One of the criminals hanging there threw insults at him: "Aren't you the Messiah? Save yourself and us!" 40 The other one, however, rebuked him, saying: "Don't you fear God? Here we are all under the same sentence. 41 Ours, however, is only right, for we are getting what we deserve for what we did; but he has done no wrong." 42 And he said to Jesus, "Remember me, Jesus, when you come as King!" 43 Jesus said to him, "I tell you this: today you will be in Paradise with me."

The Death of Jesus
(Also Matt. 27.45–56; Mark 15.33–41; John 19.28–30)

44 It was about twelve o'clock when the sun stopped shining and darkness covered the whole country until three o'clock; 45 and the curtain hanging in the Temple was torn in two. 46 Jesus cried out in a loud voice, "Father! In your hands I place my spirit!" He said this and died. 47 The army officer saw what had happened, and he praised God, saying, "Certainly he was a good man!" 48 When the people who had gathered there to watch

39 Εἷς δὲ τῶν κρεμασθέντων κακούργων ἐβλασφήμει αὐτὸν λέγων, Οὐχὶ σὺ εἶ ὁ Χριστός; σῶσον σεαυτὸν καὶ ἡμᾶς. **40** ἀποκριθεὶς δὲ ὁ ἕτερος ἐπιτιμῶν αὐτῷ ἔφη, Οὐδὲ φοβῇ σὺ τὸν θεόν, ὅτι ἐν τῷ αὐτῷ κρίματι εἶ; **41** καὶ ἡμεῖς μὲν δικαίως, ἄξια γὰρ ὧν ἐπράξαμεν ἀπολαμβάνομεν· οὗτος δὲ οὐδὲν ἄτοπον ἔπραξεν. **42** καὶ ἔλεγεν, Ἰησοῦ, μνήσθητί μου ὅταν ἔλθῃς ἐν τῇ βασιλείᾳ[7] σου. **43** καὶ εἶπεν αὐτῷ, Ἀμήν σοι λέγω, σήμερον μετ' ἐμοῦ ἔσῃ ἐν τῷ παραδείσῳ.

The Death of Jesus
(Mt 27.45–56; Mk 15.33–41; Jn 19.28–30)

44 Καὶ ἦν ἤδη ὡσεὶ ὥρα ἕκτη καὶ σκότος ἐγένετο ἐφ' ὅλην τὴν γῆν ἕως ὥρας ἐνάτης **45** τοῦ ἡλίου ἐκλιπόντος[8], ἐσχίσθη δὲ τὸ καταπέτασμα τοῦ ναοῦ μέσον. **46** καὶ φωνήσας φωνῇ μεγάλῃ ὁ Ἰησοῦς εἶπεν, Πάτερ, **εἰς χεῖράς σου παρατίθεμαι τὸ πνεῦμά μου·** τοῦτο δὲ εἰπὼν ἐξέπνευσεν. **47** Ἰδὼν δὲ ὁ ἑκατοντάρχης τὸ γενόμενον ἐδόξαζεν τὸν θεὸν λέγων, Ὄντως ὁ ἄνθρωπος οὗτος δίκαιος ἦν. **48** καὶ πάντες οἱ συμπαραγενόμενοι

---

7 42 {C} ἐν τῇ βασιλείᾳ ℵ A C K W X Δ Θ Π Ψ 0117 0124 f¹ f¹³ 28 33 565 700 892 1009 1010 1071 1079 1195 1216 1230 1241 1242 1253 1344 1365 1546 1646 2148 2174 *Byz Lect* it^a,b,q syr^c,s,p,h,pal cop^sa,bo arm? geo Origen Eusebius Chrysostom ‖ εἰς τὴν βασιλείαν 𝔓⁷⁵ B L it^aur,c,e,f,ff2,l,rl vg arm? Origen^lat Hilary ‖ ἐν τῇ ἡμέρᾳ τῆς ἐλεύσεως (*for* ὅταν ἔλθῃς ἐν τῇ βασιλείᾳ) D (it^d *in die adventus*)

8 45 {B} τοῦ ἡλίου ἐκλιπόντος 𝔓⁷⁵* ℵ C*^vid L 0124 syr^hmg geo? Origen^gr,lat Cyril-Jerusalem ‖ τοῦ ἡλίου ἐκλείποντος 𝔓⁷⁵ᶜ B l^10,12,70,185pt,211pt,299,303,950pt,1127pt (cop^sa,bomss τοῦ δέ) cop^bo ‖ καὶ ἐσκοτίσθη ὁ ἥλιος A C³ K W X Δ Θ Π Ψ 0117 f¹ f¹³ 28 565 700 892 1009 1010 1071 1079 1195mg 1216 1230 1241 1242 1253 1344 1546 1646 2148 2174 *Byz* l^60,69,70,76,80,184,185pt,211pt,547,883,950pt,1127pt,1579 it^(a),aur,(b),(c),(e),f,ff2,l,q vg syr^c,s,p,pal arm *omit* καί) eth Marcion (Diatessaron^esyr *omit* καί) Origen^lat mss^acc. to Origen ‖ ἐσκοτίσθη δὲ ὁ ἥλιος D it^d geo? ‖ τοῦ ἡλίου σκοτισθέντος syr^h geo? ‖ τοῦ ἡλίου ἐκλιπόντος καὶ ἐσκοτίσθη ὁ ἥλιος C²^vid 1365 ‖ *omit* 33 1195*

---

42 ὅταν ἔλθῃς...σου Mt 16.28   **44-45** ὡσεὶ...ἐκλιπόντος Am 8.9   **45** τὸ καταπέτασμα τοῦ ναοῦ Ex 26.31–33; 36.35   **46** εἰς χεῖρας...μου Ps 31.5 (Ac 7.59)

ὄχλοι ἐπὶ τὴν θεωρίαν ταύτην, θεωρήσαντες τὰ γενόμενα, τύπτοντες τὰ στήθη ὑπέστρεφον. **49** εἱστήκεισαν δὲ πάντες οἱ γνωστοὶ αὐτῷ ἀπὸ μακρόθεν, καὶ γυναῖκες αἱ συνακολουθοῦσαι αὐτῷ ἀπὸ τῆς Γαλιλαίας, ὁρῶσαι ταῦτα.

The Burial of Jesus
(Mt 27.57–61; Mk 15.42–47; Jn 19.38–42)

50 Καὶ ἰδοὺ ἀνὴρ ὀνόματι Ἰωσὴφ βουλευτὴς ὑπάρχων [καὶ] ἀνὴρ ἀγαθὸς καὶ δίκαιος **51** — οὗτος οὐκ ἦν συγκατατεθειμένος τῇ βουλῇ καὶ τῇ πράξει αὐτῶν — ἀπὸ Ἀριμαθαίας πόλεως τῶν Ἰουδαίων, ὃς προσεδέχετο τὴν βασιλείαν τοῦ θεοῦ, **52** οὗτος προσελθὼν τῷ Πιλάτῳ ᾐτήσατο τὸ σῶμα τοῦ Ἰησοῦ, **53** καὶ καθελὼν ἐνετύλιξεν αὐτὸ σινδόνι, καὶ ἔθηκεν αὐτὸν ἐν μνήματι λαξευτῷ οὗ οὐκ ἦν οὐδεὶς οὔπω κείμενος. **54** καὶ ἡμέρα ἦν παρασκευῆς, καὶ σάββατον ἐπέφωσκεν. **55** Κατακολουθήσασαι δὲ αἱ γυναῖκες, αἵτινες ἦσαν συνεληλυθυῖαι ἐκ τῆς Γαλιλαίας αὐτῷ, ἐθεάσαντο τὸ μνημεῖον καὶ ὡς ἐτέθη τὸ σῶμα αὐτοῦ, **56** ὑποστρέψασαι δὲ ἡτοίμασαν ἀρώματα καὶ μύρα.

The Resurrection of Jesus
(Mt 28.1–10; Mk 16.1–8; Jn 20.1–10)

Καὶ τὸ μὲν σάββατον ἡσύχασαν κατὰ τὴν ἐντολήν, **24** τῇ δὲ μιᾷ τῶν σαββάτων ὄρθρου βαθέως ἐπὶ τὸ μνῆμα ἦλθον φέρουσαι ἃ ἡτοίμασαν ἀρώματα. **2** εὗρον δὲ τὸν λίθον ἀποκεκυλισμένον ἀπὸ τοῦ μνημείου, **3** εἰσελθοῦσαι δὲ οὐχ εὗρον τὸ σῶμα τοῦ [κυρίου] Ἰησοῦ[1].

---

[1] **3** {D} τοῦ κυρίου Ἰησοῦ 𝔓75 ℵ A B C K L W X Δ Θ Π Ψ 0124 f¹ f¹³ 28 33 565 700 892 1009 1010 1079 1195 1216 1230 1242 1253 1344 1365 1546 1646 2148 2174 *Byz Lect* itaur,c,f,q vg syrh,pal copsa,bo arm eth geo Eusebius1/2 ∥ τοῦ Ἰησοῦ 1071 1241 syrc,s,p copsams,boms ∥ *omit* D ita,b,d,e,ff²,l,rl Eusebius1/2

---

48 τύπτοντες τὰ στήθη Lk 18.13   **49** εἱστήκεισαν...μακρόθεν Ps 38.11; 88.8   γυναῖκες ...Γαλιλαίας Lk 8.2; 23.55   **51** προσεδέχετο...θεοῦ Lk 2.25, 38   **53** οὗ...κείμενος Lk 19.30   **55** γυναῖκες...αὐτῷ Lk 8.2; 23.49   **56** τὸ μὲν...ἐντολήν Ex 12.16; 20..0; Dt 5.14   **24 1** τῇ δὲ...σαββάτων Jn 20.19; Ac 20.7; 1 Cor 16.2

the spectacle saw what happened, they all went back home beating their breasts. [49] All those who knew Jesus personally, including the women who had followed him from Galilee, stood off at a distance to see these things.

The Burial of Jesus
(Also Matt. 27.57–61; Mark 15.42–47; John 19.38–42)

[50-51] There was a man named Joseph, from the Jewish town of Arimathea. He was a good and honorable man, and waited for the coming of the Kingdom of God. Although a member of the Council, he had not agreed with their decision and action. [52] He went into the presence of Pilate and asked for the body of Jesus. [53] Then he took the body down, wrapped it in a linen sheet, and placed it in a grave which had been dug out of the rock — a grave which had never been used. [54] It was Friday, and the Sabbath was about to begin.

[55] The women who had followed Jesus from Galilee went with Joseph and saw the grave and how Jesus' body was laid in it. [56] Then they went back home and prepared the spices and ointments for his body.

On the Sabbath they rested, as the Law commanded.

The Resurrection
(Also Matt. 28.1–10; Mark 16.1–8; John 20.1–10)

24 Very early on Sunday morning the women went to the grave carrying the spices they had prepared. [2] They found the stone rolled away from the entrance to the grave, [3] so they went on in; but they did not find the body of the Lord

Jesus. They stood there uncertain about this, when suddenly two men in bright shining clothes stood by them. ⁵ Full of fear, the women bowed down to the ground, as the men said to them: "Why are you looking among the dead for one who is alive? ⁶ He is not here; he has risen. Remember what he said to you while he was in Galilee: ⁷ 'The Son of Man must be handed over to sinful men, be nailed to the cross and be raised to life on the third day.'" ⁸ Then the women remembered his words, ⁹ returned from the grave, and told all these things to the eleven disciples and all the rest. ¹⁰ The women were Mary Magdalene, Joanna, and Mary the mother of James; they and the other women with them told these things to the apostles. ¹¹ But the apostles thought that what the women said was nonsense, and did not believe them. ¹² But Peter got up and ran to the grave; he bent down and saw the grave cloths and nothing else. Then he went back home wondering at what had happened.¹

---

¹ **12** *Some mss. omit this verse.*

---

4 καὶ ἐγένετο ἐν τῷ ἀπορεῖσθαι αὐτὰς περὶ τούτου καὶ ἰδοὺ ἄνδρες δύο ἐπέστησαν αὐταῖς ἐν ἐσθῆτι ἀστραπτούσῃ. 5 ἐμφόβων δὲ γενομένων αὐτῶν καὶ κλινουσῶν τὰ πρόσωπα εἰς τὴν γῆν εἶπαν πρὸς αὐτάς, Τί ζητεῖτε τὸν ζῶντα μετὰ τῶν νεκρῶν; 6 οὐκ ἔστιν ὧδε, ἀλλὰ ἠγέρθη.² μνήσθητε ὡς ἐλάλησεν ὑμῖν ἔτι ὢν ἐν τῇ Γαλιλαίᾳ, 7 λέγων τὸν υἱὸν τοῦ ἀνθρώπου ὅτι δεῖ παραδοθῆναι εἰς χεῖρας ἀνθρώπων ἁμαρτωλῶν καὶ σταυρωθῆναι καὶ τῇ τρίτῃ ἡμέρᾳ ἀναστῆναι. 8 καὶ ἐμνήσθησαν τῶν ῥημάτων αὐτοῦ, 9 καὶ ὑποστρέψασαι ἀπὸ τοῦ μνημείου³ ἀπήγγειλαν ταῦτα πάντα τοῖς ἕνδεκα καὶ πᾶσιν τοῖς λοιποῖς. 10 ἦσαν δὲ⁴ ἡ Μαγδαληνὴ Μαρία καὶ Ἰωάννα καὶ Μαρία ἡ Ἰακώβου· καὶ αἱ λοιπαὶ σὺν αὐταῖς ἔλεγον πρὸς τοὺς ἀποστόλους ταῦτα. 11 καὶ ἐφάνησαν ἐνώπιον αὐτῶν ὡσεὶ λῆρος τὰ ῥήματα ταῦτα, καὶ ἠπίστουν αὐταῖς. 12 Ὁ δὲ Πέτρος ἀναστὰς ἔδραμεν ἐπὶ τὸ μνημεῖον, καὶ παρακύψας βλέπει τὰ ὀθόνια μόνα· καὶ ἀπῆλθεν πρὸς ἑαυτὸν θαυμάζων τὸ γεγονός.⁵

---

² 6 {D} οὐκ ἔστιν ὧδε, ἀλλὰ (*or* ἀλλ᾽) ἠγέρθη. 𝔭⁷⁵ ℵ A B C³ K L (W ἀνέστη) X Δ Θ Π Ψ 063 0124 *f*¹ *f*¹³ 28 33 565 700 892 1009 1010 1071 1079 1195 1216 1230 1241 1242 1253 1344 1365 1546 1646 2148 2174 *Byz Lect* it^{aur,f,q} vg syr^{c,s,h,pal} cop^{sa,bo} arm (eth) geo^{1,A} ∥ οὐκ ἔστιν ὧδε· ἠγέρθη. C* syr^p cop^{boms} Diatessaron Epiphanius ∥ ἠγέρθη. Marcion ∥ ἠγέρθη ἐκ νεκρῶν. it^c ∥ *omit* D it^{a,b,d,e,ff2,l,r1} geo^B

³ 9 {D} ἀπὸ τοῦ μνημείου 𝔭⁷⁵ ℵ A B K L W X Δ Θ Π Ψ 063 0124 *f*¹ *f*¹³ 28 33 565 700 892 1009 1010 1071 1079 1195 1216 1230 1241 1242 1253 1344 1365 1546 1646 2148 2174 *Byz Lect* it^{aur,f,q} vg syr^{c,s,p,h,pal} cop^{sa,bo} eth Tertullian Eusebius Cyril ∥ *omit* D it^{a,b,c,d,e,ff2,l,r1} arm geo

⁴ 10 {C} ἦσαν δὲ 𝔭⁷⁵ ℵ B L X Δ Θ 0124 *f*¹³ 28 33 565 700 892 1009 1071 1079 1195^{mg} 1230 1242^c 1253 1344 1546 1646 2148 *Byz* it^c syr^{p,h} cop^{boms} arm geo (Diatessaron) Eusebius ∥ ἦν δὲ K Π Ψ *f*¹ 1365 2174 it^{a,aur,b,f,ff2,l,q,r1} vg cop^{sa,boms} Cyril ∥ *omit* A D W 1010 1195* 1216 1241 1242* *Lect* it^{d,e} syr^{c,s,h with *} eth

⁵ 12 {D} *include verse 12* (*see* Jn 20.3, 5, 6, 10) 𝔭⁷⁵ ℵ A B K L W X Δ Θ Π Ψ 063 079 0124 *f*¹ *f*¹³ 28 33 565 700 892 1009 1010 1071 1079 1195 1216

---

4 καὶ ἰδού...ἀστραπτούσῃ 2 Macc 3.26; Ac 1.10   5 ἐμφόβων...αὐτῶν Lk 2.9   7 τὸν υἱὸν...ἀναστῆναι Mt 16.21; 17.22–23; 20.18–19; Mk 8.31; 9.31; 10.33–34; Lk 9.22; 17.25; 18.32–33; Ac 17.3   8 ἐμνήσθησαν...αὐτοῦ Jn 2.22   10 Μαγδαληνὴ...αὐταῖς Lk 8.2–3

The Walk to Emmaus
(Mk 16.12–13)

13 Καὶ ἰδοὺ δύο ἐξ αὐτῶν ἐν αὐτῇ τῇ ἡμέρᾳ ἦσαν πορευόμενοι εἰς κώμην ἀπέχουσαν σταδίους ἑξήκοντα[6] ἀπὸ Ἰερουσαλήμ, ᾗ ὄνομα Ἐμμαοῦς, **14** καὶ αὐτοὶ ὡμίλουν πρὸς ἀλλήλους περὶ πάντων τῶν συμβεβηκότων τούτων. **15** καὶ ἐγένετο ἐν τῷ ὁμιλεῖν αὐτοὺς καὶ συζητεῖν καὶ αὐτὸς Ἰησοῦς ἐγγίσας συνεπορεύετο αὐτοῖς, **16** οἱ δὲ ὀφθαλμοὶ αὐτῶν ἐκρατοῦντο τοῦ μὴ ἐπιγνῶναι αὐτόν. **17** εἶπεν δὲ πρὸς αὐτούς, Τίνες οἱ λόγοι οὗτοι οὓς ἀντιβάλλετε πρὸς ἀλλήλους περιπατοῦντες; καὶ ἐστάθησαν σκυθρωποί. **18** ἀποκριθεὶς δὲ εἷς ὀνόματι Κλεοπᾶς εἶπεν πρὸς αὐτόν, Σὺ μόνος παροικεῖς Ἰερουσαλὴμ καὶ οὐκ ἔγνως τὰ γενόμενα ἐν αὐτῇ ἐν ταῖς ἡμέραις ταύταις; **19** καὶ εἶπεν αὐτοῖς, Ποῖα; οἱ δὲ εἶπαν αὐτῷ, Τὰ περὶ Ἰησοῦ τοῦ Ναζαρηνοῦ[7], ὃς ἐγένετο ἀνὴρ προφήτης δυνατὸς ἐν ἔργῳ καὶ λόγῳ ἐναντίον τοῦ θεοῦ καὶ παντὸς τοῦ λαοῦ, **20** ὅπως τε παρέδωκαν αὐτὸν οἱ ἀρχιερεῖς καὶ οἱ ἄρχοντες ἡμῶν εἰς κρίμα θανάτου καὶ ἐσταύρωσαν αὐτόν. **21** ἡμεῖς δὲ ἠλπίζομεν ὅτι αὐτός ἐστιν ὁ μέλλων λυτροῦσθαι τὸν Ἰσραήλ· ἀλλά γε καὶ σὺν πᾶσιν τούτοις τρίτην

1230 1241 1242 1253 1344 1365 1546 1646 2148 2174 *Byz Lect* *l*[185m] it[aur,c,f,ff2] vg syr[c,s,p,h,palmss] cop[sa,bo] arm eth geo Eusebius[1/2] Cyril ∥ *omit verse 12* D it[a,b,d,e,l,rl] syr[palmss] Marcion Diatessaron Eusebius[1/2]

[6] **13** {B} ἑξήκοντα 𝔭[75] A B D K[2] L W X Δ Ψ 063 0124 *f*[1] *f*[13] 28 33[vid] 565 700 892 1009 1010 1071 1079[c] 1195 1216 1230 1241 1242 1253 1344 1365 1546 1646 2148 2174 *Byz Lect* *l*[185m] it[a,aur,b,c,d,f,ff2,1] vg syr[c,s,p,h] cop[sa,bo] eth geo ∥ ἕκατον ἑξήκοντα ℵ K* Θ Π 079[vid] 1079* syr[pal] arm Eusebius Jerome Sozomen ∥ ἑπτά it[e]

[7] **19** {C} Ναζαρηνοῦ 𝔭[75] ℵ B L 079 0124 it[a,aur,c,e,f,rl] vg cop[bo?] Origen ∥ Ναζωραίου Λ D K P W X Δ Θ Π Ψ 063 *f*[1] *f*[13] 28 33 565 700 892 1009 1010 1071 1079 1195 1216 1230 1241 1242 1253 1344 1365 1546 1646 2148 2174 *Byz Lect* *l*[185m] it[b,d,ff2,1] syr[c,s,p,h,pal] cop[sa,(bo?)] arm geo Origen

---

15 Mt 18.20; Mk 16.12   **19** Ἰησοῦ...προφήτης Mt 21.11   **21** ὁ μέλλων...Ἰσραήλ Lk 1.68; 2.38

The Walk to Emmaus
(Also Mark 16.12–13)

[13] On that same day two of them were going to a village named Emmaus, about seven miles from Jerusalem, [14] and they were talking to each other about all the things that had happened. [15] As they talked and discussed, Jesus himself drew near and walked along with them; [16] they saw him, but somehow did not recognize him. [17] Jesus said to them, "What are you talking about, back and forth, as you walk along?" And they stood still, with sad faces. [18] One of them, named Cleopas, asked him, "Are you the only man living in Jerusalem who does not know what has been happening there these last few days?" [19] "What things?" he asked. "The things that happened to Jesus of Nazareth," they answered. "This man was a prophet, and was considered by God and by all the people to be mighty in words and deeds. [20] Our chief priests and rulers handed him over to be sentenced to death, and they nailed him to the cross. [21] And we had hoped that he would be the one who was going to redeem Israel! Besides all that, this is

now the third day since it happened."
[22] Some of the women of our group surprised us; they went at dawn to the grave, [23] but could not find his body. They came back saying they had seen a vision of angels who told them that he is alive. [24] Some of our group went to the grave and found it exactly as the women had said, but they did not see him."

[25] Then Jesus said to them: "How foolish you are, how slow you are to believe everything the prophets said! [26] Was it not necessary for the Messiah to suffer these things and enter his glory?" [27] And Jesus explained to them what was said about him in all the Scriptures, beginning with the books of Moses and the writings of all the prophets.

[28] They came near the village to which they were going, and Jesus acted as if he were going farther; [29] but they held him back, saying, "Stay with us; the day is almost over and it is getting dark." So he went in to stay with them. [30] He sat at table with them, took the bread, and said the blessing; then he broke the bread and gave it to them. [31] Their eyes were opened and they recognized him; but he disappeared from their sight. [32] They said to each other, "Wasn't it like a fire burning in us when he talked to us on the road and explained the Scriptures to us?"

[33] They got up at once and went back

ταύτην ἡμέραν ἄγει ἀφ᾽ οὗ ταῦτα ἐγένετο. 22 ἀλλὰ καὶ γυναῖκές τινες ἐξ ἡμῶν ἐξέστησαν ἡμᾶς· [a] γενόμεναι ὀρθριναὶ ἐπὶ τὸ μνημεῖον[a] 23 καὶ μὴ εὑροῦσαι τὸ σῶμα αὐτοῦ ἦλθον λέγουσαι καὶ ὀπτασίαν ἀγγέλων ἑωρακέναι, οἳ λέγουσιν αὐτὸν ζῆν. 24 καὶ ἀπῆλθόν τινες τῶν σὺν ἡμῖν ἐπὶ τὸ μνημεῖον, καὶ εὗρον οὕτως καθὼς καὶ αἱ γυναῖκες εἶπον, αὐτὸν δὲ οὐκ εἶδον. 25 καὶ αὐτὸς εἶπεν πρὸς αὐτούς, Ὦ ἀνόητοι καὶ βραδεῖς τῇ καρδίᾳ τοῦ πιστεύειν ἐπὶ πᾶσιν οἷς ἐλάλησαν οἱ προφῆται· 26 οὐχὶ ταῦτα ἔδει παθεῖν τὸν Χριστὸν καὶ εἰσελθεῖν εἰς τὴν δόξαν αὐτοῦ; 27 καὶ ἀρξάμενος ἀπὸ Μωϋσέως καὶ ἀπὸ πάντων τῶν προφητῶν διερμήνευσεν αὐτοῖς ἐν πάσαις ταῖς γραφαῖς τὰ περὶ ἑαυτοῦ.

28 Καὶ ἤγγισαν εἰς τὴν κώμην οὗ ἐπορεύοντο, καὶ αὐτὸς προσεποιήσατο πορρώτερον πορεύεσθαι. 29 καὶ παρεβιάσαντο αὐτὸν λέγοντες, Μεῖνον μεθ᾽ ἡμῶν, ὅτι πρὸς ἑσπέραν ἐστὶν καὶ κέκλικεν ἤδη ἡ ἡμέρα. καὶ εἰσῆλθεν τοῦ μεῖναι σὺν αὐτοῖς. 30 καὶ ἐγένετο ἐν τῷ κατακλιθῆναι αὐτὸν μετ᾽ αὐτῶν λαβὼν τὸν ἄρτον εὐλόγησεν καὶ κλάσας ἐπεδίδου αὐτοῖς· 31 αὐτῶν δὲ διηνοίχθησαν οἱ ὀφθαλμοὶ καὶ ἐπέγνωσαν αὐτόν· καὶ αὐτὸς ἄφαντος ἐγένετο ἀπ᾽ αὐτῶν. 32 καὶ εἶπαν πρὸς ἀλλήλους, Οὐχὶ ἡ καρδία ἡμῶν καιομένη ἦν [ἐν ἡμῖν] ὡς ἐλάλει ἡμῖν[8] ἐν τῇ ὁδῷ, ὡς διήνοιγεν ἡμῖν τὰς γραφάς; 33 καὶ

[8] **32** {C} ἐν ἡμῖν ὡς ἐλάλει ἡμῖν ℵ (A ἐλάλησεν) (K ἐλάλη) L P W X Δ Θ Π Ψ 0196 f[1] f[13] 28 33 565 700 892 1010[mg] 1071 1079 1195 1216 1230 1241 1242 1253 1344 1365 1546 1646 2148 2174 Byz Lect l[185m] (l[211m] ὑμῖν...ὑμῖν) it[f] syr[p, h, pal] cop[sa, bo] arm eth Diatessaron Origen[gr, lat] ‖ ὡς ἐλάλει ἡμῖν 𝔭[75] B D it[d] geo Origen ‖ ἐν ἡμῖν ὡς ἐλάλει it[aur] vg ‖ ἐν ἡμῖν l[60] it[a, b, ff2, l, r1] ‖ omit it[c, e] syr[c, s]

[a a] **22** a major, a none: RSV TT Zür Seg ‖ a major, a minor: NEB Luth Jer ‖ a minor, a none: WH ‖ a minor, a major: TR AV RV ASV ‖ a minor, a minor: Bov Nes BF[2]

22–23 Mt 28.1–8; Mk 16.1–8; Lk 24.1–11 **24** Jn 20.3–8 **25** πᾶσιν...προφῆται Lk 24.44 **26** ταῦτα...Χριστόν Mt 16.21; Mk 8.31; Lk 9.22; 17.25; Ac 17.3 εἰσελθεῖν...αὐτοῦ Jn 7.39; 12.16, 23; 13.31–32; 17.1, 5; Ac 3.13 **27** Dt 18.15; Ps 22.1–18; Is 53; Lk 24.44 **30** Lk 22.19

ἀναστάντες αὐτῇ τῇ ὥρᾳ ὑπέστρεψαν εἰς Ἰερουσαλήμ, καὶ εὖρον ἠθροισμένους τοὺς ἕνδεκα καὶ τοὺς σὺν αὐτοῖς, 34 λέγοντας ὅτι[b] ὄντως ἠγέρθη ὁ κύριος καὶ ὤφθη Σίμωνι. 35 καὶ αὐτοὶ ἐξηγοῦντο τὰ ἐν τῇ ὁδῷ καὶ ὡς ἐγνώσθη αὐτοῖς ἐν τῇ κλάσει τοῦ ἄρτου.

The Appearance to the Disciples
(Mt 28.16–20; Mk 16.14–18; Jn 20.19–23; Ac 1.6–8)

36 Ταῦτα δὲ αὐτῶν λαλούντων αὐτὸς ἔστη ἐν μέσῳ αὐτῶν καὶ λέγει αὐτοῖς, Εἰρήνη ὑμῖν[9]. 37 πτοηθέντες δὲ καὶ ἔμφοβοι γενόμενοι ἐδόκουν πνεῦμα θεωρεῖν. 38 καὶ εἶπεν αὐτοῖς, Τί τεταραγμένοι ἐστέ, καὶ διὰ τί διαλογισμοὶ ἀναβαίνουσιν ἐν τῇ καρδίᾳ ὑμῶν; 39 ἴδετε τὰς χεῖράς μου καὶ τοὺς πόδας μου ὅτι ἐγώ εἰμι αὐτός· ψηλαφήσατέ με καὶ ἴδετε, ὅτι πνεῦμα σάρκα καὶ ὀστέα οὐκ ἔχει καθὼς ἐμὲ θεωρεῖτε ἔχοντα. 40 καὶ τοῦτο εἰπὼν ἔδειξεν αὐτοῖς τὰς χεῖρας καὶ τοὺς πόδας.[10] 41 ἔτι δὲ ἀπιστούντων αὐτῶν ἀπὸ τῆς χαρᾶς καὶ θαυμαζόντων εἶπεν αὐτοῖς, Ἔχετέ τι βρώσιμον ἐνθάδε; 42 οἱ δὲ ἐπέδωκαν αὐτῷ ἰχθύος ὀπτοῦ μέρος.[11] 43 καὶ λαβὼν ἐνώπιον αὐτῶν ἔφαγεν.

[9] 36 {D} καὶ λέγει αὐτοῖς, Εἰρήνη ὑμῖν (see Jn 20.19, 26) p75 ℵ A B K L X Δ Θ Π Ψ f1 f13 (28 εἶπεν for λέγει) 33 565 700 892 1009 1010 1071 1079 1195 1216 1242 1344 1365 1546 1646 2148 2174 Byz Lect l185m syrc,s copsa,bo Eusebius Chrysostom Augustine Cyril // καὶ λέγει αὐτοῖς, Εἰρήνη ὑμῖν· ἐγώ εἰμι, μὴ φοβεῖσθε P 1230 1241 1253 itaur,c,f vg syrp,h,pal copbomss arm eth geo Diatessarona,i,u Ambrose Augustine // καὶ λέγει αὐτοῖς, Ἐγώ εἰμι, μὴ φοβεῖσθε· εἰρήνη ὑμῖν W // omit D ita,b,d,e,ff2,l,r1

[10] 40 {D} include verse 40 (see Jn 20.20) p75 ℵ A B K L W X Δ Θ Π Ψ f1 f13 28 33 565 700 892 1009 1010 1071 1079 1195 1216 1230 1241 1242 1253 1344 1365 1546 1646 2148 2174 Byz Lect l185m itaur,c,f,q vg syrp,h,pal copsa,bo arm geo Eusebius Athanasius Chrysostom Cyril John-Damascus // omit verse 40 D ita,b,d,e,ff2,l,r1 syrc,s Marcion

[11] 42 {B} μέρος p75 ℵ A B D L W Π 1079 itd,e syrs copsa,bomss Clement

[b] 34 b Indirect: WH Bov Nes? BF² TT // b direct: TR Nes? AV RV ASV RSV NEB Zür Luth Jer Seg

34 1 Cor 15.4-5   36 αὐτὸς ἔστη...αὐτῶν 1 Cor 15.5   37 Mt 14.26   41 Ἔχετε... βρώσιμον Jn 21.5   42 Jn 21.9-10

---

to Jerusalem, where they found the eleven disciples gathered together with the others 34 and saying, "The Lord is risen indeed! Simon has seen him!" 35 The two then explained to them what had happened on the road, and how they had recognized the Lord when he broke the bread.

Jesus Appears to His Disciples
(Also Matt. 28.16–20; Mark 16.14–18; John 20.19–23; Acts 1.6–8)

36 While they were telling them this, suddenly the Lord himself stood among them and said to them, "Peace be with you."[2] 37 Full of fear and terror, they thought that they were seeing a ghost. 38 But he said to them: "Why are you troubled? Why are these doubts coming up in your minds? 39 Look at my hands and my feet and see that it is I, myself. Feel me, and you will see, for a ghost doesn't have flesh and bones, as you can see I have." 40 He said this and showed them his hands and his feet.[3] 41 They still could not believe, they were so full of joy and wonder; so he asked them, "Do you have anything to eat here?" 42 They gave him a piece of cooked fish, 43 which he took and ate before them.

---

[2] 36 Some mss. omit and said to them, "Peace be with you."

[3] 40 Some mss. omit this verse.

[44] Then he said to them: "These are the very things I told you while I was still with you: everything written about me in the Law of Moses, the writings of the prophets, and the Psalms had to come true." [45] Then he opened their minds to understand the Scriptures, [46] and said to them: "This is what is written: that the Messiah must suffer and be raised from death on the third day, [47] and that in his name the message about repentance and the forgiveness of sins must be preached to all nations, beginning in Jerusalem. [48] You are witnesses of these things. [49] And I myself will send upon you what my Father has

[44] Εἶπεν δὲ πρὸς αὐτούς, Οὗτοι οἱ λόγοι μου οὓς ἐλάλησα πρὸς ὑμᾶς ἔτι ὢν σὺν ὑμῖν, ὅτι[c] δεῖ πληρωθῆναι πάντα τὰ γεγραμμένα ἐν τῷ νόμῳ Μωϋσέως καὶ τοῖς προφήταις καὶ ψαλμοῖς περὶ ἐμοῦ. [45] τότε διήνοιξεν αὐτῶν τὸν νοῦν τοῦ συνιέναι τὰς γραφάς. [46] [d]καὶ εἶπεν αὐτοῖς [d]ὅτι[e] Οὕτως γέγραπται παθεῖν τὸν Χριστὸν καὶ ἀναστῆναι ἐκ νεκρῶν τῇ τρίτῃ ἡμέρᾳ, [47] καὶ κηρυχθῆναι ἐπὶ τῷ ὀνόματι αὐτοῦ μετάνοιαν καὶ[12] ἄφεσιν ἁμαρτιῶν εἰς πάντα τὰ ἔθνη —[f] ἀρξάμενοι[13] ἀπὸ Ἰερουσαλήμ·[f] [48] ὑμεῖς μάρτυρες τούτων. [49] καὶ [ἰδοὺ] ἐγὼ[14] ἀποστέλλω τὴν ἐπαγγελίαν τοῦ πατρός μου ἐφ᾽ ὑμᾶς· ὑμεῖς

Origen Eusebius Athanasius Epiphanius Cyril ∥ μέρος καὶ ἀπὸ μελισσίου κηρίου K Δ Ψ ƒ¹ 28 33 565 700 892 1009 1010 1071 1195* 1230 1241 1253 1344 1646 2148 2174 (1216 *l*⁶⁰ μέρους) Byz Lect *l*¹⁸⁵ᵐ syr^{c,p,h with *,pal} cop^{bo} arm eth geo? Justin Diatessaron Athanasius Augustine Cyril Proclus ∥ μέρος καὶ ἀπὸ μελισσίου κηρίον X Θ ƒ¹³ 1195^{mg} 1242 1365 1546 it^{(a),aur,(b),(c),f,ff²,l,(q),r¹} vg geo? Cyril-Jerusalem

[12] **47** {D} καί A C D K L W X Δ Θ Π Ψ 063 ƒ¹ ƒ¹³ 28 33 565 700 892 1009 1010 1071 1079 1195 1216 1230 1241 1242 1253 1344 1365 1546 1646 2148 2174 Byz Lect *l*¹⁸⁵ᵐ it^{a,aur,b,c,d,e,f,ff²,l,q,r¹} vg syr^{s,h,pal} arm eth geo Cyprian Eusebius ∥ εἰς 𝔭⁷⁵ ℵ B syr^p cop^{sa,bo} Diatessaron^{a,(t),v}

[13] **47** {C} ἀρξάμενοι ℵ B C* L X 33 1230 1253 cop^{sa,bo} arm eth geo² ∥ ἀρξαμένων D Δ² it^{aur,b,(d),f,ff²,q} vg Diatessaron^f ∥ ἀρξάμενον 𝔭⁷⁵ A C³ K W Δ* Π 063 ƒ¹ ƒ¹³ 28 700 892 1009 1010 1079 1195 1216 1241 1242 1344 1365 1546 1646 2148 2174 Byz Lect *l*¹⁸⁵ᵐ syr^{s,p,h,pal} Diatessaron ∥ ἀρξάμενος Θ Ψ 565 1071 *l*³⁶,⁴⁷,⁶⁰ ∥ ἀρξάμενον or ἀρξάμενος it^{a,c,e,l,r¹} geo¹

[14] **49** {C} καὶ ἰδοὺ ἐγώ A B C K X Δ Θ Π Ψ 063 ƒ¹³ 28 565 700 892 1009 1010 1071 1195 1216 1241 1242 1344 1365 1646 2148 2174 Byz Lect *l*¹⁸⁵ᵐ it^{f,q} syr^{h,pal} arm eth geo ∥ κἀγώ (𝔭⁷⁵ D καὶ ἐγώ) ℵ L 33 1230 1253 it^{a,aur,b,c,d,e,ff²,l,r¹} vg syr^{s,p} cop^{sa,bo} Diatessaron^{a,i,n} Augustine ∥ καὶ ἐγὼ ἰδού W ƒ¹ 1079 1546

---

[c] **44** *c* indirect: TR WH Bov Nes BF² AV RV ASV RSV NEB TT ∥ *c* direct: Zür Luth Jer Seg

[d] [d] **45–46** *d* number 46, *d* no number: TR^{ed} WH? Nes BF² AV RV ASV RSV NEB? TT Zür Luth Jer Seg ∥ *d* no number, *d* number 46: TR^{ed} WH? Bov NEB?

[e] **46** *e* direct: TR Nes? BF² AV RV ASV RSV NEB TT Zür Luth Jer Seg ∥ *e* indirect: WH Bov Nes?

[f] [f] **47** *f* dash, *f* major: WH Bov Nes BF² ∥ *f* major, *f* minor: (WH^{mg}) RV^{mg} ASV^{mg} (RSV^{mg}) NEB (Luth) ∥ *f* minor, *f* major: RV ASV RSV TT Zür Jer Seg ∥ *f* dash, *f* minor ∥ different text: TR AV

---

44 δεῖ...ἐμοῦ Lk 18.31; 24.27   **46** Οὕτως...Χριστόν Is 53   ἀναστῆναι...ἡμέρᾳ Ho 6.2

47 κηρυχθῆναι...ἔθνη 1 Tm 3.16   **48** Jn 15.27; Ac 1.8   **49** Jn 14.16; 15.26; 16.7; Ac 1.4

δὲ καθίσατε ἐν τῇ πόλει ἕως οὗ ἐνδύσησθε ἐξ ὕψους δύναμιν.

The Ascension of Jesus
(Mk 16.19–20; Ac 1.9–11)

50 Ἐξήγαγεν δὲ αὐτοὺς [ἔξω] ἕως πρὸς Βηθανίαν, καὶ ἐπάρας τὰς χεῖρας αὐτοῦ εὐλόγησεν αὐτούς. 51 καὶ ἐγένετο ἐν τῷ εὐλογεῖν αὐτὸν αὐτοὺς διέστη ἀπ' αὐτῶν καὶ ἀνεφέρετο εἰς τὸν οὐρανόν[15]. 52 καὶ αὐτοὶ προσκυνήσαντες αὐτὸν[16] ὑπέστρεψαν εἰς Ἰερουσαλὴμ μετὰ χαρᾶς μεγάλης, 53 καὶ ἦσαν διὰ παντὸς ἐν τῷ ἱερῷ εὐλογοῦντες[17] τὸν θεόν.[18]

promised. But you must wait in the city until the power from above comes down upon you."

Jesus Is Taken up to Heaven
(Also Mark 16.19–20; Acts 1.9–11)

50 Then he led them out of the city as far as Bethany, where he raised his hands and blessed them. 51 As he was blessing them, he departed from them and was taken up into heaven.[4] 52 They worshiped him and went back into Jerusalem, filled with great joy, 53 and spent all their time in the Temple giving thanks to God.

[4] **51** *Some mss. omit* and was taken up into heaven.

---

[15] **51** {D} καὶ ἀνεφέρετο εἰς τὸν οὐρανόν 𝔭75 ℵ° A B C K L W X Δ Θ Π Ψ 063 *f*1 *f*13 28 33 565 700 892 1000 1010 1071 1079 1195 1216 1230 1241 1242 1253 1344 1365 1546 1646 2148 2174 *Byz Lect l*185m it^aur,c,f,q,(r1) vg syr^p,h,pal cop^sa,bo arm geo² Diatessaron Augustine^2/3 Cyril Cosmos ‖ *omit* ℵ* D it^a,b,d,e,ff2,l (syr^s) geo¹ Augustine^1/3

[16] **52** {D} προσκυνήσαντες αὐτόν 𝔭75 ℵ A B C K L W X Δ Θ Π Ψ 063 *f*1 *f*13 28 33 565 892 1009 1010 1071 1079 1195 1216 1230 1241 1242 1365 1546 1646 2148 2174 *Byz Lect l*185m it^aur,f,q syr^p,h,pal cop^sa,bo arm geo ‖ προσκυνήσαντες 700 1253 1344 it^c vg ‖ *omit* D it^a,b,d,e,ff2,l syr^s Augustine

[17] **53** {C} εὐλογοῦντες 𝔭75 ℵ B C* L syr^s,pal cop^sa,bo geo ‖ αἰνοῦντες D it^a,b,d,e,ff2,l,r1 Augustine ‖ αἰνοῦντες καὶ εὐλογοῦντες A C² K W X Δ Θ Π Ψ 063 *f*1 *f*13 28 33 565 700 892 1009 1010 1071 1079 1195 1216 1230 1241 1242 1253 1344 1365 1546 1646 2148 2174 *Byz Lect l*185m it^aur,c,f,q vg syr^p,h arm Diatessaron ‖ εὐλογοῦντες καὶ αἰνοῦντες eth

[18] **53** {B} θεόν. 𝔭75 ℵ C* D L W Π* *f*1 33 1079 1365* *Lect l*70pt it^a,aur,b,d,e,ff2,(q) syr^s,pal cop^sa,bo arm geo¹ Augustine ‖ θεόν. ἀμήν. A B C² K X Δ Θ Π² Ψ 063 *f*13 28 565 700 892 1009 1010 1071 1195 1216 1230 1241 1242 1253 1344 1365^c 1546 1646 2148 2174 *Byz l*60,69,70pt,76,185m,211,1127 it^c,f,l,r1 vg syr^p,h cop^bomss eth Diatessaron

---

51 Ac 1.9   **52** ὑπέστρεψαν εἰς Ἰερουσαλήμ Ac 1.12   χαρᾶς μεγάλης Jn 14.28; 16.22

THE GOSPEL OF JOHN

The Word of Life

1 Before the world was created, the Word already existed; he was with God, and he was the same as God. [2] From the very beginning, the Word was with God. [3] Through him God made all things; not one thing in all creation was made without him. [4] The Word had life in himself,[1] and this life brought light to men. [5] The light shines in the darkness, and the darkness has never put it out.

[6] God sent his messenger, a man named John, [7] who came to tell people about the light. He came to tell them, so that all should hear the message and believe.

---

[1] **3-4** *The Word had life in himself:* or *What was made had life in union with the Word*

ΚΑΤΑ ΙΩΑΝΝΗΝ

The Word Became Flesh

1 Ἐν ἀρχῇ ἦν ὁ λόγος, καὶ ὁ λόγος ἦν πρὸς τὸν θεόν, καὶ θεὸς ἦν ὁ λόγος. **2** οὗτος ἦν ἐν ἀρχῇ πρὸς τὸν θεόν. **3** πάντα δι᾽ αὐτοῦ ἐγένετο, καὶ χωρὶς αὐτοῦ ἐγένετο οὐδὲ ἕν.[a] ὃ γέγονεν[a] **4** ἐν[1] αὐτῷ ζωὴ ἦν[2], καὶ ἡ ζωὴ ἦν τὸ φῶς τῶν ἀνθρώπων· **5** καὶ τὸ φῶς ἐν τῇ σκοτίᾳ φαίνει, καὶ ἡ σκοτία αὐτὸ οὐ κατέλαβεν.

6 Ἐγένετο ἄνθρωπος[b] ἀπεσταλμένος παρὰ θεοῦ, ὄνομα αὐτῷ Ἰωάννης· **7** οὗτος ἦλθεν εἰς μαρτυρίαν, ἵνα μαρτυρήσῃ περὶ τοῦ φωτός, ἵνα πάντες πιστεύσωσιν δι᾽ αὐτοῦ.

---

[1] **3-4** {C} οὐδὲ ἕν. ὃ γέγονεν ἐν p[75c] C L W[supp] Θ it[b] vg[ww] syr[c,(pal)] cop[sa, fay] Naassenes Theodotus[acc. to Clement] Valentinians[acc. to Irenaeus gr, lat and Clement] Diatessaron[i,n] Ptolemy Heracleon Theophilus Perateni Irenaeus Clement Tertullian Hippolytus Origen Eusebius Ambrosiaster Hilary Athanasius Cyril-Jerusalem Ambrose[2/3] Epiphanius Augustine Cyril ‖ οὐδὲ ἕν· ὃ γέγονεν· ἐν (D 1071 οὐδέν *for* οὐδὲ ἕν) 28 700 892 1195 1241 1242[c] Diatessaron[e syr] ‖ οὐδὲ ἕν ὃ γέγονεν. ἐν ℵ[c] K X Π Ψ 050 063 (f[1] οὐδέν *for* οὐδὲ ἕν) f[13] 33 565 1009 1010 1079 1216 1230 1242* 1253 1344 1365 1546 1646 *Byz Lect* vg[cl] syr[p,h] cop[bo] arm geo Adamantius Alexander Ephraem Ambrose[1/3] Didymus Epiphanius Chrysostom Jerome Nonnus Ps-Ignatius ‖ οὐδὲ ἕν ὃ γέγονεν ἐν (p[66] οὐδέν *for* οὐδὲ ἕν *and omit* ἐν) p[75*] (ℵ* οὐδέν *for* οὐδὲ ἕν) A B Δ

[2] **4** {A} ἦν (*see footnote* 1) p[66,75] A B C K L X Δ Θ Π Ψ 050 063 0234 f[1] f[13] 28 33 565 700 892 1009 1010 1071 1079 1195 1216 1230 1241 1242 1253 1344 1365 1546 1646 2148 *Byz Lect* vg syr[p,h,pal] cop[bo] arm geo Theodotus[acc. to Clement] Diatessaron Irenaeus[lat] Clement[3/5] Origen Cyprian Eusebius Chrysostom Nonnus Cyril Theodoret ‖ ἐστιν ℵ D it[a,aur,b,c,e,f,ff2,q] syr[c] cop[sa, fay] Naassenes[acc. to Hippolytus] Theodotus[acc. to Clement] Valentinians[acc. to Irenaeus] Diatessaron[l] Perateni[acc. to Hippolytus] Irenaeus[gr, lat] Clement[2/5] mss[acc. to Origen] Cyprian Ambrosiaster Victorinus-Rome Hilary Augustine ‖ *omit* W[supp]

---

[a] [a] **3** *a major, a none:* WH BF[2] RV[mg] ASV[mg] RSV[mg] NEB TT Jer Seg[mg] ‖ *a none, a major:* (TR) WH[mg] Bov Nes AV RV ASV RSV NEB[mg] (Zür) (Luth) Jer[mg] Seg

[b] **6** *b none:* TR WH AV RSV Jer Seg ‖ *b minor:* Bov Nes BF[2] RV ASV (NEB) TT Zür Luth

---

1-2 Jn 17.5; 1 Jn 1.1-2   **1** ὁ λόγος Re 19.13   **3** Wsd 9.1; Jn 1.10; 1 Cor 8.6; Col 1.16-17 He 1.2   **4** ἐν αὐτῷ ζωὴ ἦν Jn 5.26   **5** Jn 3.19   **6** Mt 3.1; Mk 1.4; Lk 1.13, 17, 76; 3.2

8 οὐκ ἦν ἐκεῖνος τὸ φῶς, ἀλλ' ἵνα μαρτυρήσῃ περὶ τοῦ φωτός. 9 Ἦν τὸ φῶς τὸ ἀληθινόν,[c] ὃ φωτίζει πάντα ἄνθρωπον,[c] ἐρχόμενον εἰς τὸν κόσμον. 10 ἐν τῷ κόσμῳ ἦν, καὶ ὁ κόσμος δι' αὐτοῦ ἐγένετο, καὶ ὁ κόσμος αὐτὸν οὐκ ἔγνω. 11 εἰς τὰ ἴδια ἦλθεν, καὶ οἱ ἴδιοι αὐτὸν οὐ παρέλαβον. 12 ὅσοι δὲ ἔλαβον αὐτόν, ἔδωκεν αὐτοῖς ἐξουσίαν τέκνα θεοῦ γενέσθαι, τοῖς πιστεύουσιν εἰς τὸ ὄνομα αὐτοῦ, 13 οἳ οὐκ[3] ἐξ αἱμάτων οὐδὲ ἐκ θελήματος σαρκὸς οὐδὲ ἐκ θελήματος ἀνδρὸς ἀλλ' ἐκ θεοῦ ἐγεννή-θησαν.[3]

14 Καὶ ὁ λόγος σὰρξ ἐγένετο καὶ ἐσκήνωσεν ἐν ἡμῖν, καὶ ἐθεασάμεθα τὴν δόξαν αὐτοῦ, δόξαν ὡς μονογενοῦς παρὰ πατρός, πλήρης χάριτος καὶ ἀληθείας. [d] 15 Ἰωάν-νης μαρτυρεῖ περὶ αὐτοῦ καὶ κέκραγεν λέγων, Οὗτος ἦν ὃν εἶπον, Ὁ ὀπίσω μου ἐρχόμενος[4] ἔμπροσθέν μου γέγονεν, ὅτι πρῶτός μου ἦν.[d] 16 ὅτι ἐκ τοῦ πληρώματος

---

[3] 13 {A} οἳ οὐκ...ἐγεννήθησαν. p[66] ℵ B[3] C D[c] K L W[supp] X Π Ψ 063 (p[75] A B* Δ 28 1071 1365 ἐγεννήθησαν) f[1] f[13] 33 565 700 892 1009 1010 1079 1195 1216 1230 1241 1242 1253 1344 1546 1646 2148[vid] Byz Lect l[69vid] it[aur,c,e,f,ff2,q] vg syr[p,h,pal] cop[sa,bo] arm geo Valentinians[acc. to Tertullian] (Clement) Origen[lat] Eusebius Hilary Athanasius Cyril-Jerusalem Chrysostom Cyril Theodoret ‖ οὐκ...ἐγεννήθησαν. D* it[a] ‖ ὃς οὐκ...ἐγεννήθη. it[b] (syr[c,pmss] οἵ [sic]) Irenaeus[lat] Tertullian Origen[lat] (Ambrose) (Sulpicius) Augustine Ps-Athanasius[vid]

[4] 15 {A} λέγων, Οὗτος ἦν ὃν εἶπον, Ὁ ὀπίσω μου ἐρχόμενος p[66c,75] (p[66*] Δ 1646* ὁ πίσω) ℵ[b] A B[3] (C[3] ὃν ἔλεγον) (D* omit λέγων) K L Θ Π Ψ 063 f[1] f[13] (28 εἶπεν) 33 565 700 892 1009 1010 1071 1079 1195 1216 1230 1241 1242 1253 1344 1365 1546 1646[c] 2148[vid] Byz Lect it[a,aur,e,ff2,q] (it[b] omit λέγων) (it[c] add ὅς) vg[cl] syr[c,p,h,pal] cop[sa,bo] arm geo Origen Nonnus ‖ λέγων, Οὗτος

c c 9 c minor, c minor: Bov Nes BF[2] RV (RV[mg1]) ASV (ASV[mg1]) (RSV) (NEB) (TT) (Zür) (Jer) (Jer[mg1]) (Seg) ‖ c none, c none: WH ‖ c minor, c none: TR AV RV[mg2] ASV[mg2] NEB[mg] Luth Jer[mg2] Seg[mg]

d d 15 d d no parens: TR Bov Nes BF[2] AV RV ASV NEB TT Zür Luth Jer Seg ‖ d parens, d parens: WH RSV

8 οὐκ...φῶς Jn 1.20   9 1 Jn 2.8   10 ἐν τῷ κόσμῳ ἦν Ju 1.14   ὁ κόσμος δι'... ἐγένετο Jn 1.3; 1 Cor 8.6; Col. 1.16; He 1.2   ὁ κόσμος αὐτὸν οὐκ ἔγνω Jn 17.25   12 Ga 3.26 13 Jn 3.3, 5, 6; Jas 1.18; 1 Pe 1.23; 1 Jn 3.9; 5.18   14 ὁ λόγος...ἐγένετο Ps Sol 7.6; Ro 1.3; Ga 4.4; Php 2.7; 1 Tm 3.16; He 2.14; 1 Jn 4.2   ἐθεασάμεθα...αὐτοῦ Is 60.1-2; Lk 9.32; Jn 2.11 15 Jn 1.30   Ὁ...ἐρχόμενος Mt 3.11; Mk 1.7; Jn 1.27   16 ἐκ...ἐλάβομεν Col 2.10

---

8 He himself was not the light; he came to tell about the light. 9 This was the real light, the light that comes into the world and shines on all men.

10 The Word, then, was in the world. God made the world through him, yet the world did not know him. 11 He came to his own country, but his own people did not receive him. 12 Some, however, did receive him and believed in him; so he gave them the right to become God's children. 13 They did not become God's children by natural means, by being born as the children of a human father; God himself was their Father.

14 The Word became a human being and lived among us. We saw his glory, full of grace and truth. This was the glory which he received as the Father's only Son.

15 John told about him. He cried out, "This is the one I was talking about when I said, 'He comes after me, but he is greater than I am, because he existed before I was born.' "

16 Out of the fulness of his grace he

has blessed us all, giving us one blessing after another. ¹⁷ God gave the Law through Moses; but grace and truth came through Jesus Christ. ¹⁸ No one has ever seen God. The only One, who is the same as God and² is at the Father's side, he has made him known.

John the Baptist's Message
(Also Matt. 3.1–12; Mark 1.1–8; Luke 3.1–18)

¹⁹ This is what John said when the Jews in Jerusalem sent priests and Levites to ask him, "Who are you?" ²⁰ John did not refuse to answer, but declared openly and clearly, "I am not the Messiah." ²¹ "Who are you, then?" they asked. "Are you Elijah?" "No, I am not," John answered. "Are you the Prophet?"

---

² 18 The only One, who is the same as God, and: *some mss. read* The only Son, who

---

αὐτοῦ ἡμεῖς πάντες ἐλάβομεν, καὶ χάριν ἀντὶ χάριτος· 17 ὅτι ὁ νόμος διὰ Μωϋσέως ἐδόθη, ἡ χάρις καὶ ἡ ἀλήθεια διὰ Ἰησοῦ Χριστοῦ ἐγένετο. 18 θεὸν οὐδεὶς ἑώρακεν πώποτε· μονογενὴς θεός⁵ ὁ ὢν εἰς τὸν κόλπον τοῦ πατρὸς ἐκεῖνος ἐξηγήσατο.

The Testimony of John the Baptist
(Mt 3.1–12; Mk 1.2–8; Lk 3.15–17)

19 Καὶ αὕτη ἐστὶν ἡ μαρτυρία τοῦ Ἰωάννου, ὅτε ἀπέστειλαν [πρὸς αὐτὸν] οἱ Ἰουδαῖοι ἐξ Ἱεροσολύμων ἱερεῖς καὶ Λευίτας ἵνα ἐρωτήσωσιν αὐτόν, Σὺ τίς εἶ; 20 καὶ ὡμολόγησεν καὶ οὐκ ἠρνήσατο, καὶ ὡμολόγησεν ὅτι Ἐγὼ οὐκ εἰμὶ ὁ Χριστός. 21 καὶ ἠρώτησαν αὐτόν, Τί οὖν σύ; Ἠλίας εἶ⁶; καὶ λέγει, Οὐκ εἰμί. Ὁ προ-

---

ἦν ὃν εἶπον ὑμῖν, Ὁ ὀπίσω μου ἐρχόμενος (Dᵇ *omit* λέγων) (Wˢᵘᵖᵖ *add* ὅς) X itᶠ vgʷʷ eth ‖ λέγων, Οὗτος ἦν ὁ. εἰπών, Ὁ ὀπίσω μου ἐρχόμενος אᵃᵛⁱᵈ B* C* Origen ‖ Οὗτος ἦν ὁ ὀπίσω μου ἐρχόμενος ὅς א*

⁵ 18 {B} μονογενὴς θεός 𝔭⁶⁶ א* B C* L (ὁ μονογενὴς θεός 𝔭⁷⁵ אᶜ 33 copᵇᵒ) syrᵖ,ʰᵐᵍ ethʳᵒ Theodotusᵃᶜᶜ. ᵗᵒ Clement Valentiniansᵃᶜᶜ. ᵗᵒ Irenaeus ᵃⁿᵈ Clement Ptolemy Diatessaronᵃ Heracleon Irenaeusˡᵃᵗ¹/³ Clement³/⁵ Origenᵍʳ,ˡᵃᵗ Ariusᵃᶜᶜ. ᵗᵒ Epiphanius Hilary Basil Apostolic Constitutions Didymus Gregory-Nyssa Epiphanius Synesiusᵃᶜᶜ. ᵗᵒ Epiphanius Jerome Cyril Ps-Ignatius ‖ ὁ μονογενὴς υἱός A C³ K Wˢᵘᵖᵖ X Δ Θ Π Ψ 063 f¹ f¹³ 28 565 700 892 1009 1010 1071 1079 1195 1216 1230 1241 1242 1253 1344 1365 1546 1646 2148 *Byz Lect* itᵃ,ᵃᵘʳ,ᵇ,ᶜ,ᵉ,ᶠ,ᶠᶠ²,¹ vg syrᶜ,ʰ,ᵖᵃˡ arm ethᵖᵖ geo Irenaeusˡᵃᵗ²/³ Clement²/⁵ Tertullian (Hippolytus) Alexander Eusebius Ambrosiaster Victorinus-Rome Hilary Athanasius Titus-Bostra Basil Gregory-Nazianzus Chrysostom Synesius Theodore Nonnus Proclus Theodoret Fulgentius Caesarius ‖ μονογενὴς υἱὸς θεοῦ itᵍ (copˢᵃ? θεός) Irenaeusˡᵃᵗ Origen ‖ ὁ μονογενής vgᵐˢ Diatessaron Origen Jacob-Nisibis Victorinus-Rome Ephraem Cyril-Jerusalem Ambrose Epiphanius Nonnus Nestorius Ps-Ignatius

⁶ 21 {D} Τί οὖν σύ; Ἠλίας εἶ (𝔭⁶⁶ τίς) 𝔭⁷⁵ C* (Wˢᵘᵖᵖ εἶ Ἠλίας) Ψ 33 it⁽ᵉ⁾,ᶠᶠ²,¹ syrᵖᵃˡ arm geo Origen ‖ Τί οὖν Ἠλίας εἶ N L itᵃ syrᵖ Cyril ‖ Τί οὖν Ἠλίας εἶ σύ A C³ K X Δ Θ Π 063ᵛⁱᵈ 0234 f¹ f¹³ 28 565 700 892 1009 1010 1079 1195 1216 1230 1241 1242 1253 1344 1365 1546 1646 2148 2174 *Byz*

---

17 ὁ νόμος...ἐδόθη Ex 31.18; 34.28; Jn 7.19   18 θεὸν...πώποτε Ex 33.20; Jn 6.46; 1 Tm 6.16; 1 Jn 4.12   μονογενὴς...ἐξηγήσατο Mt 11.27; Lk 10.22   20 Jn 3.28   21 σύ; Ἠλίας...εἰμί Mt 11.14; 17.11–13; Mk 9.13   Ὁ προφήτης εἶ σύ Dt 18.15, 18; Jn 6.14; 7.40; Ac 3.22; 7.37

φήτης εἶ σύ; καὶ ἀπεκρίθη, Οὔ. **22** εἶπαν οὖν αὐτῷ, Τίς εἶ; ἵνα ἀπόκρισιν δῶμεν τοῖς πέμψασιν ἡμᾶς· τί λέγεις περὶ σεαυτοῦ; **23** ἔφη,

Ἐγὼ φωνὴ βοῶντος ἐν τῇ ἐρήμῳ,
Εὐθύνατε τὴν ὁδὸν κυρίου,

καθὼς εἶπεν Ἠσαΐας ὁ προφήτης. **24** Καὶ ἀπεσταλμένοι ἦσαν ἐκ τῶν Φαρισαίων. **25** καὶ ἠρώτησαν αὐτὸν καὶ εἶπαν αὐτῷ, Τί οὖν βαπτίζεις εἰ σὺ οὐκ εἶ ὁ Χριστὸς οὐδὲ Ἠλίας οὐδὲ ὁ προφήτης; **26** ἀπεκρίθη αὐτοῖς ὁ Ἰωάννης λέγων, Ἐγὼ βαπτίζω ἐν ὕδατι· μέσος ὑμῶν ἕστηκεν[7] ὃν ὑμεῖς οὐκ οἴδατε, **27** ὁ ὀπίσω μου ἐρχόμενος, οὗ οὐκ εἰμὶ [ἐγὼ] ἄξιος ἵνα λύσω αὐτοῦ τὸν ἱμάντα τοῦ ὑποδήματος. **28** Ταῦτα ἐν Βηθανίᾳ ἐγένετο[8] πέραν τοῦ Ἰορδάνου, ὅπου ἦν ὁ Ἰωάννης βαπτίζων.

The Lamb of God

29 Τῇ ἐπαύριον βλέπει τὸν Ἰησοῦν ἐρχόμενον πρὸς αὐτόν, καὶ λέγει, Ἴδε ὁ ἀμνὸς τοῦ θεοῦ ὁ αἴρων τὴν

Lect *l*[698,m,70m,1858,m] it[aur,c,f,q] vg syr[h] Chrysostom ‖ Σὺ οὖν τί; Ἠλίας εἶ B ‖ Σὺ τίς εἶ; Ἠλίας εἶ 1071 ‖ Ἠλίας εἶ σύ it[b,r1] cop[sa,bo]

[7] **26** {B} ἕστηκεν 𝔭[66] A C K W[supp] X Δ Θ Π Ψ 063 0113[vid] *f*[13] 28 33 565 700 892 1009 1010 1079 1195 1216 1230 1241 1242 1253 1344 1546 1646 2148 2174 *Byz Lect l*[698,m,70m,1858,m] it[f] vg arm geo Heracleon[acc. to Origen] Origen Chrysostom Cyril ‖ ἑστήκει ℵ Origen ‖ εἱστήκει 𝔭[75] 1071 1365 Eusebius ‖ στήκει B L *f*[1] Origen Cyril ‖ *stands* it[a,aur,b,c,e,ff2,l,q] syr[c,s,p,h,pal] cop[sa,bo] Origen[lat] Cyprian

[8] **28** {C} ἐν Βηθανίᾳ ἐγένετο 𝔭[59vid,75] A B C* L W[supp] X Δ Θ Ψ[c] 063 28 565 700 892* 1009 1010 1071 1195 1216 1241 1242 1253 1344 1365* 2148 2174 *Byz*[pt] *Lect* it[aur,c,f,ff2,l,q] vg syr[p,h,palms] Heracleon[acc. to Origen] Origen mss[acc. to Origen] Ambrosiaster mss[acc. to Epiphanius] Chrysostom Nonnus Cyril ‖ ἐγένετο ἐν Βηθανίᾳ 𝔭[66] ℵ* it[a,b,e,r1] cop[bo?] ‖ ἐν Βηθαβαρᾷ ἐγένετο C[2] (K μὲν ἐν) (Π*) Π[c] Ψ*[vid] 083 0113[vid] *f*[1] *f*[13] 33 892[mg] 1079 1230 1365[c] 1546 (1646* Βιθαρᾷ) 1646[c] *Byz*[pt] *l*[70c,1231] syr[c,s,(palms)] cop[sa] arm geo Origen mss[acc. to Origen] Eusebius Epiphanius Chrysostom mss[acc. to Chrysostom] ‖ ἐν Βηθαραβᾷ ἐγένετο syr[hmg] Origen ‖ ἐγένετο ἐν Βηθαραβᾷ ℵ[b]

---

23 φωνὴ...κυρίου Is 40.3 (Mt 3.3; Mk 1.3; Lk 3.4)   **25-26** Τί...ὕδατι Mt 21.25; Mk 11.30; Lk 20.4; Jn 1.33   **27** ὁ ὀπίσω μου ἐρχόμενος Jn 1.15 ὁ ὀπίσω...ὑποδήματος Ac 13.25 **28** Mt 3.13; Jn 10.40   **29** Τῇ...θεοῦ Jn 1.36 ὁ ἀμνὸς...κόσμου Is 53.6-7; Ac 8.32; 1 Pe 1.18-19

---

they asked. "No," he replied. **22** "Tell us who you are," they said. "We have to take an answer back to those who sent us. What do you say about yourself?" **23** John answered, "This is what I am:

'The voice of one who shouts in the desert:
Make a straight path for the Lord to travel!' "

(This is what the prophet Isaiah had said.)

24 The messengers had been sent by the Pharisees. **25** They asked John, "If you are not the Messiah, nor Elijah, nor the Prophet, why do you baptize?" **26** John answered: "I baptize with water; among you stands the one you do not know. **27** He comes after me, but I am not good enough even to untie his sandals."

28 All this happened in Bethany, on the other side of the Jordan river, where John was baptizing.

The Lamb of God

29 The next day John saw Jesus coming to him and said: "Here is the Lamb of God who takes away the sin of the world! ³⁰ This is the one I was talking about when I said, 'A man comes after me, but he is greater than I am, because he existed before I was born.' ³¹ I did not know who he would be, but I came baptizing with water in order to make him known to Israel.''

³² This is the testimony that John gave: "I saw the Spirit come down like a dove from heaven and stay on him. ³³ I still did not know him, but God, who sent me to baptize with water, said to me, 'You will see the Spirit come down and stay on a man; he is the one who baptizes with the Holy Spirit.' ³⁴ I have seen it,'' said John, "and I tell you that he is the Son of God.''

The First Disciples of Jesus

³⁵ The next day John was there again with two of his disciples, ³⁶ when he saw Jesus walking by. "Here is the Lamb of God!" he said. ³⁷ The two disciples heard him say this and went with Jesus. ³⁸ Jesus turned, saw them following him, and asked, "What are you looking for?" They answered, "Where do you live, Rabbi?" (This word, translated, means "Teacher.") ³⁹ "Come and see," he answered. So they went with him and saw where he lived, and spent the rest of that day with him. (It was about four o'clock in the afternoon.)

⁴⁰ One of the two who heard John, and went with Jesus, was Andrew, Simon Peter's brother. ⁴¹ At once Andrew found

ἁμαρτίαν τοῦ κόσμου. **30** οὗτός ἐστιν ὑπὲρ οὗ ἐγὼ εἶπον, Ὀπίσω μου ἔρχεται ἀνὴρ ὃς ἔμπροσθέν μου γέγονεν, ὅτι πρῶτός μου ἦν. **31** κἀγὼ οὐκ ᾔδειν αὐτόν, ἀλλ' ἵνα φανερωθῇ τῷ Ἰσραὴλ διὰ τοῦτο ἦλθον ἐγὼ ἐν ὕδατι βαπτίζων. **32** Καὶ ἐμαρτύρησεν Ἰωάννης λέγων ὅτι Τεθέαμαι τὸ πνεῦμα καταβαῖνον ὡς περιστερὰν ἐξ οὐρανοῦ, καὶ ἔμεινεν ἐπ' αὐτόν· **33** κἀγὼ οὐκ ᾔδειν αὐτόν, ἀλλ' ὁ πέμψας με βαπτίζειν ἐν ὕδατι ἐκεῖνός μοι εἶπεν, Ἐφ' ὃν ἂν ἴδῃς τὸ πνεῦμα καταβαῖνον καὶ μένον ἐπ' αὐτόν, οὗτός ἐστιν ὁ βαπτίζων ἐν πνεύματι ἁγίῳ. **34** κἀγὼ ἑώρακα, καὶ μεμαρτύρηκα ὅτι οὗτός ἐστιν ὁ υἱὸς⁹ τοῦ θεοῦ.

The First Disciples

35 Τῇ ἐπαύριον πάλιν εἱστήκει ὁ Ἰωάννης καὶ ἐκ τῶν μαθητῶν αὐτοῦ δύο, **36** καὶ ἐμβλέψας τῷ Ἰησοῦ περιπατοῦντι λέγει, Ἴδε ὁ ἀμνὸς τοῦ θεοῦ. **37** καὶ ἤκουσαν οἱ δύο μαθηταὶ αὐτοῦ λαλοῦντος καὶ ἠκολούθησαν τῷ Ἰησοῦ. **38** στραφεὶς δὲ ὁ Ἰησοῦς καὶ θεασάμενος αὐτοὺς ἀκολουθοῦντας ᵉλέγει αὐτοῖς, ᵉΤί ζητεῖτε; οἱ δὲ εἶπαν αὐτῷ, Ῥαββί (ὃ λέγεται μεθερμηνευόμενον Διδάσκαλε), ποῦ μένεις; **39**ᵉ λέγει αὐτοῖς, Ἔρχεσθε καὶ ὄψεσθε. ἦλθαν οὖν καὶ εἶδαν ποῦ μένει, καὶ παρ' αὐτῷ ἔμειναν τὴν ἡμέραν ἐκείνην· ὥρα ἦν ὡς δεκάτη. **40**ᵉ Ἦν Ἀνδρέας ὁ ἀδελφὸς Σίμωνος Πέτρου εἷς ἐκ τῶν δύο τῶν ἀκουσάντων παρὰ Ἰωάννου καὶ ἀκολουθησάντων αὐτῷ· **41**ᵉ εὑ-

---

⁹ **34** {B} ὁ υἱός 𝔓⁶⁶,⁷⁵ ℵᶜ A B C K L P Wˢᵘᵖᵖ X Δ Θ Π Ψ 063 083 *f*¹ *f*¹³ 28 33 565 700 892 1009 1010 1071 1079 1195 1216 1230 1241 1242 1253 1344 1365 1546 1646 2148 2174 *Byz Lect*ᵐ *l*⁵⁴⁷ itᵃᵘʳ,ᶜ,ᶠ,ˡ,q vg syrᵖ,ʰ copᵇᵒ arm geo Origen Chrysostom Cyril ∥ ὁ ἐκλεκτός 𝔓⁵ᵛⁱᵈ ℵ* itᵇ,ᵉ,ff2* syrᶜ,ˢ Ambrose ∥ ὁ ἐκλεκτὸς υἱός itᵃ,ff2ᶜ syrᵖᵃˡᵐˢˢ copˢᵃ ∥ ὁ μονογενὴς υἱός syrᵖᵃˡᵐˢ

ᵉᵉᵉᵉᵉ **38–42** e no number, e no number, e number 39, e number 40, e number 41: TRᵉᵈ WH Bov Nes BF² AV RV ASV RSV NEB TT Zür Luth Jer Seg ∥ e no number, e number 39, e number 40, e number 41, e number 42: TRᵉᵈ ∥ e number 39, e no number, e number 40, e number 41, e number 42: TRᵉᵈ

---

30 Jn 1.15 **32** Τεθέαμαι...αὐτόν Mt 3.16; Mk 1.10; Lk 3.22 **34** οὗτος...θεοῦ Mt 3.17; 17.5; 27.54; Mk 9.7; 15.39; Lk 9.35; Jn 20.31; Ac 9.20 **36** Jn 1.29 **40–42** Ἦν...Ἰησοῦν Mt 4.18–20; Mk 1.16–18

ρίσκει οὗτος πρῶτον[10] τὸν ἀδελφὸν τὸν ἴδιον Σίμωνα καὶ λέγει αὐτῷ, Εὑρήκαμεν τὸν Μεσσίαν (ὅ ἐστιν μεθερμηνευόμενον Χριστός)· 42 ἤγαγεν αὐτὸν πρὸς τὸν Ἰησοῦν. ἐμβλέψας αὐτῷ ὁ Ἰησοῦς εἶπεν, Σὺ εἶ Σίμων ὁ υἱὸς Ἰωάννου[11]· σὺ κληθήσῃ Κηφᾶς (ὃ ἑρμηνεύεται Πέτρος).

The Calling of Philip and Nathanael

43 Τῇ ἐπαύριον ἠθέλησεν ἐξελθεῖν εἰς τὴν Γαλιλαίαν,[f] καὶ εὑρίσκει Φίλιππον.[f] καὶ λέγει αὐτῷ ὁ Ἰησοῦς, Ἀκολούθει μοι. 44 ἦν δὲ ὁ Φίλιππος ἀπὸ Βηθσαϊδά, ἐκ τῆς πόλεως Ἀνδρέου καὶ Πέτρου. 45 εὑρίσκει Φίλιππος τὸν Ναθαναὴλ καὶ λέγει αὐτῷ, Ὃν ἔγραψεν Μωϋσῆς ἐν τῷ νόμῳ καὶ οἱ προφῆται εὑρήκαμεν, Ἰησοῦν υἱὸν τοῦ Ἰωσὴφ τὸν ἀπὸ Ναζαρέτ. 46 καὶ εἶπεν αὐτῷ Ναθαναήλ, Ἐκ Ναζαρὲτ δύναταί τι ἀγαθὸν εἶναι; λέγει αὐτῷ Φίλιππος, Ἔρχου καὶ ἴδε. 47 εἶδεν ὁ Ἰησοῦς τὸν Ναθαναὴλ ἐρχόμενον πρὸς αὐτὸν καὶ λέγει περὶ αὐτοῦ, Ἴδε ἀληθῶς Ἰσραηλίτης ἐν ᾧ δόλος οὐκ ἔστιν. 48 λέγει αὐτῷ Ναθαναήλ, Πόθεν με γινώσκεις; ἀπεκρίθη Ἰησοῦς καὶ εἶπεν αὐτῷ, Πρὸ τοῦ σε Φίλιππον φωνῆσαι ὄντα ὑπὸ τὴν συκῆν εἶδόν σε. 49 ἀπεκρίθη αὐτῷ Ναθαναήλ,

[10] **41** {B} πρῶτον 𝔭[66,75] ℵ[c] A B X Θ Π Ψ 083 f[1] f[13] 33[vid] 892 1009 1079 1195 1216 1546 1646[c] 2174 l[1627] it[a,aur,c,f,ff2,l,q] vg syr[p,h,pal] cop[sa,bo] arm geo // πρῶτος ℵ* K L W[supp] Δ 28 565 700 1010 1071 1230 1241 1242 1253 1344 1365 1646* Byz Lect syr[pal?] Epiphanius Cyril // πρωΐ it[b,e,jvid,rlvid] // on that day syr[s] // omit 2148 syr[c] Augustine

[11] **42** {B} Ἰωάννου 𝔭[66,75] ℵ (B* Ἰωάνου) L W[supp] 33 it[a,b,f,ff2,l,r1] cop[sa,bo] eth[ro] Nonnus // Ἰωνᾶ A B³ K X Δ Π Ψ 063 f[1] f[13] 28 565 700 892 1009 1010 1071 1079 1195 1216 1230 1242 1253 1344 1365 1546 1646 2174 Byz Lect it[c,(q)] vg[cl] syr[s,p,h,pal] cop[boms] arm eth[pp] geo Diatessaron Epiphanius Chrysostom Cyril // Ἰωαννᾶ Θ (1241 Ἰωανᾶ) 2148 vg[ww] Diatessaron[f,n,t] // Bariona it[aur] // frater Andreae it[e]

f f **43** f minor, f major: Bov Nes BF² RV ASV TT Zür Seg // f major, f none: TR WH RSV NEB Jer // f minor, f minor: AV // f none, f none: Luth

41 Μεσσίαν...Χριστός Jn 4.25   **42** Σύ...Πέτρος Mt 10.2; 16.18; Mk 3.16; Lk 6.14
44 ἦν...Βηθσαϊδά Jn 12.21   **45** Ὅν...προφῆται Dt 18.18; Is 7.14; 9.6; Eze 34.23

his brother Simon and told him, "We have found the Messiah." (This word means "Christ.") 42 Then he brought Simon to Jesus. Jesus looked at him and said, "You are Simon, the son of John. Your name will be Cephas." (This is the same as Peter, and means "Rock.")

Jesus Calls Philip and Nathanael

43 The next day Jesus decided to go to Galilee. He found Philip and said to him, "Come with me!" 44 (Philip was from Bethsaida, the town where Andrew and Peter lived.) 45 So Philip found Nathanael and told him: "We have found the one of whom Moses wrote in the book of the Law, and of whom the prophets also wrote. He is Jesus, the son of Joseph, from Nazareth." 46 "Can anything good come from Nazareth?" Nathanael asked. "Come and see," answered Philip.

47 When Jesus saw Nathanael coming to him, he said about him, "Here is a real Israelite; there is nothing false in him!" 48 Nathanael asked him, "How do you know me?" Jesus answered, "I saw you when you were under the fig tree, before Philip called you." 49 "Teacher," answered Nathanael, "you are the Son

of God! You are the King of Israel!"
⁵⁰ Jesus said, "Do you believe just because I told you I saw you when you
were under the fig tree? You will see
much greater things than this!" ⁵¹ And
he said to them, "I tell you the truth:
you will see heaven open and God's angels
going up and coming down on the Son
of Man!"

The Wedding at Cana

2 Two days later there was a wedding
in the town of Cana, in Galilee. Jesus'
mother was there, ² and Jesus and his
disciples had also been invited to the
wedding. ³ When all the wine had been
drunk, Jesus' mother said to him, "They
are out of wine." ⁴ "You must not tell
me what to do, woman," Jesus replied.
"My time has not yet come." ⁵ Jesus'
mother then told the servants, "Do whatever he tells you."
⁶ The Jews have religious rules about
washing, and for this purpose six stone
water jars were there, each one large
enough to hold between twenty and thirty
gallons. ⁷ Jesus said to the servants,
"Fill these jars with water." They filled
them to the brim, ⁸ and then he told
them, "Now draw some water out and
take it to the man in charge of the
feast." They took it to him, ⁹ and he
tasted the water, which had turned into
wine. He did not know where this wine
had come from (but the servants who had
drawn out the water knew); so he called
the bridegroom ¹⁰ and said to him,
"Everyone else serves the best wine first,
and after the guests have drunk a lot he
serves the ordinary wine. But you have
kept the best wine until now!"
¹¹ Jesus performed this first of his
mighty works in Cana of Galilee; there
he revealed his glory, and his disciples
believed in him.

Ῥαββί, σὺ εἶ ὁ υἱὸς τοῦ θεοῦ, σὺ βασιλεὺς εἶ τοῦ Ἰσραήλ.
50 ἀπεκρίθη Ἰησοῦς καὶ εἶπεν αὐτῷ, Ὅτι εἶπόν σοι
ὅτι εἶδόν σε ὑποκάτω τῆς συκῆς πιστεύεις; μείζω τούτων ὄψῃ. 51 καὶ λέγει αὐτῷ, Ἀμὴν ἀμὴν λέγω ὑμῖν,
ὄψεσθε **τὸν οὐρανὸν** ἀνεῳγότα καὶ **τοὺς ἀγγέλους τοῦ
θεοῦ ἀναβαίνοντας καὶ καταβαίνοντας** ἐπὶ τὸν υἱὸν τοῦ
ἀνθρώπου.

The Wedding at Cana

2 Καὶ τῇ ἡμέρᾳ τῇ τρίτῃ γάμος ἐγένετο ἐν Κανὰ τῆς
Γαλιλαίας, καὶ ἦν ἡ μήτηρ τοῦ Ἰησοῦ ἐκεῖ· 2 ἐκλήθη
δὲ καὶ ὁ Ἰησοῦς καὶ οἱ μαθηταὶ αὐτοῦ εἰς τὸν γάμον.
3 καὶ ὑστερήσαντος οἴνου λέγει ἡ μήτηρ τοῦ Ἰησοῦ πρὸς
αὐτόν, Οἶνον οὐκ ἔχουσιν. 4 [καὶ] λέγει αὐτῇ ὁ Ἰησοῦς,
Τί ἐμοὶ καὶ σοί, γύναι; οὔπω ἥκει ἡ ὥρα μου. 5 λέγει
ἡ μήτηρ αὐτοῦ τοῖς διακόνοις, Ὅ τι ἂν λέγῃ ὑμῖν ποιήσατε. 6 ἦσαν δὲ ἐκεῖ λίθιναι ὑδρίαι ἓξ κατὰ τὸν καθα-
ρισμὸν τῶν Ἰουδαίων κείμεναι, χωροῦσαι ἀνὰ μετρητὰς
δύο ἢ τρεῖς. 7 λέγει αὐτοῖς ὁ Ἰησοῦς, Γεμίσατε τὰς
ὑδρίας ὕδατος. καὶ ἐγέμισαν αὐτὰς ἕως ἄνω. 8 καὶ
λέγει αὐτοῖς, Ἀντλήσατε νῦν καὶ φέρετε τῷ ἀρχιτρικλίνῳ·
οἱ δὲ ἤνεγκαν. 9 ὡς δὲ ἐγεύσατο ὁ ἀρχιτρίκλινος τὸ
ὕδωρ οἶνον γεγενημένον, καὶ οὐκ ᾔδει πόθεν ἐστίν, οἱ
δὲ διάκονοι ᾔδεισαν οἱ ἠντληκότες τὸ ὕδωρ, φωνεῖ τὸν
νυμφίον ὁ ἀρχιτρίκλινος 10 καὶ λέγει αὐτῷ, Πᾶς ἄνθρωπος πρῶτον τὸν καλὸν οἶνον τίθησιν, καὶ ὅταν μεθυ-
σθῶσιν τὸν ἐλάσσω· σὺ τετήρηκας τὸν καλὸν οἶνον ἕως
ἄρτι. 11 Ταύτην ἐποίησεν ἀρχὴν τῶν σημείων ὁ Ἰησοῦς
ἐν Κανὰ τῆς Γαλιλαίας καὶ ἐφανέρωσεν τὴν δόξαν αὐτοῦ,
καὶ ἐπίστευσαν εἰς αὐτὸν οἱ μαθηταὶ αὐτοῦ.

---

49 σὺ...θεοῦ Ps 2.7; Mt 3.17; 14.33; 16.16; Mk 1.11; 3.11; Lk 3.22; 4.41 Jn 11.27; Ac 13.33
βασιλεὺς...Ἰσραὴλ Zph 3.15; Mt 27.42; Mk 15.32; Jn 12.13   **51** τοὺς...καταβαίνοντας
Gn 28.12
2 1 Jn 4.46   **4** οὔπω...μου Jn 7.30; 8.20   **5** Ὅ...ποιήσατε Gn 41.55   **6** κατὰ...
Ἰουδαίων Mk 7.3–4; Jn 3.25   **11** Ταύτην...Γαλιλαίας Jn 4.54; 20.30   ἐφανέρωσεν τὴν
δόξαν αὐτοῦ Lk 9.32; Jn 1.14; 12.41

12 Μετὰ τοῦτο κατέβη εἰς Καφαρναοὺμ αὐτὸς καὶ ἡ μήτηρ αὐτοῦ καὶ οἱ ἀδελφοὶ [αὐτοῦ] καὶ οἱ μαθηταὶ αὐτοῦ, καὶ ἐκεῖ ἔμειναν[1] οὐ πολλὰς ἡμέρας.

The Cleansing of the Temple
(Mt 21.12–13; Mk 11.15–17; Lk 19.45–46)

13 Καὶ ἐγγὺς ἦν τὸ πάσχα τῶν Ἰουδαίων, καὶ ἀνέβη εἰς Ἱεροσόλυμα ὁ Ἰησοῦς. **14** καὶ εὗρεν ἐν τῷ ἱερῷ τοὺς πωλοῦντας βόας καὶ πρόβατα καὶ περιστερὰς καὶ τοὺς κερματιστὰς καθημένους, **15** καὶ ποιήσας φραγέλλιον[2] ἐκ σχοινίων πάντας ἐξέβαλεν ἐκ τοῦ ἱεροῦ, τά τε πρόβατα καὶ τοὺς βόας, καὶ τῶν κολλυβιστῶν ἐξέχεεν τὸ κέρμα καὶ τὰς τραπέζας ἀνέτρεψεν, **16** καὶ τοῖς τὰς περιστερὰς πωλοῦσιν εἶπεν, Ἄρατε ταῦτα ἐντεῦθεν, μὴ ποιεῖτε τὸν οἶκον τοῦ πατρός μου οἶκον ἐμπορίου. **17** Ἐμνήσθησαν οἱ μαθηταὶ αὐτοῦ ὅτι γεγραμμένον ἐστίν, **Ὁ ζῆλος τοῦ οἴκου σου καταφάγεταί με.** **18** ἀπεκρίθησαν οὖν οἱ Ἰουδαῖοι καὶ εἶπαν αὐτῷ, Τί σημεῖον δεικνύεις ἡμῖν, ὅτι ταῦτα ποιεῖς; **19** ἀπεκρίθη Ἰησοῦς καὶ εἶπεν αὐτοῖς, Λύσατε τὸν ναὸν τοῦτον καὶ ἐν τρισὶν ἡμέραις ἐγερῶ αὐτόν. **20** εἶπαν οὖν οἱ Ἰουδαῖοι, Τεσσαράκοντα καὶ ἓξ ἔτεσιν οἰκοδομήθη ὁ ναὸς οὗτος, καὶ σὺ ἐν τρισὶν ἡμέραις ἐγερεῖς αὐτόν; **21** ἐκεῖνος δὲ ἔλεγεν

---

[1] **12** {B} ἐκεῖ ἔμειναν 𝔭[66*,75] ℵ B K L X Δ Θ Π Ψ 063[vid] 0162 f[13] 28 33 700 892 1009 1010 1071 1079 1195 1216 1242 1344 1365 1546 2148 2174 *Byz Lect* it[n,aur,e,s,f,ff2,l,q,r1] vg syr[p,h] cop[sa,mss] eth Origen Cyril Paschal Chronicle ∥ ἐκεῖ ἔμεινεν 𝔭[66c] A f[1] 565 1241 1646 *l*[547] it[b] syr[pal] cop[sa,mss,bo,ach2] arm geo[2] Diatessaron[v] Origen Nonnus ∥ ἔμειναν W[supp] 1230 1253 ∥ ἐκεῖ ἦσαν geo[1] Chrysostom

[2] **15** {B} φραγέλλιον ℵ A B K P Δ Θ Π Ψ f[13] 28 700 1009 1071 1079 1195 1216 1230 1242 1253 1344 1365 1546 1646 2148 2174 *Byz Lect* it[l] syr[p,h] cop[sa,bo,ach2] arm geo Origen[3/4] ∥ ὡς φραγέλλιον 𝔭[66,75] L W[supp] X 0162 f[1] 33 565 892 1010 1241 it[a,vid,aur,b,c,e,f,ff2,l,q] vg syr[hmg,pal] Origen[1/4] Nonnus Cyril ∥ ὡσεὶ φραγέλλιον Cyril

---

12 Mt 4.13   **13** ἐγγὺς…Ἰουδαίων Jn 6.4; 11.55   **16** τὸν οἶκον τοῦ πατρός μου Lk 2.49   **17** Ὁ ζῆλος…με Ps 69.9   **19** Mt 26.61; 27.40; Mk 14.58; 15.29; Ac 6.14

[12] After this, Jesus and his mother, brothers, and disciples went to Capernaum, and stayed there a few days.

Jesus Goes to the Temple
(Also Matt. 21.12–13; Mark 11.15–17; Luke 19.45–46)

[13] It was almost time for the Jewish Feast of Passover, so Jesus went to Jerusalem. [14] In the Temple he found men selling cattle, sheep, and pigeons, and also the money-changers sitting at their tables. [15] He made a whip from cords and drove all the animals out of the Temple, both the sheep and the cattle; he overturned the tables of the money-changers and scattered their coins; [16] and he ordered the men who sold the pigeons, "Take them out of here! Do not make my Father's house a market place!" [17] His disciples remembered that the scripture says, "My devotion for your house, O God, burns in me like a fire." [18] The Jews came back at him with a question, "What miracle can you perform to show us that you have the right to do this?" [19] Jesus answered, "Tear down this house of God and in three days I will build it again." [20] "You are going to build it again in three days?" they asked him. "It has taken forty-six years to build this Temple!" [21] But the temple Jesus spoke of was

his body. ²² When he was raised from death, therefore, his disciples remembered that he said this; and they believed the scripture and the words that Jesus had said.

Jesus Knows All Men

²³ While Jesus was in Jerusalem during the Passover Feast, many believed in him as they saw the mighty works he did. ²⁴ But Jesus did not trust himself to them, because he knew all men well. ²⁵ There was no need for anyone to tell him about men, for he well knew what goes on in their hearts.

Jesus and Nicodemus

3 There was a man named Nicodemus, a leader of the Jews, who belonged to the party of the Pharisees. ² One night he came to Jesus and said to him: "We know, Rabbi, that you are a teacher sent by God. No one could do the mighty works you are doing unless God were with him." ³ Jesus answered, "I tell you the truth: no one can see the Kingdom of God unless he is born again."[1] ⁴ "How can a grown man be born again?" Nicodemus asked. "He certainly cannot enter his mother's womb and be born a second time!" ⁵ "I tell you the truth," replied Jesus, "that no one can enter the Kingdom of God unless he is born of water and the Spirit. ⁶ Flesh gives birth

---

[1] **3** again: *or* from above

περὶ τοῦ ναοῦ τοῦ σώματος αὐτοῦ. **22** ὅτε οὖν ἠγέρθη ἐκ νεκρῶν, ἐμνήσθησαν οἱ μαθηταὶ αὐτοῦ ὅτι τοῦτο ἔλεγεν, καὶ ἐπίστευσαν τῇ γραφῇ καὶ τῷ λόγῳ ὃν εἶπεν ὁ Ἰησοῦς.

Jesus Knows All Men

23 Ὡς δὲ ἦν ἐν τοῖς Ἱεροσολύμοις ἐν τῷ πάσχα ἐν τῇ ἑορτῇ, πολλοὶ ἐπίστευσαν εἰς τὸ ὄνομα αὐτοῦ, θεωροῦντες αὐτοῦ τὰ σημεῖα ἃ ἐποίει· **24** αὐτὸς δὲ Ἰησοῦς οὐκ ἐπίστευεν αὐτὸν αὐτοῖς διὰ τὸ αὐτὸν γινώσκειν πάντας, **25** καὶ ὅτι οὐ χρείαν εἶχεν ἵνα τις μαρτυρήσῃ περὶ τοῦ ἀνθρώπου· αὐτὸς γὰρ ἐγίνωσκεν τί ἦν ἐν τῷ ἀνθρώπῳ.

Jesus and Nicodemus

3 Ἦν δὲ ἄνθρωπος ἐκ τῶν Φαρισαίων, Νικόδημος ὄνομα αὐτῷ, ἄρχων τῶν Ἰουδαίων· **2** οὗτος ἦλθεν πρὸς αὐτὸν νυκτὸς καὶ εἶπεν αὐτῷ, Ῥαββί, οἴδαμεν ὅτι ἀπὸ θεοῦ ἐλήλυθας διδάσκαλος· οὐδεὶς γὰρ δύναται ταῦτα τὰ σημεῖα ποιεῖν ἃ σὺ ποιεῖς, ἐὰν μὴ ᾖ ὁ θεὸς μετ' αὐτοῦ. **3** ἀπεκρίθη Ἰησοῦς καὶ εἶπεν αὐτῷ, Ἀμὴν ἀμὴν λέγω σοι, ἐὰν μή τις γεννηθῇ ἄνωθεν, οὐ δύναται ἰδεῖν τὴν βασιλείαν τοῦ θεοῦ. **4** λέγει πρὸς αὐτὸν [ὁ] Νικόδημος, Πῶς δύναται ἄνθρωπος γεννηθῆναι γέρων ὤν; μὴ δύναται εἰς τὴν κοιλίαν τῆς μητρὸς αὐτοῦ δεύτερον εἰσελθεῖν καὶ γεννηθῆναι; **5** ἀπεκρίθη Ἰησοῦς, Ἀμὴν ἀμὴν λέγω σοι, ἐὰν μή τις γεννηθῇ ἐξ ὕδατος καὶ πνεύματος, οὐ δύναται εἰσελθεῖν εἰς τὴν βασιλείαν τοῦ θεοῦ[1]. **6** τὸ

---

[1] **5** {A} τοῦ θεοῦ (*see* 3.3) 𝔓^{66,75} ℵ^c A B K L W^{supp} X^{comm} Δ Θ Π Ψ 050 063^{vid} 086 f¹ f¹³ 28 33 565 700 892 1010 1071 1079 1195 1216 1230 1241 1242 1253 1344 1365 1546 1646 2148 2174 *Byz Lect* l^{698,m,70m} it^{a,aur,b,c,f,ff2,j,l,q,r1} vg syr^{c,s,p,h,pal} cop^{sa,bo,ach2,fay} goth arm geo Origen^{lat} Cyprian Gregory-Nyssa

---

21 τοῦ ναοῦ...αὐτοῦ 1 Cor 6.19   **22** Lk 24.6–8; Jn 12.16; 14.26   **23** πολλοὶ...ἐποίει Jn 7.31; 11.47–48

3 **1-2** Ἦν...νυκτός Jn 7.50; 19.39   **2** Ῥαββί...διδάσκαλος Mt 22.16   οὐδεὶς...αὐτοῦ Jn 9.16; Ac 10.38   **5** ἐάν...πνεύματος Tt 3.5

γεγεννημένον ἐκ τῆς σαρκὸς σάρξ ἐστιν, καὶ τὸ γεγεννημένον ἐκ τοῦ πνεύματος πνεῦμά ἐστιν. 7 μὴ θαυμάσῃς ὅτι εἶπόν σοι, Δεῖ ὑμᾶς γεννηθῆναι ἄνωθεν. 8 τὸ πνεῦμα ὅπου θέλει πνεῖ, καὶ τὴν φωνὴν αὐτοῦ ἀκούεις, ἀλλ' οὐκ οἶδας πόθεν ἔρχεται καὶ ποῦ ὑπάγει· οὕτως ἐστὶν πᾶς ὁ γεγεννημένος ἐκ τοῦ πνεύματος. 9 ἀπεκρίθη Νικόδημος καὶ εἶπεν αὐτῷ, Πῶς δύναται ταῦτα γενέσθαι; 10 ἀπεκρίθη Ἰησοῦς καὶ εἶπεν αὐτῷ, Σὺ εἶ ὁ διδάσκαλος τοῦ Ἰσραὴλ καὶ ταῦτα οὐ γινώσκεις; 11 ἀμὴν ἀμὴν λέγω σοι ὅτι ὃ οἴδαμεν λαλοῦμεν καὶ ὃ ἑωράκαμεν μαρτυροῦμεν, καὶ τὴν μαρτυρίαν ἡμῶν οὐ λαμβάνετε. 12 εἰ τὰ ἐπίγεια εἶπον ὑμῖν καὶ οὐ πιστεύετε, πῶς ἐὰν εἴπω ὑμῖν τὰ ἐπουράνια πιστεύσετε; 13 καὶ οὐδεὶς ἀναβέβηκεν εἰς τὸν οὐρανὸν εἰ μὴ ὁ ἐκ τοῦ οὐρανοῦ καταβάς, ὁ υἱὸς τοῦ ἀνθρώπου². 14 καὶ καθὼς Μωϋσῆς ὕψωσεν τὸν ὄφιν ἐν τῇ ἐρήμῳ, οὕτως ὑψωθῆναι δεῖ τὸν υἱὸν τοῦ ἀνθρώπου, 15 ἵνα πᾶς ὁ πιστεύων ἐν αὐτῷ³ ἔχῃ ζωὴν αἰώνιον.

to flesh, and Spirit gives birth to spirit. 7 Do not be surprised because I tell you, 'You must all be born again.'[2] 8 The wind blows wherever it wishes; you hear the sound it makes, but you do not know where it comes from or where it is going. It is the same way with everyone who is born of the Spirit." 9 "How can this be?" asked Nicodemus. 10 Jesus answered: "You are a great teacher of Israel, and you don't know this? 11 I tell you the truth: we speak of what we know, and tell what we have seen — yet none of you is willing to accept our message. 12 You do not believe me when I tell you about the things of this world; how will you ever believe me, then, when I tell you about the things of heaven? 13 And no one has ever gone up to heaven except the Son of Man, who came down from heaven."

14 As Moses lifted up the bronze snake on a pole in the desert, in the same way the Son of Man must be lifted up, 15 so that everyone who believes in him may

---

Chrysostom Cyril ∥ τῶν οὐρανῶν ℵ* 1009 *l*²⁶ ite Docetists Naassenes (Justin) Irenaeus Tertullian Hippolytus Origenlat Ps-Clement Eusebius Apostolic Constitutions Chrysostom Nonnus

² 13 {C} ἀνθρώπου 𝔭⁶⁶,⁷⁵ ℵ B L Wsupp 083 086 0113 33 1010 1241 copsa,bomss,ach2,fay eth Diatessaronearm,v Origenlat Apollinaris Didymus Cyril ∥ ἀνθρώπου ὁ ὢν ἐν τῷ οὐρανῷ (see 1.18) (A*vid omit ὤν) Ac K Δ Θ Π Ψ 050 (063 θεοῦ for ἀνθρώπου) *f*¹ *f*¹³ 28 565 700 892 1009 1071 1079 1195 1216 1230 1242 1253 1344 1365 1546 1646 2148 2174 Byz Lect *l*⁶⁹ˢ·ᵐ,⁷⁰ᵐ,⁷⁶ˢ·ᵐ, ¹⁸⁴ˢ·ᵐ,²¹¹ˢ·ᵐ,⁸⁸³ᵐ,¹⁵⁷⁹ᵐ ita,aur,b,c,f,ff2,j,l,q,rl vg syrp,h,pal copbomss arm geo Diatessarona Hippolytus Novatian Origenlat Dionysius Eustathius Jacob-Nisibis Aphraates Hilary Lucifer Basil Amphilochius Didymus Epiphanius Chrysostom Nonnus Cyril Theodoret ∥ ἀνθρώπου ὃς ἦν ἐν τῷ οὐρανῷ itc syrc,pal? ∥ ἀνθρώπου ὁ ὢν ἐκ τοῦ οὐρανοῦ 0141 80 syrs

³ 15 {B} ἐν αὐτῷ 𝔭⁷⁵ B Wsupp 0113 itaur,c,l,rl vgww syrc?s?p?h?pal? Fulgentius ∥ ἐπ' αὐτῷ 𝔭⁶⁶ L 1253 Theodoret ∥ εἰς αὐτόν 𝔭⁶³ᵛⁱᵈ ℵ K Δ Θ Π Ψ 063ᵛⁱᵈ 086 *f*¹ *f*¹³ 28 33 565 700 892 1009 1010 1071 1079 1195 1216 1230 1241 1242 1344 1365 1546 1646 2148 2174 Byz Lect *l*⁶⁹ˢ·ᵐ,⁷⁰ᵐ,⁷⁶ˢ·ᵐ,¹⁸⁴ˢ·ᵐ,¹⁸⁵ˢ·ᵐ,²¹¹ᵐ,⁸⁸³ᵐ,¹⁵⁷⁹ᵐ ita,b,e,f,ff2,j,q vgcl syrc?s?p?h?pal? copsa,bo,ach2,fay (Cyprian) Lucifer Chrysostom Cyril Theodoret ∥ ἐπ' αὐτόν A 083

---

8 τὸ...ὑπάγει Ec 11.5   11 ὃ οἴδαμεν...λαμβάνετε Jn 3.32; 8.26   12 Wsd. 9.16; Lk 22.67   13 οὐδεὶς...καταβάς Pr 30.4; Ro 10.6   14 Μωϋσῆς...ἐρήμῳ Nu 21.9 ὑψωθῆναι...ἀνθρώπου Jn 8.28; 12.34   15 Jn 20.31

---

² 7 again: or from above

have eternal life. ¹⁶ For God loved the world so much that he gave his only Son, so that everyone who believes in him may not die but have eternal life. ¹⁷ For God did not send his Son into the world to be its Judge, but to be its Savior.

¹⁸ Whoever believes in the Son is not judged; whoever does not believe has already been judged, because he has not believed in God's only Son. ¹⁹ This is how the judgment works: the light has come into the world, but men love the darkness rather than the light, because they do evil things. ²⁰ And anyone who does evil things hates the light and will not come to the light, because he does not want his evil deeds to be shown up. ²¹ But whoever does what is true comes to the light, in order that the light may show that he did his works in obedience to God.

Jesus and John

²² After this, Jesus and his disciples went to the province of Judea. He spent some time with them there, and baptized. ²³ John also was baptizing in Aenon, not far from Salim, because there was plenty of water there. People were going to him and he was baptizing them. ²⁴ (John had not yet been put in prison.)

²⁵ Some of John's disciples began arguing with a Jew about the matter of reli-

16 Οὕτως γὰρ ἠγάπησεν ὁ θεὸς τὸν κόσμον, ὥστε τὸν υἱὸν τὸν μονογενῆ ἔδωκεν, ἵνα πᾶς ὁ πιστεύων εἰς αὐτὸν μὴ ἀπόληται ἀλλ' ἔχῃ ζωὴν αἰώνιον. **17** οὐ γὰρ ἀπέστειλεν ὁ θεὸς τὸν υἱὸν εἰς τὸν κόσμον ἵνα κρίνῃ τὸν κόσμον, ἀλλ' ἵνα σωθῇ ὁ κόσμος δι' αὐτοῦ. **18** ὁ πιστεύων εἰς αὐτὸν οὐ κρίνεται· ὁ [δὲ] μὴ πιστεύων ἤδη κέκριται, ὅτι μὴ πεπίστευκεν εἰς τὸ ὄνομα τοῦ μονογενοῦς υἱοῦ τοῦ θεοῦ. **19** αὕτη δέ ἐστιν ἡ κρίσις, ὅτι τὸ φῶς ἐλήλυθεν εἰς τὸν κόσμον καὶ ἠγάπησαν οἱ ἄνθρωποι μᾶλλον τὸ σκότος ἢ τὸ φῶς, ἦν γὰρ αὐτῶν πονηρὰ τὰ ἔργα. **20** πᾶς γὰρ ὁ φαῦλα πράσσων μισεῖ τὸ φῶς καὶ οὐκ ἔρχεται πρὸς τὸ φῶς, ἵνα μὴ ἐλεγχθῇ τὰ ἔργα αὐτοῦ[4]· **21** ὁ δὲ ποιῶν τὴν ἀλήθειαν ἔρχεται πρὸς τὸ φῶς, ἵνα φανερωθῇ αὐτοῦ τὰ ἔργα ὅτι ἐν θεῷ ἐστιν εἰργασμένα.

Jesus and John the Baptist

22 Μετὰ ταῦτα ἦλθεν ὁ Ἰησοῦς καὶ οἱ μαθηταὶ αὐτοῦ εἰς τὴν Ἰουδαίαν γῆν, καὶ ἐκεῖ διέτριβεν μετ' αὐτῶν καὶ ἐβάπτιζεν. **23** ἦν δὲ καὶ ὁ Ἰωάννης βαπτίζων ἐν Αἰνὼν ἐγγὺς τοῦ Σαλείμ, ὅτι ὕδατα πολλὰ ἦν ἐκεῖ, καὶ παρεγίνοντο καὶ ἐβαπτίζοντο· **24** οὔπω γὰρ ἦν βεβλημένος εἰς τὴν φυλακὴν ὁ Ἰωάννης. **25** Ἐγένετο οὖν ζήτησις ἐκ τῶν μαθητῶν Ἰωάννου μετὰ Ἰουδαίου[5] περὶ καθαρισμοῦ.

---

[4] **20** {C} τὰ ἔργα αὐτοῦ ℵ B 050 063 083^{vid} 086 28 700 1230 1242^c 1253 1365 2148 *Byz Lect* it^{a,aur,b,e,(d),e,f,ff2,l,q} vg syr^{c,s,p,h,pal} cop^{fay} arm geo Irenaeus^{lat} Origen^{lat} Lucifer Cyril ∥ αὐτοῦ τὰ ἔργα p⁷⁵ A K W^{supp} Π *f*¹ 565 892* 1079 1546 Chrysostom ∥ τὰ ἔργα αὐτοῦ ὅτι πονηρά ἐστιν (see 3.19; 7.7) p⁶⁶ (L αὐτοῦ πονηρά ἐστιν ὅτι) Δ Θ (Ψ 1241 εἰσιν) *f*¹³ 33 (892^c αὐτὰ τὰ ἔργα) 1009 1010 1071 1195 1216 1242* 1344 1646 2174 it^{rl vid} cop^{sa,bo,ach2} (Origen^{lat}) Eusebius

[5] **25** {C} μετὰ Ἰουδαίου p⁷⁵ ℵ^c A B K L W^{supp} Δ Π Ψ 086 0193 28 33 700 892 1009 1010 1079 1195 1216 1230 1241 1242 1344 1546 1646 2148 2174

.16 Οὕτως...ἔδωκεν Ro 8.32; 1 Jn 4.9–10   ἵνα...αἰώνιον Jn 3.36; 10.28; 1 Jn 5.13   17 Jn 12.47 οὐ...κρίνῃ τὸν κόσμον Jn 5.22, 30; 8.15–16; Ac 17.31   18 ὁ πιστεύων...κρίνεται Jn 5.24   19 τὸ φῶς ἐλήλυθεν...κόσμον Jn 1.5, 9; 8.12; 9.5   20 Eph 5.11–13   21 ὁ δὲ...ἀλήθειαν Tob 4.6 LXX   22 Jn 3.26; 4.1–2   24 Mt 4.12; 14.3; Mk 1.14; 6.17; Lk 3.20

26 καὶ ἦλθον πρὸς τὸν Ἰωάννην καὶ εἶπαν αὐτῷ, Ῥαββί, ὃς ἦν μετὰ σοῦ πέραν τοῦ Ἰορδάνου, ᾧ σὺ μεμαρτύρηκας, ἴδε οὗτος βαπτίζει καὶ πάντες ἔρχονται πρὸς αὐτόν. 27 ἀπεκρίθη Ἰωάννης καὶ εἶπεν, Οὐ δύναται ἄνθρωπος λαμβάνειν οὐδὲ ἓν ἐὰν μὴ ᾖ δεδομένον αὐτῷ ἐκ τοῦ οὐρανοῦ. 28 αὐτοὶ ὑμεῖς μοι[6] μαρτυρεῖτε ὅτι εἶπον [ὅτι] Οὐκ εἰμὶ ἐγὼ ὁ Χριστός, ἀλλ᾽ ὅτι Ἀπεσταλμένος εἰμὶ ἔμπροσθεν ἐκείνου. 29 ὁ ἔχων τὴν νύμφην νυμφίος ἐστίν· ὁ δὲ φίλος τοῦ νυμφίου, ὁ ἑστηκὼς καὶ ἀκούων αὐτοῦ, χαρᾷ χαίρει διὰ τὴν φωνὴν τοῦ νυμφίου. αὕτη οὖν ἡ χαρὰ ἡ ἐμὴ πεπλήρωται. 30 ἐκεῖνον δεῖ αὐξάνειν, ἐμὲ δὲ ἐλαττοῦσθαι.

He Who Comes from Heaven

31 Ὁ ἄνωθεν ἐρχόμενος ἐπάνω πάντων ἐστίν·[a] ὁ ὢν ἐκ τῆς γῆς ἐκ τῆς γῆς ἐστιν καὶ ἐκ τῆς γῆς λαλεῖ.[a] ὁ ἐκ τοῦ οὐρανοῦ ἐρχόμενος [ἐπάνω πάντων ἐστίν·[a]] 32 ὃ ἑώρακεν καὶ ἤκουσεν τοῦτο μαρτυρεῖ[7], καὶ τὴν

Byz Lect syr[s,p,h,palmss] cop[samss,fay] arm Chrysostom Nonnus ‖ μετὰ Ἰουδαίων 𝔭[66] ℵ* Θ *f*[1] *f*[13] 565 1071 1253 1365 *l*[185] it[(a),aur,b,c,e,ff2,l] vg syr[c,palms] cop[samss,bo] goth eth geo Origen Cyril ‖ *ad Iudaeos* it[d] ‖ *et Iudaeos* it[f,j,q,(rl)]

[6] 28 {C} μοι 𝔭[66] A B D K L W[supp] Δ Θ Π Ψ 063[vid] 083 086[vid] *f*[13] 33 700 892 1010 1071 1079 1230 1241 1242 1546 1646 *Byz*[pt] *Lect* it[a,b,c,d,(e),f,ff2,l,q] vg syr[c?s?p?h?pal?] cop[samss,bo,fay] arm geo? Cyprian Eusebius Chrysostom Cyril ‖ ἐμοί *f*[1] 565 1365 *l*[547] syr[c?s?p?h?pal?] geo? ‖ *omit* 𝔭[75] ℵ 28 1009 1195 1216 1253 1344 2148 2174 *Byz*[pt] *l*[32,64,70c,76,80,159,184,210,372,381,1564,1627] it[aur] cop[samss]

[7] 31-32 {C} ἐρχόμενος ἐπάνω πάντων ἐστίν· ὃ ἑώρακεν καὶ ἤκουσεν τοῦτο μαρτυρεῖ 𝔭[36vid] (𝔭[66*] *omit* ἐρχόμενος) 𝔭[66c] (ℵ[c] *omit* τοῦτο) B L W[supp] Ψ 083 086 33 1010 1071 syr[pal] cop[bo,fay] Cyril ‖ ἐρχόμενος ἐπάνω πάντων ἐστίν· καὶ ὃ ἑώρακεν καὶ ἤκουσεν τοῦτο μαρτυρεῖ A K Δ Θ Π 063 *f*[13] (28 1365 *omit* τοῦτο) 700 892 1009 1079 1195 1216 1230 1241 1242[vid] 1253 1344 1546 1646 2148 2174 *Byz Lect* it[aur,c,f,q] vg syr[(p),h] goth (eth) Origen[gr,lat]

[a a a] 31 *a minor, a major, a minor:* Bov Nes BF[2] (NEB[mg]) (Jer[mg]) Seg ‖ *a minor, a major, a major:* TT ‖ *a major, a minor, a minor:* TR WH[ed] ‖ *a minor, a minor, a major:* AV RV ASV RSV Zür ‖ *a major, a major, a none:* Luth ‖ *a minor, a minor, a minor:* WH[ed] ‖ *different text:* NEB Jer

26 ὅς...βαπτίζει Jn 3.22; 4.1-2   27 Οὐ...οὐρανοῦ Jn 19.11; 1 Cor 4.7; He 5.4   28 Οὐκ ...Χριστός Jn 1.20 Ἀπεσταλμένος...ἐκείνου Mal 3.1; Mt 11.10; Mk 1.2   29 ὁ δὲ...νυμφίου Mt 9.15; Mk 2.19   31 Jn 8.23 ὁ ὤν...λαλεῖ 1 Jn 4.5   32 Jn 3.11   ὃ...μαρτυρεῖ Jn 8.26

gious washing. 26 So they went to John and told him: "Teacher, you remember the man who was with you on the other side of the Jordan, the one you spoke about? Well, he is baptizing now, and everyone is going to him!" 27 John answered: "No one can have anything unless God gives it to him. 28 You yourselves are my witnesses that I said, 'I am not the Messiah, but I have been sent ahead of him.' 29 The bridegroom is the one to whom the bride belongs; the bridegroom's friend stands by and listens, and he is glad when he hears the bridegroom's voice. This is how my own happiness is made complete. 30 He must become more important, while I become less important."

He who Comes from Heaven

31 He who comes from above is greater than all; he who is from the earth belongs to the earth and speaks about earthly matters. He who comes from heaven is above all. 32 He tells what he has seen

and heard, but no one accepts his message. [33] Whoever accepts his message proves by this that God is true. [34] The one whom God has sent speaks God's words; for God gives him the fulness of his Spirit. [35] The Father loves his Son and has put everything in his power. [36] Whoever believes in the Son has eternal life; whoever disobeys the Son will never have life, but God's wrath will remain on him for ever.

Jesus and the Woman of Samaria

4 The Pharisees heard that Jesus was winning and baptizing more disciples than John. [2] (Actually, Jesus himself did not baptize anyone; only his disciples did.) [3] When Jesus heard what was being said, he left Judea and went back to Galilee; [4] on his way there he had to go through Samaria.

[5] He came to a town in Samaria named Sychar, which was not far from the field that Jacob had given to his son Joseph. [6] Jacob's well was there, and Jesus, tired out by the trip, sat down by the well. It was about noon.

μαρτυρίαν αὐτοῦ οὐδεὶς λαμβάνει. **33** ὁ λαβὼν αὐτοῦ τὴν μαρτυρίαν ἐσφράγισεν ὅτι ὁ θεὸς ἀληθής ἐστιν. **34** ὃν γὰρ ἀπέστειλεν ὁ θεὸς τὰ ῥήματα τοῦ θεοῦ λαλεῖ, οὐ γὰρ ἐκ μέτρου δίδωσιν τὸ πνεῦμα. **35** ὁ πατὴρ ἀγαπᾷ τὸν υἱόν, καὶ πάντα δέδωκεν ἐν τῇ χειρὶ αὐτοῦ. **36** ὁ πιστεύων εἰς τὸν υἱὸν ἔχει ζωὴν αἰώνιον· ὁ δὲ ἀπειθῶν τῷ υἱῷ οὐκ ὄψεται ζωήν, ἀλλ' ἡ ὀργὴ τοῦ θεοῦ μένει ἐπ' αὐτόν.

Jesus and the Woman of Samaria

4 Ὡς οὖν ἔγνω ὁ Ἰησοῦς[1] ὅτι ἤκουσαν οἱ Φαρισαῖοι ὅτι Ἰησοῦς πλείονας μαθητὰς ποιεῖ καὶ βαπτίζει ἢ Ἰωάννης **2** — καίτοι γε Ἰησοῦς αὐτὸς οὐκ ἐβάπτιζεν ἀλλ' οἱ μαθηταὶ αὐτοῦ — **3** ἀφῆκεν τὴν Ἰουδαίαν καὶ ἀπῆλθεν πάλιν εἰς τὴν Γαλιλαίαν. **4** ἔδει δὲ αὐτὸν διέρχεσθαι διὰ τῆς Σαμαρείας. **5** ἔρχεται οὖν εἰς πόλιν τῆς Σαμαρείας λεγομένην Συχὰρ πλησίον τοῦ χωρίου ὃ ἔδωκεν Ἰακὼβ [τῷ] Ἰωσὴφ τῷ υἱῷ αὐτοῦ.[a] **6** ἦν δὲ ἐκεῖ πηγὴ τοῦ Ἰακώβ.[a] ὁ οὖν Ἰησοῦς κεκοπιακὼς ἐκ τῆς ὁδοιπορίας ἐκαθέζετο οὕτως ἐπὶ τῇ πηγῇ· ὥρα ἦν ὡς ἕκτη.

Chrysostom Augustine ‖ ἐρχόμενος ὃ ἑώρακεν καὶ ἤκουσεν τοῦτο μαρτυρεῖ 𝔭[75] cop[sa] Origen ‖ ἐρχόμενος ὃ ἑώρακεν καὶ ἤκουσεν μαρτυρεῖ (ℵ* ὅν for ὅ) D f[1] 565 it[a,b,d,e,ff2,j,l,rl] syr[c,(s)] arm geo Tertullian Hippolytus Hilary Ambrosiaster

[1] **1** {B} Ἰησοῦς ℵ D Θ 086 f[1] 565 1009 1010 1195 1241 1365 it[a,aur,b,c,d,e,ff2,j,l,rl] vg syr[c,p,h] cop[bo,fay] arm Diatessaron[a,n] Chrysostom ‖ κύριος 𝔭[66,75] A B C K L W[supp] Δ Π Ψ 083 f[13] 28 33 700 892 1071 1079 1216 1230 1242 1253 1344 1546 1646 2148 2174 Byz it[f,q] syr[s,hmg] cop[sa,boms] eth geo Nonnus Cyril

---

[a a] **5-6** a minor, a major: WH Bov Nes BF[2] RV ASV (NEB) ‖ a major, a minor: RSV ‖ a major, a major: TR AV TT Zür Luth Jer Seg

---

35 ὁ...υἱόν Jn 5.20; 10.17; 15.9   πάντα...αὐτοῦ Mt 11.27; Lk 10.22; Jn 13.3   **36** ὁ πιστεύων...αἰώνιον Jn 3.16; 1 Jn 5.13   ὁ δὲ...αὐτόν Eph 5.6   **4** **1-2** ἤκουσαν...αὐτοῦ Jn 3.22, 26   **4** Mt 10.5; Lk 9.52; 17.11   **5** Gn 33.19; 48.22; Jos 24.32   **6** ἦν...Ἰακώβ Jn 4.12

7 Ἔρχεται γυνὴ ἐκ τῆς Σαμαρείας ἀντλῆσαι ὕδωρ. λέγει αὐτῇ ὁ Ἰησοῦς, Δός μοι πεῖν· 8 οἱ γὰρ μαθηταὶ αὐτοῦ ἀπεληλύθεισαν εἰς τὴν πόλιν, ἵνα τροφὰς ἀγοράσωσιν. 9 λέγει οὖν αὐτῷ ἡ γυνὴ ἡ Σαμαρῖτις, Πῶς σὺ Ἰουδαῖος ὢν παρ᾽ ἐμοῦ πεῖν αἰτεῖς γυναικὸς Σαμαρίτιδος οὔσης; (οὐ γὰρ συγχρῶνται Ἰουδαῖοι Σαμαρίταις.[2]) 10 ἀπεκρίθη Ἰησοῦς καὶ εἶπεν αὐτῇ, Εἰ ᾔδεις τὴν δωρεὰν τοῦ θεοῦ καὶ τίς ἐστιν ὁ λέγων σοι, Δός μοι πεῖν, σὺ ἂν ᾔτησας αὐτὸν καὶ ἔδωκεν ἄν σοι ὕδωρ ζῶν. 11 λέγει αὐτῷ ἡ γυνή[3], Κύριε, οὔτε ἄντλημα ἔχεις καὶ τὸ φρέαρ ἐστὶν βαθύ· πόθεν οὖν ἔχεις τὸ ὕδωρ τὸ ζῶν; 12 μὴ σὺ μείζων εἶ τοῦ πατρὸς ἡμῶν Ἰακώβ, ὃς ἔδωκεν ἡμῖν τὸ φρέαρ καὶ αὐτὸς ἐξ αὐτοῦ ἔπιεν καὶ οἱ υἱοὶ αὐτοῦ καὶ τὰ θρέμματα αὐτοῦ; 13 ἀπεκρίθη Ἰησοῦς καὶ εἶπεν αὐτῇ, Πᾶς ὁ πίνων ἐκ τοῦ ὕδατος τούτου διψήσει πάλιν· 14 ὃς δ᾽ ἂν πίῃ ἐκ τοῦ ὕδατος οὗ ἐγὼ δώσω αὐτῷ, οὐ μὴ διψήσει εἰς τὸν αἰῶνα, ἀλλὰ τὸ ὕδωρ ὃ δώσω αὐτῷ γενήσεται ἐν αὐτῷ πηγὴ ὕδατος ἁλλομένου εἰς ζωὴν αἰώνιον. 15 λέγει πρὸς αὐτὸν ἡ γυνή, Κύριε, δός μοι τοῦτο τὸ ὕδωρ, ἵνα μὴ διψῶ μηδὲ διέρχωμαι ἐνθάδε ἀντλεῖν.

16 Λέγει αὐτῇ, Ὕπαγε φώνησον τὸν ἄνδρα σου καὶ ἐλθὲ ἐνθάδε. 17 ἀπεκρίθη ἡ γυνὴ καὶ εἶπεν αὐτῷ, Οὐκ

[7] A Samaritan woman came to draw some water, and Jesus said to her, "Give me a drink of water." [8] (His disciples had gone into town to buy food.) [9] The Samaritan woman answered, "You are a Jew and I am a Samaritan — how can you ask me for a drink?" (For Jews will not use the same dishes that Samaritans use.) [10] Jesus answered, "If you only knew what God gives, and who it is that is asking you for a drink, you would have asked him and he would have given you living water." [11] "Sir," the woman said, "you don't have a bucket and the well is deep. Where would you get living water? [12] Our ancestor Jacob gave us this well; he, his sons, and his flocks all drank from it. You don't claim to be greater than Jacob, do you?" [13] Jesus answered: "Whoever drinks this water will get thirsty again; [14] but whoever drinks the water that I will give him will never be thirsty again. For the water that I will give him will become in him a spring which will provide him with living water, and give him eternal life." [15] "Sir," the woman said, "give me this water! Then I will never be thirsty again, nor will I have to come here and draw water." [16] "Go call your husband," Jesus told her, "and come back here." [17] "I don't have a husband," the woman said. Jesus

[2] 9 {C} οὐ γὰρ συγχρῶνται Ἰουδαῖοι Σαμαρίταις. 𝔭63,66,75,76 ℵ[a] A B C K L W[supp] X[comm] Δ Θ Π Ψ 050 083 086 f[1] f[13] 28 33 565 700 892 (1009 1646 οἱ Ἰουδαῖοι) 1010 1071 1079 1195 1216 1230 1241 1242 1253 1344 1365 1546 2148 2174 Byz Lect (l[1127] omit Ἰουδαῖοι) it[aur,c,f,ff2,l,q,rl] vg syr[c,s,p,h,pal] cop[sa,bo,ach2] arm geo Diatessaron[a,i,n] Origen Chrysostom Nonnus Cyril ‖ omit ℵ* D it[a,b,d,e,i] cop[fay]

[3] 11 {B} αὐτῷ ἡ γυνή (𝔭66* αὐτή for αὐτῷ) 𝔭66c ℵ[c] A C D K L W[supp] X[comm] Δ Θ Π Ψ 050 083 086 f[1] f[13] 28 33 565 700 892 1009 1010 1071 1079 1195 1216 1230 1241 1242 1253 1344 1365 1546 1646 2148 2174 Byz Lect it[a,aur,b,c,d,e,f,ff2,l,q,rl] vg syr[c,p,h,pal] cop[sa,bo,fay] arm geo ‖ αὐτῷ ἐκείνη ℵ* ‖ αὐτῷ 𝔭75 B syr[s] cop[ach2]

9 οὐ...Σαμαρίταις Ezr 4.3; 9.1—10.44; Lk 9.52–53   10 τίς...λέγων σοι Jn 4.26 σὺ...ζῶν Jn 7.37–38; Re 21.6; 22.17   12 μὴ...Ἰακώβ Jn 8.53   14 ὃς...αἰῶνα Jn 6.35 τὸ...αἰώνιον Jn 7.38

replied: "You are right when you say you don't have a husband. 18 You have been married to five men, and the man you live with now is not really your husband. You have told me the truth." 19 "I see you are a prophet, sir," the woman said. 20 "My Samaritan ancestors worshiped God on this mountain, but you Jews say that Jerusalem is the place where we should worship God." 21 Jesus said to her: "Believe me, woman, the time will come when men will not worship the Father either on this mountain or in Jerusalem. 22 You Samaritans do not really know whom you worship; we Jews know whom we worship, for salvation comes from the Jews. 23 But the time is coming, and is already here, when the real worshipers will worship the Father in spirit and in truth. These are the worshipers the Father wants to worship him. 24 God is Spirit, and those who worship him must worship in spirit and in truth."

25 The woman said to him, "I know that the Messiah, called Christ, will come. When he comes he will tell us everything." 26 Jesus answered, "I am he, I who am talking with you."

27 At that moment Jesus' disciples returned; and they were greatly surprised to find him talking with a woman. But none of them said to her, "What do you want?" or asked him, "Why are you talking with her?"

28 Then the woman left her water jar, went back to town, and said to the people there, 29 "Come and see the man who

ἔχω ἄνδρα. λέγει αὐτῇ ὁ Ἰησοῦς, Καλῶς εἶπες ὅτι Ἄνδρα οὐκ ἔχω· 18 πέντε γὰρ ἄνδρας ἔσχες, καὶ νῦν ὃν ἔχεις οὐκ ἔστιν σου ἀνήρ· τοῦτο ἀληθὲς εἴρηκας. 19 λέγει αὐτῷ ἡ γυνή, Κύριε, θεωρῶ ὅτι προφήτης εἶ σύ. 20 οἱ πατέρες ἡμῶν ἐν τῷ ὄρει τούτῳ προσεκύνησαν· καὶ ὑμεῖς λέγετε ὅτι ἐν Ἱεροσολύμοις ἐστὶν ὁ τόπος ὅπου προσκυνεῖν δεῖ. 21 λέγει αὐτῇ ὁ Ἰησοῦς, Πίστευέ μοι, γύναι, ὅτι ἔρχεται ὥρα ὅτε οὔτε ἐν τῷ ὄρει τούτῳ οὔτε ἐν Ἱεροσολύμοις προσκυνήσετε τῷ πατρί. 22 ὑμεῖς προσκυνεῖτε ὃ οὐκ οἴδατε· ἡμεῖς προσκυνοῦμεν ὃ οἴδαμεν, ὅτι ἡ σωτηρία ἐκ τῶν Ἰουδαίων ἐστίν. 23 ἀλλὰ ἔρχεται ὥρα, καὶ νῦν ἐστιν, ὅτε οἱ ἀληθινοὶ προσκυνηταὶ προσκυνήσουσιν τῷ πατρὶ ἐν πνεύματι καὶ ἀληθείᾳ· καὶ γὰρ ὁ πατὴρ τοιούτους ζητεῖ τοὺς προσκυνοῦντας αὐτόν. 24 πνεῦμα ὁ θεός, καὶ τοὺς προσκυνοῦντας αὐτὸν ἐν πνεύματι καὶ ἀληθείᾳ δεῖ προσκυνεῖν. 25 λέγει αὐτῷ ἡ γυνή, Οἶδα⁴ ὅτι Μεσσίας ἔρχεται, ὁ λεγόμενος Χριστός· ὅταν ἔλθῃ ἐκεῖνος, ἀναγγελεῖ ἡμῖν ἅπαντα. 26 λέγει αὐτῇ ὁ Ἰησοῦς, Ἐγώ εἰμι, ὁ λαλῶν σοι.

27 Καὶ ἐπὶ τούτῳ ἦλθαν οἱ μαθηταὶ αὐτοῦ, καὶ ἐθαύμαζον ὅτι μετὰ γυναικὸς ἐλάλει· οὐδεὶς μέντοι εἶπεν, Τί ζητεῖς;ᵇ ἤ, Τί λαλεῖς μετ' αὐτῆς;ᵇ 28 ἀφῆκεν οὖν τὴν ὑδρίαν αὐτῆς ἡ γυνὴ καὶ ἀπῆλθεν εἰς τὴν πόλιν καὶ λέγει τοῖς ἀνθρώποις, 29 Δεῦτε ἴδετε ἄνθρωπον ὃς

---

⁴ **25** {A} οἶδα 𝔓⁶⁶*,⁷⁵ ℵ* A B C D K W^supp X^comm Δ Θ Π Ψ 086 f¹ 28 565 700 892 1009 1010 1079 1195 1216 1230 1242 1253 1344 1365 1646 2148 2174 *Byz Lect* it^a, aur, b, c, d, e, ff2, j, l, q, r¹ vg syr^c, p, h, pal cop^boms arm geo Origen Chrysostom ∥ οἴδαμεν 𝔓⁶⁶ᶜ ℵᶜ L f¹³ 33 1071 1241 1546 it^f syr^hmg cop^sa, bo, ach2, fay eth Origen Nonnus Cyril ∥ ἰδού syrˢ Ephraem

---

ᵇ ᵇ **27** ᵇ question, ᵇ question: TR WH AV RV ASV RSV NEB TT Zür Luth Jer Seg ∥ ᵇ none, ᵇ question: Bov Nes BF²

---

19 Κύριε...σύ Mt 21.46; Jn 7.40; 9.17 **20** οἱ...προσεκύνησαν Dt 11.29; Jos 8.33 ὑμεῖς...δεῖ Dt 12.5-14; Ps 122.1-5 **22** ἡ...ἐστίν Is 2.3; Ro 9.3-4 **24** πνεῦμα ὁ θεός 2 Cor 3.17 τοὺς...προσκυνεῖν Php 3.3 **25** Οἶδα...Χριστός Jn 1.41 ὅταν...ἅπαντα Jn 14.26 **26** Ἐγώ εἰμι...σοι Mk 14.61-62; Jn 9.37

εἶπέν μοι πάντα ὅσα ἐποίησα· μήτι οὗτός ἐστιν ὁ Χριστός; 30 ἐξῆλθον ἐκ τῆς πόλεως καὶ ἤρχοντο πρὸς αὐτόν.

31 Ἐν τῷ μεταξὺ ἠρώτων αὐτὸν οἱ μαθηταὶ λέγοντες, Ῥαββί, φάγε. 32 ὁ δὲ εἶπεν αὐτοῖς, Ἐγὼ βρῶσιν ἔχω φαγεῖν ἣν ὑμεῖς οὐκ οἴδατε. 33 ἔλεγον οὖν οἱ μαθηταὶ πρὸς ἀλλήλους, Μή τις ἤνεγκεν αὐτῷ φαγεῖν; 34 λέγει αὐτοῖς ὁ Ἰησοῦς, Ἐμὸν βρῶμά ἐστιν ἵνα ποιήσω τὸ θέλημα τοῦ πέμψαντός με καὶ τελειώσω αὐτοῦ τὸ ἔργον. 35 οὐχ ὑμεῖς λέγετε ὅτι Ἔτι τετράμηνός ἐστιν καὶ ὁ θερισμὸς ἔρχεται; ἰδοὺ λέγω ὑμῖν, ἐπάρατε τοὺς ὀφθαλμοὺς ὑμῶν καὶ θεάσασθε τὰς χώρας ὅτι λευκαί εἰσιν πρὸς θερισμόν.ᶜ ᵈἤδηᶜ 36ᵈ ὁ θερίζων μισθὸν λαμβάνει καὶ συνάγει καρπὸν εἰς ζωὴν αἰώνιον, ἵνα ὁ σπείρων ὁμοῦ χαίρῃ καὶ ὁ θερίζων. 37 ἐν γὰρ τούτῳ ὁ λόγος ἐστὶν ἀληθινὸς ὅτιᵉ Ἄλλος ἐστὶν ὁ σπείρων καὶ ἄλλος ὁ θερίζων. 38 ἐγὼ ἀπέστειλα ὑμᾶς θερίζειν ὃ οὐχ ὑμεῖς κεκοπιάκατε· ἄλλοι κεκοπιάκασιν, καὶ ὑμεῖς εἰς τὸν κόπον αὐτῶν εἰσεληλύθατε.

39 Ἐκ δὲ τῆς πόλεως ἐκείνης πολλοὶ ἐπίστευσαν εἰς αὐτὸν τῶν Σαμαριτῶν διὰ τὸν λόγον τῆς γυναικὸς μαρτυρούσης ὅτι Εἶπέν μοι πάντα ὅσα ἐποίησα. 40 ὡς οὖν ἦλθον πρὸς αὐτὸν οἱ Σαμαρῖται, ἠρώτων αὐτὸν μεῖναι παρ' αὐτοῖς· καὶ ἔμεινεν ἐκεῖ δύο ἡμέρας. 41 καὶ πολλῷ πλείους ἐπίστευσαν διὰ τὸν λόγον αὐτοῦ, 42 τῇ τε γυναικὶ ἔλεγον ὅτι Οὐκέτι διὰ τὴν σὴν λαλιὰν πιστεύομεν· αὐτοὶ γὰρ ἀκηκόαμεν, καὶ οἴδαμεν ὅτι οὗτός ἐστιν ἀληθῶς ὁ σωτὴρ τοῦ κόσμου.

ᶜ ᶜ **35–36** c major, c none: WH Nes BF² RVᵐᵍ ASVᵐᵍ TT Luth Jer Seg ∥ c none, c major: TR Bov AV RV ASV RSV NEB Zür

ᵈ ᵈ **35–36** d no number, d number 36: TR WH? Bov Nes BF² AV RV ASV RSV NEB TT Zür Jer ∥ d number 36, d no number: WH? Luth Seg

ᵉ **37** e direct: Nes? AV RV ASV RSV NEB Zür Luth Jer Seg ∥ e indirect: TR WH Bov Nes? BF² TT

---

29 μήτι...Χριστός Mt 12.23; Jn 7.26   **34** Ἐμὸν βρῶμα...με Jn 5.30; 6.38   τελειώσω... ἔργον Jn 5.36; 17.4   **35** θεάσασθε...θερισμόν Mt 9.37; Lk 10.2   **37** Mic 6.15   **42** αὐτοὶ... κόσμου 1 Jn 4.14

---

told me everything I have ever done. Could he be the Messiah?" 30 So they left the town and went to Jesus.

31 In the meantime the disciples were begging Jesus, "Teacher, have something to eat!" 32 But he answered, "I have food to eat that you know nothing about." 33 So the disciples started asking among themselves, "Could somebody have brought him food?" 34 "My food," Jesus said to them, "is to obey the will of him who sent me and finish the work he gave me to do.

35 "You have a saying, 'Four more months and then the harvest.' I tell you, take a good look at the fields: the crops are now ripe and ready to be harvested! 36 The man who reaps the harvest is being paid and gathers the crops for eternal life; so that the man who plants and the man who reaps will be glad together. 37 For the saying is true, 'One man plants, another man reaps.' 38 I have sent you to reap a harvest in a field where you did not work; others worked there, and you profit from their work."

39 Many of the Samaritans in that town believed in Jesus because the woman had said, "He told me everything I have ever done." 40 So when the Samaritans came to him they begged him to stay with them; and Jesus stayed there two days.

41 Many more believed because of his message, 42 and they told the woman, "We believe now, not because of what you said, but because we ourselves have heard him, and we know that he is really the Savior of the world."

Jesus Heals an Official's Son

[43] After spending two days there, Jesus left and went to Galilee. [44] For Jesus himself had said, "A prophet is not respected in his own country." [45] When he arrived in Galilee the people there welcomed him, for they themselves had gone to the Passover Feast in Jerusalem and had seen everything that he had done during the feast.

[46] So Jesus went back to Cana of Galilee, where he had turned the water into wine. There was a government official there whose son in Capernaum was sick. [47] When he heard that Jesus had come from Judea to Galilee, he went to him and asked him to go to Capernaum and heal his son, who was about to die. [48] Jesus said to him, "None of you will ever believe unless you see great and wonderful works." [49] "Sir," replied the official, "come with me before my child dies." [50] Jesus said to him, "Go, your son will live!" The man believed Jesus' words and went. [51] On his way home his servants met him with the news, "Your boy is going to live!" [52] He asked them what time it was when his son got better, and they said, "It was one o'clock yesterday afternoon when the fever left him." [53] The father remembered, then, that it was at that very hour when Jesus had told him, "Your son will live." So he and all his family believed.

[54] This was the second mighty work

The Healing of the Official's Son
(Mt 8.5–13; Lk 7.1–10)

43 Μετὰ δὲ τὰς δύο ἡμέρας ἐξῆλθεν ἐκεῖθεν εἰς τὴν Γαλιλαίαν· **44** αὐτὸς γὰρ Ἰησοῦς ἐμαρτύρησεν ὅτι προφήτης ἐν τῇ ἰδίᾳ πατρίδι τιμὴν οὐκ ἔχει. **45** ὅτε οὖν ἦλθεν εἰς τὴν Γαλιλαίαν, ἐδέξαντο αὐτὸν οἱ Γαλιλαῖοι, πάντα ἑωρακότες ὅσα ἐποίησεν ἐν Ἱεροσολύμοις ἐν τῇ ἑορτῇ, καὶ αὐτοὶ γὰρ ἦλθον εἰς τὴν ἑορτήν.

46 Ἦλθεν οὖν πάλιν εἰς τὴν Κανὰ τῆς Γαλιλαίας, ὅπου ἐποίησεν τὸ ὕδωρ οἶνον. καὶ ἦν τις βασιλικὸς οὗ ὁ υἱὸς ἠσθένει ἐν Καφαρναούμ· **47** οὗτος ἀκούσας ὅτι Ἰησοῦς ἥκει ἐκ τῆς Ἰουδαίας εἰς τὴν Γαλιλαίαν ἀπῆλθεν πρὸς αὐτὸν καὶ ἠρώτα ἵνα καταβῇ καὶ ἰάσηται αὐτοῦ τὸν υἱόν, ἤμελλεν γὰρ ἀποθνήσκειν. **48** εἶπεν οὖν ὁ Ἰησοῦς πρὸς αὐτόν, Ἐὰν μὴ σημεῖα καὶ τέρατα ἴδητε, οὐ μὴ πιστεύσητε.ᶠ **49** λέγει πρὸς αὐτὸν ὁ βασιλικός, Κύριε, κατάβηθι πρὶν ἀποθανεῖν τὸ παιδίον μου. **50** λέγει αὐτῷ ὁ Ἰησοῦς, Πορεύου· ὁ υἱός σου ζῇ. ἐπίστευσεν ὁ ἄνθρωπος τῷ λόγῳ ὃν εἶπεν αὐτῷ ὁ Ἰησοῦς καὶ ἐπορεύετο. **51** ἤδη δὲ αὐτοῦ καταβαίνοντος οἱ δοῦλοι αὐτοῦ ὑπήντησαν αὐτῷ λέγοντες ὅτι ὁ παῖς αὐτοῦ⁵ ζῇ. **52** ἐπύθετο οὖν τὴν ὥραν παρ' αὐτῶν ἐν ᾗ κομψότερον ἔσχεν· εἶπαν οὖν αὐτῷ ὅτι Ἐχθὲς ὥραν ἑβδόμην ἀφῆκεν αὐτὸν ὁ πυρετός. **53** ἔγνω οὖν ὁ πατὴρ ὅτι ἐν ἐκείνῃ τῇ ὥρᾳ ἐν ᾗ εἶπεν αὐτῷ ὁ Ἰησοῦς, Ὁ υἱός σου ζῇ, καὶ ἐπίστευσεν αὐτὸς καὶ ἡ οἰκία αὐτοῦ ὅλη. **54** Τοῦτο [δὲ] πάλιν

---

⁵ 51 {B} παῖς αὐτοῦ 𝔭⁶⁶*·⁷⁵ ℵ A B C Wˢᵘᵖᵖ arm Origen ∥ υἱὸς αὐτοῦ 1009 itᵃᵘʳ·ᶜ·ᵈ·ᶠ·ff²,¹,(ʳ¹) vg ∥ παῖς σου Δ Θ Ψ ƒ¹ 28 565 700 1010 1195 1344 1365 1646 *Byz Lect* syrʰ copˢᵃ?ᵇᵒ?ᵃᶜʰ²?ᶠᵃʸ? geo Origen Chrysostom ∥ υἱός σου 𝔭⁶⁶ᶜ Dᵍʳ K L Xᶜᵒᵐᵐ Π 33 892 1071 1079 1216 1230 1241 1242 1253 1546ᵛⁱᵈ 2148 2174 *l*²¹¹ itᵃ·ᵇ·ᵉ· q syrᶜ·ᵖ·ʰᵐᵍ,ᵖᵃˡ copˢᵃ?ᵇᵒ?ᵃᶜʰ²?ᶠᵃʸ? eth Cyril ∥ παῖς σου ὁ υἱὸς αὐτοῦ ƒ¹³

ᶠ 48 ƒ statement: TR WH Bov Nes BF² AV RV ASV RSV TT Zür Luth ∥ ƒ question: WHᵐᵍ NEB ∥ ƒ exclamation: Jer Seg

43 Μετὰ...ἡμέρας Jn 4.40 **44** Mt 13.57; Mk 6.4; Lk 4.24 **45** πάντα...ἑορτῇ Jn 2.23 **46** Κανὰ...οἶνον Jn 2.1–11 **46–47** ἦν...ἀποθνήσκειν Mt 8.5–6; Lk 7.1–3 **48** Ἐὰν... πιστεύσητε Dn 4.2, 37; Mk 13.22; 1 Cor 1.22 **50** Πορεύου...ζῇ Mt 8.13; Mk 7.29 **53** ἐπίστευσεν...ὅλη Ac 11.14; 16.14–15, 31 **54** Jn 2.11

δεύτερον σημεῖον ἐποίησεν ὁ Ἰησοῦς ἐλθὼν ἐκ τῆς Ἰουδαίας εἰς τὴν Γαλιλαίαν.

The Healing at the Pool

5 Μετὰ ταῦτα ἦν ἑορτὴ[1] τῶν Ἰουδαίων, καὶ ἀνέβη Ἰησοῦς εἰς Ἱεροσόλυμα. 2 ἔστιν δὲ ἐν τοῖς Ἱεροσολύμοις ἐπὶ τῇ προβατικῇ κολυμβήθρα[2] ἡ ἐπιλεγομένη Ἑβραϊστὶ Βηθζαθά[3], πέντε στοὰς ἔχουσα. 3 ἐν ταύταις κατέκειτο πλῆθος τῶν ἀσθενούντων, τυφλῶν, χωλῶν, ξηρῶν[4].[5] 5 ἦν δέ τις ἄνθρωπος ἐκεῖ τριάκοντα [καὶ] ὀκτὼ ἔτη ἔχων ἐν τῇ ἀσθενείᾳ αὐτοῦ· 6 τοῦτον ἰδὼν ὁ Ἰησοῦς κατακείμενον, καὶ γνοὺς ὅτι πολὺν ἤδη χρόνον ἔχει, λέγει

---

[1] **1** {A} ἑορτή p[66,75] A B D K W[supp] Θ 0125 f[13] 28 700 1195 1216 1241 1344 1646 2174 *Byz*[pt] *l*[547] arm Diatessaron[n] Origen Epiphanius Chrysostom Paschal Chronicle ‖ ἡ ἑορτή ℵ C L X[comm] Δ Π Ψ f[1] 33 892 1009 1010 1071 1079 1230 1242 1253 1365 1546 2148 *Byz*[pt] cop[sa,bo,ach2] Diatessaron Origen Cyril

[2] **2** {B} ἐπὶ τῇ προβατικῇ κολυμβήθρα p[66,75] B C K W[supp] Δ Π Ψ 063 078 0125 f[1] f[13] 28 33 565 700 892 1009 1010 1071 1079 1195 1216 1230 1241 1242 1253 1344 1365 1546 1646 2148 2174 *Byz Lect* it[c,f] vg[ww] syr[h,(pal)] cop[sa,bo,ach2] arm ‖ ἐν τῇ προβατικῇ κολυμβήθρα ℵ[c] A D L Θ it[d,q,rl] Nonnus ‖ προβατικῇ κολυμβήθρα ℵ* X[comm] *l*[57?] it[aur,e] vg[cl] eth geo Eusebius Chrysostom Theodore ‖ κολυμβήθρα it[l] syr[c,p] Diatessaron[a,n,t] Irenaeus[lat] Cyril ‖ *in inferiorem partem natatoria piscina* it[a,(b),(ff2)]

[3] **2** {D} Βηθζαθά ℵ 33 (it[l] *Betzata*) Eusebius (Cyril) ‖ Βηζαθά L it[e] ‖ *Betzetha* it[(b),ff2] ‖ Βελζεθά D it[(a),d,rl] ‖ Βηθσαϊδά (*see* 1.44) (p[66] Βηδσαϊδά) p[75] B W[supp] (Ψ Βησσαϊδά) 0125 it[aur,c] vg syr[h] cop[sa,bo,ach2] eth Diatessaron[s] Tertullian Jerome ‖ Βηθεσδά A C K X[comm] Δ Θ Π 063[vid] 078 f[1] f[13] 28 565 700 892 1009 1010 1071 1079 1195 1216 1230 1241 1242 1253[vid] 1344 1365 1546 1646 2148 2174 *Byz Lect* it[(f),q] syr[c,p,hmg,gr,pal] arm geo Diatessaron Didymus Chrysostom Cyril

[4] **3** {A} ξηρῶν p[66,75] ℵ A* B C* L 0125 it[q] syr[c] cop[sa,bomss,ach2] Diatessaron[l] ‖ ξηρῶν παραλυτικῶν ἐκδεχομένων τὴν τοῦ ὕδατος κίνησιν D it[a,aur,b,d,j,l,rl] geo[2] ‖ ξηρῶν ἐκδεχομένων τὴν τοῦ ὕδατος κίνησιν A[2] C[3] K (W[supp] X[comm] Δ Θ Π[with] * Ψ 078 f[1] f[13] 28 33 565 700 892 1009 1010 1071 1079 1195 1216 1230 1241 1242 1253 1344 1365 1546 1646 2148 2174 *Byz Lect* it[c,e,f,ff2] vg syr[p,h,pal] cop[bomss] arm eth geo[1] Diatessaron[a] Tertullian Ambrose Chrysostom Cyril

[5] **3** {A} *omit verse* 4 p[66,75] ℵ B C* D W[supp] 0125 0141 33 it[d,f,l,q] vg[ww] syr[c] cop[sa,bomss,ach2] geo Nonnus ‖ *include verse* 4 ἄγγελος γὰρ[6] κυρίου κατὰ

that Jesus did after coming from Judea to Galilee.

The Healing at the Pool

5 After this, there was a Jewish religious feast, and Jesus went to Jerusalem. 2 There is in Jerusalem, by the Sheep Gate, a pool with five porches; in the Hebrew language it is called Bethzatha. 3 A large crowd of sick people were lying on the porches — the blind, the lame, and the paralyzed. [They were waiting for the water to move; 4 for every now and then an angel of the Lord went down into the pool and stirred up the water. The first sick person to go down into the pool after the water was stirred up was healed from whatever disease he had.] 5 A man was there who had been sick for thirty-eight years. 6 Jesus saw him lying there, and he knew that the man had been sick for such a long time; so he

said to him, "Do you want to get well?"
[7] The sick man answered, "Sir, I don't have anyone here to put me in the pool when the water is stirred up; while I am trying to get in, somebody else gets there first." [8] Jesus said to him, "Get up, pick up your mat, and walk." [9] Imme-

αὐτῷ, Θέλεις ὑγιὴς γενέσθαι; 7 ἀπεκρίθη αὐτῷ ὁ ἀσθενῶν, Κύριε, ἄνθρωπον οὐκ ἔχω ἵνα ὅταν ταραχθῇ τὸ ὕδωρ βάλῃ με εἰς τὴν κολυμβήθραν· ἐν ᾧ δὲ ἔρχομαι ἐγὼ ἄλλος πρὸ ἐμοῦ καταβαίνει. 8 λέγει αὐτῷ ὁ Ἰησοῦς, Ἔγειρε ἆρον τὸν κράβαττόν σου καὶ περιπάτει. 9 καὶ

καιρὸν κατέβαινεν ἐν τῇ κολυμβήθρα[7] καὶ ἐταράσσετο[8] τὸ ὕδωρ· ὁ οὖν πρῶτος ἐμβὰς μετὰ τὴν ταραχὴν τοῦ ὕδατος[9] ὑγιὴς ἐγίνετο οἵῳ δήποτ' οὖν[10] κατείχετο νοσήματι. (with variations in mss; see footnotes 6–10) A C³ K L Xcomm Δ Θ Ψ 063 078 f¹ f¹³ 28 565 700 892 1009 1010 1071 1195 1216 1230 1241 1242 1253 1344 1365 1546 1646 2148 Byz Lect ita,aur,b, c,e,ff²,j,rl vgcl syrp,pal copbomss arm Diatessarona,earm,i,n Tertullian Ambrose Didymus Chrysostom Cyril ‖ include verse 4 with asterisks or obeli Π 047 1079 2174 syrh

---

[6] {B} γάρ (see footnote 5) A C³ K Xcomm Δ Θ Π Ψ 063 078 f¹ f¹³ 28 565 700 892 1009 1010 1071 1079 1195 1216 1230 1241 1242 1253 1344 1365 1546 1646 2148 2174 Byz Lect ite syrp,h,pal ‖ δέ L ita,aur, b,c,ff²,j,rl vgcl arm ‖ omit l⁵¹ copbomss

[7] {B} κατὰ καιρὸν κατέβαινεν ἐν τῇ κολυμβήθρα (see footnote 5) C³ (L καιρῷ) Xcomm Δ Θ 063 f¹ f¹³ 28 565 700 892 1009 1010 1071 1195 1216 1230 1242 (1344 καταβαῖνον) 1365 1646 2148 2174 Byz Lect itaur,c,e,j syrp copbomss arm ‖ κατὰ καιρὸν ἐλούετο ἐν τῇ κολυμβήθρα A K Π Ψ 1079 1241 1546 vgmss syrh eth? ‖ κατέβαινεν κατὰ καιρὸν ἐν τῇ κολυμβήθρα 239 (1253 καταβάς) vgcl syrpal ‖ κατέβαινεν ita,b,ff²

[8] {B} ἐταράσσετο (see footnote 5) C³ Π 078 1216 1242 2174c l¹²,⁶⁴, ⁶⁹,⁷⁰,⁷⁶,⁸⁰,¹⁹¹,³⁰³,³³³,³⁷²,³⁷⁴,³⁸¹,¹¹²⁷,¹²³¹,¹⁵⁶⁴,¹⁵⁷⁹,¹⁶³⁴ itc,rl vgcl syrpalmss eth ‖ ἐτάρασσε A K L Xcomm Δ Θ Ψ 063 f¹ f¹³ 28 565 700 892 1009 1010 1071 1079 1195 1230 1241 1253 1344 1365 1546 1646 2148 2174* Byz Lect ita,aur,b,e,ff²,j syrp,h,palms copbomss

[9] {A} ἐμβὰς μετὰ τὴν ταραχὴν τοῦ ὕδατος (see footnote 5) A C³ K L Xcomm Δ Θ Π Ψ 063 078 f¹ f¹³ 28 565 700 892 1009 1010 1071 1079 1195 1216 1230 1241 1242 1253 1344 1365 1546 1646 2148 2174 Byz Lect itaur,e,j syrp,h,pal copbomss (arm) ‖ descendisset in natatoria it(a,b),ff² ‖ descendisset in piscinam post motionem aquae itc,(rl) vgcl

[10] {C} οἵῳ δήποτ' οὖν (see footnote 5) A copbomss ‖ ᾧ δήποτε C³ Xcomm Δ Θ Ψ 078 f¹ f¹³ 28 565 700 892 1071 1195 1216 1230 1241 1242 1253 1344 1365 1646 2148 2174 Byz Lect ita,aur,b,c,e,ff²,j,rl vgcl ‖ ὑοδήποτε [sic] L 1009 1010 ‖ ᾧ δ' ἂν K Π 1079 1546

---

8 Mt 9.6; Mk 2.11; Lk 5.24

εὐθέως[11] ἐγένετο ὑγιὴς ὁ ἄνθρωπος, καὶ ἦρεν τὸν κράβαττον αὐτοῦ καὶ περιεπάτει.

῏Ην δὲ σάββατον ἐν ἐκείνῃ τῇ ἡμέρᾳ. 10 ἔλεγον οὖν οἱ ᾿Ιουδαῖοι τῷ τεθεραπευμένῳ, Σάββατόν ἐστιν, καὶ οὐκ ἔξεστίν σοι ἆραι τὸν κράβαττόν σου. 11 ὁ δὲ ἀπεκρίθη αὐτοῖς, ῾Ο ποιήσας με ὑγιῆ ἐκεῖνός μοι εἶπεν, ῏Αρον τὸν κράβαττόν σου καὶ περιπάτει. 12 ἠρώτησαν αὐτόν, Τίς ἐστιν ὁ ἄνθρωπος ὁ εἰπών σοι, ῏Αρον καὶ περιπάτει; 13 ὁ δὲ ἰαθεὶς οὐκ ᾔδει τίς ἐστιν, ὁ γὰρ ᾿Ιησοῦς ἐξένευσεν ὄχλου ὄντος ἐν τῷ τόπῳ. 14 μετὰ ταῦτα εὑρίσκει αὐτὸν ὁ ᾿Ιησοῦς ἐν τῷ ἱερῷ καὶ εἶπεν αὐτῷ, ῎Ιδε ὑγιὴς γέγονας· μηκέτι ἁμάρτανε, ἵνα μὴ χεῖρόν σοί τι γένηται. 15 ἀπῆλθεν ὁ ἄνθρωπος καὶ ἀνήγγειλεν τοῖς ᾿Ιουδαίοις ὅτι ᾿Ιησοῦς ἐστιν ὁ ποιήσας αὐτὸν ὑγιῆ. 16 καὶ διὰ τοῦτο ἐδίωκον οἱ ᾿Ιουδαῖοι τὸν ᾿Ιησοῦν, ὅτι ταῦτα ἐποίει ἐν σαββάτῳ. 17 ὁ δὲ ᾿Ιησοῦς[12] ἀπεκρίνατο αὐτοῖς, ῾Ο πατήρ μου ἕως ἄρτι ἐργάζεται, κἀγὼ ἐργάζομαι. 18 διὰ τοῦτο οὖν μᾶλλον ἐζήτουν αὐτὸν οἱ ᾿Ιουδαῖοι ἀποκτεῖναι, ὅτι οὐ μόνον ἔλυεν τὸ σάββατον ἀλλὰ καὶ πατέρα ἴδιον ἔλεγεν τὸν θεόν, ἴσον ἑαυτὸν ποιῶν τῷ θεῷ.

The Authority of the Son

19 ᾿Απεκρίνατο οὖν ὁ ᾿Ιησοῦς καὶ ἔλεγεν αὐτοῖς, ᾿Αμὴν ἀμὴν λέγω ὑμῖν, οὐ δύναται ὁ υἱὸς ποιεῖν ἀφ᾿ ἑαυτοῦ οὐδὲν ἐὰν μή τι βλέπῃ τὸν πατέρα ποιοῦντα· ἃ

---

[11] 9 {B} καὶ εὐθέως 𝔭[66,75] ℵ[c] A B C K L X[comm] Δ Θ Π Ψ 063 f[1] f[13] 33 700 892 1009 1010 1071 1079 1195 1216 1230 1241 1242 1253 1344 1365 1546 1646 2148 2174 Byz Lect it[a,b,c,e,f,ff2,q,r1] vg syr[c,s,p,h,pal] cop[sa,bo,ach2] eth Cyril ∥ καί D W[supp] it[aur,d,l] arm geo ∥ omit ℵ*

[12] 17 {C} δὲ ᾿Ιησοῦς 𝔭[66] A D K L X[comm] Δ Θ Π Ψ 063 f[1] f[13] 28 33 565 700 1009 1010 1079 1195 1216 1230 1242 1344 1365 1546 1646 2148 2174 Byz Lect it[a,aur,b,c,d,e,f,ff2,l,q] vg syr[c,p,h] cop[sa,bo,ach2] arm geo ∥ δὲ κύριος 1253 syr[s] ∥ δὲ ᾿Ιησοῦς κύριος syr[pal] ∥ δὲ 𝔭[75] ℵ B W 892 1071 1241 cop[boms]

---

9 ἦρεν...περιεπάτει Mk 2.12; Lk 5.25   ῏Ην...ἡμέρᾳ Lk 13.14; Jn 9.14   10 Σάββατον ...σου Jr 17.21   13 ᾿Ιησοῦς...τόπῳ Mt 8.18; 13.36; Mk 4.36; 7.17; Jn 6.2-3, 15   15 Jn 9.11 18 ἐζήτουν...ἀποκτεῖναι Mt 14.5; 26.4; Mk 14.1; Jn 7.1, 25; 8.37, 40; 11.53   ἴσον...θεῷ Jn 10.30, 33   19 οὐ...οὐδέν Jn 5.30; 8.28

---

diately the man got well; he picked up his mat, and walked.

The day this happened was a Sabbath, 10 so the Jews told the man who had been healed, "This is a Sabbath, and it is against our Law for you to carry your mat." 11 He answered, "The man who made me well told me, 'Pick up your mat and walk.' " 12 They asked him, "Who is this man who told you to pick up your mat and walk?" 13 But the man who had been healed did not know who he was, for Jesus had left, because there was a crowd in that place.

14 Afterward, Jesus found him in the Temple and said, "Look, you are well now. Quit your sins, or something worse may happen to you." 15 Then the man left and told the Jews that it was Jesus who had healed him. 16 For this reason the Jews began to persecute Jesus, because he had done this healing on a Sabbath.

17 So Jesus answered them, "My Father works always, and I too must work." 18 This saying made the Jews all the more determined to kill him; for not only had he broken the Sabbath law, but he had said that God was his own Father, and in this way had made himself equal with God.

The Authority of the Son

19 So Jesus answered them: "I tell you the truth: the Son does nothing on his own; he does only what he sees his

Father doing. What the Father does, the Son also does. ²⁰ For the Father loves the Son and shows him all that he himself is doing. He will show him even greater things than this to do, and you will all be amazed. ²¹ For even as the Father raises the dead back to life, in the same way the Son gives life to those he wants to. ²² Nor does the Father himself judge anyone. He has given his Son the full right to judge, ²³ so that all will honor the Son in the same way as they honor the Father. Whoever does not honor the Son does not honor the Father who sent him.

²⁴ "I tell you the truth: whoever hears my words, and believes in him who sent me, has eternal life. He will not be judged, but has already passed from death to life. ²⁵ I tell you the truth: the time is coming — the time has already come — when the dead will hear the voice of the Son of God, and those who hear it will live. ²⁶ Even as the Father is himself the source of life, in the same way he has made his Son to be the source of life. ²⁷ And he has given the Son the right to judge, because he is the Son of Man. ²⁸ Do not be surprised at this; for the time is coming when all the dead in the graves will hear his voice, ²⁹ and they will come out of their graves: those who have done good will be raised and live, and those who have done evil will be raised and be condemned."

Witnesses to Jesus

³⁰ "I can do nothing on my own; I judge only as God tells me, so my judgment is right, because I am not trying to do what I want, but only what he who sent me wants.

γὰρ ἂν ἐκεῖνος ποιῇ, ταῦτα καὶ ὁ υἱὸς ὁμοίως ποιεῖ. **20** ὁ γὰρ πατὴρ φιλεῖ τὸν υἱὸν καὶ πάντα δείκνυσιν αὐτῷ ἃ αὐτὸς ποιεῖ, καὶ μείζονα τούτων δείξει αὐτῷ ἔργα, ἵνα ὑμεῖς θαυμάζητε. **21** ὥσπερ γὰρ ὁ πατὴρ ἐγείρει τοὺς νεκροὺς καὶ ζῳοποιεῖ, οὕτως καὶ ὁ υἱὸς οὓς θέλει ζῳοποιεῖ. **22** οὐδὲ γὰρ ὁ πατὴρ κρίνει οὐδένα, ἀλλὰ τὴν κρίσιν πᾶσαν δέδωκεν τῷ υἱῷ, **23** ἵνα πάντες τιμῶσι τὸν υἱὸν καθὼς τιμῶσι τὸν πατέρα. ὁ μὴ τιμῶν τὸν υἱὸν οὐ τιμᾷ τὸν πατέρα τὸν πέμψαντα αὐτόν. **24** Ἀμὴν ἀμὴν λέγω ὑμῖν ὅτι ὁ τὸν λόγον μου ἀκούων καὶ πιστεύων τῷ πέμψαντί με ἔχει ζωὴν αἰώνιον, καὶ εἰς κρίσιν οὐκ ἔρχεται ἀλλὰ μεταβέβηκεν ἐκ τοῦ θανάτου εἰς τὴν ζωήν. **25** ἀμὴν ἀμὴν λέγω ὑμῖν ὅτι ἔρχεται ὥρα καὶ νῦν ἐστιν ὅτε οἱ νεκροὶ ἀκούσουσιν τῆς φωνῆς τοῦ υἱοῦ τοῦ θεοῦ καὶ οἱ ἀκούσαντες ζήσουσιν. **26** ὥσπερ γὰρ ὁ πατὴρ ἔχει ζωὴν ἐν ἑαυτῷ, οὕτως καὶ τῷ υἱῷ ἔδωκεν ζωὴν ἔχειν ἐν ἑαυτῷ·^a **27** καὶ ἐξουσίαν ἔδωκεν αὐτῷ κρίσιν ποιεῖν, ὅτι υἱὸς ἀνθρώπου ἐστίν. **28** μὴ θαυμάζετε τοῦτο, ὅτι ἔρχεται ὥρα ἐν ᾗ πάντες οἱ ἐν τοῖς μνημείοις ἀκούσουσιν τῆς φωνῆς αὐτοῦ^b **29** καὶ ἐκπορεύσονται,^b οἱ τὰ ἀγαθὰ ποιήσαντες εἰς ἀνάστασιν ζωῆς, οἱ δὲ τὰ φαῦλα πράξαντες εἰς ἀνάστασιν κρίσεως.

Witnesses to Jesus

30 Οὐ δύναμαι ἐγὼ ποιεῖν ἀπ' ἐμαυτοῦ οὐδέν· καθὼς ἀκούω κρίνω, καὶ ἡ κρίσις ἡ ἐμὴ δικαία ἐστίν, ὅτι οὐ ζητῶ τὸ θέλημα τὸ ἐμὸν ἀλλὰ τὸ θέλημα τοῦ πέμψαντός

---

^a **26** a minor: TR WH AV RV ASV RSV Luth Seg ∥ a major: Bov Nes BF² NEB TT Zür ∥ a none: Jer

^{b b} **28-29** b none, b minor: TR RSV NEB Zür Jer ∥ b minor, b major: AV RV ASV TT ∥ b major, b none: Seg ∥ b minor, b minor: Luth ∥ b none, b none: WH Bov Nes BF²

20 ὁ...υἱόν Jn 3.35; 10.17; 15.9; 17.23-24   **21** ὁ πατήρ...καὶ ζῳοποιεῖ Ro 4.17; Eph 2.5 ὁ υἱός...ζῳοποιεῖ Jn 11.25   **22** τήν...υἱῷ En 69.27; Jn 3.17; 5.27; 9.39; 12.47; Ac 10.42; 17.31 **23** ἵνα...πατέρα Php 2.10-11   ὁ...αὐτόν Lk 10.16   **24** ὁ...αἰώνιον Jn 3.15, 16; 8.51; 12.44 εἰς κρίσιν...ζωήν Jn 3.18; 1 Jn 3.14   **25** Mk 5.41; Lk 7.14; 8.54; Jn 5.28; 11.43   **26** τῷ... ἔχειν ἐν ἑαυτῷ Jn 1.4   **27** ἐξουσίαν...ποιεῖν Jn 5.22; 9.39; Ac 10.42; 17.31   **28-29** ἔρχεται... ἐκπορεύσονται Jn 5.25; 11.43   **29** Dn 12.2; Ac 24.15   **30** Οὐ δύναμαι...οὐδέν Jn 5.19 οὐ ζητῶ...με Lk 22.42; Jn 4.34; 6.38

με. **31** ἐὰν ἐγὼ μαρτυρῶ περὶ ἐμαυτοῦ, ἡ μαρτυρία μου οὐκ ἔστιν ἀληθής· **32** ἄλλος ἐστὶν ὁ μαρτυρῶν περὶ ἐμοῦ, καὶ οἶδα[13] ὅτι ἀληθής ἐστιν ἡ μαρτυρία ἣν μαρτυρεῖ περὶ ἐμοῦ. **33** ὑμεῖς ἀπεστάλκατε πρὸς Ἰωάννην, καὶ μεμαρτύρηκεν τῇ ἀληθείᾳ· **34** ἐγὼ δὲ οὐ παρὰ ἀνθρώπου τὴν μαρτυρίαν λαμβάνω, ἀλλὰ ταῦτα λέγω ἵνα ὑμεῖς σωθῆτε. **35** ἐκεῖνος ἦν ὁ λύχνος ὁ καιόμενος καὶ φαίνων, ὑμεῖς δὲ ἠθελήσατε ἀγαλλιαθῆναι πρὸς ὥραν ἐν τῷ φωτὶ αὐτοῦ. **36** ἐγὼ δὲ ἔχω τὴν μαρτυρίαν μείζω τοῦ Ἰωάννου· τὰ γὰρ ἔργα ἃ δέδωκέν μοι ὁ πατὴρ ἵνα τελειώσω αὐτά, αὐτὰ τὰ ἔργα ἃ ποιῶ, μαρτυρεῖ περὶ ἐμοῦ ὅτι ὁ πατήρ με ἀπέσταλκεν· **37** καὶ ὁ πέμψας με πατὴρ ἐκεῖνος μεμαρτύρηκεν περὶ ἐμοῦ. οὔτε φωνὴν αὐτοῦ πώποτε ἀκηκόατε οὔτε εἶδος αὐτοῦ ἑωράκατε, **38** καὶ τὸν λόγον αὐτοῦ οὐκ ἔχετε ἐν ὑμῖν μένοντα, ὅτι ὃν ἀπέστειλεν ἐκεῖνος τούτῳ ὑμεῖς οὐ πιστεύετε. **39** ἐραυνᾶτε τὰς γραφάς, ὅτι ὑμεῖς δοκεῖτε ἐν αὐταῖς ζωὴν αἰώνιον ἔχειν· καὶ ἐκεῖναί εἰσιν αἱ μαρτυροῦσαι περὶ ἐμοῦ· **40** καὶ οὐ θέλετε ἐλθεῖν πρός με ἵνα ζωὴν ἔχητε.

41 Δόξαν παρὰ ἀνθρώπων οὐ λαμβάνω, **42** ἀλλὰ ἔγνωκα ὑμᾶς ὅτι τὴν ἀγάπην τοῦ θεοῦ οὐκ ἔχετε ἐν ἑαυτοῖς. **43** ἐγὼ ἐλήλυθα ἐν τῷ ὀνόματι τοῦ πατρός μου καὶ οὐ λαμβάνετέ με· ἐὰν ἄλλος ἔλθῃ ἐν τῷ ὀνόματι τῷ ἰδίῳ, ἐκεῖνον λήμψεσθε. **44** πῶς δύνασθε ὑμεῖς πιστεῦσαι, δόξαν παρὰ ἀλλήλων λαμβάνοντες καὶ τὴν δόξαν τὴν παρὰ τοῦ μόνου θεοῦ[14] οὐ ζητεῖτε; **45** μὴ δοκεῖτε ὅτι

---

[13] **32** {B} οἶδα 𝔭[66,75] ℵ[c] A B K L W X[comm] Δ Θ Π Ψ *f*[1] *f*[13] 28 33 565 700 892 1010 1071 1070 1105 1216 1230 1241 1242 1253 1344 1365 1646 2148 2174 *Byz Lect* it[b,c,f] vg syr[p,h,pal] cop[sa,bo,ach9] eth Chrysostom Cyril ‖ οἴδαμεν 56 58 61 ‖ οἴδατε ℵ* D *l*[547] it[a,aur,d,e,q] syr[c] arm geo

[14] **44** {B} θεοῦ ℵ A D K L Δ Θ Π Ψ 0210[vid] *f*[1] *f*[13] 28 33 565 700 892 1009

31 Jn 8.13-14   **32** ἄλλος...μαρτυρῶν περὶ ἐμοῦ Jn 1.15, 34; 3.26; 5.36, 37, 39; 8.18; 10.25; 15.26; 1 Jn 5.6-9   ἀληθής...μαρτυρεῖ Jn 19.35; 21.24   **33** Jn 1.19-27   **34** ἐγώ...λαμβάνω 1 Jn 5.9   **36** ἐγώ...Ἰωάννου 1 Jn 5.9   τὰ γὰρ...περὶ ἐμοῦ Jn 10.25, 38; 14.11   **37** ὁ πέμψας...ἐμοῦ Mt 3.17; Mk 1.11; Lk 3.22; Jn 5.32; 8.18; 1 Jn 5.9   **38** τὸν...μένοντα 1 Jn 2.14   ὃν...πιστεύετε Jn 6.29   **39** Lk 24.27, 44; Ac 13.27· 1 Pe 1.10-11   **41** Jn 12.43   **42** τήν... ἑαυτοῖς 1 Jn 3.17   **44** δόξαν παρά...ζητεῖτε Jn 12.43

---

31 "If I testify on my own behalf, what I say is not to be accepted as real proof. **32** But there is someone else who testifies on my behalf, and I know that what he says about me is true. **33** You sent your messengers to John, and he spoke on behalf of the truth. **34** It is not that I must have a man's witness; I say this only in order that you may be saved. **35** John was like a lamp, burning and shining, and you were willing for a while to enjoy his light. **36** But I have a witness on my behalf even greater than the witness that John gave: the works that I do, the works my Father gave me to do, these speak on my behalf and show that the Father has sent me. **37** And the Father, who sent me, also speaks on my behalf. You have never heard his voice, you have never seen his face; **38** so you do not have his words in you, because you will not believe in the one whom he sent. **39** You study the Scriptures because you think that in them you will find eternal life. And they themselves speak about me! **40** Yet you are not willing to come to me in order to have life.

41 "I am not looking for praise from men. **42** But I know you; I know that you have no love for God in your hearts. **43** I have come with my Father's authority, but you have not received me; when someone comes with his own authority, you will receive him. **44** You like to have praise from one another, but you do not try to win praise from the only God; how, then, can you believe? **45** Do not think, however, that I will accuse you to my Father. Moses is the one who will accuse you — Moses, in whom you have hoped. ⁴⁶ If you had really believed Moses, you would have believed me, for he wrote about me. ⁴⁷ But since you do not believe what he wrote, how can you believe my words?''

Jesus Feeds the Five Thousand
(Also Matt. 14.13–21; Mark 6.30–44; Luke 9.10–17)

6 After this, Jesus went back across Lake Galilee (or, Lake Tiberias). ² A great crowd followed him, because they had seen his mighty works in healing the sick. ³ Jesus went up a hill and sat down with his disciples. ⁴ The Passover Feast of the Jews was near. ⁵ Jesus looked around and saw that a large crowd was coming to him, so he said to Philip, "Where can we buy enough food to feed all these people?" ⁶ (He said this to try Philip out; actually he already knew what he would do.) ⁷ Philip answered, "For all these people to have even a little, it would take more than two hundred dollars' worth of bread." ⁸ Another one of his disciples, Andrew, Simon Peter's brother, said: ⁹ "There is a boy here who has five loaves of barley bread and two fish. But what good are they

ἐγὼ κατηγορήσω ὑμῶν πρὸς τὸν πατέρα· ἔστιν ὁ κατηγορῶν ὑμῶν Μωϋσῆς, εἰς ὃν ὑμεῖς ἠλπίκατε. 46 εἰ γὰρ ἐπιστεύετε Μωϋσεῖ, ἐπιστεύετε ἂν ἐμοί, περὶ γὰρ ἐμοῦ ἐκεῖνος ἔγραψεν. 47 εἰ δὲ τοῖς ἐκείνου γράμμασιν οὐ πιστεύετε, πῶς τοῖς ἐμοῖς ῥήμασιν πιστεύσετε;

The Feeding of the Five Thousand
(Mt 14.13–21; Mk 6.30–44; Lk 9.10–17)

6 Μετὰ ταῦτα ἀπῆλθεν ὁ Ἰησοῦς πέραν τῆς θαλάσσης τῆς Γαλιλαίας¹ τῆς Τιβεριάδος. 2 ἠκολούθει δὲ αὐτῷ ὄχλος πολύς, ὅτι ἐθεώρουν τὰ σημεῖα ἃ ἐποίει ἐπὶ τῶν ἀσθενούντων. 3 ἀνῆλθεν δὲ εἰς τὸ ὄρος Ἰησοῦς, καὶ ἐκεῖ ἐκάθητο μετὰ τῶν μαθητῶν αὐτοῦ. 4 ἦν δὲ ἐγγὺς τὸ πάσχα, ἡ ἑορτὴ τῶν Ἰουδαίων. 5 ἐπάρας οὖν τοὺς ὀφθαλμοὺς ὁ Ἰησοῦς καὶ θεασάμενος ὅτι πολὺς ὄχλος ἔρχεται πρὸς αὐτὸν λέγει πρὸς Φίλιππον, Πόθεν ἀγοράσωμεν ἄρτους ἵνα φάγωσιν οὗτοι; 6 τοῦτο δὲ ἔλεγεν πειράζων αὐτόν, αὐτὸς γὰρ ᾔδει τί ἔμελλεν ποιεῖν. 7 ἀπεκρίθη αὐτῷ ὁ Φίλιππος, Διακοσίων δηναρίων ἄρτοι οὐκ ἀρκοῦσιν αὐτοῖς ἵνα ἕκαστος βραχύ τι λάβῃ. 8 λέγει αὐτῷ εἷς ἐκ τῶν μαθητῶν αὐτοῦ, Ἀνδρέας ὁ ἀδελφὸς Σίμωνος Πέτρου, 9 Ἔστιν παιδάριον ὧδε ὃς ἔχει πέντε ἄρτους κριθίνους καὶ δύο ὀψάρια· ἀλλὰ ταῦτα τί ἐστιν

1010 1071 1079 1195 1216 1230 1241 1242 1253 1344 1365ᶜ 1546 1646 2148 2174 *Byz Lect* itᵃᵘʳ,ᶜ,ᵈ,ᵉ,ᶠ,ff²,ʲ,ˡ,(q),(rˡ) vg syrᶜ,ᵖ,ʰ,ᵖᵃˡ copᵇᵒᵐˢˢ arm geo Origen Hilary Ephraem Basil ‖ *omit* 𝔭⁶⁶,⁷⁵ B W itᵃ,⁽ᵇ⁾ copˢᵃ,ᵇᵒᵐˢˢ,ᵃᶜʰ² Origen Adamantius Eusebius Didymus Cyril

¹ **1** {B} τῆς Γαλιλαίας 𝔭⁶⁶,⁷⁵ᵛⁱᵈ ℵ A B K Lꞌ W Δ Π Ψ 063 *f*¹ *f*¹³ 28 33 565 700 1010 1071 1079 1195 1216 1241 1242ᶜ 1365 1646 2148 *Byz Lect* itᵃ,⁽ᵃᵘʳ⁾,(ᶜ),(ff²),(ˡ),q (vg) syrᶜ,ˢ,ᵖ,ʰ,ᵖᵃˡ copˢᵃ,ᵇᵒ,ᵃᶜʰ² arm ‖ τῆς Γαλιλαίας καί V (1546 *but omit* τῆς Τιβεριάδος) itᶠ goth ‖ τῆς Γαλιλαίας εἰς τὰ μέρη D Θ 892 1009 1230 1253 itᵇ,ᵈ,ᵉ,ʳˡ geo Chrysostom ‖ *omit* 0210 1242* 1344 2174 *l*¹⁸⁴

45 ἔστιν...ἠλπίκατε Dt 31.26–27   **46** Dt 18.15; Lk 24.27; Ac 3.22; 7.37   **47** Lk 16.29–31
 6 2 ἠκολούθει...πολύς Mt 4.25; 8.1; 12.15; 19.2; 20.29; Mk 5.24; Lk 9.11   ἐθεώρουν... ἐποίει Jn 2.23; 6.14   **3** Mt 5.1; 24.3; Mk 3.13; Lk 22.39   **4** Lk 22.1; Jn 2.13; 11.55
8 Ἀνδρέας...Πέτρου Mt 4.18; 10.2; Mk 1.16; Lk 6.14; Jn 1.40   **9** ἄρτους...ὀψάρια Jn 21.9, 13

εἰς τοσούτους; **10** εἶπεν ὁ Ἰησοῦς, Ποιήσατε τοὺς ἀνθρώπους ἀναπεσεῖν. ἦν δὲ χόρτος πολὺς ἐν τῷ τόπῳ. ἀνέπεσαν οὖν οἱ ἄνδρες τὸν ἀριθμὸν ὡς πεντακισχίλιοι. **11** ἔλαβεν οὖν τοὺς ἄρτους ὁ Ἰησοῦς καὶ εὐχαριστήσας διέδωκεν τοῖς ἀνακειμένοις, ὁμοίως καὶ ἐκ τῶν ὀψαρίων ὅσον ἤθελον. **12** ὡς δὲ ἐνεπλήσθησαν λέγει τοῖς μαθηταῖς αὐτοῦ, Συναγάγετε τὰ περισσεύσαντα κλάσματα, ἵνα μή τι ἀπόληται. **13** συνήγαγον οὖν, καὶ ἐγέμισαν δώδεκα κοφίνους κλασμάτων ἐκ τῶν πέντε ἄρτων τῶν κριθίνων ἃ ἐπερίσσευσαν τοῖς βεβρωκόσιν. **14** Οἱ οὖν ἄνθρωποι ἰδόντες ὃ ἐποίησεν σημεῖον[2] ἔλεγον ὅτι Οὗτός ἐστιν ἀληθῶς ὁ προφήτης ὁ ἐρχόμενος εἰς τὸν κόσμον. **15** Ἰησοῦς οὖν γνοὺς ὅτι μέλλουσιν ἔρχεσθαι καὶ ἁρπάζειν αὐτὸν ἵνα ποιήσωσιν βασιλέα ἀνεχώρησεν[3] πάλιν εἰς τὸ ὄρος αὐτὸς μόνος.

Walking on the Water
(Mt 14.22–27; Mk 6.45–52)

16 Ὡς δὲ ὀψία ἐγένετο κατέβησαν οἱ μαθηταὶ αὐτοῦ ἐπὶ τὴν θάλασσαν, **17** καὶ ἐμβάντες εἰς πλοῖον ἤρχοντο πέραν τῆς θαλάσσης εἰς Καφαρναούμ. καὶ σκοτία ἤδη ἐγεγόνει καὶ οὔπω ἐληλύθει πρὸς αὐτοὺς ὁ Ἰησοῦς, **18** ἥ τε θάλασσα ἀνέμου μεγάλου πνέοντος διεγείρετο.

---

[2] **14** {B} ὃ ἐποίησεν σημεῖον ℵ D W it^aur,b,c,d,ff2,l vg^ww syr^c,s cop^sa, bo^ms,ach2 geo ‖ ἃ ἐποίησεν σημεῖα 𝔓75 B 086 it^a (arm τὰ σημεῖα ἃ ἐποίησεν) ‖ ὃ ἐποίησεν σημεῖον ὁ Ἰησοῦς A K L Λ Θ Π Ψ 063^vid f1 f13 28 33 565 700 892 1009 (1010 2148 σημεῖον ὃ ἐποίησεν) 1071 1079 1195 1216 1230 1241 1242 1253 1344 1365 1546 1646 2174 Byz Lect it^f,q vg^cl syr^p,h,pal goth (Cyril) ‖ ἃ ἐποίησεν σημεῖα ὁ Ἰησοῦς cop^bo

[3] **15** {B} ἀνεχώρησεν 𝔓75 ℵ^c A B D K L W Δ Θ Ψ 063 f1 f13 28 33 565 700 892 1009 1010 1071 1079 1195 1216 1230 1241 1242 1253 1344 1365 1546 1646 2148 2174 Byz Lect it^b,d,e,f,q,rl syr^(s),p,h,pal cop^sa,bo,ach2 goth arm eth geo Chrysostom Cyril ‖ φεύγει ℵ* it^a,aur,c,ff2,l vg (syr^c) Diatessaron^i,l Tertullian Augustine

---

14 ὁ προφήτης...κόσμον Dt 18.15, 18; Ac 3.22; 7.37   **15** μέλλουσιν...βασιλέα Jn 18.36   ἀνεχώρησεν...μόνος Mt 14.23; 15.29; Mk 6.46; Lk 6.12

---

for all these people?" **10** "Make the people sit down," Jesus told them. (There was a lot of grass there.) So all the people sat down; there were about five thousand men. **11** Jesus took the bread, gave thanks to God, and distributed it to the people sitting down. He did the same with the fish, and they all had as much as they wanted. **12** When they were all full, he said to his disciples, "Pick up the pieces left over; let us not waste a bit." **13** So they took them all up, and filled twelve baskets with the pieces left over from the five barley loaves which the people had eaten.

14 The people there, seeing this mighty work that Jesus had done, said, "Surely this is the Prophet who was to come to the world!" **15** Jesus knew that they were about to come and get him and make him king by force; so he went off again to the hills by himself.

Jesus Walks on the Water
(Also Matt. 14.22–33; Mark 6.45–52)

16 When evening came, his disciples went down to the lake, **17** got into the boat, and went back across the lake toward Capernaum. Night came on, and Jesus still had not come to them. **18** By now a strong wind was blowing and stirring up the water. ¹⁹ The disciples had rowed about three or four miles when they saw Jesus walking on the water, coming near the boat, and they were terrified. ²⁰ "Don't be afraid," Jesus told them, "it is I!" ²¹ They were willing to take him into the boat; and immediately the boat reached land at the place they were heading for.

The People Seek Jesus

²² Next day the crowd which had stayed on the other side of the lake saw that only one boat was left there. They knew that Jesus had not gone in the boat with his disciples, but that they had left without him. ²³ Other boats, from Tiberias, came to shore near the place where the crowd had eaten the bread, after the Lord had given thanks. ²⁴ When the

19 ἐληλακότες οὖν ὡς σταδίους εἴκοσι πέντε ἢ τριάκοντα θεωροῦσιν τὸν Ἰησοῦν περιπατοῦντα ἐπὶ τῆς θαλάσσης καὶ ἐγγὺς τοῦ πλοίου γινόμενον,[a] καὶ ἐφοβήθησαν.[a] **20** ὁ δὲ λέγει αὐτοῖς, Ἐγώ εἰμι, μὴ φοβεῖσθε. **21** ἤθελον οὖν λαβεῖν αὐτὸν εἰς τὸ πλοῖον, καὶ εὐθέως ἐγένετο τὸ πλοῖον ἐπὶ τῆς γῆς εἰς ἣν ὑπῆγον.

Jesus the Bread of Life

22 Τῇ ἐπαύριον ὁ ὄχλος ὁ ἑστηκὼς πέραν τῆς θαλάσσης εἶδον ὅτι πλοιάριον ἄλλο οὐκ ἦν ἐκεῖ εἰ μὴ ἕν[4], καὶ ὅτι οὐ συνεισῆλθεν τοῖς μαθηταῖς αὐτοῦ ὁ Ἰησοῦς εἰς τὸ πλοῖον ἀλλὰ μόνοι οἱ μαθηταὶ αὐτοῦ ἀπῆλθον· **23** ἄλλα[b] ἦλθεν πλοῖα ἐκ Τιβεριάδος[5] ἐγγὺς τοῦ τόπου ὅπου ἔφαγον τὸν ἄρτον [εὐχαριστήσαντος τοῦ κυρίου][6]. **24** ὅτε

[4] **22** {A} ἕν 𝔭75 ℵc A B L W Ψ 063 *f*1 565 1009 1010 1079 1241 1365 1546 itaur,(b),c,f,ff2,l,q,(rl) vg copbo,ach2,fay goth Nonnus ‖ ἓν ἐκεῖνο εἰς ὃ ἐνέβησαν οἱ μαθηταὶ αὐτοῦ K (Δgr ὅν for ὅ) Θ 28 700 892 1242 1344 1646 (2148 2174 ἀνέβησαν) Byz Lect (ite omit ἕν) syr(p),h (Chrysostom) (Cyril) ‖ ἓν ἐκεῖνο εἰς ὃ ἐνέβησαν οἱ μαθηταὶ τοῦ Ἰησοῦ ℵ* (Dc omit ἐκεῖνο) *f*13 (ita) (syrc,pal) copsa arm geo1,A (geoB omit ἐκεῖνο) ‖ ἓν εἰς ὃ ἐνέβησαν οἱ μαθηταὶ αὐτοῦ Ἰησοῦ Dgr* (itd omit αὐτοῦ) ‖ ἓν εἰς ὃ ἐνέβησαν οἱ μαθηταὶ αὐτοῦ 33 1071 (1195 1253 ἀνέβησαν) 1216 1230

[5] **23** {C} ἄλλα ἦλθεν πλοῖα ἐκ Τιβεριάδος 𝔭75 (B ἐκ τῆς) (ite) syrpalmss,(ms) copsa,bomss,ach2,fay geo1 ‖ ἄλλα δὲ ἦλθεν πλοιάρια ἐκ Τιβεριάδος A (W πλοῖα ἐκ τῆς) Δ Θ (Ψ πλοῖα ἦλθεν) 063 *f*13 28 700 (892 ἦν for ἦλθεν) 1010 1079 (1195 πλοιάρια ἦλθεν) (1216 ἐκ τῆς) 1241 1242 1253 1344 1365 1546 1646 2148 2174 Byz *l*76,(184),1127 syr(p),h copbomss geo2 ‖ ἄλλα δὲ ἦλθον πλοιάρια ἐκ Τιβεριάδος (086 33 omit δέ) *f*1 565 1009 *l*185 ita ‖ ἄλλα δὲ πλοιάρια ἦλθον ἐκ Τιβεριάδος K (1071 ἐκ τῆς) (*l*211 πλοῖα) (itd omit δέ) (itq) goth ‖ ἄλλα πλοιάρια ἐκ Τιβεριάδος ἦλθον L (1230 ἄλλα δέ) ‖ ἐπελθόντων οὖν τῶν πλοίων ἐκ Τιβεριάδος ℵ ‖ ἄλλων πλοιαρίων ἐλθόντων ἐκ Τιβεριάδος Dgr (syrc,s) arm ‖ aliae vero supervenerunt naves a Tiberiade itaur,c,(f),ff2,l vg ‖ et cum supervenissent aliae naves a Tiberiade itb,rl

[6] **23** {C} εὐχαριστήσαντος τοῦ κυρίου 𝔭75 ℵ A B K L W Δ Θ Ψ 063

[a] [a] **19** a minor, a major: TR WH Bov Nes BF2 AV RV ASV TT Zür Luth Seg ‖ a major, a minor: RSV NEB ‖ a major, a major: Jer

[b] **23** b ἄλλα: Bov Nes BF2 NEBmg TT ‖ b ἀλλά: WH RV ASV RSV NEB Zür Jer ‖ different text: TR AV Luth Seg

20 Ἐγώ...φοβεῖσθε Mt 14.27   **23** ἐγγὺς...κυρίου Jn 6.11

οὖν εἶδεν ὁ ὄχλος ὅτι Ἰησοῦς οὐκ ἔστιν ἐκεῖ οὐδὲ οἱ μαθηταὶ αὐτοῦ, ἐνέβησαν αὐτοὶ εἰς τὰ πλοιάρια καὶ ἦλθον εἰς Καφαρναοὺμ ζητοῦντες τὸν Ἰησοῦν. 25 καὶ εὑρόντες αὐτὸν πέραν τῆς θαλάσσης εἶπον αὐτῷ, Ῥαββί, πότε ὧδε γέγονας; 26 ἀπεκρίθη αὐτοῖς ὁ Ἰησοῦς καὶ εἶπεν, Ἀμὴν ἀμὴν λέγω ὑμῖν, ζητεῖτέ με οὐχ ὅτι εἴδετε σημεῖα ἀλλ᾽ ὅτι ἐφάγετε ἐκ τῶν ἄρτων καὶ ἐχορτάσθητε. 27 ἐργάζεσθε μὴ τὴν βρῶσιν τὴν ἀπολλυμένην ἀλλὰ τὴν βρῶσιν τὴν μένουσαν εἰς ζωὴν αἰώνιον, ἣν ὁ υἱὸς τοῦ ἀνθρώπου ὑμῖν δώσει[7]· τοῦτον γὰρ ὁ πατὴρ ἐσφράγισεν ὁ θεός. 28 εἶπον οὖν πρὸς αὐτόν, Τί ποιῶμεν ἵνα ἐργαζώμεθα τὰ ἔργα τοῦ θεοῦ; 29 ἀπεκρίθη ὁ Ἰησοῦς καὶ εἶπεν αὐτοῖς, Τοῦτό ἐστιν τὸ ἔργον τοῦ θεοῦ, ἵνα πιστεύητε εἰς ὃν ἀπέστειλεν ἐκεῖνος. 30 εἶπον οὖν αὐτῷ, Τί οὖν ποιεῖς σὺ σημεῖον, ἵνα ἴδωμεν καὶ πιστεύσωμέν σοι; τί ἐργάζῃ; 31 οἱ πατέρες ἡμῶν τὸ μάννα ἔφαγον ἐν τῇ ἐρήμῳ, καθώς ἐστιν γεγραμμένον, **Ἄρτον ἐκ τοῦ οὐρανοῦ ἔδωκεν αὐτοῖς φαγεῖν.** 32 εἶπεν οὖν αὐτοῖς ὁ Ἰησοῦς, Ἀμὴν ἀμὴν λέγω ὑμῖν, οὐ Μωϋσῆς δέδωκεν ὑμῖν τὸν ἄρτον ἐκ τοῦ οὐρανοῦ, ἀλλ᾽ ὁ πατήρ μου δίδωσιν ὑμῖν τὸν ἄρτον ἐκ τοῦ οὐρανοῦ τὸν ἀληθινόν· 33 ὁ γὰρ ἄρτος τοῦ θεοῦ ἐστιν ὁ καταβαίνων ἐκ τοῦ οὐρανοῦ καὶ ζωὴν διδοὺς τῷ κόσμῳ.

crowd saw that Jesus was not there, nor his disciples, they got into boats and went to Capernaum, looking for him.

Jesus the Bread of Life

25 When the people found Jesus on the other side of the lake they said to him, "Teacher, when did you get here?" 26 Jesus answered: "I tell you the truth: you are looking for me because you ate the bread and had all you wanted, not because you saw my works of power. 27 Do not work for food that spoils; instead, work for the food that lasts for eternal life. This food the Son of Man will give you, because God, the Father, has put his mark of approval on him." 28 They asked him then, "What can we do in order to do God's works?" 29 Jesus answered, "This is the work God wants you to do: believe in the one he sent." 30 They replied: "What sign of power will you perform so that we may see it and believe you? What will you do? 31 Our ancestors ate manna in the desert, just as the scripture says: 'He gave them bread from heaven to eat.'" 32 "I tell you the truth," Jesus said. "What Moses gave you was not the bread from heaven; it is my Father who gives you the real bread from heaven. 33 For the bread that God gives is he who comes down from heaven and gives

---

f[13] 28 33 565 700 892 1009 1010 1071 1195 1216 1230 1241 1242 1253 1344 1365 1646 2148 2174 *Byz Lect* (it[b,f,ff2,l,q,r1] *quem benedixerat (or: benedixit) Dominus*) vg syr[h,pal] cop[bo] goth geo[2?] ‖ τοῦ κυρίου εὐχαριστήσαντος *f*[1] cop[sa,ach2,fay] geo[2?] ‖ εὐχαριστήσαντος τοῦ Ἰησοῦ 1079 1546 syr[h,hmg] cop[bomss] ‖ *gratias agentes Deo* it[aur,(c)] ‖ *omit* D 086 it[a,d,e] syr[c,s] arm geo[1] Diatessaron[l,v]

7 **27** {B} ὑμῖν δώσει 𝔭[75] A B K L W Δ Θ Ψ* 063 *f*[1] 28 33 565 700 892 1010 1071 1079 1195 1216 1230 1241 1242 (1253 ἡμῖν) 1344 1365 1546 1646 2174 *Byz l*[76,185,1127] it[c] vg[ww] syr[h] Novatian Origen Cyril ‖ δώσει ὑμῖν Ψ[c] *f*[13] (1009 2148 ἡμῖν) *Lect* it[a,b,f,l,q,r1] vg[cl] syr[s,p] cop[sa,bo,ach2,fay] goth? arm geo Hilary Chrysostom ‖ δίδωσιν ὑμῖν ℵ D it[(aur),d,e,ff2,j] syr[c,pal] goth? Chrysostom

26 ἐφάγετε...ἐχορτάσθητε Jn 6.11-12 **27** τὴν βρῶσιν...αἰώνιον Jn 4.14; 6.50, 51, 54, 58
30 εἶπον...σημεῖον Jn 2.18 **31** οἱ...ἐρήμῳ Ex 16.15; Nu 11.7-9; Ne 9.15; Jn 6.49, 58
Ἄρτον...φαγεῖν Ps 78.24 (105.40) **33** ὁ γὰρ...οὐρανοῦ Jn 6.41, 51

life to the world." ³⁴ "Sir," they asked him, "give us this bread always." ³⁵ "I am the bread of life," Jesus told them. "He who comes to me will never be hungry; he who believes in me will never be thirsty.

³⁶ "Now, I told you that you had seen me but would not believe. ³⁷ Every one whom my Father gives me will come to me. I will never turn away anyone who comes to me, ³⁸ for I have come down from heaven to do the will of him who sent me, not my own will. ³⁹ This is what he who sent me wants me to do: that I should not lose any of all those he has given me, but that I should raise them all to life on the last day. ⁴⁰ For this is what my Father wants: that all who see the Son and believe in him should have eternal life; and I will raise them to life on the last day."

⁴¹ The Jews started grumbling about him, because he said, "I am the bread that came down from heaven." ⁴² So they said: "This man is Jesus the son of Joseph, isn't he? We know his father and mother. How, then, does he now say he

34 Εἶπον οὖν πρὸς αὐτόν, Κύριε, πάντοτε δὸς ἡμῖν τὸν ἄρτον τοῦτον. **35** εἶπεν αὐτοῖς ὁ Ἰησοῦς, Ἐγώ εἰμι ὁ ἄρτος τῆς ζωῆς· ὁ ἐρχόμενος πρός με οὐ μὴ πεινάσῃ, καὶ ὁ πιστεύων εἰς ἐμὲ οὐ μὴ διψήσει πώποτε. **36** ἀλλ' εἶπον ὑμῖν ὅτι καὶ ἑωράκατέ [με]⁸ καὶ οὐ πιστεύετε. **37** Πᾶν ὃ δίδωσίν μοι ὁ πατὴρ πρὸς ἐμὲ ἥξει, καὶ τὸν ἐρχόμενον πρὸς ἐμὲ οὐ μὴ ἐκβάλω ἔξω, **38** ὅτι καταβέβηκα ἀπὸ τοῦ οὐρανοῦ οὐχ ἵνα ποιῶ τὸ θέλημα τὸ ἐμὸν ἀλλὰ τὸ θέλημα τοῦ πέμψαντός με· **39** τοῦτο δέ ἐστιν τὸ θέλημα τοῦ πέμψαντός με, ἵνα πᾶν ὃ δέδωκέν μοι μὴ ἀπολέσω ἐξ αὐτοῦ ἀλλὰ ἀναστήσω αὐτὸ [ἐν] τῇ ἐσχάτῃ ἡμέρᾳ. **40** τοῦτο γάρ ἐστιν τὸ θέλημα τοῦ πατρός μου, ἵνα πᾶς ὁ θεωρῶν τὸν υἱὸν καὶ πιστεύων εἰς αὐτὸν ἔχῃ ζωὴν αἰώνιον, καὶ ἀναστήσω αὐτὸν ἐγὼ [ἐν] τῇ ἐσχάτῃ ἡμέρᾳ.

41 Ἐγόγγυζον οὖν οἱ Ἰουδαῖοι περὶ αὐτοῦ ὅτι εἶπεν, Ἐγώ εἰμι ὁ ἄρτος ὁ καταβὰς ἐκ τοῦ οὐρανοῦ, **42** καὶ ἔλεγον, Οὐχ οὗτός ἐστιν Ἰησοῦς ὁ υἱὸς Ἰωσήφ, οὗ ἡμεῖς οἴδαμεν τὸν πατέρα καὶ τὴν μητέρα⁹; πῶς νῦν¹⁰

---

⁸ **36** {C} με p⁶⁶,⁷⁵ᵛⁱᵈ B D K L (T μη [=μοι?]) W Δ Θ Π Ψ f¹ f¹³ 28 33 565 700 892 1009 1010 1071 1079 1195 1216 1230 1241 1242 1253 1344 1365 1546 1646 2148 2174 *Byz Lect* itᵃᵘʳ,ᶜ,ᵈ,ᶠ,ff²,ʲ vg syrᵖ,ʰ,ᵖᵃˡ copˢᵃ,ᵇᵒ,ᵃᶜʰ²,ᶠᵃʸ goth arm eth geo Chrysostom Cyril ∥ *omit* ℵ A itᵃ,ᵇ,ᵉ, q syrᶜ,ˢ

⁹ **42** {B} καὶ τὴν μητέρα p⁶⁶,⁷⁵ ℵᶜ A B C D K L T Δ Θ Π Ψ f¹ f¹³ 28 33 565 700 892 1009 1010 1071 1079 1195 1216 1230 1241 1242 1253 1344 1365 1546 1646 2148 2174 *Byz Lect* (l²¹¹ transposes: τὴν μητέρα καὶ τὸν πατέρα) itᵃ,ᵃᵘʳ,ᶜ,ᵈ,ᵉ,ᶠ,ff²,q,ʳˡ vg syrᵖ,ʰ,ᵖᵃˡ copˢᵃ,ᵇᵒ,ᵃᶜʰ²,ᶠᵃʸᵛⁱᵈ goth geo² ∥ *omit* ℵ* W itᵇ syrᶜ,ˢ arm geo¹ Ambrosiaster

¹⁰ **42** {C} νῦν p⁷⁵ B C T W Θ 1241 syrᵖᵃˡ copᵇᵒ goth? arm Athanasius ∥ οὖν p⁶⁶ ℵ A D K L Δ Π Ψ f¹ f¹³ 28 33 565 700 892 1009 1010 1071 1079 1195 1216 1230 1242 1253 1344 1365 1546 1646 2148 2174 *Byz Lect* itᵃᵘʳ,ᵇ,ᶜ,ᵈ,ᶠ,ff²,q,ʳˡ vg syrʰ copˢᵃᵐˢˢ goth? geo² Diatessaron Athanasius Chrysostom Cyril ∥ οὖν νῦν copᵇᵒᵐˢˢ eth ∥ *omit* 440 579 itᵃ,ᵉ syrᶜ,ˢ,(ᵖ) copˢᵃ,ᵃᶜʰ²,ᶠᵃʸᵛⁱᵈ geo¹ Diatessaronᵃ

---

34 Jn 4.15   πάντοτε...τοῦτον Mt 6.11; Lk 11.3   **35** Ἐγώ...ζωῆς Jn 6.48, 51, 58 ὁ πιστεύων...πώποτε Jn 4.14   **36** ἑωράκατε...πιστεύετε Jn 20.29   **37** Πᾶν...πατήρ Jn 17.2, 7, 24   τὸν ἐρχόμενον...ἔξω Mt 11.28   **38** οὐχ...πέμψαντός με Mt 26.39; Mk 14.36; Lk 22.42; Jn 4.34; 5.30   **39** ἵνα πᾶν...αὐτοῦ Jn 10.28, 29; 17.12; 18.9   **39, 40** ἀναστήσω... ἡμέρᾳ Jn 6.44, 54; 11.24   **41** Ἐγώ...οὐρανοῦ Jn 6.33, 35, 51, 58   **42** Οὐχ...Ἰωσήφ Mt 13.55; Mk 6.3; Lk 4.22

λέγει ὅτι Ἐκ τοῦ οὐρανοῦ καταβέβηκα; **43** ἀπεκρίθη Ἰησοῦς καὶ εἶπεν αὐτοῖς, Μὴ γογγύζετε μετ' ἀλλήλων. **44** οὐδεὶς δύναται ἐλθεῖν πρός με ἐὰν μὴ ὁ πατὴρ ὁ πέμψας με ἑλκύσῃ αὐτόν, κἀγὼ ἀναστήσω αὐτὸν ἐν τῇ ἐσχάτῃ ἡμέρᾳ. **45** ἔστιν γεγραμμένον ἐν τοῖς προφήταις, **Καὶ ἔσονται πάντες διδακτοὶ θεοῦ·** πᾶς ὁ ἀκούσας παρὰ τοῦ πατρὸς καὶ μαθὼν ἔρχεται πρὸς ἐμέ. **46** οὐχ ὅτι τὸν πατέρα ἑώρακέν τις εἰ μὴ ὁ ὢν παρὰ τοῦ θεοῦ, οὗτος ἑώρακεν τὸν πατέρα. **47** ἀμὴν ἀμὴν λέγω ὑμῖν, ὁ πιστεύων[11] ἔχει ζωὴν αἰώνιον. **48** ἐγώ εἰμι ὁ ἄρτος τῆς ζωῆς. **49** οἱ πατέρες ὑμῶν ἔφαγον ἐν τῇ ἐρήμῳ τὸ μάννα καὶ ἀπέθανον· **50** οὗτός ἐστιν ὁ ἄρτος ὁ ἐκ τοῦ οὐρανοῦ καταβαίνων ἵνα τις ἐξ αὐτοῦ φάγῃ καὶ μὴ ἀποθάνῃ. **51** ἐγώ εἰμι ὁ ἄρτος ὁ ζῶν ὁ ἐκ τοῦ οὐρανοῦ καταβάς· ἐάν τις φάγῃ ἐκ τούτου τοῦ ἄρτου ζήσει εἰς τὸν αἰῶνα· καὶ ὁ ἄρτος δὲ ὃν ἐγὼ δώσω ἡ σάρξ μού ἐστιν ὑπὲρ τῆς τοῦ κόσμου ζωῆς.

52 Ἐμάχοντο οὖν πρὸς ἀλλήλους οἱ Ἰουδαῖοι λέγοντες, Πῶς δύναται οὗτος ἡμῖν δοῦναι τὴν σάρκα [αὐτοῦ][12] φαγεῖν; **53** εἶπεν οὖν αὐτοῖς ὁ Ἰησοῦς, Ἀμὴν ἀμὴν λέγω ὑμῖν, ἐὰν μὴ φάγητε τὴν σάρκα τοῦ υἱοῦ τοῦ ἀνθρώπου καὶ πίητε αὐτοῦ τὸ αἷμα, οὐκ ἔχετε ζωὴν ἐν ἑαυτοῖς. **54** ὁ τρώγων μου τὴν σάρκα καὶ πίνων μου τὸ αἷμα ἔχει ζωὴν αἰώνιον, κἀγὼ ἀναστήσω αὐτὸν

came down from heaven?'' [43] Jesus answered: "Stop grumbling among yourselves. [44] No one can come to me unless the Father who sent me draws him to me; and I will raise him to life on the last day. [45] The prophets wrote, 'All men will be taught by God.' Everyone who hears the Father and learns from him comes to me. [46] This does not mean that anyone has seen the Father; he who is from God is the only one who has seen the Father.

[47] "I tell you the truth: he who believes has eternal life. [48] I am the bread of life. [49] Your ancestors ate the manna in the desert, but died. [50] But the bread which comes down from heaven is such that whoever eats it will not die. [51] I am the living bread which came down from heaven. If anyone eats this bread he will live for ever. And the bread which I will give him is my flesh, which I give so that the world may live."

[52] This started an angry argument among the Jews. "How can this man give us his flesh to eat?'' they asked. [53] Jesus said to them: "I tell you the truth: if you do not eat the flesh of the Son of Man and drink his blood you will not have life in yourselves. [54] Whoever eats my flesh and drinks my blood has eternal life, and I will raise him to life

---

[11] **47** {A} πιστεύων 𝔭[66,75vid] ℵ B C* L T W Θ 892 1071 it[j] cop[ach2] arm geo[1] // πιστεύων εἰς ἐμέ A C[2] D K Δ Π Ψ f[1] f[13] 28 33 565 700 1009 1010 1079 1195 1216 1230 1241 1242 1253 1344 1365 1546 1646 2148 2174 Byz it[a,aur,b,c,d,e,f,ff2,q,r1] vg syr[p,h] cop[sa,bo] goth eth geo[2] Diatessaron[a,i,n] Origen Hilary Cyril // πιστεύων εἰς τὸν θεόν syr[c,s]

[12] **52** {C} αὐτοῦ 𝔭[66] B T 892 1079 (1216 1253 1646 τὴν ἑαυτοῦ σάρκα) it[a,aur,b,c,e,f,q,r1] vg syr[c,s,p,h,pal] cop[sa,bo,ach2] arm eth geo Diatessaron[a,i,n] Origen[lat] Chrysostom Cyril Ammonius-Alexandria // omit 𝔭[75vid] ℵ C D K L W Δ Θ Π Ψ f[1] f[13] 28 33 565 700 1009 1010 1071 1195 1230 1241 1242 1344 1365 1546 2148 2174 Byz Lect it[d,ff2] goth Origen Cyril

---

44 οὐδεὶς…ἑλκύσῃ αὐτόν Jn 6.65 κἀγώ…ἡμέρᾳ Jn 6.39, 40, 54; 11.24 **45** Καὶ…θεοῦ Is 54.13; (1 Th 4.9) **46** Jn 1.18 **47** ὁ…αἰώνιον Jn 3.15, 16, 36 **48** Jn 6.35, 48, 51, 58 **49** Jn 6.31, 58 **50–51** οὗτος…αἰῶνα Jn 6.33, 58 **54** κἀγώ…ἡμέρᾳ Jn 6.39, 40, 44; 11.24

on the last day. 55 For my flesh is the
real food, my blood is the real drink.
56 Whoever eats my flesh and drinks my
blood lives in me and I live in him.
57 The living Father sent me, and because of him I live also. In the same
way, whoever eats me will live because
of me. 58 This, then, is the bread that
came down from heaven; it is not like
the bread that your ancestors ate and
then died. The one who eats this bread
will live for ever." 59 Jesus said this as
he taught in the synagogue in Capernaum.

The Words of Eternal Life

60 Many of his disciples heard this
and said, "This teaching is too hard.
Who can listen to this?" 61 Without
being told, Jesus knew that his disciples
were grumbling about this; so he said
to them: "Does this make you want to
give up? 62 Suppose, then, that you
should see the Son of Man go back up
to the place where he was before? 63 What
gives life is the Spirit; the flesh is of no
use at all. The words I have spoken to
you are Spirit and life. 64 Yet some of
you do not believe." (For Jesus knew

τῇ ἐσχάτῃ ἡμέρᾳ· **55** *ἡ γὰρ σάρξ μου ἀληθής*[13] *ἐστιν*
βρῶσις, καὶ τὸ αἷμά μου ἀληθής[13] *ἐστιν πόσις.* **56** *ὁ*
τρώγων μου τὴν σάρκα καὶ πίνων μου τὸ αἷμα ἐν ἐμοὶ
μένει κἀγὼ ἐν αὐτῷ. **57** *καθὼς ἀπέστειλέν με ὁ ζῶν*
πατὴρ κἀγὼ ζῶ διὰ τὸν πατέρα, καὶ ὁ τρώγων με
κἀκεῖνος ζήσει δι' ἐμέ. **58** *οὗτός ἐστιν ὁ ἄρτος ὁ ἐκ τοῦ*
οὐρανοῦ καταβάς, οὐ καθὼς ἔφαγον οἱ πατέρες[14] *καὶ*
ἀπέθανον· ὁ τρώγων τοῦτον τὸν ἄρτον ζήσει εἰς τὸν
αἰῶνα. **59** *Ταῦτα εἶπεν ἐν συναγωγῇ διδάσκων ἐν*
Καφαρναούμ.

The Words of Eternal Life

60 *Πολλοὶ οὖν ἀκούσαντες ἐκ τῶν μαθητῶν αὐτοῦ*
εἶπαν, Σκληρός ἐστιν ὁ λόγος οὗτος· τίς δύναται αὐτοῦ
ἀκούειν; **61** *εἰδὼς δὲ ὁ Ἰησοῦς ἐν ἑαυτῷ ὅτι γογγύ-*
ζουσιν περὶ τούτου οἱ μαθηταὶ αὐτοῦ εἶπεν αὐτοῖς,
Τοῦτο ὑμᾶς σκανδαλίζει; **62** *ἐὰν οὖν θεωρῆτε τὸν υἱὸν*
τοῦ ἀνθρώπου ἀναβαίνοντα ὅπου ἦν τὸ πρότερον; **63** *τὸ*
πνεῦμά ἐστιν τὸ ζῳοποιοῦν, ἡ σὰρξ οὐκ ὠφελεῖ οὐδέν·
τὰ ῥήματα ἃ ἐγὼ λελάληκα ὑμῖν πνεῦμά ἐστιν καὶ ζωή
ἐστιν. **64** *ἀλλ' εἰσὶν ἐξ ὑμῶν τινες οἳ οὐ πιστεύουσιν.*

---

[13] **55** {C} *ἀληθής...ἀληθής* 𝔭^{66,75} ℵ^{c} B C K L T W Π Ψ *f*^{1} 565 892 1009 1010 1071 1079 1195 1230 1241 1253 1365 1546 2174 it^{q} cop$^{sa, bo, ach^2, fay^{vid}}$ goth? arm geo Diatessaron^{l} Clement Origen$^{gr, lat3/5}$ Eusebius Basil Apollinaris Chrysostom Cyril // *ἀληθῶς...ἀληθῶς* (ℵ*) (D *omit καὶ...πόσις*) Δ Θ 0250 28 700 1216 1242 1646 2148 *Byz* *l*^{547} it$^{a, aur, b, c, d, e, f, ff^2, r^1}$ vg syr$^{c, s, p, h}$ goth? Diatessaron Origen$^{gr, lat2/5}$ Hilary Gregory-Nyssa Ambrose Augustine // *ἀληθής...ἀληθῶς* *f*^{13}

[14] **58** {A} *οἱ πατέρες* 𝔭^{66,75} ℵ B C L T W cop^{bo} Origen // *οἱ πατέρες ὑμῶν* D 33 it$^{d, e}$ syr$^{c, s}$ cop$^{sa, bo^{mss}, ach^2}$ eth Origen // *οἱ πατέρες ὑμῶν τὸ μάννα* K Δ Θ Π Ψ 0250 *f*^{1} *f*^{13} 28 565 700 892 (1009 *ἡμῶν*) 1010 1071 1079 1195 1216 1230 1241 1242 1253 1344 1365 1546 1646 2174 *Byz Lect* it$^{a, aur, b, c, f, q, r^1}$ vg syr$^{p, h, pal^{mss}}$ goth arm geo Diatessaron$^{a, n, t}$ Chrysostom Cyril // *τὸ μάννα οἱ πατέρες ὑμῶν* M (2148 *add ἐν τῷ κόσμῳ*) // *οἱ πατέρες ὑμῶν τὸ μάννα ἐν τῇ ἐρήμῳ* it$^{ff^2}$ syr$^{pal^{ms}}$ cop$^{bo^{mss}}$ (Nonnus)

---

56 *ἐν ἐμοὶ μένει...αὐτῷ* Jn 15.5; 1 Jn 3.24 **62** Ac 1.9–11 **63** *τὸ...ζῳοποιοῦν* 2 Cor 3.6

ἤδει γὰρ ἐξ ἀρχῆς ὁ Ἰησοῦς τίνες εἰσὶν οἱ μὴ πιστεύοντες καὶ[15] τίς ἐστιν ὁ παραδώσων αὐτόν. 65 καὶ ἔλεγεν, Διὰ τοῦτο εἴρηκα ὑμῖν ὅτι οὐδεὶς δύναται ἐλθεῖν πρός με ἐὰν μὴ ᾖ δεδομένον αὐτῷ ἐκ τοῦ πατρός.

66 Ἐκ τούτου [οὖν] πολλοὶ ἐκ τῶν μαθητῶν αὐτοῦ ἀπῆλθον εἰς τὰ ὀπίσω καὶ οὐκέτι μετ' αὐτοῦ περιεπάτουν. 67 εἶπεν οὖν ὁ Ἰησοῦς τοῖς δώδεκα, Μὴ καὶ ὑμεῖς θέλετε ὑπάγειν; 68 ἀπεκρίθη αὐτῷ Σίμων Πέτρος, Κύριε, πρὸς τίνα ἀπελευσόμεθα; ῥήματα ζωῆς αἰωνίου ἔχεις, 69 καὶ ἡμεῖς πεπιστεύκαμεν καὶ ἐγνώκαμεν ὅτι σὺ εἶ ὁ ἅγιος τοῦ θεοῦ[16]. 70 ἀπεκρίθη αὐτοῖς ὁ Ἰησοῦς, Οὐκ ἐγὼ ὑμᾶς τοὺς δώδεκα ἐξελεξάμην,[c] καὶ ἐξ ὑμῶν εἷς διάβολός ἐστιν;[c] 71 ἔλεγεν δὲ τὸν Ἰούδαν Σίμωνος Ἰσκαριώτου[17]. οὗτος γὰρ ἔμελλεν παραδιδόναι αὐτόν, εἷς [ὢν] ἐκ τῶν δώδεκα.

from the very beginning who were the ones that would not believe, and which one would betray him.) [65] And he added, "This is the very reason I told you that no one can come to me unless the Father makes it possible for him to do so."

[66] Because of this, many of his followers turned back and would not go with him any more. [67] So Jesus said to the twelve disciples, "And you — would you like to leave also?" [68] Simon Peter answered him: "Lord, to whom would we go? You have the words that give eternal life. [69] And now we believe and know that you are the Holy One from God." [70] Jesus answered them, "Did I not choose the twelve of you? Yet one of you is a devil!" [71] He was talking about Judas, the son of Simon Iscariot. For Judas, even though he was one of the twelve disciples, was going to betray him.

---

[15] **64** {B} τίνες εἰσὶν οἱ μὴ πιστεύοντες καὶ 𝔭[66c,75vid] B C D K L T W Δ Θ Π Ψ 0250 f[1] f[13] 28 33 565 700 892 (1009 πιστεύοντες εἰς αὐτόν) 1010 1079 1195 1230 1241 1242 1253 1344[mg] 1365 1646 2148 2174 *Byz Lect* it[a,(b),c,d,f,ff2,l,q,r1] vg[cl] syr[p,h,pal] cop[sa,bo,ach2,fay] goth arm geo ∥ τίνες οἱ μὴ πιστεύσαντες καὶ l[547] ∥ τίνες εἰσὶν οἱ πιστεύοντες καὶ ℵ X[comm] 1071 1216 1546 it[aur] vg[ww] ∥ *omit* 𝔭[66*] 1344* it[e] syr[c,s] cop[boms vid]

[16] **69** {A} ὁ ἅγιος τοῦ θεοῦ 𝔭[75] ℵ B C* D L W Ψ it[d] cop[sams,boms] Nonnus Cosmos ∥ ὁ Χριστός Tertullian ∥ ὁ Χριστὸς ὁ ἅγιος τοῦ θεοῦ 𝔭[66] cop[sa,bo,ach2] ∥ ὁ υἱὸς τοῦ θεοῦ it[b] syr[c] ∥ ὁ υἱὸς τοῦ θεοῦ τοῦ ζῶντος 17 geo[A] Cyprian ∥ ὁ Χριστὸς ὁ υἱὸς τοῦ θεοῦ (see 1.49; Mt 16.16) Θ* f[1] 33 565 1010 it[a,aur,c,e,1] vg syr[s] arm geo[1] Victorinus-Rome Cyril ∥ ὁ Χριστὸς ὁ υἱὸς τοῦ θεοῦ τοῦ ζῶντος C[3vid] K (Δ θεοῦ ζῶντος) Θ[c] Π 0250 f[13] 28 700 892 1009 1071 1079 1195 1216 1230 1241 1242 1253 1344 1365 1546 1646 2148 2174 *Byz Lect* it[f*,ff2,q,r1] syr[p,h,pal] cop[boms s] goth geo[B] Diatessaron[a] Cyprian Basil Chrysostom

[17] **71** {C} Ἰσκαριώτου 𝔭[66,75] ℵ[c] B C L W Ψ 33 892 1010 1071 1241 1344 cop[sa,ach2,fay] (geo[1] Σκαριώτου) ∥ Ἰσκαριώτην K Δ Π f[1] 28 565 700 1009 1079 1195 1216 1230 1242 1253 1365 1546 1646 2148 2174 *Byz* vg[cl] cop[bo] goth geo[2] Cyril ∥ *Iscariota* syr[c] ∥ Σκαριώθ D it[a,aur,b,d,(ff2),r1] (it[l,q] *Scariothe*, it[(c,f*),fc] vg[ww] *Scariotis*) (syr[s,p,h] arm *Scariota*) ∥ *Carioth* it[e] ∥ ἀπὸ Καρυώτου ℵ* Θ f[13] syr[hmg,gr]

[c c] **70** *c* minor, *c* question: TR AV RV ASV RSV ∥ *c* question, *c* statement: WH Bov Ne͡s BF[2] NEB TT Zür Luth Jer ∥ *c* question, *c* exclamation: Seg

64 ἤδει...αὐτόν Jn 13.11   **65** Jn 6.44   **68** ῥήματα...ἔχεις Jn 6.63   **69** σὺ...θεοῦ Mk 1.24; Lk 4.34   **71** Jn 12.4

Jesus and His Brothers

7 After this, Jesus traveled in Galilee; he did not want to travel in Judea, because the Jews there were wanting to kill him. [2] The Jewish Feast of Tabernacles was near, [3] so Jesus' brothers said to him: "Leave this place and go to Judea, so that your disciples will see the works you are doing. [4] No one hides what he is doing if he wants to be well known. Since you are doing these things, let the whole world know about you!" [5] (Not even his brothers believed in him.) [6] Jesus said to them: "The right time for me has not yet come. Any time is right for you. [7] The world cannot hate you, but it hates me, because I keep telling it that its ways are bad. [8] You go on to the feast. I am not going[1] to this feast, because the right time has not come for me." [9] He told them this, and stayed on in Galilee.

---

[1] **8** I am not going: *some mss.* read I am not yet going

The Unbelief of Jesus' Brothers

7 Καὶ μετὰ ταῦτα περιεπάτει ὁ Ἰησοῦς ἐν τῇ Γαλιλαίᾳ· οὐ γὰρ ἤθελεν[1] ἐν τῇ Ἰουδαίᾳ περιπατεῖν, ὅτι ἐζήτουν αὐτὸν οἱ Ἰουδαῖοι ἀποκτεῖναι. **2** ἦν δὲ ἐγγὺς ἡ ἑορτὴ τῶν Ἰουδαίων ἡ σκηνοπηγία. **3** εἶπον οὖν πρὸς αὐτὸν οἱ ἀδελφοὶ αὐτοῦ, Μετάβηθι ἐντεῦθεν καὶ ὕπαγε εἰς τὴν Ἰουδαίαν, ἵνα καὶ οἱ μαθηταί σου θεωρήσουσιν [σοῦ] τὰ ἔργα ἃ ποιεῖς· **4** οὐδεὶς γάρ τι ἐν κρυπτῷ ποιεῖ καὶ ζητεῖ αὐτὸς ἐν παρρησίᾳ[2] εἶναι. εἰ ταῦτα ποιεῖς, φανέρωσον σεαυτὸν τῷ κόσμῳ. **5** οὐδὲ γὰρ οἱ ἀδελφοὶ αὐτοῦ ἐπίστευον εἰς αὐτόν. **6** λέγει οὖν αὐτοῖς ὁ Ἰησοῦς, Ὁ καιρὸς ὁ ἐμὸς οὔπω πάρεστιν, ὁ δὲ καιρὸς ὁ ὑμέτερος πάντοτέ ἐστιν ἕτοιμος. **7** οὐ δύναται ὁ κόσμος μισεῖν ὑμᾶς, ἐμὲ δὲ μισεῖ, ὅτι ἐγὼ μαρτυρῶ περὶ αὐτοῦ ὅτι τὰ ἔργα αὐτοῦ πονηρά ἐστιν. **8** ὑμεῖς ἀνάβητε εἰς τὴν ἑορτήν· ἐγὼ οὐκ[3] ἀναβαίνω εἰς τὴν ἑορτὴν ταύτην, ὅτι ὁ ἐμὸς καιρὸς οὔπω πεπλήρωται. **9** ταῦτα δὲ εἰπὼν αὐτὸς[4] ἔμεινεν ἐν τῇ Γαλιλαίᾳ.

---

[1] **1** {B} ἤθελεν 𝔭[66,75] ℵ B C D K L X Δ Θ Π Ψ 0105 0250 *f*[1] *f*[13] 28 33 565 700 892 1009 1010 1071 1079 1195 1216 1230 1241 1242 1253 1344 1365 1546 1646 2148 2174 *Byz Lect* it[aur,c,d,(e),f,q] vg syr[(s),p,h,pal] cop[sa,bo,ach2] goth arm geo ∥ εἶχεν ἐξουσίαν W it[a,b,ff2,l,r1] syr[c] Chrysostom

[2] **4** {C} αὐτὸς ἐν παρρησίᾳ 𝔭[66c,75] ℵ E[c] K L X Δ Θ Π Ψ 0105 0180 0250 *f*[1] 28 33 565 700 892 1009 1010 1071 1079 1195 1216 1230 1241 1242 1253 1344 1365 1546 1646 2148 2174 *Byz Lect* it[a,aur,c,f,ff2,q,r1] vg syr[s,p,h,pal] cop[sa,ach2,fay] arm geo[2] ∥ αὐτὸ ἐν παρρησίᾳ 𝔭[66*] B W it[d] Diatessaron[n] ∥ αὐτὸν ἐν παρρησίᾳ E* 253 1093 cop[bo?] goth geo[1] ∥ ἐν παρρησίᾳ αὐτός (D[gr*] αὐτό) D[c] *f*[13] ∥ ἐν παρρησίᾳ it[b,(e)] syr[c] cop[boms?] eth

[3] **8** {C} οὐκ ℵ D K Π 1071 1079 1241 1242 1546 it[a,aur,b,c,d,e,(ff2)] vg syr[c,s] cop[bo] arm eth geo Diatessaron[esyr] Porphyry[acc. to Jerome] Ambrosiaster Epiphanius Chrysostom Cyril ∥ οὔπω 𝔭[66,75] B L T W X Δ Θ Ψ 0105 0180 0250 *f*[1] *f*[13] 28 700 892 1010 1195 1216 1230 1253 1344 1365 1646 2148 *Byz Lect* it[f,q] syr[p,hgr,pal] cop[sa,boms,ach2] goth Diatessaron Basil Nonnus

[4] **9** {B} αὐτός 𝔭[66] ℵ D* K L W X Π 0180 *f*[1] 565 1071 1079 1216 1241 1242

---

1 ἐζήτουν...ἀποκτεῖναι Jn 5.18; 7.19, 25; 8.37, 40   **2** Lv 23.34   **6** Ὁ καιρὸς... πάρεστιν Jn 2.4; 7.30; 8.20   **7** οὐ...μισεῖ Jn 15.18   τὰ ἔργα...ἐστιν Jn 3.19

Jesus at the Feast of Tabernacles

10 Ὡς δὲ ἀνέβησαν οἱ ἀδελφοὶ αὐτοῦ εἰς τὴν ἑορτήν, τότε καὶ αὐτὸς ἀνέβη, οὐ φανερῶς ἀλλ'[5] ἐν κρυπτῷ. **11** οἱ οὖν Ἰουδαῖοι ἐζήτουν αὐτὸν ἐν τῇ ἑορτῇ καὶ ἔλεγον, Ποῦ ἐστιν ἐκεῖνος; **12** καὶ γογγυσμὸς περὶ αὐτοῦ ἦν [πολὺς] ἐν τῷ ὄχλῳ[6]· οἱ μὲν ἔλεγον ὅτι Ἀγαθός ἐστιν, ἄλλοι [δὲ] ἔλεγον, Οὔ, ἀλλὰ πλανᾷ τὸν ὄχλον. **13** οὐδεὶς μέντοι παρρησίᾳ ἐλάλει περὶ αὐτοῦ διὰ τὸν φόβον τῶν Ἰουδαίων.

14 Ἤδη δὲ τῆς ἑορτῆς μεσούσης ἀνέβη Ἰησοῦς εἰς τὸ ἱερὸν καὶ ἐδίδασκεν. **15** ἐθαύμαζον οὖν οἱ Ἰουδαῖοι λέγοντες, Πῶς οὗτος γράμματα οἶδεν μὴ μεμαθηκώς; **16** ἀπεκρίθη οὖν αὐτοῖς [ὁ] Ἰησοῦς καὶ εἶπεν, Ἡ ἐμὴ διδαχὴ οὐκ ἔστιν ἐμὴ ἀλλὰ τοῦ πέμψαντός με· **17** ἐάν τις θέλῃ τὸ θέλημα αὐτοῦ ποιεῖν, γνώσεται περὶ τῆς διδαχῆς πότερον ἐκ τοῦ θεοῦ ἐστιν ἢ ἐγὼ ἀπ' ἐμαυτοῦ λαλῶ. **18** ὁ ἀφ' ἑαυτοῦ λαλῶν τὴν δόξαν τὴν ἰδίαν ζητεῖ· ὁ δὲ ζητῶν τὴν δόξαν τοῦ πέμψαντος αὐτόν, οὗτος ἀληθής ἐστιν καὶ ἀδικία ἐν αὐτῷ οὐκ ἔστιν. **19** οὐ Μωϋσῆς δέδωκεν ὑμῖν τὸν νόμον; καὶ οὐδεὶς ἐξ ὑμῶν

1546 it[aur,b,d,l] vg cop[sa,bo,ach2] arm Cyril ∥ αὐτοῖς 𝔭[75] B D[b] T Δ Θ Ψ 0105 0250 f[13] 28 33 700 892 1009 1010 1195 1230 1253 1344 1646 2148 2174 *Byz Lect* it[a,f,ff2,q,r1] syr[s,h,pal] goth eth geo[2] Basil Chrysostom ∥ ὁ Ἰησοῦς it[c] Chrysostom ∥ *omit* 1365 *l*[26] it[e] syr[c,p] geo[1] Diatessaron

5 10 {B} ἀλλ' ℵ D *l*[372] it[a,b,d,e,r1] syr[c,s] cop[sa,boms,ach2,fay] geo Diatessaron[n,v] Cyril ∥ ἀλλ' (*or* ἀλλά) ὡς 𝔭[66,75] B K L T W X Δ Θ Π Ψ 0105 0180 0238[vid] 0250 f[1] f[13] 28 33 565 700 892 1009 1010 1071 1079 1195 1216 1230 1241 1242 1253 1344 1365 1546 1646 2148 2174 *Byz Lect* it[aur,c,f,ff2,l,q] vg syr[p,h,pal] cop[bo] goth arm Basil Chrysostom

6 12 {D} τῷ ὄχλῳ 𝔭[66] ℵ D 33 it[a,aur,b,c,d,(e),(f),ff2,l,(q),r1] vg syr[c,(s),p,palms] cop[samss,bo] goth geo Diatessaron ∥ τοῖς ὄχλοις 𝔭[75] B K L T W X Δ Θ Π Ψ 0105 0180 0250 f[1] f[13] 28 565 700 892 1009 1010 1071 1079 1195 1216 1230 1241 1242 1253 1344 1365 1546 1646 2148 2174 *Byz Lect* syr[h,palms] cop[samss] arm Chrysostom Cyril

---

11 Jn 11.56   **13** διὰ...Ἰουδαίων Jn 9.22; 19.38; 20.19   **15** Mt 13.54; Lk 2.47
16 Jn 12.49; 14.10   **18** ὁ...δόξαν...ζητεῖ Jn 8.50   **19** οὐ...ὑμῖν τὸν νόμον Jn 1.17
οὐδεὶς...νόμον Ac 7.53; Ro 2.21-24

Jesus at the Feast of Tabernacles

[10] After his brothers went to the feast, Jesus also went; however, he did not go openly, but went secretly. [11] The Jews were looking for him at the feast. "Where is he?" they asked. [12] There was much whispering about him in the crowd. "He is a good man," some people said. "No," others said, "he fools the people." [13] But no one talked about him openly, because they were afraid of the Jews.

[14] The feast was nearly half over when Jesus went to the Temple and began teaching. [15] The Jews, greatly surprised, said, "How does this man know so much when he has never been to school?" [16] Jesus answered: "What I teach is not mine, but comes from God, who sent me. [17] Whoever is willing to do what God wants will know whether what I teach comes from God or whether I speak on my own authority. [18] A person who speaks on his own is trying to gain glory for himself. He who wants glory for the one who sent him, however, is honest and there is nothing false in him. [19] Moses gave you the Law, did he not? But not

one of you obeys the Law. Why are you trying to kill me?" ²⁰ The crowd answered, "You have a demon in you! Who is trying to kill you?" ²¹ Jesus answered: "I did one great work and you were all surprised. ²² Because Moses ordered you to circumcise your sons (although it was not Moses but your ancestors who started it), you will circumcise a boy on the Sabbath. ²³ If a boy is circumcised on the Sabbath so that Moses' Law will not be broken, why are you angry with me because I made a man completely well on the Sabbath? ²⁴ Stop judging by external standards, but judge by true standards."

Is He the Messiah?

²⁵ Some of the people of Jerusalem said: "Isn't this the man they are trying to kill? ²⁶ Look! He is talking in public, and nobody says anything against him! Can it be that the leaders really know that he is the Messiah? ²⁷ But when the Messiah comes, no one will know where he is from. And we all know where this man comes from."

²⁸ As Jesus taught in the Temple he said in a loud voice: "Do you really know me, and know where I am from? But I have not come on my own. He who sent me, however, is true. You do not know him, ²⁹ but I know him, for I come from him and he sent me." ³⁰ Then they tried to arrest him, but no one laid a hand on him, because his hour had not yet come. ³¹ But many in the crowd believed in him, and said, "When the

ποιεῖ τὸν νόμον. τί με ζητεῖτε ἀποκτεῖναι; 20 ἀπεκρίθη ὁ ὄχλος, Δαιμόνιον ἔχεις· τίς σε ζητεῖ ἀποκτεῖναι; 21 ἀπεκρίθη Ἰησοῦς καὶ εἶπεν αὐτοῖς, Ἓν ἔργον ἐποίησα καὶ πάντες θαυμάζετε.ᵃ 22 διὰ τοῦτοᵃ Μωϋσῆς δέδωκεν ὑμῖν τὴν περιτομήν —ᵇ οὐχ ὅτι ἐκ τοῦ Μωϋσέως ἐστὶν ἀλλ' ἐκ τῶν πατέρων —ᵇ καὶ ἐν σαββάτῳ περιτέμνετε ἄνθρωπον. 23 εἰ περιτομὴν λαμβάνει ἄνθρωπος ἐν σαββάτῳ ἵνα μὴ λυθῇ ὁ νόμος Μωϋσέως, ἐμοὶ χολᾶτε ὅτι ὅλον ἄνθρωπον ὑγιῆ ἐποίησα ἐν σαββάτῳ; 24 μὴ κρίνετε κατ' ὄψιν, ἀλλὰ τὴν δικαίαν κρίσιν κρίνετε.

Is This the Christ?

25 Ἔλεγον οὖν τινες ἐκ τῶν Ἱεροσολυμιτῶν, Οὐχ οὗτός ἐστιν ὃν ζητοῦσιν ἀποκτεῖναι; 26 καὶ ἴδε παρρησίᾳ λαλεῖ καὶ οὐδὲν αὐτῷ λέγουσιν. μήποτε ἀληθῶς ἔγνωσαν οἱ ἄρχοντες ὅτι οὗτός ἐστιν ὁ Χριστός; 27 ἀλλὰ τοῦτον οἴδαμεν πόθεν ἐστίν· ὁ δὲ Χριστὸς ὅταν ἔρχηται οὐδεὶς γινώσκει πόθεν ἐστίν. 28 ἔκραξεν οὖν ἐν τῷ ἱερῷ διδάσκων ὁ Ἰησοῦς καὶ λέγων, Κἀμὲ οἴδατεᶜ καὶ οἴδατε πόθεν εἰμί·ᶜ καὶ ἀπ' ἐμαυτοῦ οὐκ ἐλήλυθα, ἀλλ' ἔστιν ἀληθινὸς ὁ πέμψας με, ὃν ὑμεῖς οὐκ οἴδατε· 29 ἐγὼ οἶδα αὐτόν, ὅτι παρ' αὐτοῦ εἰμι κἀκεῖνός με ἀπέστειλεν. 30 Ἐζήτουν οὖν αὐτὸν πιάσαι, καὶ οὐδεὶς ἐπέβαλεν ἐπ' αὐτὸν τὴν χεῖρα, ὅτι οὔπω ἐληλύθει ἡ ὥρα αὐτοῦ. 31 Ἐκ τοῦ ὄχλου δὲ πολλοὶ ἐπίστευσαν εἰς αὐτόν, καὶ ἔλεγον,

---

ᵃ ᵃ **21-22** *a* major, *a* none: TR WH Bov Nes BF² AV RV (NEB) TT Luth? ∥ *a* none, *a* major: RVᵐᵍ ASV RSV Zür Jer Seg

ᵇ ᵇ **22** *b* dash, *b* dash: WH Bov Nes BF² TT Zür Luth Jer Seg ∥ *b* parens, *b* parens: TR AVᵉᵈ RV ASV RSV NEB ∥ *b* minor, *b* minor: AVᵉᵈ

ᶜ ᶜ **28** *c* none, *c* major: WH Bov Nes BF² TT Luth Jer ∥ *c* minor, *c* major: TR AV RV ASV NEB ∥ *c* minor, *c* question: RSV (Zür) ∥ *c* none, *c* exclamation: Seg ∥ *c* question, *c* question: NEBᵐᵍ

---

19 τί...ἀποκτεῖναι Jn 5.18; 7.1, 25; 8.37, 40 **20** Δαιμόνιον ἔχεις Jn 8.48, 52; 10.20 **21** Jn 5.16 **22** διὰ...περιτομήν Gn 17.10-13; Lv 12.3 **23** ἐμοὶ...σαββάτῳ Jn 5.8-9, 16 **24** μὴ...ὄψιν Is 11.3; Jn 8.15 τὴν...κρίνετε Lv 19.15; Is 11.4 **25** Οὐχ...ἀποκτεῖναι Jn 5.18; 7.1, 19; 8.37, 40 **27** Jn 9.29 **28-29** ὁ πέμψας...αὐτόν Jn 8.55; 17.25 **30** Jn 8.20 Ἐζήτουν...χεῖρα Jn 7.44 οὔπω...ἐληλύθει Jn 2.4; 7.6 **31** πολλοὶ...αὐτόν Jn 2.23; 8.30; 10.42; 11.45; 12.11, 42

'Ο Χριστὸς ὅταν ἔλθῃ μὴ πλείονα σημεῖα ποιήσει ὧν οὗτος ἐποίησεν[7];

Officers Sent to Arrest Jesus

32 Ἤκουσαν οἱ Φαρισαῖοι τοῦ ὄχλου γογγύζοντος περὶ αὐτοῦ ταῦτα, καὶ ἀπέστειλαν οἱ ἀρχιερεῖς καὶ οἱ Φαρισαῖοι ὑπηρέτας ἵνα πιάσωσιν αὐτόν. 33 εἶπεν οὖν ὁ Ἰησοῦς, "Ἔτι χρόνον μικρὸν μεθ' ὑμῶν εἰμι καὶ ὑπάγω πρὸς τὸν πέμψαντά με. 34 ζητήσετέ με καὶ οὐχ εὑρή-σετέ [με], καὶ ὅπου εἰμὶ ἐγὼ ὑμεῖς οὐ δύνασθε ἐλθεῖν. 35 εἶπον οὖν οἱ Ἰουδαῖοι πρὸς ἑαυτούς, Ποῦ οὗτος μέλλει πορεύεσθαι ὅτι ἡμεῖς οὐχ εὑρήσομεν αὐτόν; μὴ εἰς τὴν διασπορὰν τῶν Ἑλλήνων μέλλει πορεύεσθαι καὶ διδάσκειν τοὺς Ἕλληνας; 36 τίς ἐστιν ὁ λόγος οὗτος ὃν εἶπεν, Ζητήσετέ με καὶ οὐχ εὑρήσετέ [με], καὶ ὅπου εἰμὶ ἐγὼ ὑμεῖς οὐ δύνασθε ἐλθεῖν[8];

Rivers of Living Water

37 Ἐν δὲ τῇ ἐσχάτῃ ἡμέρᾳ τῇ μεγάλῃ τῆς ἑορτῆς εἱστήκει ὁ Ἰησοῦς καὶ ἔκραξεν λέγων, Ἐάν τις διψᾷ ἐρχέσθω πρός με[9] καὶ πινέτω.[d] 38 ὁ πιστεύων εἰς ἐμέ,[d]

---

[7] 31 {B} ἐποίησεν 𝔭66,75 ℵc B K L T W X Δ Π Ψ 0105 f1 28 33 565 700 892 1010 1071 1079 1195 1216 1230 1241 1242 1253 1344 1365 1546 1646 2148 2174 Byz itaur,b,f,l*,q syrh copsa,bo goth eth geo2 Chrysostom Cyril ‖ ποιεῖ ℵ* D Θ f13 1009 ita,c,d,e,ff2,1c,r1 vg syrc,(s),p arm geo1 Diatessarona,i,n

[8] 36 add 7.53—8.11 225 (see page 355)

[9] 37 {B} πρός με 𝔭66c (𝔭75 B ἐμέ) ℵc K L T W X Δ Θ Π Ψ 0105 f1 f13 28 33 565 700 892 1009 1010 1071 1079 1195 1216 1230 1241 1242 1253 1344 1365 1546 1646 2148 2174 Byz Lect ita,aur,e,f,ff2,l,π,q vg syre,s,p,h,pal copsa,bo,ach7 goth arm geo Origen Eusebius Victorinus-Rome Didymus Chrysostom Augustine Cyril ‖ omit 𝔭66* ℵ* D itb,d,e Cyprian Victorinus-Rome Augustine

---

d d 37-38 d major, d minor: TR WH Bov Nes BF2 AV RV ASV RSV NEBmg TT Zür Luth Seg ‖ d none, d major: RSVmg (NEB) ‖ d minor, d exclamation: Jer

---

33 Ἔτι χρόνον...εἰμι Jn 13.33; 16.5   34 Jn 8.21; 13.33 ὅπου...ἐλθεῖν Jn 13.36; 17.24
37 Ἐν...ἑορτῆς Lv 23.36 Ἐάν...πινέτω Jn 4.10, 14

Messiah comes, will he do more mighty works than this man has done?"

Guards Are Sent to Arrest Jesus

32 The Pharisees heard the crowd whispering these things about him, so they and the chief priests sent some guards to arrest Jesus. 33 Jesus said: "I shall be with you a little while longer, and then I shall go away to him who sent me. 34 You will look for me, but you will not find me; for where I shall be you cannot go." 35 The Jews said among themselves: "Where is he about to go so that we shall not find him? Will he go to the Greek cities where the Jews live, and teach the Greeks? 36 He says, 'You will look for me but you will not find me,' and, 'You cannot go where I shall be.' What does he mean?"

Streams of Living Water

37 The last day of the feast was the most important. On that day Jesus stood up and said in a loud voice: "Whoever is thirsty should come to me and drink. 38 As the scripture says, 'Whoever believes

ín me, streams of living water will pour out from his heart.' " 39 (Jesus said this about the Spirit which those who believed in him were about to receive. At that time the Spirit had not yet been given, because Jesus had not been raised to glory.)

Division among the People

40 Many of the people in the crowd heard him say this and said, "This man is really the Prophet!" 41 Others said, "He is the Messiah!" But others said, "The Messiah will not come from Galilee! 42 The scripture says that the Messiah will be a descendant of David, and will be born in Bethlehem, the town where David lived." 43 So there was a division in the crowd because of him. 44 Some wanted to arrest him, but no one laid a hand on him.

The Unbelief of the Jewish Leaders

45 The guards went back to the chief priests and Pharisees, who asked them, "Why did you not bring him along?"

καθὼς εἶπεν ἡ γραφή, ποταμοὶ ἐκ τῆς κοιλίας αὐτοῦ ῥεύσουσιν ὕδατος ζῶντος. 39 τοῦτο δὲ εἶπεν περὶ τοῦ πνεύματος ὃ ἔμελλον λαμβάνειν οἱ πιστεύσαντες[10] εἰς αὐτόν· οὔπω γὰρ ἦν πνεῦμα[11], ὅτι Ἰησοῦς οὐδέπω ἐδοξάσθη.

Division among the People

40 Ἐκ τοῦ ὄχλου οὖν ἀκούσαντες τῶν λόγων τούτων ἔλεγον, Οὗτός ἐστιν ἀληθῶς ὁ προφήτης· 41 ἄλλοι ἔλεγον, Οὗτός ἐστιν ὁ Χριστός· οἱ δὲ ἔλεγον, Μὴ γὰρ ἐκ τῆς Γαλιλαίας ὁ Χριστὸς ἔρχεται; 42 οὐχ ἡ γραφὴ εἶπεν ὅτι ἐκ **τοῦ σπέρματος** Δαυίδ, καὶ ἀπὸ **Βηθλέεμ** τῆς κώμης ὅπου ἦν Δαυίδ, ὁ Χριστὸς **ἔρχεται**; 43 σχίσμα οὖν ἐγένετο ἐν τῷ ὄχλῳ δι' αὐτόν. 44 τινὲς δὲ ἤθελον ἐξ αὐτῶν πιάσαι αὐτόν, ἀλλ' οὐδεὶς ἐπέβαλεν ἐπ' αὐτὸν τὰς χεῖρας.

The Unbelief of Those in Authority

45 Ἦλθον οὖν οἱ ὑπηρέται πρὸς τοὺς ἀρχιερεῖς καὶ Φαρισαίους, καὶ εἶπον αὐτοῖς ἐκεῖνοι, Διὰ τί οὐκ ἠγάγετε

---

[10] **39** {C} πιστεύσαντες 𝔭[66,75vid] B L T W *l*[18] (it[e]) syr[s] cop[sams,boms] geo[1] Chrysostom ‖ πιστεύσοντες cop[sams] ‖ πιστεύοντες ℵ D K X Δ Θ Π Ψ 0105 *f*[1] *f*[13] 28 33 565 700 892 1009 1010 1071 1079 1195 1216 1230 1241 1242 1253 1344 1365 1546 1646 2148 2174 *Byz Lect* it[a,aur,c,d,f,ff2,(l,q)] vg syr[c,p,h,pal] cop[samss,bo] goth Cyril-Jerusalem Didymus Chrysostom Theodore Cyril Theodoret Gelasius-Cyzicus ‖ οἳ ἐπίστευον arm

[11] **39** {A} πνεῦμα 𝔭[66c,75] ℵ K T Θ Π Ψ 1079 1546 cop[bo] arm geo[1] Rebaptism Origen[gr,lat1/3] Dionysius Cyril Hesychius ‖ πνεῦμα ἅγιον 𝔭[66*] L W X Δ 0105 *f*[1] *f*[13] 28 33 565 700 892 1009 1010 1071 1195 1216 1241 1242 1253 1344 1365 1646 2148 2174 *Byz Lect* Origen[lat1/3] Athanasius Didymus Chrysostom Cyril Theodoret ‖ πνεῦμα δεδομένον it[a,aur,b,c,ff2,l,r1] vg syr[c,s,p] cop[sa?,boms?ach2?] Eusebius Ambrosiaster Victorinus-Rome Ambrose Augustine ‖ πνεῦμα ἅγιον δεδομένον B 1230 it[e,q] (syr[h] δεδομένον with *) syr[pal] geo[2] Origen[lat1/3] ‖ τὸ πνεῦμα ἅγιον ἐπ' αὐτοῖς D* (D[b] τὸ ἅγιον ἐπ' αὐτούς) it[d,f] goth

---

38 ποταμοί...ζῶντος Pr 18.4; Is 58.11   **39** Jn 16.7; 20.22; Ac 2.4   **40** Οὗτος... προφήτης Dt 18.15; Jn 6.14; Ac 3.22; 7.37   **41** Οὗτος...Χριστός Jn 4.29; 7.26; Ac 9.22   Μὴ ...ἔρχεται Jn 7.52   **42** ἐκ...Δαυίδ 2 Sm 7.12; Ps 89.3–4   ἀπὸ Βηθλέεμ Mic 5.2; Mt 2.5–6 **43** Jn 9.16; 10.19   **44** Jn 7.30

αὐτόν; **46** ἀπεκρίθησαν οἱ ὑπηρέται, Οὐδέποτε ἐλάλησεν
οὕτως ἄνθρωπος[12]. **47** ἀπεκρίθησαν οὖν αὐτοῖς οἱ Φαρισαῖοι, Μὴ καὶ ὑμεῖς πεπλάνησθε; **48** μή τις ἐκ τῶν
ἀρχόντων ἐπίστευσεν εἰς αὐτὸν ἢ ἐκ τῶν Φαρισαίων;
49 ἀλλὰ ὁ ὄχλος οὗτος ὁ μὴ γινώσκων τὸν νόμον ἐπάρατοί
εἰσιν. **50** λέγει Νικόδημος πρὸς αὐτούς, ὁ ἐλθὼν πρὸς
αὐτὸν τὸ πρότερον, εἷς ὢν ἐξ αὐτῶν, **51** Μὴ ὁ νόμος
ἡμῶν κρίνει τὸν ἄνθρωπον ἐὰν μὴ ἀκούσῃ πρῶτον παρ'
αὐτοῦ καὶ γνῷ τί ποιεῖ; **52** ἀπεκρίθησαν καὶ εἶπαν
αὐτῷ, Μὴ καὶ σὺ ἐκ τῆς Γαλιλαίας εἶ; ἐραύνησον καὶ
ἴδε ὅτι προφήτης ἐκ τῆς Γαλιλαίας οὐκ ἐγείρεται.[13]

Jesus the Light of the World

8 **12** Πάλιν οὖν αὐτοῖς ἐλάλησεν ὁ Ἰησοῦς λέγων, Ἐγώ
εἰμι τὸ φῶς τοῦ κόσμου· ὁ ἀκολουθῶν ἐμοὶ οὐ μὴ περι-

---

[12] **46** {B} ἐλάλησεν οὕτως ἄνθρωπος 𝔓[66c,75] ℵ[c] B L T W cop[bo] Origen
Chrysostom[comm] Cyril ‖ ἐλάλησεν οὕτως ἄνθρωπος ὡς οὗτος ὁ ἄνθρωπος
X Ψ 33 1071 1241 1242 1365 ‖ οὕτως ἐλάλησεν ἄνθρωπος ὡς οὗτος ὁ
ἄνθρωπος K Δ Θ Π 0105[vid] f[1] f[13] (28 700 omit οὕτως) 565 892 1009 (1010 omit
first ἄνθρωπος) 1079 1195 1216 1230 1253 1344 1546 1646 2148 2174 Byz Lect
it[e,f,(ff2),(l),q,r1] vg syr[h] cop[sa,boms,ach2] goth arm eth geo Diatessaron[a,i,l]
Chrysostom[txt] Theodoret ‖ οὕτως ἄνθρωπος ἐλάλησεν ὡς οὗτος λαλεῖ ὁ
ἄνθρωπος 𝔓[66*] ℵ* syr[(c,s),p,pal] ‖ οὕτως ἄνθρωπος ἐλάλησεν ὡς οὗτος λαλεῖ
D it[aur,c,d]

[13] **7.53—8.11** {A} omit 7.53—8.11 (see page 413) 𝔓[66,75] ℵ A[vid] B C[vid]
L N T W X Y Δ Θ Ψ 053 0141 22 33 157 209 565 1230 1241 1242 1253 2193
Lect it[a,f,l*,q] syr[c,s,p] cop[sa,boms,ach2] goth arm geo Diatessaron[a,f] Clement[vid]
Tertullian Origen Cyprian Chrysostom Nonnus Cyril Cosmos Theophy-
lact[comm] ‖ include passage following 7.52 D (F) G H K M U Γ 28 700 892
1009 1010 1071 1079 1195 1216 1344 1365 1546 1646 2148 2174 Byz it[aur,c,d,e,]
[ff2,j,1mg,r1] vg syr[hms,pal] cop[boms] arm[mss] eth Didascalia Ambrosiaster Apostolic
Constitutions Ambrose Greek and Latin mss[acc. to Jerome] Jerome Augustine ‖ include passage with asterisks or obeli (E include 8.2–11 with
asterisks) S (Λ Π include 8.3–11 with asterisks) 1077 1443 1445 (l[185m] include
8.1–11, l[69m,70m,211m,883m,1579m] include 8.3–11 with asterisks) ‖ include passage
after 21.24 f[1] arm[mss] ‖ include passage following Lk 21.38 f[13] ‖ include
passage following Jn 7.36 225

---

48 Jn 12.42   **50** Jn 3.1–2; 19.39   **51** Dt 1.16   **52** προφήτης...ἐγείρεται Jn 1.46; 7.41
8 12 Ἐγώ...κόσμου Is 49.6; Jn 1.4, 5, 9; 9.5; 12.46

---

46 The guards answered, "Nobody has
ever talked the way this man does!"
47 "Did he fool you, too?" the Pharisees
asked them. **48** "Have you ever known
one of our leaders or one Pharisee to
believe in him? **49** This crowd does not
know the Law of Moses, so they are
under God's curse!" **50** Nicodemus was
one of them; he was the one who had
gone to see Jesus before. He said to
them, **51** "According to our Law we cannot condemn a man before hearing him
and finding out what he has done."
52 "Well," they answered, "are you also
from Galilee? Study the Scriptures and
you will learn that no prophet ever comes[2]
from Galilee."

Jesus the Light of the World

8[1] **12** Jesus spoke to them again: "I am
the light of the world. Whoever follows
me will have the light of life and will

---

[2] **52** no prophet ever comes: *one ms. reads the
Prophet will not come*

[1] **1–11** *Some mss. omit this section; others place
it after John 21.24; others place it after Luke
21.38; one ms. places it after John 7.36*

never walk in the darkness." [13] The Pharisees said to him, "Now you are testifying on your own behalf; what you say proves nothing." [14] "No," Jesus answered, "even if I do testify on my own behalf, what I say is true, because I know where I came from and where I am going. You do not know where I came from or where I am going. [15] You make judgments in a purely human way; I pass judgment on no one. [16] But if I were to pass judgment, my judging would be true, because I am not alone in this; the Father who sent me is with me. [17] It is written in your Law that when two witnesses agree, what they say is true. [18] I testify on my own behalf, and the Father who sent me also testifies on my behalf." [19] "Where is your father?" they asked him. "You know neither me nor my Father," Jesus answered. "If you knew me you would know my Father also."

[20] Jesus said all this as he taught in the Temple, in the room where the offering boxes were placed. And no one arrested him, because his hour had not come.

You Cannot Go Where I Am Going

[21] Jesus said to them again, "I will go away; you will look for me, but you will die in your sins. You cannot go where I am going." [22] So the Jews said, "He

πατήσῃ ἐν τῇ σκοτίᾳ, ἀλλ' ἕξει τὸ φῶς τῆς ζωῆς. 13 εἶπον οὖν αὐτῷ οἱ Φαρισαῖοι, Σὺ περὶ σεαυτοῦ μαρτυρεῖς· ἡ μαρτυρία σου οὐκ ἔστιν ἀληθής. 14 ἀπεκρίθη Ἰησοῦς καὶ εἶπεν αὐτοῖς, Κἂν ἐγὼ μαρτυρῶ περὶ ἐμαυτοῦ, ἀληθής ἐστιν ἡ μαρτυρία μου, ὅτι οἶδα πόθεν ἦλθον καὶ ποῦ ὑπάγω· ὑμεῖς δὲ οὐκ οἴδατε πόθεν ἔρχομαι ἢ ποῦ ὑπάγω. 15 ὑμεῖς κατὰ τὴν σάρκα κρίνετε, ἐγὼ οὐ κρίνω οὐδένα. 16 καὶ ἐὰν κρίνω δὲ ἐγώ, ἡ κρίσις ἡ ἐμὴ ἀληθινή[1] ἐστιν, ὅτι μόνος οὐκ εἰμί, ἀλλ' ἐγὼ καὶ ὁ πέμψας με πατήρ[2]. 17 καὶ ἐν τῷ νόμῳ δὲ τῷ ὑμετέρῳ γέγραπται ὅτι δύο ἀνθρώπων ἡ μαρτυρία ἀληθής ἐστιν. 18 ἐγώ εἰμι ὁ μαρτυρῶν περὶ ἐμαυτοῦ καὶ μαρτυρεῖ περὶ ἐμοῦ ὁ πέμψας με πατήρ. 19 ἔλεγον οὖν αὐτῷ, Ποῦ ἐστιν ὁ πατήρ σου; ἀπεκρίθη Ἰησοῦς, Οὔτε ἐμὲ οἴδατε οὔτε τὸν πατέρα μου· εἰ ἐμὲ ᾔδειτε, καὶ τὸν πατέρα μου ἂν ᾔδειτε. 20 Ταῦτα τὰ ῥήματα ἐλάλησεν ἐν τῷ γαζοφυλακίῳ διδάσκων ἐν τῷ ἱερῷ· καὶ οὐδεὶς ἐπίασεν αὐτόν, ὅτι οὔπω ἐληλύθει ἡ ὥρα αὐτοῦ.

Where I am Going You Cannot Come

21 Εἶπεν οὖν πάλιν αὐτοῖς, Ἐγὼ ὑπάγω καὶ ζητήσετέ με, καὶ ἐν τῇ ἁμαρτίᾳ ὑμῶν ἀποθανεῖσθε· ὅπου ἐγὼ ὑπάγω ὑμεῖς οὐ δύνασθε ἐλθεῖν. 22 ἔλεγον οὖν οἱ

[1] 16 {B} ἀληθινή p75 B D L T W X 28 33 892 1241 goth Origen ‖ ἀληθής p66 ℵ K Δ Θ Ψ 0250 f1 f13 565 700 1009 1010 1071 1079 1195 1216 1230 1253 1344 1365 1546 1646 2148 2174 Byz Lect Origen Chrysostom ‖ ἀληθινή or ἀληθής ita,aur,b,c,d,e,f,ff2,j,l,q,r1 vg syrs,p,h,pal copsa,bo,ach2 arm geo ‖ δικαία 1242 syrhmg Diatessaronn Cyril

[2] 16 {C} πατήρ p39,66,75 ℵc B K L T W X Δ Θ Ψ 0110 0250 f1 f13 28 33 565 700 892 1009 1010 1071 1079 1195 1216 1230 1241 1242 1253 1344 1365 1546 1646 2148 2174 Byz Lect ita,aur,b,c,e,f,ff2,j,l,q,r1 vg syrp,h,pal copsa,bo,ach2 goth arm geo Origen Chrysostom ‖ omit ℵ* D itd syrc,s

13 Σὺ...ἀληθής Jn 5.31   14 οἶδα...ὑπάγω Jn 13.3; 16.28   ὑμεῖς...ἔρχομαι Jn 7.28; 9.29   15 ὑμεῖς...κρίνετε 1 Sm 16.7; Jn 7.24   ἐγώ...οὐδένα Jn 12.47   16 ἡ κρίσις...ἐστιν Jn 5.30   μόνος...πατήρ Jn 5.37; 8.29   17 Dt 17.6; 19.15   18 μαρτυρεῖ...πατήρ 1 Jn 5.9   19 Οὔτε...οὔτε τὸν πατέρα μου Jn 16.3   εἰ...ᾔδειτε Jn 14.7   20 οὐδεὶς...αὐτοῦ Jn 7.30   21 Jn 7.34, 36; 13.33   22 Jn 7.35

Ἰουδαῖοι, Μήτι ἀποκτενεῖ ἑαυτόν, ὅτι λέγει, Ὅπου
ἐγὼ ὑπάγω ὑμεῖς οὐ δύνασθε ἐλθεῖν; 23 καὶ ἔλεγεν
αὐτοῖς, Ὑμεῖς ἐκ τῶν κάτω ἐστέ, ἐγὼ ἐκ τῶν ἄνω
εἰμί· ὑμεῖς ἐκ τούτου τοῦ κόσμου ἐστέ, ἐγὼ οὐκ εἰμὶ
ἐκ τοῦ κόσμου τούτου. 24 εἶπον οὖν ὑμῖν ὅτι ἀποθανεῖσθε
ἐν ταῖς ἁμαρτίαις ὑμῶν· ἐὰν γὰρ μὴ πιστεύσητε ὅτι
ἐγώ εἰμι, ἀποθανεῖσθε ἐν ταῖς ἁμαρτίαις ὑμῶν. 25 ἔλεγον
οὖν αὐτῷ, Σὺ τίς εἶ; εἶπεν αὐτοῖς ὁ Ἰησοῦς, Τὴν ἀρχὴν
ὅ τι³ καὶ λαλῶ ὑμῖν;ᵃ 26 πολλὰ ἔχω περὶ ὑμῶν λαλεῖν
καὶ κρίνειν· ἀλλ' ὁ πέμψας με ἀληθής ἐστιν, κἀγὼ ἃ
ἤκουσα παρ' αὐτοῦ ταῦτα λαλῶ εἰς τὸν κόσμον. 27 οὐκ
ἔγνωσαν ὅτι τὸν πατέρα αὐτοῖς ἔλεγεν. 28 εἶπεν οὖν
[αὐτοῖς] ὁ Ἰησοῦς, Ὅταν ὑψώσητε τὸν υἱὸν τοῦ ἀνθρώπου, τότε γνώσεσθε ὅτι ἐγώ εἰμι,ᵇ καὶ ἀπ' ἐμαυτοῦ
ποιῶ οὐδέν, ἀλλὰ καθὼς ἐδίδαξέν με ὁ πατὴρ ταῦτα
λαλῶ. 29 καὶ ὁ πέμψας με μετ' ἐμοῦ ἐστιν· οὐκ ἀφῆκέν
με μόνον, ὅτι ἐγὼ τὰ ἀρεστὰ αὐτῷ ποιῶ πάντοτε.
30 Ταῦτα αὐτοῦ λαλοῦντος πολλοὶ ἐπίστευσαν εἰς αὐτόν.

The Truth Will Make You Free

31 Ἔλεγεν οὖν ὁ Ἰησοῦς πρὸς τοὺς πεπιστευκότας
αὐτῷ Ἰουδαίους, Ἐὰν ὑμεῖς μείνητε ἐν τῷ λόγῳ τῷ

---

³ 25 {B} ὅ τι f¹ 1195ᵛⁱᵈ 1344ᵛⁱᵈ Byz ∥ ὅτι Κ Δ f¹³ 700 892 1009 1010
1071 1079 1216 1230 1241 1242 1253 1365 1546 1646 2148 2174 (itᵈ quoniam,
itᵇ vgʷʷ quia, itᵃ·ᵃᵘʳ·ᵉ·ᶠ·ff².ˡ·q·ʳˡ quod) syrˢ·ᵖ·ʰ·ᵖᵃˡ copˢᵃ·ᵇᵒ·ᵃᶜʰ² arm geo
Augustine ∥ ὅτι or ὅ τι 𝔭⁶⁶·⁷⁵ ℵ Β D L T W Χ Θ Ψ 0250 28 33 565 Lect ∥
ὅς? itᵉ vgᶜˡ Priscillian Ambrose Augustine ∥ omit eth

ᵃ 25 a question: WH Nes BF² RVᵐᵍ RSVᵐᵍ NEB TT Zür Jerᵐᵍ Seg ∥ a statement: TR WHᵐᵍ
Bov AV RV ASV RSV NEBᵐᵍ TTᵐᵍ Luth Jer Segᵐᵍ

ᵇ 28 b minor: WH Bov Nes BF² AV RV ASV RSV TT ∥ b major: TR RVᵐᵍ ASVᵐᵍ NEB ∥ b none:
Zür Luth Jer Seg

---

23 Jn 3.31; 17.14   24 ἐὰν...ἐγώ εἰμι Jn 13.19   26 ὁ...ἀληθής ἐστιν Jn 7.28   κἀγὼ
...κόσμον Jn 12.49   28 Ὅταν...ἀνθρώπου Jn 3.14; 12.32   ἀπ'...λαλῶ Jn 5.19   29 ὁ...
μόνον Jn 8.16; 16.32   30 πολλοὶ...αὐτόν Jn 2.23; 7.31; 10.42; 11.45; 12.11, 42   31 Ἐὰν...
ἐμῷ Jn 15.7

---

says, 'You cannot go where I am going.'
Does this mean that he will kill himself?"
23 Jesus answered: "You come from here
below, but I come from above. You
come from this world, but I do not come
from this world. 24 That is why I told
you that you will die in your sins. And
you will die in your sins if you do not
believe that 'I Am Who I Am'." 25 "Who
are you?" they asked him. Jesus answered: "What I have told you from the
very beginning.² 26 There are many things
I have to say and judge about you.
The one who sent me, however, is true,
and I tell the world only what I have
heard from him."
27 They did not understand that he
was talking to them about the Father.
28 So Jesus said to them: "When you
lift up the Son of Man you will know that
'I Am Who I Am'; then you will know
that I do nothing on my own, but say
only what the Father has taught me.
29 And he who sent me is with me; he
has not left me alone, because I always
do what pleases him." 30 Many who
heard Jesus say these things believed
in him.

Free Men and Slaves

31 So Jesus said to the Jews who believed in him, "If you obey my teaching

---

² 25 What I have told you from the very
beginning: or Why should I speak to you at all?

you are really my disciples; [32] you will know the truth, and the truth will make you free." [33] "We are the descendants of Abraham," they answered, "and we have never been anybody's slaves. What do you mean, then, by saying, 'You will be made free'?" [34] Jesus said to them: "I tell you the truth: everyone who sins is a slave of sin. [35] A slave does not belong to the family always; but a son belongs there for ever. [36] If the Son makes you free, then you will be really free. [37] I know you are Abraham's descendants. Yet you are trying to kill me, because you will not accept my teaching. [38] I talk about what my Father has shown me, but you do what your father has told you."

ἐμῷ, ἀληθῶς μαθηταί μού ἐστε, **32** καὶ γνώσεσθε τὴν ἀλήθειαν, καὶ ἡ ἀλήθεια ἐλευθερώσει ὑμᾶς. **33** ἀπεκρίθησαν πρὸς αὐτόν, Σπέρμα ᾿Αβραάμ ἐσμεν καὶ οὐδενὶ δεδουλεύκαμεν πώποτε· πῶς σὺ λέγεις ὅτι ᾿Ελεύθεροι γενήσεσθε; **34** ἀπεκρίθη αὐτοῖς ὁ ᾿Ιησοῦς, ᾿Αμὴν ἀμὴν λέγω ὑμῖν ὅτι πᾶς ὁ ποιῶν τὴν ἁμαρτίαν δοῦλός ἐστιν [τῆς ἁμαρτίας][4]. **35** ὁ δὲ δοῦλος οὐ μένει ἐν τῇ οἰκίᾳ εἰς τὸν αἰῶνα· ὁ υἱὸς μένει εἰς τὸν αἰῶνα. **36** ἐὰν οὖν ὁ υἱὸς ὑμᾶς ἐλευθερώσῃ, ὄντως ἐλεύθεροι ἔσεσθε. **37** οἶδα ὅτι σπέρμα ᾿Αβραάμ ἐστε· ἀλλὰ ζητεῖτέ με ἀποκτεῖναι, ὅτι ὁ λόγος ὁ ἐμὸς οὐ χωρεῖ ἐν ὑμῖν. **38** ἃ ἐγὼ ἑώρακα παρὰ τῷ πατρί[5] λαλῶ· καὶ ὑμεῖς οὖν ἃ ἠκούσατε[6] παρὰ τοῦ πατρὸς[7] ποιεῖτε.

---

[4] **34** {C} τῆς ἁμαρτίας 𝔭[66,75] ℵ B C K L W X Δ Θ Ψ 070 0250 f[1] f[13] 28 33 565 700 892 1009 1010 1071 1079 1195 1216 1230 1241 1242 1253 1344 1365 1546 1646 2148 2174 *Byz Lect* it[a,aur,c,e,f,ff2,l,q,rl] vg syr[p,h,pal] cop[sa,bo,ach2] goth arm geo Irenaeus[lat] Origen[gr,lat] Adamantius Hilary Chrysostom Cyril ∥ *omit* D it[b,d] syr[s] cop[bomss] Clement Cyprian Faustinus Gregory-Elvira

[5] **38** {B} παρὰ τῷ πατρί 𝔭[66,75] B C L X Ψ 070 1230[vid] it[l] vg[ww] syr[pal] eth[ro] Irenaeus Origen Cyril ∥ ἀπὸ τοῦ πατρός, ταῦτα W (geo[2] πατρός μου) ∥ παρὰ τῷ πατρί μου ℵ K Δ Θ 0250 f[1] f[13] 28 565 700 1009 1010 1071 1079 1195 1216 1242 1253 1344 1365 1546 1646 2148 2174 *Byz Lect* it[a,aur,e,f,ff2] vg[cl] syr[s,p,h] goth arm eth[pp] geo[1] Diatessaron Tertullian ∥ ἀπὸ τοῦ πατρός μου cop[sa?bomss?ach2?] ∥ παρὰ τῷ πατρί μου, ταῦτα D 33 892 it[b,c,d,q] cop[bo] Cyril-Jerusalem Chrysostom

[6] **38** {C} ἠκούσατε 𝔭[75] ℵ[c] B C K L W X Θ f[1] f[13] 33 565 892 1079 1242 1546 2174 it[f] syr[hmg,pal] cop[bo] goth arm eth[ro] geo Origen Chrysostom Cyril ∥ ἑωράκατε 𝔭[66] ℵ* D Δ Ψ 070 0250 28 700 1009 1010 1071 1195 1216 1253 1344 1365 1646 2148 *Byz Lect* it[a,aur,b,c,d,e,ff2,l,q,rl] vg syr[s,p,h] cop[sa,bomss,ach2] eth[pp] Diatessaron[a,i,n] Tertullian Apollinaris

[7] **38** {C} τοῦ πατρός 𝔭[66] (𝔭[75] λαλεῖτε *for* ποιεῖτε) B L W 070 Origen ∥ τῷ πατρί Ψ 1230[vid] ∥ τοῦ πατρὸς ὑμῶν ℵ C K X Θ f[1] f[13] 33 565 892 1079 1242 1365 1546 it[f] syr[pal] cop[sa?bo?ach2?] goth geo ∥ τῷ πατρὶ ὑμῶν Δ 0250 28 700 1009 1010 1071 1195 1216 1253 (1344* πατρί μου) 1344[c] 1646 2148 2174 *Byz Lect* it[a,aur,b,c,e,ff2,l,q] vg syr[s,p,h] cop[sa?bo?ach2?] arm ∥ τῷ πατρὶ ὑμῶν, ταῦτα D it[d] cop[boms] Tertullian

---

33 Σπέρμα...ἐσμεν Mt 3.9; Lk 3.8; Jn 8.39, 56   οὐδενὶ...πώποτε Ne 9.36   **34** πᾶς...ἁμαρτίας Ro 6.16, 20; 2 Pe 2.19   **35** ὁ δὲ...οἰκίᾳ εἰς τὸν αἰῶνα Ex 21.2; Dt 15.12 **37** ζητεῖτέ με ἀποκτεῖναι Jn 5.18; 7.19, 25

Your Father the Devil

39 Ἀπεκρίθησαν καὶ εἶπαν αὐτῷ, Ὁ πατὴρ ἡμῶν Ἀβραάμ ἐστιν. λέγει αὐτοῖς ὁ Ἰησοῦς, Εἰ τέκνα τοῦ Ἀβραάμ ἐστε, τὰ ἔργα τοῦ Ἀβραὰμ ἐποιεῖτε[8]· **40** νῦν δὲ ζητεῖτέ με ἀποκτεῖναι, ἄνθρωπον ὃς τὴν ἀλήθειαν ὑμῖν λελάληκα ἣν ἤκουσα παρὰ τοῦ θεοῦ· τοῦτο Ἀβραὰμ οὐκ ἐποίησεν. **41** ὑμεῖς ποιεῖτε τὰ ἔργα τοῦ πατρὸς ὑμῶν. εἶπαν [οὖν] αὐτῷ, Ἡμεῖς ἐκ πορνείας οὐ γεγεννήμεθα· ἕνα πατέρα ἔχομεν τὸν θεόν. **42** εἶπεν αὐτοῖς ὁ Ἰησοῦς, Εἰ ὁ θεὸς πατὴρ ὑμῶν ἦν, ἠγαπᾶτε ἂν ἐμέ, ἐγὼ γὰρ ἐκ τοῦ θεοῦ ἐξῆλθον καὶ ἥκω· οὐδὲ γὰρ ἀπ' ἐμαυτοῦ ἐλήλυθα, ἀλλ' ἐκεῖνός με ἀπέστειλεν. **43** διὰ τί τὴν λαλιὰν τὴν ἐμὴν οὐ γινώσκετε; ὅτι οὐ δύνασθε ἀκούειν τὸν λόγον τὸν ἐμόν. **44** ὑμεῖς ἐκ τοῦ πατρὸς τοῦ διαβόλου ἐστὲ καὶ τὰς ἐπιθυμίας τοῦ πατρὸς ὑμῶν θέλετε ποιεῖν. ἐκεῖνος ἀνθρωποκτόνος ἦν ἀπ' ἀρχῆς, καὶ ἐν τῇ ἀληθείᾳ οὐκ ἔστηκεν[9], ὅτι οὐκ ἔστιν ἀλήθεια ἐν αὐτῷ. ὅταν λαλῇ τὸ ψεῦδος, ἐκ τῶν ἰδίων λαλεῖ, ὅτι ψεύστης ἐστὶν καὶ ὁ πατὴρ αὐτοῦ. **45** ἐγὼ δὲ ὅτι τὴν ἀλήθειαν λέγω, οὐ πιστεύετέ μοι. **46** τίς ἐξ ὑμῶν ἐλέγχει με περὶ ἁμαρτίας; εἰ ἀλήθειαν λέγω, διὰ τί ὑμεῖς οὐ πιστεύετέ μοι; **47** ὁ ὢν ἐκ τοῦ θεοῦ τὰ ῥήματα

---

[8] **39** {C} ἐποιεῖτε p[75] 𝕏* B[2] D W Θ 070 0250 28 1195 1365 2148 *Byz*[pt] *Lect* it[a,aur,c,d,e,f,l,q,r1] arm geo Origen Eusebius Basil Cyril-Jerusalem Epiphanius Cyril ‖ ποιεῖτε p[66] B* 700 it[ff2] vg syr[s] Diatessaron[i,n] Origen Ps-Cyprian Eusebius Chrysostom Augustine ‖ ἐποιεῖτε ἄν 𝕏[c] C K L X Δ Π Ψ f[1] f[13] 33 565 892 1009 1010 1071 1079 1216 1230 1242 1253 1344 1546 1646 2174 *Byz*[pt] *l*[211,1127] it[b] syr[p.h] cop[sa?bo?ach2?fay]vid? goth Origen[gr.lat] Didymus Cyril

[9] **44** {D} οὐκ ἔστηκεν p[66] 𝕏 B* D L W X Δ Θ Ψ 0124 0250 f[13] 33 892 1010 1071 1079 1216 1241 1242 1344 1546 2174 *l*[211] syr[s,p,h,hmg] goth geo Didymus Cyril ‖ οὐχ ἔστηκεν p[75] B[3] C K Π f[1] 28 565 700 1009 1195 1230 1253 1365 1646 2148 *Byz Lect* syr[pal] Clement Origen Chrysostom

---

39 Ὁ πατὴρ...ἐστιν Mt 3.9; Jn 8.33   **41** ἕνα...θεόν Dt 32.6; Is 63.16; 64.8   **42** Εἰ...ἐμέ 1 Jn 5.1   ἐγώ...ἐξῆλθον Jn 13.3; 16.28; 17.8   οὐδὲ...ἀπέστειλεν Jn 7.28; 17.8   **44** ὑμεῖς...ποιεῖν 1 Jn 3.8   ὅταν...αὐτοῦ Gn 3.4   **46** τίς...ἁμαρτίας 2 Cor 5.21; 1 Pe 2.22; 1 Jn 3.5   **47** ὁ...ἀκούει Jn 18.37; 1 Jn 4.6

---

39 They answered him, "Our father is Abraham." "If you really were Abraham's children," Jesus replied, "you would do[3] the same works that he did. **40** But all I have ever done is to tell you the truth I heard from God. Yet you are trying to kill me. Abraham did nothing like this! **41** You are doing what your father did." "We are not bastards," they answered. "We have the one Father, God himself." **42** Jesus said to them: "If God really were your father, you would love me; for I came from God and now I am here. I did not come on my own, but he sent me. **43** Why do you not understand what I say? It is because you cannot bear to listen to my message. **44** You are the children of your father, the Devil, and you want to follow your father's desires. From the very beginning he was a murderer. He has never been on the side of truth, because there is no truth in him. When he tells a lie he is only doing what is natural to him, because he is a liar and the father of all lies. **45** I tell the truth, and that is why you do not believe me. **46** Which one of you can prove that I am guilty of sin? If I tell the truth, then why do you not believe me? **47** He who comes from God listens to God's words. You,

[3] **39** If you really were . . . you would do: *some mss. read* If you are . . . do

however, are not from God, and this is why you will not listen."

Jesus and Abraham

48 The Jews replied to Jesus: "Were we not right in saying that you are a Samaritan and have a demon in you?" 49 "I have no demon," Jesus answered. "I honor my Father, but you dishonor me. 50 I am not seeking honor for myself. There is one who is seeking it and who judges in my favor. 51 I tell you the truth: whoever obeys my message will never die." 52 The Jews said to him: "Now we know for sure that you have a demon! Abraham died, and the prophets died, yet you say, 'Whoever obeys my message will never die.' 53 Our father Abraham died; you do not claim to be greater than Abraham, do you? And the prophets also died. Who do you think you are?" 54 Jesus answered: "If I were to honor myself, my own honor would be worth nothing. The one who honors me is my Father — the very one you say is your God. 55 You have never known him, but I know him. If I were to say that I do not know him, I would be a liar, like you. But I do know him, and I obey his word. 56 Your father Abraham rejoiced that he was to see my day; he saw it and was glad." 57 The Jews said to him, "You are not even

τοῦ θεοῦ ἀκούει· διὰ τοῦτο ὑμεῖς οὐκ ἀκούετε, ὅτι ἐκ τοῦ θεοῦ οὐκ ἐστέ.

Before Abraham was, I am

48 Ἀπεκρίθησαν οἱ Ἰουδαῖοι καὶ εἶπαν αὐτῷ, Οὐ καλῶς λέγομεν ἡμεῖς ὅτι Σαμαρίτης εἶ σὺ καὶ δαιμόνιον ἔχεις; 49 ἀπεκρίθη Ἰησοῦς, Ἐγὼ δαιμόνιον οὐκ ἔχω, ἀλλὰ τιμῶ τὸν πατέρα μου, καὶ ὑμεῖς ἀτιμάζετέ με. 50 ἐγὼ δὲ οὐ ζητῶ τὴν δόξαν μου· ἔστιν ὁ ζητῶν καὶ κρίνων. 51 ἀμὴν ἀμὴν λέγω ὑμῖν, ἐάν τις τὸν ἐμὸν λόγον τηρήσῃ, θάνατον οὐ μὴ θεωρήσῃ εἰς τὸν αἰῶνα. 52 εἶπον [οὖν] αὐτῷ οἱ Ἰουδαῖοι, Νῦν ἐγνώκαμεν ὅτι δαιμόνιον ἔχεις. Ἀβραὰμ ἀπέθανεν καὶ οἱ προφῆται, καὶ σὺ λέγεις, Ἐάν τις τὸν λόγον μου τηρήσῃ, οὐ μὴ γεύσηται θανάτου εἰς τὸν αἰῶνα. 53 μὴ σὺ μείζων εἶ τοῦ πατρὸς ἡμῶν[10] Ἀβραάμ, ὅστις ἀπέθανεν; καὶ οἱ προφῆται ἀπέθανον· τίνα σεαυτὸν ποιεῖς; 54 ἀπεκρίθη Ἰησοῦς, Ἐὰν ἐγὼ δοξάσω ἐμαυτόν, ἡ δόξα μου οὐδέν ἐστιν· ἔστιν ὁ πατήρ μου ὁ δοξάζων με, ὃν ὑμεῖς λέγετε ὅτι θεὸς ἡμῶν[11] ἐστιν· 55 καὶ οὐκ ἐγνώκατε αὐτόν, ἐγὼ δὲ οἶδα αὐτόν. κἂν εἴπω ὅτι οὐκ οἶδα αὐτόν, ἔσομαι ὅμοιος ὑμῖν ψεύστης· ἀλλὰ οἶδα αὐτὸν καὶ τὸν λόγον αὐτοῦ τηρῶ. 56 Ἀβραὰμ ὁ πατὴρ ὑμῶν ἠγαλλιάσατο ἵνα ἴδῃ τὴν ἡμέραν τὴν ἐμήν, καὶ εἶδεν καὶ ἐχάρη. 57 εἶπον οὖν οἱ Ἰουδαῖοι πρὸς αὐτόν, Πεντήκοντα ἔτη

---

10 53 {C} πατρὸς ἡμῶν 𝔭[66,75] ℵ A B C K L X Δ Θ Π Ψ 0124 0216 f[1] f[13] 28 33 565 700 892 1009 1010 1071 1079 1195 1216 1230 1241 1242 1253 1344 1365 1546 1646 2148 2174 Byz Lect it[aur,f,q,r1] vg syr[p,h,pal] cop[sa,bo,ach2] goth arm geo Origen ‖ omit D W it[a,b,c,d,e,ff2,l] syr[s] cop[boms]

11 54 {C} ἡμῶν 𝔭[66,75] A B[2] C K L W Δ Θ Π 0124 f[1] f[13] 28 33 565 892 1195 1230 1241 1253[vid] 1344 1365 1646 2174 Byz l[76,184,1127] it[aur,f] vg[ww] syr[s,p,h] cop[sa,bo] goth arm eth geo Diatessaron ‖ ὑμῶν ℵ B* D X Ψ 700 1009 1010 1071 1079 1216 1242 1546 2148 Lect it[a,b,c,d,e,ff2,l,q] vg[cl] syr[pal] cop[boms] Diatessaron[i,l] Tertullian Chrysostom Cyril ‖ omit cop[ach2]

---

48 Οὐ...σύ Jn 4.9   δαιμόνιον ἔχεις Mk 3.21-22; Jn 7.20   50 ἐγώ...μου Jn 5.41
51 Jn 5.24   52 οὐ...θανάτου Mk 9.1   53 μὴ...Ἀβραάμ Jn 4.12   55 οὐκ ἐγνώκατε... οἶδα αὐτόν Mt 11.27; Lk 10.22; Jn 7.28-29

οὔπω ἔχεις καὶ ᾽Αβραὰμ ἑώρακας¹²; 58 εἶπεν αὐτοῖς ᾽Ιησοῦς, ᾽Αμὴν ἀμὴν λέγω ὑμῖν, πρὶν ᾽Αβραὰμ γενέσθαι ἐγὼ εἰμί. 59 ἦραν οὖν λίθους ἵνα βάλωσιν ἐπ᾽ αὐτόν· ᾽Ιησοῦς δὲ ἐκρύβη ᶜ καὶ ἐξῆλθεν ἐκ τοῦ ἱεροῦ¹³.ᶜ

The Healing of a Man Born Blind

9 Καὶ παράγων εἶδεν ἄνθρωπον τυφλὸν ἐκ γενετῆς. 2 καὶ ἠρώτησαν αὐτὸν οἱ μαθηταὶ αὐτοῦ λέγοντες, ῾Ραββί, τίς ἥμαρτεν, οὗτος ἢ οἱ γονεῖς αὐτοῦ, ἵνα τυφλὸς γεννηθῇ; 3 ἀπεκρίθη ᾽Ιησοῦς, Οὔτε οὗτος ἥμαρτεν οὔτε οἱ γονεῖς αὐτοῦ, ἀλλ᾽ ἵνα φανερωθῇ τὰ ἔργα τοῦ θεοῦ ἐν αὐτῷ. 4 ἡμᾶς δεῖ¹ ἐργάζεσθαι τὰ ἔργα τοῦ πέμψαντός

fifty years old — and have you seen Abraham?" ⁵⁸ "I tell you the truth," Jesus replied. "Before Abraham was born, 'I Am'." ⁵⁹ They picked up stones to throw at him; but Jesus hid himself and left the Temple.

Jesus Heals a Man Born Blind

9 As Jesus walked along he saw a man who had been born blind. ² His disciples asked him: "Teacher, whose sin was it that caused him to be born blind? His own or his parents' sin?" ³ Jesus answered: "His blindness has nothing to do with his sins or his parents' sins. He is blind so that God's power might be seen at work in him. ⁴ We must keep on doing the works of him who sent me,

---

¹²57 {B} ἑώρακας 𝔭⁶⁶ ℵᶜ A Bᶜ (B* W Θ 28 ἑώρακες) C D K L X Δ Π Ψ f¹ f¹³ 28 33 565 700 892 1009 1010 1071 1079 1195 1216 1230 1241 1242 1253 1344 1365 1546 1646 2148 2174 *Byz Lect* itᵃ,ᵃᵘʳ,ᵇ,ᶜ,ᵈ,ᵉ,f,ff²,l,q,rl vg syrᵖ,ʰ,ᵖᵃˡ copᵇᵒ goth arm? geo ‖ ἑώρακέν σε 𝔭⁷⁵ ℵ* 0124 syrˢ copˢᵃ,ᵇᵒᵐˢ,ᵃᶜʰ²

¹³59 {A} ἱεροῦ 𝔭⁶⁶,⁷⁵ ℵ* B D W Θ* itᵃ,ᵃᵘʳ,ᵇ,ᶜ,ᵈ,ᵉ,ff²,l,rl vg syrˢ copˢᵃ,ᵇᵒᵐˢ,ᵃᶜʰ² arm geo¹ Diatessaronf,i,n Origen Chrysostom Cyril ‖ ἱεροῦ διελθὼν διὰ μέσου αὐτῶν (*see* Lk 4.30) ℵᵇ l²¹¹ ‖ ἱεροῦ διελθὼν διὰ μέσου αὐτῶν καὶ παρῆγεν οὕτως (*see* Lk 4.30) A K Δ Θᶜ Π f¹ f¹³ 28 565 700 1009 1079 1195 1216 1230 (1242* *omit* διελθών) 1242ᶜ 1253 1365 1546 1646 2148 2174 *Byz Lect* it(f),q syrʰ goth eth Theodore-Heraclea Juliusᵃᶜᶜ. ᵗᵒ ᴬᵗʰᵃⁿᵃˢⁱᵘˢ ‖ ἱεροῦ διελθὼν διὰ μέσου αὐτῶν καὶ ἐπορεύετο καὶ παρῆγεν οὕτως (*see* Lk 4.30) 1344 ‖ ἱεροῦ καὶ διελθὼν διὰ μέσου αὐτῶν ἐπορεύετο καὶ παρῆγεν οὕτως (*see* Lk 4.30) ℵᵃ C L X Ψ 0124 33 892 1010 1071 1241 syr(p),h with *,(pal) copᵇᵒ geo² Athanasius

¹4 {C} ἡμᾶς δεῖ (*see footnote 2*) 𝔭⁶⁶,⁷⁵ ℵ* B L W 0124 syrᵖᵃˡᵐˢˢ copᵇᵒᵐˢˢ ethʳᵒ geo¹ Origen Jerome Nonnus Cyril ‖ δεῖ ἡμᾶς D itᵈ copˢᵃ ‖ ἡμᾶς syrᵖᵃˡᵐˢˢ ‖ ἐμὲ δεῖ ℵᵃ A C K X Δ Θ Π Ψ f¹ f¹³ 28 33 565 700 892 1009 1010 1071 1079 1195 1216 1230 1241 1242 1253 1344 1365 1546 1646 2148 2174 *Byz Lect* itᵃ,ᵃᵘʳ,ᵇ,ᶜ,ᵉ,f,ff²,l,q,rl vg syrˢ,ᵖ,ʰ copᵇᵒᵐˢˢ,ᵃᶜʰ² goth arm ethᵖᵖ geo² Diatessaron Chrysostom

---

ᶜ ᶜ **59** c none, c major: WH Bov Nes BF² Zür Luth Jer Seg ‖ c minor, c major: RV ASV RSV NEB TT ‖ c major, c none: NEBᵐᵍ ‖ different text: TR AV RVᵐᵍ ASVᵐᵍ

---

58 πρὶν...εἰμί Jn 1.1   **59** ἦραν...αὐτόν Jn 10.31; 11.8
9 2 τίς...γεννηθῇ Ex 20.5; Eze 18.20; Lk 13.2, 4   **3** ἵνα φανερωθῇ...αὐτῷ Jn 11.4
4 ἡμᾶς δεῖ...ἐστίν Jn 5.17

as long as it is day; the night is coming,
when no one can work. 5 While I am in
the world I am the light for the world."
6 After he said this, Jesus spat on the
ground and made some mud with the
spittle; he rubbed the mud on the man's
eyes, 7 and told him, "Go wash your
face in the Pool of Siloam." (This name
means "Sent.") So the man went, washed
his face, and came back seeing.

8 His neighbors, then, and the people
who had seen him begging before this,
asked, "Isn't this the man who used
to sit and beg?" 9 Some said, "He is the
one," but others said, "No, he is not,
he just looks like him." So the man
himself said, "I am the man." 10 "How
were your eyes opened?" they asked
him. 11 He answered, "The man named
Jesus made some mud, rubbed it on
my eyes, and told me, 'Go to Siloam and
wash your face.' So I went, and as soon

με[2] *ἕως ἡμέρα ἐστίν· ἔρχεται νὺξ ὅτε οὐδεὶς δύναται*
ἐργάζεσθαι. **5** *ὅταν ἐν τῷ κόσμῳ ὦ, φῶς εἰμι τοῦ*
κόσμου. **6** *ταῦτα εἰπὼν ἔπτυσεν χαμαὶ καὶ ἐποίησεν*
πηλὸν ἐκ τοῦ πτύσματος, καὶ ἐπέχρισεν[3] *αὐτοῦ τὸν*
πηλὸν ἐπὶ τοὺς ὀφθαλμοὺς **7** *καὶ εἶπεν αὐτῷ, Ὕπαγε*
νίψαι εἰς τὴν κολυμβήθραν τοῦ Σιλωάμ (ὃ ἑρμηνεύεται
Ἀπεσταλμένος). ἀπῆλθεν οὖν καὶ ἐνίψατο, καὶ ἦλθεν
βλέπων. **8** *Οἱ οὖν γείτονες καὶ οἱ θεωροῦντες αὐτὸν*
τὸ πρότερον ὅτι προσαίτης ἦν ἔλεγον, Οὐχ οὗτός ἐστιν
ὁ καθήμενος καὶ προσαιτῶν; **9** *ἄλλοι ἔλεγον ὅτι Οὗτός*
ἐστιν· ἄλλοι ἔλεγον, Οὐχί, ἀλλὰ ὅμοιος αὐτῷ ἐστιν.
ἐκεῖνος ἔλεγεν ὅτι Ἐγώ εἰμι. **10** *ἔλεγον οὖν αὐτῷ,*
Πῶς [οὖν] ἠνεῴχθησάν σου οἱ ὀφθαλμοί; **11** *ἀπεκρίθη*
ἐκεῖνος, Ὁ ἄνθρωπος ὁ λεγόμενος Ἰησοῦς[4] *πηλὸν ἐποί-*
ησεν καὶ ἐπέχρισέν μου τοὺς ὀφθαλμοὺς καὶ εἶπέν μοι
ὅτι Ὕπαγε εἰς τὸν Σιλωὰμ καὶ νίψαι· [a]*ἀπελθὼν οὖν καὶ*

---

[2] **4** {C} πέμψαντός με (*see footnote 1*) $\aleph^{a}$ A B C D K X Δ Θ Π Ψ 0124 f^{1} f^{13} 28 33 565 700 892 1009 1010 1071 1079 1195 1216 1230 1241 1242 1253 1344 1365 1546 1646 2148 2174 *Byz Lect* $it^{a,aur,b,c,d,e,f,ff^2,q}$ vg $syr^{s,p,h,pal}$ cop^{sa,bo^{mss},ach^2} goth arm eth^{pp} geo // πέμψαντος ἡμᾶς $\mathfrak{p}^{66,75}$ ℵ* L W cop^{bo} eth^{ro} Cyril

[3] **6** {B} ἐπέχρισεν $\mathfrak{p}^{66,75}$ ℵ A C D K L W X Δ Θ Π Ψ 0124 0216 f^{1} f^{13} 28 33 565 700 892 1009 1010 1071 1079 1195 1216 1230 1241 1242 1253 1344 1365 1546 1646 2148 2174 *Byz Lect* $it^{a,aur,b,c,d,e,f,ff^2,l,q}$ vg $syr^{s,p,h,(pal)}$ cop^{sa,bo,ach^2} goth arm geo $Irenaeus^{lat}$ // ἐπέθηκεν B $Diatessaron^{i}$ // *he made eyes from the* [*literally, his*] *clay* $Diatessaron^{e^{syr}}$

[4] **11** {C} ἀπεκρίθη ἐκεῖνος, Ὁ ἄνθρωπος ὁ λεγόμενος Ἰησοῦς $\mathfrak{p}^{66}$ ℵ B (L *omit second* ὁ) 0124 f^{1} 33 (vg ἀπεκρίθη, Ἐκεῖνος) $syr^{(s),h\ with\ *}$ cop^{sa,ach^2} goth? // ἀπεκρίθη ἐκεῖνος, Ἄνθρωπος ὁ λεγόμενος Ἰησοῦς $\mathfrak{p}^{75}$ C Θ 565 it^{aur,c,d,e,ff^2} (it^{l} Χριστός) goth? // ἀπεκρίθη ἐκεῖνος, Ἄνθρωπος λεγόμενος Ἰησοῦς D^{gr} 1242 arm goth? // ἀπεκρίθη ἐκεῖνος καὶ εἶπεν, Ἄνθρωπος λεγόμενος Ἰησοῦς A K W X Δ Π Ψ f^{13} 28 700 892 1009 1010 1079 1195 1216 1230 1241 1253 (1344 Ἰησοῦς λεγόμενος) (1365 ὁ λεγόμενος) 1546 1646 2148 2174 *Byz Lect* $it^{(a),b,f,r^1}$ (it^{q} Χριστός) $syr^{(p),h}$ $cop^{bo^{ms}}$ goth // ἀπεκρίθη ἐκεῖνος καὶ εἶπεν, Ὁ ἄνθρωπος ὁ λεγόμενος Ἰησοῦς 1071 (syr^{pal}) cop^{bo}

---

a a **11–12** *a* no number, *a* number 12: TR^{ed} WH Bov Nes BF^{2} AV RV ASV RSV NEB TT Zür Luth Jer Seg // *a* number 12, *a* no number: TR^{ed}

---

5 φῶς...κόσμου Is 49.6; Jn 1.4, 5, 9; 8.12; 12.46 **6** Mk 8.23 **7** Ὕπαγε...Σιλωάμ 2 Kgs 5.10 **8** Ac 3.10

νιψάμενος ἀνέβλεψα. **12**ᵃ καὶ εἶπαν αὐτῷ, Ποῦ ἐστιν ἐκεῖνος; λέγει, Οὐκ οἶδα.

The Pharisees Investigate the Healing

13 Ἄγουσιν αὐτὸν πρὸς τοὺς Φαρισαίους τόν ποτε τυφλόν. **14** ἦν δὲ σάββατον ἐν ᾗ ἡμέρᾳ τὸν πηλὸν ἐποίησεν ὁ Ἰησοῦς καὶ ἀνέῳξεν αὐτοῦ τοὺς ὀφθαλμούς. **15** πάλιν οὖν ἠρώτων αὐτὸν καὶ οἱ Φαρισαῖοι πῶς ἀνέβλεψεν. ὁ δὲ εἶπεν αὐτοῖς, Πηλὸν ἐπέθηκέν μου ἐπὶ τοὺς ὀφθαλμούς, καὶ ἐνιψάμην, καὶ βλέπω. **16** ἔλεγον οὖν ἐκ τῶν Φαρισαίων τινές, Οὐκ ἔστιν οὗτος παρὰ θεοῦ ὁ ἄνθρωπος, ὅτι τὸ σάββατον οὐ τηρεῖ. ἄλλοι [δὲ] ἔλεγον, Πῶς δύναται ἄνθρωπος ἁμαρτωλὸς τοιαῦτα σημεῖα ποιεῖν; καὶ σχίσμα ἦν ἐν αὐτοῖς. **17** λέγουσιν οὖν τῷ τυφλῷ πάλιν, Τί σὺ λέγεις περὶ αὐτοῦ, ὅτι ἠνέῳξέν σου τοὺς ὀφθαλμούς; ὁ δὲ εἶπεν ὅτι Προφήτης ἐστίν.

18 Οὐκ ἐπίστευσαν οὖν οἱ Ἰουδαῖοι περὶ αὐτοῦ ὅτι ἦν τυφλὸς καὶ ἀνέβλεψεν, ἕως ὅτου ἐφώνησαν τοὺς γονεῖς αὐτοῦ τοῦ ἀναβλέψαντος **19** καὶ ἠρώτησαν αὐτοὺς λέγοντες, Οὗτός ἐστιν ὁ υἱὸς ὑμῶν, ὃν ὑμεῖς λέγετε ὅτι τυφλὸς ἐγεννήθη; πῶς οὖν βλέπει ἄρτι; **20** ἀπεκρίθησαν οὖν οἱ γονεῖς αὐτοῦ καὶ εἶπαν, Οἴδαμεν ὅτι οὗτός ἐστιν ὁ υἱὸς ἡμῶν καὶ ὅτι τυφλὸς ἐγεννήθη· **21** πῶς δὲ νῦν βλέπει οὐκ οἴδαμεν, ἢ τίς ἤνοιξεν αὐτοῦ τοὺς ὀφθαλμοὺς ἡμεῖς οὐκ οἴδαμεν· αὐτὸν ἐρωτήσατε, ἡλικίαν ἔχει, αὐτὸς περὶ ἑαυτοῦ λαλήσει. **22** ταῦτα εἶπαν οἱ γονεῖς αὐτοῦ ὅτι ἐφοβοῦντο τοὺς Ἰουδαίους, ἤδη γὰρ συνετέθειντο οἱ Ἰουδαῖοι ἵνα ἐάν τις αὐτὸν ὁμολογήσῃ Χριστόν, ἀποσυνάγωγος γένηται. **23** διὰ τοῦτο οἱ γονεῖς αὐτοῦ εἶπαν ὅτι Ἡλικίαν ἔχει, αὐτὸν ἐπερωτήσατε.

24 Ἐφώνησαν οὖν τὸν ἄνθρωπον ἐκ δευτέρου ὃς ἦν τυφλὸς καὶ εἶπαν αὐτῷ, Δὸς δόξαν τῷ θεῷ· ἡμεῖς οἴδα-

---

14 Lk 13.14; Jn 5.9 **16** Οὐκ...ἄνθρωπος Jn 3.2; 9.33 τὸ...τηρεῖ Jn 5.16, 18 **Πῶς...ποιεῖν**
Jn 9.31 σχίσμα...αὐτοῖς Jn 7.43; 10.19 **17** Προφήτης ἐστίν Mt 21.46; Jn 4.19; 7.40
22 ἐφοβοῦντο τοὺς Ἰουδαίους Jn 7.13; 19.38; 20.19 ἤδη...γένηται Jn 12.42
24 Δὸς...θεῷ Jos 7.19; Re 11.13

The Pharisees Investigate the Healing

as I washed I could see." **12** "Where is he?" they asked. "I do not know," he answered.

13 Then they took the man who had been blind to the Pharisees. **14** The day that Jesus made the mud and opened the man's eyes was a Sabbath. **15** The Pharisees, then, asked the man again how he had received his sight. He told them, "He put some mud on my eyes, I washed my face, and now I can see." **16** Some of the Pharisees said, "The man who did this cannot be from God because he does not obey the Sabbath law." Others, however, said, "How could a man who is a sinner do such mighty works as these?" And there was a division among them.

17 So the Pharisees asked the man once more, "You say he opened your eyes — well, what do you say about him?" "He is a prophet," he answered. **18** The Jews, however, were not willing to believe that he had been blind and could now see, until they called the man's parents **19** and asked them: "Is this your son? Do you say that he was born blind? Well, how is it that he can see now?" **20** His parents answered: "We know that he is our son, and we know that he was born blind. **21** But we do not know how it is that he is now able to see, nor do we know who opened his eyes. Ask him; he is old enough, and he can answer for himself!" **22** His parents said this because they were afraid of the Jews; for the Jews had already agreed that if anyone professed that Jesus was the Messiah he would be put out of the synagogue. **23** That is why his parents said, "He is old enough; ask him!"

24 A second time they called back the man who had been born blind and said to him, "Promise before God that you will tell the truth! We know that this man is a sinner." 25 "I do not know if he is a sinner or not," the man replied. "One thing I do know: I was blind, and now I see." 26 "What did he do to you?" they asked. "How did he open your eyes?" 27 "I have already told you," he answered, "and you would not listen. Why do you want to hear it again? Maybe you, too, would like to be his disciples?" 28 They cursed him and said: "You are that fellow's disciple; we are Moses' disciples. 29 We know that God spoke to Moses; as for that fellow, we do not even know where he comes from!" 30 The man answered: "What a strange thing this is! You do not know where he comes from, but he opened my eyes! 31 We know that God does not listen to sinners; he does listen to people who respect him and do what he wants them to do. 32 Since the beginning of the world it has never been heard of that someone opened the eyes of a man born blind; 33 unless this man came from God, he would not be able to do a thing." 34 They answered back, "You were born and raised in sin — and you are trying to teach us?" And they threw him out of the synagogue.

Spiritual Blindness

35 Jesus heard that they had thrown him out. He found him and said, "Do you believe in the Son of Man?" 36 The man answered, "Tell me who he is, sir,

μεν ὅτι οὗτος ὁ ἄνθρωπος ἁμαρτωλός ἐστιν. 25 ἀπεκρίθη οὖν ἐκεῖνος, Εἰ ἁμαρτωλός ἐστιν οὐκ οἶδα· ἓν οἶδα, ὅτι τυφλὸς ὢν ἄρτι βλέπω. 26 εἶπον οὖν αὐτῷ, Τί ἐποίησέν σοι; πῶς ἤνοιξέν σου τοὺς ὀφθαλμούς; 27 ἀπεκρίθη αὐτοῖς, Εἶπον ὑμῖν ἤδη καὶ οὐκ ἠκούσατε· τί πάλιν θέλετε ἀκούειν; μὴ καὶ ὑμεῖς θέλετε αὐτοῦ μαθηταὶ γενέσθαι; 28 καὶ ἐλοιδόρησαν[5] αὐτὸν καὶ εἶπον, Σὺ μαθητὴς εἶ ἐκείνου, ἡμεῖς δὲ τοῦ Μωϋσέως ἐσμὲν μαθηταί· 29 ἡμεῖς οἴδαμεν ὅτι Μωϋσεῖ λελάληκεν ὁ θεός, τοῦτον δὲ οὐκ οἴδαμεν πόθεν ἐστίν. 30 ἀπεκρίθη ὁ ἄνθρωπος καὶ εἶπεν αὐτοῖς, Ἐν τούτῳ γὰρ τὸ θαυμαστόν ἐστιν ὅτι ὑμεῖς οὐκ οἴδατε πόθεν ἐστίν, καὶ ἤνοιξέν μου τοὺς ὀφθαλμούς. 31 οἴδαμεν ὅτι ἁμαρτωλῶν ὁ θεὸς οὐκ ἀκούει, ἀλλ' ἐάν τις θεοσεβὴς ᾖ καὶ τὸ θέλημα αὐτοῦ ποιῇ τούτου ἀκούει. 32 ἐκ τοῦ αἰῶνος οὐκ ἠκούσθη ὅτι ἤνοιξέν τις ὀφθαλμοὺς τυφλοῦ γεγεννημένου· 33 εἰ μὴ ἦν οὗτος παρὰ θεοῦ, οὐκ ἠδύνατο ποιεῖν οὐδέν. 34 ἀπεκρίθησαν καὶ εἶπον αὐτῷ, Ἐν ἁμαρτίαις σὺ ἐγεννήθης ὅλος, καὶ σὺ διδάσκεις ἡμᾶς; καὶ ἐξέβαλον αὐτὸν ἔξω.

Spiritual Blindness

35 Ἤκουσεν Ἰησοῦς ὅτι ἐξέβαλον αὐτὸν ἔξω, καὶ εὑρὼν αὐτὸν εἶπεν [αὐτῷ], Σὺ πιστεύεις εἰς τὸν υἱὸν τοῦ ἀνθρώπου[6]; 36 ἀπεκρίθη ἐκεῖνος καὶ εἶπεν, Καὶ

---

[5] 28 {C} καὶ ἐλοιδόρησαν 𝔭75 א* B W 0124 syrpal copsamss eth Ambrose Cyril ‖ ἐλοιδόρησαν οὖν f13 l184 itc.ff2 vgcl goth ‖ οἱ δὲ ἐλοιδόρησαν אc Dgr L Θ Ψ 0250 f1 33 565 (1071 ἐλευδόρησαν) 1241 syrs.p.h with * copbo geo172 ‖ Ad illi maledixerunt ita.d.f ‖ ἐλοιδόρησαν 𝔭66 A K X Δ 28 700 892 1009 1010 1079 1195 1216 1230 1242 1253 1344 1365 1546 1646 2148 2174 Byz Lect itaur.b,e,l,q vgww copsamss,boms,ach2,fay (arm add ἐκεῖνοι) geo17 Augustine

[6] 35 {A} ἀνθρώπου 𝔭66,75 א B D W itd syrs copsa,boms,ach2,fay ethro Chrysostom ‖ θεοῦ A K L X Δ Θ Ψ 0124 0250 f1 f13 28 33 565 700 892 1009 1010 1071 1079 1195 1216 1230 1241 1242 1253 1344 1365 1546 1646 2148 2174 Byz Lect

---

29 τοῦτον...πόθεν ἐστίν Jn 7.27, 28; 8.14　　31 οἴδαμεν...οὐκ ἀκούει Ps 66.18; Is 1.15 ἐάν...ἀκούει Ps 34.15; Pr 15.29　　33 Jn 3.2　　34 Ἐν ἁμαρτίαις...ὅλος Ps 51.5; Jn 9.2

τίς ἐστιν, κύριε⁷, ἵνα πιστεύσω εἰς αὐτόν; 37 εἶπεν αὐτῷ ὁ Ἰησοῦς, Καὶ ἑώρακας αὐτὸν καὶ ὁ λαλῶν μετὰ σοῦ ἐκεῖνός ἐστιν. 38 ὁ δὲ ἔφη, Πιστεύω, κύριε· καὶ προσεκύνησεν αὐτῷ. 39 καὶ εἶπεν ὁ Ἰησοῦς, Εἰς κρίμα ἐγὼ εἰς τὸν κόσμον τοῦτον ἦλθον, ἵνα οἱ μὴ βλέποντες βλέπωσιν καὶ οἱ βλέποντες τυφλοὶ γένωνται.

40 Ἤκουσαν ἐκ τῶν Φαρισαίων ταῦτα οἱ μετ' αὐτοῦ ὄντες, καὶ εἶπον αὐτῷ, Μὴ καὶ ἡμεῖς τυφλοί ἐσμεν; 41 εἶπεν αὐτοῖς ὁ Ἰησοῦς, Εἰ τυφλοὶ ἦτε, οὐκ ἂν εἴχετε ἁμαρτίαν· νῦν δὲ λέγετε ὅτι Βλέπομεν· ἡ ἁμαρτία ὑμῶν μένει.

The Parable of the Sheepfold

10 Ἀμὴν ἀμὴν λέγω ὑμῖν, ὁ μὴ εἰσερχόμενος διὰ τῆς θύρας εἰς τὴν αὐλὴν τῶν προβάτων ἀλλὰ ἀναβαίνων ἀλλαχόθεν ἐκεῖνος κλέπτης ἐστὶν καὶ λῃστής· 2 ὁ δὲ εἰσερχόμενος διὰ τῆς θύρας ποιμήν ἐστιν τῶν προβάτων. 3 τούτῳ ὁ θυρωρὸς ἀνοίγει, καὶ τὰ πρόβατα τῆς φωνῆς αὐτοῦ ἀκούει, καὶ τὰ ἴδια πρόβατα φωνεῖ κατ' ὄνομα καὶ ἐξάγει αὐτά. 4 ὅταν τὰ ἴδια πάντα ἐκβάλῃ, ἔμπροσθεν αὐτῶν πορεύεται, καὶ τὰ πρόβατα αὐτῷ ἀκολουθεῖ, ὅτι

itᵃ·ᵃᵘʳ·ᵇ·ᶜ·ᵉ·ᶠ·ᶠᶠ²·ˡ· q·ʳˡ vg syrᵖ·ʰ·ᵖᵃˡ copᵇᵒ goth arm ethᵖᵖ geo Tertullian Origen Chrysostom Nonnus Cyril

⁷ 36 {C} ἀπεκρίθη ἐκεῖνος καὶ εἶπεν, Καὶ τίς ἐστιν, κύριε D K X Δ Ψ (0250 εἶπεν αὐτῷ) f¹ f¹³ 28 33 565 700 892 1009 1010 1071 1195 1216 1230 1242 1253 1344 1365 1646 2148 2174 Byz Lect itᵈ syrʰ·⁽ᵖᵃˡ⁾ goth Cyril ∥ ἀπεκρίθη ἐκεῖνος καὶ εἶπεν, Κύριε, καὶ τίς ἐστιν ℵᶜ (ℵ* arm geo¹ omit second καί) (copˢᵃ·ᵃᶜʰ² omit ἀπεκρίθη ἐκεῖνος καί and second καί) ∥ ἀπεκρίθη ἐκεῖνος καὶ εἶπεν, Τίς ἐστιν, κύριε L Θ 1079 1546 itᵃᵘʳ·ᵇ·ᶜ·ᵉ·ᶠ·ᶠᶠ²·ˡ·⁽q⁾ vg (syrᵖ) (copᵇᵒᵐˢ ἐκεῖνος δὲ εἶπεν and omit ἀπεκρίθη) geoᴬ ∥ ἀπεκρίθη ἐκεῖνος, Καὶ τίς ἐστιν, ἔφη, κύριε 𝔭⁶⁶* (𝔭⁶⁶ᶜ omit ἔφη) ∥ ἀπεκρίθη ἐκεῖνος, Τίς ἐστιν, κύριε A 1241 (syrˢ) ∥ ἀπεκρίθη καὶ εἶπεν, Τίς ἐστιν, κύριε copᵇᵒ (copᶠᵃʸ omit ἀπεκρίθη) (geoᴿ omit κύριε) ∥ ἀπεκρίθη, Τίς ἐστιν itᵃ ∥ καὶ τίς ἐστιν, ἔφη, κύριε 𝔭⁷⁵ B W (0124 καὶ ἔφη, Τίς ἐστιν, κύριε)

37 Jn 4.26   39 Εἰς...ἦλθον Jn 3.17; 5.22, 27, 30; 8.15, 16; 12.47   40 Mt 15.14; 23.26
41 οὐκ...ἁμαρτίαν Jn 15.22
10 4 τὰ πρόβατα...αὐτοῦ Jn 10.27

---

so I can believe in him!" 37 Jesus said to him, "You have already seen him, and he is the one who is talking with you now." 38 "I believe, Lord!" the man said, and knelt down before Jesus.

39 Jesus said, "I come to this world to judge, so that the blind should see, and those who see should become blind." 40 Some Pharisees, who were there with him, heard him say this and asked him, "You don't mean that we are blind, too?" 41 Jesus answered, "If you were blind, then you would not be guilty; but since you say, 'We can see,' that means that you are still guilty."

The Parable of the Sheepfold

10 "I tell you the truth: the man who does not enter the sheepfold by the door, but climbs in some other way, is a thief and a robber. 2 The man who goes in by the door is the shepherd of the sheep. 3 The gatekeeper opens the gate for him; the sheep hear his voice as he calls his own sheep by name, and he leads them out. 4 When he has brought them out, he goes ahead of them, and the sheep

follow him, because they know his voice. 5 They will not follow someone else; instead, they will run away from him, because they do not know his voice.''

6 Jesus told them this parable, but they did not understand what he was telling them.

Jesus the Good Shepherd

7 So Jesus said again: "I tell you the truth: I am the door for the sheep. 8 All others who came before me are thieves and robbers; but the sheep did not listen to them. 9 I am the door. Whoever comes in by me will be saved; he will come in and go out, and find pasture. 10 The thief comes only in order to steal, kill, and destroy. I have come in order that they might have life, life in all its fulness.

11 "I am the good shepherd. The good shepherd is willing to die for the sheep. 12 The hired man, who is not a shepherd and does not own the sheep, leaves them and runs away when he sees a wolf

οἴδασιν τὴν φωνὴν αὐτοῦ· 5 ἀλλοτρίῳ δὲ οὐ μὴ ἀκολουθήσουσιν ἀλλὰ φεύξονται ἀπ' αὐτοῦ, ὅτι οὐκ οἴδασιν τῶν ἀλλοτρίων τὴν φωνήν. 6 Ταύτην τὴν παροιμίαν εἶπεν αὐτοῖς ὁ Ἰησοῦς· ἐκεῖνοι δὲ οὐκ ἔγνωσαν τίνα ἦν ἃ ἐλάλει αὐτοῖς.

Jesus the Good Shepherd

7 Εἶπεν οὖν πάλιν ὁ Ἰησοῦς, Ἀμὴν ἀμὴν λέγω ὑμῖν ὅτι ἐγώ εἰμι ἡ θύρα τῶν προβάτων. 8 πάντες ὅσοι ἦλθον [πρὸ ἐμοῦ][1] κλέπται εἰσὶν καὶ λῃσταί· ἀλλ' οὐκ ἤκουσαν αὐτῶν τὰ πρόβατα. 9 ἐγώ εἰμι ἡ θύρα· δι' ἐμοῦ ἐάν τις εἰσέλθῃ σωθήσεται καὶ εἰσελεύσεται καὶ ἐξελεύσεται καὶ νομὴν εὑρήσει. 10 ὁ κλέπτης οὐκ ἔρχεται εἰ μὴ ἵνα κλέψῃ καὶ θύσῃ καὶ ἀπολέσῃ· ἐγὼ ἦλθον ἵνα ζωὴν ἔχωσιν καὶ περισσὸν ἔχωσιν. 11 Ἐγώ εἰμι ὁ ποιμὴν ὁ καλός· ὁ ποιμὴν ὁ καλὸς τὴν ψυχὴν αὐτοῦ τίθησιν[2] ὑπὲρ τῶν προβάτων· 12 ὁ μισθωτὸς καὶ οὐκ ὢν ποιμήν, οὗ οὐκ ἔστιν τὰ πρόβατα ἴδια, θεωρεῖ τὸν λύκον ἐρχόμενον καὶ ἀφίησιν τὰ πρόβατα καὶ φεύγει —

[1] 8 {C} ἦλθον πρὸ ἐμοῦ 𝔓[66] ℵ[c] A B D K L W X Π Ψ (0250 εἰσῆλθον) f[13] 33 700 (1071 ἦλθεν) 1079 1216 1230 1241 1546 1646 2174 Byz[pt] l[883m] it[d] syr[h with *] cop[bo] eth Clement Origen Ambrosiaster Lucifer Faustus-Milevis[acc. to Augustine] Didymus Jerome Isidore Hesychius ‖ πρὸ ἐμοῦ ἦλθον Θ f[1] 565 1365 arm geo Valentinians Origen Ambrosiaster Nonnus Cyril ‖ ἦλθον 𝔓[45vid,75] ℵ* Δ 28 892 1009 1010 1195 1242 2148 Byz[pt] Lect[s,m] it[a,aur,b,c,e,f,ff2,l,q,r1] vg syr[s,p,h,pal] cop[sa,boms,ach2] goth Diatessaron[a,esyr,f,i] Manicheans[acc. to Theophylact] Theodore-Heraclea Basil Chrysostom Augustine Cyril Theophylact Euthymius ‖ omit 1344

[2] 11 {B} τίθησιν 𝔓[66,75] ℵ[c] A B K L W X Δ Θ Π Ψ 0250 f[1] f[13] 28 33 565 700 892 1009 1010 1071 1079 1195 1216 1230 1241 1242 1344 1365 1546 1646 2148 2174 Byz Lect[m] l[184,185s,m] it[a,aur,e,f,l] syr[p,h] cop[sa,ach2,fay] goth arm geo Clement Tertullian Origen[gr,lat] Eusebius Hilary Lucifer Basil Apostolic Constitutions Chrysostom Cyril Theodoret ‖ δίδωσιν 𝔓[45] ℵ* D it[(b),c,d,ff2,(r1)] vg syr[s,pal] cop[bo] Diatessaron[a,esyr,i,s] (Theodotus[acc. to Clement] ἐπιδίδωσιν) Augustine

6 Jn 16.25   8 Jr 23.1–2; Eze 34.2–3   9 Ps 118.20; Jn 14.6   11 Ἐγώ εἰμι ὁ ποιμὴν ὁ καλός Ps 23.1; Is 40.11; Eze 34.15; He 13.20; Re 7.17   τὴν...προβάτων Jn 15.13; 1 Jn 3.16

καὶ ὁ λύκος ἁρπάζει αὐτὰ καὶ σκορπίζει — **13** ὅτι μισθωτός ἐστιν καὶ οὐ μέλει αὐτῷ περὶ τῶν προβάτων. **14** Ἐγώ εἰμι ὁ ποιμὴν ὁ καλός, καὶ γινώσκω τὰ ἐμὰ καὶ γινώσκουσί με τὰ ἐμά, **15** καθὼς γινώσκει με ὁ πατὴρ κἀγὼ γινώσκω τὸν πατέρα· καὶ τὴν ψυχήν μου τίθημι[3] ὑπὲρ τῶν προβάτων. **16** καὶ ἄλλα πρόβατα ἔχω ἃ οὐκ ἔστιν ἐκ τῆς αὐλῆς ταύτης· κἀκεῖνα δεῖ με ἀγαγεῖν, καὶ τῆς φωνῆς μου ἀκούσουσιν, καὶ γενήσονται[4] μία ποίμνη, εἷς ποιμήν. **17** διὰ τοῦτό με ὁ πατὴρ ἀγαπᾷ ὅτι ἐγὼ τίθημι τὴν ψυχήν μου, ἵνα πάλιν λάβω αὐτήν. **18** οὐδεὶς αἴρει[5] αὐτὴν ἀπ' ἐμοῦ, ἀλλ' ἐγὼ τίθημι αὐτὴν ἀπ' ἐμαυτοῦ. ἐξουσίαν ἔχω θεῖναι αὐτήν, καὶ ἐξουσίαν ἔχω πάλιν λαβεῖν αὐτήν· ταύτην τὴν ἐντολὴν ἔλαβον παρὰ τοῦ πατρός μου.

19 Σχίσμα πάλιν ἐγένετο ἐν τοῖς Ἰουδαίοις διὰ τοὺς λόγους τούτους. **20** ἔλεγον δὲ πολλοὶ ἐξ αὐτῶν, Δαιμόνιον ἔχει καὶ μαίνεται· τί αὐτοῦ ἀκούετε; **21** ἄλλοι ἔλεγον, Ταῦτα τὰ ῥήματα οὐκ ἔστιν δαιμονιζομένου· μὴ δαιμόνιον δύναται τυφλῶν ὀφθαλμοὺς ἀνοῖξαι;

---

[3] **15** {C} τίθημι ℵ^c A B K L X Δ Θ Π Ψ f¹ f¹³ 28 33 565 700 892 1009 1010 1071 1079 1195 1216 1230 1241 1242 1344 1365 1546 1646 2148 2174 *Byz Lect*^m l^{184,185s.m} it^{a,aur,b,c,(e),f,ff2,l,rl} vg syr^{s,p,h,pal} cop^{sa,bo,ach2} goth arm geo Eusebius Athanasius ∥ δίδωμι 𝔭^{45,66} ℵ* D W it^d cop^{boms} Diatessaron^a

[4] **16** {C} γενήσονται 𝔭⁴⁵ ℵ^c B D L W X Θ Ψ f¹ 33 565 1071 1195^{mg} it^{d,f} syr^{hmg,pal} cop^{sa,bo,ach2} goth arm geo Clement ∥ γενήσεται 𝔭⁶⁶ ℵ* A K Δ Π f¹³ 28 700 (892 1344 γεννήσεται) 1009 1010 1079 1195* 1216 1230 1241 1242 1365 1546 1646 2148 2174 *Byz Lect*^m l^{184,185s.m} it^{a,aur,b,c,e,ff2,l,rl} vg syr^{s,p,h} Diatessaron^{a,i,n} Eusebius Basil Cyril Theodoret

[5] **18** {C} αἴρει 𝔭⁶⁶ ℵ^c A D K L W X Δ Θ Π Ψ f¹ f¹³ 28 565 700 892 1009 1010 1071 1079 1195 1216 1230 1241 1242 1344 1365 1546 1646 2148 2174 *Byz Lect* it^{a,aur,b,c,d,e,f,ff2,(l),rl} vg syr^{s,p,h,pal} cop^{sa,bo,ach2} goth arm geo Origen^{gr,lat} Cyprian Eusebius Hilary Didymus ∥ ἦρεν 𝔭⁴⁵ ℵ* B

---

12 ὁ λύκος...σκορπίζει Ac 20.29   **14** γινώσκω τὰ ἐμά Jn 10.27; 2 Tm 2.19   **15** καθὼς ...πατέρα Mt 11.27   τὴν...προβάτων Jn 15.13; 1 Jn 3.16   **16** ἄλλα...ἀγαγεῖν Is 56.8; Jn 11.52; 1 Pe 2.25   εἷς ποιμήν Eze 34.23; 37.24   **17** ἐγὼ τίθημι...αὐτήν Php 2.8–9   **18** ταύτην...ἐντολὴν...μου Jn 14.31; 15.10   **19** Jn 7.43; 9.16   **20** Δαιμόνιον...μαίνεται Mk 3.21–22; Jn 7.20; 8.48

coming; so the wolf snatches the sheep and scatters them. [13] The hired man runs away because he is only a hired man and does not care for the sheep. [14-15] I am the good shepherd. As the Father knows me and I know the Father, in the same way I know my sheep and they know me. And I am willing to die for them. [16] There are other sheep that belong to me that are not in this sheepfold. I must bring them, too; they will listen to my voice, and they will become[1] one flock with one shepherd.

[17] "The Father loves me because I am willing to give up my life, in order that I may receive it back again. [18] No one takes my life away from me. I give it up of my own free will. I have the right to give it, and I have the right to take it back. This is what my Father has commanded me to do."

[19] Again there was a division among the Jews because of these words. [20] Many of them were saying, "He has a demon! He is crazy! Why do you listen to him?" [21] But others were saying, "A man with a demon could not talk like this! How could a demon open the eyes of blind men?"

---

[1] **16** they will become: *some mss. read* there will be

Jesus Rejected by the Jews

²² The time came to celebrate the Feast of Dedication in Jerusalem; it was winter. ²³ Jesus was walking in Solomon's Porch in the Temple, ²⁴ when the Jews gathered around him and said, "How long are you going to keep us in suspense? Tell us the plain truth: are you the Messiah?" ²⁵ Jesus answered: "I have already told you, but you would not believe me. The works I do by my Father's authority speak on my behalf; ²⁶ but you will not believe because you are not my sheep. ²⁷ My sheep listen to my voice; I know them, and they follow me. ²⁸ I give them eternal life, and they shall never die; and no one can snatch them away from me. ²⁹ What my Father has given me is greater[2] than all, and no

---

[2] 29 *What my Father has given me is greater:* **some mss. read** My Father, who gave them to me, is greater

Jesus Rejected by the Jews

22 Ἐγένετο τότε[6] τὰ ἐγκαίνια ἐν τοῖς Ἱεροσολύμοις· χειμὼν ἦν, **23** καὶ περιεπάτει ὁ Ἰησοῦς ἐν τῷ ἱερῷ ἐν τῇ στοᾷ τοῦ Σολομῶνος. **24** ἐκύκλωσαν οὖν αὐτὸν οἱ Ἰουδαῖοι καὶ ἔλεγον αὐτῷ, Ἕως πότε τὴν ψυχὴν ἡμῶν αἴρεις; εἰ σὺ εἶ ὁ Χριστός, εἰπὲ ἡμῖν παρρησίᾳ. **25** ἀπεκρίθη αὐτοῖς ὁ Ἰησοῦς, Εἶπον ὑμῖν καὶ οὐ πιστεύετε· τὰ ἔργα ἃ ἐγὼ ποιῶ ἐν τῷ ὀνόματι τοῦ πατρός μου ταῦτα μαρτυρεῖ περὶ ἐμοῦ· **26** ἀλλὰ ὑμεῖς οὐ πιστεύετε, ὅτι οὐκ ἐστὲ ἐκ τῶν προβάτων τῶν ἐμῶν[7]. **27** τὰ πρόβατα τὰ ἐμὰ τῆς φωνῆς μου ἀκούουσιν, κἀγὼ γινώσκω αὐτά, καὶ ἀκολουθοῦσίν μοι, **28** κἀγὼ δίδωμι αὐτοῖς ζωὴν αἰώνιον, καὶ οὐ μὴ ἀπόλωνται εἰς τὸν αἰῶνα, καὶ οὐχ ἁρπάσει τις αὐτὰ ἐκ τῆς χειρός μου. **29** ὁ πατήρ μου ὃ δέδωκέν μοι πάντων μεῖζόν ἐστιν[8], καὶ οὐδεὶς

---

[6] **22** {C} τότε 𝔓^{66c, 75} B L W Ψ 33 1071 cop^{sa, bo mss} arm (eth) geo² ‖ δέ 𝔓^{66*} ℵ A D K X Δ Θ Π f¹³ 28 700 892 1009 1079 1195 1216 1230 1241 1242 1365 1546 1646 2148 2174 *Byz Lect* it^{aur, c, d, (e), f, ff2, (l), r1} vg syr^{p, h, pal} cop^{bo ms} goth Diatessaron Chrysostom^{1/2} Nonnus ‖ δὲ τότε 1321 cop^{sa mss, bo, ach2} ‖ *omit* f¹ 565 1010 1344 (*l*^{69m, 185m} *beginning of lection*) *l*^{70m, 1579m} it^{a, b} syr^s geo¹ Diatessaron^{a, i} Chrysostom^{1/2}

[7] **26** {B} ἐμῶν 𝔓^{66c, 75} ℵ B K L W Θ Π 33 1009 1079 1241 1546 it^{aur, c} vg cop^{sa, bo, ach2} arm geo^{1, B} ‖ ἐμῶν καθὼς εἶπον ὑμῖν (𝔓^{66*} *add* ὅτι) A D X Δ Ψ f¹ f¹³ 28 565 700 892 1010 1071 1195 1216 1230 1242 1344 1365 1646 2148 2174 *Byz Lect* *l*^{69m, 70m, 185m, 1579m} it^{(a), b, d, e, f, ff2, l, r1} syr^{s, p, h, pal} cop^{bo mss} goth eth geo^A Diatessaron^a (Chrysostom)

[8] **29** {D} ὃ δέδωκέν μοι πάντων μεῖζόν ἐστιν B* (B^c ὅς) ‖ ὃ δέδωκέν μοι μεῖζον πάντων ἐστίν it^{(a), (aur), b, c, (e), f, ff2, l, (r1)} vg cop^{bo} goth Ambrose Jerome ‖ ὃ δέδωκέν μοι πάντων μείζων ἐστίν ℵ (D δεδωκώς) L W Ψ ‖ ὃς δέδωκέν μοι μείζων πάντων ἐστίν K Δ Π f¹ 28 33 565 700 892 1009 1010 1071 1079 1195 1230 1241 1242 1365 1546 1646 2148 *Byz Lect* *l*^{69m, 70m, (76), 185m} (it^d πάντων μείζων) syr^{s, p, h} Adamantius Basil Diodore Chrysostom Nonnus Cyril ‖ ὃς δέδωκέν μοι μεῖζον πάντων ἐστίν A (X πάντων ἐστὶν μεῖζον) Θ syr^{pal} ‖ ὃς δέδωκέν μοι αὐτὰ μείζων πάντων ἐστίν f¹³ 1216

---

22 1 Macc 4.59   **23** τῇ...Σολομῶνος Ac 3.11; 5.12   **24** εἰ...παρρησίᾳ Lk 22.67   **25** τὰ ἔργα...ἐμοῦ Jn 5.36; 10.38   **26** ὑμεῖς οὐ πιστεύετε Jn 6.64; 8.45   **27** τὰ...ἀκούουσιν Jn 8.47; 10.3   **28** κἀγὼ...αἰώνιον Jn 17.2   κἀγὼ...αἰῶνα Jn 3.16   οὐ...χειρός μου Jn 6.39; 17.12; 18.9

δύναται ἁρπάζειν ἐκ τῆς χειρὸς τοῦ πατρός⁹.   30 ἐγὼ καὶ ὁ πατὴρ ἕν ἐσμεν.

31 Ἐβάστασαν πάλιν λίθους οἱ Ἰουδαῖοι ἵνα λιθάσωσιν αὐτόν. 32 ἀπεκρίθη αὐτοῖς ὁ Ἰησοῦς, Πολλὰ ἔργα καλὰ ἔδειξα ὑμῖν ἐκ τοῦ πατρός¹⁰· διὰ ποῖον αὐτῶν ἔργον ἐμὲ λιθάζετε; 33 ἀπεκρίθησαν αὐτῷ οἱ Ἰουδαῖοι, Περὶ καλοῦ ἔργου οὐ λιθάζομέν σε ἀλλὰ περὶ βλασφημίας, καὶ ὅτι σὺ ἄνθρωπος ὢν ποιεῖς σεαυτὸν θεόν. 34 ἀπεκρίθη αὐτοῖς [ὁ] Ἰησοῦς, Οὐκ ἔστιν γεγραμμένον ἐν τῷ νόμῳ ὑμῶν¹¹ ὅτι Ἐγὼ εἶπα, Θεοί ἐστε; 35 εἰ ἐκείνους εἶπεν θεοὺς πρὸς οὓς ὁ λόγος τοῦ θεοῦ ἐγένετο, ᵃκαὶ οὐ δύναται λυθῆναι ἡ γραφή,ᵃ 36 ὃν ὁ πατὴρ ἡγίασεν καὶ ἀπέστειλεν εἰς τὸν κόσμον ὑμεῖς λέγετε ὅτι Βλασφημεῖς, ὅτι εἶπον, Υἱὸς [τοῦ] θεοῦ εἰμι; 37 εἰ οὐ ποιῶ τὰ ἔργα τοῦ πατρός μου, μὴ πιστεύετέ μοι· 38 εἰ δὲ ποιῶ, κἂν ἐμοὶ μὴ πιστεύητε, τοῖς ἔργοις πιστεύετε,

---

(1344 οὕς) 2174 *l*⁵⁴⁷ cop^{sa,boᵐˢ,ach²} arm geo ‖ ὃς δέδωκέν μοι τὴν ἐξουσία[ν] μείζων πάντων ἐστίν *l*¹⁸⁴ ‖ ὃς ἔδωκέν μοι μείζων πάντων ἐστίν (p⁶⁶* omit μοι) p⁶⁶ᶜ M U Chrysostom

9 29 {C} πατρός p⁶⁶,⁷⁵ᵛⁱᵈ ℵ B L syr^{s,pal} cop^{boᵐˢ} Origen ‖ πατρός μου A D K W X Δ Θ Π Ψ *f*¹ *f*¹³ 28 33 565 700 892 1009 1010 1071 1079 1195 1216 1230 1241 1242 1344 1365 1546 1646 2148 2174 *Byz Lect* *l*⁶⁹ᵐ,⁷⁰ᵐ,¹⁸⁵ᵐ it^{a,aur,b,c,d,e,f,ff²,l,rl} vg syr^{p,h} cop^{sa,bo,ach²} goth arm geo Adamantius Basil Chrysostom Cyril ‖ *omit* τοῦ πατρός *l*⁵⁴⁷

10 32 {C} πατρός p⁴⁵ᵛⁱᵈ ℵ* B D Θ *l*⁶⁴ it^{d,e} syr^{s,pal} Hilary Athanasius ‖ πατρός μου p⁶⁶,⁷⁵ᵛⁱᵈ ℵᶜ A K L W X Δ Π Ψ *f*¹ *f*¹³ 28 33 565 700 892 1009 1010 1071 1079 1195 1216 1230 1241 1242 1344 1365 1546 1646 2148 2174 *Byz Lect* it^{a,aur,b,c,f,ff²,l,rl} vg syr^{p,h} cop^{sa,bo} goth arm geo Diatessaron Ambrosiaster Theodoret

11 34 {B} ὑμῶν p⁶⁶,⁷⁵ ℵᵃ A B K L W X Δ Π Ψ *f*¹ *f*¹³ 28 33 565 700 892 1009 1010 1071 1079 1195 1216 1230 1241 1242ᶜ 1344 1365 1546 1646 2148 2174 *Byz Lect* it^{a?f} vg syr^{p,h,pal} cop^{sa,bo,ach²} goth arm geo¹ Eusebius Athanasius Theodoret ‖ *omit* p⁴⁵ ℵ* D Θ 1242* *l*¹⁹ it^{aur,b,c,d,e,ff²,l,rl} syrˢ geo² Tertullian Cyprian Eusebius Hilary

---

ᵃ ᵃ 35 *a a* no dashes or parens: TR WH Bov Nes BF² AV ‖ *a* parens, *a* parens: RV ASV RSV TT ‖ *a* dash, *a* major: NEB Jer ‖ *a* dash, *a* dash: Zür Luth Seg

---

30 Jn 17.21   31 Jn 8.59   33 Περὶ...βλασφημίας Lv 24.16; Mt 26.65; Mk 14.64   σὺ...θεόν Jn 5.18   34 Ἐγὼ εἶπα, Θεοί ἐστε Ps 82.6   35 οὐ...γραφή Mt 5.18; Lk 16.17   36 λέγετε ...εἰμι Jn 5.17-20   38 Jn 14.10-11

---

one can snatch them away from the Father's care. 30 The Father and I are one."

31 Then the Jews once more picked up stones to throw at him. 32 Jesus said to them, "I have done many good works before you which the Father gave me to do; for which one of these do you want to stone me?" 33 The Jews answered back: "We do not want to stone you because of any good works, but because of the way in which you insult God! You are only a man, but you are trying to make yourself God!" 34 Jesus answered: "It is written in your own Law that God said, 'You are gods.' 35 We know that what the scripture says is true for ever; and God called them gods, those people to whom his message was given. 36 As for me, the Father chose me and sent me into the world. How, then, can you say that I insult God because I said that I am the Son of God? 37 Do not believe me, then, if I am not doing my Father's works. 38 But if I do them, even though you do not believe me, you should at least believe

my works, in order that you may know once and for all that the Father is in me, and I am in the Father.''

³⁹ Once more they tried to arrest him, but he slipped out of their hands.

⁴⁰ Jesus went back again across the Jordan river to the place where John had been baptizing, and stayed there. ⁴¹ Many people came to him. "John did no mighty works," they said, "but everything he said about this man was true." ⁴² And many people there believed in him.

The Death of Lazarus

11 A man named Lazarus, who lived in Bethany, became sick. Bethany was the town where Mary and her sister Martha lived. ² (This Mary was the one who poured the perfume on the Lord's feet and wiped them with her hair; it was her brother Lazarus who was sick.) ³ The sisters sent Jesus a message, "Lord, your dear friend is sick." ⁴ When Jesus heard it he said, "The final result of this sickness will not be the death of Lazarus; this has happened to bring glory to God, and will be the means by which the Son of God will receive glory."

⁵ Jesus loved Martha and her sister, and Lazarus. ⁶ When he received the news that Lazarus was sick, he stayed where he was for two more days. ⁷ Then he said to the disciples, "Let us go back to Judea." ⁸ "Teacher," the disciples answered, "just a short time ago the Jews wanted to stone you; and you plan

ἵνα γνῶτε καὶ γινώσκητε¹² ὅτι ἐν ἐμοὶ ὁ πατὴρ κἀγὼ ἐν τῷ πατρί. **39** Ἐζήτουν [οὖν] πάλιν αὐτὸν πιάσαι· καὶ ἐξῆλθεν ἐκ τῆς χειρὸς αὐτῶν.ᵇ

40 Καὶ ἀπῆλθεν πάλιν πέραν τοῦ Ἰορδάνου εἰς τὸν τόπον ὅπου ἦν Ἰωάννης τὸ πρῶτον βαπτίζων, καὶ ἔμεινεν ἐκεῖ. **41** καὶ πολλοὶ ἦλθον πρὸς αὐτὸν καὶ ἔλεγον ὅτι Ἰωάννης μὲν σημεῖον ἐποίησεν οὐδέν, πάντα δὲ ὅσα εἶπεν Ἰωάννης περὶ τούτου ἀληθῆ ἦν. **42** καὶ πολλοὶ ἐπίστευσαν εἰς αὐτὸν ἐκεῖ.

The Death of Lazarus

11 Ἦν δέ τις ἀσθενῶν, Λάζαρος ἀπὸ Βηθανίας, ἐκ τῆς κώμης Μαρίας καὶ Μάρθας τῆς ἀδελφῆς αὐτῆς. **2** ἦν δὲ Μαριὰμ ἡ ἀλείψασα τὸν κύριον μύρῳ καὶ ἐκμάξασα τοὺς πόδας αὐτοῦ ταῖς θριξὶν αὐτῆς, ἧς ὁ ἀδελφὸς Λάζαρος ἠσθένει. **3** ἀπέστειλαν οὖν αἱ ἀδελφαὶ πρὸς αὐτὸν λέγουσαι, Κύριε, ἴδε ὃν φιλεῖς ἀσθενεῖ. **4** ἀκούσας δὲ ὁ Ἰησοῦς εἶπεν, Αὕτη ἡ ἀσθένεια οὐκ ἔστιν πρὸς θάνατον ἀλλ' ὑπὲρ τῆς δόξης τοῦ θεοῦ, ἵνα δοξασθῇ ὁ υἱὸς τοῦ θεοῦ δι' αὐτῆς. **5** ἠγάπα δὲ ὁ Ἰησοῦς τὴν Μάρθαν καὶ τὴν ἀδελφὴν αὐτῆς καὶ τὸν Λάζαρον. **6** ὡς οὖν ἤκουσεν ὅτι ἀσθενεῖ, τότε μὲν ἔμεινεν ἐν ᾧ ἦν τόπῳ δύο ἡμέρας· **7** ἔπειτα μετὰ τοῦτο λέγει τοῖς μαθηταῖς, Ἄγωμεν εἰς τὴν Ἰουδαίαν πάλιν. **8** λέγουσιν αὐτῷ οἱ μαθηταί, Ῥαββί, νῦν ἐζήτουν σε λιθάσαι οἱ Ἰουδαῖοι,

---

¹² **38** {C} καὶ γινώσκητε 𝔭⁴⁵,⁶⁶,⁷⁵ B L (W X γινώσκετε) Θ f¹ 33 565 itʳˡ ᵛⁱᵈ syrᵖᵃˡ copˢᵃ,ᵇᵒ,ᵃᶜʰ² arm eth geo Hilary Athanasius Ps-Athanasius ∥ καὶ πιστεύσητε (ℵ πιστεύητε) A K Δ Π Ψ f¹³ 28 700 892 1009ᵛⁱᵈ 1010 1071 1079 1195 1216 1230 (1241 πιστεύετε) 1242 1344 1365 1546 1646 2148 2174 *Byz Lect* (*l*⁵⁴⁷) itᵃᵘʳ,ᶠ vg syrᵖ,ʰ goth Diatessaronᵃ,ⁱ,ⁿ Basil ∥ *omit* D itᵃ,ᵇ,ᶜ, ᵈ,ᵉ,ff²,¹ syrˢ Tertullian Cyprian

ᵇ **39** b major: TR WH Bov Nes BF² RV ASV RSV NEB TT Zür Jer Seg ∥ b minor: AV ∥ b none: Luth

38 ἐν ἐμοὶ...πατρί Jn 17.21   **39** Ἐζήτουν...πιάσαι Jn 7.30; 8.20   ἐξῆλθεν...αὐτῶν Lk 4.30; Jn 7.30   **40** πέραν...βαπτίζων Jn 1.28   **41** πάντα...ἀληθῆ ἦν Jn 1.29, 34; 3.27   **42** Jn 2.23; 7.31; 8.30; 11.45; 12.11, 42
11 1 Μαρίας...αὐτῆς Lk 10.38–39   **2** Μαριὰμ...αὐτῆς Jn 12.3   **3** ὃν φιλεῖς Jn 11.36   **4** ὑπὲρ τῆς δόξης...αὐτῆς Jn 9.3   **8** νῦν...Ἰουδαῖοι Jn 8.59; 10.31

καὶ πάλιν ὑπάγεις ἐκεῖ; 9 ἀπεκρίθη Ἰησοῦς, Οὐχὶ
δώδεκα ὧραί εἰσιν τῆς ἡμέρας; ἐάν τις περιπατῇ ἐν τῇ
ἡμέρᾳ, οὐ προσκόπτει, ὅτι τὸ φῶς τοῦ κόσμου τούτου
βλέπει· 10 ἐὰν δέ τις περιπατῇ ἐν τῇ νυκτί, προσκόπτει,
ὅτι τὸ φῶς οὐκ ἔστιν ἐν αὐτῷ. 11 ταῦτα εἶπεν, καὶ
μετὰ τοῦτο λέγει αὐτοῖς, Λάζαρος ὁ φίλος ἡμῶν κεκοίμηται, ἀλλὰ πορεύομαι ἵνα ἐξυπνίσω αὐτόν. 12 εἶπαν
οὖν οἱ μαθηταὶ αὐτῷ, Κύριε, εἰ κεκοίμηται σωθήσεται.
13 εἰρήκει δὲ ὁ Ἰησοῦς περὶ τοῦ θανάτου αὐτοῦ. ἐκεῖνοι
δὲ ἔδοξαν ὅτι περὶ τῆς κοιμήσεως τοῦ ὕπνου λέγει.
14 τότε οὖν εἶπεν αὐτοῖς ὁ Ἰησοῦς παρρησίᾳ, Λάζαρος
ἀπέθανεν, 15 καὶ χαίρω δι' ὑμᾶς, ἵνα πιστεύσητε, ὅτι
οὐκ ἤμην ἐκεῖ· ἀλλὰ ἄγωμεν πρὸς αὐτόν. 16 εἶπεν οὖν
Θωμᾶς ὁ λεγόμενος Δίδυμος τοῖς συμμαθηταῖς, Ἄγωμεν
καὶ ἡμεῖς ἵνα ἀποθάνωμεν μετ' αὐτοῦ.

Jesus the Resurrection and the Life

17 Ἐλθὼν οὖν ὁ Ἰησοῦς εὗρεν αὐτὸν τέσσαρας ἤδη
ἡμέρας ἔχοντα ἐν τῷ μνημείῳ. 18 ἦν δὲ ἡ Βηθανία
ἐγγὺς τῶν Ἱεροσολύμων ὡς ἀπὸ σταδίων δεκαπέντε.
19 πολλοὶ δὲ ἐκ τῶν Ἰουδαίων ἐληλύθεισαν πρὸς τὴν
Μάρθαν[1] καὶ Μαριὰμ ἵνα παραμυθήσωνται αὐτὰς περὶ
τοῦ ἀδελφοῦ. 20 ἡ οὖν Μάρθα ὡς ἤκουσεν ὅτι Ἰησοῦς
ἔρχεται ὑπήντησεν αὐτῷ· Μαριὰμ δὲ ἐν τῷ οἴκῳ ἐκαθέζετο. 21 εἶπεν οὖν ἡ Μάρθα πρὸς τὸν Ἰησοῦν, Κύριε,
εἰ ἧς ὧδε οὐκ ἂν ἀπέθανεν ὁ ἀδελφός μου· 22 [ἀλλὰ]
καὶ νῦν οἶδα ὅτι ὅσα ἂν αἰτήσῃ τὸν θεὸν δώσει σοι ὁ
θεός. 23 λέγει αὐτῇ ὁ Ἰησοῦς, Ἀναστήσεται ὁ ἀδελφός

---

[1] 19 {B} τὴν Μάρθαν 𝔭[66,75vid] ℵ B C* L W X 33 1010 1230 1241 Diatessaron[a,i,n] ‖ Μάρθαν D Andrew-Crete ‖ τὴν Μάρθαν or Μάρθαν it[a,(aur)],b,c,d,e,f,ff2,l,p,r1 vg syr[p,pal] cop[sa,bo,ach2] (arm Μάρθα) geo ‖ τὰς περὶ Μάρθαν 𝔭[45vid] A C³ K Δ Θ Π Ψ 0250 f¹ f¹³ 28 565 700 892 1000 1071 1079 1195 1216 1242 1344 1365 1546 1646 2148 2174 Byz Lect syr[hvid] goth

9-10 ἐάν τις περιπατῇ...αὐτῷ Jn 12.35   11 Λάζαρος...κεκοίμηται Mt 9.24; 27.52; Mk 5.39; Lk 8.52; Ac 7.60; 1 Cor 11.30   16 ἵνα ἀποθάνωμεν μετ' αὐτοῦ Mk 14.31; Ro 6.8   18 Mt 21.17   21 Κύριε...μου Jn 11.32

to go back there?" 9 Jesus said: "A
day has twelve hours, has it not? So
if a man walks in broad daylight he does
not stumble, because he sees the light
of this world. 10 But if he walks during
the night he stumbles, because there is
no light in him." 11 Jesus said this,
and then added, "Our friend Lazarus
has fallen asleep, but I will go wake
him up." 12 The disciples answered, "If
he is asleep, Lord, he will get well."
13 But Jesus meant that Lazarus had
died; they thought he meant natural
sleep. 14 So Jesus told them plainly,
"Lazarus is dead; 15 but for your sake
I am glad that I was not with him, so
you will believe. Let us go to him."
16 Thomas (called the Twin) said to his
fellow disciples, "Let us all go along
with the Teacher, that we may die with
him!"

Jesus the Resurrection and the Life

17 When Jesus arrived, he found that
Lazarus had been buried four days before. 18 Bethany was less than two miles
from Jerusalem, 19 and many Jews had
come to see Martha and Mary to comfort
them about their brother's death.

20 When Martha heard that Jesus was
coming, she went out to meet him; but
Mary stayed at home. 21 Martha said
to Jesus, "If you had been here, Lord,
my brother would not have died! 22 But
I know that even now God will give
you whatever you ask of him." 23 "Your
brother will be raised to life," Jesus told

her. ²⁴ "I know," she replied, "that he
will be raised to life on the last day."
²⁵ Jesus said to her: "I am the resurrection and the life. Whoever believes in me
will live, even though he dies; ²⁶ and
whoever lives and believes in me will
never die. Do you believe this?" ²⁷ "Yes,
Lord!" she answered. "I do believe that
you are the Messiah, the Son of God,
who was to come into the world."

Jesus Weeps

²⁸ After Martha said this she went
back and called her sister Mary privately.
"The Teacher is here," she told her,
"and is asking for you." ²⁹ When Mary
heard this she got up and hurried out
to meet him. ³⁰ (Jesus had not arrived
in the village yet, but was still in the
place where Martha had met him.)
³¹ The Jews who were in the house with
Mary comforting her followed her when
they saw her get up and hurry out.
They thought that she was going to
the grave, to weep there.

³² When Mary arrived where Jesus was
and saw him, she fell at his feet. "Lord,"
she said, "if you had been here, my

σου. **24** λέγει αὐτῷ ἡ Μάρθα, Οἶδα ὅτι ἀναστήσεται ἐν
τῇ ἀναστάσει ἐν τῇ ἐσχάτῃ ἡμέρᾳ. **25** εἶπεν αὐτῇ ὁ
Ἰησοῦς, Ἐγώ εἰμι ἡ ἀνάστασις καὶ ἡ ζωή². ὁ πιστεύων
εἰς ἐμὲ κἂν ἀποθάνῃ ζήσεται, **26** καὶ πᾶς ὁ ζῶν καὶ
πιστεύων εἰς ἐμὲ οὐ μὴ ἀποθάνῃ εἰς τὸν αἰῶνα· πιστεύεις τοῦτο; **27** λέγει αὐτῷ, Ναί, κύριε· ἐγὼ πεπίστευκα
ὅτι σὺ εἶ ὁ Χριστὸς ὁ υἱὸς τοῦ θεοῦ ὁ εἰς τὸν κόσμον
ἐρχόμενος.

Jesus Weeps

28 Καὶ ταῦτα εἰποῦσα ἀπῆλθεν καὶ ἐφώνησεν Μαριὰμ
τὴν ἀδελφὴν αὐτῆς[a] λάθρᾳ[a] εἰποῦσα, Ὁ διδάσκαλος
πάρεστιν καὶ φωνεῖ σε. **29** ἐκείνη δὲ ὡς ἤκουσεν ἠγέρθη
ταχὺ καὶ ἤρχετο πρὸς αὐτόν· **30** οὔπω δὲ ἐληλύθει ὁ
Ἰησοῦς εἰς τὴν κώμην, ἀλλ' ἦν ἔτι ἐν τῷ τόπῳ ὅπου
ὑπήντησεν αὐτῷ ἡ Μάρθα. **31** οἱ οὖν Ἰουδαῖοι οἱ ὄντες
μετ' αὐτῆς ἐν τῇ οἰκίᾳ καὶ παραμυθούμενοι αὐτήν,
ἰδόντες τὴν Μαριὰμ ὅτι ταχέως ἀνέστη καὶ ἐξῆλθεν,
ἠκολούθησαν αὐτῇ, δόξαντες³ ὅτι ὑπάγει εἰς τὸ μνημεῖον
ἵνα κλαύσῃ ἐκεῖ. **32** ἡ οὖν Μαριὰμ ὡς ἦλθεν ὅπου ἦν
Ἰησοῦς ἰδοῦσα αὐτὸν ἔπεσεν αὐτοῦ πρὸς τοὺς πόδας,
λέγουσα αὐτῷ, Κύριε, εἰ ἦς ὧδε οὐκ ἄν μου ἀπέθανεν

---

² **25** {B} καὶ ἡ ζωή 𝔭⁶⁶,⁷⁵ ℵ A B C D K L W X Δ Θ Π Ψ 0250 f¹ f¹³ 28
33 565 700 892 1009 1010 1071 1079 1195 1216 1230 1241 1242 1344 1365 1546
1646 2148 2174 *Byz Lect* itᵃᵘʳ,ᵇ,ᶜ,ᵈ,ᵉ,ᶠ,ff2,p,rl vg syrᵖ,ʰ,ᵖᵃˡ copˢᵃ,ᵇᵒ,ᵃᶜʰ²,ᶠᵃʸ goth
arm geo ∥ *omit* 𝔭⁴⁵ᵛⁱᵈ itˡ syrˢ Origen Cyprian Titus-Bostra

³ **31** {B} δόξαντες ℵ B C* D L W X f¹ f¹³ 33 700 1230 1241 1242 1365
1646 itᵈ syrˢ,ᵖ,ʰᵐᵍ copᵇᵒ arm eth geo Andrew-Crete ∥ δοξάζοντες 𝔭⁷⁵ ∥
λέγοντες 𝔭⁶⁶ A C² K Δ Θ Π Ψ 0250 28 892 1009 1010 1071 1079 1195 1216
1344 1546 2148 2174 *Byz Lect* itᵃ,ᵃᵘʳ,ᵇ,ᶜ,ᵉ,ᶠ,ff2,l,p,rl vg syrʰ,ᵖᵃˡ copˢᵃ,ᵃᶜʰ² goth
Diatessaronⁱ,ⁿ

---

[a][a] **28** *a* none, *a* none: TR WH Bov Nes BF² ∥ *a* none, *a* minor: AV RV ASV (Zür) (Luth) ∥
a minor, *a* none: RVᵐᵍ ASVᵐᵍ RSV NEB TT (Jer) Seg

---

24 Οἶδα...ἡμέρᾳ Dn 12.2; Jn 5.28–29; 6.39–40; Ac 24.15   **26** οὐ...αἰῶνα Jn 8.51   **27** ἐγὼ
πεπίστευκα...θεοῦ Jn 6.69   σὺ εἶ ὁ Χριστὸς...θεοῦ Mt 16.16   ὁ εἰς...ἐρχόμενος Jn 6.14
30 Jn 11.20   **32** Κύριε...ἀδελφός Jn 11.21

ὁ ἀδελφός. **33** Ἰησοῦς οὖν ὡς εἶδεν αὐτὴν κλαίουσαν καὶ τοὺς συνελθόντας αὐτῇ Ἰουδαίους κλαίοντας, ἐνεβριμήσατο τῷ πνεύματι καὶ ἐτάραξεν ἑαυτόν, **34** καὶ εἶπεν, Ποῦ τεθείκατε αὐτόν; λέγουσιν αὐτῷ, Κύριε, ἔρχου καὶ ἴδε. **35** ἐδάκρυσεν ὁ Ἰησοῦς. **36** ἔλεγον οὖν οἱ Ἰουδαῖοι, Ἴδε πῶς ἐφίλει αὐτόν. **37** τινὲς δὲ ἐξ αὐτῶν εἶπαν, Οὐκ ἐδύνατο οὗτος ὁ ἀνοίξας τοὺς ὀφθαλμοὺς τοῦ τυφλοῦ ποιῆσαι ἵνα καὶ οὗτος μὴ ἀποθάνῃ;

Lazarus Brought to Life

38 Ἰησοῦς οὖν πάλιν ἐμβριμώμενος ἐν ἑαυτῷ ἔρχεται εἰς τὸ μνημεῖον· ἦν δὲ σπήλαιον, καὶ λίθος ἐπέκειτο ἐπ' αὐτῷ. **39** λέγει ὁ Ἰησοῦς, Ἄρατε τὸν λίθον. λέγει αὐτῷ ἡ ἀδελφὴ τοῦ τετελευτηκότος Μάρθα, Κύριε, ἤδη ὄζει, τεταρταῖος γάρ ἐστιν. **40** λέγει αὐτῇ ὁ Ἰησοῦς, Οὐκ εἶπόν σοι ὅτι ἐὰν πιστεύσῃς ὄψῃ τὴν δόξαν τοῦ θεοῦ; **41** ἦραν οὖν τὸν λίθον. ὁ δὲ Ἰησοῦς ἦρεν τοὺς ὀφθαλμοὺς ἄνω καὶ εἶπεν, Πάτερ, εὐχαριστῶ σοι ὅτι ἤκουσάς μου.[b] **42** ἐγὼ δὲ ᾔδειν ὅτι πάντοτέ μου ἀκούεις· ἀλλὰ διὰ τὸν ὄχλον τὸν περιεστῶτα εἶπον, ἵνα πιστεύσωσιν ὅτι σύ με ἀπέστειλας. **43** καὶ ταῦτα εἰπὼν φωνῇ μεγάλῃ ἐκραύγασεν, Λάζαρε, δεῦρο ἔξω. **44** ἐξῆλθεν ὁ τεθνηκὼς δεδεμένος τοὺς πόδας καὶ τὰς χεῖρας κειρίαις, καὶ ἡ ὄψις αὐτοῦ σουδαρίῳ περιεδέδετο. λέγει αὐτοῖς ὁ Ἰησοῦς, Λύσατε αὐτὸν καὶ ἄφετε αὐτὸν ὑπάγειν.

The Plot to Kill Jesus
(Mt 26.1–5; Mk 14.1–2; Lk 22.1–2)

45 Πολλοὶ οὖν ἐκ τῶν Ἰουδαίων, οἱ ἐλθόντες πρὸς τὴν Μαριὰμ καὶ θεασάμενοι ἃ ἐποίησεν[4], ἐπίστευσαν εἰς

[4] **45** {B} ἃ ἐποίησεν 𝔓[6,45] ℵ A* K L W X Δ Θ Π Ψ 0250 f[13] 28 33 700

[b] **41** b major: TR Bov Nes BF² AV RV ASV RSV NEB TT Zür Luth Jer Seg ‖ b minor: WH

35 Lk 19.41   **36** Ἴδε...αὐτόν Jn 11.3   **37** οὗτος...τυφλοῦ Jn 9.6   **38** ἔρχεται... αὐτῷ Mt 27.60; Mk 15.46; Lk 23.53; 24.2; Jn 20.1   **42** διὰ τὸν ὄχλον...εἶπον Jn 12.30 ἵνα... ἀπέστειλας Jn 6.29; 17.8, 21   **44** δεδεμένος...περιεδέδετο Jn 20.6–7   **45** Lk 16.31; Jn 2.23; 7.31; 8.30; 10.42; 12.11, 42

brother would not have died!" **33** Jesus saw her weeping, and the Jews who had come with her weeping also; his heart was touched, and he was deeply moved. **34** "Where have you buried him?" he asked them. "Come and see, Lord," they answered. **35** Jesus wept. **36** So the Jews said, "See how much he loved him!" **37** But some of them said, "He opened the blind man's eyes, didn't he? Could he not have kept Lazarus from dying?"

Lazarus Brought to Life

38 Deeply moved once more, Jesus went to the tomb, which was a cave with a stone placed at the entrance. **39** "Take the stone away!" Jesus ordered. Martha, the dead man's sister, answered, "There will be a bad smell, Lord. He has been buried four days!" **40** Jesus said to her, "Didn't I tell you that you would see God's glory if you believed?" **41** They took the stone away. Jesus looked up and said: "I thank you, Father, that you listen to me. **42** I know that you always listen to me, but I say this because of the people here, so they will believe that you sent me." **43** After he had said this he called out in a loud voice, "Lazarus, come out!" **44** The dead man came out, his hands and feet wrapped in grave cloths, and a cloth around his face. "Untie him," Jesus told them, "and let him go."

The Plot against Jesus
(Also Matt 26.1–5; Mark 14.1–2; Luke 22.1–2)

45 Many of the Jews who had come to visit Mary saw what Jesus did, and believed in him. ⁴⁶ But some of them returned to the Pharisees and told them what Jesus had done. ⁴⁷ So the Pharisees and the chief priests met with the Council and said: "What shall we do? All the mighty works this man is doing! ⁴⁸ If we let him go on in this way everyone will believe in him, and the Roman authorities will take action and destroy the Temple and our whole nation!" ⁴⁹ One of them, named Caiaphas, who was High Priest that year, said: "You do not know a thing! ⁵⁰ Don't you realize that it is better for you to have one man die for the people, instead of the whole nation being destroyed?" ⁵¹ (Actually, he did not say this of his own accord; rather, as he was High Priest that year, he was prophesying that Jesus was about to die for the Jewish people, ⁵² and not only for them, but also to bring together into one body all the scattered children of God.) ⁵³ So from that day on the Jewish authorities made plans to kill Jesus. ⁵⁴ Therefore Jesus did not travel openly in Judea, but left and went to a place near the desert, to a town named Ephraim, where he stayed with the disciples.

αὐτόν· **46** τινὲς δὲ ἐξ αὐτῶν ἀπῆλθον πρὸς τοὺς Φαρισαίους καὶ εἶπαν αὐτοῖς ἃ ἐποίησεν Ἰησοῦς. **47** συνήγαγον οὖν οἱ ἀρχιερεῖς καὶ οἱ Φαρισαῖοι συνέδριον, καὶ ἔλεγον, Τί ποιοῦμεν,ᶜ ὅτι οὗτος ὁ ἄνθρωπος πολλὰ ποιεῖ σημεῖα;ᶜ **48** ἐὰν ἀφῶμεν αὐτὸν οὕτως, πάντες πιστεύσουσιν εἰς αὐτόν, καὶ ἐλεύσονται οἱ Ῥωμαῖοι καὶ ἀροῦσιν ἡμῶν καὶ τὸν τόπον καὶ τὸ ἔθνος. **49** εἷς δέ τις ἐξ αὐτῶν Καϊάφας, ἀρχιερεὺς ὢν τοῦ ἐνιαυτοῦ ἐκείνου, εἶπεν αὐτοῖς, Ὑμεῖς οὐκ οἴδατε οὐδέν, **50** οὐδὲ λογίζεσθε ὅτι συμφέρει ὑμῖν⁵ ἵνα εἷς ἄνθρωπος ἀποθάνῃ ὑπὲρ τοῦ λαοῦ καὶ μὴ ὅλον τὸ ἔθνος ἀπόληται. **51** τοῦτο δὲ ἀφ᾽ ἑαυτοῦ οὐκ εἶπεν, ἀλλὰ ἀρχιερεὺς ὢν τοῦ ἐνιαυτοῦ ἐκείνου ἐπροφήτευσεν ὅτι ἔμελλεν Ἰησοῦς ἀποθνῄσκειν ὑπὲρ τοῦ ἔθνους, **52** καὶ οὐχ ὑπὲρ τοῦ ἔθνους μόνον ἀλλ᾽ ἵνα καὶ τὰ τέκνα τοῦ θεοῦ τὰ διεσκορπισμένα συναγάγῃ εἰς ἕν. **53** ἀπ᾽ ἐκείνης οὖν τῆς ἡμέρας ἐβουλεύσαντο ἵνα ἀποκτείνωσιν αὐτόν.

54 Ὁ οὖν Ἰησοῦς οὐκέτι παρρησίᾳ περιεπάτει ἐν τοῖς Ἰουδαίοις, ἀλλὰ ἀπῆλθεν ἐκεῖθεν εἰς τὴν χώραν ἐγγὺς τῆς ἐρήμου, εἰς Ἐφραὶμ λεγομένην πόλιν, κἀκεῖ διέτριβεν μετὰ τῶν μαθητῶν.

---

892 1009 1071 1079 1195 1216 1230 1241 1242 1344 1365 1546 1646 2148 2174 *Byz Lect* itᵃ,ᵃᵘʳ,ᵇ,ᶜ,ᶠ,ff²,ˡ,π,ʳˡ vg syrˢ?ᵖ?ʰ,ᵖᵃˡ? copᵇᵒ geo? Origen Andrew-Crete ∥ ὃ ἐποίησεν 𝔭⁶⁶* ᵛⁱᵈ (𝔭⁶⁶ᶜ ὅσα) Aᶜ B C* D *f*¹ 1010 itᵈ,⁽ᵉ⁾ syrˢ?ᵖ?ᵖᵃˡ? copˢᵃ,ᵃᶜʰ² goth arm eth geo? ∥ ὃ ἐποίησεν σημεῖον C²

⁵ **50** {B} ὑμῖν 𝔭⁴⁵,⁶⁶ B D L X 1010 1241 1242 *l*¹⁸⁴,²¹⁰,²¹⁹,¹²³¹ itᵃ,ᵃᵘʳ,ᵇ,ᵈ,ᵉ,ff²,ˡ vgᶜˡ copᵇᵒ Diatessaronⁿ Origenˡᵃᵗ Chrysostom ∥ ἡμῖν A K W Δ Θ Π Ψ 065 0250 *f*¹ *f*¹³ 28 33 565 700 892 1009 1071 1079 1195 1216 1230 1344 1365 1546 1646 2148 2174 *Byz Lect* itᶜ,ᶠ,ʳˡ vgʷʷ syrˢ,ᵖ,ʰ,ᵖᵃˡ copˢᵃ,ᵃᶜʰ² arm eth geo Diatessaronᵃ,ᶠ,ⁱ Origen Eustathius Cyril ∥ *omit* ℵ copˢᵃᵐˢ,ᵇᵒᵐˢ Chrysostom Theodoret

---

ᶜ ᶜ **47** ᶜ minor, ᶜ question: (WH) Bov Nes BF² ∥ ᶜ question, ᶜ statement: TR AV RV ASV RSV NEB TT Zür Luth Jer Seg

---

49–50 Jn 18.14 **52** Jn 10.16 ἵνα…συναγάγῃ εἰς ἕν Jn 17.21 **53** ἐβουλεύσαντο… αὐτόν Mt 14.5; Jn 5.18; 7.1, 25; 8.37, 40 **54** Ὁ…Ἰουδαίοις Jn 7.1 κἀκεῖ…μαθητῶν Jn 2.12; 3.22

55 Ἦν δὲ ἐγγὺς τὸ πάσχα τῶν Ἰουδαίων, καὶ ἀνέβησαν πολλοὶ εἰς Ἱεροσόλυμα ἐκ τῆς χώρας πρὸ τοῦ πάσχα ἵνα ἁγνίσωσιν ἑαυτούς. **56** ἐζήτουν οὖν τὸν Ἰησοῦν καὶ ἔλεγον μετ᾽ ἀλλήλων ἐν τῷ ἱερῷ ἑστηκότες, Τί δοκεῖ ὑμῖν;[d] ὅτι οὐ μὴ ἔλθῃ εἰς τὴν ἑορτήν;[d] **57** δεδώκεισαν δὲ οἱ ἀρχιερεῖς καὶ οἱ Φαρισαῖοι ἐντολὴν ἵνα ἐάν τις γνῷ ποῦ ἐστιν μηνύσῃ, ὅπως πιάσωσιν αὐτόν.

The Anointing at Bethany
(Mt 26.6–13; Mk 14.3–9)

12 Ὁ οὖν Ἰησοῦς πρὸ ἓξ ἡμερῶν τοῦ πάσχα ἦλθεν εἰς Βηθανίαν, ὅπου ἦν Λάζαρος[1], ὃν ἤγειρεν ἐκ νεκρῶν Ἰησοῦς. **2** ἐποίησαν οὖν αὐτῷ δεῖπνον ἐκεῖ, καὶ ἡ Μάρθα διηκόνει, ὁ δὲ Λάζαρος εἷς ἦν ἐκ τῶν ἀνακειμένων σὺν αὐτῷ. **3** ἡ οὖν Μαριὰμ λαβοῦσα λίτραν μύρου νάρδου πιστικῆς πολυτίμου ἤλειψεν τοὺς πόδας τοῦ Ἰησοῦ καὶ ἐξέμαξεν ταῖς θριξὶν αὐτῆς τοὺς πόδας αὐτοῦ· ἡ δὲ οἰκία ἐπληρώθη ἐκ τῆς ὀσμῆς τοῦ μύρου. **4** λέγει δὲ Ἰούδας ὁ Ἰσκαριώτης εἷς τῶν μαθητῶν αὐτοῦ[2], [a]ὁ

55 The Jewish Feast of Passover was near, and many people went up from the country to Jerusalem, to perform the ceremony of purification before the feast. **56** They were looking for Jesus, and as they gathered in the Temple they asked one another, "What do you think? Surely he will not come to the feast, will he?" **57** The chief priests and the Pharisees had given orders that if anyone knew where Jesus was he must report it, so they could arrest him.

Jesus Anointed at Bethany
(Also Matt. 26.6–13; Mark 14.3–9)

12 Six days before the Passover, Jesus went to Bethany, where Lazarus lived, the man Jesus had raised from death. **2** They had prepared a dinner for him there, and Martha helped serve it, while Lazarus sat at the table with Jesus. **3** Then Mary took a whole pint of a very expensive perfume made of nard, poured it on Jesus' feet, and wiped them with her hair. The sweet smell of the perfume filled the whole house. **4** One of Jesus' disciples, Judas Iscariot —

---

[1] **1** {B} Λάζαρος א B L W X it[a,aur,c,e,rl] syr[p,pal] cop[sa,boms] eth Diatessaron[a] Chrysostom Nonnus ‖ Λάζαρος ὁ τεθνηκώς 𝔭[66] A D K Δ Θ Π Ψ 065 0217[vid] 0250 f[1] f[13] 28 33 565 700 892 1009 1010 1071 1079 1195 1216 1230 1241 1242 1344 1365 1546 1646 (2148* *omit* ὁ) 2148[c] 2174 *Byz Lect* it[b,d,f,ff2] vg syr[(s),h] cop[bo,ach,ach2] goth arm geo Paschal Chronicle

[2] **4** {C} Ἰούδας ὁ Ἰσκαριώτης εἷς τῶν μαθητῶν αὐτοῦ 𝔭[66,75vid] B L W 33 eth ‖ Ἰούδας ὁ Ἰσκαριώτης εἷς ἐκ τῶν μαθητῶν αὐτοῦ א 0217[vid] 1071 1241 syr[(s),p,pal] cop[sa,ach2] ‖ εἷς ἐκ τῶν μαθητῶν αὐτοῦ, Ἰούδας ὁ Ἰσκαριώτης f[1] (l[76] *omit* ὁ) l[185vid] vg[cl] (vg[ww] *Scariotis*) cop[bo] (arm *omit* αὐτοῦ) geo[1] (Nonnus) Augustine Cyril ‖ εἷς ἐκ τῶν μαθητῶν αὐτοῦ Ἰούδας Σίμωνος Ἰσκαριώτης A (K *omit* εἷς) X Δ Θ Π (Ψ Ἰσκαριώτου) 065 f[13] 28 (565 ὁ Σίμωνος) 700 892 1009 1010 1079 1216 1230 1242[c] 1365 1546 1646 2174 *Byz*

d d **56** *d* question, *d* question: WH Bov Nes BF[2] RV ASV RSV TT Zür Luth Jer Seg ‖ *d* minor, *d* question: TR AV ‖ *d* question, *d* statement: NEB

a a **4** *a a* no dashes or parens: TR WH Bov Nes BF[2] AV RV ASV TT Zür Luth Jer Seg ‖ *a* parens; *a* parens: RSV ‖ *a* dash, *a* dash: NEB

55 Ἦν...Ἰουδαίων Jn 2.12; 6.4   ἀνέβησαν...ἑαυτούς 2 Chr 30.17   **56** Jn 7.11
12 1 ἦλθεν...Ἰησοῦς Jn 11.1, 43–44   **2** Μάρθα διηκόνει Lk 10.40   **3** λαβοῦσα...αὐτοῦ Lk 7.37–38   **4** Ἰούδας...παραδιδόναι Jn 6.71

the one who would betray him — said,
5 "Why wasn't this perfume sold for
three hundred dollars and the money
given to the poor?" 6 He said this, not
because he cared for the poor, but because he was a thief; he carried the
money bag and would help himself from
it. 7 But Jesus said: "Leave her alone!
Let her keep what she has for the day of
my burial. 8 You will always have poor
people with you, but I will not be with
you always."

The Plot against Lazarus

9 A large crowd of the Jews heard that
Jesus was in Bethany, so they went
there; they went, not only because of
Jesus, but also to see Lazarus, whom
Jesus had raised from death. 10 So the
chief priests made plans to kill Lazarus
too; 11 because on his account many
Jews were leaving their leaders and believing in Jesus.

μέλλων αὐτὸν παραδιδόναι,ᵃ 5 Διὰ τί τοῦτο τὸ μύρον
οὐκ ἐπράθη τριακοσίων δηναρίων καὶ ἐδόθη πτωχοῖς;
6 εἶπεν δὲ τοῦτο οὐχ ὅτι περὶ τῶν πτωχῶν ἔμελεν αὐτῷ
ἀλλ' ὅτι κλέπτης ἦν καὶ τὸ γλωσσόκομον ἔχων τὰ
βαλλόμενα ἐβάσταζεν. 7 εἶπεν οὖν ὁ Ἰησοῦς, "Ἄφες
αὐτήν,ᵇ ἵνα εἰς τὴν ἡμέραν τοῦ ἐνταφιασμοῦ μου τηρήσῃ
αὐτό· 8 τοὺς πτωχοὺς γὰρ πάντοτε ἔχετε μεθ' ἑαυτῶν,
ἐμὲ δὲ οὐ πάντοτε ἔχετε.³

The Plot against Lazarus

9 Ἔγνω οὖν [ὁ] ὄχλος πολὺς ἐκ τῶν Ἰουδαίων⁴ ὅτι
ἐκεῖ ἐστιν, καὶ ἦλθον οὐ διὰ τὸν Ἰησοῦν μόνον ἀλλ'
ἵνα καὶ τὸν Λάζαρον ἴδωσιν ὃν ἤγειρεν ἐκ νεκρῶν. 10 ἐβουλεύσαντο δὲ οἱ ἀρχιερεῖς ἵνα καὶ τὸν Λάζαρον ἀποκτείνωσιν, 11 ὅτι πολλοὶ δι' αὐτὸν ὑπῆγον τῶν Ἰουδαίων
καὶ ἐπίστευον εἰς τὸν Ἰησοῦν.

---

l⁶⁹ (itᶠ *Schariotes*) syrʰ (goth ὁ Ἰσκαριώτης) geo² ∥ εἷς ἐκ τῶν μαθητῶν
αὐτοῦ Ἰούδας Σίμων ὁ Ἰσκαριώτης 1195 1242* 1344 2148 l²¹¹,¹¹²⁷ (it⁽ᵃ⁾,ʳˡ
Scarioth, it⁽ᵃᵘʳ⁾,ᵇ,⁽ff²⁾ *Scariotes*, itᶜ,⁽ᵉ⁾ *Scariotha*) copᵇᵒᵐˢˢ ∥ εἷς ἐκ τῶν
μαθητῶν αὐτοῦ Ἰούδας ἀπὸ Καρυώτου D itᵈ ∥ Ἰούδας Ἰσκαριώτης copᵇᵒᵐˢ

³ 8 {C} *include verse 8* p⁶⁶ ℵ A B K (L Θ *omit* γάρ) W X Δ Π Ψ 065
f¹ f¹³ 28 (33 ἔχετε πάντοτε) 565 700 892 1009 1010 1071 1079 1195 1216 1230
1241 1242 1344 1365 1546 1646 2148 2174 *Byz Lect* itᵃ,ᵃᵘʳ,ᵇ,ᶜ,ᵉ,ᶠ,ff²,ʳˡ vg syrᵖ,ʰ,⁽ᵖᵃˡ⁾
copˢᵃ,ᵇᵒ,ᵃᶜʰ² goth arm geo ∥ *omit* μεθ' ἑαυτῶν...ἔχετε p⁷⁵ ∥ *omit verse 8* D
itᵈ syrˢ ∥ *omit verses 7 and 8* 0250

⁴ 9 {C} Ἔγνω οὖν ὁ ὄχλος πολὺς ἐκ τῶν Ἰουδαίων ℵ B* L 28 892
1241 1242 1344 (1365 *omit* ἐκ) 1546 1646ᶜ l¹¹²⁷* (l¹¹²⁷ᶜ *omit* ὁ) ∥ Ἔγνω οὖν
ὄχλος πολὺς ἐκ τῶν Ἰουδαίων (p⁶⁶* *omit* ἐκ) p⁷⁵ A B³ K X Δ Θ Π Ψ 065
f¹ (f¹³ *omit* πολύς) 33 565 (700 ἐκ τῶν Ἰουδαίων ὄχλος πολύς) 1009 1071
1079 1195 1216 1230 1646* 2148 2174 *Byz Lect* goth Diatessaronᵃ,ⁱ ∥ Ἔγνω
οὖν ὄχλος (*or* ὁ ὄχλος) πολὺς ἐκ τῶν Ἰουδαίων itᵃᵘʳ,ᶠ,⁽ʳˡ⁾ vg syr⁽ˢ⁾,ʰ,ᵖᵃˡ
copᵇᵒᵐˢˢ (copˢᵃ,ᵇᵒᵐˢˢ,ᵃᶜʰ δέ *for* οὖν) (copᵇᵒᵐˢˢ *omit* πολύς) arm geo ∥ Ἔγνω
οὖν ὁ ὄχλος ὁ πολὺς τῶν Ἰουδαίων p⁶⁶ᶜ W 0250 (1010 ἐκ τῶν) ∥ Ὄχλος
δὲ πολὺς ἐκ τῶν Ἰουδαίων ἤκουσαν D itᵃ,ᵇ,ᶜ,ᵈ,ᵉ,ff² syrᵖ copˢᵃᵐˢˢ,ᵃᶜʰ²

ᵇ 7 b minor: WH Bov Nes BF² RVᵐᵍ ASVᵐᵍ RSV (NEB) TT (Luth) Jer ∥ b none: RV ASV
Seg ∥ different text: TR AV Zür Segᵐᵍ

5 τί...πτωχοῖς Mt 19.21; Mk 10.21; Lk 18.22　　7 ἵνα...τηρήσῃ αὐτό Jn 19.40
8 τοὺς πτωχοὺς...ἑαυτῶν Dt 15.11　　9 ἵνα...νεκρῶν Jn 11.43–44　　11 Jn 11.45

The Triumphal Entry into Jerusalem
(Mt 21.1–11; Mk 11.1–11; Lk 19.28–40)

12 Τῇ ἐπαύριον ὁ ὄχλος πολὺς ὁ[5] ἐλθὼν εἰς τὴν ἑορτήν, ἀκούσαντες ὅτι ἔρχεται ὁ Ἰησοῦς εἰς Ἱεροσόλυμα, **13** ἔλαβον τὰ βαΐα τῶν φοινίκων καὶ ἐξῆλθον εἰς ὑπάντησιν αὐτῷ, καὶ ἐκραύγαζον,

> Ὡσαννά·
> εὐλογημένος ὁ ἐρχόμενος ἐν ὀνόματι κυρίου,
>> καὶ ὁ βασιλεὺς τοῦ Ἰσραήλ.

14 εὑρὼν δὲ ὁ Ἰησοῦς ὀνάριον ἐκάθισεν ἐπ' αὐτό, καθώς ἐστιν γεγραμμένον,

15   **Μὴ φοβοῦ, θυγάτηρ Σιών·**
> ἰδοὺ ὁ βασιλεύς σου ἔρχεται,
>> καθήμενος ἐπὶ πῶλον ὄνου.

16 ταῦτα οὐκ ἔγνωσαν αὐτοῦ οἱ μαθηταὶ τὸ πρῶτον, ἀλλ' ὅτε ἐδοξάσθη Ἰησοῦς τότε ἐμνήσθησαν ὅτι ταῦτα ἦν ἐπ' αὐτῷ γεγραμμένα καὶ ταῦτα ἐποίησαν αὐτῷ. **17** ἐμαρτύρει οὖν ὁ ὄχλος ὁ ὢν μετ' αὐτοῦ ὅτε[6] τὸν Λάζαρον ἐφώνησεν ἐκ τοῦ μνημείου καὶ ἤγειρεν αὐτὸν ἐκ νεκρῶν. **18** διὰ τοῦτο [καὶ] ὑπήντησεν αὐτῷ ὁ ὄχλος ὅτι ἤκουσαν τοῦτο αὐτὸν πεποιηκέναι τὸ σημεῖον. **19** οἱ οὖν Φαρισαῖοι εἶπαν πρὸς ἑαυτούς, Θεωρεῖτε ὅτι οὐκ ὠφελεῖτε οὐδέν·[c] ἴδε ὁ κόσμος ὀπίσω αὐτοῦ ἀπῆλθεν.

---

5 12 {C} ὁ ὄχλος πολὺς ὁ 𝔭66* B L f13 1241 syrs copbo ∥ ὁ ὄχλος ὁ πολὺς ὁ 𝔭66 Θ ∥ ὄχλος πολὺς ὁ 𝔭vid אc A D K W X Π Ψ f1 28 700 1009 1010 1071 1079 1216 1230vid 1242 1344 1365 1546 1646 2148 2174 Byz Lect syrp,h,pal copsa,(boms),ach2 goth Origen ∥ ὄχλος πολύς א* Δ 565 892 1195 (itff2) ∥ turbae multae quae ita,c,e ∥ a great multitude which itaur,(b),d,f,(l),rl vg arm geo

6 17 {C} ὅτε א A B W X Δ Θ Ψ 0250 f1 f13 28 565 700 892 1009 1010 1071 1195 1216 1241 1242 1344 1365 1646 2148 2174 Byz Lect itaur,f vg syrh,pal goth eth geo1 Apollinaris ∥ ὅτι 𝔭66 D K L Π 1079 1230 1546 ita,b,c,d,e,ff2,rl syrs,p copsa,bo,ach2 arm geo2 Diatessarona Chrysostom Cyril

---

c **19** *c* minor: WH Bov Nes BF2 RV ASV RSV NEB Luth Jer Seg ∥ *c* question: TR AV ∥ *c* major: TT Zür

13 Ὡσαννά...κυρίου Ps 118.25–26   ὁ βασιλεὺς τοῦ Ἰσραήλ Mt 27.42; Mk 15.32; Jn 1.49
15 Μή...ὄνου Zch 9.9   **16** ὅτε...ἐποίησαν αὐτῷ Jn 2.22   **17** ὅτε...νεκρῶν Jn 11.43–44
19 ἴδε...ἀπῆλθεν Jn 11.48

The Triumphant Entry into Jerusalem
(Also Matt. 21.1–11; Mark 11.1–11; Luke 19.28–40)

[12] The next day the large crowd that had come to the Passover Feast heard that Jesus was coming to Jerusalem. [13] So they took branches from palm trees and went out to meet him, shouting: "Praise God! God bless him who comes in the name of the Lord! God bless the King of Israel!" [14] Jesus found a donkey and sat on it, just as the scripture says:

[15] "Do not be afraid, city of Zion!
> Now your King is coming to you,
> Riding a young donkey."

[16] His disciples did not understand this at the time; but when Jesus had been raised to glory they remembered that the scripture said this, and that they had done this for him. [17] The crowd that had been with Jesus when he called Lazarus out of the grave and raised him from death had reported what had happened. [18] That was why the crowd met him — because they heard that he had done this mighty work. [19] The Pharisees then said to each other, "You see, we are not succeeding at all! Look, the whole world is following him!"

Some Greeks Seek Jesus

20 Some Greeks were among those who went to Jerusalem to worship during the feast. 21 They came to Philip (he was from Bethsaida, in Galilee) and said, "Sir, we want to see Jesus." 22 Philip went and told Andrew, and the two of them went and told Jesus. 23 Jesus answered them: "The hour has now come for the Son of Man to be given great glory. 24 I tell you the truth: a grain of wheat is no more than a single grain unless it is dropped into the ground and dies. If it does die, then it produces many grains. 25 Whoever loves his own life will lose it; whoever hates his own life in this world will keep it for life eternal. 26 Whoever wants to serve me must follow me, so that my servant will be with me where I am. My Father will honor him who serves me."

Jesus Speaks about His Death

27 "Now my heart is troubled — and what shall I say? Shall I say, 'Father, do not let this hour come upon me'? But that is why I came, to go through this hour of suffering. 28 O Father, bring glory to your name!" Then a voice spoke from heaven, "I have brought glory to it, and I will do so again."

Some Greeks Seek Jesus

20 ῏Ησαν δὲ ῞Ελληνές τινες ἐκ τῶν ἀναβαινόντων ἵνα προσκυνήσωσιν ἐν τῇ ἑορτῇ· 21 οὗτοι οὖν προσῆλθον Φιλίππῳ τῷ ἀπὸ Βηθσαϊδὰ τῆς Γαλιλαίας, καὶ ἠρώτων αὐτὸν λέγοντες, Κύριε, θέλομεν τὸν ᾿Ιησοῦν ἰδεῖν. 22 ἔρχεται ὁ Φίλιππος καὶ λέγει τῷ ᾿Ανδρέᾳ· ἔρχεται ᾿Ανδρέας καὶ Φίλιππος καὶ λέγουσιν τῷ ᾿Ιησοῦ. 23 ὁ δὲ ᾿Ιησοῦς ἀποκρίνεται αὐτοῖς λέγων, ᾿Ελήλυθεν ἡ ὥρα ἵνα δοξασθῇ ὁ υἱὸς τοῦ ἀνθρώπου. 24 ἀμὴν ἀμὴν λέγω ὑμῖν, ἐὰν μὴ ὁ κόκκος τοῦ σίτου πεσὼν εἰς τὴν γῆν ἀποθάνῃ, αὐτὸς μόνος μένει· ἐὰν δὲ ἀποθάνῃ, πολὺν καρπὸν φέρει. 25 ὁ φιλῶν τὴν ψυχὴν αὐτοῦ ἀπολλύει αὐτήν, καὶ ὁ μισῶν τὴν ψυχὴν αὐτοῦ ἐν τῷ κόσμῳ τούτῳ εἰς ζωὴν αἰώνιον φυλάξει αὐτήν. 26 ἐὰν ἐμοί τις διακονῇ, ἐμοὶ ἀκολουθείτω, καὶ ὅπου εἰμὶ ἐγὼ ἐκεῖ καὶ ὁ διάκονος ὁ ἐμὸς ἔσται· ἐάν τις ἐμοὶ διακονῇ τιμήσει αὐτὸν ὁ πατήρ.

The Son of Man Must be Lifted Up

27 Νῦν ἡ ψυχή μου τετάρακται.[d] καὶ τί εἴπω;[d] Πάτερ, σῶσόν με ἐκ τῆς ὥρας ταύτης;[d] ἀλλὰ διὰ τοῦτο ἦλθον εἰς τὴν ὥραν ταύτην. 28 πάτερ, δόξασόν σου τὸ ὄνομα[7]. ἦλθεν οὖν φωνὴ ἐκ τοῦ οὐρανοῦ, Καὶ ἐδόξασα

---

[7] 28 {B} τὸ ὄνομα 𝔭66,75 ℵ A B K W Δ Θ Π Ψ 0250 28 565 700 892 1009 1010 1079 1195 1216 1230 1242 1344 1365 1546 1646 2148 2174 Byz Lect l698,m,70m, 211m,883m,1579m ita,aur,b,c,e,f,ff2,l,rl vg syrs,p,h,pal copsa,boms,ach2 goth geo Tertullian ‖ τὸν υἱόν (see 17.1) L X f1 f13 33 1071 1241 syrhmg copbo arm eth Origenlat Athanasius (Nonnus) ‖ τὸ ὄνομα ἐν τῇ δόξῃ ᾗ εἶχον παρὰ σοὶ πρὸ τοῦ τὸν κόσμον γένεσθαι (see 17.5) D itd

---

d d d 27 d major, d question, d question: (RVmg) (ASVmg) RSVed Zür Luth Jer Seg ‖ d major, d minor, d question: RSVed NEBmg Segmg1 ‖ d minor, d question, d major: TR WH Bov Nes BF2 AV RV ASV NEB TT (Segmg2)

---

21 Φιλίππῳ...Βηθσαϊδά Jn 1.44   θέλομεν...ἰδεῖν Lk 19.3; 23.8   23 ᾿Ελήλυθεν... ἀνθρώπου Jn 13.31–32; 17.1   24 1 Cor 15.36   25 Mt 10.39; 16.25; Mk 8.35; Lk 9.24; 17.33   26 ὅπου...ἔσται Jn 14.3; 17.24   27 ἡ...τετάρακται Ps 6.3; 42.5, 11; Mt 26.38; Mk 14.34   28 φωνὴ...οὐρανοῦ Mt 3.17; 17.5; Mk 1.11; 9.7; Lk 3.22; 9.35

καὶ πάλιν δοξάσω. **29** ὁ οὖν ὄχλος ὁ ἑστὼς καὶ ἀκούσας ἔλεγεν βροντὴν γεγονέναι· ἄλλοι ἔλεγον, Ἄγγελος αὐτῷ λελάληκεν. **30** ἀπεκρίθη καὶ εἶπεν Ἰησοῦς, Οὐ δι' ἐμὲ ἡ φωνὴ αὕτη γέγονεν ἀλλὰ δι' ὑμᾶς. **31** νῦν κρίσις ἐστὶν τοῦ κόσμου τούτου, νῦν ὁ ἄρχων τοῦ κόσμου τούτου ἐκβληθήσεται ἔξω· **32** κἀγὼ ἐὰν ὑψωθῶ ἐκ τῆς γῆς, πάντας ἑλκύσω[8] πρὸς ἐμαυτόν. **33** τοῦτο δὲ ἔλεγεν σημαίνων ποίῳ θανάτῳ ἤμελλεν ἀποθνήσκειν. **34** ἀπεκρίθη οὖν αὐτῷ ὁ ὄχλος, Ἡμεῖς ἠκούσαμεν ἐκ τοῦ νόμου ὅτι ὁ Χριστὸς μένει εἰς τὸν αἰῶνα, καὶ πῶς σὺ λέγεις ὅτι δεῖ ὑψωθῆναι τὸν υἱὸν τοῦ ἀνθρώπου; τίς ἐστιν οὗτος ὁ υἱὸς τοῦ ἀνθρώπου; **35** εἶπεν οὖν αὐτοῖς ὁ Ἰησοῦς, Ἔτι μικρὸν χρόνον τὸ φῶς ἐν ὑμῖν ἐστιν. περιπατεῖτε ὡς τὸ φῶς ἔχετε, ἵνα μὴ σκοτία ὑμᾶς καταλάβῃ· καὶ ὁ περιπατῶν ἐν τῇ σκοτίᾳ οὐκ οἶδεν ποῦ ὑπάγει. **36** ὡς τὸ φῶς ἔχετε, πιστεύετε εἰς τὸ φῶς, ἵνα υἱοὶ φωτὸς γένησθε.

The Unbelief of the Jews

Ταῦτα ἐλάλησεν Ἰησοῦς, καὶ ἀπελθὼν ἐκρύβη ἀπ' αὐτῶν. **37** Τοσαῦτα δὲ αὐτοῦ σημεῖα πεποιηκότος ἔμπροσθεν αὐτῶν οὐκ ἐπίστευον εἰς αὐτόν, **38** ἵνα ὁ λόγος Ἡσαΐου τοῦ προφήτου πληρωθῇ ὃν εἶπεν,

Κύριε, τίς ἐπίστευσεν τῇ ἀκοῇ ἡμῶν;
καὶ ὁ βραχίων κυρίου τίνι ἀπεκαλύφθη;

---

[8] **32** {D} πάντας ἑλκύσω 𝔭[75vid] ℵ[c] A B K L W X (Δ ἐκλύσω) Θ Π Ψ 0250 f[1] f[13] 28 33 565 700 892 1009 1010 1071 1079 1195 1216 1230 1241 1242 1344 1365 1546 1646 2148 2174 *Byz Lect* l[690.m, 70m, 211m, 883m, 1679m] syr[h] (cop[boms]) arm geo[2] Origen Athanasius Basil Epiphanius Chrysostom Nonnus Cyril // πάντα ἑλκύσω 𝔭[66] ℵ* it[a,aur,b,c,e,f,ff2,l,r1] vg goth geo[1] Diatessaron[f,i,n] Origen[lat] Augustine // ἑλκύσω πάντα D it[d] syr[s,p,pal] cop[sa,bo,ach2] eth

29 Ἄγγελος...λελάληκεν Ac 23.9   **30** Οὐ δι' ἐμὲ...ὑμᾶς Jn 11.42   **31** κρίσις ἐστὶν τοῦ κόσμου τούτου Jn 9.39 ὁ ἄρχων τοῦ κόσμου τούτου Jn 14.30; 16.11   **32** κἀγὼ...γῆς Jn 3.14; 8.28   **33** Jn 18.32; 21.19   **34** Ἡμεῖς...αἰῶνα Ps 89.4, 36; 110.4; Is 9.7; Dn 7.14   **35** Ἔτι...ἐστιν Jn 7.33 περιπατεῖτε...καταλάβῃ Jn 8.12; 9.4; 12.46 ὁ περιπατῶν...ὑπάγει Jn 11.10: 1 Jn 2.11   **36** ὡς...γένησθε Eph 5.8   **38** Κύριε...ἡμῶν Ro 10.16   Κύριε...ἀπεκαλύφθη Is 53.1

---

[29] The crowd standing there heard the voice and said, "It thundered!" Others said, "An angel spoke to him!" [30] But Jesus said to them: "It was not for my sake that this voice spoke, but for yours.

[31] Now is the time for the world to be judged; now the ruler of this world will be overthrown. [32] When I am lifted up from the earth, I will draw all men to me." [33] (In saying this he indicated the kind of death he was going to suffer.) [34] The crowd answered back: "Our Law tells us that the Messiah will live for ever. How, then, can you say that the Son of Man must be lifted up? Who is this Son of Man?" [35] Jesus answered: "The light will be among you a little longer. Live your lives while you have the light, so the darkness will not come upon you; because the one who lives in the dark does not know where he is going. [36] Believe in the light, then, while you have it, so that you will be the people of the light."

The Unbelief of the Jews

After Jesus said this he went off and hid himself from them. [37] Even though he had done all these mighty works before their very eyes they did not believe in him, [38] so that what the prophet Isaiah had said might come true:

"Lord, who believed the message we told?
To whom did the Lord show his power?"

[39] For this reason they were not able to believe, because Isaiah also said:
[40] "God has blinded their eyes,
He has closed their minds,
So that their eyes would not see,
Their minds would not understand,
And they would not turn to me
For me to heal them."
[41] Isaiah said this because he saw Jesus' glory, and spoke about him.
[42] Even then, many Jewish leaders believed in Jesus; but because of the Pharisees they did not talk about it openly, so as not to be put out of the synagogue. [43] They loved the approval of men rather than the approval of God.

Judgment by Jesus' Word

[44] Jesus spoke in a loud voice: "Whoever believes in me, believes not only in me but also in him who sent me. [45] Whoever sees me, also sees him who sent me. [46] I have come into the world as light, that everyone who believes in me should not remain in the darkness. [47] Whoever hears my message and does not obey it, I will not judge him. I came,

[39] διὰ τοῦτο οὐκ ἠδύναντο πιστεύειν, ὅτι πάλιν εἶπεν Ἡσαΐας,
[40] Τετύφλωκεν αὐτῶν τοὺς ὀφθαλμοὺς
καὶ ἐπώρωσεν[9] αὐτῶν τὴν καρδίαν,
ἵνα μὴ ἴδωσιν τοῖς ὀφθαλμοῖς
καὶ νοήσωσιν τῇ καρδίᾳ καὶ στραφῶσιν,
καὶ ἰάσομαι αὐτούς.
[41] ταῦτα εἶπεν Ἡσαΐας, ὅτι[10] εἶδεν τὴν δόξαν αὐτοῦ, καὶ ἐλάλησεν περὶ αὐτοῦ. [42] ὅμως μέντοι καὶ ἐκ τῶν ἀρχόντων πολλοὶ ἐπίστευσαν εἰς αὐτόν, ἀλλὰ διὰ τοὺς Φαρισαίους οὐχ ὡμολόγουν ἵνα μὴ ἀποσυνάγωγοι γένωνται· [43] ἠγάπησαν γὰρ τὴν δόξαν τῶν ἀνθρώπων μᾶλλον ἤπερ τὴν δόξαν τοῦ θεοῦ.

Judgment by Jesus' Word

[44] Ἰησοῦς δὲ ἔκραξεν καὶ εἶπεν, Ὁ πιστεύων εἰς ἐμὲ οὐ πιστεύει εἰς ἐμὲ ἀλλὰ εἰς τὸν πέμψαντά με, [45] καὶ ὁ θεωρῶν ἐμὲ θεωρεῖ τὸν πέμψαντά με. [46] ἐγὼ φῶς εἰς τὸν κόσμον ἐλήλυθα, ἵνα πᾶς ὁ πιστεύων εἰς ἐμὲ ἐν τῇ σκοτίᾳ μὴ μείνῃ. [47] καὶ ἐάν τίς μου ἀκούσῃ τῶν ῥημάτων καὶ μὴ φυλάξῃ, ἐγὼ οὐ κρίνω αὐτόν, οὐ γὰρ

---

[9] **40** {C} ἐπώρωσεν A B* L X Θ Ψ f[13] 33 1071 1230 1242* Eusebius ‖ ἐπήρωσεν p[66,75] ℵ K W Π 1079 (syr[pal?]) Didymus ‖ πεπώρωκεν B[3] Δ f[1] 565 700 892 1009 1195 1216 1241 1242[c] 1344 1365 1546 1646 2148 2174 *Byz Lect* (syr[pal?]) goth Eusebius Chrysostom Theodoret ‖ πεπήρωκεν 63 122 185 259 ‖ ἐπώρωσεν or πεπώρωκεν it[a,aur,b,c,e,f,ff2,l,q,r1] vg syr[(p),h] cop[sa,bo,ach2] geo ‖ *stupefied* arm

[10] **41** {B} ὅτι p[66,75] ℵ A B L X Θ Ψ f[1] 33 1071 1546 l[76pt,185pt] it[e] syr[pal] cop[sa,bo,ach2] arm geo[1] Origen[lat] Ambrosiaster Hilary Didymus Epiphanius Chrysostom Nonnus Cyril ‖ ὅτε D K Δ Π f[13] 565 700 892 1009 1079 1195 1216 1230 1241 1242 1344 1365 1646 2148 2174 *Byz Lect* l[76pt,185pt] it[a,aur,b,c,d,f, ff2,q,r1] vg syr[s,p,h] goth eth geo? Diatessaron[a,i,n] Origen[lat] Eusebius Ambrosiaster Hilary Basil Didymus Chrysostom ‖ ἐπεί W geo?

---

40 Τετύφλωκεν...αὐτούς Is 6.10 (Mt 13.15; Mk 4.12)   **41** εἶδεν τὴν δόξαν αὐτοῦ Is 6.1   **42** καὶ...ἐπίστευσαν εἰς αὐτόν Jn 7.48   πολλοί...αὐτόν Jn 2.23; 7.31; 8.30; 10.42; 11.45; 12.11   διὰ...γένωνται Jn 9.22   **43** Jn 5.44   **44** Ὁ πιστεύων...με Mt 10.40; Jn 5.24   **45** Jn 14.9   **46** ἐγώ...ἐλήλυθα Jn 3.19; 8.12; 9.5   ἵνα...μείνῃ Jn 12.35   **47** ἐάν...φυλάξῃ Mt 7.26   ἐγώ...σώσω τὸν κόσμον Jn 3.17; 8.15

ἦλθον ἵνα κρίνω τὸν κόσμον ἀλλ' ἵνα σώσω τὸν κόσμον. 48 ὁ ἀθετῶν ἐμὲ καὶ μὴ λαμβάνων τὰ ῥήματά μου ἔχει τὸν κρίνοντα αὐτόν· ὁ λόγος ὃν ἐλάλησα ἐκεῖνος κρινεῖ αὐτὸν ἐν τῇ ἐσχάτῃ ἡμέρᾳ· 49 ὅτι ἐγὼ ἐξ ἐμαυτοῦ οὐκ ἐλάλησα, ἀλλ' ὁ πέμψας με πατὴρ αὐτός μοι ἐντολὴν δέδωκεν τί εἴπω καὶ τί λαλήσω. 50 καὶ οἶδα ὅτι ἡ ἐντολὴ αὐτοῦ ζωὴ αἰώνιός ἐστιν. ἃ οὖν ἐγὼ λαλῶ, καθὼς εἴρηκέν μοι ὁ πατήρ, οὕτως λαλῶ.

Washing the Disciples' Feet

13 Πρὸ δὲ τῆς ἑορτῆς τοῦ πάσχα εἰδὼς ὁ Ἰησοῦς ὅτι ἦλθεν αὐτοῦ ἡ ὥρα ἵνα μεταβῇ ἐκ τοῦ κόσμου τούτου πρὸς τὸν πατέρα,[a] ἀγαπήσας τοὺς ἰδίους τοὺς ἐν τῷ κόσμῳ, εἰς τέλος ἠγάπησεν αὐτούς.[a] 2 καὶ δείπνου γινομένου[1], τοῦ διαβόλου ἤδη βεβληκότος εἰς τὴν καρδίαν ἵνα παραδοῖ αὐτὸν Ἰούδας Σίμωνος Ἰσκαριώτου[2], 3 εἰδὼς

---

[1] **2** {C} γινομένου ℵ* B L W X Ψ 0124 1241 it[d, (r1)] syr[pal] arm eth Origen[4/5] Nonnus ‖ γενομένου (𝔭[66] γεναμένου) ℵ[c] A D[gr] K Δ Θ Π f[1] f[13] 28 33 700 892 1009 1071 1079 1195 1216 1230 1242 1344 1365 1546 1646 2148 2174 *Byz Lect* it[a, aur, b, c, e, f, ff2, l, q] vg syr[s, p, h] cop[sa?bo?ach2?] Origen[1/5] Chrysostom Cyril

[2] **2** {C} Ἰούδας Σίμωνος Ἰσκαριώτου L Ψ 0124 1241 vg[cl] arm Origen ‖ Ἰούδα Σίμωνος Ἰσκαριώτου (*transposing* ἵνα αὐτὸν παραδῷ *after* Ἰσκαριώτου) A K Δ Θ Π f[1] 28 33 700 892 1009 1071 1079 1195 1216 1230 (1242* *transpose:* Ἰούδα ἵνα παραδῷ αὐτὸν Σίμωνος Ἰσκαριώτου) 1242[c] 1344 1365 1546 1646 2148 2174 *Byz Lect* (it[a, (ff2)] *Scarioth*, it[q] *Scariothe*, it[f] *Scariotis*) syr[s, p, h, (pal)] cop[sa, ach2] eth geo[2] (Origen[gr, lat]) (Cyril) ‖ Ἰούδας Σίμωνος Ἰσκαριώτης 𝔭[66] ℵ B (W Ἰσκαριώτη) X (it[r1] *Scarioth*, it[b] *Scariotes*, vg[ww] *Scariotis*) (cop[bo] Σίμων) geo[1] Origen ‖ *omit* Ἰούδας *and transpose:* Σίμωνος Ἰσκαριώτου ἵνα αὐτὸν παραδῷ f[13] it[e] cop[boms] (Origen[lat]) Ambrosiaster ‖ *transpose:* Ἰούδα Σίμωνος ἀπὸ Καρυώτου ἵνα παραδοῖ αὐτόν D it[(d), e] ‖ *transpose: Iudae ut traderet eum* it[aur]

---

[a] [a] **1** *a minor, a major:* TR (WH) Bov Nes BF2 AV RV ASV RSV TT Zür Luth Jer Seg ‖ *a major, a major:* NEB ‖ *a dash, a dash:* WH[mg]

---

49 Jn 7.17   **50** ἃ...οὕτως λαλῶ Jn 8.26, 28

13 1 ἦλθεν...ὥρα Mt 26.45; Mk 14.41; Jn 12.23; 17.1   ἵνα...πατέρα Jn 16.28   **2** τοῦ... Ἰσκαριώτης Lk 22.3; Jn 13.27

---

not to judge the world, but to save it. [48] Whoever rejects me and does not accept my message, has one who will judge him. The word I have spoken will be his judge on the last day! [49] Yes, because I have not spoken on my own, but the Father who sent me has commanded me what I must say and speak. [50] And I know that his command brings eternal life. What I say, then, is what the Father has told me to say.''

Jesus Washes His Disciples' Feet

13 It was now the day before the Feast of Passover. Jesus knew that his hour had come for him to leave this world and go to the Father. He had always loved those who were his own in the world, and he loved them to the very end.

[2] Jesus and his disciples were at supper. The Devil had already decided that Judas, the son of Simon Iscariot, would betray Jesus. [3] Jesus knew that the

Father had given him complete power; he knew that he had come from God and was going to God. ⁴ So Jesus rose from the table, took off his outer garment, and tied a towel around his waist. ⁵ Then he poured some water into a washbasin and began to wash the disciples' feet and dry them with the towel around his waist. ⁶ He came to Simon Peter, who said to him, "Are you going to wash my feet, Lord?" ⁷ Jesus answered him, "You do not know now what I am doing, but you will know later." ⁸ Peter declared, "You will never, at any time, wash my feet!" "If I do not wash your feet," Jesus answered, "you will no longer be my disciple." ⁹ Simon Peter answered, "Lord, do not wash only my feet, then! Wash my hands and head, too!" ¹⁰ Jesus said: "Whoever has taken a bath is completely clean and does not have to wash himself, except for his feet.[1] All of you are clean — all except one." ¹¹ (Jesus already knew who was going to betray him; that is why he said, "All of you, except one, are clean.")

¹² After he had washed their feet, Jesus put his outer garment back on and returned to his place at the table. "Do you understand what I have just done to you?" he asked. ¹³ "You call me

___

[1] **10** *Some mss. omit* except for his feet

___

ὅτι πάντα ἔδωκεν αὐτῷ ὁ πατὴρ εἰς τὰς χεῖρας καὶ ὅτι ἀπὸ θεοῦ ἐξῆλθεν καὶ πρὸς τὸν θεὸν ὑπάγει, **4** ἐγείρεται ἐκ τοῦ δείπνου καὶ τίθησιν τὰ ἱμάτια, καὶ λαβὼν λέντιον διέζωσεν ἑαυτόν. **5** εἶτα βάλλει ὕδωρ εἰς τὸν νιπτῆρα καὶ ἤρξατο νίπτειν τοὺς πόδας τῶν μαθητῶν καὶ ἐκμάσσειν τῷ λεντίῳ ᾧ ἦν διεζωσμένος. **6** ἔρχεται οὖν πρὸς Σίμωνα Πέτρον. λέγει αὐτῷ, Κύριε, σύ μου νίπτεις τοὺς πόδας; **7** ἀπεκρίθη Ἰησοῦς καὶ εἶπεν αὐτῷ, Ὃ ἐγὼ ποιῶ σὺ οὐκ οἶδας ἄρτι, γνώσῃ δὲ μετὰ ταῦτα. **8** λέγει αὐτῷ Πέτρος, Οὐ μὴ νίψῃς μου τοὺς πόδας εἰς τὸν αἰῶνα. ἀπεκρίθη Ἰησοῦς αὐτῷ, Ἐὰν μὴ νίψω σε, οὐκ ἔχεις μέρος μετ' ἐμοῦ. **9** λέγει αὐτῷ Σίμων Πέτρος, Κύριε, μὴ τοὺς πόδας μου μόνον ἀλλὰ καὶ τὰς χεῖρας καὶ τὴν κεφαλήν. **10** λέγει αὐτῷ ὁ Ἰησοῦς, Ὁ λελουμένος οὐκ ἔχει χρείαν εἰ μὴ τοὺς πόδας νίψασθαι³, ἀλλ' ἔστιν καθαρὸς ὅλος· καὶ ὑμεῖς καθαροί ἐστε, ἀλλ' οὐχὶ πάντες. **11** ᾔδει γὰρ τὸν παραδιδόντα αὐτόν· διὰ τοῦτο εἶπεν ὅτι Οὐχὶ πάντες καθαροί ἐστε.

12 Ὅτε οὖν ἔνιψεν τοὺς πόδας αὐτῶν [καὶ] ἔλαβεν τὰ ἱμάτια αὐτοῦ καὶ ἀνέπεσεν[b] πάλιν,[b] εἶπεν αὐτοῖς, Γινώσκετε τί πεποίηκα ὑμῖν; **13** ὑμεῖς φωνεῖτέ με

___

³ **10** {B} οὐκ ἔχει χρείαν εἰ μὴ τοὺς πόδας νίψασθαι B C* W Ψ arm Origen Augustine ‖ οὐ χρείαν ἔχει εἰ μὴ τοὺς πόδας νίψασθαι (K ἢ μή) L Π f¹³ 892 1071 1079 1216 1230 1546 1646 l⁵⁴⁷ syr^{h,pal} ‖ οὐκ ἔχει χρείαν (or οὐ χρείαν ἔχει) εἰ μὴ τοὺς πόδας νίψασθαι it^{a,b,e,f,ff²,l,q,ρ} vg^{cl} cop^{sa,bo,ach2} ‖ οὐ χρείαν ἔχει ἢ τοὺς πόδας νίψασθαι C³ E* Δ (A 1241 ἔχει χρείαν) f¹ 28 700 1009 1010 1195 (1242* *omit* ἤ) 1242^c 1344 1365 2148 2174 *Byz Lect* Cyril ‖ οὐ χρείαν ἔχει εἰ μὴ τοὺς πόδας μόνον νίψασθαι (p⁶⁶ οὐκ ἔχει χρείαν) Θ syr^{s,p} cop^{boms} geo (Chrysostom) ‖ οὐκ ἔχει χρείαν νίψασθαι ℵ it^{aur,c} vg^{ww} Tertullian Origen ‖ οὐ χρείαν ἔχει τὴν κεφαλὴν νίψασθαι εἰ μὴ τοὺς πόδας μόνον (*see* 13.9) D it^d

___

^{b b} **12** b none, b minor: WH^{mg} Bov Nes BF² AV RV ASV RSV NEB TT Zür Luth Jer Seg ‖ b minor, b none: WH ‖ b none, b none: TR

___

3 πάντα...χεῖρας Mt 11.27; Lk 10.22; Jn 3.35   ἀπὸ...ὑπάγει Jn 16.28   **5** Lk 7.44; Jn 12.3   **7** γνώσῃ...ταῦτα Jn 13.12   **10** ὑμεῖς καθαροί ἐστε Jn 15.3   **11** ᾔδει...αὐτόν Jn 6.64, 70–71   **13** Mt 23.8, 10

'Ο διδάσκαλος καὶ 'Ο κύριος, καὶ καλῶς λέγετε, εἰμὶ γάρ. **14** εἰ οὖν ἐγὼ ἔνιψα ὑμῶν τοὺς πόδας ὁ κύριος καὶ ὁ διδάσκαλος, καὶ ὑμεῖς ὀφείλετε ἀλλήλων νίπτειν τοὺς πόδας· **15** ὑπόδειγμα γὰρ δέδωκα ὑμῖν ἵνα καθὼς ἐγὼ ἐποίησα ὑμῖν καὶ ὑμεῖς ποιῆτε. **16** ἀμὴν ἀμὴν λέγω ὑμῖν, οὐκ ἔστιν δοῦλος μείζων τοῦ κυρίου αὐτοῦ οὐδὲ ἀπόστολος μείζων τοῦ πέμψαντος αὐτόν. **17** εἰ ταῦτα οἴδατε, μακάριοί ἐστε ἐὰν ποιῆτε αὐτά. **18** οὐ περὶ πάντων ὑμῶν λέγω· ἐγὼ οἶδα τίνας ἐξελεξάμην· ἀλλ' ἵνα ἡ γραφὴ πληρωθῇ, **'Ο τρώγων μου[4] τὸν ἄρτον ἐπῆρεν ἐπ' ἐμὲ τὴν πτέρναν αὐτοῦ.** **19** ἀπ' ἄρτι λέγω ὑμῖν πρὸ τοῦ γενέσθαι, ἵνα πιστεύσητε ὅταν γένηται ὅτι ἐγώ εἰμι. **20** ἀμὴν ἀμὴν λέγω ὑμῖν, ὁ λαμβάνων ἄν τινα πέμψω ἐμὲ λαμβάνει, ὁ δὲ ἐμὲ λαμβάνων λαμβάνει τὸν πέμψαντά με.

Jesus Foretells His Betrayal
(Mt 26.20—25; Mk 14.17—21; Lk 22.21—23)

21 Ταῦτα εἰπὼν ὁ 'Ιησοῦς ἐταράχθη τῷ πνεύματι καὶ ἐμαρτύρησεν καὶ εἶπεν, 'Αμὴν ἀμὴν λέγω ὑμῖν ὅτι εἷς ἐξ ὑμῶν παραδώσει με. **22** ἔβλεπον εἰς ἀλλήλους οἱ μαθηταὶ ἀπορούμενοι περὶ τίνος λέγει. **23** ἦν ἀνακείμενος εἷς ἐκ τῶν μαθητῶν αὐτοῦ ἐν τῷ κόλπῳ τοῦ 'Ιησοῦ, ὃν ἠγάπα ὁ 'Ιησοῦς· **24** νεύει οὖν τούτῳ Σίμων Πέτρος πυθέσθαι τίς ἂν εἴη περὶ οὗ λέγει[5]. **25** ἀναπεσὼν

---

[4] **18** {D} μου B C L 892 1071 1230 cop^sa eth Diatessaron^l Origen Eusebius Cyril ‖ μετ' ἐμοῦ p^66 ℵ A D K W Δ Θ Π Ψ f^1 f^13 28 33 700 1009 1010 1079 1195 1216 1241 1242 1344 1365 1546 1646 2148 2174 Byz it^a,aur,b,c,d,(e),f,ff2,l,rl vg syr^s,p,h,pal cop^bomss goth arm geo Diatessaron^a,i,n Tertullian Origen Eusebius Chrysostom Cyril Theodoret ‖ μου μετ' ἐμοῦ it^q cop^bomss,ach2

[5] **24** {B} πυθέσθαι τίς ἂν εἴη περὶ οὗ λέγει (p^66c οὗ εἶπεν) A K W Δ (Θ ἦ for εἴη) Π f^1 (f^13 1241 πείθεσθαι) 28 565 700 1009 1010 1079 1195 1216 1230 1242 1344 1365 1546 1646 2148 2174 Byz (it^rl) syr^s,p,h,pal cop^sa,bo?

---

14 Lk 22.27   εἰ...διδάσκαλος Mt 20.28   ὑμεῖς...πόδας 1 Tm 5.10   **15** Php 2.5; 1 Pe 2.21   **16** οὐκ ἔστιν δοῦλος...αὐτόν Mt 10.24; Lk 6.40; Jn 15.20   **17** Jas 1.25   **18** 'Ο τρώγων... αἱ τοῦ Ps 41.9   **19** Jn 14.29; 16.4   ἵνα πιστεύσητε...εἰμι Jn 8.24, 28   **20** ὁ λαμβάνων ...με Mt 10.40; Mk 9.37; Lk 9.48; 10.16   **23** εἷς...'Ιησοῦς Jn 19.26; 20.2; 21.7, 20   **25** Jn 21.20

Teacher and Lord, and it is right that you do so, because I am. [14] I am your Lord and Teacher, and I have just washed your feet. You, then, should wash each other's feet. [15] I have set an example for you, so that you will do just what I have done for you. [16] I tell you the truth: no slave is greater than his master; no messenger is greater than the one who sent him. [17] Now you know this truth; how happy you will be if you put it into practice!

[18] "I am not talking about all of you; I know those I have chosen. But the scripture must come true that says, 'The man who ate my food turned against me.' [19] I tell you this now before it happens, so that when it does happen you will believe that 'I Am Who I Am'. [20] I tell you the truth: whoever receives anyone I send, receives me also; and whoever receives me, receives him who sent me."

Jesus Predicts His Betrayal
(Also Matt. 26.20—25; Mark 14.17—21; Luke 22.21 23)

[21] After Jesus said this, he was deeply troubled, and declared openly: "I tell you the truth: one of you is going to betray me." [22] The disciples looked at one another, completely puzzled about whom he meant. [23] One of the disciples, whom Jesus loved, was sitting next to Jesus. [24] Simon Peter motioned to him and said, "Ask him who it is that he is talking about." [25] So that disciple moved

closer to Jesus' side and asked, "Who is it, Lord?" 26 Jesus answered, "I will dip the bread in the sauce and give it to him; he is the man." So he took a piece of bread, dipped it, and gave it to Judas, the son of Simon Iscariot. 27 As soon as Judas took the bread, Satan went into him. Jesus said to him, "Hurry and do what you must!" 28 (None of those at the table understood what Jesus said to him. 29 Since Judas was in charge of the money bag, some of the disciples thought that Jesus had told him to go to buy what they needed for the feast, or else that he had told him to give

οὖν ἐκεῖνος οὕτως ἐπὶ τὸ στῆθος τοῦ Ἰησοῦ λέγει αὐτῷ, Κύριε, τίς ἐστιν; 26 ἀποκρίνεται Ἰησοῦς, Ἐκεῖνός ἐστιν ᾧ ἐγὼ βάψω τὸ ψωμίον καὶ δώσω αὐτῷ[6]. βάψας οὖν τὸ ψωμίον [λαμβάνει καὶ] δίδωσιν[7] Ἰούδᾳ Σίμωνος Ἰσκαριώτου[8]. 27 καὶ μετὰ τὸ ψωμίον τότε εἰσῆλθεν εἰς ἐκεῖνον ὁ Σατανᾶς. λέγει οὖν αὐτῷ ὁ Ἰησοῦς, Ὃ ποιεῖς ποίησον τάχιον. 28 τοῦτο [δὲ] οὐδεὶς ἔγνω τῶν ἀνακειμένων πρὸς τί εἶπεν αὐτῷ· 29 τινὲς γὰρ ἐδόκουν, ἐπεὶ τὸ γλωσσόκομον εἶχεν Ἰούδας, ὅτι λέγει αὐτῷ [ὁ] Ἰησοῦς, Ἀγόρασον ὧν χρείαν ἔχομεν εἰς τὴν ἑορτήν,

---

goth arm geo Diatessaron[a,v] Cyril ‖ πυθέσθαι τίς ἂν εἴη οὗτος περὶ οὗ λέγει D it[d] ‖ πυθέσθαι περὶ τίνος λέγει Ψ (cop[bo?] περὶ οὗ) ‖ καὶ λέγει αὐτῷ, Εἰπὲ τίς ἐστιν περὶ οὗ λέγει B C L X 068 33 892 1071 it[f] (it[a,q] omit αὐτῷ) Origen ‖ καὶ λέγει αὐτῷ, Τίς ἐστιν περὶ οὗ λέγει it[aur] vg (Origen omit αὐτῷ) ‖ καὶ λέγει αὐτῷ, Εἰπὲ περὶ οὗ λέγει it[c] eth ‖ καὶ λέγει αὐτῷ, Εἰπὲ τίς ἐστιν 299 it[b,ff2,l] ‖ uti cognosceret a Iesu de quo dixisset it[e] ‖ πυθέσθαι τίς ἂν εἴη περὶ οὗ ἔλεγεν. καὶ λέγει αὐτῷ, Εἰπὲ τίς ἐστιν περὶ οὗ λέγει ℵ

[6] **26** {C} βάψω τὸ ψωμίον καὶ δώσω αὐτῷ (see footnote 7) B C (L δῷ) (X omit καί) 1071 1241 syr[pal] (syr[s,p,h] omit καί) cop[sa,bo,ach2] (arm omit αὐτῷ) (eth) geo? Origen (Cyril) ‖ βάψας τὸ ψωμίον ἐπιδώσω 𝔭[66] ℵ Δ Θ Ψ (A D K Π f[1] f[13] 1079 1546 ἐμβάψας) 28 33 565 700 892 1009 (1010 δώσω) (1195 ἐπιδῷ) 1216 1230 1344 1365 1646 2148 2174 Byz it[a,aur,b,c,d,(e),f,ff2,l,q,r1] vg goth Apostolic Constitutions Chrysostom (Cyril δώσω) (Theodoret) ‖ δώσω ἐμβάψας τὸ ψωμίον W

[7] **26** {C} βάψας οὖν τὸ ψωμίον λαμβάνει καὶ δίδωσιν (see footnote 6) ℵ[a] (B omit τό) C L X 33 892 1071* (1071[c] ἐμβάψας) 1241 syr[hmg] eth Origen ‖ βάψας οὖν τὸ ψωμίον δίδωσιν ℵ*,[b] it[(a),(r1)] arm? Cyril ‖ καὶ ἐμβάψας τὸ ψωμίον δίδωσιν (𝔭[66*] ψας [sic] 𝔭[66c] A K W Δ (Θ ἐπιδίδωσιν) Π* Ψ (D 1230 1646 βάψας) f[1] f[13] 28 565 700 1000 1010 1079 1195 1216 1242 1344 1365 1546 2148 2174 Byz it[aur,b,c,d,e,f,ff2,l,q] vg syr[s,p,h,pal] cop[sa,bo,ach2,fay] goth arm? geo ‖ καὶ ἐμβάψας οὖν τὸ ψωμίον ἐπιδίδωσιν Π[2]

[8] **26** {C} Ἰσκαριώτου ℵ B C L X Θ Π[2] Ψ 068 33 1010 1071 cop[sa,boms,ach2,fay] Origen ‖ Ἰσκαριώτῃ 𝔭[66] A K W Δ Π* f[1] f[13] 28 565 700 892 1009 1079 1195 1216 1230[vid] 1241 1242 1344 1365 (1546 Ἰσκαριώτην) 1646 2148 2174 Byz cop[bo] (goth Σκαριώτῃ) arm geo Origen Cyril ‖ Iscariotae vg[cl] ‖ Scarioth it[a,aur,e,ff2,r1] (it[b] Scariotae, it[c,f,l,q] Scariothae, vg[ww] Scariotis) (syr[s,p,h,pal] Scariota) ‖ ἀπὸ Καρυώτου D it[d]

---

27 τότε...Σατανᾶς Lk 22.3; Jn 13.2   29 τό...Ἰούδας Jn 12.6

ἢ τοῖς πτωχοῖς ἵνα τι δῷ. 30 λαβὼν οὖν τὸ ψωμίον ἐκεῖνος ἐξῆλθεν εὐθύς· ἦν δὲ νύξ.

The New Commandment

31 Ὅτε οὖν ἐξῆλθεν λέγει Ἰησοῦς, Νῦν ἐδοξάσθη ὁ υἱὸς τοῦ ἀνθρώπου, καὶ ὁ θεὸς ἐδοξάσθη ἐν αὐτῷ· **32** [εἰ ὁ θεὸς ἐδοξάσθη ἐν αὐτῷ][9] καὶ ὁ θεὸς δοξάσει αὐτὸν ἐν αὐτῷ[10], καὶ εὐθὺς δοξάσει αὐτόν. **33** τεκνία, ἔτι μικρὸν μεθ' ὑμῶν εἰμι· ζητήσετέ με, καὶ καθὼς εἶπον τοῖς Ἰουδαίοις ὅτι Ὅπου ἐγὼ ὑπάγω ὑμεῖς οὐ δύνασθε ἐλθεῖν, καὶ ὑμῖν λέγω ἄρτι. **34** ἐντολὴν καινὴν δίδωμι ὑμῖν, ἵνα ἀγαπᾶτε ἀλλήλους· καθὼς ἠγάπησα ὑμᾶς ἵνα καὶ ὑμεῖς ἀγαπᾶτε ἀλλήλους. **35** ἐν τούτῳ γνώσονται πάντες ὅτι ἐμοὶ μαθηταί ἐστε, ἐὰν ἀγάπην ἔχητε ἐν ἀλλήλοις.

Peter's Denial Foretold
(Mt 26.31–35; Mk 14.27–31; Lk 22.31–34)

36 Λέγει αὐτῷ Σίμων Πέτρος, Κύριε, ποῦ ὑπάγεις; ἀπεκρίθη [αὐτῷ] Ἰησοῦς, Ὅπου ὑπάγω οὐ δύνασαί μοι νῦν ἀκολουθῆσαι, ἀκολουθήσεις δὲ ὕστερον. **37** λέγει αὐτῷ ὁ Πέτρος, Κύριε[11], διὰ τί οὐ δύναμαί σοι ἀκολουθῆ-

---

[9] **32** {C} εἰ ὁ θεὸς ἐδοξάσθη ἐν αὐτῷ אᶜ A C² K Δ Θ Ψ *f*¹³ 28 565 700 1010 1195 1230 1241 1242 1344 1365 1646 2148 2174 *Byz Lect* itᵃᵘʳᵐᵍ,ᵉ,ᶠ,q,rˡ vg syrᵖ,ᵖᵃˡ copˢᵃ,ᵇᵒᵐˢˢ goth arm eth geo Diatessaron Origen Hilary (Nonnus) Cyril ∥ *omit* 𝔭⁶⁶ א* B C* D L W X Π *f*¹ 33 892 1009 1071 1079 1216 1546 itᵃ,ᵃᵘʳ*,ᵇ,ᶜ,ᵈ,ff²,ˡ syrᵃ,ʰ copᵇᵒᵐˢˢ,ᵃᶜʰ²,ᶠᵃʸ Diatessaronᶠ,ˡ Tertullian Ambrose

[10] **32** {B} ἐν αὐτῷ 2148 *l*¹⁸⁴,¹⁸⁵ syrᵖ,ʰ,ᵖᵃˡᵐˢˢ Origen ∥ ἐν αυτω 𝔭⁶⁶ א*,ᵇ B copˢᵃ,ᵇᵒ,ᵃᶜʰ²,ᶠᵃʸ ∥ ἐν ἑαυτῷ אᵃ A D K L W X Δ Θ Π Ψ *f*¹ *f*¹³ 28 33 565 700 892 1009 1010 1071 1079 1195 1216 1230 1241 1242 1344 1365 1546 1646 2174 *Byz Lect* itᵃ,ᵃᵘʳ,ᵇ,ᶜ,ᵈ,ᵉ,ᶠ,ff²,ˡ,(q),rˡ vg goth arm geo Tertullian Chrysostom Cyril ∥ *omit* syrˢ

[11] **37** {C} κύριε 𝔭⁶⁶ אᶜ A B C D K L W X Δ Θ Π Ψ *f*¹ *f*¹³ 28 700 892 1009 1010 1071 1079 1195 1216 1230 1241 1242 1344 1365 1546 1646 2148 2174 *Byz*

31–32 Jn 12.23; 17.1, 5   **33** Jn 7.33–34; 8.21   **34** Jn 15.12, 17; 1 Jn 3.23   ἐντολὴν...ὑμῖν 1 Jn 2.8; 2 Jn 5   **35** 1 Jn 3.14   **36** Κύριε, ποῦ ὑπάγεις Jn 7.35   Ὅπου...ἀκολουθῆσαι Jn 7.34, 36

---

something to the poor.) ³⁰ Judas accepted the bread and went out at once. It was night.

The New Commandment

³¹ After Judas had left, Jesus said: "Now the Son of Man's glory is revealed; now God's glory is revealed through him. ³² And if God's glory is revealed through him, then God himself will reveal the glory of the Son of Man, and he will do so at once. ³³ My children, I shall not be with you very much longer. You will look for me; but I tell you now what I told the Jews, 'You cannot go where I am going.' ³⁴ A new commandment I give you: love one another. As I have loved you, so you must love one another. ³⁵ If you have love for one another, then all will know that you are my disciples."

Jesus Predicts Peter's Denial
(Also Matt. 26.31–35; Mark 14.27–31; Luke 22.31–34)

³⁶ "Where are you going, Lord?" Simon Peter asked him. "You cannot follow me now where I am going," answered Jesus; "but later you will follow me." ³⁷ "Lord, why can't I follow you now?"

asked Peter. "I am ready to die for you!"
[38] Jesus answered: "Are you really ready
to die for me? I tell you the truth: before
the rooster crows you will say three
times that you do not know me."

Jesus the Way to the Father

14 "Do not be worried and upset,"
Jesus told them. "Believe[1] in God, and
believe also in me. [2] There are many
rooms in my Father's house, and I am
going to prepare a place for you. I
would not tell you this if it were not so.
[3] And after I go and prepare a place for
you, I will come back and take you to
myself, so that you will be where I am.
[4] You know how to get to the place
where I am going." [5] Thomas said to
him, "Lord, we do not know where you
are going; how can we know the way to
get there?" [6] Jesus answered him: "I
am the way, I am the truth, I am the
life; no one goes to the Father except by
me. [7] Now that you have known me,"

---

[1] **1** Believe: or You believe

σαι ἄρτι; τὴν ψυχήν μου ὑπὲρ σοῦ θήσω.   **38** ἀποκρίνεται Ἰησοῦς, Τὴν ψυχήν σου ὑπὲρ ἐμοῦ θήσεις; ἀμὴν
ἀμὴν λέγω σοι, οὐ μὴ ἀλέκτωρ φωνήσῃ ἕως οὗ ἀρνήσῃ
με τρίς.

Jesus the Way to the Father

14 Μὴ ταρασσέσθω ὑμῶν ἡ καρδία· πιστεύετε[a] εἰς
τὸν θεόν,[a] καὶ εἰς ἐμὲ πιστεύετε. **2** ἐν τῇ οἰκίᾳ τοῦ πατρός
μου μοναὶ πολλαί εἰσιν· εἰ δὲ μή, εἶπον ἂν ὑμῖν ὅτι[1] [b]
πορεύομαι ἑτοιμάσαι τόπον ὑμῖν;[b] **3** καὶ ἐὰν πορευθῶ
καὶ ἑτοιμάσω τόπον ὑμῖν, πάλιν ἔρχομαι καὶ παραλήμψο-
μαι ὑμᾶς πρὸς ἐμαυτόν, ἵνα ὅπου εἰμὶ ἐγὼ καὶ ὑμεῖς
ἦτε. **4** καὶ ὅπου [ἐγὼ] ὑπάγω οἴδατε τὴν ὁδόν.[2] **5** Λέγει
αὐτῷ Θωμᾶς, Κύριε, οὐκ οἴδαμεν ποῦ ὑπάγεις· πῶς
δυνάμεθα τὴν ὁδὸν εἰδέναι; **6** λέγει αὐτῷ ὁ Ἰησοῦς,
Ἐγώ εἰμι ἡ ὁδὸς καὶ ἡ ἀλήθεια καὶ ἡ ζωή· οὐδεὶς ἔρχεται πρὸς τὸν πατέρα εἰ μὴ δι' ἐμοῦ. **7** εἰ ἐγνώκατέ με[3],

---

Lect it[a, b, c, d, e, f, ff2, q, rl] syr[p, h, pal] cop[sams, bomss, ach2] goth arm geo ‖ *omit* ℵ*
33 565 it[aur] vg syr[s] cop[sams, bomss]

[1] **2** {C} ὅτι 𝔭[66c] ℵ A B C* D K L W X Π Ψ f[13] 33 565 892 1071 1079
1546 l[547] it[aur, b, c, d, ff2] vg syr[s, p, h, pal] cop[sa, bo, ach2, fay] arm geo Nonnus Cyril
Theodoret ‖ *omit* 𝔭[66*] C[2vid] Δ Θ 28 700 1009 1010 1195 1216 1230 1241 1242
1344 1365 1646 2148 2174 *Byz Lect* it[a, e, f, q] goth eth Origen[lat] Chrysostom

[2] **4** {C} τὴν ὁδόν 𝔭[66] ℵ B C* L W X 33 1071 it[a, rl vid] cop[bo] eth
Nonnus[vid] ‖ καὶ τὴν ὁδὸν οἴδατε 𝔭[66*] A C[3] D K Δ Θ Π Ψ f[1] f[13] 28 565 700
892 1009 1010 1079 1195 1216 1230 1241 1242 1344 1365 1546 1646 2148 2174
Byz Lect it[aur, b, c, d, e, f, ff2, q] vg syr[s, p, h, pal] cop[sa, ach2] goth arm geo Diatessaron[a, i, n]
Chrysostom Nonnus Cyril ‖ *omit* l[1127]

[3] **7** {C} ἐγνώκατέ με 𝔭[66] (ℵ D* ἐμέ) 1216 1365 l[185pt] it[(a), b, c, d, e, ff2] syr[s, pal]
cop[sa, bo, ach2] goth? geo Diatessaron[a] Irenaeus[lat] Novatian Victorinus-

---

[a a] **1** a none, a minor: TR WH Bov Nes BF[2] AV RV ASV RSV NEB TT (Zür) (Luth) Jer Seg ‖
a minor, a none: WH[mg]

[b b] **2** b indirect, b question: RSV NEB[mg] Zür Jer[mg] Seg[mg] ‖ b direct, b question: Luth ‖ b causal,
b statement: WH Bov Nes BF[2] RV ASV NEB TT Seg ‖ different text: TR AV Jer

---

1 Μὴ...καρδία Jn 14.27   **3** ὅπου...ἦτε Jn 12.26; 17.24   **6** Ἐγώ...ὁδός He 10.20
7 εἰ...γνώσεσθε Jn 8.19

καὶ τὸν πατέρα μου γνώσεσθε[4]· καὶ ἀπ' ἄρτι γινώσκετε
αὐτὸν καὶ ἑωράκατε αὐτόν. 8 λέγει αὐτῷ Φίλιππος,
Κύριε, δεῖξον ἡμῖν τὸν πατέρα, καὶ ἀρκεῖ ἡμῖν. 9 λέγει
αὐτῷ ὁ Ἰησοῦς, Τοσούτῳ χρόνῳ μεθ' ὑμῶν εἰμι καὶ
οὐκ ἔγνωκάς με, Φίλιππε; ὁ ἑωρακὼς ἐμὲ ἑώρακεν τὸν
πατέρα· πῶς σὺ λέγεις, Δεῖξον ἡμῖν τὸν πατέρα; 10 οὐ
πιστεύεις ὅτι ἐγὼ ἐν τῷ πατρὶ καὶ ὁ πατὴρ ἐν ἐμοί
ἐστιν; τὰ ῥήματα ἃ ἐγὼ λαλῶ ὑμῖν ἀπ' ἐμαυτοῦ οὐ
λαλῶ· ὁ δὲ πατὴρ ἐν ἐμοὶ μένων ποιεῖ τὰ ἔργα αὐτοῦ.
11 πιστεύετέ μοι ὅτι ἐγὼ ἐν τῷ πατρὶ καὶ ὁ πατὴρ ἐν
ἐμοί· εἰ δὲ μή, διὰ τὰ ἔργα αὐτὰ πιστεύετε[5]. 12 ἀμὴν
ἀμὴν λέγω ὑμῖν, ὁ πιστεύων εἰς ἐμὲ τὰ ἔργα ἃ ἐγὼ
ποιῶ κἀκεῖνος ποιήσει, καὶ μείζονα τούτων ποιήσει,
ὅτι ἐγὼ πρὸς τὸν πατέρα πορεύομαι·[c] 13 καὶ ὅ τι ἂν
αἰτήσητε ἐν τῷ ὀνόματί μου τοῦτο ποιήσω, ἵνα δοξασθῇ

Rome Hilary Augustine ‖ ἐγνώκειτέ με (A omit με) B C (D[b] ἐμέ) K L
W X Δ Θ Π Ψ f[1] f[13] 28 33 565 700 892 (1009 ἐγνώκετε) 1010 1079 1195 1230
1241 1242 1344 1546 1646 2148 2174 Byz Lect l[185pt] it[aur] vg goth? Irenaeus[lat]
Tertullian ‖ ἐγινώσκετε it[f,r1] syr[p,h] ‖ me nostis it[q]

[4] 7 {C} γνώσεσθε 𝔓[66] ℵ D W it[d] syr[s] cop[sa,bomss,ach2] goth? Victorinus-
Rome Nonnus ‖ γινώσκετε it[e,q] goth? geo[2] Irenaeus[lat] Hilary ‖ ἐγινώσκετε it[f,r1] syr[p,h,pal] ‖ ἐγνώκατε it[a,b,c,ff2] geo[1] ‖ ἐγνώκειτε ἄν Λ C[3] K
Δ (Θ γνώκειτε) Π f[13] 28 700 892 1009 1010 1071 1079 1195 1216 1230 1241
1242 1344 1546 1646 2148 2174 Byz Lect l[185pt] (l[185pt] ἐγνώκατε) it[aur] vg
Athanasius Chrysostom Ps-Athanasius ‖ ἂν ᾔδειτε B C* (L εἰδῆτε) Ψ
f[1] 33 (565 ᾔδητε) cop[bomss?] Basil Cyril Ps-Athanasius ‖ εἰδῆτε ἄν X (1365
ᾔδητε)

[5] 11 {B} πιστεύετε 𝔓[66,75] ℵ D L W 33 1071* it[aur,c,d,e,f,r1] vg syr[c,p,pal]
cop[sa,bom3,ach2] Tertullian Hilary Ambrose ‖ πιστεύετέ μοι A B K X Δ Θ
Π Ψ f[1] f[13] 28 565 700 892 1009 1010 1071[c] 1079 1195 1216 1230 1241 1242 1344
1365 1546 1646 2148 2174 Byz Lect it[a,b,ff2,q] syr[h] cop[bo] goth arm eth geo
Athanasius Chrysostom Cyril

---

[c] 12 c major: TR WH Bov Nes BF[2] AV RV ASV RSV NEB TT Luth Jer Seg ‖ c minor: WH[mg]
Zür

---

9 ὁ...πατέρα Jn 12.45; Col 1.15; He 1.3   10 ἐγὼ ἐν τῷ πατρὶ...ἐστιν Jn 10.38; 14.20;
17.21 τὰ...λαλῶ Jn 12.49; 14.24   11 διὰ...πιστεύετε Jn 10.37–38   12 ἐγὼ...πορεύομαι
Jn 7.33; 13.1; 14.28   13 ὅ τι...ποιήσω Jn 15.16; 16.23 ἵνα δοξασθῇ...υἱῷ Jn 13.31–32; 17.1

he said to them, "you will know[2] my
Father also; and from now on you do
know him, and you have seen him."

[8] Philip said to him, "Lord, show us
the Father; that is all we need." [9] Jesus
answered: "For a long time I have been
with you all; yet you do not know me,
Philip? Whoever has seen me has seen
the Father. Why, then, do you say,
'Show us the Father'? [10] Do you not
believe, Philip, that I am in the Father
and the Father is in me? The words that
I have spoken to you," Jesus said to his
disciples, "do not come from me. The
Father, who remains in me, does his
own works. [11] Believe me that I am in
the Father and the Father is in me.
If not, believe because of these works.
[12] I tell you the truth: whoever believes
in me will do the works I do — yes, he
will do even greater ones, for I am going
to the Father. [13] And I will do whatever
you ask for in my name, so that the

---

[2] 7 Now that you have known me...you
will know: some mss. read If you had known
me...you would know

Father's glory will be shown through the Son. ¹⁴ If you ask me for anything in my name, I will do it."

The Promise of the Holy Spirit

¹⁵ "If you love me, you will obey my commandments. ¹⁶ I will ask the Father, and he will give you another Helper, the Spirit of truth, to stay with you for ever. ¹⁷ The world cannot receive him, because it cannot see him or know him. But you know him, for he remains with you and lives in you.

¹⁸ "I will not leave you alone; I will come back to you. ¹⁹ In a little while the world will see me no more, but you will see me; and because I live, you also will live. ²⁰ When that day comes, you will know that I am in my Father, and that you are in me, just as I am in you.

²¹ "Whoever accepts my command-

ὁ πατὴρ ἐν τῷ υἱῷ· 14 ἐάν τι αἰτήσητέ με[7] ἐν τῷ ὀνόματί μου ἐγὼ ποιήσω.[6]

The Promise of the Spirit

15 Ἐὰν ἀγαπᾶτέ με, τὰς ἐντολὰς τὰς ἐμὰς τηρήσετε[8]· 16 κἀγὼ ἐρωτήσω τὸν πατέρα καὶ ἄλλον παράκλητον δώσει ὑμῖν ἵνα μεθ' ὑμῶν εἰς τὸν αἰῶνα ᾖ, 17 τὸ πνεῦμα τῆς ἀληθείας, ὃ ὁ κόσμος οὐ δύναται λαβεῖν, ὅτι οὐ θεωρεῖ αὐτὸ οὐδὲ γινώσκει· ὑμεῖς γινώσκετε αὐτό, ὅτι παρ' ὑμῖν μένει[9] καὶ ἐν ὑμῖν ἐστιν[9]. 18 Οὐκ ἀφήσω ὑμᾶς ὀρφανούς, ἔρχομαι πρὸς ὑμᾶς. 19 ἔτι μικρὸν καὶ ὁ κόσμος με οὐκέτι θεωρεῖ, ὑμεῖς δὲ θεωρεῖτέ με, ὅτι ἐγὼ ζῶ καὶ ὑμεῖς ζήσετε. 20 ἐν ἐκείνῃ τῇ ἡμέρᾳ γνώσεσθε ὑμεῖς ὅτι ἐγὼ ἐν τῷ πατρί μου καὶ ὑμεῖς ἐν ἐμοὶ κἀγὼ ἐν ὑμῖν. 21 ὁ ἔχων τὰς ἐντολάς μου

---

⁶ 14 {B} *include verse 14* 𝔓⁶⁶,⁷⁵ ℵ A B D K L W Δ Θ Π Ψ f¹³ 28 33 700 892 1071 1079 1195 1216 1230 1241 1242 1344 1546 1646 2148 2174 *Byz Lect* l⁶⁹⁸,ᵐ itᵃ,ᵃᵘʳ,ᶜ,ᵈ,ᵉ,f,ff²,q,rl vg syrᵖ,ʰ copˢᵃ,ᵇᵒ,ᵃᶜʰ²,ᶠᵃʸ goth ∥ *omit verse 14* X f¹ 565 1009 1010 1365 l⁷⁶,²⁵³ itᵇ vgᵐˢ syrᶜ,ˢ,ᵖᵃˡ arm geo Diatessaronᶠ,ˡ,ᵗ Nonnus

⁷ 14 {B} με (*see footnote 6*) 𝔓⁶⁶ ℵ B W Δ Θ 060 f¹³ 28 33 700 892 1230ᵛⁱᵈ 1242 1646 l⁶⁴,¹⁸⁴ᵖᵗ,²¹⁹,⁵⁴⁷,¹²³¹ itᶜ,f vg syrᵖ,ʰ goth Fulgentius ∥ τὸν πατέρα 249 397 ∥ *a patre meo* itff² eth ∥ *omit* A D K L Π Ψ 1071 1079 1195 1216 1241 1344 1546 2148 2174 *Byz Lect* l⁶⁹⁸,ᵐ,¹⁸⁴ᵖᵗ itᵃ,ᵃᵘʳ,ᵈ,ᵉ,q,rl copˢᵃ,ᵇᵒ,ᵃᶜʰ²,ᶠᵃʸ Diatessaron Victorinus-Rome Augustine Cyril Euthymius

⁸ 15 {C} τηρήσετε B L Ψ 1010 1071 1195* 2148 l³⁸¹ copˢᵃ,ᵇᵒ,ᵃᶜʰ²,ᶠᵃʸ goth? geo² Eusebius Melitius Epiphanius Chrysostom Cyril ∥ τηρήσητε 𝔓⁶⁶ ℵ 060 33 1344 1546 l¹⁸⁴,¹⁸⁵ arm geo¹⁷ ∥ τηρήσατε A D K W X Δ Θ Π f¹ f¹³ 28 565 700 892 1009 1079 1195ᵐᵍ 1216 1230 1241 1242 1365 1646 2174 *Byz Lect* l⁶⁹⁸,ᵐ itᵃ,ᵃᵘʳ,ᵇ,ᶜ,ᵈ,ᵉ,f,ff²,q,rl vg syrᶜ,ᵖ,ʰ,ᵖᵃˡ goth? eth geo¹⁷ Origenᵍʳ,ˡᵃᵗ Eusebius Chrysostom Ps-Athanasius

⁹ 17 {D} μένει...ἐστιν (B D* W μενει) f¹ 565 1365 itᵃ,ᵇ,ᶜ,ᵈ,ᵉ,f,ff²,q syrᶜ,ᵖ,ᵖᵃˡ goth Lucifer ∥ μένει...ἔσται (𝔓⁶⁶,⁷⁵ᵛⁱᵈ ℵ A Dᵇ L Δ μενει) K X Θ Π Ψ f¹³ 28 33ᵛⁱᵈ 700 892 1009 1010 1071 1079 1195 1216 1230 1241 1242 1344 1546 1646

---

15 Wsd 6.18; Jn 15.10; 1 Jn 5.3; 2 Jn 6   16 κἀγὼ...δώσει ὑμῖν Jn 14.26; 15.26; 16.7   17 τὸ...ἀληθείας Jn 15.26; 16.13   18 ἔρχομαι πρὸς ὑμᾶς Jn 14.3, 28   19 Jn 16.16 ἔτι... θεωρεῖ Jn 7.33–34, 36   ὅτι...ζήσετε Jn 6.57   20 Jn 10.38; 14.10–11; 17.21–23   21 ὁ ἔχων ...ὁ ἀγαπῶν με Jn 15.10; 1 Jn 5.3; 2 Jn 6

καὶ τηρῶν αὐτὰς ἐκεῖνός ἐστιν ὁ ἀγαπῶν με· ὁ δὲ ἀγαπῶν
με ἀγαπηθήσεται ὑπὸ τοῦ πατρός μου, κἀγὼ ἀγαπήσω
αὐτὸν καὶ ἐμφανίσω αὐτῷ ἐμαυτόν. **22** Λέγει αὐτῷ
Ἰούδας, οὐχ ὁ Ἰσκαριώτης[10], Κύριε, [καὶ] τί γέγονεν
ὅτι ἡμῖν μέλλεις ἐμφανίζειν σεαυτὸν καὶ οὐχὶ τῷ κόσμῳ;
23 ἀπεκρίθη Ἰησοῦς καὶ εἶπεν αὐτῷ, Ἐάν τις ἀγαπᾷ
με τὸν λόγον μου τηρήσει, καὶ ὁ πατήρ μου ἀγαπήσει
αὐτόν, καὶ πρὸς αὐτὸν ἐλευσόμεθα καὶ μονὴν παρ' αὐτῷ
ποιησόμεθα. **24** ὁ μὴ ἀγαπῶν με τοὺς λόγους μου οὐ
τηρεῖ· καὶ ὁ λόγος ὃν ἀκούετε οὐκ ἔστιν ἐμὸς ἀλλὰ
τοῦ πέμψαντός με πατρός.

25 Ταῦτα λελάληκα ὑμῖν παρ' ὑμῖν μένων· **26** ὁ δὲ
παράκλητος, τὸ πνεῦμα τὸ ἅγιον ὃ πέμψει ὁ πατὴρ ἐν
τῷ ὀνόματί μου, ἐκεῖνος ὑμᾶς διδάξει πάντα καὶ ὑπομνήσει
ὑμᾶς πάντα ἃ εἶπον ὑμῖν [ἐγώ]. **27** Εἰρήνην ἀφίημι ὑμῖν,
εἰρήνην τὴν ἐμὴν δίδωμι ὑμῖν· οὐ καθὼς ὁ κόσμος
δίδωσιν ἐγὼ δίδωμι ὑμῖν. μὴ ταρασσέσθω ὑμῶν ἡ
καρδία μηδὲ δειλιάτω. **28** ἠκούσατε ὅτι ἐγὼ εἶπον ὑμῖν,
Ὑπάγω καὶ ἔρχομαι πρὸς ὑμᾶς. εἰ ἠγαπᾶτέ με ἐχάρητε
ἄν, ὅτι[d] πορεύομαι πρὸς τὸν πατέρα, ὅτι ὁ πατὴρ μείζων
μού ἐστιν. **29** καὶ νῦν εἴρηκα ὑμῖν πρὶν γενέσθαι, ἵνα
ὅταν γένηται πιστεύσητε. **30** οὐκέτι πολλὰ λαλήσω μεθ'

ments and obeys them, he is the one
who loves me. My Father will love him
who loves me; I too will love him and
reveal myself to him." ²² Judas (not
Judas Iscariot) said, "Lord, how can it
be that you will reveal yourself to us and
not to the world?" ²³ Jesus answered
him: "Whoever loves me will obey my
message. My Father will love him, and
my Father and I will come to him and
live with him. ²⁴ Whoever does not love
me does not obey my words. The message
you have heard is not mine, but comes
from the Father, who sent me.

²⁵ "I have told you this while I am
still with you. ²⁶ The Helper, the Holy
Spirit whom the Father will send in my
name, will teach you everything, and
make you remember all that I have
told you.

²⁷ "Peace I leave with you; my own
peace I give you. I do not give it to you
as the world does. Do not be worried
and upset; do not be afraid. ²⁸ You
heard me say to you, 'I am leaving, but
I will come back to you.' If you loved me,
you would be glad that I am going to
the Father, because he is greater than I.
²⁹ I have told you this now, before it all
happens, so that when it does happen
you will believe. ³⁰ I cannot talk with

2148 2174 *Byz Lect* *l*⁶⁹⁸,ᵐ itʳˡ syrˢ,ʰ copᵇᵒ geo Cyril-Jerusalem Didymus
Cyril ‖ μενεῖ...ἔσται itᵃᵘʳ vg copˢᵃ,ᵇᵒᵐˢ,ᵃᶜʰ² arm eth Nonnus

10 22 {A} Ἰούδας, οὐχ ὁ Ἰσκαριώτης 𝔭⁶⁶ (𝔭⁷⁵ *omit* ὁ) ℵ A B K L W
X Δ Θ Π Ψ 0250 *f*¹ *f*¹³ 28 33 565 700 892 1009 1010 1071 1079 1195 1216 1230
1241 1242 1344 1365 1546 1646 2148 2174 *Byz Lect* *l*⁶⁹⁸,ᵐ,⁸⁸³ᵐ,¹⁵⁷⁹ᵐ (itᵃ,ᵃᵘʳ,ff²
Scarioth, itᶜ,ᵉ,q *Scariotha*, it⁽ᵇ⁾,⁽ᶠ⁾ vgʷʷ *Scariotis*) vgᶜˡ syrᵖ,ʰ,ᵖᵃˡᵐˢˢ copᵇᵒ goth
(arm οὐκ Σκαριότα) geo ‖ Ἰούδας, οὐχ ὁ ἀπὸ Καριώτου D itᵈ ‖ Ἰούδας ὁ
Κανανίτης copˢᵃ,ᵃᶜʰ²,ᶠᵃʸ ‖ Θώμας syrˢ ‖ Ἰούδας Θώμας syrᶜ

ᵈ **28** *d* causal: WH RV ASV RSV TT? ‖ *d* indirect: Bov? Nes? BF²? NEB TT? Zür Luth Jer Seg ‖
different text: TR AV

---

21 ὁ δὲ ἀγαπῶν...μου Jn 16.27   **22** ἡμῖν...κόσμῳ Ac 10.40–41   **24** ὁ λόγος...πατρός
Jn 7.16; 14.10   **26** ὁ δὲ παράκλητος...μου Jn 14.16; 15.26; 16.7   **27** Εἰρήνην ἀφίημι...
ἐμὴν δίδωμι ὑμῖν Jn 16.33   μὴ...καρδία Jn 14.1   **28** Ὑπάγω...ὑμᾶς Jn 14.3; 16.16, 17
πορεύομαι...πατέρα Jn 13.1; 14.12; 16.10, 17, 28; 20.17   **29** Jn 13.19

you much longer, for the ruler of this world is coming. He has no power over me, [31] but the world must know that I love the Father; that is why I do everything as he commands me.

"Rise, let us go from this place."

Jesus the Real Vine

15 "I am the real vine, and my Father is the gardener. [2] He takes off every branch in me that does not bear fruit, and prunes every branch that does bear fruit, so that it will be clean and bear more fruit. [3] You have been made clean already by the message I have spoken to you. [4] Remain in union with me, and I will remain in union with you. Unless you remain in me you cannot bear fruit, just as a branch cannot bear fruit unless it remains in the vine.

[5] "I am the vine, you are the branches. Whoever remains in me, and I in him, will bear much fruit; for you can do nothing without me. [6] Whoever does not remain in me is thrown out, like a branch, and dries up; such branches are gathered up and thrown into the fire, where they are burned. [7] If you remain in me, and my words remain in you, then you will ask for anything you wish, and you shall have it. [8] This is how my Father's glory is shown: by your bearing much fruit; and in this way you become my disciples. [9] I love you just as the Father loves me; remain in my love. [10] If you obey my

ὑμῶν, ἔρχεται γὰρ ὁ τοῦ κόσμου ἄρχων· [e] καὶ ἐν ἐμοὶ οὐκ ἔχει οὐδέν, [e] 31 ἀλλ' ἵνα γνῷ ὁ κόσμος ὅτι ἀγαπῶ τὸν πατέρα, καὶ καθὼς ἐνετείλατο μοι ὁ πατήρ, οὕτως ποιῶ. [e] Ἐγείρεσθε, ἄγωμεν ἐντεῦθεν.

Jesus the True Vine

15 Ἐγώ εἰμι ἡ ἄμπελος ἡ ἀληθινή, καὶ ὁ πατήρ μου ὁ γεωργός ἐστιν. 2 πᾶν κλῆμα ἐν ἐμοὶ μὴ φέρον καρπόν, αἴρει αὐτό, καὶ πᾶν τὸ καρπὸν φέρον καθαίρει αὐτὸ ἵνα καρπὸν πλείονα φέρῃ. 3 ἤδη ὑμεῖς καθαροί ἐστε διὰ τὸν λόγον ὃν λελάληκα ὑμῖν· 4 μείνατε ἐν ἐμοί, κἀγὼ ἐν ὑμῖν. καθὼς τὸ κλῆμα οὐ δύναται καρπὸν φέρειν ἀφ' ἑαυτοῦ ἐὰν μὴ μένῃ ἐν τῇ ἀμπέλῳ, οὕτως οὐδὲ ὑμεῖς ἐὰν μὴ ἐν ἐμοὶ μένητε. 5 ἐγώ εἰμι ἡ ἄμπελος, ὑμεῖς τὰ κλήματα. ὁ μένων ἐν ἐμοὶ κἀγὼ ἐν αὐτῷ οὗτος φέρει καρπὸν πολύν, ὅτι χωρὶς ἐμοῦ οὐ δύνασθε ποιεῖν οὐδέν. 6 ἐὰν μή τις μένῃ ἐν ἐμοί, ἐβλήθη ἔξω ὡς τὸ κλῆμα καὶ ἐξηράνθη, καὶ συνάγουσιν αὐτὰ καὶ εἰς τὸ πῦρ βάλλουσιν καὶ καίεται. 7 ἐὰν μείνητε ἐν ἐμοὶ καὶ τὰ ῥήματά μου ἐν ὑμῖν μείνῃ, ὃ ἐὰν θέλητε αἰτήσασθε καὶ γενήσεται ὑμῖν. 8 ἐν τούτῳ ἐδοξάσθη ὁ πατήρ μου, ἵνα καρπὸν πολὺν φέρητε καὶ γένησθε[1] ἐμοὶ μαθηταί. 9 καθὼς ἠγάπησέν με ὁ πατήρ, κἀγὼ ὑμᾶς ἠγάπησα· [a] μείνατε ἐν τῇ ἀγάπῃ τῇ ἐμῇ. 10 ἐὰν

---

[1] 8 {D} γένησθε 𝔓[66vid] B D L X Θ Π 0250 f[1] 565 1079 1195 1230 1242 1646 it[a, aur, b, c, d, e, f, ff2, q, rl] vg cop[sa, bo, ach2] Amphilochius // γενήσεσθε ℵ A K Δ Ψ f[13] 28 33 700 892 1009 1010 1071 1216 1241 1344 1365 1546 2148 2174 *Byz Lect* l[698, m] syr[s, p, h, pal] goth Chrysostom Cyril

[e e e] **30-31** *e* major, *e* minor, *e* major: (TR) WH Bov Nes BF2 RV ASV RSV Zür Luth Jer // *e* minor, *e* major, *e* major: AV NEB[mg] TT // *e* major, *e* minor, *e* minor: NEB // *e* major, *e* major, *e* major: ASV[mg] Seg
[a] **9** *a* major: TR WH[mg] Bov Nes BF2 AV RV ASV RSV NEB TT Zür Luth Jer Seg // *a* minor: WH

30 ὁ...ἄρχων Jn 12.31; 16.11 **31** καθὼς...ποιῶ Jn 12.49; 15.10 Ἐγείρεσθε, ἄγωμεν Mt 26.46; Mk 14.42
15 2 πᾶν κλῆμα...αἴρει αὐτό Mt 3.10; 15.13 3 ἤδη ὑμεῖς καθαροί ἐστε Jn 13.10 4 Ro 11.17-18; 2 Cor 3.5 μείνατε...ὑμῖν Jn 6.56 5 ἐγώ...κλήματα 1 Cor 12.12, 27 οὗτος...πολύν Jn 15.16 χωρὶς...οὐδέν 2 Cor 3.5 6 εἰς...βάλλουσιν Mt 3.10; 7.19; 13.42 7 ὃ ἐὰν θέλητε...ὑμῖν Mk 11.24; Jn 14.13; 16.23 8 ἐν...φέρητε Mt 5.16 10 ἐὰν...ἀγάπῃ μου Jn 14.15; 1 Jn 2.5; 5.3

τὰς ἐντολάς μου τηρήσητε, μενεῖτε ἐν τῇ ἀγάπῃ μου, καθὼς ἐγὼ τὰς ἐντολὰς τοῦ πατρός μου τετήρηκα καὶ μένω αὐτοῦ ἐν τῇ ἀγάπῃ.

11 Ταῦτα λελάληκα ὑμῖν ἵνα ἡ χαρὰ ἡ ἐμὴ ἐν ὑμῖν ᾖ καὶ ἡ χαρὰ ὑμῶν πληρωθῇ. **12** αὕτη ἐστὶν ἡ ἐντολὴ ἡ ἐμή, ἵνα ἀγαπᾶτε ἀλλήλους καθὼς ἠγάπησα ὑμᾶς· **13** μείζονα ταύτης ἀγάπην οὐδεὶς ἔχει, ἵνα τις τὴν ψυχὴν αὐτοῦ θῇ ὑπὲρ τῶν φίλων αὐτοῦ. **14** ὑμεῖς φίλοι μού ἐστε ἐὰν ποιῆτε ἃ ἐγὼ ἐντέλλομαι ὑμῖν. **15** οὐκέτι λέγω ὑμᾶς δούλους, ὅτι ὁ δοῦλος οὐκ οἶδεν τί ποιεῖ αὐτοῦ ὁ κύριος· ὑμᾶς δὲ εἴρηκα φίλους, ὅτι πάντα ἃ ἤκουσα παρὰ τοῦ πατρός μου ἐγνώρισα ὑμῖν. **16** οὐχ ὑμεῖς με ἐξελέξασθε, ἀλλ' ἐγὼ ἐξελεξάμην ὑμᾶς καὶ ἔθηκα ὑμᾶς ἵνα ὑμεῖς ὑπάγητε καὶ καρπὸν φέρητε καὶ ὁ καρπὸς ὑμῶν μένῃ, ἵνα ὅ τι ἂν αἰτήσητε τὸν πατέρα ἐν τῷ ὀνόματί μου δῷ ὑμῖν. **17** ταῦτα ἐντέλλομαι ὑμῖν, ἵνα ἀγαπᾶτε ἀλλήλους.

The World's Hatred

18 Εἰ ὁ κόσμος ὑμᾶς μισεῖ, γινώσκετε ὅτι ἐμὲ πρῶτον ὑμῶν μεμίσηκεν. **19** εἰ ἐκ τοῦ κόσμου ἦτε, ὁ κόσμος ἂν τὸ ἴδιον ἐφίλει· ὅτι δὲ ἐκ τοῦ κόσμου οὐκ ἐστέ, ἀλλ' ἐγὼ ἐξελεξάμην ὑμᾶς ἐκ τοῦ κόσμου, διὰ τοῦτο μισεῖ ὑμᾶς ὁ κόσμος. **20** μνημονεύετε τοῦ λόγου οὗ ἐγὼ εἶπον ὑμῖν, Οὐκ ἔστιν δοῦλος μείζων τοῦ κυρίου αὐτοῦ. εἰ ἐμὲ ἐδίωξαν, καὶ ὑμᾶς διώξουσιν· εἰ τὸν λόγον μου ἐτήρησαν, καὶ τὸν ὑμέτερον τηρήσουσιν. **21** ἀλλὰ ταῦτα πάντα ποιήσουσιν εἰς ὑμᾶς διὰ τὸ ὄνομά μου, ὅτι οὐκ οἴδασιν τὸν πέμψαντά με. **22** εἰ μὴ ἦλθον καὶ ἐλάλησα αὐτοῖς, ἁμαρτίαν οὐκ εἴχοσαν· νῦν δὲ πρόφασιν οὐκ

11 Jn 17.13; 1 Jn 1.4   **12** Jn 13.34; 1 Jn 3.11, 23; 2 Jn 5   **13** Jn 10.11; Ro 5.8; 1 Jn 3.16
14 ὑμεῖς φίλοι μού ἐστε Lk 12.4   **16** ἐγὼ ἐξελεξάμην ὑμᾶς Jn 6.70; 13.18   ἵνα ὑμεῖς...
φέρητε Jn 15.5   ἵνα ὅ τι...δῷ ὑμῖν Jn 14.13, 14; 16.23   **17** Jn 13.34; 1 Jn 3.11, 23; 2 Jn 5
18 Εἰ...μισεῖ Mt 10.22; 24.9; Mk 13.13, Lk 6.22; Jn 17.14; 1 Jn 3.13   ἐμὲ...μεμίσηκεν Ju 7.7
19 εἰ...ἐφίλει 1 Jn 4.5   ὅτι...κόσμος Jn 17.14   **20** Οὐκ ἔστιν δοῦλος...αὐτοῦ Mt 10.24;
Lk 6.40; Jn 13.16   **21** Jn 16.3   ταῦτα...ὄνομά μου Mt 5.11   **22** ἁμαρτίαν οὐκ εἴχοσαν
Jn 9.41

commands, you will remain in my love, in the same way that I have obeyed my Father's commands and remain in his love.

[11] "I have told you this so that my joy may be in you, and that your joy may be complete. [12] This is my commandment: love one another, just as I love you. [13] The greatest love a man can have for his friends is to give his life for them. [14] And you are my friends, if you do what I command. [15] I do not call you servants any longer, because a servant does not know what his master is doing. Instead, I call you friends, because I have told you everything I heard from my Father. [16] You did not choose me; I chose you, and appointed you to go and bear much fruit, the kind of fruit that endures. And the Father will give you whatever you ask of him in my name. [17] This, then, is what I command you: love one another."

The World's Hatred

[18] "If the world hates you, you must remember that it has hated me first. [19] If you belonged to the world, then the world would love you as its own. But I chose you from this world, and you do not belong to it; this is why the world hates you. [20] Remember what I told you: 'No slave is greater than his master.' If they persecuted me, they will persecute you too; if they obeyed my message, they will obey yours too. [21] But they will do all this to you because you are mine; for they do not know him who sent me. [22] They would not have been guilty of sin if I had not come and spoken to them; as it is, they no longer

have any excuse for their sin. [23] Whoever
hates me hates my Father also. [24] They
would not have been guilty of sin if I
had not done the works among them that
no one else ever did; as it is, they have
seen what I did and they hate both me
and my Father. [25] This must be, however, so that what is written in their
Law may come true, 'They hated me for
no reason at all.'

[26] "The Helper will come — the Spirit
of truth, who comes from the Father.
I will send him from the Father, and he
will speak about me. [27] And you, too,
will speak about me, for you have been
with me from the very beginning.

16 "I have told you this so that you
will not fall away. [2] They will put you
out of their synagogues. And the time
will come when anyone who kills you will
think that by doing this he is serving
God. [3] They will do these things to you
because they have not known either the
Father or me. [4] But I have told you this,
so that when the time comes for them
to do these things, you will remember
that I told you."

ἔχουσιν περὶ τῆς ἁμαρτίας αὐτῶν. **23** ὁ ἐμὲ μισῶν καὶ
τὸν πατέρα μου μισεῖ. **24** εἰ τὰ ἔργα μὴ ἐποίησα ἐν
αὐτοῖς ἃ οὐδεὶς ἄλλος ἐποίησεν, ἁμαρτίαν οὐκ εἴχοσαν·
νῦν δὲ καὶ ἑωράκασιν καὶ μεμισήκασιν καὶ ἐμὲ καὶ τὸν
πατέρα μου. **25** ἀλλ' ἵνα πληρωθῇ ὁ λόγος ὁ ἐν τῷ
νόμῳ αὐτῶν γεγραμμένος ὅτι **Ἐμίσησάν με δωρεάν.**

26 Ὅταν ἔλθῃ ὁ παράκλητος ὃν ἐγὼ πέμψω ὑμῖν
παρὰ τοῦ πατρός, τὸ πνεῦμα τῆς ἀληθείας ὃ παρὰ τοῦ
πατρὸς ἐκπορεύεται, ἐκεῖνος μαρτυρήσει περὶ ἐμοῦ·
27 καὶ ὑμεῖς δὲ μαρτυρεῖτε, ὅτι ἀπ' ἀρχῆς μετ' ἐμοῦ
ἐστε.

16 Ταῦτα λελάληκα ὑμῖν ἵνα μὴ σκανδαλισθῆτε.
2 ἀποσυναγώγους ποιήσουσιν ὑμᾶς· ἀλλ' ἔρχεται ὥρα
ἵνα πᾶς ὁ ἀποκτείνας ὑμᾶς δόξῃ λατρείαν προσφέρειν
τῷ θεῷ. **3** καὶ ταῦτα ποιήσουσιν[1] ὅτι οὐκ ἔγνωσαν τὸν
πατέρα οὐδὲ ἐμέ. **4** ἀλλὰ ταῦτα λελάληκα ὑμῖν ἵνα
ὅταν ἔλθῃ ἡ ὥρα αὐτῶν μνημονεύητε αὐτῶν[2] ὅτι ἐγὼ
εἶπον ὑμῖν.

---

[1] **3** {C} ποιήσουσιν Α Β Κ Δ Π 700 892 1010 1079 1216 1230 1241 1242
1344 1646 2148 2174 *l*[32,64,69,76,80,185,191,219,303,3³³,372,374,381,1127,1231,1579,1634,1642] it[aur,b,e,l]
vg[ww] syr[p,h] goth? geo[A] Diatessaron[a,f] Cyprian Lucifer Chrysostom ‖
ποιοῦσιν Θ it[q] goth? ‖ ποιήσουσιν ὑμῖν D L Ψ *f*[1] *f*[13] 565 1071 1195 1365
Byz Lect it[a,d,f,ff2] vg[cl] syr[h with *] cop[sa,bo,ach2] arm eth geo[B] ‖ ποιοῦσιν ὑμῖν
it[e] syr[pal] geo[1] ‖ ποιήσωσιν ὑμῖν ℵ (1009 1546 *omit* ὑμῖν) ‖ ποιήσωσιν εἰς
ὑμᾶς 33 ‖ ποιήσουσιν ὑμᾶς 73 259

[2] **4** {C} ὥρα αὐτῶν μνημονεύητε αὐτῶν p[66vid] Α Β Θ (Π* μνημονεύσητε)
33 1009 1071 1079 1195 1230 1546 1646 syr[p,h] goth ‖ ὥρα αὐτῶν μνημονεύητε
ℵ[a] (L μνημονεύετε) Π² (*f*[13] μνημονεύσητε) *Lect* it[aur,b,c,e,f,l,q,r1] vg cop[boms]
Cyprian ‖ ὥρα μνημονεύητε αὐτῶν Κ Ψ 054 (Δ 1216 1241 1242 1344
μνημονεύετε) *f*[1] 565 700 892 1010 1365 2174 *Byz l*[64,69,76,184,185,1127] it[ff2] syr[pal]
cop[boms] geo Diatessaron[1] (Chrysostom τούτων) ‖ ὥρα μνημονεύητε ℵ* (D*
2148 μνημονεύετε) (D[b] μνημονεύσητε) it[a,d] syr[s] cop[sa,boms,ach2] arm Cyril

---

23 Lk 10.16; Jn 5.23; 1 Jn 2.23   **24** εἰ...εἴχοσαν Jn 14.11   ἁμαρτίαν οὐκ εἴχοσαν Jn 9.41
25 Ἐμίσησάν με δωρεάν Ps 35.19; 69.4   **26** ὁ παράκλητος...ἐκπορεύεται Jn 14.26
27 ὑμεῖς δὲ μαρτυρεῖτε Ac 1.8; 5.32; 1 Jn 4.14   ἀπ' ἀρχῆς μετ' ἐμοῦ ἐστε Lk 1.2; Ac 1.21-22
16 2 ἀποσυναγώγους...ὑμᾶς Jn 9.22   **3** Jn 15.21   **4** ταῦτα λελάληκα ὑμῖν Jn 13.19;
16.25

The Work of the Spirit

Ταῦτα δὲ ὑμῖν ἐξ ἀρχῆς οὐκ εἶπον, ὅτι μεθ' ὑμῶν ἤμην. 5 νῦν δὲ ὑπάγω πρὸς τὸν πέμψαντά με, καὶ οὐδεὶς ἐξ ὑμῶν ἐρωτᾷ με, Ποῦ ὑπάγεις; 6 ἀλλ' ὅτι ταῦτα λελάληκα ὑμῖν ἡ λύπη πεπλήρωκεν ὑμῶν τὴν καρδίαν. 7 ἀλλ' ἐγὼ τὴν ἀλήθειαν λέγω ὑμῖν, συμφέρει ὑμῖν ἵνα ἐγὼ ἀπέλθω. ἐὰν γὰρ μὴ ἀπέλθω, ὁ παράκλητος οὐκ ἐλεύσεται πρὸς ὑμᾶς· ἐὰν δὲ πορευθῶ, πέμψω αὐτὸν πρὸς ὑμᾶς. 8 καὶ ἐλθὼν ἐκεῖνος ἐλέγξει τὸν κόσμον περὶ ἁμαρτίας καὶ περὶ δικαιοσύνης καὶ περὶ κρίσεως· 9 περὶ ἁμαρτίας μέν, ὅτι οὐ πιστεύουσιν εἰς ἐμέ· 10 περὶ δικαιοσύνης δέ, ὅτι πρὸς τὸν πατέρα ὑπάγω καὶ οὐκέτι θεωρεῖτέ με· 11 περὶ δὲ κρίσεως, ὅτι ὁ ἄρχων τοῦ κόσμου τούτου κέκριται.

12 Ἔτι πολλὰ ἔχω ὑμῖν λέγειν, ἀλλ' οὐ δύνασθε βαστάζειν ἄρτι· 13 ὅταν δὲ ἔλθῃ ἐκεῖνος, τὸ πνεῦμα τῆς ἀληθείας, ὁδηγήσει ὑμᾶς ἐν τῇ ἀληθείᾳ πάσῃ³· οὐ γὰρ λαλήσει ἀφ' ἑαυτοῦ, ἀλλ' ὅσα ἀκούσει λαλήσει, καὶ τὰ ἐρχόμενα ἀναγγελεῖ ὑμῖν. 14 ἐκεῖνος ἐμὲ δοξάσει, ὅτι ἐκ τοῦ ἐμοῦ λήμψεται καὶ ἀναγγελεῖ ὑμῖν. 15 πάντα ὅσα ἔχει ὁ πατὴρ ἐμά ἐστιν· διὰ τοῦτο εἶπον ὅτι ἐκ τοῦ ἐμοῦ λαμβάνει καὶ ἀναγγελεῖ ὑμῖν.

---

³ 13 {B} ὁδηγήσει ὑμᾶς ἐν τῇ ἀληθείᾳ πάσῃ (ℵ* omit πάσῃ) ℵ^a L W f¹ 33 565 1071 it^b cop^sa?bo?ach²? (cop^boms omit πάσῃ) goth? geo¹ Victorinus-Rome mss^acc. to Augustine Nonnus Cyril ∥ ὁδηγήσει ὑμᾶς ἐν πάσῃ τῇ ἀληθείᾳ (Θ ὁδηγήσει) it^ff2 syr^h arm goth? ∥ ὁδηγήσει ὑμᾶς εἰς τὴν ἀλήθειαν πᾶσαν A B 054 it^e Origen Didymus (Cyril ἐπί) ∥ ὁδηγήσει ὑμᾶς εἰς πᾶσαν τὴν ἀλήθειαν Κ Δ Π Ψ 068 f¹³ 28 700 892 1009 1010 1079 1195 1216 1230 1241 1242 1344 1365 1546 1646 2148 2174 Byz Lect it^f,q,rl geo² Tertullian Basil Epiphanius Chrysostom Theodore Theodoret ∥ διηγήσεται ὑμῖν τὴν ἀλήθειαν πᾶσαν it^aur,c vg Eusebius Cyril-Jerusalem ∥ ἐκεῖνος ὑμᾶς ὁδηγήσει ἐν τῇ ἀληθείᾳ πάσῃ D it^d syr^s,p,pal cop^boms ∥ ἐκεῖνος ὑμᾶς

---

5 νῦν...πέμψαντά με Jn 7.33 οὐδεὶς...ὑπάγεις Jn 13.36; 14.5   6 Jn 16.22   7 πέμψω ...ὑμᾶς Jn 14.16, 26; 15.26   8 περὶ δικαιοσύνης...κρίσεως Ac 24.25   9 ὅτι οὐ πιστεύουσιν εἰς ἐμέ Jn 5.38; 6.36, 64; 7.5; 10.26; 12.37   10 πρὸς...ὑπάγω Jn 13.1; 14.12, 28; 16.28; 20.17   11 ὁ ἄρχων...τούτου Jn 12.31; 14.30   12 1 Cor 3.1   13 τὸ...ἀληθείας Jn 14.17; 15.26 ὁδηγήσει...πάσῃ Jn 14.26; 1 Jn 2.27   15 πάντα...ἐστιν Jn 17 10

The Work of the Holy Spirit

"I did not tell you these things at the beginning, because I was with you. 5 But now I am going to him who sent me; but none of you asks me, 'Where are you going?' 6 And now that I have told you, sadness has filled your hearts. 7 But I tell you the truth: it is better for you that I go away, because if I do not go, the Helper will not come to you. But if I do go away, then I will send him to you. 8 And when he comes he will prove to the people of the world that they are wrong about sin, and about what is right, and about God's judgment. 9 They are wrong about sin, because they do not believe in me; 10 about what is right, because I am going to the Father and you will not see me any more; 11 about judgment, because the ruler of this world has already been judged.

12 "I have much more to tell you, but now it would be too much for you to bear. 13 But when the Spirit of truth comes, he will lead you into all the truth. He will not speak on his own, but he will tell you what he hears, and will speak of things to come. 14 He will give me glory, for he will take what I have to say and tell it to you. 15 All that my Father has is mine; that is why I said that the Spirit will take what I give him and tell it to you."

Sadness and Gladness

[16] "In a little while you will not see me any more; and then a little while later you will see me." [17] Some of his disciples said to the others: "What does this mean? He tells us, 'In a little while you will not see me, and then a little while later you will see me'; and he also says, 'It is because I am going to the Father.' [18] What does this 'a little while' mean?" they asked. "We do not know what he is talking about!" [19] Jesus knew that they wanted to ask him, so he said to them: "I said, 'In a little while you will not see me, and then a little while later you will see me.' Is this what you are asking about among yourselves? [20] I tell you the truth: you will cry and weep, but the world will be glad; you will be sad, but your sadness will turn into gladness. [21] When a woman is about to give birth to a child she is sad, because her hour of suffering has come; but when the child is born she forgets her suffering, because she is happy that a baby has been born into the world. [22] That is the way it is with you: now you are sad, but I will see you again, and your hearts will be filled with gladness, the kind of gladness that no one can take away from you.

[23] "When that day comes you will not ask me for a thing. I tell you the truth: the Father will give you anything you

Sorrow Will Turn into Joy

16 Μικρὸν καὶ οὐκέτι θεωρεῖτέ με, καὶ πάλιν μικρὸν καὶ ὄψεσθέ με. [17] εἶπαν οὖν ἐκ τῶν μαθητῶν αὐτοῦ πρὸς ἀλλήλους, Τί ἐστιν τοῦτο ὃ λέγει ἡμῖν, Μικρὸν καὶ οὐ θεωρεῖτέ με, καὶ πάλιν μικρὸν καὶ ὄψεσθέ με; καί, Ὅτι ὑπάγω πρὸς τὸν πατέρα; [18] ἔλεγον οὖν, Τί ἐστιν τοῦτο [ὃ λέγει], τὸ μικρόν; οὐκ οἴδαμεν τί λαλεῖ. [19] ἔγνω [ὁ] Ἰησοῦς ὅτι ἤθελον αὐτὸν ἐρωτᾶν, καὶ εἶπεν αὐτοῖς, Περὶ τούτου ζητεῖτε μετ᾽ ἀλλήλων ὅτι εἶπον, Μικρὸν καὶ οὐ θεωρεῖτέ με, καὶ πάλιν μικρὸν καὶ ὄψεσθέ με; [20] ἀμὴν ἀμὴν λέγω ὑμῖν ὅτι κλαύσετε καὶ θρηνήσετε ὑμεῖς, ὁ δὲ κόσμος χαρήσεται· ὑμεῖς λυπηθήσεσθε, ἀλλ᾽ ἡ λύπη ὑμῶν εἰς χαρὰν γενήσεται. [21] ἡ γυνὴ ὅταν τίκτῃ λύπην ἔχει, ὅτι ἦλθεν ἡ ὥρα αὐτῆς· ὅταν δὲ γεννήσῃ τὸ παιδίον, οὐκέτι μνημονεύει τῆς θλίψεως διὰ τὴν χαρὰν ὅτι ἐγεννήθη ἄνθρωπος εἰς τὸν κόσμον. **22** καὶ ὑμεῖς οὖν νῦν μὲν λύπην ἔχετε[4]· πάλιν δὲ ὄψομαι ὑμᾶς, καὶ χαρήσεται ὑμῶν ἡ καρδία, καὶ τὴν χαρὰν ὑμῶν οὐδεὶς αἴρει[5] ἀφ᾽ ὑμῶν. **23** καὶ ἐν ἐκείνῃ τῇ ἡμέρᾳ ἐμὲ οὐκ ἐρωτήσετε οὐδέν.[a] ἀμὴν ἀμὴν λέγω ὑμῖν, ἄν τι αἰτήσητε τὸν πατέρα ἐν τῷ ὀνόματί μου

ὁδηγήσει εἰς πᾶσαν τὴν ἀλήθειαν it[a] Tertullian Novatian Hilary // *docebit vos in veritate omnia* it[l]

4 22 {C} ἔχετε p[22] ℵ* B C K W[c] Δ Π 054 *f*[1] *f*[13] 28 565 700 892 1009 1010 1071 1216 1230 1241 1242 1344 1365 1646 2148 2174[vid] Byz *Lect* it[aur,c,f,ff2,q] vg syr[s,p,h,pal] cop[sa,boms,ach2] arm eth geo Diatessaron[a,i,n] Hilary Cyril // ἕξετε p[66] ℵ[c] A D (L ἔξητε) W* X[comm] Θ Ψ 33 1079 1195 1546 *l*[32,184pt] it[a,b,d,e,rl] cop[bo] Chrysostom Antiochus

5 22 {C} αἴρει p[22,66vid] ℵ A C D[b] K L Δ Θ Π Ψ 054 *f*[1] *f*[13] 28 565 700 892 1010 1071 1079 1195 1216 1230 1241 1242 1344 1365 1546 1646 2148 2174 Byz *Lect* it[b,e,f,q] syr[p,h] Chrysostom Cyril Antiochus // ἀρεῖ p[5] B D* 33 1009 it[a,aur,c,d,ff2,rl] vg cop[sa,bo,ach27] arm eth geo Diatessaron[a,i,n] Hippolytus Origen[gr,lat] Cyprian Hilary // αἴρει or ἀρεῖ syr[s,pal] goth // αφερει [=ἀφαίρει] W

[a] **23** *a major:* TR WH[mg] Bov Nes BF² AV RV ASV RSV NEB TT Zür Luth Jer Seg // *a minor:* WH

16 Jn 14.19   **21** ἡ γυνὴ...ἔχει Is 13.8; 21.3; 26.17; Mic 4.9; 1 Th 5.3   **22** καὶ χαρήσεται ...καρδία Is 66.14   **23** ἄν...δώσει ὑμῖν Jn 14.13, 14; 15.16; 1 Jn 5.14–15

δώσει ὑμῖν⁶. **24** ἕως ἄρτι οὐκ ᾐτήσατε οὐδὲν ἐν τῷ ὀνόματί μου· αἰτεῖτε καὶ λήμψεσθε, ἵνα ἡ χαρὰ ὑμῶν ᾖ πεπληρωμένη.

I Have Overcome the World

25 Ταῦτα ἐν παροιμίαις λελάληκα ὑμῖν· ἔρχεται ὥρα ὅτε οὐκέτι ἐν παροιμίαις λαλήσω ὑμῖν ἀλλὰ παρρησίᾳ περὶ τοῦ πατρὸς ἀπαγγελῶ ὑμῖν. **26** ἐν ἐκείνῃ τῇ ἡμέρᾳ ἐν τῷ ὀνόματί μου αἰτήσεσθε, καὶ οὐ λέγω ὑμῖν ὅτι ἐγὼ ἐρωτήσω τὸν πατέρα περὶ ὑμῶν· **27** αὐτὸς γὰρ ὁ πατὴρ φιλεῖ ὑμᾶς, ὅτι ὑμεῖς ἐμὲ πεφιλήκατε καὶ πεπιστεύκατε ὅτι ἐγὼ παρὰ [τοῦ] θεοῦ⁷ ἐξῆλθον. **28** ἐξῆλθον παρὰ τοῦ πατρὸς⁸ καὶ ἐλήλυθα εἰς τὸν κόσμον· πάλιν ἀφίημι τὸν κόσμον καὶ πορεύομαι πρὸς τὸν πατέρα. **29** Λέγουσιν οἱ μαθηταὶ αὐτοῦ, Ἴδε νῦν ἐν παρρησίᾳ λαλεῖς, καὶ παροιμίαν οὐδεμίαν λέγεις. **30** νῦν οἴδαμεν ὅτι οἶδας πάντα καὶ οὐ χρείαν ἔχεις ἵνα τίς σε ἐρωτᾷ· ἐν τούτῳ πιστεύομεν ὅτι ἀπὸ θεοῦ ἐξῆλθες. **31** ἀπεκρίθη

ask of him in my name.[1] **24** Until now you have not asked for anything in my name; ask and you will receive, so that your happiness may be complete."

Victory over the World

25 "I have told you these things by means of parables. But the time will come when I will use parables no more, but I will speak to you in plain words about the Father. **26** When that day comes you will ask him in my name; and I do not say that I will ask him on your behalf, **27** for the Father himself loves you. He loves you because you love me and have believed that I came from God. **28** I did come from the Father and I came into the world; and now I am leaving the world and going to the Father." **29** Then his disciples said to him: "Look, you are speaking very plainly now, without using parables. **30** We know now that you know everything; you do not need someone to ask you questions. This makes us believe that you came from God." **31** Jesus answered them:

---

⁶ **23** {C} ἐν τῷ ὀνόματί μου δώσει ὑμῖν 𝔭²²ᵛⁱᵈ A C³ᵛⁱᵈ D K W Θ Π Ψ f¹ f¹³ 28 (33 δῷη) 565 700 892 1009 1010 1071 1079 1195 1216 1230 1241 1242 1344 1365 1646 2148 2174 *Byz Lect* itᵃ,ᵃᵘʳ,ᵇ,ᶜ,ᵈ,(ᵉ),f,ff²,q,ʳˡ vg syrˢ,ᵖ,ʰ,ᵖᵃˡ copᵇᵒ goth arm eth geo Diatessaronᵃ,ⁱ,ⁿ Chrysostom Cyril ‖ δώσει ὑμῖν ἐν τῷ ὀνόματί μου 𝔭⁵ᵛⁱᵈ ℵ B C* L X Δ 054 copˢᵃ,ᵃᶜʰ² Origen Cyril ‖ δώσει ὑμῖν 1546

⁷ **27** {C} τοῦ θεοῦ C³ K W Δ Π Ψ 054 f¹ f¹³ 28 565 700 892 1009 1010 1071 1195 1216 1230 1241 1242 1344 1365 1546 1646 2148 2174 *Byz Lect* l¹⁸⁵ᵖᵗ Chrysostom ‖ θεοῦ 𝔭⁵ ℵ*,ᵇ A Θ 33 1079 l⁷⁶ Chrysostom ‖ θεοῦ or τοῦ θεοῦ itᵃ,ᵃᵘʳ,ᵇ,ᶜ,ᵉ,f,q,ʳˡ vg syrˢ,ᵖ,ʰ,ᵖᵃˡ goth arm eth geo Origenˡᵃᵗ Hilary Cyril ‖ τοῦ πατρός (ℵᵃ *omit* τοῦ) B C* D L X l¹⁸⁵ᵖᵗ itᵈ copˢᵃ,ᵇᵒ,ᵃᶜʰ² Diatessaronᵃ,ⁱ Didymus Cyril ‖ *a deo patre* itff²

⁸ **28** {C} ἐξῆλθον παρὰ τοῦ πατρός 𝔭⁵,²² ℵ A C² K Δ Θ Π 054 f¹ f¹³ 28 565 700 892 1009 1010 1071 1079 1195 1216 1230 1241 1242 1344 1365 1546 1646 2148 2174 *Byz Lect* goth Diatessaron (Chrysostom ἀπό) Cyril ‖ ἐξῆλθον ἐκ τοῦ πατρός B C* L X Ψ 33 syrᵖ,ʰ,ᵖᵃˡ Epiphanius ‖ ἐξῆλθον ἐκ (or παρά) τοῦ πατρός itᵃᵘʳ,ᶜ,f,q vg copˢᵃ,ᵇᵒ arm geo Hilary ‖ παρὰ (or ἐκ) τοῦ πατρός it(ᵃ),ᵉ,ʳˡ ‖ *omit* D W itᵇ,ᵈ,ff² syrˢ copᵃᶜʰ²

---

24 ἵνα...πεπληρωμένη Jn 15.11; 1 Jn 1.4   **25** Ταῦτα...λελάληκα ὑμῖν Mt 13.34; Mk 4.33–34; Jn 16.4   **27** αὐτὸς...φιλεῖ ὑμᾶς Jn 14.21, 23   ἐγώ...ἐξῆλθον Jn 3.2; 8.42; 13.3; 17.8   **28** Jn 13.3   **30** οἴδαμεν...ἐρωτᾷ Jn 2.24–25

---

[1] **23** The Father will give you anything you ask of him in my name: *some mss. read* if you ask the Father for anything, he will give it to you in my name

"Do you believe now? [32] The time is coming, and is already here, when all of you will be scattered, each one to his own home, and I will be left all alone. But I am not really alone, because the Father is with me. [33] I have told you this so that you will have peace through your union with me. The world will make you suffer. But be brave! I have defeated the world!"

Jesus Prays for His Disciples

17 After Jesus finished saying this, he looked up to heaven and said: "Father, the hour has come. Give glory to your Son, that the Son may give glory to you. [2] For you gave him authority over all men, so that he might give eternal life to all those you gave him. [3] And this is eternal life: for men to know you, the only true God, and to know Jesus Christ, whom you sent. [4] I showed your glory on earth; I finished the work you gave me to do. [5] O Father! Give me glory in your presence now, the same glory I had with you before the world was made.

[6] "I have made you known to the men you gave me out of the world. They belonged to you, and you gave them to me. They have obeyed your word, [7] and now they know that everything you gave me comes from you. [8] For I gave them the message that you gave me, and they

αὐτοῖς Ἰησοῦς, "Ἄρτι πιστεύετε;[b] **32** ἰδοὺ ἔρχεται ὥρα καὶ ἐλήλυθεν ἵνα σκορπισθῆτε ἕκαστος εἰς τὰ ἴδια κἀμὲ μόνον ἀφῆτε· καὶ οὐκ εἰμὶ μόνος, ὅτι ὁ πατὴρ μετ' ἐμοῦ ἐστιν. **33** ταῦτα λελάληκα ὑμῖν ἵνα ἐν ἐμοὶ εἰρήνην ἔχητε· ἐν τῷ κόσμῳ θλῖψιν ἔχετε, ἀλλὰ θαρσεῖτε, ἐγὼ νενίκηκα τὸν κόσμον.

The Prayer of Jesus

17 Ταῦτα ἐλάλησεν Ἰησοῦς, καὶ ἐπάρας τοὺς ὀφθαλμοὺς αὐτοῦ εἰς τὸν οὐρανὸν εἶπεν, Πάτερ, ἐλήλυθεν ἡ ὥρα· δόξασόν σου τὸν υἱόν, ἵνα ὁ υἱός[1] δοξάσῃ σέ, **2** καθὼς ἔδωκας αὐτῷ ἐξουσίαν πάσης σαρκός, ἵνα πᾶν ὃ δέδωκας αὐτῷ δώσῃ αὐτοῖς ζωὴν αἰώνιον. **3** αὕτη δέ ἐστιν ἡ αἰώνιος ζωή, ἵνα γινώσκωσιν σὲ τὸν μόνον ἀληθινὸν θεὸν καὶ ὃν ἀπέστειλας Ἰησοῦν Χριστόν. **4** ἐγώ σε ἐδόξασα ἐπὶ τῆς γῆς, τὸ ἔργον τελειώσας ὃ δέδωκάς μοι ἵνα ποιήσω· **5** καὶ νῦν δόξασόν με σύ, πάτερ, παρὰ σεαυτῷ τῇ δόξῃ ᾗ εἶχον πρὸ τοῦ τὸν κόσμον εἶναι παρὰ σοί.

6 Ἐφανέρωσά σου τὸ ὄνομα τοῖς ἀνθρώποις οὓς ἔδωκάς μοι ἐκ τοῦ κόσμου. σοὶ ἦσαν κἀμοὶ αὐτοὺς ἔδωκας, καὶ τὸν λόγον σου τετήρηκαν. **7** νῦν ἔγνωκαν ὅτι πάντα ὅσα δέδωκάς μοι παρὰ σοῦ εἰσιν· **8** ὅτι τὰ ῥήματα ἃ ἔδωκάς μοι δέδωκα αὐτοῖς, καὶ αὐτοὶ ἔλαβον

---

[1] **1** {C} ὁ υἱός 𝔭[60vid] א B C* W 0109 it[d,e,ff2] cop[boms] Origen Victorinus-Rome Hilary ‖ ὁ υἱός σου A (C² καὶ ὁ υἱός) C³ D[gr] (K *omit* ὁ) L X Δ Θ Π Ψ 054 0250 f¹ f¹³ 28 33 565 700 892 1009 1010 1071 1079 1195 1216 1230 1241 1242 1344 1365 1546 1646 2148 2174 *Byz Lect* it[a,aur,b,c,f,q,r1] vg syr[s,p,h,pal] cop[sa,bo,ach2] goth arm geo Diatessaron[a,i,n] Origen[gr,lat] Hilary

[b] **31** *b* question: TR WH Bov Nes BF² AV RV ASV RSV NEB TT Zür Luth Jer Seg ‖ *b* statement: NEB[mg]

32 ἵνα...ἀφῆτε Zch 13.7; Mt 26.31, 56; Mk 14.27, 50   οὐκ εἰμὶ μόνος...ἐστιν Jn 8.29 **33** ταῦτα...ἔχητε Jn 14.27   ἐν τῷ...ἔχετε 2 Tm 3.12   ἐγὼ...κόσμον 1 Jn 5.4 **17 1** ἐπάρας...οὐρανόν Jn 11.41   ἐλήλυθεν ἡ ὥρα Mt 26.45; Mk 14.41; Jn 12.23; 13.1 δόξασον...σέ Jn 13.31-32   **2** καθὼς...σαρκός Mt 28.18   **3** αὕτη...θεόν Wsd 15.3   ἵνα... θεόν 1 Th 1.9; 1 Jn 5.20   **4** ἐγώ...γῆς Jn 13.31-32; 14.13   τὸ...ποιήσω Jn 4.34   **5** πρὸ... κόσμον...σοί Jn 1.1-2; 8.58; 17.24   **6** Ἐφανέρωσα...κόσμου Jn 17.26

καὶ ἔγνωσαν ἀληθῶς ὅτι παρὰ σοῦ ἐξῆλθον, καὶ ἐπίστευσαν ὅτι σύ με ἀπέστειλας. 9 ἐγὼ περὶ αὐτῶν ἐρωτῶ· οὐ περὶ τοῦ κόσμου ἐρωτῶ ἀλλὰ περὶ ὧν δέδωκάς μοι, ὅτι σοί εἰσιν, 10 καὶ τὰ ἐμὰ πάντα σά ἐστιν καὶ τὰ σὰ ἐμά, καὶ δεδόξασμαι ἐν αὐτοῖς. 11 καὶ οὐκέτι εἰμὶ ἐν τῷ κόσμῳ, καὶ αὐτοὶ ἐν τῷ κόσμῳ εἰσίν, κἀγὼ πρὸς σὲ ἔρχομαι. Πάτερ ἅγιε, τήρησον αὐτοὺς ἐν τῷ ὀνόματί σου ᾧ δέδωκάς μοι[2], ἵνα ὦσιν ἓν καθὼς ἡμεῖς. 12 ὅτε ἤμην μετ' αὐτῶν ἐγὼ ἐτήρουν αὐτοὺς ἐν τῷ ὀνόματί σου ᾧ δέδωκάς μοι, καὶ[3] ἐφύλαξα, καὶ οὐδεὶς ἐξ αὐτῶν ἀπώλετο εἰ μὴ ὁ υἱὸς τῆς ἀπωλείας, ἵνα ἡ γραφὴ πληρωθῇ. 13 νῦν δὲ πρὸς σὲ ἔρχομαι, καὶ ταῦτα λαλῶ ἐν τῷ κόσμῳ ἵνα ἔχωσιν τὴν χαρὰν τὴν ἐμὴν πεπληρωμένην ἐν αὐτοῖς. 14 ἐγὼ δέδωκα αὐτοῖς τὸν λόγον σου, καὶ ὁ κόσμος ἐμίσησεν αὐτούς, ὅτι οὐκ εἰσὶν ἐκ τοῦ κόσμου καθὼς ἐγὼ οὐκ εἰμὶ ἐκ τοῦ κόσμου. 15 οὐκ ἐρωτῶ ἵνα ἄρῃς αὐτοὺς ἐκ τοῦ κόσμου ἀλλ' ἵνα τηρήσῃς αὐτοὺς ἐκ τοῦ πονηροῦ. 16 ἐκ τοῦ κόσμου οὐκ εἰσὶν καθὼς ἐγὼ οὐκ εἰμὶ ἐκ τοῦ κόσμου. 17 ἁγίασον αὐτοὺς ἐν τῇ

---

[2] **11** {C} ᾧ δέδωκάς μοι 𝔭60vid (𝔭66* omit ἵνα ὦσιν ἓν καθὼς ἡμεῖς) 𝔭66c vid (א L W ἔδωκας) A B C K Δ Θ Π Ψ 054 f¹ f¹³ 28 565 700 1010 1071 1079 1216 1241 1242vid 1344 1365 1546 2174 Byz Lect l698,m,211m,1127pt,1579m arm geo¹ Athanasiusmss Cyril ‖ ὃ δέδωκάς μοι D* X 2148 l159,183,1127pt itd ‖ ᾧ (or ὃ) δέδωκάς μοι syrp,h,pal copsa,bo ‖ οὓς δέδωκάς μοι Db 892vid 1009 1195 1230 1646 l185 itaur,f,q vg copsamss goth eth geo² Diatessaroni Athanasiused ‖ omit ᾧ δέδωκάς μοι, ἵνα ὦσιν ἓν καθὼς ἡμεῖς ita,b,c,e,ff2,rl syrs copach² Hilary Chrysostom Nonnus

[3] **12** {C} ᾧ δέδωκάς μοι, καί 𝔭66c vid B (C* ἔδωκας) L W 33 arm (geo¹ omit καί) Cyril ‖ ὃ δέδωκάς μοι καί אc ‖ ᾧ (or ὃ) δέδωκάς μοι, καί syrpalmss copsa,bo,ach² ‖ οὓς δέδωκάς μοι A (C³ ἔδωκας) Dgr K X Δ Θ Π Ψ 054 f¹ f¹³ 28 565 700 1009 1010 1071 1079 1195 1216 1230 1241 1242 1344 1365 1546 1646 2148 1274 Byz Lect l698,m,211m,1579m ita,aur,b,c,e,f,ff2,q,rl (itd add καί) vg syrp,h goth eth geo² nub Origenlat ‖ καί 𝔭66* א* syrs

---

8 ἔγνωσαν...ἐξῆλθον Jn 3.2; 16.30   **10** τὰ ἐμὰ πάντα σά ἐστιν Lk 15.31   τὰ σὰ ἐμά Jn 16.15   **11** αὐτοὶ ἐν τῷ κόσμῳ εἰσίν Jn 13.1   κἀγὼ...ἔρχομαι Jn 13.1, 3; 16.28   ἵνα ὦσιν ἕν,,,ἡμεῖς Jn 10.30; 17.21; Ga 3.28   **12** οὐδεὶς...ἀπώλετο Jn 6.39· 18.9   οὐδεὶς πληρωθῇ Ps 41.9; 109.4, 5, 7, 8   ὁ...ἀπωλείας 2 Th 2.3   **13** ταῦτα λαλῶ...αὐτοῖς Jn 15.11; 1 Jn 1.4   **14** ὁ...εἰσὶν ἐκ τοῦ κόσμου Jn 15.18-19   ἐγὼ οὐκ...κόσμου Jn 8.23   **15** ἵνα...πονηροῦ Mt 6.13; 2 Th 3.3; 1 Jn 5.18

received it; they know that it is true that I came from you, and they believe that you sent me.

9 "I pray for them. I do not pray for the world, but for the men you gave me, because they belong to you. 10 All I have is yours, and all you have is mine; and my glory is shown through them. 11 And now I am coming to you; I am no longer in the world, but they are in the world. O holy Father! Keep them safe by the power of your name, the name you gave me,[1] so they may be one just as you and I are one. 12 While I was with them I kept them safe by the power of your name, the name you gave me.[2] I protected them, and not one of them was lost, except the man who was bound to be lost — that the scripture might come true. 13 And now I am coming to you, and I say these things in the world so that they might have my joy in their hearts, in all its fulness. 14 I gave them your message and the world hated them, because they do not belong to the world, just as I do not belong to the world. 15 I do not ask you to take them out of the world, but I do ask you to keep them safe from the Evil One. 16 Just as I do not belong to the world, they do not belong to the world. 17 Make them your

---

[1] **11** keep them safe by the power of your name, the name you gave me: *some mss. read* by the power of your name keep safe those you have given me

[2] **12** I kept them safe by the power of your name, the name you gave me: *some mss. read* by the power of your name I kept safe those you have given me

own, by means of the truth; your word is truth. 18 I sent them into the world just as you sent me into the world. 19 And for their sake I give myself to you, in order that they, too, may truly belong to you.

20 "I do not pray only for them, but also for those who believe in me because of their message. 21 I pray that they may all be one. O Father! May they be in us, just as you are in me and I am in you. May they be one, so that the world will believe that you sent me. 22 I gave them the same glory you gave me, so that they may be one, just as you and I are one: 23 I in them and you in me, so they may be completely one, in order that the world may know that you sent me and that you love them as you love me.

24 "O Father! You have given them to me, and I want them to be with me where I am, so they may see my glory, the glory you gave me; for you loved me before the world was made. 25 O righteous Father! The world does not know you, but I know you, and these know that you sent me. 26 I made you known to them and I will continue to do so, in order that the love you have for me may be in them, and I may be in them."

ἀληθείᾳ· ὁ λόγος ὁ σὸς ἀλήθειά ἐστιν. 18 καθὼς ἐμὲ ἀπέστειλας εἰς τὸν κόσμον, κἀγὼ ἀπέστειλα αὐτοὺς εἰς τὸν κόσμον· 19 καὶ ὑπὲρ αὐτῶν [ἐγὼ] ἁγιάζω ἐμαυτόν, ἵνα ὦσιν καὶ αὐτοὶ ἡγιασμένοι ἐν ἀληθείᾳ.

20 Οὐ περὶ τούτων δὲ ἐρωτῶ μόνον, ἀλλὰ καὶ περὶ τῶν πιστευόντων διὰ τοῦ λόγου αὐτῶν εἰς ἐμέ, 21 ἵνα πάντες ἓν ὦσιν, καθὼς σύ, πάτερ, ἐν ἐμοὶ κἀγὼ ἐν σοί, ἵνα καὶ αὐτοὶ ἐν ἡμῖν ὦσιν[4], ἵνα ὁ κόσμος πιστεύῃ ὅτι σύ με ἀπέστειλας. 22 κἀγὼ τὴν δόξαν ἣν δέδωκάς μοι δέδωκα αὐτοῖς, ἵνα ὦσιν ἓν καθὼς ἡμεῖς ἕν, 23 ἐγὼ ἐν αὐτοῖς καὶ σὺ ἐν ἐμοί, ἵνα ὦσιν τετελειωμένοι εἰς ἕν, ἵνα γινώσκῃ ὁ κόσμος ὅτι σύ με ἀπέστειλας καὶ ἠγάπησας αὐτοὺς καθὼς ἐμὲ ἠγάπησας. 24 Πάτερ, ὃ δέδωκάς μοι[5], θέλω ἵνα ὅπου εἰμὶ ἐγὼ κἀκεῖνοι ὦσιν μετ' ἐμοῦ, ἵνα θεωρῶσιν τὴν δόξαν τὴν ἐμὴν[a] ἣν δέδωκάς μοι,[a] ὅτι ἠγάπησάς με πρὸ καταβολῆς κόσμου. 25 πάτερ δίκαιε, καὶ ὁ κόσμος σε οὐκ ἔγνω, ἐγὼ δέ σε ἔγνων, καὶ οὗτοι ἔγνωσαν ὅτι σύ με ἀπέστειλας, 26 καὶ ἐγνώρισα αὐτοῖς τὸ ὄνομά σου καὶ γνωρίσω, ἵνα ἡ ἀγάπη ἣν ἠγάπησάς με ἐν αὐτοῖς ᾖ κἀγὼ ἐν αὐτοῖς.

---

4 21 {C} ὦσιν 𝔓66vid B C* D W ita,b,c,d,e,(r1) syrs copsa,bomss,ach2 arm geo Clement Origen Eusebius Hilary Athanasius ‖ ἐν ὦσιν ℵ A C3 K L X Δ Θ Π Ψ 054 f1 f13 28 33 565 700 892 1009 1010 1071 1079 1195 1216 1230 1241 1242 1344 1365 1546 1646 2148 2174 *Byz Lect* l69s,m,211m,1579m itaur,f,q vg syrp,h,pal copbo goth eth Clement Origengr,lat Cyprian Eusebius Hilary Basil Athanasius Cyril Theodoret

5 24 {B} ὃ δέδωκάς μοι 𝔓60 ℵ B D W itd syrs,pal copbo goth geo1 ‖ οὗ δέδωκάς μοι Θ ‖ οὓς δέδωκάς μοι A C K L X Δ Π Ψ 054 f1 f13 28 33 565 700 892 1009 1010 1071 (1079 ἔδωκας) 1195 1216 1230 1241 1242 1344 1365 1546 1646 2148 2174 *Byz Lect* ita,aur,b,c,e,f,(q),r1 vg syrp,h copsa,boms arm eth geo2 Diatessarona,i,n Clement Cyprian Eusebius Ambrosiaster1/4 Chrysostom Nonnus Cyril Theodoret ‖ *omit* Ambrosiaster3/4

---

a a **24** a none, a minor: WH (Zür) Jer ‖ a minor, a major: AV RV ASV Luth ‖ a minor, a none: Bov Nes BF2 NEB TT ‖ a minor, a minor: TR Seg ‖ a none, a none: RSV

---

18 Jn 20.21   **20** Οὐ...ἐρωτῶ μόνον Jn 17.9   **21** ἵνα...ἓν ὦσιν Ga 3.28   καθὼς... κἀγὼ ἐν σοί Jn 10.38   **22** ἵνα...ἡμεῖς ἕν Jn 17.11   **24** θέλω...ἐμοῦ Jn 12.26   ἵνα θεωρῶσιν...ἐμὴν Jn 1.14   τὴν δόξαν...κόσμου Jn 17.5   **25** ὁ...ἔγνω Jn 1.10; 8.55   ἐγὼ...ἔγνων Mt 11.27; Lk 10.22; Jn 8.55   **26** ἐγνώρισα...σου Jn 17.6

The Betrayal and Arrest of Jesus
(Mt 26.47–56; Mk 14.43–50; Lk 22.47–53)

18 Ταῦτα εἰπὼν Ἰησοῦς ἐξῆλθεν σὺν τοῖς μαθηταῖς αὐτοῦ πέραν τοῦ χειμάρρου τοῦ Κεδρὼν ὅπου ἦν κῆπος, εἰς ὃν εἰσῆλθεν αὐτὸς καὶ οἱ μαθηταὶ αὐτοῦ. 2 ᾔδει δὲ καὶ Ἰούδας ὁ παραδιδοὺς αὐτὸν τὸν τόπον, ὅτι πολλάκις συνήχθη Ἰησοῦς ἐκεῖ μετὰ τῶν μαθητῶν αὐτοῦ. 3 ὁ οὖν Ἰούδας λαβὼν τὴν σπεῖραν καὶ ἐκ τῶν ἀρχιερέων καὶ [ἐκ] τῶν Φαρισαίων ὑπηρέτας ἔρχεται ἐκεῖ μετὰ φανῶν καὶ λαμπάδων καὶ ὅπλων. 4 Ἰησοῦς οὖν εἰδὼς πάντα τὰ ἐρχόμενα ἐπ᾽ αὐτὸν ἐξῆλθεν καὶ λέγει αὐτοῖς, Τίνα ζητεῖτε; 5 ἀπεκρίθησαν αὐτῷ, Ἰησοῦν τὸν Ναζωραῖον. λέγει αὐτοῖς, Ἐγώ εἰμι[1]. εἱστήκει δὲ καὶ Ἰούδας ὁ παραδιδοὺς αὐτὸν μετ᾽ αὐτῶν. 6 ὡς οὖν εἶπεν αὐτοῖς, Ἐγώ εἰμι, ἀπῆλθον εἰς τὰ ὀπίσω καὶ ἔπεσαν χαμαί. 7 πάλιν οὖν ἐπηρώτησεν αὐτούς, Τίνα ζητεῖτε; οἱ δὲ εἶπαν, Ἰησοῦν τὸν Ναζωραῖον. 8 ἀπεκρίθη Ἰησοῦς, Εἶπον ὑμῖν ὅτι ἐγώ εἰμι· εἰ οὖν ἐμὲ ζητεῖτε, ἄφετε τούτους ὑπάγειν· 9 ἵνα πληρωθῇ ὁ λόγος ὃν εἶπεν ὅτι Οὓς δέδωκάς μοι οὐκ ἀπώλεσα ἐξ αὐτῶν οὐδένα. 10 Σίμων οὖν Πέτρος ἔχων μάχαιραν εἵλκυσεν αὐτὴν καὶ ἔπαισεν τὸν τοῦ ἀρχιερέως δοῦλον καὶ ἀπέκοψεν αὐτοῦ τὸ ὠτάριον τὸ δεξιόν. ἦν δὲ ὄνομα τῷ δούλῳ Μάλχος. 11 εἶπεν οὖν ὁ Ἰησοῦς τῷ Πέτρῳ, Βάλε τὴν μάχαιραν εἰς τὴν θήκην· τὸ ποτήριον ὃ δέδωκέν μοι ὁ πατὴρ οὐ μὴ πίω αὐτό;

---

[1] 5 {C} Ἐγώ εἰμι p60 D l150,253 itb,e,r1 syrs,palms copbo,mss Origen ‖ ὁ Ἰησοῦς, Ἐγώ εἰμι (ℵ omit ὁ) A C K L W X Δ Θ Π Ψ 054 0250 f1 f13 28 33 565 700 892 1009 1010 1071 1079 1195 1216 1230 1241 1242 1344 1365 1546 1646 2148 2174 Byz Lect itaur,c,f,q vg syrp,h,palmss copsa,bo,ach2 goth arm geo ‖ Ἐγώ εἰμι Ἰησοῦς B ‖ Ego sum. Iesus autem . . . ita

---

1 Mt 26.36; Mk 14.32   2 πολλάκις...αὐτοῦ Lk 21.37; 22.39   3 ἐκ τῶν ἀρχιερέων ...ὑπηρέτας Jn 7.32, 45   9 Jn 6.39; 17.12   10 Σίμων...μάχαιραν Lk 22.36, 38   11 τὸ ποτήριον...αὐτό Mt 20.22; 26.39; Mk 10.38; 14.36; Lk 22.42

The Arrest of Jesus
(Also Matt. 26.47–56; Mark 14.43–50; Luke 22.47–53)

18 After Jesus had said this prayer he left with his disciples and went across the brook Kidron. There was a garden in that place, and Jesus and his disciples went in. [2] Judas, the traitor, knew where it was, because many times Jesus had met there with his disciples. [3] So Judas went to the garden, taking with him a group of soldiers and some Temple guards sent by the chief priests and the Pharisees; they were armed and carried lanterns and torches. [4] Jesus knew everything that was going to happen to him; so he stepped forward and said to them, "Who is it you are looking for?" [5] "Jesus of Nazareth," they answered. "I am he," he said.

Judas, the traitor, was standing there with them. [6] When Jesus said to them, "I am he," they moved back and fell to the ground. [7] Jesus asked them again, "Who is it you are looking for?" "Jesus of Nazareth," they said. [8] "I have already told you that I am he," Jesus said. "If, then, you are looking for me, let these others go." [9] (He said this so that what he had said might come true: "Not a single one was lost, Father, of all those you gave me.") [10] Simon Peter had a sword; he drew it and struck the High Priest's slave, cutting off his right ear. The name of the slave was Malchus. [11] Jesus said to Peter, "Put your sword back in its place! Do you think that I will not drink the cup of suffering my Father has given me?"

Jesus before Annas

[12] The group of soldiers with their commanding officer and the Jewish guards arrested Jesus, tied him up, [13] and took him first to Annas. He was the father-in-law of Caiaphas, who was High Priest that year. [14] It was Caiaphas who had advised the Jews that it was better that one man die for all the people.

Peter Denies Jesus
(Also Matt. 26.69–70; Mark 14.66–68; Luke 22.55–57)

[15] Simon Peter and another disciple followed Jesus. That other disciple was well known to the High Priest, so he went with Jesus into the courtyard of the High Priest's house. [16] Peter stayed outside by the gate. The other disciple, who was well known to the High Priest, went back out, spoke to the girl at the gate and brought Peter inside. [17] The girl at the gate said to Peter, "Aren't you one of the disciples of that man?" "No, I am not," answered Peter.

[18] It was cold, so the servants and guards had built a charcoal fire and were standing around it, warming themselves. Peter went over and stood with them, warming himself.

Jesus before the High Priest
(Mt 26.57–58; Mk 14.53–54; Lk 22.54)

12 Ἡ οὖν σπεῖρα καὶ ὁ χιλίαρχος καὶ οἱ ὑπηρέται τῶν Ἰουδαίων συνέλαβον τὸν Ἰησοῦν καὶ ἔδησαν αὐτὸν **13** ²καὶ ἤγαγον πρὸς Ἄνναν πρῶτον· ἦν γὰρ πενθερὸς τοῦ Καϊάφα, ὃς ἦν ἀρχιερεὺς τοῦ ἐνιαυτοῦ ἐκείνου· **14** ἦν δὲ Καϊάφας ὁ συμβουλεύσας τοῖς Ἰουδαίοις ὅτι συμφέρει ἕνα ἄνθρωπον ἀποθανεῖν ὑπὲρ τοῦ λαοῦ.

Peter's Denial of Jesus
(Mt 26.69–70; Mk 14.66–68; Lk 22.55–57)

15 Ἠκολούθει δὲ τῷ Ἰησοῦ Σίμων Πέτρος καὶ ἄλλος μαθητής. ὁ δὲ μαθητὴς ἐκεῖνος ἦν γνωστὸς τῷ ἀρχιερεῖ, καὶ συνεισῆλθεν τῷ Ἰησοῦ εἰς τὴν αὐλὴν τοῦ ἀρχιερέως, **16** ὁ δὲ Πέτρος εἱστήκει πρὸς τῇ θύρᾳ ἔξω. ἐξῆλθεν οὖν ὁ μαθητὴς ὁ ἄλλος ὁ γνωστὸς τοῦ ἀρχιερέως³ καὶ εἶπεν τῇ θυρωρῷ καὶ εἰσήγαγεν τὸν Πέτρον. **17** λέγει οὖν τῷ Πέτρῳ ἡ παιδίσκη ἡ θυρωρός, Μὴ καὶ σὺ ἐκ τῶν μαθητῶν εἶ τοῦ ἀνθρώπου τούτου; λέγει ἐκεῖνος, Οὐκ εἰμί. **18** εἱστήκεισαν δὲ οἱ δοῦλοι καὶ οἱ ὑπηρέται ἀνθρακιὰν πεποιηκότες, ὅτι ψῦχος ἦν, καὶ ἐθερμαίνοντο· ἦν δὲ καὶ ὁ Πέτρος μετ' αὐτῶν ἑστὼς καὶ θερμαινόμενος.

---

² **13** *See footnote 4 page 401.*

³ **16** {C} ὁ μαθητὴς ὁ ἄλλος ὁ γνωστὸς τοῦ ἀρχιερέως B C*vid L (syrˢ) ‖ ὁ μαθητὴς ὃς ἦν γνωστὸς τοῦ ἀρχιερέως 𝔭66vid (copsa,bo,ach2) ‖ ὁ μαθητὴς ὁ ἄλλος ὃς ἦν γνωστὸς τῷ ἀρχιερεῖ ℵ A C² Dsupp Kᶜ W (X τοῦ ἀρχιερέως) Δ Θ Π (054 *omit* ὁ ἄλλος) *f*¹ 33 565 700 892 (1009 *l*⁷⁶ ὁ ἄλλος μαθητής) 1010 1071 1079 1195 1216 1230 1242 1344 1365 (1546 *omit* ὃς... ἀρχιερεῖ) 1646 2174 *Byz Lect* vg syrp,h,pal goth arm geo¹ Diatessarona,i,n Cyril ‖ ὁ μαθητὴς ἐκεῖνος ὃς ἦν γνωστὸς τῷ ἀρχιερεῖ K*vid Ψ *f*¹³ 1241 2148 itaur (itᵍ *omit* ὃς ἦν) eth geo²? ‖ *discipulus ille alius, qui erat notus principi sacerdotum* ita,b,(c),f,(ff2),rl

---

13 Lk 3.2; Jn 18.24   **13–14** Καϊάφα...λαοῦ Jn 11.49–51   **15** Σίμων...μαθητής Jn 20.3
15–16 συνεισῆλθεν...Πέτρον Mt 26.58; Mk 14.54; Lk 22.54–55   **17** Μὴ καὶ σὺ...Οὐκ εἰμί Jn 18.25

The High Priest Questions Jesus
(Mt 26.59—66; Mk 14.55—64; Lk 22.66—71)

19 Ὁ οὖν ἀρχιερεὺς ἠρώτησεν τὸν Ἰησοῦν περὶ τῶν μαθητῶν αὐτοῦ καὶ περὶ τῆς διδαχῆς αὐτοῦ. **20** ἀπεκρίθη αὐτῷ Ἰησοῦς, Ἐγὼ παρρησίᾳ λελάληκα τῷ κόσμῳ· ἐγὼ πάντοτε ἐδίδαξα ἐν συναγωγῇ καὶ ἐν τῷ ἱερῷ, ὅπου πάντες οἱ Ἰουδαῖοι συνέρχονται, καὶ ἐν κρυπτῷ ἐλάλησα οὐδέν. **21** τί με ἐρωτᾷς; ἐρώτησον τοὺς ἀκηκοότας τί ἐλάλησα αὐτοῖς· ἴδε οὗτοι οἴδασιν ἃ εἶπον ἐγώ. **22** ταῦτα δὲ αὐτοῦ εἰπόντος εἷς παρεστηκὼς τῶν ὑπηρετῶν ἔδωκεν ῥάπισμα τῷ Ἰησοῦ εἰπών, Οὕτως ἀποκρίνῃ τῷ ἀρχιερεῖ; **23** ἀπεκρίθη αὐτῷ Ἰησοῦς, Εἰ κακῶς ἐλάλησα, μαρτύρησον περὶ τοῦ κακοῦ· εἰ δὲ καλῶς, τί με δέρεις; **24** ἀπέστειλεν οὖν αὐτὸν ὁ Ἄννας δεδεμένον πρὸς Καιάφαν τὸν ἀρχιερέα.

Peter Denies Jesus Again
(Mt 26.71—75; Mk 14.69—72; Lk 22.58—62)

25 Ἦν δὲ Σίμων Πέτρος ἑστὼς καὶ θερμαινόμενος. εἶπον οὖν αὐτῷ, Μὴ καὶ σὺ ἐκ τῶν μαθητῶν αὐτοῦ εἶ; ἠρνήσατο ἐκεῖνος καὶ εἶπεν, Οὐκ εἰμί. **26** λέγει εἷς ἐκ τῶν δούλων τοῦ ἀρχιερέως, συγγενὴς ὢν οὗ ἀπέκοψεν Πέτρος τὸ ὠτίον, Οὐκ ἐγώ σε εἶδον ἐν τῷ κήπῳ μετ' αὐτοῦ; **27** πάλιν οὖν ἠρνήσατο Πέτρος· καὶ εὐθέως ἀλέκτωρ ἐφώνησεν.[4]

---

[4] **13—27** {A} *verses 13—27* 𝔓⁶⁰,⁶⁶ ℵ A B C (D vs 13 *and* Dˢᵘᵖᵖ vs 14—27) K L W X Δ Θ Π Ψ 054 *f*¹ *f*¹³ 28 33 565 700 892 1000 1010 1071 1079 1216 1230 1241 1242 1344 1365 1546 1646 2148 2174 *Byz Lect* itᵃ,ᵃᵘʳ,ᵇ,ᶜ,ᶠ,ᶠᶠ²,�q,ʳ¹ vg syrᵖ,ʰ,ᵖᵃˡᵐˢˢ copˢᵃ,ᵇᵒ,ᵃᶜʰ² goth arm geo ‖ *verses 13, 24, 14, 15, 19—23, 16—18, 25b—27* syrˢ ‖ *verses 13, 24, 14—23, 24, 25—27* 1195 syrᵖᵃˡᵐˢ Cyril ‖ *verses 13a, 24, 13b—23, 24, 25—27* 225

---

20 Ἐγὼ παρρησίᾳ...κόσμῳ Jn 7.26   ἐγὼ πάντοτε...ἱερῷ Mt 4.23; 26.55; Jn 6.59; 7.14   **22** Ac 23.2   ἔδωκεν...Ἰησοῦ Jn 19.3   **24** Lk 3.2; Jn 18.13   **25** εἶπον...εἰμί Jn 18.17   **26** συγγενὴς...ὠτίον Mt 26.51; Mk 14.47; Lk 22.49—50; Jn 18.10   Οὐκ ἐγώ σε εἶδον...μετ' αὐτοῦ Jn 18.1   **27** Mt 26.34; Mk 14.30; Lk 22.34; Jn 13.38

The High Priest Questions Jesus
(Also Matt. 26.59—66; Mark 14.55—64; Luke 22.66—71)

19 The High Priest questioned Jesus about his disciples and about his teaching. **20** Jesus answered: "I have always spoken publicly to everyone; all my teaching was done in the synagogues and in the Temple, where all the Jews come together. I have never said anything in secret. **21** Why, then, do you question me? Question the people who heard me. Ask them what I told them — they know what I said." **22** When Jesus said this, one of the guards there slapped him and said, "How dare you talk like this to the High Priest!" **23** Jesus answered him: "If I have said something wrong, tell everyone here what it was. But if I am right in what I have said, why do you hit me?"

24 So Annas sent him, still tied up, to Caiaphas the High Priest.

Peter Denies Jesus again
(Also Matt. 26.71—75; Mark 14.69—72; Luke 22.58—62)

25 Peter was still standing there keeping himself warm. So the others said to him, "Aren't you one of the disciples of that man?" But Peter denied it. "No, I am not," he said. **26** One of the High Priest's slaves, a relative of the man whose ear Peter had cut off, spoke up. "Didn't I see you with him in the garden?" he asked. **27** Again Peter said "No" — and at once a rooster crowed.

Jesus before Pilate
(Also Matt. 27.1–2, 11–14; Mark 15.1–5; Luke 23.1–5)

28 They took Jesus from Caiaphas' house to the Governor's palace. It was early in the morning. The Jews did not go inside the palace because they wanted to keep themselves ritually clean, in order to be able to eat the Passover meal. 29 So Pilate went outside to meet them and said, "What do you accuse this man of?" 30 Their answer was, "We would not have brought him to you if he had not committed a crime." 31 Pilate said to them, "You yourselves take him and try him according to your own law." The Jews replied, "We are not allowed to put anyone to death." 32 (This happened to make come true what Jesus had said when he indicated the kind of death he would die.) 33 Pilate went back into the palace and called Jesus. "Are you the king of the Jews?" he asked him. 34 Jesus answered, "Does this question come from you or have others told you about me?" 35 Pilate replied: "Do you think I am a Jew? It was your own people and their chief priests who handed you over to me. What have you done?" 36 Jesus said: "My kingdom does not belong to this world; if my kingdom belonged to this world, my followers would fight to keep me from being handed over to the Jews. No, my kingdom does not belong here!" 37 So Pilate asked him, "Are you a king, then?" Jesus

Jesus before Pilate
(Mt 27.1–2, 11–14; Mk 15.1–5; Lk 23.1–5)

28 Ἄγουσιν οὖν τὸν Ἰησοῦν ἀπὸ τοῦ Καϊάφα εἰς τὸ πραιτώριον· ἦν δὲ πρωΐ· καὶ αὐτοὶ οὐκ εἰσῆλθον εἰς τὸ πραιτώριον, ἵνα μὴ μιανθῶσιν ἀλλὰ φάγωσιν τὸ πάσχα. 29 ἐξῆλθεν οὖν ὁ Πιλᾶτος ἔξω πρὸς αὐτοὺς καὶ φησίν, Τίνα κατηγορίαν φέρετε κατὰ τοῦ ἀνθρώπου τούτου; 30 ἀπεκρίθησαν καὶ εἶπαν αὐτῷ, Εἰ μὴ ἦν οὗτος κακὸν ποιῶν[5], οὐκ ἄν σοι παρεδώκαμεν αὐτόν. 31 εἶπεν οὖν αὐτοῖς ὁ Πιλᾶτος, Λάβετε αὐτὸν ὑμεῖς, καὶ κατὰ τὸν νόμον ὑμῶν κρίνατε αὐτόν. εἶπον [οὖν] αὐτῷ οἱ Ἰουδαῖοι, Ἡμῖν οὐκ ἔξεστιν ἀποκτεῖναι οὐδένα· 32 ἵνα ὁ λόγος τοῦ Ἰησοῦ πληρωθῇ ὃν εἶπεν σημαίνων ποίῳ θανάτῳ ἤμελλεν ἀποθνῄσκειν. 33 Εἰσῆλθεν οὖν πάλιν εἰς τὸ πραιτώριον ὁ Πιλᾶτος καὶ ἐφώνησεν τὸν Ἰησοῦν καὶ εἶπεν αὐτῷ, Σὺ εἶ ὁ βασιλεὺς τῶν Ἰουδαίων; 34 ἀπεκρίθη Ἰησοῦς, Ἀπὸ σεαυτοῦ σὺ τοῦτο λέγεις ἢ ἄλλοι εἶπόν σοι περὶ ἐμοῦ; 35 ἀπεκρίθη ὁ Πιλᾶτος, Μήτι ἐγὼ Ἰουδαῖός εἰμι; τὸ ἔθνος τὸ σὸν καὶ οἱ ἀρχιερεῖς παρέδωκάν σε ἐμοί· τί ἐποίησας; 36 ἀπεκρίθη Ἰησοῦς, Ἡ βασιλεία ἡ ἐμὴ οὐκ ἔστιν ἐκ τοῦ κόσμου τούτου· εἰ ἐκ τοῦ κόσμου τούτου ἦν ἡ βασιλεία ἡ ἐμή, οἱ ὑπηρέται οἱ ἐμοὶ ἠγωνίζοντο [ἄν], ἵνα μὴ παραδοθῶ τοῖς Ἰουδαίοις· νῦν δὲ ἡ βασιλεία ἡ ἐμὴ οὐκ ἔστιν ἐντεῦθεν. 37 εἶπεν οὖν αὐτῷ ὁ Πιλᾶτος, Οὐκοῦν βασιλεὺς εἶ σύ; ἀπεκρίθη ὁ Ἰησοῦς, Σὺ λέγεις ὅτι βασιλεὺς

---

5 **30** {B} κακὸν ποιῶν ‭א‬c B L W ite syrh, pal copsa?boms?ach2? geo? (Nonnus) ‖ κακὸν ποιήσας ‭א‬* copsa?boms?ach2? ‖ κακοποιῶν C* Ψ 33 l63 ita, (rl) copbo? geo? Cyril ‖ κακοποιός A C3 Dsupp K X Δ Θ Π 054 f1 f13 28 565 700 892 1009 1010 1071 1079 1195 1216 1230 1241 1242 1365 1546 1646 2148 2174 Byz Lect itb, c, f, ff2, q vg syrs, p copbo? goth (arm?) geo? Eusebius Athanasius Chrysostom Cyril

---

31 Jn 19.6–7 Λάβετε αὐτὸν ὑμεῖς Jn 19.6 Λάβετε...κρίνατε αὐτόν Ac 18.15
32 Mt 20.19; 26.2; Jn 3.14; 8.28; 12.33 **35** τὸ ἔθνος...ἐμοί Jn 1.11

εἰμι.[a] ἐγὼ εἰς τοῦτο γεγέννημαι καὶ εἰς τοῦτο ἐλήλυθα εἰς τὸν κόσμον, ἵνα μαρτυρήσω τῇ ἀληθείᾳ· πᾶς ὁ ὢν ἐκ τῆς ἀληθείας ἀκούει μου τῆς φωνῆς. **38** λέγει αὐτῷ ὁ Πιλᾶτος, Τί ἐστιν ἀλήθεια;

Jesus Sentenced to Die
(Mt 27.15–31; Mk 15.6–20; Lk 23.13–25)

Καὶ τοῦτο εἰπὼν πάλιν ἐξῆλθεν πρὸς τοὺς Ἰουδαίους, καὶ λέγει αὐτοῖς, Ἐγὼ οὐδεμίαν εὑρίσκω ἐν αὐτῷ αἰτίαν. **39** ἔστιν δὲ συνήθεια ὑμῖν ἵνα ἕνα ἀπολύσω ὑμῖν ἐν τῷ πάσχα· βούλεσθε οὖν ἀπολύσω ὑμῖν τὸν βασιλέα τῶν Ἰουδαίων; **40** ἐκραύγασαν οὖν πάλιν λέγοντες, Μὴ τοῦτον ἀλλὰ τὸν Βαραββᾶν. ἦν δὲ ὁ Βαραββᾶς λῃστής.

19 Τότε οὖν ἔλαβεν ὁ Πιλᾶτος τὸν Ἰησοῦν καὶ ἐμαστίγωσεν. **2** καὶ οἱ στρατιῶται πλέξαντες στέφανον ἐξ ἀκανθῶν ἐπέθηκαν αὐτοῦ τῇ κεφαλῇ, καὶ ἱμάτιον πορφυροῦν περιέβαλον αὐτόν, **3** καὶ ἤρχοντο πρὸς αὐτὸν καὶ ἔλεγον, Χαῖρε, ὁ βασιλεὺς τῶν Ἰουδαίων· καὶ ἐδίδοσαν αὐτῷ ῥαπίσματα. **4** Καὶ ἐξῆλθεν πάλιν ἔξω ὁ Πιλᾶτος καὶ λέγει αὐτοῖς, Ἴδε ἄγω ὑμῖν αὐτὸν ἔξω, ἵνα γνῶτε ὅτι οὐδεμίαν αἰτίαν εὑρίσκω ἐν αὐτῷ. **5** ἐξῆλθεν οὖν ὁ Ἰησοῦς ἔξω, φορῶν τὸν ἀκάνθινον στέφανον καὶ τὸ πορφυροῦν ἱμάτιον. καὶ λέγει αὐτοῖς, Ἰδοὺ ὁ ἄνθρωπος. **6** ὅτε οὖν εἶδον αὐτὸν οἱ ἀρχιερεῖς καὶ οἱ ὑπηρέται ἐκραύγασαν λέγοντες, Σταύρωσον σταύρωσον. λέγει αὐτοῖς ὁ Πιλᾶτος, Λάβετε αὐτὸν ὑμεῖς καὶ σταυρώσατε, ἐγὼ γὰρ οὐχ εὑρίσκω ἐν αὐτῷ αἰτίαν. **7** ἀπεκρίθησαν αὐτῷ οἱ Ἰουδαῖοι, Ἡμεῖς νόμον ἔχομεν, καὶ κατὰ τὸν νόμον ὀφείλει ἀποθανεῖν, ὅτι υἱὸν θεοῦ ἑαυτὸν ἐποίησεν.

[a] *37 a* statement: TR WH Bov Nes BF² AV RV ASV RSV NEB TT Zür Luth Jer Seg *‖ a* question: WHᵐᵍ

37 ἐγώ...φωνῆς 1 Tm 6.13   ἵνα...ἀληθείᾳ Jn 3.32–33   πᾶς...φωνῆς Jn 8.47; 1 Jn 4.6
40 Ac 3.14
19 2 ἱμάτιον...αὐτόν Lk 23.11   **3** ἐδίδοσαν αὐτῷ ῥαπίσματα Jn 18.22   **4** Lk 23.4; Jn 18.38   **6** Λάβετε αὐτὸν ὑμεῖς Jn 18.31   **7** Lv 24.16   Ἡμεῖς...ἀποθανεῖν Jn 18.31   υἱὸν...ἐποίησεν Jn 5.18; 10.33

answered: "You say that I am a king. I was born and came into the world for this one purpose, to speak about the truth. Whoever belongs to the truth listens to me." ³⁸ "And what is truth?" Pilate asked.

Jesus Sentenced to Death
(Also Matt. 27.15–31; Mark 15.6–20; Luke 23.13–25)

Then Pilate went back outside to the Jews and said to them: "I cannot find any reason to condemn him. ³⁹ But according to the custom you have, I always set free a prisoner for you during the Passover. Do you want me to set the king of the Jews free for you?" ⁴⁰ They answered him with a shout, "No, not him! We want Barabbas!" (Barabbas was a bandit.)

19 Then Pilate took Jesus and had him whipped. ² The soldiers made a crown of thorny branches and put it on his head; they put a purple robe on him, ³ and came to him and said, "Long live the King of the Jews!" And they went up and slapped him.

⁴ Pilate went back out once more and said to the crowd, "Look, I will bring him out here to you, to let you see that I cannot find any reason to condemn him." ⁵ So Jesus went outside, wearing the crown of thorns and the purple robe. Pilate said to them, "Look! Here is the man!" ⁶ When the chief priests and the guards saw him they shouted, "Nail him to the cross! Nail him to the cross!" Pilate said to them, "You take him, then, and nail him to the cross. I find no reason to condemn him." ⁷ The Jews answered back, "We have a law that says he ought to die, because he claimed to be the Son of God."

⁸ When Pilate heard them say this, he was even more afraid. ⁹ He went back into the palace and said to Jesus, "Where do you come from?" But Jesus gave him no answer. ¹⁰ Pilate said to him, "You will not speak to me? Remember, I have the authority to set you free, and also the authority to have you nailed to the cross." ¹¹ Jesus answered, "You have authority over me only because it was given to you by God. So the man who handed me over to you is guilty of a worse sin." ¹² When Pilate heard this he was all the more anxious to set him free. But the Jews shouted back, "If you set him free that means you are not the Emperor's friend! Anyone who claims to be a king is the Emperor's enemy!" ¹³ When Pilate heard these words, he took Jesus outside and sat down on the judge's seat in the place called "The Stone Pavement." (In Hebrew the name is "Gabbatha.")

¹⁴ It was then almost noon of the day before the Passover. Pilate said to the Jews, "Here is your king!" ¹⁵ They shouted back, "Kill him! Kill him! Nail him to the cross!" Pilate asked them, "Do you want me to nail your king to the cross?" The chief priests answered, "The only king we have is the Emperor!" ¹⁶ Then Pilate handed Jesus over to them to be nailed to the cross.

Jesus Nailed to the Cross
(Also Matt. 27.32–44; Mark 15.21–32; Luke 23.26–43)

So they took charge of Jesus. ¹⁷ He went out, carrying his own cross, and came to "The Place of the Skull," as it is called. (In Hebrew it is called "Golgotha.") ¹⁸ There they nailed him to the cross; they also nailed two other men to crosses, one on each side, with Jesus between them. ¹⁹ Pilate wrote a notice and had it put on the cross. "Jesus of Nazareth, the King of the Jews," is what he wrote. ²⁰ Many Jews read this, because the place where Jesus

8 Ὅτε οὖν ἤκουσεν ὁ Πιλᾶτος τοῦτον τὸν λόγον, μᾶλλον ἐφοβήθη, 9 καὶ εἰσῆλθεν εἰς τὸ πραιτώριον πάλιν καὶ λέγει τῷ Ἰησοῦ, Πόθεν εἶ σύ; ὁ δὲ Ἰησοῦς ἀπόκρισιν οὐκ ἔδωκεν αὐτῷ. 10 λέγει οὖν αὐτῷ ὁ Πιλᾶτος, Ἐμοὶ οὐ λαλεῖς; οὐκ οἶδας ὅτι ἐξουσίαν ἔχω ἀπολῦσαί σε καὶ ἐξουσίαν ἔχω σταυρῶσαί σε; 11 ἀπεκρίθη αὐτῷ ὁ Ἰησοῦς, Οὐκ εἶχες ἐξουσίαν κατ' ἐμοῦ οὐδεμίαν εἰ μὴ ἦν δεδομένον σοι ἄνωθεν· διὰ τοῦτο ὁ παραδούς μέ σοι μείζονα ἁμαρτίαν ἔχει. 12 ἐκ τούτου ὁ Πιλᾶτος ἐζήτει ἀπολῦσαι αὐτόν· οἱ δὲ Ἰουδαῖοι ἐκραύγαζον λέγοντες, Ἐὰν τοῦτον ἀπολύσῃς, οὐκ εἶ φίλος τοῦ Καίσαρος· πᾶς ὁ βασιλέα ἑαυτὸν ποιῶν ἀντιλέγει τῷ Καίσαρι.

13 Ὁ οὖν Πιλᾶτος ἀκούσας τῶν λόγων τούτων ἤγαγεν ἔξω τὸν Ἰησοῦν, καὶ ἐκάθισεν ἐπὶ βήματος εἰς τόπον λεγόμενον Λιθόστρωτον, Ἑβραϊστὶ δὲ Γαββαθα. 14 ἦν δὲ παρασκευὴ τοῦ πάσχα, ὥρα ἦν ὡς ἕκτη. καὶ λέγει τοῖς Ἰουδαίοις, Ἴδε ὁ βασιλεὺς ὑμῶν. 15 ἐκραύγασαν οὖν ἐκεῖνοι, Ἆρον ἆρον, σταύρωσον αὐτόν. λέγει αὐτοῖς ὁ Πιλᾶτος, Τὸν βασιλέα ὑμῶν σταυρώσω; ἀπεκρίθησαν οἱ ἀρχιερεῖς, Οὐκ ἔχομεν βασιλέα εἰ μὴ Καίσαρα. 16 τότε οὖν παρέδωκεν αὐτὸν αὐτοῖς ἵνα σταυρωθῇ.

The Crucifixion of Jesus
(Mt 27.32–44; Mk 15.21–32; Lk 23.26–43)

Παρέλαβον οὖν τὸν Ἰησοῦν· 17 καὶ βαστάζων αὑτῷ τὸν σταυρὸν ἐξῆλθεν εἰς τὸν λεγόμενον Κρανίου Τόπον, ὃ λέγεται Ἑβραϊστὶ Γολγοθα, 18 ὅπου αὐτὸν ἐσταύρωσαν, καὶ μετ' αὐτοῦ ἄλλους δύο ἐντεῦθεν καὶ ἐντεῦθεν, μέσον δὲ τὸν Ἰησοῦν. 19 ἔγραψεν δὲ καὶ τίτλον ὁ Πιλᾶτος καὶ ἔθηκεν ἐπὶ τοῦ σταυροῦ· ἦν δὲ γεγραμμένον, Ἰησοῦς ὁ Ναζωραῖος ὁ βασιλεὺς τῶν Ἰουδαίων. 20 τοῦτον οὖν τὸν τίτλον πολλοὶ ἀνέγνωσαν τῶν Ἰουδαίων, ὅτι ἐγγὺς ἦν ὁ τόπος τῆς πόλεως ὅπου ἐσταυρώθη ὁ Ἰησοῦς·

9 ὁ...αὐτῷ Mt 26.62–63; 27.12, 14; Mk 14.61; Lk 23.9   11 Οὐκ...ἄνωθεν Jn 10.18; Ro 13.1   12 πᾶς...ποιῶν Lk 23.2; Jn 18.37; Ac 17.7

καὶ ἦν γεγραμμένον Ἑβραϊστί, Ῥωμαϊστί, Ἑλληνιστί. **21** ἔλεγον οὖν τῷ Πιλάτῳ οἱ ἀρχιερεῖς τῶν Ἰουδαίων, Μὴ γράφε, Ὁ βασιλεὺς τῶν Ἰουδαίων, ἀλλ' ὅτι ἐκεῖνος εἶπεν, Βασιλεύς εἰμι τῶν Ἰουδαίων. **22** ἀπεκρίθη ὁ Πιλᾶτος, Ὃ γέγραφα, γέγραφα.

23 Οἱ οὖν στρατιῶται ὅτε ἐσταύρωσαν τὸν Ἰησοῦν ἔλαβον τὰ ἱμάτια αὐτοῦ καὶ ἐποίησαν τέσσαρα μέρη, ἑκάστῳ στρατιώτῃ μέρος, καὶ τὸν χιτῶνα. ἦν δὲ ὁ χιτὼν ἄραφος, ἐκ τῶν ἄνωθεν ὑφαντὸς δι' ὅλου. **24** εἶπαν οὖν πρὸς ἀλλήλους, Μὴ σχίσωμεν αὐτόν, ἀλλὰ λάχωμεν περὶ αὐτοῦ τίνος ἔσται· ἵνα ἡ γραφὴ πληρωθῇ ἡ λέγουσα,

Διεμερίσαντο τὰ ἱμάτιά μου ἑαυτοῖς
καὶ ἐπὶ τὸν ἱματισμόν μου ἔβαλον κλῆρον.

Οἱ μὲν οὖν στρατιῶται ταῦτα ἐποίησαν. **25** εἱστήκεισαν δὲ παρὰ τῷ σταυρῷ τοῦ Ἰησοῦ ἡ μήτηρ αὐτοῦ καὶ ἡ ἀδελφὴ τῆς μητρὸς αὐτοῦ, Μαρία ἡ τοῦ Κλωπᾶ καὶ Μαρία ἡ Μαγδαληνή. **26** Ἰησοῦς οὖν ἰδὼν τὴν μητέρα καὶ τὸν μαθητὴν παρεστῶτα ὃν ἠγάπα, λέγει τῇ μητρί, Γύναι, ἴδε ὁ υἱός σου. **27** εἶτα λέγει τῷ μαθητῇ, Ἴδε ἡ μήτηρ σου. καὶ ἀπ' ἐκείνης τῆς ὥρας ἔλαβεν αὐτὴν ὁ μαθητὴς εἰς τὰ ἴδια.

The Death of Jesus
(Mt 27.45—56; Mk 15.33—41; Lk 23.44—49)

28 Μετὰ τοῦτο εἰδὼς ὁ Ἰησοῦς ὅτι ἤδη πάντα τετέλεσται,[a] ἵνα τελειωθῇ ἡ γραφή,[a] λέγει, Διψῶ. **29** σκεῦος ἔκειτο ὄξους μεστόν· σπόγγον οὖν μεστὸν τοῦ ὄξους ὑσσώπῳ[1] περιθέντες προσήνεγκαν αὐτοῦ τῷ στόματι.

[1] **29** |A| ὑσσώπῳ 𝔭66vid ℵ A B Dsupp K L W X Π Ψ 054 f1 28 565 700 1009 1010 1071 1079 1216 1230 1241 1365 1546 1646 2148 *Byz Lect* (l127) ita,aur,e,f vg syrp copsa,bo,ach2 (eth) ‖ ὑσσῷ 1242 ‖ *perticae* itb,ff2,n,v ‖ μετὰ χολῆς καὶ ὑσσώπου (*see* Mt 27.34) Θ 892 1195 2174 l547 itr1 syrh,palmss arm geo Eusebius ‖ μετὰ χολῆς καὶ ὑσσώπῳ f13 (ita) ‖ *cum felle permixtum* itr

[a a] **28** a minor, a minor: TR Bov Nes BF2 AV RV ASV Luth ‖ a none, a none: WH ‖ a parens, a parens: RSV ‖ a minor, a none: NEB TT Zür Jer Seg

24 Διεμερίσαντο...κλῆρον Ps 22.18   **25** Mt 27.55—56; Mk 15.40—41; Lk 23.49   **26** τὸν ...ἠγάπα Jn 13.23; 20.2; 21.7, 20   **28** ἵνα...Διψῶ Ps 22.15   **29** Ps 69.21

was nailed to the cross was not far from the city. The notice was written in Hebrew, Latin, and Greek. ²¹ The Jewish chief priests said to Pilate, "Do not write 'The King of the Jews,' but rather, 'This man said, I am the King of the Jews.'" ²² Pilate answered, "What I have written stays written."

²³ After the soldiers had nailed Jesus to the cross, they took his clothes and divided them into four parts, one part for each soldier. They also took the robe, which was made of one piece of woven cloth, without any seams in it. ²⁴ The soldiers said to each other, "Let us not tear it; let us throw dice to see who will get it." This happened to make the scripture come true:

"They divided my clothes among themselves,
They gambled for my robe."

So the soldiers did this.

²⁵ Standing close to Jesus' cross were his mother, his mother's sister, Mary the wife of Clopas, and Mary Magdalene. ²⁶ Jesus saw his mother and the disciple he loved standing there; so he said to his mother, "Woman, here is your son." ²⁷ Then he said to the disciple, "Here is your mother." And from that time the disciple took her to live in his home.

The Death of Jesus
(Also Matt. 27.45—56; Mark 15.33—41; Luke 23.44—49)

²⁸ Jesus knew that by now everything had been completed; and in order to make the scripture come true he said, "I am thirsty." ²⁹ A bowl was there, full of cheap wine; they soaked a sponge in the wine, put it on a branch of hyssop,

and lifted it up to his lips. ³⁰ Jesus took the wine and said, "It is finished!" Then he bowed his head and died.

Jesus' Side Pierced

³¹ Then the Jews asked Pilate to allow them to break the legs of the men who had been put to death, and take them down from the crosses. They did this because it was Friday, and they did not want the bodies to stay on the crosses on the Sabbath day, since the coming Sabbath was especially holy. ³² So the soldiers went and broke the legs of the first man and then of the other man who had been put to death with Jesus. ³³ But when they came to Jesus they saw that he was already dead, so they did not break his legs. ³⁴ One of the soldiers, however, plunged his spear into Jesus' side, and at once blood and water poured out. ³⁵ The one who saw this happen has spoken of it. We know that what he said is true, and he also knows that he speaks the truth, so that you also may believe. ³⁶ This was done to make the scripture come true, "Not one of his bones will be broken." ³⁷ And there is another scripture that says, "People will look at him whom they pierced."

The Burial of Jesus
(Also Matt. 27.57–61; Mark 15.42–47; Luke 23.50–56)

³⁸ After this, Joseph, who was from the town of Arimathea, asked Pilate if he could take Jesus' body. (Joseph was a follower of Jesus, but in secret, because he was afraid of the Jews.) Pilate told him he could have the body, so Joseph went and took it away. ³⁹ Nicodemus, who at first had gone to see Jesus at night, went with Joseph, taking with him about one hundred pounds of spices, a

30 ὅτε οὖν ἔλαβεν τὸ ὄξος [ὁ] ᾽Ιησοῦς εἶπεν, Τετέλεσται· καὶ κλίνας τὴν κεφαλὴν παρέδωκεν τὸ πνεῦμα.

The Piercing of Jesus' Side

31 Οἱ οὖν ᾽Ιουδαῖοι, ἐπεὶ παρασκευὴ ἦν, ἵνα μὴ μείνῃ ἐπὶ τοῦ σταυροῦ τὰ σώματα ἐν τῷ σαββάτῳ, ἦν γὰρ μεγάλη ἡ ἡμέρα ἐκείνου τοῦ σαββάτου, ἠρώτησαν τὸν Πιλᾶτον ἵνα κατεαγῶσιν αὐτῶν τὰ σκέλη καὶ ἀρθῶσιν. **32** ἦλθον οὖν οἱ στρατιῶται, καὶ τοῦ μὲν πρώτου κατέαξαν τὰ σκέλη καὶ τοῦ ἄλλου τοῦ συσταυρωθέντος αὐτῷ· **33** ἐπὶ δὲ τὸν ᾽Ιησοῦν ἐλθόντες, ὡς εἶδον ἤδη αὐτὸν τεθνηκότα, οὐ κατέαξαν αὐτοῦ τὰ σκέλη, **34** ἀλλ᾽ εἷς τῶν στρατιωτῶν λόγχῃ αὐτοῦ τὴν πλευρὰν ἔνυξεν, καὶ ἐξῆλθεν εὐθὺς αἷμα καὶ ὕδωρ. **35** καὶ ὁ ἑωρακὼς μεμαρτύρηκεν,[b] καὶ ἀληθινὴ αὐτοῦ ἐστιν ἡ μαρτυρία, καὶ ἐκεῖνος οἶδεν ὅτι ἀληθῆ λέγει,[b] ἵνα καὶ ὑμεῖς πιστεύσητε. **36** ἐγένετο γὰρ ταῦτα ἵνα ἡ γραφὴ πληρωθῇ, **Ὀστοῦν οὐ συντριβήσεται αὐτοῦ. 37** καὶ πάλιν ἑτέρα γραφὴ λέγει, **Ὄψονται εἰς ὃν ἐξεκέντησαν.**

The Burial of Jesus
(Mt 27.57–61; Mk 15.42–47; Lk 23.50–56)

38 Μετὰ δὲ ταῦτα ἠρώτησεν τὸν Πιλᾶτον ᾽Ιωσὴφ ὁ ἀπὸ ᾽Αριμαθαίας, ὢν μαθητὴς τοῦ ᾽Ιησοῦ κεκρυμμένος δὲ διὰ τὸν φόβον τῶν ᾽Ιουδαίων, ἵνα ἄρῃ τὸ σῶμα τοῦ ᾽Ιησοῦ· καὶ ἐπέτρεψεν ὁ Πιλᾶτος. ἦλθεν οὖν καὶ ἦρεν τὸ σῶμα αὐτοῦ. **39** ἦλθεν δὲ καὶ Νικόδημος, ὁ ἐλθὼν πρὸς αὐτὸν νυκτὸς τὸ πρῶτον, φέρων μίγμα² σμύρνης

---

² **39** {C} μίγμα 𝔭⁶⁶ᵛⁱᵈ ℵᶜ A Dˢᵘᵖᵖ K L X Δ Θ Π 054 f¹ f¹³ 28 33 565 700 1009 1010 1071 1079 1195 1216 1230 1241 1242ᶜ 1365 1546 1646 2148 *Byz Lect*

ᵇ ᵇ **35** b b no dashes: TR WH Bov Nes BF² AV RV ASV (NEB) TT Zür Luth Seg ‖ b dash, b dash: RSV Jer

30 ὁ...Τετέλεσται Job 19.26, 27 LXX   **31** ἵνα...σαββάτῳ Dt 21.22–23   **34** αἷμα καὶ ὕδωρ 1 Jn 5.6, 8   **35** ὁ...λέγει Jn 21.24   **36** Ὀστοῦν...αὐτοῦ Ex 12.46; Nu 9.12; Ps 34.20   **37** Ὄψονται...ἐξεκέντησαν Zch 12.10 (Re 1.7)   **38** διὰ...᾽Ιουδαίων Jn 7.13; 9.22; 20.19   **39** ἦλθεν...πρῶτον Jn 3.1–2; 7.50

καὶ ἀλόης ὡς λίτρας ἑκατόν. **40** ἔλαβον οὖν τὸ σῶμα τοῦ Ἰησοῦ καὶ ἔδησαν αὐτὸ ὀθονίοις μετὰ τῶν ἀρωμάτων, καθὼς ἔθος ἐστὶν τοῖς Ἰουδαίοις ἐνταφιάζειν. **41** ἦν δὲ ἐν τῷ τόπῳ ὅπου ἐσταυρώθη κῆπος, καὶ ἐν τῷ κήπῳ μνημεῖον καινὸν ἐν ᾧ οὐδέπω οὐδεὶς ἦν τεθειμένος· **42** ἐκεῖ οὖν διὰ τὴν παρασκευὴν τῶν Ἰουδαίων, ὅτι ἐγγὺς ἦν τὸ μνημεῖον, ἔθηκαν τὸν Ἰησοῦν.

The Resurrection of Jesus
(Mt 28.1–10; Mk 16.1–8; Lk 24.1–12)

20 Τῇ δὲ μιᾷ τῶν σαββάτων Μαρία ἡ Μαγδαληνὴ ἔρχεται πρωῒ σκοτίας ἔτι οὔσης εἰς τὸ μνημεῖον, καὶ βλέπει τὸν λίθον ἠρμένον ἐκ τοῦ μνημείου. **2** τρέχει οὖν καὶ ἔρχεται πρὸς Σίμωνα Πέτρον καὶ πρὸς τὸν ἄλλον μαθητὴν ὃν ἐφίλει ὁ Ἰησοῦς, καὶ λέγει αὐτοῖς, Ἦραν τὸν κύριον ἐκ τοῦ μνημείου, καὶ οὐκ οἴδαμεν ποῦ ἔθηκαν αὐτόν. **3** Ἐξῆλθεν οὖν ὁ Πέτρος καὶ ὁ ἄλλος μαθητής, καὶ ἤρχοντο εἰς τὸ μνημεῖον. **4** ἔτρεχον δὲ οἱ δύο ὁμοῦ· καὶ ὁ ἄλλος μαθητὴς προέδραμεν τάχιον τοῦ Πέτρου καὶ ἦλθεν πρῶτος εἰς τὸ μνημεῖον, **5** καὶ παρακύψας βλέπει κείμενα τὰ ὀθόνια, οὐ μέντοι εἰσῆλθεν. **6** ἔρχεται οὖν καὶ Σίμων Πέτρος ἀκολουθῶν αὐτῷ, καὶ εἰσῆλθεν εἰς τὸ μνημεῖον· καὶ θεωρεῖ τὰ ὀθόνια κείμενα, **7** καὶ τὸ σουδάριον, ὃ ἦν ἐπὶ τῆς κεφαλῆς αὐτοῦ, οὐ μετὰ τῶν ὀθονίων κείμενον ἀλλὰ χωρὶς ἐντετυλιγμένον εἰς ἕνα τόπον. **8** τότε οὖν εἰσῆλθεν καὶ ὁ ἄλλος μαθητὴς ὁ ἐλθὼν πρῶτος εἰς τὸ μνημεῖον, καὶ εἶδεν καὶ ἐπίστευσεν· **9** οὐδέπω γὰρ ᾔδεισαν τὴν γραφὴν ὅτι δεῖ αὐτὸν ἐκ νεκρῶν ἀναστῆναι. **10** ἀπῆλθον οὖν πάλιν πρὸς αὐτοὺς οἱ μαθηταί.

---

it^a,aur,b,c,f,ff2,n,q,rl vg syr^p,h cop^sa,bo arm geo ‖ ἔλιγμα ℵ* B W cop^boms ‖ σμίγμα Ψ 892 2174 *l*^47 ‖ σμῆγμα 1242* *l*^181 syr^pal ‖ *malagmani* it^e

1 Τῇ...σαββάτων Jn 20.19; Ac 20.7   **2** τὸν ἄλλον...Ἰησοῦς Jn 13.23; 19.26; 21.7, 20 Ἦραν...αὐτόν Jn 20.13   **6–7** θεωρεῖ...αὐτοῦ Jn 11.44   **9** Ps 16.9; Lk 24.26–27; Ac 2.27, 31; 1 Cor 15.4

mixture of myrrh and aloes. [40] The two men took Jesus' body and wrapped it in linen cloths with the spices; for this is how the Jews prepare a body for burial. [41] There was a garden in the place where Jesus had been put to death, and in it there was a new tomb where no one had ever been laid. [42] Since it was the day before the Jewish Sabbath, and because the tomb was close by, they laid Jesus there.

The Empty Tomb
(Also Matt. 28.1–8; Mark 16.1–8; Luke 24.1–12)

20 Early on Sunday morning, while it was still dark, Mary Magdalene went to the tomb and saw that the stone had been taken away from the entrance. [2] She ran and went to Simon Peter and the other disciple, whom Jesus loved, and told them, "They have taken the Lord from the tomb and we don't know where they have put him!" [3] Then Peter and the other disciple left and went to the tomb. [4] The two of them were running, but the other disciple ran faster than Peter and reached the tomb first. [5] He bent over and saw the linen cloths, but he did not go in. [6] Behind him came Simon Peter, and he went straight into the tomb. He saw the linen cloths lying there [7] and the cloth which had been around Jesus' head. It was not lying with the linen cloths but was rolled up by itself. [8] Then the other disciple, who had reached the tomb first, also went in; he saw and believed. [9] (They still did not understand the scripture which said that he must be raised from death.) [10] Then the disciples went back home.

Jesus Appears to Mary Magdalene
(Also Matt. 28.9–10; Mark 16.9–11)

[11] Mary stood crying outside the tomb. Still crying, she bent over and looked in the tomb, [12] and saw two angels there, dressed in white, sitting where the body of Jesus had been, one at the head, the other at the feet. [13] "Woman, why are you crying?" they asked her. She answered, "They have taken my Lord away, and I do not know where they have put him!" [14] When she had said this, she turned around and saw Jesus standing there; but she did not know that it was Jesus. [15] "Woman, why are you crying?" Jesus asked her. "Who is it that you are looking for?" She thought he was the gardener, so she said to him, "If you took him away, sir, tell me where you have put him, and I will go and get him." [16] Jesus said to her, "Mary!" She turned toward him and said in Hebrew, "Rabboni!" (This means "Teacher.") [17] "Do not hold on to me," Jesus told her, "because I have not yet gone back up to the Father. But go to my brothers

The Appearance of Jesus to Mary Magdalene
(Mk 16.9–11)

11 Μαρία δὲ εἱστήκει πρὸς τῷ μνημείῳ ἔξω κλαίουσα[1]. ὡς οὖν ἔκλαιεν παρέκυψεν εἰς τὸ μνημεῖον, **12** καὶ θεωρεῖ δύο ἀγγέλους ἐν λευκοῖς καθεζομένους, ἕνα πρὸς τῇ κεφαλῇ καὶ ἕνα πρὸς τοῖς ποσίν, ὅπου ἔκειτο τὸ σῶμα τοῦ Ἰησοῦ. **13** καὶ λέγουσιν αὐτῇ ἐκεῖνοι, Γύναι, τί κλαίεις; λέγει αὐτοῖς ὅτι[a] Ἦραν τὸν κύριόν μου, καὶ οὐκ οἶδα ποῦ ἔθηκαν αὐτόν. **14** ταῦτα εἰποῦσα ἐστράφη εἰς τὰ ὀπίσω, καὶ θεωρεῖ τὸν Ἰησοῦν ἑστῶτα, καὶ οὐκ ᾔδει ὅτι Ἰησοῦς ἐστιν. **15** λέγει αὐτῇ Ἰησοῦς, Γύναι, τί κλαίεις; τίνα ζητεῖς; ἐκείνη δοκοῦσα ὅτι ὁ κηπουρός ἐστιν λέγει αὐτῷ, Κύριε, εἰ σὺ ἐβάστασας αὐτόν, εἰπέ μοι ποῦ ἔθηκας αὐτόν, κἀγὼ αὐτὸν ἀρῶ. **16** λέγει αὐτῇ Ἰησοῦς, Μαρία. στραφεῖσα ἐκείνη λέγει αὐτῷ Ἑβραϊστί, Ραββουνι (ὃ λέγεται Διδάσκαλε[2]). **17** λέγει αὐτῇ Ἰησοῦς, Μή μου ἅπτου, οὔπω γὰρ ἀναβέβηκα πρὸς τὸν πατέρα[3]· πορεύου δὲ πρὸς τοὺς ἀδελ-

---

[1] **11** {C} ἔξω κλαίουσα ℵc B W X Δ 050 *f*1 33 565 itaur,d,f vg syrpal (copsa?bo) arm eth geo Gregory-Nyssa Ambrose Augustine Cyril ‖ κλαίουσα ἔξω Dgrsupp K L Θ Π Ψ *f*13 28 700 892 1009 1010 1071 1079 1195 1216 1230 1241 1242 1365 1546 1646 2148 2174 *Byz Lect* *l*70m itq syrh Severus ‖ κλαίουσα ℵ* A ita,b,c,e,ff2,r1,v syrs,p Diatessarona,s,t

[2] **16** {B} διδάσκαλε ℵ*,b A B K L W X Δ Π 050 0250 *f*1 28 33 565 700 892 1009 1010 1071 1079 1195mg 1216 1241 1242 1365 1546 1646 2148 2174 *Byz Lect* *l*70m itaur,b,c,f,q vg syrp copsa,bo arm geo1 ‖ κύριε ita,r1 ‖ κύριε διδάσκαλε D itd ‖ διδάσκαλε, κύριε it(e),ff2 ‖ διδάσκαλε, καὶ προσέδραμεν ἅψασθαι αὐτοῦ ℵa Θ Ψ (*f*13 ἅψεσθαι) 1195* 1230 syrs,h,pal geo2 Cyril

[3] **17** {C} πατέρα ℵ B D W itb,d,e syrpal Irenaeuslat Origen Epiphanius Chrysostom Maximus ‖ πατέρα μου p66 A K L X Δ Θ Π Ψ 050 *f*1 *f*13 28 33 565 700 892 1009 1010 1071 1079 1195 1216 1230 1241 1242 1365 1546 1646 2148 2174 *Byz Lect* *l*70m ita,aur,c,f,ff2,q,r1 vg syrs,p,h copsa,bo arm eth geo Tertullian Origen Eusebius Gregory-Nyssa Nonnus Cyril Theodoret Severus

---

[a] **13** *a* direct: TR? WH Nes? BF2 NEB TT Zür Luth Jer ‖ *a* causal: TR? WHmg Bov AV RV ASV RSV Seg ‖ *a* indirect: Nes?

---

13 Ἦραν...αὐτόν Jn 20.2   **14** οὐκ ᾔδει ὅτι Ἰησοῦς ἐστιν Lk 24.16; Jn 21.4 **17** τοὺς ἀδελφούς μου Ro 8.29; He 2.11–12

φούς μου καὶ εἰπὲ αὐτοῖς, 'Αναβαίνω πρὸς τὸν πατέρα μου καὶ πατέρα ὑμῶν καὶ θεόν μου καὶ θεὸν ὑμῶν. **18** ἔρχεται Μαρία ἡ Μαγδαληνὴ ἀγγέλλουσα τοῖς μαθηταῖς ὅτι 'Εώρακα τὸν κύριον, καὶ ταῦτα εἶπεν αὐτῇ.

The Appearance of Jesus to the Disciples
(Mt 28.16–20; Mk 16.14–18; Lk 24.36–49)

19 Οὔσης οὖν ὀψίας τῇ ἡμέρα ἐκείνῃ τῇ μιᾷ σαββάτων, καὶ τῶν θυρῶν κεκλεισμένων ὅπου ἦσαν οἱ μαθηταὶ διὰ τὸν φόβον τῶν 'Ιουδαίων, ἦλθεν ὁ 'Ιησοῦς καὶ ἔστη εἰς τὸ μέσον καὶ λέγει αὐτοῖς, Εἰρήνη ὑμῖν. **20** καὶ τοῦτο εἰπὼν ἔδειξεν τὰς χεῖρας καὶ τὴν πλευρὰν αὐτοῖς. ἐχάρησαν οὖν οἱ μαθηταὶ ἰδόντες τὸν κύριον. **21** εἶπεν οὖν αὐτοῖς πάλιν, Εἰρήνη ὑμῖν· καθὼς ἀπέσταλκέν με ὁ πατήρ, κἀγὼ πέμπω ὑμᾶς. **22** καὶ τοῦτο εἰπὼν ἐνεφύσησεν καὶ λέγει αὐτοῖς, Λάβετε πνεῦμα ἅγιον· **23** ἄν τινων ἀφῆτε τὰς ἁμαρτίας ἀφέωνται[4] αὐτοῖς, ἄν τινων κρατῆτε κεκράτηνται.

Jesus and Thomas

24 Θωμᾶς δὲ εἷς ἐκ τῶν δώδεκα, ὁ λεγόμενος Δίδυμος, οὐκ ἦν μετ' αὐτῶν ὅτε ἦλθεν 'Ιησοῦς. **25** ἔλεγον οὖν αὐτῷ οἱ ἄλλοι μαθηταί, Ἑωράκαμεν τὸν κύριον. ὁ δὲ εἶπεν αὐτοῖς, Ἐὰν μὴ ἴδω ἐν ταῖς χερσὶν αὐτοῦ τὸν τύπον τῶν ἥλων καὶ βάλω τὸν δάκτυλόν μου εἰς τὸν τύπον τῶν ἥλων καὶ βάλω μου τὴν χεῖρα εἰς τὴν πλευρὰν

---

[4] **23** {B} ἀφέωνται ‭א‬ᶜ A D (L ἀφέονται) X 050 f¹ f¹³ 33ᵛⁱᵈ 565 1365 Chrysostom Cyril ‖ ἀφίονται (B* ἀφείωνται) Ψ ‖ ἀφίενται B³ K W Δ Θ Π 078 700 892 1009 1010 1071 1079 1195 1216 1230 1241 1242 1546 1646 2148 2174 *Byz Lect* l¹¹²⁷ itᵃᵘʳ,ᵇ,ᶜ,ᶠ vg copᵇᵒ geo Origenᵍʳ,ˡᵃᵗ Eusebius Basil Cyril-Jerusalem Cyril Ps-Athanasius ‖ ἀφεθήσεται ‭א‬* it⁽ᵃ⁾,⁽ᵈ⁾,⁽ᵉ,ff²⁾,q,⁽ʳ¹⁾ syr⁽ˢ,ᵖ,ʰ⁾,ᵖᵃˡ copˢᵃ,ᵇᵒᵐˢ arm eth Diatessaronᵃ,ⁱ,ⁿ (Novatian) Cyprian ‖ ἀφίεται 69* 127

---

19 τῇ μιᾷ σαββάτων Jn 20.1; Ac 20.7   τῶν θυρῶν...ὑμῖν Jn 20.26   διὰ...'Ιουδαίων Jn 7.13; 9.22; 19.38   **20** ἔδειξεν...αὐτοῖς Jn 19.34; 20.25, 27   ἐχάρησαν...κύριον Jn 16.20, 22   **21** καθὼς ἀπέσταλκέν με...ὑμᾶς Jn 17.18   **23** Mt 16.19; 18.18   **24** Θωμᾶς...Δίδυμος Jn 11.16; 21.2   **25** Ἐὰν...πλευρὰν αὐτοῦ Jn 19.34; 20.20

---

and tell them for me, 'I go back up to him who is my Father and your Father, my God and your God.'" [18] So Mary Magdalene told the disciples that she had seen the Lord, and that he had told her this.

Jesus Appears to His Disciples
(Also Matt. 28.16–20; Mark 16.14–18; Luke 24.36–49)

[19] It was late that Sunday evening, and the disciples were gathered together behind locked doors, because they were afraid of the Jews. Then Jesus came and stood among them. "Peace be with you," he said. [20] After saying this, he showed them his hands and his side. The disciples were filled with joy at seeing the Lord. [21] Then Jesus said to them again, "Peace be with you. As the Father sent me, so I send you." [22] He said this, and then he breathed on them and said, "Receive the Holy Spirit. [23] If you forgive men's sins, then they are forgiven; if you do not forgive them, then they are not forgiven."

Jesus and Thomas

[24] One of the disciples, Thomas (called the Twin), was not with them when Jesus came. [25] So the other disciples told him, "We saw the Lord!" Thomas said to them, "If I do not see the scars of the nails in his hands, and put my finger where the nails were, and my hand in his side, I will not believe."

²⁶ A week later the disciples were together indoors again, and Thomas was with them. The doors were locked, but Jesus came and stood among them and said, "Peace be with you." ²⁷ Then he said to Thomas, "Put your finger here, and look at my hands; then stretch out your hand and put it in my side. Stop your doubting and believe!" ²⁸ Thomas answered him, "My Lord and my God!" ²⁹ Jesus said to him, "Do you believe because you see me? How happy are those who believe without seeing me!"

The Purpose of this Book

³⁰ Jesus did many other mighty works in his disciples' presence which are not written down in this book. ³¹ These have been written that you may believe[1] that Jesus is the Messiah, the Son of God, and that through this faith you may have life in his name.

Jesus Appears to Seven Disciples

21 After this, Jesus showed himself once more to his disciples at Lake Tiberias. This is how he did it. ² Simon Peter, Thomas (called the Twin), Nathanael (the one from Cana in Galilee),

---

[1] **31** you may believe: *some mss. read* you may keep on believing

αὐτοῦ, οὐ μὴ πιστεύσω. **26** Καὶ μεθ' ἡμέρας ὀκτὼ πάλιν ἦσαν ἔσω οἱ μαθηταὶ αὐτοῦ καὶ Θωμᾶς μετ' αὐτῶν. ἔρχεται ὁ Ἰησοῦς τῶν θυρῶν κεκλεισμένων, καὶ ἔστη εἰς τὸ μέσον καὶ εἶπεν, Εἰρήνη ὑμῖν. **27** εἶτα λέγει τῷ Θωμᾷ, Φέρε τὸν δάκτυλόν σου ὧδε καὶ ἴδε τὰς χεῖράς μου, καὶ φέρε τὴν χεῖρά σου καὶ βάλε εἰς τὴν πλευράν μου, καὶ μὴ γίνου ἄπιστος ἀλλὰ πιστός. **28** ἀπεκρίθη Θωμᾶς καὶ εἶπεν αὐτῷ, Ὁ κύριός μου καὶ ὁ θεός μου. **29** λέγει αὐτῷ ὁ Ἰησοῦς, Ὅτι ἑώρακάς με πεπίστευκας;[b] μακάριοι οἱ μὴ ἰδόντες καὶ πιστεύσαντες.

The Purpose of the Book

30 Πολλὰ μὲν οὖν καὶ ἄλλα σημεῖα ἐποίησεν ὁ Ἰησοῦς ἐνώπιον τῶν μαθητῶν [αὐτοῦ][5], ἃ οὐκ ἔστιν γεγραμμένα ἐν τῷ βιβλίῳ τούτῳ· **31** ταῦτα δὲ γέγραπται ἵνα πιστεύσητε[6] ὅτι Ἰησοῦς ἐστιν ὁ Χριστὸς ὁ υἱὸς τοῦ θεοῦ, καὶ ἵνα πιστεύοντες ζωὴν ἔχητε ἐν τῷ ὀνόματι αὐτοῦ.

The Appearance of Jesus to the Seven Disciples

21 Μετὰ ταῦτα ἐφανέρωσεν ἑαυτὸν πάλιν ὁ Ἰησοῦς τοῖς μαθηταῖς ἐπὶ τῆς θαλάσσης τῆς Τιβεριάδος· ἐφανέρωσεν δὲ οὕτως. **2** ἦσαν ὁμοῦ Σίμων Πέτρος καὶ Θωμᾶς ὁ λεγόμενος Δίδυμος καὶ Ναθαναὴλ ὁ ἀπὸ Κανὰ τῆς

---

[5] **30** {C} μαθητῶν αὐτοῦ 𝔓⁶⁶ ℵ C D L W X Θ Ψ f¹ f¹³ 33 565 700 892 1009 1071 1230 1241 1242 1646 2148 2174 *Byz Lect* l⁷⁰ᵐ itᵃ·ᵃᵘʳ·ᵇ·ᶜ·ᵈ·π·q·rˡ vg syrˢ·ᵖ·ʰ with *,pal copˢᵃ·ᵇᵒ arm eth geo Diatessaronᵃ·ⁱ·ⁿ Chrysostom Cyril ∥ μαθητῶν A B K Δ Π 0250 1010 1079 1195 1216 1546 itᶠ syrʰ ∥ *discipulis suis, postquam resurrexit a mortuis* itᵉ

[6] **31** {C} πιστεύσητε ℵᶜ A C D K L W X Δ Π Ψ 0100 f¹ f¹³ 33 565 700 1009 1010 1071 1079 1195 1216 1230 1241 1242 1546 1646 2148 2174 *Byz Lect* l⁷⁰ᵐ syrˢ·ᵖ·ʰ·ᵖᵃˡ Cyril ∥ πιστεύητε 𝔓⁶⁶ᵛⁱᵈ ℵ* B Θ 0250 892

---

[b] **29** b question: WH Bov Nes BF² RVᵐᵍ ASVᵐᵍ RSV TT ∥ b statement: TR AV RV ASV NEB Zür Luth Jer Seg

---

26 ἔρχεται...ὑμῖν Jn 20.19   **27** Φέρε...πλευράν μου Jn 19.34; 20.20, 25   **29** μακάριοι ...πιστεύσαντες 1 Pe 1.8   **30** Jn 21.25   **31** ἵνα πιστεύοντες...αὐτοῦ Jn 3.15; 1 Jn 5.13   **21** 2 Θωμᾶς...Δίδυμος Jn 11.16; 20.24

Γαλιλαίας καὶ οἱ τοῦ Ζεβεδαίου καὶ ἄλλοι ἐκ τῶν μαθη- τῶν αὐτοῦ δύο. 3 λέγει αὐτοῖς Σίμων Πέτρος, Ὑπάγω ἁλιεύειν. λέγουσιν αὐτῷ, Ἐρχόμεθα καὶ ἡμεῖς σὺν σοί. ἐξῆλθον καὶ ἐνέβησαν εἰς τὸ πλοῖον, καὶ ἐν ἐκείνῃ τῇ νυκτὶ ἐπίασαν οὐδέν. 4 πρωΐας δὲ ἤδη γενομένης ἔστη Ἰησοῦς εἰς τὸν αἰγιαλόν· οὐ μέντοι ᾔδεισαν οἱ μαθηταὶ ὅτι Ἰησοῦς ἐστιν. 5 λέγει οὖν αὐτοῖς [ὁ] Ἰησοῦς, Παιδία, μή τι προσφάγιον ἔχετε; ἀπεκρίθησαν αὐτῷ, Οὔ. 6 ὁ δὲ εἶπεν αὐτοῖς, Βάλετε εἰς τὰ δεξιὰ μέρη τοῦ πλοίου τὸ δίκτυον, καὶ εὑρήσετε. ἔβαλον οὖν, καὶ οὐκέτι αὐτὸ ἑλκύσαι ἴσχυον ἀπὸ τοῦ πλήθους τῶν ἰχθύων. 7 λέγει οὖν ὁ μαθητὴς ἐκεῖνος ὃν ἠγάπα ὁ Ἰησοῦς τῷ Πέτρῳ, Ὁ κύριός ἐστιν. Σίμων οὖν Πέτρος, ἀκούσας ὅτι ὁ κύριός ἐστιν, τὸν ἐπενδύτην διεζώσατο, ἦν γὰρ γυμνός, καὶ ἔβαλεν ἑαυτὸν εἰς τὴν θάλασσαν· 8 οἱ δὲ ἄλλοι μαθηταὶ τῷ πλοιαρίῳ ἦλθον, οὐ γὰρ ἦσαν μακρὰν ἀπὸ τῆς γῆς ἀλλὰ ὡς ἀπὸ πηχῶν διακοσίων, σύροντες τὸ δίκτυον τῶν ἰχθύων. 9 ὡς οὖν ἀπέβησαν εἰς τὴν γῆν βλέπουσιν ἀνθρακιὰν κειμένην καὶ ὀψάριον ἐπικείμενον καὶ ἄρτον. 10 λέγει αὐτοῖς ὁ Ἰησοῦς, Ἐνέγκατε ἀπὸ τῶν ὀψαρίων ὧν ἐπιάσατε νῦν. 11 ἀνέβη οὖν Σίμων Πέτρος καὶ εἵλκυσεν τὸ δίκτυον εἰς τὴν γῆν μεστὸν ἰχθύων μεγάλων ἑκατὸν πεντήκοντα τριῶν· καὶ τοσούτων ὄντων οὐκ ἐσχίσθη τὸ δίκτυον. 12 λέγει αὐτοῖς ὁ Ἰησοῦς, Δεῦτε ἀριστήσατε. οὐδεὶς δὲ ἐτόλμα τῶν μαθητῶν ἐξετάσαι αὐτόν, Σὺ τίς εἶ; εἰδότες ὅτι ὁ κύριός ἐστιν. 13 ἔρχεται Ἰησοῦς καὶ λαμβάνει τὸν ἄρτον καὶ δίδωσιν αὐτοῖς, καὶ τὸ ὀψάριον ὁμοίως. 14 τοῦτο ἤδη τρίτον ἐφανερώθη Ἰησοῦς τοῖς μαθηταῖς ἐγερθεὶς ἐκ νεκρῶν.

Jesus and Peter

15 Ὅτε οὖν ἠρίστησαν λέγει τῷ Σίμωνι Πέτρῳ ὁ Ἰησοῦς, Σίμων Ἰωάννου, ἀγαπᾷς με πλέον τούτων;

4 οὐ μέντοι ᾔδεισαν...ἐστιν Lk 24.16; Jn 20.14   5 μή...ἔχετε Lk 24.41   6 Lk 5.4-7
7 ὁ μαθητής...Ἰησοῦς Jn 13.23; 19.26; 20.2; 21.20   Σίμων...θάλασσαν Mt 14.29
11 μεστὸν...δίκτυον Lk 5.6   13 Mt 14.19; 15.36; Mk 6.41; 8.6; Lk 9.16; Jn 6.11   14 Jn 20.19, 26

the sons of Zebedee, and two other disciples of Jesus were all together. [3] Simon Peter said to the others, "I am going fishing." "We will come with you," they told him. So they went and got into the boat; but all that night they did not catch a thing. [4] As the sun was rising, Jesus stood at the water's edge, but the disciples did not know that it was Jesus. [5] Then he said to them, "Young men, haven't you caught anything?" "Not a thing," they answered. [6] He said to them, "Throw your net out on the right side of the boat, and you will find some." So they threw the net out, and could not pull it back in, because they had caught so many fish. [7] The disciple whom Jesus loved said to Peter, "It is the Lord!" When Simon Peter heard that it was the Lord, he wrapped his outer garment around him (for he had taken his clothes off) and jumped into the water. [8] The rest of the disciples came to shore in the boat, pulling the net full of fish. They were not very far from land, about a hundred yards away. [9] When they stepped ashore they saw a charcoal fire there with fish and bread on it. [10] Then Jesus said to them, "Bring some of the fish you have just caught." [11] Simon Peter went aboard and dragged the net ashore, full of big fish, a hundred and fifty-three in all; even though there were so many, still the net did not tear. [12] Jesus said to them, "Come and eat." None of the disciples dared ask him, "Who are you?" because they knew it was the Lord. [13] So Jesus went over, took the bread, and gave it to them; he did the same with the fish.

[14] This, then, was the third time Jesus showed himself to the disciples after he was raised from death.

Jesus and Peter

[15] After they had eaten, Jesus said to Simon Peter, "Simon, son of John, do

you love me more than these?'' ''Yes, Lord,'' he answered, ''you know that I love you.'' Jesus said to him, ''Take care of my lambs.'' [16] A second time Jesus said to him, ''Simon, son of John, do you love me?'' ''Yes, Lord,'' he answered, ''you know that I love you.'' Jesus said to him, ''Take care of my sheep.'' [17] A third time Jesus said, ''Simon, son of John, do you love me?'' Peter became sad because Jesus asked him the third time, ''Do you love me?'' and said to him, ''Lord, you know everything; you know that I love you!'' Jesus said to him: ''Take care of my sheep. [18] I tell you the truth: when you were young you used to fasten your belt and go anywhere you wanted to; but when you are old you will stretch out your hands and someone else will tie them and take you where you don't want to go.'' [19] (In saying this Jesus was indicating the way in which Peter would die and bring glory to God.) Then Jesus said to him, ''Follow me!''

Jesus and the Other Disciple

[20] Peter turned around and saw behind him that other disciple, whom Jesus loved — the one who had leaned close to Jesus at the meal and asked, ''Lord, who is going to betray you?'' [21] When Peter saw him, he said to Jesus, ''Lord, what about this man?'' [22] Jesus answered him, ''If I want him to live on until I come, what is that to you? Follow me!'' [23] So a report spread among the followers

λέγει αὐτῷ, Ναί, κύριε, σὺ οἶδας ὅτι φιλῶ σε. λέγει αὐτῷ, Βόσκε τὰ ἀρνία μου. 16 λέγει αὐτῷ πάλιν δεύτερον, Σίμων Ἰωάννου, ἀγαπᾷς με; λέγει αὐτῷ, Ναί, κύριε, σὺ οἶδας ὅτι φιλῶ σε. λέγει αὐτῷ, Ποίμαινε τὰ πρόβατά μου. 17 λέγει αὐτῷ τὸ τρίτον, Σίμων Ἰωάννου, φιλεῖς με; ἐλυπήθη ὁ Πέτρος ὅτι εἶπεν αὐτῷ τὸ τρίτον, Φιλεῖς με; καὶ λέγει αὐτῷ, Κύριε, πάντα σὺ οἶδας, σὺ γινώσκεις ὅτι φιλῶ σε. λέγει αὐτῷ, Βόσκε τὰ πρόβατά μου. 18 ἀμὴν ἀμὴν λέγω σοι, ὅτε ἦς νεώτερος, ἐζώννυες σεαυτὸν καὶ περιεπάτεις ὅπου ἤθελες· ὅταν δὲ γηράσῃς, ἐκτενεῖς τὰς χεῖράς σου, καὶ ἄλλος σε ζώσει καὶ οἴσει[1] ὅπου οὐ θέλεις. 19 ᵃτοῦτο δὲ εἶπεν σημαίνων ποίῳ θανάτῳ δοξάσει τὸν θεόν.ᵃ καὶ τοῦτο εἰπὼν λέγει αὐτῷ, Ἀκολούθει μοι.

Jesus and the Beloved Disciple

20 Ἐπιστραφεὶς ὁ Πέτρος βλέπει τὸν μαθητὴν ὃν ἠγάπα ὁ Ἰησοῦς ἀκολουθοῦντα, ὃς καὶ ἀνέπεσεν ἐν τῷ δείπνῳ ἐπὶ τὸ στῆθος αὐτοῦ καὶ εἶπεν, Κύριε, τίς ἐστιν ὁ παραδιδούς σε; 21 τοῦτον οὖν ἰδὼν ὁ Πέτρος λέγει τῷ Ἰησοῦ, Κύριε, οὗτος δὲ τί; 22 λέγει αὐτῷ ὁ Ἰησοῦς, Ἐὰν αὐτὸν θέλω μένειν ἕως ἔρχομαι, τί πρὸς σέ; σύ μοι ἀκολούθει. 23 ἐξῆλθεν οὖν οὗτος ὁ λόγος εἰς τοὺς

---

[1] **18** {C} ἄλλος σε ζώσει καὶ οἴσει (B C*ᵛⁱᵈ ζώσει σε) K X Δ Θ Ψ f¹³ 700 (892 ἀποίσῃ) 1009 1010 1071 1195 1216 1230 1241 1242 1646 2148 2174 *Byz Lect* l⁸⁸³ᵐ itᵃᵘʳ,ᵇ,ᵉ,ᶠ,ʳˡ vg copˢᵃ?ᵇᵒ? ‖ ἄλλος σε ζώσει καὶ οἴσει σε A itᵃ,ᶜ,ᶠᶠ² syr⁽ˢ⁾,ᵖ,ʰ copˢᵃ?ᵇᵒ? eth ‖ ἄλλοι σε ζώσουσιν καὶ οἴσουσιν (Π f¹ ἀποίσουσιν) 33ᵛⁱᵈ (syrʰᵐᵍ,ᵖᵃˡ *add* σε) arm Chrysostom ‖ ἄλλοι ζώσουσίν σε καὶ οἴσουσιν C² copᵇᵒᵐˢ ‖ ἄλλοι ζώσουσίν σε καὶ ἀποίσουσίν σε ℵᶜ (ℵ* ποιήσουσιν *and* ὅσα *for* ὅπου) (W 565ᵛⁱᵈ σε ζώσουσιν) (1079 1546 *omit second* σε) geo ‖ ἄλλοι σε ζώσουσιν καὶ ἀπάγουσίν σε D itᵈ

ᵃ ᵃ **19** *a a no parens:* TR WH Bov Nes BF² AV RV ASV NEB TT Zür Luth Jer Seg ‖ *a parens,* *a parens:* RSV

---

16 Ποίμαινε...μου Ac 20.28; 1 Pe 5.2　　**17** πάντα σὺ οἶδας Jn 16.30　　**18** ὅταν...θέλεις 2 Pe 1.14　　**19** τοῦτο...θεόν Jn 12.33; 18.32　　**20** τὸν...Ἰησοῦς Jn 13.23; 19.26; 20.2; 21.7 ὃς καὶ ἀνέπεσεν Jn 13.25　　**22** Ἐὰν...ἔρχομαι Mt 16.28

ἀδελφοὺς ὅτι ὁ μαθητὴς ἐκεῖνος οὐκ ἀποθνῄσκει. οὐκ εἶπεν δὲ αὐτῷ ὁ Ἰησοῦς ὅτι οὐκ ἀποθνῄσκει, ἀλλ᾽, Ἐὰν αὐτὸν θέλω μένειν ἕως ἔρχομαι [, τί πρὸς σέ];

24 Οὗτός ἐστιν ὁ μαθητὴς ὁ μαρτυρῶν περὶ τούτων καὶ γράψας ταῦτα, καὶ οἴδαμεν ὅτι ἀληθὴς αὐτοῦ ἡ μαρτυρία ἐστίν.²

25 Ἔστιν δὲ καὶ ἄλλα πολλὰ ἃ ἐποίησεν ὁ Ἰησοῦς, ἅτινα ἐὰν γράφηται καθ᾽ ἕν, οὐδ᾽ αὐτὸν οἶμαι τὸν κόσμον χωρῆσαι τὰ γραφόμενα βιβλία.

The Woman Caught in Adultery
Jn 7.53—8.11

7 **53** ¹Καὶ ἐπορεύθησαν ἕκαστος εἰς τὸν οἶκον αὐτοῦ,
8 Ἰησοῦς δὲ ἐπορεύθη εἰς τὸ Ὄρος τῶν Ἐλαιῶν. **2** Ὄρθρου δὲ πάλιν παρεγένετο εἰς τὸ ἱερόν, καὶ πᾶς ὁ λαὸς ἤρχετο πρὸς αὐτόν, καὶ καθίσας ἐδίδασκεν αὐτούς².

---

² **24** *add 7.53—8.11* f¹ arm^mss (*see note 1 below*)

¹ **7.53—8.11** {A} *omit 7.53—8.11* (*see page 355*) 𝔓⁶⁶,⁷⁵ ℵ A^vid B C^vid L N T W X Y Δ Θ Ψ 053 0141 22 33 157 209 565 1230 1241 1242 1253 2193 *Lect* it^a,f,l*,q syr^c,s,p cop^sa,bomss,ach² goth arm geo Diatessaron^a,f Clement^vid Tertullian Origen Cyprian Chrysostom Nonnus Cyril Cosmos Theophylact^comm ∥ *include passage following 7.52* D (F) G H K M U Γ 28 700 892 1009 1010 1071 1079 1195 1216 1344 1365 1546 1646 2148 2174 *Byz* it^aur,c,d,e,ff²,j,1mg,r1 vg syr^hms,pal cop^bomss arm^mss eth Didascalia Ambrosiaster Apostolic Constitutions Ambrose Greek and Latin mss^acc. to Jerome Jerome Augustine ∥ *include passage with asterisks or obeli* (E *include 8.2–11 with asterisks*) S (Λ Π *include 8.3–11 with asterisks*) 1077 1443 1445 (l^185m *include 8.1–11,* l^69m,70m,211m,883m,1579m *include 8.3–11, with asterisks*) ∥ *include passage after 21.24* f¹ arm^mss ∥ *include passage following Lk 21.38* f¹³ ∥ *include passage following Jn 7.36* 225

² **2** {B} καὶ πᾶς ὁ λαὸς ἤρχετο πρὸς αὐτόν, καὶ καθίσας ἐδίδασκεν αὐτούς M (Γ *omit ὁ λαός*) (S U Λ 28 700 1216 πᾶς ὁ ὄχλος) f¹ 225 892 1009 1010 1077 1344 1365 1443 1445 1646 2174 *Byz*^pt *Lect*^mpt it^aur,c,e,ff²,1mg,r1 vg syr^hms,pal

---

24 Jn 19.35   **25** Jn 20.30
8 **1** Lk 21.37   **2** *καθίσας...αὐτούς* Mt 26.55

---

of Jesus that this disciple would not die. But Jesus did not say that he would not die; he said, "If I want him to live on until I come, what is that to you?"

²⁴ He is the disciple who spoke of these things, the one who also wrote them down; and we know that what he said is true.

Conclusion

²⁵ Now, there are many other things that Jesus did. If they were all written down one by one, I suppose that the whole world could not hold the books that would be written.

The Woman Caught in Adultery

8 [Then everyone went home, but Jesus went to the Mount of Olives. ² Early the next morning he went back to the Temple. The whole crowd gathered around him, and he sat down and began to teach them. ³ The teachers of the Law and the Pharisees brought in a woman who had been caught commiting adultery, and made her stand before them all. ⁴ "Teacher," they said to Jesus, "this woman was caught in the very act of committing adultery. ⁵ In our Law Moses gave a commandment that such a woman must be stoned to death. Now, what do you say?" ⁶ They said this to trap him, so they could accuse him. But Jesus bent over and wrote on the ground with his finger. ⁷ As they stood there asking questions, Jesus straightened up and said to them, "Whichever one of you has committed no sin may throw the first stone at her." ⁸ Then he bent over again and wrote on the ground. ⁹ When they heard this they all left, one by one, the older ones

3 ἄγουσιν δὲ οἱ γραμματεῖς καὶ οἱ Φαρισαῖοι γυναῖκα ἐπὶ μοιχείᾳ³ κατειλημμένην, καὶ στήσαντες αὐτὴν ἐν μέσῳ 4 λέγουσιν αὐτῷ⁴, Διδάσκαλε, αὕτη ἡ γυνὴ κατείληπται ἐπ' αὐτοφώρῳ μοιχευομένη· 5 ἐν δὲ τῷ νόμῳ ἡμῖν Μωϋσῆς ἐνετείλατο τὰς τοιαύτας λιθάζειν· σὺ οὖν τί λέγεις; 6 τοῦτο δὲ ἔλεγον πειράζοντες αὐτόν, ἵνα ἔχωσιν κατηγορεῖν αὐτοῦ. ὁ δὲ Ἰησοῦς κάτω κύψας τῷ δακτύλῳ κατέγραφεν εἰς τὴν γῆν. 7 ὡς δὲ ἐπέμενον ἐρωτῶντες [αὐτόν], ἀνέκυψεν καὶ εἶπεν αὐτοῖς, Ὁ ἀναμάρτητος ὑμῶν πρῶτος ἐπ' αὐτὴν βαλέτω λίθον· 8 καὶ πάλιν κατακύψας ἔγραφεν εἰς τὴν γῆν⁵. 9 οἱ δὲ ἀκούσαντες ἐξήρχοντο εἷς καθ' εἷς⁶ ἀρξάμενοι ἀπὸ τῶν πρεσβυτέ-

---

cop^bomss ‖ καὶ πᾶς ὁ λαὸς ἤρχετο καὶ καθίσας ἐδίδασκεν αὐτούς E (G πᾶς ὁ ὄχλος) H K Π 1079 1195 1546 2148 Byz^pt ‖ καὶ πᾶς ὁ λαὸς ἤρχετο πρὸς αὐτόν D 1071 it^d ‖ καὶ καθίσας ἐδίδασκεν αὐτούς l^185m ‖ omit f^13 l^185

³ 3 {C} γυναῖκα ἐπὶ μοιχείᾳ M S U Γ Λ f¹ f^13 28 225 700 892 1009 1010 1077 1216 1443 Byz^pt Lect it^aur,e,1mg,rl vg (syr^hms) ‖ γυναῖκα ἐπὶ ἀμαρτίᾳ 1071 ‖ ἐπὶ ἀμαρτίᾳ γυναῖκα D it^d ‖ πρὸς αὐτὸν γυναῖκα ἐν μοιχείᾳ E G H K Π 1079 1195 (1344 1365 1445 1646 2174 ἐπὶ μοιχείᾳ) 1546 2148 Byz^pt (l^12m,32m beginning of lection) it^c,(ff2) cop^bomss (eth) ‖ πρὸς Ἰησοῦν γυναῖκα ἐν μοιχείᾳ (syr^pal)

⁴ 4 {A} αὐτῷ (M see below) S U Γ Λ f¹ f^13 28 225 700 892 1009 1010 1077 1195 1216 1344 1365 1445 1646 2174 Byz^pt Lect it^aur,e,1mg,rl vg syr^hms,pal cop^bomss eth ‖ ad Iesum it^c,ff2 ‖ αὐτῷ πειράζοντες E G H K Π 1079 1443 1546 2148 Byz^pt ‖ αὐτῷ ἐκπειράζοντες αὐτὸν οἱ ἱερεῖς ἵνα ἔχωσιν κατηγορείαν αὐτοῦ and omit τοῦτο...αὐτοῦ in 8.6 D (1071 ἀρχιερεῖς and κατηγορεῖν) (it^d κατηγορεῖν) ‖ omit τοῦτο...αὐτοῦ in 8.6 and add τοῦτο δὲ εἶπαν πειράζοντες αὐτόν, ἵνα ἔχωσι κατηγορίαν κατ' αὐτοῦ after 8.11 M

⁵ 8 {A} γῆν D E G H K M S Γ Λ f¹ f^13 28 225 892 1009 1010 1071 1077 1079 1195 1216 1344 1365 1443 1445 1546 1646 2148 2174 Byz Lect^m it^aur,c,d,e,ff2,1mg vg syr^hms,pal cop^bomss ‖ γῆν ἑνὸς ἑκάστου αὐτῶν τὰς ἀμαρτίας U 700

⁶ 9 {A} οἱ δὲ ἀκούσαντες ἐξήρχοντο εἷς καθ' εἷς S U Γ 28 225 700 1010 1077 1195 1216 1344 Byz^pt l^69m,70m,211m,1579m,1642m it^(aur),(c),e,(ff2),1mg (vg) syr^hms eth ‖ οἱ δὲ ἀκούσαντες εἷς καθ' εἷς ἀνεχώρησαν M (1009 omit καθ' εἷς) ‖ ἀκούσαντες δὲ ἐξήρχοντο εἷς ἕκαστος f¹ (892 εἷς καθ' εἷς) ‖ ἐξῆλθεν εἷς καθ' εἷς Λ ‖ καὶ ἐξῆλθον εἷς καθ' εἷς f^13 syr^pal ‖ ἕκαστος δὲ τῶν Ἰουδαίων ἐξήρχετο D 1071 it^d ‖ οἱ δὲ ἀκούσαντες καὶ ὑπὸ τῆς συνειδήσεως ἐλεγ-

---

5 ἐν...λιθάζειν Lv 20.10; Dt 22.22 6 τοῦτο...αὐτοῦ Mt 22.15 7 Ὁ...λίθον Dt 17.7
9 οἱ...καθ' εἷς Mt 22.22

ρων[7], καὶ κατελείφθη μόνος, καὶ ἡ γυνὴ ἐν μέσῳ οὖσα.
10 ἀνακύψας δὲ ὁ Ἰησοῦς[8] εἶπεν αὐτῇ, Γύναι, ποῦ εἰσιν[9];
οὐδείς σε κατέκρινεν;   **11** ἡ δὲ εἶπεν, Οὐδείς, κύριε.
εἶπεν δὲ ὁ Ἰησοῦς, Οὐδὲ ἐγώ σε κατακρίνω· πορεύου,
[καὶ] ἀπὸ τοῦ νῦν μηκέτι ἁμάρτανε.]]

first. Jesus was left alone, with the woman
still standing there.   [10] He straightened
up and said to her, "Where are they,
woman? Is there no one left to condemn
you?"   [11] "No one, sir," she answered.
"Well, then," Jesus said, "I do not
condemn you either. You may leave,
but do not sin again."]

χόμενοι ἐξήρχοντο εἷς καθ᾽ εἷς E G H K 1079 1365 (1443 ἐξήρχοντο εἷς
ἕκαστος αὐτῶν) 1445 1546 1646 2148 2174 *Byz*[pt] *l*[32m,883m] (*l*[185m] τῆς ἰδίας
συνειδήσεως) (cop[bomss])

[7] **9** {A} πρεσβυτέρων E G H K M Γ *f*[1] 892 1009 1079 1195 1546 2148
Byz[pt] *Lect*[m] it[aur,e,lmg] vg syr[hms] ‖ πρεσβυτέρων ἕως τῶν ἐσχάτων S U Λ
f[13] 28 225 700 1010 1077 1216 1344 1365 1443 1445 1646 2174 *Byz*[pt] *l*[185m,883m]
syr[pal] eth ‖ πρεσβυτέρων ὥστε πάντας ἐξελθεῖν D 1071 it[d] ‖ πρεσβυτέρων
πάντες ἀνεχώρησαν it[c,ff2] cop[boms,(mss)]

[8] **10** {A} Ἰησοῦς D M S Γ *f*[1] 28 892 1009 1010 1071 1195 1365 *Byz*[pt]
Lect[m] it[aur,c,d,e,ff2,lmg,rl] vg syr[hms,pal] cop[bomss] ‖ Ἰησοῦς καὶ μηδένα θεασάμενος πλὴν τῆς γυναικός E F[vid] G H K 1079 1210 1344 1445 1546 1646
2148 2174 *Byz*[pt] *l*[883m] ‖ Ἰησοῦς εἶδεν αὐτὴν καί U Λ *f*[13] 225 700 1077 1443
l[185m] eth

[9] **10** {A} ποῦ εἰσιν D M Γ Λ *f*[1] 892 1010 1071 1077 1195 *Lect*[m] it[c,d,e]
vg[ww] syr[hms,pal] cop[boms] ‖ ποῦ εἰσιν ἐκεῖνοι οἱ κατήγοροί σου E F G K
1079 1445 1546 1646 2148 *Byz*[pt] *l*[883m] ‖ ποῦ εἰσιν οἱ κατήγοροί σου H S U
f[13] 28 225 700 1009 1216 1344 1365 1443 2174 *Byz*[pt] *l*[185m] it[aur,(ff2),lmg,rl] vg[cl]
cop[bomss] eth Jerome ‖ *omit* 118 209

---

11 ἀπὸ...ἁμάρτανε Jn 5.14

THE ACTS
OF THE APOSTLES

1 Dear Theophilus:
In my first book I wrote about all the things that Jesus did and taught, from the time he began his work ² until the day he was taken up to heaven. Before he was taken up he gave instructions by the power of the Holy Spirit to the men he had chosen as his apostles. ³ For forty days after his death he showed himself to them many times, in ways that proved beyond doubt that he was alive; he was seen by them, and talked with them about the Kingdom of God. ⁴ And when they came together, he gave them this order: "Do not leave Jerusalem, but wait for the gift my Father promised, that I told you about. ⁵ For John baptized with water, but in a few days you will be baptized with the Holy Spirit."

Jesus Is Taken up to Heaven

⁶ When the apostles met together with Jesus they asked him, "Lord, will you at this time give the Kingdom back to Israel?" ⁷ Jesus said to them: "The times and occasions are set by my Father's own authority, and it is not for you to know when they will be. ⁸ But you will be filled with power when the Holy Spirit comes on you, and you will be witnesses for me in Jerusalem, in all of Judea and Samaria, and to the ends of the earth." ⁹ After saying this, he was taken up into heaven as they watched him, and a cloud hid him from their sight.

416

ΠΡΑΞΕΙΣ ΑΠΟΣΤΟΛΩΝ

The Promise of the Holy Spirit

1 Τὸν μὲν πρῶτον λόγον ἐποιησάμην περὶ πάντων, ὦ Θεόφιλε, ὧν ἤρξατο ὁ Ἰησοῦς ποιεῖν τε καὶ διδάσκειν **2** ἄχρι ἧς ἡμέρας ἐντειλάμενος τοῖς ἀποστόλοις διὰ πνεύματος ἁγίου οὓς ἐξελέξατο ἀνελήμφθη· **3** οἷς καὶ παρέστησεν ἑαυτὸν ζῶντα μετὰ τὸ παθεῖν αὐτὸν ἐν πολλοῖς τεκμηρίοις, δι᾽ ἡμερῶν τεσσαράκοντα ὀπτανόμενος αὐτοῖς καὶ λέγων τὰ περὶ τῆς βασιλείας τοῦ θεοῦ. **4** καὶ συναλιζόμενος παρήγγειλεν αὐτοῖς ᵃἀπὸ Ἱεροσολύμων μὴ χωρίζεσθαι, ἀλλὰ ᵃπεριμένειν τὴν ἐπαγγελίαν τοῦ πατρὸς ᵃἣν ἠκούσατέ μου· **5** ὅτι Ἰωάννης μὲν ἐβάπτισεν ὕδατι, ὑμεῖς δὲ ἐν πνεύματι βαπτισθήσεσθε ἁγίῳ οὐ μετὰ πολλὰς ταύτας ἡμέρας.

The Ascension of Jesus

6 Οἱ μὲν οὖν συνελθόντες ἠρώτων αὐτὸν λέγοντες, Κύριε, εἰ ἐν τῷ χρόνῳ τούτῳ ἀποκαθιστάνεις τὴν βασιλείαν τῷ Ἰσραήλ; **7** εἶπεν δὲ πρὸς αὐτούς, Οὐχ ὑμῶν ἐστιν γνῶναι χρόνους ἢ καιροὺς οὓς ὁ πατὴρ ἔθετο ἐν τῇ ἰδίᾳ ἐξουσίᾳ· **8** ἀλλὰ λήμψεσθε δύναμιν ἐπελθόντος τοῦ ἁγίου πνεύματος ἐφ᾽ ὑμᾶς, καὶ ἔσεσθέ μου μάρτυρες ἔν τε Ἱερουσαλὴμ καὶ ἐν πάσῃ τῇ Ἰουδαίᾳ καὶ Σαμαρείᾳ καὶ ἕως ἐσχάτου τῆς γῆς. **9** καὶ ταῦτα εἰπὼν βλεπόντων αὐτῶν ἐπήρθη, καὶ νεφέλη ὑπέλαβεν αὐτὸν¹ ἀπὸ τῶν

---

¹ **9** {B} εἰπὼν βλεπόντων αὐτῶν ἐπήρθη, καὶ νεφέλη ὑπέλαβεν αὐτὸν

ᵃ ᵃ ᵃ **4** a indirect, a indirect, a indirect: WH Bov Nes? BF² ∥ a indirect, a indirect, a direct: TR Nes? AV RV ASV RSV TT Zür Luth Jer Seg ∥ a indirect, a direct, a direct: NEB ∥ a direct, a direct, a direct

1 Lk 1.3   **2** Mk 16.19; Lk 24.49–51   **3** οἷς...τεκμηρίοις Lk 24.36–42; Jn 20.19–20, 26–27 λέγων...θεοῦ Mt 28.18–20; Lk 24.46–49; Jn 20.21–23   **4** παρήγγειλεν...πατρός Lk 24.49 τὴν ἐπαγγελίαν...μου Jn 14.16–17; 15.26; Ac 2.33   **5** Ἰωάννης...ἁγίῳ Mt 3.11; Mk 1.8; Lk 3.16; Jn 1.33   **6** Κύριε...Ἰσραήλ Lk 24.21   **7** Οὐχ...ἐξουσίᾳ Mk 13.32   **8** λήμψεσθε ...ὑμᾶς Eph 3.16   ἔσεσθέ μου μάρτυρες Lk 24.48; Jn 15.27; Ac 2.32; 3.15; 5.32   **9** ταῦτα... ἐπήρθη Mk 16.19; Jn 6.62

ὀφθαλμῶν αὐτῶν. **10** καὶ ὡς ἀτενίζοντες ἦσαν εἰς τὸν οὐρανὸν πορευομένου αὐτοῦ, καὶ ἰδοὺ ἄνδρες δύο παρειστή-κεισαν αὐτοῖς ἐν ἐσθήσεσι λευκαῖς, **11** οἳ καὶ εἶπαν, ″Ανδρες Γαλιλαῖοι, τί ἑστήκατε βλέποντες εἰς τὸν οὐρα-νόν; οὗτος ὁ Ἰησοῦς ὁ ἀναλημφθεὶς ἀφ' ὑμῶν εἰς τὸν οὐρανὸν² οὕτως ἐλεύσεται ὃν τρόπον ἐθεάσασθε αὐτὸν πορευόμενον εἰς τὸν οὐρανόν.

The Choice of Judas' Successor

12 Τότε ὑπέστρεψαν εἰς Ἰερουσαλὴμ ἀπὸ ὄρους τοῦ καλουμένου Ἐλαιῶνος, ὅ ἐστιν ἐγγὺς Ἰερουσαλὴμ σαβ-βάτου ἔχον ὁδόν. **13** καὶ ὅτε εἰσῆλθον, εἰς τὸ ὑπερῷον ἀνέβησαν οὗ ἦσαν καταμένοντες, ὅ τε Πέτρος καὶ Ἰωάννης καὶ Ἰάκωβος καὶ Ἀνδρέας, Φίλιππος καὶ Θωμᾶς, Βαρθολομαῖος καὶ Μαθθαῖος, Ἰάκωβος Ἀλφαίου καὶ Σίμων ὁ ζηλωτὴς καὶ Ἰούδας Ἰακώβου. **14** οὗτοι πάντες ἦσαν προσκαρτεροῦντες ὁμοθυμαδὸν τῇ προσευχῇ σὺν γυναιξὶν καὶ Μαριὰμ τῇ μητρὶ τοῦ Ἰησοῦ καὶ τοῖς ἀδελφοῖς αὐτοῦ.

15 Καὶ ἐν ταῖς ἡμέραις ταύταις ἀναστὰς Πέτρος ἐν μέσῳ τῶν ἀδελφῶν εἶπεν (ᵇἦν τε ὄχλος ὀνομάτων ἐπὶ τὸ αὐτὸ ὡς ἑκατὸν εἴκοσι)ᵇ, **16** ″Ανδρες ἀδελφοί, ἔδει

[10] They still had their eyes fixed on the sky as he went away, when two men dressed in white suddenly stood beside them. [11] "Men of Galilee," they said, "why do you stand there looking up at the sky? This Jesus, who was taken up from you into heaven, will come back in the same way that you saw him go to heaven."

Judas' Successor

[12] Then the apostles went back to Jerusalem from the Mount of Olives, which is about half a mile away from the city. [13] They entered Jerusalem and went up to the room where they were staying: Peter, John, James and Andrew, Philip and Thomas, Bartholomew and Matthew, James the son of Alphaeus, Simon the patriot, and Judas the son of James. [14] They all joined together in a group to pray frequently, together with the women, and Mary the mother of Jesus, and his brothers. [15] A few days later there was a meeting of the believers, about one hundred and twenty in all, and Peter stood up to speak. [16] "My brothers," he said, "the

---

(א* εἰπόντων) אᶜ A (B εἰπὼν αὐτῶν βλεπόντων) C E Ψ 049 056 0142 33 81 88 104 181 326 330 436 451 614 629 630 945 1241 1505 1739 1877 2127 2412 2492 2495 *Byz Lect* itᵃʳ,ᵉ,ᵍⁱᵍ vg syr⁽ᵖ⁾,ʰ copᵇᵒ arm geo ∥ εἰπόντος αὐτοῦ νεφέλη ὑπέλαβεν αὐτὸν καὶ ἀπήρθη (D ὑπέβαλεν) itᵈ copᵃᵃ Augustine

² **11** {C} εἰς τὸν οὐρανόν א A B C E Ψ 049 056 0142 33 81 88 104 181 326ᵐᵍ 330 436 451 614 629 630 945 1241 1505 1739 1877 2127 2412 2492 *Byz Lect* itᵃʳ,ᵉ,ᵖʰ vg syrᵖ,ʰ copˢᵃ,ᵇᵒ arm geo Ignatius Origenˡᵃᵗ Epiphanius Chrysostom Cyril Theodoret Cosmos ∥ *omit* D 326* 2495 *l*⁶⁰ itᵈ,ᵍⁱᵍ copᵇᵒᵐˢˢ Augustine Vigilius

ᵇ ᵇ **15** *b* parens, *b* parens: WH AV RV ASV RSV ∥ *b* dash, *b* dash: Zür Luth Jer Seg ∥ *b b* no dashes or parens: TR Bov Nes BF² NEB TT

---

10 ἰδού...λευκαῖς Lk 24.4   **11** οὗτος...πορευόμενον εἰς τὸν οὐρανόν Mt 26.64; Lk 21.27; Re 1.7   **12** Lk 24.50, 52   **13** Πέτρος...Ἰούδας Ἰακώβου Mt 10.2–4; Mk 3.16–19; Lk 6.14–16

scripture had to come true in which the Holy Spirit, speaking through David, predicted about Judas, who was the guide of the men who arrested Jesus. ¹⁷ Judas was a member of our group, for he had been chosen to have a part in our work."

¹⁸ (With the money that Judas got for his evil act he bought a field, where he fell to his death; he burst open and all his insides spilled out. ¹⁹ All the people living in Jerusalem heard about it, and so in their own language they call that field Akeldama, which means "Field of Blood.")

²⁰ "For it is written in the book of Psalms,

'May his house become empty,
　　Let no one live in it.'

It is also written,

'May someone else take his place of
　　service.'

²¹⁻²² "So then, a man must join us as a witness to the resurrection of the Lord Jesus. He must be one of those who were in our group during the whole time that the Lord Jesus traveled about with us, beginning from the time John preached his baptism until the day Jesus was taken up from us into heaven." ²³ So they proposed two men: Joseph, who was called Barsabbas (he was also called Justus), and Matthias. ²⁴ Then they prayed: "Lord, you know the hearts of all men. And so, Lord, show us which one of these two you have chosen ²⁵ to take this place of service as an apostle

πληρωθῆναι τὴν γραφὴν ἣν προεῖπεν τὸ πνεῦμα τὸ ἅγιον διὰ στόματος Δαυὶδ περὶ Ἰούδα τοῦ γενομένου ὁδηγοῦ τοῖς συλλαβοῦσιν Ἰησοῦν, **17** ὅτι κατηριθμημένος ἦν ἐν ἡμῖν καὶ ἔλαχεν τὸν κλῆρον τῆς διακονίας ταύτης.ᶜ **18** Οὗτος μὲν οὖν ἐκτήσατο χωρίον ἐκ μισθοῦ τῆς ἀδικίας, καὶ πρηνὴς γενόμενος³ ἐλάκησεν μέσος, καὶ ἐξεχύθη πάντα τὰ σπλάγχνα αὐτοῦ. **19** καὶ γνωστὸν ἐγένετο πᾶσι τοῖς κατοικοῦσιν Ἰερουσαλήμ, ὥστε κληθῆναι τὸ χωρίον ἐκεῖνο τῇ [ἰδίᾳ] διαλέκτῳ αὐτῶν Ἀκελδαμάχ, τοῦτ' ἔστιν, Χωρίον Αἵματος.ᶜ **20** Γέγραπται γὰρ ἐν βίβλῳ ψαλμῶν,

**Γενηθήτω ἡ ἔπαυλις αὐτοῦ ἔρημος
　　καὶ μὴ ἔστω ὁ κατοικῶν ἐν αὐτῇ,**

καί,

Τὴν ἐπισκοπὴν αὐτοῦ λαβέτω ἕτερος.

21 δεῖ οὖν τῶν συνελθόντων ἡμῖν ἀνδρῶν ἐν παντὶ χρόνῳ ᾧ εἰσῆλθεν καὶ ἐξῆλθεν ἐφ' ἡμᾶς ὁ κύριος Ἰησοῦς, **22** ἀρξάμενος ἀπὸ τοῦ βαπτίσματος Ἰωάννου ἕως τῆς ἡμέρας ἧς ἀνελήμφθη ἀφ' ἡμῶν, μάρτυρα τῆς ἀναστάσεως αὐτοῦ σὺν ἡμῖν γενέσθαι ἕνα τούτων. **23** καὶ ἔστησαν δύο, Ἰωσὴφ τὸν καλούμενον Βαρσαββᾶν, ὃς ἐπεκλήθη Ἰοῦστος, καὶ Μαθθίαν. **24** καὶ προσευξάμενοι εἶπαν, Σὺ κύριε, καρδιογνῶστα πάντων, ἀνάδειξον ὃν ἐξελέξω ἐκ τούτων τῶν δύο ἕνα **25** λαβεῖν τὸν τόπον⁴ τῆς δια-

---

³ **18** {A} *πρηνὴς γενόμενος* ℵ A B C Dᵍʳ Eᵍʳ Ψ 049 056 0142 33 81 88 104 181 326 330 436 451 614 629 630 945 1241 1505 1739 1877 2127 2412 2492 2495 *Byz* syr⁽ᵖ⁾,ʰ copˢᵃ,ᵇᵒ ‖ *πεπρησμένος cj* (see Nu 5.21–27) geo? ‖ *πρησθείς* geo? Papias ‖ *pronus factus* itᵈ,ᵉ,ᵖ* ‖ *in faciem prostratus* itᵍⁱᵍ Ambrose ‖ *suspensus* itᵃʳ,ᶜ,ᵖᶜ,ᵗ vg Bede ‖ *swollen* arm

⁴ **25** {B} *τόπον* 𝔭⁷⁴ A B C* D Ψ itᵃʳ,ᵈ,ᵍⁱᵍ vg syrʰᵐᵍ copˢᵃ,ᵇᵒ arm geo Augustine ‖ *κλῆρον* (see 1.17) ℵ C³ E 049 056 0142 33 81 88 104 181 326 330

ᶜ ᶜ **17–19** c c no dashes or parens: TR Bov Nes BF² AV TT Zür Luth Seg ‖ c parens, c parens: RV ASV RSV NEB ‖ c dash, c dash: WH ‖ c major, c dash: Jer

---

16 *τὴν…Ἰησοῦν* Ps 41.9　　**18** Mt 27.3–8　　**20** *Γενηθήτω…αὐτῇ* Ps 69.25　　**Τὴν…** *ἕτερος* Ps 109.8　　**21–22** *τῶν…Ἰωάννου* Lk 1.2; Jn 15.27　　**22** *τοῦ…Ἰωάννου* Mt 3.13–15; Mk 1.9; Lk 3.21　　*ἕως…ἀνελήμφθη…ἡμῶν* Mk 16.19; Ac 1.9　　**24** *κύριε…πάντων* Jn 2.24–25

κονίας ταύτης καὶ ἀποστολῆς, ἀφ' ἧς παρέβη Ἰούδας πορευθῆναι εἰς τὸν τόπον τὸν ἴδιον. 26 καὶ ἔδωκαν κλήρους αὐτοῖς⁵, καὶ ἔπεσεν ὁ κλῆρος ἐπὶ Μαθθίαν, καὶ συγκατεψηφίσθη μετὰ τῶν ἔνδεκα⁶ ἀποστόλων.

The Coming of the Holy Spirit

2 Καὶ ἐν τῷ συμπληροῦσθαι τὴν ἡμέραν τῆς πεντηκοστῆς ἦσαν πάντες ὁμοῦ ἐπὶ τὸ αὐτό. 2 καὶ ἐγένετο ἄφνω ἐκ τοῦ οὐρανοῦ ἦχος ὥσπερ φερομένης πνοῆς βιαίας καὶ ἐπλήρωσεν ὅλον τὸν οἶκον οὗ ἦσαν καθήμενοι· 3 καὶ ὤφθησαν αὐτοῖς διαμεριζόμεναι γλῶσσαι ὡσεὶ πυρός, καὶ ἐκάθισεν ἐφ' ἕνα ἕκαστον αὐτῶν, 4 καὶ ἐπλήσθησαν πάντες πνεύματος ἁγίου, καὶ ἤρξαντο λαλεῖν ἑτέραις γλώσσαις καθὼς τὸ πνεῦμα ἐδίδου ἀποφθέγγεσθαι αὐτοῖς.

5 Ἦσαν δὲ ἐν Ἰερουσαλὴμ κατοικοῦντες Ἰουδαῖοι, ἄνδρες εὐλαβεῖς¹ ἀπὸ παντὸς ἔθνους τῶν ὑπὸ τὸν οὐρανόν·

which Judas left to go to the place where he belongs." 26 After this they drew lots to choose between the two names. The name chosen was that of Matthias, and he was added to the group of the eleven apostles.

The Coming of the Holy Spirit

2 When the day of Pentecost arrived, all the believers were gathered together in one place. 2 Suddenly there was a noise from the sky which sounded like a strong wind blowing, and it filled the whole house where they were sitting. 3 Then they saw what looked like tongues of fire spreading out; and each person there was touched by a tongue. 4 They were all filled with the Holy Spirit and began to talk in other languages, as the Spirit enabled them to speak.

5 There were Jews living in Jerusalem, religious men who had come from every

---

436 451 614 629 630 945 1241 1505 1739 1877 2127 2412 2492 2495 *Byz Lect* itᵉ syrᵖ˒ʰ Eusebius Basil Chrysostom

⁵ **26** ⸆{B} αὐτοῖς ℵ A B C Dᵇ 33 81 88 104 945 1739 vg copˢᵃˑᵇᵒ arm? eth geo Chrysostom ‖ αὐτῶν D* E Ψ 049 056 0142 181 326 330 436 451 614 629 630 1241 1505 1877 2127 2412 2492 2495 *Byz Lect* itᵃʳˑ⁽ᵈ⁾ˑᵉˑᵍⁱᵍˑᵖˑᵗ syrʰ arm? Chrysostom Augustine ‖ *omit* syrᵖ

⁶ **26** {A} ἔνδεκα ℵ Λ B C E Ψ 049 056 0142 33 81 88 104 181 326 330 436 451 614 629 630 945 1241 1505 1739 1877 2127 2412 2492 2495 *Byz Lect* itᵃʳˑᵉˑᵍⁱᵍ vg syrᵖˑʰ copˢᵃˑᵇᵒ arm geo Origenˡᵃᵗ ‖ δώδεκα D itᵈ Eusebius (Augustine)

¹ **5** {B} κατοικοῦντες Ἰουδαῖοι, ἄνδρες εὐλαβεῖς A B (C *transposes*: C* κατοικοῦντες ἐν Ἰερουσαλὴμ ἄνδρες Ἰουδαῖοι, C³ Ἰουδαῖοι ἄνδρες) (D εὐλαβεῖς ἄνδρες) (E Ἰουδαῖοι κατοικοῦντες) Ψ 049 056 0142 33 81 88 104 181 326 330 436 451 614 629 630 945 1241 1505 1739 1877 2127 2412 2492 2495 *Byz Lect* (l¹⁵⁹⁰ᶜ οἱ κατοικοῦντες) itᵃʳˑ⁽ᵈ⁾ˑ⁽ᵉ⁾ˑᵍⁱᵍˑʳ vg syrᵖˑʰ copˢᵃˑᵇᵒ arm geo ‖ κατοικοῦντες ἄνδρες εὐλαβεῖς ℵ itᵖʰ ‖ κατοικοῦντες Ἰουδαῖοι l⁶⁰³*

---

26 Pr 16.33
2 1 τὴν...πεντηκοστῆς Lv 23.15–21; Dt 16.9–11 **3–4** ὤφθησαν...ἁγίου Mt 3.11;
Lk 3.16 **4** ἐπλήσθησαν...ἁγίου Ac 4.31; 10.44–45; 19 6 ἤρξαντο...γλώσσαις Mk 16.17;
Ac 10.46; 19.6; 1 Cor 13 1

country in the world. 6 When they heard this noise, a whole crowd gathered. They were all excited, because each one of them heard the believers talking in his own language. 7 In amazement and wonder they exclaimed: "These men who are talking like this — they are all Galileans! 8 How is it, then, that all of us hear them speaking in our own native language? 9 We are from Parthia, Media, and Elam; from Mesopotamia, Judea, and Cappadocia; from Pontus and Asia, 10 from Phrygia and Pamphylia, from Egypt and the regions of Libya near Cyrene; some of us are from Rome, 11 both Jews and Gentiles converted to Judaism; and some of us are from Crete and Arabia — yet all of us hear them speaking in our own languages of the great things that God has done!" 12 Amazed and confused they all kept asking each other, "What does this mean?" 13 But others made fun of the believers, saying, "These men are drunk!"

Peter's Message

14 Then Peter stood up with the other eleven apostles, and in a loud voice began to speak to the crowd: "Fellow Jews, and all of you who live in Jerusalem, listen to me and pay attention to what I am about to say. 15 These men are not drunk, as you suppose; it is only nine o'clock in the morning. 16 Rather, this is what the prophet Joel spoke about:

6 γενομένης δὲ τῆς φωνῆς ταύτης συνῆλθεν τὸ πλῆθος καὶ συνεχύθη, ὅτι ἤκουον εἷς ἕκαστος τῇ ἰδίᾳ διαλέκτῳ λαλούντων αὐτῶν. 7 ἐξίσταντο δὲ καὶ ἐθαύμαζον λέγοντες[2], Οὐχ ἰδοὺ ἅπαντες οὗτοί εἰσιν οἱ λαλοῦντες Γαλιλαῖοι; 8 καὶ πῶς ἡμεῖς ἀκούομεν ἕκαστος τῇ ἰδίᾳ διαλέκτῳ ἡμῶν ἐν ᾗ ἐγεννήθημεν;[a] 9 Πάρθοι καὶ Μῆδοι καὶ Ἐλαμῖται, καὶ οἱ κατοικοῦντες τὴν Μεσοποταμίαν, Ἰουδαίαν τε καὶ Καππαδοκίαν, Πόντον καὶ τὴν Ἀσίαν, 10 Φρυγίαν τε καὶ Παμφυλίαν, Αἴγυπτον καὶ τὰ μέρη τῆς Λιβύης τῆς κατὰ Κυρήνην, καὶ οἱ ἐπιδημοῦντες Ῥωμαῖοι, 11[b] Ἰουδαῖοί τε καὶ προσήλυτοι, [b]Κρῆτες καὶ Ἄραβες,[a] ἀκούομεν λαλούντων αὐτῶν ταῖς ἡμετέραις γλώσσαις τὰ μεγαλεῖα τοῦ θεοῦ.[a] 12 ἐξίσταντο δὲ πάντες καὶ διηπόρουν, ἄλλος πρὸς ἄλλον λέγοντες, Τί θέλει τοῦτο εἶναι; 13 ἕτεροι δὲ διαχλευάζοντες ἔλεγον ὅτι Γλεύκους μεμεστωμένοι εἰσίν.

Peter's Speech at Pentecost

14 Σταθεὶς δὲ ὁ Πέτρος σὺν τοῖς ἕνδεκα ἐπῆρεν τὴν φωνὴν αὐτοῦ καὶ ἀπεφθέγξατο αὐτοῖς, Ἄνδρες Ἰουδαῖοι καὶ οἱ κατοικοῦντες Ἰερουσαλὴμ πάντες, τοῦτο ὑμῖν γνωστὸν ἔστω καὶ ἐνωτίσασθε τὰ ῥήματά μου. 15 οὐ γὰρ ὡς ὑμεῖς ὑπολαμβάνετε οὗτοι μεθύουσιν, ἔστιν γὰρ ὥρα τρίτη τῆς ἡμέρας, 16 ἀλλὰ τοῦτό ἐστιν τὸ εἰρημένον διὰ τοῦ προφήτου Ἰωήλ[3],

---

[2] 7 {B} λέγοντες 𝔓74 ℵ A B C* 81 itar,r vg copsa,bo eth Chrysostom ‖ πρὸς ἀλλήλους 33 ‖ λέγοντες πρὸς ἀλλήλους C3 D E 049 056 096 0142 88 104 181 326 330 436 451 614 629 630 945 1241 1505 1739 1877 2127 2412 2492 2495 Byz Lect itd,e syrp,h arm geo Augustine ‖ πρὸς ἀλλήλους λέγοντες Ψ itgig

[3] 16 {D} προφήτου Ἰωήλ ℵ A B C E P Ψ 049 056 076 096 0142 33 81

[a a a] 8-11 a question, a minor, a statement: WH AV RV ASV RSV NEB Luth ‖ a major, a dash, a statement: Zür ‖ a minor, a minor, a question: TR Bov Nes BF2 ‖ a question, a minor, a exclamation: Jer ‖ a question, a minor, a exclamation: Seg ‖ a minor, a question, a question: TT

[b b] 10-11 b number 11, b no number: TRed WH? Bov Nes BF2 NEB? TT Luth Jer ‖ b no number, b number 11: TRed WH? AV RV ASV RSV NEB? Zür Seg

---

7 Οὐχ...Γαλιλαῖοι Ac 1.11

17 Καὶ ἔσται ἐν ταῖς ἐσχάταις ἡμέραις, λέγει ὁ θεός,
    ἐκχεῶ ἀπὸ τοῦ πνεύματός μου ἐπὶ πᾶσαν σάρκα,
        καὶ προφητεύσουσιν οἱ υἱοὶ ὑμῶν καὶ αἱ
            θυγατέρες ὑμῶν,
    καὶ οἱ νεανίσκοι ὑμῶν ὁράσεις ὄψονται,
        καὶ οἱ πρεσβύτεροι ὑμῶν ἐνυπνίοις ἐνυπνιασθή-
            σονται·
18 καί γε ἐπὶ τοὺς δούλους μου καὶ ἐπὶ τὰς δούλας μου
    ἐν ταῖς ἡμέραις ἐκείναις[4] ἐκχεῶ ἀπὸ τοῦ πνεύ-
        ματός μου,
        καὶ προφητεύσουσιν[5].
19 καὶ δώσω τέρατα ἐν τῷ οὐρανῷ ἄνω
    καὶ σημεῖα ἐπὶ τῆς γῆς κάτω,
        αἷμα καὶ πῦρ καὶ ἀτμίδα καπνοῦ[6]·
20 ὁ ἥλιος μεταστραφήσεται εἰς σκότος
    καὶ ἡ σελήνη εἰς αἷμα
        πρὶν ἐλθεῖν ἡμέραν κυρίου τὴν μεγάλην [καὶ
            ἐπιφανῆ].

17 'This is what I will do in the last
    days, God says:
    I will pour out my Spirit upon all
        men;
    Your sons and your daughters will
        prophesy,
    Your young men will see visions,
    And your old men will dream dreams.
18 Yes, even on my slaves, both men
        and women,
    I will pour out my Spirit in those
        days,
    And they will prophesy.
19 I will perform miracles in the sky
        above,
    And marvels on the earth below:
    There will be blood and fire and thick
        smoke;
20 The sun will become dark,
    And the moon red as blood,
    Before the great and glorious Day
        of the Lord arrives.

---

88 104 181 326 330 436 451 614 629 630 945 1241 1505 1739 1877 2127 2412 2492
2495 *Byz Lect* it[ar,e] vg syr[h] cop[bo] arm geo Dionysius[acc. to Paul-Samosata] Basil
Cyril-Jerusalem Chrysostom ‖ Ἰωὴλ προφήτου it[gig] syr[p] cop[sa] eth
Dionysius Gaudentius ‖ προφήτου D it[d,r] Irenaeus[lat] Rebaptism Ephraem
Hilary Priscillian Gregory-Elvira Augustine

[4] **18** {C} ἐν ταῖς ἡμέραις ἐκείναις p[74] ℵ A B C E P Ψ* 049 056 076
0142 33 81 88 104 181 326 330 436 451 614 629 630 945 1241 1505 1739 1877
2127 2412 2492 2495 *Byz Lect* (l[1021] ἡμέραις ταύταις) it[ar,e] vg syr[p,h] cop[sa,bo]
(cop[bomss] ἐν τῇ ἡμέρᾳ ἐκείνῃ) arm geo ‖ *omit* D it[d,gig,r] Rebaptism
Priscillian

[5] **18** {B} καὶ προφητεύσουσιν p[74] ℵ A B C E P Ψ 049 056 0142 (076 88
l[680] προφητεύσωσιν) 33 81 104 181 326 330 436 451 614 629 630 945 1241 1505
1739 1877 2127 2412 2492 2495 *Byz Lect* it[ar,e,gig,r] vg syr[p,h] cop[sa,bo] arm geo ‖
omit D it[d,p] Tertullian Rebaptism Priscillian

[6] **19** {B} αἷμα καὶ πῦρ καὶ ἀτμίδα καπνοῦ p[74vid] ℵ A B C E P Ψ 049
056 076 0142 33 81 88 104 181 326 330 436 451 614 629 630 945 1241 1505 1739
1877 2127 2412 2492 2495 *Byz Lect* it[ar,e] vg syr[p,h] cop[sa,bo] arm geo Didymus ‖
omit D it[d,gig,p,r] Priscillian

17-21 Jl 2.28–32 (3.1–5 LXX)

²¹ And then, whoever calls on the name of the Lord will be saved.'

²² "Listen to these words, men of Israel! Jesus of Nazareth was a man whose divine mission was clearly shown to you by the miracles, wonders, and signs which God did through him; you yourselves know this, for it took place here among you. ²³ God, in his own will and knowledge, had already decided that Jesus would be handed over to you; and you killed him, by letting sinful men nail him to the cross. ²⁴ But God raised him from the dead, he set him free from the pains of death, for it was impossible that death should hold him prisoner. ²⁵ For David said about him:

'I saw the Lord before me at all times,
For he is by my right side, so that I will not be troubled.
²⁶ Because of this my heart is glad and my words are full of joy;
And I, mortal though I am, will rest assured in hope,
²⁷ For you will not abandon my soul in the world of the dead,
You will not allow your devoted servant to suffer decay.
²⁸ You have shown me the paths that lead to life,
And by your presence you will fill me with joy.'

²⁹ "Brothers: I must speak to you quite plainly about our patriarch David. He died and was buried, and his grave is here with us to this very day. ³⁰ He was a prophet, and he knew God's promise to him: God made a vow that he would

21 καὶ ἔσται πᾶς ὃς ἐὰν ἐπικαλέσηται τὸ ὄνομα κυρίου σωθήσεται.

22 "Ἄνδρες Ἰσραηλῖται, ἀκούσατε τοὺς λόγους τούτους· Ἰησοῦν τὸν Ναζωραῖον, ἄνδρα ἀποδεδειγμένον ἀπὸ τοῦ θεοῦ εἰς ὑμᾶς δυνάμεσι καὶ τέρασι καὶ σημείοις οἷς ἐποίησεν δι' αὐτοῦ ὁ θεὸς ἐν μέσῳ ὑμῶν, καθὼς αὐτοὶ οἴδατε, **23** τοῦτον τῇ ὡρισμένῃ βουλῇ καὶ προγνώσει τοῦ θεοῦ ἔκδοτον διὰ χειρὸς ἀνόμων προσπήξαντες ἀνείλατε, **24** ὃν ὁ θεὸς ἀνέστησεν λύσας τὰς ὠδῖνας τοῦ θανάτου[7], καθότι οὐκ ἦν δυνατὸν κρατεῖσθαι αὐτὸν ὑπ' αὐτοῦ· **25** Δαυὶδ γὰρ λέγει εἰς αὐτόν,

Προορώμην τὸν κύριον ἐνώπιόν μου διὰ παντός,
ὅτι ἐκ δεξιῶν μού ἐστιν ἵνα μὴ σαλευθῶ.
26 διὰ τοῦτο ηὐφράνθη ἡ καρδία μου καὶ ἠγαλλιάσατο ἡ γλῶσσά μου,
ἔτι δὲ καὶ ἡ σάρξ μου κατασκηνώσει ἐπ' ἐλπίδι·
27 ὅτι οὐκ ἐγκαταλείψεις τὴν ψυχήν μου εἰς ᾅδην,
οὐδὲ δώσεις τὸν ὅσιόν σου ἰδεῖν διαφθοράν.
28 ἐγνώρισάς μοι ὁδοὺς ζωῆς,
πληρώσεις με εὐφροσύνης μετὰ τοῦ προσώπου σου.

29 "Ἄνδρες ἀδελφοί, ἐξὸν εἰπεῖν μετὰ παρρησίας πρὸς ὑμᾶς περὶ τοῦ πατριάρχου Δαυίδ, ὅτι καὶ ἐτελεύτησεν καὶ ἐτάφη καὶ τὸ μνῆμα αὐτοῦ ἐστιν ἐν ἡμῖν ἄχρι τῆς ἡμέρας ταύτης· **30** προφήτης οὖν ὑπάρχων, καὶ εἰδὼς ὅτι ὅρκῳ **ὤμοσεν αὐτῷ** ὁ θεὸς **ἐκ καρποῦ τῆς ὀσφύος**

---

[7] **24** {B} θανάτου 𝔓[74vid] ℵ A B C E[gr] P Ψ 049 056 0142 33 81 88 104 181 326 330 436 451 614 629 630 945 1241 1505 1739 1877 2127 2412 2492 2495 *Byz Lect* syr[h] cop[sa] arm eth geo Eusebius Athanasius Cyril Theodotus-Ancyra Theodoret Cosmos ∥ ᾅδου (*see* 2.27, 31) D it[ar,d,e,gig] vg syr[p] cop[bo] Polycarp Irenaeus[lat] Ephraem Ps-Athanasius Epiphanius Augustine Theodoret Facundus

---

21 πᾶς...σωθήσεται Ro 10.13   **22** Ἰησοῦν...ὑμῶν Jn 3.2   **23** τοῦτον...ἔκδοτον Ac 4.28   διὰ...ἀνείλατε Mt 27.35, 50; Mk 15.24, 37; Lk 23.33, 46; Jn 19.18, 30; Ac 3.15   **24** ὃν ...ἀνέστησεν Mt 28.6; Mk 16.6; Lk 24.5; Ac 3.15   ὠδῖνας τοῦ θανάτου 2 Sm 22.6; Ps 18.4; 116.3   **25-28** Προορώμην...σου Ps 16.8-11   **27** οὐδὲ...διαφθοράν Ac 13.35   **29** περὶ...ἐτάφη 1 Kgs 2.10; Ac 13.36   **30** ὤμοσεν...θρόνον αὐτοῦ Ps 132.11; 2 Sm 7.12-13

αὐτοῦ **καθίσαι**[8] ἐπὶ τὸν θρόνον αὐτοῦ, 31 προϊδὼν ἐλάλησεν περὶ τῆς ἀναστάσεως τοῦ Χριστοῦ ὅτι

     οὔτε ἐγκατελείφθη εἰς ᾅδην

       οὔτε ἡ σὰρξ αὐτοῦ εἶδεν διαφθοράν.

32 τοῦτον τὸν Ἰησοῦν ἀνέστησεν ὁ θεός, οὗ πάντες ἡμεῖς ἐσμεν μάρτυρες. 33 τῇ δεξιᾷ οὖν τοῦ θεοῦ ὑψωθεὶς τήν τε ἐπαγγελίαν τοῦ πνεύματος τοῦ ἁγίου λαβὼν παρὰ τοῦ πατρὸς ἐξέχεεν τοῦτο ὃ ὑμεῖς [καὶ] βλέπετε καὶ ἀκούετε. 34 οὐ γὰρ Δαυὶδ ἀνέβη εἰς τοὺς οὐρανούς, λέγει δὲ αὐτός,

     Εἶπεν κύριος τῷ κυρίῳ μου,

     Κάθου ἐκ δεξιῶν μου

35   **ἕως ἂν θῶ τοὺς ἐχθρούς σου ὑποπόδιον τῶν ποδῶν σου.**

36 ἀσφαλῶς οὖν γινωσκέτω πᾶς οἶκος Ἰσραὴλ ὅτι καὶ κύριον αὐτὸν καὶ Χριστὸν ἐποίησεν ὁ θεός, τοῦτον τὸν Ἰησοῦν ὃν ὑμεῖς ἐσταυρώσατε.

37 Ἀκούσαντες δὲ κατενύγησαν τὴν καρδίαν, εἶπόν τε πρὸς τὸν Πέτρον καὶ τοὺς λοιπούς[9] ἀποστόλους, Τί ποιήσωμεν, ἄνδρες ἀδελφοί; 38 Πέτρος δὲ πρὸς αὐτούς, Μετανοήσατε, καὶ βαπτισθήτω ἕκαστος ὑμῶν ἐπὶ τῷ

---

[8] **30** {B} καθίσαι p[74vid] ℵ A B C (D[b] καὶ καθίσαι) 81 629* it[ar,gig,r] vg syr[p,pal] cop[sa,bo] arm eth Irenaeus[lat] Eusebius Victorinus-Rome Cyril Fulgentius ‖ τὸ κατὰ σάρκα ἀναστήσειν τὸν Χριστὸν καθίσαι P 049 056 0142 (Ψ 104 καὶ καθίσαι) (33 88 181 1877 ἀναστῆσαι) 326 330 436 451 614 629[mg] 630 945 1241 1505 2127 2412 2492 2495 Byz Lect it[d] syr[h] Origen Eusebius Chrysostom ‖ κατὰ σάρκα ἀναστῆσαι τὸν Χριστὸν καὶ καθίσαι D[gr*] (242 429 460 l[6c] τὸ κατά) ‖ καθίσαι τὸν Χριστὸν κατὰ σάρκα Athanasius ‖ ἀναστῆσαι τὸν Χριστὸν καὶ καθίσαι E it[o] ‖ ἀναστήσειν τὸν Χριστὸν καθίσαι 1739 geo

[9] **37** {B} λοιπούς p[74vid] ℵ A B C E P Ψ 049 056 0142 33 81 88 104 181 326 330 436 451 614 629 630 945 1241 1505 1739 1877 2127 2412 2492 2495 Byz it[ar,e] vg syr[p,h] cop[sa,bo] arm geo ‖ omit D it[d,gig,r] cop[bomss] Hippolytus[arm] Augustine

---

31 οὔτε ἐγκατελείφθη…διαφθοράν Ps 16.10   **32** οὗ…μάρτυρες Lk 24.48; Ac 1.8   **33** τῇ…ὑψωθείς Mk 16.19; Ac 7.55, 56; Ro 8.34; Col 3.1; He 1.3; 8.1; 10.12; 12.2; 1 Pe 3.22 τήν…πατρός Jn 14.16-17; 15.26; Ac 1.4   **34-35** Εἶπεν…ποδῶν σου Ps 110.1 (Mt 22.44; Mk 12.36; Lk 20.42-43; He 1.13)   **36** Ac 5.30-31   **37** Τί ποιήσωμεν Lk 3.10, 12, 14   **38** Μετανοήσατε…ἁμαρτιῶν ὑμῶν Ac 3.19

---

make one of David's descendants a king, just as he was. [31] David saw what God was going to do, and so he spoke about the resurrection of the Messiah when he said:

'He was not abandoned in the world of the dead,
His flesh did not decay.'

[32] God has raised this very Jesus from the dead, and we are all witnesses to this fact. [33] He has been raised to the right side of God and received from him the Holy Spirit, as his Father had promised; and what you now see and hear is his gift that he has poured out on us. [34] For David himself did not go up into heaven; rather he said:

"The Lord said to my Lord:
Sit here at my right side,
[35] Until I put your enemies
As a footstool under your feet.'

[36] "All the people of Israel, then, are to know for sure that it is this Jesus, whom you nailed to the cross, that God has made Lord and Messiah!"

[37] When the people heard this, they were deeply troubled, and said to Peter and the other apostles, "What shall we do, brothers?" [38] Peter said to them: "Turn away from your sins, each one of you, and be baptized in the name of

Jesus Christ, so that your sins will be forgiven; and you will receive God's gift, the Holy Spirit. ³⁹ For God's promise was made to you and your children, and to all who are far away — all whom the Lord our God calls to himself.''

⁴⁰ Peter made his appeal to them and with many other words he urged them, saying, "Save yourselves from the punishment coming to this wicked people!" ⁴¹ Many of them believed his message and were baptized; about three thousand people were added to the group that day. ⁴² They spent their time in learning from the apostles, taking part in the fellowship, and sharing in the fellowship meals and the prayers.

Life among the Believers

⁴³ Many miracles and wonders were done through the apostles, which caused everyone to be filled with awe. ⁴⁴ All the believers continued together in close fellowship, and shared their belongings with one another. ⁴⁵ They would sell their property and possessions and dis-

ὀνόματι Ἰησοῦ Χριστοῦ εἰς ἄφεσιν τῶν ἁμαρτιῶν ὑμῶν, καὶ λήμψεσθε τὴν δωρεὰν τοῦ ἁγίου πνεύματος· **39** ὑμῖν γάρ ἐστιν ἡ ἐπαγγελία καὶ τοῖς τέκνοις ὑμῶν καὶ πᾶσιν τοῖς εἰς μακρὰν ὅσους ἂν προσκαλέσηται κύριος ὁ θεὸς ἡμῶν. **40** ἑτέροις τε λόγοις πλείοσιν διεμαρτύρατο, καὶ παρεκάλει αὐτοὺς λέγων, Σώθητε ἀπὸ τῆς γενεᾶς τῆς σκολιᾶς ταύτης. **41** οἱ μὲν οὖν ἀποδεξάμενοι τὸν λόγον αὐτοῦ ἐβαπτίσθησαν, καὶ προσετέθησαν ἐν τῇ ἡμέρᾳ ἐκείνῃ ψυχαὶ ὡσεὶ τρισχίλιαι. **42** ἦσαν δὲ προσκαρτεροῦντες τῇ διδαχῇ τῶν ἀποστόλων καὶ τῇ κοινωνίᾳ,ᶜ τῇ κλάσει τοῦ ἄρτουᶜ καὶ ταῖς προσευχαῖς.

Life among the Believers

43 Ἐγίνετο δὲ πάσῃ ψυχῇ φόβος, πολλά τε τέρατα καὶ σημεῖα διὰ τῶν ἀποστόλων ἐγίνετο¹⁰. **44** πάντες δὲ οἱ πιστεύσαντες ἦσαν ἐπὶ τὸ αὐτὸ καὶ¹¹ εἶχον ἅπαντα κοινά, **45** καὶ τὰ κτήματα καὶ τὰς ὑπάρξεις ἐπίπρασκον καὶ

¹⁰ **43** {C} διὰ τῶν ἀποστόλων ἐγίνετο B (D *reads* ἀποστόλων ἐν Ἰερουσαλήμ *in* 2.42) P 049 (81 *add* καί) 330 436 451 614 630 945 1241 1505 1739 1877 2412 (056 0142 2492 *l*⁶⁰,⁵⁹⁸,⁶⁸⁰,¹⁰²¹,¹³⁵⁶,¹⁵⁹⁰ ἐγένετο) *Byz Lect* it^d,gig,p*,r syr^h cop^sa arm ∥ διὰ τῶν ἀποστόλων ἐγίνετο εἰς Ἰερουσαλήμ 33 (syr^p) ∥ διὰ τῶν ἀποστόλων ἐγίνετο ἐν Ἰερουσαλήμ φόβος τε ἦν μέγας ἐπὶ πάντας καί p^74vid ℵ (A C 2127 *l*⁶¹¹ ἐγένετο διὰ τῶν ἀποστόλων ἐν) 88 (326 *omit* καί) (2495 ἐγένετο *for* ἐγίνετο *and* δέ *for* τε *and omit* καί) it^ar vg geo ∥ διὰ τῶν ἀποστόλων ἐν Ἰερουσαλήμ ἐγίνοντο καὶ φόβος ἦν μέγας ἐπὶ πάντας τοὺς ἀνθρώπους 629 ∥ διὰ τῶν χειρῶν τῶν ἀποστόλων ἐγίνοντο ἐν Ἰερουσαλήμ φόβος τε ἦν μέγας ἐπὶ πάντας αὐτούς Ψ cop^bo ∥ διὰ τῶν χειρῶν τῶν ἀποστόλων ἐγίνετο ἐν Ἰερουσαλήμ (E it^e ἐγίνοντο) 104 (181 *add* καί) (eth ἐγίνετο διὰ τῶν χειρῶν τῶν ἀποστόλων καὶ ἐν)

¹¹ **44** {D} ἦσαν ἐπὶ τὸ αὐτὸ καί p^74 ℵ A C D E P Ψ 049 056 0142 33 81 88 104 181 326 330 436 451 614 629 630 945 1241 1505 1739 1877 2127 2412 2492 *Byz* it^ar,d,e vg syr^p,h cop^sa,bo arm geo ∥ ἐπὶ τὸ αὐτὸ καί 2495 ∥ ἐπὶ τὸ αὐτό B it^m,p Origen Salvian ∥ *omit* it^gig

ᶜᶜ **42** *c minor, c none:* WH Bov Nes BF² RV ASV RSV TT Zür Jer Seg ∥ *c minor, c minor:* WH^mg NEB ∥ *different text:* TR AV Luth

39 τοῖς εἰς μακράν Is 57.19   ὅσους...κύριος Jl 2.32; Ro 10.13   **40** τῆς γενεᾶς...ταύτης Dt 32.5; Ps 78.8; Php 2.15   **41** Ac 2.47; 4.4; 5.14; 6.7; 11.21, 24; 21.20   **42** τῇ κλάσει τοῦ ἄρτου Ac 2.46; 20.7   **43** Ἐγίνετο...φόβος Ac 5.5, 11; 19.17   πολλά...ἐγίνετο Ac 5.12; 6.8; 14.3; 15.12   **44** Ac 4.32   **45** Ac 4.34–35

διεμέριζον αὐτὰ πᾶσιν καθότι ἄν τις χρείαν εἶχεν· **46** καθ’ ἡμέραν τε προσκαρτεροῦντες ὁμοθυμαδὸν ἐν τῷ ἱερῷ, κλῶντές τε κατ’ οἶκον ἄρτον, μετελάμβανον τροφῆς ἐν ἀγαλλιάσει καὶ ἀφελότητι καρδίας, **47** αἰνοῦντες τὸν θεὸν καὶ ἔχοντες χάριν πρὸς ὅλον τὸν λαόν. ὁ δὲ κύριος προσετίθει τοὺς σῳζομένους καθ’ ἡμέραν [d]ἐπὶ τὸ αὐτό.

The Lame Man Healed at the Gate of the Temple

3 [d] Πέτρος δὲ[1] καὶ Ἰωάννης ἀνέβαινον εἰς τὸ ἱερὸν ἐπὶ τὴν ὥραν τῆς προσευχῆς τὴν ἐνάτην. **2** καί τις ἀνὴρ χωλὸς ἐκ κοιλίας μητρὸς αὐτοῦ ὑπάρχων ἐβαστάζετο, ὃν ἐτίθουν καθ’ ἡμέραν πρὸς τὴν θύραν τοῦ ἱεροῦ τὴν λεγομένην Ὡραίαν τοῦ αἰτεῖν ἐλεημοσύνην παρὰ τῶν εἰσπορευομένων εἰς τὸ ἱερόν· **3** ὃς ἰδὼν Πέτρον καὶ Ἰωάννην μέλλοντας εἰσιέναι εἰς τὸ ἱερὸν ἠρώτα ἐλεημοσύνην [λαβεῖν]. **4** ἀτενίσας δὲ Πέτρος εἰς αὐτὸν σὺν τῷ Ἰωάννῃ εἶπεν, Βλέψον εἰς ἡμᾶς. **5** ὁ δὲ ἐπεῖχεν αὐτοῖς προσδοκῶν τι παρ’ αὐτῶν λαβεῖν. **6** εἶπεν δὲ Πέτρος, Ἀργύριον καὶ χρυσίον οὐχ ὑπάρχει μοι, ὃ δὲ ἔχω τοῦτό σοι δίδωμι· ἐν τῷ ὀνόματι Ἰησοῦ Χριστοῦ

---

[1] **2.47—3.1** {B} ἐπὶ τὸ αὐτό. Πέτρος δέ 𝔭74 ℵ A B C 81 it[ar,gig] vg cop[sa,bo] arm eth Lucifer Cyril ‖ Ἐπὶ τὸ αὐτὸ δὲ Πέτρος Ψ ‖ τῇ ἐκκλησίᾳ. Πέτρος δέ 1505 geo ‖ τῇ ἐκκλησίᾳ. Ἐπὶ τὸ αὐτὸ δὲ Πέτρος E P 049 056 0142 33 88 (104 ἐν τῇ and add καί) 181 326 330 436 451 614 1241 1877 2412 2492 Byz it[e] syr[(p),h] Basil Chrysostom ‖ τῇ ἐκκλησίᾳ ἐπὶ τὸ αὐτό· Πέτρος δὲ καὶ (629 καὶ ἐκκλησίᾳ, 629* omit ἐπὶ τό) (630 τῆς ἐκκλησίας) (945 omit καί) 1739 (2127 ἐπὶ τὸ αὐτὸ τῇ ἐκκλησίᾳ) (2495 τῆς ἐκκλησίας and omit δέ) ‖ ἐπὶ τὸ αὐτὸ ἐν τῇ ἐκκλησίᾳ. Ἐν δὲ ταῖς ἡμέραις ταύταις Πέτρος D it[d] (it[r] omit ἐν τῇ ἐκκλησίᾳ)

[d d] **2.47—3.1** d no number, d number 1: Bov Nes BF² RV ASV RSV NEB TT Zür Luth Jer Seg ‖ d number 1, d no number: TR WH AV

---

46 καθ’...ἱερῷ Lk 24.53　κλῶντες...ἄρτον Ac 2.42　**47** ὁ...προσετίθει...αὐτό Ac 2.41; 4.4; 5.14; 6.7; 11 21, 24; 21.20
3 1 ἐπὶ...προσευχῆς τὴν ἐνάτην Ac 10.3, 9, 30　**2** χωλὸς...αὐτοῦ Jn 9.1; Ac´14.8
4 ἀτενίσας...αὐτόν Ac 6.15; 13.9; 14.9; 23.1　**6** ἐν...περιπάτει Ac 3.16; 4.10; 16.18

tribute the money among all, according to what each one needed. **46** Every day they continued to meet as a group in the Temple, and they had their meals together in their homes, eating the food with glad and humble hearts, **47** praising God, and enjoying the good will of all the people. And every day the Lord added to their group those who were being saved.

The Lame Man Healed

3 One day Peter and John went to the Temple at three o'clock in the afternoon, the hour for prayers. **2** There, at the "Beautiful Gate," as it was called, was a man who had been lame all his life. Every day he was carried to this gate to beg for money from the people who were going into the Temple. **3** When he saw Peter and John going in, he begged them to give him something. **4** They looked straight at him and Peter said, "Look at us!" **5** So he looked at them, expecting to get something from them. **6** And Peter said to him, "I have no money at all, but I will give you what I have: in the name of Jesus Christ of Nazareth I order you to walk!'' ⁷ Then he took him by his right hand and helped him up. At once the man's feet and ankles became strong; ⁸ he jumped up, stood on his feet and started walking around. Then he went into the Temple with them, walking and jumping and praising God. ⁹ The whole crowd saw him walking and praising God; ¹⁰ and when they recognized him as the beggar who sat at the Temple's "Beautiful Gate," they were all filled with surprise and amazement at what had happened to him.

Peter's Message in the Temple

¹¹ As the man held on to Peter and John, all the people were amazed and ran to them in "Solomon's Porch," as it was called. ¹² When Peter saw the people, he said to them: "Men of Israel, why are you surprised at this, and why do you stare at us? Do you think that it was by means of our own power or godliness that we made this man walk? ¹³ The God of Abraham, Isaac, and Jacob, the God of our ancestors, has given divine glory to his Servant Jesus. You handed him over to the authorities, and you rejected him in Pilate's presence, even after Pilate had decided to set him free. ¹⁴ He was holy

τοῦ Ναζωραίου περιπάτει². 7 καὶ πιάσας αὐτὸν τῆς δεξιᾶς χειρὸς ἤγειρεν αὐτόν· παραχρῆμα δὲ ἐστερεώθησαν αἱ βάσεις αὐτοῦ καὶ τὰ σφυδρά, 8 καὶ ἐξαλλόμενος ἔστη καὶ περιεπάτει, καὶ εἰσῆλθεν σὺν αὐτοῖς εἰς τὸ ἱερὸν περιπατῶν καὶ ἁλλόμενος καὶ αἰνῶν τὸν θεόν. 9 καὶ εἶδεν πᾶς ὁ λαὸς αὐτὸν περιπατοῦντα καὶ αἰνοῦντα τὸν θεόν, 10 ἐπεγίνωσκον δὲ αὐτὸν ὅτι αὐτὸς ἦν ὁ πρὸς τὴν ἐλεημοσύνην καθήμενος ἐπὶ τῇ Ὡραίᾳ Πύλῃ τοῦ ἱεροῦ, καὶ ἐπλήσθησαν θάμβους καὶ ἐκστάσεως ἐπὶ τῷ συμβεβηκότι αὐτῷ.

Peter's Speech in Solomon's Portico

11 Κρατοῦντος δὲ αὐτοῦ τὸν Πέτρον καὶ τὸν Ἰωάννην συνέδραμεν πᾶς ὁ λαὸς πρὸς αὐτοὺς ἐπὶ τῇ στοᾷ τῇ καλουμένῃ Σολομῶντος ἔκθαμβοι. 12 ἰδὼν δὲ ὁ Πέτρος ἀπεκρίνατο πρὸς τὸν λαόν, Ἄνδρες Ἰσραηλῖται, τί θαυμάζετε ἐπὶ τούτῳ, ἢ ἡμῖν τί ἀτενίζετε ὡς ἰδίᾳ δυνάμει ἢ εὐσεβείᾳ πεποιηκόσιν τοῦ περιπατεῖν αὐτόν; 13 ὁ θεὸς Ἀβραὰμ καὶ [ὁ θεὸς] Ἰσαὰκ καὶ [ὁ θεὸς] Ἰακώβ³, ὁ θεὸς τῶν πατέρων ἡμῶν, ἐδόξασεν τὸν παῖδα αὐτοῦ Ἰησοῦν, ὃν ὑμεῖς μὲν παρεδώκατε καὶ ἠρνήσασθε κατὰ πρόσωπον Πιλάτου, κρίναντος ἐκείνου ἀπολύειν· 14 ὑμεῖς

---

² 6 {B} περιπάτει ℵ B D itᵈ copˢᵃ Athanasius ∥ ἔγειρε καὶ περιπάτει A C E P Ψ 049 056 095 0142 33 81 88 104 181 326 330 436 451 614 629 630 945 1241 1505 1739 1877 2127 2412 2492 2495 Byz Lect (l⁶⁰,⁶¹¹,⁸⁰⁹,¹¹⁵³ᵃ,¹³⁵⁶,¹⁴³⁹ ἔγειραι) itᵃʳ,ᵉ,ᵍⁱᵍ,ʰ,ʳ vg syrᵖ,ʰ copᵇᵒ arm eth geo Irenaeusˡᵃᵗ Origenˡᵃᵗ Cyprian Eusebius Lucifer Basil Chrysostom Eutherius Theodoret Severus

³ 13 {C} ὁ θεὸς Ἰσαὰκ καὶ ὁ θεὸς Ἰακώβ 𝔭⁷⁴ ℵ C 88 104 629 l⁵³ arm Chrysostom ∥ θεὸς Ἰσαὰκ καὶ θεὸς Ἰακώβ A D ∥ ὁ θεὸς (or θεὸς) Ἰσαὰκ καὶ ὁ θεὸς (or θεὸς) Ἰακώβ itᵃʳ,ᵈ,ʳ vg copˢᵃᵐˢ,ᵇᵒ eth geo Irenaeusˡᵃᵗ ∥ ὁ θεὸς Ἰσαὰκ καὶ Ἰακώβ 049 ∥ Ἰσαὰκ καὶ Ἰακώβ B E P Ψ 056 0142 0236 33 81 181 326 330 436 451 614 630 945 1241 1505 1739 1877 2127 2412 2492 2495 Byz Lect itᵉ,ᵍⁱᵍ,ʰ syrᵖ,ʰ copˢᵃ Severian Theodotus-Ancyra ∥ omit ὁ θεὸς Ἀβραάμ...Ἰακώβ l¹⁰²¹

---

8 ἐξαλλόμενος...περιεπάτει Ac 14.10   εἰσῆλθεν...ἱερόν Jn 5.14   10 ἐπεγίνωσκον...καθήμενος Jn 9.8   11 ἐπὶ...Σολομῶντος Jn 10.23; Ac 5.12   13 ὁ θεὸς Ἀβραάμ...ἡμῶν Ex 3.6, 15; Mt 22.32; Mk 12.26; Ac 7.32   ἐδόξασεν...Ἰησοῦν Is 52.13; Jn 13.32   ὃν...ἀπολύειν Lk 23.14–23; Jn 18.38–40; 19.12–15   14 Mt 27.20–21; Mk 15 7, 11–12

δὲ τὸν ἅγιον καὶ δίκαιον ἠρνήσασθε, καὶ ἠτήσασθε ἄνδρα φονέα χαρισθῆναι ὑμῖν, **15** τὸν δὲ ἀρχηγὸν τῆς ζωῆς ἀπεκτείνατε, ὃν ὁ θεὸς ἤγειρεν ἐκ νεκρῶν, οὗ ἡμεῖς μάρτυρές ἐσμεν. **16** καὶ ἐπὶ τῇ πίστει τοῦ ὀνόματος αὐτοῦ τοῦτον ὃν θεωρεῖτε καὶ οἴδατε ἐστερέωσεν τὸ ὄνομα αὐτοῦ, καὶ ἡ πίστις ἡ δι᾽ αὐτοῦ ἔδωκεν αὐτῷ τὴν ὁλοκληρίαν ταύτην ἀπέναντι πάντων ὑμῶν. **17** καὶ νῦν, ἀδελφοί, οἶδα ὅτι κατὰ ἄγνοιαν ἐπράξατε, ὥσπερ καὶ οἱ ἄρχοντες ὑμῶν· **18** ὁ δὲ θεὸς ἃ προκατήγγειλεν διὰ στόματος πάντων τῶν προφητῶν παθεῖν τὸν Χριστὸν αὐτοῦ ἐπλήρωσεν οὕτως. **19** μετανοήσατε οὖν καὶ ἐπιστρέψατε εἰς τὸ ἐξαλειφθῆναι ὑμῶν τὰς ἁμαρτίας, **20**^{a} ὅπως ἂν ἔλθωσιν καιροὶ ἀναψύξεως ἀπὸ προσώπου τοῦ κυρίου ^{a}καὶ ἀποστείλῃ τὸν προκεχειρισμένον ὑμῖν Χριστόν,^{b} Ἰησοῦν, **21** ὃν δεῖ οὐρανὸν μὲν δέξασθαι ἄχρι χρόνων ἀποκαταστάσεως πάντων ὧν ἐλάλησεν ὁ θεὸς διὰ στόματος τῶν ἁγίων ἀπ᾽ αἰῶνος αὐτοῦ προφητῶν[4]. **22** Μωϋσῆς μὲν εἶπεν[5] ὅτι **Προφήτην ὑμῖν ἀναστήσει κύριος ὁ θεὸς ὑμῶν**[6]

---

[4] **21** {C} ἀπ᾽ αἰῶνος αὐτοῦ προφητῶν 𝔭^{74vid} ℵ* A B* C (ℵ^c B^3 E 945 τῶν ἀπ᾽) 81 630 1739 it^e Cosmos ‖ αὐτοῦ προφητῶν ἀπ᾽ αἰῶνος P (Ψ τῶν ἀπ᾽) 049 056 0142 104 181 326 330 436 451 1241 1505 1877 2127 2492 2495 *Byz Lect* syr^{p,h} eth Chrysostom ‖ τῶν ἀπ᾽ αἰώνων προφητῶν τῶν αὐτῶν *l*^{60} ‖ *transpose* ἁγίων: προφητῶν ἁγίων αὐτοῦ ἀπ᾽ αἰῶνος (614 τῶν προφητῶν) 2412 ‖ αὐτοῦ ἀπ᾽ αἰῶνος προφητῶν (88 αὐτοῦ τοῦ) it^{ar} vg Origen ‖ προφητῶν αὐτοῦ ἀπ᾽ αἰῶνος 209 *l*^{368} ‖ αὐτοῦ τῶν προφητῶν D (629 *omit* τῶν) it^{d,gig,h} arm geo Irenaeus^{lat} Tertullian Origen^{lat} Cosmos

[5] **22** {B} εἶπεν ℵ A B C 81 629 2127 *l*^{60} it^{ar} vg syr^p cop^{bo} geo ‖ πρὸς τοὺς πατέρας εἶπεν P 049 056 0142 104 181 326 436 1241 1505 1877 2412 2492 *Byz Lect* syr^h Theophylact ‖ εἶπεν πρὸς τοὺς πατέρας Ψ 630 945 1739 ‖ εἶπεν πρὸς τοὺς πατέρας ἡμῶν D 33 88 326 (2495 εἶπεν μέν) it^{d,gig,p} cop^{sa} arm eth Irenaeus^{lat} ‖ εἶπεν πρὸς τοὺς πατέρας ὑμῶν E it^e Greek mss$^{acc.\ to\ Bede}$

[6] **22** {C} θεὸς ὑμῶν ℵ^c A D 049 056 0142 81 88 104 181 330 451 945 1505

$^{a\ a}$ **19-20** *a* number 20, *a* no number: TR^{ed} WH Bov Nes BF^2 TT Zür Luth Jer Seg ‖ *a* no number, *a* number 20: TR^{ed} AV RV ASV RSV NEB

^{b} **20** *b* minor: RV ASV RSV NEB TT Luth Jer Seg ‖ *b* none: Bov BF^2 Zür ‖ χριστὸν Ἰησοῦν: WH Nes ‖ Ἰησοῦν Χριστόν: TR AV

---

15 τὸν...νεκρῶν Ac 4.10; 5.30 οὗ ἡμεῖς μάρτυρές ἐσμεν Lk 24.48; Ac 1.8; 2.32 **17** Lk 23.34; 1 Tm 1.13 **18** Lk 24.27, 44, 46 **19** Ac 2.38 **22** Dt 18.15–16 (Ac 7.37)

---

and good, but you rejected him and instead you asked Pilate to do you the favor of turning loose a murderer. **15** And so you killed the Author of life. But God raised him from the dead — and we are witnesses to this. **16** It was the power of his name that gave strength to this lame man. What you see and know was done by faith in his name; it was faith in Jesus that made him well like this before you all.

17 "And now, my brothers, I know that what you and your leaders did to Jesus was done because of your ignorance. **18** God long ago announced by means of all the prophets that his Messiah had to suffer; and he made it come true in this way. **19** Repent, then, and turn to God, so that he will wipe away your sins, **20** so that times of spiritual strength may come from the Lord's presence, and that he may send Jesus, who is the Messiah he has already chosen for you. **21** He must remain in heaven until the time comes for all things to be made new, as God announced by means of his holy prophets of long ago. **22** For Moses said: 'The Lord your God will send you a prophet, just as he sent me,[1] who will be

---

[1] **22** just as he sent me: *or* like me

of your own people. You must listen to everything that he tells you. ²³ Anyone who does not listen to what that prophet says will be separated from God's people and destroyed.' ²⁴ And the prophets, including Samuel and those who came after him, all of them who had a message, also announced these present days. ²⁵ The promises of God through his prophets are for you, and you share in the covenant which God made with your ancestors. As he said to Abraham, 'Through your descendants I will bless all the people on earth.' ²⁶ And so God chose and sent his Servant to you first, to bless you by making all of you turn away from your wicked ways.''

Peter and John before the Council

4 Peter and John were still speaking to the people when the priests,[1] the officer in charge of the Temple guards, and the Sadducees came up to them. ² They were annoyed because the two apostles were teaching the people that Jesus had been raised from death, which proved that the dead will be raised to life.

---

[1] **1** priests: *some mss. read* chief priests

ἐκ τῶν ἀδελφῶν ὑμῶν ὡς ἐμέ· αὐτοῦ ἀκούσεσθε κατὰ πάντα ὅσα ἂν λαλήσῃ πρὸς ὑμᾶς. 23 ἔσται δὲ πᾶσα ψυχὴ ἥτις ἐὰν μὴ ἀκούσῃ τοῦ προφήτου ἐκείνου ἐξολεθρευθήσεται ἐκ τοῦ λαοῦ. 24 καὶ πάντες δὲ οἱ προφῆται ἀπὸ Σαμουὴλ καὶ τῶν καθεξῆς ὅσοι ἐλάλησαν ͨ καὶ κατήγγειλαν τὰς ἡμέρας ταύτας. 25 ὑμεῖς ἐστε οἱ υἱοὶ τῶν προφητῶν καὶ τῆς διαθήκης ἧς διέθετο ὁ θεὸς πρὸς τοὺς πατέρας ὑμῶν⁷, λέγων πρὸς Ἀβραάμ, **Καὶ ἐν τῷ σπέρματί σου ἐνευλογηθήσονται πᾶσαι αἱ πατριαὶ τῆς γῆς.** 26 ὑμῖν πρῶτον ἀναστήσας ὁ θεὸς τὸν παῖδα αὐτοῦ ἀπέστειλεν αὐτὸν εὐλογοῦντα ὑμᾶς ἐν τῷ ἀποστρέφειν ἕκαστον ἀπὸ τῶν πονηριῶν ὑμῶν.

Peter and John before the Council

4 Λαλούντων δὲ αὐτῶν πρὸς τὸν λαὸν ἐπέστησαν αὐτοῖς οἱ ἱερεῖς[1] καὶ ὁ στρατηγὸς τοῦ ἱεροῦ καὶ οἱ Σαδδουκαῖοι, 2 διαπονούμενοι διὰ τὸ διδάσκειν αὐτοὺς τὸν λαὸν καὶ καταγγέλλειν ἐν τῷ Ἰησοῦ τὴν ἀνάστασιν τὴν ἐκ νεκρῶν,

---

1739 2127 *Byz*ᵖᵗ *Lect* itᵃʳ·ᵈ·ᵍⁱᵍ vg geo Irenaeusˡᵃᵗ Origen ‖ θεὸς ἡμῶν ℵ* C E P Ψ 33 326 436 614 629 630 1241 1877 2412 2492 2495 *Byz*ᵖᵗ *l*⁶⁰·⁵⁹⁸·¹²⁹⁴·¹³⁵⁶· ¹³⁶⁴·¹³⁶⁵·¹⁴⁴⁰ itᵉ syrʰ copˢᵃ arm eth Justin Origen ‖ θεός 𝔭⁷⁴ᵛⁱᵈ B *l*⁶⁸⁰ itʰ·ᵖ copˢᵃᵐˢ·ᵇᵒ Chrysostom Cosmos Paschal Chronicle ‖ *omit* syrᵖ

7 25 {C} ὑμῶν 𝔭⁷⁴ ℵᶜ A B E 81 88 104 630 945 1505 1739 2127 2492 *l*⁶¹¹·¹¹⁴¹·¹³⁰⁰ itᵉ vgʷʷ copˢᵃ geo Chrysostom Theophylact ‖ ἡμῶν ℵ* C D P Ψ 049 056 0142 0165 181 326 330 436 451 614 629 1241 1877 2412 2495 *Byz Lect* itᵃʳ·ᵈ·ᵍⁱᵍ·ʰ·ᵖʰ vgᶜˡ syrᵖ·ʰ copˢᵃᵐˢˢ·ᵇᵒ arm eth Irenaeusˡᵃᵗ Chrysostom Cosmos

1 1 {C} ἱερεῖς ℵ A D E P Ψ 049 056 0142 0165 33 81 88 104 181 326 330 436 451 614 629 630 945 1241 1505 1739 1877 2127 2412 2492 2495 *Byz Lect* itᵃʳ·ᵈ·ᵉ·(ᵍⁱᵍ?)·ʰ vg syrᵖ·ʰ copˢᵃ·ᵇᵒ geo Lucifer Chrysostom ‖ ἀρχιερεῖς B C arm eth

---

ͨ **24** *c none:* WH Bov Nes BF² ‖ *c minor:* TR AV RV ASV RSV NEB TT Zür Luth Jer Seg

---

23 Dt 18.19; Lv 23.29   **24** Lk 24.27   **25** Καὶ ἐν...γῆς Gn 22.18; 26.4 (12.3; 18.18; Ga 3.8) **26** ὑμῖν πρῶτον...αὐτόν Ac 13.46; Ro 1.16
4 1 οἱ ἱερεῖς...ἱεροῦ Lk 22.4, 52; Ac 5.24   **1-2** οἱ Σαδδουκαῖοι...νεκρῶν Mt 22.23; Mk 12.18; Lk 20.27; Ac 23.8   **2** καταγγέλλειν...νεκρῶν Ac 4.33; 17.18; 26.23

3 καὶ ἐπέβαλον αὐτοῖς τὰς χεῖρας καὶ ἔθεντο εἰς τήρησιν εἰς τὴν αὔριον· ἦν γὰρ ἑσπέρα ἤδη. 4 πολλοὶ δὲ τῶν ἀκουσάντων τὸν λόγον ἐπίστευσαν, καὶ ἐγενήθη ἀριθμὸς τῶν ἀνδρῶν [ὡς] χιλιάδες πέντε.

5 Ἐγένετο δὲ ἐπὶ τὴν αὔριον συναχθῆναι αὐτῶν τοὺς ἄρχοντας καὶ τοὺς πρεσβυτέρους καὶ τοὺς γραμματεῖς ἐν Ἰερουσαλήμ (ᵃ6 καὶ Ἄννας ὁ ἀρχιερεὺς καὶ Καϊάφας καὶ Ἰωάννης² καὶ Ἀλέξανδρος καὶ ὅσοι ἦσαν ἐκ γένους ἀρχιερατικοῦ)ᵃ 7 καὶ στήσαντες αὐτοὺς ἐν τῷ μέσῳ ἐπυνθάνοντο, Ἐν ποίᾳ δυνάμει ἢ ἐν ποίῳ ὀνόματι ἐποιήσατε τοῦτο ὑμεῖς; 8 τότε Πέτρος πλησθεὶς πνεύματος ἁγίου εἶπεν πρὸς αὐτούς, Ἄρχοντες τοῦ λαοῦ καὶ πρεσβύτεροι³, 9 εἰ ἡμεῖς σήμερον ἀνακρινόμεθα ἐπὶ εὐεργεσίᾳ ἀνθρώπου ἀσθενοῦς, ἐν τίνι οὗτος σέσωσται, 10 γνωστὸν ἔστω πᾶσιν ὑμῖν καὶ παντὶ τῷ λαῷ Ἰσραὴλ ὅτι ἐν τῷ ὀνόματι Ἰησοῦ Χριστοῦ τοῦ Ναζωραίου, ὃν ὑμεῖς ἐσταυρώσατε, ὃν ὁ θεὸς ἤγειρεν ἐκ νεκρῶν, ἐν τούτῳ οὗτος παρέστηκεν ἐνώπιον ὑμῶν ὑγιής⁴. 11 οὗτός ἐστιν

---

² 6 {B} Ἰωάννης 𝔓⁷⁴ ℵ A B 0165 81 (E P Ψ 049 056 0142 33 104 181 326 330 436 451 614 629 630 945 1241 1505 1739 1877 2127 2412 2492 2495 *Byz Lect* itᵉ Chrysostom Ἰωάννην) itᵃʳ,ʰ vg syrᵖ,ʰ copˢᵃ,ᵇᵒ arm geo ‖ Ἰωνάθας D itᵈᶜ (itᵈ* *Ioathas*, itᵍⁱᵍ,(ᵖ) *Ionathan*)

³ 8 {C} πρεσβύτεροι 𝔓⁷⁴ ℵ A B 0165 629 itᵃʳ,(ᵖʰ) vg copˢᵃ,ᵇᵒ eth Cyril Fulgentius ‖ πρεσβύτεροι τοῦ Ἰσραήλ D E P Ψ 049 056 0142 33 88 104 181 330 436 451 614 630 945 1241 1505 1739 1877 2127 2412 2492 2495 *Byz Lect* itᵈ,ᵉ,ᵍⁱᵍ,ʰ syrᵖ,ʰ arm geo Irenaeusˡᵃᵗ Cyprian Chrysostom ‖ πρεσβύτεροι τοῦ λαοῦ Ἰσραήλ 326

⁴ 10 {A} ὑγιής 𝔓⁷⁴ ℵ A B D P Ψ 049 056 0142 0165 33 88 104 181 326 330 436 451 614 629 630 945 1241 1505 1739 1877 2127 2412 2492 2495 *Byz Lect* itᵃʳ,ᵈ,ᵍⁱᵍ vg syrᵖ,ʰ copˢᵃ,ᵇᵒ arm geo Irenaeusˡᵃᵗ Cyril ‖ ὑγιὴς καὶ ἐν ἄλλῳ οὐδενί (*see* 4.12) E itᵉ,(ʰ) (syrʰᵐᵍ) (Cyprian) Greekᵃᶜᶜ· ᵗᵒ Bede

---

ᵃ ᵃ 5–6 *a parens, a parens*: WH ‖ *a major, a major*: NEB Jer ‖ *a minor, a major*: TR AV RV ASV RSV TT (Zür) Seg ‖ *a minor, a minor*: Bov Nes BF² (Luth)

---

3 ἐπέβαλον...τήρησιν Ac 5.18   ἦν γὰρ ἑσπέρα ἤδη Ac 3.1   4 Ac 2.41, 47; 5.14; 6.7; 11.21, 24; 21.20   7 Ἐν ποίᾳ δυνάμει...ὑμεῖς Mt 21.23; Mk 11.28; Lk 20.2   8 τότε... πλησθεὶς πνεύματος...αὐτούς Mt 10.19–20; Mk 13.11; Lk 12.11–12   πλησθεὶς...ἁγίου Ac 6.3, 5; 7.55; 9.17; 11.24; 13.9   10 ἐν τῷ...Ναζωραίου Ac 3.6   ὃν ὑμεῖς ἐσταυρώσατε Ac 2.36; 5.30; 10.39   ὃν ὁ...νεκρῶν Ac 2.24, 32; 3.15; 5.30; 10.40; 13.30; 17.31

---

3 So they arrested them and put them in jail until the next day, since it was already late. 4 But many who heard the message believed; and the number of men came to about five thousand.

5 The next day the Jewish leaders, the elders, and the teachers of the Law gathered in Jerusalem. 6 They met with the High Priest Annas, and Caiaphas, and John, and Alexander, and the others who were members of the High Priest's family. 7 They made the apostles stand before them and asked them, "How did you do this? What power do you have, or whose name did you use?" 8 Peter, full of the Holy Spirit, answered them: "Leaders of the people and elders: 9 if we are being questioned today about the good deed done to the lame man and how he was made well, 10 then you should all know, and all the people of Israel should know, that this man stands here before you completely well by the power of the name of Jesus Christ of Nazareth — whom you crucified and God raised from death. 11 Jesus is the one of whom the scripture says,

'The stone that you the builders despised
Turned out to be the most important stone.'

[12] Salvation is to be found through him alone; for there is no one else in all the world, whose name God has given to men, by whom we can be saved.''

[13] The members of the Council were amazed to see how bold Peter and John were, and to learn that they were ordinary men of no education. They realized then that they had been companions of Jesus. [14] But there was nothing that they could say, for they saw the man who had been made well standing there with Peter and John. [15] So they told them to leave the Council room, and started discussing among themselves. [16] "What shall we do with these men?'' they asked. "Everyone living in Jerusalem knows that this extraordinary miracle has been performed by them, and we cannot deny it. [17] But to keep this matter from spreading any further among the people, let us warn them never again to speak to anyone in the name of Jesus.'' [18] So they called them back in and told them that under no condition were they to speak or to teach in the name of Jesus.

[19] But Peter and John answered them: "You yourselves judge which is right in God's sight, to obey you or to obey God. [20] For we cannot stop speaking of what we ourselves have seen and heard.'' [21] The Council warned them even more strongly, and then set them free. They could find no reason for punishing them, for the people were all praising God for what had happened. [22] The man on whom this miracle of healing had been performed was over forty years old.

ὁ λίθος ὁ ἐξουθενηθεὶς ὑφ' ὑμῶν τῶν οἰκοδόμων,
ὁ γενόμενος εἰς κεφαλὴν γωνίας.

12 καὶ οὐκ ἔστιν ἐν ἄλλῳ οὐδενὶ ἡ σωτηρία[5], οὐδὲ γὰρ ὄνομά ἐστιν ἕτερον ὑπὸ τὸν οὐρανὸν τὸ δεδομένον ἐν ἀνθρώποις ἐν ᾧ δεῖ σωθῆναι ἡμᾶς. **13** Θεωροῦντες δὲ τὴν τοῦ Πέτρου παρρησίαν καὶ Ἰωάννου, καὶ καταλαβόμενοι ὅτι ἄνθρωποι ἀγράμματοί εἰσιν καὶ ἰδιῶται, ἐθαύμαζον ἐπεγίνωσκόν τε αὐτοὺς ὅτι σὺν τῷ Ἰησοῦ ἦσαν· **14** τόν τε ἄνθρωπον βλέποντες σὺν αὐτοῖς ἑστῶτα τὸν τεθεραπευμένον οὐδὲν εἶχον ἀντειπεῖν. **15** κελεύσαντες δὲ αὐτοὺς ἔξω τοῦ συνεδρίου ἀπελθεῖν συνέβαλλον πρὸς ἀλλήλους **16** λέγοντες, Τί ποιήσωμεν τοῖς ἀνθρώποις τούτοις; ὅτι μὲν γὰρ γνωστὸν σημεῖον γέγονεν δι' αὐτῶν πᾶσιν τοῖς κατοικοῦσιν Ἰερουσαλὴμ φανερόν, καὶ οὐ δυνάμεθα ἀρνεῖσθαι· **17** ἀλλ' ἵνα μὴ ἐπὶ πλεῖον διανεμηθῇ εἰς τὸν λαόν, ἀπειλησώμεθα αὐτοῖς μηκέτι λαλεῖν ἐπὶ τῷ ὀνόματι τούτῳ μηδενὶ ἀνθρώπων. **18** καὶ καλέσαντες αὐτοὺς παρήγγειλαν τὸ καθόλου μὴ φθέγγεσθαι μηδὲ διδάσκειν ἐπὶ τῷ ὀνόματι τοῦ Ἰησοῦ. **19** ὁ δὲ Πέτρος καὶ Ἰωάννης ἀποκριθέντες εἶπον πρὸς αὐτούς, Εἰ δίκαιόν ἐστιν ἐνώπιον τοῦ θεοῦ ὑμῶν ἀκούειν μᾶλλον ἢ τοῦ θεοῦ, κρίνατε, **20** οὐ δυνάμεθα γὰρ ἡμεῖς ἃ εἴδαμεν καὶ ἠκούσαμεν μὴ λαλεῖν. **21** οἱ δὲ προσαπειλησάμενοι ἀπέλυσαν αὐτούς, μηδὲν εὑρίσκοντες τὸ πῶς κολάσωνται αὐτούς, διὰ τὸν λαόν, ὅτι πάντες ἐδόξαζον τὸν θεὸν ἐπὶ τῷ γεγονότι· **22** ἐτῶν γὰρ ἦν πλειόνων τεσσαράκοντα ὁ ἄνθρωπος ἐφ' ὃν γεγόνει τὸ σημεῖον τοῦτο τῆς ἰάσεως.

---

[5] **12** {A} καὶ οὐκ ἔστιν ἐν ἄλλῳ οὐδενὶ ἡ σωτηρία 𝔭[74vid] ℵ A B E P Ψ 049 056 0142 0165 33 88 (104 1877 2495 *omit* ἡ) 181 326 (330 *omit* ἄλλῳ) 436 451 614 629 630 945 1241 1505 1739 (2127 οὐδέν) 2412 2492 *Byz* it[ar,e,gig] vg syr[p,h] cop[sa,bo] arm ‖ καὶ οὐκ ἔστιν ἐν ἄλλῳ οὐδενί D it[d,p] ‖ *omit* (see 4.10) it[h] vg[ms] geo Irenaeus[lat] Cyprian Augustine

---

11 ὁ λίθος...γωνίας Ps 118.22; Mt 21.42; Mk 12.10; Lk 20.17; 1 Pe 2.4, 7   **12** οὐδὲ γὰρ ὄνομα...ἡμᾶς Mt 1.21   **15** Ac 5.34–35   **16** Τί...φανερόν Jn 11.47   **17–18** Ac 5.28   **19** Ac 5.29

The Believers Pray for Boldness

23 Ἀπολυθέντες δὲ ἦλθον πρὸς τοὺς ἰδίους καὶ ἀπήγγειλαν ὅσα πρὸς αὐτοὺς οἱ ἀρχιερεῖς καὶ οἱ πρεσβύτεροι εἶπαν. 24 οἱ δὲ ἀκούσαντες ὁμοθυμαδὸν ἦραν φωνὴν πρὸς τὸν θεὸν καὶ εἶπαν, Δέσποτα, σύ[6] ὁ **ποιήσας τὸν οὐρανὸν καὶ τὴν γῆν καὶ τὴν θάλασσαν καὶ πάντα τὰ ἐν αὐτοῖς,** 25 ὁ τοῦ πατρὸς ἡμῶν διὰ πνεύματος ἁγίου στόματος Δαυὶδ παιδός σου εἰπών[7],

> Ἱνατί ἐφρύαξαν ἔθνη
> καὶ λαοὶ ἐμελέτησαν κενά;
> 26   παρέστησαν οἱ βασιλεῖς τῆς γῆς
> καὶ οἱ ἄρχοντες συνήχθησαν ἐπὶ τὸ αὐτὸ
> κατὰ τοῦ κυρίου καὶ κατὰ τοῦ Χριστοῦ αὐτοῦ.[b]

27 συνήχθησαν γὰρ ἐπ' ἀληθείας ἐν τῇ πόλει ταύτῃ ἐπὶ τὸν ἅγιον παῖδά σου Ἰησοῦν, ὃν ἔχρισας, Ἡρῴδης τε καὶ Πόντιος Πιλᾶτος σὺν ἔθνεσιν καὶ λαοῖς Ἰσραήλ, 28 ποιῆσαι ὅσα ἡ χείρ σου καὶ ἡ βουλή σου προώρισεν

The Believers Pray for Boldness

[23] As soon as they were set free, Peter and John returned to their group and told them what the chief priests and the elders had said. [24] When they heard it, they all joined together in prayer to God: "Master and Creator of heaven, and earth, and sea, and all that is in them! [25] By means of the Holy Spirit you spoke through our ancestor David, your servant, when he said:

> 'Why were the Gentiles furious,
> Why did the peoples plot in vain?
> [26] The kings of the earth prepared
> themselves,
> And the rulers met together
> Against the Lord and his Messiah.'

[27] For indeed Herod and Pontius Pilate met together in this city with the Gentiles and the peoples of Israel against Jesus, your holy Servant, whom you made Messiah. [28] They gathered to do everything that you, by your power and will, had already decided would take place.

---

[6] **24** {B} σύ 𝔭[74] ℵ A B 2495 it[t] vg[ww] cop[bo] Athanasius Didymus ‖ σὺ εἶ vg[cl] Hilary Augustine ‖ σὺ ὁ θεός D E P Ψ 049 056 0142 104 326 330 436 451 614 629 945 1241 1505 1739 2412 2492 *Byz Lect* it[e.gig] geo Lucifer ‖ σὺ εἶ ὁ θεός 2127 *l*[680,1443] it[d] cop[sa] Irenaeus[lat] Theophylact ‖ κύριε ὁ θεός (*see* Ex 20.11; Ps 146.6) 33 (88 κύριε σύ) 181 1877 syr[p.h] (arm σὺ κύριος) ‖ κύριε it[ar]

[7] **25** {D} ὁ τοῦ πατρὸς ἡμῶν διὰ πνεύματος ἁγίου στόματος Δαυὶδ παιδός σου εἰπών 𝔭[74] ℵ A B E Ψ 33 88 (945 ὁ διὰ τοῦ πατρὸς ἡμῶν ἐν πνεύματι ἁγίῳ) 1739 *l*[60] it[e] (syr[h?]) geo Athanasius ‖ ὁ πνεύματι ἁγίῳ διὰ στόματος τοῦ πατρὸς ἡμῶν Δαυὶδ τοῦ παιδός σου εἰπόν [= εἰπών] 629 it[ar.gig] vg syr[p.(h?)] cop[bomss] ‖ ὃς διὰ πνεύματος ἁγίου διὰ τοῦ στόματος λαλήσας Δαυὶδ παιδός σου D (it[d] *puero tuo*) cop[(sa).bomss] (Irenaeus[lat]) ‖ ὁ διὰ στόματος Δαυὶδ τοῦ παιδός σου εἰπών 049 056 0142 326 330 451 1505 1877 2495 (P 104 181 436 614 1241 2127 2412 2492 *Lect omit* τοῦ) *Byz* Athanasius Chrysostom ‖ *Thou, who hast spoken through the mouth of our father, thy servant David, and hast said by the Holy Spirit* arm

---

[b] **26** *b* major: TR WH Bov Nes BF[2] AV NEB TT Zür Jer Seg ‖ *b* minor: RV ASV Luth ‖ *b* dash: RSV

---

24 ὁ ποιήσας...αὐτοῖς Ex 20.11; Ps 146.6   **25–26** Ἱνατί...αὐτοῦ Ps 2.1-2   **27** τὸν... Ἰησοῦν Ac 3.13   ὃν ἔχρισας Is 61.1   **28** Ac 2.23

[29] And now, Lord, take notice of the threats they made and allow us, your servants, to speak your message with all boldness. [30] Stretch out your hand to heal, and grant that wonders and miracles may be performed through the name of your holy Servant Jesus." [31] When they finished praying, the place where they were meeting was shaken. They were all filled with the Holy Spirit and began to speak God's message with boldness.

All Things Together

[32] The group of believers was one in mind and heart. No one said that any of his belongings was his own, but they all shared with one another everything they had. [33] With great power the apostles gave witness of the resurrection of the Lord Jesus, and God poured rich blessings on them all. [34] There was no one in the group who was in need. Those who owned fields or houses would sell them, bring the money received from the sale, [35] and turn it over to the apostles; and the money was distributed to each one according to his need.

[36] And so it was that Joseph, a Levite born in Cyprus, whom the apostles called Barnabas (which means "One who Encourages"), [37] sold a field he owned, brought the money, and turned it over to the apostles.

γενέσθαι. **29** καὶ τὰ νῦν, κύριε, ἔπιδε ἐπὶ τὰς ἀπειλὰς αὐτῶν, καὶ δὸς τοῖς δούλοις σου μετὰ παρρησίας πάσης λαλεῖν τὸν λόγον σου, **30** ἐν τῷ τὴν χεῖρά σου ἐκτείνειν σε εἰς ἴασιν καὶ σημεῖα καὶ τέρατα γίνεσθαι διὰ τοῦ ὀνόματος τοῦ ἁγίου παιδός σου Ἰησοῦ. **31** καὶ δεηθέντων αὐτῶν ἐσαλεύθη ὁ τόπος ἐν ᾧ ἦσαν συνηγμένοι, καὶ ἐπλήσθησαν ἅπαντες τοῦ ἁγίου πνεύματος, καὶ ἐλάλουν τὸν λόγον τοῦ θεοῦ μετὰ παρρησίας.

All Things in Common

32 Τοῦ δὲ πλήθους τῶν πιστευσάντων ἦν καρδία καὶ ψυχὴ μία, καὶ οὐδὲ εἷς τι τῶν ὑπαρχόντων αὐτῷ ἔλεγεν ἴδιον εἶναι, ἀλλ' ἦν αὐτοῖς πάντα κοινά. **33** καὶ δυνάμει μεγάλῃ ἀπεδίδουν τὸ μαρτύριον οἱ ἀπόστολοι τῆς ἀναστάσεως τοῦ κυρίου Ἰησοῦ[8], χάρις τε μεγάλη ἦν ἐπὶ πάντας αὐτούς. **34** οὐδὲ γὰρ ἐνδεής τις ἦν ἐν αὐτοῖς· ὅσοι γὰρ κτήτορες χωρίων ἢ οἰκιῶν ὑπῆρχον, πωλοῦντες ἔφερον τὰς τιμὰς τῶν πιπρασκομένων **35** καὶ ἐτίθουν παρὰ τοὺς πόδας τῶν ἀποστόλων· διεδίδετο δὲ ἑκάστῳ καθότι ἄν τις χρείαν εἶχεν. **36** Ἰωσὴφ δὲ ὁ ἐπικληθεὶς Βαρναβᾶς ἀπὸ τῶν ἀποστόλων, ὅ ἐστιν μεθερμηνευόμενον υἱὸς παρακλήσεως, Λευίτης, Κύπριος τῷ γένει, **37** ὑπάρχοντος αὐτῷ ἀγροῦ πωλήσας ἤνεγκεν τὸ χρῆμα καὶ ἔθηκεν παρὰ τοὺς πόδας τῶν ἀποστόλων.

---

[8] **33** {C} τῆς ἀναστάσεως τοῦ κυρίου Ἰησοῦ 𝔭[8] P Ψ 049 056 0142 88 104 181 326 330 451 614 1241 1505 1877 2127 2412 2492 *Byz* it^gig syr^h cop^sa eth^pp Irenaeus^lat Augustine Theophylact ‖ τοῦ κυρίου Ἰησοῦ τῆς ἀναστάσεως B ‖ τῆς ἀναστάσεως Ἰησοῦ Χριστοῦ 808 1522 syr^p cop^bomss ‖ τῆς ἀναστάσεως τοῦ κυρίου Ἰησοῦ Χριστοῦ D E 436 945 1739 2495 it^d,e,r arm Chrysostom ‖ τῆς ἀναστάσεως Ἰησοῦ Χριστοῦ τοῦ κυρίου ℵ A it^ar vg^ww cop^bomss ‖ τῆς ἀναστάσεως Ἰησοῦ Χριστοῦ τοῦ κυρίου ἡμῶν 629 vg^cl cop^boms ‖ τῆς ἀναστάσεως τοῦ κυρίου ἡμῶν Ἰησοῦ Χριστοῦ it^ph eth^ro geo

---

29 μετὰ...λόγον σου Eph 6.19   **31** ἐπλήσθησαν...πνεύματος Ac 2.4   **32** οὐδὲ... κοινά Ac 2.44   **33** ἀπεδίδουν...Ἰησοῦ Ac 4.2   χάρις...αὐτούς Ac 2.47   **34–35** Ac 2.45

Ananias and Sapphira

5 Ἀνὴρ δέ τις Ἀνανίας ὀνόματι σὺν Σαπφείρῃ τῇ γυναικὶ αὐτοῦ ἐπώλησεν κτῆμα **2** καὶ ἐνοσφίσατο ἀπὸ τῆς τιμῆς, συνειδυίης καὶ τῆς γυναικός, καὶ ἐνέγκας μέρος τι παρὰ τοὺς πόδας τῶν ἀποστόλων ἔθηκεν. **3** εἶπεν δὲ ὁ Πέτρος, Ἀνανία, διὰ τί ἐπλήρωσεν[1] ὁ Σατανᾶς τὴν καρδίαν σου ψεύσασθαί σε τὸ πνεῦμα τὸ ἅγιον καὶ νοσφίσασθαι ἀπὸ τῆς τιμῆς τοῦ χωρίου; **4** οὐχὶ μένον σοὶ ἔμενεν[a] καὶ πραθὲν ἐν τῇ σῇ ἐξουσίᾳ ὑπῆρχεν;[a] τί ὅτι ἔθου ἐν τῇ καρδίᾳ σου τὸ πρᾶγμα τοῦτο; οὐκ ἐψεύσω ἀνθρώποις ἀλλὰ τῷ θεῷ. **5** ἀκούων δὲ ὁ Ἀνανίας τοὺς λόγους τούτους πεσὼν ἐξέψυξεν· καὶ ἐγένετο φόβος μέγας ἐπὶ πάντας τοὺς ἀκούοντας. **6** ἀναστάντες δὲ οἱ νεώτεροι συνέστειλαν αὐτὸν καὶ ἐξενέγκαντες ἔθαψαν.

7 Ἐγένετο δὲ ὡς ὡρῶν τριῶν διάστημα καὶ ἡ γυνὴ αὐτοῦ μὴ εἰδυῖα τὸ γεγονὸς εἰσῆλθεν. **8** ἀπεκρίθη δὲ πρὸς αὐτὴν Πέτρος, Εἰπέ μοι, εἰ τοσούτου τὸ χωρίον ἀπέδοσθε; [b]ἡ δὲ εἶπεν, Ναί, τοσούτου. **9**[b] ὁ δὲ Πέτρος πρὸς αὐτήν, Τί ὅτι συνεφωνήθη ὑμῖν πειράσαι τὸ πνεῦμα κυρίου; ἰδοὺ οἱ πόδες τῶν θαψάντων τὸν ἄνδρα σου ἐπὶ τῇ θύρᾳ καὶ ἐξοίσουσίν σε. **10** ἔπεσεν δὲ παραχρῆμα πρὸς τοὺς πόδας αὐτοῦ καὶ ἐξέψυξεν· εἰσελθόντες δὲ οἱ νεανίσκοι εὗρον αὐτὴν νεκράν, καὶ ἐξενέγκαντες ἔθαψαν πρὸς τὸν ἄνδρα αὐτῆς. **11** καὶ ἐγένετο φόβος

---

1 3 {C} ἐπλήρωσεν p⁸ א^c A B D E P Ψ 049 056 0142 0189 88 104 181 326 436 614 629 630 945 1241 1505 1739 1877 2127 2412 2495 *Byz Lect* it^{dvid,e,gig,r} syr^{p,h} cop^{sa,bo} arm geo Origen Cyprian Lucifer Athanasius Cyril-Jerusalem Didymus Epiphanius^{1/3} Chrysostom Leontius ‖ ἐπείρασεν p⁷⁴ it^{ar,ph} vg Athanasius Didymus Epiphanius^{2/3} Fulgentius Greek ms^{acc. to Bede} ‖ ἐπήρωσεν א* 330 451 ‖ ἐπώρωσεν 2492

ᵃ ᵃ **4** a none, a question: (TR) WH Bov Nes BF (TT) (Zür) (Jer) ‖ a question, a question: AV RV ASV RSV NEB Seg ‖ a statement, a statement: Luth

ᵇ ᵇ **8–9** b no number, b number 9: TR^{ed} WH? Bov Nes BF² AV RV ASV RSV NEB TT Zür Luth Jer Seg ‖ b number 9, b no number: TR^{ed} WH?

---

2 ἐνέγκας...ἔθηκεν Ac 4.34–35, 37   **3** ἐπλήρωσεν...σου Jn 13.2   **5** ἐγένετο...ἀκούοντας Ac 2.43; 5.11; 19.17   **9** πειράσαι...κυρίου 1 Cor 10.9   **11** Ac 2.43; 5.5; 19.17

Ananias and Sapphira

5 But there was a man named Ananias, whose wife's name was Sapphira. He sold some property that belonged to them, **2** but kept part of the money for himself, as his wife knew, and turned the rest over to the apostles. **3** Peter said to him: "Ananias, why did you let Satan take control of your heart and make you lie to the Holy Spirit by keeping part of the money you received for the property? **4** Before you sold the property it belonged to you, and after you sold it the money was yours. Why, then, did you decide in your heart that you would do such a thing? You have not lied to men — you have lied to God!" **5** As soon as Ananias heard this he fell down dead; and all who heard about it were filled with fear. **6** The young men came in, wrapped up his body, took him out, and buried him.

7 About three hours later his wife came in, but she did not know what had happened. **8** Peter said to her, "Tell me, was this the full amount you and your husband received for your property?" "Yes," she answered, "the full amount." **9** So Peter said to her, "Why did you and your husband decide to put the Lord's Spirit to the test? The men who buried your husband are at the door right now, and they will carry you out too!" **10** At once she fell down at his feet and died. The young men came in and saw that she was dead, so they carried her out and buried her beside her husband. **11** The whole church and all the others who heard of this were filled with great fear.

Miracles and Wonders

[12] Many miracles and wonders were being performed among the people by the apostles. All the believers met together in a group in Solomon's Porch. [13] Nobody outside the group dared join them, even though the people spoke highly of them. [14] But more and more people were added to the group — a crowd of men and women who believed in the Lord. [15] As a result of what the apostles were doing, the sick people were carried out in the streets and placed on beds and mats so that, when Peter walked by, at least his shadow might pass over some of them. [16] And crowds of people came in from the towns around Jerusalem, bringing their sick and those who had evil spirits in them; and they were all healed.

The Apostles Persecuted

[17] Then the High Priest and all his companions, members of the local party of the Sadducees, became extremely jealous of the apostles; so they decided to take action. [18] They arrested the apostles and placed them in the public jail. [19] But that night an angel of the Lord opened the prison gates, led the apostles out, and said to them, [20] "Go and stand in the Temple, and tell the people all about this new life." [21] The apostles obeyed, and at dawn they entered the Temple and started teaching.

μέγας ἐφ' ὅλην τὴν ἐκκλησίαν καὶ ἐπὶ πάντας τοὺς ἀκούοντας ταῦτα.

Many Signs and Wonders Performed

12 Διὰ δὲ τῶν χειρῶν τῶν ἀποστόλων ἐγίνετο σημεῖα καὶ τέρατα πολλὰ ἐν τῷ λαῷ· καὶ ἦσαν ὁμοθυμαδὸν ἅπαντες ἐν τῇ Στοᾷ Σολομῶντος. 13 τῶν δὲ λοιπῶν οὐδεὶς ἐτόλμα κολλᾶσθαι αὐτοῖς, ἀλλ' ἐμεγάλυνεν αὐτοὺς ὁ λαός· 14 μᾶλλον δὲ προσετίθεντο πιστεύοντες τῷ κυρίῳ πλήθη ἀνδρῶν τε καὶ γυναικῶν, 15 ὥστε καὶ εἰς τὰς πλατείας ἐκφέρειν τοὺς ἀσθενεῖς καὶ τιθέναι ἐπὶ κλιναρίων καὶ κραβάττων, ἵνα ἐρχομένου Πέτρου κἂν ἡ σκιὰ ἐπισκιάσῃ τινὶ αὐτῶν. 16 συνήρχετο δὲ καὶ τὸ πλῆθος τῶν πέριξ πόλεων Ἰερουσαλήμ², φέροντες ἀσθενεῖς καὶ ὀχλουμένους ὑπὸ πνευμάτων ἀκαθάρτων, οἵτινες ἐθεραπεύοντο ἅπαντες.

Persecution of the Apostles

17 Ἀναστὰς δὲ ὁ ἀρχιερεὺς καὶ πάντες οἱ σὺν αὐτῷ, ἡ οὖσα αἵρεσις τῶν Σαδδουκαίων, ἐπλήσθησαν ζήλου 18 καὶ ἐπέβαλον τὰς χεῖρας ἐπὶ τοὺς ἀποστόλους καὶ ἔθεντο αὐτοὺς ἐν τηρήσει δημοσίᾳ. 19 ἄγγελος δὲ κυρίου διὰ νυκτὸς ἤνοιξε τὰς θύρας τῆς φυλακῆς ἐξαγαγών τε αὐτοὺς εἶπεν, 20 Πορεύεσθε καὶ σταθέντες λαλεῖτε ἐν τῷ ἱερῷ τῷ λαῷ πάντα τὰ ῥήματα τῆς ζωῆς ταύτης. 21 ἀκούσαντες δὲ εἰσῆλθον ὑπὸ τὸν ὄρθρον εἰς τὸ ἱερὸν καὶ ἐδίδασκον. Παραγενόμενος δὲ ὁ ἀρχιερεὺς καὶ οἱ

---

² 16 {C} Ἰερουσαλήμ 𝔓⁷⁴ ℵ A B 0142 0189 *l*¹³⁶⁴ it^{ar,gig,ph} vg (syr^{p,h}) (cop^{sa}) (eth) Lucifer ∥ εἰς Ἰερουσαλήμ D E P Ψ 049 056 88 104 181 326 330 436 451 614 629 630 945 1241 1505 1739 1877 2127 2412 2492 2495 *Byz Lect* it^{c,d,e} cop^{bo} arm geo Chrysostom ∥ ἐν Ἰερουσαλήμ 467 547

12 Διὰ...τέρατα πολλά Ac 2.43; 6.8; 14.3; 15.12   ἐν τῇ Στοᾷ Σολομῶντος Jn 10.23; Ac 3.11   13 ἐμεγάλυνεν...λαός Ac 2.47   14 Ac 2.41, 47; 4.4; 6.7; 11.21, 24; 21.20   15-16 Mk 6.56; Ac 19.11-12   17 Ac 4.1, 6   18 Ac 4.3   19 Ac 12.7-10

σὺν αὐτῷ συνεκάλεσαν τὸ συνέδριον καὶ πᾶσαν τὴν γερουσίαν τῶν υἱῶν Ἰσραήλ, καὶ ἀπέστειλαν εἰς τὸ δεσμωτήριον ἀχθῆναι αὐτούς. 22 οἱ δὲ παραγενόμενοι ὑπηρέται οὐχ εὗρον αὐτοὺς ἐν τῇ φυλακῇ, ἀναστρέψαντες δὲ ἀπήγγειλαν 23 λέγοντες ὅτι Τὸ δεσμωτήριον εὕρομεν κεκλεισμένον ἐν πάσῃ ἀσφαλείᾳ καὶ τοὺς φύλακας ἑστῶτας ἐπὶ τῶν θυρῶν, ἀνοίξαντες δὲ ἔσω, οὐδένα εὕρομεν. 24 ὡς δὲ ἤκουσαν τοὺς λόγους τούτους ὅ τε στρατηγὸς τοῦ ἱεροῦ καὶ οἱ ἀρχιερεῖς, διηπόρουν περὶ αὐτῶν τί ἂν γένοιτο τοῦτο. 25 παραγενόμενος δέ τις ἀπήγγειλεν αὐτοῖς ὅτι Ἰδοὺ οἱ ἄνδρες οὓς ἔθεσθε ἐν τῇ φυλακῇ εἰσὶν ἐν τῷ ἱερῷ ἑστῶτες καὶ διδάσκοντες τὸν λαόν. 26 τότε ἀπελθὼν ὁ στρατηγὸς σὺν τοῖς ὑπηρέταις ἦγεν αὐτούς, οὐ μετὰ βίας, ἐφοβοῦντο γὰρ τὸν λαόν, μὴ λιθασθῶσιν.

27 Ἀγαγόντες δὲ αὐτοὺς ἔστησαν ἐν τῷ συνεδρίῳ. καὶ ἐπηρώτησεν αὐτοὺς ὁ ἀρχιερεὺς 28 λέγων, Παραγγελίᾳ[3] παρηγγείλαμεν ὑμῖν μὴ διδάσκειν ἐπὶ τῷ ὀνόματι τούτῳ, καὶ ἰδοὺ πεπληρώκατε τὴν Ἰερουσαλὴμ τῆς διδαχῆς ὑμῶν, καὶ βούλεσθε ἐπαγαγεῖν ἐφ᾽ ἡμᾶς τὸ αἷμα τοῦ ἀνθρώπου τούτου. 29 ἀποκριθεὶς δὲ Πέτρος καὶ οἱ ἀπόστολοι εἶπαν, Πειθαρχεῖν δεῖ θεῷ μᾶλλον ἢ ἀνθρώποις. 30 ὁ θεὸς τῶν πατέρων ἡμῶν ἤγειρεν Ἰησοῦν, ὃν ὑμεῖς διεχειρίσασθε κρεμάσαντες ἐπὶ ξύλου· 31 τοῦτον ὁ θεὸς ἀρχηγὸν καὶ σωτῆρα ὕψωσεν τῇ δεξιᾷ αὐτοῦ, δοῦναι μετάνοιαν τῷ Ἰσραὴλ καὶ ἄφεσιν ἁμαρτιῶν.

[3] 28 {C} παραγγελίᾳ 𝔭[74] ℵ* A B *l*[147] it[ar,d,gig] vg cop[sams,bo] geo Lucifer Athanasius[1/2] Cyril[1/2] ‖ οὐ παραγγελίᾳ ℵ[c] D[gr] E P (Ψ οὐχί) 049 056 0142 88 104 181 326 330 436 451 614 629 630 945 1241 1505 1739 1877 2127 2412 2492 2495 *Byz Lect* it[e,h,p] syr[p,h] cop[sa] arm eth Athanasius[1/2] Basil Chrysostom Cyril[1/2] Theodoret

21 ἀπέστειλαν...αὐτούς Ac 12.19   24 ὁ...ἀρχιερεῖς Lk 22.4, 52; Ac 4.1   26 ἐφο βοῦντο...λαόν Mt 14.5; 21.26, 46; Mk 11.32; 12.12; Lk 20.19; 22.2   28 μὴ...ὀνόματι τούτῳ Ac 4.18 βούλεσθε...τούτου Mt 27.25   29 Ac 4.19   30 ὁ θεός...ἤγειρεν Ἰησοῦν Ac 2.24, 32; 3.15; 4.10; 10.40; 13.30; 17.31 ὃν ὑμεῖς διεχειρίσασθε...ἐπὶ ξύλου Ac 2.23, 36; 3.15; 4.10; 10.39   31 ἀρχηγὸν καὶ σωτῆρα He 2.10 ὕψωσεν...αὐτοῦ Ac 2.33 δοῦναι...ἁμαρτιῶν Lk 24.47; Ac 2.38

The High Priest and his companions called together all the Jewish elders for a full meeting of the Council; then they sent orders to the prison to have the apostles brought before them. 22 But when the officials arrived, they did not find the apostles in prison; so they returned to the Council and reported: 23 "When we arrived at the jail we found it locked up tight and all the guards on watch at the gates; but when we opened the gates we did not find anyone inside!" 24 When the officer in charge of the Temple guards and the chief priests heard this, they wondered what had happened to the apostles. 25 Then a man came in who said to them, "Listen! The men you put in prison are standing in the Temple teaching the people!" 26 So the officer went off with his men and brought the apostles back. They did not use force, however, because they were afraid that the people might stone them.

27 They brought the apostles in and made them stand before the Council, and the High Priest questioned them. 28 "We gave you strict orders not to teach in the name of this man," he said; "but see what you have done! You have spread your teaching all over Jerusalem, and you want to make us responsible for his death!" 29 Peter and the other apostles answered back: "We must obey God, not men. 30 The God of our fathers raised Jesus from death, after you had killed him by nailing him to a cross. 31 And God raised him to his right side as Leader and Savior, to give to the people of Israel the opportunity to repent

and have their sins forgiven. [32] We are witnesses to these things — we and the Holy Spirit, who is God's gift to those who obey him.''

[33] When the members of the Council heard this they were so furious that they decided to have the apostles put to death. [34] But one of them, a Pharisee named Gamaliel, a teacher of the Law who was highly respected by all the people, stood up in the Council. He ordered the apostles to be taken out, [35] and then said to the Council: "Men of Israel, be careful what you are about to do to these men. [36] Some time ago Theudas appeared, claiming that he was somebody great; and about four hundred men joined him. But he was killed, all his followers were scattered, and his movement died out. [37] After this, Judas the Galilean appeared during the time of the census; he also drew a crowd after him, but he also was killed and all his

32 καὶ ἡμεῖς ἐσμεν μάρτυρες[4] τῶν ῥημάτων τούτων, καὶ τὸ πνεῦμα τὸ ἅγιον ὃ[5] ἔδωκεν ὁ θεὸς τοῖς πειθαρχοῦσιν αὐτῷ.

33 Οἱ δὲ ἀκούσαντες διεπρίοντο καὶ ἐβουλεύοντο[6] ἀνελεῖν αὐτούς. **34** ἀναστὰς δέ τις ἐν τῷ συνεδρίῳ Φαρισαῖος ὀνόματι Γαμαλιήλ, νομοδιδάσκαλος τίμιος παντὶ τῷ λαῷ, ἐκέλευσεν ἔξω βραχὺ τοὺς ἀνθρώπους ποιῆσαι, **35** εἶπέν τε πρὸς αὐτούς, Ἄνδρες Ἰσραηλῖται, προσέχετε ἑαυτοῖς ἐπὶ τοῖς ἀνθρώποις τούτοις τί μέλλετε πράσσειν. **36** πρὸ γὰρ τούτων τῶν ἡμερῶν ἀνέστη Θευδᾶς, λέγων εἶναί τινα ἑαυτόν, ᾧ προσεκλίθη ἀνδρῶν ἀριθμὸς ὡς τετρακοσίων· ὃς ἀνῃρέθη, καὶ πάντες ὅσοι ἐπείθοντο αὐτῷ διελύθησαν καὶ ἐγένοντο εἰς οὐδέν. **37** μετὰ τοῦτον ἀνέστη Ἰούδας ὁ Γαλιλαῖος ἐν ταῖς ἡμέραις τῆς ἀπογραφῆς καὶ ἀπέστησεν λαὸν[7] ὀπίσω αὐτοῦ· κἀκεῖνος ἀπώλετο, καὶ πάντες[8] ὅσοι ἐπείθοντο αὐτῷ διεσκορπίσθησαν.

---

[4] **32** {C} ἐσμεν μάρτυρες p74 ℵ Dgr* 88 104 181 614 629 1877 2412 *l*60,680,1441 (*l*597 μὲν μάρτυρες) itar vg copsa,bo arm Didymus ‖ μάρτυρές ἐσμεν A itd,gig,h syrp ‖ ἐσμεν αὐτοῦ μάρτυρες Db E P (Ψ μὲν αὐτοῦ μάρτυρές ἐσμεν) 049 056 0142 326 330 (436 ἐσμεν μάρτυρες αὐτοῦ) 451 1241 1505 2127 2492 2495 *Byz Lect* ite syrh eth geo ‖ ἐν αὐτῷ ἐσμεν μάρτυρες (B omit ἐσμεν) (69 1518 ἐσμεν αὐτῷ and omit ἐν) 630 945 1739 copboms Irenaeuslat

[5] **32** {B} ὃ p45 ℵ A Db (D* E ὅν) P Ψ 049 056 0142 88 104 181 330 451 614 629 630 945 1241 1505 1739 1877 2127 2412 2492 2495 *Byz Lect* itar,d,e,gig,h vg syrp,h arm geo ‖ omit B 436 copsa,bo

[6] **33** {C} ἐβουλεύοντο ℵ D P 056 0142 181 326 330 436 451 629 630 945 1505 1739 1877 2127 2495 *Byz* itar,d,e,gig vg syrp,h arm Lucifer ‖ ἐβούλοντο p74vid A B Egr Ψ 049 104 614 2412 2492 copsa,bo eth Chrysostom ‖ ἐβουλεύσαντο 88 1241 geo Theophylactb

[7] **37** {B} λαόν p74 ℵ A* B 88 1241 itar,d vg copsa,bo? Eusebius Cyril1/2 ‖ λαὸν ἱκανόν A2 P Ψ 049 056 0142 104 330 436 451 629 630 945 1505 1739 (1877 ὄχλον ἱκανόν) 2127 2492 2495 *Byz* itgig?p? syrp,h copsamss? arm eth Cyril1/2 ‖ ἱκανὸν λαόν E 33 181 326 614 2412 ite,h Eusebius ‖ λαὸν πολύν (C* λαὸν πολύ) C3 Dgr itgig?p? copsamss? geo Eusebius

[8] **37** {C} πάντες p74 ℵ A B C E P Ψ 049 056 0142 88 104 181 326 330 436

---

32 ἡμεῖς...μάρτυρες...τούτων Lk 24.48; Jn 15.27; Ac 1.8; 2.32; 3.15   ἡμεῖς...πνεῦμα τὸ ἅγιον Jn 15.26   **33** Ac 7.54   **34** Φαρισαῖος...λαῷ Ac 22.3   ἐκέλευσεν...ποιῆσαι Ac 4.15   **36** Ac 21.38   **37** Lk 13.1-2

38 καὶ τὰ νῦν λέγω ὑμῖν, ἀπόστητε ἀπὸ τῶν ἀνθρώπων τούτων καὶ ἄφετε αὐτούς·[c] ὅτι ἐὰν ᾖ ἐξ ἀνθρώπων ἡ βουλὴ αὕτη ἢ τὸ ἔργον τοῦτο, καταλυθήσεται· 39 εἰ δὲ ἐκ θεοῦ ἐστιν, οὐ δυνήσεσθε καταλῦσαι αὐτούς — [c] μήποτε καὶ θεομάχοι εὑρεθῆτε. [d]ἐπείσθησαν δὲ αὐτῷ, 40[d] καὶ προσκαλεσάμενοι τοὺς ἀποστόλους δείραντες παρήγγειλαν μὴ λαλεῖν ἐπὶ τῷ ὀνόματι τοῦ Ἰησοῦ καὶ ἀπέλυσαν. 41 Οἱ μὲν οὖν ἐπορεύοντο χαίροντες ἀπὸ προσώπου τοῦ συνεδρίου ὅτι κατηξιώθησαν ὑπὲρ τοῦ ὀνόματος ἀτιμασθῆναι· 42 πᾶσάν τε ἡμέραν ἐν τῷ ἱερῷ καὶ κατ' οἶκον οὐκ ἐπαύοντο διδάσκοντες καὶ εὐαγγελιζόμενοι τὸν Χριστόν,[e] Ἰησοῦν.

The Appointment of the Seven

6 Ἐν δὲ ταῖς ἡμέραις ταύταις πληθυνόντων τῶν μαθητῶν ἐγένετο γογγυσμὸς τῶν Ἑλληνιστῶν πρὸς τοὺς Ἑβραίους, ὅτι[a] παρεθεωροῦντο ἐν τῇ διακονίᾳ τῇ καθημερινῇ αἱ χῆραι αὐτῶν. 2 προσκαλεσάμενοι δὲ οἱ δώδεκα τὸ πλῆθος τῶν μαθητῶν εἶπαν, Οὐκ ἀρεστόν ἐστιν ἡμᾶς καταλείψαντας τὸν λόγον τοῦ θεοῦ διακονεῖν τραπέζαις· 3 ἐπισκέψασθε δὲ[1], ἀδελφοί, ἄνδρας ἐξ ὑμῶν μαρτυρου-

---

451 614 629 630 945 1241 1505 1739 1877 2127 2412 2492 2495 *Byz* it[ar,e] vg syr[p,h] cop[sa,bo] arm geo Eusebius ‖ *omit* 𝔓[45] D it[d,gig,h,p]

[1] **3** {C} δέ ℵ B cop[sa] ‖ δή A ‖ οὖν C E P Ψ 049 056 0142 33 88 104 181 326 330 436 451 614 629 630 945 1241 1505 1739 1877 2127 2412 2492 2495 *Byz Lect* it[ar,(d),e,gig] vg syr[p,h] cop[bo] Origen Didymus Chrysostom ‖ δὲ οὖν 1175 ‖ *omit* 𝔓[74] (D[gr]) (it[h]) cop[sams] arm eth geo Basil

[c c] **38-39** *c* major, *c* dash ‖ *c* exclamation, *c* major: Zür ‖ *c* major, *c* major: TR Jer Seg ‖ *c* major, *c* minor: Bov Nes BF² AV RV ASV NEB Luth ‖ *c* minor, *c* major: RSV TT ‖ *c* parens, *c* parens: WH
[d d] **39-40** *d* no number, *d* number 40: TR[ed] WH? Bov Nes BF² NEB? TT Zür Jer Seg ‖ *d* number 40, *d* no number: TR[ed] WH? AV RV ASV NEB? Luth
[e] **42** *e* minor: (RV) (ASV) (RSV) (NEB) (TT) (Zür) Seg[mg] ‖ χριστὸν Ἰησοῦν: WH Nes ‖ Χριστὸν Ἰησοῦν: Bov BF² Jer Seg ‖ Ἰησοῦν τὸν Χριστόν: TR AV Luth
[a] **1** *a* causal: TR? Bov? Nes? BF²? AV RV ASV RSV TT Zür Luth Seg ‖ *a* indirect: WH? NEB Jer

---

39 Wsd 12.13-14   **40** παρήγγειλαν...Ἰησοῦ Ac 4.18   **41** Mt 5.10-12; 1 Pe 4.13
42 πᾶσαν...οἶκον Ac 2.46   διδάσκοντες...Ἰησοῦν Ac 17.3; 18.5, 28
6 1 τῇ διακονίᾳ τῇ καθημερινῇ Ac 2.45; 4.35   **3** μαρτυρουμένους Ac 10.22; 16.2; 22.12; 1 Tm 3.7; 3 Jn 12

---

followers were scattered. [38] And so in this case now, I tell you, do not take any action against these men. Leave them alone, for if this plan and work of theirs is a man-made thing, it will disappear; [39] but if it comes from God you cannot possibly defeat them. You could find yourselves fighting against God!" The Council followed Gamaliel's advice. [40] They called the apostles in, had them whipped, and ordered them never again to speak in the name of Jesus; and then they set them free. [41] The apostles left the Council, full of joy that God had considered them worthy to suffer disgrace for the name of Jesus. [42] And every day in the Temple and in people's homes they continued to teach and preach the Good News about Jesus the Messiah.

The Seven Helpers

6 Some time later, as the number of disciples kept growing, there was a quarrel between the Greek-speaking Jews and the native Jews. The Greek-speaking Jews said that their widows were being neglected in the daily distribution of funds. [2] So the twelve apostles called the whole group of disciples together and said: "It is not right for us to neglect the preaching of God's word in order to handle finances. [3] So then, brothers, choose seven men among you who are known to be full of the Holy Spirit and wisdom, and we will put them in charge of this matter." [4] We ourselves, then, will give our full time to prayers and the work of preaching." [5] The whole group was pleased with the apostles' proposal; so they chose Stephen, a man full of faith and the Holy Spirit, and Philip, Prochorus, Nicanor, Timon, Parmenas, and Nicolaus from Antioch, a Gentile who had been converted to Judaism. [6] The group presented them to the apostles, who prayed and placed their hands on them.

[7] And so the word of God continued to spread. The number of disciples in Jerusalem grew larger and larger, and a great number of priests accepted the faith.

The Arrest of Stephen

[8] Stephen, a man richly blessed by God and full of power, performed great miracles and wonders among the people. [9] But some men opposed him; they were members of the synagogue of the Free Men (as it was called), which had Jews from Cyrenia and Alexandria. They and other Jews from Cilicia and Asia started arguing with Stephen. [10] But the Spirit gave Stephen such wisdom that when he spoke they could not resist him. [11] So they paid some men to say, "We heard him speaking against Moses and against God!" [12] In this way they stirred up the people, the elders, and the teachers of the Law. They came to Stephen, seized him, and took him before the Council. [13] Then they brought in some men to

μένους ἑπτὰ πλήρεις πνεύματος καὶ σοφίας, οὓς καταστήσομεν ἐπὶ τῆς χρείας ταύτης· **4** ἡμεῖς δὲ τῇ προσευχῇ καὶ τῇ διακονίᾳ τοῦ λόγου προσκαρτερήσομεν. **5** καὶ ἤρεσεν ὁ λόγος ἐνώπιον παντὸς τοῦ πλήθους, καὶ ἐξελέξαντο Στέφανον, ἄνδρα πλήρης πίστεως καὶ πνεύματος ἁγίου, καὶ Φίλιππον καὶ Πρόχορον καὶ Νικάνορα καὶ Τίμωνα καὶ Παρμενᾶν καὶ Νικόλαον προσήλυτον Ἀντιοχέα, **6** οὓς ἔστησαν ἐνώπιον τῶν ἀποστόλων, καὶ προσευξάμενοι ἐπέθηκαν αὐτοῖς τὰς χεῖρας.

7 Καὶ ὁ λόγος τοῦ θεοῦ[2] ηὔξανεν, καὶ ἐπληθύνετο ὁ ἀριθμὸς τῶν μαθητῶν ἐν Ἰερουσαλὴμ σφόδρα, πολύς τε ὄχλος τῶν ἱερέων ὑπήκουον τῇ πίστει.

The Arrest of Stephen

8 Στέφανος δὲ πλήρης χάριτος καὶ δυνάμεως ἐποίει τέρατα καὶ σημεῖα μεγάλα ἐν τῷ λαῷ. **9** ἀνέστησαν δέ τινες τῶν ἐκ τῆς συναγωγῆς τῆς λεγομένης[3] Λιβερτίνων καὶ Κυρηναίων καὶ Ἀλεξανδρέων καὶ τῶν ἀπὸ Κιλικίας καὶ Ἀσίας συζητοῦντες τῷ Στεφάνῳ, **10** καὶ οὐκ ἴσχυον ἀντιστῆναι τῇ σοφίᾳ καὶ τῷ πνεύματι ᾧ ἐλάλει. **11** τότε ὑπέβαλον ἄνδρας λέγοντας ὅτι Ἀκηκόαμεν αὐτοῦ λαλοῦντος ῥήματα βλάσφημα εἰς Μωϋσῆν καὶ τὸν θεόν· **12** συνεκίνησάν τε τὸν λαὸν καὶ τοὺς πρεσβυτέρους καὶ τοὺς γραμματεῖς, καὶ ἐπιστάντες συνήρπασαν αὐτὸν καὶ ἤγαγον εἰς τὸ συνέδριον, **13** ἔστησάν τε μάρτυρας ψευδεῖς

---

[2] **7** {B} θεοῦ 𝔓[74] ℵ A B C P 049 056 0142 33 88 104 181 326 330 436 451 629 630 945 1241 1505 1739 1877 2127 2492 2495 *Byz Lect* it[ar,gig] vg[ww] syr[p] cop[sa,bo] arm Chrysostom ∥ κυρίου D E Ψ 614 2412 it[c,d,e,h,p,ph,t] vg[cl] syr[h] geo Origen[lat] Chrysostom

[3] **9** {B} τῆς λεγομένης 𝔓[8,74] B C D E P Ψ 049 056 0142 88 104 330 436 451 614 629 630 1241 1505 1739 1877 2127 2412 2492 *Byz Lect* it[ar,d,e,h] vg syr[p,h] arm eth geo Chrysostom Proclus ∥ τῶν λεγομένων ℵ A 0175 33 181 326 2495 it[gig] cop[sa,bo] Chrysostom ∥ *omit* 945

---

3 πλήρεις...σοφίας Ac 6.10   **5** ἄνδρα...πνεύματος ἁγίου Ac 11.24   **6** προσευξάμενοι ...χεῖρας Ac 1.24; 13.3; 14.23   **7** ὁ λόγος...ηὔξανεν Ac 12.24; 19.20   ἐπληθύνετο...σφόδρα Ac 2.41, 47; 4.4; 5.14; 11.21, 24; 16.5; 21.20   **8** ἐποίει...μεγάλα Ac 2.43; 5.12; 14.3; 15.12   **10** Lk 21.15   τῇ σοφίᾳ...ἐλάλει Ac 6.3   **11** Mt 26.59–61; Mk 14.55–58

λέγοντας, Ὁ ἄνθρωπος οὗτος οὐ παύεται λαλῶν ῥήματα κατὰ τοῦ τόπου τοῦ ἁγίου [τούτου] καὶ τοῦ νόμου· 14 ἀκηκόαμεν γὰρ αὐτοῦ λέγοντος ὅτι Ἰησοῦς ὁ Ναζωραῖος οὗτος καταλύσει τὸν τόπον τοῦτον καὶ ἀλλάξει τὰ ἔθη ἃ παρέδωκεν ἡμῖν Μωϋσῆς. 15 καὶ ἀτενίσαντες εἰς αὐτὸν πάντες οἱ καθεζόμενοι ἐν τῷ συνεδρίῳ εἶδον τὸ πρόσωπον αὐτοῦ ὡσεὶ πρόσωπον ἀγγέλου.

Stephen's Speech

7 Εἶπεν δὲ ὁ ἀρχιερεύς, Εἰ ταῦτα οὕτως ἔχει; 2 ὁ δὲ ἔφη, Ἄνδρες ἀδελφοὶ καὶ πατέρες, ἀκούσατε. Ὁ θεὸς τῆς δόξης ὤφθη τῷ πατρὶ ἡμῶν Ἀβραὰμ ὄντι ἐν τῇ Μεσοποταμίᾳ πρὶν ἢ κατοικῆσαι αὐτὸν ἐν Χαρράν, **3 καὶ εἶπεν πρὸς αὐτόν, Ἔξελθε ἐκ τῆς γῆς σου καὶ ἐκ τῆς συγγενείας σου, καὶ δεῦρο εἰς τὴν γῆν ἣν ἄν σοι δείξω.** 4 τότε ἐξελθὼν ἐκ γῆς Χαλδαίων κατῴκησεν ἐν Χαρράν. κἀκεῖθεν μετὰ τὸ ἀποθανεῖν τὸν πατέρα αὐτοῦ μετῴκισεν αὐτὸν εἰς τὴν γῆν ταύτην εἰς ἣν ὑμεῖς νῦν κατοικεῖτε, 5 καὶ οὐκ ἔδωκεν αὐτῷ κληρονομίαν ἐν αὐτῇ οὐδὲ βῆμα ποδός, καὶ ἐπηγγείλατο **δοῦναι αὐτῷ εἰς κατάσχεσιν αὐτὴν καὶ τῷ σπέρματι αὐτοῦ μετ᾿ αὐτόν,** οὐκ ὄντος αὐτῷ τέκνου. 6 ἐλάλησεν δὲ οὕτως ὁ θεὸς ὅτι **ἔσται τὸ σπέρμα αὐτοῦ πάροικον ἐν γῇ ἀλλοτρίᾳ, καὶ δουλώσουσιν αὐτὸ καὶ κακώσουσιν ἔτη τετρακόσια· 7 καὶ τὸ ἔθνος ᾧ ἐὰν δουλεύσουσιν κρινῶ ἐγώ,** ὁ θεὸς εἶπεν, **καὶ μετὰ ταῦτα ἐξελεύσονται καὶ λατρεύσουσίν μοι ἐν τῷ τόπῳ τούτῳ.** 8 καὶ ἔδωκεν αὐτῷ διαθήκην περιτομῆς· καὶ οὕτως ἐγέννησεν τὸν Ἰσαὰκ καὶ περιέτεμεν αὐτὸν τῇ ἡμέρᾳ τῇ ὀγδόῃ, καὶ Ἰσαὰκ τὸν Ἰακώβ, καὶ Ἰακὼβ τοὺς δώδεκα πατριάρχας.

---

13 Ὁ ἄνθρωπος...ἁγίου τούτου Jr 26.11   14 Ac 21.21
7 2 Ἄνδρες...ἀκούσατε Ac 22.1   Ὁ θεὸς τῆς δόξης Ps 29.3   Ὁ θεὸς...Χαρράν Gn 11.31—12.1   3 Gn 12.1   4 Gn 11.31—12.1, 5; 15.7   5 οὐκ...ποδός Dt 2.5 ἐπηγγείλατο... αὐτόν Gn 12.7; 13.15; 15.2, 18; 17.8; 24.7; 48.4   οὐκ ὄντος αὐτῷ τέκνου Gn 16.1   6-7 ἔσται τὸ σπέρμα...τούτῳ Gn 15.13-14   7 ἐξελεύσονται...τούτῳ Ex 3.12   8 ἔδωκεν...περιτομῆς Gn 17.10-14   οὕτως...ὀγδόῃ Gn 21.4

tell lies about him. "This man," they said, "is always talking against our sacred Temple and the Law of Moses. 14 For we heard him say that this Jesus of Nazareth will tear down the Temple and change all the customs which have come down to us from Moses!" 15 All those sitting in the Council fixed their eyes on Stephen and saw that his face looked like the face of an angel.

Stephen's Speech

7 The High Priest asked Stephen, "Is this really so?" 2 And Stephen answered: "Brothers and fathers! Listen to me! The God of glory appeared to our ancestor Abraham while he was living in Mesopotamia, before he had gone to live in Haran, 3 and said to him, 'Leave your family and country and go to the land that I will show you.' 4 And so he left the land of Chaldea and went to live in Haran. After Abraham's father died, God made him move to this country, where you now live. 5 God did not then give Abraham any part of it as his own, not even a square foot of ground; but God promised that he would give it to him, and that it would belong to him and his descendants after him. At the time God made this promise Abraham had no children. 6 This is what God said to him: 'Your descendants will live in a foreign country, where they will be slaves and will be badly treated for four hundred years. 7 But I will pass judgment on the people that they will serve,' God said, 'and afterward they will come out of that country and will worship me in this place.' 8 Then God gave to Abraham the ceremony of circumcision as a sign of the covenant. So Abraham circumcised Isaac a week after he was born; Isaac circumcised Jacob, and Jacob circumcised the twelve patriarchs.

⁹ "The patriarchs were jealous of Joseph, and sold him as a slave in Egypt. But God was with him, ¹⁰ and brought him safely through all his troubles. When Joseph appeared before Pharaoh, the king of Egypt, God gave him a pleasing manner and wisdom. Pharaoh made Joseph governor over the country and the royal household. ¹¹ Then there was a famine in all of Egypt and Canaan, which caused much suffering. Our ancestors could not find any food. ¹² So when Jacob heard that there was grain in Egypt, he sent our ancestors on their first visit there. ¹³ On the second visit Joseph made himself known to his brothers, and Pharaoh came to know about Joseph's family. ¹⁴ So Joseph sent a message to his father Jacob, telling him and the whole family to come to Egypt; there were seventy-five people in all. ¹⁵ Then Jacob went down to Egypt, where he and our ancestors died. ¹⁶ Their bodies were moved to Shechem, where they were buried in the grave which Abraham had bought from the tribe of Hamor for a sum of money.

¹⁷ "When the time drew near for God to keep the promise he had made to Abraham, the number of our people in Egypt had grown much larger. ¹⁸ At last a different king, who had not known

9 Καὶ οἱ πατριάρχαι ζηλώσαντες τὸν Ἰωσὴφ ἀπέδοντο εἰς Αἴγυπτον· καὶ ἦν ὁ θεὸς μετ' αὐτοῦ, **10** καὶ ἐξείλατο αὐτὸν ἐκ πασῶν τῶν θλίψεων αὐτοῦ, καὶ **ἔδωκεν αὐτῷ χάριν** καὶ σοφίαν **ἐναντίον Φαραὼ βασιλέως Αἰγύπτου, καὶ κατέστησεν αὐτὸν ἡγούμενον ἐπ' Αἴγυπτον καὶ [ἐφ'] ὅλον τὸν οἶκον αὐτοῦ.** **11** ἦλθεν δὲ λιμὸς ἐφ' ὅλην τὴν **Αἴγυπτον** καὶ **Χανάαν** καὶ θλῖψις μεγάλη, καὶ οὐχ ηὕρισκον χορτάσματα οἱ πατέρες ἡμῶν. **12** ἀκούσας δὲ Ἰακὼβ ὄντα σιτία εἰς Αἴγυπτον ἐξαπέστειλεν τοὺς πατέρας ἡμῶν πρῶτον· **13** καὶ ἐν τῷ δευτέρῳ ἀνεγνωρίσθη Ἰωσὴφ τοῖς ἀδελφοῖς αὐτοῦ, καὶ φανερὸν ἐγένετο τῷ Φαραὼ τὸ γένος [τοῦ] Ἰωσήφ. **14** ἀποστείλας δὲ Ἰωσὴφ μετεκαλέσατο Ἰακὼβ τὸν πατέρα αὐτοῦ καὶ πᾶσαν τὴν συγγένειαν ἐν ψυχαῖς ἑβδομήκοντα πέντε, **15** καὶ κατέβη Ἰακὼβ εἰς Αἴγυπτον. καὶ ἐτελεύτησεν αὐτὸς καὶ οἱ πατέρες ἡμῶν, **16** καὶ μετετέθησαν εἰς Συχὲμ καὶ ἐτέθησαν ἐν τῷ μνήματι ᾧ ὠνήσατο Ἀβραὰμ τιμῆς ἀργυρίου παρὰ τῶν υἱῶν Ἐμμὼρ ἐν Συχέμ¹.

17 Καθὼς δὲ ἤγγιζεν ὁ χρόνος τῆς ἐπαγγελίας ἧς ὡμολόγησεν² ὁ θεὸς τῷ Ἀβραάμ, ηὔξησεν ὁ λαὸς καὶ ἐπληθύνθη ἐν Αἰγύπτῳ, **18** ἄχρι οὗ ἀνέστη βασιλεὺς

---

¹ **16** {D} ἐν Συχέμ ℵ* B C 88 181 630 945 1739 1877 2495 copˢᵃ,ᵇᵒ,ᶠᵃʸ arm geo ∥ τοῦ Συχέμ p⁷⁴ Dᵍʳ (Ρ τοῦ χέμ) Ψ 049 056 0142 104 326 330 436 451 614 1241 1505 2127 2412 2492 *Byz* itᵃʳ,ᵖ vg eth Chrysostom ∥ τοῦ ἐν Συχέμ ℵᶜ A E (629 τοῦ υἱοῦ ἐν Συχέμ) (itᵉ) ∥ *who was from Shechem* syrʰ ∥ *et Sychem* itᵈ ∥ *omit* syrᵖ

² **17** {C} ὡμολόγησεν p⁷⁴ ℵ A B C itᵃʳ vg syrᵖ,ʰᵐᵍ copˢᵃ eth ∥ ὤμοσεν Ρ Ψ 049 056 0142 81 88 104 181 326 330 436 451 614 629 630 945 1241 1505 1739 1877 2127 2412 2492 2495 *Byz* itᵍⁱᵍ syrʰ copᵇᵒ,ᶠᵃʸ Chrysostom ∥ ἐπηγγείλατο p⁴⁵ D E itᵈ,ᵉ,ᵖ arm geo Greekᵃᶜᶜ·ᵗᵒ ᴮᵉᵈᵉ

---

9 οἱ...Ἰωσήφ Gn 37.11   ἀπέδοντο εἰς Αἴγυπτον Gn 37.28; 45.4   ἦν ὁ θεὸς μετ' αὐτοῦ Gn 39.2, 3, 21, 23   **10** ἔδωκεν...Αἰγύπτου Gn 41.37–39   κατέστησεν...αὐτοῦ Gn 41.40–44; Ps 105.21   **11** ἦλθεν...Χανάαν Gn 41.54; 42.5   **12** Gn 42.1–2   **13** ἐν...ἀδελφοῖς αὐτοῦ Gn 45.3–4   φανερὸν...Ἰωσήφ Gn 45.16   **14** Gn 45.9–11, 18–19   πᾶσαν...ἑβδομήκοντα πέντε Gn 46.27 ʟxx; Ex 1.5 ʟxx; Dt 10.22   **15** κατέβη...Αἴγυπτον Gn 46.5–6   ἐτελεύτησεν...ἡμῶν Gn 49.33; Ex 1.6   **16** Gn 23.2–20; 33.19; 49.29–30; 50.7–13; Jos 24.32   **17–18** ηὔξησεν...Ἰωσήφ Ex 1.7–8

ἕτερος [ἐπ' Αἴγυπτον][3] ὃς οὐκ ᾔδει τὸν Ἰωσήφ. 19 οὗτος κατασοφισάμενος τὸ γένος ἡμῶν ἐκάκωσεν τοὺς πατέρας[4] τοῦ ποιεῖν τὰ βρέφη ἔκθετα αὐτῶν εἰς τὸ μὴ ζῳογονεῖσθαι. 20 ἐν ᾧ καιρῷ ἐγεννήθη Μωϋσῆς, καὶ ἦν ἀστεῖος τῷ θεῷ· ὃς ἀνετράφη μῆνας τρεῖς ἐν τῷ οἴκῳ τοῦ πατρός· 21 ἐκτεθέντος δὲ αὐτοῦ ἀνείλατο αὐτὸν ἡ θυγάτηρ Φαραὼ καὶ ἀνεθρέψατο αὐτὸν ἑαυτῇ εἰς υἱόν. 22 καὶ ἐπαιδεύθη Μωϋσῆς [ἐν] πάσῃ σοφίᾳ Αἰγυπτίων, ἦν δὲ δυνατὸς ἐν λόγοις καὶ ἔργοις αὐτοῦ.

23 Ὡς δὲ ἐπληροῦτο αὐτῷ τεσσαρακονταετὴς χρόνος, ἀνέβη ἐπὶ τὴν καρδίαν αὐτοῦ ἐπισκέψασθαι τοὺς ἀδελφοὺς αὐτοῦ τοὺς υἱοὺς Ἰσραήλ. 24 καὶ ἰδών τινα ἀδικούμενον ἠμύνατο καὶ ἐποίησεν ἐκδίκησιν τῷ καταπονουμένῳ πατάξας τὸν Αἰγύπτιον. 25 ἐνόμιζεν δὲ συνιέναι τοὺς ἀδελφοὺς αὐτοῦ ὅτι ὁ θεὸς διὰ χειρὸς αὐτοῦ δίδωσιν σωτηρίαν αὐτοῖς, οἱ δὲ οὐ συνῆκαν. 26 τῇ τε ἐπιούσῃ ἡμέρᾳ ὤφθη αὐτοῖς μαχομένοις καὶ συνήλλασσεν αὐτοὺς εἰς εἰρήνην εἰπών, Ἄνδρες, ἀδελφοί ἐστε· ἱνατί ἀδικεῖτε ἀλλήλους; 27 ὁ δὲ ἀδικῶν τὸν πλησίον ἀπώσατο αὐτὸν εἰπών, **Τίς σε κατέστησεν ἄρχοντα καὶ δικαστὴν ἐφ' ἡμῶν; 28 μὴ ἀνελεῖν με σὺ θέλεις ὃν τρόπον ἀνεῖλες ἐχθὲς τὸν Αἰγύπτιον;** 29 ἔφυγεν δὲ Μωϋσῆς ἐν τῷ λόγῳ τούτῳ, καὶ ἐγένετο πάροικος ἐν γῇ Μαδιάμ, οὗ ἐγέννησεν υἱοὺς δύο.

30 Καὶ πληρωθέντων ἐτῶν τεσσαράκοντα **ὤφθη αὐτῷ**

---

[3] 18 {C} ἐπ' Αἴγυπτον p[58,74] ℵ Λ B C 88 104 (181 Ἔγυπτον) 630 945 1505 1739 1877[mg] (1877* it[ar,p] vg ἐν Ἀιγύπτῳ) cop[sa,bo,fay] syr[p,hmg] arm eth geo ‖ omit p[45vid] D E P Ψ 049 056 0142 81 320 330 436 451 614 629 1241 2127 2412 2492 2495 Byz it[d,e,gig] syr[h] Chrysostom

[4] 19 {C} πατέρας p[74] ℵ B D 1505 it[d] vg[ww] ‖ πατέρας ἡμῶν A C E P Ψ 049 056 0142 81 88 104 181 326 330 436 451 614 629 630 945 1241 1739 1877 2127 2412 2492 2495 Byz it[arvid,c,e,gig,ph] vg[cl] syr[p,h] cop[sa,bo,fay] arm eth geo Chrysostom

---

19 οὗτος...πατέρας Ex 1.10–11   τοῦ...ζῳογονεῖσθαι Ex 1.22   **20** Ex 2.2; He 11.23 **21** Ex 2.3–10   **23–24** Ex 2.11–12   **26–28** Ex 2.13–14   **27** Τίς σε κατέστησεν...ἡμῶν Lk 12.14   **29** ἔφυγεν...Μαδιάμ Ex 2.15   ἐγένετο...υἱοὺς δύο Ex 2.21–22; 18.3–4   **30–31** ὤφθη ...ὅραμα Ex 3.2–3

Joseph, began to rule in Egypt. [19] He tricked our people and was cruel to our ancestors, forcing them to put their babies out of their homes, so that they would die. [20] It was at this time that Moses was born, a very beautiful child. He was brought up at home for three months, [21] and when he was put out of his home the daughter of Pharaoh adopted him and brought him up as her own son. [22] He was taught all the wisdom of the Egyptians, and became a great man in words and deeds.

[23] "When Moses was forty years old he decided to visit his fellow Israelites. [24] He saw one of them being mistreated by an Egyptian; so he went to his help and took revenge on the Egyptian by killing him. [25] (He thought that his own people would understand that God was going to use him to set them free; but they did not understand.) [26] The next day he saw two Israelites fighting, and he tried to make peace between them. 'Listen, men,' he said, 'you are brothers; why do you mistreat each other?' [27] But the one who was mistreating the other pushed Moses aside. 'Who made you ruler and judge over us?' he asked. [28] 'Do you want to kill me, just as you killed that Egyptian yesterday?' [29] When Moses heard this he fled from Egypt and started living in the land of Midian. There he had two sons.

[30] "After forty years had passed, an angel appeared to Moses in the flames

of a burning bush in the desert near Mount Sinai. ³¹ Moses was amazed by what he saw, and went near the bush to look at it closely. But he heard the Lord's voice: ³² 'I am the God of your ancestors, the God of Abraham and Isaac and Jacob.' Moses trembled with fear and dared not look. ³³ And the Lord said to him: 'Take your sandals off, for the place where you are standing is holy ground. ³⁴ I have looked and seen the cruel suffering of my people in Egypt. I have heard their groans, and I have come down to save them. Come now, I will send you to Egypt.'

³⁵ "This is the Moses who was rejected by the people of Israel. 'Who made you ruler and judge over us?' they asked. He is the one whom God sent as ruler and savior, with the help of the angel he saw in the burning bush. ³⁶ He led the people out of Egypt, performing miracles and wonders in Egypt and the Red Sea, and in the desert for forty years. ³⁷ He is the Moses who said to the people of Israel, 'God will send you a prophet, just as he sent me,[1] who will be of your own people.' ³⁸ He is the one who was with the people of Israel assembled in the desert; he was there with our ancestors and with the angel who spoke to him on Mount Sinai; he received God's living messages to pass on to us.

³⁹ "But our ancestors refused to obey him; they pushed him aside and wished

---

[1] **37** just as he sent me: *or* like me

ἐν τῇ ἐρήμῳ τοῦ ὄρους Σινᾶ ἄγγελος ἐν φλογὶ πυρὸς βάτου. 31 ὁ δὲ Μωϋσῆς ἰδὼν ἐθαύμαζεν τὸ ὅραμα· προσερχομένου δὲ αὐτοῦ κατανοῆσαι ἐγένετο φωνὴ κυρίου, 32 Ἐγὼ ὁ θεὸς τῶν πατέρων σου, ὁ θεὸς Ἀβραὰμ καὶ Ἰσαὰκ καὶ Ἰακώβ⁵. ἔντρομος δὲ γενόμενος Μωϋσῆς οὐκ ἐτόλμα κατανοῆσαι. 33 εἶπεν δὲ αὐτῷ ὁ κύριος, Λῦσον τὸ ὑπόδημα τῶν ποδῶν σου, ὁ γὰρ τόπος ἐφ' ᾧ ἕστηκας γῆ ἁγία ἐστίν. 34 ἰδὼν εἶδον τὴν κάκωσιν τοῦ λαοῦ μου τοῦ ἐν Αἰγύπτῳ, καὶ τοῦ στεναγμοῦ αὐτῶν ἤκουσα, καὶ κατέβην ἐξελέσθαι αὐτούς· καὶ νῦν δεῦρο ἀποστείλω σε εἰς Αἴγυπτον. 35 Τοῦτον τὸν Μωϋσῆν, ὃν ἠρνήσαντο εἰπόντες, Τίς σε κατέστησεν ἄρχοντα καὶ δικαστήν;ᵃ τοῦτον ὁ θεὸς [καὶ] ἄρχοντα καὶ λυτρωτὴν ἀπέσταλκεν σὺν χειρὶ ἀγγέλου τοῦ ὀφθέντος αὐτῷ ἐν τῇ βάτῳ. 36 οὗτος ἐξήγαγεν αὐτοὺς ποιήσας τέρατα καὶ σημεῖα ἐν γῇ Αἰγύπτῳ καὶ ἐν Ἐρυθρᾷ Θαλάσσῃ καὶ ἐν τῇ ἐρήμῳ ἔτη τεσσαράκοντα. 37 οὗτός ἐστιν ὁ Μωϋσῆς ὁ εἴπας τοῖς υἱοῖς Ἰσραήλ, Προφήτην ὑμῖν ἀναστήσει ὁ θεὸς ἐκ τῶν ἀδελφῶν ὑμῶν ὡς ἐμέ. 38 οὗτός ἐστιν ὁ γενόμενος ἐν τῇ ἐκκλησίᾳ ἐν τῇ ἐρήμῳ μετὰ τοῦ ἀγγέλου τοῦ λαλοῦντος αὐτῷ ἐν τῷ ὄρει Σινᾶ καὶ τῶν πατέρων ἡμῶν, ὃς ἐδέξατο λόγια ζῶντα δοῦναι ἡμῖν⁶, 39 ᾧ οὐκ ἠθέλησαν ὑπήκοοι γενέσθαι οἱ πατέρες ἡμῶν ἀλλὰ ἀπώσαντο καὶ ἐστράφησαν

---

⁵ 32 {C} καὶ Ἰσαὰκ καὶ Ἰακώβ 𝔭⁷⁴ ℵ A B C Ψ 81 181 614 1877 2412 syrᵖˑʰ copˢᵃ arm ∥ καὶ ὁ θεὸς Ἰσαὰκ καὶ ὁ θεὸς Ἰακώβ E P 049 056 0142 33 88 104 326 330 436 451 629 630 945 1241 1505 1739 2127 2492 2495 *Byz* l¹⁴³⁹ᵐˑ¹⁴⁴¹ᵐ Chrysostom ∥ καὶ θεὸς Ἰσαὰκ καὶ θεὸς Ἰακώβ Dᵍʳ ∥ καὶ (*or* καὶ ὁ) θεὸς Ἰσαὰκ καὶ (*or* καὶ ὁ) θεὸς Ἰακώβ it⁽ᵃʳ⁾ˑᵈˑᵉˑᵍⁱᵍ vg copˢᵃᵐˢˑᵇᵒ geo

⁶ 38 {B} ἡμῖν A C D E P Ψ 049 056 0142 33 81 88 104 181 326 330 436 451 614 629 630 945 1241 1505 1739 2127 2412 *Byz* itᵃʳˑᵈˑᵉˑᵍⁱᵍ vg syrᵖˑʰ arm ∥ ὑμῖν 𝔭⁷⁴ ℵ B 2492 2495 l¹⁴³⁹ᵐ itᵖ copˢᵃˑᵇᵒ geo Irenaeus

---

ᵃ 35 *a* question: TR Bov Nes BF² AV RV ASV RSV NEB TT Zür Luth Jer Seg ∥ *a minor:* WH

31–34 προσερχομένου...Αἴγυπτον Ex 3.4–10   **35** Τίς...δικαστήν Ex 2.14 ἀγγέλου... βάτῳ Ex 3.2   **36** ποιήσας...Αἰγύπτῳ Ex 7.3   ἐν Ἐρυθρᾷ Θαλάσσῃ Ex 14.21   ἐν τῇ ἐρήμῳ ἔτη τεσσαράκοντα Nu 14.33   **37** Προφήτην...ἐμέ Dt 18.15 (Ac 3.22)   **38** μετὰ τοῦ ἀγγέλου...Σινᾶ Ac 7.53   ὃς ἐδέξατο...ἡμῖν Ex 19.1–6; 20.1–17; Dt 5.4–22; 9.10 **39** ἐστράφησαν...Αἴγυπτον Nu 14.3

ἐν ταῖς καρδίαις αὐτῶν εἰς Αἴγυπτον, 40 εἰπόντες τῷ Ἀαρών, **Ποίησον ἡμῖν θεοὺς οἳ προπορεύσονται ἡμῶν·** ὁ γὰρ Μωϋσῆς οὗτος, ὃς ἐξήγαγεν ἡμᾶς ἐκ γῆς Αἰγύπτου, οὐκ οἴδαμεν τί ἐγένετο αὐτῷ. 41 καὶ ἐμοσχοποίησαν ἐν ταῖς ἡμέραις ἐκείναις καὶ ἀνήγαγον θυσίαν τῷ εἰδώλῳ, καὶ εὐφραίνοντο ἐν τοῖς ἔργοις τῶν χειρῶν αὐτῶν. 42 ἔστρεψεν δὲ ὁ θεὸς καὶ παρέδωκεν αὐτοὺς λατρεύειν τῇ στρατιᾷ τοῦ οὐρανοῦ, καθὼς γέγραπται ἐν βίβλῳ τῶν προφητῶν,

Μὴ σφάγια καὶ θυσίας προσηνέγκατέ μοι
ἔτη τεσσαράκοντα ἐν τῇ ἐρήμῳ, οἶκος Ἰσραήλ; [b]
43 **καὶ ἀνελάβετε τὴν σκηνὴν τοῦ Μολὸχ**
  καὶ τὸ ἄστρον τοῦ θεοῦ [ὑμῶν] Ῥαιφάν,
    τοὺς τύπους οὓς ἐποιήσατε προσκυνεῖν
      αὐτοῖς· [b]
καὶ μετοικιῶ ὑμᾶς ἐπέκεινα Βαβυλῶνος.

44 Ἡ σκηνὴ τοῦ μαρτυρίου ἦν τοῖς πατράσιν ἡμῶν ἐν τῇ ἐρήμῳ, καθὼς διετάξατο ὁ λαλῶν τῷ Μωϋσῇ ποιῆσαι αὐτὴν κατὰ τὸν τύπον ὃν ἑωράκει, 45 ἣν καὶ εἰσήγαγον διαδεξάμενοι οἱ πατέρες ἡμῶν μετὰ Ἰησοῦ ἐν τῇ κατασχέσει τῶν ἐθνῶν ὧν ἐξῶσεν ὁ θεὸς ἀπὸ προσώπου τῶν πατέρων ἡμῶν[c] ἕως τῶν ἡμερῶν Δαυίδ,[c] 46 ὃς εὗρεν χάριν ἐνώπιον τοῦ θεοῦ καὶ ᾐτήσατο εὑρεῖν σκήνωμα τῷ οἴκῳ[7] Ἰακώβ. 47 Σολομῶν δὲ οἰκοδόμησεν αὐτῷ οἶκον.

---

[7] **46** {C} οἴκῳ 𝔭74 ℵ* B D 049 it[d] cop[sams] ‖ θεῷ (see Ps 132.5) ℵ[c] A C E P Ψ 056 0142 33 81 88 104 181 326 330 436 451 614 629 630 945 1241 1505 1739 1877 2127 2412 2492 2495 *Byz* it[ar,e,gig,h] vg syr[p,h] cop[sa,bo] arm eth geo Chrysostom

[b b] **42–43** b question, b statement: TR WH Bov AV RV ASV RSV NEB TT Zür Luth Jer ‖ b minor, b question: Nes BF² ‖ b question with ellipsis, b exclamation: Seg

[c c] **45** c none, c minor ‖ c none, c major: WH ‖ c minor, c major: TR Bov Nes BF² AV RV ASV NEB Zür Luth Jer ‖ c major, c minor: RSV Seg ‖ c major, c major: TT

40 Ποίησον...αὐτῷ Ex 32.1, 23 **41** Ex 32.4–6 **42** λατρεύειν...οὐρανοῦ Jr 7.18 LXX; 8.2; 19.13 **42–43** Μὴ...Βαβυλῶνος Am 5.25–27 **44** Ἡ...ἐρήμῳ Ex 27.21; Nu 1.50 διετάξατο...ἑωράκει Ex 25.9, 40 **45** ἣν καὶ εἰσήγαγον...Ἰησοῦ Jos 3.14–17; 18.1 ἐν... πατέρων ἡμῶν Jos 23.9; 24.18 **45–46** Δαυίδ...Ἰακώβ 2 Sm 7.2–16; 1 Kgs 8.17–18; 1 Chr 17.1–14; 2 Chr 6.7–8; Ps 132.1–5 **47** 1 Kgs 6.1, 14; 8.19–20; 2 Chr 3.1; 5.1; 6.2, 10

---

that they could go back to Egypt. 40 So they said to Aaron: 'Make us some gods who will go in front of us. We do not know what has happened to that Moses who brought us out of Egypt.' 41 It was then that they made an idol in the shape of a calf and offered sacrifice to it, and had a feast in honor of what they themselves had made. 42 But God turned away from them, and gave them over to worship the stars of heaven, as it is written in the book of the prophets:

'People of Israel! It was not to me
That you slaughtered and sacrificed animals
For forty years in the desert.
43 It was the tent of the god Moloch that you carried,
And the image of the star of your god Rephan;
They were idols that you had made to worship.
And so I will send you away beyond Babylon.'

44 "Our ancestors had the tent of God's presence with them in the desert. It had been made as God had told Moses to make it, according to the pattern that Moses had been shown. 45 Later on, our ancestors who received the tent from their fathers carried it with them when they went with Joshua and took over the land from the nations that God drove out before them. And it stayed there until the time of David. 46 He won God's favor, and asked God to allow him to provide a house for the God[2] of Jacob. 47 But it was Solomon who built him a house.

---

[2] **46** a house for the God: *some mss. read* a dwelling place for the house

48 "But the Most High God does not live in houses built by men; as the prophet says:
49 'Heaven is my throne, says the Lord, And earth is my footstool. What kind of house would you build for me? Where is the place for me to rest?
50 Did not I myself make all these things?'
51 "How stubborn you are! How heathen your hearts, how deaf you are to God's message! You are just like your ancestors: you too have always resisted the Holy Spirit! 52 Was there a single prophet that your ancestors did not persecute? They killed God's messengers, who long ago announced the coming of his righteous Servant. And now you have betrayed and murdered him. 53 You are the ones who received God's law, that was handed down by angels — yet you have not obeyed it!"

The Stoning of Stephen

54 As the members of the Council listened to Stephen they became furious and ground their teeth at him in anger. 55 But Stephen, full of the Holy Spirit, looked up to heaven and saw God's glory, and Jesus standing at the right side of God. 56 "Look!" he said. "I see heaven opened and the Son of Man standing at the right side of God!" 57 With a loud cry they stopped up their ears, and all rushed together at him at once. 58 They threw him out of the city and stoned him. The witnesses left their cloaks in charge of a young man named Saul. 59 They kept on stoning Stephen as he called on the Lord, "Lord Jesus, receive my spirit!" 60 He knelt down and

48 ἀλλ' οὐχ ὁ ὕψιστος ἐν χειροποιήτοις κατοικεῖ· καθὼς ὁ προφήτης λέγει,
49 Ὁ οὐρανός μοι θρόνος, ἡ δὲ γῆ ὑποπόδιον τῶν ποδῶν μου· ποῖον οἶκον οἰκοδομήσετέ μοι, λέγει κύριος, ἢ τίς τόπος τῆς καταπαύσεώς μου;
50 οὐχὶ ἡ χείρ μου ἐποίησεν ταῦτα πάντα;
51 Σκληροτράχηλοι καὶ ἀπερίτμητοι καρδίαις καὶ τοῖς ὠσίν, ὑμεῖς ἀεὶ τῷ πνεύματι τῷ ἁγίῳ ἀντιπίπτετε, ὡς οἱ πατέρες ὑμῶν καὶ ὑμεῖς. 52 τίνα τῶν προφητῶν οὐκ ἐδίωξαν οἱ πατέρες ὑμῶν; καὶ ἀπέκτειναν τοὺς προκαταγγείλαντας περὶ τῆς ἐλεύσεως τοῦ δικαίου οὗ νῦν ὑμεῖς προδόται καὶ φονεῖς ἐγένεσθε, 53 οἵτινες ἐλάβετε τὸν νόμον εἰς διαταγὰς ἀγγέλων, καὶ οὐκ ἐφυλάξατε.

The Stoning of Stephen

54 Ἀκούοντες δὲ ταῦτα διεπρίοντο ταῖς καρδίαις αὐτῶν καὶ ἔβρυχον τοὺς ὀδόντας ἐπ' αὐτόν. 55 ὑπάρχων δὲ πλήρης πνεύματος ἁγίου ἀτενίσας εἰς τὸν οὐρανὸν εἶδεν δόξαν θεοῦ καὶ Ἰησοῦν ἑστῶτα ἐκ δεξιῶν τοῦ θεοῦ, 56 καὶ εἶπεν, Ἰδοὺ θεωρῶ τοὺς οὐρανοὺς διηνοιγμένους καὶ τὸν υἱὸν τοῦ ἀνθρώπου ἐκ δεξιῶν ἑστῶτα τοῦ θεοῦ. 57 κράξαντες δὲ φωνῇ μεγάλῃ συνέσχον τὰ ὦτα αὐτῶν, καὶ ὥρμησαν ὁμοθυμαδὸν ἐπ' αὐτόν, 58 καὶ ἐκβαλόντες ἔξω τῆς πόλεως ἐλιθοβόλουν. καὶ οἱ μάρτυρες ἀπέθεντο τὰ ἱμάτια αὐτῶν παρὰ τοὺς πόδας νεανίου καλουμένου Σαύλου. 59 καὶ ἐλιθοβόλουν τὸν Στέφανον ἐπικαλούμενον καὶ λέγοντα, Κύριε Ἰησοῦ, δέξαι τὸ πνεῦμά μου. 60 θεὶς

49-50 Is 66.1-2   **51** Σκληροτράχηλοι Ex 32.9; 33.3, 5   ἀπερίτμητοι...ὠσίν Lv 26.41; Jr 9.26; 6.10   ὑμεῖς ἀεὶ...ἀντιπίπτετε Is 63.10   **52** τίνα τῶν προφητῶν...ὑμῶν 2 Chr 36.16   ἀπέκτειναν...δικαίου Mt 23.31   **53** οἵτινες...ἀγγέλων Ac 7.38; Ga 3.19; He 2.2   **54** διεπρίοντο...αὐτῶν Ac 5.33   ἔβρυχον...αὐτόν Job 16.9; Ps 35.16; 37.12; 112.10   **55** ὑπάρχων...ἁγίου Ac 4.8; 6.3, 5; 9.17; 11.24; 13.9   Ἰησοῦν...ἐκ δεξιῶν τοῦ θεοῦ Mt 22.44; 26.64; Mk 12.36; 14.62; 16.19; Lk 20.42; 22.69; Ac 2.34; Ro 8.34; Eph 1.20; Col 3.1; He 1.3, 13; 8.1; 10.12; 12.2; 1 Pe 3.22   **56** τοὺς...διηνοιγμένους Mt 3.16; Lk 3.21; Jn 1.51; Ac 10.11; Re 19.11   **58** οἱ μάρτυρες...Σαύλου Ac 22.20   **59** Κύριε...δέξαι...μου Ps 31.5; Lk 23.46

δὲ τὰ γόνατα ἔκραξεν φωνῇ μεγάλῃ, Κύριε, μὴ στήσῃς αὐτοῖς ταύτην τὴν ἁμαρτίαν. καὶ τοῦτο εἰπὼν ἐκοιμήθη. **8** Σαῦλος δὲ ἦν συνευδοκῶν τῇ ἀναιρέσει αὐτοῦ.

Saul Persecutes the Church

Ἐγένετο δὲ ἐν ἐκείνῃ τῇ ἡμέρᾳ διωγμὸς μέγας ἐπὶ τὴν ἐκκλησίαν τὴν ἐν Ἱεροσολύμοις· πάντες δὲ διεσπάρησαν κατὰ τὰς χώρας τῆς Ἰουδαίας καὶ Σαμαρείας πλὴν τῶν ἀποστόλων. 2 συνεκόμισαν δὲ τὸν Στέφανον ἄνδρες εὐλαβεῖς καὶ ἐποίησαν κοπετὸν μέγαν ἐπ᾽ αὐτῷ. 3 Σαῦλος δὲ ἐλυμαίνετο τὴν ἐκκλησίαν κατὰ τοὺς οἴκους εἰσπορευόμενος, σύρων τε ἄνδρας καὶ γυναῖκας παρεδίδου εἰς φυλακήν.

The Gospel Preached in Samaria

4 Οἱ μὲν οὖν διασπαρέντες διῆλθον εὐαγγελιζόμενοι τὸν λόγον. 5 Φίλιππος δὲ κατελθὼν εἰς [τὴν] πόλιν τῆς Σαμαρείας ἐκήρυσσεν αὐτοῖς τὸν Χριστόν. 6 προσεῖχον δὲ οἱ ὄχλοι τοῖς λεγομένοις ὑπὸ τοῦ Φιλίππου ὁμοθυμαδὸν ἐν τῷ ἀκούειν αὐτοὺς καὶ βλέπειν τὰ σημεῖα ἃ ἐποίει· 7 πολλοὶ γὰρ τῶν ἐχόντων πνεύματα ἀκάθαρτα βοῶντα φωνῇ μεγάλῃ ἐξήρχοντο, πολλοὶ δὲ παραλελυμένοι καὶ χωλοὶ ἐθεραπεύθησαν· 8 ἐγένετο δὲ πολλὴ χαρὰ ἐν τῇ πόλει ἐκείνῃ. 9 Ἀνὴρ δέ τις ὀνόματι Σίμων προϋπῆρχεν ἐν τῇ πόλει μαγεύων καὶ ἐξιστάνων τὸ ἔθνος τῆς Σαμαρείας, λέγων εἶναί τινα ἑαυτὸν μέγαν, 10 ᾧ προσεῖχον πάντες ἀπὸ μικροῦ ἕως μεγάλου λέγοντες, Οὗτός ἐστιν ἡ δύναμις τοῦ θεοῦ ἡ καλουμένη[1] Μεγάλη. 11 προσεῖχον δὲ αὐτῷ

---

[1] **10** {B} καλουμένη 𝔭74 ℵ A B C D E 33 81 181 945 1739 *l*611 it^{ar,d,e,gig,r} vg syr^h cop^{bo} arm eth^{ro} geo Irenaeus^{lat} Origen ∥ λεγομένη 614 2412 ∥ *omit*

60 ἔκραξεν φωνῇ μεγάλῃ Mt 27.46, 50; Mk 15.34; Lk 23.46   Κύριε...ἁμαρτίαν Lk 23.34
8 1 Σαῦλος...αὐτοῦ Ac 7.58; 22.20   Ἐγένετο...ἀποστόλων Ac 8.4; 11.19   **2** συνεκόμισαν...εὐλαβεῖς Mt 14.12; Mk 6.29   **3** Ac 9.1, 13; 22.4; 26.9–11   **4** Ac 8.1; 11.19
7 πνεύματα...ἐξήρχοντο Mt 10.1; Mk 6.7; 16.17

---

cried in a loud voice, "Lord! Do not remember this sin against them!" He said this and died.

8 And Saul approved of his murder.

Saul Persecutes the Church

That very day the church in Jerusalem began to suffer a cruel persecution. All the believers, except the apostles, were scattered throughout the provinces of Judea and Samaria. 2 Some devout men buried Stephen, weeping for him with loud cries.

3 But Saul tried to destroy the church; going from house to house, he dragged the believers out, both men and women, and threw them into jail.

The Gospel Preached in Samaria

4 The believers who were scattered went everywhere, preaching the message. 5 Philip went to the city of Samaria and preached the Messiah to the people there. 6 The crowds paid close attention to what Philip said. They all listened to him and saw the miracles that he performed. 7 Evil spirits came out with a loud cry from many people; many paralyzed and lame people were also healed. 8 And there was great joy in Samaria.

9 In that city lived a man named Simon, who for some time had astounded the Samaritans with his magic. He claimed that he was someone great, 10 and everyone in the city, from all classes of society, paid close attention to him. "He is that power of God known as 'The Great Power.'" they said. 11 He had astounded them with his magic for

such a long time that they paid close attention to him. ¹² But when they believed Philip's message about the Good News of the Kingdom of God and the name of Jesus Christ, they were baptized, both men and women. ¹³ Simon himself also believed; and after being baptized he stayed close to Philip, and was astounded when he saw the great wonders and miracles that were being performed.

¹⁴ The apostles in Jerusalem heard that the people of Samaria had received the word of God; so they sent Peter and John to them. ¹⁵ When they arrived, they prayed for the believers that they might receive the Holy Spirit. ¹⁶ For the Holy Spirit had not yet come down on any of them; they had only been baptized in the name of the Lord Jesus. ¹⁷ Then Peter and John placed their hands on them, and they received the Holy Spirit.

¹⁸ Simon saw that the Spirit had been given to them when the apostles placed their hands on them. So he offered money to Peter and John, ¹⁹ and said, "Give this power to me too, so that anyone I place my hands on will receive the Holy Spirit." ²⁰ But Peter answered him: "May you and your money go to hell, for thinking that you can buy God's gift with money! ²¹ You have no part or share in our work, because your heart is not right in God's sight. ²² Repent, then, from this evil plan of yours, and pray to the Lord that he will forgive you for thinking such a thing as this. ²³ For I see that you are full of bitter envy, and are a prisoner of sin." ²⁴ Simon said to Peter and John, "Please pray to the Lord for

διὰ τὸ ἱκανῷ χρόνῳ ταῖς μαγείαις ἐξεστακέναι αὐτούς. 12 ὅτε δὲ ἐπίστευσαν τῷ Φιλίππῳ εὐαγγελιζομένῳ περὶ τῆς βασιλείας τοῦ θεοῦ καὶ τοῦ ὀνόματος Ἰησοῦ Χριστοῦ, ἐβαπτίζοντο ἄνδρες τε καὶ γυναῖκες. 13 ὁ δὲ Σίμων καὶ αὐτὸς ἐπίστευσεν, καὶ βαπτισθεὶς ἦν προσκαρτερῶν τῷ Φιλίππῳ, θεωρῶν τε σημεῖα καὶ δυνάμεις μεγάλας γινομένας ἐξίστατο.

14 Ἀκούσαντες δὲ οἱ ἐν Ἱεροσολύμοις ἀπόστολοι ὅτι δέδεκται ἡ Σαμάρεια τὸν λόγον τοῦ θεοῦ ἀπέστειλαν πρὸς αὐτοὺς Πέτρον καὶ Ἰωάννην, 15 οἵτινες καταβάντες προσηύξαντο περὶ αὐτῶν ὅπως λάβωσιν πνεῦμα ἅγιον· 16 οὐδέπω γὰρ ἦν ἐπ᾽ οὐδενὶ αὐτῶν ἐπιπεπτωκός, μόνον δὲ βεβαπτισμένοι ὑπῆρχον εἰς τὸ ὄνομα τοῦ κυρίου Ἰησοῦ. 17 τότε ἐπετίθουν τὰς χεῖρας ἐπ᾽ αὐτούς, καὶ ἐλάμβανον πνεῦμα ἅγιον. 18 ἰδὼν δὲ ὁ Σίμων ὅτι διὰ τῆς ἐπιθέσεως τῶν χειρῶν τῶν ἀποστόλων δίδοται τὸ πνεῦμα², προσήνεγκεν αὐτοῖς χρήματα 19 λέγων, Δότε κἀμοὶ τὴν ἐξουσίαν ταύτην ἵνα ᾧ ἐὰν ἐπιθῶ τὰς χεῖρας λαμβάνῃ πνεῦμα ἅγιον. 20 Πέτρος δὲ εἶπεν πρὸς αὐτόν, Τὸ ἀργύριόν σου σὺν σοὶ εἴη εἰς ἀπώλειαν, ὅτι τὴν δωρεὰν τοῦ θεοῦ ἐνόμισας διὰ χρημάτων κτᾶσθαι. 21 οὐκ ἔστιν σοι μερὶς οὐδὲ κλῆρος ἐν τῷ λόγῳ τούτῳ, ἡ γὰρ καρδία σου οὐκ ἔστιν εὐθεῖα ἔναντι τοῦ θεοῦ. 22 μετανόησον οὖν ἀπὸ τῆς κακίας σου ταύτης, καὶ δεήθητι τοῦ κυρίου εἰ ἄρα ἀφεθήσεταί σοι ἡ ἐπίνοια τῆς καρδίας σου· 23 εἰς γὰρ χολὴν πικρίας καὶ σύνδεσμον ἀδικίας ὁρῶ σε ὄντα. 24 ἀποκριθεὶς δὲ ὁ Σίμων εἶπεν,

---

P Ψ 049 056 0142 88 104 326 330 436 451 629 630 1241 1505 1877 2127 2492 2495 *Byz Lect* syrᵖ copˢᵃ ethᵖᵖ Chrysostom

² 18 {C} πνεῦμα ℵ B copˢᵃ Apostolic Constitutions ‖ πνεῦμα τὸ ἅγιον 𝔭⁴⁵,⁷⁴ A C D E P Ψ 049 056 0142 33 81 88 104 181 326 330 436 451 614 629 630 945 1241 1505 1739 1877 2127 2412 2492 2495 *Byz Lect* itᵃʳ,ᵈ,(ᵉ),ᵍⁱᵍ,ʳ vg syrᵖ,ʰ copᵇᵒ arm eth geo Basil Chrysostom

---

17 Ac 19.6   21 ἡ γὰρ καρδία...θεοῦ Ps 78.37   23 χολὴν πικρίας Dt 29.18; Lm 3.15 LXX σύνδεσμον ἀδικίας Is 58.6

Δεήθητε ὑμεῖς ὑπὲρ ἐμοῦ πρὸς τὸν κύριον ὅπως μηδὲν ἐπέλθη ἐπ’ ἐμὲ ὧν εἰρήκατε.

25 Οἱ μὲν οὖν διαμαρτυράμενοι καὶ λαλήσαντες τὸν λόγον τοῦ κυρίου ὑπέστρεφον εἰς Ἱεροσόλυμα, πολλάς τε κώμας τῶν Σαμαριτῶν εὐηγγελίζοντο.

Philip and the Ethiopian Eunuch

26 Ἄγγελος δὲ κυρίου ἐλάλησεν πρὸς Φίλιππον λέγων, Ἀνάστηθι καὶ πορεύου κατὰ μεσημβρίαν ἐπὶ τὴν ὁδὸν τὴν καταβαίνουσαν ἀπὸ Ἱερουσαλὴμ εἰς Γάζαν· αὕτη ἐστὶν ἔρημος. **27** καὶ ἀναστὰς ἐπορεύθη·[a] καὶ ἰδοὺ ἀνὴρ Αἰθίοψ εὐνοῦχος δυνάστης Κανδάκης βασιλίσσης Αἰθιόπων, ὃς ἦν ἐπὶ πάσης τῆς γάζης αὐτῆς, ὃς ἐληλύθει προσκυνήσων εἰς Ἱερουσαλήμ, **28** ἦν τε ὑποστρέφων καὶ καθήμενος ἐπὶ τοῦ ἅρματος αὐτοῦ καὶ ἀνεγίνωσκεν τὸν προφήτην Ἡσαΐαν. **29** εἶπεν δὲ τὸ πνεῦμα τῷ Φιλίππῳ, Πρόσελθε καὶ κολλήθητι τῷ ἅρματι τούτῳ. **30** προσδραμὼν δὲ ὁ Φίλιππος ἤκουσεν αὐτοῦ ἀναγινώσκοντος Ἡσαΐαν τὸν προφήτην, καὶ εἶπεν, Ἆρά γε γινώσκεις ἃ ἀναγινώσκεις; **31** ὁ δὲ εἶπεν, Πῶς γὰρ ἂν δυναίμην ἐὰν μή τις ὁδηγήσει με; παρεκάλεσέν τε τὸν Φίλιππον ἀναβάντα καθίσαι σὺν αὐτῷ. **32** ἡ δὲ περιοχὴ τῆς γραφῆς ἣν ἀνεγίνωσκεν ἦν αὕτη·

Ὡς πρόβατον ἐπὶ σφαγὴν ἤχθη,

     καὶ ὡς ἀμνὸς ἐναντίον τοῦ κείραντος αὐτὸν ἄφωνος,

     οὕτως οὐκ ἀνοίγει τὸ στόμα αὐτοῦ.

33   Ἐν τῇ ταπεινώσει ἡ κρίσις αὐτοῦ ἤρθη·

     τὴν γενεὰν αὐτοῦ τίς διηγήσεται;

     ὅτι αἴρεται ἀπὸ τῆς γῆς ἡ ζωὴ αὐτοῦ.

34 Ἀποκριθεὶς δὲ ὁ εὐνοῦχος τῷ Φιλίππῳ εἶπεν, Δέο-

---

[a] **27** a major: Bov Nes BF² RSV TT Zür Luth Jer Seg ∥ a minor: TR WH AV RV ASV ∥ a none: NEB

24 Δεήθητε...κύριον Ex 8.4 LXX, 24 LXX; 9.28 LXX   **31** Πῶς...ὁδηγήσει με Jn 16.13
32-33 Ὡς...ζωὴ αὐτοῦ Is 53.7-8 LXX

---

me, so that none of these things you said might happen to me.”

25 After they had given their testimony and spoken the Lord’s message, Peter and John went back to Jerusalem. On their way they preached the Good News in many villages of Samaria.

Philip and the Ethiopian Official

26 An angel of the Lord spoke to Philip: “Get yourself ready and go south to the road that goes from Jerusalem to Gaza.” (This road is no longer used.)[1] 27-28 So Philip got ready and went. Now an Ethiopian eunuch was on his way home. This man was an important official in charge of the treasury of the Queen, or Candace, of Ethiopia. He had been to Jerusalem to worship God, and was going back in his carriage. As he rode along he was reading from the book of the prophet Isaiah. 29 The Holy Spirit said to Philip, “Go over and stay close to that carriage.” 30 Philip ran over and heard him reading from the book of the prophet Isaiah; so he asked him, “Do you understand what you are reading?” 31 “How can I understand,” the official replied, “unless someone explains it to me?” And he invited Philip to climb up and sit in the carriage with him. 32 The passage of scripture which he was reading was this:

     “He was like a sheep that is taken to be slaughtered,

     He was like a lamb that makes no sound when its wool is cut off.

     He did not say a word.

33 He was humiliated, and justice was denied him.

     No one will be able to tell about his descendants,

     For his life on earth has come to an end.”

34 The official said to Philip, “Tell me,

---

[1] **26** This road is no longer used: *or* This is the desert road.

of whom is the prophet saying this? Of himself or of someone else?" ³⁵ Philip began to speak; starting from this very passage of scripture, he told him the Good News about Jesus. ³⁶ As they traveled down the road they came to a place where there was some water, and the official said, "Here is some water. What is to keep me from being baptized?" [³⁷ Philip said to him, "You may be baptized if you believe with all your heart." "I do," he answered; "I believe that Jesus Christ is the Son of God."] ³⁸ The official ordered the carriage to stop; and both of them, Philip and the official, went down into the water, and Philip baptized him. ³⁹ When they came up out of the water the Spirit of the Lord took Philip away. The official did not see him again, but continued on his way, full of joy. ⁴⁰ Philip found himself in Ashdod; and he went through all the towns preaching the Good News, until he arrived at Caesarea.

The Conversion of Saul
(Also Acts 22.6–16; 26.12–18)

9 In the meantime Saul kept up his violent threats of murder against the disciples of the Lord. He went to the

μαί σου, περὶ τίνος ὁ προφήτης λέγει τοῦτο;ᵇ περὶ ἑαυτοῦ ἢ περὶ ἑτέρου τινός;ᵇ 35 ἀνοίξας δὲ ὁ Φίλιππος τὸ στόμα αὐτοῦ καὶ ἀρξάμενος ἀπὸ τῆς γραφῆς ταύτης εὐηγγελίσατο αὐτῷ τὸν Ἰησοῦν. 36 ὡς δὲ ἐπορεύοντο κατὰ τὴν ὁδόν, ἦλθον ἐπί τι ὕδωρ, καί φησιν ὁ εὐνοῦχος, Ἰδοὺ ὕδωρ· τί κωλύει με βαπτισθῆναι;³ 38 καὶ ἐκέλευσεν στῆναι τὸ ἅρμα, καὶ κατέβησαν ἀμφότεροι εἰς τὸ ὕδωρ ὅ τε Φίλιππος καὶ ὁ εὐνοῦχος, καὶ ἐβάπτισεν αὐτόν. 39 ὅτε δὲ ἀνέβησαν ἐκ τοῦ ὕδατος, πνεῦμα κυρίου ἥρπασεν τὸν Φίλιππον, καὶ οὐκ εἶδεν αὐτὸν οὐκέτι ὁ εὐνοῦχος· ἐπορεύετο γὰρ τὴν ὁδὸν αὐτοῦ χαίρων. 40 Φίλιππος δὲ εὑρέθη εἰς Ἄζωτον, καὶ διερχόμενος εὐηγγελίζετο τὰς πόλεις πάσας ἕως τοῦ ἐλθεῖν αὐτὸν εἰς Καισάρειαν.

The Conversion of Saul
(Ac 22.6–16; 26.12–18)

9 Ὁ δὲ Σαῦλος, ἔτι ἐμπνέων ἀπειλῆς καὶ φόνου εἰς τοὺς μαθητὰς τοῦ κυρίου, προσελθὼν τῷ ἀρχιερεῖ

---

³ 36 {A} *omit verse 37* 𝔭⁴⁵,⁷⁴ ℵ A B C P Ψ 049 056 0142 33? 81 88* 104 181 326 330 436 451 614 1241 1505 2127 2412 2492 2495 *Byz Lect* vgᵂᵂ syrᵖ,ʰ copˢᵃ,ᵇᵒ eth Chrysostom Theophylactᵃ ‖ *add verse 37* εἶπε δὲ ὁ Φίλιππος, Εἰ πιστεύεις ἐξ ὅλης τῆς καρδίας, ἔξεστιν· ἀποκριθεὶς δὲ εἶπε, Πιστεύω τὸν υἱὸν τοῦ θεοῦ εἶναι τὸν Ἰησοῦν Χριστόν. (88ᶜ *omit* ὁ Φίλιππος…*add* ὁ εὐνοῦχος *after second* δὲ…*add* αὐτῷ *after second* εἶπεν…*omit second* τόν) 104 (630 945 1739 1877 αὐτῷ *for* ὁ Φίλιππος…*add* σου *after* καρδίας… *omit* τόν *before* Ἰησοῦν, 1877 καὶ ἀποκριθεὶς *for* ἀποκριθεὶς δέ) *l*⁵⁹ itᶜ?ˡ,(ᵐ),ʳ (itᵃʳ,ᵖʰ *omit* Χριστόν, itᵍⁱᵍ *omit* ἔξεστιν) vgᶜˡ syrʰ ʷⁱᵗʰ * arm geo (Irenaeus) Tertullian (Cyprian) Ambrosiaster Pacian Ambrose Augustine Theophylactᵇ ‖ *add verse 37* εἶπε δὲ αὐτῷ ὁ Φίλιππος, Ἐὰν πιστεύεις ἐξ ὅλης τῆς καρδίας σου, σωθήσει· ἀποκριθεὶς δὲ εἶπε, Πιστεύω εἰς τὸν Χριστὸν τὸν υἱὸν τοῦ θεοῦ. E itᵉ Greek msᵃᶜᶜ· ᵗᵒ ᴮᵉᵈᵉ ‖ *add verse 37* εἶπεν δὲ Φίλιππος, Ἐὰν πιστεύσῃς ἐξ ὅλης καρδίας· καὶ ἀπεκρίθη ὁ εὐνοῦχος αὐτῷ, Πιστεύω τοῦ θεοῦ υἱὸν εἶναι Ἰησοῦν Χριστόν. 629

ᵇ ᵇ **34** *b* question, *b* question: TR WH Bov Nes BF² AV RV ASV TT Zür Jer Seg ‖ *b* minor, *b* question: RSV NEB Luth

---

36 Ἰδοὺ…βαπτισθῆναι Ac 10.47   **39** πνεῦμα…εὐνοῦχος 1 Kgs 18.12   **40** Ac 21.8
9 1 Ὁ δὲ Σαῦλος…κυρίου Ac 8.3; 9.13   **1-2** προσελθών…Ἱερουσαλήμ Ac 9.14

2 ἠτήσατο παρ' αὐτοῦ ἐπιστολὰς εἰς Δαμασκὸν πρὸς τὰς συναγωγάς, ὅπως ἐάν τινας εὕρῃ τῆς ὁδοῦ ὄντας, ἄνδρας τε καὶ γυναῖκας, δεδεμένους ἀγάγῃ εἰς Ἰερουσαλήμ. 3 ἐν δὲ τῷ πορεύεσθαι ἐγένετο αὐτὸν ἐγγίζειν τῇ Δαμασκῷ, ἐξαίφνης τε αὐτὸν περιήστραψεν φῶς ἐκ τοῦ οὐρανοῦ, 4 καὶ πεσὼν ἐπὶ τὴν γῆν ἤκουσεν φωνὴν λέγουσαν αὐτῷ, Σαοὺλ Σαούλ, τί με διώκεις;[1] 5 εἶπεν δέ, Τίς εἶ, κύριε; ὁ δέ, Ἐγώ εἰμι Ἰησοῦς ὃν σὺ διώκεις· 6 ἀλλὰ[2] ἀνάστηθι καὶ εἴσελθε εἰς τὴν πόλιν, καὶ λαληθήσεταί σοι ὅ τί σε δεῖ ποιεῖν. 7 οἱ δὲ ἄνδρες οἱ συνοδεύοντες αὐτῷ εἱστήκεισαν ἐνεοί, ἀκούοντες μὲν τῆς φωνῆς μηδένα δὲ θεωροῦντες. 8 ἠγέρθη δὲ Σαῦλος ἀπὸ τῆς γῆς, ἀνεῳγμένων δὲ τῶν ὀφθαλμῶν αὐτοῦ οὐδὲν ἔβλεπεν· χειραγωγοῦντες δὲ αὐτὸν εἰσήγαγον εἰς Δαμασκόν. 9 καὶ ἦν ἡμέρας τρεῖς μὴ βλέπων, καὶ οὐκ ἔφαγεν οὐδὲ ἔπιεν.

10 Ἦν δέ τις μαθητὴς ἐν Δαμασκῷ ὀνόματι Ἁνανίας, καὶ εἶπεν πρὸς αὐτὸν ἐν ὁράματι ὁ κύριος, Ἁνανία. ὁ δὲ εἶπεν, Ἰδοὺ ἐγώ, κύριε. 11 ὁ δὲ κύριος πρὸς αὐτόν, Ἀναστὰς πορεύθητι ἐπὶ τὴν ῥύμην τὴν καλουμένην Εὐθεῖαν καὶ ζήτησον ἐν οἰκίᾳ Ἰούδα Σαῦλον ὀνόματι Ταρσέα· ἰδοὺ γὰρ προσεύχεται, 12 καὶ εἶδεν ἄνδρα [ἐν

---

[1] 4 {A} διώκεις (see footnote 2) 𝔭[45vid,74vid] ℵ A B C P Ψ 049 056 0142 33 81 88 104 181 326 330 436 451 614 629 630 945 1241 1505 1739 1877 2127 2412 2492 2495 Byz Lect it[ar,gig,h,r] vg syr[h] cop[sa,bo] arm ∥ διώκεις. σκληρόν σοι πρὸς κέντρα λακτίζειν (see 26.14) E it[e,l,ph] syr[p,h with *] geo Augustine

[2] 5–6 {A} διώκεις· ἀλλά (see footnote 1) 𝔭[74] ℵ A B C E P Ψ 049 056 0142 33 81 88 104 181 326 330 436 451 614 630 945 1241 1505 1739 1877 2127 2412 2402 2405 Byz Lect (l[597] ἀλλ') it[e] vg[ww] syr[p,h] cop[sa,bo] arm geo Chrysostom Theophylact[a] ∥ διώκεις· σκληρόν σοι πρὸς κέντρα λακτίζειν. 629[gr] it[gig,r] ∥ persequeris, durum est tibi contra stimulum calcitrare. 6 Et tremens ac stupens dixit: Domine, quid me vis facere? Et dominus ad eum: 629[lat] it[ar,c,h,l,p,ph,t] vg[cl] syr[h with *] (eth) Lucifer Ephraem Ambrose Theophylact[b]

---

5 1 Cor 15.8 7 Wsd 18.1 8 ἀνεῳγμένων...αὐτόν Ac 13.11 11 Σαῦλον...Ταρσέα Ac 21.39

High Priest [2] and asked for letters of introduction to the Jewish synagogues in Damascus, so that if he should find any followers of the Way of the Lord there, he would be able to arrest them, both men and women, and take them back to Jerusalem.

[3] On his way to Damascus, as he came near the city, a light from the sky suddenly flashed all around him. [4] He fell to the ground and heard a voice saying to him, "Saul, Saul! Why do you persecute me?" [5] "Who are you, Lord?" he asked. "I am Jesus, whom you persecute," the voice said. [6] "But get up and go into the city, where you will be told what you must do." [7] Now the men who were traveling with Saul had stopped, not saying a word; they heard the voice but could not see anyone. [8] Saul got up from the ground and opened his eyes, but could not see a thing. So they took him by the hand and led him into Damascus. [9] For three days he was not able to see, and during that time he did not eat or drink anything.

[10] There was a disciple in Damascus named Ananias. He had a vision, in which the Lord said to him, "Ananias!" "Here I am, Lord," he answered. [11] The Lord said to him: "Get ready and go to Straight Street, and in the house of Judas ask for a man from Tarsus named Saul. He is praying, [12] and in a vision

he saw a man named Ananias come in and place his hands on him so that he might see again." [13] Ananias answered: "Lord, many people have told me about this man, about all the terrible things he has done to your people in Jerusalem. [14] And he has come to Damascus with authority from the chief priests to arrest all who call on your name." [15] The Lord said to him: "Go, for I have chosen him to serve me, to make my name known to Gentiles and kings, and to the people of Israel. [16] And I myself will show him all that he must suffer for my sake."

[17] So Ananias went, entered the house and placed his hands on Saul. "Brother Saul," he said, "the Lord has sent me — Jesus himself, whom you saw on the road as you were coming here. He sent me so that you might see again and be filled with the Holy Spirit." [18] At once something like fish scales fell from Saul's eyes and he was able to see again. He stood up and was baptized; [19] and after he had eaten, his strength came back.

Saul Preaches in Damascus

Saul stayed for a few days with the disciples in Damascus. [20] He went straight to the synagogues and began to preach about Jesus. "He is the Son of God," he said. [21] All who heard him were amazed, and asked, "Isn't this the man who in Jerusalem was killing those who call on this name? And didn't he come here for the very purpose of arresting them and taking them back to the chief priests?"

[22] But Saul's preaching became even more powerful, and his proofs that Jesus

ὁράματι]³ Ἀνανίαν ὀνόματι εἰσελθόντα καὶ ἐπιθέντα αὐτῷ [τὰς] χεῖρας ὅπως ἀναβλέψῃ. **13** ἀπεκρίθη δὲ Ἀνανίας, Κύριε, ἤκουσα ἀπὸ πολλῶν περὶ τοῦ ἀνδρὸς τούτου, ὅσα κακὰ τοῖς ἁγίοις σου ἐποίησεν ἐν Ἰερουσαλήμ· **14** καὶ ὧδε ἔχει ἐξουσίαν παρὰ τῶν ἀρχιερέων δῆσαι πάντας τοὺς ἐπικαλουμένους τὸ ὄνομά σου. **15** εἶπεν δὲ πρὸς αὐτὸν ὁ κύριος, Πορεύου, ὅτι σκεῦος ἐκλογῆς ἐστίν μοι οὗτος τοῦ βαστάσαι τὸ ὄνομά μου ἐνώπιον ἐθνῶν τε καὶ βασιλέων υἱῶν τε Ἰσραήλ· **16** ἐγὼ γὰρ ὑποδείξω αὐτῷ ὅσα δεῖ αὐτὸν ὑπὲρ τοῦ ὀνόματός μου παθεῖν. **17** Ἀπῆλθεν δὲ Ἀνανίας καὶ εἰσῆλθεν εἰς τὴν οἰκίαν, καὶ ἐπιθεὶς ἐπ' αὐτὸν τὰς χεῖρας εἶπεν, Σαοὺλ ἀδελφέ, ὁ κύριος ἀπέσταλκέν με, Ἰησοῦς ὁ ὀφθείς σοι ἐν τῇ ὁδῷ ᾗ ἤρχου, ὅπως ἀναβλέψῃς καὶ πλησθῇς πνεύματος ἁγίου. **18** καὶ εὐθέως ἀπέπεσαν αὐτοῦ ἀπὸ τῶν ὀφθαλμῶν ὡς λεπίδες, ἀνέβλεψέν τε, καὶ ἀναστὰς ἐβαπτίσθη, **19** καὶ λαβὼν τροφὴν ἐνίσχυσεν.

Saul Preaches at Damascus

Ἐγένετο δὲ μετὰ τῶν ἐν Δαμασκῷ μαθητῶν ἡμέρας τινάς, **20** καὶ εὐθέως ἐν ταῖς συναγωγαῖς ἐκήρυσσεν τὸν Ἰησοῦν ὅτι οὗτός ἐστιν ὁ υἱὸς τοῦ θεοῦ. **21** ἐξίσταντο δὲ πάντες οἱ ἀκούοντες καὶ ἔλεγον, Οὐχ οὗτός ἐστιν ὁ πορθήσας ἐν Ἰερουσαλὴμ τοὺς ἐπικαλουμένους τὸ ὄνομα τοῦτο,ᵃ καὶ ὧδε εἰς τοῦτο ἐληλύθει ἵνα δεδεμένους αὐτοὺς ἀγάγῃ ἐπὶ τοὺς ἀρχιερεῖς;ᵃ **22** Σαῦλος δὲ μᾶλλον ἐνεδυνα-

---

³ **12** {C} ἄνδρα ἐν ὁράματι B C *l*⁶⁰ cop^{boms} ‖ ἐν ὁράματι ἄνδρα E P 049 056 0142 33 88ᶜ 104 181 326 330 436 451 614 630 945 1241 1505 1739 1877^{mg} 2127 2412 2492 2495 *Byz Lect* it^{ar,e} syr^{p,h} arm geo Chrysostom ‖ ἄνδρα 𝔓⁷⁴ ℵ A 81 629 1877* it^{gig,l,r} vg cop^{sa,bo} eth ‖ ἐν ὁράματι Ψ

ᵃ ᵃ **21** *a* minor, *a* question: TR WH Bov Nes BF² AV TT Zür Luth Jer Seg ‖ *a* question, *a* statement: RV ASV RSV ‖ *a* question, *a* question: NEB

12 ἐπιθέντα...ἀναβλέψῃ Mk 8.23-25   **13** ὅσα...Ἰερουσαλήμ Ac 8.3; 9.1   **14** Ac 9.1-2, 21; 26.10   τοὺς...ὄνομά σου Ac 9.21; 22.16; 1 Cor 1.2; 2 Tm 2.22   **15** τοῦ...βασιλέων Ro 1.5; Ac 26.1; 27.24   **16** ὅσα...παθεῖν 2 Cor 11.23-28   **21** Οὐχ...ὄνομα τοῦτο Ac 8.1; 9.1, 14; 26.10

μοῦτο καὶ συνέχυννεν [τοὺς] Ἰουδαίους τοὺς κατοικοῦντας ἐν Δαμασκῷ, συμβιβάζων ὅτι οὗτός ἐστιν ὁ
Χριστός.

Saul Escapes from the Jews

23 Ὡς δὲ ἐπληροῦντο ἡμέραι ἱκαναί, συνεβουλεύσαντο
οἱ Ἰουδαῖοι ἀνελεῖν αὐτόν· **24** ἐγνώσθη δὲ τῷ Σαύλῳ
ἡ ἐπιβουλὴ αὐτῶν. παρετηροῦντο δὲ καὶ τὰς πύλας
ἡμέρας τε καὶ νυκτὸς ὅπως αὐτὸν ἀνέλωσιν· **25** λαβόντες
δὲ οἱ μαθηταὶ αὐτοῦ νυκτὸς διὰ τοῦ τείχους καθῆκαν
αὐτὸν χαλάσαντες ἐν σπυρίδι.

Saul at Jerusalem

26 Παραγενόμενος δὲ εἰς Ἰερουσαλὴμ ἐπείραζεν κολλᾶσθαι τοῖς μαθηταῖς· καὶ πάντες ἐφοβοῦντο αὐτόν, μὴ
πιστεύοντες ὅτι ἐστὶν μαθητής. **27** Βαρναβᾶς δὲ ἐπιλαβόμενος αὐτὸν ἤγαγεν πρὸς τοὺς ἀποστόλους, καὶ διηγήσατο αὐτοῖς πῶς ἐν τῇ ὁδῷ εἶδεν τὸν κύριον καὶ ὅτι
ἐλάλησεν αὐτῷ, καὶ πῶς ἐν Δαμασκῷ ἐπαρρησιάσατο ἐν
τῷ ὀνόματι Ἰησοῦ. **28** καὶ ἦν μετ' αὐτῶν εἰσπορευόμενος
καὶ ἐκπορευόμενος εἰς Ἰερουσαλήμ, παρρησιαζόμενος ἐν
τῷ ὀνόματι τοῦ κυρίου, **29** ἐλάλει τε καὶ συνεζήτει πρὸς
τοὺς Ἑλληνιστάς· οἱ δὲ ἐπεχείρουν ἀνελεῖν αὐτόν.
30 ἐπιγνόντες δὲ οἱ ἀδελφοὶ κατήγαγον αὐτὸν εἰς Καισάρειαν καὶ ἐξαπέστειλαν αὐτὸν εἰς Ταρσόν.

31 Ἡ⁴ μὲν οὖν ἐκκλησία⁴ καθ' ὅλης τῆς Ἰουδαίας καὶ
Γαλιλαίας καὶ Σαμαρείας εἶχεν⁴ εἰρήνην,ᵇ οἰκοδομουμένηᵇ
καὶ πορευομένη⁴ τῷ φόβῳ τοῦ κυρίου,ᵇ καὶ τῇ παρακλήσει
τοῦ ἁγίου πνεύματοςᵇ ἐπληθύνετο.⁴

---

⁴ **31** {B} ἡ...ἐκκλησία...εἶχεν...οἰκοδομουμένη καὶ πορευομένη...ἐπλη-

ᵇ ᵇ ᵇ ᵇ **31** ᵇ minor, ᵇ none, ᵇ minor, ᵇ none: TR (TT) Zür Jer ∥ ᵇ major, ᵇ minor, ᵇ none, ᵇ none:
(Luth) Seg ∥ ᵇ none, ᵇ minor, ᵇ none, ᵇ none: WH (RV) (ASV) RSV (NEB) ∥ ᵇ none, ᵇ none, ᵇ minor,
ᵇ none: Bov Nes BF² ∥ ᵇ minor, ᵇ major, ᵇ minor, ᵇ minor: AV

22 συμβιβάζων...Χριστός Ac 17.3; 18.5, 28   **23** συνεβουλεύσαντο...αὐτόν Ac 23.12
24 ἐγνώσθη...αὐτῶν Ac 23.16   **25** διὰ τοῦ τείχους...σπυρίδι 2 Cor 11.33   **26–27** Παραγενόμενος...ἀποστόλους Ga 1.18   **27** ἐν τῇ ὁδῷ...κύριον 1 Cor 9.1; 15.8   ἐλάλησεν
αὐτῷ Ac 9.4; 22.7; 26.14   ἐν Δαμασκῷ...Ἰησοῦ Ac 9.20   **30** ἐξαπέστειλαν...Ταρσόν Ac 11.25

---

was the Messiah were so strong that
the Jews who lived in Damascus could
not answer him.

[23] After many days had gone by, the
Jews gathered and made plans to kill
Saul; [24] but he was told of what they
planned to do. Day and night they
watched the city gates in order to kill
him. [25] But one night Saul's followers
took him and let him down through an
opening in the wall, lowering him in a
basket.

Saul in Jerusalem

[26] Saul went to Jerusalem and tried
to join the disciples. They would not
believe, however, that he was a disciple,
and they were all afraid of him. [27] Then
Barnabas came to his help and took him
to the apostles. He explained to them
how Saul had seen the Lord on the road,
and that the Lord had spoken to him.
He also told them how boldly Saul had
preached in the name of Jesus in Damascus. [28] And so Saul stayed with them
and went all over Jerusalem, boldly
preaching in the name of the Lord.
[29] He also talked and disputed with the
Greek-speaking Jews, but they tried to
kill him. [30] When the brothers found
out about this, they took Saul down to
Caesarea and sent him away to Tarsus.

[31] And so it was that the church
throughout all of Judea and Galilee and
Samaria had a time of peace. It was
built up and grew in numbers through
the help of the Holy Spirit, as it lived its
life in reverence for the Lord.

Peter in Lydda and Joppa

32 Peter traveled everywhere, and one time he went to visit God's people who lived in Lydda. **33** There he met a man named Aeneas, who was paralyzed and had not been able to get out of bed for eight years. **34** "Aeneas," Peter said to him, "Jesus Christ makes you well. Get up and make your bed." At once Aeneas got up. **35** All the people living in Lydda and Sharon saw him, and they turned to the Lord.

36 In Joppa there was a woman named Tabitha, who was a believer. (Her name in Greek is Dorcas, meaning a deer.) She spent all her time doing good and helping the poor. **37** At that time she got sick and died. Her body was washed and laid in a room upstairs. **38** Joppa was not very far from Lydda, and when the disciples in Joppa heard that Peter was in Lydda, they sent two men to him with the message, "Please hurry and come to us." **39** So Peter got ready and went with them. When he arrived he was taken to the room upstairs. All the widows crowded around him, crying and showing him the shirts and coats that Dorcas had made while she was alive. **40** Peter put them all out of the room, and knelt down and prayed; then he turned to the body and said, "Tabitha, get up!" She opened

The Healing of Aeneas

32 Ἐγένετο δὲ Πέτρον διερχόμενον διὰ πάντων κατελθεῖν καὶ πρὸς τοὺς ἁγίους τοὺς κατοικοῦντας Λύδδα. **33** εὗρεν δὲ ἐκεῖ ἄνθρωπόν τινα ὀνόματι Αἰνέαν ἐξ ἐτῶν ὀκτὼ κατακείμενον ἐπὶ κραβάττου, ὃς ἦν παραλελυμένος. **34** καὶ εἶπεν αὐτῷ ὁ Πέτρος, Αἰνέα, ἰαταί σε Ἰησοῦς Χριστός· ἀνάστηθι καὶ στρῶσον σεαυτῷ. καὶ εὐθέως ἀνέστη. **35** καὶ εἶδαν αὐτὸν πάντες οἱ κατοικοῦντες Λύδδα καὶ τὸν Σαρῶνα, οἵτινες ἐπέστρεψαν ἐπὶ τὸν κύριον.

Dorcas Restored to Life

36 Ἐν Ἰόππῃ δέ τις ἦν μαθήτρια ὀνόματι Ταβιθά, ἣ διερμηνευομένη λέγεται Δορκάς· αὕτη ἦν πλήρης ἔργων ἀγαθῶν καὶ ἐλεημοσυνῶν ὧν ἐποίει. **37** ἐγένετο δὲ ἐν ταῖς ἡμέραις ἐκείναις ἀσθενήσασαν αὐτὴν ἀποθανεῖν· λούσαντες δὲ [αὐτὴν] ἔθηκαν ἐν ὑπερῴῳ. **38** ἐγγὺς δὲ οὔσης Λύδδας τῇ Ἰόππῃ οἱ μαθηταὶ ἀκούσαντες ὅτι Πέτρος ἐστὶν ἐν αὐτῇ ἀπέστειλαν δύο ἄνδρας πρὸς αὐτὸν παρακαλοῦντες, Μὴ ὀκνήσῃς διελθεῖν ἕως ἡμῶν. **39** ἀναστὰς δὲ Πέτρος συνῆλθεν αὐτοῖς· ὃν παραγενόμενον ἀνήγαγον εἰς τὸ ὑπερῷον, καὶ παρέστησαν αὐτῷ πᾶσαι αἱ χῆραι κλαίουσαι καὶ ἐπιδεικνύμεναι χιτῶνας καὶ ἱμάτια ὅσα ἐποίει μετ' αὐτῶν οὖσα ἡ Δορκάς. **40** ἐκβαλὼν δὲ ἔξω πάντας ὁ Πέτρος καὶ θεὶς τὰ γόνατα προσηύξατο, καὶ ἐπιστρέψας πρὸς τὸ σῶμα εἶπεν, Ταβιθά, ἀνάστηθι.

θύνετο. 𝔭⁷⁴ ℵ A B C 33? 81 88 181 945 1739 1877 itᵖʰ vg syrᵖ copˢᵃ,⁽ᵇᵒ, ᶠᵃʸ⁾ arm eth Dionysius Theophylactᵇ ‖ ἡ...ἐκκλησία...εἶχον...οἰκοδομήμενοι καὶ πορευόμενοι...ἐπληθύνετο [sic] Ψ ‖ αἱ...ἐκκλησίαι...εἶχον... οἰκοδομούμεναι καὶ πορευόμεναι...ἐπληθύνοντο. P 049 056 0142 104 326 330 436 451 614 629 630 1241 1505 2127 2412 2492 2495 *Byz Lect* (*l*⁶⁸⁰ ληται- βόμενοι [sic] *for* πορευόμεναι) itᵃʳ·ᵍⁱᵍ syrʰ copᵇᵒᵐˢˢ geo Chrysostom Augustine Theophylactᵃ ‖ αἱ...ἐκκλησίαι πᾶσαι...εἶχον...οἰκοδομούμενοι καὶ πορευόμενοι...ἐπληθύνοντο. E itᵉ

---

39 ἀναστὰς...αὐτοῖς Ac 10.23   **40** ἐκβαλὼν...ἀνάστηθι Mk 5.40–41

ἡ δὲ ἤνοιξεν τοὺς ὀφθαλμοὺς αὐτῆς, καὶ ἰδοῦσα τὸν Πέτρον ἀνεκάθισεν. **41** δοὺς δὲ αὐτῇ χεῖρα ἀνέστησεν αὐτήν, φωνήσας δὲ τοὺς ἁγίους καὶ τὰς χήρας παρέστησεν αὐτὴν ζῶσαν. **42** γνωστὸν δὲ ἐγένετο καθ᾽ ὅλης [τῆς] Ἰόππης, καὶ ἐπίστευσαν πολλοὶ ἐπὶ τὸν κύριον. **43** Ἐγένετο δὲ ἡμέρας ἱκανὰς μεῖναι ἐν Ἰόππῃ παρά τινι Σίμωνι βυρσεῖ.

Peter and Cornelius

10 Ἀνὴρ δέ τις ἐν Καισαρείᾳ ὀνόματι Κορνήλιος, ἑκατοντάρχης ἐκ σπείρης τῆς καλουμένης Ἰταλικῆς, **2** εὐσεβὴς καὶ φοβούμενος τὸν θεὸν σὺν παντὶ τῷ οἴκῳ αὐτοῦ, ποιῶν ἐλεημοσύνας πολλὰς τῷ λαῷ καὶ δεόμενος τοῦ θεοῦ διὰ παντός, **3** εἶδεν ἐν ὁράματι φανερῶς ὡσεὶ περὶ ὥραν ἐνάτην τῆς ἡμέρας ἄγγελον τοῦ θεοῦ εἰσελθόντα πρὸς αὐτὸν καὶ εἰπόντα αὐτῷ, Κορνήλιε. **4** ὁ δὲ ἀτενίσας αὐτῷ καὶ ἔμφοβος γενόμενος εἶπεν, Τί ἐστιν, κύριε; εἶπεν δὲ αὐτῷ, Αἱ προσευχαί σου καὶ αἱ ἐλεημοσύναι σου ἀνέβησαν εἰς μνημόσυνον ἔμπροσθεν τοῦ θεοῦ. **5** καὶ νῦν πέμψον ἄνδρας εἰς Ἰόππην καὶ μετάπεμψαι Σίμωνά τινα[1] ὃς ἐπικαλεῖται Πέτρος· **6** οὗτος ξενίζεται παρά τινι Σίμωνι βυρσεῖ, ᾧ ἐστιν οἰκία παρὰ θάλασσαν. **7** ὡς δὲ ἀπῆλθεν ὁ ἄγγελος ὁ λαλῶν αὐτῷ, φωνήσας δύο τῶν οἰκετῶν καὶ στρατιώτην εὐσεβῆ τῶν προσκαρτερούντων αὐτῷ, **8** καὶ ἐξηγησάμενος ἅπαντα αὐτοῖς ἀπέστειλεν αὐτοὺς εἰς τὴν Ἰόππην.

9 Τῇ δὲ ἐπαύριον ὁδοιπορούντων ἐκείνων καὶ τῇ πόλει ἐγγιζόντων ἀνέβη Πέτρος ἐπὶ τὸ δῶμα προσεύξασθαι

---

[1] **5** {B} τινα 𝔭⁷⁴ A B C 0142 81 88 630 945 1739 1877 itᵃʳ vg syrʰᵐᵍ copᵇᵒ arm ‖ τόν (and omit ὅς) l⁶⁰ ‖ omit ℵ E P Ψ 049 056 33 104 181 326 330 436 451 614 629 1241 1505 2127 2412 2492 2495 Byz Lect itᵈ·ᵉ·ᵍⁱᵍ·ˡ·ᵖ syrᵖ·ʰ copˢᵃ eth geo Irenaeusˡᵃᵗ Origen Chrysostom

43 Aē 10.6, 32
10 **1-8** Ac 10.30-33   **1-2** ἑκατοντάρχης…λαῷ Lk 7.2, 5; Ac 27.1, 3   **3** περὶ…ἡμέρας Ac 3.1   **5** Σίμωνα…Πέτρος Mt 10.2; Mk 3.16; Lk 6.14; Jn 1.42; Ac 10.18; 11.13   **6** οὗτος …βυρσεῖ Ac 9.43; 10.32

---

her eyes, and when she saw Peter she sat up. [41] Peter reached over and helped her get up. Then he called the believers and the widows, and presented her alive to them. [42] The news about this spread all over Joppa, and many people believed in the Lord. [43] Peter stayed on in Joppa for many days with a leather-worker named Simon.

Peter and Cornelius

10 There was a man in Caesarea named Cornelius, a captain in the Roman army regiment called "The Italian Regiment." [2] He was a religious man; he and his whole family worshiped God. He did much to help the Jewish poor people, and was constantly praying to God. [3] It was about three o'clock one afternoon when he had a vision, in which he clearly saw an angel of God come in and say to him, "Cornelius!" [4] He stared at the angel in fear and said, "What is it, sir?" The angel answered: "God has accepted your prayers and works of charity, and has remembered you. [5] And now send some men to Joppa to call for a certain man whose full name is Simon Peter. [6] He is a guest in the home of a leather-worker named Simon, who lives by the sea." [7] Then the angel who was speaking to him went away, and Cornelius called two of his house servants and a soldier, a religious man who was one of his personal attendants. [8] He told them what had happened and sent them off to Joppa.

[9] The next day, as they were on their way and coming near Joppa, Peter went up on the roof of the house about noon

in order to pray. ¹⁰ He became hungry, and wanted to eat; while the food was being prepared he had a vision. ¹¹ He saw heaven opened and something coming down that looked like a large sheet being lowered by its four corners to the earth. ¹² In it were all kinds of land animals, reptiles, and wild birds. ¹³ A voice said to him, "Get up, Peter; kill and eat!" ¹⁴ But Peter said, "Certainly not, Lord! I have never eaten anything considered defiled or unclean." ¹⁵ The voice spoke to him again: "Do not consider anything unclean that God has declared clean." ¹⁶ This happened three times; and then the thing was taken back up into heaven.

περὶ ὥραν ἕκτην. **10** ἐγένετο δὲ πρόσπεινος καὶ ἤθελεν γεύσασθαι· παρασκευαζόντων δὲ αὐτῶν ἐγένετο ἐπ᾽ αὐτὸν ἔκστασις, **11** καὶ θεωρεῖ τὸν οὐρανὸν ἀνεῳγμένον καὶ καταβαῖνον σκεῦός τι ὡς ὀθόνην μεγάλην τέσσαρσιν ἀρχαῖς καθιέμενον² ἐπὶ τῆς γῆς, **12** ἐν ᾧ ὑπῆρχεν πάντα τὰ τετράποδα καὶ ἑρπετὰ τῆς γῆς³ καὶ πετεινὰ τοῦ οὐρανοῦ. **13** καὶ ἐγένετο φωνὴ πρὸς αὐτόν, Ἀναστάς, Πέτρε, θῦσον καὶ φάγε. **14** ὁ δὲ Πέτρος εἶπεν, Μηδαμῶς, κύριε, ὅτι οὐδέποτε ἔφαγον πᾶν κοινὸν καὶ ἀκάθαρτον. **15** καὶ φωνὴ πάλιν ἐκ δευτέρου πρὸς αὐτόν, Ἃ ὁ θεὸς ἐκαθάρισεν σὺ μὴ κοίνου. **16** τοῦτο δὲ ἐγένετο ἐπὶ τρίς, καὶ εὐθὺς ἀνελήμφθη⁴ τὸ σκεῦος εἰς τὸν οὐρανόν.

---

² **11** {C} καὶ καταβαῖνον σκεῦός τι ὡς ὀθόνην μεγάλην τέσσαρσιν ἀρχαῖς καθιέμενον 𝔭⁷⁴ ℵ A B (C² *omit* μεγάλην) (E τέτρασιν) (88 καταβαίνοντα) (181 καταβαίνοντα *and* καθιεμένην) (1877 καθιεμένην) itᵃʳ,ᵉ vg geo (Origen) ‖ καὶ καταβαῖνον σκεῦός τι ὡς ὀθόνην μεγάλην τέσσαρσιν ἀρχαῖς δεδεμένον καὶ καθιέμενον 81 629ᶜ 630 (945 τὸ καταβαῖνον) 1739 (syrᵖ) ‖ καὶ καταβαῖνον ἐπ᾽ αὐτὸν σκεῦός τι ὡς ὀθόνην μεγάλην, τέσσαρσιν ἀρχαῖς δεδεμένον καὶ καθιέμενον P 049 056 0142 (326 ἐπ᾽ αὐτῷ *and* καὶ τέσσαρσιν) 330 436 451 614 1241 (1505 *l*⁶¹¹ δεδεμένην) 2127 2412 2492 (104 2495 *l*⁵⁹⁷,¹⁴⁴¹ καθήμενον) Byz Lect (*l*⁶⁰*,¹⁵⁹⁰* *omit* καὶ καταβαῖνον, *l*⁶⁰ᶜ καὶ σκεῦος *and omit* δεδεμένον) Chrysostom ‖ καὶ τέσσαρσιν ἀρχαῖς δεδεμένον σκεῦός τι ὡς ὀθόνην μεγάλην καταβαῖνον καὶ καθιέμενον Ψ 33 it⁽ᵈ⁾,⁽ᵍⁱᵍ⁾,⁽ˡ⁾ (syrʰ) (copˢᵃ,ᵇᵒ *omit* καταβαῖνον καί) arm Theophylact ‖ καὶ τέσσαρσιν ἀρχαῖς δεδεμένον σκεῦός τι καθιέμενον 𝔭⁴⁵ ‖ καί τι σκεῦος τέσσαρσιν ἀρχαῖς ἐκδεδεμένον Clement

³ **12** {B} τετράποδα καὶ ἑρπετὰ τῆς γῆς 𝔭⁷⁴ ℵ A B C²ᵛⁱᵈ 81 (181 τὰ ἑρπετά) 326 630 (945 1739 1877 τὰ ἑρπετά) it⁽ᵃʳ⁾,ᵍⁱᵍ,⁽ˡ⁾ vg syrᵖ copᵇᵒᵐˢˢ arm geo (Clement) Origen Apostolic Constitutions Augustine ‖ τετράποδα καὶ τὰ ἑρπετά itᵈ copˢᵃᵐˢ Origenˡᵃᵗ ‖ θηρία καὶ ἑρπετὰ τῆς γῆς (𝔭⁴⁵ᵛⁱᵈ) copˢᵃ,ᵇᵒᵐˢˢ ‖ τετράποδα καὶ ἑρπετὰ τῆς γῆς καὶ τὰ θηρία E (itᵉ) ‖ τετράποδα τῆς γῆς καὶ τὰ θηρία καὶ τὰ ἑρπετά P Ψ 049 056 0142 104 330 436 451 614 629ᶜ 1241 1505 2127 2412 2492 2495 Byz Lect syrʰ Chrysostom ‖ τετράποδα καὶ τὰ θηρία καὶ τὰ ἑρπετὰ τῆς γῆς C*ᵛⁱᵈ 33 Clement (Origen) Apostolic Constitutions ‖ τετράποδα καὶ ἑρπετὰ καὶ θηρία τῆς γῆς Origen ‖ τὰ θηρία καὶ τὰ τετράποδα καὶ τὰ ἑρπετὰ τῆς γῆς 88

⁴ **16** {C} εὐθὺς ἀνελήμφθη 𝔭⁷⁴ ℵ A B C Eᵍʳ 81 88 (181 εὐθέως) 1877 itᵃʳ vg syrʰᵐᵍ copᵇᵒ ethʳᵒ ‖ ἀνελήμφθη 𝔭⁴⁵ itᵈ syrᵖ copˢᵃᵐˢ,ᵇᵒᵐˢ arm ethᵖᵖ

11–20 Ac 11.5–12　　**14** οὐδέποτε...ἀκάθαρτον Lv 11.1–47; Eze 4.14　　**15** Ἃ...ἐκαθάρισεν...κοίνου Mk 7.15, 19

17 Ὡς δὲ ἐν ἑαυτῷ[5] διηπόρει ὁ Πέτρος τί ἂν εἴη τὸ ὅραμα ὃ εἶδεν, ἰδοὺ οἱ ἄνδρες οἱ ἀπεσταλμένοι ὑπὸ τοῦ Κορνηλίου διερωτήσαντες τὴν οἰκίαν τοῦ Σίμωνος ἐπέστησαν ἐπὶ τὸν πυλῶνα, **18** καὶ φωνήσαντες ἐπυνθάνοντο εἰ Σίμων ὁ ἐπικαλούμενος Πέτρος ἐνθάδε ξενίζεται. **19** τοῦ δὲ Πέτρου διενθυμουμένου περὶ τοῦ ὁράματος εἶπεν [αὐτῷ] τὸ πνεῦμα, Ἰδοὺ ἄνδρες [δύο][6] ζητοῦσίν σε· **20** ἀλλὰ ἀναστὰς κατάβηθι καὶ πορεύου σὺν αὐτοῖς μηδὲν διακρινόμενος, ὅτι ἐγὼ ἀπέσταλκα αὐτούς. **21** καταβὰς δὲ Πέτρος πρὸς τοὺς ἄνδρας εἶπεν, Ἰδοὺ ἐγώ εἰμι ὃν ζητεῖτε· τίς ἡ αἰτία δι' ἣν πάρεστε; **22** οἱ δὲ εἶπαν, Κορνήλιος ἑκατοντάρχης, ἀνὴρ δίκαιος καὶ φοβούμενος τὸν θεὸν μαρτυρούμενός τε ὑπὸ ὅλου τοῦ ἔθνους τῶν Ἰουδαίων, ἐχρηματίσθη ὑπὸ ἀγγέλου ἁγίου μεταπέμψασθαί σε εἰς τὸν οἶκον αὐτοῦ καὶ ἀκοῦσαι ῥήματα παρὰ σοῦ. **23** εἰσκαλεσάμενος οὖν αὐτοὺς ἐξένισεν.

Τῇ δὲ ἐπαύριον ἀναστὰς ἐξῆλθεν σὺν αὐτοῖς, καί τινες τῶν ἀδελφῶν τῶν ἀπὸ Ἰόππης συνῆλθον αὐτῷ. **24** τῇ δὲ ἐπαύριον εἰσῆλθεν[7] εἰς τὴν Καισάρειαν· ὁ δὲ Κορνήλιος

[17] Peter wondered to himself about the meaning of this vision that he had seen. In the meantime the men sent by Cornelius had learned where Simon's house was, and were now standing in front of the gate. [18] They called out and asked, "Is there a guest here by the name of Simon Peter?" [19] Peter was still trying to understand what the vision meant when the Spirit said: "Listen! Three[1] men are here looking for you. [20] So get yourself ready and go down, and do not hesitate to go with them, for I have sent them." [21] So Peter went down and said to the men, "I am the man you are looking for. Why have you come?" [22] "Captain Cornelius sent us," they answered. "He is a good man who worships God and is highly respected by all the Jewish people. He was told by one of God's angels to invite you to his house, so he could hear what you have to say." [23] Peter invited the men in and had them spend the night there.

The next day he got ready and went with them; and some of the brothers from Joppa went along with him. [24] The following day he arrived in Caesarea, where Cornelius was waiting for him, together

Origen[lat] Apostolic Constitutions Ambrose ‖ πάλιν ἀνελήμφθη P Ψ 049 056 0142 104 330 436 451 614 629 630 945 1241 1505 1739 2127 2412 2492 2495 *Byz* (*Lect* ἀνελήφθη) it[e, (gig)] syr[h] cop[samss] geo Chrysostom ‖ ἀνελήμφθη πάλιν D[gr] ‖ εὐθέως ἀνελήμφθη πάλιν 326

[5] **17** {C} ἑαυτῷ p[74] ℵ A B C E P Ψ 049 056 0142 33 81 88 104 181 326 (330 451 2127 αὐτῷ) 436 614 629 630 945 1241 1505 1739 1877 2412 2492 (2495 αὐτῷ) *Byz* l[597] it[ar,e,gig] vg syr[p,h] cop[sa,bo] arm geo ‖ ἑαυτῷ ἐγένετο D it[d,p]

[6] **19** {C} δύο (see 10.7) B ‖ τρεῖς (see 11.11) p[74] ℵ A C E 33 81 88 104 181 629 630 945 1739 1877[c] *Byz*[pt] it[ar,e,gig] vg syr[p,hmg] cop[sa,bo] eth geo Didymus Theophylact[b] ‖ τινες arm ‖ *omit* D P Ψ 049 056 0142 326 330 436 451 614 1241 1505 1877* 2127 2412 2492 2495 *Byz*[pt] l[597] it[d,l,m,p*] syr[h] Apostolic Constitutions Cyril-Jerusalem Ambrose Chrysostom Augustine Theophylact[a]

[7] **24** {C} εἰσῆλθεν B D Ψ 049 81 181 330 451 614 2412 l[147,597,598,809,1141, 1153a,1356,1364,1439,1443] it[ar,d,l] vg syr[p,h] cop[sa] eth Theophylact[a] ‖ εἰσῆλθον p[74] ℵ A C E P 056 0142 88 104 326 436 629 (630 ἦλθον) 945 1241 1505 1739 1877 2127

18 Σίμων...Πέτρος Mt 10.2; Mk 3.16; Lk 6.14; Jn 1.42; Ac 10.5, 32; 11.13   **19** εἶπεν... πνεῦμα Ac 11.12; 13.2   **22** Ac 10.1-2, 5   μαρτυρούμενος...Ἰουδαίων Lk 7.5   **23** τινες... ἀπὸ Ἰόππης...αὐτῷ Ac 10.45; 11.12

[1] **19** Three: *one ms. reads* Two; *other mss. read* Some

with relatives and close friends that he had invited. 25 As Peter was about to go in, Cornelius met him, fell at his feet and bowed down before him. 26 But Peter made him rise. "Stand up," he said, "for I myself am only a man." 27 Peter kept on talking to Cornelius as he went into the house, where he found many people gathered. 28 He said to them: "You yourselves know very well that a Jew is not allowed by his religion to visit or associate with a Gentile. But God has shown me that I must not consider any man unclean or defiled. 29 And so when you sent for me I came without any objection. I ask you, then, why did you send for me?"

30 Cornelius said: "It was about this time three days ago that I was praying in my house at three o'clock in the afternoon. Suddenly a man dressed in shining clothes stood in front of me 31 and said: 'Cornelius! God has heard your prayer, and has remembered your works of charity. 32 Send someone to Joppa to call for a man whose full name is Simon Peter. He is a guest in the home of Simon the leather-worker, who lives by the sea.'

ἦν προσδοκῶν αὐτούς, συγκαλεσάμενος τοὺς συγγενεῖς αὐτοῦ καὶ τοὺς ἀναγκαίους φίλους. 25 ὡς δὲ ἐγένετο τοῦ εἰσελθεῖν τὸν Πέτρον, συναντήσας αὐτῷ ὁ Κορνήλιος πεσὼν ἐπὶ τοὺς πόδας προσεκύνησεν. 26 ὁ δὲ Πέτρος ἤγειρεν αὐτὸν λέγων, Ἀνάστηθι· καὶ ἐγὼ αὐτὸς ἄνθρωπός εἰμι. 27 καὶ συνομιλῶν αὐτῷ εἰσῆλθεν, καὶ εὑρίσκει συνεληλυθότας πολλούς, 28 ἔφη τε πρὸς αὐτούς, Ὑμεῖς ἐπίστασθε ὡς ἀθέμιτόν ἐστιν ἀνδρὶ Ἰουδαίῳ κολλᾶσθαι ἢ προσέρχεσθαι ἀλλοφύλῳ· κἀμοὶ ὁ θεὸς ἔδειξεν μηδένα κοινὸν ἢ ἀκάθαρτον λέγειν ἄνθρωπον· 29 διὸ καὶ ἀναντιρρήτως ἦλθον μεταπεμφθείς. πυνθάνομαι οὖν τίνι λόγῳ μετεπέμψασθέ με;[a] 30 καὶ ὁ Κορνήλιος ἔφη, Ἀπὸ τετάρτης ἡμέρας μέχρι ταύτης τῆς ὥρας ἤμην τὴν ἐνάτην[8] προσευχόμενος ἐν τῷ οἴκῳ μου, καὶ ἰδοὺ ἀνὴρ ἔστη ἐνώπιόν μου ἐν ἐσθῆτι λαμπρᾷ 31 καὶ φησίν, Κορνήλιε, εἰσηκούσθη σου ἡ προσευχὴ καὶ αἱ ἐλεημοσύναι σου ἐμνήσθησαν ἐνώπιον τοῦ θεοῦ. 32 πέμψον οὖν εἰς Ἰόππην καὶ μετακάλεσαι Σίμωνα ὃς ἐπικαλεῖται Πέτρος· οὗτος ξενίζεται ἐν οἰκίᾳ Σίμωνος βυρσέως παρὰ θάλασσαν[9].

2492 2495 *Byz* *l*[60,611,680,1021,1291,1294,1298,1300,1365,1440,1441] it[e,gig] syr[hmg] cop[sams,bo] arm geo Chrysostom

[8] **30** {D} τὴν ἐνάτην p[74] ℵ A* B C 81 630 945 1739 *l*[60] vg cop[bo] arm eth geo ‖ νηστεύων καὶ τὴν ἐνάτην p[50] A[2] (E) (D[gr]* νηστεύων τὴν ἐνάτην τε, D[c] *omit* τε) P Ψ 049 056 0142 88 104 (181 νηστεύων τὴν ἐνάτην καί) 326 330 436 451 614 629 1241 1505 1877 2127 2412 2492 2495 *Byz Lect* syr[p,h] cop[sa] Chrysostom ‖ *include* νηστεύων *but with syntactical and other differences in the sentence* it[ar,d,e,gig,l,p,ph]

[9] **32** {C} θάλασσαν p[45,74] ℵ A B 81 629 vg cop[bo] eth[ro] ‖ θάλασσαν ὃς παραγενόμενος λαλήσει σοι C D E P Ψ 049 056 0142 88 104 181 326 330 436 451 614 630 945 1241 1505 1739 1877 2127 2412 2492 2495 *Byz Lect* it[ar,d,e,gig,l,ph,t] syr[p,h,pal] cop[sa] arm eth[pp] geo Chrysostom Greek[acc. to Bede] ‖ *omit* παρὰ θάλασσαν *l*[1021]

---

[a] **29** *a question*: TR Bov Nes BF[2] AV NEB TT Zür Jer ‖ *a statement*: WH RV ASV RSV Luth Seg

---

25-26 πεσὼν...εἰμι Ac 14.13-15; Re 19.10   **26** καὶ ἐγὼ αὐτὸς ἄνθρωπός εἰμι Wsd 7.1   **28** κἀμοὶ...ἄνθρωπον Ac 10.15; 11.9   **30-33** Ac 10.1-8   **30** ἤμην...προσευχόμενος Ac 3.1   ἀνὴρ...λαμπρᾷ Lk 24.4; Ac 1.10   **32** Σίμωνα...Πέτρος Mt 10.2; Mk 3.16; Lk 6.14; Jn 1.42; Ac 10.18; 11.13   οὗτος...θάλασσαν Ac 9.43; 10.6

33 ἐξαυτῆς οὖν ἔπεμψα πρὸς σέ, σύ τε καλῶς ἐποίησας παραγενόμενος. νῦν οὖν πάντες ἡμεῖς ἐνώπιον τοῦ θεοῦ[10] πάρεσμεν ἀκοῦσαι πάντα τὰ προστεταγμένα σοι ὑπὸ τοῦ κυρίου[11].

Peter Speaks in Cornelius' House

34 Ἀνοίξας δὲ Πέτρος τὸ στόμα εἶπεν, Ἐπ' ἀληθείας καταλαμβάνομαι ὅτι οὐκ ἔστιν προσωπολήμπτης ὁ θεός, **35** ἀλλ' ἐν παντὶ ἔθνει ὁ φοβούμενος αὐτὸν καὶ ἐργαζόμενος δικαιοσύνην δεκτὸς αὐτῷ ἐστιν. **36** τὸν λόγον [ὃν][12] ἀπέστειλεν τοῖς υἱοῖς Ἰσραὴλ εὐαγγελιζόμενος εἰρήνην διὰ Ἰησοῦ Χριστοῦ —[b] οὗτός ἐστιν πάντων κύριος —[b] **37** ὑμεῖς οἴδατε,[c] τὸ γενόμενον ῥῆμα καθ' ὅλης τῆς Ἰουδαίας, ἀρξάμενος ἀπὸ τῆς Γαλιλαίας μετὰ τὸ βάπτισμα ὃ ἐκήρυξεν Ἰωάννης, **38** Ἰησοῦν τὸν ἀπὸ Ναζαρέθ, ὡς ἔχρισεν αὐτὸν ὁ θεὸς πνεύματι ἁγίῳ καὶ δυνάμει, ὃς διῆλθεν εὐεργετῶν καὶ ἰώμενος πάντας τοὺς καταδυναστευομένους ὑπὸ τοῦ διαβόλου, ὅτι ὁ θεὸς ἦν μετ' αὐτοῦ.

[10] **33** {C} ἐνώπιον τοῦ θεοῦ 𝔭[74] ℵ Λ B C D[b] E P Ψ 049 056 0142 81 88 104 181 326 330 436 451 614 630 945 1241 1505 1739 1877 2127 2412 2492 2495 *Byz Lect* it[e,gig] syr[h] cop[bo] Chrysostom ∥ ἐνώπιον τοῦ κυρίου 323 327 441 1518 ∥ ἐνώπιόν σου D* 629 it[ar,d,l,p] vg syr[p] cop[sa] arm geo

[11] **33** {C} τοῦ κυρίου 𝔭[45] ℵ A B C E Ψ (81* *omit* τοῦ) 181 614 630 945 1739 2412 *l*[60,597] it[ar,e,gig,l] vg syr[h] cop[bo] arm geo ∥ τοῦ θεοῦ 𝔭[74] D P 049 056 0142 81[c] 88 104 326 330 436 451 629 1241 1505 1877 2127 2492 2495 *Byz Lect* it[d,p] syr[p,pal] cop[sa,boms] Chrysostom

[12] **36** {C} ὅν 𝔭[74] ℵ* C D[gr] E P Ψ 049 056 0142 88 104 181 326 330 436 451 629 630 945 1241 1505 1877 2127 2492 2495 *Byz Lect* it[e] syr[p,h] geo Cyril-Jerusalem Chrysostom ∥ *omit* ℵ[a] A B 81 614 1739 2412 it[ar,d,gig,l,m,ph] vg cop[sa,bo] arm eth Hippolytus Athanasius Cyril-Jerusalem

[b b] **36** *b* dash, *b* dash: Bov Zür ∥ *b* dash, *b* major: TT ∥ *b* parens, *b* parens: WH[mg] AV RV ASV RSV ∥ *b b* no dashes or parens: TR WH Nes BF[2] NEB Luth Jer Seg

[c] **37** *c* minor: AV RV ASV RSV Zür Luth Jer[mg?] ∥ *c* none: TR Bov Nes BF[2] TT ∥ different text ln 36: WH NEB Jer Seg

34 οὐκ...προσωπολήμπτης ὁ θεός Dt 10.17; 2 Chr 19.7; Ro 2.11; Ga 2.6; Eph 6.9; Col 3.25; 1 Pe 1.17   **35** Jn 9.31   **36** τὸν...ἀπέστειλεν Ps 107.20; 147.18   εὐαγγελιζόμενος εἰρήνην Is 52.7; Na 1.15   διὰ...κύριος Re 17.14; 19.16   **37** Mt 4.12, 17; Mk 1.14   **38** ἔχρισεν... πνεύματι ἁγίῳ Is 61.1; Lk 4.18   ὁ θεὸς ἦν μετ' αὐτοῦ Jn 3.2

---

[33] And so I sent for you at once, and you have been good enough to come. Now we are all here in the presence of God, waiting to hear anything that the Lord has ordered you to say."

Peter's Speech

[34] Peter began to speak: "I now realize that it is true that God treats all men alike. [35] Whoever fears him and does what is right is acceptable to him, no matter what race he belongs to. [36] You know the message he sent to the people of Israel, proclaiming the Good News of peace through Jesus Christ, who is Lord of all men. [37] You know of the great event that took place throughout all of Judea, beginning in Galilee, after the baptism that John preached. [38] You know about Jesus of Nazareth, how God poured out on him the Holy Spirit and power. He went everywhere, doing good and healing all who were under the power of the Devil, for God was with

him. ³⁹ We are witnesses of all that he
did in the country of the Jews and in
Jerusalem. They put him to death by
nailing him to the cross. ⁴⁰ But God
raised him from death on the third day,
and caused him to appear. ⁴¹ He was
not seen by all the people, but only by
us who are the witnesses that God had
already chosen. We ate and drank with
him after God raised him from death.
⁴² And he commanded us to preach the
gospel to the people, and to testify that
he is the one whom God has appointed
Judge of the living and the dead. ⁴³ All
the prophets spoke about him, saying
that everyone who believes in him will
have his sins forgiven through the power
of his name.''

The Gentiles Receive the Holy Spirit

⁴⁴ While Peter was still speaking, the
Holy Spirit came down upon all those
who were listening to the message. ⁴⁵ The
Jewish believers who had come from
Joppa with Peter were amazed that God
had poured out his gift of the Holy
Spirit upon the Gentiles also. ⁴⁶ For they
heard them speaking with strange sounds
and praising God's greatness. Peter spoke
up: ⁴⁷ "These people have received the
Holy Spirit, just as we also did. Can
anyone, then, stop them from being
baptized with water?" ⁴⁸ So he ordered
them to be baptized in the name of
Jesus Christ. Then they asked him to
stay with them for a few days.

39 καὶ ἡμεῖς μάρτυρες πάντων ὧν ἐποίησεν ἔν τε τῇ
χώρᾳ τῶν Ἰουδαίων καὶ Ἰερουσαλήμ· ὃν καὶ ἀνεῖλαν
κρεμάσαντες ἐπὶ ξύλου. **40** τοῦτον ὁ θεὸς ἤγειρεν τῇ
τρίτῃ ἡμέρᾳ¹³ καὶ ἔδωκεν αὐτὸν ἐμφανῆ γενέσθαι, **41** οὐ
παντὶ τῷ λαῷ ἀλλὰ μάρτυσιν τοῖς προκεχειροτονημένοις
ὑπὸ τοῦ θεοῦ, ἡμῖν, οἵτινες συνεφάγομεν καὶ συνεπίομεν
αὐτῷ μετὰ τὸ ἀναστῆναι αὐτὸν ἐκ νεκρῶν· **42** καὶ
παρήγγειλεν ἡμῖν κηρύξαι τῷ λαῷ καὶ διαμαρτύρασθαι
ὅτι οὗτός ἐστιν ὁ ὡρισμένος ὑπὸ τοῦ θεοῦ κριτὴς ζώντων
καὶ νεκρῶν. **43** τούτῳ πάντες οἱ προφῆται μαρτυροῦσιν,
ἄφεσιν ἁμαρτιῶν λαβεῖν διὰ τοῦ ὀνόματος αὐτοῦ πάντα
τὸν πιστεύοντα εἰς αὐτόν.

Gentiles Receive the Holy Spirit

44 Ἔτι λαλοῦντος τοῦ Πέτρου τὰ ῥήματα ταῦτα
ἐπέπεσεν τὸ πνεῦμα τὸ ἅγιον ἐπὶ πάντας τοὺς ἀκούοντας
τὸν λόγον. **45** καὶ ἐξέστησαν οἱ ἐκ περιτομῆς πιστοὶ
ὅσοι συνῆλθαν τῷ Πέτρῳ, ὅτι καὶ ἐπὶ τὰ ἔθνη ἡ δωρεὰ
τοῦ πνεύματος τοῦ ἁγίου ἐκκέχυται· **46** ἤκουον γὰρ
αὐτῶν λαλούντων γλώσσαις καὶ μεγαλυνόντων τὸν θεόν.
τότε ἀπεκρίθη Πέτρος, **47** Μήτι τὸ ὕδωρ δύναται κωλῦσαί
τις τοῦ μὴ βαπτισθῆναι τούτους οἵτινες τὸ πνεῦμα τὸ
ἅγιον ἔλαβον ὡς καὶ ἡμεῖς; **48** προσέταξεν δὲ αὐτοὺς
ἐν τῷ ὀνόματι Ἰησοῦ Χριστοῦ¹⁴ βαπτισθῆναι. τότε
ἠρώτησαν αὐτὸν ἐπιμεῖναι ἡμέρας τινάς.

---

¹³ **40** {C} τῇ τρίτῃ ἡμέρᾳ 𝔭⁷⁴ ℵᶜ A B Dᵇ E P Ψ 049 056 0142 33 81 104
326 330 436 451 614 629 945 1241 1505 1739 1877 2127 2412 2492 2495 *Byz Lect*
itᵃʳ,ᵉ,ᵍⁱᵍ,ᵖʰ vg syrᵖ Chrysostom ‖ ἐν τῇ τρίτῃ ἡμέρᾳ ℵ* C 88 181 630 syrʰ ‖
τῇ (or ἐν τῇ) τρίτῃ ἡμέρᾳ copˢᵃ,ᵇᵒ arm geo ‖ μετὰ τὴν τρίτην ἡμέραν
D* itᵈ,¹,ᵗ

¹⁴ **48** {C} Ἰησοῦ Χριστοῦ 𝔭⁷⁴ ℵ A B E (Ψ *transposes:* βαπτισθῆναι
ἐν ὀνόματι Ἰησοῦ Χριστοῦ) 33 81ᶜ 181 326 614 629 630 945 1739 2412 𝑙⁶⁰

39 κρεμάσαντες ἐπὶ ξύλου Dt 21.22   **40–41** ἔδωκεν…ἡμῖν Jn 14.19, 22   **41** ἡμῖν…
νεκρῶν Lk 24.30, 42; Jn 21.12–13; Ac 1.4   **42** οὗτος…νεκρῶν Ac 17.31; Ro 14.9; 2 Tm 4.1; 1 Pe 4.5
43 Is 33.24; 53.5–6; Jr 31.34; Dn 9.24   **44** Ac 11.15; 15.8   **46** ἤκουον…θεόν Mk 16.17; Ac 2.4,
11; 19.6   **47** Μήτι…βαπτισθῆναι τούτους Ac 8.36   **48** προσέταξεν…βαπτισθῆναι Ac 19.5
τότε…ἐπιμεῖναι ἡμέρας τινάς Jn 4.40

Peter's Report to the Church at Jerusalem

11 Ἤκουσαν δὲ οἱ ἀπόστολοι καὶ οἱ ἀδελφοὶ οἱ ὄντες κατὰ τὴν Ἰουδαίαν ὅτι καὶ τὰ ἔθνη ἐδέξαντο τὸν λόγον τοῦ θεοῦ. 2 ὅτε δὲ ἀνέβη Πέτρος εἰς Ἰερουσαλήμ, διεκρίνοντο πρὸς αὐτὸν οἱ ἐκ περιτομῆς 3 λέγοντες ὅτι[a] Εἰσῆλθες πρὸς ἄνδρας ἀκροβυστίαν ἔχοντας καὶ συνέφαγες αὐτοῖς. 4 ἀρξάμενος δὲ Πέτρος ἐξετίθετο αὐτοῖς καθεξῆς λέγων, 5 Ἐγὼ ἤμην ἐν πόλει Ἰόππῃ προσευχόμενος καὶ εἶδον ἐν ἐκστάσει ὅραμα, καταβαῖνον σκεῦός τι ὡς ὀθόνην μεγάλην τέσσαρσιν ἀρχαῖς καθιεμένην ἐκ τοῦ οὐρανοῦ, καὶ ἦλθεν ἄχρι ἐμοῦ· 6 εἰς ἣν ἀτενίσας κατενόουν καὶ εἶδον τὰ τετράποδα τῆς γῆς καὶ τὰ θηρία καὶ τὰ ἑρπετὰ καὶ τὰ πετεινὰ τοῦ οὐρανοῦ. 7 ἤκουσα δὲ καὶ φωνῆς λεγούσης μοι, Ἀναστάς, Πέτρε, θῦσον καὶ φάγε. 8 εἶπον δέ, Μηδαμῶς, κύριε, ὅτι κοινὸν ἢ ἀκάθαρτον οὐδέποτε εἰσῆλθεν εἰς τὸ στόμα μου. 9 ἀπεκρίθη δὲ φωνὴ ἐκ δευτέρου ἐκ τοῦ οὐρανοῦ[1], Ἃ ὁ θεὸς ἐκαθάρισεν σὺ μὴ κοίνου. 10 τοῦτο δὲ ἐγένετο ἐπὶ τρίς, καὶ ἀνεσπάσθη πάλιν ἅπαντα εἰς τὸν οὐρανόν. 11 καὶ ἰδοὺ ἐξαυτῆς τρεῖς

---

it[ar,e,gig,(ph)] vg[ww] syr[h] cop[sa,bo] arm Rebaptism Cyril-Jerusalem Chrysostom ‖ τοῦ κυρίου P 049 056 0142 88 104 330 451 1505 1877 2127 2492 2495 Byz[pt] l[611,1356,1443] ‖ τοῦ κυρίου Ἰησοῦ 436 1241 Byz[pt] Lect ‖ τοῦ κυρίου Ἰησοῦ Χριστοῦ D 81* it[d,p] vg[cl] (syr[p] κυρίου ἡμῶν) geo

[1] 9 {C} ἀπεκρίθη δὲ φωνὴ ἐκ δευτέρου ἐκ τοῦ οὐρανοῦ 𝔓[45,74] ℵ A 049 056 81 181 630 945 1739 it[(ar),gig] vg cop[sa,bo] ‖ ἀπεκρίθη δέ μοι φωνὴ ἐκ δευτέρου ἐκ τοῦ οὐρανοῦ P Ψ (0142 omit ἐκ δευτέρου) 104 326 330 436 451 614 1241 1505 1877 2127 2412 2492 2495 Byz Lect Epiphanius ‖ ἀπεκρίθη δὲ ἐκ δευτέρου φωνὴ ἐκ τοῦ οὐρανοῦ B ‖ ἀπεκρίθη δέ μοι ἐκ δευτέρου φωνὴ ἐκ τοῦ οὐρανοῦ E it[e] syr[p,h] (arm omit δέ) eth Chrysostom ‖ ἀπεκρίθη δέ μοι φωνὴ ἐκ δευτέρου ἐκ τοῦ οὐρανοῦ λέγουσα 33 88 (629 λέγων) ‖ ἐγένετο φωνὴ ἐκ τοῦ οὐρανοῦ πρός με D* (D[b] ἐγένετο δέ) (it[d] ἀπεκρίθη δὲ φωνή) cop[sams] geo

---

[a] 3 a direct: TR WH[mg] Nes BF[2] AV RV ASV TT Zür ‖ a direct with exclamation: NEB Luth Seg ‖ a interrogative: RSV Jer ‖ different text: WH Bov

---

3 Εἰσῆλθες...αὐτοῖς Ac 10.28; Ga 2.12   5–12 Ἐγώ...διακρίναντα Ac 10.9–20

Peter's Report to the Church at Jerusalem

11 The apostles and the brothers throughout all of Judea heard that the Gentiles also had received the word of God. 2 When Peter went up to Jerusalem, those who were in favor of circumcising Gentiles criticized him: 3 "You were a guest in the home of uncircumcised Gentiles, and you even ate with them!" 4 So Peter gave them a full account of what had happened, from the very beginning:

5 "I was praying in the city of Joppa, and I had a vision. I saw something coming down that looked like a large sheet being lowered by its four corners from heaven, and it stopped next to me. 6 I looked closely inside and saw four-footed animals, and beasts, and reptiles, and wild birds. 7 Then I heard a voice saying to me, 'Get up, Peter; kill and eat!' 8 But I said, 'Certainly not, Lord! No defiled or unclean food has ever entered my mouth.' 9 The voice spoke again from heaven, 'Do not consider anything unclean that God has declared clean.' 10 This happened three times, and finally the whole thing was drawn back up into heaven. 11 At that very moment three men who had been sent to me from

Caesarea arrived at the house where I was staying. ¹²The Spirit told me to go with them without hesitation. These six brothers also went with me to Caesarea, and we all went into the house of Cornelius. ¹³He told us how he had seen an angel standing in his house who said to him, 'Send someone to Joppa to call for a man whose full name is Simon Peter. ¹⁴He will speak words to you by which you and all your family will be saved.' ¹⁵And when I began to speak, the Holy Spirit came down on them just as on us at the beginning. ¹⁶Then I remembered what the Lord had said: 'John baptized with water, but you will be baptized with the Holy Spirit.' ¹⁷It is clear that God gave those Gentiles the same gift that he gave us when we believed in the Lord Jesus Christ; who was I, then, to try to stop God!'' ¹⁸When they heard this, they stopped their criticism and praised God, saying, "Then God has given to the Gentiles also the opportunity to repent and live!''

The Church at Antioch

¹⁹The believers were scattered by the persecution which took place when Stephen was killed. Some of them went as far as Phoenicia and Cyprus and Antioch, telling the message to Jews only. ²⁰But some of the believers, men from Cyprus and Cyrene, went to Antioch

ἄνδρες ἐπέστησαν ἐπὶ τὴν οἰκίαν ἐν ᾗ ἤμην², ἀπεσταλμένοι ἀπὸ Καισαρείας πρός με. **12** εἶπεν δὲ τὸ πνεῦμά μοι συνελθεῖν αὐτοῖς μηδὲν διακρίναντα³. ἦλθον δὲ σὺν ἐμοὶ καὶ οἱ ἓξ ἀδελφοὶ οὗτοι, καὶ εἰσήλθομεν εἰς τὸν οἶκον τοῦ ἀνδρός. **13** ἀπήγγειλεν δὲ ἡμῖν πῶς εἶδεν τὸν ἄγγελον ἐν τῷ οἴκῳ αὐτοῦ σταθέντα καὶ εἰπόντα, Ἀπόστειλον εἰς Ἰόππην καὶ μετάπεμψαι Σίμωνα τὸν ἐπικαλούμενον Πέτρον, **14** ὃς λαλήσει ῥήματα πρὸς σὲ ἐν οἷς σωθήσῃ σὺ καὶ πᾶς ὁ οἶκός σου. **15** ἐν δὲ τῷ ἄρξασθαί με λαλεῖν ἐπέπεσεν τὸ πνεῦμα τὸ ἅγιον ἐπ' αὐτοὺς ὥσπερ καὶ ἐφ' ἡμᾶς ἐν ἀρχῇ. **16** ἐμνήσθην δὲ τοῦ ῥήματος τοῦ κυρίου ὡς ἔλεγεν, Ἰωάννης μὲν ἐβάπτισεν ὕδατι, ὑμεῖς δὲ βαπτισθήσεσθε ἐν πνεύματι ἁγίῳ. **17** εἰ οὖν τὴν ἴσην δωρεὰν ἔδωκεν αὐτοῖς ὁ θεὸς ὡς καὶ ἡμῖν πιστεύσασιν ἐπὶ τὸν κύριον Ἰησοῦν Χριστόν, ἐγὼ τίς ἤμην δυνατὸς κωλῦσαι τὸν θεόν; **18** ἀκούσαντες δὲ ταῦτα ἡσύχασαν καὶ ἐδόξασαν τὸν θεὸν λέγοντες, Ἄρα καὶ τοῖς ἔθνεσιν ὁ θεὸς τὴν μετάνοιαν εἰς ζωὴν ἔδωκεν.

The Church at Antioch

19 Οἱ μὲν οὖν διασπαρέντες ἀπὸ τῆς θλίψεως τῆς γενομένης ἐπὶ Στεφάνῳ διῆλθον ἕως Φοινίκης καὶ Κύπρου καὶ Ἀντιοχείας, μηδενὶ λαλοῦντες τὸν λόγον εἰ μὴ μόνον Ἰουδαίοις. **20** ἦσαν δέ τινες ἐξ αὐτῶν ἄνδρες Κύπριοι καὶ Κυρηναῖοι, οἵτινες ἐλθόντες εἰς Ἀντιόχειαν ἐλάλουν

---

² 11 {C} ἤμην 𝔭⁴⁵ E P Ψ 049 056 0142 33 81 88 104 326 330 436 451 614 629 630 945 1241 1505 1739 1877 2127 2412 2492 2495 *Byz* it^(e,gig,l) vg syr^(p,h) cop^(sa,bo) arm eth geo Chrysostom ‖ ἤμεν 𝔭⁷⁴ ℵ A B D^(gr) 181 it^(ar) ‖ ἦσαν it^d

³ 12 {C} μηδὲν διακρίναντα (𝔭⁷⁴ ἀνακρίναντα) ℵ^c A B 33 81 181 630 945 1739 ‖ μηδὲν διακρίνοντα ℵ* E^(gr) Ψ ‖ μηδὲν διακρινόμενον P 049 056 (0142 326 1241 διακρινόμενος) 88 104 330 436 451 614 629 1505 1877 2127 2412 2492 2495 *Byz* Chrysostom ‖ μηδὲν διακριν (–αντα, –οντα, –ομενον) it^(ar,e,gig) vg syr^p cop^(sa,bo) eth geo ‖ omit 𝔭^(45vid) D it^(d,l,p*) syr^h

12 ἦλθον...οὗτοι Ac 10.23, 45   13 Ac 10.3–5, 22, 30–32   14 ὃς λαλήσει ῥήματα πρὸς σέ Ac 10.22 σωθήσῃ...σου Ac 16.31   15 Ac 10.44   ἐπέπεσεν...ἀρχῇ Ac 2.4   16 Ac 1.5   18 Ἄρα...ἔδωκεν Ac 13.48; 14.27   19 Ac 8.1–4   20 ἐλάλουν...Ἰησοῦν Jn 7.35

καὶ πρὸς τοὺς ῞Ελληνας[4], εὐαγγελιζόμενοι τὸν κύριον Ἰησοῦν. 21 καὶ ἦν χεὶρ κυρίου μετ᾽ αὐτῶν, πολύς τε ἀριθμὸς ὁ πιστεύσας ἐπέστρεψεν ἐπὶ τὸν κύριον. 22 ἠκούσθη δὲ ὁ λόγος εἰς τὰ ὦτα τῆς ἐκκλησίας τῆς οὔσης ἐν Ἰερουσαλὴμ περὶ αὐτῶν, καὶ ἐξαπέστειλαν Βαρναβᾶν ἕως Ἀντιοχείας· 23 ὃς παραγενόμενος καὶ ἰδὼν τὴν χάριν [τὴν] τοῦ θεοῦ ἐχάρη καὶ παρεκάλει πάντας τῇ προθέσει τῆς καρδίας προσμένειν τῷ κυρίῳ[5], 24 ὅτι ἦν ἀνὴρ ἀγαθὸς καὶ πλήρης πνεύματος ἁγίου καὶ πίστεως. καὶ προσετέθη ὄχλος ἱκανὸς τῷ κυρίῳ. 25 ἐξῆλθεν δὲ εἰς Ταρσὸν ἀναζητῆσαι Σαῦλον, 26[b] καὶ εὑρὼν ἤγαγεν εἰς Ἀντιόχειαν. [b]ἐγένετο δὲ αὐτοῖς καὶ ἐνιαυτὸν ὅλον συναχθῆναι ἐν τῇ ἐκκλησίᾳ καὶ διδάξαι ὄχλον ἱκανόν, χρηματίσαι τε πρώτως ἐν Ἀντιοχείᾳ τοὺς μαθητὰς Χριστιανούς.

27 Ἐν ταύταις δὲ ταῖς ἡμέραις κατῆλθον ἀπὸ Ἱεροσολύμων προφῆται εἰς Ἀντιόχειαν· 28 ἀναστὰς δὲ εἷς ἐξ αὐτῶν ὀνόματι ῞Αγαβος ἐσήμανεν διὰ τοῦ πνεύματος λιμὸν μεγάλην μέλλειν ἔσεσθαι ἐφ᾽ ὅλην τὴν οἰκουμένην· ἥτις ἐγένετο ἐπὶ Κλαυδίου. 29 τῶν δὲ μαθητῶν καθὼς εὐπορεῖτό τις ὥρισαν ἕκαστος αὐτῶν εἰς διακονίαν πέμψαι τοῖς κατοικοῦσιν ἐν τῇ Ἰουδαίᾳ ἀδελφοῖς· 30 ὃ

and told the message to Gentiles also, preaching to them the Good News about the Lord Jesus. 21 The Lord's power was with them, and a great number of people believed and turned to the Lord.

22 The news about this reached the church in Jerusalem, so they sent Barnabas to Antioch. 23 When he arrived and saw how God had blessed the people, he was glad and urged them all to be faithful and true to the Lord with all their hearts. 24 Barnabas was a good man, full of the Holy Spirit and faith. Many people were brought to the Lord.

25 Then Barnabas went to Tarsus to look for Saul. 26 When he found him, he brought him to Antioch. For a whole year the two met with the people of the church and taught a large group. It was at Antioch that the disciples were first called Christians.

27 About that time some prophets went down from Jerusalem to Antioch. 28 One of them, named Agabus, stood up and by the power of the Spirit predicted that a great famine was about to come over all the earth. (It came when Claudius was Emperor.) 29 The disciples decided that each of them would send as much as he could to help their brothers who lived in Judea. 30 They did this, then,

---

4 20 {C} ῞Ελληνας 𝔭[74] ℵ[c] A D* arm Eusebius Chrysostom Ps-Oecumenius Theophylact[b] ∥ Ἑλληνιστάς B D[b] E P Ψ 049 056 0142 81 88 104 181 326 330 436 451 614 629 630 945 1241 1505 1739 1877 2127 2412 2492 2495 *Byz Lect* Chrysostom ∥ ῞Ελληνας or Ἑλληνιστάς it[ar,d,e,gig] vg syr[p,h] cop[sa,bo] eth geo ∥ εὐαγγελίστας ℵ*

5 23 {B} τῷ κυρίῳ 𝔭[74] ℵ Λ D E P 049 056 0142 81 88 104 330 436 451 614 629 630 945 1241 1505 1739 1877 2127 2412 2492 2495 *Byz Lect* it[d] syr[p,h] cop[sa,ms] geo ∥ ἐν τῷ κυρίῳ B Ψ 181 326 it[ar,e,gig,ph] vg cop[sa,bo] arm

---

b b **25–26** b number 26, b no number: TR[ed] WH Bov Nes BF[2] AV RV ASV RSV NEB TT Zür Luth Jer Seg ∥ b no number, b number 26: TR[ed]

---

21 πολύς...κύριον Ac 2.41; 4.4; 5.14; 6.7; 11.24; 21.20 **23** παρεκάλει...κυρίῳ Ac 13.43; 14.22 **24** ἀνὴρ...πίστεως Ac 6.5 προσετέθη...κυρίῳ Ac 2.41; 4.4; 5.14; 6.7; 11.21; 21.20 **25** ἐξῆλθεν...Σαῦλον Ac 9.30 **27** προφῆται εἰς Ἀντιόχειαν Ac 13.1; 15.32 **28** εἰς...῞Αγαβος Ac 21.10 **30** Ac 12.25

and sent the money to the church elders by Barnabas and Saul.

More Persecution

12 About this time King Herod began to persecute some members of the church. [2] He had James, the brother of John, put to death by the sword. [3] When he saw that this pleased the Jews, he went ahead and had Peter arrested. (This happened during the time of the Feast of Unleavened Bread.) [4] After his arrest Peter was put in jail, where he was handed over to be guarded by four groups of four soldiers each. Herod planned to bring him out to the Jewish people after Passover. [5] So Peter was kept in jail, but the people of the church were praying earnestly to God for him.

Peter Set Free from Prison

[6] The night before Herod was going to bring him out to the people, Peter was sleeping between two guards. He was tied with two chains, and there were guards on duty at the prison gate. [7] Suddenly an angel of the Lord stood there, and a light shone in the cell. The angel shook Peter by the shoulder, woke him up and said, "Hurry! Get up!" And at once the chains fell off his hands. [8] Then the angel said, "Tighten your belt and tie on your sandals." Peter did so, and the angel said, "Put your cloak around you and come with me." [9] Peter followed him out of the prison. He did not know, however, if what the angel was doing was real; he thought he was seeing a vision. [10] They passed by the first guard station, and then the second, and came at last to the iron

καὶ ἐποίησαν ἀποστείλαντες πρὸς τοὺς πρεσβυτέρους διὰ χειρὸς Βαρναβᾶ καὶ Σαύλου.

James Killed and Peter Imprisoned

12 Κατ' ἐκεῖνον δὲ τὸν καιρὸν ἐπέβαλεν Ἡρῴδης ὁ βασιλεὺς τὰς χεῖρας κακῶσαί τινας τῶν ἀπὸ τῆς ἐκκλησίας. **2** ἀνεῖλεν δὲ Ἰάκωβον τὸν ἀδελφὸν Ἰωάννου μαχαίρῃ. **3** ἰδὼν δὲ ὅτι ἀρεστόν ἐστιν τοῖς Ἰουδαίοις προσέθετο συλλαβεῖν καὶ Πέτρον (ᵃἦσαν δὲ ἡμέραι τῶν ἀζύμων)ᵃ, **4** ὃν καὶ πιάσας ἔθετο εἰς φυλακήν, παραδοὺς τέσσαρσιν τετραδίοις στρατιωτῶν φυλάσσειν αὐτόν, βουλόμενος μετὰ τὸ πάσχα ἀναγαγεῖν αὐτὸν τῷ λαῷ. **5** ὁ μὲν οὖν Πέτρος ἐτηρεῖτο ἐν τῇ φυλακῇ· προσευχὴ δὲ ἦν ἐκτενῶς γινομένη ὑπὸ τῆς ἐκκλησίας πρὸς τὸν θεὸν περὶ αὐτοῦ.

Peter Delivered from Prison

6 Ὅτε δὲ ἤμελλεν προαγαγεῖν αὐτὸν ὁ Ἡρῴδης, τῇ νυκτὶ ἐκείνῃ ἦν ὁ Πέτρος κοιμώμενος μεταξὺ δύο στρατιωτῶν δεδεμένος ἁλύσεσιν δυσίν, φύλακές τε πρὸ τῆς θύρας ἐτήρουν τὴν φυλακήν. **7** καὶ ἰδοὺ ἄγγελος κυρίου ἐπέστη, καὶ φῶς ἔλαμψεν ἐν τῷ οἰκήματι· πατάξας δὲ τὴν πλευρὰν τοῦ Πέτρου ἤγειρεν αὐτὸν λέγων, Ἀνάστα ἐν τάχει. καὶ ἐξέπεσαν αὐτοῦ αἱ ἁλύσεις ἐκ τῶν χειρῶν. **8** εἶπεν δὲ ὁ ἄγγελος πρὸς αὐτόν, Ζῶσαι καὶ ὑπόδησαι τὰ σανδάλιά σου. ἐποίησεν δὲ οὕτως. καὶ λέγει αὐτῷ, Περιβαλοῦ τὸ ἱμάτιόν σου καὶ ἀκολούθει μοι. **9** καὶ ἐξελθὼν ἠκολούθει, καὶ οὐκ ᾔδει ὅτι ἀληθές ἐστιν τὸ γινόμενον διὰ τοῦ ἀγγέλου, ἐδόκει δὲ ὅραμα βλέπειν. **10** διελθόντες δὲ πρώτην φυλακὴν καὶ δευτέραν ἦλθαν ἐπὶ τὴν πύλην τὴν

ᵃ ᵃ **3** a parens, a parens: WH AV ∥ a dash, a dash: Seg ∥ a a no dash or parens: TR Bov Nes BF² RV ASV RSV NEB TT Zür Luth Jer

4 ὃν...φυλακήν Ac 4.3   **5** προσευχὴ...αὐτοῦ Jas 5.16   **6** φύλακες...φυλακήν Ac 5.23   **10** Ac 5.19

σιδηρᾶν τὴν φέρουσαν εἰς τὴν πόλιν, ἥτις αὐτομάτη ἠνοίγη αὐτοῖς, καὶ ἐξελθόντες προῆλθον ῥύμην μίαν, καὶ εὐθέως ἀπέστη ὁ ἄγγελος ἀπ᾽ αὐτοῦ. **11** καὶ ὁ Πέτρος ἐν ἑαυτῷ γενόμενος εἶπεν, Νῦν οἶδα ἀληθῶς ὅτι ἐξαπέστειλεν [ὁ] κύριος τὸν ἄγγελον αὐτοῦ καὶ ἐξείλατό με ἐκ χειρὸς Ἡρῴδου καὶ πάσης τῆς προσδοκίας τοῦ λαοῦ τῶν Ἰουδαίων. **12** συνιδών τε ἦλθεν ἐπὶ τὴν οἰκίαν τῆς Μαρίας τῆς μητρὸς Ἰωάννου τοῦ ἐπικαλουμένου Μάρκου, οὗ ἦσαν ἱκανοὶ συνηθροισμένοι καὶ προσευχόμενοι. **13** κρούσαντος δὲ αὐτοῦ τὴν θύραν τοῦ πυλῶνος προσῆλθεν παιδίσκη ὑπακοῦσαι ὀνόματι Ῥόδη· **14** καὶ ἐπιγνοῦσα τὴν φωνὴν τοῦ Πέτρου ἀπὸ τῆς χαρᾶς οὐκ ἤνοιξεν τὸν πυλῶνα, εἰσδραμοῦσα δὲ ἀπήγγειλεν ἑστάναι τὸν Πέτρον πρὸ τοῦ πυλῶνος. **15** οἱ δὲ πρὸς αὐτὴν εἶπαν, Μαίνῃ. ἡ δὲ διϊσχυρίζετο οὕτως ἔχειν. οἱ δὲ ἔλεγον, Ὁ ἄγγελός ἐστιν αὐτοῦ. **16** ὁ δὲ Πέτρος ἐπέμενεν κρούων· ἀνοίξαντες δὲ εἶδαν αὐτὸν καὶ ἐξέστησαν. **17** κατασείσας δὲ αὐτοῖς τῇ χειρὶ σιγᾶν διηγήσατο [αὐτοῖς] πῶς ὁ κύριος αὐτὸν ἐξήγαγεν ἐκ τῆς φυλακῆς, εἶπέν τε, Ἀπαγγείλατε Ἰακώβῳ καὶ τοῖς ἀδελφοῖς ταῦτα. καὶ ἐξελθὼν ἐπορεύθη εἰς ἕτερον τόπον.

18 Γενομένης δὲ ἡμέρας ἦν τάραχος οὐκ ὀλίγος[1] ἐν τοῖς στρατιώταις, τί ἄρα ὁ Πέτρος ἐγένετο. **19** Ἡρῴδης δὲ ἐπιζητήσας αὐτὸν καὶ μὴ εὑρὼν ἀνακρίνας τοὺς φύλακας ἐκέλευσεν ἀπαχθῆναι, καὶ κατελθὼν ἀπὸ τῆς Ἰουδαίας εἰς Καισάρειαν διέτριβεν.

The Death of Herod

20 Ἦν δὲ θυμομαχῶν Τυρίοις καὶ Σιδωνίοις· ὁμοθυμαδὸν δὲ παρῆσαν πρὸς αὐτόν, καὶ πείσαντες Βλάστον

---

[1] **18** {C} οὐκ ὀλίγος 𝔭⁴⁵,⁷⁴ ℵ A B E P Ψ 049 056 0142 33 81 88 104 181 326 330 436 451 614 629 630 945 1241 1505 1739 1877 2127 2412 2492 2495 *Byz* it^{ar,e} vg syr^h cop^bo geo ‖ μέγας 36 94 307 431 1175 (syr^p) cop^{sa,bomss} arm ‖ *omit* D it^{d,gig,p} Lucifer

12 Ἰωάννου...Μάρκου Ac 12.25; 15.37   **15** οἱ...Μαίνῃ Ac 26.24   Ὁ ἄγγελός ἐστιν αὐτοῦ Mt 18.10   **17** κατασείσας...σιγᾶν Ac 13.16; 19.33; 21.40   **18–19** ἦν...εὑρών Ac 5.22–24

gate that opens into the city. The gate opened for them by itself, and they went out. They walked down a street, and suddenly the angel left Peter. [11] Then Peter realized what had happened to him, and said: "Now I know that it is really true! The Lord sent his angel, and he rescued me from Herod's power and from all the things the Jewish people expected to do." [12] Aware of his situation, he went to the home of Mary, the mother of John Mark. Many people had gathered there and were praying. [13] Peter knocked at the outside door, and a servant girl named Rhoda came to answer it. [14] She recognized Peter's voice and was so happy that she ran back in without opening the door, and announced that Peter was standing outside. [15] "You are crazy!" they told her. But she insisted that it was true. So they answered, "It is his angel." [16] Meanwhile, Peter kept on knocking. They opened the door at last and when they saw him they were amazed. [17] He motioned with his hand for them to be quiet, and explained to them how the Lord had brought him out of prison. "Tell this to James and the rest of the brothers," he said; then he left and went somewhere else.

[18] When morning came, there was a tremendous confusion among the guards: what had happened to Peter? [19] Herod gave orders to search for him, but they could not find him. So he had the guards questioned and ordered them to be put to death.

After this Herod went down from Judea and spent some time in Caesarea.

The Death of Herod

[20] Herod was very angry with the people of Tyre and Sidon; so they went in a group to see Herod. First they won

Blastus over to their side; he was in charge of the palace. Then they went to Herod and asked him for peace, because their country got its food supplies from the king's country.

21 On a chosen day Herod put on his royal robes, sat on his throne, and made a speech to the people. 22 "It isn't a man speaking, but a god!" they shouted. 23 At once the angel of the Lord struck Herod down, because he did not give honor to God. He was eaten by worms and died.

24 The word of God continued to spread and grow.

25 Barnabas and Saul finished their mission and returned from[1] Jerusalem, taking John Mark with them.

Barnabas and Saul Chosen and Sent

13 In the church at Antioch there were some prophets and teachers: Barnabas, Simeon (called the Black), Lucius (from Cyrene), Manaen (who had been brought up with Governor Herod), and Saul. 2 While they were serving the Lord and fasting, the Holy Spirit said to them, "Set apart for me Barnabas and Saul, to do the work to which I have called them." 3 They fasted and prayed, placed their hands on them and sent them off.

---

[1] **25** from: *some mss. read* to

τὸν ἐπὶ τοῦ κοιτῶνος τοῦ βασιλέως ἠτοῦντο εἰρήνην, διὰ τὸ τρέφεσθαι αὐτῶν τὴν χώραν ἀπὸ τῆς βασιλικῆς. 21 τακτῇ δὲ ἡμέρᾳ ὁ Ἡρῴδης ἐνδυσάμενος ἐσθῆτα βασιλικὴν [καὶ] καθίσας ἐπὶ τοῦ βήματος ἐδημηγόρει πρὸς αὐτούς· 22 ὁ δὲ δῆμος ἐπεφώνει, Θεοῦ φωνὴ καὶ οὐκ ἀνθρώπου. 23 παραχρῆμα δὲ ἐπάταξεν αὐτὸν ἄγγελος κυρίου ἀνθ' ὧν οὐκ ἔδωκεν τὴν δόξαν τῷ θεῷ, καὶ γενόμενος σκωληκόβρωτος ἐξέψυξεν.

24 Ὁ δὲ λόγος τοῦ θεοῦ ηὔξανεν καὶ ἐπληθύνετο. 25 Βαρναβᾶς δὲ καὶ Σαῦλος ὑπέστρεψαν εἰς Ἰερουσαλὴμ[2] πληρώσαντες τὴν διακονίαν, συμπαραλαβόντες Ἰωάννην τὸν ἐπικληθέντα Μᾶρκον.

Barnabas and Saul Commissioned

13 Ἦσαν δὲ ἐν Ἀντιοχείᾳ κατὰ τὴν οὖσαν ἐκκλησίαν προφῆται καὶ διδάσκαλοι ὅ τε Βαρναβᾶς καὶ Συμεὼν ὁ καλούμενος Νίγερ, καὶ Λούκιος ὁ Κυρηναῖος, Μαναήν τε Ἡρῴδου τοῦ τετραάρχου σύντροφος καὶ Σαῦλος. 2 λειτουργούντων δὲ αὐτῶν τῷ κυρίῳ καὶ νηστευόντων εἶπεν τὸ πνεῦμα τὸ ἅγιον, Ἀφορίσατε δή μοι τὸν Βαρναβᾶν καὶ Σαῦλον εἰς τὸ ἔργον ὃ προσκέκλημαι αὐτούς. 3 τότε νηστεύσαντες καὶ προσευξάμενοι καὶ ἐπιθέντες τὰς χεῖρας αὐτοῖς ἀπέλυσαν.

---

[2] **25** {D} εἰς Ἰερουσαλήμ ℵ B P 049 056 0142 81 88 104 326 330 451 629 1241 1505 1877 2492 2495 *Byz Lect* syr^hmg eth^ro Chrysostom Theophylact ‖ ἐξ Ἰερουσαλήμ p^74 A 33 630 945 1739 2127 syr^h? cop^bo eth^pp Chrysostom ‖ ἀπὸ Ἰερουσαλήμ D Ψ 181 436 614 2412 *l*^147,809,1021,1141,1364,1439 it^ar,d,gig vg syr^h? Chrysostom ‖ εἰς Ἀντιοχείαν 97^mg 110 328 424^mg 425^c (*l*^38 εἰς τὴν) ‖ ἐξ Ἰερουσαλὴμ εἰς Ἀντιοχείαν (E ἀπό *for* ἐξ) 322 323 429 it^e,p syr^p cop^sa geo ‖ εἰς Ἰερουσαλὴμ εἰς Ἀντιοχείαν cop^sams

---

20 διὰ...βασιλικῆς 1 Kgs 5.11; Eze 27.17   **22** Eze 28.2   **23** ἐπάταξεν...θεῷ Dn 5.20 **24** Ac 6.7; 19.20   **25** Βαρναβᾶς...διακονίαν Ac 11.29–30   Ἰωάννην...Μᾶρκον Ac 12.12; 15.37
13 1 Ἦσαν...προφῆται Ac 11.27; 15.32   **2** Ἀφορίσατε...αὐτούς Ac 9.15; Ga 1.15–16 **3** νηστεύσαντες...αὐτοῖς Ac 6.6; 14.23

The Apostles Preach in Cyprus

4 Αὐτοὶ μὲν οὖν ἐκπεμφθέντες ὑπὸ τοῦ ἁγίου πνεύματος κατῆλθον εἰς Σελεύκειαν, ἐκεῖθέν τε ἀπέπλευσαν εἰς Κύπρον, **5** καὶ γενόμενοι ἐν Σαλαμῖνι κατήγγελλον τὸν λόγον τοῦ θεοῦ ἐν ταῖς συναγωγαῖς τῶν Ἰουδαίων· εἶχον δὲ καὶ Ἰωάννην ὑπηρέτην. **6** διελθόντες δὲ ὅλην τὴν νῆσον ἄχρι Πάφου εὗρον ἄνδρα τινὰ μάγον ψευδοπροφήτην Ἰουδαῖον ᾧ ὄνομα Βαριησοῦ, **7** ὃς ἦν σὺν τῷ ἀνθυπάτῳ Σεργίῳ Παύλῳ, ἀνδρὶ συνετῷ. οὗτος προσκαλεσάμενος Βαρναβᾶν καὶ Σαῦλον ἐπεζήτησεν ἀκοῦσαι τὸν λόγον τοῦ θεοῦ· **8** ἀνθίστατο δὲ αὐτοῖς Ἐλύμας ὁ μάγος, οὕτως γὰρ μεθερμηνεύεται τὸ ὄνομα αὐτοῦ, ζητῶν διαστρέψαι τὸν ἀνθύπατον ἀπὸ τῆς πίστεως. **9** Σαῦλος δέ, ὁ καὶ Παῦλος, πλησθεὶς πνεύματος ἁγίου ἀτενίσας εἰς αὐτὸν **10** εἶπεν, Ὦ πλήρης παντὸς δόλου καὶ πάσης ῥᾳδιουργίας, υἱὲ διαβόλου, ἐχθρὲ πάσης δικαιοσύνης, οὐ παύσῃ διαστρέφων τὰς ὁδοὺς [τοῦ] κυρίου τὰς εὐθείας; **11** καὶ νῦν ἰδοὺ χεὶρ κυρίου ἐπὶ σέ, καὶ ἔσῃ τυφλὸς μὴ βλέπων τὸν ἥλιον ἄχρι καιροῦ. παραχρῆμά τε ἔπεσεν ἐπ' αὐτὸν ἀχλὺς καὶ σκότος, καὶ περιάγων ἐζήτει χειραγωγούς. **12** τότε ἰδὼν ὁ ἀνθύπατος τὸ γεγονὸς ἐπίστευσεν ἐκπλησσόμενος ἐπὶ τῇ διδαχῇ τοῦ κυρίου.

Paul and Barnabas at Antioch of Pisidia

13 Ἀναχθέντες δὲ ἀπὸ τῆς Πάφου οἱ περὶ Παῦλον ἦλθον εἰς Πέργην τῆς Παμφυλίας· Ἰωάννης δὲ ἀποχωρήσας ἀπ' αὐτῶν ὑπέστρεψεν εἰς Ἱεροσόλυμα. **14** αὐτοὶ δὲ διελθόντες ἀπὸ τῆς Πέργης παρεγένοντο εἰς Ἀντιόχειαν τὴν Πισιδίαν[1], καὶ εἰσελθόντες εἰς τὴν συναγωγὴν

---

[1] **14** {B} τὴν Πισιδίαν 𝔭[45,74] ℵ A B C ‖ τῆς Πισιδίας D E P Ψ 049 056 0142 33 81 88 104 181 326 330 436 451 614 629 630 945 1241 1505 1739 1877 2127 2412 2492 2495 *Byz Lect* it[ar,d,e,gig,(ph)] vg syr[p,h] cop[sa,bo] arm geo Chrysostom

---

4 ἀπέπλευσαν εἰς Κύπρον Ac 15.39   **5** εἶχον...ὑπηρέτην Ac 12.25; 13.13; 15.39
8 2 Tm 3.8   **10** διαστρέφων τὰς ὁδούς Pr 10.9   τὰς ὁδοὺς...εὐθείας Ho 14.9   **11** Ac 9.8;
22.11   **13** Ἰωάννης...Ἱεροσόλυμα Ac 13.5; 15.38

4 Barnabas and Saul, then, having been sent by the Holy Spirit, went down to Seleucia and sailed from there to the island of Cyprus. **5** When they arrived at Salamis, they preached the word of God in the Jewish synagogues. They had John Mark with them to help in the work.

6 They went all the way across the island to Paphos, where they met a certain magician named Bar-Jesus, a Jew who claimed to be a prophet. **7** He was a friend of the Governor of the island, Sergius Paulus, who was an intelligent man. The Governor called Barnabas and Saul before him because he wanted to hear the word of God. **8** But they were opposed by the magician Elymas (this is his name in Greek); he tried to turn the Governor away from the faith. **9** Then Saul — also known as Paul — was filled with the Holy Spirit; he looked straight at the magician **10** and said: "You son of the Devil! You are the enemy of everything that is good; you are full of all kinds of evil tricks, and you always keep trying to turn the Lord's truths into lies! **11** The Lord's hand will come down on you now; you will be blind, and will not see the light of day for a time." At once Elymas felt a black mist cover his eyes, and he walked around trying to find someone to lead him by the hand. **12** The Governor believed, when he saw what had happened; he was greatly amazed at the teaching about the Lord.

In Antioch of Pisidia

13 Paul and his companions sailed from Paphos and came to Perga, in Pamphylia; but John Mark left them there and went back to Jerusalem. **14** They went on from Perga and came to Antioch of Pisidia; and on the Sabbath day they

went into the synagogue and sat down.
[15] After the reading from the Law of
Moses and the writings of the prophets,
the officials of the synagogue sent them
a message: "Brothers: we want you to
speak to the people if you have a message of encouragement for them." [16] Paul
stood up, motioned with his hand and
began to speak:

"Fellow Israelites and all Gentiles here
who worship God: hear me! [17] The God
of this people of Israel chose our ancestors, and made the people great during
the time they lived as foreigners in the
land of Egypt. God brought them out of
Egypt by his great power, [18] and for
forty years he endured[1] them in the
desert. [19] He destroyed seven nations in
the land of Canaan and made his people
the owners of the land [20] for about four
hundred and fifty years.

"After this he gave them judges, until

---

[1] **18** endured: *some mss. read* took care of

τῇ ἡμέρᾳ τῶν σαββάτων ἐκάθισαν. **15** μετὰ δὲ τὴν
ἀνάγνωσιν τοῦ νόμου καὶ τῶν προφητῶν ἀπέστειλαν οἱ
ἀρχισυνάγωγοι πρὸς αὐτοὺς λέγοντες, Ἄνδρες ἀδελφοί,
εἴ τίς ἐστιν ἐν ὑμῖν λόγος παρακλήσεως πρὸς τὸν λαόν,
λέγετε. **16** ἀναστὰς δὲ Παῦλος καὶ κατασείσας τῇ χειρὶ
εἶπεν·

Ἄνδρες Ἰσραηλῖται καὶ οἱ φοβούμενοι τὸν θεόν,
ἀκούσατε. **17** ὁ θεὸς τοῦ λαοῦ τούτου Ἰσραὴλ ἐξελέξατο
τοὺς πατέρας ἡμῶν, καὶ τὸν λαὸν ὕψωσεν ἐν τῇ παροικίᾳ
ἐν γῇ Αἰγύπτου, καὶ μετὰ βραχίονος ὑψηλοῦ ἐξήγαγεν
αὐτοὺς ἐξ αὐτῆς, **18** καὶ ὡς τεσσαρακονταετῆ χρόνον
ἐτροποφόρησεν[2] αὐτοὺς ἐν τῇ ἐρήμῳ, **19** καὶ καθελὼν
ἔθνη ἑπτὰ ἐν γῇ Χανάαν κατεκληρονόμησεν τὴν[3] γῆν
αὐτῶν[a] **20** ὡς ἔτεσιν τετρακοσίοις καὶ πεντήκοντα.[a] καὶ
μετὰ ταῦτα[4] ἔδωκεν κριτὰς ἕως Σαμουὴλ [τοῦ] προ-

---

[2] **18** {D} ἐτροποφόρησεν ℵ B C² Dᵍʳ P 049 (056 0142 ἐτροποφόρησαν)
81 88 104 326 330 436 451 614 629 630 945 1241 1505 1739 1877 2412 2495 *Byz
Lect* itᵃʳ vg syrʰᵍʳ Chrysostom Cosmos Ps-Oecumenius Theophylact ∥
ἐτροφοφόρησεν (*see* Dt 1.31) 𝔭⁷⁴ A C* E Ψ 33 181 2127 2492 *l*⁸⁰⁹,¹³⁶⁴ itᵈ,ᵉ,ᵍⁱᵍ
syrᵖ,ʰ copˢᵃ,ᵇᵒ arm eth geo Apostolic Constitutions Hesychius-Salonitan
Ps-Chrysostom

[3] **19** {C} τήν 𝔭⁷⁴ ℵ B Dᵍʳ* Ψ 33 81 181 copˢᵃᵐˢ Cosmos ∥ αὐτοῖς τήν
A C Dᵇ E P 049 056 0142 104 326 330 436 451 614 629 630 945 1241 1505 1739
1877 2127 2412 2492 2495 (88 *l*¹³⁵⁶ αὐτούς) *Byz Lect* itᵃʳ,ᵉ,ᵍⁱᵍ vg syrᵖ,ʰ copˢᵃ,ᵇᵒ?
arm geo Chrysostom ∥ *possidere eos fecit terram allophoelorum* itᵈ

[4] **20** {D} ὡς ἔτεσιν τετρακοσίοις καὶ πεντήκοντα. καὶ μετὰ ταῦτα
𝔭⁷⁴ ℵ A B C 33 81 181 itᵃʳ,ᵉ vg (copˢᵃ *omit* μετὰ ταῦτα, copᵇᵒ *omit* καὶ
πεντήκοντα) arm geo Cosmos ∥ καὶ μετὰ ταῦτα ὡς ἔτεσιν τετρακοσίοις
καὶ πεντήκοντα Dᵇ E P Ψ 049 056 0142 88 104 326 330 436 451 629 630 945
1241 1505 1739 1877ᶜ 2127 2492 2495 *Byz Lect* (*l*⁶⁰³ τριακοσίοις) itᵉ ethᵖᵖ
Greekᵃᶜᶜ· ᵗᵒ ᴮᵉᵈᵉ ∥ καὶ ἕως ἔτεσιν τετρακοσίοις καὶ πεντήκοντα Dᵍʳ* itᵍⁱᵍ
(itᵈ syrʰ ὡς) ∥ ἔτεσιν τετρακοσίοις καὶ πεντήκοντα 614 (2412 *add* καί)
(syrᵖ ethʳᵒ καὶ ἔτεσιν) ∥ καὶ μετὰ ταῦτα 1877*

[a a] **19–20** *a none, a major*: WH Bov Nes BF² (NEB) ∥ *a minor, a major*: RV ASV RSV TT Luth
Jer Seg ∥ *different text*: TR AV Zür Jerᵐᵍ Segᵐᵍ

---

15 τὴν ἀνάγνωσιν τοῦ νόμου Ac 15.21   **16** κατασείσας τῇ χειρί Ac 12.17; 19.33; 21.40
Ἄνδρες...θεόν Ac 13.26   **17** μετὰ...ἐξήγαγεν...αὐτῆς Ex 6.1, 6; 12.51   **18** Ex 16.35; Nu 14.34
19 Dt 7.1   κατεκληρονόμησεν...αὐτῶν Jos 14.1   **20** μετὰ...κριτάς Jdg 2.16   ἕως...
προφήτου 1 Sm 3.20

φήτου. **21** κἀκεῖθεν ᾐτήσαντο βασιλέα, καὶ ἔδωκεν αὐτοῖς ὁ θεὸς τὸν Σαοὺλ υἱὸν Κίς, ἄνδρα ἐκ φυλῆς Βενιαμείν, ἔτη τεσσαράκοντα. **22** καὶ μεταστήσας αὐτὸν ἤγειρεν τὸν Δαυὶδ αὐτοῖς εἰς βασιλέα, ᾧ καὶ εἶπεν μαρτυρήσας, **Εὗρον Δαυὶδ** τὸν τοῦ Ἰεσσαί, **ἄνδρα κατὰ τὴν καρδίαν μου**, ὃς ποιήσει πάντα τὰ θελήματά μου. **23** τούτου ὁ θεὸς ἀπὸ τοῦ σπέρματος κατ' ἐπαγγελίαν ἤγαγεν[5] τῷ Ἰσραὴλ σωτῆρα Ἰησοῦν, **24** προκηρύξαντος Ἰωάννου πρὸ προσώπου τῆς εἰσόδου αὐτοῦ βάπτισμα μετανοίας παντὶ τῷ λαῷ Ἰσραήλ. **25** ὡς δὲ ἐπλήρου Ἰωάννης τὸν δρόμον, ἔλεγεν, Τί ἐμὲ ὑπονοεῖτε εἶναι;[b] οὐκ εἰμὶ ἐγώ· ἀλλ' ἰδοὺ ἔρχεται μετ' ἐμὲ οὗ οὐκ εἰμὶ ἄξιος τὸ ὑπόδημα τῶν ποδῶν λῦσαι.

26 Ἄνδρες ἀδελφοί, υἱοὶ γένους Ἀβραὰμ καὶ οἱ ἐν ὑμῖν φοβούμενοι τὸν θεόν, ἡμῖν[6] ὁ λόγος τῆς σωτηρίας ταύτης ἐξαπεστάλη. **27** οἱ γὰρ κατοικοῦντες ἐν Ἰερουσαλὴμ καὶ οἱ ἄρχοντες αὐτῶν τοῦτον ἀγνοήσαντες καὶ τὰς φωνὰς τῶν προφητῶν τὰς κατὰ πᾶν σάββατον ἀναγινωσκομένας κρίναντες ἐπλήρωσαν, **28** καὶ μηδεμίαν αἰτίαν θανάτου εὑρόντες ᾐτήσαντο Πιλᾶτον ἀναιρεθῆναι

[5] **23** {B} ἤγαγεν 𝔭74 ℵ A B E P Ψ 049 056 0142 81 326 330 436 451 629 1505 1877 2127 2492 2495 *Byz Lect* it[ar, e] vg cop[bo] eth Athanasius Chrysostom[1/2] Cosmos Theophylact[a] ∥ ἤγειρε C D 33 88 104 181 614 630 945 1241 2412 it[d, gig] syr[p, h] cop[sa] arm geo Chrysostom[1/2] Theodoret Theophylact[b] ∥ *omit* 1739

[6] **26** {B} ἡμῖν 𝔭74 ℵ A B D 33 81 326 614 2412 it[d] syr[hmg] cop[sa] Cosmos ∥ ὑμῖν 𝔭45 C E P Ψ 049 056 0142 88 104 181 330 436 451 629 630 945 1241 1505 1739 1877 2127 2492 2495 *Byz Lect*[m] *l*[1443] it[ar, e, gig] vg syr[p, h] cop[bo] arm eth geo Chrysostom

[b] **25** *b* question: TR WH AV RV ASV RSV ∥ *b* minor: WH[mg] Bov Nes BF² (NEB) (TT) Zür Luth Jer (Seg)

21 κἀκεῖθεν...βασιλέα 1 Sm 8.5, 19   ἔδωκεν...Βενιαμείν 1 Sm 10.20-21, 24; 11.15 **22** μεταστήσας αὐτόν 1 Sm 13.14   ἤγειρεν...βασιλέα 1 Sm 16.12-13   Εὗρον Δαυίδ Ps 89.20   ἄνδρα...καρδίαν μου 1 Sm 13.14   ὃς...θελήματά μου Is 44.28 **23** τούτου...σωτῆρα 2 Sm 7.12; Is 11.1   **24** Mt 3.1-2, 5, Mk 1.4-5; Lk 3.3   **25** Τί...εἰμὶ ἐγώ Jn 1.20   ἔρχεται...λῦσαι Mt 3.11; Mk 1.7; Lk 3.16; Jn 1.27   **26** Ἄνδρες...θεόν Ac 13.16   **27** Ac 3.17   **28** μηδεμίαν ...εὑρόντες Mt 26.60; Mk 14.55, 56, 59; 15.14; Lk 23.4, 14, 15, 22; Jn 18.38; 19.4, 6   ᾐτήσαντο... αὐτόν Mt 27.22-23; Mk 15.13-14; Lk 23.21, 23; Jn 19.6, 7, 15

the time of the prophet Samuel. **21** And when they asked for a king, God gave them Saul, the son of Kish, from the tribe of Benjamin, to be their king for forty years. **22** After removing him, God made David their king. This is what God said about him: 'I have found that David, the son of Jesse, is the kind of man I like, a man who will do all I want him to do.' **23** It was Jesus, one of the descendants of David, that God made the Savior of the people of Israel, as he had promised. **24** Before the coming of Jesus, John preached to all the people of Israel that they should turn from their sins and be baptized. **25** And as John was about to finish his mission, he said to the people: 'Who do you think I am? I am not the one you are waiting for. But look! He is coming after me, and I am not good enough to take his sandals off his feet.'

26 "My brothers, descendants of Abraham, and all Gentiles here who worship God: it is to us that this message of salvation has been sent! **27** For the people who live in Jerusalem, and their leaders, did not know that he is the Savior, nor did they understand the words of the prophets that are read every Sabbath day. Yet they made the prophets' words come true by condemning Jesus. **28** And even though they could find no reason to pass the death sentence on him, they asked Pilate to have him put to death.

[29] And after they had done everything that the Scriptures say about him, they took him down from the cross and placed him in a grave. [30] But God raised him from the dead, [31] and for many days he was seen by those who had traveled with him from Galilee to Jerusalem. They are now witnesses for him to the people of Israel. [32-33] And we are here to bring the Good News to you: what God promised our ancestors he would do, he has now done for us, who are their descendants, by raising Jesus to life. As it is written in the second Psalm:

> 'You are my Son,
> Today I have become your Father.'

[34] And this is what God said about raising him from the dead, never again to return to decay:

> 'I will give you the sacred and sure blessings
> That I promised to David.'

[35] As indeed he says in another passage,

> 'You will not allow your devoted servant to suffer decay.'

[36] For David served God's purposes in his own time; and then he died, and was buried beside his ancestors, and suffered

αὐτόν· **29** ὡς δὲ ἐτέλεσαν πάντα τὰ περὶ αὐτοῦ γεγραμμένα, καθελόντες ἀπὸ τοῦ ξύλου ἔθηκαν εἰς μνημεῖον. **30** ὁ δὲ θεὸς ἤγειρεν αυτον εκ νεκρῶν· **31** ὃς ὤφθη ἐπὶ ἡμέρας πλείους τοῖς συναναβάσιν αὐτῷ ἀπὸ τῆς Γαλιλαίας εἰς Ἰερουσαλήμ, οἵτινες [νῦν] εἰσιν μάρτυρες αὐτοῦ πρὸς τὸν λαόν. **32** καὶ ἡμεῖς ὑμᾶς εὐαγγελιζόμεθα τὴν πρὸς τοὺς πατέρας ἐπαγγελίαν γενομένην, **33**ᶜ ὅτι ταύτην ὁ θεὸς ἐκπεπλήρωκεν τοῖς τέκνοις ἡμῖν[7] ἀναστήσας Ἰησοῦν, ᶜὡς καὶ ἐν τῷ ψαλμῷ γέγραπται τῷ δευτέρῳ[8],

> **Υἱός μου εἶ σύ,**
> **ἐγὼ σήμερον γεγέννηκά σε.**

34 ὅτι δὲ ἀνέστησεν αὐτὸν ἐκ νεκρῶν μηκέτι μέλλοντα ὑποστρέφειν εἰς διαφθοράν, οὕτως εἴρηκεν ὅτι

> **Δώσω ὑμῖν τὰ ὅσια Δαυὶδ τὰ πιστά.**

35 διότι καὶ ἐν ἑτέρῳ λέγει,

> **Οὐ δώσεις τὸν ὅσιόν σου ἰδεῖν διαφθοράν.**

36 Δαυὶδ μὲν γὰρ ἰδίᾳ γενεᾷ ὑπηρετήσας[d] τῇ τοῦ θεοῦ βουλῇ[d] ἐκοιμήθη καὶ προσετέθη πρὸς τοὺς πατέρας αὐτοῦ

---

[7] **33** {D} ἡμῖν 142 ‖ ἡμῶν p74 ℵ A B C* D Ψ itᵃʳ,ᶜ,ᵈ,ᵗ vg eth Hilary Ambrose Cosmos ‖ αὐτῶν 629 itᵍⁱᵍ copˢᵃ,ᵇᵒᵐˢˢ Ambrose ‖ αὐτῶν ἡμῖν C³ E P 049 056 0142 33 81 88 104 181 326 330 436 451 614 630 945 1241 1505 1739 1877 2127 2412 2492 2495 Byz Lectᵐ l¹⁴⁴³ itᵉ (syrᵖ·ʰ) arm geo Chrysostom Cosmos Greekᵃᶜᶜ· ᵗᵒ ᴮᵉᵈᵉ Theophylact ‖ omit copᵇᵒᵐˢˢ

[8] **33** {D} τῷ ψαλμῷ γέγραπται τῷ δευτέρῳ p74 ℵ A B C Ψ 33 81 181 326 630 945 1739 syrᵖ?ʰ? copˢᵃ?ᵇᵒ? arm eth? geo ‖ τῷ ψαλμῷ τῷ δευτέρῳ γέγραπται E P 049 (056 0142 l¹⁴⁴³ τῷ δευτέρῳ ψαλμῷ) 88 104 330 436 451 614 629 1241 1505 1877 2127 2412 2492 2495 Byz itᵃʳ,ᵉ vg syrᵖ?ʰ? copˢᵃ?ᵇᵒ? eth? Ambrose Chrysostom Cosmos ‖ τῷ πρώτῳ ψαλμῷ γέγραπται D itᵈ,ᵍⁱᵍ,ᵖʰᵐᵍ Origen Hilary Ps-Jerome Latin mssᵃᶜᶜ· ᵗᵒ ᴮᵉᵈᵉ ‖ τοῖς ψαλμοῖς γέγραπται p45 Tertullianᵖᵗ ‖ τῷ ψαλμῷ γέγραπται 522 1175 Hilary Hesychius Bede

---

ᶜᶜ **32-33** c number 33, c no number: TRᵉᵈ WH Bov Nes BF² AV RV ASV RSV NEB (TT) Zür Luth Jer Seg ‖ c no number, c number 33: TRᵉᵈ

ᵈ ᵈ **36** d none, d none: TR WH Bov Nes BF² ‖ d none, d minor: AV RV ASV RSV NEB TT Luth Jer Seg ‖ d minor, d none: RVᵐᵍ ASVᵐᵍ Zür

---

29 καθελόντες...μνημεῖον Mt 27.59–60; Mk 15.46; Lk 23.53; Jn 19.38, 41–42   **30** ὁ δὲ... νεκρῶν Ac 2.24, 32; 3.15; 4.10; 5.30; 10.40; 17.31   **31** ὃς ὤφθη...Ἰερουσαλήμ Ac 1.3 οἵτινες...μάρτυρες αὐτοῦ Lk 24.48; Ac 1.8; 2.32; 3.15; 5.32; 10.39, 41   **32-33** ἡμεῖς...Ἰησοῦν Ac 13.23   **33** Υἱός...σε Ps 2.7 (He 1.5; 5.5)   **34** Δώσω...πιστά Is 55.3 ʟxx   **35** Οὐ... διαφθοράν Ps 16.10 ʟxx   **36** Δαυὶδ...αὐτοῦ 1 Kgs 2.10; Ac 2.29   προσετέθη...αὐτοῦ Jdg 2.10

καὶ εἶδεν διαφθοράν, **37** ὃν δὲ ὁ θεὸς ἤγειρεν οὐκ εἶδεν διαφθοράν. **38** γνωστὸν οὖν ἔστω ὑμῖν, ἄνδρες ἀδελφοί, ὅτι διὰ τούτου ὑμῖν ἄφεσις ἁμαρτιῶν καταγγέλλεται[, *ᵉκαὶ*] ἀπὸ πάντων ὧν οὐκ ἠδυνήθητε ἐν νόμῳ Μωϋσέως δικαιωθῆναι **39**ᵉ ἐν τούτῳ πᾶς ὁ πιστεύων δικαιοῦται. **40** βλέπετε οὖν μὴ ἐπέλθῃ⁹ τὸ εἰρημένον ἐν τοῖς προφήταις,

41 Ἴδετε, οἱ καταφρονηταί,
    καὶ θαυμάσατε καὶ ἀφανίσθητε,
    ὅτι ἔργον ἐργάζομαι ἐγὼ ἐν ταῖς ἡμέραις ὑμῶν,
    ἔργον ὃ οὐ μὴ πιστεύσητε ἐάν τις ἐκδιηγῆται ὑμῖν.

42 Ἐξιόντων δὲ αὐτῶν¹⁰ παρεκάλουν εἰς τὸ μεταξὺ σάββατον¹¹ λαληθῆναι αὐτοῖς τὰ ῥήματα ταῦτα. **43** λυθείσης δὲ τῆς συναγωγῆς ἠκολούθησαν πολλοὶ τῶν Ἰουδαίων καὶ τῶν σεβομένων προσηλύτων τῷ Παύλῳ καὶ τῷ Βαρναβᾷ, οἵτινες προσλαλοῦντες αὐτοῖς ἔπειθον αὐτοὺς προσμένειν τῇ χάριτι τοῦ θεοῦ.

44 Τῷ δὲ ἐρχομένῳ σαββάτῳ σχεδὸν πᾶσα ἡ πόλις

⁹ **40** {C} ἐπέλθῃ 𝔭⁷⁴ (ℵ* ἀπέλθῃ) ℵᶜ B D 33 436 614 2412 itᵈ (Chrysostom ἐπελθοί) ‖ ἐπέλθῃ ἐφ' ὑμᾶς A C E P Ψ 049 056 097 0142 81 88 104 181 326 330 451 629 630 945 1241 1505 1739 1877 2127 2492 2495 *Byz* itᵃʳ,ᶜ,ᵉ,ᵍⁱᵍ vg syrᵖ,ʰ copˢᵃ,ᵇᵒ arm eth geo Cosmos

¹⁰ **42** {A} αὐτῶν 𝔭⁷⁴ ℵ A B C D E Ψ 097 33ᵛⁱᵈ? 81 104 181 326 436 614 629 630 945 1739 2412 itᵃʳ,ᵈ,ᵉ,ᵍⁱᵍ vg syr⁽ᵖ⁾,ʰ copˢᵃ,ᵇᵒ arm (eth) geo Chrysostom ‖ αὐτῶν ἐκ τῆς συναγωγῆς 241 489 927 1873 ‖ ἐκ τῆς συναγωγῆς τῶν Ἰουδαίων P 056 0142 330 451 1505 2127 2495 *Byz*ᵖᵗ Theophylactᵃ ‖ αὐτῶν ἐκ τῆς συναγωγῆς τῶν Ἰουδαίων 049 88 1241 1877 2492 *Byz*ᵖᵗ Theophylactᵇ

¹¹ **42** {C} παρεκάλουν εἰς τὸ μεταξὺ σάββατον 𝔭⁷⁴ ℵ A C (D τὸ ἑξῆς σάββατον) Ψ 097 0142 33 81 104 181 326 436 614 629 630 945 1739 2412 itᵃʳ,ᵈ,ᵍⁱᵍ vg syrᵖ,ʰ copˢᵃ arm eth Chrysostom ‖ παρεκάλουν τὰ ἔθνη εἰς τὸ μεταξὺ σάββατον P 049 056 88 330 451 1241 1505 1877 2127 2492 2495 *Byz* geo ‖ εἰς τὸ μεταξὺ σάββατον ἠξίουν B copᵇᵒ ‖ εἰς τὸ μεταξὺ σάββατον E itᵉ

ᵉ ᵉ **38–39** *e* no number, *e* number 39: TRᵉᵈ Bov Nes BF² Zür Luth Jer ‖ *e* number 39, *e* no number: TRᵉᵈ WH (AV) (RV) (ASV) (RSV) (NEB) (TT) Seg

38 διὰ...καταγγέλλεται Ac 10.43   ἀπὸ...δικαιωθῆναι He 9.9   **39** ἐν...δικαιοῦται Ro 4.25; 6.7; 10.4   **41** Hab 1.5   **43** ἔπειθον...θεοῦ Ac 11.23; 14.22

decay. **37** But the one whom God raised from the dead did not suffer decay. **38-39** All of you, my brothers, are to know for sure that it is through Jesus that the message about forgiveness of sins is preached to you; you are to know that everyone who believes in him is set free from all the sins from which the Law of Moses could not set you free. **40** Take care, then, so that what the prophets said may not happen to you:

41 'Look, you scorners! Wonder and die!
    For the work that I am doing in your own day
    Is something that you will not believe,
    Even when someone explains it to you!' "

42 As Paul and Barnabas were leaving the synagogue, the people invited them to come back the next Sabbath and tell them more about these things. **43** After the people had left the meeting, Paul and Barnabas were followed by many Jews and many Gentiles converted to Judaism. The apostles spoke to them and encouraged them to keep on living in the grace of God.

44 The next Sabbath day nearly everyone in the town came to hear the word of the Lord. ⁴⁵ When the Jews saw the crowds, they were filled with jealousy; they spoke against what Paul was saying and insulted him. ⁴⁶ But Paul and Barnabas spoke out even more boldly: "It was necessary that the word of God should be spoken first to you. But since you reject it, and do not consider yourselves worthy of eternal life, we will leave you and go to the Gentiles. ⁴⁷ For this is the commandment that the Lord has given us:

'I have set you to be a light for the Gentiles,
To be the way of salvation for the whole world.' "

⁴⁸ When the Gentiles heard this they rejoiced and praised the Lord's message; and those who had been chosen for eternal life became believers.

⁴⁹ The word of the Lord spread everywhere in that region. ⁵⁰ But the Jews stirred up the leading men of the city and the Gentile women of high society who worshiped God. They started a persecution against Paul and Barnabas, and threw them out of their region. ⁵¹ The apostles shook the dust off their feet against them and went on to Iconium. ⁵² The disciples in Antioch were full of joy and the Holy Spirit.

συνήχθη ἀκοῦσαι τὸν λόγον τοῦ κυρίου¹². **45** ἰδόντες δὲ οἱ Ἰουδαῖοι τοὺς ὄχλους ἐπλήσθησαν ζήλου καὶ ἀντέλεγον τοῖς ὑπὸ Παύλου λαλουμένοις βλασφημοῦντες¹³. **46** παρρησιασάμενοί τε ὁ Παῦλος καὶ ὁ Βαρναβᾶς εἶπαν, Ὑμῖν ἦν ἀναγκαῖον πρῶτον λαληθῆναι τὸν λόγον τοῦ θεοῦ· ἐπειδὴ ἀπωθεῖσθε αὐτὸν καὶ οὐκ ἀξίους κρίνετε ἑαυτοὺς τῆς αἰωνίου ζωῆς, ἰδοὺ στρεφόμεθα εἰς τὰ ἔθνη. **47** οὕτως γὰρ ἐντέταλται ἡμῖν ὁ κύριος,

Τέθεικά σε εἰς φῶς ἐθνῶν
  τοῦ εἶναί σε εἰς σωτηρίαν ἕως ἐσχάτου τῆς γῆς.

48 ἀκούοντα δὲ τὰ ἔθνη ἔχαιρον καὶ ἐδόξαζον τὸν λόγον τοῦ κυρίου¹⁴, καὶ ἐπίστευσαν ὅσοι ἦσαν τεταγμένοι εἰς ζωὴν αἰώνιον· **49** διεφέρετο δὲ ὁ λόγος τοῦ κυρίου δι᾽ ὅλης τῆς χώρας. **50** οἱ δὲ Ἰουδαῖοι παρώτρυναν τὰς σεβομένας γυναῖκας τὰς εὐσχήμονας καὶ τοὺς πρώτους τῆς πόλεως καὶ ἐπήγειραν διωγμὸν ἐπὶ τὸν Παῦλον καὶ Βαρναβᾶν, καὶ ἐξέβαλον αὐτοὺς ἀπὸ τῶν ὁρίων αὐτῶν. **51** οἱ δὲ ἐκτιναξάμενοι τὸν κονιορτὸν τῶν ποδῶν ἐπ᾽ αὐτοὺς ἦλθον εἰς Ἰκόνιον, **52** οἵ τε μαθηταὶ ἐπληροῦντο χαρᾶς καὶ πνεύματος ἁγίου.

---

¹² **44** {C} τὸν λόγον τοῦ κυρίου 𝔭⁷⁴ ℵ A B³ 81 181 326 630 945 1739 itᵃʳ,ᵍⁱᵍ vgʷʷ copˢᵃ geo ‖ τὸν λόγον τοῦ θεοῦ (*see* 13.46) B* C E P Ψ 049 056 0142 88 104 330 436 451 614 629 1241 1505 1877 2127 2412 (2492 τῶν λόγων) 2495 *Byz* itᵉ,ᵖʰ vgᵉˡ syrᵖ,ʰ copᵇᵒ arm eth Chrysostom ‖ Παύλου πολύν τε λόγον ποιησαμένου περὶ τοῦ κυρίου D (itᵈ)

¹³ **45** {B} βλασφημοῦντες 𝔭⁷⁴ ℵ A B C Ψ 097 33 81 88 326 436* 629 630 945 1505 1739 2495 itᵃʳ vg syrᵖ copˢᵃ,ᵇᵒ arm eth geo ‖ ἀντιλέγοντες καὶ βλασφημοῦντες D P 049 056 0142 104 181 330 436ᶜ 451 614 1241 1877 2127 2412 2492 *Byz* itᵈ syrʰ Chrysostom Theophylact ‖ ἐναντιούμενοι καὶ βλασφημοῦντες E itᵉ,ᵍⁱᵍ

¹⁴ **48** {C} τὸν λόγον τοῦ κυρίου 𝔭⁴⁵,⁷⁴ ℵ A C P Ψ 056 0142 33 81 104 181 (326 καὶ τόν) 330 436 451 (629 τοῦ κυρίου τὸν λόγον) 630 945 1241 1505 1739 1877 2127 2495 *Byz* itᵈ,ᵉ,ᵍⁱᵍ vg copˢᵃ arm geo Chrysostom ‖ τὸν λόγον τοῦ θεοῦ B Dᵍʳ Eᵍʳ 049 88 2492 copˢᵃᵐˢ,ᵇᵒ Augustine ‖ τὸν θεόν 614 2412 syrᵖ,ʰ eth ‖ τὸν κύριον itᵃʳ

---

45 Ac 14.2　　**46** Ὑμῖν...θεοῦ Ac 3.26; Ro 1.16　ἐπειδὴ...ζωῆς Lk 7.30　ἐπειδὴ...ἔθνη Ac 18.6　　**47** Τέθεικα...γῆς Is 49.6　　**48** Ac 11.18　　**50** γυναῖκας...πρώτους Ac 17.4, 12　**51** ἐκτιναξάμενοι...αὐτούς Mt 10.14; Mk 6.11; Lk 9.5; 10.11; Ac 18.6

Paul and Barnabas at Iconium

14 Ἐγένετο δὲ ἐν Ἰκονίῳ κατὰ τὸ αὐτὸ εἰσελθεῖν αὐτοὺς εἰς τὴν συναγωγὴν τῶν Ἰουδαίων καὶ λαλῆσαι οὕτως ὥστε πιστεῦσαι Ἰουδαίων τε καὶ Ἑλλήνων πολὺ πλῆθος. **2** οἱ δὲ ἀπειθήσαντες Ἰουδαῖοι ἐπήγειραν καὶ ἐκάκωσαν τὰς ψυχὰς τῶν ἐθνῶν κατὰ τῶν ἀδελφῶν. **3** ἱκανὸν μὲν οὖν χρόνον διέτριψαν παρρησιαζόμενοι ἐπὶ τῷ κυρίῳ τῷ μαρτυροῦντι τῷ λόγῳ τῆς χάριτος αὐτοῦ, διδόντι σημεῖα καὶ τέρατα γίνεσθαι διὰ τῶν χειρῶν αὐτῶν. **4** ἐσχίσθη δὲ τὸ πλῆθος τῆς πόλεως, καὶ οἱ μὲν ἦσαν σὺν τοῖς Ἰουδαίοις οἱ δὲ σὺν τοῖς ἀποστόλοις. **5** ὡς δὲ ἐγένετο ὁρμὴ τῶν ἐθνῶν τε καὶ Ἰουδαίων σὺν τοῖς ἄρχουσιν αὐτῶν ὑβρίσαι καὶ λιθοβολῆσαι αὐτούς, **6** συνιδόντες κατέφυγον εἰς τὰς πόλεις τῆς Λυκαονίας Λύστραν καὶ Δέρβην καὶ τὴν περίχωρον, **7** κἀκεῖ εὐαγγελιζόμενοι ἦσαν.

Paul and Barnabas at Lystra

8 Καί τις ἀνὴρ ἀδύνατος ἐν Λύστροις τοῖς ποσὶν ἐκάθητο, χωλὸς ἐκ κοιλίας μητρὸς αὐτοῦ, ὃς οὐδέποτε περιεπάτησεν. **9** οὗτος ἤκουσεν τοῦ Παύλου λαλοῦντος· ὃς ἀτενίσας αὐτῷ καὶ ἰδὼν ὅτι ἔχει πίστιν τοῦ σωθῆναι **10** εἶπεν μεγάλῃ φωνῇ, Ἀνάστηθι ἐπὶ τοὺς πόδας σου ὀρθός. καὶ ἥλατο καὶ περιεπάτει. **11** οἵ τε ὄχλοι ἰδόντες ὃ ἐποίησεν Παῦλος ἐπῆραν τὴν φωνὴν αὐτῶν Λυκαονιστὶ λέγοντες, Οἱ θεοὶ ὁμοιωθέντες ἀνθρώποις κατέβησαν πρὸς ἡμᾶς· **12** ἐκάλουν τε τὸν Βαρναβᾶν Δία, τὸν δὲ Παῦλον Ἑρμῆν, ἐπειδὴ αὐτὸς ἦν ὁ ἡγούμενος τοῦ λόγου. **13** ὅ τε ἱερεὺς τοῦ Διὸς τοῦ ὄντος πρὸ τῆς πόλεως ταύρους καὶ στέμματα ἐπὶ τοὺς πυλῶνας ἐνέγκας σὺν τοῖς ὄχλοις ἤθελεν θύειν. **14** ἀκούσαντες δὲ οἱ ἀπόστολοι Βαρναβᾶς

2 Ac 13.45　**3** ἐπὶ...αὐτῶν Mk 16.20; Ac 19.11; He 2.4　**5** ὁρμὴ...αὐτούς Ac 14.19; 2 Tm 3.11　**6** Mt 10.23　**8** χωλὸς...αὐτοῦ Jn 9.1; Ac 3.2　**9** ἰδὼν...σωθῆναι Mt 9.28　**11** Οἱ θεοὶ...ἡμᾶς Ac 28.6

In Iconium

14 The same thing happened in Iconium: Paul and Barnabas went to the Jewish synagogue and spoke in such a way that a great number of Jews and Gentiles became believers. [2] But the Jews who would not believe stirred up the Gentiles and turned their feelings against the brothers. [3] The apostles stayed there for a long time. They spoke boldly about the Lord, who proved that their message about his grace was true by giving them the power to perform miracles and wonders. [4] The crowd in the city was divided: some were for the Jews, others for the apostles.

[5] Then the Gentiles and the Jews, together with their leaders, decided to mistreat the apostles and stone them. [6] When the apostles learned about it they fled to Lystra and Derbe, cities in Lycaonia, and to the surrounding territory. [7] There they preached the Good News.

In Lystra and Derbe

[8] There was a man sitting in Lystra whose feet were crippled; he had been lame from birth and had never been able to walk. [9] He listened to Paul's words. Paul saw that he believed and could be healed, so he looked straight at him [10] and said in a loud voice, "Stand up straight on your feet!" The man jumped up and started walking around. [11] When the crowds saw what Paul had done, they started to shout in their own Lycaonian language, "The gods have become like men and have come down to us!" [12] They gave Barnabas the name Zeus, and Paul the name Hermes, because he was the one who did the speaking. [13] The priest of the god Zeus, whose temple stood just outside the town, brought bulls and flowers to the gate. He and the crowds wanted to offer sacrifice to the apostles. [14] When Barnabas and Paul heard what

they were about to do, they tore their clothes and ran into the middle of the crowd, shouting: [15] "Why are you doing this, men? We are just men, human beings like you! We are here to announce the Good News, to turn you away from these worthless things to the living God, who made heaven, earth, sea, and all that is in them. [16] In the past he allowed all peoples to go their own way. [17] But he has always given proof of himself by the good things he does: he gives you rain from heaven and crops at the right times; he gives you food and fills your hearts with happiness." [18] Even with these words the apostles could hardly keep the crowds from offering a sacrifice to them.

[19] Some Jews came from Antioch of Pisidia and from Iconium; they won the crowds to their side, stoned Paul and dragged him out of town, thinking that he was dead. [20] But when the believers gathered around him, he got up and went back into the town. The next day he and Barnabas went to Derbe.

καὶ Παῦλος, διαρρήξαντες τὰ ἱμάτια αὐτῶν ἐξεπήδησαν εἰς τὸν ὄχλον, κράζοντες 15 καὶ λέγοντες, Ἄνδρες, τί ταῦτα ποιεῖτε; καὶ ἡμεῖς ὁμοιοπαθεῖς ἐσμεν ὑμῖν ἄνθρωποι, εὐαγγελιζόμενοι ὑμᾶς ἀπὸ τούτων τῶν ματαίων ἐπιστρέφειν ἐπὶ θεὸν ζῶντα **ὃς ἐποίησεν τὸν οὐρανὸν καὶ τὴν γῆν καὶ τὴν θάλασσαν καὶ πάντα τὰ ἐν αὐτοῖς·** 16 ὃς ἐν ταῖς παρῳχημέναις γενεαῖς εἴασεν πάντα τὰ ἔθνη πορεύεσθαι ταῖς ὁδοῖς αὐτῶν· 17 καίτοι οὐκ ἀμάρτυρον αὐτὸν ἀφῆκεν ἀγαθουργῶν, οὐρανόθεν ὑμῖν ὑετοὺς διδοὺς καὶ καιροὺς καρποφόρους, ἐμπιπλῶν τροφῆς καὶ εὐφροσύνης τὰς καρδίας ὑμῶν. 18 καὶ ταῦτα λέγοντες μόλις κατέπαυσαν τοὺς ὄχλους τοῦ μὴ θύειν αὐτοῖς[1].

19 Ἐπῆλθαν δὲ[2] ἀπὸ Ἀντιοχείας καὶ Ἰκονίου Ἰουδαῖοι, καὶ πείσαντες τοὺς ὄχλους[3] καὶ λιθάσαντες τὸν Παῦλον ἔσυρον ἔξω τῆς πόλεως, νομίζοντες αὐτὸν τεθνηκέναι. 20 κυκλωσάντων δὲ τῶν μαθητῶν αὐτὸν ἀναστὰς εἰσῆλθεν εἰς τὴν πόλιν. καὶ τῇ ἐπαύριον ἐξῆλθεν σὺν τῷ Βαρναβᾷ εἰς Δέρβην.

---

[1] **18** {C} αὐτοῖς 𝔓45vid,74 ℵ A B D E P Ψ 049 056 0142 181 330 451 629 945 1241 1505 1739 1877* 2127 2492 2495 *Byz Lect* (*l*1021 αὐτούς) itar,d,e,gig vg syrp,h copsa,bo ‖ αὐτοῖς ἀλλὰ πορεύεσθαι ἕκαστον εἰς τὰ ἴδια C 33 81 88 104 326 436 614 630 1877c 2412 (ith) syrhmg arm geo

[2] **19** {C} ἐπῆλθαν δέ (𝔓45 ἀπῆλθον) 𝔓74vid ℵ A B P Ψ 049 056 0142 104 330 451 614 629 1241 1505 2127 2412 2492 2495 *Byz* itar,gig vg syrp,h copsa,bo eth Chrysostom ‖ διατριβόντων δὲ αὐτῶν καὶ διδασκόντων ἐπῆλθον (C *omit* καί) (Dgr* *omit* δέ) (E *add* τινες) 33 81 88 326 436 630 945 1739 1877 it(d),e syrhmg arm geo Cassiodorus Greekacc. to Bede ‖ διατριβόντων δὲ αὐτῶν ἐκεῖ καὶ διδασκόντων ἐπῆλθον 181

[3] **19** {C} καὶ πείσαντες τοὺς ὄχλους 𝔓45vid,74 ℵ A B (D ἐπεισείσαντες) E P Ψ 049 056 0142 33 330 451 614 629 1241 1505 1877 (2127 *omit* καί) 2412 2492 2495 *Byz* itar,(d),e,gig vg syrp,h copsa,bo ‖ καὶ διαλεγομένων αὐτῶν παρρησίᾳ ἔπεισαν τοὺς ὄχλους ἀποστῆναι ἀπ' αὐτῶν λέγοντες, ὅτι οὐδὲν ἀληθὲς λέγουσιν ἀλλὰ πάντα ψεύδονται C (81 ἀνέπεισαν and ἄπαντα) (88 καὶ πείσαντες) (104 ἀλήθειαν) (181 630 945 ἀνέπεισαν) (326 ἀνέπεισαν and *omit* ἀπ') (436 καὶ πείσαντες and *omit* πάντα) 1739 (ith) syrhmg arm geo

---

15 ἡμεῖς...ἄνθρωποι Ac 10.26; Jas 5.17   θεὸν...αὐτοῖς Ex 20.11; Ps 146.6   **16** Ac 17.30   **17** οὐρανόθεν...καρποφόρους Ps 147.8; Jr 5.24   **19** Ἐπῆλθαν...ὄχλους Ac 17.13   λιθάσαντες τὸν Παῦλον 2 Cor 11.25; 2 Tm 3.11

The Return to Antioch in Syria

21 Εὐαγγελισάμενοί τε τὴν πόλιν ἐκείνην καὶ μαθητεύσαντες ἱκανοὺς ὑπέστρεψαν εἰς τὴν Λύστραν καὶ εἰς Ἰκόνιον καὶ εἰς Ἀντιόχειαν, **22** ἐπιστηρίζοντες τὰς ψυχὰς τῶν μαθητῶν, παρακαλοῦντες ἐμμένειν τῇ πίστει, καὶ ὅτι[a] διὰ πολλῶν θλίψεων δεῖ ἡμᾶς εἰσελθεῖν εἰς τὴν βασιλείαν τοῦ θεοῦ. **23** χειροτονήσαντες δὲ αὐτοῖς κατ' ἐκκλησίαν πρεσβυτέρους προσευξάμενοι μετὰ νηστειῶν παρέθεντο αὐτοὺς τῷ κυρίῳ εἰς ὃν πεπιστεύκεισαν. **24** καὶ διελθόντες τὴν Πισιδίαν ἦλθον εἰς τὴν Παμφυλίαν, **25** καὶ λαλήσαντες ἐν Πέργῃ τὸν λόγον κατέβησαν εἰς Ἀττάλειαν. **26** κἀκεῖθεν ἀπέπλευσαν εἰς Ἀντιόχειαν, ὅθεν ἦσαν παραδεδομένοι τῇ χάριτι τοῦ θεοῦ εἰς τὸ ἔργον ὃ ἐπλήρωσαν. **27** παραγενόμενοι δὲ καὶ συναγαγόντες τὴν ἐκκλησίαν ἀνήγγελλον ὅσα ἐποίησεν ὁ θεὸς μετ' αὐτῶν καὶ ὅτι ἤνοιξεν τοῖς ἔθνεσιν θύραν πίστεως. **28** διέτριβον δὲ χρόνον οὐκ ὀλίγον σὺν τοῖς μαθηταῖς.

The Council at Jerusalem

15 Καί τινες κατελθόντες ἀπὸ τῆς Ἰουδαίας ἐδίδασκον τοὺς ἀδελφοὺς ὅτι Ἐὰν μὴ περιτμηθῆτε τῷ ἔθει τῷ Μωϋσέως, οὐ δύνασθε σωθῆναι. **2** γενομένης δὲ στάσεως καὶ ζητήσεως οὐκ ὀλίγης τῷ Παύλῳ καὶ τῷ Βαρναβᾷ πρὸς αὐτοὺς ἔταξαν ἀναβαίνειν Παῦλον καὶ Βαρναβᾶν καί τινας ἄλλους ἐξ αὐτῶν πρὸς τοὺς ἀποστόλους καὶ πρεσβυτέρους εἰς Ἰερουσαλὴμ περὶ τοῦ ζητήματος τούτου. **3** Οἱ μὲν οὖν προπεμφθέντες ὑπὸ τῆς ἐκκλησίας διήρχοντο

---

a **22** *a* indirect: WH Bov Nes? BF² AV RV ASV RSV NEB Zür Luth ǁ *a* causal and direct: TR Jer ǁ *a* direct: Nes? TT Seg

22 1 Th 3.3   ἐπιστηρίζοντες...μαθητῶν Ac 15.32; 18.23   παρακαλοῦντες...πίστει Ac 11.23; 13.43   **23** προσευξάμενοι μετὰ νηστειῶν Ac 13.3   **26** εἰς Ἀντιόχειαν... ἐπλήρωσαν Ac 13.1-2; 15.40   **27** παραγενόμενοι...αὐτῶν Ac 15.4, 12   ἤνοιξεν...πίστεως Ac 11.18; 13.47-48   **15** 1 Ga 5.2 Ἐὰν...Μωϋσέως Lv 12.3   **2** ἔταξαν...Ἰερουσαλήμ Ac 11.30; Ga 2.1

The Return to Antioch in Syria

21 Paul and Barnabas preached the Good News in Derbe, and won many disciples. Then they went back to Lystra, then to Iconium, and then to Antioch of Pisidia. **22** They strengthened the believers and encouraged them to remain true to the faith. "We must pass through many troubles to enter the Kingdom of God," they taught. **23** In each church they appointed elders for them; and with prayers and fasting they commended them to the Lord in whom they had put their trust.

24 After going through the territory of Pisidia, they came to Pamphylia. **25** They preached the message in Perga and then went down to Attalia, **26** and from there they sailed back to Antioch, the place where they had been commended to the care of God's grace for the work they had now completed.

27 When they arrived in Antioch they gathered the people of the church together and told them of all that God had done with them, and how he had opened the way for the Gentiles to believe. **28** They stayed a long time there with the believers.

The Meeting at Jerusalem

15 Some men came from Judea to Antioch and started teaching the brothers: "You cannot be saved unless you are circumcised as the Law of Moses requires." **2** Paul and Barnabas had a fierce argument and dispute with them about this; so it was decided that Paul and Barnabas and some of the others in Antioch should go to Jerusalem and see the apostles and elders about this matter.

3 They were sent on their way by the

church, and as they went through Phoenicia and Samaria they reported how the Gentiles had turned to God; this news brought great joy to all the brothers. [4] When they arrived in Jerusalem, they were welcomed by the church, the apostles, and the elders, to whom they told all that God had done with them. [5] But some of the believers who belonged to the party of the Pharisees stood up and said, "They have to be circumcised and told to obey the Law of Moses."

[6] The apostles and the elders met together to consider this question. [7] After a long debate Peter stood up and said: "My brothers, you know that a long time ago God chose me from among you to preach the message of Good News to the Gentiles, so that they could hear and believe. [8] And God, who knows the hearts of men, showed his approval of the Gentiles by giving the Holy Spirit to them, just as he had to us. [9] He made no difference between us and them; he forgave them their sins because they believed. [10] So then, why do you want to put God to the test now by laying a load on the backs of the believers which neither our ancestors nor we ourselves were able to carry? [11] No! We believe and are saved by the grace of the Lord Jesus, just as they are."

[12] The whole group was silent as they heard Barnabas and Paul report all the wonders and miracles that God had done through them among the

τήν τε Φοινίκην καὶ Σαμάρειαν ἐκδιηγούμενοι τὴν ἐπιστροφὴν τῶν ἐθνῶν, καὶ ἐποίουν χαρὰν μεγάλην πᾶσιν τοῖς ἀδελφοῖς. **4** παραγενόμενοι δὲ εἰς Ἰερουσαλὴμ παρεδέχθησαν ἀπὸ τῆς ἐκκλησίας καὶ τῶν ἀποστόλων καὶ τῶν πρεσβυτέρων, ἀνήγγειλάν τε ὅσα ὁ θεὸς ἐποίησεν μετ' αὐτῶν. **5** ἐξανέστησαν δέ τινες τῶν ἀπὸ τῆς αἱρέσεως τῶν Φαρισαίων πεπιστευκότες, λέγοντες ὅτι[a] δεῖ περιτέμνειν αὐτοὺς παραγγέλλειν τε τηρεῖν τὸν νόμον Μωϋσέως.

6 Συνήχθησαν δὲ οἱ ἀπόστολοι καὶ οἱ πρεσβύτεροι ἰδεῖν περὶ τοῦ λόγου τούτου. **7** πολλῆς δὲ ζητήσεως γενομένης ἀναστὰς Πέτρος εἶπεν πρὸς αὐτούς, Ἄνδρες ἀδελφοί, ὑμεῖς ἐπίστασθε ὅτι ἀφ' ἡμερῶν ἀρχαίων ἐν ὑμῖν ἐξελέξατο ὁ θεὸς[1] διὰ τοῦ στόματός μου ἀκοῦσαι τὰ ἔθνη τὸν λόγον τοῦ εὐαγγελίου καὶ πιστεῦσαι· **8** καὶ ὁ καρδιογνώστης θεὸς ἐμαρτύρησεν αὐτοῖς δοὺς τὸ πνεῦμα τὸ ἅγιον καθὼς καὶ ἡμῖν, **9** καὶ οὐθὲν διέκρινεν μεταξὺ ἡμῶν τε καὶ αὐτῶν, τῇ πίστει καθαρίσας τὰς καρδίας αὐτῶν. **10** νῦν οὖν τί πειράζετε τὸν θεόν, ἐπιθεῖναι ζυγὸν ἐπὶ τὸν τράχηλον τῶν μαθητῶν ὃν οὔτε οἱ πατέρες ἡμῶν οὔτε ἡμεῖς ἰσχύσαμεν βαστάσαι; **11** ἀλλὰ διὰ τῆς χάριτος τοῦ κυρίου Ἰησοῦ πιστεύομεν σωθῆναι καθ' ὃν τρόπον κἀκεῖνοι.

12 Ἐσίγησεν δὲ πᾶν τὸ πλῆθος, καὶ ἤκουον Βαρναβᾶ καὶ Παύλου ἐξηγουμένων ὅσα ἐποίησεν ὁ θεὸς σημεῖα καὶ

---

[1] **7** {B} ἐν ὑμῖν ἐξελέξατο ὁ θεός 𝔭[74] ℵ A B C 33 81 88 181 436 630 945 1739 *l*[147] it[ar] (cop[bo]) arm geo (Irenaeus[lat]) Apostolic Constitutions Chrysostom ∥ ὁ θεὸς ἐν ἡμῖν ἐξελέξατο E P 049 (056 0142 *omit ἐν*) 104 330 451 1241 1505 1877 2127 2495 *Byz Lect* it[e] vg[cl] syr[h] ∥ ἡμῖν ὁ θεὸς ἐξελέξατο D[gr*] (D[c] it[d.gig] ἐν ἡμῖν) 614 2412 ∥ ἐν ἡμῖν ἐξελέξατο ὁ θεός Ψ 326 629 it[l] vg[ww] (Rebaptism) ∥ ὁ θεὸς ἐξελέξατο 2492 *l*[1356] vg[mss] syr[p] cop[sa] eth

---

[a] **5** *a* indirect: WH Bov Nes? BF[2] AV? Jer Seg ∥ *a* direct: TR AV? RV ASV RSV NEB TT Zür Luth

---

4 Ac 14.27; 15.12   **7–8** ἀναστὰς...ἡμῖν Ac 2.4; 10.44; 11.15   **9** οὐθὲν...καὶ αὐτῶν Ac 10.34–35   **10** ἐπιθεῖναι...μαθητῶν Ac 15.19; Ga 5.1   **11** Ga 2.16; Eph 2.5–8   **12** ἤκουον ...αὐτῶν Ac 14.27; 15.4

τέρατα ἐν τοῖς ἔθνεσιν δι' αὐτῶν. 13 Μετὰ δὲ τὸ σιγῆσαι αὐτοὺς ἀπεκρίθη Ἰάκωβος λέγων, Ἄνδρες ἀδελφοί, ἀκούσατέ μου. 14 Συμεὼν ἐξηγήσατο καθὼς πρῶτον ὁ θεὸς ἐπεσκέψατο λαβεῖν ἐξ ἐθνῶν λαὸν τῷ ὀνόματι αὐτοῦ. 15 καὶ τούτῳ συμφωνοῦσιν οἱ λόγοι τῶν προφητῶν, καθὼς γέγραπται,

16   Μετὰ ταῦτα ἀναστρέψω
     καὶ ἀνοικοδομήσω τὴν σκηνὴν Δαυὶδ τὴν πεπτωκυῖαν,
     καὶ τὰ κατεσκαμμένα αὐτῆς ἀνοικοδομήσω
      καὶ ἀνορθώσω αὐτήν,

17   ὅπως ἂν ἐκζητήσωσιν οἱ κατάλοιποι τῶν ἀνθρώπων
      τὸν κύριον,
     καὶ πάντα τὰ ἔθνη ἐφ' οὓς ἐπικέκληται τὸ ὄνομά
      μου ἐπ' αὐτούς,
       λέγει κύριος ποιῶν ταῦτα 18 γνωστὰ ἀπ'
       αἰῶνος[2].

19 διὸ ἐγὼ κρίνω μὴ παρενοχλεῖν τοῖς ἀπὸ τῶν ἐθνῶν ἐπιστρέφουσιν ἐπὶ τὸν θεόν, 20 ἀλλὰ ἐπιστεῖλαι αὐτοῖς τοῦ ἀπέχεσθαι τῶν ἀλισγημάτων τῶν εἰδώλων καὶ τῆς πορνείας[3] καὶ τοῦ πνικτοῦ[4] καὶ τοῦ αἵματος[5]· 21 Μωϋσῆς

---

[2] 18 {C} γνωστὰ ἀπ' αἰῶνος ℵ B C Ψ 33 81 630 1505 1739 2495 cop[sa,bo] arm (geo? γνωστὰ πάντα) Didascalia ‖ ἅ ἐστιν γνωστὰ αὐτῷ ἀπ' αἰῶνος 945 (eth) ‖ πάντα τὰ ἔργα αὐτοῦ 2127 ‖ γνωστά ἐστιν κυρίῳ τὰ ἔργα αὐτοῦ 629* ‖ γνωστά ἐστιν ἀπ' αἰῶνος τῷ κυρίῳ τὰ ἔργα αὐτοῦ 629[c] ‖ γνωστὸν ἀπ' αἰῶνός ἐστιν τῷ κυρίῳ τὸ ἔργον αὐτοῦ (𝔭[74] A omit ἐστιν) D it[d.1] vg (syr[hmg]) (Irenaeus[lat]) ‖ γνωστὰ ἀπ' αἰῶνός ἐστι τῷ θεῷ πάντα τὰ ἔργα αὐτοῦ E P 049 056 0142 88 (104 ἀπὸ τοῦ) (181 1877 omit πάντα) 326 330 436 451 614 1241 2412 2492 Byz it[e.(gig)] syr[(p),h] Apostolic Constitutions Chrysostom

[3] 20 {B} καὶ τῆς πορνείας (see footnotes 4 and 5) 𝔭[74] ℵ A B C D E P Ψ 049 056 0142 33 81 88 104 181 326 330 436 451 614 629 (630 1739 transpose: καὶ τοῦ αἵματος καὶ τοῦ πνικτοῦ καὶ τῆς πορνείας) 945 1241 1505 1877 2127 2412 2492 2495 Byz it[ar.d.e,gig,1] vg syr[p.h] cop[sa,bo] eth[pp] geo ‖ omit 𝔭[45] arm eth[ro] Origen?

[4] 20 {C} καὶ τοῦ πνικτοῦ (see footnotes 3 and 5) 𝔭[45] ℵ C E P 049

---

14 Ac 15.7–9 ὁ θεὸς...λαόν Lk 1.68   16–17 Am 9.11–12   18 γνῶστα ἀπ' αἰῶνος Is 45.21   19 Ac 15.10   20 τοῦ αἵματος Gn 9.4; Lv 3.17; 17.10–14   21 Ac 13.15

Gentiles. 13 When they finished speaking, James spoke up: "Listen to me, brothers! 14 Simon has just explained how God first showed his care for the Gentiles by taking from among them a people to be all his own. 15 The words of the prophets agree completely with this. As the scripture says:

16 'After this I will return, says the
     Lord,
   And I will raise David's fallen house;
   I will restore its ruins
   And build it up again.
17 And so all other people will seek the
     Lord,
   All the nations whom I have called
     to be my own.
18 So says the Lord, who made this
     known long ago.'

19 "It is my opinion," James went on, "that we should not trouble the Gentiles who are turning to God. 20 Instead, we should write a letter telling them not to eat any food that is unclean because it has been offered to idols; to keep themselves from immorality; not to eat any animal that has been strangled, or any blood. 21 For the Law of Moses has been

read for a very long time in the synagogues every Sabbath, and his words are
preached in every town."

The Letter to the Gentile Believers

[22] Then the apostles and the elders,
together with the whole church, decided
to choose some men from the group and
send them to Antioch with Paul and
Barnabas. They chose Judas, called
Barsabbas, and Silas, two men who
were highly respected by the brothers.
[23] They sent the following letter by them:
"The apostles and the elders, your

γὰρ ἐκ γενεῶν ἀρχαίων κατὰ πόλιν τοὺς κηρύσσοντας
αὐτὸν ἔχει ἐν ταῖς συναγωγαῖς κατὰ πᾶν σάββατον
ἀναγινωσκόμενος.

The Reply of the Council

22 Τότε ἔδοξε τοῖς ἀποστόλοις καὶ τοῖς πρεσβυτέροις
σὺν ὅλῃ τῇ ἐκκλησίᾳ ἐκλεξαμένους ἄνδρας ἐξ αὐτῶν
πέμψαι εἰς Ἀντιόχειαν σὺν τῷ Παύλῳ καὶ Βαρναβᾷ,
Ἰούδαν τὸν καλούμενον Βαρσαββᾶν καὶ Σίλαν, ἄνδρας
ἡγουμένους ἐν τοῖς ἀδελφοῖς, **23** γράψαντες διὰ χειρὸς
αὐτῶν[6], Οἱ ἀπόστολοι καὶ οἱ πρεσβύτεροι[b] ἀδελφοί[7] [b]

056 0142 88 104 181 326 330 436 451 614 629 (630) 945 1241 1505 (1739) 1877
2127 2412 2492 2495 *Byz* Chrysostom ∥ καὶ πνικτοῦ 𝔭[74] A B Ψ 33 81 (Apostolic
Constitutions) ∥ καὶ (*or* καὶ τοῦ) πνικτοῦ it[ar,e,l] vg syr[p,h] cop[sa,bo] arm geo ∥
omit D it[d,gig] Aristides Irenaeus[lat] Ambrosiaster Ephraem Ambrose
Augustine

[5] **20** {A} αἵματος (*see footnotes 3 and 4*) 𝔭[45,74] ℵ A B C E P Ψ 049
056 0142 33 81 88 104 181 326 330 436 451 614 629 1241 1505 1877 2127 2412 2492
2495 *Byz* it[e,gig,l] vg syr[p,h] cop[bo] arm geo ∥ αἵματος καὶ ὅσα ἂν μὴ θέλωσιν
ἑαυτοῖς γίνεσθαι ἑτέροις μὴ ποιεῖν (*see* 15.29 *mg*) (D ὅσα μὴ θέλωσιν...
ποιεῖτε) (630) (945 αὐτοῖς) (1739) it[ar,(d)] (cop[sa]) eth Aristides Irenaeus[lat]
Porphyry Eusebius Ephraem

[6] **23** {B} διὰ χειρὸς αὐτῶν 𝔭[33vid,45vid,74] ℵ* A B 629 it[l] vg cop[bo] eth[ro] ∥
διὰ χειρὸς αὐτῶν τάδε ℵ[c] E P 049 056 0142 (33 χειρῶν) 81 88 104 181 326
330 436 451 630 945 1241 (1505 2495 ταῦτα *for* τάδε) 1739 1877 2127 2492
Byz it[e] syr[p,h] arm Apostolic Constitutions Chrysostom ∥ διὰ χειρὸς
αὐτῶν ἐπιστολὴν περιέχουσαν τάδε C it[ar,c,gig,w] (cop[sa] *omit* περιέχουσαν)
eth[pp] geo ∥ ἐπιστολὴν διὰ χειρὸς αὐτῶν περιέχουσαν τάδε D it[d] ∥ διὰ
χειρὸς αὐτῶν ἐπιστολὴν καὶ πέμψαντες περιέχουσαν τάδε 614 2412
syr[hmg] ∥ ἐπιστολὴν διὰ χειρὸς αὐτῶν ἔχουσαν τὸν τύπον τοῦτον (*see*
23.25) Ψ

[7] **23** {B} ἀδελφοί 𝔭[33,74] ℵ* A B C D 33 81 it[(ar),d,gig,l] vg cop[bo]? Irenaeus[lat]
Origen Athanasius Pacian Vigilius ∥ καὶ οἱ ἀδελφοί ℵ[c] E P Ψ 049 056
0142 88 104 181 326 330 436 451 614 (629 *omit* οἱ) 630 945 1241 1505 1739 1877
2127 2412 2492 2495 *Byz* it[e] syr[p,h] cop[bomss] arm eth geo Apostolic Constitutions Chrysostom ∥ *omit* 61 467 2138[c] cop[sa] Origen[lat]

---

b b **23** *b* none, *b* none: WH Bov Nes BF² RV ASV[mg] TT ∥ *b* minor, *b* minor: ASV RSV NEB Zür
Luth Jer Seg ∥ different text: TR AV

τοῖς κατὰ τὴν ᾿Αντιόχειαν καὶ Συρίαν καὶ Κιλικίαν ἀδελφοῖς τοῖς ἐξ ἐθνῶν χαίρειν. 24 ᾿Επειδὴ ἠκούσαμεν ὅτι τινὲς ἐξ ἡμῶν [ἐξελθόντες][8] ἐτάραξαν ὑμᾶς λόγοις ἀνασκευάζοντες τὰς ψυχὰς ὑμῶν[9], οἷς οὐ διεστειλάμεθα, 25 ἔδοξεν ἡμῖν γενομένοις ὁμοθυμαδὸν ἐκλεξαμένους[10] ἄνδρας πέμψαι πρὸς ὑμᾶς σὺν τοῖς ἀγαπητοῖς ἡμῶν Βαρναβᾷ καὶ Παύλῳ, 26 ἀνθρώποις παραδεδωκόσι τὰς ψυχὰς αὐτῶν ὑπὲρ τοῦ ὀνόματος τοῦ κυρίου ἡμῶν ᾿Ιησοῦ Χριστοῦ. 27 ἀπεστάλκαμεν οὖν ᾿Ιούδαν καὶ Σίλαν, καὶ αὐτοὺς διὰ λόγου ἀπαγγέλλοντας τὰ αὐτά. 28 ἔδοξεν γὰρ τῷ πνεύματι τῷ ἁγίῳ καὶ ἡμῖν μηδὲν πλέον ἐπιτίθεσθαι ὑμῖν βάρος πλὴν τούτων τῶν ἐπάναγκες, 29 ἀπέχεσθαι εἰδωλοθύτων καὶ αἵματος καὶ πνικτῶν[11] καὶ

brothers, send their greetings to all brothers of Gentile birth who live in Antioch and Syria and Cilicia. 24 We have heard that some men of our group went out and troubled and upset you by what they said; they had not, however, received any instructions from us to do this. 25 And so we have met together and have all agreed to choose some messengers and send them to you. They will go with our dear friends Barnabas and Paul, 26 who have risked their lives in the service of our Lord Jesus Christ. 27 We send you, then, Judas and Silas, who will tell you in person the same things we are writing. 28 For the Holy Spirit and we have agreed not to put any other burden on you besides these necessary rules: 29 Eat no food that has been offered to idols; eat no blood; eat no animal that has been strangled; and keep

---

[8] **24** {C} ἐξελθόντες p[33,74] ℵ[c] A C D E P Ψ 049 056 0142 33 81 104 181 326 330 436 451 614 629 630 945 1241 1505 1739 1877 2127 2412 2492 2495 *Byz* it[ar,d,e,gig,l] vg syr[p,h] cop[sa,bo] eth[pp] geo Irenaeus[lat] Origen[lat] Pacian ‖ *omit* ℵ* B 88 vg[mss] arm eth[ro] Athanasius Apostolic Constitutions Chrysostom Vigilius

[9] **24** {B} ὑμῶν p[33,45vid,74] ℵ A B D 33 81 614 629 945 it[ar,d,l] vg cop[sa,(bo)] eth[ro] Origen[lat] Athanasius[lat] Apostolic Constitutions Epiphanius Vigilius ‖ ὑμῶν λέγοντες περιτέμνεσθαι καὶ τηρεῖν τὸν νόμον C (E περιτέμνεσθαι δεῖ) P Ψ 049 056 (0142 ἡμῶν) 88 104 181 326 330 436 451 630 1241 (1505 2495 τὸν λόγον) 1739 1877 2127 2412 2492 *Byz* (it[e] περιτέμνεσθαι δεῖ) (it[gig]) syr[p,h] arm eth[pp] geo (Irenaeus[lat]) (Chrysostom) Greek[acc. to Bede] Theophylact

[10] **25** {C} ἐκλεξαμένους ℵ C D E[gr] P 049 056 0142 33 88 104 181 326 330 451 629 1241 (1505 ἐξελεξαμένους) 1877 2127 2492 2495 *Byz* it[d] arm Irenaeus[lat] Apostolic Constitutions Chrysostom ‖ ἐκλεξαμένοις p[45vid] A B Ψ 81 436[vid?] 614 630 945 1739 2412

[11] **29** {B} καὶ πνικτῶν ℵ* Λ* B C 81 614 2412 cop[sa,bo] Clement Origen Gaudentius mss[acc. to Jerome] ‖ καὶ πνικτοῦ p[74] ℵ[c] A[2] E P Ψ 049 056 0142 33 88 104 181 326 330 436 451 629 630 945 1241 1505 1739 1877 2127 2492 2495 *Byz* it[ar,e,gig] vg[cl] syr[p,h] arm Apostolic Constitutions Didymus Epiphanius Chrysostom Theodoret ‖ πνικτοῦ it[ph] vg[ww with [ ]] Athanasius[lat] ‖ *omit* D it[d,l] vg[mss] geo Irenaeus[lat] Tertullian Cyprian Ambrosiaster Ephraem Pacian Jerome Augustine

---

24 τινὲς...λόγοις Ac 15.1 **28** μηδὲν...βάρος Mt 23.4 **29** αἵματος Gn 9.4; Lv 3.17; 17.10–14

yourselves from immorality. You will
do well if you keep yourselves from doing
these things. Good-bye.''

30 The messengers were sent off and
went to Antioch, where they gathered
the whole group of believers and gave
them the letter. 31 When the people read
the letter, they were filled with joy by
the message of encouragement. 32 Judas
and Silas, who were themselves prophets,
spoke a long time with the brothers,
giving them courage and strength. 33 After spending some time there, they were
sent off in peace by the brothers, and
went back to those who had sent them.
[34 But Silas decided to stay there.]

35 Paul and Barnabas spent some time
in Antioch. Together with many others,
they taught and preached the word of
the Lord.

πορνείας[12]· ἐξ ὧν διατηροῦντες ἑαυτοὺς εὖ πράξετε[13].
Ἔρρωσθε.

30 Οἱ μὲν οὖν ἀπολυθέντες κατῆλθον εἰς Ἀντιόχειαν,
καὶ συναγαγόντες τὸ πλῆθος ἐπέδωκαν τὴν ἐπιστολήν·
31 ἀναγνόντες δὲ ἐχάρησαν ἐπὶ τῇ παρακλήσει. 32 Ἰούδας
τε καὶ Σίλας, καὶ αὐτοὶ προφῆται ὄντες, διὰ λόγου πολλοῦ
παρεκάλεσαν τοὺς ἀδελφοὺς καὶ ἐπεστήριξαν· 33 ποιήσαντες δὲ χρόνον ἀπελύθησαν μετ' εἰρήνης ἀπὸ τῶν
ἀδελφῶν πρὸς τοὺς ἀποστείλαντας αὐτούς.[14] 35 Παῦλος
δὲ καὶ Βαρναβᾶς διέτριβον ἐν Ἀντιοχείᾳ διδάσκοντες καὶ
εὐαγγελιζόμενοι μετὰ καὶ ἑτέρων πολλῶν τὸν λόγον
τοῦ κυρίου.

---

[12] **29** {B} καὶ πορνείας 𝔭[33,74] ℵ A B C E P Ψ 049 056 0142 33 81 88 104
181 326 330 436 451 629 1241 1505 1877 2127 2492 2495 *Byz* it[e,gig] vg syr[p,h]
cop[bo] arm geo Clement Tertullian Origen[lat] Athanasius[lat] Apostolic
Constitutions Didymus ‖ καὶ πορνείας, καὶ ὅσα μὴ θέλετε ἑαυτοῖς
γίνεσθαι ἑτέροις μὴ ποιεῖν (see 15.20 mg) (D ἑτέρῳ) (614 2412 αὐτοῖς
and ἑτέρῳ μὴ ποιετε [= ποιῆτε]) (630 θέλητε) 945 1739 it[ar,l,p,ph] (it[d] ἑτέρῳ)
vg[mss] syr[h with *] cop[sa] eth (Irenaeus[lat]) (Cyprian) Porphyry Eusebius
(Ambrosiaster) ‖ *omit* vg[ms*] Origen[pt] Gaudentius Vigilius

[13] **29** {B} πράξετε 𝔭[33] ℵ A B P Ψ 049 056 0142 33 81 88 104 181 330 451
614 629 630 945 1241 1505 1739* 2127 2412 2492 2495 *Byz* it[e,gig] vg syr[p,h]
cop[sa,bo] geo Clement Origen[lat] Apostolic Constitutions Pacian Didymus ‖
πράξατε 𝔭[74] C 326 it[ar] arm eth[ro] ‖ πράξητε E[gr] 436 1877 ‖ πράξατε
φερόμενοι ἐν τῷ ἁγίῳ πνεύματι D (1739[mg] πράξετε *and omit* τῷ) it[d,(l)]
Irenaeus[lat] Tertullian Ephraem

[14] **33** {B} *omit verse 34* 𝔭[74] ℵ A B E P Ψ 049 056 0142 81 104 330 451 629
1241 1505 1877 2127 2492 2495 *Byz*[pt] it[e,p] vg[ww] syr[p,h] cop[bo] Chrysostom
Theophylact[a] ‖ *add verse 34* ἔδοξε δὲ τῷ Σίλᾳ ἐπιμεῖναι αὐτοῦ. (C αὐτούς)
33 88 181 (326 *omit* δέ) (436 αὐτοῖς) 614 (630 945 αὐτόθι) 1739 2412 *Byz*[pt]
it[c] syr[h with *] cop[sa,bo mss] arm eth geo Cassiodorus Theophylact[b] ‖ *add
verse 34* ἔδοξε δὲ τῷ Σίλᾳ ἐπιμεῖναι αὐτούς, μόνος δὲ Ἰούδας ἐπορεύθη.
(D[gr*] Σείλεα) (D[c] πρὸς αὐτούς) it[d] (it[ar,gig,l,ph] ἐπιμεῖναι αὐτοῦ) ‖ *add
verse 34* ἔδοξε δὲ τῷ Σίλᾳ ἐπιμεῖναι αὐτοῦ, μόνος δὲ Ἰούδας ἐπορεύθη εἰς
Ἰερουσαλήμ. it[w] vg[cl]

---

32 Ἰούδας...ὄντες Ac 11.27; 13.1   παρεκάλεσαν...ἐπεστήριξαν Ac 14.22; 18.23

Paul and Barnabas Separate

36 Μετὰ δέ τινας ἡμέρας εἶπεν πρὸς Βαρναβᾶν Παῦλος, Ἐπιστρέψαντες δὴ ἐπισκεψώμεθα τοὺς ἀδελφοὺς κατὰ πόλιν πᾶσαν ἐν αἷς κατηγγείλαμεν τὸν λόγον τοῦ κυρίου, πῶς ἔχουσιν. **37** Βαρναβᾶς δὲ ἐβούλετο συμπαραλαβεῖν καὶ τὸν Ἰωάννην τὸν καλούμενον Μᾶρκον· **38** Παῦλος δὲ ἠξίου τὸν ἀποστάντα ἀπ' αὐτῶν ἀπὸ Παμφυλίας καὶ μὴ συνελθόντα αὐτοῖς εἰς τὸ ἔργον μὴ συμπαραλαμβάνειν τοῦτον. **39** ἐγένετο δὲ παροξυσμὸς ὥστε ἀποχωρισθῆναι αὐτοὺς ἀπ' ἀλλήλων, τόν τε Βαρναβᾶν παραλαβόντα τὸν Μᾶρκον ἐκπλεῦσαι εἰς Κύπρον. **40** Παῦλος δὲ ἐπιλεξάμενος Σίλαν ἐξῆλθεν παραδοθεὶς τῇ χάριτι τοῦ κυρίου ὑπὸ τῶν ἀδελφῶν, **41** διήρχετο δὲ τὴν Συρίαν καὶ τὴν Κιλικίαν ἐπιστηρίζων τὰς ἐκκλησίας.

Timothy Accompanies Paul and Silas

16 Κατήντησεν δὲ εἰς Δέρβην καὶ εἰς Λύστραν. καὶ ἰδοὺ μαθητής τις ἦν ἐκεῖ ὀνόματι Τιμόθεος, υἱὸς γυναικὸς Ἰουδαίας πιστῆς πατρὸς δὲ Ἕλληνος, **2** ὃς ἐμαρτυρεῖτο ὑπὸ τῶν ἐν Λύστροις καὶ Ἰκονίῳ ἀδελφῶν. **3** τοῦτον ἠθέλησεν ὁ Παῦλος σὺν αὐτῷ ἐξελθεῖν, καὶ λαβὼν περιέτεμεν αὐτὸν διὰ τοὺς Ἰουδαίους τοὺς ὄντας ἐν τοῖς τόποις ἐκείνοις, ᾔδεισαν γὰρ ἅπαντες τὸν πατέρα αὐτοῦ ὅτι Ἕλλην ὑπῆρχεν. **4** ὡς δὲ διεπορεύοντο τὰς πόλεις, παρεδίδοσαν αὐτοῖς φυλάσσειν τὰ δόγματα τὰ κεκριμένα ὑπὸ τῶν ἀποστόλων καὶ πρεσβυτέρων τῶν ἐν Ἱεροσολύμοις. **5** αἱ μὲν οὖν ἐκκλησίαι ἐστερεοῦντο τῇ πίστει καὶ ἐπερίσσευον τῷ ἀριθμῷ καθ' ἡμέραν.

---

37 Ἰωάννην...Μᾶρκον Ac 12.12, 25   **38** τὸν...ἔργον Ac 13.13; Col 4.10   **39** τόν τε... Κύπρον Ac 4.36; 13.4   **40** παραδοθεὶς...κυρίου Ac 14.26
16 **1** Κατήντησεν...Δέρβην Ac 14.6   Τιμόθεος...πιστῆς 2 Tm 1.5   **2** Php 2.20, 22   **3** λαβὼν...ἐκείνοις Ga 2.3–5   **4** τὰ δόγματα...Ἱεροσολύμοις Ac 15.23–29   **5** Ac 2.47; 5.14; 6.7

Paul and Barnabas Separate

[36] Some time later Paul said to Barnabas, "Let us go back and visit the brothers in every city where we preached the word of the Lord, and find out how they are getting along." [37] Barnabas wanted to take John Mark with them, [38] but Paul did not think it was right to take him, because he had not stayed with them to the end of their mission, but had turned back and left them in Pamphylia. [39] They had a sharp argument between them, and separated from each other. Barnabas took Mark and sailed off for Cyprus, [40] while Paul chose Silas and left, commended by the brothers to the care of God's grace. [41] He went through Syria and Cilicia, strengthening the churches.

Timothy Goes with Paul and Silas

16 Paul traveled on to Derbe and Lystra. A believer named Timothy lived there; his mother, also a believer, was Jewish, but his father was Greek. [2] All the brothers in Lystra and Iconium spoke well of Timothy. [3] Paul wanted to take Timothy along with him, so he circumcised him. He did so because all the Jews who lived in those places knew that Timothy's father was a Greek. [4] As they went through the towns they delivered to the believers the rules decided upon by the apostles and elders in Jerusalem, and told them to obey these rules. [5] So the churches were made stronger in the faith and grew in numbers every day.

In Troas: Paul's Vision

[6] They traveled through the region of Phrygia and Galatia; the Holy Spirit did not let them preach the message in the province of Asia. [7] When they reached the border of Mysia, they tried to go into the province of Bithynia, but the Spirit of Jesus did not allow them. [8] So they traveled right on through[1] Mysia and went down to Troas. [9] Paul had a vision that night in which he saw a man of Macedonia standing and begging him, "Come over to Macedonia and help us!" [10] As soon as Paul had this vision, we got ready to leave for Macedonia, for we decided that God had called us to preach the Good News to the people there.

In Philippi: the Conversion of Lydia

[11] We left by ship from Troas and sailed straight across to Samothrace, and the next day to Neapolis. [12] From there we went inland to Philippi, a city of the first district of Macedonia;[2] it is also a Roman colony. We spent several days in that city. [13] On the Sabbath day we went out of the city to the riverside, where we thought there would be a Jewish place for prayer. We sat down and talked to the women who gathered

---

[1] **8** traveled right on through: *or* passed by

[2] **12** a city of the first district of Macedonia: *some mss. read* the main city of the district of Macedonia; *or* the main city of that district in Macedonia

Paul's Vision of the Man of Macedonia

6 Διῆλθον δὲ τὴν Φρυγίαν καὶ Γαλατικὴν χώραν, κωλυθέντες ὑπὸ τοῦ ἁγίου πνεύματος λαλῆσαι τὸν λόγον ἐν τῇ Ἀσίᾳ· **7** ἐλθόντες δὲ κατὰ τὴν Μυσίαν ἐπείραζον εἰς τὴν Βιθυνίαν πορευθῆναι, καὶ οὐκ εἴασεν αὐτοὺς τὸ πνεῦμα Ἰησοῦ· **8** παρελθόντες δὲ τὴν Μυσίαν κατέβησαν εἰς Τρῳάδα. **9** καὶ ὅραμα διὰ [τῆς] νυκτὸς τῷ Παύλῳ ὤφθη, ἀνὴρ Μακεδών τις ἦν ἑστὼς καὶ παρακαλῶν αὐτὸν καὶ λέγων, Διαβὰς εἰς Μακεδονίαν βοήθησον ἡμῖν. **10** ὡς δὲ τὸ ὅραμα εἶδεν, εὐθέως ἐζητήσαμεν ἐξελθεῖν εἰς Μακεδονίαν, συμβιβάζοντες ὅτι προσκέκληται ἡμᾶς ὁ θεὸς[1] εὐαγγελίσασθαι αὐτούς.

The Conversion of Lydia

11 Ἀναχθέντες δὲ ἀπὸ Τρῳάδος εὐθυδρομήσαμεν εἰς Σαμοθράκην, τῇ δὲ ἐπιούσῃ εἰς Νέαν Πόλιν, **12** κἀκεῖθεν εἰς Φιλίππους, ἥτις ἐστὶν πρώτης μερίδος τῆς[2] Μακεδονίας πόλις, κολωνία. ἦμεν δὲ ἐν ταύτῃ τῇ πόλει διατρίβοντες ἡμέρας τινάς. **13** τῇ τε ἡμέρᾳ τῶν σαββάτων ἐξήλθομεν ἔξω τῆς πύλης παρὰ ποταμὸν οὗ ἐνομίζομεν προσευχὴν[3] εἶναι, καὶ καθίσαντες ἐλαλοῦμεν ταῖς συν-

---

[1] **10** {B} θεός 𝔭74 ℵ A B C E Ψ 33 81 181 326 630 945 1739 it[ar, e, l] vg cop[bo] geo Theophylact[b] ‖ κύριος D P 049 056 0142 88 104 330 436 451 614 629 1241 1505 1877 2127 2412 2492 2495 *Byz* it[c, d, gig] syr[p, h] cop[sa] arm Irenaeus[lat] Chrysostom Theophylact[a]

[2] **12** {D} πρώτης μερίδος τῆς cj, (vg[3 mss] *primae partis*) Provençal Old German ‖ πρώτη τῆς μερίδος 𝔭74 ℵ A C Ψ 33 81 88 181 326 630 945 ‖ πρώτη τῆς μερίδος τῆς (B *omit first* τῆς) P 049 056 0142 104 330 436 451 629 1877 2127 *Byz* cop[sa, bo] Chrysostom ‖ πρώτη τῆς μερίδος (*or add* τῆς) it[ar, e, gig, (l)] vg ‖ πρώτη μερίς E[gr] it[ph] cop[sa mss] arm geo ‖ πρώτη τῆς 614 1241 1505 1739 2412 2492 2495 l[1439m] syr[h] eth Chrysostom ‖ κεφαλὴ τῆς D it[d] syr[p]

[3] **13** {D} ἐνομίζομεν προσευχήν A[2] (B 181 προσευχή) (C ἐνομίζαμεν) Ψ 33 81 cop[sa, bo] (arm ἐνομίζοντο) eth[ro] ‖ ἐνομίζετο προσευχή E[gr] P 049 056 0142 (A[*vid?] 326 προσευχήν) 88 104 330 436 451 614 629 630 945 1241 1505 1739 1877 2127 2412 (2492 εὐχή) 2495 *Byz* l[1439m] Chrysostom Ammonius-Alexandria Theophylact[a, b] ‖ ἐνόμιζεν προσευχήν (𝔭74 προσευχή) ℵ ‖ ἐδόκει προσευχή D it[ar, d, e, gig, l] vg ‖ ἐνομίζετο (*or* ἐδόκει) προσευχή syr[p, h] geo

ἐλθούσαις γυναιξίν. 14 καί τις γυνὴ ὀνόματι Λυδία, πορφυρόπωλις πόλεως Θυατίρων σεβομένη τὸν θεόν, ἤκουεν, ἧς ὁ κύριος διήνοιξεν τὴν καρδίαν προσέχειν τοῖς λαλουμένοις ὑπὸ τοῦ Παύλου. 15 ὡς δὲ ἐβαπτίσθη καὶ ὁ οἶκος αὐτῆς, παρεκάλεσεν λέγουσα, Εἰ κεκρίκατέ με πιστὴν τῷ κυρίῳ εἶναι, εἰσελθόντες εἰς τὸν οἶκόν μου μένετε· καὶ παρεβιάσατο ἡμᾶς.

The Imprisonment at Philippi

16 Ἐγένετο δὲ πορευομένων ἡμῶν εἰς τὴν προσευχὴν παιδίσκην τινὰ ἔχουσαν πνεῦμα πύθωνα ὑπαντῆσαι ἡμῖν, ἥτις ἐργασίαν πολλὴν παρεῖχεν τοῖς κυρίοις αὐτῆς μαντευομένη. 17 αὕτη κατακολουθοῦσα τῷ Παύλῳ καὶ ἡμῖν ἔκραζεν λέγουσα, Οὗτοι οἱ ἄνθρωποι δοῦλοι τοῦ θεοῦ τοῦ ὑψίστου εἰσίν, οἵτινες καταγγέλλουσιν ὑμῖν[4] ὁδὸν σωτηρίας. 18 τοῦτο δὲ ἐποίει ἐπὶ πολλὰς ἡμέρας. διαπονηθεὶς δὲ Παῦλος καὶ ἐπιστρέψας τῷ πνεύματι εἶπεν, Παραγγέλλω σοι ἐν ὀνόματι Ἰησοῦ Χριστοῦ ἐξελθεῖν ἀπ' αὐτῆς· καὶ ἐξῆλθεν αὐτῇ τῇ ὥρᾳ. 19 ἰδόντες δὲ οἱ κύριοι αὐτῆς ὅτι ἐξῆλθεν ἡ ἐλπὶς τῆς ἐργασίας αὐτῶν ἐπιλαβόμενοι τὸν Παῦλον καὶ τὸν Σίλαν εἵλκυσαν εἰς τὴν ἀγορὰν ἐπὶ τοὺς ἄρχοντας, 20 καὶ προσαγαγόντες αὐτοὺς τοῖς στρατηγοῖς εἶπαν, Οὗτοι οἱ ἄνθρωποι ἐκταράσσουσιν ἡμῶν τὴν πόλιν Ἰουδαῖοι ὑπάρχοντες, 21 καὶ καταγγέλλουσιν ἔθη ἃ οὐκ ἔξεστιν ἡμῖν παραδέχεσθαι οὐδὲ ποιεῖν Ῥωμαίοις οὖσιν. 22 καὶ συνεπέστη ὁ ὄχλος κατ' αὐτῶν, καὶ οἱ στρατηγοὶ περιρήξαντες αὐτῶν τὰ ἱμάτια ἐκέλευον ῥαβδίζειν, 23 πολλάς τε

---

4 **17** {B} ὑμῖν 𝔭74 ℵ B D Egr 104 330 451 629 630 1739 2127 itar.d.gig.l vg syrp.h copbo arm ethpp geo Theodoret ‖ ἡμῖν A C P Ψ 049 056 0142 33 81 88 181 326 436 614 945 1241 1505 1877 2412 2492 2495 *Byz Lect* ite.ph copsa ethro Origen Eustathius Lucifer Chrysostom ‖ *omit* Origenlat

---

15 ἐβαπτίσθη...αὐτῆς Ac 16.33; 18.8   **16** ἐργασίαν...αὐτῆς Ac 19.24   **17** Οὗτοι... δοῦλοι...εἰσίν Mk 1.24, 34; Lk 4.34, 41   **18** διαπονηθεὶς...αὐτῆς Mk 16.17; Ac 19.13   **20** Ac 17.6   ἐκταράσσουσιν...πόλιν 1 Kgs 18.17   **22–23** Php 1.30; 1 Th 2.2   **22** ἐκέλευον ῥαβδίζειν 2 Cor 11.25

there. 14 One of those who heard us was Lydia, from Thyatira, who was a dealer in purple goods. She was a woman who worshiped God, and the Lord opened her mind to pay attention to what Paul was saying. 15 She and the people of her house were baptized. Then she invited us: "Come and stay in my house, if you have decided that I am a true believer in the Lord." And she persuaded us to go.

In Prison at Philippi

16 One day as we were going to the place of prayer, we were met by a slave girl who had an evil spirit in her that made her guess the future. She earned much money for her owners by telling fortunes. 17 She followed Paul and us, shouting, "These men are servants of the Most High God! They announce to you how you can be saved!" 18 She did this for many days, until Paul became so upset that he turned around and said to the spirit, "In the name of Jesus Christ I order you to come out of her!" The spirit went out of her that very moment. 19 When her owners realized that their chance of making money was gone, they grabbed Paul and Silas and dragged them to the authorities in the public square. 20 They brought them before the Roman officials and said: "These men are Jews, and they are causing trouble in our city. 21 They are teaching customs that are against our law; we are Romans and cannot follow those customs!" 22 The crowd joined the attack against them; the officials tore the clothes off Paul and Silas, and ordered them to be whipped. 23 After a severe

beating they were thrown into jail, and the jailer was ordered to lock them up tight. ²⁴ Upon receiving this order, the jailer threw them into the inner cell and fastened their feet between heavy blocks of wood.

²⁵ About midnight Paul and Silas were praying and singing hymns to God, and the other prisoners were listening to them. ²⁶ Suddenly there was a violent earthquake, which shook the prison to its foundations. At once all the doors opened, and the chains fell off all the prisoners. ²⁷ The jailer woke up, and when he saw the prison doors open he thought that all the prisoners had escaped; so he pulled out his sword and was about to kill himself. ²⁸ But Paul shouted at the top of his voice, "Don't harm yourself! We are all here!" ²⁹ The jailer called for a light, rushed in, and fell trembling at the feet of Paul and Silas. ³⁰ Then he led them out and asked, "What must I do, sirs, to be saved?" ³¹ "Believe in the Lord Jesus," they said, "and you will be saved — you and your family." ³² And they preached the word of the Lord to him and to all the others in his house. ³³ At that very hour of the night the jailer took them and washed off their wounds; and he and all his family were baptized at once. ³⁴ He took Paul and Silas up into his house and gave them some food to eat. He and his family were filled with joy, because they now believed in God.

³⁵ The next morning the Roman authorities sent an order to the police officers: "Let those men go." ³⁶ So the jailer told it to Paul: "The officials have sent an order for you and Silas to be

ἐπιθέντες αὐτοῖς πληγὰς ἔβαλον εἰς φυλακήν, παραγγείλαντες τῷ δεσμοφύλακι ἀσφαλῶς τηρεῖν αὐτούς· 24 ὃς παραγγελίαν τοιαύτην λαβὼν ἔβαλεν αὐτοὺς εἰς τὴν ἐσωτέραν φυλακὴν καὶ τοὺς πόδας ἠσφαλίσατο αὐτῶν εἰς τὸ ξύλον.

25 Κατὰ δὲ τὸ μεσονύκτιον Παῦλος καὶ Σίλας προσευχόμενοι ὕμνουν τὸν θεόν, ἐπηκροῶντο δὲ αὐτῶν οἱ δέσμιοι· 26 ἄφνω δὲ σεισμὸς ἐγένετο μέγας ὥστε σαλευθῆναι τὰ θεμέλια τοῦ δεσμωτηρίου, ἠνεῴχθησαν δὲ παραχρῆμα αἱ θύραι πᾶσαι, καὶ πάντων τὰ δεσμὰ ἀνέθη. 27 ἔξυπνος δὲ γενόμενος ὁ δεσμοφύλαξ καὶ ἰδὼν ἀνεῳγμένας τὰς θύρας τῆς φυλακῆς, σπασάμενος [τὴν] μάχαιραν ἤμελλεν ἑαυτὸν ἀναιρεῖν, νομίζων ἐκπεφευγέναι τοὺς δεσμίους. 28 ἐφώνησεν δὲ Παῦλος μεγάλῃ φωνῇ λέγων, Μηδὲν πράξῃς σεαυτῷ κακόν, ἅπαντες γάρ ἐσμεν ἐνθάδε. 29 αἰτήσας δὲ φῶτα εἰσεπήδησεν, καὶ ἔντρομος γενόμενος προσέπεσεν τῷ Παύλῳ καὶ [τῷ] Σίλᾳ, 30 καὶ προαγαγὼν αὐτοὺς ἔξω ἔφη, Κύριοι, τί με δεῖ ποιεῖν ἵνα σωθῶ; 31 οἱ δὲ εἶπαν, Πίστευσον ἐπὶ τὸν κύριον Ἰησοῦν, καὶ σωθήσῃ σὺ καὶ ὁ οἶκός σου. 32 καὶ ἐλάλησαν αὐτῷ τὸν λόγον τοῦ κυρίου⁵ σὺν πᾶσιν τοῖς ἐν τῇ οἰκίᾳ αὐτοῦ. 33 καὶ παραλαβὼν αὐτοὺς ἐν ἐκείνῃ τῇ ὥρᾳ τῆς νυκτὸς ἔλουσεν ἀπὸ τῶν πληγῶν, καὶ ἐβαπτίσθη αὐτὸς καὶ οἱ αὐτοῦ πάντες παραχρῆμα, 34 ἀναγαγών τε αὐτοὺς εἰς τὸν οἶκον παρέθηκεν τράπεζαν, καὶ ἠγαλλιάσατο πανοικεὶ πεπιστευκὼς τῷ θεῷ.

35 Ἡμέρας δὲ γενομένης ἀπέστειλαν οἱ στρατηγοὶ τοὺς ῥαβδούχους λέγοντες, Ἀπόλυσον τοὺς ἀνθρώπους ἐκείνους. 36 ἀπήγγειλεν δὲ ὁ δεσμοφύλαξ τοὺς λόγους πρὸς τὸν Παῦλον, ὅτι Ἀπέσταλκαν οἱ στρατηγοὶ ἵνα

---

⁵ 32 {B} τοῦ κυρίου 𝔭⁴⁵,⁷⁴ ℵᶜ A C (D omit τοῦ) E P Ψ 049 056 0142 33 81 88 104 181 326 330 436 451 614 629 630 945 1241 1505 1739 1877 2127 2412 2492 2495 Byz Lect itᵈ,ᵉ,ᵍⁱᵍ,ˡ vg syrᵖ,ʰ copˢᵃ,ᵇᵒ arm geo Lucifer Chrysostom ‖ τοῦ θεοῦ ℵ* B l¹⁴³⁹ ‖ omit itᵃʳ

---

27 Ac 12.18–19   30 Κύριοι...σωθῶ Ac 2.37   33 ἐβαπτίσθη...πάντες Ac 16.15

ἀπολυθῆτε· νῦν οὖν ἐξελθόντες πορεύεσθε ἐν εἰρήνῃ[6]. 37 ὁ δὲ Παῦλος ἔφη πρὸς αὐτούς, Δείραντες ἡμᾶς δημοσίᾳ ἀκατακρίτους, ἀνθρώπους Ῥωμαίους ὑπάρχοντας, ἔβαλαν εἰς φυλακήν· καὶ νῦν λάθρα ἡμᾶς ἐκβάλλουσιν; οὐ γάρ, ἀλλὰ ἐλθόντες αὐτοὶ ἡμᾶς ἐξαγαγέτωσαν. 38 ἀπήγγειλαν δὲ τοῖς στρατηγοῖς οἱ ῥαβδοῦχοι τὰ ῥήματα ταῦτα. ἐφοβήθησαν δὲ ἀκούσαντες ὅτι Ῥωμαῖοί εἰσιν, 39 καὶ ἐλθόντες παρεκάλεσαν αὐτούς, καὶ ἐξαγαγόντες ἠρώτων ἀπελθεῖν ἀπὸ τῆς πόλεως. 40 ἐξελθόντες δὲ ἀπὸ τῆς φυλακῆς εἰσῆλθον πρὸς τὴν Λυδίαν, καὶ ἰδόντες παρεκάλεσαν τοὺς ἀδελφοὺς καὶ ἐξῆλθαν.

The Uproar in Thessalonica

17 Διοδεύσαντες δὲ τὴν Ἀμφίπολιν καὶ τὴν Ἀπολλωνίαν ἦλθον εἰς Θεσσαλονίκην, ὅπου ἦν συναγωγὴ τῶν Ἰουδαίων. 2 κατὰ δὲ τὸ εἰωθὸς τῷ Παύλῳ εἰσῆλθεν πρὸς αὐτοὺς καὶ ἐπὶ σάββατα τρία διελέξατο αὐτοῖς[a] ἀπὸ τῶν γραφῶν,[a] 3 διανοίγων καὶ παρατιθέμενος ὅτι τὸν Χριστὸν ἔδει παθεῖν καὶ ἀναστῆναι ἐκ νεκρῶν, καὶ ὅτι[b] οὗτός ἐστιν ὁ Χριστός, [ὁ] Ἰησοῦς[1], ὃν ἐγὼ καταγγέλλω ὑμῖν. 4 καί τινες ἐξ αὐτῶν ἐπείσθησαν καὶ προσεκληρώθησαν τῷ Παύλῳ καὶ τῷ Σίλᾳ, τῶν τε

---

[6] 36 {B} ἐν εἰρήνῃ p[45vid,74] (ℵ εἰς εἰρήνην) A B C E P Ψ 049 056 0120 0142 33 81 88 104 181 326 330 436 451 614 629 630 945 1241 1505 1739 1877 2127 2412 2492 2495 *Byz* it[ar,e,l] vg syr[p,h] cop[sa,bo] arm geo ∥ *omit* D it[d,gig]

[1] 3 {D} ὁ Χριστός, ὁ Ἰησοῦς B cop[sa?] ∥ ὁ Χριστὸς Ἰησοῦς P Ψ 049 056 0142 88 104 181 326 330 436 451 629 630 945 1241 1739 1877 2492 *Byz Lect* cop[sa?] Theophylact ∥ Χριστός, Ἰησοῦς p[74] A D 33[vid] 81 it[d,gig,l]* vg[ww] syr[h] arm eth Chrysostom ∥ Ἰησοῦς Χριστός ℵ 614 1505 2127 2412 2495 it[ar,e?l2,ph] vg[cl] syr[p] cop[bo?] ∥ Ἰησοῦς ὁ Χριστός E *l*[680,1441,1590] it[e?] cop[bo?] Chrysostom ∥ ὁ Χριστός *l*[1021] geo

[a a] 2 *a* none, *a* minor: TR WH Bov Nes BF[2] AV RV ASV RSV TT Zür Luth Jer Seg ∥ *a* minor, *a* none: NEB
[b] 3 *b* indirect: WH Bov Nes? BF[2] AV RV ASV Zür Luth ∥ *b* direct: TR? Nes? RSV NEB TT Jer Seg

37 Δείραντες...ὑπάρχοντας Ac 22.25   39 Mt 8.34
17 1-9 1 Th 2.1-2   2 κατὰ δὲ τὸ εἰωθὸς...αὐτούς Lk 4.16; Ac 9.20; 17.10, 17   3 τὸν...παθεῖν Lk 24.26; Ac 3.18   τὸν...νεκρῶν Lk 24.46   οὗτος...ὑμῖν Ac 9.22; 18.5, 28   4 τῶν τε...ὀλίγαι Ac 13.50; 17.12

---

released. You may leave, then, and go quietly away." 37 But Paul said to the police officers: "We were not found guilty of any crime, yet they whipped us in public — and we are Roman citizens! Then they threw us in prison. And now they want to send us away secretly? Not at all! The Roman officials themselves must come here and let us out." 38 The police officers reported these words to the Roman officials; and when they heard that Paul and Silas were Roman citizens, they were afraid. 39 So they went and apologized to them; then they led them out of the prison and asked them to leave the city. 40 Paul and Silas left the prison and went to Lydia's house. There they met the brothers, spoke words of encouragement to them, and left.

In Thessalonica

17 They traveled on through Amphipolis and Apollonia, and came to Thessalonica, where there was a Jewish synagogue. 2 According to his usual habit, Paul went to the synagogue. There during three Sabbath days he argued with the people from the Scriptures, 3 explaining them and proving from them that the Messiah had to suffer and be raised from death. "This Jesus whom I announce to you," Paul said, "is the Messiah." 4 Some of them were convinced and joined Paul and Silas;

so did a large group of Greeks who worshiped God, and many of the leading women.

⁵ But the Jews were jealous and gathered some of the worthless loafers from the streets and formed a mob. They set the whole city in an uproar, and attacked the home of Jason, trying to find Paul and Silas and bring them out to the people. ⁶ But when they did not find them, they dragged Jason and some other brothers to the city authorities and shouted: "These men have caused trouble everywhere! Now they have come to our city, ⁷ and Jason has kept them in his house. They are all breaking the laws of the Emperor, saying that there is another king, by the name of Jesus." ⁸ With these words they threw the crowd and the city authorities in an uproar. ⁹ The authorities made Jason and the others pay the required amount of money to be released, and then let them go.

In Berea

¹⁰ As soon as night came, the brothers sent Paul and Silas to Berea. When they arrived, they went to the Jewish synagogue. ¹¹ The people there were more open-minded than the people in Thessalonica. They listened to the message with great eagerness, and every day they studied the Scriptures to see if what Paul said was really true. ¹² Many of them believed; and many Greek women of high society and many Greek men also believed. ¹³ But when the Jews in Thessalonica heard that Paul had preached the word of God in Berea also, they came there and started exciting and

σεβομένων Ἑλλήνων πλῆθος πολὺ γυναικῶν τε² τῶν πρώτων οὐκ ὀλίγαι. 5 Ζηλώσαντες δὲ οἱ Ἰουδαῖοι καὶ προσλαβόμενοι τῶν ἀγοραίων ἄνδρας τινὰς πονηροὺς καὶ ὀχλοποιήσαντες ἐθορύβουν τὴν πόλιν, καὶ ἐπιστάντες τῇ οἰκίᾳ Ἰάσονος ἐζήτουν αὐτοὺς προαγαγεῖν εἰς τὸν δῆμον. 6 μὴ εὑρόντες δὲ αὐτοὺς ἔσυρον Ἰάσονα καί τινας ἀδελφοὺς ἐπὶ τοὺς πολιτάρχας, βοῶντες ὅτι Οἱ τὴν οἰκουμένην ἀναστατώσαντες οὗτοι καὶ ἐνθάδε πάρεισιν, 7 οὓς ὑποδέδεκται Ἰάσων· καὶ οὗτοι πάντες ἀπέναντι τῶν δογμάτων Καίσαρος πράσσουσι, βασιλέα ἕτερον λέγοντες εἶναι Ἰησοῦν. 8 ἐτάραξαν δὲ τὸν ὄχλον καὶ τοὺς πολιτάρχας ἀκούοντας ταῦτα, 9 καὶ λαβόντες τὸ ἱκανὸν παρὰ τοῦ Ἰάσονος καὶ τῶν λοιπῶν ἀπέλυσαν αὐτούς.

The Apostles at Beroea

10 Οἱ δὲ ἀδελφοὶ εὐθέως διὰ νυκτὸς ἐξέπεμψαν τόν τε Παῦλον καὶ τὸν Σίλαν εἰς Βέροιαν, οἵτινες παραγενόμενοι εἰς τὴν συναγωγὴν τῶν Ἰουδαίων ἀπῄεσαν. 11 οὗτοι δὲ ἦσαν εὐγενέστεροι τῶν ἐν Θεσσαλονίκῃ, οἵτινες ἐδέξαντο τὸν λόγον μετὰ πάσης προθυμίας, καθ᾽ ἡμέραν ἀνακρίνοντες τὰς γραφὰς εἰ ἔχοι ταῦτα οὕτως. 12 πολλοὶ μὲν οὖν ἐξ αὐτῶν ἐπίστευσαν, καὶ τῶν Ἑλληνίδων γυναικῶν τῶν εὐσχημόνων καὶ ἀνδρῶν οὐκ ὀλίγοι. 13 Ὡς δὲ ἔγνωσαν οἱ ἀπὸ τῆς Θεσσαλονίκης Ἰουδαῖοι ὅτι καὶ ἐν τῇ Βεροίᾳ κατηγγέλη ὑπὸ τοῦ Παύλου ὁ λόγος τοῦ θεοῦ, ἦλθον κἀκεῖ σαλεύοντες καὶ ταράσσοντες τοὺς ὄχλους³.

---

² **4** {B} γυναικῶν τε p⁷⁴ ℵ A B E P Ψ 049 056 0120 0142 33 81 88 (104 add καὶ) 181 326 330 436 451 614 629 630 945 1241 1505 1739 1877 2127 2412 2492 2495 *Byz Lect* itᵃʳ?ᵉ? copᵇᵒ ‖ καὶ γυναῖκες D itᵈ?ᵍⁱᵍ?ˡ? vg syrᵖ·ʰ copˢᵃ geo ‖ γυναικῶν δὲ *l*¹⁰²¹ ‖ γυναικῶν *l*⁶⁸⁰ copᵇᵒᵐˢˢ

³ **13** {B} καὶ ταράσσοντες τοὺς ὄχλους p⁷⁴ ℵ A B 33 81 104 181 326 436 614 629 630 945 1505 1739 2412 2495 itᵃʳ·ᵍⁱᵍ vg syrʰ copˢᵃ arm geo ‖ τοὺς

5-6 1 Th 2.14　　**6** Οἱ...πάρεισιν Ac 16.20　　**7** ἀπέναντι...πράσσουσι Lk 23.2 βασιλέα...᾽Ιησοῦν Jn 19.12　　**11** ἀνακρίνοντες...οὕτως Jn 5.39　　**12** τῶν Ἑλληνίδων... ὀλίγοι Ac 13.50; 17.4　　**13** Ac 14.19

14 εὐθέως δὲ τότε τὸν Παῦλον ἐξαπέστειλαν οἱ ἀδελφοὶ πορεύεσθαι ἕως[4] ἐπὶ τὴν θάλασσαν· ὑπέμεινάν τε ὅ τε Σίλας καὶ ὁ Τιμόθεος ἐκεῖ. **15** οἱ δὲ καθιστάνοντες τὸν Παῦλον ἤγαγον ἕως Ἀθηνῶν, καὶ λαβόντες ἐντολὴν πρὸς τὸν Σίλαν καὶ τὸν Τιμόθεον ἵνα ὡς τάχιστα ἔλθωσιν πρὸς αὐτὸν ἐξῄεσαν.

Paul at Athens

16 Ἐν δὲ ταῖς Ἀθήναις ἐκδεχομένου αὐτοὺς τοῦ Παύλου, παρωξύνετο τὸ πνεῦμα αὐτοῦ ἐν αὐτῷ θεωροῦντος κατείδωλον οὖσαν τὴν πόλιν. **17** διελέγετο μὲν οὖν ἐν τῇ συναγωγῇ τοῖς Ἰουδαίοις καὶ τοῖς σεβομένοις καὶ ἐν τῇ ἀγορᾷ κατὰ πᾶσαν ἡμέραν πρὸς τοὺς παρατυγχάνοντας. **18** τινὲς δὲ καὶ τῶν Ἐπικουρείων καὶ Στοϊκῶν φιλοσόφων συνέβαλλον αὐτῷ, καί τινες ἔλεγον, Τί ἂν θέλοι ὁ σπερμολόγος οὗτος λέγειν; οἱ δέ, Ξένων δαιμονίων δοκεῖ καταγγελεὺς εἶναι· ὅτι τὸν Ἰησοῦν καὶ τὴν [c]ἀνάστασιν εὐηγγελίζετο. **19** ἐπιλαβόμενοί τε αὐτοῦ ἐπὶ τὸν Ἄρειον Πάγον ἤγαγον, λέγοντες, Δυνάμεθα γνῶναι τίς ἡ καινὴ αὕτη ἡ ὑπὸ σοῦ λαλουμένη διδαχή; **20** ξενίζοντα γάρ τινα εἰσφέρεις εἰς τὰς ἀκοὰς ἡμῶν· βουλόμεθα οὖν γνῶναι τίνα θέλει ταῦτα εἶναι. **21** Ἀθηναῖοι δὲ πάντες καὶ οἱ ἐπιδημοῦντες ξένοι εἰς οὐδὲν ἕτερον ηὐκαίρουν ἢ λέγειν τι ἢ ἀκούειν τι καινότερον.

ὄχλους καὶ ταράσσοντες Ψ cop[bo?] ‖ καὶ ταράσσοντες τοὺς ὄχλους οὐ διελίμπανον D it[d] syr[p] ‖ τοὺς ὄχλους p[45] E P 049 056 0120 0142 88 330 451 1877 2127 2492 *Byz* it[e] eth Chrysostom

[4] **14** {B} ἕως p[74] ℵ A B E 33 81 104 181 945 1739 it[ar, e, l] vg cop[sa, bomss] arm ‖ ὡς P Ψ 056 0120 0142 326 330 436 451 614 629 630 1505 1877 2127 2412 2492 2495 *Byz* syr[h] Chrysostom ‖ *omit* D 049 88 it[d, gig] syr[p] cop[samss, bomss] eth geo

[c] **18** [c] ἀνάστασιν: TR WH Bov Nes BF² AV RV ASV RSV Zür Luth Jer Seg ‖ [c] Ἀνάστασιν: NEB TT Jer[mg] Seg[mg]

17 διελέγετο...Ἰουδαίοις Ac 18.19

---

stirring up the mobs. [14] At once the brothers sent Paul away to the coast, but both Silas and Timothy stayed in Berea. [15] The men who were taking Paul went with him as far as Athens. Then they went back to Berea with instructions from Paul that Silas and Timothy join him as soon as possible.

In Athens

[16] While Paul was waiting in Athens for Silas and Timothy, he was greatly upset when he noticed how full of idols the city was. [17] So he argued in the synagogue with the Jews and the Gentiles who worshiped God, and in the public square every day with the people who happened to come by. [18] Certain Epicurean and Stoic teachers also debated with him. Some said, "What is this ignorant show-off trying to say?" Others said, "He seems to be talking about foreign gods." They said this because Paul was preaching about Jesus and the resurrection. [19] So they took Paul, brought him before the meeting of the Areopagus, and said: "We would like to know this new teaching that you are talking about. [20] Some of the things we hear you say sound strange to us, and we would like to know what they mean." [21] (For all the citizens of Athens and the foreigners who lived there liked to spend all their time telling and hearing the latest new thing.)

22 Paul stood up in front of the meeting of the Areopagus and said: "Men of Athens! I see that in every way you are very religious. 23 For as I walked through your city and looked at the places where you worship, I found also an altar on which is written, 'To an Unknown God.' That which you worship, then, even though you do not know it, is what I now proclaim to you. 24 God, who made the world and everything in it, is Lord of heaven and earth, and does not live in temples made by men. 25 Nor does he need anything that men can supply by working for him, since it is he himself who gives life and breath and everything else to all men. 26 From the one man he created all races of men, and made them live over the whole earth. He himself fixed beforehand the exact times and the limits of the places where they would live. 27 He did this so that they would look for him, and perhaps find him as they felt around for him.

22 Σταθεὶς δὲ ⌊ὁ⌋ Παῦλος ἐν μέσῳ τοῦ Ἀρείου Πάγου ἔφη, Ἄνδρες Ἀθηναῖοι, κατὰ πάντα ὡς δεισιδαιμονεστέρους ὑμᾶς θεωρῶ· 23 διερχόμενος γὰρ καὶ ἀναθεωρῶν τὰ σεβάσματα ὑμῶν εὗρον καὶ βωμὸν ἐν ᾧ ἐπεγέγραπτο, Ἀγνώστῳ θεῷ. ὃ οὖν ἀγνοοῦντες εὐσεβεῖτε, τοῦτο ἐγὼ καταγγέλλω ὑμῖν. 24 ὁ θεὸς ὁ ποιήσας τὸν κόσμον καὶ πάντα τὰ ἐν αὐτῷ, οὗτος οὐρανοῦ καὶ γῆς ὑπάρχων κύριος οὐκ ἐν χειροποιήτοις ναοῖς κατοικεῖ 25 οὐδὲ ὑπὸ χειρῶν ἀνθρωπίνων θεραπεύεται προσδεόμενός τινος, αὐτὸς διδοὺς πᾶσι ζωὴν καὶ πνοὴν καὶ τὰ πάντα· 26 ἐποίησέν τε ἐξ ἑνός[5] πᾶν ἔθνος ἀνθρώπων κατοικεῖν ἐπὶ παντὸς προσώπου τῆς γῆς, ὁρίσας προστεταγμένους καιροὺς καὶ τὰς ὁροθεσίας τῆς κατοικίας αὐτῶν, 27 ζητεῖν τὸν θεὸν εἰ ἄρα γε ψηλαφήσειαν αὐτὸν[6] καὶ εὕροιεν, καί γε οὐ μακρὰν ἀπὸ ἑνὸς ἑκάστου ἡμῶν ὑπάρχοντα[7].

---

[5] 26 {D} ἐξ ἑνός 𝔓[74] ℵ A B 33 81 181 629 630 1739 vg cop[sa,bo] eth[pp] Clement Cosmos ∥ ἐξ ἑνὸς αἵματος D E P Ψ 049 056 0142 88 104 326 330 436 451 614 945 1241 1505 1877 2127 2412 2492 2495 Byz Lect (l[603] στόματος) l[147mg,597m, 1356m,1439m] it[ar,d,e,gig] syr[p,h] arm geo Irenaeus[lat] Ephraem Chrysostom Theodoret Cosmos Greek[acc. to Bede] Theophylact ∥ omit eth[ro]

[6] 27 {C} τὸν θεὸν εἰ ἄρα γε ψηλαφήσειαν αὐτόν 𝔓[74] ℵ A B 049 056 0142 81 88 104 181 326 330 451 614 629 630 (945 ψηλαφήσαιεν) 1241 (1505 2495 omit τόν) 1739 2412 2492 Byz[pt] l[1356m pt,1441] it[ar] vg syr[p,h] cop[sa,bo] arm geo Chrysostom ∥ τὸν κύριον εἰ ἄρα γε ψηλαφήσειαν αὐτόν E P Ψ 436 1877 2127 Byz[pt] Lect (l[597m] ψηλαφήσειεν) l[147mg,1356m pt,1439m] it[e] ∥ τὸ θεῖον εἰ ἄρα γε ψηλαφήσειαν αὐτό it[gig] Ambrose ∥ τὸ θεῖόν ἐστιν εἰ ἄρα γε ψηλαφήσαισαν αὐτόν (see footnote 7) D (it[d] αὐτό) Irenaeus[lat] ∥ τὸ θεῖον εἰ ἄρα γε ψηλαφήσειαν Clement

[7] 27 {C} ἀπὸ ἑνὸς ἑκάστου ἡμῶν ὑπάρχοντα 𝔓[74] ℵ A[c] B (E 0120[vid] ὑπάρχοντος) P 049 056 0142 33[vid] 81 88 104 181 326 330 436 451 614 629 (630 945 ἀφ' ἑνός) 1241 (1739 ἀφ' ἑνός and ἀπέχοντα) 2412 2492 2495 Byz Lect (l[147mg,1356m,1439m,1441,1443] ὑπάρχοντος) it[(e),gig] vg syr[p,h] cop[sa?bo?] geo (Clement ὑπάρχοντος) Didymus ∥ ἀπὸ ἑνὸς ἑκάστου ὑμῶν ὑπάρχοντα A* (Ψ omit ἀπό) 1505 (1877 l[597m] ὑπάρχοντος) 2127 it[ar] ∥ ὧν ἀφ' ἑνὸς ἑκάστου ἡμῶν

---

24 ὁ θεὸς...κύριος Ps 146.6; Is 42.5   οὗτος...κύριος Mt 11.25   οὐκ...κατοικεῖ 1 Kgs 8.27; Ac 7.48   25 οὐδὲ...προσδεόμενός τινος Ps 50.12   αὐτὸς...πάντα Is 42.5   26 τὰς ὁροθεσίας ...αὐτῶν Dt 32.8   27 ζητεῖν...εὕροιεν Is 55.6   οὐ...ὑπάρχοντα Ps 145.18; Jr 23.23

28 Ἐν αὐτῷ γὰρ ζῶμεν καὶ κινούμεθα καὶ ἐσμέν, ὡς καί τινες τῶν καθ᾽ ὑμᾶς ποιητῶν⁸ εἰρήκασιν,

　Τοῦ γὰρ καὶ γένος ἐσμέν.

29 γένος οὖν ὑπάρχοντες τοῦ θεοῦ οὐκ ὀφείλομεν νομίζειν χρυσῷ ἢ ἀργύρῳ ἢ λίθῳ, χαράγματι τέχνης καὶ ἐνθυμήσεως ἀνθρώπου, τὸ θεῖον εἶναι ὅμοιον. **30** τοὺς μὲν οὖν χρόνους τῆς ἀγνοίας ὑπεριδὼν ὁ θεὸς τὰ νῦν παραγγέλλει⁹ τοῖς ἀνθρώποις πάντας πανταχοῦ μετανοεῖν, **31** καθότι ἔστησεν ἡμέραν ἐν ᾗ μέλλει κρίνειν τὴν οἰκουμένην ἐν δικαιοσύνῃ ἐν ἀνδρὶ ᾧ ὥρισεν, πίστιν παρασχὼν πᾶσιν ἀναστήσας αὐτὸν ἐκ νεκρῶν.

32 Ἀκούσαντες δὲ ἀνάστασιν νεκρῶν οἱ μὲν ἐχλεύαζον, οἱ δὲ εἶπαν, Ἀκουσόμεθά σου περὶ τούτου καὶ πάλιν. **33** οὕτως ὁ Παῦλος ἐξῆλθεν ἐκ μέσου αὐτῶν. **34** τινὲς δὲ ἄνδρες κολληθέντες αὐτῷ ἐπίστευσαν, ἐν οἷς καὶ Διονύσιος ὁ Ἀρεοπαγίτης καὶ γυνὴ ὀνόματι Δάμαρις καὶ ἕτεροι σὺν αὐτοῖς.

Paul at Corinth

18 Μετὰ ταῦτα χωρισθεὶς ἐκ¹ τῶν Ἀθηνῶν ἦλθεν εἰς Κόρινθον. **2** καὶ εὑρών τινα Ἰουδαῖον ὀνόματι Ἀκύλαν,

(D* ὅν) (Dᵇ ἡμῶν ὑπάρχων) (itᵈ) copˢᵃˀᵇᵒˀ Irenaeusˡᵃᵗ ‖ ἀπὸ ἑκάστου ἑνὸς ἡμῶν arm

⁸ **28** {C} τινες τῶν καθ᾽ ὑμᾶς ποιητῶν ℵ A E P Ψ 056 0120 33ᵛⁱᵈ 88 (104 ὑμῶν) 181 326 330 436 451 629 630 945 1241 1505 1739 1877 2127 2492 2495 Byz Lect l¹⁴⁷ᵐᵍ,⁵⁹⁷ᵐ,¹³⁵⁶ᵐ,¹⁴³⁹ᵐᵖᵗ itᵃʳ,ᶜ,ᵉ vg syrᵖ,ʰ copˢᵃ,ᵇᵒ arm geoᴬ,ᴮᶜ Clement Origen Didymus ‖ τινες τῶν καθ᾽ ἡμᾶς ποιητῶν 𝔭⁷⁴ B 049 614 2412 l⁵⁹⁹,¹⁴³⁹ᵐᵖᵗ ‖ τῶν καθ᾽ ὑμᾶς τινες D it⁽ᵈ⁾,⁽ᵍⁱᵍ⁾ eth? Irenaeusˡᵃᵗ? Ambrose? ‖ τινες τῶν καθ᾽ ὑμᾶς eth? geoᴮ* Irenaeusˡᵃᵗ? Ambrosiaster Pacian Ambrose? Pelagius Augustine

⁹ **30** {C} παραγγέλλει 𝔭⁴¹,⁷⁴ ℵᶜ A Dᵍʳ Eᵍʳ P Ψ 049 056 0142 88 104 181 326 330 436 451 614 629 630 945 1241 1505 1739 1877 2127 2412 2492 2495 Byz Lectᵐ (l⁶⁸⁰,¹³⁵⁶,¹⁴³⁹,¹⁴⁴³ παραγγέλει, l¹³⁶⁴ παραγγέλλω) itᵐ syrᵖ,ʰ copˢᵃ arm Athanasius Cyril ‖ ἀπαγγέλλει ℵ* B itᵃʳ,ᵈ,ᵉ,ᵍⁱᵍ,ᵖʰ vg copᵇᵒ Athanasius

¹ **1** {B} ἐκ 𝔭⁴¹,⁷⁴ ℵ B (D itᵈ ἀναχωρήσας δὲ ἀπό) 33 itᵃʳ,ᵍⁱᵍ vg copˢᵃ,ᵇᵒ ‖

28 Τοῦ...ἐσμέν Cleanthes? Aratus, *Phaenomena* 5 **29** γένος...θεοῦ Gn 1.27 οὐκ...ὅμοιον Is 40.18–20; 44.10–17; Ac 19.26 **30** τοὺς...ὑπεριδὼν ὁ θεός Ac 14.16; 17.23 **31** μέλλει ...δικαιοσύνῃ Ps 9.8; 96.13; 98.9 μέλλει...ὥρισεν Ac 10.42

18 2 τινα Ἰουδαῖον...αὐτοῦ Ro 16.3

Yet God is actually not far from any one of us; ²⁸ for

'In him we live and move and are.'
It is as some of your poets have also said,
'We too are his children.'

²⁹ Since we are his children, we should not suppose that God's nature is anything like an image of gold or silver or stone, shaped by the art and skill of man. ³⁰ God has overlooked the times when men did not know, but now he commands all men everywhere to turn away from their evil ways. ³¹ For he has fixed a day in which he will judge the whole world with justice, by means of a man he has chosen. He has given proof of this to everyone by raising that man from death!"

³² When they heard Paul speak about a raising from death, some of them made fun of him, but others said, "We want to hear you speak about this again." ³³ And so Paul left the meeting. ³⁴ Some men joined him and believed; among them was Dionysius, a member of the Areopagus, a woman named Damaris, and some others.

In Corinth

18 After this, Paul left Athens and went on to Corinth. ² There he met a Jew named Aquila, born in Pontus, who had just come from Italy with his wife Priscilla — because Emperor Claudius had ordered all the Jews to leave Rome. Paul went to see them, [3] and stayed and worked with them, because he earned his living by making tents, just as they did. [4] He argued in the synagogue every Sabbath, trying to convince both Jews and Greeks.

[5] When Silas and Timothy arrived from Macedonia, Paul gave his whole time to preaching the message, testifying to the Jews that Jesus is the Messiah. [6] When they opposed him and said evil things about him, he protested by shaking the dust from his clothes and saying to them: "If you are lost, you yourselves must take the blame for it! I am not responsible. From now on I will go to the Gentiles." [7] So he left them and went to live in the house of a Gentile named Titius Justus, who worshiped God;

Ποντικὸν τῷ γένει, προσφάτως ἐληλυθότα ἀπὸ τῆς Ἰταλίας καὶ Πρίσκιλλαν γυναῖκα αὐτοῦ διὰ τὸ διατεταχέναι Κλαύδιον χωρίζεσθαι πάντας τοὺς Ἰουδαίους ἀπὸ τῆς Ῥώμης, προσῆλθεν αὐτοῖς, 3 καὶ διὰ τὸ ὁμότεχνον εἶναι ἔμενεν παρ' αὐτοῖς καὶ ἠργάζετο[2]· ἦσαν γὰρ σκηνοποιοὶ τῇ τέχνῃ. 4 διελέγετο δὲ ἐν τῇ συναγωγῇ κατὰ πᾶν σάββατον, ἔπειθέν τε Ἰουδαίους καὶ Ἕλληνας.

5 Ὡς δὲ κατῆλθον ἀπὸ τῆς Μακεδονίας ὅ τε Σίλας καὶ ὁ Τιμόθεος, συνείχετο τῷ λόγῳ[3] ὁ Παῦλος, διαμαρτυρόμενος τοῖς Ἰουδαίοις εἶναι τὸν Χριστόν, Ἰησοῦν. 6 ἀντιτασσομένων δὲ αὐτῶν καὶ βλασφημούντων ἐκτιναξάμενος τὰ ἱμάτια εἶπεν πρὸς αὐτούς, Τὸ αἷμα ὑμῶν ἐπὶ τὴν κεφαλὴν ὑμῶν· καθαρὸς ἐγώ·[a] ἀπὸ τοῦ νῦν[a] εἰς τὰ ἔθνη πορεύσομαι. 7 καὶ μεταβὰς ἐκεῖθεν εἰσῆλθεν εἰς οἰκίαν τινὸς ὀνόματι Τιτίου Ἰούστου[4] σεβομένου τὸν θεόν,

---

ὁ Παῦλος ἐκ A E P Ψ 049 056 0142 88 104 181 326 330 436 451 614 629 630 945 1241 1505 1739 1877 2127 2412 2492 2495 *Byz Lect*[m] it[e, h] syr[p, h] cop[boms] arm eth geo Origen[lat] Chrysostom

[2] **3** {B} ἠργάζετο (or εἰργάζετο) p[74] א[c] A D E P Ψ 049 056 0142 33 88 104 181 326 330 436 451 614 629 630 945 1241 1505 1739 1877 2127 2412 2492 2495 *Byz Lect*[m] it[ar, d, e, gig, m] vg syr[h] cop[sa] arm geo Chrysostom ∥ ἠργάζοντο א* B* (B[3] εἰργάζοντο) cop[samss, bo] Origen ∥ ἠργάζετο σὺν αὐτοῖς syr[p, h with *]

[3] **5** {B} λόγῳ p[74] א A B D E Ψ 33 181 436 614 629 1505 2412 2495 it[ar, c, d, e, gig] vg syr[p, h] cop[sa, bo] eth Basil Theodoret ∥ πνεύματι P 049 056 0142 88 104 326 330 451 630 945 1241 1739 1877 2127 2492 *Byz* syr[hmg] arm geo Chrysostom

[4] **7** {D} Τιτίου Ἰούστου p[74] B* D[b] it[ar?e?gig?] vg? syr[h] geo ∥ Τίτου Ἰούστου א E 630 945 1739 it[ar?e?gig?] vg? cop[bo] arm Bede Theophylact[b] ∥ Ἰούστου A B[3] D[gr*] P Ψ 049 056 0142 33 88 104 181 326 330 436 451 614 629 1241 1505 1877 2127 2412 2492 2495 *Byz* it[d] eth Chrysostom Theophylact[a] ∥ Τίτου vg[mss] syr[p] cop[sa, boms] ∥ *omit* 2 325

[a a] **6** *a* major, *a* none: WH AV RV ASV RSV NEB Zür (Jer) (Seg) ∥ *a* none, *a* none: TR Bov Nes BF[2] TT Luth

---

3 ἔμενεν...τέχνῃ Ac 20.34; 1 Cor 4.12   **5** Ὡς...Τιμόθεος Ac 17.14–15 διαμαρτυρόμενος ...Ἰησοῦν Ac 9.22; 17.3; 18.28   **6** Ac 13.45–46 ἐκτιναξάμενος τὰ ἱμάτια Mt 10.14; Mk 6.11; Lk 9.5; 10.10–11; Ac 13.51   Τὸ αἷμα...καθαρὸς ἐγώ Ac 20.26

οὗ ἡ οἰκία ἦν συνομοροῦσα τῇ συναγωγῇ. **8** Κρίσπος δὲ ὁ ἀρχισυνάγωγος ἐπίστευσεν τῷ κυρίῳ σὺν ὅλῳ τῷ οἴκῳ αὐτοῦ, καὶ πολλοὶ τῶν Κορινθίων ἀκούοντες ἐπίστευον καὶ ἐβαπτίζοντο. **9** εἶπεν δὲ ὁ κύριος ἐν νυκτὶ δι᾽ ὁράματος τῷ Παύλῳ, Μὴ φοβοῦ, ἀλλὰ λάλει καὶ μὴ σιωπήσῃς, **10** διότι ἐγώ εἰμι μετὰ σοῦ καὶ οὐδεὶς ἐπιθήσεταί σοι τοῦ κακῶσαί σε, διότι λαός ἐστί μοι πολὺς ἐν τῇ πόλει ταύτῃ. **11** Ἐκάθισεν δὲ ἐνιαυτὸν καὶ μῆνας ἓξ διδάσκων ἐν αὐτοῖς τὸν λόγον τοῦ θεοῦ.

12 Γαλλίωνος δὲ ἀνθυπάτου ὄντος τῆς Ἀχαΐας κατεπέστησαν ὁμοθυμαδὸν οἱ Ἰουδαῖοι τῷ Παύλῳ καὶ ἤγαγον αὐτὸν ἐπὶ τὸ βῆμα, **13**^b λέγοντες ^bὅτι Παρὰ τὸν νόμον ἀναπείθει οὗτος τοὺς ἀνθρώπους σέβεσθαι τὸν θεόν. **14** μέλλοντος δὲ τοῦ Παύλου ἀνοίγειν τὸ στόμα εἶπεν ὁ Γαλλίων πρὸς τοὺς Ἰουδαίους, Εἰ μὲν ἦν ἀδίκημά τι ἢ ῥᾳδιούργημα πονηρόν, ὦ Ἰουδαῖοι, κατὰ λόγον ἂν ἀνεσχόμην ὑμῶν· **15** εἰ δὲ ζητήματά ἐστιν περὶ λόγου καὶ ὀνομάτων καὶ νόμου τοῦ καθ᾽ ὑμᾶς, ὄψεσθε αὐτοί· κριτὴς ἐγὼ τούτων οὐ βούλομαι εἶναι. **16** καὶ ἀπήλασεν αὐτοὺς ἀπὸ τοῦ βήματος. **17** ἐπιλαβόμενοι δὲ πάντες⁵ Σωσθένην τὸν ἀρχισυνάγωγον ἔτυπτον ἔμπροσθεν τοῦ βήματος· καὶ οὐδὲν τούτων τῷ Γαλλίωνι ἔμελεν.

Paul's Return to Antioch

18 Ὁ δὲ Παῦλος ἔτι προσμείνας ἡμέρας ἱκανὰς τοῖς ἀδελφοῖς ἀποταξάμενος ἐξέπλει εἰς τὴν Συρίαν, καὶ σὺν αὐτῷ Πρίσκιλλα καὶ Ἀκύλας, κειράμενος ἐν Κεγχρεαῖς

^b **17** {C} πάντες 𝔭⁷⁴ ℵ A B 629 vg cop^{bo} ∥ πάντες οἱ Ἕλληνες D E P Ψ 049 056 0120 0142 33 88 104 181 326 330 436 451 614 630 945 1241 1505 1739 1877 2127 2412 2492 2495 Byz it^{ar,d,e,gig,(h)} syr^{p,h} cop^{sa} arm eth geo Ephraem Chrysostom Greek^{acc. to Bede} ∥ πάντες οἱ Ἰουδαῖοι 307 431

^{b b} **12–13** b number 13, b no number: TR^{ed} WH Bov Nes BF² AV RV ASV RSV NEB? TT Luth Jer Seg ∥ b no number, b number 13: TR^{ed} NEB? Zür

8 1 Cor 1 14 ἐπίστευσεν...αὐτοῦ Ac 16.15, 33   **9–10** εἶπεν...σε 1 Cor 2.3   **9–10** Μὴ φοβοῦ...κακῶσαί σε Is 41.10; 43.5; Jr 1.8   **14–15** ὁ Γαλλίων...εἶναι Ac 23.29; 25.18–19   **15** Jn 18.31   **18** κειράμενος...εὐχήν Nu 6.18; Ac 21.24

his house was next to the synagogue. **8** Crispus, the leader of the synagogue, believed in the Lord, he and all his family; and many other people in Corinth heard the message, believed, and were baptized. **9** One night Paul had a vision, in which the Lord said to him: "Do not be afraid, but keep on speaking and do not give up, **10** for I am with you. No one will be able to harm you, because many in this city are my people." **11** So Paul stayed there for a year and a half, teaching the people the word of God. **12** When Gallio was made the Roman governor of Greece, the Jews got together, seized Paul and took him into court. **13** "This man," they said, "is trying to persuade people to worship God in a way that is against the law!" **14** Paul was about to speak when Gallio said to the Jews: "If this were a matter of some wrong or evil crime that has been committed, it would be reasonable for me to be patient with you Jews. **15** But since it is an argument about words and names and your own law, you yourselves must settle it. I will not be the judge of such things!" **16** And he drove them out of the court. **17** They all grabbed Sosthenes, the leader of the synagogue, and beat him in front of the court. But that did not bother Gallio a bit.

The Return to Antioch

18 Paul stayed on in Corinth with the brothers for many days, then left them and sailed off with Priscilla and Aquila for Syria. Before sailing he made a vow in Cenchreae and had his head shaved.

¹⁹ They arrived in Ephesus, where Paul left Priscilla and Aquila. He went into the synagogue and argued with the Jews. ²⁰ They asked him to stay with them a long time, but he would not consent. ²¹ Instead, he told them as he left, "If it is the will of God, I will come back to you." And so he sailed from Ephesus. ²² When he arrived at Caesarea he

τὴν κεφαλήν, εἶχεν γὰρ εὐχήν. 19 κατήντησαν⁶ δὲ εἰς Ἔφεσον, κἀκείνους κατέλιπεν αὐτοῦ⁷, αὐτὸς δὲ εἰσελθὼν εἰς τὴν συναγωγὴν διελέξατο τοῖς Ἰουδαίοις. 20 ἐρωτώντων δὲ αὐτῶν ἐπὶ πλείονα χρόνον μεῖναι οὐκ ἐπένευσεν, 21 ἀλλὰ ἀποταξάμενος καὶ εἰπών,⁸ Πάλιν ἀνακάμψω πρὸς ὑμᾶς τοῦ θεοῦ θέλοντος,ᶜ ἀνήχθη ἀπὸ τῆς Ἐφέσου·ᶜ 22 καὶ κατελθὼν⁹ εἰς Καισάρειαν, ἀναβὰς

---

⁶ **19** {B} κατήντησαν ℵ A B E 33 181 itᶜ·ᵈ·ᵉ syrᵖ copˢᵃ ethᵖᵖ ‖ καταντήσας Dᵍʳ itʰ arm ‖ κατήντησε 𝔭⁷⁴ P Ψ 049 056 0120 0142 88 104 326 330 436 451 614 629 630 945 1241 1505 1739 1877 2127 2412 2492 2495 *Byz* itᵃʳ·ᵍⁱᵍ vg syrʰ copᵇᵒ ethʳᵒ geo Chrysostom

⁷ **19** {C} κἀκείνους κατέλιπεν αὐτοῦ B 0120 630 945 1505 1739 2495 *Byz*ᵖᵗ copᵇᵒ ‖ καὶ ἐκείνους κατέλειπεν αὐτοῦ P Ψ 049 (0142 ἐκείνου κατέλιπεν) (056 330 451 629 κατέλιπεν) 88 1877 2127 2492 *Byz*ᵖᵗ Chrysostom Theophylactᵃ ‖ κἀκείνους κατέλειπεν ἐκεῖ A 33 (104 καὶ ἔκλειπεν) 181 326 arm ‖ κἀκείνους (or καὶ ἐκείνους) κατέλιπεν αὐτοῦ (or ἐκεῖ) itᵃʳ·ᵉ·ᵍⁱᵍ vg geo ‖ κἀκείνους κατέλιπεν ἐκεῖ 𝔭⁷⁴ᵛⁱᵈ ℵ E 436 1241 syrʰ ‖ κἀκεῖ κατέλιπεν αὐτούς 489 ‖ τῷ ἐπιόντι σαββάτῳ copˢᵃ ‖ καὶ τῷ ἐπιόντι σαββάτῳ ἐκείνους κατέλιπεν ἐκεῖ D (itᵈ) ‖ τῷ ἐπιόντι σαββάτῳ κἀκείνους κατέλιπεν αὐτοῦ (614 2412 κἀκείνος) syrʰ ʷⁱᵗʰ * ‖ omit (see footnote 9) syrᵖ

⁸ **21** {B} εἰπών 𝔭⁷⁴ ℵ A B E 33 945 1739 itᵉ vg copˢᵃ·ᵇᵒ arm geo ‖ εἰπών, Δεῖ με πάντως τὴν ἑορτὴν τὴν ἐρχομένην ποιῆσαι εἰς Ἱεροσόλυμα. (D* δέ for με, D ἡμέραν for second τήν) P Ψ 049 056 0120 0142 88 104 181 326 330 436 451 614 629 630 1241 1505 (1877 τὴν ἐρχομένην ἑορτήν) 2127 2412 2492 (2495 μεῖναι εἰς Ἱερουσαλήμ) *Byz* itᵃʳ·ᵍⁱᵍ·ᵖʰ (itᵈ ἡμέραν for second τήν) vgᵐˢˢ syrᵖ·ʰ Ephraem Chrysostom Theophylact

⁹ **21–22** {B} ἀνήχθη ἀπὸ τῆς Ἐφέσου· καὶ κατελθών 𝔭⁷⁴ ℵᶜ (ℵ* ἀνήχθη δέ) A B Dᶜ (D* τοῦ Ἐφέσου) 630 945 1739 itᵃʳ·ᵈ vg syrʰ copˢᵃ·ᵇᵒ arm geo ‖ καὶ ἀνήχθη ἀπὸ τῆς Ἐφέσου· καὶ κατελθών E P Ψ 049 0120 (056 0142 καὶ καταβάς) (33 ἀπήχθη) 88 104 181 326 330 436 451 629 1241 1505 1877 2127 2492 2495 *Byz* itᵉ·ᵍⁱᵍ ‖ καὶ ἀνήχθη ἀπὸ τῆς Ἐφέσου· τὸν δὲ Ἀκύλαν εἴασεν ἐν Ἐφέσῳ· αὐτὸς δὲ ἀναχθεὶς ἦλθεν (614 omit καί) 2412 ‖ *but he left Aquila in Ephesus; embarking on a boat, he came* syrʰᵐᵍ ‖ *and he left Aquila and Priscilla at Ephesus, and he travelled by sea and came (see footnote 7)* syrᵖ copᵇᵒᵐˢ

ᶜ ᶜ **21** *c* minor, *c* major: (WH) RV ASV RSV NEB TT Zür ‖ *c* major, *c* minor: TR (Luth) (Seg) ‖ *c* minor, *c* minor: Bov Nes BF² ‖ *c* major, *c* major: AV Jer

---

19 αὐτὸς...Ἰουδαίοις Ac 17.17   **21** Πάλιν...θέλοντος Ro 1.10; 1 Cor 4.19

καὶ ἀσπασάμενος τὴν ἐκκλησίαν, κατέβη εἰς Ἀντιόχειαν, **23** καὶ ποιήσας χρόνον τινὰ ἐξῆλθεν, διερχόμενος καθεξῆς τὴν Γαλατικὴν χώραν καὶ Φρυγίαν, ἐπιστηρίζων πάντας τοὺς μαθητάς.

Apollos Preaches at Ephesus

24 Ἰουδαῖος δέ τις Ἀπολλῶς ὀνόματι, Ἀλεξανδρεὺς τῷ γένει, ἀνὴρ λόγιος, κατήντησεν εἰς Ἔφεσον, δυνατὸς ὢν ἐν ταῖς γραφαῖς. **25** οὗτος ἦν κατηχημένος τὴν ὁδὸν τοῦ κυρίου, καὶ ζέων τῷ πνεύματι ἐλάλει καὶ ἐδίδασκεν ἀκριβῶς τὰ περὶ τοῦ Ἰησοῦ[10], ἐπιστάμενος μόνον τὸ βάπτισμα Ἰωάννου. **26** οὗτός τε ἤρξατο παρρησιάζεσθαι ἐν τῇ συναγωγῇ· ἀκούσαντες δὲ αὐτοῦ Πρίσκιλλα καὶ Ἀκύλας προσελάβοντο αὐτὸν καὶ ἀκριβέστερον αὐτῷ ἐξέθεντο τὴν ὁδὸν τοῦ θεοῦ[11]. **27** βουλομένου δὲ αὐτοῦ διελθεῖν εἰς τὴν Ἀχαΐαν προτρεψάμενοι οἱ ἀδελφοὶ ἔγραψαν τοῖς μαθηταῖς ἀποδέξασθαι αὐτόν· ὃς παραγενόμενος συνεβάλετο πολὺ τοῖς πεπιστευκόσιν διὰ τῆς χάριτος· **28** εὐτόνως γὰρ τοῖς Ἰουδαίοις διακατηλέγχετο δημοσίᾳ ἐπιδεικνὺς διὰ τῶν γραφῶν εἶναι τὸν Χριστὸν Ἰησοῦν.

---

[10] **25** {B} τοῦ Ἰησοῦ 𝔭74vid ℵ A B E Ψ 0120 181 436 614 629 630 945 1241 1505 1739 2412 2495 arm Theophylact[b] ‖ Ἰησοῦ D 33 l598,(1153a?) ‖ τοῦ Ἰησοῦ or Ἰησοῦ itar,d,e,gig vg syrp,h copsa,bo eth geo ‖ τοῦ κυρίου P 049 056 0142 88 104 330 451 1877 2127 2492 *Byz Lect* Chrysostom Theophylact[a] ‖ τοῦ Χριστοῦ 326 ‖ τοῦ Χριστοῦ Ἰησοῦ 𝔭41vid ‖ τοῦ κυρίου Ἰησοῦ l680,1298

[11] **26** {C} τὴν ὁδὸν τοῦ θεοῦ 𝔭74 ℵ A B 33 88 181 326 436 614 (629* *omit* τοῦ) 629c 2412 l60,1356 itar vgww syrh copsa,bo arm geo Theophylact[b] ‖ τὴν ὁδὸν τοῦ κυρίου E 1505 2495 l598 (l599 τοῦ κυρίου ὁδόν) itc,e,p,ph vgcl syrp Augustine ‖ τὸν λόγον τοῦ κυρίου (630 τοῦ θεοῦ) 945 1739 ‖ τὴν τοῦ θεοῦ ὁδόν P Ψ 049 056 0142 104 330 451 1241 1877 2127 2492 *Byz Lect* (l1298 τῇ τοῦ θεοῦ ὁδῷ) Chrysostom ‖ τὴν ὁδόν D itd,gig

---

25 ζέων τῷ πνεύματι Ro 12.11　ἐπιστάμενος...Ἰωάννου Ac 19.3　**26** ἤρξατο... συναγωγῇ Ac 19.8　**27** βουλομένου...αὐτόν 2 Cor 3.1　**28** Ac 9.22: 17.3

---

went to Jerusalem and greeted the church, and then went to Antioch. [23] After spending some time there he left. He went through the region of Galatia and Phrygia, strengthening all the believers.

Apollos in Ephesus and Corinth

[24] A certain Jew named Apollos, born in Alexandria, came to Ephesus. He was an eloquent speaker and had a thorough knowledge of the Scriptures. [25] He had been instructed in the Way of the Lord, and with great enthusiasm spoke and taught correctly the facts about Jesus. However, he knew only the baptism of John. [26] He began to speak boldly in the synagogue. When Priscilla and Aquila heard him, they took him home with them and explained to him more correctly the Way of God. [27] Apollos decided to go to Greece, so the believers in Ephesus helped him by writing to their brothers in Greece, urging them to welcome him there. When he arrived, he was a great help to those who through God's grace had become believers. [28] For with his strong arguments he defeated the Jews in public debates, proving from the Scriptures that Jesus is the Messiah.

Paul in Ephesus

19 While Apollos was in Corinth, Paul traveled through the interior of the province and arrived in Ephesus. There he found some disciples, [2] and asked them, "Did you receive the Holy Spirit when you believed?" "We have not even heard that there is a Holy Spirit," they answered. [3] "Well, then, what kind of baptism did you receive?" Paul asked. "The baptism of John," they answered. [4] Paul said: "The baptism of John was for those who turned from their sins; and he told the people of Israel that they should believe in the one who was coming after him — that is, in Jesus." [5] When they heard this, they were baptized in the name of the Lord Jesus. [6] Paul placed his hands on them, and the Holy Spirit came upon them; they talked with strange sounds and also spoke God's word. [7] They were about twelve men in all.

[8] Paul went into the synagogue, and for three months spoke boldly with the people, arguing with them and trying to convince them about the Kingdom of God. [9] But some of them were stubborn and would not believe, and said evil things about the Way of the Lord before the whole group. So Paul left them and took the disciples with him; and every day[1] he held discussions in the lecture hall of Tyrannus. [10] This went on for two years, so that all the people who lived in the province of Asia, both Jews and Gentiles, heard the word of the Lord.

---

[1] **9** every day: *some mss. add* from 11:00 A.M. until 4:00 P.M.

Paul at Ephesus

19 Ἐγένετο δὲ ἐν τῷ τὸν Ἀπολλῶ εἶναι ἐν Κορίνθῳ Παῦλον διελθόντα τὰ ἀνωτερικὰ μέρη ἐλθεῖν εἰς Ἔφεσον καὶ εὑρεῖν τινας μαθητάς, 2 εἶπέν τε πρὸς αὐτούς, Εἰ πνεῦμα ἅγιον ἐλάβετε πιστεύσαντες; οἱ δὲ πρὸς αὐτόν, Ἀλλ' οὐδ' εἰ πνεῦμα ἅγιον ἔστιν[1] ἠκούσαμεν. 3 ὁ δὲ εἶπεν, Εἰς τί οὖν ἐβαπτίσθητε; οἱ δὲ εἶπαν, Εἰς τὸ Ἰωάννου βάπτισμα. 4 εἶπεν δὲ Παῦλος, Ἰωάννης ἐβάπτισεν βάπτισμα μετανοίας, τῷ λαῷ λέγων εἰς τὸν ἐρχόμενον μετ' αὐτὸν ἵνα πιστεύσωσιν, τοῦτ' ἔστιν εἰς τὸν Ἰησοῦν. 5 ἀκούσαντες δὲ ἐβαπτίσθησαν εἰς τὸ ὄνομα τοῦ κυρίου Ἰησοῦ· 6 καὶ ἐπιθέντος αὐτοῖς τοῦ Παύλου χεῖρας ἦλθε τὸ πνεῦμα τὸ ἅγιον ἐπ' αὐτούς, ἐλάλουν τε γλώσσαις καὶ ἐπροφήτευον. 7 ἦσαν δὲ οἱ πάντες ἄνδρες ὡσεὶ δώδεκα.

8 Εἰσελθὼν δὲ εἰς τὴν συναγωγὴν ἐπαρρησιάζετο ἐπὶ μῆνας τρεῖς διαλεγόμενος καὶ πείθων περὶ τῆς βασιλείας τοῦ θεοῦ. 9 ὡς δέ τινες ἐσκληρύνοντο καὶ ἠπείθουν κακολογοῦντες τὴν ὁδὸν ἐνώπιον τοῦ πλήθους, ἀποστὰς ἀπ' αὐτῶν ἀφώρισεν τοὺς μαθητάς, καθ' ἡμέραν διαλεγόμενος ἐν τῇ σχολῇ Τυράννου[2]. 10 τοῦτο δὲ ἐγένετο ἐπὶ ἔτη δύο, ὥστε πάντας τοὺς κατοικοῦντας τὴν Ἀσίαν ἀκοῦσαι τὸν λόγον τοῦ κυρίου, Ἰουδαίους τε καὶ Ἕλληνας.

---

[1] **2** {B} ἔστιν 𝔭74 ℵ A B D^b E P Ψ 049 056 0142 33 88 104 181 326 330 436 451 614 629 630 945 1241 1505 1739 1877 2127 2412 2492 2495 *Byz Lect* it^ar,dᶜ,e,gig,p* vg syr^p,h cop^bo arm geo ‖ λαμβάνουσίν τινες 𝔭38,(41) D* it^d* syr^hmg cop^sa

[2] **9** {B} Τυράννου 𝔭74 ℵ A B 945 1739 it^r vg^ww syr^p cop^sa,bo geo? ‖ Τυράννου τινός E P Ψ 049 056 0142 (88 ἑνός) 104 (181 Τυρρανίου) 326 330 436 451 629 630 1241 1505 1877 2127 2492 2495 *Byz* it^c,e vg^cl syr^h arm geo? Chrysostom ‖ Τυράννου τινὸς ἀπὸ ὥρας ε' ἕως δεκάτης D (614 2412 ἕως ὥρας δεκάτης) it^(ar),d,gig,ph vg^mss syr^h with * (Ambrosiaster)

---

2 Εἰ...πιστεύσαντες Ac 2.38   οὐδ'...ἠκούσαμεν Jn 7.39 Ac 8.16   4 Ἰωάννης... πιστεύσωσιν Mt 3.11; Mk 1.4, 7–8   6 ἐπιθέντος...αὐτούς Ac 8.17; 10.44   ἐλάλουν... ἐπροφήτευον Ac 10.46   8 Εἰσελθὼν...ἐπαρρησιάζετο Ac 18.26   9 ἀποστὰς...μαθητάς 2 Cor 6.17

The Sons of Sceva

11 Δυνάμεις τε οὐ τὰς τυχούσας ὁ θεὸς ἐποίει διὰ τῶν χειρῶν Παύλου, 12 ὥστε καὶ ἐπὶ τοὺς ἀσθενοῦντας ἀποφέρεσθαι ἀπὸ τοῦ χρωτὸς αὐτοῦ σουδάρια ἢ σιμικίνθια καὶ ἀπαλλάσσεσθαι ἀπ' αὐτῶν τὰς νόσους, τά τε πνεύματα τὰ πονηρὰ ἐκπορεύεσθαι. 13 ἐπεχείρησαν δέ τινες καὶ τῶν περιερχομένων Ἰουδαίων ἐξορκιστῶν ὀνομάζειν ἐπὶ τοὺς ἔχοντας τὰ πνεύματα τὰ πονηρὰ τὸ ὄνομα τοῦ κυρίου Ἰησοῦ λέγοντες, Ὁρκίζω ὑμᾶς τὸν Ἰησοῦν ὃν Παῦλος κηρύσσει. 14 ἦσαν δέ τινος Σκευᾶ Ἰουδαίου ἀρχιερέως ἑπτὰ υἱοὶ τοῦτο ποιοῦντες. 15 ἀποκριθὲν δὲ τὸ πνεῦμα τὸ πονηρὸν εἶπεν αὐτοῖς, Τὸν [μὲν] Ἰησοῦν γινώσκω καὶ τὸν Παῦλον ἐπίσταμαι, ὑμεῖς δὲ τίνες ἐστέ; 16 καὶ ἐφαλόμενος ὁ ἄνθρωπος ἐπ' αὐτοὺς ἐν ᾧ ἦν τὸ πνεῦμα τὸ πονηρὸν κατακυριεύσας ἀμφοτέρων ἴσχυσεν κατ' αὐτῶν, ὥστε γυμνοὺς καὶ τετραυματισμένους ἐκφυγεῖν ἐκ τοῦ οἴκου ἐκείνου. 17 τοῦτο δὲ ἐγένετο γνωστὸν πᾶσιν Ἰουδαίοις τε καὶ Ἕλλησιν τοῖς κατοικοῦσιν τὴν Ἔφεσον, καὶ ἐπέπεσεν φόβος ἐπὶ πάντας αὐτούς, καὶ ἐμεγαλύνετο τὸ ὄνομα τοῦ κυρίου Ἰησοῦ. 18 πολλοί τε τῶν πεπιστευκότων ἤρχοντο ἐξομολογούμενοι καὶ ἀναγγέλλοντες τὰς πράξεις αὐτῶν. 19 ἱκανοὶ δὲ τῶν τὰ περίεργα πραξάντων συνενέγκαντες τὰς βίβλους κατέκαιον ἐνώπιον πάντων· καὶ συνεψήφισαν τὰς τιμὰς αὐτῶν καὶ εὗρον ἀργυρίου μυριάδας πέντε. 20 Οὕτως κατὰ κράτος τοῦ κυρίου ὁ λόγος[3] ηὔξανεν καὶ ἴσχυεν.

The Sons of Sceva

[11] God was performing unusual miracles through Paul. [12] Even handkerchiefs and aprons he had used were taken to the sick, and their diseases were driven away and the evil spirits would go out of them. [13] Some Jews who traveled around and drove out evil spirits also tried to use the name of the Lord Jesus to do this. They said to the evil spirits, "I command you in the name of Jesus, whom Paul preaches." [14] It was the seven sons of a Jewish High Priest named Sceva who were doing so. [15] But the evil spirit said to them, "I know Jesus and I know about Paul; but you — who are you?" [16] The man who had the evil spirit in him attacked them with such violence that he defeated them. They all ran away from his house wounded and with their clothes torn off. [17] All the Jews and Gentiles who lived in Ephesus heard about this; they were all filled with fear, and the name of the Lord Jesus was given greater honor. [18] Many of the believers came, publicly admitting and revealing what they had done. [19] Many of those who had practiced magic brought their books together and burned them in the presence of everyone. They added up the price of the books and the total came to fifty thousand dollars. [20] In this powerful way the word of the Lord kept spreading and growing stronger.

---

[3] 20 {C} τοῦ κυρίου ὁ λόγος ℵ* A B ‖ ὁ λόγος τοῦ κυρίου 𝔭[74] ℵ[c] P Ψ 049 056 0142 33 104 181 326 330 451 614 629 630 945 1241 1505 1739 1877 2127 2412 2492 2495 Byz syr[h] cop[sa,bo] arm eth geo Chrysostom ‖ ὁ λόγος τοῦ θεοῦ E 88 436 it[ar,c,e,gig,p] vg cop[sams] ‖ ἡ πίστις τοῦ θεοῦ D it[d] syr[p]

---

11 Ac 14.3　　12 Ac 5.15–16　　13 ἐπεχείρησαν...Ἰησοῦ Mk 9.38; Lk 9.49　　15 ἀποκριθὲν ...γινώσκω Mk 1.24, 34; Lk 4.34, 41　　17 ἐπέπεσεν...αὐτούς Ac 5 5, 11　　20 Ac 6.7; 12.24

The Riot in Ephesus

²¹ After these things had happened, Paul made up his mind² to travel through Macedonia and Greece and go on to Jerusalem. "After I go there," he said, "I must also see Rome." ²² So he sent Timothy and Erastus, two of his helpers, to Macedonia, while he spent more time in the province of Asia.

²³ It was at this time that there was serious trouble in Ephesus because of the Way of the Lord. ²⁴ A certain silversmith named Demetrius made silver models of the temple of the goddess Artemis, and his business brought a great deal of profit to the workers. ²⁵ So he called them all together, with others whose work was like theirs, and said to them: "Men, you know that our prosperity comes from this work. ²⁶ You can see and hear for yourselves what this fellow Paul is doing. He says that gods made by men are not gods at all, and has succeeded in convincing many people, both here in Ephesus and in nearly the whole province of Asia. ²⁷ There is the danger, then, that this business of ours will get a bad name. Not only that, there is also the danger that the temple of the great goddess Artemis will come to mean nothing, and that her greatness will be destroyed — the goddess worshiped by everyone in Asia and in all the world!"

²⁸ As the crowd heard these words they became furious, and started shouting: "Great is Artemis of Ephesus!" ²⁹ The uproar spread throughout the whole city. The mob grabbed Gaius and Aristarchus, two Macedonians who were traveling with Paul, and rushed with them to the theater. ³⁰ Paul himself wanted to go before the crowd, but the believers would not let him. ³¹ Some of the provincial authorities, who were his friends, also sent him a message begging him not to show himself in the theater. ³² Meanwhile, the whole meeting was in an uproar: some people were shouting one thing, others were shouting something else, for most of them did not even know why they had come together. ³³ Some of

---

² 21 *Paul made up his mind*: or *Paul, led by the Spirit, decided*

The Riot at Ephesus

21 Ὡς δὲ ἐπληρώθη ταῦτα, ἔθετο ὁ Παῦλος ἐν τῷ πνεύματι διελθὼν τὴν Μακεδονίαν καὶ Ἀχαΐαν πορεύεσθαι εἰς Ἱεροσόλυμα, εἰπὼν ὅτι Μετὰ τὸ γενέσθαι με ἐκεῖ δεῖ με καὶ Ῥώμην ἰδεῖν. 22 ἀποστείλας δὲ εἰς τὴν Μακεδονίαν δύο τῶν διακονούντων αὐτῷ, Τιμόθεον καὶ Ἔραστον, αὐτὸς ἐπέσχεν χρόνον εἰς τὴν Ἀσίαν.

23 Ἐγένετο δὲ κατὰ τὸν καιρὸν ἐκεῖνον τάραχος οὐκ ὀλίγος περὶ τῆς ὁδοῦ. 24 Δημήτριος γάρ τις ὀνόματι, ἀργυροκόπος, ποιῶν ναοὺς ἀργυροῦς Ἀρτέμιδος παρείχετο τοῖς τεχνίταις οὐκ ὀλίγην ἐργασίαν, 25 οὓς συναθροίσας καὶ τοὺς περὶ τὰ τοιαῦτα ἐργάτας εἶπεν, Ἄνδρες, ἐπίστασθε ὅτι ἐκ ταύτης τῆς ἐργασίας ἡ εὐπορία ἡμῖν ἐστιν, 26 καὶ θεωρεῖτε καὶ ἀκούετε ὅτι οὐ μόνον Ἐφέσου ἀλλὰ σχεδὸν πάσης τῆς Ἀσίας ὁ Παῦλος οὗτος πείσας μετέστησεν ἱκανὸν ὄχλον, λέγων ὅτι οὐκ εἰσὶν θεοὶ οἱ διὰ χειρῶν γινόμενοι. 27 οὐ μόνον δὲ τοῦτο κινδυνεύει ἡμῖν τὸ μέρος εἰς ἀπελεγμὸν ἐλθεῖν, ἀλλὰ καὶ τὸ τῆς μεγάλης θεᾶς Ἀρτέμιδος ἱερὸν εἰς οὐθὲν λογισθῆναι, μέλλειν τε καὶ καθαιρεῖσθαι τῆς μεγαλειότητος αὐτῆς, ἣν ὅλη ἡ Ἀσία καὶ ἡ οἰκουμένη σέβεται.

28 Ἀκούσαντες δὲ καὶ γενόμενοι πλήρεις θυμοῦ ἔκραζον λέγοντες, Μεγάλη ἡ Ἄρτεμις Ἐφεσίων. 29 καὶ ἐπλήσθη ἡ πόλις τῆς συγχύσεως, ὥρμησάν τε ὁμοθυμαδὸν εἰς τὸ θέατρον συναρπάσαντες Γάϊον καὶ Ἀρίσταρχον Μακεδόνας, συνεκδήμους Παύλου. 30 Παύλου δὲ βουλομένου εἰσελθεῖν εἰς τὸν δῆμον οὐκ εἴων αὐτὸν οἱ μαθηταί· 31 τινὲς δὲ καὶ τῶν Ἀσιαρχῶν, ὄντες αὐτῷ φίλοι, πέμψαντες πρὸς αὐτὸν παρεκάλουν μὴ δοῦναι ἑαυτὸν εἰς τὸ θέατρον. 32 ἄλλοι μὲν οὖν ἄλλο τι ἔκραζον, ἦν γὰρ ἡ ἐκκλησία συγκεχυμένη, καὶ οἱ πλείους οὐκ ᾔδεισαν τίνος ἕνεκα συνεληλύθεισαν. 33 ἐκ δὲ τοῦ ὄχλου συνεβίβα-

---

21 Μετὰ...Ῥώμην ἰδεῖν Ac 23.11; Ro 1.13   23 2 Cor 1.8   24 παρείχετο...ἐργασίαν Ac 16.16   26 λέγων...γινόμενοι Ac 17.29

σαν[4] Ἀλέξανδρον, προβαλόντων αὐτὸν τῶν Ἰουδαίων· ὁ δὲ Ἀλέξανδρος κατασείσας τὴν χεῖρα ἤθελεν ἀπολογεῖσθαι τῷ δήμῳ. 34 ἐπιγνόντες δὲ ὅτι Ἰουδαῖός ἐστιν φωνὴ ἐγένετο μία ἐκ πάντων ὡς ἐπὶ ὥρας δύο κραζόντων, Μεγάλη ἡ Ἄρτεμις Ἐφεσίων. 35 καταστείλας δὲ ὁ γραμματεὺς τὸν ὄχλον φησίν, Ἄνδρες Ἐφέσιοι, τίς γάρ ἐστιν ἀνθρώπων ὃς οὐ γινώσκει τὴν Ἐφεσίων πόλιν νεωκόρον οὖσαν τῆς μεγάλης Ἀρτέμιδος καὶ τοῦ διοπετοῦς; 36 ἀναντιρρήτων οὖν ὄντων τούτων δέον ἐστὶν ὑμᾶς κατεσταλμένους ὑπάρχειν καὶ μηδὲν προπετὲς πράσσειν. 37 ἠγάγετε γὰρ τοὺς ἄνδρας τούτους οὔτε ἱεροσύλους οὔτε βλασφημοῦντας τὴν θεὸν ἡμῶν[5]. 38 εἰ μὲν οὖν Δημήτριος καὶ οἱ σὺν αὐτῷ τεχνῖται ἔχουσι πρός τινα λόγον, ἀγοραῖοι ἄγονται καὶ ἀνθύπατοί εἰσιν· ἐγκαλείτωσαν ἀλλήλοις. 39 εἰ δέ τι περαιτέρω[6] ἐπιζητεῖτε, ἐν τῇ ἐννόμῳ ἐκκλησίᾳ ἐπιλυθήσεται. 40 καὶ γὰρ κινδυνεύομεν ἐγκαλεῖσθαι στάσεως περὶ τῆς σήμερον,[a] μηδενὸς αἰτίου ὑπάρχοντος,[a] περὶ οὗ [οὐ][7] δυνησόμεθα

the people concluded that Alexander was responsible, since the Jews made him go up to the front. Then Alexander motioned with his hand and tried to make a speech of defense before the people. 34 But when they recognized that he was a Jew, they all shouted together the same thing for two hours: "Great is Artemis of Ephesus!"

35 At last the city clerk was able to calm the crowd. "Men of Ephesus!" he said. "Everyone knows that the city of Ephesus is the keeper of the temple of the great Artemis and of the sacred stone that fell down from heaven. 36 Nobody can deny these things. So then, you must calm down and not do anything reckless. 37 You have brought these men here, even though they have not robbed temples or said evil things about our goddess. 38 If Demetrius and his workers have an accusation against someone, there are the regular days for court and there are the authorities; they can accuse each other there. 39 But if there is something more that you want, it will have to be settled in the legal meeting of citizens. 40 For there is the danger that we will be accused of a riot in what has happened today. There is no excuse for all this uproar, and we would not be able

---

[4] 33 {B} συνεβίβασαν 𝔭74 ℵ A B Egr 33 630 945 1739 syrpal ∥ προεβίβασαν Db P Ψ 049 056 0142 88 104 181 326 330 436 451 614 (629 προσεβίβασαν) 1241 1505 1877 2127 2412 2492 2495 Byz syr(p),h arm geo Chrysostom ∥ κατεβίβασαν Dgr* ∥ detraxerunt itar,e,gig vg ∥ distraxerunt itd

[5] 37 {B} ἡμῶν 𝔭74 ℵ A B D E2 Ψ 181 330 451 945 1739 itd,e,gig syrp copsa,boms arm ethpp geo Chrysostom Theophylacta ∥ ὑμῶν Egr P 049 056 0142 88 104 326 436 614 629 630 1241 1505 1877 2127 2412 2492 2495 Byz itar vg syrh copbo ethro Chrysostom Theophylactb

[6] 39 {C} περαιτέρω 𝔭74 B 33 945 1739 itd,gig ∥ περὶ ἑτέρων ℵ A Dgr P Ψ 049 050 0142 88 104 181 326 330 436 451 614 629 630 1241 1505 1877 2127 2412 2492 2495 Byz itar,e vg syrp,h copsa,bo arm eth Ephraem Chrysostom ∥ περ' ἕτερον Egr geo

[7] 40 {D} οὐ ℵ A B P Ψ 049 056 0142 33 88 104 181 326 330 436 451 614 629 1241 1505 1739 1877 2127 2412 2492 2495 Byz itp* syrp,h arm ethvid geo Chrysostom Theophylacta ∥ omit 𝔭74 D E 630 945 itar,d,e,gig vg copsa?bo? Chrysostom Theophylactb

---

a a 40 a minor, a minor: Bov Nes BF2 ∥ a none, a minor: WH ∥ a major, a minor: NEB TT ∥ a minor, a major: RV ASV ∥ different text: TR AV RSV Zür Luth Jer Seg

33 κατασείσας τὴν χεῖρα Ac 12.17; 13.16; 21.40

to give a good reason for it.'' [41] After
saying this, he dismissed the meeting.

To Macedonia and Greece

20 After the uproar died down, Paul
called together the believers, and with
words of encouragement said good-bye
to them. Then he left and went on to
Macedonia. [2] He went through those
regions and encouraged the people with
many messages. Then he came to Greece,
[3] where he stayed three months. He was
getting ready to go to Syria when he
discovered that the Jews were plotting
against him; so he decided to go back
through Macedonia. [4] Sopater, the son
of Pyrrhus, from Berea, went with him;
so did Aristarchus and Secundus, from
Thessalonica; Gaius, from Derbe; Timothy; and Tychicus and Trophimus, from
the province of Asia. [5] They went ahead
and waited for us in Troas. [6] We sailed

ἀποδοῦναι λόγον περὶ τῆς συστροφῆς ταύτης. [b]καὶ
ταῦτα εἰπὼν ἀπέλυσεν τὴν ἐκκλησίαν.

Paul's Journey to Macedonia and Greece

20 Μετὰ δὲ τὸ παύσασθαι τὸν θόρυβον μεταπεμψά-
μενος ὁ Παῦλος τοὺς μαθητὰς καὶ παρακαλέσας, ἀσπασάμενος ἐξῆλθεν πορεύεσθαι εἰς Μακεδονίαν. **2** διελθὼν
δὲ τὰ μέρη ἐκεῖνα καὶ παρακαλέσας αὐτοὺς λόγῳ πολλῷ
ἦλθεν εἰς τὴν Ἑλλάδα, **3** ποιήσας τε μῆνας τρεῖς γενομένης ἐπιβουλῆς αὐτῷ ὑπὸ τῶν Ἰουδαίων μέλλοντι ἀνάγεσθαι εἰς τὴν Συρίαν ἐγένετο γνώμης τοῦ ὑποστρέφειν
διὰ Μακεδονίας. **4** συνείπετο δὲ αὐτῷ[1] Σώπατρος Πύρρου[2]
Βεροιαῖος, Θεσσαλονικέων δὲ Ἀρίσταρχος καὶ Σε-
κοῦνδος, καὶ Γάϊος Δερβαῖος[3] καὶ Τιμόθεος, Ἀσιανοὶ
δὲ Τυχικὸς καὶ Τρόφιμος. **5** οὗτοι δὲ προελθόντες[4]
ἔμενον ἡμᾶς ἐν Τρῳάδι· **6** ἡμεῖς δὲ ἐξεπλεύσαμεν μετὰ

[1] 4 {C} συνείπετο δὲ αὐτῷ p⁷⁴ ℵ B 33 629 itᵃʳ vg syrᵖᵃˡ copˢᵃ,ᵇᵒ eth ∥
συνείπετο δὲ αὐτῷ ἄχρι τῆς Ἀσίας A E P 049 056 0142 88 (104 μέχρι)
181 326 330 436 451 614 630 945 1241 1505 1739 1877 2127 2412 2492 2495 Byz
itᵉ,ᵍⁱᵍ syrʰ arm geo Chrysostom ∥ συνείποντο δὲ αὐτῷ ἄχρι τῆς Ἀσίας
Ψ (syrᵖ omit δέ) ∥ μέλλοντος οὖν ἐξιέναι αὐτοῦ μέχρι τῆς Ἀσίας D itᵈ ∥
When he was about to go, they accompanied him to Asia syrʰᵐᵍ

[2] 4 {B} Πύρρου p⁷⁴ ℵ A B D E Ψ (33 Πύρου) 104 181 436 630 945 1739
it⁽ᵃʳ⁾,ᶜ,ᵉ,ᵍⁱᵍ,ᵖ,ᵖʰ (itᵈ virri) vg syrʰᵐᵍ copˢᵃ,ᵇᵒ (copˢᵃᵐˢ Πύρρα) arm geo Origenˡᵃᵗ
Theophylactᵇ ∥ Πυθίου 88 ∥ υἱὸς Βέρου syrᵖᵃˡ copˢᵃᵐˢ ∥ omit P 049 056
0142 326 330 451 614 629 1241 1505 1877 2127 2412 2492 2495 Byz syrᵖ,ʰ eth
Chrysostom Theophylactᵃ

[3] 4 {C} Δερβαῖος p⁷⁴ ℵ Dᶜ E P Ψ 049 056 0142 88 104 181 326 330 436
451 614 629 630 945 1241 1505 1739 1877 2127 2412 2492 2495 Byz itᵃʳ,ᵉ vg
syrᵖ,ʰ,ᵖᵃˡ copˢᵃ arm? geo? ∥ ὁ Δερβαῖος A B 33 copᵇᵒ? arm? geo? ∥ Δουβέριος
D*ᵛⁱᵈ (itᵈ Doverius, itᵍⁱᵍ Doberius)

[4] 5 {C} προελθόντες p⁷⁴ B³ D 104 326 330 451 614 629ᶜ 630 2412 2492
Byzᵖᵗ itᵃʳ,ᵈ,ᵉ,ᵍⁱᵍ vg syrᵖ,ʰ copˢᵃ,ᵇᵒ arm eth geo Chrysostom ∥ προσελθόντες
ℵ B* Eᵍʳ P Ψ 049 056 0142 88 181 436 629* 945 1241 1505 1739 1877 2127 2495
Byzᵖᵗ

[b] 40 (41) b no number: TRᵉᵈ WHᵉᵈ Bov Nes BF² TT Zür Luth Jer Seg ∥ b number 41: TRᵉᵈ WHᵉᵈ
AV RV ASV RSV NEB

τὰς ἡμέρας τῶν ἀζύμων ἀπὸ Φιλίππων, καὶ ἤλθομεν πρὸς αὐτοὺς εἰς τὴν Τρῳάδα ἄχρι ἡμερῶν πέντε, οὗ διετρίψαμεν ἡμέρας ἑπτά.

Paul's Farewell Visit to Troas

7 Ἐν δὲ τῇ μιᾷ τῶν σαββάτων συνηγμένων ἡμῶν κλάσαι ἄρτον ὁ Παῦλος διελέγετο αὐτοῖς, μέλλων ἐξιέναι τῇ ἐπαύριον, παρέτεινέν τε τὸν λόγον μέχρι μεσονυκτίου. **8** ἦσαν δὲ λαμπάδες ἱκαναὶ ἐν τῷ ὑπερῴῳ οὗ ἦμεν συνηγμένοι· **9** καθεζόμενος δέ τις νεανίας ὀνόματι Εὔτυχος ἐπὶ τῆς θυρίδος, καταφερόμενος ὕπνῳ βαθεῖ διαλεγομένου τοῦ Παύλου^a ἐπὶ πλεῖον,^{a} κατενεχθεὶς ἀπὸ τοῦ ὕπνου ἔπεσεν ἀπὸ τοῦ τριστέγου κάτω καὶ ἤρθη νεκρός. **10** καταβὰς δὲ ὁ Παῦλος ἐπέπεσεν αὐτῷ καὶ συμπεριλαβὼν εἶπεν, Μὴ θορυβεῖσθε, ἡ γὰρ ψυχὴ αὐτοῦ ἐν αὐτῷ ἐστιν. **11** ἀναβὰς δὲ καὶ κλάσας τὸν ἄρτον καὶ γευσάμενος ἐφ' ἱκανόν τε ὁμιλήσας ἄχρι αὐγῆς οὕτως ἐξῆλθεν. **12** ἤγαγον δὲ τὸν παῖδα ζῶντα, καὶ παρεκλήθησαν οὐ μετρίως.

The Voyage from Troas to Miletus

13 Ἡμεῖς δὲ προελθόντες ἐπὶ τὸ πλοῖον^b ἀνήχθημεν ἐπὶ τὴν Ἆσσον, ἐκεῖθεν μέλλοντες ἀναλαμβάνειν τὸν Παῦλον, οὕτως γὰρ διατεταγμένος ἦν μέλλων αὐτὸς πεζεύειν. **14** ὡς δὲ συνέβαλεν ἡμῖν εἰς τὴν Ἆσσον,

---

5 13 {C} προελθόντες...πλοῖον 𝔭74 ℵ B³ C Ψ 33 181 436 614 945 1505 1739 2412 2495 cop^sa?bo? geo Theophylact^b ‖ προσελθόντες...πλοῖον A B* E P 049 056 0142 88 104 326 330 451 629 (630^vid add καί) 1241 1877 2127 2492 Byz it^ar,e arm Chrysostom Theophylact^a ‖ προ- (or προσ-) ελθόντες... πλοῖον vg syr^h (syr^pal πλοῖον καί) ‖ κατελθόντες...πλοῖον D^gr (syr^p πλοῖον καί) ‖ προήλθομεν...πλοῖον καί 𝔭41^vid ‖ descendimus ad navem et it^gig ‖ ascendimus in navem it^d

---

$^{a\ a}$ **9** a none, a minor: TR WH Bov Nes BF² AV RV ASV RSV (NEB) (TT) Zür Luth (Jer) Seg ‖ a minor, a none: WH^mg

---

7 συνηγμένων...ἄρτον Ac 2.42, 46   **10** 1 Kgs 17.21

Paul's Last Visit in Troas

7 On Saturday[1] evening we gathered together for the fellowship meal. Paul spoke to the people, and kept on speaking until midnight, since he was going to leave the next day. **8** There were many lamps in the upstairs room where we were meeting. **9** A young man named Eutychus was sitting in the window; and as Paul kept on talking, Eutychus got sleepier and sleepier, until he finally went sound asleep and fell from the third story to the ground. They picked him up, and he was dead. **10** But Paul went down and threw himself on him and hugged him. "Don't worry," he said, "he is still alive!" **11** Then he went back upstairs, broke bread, and ate. After talking with them for a long time until sunrise, Paul left. **12** They took the young man home alive, and were greatly comforted.

From Troas to Miletus

13 We went on ahead to the ship and sailed off to Assos, where we were going to take Paul aboard. He had told us to do this, because he was going there by land. **14** When he met us in Assos, we

---

[1] **7** Saturday: or Sunday

took him aboard and went on to Mitylene.
15 We sailed from there and arrived off
Chios the next day. A day later we came
to Samos, and the following day we
reached Miletus. 16 Paul had decided to
sail on by Ephesus, so as not to lose any
time in the province of Asia. He was in a
hurry to arrive in Jerusalem, if at all
possible, by the day of Pentecost.

Paul's Farewell Speech to the Elders of Ephesus

17 Paul sent a message from Miletus
to Ephesus, asking the elders of the
church to meet him. 18 When they came
he said to them: "You know how I
spent the whole time I was with you,
from the first day I arrived in the province
of Asia. 19 With all humility and tears
I did my work as the Lord's servant,
through the hard times that came to
me because of the plots of the Jews.
20 You know that I did not hold back
anything that would be of help to you
as I preached and taught you in public
and in your homes. 21 To Jews and
Gentiles alike I gave solemn warning that
they should turn from their sins to God,
and believe in our Lord Jesus. 22 And
now, in obedience to the Holy Spirit,
I am going to Jerusalem, not knowing

ἀναλαβόντες αὐτὸν ἤλθομεν εἰς Μιτυλήνην, 15 κἀκεῖθεν
ἀποπλεύσαντες τῇ ἐπιούσῃ κατηντήσαμεν ἄντικρυς Χίου,
τῇ δὲ ἑτέρᾳ παρεβάλομεν εἰς Σάμον, τῇ δὲ⁶ ἐχομένῃ
ἤλθομεν εἰς Μίλητον· 16 κεκρίκει γὰρ ὁ Παῦλος παρα-
πλεῦσαι τὴν Ἔφεσον, ὅπως μὴ γένηται αὐτῷ χρονοτρι-
βῆσαι ἐν τῇ Ἀσίᾳ, ἔσπευδεν γὰρ εἰ δυνατὸν εἴη αὐτῷ
τὴν ἡμέραν τῆς πεντηκοστῆς γενέσθαι εἰς Ἰεροσόλυμα.

Paul Speaks to the Ephesian Elders

17 Ἀπὸ δὲ τῆς Μιλήτου πέμψας εἰς Ἔφεσον μετεκαλέσατο τοὺς πρεσβυτέρους τῆς ἐκκλησίας. 18 ὡς δὲ
παρεγένοντο πρὸς αὐτὸν εἶπεν αὐτοῖς, Ὑμεῖς ἐπίστασθε
ἀπὸ πρώτης ἡμέρας ἀφ' ἧς ἐπέβην εἰς τὴν Ἀσίαν πῶς
μεθ' ὑμῶν τὸν πάντα χρόνον ἐγενόμην, 19 δουλεύων τῷ
κυρίῳ μετὰ πάσης ταπεινοφροσύνης καὶ δακρύων καὶ
πειρασμῶν τῶν συμβάντων μοι ἐν ταῖς ἐπιβουλαῖς τῶν
Ἰουδαίων· 20 ὡς οὐδὲν ὑπεστειλάμην τῶν συμφερόντων
τοῦ μὴ ἀναγγεῖλαι ὑμῖν καὶ διδάξαι ὑμᾶς δημοσίᾳ καὶ
κατ' οἴκους, 21 διαμαρτυρόμενος Ἰουδαίοις τε καὶ
Ἕλλησιν τὴν εἰς θεὸν μετάνοιαν καὶ πίστιν εἰς τὸν κύριον
ἡμῶν Ἰησοῦν⁷. 22 καὶ νῦν ἰδοὺ δεδεμένος ἐγὼ τῷ πνεύματι πορεύομαι εἰς Ἰερουσαλήμ, τὰ ἐν αὐτῇ συναντήσοντά

⁶15 {C} τῇ δέ 𝔭⁷⁴ ℵ A B C Eᵍʳ 33 630 1739 ‖ καὶ τῇ 436 629 itᵃʳᵛⁱᵈ vg
arm geo ‖ τῇ itᵉ copᵇᵒ ethᵖᵖ ‖ καὶ μείναντες ἐν Τρωγυλλίῳ τῇ 𝔭ᵈⁱᵛⁱᵈ D P
049 (056 0142 Στρογγυλίῳ) 88 (104 Στογυλίῳ) 181 326 330 451 614 945
1241 1505 1877 2127 2412 2492 2495 Byz itᵈ·ᵍⁱᵍ syrᵖ·ʰ copˢᵃ Chrysostom
Theophylact ‖ μείνοντες εἰς τὸ Γύλλιον· τῇ Ψ

⁷ 21 {B} εἰς τὸν κύριον ἡμῶν Ἰησοῦν B P Ψ 056 0142 614 1877 2127
2412 2492 Byzᵖᵗ itᵍⁱᵍ syrʰ copˢᵃ ethʳᵒ Lucifer Basil Theophylactᵃ ‖ εἰς τὸν
κύριον ἡμῶν Ἰησοῦν Χριστόν 𝔭⁷⁴ ℵ A C (E omit ἡμῶν) 049 33 88 104 181
326 330 436 451 629 630 945 1241 1505 1739 2495 Byzᵖᵗ l⁵⁹⁹ itᵃʳ·ᵈ (itᵉ copᵇᵒᵐˢˢ omit
ἡμῶν) vg syrᵖ copᵇᵒ arm ethᵖᵖ geo Chrysostom Theophylactᵇ ‖ διὰ τοῦ
κυρίου ἡμῶν Ἰησοῦ Χριστοῦ Dᵍʳ itᵖʰ

17 Ac 18.21   18 ἀπὸ...ἐγενόμην Ac 18.19; 19.10   19 ταῖς...Ἰουδαίων Ac 20.3
22 δεδεμένος...Ἰερουσαλήμ Ac 19.21

μοι μὴ εἰδώς, **23** πλὴν ὅτι τὸ πνεῦμα τὸ ἅγιον κατὰ πόλιν διαμαρτύρεταί μοι λέγον ὅτι δεσμὰ καὶ θλίψεις με μένουσιν. **24** ἀλλ' οὐδενὸς λόγου ποιοῦμαι τὴν ψυχὴν τιμίαν ἐμαυτῷ ὡς τελειώσω τὸν δρόμον μου καὶ τὴν διακονίαν ἣν ἔλαβον παρὰ τοῦ κυρίου Ἰησοῦ, διαμαρτύρασθαι τὸ εὐαγγέλιον τῆς χάριτος τοῦ θεοῦ.

25 Καὶ νῦν ἰδοὺ ἐγὼ οἶδα ὅτι οὐκέτι ὄψεσθε τὸ πρόσωπόν μου ὑμεῖς πάντες ἐν οἷς διῆλθον κηρύσσων τὴν βασιλείαν· **26** διότι μαρτύρομαι ὑμῖν ἐν τῇ σήμερον ἡμέρᾳ ὅτι καθαρός εἰμι ἀπὸ τοῦ αἵματος πάντων, **27** οὐ γὰρ ὑπεστειλάμην τοῦ μὴ ἀναγγεῖλαι πᾶσαν τὴν βουλὴν τοῦ θεοῦ ὑμῖν. **28** προσέχετε ἑαυτοῖς καὶ παντὶ τῷ ποιμνίῳ, ἐν ᾧ ὑμᾶς τὸ πνεῦμα τὸ ἅγιον ἔθετο ἐπισκόπους, ποιμαίνειν τὴν ἐκκλησίαν τοῦ θεοῦ[8], ἣν περιεποιήσατο διὰ τοῦ αἵματος τοῦ ἰδίου[9]. **29** ἐγὼ οἶδα ὅτι εἰσελεύσονται μετὰ τὴν ἄφιξίν μου λύκοι βαρεῖς εἰς ὑμᾶς μὴ φειδόμενοι τοῦ ποιμνίου, **30** καὶ ἐξ ὑμῶν αὐτῶν ἀναστήσονται ἄνδρες λαλοῦντες διεστραμμένα τοῦ ἀποσπᾶν τοὺς μαθητὰς ὀπίσω αὐτῶν. **31** διὸ γρηγορεῖτε, μνημονεύοντες ὅτι τριετίαν

what will happen to me there. [23] I only know that in every city the Holy Spirit has warned me that prison and troubles wait for me. [24] But I reckon my own life to be worth nothing to me, in order that I may complete my mission and finish the work that the Lord Jesus gave me to do, which is to declare the Good News of the grace of God.

[25] "I have gone about among all of you, preaching the Kingdom of God. And now I know that none of you will ever see me again. [26] So I solemnly declare to you this very day: if any of you should be lost, I am not responsible. [27] For I have not held back from announcing to you the whole purpose of God. [28] Keep watch over yourselves and over all the flock which the Holy Spirit has placed in your charge. Be shepherds of the church of God,[2] which he made his own through the death of his own Son.[3] [29] For I know that after I leave, fierce wolves will come among you, and they will not spare the flock. [30] And the time will come when some men from your own group will tell lies to lead the believers away after them. [31] Watch, then, and remember that with many tears, day

---

[8] 28 {C} θεοῦ ℵ B 056 0142 104 614 629 1505 1877* 2412 2495 *l*[60,368,598,603,611,1021,1291,1439] it[ar,c] vg syr[p,h] cop[boms] geo Basil Orsisius Ambrose Epiphanius Chrysostom Theodore Caelestinus Cyril Ps-Athanasius Primasius Antiochus Theophylact[b] ∥ κυρίου 𝔭[74] A C* D E Ψ 33 181 436 451 630 945 1739 *l*[164,599] it[d,e,gig,p] syr[hmg] cop[sa,bo] arm Irenaeus[lat] Ambrosiaster Lucifer Athanasius Apostolic Constitutions Didymus Chrysostom Jerome Theophylact[c] ∥ κυρίου καὶ θεοῦ C[3] P 049 326 2127 2492 Byz[pt] Lect Theophylact[a] ∥ κυρίου τοῦ θεοῦ 88 330 1241 1877[c] Byz[pt] ∥ κυρίου Ἰησοῦ Ambrosiaster ∥ Ἰησοῦ Χριστοῦ it[m] ∥ Χριστοῦ Athanasius Theodoret

[9] 28 {B} αἵματος τοῦ ἰδίου 𝔭[74] ℵ A B C D E Ψ 33 181 326 436 630 945 1739 *l*[60] syr[p,h,hgr] arm geo Didymus ∥ ἰδίου αἵματος P 049 056 0142 88 104 330 451 614 629 1241 1505 1877 2127 2412 2492 2495 Byz Lect Athanasius Didymus Chrysostom (Caelestinus) Maximus Antiochus Ps-Oecumenius Anthony Theophylact

2 28 God: *some mss. read* the Lord

3 28 the death of his own Son: *or* his own death

---

23 Ac 21.4, 11   θλίψεις με μένουσιν Ac 9.16   **24** Lk 21.19   ὡς τελειώσω τὸν δρόμον μου 2 Tm 4.7   **26** καθαρός...πάντων Ac 18.6   **28** προσέχετε...θεοῦ 1 Pe 5.2   τὴν...περιεποιήσατο Ps 74.2   **29** λύκοι βαρεῖς Mt 7.15; Jn 10.12   **30** ἐξ...διεστραμμένα 1 Jn 2.19   **31** Ac 19.10

and night, I taught every one of you for three years.

32 "And now I place you in the care of God and the message of his grace. He is able to build you up and give you the blessings he keeps for all his people. 33 I have not coveted anyone's silver or gold or clothing. 34 You yourselves know that with these hands of mine I have worked and provided everything that my companions and I have needed. 35 I have shown you in all things that by working hard in this way we must help the weak, remembering the words that the Lord Jesus himself said, 'There is more happiness in giving than in receiving.'"

36 When Paul finished, he knelt down with them all and prayed. 37 They were all crying as they hugged him and kissed him good-bye. 38 They were especially sad at the words he had said that they would never see him again. And so they went with him to the ship.

Paul Goes to Jerusalem

21 We said good-bye to them and left. After sailing straight across, we came to Cos; the next day we reached Rhodes, and from there we went on to Patara. 2 There we found a ship that was going

νύκτα καὶ ἡμέραν οὐκ ἐπαυσάμην μετὰ δακρύων νουθετῶν ἕνα ἕκαστον. 32 καὶ τὰ νῦν παρατίθεμαι ὑμᾶς τῷ θεῷ[10] καὶ τῷ λόγῳ τῆς χάριτος αὐτοῦ τῷ δυναμένῳ οἰκοδομῆσαι καὶ δοῦναι τὴν κληρονομίαν ἐν τοῖς ἡγιασμένοις πᾶσιν. 33 ἀργυρίου ἢ χρυσίου ἢ ἱματισμοῦ οὐδενὸς ἐπεθύμησα· 34 αὐτοὶ γινώσκετε ὅτι ταῖς χρείαις μου καὶ τοῖς οὖσιν μετ' ἐμοῦ ὑπηρέτησαν αἱ χεῖρες αὗται.[b] 35 πάντα[b] ὑπέδειξα ὑμῖν ὅτι οὕτως κοπιῶντας δεῖ ἀντιλαμβάνεσθαι τῶν ἀσθενούντων, μνημονεύειν τε τῶν λόγων τοῦ κυρίου Ἰησοῦ ὅτι αὐτὸς εἶπεν, Μακάριόν ἐστιν μᾶλλον διδόναι ἢ λαμβάνειν.

36 Καὶ ταῦτα εἰπὼν θεὶς τὰ γόνατα αὐτοῦ σὺν πᾶσιν αὐτοῖς προσηύξατο. 37 ἱκανὸς δὲ κλαυθμὸς ἐγένετο πάντων, καὶ ἐπιπεσόντες ἐπὶ τὸν τράχηλον τοῦ Παύλου κατεφίλουν αὐτόν, 38 ὀδυνώμενοι μάλιστα ἐπὶ τῷ λόγῳ ᾧ εἰρήκει ὅτι οὐκέτι μέλλουσιν τὸ πρόσωπον αὐτοῦ θεωρεῖν. προέπεμπον δὲ αὐτὸν εἰς τὸ πλοῖον.

Paul's Journey to Jerusalem

21 Ὡς δὲ ἐγένετο ἀναχθῆναι ἡμᾶς ἀποσπασθέντας ἀπ' αὐτῶν, εὐθυδρομήσαντες ἤλθομεν εἰς τὴν Κῶ, τῇ δὲ ἑξῆς εἰς τὴν Ῥόδον, κἀκεῖθεν εἰς Πάταρα[1]· 2 καὶ

[10] 32 {B} θεῷ p[74] ℵ A C D[gr] E P Ψ 049 056 0142 88 104 181 436 614 629 630 945 1241 1505 1739 1877 2127 2412 2492 2495 Byz Lect (l[60] ὑμᾶς, ἀδελφοί, τῷ θεῷ) it[ar,e] vg syr[p,h] cop[sa] arm geo ∥ κυρίῳ B 326 330 451 l[599] it[gig] cop[sa mss,bo]

[1] 1 {C} Πάταρα (p[74] A C Πάτερα) ℵ B E P Ψ 049 056 0142 33 88 104 181 326 330 436 451 614 629 630 945 1241 1505 1739 1877 2127 2412 2492 2495 Byz it[ar,e] vg syr[p,h,gr] cop[bo] arm geo ∥ Πάταρα καὶ Μύρα (see 27.5) (p[41vid] εἰς Μύρα) D[gr] it[gig] (it[ph] Hyram) vg[mss] cop[sa]

[b b] 34-35 b major, b none: TR WH Bov Nes BF² AV RV ASV RSV TT Zür Luth Jer Seg ∥ b none, b minor: NEB

31 οὐκ...ἕκαστον 1 Th 2.11   32 κληρονομίαν...πᾶσιν Dt 33.3-4; Wsd 5.5; Ac 26.18 33 1 Sm 12.3; 1 Cor 9.11   34 Ac 18.3; 1 Cor 4.12; 1 Th 2.9   35 Μακάριον...λαμβάνειν Mt 10.8   36 Ac 21.5   37 ἐπιπεσόντες...αὐτόν Ac 21.5; Ro 16.16; 1 Pe 5.14   38 ἐπί...θεωρεῖν Ac 20.25

εὑρόντες πλοῖον διαπερῶν εἰς Φοινίκην ἐπιβάντες ἀνήχθημεν. 3 ἀναφάναντες δὲ τὴν Κύπρον καὶ καταλιπόντες
αὐτὴν εὐώνυμον ἐπλέομεν εἰς Συρίαν, καὶ κατήλθομεν
εἰς Τύρον, ἐκεῖσε γὰρ τὸ πλοῖον ἦν ἀποφορτιζόμενον
τὸν γόμον. 4 ἀνευρόντες δὲ τοὺς μαθητὰς ἐπεμείναμεν
αὐτοῦ ἡμέρας ἑπτά, οἵτινες τῷ Παύλῳ ἔλεγον διὰ τοῦ
πνεύματος μὴ ἐπιβαίνειν εἰς Ἱεροσόλυμα. 5 ὅτε δὲ
ἐγένετο ἡμᾶς ἐξαρτίσαι τὰς ἡμέρας, ἐξελθόντες ἐπορευό-
μεθα προπεμπόντων ἡμᾶς πάντων σὺν γυναιξὶ καὶ τέκνοις
ἕως ἔξω τῆς πόλεως, καὶ θέντες τὰ γόνατα ἐπὶ τὸν αἰγιαλὸν
προσευξάμενοι 6 ἀπησπασάμεθα ἀλλήλους, καὶ ἐνέβημεν
εἰς τὸ πλοῖον, ἐκεῖνοι δὲ ὑπέστρεψαν εἰς τὰ ἴδια.

7 Ἡμεῖς δὲ τὸν πλοῦν διανύσαντες ἀπὸ Τύρου κατηντήσαμεν εἰς Πτολεμαΐδα, καὶ ἀσπασάμενοι τοὺς ἀδελφοὺς
ἐμείναμεν ἡμέραν μίαν παρ' αὐτοῖς. 8 τῇ δὲ ἐπαύριον
ἐξελθόντες ἤλθομεν² εἰς Καισάρειαν, καὶ εἰσελθόντες εἰς
τὸν οἶκον Φιλίππου τοῦ εὐαγγελιστοῦ ὄντος ἐκ τῶν ἑπτὰ
ἐμείναμεν παρ' αὐτῷ. 9 τούτῳ δὲ ἦσαν θυγατέρες τέσσαρες παρθένοι προφητεύουσαι. 10 ἐπιμενόντων δὲ ἡμέρας πλείους κατῆλθέν τις ἀπὸ τῆς Ἰουδαίας προφήτης
ὀνόματι Ἄγαβος, 11 καὶ ἐλθὼν πρὸς ἡμᾶς καὶ ἄρας τὴν
ζώνην τοῦ Παύλου δήσας ἑαυτοῦ τοὺς πόδας καὶ τὰς
χεῖρας εἶπεν, Τάδε λέγει τὸ πνεῦμα τὸ ἅγιον, Τὸν ἄνδρα
οὗ ἐστιν ἡ ζώνη αὕτη οὕτως δήσουσιν ἐν Ἱερουσαλὴμ οἱ
Ἰουδαῖοι καὶ παραδώσουσιν εἰς χεῖρας ἐθνῶν. 12 ὡς
δὲ ἠκούσαμεν ταῦτα, παρεκαλοῦμεν ἡμεῖς τε καὶ οἱ
ἐντόπιοι τοῦ μὴ ἀναβαίνειν αὐτὸν εἰς Ἱερουσαλήμ.

to Phoenicia; so we went aboard and sailed away. 3 We came to where we could see Cyprus, and sailed south of it on to Syria. We went ashore at Tyre, where the ship was going to unload its cargo. 4 We found some believers there, and stayed with them a week. By the power of the Spirit they told Paul not to go to Jerusalem. 5 But when our time with them was over, we left and went on our way. All of them, with their wives and children, went with us out of the city. We all knelt down on the beach and prayed. 6 Then we said good-bye to one another, and we went on board the ship while they went back home.

7 We continued our voyage, sailing from Tyre to Ptolemais, where we greeted the brothers and stayed with them for a day. 8 On the following day we left and arrived in Caesarea. There we went to the house of the evangelist Philip, and stayed with him. He was one of the seven men who had been chosen in Jerusalem. 9 He had four unmarried daughters who preached God's word. 10 We had been there for several days when a prophet named Agabus arrived from Judea. 11 He came to us, took Paul's belt, tied up his own feet and hands with it, and said: "This is what the Holy Spirit says: The owner of this belt will be tied up in this way by the Jews in Jerusalem, and they will hand him over to the Gentiles." 12 When we heard this, we and the people there begged Paul not to go to Jerusalem.

---

² 8 {A} ἤλθομεν 𝔭⁷⁴ ℵ A B C E Ψ 33 (104 εἰσήλθομεν) 181 436 014 029 630 945 1505 1739 2412 2495 itᵃʳ,ᵉ,ᵍⁱᵍ vg syrᵖ,ʰ,ᵖᵃˡ copˢᵃ,ᵇᵒ arm ethᵖᵖ geo Eusebius Chrysostom Theophylactᵇ ∥ οἱ περὶ τὸν Παῦλον ἤλθομεν 056 0142 326 ethʳᵒ ∥ οἱ περὶ τὸν Παῦλον ἤλθον P 049 88 330 451 1241 1877 2127 2492 *Byz Lect* Theophylactᵃ

---

4 οἵτινες...Ἱεροσόλυμα Ac 20.23   5 θέντες...προσευξάμενοι Ac 20.30   8 Φιλίππου τοῦ εὐαγγελιστοῦ Ac 8.40   Φιλίππου...ἑπτά Ac 6.5   9 θυγατέρες...προφητεύουσαι Jl 2.28; Ac 2.17   10 κατῆλθεν...Ἄγαβος Ac 11.28   11 Jn 21.18; Ac 20.23; 21.33 12 παρεκαλοῦμεν...Ἱερουσαλήμ Mt 16.22

[13] But he answered: "What are you doing, crying like this and breaking my heart? I am ready not only to be tied up in Jerusalem but even to die for the sake of the Lord Jesus." [14] We could not convince him. So we gave up and said, "May the Lord's will be done."

[15] After spending some time there, we got our things ready and left for Jerusalem. [16] Some of the disciples from Caesarea also went with us, and took us to the house of the man we were going to stay with — Mnason, from Cyprus, who had been a believer since the early days.

Paul Visits James

[17] When we arrived in Jerusalem the brothers welcomed us warmly. [18] The next day Paul went with us to see James; and all the church elders were present. [19] Paul greeted them and gave a complete report of everything that God had done among the Gentiles through his work.
[20] After hearing him, they all praised God. Then they said to Paul: "You can see how it is, brother. There are thousands of Jews who have become believers, and they are all very devoted to the Law. [21] They have been told about you that you have been teaching all the Jews who live in Gentile countries to abandon the Law of Moses, and have been telling them not to circumcise their

[13] τότε ἀπεκρίθη[3] ὁ Παῦλος, Τί ποιεῖτε κλαίοντες καὶ συνθρύπτοντές μου τὴν καρδίαν; ἐγὼ γὰρ οὐ μόνον δεθῆναι ἀλλὰ καὶ ἀποθανεῖν εἰς Ἰερουσαλὴμ ἑτοίμως ἔχω ὑπὲρ τοῦ ὀνόματος τοῦ κυρίου Ἰησοῦ. [14] μὴ πειθομένου δὲ αὐτοῦ ἡσυχάσαμεν εἰπόντες, Τοῦ κυρίου τὸ θέλημα γινέσθω.

[15] Μετὰ δὲ τὰς ἡμέρας ταύτας ἐπισκευασάμενοι ἀνεβαίνομεν εἰς Ἱεροσόλυμα· [16] συνῆλθον δὲ καὶ τῶν μαθητῶν ἀπὸ Καισαρείας σὺν ἡμῖν, ἄγοντες παρ' ᾧ ξενισθῶμεν Μνάσωνί τινι Κυπρίῳ, ἀρχαίῳ μαθητῇ.

Paul Visits James

[17] Γενομένων δὲ ἡμῶν εἰς Ἱεροσόλυμα ἀσμένως ἀπεδέξαντο ἡμᾶς οἱ ἀδελφοί. [18] τῇ δὲ ἐπιούσῃ εἰσῄει ὁ Παῦλος σὺν ἡμῖν πρὸς Ἰάκωβον, πάντες τε παρεγένοντο οἱ πρεσβύτεροι. [19] καὶ ἀσπασάμενος αὐτοὺς ἐξηγεῖτο καθ' ἓν ἕκαστον ὧν ἐποίησεν ὁ θεὸς ἐν τοῖς ἔθνεσιν διὰ τῆς διακονίας αὐτοῦ. [20] οἱ δὲ ἀκούσαντες ἐδόξαζον τὸν θεόν, εἶπάν τε αὐτῷ, Θεωρεῖς, ἀδελφέ, πόσαι μυριάδες εἰσὶν ἐν τοῖς Ἰουδαίοις[4] τῶν πεπιστευκότων, καὶ πάντες ζηλωταὶ τοῦ νόμου ὑπάρχουσιν· [21] κατηχήθησαν δὲ περὶ σοῦ ὅτι ἀποστασίαν διδάσκεις ἀπὸ Μωϋσέως τοὺς κατὰ τὰ ἔθνη πάντας Ἰουδαίους, λέγων μὴ περιτέμνειν αὐτοὺς

[3] **13** {B} . τότε ἀπεκρίθη (p74 B omit ὁ) ℵ A C2 E 436 itar,e vg syrp,pal copsa,bo arm geo ‖ τότε. ἀπεκρίθη δέ C* 33 ‖ . ἀπεκρίθη τε P 049 056 0142 104 330 451 629 1241 2127 2492 Byzpt Lect eth Theophylact ‖ . ἀπεκρίθη δέ Ψ 88 326 614 630 945 1505 1739 1877 2412 2495 Byzpt l60,598,603 syrh Basil Chrysostom ‖ . εἶπεν δὲ πρὸς ἡμᾶς Dgr (itd ἀπεκρίθη δέ) ‖ τότε. ἀποκριθεὶς δὲ ὁ Παῦλος εἶπεν 181 ‖ . Qui respondit et dixit nobis itgig

[4] **20** {B} ἐν τοῖς Ἰουδαίοις (p74 omit ἐν) A B C E 33 181 326 630 945 1739 it(ar),e vg copbo eth geo Ambrosiaster ‖ ἐν τῇ Ἰουδαίᾳ D itd,gig syrp copsa Ambrosiaster Jerome Augustine ‖ Ἰουδαίων P Ψ 049 056 0142 88 104 330 436 451 614 629 1241 1505 1877 2127 2412 2492 2495 Byz syrh arm Chrysostom Theodoret Theophylacta,(b) ‖ omit ℵ

13 ἐγὼ...Ἰησοῦ Ac 20.24 **14** Τοῦ...γινέσθω Mt 26.39; Mk 14.36; Lk 22.42 **18** Ac 15.2 εἰσῄει...Ἰάκωβον Ac 15.13; Ga 1.19 **19** ἐξηγεῖτο...αὐτοῦ Ac 15.12 **20** πόσαι...ὑπάρχουσιν Ac 15.1, 5 **21** Ac 15.30; Ac 16.3; 21.28; Ga 2.3

τὰ τέκνα μηδὲ τοῖς ἔθεσιν περιπατεῖν. **22** τί οὖν ἐστιν; πάντως ἀκούσονται[5] ὅτι ἐλήλυθας. **23** τοῦτο οὖν ποίησον ὅ σοι λέγομεν· εἰσὶν ἡμῖν ἄνδρες τέσσαρες εὐχὴν ἔχοντες ἐφ᾽[6] ἑαυτῶν. **24** τούτους παραλαβὼν ἁγνίσθητι σὺν αὐτοῖς καὶ δαπάνησον ἐπ᾽ αὐτοῖς ἵνα ξυρήσονται τὴν κεφαλήν, καὶ γνώσονται πάντες ὅτι ὧν κατήχηνται περὶ σοῦ οὐδέν ἐστιν, ἀλλὰ στοιχεῖς καὶ αὐτὸς φυλάσσων τὸν νόμον. **25** περὶ δὲ τῶν πεπιστευκότων ἐθνῶν ἡμεῖς ἐπεστείλαμεν[7] κρίναντες φυλάσσεσθαι αὐτούς[8] τό τε εἰδωλόθυτον καὶ αἷμα καὶ πνικτὸν καὶ πορνείαν[9]. **26** τότε ὁ Παῦλος παρα-

---

[5] **22** {C} ἀκούσονται Β C* 436 614 630 1505 1739* 2127 2412 2495 syr[(p),h] cop[sa,bo] arm eth geo Origen ‖ δεῖ συνελθεῖν πλῆθος ἀκούσονται γάρ 𝔭[74] (א* C² *omit* γάρ) א[c] A E 33 88 181 326 629 945 1739[c] it[(ar),e,gig] vg ‖ δεῖ πλῆθος συνελθεῖν ἀκούσονται γάρ D P Ψ 049 056 0142 104 330 451 1241 (1877 ἀκούσοντες) *Byz* it[d] Chrysostom

[6] **23** {D} ἐφ᾽ 𝔭[74] A C D E P Ψ 049 056 0142 88 104 181 326 330 436 451 614 629 630 945 1241 1505 1739 1877 2127 2412 2495 *Byz* it[ar,d,e,(gig)] vg syr[p,h] cop[sa?] ‖ ἀφ᾽ א B 33 cop[bo?] Origen

[7] **25** {C} ἐπεστείλαμεν 𝔭[74] א A C² E[gr] P 056 0142 33 88 104 326 330 436 451 629 630 945 1241 1505 1739 2492 *Byz* it[ar,d,gig] vg syr[p?h?] cop[sa] (eth) geo? Chrysostom ‖ ἀπεστείλαμεν B C* D[gr] Ψ 049 181 614 2127 2412 2495 syr[p?h?] cop[bo] arm geo? ‖ *destinavimus* it[e]

[8] **25** {C} κρίναντες φυλάσσεσθαι αὐτούς 𝔭[74] א Λ B 33 88 it[ar] vg syr[p] cop[sa,bo] ‖ κρίναντες μηδὲν τοιοῦτον τηρεῖν αὐτοὺς ἀλλὰ φυλάσσεσθαι (181 εἰ μή *for* ἀλλά) 630 (945 κρίνοντες *and* τοιοῦτο) (1739 τοιοῦτο) ‖ κρίναντες μηδὲν τοιοῦτον τηρεῖν αὐτοὺς εἰ μὴ φυλάσσεσθαι αὐτούς (D* κρίνοντες) D[c] P Ψ 049 056 0142 (C E 1505 2495 τοιοῦτο) 104 326 330 436 451 614 629[c] 1241 1877 2127 2412 2492 *Byz* it[d,e,gig] syr[h] arm (eth) geo Chrysostom Augustine Greek[acc. to Bede]

[9] **25** {C} τό τε εἰδωλόθυτον καὶ αἷμα καὶ πνικτὸν καὶ πορνείαν (𝔭[74] *omit* τε) א A B C 33 436 630 945 1739 ‖ τό τε εἰδωλόθυτον καὶ τὸ αἷμα καὶ πνικτὸν καὶ πορνείαν P 049 056 0142 (Ψ 614 1505 2412 *omit* τε) 88 104 (181 τὸ πνικτόν *and omit* τε) 326 330 451 629[c] 1241 1877 2127 (2492 τὸ πνικτόν καὶ τήν) 2495 *Byz* cop[sa?] arm (Chrysostom τὸ πνικτόν *and omit* τε) (Theophylact[b] τὸ πνικτόν) ‖ τό τε εἰδωλόθυτον καὶ πορνείαν καὶ πνικτὸν καὶ αἷμα (*see* 15.20) syr[p?] eth[pp] ‖ ἀπὸ εἰδωλοθύτων καὶ αἵματος καὶ πνικτοῦ καὶ πορνείας E it[ar,(e)] vg syr[p?h] cop[bo?] ‖ τὸ εἰδωλόθυτον καὶ αἷμα καὶ πορνείαν (*see* 15.20) D it[d,gig] geo (Ambrosiaster) Augustine

---

23–24 ἄνδρες...κεφαλήν Nu 6.5, 13–18, 21; Ac 18.18   **25** Ac 15.19–20, 28–29   **26** ὁ... ἱερόν 1 Cor 9.20

---

children or follow the Jewish customs. **22** They are sure to hear that you have arrived. What should be done, then? **23** Do what we tell you. There are four men here who have taken a vow. **24** Go along with them and join them in the ceremony of purification and pay their expenses; then they will be able to shave their heads. In this way everybody will know that there is no truth in any of the things they have been told about you, but that you yourself live in accordance with the Law of Moses. **25** But as to the Gentiles who have become believers, we have sent them a letter telling them we decided that they must not eat any food that has been offered to idols, or any blood, or any animal that has been strangled, and that they must keep themselves from immorality." **26** Then Paul took the men and the next day performed the ceremony of purification with them. Then he went into the Temple and gave notice of how many days it would be until the end of the period of purification, when the sacrifice for each one of them would be offered.

Paul Arrested in the Temple

27 When the seven days were about to come to an end, some Jews from the province of Asia saw Paul in the Temple. They stirred up the whole crowd and grabbed Paul. 28 "Men of Israel!" they shouted. "Help! This is the man who goes everywhere teaching everyone against the people of Israel, the Law of Moses, and this Temple. And now he has even brought some Gentiles into the Temple and defiled this holy place!" 29 (They said this because they had seen Trophimus from Ephesus with Paul in the city, and they thought that Paul had taken him into the Temple.) 30 Confusion spread through the whole city, and the people all ran together, grabbed Paul, and dragged him out of the Temple. At once the Temple doors were closed. 31 The mob was trying to kill Paul when a report was sent up to the commander of the Roman troops that all of Jerusalem was rioting. 32 At once the commander took some officers and soldiers and rushed down to the crowd. When the people saw him with the soldiers, they stopped beating Paul. 33 The commander went over to Paul, arrested him, and ordered him to be tied up with two chains. Then he asked, "Who is this man, and what has he done?" 34 Some in the crowd shouted one thing, others something else. There was such confusion that the commander could not find out exactly what had happened; so he ordered his men to take Paul up into the fort. 35 They got with him to the steps, and then the soldiers had to carry him because the mob was so wild. 36 They were all coming after him and screaming, "Kill him!"

λαβὼν τοὺς ἄνδρας,ᵃ τῇ ἐχομένῃ ἡμέρᾳᵃ σὺν αὐτοῖς ἁγνισθεὶς εἰσῄει εἰς τὸ ἱερόν, διαγγέλλων τὴν ἐκπλήρωσιν τῶν ἡμερῶν τοῦ ἁγνισμοῦ ἕως οὗ προσηνέχθη ὑπὲρ ἑνὸς ἑκάστου αὐτῶν ἡ προσφορά.

Paul Arrested in the Temple

27 Ὡς δὲ ἔμελλον αἱ ἑπτὰ ἡμέραι συντελεῖσθαι, οἱ ἀπὸ τῆς Ἀσίας Ἰουδαῖοι θεασάμενοι αὐτὸν ἐν τῷ ἱερῷ συνέχεον πάντα τὸν ὄχλον καὶ ἐπέβαλον ἐπ᾽ αὐτὸν τὰς χεῖρας, 28 κράζοντες, Ἄνδρες Ἰσραηλῖται, βοηθεῖτε· οὗτός ἐστιν ὁ ἄνθρωπος ὁ κατὰ τοῦ λαοῦ καὶ τοῦ νόμου καὶ τοῦ τόπου τούτου πάντας πανταχῇ διδάσκων, ἔτι τε καὶ Ἕλληνας εἰσήγαγεν εἰς τὸ ἱερὸν καὶ κεκοίνωκεν τὸν ἅγιον τόπον τοῦτον. 29 ἦσαν γὰρ προεωρακότες Τρόφιμον τὸν Ἐφέσιον ἐν τῇ πόλει σὺν αὐτῷ, ὃν ἐνόμιζον ὅτι εἰς τὸ ἱερὸν εἰσήγαγεν ὁ Παῦλος. 30 ἐκινήθη τε ἡ πόλις ὅλη καὶ ἐγένετο συνδρομὴ τοῦ λαοῦ, καὶ ἐπιλαβόμενοι τοῦ Παύλου εἷλκον αὐτὸν ἔξω τοῦ ἱεροῦ, καὶ εὐθέως ἐκλείσθησαν αἱ θύραι. 31 ζητούντων τε αὐτὸν ἀποκτεῖναι ἀνέβη φάσις τῷ χιλιάρχῳ τῆς σπείρης ὅτι ὅλη συγχύννεται Ἰερουσαλήμ, 32 ὃς ἐξαυτῆς παραλαβὼν στρατιώτας καὶ ἑκατοντάρχας κατέδραμεν ἐπ᾽ αὐτούς· οἱ δὲ ἰδόντες τὸν χιλίαρχον καὶ τοὺς στρατιώτας ἐπαύσαντο τύπτοντες τὸν Παῦλον. 33 τότε ἐγγίσας ὁ χιλίαρχος ἐπελάβετο αὐτοῦ καὶ ἐκέλευσεν δεθῆναι ἁλύσεσι δυσί, καὶ ἐπυνθάνετο τίς εἴη καὶ τί ἐστιν πεποιηκώς. 34 ἄλλοι δὲ ἄλλο τι ἐπεφώνουν ἐν τῷ ὄχλῳ· μὴ δυναμένου δὲ αὐτοῦ γνῶναι τὸ ἀσφαλὲς διὰ τὸν θόρυβον ἐκέλευσεν ἄγεσθαι αὐτὸν εἰς τὴν παρεμβολήν. 35 ὅτε δὲ ἐγένετο ἐπὶ τοὺς ἀναβαθμούς, συνέβη βαστάζεσθαι αὐτὸν ὑπὸ τῶν στρατιωτῶν διὰ τὴν βίαν τοῦ ὄχλου, 36 ἠκολούθει γὰρ τὸ πλῆθος τοῦ λαοῦ κράζοντες, Αἶρε αὐτόν.

ᵃ ᵃ **26** *a* minor, *a* none: AV RV ASV RSV NEB Zür (Luth) ∥ *a* none, *a* minor: RVᵐᵍ ASVᵐᵍ TT ∥ *a* none, *a* none: TR WH Bov Nes BF² (Jer) (Seg)

26 σὺν...προσφορά Nu 6.2–5, 13–21   **28** οὗτος...διδάσκων Ac 6.13; 21.21   Ἕλληνας...τοῦτον Eze 44.7   **33** ἐκέλευσεν...δυσί Ac 20.23; 21.11   **36** τὸ πλῆθος...Αἶρε αὐτόν Lk 23.18; Jn 19.15; Ac 22.22

Paul Defends Himself

37 Μέλλων τε εἰσάγεσθαι εἰς τὴν παρεμβολὴν ὁ Παῦλος λέγει τῷ χιλιάρχῳ, Εἰ ἔξεστίν μοι εἰπεῖν τι πρὸς σέ; ὁ δὲ ἔφη, Ἑλληνιστὶ γινώσκεις; **38** οὐκ ἄρα σὺ εἶ ὁ Αἰγύπτιος ὁ πρὸ τούτων τῶν ἡμερῶν ἀναστατώσας καὶ ἐξαγαγὼν εἰς τὴν ἔρημον τοὺς τετρακισχιλίους ἄνδρας τῶν σικαρίων; **39** εἶπεν δὲ ὁ Παῦλος, Ἐγὼ ἄνθρωπος μέν εἰμι Ἰουδαῖος, Ταρσεὺς[b] τῆς Κιλικίας,[b] οὐκ ἀσήμου πόλεως πολίτης· δέομαι δέ σου, ἐπίτρεψόν μοι λαλῆσαι πρὸς τὸν λαόν. **40** ἐπιτρέψαντος δὲ αὐτοῦ ὁ Παῦλος ἑστὼς ἐπὶ τῶν ἀναβαθμῶν κατέσεισεν τῇ χειρὶ τῷ λαῷ· πολλῆς δὲ σιγῆς γενομένης προσεφώνησεν τῇ Ἑβραΐδι διαλέκτῳ λέγων, **22** Ἄνδρες ἀδελφοὶ καὶ πατέρες, ἀκούσατέ μου τῆς πρὸς ὑμᾶς νυνὶ ἀπολογίας —[a] **2** ἀκούσαντες δὲ ὅτι τῇ Ἑβραΐδι διαλέκτῳ προσεφώνει αὐτοῖς μᾶλλον παρέσχον ἡσυχίαν. καὶ φησίν —[a] **3** Ἐγώ εἰμι ἀνὴρ Ἰουδαῖος, γεγεννημένος ἐν Ταρσῷ τῆς Κιλικίας, ἀνατεθραμμένος δὲ ἐν τῇ πόλει ταύτῃ,[b] παρὰ τοὺς πόδας Γαμαλιὴλ[b] πεπαιδευμένος κατὰ ἀκρίβειαν τοῦ πατρῴου νόμου, ζηλωτὴς ὑπάρχων τοῦ θεοῦ καθὼς πάντες ὑμεῖς ἐστε σήμερον· **4** ὃς ταύτην τὴν ὁδὸν ἐδίωξα ἄχρι θανάτου, δεσμεύων καὶ παραδιδοὺς εἰς φυλακὰς ἄνδρας τε καὶ γυναῖκας, **5** ὡς καὶ ὁ ἀρχιερεὺς μαρτυρεῖ μοι καὶ πᾶν τὸ πρεσβυτέριον· παρ' ὧν καὶ ἐπιστολὰς δεξάμενος πρὸς τοὺς ἀδελφοὺς εἰς Δαμασκὸν ἐπορευόμην ἄξων καὶ τοὺς ἐκεῖσε ὄντας δεδεμένους εἰς Ἱερουσαλὴμ ἵνα τιμωρηθῶσιν.

---

[b][b] **39** b none, b minor: WH RV ASV RSV NEB Zür Jer ∥ b minor, b none: Bov Nes BF² TT Luth ∥ b none, b none: TR ∥ b minor, b minor: AV Seg

[a][a] **1-2** a dash, a dash: WH Bov Nes BF² ∥ a parens, a parens: AV ∥ a a no dash or parens: TR RV ASV RSV NEB TT Zür Luth Jer Seg

[b][b] **3** b minor, b none: Bov Nes BF² NEB TT Zür Luth Jer (Seg) ∥ b none, b minor: TR WH AV (RV) (ASV) RSV

---

38 Ac 5.36 37   **39** Ἐγώ...πολίτης Ac 9.11; 22.3   **40** κατέσεισεν...γενομένης Ac 12.17; 13.16; 19.33   προσεφώνησεν...διαλέκτῳ Ac 26.14

22 **1** Ἄνδρες...μου Ac 7.2   **3** Ἐγώ...Κιλικίας Ac 21.39   ἀνατεθραμμένος...νόμου Ac 5.34   ζηλωτὴς...σήμερον Ro 10.2   **4** Ac 8.3; 22.19; 26.9–11

Paul Defends Himself

[37] As they were about to take Paul into the fort, he spoke to the commander: "May I say something to you?" "Do you speak Greek?" the commander asked. [38] "Then you are not that Egyptian fellow who some time ago started a revolution and led four thousand armed terrorists out into the desert?" [39] Paul answered: "I am a Jew, born in Tarsus of Cilicia, a citizen of an important city. Please, let me speak to the people." [40] The commander gave him permission, so Paul stood on the steps and motioned with his hand to the people. When they were quiet, Paul spoke to them in Hebrew: **22** "Men, brothers and fathers, listen to me as I make my defense before you!" [2] When they heard him speaking to them in Hebrew, they were even quieter; and Paul went on:

[3] "I am a Jew, born in Tarsus of Cilicia, but brought up here in Jerusalem as a student of Gamaliel. I received strict instruction in the Law of our ancestors, and was just as dedicated to God as all of you here today are. [4] I persecuted to the death the people who followed this Way. I arrested men and women and threw them into prison. [5] The High Priest and the whole Council can prove that I am telling the truth. I received from them letters written to the Jewish brothers in Damascus, so I went there to arrest these people and bring them back in chains to Jerusalem to be punished."

Paul Tells of His Conversion
(Acts 9.1–19; 26.12–18)

[6] "And as I was traveling and coming near Damascus, about midday a bright light suddenly flashed from the sky around me. [7] I fell to the ground and heard a voice saying to me, 'Saul, Saul! Why do you persecute me?' [8] 'Who are you, Lord?' I asked. 'I am Jesus of Nazareth, whom you persecute,' he said to me. [9] The men with me saw the light but did not hear the voice of the one who was speaking to me. [10] I asked, 'What shall I do, Lord?' and the Lord said to me, 'Get up and go into Damascus, and there you will be told everything that God has determined for you to do.' [11] I was blind because of the bright light, and so my companions took me by the hand and led me into Damascus.

[12] "There was a man named Ananias, a religious man who obeyed our Law and was highly respected by all the Jews living in Damascus. [13] He came to me, stood by me and said, 'Brother Saul, see again!' At that very moment I saw again and looked at him. [14] He said: 'The God of our ancestors has chosen you to know his will, to see his righteous

Paul Tells of His Conversion
(Ac 9.1–19; 26.12–18)

6 Ἐγένετο δέ μοι πορευομένῳ καὶ ἐγγίζοντι τῇ Δαμασκῷ περὶ μεσημβρίαν ἐξαίφνης ἐκ τοῦ οὐρανοῦ περιαστράψαι φῶς ἱκανὸν περὶ ἐμέ, **7** ἔπεσά τε εἰς τὸ ἔδαφος καὶ ἤκουσα φωνῆς λεγούσης μοι, Σαοὺλ Σαούλ, τί με διώκεις; **8** ἐγὼ δὲ ἀπεκρίθην, Τίς εἶ, κύριε; εἶπέν τε πρός με, Ἐγώ εἰμι Ἰησοῦς ὁ Ναζωραῖος ὃν σὺ διώκεις. **9** οἱ δὲ σὺν ἐμοὶ ὄντες τὸ μὲν φῶς ἐθεάσαντο[1] τὴν δὲ φωνὴν οὐκ ἤκουσαν τοῦ λαλοῦντός μοι. **10** εἶπον δέ, Τί ποιήσω, κύριε; ὁ δὲ κύριος εἶπεν πρός με, Ἀναστὰς πορεύου εἰς Δαμασκόν, κἀκεῖ σοι λαληθήσεται περὶ πάντων ὧν τέτακταί σοι ποιῆσαι. **11** ὡς δὲ οὐκ ἐνέβλεπον ἀπὸ τῆς δόξης τοῦ φωτὸς ἐκείνου, χειραγωγούμενος ὑπὸ τῶν συνόντων μοι ἦλθον εἰς Δαμασκόν.

12 Ἀνανίας δέ τις,[c] ἀνὴρ εὐλαβὴς κατὰ τὸν νόμον, μαρτυρούμενος ὑπὸ πάντων τῶν κατοικούντων Ἰουδαίων[2], **13** ἐλθὼν πρός με καὶ ἐπιστὰς εἶπέν μοι, Σαοὺλ ἀδελφέ, ἀνάβλεψον· κἀγὼ αὐτῇ τῇ ὥρᾳ ἀνέβλεψα εἰς αὐτόν[3]. **14** ὁ δὲ εἶπεν, Ὁ θεὸς τῶν πατέρων ἡμῶν προεχειρίσατό

---

[1] **9** {C} ἐθεάσαντο p⁷⁴ ℵᶜ (ℵ* ἐθέατο) A B 049 33 181 326 1241 2492 itᵃʳ vg syrᵖ copᵇᵒ arm geo ‖ *transpose:* τὸ φῶς τοῦ λαλοῦντός μοι οὐκ ἤκουσαν 629ᶜ ‖ ἐθεάσαντο καὶ ἔμφοβοι ἐγένοντο Dᵍʳ E P Ψ 056 0142 88 104 330 436 451 614 630 945 1505 1739 1877 2127 2412 2495 *Byz* itᵉ·ᵍⁱᵍ syrʰ copˢᵃ eth Chrysostom Greekᵃᶜᶜ·ᵗᵒ ᴮᵉᵈᵉ

[2] **12** {C} κατοικούντων Ἰουδαίων p⁷⁴ ℵ A B E P 88 1877* *Byz*ᵖᵗ itᵉ·⁽ᵍⁱᵍ⁾ vg syrᵖ copᵇᵒ ‖ Ἰουδαίων 629 itᵈ Chrysostom ‖ κατοικούντων ἐν Δαμάσκῳ Ἰουδαίων (p⁴¹ᵛⁱᵈ ἐν τῇ) Ψ 049 056 0142 33 104 181 326 (330 451 εἰς Δαμάσκον) (436 Ἰουδαίων ἐν Δαμάσκῳ) 614 630 945 1241 1505 1739 1877ᶜ 2127 2412 2492 2495 *Byz*ᵖᵗ itᶜ·ᵖᶜ syrʰ copˢᵃ arm eth geo Theophylact

[3] **13** {C} εἰς αὐτόν p⁷⁴ ℵ A B E P Ψ 049 056 0142 33 88 104 181 326 330 436 451 614 629 630 945 1241 1505 1739 1877 2127 (2412 *omit* εἰς) 2492 2495 *Byz* itᵃʳ·ᵉ·ᵍⁱᵍ vg syrᵖ·ʰ copᵇᵒ arm geoᴮ ‖ *omit* p⁴¹ 5 itᵈ copˢᵃ geoᴬ

---

[c] **12** c minor: Bov Nes BF² AV RV ASV RSV NEB TT Zür Jer Seg ‖ c none: TR WH (Luth)

---

9 Wsd 18.1

σε γνῶναι τὸ θέλημα αὐτοῦ καὶ ἰδεῖν τὸν δίκαιον καὶ ἀκοῦσαι φωνὴν ἐκ τοῦ στόματος αὐτοῦ, 15 ὅτι ἔσῃ μάρτυς αὐτῷ πρὸς πάντας ἀνθρώπους ὧν ἑώρακας καὶ ἤκουσας. 16 καὶ νῦν τί μέλλεις; ἀναστὰς βάπτισαι καὶ ἀπόλουσαι τὰς ἁμαρτίας σου ἐπικαλεσάμενος τὸ ὄνομα αὐτοῦ.

Paul Sent to the Gentiles

17 Ἐγένετο δέ μοι ὑποστρέψαντι εἰς Ἰερουσαλὴμ καὶ προσευχομένου μου ἐν τῷ ἱερῷ γενέσθαι με ἐν ἐκστάσει 18 καὶ ἰδεῖν αὐτὸν λέγοντά μοι, Σπεῦσον καὶ ἔξελθε ἐν τάχει ἐξ Ἰερουσαλήμ, διότι οὐ παραδέξονταί σου μαρτυρίαν περὶ ἐμοῦ. 19 κἀγὼ εἶπον, Κύριε, αὐτοὶ ἐπίστανται ὅτι ἐγὼ ἤμην φυλακίζων καὶ δέρων κατὰ τὰς συναγωγὰς τοὺς πιστεύοντας ἐπὶ σέ· 20 καὶ ὅτε ἐξεχύννετο τὸ αἷμα Στεφάνου τοῦ μάρτυρός σου, καὶ αὐτὸς ἤμην ἐφεστὼς καὶ συνευδοκῶν καὶ φυλάσσων τὰ ἱμάτια τῶν ἀναιρούντων αὐτόν. 21 καὶ εἶπεν πρός με, Πορεύου, ὅτι ἐγὼ εἰς ἔθνη μακρὰν ἐξαποστελῶ σε.

Paul and the Roman Tribune

22 Ἤκουον δὲ αὐτοῦ ἄχρι τούτου τοῦ λόγου καὶ ἐπῆραν τὴν φωνὴν αὐτῶν λέγοντες, Αἶρε ἀπὸ τῆς γῆς τὸν τοιοῦτον, οὐ γὰρ καθῆκεν αὐτὸν ζῆν. 23 κραυγαζόντων τε αὐτῶν καὶ ῥιπτούντων τὰ ἱμάτια καὶ κονιορτὸν βαλλόντων εἰς τὸν ἀέρα, 24 ἐκέλευσεν ὁ χιλίαρχος εἰσάγεσθαι αὐτὸν εἰς τὴν παρεμβολήν, εἴπας μάστιξιν ἀνετάζεσθαι αὐτὸν ἵνα ἐπιγνῷ δι᾽ ἣν αἰτίαν οὕτως ἐπεφώνουν αὐτῷ. 25 ὡς δὲ προέτειναν αὐτὸν τοῖς ἱμᾶσιν εἶπεν πρὸς τὸν ἑστῶτα ἑκατόνταρχον ὁ Παῦλος, Εἰ ἄνθρωπον Ῥωμαῖον καὶ ἀκατάκριτον ἔξεστιν ὑμῖν μαστίζειν;

16 ἀπόλουσαι...αὐτοῦ Jl 2.32; Ac 2.21; Ro 10.13   18 Ac 9.29–30   19 ἐγὼ ἤμην φυλακίζων...ἐπὶ σέ Ac 8.3; 22.4–5; 26.9–11   20 Ac 7.58; 8.1   21 ἐγὼ εἰς ἔθνη...σε Ac 9.15; 13.2; Ga 2.7–9   22 ἐπῆραν...ζῆν Ac 21.36   25 Εἰ...μαστίζειν Ac 16.37; 23.27

Servant, and hear him speaking with his own voice. 15 For you will be a witness for him to tell all men what you have seen and heard. 16 And now, why wait any longer? Get up and be baptized and have your sins washed away by calling on his name.' "

Paul's Call to Preach to the Gentiles

17 "I went back to Jerusalem, and while I was praying in the Temple I had a vision, 18 in which I saw the Lord as he said to me, 'Hurry and leave Jerusalem quickly, because the people here will not accept your witness about me.' 19 'Lord,' I answered, 'they know very well that I went to the synagogues and arrested and beat those who believe in you. 20 And when your witness Stephen was put to death, I myself was there, approving of his murder and taking care of the cloaks of his murderers.' 21 'Go,' the Lord said to me, 'for I will send you far away to the Gentiles.' "

22 The people listened to Paul until he said this; but then they started shouting at the top of their voices, "Away with him! Kill him! He's not fit to live!" 23 They were screaming and waving their clothes and throwing dust up in the air. 24 The Roman commander ordered his men to take Paul into the fort, and told them to whip him to find out why the Jews were screaming like this against him. 25 But when they had tied him up to be whipped, Paul said to the officer standing there, "Is it lawful for you to whip a Roman citizen who hasn't even

been tried for any crime?" ²⁶ When the officer heard this, he went to the commander and asked him, "What are you doing? That man is a Roman citizen!" ²⁷ So the commander went to Paul and asked him, "Tell me, are you a Roman citizen?" "Yes," answered Paul. ²⁸ The commander said, "I became one by paying a large amount of money." "But I am one by birth," Paul answered. ²⁹ At once the men who were going to question Paul drew back from him; and the commander was afraid when he realized that Paul was a Roman citizen, and that he had put him in chains.

Paul before the Council

³⁰ The commander wanted to find out for sure what the Jews were accusing Paul of; so the next day he had Paul's chains taken off and ordered the chief priests and the whole Council to meet. Then he took Paul, and made him stand before them.

23 Paul looked straight at the Council and said, "My brothers! My conscience is perfectly clear about my whole life before God, to this very day." ² The High Priest Ananias ordered those who were standing close to Paul to strike him on the mouth. ³ Paul said to him: "God will certainly strike you — you whitewashed wall! You sit there to judge me according to the Law, yet you break the Law by ordering them to strike me!" ⁴ The men close to Paul said to him, "You are insulting God's High Priest!" ⁵ Paul answered; "I did not know, my brothers, that he was the High Priest. For the scripture says, 'You must not speak evil of the ruler of your people.'"

⁶ When Paul saw that some of the group were Sadducees and that others

26 ἀκούσας δὲ ὁ ἑκατοντάρχης προσελθὼν τῷ χιλιάρχῳ ἀπήγγειλεν λέγων, Τί⁴ μέλλεις ποιεῖν; ὁ γὰρ ἄνθρωπος οὗτος Ῥωμαῖός ἐστιν. 27 προσελθὼν δὲ ὁ χιλίαρχος εἶπεν αὐτῷ, Λέγε μοι, σὺ Ῥωμαῖος εἶ; ὁ δὲ ἔφη, Ναί. 28 ἀπεκρίθη δὲ ὁ χιλίαρχος, Ἐγὼ πολλοῦ κεφαλαίου τὴν πολιτείαν ταύτην ἐκτησάμην. ὁ δὲ Παῦλος ἔφη, Ἐγὼ δὲ καὶ γεγέννημαι. 29 εὐθέως οὖν ἀπέστησαν ἀπ' αὐτοῦ οἱ μέλλοντες αὐτὸν ἀνετάζειν· καὶ ὁ χιλίαρχος δὲ ἐφοβήθη ἐπιγνοὺς ὅτι Ῥωμαῖός ἐστιν καὶ ὅτι αὐτὸν ἦν δεδεκώς.

Paul before the Council

30 Τῇ δὲ ἐπαύριον βουλόμενος γνῶναι τὸ ἀσφαλὲς τὸ τί κατηγορεῖται ὑπὸ τῶν Ἰουδαίων ἔλυσεν αὐτόν, καὶ ἐκέλευσεν συνελθεῖν τοὺς ἀρχιερεῖς καὶ πᾶν τὸ συνέδριον, καὶ καταγαγὼν τὸν Παῦλον ἔστησεν εἰς αὐτούς. **23** ἀτενίσας δὲ τῷ συνεδρίῳ ὁ Παῦλος εἶπεν, Ἄνδρες ἀδελφοί, ἐγὼ πάσῃ συνειδήσει ἀγαθῇ πεπολίτευμαι τῷ θεῷ ἄχρι ταύτης τῆς ἡμέρας. 2 ὁ δὲ ἀρχιερεὺς Ἀνανίας ἐπέταξεν τοῖς παρεστῶσιν αὐτῷ τύπτειν αὐτοῦ τὸ στόμα. 3 τότε ὁ Παῦλος πρὸς αὐτὸν εἶπεν, Τύπτειν σε μέλλει ὁ θεός, τοῖχε κεκονιαμένε· καὶ σὺ κάθῃ κρίνων με κατὰ τὸν νόμον, καὶ παρανομῶν κελεύεις με τύπτεσθαι; 4 οἱ δὲ παρεστῶτες εἶπαν, Τὸν ἀρχιερέα τοῦ θεοῦ λοιδορεῖς; 5 ἔφη τε ὁ Παῦλος, Οὐκ ᾔδειν, ἀδελφοί, ὅτι ἐστὶν ἀρχιερεύς· γέγραπται γὰρ ὅτι **Ἄρχοντα τοῦ λαοῦ σου οὐκ ἐρεῖς κακῶς.** 6 Γνοὺς δὲ ὁ Παῦλος ὅτι τὸ ἓν μέρος ἐστὶν Σαδδου-

---

⁴ 26 {B} τί 𝔓⁷⁴ ℵ A B C E Ψ 33 181 436 614 945* 1505 1739 2412 2495 itᵉ vg syrᵖ·ʰ copᵇᵒ arm geo ∥ ὅρα τί D P 049 056 0142 88 104 326 330 451 629 630 945ᶜ 1241 1877 2127 2492 Byz itᵍⁱᵍ·ᵖ copˢᵃ eth Chrysostom

---

29 ὁ χιλίαρχος...ἐστιν Ac 16.38
23 **1** ἐγὼ...ἡμέρας Ac 24.16   **2-3** Jn 18.22-23   **3** τοῖχε κεκονιαμένε Eze 13.10-15 σὺ...τύπτεσθαι Lv 19.15   **5** Ἄρχοντα...κακῶς Ex 22.28   **6** Ac 4.2

καίων τὸ δὲ ἕτερον Φαρισαίων ἔκραζεν ἐν τῷ συνεδρίῳ, "Ανδρες ἀδελφοί, ἐγὼ Φαρισαῖός εἰμι, υἱὸς Φαρισαίων· περὶ ἐλπίδος καὶ ἀναστάσεως νεκρῶν ἐγὼ κρίνομαι. 7 τοῦτο δὲ αὐτοῦ λαλοῦντος ἐγένετο στάσις τῶν Φαρισαίων καὶ Σαδδουκαίων, καὶ ἐσχίσθη τὸ πλῆθος. 8 Σαδδουκαῖοι μὲν γὰρ λέγουσιν μὴ εἶναι ἀνάστασιν μήτε ἄγγελον μήτε πνεῦμα, Φαρισαῖοι δὲ ὁμολογοῦσιν τὰ ἀμφότερα. 9 ἐγένετο δὲ κραυγὴ μεγάλη, καὶ ἀναστάντες τινὲς τῶν γραμματέων τοῦ μέρους τῶν Φαρισαίων διεμάχοντο λέγοντες, Οὐδὲν κακὸν εὑρίσκομεν ἐν τῷ ἀνθρώπῳ τούτῳ· εἰ δὲ πνεῦμα ἐλάλησεν αὐτῷ ἢ ἄγγελος —ᵃ 10 Πολλῆς δὲ γινομένης στάσεως φοβηθεὶς ὁ χιλίαρχος μὴ διασπασθῇ ὁ Παῦλος ὑπ' αὐτῶν ἐκέλευσεν τὸ στράτευμα καταβὰν ἁρπάσαι αὐτὸν ἐκ μέσου αὐτῶν, ἄγειν τε εἰς τὴν παρεμβολήν.

11 Τῇ δὲ ἐπιούσῃ νυκτὶ ἐπιστὰς αὐτῷ ὁ κύριος εἶπεν, Θάρσει, ὡς γὰρ διεμαρτύρω τὰ περὶ ἐμοῦ εἰς Ἰερουσαλὴμ οὕτω σε δεῖ καὶ εἰς Ῥώμην μαρτυρῆσαι.

The Plot against Paul's Life

12 Γενομένης δὲ ἡμέρας ποιήσαντες συστροφὴν οἱ Ἰουδαῖοι¹ ἀνεθεμάτισαν ἑαυτοὺς λέγοντες μήτε φαγεῖν μήτε πίειν ἕως οὗ ἀποκτείνωσιν τὸν Παῦλον. 13 ἦσαν

---

¹ 12 {B} συστροφὴν οἱ Ἰουδαῖοι 𝔭⁷⁴ ℵ A B C E 33 81 181 436 630 945 1739 itᵉ copᵇᵒ (arm τῶν Ἰουδαίων) eth geo ‖ οἱ Ἰουδαῖοι συστροφὴν Ψ 614 (1505 2495 ἀναστροφήν) 2412 syrʰ Chrysostom Theophylactᵇ ‖ τινες τῶν Ἰουδαίων συστροφὴν P 049 056 0142 104 326 330 451 629 1241 1877 2127 2492 Byz copˢᵃ Theophylactᵃ ‖ συστροφήν τινες τῶν Ἰουδαίων (𝔭⁴⁸ βοήθειαν συσραφέντες) 88 it⁽ᵃʳ⁾·ᵍⁱᵍ·ʰ vg syrᵖ Lucifer ‖ τινες τῶν Ἰουδαίων (copˢᵃᵐˢˢ omit ποιήσαντες)

ᵃ 9 a dash: WH Nes BF² ‖ a dash with question: Zür ‖ a question: Bov RV ASV RSV TT Jer Seg ‖ a statement: NEB Luth ‖ different text: TR AV

---

6 ἐγὼ...Φαρισαίων Ac 26.5; Php 3.5   περὶ...κρίνομαι Ac 24.15, 21   8 Σαδδουκαῖοι ...πνεῦμα Mt 22.23   9 Οὐδὲν κακὸν...τούτῳ Lk 23.4, 14, 22; Jn 18.38; 19.4, 6; Ac 25.25   11 Τῇ δὲ ἐπιούσῃ...Θάρσει Ac 18.9   ὡς...μαρτυρῆσαι Ac 19.21; 27.24; 28.16, 23

were Pharisees, he called out in the Council: "My brothers! I am a Pharisee, the son of Pharisees. I am on trial here because I hope that the dead will be raised to life!" 7 As soon as he said this, the Pharisees and Sadducees started to quarrel, and the group was divided. 8 (For the Sadducees say that people will not be raised from death, and that there are no angels or spirits — but the Pharisees believe in all three.) 9 So the shouting became louder, and some of the teachers of the Law who belonged to the party of the Pharisees stood up and protested strongly: "We cannot find a thing wrong with this man! Perhaps a spirit or an angel really did speak to him!"

10 The argument became so violent that the commander was afraid that Paul would be torn to pieces by them. So he ordered his soldiers to go down into the group and get Paul away from them, and take him into the fort.

11 The following night the Lord stood by Paul and said: "Courage! You have given your witness to me here in Jerusalem, and you must do the same in Rome also."

The Plot against Paul's Life

12 The next morning the Jews met together and made a plan. They took a vow that they would not eat or drink anything until they had killed Paul. 13 There were more than forty of them

who planned this together. ¹⁴ Then they went to the chief priests and elders and said: "We have taken a solemn vow together not to eat a thing until we kill Paul. ¹⁵ Now then, you and the Council send word to the Roman commander to bring Paul down to you, pretending that you want to get more accurate information about him. But we will be ready to kill him before he ever gets here."

¹⁶ But the son of Paul's sister heard of the plot; so he went and entered the fort and told it to Paul. ¹⁷ Then Paul called one of the officers and said to him, "Take this young man to the commander; he has something to tell him." ¹⁸ The officer took him, led him to the commander and said, "The prisoner Paul called me and asked me to bring this young man to you, for he has something to say to you." ¹⁹ The commander took him by the hand, led him off by himself and asked him, "What do you have to tell me?" ²⁰ He said: "The Jews have agreed to ask you tomorrow to take Paul down to the Council, pretending that the Council wants to get more accurate information about him. ²¹ But don't listen to them, because there are more than forty men who will be hiding and waiting for him. They have all taken a vow not to eat or drink until they kill him. They are now ready to do it, and are waiting for your decision." ²² The commander said, "Don't tell anyone that you have reported this to me." And he sent the young man away.

δὲ πλείους τεσσαράκοντα οἱ ταύτην τὴν συνωμοσίαν ποιησάμενοι· **14** οἵτινες προσελθόντες τοῖς ἀρχιερεῦσιν καὶ τοῖς πρεσβυτέροις εἶπαν, ᾿Αναθέματι ἀνεθεματίσαμεν ἑαυτοὺς μηδενὸς γεύσασθαι ἕως οὗ ἀποκτείνωμεν τὸν Παῦλον. **15** νῦν οὖν ὑμεῖς ἐμφανίσατε τῷ χιλιάρχῳ σὺν τῷ συνεδρίῳ ὅπως καταγάγῃ αὐτὸν εἰς ὑμᾶς ὡς μέλλοντας διαγινώσκειν ἀκριβέστερον τὰ περὶ αὐτοῦ· ἡμεῖς δὲ πρὸ τοῦ ἐγγίσαι αὐτὸν ἕτοιμοί ἐσμεν τοῦ ἀνελεῖν αὐτόν. **16** ᾿Ακούσας δὲ ὁ υἱὸς τῆς ἀδελφῆς Παύλου τὴν ἐνέδραν παραγενόμενος καὶ εἰσελθὼν εἰς τὴν παρεμβολὴν ἀπήγγειλεν τῷ Παύλῳ. **17** προσκαλεσάμενος δὲ ὁ Παῦλος ἕνα τῶν ἑκατονταρχῶν ἔφη, Τὸν νεανίαν τοῦτον ἀπάγαγε πρὸς τὸν χιλίαρχον, ἔχει γὰρ ἀπαγγεῖλαί τι αὐτῷ. **18** ὁ μὲν οὖν παραλαβὼν αὐτὸν ἤγαγεν πρὸς τὸν χιλίαρχον καὶ φησίν, ῾Ο δέσμιος Παῦλος προσκαλεσάμενός με ἠρώτησεν τοῦτον τὸν νεανίσκον ἀγαγεῖν πρὸς σέ, ἔχοντά τι λαλῆσαί σοι. **19** ἐπιλαβόμενος δὲ τῆς χειρὸς αὐτοῦ ὁ χιλίαρχος καὶ ἀναχωρήσας κατ᾿ ἰδίαν ἐπυνθάνετο, Τί ἐστιν ὃ ἔχεις ἀπαγγεῖλαί μοι; **20** εἶπεν δὲ ὅτι Οἱ ᾿Ιουδαῖοι συνέθεντο τοῦ ἐρωτῆσαί σε ὅπως αὔριον τὸν Παῦλον καταγάγῃς εἰς τὸ συνέδριον ὡς μέλλον² τι ἀκριβέστερον πυνθάνεσθαι περὶ αὐτοῦ. **21** σὺ οὖν μὴ πεισθῇς αὐτοῖς· ἐνεδρεύουσιν γὰρ αὐτὸν ἐξ αὐτῶν ἄνδρες πλείους τεσσαράκοντα, οἵτινες ἀνεθεμάτισαν ἑαυτοὺς μήτε φαγεῖν μήτε πιεῖν ἕως οὗ ἀνέλωσιν αὐτόν, καὶ νῦν εἰσιν ἕτοιμοι προσδεχόμενοι τὴν ἀπὸ σοῦ ἐπαγγελίαν. **22** ὁ μὲν οὖν χιλίαρχος ἀπέλυσε τὸν νεανίσκον παραγγείλας μηδενὶ ἐκλαλῆσαι ὅτι ταῦτα ἐνεφάνισας πρός με.

---

² **20** {C} μέλλον ℵ* 33 181 arm? ∥ μέλλων 𝔭⁷⁴ A B E 81 itᵉ copᵇᵒ arm? eth ∥ μέλλοντα P 049 056 0142 88 104 326 330 451 1241 *Byz*ᵖᵗ Theophylactᵃ ∥ μέλλοντες 630 1877 2492 *Byz*ᵖᵗ itᵃʳ,ᵍⁱᵍ,ʰ,ˢ vg syrᵖ,ʰ copˢᵃ Lucifer Theophylactᵇ ∥ μελλόντων ℵᶜ Ψ 436 614 629ᶜ 945 1505 1739 2412 2495 Chrysostom ∥ μέλλοντας 2127

14–15 Ac 25.3

Paul Sent to Felix the Governor

23 Καὶ προσκαλεσάμενος δύο τινὰς τῶν ἑκατονταρχῶν εἶπεν, Ἑτοιμάσατε στρατιώτας διακοσίους ὅπως πορευθῶσιν ἕως Καισαρείας, καὶ ἱππεῖς ἑβδομήκοντα καὶ δεξιολάβους διακοσίους, ἀπὸ τρίτης ὥρας τῆς νυκτός, **24** κτήνη τε παραστῆσαι ἵνα ἐπιβιβάσαντες τὸν Παῦλον διασώσωσι πρὸς Φήλικα τὸν ἡγεμόνα, **25** γράψας ἐπιστολὴν ἔχουσαν τὸν τύπον τοῦτον· **26** Κλαύδιος Λυσίας τῷ κρατίστῳ ἡγεμόνι Φήλικι χαίρειν. **27** Τὸν ἄνδρα τοῦτον συλλημφθέντα ὑπὸ τῶν Ἰουδαίων καὶ μέλλοντα ἀναιρεῖσθαι ὑπ' αὐτῶν ἐπιστὰς σὺν τῷ στρατεύματι ἐξειλάμην, μαθὼν ὅτι Ῥωμαῖός ἐστιν·[b] **28** βουλόμενός τε ἐπιγνῶναι τὴν αἰτίαν δι' ἣν ἐνεκάλουν αὐτῷ κατήγαγον εἰς τὸ συνέδριον αὐτῶν[3]· **29** ὃν εὗρον ἐγκαλούμενον περὶ ζητημάτων τοῦ νόμου αὐτῶν, μηδὲν δὲ ἄξιον θανάτου ἢ δεσμῶν ἔχοντα ἔγκλημα. **30** μηνυθείσης δέ μοι ἐπιβουλῆς εἰς τὸν ἄνδρα ἔσεσθαι ἐξ αὐτῶν[4] ἔπεμψα πρὸς σέ, παραγγείλας καὶ τοῖς κατηγόροις λέγειν πρὸς αὐτὸν ἐπὶ σοῦ.[5]

---

[3] **28** {C} κατήγαγον εἰς τὸ συνέδριον αὐτῶν 𝔭[74] ℵ A 33 436 614 (630 ἤγαγον) 945 1739 2412 vg[mss] geo ‖ κατήγαγον αὐτὸν εἰς τὸ συνέδριον αὐτῶν (𝔭[48] omit αὐτῶν) B[2ⁿᵍ] E P Ψ 049 056 0142 88 104 181 326 330 451 629 1241 1505 1877 2127 2492 2495 Byz it[ar,e,(gig)] vg syr[p,h] cop[sa,bo] arm Chrysostom ‖ κατήγαγον eth ‖ omit B* 81

[4] **30** {C} ἔσεσθαι ἐξ αὐτῶν ℵ A E 33 81 181 436 1739 2495 l[1504m] it[(ar),e] (vg) syr[h] arm ‖ ἔσεσθαι, ἐξαυτῆς 𝔭[74] B Ψ 614 2412 cop[bo] geo ‖ ἔσεσθαι ἐξ αὐτῶν, ἐξαυτῆς cop[boms] ‖ μέλλειν ἔσεσθαι ἐξ αὐτῶν 945 1505 ‖ μέλλειν ἔσεσθαι ἐξαυτῆς 630 ‖ μέλλειν ἔσεσθαι ὑπὸ τῶν Ἰουδαίων, ἐξαυτῆς P 049 056 0142 88 104 326 330 451 629[c] 1241 1877 2127 2492 Byz (it[gig?]) syr[p] cop[sa] (Chrysostom)

[5] **30** {C} σοῦ. 𝔭[74vid] A B 33 it[gig] vg[ww] cop[sa,bo] eth[ro] ‖ σοῦ· ἔρρωσο. ℵ E Ψ 056 0142 (81 omit ἐπὶ σοῦ) 104 181 436 614 630 945 1241 1505 1739 2127 2412 2495 Byz[pt] it[ar,e] vg[cl] syr[p,h] arm eth[pp] geo Chrysostom Theophylact ‖ σοῦ· ἔρρωσθε. P 049 88 326 330 451 1877 2492 Byz[pt] Chrysostom

---

[b] **27** b major: TR Bov Nes BF² AV RV ASV RSV NEB TT Zür Luth Jer Seg ‖ b minor: WII

27 Τὸν...ἐξειλάμην Ac 21.30–33 μαθὼν...ἐστιν Ac 22.27 **28** Ac 22.30 **29** Ac 18.14–15; 25.18–19 ἐγκαλούμενον...αὐτῶν Ac 23.6 μηδὲν...ἔγκλημα Ac 23.9; 26.31; 28.18 **30** παραγγείλας...σοῦ Ac 24.5–8; 25.5

Paul Sent to Governor Felix

[23] Then the commander called two of his officers and said: "Get two hundred soldiers ready to go to Caesarea, together with seventy horsemen and two hundred spearmen, and be ready to leave by nine o'clock tonight. [24] Provide some horses for Paul to ride, and get him safely through to Governor Felix." [25] Then the commander wrote a letter that went like this:

[26] "Claudius Lysias to his Excellency, the Governor Felix: Greetings. [27] The Jews seized this man and were about to kill him. I learned that he is a Roman citizen, so I went with my soldiers and rescued him. [28] I wanted to know what they were accusing him of, so I took him down to their Council. [29] I found out that he had not done a thing for which he deserved to die or be put in prison; the accusation against him had to do with questions about their own law. [30] And when I was informed that the Jews are making a plot against him, I decided to send him to you. I told his accusers to make their charges against him before you."

31 The soldiers carried out their orders. They took Paul and brought him that night as far as Antipatris. 32 The next day the foot soldiers returned to the fort and left the horsemen to go on with him. 33 They took him to Caesarea and delivered the letter to the Governor and turned Paul over to him. 34 The Governor read the letter and asked Paul what province he was from. When he found out that he was from Cilicia, 35 he said, "I will hear you when your accusers arrive." Then he gave orders that Paul be kept under guard in Herod's palace.

Paul Accused by the Jews

24 After five days the High Priest Ananias went to Caesarea with some elders and a lawyer named Tertullus. They appeared before Governor Felix and made their charges against Paul. 2 Tertullus was called and began to accuse Paul as follows:

"Your Excellency! Your wise leadership has brought us a long period of peace, and many necessary reforms are being made for the good of our country. 3 We welcome this everywhere at all times, and we are deeply grateful to you. 4 I do not want to take up too much of your time, however, so I beg you to be kind and listen to our brief account. 5 We found this man to be a dangerous nuisance; he starts riots among the Jews all over the world, and is a leader of the party of the Nazarenes. 6 He also tried to defile the Temple, and we arrested him. [We planned to judge him according to our own Law, 7 but the commander Lysias came in and with great violence took him from us. 8 Then Lysias gave orders that his accusers

31 Οἱ μὲν οὖν στρατιῶται κατὰ τὸ διατεταγμένον αὐτοῖς ἀναλαβόντες τὸν Παῦλον ἤγαγον διὰ νυκτὸς εἰς τὴν Ἀντιπατρίδα· 32 τῇ δὲ ἐπαύριον ἐάσαντες τοὺς ἱππεῖς ἀπέρχεσθαι σὺν αὐτῷ ὑπέστρεψαν εἰς τὴν παρεμβολήν· 33 οἵτινες εἰσελθόντες εἰς τὴν Καισάρειαν καὶ ἀναδόντες τὴν ἐπιστολὴν τῷ ἡγεμόνι παρέστησαν καὶ τὸν Παῦλον αὐτῷ. 34 ἀναγνοὺς δὲ καὶ ἐπερωτήσας ἐκ ποίας ἐπαρχείας ἐστὶν καὶ πυθόμενος ὅτι ἀπὸ Κιλικίας, 35 Διακούσομαί σου, ἔφη, ὅταν καὶ οἱ κατήγοροί σου παραγένωνται· κελεύσας ἐν τῷ πραιτωρίῳ τοῦ Ἡρῴδου φυλάσσεσθαι αὐτόν.

The Case against Paul

24 Μετὰ δὲ πέντε ἡμέρας κατέβη ὁ ἀρχιερεὺς Ἀνανίας μετὰ πρεσβυτέρων τινῶν καὶ ῥήτορος Τερτύλλου τινός, οἵτινες ἐνεφάνισαν τῷ ἡγεμόνι κατὰ τοῦ Παύλου. 2 κληθέντος δὲ αὐτοῦ ἤρξατο κατηγορεῖν ὁ Τέρτυλλος λέγων, ᵃΠολλῆς εἰρήνης τυγχάνοντες διὰ σοῦ καὶ διορθωμάτων γινομένων τῷ ἔθνει τούτῳ διὰ τῆς σῆς προνοίας,ᵇ 3 ᵃ πάντῃ τε καὶ πανταχοῦᵇ ἀποδεχόμεθα, κράτιστε Φῆλιξ, μετὰ πάσης εὐχαριστίας. 4 ἵνα δὲ μὴ ἐπὶ πλεῖόν σε ἐγκόπτω, παρακαλῶ ἀκοῦσαί σε ἡμῶν συντόμως τῇ σῇ ἐπιεικείᾳ. 5 εὑρόντες γὰρ τὸν ἄνδρα τοῦτον λοιμὸν καὶ κινοῦντα στάσεις πᾶσιν τοῖς Ἰουδαίοις τοῖς κατὰ τὴν οἰκουμένην πρωτοστάτην τε τῆς τῶν Ναζωραίων αἱρέσεως, 6 ὃς καὶ τὸ ἱερὸν ἐπείρασεν βεβηλῶσαι, ὃν καὶ ἐκρατήσαμεν,[1] 8 παρ' οὗ δυνήσῃ αὐτὸς ἀνακρίνας περὶ

---

[1] **6-8** {D} ἐκρατήσαμεν, p74 ℵ A B P 049 81 326 330 451 629gr 1241 1877 2127 2492 Byzpt itp*,s vgww copsa,bo geo ‖ add verses 6b–8a ἐκρατήσαμεν καὶ κατὰ

ᵃ ᵃ **2-3** a no number, a number 3: TRed WH Bov Nes BF2 AV RV ASV RSV (NEB) TT Zür Jer Seg ‖ a number 3, a no number: TRed Luth
ᵇ ᵇ **2-3** b minor, b none: Bov Nes BF2 AV RV ASV RSV (TT) Luth Jer Seg ‖ b none, b minor: TR NEB Zür ‖ b none, b none: WH

34 πυθόμενος...Κιλικίας Ac 22.3
24 1 Ac 25.2   **5** εὑρόντες...οἰκουμένην Ac 17.6   τῆς...αἱρέσεως Ac 24.14   **6** ὃς... βεβηλῶσαι Ac 21.28   ὃν καὶ ἐκρατήσαμεν Ac 21.30

πάντων τούτων ἐπιγνῶναι ὧν ἡμεῖς κατηγοροῦμεν αὐτοῦ.
9 συνεπέθεντο δὲ καὶ οἱ Ἰουδαῖοι φάσκοντες ταῦτα οὕτως
ἔχειν.

Paul Defends Himself before Felix

10 Ἀπεκρίθη τε ὁ Παῦλος νεύσαντος αὐτῷ τοῦ ἡγεμόνος λέγειν, Ἐκ πολλῶν ἐτῶν ὄντα σε κριτὴν τῷ ἔθνει
τούτῳ ἐπιστάμενος εὐθύμως τὰ περὶ ἐμαυτοῦ ἀπολογοῦμαι,
11 δυναμένου σου ἐπιγνῶναι ὅτι[c] οὐ πλείους εἰσίν μοι
ἡμέραι δώδεκα ἀφ' ἧς ἀνέβην προσκυνήσων εἰς Ἰερουσαλήμ, 12 καὶ οὔτε ἐν τῷ ἱερῷ εὗρόν με πρός τινα διαλεγό-
μενον ἢ ἐπίστασιν ποιοῦντα ὄχλου οὔτε ἐν ταῖς συναγωγαῖς
οὔτε κατὰ τὴν πόλιν, 13 οὐδὲ παραστῆσαι δύνανταί σοι
περὶ ὧν νυνὶ κατηγοροῦσίν μου. 14 ὁμολογῶ δὲ τοῦτό σοι
ὅτι κατὰ τὴν ὁδὸν[d] ἣν λέγουσιν αἵρεσιν[d] οὕτως λατρεύω
τῷ πατρῴῳ θεῷ, πιστεύων πᾶσι τοῖς κατὰ τὸν νόμον
καὶ τοῖς ἐν τοῖς προφήταις γεγραμμένοις, 15 ἐλπίδα
ἔχων εἰς τὸν θεόν, ἣν καὶ αὐτοὶ οὗτοι προσδέχονται,
ἀνάστασιν μέλλειν ἔσεσθαι[2] δικαίων τε καὶ ἀδίκων.

τὸν ἡμέτερον νόμον ἐβουλήθημεν ἀνελεῖν. 7 παρελθὼν δὲ Λυσίας ὁ χιλίαρχος ἥρπασεν αὐτὸν ἐκ τῶν χειρῶν ἡμῶν, 8 πέμψας πρὸς σέ, 483 ‖ add
verses 6b–8a ἐκρατήσαμεν καὶ κατὰ τὸν ἡμέτερον νόμον ἠθελήσαμεν κρῖναι.
7 παρελθὼν δὲ Λυσίας ὁ χιλίαρχος μετὰ πολλῆς βίας ἐκ τῶν χειρῶν
ἡμῶν ἀπήγαγε, 8 κελεύσας τοὺς κατηγόρους αὐτοῦ ἔρχεσθαι ἐπὶ σέ.
(Ε πρὸς σέ) Ψ (056 0142 ἐπὶ σοῦ and omit καὶ) 33 88 (104 ἐπὶ σοῦ) (181
νόμον ἐβουλήθημεν and ἐπὶ σοῦ) 436 (614 2412 2495 κρίνειν and ἐπὶ σοῦ)
629lat 630 945 (1505 κρίνειν) 1739 Byzpt itar,c,e,(gig),pc,ph (vgcl) syrp.h arm eth
Chrysostom Greekacc. to Bede Theophylact ‖ add verses 6b–8a ἐκρατήσαμεν
καὶ κατὰ τὸν ἡμέτερον νόμον, ἠβουλήθημεν κρίναι κατὰ τὸν ἡμέτερον
νόμον. 7 ἐλθὼν δὲ ὁ χιλίαρχος Λυσίας βίᾳ πολλῇ ἐκ τῶν χειρῶν ἡμῶν
ἀφίλετο καὶ πρός σε ἀπέστειλε, 8 κελεύσας τοὺς κατηγόρους αὐτοῦ
ἔρχεσθαι πρὸς σέ. 424*

[2] 15 {A} ἔσεσθαι 𝔓74 ℵ A B C 33 81 181 436 629 945 1739 itarc,gig,s vg

[c] 11 c indirect: TR Bov Nes BF² AV RV ASV RSV NEB TT Zur Luth Jer Seg ‖ c causal: WH
[d d] 14 d none, d none: (TR) WH Bov Nes BF² (AV) (RV) (ASV) (Seg) ‖ d minor, d minor: RSV
TT Zür? Luth? Jer ‖ d parens, d parens: NEB

11 οὐ...Ἰερουσαλήμ Ac 21.17   ἀνέβην...Ἰερουσαλήμ Ac 8.27   14 κατὰ τὴν...θεῷ
Ac 24.5   15 Dn 12.2; Jn 5.28–29; Ac 23.6

should come before you.] If you question this man, you yourself will be able
to learn from him all the things that
we are accusing him of." 9 The Jews also
joined in the accusation and said that
all this was true.

Paul's Defense before Felix

10 The Governor then motioned to Paul
to speak, and Paul said:
"I know that you have been a judge
over this nation for many years, and so
I am happy to defend myself before you.
11 As you can find out for yourself, it
was no more than twelve days ago that
I went up to Jerusalem to worship.
12 The Jews did not find me arguing with
anyone in the Temple, nor did they
find me stirring up the people, either in
their synagogues or anywhere else in the
city. 13 Nor can they give you proof of
the accusations they now bring against
me. 14 I do admit this to you: I worship
the God of our ancestors by following
that Way which they say is false. But I
also believe in all the things written in
the Law of Moses and the books of the
prophets. 15 I have the same hope in
God that these themselves hold, that all
men, both the good and the bad, will be

raised from death. ¹⁶ And so I do my best always to have a clear conscience before God and men.

¹⁷ "After being away from Jerusalem for several years, I went there to take some money to my own people and to offer sacrifices. ¹⁸ It was while I was doing this that they found me in the Temple, after I had completed the ceremony of purification. There was no crowd with me, and no disorder. ¹⁹ But some Jews from the province of Asia were there; they themselves ought to come before you and make their accusations, if they have anything against me. ²⁰ Or let these men here tell what crime they found me guilty of when I stood before the Council — ²¹ except for the one thing I called out when I stood before them: 'I am being judged by you today for believing that the dead will be raised to life.'"

²² Then Felix, who was well informed about the Way, brought the hearing to a close. "I will decide your case," he told them, "when the commander Lysias arrives." ²³ He ordered the officer in charge of Paul to keep him under guard, but to give him some freedom and allow his friends to provide for his needs.

Paul before Felix and Drusilla

²⁴ After some days Felix came with his wife Drusilla, who was Jewish. He sent for Paul and listened to him as he talked about faith in Christ Jesus. ²⁵ But as Paul went on discussing about goodness, self-control, and the coming Day of

16 ἐν τούτῳ καὶ αὐτὸς ἀσκῶ ἀπρόσκοπον συνείδησιν ἔχειν πρὸς τὸν θεὸν καὶ τοὺς ἀνθρώπους διὰ παντός. 17 δι' ἐτῶν δὲ πλειόνων ἐλεημοσύνας ποιήσων εἰς τὸ ἔθνος μου παρεγενόμην καὶ προσφοράς, 18 ἐν αἷς εὗρόν με ἡγνισμένον ἐν τῷ ἱερῷ, οὐ μετὰ ὄχλου οὐδὲ μετὰ θορύβου·ᵉ 19ᶠ τινὲς δὲ ἀπὸ τῆς Ἀσίας Ἰουδαῖοι,ᵉ ᶠοὓς ἔδει ἐπὶ σοῦ παρεῖναι καὶ κατηγορεῖν εἴ τι ἔχοιεν πρὸς ἐμέ—ᵉ 20 ἢ αὐτοὶ οὗτοι εἰπάτωσαν τί εὗρον ἀδίκημα³ στάντος μου ἐπὶ τοῦ συνεδρίου 21 ἢ περὶ μιᾶς ταύτης φωνῆς ἧς ἐκέκραξα ἐν αὐτοῖς ἑστὼς ὅτι Περὶ ἀναστάσεως νεκρῶν ἐγὼ κρίνομαι σήμερον ἐφ' ὑμῶν.

22 Ἀνεβάλετο δὲ αὐτοὺς ὁ Φῆλιξ, ἀκριβέστερον εἰδὼς τὰ περὶ τῆς ὁδοῦ, εἴπας, Ὅταν Λυσίας ὁ χιλίαρχος καταβῇ διαγνώσομαι τὰ καθ' ὑμᾶς, 23 διαταξάμενος τῷ ἑκατοντάρχῃ τηρεῖσθαι αὐτὸν ἔχειν τε ἄνεσιν καὶ μηδένα κωλύειν τῶν ἰδίων αὐτοῦ ὑπηρετεῖν αὐτῷ.

Paul Held in Custody

24 Μετὰ δὲ ἡμέρας τινὰς παραγενόμενος ὁ Φῆλιξ σὺν Δρουσίλλῃ τῇ ἰδίᾳ γυναικὶ οὔσῃ Ἰουδαίᾳ μετεπέμψατο τὸν Παῦλον καὶ ἤκουσεν αὐτοῦ περὶ τῆς εἰς Χριστὸν Ἰησοῦν⁴ πίστεως. 25 διαλεγομένου δὲ αὐτοῦ περὶ δικαιο-

cop^{sa,bo} arm geo Chrysostom Theophylact^b ‖ ἔσεσθαι νεκρῶν E P Ψ 049 056 0142 88 326 330 451 614 630 1241 1505 1877 2127 2412 2492 2495 *Byz* it^{ar*,e} syr^{p,h} eth Theophylact^a

³ **20** {B} εὗρον ἀδίκημα 𝔭⁷⁴ ℵ A B 33 81 181 945 ‖ εὗρον ἐν ἐμοὶ ἀδίκημα C E P Ψ 049 056 0142 88 104 326 330 436 451 614 629 (630 1739 ἀδίκημα ἐν ἐμοί) 1241 1505 1877 2127 2412 2492 2495 *Byz* it^{ar,e,gig} vg syr^{p,h} cop^{sa,bo} arm geo Chrysostom

⁴ **24** {C} Χριστὸν Ἰησοῦν 𝔭⁷⁴ ℵ* B E (Ψ τὸν Χριστὸν Ἰησοῦν) 049

^{e e e} **18-19** *e* major, *e* minor, *e* dash ‖ *e* minor, *e* minor, *e* dash: WH ‖ *e* major, *e* dash, *e* major: RV ASV RSV ‖ *e* major, *e* ellipsis, *e* major: (Jer) Seg ‖ *e* minor, *e* minor, *e* major: TR Bov Nes BF² (AV) Luth ‖ *e* major, *e* minor, *e* major: NEB TT Zür

^{f f} **18-19** *f* verse 19, *f* no number: TR^{ed} WH? Bov Nes BF² TT Zür Luth Jer Seg ‖ *f* no number, *f* verse 19: TR^{ed} WH? AV RV ASV RSV NEB

16 Ac 23.1   17 Ac 11.29-30; Ro 15.25-26; Ga 2.10   **18-19** ἐν αἷς...Ἰουδαῖοι Ac 21.26-27   21 Ac 23.6; 24.15   23 Ac 27.3; 28.16, 30   25 περὶ...μέλλοντος Jn 16.8

σύνης καὶ ἐγκρατείας καὶ τοῦ κρίματος τοῦ μέλλοντος ἔμφοβος γενόμενος ὁ Φῆλιξ ἀπεκρίθη, Τὸ νῦν ἔχον πορεύου, καιρὸν δὲ μεταλαβὼν μετακαλέσομαί σε· **26** ἅμα καὶ ἐλπίζων ὅτι χρήματα δοθήσεται αὐτῷ ὑπὸ τοῦ Παύλου· διὸ καὶ πυκνότερον αὐτὸν μεταπεμπόμενος ὡμίλει αὐτῷ.

27 Διετίας δὲ πληρωθείσης ἔλαβεν διάδοχον ὁ Φῆλιξ Πόρκιον Φῆστον· θέλων τε χάριτα καταθέσθαι τοῖς Ἰουδαίοις ὁ Φῆλιξ κατέλιπε τὸν Παῦλον δεδεμένον.

Paul Appeals to Caesar

25 Φῆστος οὖν ἐπιβὰς τῇ ἐπαρχείᾳ μετὰ τρεῖς ἡμέρας ἀνέβη εἰς Ἱεροσόλυμα ἀπὸ Καισαρείας, **2** ἐνεφάνισάν τε αὐτῷ οἱ ἀρχιερεῖς καὶ οἱ πρῶτοι τῶν Ἰουδαίων κατὰ τοῦ Παύλου, καὶ παρεκάλουν αὐτὸν **3** αἰτούμενοι χάριν κατ᾽ αὐτοῦ ὅπως μεταπέμψηται αὐτὸν εἰς Ἱερουσαλήμ, ἐνέδραν ποιοῦντες ἀνελεῖν αὐτὸν κατὰ τὴν ὁδόν. **4** ὁ μὲν οὖν Φῆστος ἀπεκρίθη τηρεῖσθαι τὸν Παῦλον εἰς Καισάρειαν, ἑαυτὸν δὲ μέλλειν ἐν τάχει ἐκπορεύεσθαι· **5** Οἱ οὖν ἐν ὑμῖν, φησίν, δυνατοὶ συγκαταβάντες εἴ τί ἐστιν ἐν τῷ ἀνδρὶ ἄτοπον κατηγορείτωσαν αὐτοῦ.

6 Διατρίψας δὲ ἐν αὐτοῖς ἡμέρας οὐ πλείους ὀκτὼ ἢ δέκα, καταβὰς εἰς Καισάρειαν, τῇ ἐπαύριον καθίσας ἐπὶ τοῦ βήματος ἐκέλευσεν τὸν Παῦλον ἀχθῆναι. **7** παραγενομένου δὲ αὐτοῦ περιέστησαν αὐτὸν οἱ ἀπὸ Ἱεροσολύμων καταβεβηκότες Ἰουδαῖοι, πολλὰ καὶ βαρέα αἰτιώματα καταφέροντες ἃ οὐκ ἴσχυον ἀποδεῖξαι, **8** τοῦ Παύλου ἀπολογουμένου ὅτι Οὔτε εἰς τὸν νόμον τῶν Ἰουδαίων οὔτε εἰς τὸ ἱερὸν οὔτε εἰς Καίσαρά τι ἥμαρτον.

093 33 81 104 181 326 629 630 945 1505 1739 1877ᶜ 2127 2492 2495 itᵃʳ,ᵉ,ᵍⁱᵍ, ˢ vgᶜˡ syrʰ copˢᵃᵐˢ,ᵇᵒ geo Chrysostom Theophylactᵇ ‖ Ἰησοῦν Χριστόν vgʷʷ arm eth ‖ Χριστόν ℵᶜ A P 056 0142 88 330 436 451 614 1241 1877* 2412 *Byz* syrᵖ copˢᵃ Theophylactᵃ

27 θέλων…Ἰουδαίοις Ac 25.9
25 2 ἐνεφάνισαν…Παύλου Ac 24.1; 25.15   **3** Ac 23.15   **5** Ac 23.30   **6** τῇ…ἀχθῆναι Ac 25.17   **7** πολλὰ…καταφέροντες Ac 24.5–6   ἃ…ἀποδεῖξαι Ac 24.13

Judgment, Felix was afraid and said, "You may leave now. I will call you again when I get the chance." [26] At the same time he was hoping that Paul would give him some money; and for this reason he would call for him often and talk with him.

[27] After two years had passed, Porcius Festus took the place of Felix as Governor. Felix wanted to gain favor with the Jews, so he left Paul in prison.

Paul Appeals to the Emperor

25 Three days after Festus arrived in the province, he went from Caesarea to Jerusalem. [2] There the chief priests and the Jewish leaders brought their charges against Paul. They begged Festus [3] to do them the favor of having Paul come to Jerusalem, because they had made a plot to kill him on the way. [4] Festus answered: "Paul is being kept a prisoner in Caesarea, and I myself will be going back there soon. [5] Let your leaders go to Caesarea with me and accuse the man, if he has done anything wrong."

[6] Festus spent another eight or ten days with them, and then went to Caesarea. On the next day he sat down in the judgment court, and ordered Paul to be brought in. [7] When Paul arrived, the Jews who had come from Jerusalem stood around him and started making many serious charges against him, which they were not able to prove. [8] But Paul defended himself: "I have done nothing wrong against the Law of the Jews, or the Temple, or the Roman Emperor."

⁹ Festus wanted to gain favor with the Jews, so he asked Paul, "Would you want to go to Jerusalem and be tried on these charges before me there?" ¹⁰ Paul said: "I am standing before the Emperor's own judgment court, where I should be tried. I have done no wrong to the Jews, as you yourself well know. ¹¹ If I have broken the law and done something for which I deserve the death penalty, I do not ask to escape it. But if there is no truth in the charges they bring against me, no one can hand me over to them. I appeal to the Emperor." ¹² Then Festus, after conferring with his advisers, answered, "You have appealed to the Emperor, so to the Emperor you will go."

Paul before Agrippa and Bernice

¹³ Some time later King Agrippa and Bernice came to Caesarea to pay a visit of welcome to Festus. ¹⁴ After they had been there several days, Festus explained Paul's situation to the king: "There is a man here who was left a prisoner by Felix; ¹⁵ and when I went to Jerusalem, the Jewish chief priests and elders brought charges against him and asked me to condemn him. ¹⁶ But I told them that the Romans are not in the habit of handing over any man accused of a crime before he has met his accusers face to face, and has the chance of defending himself against the accusation. ¹⁷ When they all came here, then, I lost no time, but on the very next day I sat in the judgment court and ordered the man to be brought in. ¹⁸ His opponents stood up, but they did not accuse him of any of the evil crimes that I thought they

9 ὁ Φῆστος δὲ θέλων τοῖς Ἰουδαίοις χάριν καταθέσθαι ἀποκριθεὶς τῷ Παύλῳ εἶπεν, Θέλεις εἰς Ἱεροσόλυμα ἀναβὰς ἐκεῖ περὶ τούτων κριθῆναι ἐπ' ἐμοῦ; **10** εἶπεν δὲ ὁ Παῦλος, Ἑστὼς ἐπὶ τοῦ βήματος Καίσαρός εἰμι, οὗ με δεῖ κρίνεσθαι. Ἰουδαίους οὐδὲν ἠδίκησα, ὡς καὶ σὺ κάλλιον ἐπιγινώσκεις. **11** εἰ μὲν οὖν ἀδικῶ καὶ ἄξιον θανάτου πέπραχά τι, οὐ παραιτοῦμαι τὸ ἀποθανεῖν· εἰ δὲ οὐδέν ἐστιν ὧν οὗτοι κατηγοροῦσίν μου, οὐδείς με δύναται αὐτοῖς χαρίσασθαι· Καίσαρα ἐπικαλοῦμαι. **12** τότε ὁ Φῆστος συλλαλήσας μετὰ τοῦ συμβουλίου ἀπεκρίθη, Καίσαρα ἐπικέκλησαι, ἐπὶ Καίσαρα πορεύσῃ.

Paul Brought before Agrippa and Bernice

13 Ἡμερῶν δὲ διαγενομένων τινῶν Ἀγρίππας ὁ βασιλεὺς καὶ Βερνίκη κατήντησαν εἰς Καισάρειαν ἀσπασάμενοι¹ τὸν Φῆστον. **14** ὡς δὲ πλείους ἡμέρας διέτριβον ἐκεῖ, ὁ Φῆστος τῷ βασιλεῖ ἀνέθετο τὰ κατὰ τὸν Παῦλον λέγων, Ἀνήρ τίς ἐστιν καταλελειμμένος ὑπὸ Φήλικος δέσμιος, **15** περὶ οὗ γενομένου μου εἰς Ἱεροσόλυμα ἐνεφάνισαν οἱ ἀρχιερεῖς καὶ οἱ πρεσβύτεροι τῶν Ἰουδαίων, αἰτούμενοι κατ' αὐτοῦ καταδίκην· **16** πρὸς οὓς ἀπεκρίθην ὅτι οὐκ ἔστιν ἔθος Ῥωμαίοις χαρίζεσθαί τινα ἄνθρωπον πρὶν ἢ ὁ κατηγορούμενος κατὰ πρόσωπον ἔχοι τοὺς κατηγόρους τόπον τε ἀπολογίας λάβοι περὶ τοῦ ἐγκλήματος. **17** συνελθόντων οὖν ἐνθάδε ἀναβολὴν μηδεμίαν ποιησάμενος τῇ ἑξῆς καθίσας ἐπὶ τοῦ βήματος ἐκέλευσα ἀχθῆναι τὸν ἄνδρα· **18** περὶ οὗ σταθέντες οἱ κατήγοροι οὐδεμίαν αἰτίαν ἔφερον ὧν ἐγὼ ὑπενόουν πονηρῶν²,

---

¹ **13** {B} ἀσπασάμενοι 𝔭⁷⁴ ℵ A B C² Eᵍʳ P 049 33 326 330 451 614 629 1241 2127 2412 2492 *Lect* copᵇᵒ eth Theophylactᵃ ‖ ἀσπασόμενοι Ψ 056 0142 81 88 104 181 436 630 945 1505 1739 1877 2495 *Byz* *l*⁶⁸⁰,¹¹⁵³ᵃ,¹²⁹⁸,¹⁴⁴¹ itᵃʳ,ᵉ,ᵍⁱᵍ vg syrᵖ,ʰ,ᵖᵃˡ copˢᵃ arm geo Chrysostom Theophylactᵇ

² **18** {C} πονηρῶν ℵᶜ B E 81 104 436 *l*¹⁵⁰⁴ itᵉ syrᵖᵃˡ copᵇᵒ? ‖ πονηράν

---

9 θέλων...καταθέσθαι Ac 24.27   **14** Ἀνήρ...δέσμιος Ac 24.27   **15** γενομένου... Ἰουδαίων Ac 25.1-2   **17** Ac 25.6   **18-19** περὶ οὗ...πρὸς αὐτόν Ac 18.14-15; 23.29

19 ζητήματα δέ τινα περὶ τῆς ἰδίας δεισιδαιμονίας εἶχον πρὸς αὐτὸν καὶ περί τινος Ἰησοῦ τεθνηκότος, ὃν ἔφασκεν ὁ Παῦλος ζῆν. 20 ἀπορούμενος δὲ ἐγὼ τὴν περὶ τούτων ζήτησιν ἔλεγον εἰ βούλοιτο πορεύεσθαι εἰς Ἰεροσόλυμα κἀκεῖ κρίνεσθαι περὶ τούτων. 21 τοῦ δὲ Παύλου ἐπικαλεσαμένου τηρηθῆναι αὐτὸν εἰς τὴν τοῦ Σεβαστοῦ διάγνωσιν, ἐκέλευσα τηρεῖσθαι αὐτὸν ἕως οὗ ἀναπέμψω αὐτὸν πρὸς Καίσαρα. 22 Ἀγρίππας δὲ πρὸς τὸν Φῆστον, Ἐβουλόμην καὶ αὐτὸς τοῦ ἀνθρώπου ἀκοῦσαι. Αὔριον, φησίν, ἀκούσῃ αὐτοῦ.

23 Τῇ οὖν ἐπαύριον ἐλθόντος τοῦ Ἀγρίππα καὶ τῆς Βερνίκης μετὰ πολλῆς φαντασίας καὶ εἰσελθόντων εἰς τὸ ἀκροατήριον σύν τε χιλιάρχοις καὶ ἀνδράσιν τοῖς κατ᾽ ἐξοχὴν τῆς πόλεως, καὶ κελεύσαντος τοῦ Φήστου ἤχθη ὁ Παῦλος. 24 καὶ φησιν ὁ Φῆστος, Ἀγρίππα βασιλεῦ καὶ πάντες οἱ συμπαρόντες ἡμῖν ἄνδρες, θεωρεῖτε τοῦτον περὶ οὗ ἅπαν τὸ πλῆθος τῶν Ἰουδαίων ἐνέτυχόν μοι ἔν τε Ἰεροσολύμοις καὶ ἐνθάδε, βοῶντες μὴ δεῖν αὐτὸν ζῆν μηκέτι. 25 ἐγὼ δὲ κατελαβόμην μηδὲν ἄξιον αὐτὸν θανάτου πεπραχέναι, αὐτοῦ δὲ τούτου ἐπικαλεσαμένου τὸν Σεβαστὸν ἔκρινα πέμπειν. 26 περὶ οὗ ἀσφαλές τι γράψαι τῷ κυρίῳ οὐκ ἔχω· διὸ προήγαγον αὐτὸν ἐφ᾽ ὑμῶν καὶ μάλιστα ἐπὶ σοῦ, βασιλεῦ Ἀγρίππα, ὅπως τῆς ἀνακρίσεως γενομένης σχῶ τί γράψω· 27 ἄλογον γάρ μοι δοκεῖ πέμποντα δέσμιον μὴ καὶ τὰς κατ᾽ αὐτοῦ αἰτίας σημᾶναι.

Paul Defends Himself before Agrippa

26 Ἀγρίππας δὲ πρὸς τὸν Παῦλον ἔφη, Ἐπιτρέπεταί σοι περὶ σεαυτοῦ λέγειν. τότε ὁ Παῦλος ἐκτείνας τὴν

𝔓74 A C* Ψ 33vid 88 181 614 630 945 1505 1739 2412 2495 *l*598 itgig vgww syrp,h arm eth geo Theophylactb ‖ πονηρόν itar,v* vgcl copsa ‖ πονηρά ℵ* C2 ‖ *omit* P 049 056 0142 326 330 451 629c 1241 1877 2127 2492 *Byz Lect* Chrysostom Theophylacta

20 ἔλεγον...τούτων Ac 25.9   21 Ac 25.11–12   22 Ἐβουλόμην...ἀκοῦσαι Lk 23.8
23 Mt 10.18; Mk 13.9; Lk 21.12   24 τοῦτον...ἐνθάδε Ac 25.2, 7, 15   βοῶντες...μηκέτι Ac 22.22

would. 19 All they had were some arguments with him about their own religion and about a certain dead man named Jesus; Paul claims that he is alive. 20 I was undecided about how I could get information on these matters, so I asked Paul if he would be willing to go to Jerusalem and be tried there on these charges. 21 But Paul appealed; he asked to be kept under guard and let the Emperor decide his case. So I gave orders for him to be kept under guard until I could send him to the Emperor." 22 Agrippa said to Festus, "I myself would like to hear this man." "You will hear him tomorrow," Festus answered.

23 The next day Agrippa and Bernice came with much ceremony and honor, and entered the audience hall with the military chiefs and the leading men of the city. Festus gave the order and Paul was brought in. 24 Festus said: "King Agrippa, and all who are here with us: You see this man against whom all the Jewish people, both here and in Jerusalem, have brought complaints to me. They scream that he should not live any longer. 25 But I could not find that he had done anything for which he deserved the death sentence. And since he himself made an appeal to the Emperor, I have decided to send him. 26 But I do not have anything definite about him to write to the Emperor. So I have brought him here before you — and especially before you, King Agrippa! — so that, after investigating his case, I may have something to write. 27 For it seems unreasonable to me to send a prisoner without clearly indicating the charges against him."

Paul Defends Himself before Agrippa

26 Agrippa said to Paul, "You have permission to speak on your own behalf." Paul stretched out his hand and defended himself as follows:

² "King Agrippa! I consider myself fortunate that today I am to defend myself before you from all the things the Jews accuse me of. ³ This is especially true because you know so well all the Jewish customs and questions. I ask you, then, to listen to me with patience.

⁴ "All the Jews know how I have lived ever since I was young. They know that from the beginning I have spent my whole life in my own country and in Jerusalem. ⁵ They have always known, if they are willing to testify, that from the very first I have lived as a member of the strictest party of our religion, the Pharisees. ⁶ And now I stand here to be tried because I hope in the promise that God made to our ancestors — ⁷ the very promise that all twelve tribes of our people hope to receive, as they worship God day and night. And it is because of this hope, your Majesty, that I am being accused by the Jews! ⁸ Why do you Jews find it impossible to believe that God raises the dead?

⁹ "I myself thought that I should do everything I could against the name of Jesus of Nazareth. ¹⁰ That is what I did in Jerusalem. I received authority from the chief priests and put many of God's people in prison; and when they were sentenced to death, I also voted for it. ¹¹ Many times I had them punished in all the synagogues, and tried to make them deny their faith. I was so furious with them that I even went to foreign cities to persecute them."

Paul Tells of His Conversion
(Also Acts 9.1–19; 22.6–16)

¹² "It was for this purpose that I went to Damascus with the authority and orders from the chief priests. ¹³ It was on the road at midday, your Majesty, that I saw a light much brighter than the sun shining from the sky around me and the men traveling with me. ¹⁴ All of us fell to the ground, and I heard a voice say to me in the Hebrew language, 'Saul, Saul! Why are you persecuting me? You hurt yourself by hitting back, like an ox kicking against its owner's stick.'

χεῖρα ἀπελογεῖτο, **2** Περὶ πάντων ὧν ἐγκαλοῦμαι ὑπὸ Ἰουδαίων, βασιλεῦ Ἀγρίππα, ἥγημαι ἐμαυτὸν μακάριον ἐπὶ σοῦ μέλλων σήμερον ἀπολογεῖσθαι, **3** μάλιστα γνώστην ὄντα σε πάντων τῶν κατὰ Ἰουδαίους ἐθῶν τε καὶ ζητημάτων· διὸ δέομαι μακροθύμως ἀκοῦσαί μου. **4** Τὴν μὲν οὖν βίωσίν μου ἐκ νεότητος τὴν ἀπ' ἀρχῆς γενομένην ἐν τῷ ἔθνει μου ἔν τε Ἱεροσολύμοις ἴσασι πάντες Ἰουδαῖοι, **5** προγινώσκοντές με ἄνωθεν, ἐὰν θέλωσι μαρτυρεῖν, ὅτι κατὰ τὴν ἀκριβεστάτην αἵρεσιν τῆς ἡμετέρας θρησκείας ἔζησα Φαρισαῖος. **6** καὶ νῦν ἐπ' ἐλπίδι τῆς εἰς τοὺς πατέρας ἡμῶν ἐπαγγελίας γενομένης ὑπὸ τοῦ θεοῦ ἕστηκα κρινόμενος, **7** εἰς ἣν τὸ δωδεκάφυλον ἡμῶν ἐν ἐκτενείᾳ νύκτα καὶ ἡμέραν λατρεῦον ἐλπίζει καταντῆσαι· περὶ ἧς ἐλπίδος ἐγκαλοῦμαι ὑπὸ Ἰουδαίων, βασιλεῦ. **8** τί ἄπιστον κρίνεται παρ' ὑμῖν εἰ ὁ θεὸς νεκροὺς ἐγείρει; **9** ἐγὼ μὲν οὖν ἔδοξα ἐμαυτῷ πρὸς τὸ ὄνομα Ἰησοῦ τοῦ Ναζωραίου δεῖν πολλὰ ἐναντία πρᾶξαι· **10** ὃ καὶ ἐποίησα ἐν Ἱεροσολύμοις, καὶ πολλούς τε τῶν ἁγίων ἐγὼ ἐν φυλακαῖς κατέκλεισα τὴν παρὰ τῶν ἀρχιερέων ἐξουσίαν λαβών, ἀναιρουμένων τε αὐτῶν κατήνεγκα ψῆφον, **11** καὶ κατὰ πάσας τὰς συναγωγὰς πολλάκις τιμωρῶν αὐτοὺς ἠνάγκαζον βλασφημεῖν, περισσῶς τε ἐμμαινόμενος αὐτοῖς ἐδίωκον ἕως καὶ εἰς τὰς ἔξω πόλεις.

Paul Tells of His Conversion
(Ac 9.1–19; 22.6–16)

12 Ἐν οἷς πορευόμενος εἰς τὴν Δαμασκὸν μετ' ἐξουσίας καὶ ἐπιτροπῆς τῆς τῶν ἀρχιερέων **13** ἡμέρας μέσης κατὰ τὴν ὁδὸν εἶδον, βασιλεῦ, οὐρανόθεν ὑπὲρ τὴν λαμπρότητα τοῦ ἡλίου περιλάμψαν με φῶς καὶ τοὺς σὺν ἐμοὶ πορευομένους· **14** πάντων τε καταπεσόντων ἡμῶν εἰς τὴν γῆν ἤκουσα φωνὴν λέγουσαν πρός με τῇ Ἑβραΐδι διαλέκτῳ, Σαοὺλ Σαούλ, τί με διώκεις; σκληρόν σοι πρὸς κέντρα

---

5 κατὰ...Φαρισαῖος Php 3.5–6   **6** Ac 23.6; 24.15, 21; 28.20   **9–11** Ac 8.3; 22.4–5

λακτίζειν. **15** ἐγὼ δὲ εἶπα, Τίς εἶ, κύριε; ὁ δὲ κύριος εἶπεν, Ἐγώ εἰμι Ἰησοῦς ὃν σὺ διώκεις. **16** ἀλλὰ ἀνάστηθι καὶ στῆθι ἐπὶ τοὺς πόδας σου· εἰς τοῦτο γὰρ ὤφθην σοι, προχειρίσασθαί σε ὑπηρέτην καὶ μάρτυρα ὧν τε εἶδές με[1] ὧν τε ὀφθήσομαί σοι, **17** ἐξαιρούμενός σε ἐκ τοῦ λαοῦ καὶ ἐκ τῶν ἐθνῶν, εἰς οὓς ἐγὼ ἀποστέλλω σε **18** ἀνοῖξαι ὀφθαλμοὺς αὐτῶν, τοῦ ἐπιστρέψαι ἀπὸ σκότους εἰς φῶς καὶ τῆς ἐξουσίας τοῦ Σατανᾶ ἐπὶ τὸν θεόν, τοῦ λαβεῖν αὐτοὺς ἄφεσιν ἁμαρτιῶν καὶ κλῆρον ἐν τοῖς ἡγιασμένοις πίστει τῇ εἰς ἐμέ.

Paul's Testimony to Jews and Gentiles

19 Ὅθεν, βασιλεῦ Ἀγρίππα, οὐκ ἐγενόμην ἀπειθὴς τῇ οὐρανίῳ ὀπτασίᾳ, **20** ἀλλὰ τοῖς ἐν Δαμασκῷ πρῶτόν τε καὶ Ἱεροσολύμοις,[a] πᾶσάν τε τὴν χώραν τῆς Ἰουδαίας[a] καὶ τοῖς ἔθνεσιν ἀπήγγελλον μετανοεῖν καὶ ἐπιστρέφειν ἐπὶ τὸν θεόν, ἄξια τῆς μετανοίας ἔργα πράσσοντας. **21** ἕνεκα τούτων με Ἰουδαῖοι συλλαβόμενοι [ὄντα] ἐν τῷ ἱερῷ ἐπειρῶντο διαχειρίσασθαι. **22** ἐπικουρίας οὖν τυχὼν τῆς ἀπὸ τοῦ θεοῦ ἄχρι τῆς ἡμέρας ταύτης ἕστηκα μαρτυρόμενος μικρῷ τε καὶ μεγάλῳ, οὐδὲν ἐκτὸς λέγων ὧν τε οἱ προφῆται ἐλάλησαν μελλόντων γίνεσθαι καὶ Μωϋσῆς, **23** εἰ παθητὸς ὁ Χριστός, εἰ πρῶτος ἐξ ἀναστάσεως νεκρῶν φῶς μέλλει καταγγέλλειν τῷ τε λαῷ καὶ τοῖς ἔθνεσιν.

---

[1] **16** {C} με B C*vid? 88 614 945 1505 1739 2412 2495 l60m syrp, h copsa arm geo Ambrose Augustine // omit 𝔓74 ℵ A C² E Γ Ψ 049 056 096 0142 81 104 181 326 330 436 451 629 630 1241 1877 2127 2492 Byz Lectm itar, e, gig vg copbo

---

a a **20** a minor, a none: Nes TT // a none, a minor: RSV NEB Jer // a minor, a minor: TR WH AV RV ASV Seg // a none, a none: Bov BF² Zür Luth

---

16 στῆθι...σου Eze 2.1 **17** ἐξαιρούμενος...ἐθνῶν 1 Chr 16.35 εἰς...ἀποστέλλω σε Jr 1.7 **18** ἀνοῖξαι...αὐτῶν Is 35.5; 42.7; 61.1 LXX τοῦ ἐπιστρέψαι...φῶς Is 42.16 τῆς...Σατανᾶ Eph 2.2; Col 1.13 κλῆρον...ἡγιασμένοις Dt 33.3-4; Wsd 5.5; Ac 20.32 **20** τοῖς ἐν Δαμασκῷ πρῶτον Ac 9.19 ἄξια...πράσσοντας Mt 3.8 **21** Ac 21.30-31 **22** ὧν...Μωϋσῆς Lk 24.44 **23** Lk 24.46-47 φῶς...ἔθνεσιν Is 42.6; 49.6

---

15 'Who are you, Lord?' I asked. And the Lord said: 'I am Jesus, whom you persecute. 16 But get up and stand on your feet. I have appeared to you to appoint you as my servant; you are to tell others what you have seen of me today, and what I will show you in the future. 17 I will save you from the people of Israel and from the Gentiles, to whom I will send you. 18 You are to open their eyes and turn them from the darkness to the light, and from the power of Satan to God, so that through their faith in me they will have their sins forgiven and receive their place among God's chosen people.' "

Paul Tells of His Work

19 "And so, King Agrippa, I did not disobey the vision I had from heaven. 20 First in Damascus and in Jerusalem, and then in the whole country of Judea and among the Gentiles, I preached that they must repent of their sins and turn to God, and do the things that would show they had repented. 21 It was for this reason that the Jews seized me while I was in the Temple, and tried to kill me. 22 But to this very day I have been helped by God, and so I stand here giving my witness to all, to the small and great alike. What I say is the very same thing the prophets and Moses said was going to happen: 23 that the Messiah must suffer and be the first one to rise from death, to announce the light of salvation to the Jews and to the Gentiles."

²⁴ As Paul defended himself in this way, Festus shouted at him, "You are mad, Paul! Your great learning is driving you mad!" ²⁵ Paul answered: "I am not mad, your Excellency! The words I speak are true and sober. ²⁶ King Agrippa! I can speak to you with all boldness, because you know about these things. I am sure that you have taken notice of every one of them, for this thing has not happened hidden away in a corner. ²⁷ King Agrippa, do you believe the prophets? I know that you do!" ²⁸ Agrippa said to Paul, "In this short time you think you will make me a Christian?" ²⁹ "Whether a short time or a long time," Paul answered, "my prayer to God is that you and all the rest of you who are listening to me today might become what I am — except, of course; for these chains!"

³⁰ Then the king, the Governor, Bernice, and all the others got up, ³¹ and after leaving they said to each other, "This man has not done anything for which he should die or be put in prison." ³² And Agrippa said to Festus, "This man could have been released if he had not appealed to the Emperor."

Paul Sails for Rome

27 When it was decided that we should sail to Italy, they handed Paul and some other prisoners over to Julius, an officer in the Roman army regiment called "The Emperor's Regiment." ² We went aboard a ship from Adramyttium, which was

Paul Appeals to Agrippa to Believe

24 Ταῦτα δὲ αὐτοῦ ἀπολογουμένου ὁ Φῆστος μεγάλῃ τῇ φωνῇ φησιν, Μαίνῃ, Παῦλε· τὰ πολλά σε γράμματα εἰς μανίαν περιτρέπει. **25** ὁ δὲ Παῦλος, Οὐ μαίνομαι, φησίν, κράτιστε Φῆστε, ἀλλὰ ἀληθείας καὶ σωφροσύνης ῥήματα ἀποφθέγγομαι. **26** ἐπίσταται γὰρ περὶ τούτων ὁ βασιλεύς, πρὸς ὃν καὶ παρρησιαζόμενος λαλῶ· λανθάνειν γὰρ αὐτὸν τούτων οὐ πείθομαι οὐθέν, οὐ γάρ ἐστιν ἐν γωνίᾳ πεπραγμένον τοῦτο. **27** πιστεύεις, βασιλεῦ Ἀγρίππα, τοῖς προφήταις; οἶδα ὅτι πιστεύεις. **28** ὁ δὲ Ἀγρίππας πρὸς τὸν Παῦλον, Ἐν ὀλίγῳ με πείθεις Χριστιανὸν ποιῆσαι². **29** ὁ δὲ Παῦλος, Εὐξαίμην ἂν τῷ θεῷ καὶ ἐν ὀλίγῳ καὶ ἐν μεγάλῳ οὐ μόνον σὲ ἀλλὰ καὶ πάντας τοὺς ἀκούοντάς μου σήμερον γενέσθαι τοιούτους ὁποῖος καὶ ἐγώ εἰμι, παρεκτὸς τῶν δεσμῶν τούτων.

30 Ἀνέστη τε ὁ βασιλεὺς καὶ ὁ ἡγεμὼν ἥ τε Βερνίκη καὶ οἱ συγκαθήμενοι αὐτοῖς, **31** καὶ ἀναχωρήσαντες ἐλάλουν πρὸς ἀλλήλους λέγοντες ὅτι Οὐδὲν θανάτου ἢ δεσμῶν ἄξιον πράσσει ὁ ἄνθρωπος οὗτος. **32** Ἀγρίππας δὲ τῷ Φήστῳ ἔφη, Ἀπολελύσθαι ἐδύνατο ὁ ἄνθρωπος οὗτος εἰ μὴ ἐπεκέκλητο Καίσαρα.

Paul Sails for Rome

27 Ὡς δὲ ἐκρίθη τοῦ ἀποπλεῖν ἡμᾶς εἰς τὴν Ἰταλίαν, παρεδίδουν τόν τε Παῦλον καί τινας ἑτέρους δεσμώτας ἑκατοντάρχῃ ὀνόματι Ἰουλίῳ σπείρης Σεβαστῆς. **2** ἐπιβάντες δὲ πλοίῳ Ἀδραμυττηνῷ μέλλοντι πλεῖν εἰς τοὺς

---

² **28** {B} ποιῆσαι 𝔭⁷⁴ ℵ A B 048 33 81 181 syrʰᵐᵍ·ᵖᵃˡ copˢᵃ·ᵇᵒ (ethᵖᵖ) geo (Cassiodorus) ‖ γενέσθαι (see 26.29) E P Ψ 049 056 0142 88 104 326 330 436 451 614 629 630 945 1241 1505 1739 1877 2127 2412 2492 2495 Byz itᵃʳ·ᵉ·ᵍⁱᵍ·ᵖʰ·ˢ vg syrᵖ·ʰ arm Cyril-Jerusalem Chrysostom

26 Jn 18.20   **31** Οὐδὲν θανάτου...οὗτος Ac 23.29   **32** εἰ...Καίσαρα Ac 25.11
27 1 Ὡς...Ἰταλίαν Ac 25.12

κατὰ τὴν ᾿Ασίαν τόπους ἀνήχθημεν, ὄντος σὺν ἡμῖν ᾿Αριστάρχου Μακεδόνος Θεσσαλονικέως· 3 τῇ τε ἑτέρᾳ κατήχθημεν εἰς Σιδῶνα, φιλανθρώπως τε ὁ ᾿Ιούλιος τῷ Παύλῳ χρησάμενος ἐπέτρεψεν πρὸς τοὺς φίλους πορευθέντι ἐπιμελείας τυχεῖν. 4 κἀκεῖθεν ἀναχθέντες ὑπεπλεύσαμεν τὴν Κύπρον διὰ τὸ τοὺς ἀνέμους εἶναι ἐναντίους, 5 τό τε πέλαγος τὸ κατὰ τὴν Κιλικίαν καὶ Παμφυλίαν διαπλεύσαντες κατήλθομεν[1] εἰς Μύρα τῆς Λυκίας. 6 κἀκεῖ εὑρὼν ὁ ἑκατοντάρχης πλοῖον ᾿Αλεξανδρῖνον πλέον εἰς τὴν ᾿Ιταλίαν ἐνεβίβασεν ἡμᾶς εἰς αὐτό. 7 ἐν ἱκαναῖς δὲ ἡμέραις βραδυπλοοῦντες καὶ μόλις γενόμενοι κατὰ τὴν Κνίδον, μὴ προσεῶντος ἡμᾶς τοῦ ἀνέμου, ὑπεπλεύσαμεν τὴν Κρήτην κατὰ Σαλμώνην, 8 μόλις τε παραλεγόμενοι αὐτὴν ἤλθομεν εἰς τόπον τινὰ καλούμενον Καλοὺς Λιμένας, ᾧ ἐγγὺς πόλις ἦν Λασαία.

9 ᾿Ικανοῦ δὲ χρόνου διαγενομένου καὶ ὄντος ἤδη ἐπισφαλοῦς τοῦ πλοὸς διὰ τὸ καὶ τὴν νηστείαν ἤδη παρεληλυθέναι, παρῄνει ὁ Παῦλος 10 λέγων αὐτοῖς, ῎Ανδρες, θεωρῶ ὅτι μετὰ ὕβρεως καὶ πολλῆς ζημίας οὐ μόνον τοῦ φορτίου καὶ τοῦ πλοίου ἀλλὰ καὶ τῶν ψυχῶν ἡμῶν μέλλειν ἔσεσθαι τὸν πλοῦν. 11 ὁ δὲ ἑκατοντάρχης τῷ κυβερνήτῃ καὶ τῷ ναυκλήρῳ μᾶλλον ἐπείθετο ἢ τοῖς ὑπὸ Παύλου λεγομένοις. 12 ἀνευθέτου δὲ τοῦ λιμένος ὑπάρχοντος πρὸς παραχειμασίαν οἱ πλείονες ἔθεντο βουλὴν ἀναχθῆναι ἐκεῖθεν, εἴ πως δύναιντο καταντήσαντες εἰς Φοίνικα παραχειμάσαι, λιμένα τῆς Κρήτης βλέποντα κατὰ λίβα καὶ κατὰ χῶρον.

---

[1] 5 {B} κατήλθομεν p74 ℵ A B P Ψ 049 056 33 81 (88 κατηντήσαμεν) 181 326 330 436 629 630 945 1241 1505 1739 1877 2127 2492 2495 Byz Lect (l1356 κατήχθημεν) itgig,s syrp,h arm geo ‖ ἤλθομεν 104 (451 ἤλθαμεν) vg copsa,bo ‖ δι᾿ ἡμερῶν δεκάπεντε κατήλθομεν 614 2412 itar,hvid,ph? vgmss syrh with * ‖ κατήλθομεν δι᾿ ἡμερῶν δεκάπεντε 0142

---

2 ᾿Αριστάρχου...Θεσσαλονικέως Ac 19.29; 20.4 3 φιλανθρώπως...χρησάμενος Ac 28.2 ἐπέτρεψεν...πορευθέντι Ac 24.23 9–10 2 Cor 11.26 9 διὰ...παρεληλυθέναι Lv 16.29 10 Ac 27.22

ready to leave for the seaports of the province of Asia, and sailed away. Aristarchus, a Macedonian from Thessalonica, was with us. [3] The next day we arrived at Sidon. Julius was kind to Paul and allowed him to go and see his friends, to be given what he needed. [4] We went on from there, and because the winds were blowing against us we sailed on the sheltered side of the island of Cyprus. [5] We crossed over the sea off Cilicia and Pamphylia, and came to Myra, in Lycia. [6] There the officer found a ship from Alexandria that was going to sail for Italy, so he put us aboard.

[7] We sailed slowly for several days, and with great difficulty finally arrived off the town of Cnidus. The wind would not let us go any farther in that direction, so we sailed down the sheltered side of the island of Crete, passing by Cape Salmone. [8] We kept close to the coast, and with great difficulty came to a place called Safe Harbors, not far from the town of Lasea.

[9] We spent a long time there, until it became dangerous to continue the voyage, because by now the day of Atonement was already past. So Paul gave them this advice: [10] "Men, I see that our voyage from here on will be dangerous; there will be great damage to the cargo and to the ship, and loss of life as well." [11] But the army officer was convinced by what the captain and the owner of the ship said, and not by what Paul said. [12] The harbor was not a good one to spend the winter in; so most of the men were in favor of putting out to sea and trying to reach Phoenix, if possible. It is a harbor in Crete that faces southwest and northwest, and they could spend the winter there.

The Storm at Sea

[13] A soft wind from the south began to blow, and the men thought that they could carry out their plan; so they pulled up the anchor and sailed as close as possible along the coast of Crete. [14] But soon a very strong wind — the one called "Northeaster" — blew down from the island. [15] It hit the ship, and since it was impossible to keep the ship headed into the wind, we gave up trying and let it be carried along by the wind. [16] We got some shelter when we passed to the south of the little island of Cauda. There, with some difficulty, we managed to make the ship's boat secure. [17] They pulled it aboard, and then fastened some ropes tight around the ship. They were afraid that they might run into the sandbanks off the coast of Libya; so they lowered the sail and let the ship be carried by the wind. [18] The violent storm continued, so on the next day they began to throw the ship's cargo overboard, [19] and on the following day they threw the ship's equipment overboard with their own hands. [20] For many days we could not see the sun or the stars, and the wind kept on blowing very hard. We finally gave up all hope of being saved.

[21] After the men had gone a long time without food, Paul stood before them and said: "Men, you should have listened to me and not have sailed from Crete; then we would have avoided all this damage and loss. [22] But now I beg you, take courage! Not one of you will lose his life; only the ship will be lost. [23] For last night an angel of the God to whom I belong and whom I worship came to me

The Storm at Sea

13 Ὑποπνεύσαντος δὲ νότου δόξαντες τῆς προθέσεως κεκρατηκέναι, ἄραντες ἆσσον παρελέγοντο τὴν Κρήτην. 14 μετ' οὐ πολὺ δὲ ἔβαλεν κατ' αὐτῆς ἄνεμος τυφωνικὸς ὁ καλούμενος Εὐρακύλων[2]· 15 συναρπασθέντος δὲ τοῦ πλοίου καὶ μὴ δυναμένου ἀντοφθαλμεῖν τῷ ἀνέμῳ ἐπιδόντες ἐφερόμεθα. 16 νησίον δέ τι ὑποδραμόντες καλούμενον Καῦδα[3] ἰσχύσαμεν μόλις περικρατεῖς γενέσθαι τῆς σκάφης, 17 ἣν ἄραντες βοηθείαις ἐχρῶντο ὑποζωννύντες τὸ πλοῖον· φοβούμενοί τε μὴ εἰς τὴν Σύρτιν ἐκπέσωσιν, χαλάσαντες τὸ σκεῦος, οὕτως ἐφέροντο. 18 σφοδρῶς δὲ χειμαζομένων ἡμῶν τῇ ἑξῆς ἐκβολὴν ἐποιοῦντο, 19 καὶ τῇ τρίτῃ αὐτόχειρες τὴν σκευὴν τοῦ πλοίου ἔρριψαν. 20 μήτε δὲ ἡλίου μήτε ἄστρων ἐπιφαινόντων ἐπὶ πλείονας ἡμέρας, χειμῶνός τε οὐκ ὀλίγου ἐπικειμένου, λοιπὸν περιῃρεῖτο ἐλπὶς πᾶσα τοῦ σῴζεσθαι ἡμᾶς.

21 Πολλῆς τε ἀσιτίας ὑπαρχούσης τότε σταθεὶς ὁ Παῦλος ἐν μέσῳ αὐτῶν εἶπεν, Ἔδει μέν, ὦ ἄνδρες, πειθαρχήσαντάς μοι μὴ ἀνάγεσθαι ἀπὸ τῆς Κρήτης κερδῆσαί τε τὴν ὕβριν ταύτην καὶ τὴν ζημίαν. 22 καὶ τὰ νῦν παραινῶ ὑμᾶς εὐθυμεῖν, ἀποβολὴ γὰρ ψυχῆς οὐδεμία ἔσται ἐξ ὑμῶν πλὴν τοῦ πλοίου· 23 παρέστη γάρ μοι ταύτῃ τῇ νυκτὶ τοῦ θεοῦ οὗ εἰμι [ἐγώ], ᾧ καὶ

---

[2] 14 {B} Εὐρακύλων 𝔓74 ℵ A B* (it^{ar,gig,s} vg Euroaquilo) syr^{pal} cop^{sa,bo} (arm Εὐρακύκλων) (eth^{pp} Eurakis) (Cassiodorus Euroaquilo) ‖ Εὐροκλύδων P^{mg} Ψ 049 056 0142 (33 Εὐροκοίδον) (81 Εὐροκλύδω) 88 104 (181* Εὐροκλύδων, B³ 181^c Εὐρυκλύδων) 326 330 436 451 614 629 630 945 1241 1505 1739 1877 (2127 Εὐρωκλύδων) 2412 2492 2495 Byz Lect syr^{p,h,hmg,gr} (geo? Εὐρυκλύδων) Chrysostom ‖ omit ὁ καλούμενος Εὐροκλύδων P*

[3] 16 {B} Καῦδα 𝔓74 ℵ^c B it^s (it^{gig} Caudae) vg (syr^p) eth geo Jerome Bede ‖ Κλαῦδα ℵ* A^{vid} 33 81 181 614 945 1505 1739 2412 2495 it^{ar} syr^{h,hgr} cop^{sa,bo} arm ‖ Κλαῦδαν 88 104 l^{60} ‖ Κλαύδην P 049 (330 451 l^{1439} Κλαύδιον) 436 629 630 1241 1877 2127 2492 Byz Lect (l^{598} Κλαύδη) (l^{1356} Κλάδιν) Chrysostom ‖ Γαύδην Ψ Cassiodorus ‖ omit καλούμενον Καῦδα 326

---

22 ἀποβολὴ...πλοίου Ac 27.10, 31

λατρεύω, ἄγγελος 24 λέγων, Μὴ φοβοῦ, Παῦλε· Καίσαρί σε δεῖ παραστῆναι, καὶ ἰδοὺ κεχάρισταί σοι ὁ θεὸς πάντας τοὺς πλέοντας μετὰ σοῦ. 25 διὸ εὐθυμεῖτε, ἄνδρες· πιστεύω γὰρ τῷ θεῷ ὅτι οὕτως ἔσται καθ᾽ ὃν τρόπον λελάληταί μοι. 26 εἰς νῆσον δέ τινα δεῖ ἡμᾶς ἐκπεσεῖν.

27 Ὡς δὲ τεσσαρεσκαιδεκάτη νὺξ ἐγένετο διαφερο-μένων ἡμῶν ἐν τῷ Ἀδρίᾳ, κατὰ μέσον τῆς νυκτὸς ὑπενόουν οἱ ναῦται προσάγειν[4] τινὰ αὐτοῖς χώραν. 28 καὶ βολίσαντες εὗρον ὀργυιὰς εἴκοσι, βραχὺ δὲ διαστήσαντες καὶ πάλιν βολίσαντες εὗρον ὀργυιὰς δεκαπέντε· 29 φοβού-μενοί τε μή που κατὰ τραχεῖς τόπους ἐκπέσωμεν, ἐκ πρύμνης ῥίψαντες ἀγκύρας τέσσαρας ηὔχοντο ἡμέραν γενέσθαι. 30 τῶν δὲ ναυτῶν ζητούντων φυγεῖν ἐκ τοῦ πλοίου καὶ χαλασάντων τὴν σκάφην εἰς τὴν θάλασσαν προφάσει ὡς ἐκ πρῴρης ἀγκύρας μελλόντων ἐκτείνειν, 31 εἶπεν ὁ Παῦλος τῷ ἑκατοντάρχῃ καὶ τοῖς στρατιώταις, Ἐὰν μὴ οὗτοι μείνωσιν ἐν τῷ πλοίῳ, ὑμεῖς σωθῆναι οὐ δύνασθε. 32 τότε ἀπέκοψαν οἱ στρατιῶται τὰ σχοινία τῆς σκάφης καὶ εἴασαν αὐτὴν ἐκπεσεῖν.

33 Ἄχρι δὲ οὗ ἡμέρα ἤμελλεν γίνεσθαι παρεκάλει ὁ Παῦλος ἅπαντας μεταλαβεῖν τροφῆς λέγων, Τεσσαρεσκαι-δεκάτην σήμερον ἡμέραν προσδοκῶντες ἄσιτοι διατελεῖτε, μηθὲν προσλαβόμενοι· 34 διὸ παρακαλῶ ὑμᾶς μεταλαβεῖν τροφῆς, τοῦτο γὰρ πρὸς τῆς ὑμετέρας[5] σωτηρίας ὑπάρχει· οὐδενὸς γὰρ ὑμῶν θρὶξ ἀπὸ τῆς κεφαλῆς ἀπολεῖται.

[24] and said, 'Don't be afraid, Paul! You must stand before the Emperor; and God, in his goodness, has given you the lives of all those who are sailing with you.' [25] And so, men, take courage! For I trust in God that it will be just as I was told. [26] But we will be driven ashore on some island."

[27] It was the fourteenth night, and we were being driven by the storm on the Mediterranean. About midnight the sailors suspected that we were getting close to land. [28] So they dropped a line with a weight tied to it and found that the water was one hundred and twenty feet deep; a little later they did the same and found that it was ninety feet deep. [29] They were afraid that our ship would go on the rocks, so they lowered four anchors from the back of the ship and prayed for daylight. [30] The sailors tried to escape from the ship; they lowered the boat into the water and pretended that they were going to put out some anchors from the front of the ship. [31] But Paul said to the army officer and soldiers, "If these sailors don't stay on board, you cannot be saved." [32] So the soldiers cut the ropes that held the boat and let it go.

[33] Day was about to come, and Paul begged them all to eat some food: "You have been waiting for fourteen days now, and all this time you have not eaten a thing. [34] I beg you, then, eat some food; you need it in order to survive. Not even a hair of your heads will be lost."

---

[4] 27 {D} προσάγειν p⁷⁴ א^c A C P Ψ 049 056 0142 33 81 88 326 330 436 451 629 630 945 1241 1739 1877 2492 Byz Lect syr^{p?h?} cop^{sa?bo?} geo Chrysostom Theophylact^a ‖ προσαχεῖν B* it^{gig,s} ‖ προάγειν 104 2127 syr^{p?h?} Theo-phylact^b ‖ προαγαγεῖν א* ‖ προσαγαγεῖν 181 ‖ προσανέχειν B³ ‖ προσεγγίζειν 614 1505 2412 2495 syr^{p?h?} cop^{sa?bo?} ‖ apparere it^{ar} vg ‖ προσέρχεσθαι arm

[5] 34 {B} ὑμετέρας p⁷⁴ א B C Ψ 049 056 0142 33 81 88 104 330 436 451 629 630 945 1241 1505 1739 1877 2127 2495 Byz Lect it^{ar.gig} vg syr^p cop^{sa.bo} arm eth^{pp} geo Chrysostom Theophylact^a ‖ ἡμετέρας A P (181 ἡμέρας) 326 614 2412 2492 l^{1439} syr^h Theophylact^b

---

24 Μὴ...παραστῆναι Ac 23.11   26 Ac 28.1   31 Ἐὰν...δύνασθε Ac 27.22
34 οὐδενὸς...ἀπολεῖται 1 Sm 14.45; 2 Sm 14.11; Mt 10.30; Lk 12.7

[35] After saying this, Paul took some bread, gave thanks to God before them all, broke it, and began to eat. [36] They took courage, and every one of them also ate some food. [37] There was a total of two hundred and seventy-six[1] of us on board. [38] After everyone had eaten enough, they lightened the ship by throwing the wheat into the sea.

The Shipwreck

[39] When day came, the sailors did not recognize the coast, but they noticed a bay with a beach and decided that, if possible, they would run the ship aground there. [40] So they cut off the anchors and left them in the water, and at the same time they untied the ropes that held the steering oars. Then they raised the sail at the front of the ship so that the wind would blow the ship forward, and headed for shore. [41] But the ship ran into a sandbank and went aground; the front part of the ship got stuck and could not move, while the back part was being broken to pieces by the violence of the waves.

[42] The soldiers made a plan to kill all the prisoners, so that none of them would swim ashore and escape. [43] But the army

---

[1] **37** two hundred and seventy-six: *some mss. read* two hundred and seventy-five; *others read* seventy-six; *others read* about seventy-six

35 εἴπας δὲ ταῦτα καὶ λαβὼν ἄρτον εὐχαρίστησεν τῷ θεῷ ἐνώπιον πάντων καὶ κλάσας ἤρξατο ἐσθίειν. **36** εὔθυμοι δὲ γενόμενοι πάντες καὶ αὐτοὶ προσελάβοντο τροφῆς. ᵃ**37** ἤμεθα δὲ αἱ πᾶσαι ψυχαὶ ἐν τῷ πλοίῳ διακόσιαι ἑβδομήκοντα ἕξ⁶.ᵃ **38** κορεσθέντες δὲ τροφῆς ἐκούφιζον τὸ πλοῖον ἐκβαλλόμενοι τὸν σῖτον εἰς τὴν θάλασσαν.

The Shipwreck

39 Ὅτε δὲ ἡμέρα ἐγένετο, τὴν γῆν οὐκ ἐπεγίνωσκον, κόλπον δέ τινα κατενόουν ἔχοντα αἰγιαλὸν εἰς ὃν ἐβουλεύοντο εἰ δύναιντο ἐξῶσαι⁷ τὸ πλοῖον. **40** καὶ τὰς ἀγκύρας περιελόντες εἴων εἰς τὴν θάλασσαν, ἅμα ἀνέντες τὰς ζευκτηρίας τῶν πηδαλίων, καὶ ἐπάραντες τὸν ἀρτέμωνα τῇ πνεούσῃ κατεῖχον εἰς τὸν αἰγιαλόν. **41** περιπεσόντες δὲ εἰς τόπον διθάλασσον ἐπέκειλαν τὴν ναῦν, καὶ ἡ μὲν πρῷρα ἐρείσασα ἔμεινεν ἀσάλευτος, ἡ δὲ πρύμνα ἐλύετο ὑπὸ τῆς βίας [τῶν κυμάτων]⁸. **42** τῶν δὲ στρατιωτῶν βουλὴ ἐγένετο ἵνα τοὺς δεσμώτας ἀποκτείνωσιν, μή τις ἐκκολυμβήσας διαφύγῃ· **43** ὁ δὲ ἑκατον-

---

⁶ **37** {B} διακόσιαι ἑβδομήκοντα ἕξ ℵ C P Ψ 049 056 0142 33 81 88 104 181 326 330 436 451 614 629 630 945 1241 1505 1739 1877 2127 2412 2492 2495 *Byz Lect* itᵃʳ,ᵍⁱᵍ,ᵖʰ vg syrᵖ,ʰ copᵇᵒ (copᵇᵒᵐˢˢ ἕκατον for διακόσιαι) arm geo ∥ διακόσιαι ἑβδομήκοντα πέντε A copˢᵃᵐˢ? ∥ ὡς ἑβδομήκοντα ἕξ B copˢᵃ ∥ ὡς ἑβδομήκοντα Epiphanius ∥ διακόσιαι ἑβδομήκοντα 69 ∥ ἑβδομήκοντα ἕξ 522 *l*⁶⁸⁰

⁷ **39** {B} ἐξῶσαι ℵ A Bᶜ P Ψ (049 ἐξέωσαι) 056 0142 33 81 104 181 326 330 436 451 614 629 630 945 1241 1505 1739 1877 2127 2412 2492 2495 *Byz Lect* itᵃʳ,ᵍⁱᵍ vg syrᵖ,ʰ geo ∥ ἐκσῶσαι B* C 88 copˢᵃ,ᵇᵒ arm

⁸ **41** {C} ὑπὸ τῆς βίας τῶν κυμάτων 𝔭⁷⁴ C P 049 056 0142 (ℵᶜ 104 ἀπό) 33 81 88 181 326 330 436 451 614 (629 τῶν ἀνέμων) 630 945 1241 1505 1739 1877 2127 2412 2492 2495 *Byz Lect* syrᵖ,ʰ cop⁽ˢᵃ⁾,ᵇᵒ ethᵖᵖ Chrysostom ∥ *a vi maris* itᵃʳ,ᵍⁱᵍ vg ∥ ὑπὸ τῆς βίας ℵ* A B arm geo ∥ ὑπὸ τῶν κυμάτων Ψ (*l*¹⁴⁴¹ τῶν κυμάτων *with obeli and omit* ὑπό)

ᵃ ᵃ **37** *a a* no parens: TR WH Bov Nes BF² AV RV ASV NEB TT Zür Luth Jer Seg ∥ *a* parens: RSV

35 λαβών...κλάσας Mt 15.36; Mk 8.6; Lk 22.19; 1 Cor 11.23–24   **41** Ac 27.22   **43–44** Ac 27.22, 24

τάρχης βουλόμενος διασῶσαι τὸν Παῦλον ἐκώλυσεν αὐτοὺς τοῦ βουλήματος, ἐκέλευσέν τε τοὺς δυναμένους κολυμβᾶν ἀπορίψαντας πρώτους ἐπὶ τὴν γῆν ἐξιέναι, 44 καὶ τοὺς λοιποὺς οὓς μὲν ἐπὶ σανίσιν οὓς δὲ ἐπί τινων τῶν ἀπὸ τοῦ πλοίου· καὶ οὕτως ἐγένετο πάντας διασωθῆναι ἐπὶ τὴν γῆν.

Paul on the Island of Malta

28 Καὶ διασωθέντες τότε ἐπέγνωμεν ὅτι Μελίτη[1] ἡ νῆσος καλεῖται. 2 οἵ τε βάρβαροι παρεῖχον οὐ τὴν τυχοῦσαν φιλανθρωπίαν ἡμῖν, ἅψαντες γὰρ πυρὰν προσελάβοντο πάντας ἡμᾶς διὰ τὸν ὑετὸν τὸν ἐφεστῶτα καὶ διὰ τὸ ψῦχος. 3 συστρέψαντος δὲ τοῦ Παύλου φρυγάνων τι πλῆθος καὶ ἐπιθέντος ἐπὶ τὴν πυράν, ἔχιδνα ἀπὸ τῆς θέρμης ἐξελθοῦσα καθῆψεν τῆς χειρὸς αὐτοῦ. 4 ὡς δὲ εἶδον οἱ βάρβαροι κρεμάμενον τὸ θηρίον ἐκ τῆς χειρὸς αὐτοῦ, πρὸς ἀλλήλους ἔλεγον, Πάντως φονεύς ἐστιν ὁ ἄνθρωπος οὗτος ὃν διασωθέντα ἐκ τῆς θαλάσσης ἡ δίκη ζῆν οὐκ εἴασεν. 5 ὁ μὲν οὖν ἀποτινάξας τὸ θηρίον εἰς τὸ πῦρ ἔπαθεν οὐδὲν κακόν· 6 οἱ δὲ προσεδόκων αὐτὸν μέλλειν πίμπρασθαι ἢ καταπίπτειν ἄφνω νεκρόν. ἐπὶ πολὺ δὲ αὐτῶν προσδοκώντων καὶ θεωρούντων μηδὲν ἄτοπον εἰς αὐτὸν γινόμενον, μεταβαλόμενοι ἔλεγον αὐτὸν εἶναι θεόν. 7 Ἐν δὲ τοῖς περὶ τὸν τόπον ἐκεῖνον ὑπῆρχεν χωρία τῷ πρώτῳ τῆς νήσου ὀνόματι Ποπλίῳ, ὃς ἀναδεξάμενος ἡμᾶς τρεῖς ἡμέρας φιλοφρόνως ἐξένισεν. 8 ἐγένετο δὲ τὸν πατέρα τοῦ Ποπλίου πυρετοῖς καὶ δυσεντερίῳ συνεχόμενον κατακεῖσθαι, πρὸς ὃν ὁ Παῦλος εἰσελθὼν καὶ

---

¹ 1 {B} Μελίτη 𝔭⁷⁴ ℵ A B³ C P Ψ 049 056 0142 33 81 88 104 181 326 330 436 451 614 629 630 945 1241 1505 1739 1877 2127 2412 2492 2495 *Byz Lect* (vg^ol *Melita*) syr^p cop^sa geo Chrysostom ∥ Μελιτήνη B* (*l*⁶⁰˒⁵⁹⁹ Μελιτίνη, *l*⁶⁸⁰ Μελητήνη) (it^ar *Militinae*, it^gig *Mililenae*, vg^ww *Militene*) syr^h.hgr cop^bo arm (Jerome) ∥ Μυτιλήνη it^c.p² (it^ph *Mitilene*) vg^mss

---

2 διὰ τὸ ψῦχος 2 Cor 11.27   5 Mk 16.18   6 ἔλεγον...θεόν Ac 14.11

---

officer wanted to save Paul, so he stopped them from doing this. Instead, he ordered all the men who could swim to jump overboard first and swim ashore; [44] the rest were to follow, holding on to the planks or to some broken pieces of the ship. And this was how we all got safely ashore.

In Malta

28 When we were safely ashore, we learned that the island was called Malta. [2] The natives there were very friendly to us. It had started raining and was cold, so they built a fire and made us all welcome. [3] Paul gathered up a bundle of sticks and was putting them on the fire when a snake came out, on account of the heat, and fastened itself to his hand. [4] The natives saw the snake hanging on Paul's hand and said to one another, "This man must be a murderer, but Fate will not let him live, even though he escaped from the sea." [5] But Paul shook the snake off into the fire without being harmed at all. [6] They were waiting for him to swell up or suddenly fall down dead. But after waiting for a long time and not seeing anything unusual happening to him, they changed their minds and said, "He is a god!"

[7] Not far from that place were some fields that belonged to Publius, the chief of the island. He welcomed us kindly and for three days we were his guests. [8] Publius' father was in bed sick with fever and dysentery. Paul went into his

room, prayed, placed his hands on him,
and healed him. [9] When this happened,
all the other sick people on the island
came and were healed. [10] They gave us
many gifts, and when we sailed they
put on board what we needed for the
voyage.

From Malta to Rome

[11] After three months we sailed away
on a ship from Alexandria, called "The
Twin Gods," which had spent the winter
in the island. [12] We arrived in the city
of Syracuse and stayed there for three
days. [13] From there we sailed on and
arrived in the city of Rhegium. The next
day a wind began to blow from the
south, and in two days we came to the
town of Puteoli. [14] We found some believers there who asked us to stay with
them a week. And so we came to Rome.
[15] The brothers in Rome heard about us
and came as far as Market of Appius
and Three Inns to meet us. When Paul
saw them, he thanked God and took
courage.

In Rome

[16] When we arrived in Rome, Paul was
allowed to live by himself with a soldier
guarding him.

προσευξάμενος ἐπιθεὶς τὰς χεῖρας αὐτῷ ἰάσατο αὐτόν.
[9] τούτου δὲ γενομένου καὶ οἱ λοιποὶ οἱ ἐν τῇ νήσῳ ἔχοντες
ἀσθενείας προσήρχοντο καὶ ἐθεραπεύοντο, [10] οἳ καὶ πολλαῖς τιμαῖς ἐτίμησαν ἡμᾶς καὶ ἀναγομένοις ἐπέθεντο
τὰ πρὸς τὰς χρείας.

Paul Arrives at Rome

[11] Μετὰ δὲ τρεῖς μῆνας ἀνήχθημεν ἐν πλοίῳ παρακε-
χειμακότι ἐν τῇ νήσῳ Ἀλεξανδρίνῳ, παρασήμῳ Διοσκού-
ροις. [12] καὶ καταχθέντες εἰς Συρακούσας ἐπεμείναμεν
ἡμέρας τρεῖς, [13] ὅθεν περιελόντες[2] κατηντήσαμεν εἰς
Ῥήγιον. καὶ μετὰ μίαν ἡμέραν ἐπιγενομένου νότου
δευτεραῖοι ἤλθομεν εἰς Ποτιόλους, [14] οὗ εὑρόντες ἀδελφοὺς παρεκλήθημεν παρ' αὐτοῖς ἐπιμεῖναι[3] ἡμέρας ἑπτά·
καὶ οὕτως εἰς τὴν Ῥώμην ἤλθαμεν. [15] κἀκεῖθεν οἱ
ἀδελφοὶ ἀκούσαντες τὰ περὶ ἡμῶν ἦλθαν εἰς ἀπάντησιν
ἡμῖν ἄχρι Ἀππίου Φόρου καὶ Τριῶν Ταβερνῶν, οὓς
ἰδὼν ὁ Παῦλος εὐχαριστήσας τῷ θεῷ ἔλαβε θάρσος.

[16] Ὅτε δὲ εἰσήλθομεν εἰς Ῥώμην, ἐπετράπη τῷ
Παύλῳ[4] μένειν καθ' ἑαυτὸν σὺν τῷ φυλάσσοντι αὐτὸν
στρατιώτῃ.

---

[2] **13** {D} περιελόντες (see 27.40) ℵ* B Ψ cop[sa,(bo)] ‖ περιελθόντες 𝔭[74]
ℵ[c] A P 048 056 066 0142 81 88 104 181 326 330 436 451 614 629 630 945 1241
1505 1739 1877 2127 2412 2492 2495 Byz Lect (l[680] παρελθόντες) syr[p,h] arm
geo ‖ προσελθόντες 049 ‖ προελθόντες l[1441] ‖ circumlegentes vg ‖ circum-
navigantes it[ar] ‖ tulimus it[gig]

[3] **14** {C} ἐπιμεῖναι 𝔭[74] ℵ A B P 066 81 88 104 181 330 436 451 945 1241
1739 1877 2127 2492 Byz Lect it[ar] vg cop[sa,bo] arm geo ‖ ἐπιμείναντες Ψ 049
326 614 630 1505 2412 2495 l[598,1441] it[gig] syr[h] Theophylact ‖ ἐπιμεῖναι παρ'
αὐτοῖς 048 ‖ μείναντες ἐπ' αὐτοῖς 629 ‖ ἐπί 056 0142 syr[p]

[4] **16** {B} ἐπετράπη τῷ Παύλῳ ℵ A B Ψ 048 81 181 629* (629[c] add δέ)
1505 1739 2495 l[60] it[ar] vg syr[p,h] cop[bo] arm geo Chrysostom ‖ ὁ ἑκατόνταρχος
παρέδωκε τοὺς δεσμίους τῷ στρατοπεδάρχῳ τῷ δὲ Παύλῳ ἐπετράπη
P 049 326 (330 451 στρατοπεδάρχῃ Παύλῳ ἐπετράπη) 1241 (056 0142 88
104 436 614 630 945 1877 2412 2495 Byz Lect στρατοπεδάρχῃ) (l[599] ἑκατοντάρχης...δεσμώτας...ἐτράπει) l[1443] it[gig] (syr[h with *]) cop[sa] (eth) Theophylact[a,(b)]

16 ἐπετράπη...στρατιώτῃ Ac 24.23; 28.30

Paul Preaches in Rome

17 Ἐγένετο δὲ μετὰ ἡμέρας τρεῖς συγκαλέσασθαι αὐτὸν τοὺς ὄντας τῶν Ἰουδαίων πρώτους· συνελθόντων δὲ αὐτῶν ἔλεγεν πρὸς αὐτούς, Ἐγώ, ἄνδρες ἀδελφοί, οὐδὲν ἐναντίον ποιήσας τῷ λαῷ ἢ τοῖς ἔθεσι τοῖς πατρῴοις δέσμιος ἐξ Ἱεροσολύμων παρεδόθην εἰς τὰς χεῖρας τῶν Ῥωμαίων, **18** οἵτινες ἀνακρίναντές με ἐβούλοντο ἀπολῦσαι διὰ τὸ μηδεμίαν αἰτίαν θανάτου ὑπάρχειν ἐν ἐμοί· **19** ἀντιλεγόντων δὲ τῶν Ἰουδαίων ἠναγκάσθην ἐπικαλέσασθαι Καίσαρα, οὐχ ὡς τοῦ ἔθνους μου ἔχων τι κατηγορεῖν. **20** διὰ ταύτην οὖν τὴν αἰτίαν παρεκάλεσα ὑμᾶς ἰδεῖν καὶ προσλαλῆσαι, ἕνεκεν γὰρ τῆς ἐλπίδος τοῦ Ἰσραὴλ τὴν ἅλυσιν ταύτην περίκειμαι. **21** οἱ δὲ πρὸς αὐτὸν εἶπαν, Ἡμεῖς οὔτε γράμματα περὶ σοῦ ἐδεξάμεθα ἀπὸ τῆς Ἰουδαίας, οὔτε παραγενόμενός τις τῶν ἀδελφῶν ἀπήγγειλεν ἢ ἐλάλησέν τι περὶ σοῦ πονηρόν. **22** ἀξιοῦμεν δὲ παρὰ σοῦ ἀκοῦσαι ἃ φρονεῖς, περὶ μὲν γὰρ τῆς αἱρέσεως ταύτης γνωστὸν ἡμῖν ἐστιν ὅτι πανταχοῦ ἀντιλέγεται.

23 Ταξάμενοι δὲ αὐτῷ ἡμέραν ἦλθον πρὸς αὐτὸν εἰς τὴν ξενίαν πλείονες, οἷς ἐξετίθετο διαμαρτυρόμενος τὴν βασιλείαν τοῦ θεοῦ πείθων τε αὐτοὺς περὶ τοῦ Ἰησοῦ ἀπό τε τοῦ νόμου Μωϋσέως καὶ τῶν προφητῶν ἀπὸ πρωῒ ἕως ἑσπέρας. **24** καὶ οἱ μὲν ἐπείθοντο τοῖς λεγομένοις, οἱ δὲ ἠπίστουν· **25** ἀσύμφωνοι δὲ ὄντες πρὸς ἀλλήλους ἀπελύοντο, εἰπόντος τοῦ Παύλου ῥῆμα ἓν ὅτι Καλῶς τὸ πνεῦμα τὸ ἅγιον ἐλάλησεν διὰ Ἡσαΐου τοῦ προφήτου πρὸς τοὺς πατέρας ὑμῶν[5] **26** λέγων,

---

5 25 {B} ὑμῶν 𝔭[74] ℵ A B Ψ 049 056 0142 33 81 104 181 326 945 1739 2492 *l*[597,598,680,1443] it[p.s] syr[p] cop[sa,bo] geo Ambrosiaster Athanasius Basil Cyril-Jerusalem Didymus Cyril Ammonius-Alexandria Vigilius ‖ ἡμῶν P 88 330 436 451 614 629 630 1241 1505 1877 2127 2412 2495 *Byz Lect* it[gig] vg cop[boms] arm eth[pp] Ambrose Chrysostom ‖ *omit* syr[h]

---

17 Ἐγώ...πατρῴοις Ac 24.12–13; 25.8   **18** Ac 23.29; 25.25; 26.31–32   **19** ἠναγκάσθην ...Καίσαρα Ac 25.11   **20** Lk 2.34   ἕνεκεν...Ἰσραήλ Ac 24.15; 26.6–7   **22** τῆς αἱρέσεως ταύτης Ac 24.14

[17] After three days Paul called the local Jewish leaders to a meeting. When they gathered, he said to them: "My brothers! Even though I did nothing against our people or the customs that we received from our ancestors, I was made a prisoner in Jerusalem and handed over to the Romans. [18] They questioned me and wanted to release me, because they found that I had done nothing for which I deserved to die. [19] But when the Jews opposed this, I was forced to appeal to the Emperor, even though I had no accusation to make against my own people. [20] That is why I asked to see you and talk with you; because I have this chain on me for the sake of him for whom the people of Israel hope." [21] They said to him: "We have not received any letters from Judea about you, nor have any of our brothers come from there with any news, or to say anything bad about you. [22] But we would like to hear your ideas, for we do know that everywhere people speak against this party that you belong to."

[23] So they set a date with Paul, and a larger number of them came that day to where Paul was staying. From morning till night he explained and gave them his message about the Kingdom of God. He tried to convince them about Jesus by quoting from the Law of Moses and the writings of the prophets. [24] Some of them were convinced by his words, but others would not believe. [25] So they left, disagreeing among themselves, after Paul had said this one thing: "How well the Holy Spirit spoke through the prophet Isaiah to your ancestors! [26] For he said:

'Go and say to this people:
    You will listen and listen, but not
        understand;
    You will look and look, but not see.
27 Because this people's mind is dull;
    They have stopped up their ears,
    And they have closed their eyes.
    Otherwise, their eyes might see,
    Their ears might hear,
    Their minds might understand,
    And they might turn to me, says God,
    And I would heal them.' "
28 And Paul added: "You are to know,
then, that God's message of salvation has
been sent to the Gentiles. They will
listen!" [29 After Paul said this, the
Jews left, arguing violently among themselves.]
    30 For two years Paul lived there in a
place he rented for himself, and welcomed
all who came to see him. 31 He preached
about the Kingdom of God and taught
about the Lord Jesus Christ, speaking
with all boldness and freedom.

Πορεύθητι πρὸς τὸν λαὸν τοῦτον καὶ εἰπόν,
    'Ακοῇ ἀκούσετε καὶ οὐ μὴ συνῆτε,
        καὶ βλέποντες βλέψετε καὶ οὐ μὴ ἴδητε·
27 ἐπαχύνθη γὰρ ἡ καρδία τοῦ λαοῦ τούτου,
    καὶ τοῖς ὠσὶν βαρέως ἤκουσαν,
        καὶ τοὺς ὀφθαλμοὺς αὐτῶν ἐκάμμυσαν·
    μήποτε ἴδωσιν τοῖς ὀφθαλμοῖς
    καὶ τοῖς ὠσὶν ἀκούσωσιν
καὶ τῇ καρδίᾳ συνῶσιν καὶ ἐπιστρέψωσιν,
    καὶ ἰάσομαι αὐτούς.
28 γνωστὸν οὖν ἔστω ὑμῖν ὅτι τοῖς ἔθνεσιν ἀπεστάλη
τοῦτο τὸ σωτήριον τοῦ θεοῦ· αὐτοὶ καὶ ἀκούσονται.[6]

    30 'Ενέμεινεν δὲ διετίαν ὅλην ἐν ἰδίῳ μισθώματι, καὶ
ἀπεδέχετο πάντας τοὺς εἰσπορευομένους πρὸς αὐτόν,
31 κηρύσσων τὴν βασιλείαν τοῦ θεοῦ καὶ διδάσκων τὰ
περὶ τοῦ κυρίου 'Ιησοῦ Χριστοῦ μετὰ πάσης παρρησίας
ἀκωλύτως.

---

[6] 28 {B} omit verse 29 p[74vid] ℵ A B E Ψ 048 33 81 181 629[lat] 1739 l[6,60]
it[e,s] vg[ww] syr[p,h] cop[sa,bo] arm eth[pp] geo ∥ add verse 29 καὶ ταῦτα αὐτοῦ
εἰπόντος ἀπῆλθον οἱ Ἰουδαῖοι, πολλὴν ἔχοντες ἐν ἑαυτοῖς συζήτησιν.
P 049 056 0142 88 326 (330 ἔχειν) 436 451 614 629[gr] 630 945 1241 (1505 2495
εἰπόντος αὐτοῦ) 1877 2127 2412 2492 (104 l[599] ζήτησιν) Byz Lect (l[597] omit
ἐν ἑαυτοῖς) it[ar,c,gig,p,ph] vg[cl] syr[h with] * (Chrysostom πάλιν for πολλήν)
(Euthalius ζήτησιν) Theophylact

26-27 Πορεύθητι...αὐτούς Is 6.9-10   28 τοῖς...θεοῦ Ps 67.2; 98.3; Is 40.5 LXX; Lk 3.6;
Ac 13.46; 18.6   30 Ac 28.16

PAUL'S LETTER TO THE ROMANS

Salutation

1 Παῦλος δοῦλος Χριστοῦ Ἰησοῦ, κλητὸς ἀπόστολος, ἀφωρισμένος εἰς εὐαγγέλιον θεοῦ, **2** ὃ προεπηγγείλατο διὰ τῶν προφητῶν αὐτοῦ ἐν γραφαῖς ἁγίαις,[a] **3** περὶ τοῦ υἱοῦ αὐτοῦ[a] τοῦ γενομένου ἐκ σπέρματος Δαυὶδ κατὰ σάρκα, **4** τοῦ ὁρισθέντος υἱοῦ θεοῦ ἐν δυνάμει κατὰ πνεῦμα ἁγιωσύνης ἐξ ἀναστάσεως νεκρῶν, Ἰησοῦ Χριστοῦ τοῦ κυρίου ἡμῶν, **5** δι᾽ οὗ ἐλάβομεν χάριν καὶ ἀποστολὴν εἰς ὑπακοὴν πίστεως ἐν πᾶσιν τοῖς ἔθνεσιν ὑπὲρ τοῦ ὀνόματος αὐτοῦ, **6** ἐν οἷς ἐστε καὶ ὑμεῖς κλητοὶ Ἰησοῦ Χριστοῦ, **7** πᾶσιν τοῖς οὖσιν ἐν Ῥώμῃ[1] ἀγαπητοῖς θεοῦ[2], κλητοῖς ἁγίοις· χάρις ὑμῖν καὶ εἰρήνη ἀπὸ θεοῦ πατρὸς ἡμῶν καὶ κυρίου Ἰησοῦ Χριστοῦ.

Paul's Desire to Visit Rome

8 Πρῶτον μὲν εὐχαριστῶ τῷ θεῷ μου διὰ Ἰησοῦ Χριστοῦ περὶ πάντων ὑμῶν, ὅτι ἡ πίστις ὑμῶν καταγγέλλεται ἐν ὅλῳ τῷ κόσμῳ. **9** μάρτυς γάρ μού ἐστιν ὁ

---

1 From Paul, a servant of Christ Jesus, and an apostle chosen and called by God to preach his Good News.

[2] The Good News was promised long ago by God through his prophets, and written in the Holy Scriptures. [3] It is about his Son, our Lord Jesus Christ: as to his humanity, he was born a descendant of David; [4] as to his divine holiness, he was shown with great power to be the Son of God, by being raised from death. [5] Through him God gave me the privilege of being an apostle, for the sake of Christ, in order to lead people of all nations to believe and obey. [6] This also includes you who are in Rome, whom God has called to belong to Jesus Christ.

[7] And so I write to all of you in Rome whom God loves and has called to be his own people:

May God our Father and the Lord Jesus Christ give you grace and peace.

Prayer of Thanksgiving

[8] First, I thank my God, through Jesus Christ, for all of you; because the whole world is hearing of your faith. [9] God can prove that what I say is true — the

---

[1] **7** {B} ἐν Ῥώμῃ 𝔭[10,26vid] ℵ A B C D[abs1] K P Ψ 33 81 88 104 181 330 436 451 614 629 630 1241 1739[txt] 1877 1881 1962 1984 1985 2127 2492 2495 *Byz Lect* it[ar,d,dem,e,x,z] vg syr[p,h,pal] cop[sa,bo] arm Origen[gr,lat] Ambrosiaster Augustine // *omit* G 1739[mg] 1908[mg] it[g] Origen

[2] **7** {B} ἀγαπητοῖς θεοῦ 𝔭[10,26] ℵ A B C K P Ψ 81 88 104 181 330 436 451 614 629 630 1241 1739 1877 1881 1962 1984 1985 2127 2492 2495 *Byz Lect* it[dem,x,z] vg syr[p,h,pal] cop[sa,bo] arm Origen[gr,lat] Ambrosiaster[mss] Augustine // ἐν ἀγάπῃ θεοῦ G it[ar,d*,g] Ambrosiaster Pelagius // *omit* D[abs1] it[e]

[a a] **2-3** *a* minor, *a* none: (NEB) (Seg) // *a* none, *a* minor: WH Bov TT // *a* minor, *a* minor: TR (AV) RV ASV RSV Zür Luth Jer // *a* none, *a* none: Nes BF²

---

1 ἀφωρισμένος...θεοῦ Ac 9.15; 13.2; Ga 1.15　**2** Ro 16.25-26; Tt 1.2　**3** τοῦ γενομένου ...Δαυίδ Mt 22.42; 2 Tm 2.8　κατὰ σάρκα Ro 9.5　**4** τοῦ ὁρισθέντος...νεκρῶν Ac 13.33　**5** Ac 26.16-18; Ro 15.18; Ga 2.7, 9　**7** κλητοῖς ἁγίοις 1 Cor 1.2; 2 Cor 1.1　χάρις...Χριστοῦ Nu 6.25-26; 1 Cor 1.3; 2 Cor 1.2　**8** ἡ πίστις...κόσμῳ 1 Th 1.8　**9** μάρτυς...θεός Php 1.8; 1 Th 2.5. 10

God whom I serve with all my heart by preaching the Good News about his Son. God knows that I always remember you ¹⁰ every time I pray. I ask that God, in his good will, may at last make it possible for me to visit you now. ¹¹ For I want very much to see you in order to share a spiritual blessing with you, to make you strong. ¹² What I mean is that both you and I will be helped at the same time: you by my faith and I by your faith.

¹³ You must remember this, my brothers: many times I have planned to visit you, but something has always kept me from doing so. I have wanted to win converts among you, too, as I have among other Gentiles. ¹⁴ For I have an obligation to all peoples, to the civilized and to the savage, to the educated and to the ignorant. ¹⁵ Therefore, I am eager to preach the Good News to you also who live in Rome.

The Power of the Gospel

¹⁶ For I have complete confidence in the gospel: it is God's power to save all who believe, first the Jews and also the Gentiles. ¹⁷ For the gospel reveals how God puts men right with himself: it is through faith alone, from beginning to end. As the scripture says, "He who is put right with God through faith shall live."¹

¹ **17** put right with God through faith shall live: *or* put right with God shall live through faith

θεός, ᾧ λατρεύω ἐν τῷ πνεύματί μου ἐν τῷ εὐαγγελίῳ τοῦ υἱοῦ αὐτοῦ, ὡς ἀδιαλείπτως μνείαν ὑμῶν ποιοῦμαι[b] **10** πάντοτε ἐπὶ τῶν προσευχῶν μου,[b] δεόμενος[b] εἴ πως ἤδη ποτὲ εὐοδωθήσομαι ἐν τῷ θελήματι τοῦ θεοῦ ἐλθεῖν πρὸς ὑμᾶς. **11** ἐπιποθῶ γὰρ ἰδεῖν ὑμᾶς, ἵνα τι μεταδῶ χάρισμα ὑμῖν πνευματικὸν εἰς τὸ στηριχθῆναι ὑμᾶς, **12** τοῦτο δέ ἐστιν συμπαρακληθῆναι ἐν ὑμῖν διὰ τῆς ἐν ἀλλήλοις πίστεως ὑμῶν τε καὶ ἐμοῦ. **13** οὐ θέλω[3] δὲ ὑμᾶς ἀγνοεῖν, ἀδελφοί, ὅτι πολλάκις προεθέμην ἐλθεῖν πρὸς ὑμᾶς, καὶ ἐκωλύθην ἄχρι τοῦ δεῦρο, ἵνα τινὰ καρπὸν σχῶ καὶ ἐν ὑμῖν καθὼς καὶ ἐν τοῖς λοιποῖς ἔθνεσιν. **14** Ἕλλησίν τε καὶ βαρβάροις, σοφοῖς τε καὶ ἀνοήτοις ὀφειλέτης εἰμί· **15** οὕτως τὸ κατ' ἐμὲ πρόθυμον καὶ ὑμῖν τοῖς ἐν Ῥώμῃ[4] εὐαγγελίσασθαι.

The Power of the Gospel

16 Οὐ γὰρ ἐπαισχύνομαι τὸ εὐαγγέλιον, δύναμις γὰρ θεοῦ ἐστιν εἰς σωτηρίαν παντὶ τῷ πιστεύοντι, Ἰουδαίῳ τε πρῶτον καὶ Ἕλληνι· **17** δικαιοσύνη γὰρ θεοῦ ἐν αὐτῷ ἀποκαλύπτεται ἐκ πίστεως εἰς πίστιν, καθὼς γέγραπται, Ὁ δὲ δίκαιος ἐκ πίστεως ζήσεται.

---

³ **13** {A} οὐ θέλω 𝔓²⁶ᵛⁱᵈ ℵ A B C Dᶜ K P Ψ 88 104 181 330 436 451 614 629 630 1241 1739 1877 1881 1962 1984 1985 2127 2492 2495 *Byz Lect* itᵃʳ,ᵈᵉᵐ,ˣ,ᶻ vg syr⁽ᵖ⁾,ʰ cop⁽ˢᵃ⁾,ᵇᵒ arm Origenˡᵃᵗ Chrysostom Theodoret John-Damascus ∥ οὐκ οἴομαι D* G itᵈ,ᵉ,ᵍ Ambrosiaster Pelagius ∥ οὐκ οἴομαι Dᵈ Dᵃᵇˢˡ ∥ οὐ θέλομεν 81

⁴ **15** {B} τοῖς ἐν Ῥώμῃ 𝔓²⁶ᵛⁱᵈ ℵ A B C D K P Ψ 33 81 88 104 181 330 436 451 614 629 630 1241 1739 1877 1881 1962 1984 1985 2127 2492 2495 *Byz Lect* itᵃʳ,ᵈ,ᵈᵉᵐ,ᵉ,ˣ,ᶻ vg syrᵖ,ʰ copˢᵃ,ᵇᵒ arm ∥ *omit* G itᵍ Origenˡᵃᵗ

ᵇ ᵇ ᵇ **9–10** *b* none, *b* minor, *b* none: WH Nes BF² AVᵉᵈ (AVᵉᵈ) RSV NEB TT Seg ∥ *b* minor; *b* none, *b* minor: TR (Bov) RV ASV Zür (Luth) (Jer)

---

9 ἀδιαλείπτως...ποιοῦμαι Eph 1.16   **10** δεόμενος...ὑμᾶς Ac 19.21; Ro 15.23, 32   **13** τινὰ καρπὸν σχῶ Jn 15.16   **16** Οὐ...εὐαγγέλιον Ps 119.46; Mk 8.38   δύναμις...πιστεύοντι 1 Cor 1.18, 24   Ἰουδαίῳ...Ἕλληνι Ac 13.46   **17** δικαιοσύνη...πίστιν Ro 3.21-22   Ὁ δὲ...ζήσεται Hab 2.4 (Ga 3.11; He 10.38)

The Guilt of Mankind

18 Ἀποκαλύπτεται γὰρ ὀργὴ θεοῦ ἀπ᾽ οὐρανοῦ ἐπὶ πᾶσαν ἀσέβειαν καὶ ἀδικίαν ἀνθρώπων τῶν τὴν ἀλήθειαν ἐν ἀδικίᾳ κατεχόντων, **19** διότι τὸ γνωστὸν τοῦ θεοῦ φανερόν ἐστιν ἐν αὐτοῖς· ὁ θεὸς γὰρ αὐτοῖς ἐφανέρωσεν. **20** τὰ γὰρ ἀόρατα αὐτοῦ ἀπὸ κτίσεως κόσμου τοῖς ποιήμασιν νοούμενα καθορᾶται, ἥ τε ἀΐδιος αὐτοῦ δύναμις καὶ θειότης, εἰς τὸ εἶναι αὐτοὺς ἀναπολογήτους· **21** διότι γνόντες τὸν θεὸν οὐχ ὡς θεὸν ἐδόξασαν ἢ ηὐχαρίστησαν, ἀλλ᾽ ἐματαιώθησαν ἐν τοῖς διαλογισμοῖς αὐτῶν καὶ ἐσκοτίσθη ἡ ἀσύνετος αὐτῶν καρδία. [c] **22** φάσκοντες εἶναι σοφοὶ ἐμωράνθησαν, **23** καὶ ἤλλαξαν τὴν δόξαν τοῦ ἀφθάρτου θεοῦ ἐν ὁμοιώματι εἰκόνος φθαρτοῦ ἀνθρώπου καὶ πετεινῶν καὶ τετραπόδων καὶ ἑρπετῶν. [d]

24 Διὸ παρέδωκεν αὐτοὺς ὁ θεὸς ἐν ταῖς ἐπιθυμίαις τῶν καρδιῶν αὐτῶν εἰς ἀκαθαρσίαν τοῦ ἀτιμάζεσθαι τὰ σώματα αὐτῶν ἐν αὐτοῖς, [d] **25** οἵτινες μετήλλαξαν τὴν ἀλήθειαν τοῦ θεοῦ ἐν τῷ ψεύδει, καὶ ἐσεβάσθησαν καὶ ἐλάτρευσαν τῇ κτίσει παρὰ τὸν κτίσαντα, ὅς ἐστιν εὐλογητὸς εἰς τοὺς αἰῶνας· ἀμήν. **26** διὰ τοῦτο παρέδωκεν αὐτοὺς ὁ θεὸς εἰς πάθη ἀτιμίας· αἵ τε γὰρ θήλειαι αὐτῶν μετήλλαξαν τὴν φυσικὴν χρῆσιν εἰς τὴν παρὰ φύσιν, **27** ὁμοίως τε καὶ οἱ ἄρσενες ἀφέντες τὴν φυσικὴν χρῆσιν τῆς θηλείας ἐξεκαύθησαν ἐν τῇ ὀρέξει αὐτῶν εἰς ἀλλήλους, [e] ἄρσενες ἐν ἄρσεσιν[e] τὴν ἀσχημοσύνην κατεργαζόμενοι καὶ τὴν ἀντιμισθίαν ἣν ἔδει τῆς πλάνης αὐτῶν ἐν ἑαυτοῖς ἀπολαμβάνοντες. **28** καὶ καθὼς οὐκ

---

[c] **21** c major: Bov Nes BF² AV RV ASV RSV NEB TT Zür Luth Seg ∥ c minor: TR WH Jer

[d] **23-24** d paragraph, d minor: WH Bov AVᵉᵈ RV ASV RSV NEB Luth Jer Seg ∥ d major, d minor: TR AVᵉᵈ Zür ∥ d major, d paragraph: Nes BF² TT

[e] **27** e minor, e none: TR Bov Nes BF² AV RV ASV RSV NEB TT Zür (Luth) Jer Seg ∥ e none, e minor: WH

---

18 Ἀποκαλύπτεται...ἀνθρώπων Eph 5.6; Col 3.6   τῶν τὴν...κατεχόντων 2 Th 2.12   **19** Ac 14.15-17; 17.24-28   **20** τὰ γὰρ...θειότης Job 12.7-9; Ps 19.1   **21** ἐματαιώθησαν ...καρδία Eph 4.17-18   **22** Jr 10.14; 1 Cor 1.20   **23** Dt 4.15-19; Ps 106.20   **24** Ac 14.16   **25** οἵτινες...ψεύδει Jr 13.25; 16.19   τὸν κτίσαντα...αἰῶνας Ro 9.5   **27** Lv 18.22; 20.13; 1 Cor 6.9

The Guilt of Mankind

[18] God's wrath is revealed coming down from heaven upon all the sin and evil of men, whose evil ways prevent the truth from being known. [19] God punishes them, because what men can know about God is plain to them. God himself made it plain to them. [20] Ever since God created the world, his invisible qualities, both his eternal power and his divine nature, have been clearly seen. Men can perceive them in the things that God has made. So they have no excuse at all! [21] They know God, but they do not give him the honor that belongs to him, nor do they thank him. Instead, their thoughts have become complete nonsense and their empty minds are filled with darkness. [22] They say they are wise, but they are fools; [23] instead of worshiping the immortal God, they worship images made to look like mortal man or birds or animals or reptiles.

[24] Because men are such fools, God has given them over to do the filthy things their hearts desire, and they do shameful things with each other. [25] They exchange the truth about God for a lie; they worship and serve what God has created instead of the Creator himself, who is to be praised for ever! Amen.

[26] Because of what men do, God has given them over to shameful passions. Even the women pervert the natural use of their sex by unnatural acts. [27] In the same way the men give up natural sexual relations with women and burn with passion for each other. Men do shameful things with each other, and as a result they receive in themselves the punishment they deserve for their wrongdoing.

[28] Because men refuse to keep in mind

the true knowledge about God, he has given them over to corrupted minds, so that they do the things that they should not. ²⁹ They are filled with all kinds of wickedness, evil, greed, and vice; they are full of jealousy, murder, fighting, deceit, and malice. They gossip, ³⁰ and speak evil of one another; they are hateful to God, insolent, proud, and boastful; they think of more ways to do evil; they disobey their parents; ³¹ they are immoral; they do not keep their promises, and they show no kindness or pity to others. ³² They know that God's law says that people who live in this way deserve death. Yet they continue to do these very things — and worse still, they approve of others who do them also.

God's Judgment

2 Do you, my friend, pass judgment on others? You have no excuse at all, whoever you are. For when you judge others, but do the same things that they do, you condemn yourself. ² We know that God is right when he judges the people who do such things as these. ³ But you, my friend, do these very things yourself

ἐδοκίμασαν τὸν θεὸν ἔχειν ἐν ἐπιγνώσει, παρέδωκεν αὐτοὺς ὁ θεὸς εἰς ἀδόκιμον νοῦν, ποιεῖν τὰ μὴ καθήκοντα, 29 πεπληρωμένους πάσῃ ἀδικίᾳ πονηρίᾳ πλεονεξίᾳ κακίᾳ⁵, μεστοὺς φθόνου φόνου ἔριδος δόλου κακοηθείας, ʄψιθυριστάς, 30 ʄ καταλάλους, θεοστυγεῖς, ὑβριστάς, ὑπερηφάνους, ἀλαζόνας, ἐφευρετὰς κακῶν, γονεῦσιν ἀπειθεῖς, 31 ἀσυνέτους, ἀσυνθέτους, ἀστόργους, ἀνελεήμονας· 32 οἵτινες τὸ δικαίωμα τοῦ θεοῦ ἐπιγνόντες, ὅτι οἱ τὰ τοιαῦτα πράσσοντες ἄξιοι θανάτου εἰσίν, οὐ μόνον αὐτὰ ποιοῦσιν ἀλλὰ καὶ συνευδοκοῦσιν τοῖς πράσσουσιν.

The Righteous Judgment of God

2 Διὸ ἀναπολόγητος εἶ, ὦ ἄνθρωπε πᾶς ὁ κρίνων· ἐν ᾧ γὰρ κρίνεις τὸν ἕτερον, σεαυτὸν κατακρίνεις, τὰ γὰρ αὐτὰ πράσσεις ὁ κρίνων. 2 οἴδαμεν δὲ¹ ὅτι τὸ κρίμα τοῦ θεοῦ ἐστιν κατὰ ἀλήθειαν ἐπὶ τοὺς τὰ τοιαῦτα πράσσοντας. 3 λογίζῃ δὲ τοῦτο, ὦ ἄνθρωπε ὁ κρίνων τοὺς τὰ τοιαῦτα

---

⁵ **29** {C} *πονηρίᾳ πλεονεξίᾳ κακίᾳ* B 0172ᵛⁱᵈ 1739 1881 Origen Basil Gregory-Nyssa Chrysostom Theodoret Ps-Oecumenius Theophylact ∥ *πονηρίᾳ κακίᾳ πλεονεξίᾳ* ℵ A copᵇᵒᵐˢˢ ∥ *κακίᾳ πονηρίᾳ πλεονεξίᾳ* C 33 81 copˢᵃˑᵇᵒ eth John-Damascus ∥ *κακίᾳ πορνείᾳ πλεονεξίᾳ* D* (Dᶜ *πορνείᾳ πονηρίᾳ*) G (629 *add πονηρίᾳ*) itᵈˑᵉˑᵍ ∥ *πορνείᾳ πονηρίᾳ πλεονεξίᾳ κακίᾳ* Ψ (88 *add καί after each word*) (181 *ἀδικίᾳ for πονηρίᾳ*) 326 330 436 451 614 630 1241 1877 1962 1984 1985 2127 2492 2495 *Byz Lect* syrʰ arm (syrᵖ Ephraem *κακίᾳ πλεονεξίᾳ*) Basil Gregory-Nyssa Euthalius Theodoret ∥ *πονηρίᾳ πορνείᾳ πλεονεξίᾳ κακίᾳ* 104 itᵃʳˀ⁾ᵈᵉᵐˀˣˀ⁽ᶻˀ⁾ vg? ∥ *καὶ πορνείᾳ πλεονεξίᾳ κακίᾳ* P ∥ *πλεονεξίᾳ κακίᾳ* K

¹ **2** {B} *δέ* A B Dᵍʳ G K P Ψ 81 88 104 181 326 330 451 614 629 630 1241 1739 1877 1881 1984 1985 2495 *Byz Lect* itᵃʳᵛⁱᵈˑᵍˑᵐ syr⁽ᵖ⁾ˑʰ copˢᵃᵐˢ Marcion Tertullian Origenˡᵃᵗ Ambrosiaster Theodoret John-Damascus ∥ *γάρ* ℵ C 33 436 1962 2127 2492 itᵈˑᵈᵉᵐˑᵉˑˣˑᶻ vg copˢᵃˑᵇᵒ arm Chrysostom ∥ *omit* 1906 eth

---

ʄ ʄ **29–30** ʄ no number, ʄ number 30: TRᵉᵈ WH? Bov Nes BF² AV RV ASV RSV NEB? TT Zür Luth Jer ∥ ʄ number 30, ʄ no number: TRᵉᵈ WH? NEB? Seg

---

1 *ἐν...κατακρίνεις* Mt 7.2; Lk 6.37; Jn 8.7

πράσσοντας καὶ ποιῶν αὐτά, ὅτι σὺ ἐκφεύξῃ τὸ κρίμα τοῦ θεοῦ; 4 ἢ τοῦ πλούτου τῆς χρηστότητος αὐτοῦ καὶ τῆς ἀνοχῆς καὶ τῆς μακροθυμίας καταφρονεῖς, ἀγνοῶν ὅτι τὸ χρηστὸν τοῦ θεοῦ εἰς μετάνοιάν σε ἄγει; 5 κατὰ δὲ τὴν σκληρότητά σου καὶ ἀμετανόητον καρδίαν θησαυρίζεις σεαυτῷ ὀργὴν ἐν ἡμέρᾳ ὀργῆς καὶ ἀποκαλύψεως δικαιοκρισίας τοῦ θεοῦ, 6 ὃς ἀποδώσει ἑκάστῳ κατὰ τὰ ἔργα αὐτοῦ, 7 τοῖς μὲν καθ᾽ ὑπομονὴν ἔργου ἀγαθοῦ δόξαν καὶ τιμὴν καὶ ἀφθαρσίαν ζητοῦσιν, ζωὴν αἰώνιον· 8 τοῖς δὲ ἐξ ἐριθείας καὶ ἀπειθοῦσι τῇ ἀληθείᾳ πειθομένοις δὲ τῇ ἀδικίᾳ, ὀργὴ καὶ θυμός —[a] 9 θλῖψις καὶ στενοχωρία[a] ἐπὶ πᾶσαν ψυχὴν ἀνθρώπου τοῦ κατεργαζομένου τὸ κακόν, Ἰουδαίου τε πρῶτον καὶ Ἕλληνος· 10 δόξα δὲ καὶ τιμὴ καὶ εἰρήνη παντὶ τῷ ἐργαζομένῳ τὸ ἀγαθόν, Ἰουδαίῳ τε πρῶτον καὶ Ἕλληνι· 11 οὐ γὰρ ἐστιν προσωπολημψία παρὰ τῷ θεῷ. 12 ὅσοι γὰρ ἀνόμως ἥμαρτον, ἀνόμως καὶ ἀπολοῦνται· καὶ ὅσοι ἐν νόμῳ ἥμαρτον, διὰ νόμου κριθήσονται·[b] 13 οὐ γὰρ οἱ ἀκροαταὶ νόμου δίκαιοι παρὰ τῷ θεῷ, ἀλλ᾽ οἱ ποιηταὶ νόμου δικαιωθήσονται.[b] 14 ὅταν γὰρ ἔθνη τὰ μὴ νόμον ἔχοντα φύσει τὰ τοῦ νόμου ποιῶσιν, οὗτοι νόμον μὴ ἔχοντες ἑαυτοῖς εἰσιν νόμος· 15 οἵτινες ἐνδείκνυνται τὸ ἔργον τοῦ νόμου γραπτὸν ἐν ταῖς καρδίαις αὐτῶν,[b] συμμαρτυρούσης αὐτῶν τῆς συνειδήσεως καὶ μεταξὺ ἀλλήλων τῶν λογισμῶν κατηγορούντων ἢ καὶ ἀπολογουμένων,[b] 16 ἐν ᾗ ἡμέρᾳ κρίνει ὁ θεὸς τὰ κρυπτὰ τῶν ἀνθρώπων κατὰ τὸ εὐαγγέλιόν μου διὰ Ἰησοῦ Χριστοῦ.

[a a] **8-9** *a* dash, *a* none // *a* major, *a* none: Bov Nes BF² RSV NEB TT Zür Luth Jer Seg // *a* minor, *a* minor: (TR) WH (AV) RV ASV

[b b b b] **12-15** *b* major, *b* major, *b* minor, *b* minor: TR WH Bov Nes BF² RV (RSV) (NEB) Luth (Seg) // *b* minor, *b* major, *b* minor, *b* ellipsis: Jer // *b* parens, *b* major, *b* minor, *b* parens: AV // *b* minor, *b* parens, *b* minor, *b* parens: ASV // *b* minor, *b* dash, *b* minor, *b* dash: Zür // *b* major, *b* major, *b* parens, *b* parens: TT

---

4 τὸ χρηστὸν...ἄγει 2 Pe 3.15   **6** Ps 62.12; Pr 24.12; Sir 16.14; Mt 16.27; Jn 5.29; 2 Cor 5.10   **9** θλῖψις...Ἕλληνος Ro 1.16   **11** Dt 10.17; 2 Chr 19.7; Ac 10.34; Ga 2.6; Eph 6.9; Col 3.25; 1 Pe 1.17   **13** Mt 7.21; Jas 1.22, 25; 1 Jn 3.7   **14** Ac 10.35   **16** κατὰ τὸ εὐαγγέλιόν μου 2 Tm 2.8

for which you pass judgment on others! Do you think you will escape God's judgment? [4] Or perhaps you despise his great kindness, and tolerance, and patience. Surely you know that God is kind because he is trying to lead you to repent! [5] But you have a hard and stubborn heart. Therefore, you are making your own punishment even greater on the Day when God's wrath and right judgments will be revealed. [6] For God will reward every person according to what he has done. [7] Some men keep on doing good, and seek glory, honor, and immortal life: to them God will give eternal life. [8] Other men are selfish and reject what is right, to follow what is wrong: on them God will pour his wrath and anger. [9] There will be suffering and pain for all men who do what is evil, for the Jews first and also for the Gentiles. [10] But God will give glory, honor, and peace to all who do what is good, to the Jews first, and also to the Gentiles. [11] For God treats all men alike.

[12] The Gentiles do not have the Law of Moses; they sin and are lost apart from the Law. The Jews have the Law; they sin and are judged by the Law. [13] For it is not by hearing the Law that men are put right with God, but by doing what the Law commands. [14] The Gentiles do not have the Law; but whenever of their own free will they do what the Law commands, they are a law to themselves, even though they do not have the Law. [15] Their conduct shows that what the Law commands is written in their hearts. Their consciences also show that this is true, since their thoughts sometimes accuse them and sometimes defend them. [16] This, according to the Good News I preach, is how it will be on that Day when God, through Jesus Christ, will judge all the secret thoughts in men's hearts.

The Jews and the Law

17 What about you? You call yourself a Jew; you depend on the Law and boast about God; 18 you know what God wants you to do, and you have learned from the Law to choose what is right; 19 you are sure that you are a guide for the blind, a light for those who are in darkness, 20 an instructor for the foolish, and a teacher for the young. You are certain that in the Law you have the full content of knowledge and of truth. 21 You teach others — why don't you teach yourself? You preach, "Do not steal" — but do you yourself steal? 22 You say, "Do not commit adultery" — but do you commit adultery? You detest idols — but do you rob temples? 23 You boast about having God's law — but do you bring shame on God by breaking his law? 24 For the scripture says, "Because of you Jews, the Gentiles speak evil of God's name."

25 If you obey the Law, your circumcision is of value; but if you disobey the Law, you might as well never have been circumcised. 26 If the Gentile, who is not circumcised, obeys the commands of the Law, will not God regard him as though he were circumcised? 27 And you Jews will be condemned by the Gentiles. For you break the Law, even though you have it written down and are circumcised, while they obey the Law, even though they are not physically circumcised. 28 After all, who is a real Jew, truly circumcised? Not the man who is a Jew on the outside, whose circumcision is a physical thing. 29 Rather, the real Jew is the man who is a Jew on the inside, that is, whose heart has been circumcised, which is the work of God's Spirit, not of the written Law. This man receives his praise from God, not from men.

3 Do the Jews have any advantage over the Gentiles, then? Or is there any value in being circumcised? 2 Much, indeed, in every way! In the first place, God trusted his message to the Jews. 3 What

The Jews and the Law

17 Εἰ δὲ σὺ Ἰουδαῖος ἐπονομάζῃ καὶ ἐπαναπαύῃ νόμῳ καὶ καυχᾶσαι ἐν θεῷ 18 καὶ γινώσκεις τὸ θέλημα καὶ δοκιμάζεις τὰ διαφέροντα κατηχούμενος ἐκ τοῦ νόμου, 19 πέποιθάς τε σεαυτὸν ὁδηγὸν εἶναι τυφλῶν, φῶς τῶν ἐν σκότει, 20 παιδευτὴν ἀφρόνων, διδάσκαλον νηπίων, ἔχοντα τὴν μόρφωσιν τῆς γνώσεως καὶ τῆς ἀληθείας ἐν τῷ νόμῳ — 21 ὁ οὖν διδάσκων ἕτερον σεαυτὸν οὐ διδάσκεις; ὁ κηρύσσων μὴ κλέπτειν κλέπτεις; 22 ὁ λέγων μὴ μοιχεύειν μοιχεύεις; ὁ βδελυσσόμενος τὰ εἴδωλα ἱεροσυλεῖς; 23 ὃς ἐν νόμῳ καυχᾶσαι, διὰ τῆς παραβάσεως τοῦ νόμου τὸν θεὸν ἀτιμάζεις; 24 **τὸ γὰρ ὄνομα τοῦ θεοῦ δι' ὑμᾶς βλασφημεῖται ἐν τοῖς ἔθνεσιν,** καθὼς γέγραπται. 25 περιτομὴ μὲν γὰρ ὠφελεῖ ἐὰν νόμον πράσσῃς· ἐὰν δὲ παραβάτης νόμου ᾖς, ἡ περιτομή σου ἀκροβυστία γέγονεν. 26 ἐὰν οὖν ἡ ἀκροβυστία τὰ δικαιώματα τοῦ νόμου φυλάσσῃ, οὐχὶ ἡ ἀκροβυστία αὐτοῦ εἰς περιτομὴν λογισθήσεται; 27 καὶ κρινεῖ ἡ ἐκ φύσεως ἀκροβυστία τὸν νόμον τελοῦσα σὲ τὸν διὰ γράμματος καὶ περιτομῆς παραβάτην νόμου.^{c} 28 οὐ γὰρ ὁ ἐν τῷ φανερῷ Ἰουδαῖός ἐστιν, οὐδὲ ἡ ἐν τῷ φανερῷ ἐν σαρκὶ περιτομή· 29 ἀλλ' ὁ ἐν τῷ κρυπτῷ Ἰουδαῖος, καὶ περιτομὴ καρδίας ἐν πνεύματι οὐ γράμματι, οὗ ὁ ἔπαινος οὐκ ἐξ ἀνθρώπων ἀλλ' ἐκ τοῦ θεοῦ.

3 Τί οὖν τὸ περισσὸν τοῦ Ἰουδαίου,^{a} ἢ τίς ἡ ὠφέλεια τῆς περιτομῆς;^{a} 2 πολὺ κατὰ πάντα τρόπον. πρῶτον μὲν [γὰρ] ὅτι ἐπιστεύθησαν τὰ λόγια τοῦ θεοῦ. 3 τί

---

^{c} **27** *c* statement: WH Bov Nes BF² RSV NEB TT Luth Jer ∥ *c* question: TR AV RV ASV Zür Seg
$^{a\ a}$ **1** *a* minor, *a* question: TR WH Bov Nes BF² Luth Seg ∥ *a* question, *a* question: AV RV ASV RSV NEB TT Zür Jer

---

18 δοκιμάζεις τὰ διαφέροντα Php 1.10   **19** πέποιθας...τυφλῶν Mt 15.14; Lk 18.9
20 ἔχοντα...νόμῳ 2 Tm 3.15   **21** Ps 50.16–21; Mt 23.3–4   **24** τὸ...ἔθνεσιν Is 52.5; Eze 36.20
25 ἐὰν δὲ...ἀκροβυστία Jr 4.4: 9.25   **26** Ga 5.6   **28** Jn 7.24; 8.15, 39   **29** περιτομὴ... πνεύματι Dt 30.6: Col 2.11   ὁ ἔπαινος...θεοῦ 1 Cor 4.5; 2 Cor 10.18
3 2 ἐπιστεύθησαν...θεοῦ Dt 4.7–8; Ps 103.7; 147.19–20; Ro 9.4

γὰρ[b] εἰ ἠπίστησάν τινες;[b] μὴ ἡ ἀπιστία αὐτῶν τὴν πίστιν τοῦ θεοῦ καταργήσει;[b] **4** μὴ γένοιτο· γινέσθω δὲ ὁ θεὸς ἀληθής, πᾶς δὲ ἄνθρωπος ψεύστης, καθὼς γέγραπται,

Ὅπως ἂν δικαιωθῇς ἐν τοῖς λόγοις σου
καὶ νικήσεις ἐν τῷ κρίνεσθαί σε.

5 εἰ δὲ ἡ ἀδικία ἡμῶν θεοῦ δικαιοσύνην συνίστησιν, τί ἐροῦμεν; μὴ ἄδικος ὁ θεὸς ὁ ἐπιφέρων τὴν ὀργήν; κατὰ ἄνθρωπον λέγω. **6** μὴ γένοιτο· ἐπεὶ πῶς κρινεῖ ὁ θεὸς τὸν κόσμον; **7** εἰ γὰρ[1] ἡ ἀλήθεια τοῦ θεοῦ ἐν τῷ ἐμῷ ψεύσματι ἐπερίσσευσεν εἰς τὴν δόξαν αὐτοῦ, τί ἔτι κἀγὼ ὡς ἁμαρτωλὸς κρίνομαι;[c] **8** καὶ μὴ καθὼς βλασφημούμεθα καὶ καθώς φασίν τινες ἡμᾶς λέγειν ὅτι Ποιήσωμεν τὰ κακὰ ἵνα ἔλθῃ τὰ ἀγαθά; ὧν τὸ κρίμα ἔνδικόν ἐστιν.

There is None Righteous

9 Τί οὖν; προεχόμεθα; οὐ πάντως,[2] προῃτιασάμεθα γὰρ Ἰουδαίους τε καὶ Ἕλληνας πάντας ὑφ᾽ ἁμαρτίαν εἶναι, **10** καθὼς γέγραπται ὅτι

Οὐκ ἔστιν δίκαιος οὐδὲ εἷς,

---

[1] **7** {C} γάρ B D G K P Ψ 33 88 104 181 326 330 436 451 614 629 630 1241 1739 1877 1881 1962 1984 1985 2492 2495 *Byz Lect* it[ar,d,dem,e,g] vg syr[p,h] cop[sa] Origen[lat] Ambrosiaster Chrysostom Theodoret ∥ δέ ℵ A 81 2127 it[x,z] cop[bo] arm John-Damascus

[2] **9** {B} προεχόμεθα; οὐ πάντως, ℵ B (D[c] προκατεχόμεθα) K 33 81 88 181 326 (330 προσευχόμεθα) 436 451 614 629 630 1241 1739 1877 1881 1962 1984 1985 (2127 προσερχόμεθα) 2492 *Byz Lect* it[dem,e,x,z] vg syr[hmg] cop[sa?bo] ∥ προεχόμεθα; οὐ πάντως· A arm ∥ προκατέχομεν περισσόν; D* G Ψ 104 (2495 κατέχομεν) it[(ar),d,g] (syr[p,h]) Origen[lat] Ambrosiaster Chrysostom (Severian) Pelagius Theodore (Theodoret) ∥ προεχόμεθα; P eth Origen Ephraem

---

[b b b] **3** *b* none, *b* question, *b* question: TR (Bov) AV RV ASV RSV NEB Luth ∥ *b* question, *b* minor, *b* question: WH Nes BF² TT Zür Jer ∥ *b* exclamation, *b* minor, *b* question: Seg

[c] **7** *c* question: TR Bov Nes BF² AV RV ASV RSV NEB TT Zür Luth Jer Seg ∥ *c* minor: WH

---

3 μὴ...καταργήσει Ro 9.6; 11.29; 2 Tm 2.13   **4** πᾶς...ψεύστης Ps 116.11 Ὅπως... κρίνεσθαί σε Ps 51.4   **8** Ποιήσωμεν...ἀγαθά Ro 6.1   **9** προῃτιασάμεθα...εἶναι Ro 1.18—2.24; 3.23   **10–12** Οὐκ...ἑνός Ps 14.1–3; 53.1–3; Ec 7.20

---

if some of them were not faithful? Does it mean that for this reason God will not be faithful? **4** Certainly not! God must be true, even though every man is a liar. As the scripture says:

"You must be shown to be right
when you speak,
You must win your case when you
are being tried."

5 But what if our doing wrong serves to show up more clearly God's doing right? What can we say? That God does wrong when he punishes us? (I speak here as men do.) **6** By no means! If God is not just, how can he judge the world?

7 But what if my untruth serves God's glory by making his truth stand out more clearly? Why should I still be condemned as a sinner? **8** Why not say, then, "Let us do evil that good may come"? Some people, indeed, have insulted me by accusing me of saying this very thing! They will be condemned, as they should be.

No Man Is Righteous

9 Well then, are we Jews in any better condition than the Gentiles? Not at all! I have already shown that Jews and Gentiles alike are all under the power of sin. **10** As the Scriptures say:

"There is not a single man who is
righteous,

[11] There is not one who understands,
Or who seeks for God.
[12] All men have turned away from God,
They have all gone wrong.
No one does what is good, not even
one.
[13] Their throat is like an open grave.
Wicked lies roll off their tongues,
And deadly words, like snake's poison, from their lips;
[14] Their mouths are full of bitter curses.
[15] They are quick to hurt and kill;
[16] They leave ruin and misery wherever
they go.
[17] They have not known the path of
peace,
[18] Nor have they learned to fear God."
[19] Now we know that everything in the
Law applies to those who live under the
Law, in order to stop all human excuses
and bring the whole world under God's
judgment. [20] For no man is put right in
God's sight by doing what the Law requires; what the Law does is to make
man know that he has sinned.

How God Puts Men Right

[21] But now God's way of putting men
right with himself has been revealed,
and it has nothing to do with law. The
Law and the prophets gave their witness
to it: [22] God puts men right through
their faith in Jesus Christ. God does
this to all who believe in Christ, for there

11   οὐκ ἔστιν ὁ συνίων,
οὐκ ἔστιν ὁ ἐκζητῶν τὸν θεόν.

12 πάντες ἐξέκλιναν, ἅμα ἠχρειώθησαν·
οὐκ ἔστιν ποιῶν χρηστότητα,
οὐκ ἔστιν[3] ἕως ἑνός.

13 τάφος ἀνεῳγμένος ὁ λάρυγξ αὐτῶν,
ταῖς γλώσσαις αὐτῶν ἐδολιοῦσαν,
ἰὸς ἀσπίδων ὑπὸ τὰ χείλη αὐτῶν,

14   ὧν τὸ στόμα ἀρᾶς καὶ πικρίας γέμει·

15 ὀξεῖς οἱ πόδες αὐτῶν ἐκχέαι αἷμα,

16   σύντριμμα καὶ ταλαιπωρία ἐν ταῖς ὁδοῖς αὐτῶν,

17 καὶ ὁδὸν εἰρήνης οὐκ ἔγνωσαν.

18   οὐκ ἔστιν φόβος θεοῦ ἀπέναντι τῶν ὀφθαλμῶν
αὐτῶν.

19 Οἴδαμεν δὲ ὅτι ὅσα ὁ νόμος λέγει τοῖς ἐν τῷ νόμῳ
λαλεῖ, ἵνα πᾶν στόμα φραγῇ καὶ ὑπόδικος γένηται πᾶς ὁ
κόσμος τῷ θεῷ· **20** διότι ἐξ ἔργων νόμου **οὐ δικαιωθήσεται πᾶσα σὰρξ** ἐνώπιον αὐτοῦ, διὰ γὰρ νόμου ἐπίγνωσις
ἁμαρτίας.

Righteousness through Faith

21 Νυνὶ δὲ χωρὶς νόμου δικαιοσύνη θεοῦ πεφανέρωται,
μαρτυρουμένη ὑπὸ τοῦ νόμου καὶ τῶν προφητῶν, **22** δικαιοσύνη δὲ θεοῦ διὰ πίστεως Ἰησοῦ Χριστοῦ, εἰς
πάντας[4] τοὺς πιστεύοντας·[d] οὐ γάρ ἐστιν διαστολή·[d]

---

[3] **12** {C} οὐκ ἔστιν ℵ A D G K P Ψ 33 81 88 104 181 326 330 436 451
614 629 630 1241 1877 1881 1962 1984 1985 2127 2492 2495 *Byz Lect* it[ar,d,dem,]
[e,g,x,z] vg syr[h] cop[sa,bo] arm Origen[lat] Ambrosiaster // *omit* B 1739 syr[p] Origen

[4] **22** {B} εἰς πάντας 𝔭[40] ℵ* A B C P Ψ 81 88 104 436 630 1739 1881 *l*[598,599]
syr[pal] cop[sa,bo] arm eth Clement Origen[gr,lat] Augustine Cyril // ἐπὶ πάντας

[d d d] **22-23** d major, d major, d minor: TR Bov Nes BF[2] AV (RV) (ASV) // d major, d minor,
d major: TT // d major, d minor, d minor: RSV (Zür) Luth Seg // d minor, d major, d minor:
WH // d dash, d major, d minor: NEB // d dash, d major, d dash: Jer

---

13 τάφος...ἐδολιοῦσαν Ps 5.9   ἰὸς...αὐτῶν Ps 140.3   **14** Ps 10.7   **15-17** Is 59.7-8;
Pr 1.16   **18** Ps 36.1   **20** οὐ δικαιωθήσεται...αὐτοῦ Ps 143.2; Ga 2.16   διὰ...ἁμαρτίας Ro 7.7
21 μαρτυρουμένη...προφητῶν Ac 10.43   **22** δικαιοσύνη...πιστεύοντας Ro 1.17; Ga 2.16

23 πάντες γὰρ ἥμαρτον καὶ ὑστεροῦνται τῆς δόξης τοῦ θεοῦ,[a] 24 δικαιούμενοι δωρεὰν τῇ αὐτοῦ χάριτι διὰ τῆς ἀπολυτρώσεως τῆς ἐν Χριστῷ Ἰησοῦ·[e] 25 ὃν προέθετο ὁ θεὸς ἱλαστήριον[e] διὰ πίστεως[5] [e] ἐν τῷ αὐτοῦ αἵματι εἰς ἔνδειξιν τῆς δικαιοσύνης αὐτοῦ διὰ τὴν πάρεσιν τῶν προγεγονότων ἁμαρτημάτων 26 ἐν τῇ ἀνοχῇ τοῦ θεοῦ, πρὸς τὴν ἔνδειξιν τῆς δικαιοσύνης αὐτοῦ ἐν τῷ νῦν καιρῷ, εἰς τὸ εἶναι αὐτὸν δίκαιον καὶ δικαιοῦντα τὸν ἐκ πίστεως Ἰησοῦ[6].

27 Ποῦ οὖν ἡ καύχησις; ἐξεκλείσθη. διὰ ποίου νόμου; τῶν ἔργων; οὐχί, ἀλλὰ διὰ νόμου πίστεως. 28 λογιζόμεθα γὰρ[7] δικαιοῦσθαι πίστει ἄνθρωπον χωρὶς ἔργων

---

it[zvid] vg[ww] Pelagius John-Damascus ∥ εἰς πάντας καὶ ἐπὶ πάντας ℵ[c] D G K 33 181 326 330 451 614 629 1241 1877 1962 1984 1985 2127 2492 2495 Byz Lect it[ar,d,(dem),e,f,g,gig,x] vg[cl] syr[p,h] Origen[lat] Ambrosiaster Chrysostom Chromatius Euthalius Theodoret Gennadius Ps-Oecumenius Theophylact

[5] 25 {B} διὰ πίστεως ℵ C* D* G 88 104 436 1739 1881 1962 1984 1985 2495 Origen Eusebius Basil Cyril John-Damascus Theophylact ∥ διὰ τῆς πίστεως B C³ D[c] K P Ψ 33 81 181 326 330 451 614 629 630 1241 1877 2492 Byz Lect Basil Chrysostom Euthalius Theodoret Ps-Oecumenius ∥ διὰ (or διὰ τῆς) πίστεως it[ar,d,dem,e,f,g,gig,x,z] vg syr[p,h] cop[sa,bo] arm Origen[lat] Ambrosiaster Ambrose Augustine ∥ omit A 2127

[6] 26 {C} Ἰησοῦ ℵ A B C K P 81 88 104 181 630 1241 1739 1877 1962 2495 Byz l[598,599,603] it[d2,x] vg[ww] syr[h] cop[sa,boms] arm eth Chrysostom Orosius Augustine Euthalius Theophylact ∥ Ἰησοῦν D[gr] Ψ 33 326 330 436 451 614 1881 1985 2127 2492 Lect Clement ∥ Ἰησοῦν Χριστόν 1984 ∥ Ἰησοῦ Χριστοῦ 629 it[ar,c,(d*),dem,gig,z] vg[cl] syr[pal] cop[bo] Origen[lat] Ambrosiaster Ephraem Pelagius Theodoret ∥ κυρίου ἡμῶν Ἰησοῦ Χριστοῦ syr[v] ∥ omit G it[e,f,g]

[7] 28 {C} γάρ ℵ A D* G Ψ 81 326 436 630 1739 1881 1962 2127 2492 it[ar,vid,d,dem,e,f,g,x,z] vg syr[pal] cop[sa,bo] arm (eth) Origen[lat] Ambrosiaster Augustine John-Damascus ∥ οὖν B C D[c] K P 33 88 104 181 330 451 614 629 1241 1877 1984 1985 2495 Byz syr[p,h] Ephraem Chrysostom Euthalius Theodoret Ps-Oecumenius Theophylact ∥ omit Lect

---

[e e e] 24-25 e major, e none, e none: (TR) WH Bov Nes BF² AV Zür Luth Jer Seg ∥ e major, e minor, e minor: RV ASV (RSV) (NEB) ∥ e major, e minor, e none: RV[mg] ∥ e major, e none, e minor: TT

---

23 Ro 3.9   24 δικαιούμενοι...χάριτι Eph 2.8   διὰ...Ἰησοῦ Ro 5.1   25 προέθετο...αἵματι Eph 1.7   27 Ποῦ...ἐξεκλείσθη 1 Cor 1.31   28 Ga 2.16

is no difference at all: 23 all men have sinned and are far away from God's saving presence. 24 But by the free gift of God's grace they are all put right with him through Christ Jesus, who sets them free. 25 God offered him so that by his death he should become the means by which men's sins are forgiven, through their faith in him. God offered Christ to show how he puts men right with himself. In the past, God was patient and overlooked men's sins; 26 but now in the present time he deals with men's sins, to prove that he puts men right with himself. In this way God shows that he himself is righteous and that he puts right everyone who believes in Jesus.

27 What, then, is there to boast about? Nothing! For what reason? Because a man obeys the Law? No, but because he believes. 28 For we conclude that a man is put right with God only through faith, and not by doing what the Law com-

mands. ²⁹ Or is God only the God of the Jews? Is he not the God of the Gentiles also? Of course he is. ³⁰ God is one, and he will put the Jews right with himself on the basis of their faith, and the Gentiles right through their faith. ³¹ Does this mean that we do away with the Law by this faith? No, not at all; instead, we uphold the Law.

The Example of Abraham

4 What shall we say, then, of Abraham, our racial ancestor? What did he find? ² If he was put right with God by the things he did, he would have something to boast about. But he cannot boast before God. ³ The scripture says, "Abraham believed God, and because of his faith God accepted him as righteous." ⁴ A man who works is paid; his wages are not regarded as a gift but as something that he has earned. ⁵ As for the man who does not work, however, but simply puts his faith in God, who declares the guilty to be innocent, it is his faith that God takes into account in order to put him right with himself. ⁶ This is what David meant when he spoke of the happiness of the man whom God accepts as righteous, apart from any works:

⁷ "How happy are those whose wrongs
    God has forgiven,
  Whose sins he has covered over!
⁸ How happy is the man whose sins the
    Lord will not keep account of!"

⁹ Does this happiness that David spoke of belong only to those who are circumcised? No. It belongs also to those who are not circumcised. For we have quoted the scripture, "Abraham believed God, and because of his faith God accepted him as righteous." ¹⁰ When did this take place? Was it before or after Abraham

νόμου. 29 ἢ Ἰουδαίων ὁ θεὸς μόνον; οὐχὶ καὶ ἐθνῶν; ναὶ καὶ ἐθνῶν, 30 εἴπερ εἷς ὁ θεός, ὃς δικαιώσει περιτομὴν ἐκ πίστεως καὶ ἀκροβυστίαν διὰ τῆς πίστεως. 31 νόμον οὖν καταργοῦμεν διὰ τῆς πίστεως; μὴ γένοιτο, ἀλλὰ νόμον ἱστάνομεν.

The Example of Abraham

4 Τί οὖν ἐροῦμεν εὑρηκέναι Ἀβραὰμ τὸν προπάτορα ἡμῶν¹ κατὰ σάρκα; 2 εἰ γὰρ Ἀβραὰμ ἐξ ἔργων ἐδικαιώθη, ἔχει καύχημα· ἀλλ' οὐ πρὸς θεόν. 3 τί γὰρ ἡ γραφὴ λέγει; Ἐπίστευσεν δὲ Ἀβραὰμ τῷ θεῷ, καὶ ἐλογίσθη αὐτῷ εἰς δικαιοσύνην. 4 τῷ δὲ ἐργαζομένῳ ὁ μισθὸς οὐ λογίζεται κατὰ χάριν ἀλλὰ κατὰ ὀφείλημα· 5 τῷ δὲ μὴ ἐργαζομένῳ, πιστεύοντι δὲ ἐπὶ τὸν δικαιοῦντα τὸν ἀσεβῆ, λογίζεται ἡ πίστις αὐτοῦ εἰς δικαιοσύνην, 6 καθάπερ καὶ Δαυὶδ λέγει τὸν μακαρισμὸν τοῦ ἀνθρώπου ᾧ ὁ θεὸς λογίζεται δικαιοσύνην χωρὶς ἔργων,

7   Μακάριοι ὧν ἀφέθησαν αἱ ἀνομίαι
        καὶ ὧν ἐπεκαλύφθησαν αἱ ἁμαρτίαι·
8   μακάριος ἀνὴρ οὗ οὐ μὴ λογίσηται κύριος ἁμαρτίαν.
9 ὁ μακαρισμὸς οὖν οὗτος ἐπὶ τὴν περιτομὴν ἢ καὶ ἐπὶ τὴν ἀκροβυστίαν; λέγομεν γάρ, Ἐλογίσθη τῷ Ἀβραὰμ ἡ πίστις εἰς δικαιοσύνην. 10 πῶς οὖν ἐλογίσθη; ἐν περιτομῇ ὄντι ἢ ἐν ἀκροβυστίᾳ; οὐκ ἐν περιτομῇ ἀλλ'

---

¹ 1 {B} εὑρηκέναι Ἀβραὰμ τὸν προπάτορα ἡμῶν ℵ*·ᶜ A C* 81 330 2127 syrᵖᵃˡ copˢᵃ,⁽ᵇᵒ⁾ arm Cyril John-Damascus ‖ εὑρηκέναι Ἀβραὰμ τὸν πατέρα ἡμῶν ℵᵃ C³ D G Ψ (451 Ἀβραὰμ εὑρηκέναι) 629 l⁵⁹⁸,⁵⁹⁹,¹³⁶⁴ itᵃʳᵛⁱᵈ,ᵈ,ᵈᵉᵐ,ᵉ,f,g,x,z vg Origenˡᵃᵗ ‖ Ἀβραὰμ τὸν πατέρα ἡμῶν εὑρηκέναι K P 33 88 104 181 326 436 614 630 1241 1877 1881 1962 1984 1985 2492 2495 *Byz Lect* syr⁽ᵖ⁾,ʰ Chrysostom Euthalius Theodoret Ps-Oecumenius Theophylact ‖ Ἀβραὰμ τὸν προπάτορα ἡμῶν B (1739 πατέρα) Origen Ephraem (Chrysostomᶜᵒᵐᵐ πατέρα)

---

29 Ro 10.12   30 εἷς ὁ θεός Dt 6.4; Ga 3.20   ὃς...πίστεως Ro 4.11-12   31 Mt 5.17; Ro 4.3; 8.4
4 3 Ἐπίστευσεν...δικαιοσύνην Gn 15.6 (Ga 3.6; Jas 2.23)   4 Ro 11.6   7-8 Ps 32.1-2
9 Ἐλογίσθη...δικαιοσύνην Gn 15.6 (Ro 4.3; Ga 3.6; Jas 2.23)

ἐν ἀκροβυστίᾳ· 11 καὶ σημεῖον ἔλαβεν περιτομῆς, σφραγῖδα τῆς δικαιοσύνης τῆς πίστεως τῆς ἐν τῇ ἀκροβυστίᾳ, εἰς τὸ εἶναι αὐτὸν πατέρα πάντων τῶν πιστευόντων δι' ἀκροβυστίας, εἰς τὸ λογισθῆναι[2] αὐτοῖς [τὴν] δικαιοσύνην, 12 καὶ πατέρα περιτομῆς τοῖς οὐκ ἐκ περιτομῆς μόνον ἀλλὰ καὶ τοῖς στοιχοῦσιν τοῖς ἴχνεσιν τῆς ἐν ἀκροβυστίᾳ πίστεως τοῦ πατρὸς ἡμῶν Ἀβραάμ.

The Promise Realized through Faith

13 Οὐ γὰρ διὰ νόμου ἡ ἐπαγγελία τῷ Ἀβραὰμ ἢ τῷ σπέρματι αὐτοῦ, τὸ κληρονόμον αὐτὸν εἶναι κόσμου, ἀλλὰ διὰ δικαιοσύνης πίστεως· 14 εἰ γὰρ οἱ ἐκ νόμου κληρονόμοι, κεκένωται ἡ πίστις καὶ κατήργηται ἡ ἐπαγγελία· 15 ὁ γὰρ νόμος ὀργὴν κατεργάζεται· οὗ δὲ οὐκ ἔστιν νόμος, οὐδὲ παράβασις. 16 διὰ τοῦτο ἐκ πίστεως, ἵνα κατὰ χάριν, εἰς τὸ εἶναι βεβαίαν τὴν ἐπαγγελίαν παντὶ τῷ σπέρματι,[a] οὐ τῷ ἐκ τοῦ νόμου μόνον ἀλλὰ καὶ τῷ ἐκ πίστεως Ἀβραάμ ([a]ὅς ἐστιν πατὴρ πάντων ἡμῶν,[a] 17 καθὼς γέγραπται ὅτι **Πατέρα πολλῶν ἐθνῶν τέθεικά σε**)[a] κατέναντι οὗ ἐπίστευσεν θεοῦ τοῦ ζωοποιοῦντος τοὺς νεκροὺς καὶ καλοῦντος τὰ μὴ ὄντα ὡς ὄντα· 18 ὃς παρ' ἐλπίδα ἐπ' ἐλπίδι ἐπίστευσεν εἰς τὸ γενέσθαι αὐτὸν **πατέρα πολλῶν ἐθνῶν** κατὰ τὸ εἰρημένον, **Οὕτως ἔσται τὸ σπέρμα σου·** 19 καὶ μὴ ἀσθενήσας τῇ

---

[2] 11 {C} λογισθῆναι ℵ* A B Ψ 81 330 630 1739 1881 it[ar, x] cop[sa ms, bo] Origen Cyril John-Damascus ∥ λογισθῆναι καί ℵ[c] C D G K P 88 104 181 326 436 614 629 1241 1877 1962 1984 1985 2127 2492 2495 *Byz Lect* it[d, (dem), e, f, g, z] vg syr[p, h, pal] cop[sa] arm eth Origen[lat] Theodoret Ps Oecumenius Theophylact ∥ λογισθῆναι αὐτόν 451

[a a a a] 16–17 a minor, a parens, a minor, a parens: WH Bov ∥ a minor, a minor, a parens, a parens: TR AV RV ASV (TT) Zür ∥ a dash, a minor, a minor, a dash: RSV ∥ a minor, a major, a dash, a dash: Luth ∥ a minor, a minor, a minor, a dash: Jer ∥ a minor, a minor, a minor, a minor: Nes BF² (NEB) (Seg)

11 σημεῖον...ἀκροβυστίᾳ Gn 17.10–11   13 ἡ ἐπαγγελία...κόσμου Gn 18.18; 22.17–18 τῷ σπέρματι αὐτοῦ Ga 3.29   14 Ga 3.18   15 οὖ...παράβασις Ro 3.20; 5.13; 7.8   16 τῷ ἐκ πίστεως...ἡμῶν Ga 3.7   17 Πατέρα...σε Gn 17.5   καλοῦντος...ὡς ὄντα Is 48.13 18 Οὕτως...σπέρμα σου Gn 15.5

---

was circumcised? Before, not after. 11 He was circumcised later, and his circumcision was a sign to prove that because of Abraham's faith God had accepted him as righteous before he had been circumcised. And so Abraham is the spiritual father of all who believe in God and are accepted as righteous by him, even though they are not circumcised. 12 He is also the father of those who are circumcised, not just because they are circumcised, but because they live the same life of faith that our father Abraham lived before he was circumcised.

God's Promise Received through Faith

13 God promised Abraham and his descendants that the world would belong to him. This promise was made, not because Abraham obeyed the Law, but because he believed and was accepted as righteous by God. 14 For if what God promises is to be given to those who obey the Law, then man's faith means nothing and God's promise is worthless. 15 The Law brings down God's wrath; but where there is no law, there is no disobeying of the law either.

16 The promise was based on faith, then, in order that the promise should be guaranteed as God's free gift to all of Abraham's descendants — not just those who obey the Law, but also those who believe as Abraham did. For Abraham is the spiritual father of us all. 17 As the scripture says, "I have made you father of many nations." So the promise is good in the sight of God, in whom Abraham believed — the God who brings the dead to life and whose command brings into being what did not exist. 18 Abraham believed and hoped, when there was no hope, and so became "the father of many nations." Just as the scripture says, "Your descendants will be this many." 19 He was almost one

hundred years old; but his faith did not weaken when he thought of his body, which was already practically dead, or of the fact that Sarah could not have children. [20] His faith did not leave him, and he did not doubt God's promise; his faith filled him with power, and he gave praise to God. [21] For he was absolutely sure that God would be able to do what he had promised. [22] That is why Abraham, through faith, "was accepted as righteous by God." [23] The words "he was accepted as righteous" were not written for him alone. [24] They were written also for us who are to be accepted as righteous, who believe in him who raised Jesus our Lord from death. [25] He was given over to die because of our sins, and was raised to life to put us right with God.

Right with God

5 Now that we have been put right with God through faith, we have peace[1] with God through our Lord Jesus Christ. [2] He has brought us, by faith, into the

[1] **1** we have peace: *some mss. read* let us have peace

πίστει κατενόησεν[3] τὸ ἑαυτοῦ σῶμα ἤδη[4] νενεκρωμένον, ἑκατονταετής που ὑπάρχων, καὶ τὴν νέκρωσιν τῆς μήτρας Σάρρας, 20 εἰς δὲ τὴν ἐπαγγελίαν τοῦ θεοῦ οὐ διεκρίθη τῇ ἀπιστίᾳ ἀλλ' ἐνεδυναμώθη τῇ πίστει, δοὺς δόξαν τῷ θεῷ 21 καὶ πληροφορηθεὶς ὅτι ὃ ἐπήγγελται δυνατός ἐστιν καὶ ποιῆσαι. 22 διὸ καὶ[5] **ἐλογίσθη αὐτῷ εἰς δικαιοσύνην.** 23 Οὐκ ἐγράφη δὲ δι' αὐτὸν μόνον ὅτι ἐλογίσθη αὐτῷ, 24 ἀλλὰ καὶ δι' ἡμᾶς οἷς μέλλει λογίζεσθαι, τοῖς πιστεύουσιν ἐπὶ τὸν ἐγείραντα Ἰησοῦν τὸν κύριον ἡμῶν ἐκ νεκρῶν, 25 ὃς παρεδόθη διὰ τὰ παραπτώματα ἡμῶν καὶ ἠγέρθη διὰ τὴν δικαίωσιν ἡμῶν.

Results of Justification

5 Δικαιωθέντες οὖν ἐκ πίστεως εἰρήνην ἔχομεν[1] πρὸς τὸν θεὸν διὰ τοῦ κυρίου ἡμῶν Ἰησοῦ Χριστοῦ, 2 δι' οὗ

[3] **19** {C} κατενόησεν ℵ A B C 81 88 1739 2127 it[x] vg[ww] syr[p] cop[sa, bo, fay] arm Origen[lat1/3] (Chrysostom) Julian-Eclanum[acc. to Augustine] John-Damascus // οὐ κατενόησεν D G K P Ψ 33 104 181 326 330 436 451 629 630 1241 1877 1881 1962 1984 1985 2492 2495 *Byz Lect* it[ar,c,d,dem,e,f,g,z vid?] vg[cl] syr[h] Origen[lat 2/3] Ambrosiaster Ephraem Epiphanius Chrysostom Pelagius Cosmos Paschal Chronicle Ps-Oecumenius Theophylact // ἀλλὰ κατενόησεν syr[pal]

[4] **19** {C} ἤδη ℵ A C D[gr] K P Ψ 33 81 88 104 181 326 330 436 451 629 1241 1877 1962 1984 1985 2127 2492 2495 *Byz Lect* it[gig] syr[h with *] cop[bo] arm Origen[lat] Euthalius Theodoret Paschal Chronicle John-Damascus Ps-Oecumenius Theophylact // *omit* B G 630 1739 1881 it[ar,d,dem,e,f,g,x,z] vg[(cl),ww] syr[p,h,pal] cop[sa, fayvid] eth Origen[lat] Ephraem Epiphanius Chrysostom

[5] **22** {C} καί ℵ A C D[b,c] K P Ψ 33 81 88 104 181 326 330 436 451 629 630 1241 1739 1877 1881 1962 1985 2127 2492 2495 *Byz Lect* it[arvid,d?dem,x,z] vg syr[h] Origen[lat] Ambrosiaster Euthalius Theodoret Paschal Chronicle John-Damascus // *omit* B D[gr*] G 1984 it[e,f,g] syr[p,pal] cop[sa,bo] arm

[1] **1** {C} ἔχομεν ℵ[a] B[3] G[gr] P Ψ 0220[vid] 88 104 326 330 451 629 1241 1739 1877 1881 1984 2127 2492 2495 *Byz Lect* it[arvid?z*] syr[h] cop[sa] Ephraem Didymus Epiphanius Cyril[3/4] Sedulius-Scotus // ἔχωμεν ℵ* A B* C D K

19 ἑκατονταετὴς που ὑπάρχων Gn 17.17   **22** ἐλογίσθη...δικαιοσύνην Gn 15.6 **23-24** Οὐκ...ἡμᾶς Ro 15.4   **24** τὸν ἐγείραντα...νεκρῶν 1 Pe 1.21   **25** ὅς...παραπτώματα ἡμῶν Is 53.4-5 ἠγέρθη...ἡμῶν 1 Cor 15.17

5 1 Δικαιωθέντες...πίστεως Ro 3.24, 28   **2** δι' οὗ...ἐσχήκαμεν Eph 2.18; 3.12

καὶ τὴν προσαγωγὴν ἐσχήκαμεν [τῇ πίστει]² εἰς τὴν χάριν ταύτην ἐν ᾗ ἐστήκαμεν, καὶ καυχώμεθα ἐπ’ ἐλπίδι τῆς δόξης τοῦ θεοῦ. 3 οὐ μόνον δέ, ἀλλὰ καὶ καυχώμεθα ἐν ταῖς θλίψεσιν, εἰδότες ὅτι ἡ θλῖψις ὑπομονὴν κατεργάζεται, 4 ἡ δὲ ὑπομονὴ δοκιμήν, ἡ δὲ δοκιμὴ ἐλπίδα· 5 ἡ δὲ ἐλπὶς οὐ καταισχύνει, ὅτι ἡ ἀγάπη τοῦ θεοῦ ἐκκέχυται ἐν ταῖς καρδίαις ἡμῶν διὰ πνεύματος ἁγίου τοῦ δοθέντος ἡμῖν, 6 ἔτι γὰρ³ Χριστὸς ὄντων ἡμῶν ἀσθενῶν ἔτι³ κατὰ καιρὸν ὑπὲρ ἀσεβῶν ἀπέθανεν. 7 μόλις γὰρ ὑπὲρ δικαίου τις ἀποθανεῖται· ὑπὲρ γὰρ τοῦ ἀγαθοῦ τάχα τις καὶ τολμᾷ ἀποθανεῖν· 8 συνίστησιν δὲ τὴν ἑαυτοῦ ἀγάπην εἰς ἡμᾶς ὁ θεὸς ὅτι ἔτι ἁμαρτωλῶν ὄντων ἡμῶν Χριστὸς ὑπὲρ ἡμῶν ἀπέθανεν. 9 πολλῷ οὖν μᾶλλον δικαιωθέντες νῦν ἐν τῷ αἵματι αὐτοῦ σωθησόμεθα δι’ αὐτοῦ ἀπὸ τῆς ὀργῆς. 10 εἰ γὰρ ἐχθροὶ ὄντες κατηλλάγημεν τῷ θεῷ διὰ τοῦ θανάτου τοῦ υἱοῦ αὐτοῦ, πολλῷ μᾶλλον καταλλαγέντες σωθησόμεθα ἐν τῇ ζωῇ αὐτοῦ· 11 οὐ μόνον δέ, ἀλλὰ καὶ καυχώμενοι ἐν τῷ θεῷ διὰ τοῦ κυρίου ἡμῶν Ἰησοῦ Χριστοῦ, δι’ οὗ νῦν τὴν καταλλαγὴν ἐλάβομεν.

grace of God in which we now stand. We rejoice,[2] then, in the hope we have of sharing God's glory! [3] And we also rejoice[3] in our troubles, for we know that trouble produces endurance, [4] endurance brings God's approval, and his approval creates hope. [5] This hope does not disappoint us, for God has poured out his love into our hearts by means of the Holy Spirit, who is God's gift to us.

[6] For when we were still helpless, Christ died for the wicked, at the time that God chose. [7] It is a difficult thing for someone to die for a righteous person. It may be that someone might dare to die for a good person. [8] But God has shown us how much he loves us: it was while we were still sinners that Christ died for us! [9] By his death we are now put right with God; how much more, then, will we be saved by him from God's wrath. [10] We were God's enemies, but he made us his friends through the death of his Son. Now that we are God's friends, how much more will we be saved by Christ's life! [11] But that is not all; we rejoice in God through our Lord Jesus Christ, who has now made us God's friends.

33 81 181 436 630 1962 1985 *l*⁵⁹⁷,⁵⁹⁹ it^{d,dem,e,f,g,t,x} vg syr^{p,pal} cop^{bo} arm eth Marcion Tertullian Origen^{lat} Ambrosiaster Titus-Bostra Chrysostom Cyril^{1/4} Euthalius Theodoret John-Damascus

² 2 {C} τῇ πίστει ℵ*,ᶜ C K P Ψ 33 81 104 181 326 330 436 451 629 630 1241 1739 1877 1881 1984 1985 2127 2492 2495 *Byz Lect* arm Chrysostom Cyril Euthalius Theodoret John-Damascus ∥ ἐν τῇ πίστει ℵᵃ A 88 1962 *l*⁵⁹⁷ Titus-Bostra Chrysostom ∥ ἐν τῇ πίστει or τῇ πίστει (it^{ar,d⁶,dem,gig,z} vg^{cl} *per fidem*, it^{t,x} *fidei*, vg^{ww} *fide*) syr^{p,h,pal} cop^{bo} eth^{pp} Origen^{lat} Ambrosiaster ∥ *omit* B D G 0220 it^{d*,e,f,g} cop^{sa} eth^{ro} Origen^{lat} Ephraem

³ 6 {D} ἔτι γάρ...ἔτι ℵ A C D^{gr*} 81 104 1241 2127 2492 syr^h Marcion Origen^{lat} (Epiphanius) John-Damascus ∥ ἔτι γάρ...*omit* D^c K P Ψ 33 88^{vid} 181 326 330 436 451 614 629 630 1739 1877 1881 1962 1984 1985 2495 *Byz Lect* arm eth Origen^{lat} Chrysostom ∥ εἰ γάρ...*omit* Isidore ∥ εἰ δέ...*omit* syr^p Augustine ∥ εἴ γε...ἔτι B cop^{sa} ∥ εἰ γάρ...ἔτι syr^{pal} cop^{bo} ∥ εἰς τί γάρ...ἔτι D^b G it^{ar,d,dem,e,f,g,t,x,z} vg Irenaeus^{lat} Faustinus

3 καυχώμεθα...κατεργάζεται Jas 1.2–3; 1 Pe 1.5–7   5 ἡ δέ...καταισχύνει Ps 22.5; 25.20; He 6.18–19   8 Jn 3.16; 1 Jn 4.10   9 σωθησόμεθα...ὀργῆς Ro 1.18; 2.5, 8   10 Ro 8.7–8

² 2 we rejoice: *or* let us rejoice
³ 3 we also rejoice: *or* let us also rejoice

Adam and Christ

[12] Sin came into the world through one man, and his sin brought death with it. As a result, death spread to the whole human race, because all men sinned. [13] There was sin in the world before the Law was given; but since there was no law, no account was kept of sins. [14] But from the time of Adam to the time of Moses death ruled over all men, even over those who did not sin as Adam did by disobeying God's command.

Adam was a figure of the one who was to come. [15] But the two are not the same; for the free gift of God is not like Adam's sin. It is true that many men died because of the sin of that one man. But God's grace is much greater, and so is his free gift to so many men through the grace of the one man, Jesus Christ. [16] And there is a difference between God's gift and the sin of one man. After the one sin came the judgment of "Guilty"; but after so many sins comes the undeserved gift of "Not guilty!" [17] It is true that through the sin of one man death began to rule, because of that one man. But how much greater is the result of what was done by the one man, Jesus Christ! All who receive God's abundant grace and the free gift of his righteousness will rule in life through Christ.

[18] So then, as the one sin condemned all men, in the same way the one righteous

Adam and Christ

12 Διὰ τοῦτο ὥσπερ δι' ἑνὸς ἀνθρώπου ἡ ἁμαρτία εἰς τὸν κόσμον εἰσῆλθεν καὶ διὰ τῆς ἁμαρτίας ὁ θάνατος, καὶ οὕτως εἰς πάντας ἀνθρώπους ὁ θάνατος διῆλθεν[4], ἐφ' ᾧ πάντες ἥμαρτον — **13** ἄχρι γὰρ νόμου ἁμαρτία ἦν ἐν κόσμῳ, ἁμαρτία δὲ οὐκ ἐλλογεῖται μὴ ὄντος νόμου· **14** ἀλλὰ ἐβασίλευσεν ὁ θάνατος ἀπὸ Ἀδὰμ μέχρι Μωϋσέως καὶ ἐπὶ τοὺς μὴ ἁμαρτήσαντας ἐπὶ τῷ ὁμοιώματι τῆς παραβάσεως Ἀδάμ, ὅς ἐστιν τύπος τοῦ μέλλοντος.

15 Ἀλλ' οὐχ ὡς τὸ παράπτωμα, οὕτως καὶ τὸ χάρισμα· εἰ γὰρ τῷ τοῦ ἑνὸς παραπτώματι οἱ πολλοὶ ἀπέθανον, πολλῷ μᾶλλον ἡ χάρις τοῦ θεοῦ καὶ ἡ δωρεὰ ἐν χάριτι τῇ τοῦ ἑνὸς ἀνθρώπου Ἰησοῦ Χριστοῦ εἰς τοὺς πολλοὺς ἐπερίσσευσεν. **16** καὶ οὐχ ὡς δι' ἑνὸς ἁμαρτήσαντος τὸ δώρημα· τὸ μὲν γὰρ κρίμα ἐξ ἑνὸς εἰς κατάκριμα, τὸ δὲ χάρισμα ἐκ πολλῶν παραπτωμάτων εἰς δικαίωμα. **17** εἰ γὰρ τῷ τοῦ ἑνὸς παραπτώματι ὁ θάνατος ἐβασίλευσεν διὰ τοῦ ἑνός, πολλῷ μᾶλλον οἱ τὴν περισσείαν τῆς χάριτος καὶ τῆς δωρεᾶς[5] τῆς δικαιοσύνης λαμβάνοντες ἐν ζωῇ βασιλεύσουσιν διὰ τοῦ ἑνὸς Ἰησοῦ Χριστοῦ. **18** Ἄρα οὖν ὡς δι' ἑνὸς παραπτώματος εἰς πάντας ἀνθρώπους εἰς κατάκριμα, οὕτως καὶ δι' ἑνὸς δικαιώ-

---

[4] **12** {C} ὁ θάνατος διῆλθεν ℵ A B C K P 0220[vid] 33 81 88 104 181 326 330 436 451 614 629 630 1241 1739 1877 (1881 εἰσῆλθεν) 1962 1984 1985 2127 2492 *Byz Lect* it[ar,dem,x,z] vg syr[p,h with *,pal] cop[sa,bo] Origen[gr,lat] Augustine Euthalius ‖ διῆλθεν ὁ θάνατος Ψ arm Chrysostom Theodoret (John-Damascus εἰσῆλθεν) ‖ διῆλθεν D G 2495 it[d,e,f,g] syr[h] eth Origen Aphraates Ambrosiaster Pacian Ambrose Augustine Leo Bede

[5] **17** {B} τῆς δωρεᾶς 𝔭[46] ℵ A C D G K P 33 81[vid] 181 326 436 614 629 630 1241 1739 1877 1881 1962 *Byz Lect* it[d,e,f,g] cop[bo,fay] arm ‖ τῆς δωρεᾶς καὶ Ψ 0221 330 451 2127 2492 2495 it[ar vid,dem,r3,x,z] vg syr[p,h] Ambrosiaster Chrysostom Isidore Theodoret ‖ τὴν δωρεάν 88 104 1984 1985 Origen[lat] Theophylact ‖ *omit* B cop[sa] Irenaeus[lat] Origen Ephraem Chrysostom Augustine

---

12 δι' ἑνὸς...εἰσῆλθεν Gn 2.17; 3.6, 19   διὰ...θάνατος Ro 6.23   **13** ἁμαρτία...νόμου Ro 4.15   **14** ὅς...μέλλοντος 1 Cor 15.21–22, 45   **18** 1 Cor 15.22

ματος εἰς πάντας ἀνθρώπους εἰς δικαίωσιν ζωῆς· **19** ὥσπερ γὰρ διὰ τῆς παρακοῆς τοῦ ἑνὸς ἀνθρώπου ἁμαρτωλοὶ κατεστάθησαν οἱ πολλοί, οὕτως καὶ διὰ τῆς ὑπακοῆς τοῦ ἑνὸς δίκαιοι κατασταθήσονται οἱ πολλοί. **20** νόμος δὲ παρεισῆλθεν ἵνα πλεονάσῃ τὸ παράπτωμα· οὗ δὲ ἐπλεόνασεν ἡ ἁμαρτία, ὑπερεπερίσσευσεν ἡ χάρις, **21** ἵνα ὥσπερ ἐβασίλευσεν ἡ ἁμαρτία ἐν τῷ θανάτῳ, οὕτως καὶ ἡ χάρις βασιλεύσῃ διὰ δικαιοσύνης εἰς ζωὴν αἰώνιον διὰ Ἰησοῦ Χριστοῦ τοῦ κυρίου ἡμῶν.

Dead to Sin but Alive in Christ

6 Τί οὖν ἐροῦμεν; ἐπιμένωμεν τῇ ἁμαρτίᾳ, ἵνα ἡ χάρις πλεονάσῃ; **2** μὴ γένοιτο· οἵτινες ἀπεθάνομεν τῇ ἁμαρτίᾳ, πῶς ἔτι ζήσομεν ἐν αὐτῇ; **3** ἢ ἀγνοεῖτε ὅτι ὅσοι ἐβαπτίσθημεν εἰς Χριστὸν Ἰησοῦν εἰς τὸν θάνατον αὐτοῦ ἐβαπτίσθημεν; **4** συνετάφημεν οὖν αὐτῷ διὰ τοῦ βαπτίσματος εἰς τὸν θάνατον, ἵνα ὥσπερ ἠγέρθη Χριστὸς ἐκ νεκρῶν διὰ τῆς δόξης τοῦ πατρός, οὕτως καὶ ἡμεῖς ἐν καινότητι ζωῆς περιπατήσωμεν. **5** εἰ γὰρ σύμφυτοι γεγόναμεν τῷ ὁμοιώματι τοῦ θανάτου αὐτοῦ, ἀλλὰ καὶ τῆς ἀναστάσεως ἐσόμεθα· **6** τοῦτο γινώσκοντες, ὅτι ὁ παλαιὸς ἡμῶν ἄνθρωπος συνεσταυρώθη, ἵνα καταργηθῇ τὸ σῶμα τῆς ἁμαρτίας, τοῦ μηκέτι δουλεύειν ἡμᾶς τῇ ἁμαρτίᾳ· **7** ὁ γὰρ ἀποθανὼν δεδικαίωται ἀπὸ τῆς ἁμαρτίας. **8** εἰ δὲ ἀπεθάνομεν σὺν Χριστῷ, πιστεύομεν ὅτι καὶ συζήσομεν αὐτῷ· **9** εἰδότες ὅτι Χριστὸς ἐγερθεὶς ἐκ νεκρῶν οὐκέτι ἀποθνῄσκει, θάνατος αὐτοῦ οὐκέτι κυριεύει. **10** ὃ γὰρ ἀπέθανεν, τῇ ἁμαρτίᾳ ἀπέθανεν ἐφάπαξ· ὃ δὲ ζῇ, ζῇ τῷ θεῷ. **11** οὕτως καὶ ὑμεῖς λογίζεσθε ἑαυτοὺς [εἶναι]

---

19 διὰ τῆς ὑπακοῆς...πολλοί Is 53.11   **20** νόμος...παράπτωμα Ro 4.15; 7.8; Ga 3.19 **21** Ro 6.23
6 1 ἐπιμένωμεν...πλεονάσῃ Ro 3.5-8   **2** οἵτινες...αὐτῇ 1 Pe 4.1   **3** ὅσοι ἐβαπτίσθημεν Ga 3.27   **4** Col 2.12   **5** Php 3.10-11   **6** ὁ παλαιὸς...συνεσταυρώθη Ga 5.24 **7** 1 Pe 4.1   **10** τῇ ἁμαρτίᾳ...ἐφάπαξ He 9.26-28; 1 Pe 3.18   ὃ δὲ ζῇ...θεῷ Ga 2.19 **11** 2 Cor 5.15; 1 Pe 2.24

act sets all men free and gives them life. ¹⁹ And just as many men were made sinners as the result of the disobedience of one man, in the same way many will be put right with God as the result of the obedience of the one man.

²⁰ Law was introduced in order to increase wrongdoing; but where sin increased, God's grace increased much more. ²¹ So then, just as sin ruled by means of death, so also God's grace rules by means of righteousness, leading us to eternal life through Jesus Christ our Lord.

Dead to Sin but Alive in Christ

6 What shall we say, then? That we should continue to live in sin so that God's grace will increase? ² Certainly not! We have died to sin — how then can we go on living in it? ³ For surely you know this: when we were baptized into union with Christ Jesus, we were baptized into union with his death. ⁴ By our baptism, then, we were buried with him and shared his death, in order that, just as Christ was raised from death by the glorious power of the Father, so also we might live a new life.

⁵ For if we became one with him in dying as he did, in the same way we shall be one with him by being raised to life as he was. ⁶ For we know this: our old being has been put to death with Christ on his cross, in order that the power of the sinful self might be destroyed, so that we should no longer be the slaves of sin. ⁷ For when a person dies he is set free from the power of sin. ⁸ If we have died with Christ, we believe that we will also live with him. ⁹ For we know that Christ has been raised from death and will never die again — death has no more power over him. ¹⁰ The death he died was death to sin, once and for all; and the life he now lives is life to God. ¹¹ In the same way you are to

think of yourselves as dead to sin but alive to God in union with Christ Jesus.
[12] Sin must no longer rule in your mortal bodies, so that you obey the desires of your natural self. [13] Nor must you surrender any part of yourselves to sin, to be used for wicked purposes. Instead, give yourselves to God, as men who have been brought from death to life, and surrender your whole being to him to be used for righteous purposes. [14] For sin must not rule over you; you do not live under law but under God's grace.

Slaves of Righteousness

[15] What, then? Shall we sin, because we are not under law but under God's grace? By no means! [16] For surely you know this: when you surrender yourselves as slaves to obey someone, you are in fact the slaves of the master you obey — either of sin, which results in death, or of obedience, which results in

νεκροὺς μὲν τῇ ἁμαρτίᾳ ζῶντας δὲ τῷ θεῷ ἐν Χριστῷ Ἰησοῦ[1].

12 Μὴ οὖν βασιλευέτω ἡ ἁμαρτία ἐν τῷ θνητῷ ὑμῶν σώματι εἰς τὸ ὑπακούειν ταῖς ἐπιθυμίαις αὐτοῦ[2], **13** μηδὲ παριστάνετε τὰ μέλη ὑμῶν ὅπλα ἀδικίας τῇ ἁμαρτίᾳ, ἀλλὰ παραστήσατε ἑαυτοὺς τῷ θεῷ ὡσεὶ ἐκ νεκρῶν ζῶντας καὶ τὰ μέλη ὑμῶν ὅπλα δικαιοσύνης τῷ θεῷ· **14** ἁμαρτία γὰρ ὑμῶν οὐ κυριεύσει, οὐ γάρ ἐστε ὑπὸ νόμον ἀλλὰ ὑπὸ χάριν.

Slaves of Righteousness

15 Τί οὖν; ἁμαρτήσωμεν ὅτι οὐκ ἐσμὲν ὑπὸ νόμον ἀλλὰ ὑπὸ χάριν; μὴ γένοιτο. **16** οὐκ οἴδατε ὅτι ᾧ παριστάνετε ἑαυτοὺς δούλους εἰς ὑπακοήν, δοῦλοί ἐστε ᾧ ὑπακούετε, ἤτοι ἁμαρτίας εἰς θάνατον[3] ἢ ὑπακοῆς εἰς

---

[1] **11** {B} ἐν Χριστῷ Ἰησοῦ 𝔭⁴⁶ A B D G Ψ 629 630 1739* it^{ar,d,e,f,g,m,x,z} vg^{ww} syr^h cop^{sa} eth Tertullian Origen Hilary Basil Pelagius Augustine Cyril Theodoret Ps-Oecumenius^{comm} Theophylact ∥ ἐν Χριστῷ Ἰησοῦ τῷ κυρίῳ ἡμῶν ℵ C K P 33 81 88 (104 *omit* Ἰησοῦ) 181 326 330 436 451 614 1241 1739^c 1877 1881 1962 1984 1985 2127 2492 2495 *Byz Lect* (it^{dem} [τῷ κυρίῳ ἡμῶν]) vg^{cl} (syr^p) cop^{bo} arm Origen^{lat} Ambrosiaster Didymus Chrysostom Euthalius John-Damascus Ps-Oecumenius^{txt} Theophylact ∥ *omit* it^{r3}

[2] **12** {C} ταῖς ἐπιθυμίαις αὐτοῦ ℵ A B C* 81 326 330 436 451 630 1739 1881 1962 2127 *l*^{597} it^{ar,dc,dem,r3,t,x,z} vg syr^p cop^{sa,bo} arm eth Origen^{gr,lat} Methodius Ambrosiaster Jerome Augustine Antiochus John-Damascus ∥ αὐτῇ 𝔭⁴⁶ D G it^{d*,f,g,m} Irenaeus^{lat} Tertullian Origen^{lat} Victor-Tunis ∥ αὐτῇ ἐν ταῖς ἐπιθυμίαις αὐτοῦ C³ K P Ψ (33 αὐτοῦ *for* αὐτῇ) 88 104 181 614 629 1241 1877 1984 (1985 αὐτῶν *for* αὐτοῦ) 2492 2495 *Byz Lect* syr^h Basil Chrysostom Euthalius (Theodoret) Ps-Oecumenius Theophylact ∥ *omit* 618 it^e

[3] **16** {C} εἰς θάνατον ℵ A B C G K P Ψ 33 81 88 104 181 326 330 436 451 614 629 630 1241 1739^{mg} 1877 1881 1962 1984 1985 2127 2492 2495 *Byz Lect* it^{ar,dem,f,g,t,x,z} vg^{cl} syr^{h,pal} cop^{bo} eth Origen^{lat} Basil Chrysostom Theodoret John-Damascus ∥ *omit* D 1739* it^{d,e,r3} vg^{ww} syr^p cop^{sa} arm Origen^{lat} Ambrosiaster Ephraem

---

12 Gn 4.7   **13** παραστήσατε...δικαιοσύνης τῷ θεῷ Ro 12.1   ἐκ νεκρῶν ζῶντας Eph 2.5; 5.14   **14** ἁμαρτία...κυριεύσει 1 Jn 3.6   **15** ἁμαρτήσωμεν...γένοιτο Ro 5.17, 21 **16** Jn 8.34; 2 Pe 2.19

δικαιοσύνην; 17 χάρις δὲ τῷ θεῷ ὅτι ἦτε δοῦλοι τῆς ἁμαρτίας ὑπηκούσατε δὲ ἐκ καρδίας εἰς ὃν παρεδόθητε τύπον διδαχῆς, 18 ἐλευθερωθέντες δὲ ἀπὸ τῆς ἁμαρτίας ἐδουλώθητε τῇ δικαιοσύνῃ· 19 ἀνθρώπινον λέγω διὰ τὴν ἀσθένειαν τῆς σαρκὸς ὑμῶν. ὥσπερ γὰρ παρεστήσατε τὰ μέλη ὑμῶν δοῦλα τῇ ἀκαθαρσίᾳ καὶ τῇ ἀνομίᾳ εἰς τὴν ἀνομίαν, οὕτως νῦν παραστήσατε τὰ μέλη ὑμῶν δοῦλα τῇ δικαιοσύνῃ εἰς ἁγιασμόν. 20 ὅτε γὰρ δοῦλοι ἦτε τῆς ἁμαρτίας, ἐλεύθεροι ἦτε τῇ δικαιοσύνῃ. 21 τίνα οὖν καρπὸν εἴχετε τότε[a] ἐφ᾽ οἷς νῦν ἐπαισχύνεσθε;[a] τὸ γὰρ τέλος ἐκείνων θάνατος. 22 νυνὶ δέ,[b] ἐλευθερωθέντες ἀπὸ τῆς ἁμαρτίας δουλωθέντες δὲ τῷ θεῷ, ἔχετε τὸν καρπὸν ὑμῶν εἰς ἁγιασμόν, τὸ δὲ τέλος ζωὴν αἰώνιον. 23 τὰ γὰρ ὀψώνια τῆς ἁμαρτίας θάνατος, τὸ δὲ χάρισμα τοῦ θεοῦ ζωὴ αἰώνιος ἐν Χριστῷ Ἰησοῦ τῷ κυρίῳ ἡμῶν.

An Analogy from Marriage

7 Ἢ ἀγνοεῖτε, ἀδελφοί, γινώσκουσιν γὰρ νόμον λαλῶ, ὅτι ὁ νόμος κυριεύει τοῦ ἀνθρώπου ἐφ᾽ ὅσον χρόνον ζῇ; 2 ἡ γὰρ ὕπανδρος γυνὴ τῷ ζῶντι ἀνδρὶ δέδεται νόμῳ· ἐὰν δὲ ἀποθάνῃ ὁ ἀνήρ, κατήργηται ἀπὸ τοῦ νόμου τοῦ ἀνδρός. 3 ἄρα οὖν ζῶντος τοῦ ἀνδρὸς μοιχαλὶς χρηματίσει ἐὰν γένηται ἀνδρὶ ἑτέρῳ· ἐὰν δὲ ἀποθάνῃ ὁ ἀνήρ, ἐλευθέρα ἐστὶν ἀπὸ τοῦ νόμου, τοῦ μὴ εἶναι αὐτὴν μοιχαλίδα γενομένην ἀνδρὶ ἑτέρῳ. 4 ὥστε, ἀδελφοί μου, καὶ ὑμεῖς ἐθανατώθητε τῷ νόμῳ διὰ τοῦ σώματος τοῦ Χριστοῦ, εἰς τὸ γενέσθαι ὑμᾶς ἑτέρῳ,[a] τῷ ἐκ νεκρῶν ἐγερθέντι,[a]

[a a] **21** a none, a question: TR WH AV RV ASV RSV Jer ∥ a question, a minor: Bov Nes BF² NEB TT Zür Luth Seg
    [b] **22** b minor: WH NEB Zür Jer Seg ∥ b none: TR Bov Nes BF² AV RV ASV RSV TT Luth
[a a] **4** a minor, a minor: TR Bov Nes BF² AV RV ASV TT Zür Luth Seg ∥ a minor, a none: WH RSV Jer ∥ a none, a minor: NEB

18 ἐλευθερωθέντες...ἁμαρτίας Jn 8.32   **21** ἐφ᾽...ἐπαισχύνεσθε Eze 16.61, 63   τὸ γὰρ ...θάνατος Ro 7.5; 8.6, 13   **22** τὸ δὲ...αἰώνιον 1 Pe 1.9   **23** Ro 5.12, 15
7 4 ὑμεῖς...Χριστοῦ Col 2.14

---

being put right with God. [17] But thanks be to God! For at one time you were slaves to sin, but now you obey with all your heart the truths found in the teaching you received. [18] You were set free from sin and became the slaves of righteousness. [19] I use ordinary words because of the weakness of your natural selves. At one time you surrendered yourselves entirely as slaves to impurity and wickedness, for wicked purposes. In the same way you must now surrender yourselves entirely as slaves of righteousness, for holy purposes.

[20] When you were the slaves of sin, you were free from righteousness. [21] Well, what good did you receive from doing the things that you are ashamed of now? The result of those things is death! [22] But now you have been set free from sin and are the slaves of God; as a result your life is fully dedicated to him, and at the last you will have eternal life. [23] For sin pays its wage — death; but God's free gift is eternal life in union with Christ Jesus our Lord.

An Illustration from Marriage

7 Certainly you understand what I am about to say, my brothers, for all of you know about law: the law rules over a man only as long as he lives. [2] A married woman, for example, is bound by the law to her husband as long as he lives; but if he dies, then she is free from the law that bound her to him. [3] So then, if she lives with another man while her husband is alive, she will be called an adulteress; but if her husband dies, she is legally a free woman, and does not commit adultery if she marries another man. [4] That is the way it is with you, too, my brothers. You also have died, as far as the Law is concerned, because you are part of the body of Christ; and now you belong to him who was raised from death in order that we might live

useful lives for God. [5] For when we lived according to our human nature, the sinful desires stirred up by the Law were at work in our bodies, and produced death. [6] Now, however, we are free from the Law, because we died to that which once held us prisoners. No longer do we serve in the old way of a written law, but in the new way of the Spirit.

Law and Sin

[7] What shall we say, then? That the Law itself is sinful? Of course not! But it was the Law that made me know what sin is. For I would not have known what it is to covet if the Law had not said, "Do not covet." [8] Sin found its chance to stir up all kinds of covetousness in me by working through the commandment. For sin is a dead thing apart from law. [9] I myself was once alive apart from law; but when the commandment came, sin sprang to life, [10] and I died. And the commandment which was meant to bring life, in my case brought death. [11] For sin found its chance and deceived me by working through the commandment; by means of the commandment sin killed me.

[12] The Law itself is holy, and the commandment is holy, and right, and good. [13] Does this mean that what is good brought about my death? By no means! It was sin that did it; by using what is good, sin brought death to me in order that its true nature as sin might be revealed. And so, by means of the commandment, sin becomes even more terribly sinful.

The Two Natures in Man

[14] We know that the Law is spiritual; but I am mortal man, sold as a slave to

ἵνα καρποφορήσωμεν τῷ θεῷ. **5** ὅτε γὰρ ἦμεν ἐν τῇ σαρκί, τὰ παθήματα τῶν ἁμαρτιῶν τὰ διὰ τοῦ νόμου ἐνηργεῖτο ἐν τοῖς μέλεσιν ἡμῶν εἰς τὸ καρποφορῆσαι τῷ θανάτῳ· **6** νυνὶ δὲ κατηργήθημεν ἀπὸ τοῦ νόμου, ἀποθανόντες[1] ἐν ᾧ κατειχόμεθα, ὥστε δουλεύειν ἡμᾶς ἐν καινότητι πνεύματος καὶ οὐ παλαιότητι γράμματος.

The Problem of Indwelling Sin

7 Τί οὖν ἐροῦμεν; ὁ νόμος ἁμαρτία; μὴ γένοιτο· ἀλλὰ τὴν ἁμαρτίαν οὐκ ἔγνων εἰ μὴ διὰ νόμου, τήν τε γὰρ ἐπιθυμίαν οὐκ ᾔδειν εἰ μὴ ὁ νόμος ἔλεγεν, **Οὐκ ἐπιθυμήσεις.** **8** ἀφορμὴν δὲ λαβοῦσα ἡ ἁμαρτία διὰ τῆς ἐντολῆς κατειργάσατο ἐν ἐμοὶ πᾶσαν ἐπιθυμίαν· χωρὶς γὰρ νόμου ἁμαρτία νεκρά. **9** ἐγὼ δὲ ἔζων χωρὶς νόμου ποτέ· ἐλθούσης δὲ τῆς ἐντολῆς ἡ ἁμαρτία ἀνέζησεν, **10** ἐγὼ δὲ ἀπέθανον, καὶ εὑρέθη μοι ἡ ἐντολὴ ἡ εἰς ζωὴν αὕτη εἰς θάνατον· **11** ἡ γὰρ ἁμαρτία ἀφορμὴν λαβοῦσα διὰ τῆς ἐντολῆς ἐξηπάτησέν με καὶ δι' αὐτῆς ἀπέκτεινεν. **12** ὥστε ὁ μὲν νόμος ἅγιος, καὶ ἡ ἐντολὴ ἁγία καὶ δικαία καὶ ἀγαθή.

13 Τὸ οὖν ἀγαθὸν ἐμοὶ ἐγένετο θάνατος; μὴ γένοιτο· ἀλλὰ ἡ ἁμαρτία, ἵνα φανῇ ἁμαρτία,[b] διὰ τοῦ ἀγαθοῦ μοι κατεργαζομένη θάνατον· ἵνα γένηται καθ' ὑπερβολὴν ἁμαρτωλὸς ἡ ἁμαρτία διὰ τῆς ἐντολῆς. **14** οἴδαμεν γὰρ

---

[1] **6** {B} ἀποθανόντες ℵ A B C K P Ψ 33 81 88 104 181 326 330 436 451 614 629 630 1241 1739 1877 1881 1962 1984 1985 2127 2492 2495 *Byz Lect* it^x vg^{ww} syr^{p,h,pal} cop^{(sa),bo} goth arm eth Tertullian Origen^{lat} Basil Didymus Chrysostom Cyril Euthalius Theodoret John-Damascus // τοῦ θανάτου D G it^{ar,d,dem,e,f,g,z} vg^{el} mss^{acc. to} Origen^{lat} Ambrosiaster Pelagius Augustine

---

[b] **13** b minor: TR Bov Nes BF² AV RV ASV RSV NEB TT Zür Luth Jer Seg // b none: WH

---

5 εἰς...θανάτῳ Ro 5.21; 8.6, 13   **6** νυνὶ...νόμου Ro 8.2   ὥστε...γράμματος Ro 6.4
7 Οὐκ ἐπιθυμήσεις Ex 20.17; Dt 5.21 (4 Macc 2.5; Ro 13.9)   **8** χωρὶς...νεκρά Ro 5.13
10 ἡ ἐντολὴ...αὕτη Lv 18.5   **11** ἡ γὰρ...ἐξηπάτησέν με Gn 3.13; He 3.13   **12** 1 Tm 1.8
13 ἡ ἁμαρτία...ἐντολῆς Ro 5.20

ὅτι ὁ νόμος πνευματικός ἐστιν· ἐγὼ δὲ σάρκινός εἰμι, πεπραμένος ὑπὸ τὴν ἁμαρτίαν. **15** ὃ γὰρ κατεργάζομαι οὐ γινώσκω· οὐ γὰρ ὃ θέλω τοῦτο πράσσω, ἀλλ' ὃ μισῶ τοῦτο ποιῶ. **16** εἰ δὲ ὃ οὐ θέλω τοῦτο ποιῶ, σύμφημι τῷ νόμῳ ὅτι καλός. **17** νυνὶ δὲ οὐκέτι ἐγὼ κατεργάζομαι αὐτὸ ἀλλὰ ἡ οἰκοῦσα ἐν ἐμοὶ ἁμαρτία. **18** οἶδα γὰρ ὅτι οὐκ οἰκεῖ ἐν ἐμοί, τοῦτ' ἔστιν ἐν τῇ σαρκί μου, ἀγαθόν· τὸ γὰρ θέλειν παράκειταί μοι, τὸ δὲ κατεργάζεσθαι τὸ καλὸν οὔ[2]· **19** οὐ γὰρ ὃ θέλω ποιῶ ἀγαθόν, ἀλλὰ ὃ οὐ θέλω κακὸν τοῦτο πράσσω. **20** εἰ δὲ ὃ οὐ θέλω [ἐγὼ] τοῦτο ποιῶ, οὐκέτι ἐγὼ κατεργάζομαι αὐτὸ ἀλλὰ ἡ οἰκοῦσα ἐν ἐμοὶ ἁμαρτία. **21** Εὑρίσκω ἄρα τὸν νόμον τῷ θέλοντι ἐμοὶ ποιεῖν τὸ καλὸν ὅτι ἐμοὶ τὸ κακὸν παράκειται· **22** συνήδομαι γὰρ τῷ νόμῳ τοῦ θεοῦ κατὰ τὸν ἔσω ἄνθρωπον, **23** βλέπω δὲ ἕτερον νόμον ἐν τοῖς μέλεσίν μου ἀντιστρατευόμενον τῷ νόμῳ τοῦ νοός μου καὶ αἰχμαλωτίζοντά με ἐν[3] τῷ νόμῳ τῆς ἁμαρτίας τῷ ὄντι ἐν τοῖς μέλεσίν μου. **24** ταλαίπωρος ἐγὼ ἄνθρωπος· τίς με ῥύσεται ἐκ τοῦ σώματος τοῦ θανάτου τούτου; **25** χάρις δὲ τῷ θεῷ[4] διὰ Ἰησοῦ Χριστοῦ τοῦ κυρίου ἡμῶν. ἄρα

sin. [15] I do not understand what I do; for I don't do what I would like to do, but instead I do what I hate. [16] When I do what I don't want to do, this shows that I agree that the Law is right. [17] So I am not really the one who does this thing; rather it is the sin that lives in me. [18] I know that good does not live in me — that is, in my human nature. For even though the desire to do good is in me, I am not able to do it. [19] I don't do the good I want to do; instead, I do the evil that I do not want to do. [20] If I do what I don't want to do, this means that no longer am I the one who does it; instead, it is the sin that lives in me.

[21] So I find that this law is at work: when I want to do what is good, what is evil is the only choice I have. [22] My inner being delights in the law of God. [23] But I see a different law at work in my body — a law that fights against the law that my mind approves of. It makes me a prisoner to the law of sin which is at work in my body. [24] What an unhappy man I am! Who will rescue me from this body that is taking me to death? [25] Thanks be to God, through our Lord Jesus Christ!

---

[2] **18** {C} οὔ ℵ A B C 81 436 1739 1881 cop[sa,bo] goth arm Origen Methodius Greek mss[acc. to Augustine] Augustine Cyril ‖ οὐχ εὑρίσκω D G K P Ψ 33 88* 104 181 326 330 451 614 629 1241 1877 1962 1984 1985 2492 2495 *Byz Lect* it[ar,d,dem,e,f,g,t,x,z] vg syr[p,h] (eth) Origen[lat] Ambrosiaster Chrysostom Jerome Euthalius Theodoret John-Damascus ‖ οὐ γινώσκω 88[mg] 2127

[3] **23** {B} ἐν ℵ B D G K P Ψ 33 88 181 1877 1881 2492 *Lect* it[ar,d,dem,e,f,g,t,x,z] vg cop[sa,bo] goth Clement Origen[lat] Ambrosiaster Euthalius Theodoret ‖ omit A C 81 104 326 330 436 451 614 629 630 1241 1739 1962 1984 1985 2127 2495 *Byz* arm Methodius Caesarius-Nazianzus Chrysostom Cyril John-Damascus

[4] **25** {C} χάρις δὲ τῷ θεῷ ℵ[a] C[2] Ψ 33 81 88 104 436 2127 cop[bo] arm Origen Methodius Ephraem Didymus Cyril John-Damascus ‖ χάρις τῷ θεῷ B cop[sa] Origen Methodius Epiphanius Jerome[1/2] ‖ ἡ χάρις τοῦ θεοῦ D it[ar,d,dem,e,t,x,z] vg Irenaeus Origen[lat] Ambrosiaster Jerome[1/2] ‖ ἡ χάρις κυρίου G it[f,g] (Irenaeus[lat]) ‖ εὐχαριστῶ τῷ θεῷ ℵ* A K P 181 326 330

14 ἐγὼ…ἁμαρτίαν Ps 51.5; Jn 3.6   **18** οἶδα…ἀγαθόν Gn 6.5; 8.21   **23** ἕτερον…νοός μου Ga 5.17; Jas 4.1; 1 Pe 2.11   **25** χάρις…ἡμῶν 1 Cor 15.57

This, then, is my condition: by myself I can serve God's law only with my mind, while my human nature serves the law of sin.

Life in the Spirit

8 There is no condemnation now for those who live in union with Christ Jesus. [2] For the law of the Spirit, which brings us life in union with Christ Jesus, has set me[1] free from the law of sin and death. [3] What the Law could not do, because human nature was weak, God did. He condemned sin in human nature by sending his own Son, who came with a nature like man's sinful nature to do away with sin. [4] God did this so that the righteous demands of the Law might be fully satisfied in us who live according to the Spirit, not according to human nature. [5] For those who live as their human nature tells them to live, have their minds controlled by what human nature wants. Those who live as the Spirit tells them to live, have their minds controlled by what the Spirit wants. [6] To have your mind controlled by what human nature wants will result in death; to have your mind controlled by what the Spirit wants will result in life and peace. [7] And so a man becomes an enemy of God when his mind is controlled by what human nature wants; for he does not obey God's law, and in fact he cannot obey it. [8] Those who

---

[1] **2** me: *some mss. read* you

οὖν αὐτὸς ἐγὼ τῷ μὲν νοΐ δουλεύω νόμῳ θεοῦ, τῇ δὲ σαρκὶ νόμῳ ἁμαρτίας.

Life in the Spirit

8 Οὐδὲν ἄρα νῦν κατάκριμα τοῖς ἐν Χριστῷ Ἰησοῦ[1]. [2] ὁ γὰρ νόμος τοῦ πνεύματος τῆς ζωῆς ἐν Χριστῷ Ἰησοῦ ἠλευθέρωσέν με[2] ἀπὸ τοῦ νόμου τῆς ἁμαρτίας καὶ τοῦ θανάτου. [3] τὸ γὰρ ἀδύνατον τοῦ νόμου, ἐν ᾧ ἠσθένει διὰ τῆς σαρκός, ὁ θεὸς τὸν ἑαυτοῦ υἱὸν πέμψας ἐν ὁμοιώματι σαρκὸς ἁμαρτίας καὶ περὶ ἁμαρτίας κατέκρινεν τὴν ἁμαρτίαν ἐν τῇ σαρκί, [4] ἵνα τὸ δικαίωμα τοῦ νόμου πληρωθῇ ἐν ἡμῖν τοῖς μὴ κατὰ σάρκα περιπατοῦσιν ἀλλὰ κατὰ πνεῦμα. [5] οἱ γὰρ κατὰ σάρκα ὄντες τὰ τῆς σαρκὸς φρονοῦσιν, οἱ δὲ κατὰ πνεῦμα τὰ τοῦ πνεύματος. [6] τὸ γὰρ φρόνημα τῆς σαρκὸς θάνατος, τὸ δὲ φρόνημα τοῦ πνεύματος ζωὴ καὶ εἰρήνη· [7] διότι τὸ φρόνημα τῆς σαρκὸς ἔχθρα εἰς θεόν, τῷ γὰρ νόμῳ τοῦ θεοῦ οὐχ ὑποτάσσεται, οὐδὲ γὰρ δύναται· [8] οἱ δὲ ἐν σαρκὶ ὄντες θεῷ

---

451 614 629 630 1241 1739 1877 1881 1962 1984 1985 2492 2495 *Byz Lect* syr[p,h] goth Marcion Origen Chrysostom Euthalius Theodoret

[1] **1** {A} Ἰησοῦ ℵ* B C[2] D* G 1739 1881 it[d*,g] cop[sa,bo] eth Marcion Origen[lat] Adamantius Ambrosiaster Athanasius Augustine Cyril ∥ Ἰησοῦ μὴ κατὰ σάρκα περιπατοῦσιν (see 8.4) A D[b] Ψ 81 629 2127 it[dc,dem,f,m,x,z] vg syr[p] goth arm Victorinus-Rome Ambrosiaster[mss] Ephraem Basil Chrysostom ∥ Ἰησοῦ μὴ κατὰ σάρκα περιπατοῦσιν ἀλλὰ κατὰ πνεῦμα (see 8.4) ℵc D[c] K P 33 88 104 181 326 330 (436 *omit* μή) 451 614 630 1241 1877 1962 1984 1985 2492 2495 *Byz Lect* it[ar,evid] syr[h] Theodoret Ps-Oecumenius Theophylact

[2] **2** {C} με A C[2vid] D K P 81 88 104 181 326 330 436 451 614 629 630 1241 1739c 1877 1881 1962 1984 1985 2127 2492 2495 *Byz Lect* it[d,dem,e,x,z] vg syr[h] cop[sa] goth arm Clement Tertullian Origen[lat] Athanasius Didymus Chrysostom Theodoret John-Damascus ∥ σε ℵ B G 1739* it[ar,f,g,m] syr[p] Tertullian Ambrosiaster Ephraem Chrysostom Pelagius Augustine ∥ ἡμᾶς Ψ syr[pal] cop[bo] eth Marcion Origen Adamantius Methodius ∥ *omit* Origen

---

2 Ro 7.23, 24 ὁ γὰρ...Ἰησοῦ Ro 3.27   **3** τὸ γὰρ...σαρκός Ac 13.38; 15.10   ὁ θεὸς...ἁμαρτίας Jn 1.14; Php 2.7; He 2.17; 4.15   **4** ἡμῖν...πνεῦμα Ga 5.16, 25   **6** τὸ γὰρ...θάνατος Ro 6.21; 7.5; 8.13   **7** τὸ φρόνημα...θεόν Jas 4.4   τῷ γὰρ...δύναται Mt 12.34; Jn 8.43; 12.39

ἀρέσαι οὐ δύνανται. 9 ὑμεῖς δὲ οὐκ ἐστὲ ἐν σαρκὶ ἀλλὰ ἐν πνεύματι, εἴπερ πνεῦμα θεοῦ οἰκεῖ ἐν ὑμῖν. εἰ δέ τις πνεῦμα Χριστοῦ οὐκ ἔχει, οὗτος οὐκ ἔστιν αὐτοῦ. 10 εἰ δὲ Χριστὸς ἐν ὑμῖν, τὸ μὲν σῶμα νεκρὸν διὰ ἁμαρτίαν, τὸ δὲ πνεῦμα ζωὴ διὰ δικαιοσύνην. 11 εἰ δὲ τὸ πνεῦμα τοῦ ἐγείραντος τὸν Ἰησοῦν ἐκ νεκρῶν οἰκεῖ ἐν ὑμῖν, ὁ ἐγείρας [τὸν] Χριστὸν ἐκ νεκρῶν[3] ζῳοποιήσει καὶ τὰ θνητὰ σώματα ὑμῶν διὰ τοῦ ἐνοικοῦντος αὐτοῦ πνεύματος[4] ἐν ὑμῖν.

12 Ἄρα οὖν, ἀδελφοί, ὀφειλέται ἐσμέν, οὐ τῇ σαρκὶ τοῦ κατὰ σάρκα ζῆν· 13 εἰ γὰρ κατὰ σάρκα ζῆτε μέλλετε ἀποθνῄσκειν, εἰ δὲ πνεύματι τὰς πράξεις τοῦ σώματος θανατοῦτε ζήσεσθε. 14 ὅσοι γὰρ πνεύματι θεοῦ ἄγονται,

obey their human nature cannot please God.

⁹ But you do not live as your human nature tells you to; you live as the Spirit tells you to — if, in fact, God's Spirit lives in you. Whoever does not have the Spirit of Christ does not belong to him. ¹⁰ But if Christ lives in you, although your body is dead because of sin, yet the Spirit is life for you² because you have been put right with God. ¹¹ If the Spirit of God, who raised Jesus from death, lives in you, then he who raised Christ from death will also give life to your mortal bodies by the presence of his Spirit in you.

¹² So then, my brothers, we have an obligation, but not to live as our human nature wants us to. ¹³ For if you live according to your human nature, you are going to die; but if, by the Spirit, you kill your sinful actions, you will live. ¹⁴ Those who are led by God's Spirit

---

[3] **11** {D} τὸν Χριστὸν ἐκ νεκρῶν ℵ^u K P Ψ 33 88 181 326 330 451 614 1241 1877 1984 2492 2495 *Byz Lect* arm Methodius Severian Theodoret Ps-Athanasius Ps-Oecumenius Theophylact ∥ Χριστὸν ἐκ νεκρῶν B D° G 1985 2127 *l*^{62,1365} Valentinians Methodius Basil Epiphanius Ps-Athanasius ∥ τὸν (or omit τόν) Χριστὸν ἐκ νεκρῶν it^{f,g,m} cop^{sa} eth^{pp} Irenaeus^{lat} Tertullian Origen^{lat} Ambrosiaster Hilary ∥ Ἰησοῦν ἐκ νεκρῶν *l*⁸⁰⁹ it^z syr^h Tertullian Cyril-Jerusalem ∥ Χριστὸν Ἰησοῦν ἐκ νεκρῶν D* it^{d,e} cop^{bo} (Hippolytus) Athanasius Didymus ∥ Ἰησοῦν Χριστὸν ἐκ νεκρῶν 104 it^{dem,x} vg syr^{pal} (syr^p *our Lord Jesus Christ*) cop^{bomss} eth^{ro} Origen^{lat} Athanasius Didymus Augustine Cyril ∥ ἐκ νεκρῶν Χριστὸν Ἰησοῦν ℵ* A 630 1739 1881 Cyril John-Damascus ∥ ἐκ νεκρῶν Ἰησοῦν Χριστόν C 81 Cyril ∥ τὸν Χριστόν 103 Chrysostom ∥ *omit* ὁ ἐγείρας ἐκ νεκρῶν Χριστὸν Ἰησοῦν 436 629 it^{ar}

[4] **11** {C} τοῦ ἐνοικοῦντος αὐτοῦ πνεύματος ℵ A C P² 81 88 104 326 436 1962 2127 2495 *l*¹³⁶⁵ it^{ar?f} syr^{h,pal} cop^{sa,bo} arm eth Clement Hippolytus Methodius Athanasius Basil Cyril-Jerusalem Didymus^{gr,lat} Apollinaris Macarius Epiphanius Chrysostom^{1/2} Augustine Cyril mss^{acc. to Theodoret} Vigilius mss^{acc. to Ps-Athanasius} John-Damascus ∥ τὸ ἐνοικοῦν αὐτοῦ πνεῦμα B D G K P* Ψ 33 181 330 451 (614 αὐτῷ *for* αὐτοῦ) 629 630 1241 1739 (1877 οἰκοῦν) 1881 1984 1985 2492 *Byz Lect* it^{ar?d,dem,e,g,m,x,z} vg syr^p Irenaeus^{lat} Tertullian Origen^{gr,lat} Methodius Ambrosiaster Hilary Ephraem Chrysostom^{1/2} Severian Niceta mss^{acc. to Theodoret} Theodoret Euthalius mss^{acc. to Ps-Athanasius}

---

9 πνεῦμα...ὑμῖν 1 Cor 3.16   εἰ δέ τις...αὐτοῦ 1 Cor 12.3   **10** Ga 2.20; 1 Pe 4.6
12 Ro 6.7, 18   **13** Ga 6.8

---

² **10** the Spirit is life for you: *or* your spirit is alive

are God's sons. 15 For the Spirit that God has given you does not make you a slave and cause you to be afraid; instead, the Spirit makes you God's sons, and by the Spirit's power we cry to God, "Father! my Father!" 16 God's Spirit joins himself to our spirits to declare that we are God's children. 17 Since we are his children, we will possess the blessings he keeps for his people, and we will also possess with Christ what God has kept for him; for if we share Christ's suffering, we will also share his glory.

The Future Glory

18 I consider that what we suffer at this present time cannot be compared at all with the glory that is going to be revealed to us. 19 All of creation waits with eager longing for God to reveal his sons. 20 For creation was condemned to become worthless, not of its own will, but because God willed it to be so. Yet there was this hope: 21 that creation itself would one day be set free from its slavery to decay, and share the glorious freedom of the children of God. 22 For we know that up to the present time all of creation groans with pain like the pain of childbirth. 23 But not just creation alone; we who have the Spirit as the first of God's gifts, we also groan within ourselves as we wait for God to make us his sons and set our whole being free.

οὗτοι υἱοὶ θεοῦ εἰσιν. 15 οὐ γὰρ ἐλάβετε πνεῦμα δουλείας πάλιν εἰς φόβον, ἀλλὰ ἐλάβετε πνεῦμα υἱοθεσίας,ᵃ ἐν ᾧ κράζομεν, Αββα ὁ πατήρ·ᵃ 16 αὐτὸ τὸ πνεῦμα συμμαρτυρεῖ τῷ πνεύματι ἡμῶν ὅτι ἐσμὲν τέκνα θεοῦ. 17 εἰ δὲ τέκνα, καὶ κληρονόμοι· κληρονόμοι μὲν θεοῦ, συγκληρονόμοι δὲ Χριστοῦ, εἴπερ συμπάσχομεν ἵνα καὶ συνδοξασθῶμεν.

The Glory That is to be

18 Λογίζομαι γὰρ ὅτι οὐκ ἄξια τὰ παθήματα τοῦ νῦν καιροῦ πρὸς τὴν μέλλουσαν δόξαν ἀποκαλυφθῆναι εἰς ἡμᾶς. 19 ἡ γὰρ ἀποκαραδοκία τῆς κτίσεως τὴν ἀποκάλυψιν τῶν υἱῶν τοῦ θεοῦ ἀπεκδέχεται· 20 τῇ γὰρ ματαιότητι ἡ κτίσις ὑπετάγη,ᵇ οὐχ ἑκοῦσα ἀλλὰ διὰ τὸν ὑποτάξαντα,ᵇ ᶜἐφ' ἐλπίδιᵇ 21 ᶜὅτι⁵ καὶ αὐτὴ ἡ κτίσις ἐλευθερωθήσεται ἀπὸ τῆς δουλείας τῆς φθορᾶς εἰς τὴν ἐλευθερίαν τῆς δόξης τῶν τέκνων τοῦ θεοῦ. 22 οἴδαμεν γὰρ ὅτι πᾶσα ἡ κτίσις συστενάζει καὶ συνωδίνει ἄχρι τοῦ νῦν· 23 οὐ μόνον δέ, ἀλλὰ καὶ αὐτοὶ τὴν ἀπαρχὴν τοῦ πνεύματος ἔχοντες ἡμεῖς καὶ αὐτοὶ ἐν ἑαυτοῖς στενάζομενᵈ υἱοθεσίαν⁶ ἀπεκδεχόμενοι,ᵈ τὴν ἀπολύτρωσιν τοῦ

---

⁵ **21** {C} ὅτι 𝔭⁴⁶ A B C Dᶜ K P Ψ 33 81 88 104 181 326 436 614 629 630 1739 1877 1881 1962 1984 1985 2492 2495 *Byz Lect* syrᵖ arm Theodotusᵃᶜᶜ· ᵗᵒ Clement Origen Methodius Chrysostom Theodoret John-Damascus ∥ διότι ℵ D* G 330 451 2127 syrʰ·ᵖᵃˡ ∥ ὅτι or διότι itᵃʳ·ᵈ·ᵈᵉᵐ·ᶠ·ᵍ·ˣ·ᶻ vg copˢᵃ·ᵇᵒ ∥ *omit* 1241

⁶ **23** {C} υἱοθεσίαν ℵ A B C K P Ψ 33 81 88 104 181 326 330 436 451

ᵃ ᵃ **15** *a* minor, *a* major: TR WH Bov Nes BF² AV RV ASV NEB (TT) Zür Luth (Jer) Seg ∥ *a* major, *a* minor: WHᵐᵍ RSV

ᵇ ᵇ ᵇ **20** *b* minor, *b* minor: WH Bov Nes BF² RV ASV (NEB) TT (Zür) ∥ *b* minor, *b* none, *b* minor: AVᵉᵈ RSV ∥ *b* minor, *b* minor, *b* minor: AVᵉᵈ RVᵐᵍ ASVᵐᵍ ∥ *b* none, *b* minor, *b* minor: TR ∥ *b* dash, *b* dash, *b* none: Jer ∥ *b* dash, *b* dash, *b* major: Luth Seg

ᶜ ᶜ **20–21** *c* no number, *c* number 21: TRᵉᵈ WH Bov Nes BF² AV RV ASV RSV NEB TT Luth Jer Segᵉᵈ ∥ *c* number 21, *c* no number: TRᵉᵈ Segᵉᵈ Zür

ᵈ ᵈ **23** *d* none, *d* minor: TR Bov Nes BF² RSV TT Zür ∥ *d* minor, *d* none: WH ∥ *d* minor, *d* minor: AV RV ASV Seg ∥ *d* none, *d* none: NEB Luth Jerᵐᵍ ∥ different text: Jer

---

15 οὐ γὰρ...φόβον 2 Tm 1.7   ἐλάβετε...πατήρ Ga 4.5–6   Αββα ὁ πατήρ Mk 14.36   **16** 2 Cor 1.22   **17** εἰ...θεοῦ Ga 4.7; Re 21.7   **18** 2 Cor 4.17   **19** τὴν ἀποκάλυψιν...θεοῦ Col 3.4   **20** Gn 3.17–19; 5.29; Ec 1.2   **21** αὐτὴ...φθορᾶς 2 Pe 3.13   τῆς δόξης...θεοῦ 1 Jn 3.2   **23** 2 Cor 5.2–4; Ga 5.5

σώματος ἡμῶν. **24** τῇ γὰρ ἐλπίδι ἐσώθημεν· ἐλπὶς δὲ βλεπομένη οὐκ ἔστιν ἐλπίς· ὃ γὰρ βλέπει τίς[7] ἐλπίζει[8]; **25** εἰ δὲ ὃ οὐ βλέπομεν ἐλπίζομεν, δι᾽ ὑπομονῆς ἀπεκδεχόμεθα.

26 Ὡσαύτως δὲ καὶ τὸ πνεῦμα συναντιλαμβάνεται τῇ ἀσθενείᾳ ἡμῶν· τὸ γὰρ τί προσευξώμεθα καθὸ δεῖ οὐκ οἴδαμεν, ἀλλὰ αὐτὸ τὸ πνεῦμα ὑπερεντυγχάνει[9] στεναγμοῖς ἀλαλήτοις· **27** ὁ δὲ ἐραυνῶν τὰς καρδίας οἶδεν τί τὸ φρόνημα τοῦ πνεύματος, ὅτι κατὰ θεὸν ἐντυγχάνει ὑπὲρ ἁγίων. **28** οἴδαμεν δὲ ὅτι τοῖς ἀγαπῶσιν τὸν θεὸν πάντα συνεργεῖ[10] εἰς ἀγαθόν, τοῖς κατὰ πρόθεσιν κλητοῖς

---

24 For it was by hope that we were saved; but if we see what we hope for, then it is not really hope. For who hopes for something that he sees? 25 But if we hope for what we do not see, we wait for it with patience.

26 In the same way the Spirit also comes to help us, weak that we are. For we do not know how we ought to pray; the Spirit himself pleads with God for us, in groans that words cannot express. 27 And God, who sees into the hearts of men, knows what the thought of the Spirit is; for the Spirit pleads with God on behalf of his people, and in accordance with his will.

28 For we know that in all things God works for good with those who love him,[3] those whom he has called according to his

---

629 630 1241 1739 1877 1881 1962 1984 1985 2127 2492 2495 *Byz Lect* it[ar,dem,x,z] vg syr[p,h] cop[sa,bo] arm Origen[lat] Methodius Augustine ‖ *omit* p[46vid] D G 614 it[d,f,g,t] Ambrosiaster Ephraem Ambrose Pelagius

[7] **24** {C} τίς (*see footnote 8*) p[46] B* 1739[mg] cop[bo] Origen ‖ τις, τί B[2] D G 1877 it[ar,d,dem,f,g,t,x,z] vg syr[p] Origen[p] Cyprian Ambrosiaster Chrysostom ‖ τίς καί ℵ* (1739* τις καί) Origen ‖ τις, τί καί ℵ[c] A C K P Ψ 33 81 88 104 181 326 330 436 451 614 629 630 1241 1881 1962 1984 1985 2127 2492 2495 *Byz Lect* syr[h] cop[sa] arm (eth) Clement Chrysostom Theodoret John-Damascus

[8] **24** {C} ἐλπίζει (*see footnote 7*) p[46] ℵ[c] B C D G K P Ψ 33 81 88 104 181 326 330 436 451 614 629 630 1241 1739* 1877 1881 1962 1984 1985 2127 2492 2495 *Byz Lect* it[ar,d,dem,f,g,t,x,z] vg syr[p,h] cop[boms] arm eth Clement Origen[lat] Cyprian Ambrosiaster Chrysostom Theodoret John-Damascus ‖ ὑπομένει ℵ* A 1739[mg] cop[sa,bo] Origen Ephraem

[9] **26** {B} ὑπερεντυγχάνει p[27vid] ℵ* A B D G 81 1739 1881 2127 it[d*,g] arm Origen Epiphanius Augustine John-Damascus ‖ ὑπερεντυγχάνει ὑπὲρ ἡμῶν ℵ[c] C K P Ψ 33 88 104 181 326 330 436 451 614 (629 ἐντυγχάνει) 1241 1877 1962 1984 1985 2492 2495 *Byz Lect* it[ar,dc,dem,f,t,x,z] vg syr[p,h] cop[sa,bo] Origen[lat] Hieracus Eusebius (Ephraem) Cyril-Jerusalem Didymus[gr,lat] Epiphanius (Chrysostom) Augustine Theodoret ‖ ὑπὲρ ἡμῶν ἐντυγχάνει 630

[10] **28** {C} συνεργεῖ ℵ C D G K P Ψ 33 88 104 181 326 330 436 451 614 629 630 1241 1739 1877 1881 1962 1984 1985 2127 2492 2495 *Byz Lect* it[ar,d,dem,f,g,t,x,z] vg syr[p,h] cop[bo] arm Clement Origen[gr3/5,lat] Eusebius Lucifer Cyril-Jerusalem Chrysostom Augustine Cyril Theodoret John-Damascus ‖ συνεργεῖ ὁ θεός p[46] A B 81 cop[sa] (eth) Origen[gr2/5]

---

[3] **28** in all things God works for good with those who love him: *some mss. read* all things work for good for those who love God

---

24 τῇ γὰρ...ἔστιν ἐλπίς 2 Cor 5.7   **27** ὁ δὲ...καρδίας Ps 139.1; 1 Cor 4.5   **28** τοῖς ἀγαπῶσιν...ἀγαθόν Eph 1.11; 3.11

purpose. 29 For those whom God had already chosen he had also set apart to become like his Son, so that the Son should be the first among many brothers.

30 And so God called those whom he had set apart; not only did he call them, but he also put them right with himself; not only did he put them right with himself, but he also shared his glory with them.

God's Love in Christ Jesus

31 Faced with all this, what can we say? If God is for us, who can be against us? 32 He did not even keep back his own Son, but offered him for us all! He gave us his Son — will he not also freely give us all things? 33 Who will accuse God's chosen people? God himself declares them not guilty! 34 Can anyone, then, condemn them? Christ Jesus is the one who died, or rather, who was raised to life and is at the right side of God. He pleads with God for us! 35 Who, then, can separate us from the love of Christ? Can trouble do it, or hardship, or persecution, or hunger, or poverty, or danger, or death? 36 As the scripture says,

"For your sake we are in danger of
     death the whole day long,
We are treated like sheep that are
     going to be slaughtered."

God is for us.

οὖσιν. 29 ὅτι οὓς προέγνω, καὶ προώρισεν συμμόρφους τῆς εἰκόνος τοῦ υἱοῦ αὐτοῦ, εἰς τὸ εἶναι αὐτὸν πρωτότοκον ἐν πολλοῖς ἀδελφοῖς· 30 οὓς δὲ προώρισεν, τούτους καὶ ἐκάλεσεν· καὶ οὓς ἐκάλεσεν, τούτους καὶ ἐδικαίωσεν· οὓς δὲ ἐδικαίωσεν, τούτους καὶ ἐδόξασεν.

God's Love

31 Τί οὖν ἐροῦμεν πρὸς ταῦτα; εἰ ὁ θεὸς ὑπὲρ ἡμῶν, τίς καθ' ἡμῶν; 32 ὅς γε τοῦ ἰδίου υἱοῦ οὐκ ἐφείσατο, ἀλλὰ ὑπὲρ ἡμῶν πάντων παρέδωκεν αὐτόν, πῶς οὐχὶ καὶ σὺν αὐτῷ τὰ πάντα ἡμῖν χαρίσεται; 33 τίς ἐγκαλέσει κατὰ ἐκλεκτῶν θεοῦ; θεὸς ὁ δικαιῶν· [e] 34 τίς ὁ κατακρινῶν; Χριστὸς ['Ιησοῦς] ὁ ἀποθανών, μᾶλλον δὲ ἐγερθείς[11], ὃς καί ἐστιν ἐν δεξιᾷ τοῦ θεοῦ, ὃς καὶ ἐντυγχάνει ὑπὲρ ἡμῶν.[f] 35 τίς ἡμᾶς χωρίσει ἀπὸ τῆς ἀγάπης τοῦ Χριστοῦ[12]; θλῖψις ἢ στενοχωρία ἢ διωγμὸς ἢ λιμὸς ἢ γυμνότης ἢ κίνδυνος ἢ μάχαιρα; 36 καθὼς γέγραπται ὅτι

Ἕνεκεν σοῦ θανατούμεθα ὅλην τὴν ἡμέραν,
     ἐλογίσθημεν ὡς πρόβατα σφαγῆς.

[11] 34 {C} ἐγερθείς p[27vid,46] ℵ[a] B D G K 181 614 629 630 1241 1739 1877 1881 1984 1985 2127 2492 2495 *Byz Lect* it[ar,d,dem,e,f,g,t,x,z] vg syr[p,h] arm Irenaeus[lat] Origen[lat] Cyril ‖ ἐγερθεὶς ἐκ νεκρῶν ℵ[*,c] A C Ψ 33 81 88 104 326 330 436 451 1962 cop[sa,bo] eth Didymus Chrysostom John-Damascus

[12] 35 {B} Χριστοῦ A C D G K Ψ 33 81 88 104 181 436 614 629 630 1241 1739 1877 1881 1962 2127 2492 2495 *Byz Lect* it[ar,d,dem,e,f,g,t,x,z] vg syr[p,h] cop[bo] goth arm eth Tertullian Origen[gr2/3,lat1/7] Cyprian Methodius Eusebius[2/6] Ambrosiaster Hilary[1/2] Lucifer Athanasius Ephraem Basil[4/6] Cyril-Jerusalem Chrysostom Augustine Cyril Theodoret ‖ θεοῦ ℵ 326 330 451 1984 1985 l[598] cop[sa] Origen[gr1/3,lat4/7] Eusebius[4/6] Hilary[1/2] Ephraem Basil[2/6] Epiphanius Jerome Antiochus ‖ θεοῦ τῆς ἐν Χριστῷ 'Ιησοῦ (*see* 8.39) B Origen[lat2/7]

[e] 33 *e* statement: TR WH Bov Nes BF[2] AV RV ASV RSV NEB TT Zür Luth Jer ‖ *e* question: RV[mg] ASV[mg] (NEB[mg]) ‖ *e* exclamation: Seg
[f] 34 *f* statement: TR WH Bov Nes BF[2] AV RV ASV RSV[mg] NEB TT Zür Luth ‖ *f* question: RV[mg] ASV[mg] RSV (NEB[mg]) Jer ‖ *f* exclamation: Seg

29 πρωτότοκον...ἀδελφοῖς Col 1.18: He 1.6   31 εἰ ὁ θεὸς ὑπὲρ ἡμῶν Ps 118.6   32 ὅς ...παρέδωκεν αὐτόν Jn 3.16   33 Is 50.8   34 ὅς...δεξιᾷ τοῦ θεοῦ Ps 110.1   ὃς καὶ ἐντυγχάνει ὑπὲρ ἡμῶν 1 Jn 2.1   36 Ἕνεκεν...σφαγῆς Ps 44.22 (2 Cor 4.11)

37 ἀλλ' ἐν τούτοις πᾶσιν ὑπερνικῶμεν διὰ τοῦ ἀγαπήσαντος ἡμᾶς. 38 πέπεισμαι γὰρ ὅτι οὔτε θάνατος οὔτε ζωὴ οὔτε ἄγγελοι οὔτε ἀρχαὶ οὔτε ἐνεστῶτα οὔτε μέλλοντα οὔτε δυνάμεις 39 οὔτε ὕψωμα οὔτε βάθος οὔτε τις κτίσις ἑτέρα δυνήσεται ἡμᾶς χωρίσαι ἀπὸ τῆς ἀγάπης τοῦ θεοῦ τῆς ἐν Χριστῷ Ἰησοῦ τῷ κυρίῳ ἡμῶν.

God's Election of Israel

9 Ἀλήθειαν λέγω ἐν Χριστῷ, οὐ ψεύδομαι, συμμαρτυρούσης μοι τῆς συνειδήσεώς μου ἐν πνεύματι ἁγίῳ, 2 ὅτι λύπη μοί ἐστιν μεγάλη καὶ ἀδιάλειπτος ὀδύνη τῇ καρδίᾳ μου. 3 ηὐχόμην γὰρ ἀνάθεμα εἶναι αὐτὸς ἐγὼ ἀπὸ τοῦ Χριστοῦ ὑπὲρ τῶν ἀδελφῶν μου τῶν συγγενῶν μου κατὰ σάρκα, 4 οἵτινές εἰσιν Ἰσραηλῖται, ὧν ἡ υἱοθεσία καὶ ἡ δόξα καὶ αἱ διαθῆκαι[1] καὶ ἡ νομοθεσία καὶ ἡ λατρεία καὶ αἱ ἐπαγγελίαι, 5 ὧν οἱ πατέρες, καὶ ἐξ ὧν ὁ Χριστὸς τὸ κατὰ σάρκα·[a] ὁ ὢν ἐπὶ πάντων[a] θεὸς[a] εὐλογητὸς εἰς τοὺς αἰῶνας, ἀμήν.

6 Οὐχ οἷον δὲ ὅτι ἐκπέπτωκεν ὁ λόγος τοῦ θεοῦ. οὐ γὰρ πάντες οἱ ἐξ Ἰσραήλ, οὗτοι Ἰσραήλ· 7 οὐδ' ὅτι εἰσὶν σπέρμα Ἀβραάμ, πάντες τέκνα, ἀλλ', **Ἐν Ἰσαὰκ κληθήσεταί σοι σπέρμα.** 8 τοῦτ' ἔστιν, οὐ τὰ τέκνα τῆς

---

1 **4** {B} αἱ διαθῆκαι ℵ C K Ψ 33 81 88 104 181 326 330 436 451 614 629 630 1241 1739 1877 1881 (1962 *omit* αἱ) 1984 1985 2127 2492 2495 *Byz Lect* it[d,e,f,g,x,z] vg[ww] syr[p,h,hgr] cop[bo] goth arm Origen[lat] Ambrosiaster Hilary Epiphanius Chrysostom Augustine Euthalius Theodoret John-Damascus Photius ‖ ἡ διαθήκη 𝔭[46] B D[gr] G[gr] it[ar,vid?,c,dem] vg[cl] cop[sa,bomss] eth Origen Cyprian Chrysostom Jerome Theodore Cyril Ps-Athanasius

---

a a a **5** *a major, a none, a none:* WH[mg] Nes BF² RV[mg1] RSV TT Seg[mg] ‖ *a minor, a none, a none:* TR Bov ‖ *a minor, a minor, a none:* WH AV RV ASV NEB[mg1] Jer (Seg) ‖ *a major, a minor, a minor:* ASV[mg] NEB Zür ‖ *a minor, a none, a minor:* RSV[mg] Zür[mg] Luth ‖ *a major, a none, a none:* RV[mg2] ‖ *a minor, a major, a none:* RV[mg3] NEB[mg2]

---

37 Jn 16.33
9 3 Ex 32.32   4 Ἰσραηλῖται...υἱοθεσία Ex 4.22; Dt 7.6: 14.1-2   5 ἐξ...σάρκα Mt 1.1-16; Lk 3.23-38   ὁ ὢν ἐπὶ πάντων Jn 1.1   θεὸς...ἀμήν Ps 41.13; Ro 1.25   6 Οὐχ...θεοῦ Nu 23.19   οὐ...Ἰσραήλ Ro 2.28   7 Ἐν...σπέρμα Gn 21.12   8 Ga 4.23

---

[37] No, in all these things we have complete victory through him who loved us! [38] For I am certain that nothing can separate us from his love: neither death nor life; neither angels nor other heavenly rulers or powers; neither the present nor the future; [39] neither the world above nor the world below — there is nothing in all creation that will ever be able to separate us from the love of God which is ours through Christ Jesus our Lord.

God and His Chosen People

9 What I say is true; I belong to Christ and I do not lie. My conscience, ruled by the Holy Spirit, also assures me that I am not lying. [2] How great is my sorrow, how endless the pain in my heart for my people, my own flesh and blood! [3] For their sake I could wish that I myself were under God's curse and separated from Christ. [4] They are God's chosen people; he made them his sons and shared his glory with them; he made his covenants with them and gave them the Law; they have the true worship; they have received God's promises; [5] they are descended from the patriarchs, and Christ, as a human being, belongs to their race. May God, who rules over all, be praised for ever![1] Amen.

[6] I am not saying that the promise of God has failed; for not all the people of Israel are the chosen people of God. [7] Neither are all Abraham's descendants the children of God; for God said to Abraham, "Only the descendants of Isaac will be counted as yours." [8] This means that the children born in the natural way are not the children of God; instead, the

---

1 **5** *May God, who rules over all, be praised for ever: or* And may he, who is God ruling over all, be praised for ever

children born as a result of God's promise are regarded as the true descendants. ⁹ For God's promise was made in these words: "At the right time I will come back and Sarah will have a son."

¹⁰ And this is not all. For Rebecca's two sons had the same father, our ancestor Isaac. ¹¹⁻¹² But in order that the choice of one son might be completely the result of God's own purpose, God said to her, "The older will serve the younger." He said this before they were born, before they had done anything either good or bad; so God's choice was based on his call, and not on anything they did. ¹³ As the scripture says, "I loved Jacob, but I hated Esau."

¹⁴ What shall we say, then? That God is unjust? Not at all. ¹⁵ For he said to Moses, "I will have mercy on whom I wish, I will take pity on whom I wish." ¹⁶ So then, it does not depend on what man wants or does, but only on God's mercy. ¹⁷ For the scripture says to Pharaoh, "I made you king for this very purpose, to use you to show my power, and to make my name known in all the world." ¹⁸ So then, God has mercy on whom he wishes, and he makes stubborn whom he wishes.

God's Wrath and Mercy

¹⁹ One of you, then, will say to me, "If this is so, how can God find fault with a man? For who can resist God's will?" ²⁰ But who are you, my friend, to talk back to God? A clay pot does not ask the man who made it, "Why did you make me like this?" ²¹ After all, the man who makes the pots has the right to use the clay as he wishes, and to

σαρκὸς ταῦτα τέκνα τοῦ θεοῦ, ἀλλὰ τὰ τέκνα τῆς ἐπαγγελίας λογίζεται εἰς σπέρμα· 9 ἐπαγγελίας γὰρ ὁ λόγος οὗτος, **Κατὰ τὸν καιρὸν τοῦτον ἐλεύσομαι καὶ ἔσται τῇ Σάρρᾳ υἱός.** 10 οὐ μόνον δέ, ἀλλὰ καὶ Ῥεβέκκα ἐξ ἑνὸς κοίτην ἔχουσα, Ἰσαὰκ τοῦ πατρὸς ἡμῶν·ᵇ 11 μήπω γὰρ γεννηθέντων μηδὲ πραξάντων τι ἀγαθὸν ἢ φαῦλον,ᵇ ἵνα ἡ κατ' ἐκλογὴν πρόθεσις τοῦ θεοῦ μένῃ, 12ᶜ οὐκ ἐξ ἔργων ἀλλ' ἐκ τοῦ καλοῦντος,ᵇ ᶜἐρρέθη αὐτῇ ὅτι **Ὁ μείζων δουλεύσει τῷ ἐλάσσονι·** 13 καθὼς γέγραπται,
Τὸν Ἰακὼβ ἠγάπησα,
τὸν δὲ Ἠσαῦ ἐμίσησα.
14 Τί οὖν ἐροῦμεν; μὴ ἀδικία παρὰ τῷ θεῷ; μὴ γένοιτο· 15 τῷ Μωϋσεῖ γὰρ λέγει,
Ἐλεήσω ὃν ἂν ἐλεῶ,
καὶ οἰκτιρήσω ὃν ἂν οἰκτίρω.
16 ἄρα οὖν οὐ τοῦ θέλοντος οὐδὲ τοῦ τρέχοντος, ἀλλὰ τοῦ ἐλεῶντος θεοῦ. 17 λέγει γὰρ ἡ γραφὴ τῷ Φαραὼ ὅτι **Εἰς αὐτὸ τοῦτο ἐξήγειρά σε ὅπως ἐνδείξωμαι ἐν σοὶ τὴν δύναμίν μου, καὶ ὅπως διαγγελῇ τὸ ὄνομά μου ἐν πάσῃ τῇ γῇ.** 18 ἄρα οὖν ὃν θέλει ἐλεεῖ, ὃν δὲ θέλει σκληρύνει.

God's Wrath and Mercy

19 Ἐρεῖς μοι οὖν, Τί [οὖν] ἔτι μέμφεται; τῷ γὰρ βουλήματι αὐτοῦ τίς ἀνθέστηκεν; 20 ὦ ἄνθρωπε, μενοῦνγε σὺ τίς εἶ ὁ ἀνταποκρινόμενος τῷ θεῷ; μὴ ἐρεῖ **τὸ πλάσμα τῷ πλάσαντι, Τί με ἐποίησας οὕτως;** 21 ἢ οὐκ ἔχει ἐξουσίαν ὁ κεραμεὺς τοῦ πηλοῦ ἐκ τοῦ αὐτοῦ

ᵇ ᵇ ᵇ **10-12** b major, b minor, b minor: TR WH Bov Nes BF² RSV NEB TT Jer ∥ b parens, b minor, b parens: AV ∥ b dash, b minor, b minor: RV ASV ∥ b major, b dash, b dash: Zür Luth Seg ∥ b dash, b minor, b dash

ᶜ ᶜ **11-12** c number 12, c no number: TRᵉᵈ WH? Bov Nes BF² TT Zür Luth Jer ∥ c no number; c number 12: TRᵉᵈ WH? AV RV ASV RSV NEB Seg

9 Κατὰ...υἱός Gn 18.10, 14   **10** Gn 25.21   **12** Ὁ μείζων...ἐλάσσονι Gn 25.23   **13** Τὸν Ἰακὼβ...ἐμίσησα Mal 1.2-3   **14** μὴ ἀδικία...γένοιτο Dt 32.4   **15** Ἐλεήσω...οἰκτίρω Ex 33.19   **16** Eph 2.8   **17** Εἰς...γῇ Ex 9.16   **18** ὃν δὲ θέλει σκληρύνει Ex 4.21; 7.3; 9.12; 14.4, 17   **20** μὴ ἐρεῖ...πλάσαντι Is 29.16; 45.9; Wsd 12.12   **21** οὐκ...πηλοῦ Jr 18.6 ἐκ τοῦ...ἀτιμίαν Wsd 15.7

φυράματος ποιῆσαι ὃ μὲν εἰς τιμὴν σκεῦος, ὃ δὲ εἰς
ἀτιμίαν; 22 εἰ δὲ θέλων ὁ θεὸς ἐνδείξασθαι τὴν ὀργὴν
καὶ γνωρίσαι τὸ δυνατὸν αὐτοῦ ἤνεγκεν ἐν πολλῇ μακροθυμίᾳ σκεύη ὀργῆς κατηρτισμένα εἰς ἀπώλειαν, 23 καὶ
ἵνα² γνωρίσῃ τὸν πλοῦτον τῆς δόξης αὐτοῦ ἐπὶ σκεύη
ἐλέους, ἃ προητοίμασεν εἰς δόξαν,ᵈ 24 οὓς καὶ ἐκάλεσεν
ἡμᾶς οὐ μόνον ἐξ Ἰουδαίων ἀλλὰ καὶ ἐξ ἐθνῶν;ᵈ
25 ὡς καὶ ἐν τῷ Ὡσηὲ λέγει,

> **Καλέσω τὸν οὐ λαόν μου λαόν μου**
> **καὶ τὴν οὐκ ἠγαπημένην ἠγαπημένην·**

26 **καὶ ἔσται ἐν τῷ τόπῳ οὗ ἐρρέθη αὐτοῖς, Οὐ λαός μου**
> **ὑμεῖς,**
> **ἐκεῖ κληθήσονται υἱοὶ θεοῦ ζῶντος.**

27 Ἡσαΐας δὲ κράζει ὑπὲρ τοῦ Ἰσραήλ, Ἐὰν ᾖ ὁ ἀριθμὸς
τῶν υἱῶν Ἰσραὴλ ὡς ἡ ἄμμος τῆς θαλάσσης, τὸ ὑπό-
λειμμα σωθήσεται· 28 λόγον γὰρ συντελῶν καὶ συν-
τέμνων³ ποιήσει κύριος ἐπὶ τῆς γῆς. 29 καὶ καθὼς
προείρηκεν Ἡσαΐας,

> **Εἰ μὴ κύριος Σαβαὼθ ἐγκατέλιπεν ἡμῖν σπέρμα,**
> **ὡς Σόδομα ἂν ἐγενήθημεν**
> **καὶ ὡς Γόμορρα ἂν ὡμοιώθημεν.**

make two pots from the same lump of
clay, an expensive pot and a cheap one.
²² And the same is true of what God
has done. He wanted to show his wrath
and to make his power known. So he
was very patient in enduring those who
were the objects of his wrath, who were
ready to be destroyed. ²³ And he wanted
also to reveal his rich glory, which was
poured out on us who are the objects of
his mercy, those of us whom he has
prepared to receive his glory. ²⁴ For we
are the ones whom he called, not only
from among the Jews but also from
among the Gentiles. ²⁵ For this is what
he says in the book of Hosea:

> "The people who were not mine,
>   I will call 'My People,'
> The nation that I did not love,
>   I will call 'My Beloved.'
> ²⁶ And in the very place where they
>   were told, 'You are not my
>   people,'
> There they will be called the sons
>   of the living God."

²⁷ And Isaiah exclaims about Israel:
"Even if the people of Israel are as many
as the grains of sand by the sea, yet
only a few of them will be saved; ²⁸ for
the Lord will quickly settle his full
account with all the world." ²⁹ It is
as Isaiah had said before, "If the Lord
Almighty had not left us some descendants, we would have become like Sodom,
we would have been like Gomorrah."

---

² **23** {B} καὶ ἵνα 𝔭⁴⁶ᵛⁱᵈ ℵ A D G K P Ψ 33 81 88 104 181 330 451 614 629
630 1241 1739* 1877 1881 1962 1984 1985 2127 2492 2495 *Byz Lect* itᵈ,ᵉ,ᶠ,ᵍ,ˣ
syrᵖ,ʰ copᵇᵒᵐˢˢ eth Ambrosiaster Chrysostom Augustine Julian-Eclanumᵃᶜᶜ·
ᵗᵒ ᴬᵘᵍᵘˢᵗⁱⁿᵉ Theodoret John-Damascus // ἵνα B 326 436 1739ᵐᵍ itᵃʳ,ᶜ,ᵈᵉᵐ,ᶻ vg
copˢᵃ,ᵇᵒᵐˢˢ goth arm Origenᵍʳ,ˡᵃᵗ Fulgentius

³ **28** {A} συντέμνων 𝔭⁴⁶ᵛⁱᵈ ℵ* A B 1739 1881 (2127 συντετμημένον) syrᵖ
copˢᵃ,ᵇᵒ eth Crigen Eusebius²/³ Augustine (Theodoret) John-Damascus //
συντέμνων ἐν δικαιοσύνῃ 81 436 // συντέμνων ἐν δικαιοσύνῃ, ὅτι λόγον
συντετμημένον (see Is 10.22–23) ℵᶜ D G K P Ψ 33 88 104 181 326 330 451
614 629 630 1241 1877 1962 1984 1985 (2492 συντέμνων καὶ συντέμνων) 2495
Byz Lect itᵃʳ,ᵈ,ᵈᵉᵐ,ᵉ,ᶠ,ᵍ,ˣ,ᶻ vg syrʰ goth arm Eusebius¹/³ Ambrosiaster
Chrysostom Euthalius Ps-Oecumenius Theophylact

ᵈ ᵈ **23-24** *d* minor, *d* question: Bov Nes BF² AV RV ASV RSV TT // *d* minor, *d* dash and question:
WH // *d* minor, *d* ellipsis: Jer // *d* question, *d* minor: TR NEB Zür Seg // *d* major, *d* major: Luth

---

22 ἤνεγκεν...ὀργῆς Jr 50.25   **23** Eph 1.3–12   **25** Καλέσω...ἠγαπημένην Ho 2.23
26 Ho 1.10   **27-28** Ἐὰν...γῆς Is 10.22–23; Ho 1.10   **29** Εἰ...ὡμοιώθημεν Is 1.9

REMNANT MOTIF

Israel and the Gospel

30 What shall we say, then? This: that the Gentiles, who were not trying to put themselves right with God, were put right with him through faith; **31** while the chosen people, who were seeking a law that would put them right with God, did not find it. **32** And why not? Because what they did was not based on faith but on works. They stumbled over the "stumbling stone" **33** that the scripture speaks of:

"See, I put in Zion a stone that will
      make people stumble,
A rock on which they will trip.
But the one who believes in him will
      not be disappointed."

10 My brothers, how I wish with all my heart that my own people might be saved! How I pray to God for them! **2** For I can be a witness for them that they are deeply devoted to God. But their devotion is not based on true knowledge. **3** For they have not known the way in which God puts men right with himself, and have tried to set up

Israel and the Gospel

30 Τί οὖν ἐροῦμεν; ὅτι ἔθνη τὰ μὴ διώκοντα δικαιοσύνην κατέλαβεν δικαιοσύνην, δικαιοσύνην δὲ τὴν ἐκ
πίστεως· **31** Ἰσραὴλ δὲ διώκων νόμον δικαιοσύνης εἰς
νόμον οὐκ ἔφθασεν. **32** διὰ τί; ὅτι οὐκ ἐκ πίστεως ἀλλ᾽
ὡς ἐξ ἔργων[4]. ᵉ προσέκοψαν τῷ λίθῳ τοῦ προσκόμματος,
33 καθὼς γέγραπται,

      Ἰδοὺ τίθημι ἐν Σιὼν λίθον προσκόμματος καὶ πέτραν
            σκανδάλου,
            καὶ[5] ὁ πιστεύων ἐπ᾽ αὐτῷ οὐ καταισχυνθήσεται.

10 Ἀδελφοί, ἡ μὲν εὐδοκία τῆς ἐμῆς καρδίας καὶ ἡ
δέησις πρὸς τὸν θεὸν ὑπὲρ αὐτῶν[1] εἰς σωτηρίαν. **2** μαρτυρῶ
γὰρ αὐτοῖς ὅτι ζῆλον θεοῦ ἔχουσιν, ἀλλ᾽ οὐ κατ᾽ ἐπίγνωσιν·
3 ἀγνοοῦντες γὰρ τὴν τοῦ θεοῦ δικαιοσύνην, καὶ τὴν

---

[4] **32** {B} ἔργων 𝔭[46vid] ℵ* A B G 629 630 1739 1881 it[ar,dem,f,g,x,z] vg cop[sa,bo] Origen[gr,lat] Ambrosiaster Jerome Augustine ∥ ἔργων νόμου ℵ[c] D K P Ψ 33 81 88 104 181 326 330 436 451 614 1241 1877 1962 1984 1985 2127 2492 2495 *Byz Lect* it[d,e] syr[p,h,pal] goth arm Ephraem Chrysostom Theodore Theodoret John-Damascus

[5] **33** {B} καί ℵ A B D G 81 1881 it[d*,e,f,g] syr[p,pal] cop[sa,bo] goth eth Origen[gr,lat] Ambrosiaster Augustine Cyril John-Damascus ∥ καὶ πᾶς (*see* 10.11) K P Ψ 33 88 104 181 326 330 436 451 614 629 630 1241 1739 1877 1962 1984 1985 2127 2492 2495 *Byz Lect* it[ar,dc,dem,x,z] vg syr[h] arm Didymus Chrysostom Jerome Theodore Euthalius Theodoret

[1] **1** {A} αὐτῶν 𝔭[46] ℵ* A B D G 1739 1881 1962 2127 𝑙[60] it[d*,e,f,g] syr[p,pal] cop[sa,bo] goth (eth) Augustine Cyril John-Damascus ∥ αὐτῶν ἐστιν ℵ[c] P Ψ 33 88 2495 it[ar] syr[h] (arm αὐτῶν εἰσιν) Chrysostom ∥ *fit pro illis* it[dc,dem,x,z] vg Origen[lat] Ambrosiaster (Augustine) ∥ τοῦ Ἰσραὴλ ἐστιν K 81 104 181 326 330 436 451 614 629 630 1241 1877 1984 1985 2492 *Byz Lect* (it[p] Marcion *omit* ἐστιν) Theodoret Ps-Oecumenius Theophylact

---

ᵉ **32** *e* major: TR WH Bov Nes BF² AV RV ASV RSV NEB TT Zür Luth Jer Seg ∥ *e* minor: WH[mg] RV[mg] ASV[mg]

---

30 Ro 10.20   **31** Wsd 2.11; Ro 10.2-3   **32** τῷ λίθῳ τοῦ προσκόμματος Is 8.14
33 Ἰδού...καταισχυνθήσεται Is 28.16 (Ro 10.11; 1 Pe 2.6, 8)
10 **2** ζῆλον θεοῦ ἔχουσιν Ac 22.3   **3** Ro 9.31-32

ἰδίαν ζητοῦντες στῆσαι, τῇ δικαιοσύνῃ τοῦ θεοῦ οὐχ ὑπετάγησαν· 4 τέλος γὰρ νόμου Χριστὸς εἰς δικαιοσύνην παντὶ τῷ πιστεύοντι.

Salvation for All

5 Μωϋσῆς γὰρ γράφει τὴν δικαιοσύνην τὴν ἐκ τοῦ νόμου ὅτι[2] [a] ὁ **ποιήσας ἄνθρωπος ζήσεται ἐν αὐτῇ**[3]. 6 ἡ δὲ ἐκ πίστεως δικαιοσύνη οὕτως λέγει, **Μὴ εἴπῃς ἐν τῇ καρδίᾳ σου, Τίς ἀναβήσεται εἰς τὸν οὐρανόν;** τοῦτ᾽ ἔστιν Χριστὸν καταγαγεῖν· 7 ἤ, **Τίς καταβήσεται εἰς τὴν ἄβυσσον;** τοῦτ᾽ ἔστιν Χριστὸν ἐκ νεκρῶν ἀναγαγεῖν. 8 ἀλλὰ τί λέγει;

Ἐγγύς σου τὸ ῥῆμά ἐστιν, ἐν τῷ στόματί σου καὶ ἐν τῇ καρδίᾳ σου·

τοῦτ᾽ ἔστιν τὸ ῥῆμα τῆς πίστεως ὃ κηρύσσομεν.[b] 9 ὅτι

Salvation Is for All

5 This is what Moses wrote about being put right with God by obeying the Law: "The man who does what the Law commands will live by it." 6 But this is what is said about being put right with God through faith: "Do not say to yourself, Who will go up into heaven?" (that is, to bring Christ down). 7 "Do not say either, Who will go down into the world below?" (that is, to bring Christ up from the dead). 8 This is what it says: "God's message is near you, on your lips and in your heart" — that is, the message of faith that we preach. 9 If you declare with your lips, "Jesus is

---

[2] **5** {C} τὴν δικαιοσύνην τὴν ἐκ τοῦ νόμου ὅτι 𝔭46 (ℵc B Ψ omit τοῦ) Dc G K P 33c 88 104 181 326 330 436 451 614 629 1241 1877 1962 1985 2127 2492 2495 *Byz Lect* itar,d,e,f,g syr(p),h,palms goth arm Ambrosiaster Chrysostom Pelagius Theodoret ‖ ὅτι τὴν δικαιοσύνην τὴν ἐκ τοῦ νόμου (ℵ* omit τοῦ) (D* τῆς ἐκ) 33* 81 630 1739 1881 itdem,x,z vg syrpalms copsa,bo Origen Ambrosiastermss Cassiodorus John-Damascus ‖ τὴν δικαιοσύνην τὴν ἐκ τοῦ νόμου 1984 ‖ ὅτι τὴν δικαιοσύνην τὴν ἐκ πίστεως A ‖ ὅτι eth

[3] **5** {C} ὁ ποιήσας ἄνθρωπος ζήσεται ἐν αὐτῇ ℵ* A 81 630 1739 itdem,z vg copsa?bo? Origengr,lat John-Damascus ‖ ὁ ποιήσας ἄνθρωπος ζήσεται ἐν αὐτοῖς Dgr ‖ ὁ ποιήσας αὐτὰ ἄνθρωπος ζήσεται ἐν αὐτῇ B (33* ταῦτα) 33c 436 1881 itx ‖ ὁ ποιήσας αὐτὰ ἄνθρωπος ζήσεται ἐν αὐτοῖς 𝔭46 ℵc K P Ψ 88 104 181 326 330 451 614 629 1241 1877 1962 1985 2127 2492 2495 *Byz Lect* itd* syrh Pelagius Theodoret ‖ ὁ ποιήσας αὐτὰ ζήσεται ἐν αὐτοῖς (see Lv 18.5; Ga 3.12) G 1984 itf,g syrp Ambrosiaster Chrysostom ‖ ὁ ποιήσας αὐτὴν ἄνθρωπος ζήσεται ἐν αὐτῇ itdc,e copsa?bo? goth arm Cassiodorus

---

[a] **5** *a* indirect: Bov Jer ‖ *a* direct: TR AV NEB Luth Seg ‖ different text: WH Nes BF2 RV ASV RSV TT Zür

[b] **8** *b* major: WH Bov Nes BF2 NEB TT Zür Luth Jer Seg ‖ *b* minor: TR AV RV ASV RSV

---

4 Mt 5.17; Jn 3.18; He 8.13 **5** Lv 18.5; Ga 3.12 **6-8** Μὴ εἴπῃς...καρδίᾳ σου Dt 9.4; 30.12-14

Lord," and believe in your heart that God raised him from the dead, you will be saved. [10] For we believe in our hearts and are put right with God; we declare with our lips and are saved. [11] For the scripture says, "Whoever believes in him will not be disappointed." [12] This includes everyone, for there is no difference between Jews and Gentiles; God is the same Lord of all, and richly blesses all who call on him. [13] As the scripture says, "Everyone who calls on the name of the Lord will be saved."

[14] But how can they call on him, if they have not believed? And how can they believe, if they have not heard the message? And how can they hear, if the message is not preached? [15] And how can the message be preached, if the messengers are not sent out? As the scripture says, "How wonderful is the coming of those who bring good news!" [16] But they have not all accepted the Good News. Isaiah himself said, "Lord, who believed our message?" [17] So then, faith comes from hearing the message, and the message comes through preaching Christ.

[18] But I ask: Is it true that they did not hear the message? Of course they did — as the scripture says:

ἐὰν ὁμολογήσῃς ἐν τῷ στόματί σου κύριον Ἰησοῦν[4], καὶ πιστεύσῃς ἐν τῇ καρδίᾳ σου ὅτι ὁ θεὸς αὐτὸν ἤγειρεν ἐκ νεκρῶν, σωθήσῃ· 10 καρδίᾳ γὰρ πιστεύεται εἰς δικαιοσύνην, στόματι δὲ ὁμολογεῖται εἰς σωτηρίαν. 11 λέγει γὰρ ἡ γραφή, **Πᾶς ὁ πιστεύων ἐπ᾽ αὐτῷ οὐ καταισχυνθήσεται.** 12 οὐ γάρ ἐστιν διαστολὴ Ἰουδαίου τε καὶ Ἕλληνος, ὁ γὰρ αὐτὸς κύριος πάντων, πλουτῶν εἰς πάντας τοὺς ἐπικαλουμένους αὐτόν· 13 **Πᾶς** γὰρ **ὃς ἂν ἐπικαλέσηται τὸ ὄνομα κυρίου σωθήσεται.**

14 *Πῶς* οὖν ἐπικαλέσωνται εἰς ὃν οὐκ ἐπίστευσαν; πῶς δὲ πιστεύσωσιν οὗ οὐκ ἤκουσαν; πῶς δὲ ἀκούσωσιν χωρὶς κηρύσσοντος; 15 πῶς δὲ κηρύξωσιν ἐὰν μὴ ἀποσταλῶσιν; καθὼς γέγραπται, **Ὡς ὡραῖοι οἱ πόδες[5] τῶν εὐαγγελιζομένων ἀγαθά.** 16 Ἀλλ᾽ οὐ πάντες ὑπήκουσαν τῷ εὐαγγελίῳ· Ἠσαΐας γὰρ λέγει, **Κύριε, τίς ἐπίστευσεν τῇ ἀκοῇ ἡμῶν;** 17 ἄρα ἡ πίστις ἐξ ἀκοῆς, ἡ δὲ ἀκοὴ διὰ ῥήματος Χριστοῦ[6]. 18 ἀλλὰ λέγω, μὴ οὐκ ἤκουσαν; μενοῦνγε,

---

[4] **9** {B} ἐν τῷ στόματί σου κύριον Ἰησοῦν ℵ D G K P Ψ 33 88 104 181 330 436 451 614 629 630 1241 1739 1877 1881 1962 1984 1985 2127 2492 2495 *Byz Lect* it[(ar),d,dem,e,f,g,x,z] vg syr[p,h] goth arm Irenaeus[lat] Origen[lat] Ambrosiaster Chrysostom Theodoret John-Damascus ∥ ἐν τῷ στόματί σου κύριον Ἰησοῦν Χριστόν p[46vid] A it[t] ∥ ἐν τῷ στόματί σου ὅτι κύριος Ἰησοῦς 81 syr[pal] cop[bo] Hilary (Cyril-Jerusalem *add* Χριστός) Augustine ∥ τὸ ῥῆμα ἐν τῷ στόματί σου ὅτι κύριος Ἰησοῦς B cop[sa] Clement (Peter-Alexandria) (Cyril)

[5] **15** {A} πόδες p[46] ℵ* A B C 81 630 1739 1881 it[ar] cop[sa,bo] eth Clement Origen[gr,lat] Epiphanius Theodore Cyril Euthalius John-Damascus ∥ πόδες τῶν εὐαγγελιζομένων εἰρήνην (*see* Is 52.7) ℵ[c] D G K P Ψ 33 88 104 181 330 436 451 614 629 1241 1877 1962 1984 1985 2127 2492 2495 *Byz Lect* it[d,dem,e,f,g,x,z] vg syr[p,h] goth (arm *add* καί) Marcion Irenaeus[gr,lat] Tertullian Hilary Ambrose Chrysostom Euthalius Theodoret Ps-Cecumenius Theophylact

[6] **17** {B} Χριστοῦ p[46vid] ℵ* B C D* 81 629 1739 it[ar,d,dem,e,x,z] vg cop[sa,bo,fay] goth arm eth[ro] Origen[lat] Ambrosiaster[mss] Pelagius Augustine ∥ θεοῦ ℵ[c] A D[b,c] K P Ψ 33 88 104 181 330 436 451 614 630 1241 1877 1881 1962 1984

---

11 ὁ πιστεύων...καταισχυνθήσεται Is 28.16 (Ro 9.33) **12** οὐ...Ἕλληνος Ac 10.34; 15.9 **13** Πᾶς...σωθήσεται Jl 2.32 **15** Ὡς...ἀγαθά Is 52.7; Na 1.15; Eph 6.15 **16** Κύριε...ἡμῶν Is 53.1; Jn 12.38 **17** ἡ πίστις ἐξ ἀκοῆς Jn 17.20

Εἰς πᾶσαν τὴν γῆν ἐξῆλθεν ὁ φθόγγος αὐτῶν,
　　καὶ εἰς τὰ πέρατα τῆς οἰκουμένης τὰ ῥήματα
　　αὐτῶν.
19 ἀλλὰ λέγω, μὴ Ἰσραὴλ οὐκ ἔγνω; πρῶτος Μωϋσῆς
λέγει,
　　Ἐγὼ παραζηλώσω ὑμᾶς ἐπ᾽ οὐκ ἔθνει,
　　ἐπ᾽ ἔθνει ἀσυνέτῳ παροργιῶ ὑμᾶς.
20 Ἡσαΐας δὲ ἀποτολμᾷ καὶ λέγει,
　　Εὑρέθην [ἐν] τοῖς ἐμὲ μὴ ζητοῦσιν,
　　ἐμφανὴς ἐγενόμην τοῖς ἐμὲ μὴ ἐπερωτῶσιν.
21 πρὸς δὲ τὸν Ἰσραὴλ λέγει, Ὅλην τὴν ἡμέραν ἐξεπέ-
τασα τὰς χεῖράς μου πρὸς λαὸν ἀπειθοῦντα καὶ ἀντι-
λέγοντα.

The Remnant of Israel

11 Λέγω οὖν, μὴ ἀπώσατο ὁ θεὸς τὸν λαὸν[1] αὐτοῦ;
μὴ γένοιτο· καὶ γὰρ ἐγὼ Ἰσραηλίτης εἰμί, ἐκ σπέρματος
Ἀβραάμ, φυλῆς Βενιαμείν. 2 οὐκ ἀπώσατο ὁ θεὸς τὸν
λαὸν αὐτοῦ ὃν προέγνω. ἢ οὐκ οἴδατε ἐν Ἠλίᾳ τί λέγει
ἡ γραφή;[a] ὡς ἐντυγχάνει τῷ θεῷ κατὰ τοῦ Ἰσραήλ,[a]
3 Κύριε, τοὺς προφήτας σου ἀπέκτειναν, τὰ θυσιαστήριά
σου κατέσκαψαν, κἀγὼ ὑπελείφθην μόνος, καὶ ζητοῦσιν
τὴν ψυχήν μου.[a] 4 ἀλλὰ τί λέγει αὐτῷ ὁ χρηματισμός;

1985 2127 2492 2495 *Byz Lect* syr[p,h] eth[pp] Clement Chrysostom Theodore Ambrosiaster[ms] Theodoret Ps-Athanasius John-Damascus Sedulius-Scotus ∥ *omit* G it[f.g] Ambrosiaster Hilary Pelagius

　[1] **1** {B} τὸν λαόν ℵ A B C D P Ψ 33 81 88 104 181 330 436 451 614 629 630 1241 1739 1877 1881 1962 1984 1985 2127 2492 2495 *Byz Lect* it[ar,d,dem,e,z] vg syr[p,h] cop[sa,bo] arm Origen[lat] Eusebius Chrysostom Augustine Theodoret ∥ τὴν κληρονομίαν 𝔭[46] G it[f.g.x] goth Ambrosiaster Ambrose Pelagius

---

　[a a a] **2-3** *a* question, *a* minor, *a* major: (TR) (AV) RV ASV (NEB) ∥ *a* minor, *a* question, *a* major: WH Bov Nes BF² RSV Zür ∥ *a* minor, *a* minor, *a* question: TT Luth (Seg) ∥ *a* minor, *a* minor, *a* exclamation: Jer

---

　18 Εἰς πᾶσαν...αὐτῶν Ps 19.4　　**19** Ἐγώ...παροργιῶ ὑμᾶς Dt 32.21　　**20** Εὑρέθην... ἐπερωτῶσιν Is 65.1　　**21** Ὅλην...ἀντιλέγοντα Is 65.2
　11 1 ἐγώ...Βενιαμείν Php 3.5　　**1-2** μὴ γένοιτο...λαὸν αὐτοῦ 1 Sm 12.22; Ps 94.14
3 Κύριε...μου 1 Kgs 19.10, 14

"The sound of their voices went out
　　over all the earth,
Their words reached the very ends
　　of the world."
19 Again I ask: Did the people of Israel not know? Moses himself is the first one to answer:
　　"I will make you jealous of a people
　　　who are not a real nation,
　　I will make you angry with a nation
　　　of foolish people."
20 And Isaiah is bolder when he says:
　　"I was found by those who were not
　　　looking for me,
　　I appeared to those who were not
　　　asking for me."
21 But concerning Israel he says: "I held out my hands the whole day long to a disobedient and rebellious people."

God's Mercy on Israel

11 I ask, then: Did God reject his own people? Certainly not! I myself am an Israelite, a descendant of Abraham, a member of the tribe of Benjamin. 2 God has not rejected his people, whom he chose from the beginning. You know what the scripture says in the passage where Elijah pleads with God against Israel: 3 "Lord, they have killed your prophets and torn down your altars; I am the only one left, and they are trying to kill me." 4 What answer did God give him? "I have kept for myself seven thousand men who have not worshiped the false god Baal." [5] It is the same way now at this time: there is a small number of those whom God has chosen, because of his mercy. [6] His choice is based on his mercy, not on what they have done. For if God's choice were based on what men do, then his mercy would not be true mercy.

[7] What then? The people of Israel did not find what they were looking for. It was the small group that God chose who found it; the rest grew deaf to God's call. [8] As the scripture says, "God made them dull of heart and mind; to this very day they cannot see with their eyes or hear with their ears." [9] And David says:

"May they be caught and trapped
at their feasts,
May they fall, may they be punished!
[10] May their eyes be closed so that they
cannot see;
And make them bend under their
troubles at all times."

[11] I ask, then: When the Jews stumbled, did they fall to their ruin? By no means! Because they sinned, salvation has come to the Gentiles, to make the Jews jealous of them. [12] The sin of the Jews brought rich blessings to the world, and their spiritual poverty brought rich blessings to the Gentiles. How much greater the blessings will be, then, when the complete number of Jews is included!

Κατέλιπον ἐμαυτῷ ἑπτακισχιλίους ἄνδρας, οἵτινες οὐκ ἔκαμψαν γόνυ τῇ Βάαλ. 5 οὕτως οὖν καὶ ἐν τῷ νῦν καιρῷ λεῖμμα κατ' ἐκλογὴν χάριτος γέγονεν· 6 εἰ δὲ χάριτι, οὐκέτι ἐξ ἔργων, ἐπεὶ ἡ χάρις οὐκέτι γίνεται χάρις[2]. 7 τί οὖν; ὃ ἐπιζητεῖ Ἰσραήλ, τοῦτο οὐκ ἐπέτυχεν, ἡ δὲ ἐκλογὴ ἐπέτυχεν· οἱ δὲ λοιποὶ ἐπωρώθησαν, 8 καθὼς γέγραπται,

Ἔδωκεν αὐτοῖς ὁ θεὸς πνεῦμα κατανύξεως,
ὀφθαλμοὺς τοῦ μὴ βλέπειν
καὶ ὦτα τοῦ μὴ ἀκούειν,
ἕως τῆς σήμερον ἡμέρας.

9 καὶ Δαυὶδ λέγει,

Γενηθήτω ἡ τράπεζα αὐτῶν εἰς παγίδα καὶ εἰς θήραν
καὶ εἰς σκάνδαλον καὶ εἰς ἀνταπόδομα αὐτοῖς,
10 σκοτισθήτωσαν οἱ ὀφθαλμοὶ αὐτῶν τοῦ μὴ βλέπειν,
καὶ τὸν νῶτον αὐτῶν διὰ παντὸς σύγκαμψον.

The Salvation of the Gentiles

11 Λέγω οὖν, μὴ ἔπταισαν ἵνα πέσωσιν; μὴ γένοιτο· ἀλλὰ τῷ αὐτῶν παραπτώματι ἡ σωτηρία τοῖς ἔθνεσιν, εἰς τὸ παραζηλῶσαι αὐτούς. 12 εἰ δὲ τὸ παράπτωμα αὐτῶν πλοῦτος κόσμου καὶ τὸ ἥττημα αὐτῶν πλοῦτος ἐθνῶν, πόσῳ μᾶλλον τὸ πλήρωμα αὐτῶν.[b]

---

[2] 6 {A} χάρις p[46] ℵ* A C D G P (81 transposes: χάρις γίνεται) 629 630 1739 1881 it[ar,d,dem,e,f,g,x,z] vg cop[sa,bo] arm Origen[lat] Ambrosiaster Chrysostom[comm] Theodoret[comm] John-Damascus ∥ χάρις. εἰ δὲ ἐξ ἔργων οὐκέτι ἐστὶ χάρις 1877 ∥ χάρις. ἐπεὶ τὸ ἔργον οὐκέτι ἐστὶν ἔργον 2127 ∥ χάρις. εἰ δὲ ἐξ ἔργων οὐκέτι ἐστὶ χάρις ἐπεὶ τὸ ἔργον οὐκέτι ἐστὶν ἔργον ℵ[c] (B omit first ἐστί and read χάρις for final ἔργον) Ψ 88 104 181 330 436 451 614 1241 (1962 ἤ for ἐπεί) 1984 1985 2492 (2495 χάρις γίνεται. εἰ δὲ... οὐκέτι χάρις ἐστὶν ἐπεί) Byz Lect syr[p,h] (eth) Chrysostom[txt] Theodoret[txt] Gennadius Ps-Oecumenius Theophylact

[b] 12 b statement: WH Bov Nes BF[2] ∥ b exclamation: RSV NEB TT Luth Jer ∥ b question: TR AV RV ASV Zür Seg

---

4 Κατέλιπον...Βάαλ 1 Kgs 19.18   5 Ro 9.27   6 Ga 3.18   7 ὃ...ἐπέτυχεν Ro 9.31
8 Ἔδωκεν...ἡμέρας Dt 29.4; Is 29.10   9–10 Γενηθήτω...σύγκαμψον Ps 69.22–23; 35.8
11 τῷ αὐτῶν...ἔθνεσιν Ac 13.46   εἰς...αὐτούς Dt 32.21; Ro 10.19

13 Ὑμῖν δὲ λέγω τοῖς ἔθνεσιν. ἐφ᾽ ὅσον μὲν οὖν εἰμι ἐγὼ ἐθνῶν ἀπόστολος, τὴν διακονίαν μου δοξάζω, 14 εἴ πως παραζηλώσω μου τὴν σάρκα καὶ σώσω τινὰς ἐξ αὐτῶν. 15 εἰ γὰρ ἡ ἀποβολὴ αὐτῶν καταλλαγὴ κόσμου, τίς ἡ πρόσλημψις εἰ μὴ ζωὴ ἐκ νεκρῶν; 16 εἰ δὲ ἡ ἀπαρχὴ ἁγία, καὶ τὸ φύραμα· καὶ εἰ[3] ἡ ῥίζα ἁγία, καὶ οἱ κλάδοι.

17 Εἰ δέ τινες τῶν κλάδων ἐξεκλάσθησαν, σὺ δὲ ἀγριέλαιος ὢν ἐνεκεντρίσθης ἐν αὐτοῖς καὶ συγκοινωνὸς τῆς ῥίζης τῆς πιότητος[4] τῆς ἐλαίας ἐγένου, 18 μὴ κατακαυχῶ τῶν κλάδων· εἰ δὲ κατακαυχᾶσαι, οὐ σὺ τὴν ῥίζαν βαστάζεις ἀλλὰ ἡ ῥίζα σέ. 19 ἐρεῖς οὖν, Ἐξεκλάσθησαν κλάδοι ἵνα ἐγὼ ἐγκεντρισθῶ. 20 καλῶς· τῇ ἀπιστίᾳ ἐξεκλάσθησαν, σὺ δὲ τῇ πίστει ἕστηκας. μὴ ὑψηλὰ φρόνει, ἀλλὰ φοβοῦ· 21 εἰ γὰρ ὁ θεὸς τῶν κατὰ φύσιν κλάδων οὐκ ἐφείσατο, οὐδὲ[5] σοῦ φείσεται. 22 ἴδε οὖν χρηστότητα καὶ ἀποτομίαν θεοῦ· ἐπὶ μὲν τοὺς πεσόντας ἀποτομία, ἐπὶ δὲ σὲ χρηστότης θεοῦ, ἐὰν ἐπιμένῃς τῇ χρηστότητι, ἐπεὶ καὶ σὺ ἐκκοπήσῃ. 23 κἀκεῖνοι δέ, ἐὰν μὴ ἐπιμένωσιν τῇ ἀπιστίᾳ, ἐγκεντρισθήσονται· δυνατὸς γάρ ἐστιν ὁ θεὸς πάλιν ἐγκεντρίσαι αὐτούς.

---

[3] 16 {B} εἰ ℵ A B C D P^c Ψ 33 81 104 181 326 330 451 614 629 630 1739 1877 1984^c 2492 2495 Byz l^{598,1364} it^{ar,d,dem,x,z} vg syr^{p,h} cop^{sa,bo} goth Ephraem // omit 𝔭^{46} G P* 88 436 1241 1881 1962 1984* 1985 2127 Lect it^{f,g} arm eth Chrysostom

[4] 17 {C} τῆς ῥίζης τῆς πιότητος ℵ* B C Ψ John-Damascus // τῆς ῥίζης καὶ τῆς πιότητος ℵ^c A D^{b,c} P 33 81 88 104 181 326 330 436 451 614 629 630 1241 1739 1877 1881 1962 1984 1985 2127 2492 2495 Byz Lect it^{ar vid? dem,x,z} vg syr^{p,h} goth arm eth Origen^{lat} Chrysostom Theodoret Antiochus // τῆς πιότητος 𝔭^{46} D* G it^{d,f,g} cop^{boms,fay} Irenaeus^{lat} Aphraates Augustine // τῆς πιότητος τῆς ῥίζης cop^{sa,bo} // τῆς πιότητος καὶ τῆς ῥίζης Pelagius

[5] 21 {C} οὐδὲ ℵ A B C P 81 436 630 1739 1881 2127 cop^{sa,bo,fay} Origen^{lat} Orsisius Augustine Antiochus John-Damascus // μή πως οὐδέ 𝔭^{46} D G Ψ 33 88 104 181 326 330 451 614 629 1241 1877 1962 1984 1985 2492 2495 Byz Lect it^{ar,d,dem,f,g,x,z} vg syr^{p,h} goth arm (eth) Irenaeus^{lat} Cyprian Ambrosiaster Chrysostom Theodoret Antiochus Ps-Oecumenius Theophylact

---

16 εἰ δὲ...φύραμα Nu 15.17–21; Ne 10.37; Eze 44.30   17 Eph 2.11–19   18 οὐ...ῥίζα σέ Jn 4.22   20 μὴ ὑψηλὰ φρόνει Ro 12.16   22 Jn 15.2, 4 ἐὰν...χρηστότητι He 3.14

The Salvation of the Gentiles

[13] I am speaking now to you Gentiles: as long as I am an apostle to the Gentiles I will take pride in my work. [14] Perhaps I can make the people of my own race jealous, and so be able to save some of them. [15] For when they were rejected, the world was made friends with God. What will it be, then, when they are accepted? It will be life for the dead!

[16] If the first piece of bread is given to God, then the whole loaf is his also; and if the roots of a tree are offered to God, the branches are his also. [17] Some of the branches of the cultivated olive tree have been broken off, and the branch of a wild olive tree has been joined to it. You Gentiles are like that wild olive tree, and now you share the strength and rich life of the Jews. [18] Therefore you must not despise those who were broken off like branches. How can you be proud? You are just a branch; you don't support the root — the root supports you.

[19] But you will say, "Yes, but the branches were broken off to make room for me." [20] This is true. They were broken off because they did not believe, while you remain in place because you believe. But do not have proud thoughts about it; instead, be afraid. [21] God did not spare the Jews, who are like natural branches; do you think he will spare you? [22] Here we see how kind and how severe God is. He is severe toward those who have fallen, but kind to you — if you continue in his kindness; but if you do not, you too will be broken off. [23] And the Jews, if they abandon their unbelief, will be put back in the place where they were, for God is able to put

them back again. 24 You Gentiles are like the branch of a wild olive tree that is broken off, and then, contrary to nature, is joined to the cultivated olive tree. The Jews are like this cultivated tree; and it will be much easier, then, for God to join these broken-off branches back to their own tree.

God's Mercy on All

25 There is a secret truth, my brothers, which I want you to know. It will keep you from thinking how wise you are. It is this: the stubbornness of the people of Israel is not permanent, but will last only until the complete number of Gentiles comes to God. 26 And this is how all Israel will be saved. As the scripture says:

"The Savior will come from Zion,
He will remove all wickedness from the descendants of Jacob.
27 I will make this covenant with them,
When I take away their sins."

28 Because they reject the Good News, the Jews are God's enemies for the sake of you, the Gentiles. But because of God's choice, they are his friends for the sake of the patriarchs. 29 For God does not change his mind about whom he chooses and blesses. 30 As for you Gentiles, you disobeyed God in the past; but now you have received God's mercy because the Jews disobeyed. 31 In the same way, because of the mercy that you have received, the Jews now disobey God, in order that they also may now receive God's mercy. 32 For God has made all men prisoners of disobedience, that he might show mercy to them all.

24 εἰ γὰρ σὺ ἐκ τῆς κατὰ φύσιν ἐξεκόπης ἀγριελαίου καὶ παρὰ φύσιν ἐνεκεντρίσθης εἰς καλλιέλαιον, πόσῳ μᾶλλον οὗτοι οἱ κατὰ φύσιν ἐγκεντρισθήσονται τῇ ἰδίᾳ ἐλαίᾳ.[c]

The Restoration of Israel

25 Οὐ γὰρ θέλω ὑμᾶς ἀγνοεῖν, ἀδελφοί, τὸ μυστήριον τοῦτο, ἵνα μὴ ἦτε [ἐν] ἑαυτοῖς φρόνιμοι, ὅτι πώρωσις ἀπὸ μέρους τῷ Ἰσραὴλ γέγονεν ἄχρις οὗ τὸ πλήρωμα τῶν ἐθνῶν εἰσέλθῃ, 26 καὶ οὕτως πᾶς Ἰσραὴλ σωθήσεται· καθὼς γέγραπται,

Ἥξει ἐκ Σιὼν ὁ ῥυόμενος,
ἀποστρέψει ἀσεβείας ἀπὸ Ἰακώβ·
27 καὶ αὕτη αὐτοῖς ἡ παρ' ἐμοῦ διαθήκη,
ὅταν ἀφέλωμαι τὰς ἁμαρτίας αὐτῶν.

28 κατὰ μὲν τὸ εὐαγγέλιον ἐχθροὶ δι' ὑμᾶς, κατὰ δὲ τὴν ἐκλογὴν ἀγαπητοὶ διὰ τοὺς πατέρας· 29 ἀμεταμέλητα γὰρ τὰ χαρίσματα καὶ ἡ κλῆσις τοῦ θεοῦ. 30 ὥσπερ γὰρ ὑμεῖς ποτε ἠπειθήσατε τῷ θεῷ, νῦν δὲ ἠλεήθητε τῇ τούτων ἀπειθείᾳ, 31 οὕτως καὶ οὗτοι νῦν ἠπείθησαν τῷ ὑμετέρῳ ἐλέει ἵνα καὶ αὐτοὶ νῦν[6] ἐλεηθῶσιν· 32 συνέκλεισεν γὰρ ὁ θεὸς τοὺς πάντας[7] εἰς ἀπείθειαν ἵνα τοὺς πάντας ἐλεήσῃ.

---

6 31 {B} νῦν ℵ B Dᵍʳ*,d (𝑙⁸⁰⁹ νῦν δέ) 𝑙¹³⁶⁴ copᵇᵒ,ᶠᵃʸᵐˢ John-Damascus // ὕστερον 33 88 1962 2127 copˢᵃ,ᶠᵃʸᵐˢ // omit 𝔭⁴⁶ᵛⁱᵈ A Dᵇ,ᶜ G Ψ 81 104 181 326 330 436 451 614 629 630 1241 1739 1877 1881 1984 1985 2492 2495 Byz Lect itᵃʳ,d,dem,e,f,g,t,x,z vg syrᵖ,ʰ goth arm eth Origenˡᵃᵗ Ambrosiaster Chrysostom Theodoret

7 32 {B} τοὺς πάντας ℵ A B Dᵇ,ᶜ Ψ 33 81 88 104 181 326 330 436 451 614 629 630 1241 1739 1877 1881 1962 1984 1985 2127 2492 2495 Byz Lect syrᵖ,ʰ copˢᵃ,ᵇᵒ,ᶠᵃʸ goth arm Origenˡᵃᵗ Chrysostom Augustine Theodoret John-

c 24 c statement: WH Bov Nes BF² RSV Seg // c question: TR AV RV ASV // c exclamation: NEB TT Zür Luth Jer

25 μὴ...φρόνιμοι Ro 12.16   τὸ πλήρωμα...εἰσέλθῃ Lk 21.24; Jn 10.16   26 πᾶς Ἰσραὴλ σωθήσεται Mt 23.39   26–27 Ἥξει...διαθήκη Is 59.20–21 (Ps 14.7)   27 ὅταν...αὐτῶν Is 27.9; Jr 31.33–34   32 Ga 3.22; 1 Tm 2.4

33 ῏Ω βάθος πλούτου καὶ σοφίας καὶ γνώσεως θεοῦ·
ὡς ἀνεξεραύνητα τὰ κρίματα αὐτοῦ καὶ ἀνεξιχνίαστοι
αἱ ὁδοὶ αὐτοῦ.

34   Τίς γὰρ ἔγνω νοῦν κυρίου; [d]
        ἢ τίς σύμβουλος αὐτοῦ ἐγένετο; [d]

35   ἢ τίς προέδωκεν αὐτῷ,
        καὶ ἀνταποδοθήσεται αὐτῷ;

36 ὅτι ἐξ αὐτοῦ καὶ δι᾽ αὐτοῦ καὶ εἰς αὐτὸν τὰ πάντα·
αὐτῷ ἡ δόξα εἰς τοὺς αἰῶνας· ἀμήν.

The New Life in Christ

12 Παρακαλῶ οὖν ὑμᾶς, ἀδελφοί, διὰ τῶν οἰκτιρμῶν
τοῦ θεοῦ,[a] παραστῆσαι τὰ σώματα ὑμῶν θυσίαν ζῶσαν
ἁγίαν εὐάρεστον τῷ θεῷ, τὴν λογικὴν λατρείαν ὑμῶν·
2 καὶ μὴ συσχηματίζεσθε τῷ αἰῶνι τούτῳ, ἀλλὰ μεταμορφοῦσθε τῇ ἀνακαινώσει τοῦ νοός, εἰς τὸ δοκιμάζειν
ὑμᾶς τί τὸ θέλημα τοῦ θεοῦ,[b] τὸ ἀγαθὸν καὶ εὐάρεστον
καὶ τέλειον.

3 Λέγω γὰρ διὰ τῆς χάριτος τῆς δοθείσης μοι παντὶ
τῷ ὄντι ἐν ὑμῖν μὴ ὑπερφρονεῖν παρ᾽ ὃ δεῖ φρονεῖν, ἀλλὰ
φρονεῖν εἰς τὸ σωφρονεῖν, ἑκάστῳ ὡς ὁ θεὸς ἐμέρισεν
μέτρον πίστεως. 4 καθάπερ γὰρ ἐν ἑνὶ σώματι πολλὰ
μέλη ἔχομεν, τὰ δὲ μέλη πάντα οὐ τὴν αὐτὴν ἔχει πρᾶξιν,
5 οὕτως οἱ πολλοὶ ἓν σῶμά ἐσμεν ἐν Χριστῷ, τὸ δὲ

Damascus ∥ τὰ πάντα p[46vid] D* (G *omit* τά) it[ar,d,dem,e,f,g,t,x,z] vg (Irenaeus[gr.lat]) Ambrose

[d][d] **34** d question· d question· TR WH Bov Nes BF² AV RV ASV NEB TT Jer ∥ d minor,
d question: RSV Zür Luth Seg
[a] **1** minor: TR Bov Nes BF² AV RV ASV RSV (NEB) TT Zür Luth Jer Seg ∥ a none: WH
[b] **2** b minor: WH Bov Nes BF² RV[mg] ASV[mg] RSV NEB Zür Luth Jer Seg ∥ b none: TR AV RV
ASV RSV[mg] TT

33 ἀνεξιχνίαστοι...αὐτοῦ Is 45.15; 55.8   **34** Is 40.13; Job 15.8; Jr 23.18; 1 Cor 2.16
35 Job 41.11   **36** ἐξ...πάντα 1 Cor 8.6
12 1-2 παραστῆσαι...εὐάρεστον Ro 6.11, 13; 1 Pe 2.5   **2** μεταμορφοῦσθε...νοός
Eph 4.23   εἰς...τέλειον Eph 5.10, 17   **3** ἑκάστῳ...πίστεως 1 Cor 12.11; Eph 4.7
4 1 Cor 12.12   **5** 1 Cor 12.27; Eph 4.25

Praise to God

33 How great are God's riches! How
deep are his wisdom and knowledge!
Who can explain his decisions? Who can
understand his ways? 34 As the scripture
says:

"Who knows the mind of the Lord?
Who is able to give him advice?
35 Who has ever given him anything,
To be paid back by him?"

36 For all things were created by him,
and all things exist through him and for
him. To God be the glory for ever! Amen.

Life in God's Service

12 So then, my brothers, because of
God's many mercies to us, I make this
appeal to you: Offer yourselves as a
living sacrifice to God, dedicated to his
service and pleasing to him. This is
the true worship that you should offer.
2 Do not conform outwardly to the
standards of this world, but let God
transform you inwardly by a complete
change of your mind. Then you will be
able to know the will of God — what is
good, and is pleasing to him, and is
perfect.

3 For because of God's gracious gift
to me, I say to all of you: Do not think
of yourselves more highly than you
should. Instead, be modest in your
thinking, and each one of you judge
himself according to the amount of faith
that God has given him. 4 We have
many parts in the one body, and all
these parts have different functions. 5 In
the same way, though we are many, we
are one body in union with Christ and
we are all joined to each other as different

parts of one body. ⁶ So we are to use our different gifts in accordance with the grace that God has given us. If our gift is to preach God's message, we must do it according to the faith that we have. ⁷ If it is to serve, we must serve. If it is to teach, we must teach. ⁸ If it is to encourage others, we must do so. Whoever shares what he has with others, must do it generously; whoever has authority, must work hard; whoever shows kindness to others, must do it cheerfully.

⁹ Love must be completely sincere. Hate what is evil, hold on to what is good. ¹⁰ Love one another warmly as brothers in Christ, and be eager to show respect for one another. ¹¹ Work hard, and do not be lazy. Serve the Lord with a heart full of devotion. ¹² Let your hope keep you joyful, be patient in your troubles, and pray at all times. ¹³ Share your belongings with your needy brothers, and open your homes to strangers.

¹⁴ Ask God to bless those who persecute you; yes, ask him to bless, not to curse. ¹⁵ Rejoice with those who rejoice, weep with those who weep. ¹⁶ Show the same spirit toward all alike. Do not be proud,

καθ' εἷς ἀλλήλων μέλη. **6** ἔχοντες δὲ χαρίσματα κατὰ τὴν χάριν τὴν δοθεῖσαν ἡμῖν διάφορα, εἴτε προφητείαν κατὰ τὴν ἀναλογίαν τῆς πίστεως, **7** εἴτε διακονίαν ἐν τῇ διακονίᾳ, εἴτε ὁ διδάσκων ἐν τῇ διδασκαλίᾳ, **8** εἴτε ὁ παρακαλῶν ἐν τῇ παρακλήσει, ὁ μεταδιδοὺς ἐν ἁπλότητι, ὁ προϊστάμενος ἐν σπουδῇ, ὁ ἐλεῶν ἐν ἱλαρότητι.

Rules of the Christian Life

9 Ἡ ἀγάπη ἀνυπόκριτος. ἀποστυγοῦντες τὸ πονηρόν, κολλώμενοι τῷ ἀγαθῷ· **10** τῇ φιλαδελφίᾳ εἰς ἀλλήλους φιλόστοργοι, τῇ τιμῇ ἀλλήλους προηγούμενοι, **11** τῇ σπουδῇ μὴ ὀκνηροί, τῷ πνεύματι ζέοντες, τῷ κυρίῳ¹ δουλεύοντες, **12** τῇ ἐλπίδι χαίροντες, τῇ θλίψει ὑπομένοντες, τῇ προσευχῇ προσκαρτεροῦντες, **13** ταῖς χρείαις τῶν ἁγίων κοινωνοῦντες, τὴν φιλοξενίαν διώκοντες. **14** εὐλογεῖτε τοὺς διώκοντας², εὐλογεῖτε καὶ μὴ καταρᾶσθε. **15** χαίρειν μετὰ χαιρόντων, κλαίειν μετὰ κλαιόντων. **16** τὸ αὐτὸ εἰς ἀλλήλους φρονοῦντες, μὴ τὰ ὑψηλὰ φρονοῦντες ἀλλὰ τοῖς ταπεινοῖς συναπαγόμενοι.

---

¹ **11** {A} κυρίῳ 𝔭⁴⁶ ℵ A B Dᵇ,ᶜ P Ψ 33 81 88 104 181 326 330 436 451 614 629 630 1241 1739 1877 1881 1962 1984 1985 2127 2492 2495 *Byz Lect* itᵃʳ,ᵈᶜ,ᵈᵉᵐ, ᵉ,ᶠ,ˣ,ᶻ (itᵗ *deo*) vg syrᵖ,ʰ,ᵖᵃˡ copˢᵃ,ᵇᵒ,ᶠᵃʸ goth arm eth Theophilus Clement Origenᵍʳ,ˡᵃᵗ Greek mssᵃᶜᶜ· ᵗᵒ Origenˡᵃᵗ,ᴬᵐᵇʳᵒˢⁱᵃˢᵗᵉʳ Athanasius Basil Chrysostom Jerome Greek mssᵃᶜᶜ· ᵗᵒ ᴶᵉʳᵒᵐᵉ Theodoret Antiochus John-Damascus Ps-Oecumenius Theophylact ‖ καιρῷ D* G itᵈ*,ᵍ Origenˡᵃᵗ Latin mssᵃᶜᶜ· ᵗᵒ Origenˡᵃᵗ Cyprian Ambrosiaster Jerome Latin mssᵃᶜᶜ· ᵗᵒ ᴶᵉʳᵒᵐᵉ

² **14** {C} διώκοντας 𝔭⁴⁶ B 1739 vgʷʷ Clement Origen ‖ διώκοντας ὑμᾶς ℵ A D P Ψ 81 88 104 181 326 330 436 451 614 629 630 1241 1877 1881 1962 (1984 ἡμᾶς) 1985 2127 2492 2495 *Byz Lect* itᵈ,ᵈᵉᵐ,(ᵉ),ᵍⁱᵍ,ᵗ,ˣ,ᶻᵛⁱᵈ vgᶜˡ syrᵖ,ʰ copˢᵃ,ᵇᵒ,ᶠᵃʸ goth arm Origenˡᵃᵗ Ambrosiaster Basil Chrysostom Augustine Theodoret John-Damascus ‖ ἐχθροὺς ὑμῶν Origen

6–8 1 Cor 12.4–11; 1 Pe 4.10–11   **8** ὁ μεταδιδοὺς ἐν ἁπλότητι 2 Cor 9.7   **9** Ἡ ἀγάπη ἀνυπόκριτος 1 Tm 1.5; 1 Pe 1.22   ἀποστυγοῦντες...ἀγαθῷ Am 5.15   **10** τῇ φιλαδελφίᾳ... φιλόστοργοι 2 Pe 1.7   τῇ τιμῇ...προηγούμενοι Php 2.3   **11** τῷ πνεύματι ζέοντες Ac 18.25; Re 3.15   **12** τῇ προσευχῇ προσκαρτεροῦντες 1 Th 5.17   **13** τὴν φιλοξενίαν διώκοντες He 13.2   **14** Mt 5.44; Lk 6.28; Ac 7.60; 1 Cor 4.12   **15** κλαίειν μετὰ κλαιόντων Ps 35.13   **16** τὸ αὐτὸ...φρονοῦντες Ro 15.5

μὴ γίνεσθε φρόνιμοι παρ' ἑαυτοῖς. 17 μηδενὶ κακὸν ἀντὶ κακοῦ ἀποδιδόντες· **προνοούμενοι καλὰ ἐνώπιον πάντων ἀνθρώπων·** 18 εἰ δυνατόν, τὸ ἐξ ὑμῶν μετὰ πάντων ἀνθρώπων εἰρηνεύοντες· 19 μὴ ἑαυτοὺς ἐκδικοῦντες, ἀγαπητοί, ἀλλὰ δότε τόπον τῇ ὀργῇ, γέγραπται γάρ, Ἐμοὶ ἐκδίκησις, ἐγὼ ἀνταποδώσω, λέγει κύριος. 20 ἀλλὰ **ἐὰν πεινᾷ ὁ ἐχθρός σου, ψώμιζε αὐτόν· ἐὰν διψᾷ, πότιζε αὐτόν· τοῦτο γὰρ ποιῶν ἄνθρακας πυρὸς σωρεύσεις ἐπὶ τὴν κεφαλὴν αὐτοῦ.** 21 μὴ νικῶ ὑπὸ τοῦ κακοῦ, ἀλλὰ νίκα ἐν τῷ ἀγαθῷ τὸ κακόν.

Obedience to Rulers

13 Πᾶσα ψυχὴ ἐξουσίαις ὑπερεχούσαις ὑποτασσέσθω[1]. οὐ γὰρ ἔστιν ἐξουσία εἰ μὴ ὑπὸ θεοῦ, αἱ δὲ οὖσαι ὑπὸ θεοῦ τεταγμέναι εἰσίν· 2 ὥστε ὁ ἀντιτασσόμενος τῇ ἐξουσίᾳ τῇ τοῦ θεοῦ διαταγῇ ἀνθέστηκεν, οἱ δὲ ἀνθεστηκότες ἑαυτοῖς κρίμα λήμψονται. 3 οἱ γὰρ ἄρχοντες οὐκ εἰσὶν φόβος τῷ ἀγαθῷ ἔργῳ ἀλλὰ τῷ κακῷ. θέλεις δὲ μὴ φοβεῖσθαι τὴν ἐξουσίαν; τὸ ἀγαθὸν ποίει, καὶ ἕξεις ἔπαινον ἐξ αὐτῆς· 4 θεοῦ γὰρ διάκονός ἐστιν σοὶ εἰς τὸ ἀγαθόν. ἐὰν δὲ τὸ κακὸν ποιῇς, φοβοῦ· οὐ γὰρ εἰκῇ τὴν μάχαιραν φορεῖ· θεοῦ γὰρ διάκονός ἐστιν, ἔκδικος εἰς ὀργὴν τῷ τὸ κακὸν πράσσοντι. 5 διὸ ἀνάγκη ὑπο-

---

[1] 1 {C} πᾶσα ψυχὴ ἐξουσίαις ὑπερεχούσαις ὑποτασσέσθω ℵ A B D^{b,c} P Ψ 33 81 88 104 181 326 330 436 451 614 629 630 1241 1739 1877 1881 1962 1984 1985 2127 2492 2495 *Byz Lect* it^{de,dem,e,gue,x,z} vg syr^{p,h,pal} cop^{sa,(bo)} goth arm eth Origen^{gr,lat} Acacius Basil Didymus^{lat} Chrysostom Augustine Theodoret Gennadius Cassiodorus John-Damascus ∥ πάσαις ἐξουσίαις ὑπερεχούσαις ὑποτάσσεσθε p^{46} D* G it^{ar,d*,f,g,m,t} Irenaeus^{lat} Tertullian Ambrosiaster

16 μὴ γίνεσθε...ἑαυτοῖς Pr 3.7; Is 5.21; Ro 11.20   17 μηδενὶ...ἀποδιδόντες 1 Th 5.15 προνοούμενοι...ἀνθρώπων Pr 3.4 lxx   18 Mk 9.50; He 12.14   19 μὴ ἑαυτοὺς ἐκδικοῦντες Lv 19.18; Mt 5.39 δότε...ὀργῇ Ro 13.4; 2 Th 1.6-7 Ἐμοὶ...ἀνταποδώσω Dt 32.35 (He 10.30) 20 ἐὰν...αὐτοῦ Pr 25.21-22; Mt 5.44
13 1 Πᾶσα...ὑποτασσέσθω Tt 3.1   οὐ γὰρ...τεταγμέναι εἰσίν Pr 8.15; Jn 19.11 3 οἱ γὰρ...κακῷ 1 Pe 2.13-14; 3.13   4 ἔκδικος...πράσσοντι Ro 12.19

---

but accept humble duties.[1] Do not think of yourselves as wise.

17 If someone does evil to you, do not pay him back with evil. Try to do what all men consider to be good. 18 Do everything possible, on your part, to live at peace with all men. 19 Never take revenge, my friends, but instead let God's wrath do it. For the scripture says, "I will take revenge, I will pay back, says the Lord." 20 Instead, as the scripture says: "If your enemy is hungry, feed him; if he is thirsty, give him to drink; for by doing this you will heap burning coals on his head." 21 Do not let evil defeat you; instead, conquer evil with good.

Duties toward the State Authorities

13 Everyone must obey the state authorities; for no authority exists without God's permission, and the existing authorities have been put there by God. 2 Whoever opposes the existing authority opposes what God has ordered; and anyone who does so will bring judgment on himself. 3 For rulers are not to be feared by those who do good but by those who do evil. Would you like to be unafraid of the man in authority? Then do what is good, and he will praise you. 4 For he is God's servant working for your own good. But if you do evil, be afraid of him, for his power to punish is real. He is God's servant and carries out God's wrath on those who do evil. 5 For this reason you must obey the

---

[1] 16 accept humble duties: *or* make friends with the lowly

authorities — not just because of God's wrath, but also as a matter of conscience.

⁶ This is also the reason that you pay taxes; for the authorities are working for God when they fulfil their duties. ⁷ Pay, then, what you owe them; pay them your personal and property taxes, and show respect and honor for them all.

Duties toward One Another

⁸ Be in debt to no one — the only debt you should have is to love one another. Whoever loves his fellow man has obeyed the Law. ⁹ The commandments, "Do not commit adultery; do not murder; do not steal; do not covet" — all these, and any others besides, are summed up in the one command, "Love your neighbor as yourself." ¹⁰ Whoever loves his neighbor will never do him wrong. To love, then, is to obey the whole Law.

¹¹ You must do this, because you know what hour it is: the time has come for you to wake up from your sleep. For the moment when we will be saved is closer

τάσσεσθαι², οὐ μόνον διὰ τὴν ὀργὴν ἀλλὰ καὶ διὰ τὴν συνείδησιν. 6 διὰ τοῦτο γὰρ καὶ φόρους τελεῖτε, λειτουργοὶ γὰρ θεοῦ εἰσιν εἰς αὐτὸ τοῦτο προσκαρτεροῦντες. 7 ἀπόδοτε πᾶσιν τὰς ὀφειλάς, τῷ τὸν φόρον τὸν φόρον, τῷ τὸ τέλος τὸ τέλος, τῷ τὸν φόβον τὸν φόβον, τῷ τὴν τιμὴν τὴν τιμήν.

Brotherly Love

8 Μηδενὶ μηδὲν ὀφείλετε, εἰ μὴ τὸ ἀλλήλους ἀγαπᾶν· ὁ γὰρ ἀγαπῶν τὸν ἕτερον νόμον πεπλήρωκεν. 9 τὸ γὰρ **Οὐ μοιχεύσεις, Οὐ φονεύσεις, Οὐ κλέψεις, Οὐκ ἐπιθυμήσεις³**, καὶ εἴ τις ἑτέρα ἐντολή, ἐν τῷ λόγῳ τούτῳ ἀνακεφαλαιοῦται, [ἐν τῷ] **Ἀγαπήσεις τὸν πλησίον σου ὡς σεαυτόν.** 10 ἡ ἀγάπη τῷ πλησίον κακὸν οὐκ ἐργάζεται· πλήρωμα οὖν νόμου ἡ ἀγάπη.

The Approach of the Day of Christ

11 Καὶ τοῦτο εἰδότες τὸν καιρόν, ὅτι ὥρα ἤδη ὑμᾶς⁴ ἐξ ὕπνου ἐγερθῆναι, νῦν γὰρ ἐγγύτερον ἡμῶν ἡ σωτηρία

---

² 5 {B} ἀνάγκη ὑποτάσσεσθαι ℵ A B P Ψ 048 33 81 88 104 181 326 330 436 451 614 629 630 1241 1739 1877 1881 1962 1984 1985 2127 2492 2495 *Byz Lect* itᵃʳ,ᵈᵉᵐ,ᵗ,ˣ,ᶻᵛⁱᵈ vg syrᵖ,ʰ,ᵖᵃˡ copˢᵃ,ᵇᵒ arm eth Origenˡᵃᵗ Ambrosiasterᵐˢˢ Augustine ∥ καὶ ὑποτάσσεσθε (p⁴⁶* ὑποτάσεσθε) p⁴⁶ᶜ ∥ ὑποτάσσεσθε D G itᵈ,ᵉ,ᶠ,ᵍ,ᵍᵘᵉ,ᵐ goth Irenaeusˡᵃᵗ Ambrosiaster

³ 9 {B} οὐ κλέψεις, οὐκ ἐπιθυμήσεις p⁴⁶ A B D G 33 181 614 630 1241 1739 1877 1881 1985 2492 *Lect* itᵈ,ᵉ,ᶠ,ᵍ,ˣ vgʷʷ syrᵖ copˢᵃ goth Ambrosiaster Ambrose Augustine Cyril Theodoret John-Damascus ∥ οὐ κλέψεις 1984* Clement Origenᵍʳ,ˡᵃᵗ Adamantius ∥ οὐ κλέψεις, οὐ ψευδομαρτυρήσεις Chrysostom ∥ οὐ κλέψεις, οὐκ ἐπιθυμήσεις, οὐ ψευδομαρτυρήσεις 2495 syrʰ ∥ οὐ κλέψεις, οὐ ψευδομαρτυρήσεις, οὐκ ἐπιθυμήσεις (*see* Dt 5.19–20) ℵ (P κλεψης...ψευδομαρτυρησης...επιθυμησης) Ψ 048 81 88 104 326 330 436 451 629 1962 1984ᶜ 2127 *Byz* l⁵⁹⁷,⁵⁹⁸,⁵⁹⁹ itᵃʳ,ᶜ,ᵈᵉᵐ,ᵍⁱᵍ,ᶻ vgᶜˡ copᵇᵒ arm eth Origenˡᵃᵗ

⁴ 11 {C} ὑμᾶς ℵ* A B C P 81 326 330 (451 ὑμεῖς) 1881 1962 1984* 1985

---

7 ἀπόδοτε...φόρον Mt 22.21; Mk 12.17; Lk 20.25 8 ὁ γὰρ...πεπλήρωκεν Ga 5.14; 1 Tm 1.5 9 Οὐ μοιχεύσεις...ἐπιθυμήσεις Ex 20.13-15, 17; Dt 5.17-19, 21 (Mt 19.18) Ἀγαπήσεις... σεαυτόν Lv 19.18 (Mt 5.43; 19.19; 22.39; Mk 12.31; Lk 10.27; Ga 5.14; Jas 2.8) 10 πλήρωμα... ἀγάπη Mt 22.40 11 εἰδότες...ἐγερθῆναι Eph 5.14; 1 Th 5.6-7

ἢ ὅτε ἐπιστεύσαμεν. 12 ἡ νὺξ προέκοψεν, ἡ δὲ ἡμέρα ἤγγικεν. ἀποθώμεθα οὖν τὰ ἔργα τοῦ σκότους, ἐνδυσώμεθα δὲ τὰ ὅπλα τοῦ φωτός. 13 ὡς ἐν ἡμέρᾳ εὐσχημόνως περιπατήσωμεν, μὴ κώμοις καὶ μέθαις, μὴ κοίταις καὶ ἀσελγείαις, μὴ ἔριδι καὶ ζήλῳ· 14 ἀλλὰ ἐνδύσασθε τὸν κύριον Ἰησοῦν Χριστόν, καὶ τῆς σαρκὸς πρόνοιαν μὴ ποιεῖσθε εἰς ἐπιθυμίας.

Do Not Judge Your Brother

14 Τὸν δὲ ἀσθενοῦντα τῇ πίστει προσλαμβάνεσθε, μὴ εἰς διακρίσεις διαλογισμῶν. 2 ὃς μὲν πιστεύει φαγεῖν πάντα, ὁ δὲ ἀσθενῶν λάχανα ἐσθίει. 3 ὁ ἐσθίων τὸν μὴ ἐσθίοντα μὴ ἐξουθενείτω, ὁ δὲ μὴ ἐσθίων τὸν ἐσθίοντα μὴ κρινέτω, ὁ θεὸς γὰρ αὐτὸν προσελάβετο. 4 σὺ τίς εἶ ὁ κρίνων ἀλλότριον οἰκέτην; τῷ ἰδίῳ κυρίῳ στήκει ἢ πίπτει· σταθήσεται δέ, δυνατεῖ γὰρ ὁ κύριος[1] στῆσαι αὐτόν. 5 ὃς μὲν [γὰρ][2] κρίνει ἡμέραν παρ᾽ ἡμέραν, ὃς δὲ κρίνει πᾶσαν ἡμέραν· ἕκαστος ἐν τῷ ἰδίῳ νοῒ πληροφορείσθω. 6 ὁ φρονῶν τὴν ἡμέραν κυρίῳ φρονεῖ· καὶ

2127 2492 cop[bo] Clement Origen Chrysostom Cyril ‖ ἡμᾶς 𝔭[46vid] ℵ[c] D G Ψ 33 88 104 181 436 614 629 630 1241 1739 1877 1984[c] 2495 Byz it[ar,d,e,f,g,t,x,z] vg syr[p] cop[sa] goth arm Aphraates Chrysostom Theodoret John-Damascus ‖ omit syr[h] eth Origen[lat] Cyril

[1] 4 {A} κύριος 𝔭[46] ℵ A B C P Ψ cop[sa,bo] goth arm eth Basil Orsisius Optatus Augustine ‖ θεός (see 14.3) D G 048 33 81 88 104 181 326 330 436 451 614 629 630 1241 1739 1877[vid] 1881 1962 1984 1985 2127 2492 2495 Byz Lect it[ar,d,dem,e,f,g,x,z] vg syr[h] Origen[lat] Cyprian Ambrosiaster Ephraem Basil Chrysostom Augustine Theodoret John-Damascus ‖ κύριος αὐτοῦ syr[p]

[2] 5 {C} γὰρ ℵ* A C[2] P 104 326 2127 it[ar,d,dem,e,f,g,x,z] vg cop[bo] Ambrosiaster Basil John-Damascus ‖ omit 𝔭[46] ℵ[c] B D[gr] G[gr] Ψ 048 33 81 88 181 330 436 451 614 629 630 1241 1739 1877 1881 1962 1984 1985 2492 2495 Byz syr[p,h] cop[sa] arm eth Origen[lat] (Adamantius) Ephraem Chrysostom Augustine Theodoret

---

12 ἡ νὺξ...ἤγγικεν 1 Jn 2.8   ἀποθώμεθα...σκότους Eph 5.11   13 ὡς...μέθαις Lk 21.34; Eph 5.18   14 ἐνδύσασθε...Χριστόν Ga 3.27

14 1 Τὸν δὲ...προσλαμβάνεσθε Ro 15.7   2 Gn 1.29; 9.3   3 Col 2.16   4 σὺ...κρίνων Mt 7.11; Jas 4.11-12   5 ὃς μὲν...ἡμέραν Ga 4.10

---

now than it was when we first believed. [12] The night is nearly over, day is almost here. Let us stop doing the things that belong to the dark. Let us take up the weapons for fighting in the light. [13] Let us conduct ourselves properly, as people who live in the light of day; no orgies or drunkenness, no immorality or indecency, no fighting or jealousy. [14] But take up the weapons of the Lord Jesus Christ, and stop giving attention to your sinful nature, to satisfy its desires.

Do Not Judge Your Brother

14 Accept among you the man who is weak in the faith, but do not argue with him about his personal opinions. [2] One man's faith allows him to eat anything, but the man who is weak in the faith eats only vegetables. [3] The man who will eat anything is not to despise the man who doesn't; while the one who eats only vegetables is not to pass judgment on the one who eats anything, for God has accepted him. [4] Who are you to judge the servant of someone else? It is his own Master who will decide whether he succeeds or fails. And he will succeed, for the Lord is able to make him succeed.

[5] One man thinks that a certain day is more important than the others, while another man thinks that all days are the same. Each one should have his own mind firmly made up. [6] He who thinks highly of a certain day does it in honor of the Lord; he who eats anything does it in honor of the Lord, for he gives thanks to God for the food. He who

---

[handwritten notes]

Ch.14   Do not Judge.
Do not change another's Faith
Sin is whatever does not proceed from Faith
Conclusion in Ch 15.

14.3 God has accepted him
.4 Only God will Judge

.9 God of living & dead
10-12

13-23

.20

refuses to eat certain things does so in honor of the Lord, and he gives thanks to God. [7] For none of us lives for himself only, none of us dies for himself only; if we live, it is for the Lord that we live, [8] and if we die, it is for the Lord that we die. Whether we live or die, then, we belong to the Lord. [9] For Christ died and rose to life in order to be the Lord of the living and of the dead. [10] You, then — why do you pass judgment on your brother? And you — why do you despise your brother? All of us will stand before God, to be judged by him. [11] For the scripture says,

"As I live, says the Lord, everyone
    will kneel before me,
And everyone will declare that I
    am God."

[12] Every one of us, then, will have to give an account of himself to God.

ὁ ἐσθίων κυρίῳ ἐσθίει, εὐχαριστεῖ γὰρ τῷ θεῷ· καὶ ὁ μὴ ἐσθίων κυρίῳ οὐκ ἐσθίει, καὶ εὐχαριστεῖ τῷ θεῷ. **7** οὐδεὶς γὰρ ἡμῶν ἑαυτῷ ζῇ, καὶ οὐδεὶς ἑαυτῷ ἀποθνῄσκει· **8** ἐάν τε γὰρ ζῶμεν, τῷ κυρίῳ ζῶμεν, ἐάν τε ἀποθνῄσκωμεν, τῷ κυρίῳ ἀποθνῄσκομεν. ἐάν τε οὖν ζῶμεν ἐάν τε ἀποθνῄσκωμεν, τοῦ κυρίου ἐσμέν. **9** εἰς τοῦτο γὰρ Χριστὸς ἀπέθανεν καὶ ἔζησεν[3] ἵνα καὶ νεκρῶν καὶ ζώντων κυριεύσῃ. **10** σὺ δὲ τί κρίνεις τὸν ἀδελφόν σου; ἢ καὶ σὺ τί ἐξουθενεῖς τὸν ἀδελφόν σου; πάντες γὰρ παραστησόμεθα τῷ βήματι τοῦ θεοῦ[4]· **11** γέγραπται γάρ,

    Ζῶ ἐγώ, λέγει κύριος, ὅτι ἐμοὶ κάμψει πᾶν γόνυ,
    καὶ πᾶσα γλῶσσα ἐξομολογήσεται τῷ θεῷ.

12 ἄρα [οὖν] ἕκαστος ἡμῶν περὶ ἑαυτοῦ λόγον δώσει τῷ θεῷ[5].

---

[3] 9 {B} ἀπέθανεν καὶ ἔζησεν ℵ* A B C 1739 (1881 καὶ ἀπέθανεν) 2127 cop[sa, bo] arm eth Origen[lat] Cyril-Jerusalem Chrysostom[1/2] Cyril[3/5] Anastasius John-Damascus ‖ ἀπέθανεν καὶ ἀνέστη G it[dem, f, g, gig] vg[ol] Origen Ambrosiaster Pelagius Cyril[2/5] ‖ καὶ ἀπέθανεν καὶ ἀνέστη 629 it[do?x, (z)] vg[ww] Fulgentius ‖ καὶ ἀπέθανεν καὶ ἀνέστη καὶ ἔζησεν ℵ[c] D[b] 0209[vid] (P Ψ 326 330 451 630 1985 *omit first* καὶ) 81 104 181 436 614 1241 1877 1984 2492 2495 *Byz Lect* syr[h] Ephraem Chrysostom[1/2] Ps-Oecumenius Theophylact ‖ καὶ ἀπέθανεν καὶ ἀνέστη καὶ ἀνέζησεν 33 88 (syr[p]) Theodoret ‖ καὶ ἔζησεν καὶ ἀπέθανεν καὶ ἀνέστη it[d*, e] Irenaeus[lat] ‖ ἔζησεν καὶ ἀπέθανεν καὶ ἀνέστη D[gr*, c] (Methodius) Gaudentius ‖ ἀπέθανεν καὶ ἔζησεν καὶ ἀνέστη 1962

[4] 10 {B} θεοῦ ℵ* A B C* D G 630 1739 it[ar, d, e, f, g, x, z] vg[ww] cop[sa, bo] Origen[lat] Augustine Fulgentius John-Damascus Sedulius-Scotus ‖ Χριστοῦ (see 2 Cor 5.10) ℵ[c] C[2vid] P Ψ 048 0209[vid] 33 81 88 104 181 326 330 436 451 614 629 1241 1877 1881 1962 1984 1985 2127 2492 2495 *Byz* l[603, 1364] it[dem, gue, r1] vg[ol] syr[p, h] arm Marcion Polycarp Tertullian Origen Ambrosiaster Didymus Chrysostom Theodore Cyril Theodoret Gennadius Antiochus

[5] 12 {C} τῷ θεῷ ℵ A C D P Ψ 048 0209 33 81 88 104 181 326 330 436 451 614 629 1241 1877 1962 1985 2127 2492 2495 *Byz Lect* it[d, dem, e, gue, x, z] vg syr[p, h] cop[sa, bo] goth arm Origen[lat] Ambrosiaster Chrysostom Theodoret Antiochus John-Damascus ‖ *omit* B G 630 1739 1881 1984 l[603] it[f, g, r1] Polycarp Tertullian Cyprian Pelagius Augustine

---

    8 Lk 20.38; Ga 2.20; 1 Th 5.10   **10** πάντες...θεοῦ Mt 25.31–32; Ac 17.31; 2 Cor 5.10
    11 Ζῶ...θεῷ Is 49.18; 45.23 (Php 2.10–11)   **12** Ga 6.5

Do Not Make Your Brother Stumble

13 Μηκέτι οὖν ἀλλήλους κρίνωμεν· ἀλλὰ τοῦτο κρίνατε μᾶλλον, τὸ μὴ τιθέναι πρόσκομμα τῷ ἀδελφῷ ἢ σκάνδαλον. **14** οἶδα καὶ πέπεισμαι ἐν κυρίῳ Ἰησοῦ ὅτι οὐδὲν κοινὸν δι᾽ ἑαυτοῦ· εἰ μὴ τῷ λογιζομένῳ τι κοινὸν εἶναι, ἐκείνῳ κοινόν. **15** εἰ γὰρ διὰ βρῶμα ὁ ἀδελφός σου λυπεῖται, οὐκέτι κατὰ ἀγάπην περιπατεῖς. μὴ τῷ βρώματί σου ἐκεῖνον ἀπόλλυε ὑπὲρ οὗ Χριστὸς ἀπέθανεν. **16** μὴ βλασφημείσθω οὖν ὑμῶν[6] τὸ ἀγαθόν. **17** οὐ γάρ ἐστιν ἡ βασιλεία τοῦ θεοῦ βρῶσις καὶ πόσις, ἀλλὰ δικαιοσύνη καὶ εἰρήνη καὶ χαρὰ ἐν πνεύματι ἁγίῳ· **18** ὁ γὰρ ἐν τούτῳ δουλεύων τῷ Χριστῷ εὐάρεστος τῷ θεῷ καὶ δόκιμος τοῖς ἀνθρώποις. **19** ἄρα οὖν τὰ τῆς εἰρήνης διώκωμεν[7] καὶ τὰ τῆς οἰκοδομῆς τῆς εἰς ἀλλήλους· **20** μὴ ἕνεκεν βρώματος κατάλυε τὸ ἔργον τοῦ θεοῦ. πάντα μὲν καθαρά, ἀλλὰ κακὸν τῷ ἀνθρώπῳ τῷ διὰ προσκόμματος ἐσθίοντι. **21** καλὸν τὸ μὴ φαγεῖν κρέα μηδὲ πιεῖν οἶνον μηδὲ ἐν ᾧ ὁ ἀδελφός σου προσκόπτει[8].

Do Not Make Your Brother Fall

[13] So then, let us stop judging one another. Instead, this is what you should decide: not to do anything that would make your brother stumble, or fall into sin. [14] My union with the Lord Jesus makes me know for certain that nothing is unclean of itself; but if a man believes that something is unclean, then it becomes unclean for him. [15] If you hurt your brother because of something you eat, then you are no longer acting from love. Do not let the food that you eat ruin the man for whom Christ died! [16] Do not let what you regard as good acquire a bad name. [17] For God's Kingdom is not a matter of eating and drinking, but of the righteousness and peace and joy that the Holy Spirit gives. [18] And whoever serves Christ in this way wins God's pleasure and man's approval.

[19] So then, we must always aim at those things that bring peace, and that help strengthen one another. [20] Do not, because of food, destroy what God has done. All foods may be eaten, but it is wrong to eat anything that will cause someone else to fall into sin. [21] The right thing to do is to keep from eating meat, drinking wine, or doing anything else

[6] **16** {C} ὑμῶν ℵ A B C P 048 0209 33 81 88 104 181 326 330 436 451 614 629 630 1241 1739 1877 1881 1962 1984 1985 2127 2492 2495 *Byz* *l*[603,1364] it[f] syr[h] cop[bo] Chrysostom Theodoret ∥ ἡμῶν D G Ψ it[ar,d,dem,e,g,gue?m,rl,x,z] vg syr[p] cop[sa] goth arm Clement Origen[lat] Ambrosiaster Athanasius Augustine John-Damascus ∥ *our good and your good* cop[bomss] ∥ σου syr[pal]

[7] **19** {D} διώκωμεν C D Ψ 33 81 104 181 436 614 630 1241 1739 1877 1881 1962 2127 2492 2495 *Byz Lect* it[ar,d,dem,e,f,g,gue,m,rl,x,z] vg syr[p,h,pal] cop[sa,bo] goth Origen[lat] Ambrosiaster Chrysostom Theodoret John-Damascus ∥ διώκομεν ℵ A B G[gr] P 048 0209 88 326 330 451 629 1984 1985 *l*[507,603] arm Chrysostom

[8] **21** {C} προσκόπτει ℵ[a] A C 048 81 1739 it[rl] syr[p] cop[bo] eth Marcion Origen[gr,lat] Ephraem Augustine John-Damascus ∥ λυπεῖται ℵ* ∥ προσκόπτει ἢ ἀσθενεῖ syr[pal] ∥ λυπεῖται ἢ σκανδαλίζεται ἢ ἀσθενεῖ P ∥ προσκόπτει ἢ σκανδαλίζεται ἢ ἀσθενεῖ ℵ[c] B D G Ψ 0209[vid] 33 88 104 181 326 330 436 451 614 629 630 (1241 *transposes*: προσκόπτει ὁ ἀδελφός σου) 1877 1881 1962 2127 2492 2495 *Byz Lect* it[ar,d,demvid,e,f,g,x,z] vg syr[h] cop[sa] arm Ambrosiaster Basil Chrysostom Theodoret ∥ σκανδαλίζεται ἢ προσκόπτει ἢ ἀσθενεῖ 1984 1985 it[m] Chrysostom

14 Ac 10.15; Tt 1.15   **15** μὴ...ἀπέθανεν 1 Cor 8.11-13   **16** Tt 2.5   **19** τὰ τῆς εἰρήνης διώκωμεν Ro 12.18   τὰ τῆς οἰκοδομῆς...ἀλλήλους Ro 15.2   **21** 1 Cor 8.13

that will make your brother fall. ²² Keep what you believe about this matter, then, between yourself and God. Happy is the man who does not feel himself condemned when he does what he approves of! ²³ But if he has doubts about what he eats, God condemns him when he eats it, because his action is not based on faith. And anything that is not based on faith is sin.

Please Others, Not Yourselves

15 We who are strong in the faith ought to help the weak to carry their burdens. We should not please ourselves. ² Instead, each of us should please his brother for his own good, in order to build him up in the faith. ³ For Christ did not please himself. Instead, as the scripture says, "The insults spoken by those who insulted you have fallen on me." ⁴ For everything written in the Scriptures was written to teach us, in order that we might have hope through the patience and encouragement the Scriptures give us. ⁵ And may God, the source of patience and encouragement, enable you to have the same point of view among yourselves by following the example of Christ Jesus, ⁶ so that all of you together, with one voice, may praise the God and Father of our Lord Jesus Christ.

Paul is one of the "strong in faith"

22 σὺ πίστιν [ἣν] ἔχεις⁹ κατὰ σεαυτὸν ἔχε ἐνώπιον τοῦ θεοῦ. μακάριος ὁ μὴ κρίνων ἑαυτὸν ἐν ᾧ δοκιμάζει· 23 ὁ δὲ διακρινόμενος ἐὰν φάγῃ κατακέκριται, ὅτι οὐκ ἐκ πίστεως· πᾶν δὲ ὃ οὐκ ἐκ πίστεως ἁμαρτία ἐστίν¹⁰.

Please Your Fellow Men, Not Yourself

15 Ὀφείλομεν δὲ ἡμεῖς οἱ δυνατοὶ τὰ ἀσθενήματα τῶν ἀδυνάτων βαστάζειν, καὶ μὴ ἑαυτοῖς ἀρέσκειν. 2 ἕκαστος ἡμῶν τῷ πλησίον ἀρεσκέτω εἰς τὸ ἀγαθὸν πρὸς οἰκοδομήν· 3 καὶ γὰρ ὁ Χριστὸς οὐχ ἑαυτῷ ἤρεσεν· ἀλλὰ καθὼς γέγραπται, **Οἱ ὀνειδισμοὶ τῶν ὀνειδιζόντων σε ἐπέπεσαν ἐπ᾽ ἐμέ.** 4 ὅσα γὰρ προεγράφη, εἰς τὴν ἡμετέραν διδασκαλίαν ἐγράφη, ἵνα διὰ τῆς ὑπομονῆς καὶ διὰ τῆς παρακλήσεως τῶν γραφῶν τὴν ἐλπίδα ἔχωμεν. 5 ὁ δὲ θεὸς τῆς ὑπομονῆς καὶ τῆς παρακλήσεως δῴη ὑμῖν τὸ αὐτὸ φρονεῖν ἐν ἀλλήλοις κατὰ Χριστὸν Ἰησοῦν, 6 ἵνα ὁμοθυμαδὸν ἐν ἑνὶ στόματι δοξάζητε τὸν θεὸν καὶ πατέρα τοῦ κυρίου ἡμῶν Ἰησοῦ Χριστοῦ.

---

⁹ **22** {C} ἣν ἔχεις ℵ A B C 048 it^{ar,c,rl} Origen^lat Pelagius Augustine ∥ ἔχεις; D G P Ψ 0209^vid 81 88 104 181 326 330 436 451 614 629 630 1241 1739 1877 1881 1962 1984 1985 2127 2492 2495 *Byz Lect* it^{d,dem,e,f,g,x,z} vg syr^{p,h} cop^{sa,bo} arm eth Ambrosiaster Chrysostom Augustine Theodoret John-Damascus

¹⁰ **23** {A} ἐστίν (*see* 15.33; 16.25) ℵ B C D D^{abs1} 048 81 436 630 1739 1962 2127 it^{ar,d*,e,f,rl,x,z} vg syr^{p.pal} cop^{sa,bo} eth Clement Origen^lat Ambrosiaster ∥ ἐστίν *plus* 16.25–27 *here only* L Ψ 0209^vid 181 326 330 451 614 1241 1877 1881 1984 1985 2492 2495 *Byz Lect* it^dem syr^h mss^{acc. to Origen^lat} Chrysostom (Theodore) Cyril Theodoret John-Damascus ∥ ἐστίν *plus* 16.25–27 *both here and at* 16.25 A P 5 33 88 104 460^lat arm ∥ ἐστίν *plus* 16.25–27 *at* 15.33 *only* 𝔭⁴⁶ ∥ *omit* 16.25–27 *here and at* 16.25 F^gr (G *omits but leaves space*) 629 it^{d?(g)} Marcion^{acc. to Origen^lat} mss^{acc. to Jerome^vid}

---

23 Tt 1.15
15 **2** Ro 14.19; 1 Cor 9.19; 10.24, 33 **3** Οἱ...ἐμέ Ps 69.9 **4** Ro 4.23–24; 1 Cor 10.11

The Gospel for Jews and Gentiles Alike

7 Διὸ προσλαμβάνεσθε ἀλλήλους, καθὼς καὶ ὁ Χριστὸς προσελάβετο ὑμᾶς[1],[a] εἰς δόξαν τοῦ θεοῦ. **8** λέγω γὰρ Χριστὸν διάκονον γεγενῆσθαι περιτομῆς ὑπὲρ ἀληθείας θεοῦ, εἰς τὸ βεβαιῶσαι τὰς ἐπαγγελίας τῶν πατέρων, **9** τὰ δὲ ἔθνη ὑπὲρ ἐλέους δοξάσαι τὸν θεόν· καθὼς γέγραπται,

Διὰ τοῦτο ἐξομολογήσομαί σοι ἐν ἔθνεσιν,
καὶ τῷ ὀνόματί σου ψαλῶ.

10 καὶ πάλιν λέγει,

Εὐφράνθητε, ἔθνη, μετὰ τοῦ λαοῦ αὐτοῦ.

11 καὶ πάλιν,

Αἰνεῖτε, πάντα τὰ ἔθνη, τὸν κύριον,
καὶ ἐπαινεσάτωσαν αὐτὸν πάντες οἱ λαοί.

12 καὶ πάλιν Ἡσαΐας λέγει,

Ἔσται ἡ ῥίζα τοῦ Ἰεσσαί,
καὶ ὁ ἀνιστάμενος ἄρχειν ἐθνῶν·
ἐπ᾽ αὐτῷ ἔθνη ἐλπιοῦσιν.

13 ὁ δὲ θεὸς τῆς ἐλπίδος πληρώσαι ὑμᾶς πάσης χαρᾶς καὶ εἰρήνης ἐν τῷ πιστεύειν, εἰς τὸ περισσεύειν ὑμᾶς ἐν τῇ ἐλπίδι ἐν δυνάμει πνεύματος ἁγίου.

Paul's Missionary Commission

14 Πέπεισμαι δέ, ἀδελφοί μου, καὶ αὐτὸς ἐγὼ περὶ ὑμῶν, ὅτι καὶ αὐτοὶ μεστοί ἐστε ἀγαθωσύνης, πεπληρωμένοι πάσης [τῆς] γνώσεως, δυνάμενοι καὶ ἀλλήλους

The Gospel to the Gentiles

[7] Accept one another, then, for the glory of God, as Christ has accepted you. [8] For I tell you that Christ became a servant of the Jews to show that God is faithful, to make God's promises to the patriarchs come true, [9] and also to enable the Gentiles to praise God for his mercy. As the scripture says,

"Therefore I will give thanks to you among the Gentiles,
I will sing praises to your name."

[10] Again it says,

"Rejoice, Gentiles, with God's chosen people!"

[11] And again,

"Praise the Lord, all Gentiles,
Praise him greatly, all peoples!"

[12] And again, Isaiah says,

"A descendant of Jesse will come;
He will be raised to rule the Gentiles,
And they will put their hope in him."

[13] May God, the source of hope, fill you with all joy and peace by means of your faith in him, so that your hope will continue to grow by the power of the Holy Spirit.

Paul's Reason for Writing So Boldly

[14] My brothers: I myself feel sure that you are full of goodness, that you are filled with all knowledge and are able to

---

[1] **7** {B} ὑμᾶς א A C Dᵇ·ᶜ G Ψ 33 81 88 181 326 330 436 451 630 1241 1739 1881 1962 2127ᶜ 2492ᶜ 2495 *Byz Lect* itᵈᶜ,ᵈᵉᵐ,ᵉ,f,g,gue,m,x,z vg syrᵖ·ʰ copᵇᵒ goth arm eth Origenˡᵃᵗ Ambrosiaster Chrysostom ∥ ἡμᾶς B D* P 048 104 614 629 1877 1984 1985 2127* 2492* *l*⁵⁹⁷ itᵃʳ·ᵈ*·ʳˡ copˢᵃ Theodoret John-Damascus

[a] **7** *a minor:* WH AVᵉᵈ RV ASV RSV NEB Zür Seg ∥ *a none:* TR Bov Nes BF² AVᵉᵈ TT Luth Jer

7 προσλαμβάνεσθε ἀλλήλους Ro 14.1   **8** Χριστὸν...θεοῦ Mt 15.24   τὰς ἐπαγγελίας τῶν πατέρων Mic 7.20; Ac 3.25   **9** τὰ δὲ...θεόν Ro 11.30   Διὰ...ψαλῶ Ps 18.49 (2 Sm 22.50)   **10** Εὐφράνθητε...αὐτοῦ Dt 32.43   **11** Αἰνεῖτε...λαοί Ps 117.1   **12** Ἔσται...ἐλπιοῦσιν Is 11.10; Re 5.5

teach one another. ¹⁵ But in this letter
I have been quite bold about certain
subjects of which I have reminded you.
I have been bold because of the privilege
God has given me ¹⁶ of being a servant
of Christ Jesus to work for the Gentiles.
I serve as a priest in preaching the Good
News from God, in order that the Gentiles may be an offering acceptable to
God, dedicated to him by the Holy
Spirit. ¹⁷ In union with Christ Jesus,
then, I can be proud of my service for
God. ¹⁸ I will be bold and speak only of
what Christ has done through me to
lead the Gentiles to obey God, by means
of words and deeds, ¹⁹ by the power of
signs and miracles, and by the power of
the Spirit. And so, in traveling all the
way from Jerusalem to Illyricum, I have
proclaimed fully the Good News about
Christ. ²⁰ My ambition has always been
to proclaim the Good News in places
where Christ has not been heard of, so as
not to build on the foundation laid by
someone else. ²¹ As the scripture says,
"Those who were not told about
    him will see,
And those who have not heard will
    understand."

Paul's Plan to Visit Rome

²² For this reason I have been prevented
many times from coming to you. ²³ But
now that I have finished my work in these
regions, and since I have been wanting
for so many years to come to see you,

νουθετεῖν. 15 τολμηρότερον δὲ ἔγραψα ὑμῖν ἀπὸ μέρους,ᵇ
ὡς ἐπαναμιμνῄσκων ὑμᾶςᵇ διὰ τὴν χάριν τὴν δοθεῖσάν μοι
ὑπὸ τοῦ θεοῦ 16 εἰς τὸ εἶναί με λειτουργὸν Χριστοῦ Ἰησοῦ
εἰς τὰ ἔθνη, ἱερουργοῦντα τὸ εὐαγγέλιον τοῦ θεοῦ, ἵνα
γένηται ἡ προσφορὰ τῶν ἐθνῶν εὐπρόσδεκτος, ἡγιασμένη
ἐν πνεύματι ἁγίῳ. 17 ἔχω οὖν [τὴν] καύχησιν ἐν
Χριστῷ Ἰησοῦ τὰ πρὸς τὸν θεόν· 18 οὐ γὰρ τολμήσω
τι λαλεῖν ὧν οὐ κατειργάσατο Χριστὸς δι᾽ ἐμοῦ εἰς
ὑπακοὴν ἐθνῶν, λόγῳ καὶ ἔργῳ, 19 ἐν δυνάμει σημείων
καὶ τεράτων, ἐν δυνάμει πνεύματος². ὥστε με ἀπὸ
Ἰερουσαλὴμ καὶ κύκλῳ μέχρι τοῦ Ἰλλυρικοῦ πεπληρω-
κέναι τὸ εὐαγγέλιον τοῦ Χριστοῦ, 20 οὕτως δὲ φιλοτι-
μούμενον εὐαγγελίζεσθαι οὐχ ὅπου ὠνομάσθη Χριστός,
ἵνα μὴ ἐπ᾽ ἀλλότριον θεμέλιον οἰκοδομῶ, 21 ἀλλὰ καθὼς
γέγραπται,

Οἷς οὐκ ἀνηγγέλη περὶ αὐτοῦ ὄψονται,
καὶ οἳ οὐκ ἀκηκόασιν συνήσουσιν.

Paul's Plan to Visit Rome

22 Διὸ καὶ ἐνεκοπτόμην τὰ πολλὰ τοῦ ἐλθεῖν πρὸς
ὑμᾶς· 23 νυνὶ δὲ μηκέτι τόπον ἔχων ἐν τοῖς κλίμασι
τούτοις, ἐπιποθίαν δὲ ἔχων τοῦ ἐλθεῖν πρὸς ὑμᾶς ἀπὸ

---

² 19 {C} πνεύματος B (Pelagiusᶜᵒᵐᵐ) Vigilius ‖ πνεύματος ἁγίου
A Dˣ·ᶜ G 33 81 104 630 1739 1881 1962 2127 itᵃʳ·ᵈ·ᵈᵉᵐ·ᵉ·ᶠ·ᵍ·ᵐ·ˣ·ᶻ vg syrʰᵐᵍ·ᵖᵃˡ
copˢᵃ·ᵇᵒ arm Adamantius Ambrosiaster Athanasius Basil Apollinaris
Didymus Augustine Cyrilᵃᶜᶜ· ᵗᵒ ᵀʰᵉᵒᵈᵒʳᵉᵗ ‖ πνεύματος θεοῦ 𝔭⁴⁶ ℵ Dᵇ P Ψ
88 181 326 436 614 629 1241 1877 1984 1985 2492 2495 Byz Lect syrᵖ·ʰ eth
Origenˡᵃᵗ Chrysostom Cyril Euthalius Theodoret John-Damascus Ps-
Oecumenius Theophylact ‖ πνεύματος θεοῦ ἁγίου 330 451

ᵇ ᵇ 15 b minor, b none: Bov Nes BF² Zür Luth ‖ b none, b minor: TR RSV ‖ b minor, b minor:
WH AV RV ASV (NEB) TT Jer Seg

---

15 διὰ…θεοῦ Ro 1.5; 12.3   16 εἰς…ἔθνη Ro 11.13   γένηται…εὐπρόσδεκτος Php 2.17
18 οὐ γὰρ…ἐμοῦ 2 Cor 3.5   20 2 Cor 10.15-16   21 ὄψονται…συνήσουσιν Is 52.15
22 Ro 1.10-13

πολλῶν³ ἐτῶν,   24 ὡς ἂν πορεύωμαι εἰς τὴν Σπανίαν·
ἐλπίζω γὰρ διαπορευόμενος θεάσασθαι ὑμᾶς καὶ ὑφ'
ὑμῶν προπεμφθῆναι ἐκεῖ ἐὰν ὑμῶν πρῶτον ἀπὸ μέρους
ἐμπλησθῶ — 25 νυνὶ δὲ πορεύομαι εἰς Ἰερουσαλὴμ
διακονῶν τοῖς ἁγίοις. 26 ηὐδόκησαν γὰρ Μακεδονία
καὶ Ἀχαΐα κοινωνίαν τινὰ ποιήσασθαι εἰς τοὺς πτωχοὺς
τῶν ἁγίων τῶν ἐν Ἰερουσαλήμ. 27 ηὐδόκησαν γάρ, καὶ
ὀφειλέται εἰσὶν αὐτῶν· εἰ γὰρ τοῖς πνευματικοῖς αὐτῶν
ἐκοινώνησαν τὰ ἔθνη, ὀφείλουσιν καὶ ἐν τοῖς σαρκικοῖς
λειτουργῆσαι αὐτοῖς. 28 τοῦτο οὖν ἐπιτελέσας, καὶ
σφραγισάμενος αὐτοῖς τὸν καρπὸν τοῦτον, ἀπελεύσομαι
δι' ὑμῶν εἰς Σπανίαν· 29 οἶδα δὲ ὅτι ἐρχόμενος πρὸς
ὑμᾶς ἐν πληρώματι εὐλογίας Χριστοῦ⁴ ἐλεύσομαι.

30 Παρακαλῶ δὲ ὑμᾶς [, ἀδελφοί,] διὰ τοῦ κυρίου
ἡμῶν Ἰησοῦ Χριστοῦ καὶ διὰ τῆς ἀγάπης τοῦ πνεύματος, συναγωνίσασθαί μοι ἐν ταῖς προσευχαῖς ὑπὲρ ἐμοῦ
πρὸς τὸν θεόν, 31 ἵνα ῥυσθῶ ἀπὸ τῶν ἀπειθούντων ἐν τῇ
Ἰουδαίᾳ καὶ ἡ διακονία⁵ μου ἡ εἰς Ἰερουσαλὴμ εὐπρόσδεκτος τοῖς ἁγίοις γένηται, 32 ἵνα ἐν χαρᾷ ἐλθὼν

24 I hope to do so now. I would like to see you on my way to Spain, and be helped by you to go there, after I have enjoyed visiting you for a while. 25 Right now, however, I am going to Jerusalem in the service of God's people there. 26 For the churches in Macedonia and Greece have freely decided to give an offering to help the poor among God's people in Jerusalem. 27 They themselves decided to do it. But, as a matter of fact, they have an obligation to help those poor; for the Jews shared their spiritual blessings with the Gentiles, and so the Gentiles ought to serve the Jews with their material blessings. 28 When I have finished this task, and have turned over to them the full amount of money that has been raised for them, I shall leave for Spain and visit you on my way there. 29 When I come to you, I know that I shall come with a full measure of the blessing of Christ.

30 I urge you, brothers, by our Lord Jesus Christ and by the love that the Spirit gives: join me in praying fervently to God for me. 31 Pray that I may be kept safe from the unbelievers in Judea, and that my service in Jerusalem may be acceptable to God's people there. 32 And so I will come to you full of joy,

---

³ 23 {B} πολλῶν 𝔭⁴⁶ ℵ A D G Ψ 33 88 104 181 330 436 451 629 630 1241 1739 1877 1881 1984 1985 2492 2495 *Byz Lect* Chrysostom Theodoret ∥ ἱκανῶν B C P 81 326 1962 2127 John-Damascus

⁴ 29 {B} Χριστοῦ 𝔭⁴⁶ ℵ* A B C D G P 81 629 630 1739 1881 it^ar,d,e,f,g,x,z vg^ww cop^sa,bo arm Clement Origen^lat Ambrosiaster Pelagius Sedulius-Scotus ∥ τοῦ εὐαγγελίου τοῦ Χριστοῦ ℵ^c Ψ 33 88 104 181 326 330 436 451 614 1241 1877 1962 1984 2127 2492 2495 *Byz Lect* (it^dem) vg^cl syr^p,h (Ephraem) Chrysostom Theodoret (John-Damascus) ∥ τῆς διδαχῆς τοῦ Χριστοῦ eth^ro

⁵ 31 {B} διακονία 𝔭⁴⁶ ℵ Λ C D^c P Ψ 33 81 88 104 181 326 330 436 451 614 629 630 1241 1739 1877 1881 1962 1984 1985 2127 2492 2495 *Byz Lect* it^dc,f,g syr^p,h cop^sa,bo arm eth Origen^lat Chrysostom Theodoret John-Damascus ∥ δωροφορία B D* G^gr (it^ar,d* *remuneratio*) Ambrosiaster Ephraem ∥ *obsequii mei oblatio* it^demvid,x,z vg ∥ *oblatio et remuneratio* it^e

---

24 ἐλπίζω...ἐμπλησθῶ 1 Cor 16.6   25 Ac 19.21; 20.22   26 κοινωνίαν...Ἰερουσαλήμ 1 Cor 16.1; 2 Cor 8.1; 9.2, 12   27 τοῖς πνευματικοῖς...ἔθνη Ro 9.4   εἰ γὰρ...λειτουργῆσαι αὐτοῖς 1 Cor 9.11   30 2 Cor 1.11; Php 1.27; Col 4.3; 2 Th 3.1

if it is God's will, and enjoy a refreshing visit with you. ³³ May God, our source of peace, be with all of you. Amen.

Personal Greetings

16 I recommend to you our sister Phoebe, who serves the church at Cenchreae. ² Receive her in the Lord's name, as God's people should, and give her any help she may need from you; for she herself has been a good friend to many people and also to me.

³ I send greetings to Prisca and Aquila, my fellow workers in the service of Christ Jesus, ⁴ who risked their lives for me. I am grateful to them — not only I, but all the Gentile churches as well. ⁵ Greetings also to the church that meets in their house.

Greetings to my dear friend Epaenetus, who was the first man in the province of Asia to believe in Christ. ⁶ Greetings to Mary, who has worked so hard for you. ⁷ Greetings to Andronicus and Junias,

πρὸς ὑμᾶς διὰ θελήματος θεοῦ συναναπαύσωμαι ὑμῖν[6]. 33 ὁ δὲ θεὸς τῆς εἰρήνης μετὰ πάντων ὑμῶν· ἀμήν.[7]

Personal Greetings

16 Συνίστημι δὲ ὑμῖν Φοίβην τὴν ἀδελφὴν ἡμῶν, οὖσαν [καὶ] διάκονον τῆς ἐκκλησίας τῆς ἐν Κεγχρεαῖς, 2 ἵνα προσδέξησθε αὐτὴν ἐν κυρίῳ ἀξίως τῶν ἁγίων, καὶ παραστῆτε αὐτῇ ἐν ᾧ ἂν ὑμῶν χρῄζῃ πράγματι, καὶ γὰρ αὐτὴ προστάτις πολλῶν ἐγενήθη καὶ ἐμοῦ αὐτοῦ.

3 Ἀσπάσασθε Πρίσκαν καὶ Ἀκύλαν τοὺς συνεργούς μου ἐν Χριστῷ Ἰησοῦ, 4 οἵτινες ὑπὲρ τῆς ψυχῆς μου τὸν ἑαυτῶν τράχηλον ὑπέθηκαν, οἷς οὐκ ἐγὼ μόνος εὐχαριστῶ ἀλλὰ καὶ πᾶσαι αἱ ἐκκλησίαι τῶν ἐθνῶν, 5 καὶ τὴν κατ' οἶκον αὐτῶν ἐκκλησίαν. ἀσπάσασθε Ἐπαίνετον τὸν ἀγαπητόν μου, ὅς ἐστιν ἀπαρχὴ τῆς Ἀσίας εἰς Χριστόν. 6 ἀσπάσασθε Μαριάμ, ἥτις πολλὰ ἐκοπίασεν εἰς ὑμᾶς. 7 ἀσπάσασθε Ἀνδρόνικον καὶ Ἰουνιᾶν[1] τοὺς

---

6 32 {C} ἐν χαρᾷ ἐλθὼν πρὸς ὑμᾶς διὰ θελήματος θεοῦ συναναπαύσωμαι ὑμῖν A C (33 88 181* 326* θεοῦ καί) 81 630 1739 (1881* ἀναπαύσομαι) 1881ᶜ 2127 2495 copˢᵃ arm ‖ ἐλθὼν ἐν χαρᾷ πρὸς ὑμᾶς διὰ θελήματος Ἰησοῦ Χριστοῦ συναναπαύσωμαι ὑμῖν ℵ* (Origenᵍʳ·ˡᵃᵗ θεοῦ for Ἰησοῦ Χριστοῦ) ‖ ἐν χαρᾷ ἔλθω πρὸς ὑμᾶς διὰ θελήματος θεοῦ καὶ συναναπαύσωμαι ὑμῖν ℵᶜ (P Ψ συναναπαύσομαι) 104 181ᶜ 326ᶜ 330 436 451 614 (629 ἔλθω πρὸς ὑμᾶς ἐν χαρᾷ) 1241 1877 1962 1984 1985 2492 Byz Lect it⁽ᵈᵉᵐ⁾·ᵍⁱᵍ·ᶻ (vg) syr⁽ᵖ⁾·ʰ copᵇᵒ (eth κυρίου for θεοῦ) Chrysostom Theodoret (John-Damascus omit καί) ‖ ἐν χαρᾷ ἔλθω πρὸς ὑμᾶς διὰ θελήματος Χριστοῦ Ἰησοῦ καὶ ἀναψύξω μεθ' ὑμῶν D* (Dᶜ itᵈᶜ θεοῦ for Χριστοῦ Ἰησοῦ) (G ἀναψύχω) it⁽ᵃʳ⁾·ᵈ*·ᵉ·ᶠ·ᵍ·⁽ˣ⁾ Ambrosiaster ‖ ἐν χαρᾷ ἔλθω πρὸς ὑμᾶς διὰ θελήματος θεοῦ 𝔭⁴⁶ (B κυρίου Ἰησοῦ for θεοῦ)

7 33 {A} ἀμήν. (see 14.23; 16.25) ℵ B C D P Ψ 33 81 88 104 181 326 614 629 1241 1877 1962 1984 1985 2127 2492 2495 Byz Lect itᵃʳ·ᵈ·ᵈᵉᵐ·ᵉ·ᶻ vg syrᵖ·ʰ copˢᵃ·ᵇᵒ arm eth Origenˡᵃᵗ Chrysostom Theodoret John-Damascus ‖ omit A G 330 436 451 630 1739 1881 itᶠ·ᵍ·ˣ ‖ omit ἀμήν, add 16.25–27 𝔭⁴⁶

1 7 {A} Ἰουνιᾶν ℵ A B C D G P Ψ 33 81 88 104 181 326 330 436 451 614 629 630 1241 1739 1877 1881 1962 1984 1985 2127 2492 2495 Byz Lect

---

3 Πρίσκαν καὶ Ἀκύλαν Ac 18.2, 18, 26　　　**5** τὴν κατ'...ἐκκλησίαν 1 Cor 16.19
ἀπαρχὴ...Χριστόν 1 Cor 16.15

συγγενεῖς μου καὶ συναιχμαλώτους μου, οἵτινές εἰσιν
ἐπίσημοι ἐν τοῖς ἀποστόλοις, οἳ καὶ πρὸ ἐμοῦ γέγοναν[2]
ἐν Χριστῷ. 8 ἀσπάσασθε Ἀμπλιᾶτον τὸν ἀγαπητόν μου
ἐν κυρίῳ. 9 ἀσπάσασθε Οὐρβανὸν τὸν συνεργὸν ἡμῶν
ἐν Χριστῷ καὶ Στάχυν τὸν ἀγαπητόν μου. 10 ἀσπάσασθε
Ἀπελλῆν τὸν δόκιμον ἐν Χριστῷ. ἀσπάσασθε τοὺς ἐκ
τῶν Ἀριστοβούλου. 11 ἀσπάσασθε Ἡρῳδίωνα τὸν συγ-
γενῆ μου. ἀσπάσασθε τοὺς ἐκ τῶν Ναρκίσσου τοὺς ὄντας
ἐν κυρίῳ. 12 ἀσπάσασθε Τρύφαιναν καὶ Τρυφῶσαν τὰς
κοπιώσας ἐν κυρίῳ. ἀσπάσασθε Περσίδα τὴν ἀγαπητήν,
ἥτις πολλὰ ἐκοπίασεν ἐν κυρίῳ. 13 ἀσπάσασθε Ῥοῦφον
τὸν ἐκλεκτὸν ἐν κυρίῳ καὶ τὴν μητέρα αὐτοῦ καὶ ἐμοῦ.
14 ἀσπάσασθε Ἀσύγκριτον, Φλέγοντα, Ἑρμῆν, Πατρο-
βᾶν, Ἑρμᾶν, καὶ τοὺς σὺν αὐτοῖς ἀδελφούς. 15 ἀσπάσασθε Φιλόλογον καὶ Ἰουλίαν[3], Νηρέα καὶ τὴν ἀδελφὴν
αὐτοῦ, καὶ Ὀλυμπᾶν, καὶ τοὺς σὺν αὐτοῖς πάντας ἁγίους.
16 Ἀσπάσασθε ἀλλήλους ἐν φιλήματι ἁγίῳ. Ἀσπάζονται
ὑμᾶς αἱ ἐκκλησίαι πᾶσαι τοῦ Χριστοῦ.

17 Παρακαλῶ δὲ ὑμᾶς, ἀδελφοί, σκοπεῖν τοὺς τὰς
διχοστασίας καὶ τὰ σκάνδαλα παρὰ τὴν διδαχὴν ἣν ὑμεῖς
ἐμάθετε ποιοῦντας, καὶ ἐκκλίνετε ἀπ᾽ αὐτῶν· 18 οἱ γὰρ
τοιοῦτοι τῷ κυρίῳ ἡμῶν Χριστῷ οὐ δουλεύουσιν ἀλλὰ
τῇ ἑαυτῶν κοιλίᾳ, καὶ διὰ τῆς χρηστολογίας καὶ εὐλο-

fellow Jews who were in prison with me;
they are well known among the apostles,
and they became Christians before I did.

8 My greetings to Ampliatus, my dear
friend in the fellowship of the Lord.
9 Greetings to Urbanus, our fellow worker
in Christ's service, and to Stachys, my
dear friend. 10 Greetings to Apelles, whose
loyalty to Christ has been proved. Greetings to those who belong to the family of
Aristobulus. 11 Greetings to Herodion,
a fellow Jew, and to the Christian brothers
in the family of Narcissus.

12 My greetings to Tryphaena and
Tryphosa, who work in the Lord's service,
and to my dear friend Persis, who has
done so much work for the Lord. 13 I
send greetings to Rufus, that outstanding
worker in the Lord's service, and to his
mother, who has always treated me like
a son. 14 My greetings to Asyncritus,
Phlegon, Hermes, Patrobas, Hermas, and
all the other Christian brothers with
them. 15 Greetings to Philologus and
Julia, to Nereus and his sister, to Olympas
and to all of God's people who are with
them.

16 Greet one another with a brotherly
kiss. All the churches of Christ send you
their greetings.

---

it[d,dem,e,f,g] vg syr[p,h] cop[sa] arm ‖ Ἰουλίαν (see 16.15) 𝔭[46] it[ar,c,gig,x,z] cop[bo]
eth Ambrosiaster

2 7 {C} οἳ καὶ πρὸ ἐμοῦ γέγοναν (ℵ* omit οἵ) ℵ[c] Λ Β 630 1739 1881 ‖
οἳ καὶ πρὸ ἐμοῦ γεγόνασιν C P Ψ 33 81 88 104 181 326 330 436 451 614 629
1241 1877 1062 1084 1085 2127 2492 2495 Byz Lect ‖ οἳ καὶ πρὸ ἐμοῦ γέγοναν
(or γεγόνασιν) it[d,dem,t,x,z] vg syr[(p),h] cop[sa] arm ‖ ὃς καὶ πρὸ ἐμοῦ γέγονεν
𝔭[46] ‖ τοῖς πρὸ ἐμοῦ D G (it[ar,d*,e,g,gig]) cop[bo?] Ambrosiaster

3 15 {A} Ἰουλίαν (𝔭[46] Βηρέα καὶ Ἀουλίαν for Ἰουλίαν, Νηρέα) ℵ A B
C[2] D P Ψ 33 81 88 104 181 326 330 436 451 614 629 630 1241 1739 1877 1881 1962
1084 1985 2127 2492 2495 Byz Lect it[ar,d,dem,o,f,g,x,z] vg syr[p,h] cop[sa,bo] arm
Chrysostom ‖ Ἰουνιαν (Ἰουνίαν fem or Ἰουνιᾶν masc: see 16.7) C* G[gr]

---

13 Ῥοῦφον Mk 15.21   16 Ἀσπάσασθε...ἁγίῳ 1 Cor 16.20; 1 Pe 5.14   17 σκοπεῖν...
αὐτῶν Mt 7.15; Tt 3.10   18 οἱ γὰρ...κοιλίᾳ Php 3.19   διὰ...ἀκάκων Col 2.4; 2 Pe 2.3

Final Instructions

17 I urge you, my brothers: watch out
for those who cause divisions and upset
people's faith, who go against the teaching which you have received; keep away
from them. 18 For those who do such
things are not serving Christ our Lord,
but their own appetites. By their fine
words and flattering speech they deceive

the minds of innocent people. ¹⁹ Everyone has heard of your loyalty to the gospel, and for this reason I am happy about you. I want you to be wise about what is good, but innocent in what is evil. ²⁰ And God, our source of peace, will soon crush Satan under your feet.

The grace of our Lord Jesus be with you.

²¹ Timothy, my fellow worker, sends you his greetings; and so do Lucius, Jason, and Sosipater, fellow Jews.

²² I, Tertius, the writer of this letter, send you Christian greetings.

²³ My host Gaius, in whose house the church meets, sends you his greetings; Erastus, the city treasurer, and our brother Quartus, send you their greetings.

[²⁴ The grace of our Lord Jesus Christ be with you all. Amen.]

Concluding Prayer of Praise

²⁵ Let us give glory to God! He is able to make you stand firm in your faith, according to the Good News I preach, the message about Jesus Christ, and according to the revelation of the secret truth which was hidden for long ages in the past. ²⁶ Now, however, that

γίας ἐξαπατῶσιν τὰς καρδίας τῶν ἀκάκων. **19** ἡ γὰρ ὑμῶν ὑπακοὴ εἰς πάντας ἀφίκετο· ἐφ' ὑμῖν οὖν χαίρω, θέλω δὲ ὑμᾶς σοφοὺς εἶναι εἰς τὸ ἀγαθόν, ἀκεραίους δὲ εἰς τὸ κακόν. **20** ὁ δὲ θεὸς τῆς εἰρήνης συντρίψει τὸν Σατανᾶν ὑπὸ τοὺς πόδας ὑμῶν ἐν τάχει. ἡ χάρις τοῦ κυρίου ἡμῶν Ἰησοῦ μεθ' ὑμῶν⁴.

21 Ἀσπάζεται ὑμᾶς Τιμόθεος ὁ συνεργός μου, καὶ Λούκιος καὶ Ἰάσων καὶ Σωσίπατρος οἱ συγγενεῖς μου. **22** ἀσπάζομαι ὑμᾶς ἐγὼ Τέρτιος ὁ γράψας τὴν ἐπιστολήνᵃ ἐν κυρίῳ. **23** ἀσπάζεται ὑμᾶς Γάϊος ὁ ξένος μου καὶ ὅλης τῆς ἐκκλησίας. ἀσπάζεται ὑμᾶς Ἔραστος ὁ οἰκονόμος τῆς πόλεως καὶ Κούαρτος ὁ ἀδελφός.⁵

Doxology

25 Τῷ δὲ δυναμένῳ ὑμᾶς στηρίξαι κατὰ τὸ εὐαγγέλιόν μου καὶ τὸ κήρυγμα Ἰησοῦ Χριστοῦ, κατὰ ἀποκάλυψιν μυστηρίου χρόνοις αἰωνίοις σεσιγημένου **26** φανερω-

---

⁴ **20** {B} ἡ χάρις τοῦ κυρίου ἡμῶν Ἰησοῦ μεθ' ὑμῶν 𝔭⁴⁶ ℵ B 1881 ‖ ἡ χάρις τοῦ κυρίου ἡμῶν Ἰησοῦ Χριστοῦ μεθ' ὑμῶν A C P Ψ 33 81 88 104 181 326 (330 μεθ' ἡμῶν) 436 451 614 629 630 1241 1739 1877 1962 1984 1985 2127 2492 2495 *Byz Lect* itᵃʳ,ᵈᵉᵐ,ᵗ,ᶻ (itᵈᶜ *omit* ἡμῶν) vg syrᵖ,ʰ copˢᵃ,ᵇᵒ arm eth Origenˡᵃᵗ Ambrosiaster Chrysostom Theodoret John-Damascus ‖ *omit* (see 16.24) D G itᵈ*,ᵉ,ᶠ,ᵍ,ˣ Sedulius-Scotus

⁵ **23** {B} *omit verse 24* 𝔭⁴⁶,⁶¹ᵛⁱᵈ ℵ A B C 5 81 263 623 1739 1838 1962 2127 itᶻ vgʷʷ copˢᵃ,ᵇᵒ ethʳᵒ Origenˡᵃᵗ ‖ *include verse 24 here* ἡ χάρις τοῦ κυρίου ἡμῶν Ἰησοῦ Χριστοῦ μετὰ πάντων ὑμῶν. ἀμήν. (see 16.20; 2 Th 3.18) D (G *omit* Ἰησοῦ Χριστοῦ) Ψ 88 181 326 330 451 614 629 (630 *omit* πάντων *and* ἀμήν) 1241 1877 1881 1984 1985 2492 2495 *Byz Lect* itᵃʳ,ᵈ,ᵈᵉᵐ,ᵍⁱᵍ (itᵉ,ˣ *omit* ἡμῶν, itᶠ,ᵍ *omit* Ἰησοῦ Χριστοῦ) vgᶜˡ syrʰ (goth μετὰ τοῦ πνεύματος ὑμῶν) (Chrysostom *omit* πάντων) Euthalius Theodoret John-Damascus ‖ *include verse 24 following 16.27* P 33 104 256 436 1319 1837 syrᵖ arm ethᵖᵖ Ambrosiaster

---

ᵃ **22** *a none:* TR WH Bov Nes BF² RVᵐᵍ ASVᵐᵍ TT Seg ‖ *a minor:* AV RV ASV RSV NEB Zür Luth Jer

---

19 ἡ γὰρ...ἀφίκετο Ro 1.8   θέλω...κακόν Mt 10.16; 1 Cor 14.20   **20** Gn 3.15   ὁ δὲ... εἰρήνης Ro 15.33   **21** Τιμόθεος Ac 16.1; 19.22; 20.4; Php 2.19   **23** Γάϊος Ac 19.29; 1 Cor 1.14 Ἔραστος 2 Tm 4.20   **25** ἀποκάλυψιν...σεσιγημένου Eph 1.9; 3.5, 9; Col 1.26

θέντος δὲ νῦν διά τε γραφῶν προφητικῶν κατ' ἐπιταγὴν τοῦ αἰωνίου θεοῦ εἰς ὑπακοὴν πίστεως εἰς πάντα τὰ ἔθνη γνωρισθέντος, 27 μόνῳ σοφῷ θεῷ διὰ 'Ιησοῦ Χριστοῦ [ᾧ][7] ἡ δόξα εἰς τοὺς αἰῶνας[8]· ἀμήν.[6]

truth has been brought out into the open through the writings of the prophets; and by the command of the eternal God it is made known to all nations, so that all may believe and obey.

27 To the only God, who alone is all-wise, be the glory through Jesus Christ for ever! Amen.

---

[6] **25–27** {C} *include 16.25–27 here (see 14.23; 15.33)* p[61] ℵ B C D D[abs1] 81 436 630 1739 1962 2127 it[ar,d,e,f,gig,x,z] vg syr[p] cop[sa,bo] eth Clement Origen[lat] mss[acc. to Origen][lat] Ambrosiaster ‖ *include 16.25–27 here and following 14.23* A P 5 33 (88 *includes here only* 16.25 τῷ δὲ...ἀποκάλυψιν) 104 (460[lat*]) arm ‖ *include 16.25–27 following 14.23 only* L Ψ 0209[vid] 181 326 330 451 460[latc] 614 1241 1877 1881 1984 1985 2492 2495 *Byz* it[dem] syr[h] mss[acc. to Origen][lat] Chrysostom (Theodore) Cyril Theodoret Ps-Theodulus Ps-Oecumenius John-Damascus ‖ *include 16.25–27 following 15.33* p[46] ‖ *omit 16.25–27* F[gr] (G *has space at* 14.23) 629 it[g] goth Marcion[acc. to Origen][lat] mss[acc. to Jerome]

[7] **27** {C} ᾧ (*see footnote 6*) p[46] ℵ A C D Ψ 33 88 181 326 330 451 614 1241 1739 1877 1881 1984 1985 2127 2495 *Byz* it[ar,d,e,x,z] vg cop[sa,bo] ‖ αὐτῷ Γ 81 104 436 1962 2492 syr[h] arm Chrysostom ‖ *omit* B 630 it[f] syr[p] Origen[lat]

[8] **27** {C} αἰῶνας (*see footnote 6*) p[46] B C Ψ 33 88 104 181 326 330 451 614 630 1241 1739 1877 1881 1984 1985 2127 2495 *Byz* syr[h] cop[sa] Chrysostom Cyril Theodoret ‖ αἰῶνας τῶν αἰώνων p[61vid] ℵ A D P 81 436 1962 2492 it[ar,d,e,f,x,z] vg syr[p] cop[bo] arm eth Origen[lat] Ambrosiaster Hilary John-Damascus

---

26 εἰς ὑπακοὴν πίστεως Ro 1.5   **27** 1 Tm 1.17; Jd 25

PAUL'S FIRST LETTER TO THE CORINTHIANS

1 From Paul, who by the will of God was called to be an apostle of Christ Jesus, and from our brother Sosthenes —

[2] To the church of God which is in Corinth, to all who are called to be God's people, who belong to him in union with Christ Jesus, together with all people everywhere who call on the name of our Lord Jesus Christ, their Lord and ours:

[3] May God our Father and the Lord Jesus Christ give you grace and peace.

Blessings in Christ

[4] I always give thanks to my God for you, because of the grace he has given you through Christ Jesus. [5] For in union with Christ you have become rich in all things, including all speech and all knowledge. [6] The message about Christ has become so firmly fixed in you, [7] that you have not failed to receive a single blessing, as you wait for our Lord Jesus Christ to be revealed. [8] He will also keep you firm to the end, so that you will be found without fault in the Day of our Lord Jesus Christ. [9] God is to be trusted, the God who called you to have fellowship with his Son Jesus Christ, our Lord.

[handwritten: greeting]

[handwritten: Thanksgiving]

[handwritten: vs 5–7 doesn't fit enunciates theme of letter]

578

ΠΡΟΣ ΚΟΡΙΝΘΙΟΥΣ Α

Greeting and Thanksgiving

1 Παῦλος κλητὸς ἀπόστολος Χριστοῦ Ἰησοῦ διὰ θελήματος θεοῦ, καὶ Σωσθένης ὁ ἀδελφός, **2** τῇ ἐκκλησίᾳ τοῦ θεοῦ τῇ οὔσῃ ἐν Κορίνθῳ, ἡγιασμένοις ἐν Χριστῷ Ἰησοῦ, κλητοῖς ἁγίοις,[a] σὺν πᾶσιν τοῖς ἐπικαλουμένοις τὸ ὄνομα τοῦ κυρίου ἡμῶν Ἰησοῦ Χριστοῦ ἐν παντὶ τόπῳ, αὐτῶν καὶ ἡμῶν· **3** χάρις ὑμῖν καὶ εἰρήνη ἀπὸ θεοῦ πατρὸς ἡμῶν καὶ κυρίου Ἰησοῦ Χριστοῦ.

4 Εὐχαριστῶ τῷ θεῷ μου[1] πάντοτε περὶ ὑμῶν ἐπὶ τῇ χάριτι τοῦ θεοῦ τῇ δοθείσῃ ὑμῖν ἐν Χριστῷ Ἰησοῦ, **5** ὅτι ἐν παντὶ ἐπλουτίσθητε ἐν αὐτῷ, ἐν παντὶ λόγῳ καὶ πάσῃ γνώσει, **6** καθὼς τὸ μαρτύριον τοῦ Χριστοῦ ἐβεβαιώθη ἐν ὑμῖν, **7** ὥστε ὑμᾶς μὴ ὑστερεῖσθαι ἐν μηδενὶ χαρίσματι, ἀπεκδεχομένους τὴν ἀποκάλυψιν τοῦ κυρίου ἡμῶν Ἰησοῦ Χριστοῦ· **8** ὃς καὶ βεβαιώσει ὑμᾶς ἕως τέλους ἀνεγκλήτους ἐν τῇ ἡμέρᾳ τοῦ κυρίου ἡμῶν Ἰησοῦ [Χριστοῦ][2]. **9** πιστὸς ὁ θεὸς δι' οὗ ἐκλήθητε εἰς κοινωνίαν τοῦ υἱοῦ αὐτοῦ Ἰησοῦ Χριστοῦ τοῦ κυρίου ἡμῶν.

---

[1] **4** {B} θεῷ μου א[a] A C D G P Ψ 33 81 104 181 326 330 436 451 614 629 630 1241 1739 1877 1881 1962 2127 2492 2495 *Byz Lect* it[(ar),d,dem,e,f,g,(r1),t,x,z] vg syr[p,h] cop[sa,bo] arm Origen Chrysostom Cyril Theodoret ‖ θεῷ ἡμῶν 491 ‖ θεῷ א* B eth Ephraem ‖ *omit* τῷ θεῷ μου 1984

[2] **8** {C} Χριστοῦ א A C D G P Ψ 33 81[vid] 88 104 181 326 330 436 451 614 629 630 1241 1739 1877 1881 1962 1984 2127 2492 2495 *Byz Lect* it[ar,d,dem, e,f,g,r1,t,x,z] vg syr[p,h,pal] cop[sa,bo] arm Origen ‖ *omit* 𝔭[46] B

---

[a] **2** *a* minor: TR WH Bov Nes BF² AV RV ASV NEB TT Zür Seg ‖ *a* none: RSV Luth Jer

2 τῇ ἐκκλησίᾳ...Ἰησοῦ 1 Cor 6.11   πᾶσιν...Χριστοῦ Ac 9.14   **3** Ro 1.7   **7** τὴν ἀποκάλυψιν...Χριστοῦ Lk 17.30; 2 Th 1.7; Tt 2.13   **8** Php 1.6; 1 Th 3.13; 5.23   **9** πιστὸς ὁ θεός Dt 7.9; 1 Cor 10.13; 1 Th 5.24   κοινωνίαν...ἡμῶν 1 Jn 1.3

Divisions in the Church

10 Παρακαλῶ δὲ ὑμᾶς, ἀδελφοί, διὰ τοῦ ὀνόματος τοῦ κυρίου ἡμῶν Ἰησοῦ Χριστοῦ, ἵνα τὸ αὐτὸ λέγητε πάντες, καὶ μὴ ᾖ ἐν ὑμῖν σχίσματα, ἦτε δὲ κατηρτισμένοι ἐν τῷ αὐτῷ νοῒ καὶ ἐν τῇ αὐτῇ γνώμῃ. **11** ἐδηλώθη γάρ μοι περὶ ὑμῶν, ἀδελφοί μου, ὑπὸ τῶν Χλόης ὅτι ἔριδες ἐν ὑμῖν εἰσιν. **12** λέγω δὲ τοῦτο, ὅτι ἕκαστος ὑμῶν λέγει, Ἐγὼ μέν εἰμι Παύλου, Ἐγὼ δὲ Ἀπολλῶ, Ἐγὼ δὲ Κηφᾶ, Ἐγὼ δὲ Χριστοῦ. **13** μεμέρισται[3] ὁ Χριστός;[b] μὴ Παῦλος ἐσταυρώθη ὑπὲρ ὑμῶν,[c] ἢ εἰς τὸ ὄνομα Παύλου ἐβαπτίσθητε;[c] **14** εὐχαριστῶ[4] ὅτι οὐδένα ὑμῶν ἐβάπτισα εἰ μὴ Κρίσπον καὶ Γάϊον, **15** ἵνα μή τις εἴπῃ ὅτι εἰς τὸ ἐμὸν ὄνομα ἐβαπτίσθητε.[d] **16** ἐβάπτισα δὲ καὶ τὸν Στεφανᾶ οἶκον· λοιπὸν οὐκ οἶδα εἴ τινα ἄλλον ἐβάπτισα.[d] **17** οὐ γὰρ ἀπέστειλέν με Χριστὸς βαπτίζειν ἀλλὰ εὐαγγελίζεσθαι, οὐκ ἐν σοφίᾳ λόγου, ἵνα μὴ κενωθῇ ὁ σταυρὸς τοῦ Χριστοῦ.

Divisions in the Church

[10] I appeal to you, brothers, by the authority of our Lord Jesus Christ: agree, all of you, in what you say, so there will be no divisions among you; be completely united, with only one thought and one purpose. [11] For some people from Chloe's family have told me quite plainly, my brothers, that there are quarrels among you. [12] Let me put it this way: each one of you says something different. One says, "I am with Paul"; another, "I am with Apollos"; another, "I am with Peter"; and another, "I am with Christ." [13] Christ has been split up into groups! Was it Paul who died on the cross for you? Were you baptized as Paul's disciples?

[14] I thank God that I did not baptize any of you except Crispus and Gaius. [15] No one can say, then, that you were baptized as my disciples. [16] (Oh yes, I also baptized Stephanas and his family; but I can't remember whether I baptized anyone else.) [17] Christ did not send me to baptize. He sent me to tell the Good News, and to tell it without using the language of men's wisdom, for that would rob Christ's death on the cross of all its power.

---

[3] **13** {C} μεμέρισται ℵ A B C D G P Ψ 33 81 88 104 181 330 436 451 614 629 630 1241 1739 1877 1881 1984 2127 2492 2495 *Byz Lect* it[ar,d,dem,e,f,g,r1,x,z] vg syr[h] cop[bo] goth Adamantius ∥ μὴ μεμέρισται p[46] 326 1962 *l*[599] syr[p,pal] cop[sa] arm Optatus

[4] **14** {B} εὐχαριστῶ ℵ* B 1739 cop[sa mss,bo] Clement Origen Chrysostom[1/2] John-Damascus ∥ εὐχαριστῶ τῷ θεῷ ℵ[c] C D G P Ψ 88 104 181 614 629 630 1241 1877 1881 1962 1984 2127 2492 2495 *Byz Lect* it[d,e,f,g,r1,z] vg syr[h] cop[bo mss] goth eth Tertullian Origen[lat] Ambrosiaster Ephraem Chrysostom[1/2] ∥ εὐχαριστῶ τῷ θεῷ μου (*see* 1.4) Λ 33 81 326 330 436 451 it[ar,c,dem vid,gig,x] syr[p,h with *,pal] cop[sa,bo mss] (cop[bo mss] εὐχαριστῶ γάρ) arm Origen[lat] Pelagius Theodoret.

---

[b] **13** *b* question: TR WH[mg] Bov Nes BF[2] AV RV ASV RSV TT Zür Luth Jer Seg ∥ *b* exclamation: ASV[mg] NEB ∥ *b* statement: WH RV[mg]

[cc] **13** *c* minor, *c* question: TR WH Bov Nes BF[2] Zür Seg ∥ *c* question, *c* question: AV RV ASV RSV NEB TT Luth Jer

[dd] **15-16** *d* major, *d* major: TR Bov Nes BF[2] AV RV ASV TT Zür Luth Jer Seg ∥ *d* minor, *d* major: WH ∥ *d* major and dash, *d* major: NEB ∥ *d* parens, *d* parens: RSV

---

10 ἦτε...νοῒ Php 2.2   **12** 1 Cor 3.4 Ἀπολλῶ Ac 18.24–28 Κηφᾶ Jn 1.42   **14** Κρίσπον Ac 18.8 Γάϊον Ac 19.29; Ro 16.23   **16** τὸν Στεφανᾶ οἶκον 1 Cor 16.15   **17** οὐ γάρ... εὐαγγελίζεσθαι Mt 28.19; Jn 4.2

Christ the Power and the Wisdom of God

¹⁸ For the message about Christ's death on the cross is nonsense to those who are being lost; but for us who are being saved, it is God's power. ¹⁹ For the scripture says,

"I will destroy the wisdom of the wise,
I will set aside the understanding of the scholars."

²⁰ So then, where does that leave the wise men? Or the scholars? Or the skillful debaters of this world? God has shown that this world's wisdom is foolishness! ²¹ For God in his wisdom made it impossible for men to know him by means of their own wisdom. Instead, God decided to save those who believe, by means of the "foolish" message we preach. ²² Jews want miracles for proof, and Greeks look for wisdom. ²³ As for us, we proclaim Christ on the cross, a message that is offensive to the Jews and nonsense to the Gentiles; ²⁴ but for those whom God has called, both Jews and Gentiles, this message is Christ, who is the power of God and the wisdom of God. ²⁵ For what seems to be God's foolishness is wiser than men's wisdom, and what seems to be God's weakness is stronger than men's strength.

²⁶ Now remember what you were, brothers, when God called you. Few of you were wise, or powerful, or of high social status, from the human point of view. ²⁷ God purposely chose what the world considers nonsense in order to put wise men to shame, and what the world considers weak in order to put powerful men to shame. ²⁸ He chose what the world looks down on, and despises, and thinks is nothing, in order to destroy what the world thinks is important.

Christ the Power and Wisdom of God

18 Ὁ λόγος γὰρ ὁ τοῦ σταυροῦ τοῖς μὲν ἀπολλυμένοις μωρία ἐστίν, τοῖς δὲ σῳζομένοις ἡμῖν δύναμις θεοῦ ἐστιν. **19** γέγραπται γάρ,

**Ἀπολῶ τὴν σοφίαν τῶν σοφῶν,
καὶ τὴν σύνεσιν τῶν συνετῶν ἀθετήσω.**

20 ποῦ σοφός; ποῦ γραμματεύς; ποῦ συζητητὴς τοῦ αἰῶνος τούτου; οὐχὶ ἐμώρανεν ὁ θεὸς τὴν σοφίαν τοῦ κόσμου; **21** ἐπειδὴ γὰρ ἐν τῇ σοφίᾳ τοῦ θεοῦ οὐκ ἔγνω ὁ κόσμος διὰ τῆς σοφίας τὸν θεόν, εὐδόκησεν ὁ θεὸς διὰ τῆς μωρίας τοῦ κηρύγματος σῶσαι τοὺς πιστεύοντας. **22** ἐπειδὴ καὶ Ἰουδαῖοι σημεῖα αἰτοῦσιν καὶ Ἕλληνες σοφίαν ζητοῦσιν, **23** ἡμεῖς δὲ κηρύσσομεν Χριστὸν ἐσταυρωμένον, Ἰουδαίοις μὲν σκάνδαλον ἔθνεσιν δὲ μωρίαν, **24** αὐτοῖς δὲ τοῖς κλητοῖς, Ἰουδαίοις τε καὶ Ἕλλησιν, Χριστὸν θεοῦ δύναμιν καὶ θεοῦ σοφίαν· **25** ὅτι τὸ μωρὸν τοῦ θεοῦ σοφώτερον τῶν ἀνθρώπων ἐστίν, καὶ τὸ ἀσθενὲς τοῦ θεοῦ ἰσχυρότερον τῶν ἀνθρώπων.

26 Βλέπετε γὰρ τὴν κλῆσιν ὑμῶν, ἀδελφοί, ὅτι οὐ πολλοὶ σοφοὶ κατὰ σάρκα, οὐ πολλοὶ δυνατοί, οὐ πολλοὶ εὐγενεῖς· **27** ἀλλὰ τὰ μωρὰ τοῦ κόσμου ἐξελέξατο ὁ θεὸς ἵνα καταισχύνῃ τοὺς σοφούς, καὶ τὰ ἀσθενῆ τοῦ κόσμου ἐξελέξατο ὁ θεὸς ἵνα καταισχύνῃ τὰ ἰσχυρά, **28** καὶ τὰ ἀγενῆ τοῦ κόσμου καὶ τὰ ἐξουθενημένα ἐξελέξατο ὁ θεός, τὰ μὴ ὄντα[5], ἵνα τὰ ὄντα καταργήσῃ,

---

[5] **28** {C} τὰ μὴ ὄντα 𝔭46 ℵ* A C* D* G 0129 33 1739 it^{d,e,g,m} cop^{sams} eth^{ro} Marcion Tertullian Origen^{gr1/7} Ambrosiaster Tyconius Pelagius Euthalius ∥ καὶ τὰ μὴ ὄντα ℵc B C3 Db P Ψ 81 88 104 326 330 436 451 614 629 630 1241 1877 1881 1962 1984 2127 2495 *Byz Lect* it^{ar,dem vid,f,rl,x,z} vg syr^{p,h} cop^{sa,bo} arm eth^{pp} Origen^{gr6/7,lat} Pamphilus Eusebius Aphraates Chrysostom Theodoret John-Damascus ∥ *omit* 2492

18 2 Cor 4.3; Ro 1.16   **19** Ἀπολῶ...ἀθετήσω Is 29.14   **20** ποῦ σοφός Is 19.12   ποῦ γραμματεύς Is 33.18   οὐχί...κόσμου Is 44.25   **21** Mt 11.25   **22** Ἰουδαῖοι σημεῖα αἰτοῦσιν Mt 12.38; Jn 4.48   Ἕλληνες σοφίαν ζητοῦσιν Ac 17.18, 32   **23** Ἰουδαίοις μὲν σκάνδαλον Ro 9.32   ἔθνεσιν δὲ μωρίαν 1 Cor 2.14   **24** Χριστόν...σοφίαν Col 2.3   **25** τὸ ἀσθενές...ἀνθρώπων 2 Cor 13.4   **26** Mt 11.25; Jn 7.48; Jas 2.1–5

29 ὅπως μὴ καυχήσηται πᾶσα σὰρξ ἐνώπιον τοῦ θεοῦ. **30** ἐξ αὐτοῦ δὲ ὑμεῖς ἐστε ἐν Χριστῷ Ἰησοῦ, ὃς ἐγενήθη σοφία ἡμῖν ἀπὸ θεοῦ, δικαιοσύνη τε καὶ ἁγιασμὸς καὶ ἀπολύτρωσις, **31** ἵνα καθὼς γέγραπται, **Ὁ καυχώμενος ἐν κυρίῳ καυχάσθω.**

Proclaiming Christ Crucified

2 Κἀγὼ ἐλθὼν πρὸς ὑμᾶς, ἀδελφοί, ἦλθον οὐ καθ' ὑπεροχὴν λόγου ἢ σοφίας καταγγέλλων ὑμῖν τὸ μυστήριον[1] τοῦ θεοῦ. **2** οὐ γὰρ ἔκρινά τι εἰδέναι ἐν ὑμῖν εἰ μὴ Ἰησοῦν Χριστὸν καὶ τοῦτον ἐσταυρωμένον. **3** κἀγὼ ἐν ἀσθενείᾳ καὶ ἐν φόβῳ καὶ ἐν τρόμῳ πολλῷ ἐγενόμην πρὸς ὑμᾶς, **4** καὶ ὁ λόγος μου καὶ τὸ κήρυγμά μου οὐκ ἐν πειθοῖ[ς] σοφίας [λόγοις][2] ἀλλ' ἐν ἀποδείξει πνεύματος καὶ δυνάμεως, **5** ἵνα ἡ πίστις ὑμῶν μὴ ᾖ ἐν σοφίᾳ ἀνθρώπων ἀλλ' ἐν δυνάμει θεοῦ.

---

[1] **1** {C} μυστήριον 𝔓[46vid?] ℵ* A C 88 436 it[ar,r1] syr[p] cop[bo] Hippolytus Ambrosiaster Ephraem Ambrose Pelagius Augustine Antiochus ∥ μαρτύριον ℵ[c] B D G P Ψ 33 81 104 181 326 330 451 614 629 630 1241 1739 1877 1881 1962 1984 2127 2492 2495 *Byz Lect* l[598pt] it[d,dem,e,f,g,x,z] vg syr[h] cop[sa] arm eth Origen Chrysostom Pelagius Cyril John-Damascus ∥ εὐαγγέλιον Theodoret ∥ σωτήριον 489 l[598pt,599]

[2] **4** {D} πειθοῖς σοφίας λόγοις (ℵ* λόγος) B (D[gr*] 33 πιθοῖς) D[c] 181 1739 1877 1881 it[r1] vg[ww] eth Origen[gr,lat] Eusebius Cyril-Jerusalem Chrysostom Severian Jerome Cyril Theodoret John-Damascus ∥ πειθοῖς ἀνθρωπίνης σοφίας λόγοις 131 ∥ πειθοῖς ἀνθρωπίνης σοφίας καὶ λόγοις ℵ[c] C Ψ (A P 326 330 πιθοῖς) 81 88 104 436 451 614 629 (630 *omit* λόγοις) 1241 1984 2127 2492 *Byz* it[(ar),c,gig,x,zvid] vg[cl] syr[h] cop[bo] Origen Eusebius Ambrosiaster Athanasius Basil Cyril-Jerusalem ∥ πειθοῖ σοφίας ἀνθρωπίνης λόγοις (1962 πιθοῖς) 2495 ∥ πειθοῖ σοφίας λόγου ἀνθρώπου cop[bomss?] eth[pp] ∥ πειθοῖ σοφίας λόγοις 1 18 42 205 209 216* 234 605[c] 1518 ∥ πειθοῖ σοφίας λόγων 440 (it[d,e]) syr[p] cop[sa] Origen? ∥ πειθοῖς σοφίας 𝔓[46] G[gr] ∥ πειθοῖ σοφίας 35* it[f,g] ∥ πειθοῖ λόγου eth[ro] ∥ πειθὸς λόγοις σοφίας *and omit* ἐν arm

---

29 Ro 3.27; Eph 2.9   **30** ὃς...ἀπολύτρωσις Jr 23.5–6; Jn 17.19; 2 Cor 5.21   **31** Ὁ καυχώμενος...καυχάσθω Jr 9.24 (2 Cor 10.17)
2 1 1 Cor 1.17   **2** Ga 6.14   **3** Ac 18.9; 2 Cor 10.1   **4** 1 Th 1.5

---

29 This means that no single person can boast in God's presence. **30** But God has brought you into union with Christ Jesus, and God has made Christ to be our wisdom; by him we are put right with God, we become God's own people, and are set free. **31** Therefore, as the scripture says, "Whoever wants to boast must boast of what the Lord has done."

The Message about Christ on the Cross

2 When I came to you, my brothers, to preach God's secret truth[1] to you, I did not use long words and great learning. **2** For I made up my mind to forget everything while I was with you except Jesus Christ, and especially his death on the cross. **3** So when I came to you I was weak and trembled all over with fear, **4** and my speech and message were not delivered with skillful words of human wisdom, but with convincing proof of the power of God's Spirit. **5** Your faith, then, does not rest on man's wisdom, but on God's power.

---

[1] **1** secret truth: *some mss. read* testimony

God's Wisdom

⁶ Yet I do speak wisdom to those who *Sarcasm* are spiritually mature. But it is not the wisdom that belongs to this world, or to the powers that rule this world — powers which are losing their power. ⁷ The wisdom I speak is God's secret wisdom, hidden from men, which God had already chosen for our glory, even before the world was made. ⁸ None of the rulers of this world knew this wisdom. If they had known it, they would not have nailed the Lord of glory to the cross. ⁹ However, as the scripture says,

"What no man ever saw or heard,
What no man ever thought could happen,
Is the very thing God prepared for those who love him."

¹⁰ But it was to us that God made known his secret, by means of his Spirit. The Spirit searches everything, even the hidden depths of God's purposes. ¹¹ As for a man, it is his own spirit within him that knows all about him; in the same way, only God's Spirit knows all about God. ¹² We have not received this world's spirit; we have received the Spirit sent by God, that we may know all that God has given us. ¹³ So then, we do not speak in words taught by human wisdom, but in words taught by the Spirit, as we explain spiritual truths to those who have the Spirit.² ¹⁴ But the man who does not

---

² 13 to those who have the Spirit: *or* with words given by the Spirit

The Revelation by God's Spirit

6 Σοφίαν δὲ λαλοῦμεν ἐν τοῖς τελείοις, σοφίαν δὲ οὐ τοῦ αἰῶνος τούτου οὐδὲ τῶν ἀρχόντων τοῦ αἰῶνος τούτου τῶν καταργουμένων· **7** ἀλλὰ λαλοῦμεν θεοῦ σοφίαν ἐν μυστηρίῳ, τὴν ἀποκεκρυμμένην, ἣν προώρισεν ὁ θεὸς πρὸ τῶν αἰώνων εἰς δόξαν ἡμῶν· **8** ἣν οὐδεὶς τῶν ἀρχόντων τοῦ αἰῶνος τούτου ἔγνωκεν, εἰ γὰρ ἔγνωσαν, οὐκ ἂν τὸν κύριον τῆς δόξης ἐσταύρωσαν. **9** ἀλλὰ καθὼς γέγραπται,

Ἃ ὀφθαλμὸς οὐκ εἶδεν καὶ οὖς οὐκ ἤκουσεν
    καὶ ἐπὶ καρδίαν ἀνθρώπου οὐκ ἀνέβη,
    ἃ ἡτοίμασεν ὁ θεὸς τοῖς ἀγαπῶσιν αὐτόν.ᵃ
10 ἡμῖν δὲ³ ἀπεκάλυψεν ὁ θεὸς διὰ τοῦ πνεύματος·ᵃ τὸ γὰρ πνεῦμα πάντα ἐραυνᾷ, καὶ τὰ βάθη τοῦ θεοῦ. **11** τίς γὰρ οἶδεν ἀνθρώπων τὰ τοῦ ἀνθρώπου εἰ μὴ τὸ πνεῦμα τοῦ ἀνθρώπου τὸ ἐν αὐτῷ; οὕτως καὶ τὰ τοῦ θεοῦ οὐδεὶς ἔγνωκεν εἰ μὴ τὸ πνεῦμα τοῦ θεοῦ. **12** ἡμεῖς δὲ οὐ τὸ πνεῦμα τοῦ κόσμου ἐλάβομεν ἀλλὰ τὸ πνεῦμα τὸ ἐκ τοῦ θεοῦ, ἵνα εἰδῶμεν τὰ ὑπὸ τοῦ θεοῦ χαρισθέντα ἡμῖν· **13** ἃ καὶ λαλοῦμεν οὐκ ἐν διδακτοῖς ἀνθρωπίνης σοφίας λόγοις ἀλλ' ἐν διδακτοῖς πνεύματος, πνευματικοῖς πνευματικὰ συγκρίνοντες. **14** ψυχικὸς δὲ ἄνθρωπος οὐ δέχεται

---

³ **10** {C} δὲ ℵ A C D G P Ψ 33 81 104 330 436 451 614 629 630 1241 1881 1962 1984 1985 2495 *Byz* itᵃʳᵛⁱᵈ,ᵈ,ᵈᵉᵐ,ᵉ,f,g,rlᵛⁱᵈ,x,z vg syrᵖ·ʰ copᵇᵒᵐˢˢ arm eth Origenᵍʳ·ˡᵃᵗ Ambrosiaster Hilary Athanasius Apollinaris Didymusᵍʳ·ˡᵃᵗ Macarius Epiphanius Chrysostom Pelagius Theodoret John-Damascus ∥ γάρ 𝔭⁴⁶ B 88 181 326 1739 1877 2127 2492 itᵐ copˢᵃ·ᵇᵒᵐˢˢ Clement Origen Basil Euthalius Antiochus ∥ *omit* Lect copᵇᵒᵐˢ

ᵃ ᵃ **9–10** a major, a minor: TR AV RV ASV Zür Luth ∥ a minor, a major: RSV NEB ∥ a major, a major: Seg ∥ a major with different text, a minor: WH Bov Nes BF² RVᵐᵍ ASVᵐᵍ (TT) Jer

6 Σοφίαν...τελείοις Eph 4.13; Php 3.15   **7** θεοῦ...ἀποκεκρυμμένην Ro 16.25; Col 1.26   **8** Lk 23.34   τὸν κύριον τῆς δόξης Jas 2.1   **9** Ἃ...ἤκουσεν...αὐτόν Is 64.4; 52.15   τοῖς ἀγαπῶσιν αὐτόν Sir 1.10   **10** ἡμῖν...πνεύματος Mt 13.11   **11** τίς...αὐτῷ Pr 20.27   **12** τὸ πνεῦμα τοῦ...ἡμῖν Jn 16.13–14   **13** 1 Cor 2.4   **14** Jn 8.47; 14.17

After humiliation theme 1.   comes this sarcastic section, building up their pride

τὰ τοῦ πνεύματος τοῦ θεοῦ[4], μωρία γὰρ αὐτῷ ἐστιν,
καὶ οὐ δύναται γνῶναι, ὅτι πνευματικῶς ἀνακρίνεται·
15 ὁ δὲ πνευματικὸς ἀνακρίνει [τὰ] πάντα[5], αὐτὸς δὲ
ὑπ' οὐδενὸς ἀνακρίνεται.
16 τίς γὰρ ἔγνω νοῦν κυρίου,
  ὃς συμβιβάσει αὐτόν;
ἡμεῖς δὲ νοῦν Χριστοῦ ἔχομεν.

Fellow Workmen for God

3 Κἀγώ, ἀδελφοί, οὐκ ἠδυνήθην λαλῆσαι ὑμῖν ὡς
πνευματικοῖς ἀλλ' ὡς σαρκίνοις, ὡς νηπίοις ἐν Χριστῷ.
2 γάλα ὑμᾶς ἐπότισα, οὐ βρῶμα, οὔπω γὰρ ἐδύνασθε.[a]
ἀλλ' οὐδὲ ἔτι νῦν δύνασθε,[a] 3 ἔτι γὰρ σαρκικοί ἐστε.
ὅπου γὰρ ἐν ὑμῖν ζῆλος καὶ ἔρις[1], οὐχὶ σαρκικοί ἐστε

---

4 14 {C} τοῦ θεοῦ p[11vid,46] ℵ A B C D G P Ψ 33 81 88 104 181 326 436
614 629 630 1241 1739 1877 1881 1962 1984 1985 2127 2492 2495 *Byz Lect*
it[ar,d,dem,e,f,g,m,r1,x,z] vg syr[h] cop[sa,bo,fay] arm Naassenes and Valentinians[acc.]
[to Hippolytus] Clement Origen[gr,lat] Eusebius Ambrosiaster Hilary Ambrose
Didymus Augustine ∥ ἁγίου eth ∥ *omit* 330 451 syr[p] Valentinians[acc.]
[to Irenaeus] Irenaeus[gr,lat] Clement Tertullian Origen Hilary Athanasius
Epiphanius Chrysostom Jerome Theodotus-Ancyra

5 15 {D} τὰ πάντα p[46] A C D* arm eth Valentinians Irenaeus[grms]
Clement Origen ∥ πάντα G Irenaeus[gr] Clement Origen Theodoret ∥ τὰ
πάντα *or* πάντα it[ar,d,dem,e,f,g,m,r1,x,z0] vg syr[p] cop[sams,bo,fay] Irenaeus[lat]
Origen[lat] ∥ μὲν πάντα ℵ[a] B D[b] Ψ 104 181 326 330 436 451 614 629 1241 1877
1881 1962 1984 1985 2492 2495 *Byz Lect* syr[h] cop[samss?] Macarius (Didymus
Theodoret πάντας) ∥ μὲν τὰ πάντα P 33 81 88 630 1739 2127 cop[samss?]
Chrysostom

1 3 {C} ἔρις p[11vid] ℵ (A ἔρεις) B C P Ψ 81 181* 630 1739 1877 1881 it[dem,]
[m,r1,x,z] vg cop[sa,bo,fay] arm eth Clement Origen (Eusebius ἔρεις) Cyril
Euthalius ∥ ἔρις διχοστασία 623 Chrysostom ∥ ἔρις καὶ διχοστασίαι
p[46] D (G ἔρεις) 33 88 104 181[mg] 326 330 436 451 614 629 1241 (1962 ἀρχοστασία)

[a a] **2** *a* major, *a* minor: WH Bov Nes BF[2] RV ASV RSV NEB TT Zür Luth Jer Seg ∥ *a* minor,
a major: AV ∥ *a* major, *a* major: TR

---

14 μωρία...ἐστιν 1 Cor 1.23   **15** ὁ δὲ...πάντα 1 Jn 2.20   **16** τίς...συμβιβάσει αὐτόν
Is 40.13 (Ro 11.34)
  3 1 Jn 16.12   **2** γάλα...βρῶμα He 5.12–13; 1 Pe 2.2   **3** ἐν ὑμῖν...ἔρις 1 Cor 1.10–11;
11.18

---

have the Spirit cannot receive the gifts
that come from God's Spirit. He really
does not understand them; they are nonsense to him, because their value can be
judged only on a spiritual basis. [15] The
man who has the Spirit is able to judge
the value of everything, but no one is
able to judge him. [16] As the scripture
says,
  "Who knows the mind of the Lord?
  Who is able to give him advice?"
We, however, have the mind of Christ.

Servants of God

3 As a matter of fact, brothers, I could
not talk to you as I talk to men who
have the Spirit; I had to talk to you as
men of this world, as children in the
Christian faith. [2] I had to feed you
milk, not solid food, because you were
not ready for it. And even now you are
not ready for it, [3] because you still live
as men of this world. When there is
jealousy among you, and you quarrel
with one another, doesn't this prove that
you are men of this world, living by this

Ch 3 knocks down their false pride

world's standards? [4] When one of you says, "I am with Paul," and another, "I am with Apollos" — aren't you acting like worldly men?

[5] After all, who is Apollos? And who is Paul? We are simply God's servants, by whom you were led to believe. Each one of us does the work the Lord gave him to do: [6] I planted the seed, Apollos watered the plant, but it was God who made the plant grow. [7] The one who plants and the one who waters really do not matter. It is God who matters, for he makes the plant grow. [8] There is no difference between the man who plants and the man who waters; God will reward each one according to the work he has done. [9] For we are partners working together for God, and you are God's field.

You are also God's building. [10] Using the gift that God gave me, I did the work of an expert builder and laid the foundation, and another man is building upon it. But each one must be careful how he builds. [11] For God has already placed Jesus Christ as the one and only foundation, and no other foundation can be laid. [12] Some will use gold, or silver, or precious stones in building upon the foundation; others will use wood, or grass, or straw. [13] And the quality of each man's work will be seen when the Day of Christ exposes it. For that Day's fire will reveal every man's work: the fire will test it and show its real quality. [14] If what a man built on the foundation survives the fire, he will receive a reward. [15] But if any man's work is burnt up, then he will lose it; but he himself will be saved, as if he had escaped through the fire.

[16] Surely you know that you are God's temple, and that God's Spirit lives in

καὶ κατὰ ἄνθρωπον περιπατεῖτε; **4** ὅταν γὰρ λέγῃ τις, Ἐγὼ μέν εἰμι Παύλου, ἕτερος δέ, Ἐγὼ Ἀπολλῶ, οὐκ ἄνθρωποί ἐστε; **5** τί οὖν ἐστιν Ἀπολλῶς; τί δέ ἐστιν Παῦλος; διάκονοι δι᾿ ὧν ἐπιστεύσατε, καὶ ἑκάστῳ ὡς ὁ κύριος ἔδωκεν. **6** ἐγὼ ἐφύτευσα, Ἀπολλῶς ἐπότισεν, ἀλλὰ ὁ θεὸς ηὔξανεν· **7** ὥστε οὔτε ὁ φυτεύων ἐστίν τι οὔτε ὁ ποτίζων, ἀλλ᾿ ὁ αὐξάνων θεός. **8** ὁ φυτεύων δὲ καὶ ὁ ποτίζων ἕν εἰσιν, ἕκαστος δὲ τὸν ἴδιον μισθὸν λήμψεται κατὰ τὸν ἴδιον κόπον. **9** θεοῦ γάρ ἐσμεν συνεργοί· θεοῦ γεώργιον,[b] θεοῦ οἰκοδομή ἐστε.[b]

10 Κατὰ τὴν χάριν τοῦ θεοῦ[2] τὴν δοθεῖσάν μοι ὡς σοφὸς ἀρχιτέκτων θεμέλιον ἔθηκα, ἄλλος δὲ ἐποικοδομεῖ. ἕκαστος δὲ βλεπέτω πῶς ἐποικοδομεῖ· **11** θεμέλιον γὰρ ἄλλον οὐδεὶς δύναται θεῖναι παρὰ τὸν κείμενον, ὅς ἐστιν Ἰησοῦς Χριστός. **12** εἰ δέ τις ἐποικοδομεῖ ἐπὶ τὸν θεμέλιον χρυσόν, ἄργυρον, λίθους τιμίους, ξύλα, χόρτον, καλάμην, **13** ἑκάστου τὸ ἔργον φανερὸν γενήσεται, ἡ γὰρ ἡμέρα δηλώσει· ὅτι ἐν πυρὶ ἀποκαλύπτεται, καὶ ἑκάστου τὸ ἔργον ὁποῖόν ἐστιν τὸ πῦρ [αὐτὸ] δοκιμάσει. **14** εἴ τινος τὸ ἔργον μενεῖ ὃ ἐποικοδόμησεν, μισθὸν λήμψεται· **15** εἴ τινος τὸ ἔργον κατακαήσεται, ζημιωθήσεται, αὐτὸς δὲ σωθήσεται, οὕτως δὲ ὡς διὰ πυρός. **16** οὐκ οἴδατε ὅτι ναὸς θεοῦ ἐστε καὶ τὸ πνεῦμα τοῦ θεοῦ

1984 1985 2127 2492 2495 *Byz Lect* it[ar,d,e,f,g] syr[p,h] Marcion Irenaeus[gr,lat] Origen[lat] Cyprian Ephraem Ambrose Pelagius Jerome Augustine Theodoret

[2] 10 {C} *τοῦ θεοῦ* ℵ A B C D P Ψ 33 88 104 181 326 330 436 451 614 629 630 1241 1739 1877 1881 1984[mg] 1985 2127 2492 *Byz Lect* it[ar,d,e,t,x,z] vg syr[p,h] cop[sa,bo,fay] arm ‖ *omit* 𝔓46 81 1962 2495 it[c,dem vid,f] Clement Augustine Cyril Theodoret

---

[b b] **9** *b* minor, *b* paragraph: TR WH Bov Nes BF[2] AV[ed] RV ASV RSV TT Jer Seg ‖ *b* minor, *b* major: AV[ed] Zür (Luth) ‖ *b* paragraph, *b* major: NEB

---

4 λέγῃ...Ἀπολλῶ 1 Cor 1.12   **5** τί...Ἀπολλῶς Ac 18.24, 27   **6** ἐγὼ ἐφύτευσα Ac 18.4, 11   Ἀπολλῶς ἐπότισεν Ac 18.24–28   **9** θεοῦ γεώργιον Mt 13.3–9   θεοῦ οἰκοδομή Eph 2.20   **10** Κατὰ...δοθεῖσάν μοι 1 Cor 15.10   σοφὸς ἀρχιτέκτων 2 Pe 3.15   **11** Is 28.16; 1 Pe 2.4–6   **13** 1 Cor 4.5; 2 Th 1.7–10   **16** 1 Cor 6.19; 2 Cor 6.16

οἰκεῖ ἐν ὑμῖν;   **17** εἴ τις τὸν ναὸν τοῦ θεοῦ φθείρει, φθερεῖ[3] τοῦτον ὁ θεός· ὁ γὰρ ναὸς τοῦ θεοῦ ἅγιός ἐστιν, οἵτινές ἐστε ὑμεῖς.

18 Μηδεὶς ἑαυτὸν ἐξαπατάτω· εἴ τις δοκεῖ σοφὸς εἶναι ἐν ὑμῖν ἐν τῷ αἰῶνι τούτῳ, μωρὸς γενέσθω, ἵνα γένηται σοφός.   **19** ἡ γὰρ σοφία τοῦ κόσμου τούτου μωρία παρὰ τῷ θεῷ ἐστιν· γέγραπται γάρ,

Ὁ δρασσόμενος τοὺς σοφοὺς ἐν τῇ πανουργίᾳ αὐτῶν·
20 καὶ πάλιν,

Κύριος γινώσκει τοὺς διαλογισμοὺς τῶν σοφῶν
ὅτι εἰσὶν μάταιοι.

21 ὥστε μηδεὶς καυχάσθω ἐν ἀνθρώποις· πάντα γὰρ ὑμῶν ἐστιν,   **22** εἴτε Παῦλος εἴτε Ἀπολλῶς εἴτε Κηφᾶς εἴτε κόσμος εἴτε ζωὴ εἴτε θάνατος εἴτε ἐνεστῶτα εἴτε μέλλοντα, πάντα ὑμῶν,   **23** ὑμεῖς δὲ Χριστοῦ, Χριστὸς δὲ θεοῦ.

The Ministry of the Apostles

4 Οὕτως ἡμᾶς λογιζέσθω ἄνθρωπος ὡς ὑπηρέτας Χριστοῦ καὶ οἰκονόμους μυστηρίων θεοῦ.   **2** ὧδε λοιπὸν ζητεῖται ἐν τοῖς οἰκονόμοις ἵνα πιστός τις εὑρεθῇ.   **3** ἐμοὶ δὲ εἰς ἐλάχιστόν ἐστιν ἵνα ὑφ᾽ ὑμῶν ἀνακριθῶ ἢ ὑπὸ ἀνθρωπίνης ἡμέρας· ἀλλ᾽ οὐδὲ ἐμαυτὸν ἀνακρίνω·   **4** οὐδὲν γὰρ ἐμαυτῷ σύνοιδα, ἀλλ᾽ οὐκ ἐν τούτῳ δεδικαίωμαι, ὁ δὲ ἀνακρίνων με κύριός ἐστιν.   **5** ὥστε μὴ πρὸ καιροῦ τι κρίνετε, ἕως ἂν ἔλθῃ ὁ κύριος, ὃς καὶ φωτίσει τὰ κρυπτὰ τοῦ σκότους καὶ φανερώσει τὰς βουλὰς τῶν

---

[3] **17** {C} φθερεῖ 𝔭⁴⁶ ℵ A B C Ψ 104 436 629 630 1739 1877 1881 1962 1984 1985 2127 2492 2495 *Byz Lect* it^ar,d,dem,e,f,g,m,t,x vg cop^sa,bo arm Irenaeus^lat Origen^gr,lat Cyprian Eusebius Ambrosiaster Hilary Didymus Cyril ∥ φθείρει D^gr G^gr P (33 φθηρεῖ) 81 (88 181 614 φθειρεῖ) (330 451 1241 φθειρῇ) *l*⁸⁰⁹ it^z syr^p,h Ephraem

---

19 Ὁ δρασσόμενος...αὐτῶν Job 5.13   **20** Κύριος...μάταιοι Ps 94.11
4 2 Lk 12.42   **4** οὐκ...δεδικαίωμαι Ps 143.2

you!   **17** So if anyone destroys God's temple, God will destroy him. For God's temple is holy, and you yourselves are his temple.

18 No one should fool himself. If anyone among you thinks that he is a wise man by this world's standards, he should become a fool, in order to be really wise. **19** For what this world considers to be wisdom is nonsense in God's sight. As the scripture says, "God traps the wise men in their cleverness"; **20** and another scripture says, "The Lord knows that the thoughts of the wise are worthless." **21** No one, then, should boast about what men can do. Actually everything belongs to you: **22** Paul, Apollos, and Peter; this world, life and death, the present and the future; all of these are yours, **23** and you belong to Christ, and Christ belongs to God.

Apostles of Christ

4 You should look on us as Christ's servants who have been put in charge of God's secret truths. **2** The one thing required of the man in charge is that he be faithful to his master. **3** Now, I am not at all concerned about being judged by you, or by any human standard; I don't even pass judgment on myself. **4** My conscience is clear, but that does not prove that I am really innocent. The Lord is the one who passes judgment on me. **5** So you should not pass judgment on anyone before the right time comes. Final judgment must wait until the Lord comes: he will bring to light the dark secrets and expose the hidden purposes of men's hearts. And then every man will receive from God the praise he deserves.

6 For your sake, brothers, I have applied all this to Apollos and me. I have used us as an example, that you may learn what the saying means, "Observe the proper rules." None of you should be proud of one man and despise the other. 7 Who made you superior to the others? Didn't God give you everything you have? Well, then, how can you brag, as if what you have were not a gift? 8 Already you have everything you need! Already you are rich! You have become kings, even though we are not! Well, I wish you really were kings, so that we could be kings together with you. 9 For it seems to me that God has given us apostles the very last place, like men condemned to die in public, as a spectacle for the whole world of angels and of men. 10 For Christ's sake we are fools; but you are wise in Christ! We are weak, but you are strong! We are despised, but you are honored! 11 To this very hour we go hungry and thirsty; we are clothed in rags; we are beaten; we wander from place to place; 12 we work hard to support ourselves. When we are cursed, we bless; when we are persecuted, we endure; 13 when we are insulted, we answer back with kind words. We are no more than this world's garbage; we are the scum of the earth to this very hour!

14 I write like this to you, not because I want to make you feel ashamed; I do it to instruct you as my own dear children. 15 For even if you have ten thousand teachers in your life in Christ, you have only one father. For in your life in Christ Jesus I have become your father, by bringing the Good News to you. 16 I beg you, then, follow my example. 17 For this purpose I am send-

[handwritten marginal note: "antitheses"]

[handwritten marginal note: "midrash on Beatitudes"]

καρδιῶν· καὶ τότε ὁ ἔπαινος γενήσεται ἑκάστῳ ἀπὸ τοῦ θεοῦ.

6 Ταῦτα δέ, ἀδελφοί, μετεσχημάτισα εἰς ἐμαυτὸν καὶ Ἀπολλῶν δι᾽ ὑμᾶς, ἵνα ἐν ἡμῖν μάθητε τὸ ᵃΜὴ ὑπὲρ ἃ γέγραπται, ἵνα μὴ εἷς ὑπὲρ τοῦ ἑνὸς φυσιοῦσθε κατὰ τοῦ ἑτέρου. 7 τίς γάρ σε διακρίνει; τί δὲ ἔχεις ὃ οὐκ ἔλαβες; εἰ δὲ καὶ ἔλαβες, τί καυχᾶσαι ὡς μὴ λαβών; 8 ἤδη κεκορεσμένοι ἐστέ·ᵇ ἤδη ἐπλουτήσατε·ᵇ χωρὶς ἡμῶν ἐβασιλεύσατε·ᵇ καὶ ὄφελόν γε ἐβασιλεύσατε, ἵνα καὶ ἡμεῖς ὑμῖν συμβασιλεύσωμεν. 9 δοκῶ γάρ, ὁ θεὸς ἡμᾶς τοὺς ἀποστόλους ἐσχάτους ἀπέδειξενᶜ ὡς ἐπιθανατίους,ᶜ ὅτι θέατρον ἐγενήθημεν τῷ κόσμῳ καὶ ἀγγέλοις καὶ ἀνθρώποις. 10 ἡμεῖς μωροὶ διὰ Χριστόν, ὑμεῖς δὲ φρόνιμοι ἐν Χριστῷ· ἡμεῖς ἀσθενεῖς, ὑμεῖς δὲ ἰσχυροί· ὑμεῖς ἔνδοξοι, ἡμεῖς δὲ ἄτιμοι. 11 ἄχρι τῆς ἄρτι ὥρας καὶ πεινῶμεν καὶ διψῶμεν καὶ γυμνιτεύομεν καὶ κολαφιζόμεθα καὶ ἀστατοῦμεν 12 καὶ κοπιῶμεν ἐργαζόμενοι ταῖς ἰδίαις χερσίν· λοιδορούμενοι εὐλογοῦμεν, διωκόμενοι ἀνεχόμεθα, 13 δυσφημούμενοι παρακαλοῦμεν· ὡς περικαθάρματα τοῦ κόσμου ἐγενήθημεν, πάντων περίψημα, ἕως ἄρτι.

14 Οὐκ ἐντρέπων ὑμᾶς γράφω ταῦτα, ἀλλ᾽ ὡς τέκνα μου ἀγαπητὰ νουθετῶν· 15 ἐὰν γὰρ μυρίους παιδαγωγοὺς ἔχητε ἐν Χριστῷ, ἀλλ᾽ οὐ πολλοὺς πατέρας, ἐν γὰρ Χριστῷ Ἰησοῦ διὰ τοῦ εὐαγγελίου ἐγὼ ὑμᾶς ἐγέννησα. 16 παρακαλῶ οὖν ὑμᾶς, μιμηταί μου γίνεσθε. 17 διὰ

ᵃ 6 a direct: WH Bov Nes? BF² NEB TT Zür? Luth Jer ∥ a indirect: RV ASV RSV Seg ∥ different text: TR AV

ᵇ ᵇ ᵇ 8 b major, b major, b major: Bov Nes BF² NEB ∥ b minor, b minor, b major: TR AV RV ASV ∥ b question, b question, b question: WH Luth ∥ b exclamation, b exclamation, b exclamation: RSV TT Jer ∥ b minor, b minor, b exclamation: Zür Seg

ᶜ ᶜ 9 c none, c minor: TR WH Bov Nes BF² ∥ c minor, c major: AV RV ASV RSV Zür Luth Jer ∥ c major, c minor: NEB ∥ c minor, c minor: WHᵐᵍ TT Seg

5 ὁ ἔπαινος...θεοῦ 1 Cor 3.8   6 μάθητε...ἑτέρου Ro 12.3   7 τί δὲ...ἔλαβες Ro 12.6
8 ἤδη...ἐβασιλεύσατε Re 3.17   ὄφελον...συμβασιλεύσωμεν Re 3.21   9 ὁ θεὸς...ἐπιθανατίους Ro 8.36; He 10.33   10 1 Cor 3.18   11 2 Cor 11.23–27   12 κοπιῶμεν...χερσίν Ac 18.3; 20.34; 1 Th 2.9; 2 Th 3.8; 1 Cor 9.14–15   λοιδορούμενοι εὐλογοῦμεν Ps 109.28; Mt 5.44; Lk 6.28; Ac 7.60; Ro 12.14   13 ὡς...ἐγενήθημεν Lm 3.45   15 ἐν γὰρ...ἐγέννησα Ga 4.19   16 μιμηταί μου γίνεσθε 1 Cor 11.1; Php 3.17; 1 Th 1.6

[handwritten notes at bottom of page:]

4.8–13 antitheses — theme of wise-foolish paradox of 1.26
4.15,16 – return to the "who I belong to" theme of 1.12 Spiritual Father

τοῦτο[1] ἔπεμψα ὑμῖν Τιμόθεον, ὅς ἐστίν μου τέκνον ἀγαπητὸν καὶ πιστὸν ἐν κυρίῳ, ὃς ὑμᾶς ἀναμνήσει τὰς ὁδούς μου τὰς ἐν Χριστῷ ['Ιησοῦ], καθὼς πανταχοῦ ἐν πάσῃ ἐκκλησίᾳ διδάσκω. **18** ὡς μὴ ἐρχομένου δέ μου πρὸς ὑμᾶς ἐφυσιώθησάν τινες· **19** ἐλεύσομαι δὲ ταχέως πρὸς ὑμᾶς, ἐὰν ὁ κύριος θελήσῃ, καὶ γνώσομαι οὐ τὸν λόγον τῶν πεφυσιωμένων ἀλλὰ τὴν δύναμιν, **20** οὐ γὰρ ἐν λόγῳ ἡ βασιλεία τοῦ θεοῦ ἀλλ' ἐν δυνάμει. **21** τί θέλετε; ἐν ῥάβδῳ ἔλθω πρὸς ὑμᾶς, ἢ ἐν ἀγάπῃ πνεύματί τε πραΰτητος;

Judgment against Immorality

5 Ὅλως ἀκούεται ἐν ὑμῖν πορνεία, καὶ τοιαύτη πορνεία ἥτις οὐδὲ ἐν τοῖς ἔθνεσιν, ὥστε γυναῖκά τινα τοῦ πατρὸς ἔχειν. **2** καὶ ὑμεῖς πεφυσιωμένοι ἐστέ,[a] καὶ οὐχὶ μᾶλλον ἐπενθήσατε,[a] ἵνα ἀρθῇ ἐκ μέσου ὑμῶν ὁ τὸ ἔργον τοῦτο ποιήσας;[a] **3** ἐγὼ μὲν γάρ, ἀπὼν τῷ σώματι παρὼν δὲ τῷ πνεύματι, ἤδη κέκρικα ὡς παρὼν τὸν οὕτως τοῦτο κατεργασάμενον[b] **4** ἐν τῷ ὀνόματι τοῦ κυρίου [ἡμῶν] 'Ιησοῦ[1],[b] συναχθέντων ὑμῶν καὶ τοῦ ἐμοῦ πνεύματος[c]

---

[1] **17** {C} τοῦτο 𝔭46,68 ℵc B C D G Ψ 88 104 326 614 629 630 1241 1739 1881 1962 1984 1985 2127 2492 *Byz Lect* itar,d,demvid,e,f,g,x,z vg syrp copsa,bo arm Origen Chrysostom Theodoret John-Damascus ∥ τοῦτο αὐτό 𝔭11vid ℵ* A P 33 81 181 330 436 451 1877 2495 syrh Euthalius

[1] **4** {D} ἡμῶν 'Ιησοῦ B D* 1739 itd ∥ 'Ιησοῦ A Ψ 2495 syrh ethro Lucifer ∥

---

a a a **2** a minor, a minor, a question: TR WH Bov Neo BF2 (Zür) (Luth) ∥ a question, a minor, a question: RVmg ASVmg TT ∥ a exclamation, a minor, a exclamation: Jer Seg ∥ a exclamation, a question, a statement: RSV ∥ a exclamation, a minor, a statement: NEB ∥ a minor, a minor, a statement: AV RV ASV

b b **3–4** b none, b minor: TR WH (RSV) ∥ b major, b none: NEB Zür Luth Jer ∥ b major, b minor: TT Seg ∥ b minor, b minor: AV RV ASV ∥ b none, b none: Bov Nes BF2

c c **4** c none, c minor: WH Zür Luth ∥ c minor, c minor: TR AV RV ASV RSV NEB TT Jer Seg ∥ c none, c none: Bov Nes BF2

---

17 ἔπεμψα...Χριστῷ Ac 19.22; Php 2.19–22   **19** ἐλεύσομαι...θελήσῃ Ac 18.21; Jas 4.15   **20** 1 Cor 2.4

5 1 γυναῖκα...ἔχειν Lv 18.7–8; Dt 22.30; 27.20   **3** ἀπὼν...πνεύματι Col 2.5

ing Timothy to you. He is my own dear and faithful son in the Lord. He will remind you of the principles which I follow in the new life in Christ Jesus, and which I teach in all the churches everywhere.

[18] Some of you have become proud, thinking that I would not be coming to visit you. [19] If the Lord is willing, however, I will come to you soon, and then I will find out for myself what these proud ones can do, and not just what they can say! [20] For the Kingdom of God is not a matter of words, but of power. [21] Which do you prefer? Shall I come to you with a whip, or with a heart of love and gentleness?

Immorality in the Church

5 Now, it is actually being said that there is sexual immorality among you so terrible that not even the heathen would be guilty of it; for I am told that a man is living with his stepmother! [2] How then, can you be proud? On the contrary, you should be filled with sadness, and the man who has done such a thing should be put out of your group! [3] As for me, even though I am far away from you in body, still I am there with you in spirit; and in the name of our Lord Jesus I have already passed judgment on the man who has done this terrible thing, as though I were there with you. [4] As you meet together, and I meet with you in my spirit, by the power of our

Lord Jesus present with us, ⁵ you are to hand this man over to Satan for his body to be destroyed, so that his spirit may be saved in the Day of the Lord.

⁶ It is not right for you to be proud! You know the saying, "A little bit of yeast makes the whole batch of dough rise." ⁷ You must take out this old yeast of sin so that you will be entirely pure. Then you will be like a new batch of dough without any yeast, as indeed I know you actually are. For our Passover feast is ready, now that Christ, our Passover lamb, has been sacrificed. ⁸ Let us celebrate our feast, then, not with bread having the old yeast, the yeast of sin and immorality, but with the bread that has no yeast, the bread of purity and truth.

⁹ In the letter that I wrote you I told you not to associate with immoral people. ¹⁰ Now, I did not mean pagans who are immoral, or greedy, or law-breakers, or who worship idols. To avoid them you would have to get out of the world completely! ¹¹ What I meant was that you should not associate with a man who calls himself a brother but is immoral, or greedy, or worships idols, or is a slanderer, or a drunkard, or a lawbreaker. Don't even sit down to eat with such a person.

¹²⁻¹³ After all, it is none of my business to judge outsiders. God will judge them. But should you not judge the members of your own fellowship? As the scripture

σὺν τῇ δυνάμει τοῦ κυρίου ἡμῶν Ἰησοῦ,ᶜ 5 παραδοῦναι τὸν τοιοῦτον τῷ Σατανᾷ εἰς ὄλεθρον τῆς σαρκός, ἵνα τὸ πνεῦμα σωθῇ ἐν τῇ ἡμέρᾳ τοῦ κυρίου². 6 Οὐ καλὸν τὸ καύχημα ὑμῶν. οὐκ οἴδατε ὅτι μικρὰ ζύμη ὅλον τὸ φύραμα ζυμοῖ; 7 ἐκκαθάρατε τὴν παλαιὰν ζύμην, ἵνα ἦτε νέον φύραμα, καθώς ἐστε ἄζυμοι. καὶ γὰρ τὸ πάσχα ἡμῶν ἐτύθη Χριστός· 8 ὥστε ἑορτάζωμεν, μὴ ἐν ζύμῃ παλαιᾷ μηδὲ ἐν ζύμῃ κακίας καὶ πονηρίας, ἀλλ᾽ ἐν ἀζύμοις εἰλικρινείας καὶ ἀληθείας.

9 Ἔγραψα ὑμῖν ἐν τῇ ἐπιστολῇ μὴ συναναμίγνυσθαι πόρνοις, 10 οὐ πάντως τοῖς πόρνοις τοῦ κόσμου τούτου ἢ τοῖς πλεονέκταις καὶ ἅρπαξιν ἢ εἰδωλολάτραις, ἐπεὶ ὠφείλετε ἄρα ἐκ τοῦ κόσμου ἐξελθεῖν. 11 νῦν δὲ ἔγραψα ὑμῖν μὴ συναναμίγνυσθαι ἐάν τις ἀδελφὸς ὀνομαζόμενος ἢ πόρνος ἢ πλεονέκτης ἢ εἰδωλολάτρης ἢ λοίδορος ἢ μέθυσος ἢ ἅρπαξ, τῷ τοιούτῳ μηδὲ συνεσθίειν. 12 τί γάρ μοι τοὺς ἔξω κρίνειν; οὐχὶ τοὺς ἔσω ὑμεῖς κρίνετε;ᵈ

Ἰησοῦ Χριστοῦ ℵ ∥ ἡμῶν Ἰησοῦ Χριστοῦ 𝔭⁴⁶ Dᶜ G P 33 88 104 181 326 330 436 451 614 629 630 1241 1877 1881 1962 1984 1985 2127 2492 *Byz Lect* itᵃʳ,ᵉ,f,g,x,z vg syrᵖ,ʰ with * copˢᵃ,ᵇᵒ goth arm ethᵖᵖ Adamantius Ambrosiaster Basil Chrysostom Theodoret John-Damascus ∥ Ἰησοῦ Χριστοῦ τοῦ κυρίου ἡμῶν 81

² 5 {C} κυρίου 𝔭⁴⁶ B 630 1739 Marcion Tertullian Origenᵍʳ⁴/⁵,ˡᵃᵗ Manes Eusebius Hilary Pacian Epiphanius Jerome Augustine ∥ κυρίου Ἰησοῦ ℵ Ψ 81 181 326 614 1877 1985 2492 2495 *Byz Lect* vgʷʷ syrʰ goth Origenˡᵃᵗ Basil Chrysostom Augustine Euthalius Ps-Oecumenius Theophylact ∥ κυρίου Ἰησοῦ Χριστοῦ D 1984 itᵈ,ᵈᵉᵐᵛⁱᵈ,ᵉ Ambrosiaster ∥ κυρίου ἡμῶν Ἰησοῦ 048ᵛⁱᵈ? copᵇᵒᵐˢ eth ∥ κυρίου ἡμῶν Ἰησοῦ Χριστοῦ A G P 33 88 104 330 436 451 629 1241 1881 1962 2127 itᵃʳ,ᶜ,f,g,x,zᵛⁱᵈ vgᶜˡ syrᵖ,ʰ with * copˢᵃ,ᵇᵒ arm Origenᵍʳ¹/⁵,ˡᵃᵗ Lucifer Ephraem Ambrose Chrysostom Pelagius Theodore Theodoret John-Damascus

---

ᵈ ᵈ **12-13** d question, d statement: Bov Nes BF² AV ASV RSV TT Zür Luth Jer Seg ∥ d minor, d question: TR WH RV ∥ d statement, d statement: NEB

---

4 σὺν...Ἰησοῦ Mt 16.19; 18.18; 2 Cor 13.10   5 παραδοῦναι...σαρκός 1 Tm 1.20; 1 Pe 4.6   6 οὐκ...ζυμοῖ Ga 5.9   7 ἐκκαθάρατε...ἄζυμοι Ex 13.7   τὸ πάσχα...Χριστός Ex 12.21; Is 53.7; 1 Pe 1.19   8 Ex 12.3-20; 13.7; Dt 16.3   9 μὴ συναναμίγνυσθαι πόρνοις Mt 18.17; 2 Th 3.14   11 μὴ...συνεσθίειν 2 Th 3.6; Tt 3.10; 2 Jn 10   12 τοὺς ἔξω Mk 4.11

13 τοὺς δὲ ἔξω ὁ θεὸς κρινεῖ[3].[d] **ἐξάρατε τὸν πονηρὸν ἐξ ὑμῶν αὐτῶν.**

says, "Take the evil man out of your group."

Going to Law before Unbelievers

6 Τολμᾷ τις ὑμῶν πρᾶγμα ἔχων πρὸς τὸν ἕτερον κρίνεσθαι ἐπὶ τῶν ἀδίκων, καὶ οὐχὶ ἐπὶ τῶν ἁγίων; **2** ἢ οὐκ οἴδατε ὅτι οἱ ἅγιοι τὸν κόσμον κρινοῦσιν; καὶ εἰ ἐν ὑμῖν κρίνεται ὁ κόσμος, ἀνάξιοί ἐστε κριτηρίων ἐλαχίστων; **3** οὐκ οἴδατε ὅτι ἀγγέλους κρινοῦμεν,[a] μήτιγε βιωτικά;[a] **4** βιωτικὰ μὲν οὖν κριτήρια ἐὰν ἔχητε, τοὺς ἐξουθενημένους ἐν τῇ ἐκκλησίᾳ τούτους καθίζετε;[b] **5** πρὸς ἐντροπὴν ὑμῖν λέγω. οὕτως οὐκ ἔνι ἐν ὑμῖν οὐδεὶς σοφὸς ὃς δυνήσεται διακρῖναι ἀνὰ μέσον τοῦ ἀδελφοῦ αὐτοῦ;[c] **6** ἀλλὰ ἀδελφὸς μετὰ ἀδελφοῦ κρίνεται, καὶ τοῦτο ἐπὶ ἀπίστων;[c] **7** ἤδη μὲν [οὖν] ὅλως ἥττημα ὑμῖν ἐστιν ὅτι κρίματα ἔχετε μεθ' ἑαυτῶν· διὰ τί οὐχὶ μᾶλλον ἀδικεῖσθε; διὰ τί οὐχὶ μᾶλλον ἀποστερεῖσθε; **8** ἀλλὰ ὑμεῖς ἀδικεῖτε καὶ ἀποστερεῖτε, καὶ τοῦτο ἀδελφούς. **9** ἢ οὐκ οἴδατε ὅτι ἄδικοι θεοῦ βασιλείαν οὐ κληρονομήσουσιν; μὴ πλανᾶσθε· οὔτε πόρνοι οὔτε εἰδωλολάτραι οὔτε μοιχοὶ οὔτε μαλακοὶ οὔτε ἀρσενοκοῖται **10** οὔτε κλέπται οὔτε πλεονέκται, οὐ μέθυσοι, οὐ λοίδοροι, οὐχ ἅρπαγες βασιλείαν θεοῦ κληρονομήσουσιν. **11** καὶ ταῦτά τινες ἦτε· ἀλλὰ ἀπε-

---

[3] **13** {C} κρινεῖ B[3] P 33 81 88 104 181 326 436 614 630 1739 1877 1881 1962 1984 1985 2127 2492 *Byz* it[ar,dem,f,g,x,z] vg cop[sa,bo] arm Ambrosiaster Augustine ‖ κρίνει 𝔭[46] ℵ A B* C D[gr*] G[gr] goth ‖ κρίνει D[c] Ψ 330 451 629 1241 2495 *Lect* it[d,e] syr[p,h]

[a] [a] **3** *a minor, a question:* TR WH Bov Nes BF[2] TT ‖ *a question, a exclamation:* RSV NEB Zür (Luth) Jer ‖ *a question, a question:* AV RV ASV Seg

[b] **4** *b question:* WH Nes BF[2] RV ASV RSV NEB TT ‖ *b command:* AV RV[mg] ASV[mg] Luth ‖ *b exclamation:* Zür Jer Seg ‖ *b command or statement:* TR Bov

[c] [c] **5–6** *c question, c question:* TR Bov Nes BF[2] NEB TT ‖ *c exclamation, c exclamation:* Jer Seg ‖ *c question, c exclamation:* Luth ‖ *c minor, c exclamation:* WH RV ASV RSV Zür ‖ *c question, c statement:* AV

---

13 ἐξάρατε...αὐτῶν Dt 17.7; 19.19; 22.21, 24; 24.7
6 2 οἱ ἅγιοι...κρινοῦσιν Dn 7.22; Wsd 3.8; Re 3.21   **7** ἤδη...ἑαυτῶν Mt 5.39; 1 Th 5.15;
1 Pe 3.9   **9–10** Ga 5.19–21; Eph 5.5; Re 22.15   **11** Tt 3.3–7

Lawsuits against Brothers

6 If one of you has a dispute with a brother, how dare he go before heathen judges, instead of letting God's people settle the matter? [2] Don't you know that God's people will judge the world? Well, then, if you are to judge the world, aren't you capable of judging small matters? [3] Do you not know that we shall judge the angels? How much more, then, the things of this life! [4] If, then, such matters come up, are you going to take them to be settled by people who have no standing in the church? [5] Shame on you! Surely there is at least one wise man in your fellowship who can settle a dispute between the brothers! [6] Instead, one brother goes to court against another, and lets unbelievers judge the case!

[7] The very fact that you have legal disputes among yourselves shows that you have failed completely. Would it not be better for you to be wronged? Would it not be better for you to be robbed? [8] Instead, you yourselves wrong one another, and rob one another, even your very brothers! [9] Surely you know that the wicked will not receive God's Kingdom. Do not fool yourselves: people who are immoral, or worship idols, or are adulterers, or homosexual perverts, [10] or who rob, or are greedy, or are drunkards, or who slander others, or are lawbreakers — none of these will receive God's Kingdom. [11] Some of you were like that. But you have been cleansed from sin; you have been dedicated to God; you have been put right with God

— civil courts tied up with civil religion
— to go outside the ✗ community for settlement ignores the office of Christ as judge.

through the name of the Lord Jesus
Christ and by the Spirit of our God.

Use Your Bodies for God's Glory

[12] Someone will say, "I am allowed to
do anything." Yes; but not everything
is good for you. I could say, "I am
allowed to do anything"; but I am not
going to let anything make a slave of
me. [13] Someone else will say, "Food is
for the stomach, and the stomach is for
food." Yes; but God will put an end to
both. A man's body is not meant for
immorality, but for the Lord; and the
Lord is for the body. [14] God raised the
Lord from death, and he will also raise
us by his power.

[15] You know that your bodies are parts
of the body of Christ. Shall I take a
part of Christ's body and make it part
of the body of a prostitute? Impossible!
[16] Or perhaps you don't know that the
man who joins his body to a prostitute
becomes physically one with her? The
scripture says quite plainly, "The two
will become one body." [17] But he who
joins himself to the Lord becomes spiritually one with him.

[18] Avoid immorality. Any other sin a
man commits does not affect his body;
but the man who commits immorality
sins against his own body. [19] Don't you
know that your body is the temple of
the Holy Spirit, who lives in you, the
Spirit given you by God? You do not

λούσασθε, ἀλλὰ ἡγιάσθητε, ἀλλὰ ἐδικαιώθητε ἐν τῷ
ὀνόματι τοῦ κυρίου ᾽Ιησοῦ Χριστοῦ[1] καὶ ἐν τῷ πνεύματι
τοῦ θεοῦ ἡμῶν.

Glorify God in Your Body

12 Πάντα μοι ἔξεστιν, ἀλλ᾽ οὐ πάντα συμφέρει. πάντα
μοι ἔξεστιν, ἀλλ᾽ οὐκ ἐγὼ ἐξουσιασθήσομαι ὑπό τινος.
13 τὰ βρώματα τῇ κοιλίᾳ, καὶ ἡ κοιλία τοῖς βρώμασιν·[d]
ὁ δὲ θεὸς καὶ ταύτην καὶ ταῦτα καταργήσει. τὸ δὲ σῶμα
οὐ τῇ πορνείᾳ ἀλλὰ τῷ κυρίῳ, καὶ ὁ κύριος τῷ σώματι·
14 ὁ δὲ θεὸς καὶ τὸν κύριον ἤγειρεν καὶ ἡμᾶς ἐξεγερεῖ διὰ
τῆς δυνάμεως αὐτοῦ. **15** οὐκ οἴδατε ὅτι τὰ σώματα
ὑμῶν μέλη Χριστοῦ ἐστιν; ἄρας οὖν τὰ μέλη τοῦ Χριστοῦ
ποιήσω πόρνης μέλη; μὴ γένοιτο. **16** [ἢ] οὐκ οἴδατε ὅτι
ὁ κολλώμενος τῇ πόρνῃ ἓν σῶμά ἐστιν; Ἔσονται γάρ,
φησίν, **οἱ δύο εἰς σάρκα μίαν.** **17** ὁ δὲ κολλώμενος τῷ
κυρίῳ ἓν πνεῦμά ἐστιν. **18** φεύγετε τὴν πορνείαν· πᾶν
ἁμάρτημα ὃ ἐὰν ποιήσῃ ἄνθρωπος ἐκτὸς τοῦ σώματός
ἐστιν, ὁ δὲ πορνεύων εἰς τὸ ἴδιον σῶμα ἁμαρτάνει.
19 ἢ οὐκ οἴδατε ὅτι τὸ σῶμα ὑμῶν ναὸς τοῦ ἐν ὑμῖν
ἁγίου πνεύματός ἐστιν, οὗ ἔχετε ἀπὸ θεοῦ,[e] καὶ οὐκ

---

[1] **11** {C} ᾽Ιησοῦ Χριστοῦ 𝔓[11vid,46] ℵ D* (𝑙[603pt] Χριστοῦ ᾽Ιησοῦ) it[d,e]
Irenaeus[lat] Tertullian Didymus ∥ ᾽Ιησοῦ A D[c] Ψ 88 614 1241 1984 2495 *Byz
Lect* 𝑙[603pt] syr[h] John-Damascus ∥ ἡμῶν ᾽Ιησοῦ cop[sa] ∥ ἡμῶν ᾽Ιησοῦ Χριστοῦ
B C[vid] P 33 81 104 181 326 330 436 451 629 630 1739 1877 1881 1962 2127
it[ar,dem,f,m,r1,x,z] vg syr[p,h with *] cop[bo] arm eth Irenaeus[lat] Origen[lat] Cyprian
Adamantius Athanasius[gr,lat] Didymus[gr,(lat)] Epiphanius Chrysostom
Euthalius Theodoret Ps-Athanasius ∥ *omit* 2492

---

d **13** *d* minor: TR WH Nes BF² AV RV ASV TT Zür Luth Jer Seg ∥ *d* dash: RSV ∥ *d* ellipsis:
Bov (NEB)

e e **19** *e* minor, *e* question: TR Bov Nes BF² AV TT Zür Luth Seg ∥ *e* question, *e* minor: WH RV
ASV RSV NEB ∥ *e* question, *e* question: Jer

---

12 Πάντα…συμφέρει Slr 37.28; 1 Cor 10.23   **13** τὸ δὲ…σώματι 1 Th 4.3–5   **14** Ro 8.11;
1 Cor 15.15, 20; 2 Cor 4.14   **15** τὰ σώματα…ἐστιν Ro 12.5; 1 Cor 12.27   **16** Ἔσονται…οἱ
δύο…μίαν Gn 2.24 (Mt 19.5)   **17** Jn 17.21–23; Ro 8.9–11; Ga 2.20   **19** τὸ σῶμα…ἐστιν
1 Cor 3.16; 2 Cor 6.16

---

handwritten notes:

– all things are lawful but
you can become enslaved

– Body = spiritual body w/
is incarnate in
flesh.

ἐστὲ ἑαυτῶν;[e] **20** ἠγοράσθητε γὰρ τιμῆς· δοξάσατε δὴ τὸν θεὸν ἐν τῷ σώματι ὑμῶν[2].

Problems concerning Marriage

7 Περὶ δὲ ὧν ἐγράψατε, καλὸν ἀνθρώπῳ γυναικὸς μὴ ἅπτεσθαι· **2** διὰ δὲ τὰς πορνείας ἕκαστος τὴν ἑαυτοῦ γυναῖκα ἐχέτω, καὶ ἑκάστη τὸν ἴδιον ἄνδρα ἐχέτω. **3** τῇ γυναικὶ ὁ ἀνὴρ τὴν ὀφειλὴν ἀποδιδότω, ὁμοίως δὲ καὶ ἡ γυνὴ τῷ ἀνδρί. **4** ἡ γυνὴ τοῦ ἰδίου σώματος οὐκ ἐξουσιάζει ἀλλὰ ὁ ἀνήρ· ὁμοίως δὲ καὶ ὁ ἀνὴρ τοῦ ἰδίου σώματος οὐκ ἐξουσιάζει ἀλλὰ ἡ γυνή. **5** μὴ ἀποστερεῖτε ἀλλήλους, εἰ μήτι ἂν ἐκ συμφώνου πρὸς καιρὸν ἵνα σχολάσητε τῇ προσευχῇ[1] καὶ πάλιν ἐπὶ τὸ αὐτὸ ἦτε, ἵνα μὴ πειράζῃ ὑμᾶς ὁ Σατανᾶς διὰ τὴν ἀκρασίαν ὑμῶν. **6** τοῦτο δὲ λέγω κατὰ συγγνώμην, οὐ κατ᾽ ἐπιταγήν. **7** θέλω δὲ[2] πάντας ἀνθρώπους εἶναι ὡς καὶ ἐμαυτόν·

belong to yourselves but to God; [20] he bought you for a price. So use your bodies for God's glory.

Questions about Marriage

7 Now, to deal with the matters you wrote about.

A man does well not to marry. [2] But because there is so much immorality, every man should have his own wife, and every woman should have her own husband. [3] A man should fulfil his duty as a husband and a woman should fulfil her duty as a wife, and each should satisfy the other's needs. [4] The wife is not the master of her own body, but the husband is; in the same way the husband is not the master of his own body, but the wife is. [5] Do not deny yourselves to each other, unless you first agree to do so for a while, in order to spend your time in prayer; but then resume normal marital relations, so that your lack of self-control will not make you give in to Satan's temptation.

[6] I tell you this not as an order, but simply as a permission. [7] Actually I would prefer that all were as I am; but each one has the special gift that God

---

[2] **20** {A} ὑμῶν p[46] ℵ A B C* D* G 33 81 181 629 1739* 1877 1962 *l*[597,603] it[ar,d,] dem,e,f,g,m[vid],rl,t,x,z vg cop[sa,bo,fay] eth Irenaeus[lat] Tertullian Origen Cyprian Adamantius Methodius Ambrosiaster Lucifer Basil Didymus Cyril Euthalius John-Damascus ∥ ὑμῶν καὶ ἐν τῷ πνεύματι ὑμῶν arm ∥ ὑμῶν καὶ ἐν τῷ πνεύματι ὑμῶν, ἅτινά ἐστιν τοῦ θεοῦ C[3] D[c] K P Ψ 88 104 326 330 (436 *omit second* ὑμῶν) 451 614 630 (1241 1881 ἡμῶν *for first* ὑμῶν) 1739[mg] 1984 1985 2127 2492 2495 *Byz Lect* syr[p,h] Chrysostom Theodoret

[1] **5** {A} τῇ προσευχῇ p[11vid,46] ℵ* A B C D G P Ψ 33 81 104 181 629 630 1739 1877 1881 1962 it[ar,d,dem,e,f,g,rl,t,x,z] vg cop[sa,bo,fay] arm eth (Clement) Origen[gr,lat] Cyprian Dionysius Methodius Ambrosiaster Epiphanius Chrysostom[comm] Augustine Euthalius ∥ τῇ νηστείᾳ καὶ τῇ προσευχῇ (*see* Mk 9.29 mg) ℵ[c] K 88 326 436 614 1241 1984 1985 2127 2492 2495 *Byz Lect* syr[p,h] goth Dionysius Ephraem Chrysostom[txt] Theodoret ∥ τῇ προσευχῇ καὶ νηστείᾳ (*see* Mk 9.29 mg) 330 451 John-Damascus

[2] **7** {B} δέ p[46] ℵ* A C D* G 33[vid] 81 181 326 629 1877 1962 1985 it[ar,vid,d,] dem[vid],e,f,g,rl,t,x,z vg[ww] cop[bo] goth Tertullian Origen[2/3] Cyprian Ambrosiaster Chrysostom[1/2] Cyril Euthalius John-Damascus ∥ γάρ ℵ[c] B D[b,c] K P Ψ 88 104 330 436 451 614 630 1241 1739 1881 1984 2127 2492 2495 *Byz Lect* vg[cl] syr[p,h] cop[sa] arm eth Origen[1/3] Chrysostom[1/2] Theodoret

---

20 ἠγοράσθητε γὰρ τιμῆς 1 Cor 7.23; 1 Pe 1.18–19   δοξάσατε...ὑμῶν Php 1.20
7 7 Mt 19.11–12

has given him, one man this gift, another man that.

8 Now, I say this to the unmarried and to the widows: it would be better for you to continue to live alone, as I do. 9 But if you cannot restrain your desires, go on and marry — it is better to marry than to burn with passion.

10 For married people I have a command, not my own but the Lord's: a married woman must not leave her husband; 11 if she does, she must remain single or else be reconciled to her husband; and a husband must not divorce his wife.

12 To the others I say (I, myself, not the Lord): if a Christian man has a wife who is an unbeliever and she agrees to go on living with him, he must not divorce her. 13 And if a Christian woman is married to a man who is an unbeliever, and he agrees to go on living with her, she must not divorce him. 14 For the unbelieving husband is made acceptable to God by being united to his wife, and the unbelieving wife is made acceptable to God by being united to her Christian husband. If this were not so, their children would be like pagan children; but as it is, they are acceptable to God. 15 However, if the one who is not a believer wishes to leave the Christian partner, let him do so. In such cases the Christian partner, whether husband or wife, is free to choose; for God has called you to live in peace. 16 How can you be sure, Christian wife, that you will not save your husband? Or how can you be sure, Christian husband, that you will not save your wife?

ἀλλὰ ἕκαστος ἴδιον ἔχει χάρισμα ἐκ θεοῦ, ὁ μὲν οὕτως, ὁ δὲ οὕτως.

8 Λέγω δὲ τοῖς ἀγάμοις καὶ ταῖς χήραις, καλὸν αὐτοῖς ἐὰν μείνωσιν ὡς κἀγώ· 9 εἰ δὲ οὐκ ἐγκρατεύονται γαμησάτωσαν, κρεῖττον γάρ ἐστιν γαμῆσαι ἢ πυροῦσθαι. 10 τοῖς δὲ γεγαμηκόσιν παραγγέλλω, οὐκ ἐγὼ ἀλλὰ ὁ κύριος, γυναῖκα ἀπὸ ἀνδρὸς μὴ χωρισθῆναι 11 — ἐὰν δὲ καὶ χωρισθῇ, μενέτω ἄγαμος ἢ τῷ ἀνδρὶ καταλλαγήτω — καὶ ἄνδρα γυναῖκα μὴ ἀφιέναι. 12 Τοῖς δὲ λοιποῖς λέγω ἐγώ, οὐχ ὁ κύριος· εἴ τις ἀδελφὸς γυναῖκα ἔχει ἄπιστον, καὶ αὕτη συνευδοκεῖ οἰκεῖν μετ᾽ αὐτοῦ, μὴ ἀφιέτω αὐτήν· 13 καὶ γυνὴ εἴ τις[3] ἔχει ἄνδρα ἄπιστον, καὶ οὗτος συνευδοκεῖ οἰκεῖν μετ᾽ αὐτῆς, μὴ ἀφιέτω τὸν ἄνδρα. 14 ἡγίασται γὰρ ὁ ἀνὴρ ὁ ἄπιστος ἐν τῇ γυναικί, καὶ ἡγίασται ἡ γυνὴ ἡ ἄπιστος ἐν τῷ ἀδελφῷ[4]· ἐπεὶ ἄρα τὰ τέκνα ὑμῶν ἀκάθαρτά ἐστιν, νῦν δὲ ἅγιά ἐστιν. 15 εἰ δὲ ὁ ἄπιστος χωρίζεται, χωριζέσθω· οὐ δεδούλωται ὁ ἀδελφὸς ἢ ἡ ἀδελφὴ ἐν τοῖς τοιούτοις· ἐν δὲ εἰρήνῃ κέκληκεν ὑμᾶς[5] ὁ θεός. 16 τί γὰρ οἶδας, γύναι, εἰ τὸν ἄνδρα σώσεις; ἢ τί οἶδας, ἄνερ, εἰ τὴν γυναῖκα σώσεις;

---

3 13 {D} εἴ τις 𝔭46 ℵ D* G P 1984 1985 2495 Lect (l809 *beginning of lection*) itar,d,dem,e,f,g,t,x,z vg copsa Ambrosiaster Chrysostom Augustine Theodoret John-Damascus Theophylact ∥ ἥτις A B Dᶜ K Ψ 33 81 88 104 181 326 330 436 451 614 (629 *transposes:* ἢ τις γυνή) 630 1241 1739 1877 1881 1962 2127 2492 *Byz* syrp,h copsams,bo,fay goth arm Chrysostom Cyril Theodoret

4 14 {B} ἀδελφῷ 𝔭46 ℵ* A B C D* G P Ψ 33 181 1739 1877 1962 itd,e,f,g copsa,bo,fay Augustine ∥ ἀνδρί ℵᶜ Dᶜ K 81 88 104 326 330 436 451 614 630 1241 1881 1984 1985 2127 2492 2495 *Byz Lect* syrh goth arm eth (Clement) Ephraem Chrysostom Euthalius Theodoret John-Damascus ∥ ἀνδρὶ τῷ πιστῷ 629 itar,c,dem,t,x,z vg syrp Irenaeuslat Tertullian Ambrosiaster

5 15 {C} ὑμᾶς ℵ* A C K 81 181 326 1877 1984 2127 copbo Pelagius Euthalius John-Damascus Theophylact ∥ ἡμᾶς 𝔭46 ℵᶜ B D G Ψ 33 104 330 436 451 614 629 630 1241 1739 1881 1962 1985 2492 2495 *Byz Lect* itar,d,dem,e,f,g,x,z vg syrp,h copsa,fay goth arm eth Origen Ambrosiaster Gregory-Nyssa Chrysostom Pelagius Theodoret Ps-Jerome Cassiodorus Photius Ps-Oecumenius

---

9 εἰ...γαμησάτωσαν 1 Tm 5.14   10–11 γυναῖκα...ἀφιέναι Mt 5.32; 19.9; Mk 10.11–12; Lk 16.18   14 Ro 11.16   15 ἐν δὲ...θεός Ro 14.19   16 τί γὰρ...σώσεις 1 Pe 3.1

The Life Which the Lord Has Assigned

17 Εἰ μὴ ἑκάστῳ ὡς ἐμέρισεν ὁ κύριος, ἕκαστον ὡς κέκληκεν ὁ θεός, οὕτως περιπατείτω· καὶ οὕτως ἐν ταῖς ἐκκλησίαις πάσαις διατάσσομαι. 18 περιτετμημένος τις ἐκλήθη;[a] μὴ ἐπισπάσθω. ἐν ἀκροβυστίᾳ κέκληταί τις;[b] μὴ περιτεμνέσθω. 19 ἡ περιτομὴ οὐδέν ἐστιν, καὶ ἡ ἀκροβυστία οὐδέν ἐστιν, ἀλλὰ τήρησις ἐντολῶν θεοῦ. 20 ἕκαστος ἐν τῇ κλήσει ᾗ ἐκλήθη ἐν ταύτῃ μενέτω. 21 δοῦλος ἐκλήθης;[c] μή σοι μελέτω· ἀλλ' εἰ καὶ δύνασαι ἐλεύθερος γενέσθαι, μᾶλλον χρῆσαι. 22 ὁ γὰρ ἐν κυρίῳ κληθεὶς δοῦλος ἀπελεύθερος κυρίου ἐστίν· ὁμοίως ὁ ἐλεύθερος κληθεὶς δοῦλός ἐστιν Χριστοῦ. 23 τιμῆς ἠγοράσθητε· μὴ γίνεσθε δοῦλοι ἀνθρώπων. 24 ἕκαστος ἐν ᾧ ἐκλήθη, ἀδελφοί, ἐν τούτῳ μενέτω παρὰ θεῷ.

The Unmarried and Widows

25 Περὶ δὲ τῶν παρθένων ἐπιταγὴν κυρίου οὐκ ἔχω, γνώμην δὲ δίδωμι ὡς ἠλεημένος ὑπὸ κυρίου πιστὸς εἶναι. 26 Νομίζω οὖν τοῦτο καλὸν ὑπάρχειν διὰ τὴν ἐνεστῶσαν ἀνάγκην, ὅτι καλὸν ἀνθρώπῳ τὸ οὕτως εἶναι. 27 δέδεσαι γυναικί;[d] μὴ ζήτει λύσιν· λέλυσαι ἀπὸ γυναικός;[e] μὴ ζήτει γυναῖκα. 28 ἐὰν δὲ καὶ γαμήσῃς, οὐχ ἥμαρτες· καὶ ἐὰν γήμῃ ἡ παρθένος, οὐχ ἥμαρτεν. θλῖψιν δὲ τῇ σαρκὶ ἕξουσιν οἱ τοιοῦτοι, ἐγὼ δὲ ὑμῶν φείδομαι. 29 τοῦτο δέ φημι, ἀδελφοί, ὁ καιρὸς συνεσταλμένος ἐστίν·[f] τὸ λοιπὸν[f] ἵνα καὶ οἱ ἔχοντες γυναῖκας

---

a 18 a question: TR WH Bov Nes BF² AV RV ASV RSV NEB TT Jer // a minor: Zür Luth Seg
b 18 b question: TR WH Bov Nes BF² AV RV ASV RSV NEB TT Jer // b minor: Zür Luth Seg
c 21 c question: TR WH Bov Nes BF² AV RV ASV RSV NEB TT Jer // c minor: Zür Luth Seg
d 27 d question: TR WH Bov Nes BF² AV RV ASV RSV NEB TT Jer // d minor: Zür Luth Seg
e 27 e question: TR WH Bov Nes BF² AV RV ASV RSV NEB TT Jer // e minor: Zür Luth Seg
f f 29 f minor, f none: WH Bov Nes BF² RV ASV (RSV) (NEB) TT Zür (Luth) (Jer) Seg //
f none, f minor: WHᵐᵍ RVᵐᵍ ASVᵐᵍ // different text: TR AV

17 ἕκαστον...περιπατείτω 1 Cor 7.20, 24   19 Ro 2.25; Ga 5.6; 6.15   22 ὁ γὰρ...ἐστίν Phm 16   ὁ ἐλεύθερος...Χριστοῦ Eph 6.6; 1 Pe 2.16   25 ἠλεημένος...εἶναι 1 Tm 1.12–13 28 θλῖψιν...τοιοῦτοι Lk 21.23   29 ὁ καιρὸς συνεσταλμένος ἐστίν Ro 13.11

Live as God Called You

17 Each one should go on living according to the Lord's gift to him, and as he was when God called him. This is the rule I teach in all the churches. 18 If a circumcised man has accepted God's call, he should not try to remove the marks of circumcision; if an uncircumcised man has accepted God's call, he should not get circumcised. 19 Because being circumcised or not means nothing. What matters is to obey God's commandments. 20 Every man should remain as he was when he accepted God's call. 21 Were you a slave when God called you? Well, never mind; but if you do have a chance to become a free man, use it. 22 For a slave who has been called by the Lord is the Lord's free man; in the same way a free man who has been called by Christ is his slave. 23 God bought you for a price; so do not become men's slaves. 24 Brothers, each one should remain in fellowship with God as he was when he was called.

Questions about the Unmarried and the Widows

25 Now, the matter about the unmarried: I do not have a command from the Lord, but I give my opinion as one who by the Lord's mercy is worthy of trust. 26 Considering the present distress, I think it is better for a man to stay as he is. 27 Do you have a wife? Then don't try to get rid of her. Are you unmarried? Then don't look for a wife. 28 But if you do marry, you haven't committed a sin; and if an unmarried woman marries, she hasn't committed a sin. But I would rather spare you the everyday troubles that such people will have.
29 This is what I mean, brothers: there is not much time left, and from now on

married men should live as though they were not married; ³⁰ those who weep, as though they were not sad; those who laugh, as though they were not happy; those who buy, as though they did not own what they bought; ³¹ those who deal in worldly goods, as though they were not fully occupied with them. For this world, as it is now, will not last much longer.

³² I would like you to be free from worry. An unmarried man concerns himself with the Lord's work, because he is trying to please the Lord; ³³ but a married man concerns himself with worldly matters, because he wants to please his wife, ³⁴ and so he is pulled in two directions. An unmarried woman or a virgin concerns herself with the Lord's work, because she wants to be dedicated both in body and spirit; but a married woman concerns herself with worldly matters, because she wants to please her husband.

³⁵ I am saying this because I want to help you. I am not trying to put restrictions on you. Instead I want you to do what is right and proper, and give yourselves completely to the Lord's service without any reservation.

³⁶ In the case of an engaged couple who have decided not to marry: if the man feels that he is not acting properly toward the girl; if his passions are too strong, and he feels that they ought to marry, then they should get married, as he wants to. There is no sin in this. ³⁷ But if a man, without being forced to do so, has firmly made up his mind not to marry; if he has his will under complete control, and has already decided in his own mind what to do — then he does well not to marry the girl. ³⁸ So the man who marries his girl does well, but the one who does not marry her will do even better.[1]

---

[1] **36–38** The man *and* the girl *in this passage may be* a father and his daughter, *instead of* an engaged couple who have decided not to marry

ὡς μὴ ἔχοντες ὦσιν, 30 καὶ οἱ κλαίοντες ὡς μὴ κλαίοντες, καὶ οἱ χαίροντες ὡς μὴ χαίροντες, καὶ οἱ ἀγοράζοντες ὡς μὴ κατέχοντες, 31 καὶ οἱ χρώμενοι τὸν κόσμον ὡς μὴ καταχρώμενοι· παράγει γὰρ τὸ σχῆμα τοῦ κόσμου τούτου. 32 θέλω δὲ ὑμᾶς ἀμερίμνους εἶναι. ὁ ἄγαμος μεριμνᾷ τὰ τοῦ κυρίου, πῶς ἀρέσῃ τῷ κυρίῳ· 33 ὁ δὲ γαμήσας μεριμνᾷ τὰ τοῦ κόσμου, πῶς ἀρέσῃ τῇ γυναικί, 34 ^g καὶ μεμέρισται. ^g καὶ ἡ γυνὴ ἡ ἄγαμος καὶ ἡ παρθένος[6] μεριμνᾷ τὰ τοῦ κυρίου, ^g ἵνα ᾖ ἁγία [καὶ] τῷ σώματι καὶ τῷ πνεύματι· ἡ δὲ γαμήσασα μεριμνᾷ τὰ τοῦ κόσμου, πῶς ἀρέσῃ τῷ ἀνδρί. 35 τοῦτο δὲ πρὸς τὸ ὑμῶν αὐτῶν σύμφορον λέγω, οὐχ ἵνα βρόχον ὑμῖν ἐπιβάλω, ἀλλὰ πρὸς τὸ εὔσχημον καὶ εὐπάρεδρον τῷ κυρίῳ ἀπερισπάστως.

36 Εἰ δέ τις ἀσχημονεῖν ἐπὶ τὴν παρθένον αὐτοῦ νομίζει ἐὰν ᾖ ὑπέρακμος, καὶ οὕτως ὀφείλει γίνεσθαι, ὃ θέλει ποιείτω· οὐχ ἁμαρτάνει· γαμείτωσαν. 37 ὃς δὲ ἕστηκεν ἐν τῇ καρδίᾳ αὐτοῦ ἑδραῖος, μὴ ἔχων ἀνάγκην, ἐξουσίαν δὲ ἔχει περὶ τοῦ ἰδίου θελήματος, καὶ τοῦτο κέκρικεν ἐν τῇ ἰδίᾳ καρδίᾳ, τηρεῖν τὴν ἑαυτοῦ παρθένον, καλῶς ποιήσει· 38 ὥστε καὶ ὁ γαμίζων τὴν ἑαυτοῦ παρθένον καλῶς ποιεῖ, καὶ ὁ μὴ γαμίζων κρεῖσσον ποιήσει.

---

[6] **34** {D} καὶ μεμέρισται. καὶ ἡ γυνὴ ἡ ἄγαμος καὶ ἡ παρθένος 𝔭¹⁵ B P 104 (181* *omit* καὶ ἡ παρθένος) 181^c 1962 2495 it^{t,x,z} vg cop^{sa,bo} Eusebius ‖ μεμέρισται καὶ ἡ γυνὴ καὶ ἡ παρθένος ἡ ἄγαμος D^c G K Ψ 326 330 436 451 614 630 1984 1985 2492 *Byz* it^{d?e,g,m} ‖ καὶ μεμέρισται. καὶ ἡ γυνὴ ἡ ἄγαμος καὶ ἡ παρθένος ἡ ἄγαμος 𝔭⁴⁶ ℵ A 33 81 1739 1877 1881 eth ‖ καὶ μεμέρισται ἡ γυνή· καὶ ἡ παρθένος ἡ ἄγαμος D^{gr*} 629 1241 arm? ‖ μεμέρισται ἡ γυνὴ καὶ ἡ παρθένος ἡ ἄγαμος D^{abs1} *Lect* ‖ μεμέρισται δὲ ἡ γυνὴ καὶ ἡ παρθένος ἡ ἄγαμος syr^p ‖ καὶ μεμέρισται ἡ γυνὴ ἡ ἄγαμος καὶ ἡ παρθένος 88 2127 it^{demvid} ‖ καὶ μεμέρισται καὶ ἡ γυνὴ καὶ ἡ παρθένος· ἡ ἄγαμος syr^h ‖ καὶ μεμέρισται καὶ ἡ γυνὴ καὶ ἡ παρθένος it^{(f),gig}

---

^{g g g} **33-34** *g* number 34, *g* no number, *g* no number: (TR^{ed}) Bov Nes BF² AV RV ASV RSV NEB? TT Zür Jer Seg ‖ *g* no number, *g* number 34, *g* no number: (TR^{ed}) NEB? Luth ‖ *g* no number, *g* no number, *g* number 34: WH

---

31 παράγει...τούτου 1 Jn 2.17

39 Γυνὴ δέδεται ἐφ' ὅσον χρόνον ζῇ ὁ ἀνὴρ αὐτῆς· ἐὰν δὲ κοιμηθῇ ὁ ἀνήρ, ἐλευθέρα ἐστὶν ᾧ θέλει γαμηθῆναι, μόνον ἐν κυρίῳ. **40** μακαριωτέρα δέ ἐστιν ἐὰν οὕτως μείνῃ, κατὰ τὴν ἐμὴν γνώμην, δοκῶ δὲ κἀγὼ πνεῦμα θεοῦ ἔχειν.

Food Offered to Idols

8 Περὶ δὲ τῶν εἰδωλοθύτων, οἴδαμεν ὅτι πάντες γνῶσιν ἔχομεν. ἡ γνῶσις φυσιοῖ, ἡ δὲ ἀγάπη οἰκοδομεῖ. **2** εἴ τις δοκεῖ ἐγνωκέναι τι[1], οὔπω ἔγνω καθὼς δεῖ γνῶναι· **3** εἰ δέ τις ἀγαπᾷ τὸν θεόν[2], οὗτος ἔγνωσται ὑπ' αὐτοῦ[3]. **4** Περὶ τῆς βρώσεως οὖν τῶν εἰδωλοθύτων οἴδαμεν ὅτι οὐδὲν εἴδωλον ἐν κόσμῳ, καὶ ὅτι οὐδεὶς θεὸς εἰ μὴ εἷς. **5** καὶ γὰρ εἴπερ εἰσὶν λεγόμενοι θεοὶ εἴτε ἐν οὐρανῷ εἴτε ἐπὶ γῆς, ὥσπερ εἰσὶν θεοὶ πολλοὶ καὶ κύριοι πολλοί, **6** ἀλλ' ἡμῖν εἷς θεὸς ὁ πατήρ, ἐξ οὗ τὰ πάντα καὶ ἡμεῖς εἰς αὐτόν, καὶ εἷς κύριος Ἰησοῦς Χριστός, δι' οὗ τὰ πάντα καὶ ἡμεῖς δι' αὐτοῦ.

7 Ἀλλ' οὐκ ἐν πᾶσιν ἡ γνῶσις· τινὲς δὲ τῇ συνηθείᾳ[4]

---

1 2 {B} τι (see footnotes 2 and 3) 𝔭[15] ℵ A B D G K P Ψ 33 81 88 104 181 326 330 436 451 614 629 630 1241 1739 1877 1881 1962 1984 1985 2492 2495 Byz Lect it[ar,d,dem,e,f,g,x,z] vg syr[p,h] cop[sa,bo,fay] arm // omit 𝔭[46] Tertullian Origen[lat] Ambrosiaster Hilary

2 3 {B} τὸν θεόν (see footnotes 1 and 3) 𝔭[15] ℵ A B D G K P Ψ 33 81 88 104 181 326 330 436 451 614 629 630 1241 1739 1877 1881 1962 1984 1985 2492 2495 Byz Lect it[ar,d,dem,e,f,g,x,z] vg syr[p,h] cop[sa,bo,fay] arm // omit 𝔭[46] Clement (Ephraem)

3 3 {C} ὑπ' αὐτοῦ (see footnotes 1 and 2) 𝔭[15vid] ℵ[c] A B D G K P Ψ 81 88 104 181 326 330 436 451 614 629 630 1241 1739 1877 1881 1962 1984 1985 2492 2495 Byz Lect it[ar,d,dem,e,f,g,x,z] vg syr[p,h] cop[sa,bo,fay] arm // omit 𝔭[46] ℵ* 33 Clement (Ephraem)

4 7 {B} συνηθείᾳ ℵ* A B P Ψ 33 81 181 436 630 1739 1877 1881 1962 syr[hmg] cop[sa,bo,fay] eth Euthalius John-Damascus // συνειδήσει ℵ[c] D G 88 104 326 330 451 614 629 1241 1984 1985 2127 2492 2495 Byz Lect it[ar,d,dem,e,f,g,x,z] vg syr[p,h] arm Tertullian Ambrosiaster Chrysostom Augustine Theodoret

---

39 Ro 7.2 3

8 1 Περὶ...εἰδωλοθύτων Ac 15.29   **2** Ga 6.3   **3** Ga 4.9   **4** Περὶ...κόσμῳ 1 Cor 10.19 οὐδεὶς...εἷς Dt 4.35, 39; 6.4   **6** εἷς θεός...πάντα Mal 2.10; 1 Cor 12.6; Eph 4.6   εἷς κύριος... αὐτοῦ Jn 1.3; 1 Cor 12.5; Eph 4.5; Col 1.16

[39] A married woman is not free as long as her husband lives; but if her husband dies, then she is free to be married to the man she wants; but it must be a Christian marriage. [40] She will be happier, however, if she stays as she is. That is my opinion, and I think that I too have God's Spirit.

The Question about Food Offered to Idols

8 Now, the matter about food offered to idols.

It is true, of course, that "all of us have knowledge," as they say. Such knowledge, however, puffs a man up with pride; but love builds up. [2] The person who thinks he knows something really doesn't know as he ought to know. [3] But the man who loves God is known by him.

[4] So then, about eating the food offered to idols: we know that an idol stands for something that does not really exist; we know that there is only the one God. [5] Even if there are so-called "gods," whether in heaven or on earth, and even though there are many of these "gods" and "lords," [6] yet there is for us only one God, the Father, who is the creator of all things, and for whom we live; and there is only one Lord, Jesus Christ, through whom all things were created, and through whom we live.

[7] But not everyone knows this truth. Certain people are so used to idols that to this very day when they eat such food they still think of it as food that belongs to an idol; their conscience is

weak and they feel they are defiled by the food. [8] Food, however, will not bring us any closer to God; we shall not lose anything if we do not eat, nor shall we gain anything if we do eat.

[9] Be careful, however, and do not let your freedom of action make those who are weak in the faith fall into sin. [10] For if a man whose conscience is weak in this matter sees you, who have "knowledge," eating in the temple of an idol, will not this encourage him to eat food offered to idols? [11] And so this weak man, your brother for whom Christ died, will perish because of your "knowledge"! [12] And in this way you will be sinning against Christ by sinning against your brothers and wounding their weak conscience. [13] If food makes my brother sin, I myself will never eat meat again, so as not to make my brother fall into sin.

Rights and Duties of an Apostle

9 Am I not a free man? Am I not an apostle? Haven't I seen Jesus our Lord? And aren't you the result of my work for the Lord? [2] Even if others do not accept me as an apostle, surely you do! You yourselves, because of your life in the Lord, are proof of the fact that I am an apostle.

[3] When people criticize me, this is how I defend myself: [4] Don't I have the right to be given food and drink for my work? [5] Don't I have the right to do what the other apostles do, and the Lord's brothers, and Peter, and take a Christian wife with me on my trips? [6] Or are Barnabas and I the only ones who have to work for our living? [7] Who ever heard of a soldier who paid his own expenses in the army? Or of a farmer who did not eat the grapes from his own vineyard? Or of a shepherd who did not use the milk from his own sheep?

ἕως ἄρτι τοῦ εἰδώλου ὡς εἰδωλόθυτον ἐσθίουσιν, καὶ ἡ συνείδησις αὐτῶν ἀσθενὴς οὖσα μολύνεται. 8 βρῶμα δὲ ἡμᾶς οὐ παραστήσει τῷ θεῷ· οὔτε ἐὰν μὴ φάγωμεν ὑστερούμεθα, οὔτε ἐὰν φάγωμεν περισσεύομεν. 9 βλέπετε δὲ μή πως ἡ ἐξουσία ὑμῶν αὕτη πρόσκομμα γένηται τοῖς ἀσθενέσιν. 10 ἐὰν γάρ τις ἴδῃ σὲ τὸν ἔχοντα γνῶσιν ἐν εἰδωλείῳ κατακείμενον, οὐχὶ ἡ συνείδησις αὐτοῦ ἀσθενοῦς ὄντος οἰκοδομηθήσεται εἰς τὸ τὰ εἰδωλόθυτα ἐσθίειν; 11 ἀπόλλυται γὰρ ὁ ἀσθενῶν ἐν τῇ σῇ γνώσει, ὁ ἀδελφὸς δι' ὃν Χριστὸς ἀπέθανεν. 12 οὕτως δὲ ἁμαρτάνοντες εἰς τοὺς ἀδελφοὺς καὶ τύπτοντες αὐτῶν τὴν συνείδησιν ἀσθενοῦσαν[5] εἰς Χριστὸν ἁμαρτάνετε. 13 διόπερ εἰ βρῶμα σκανδαλίζει τὸν ἀδελφόν μου, οὐ μὴ φάγω κρέα εἰς τὸν αἰῶνα, ἵνα μὴ τὸν ἀδελφόν μου σκανδαλίσω.

The Rights of an Apostle

9 Οὐκ εἰμὶ ἐλεύθερος; οὐκ εἰμὶ ἀπόστολος; οὐχὶ Ἰησοῦν τὸν κύριον ἡμῶν ἑώρακα; οὐ τὸ ἔργον μου ὑμεῖς ἐστε ἐν κυρίῳ; 2 εἰ ἄλλοις οὐκ εἰμὶ ἀπόστολος, ἀλλά.γε ὑμῖν εἰμι· ἡ γὰρ σφραγίς μου τῆς ἀποστολῆς ὑμεῖς ἐστε ἐν κυρίῳ.

3 Ἡ ἐμὴ ἀπολογία τοῖς ἐμὲ ἀνακρίνουσίν ἐστιν αὕτη. 4 μὴ οὐκ ἔχομεν ἐξουσίαν φαγεῖν καὶ πεῖν; 5 μὴ οὐκ ἔχομεν ἐξουσίαν ἀδελφὴν γυναῖκα περιάγειν, ὡς καὶ οἱ λοιποὶ ἀπόστολοι καὶ οἱ ἀδελφοὶ τοῦ κυρίου καὶ Κηφᾶς; 6 ἢ μόνος ἐγὼ καὶ Βαρναβᾶς οὐκ ἔχομεν ἐξουσίαν μὴ ἐργάζεσθαι; 7 τίς στρατεύεται ἰδίοις ὀψωνίοις ποτέ; τίς φυτεύει ἀμπελῶνα καὶ τὸν καρπὸν αὐτοῦ οὐκ ἐσθίει; ἢ τίς ποιμαίνει ποίμνην καὶ ἐκ τοῦ γάλακτος τῆς ποίμνης

---

[5] **12** {A} ἀσθενοῦσαν ℵ A B D G K P Ψ 33 81 88 104 181 326 330 436 451 614 629 630 1241 1739 1877 1881 1962 1984 1985 2127 2492 2495 *Byz Lect* it^ar, d, dem, e, f, g, x, z vg syr^p, h cop^sa, bo, fay goth arm // *omit* 𝔭^46 Clement

---

8 Ro 14.17   **9** Ro 14.13, 15, 21; Ga 5.13   **11** Ro 14.15, 20   **13** Ro 14.21
9 **1** οὐχὶ...ἑώρακα Ac 22.17–18; 26.16; 1 Cor 15.8   **2** ἡ γάρ...κυρίῳ 2 Cor 3.2–3   **4** Lk 10.8; 1 Cor 9.13–14   **5** Κηφᾶς Jn 1.42

οὐκ ἐσθίει; 8 Μὴ κατὰ ἄνθρωπον ταῦτα λαλῶ,[a] ἢ καὶ ὁ νόμος ταῦτα οὐ λέγει;[a] 9 ἐν γὰρ τῷ Μωϋσέως νόμῳ γέγραπται, **Οὐ κημώσεις βοῦν ἀλοῶντα.** μὴ τῶν βοῶν μέλει τῷ θεῷ;[b] 10 ἢ δι' ἡμᾶς πάντως λέγει;[b] δι' ἡμᾶς γὰρ ἐγράφη, ὅτι ὀφείλει ἐπ' ἐλπίδι ὁ ἀροτριῶν ἀροτριᾶν, καὶ ὁ ἀλοῶν ἐπ' ἐλπίδι τοῦ μετέχειν. 11 εἰ ἡμεῖς ὑμῖν τὰ πνευματικὰ ἐσπείραμεν, μέγα εἰ ἡμεῖς ὑμῶν τὰ σαρκικὰ θερίσομεν; 12 εἰ ἄλλοι τῆς ὑμῶν ἐξουσίας μετέχουσιν, οὐ μᾶλλον ἡμεῖς;

Ἀλλ' οὐκ ἐχρησάμεθα τῇ ἐξουσίᾳ ταύτῃ, ἀλλὰ πάντα στέγομεν ἵνα μή τινα ἐγκοπὴν δῶμεν τῷ εὐαγγελίῳ τοῦ Χριστοῦ. 13 οὐκ οἴδατε ὅτι οἱ τὰ ἱερὰ ἐργαζόμενοι [τὰ] ἐκ τοῦ ἱεροῦ ἐσθίουσιν,[c] οἱ τῷ θυσιαστηρίῳ παρεδρεύοντες τῷ θυσιαστηρίῳ συμμερίζονται;[c] 14 οὕτως καὶ ὁ κύριος διέταξεν τοῖς τὸ εὐαγγέλιον καταγγέλλουσιν ἐκ τοῦ εὐαγγελίου ζῆν. 15 ἐγὼ δὲ οὐ κέχρημαι οὐδενὶ τούτων. οὐκ ἔγραψα δὲ ταῦτα ἵνα οὕτως γένηται ἐν ἐμοί, καλὸν γάρ μοι μᾶλλον ἀποθανεῖν ἢ — τὸ καύχημά μου οὐδεὶς κενώσει[1]. 16 ἐὰν γὰρ εὐαγγελίζωμαι, οὐκ ἔστιν μοι καύχημα· ἀνάγκη γάρ μοι ἐπίκειται· οὐαὶ γάρ μοι

---

[1] 15 {C} οὐδεὶς κενώσει 𝔓46 ℵ* B D*,ᵉ 33 1739 1881 itd.e syrᵖ copsa?fay? arm Tertullianᵛⁱᵈ Ambrosiaster ∥ οὐθεὶς μὴ κενώσει A ∥ τίς κενώσει G itᵍ syrʰ ∥ ἵνα τις κενώσῃ K Ψ (ℵᶜ C Dᵇˑᶜ P 326 614 1241 1877 1962 1985 2127 κενώσει) 81 88 104 330 436 451 629 630 1984 2492 2495 Byz Lect itar,dem,f,t,z vg copᵇᵒ? Ambrosiaster Ephraem Basil Chrysostom Jerome Augustine Theodoret John-Damascus ∥ ἵνα τις μὴ κενώσει 181 ∥ ἵνα τις οὐ μὴ κενώσῃ 917 1836 1898

ᵃ ᵃ **8** a minor, a question: WH Bov Nes BF² Zür ∥ a question, a question· TR AV RV ASV RSV TT Luth Jer Seg ∥ a a paraphrased: NEB

ᵇ ᵇ **9-10** b question, b question: Bov Nes BF² AV RSV NEB TT Luth Jer ∥ b minor, b question: TR WH RV ASV Zür Seg

ᶜ ᶜ **13** c minor, c question: TR WH Bov Nes BF² RV ASV RSV (NEB) TT Luth Jer Seg ∥ c question, c question: AV Zür

9 Οὐ...ἀλοῶντα Dt 25.4 (1 Tm 5.18)   **10** ἐπ'...μετέχειν 2 Tm 2.6   **11** Ro 15.27   **12** οὐκ...ταύτῃ Ac 20.24–35, 2 Cor 11.9   πάντα στέγομεν 1 Cor 13.7   **13** Lv 6.16, 26; Nu 18.8, 31; Dt 18.1-3   **14** Mt 10.10; Lk 10.7; Ga 6.6   **15** ἐγὼ...τούτων Ac 18.3   **16** ἀνάγκη... εὐαγγελίσωμαι Jr 20.9

---

[8] I don't have to limit myself to these everyday examples, for the Law says the same thing. [9] We read in the Law of Moses, "Do not tie up the mouth of the ox when it treads out the grain." Now, is God concerned about oxen? [10] Or did he not really mean us when he said this? Of course this was written for us! The man who plows and the man who reaps should do their work in the hope of getting a share of the crop. [11] We have sown spiritual seed among you. Is it too much if we reap material benefits from you? [12] If others have the right to expect this from you, don't we have an even greater right?

But we haven't made use of this right. Instead, we have endured everything in order not to put any obstacle in the way of the Good News about Christ. [13] Surely you know that the men who work in the Temple get their food from the Temple, and that those who offer the sacrifices on the altar get a share of the sacrifices. [14] In the same way, the Lord has ordered that those who preach the gospel should get their living from it.

[15] But I haven't made use of any of these rights, nor am I writing this now in order to claim such rights for myself. I would rather die first! Nobody is going to turn my rightful boast into empty words! [16] I have no right to boast just because I preach the gospel. After all, I am under orders to do so. And how terrible it would be for me if I

did not preach the gospel! ¹⁷ If I did my work as a matter of free choice, then I could expect to be paid; but since I do it as a matter of duty, it means that I do it as a job given me to do. ¹⁸ What pay do I get, then? It is the privilege of preaching the Good News without charging for it, without claiming my rights in my work for the gospel.

¹⁹ I am a free man, nobody's slave; but I make myself everybody's slave in order to win as many as possible. ²⁰ While working with the Jews, I live like a Jew in order to win them; and even though I myself am not subject to the Law of Moses, I live as though I were, when working with those who are, in order to win them. ²¹ In the same way, when with Gentiles I live like a Gentile, outside the Jewish Law, in order to win Gentiles. This does not mean that I don't obey God's law, for I am really under Christ's law. ²² Among the weak in faith I become weak like one of them, in order to win them. So I become all things to all men, that I may save some of them by any means possible.

²³ All this I do for the gospel's sake, in order to share in its blessings. ²⁴ Surely you know that in a race all the runners take part in it, but only one of them wins the prize. Run, then, in such a way as to win the prize. ²⁵ Every athlete in training submits to strict discipline; he does so in order to be crowned with a wreath that will not last; but we do it for one that will last for ever. ²⁶ That is why I run straight for the finish line; that is why I am like a boxer, who does not waste his punches. ²⁷ I harden my body with blows and bring it under complete control, to keep from being rejected myself after having called others to the contest.

ἐστιν ἐὰν μὴ εὐαγγελίσωμαι. 17 εἰ γὰρ ἑκὼν τοῦτο πράσσω, μισθὸν ἔχω· εἰ δὲ ἄκων, οἰκονομίαν πεπίστευμαι. 18 τίς οὖν μού ἐστιν ὁ μισθός; ἵνα εὐαγγελιζόμενος ἀδάπανον θήσω τὸ εὐαγγέλιον, εἰς τὸ μὴ καταχρήσασθαι τῇ ἐξουσίᾳ μου ἐν τῷ εὐαγγελίῳ.

19 Ἐλεύθερος γὰρ ὢν ἐκ πάντων πᾶσιν ἐμαυτὸν ἐδούλωσα, ἵνα τοὺς πλείονας κερδήσω· 20 καὶ ἐγενόμην τοῖς Ἰουδαίοις ὡς Ἰουδαῖος, ἵνα Ἰουδαίους κερδήσω· τοῖς ὑπὸ νόμον ὡς ὑπὸ νόμον, μὴ ὢν αὐτὸς ὑπὸ νόμον², ἵνα τοὺς ὑπὸ νόμον κερδήσω· 21 τοῖς ἀνόμοις ὡς ἄνομος, μὴ ὢν ἄνομος θεοῦ ἀλλ' ἔννομος Χριστοῦ, ἵνα κερδάνω τοὺς ἀνόμους· 22 ἐγενόμην τοῖς ἀσθενέσιν ἀσθενής, ἵνα τοὺς ἀσθενεῖς κερδήσω· τοῖς πᾶσιν γέγονα πάντα, ἵνα πάντως τινὰς σώσω. 23 πάντα δὲ ποιῶ διὰ τὸ εὐαγγέλιον, ἵνα συγκοινωνὸς αὐτοῦ γένωμαι.

24 Οὐκ οἴδατε ὅτι οἱ ἐν σταδίῳ τρέχοντες πάντες μὲν τρέχουσιν, εἷς δὲ λαμβάνει τὸ βραβεῖον; οὕτως τρέχετε ἵνα καταλάβητε. 25 πᾶς δὲ ὁ ἀγωνιζόμενος πάντα ἐγκρατεύεται, ἐκεῖνοι μὲν οὖν ἵνα φθαρτὸν στέφανον λάβωσιν, ἡμεῖς δὲ ἄφθαρτον. 26 ἐγὼ τοίνυν οὕτως τρέχω ὡς οὐκ ἀδήλως, οὕτως πυκτεύω ὡς οὐκ ἀέρα δέρων· 27 ἀλλὰ ὑπωπιάζω μου τὸ σῶμα καὶ δουλαγωγῶ, μή πως ἄλλοις κηρύξας αὐτὸς ἀδόκιμος γένωμαι.

---

² **20** {A} μὴ ὢν αὐτὸς ὑπὸ νόμον 𝔓⁴⁶ᵛⁱᵈ? ℵ A B C D* G P 33 104 181 436 629*ᵛⁱᵈ 630 1739 1877 2127 2495 itᵃʳ,ᵈ,ᵈᵉᵐ,ᵉ,f,g,x,z vg syrʰ copˢᵃ,ᵇᵒ goth arm Clement Origenᵍʳ,ˡᵃᵗ Ambrosiaster Chrysostomᵗˣᵗ Augustine Cyril John-Damascus ‖ omit Dᶜ K Ψ 81 88 326 330 451 614 629ᶜ 1241 1881 1984 1985 2492 Byz Lect syrᵖ eth Origen Chrysostomᶜᵒᵐᵐ Nestoriusᵃᶜᶜ· ᵗᵒ ᴹᵃʳⁱᵘˢ ᴹᵉʳᶜᵃᵗᵒʳ Theodoret Ps-Oecumenius Theophylact

---

17 οἰκονομίαν πεπίστευμαι 1 Cor 4.1   **19** πᾶσιν ἐμαυτὸν ἐδούλωσα Mt 20.26-27 **20** ἐγενόμην...Ἰουδαῖος Ac 16.3; 21.20-26   **21** τοῖς ἀνόμοις ὡς ἄνομος Ga 2.3   **22** ἐγενόμην ...ἀσθενής 2 Cor 11.29   ἵνα πάντως τινὰς σώσω Ro 11.14   **24** οὕτως...καταλάβητε Php 3.14; 2 Tm 4.7   **25** πᾶς...ἐγκρατεύεται 2 Tm 2.4-5   ἡμεῖς δὲ ἄφθαρτον 2 Tm 4.8; Jas 1.12; 1 Pe 5.4   **27** ὑπωπιάζω...δουλαγωγῶ Ro 8.13; 13.14

Warning against Idolatry

10 Οὐ θέλω γὰρ ὑμᾶς ἀγνοεῖν, ἀδελφοί, ὅτι οἱ πατέρες ἡμῶν πάντες ὑπὸ τὴν νεφέλην ἦσαν καὶ πάντες διὰ τῆς θαλάσσης διῆλθον, 2 καὶ πάντες εἰς τὸν Μωϋσῆν ἐβαπτί-σαντο[1] ἐν τῇ νεφέλῃ καὶ ἐν τῇ θαλάσσῃ, 3 καὶ πάντες τὸ αὐτὸ πνευματικὸν βρῶμα ἔφαγον, 4 καὶ πάντες τὸ αὐτὸ πνευματικὸν ἔπιον πόμα· ἔπινον γὰρ ἐκ πνευμα-τικῆς ἀκολουθούσης πέτρας· ἡ πέτρα δὲ ἦν ὁ Χριστός. 5 ἀλλ᾽ οὐκ ἐν τοῖς πλείοσιν αὐτῶν εὐδόκησεν ὁ θεός, κατεστρώθησαν γὰρ ἐν τῇ ἐρήμῳ. 6 ταῦτα δὲ τύποι ἡμῶν ἐγενήθησαν, εἰς τὸ μὴ εἶναι ἡμᾶς ἐπιθυμητὰς κακῶν, καθὼς κἀκεῖνοι ἐπεθύμησαν. 7 μηδὲ εἰδωλολάτραι γίνεσθε, καθώς τινες αὐτῶν· ὥσπερ γέγραπται, **Ἐκά-θισεν ὁ λαὸς φαγεῖν καὶ πεῖν, καὶ ἀνέστησαν παίζειν.** 8 μηδὲ πορνεύωμεν, καθώς τινες αὐτῶν ἐπόρνευσαν, καὶ ἔπεσαν μιᾷ ἡμέρᾳ εἴκοσι τρεῖς χιλιάδες. 9 μηδὲ ἐκπει-ράζωμεν τὸν κύριον[2], καθώς τινες αὐτῶν ἐξεπείρασαν, καὶ ὑπὸ τῶν ὄφεων ἀπώλλυντο. 10 μηδὲ γογγύζετε[3],

[1] **2** {C} ἐβαπτίσαντο p[46c] B K P 614 629 1241 1739 1881 1984 2492 *Byz Lect* (*l[603vid]*) syr[p, h] arm Origen Chrysostom Theodoret John-Damascus Photius Ps-Oecumenius ‖ ἐβαπτίζοντο p[46*] ‖ ἐβαπτίσθησαν ℵ A C D G Ψ 33 81 88 104 181 326 330 436 451 630 1877 1985 2127 2495 *l[597]* syr[pal] Marcion Irenaeus Adamantius Basil Didymus Chrysostom Cyril Euthalius Theodoret ‖ ἐβαπτίζοντο or ἐβαπτίσθησαν it[ar, d, dem, e, f, g, x, z] vg cop[sa, bo] goth

[2] **9** {C} κύριον ℵ B C P 33 104 181 326 436 1877 2127 syr[hmg] arm eth Epiphanius Chrysostom[1/1] Theodoret Cassiodorus John-Damascus Sedulius-Scotus ‖ Χριστόν p[46] D G K Ψ 88 330 451 614 629 630 1241 1739 1881 1984 2492 2495 *Byz Lect* it[ar, d, dem, e, f, g, x, z] vg syr[p, h] cop[sa, bo] Marcion Theotecnus Irenaeus[lat] Clement Origen Ambrosiaster Ephraem Chrysostom[3/4] Pelagius Augustine Ps-Oecumenius Theophylact ‖ θεόν A 81 Euthalius ‖ *omit τὸν κύριον* 1985

[3] **10** {C} γογγύζετε A B C K P Ψ 81[vid] 88 104 181 326 330 436 451 614

1 οἱ πατέρες...ἦσαν Ex 13.21–22   πάντες...διῆλθον Ex 14.22–29   **3** Ex 16.4, 35; Dt 8.3; Ps 78.24–29   4 πάντες...ἔπιον Ex 17.6, Nu 20.11, Ps 78.15   **5** Nu 14.16, 29, 30; Ps 78.31; He 3.17; Jd 5   **6** ταῦτα... ἐγενήθησαν 1 Cor 10.11   καθὼς κἀκεῖνοι ἐπεθύμησαν Nu 11.4, 34; Ps 106.14   **7** Ἐκάθισεν...παίζειν Ex 32.6   8 τινες...χιλιάδες Nu 25.1, 9   9 Nu 21.5–6   **10** Nu 14.2, 36; 16.41–49; Ps 106.25–27; He 3.11, 17

Warning against Idols

10 I want you to remember, brothers, what happened to our ancestors who followed Moses. They were all under the protection of the cloud, and all passed safely through the Red Sea. 2 In the cloud and in the sea they were all baptized as followers of Moses. 3 All ate the same spiritual bread, 4 and all drank the same spiritual drink; for they drank from that spiritual rock that went along with them; and that rock was Christ himself. 5 But even then God was not pleased with most of them, and so their dead bodies were scattered over the desert.

6 Now, all these things are examples for us, to warn us not to desire evil things, as they did, 7 nor to worship idols, as some of them did. As the scripture says, "The people sat down to eat and drink, and got up to dance." 8 We must not commit sexual immorality, as some of them did — and in one day twenty-three thousand of them fell dead. 9 We must not put the Lord to the test, as some of them did — and they were killed by the snakes. 10 You must not

transition
— ethics
— sacramental notion of body
— freedom ; rel. both these 3

complain, as some of them did — and they were destroyed by the Angel of Death.

¹¹ All these things happened to them as examples for others, and they were written down as a warning for us. For we live at the time when the end is about to come.

¹² The one who thinks he is standing up better be careful that he does not fall. ¹³ Every temptation that has come your way is the kind that normally comes to people. For God keeps his promise, and he will not allow you to be tempted beyond your power to resist; but at the time you are tempted he will give you the strength to endure it, and so provide you with a way out.

¹⁴ So then, my dear friends, keep away from the worship of idols. ¹⁵ I speak to you as sensible people; judge for yourselves what I say. ¹⁶ The cup of blessing for which we give thanks to God: do we not share in the blood of Christ when we drink from this cup? And the bread we break: do we not share in the body of Christ when we eat this bread? ¹⁷ Because there is the one bread, all of us, though many, are one body; for we all share the same loaf.

¹⁸ Consider the Hebrew people: those who eat what is offered in sacrifice share in the altar's service to God. ¹⁹ What do I mean? That an idol or the food offered to it really amounts to anything? ²⁰ No! What I am saying is that what is sacrificed on pagan altars is offered to demons, not to God. And I do not want you to

καθάπερ τινὲς αὐτῶν ἐγόγγυσαν, καὶ ἀπώλοντο ὑπὸ τοῦ ὀλοθρευτοῦ. 11 ταῦτα δὲ⁴ τυπικῶς συνέβαινεν ἐκείνοις, ἐγράφη δὲ πρὸς νουθεσίαν ἡμῶν, εἰς οὓς τὰ τέλη τῶν αἰώνων κατήντηκεν. 12 ὥστε ὁ δοκῶν ἑστάναι βλεπέτω μὴ πέσῃ. 13 πειρασμὸς ὑμᾶς οὐκ εἴληφεν εἰ μὴ ἀνθρώπινος· πιστὸς δὲ ὁ θεός, ὃς οὐκ ἐάσει ὑμᾶς πειρασθῆναι ὑπὲρ ὃ δύνασθε, ἀλλὰ ποιήσει σὺν τῷ πειρασμῷ καὶ τὴν ἔκβασιν τοῦ δύνασθαι ὑπενεγκεῖν.

14 Διόπερ, ἀγαπητοί μου, φεύγετε ἀπὸ τῆς εἰδωλολατρίας. 15 ὡς φρονίμοις λέγω· κρίνατε ὑμεῖς ὅ φημι. 16 τὸ ποτήριον τῆς εὐλογίας ὃ εὐλογοῦμεν, οὐχὶ κοινωνία ἐστὶν τοῦ αἵματος τοῦ Χριστοῦ; τὸν ἄρτον ὃν κλῶμεν, οὐχὶ κοινωνία τοῦ σώματος τοῦ Χριστοῦ ἐστιν; 17 ὅτι εἷς ἄρτος, ἓν σῶμα οἱ πολλοί ἐσμεν, οἱ γὰρ πάντες ἐκ τοῦ ἑνὸς ἄρτου μετέχομεν. 18 βλέπετε τὸν Ἰσραὴλ κατὰ σάρκα· οὐχ οἱ ἐσθίοντες τὰς θυσίας κοινωνοὶ τοῦ θυσιαστηρίου εἰσίν; 19 τί οὖν φημι; ὅτι εἰδωλόθυτόν τί ἐστιν;ᵃ ἢ ὅτι εἴδωλόν τί ἐστιν;ᵃ 20 ἀλλ' ὅτι ἃ θύουσιν [τὰ ἔθνη], δαιμονίοις καὶ οὐ θεῷ θύουσιν⁵, οὐ θέλω δὲ

---

629 630 1241 1739 1877 1881 1984 1985 2127 2492 2495 *Byz Lect* it^{ar,dem,f,x,z} vg syr^{p,h} cop^{sa} eth Irenaeus^{lat} Origen^{lat} Eusebius Ambrosiaster Basil Chrysostom Augustine Euthalius Theodoret John-Damascus ‖ γογγύζωμεν ℵ D G^{gr} 33 it^{d,e} cop^{bo} arm Origen Chrysostom Augustine ‖ *murmuraverunt* it^g

⁴ 11 {C} ταῦτα δέ A B 33 630 1739 1881 cop^{sa} Marcion Irenaeus^{lat} Tertullian Hippolytus Origen^{gr,lat} Adamantius Basil Cyril-Jerusalem Pacian Chrysostom Cyril ‖ ταῦτα δὲ πάντα C K P Ψ 88 104 326 330 436 451 614 629 1241 1877 1984 (1985 τὰ πάντα) 2127 2492 2495 *Byz Lect* it^{ar,d,dem,e,x,z} vg syr^{p,h} cop^{bo} arm Irenaeus^{lat} Origen^{lat} Ambrosiaster Chrysostom Euthalius Theodoret John-Damascus ‖ πάντα δὲ ταῦτα ℵ D^{gr} G 81 181 it^{f,g} eth Irenaeus^{lat} Origen^{gr,lat} Chrysostom Augustine

⁵ 20 {C} ἃ θύουσιν τὰ ἔθνη, δαιμονίοις καὶ οὐ θεῷ θύουσιν 𝔓^{46vid} ℵ A

ᵃ ᵃ 19 a question, a question: TR Bov Nes BF² NEB TT Luth Jer Seg ‖ a minor, a question: WH AV RV ASV RSV (Zür)

---

11 ταῦτα...ἐκείνοις 1 Cor 10.6   εἰς...κατήντηκεν 1 Pe 4.7   13 πιστὸς...θεός Dt 7.9; 1 Cor 1.9; 1 Th 5.24   14 1 Jn 5.21   16 Mt 26.26–28; Mk 14.22–24; Lk 22.19–20   τὸν ἄρτον ὃν κλῶμεν Ac 2.42   17 ἕν...ἐσμεν Ro 12.5; 1 Cor 12.27; Eph 4.16; Col 3.15   18 οὐχ οἱ ἐσθίοντες ...εἰσίν Lv 7.6, 15   19 1 Cor 8.4   20 δαιμονίοις...θύουσιν Dt 32.17; Ps 106.37; Bar 4.7; Re 9.20

ὑμᾶς κοινωνοὺς τῶν δαιμονίων γίνεσθαι. **21** οὐ δύνασθε ποτήριον κυρίου πίνειν καὶ ποτήριον δαιμονίων· οὐ δύνασθε τραπέζης κυρίου μετέχειν καὶ τραπέζης δαιμονίων. **22** ἢ παραζηλοῦμεν τὸν κύριον; μὴ ἰσχυρότεροι αὐτοῦ ἐσμεν;

Do All to the Glory of God

23 Πάντα ἔξεστιν, ἀλλ' οὐ πάντα συμφέρει. πάντα ἔξεστιν, ἀλλ' οὐ πάντα οἰκοδομεῖ. **24** μηδεὶς τὸ ἑαυτοῦ ζητείτω ἀλλὰ τὸ τοῦ ἑτέρου. **25** Πᾶν τὸ ἐν μακέλλῳ πωλούμενον ἐσθίετε μηδὲν ἀνακρίνοντες διὰ τὴν συνείδησιν, **26** τοῦ κυρίου γὰρ ἡ γῆ καὶ τὸ πλήρωμα αὐτῆς. **27** εἴ τις καλεῖ ὑμᾶς τῶν ἀπίστων καὶ θέλετε πορεύεσθαι, πᾶν τὸ παρατιθέμενον ὑμῖν ἐσθίετε μηδὲν ἀνακρίνοντες διὰ τὴν συνείδησιν. **28** ἐὰν δέ τις ὑμῖν εἴπῃ, Τοῦτο ἱερόθυτόν ἐστιν, μὴ ἐσθίετε δι' ἐκεῖνον τὸν μηνύσαντα καὶ τὴν συνείδησιν[6] — **29** συνείδησιν δὲ λέγω οὐχὶ τὴν ἑαυτοῦ ἀλλὰ τὴν τοῦ ἑτέρου. ἱνατί γὰρ ἡ ἐλευθερία μου κρίνεται ὑπὸ ἄλλης συνειδήσεως; **30** εἰ ἐγὼ χάριτι μετέχω, τί βλασφημοῦμαι ὑπὲρ οὗ ἐγὼ

be partners with demons. [21] You cannot drink from the Lord's cup and also from the cup of demons; you cannot eat at the Lord's table and also at the table of demons. [22] Or do we want to make the Lord jealous? Do you think that we are stronger than he?

[23] "We are allowed to do anything," so they say. Yes, but not everything is good. "We are allowed to do anything" — but not everything is helpful. [24] No one should be looking out for his own interests, but for the interests of others.

[25] You are free to eat anything sold in the meat market, without asking any questions because of conscience. [26] For, as the scripture says, "The earth and everything in it belong to the Lord."

[27] If an unbeliever invites you to a meal and you decide to go, eat what is set before you without asking any questions because of conscience. [28] But if someone tells you, "This is food that was offered to idols," then do not eat that food, for the sake of the one who told you so and for conscience' sake — [29] that is, not your own conscience, but the other man's conscience.

"Well, then," someone asks, "why should my freedom to act be limited by another person's conscience? [30] If I thank God for my food, why should anyone criticize me about food for which I give thanks?"

C P Ψ 33 81 181 630 1241 1739 1877 2127 (104 330 451 2495 *transpose*: θύουσιν καὶ οὐ θεῷ) arm Origen Euthalius ∥ ἃ θύει τὰ ἔθνη, δαιμονίοις θύει καὶ οὐ θεῷ K 88 326 436 614 629 1881 1984 1985 2492 *Byz Lect* it(ar),dem,f,g,t,x,z vg syrp,h copsa?bo? goth eth? Chrysostom Theodoret John-Damascus ∥ ἃ θύουσιν, δαιμονίοις θύουσιν καὶ οὐ θεῷ D Ggr itd,e ∥ ἃ θύουσιν, δαιμονίοις καὶ οὐ θεῷ θύουσιν B ∥ ἃ θύουσιν, δαιμονίοις θύουσιν itm Tertullian Ambrosiaster

[6] **28** {A} συνείδησιν ℵ A B C D G H* P 33 81 181 436 629 630 1241 1739 1877 1881 1962 2127 itar,d,dem,e,f,g,x,z vg syrp copsa,bo arm eth Ambrosiaster Augustine John-Damascus ∥ συνείδησιν — τοῦ γὰρ κυρίου ἡ γῆ καὶ τὸ πλήρωμα αὐτῆς (*see* 10.26) Hc K Ψ (88 κυρίου γάρ) 104 326 330 451 614 1984 2492 2495 *Byz Lect* syrh goth Ephraem Chrysostom Euthalius Theodoret Photiusacc. to Ps-Oecumenius Ps-Oecumenius Theophylact

21 οὐ...δαιμονίων Mal 1.7, 12; 2 Cor 6.15, 16   **22** παραζηλοῦμεν τὸν κύριον Dt 32.21   **23** Πάντα ἔξεστιν...συμφέρει 1 Cor 6.12   **24** Ro 15.2   **26** Ps 24.1; 50.12; 89.11   **27** Lk 10.8   **28** 1 Cor 8.7   **30** 1 Tm 4.4

³¹ Well, whatever you do, whether you eat or drink, do it all for God's glory. ³² Live in such a way as to cause no trouble either to Jews, or Gentiles, or to the church of God. ³³ Just do as I do: I try to please everyone in all that I do, with no thought of my own good, but for the good of all, so they might be saved.

11
Imitate me, then, just as I imitate Christ.

Covering the Head in Worship

² I do praise you because you always remember me and follow the teachings that I have handed on to you. ³ But I want you to understand that Christ is supreme over every man, the husband is supreme over his wife, and God is supreme over Christ. ⁴ So a man who in public worship prays or speaks God's message with his head covered disgraces Christ. ⁵ And any woman who in public worship prays or speaks God's message with nothing on her head disgraces her husband; there is no difference between her and a woman whose head has been shaved. ⁶ If the woman does not cover her head, she might as well cut her hair. And since it is a shameful thing for a woman to shave her head or cut her hair, she should cover her head. ⁷ A man has no need to cover his head, because he reflects the image and glory of God. But woman reflects the glory of man; ⁸ for man was not created from woman, but woman from man. ⁹ Nor was man created for woman's sake, but woman was created for man's sake. ¹⁰ On account of the angels, then, a woman should have a covering over her head to

εὐχαριστῶ; **31** εἴτε οὖν ἐσθίετε εἴτε πίνετε εἴτε τι ποιεῖτε, πάντα εἰς δόξαν θεοῦ ποιεῖτε. **32** ἀπρόσκοποι καὶ Ἰουδαίοις γίνεσθε καὶ Ἕλλησιν καὶ τῇ ἐκκλησίᾳ τοῦ θεοῦ, **33** καθὼς κἀγὼ πάντα πᾶσιν ἀρέσκω, μὴ ζητῶν τὸ ἐμαυτοῦ σύμφορον ἀλλὰ τὸ τῶν πολλῶν, ἵνα σωθῶσιν. **11** μιμηταί μου γίνεσθε, καθὼς κἀγὼ Χριστοῦ.

Covering the Head in Worship

2 Ἐπαινῶ δὲ ὑμᾶς ὅτι πάντα μου μέμνησθε καὶ καθὼς παρέδωκα ὑμῖν τὰς παραδόσεις κατέχετε. **3** θέλω δὲ ὑμᾶς εἰδέναι ὅτι παντὸς ἀνδρὸς ἡ κεφαλὴ ὁ Χριστός ἐστιν, κεφαλὴ δὲ γυναικὸς ὁ ἀνήρ, κεφαλὴ δὲ τοῦ Χριστοῦ ὁ θεός. **4** πᾶς ἀνὴρ προσευχόμενος ἢ προφητεύων κατὰ κεφαλῆς ἔχων καταισχύνει τὴν κεφαλὴν αὐτοῦ· **5** πᾶσα δὲ γυνὴ προσευχομένη ἢ προφητεύουσα ἀκατακαλύπτῳ τῇ κεφαλῇ καταισχύνει τὴν κεφαλὴν αὐτῆς· ἓν γάρ ἐστιν καὶ τὸ αὐτὸ τῇ ἐξυρημένῃ. **6** εἰ γὰρ οὐ κατακαλύπτεται γυνή, καὶ κειράσθω· εἰ δὲ αἰσχρὸν γυναικὶ τὸ κείρασθαι ἢ ξυρᾶσθαι, κατακαλυπτέσθω. **7** ἀνὴρ μὲν γὰρ οὐκ ὀφείλει κατακαλύπτεσθαι τὴν κεφαλήν, εἰκὼν καὶ δόξα θεοῦ ὑπάρχων· ἡ γυνὴ δὲ δόξα ἀνδρός ἐστιν. ᵃ**8** οὐ γάρ ἐστιν ἀνὴρ ἐκ γυναικός, ἀλλὰ γυνὴ ἐξ ἀνδρός· **9** καὶ γὰρ οὐκ ἐκτίσθη ἀνὴρ διὰ τὴν γυναῖκα, ἀλλὰ γυνὴ διὰ τὸν ἄνδρα.ᵃ **10** διὰ τοῦτο ὀφείλει ἡ γυνὴ ἐξουσίαν¹ ἔχειν

¹ **10** {A} ἐξουσίαν 𝔭⁴⁶ ℵ A B C D G H K P Ψ 33 81 88 104 181 326 330 436 451 614 629 630 1241 1739 1877 1881 1962 1984 1985 2127 2492 2495 *Byz Lect* it^{ar,d,dem,e,f,g,x,z} vg syr^{p,h} cop^{sa,bomss} Clement^{from Theodotus} Tertullian Ambrosiaster ‖ κάλυμμα it^c cop^{bomss} arm? eth^{ro} Valentinians^{acc. to Irenaeus} Ptolemy^{acc. to Irenaeus} Irenaeus^{gr,lat} Tertullian Jerome Augustine ‖ κάλυμμα καὶ ἐξουσίαν Origen^{lat}

ᵃ ᵃ **8-9** *a a* no parens: TR WH Bov Nes BF² AV RV ASV NEB TT Zür Luth Jer Seg ‖ *a* parens; *a* parens: RSV

31 Col 3.17   **32** Ro 14.13   **33** 1 Cor 9.20-22
11 1 1 Cor 4.16; Php 3.17   **3** παντὸς...ἐστιν Eph 5.23   κεφαλὴ δὲ γυναικὸς ὁ ἀνήρ Gn 3.16; Eph 5.23   κεφαλὴ δὲ τοῦ Χριστοῦ ὁ θεός 1 Cor 3.23   **7** εἰκὼν...ὑπάρχων Gn 1.27; 5.1; 9.6; Wsd 2.23; Jas 3.9   **8** Gn 2.21-23; 1 Tm 2.13   **9** Gn 2.18

ἐπὶ τῆς κεφαλῆς διὰ τοὺς ἀγγέλους. [b]11 πλὴν οὔτε γυνὴ χωρὶς ἀνδρὸς οὔτε ἀνὴρ χωρὶς γυναικὸς ἐν κυρίῳ· 12 ὥσπερ γὰρ ἡ γυνὴ ἐκ τοῦ ἀνδρός, οὕτως καὶ ὁ ἀνὴρ διὰ τῆς γυναικός· τὰ δὲ πάντα ἐκ τοῦ θεοῦ.[b] 13 ἐν ὑμῖν αὐτοῖς κρίνατε· πρέπον ἐστὶν γυναῖκα ἀκατακάλυπτον τῷ θεῷ προσεύχεσθαι; 14 οὐδὲ ἡ φύσις αὐτὴ διδάσκει ὑμᾶς ὅτι ἀνὴρ μὲν ἐὰν κομᾷ ἀτιμία αὐτῷ ἐστιν, 15 γυνὴ δὲ ἐὰν κομᾷ δόξα αὐτῇ ἐστιν; ὅτι ἡ κόμη ἀντὶ περιβολαίου δέδοται [αὐτῇ]. 16 Εἰ δέ τις δοκεῖ φιλόνεικος εἶναι, ἡμεῖς τοιαύτην συνήθειαν οὐκ ἔχομεν, οὐδὲ αἱ ἐκκλησίαι τοῦ θεοῦ.

Abuses at the Lord's Supper

17 Τοῦτο δὲ παραγγέλλων οὐκ ἐπαινῶ ὅτι οὐκ εἰς τὸ κρεῖσσον ἀλλὰ εἰς τὸ ἧσσον συνέρχεσθε. 18 πρῶτον μὲν γὰρ συνερχομένων ὑμῶν ἐν ἐκκλησίᾳ ἀκούω σχίσματα ἐν ὑμῖν ὑπάρχειν, καὶ μέρος τι πιστεύω. 19 δεῖ γὰρ καὶ αἱρέσεις ἐν ὑμῖν εἶναι, ἵνα [καὶ] οἱ δόκιμοι φανεροὶ γένωνται ἐν ὑμῖν. 20 Συνερχομένων οὖν ὑμῶν ἐπὶ τὸ αὐτὸ οὐκ ἔστιν κυριακὸν δεῖπνον φαγεῖν, 21 ἕκαστος γὰρ τὸ ἴδιον δεῖπνον προλαμβάνει ἐν τῷ φαγεῖν, καὶ ὃς μὲν πεινᾷ, ὃς δὲ μεθύει. 22 μὴ γὰρ οἰκίας οὐκ ἔχετε εἰς τὸ ἐσθίειν καὶ πίνειν; ἢ τῆς ἐκκλησίας τοῦ θεοῦ καταφρονεῖτε, καὶ καταισχύνετε τοὺς μὴ ἔχοντας; τί εἴπω ὑμῖν; ἐπαινέσω ὑμᾶς; [c]ἐν τούτῳ[c] οὐκ ἐπαινῶ.

The Institution of the Lord's Supper
(Mt 26.26–29; Mk 14.22–25; Lk 22.14–20)

23 Ἐγὼ γὰρ παρέλαβον ἀπὸ τοῦ κυρίου, ὃ καὶ παρέδωκα ὑμῖν, ὅτι ὁ κύριος Ἰησοῦς ἐν τῇ νυκτὶ ᾗ παρεδίδετο

b b **11-12** b b no parens: TR WH Bov Nes BF² AV RV ASV NEB TT Zür Luth Jer Seg ∥ b parens, b parens: RSV

c c **22** c question, c none: WH Bov Nes BF² RVmg ASV (NEB) TT Zür Luth (Jer) (Seg) ∥ c none, c question: TR AV RV ASVmg RSV

18 ἀκούω...ὑπάρχειν 1 Cor 1.10–12; 3.3   **19** ἵνα καὶ οἱ δόκιμοι...ὑμῖν Dt 13.3; 1 Jn 2.19   **22** καταισχύνετε...ἔχοντας Jas 2.5–6   **23-25** Mt 26.26–28; Mk 14.22–24; Lk 22.19–20

show that she is under her husband's authority. 11 In our life in the Lord, however, woman is not independent of man, nor is man independent of woman. 12 For as woman was made from man, in the same way man is born of woman; and all things come from God.

13 Judge for yourselves: is it proper for a woman to pray to God in public worship with nothing on her head? 14 Why, nature herself teaches you that long hair is a disgraceful thing for a man, 15 but is a woman's pride. Her long hair has been given her to serve as a covering. 16 But if anyone wants to argue about it, all I have to say is that neither we nor the churches of God have any other custom in worship.

The Lord's Supper

17 In the following instructions, however, I do not praise you; for your church meetings actually do more harm than good. 18 In the first place, I have been told that there are opposing groups in your church meetings; and this I believe is partly true. 19 (No doubt there must be divisions among you so that the ones who are in the right may be clearly seen.) 20 When you meet together as a group, you do not come to eat the Lord's Supper. 21 For as you eat, each one goes ahead with his own meal, so that some are hungry while others get drunk. 22 Don't you have your own homes in which to eat and drink? Or would you rather despise the church of God and put to shame the people who are in need? What do you expect me to say to you about this? Should I praise you? Of course I do not praise you!

23 For from the Lord I received the teaching that I passed on to you: that

the Lord Jesus, on the night he was betrayed, took the bread, [24] gave thanks to God, broke it, and said, "This is my body, which is for you. Do this in memory of me." [25] In the same way, he took the cup after the supper and said, "This cup is God's new covenant, sealed with my blood. Whenever you drink it, do it in memory of me." [26] For until the Lord comes, you proclaim his death whenever you eat this bread and drink from this cup.

[27] It follows, then, that if anyone eats the Lord's bread or drinks from his cup in an improper manner, he is guilty of sin against the Lord's body and blood. [28] Everyone should examine himself, therefore, and with this attitude eat the bread and drink from the cup. [29] For if he does not recognize the meaning of the Lord's body when he eats the bread and drinks from the cup, he brings judgment on himself as he eats and drinks. [30] That is why many of you

ἔλαβεν ἄρτον 24 καὶ εὐχαριστήσας ἔκλασεν καὶ εἶπεν, Τοῦτό μού ἐστιν τὸ σῶμα τὸ ὑπὲρ ὑμῶν[2]· τοῦτο ποιεῖτε εἰς τὴν ἐμὴν ἀνάμνησιν. 25 ὡσαύτως καὶ τὸ ποτήριον μετὰ τὸ δειπνῆσαι, λέγων, Τοῦτο τὸ ποτήριον ἡ καινὴ διαθήκη ἐστὶν ἐν τῷ ἐμῷ αἵματι· τοῦτο ποιεῖτε, ὁσάκις ἐὰν πίνητε, εἰς τὴν ἐμὴν ἀνάμνησιν. 26 ὁσάκις γὰρ ἐὰν ἐσθίητε τὸν ἄρτον τοῦτον καὶ τὸ ποτήριον πίνητε, τὸν θάνατον τοῦ κυρίου καταγγέλλετε, ἄχρις οὗ ἔλθῃ.

Partaking of the Supper Unworthily

27 Ὥστε ὃς ἂν ἐσθίῃ τὸν ἄρτον ἢ πίνῃ τὸ ποτήριον τοῦ κυρίου ἀναξίως, ἔνοχος ἔσται τοῦ σώματος καὶ τοῦ αἵματος τοῦ κυρίου. 28 δοκιμαζέτω δὲ ἄνθρωπος ἑαυτόν, καὶ οὕτως ἐκ τοῦ ἄρτου ἐσθιέτω καὶ ἐκ τοῦ ποτηρίου πινέτω· 29 ὁ γὰρ ἐσθίων καὶ πίνων[3] κρίμα ἑαυτῷ ἐσθίει καὶ πίνει μὴ διακρίνων τὸ σῶμα[4]. 30 διὰ τοῦτο

---

2 24 {B} ὑμῶν 𝔭[46] ℵ* A B C* 33 1739* arm Origen Cyprian Athanasius[acc. to Theodoret] Pelagius Cyril Fulgentius ∥ ὑμῶν κλώμενον ℵ[c] C³ D[b,c] G K P Ψ 81 88 104 181 326 330 436 451 614 629 630 1241 1739[mg] 1877 1881 1962 1984 1985 2127 2492 2495 *Byz Lect* it[d,e,g] syr[p,h] goth Ambrosiaster Basil Chrysostom Euthalius Theodoret John-Damascus ∥ ὑμῶν θρυπτόμενον D[gr*] ∥ ὑμῶν διδόμενον (see Lk 22.19) (it[c,dem,f,t,x,z[c]] vg *tradetur*, it[ar] *quod tradidi pro vobis*, it[z*] *quod pro vobis traditur*) cop[sa,bo] eth Euthalius

3 29 {C} πίνων 𝔭[46] ℵ* A B C* 33 1739 cop[sa,bo] eth[ro] Ambrosiaster Pelagius ∥ πίνων ἀναξίως (see 11.27) ℵ[c] C³ D G K P Ψ 81 88 (104 *transposes* ἀναξίως *after* γάρ) 181 326 330 436 451 614 (629 πένων) 630 1241 1877 1881 1962 1984 1985 2127 2492 2495 *Byz Lect* it[ar,d,e,f,g,t,x,z] vg syr[p,h,pal] goth arm eth[pp] Ambrosiaster Athanasius Ephraem Basil Chrysostom Augustine Euthalius Theodoret John-Damascus

4 29 {C} σῶμα 𝔭[46] ℵ* A B C* 33 1739 it[z] vg[ww] cop[sa,bo] (eth) ∥ σῶμα τοῦ κυρίου ℵ[c] C³ D G K P (Ψ *add* Ἰησοῦ) 81 88 104 181 326 330 436 451 614 629 630 1877 1881 1962 1984 1985 2127 2492 2495 *Byz Lect* it[ar,d,dem,e,f,g,gig,t,x] vg[cl] syr[p,h,pal] goth arm Ambrosiaster Basil Chrysostom Augustine Euthalius Theodoret John-Damascus ∥ αἷμα τοῦ κυρίου 1241

---

25 ἡ καινὴ διαθήκη Ex 24.8; Jr 31.31; 32.40; 2 Cor 3.6; He 8.8–13   διαθήκη...αἵματι Ex 24.6–8; Zch 9.11   **26** Mt 26.29   **27** He 10.29   **28** δοκιμαζέτω...ἑαυτόν Mt 26.22; 2 Cor 13.5

ἐν ὑμῖν πολλοὶ ἀσθενεῖς καὶ ἄρρωστοι καὶ κοιμῶνται ἱκανοί. 31 εἰ δὲ ἑαυτοὺς διεκρίνομεν, οὐκ ἂν ἐκρινόμεθα· 32 κρινόμενοι δὲ ὑπὸ [τοῦ] κυρίου παιδευόμεθα, ἵνα μὴ σὺν τῷ κόσμῳ κατακριθῶμεν. 33 ὥστε, ἀδελφοί μου, συνερχόμενοι εἰς τὸ φαγεῖν ἀλλήλους ἐκδέχεσθε.ᵈ 34 εἴ τις πεινᾷ, ἐν οἴκῳ ἐσθιέτω,ᵈ ἵνα μὴ εἰς κρίμα συνέρχησθε. Τὰ δὲ λοιπὰ ὡς ἂν ἔλθω διατάξομαι.

Spiritual Gifts

12 Περὶ δὲ τῶν πνευματικῶν, ἀδελφοί, οὐ θέλω ὑμᾶς ἀγνοεῖν. 2 Οἴδατε ὅτι ὅτε ἔθνη ἦτε πρὸς τὰ εἴδωλα τὰ ἄφωνα ὡς ἂν ἤγεσθε ἀπαγόμενοι. 3 διὸ γνωρίζω ὑμῖν ὅτι οὐδεὶς ἐν πνεύματι θεοῦ λαλῶν λέγει, Ἀνάθεμα Ἰησοῦς, καὶ οὐδεὶς δύναται εἰπεῖν, Κύριος Ἰησοῦς, εἰ μὴ ἐν πνεύματι ἁγίῳ.

4 Διαιρέσεις δὲ χαρισμάτων εἰσίν, τὸ δὲ αὐτὸ πνεῦμα· 5 καὶ διαιρέσεις διακονιῶν εἰσιν, καὶ ὁ αὐτὸς κύριος· 6 καὶ διαιρέσεις ἐνεργημάτων εἰσίν, ὁ δὲ αὐτὸς θεός, ὁ ἐνεργῶν τὰ πάντα ἐν πᾶσιν. 7 ἑκάστῳ δὲ δίδοται ἡ φανέρωσις τοῦ πνεύματος πρὸς τὸ συμφέρον. 8 ᾧ μὲν γὰρ διὰ τοῦ πνεύματος δίδοται λόγος σοφίας, ἄλλῳ δὲ λόγος γνώσεως κατὰ τὸ αὐτὸ πνεῦμα, 9 ἑτέρῳ πίστις ἐν τῷ αὐτῷ πνεύματι, ἄλλῳ δὲ χαρίσματα ἰαμάτων ἐν τῷ ἑνὶ πνεύματι¹, 10 ἄλλῳ δὲ ἐνεργήματα δυνάμεων,

---

¹ **9** {B} ἐν τῷ ἑνὶ πνεύματι A B 33 81 104 436 630 (1739 *omit* τῷ) 1881 it^{ar, d, dem, e, f, m, t, x, z} vg Ambrose Hilary Basil Didymus Augustine Euthalius John-Damascus // ἐν τῷ αὐτῷ πνεύματι ℵ C³ D^{gr} G K P 0201 88 181 330 451 614 629 1241 1877 1962 1984 1985 2127 2492 2495 *Byz Lect* it^g syr^{p, h} cop^{sa, bo} arm Marcion Clement Origen Hilary Basil Cyril-Jerusalem Chrysostom Theodoret // ἐν τῷ πνεύματι p⁴⁶ // *omit* C* Tertullian Eusebius // *omit* ἰαμάτων...πνεύματι Ψ

ᵈ ᵈ **33-34** *d* major, *d* minor: WH Bov Nes BF² AV RV ASV NEB TT Zür Luth Jer Seg // *d* minor, *d* minor: Tif // *d* dash, *d* dash: RSV

---

30 κοιμῶνται ἱκανοί Ac 7.60; 1 Cor 15.20; Eph 5.14; 1 Th 5.6   **32** He 12.5-6
12 **2** τὰ εἴδωλα τὰ ἄφωνα Hab 2.18-19   **3** οὐδεὶς...ἁγίῳ Mk 9.39; 1 Jn 4.2-3
4 Διαιρέσεις...εἰσίν Ro 12.6   τὸ δὲ αὐτὸ πνεῦμα Eph 4.4   **5** διαιρέσεις διακονιῶν εἰσιν Eph 4.11   **7** πρὸς τὸ συμφέρον 1 Cor 14.26; Eph 4.12

---

are sick and weak, and several have died. 31 If we would examine ourselves first, we would not come under God's judgment. 32 But we are judged and punished by the Lord, so that we shall not be condemned along with the world.

33 So then, my brothers, when you gather together to eat the Lord's meal, wait for one another. 34 And if anyone is hungry, he should eat at home, so that you will not come under God's judgment as you meet together. As for the other matters, I will settle them when I come.

Gifts from the Holy Spirit

12 Now, the matter about the gifts from the Holy Spirit.

I want you to know the truth about them, my brothers. 2 You know that while you were still heathen you were controlled by dead idols, who always led you astray. 3 You must realize, then, that no one who is led by God's Spirit can say, "A curse on Jesus!", and no one can confess "Jesus is Lord," unless he is guided by the Holy Spirit.

4 There are different kinds of spiritual gifts, but the same Spirit gives them. 5 There are different ways of serving, but the same Lord is served. 6 There are different abilities to perform service, but the same God gives ability to everyone for all services. 7 Each one is given some proof of the Spirit's presence for the good of all. 8 The Spirit gives one man a message of wisdom, while to another man the same Spirit gives a message of knowledge. 9 One and the same Spirit gives faith to one man, while to another man he gives the power to heal. 10 The Spirit gives one man the power to work

miracles; to another, the gift of speaking God's message; and to yet another, the ability to tell the difference between gifts that come from the Spirit and those that do not. To one man he gives the ability to speak with strange sounds; to another, he gives the ability to explain what these sounds mean. 11 But it is one and the same Spirit who does all this; he gives a different gift to each man, as he wishes.

One Body with Many Parts

12 For Christ is like a single body, which has many parts; it is still one body, even though it is made up of different parts. 13 In the same way, all of us, Jews and Gentiles, slaves and free men, have been baptized into the one body by the same Spirit, and we have all been given the one Spirit to drink.

14 For the body itself is not made up of only one part, but of many parts. 15 If the foot were to say, "Because I am not a hand, I don't belong to the body," that would not make it stop being a part of the body. 16 And if the ear were to say, "Because I am not an eye, I don't belong to the body," that would not make it stop being a part of the body. 17 If the whole body were just an eye, how could it hear? And if it were only an ear, how could it smell? 18 As it is, however, God put every different part in the body just as he wished. 19 There would not be a body if it were all only one part! 20 As it is, there are many parts, and one body.

21 So then, the eye cannot say to the hand, "I don't need you!" Nor can the head say to the feet, "Well, I don't need you!" 22 On the contrary; we cannot get along without the parts of the body that seem to be weaker, 23 and those parts that we think aren't worth very much are the ones which we treat with greater care; while the parts of the body which don't look very nice receive special attention, 24 which the more beautiful parts of our body do not need. God himself has put our bodies together in such a way as to give greater honor to those parts that lack it. 25 And so there is no division in the body, but

ἄλλῳ [δὲ] προφητεία, ἄλλῳ [δὲ] διακρίσεις πνευμάτων, ἑτέρῳ γένη γλωσσῶν, ἄλλῳ δὲ ἑρμηνεία γλωσσῶν· 11 πάντα δὲ ταῦτα ἐνεργεῖ τὸ ἓν καὶ τὸ αὐτὸ πνεῦμα, διαιροῦν ἰδίᾳ ἑκάστῳ καθὼς βούλεται.

One Body with Many Members

12 Καθάπερ γὰρ τὸ σῶμα ἕν ἐστιν καὶ μέλη πολλὰ ἔχει, πάντα δὲ τὰ μέλη τοῦ σώματος πολλὰ ὄντα ἕν ἐστιν σῶμα, οὕτως καὶ ὁ Χριστός· 13 καὶ γὰρ ἐν ἑνὶ πνεύματι ἡμεῖς πάντες εἰς ἓν σῶμα ἐβαπτίσθημεν, εἴτε Ἰουδαῖοι εἴτε Ἕλληνες, εἴτε δοῦλοι εἴτε ἐλεύθεροι, καὶ πάντες ἓν πνεῦμα ἐποτίσθημεν. 14 καὶ γὰρ τὸ σῶμα οὐκ ἔστιν ἓν μέλος ἀλλὰ πολλά. 15 ἐὰν εἴπῃ ὁ πούς, Ὅτι οὐκ εἰμὶ χείρ, οὐκ εἰμὶ ἐκ τοῦ σώματος, οὐ παρὰ τοῦτο οὐκ ἔστιν ἐκ τοῦ σώματος· [a] 16 καὶ ἐὰν εἴπῃ τὸ οὖς, Ὅτι οὐκ εἰμὶ ὀφθαλμός, οὐκ εἰμὶ ἐκ τοῦ σώματος, οὐ παρὰ τοῦτο οὐκ ἔστιν ἐκ τοῦ σώματος· [b] 17 εἰ ὅλον τὸ σῶμα ὀφθαλμός, ποῦ ἡ ἀκοή; εἰ ὅλον ἀκοή, ποῦ ἡ ὄσφρησις; 18 νυνὶ δὲ ὁ θεὸς ἔθετο τὰ μέλη, ἓν ἕκαστον αὐτῶν, ἐν τῷ σώματι καθὼς ἠθέλησεν. 19 εἰ δὲ ἦν τὰ πάντα ἓν μέλος, ποῦ τὸ σῶμα; 20 νῦν δὲ πολλὰ μὲν μέλη, ἓν δὲ σῶμα. 21 οὐ δύναται δὲ ὁ ὀφθαλμὸς εἰπεῖν τῇ χειρί, Χρείαν σου οὐκ ἔχω, ἢ πάλιν ἡ κεφαλὴ τοῖς ποσίν, Χρείαν ὑμῶν οὐκ ἔχω· 22 ἀλλὰ πολλῷ μᾶλλον τὰ δοκοῦντα μέλη τοῦ σώματος ἀσθενέστερα ὑπάρχειν ἀναγκαῖά ἐστιν, 23 καὶ ἃ δοκοῦμεν ἀτιμότερα εἶναι τοῦ σώματος, τούτοις τιμὴν περισσοτέραν περιτίθεμεν, καὶ τὰ ἀσχήμονα ἡμῶν εὐσχημοσύνην περισσοτέραν ἔχει, 24 τὰ δὲ εὐσχήμονα ἡμῶν οὐ χρείαν ἔχει. ἀλλὰ ὁ θεὸς συνεκέρασεν τὸ σῶμα, τῷ ὑστερουμένῳ περισσοτέραν δοὺς τιμήν, 25 ἵνα μὴ ᾖ σχίσμα ἐν τῷ σώματι, ἀλλὰ

---

[a] 15 a statement: TR WH Bov Nes BF² RV ASV RSV NEB TT Zür Seg ∥ a question: AV Luth Jer
[b] 16 b statement: TR WH Bov Nes BF² RV ASV RSV NEB TT Zür Seg ∥ b question: AV Luth Jer

10 ἑτέρῳ γένη γλωσσῶν Ac 2.4; 1 Cor 14.5   11 διαιροῦν...βούλεται Ro 12.3; 1 Cor 7.7 ; Eph 4.7   12 τὸ σῶμα...σῶμα Ro 12.4–5; 1 Cor 10.17   13 ἐν...ἐλεύθεροι Ga 3.28

τὸ αὐτὸ ὑπὲρ ἀλλήλων μεριμνῶσιν τὰ μέλη. 26 καὶ εἴτε πάσχει ἓν μέλος, συμπάσχει πάντα τὰ μέλη· εἴτε δοξάζεται ἓν μέλος, συγχαίρει πάντα τὰ μέλη.

27 Ὑμεῖς δέ ἐστε σῶμα Χριστοῦ καὶ μέλη ἐκ μέρους. 28 καὶ οὓς μὲν ἔθετο ὁ θεὸς ἐν τῇ ἐκκλησίᾳ πρῶτον ἀποστόλους, δεύτερον προφήτας, τρίτον διδασκάλους, ἔπειτα δυνάμεις, ἔπειτα χαρίσματα ἰαμάτων, ἀντιλήμψεις, κυβερνήσεις, γένη γλωσσῶν. 29 μὴ πάντες ἀπόστολοι; μὴ πάντες προφῆται; μὴ πάντες διδάσκαλοι; μὴ πάντες δυνάμεις; 30 μὴ πάντες χαρίσματα ἔχουσιν ἰαμάτων; μὴ πάντες γλώσσαις λαλοῦσιν; μὴ πάντες διερμηνεύουσιν;[c] 31 ζηλοῦτε δὲ τὰ χαρίσματα τὰ μείζονα.[c]

Love

Καὶ ἔτι καθ᾽ ὑπερβολὴν ὁδὸν ὑμῖν δείκνυμι.[c] **13** Ἐὰν ταῖς γλώσσαις τῶν ἀνθρώπων λαλῶ καὶ τῶν ἀγγέλων, ἀγάπην δὲ μὴ ἔχω, γέγονα χαλκὸς ἠχῶν ἢ κύμβαλον ἀλαλάζον. 2 καὶ ἐὰν ἔχω προφητείαν καὶ εἰδῶ τὰ μυστήρια πάντα καὶ πᾶσαν τὴν γνῶσιν, κἂν ἔχω πᾶσαν τὴν πίστιν ὥστε ὄρη μεθιστάναι, ἀγάπην δὲ μὴ ἔχω, οὐθέν εἰμι. 3 κἂν ψωμίσω πάντα τὰ ὑπάρχοντά μου, καὶ ἐὰν παραδῶ τὸ σῶμά μου ἵνα καυχήσωμαι[1], ἀγάπην δὲ μὴ ἔχω, οὐδὲν ὠφελοῦμαι.

---

¹ 3 {C} καυχήσωμαι 𝔭⁴⁶ ℵ A B 33 1739* cop^sa,bo goth^mg eth^ro Clement Origen (Pelagius^comm) Jerome Greek mss^acc. to Jerome ‖ καυθήσωμαι K Ψ 181 326 (330* καθήσωμαι) 330^c 451 614 629 1739^c 1881 1962 1984 Byz l⁵⁹⁸ Origen Chrysostom Cyril Theodoret John-Damascus ‖ καυθήσομαι C D G 81 88^vid 104 436 630 1085 l⁵⁹⁷,⁵⁹⁹,¹³⁶⁴,¹³⁶⁵ (Methodius) Basil Chrysostom Cyril Euthalius Maximus-Confessor ‖ καυθήσομαι or καυθήσωμαι it^ar,d,dem,e,f,g,m,t,x vg syr^p,h goth^txt arm eth^pp Tertullian Rebaptism Cyprian

---

ᶜ ᶜ ᶜ 12.30—13.1 c no paragraph, c paragraph, c no paragraph: WH Bov Nes BF² ‖ c no paragraph, c paragraph, c no paragraph: RSV NEB TT Luth ‖ c no paragraph, c no paragraph, c paragraph: TR AV RV ASV Zür ‖ c paragraph, c no paragraph, c paragraph: Jer Seg

---

27 Ro 12.5; Eph 5.30   28 ἔθετο...διδασκάλους Eph 4.11–12   31 1 Cor 14.1
13 2 ἔχω πᾶσαν...μεθιστάναι Mt 17.20; 21.21; Mk 11.23   3 ψωμίσω...μου Mt 6.2

all its different parts have the same concern for one another. 26 If one part of the body suffers, all the other parts suffer with it; if one part is praised, all the other parts share its happiness.

27 All of you, then, are Christ's body, and each one is a part of it. 28 In the church, then, God has put all in place: in the first place, apostles, in the second place, prophets, and in the third place, teachers; then those who perform miracles, followed by those who are given the power to heal, or to help others, or to direct them, or to speak with strange sounds. 29 They are not all apostles, or prophets, or teachers. Not all have the power to work miracles, 30 or to heal diseases, or to speak with strange sounds, or to explain what these sounds mean. 31 Set your hearts, then, on the more important gifts.

Best of all, however, is the following way.

Love

13 I may be able to speak the languages of men and even of angels, but if I have not love, my speech is no more than a noisy gong or a clanging bell. 2 I may have the gift of inspired preaching; I may have all knowledge and understand all secrets; I may have all the faith needed to move mountains — but if I have not love, I am nothing. 3 I may give away everything I have, and even give up my body to be burned[1] — but if I have not love, it does me no good.

---

¹ **3** to be burned: *some mss. read* in order to boast

[4] Love is patient and kind; love is not jealous, or conceited, or proud; [5] love is not ill-mannered, or selfish, or irritable; love does not keep a record of wrongs; [6] love is not happy with evil, but is happy with the truth. [7] Love never gives up: its faith, hope, and patience never fail.

[8] Love is eternal. There are inspired messages, but they are temporary; there are gifts of speaking, but they will cease; there is knowledge, but it will pass. [9] For our gifts of knowledge and of inspired messages are only partial; [10] but when what is perfect comes, then what is partial will disappear.

[11] When I was a child, my speech, feelings, and thinking were all those of a child; now that I am a man, I have no more use for childish ways. [12] What we see now is like the dim image in a mirror; then we shall see face to face. What I know now is only partial; then it will be complete, as complete as God's knowledge of me.

[13] Meanwhile these three remain: faith, hope, and love; and the greatest of these is love.

More about Gifts from the Spirit

14 It is love, then, that you should strive for. Set your hearts on spiritual gifts, especially the gift of speaking God's message. [2] The one who speaks with strange sounds does not speak to men but to God, because no one understands him. He is speaking secret truths by the power of the Spirit. [3] But the one who speaks God's message speaks to men, and gives them help, encouragement, and comfort. [4] The man who speaks with strange sounds helps only himself, but the one who speaks God's message helps the whole church.

[4] Ἡ ἀγάπη μακροθυμεῖ, χρηστεύεται[a] ἡ ἀγάπη,[a] οὐ ζηλοῖ, οὐ περπερεύεται, οὐ φυσιοῦται, [5] οὐκ ἀσχημονεῖ, οὐ ζητεῖ τὰ ἑαυτῆς, οὐ παροξύνεται, οὐ λογίζεται τὸ κακόν, [6] οὐ χαίρει ἐπὶ τῇ ἀδικίᾳ, συγχαίρει δὲ τῇ ἀληθείᾳ· [7] πάντα στέγει, πάντα πιστεύει, πάντα ἐλπίζει, πάντα ὑπομένει.

[8] Ἡ ἀγάπη οὐδέποτε πίπτει. εἴτε δὲ προφητεῖαι, καταργηθήσονται· εἴτε γλῶσσαι, παύσονται· εἴτε γνῶσις, καταργηθήσεται. [9] ἐκ μέρους γὰρ γινώσκομεν καὶ ἐκ μέρους προφητεύομεν· [10] ὅταν δὲ ἔλθῃ τὸ τέλειον, τὸ ἐκ μέρους καταργηθήσεται. [11] ὅτε ἤμην νήπιος, ἐλάλουν ὡς νήπιος, ἐφρόνουν ὡς νήπιος, ἐλογιζόμην ὡς νήπιος· ὅτε γέγονα ἀνήρ, κατήργηκα τὰ τοῦ νηπίου. [12] βλέπομεν γὰρ ἄρτι δι' ἐσόπτρου ἐν αἰνίγματι, τότε δὲ πρόσωπον πρὸς πρόσωπον· ἄρτι γινώσκω ἐκ μέρους, τότε δὲ ἐπιγνώσομαι καθὼς καὶ ἐπεγνώσθην. [13] νυνὶ δὲ μένει πίστις, ἐλπίς, ἀγάπη,[b] τὰ τρία ταῦτα·[b] μείζων δὲ τούτων ἡ ἀγάπη.

Tongues and Prophecy

14 Διώκετε τὴν ἀγάπην, ζηλοῦτε δὲ τὰ πνευματικά, μᾶλλον δὲ ἵνα προφητεύητε. [2] ὁ γὰρ λαλῶν γλώσσῃ οὐκ ἀνθρώποις λαλεῖ ἀλλὰ θεῷ, οὐδεὶς γὰρ ἀκούει, πνεύματι δὲ λαλεῖ μυστήρια· [3] ὁ δὲ προφητεύων ἀνθρώποις λαλεῖ οἰκοδομὴν καὶ παράκλησιν καὶ παραμυθίαν. [4] ὁ λαλῶν γλώσσῃ ἑαυτὸν οἰκοδομεῖ· ὁ δὲ προφητεύων

Methodius Jacob-Nisibis Aphraates Ambrosiaster Ephraem Basil Petilianus[acc. to Augustine] Greek and Latin mss[acc. to Jerome] Augustine ‖ καυθήσεται 1877 2492 Clement

---

[a a] **4** a none, a minor: Nes BF[2] (NEB) TT Jer Seg ‖ a minor, a none: TR WH Bov AV RV ASV RSV Zür Luth

[b b] **13** b mlnor, b major: TR Bov Nes BF[2] AV RV ASV RSV (NEB) (TT) Zür Luth (Jer) (Seg) ‖ b major, b mlnor: WH

---

5 οὐ ζητεῖ τὰ ἑαυτῆς Php 2.4   οὐ λογίζεται τὸ κακόν Zch 8.17   **6** Ro 12.9   **7** πάντα στέγει Pr 10.12; Ro 15.1; 1 Pe 4.8   πάντα ὑπομένει 1 Cor 9.12   **12** βλέπομεν...αἰνίγματι 2 Cor 5.7; Jas 1.23   **13** νυνὶ...ἐλπίς, ἀγάπη 1 Th 1.3   μείζων...ἀγάπη 1 Jn 4.16
   14 **1** ζηλοῦτε...πνευματικά 1 Cor 12.31; 14.39

ἐκκλησίαν οἰκοδομεῖ. 5 θέλω δὲ πάντας ὑμᾶς λαλεῖν γλώσσαις, μᾶλλον δὲ ἵνα προφητεύητε· μείζων δὲ ὁ προφητεύων ἢ ὁ λαλῶν γλώσσαις, ἐκτὸς εἰ μὴ διερμηνεύῃ, ἵνα ἡ ἐκκλησία οἰκοδομὴν λάβῃ.

6 Νῦν δέ, ἀδελφοί, ἐὰν ἔλθω πρὸς ὑμᾶς γλώσσαις λαλῶν, τί ὑμᾶς ὠφελήσω, ἐὰν μὴ ὑμῖν λαλήσω ἢ ἐν ἀποκαλύψει ἢ ἐν γνώσει ἢ ἐν προφητείᾳ ἢ ἐν διδαχῇ; 7 ὅμως τὰ ἄψυχα φωνὴν διδόντα, εἴτε αὐλὸς εἴτε κιθάρα, ἐὰν διαστολὴν τοῖς φθόγγοις μὴ δῷ, πῶς γνωσθήσεται τὸ αὐλούμενον ἢ τὸ κιθαριζόμενον; 8 καὶ γὰρ ἐὰν ἄδηλον σάλπιγξ φωνὴν δῷ, τίς παρασκευάσεται εἰς πόλεμον; 9 οὕτως καὶ ὑμεῖς διὰ τῆς γλώσσης ἐὰν μὴ εὔσημον λόγον δῶτε, πῶς γνωσθήσεται τὸ λαλούμενον; ἔσεσθε γὰρ εἰς ἀέρα λαλοῦντες. 10 τοσαῦτα εἰ τύχοι γένη φωνῶν εἰσιν ἐν κόσμῳ, καὶ οὐδὲν ἄφωνον· 11 ἐὰν οὖν μὴ εἰδῶ τὴν δύναμιν τῆς φωνῆς, ἔσομαι τῷ λαλοῦντι βάρβαρος καὶ ὁ λαλῶν ἐν ἐμοὶ βάρβαρος. 12 οὕτως καὶ ὑμεῖς, ἐπεὶ ζηλωταί ἐστε πνευμάτων, πρὸς τὴν οἰκοδομὴν τῆς ἐκκλησίας ζητεῖτε ἵνα περισσεύητε. 13 διὸ ὁ λαλῶν γλώσσῃ προσευχέσθω ἵνα διερμηνεύῃ. 14 ἐὰν [γὰρ] προσεύχωμαι γλώσσῃ, τὸ πνεῦμά μου προσεύχεται, ὁ δὲ νοῦς μου ἄκαρπός ἐστιν. 15 τί οὖν ἐστιν; προσεύξομαι τῷ πνεύματι, προσεύξομαι δὲ καὶ τῷ νοΐ· ψαλῶ τῷ πνεύματι, ψαλῶ δὲ καὶ τῷ νοΐ. 16 ἐπεὶ ἐὰν εὐλογῇς ἐν πνεύματι, ὁ ἀναπληρῶν τὸν τόπον τοῦ ἰδιώτου πῶς ἐρεῖ τὸ Ἀμὴν ἐπὶ τῇ σῇ εὐχαριστίᾳ,[a] ἐπειδὴ τί λέγεις οὐκ οἶδεν;[a] 17 σὺ μὲν γὰρ καλῶς εὐχαριστεῖς, ἀλλ' ὁ ἕτερος οὐκ οἰκοδομεῖται. 18 εὐχαριστῶ τῷ θεῷ, πάντων ὑμῶν μᾶλλον γλώσσαις λαλῶ· 19 ἀλλὰ ἐν ἐκκλησίᾳ θέλω πέντε λόγους τῷ νοΐ μου λαλῆσαι[1], ἵνα καὶ ἄλλους κατηχήσω, ἢ μυρίους λόγους ἐν γλώσσῃ.

---

1 19 {B} πέντε λόγους τῷ νοΐ μου λαλῆσαι (p46 ἐν τῷ) ℵ A B Dgr P Ψ

a a 16 a minor, a question: TR AV RV ASV (RSV) NEB TT Luth Jer Seg ‖ a question, a statement: WH Bov Nes BF2 Zür

---

5 μᾶλλον...προφητεύητε Nu 11.29   15 ψαλῶ τῷ πνεύματι Eph 5.19

---

5 I would like for all of you to speak with strange sounds; but I would rather that all of you had the gift of speaking God's message. For the man who speaks God's message is of greater value than the one who speaks with strange sounds — unless there is someone present who can explain what he says, so that the whole church may be helped. 6 So when I come to you, brothers, what use will I be to you if I speak with strange sounds? Not a bit, unless I bring you some revelation from God, or some knowledge, or some inspired message or teaching.

7 Even such lifeless musical instruments as the flute and the harp — how will anyone know the tune that is being played unless the notes are sounded distinctly? 8 And if the man who plays the bugle does not sound a clear call, who will prepare for battle? 9 In the same way, how will anyone understand what you are talking about if your message by means of strange sounds is not clear? Your words will vanish in the air! 10 There are many different languages in the world, yet not a single one of them is without meaning. 11 But if I do not know the language being spoken, the man who uses it will be a foreigner to me and I will be a foreigner to him. 12 Since you are eager to have the gifts of the Spirit, above everything else you must try to make greater use of those which help build up the church.

13 The man who speaks with strange sounds, then, must pray for the gift to explain what they mean. 14 For if I pray in this way, my spirit prays indeed, but my mind has no part in it. 15 What should I do, then? I will pray with my spirit, but I will pray also with my mind; I will sing with my spirit, but I will sing also with my mind. 16 When you give thanks to God in spirit only, how can an ordinary man taking part in the meeting say "Amen" to your prayer of thanksgiving? He has no way of knowing what you are saying. 17 Even if your prayer of thanks to God is quite good, the other man is not helped at all. 18 I thank God that I speak with strange sounds much more than any of you. 19 But in church worship I would rather speak five words that can be understood, in order to teach others, than speak thousands of words with strange sounds.

²⁰ Do not be like children in your thinking, brothers; be children so far as evil is concerned, but be mature in your thinking. ²¹ In the Scriptures it is written:

"I will speak to this people, says the
    Lord:
I will speak through men of foreign
    languages,
And through the lips of foreigners.
But even then my people will not
    listen to me."

²² So then, the gift of speaking with strange sounds is proof for unbelievers, not for believers, while the gift of speaking God's message is proof for believers, not for unbelievers.

²³ If, then, the whole church meets together and everyone starts speaking with strange sounds — if some ordinary people or unbelievers come in, won't they say that you are all crazy? ²⁴ But if all speak God's message, when some unbeliever or ordinary person comes in he will be convinced of his sin by what he hears. He will be judged by all he hears, ²⁵ his secret thoughts will be brought into the open, and he will bow down and worship God, confessing, "Truly God is here with you!"

Order in the Church

²⁶ What do I mean, my brothers? When you meet for worship, one man has a hymn, another a teaching, another a revelation from God, another a message with strange sounds, and still another the explanation of what it means. Everything must be of help to the church. ²⁷ If someone is going to speak with strange sounds, two or three at the most should speak, one after the other, and someone else must explain what is being said. ²⁸ If no person is there who

20 Ἀδελφοί, μὴ παιδία γίνεσθε ταῖς φρεσίν, ἀλλὰ τῇ κακίᾳ νηπιάζετε, ταῖς δὲ φρεσὶν τέλειοι γίνεσθε. **21** ἐν τῷ νόμῳ γέγραπται ὅτι

Ἐν ἑτερογλώσσοις
    καὶ ἐν χείλεσιν ἑτέρων
λαλήσω τῷ λαῷ τούτῳ,
    καὶ οὐδ' οὕτως **εἰσακούσονταί** μου,

λέγει κύριος. **22** ὥστε αἱ γλῶσσαι εἰς σημεῖόν εἰσιν οὐ τοῖς πιστεύουσιν ἀλλὰ τοῖς ἀπίστοις, ἡ δὲ προφητεία οὐ τοῖς ἀπίστοις ἀλλὰ τοῖς πιστεύουσιν. **23** Ἐὰν οὖν συνέλθῃ ἡ ἐκκλησία ὅλη ἐπὶ τὸ αὐτὸ καὶ πάντες λαλῶσιν γλώσσαις, εἰσέλθωσιν δὲ ἰδιῶται ἢ ἄπιστοι, οὐκ ἐροῦσιν ὅτι μαίνεσθε; **24** ἐὰν δὲ πάντες προφητεύωσιν, εἰσέλθῃ δέ τις ἄπιστος ἢ ἰδιώτης, ἐλέγχεται ὑπὸ πάντων, ἀνακρίνεται ὑπὸ πάντων, **25** τὰ κρυπτὰ τῆς καρδίας αὐτοῦ φανερὰ γίνεται, καὶ οὕτως πεσὼν ἐπὶ πρόσωπον προσκυνήσει τῷ θεῷ, ἀπαγγέλλων ὅτι Ὄντως ὁ θεὸς ἐν ὑμῖν ἐστιν.

All Things to be Done in Order

26 Τί οὖν ἐστιν, ἀδελφοί; ὅταν συνέρχησθε, ἕκαστος ψαλμὸν ἔχει, διδαχὴν ἔχει, ἀποκάλυψιν ἔχει, γλῶσσαν ἔχει, ἑρμηνείαν ἔχει· πάντα πρὸς οἰκοδομὴν γινέσθω. **27** εἴτε γλώσσῃ τις λαλεῖ, κατὰ δύο ἢ τὸ πλεῖστον τρεῖς, καὶ ἀνὰ μέρος, καὶ εἷς διερμηνευέτω· **28** ἐὰν δὲ μὴ

0243 (33 τῷ νοΐ μου πέντε λόγους λαλῆσαι) 81 104 326 436 630 1241 1739 1877 1881 (1962 λαλῆσαι τῷ νοΐ μου) 2127 it^{dem,(f),(x)} vg (syr^p) cop^{sa,bo} (arm *omit μου*) Marcion Gregory-Nyssa Ambrose Euthalius John-Damascus ‖ πένται λόγους λαλή ομεν [*sic*] τῷ νοΐ μου G (it^g *loqui*) ‖ πέντε λόγους διὰ τοῦ νοός μου λαλῆσαι K 048 88 181 330 451 614 629 1984 1985 2492 2495 *Byz Lect* it^{d,e} (syr^h) Ambrosiaster^{edpt} Macarius Chrysostom Theodoret Maximus-Confessor Photius ‖ πέντε λόγους διὰ τὸν νόμον λαλῆσαι Marcion Pelagius ‖ *quinque verba sensu meo loqui per legem* it^{ar,(z)} Ambrosiaster^{edpt} (Paulinus-Nola *in lege*)

20 μὴ...φρεσίν Eph 4.14   ταῖς δὲ...γίνεσθε Php 3.15   **21** Ἐν...εἰσακούσονται Is 28.11–12; Dt 28.49   **23** Ac 2.13   **24** ἀνακρίνεται ὑπὸ πάντων Jn 16.8   **25** Ὄντως... ἐστιν Is 45.14; Dn 2.47; Zch 8.23; Jn 4.19   **26** ὅταν...ἑρμηνείαν 1 Cor 11.18; 12.8–10   πάντα ...γινέσθω Eph 4.12

ἢ διερμηνευτής, σιγάτω ἐν ἐκκλησίᾳ, ἑαυτῷ δὲ λαλείτω καὶ τῷ θεῷ. 29 προφῆται δὲ δύο ἢ τρεῖς λαλείτωσαν, καὶ οἱ ἄλλοι διακρινέτωσαν· 30 ἐὰν δὲ ἄλλῳ ἀποκαλυφθῇ καθημένῳ, ὁ πρῶτος σιγάτω. 31 δύνασθε γὰρ καθ᾽ ἕνα πάντες προφητεύειν, ἵνα πάντες μανθάνωσιν καὶ πάντες παρακαλῶνται, ᵇ32 καὶ πνεύματα προφητῶν προφήταις ὑποτάσσεται· 33 οὐ γάρ ἐστιν ἀκαταστασίας ὁ θεὸς ἀλλὰ εἰρήνης.ᵇ ᶜ

Ὡς ἐν πάσαις ταῖς ἐκκλησίαις τῶν ἁγίων,ᶜ 34 αἱ γυναῖκες ἐν ταῖς ἐκκλησίαις σιγάτωσαν, οὐ γὰρ ἐπιτρέπεται αὐταῖς λαλεῖν· ἀλλὰ ὑποτασσέσθωσαν, καθὼς καὶ ὁ νόμος λέγει.² 35 εἰ δέ τι μαθεῖν θέλουσιν, ἐν οἴκῳ τοὺς ἰδίους ἄνδρας ἐπερωτάτωσαν, αἰσχρὸν γάρ ἐστιν γυναικὶ λαλεῖν ἐν ἐκκλησίᾳ.² 36 ἢ ἀφ᾽ ὑμῶν ὁ λόγος τοῦ θεοῦ ἐξῆλθεν, ἢ εἰς ὑμᾶς μόνους κατήντησεν;

37 Εἴ τις δοκεῖ προφήτης εἶναι ἢ πνευματικός, ἐπιγινωσκέτω ἃ γράφω ὑμῖν ὅτι κυρίου ἐστὶν ἐντολή³. 38 εἰ δέ τις ἀγνοεῖ, ἀγνοεῖται⁴. 39 ὥστε, ἀδελφοί [μου],

can explain, then no one should speak out in the meeting, but only to himself and to God. 29 Two or three who are given God's message should speak, while the others judge what they say. 30 But if someone sitting in the meeting receives a message from God, the one who is speaking should stop. 31 All of you may speak God's message, one by one, so that all will learn and be encouraged. 32 The gift of speaking God's message should be under the speaker's control; 33 for God has not called us to be disorderly, but peaceful.

As in all the churches of God's people, 34 the women should keep quiet in the church meetings. They are not allowed to speak; as the Jewish Law says, they must not be in charge. 35 If they want to find out about something, they should ask their husbands at home. It is a disgraceful thing for a woman to speak in a church meeting.

36 Or could it be that the word of God came from you? Or are you the only ones to whom it came? 37 If anyone supposes he is God's messenger or has a spiritual gift, he must realize that what I am writing you is the Lord's command. 38 But if he does not pay attention to this, pay no attention to him.

39 So then, my brothers, set your heart

---

² **34-35** {B} *include verses 34-35 here* 𝔭⁴⁶ ℵ A B K Ψ 0243 33 81 88ᵐᵍ 104 181 326 330 436 451 614 629 630 1241 1739 1877 1881 1962 1984 1985 2127 2492 2495 *Byz Lect* itᵈᵉᵐ,ˣ,ᶻ vg syrᵖ,ʰ,ᵖᵃˡ copˢᵃ,ᵇᵒ,ᶠᵃʸ arm ‖ *transpose verses 34-35 following 14.40* D G 88* itᵃʳ,ᵈ,ᵉ,ᶠ,ᵍ Ambrosiaster Sedulius-Scotus

³ **37** {C} ἐστὶν ἐντολή 𝔭⁴⁶ ℵᶜ A B 048 0243 33 1241 1739 1881 syrᵖᵃˡ copᵇᵒ eth Augustine ‖ ἐντολή ἐστιν ℵ* ‖ εἰσὶν ἐντολαί Dᵇ,ᶜ K Ψ 88 104 181 326 330 451 614 629 630 1877 1984 1985 2492 2495 *Byz Lect* itᵃʳ,ᵈᵉᵐ,ˣ,ᶻ vg syrᵖ,ʰ copˢᵃ,ᶠᵃʸ Ambrosiaster (Chrysostom αἱ ἐντολαί) Theodoret John-Damascus ‖ ἐντολαί εἰσιν 81ᵛⁱᵈ 436 1962 itᶠ arm Euthalius ‖ ἐντολαὶ κυρίου εἰσιν 2127 ‖ ἐστίν D* G (itᵈ,ᵉ,ᵍ) Origenᵍʳ,ˡᵃᵗ Ambrosiaster Hilary Pelagius

⁴ **38** {B} ἀγνοεῖται ℵ* A*ᵛⁱᵈ (Gᵍʳ ἠγνοεῖται) 048 0243 33 1739 itᵈ,ᵉ syrᵖᵃˡ copˢᵃ,ᵇᵒ,ᶠᵃʸ Origenᵍʳ Hilary Ephraem Jerome ‖ ἀγνοεῖτε Dᵍʳ* ‖ ἀγνοείτω 𝔭⁴⁶ ℵᶜ A² B Dᵇ,ᶜ K Ψ 81 88 104 181 326 330 436 451 614 629 630 1241 1877 1881 1962 1984 1985 2127 2492 2495 *Byz Lect* syrᵖ,ʰ arm eth Origen Chrysostom

---

ᵇ ᵇ **32-33** *b b no parens:* TR WHᵐᵍ Bov Nes BF² AV RV ASV RSV NEB TT Zür Luth Jer Seg ‖ *b parens, b parens:* WH

ᶜ ᶜ **33-34** *c paragraph, c minor:* WHᵐᵍ Bov Nes BF² ASV RSV NEB TT (Zür) (Luth) Jer Seg ‖ *c minor, c paragraph:* TR WH AV RV NEBᵐᵍ

---

29 οἱ ἄλλοι διακρινέτωσαν Ac 17.11; 1 Th 5.21   **34** ἀλλά...λέγει Gn 3.16; 1 Cor 11.3; Eph 5.22; 1 Tm 2.12; Tt 2.5   **37** ἃ...ἐντολή 1 Jn 4.6

on speaking God's message, but do not forbid the speaking with strange sounds. 40 Everything must be done in a proper and orderly way.

The Resurrection of Christ

15 And now I want to remind you, brothers, of the Good News which I preached to you, which you received, and on which your faith stands firm. 2 That is the gospel, the message that I preached to you. You are saved by the gospel if you hold firmly to it — unless it was for nothing that you believed.

3 I passed on to you what I received, which is of the greatest importance: that Christ died for our sins, as written in the Scriptures; 4 that he was buried and raised to life on the third day, as written in the Scriptures; 5 that he appeared to Peter, and then to all twelve apostles. 6 Then he appeared to more than five hundred of his followers at once, most of whom are still alive, although some have died. 7 Then he appeared to James, and then to all the apostles.

8 Last of all he appeared also to me — even though I am like one who was born in a most unusual way. 9 For I am the least of all the apostles — I do not even

ζηλοῦτε τὸ προφητεύειν, καὶ τὸ λαλεῖν μὴ κωλύετε γλώσσαις[5]· 40 πάντα δὲ εὐσχημόνως καὶ κατὰ τάξιν γινέσθω.[6]

The Resurrection of Christ

15 Γνωρίζω δὲ ὑμῖν, ἀδελφοί, τὸ εὐαγγέλιον ὃ εὐηγγελισάμην ὑμῖν, ὃ καὶ παρελάβετε, ἐν ᾧ καὶ ἑστήκατε, 2 δι' οὗ καὶ σῴζεσθε, τίνι λόγῳ εὐηγγελισάμην ὑμῖν[a] εἰ κατέχετε,[a] ἐκτὸς εἰ μὴ εἰκῇ ἐπιστεύσατε. 3 παρέδωκα γὰρ ὑμῖν ἐν πρώτοις, ὃ καὶ παρέλαβον, ὅτι Χριστὸς ἀπέθανεν ὑπὲρ τῶν ἁμαρτιῶν ἡμῶν κατὰ τὰς γραφάς, 4 καὶ ὅτι ἐτάφη, καὶ ὅτι ἐγήγερται τῇ ἡμέρᾳ τῇ τρίτῃ κατὰ τὰς γραφάς, 5 καὶ ὅτι ὤφθη Κηφᾷ, εἶτα τοῖς δώδεκα· 6 ἔπειτα ὤφθη ἐπάνω πεντακοσίοις ἀδελφοῖς ἐφάπαξ, ἐξ ὧν οἱ πλείονες μένουσιν ἕως ἄρτι, τινὲς δὲ ἐκοιμήθησαν· 7 ἔπειτα ὤφθη Ἰακώβῳ, εἶτα τοῖς ἀποστόλοις πᾶσιν· 8 ἔσχατον δὲ πάντων ὡσπερεὶ τῷ ἐκτρώματι ὤφθη κἀμοί. 9 Ἐγὼ γάρ εἰμι ὁ ἐλάχιστος τῶν ἀποστόλων, ὃς οὐκ εἰμὶ ἱκανὸς καλεῖσθαι ἀπόστολος,

---

Euthalius Theodoret John-Damascus ‖ *ignorabitur* it[arvid,dem,f,g,x,z] vg Origen[lat] Ambrosiaster Ambrose

[5] **39** {D} τὸ λαλεῖν μὴ κωλύετε γλώσσαις ℵ A P (0243 630 1739 1881 *omit* τό) 33 81 326 1241 1962 Euthalius John-Damascus ‖ λαλεῖν μὴ κωλύετε ἐν γλώσσαις 𝔭[46] B cop[sa?bo?] ‖ τὸ λαλεῖν ἐν γλώσσαις μὴ κωλύετε D* G it[d,e,g] syr[p,h,pal] ‖ τὸ λαλεῖν γλώσσαις μὴ κωλύετε D[c] K Ψ 88 104 181 (330 451 2492 *omit* τό) 436 614 629 1877 (1984 τοῦ λαλεῖν) 1985 2127 2495 *Byz Lect* (*l*[809] κωλυέτω) it[ar,dem,f,x,z] vg arm eth? Ambrosiaster Chrysostom Theodoret

[6] **40** {B} *omit verses 34–35 here* 𝔭[46] ℵ A B K Ψ 0243 33 81 88[mg] 104 181 326 330 436 451 614 629 630 1241 1739 1877 1881 1962 1984 1985 2127 2492 2495 *Byz Lect* it[dem,x,z] vg syr[p,h,pal] cop[sa,bo,fay] arm ‖ *include verses 34–35 here* D G 88* it[ar,d,e,f,g] Ambrosiaster Sedulius-Scotus

---

[a a] **2** *a none, a minor:* TR Bov Nes BF[2] AV RV[mg] ASV Seg ‖ *a minor, a minor:* WH RV Luth ‖ *a minor, a dash:* (RSV) (TT) Zür ‖ *a none, a ellipsis:* Jer ‖ *a none, a question:* NEB

---

40 1 Cor 14.33; Col 2.5

15 3 Χριστὸς...γραφάς Is 53.8-9   **4** ἐγήγερται...γραφάς Ps 16.10; Ho 6.2; Jon 1.17; Mt 12.40; Ac 2.24-32   **5** ὤφθη Κηφᾷ Lk 24.34   τοῖς δώδεκα Mt 28.16-17; Mk 16.14; Lk 24.36; Jn 20.19   **7** τοῖς ἀποστόλοις πᾶσιν Lk 24.50   **8** Ac 9.3-6; 1 Cor 9.1   **9** Ἐγὼ...ἀποστόλων Eph 3.8; 1 Tm 1.15; Mt 5.19

[handwritten notes:]

Creed or 4 separate formulae ὅτι

15.3-5 early Aramaic creed

the 12 ≠ the apostles

κατα γραφας - not Aramaic

2 competing traditions?
① Peter & the 12
② James & the apostles

διότι ἐδίωξα τὴν ἐκκλησίαν τοῦ θεοῦ· 10 χάριτι δὲ θεοῦ εἰμι ὅ εἰμι, καὶ ἡ χάρις αὐτοῦ ἡ εἰς ἐμὲ οὐ κενὴ ἐγενήθη, ἀλλὰ περισσότερον αὐτῶν πάντων ἐκοπίασα, οὐκ ἐγὼ δὲ ἀλλὰ ἡ χάρις τοῦ θεοῦ [ἡ] σὺν ἐμοί[1]. 11 εἴτε οὖν ἐγὼ εἴτε ἐκεῖνοι, οὕτως κηρύσσομεν καὶ οὕτως ἐπιστεύσατε.

The Resurrection of the Dead

12 Εἰ δὲ Χριστὸς κηρύσσεται ὅτι ἐκ νεκρῶν ἐγήγερται, πῶς λέγουσιν ἐν ὑμῖν τινες ὅτι ἀνάστασις νεκρῶν οὐκ ἔστιν; 13 εἰ δὲ ἀνάστασις νεκρῶν οὐκ ἔστιν, οὐδὲ Χριστὸς ἐγήγερται· 14 εἰ δὲ Χριστὸς οὐκ ἐγήγερται, κενὸν ἄρα [καὶ] τὸ κήρυγμα ἡμῶν, κενὴ καὶ ἡ πίστις ὑμῶν[2], 15 εὑρισκόμεθα δὲ καὶ ψευδομάρτυρες τοῦ θεοῦ, ὅτι ἐμαρτυρήσαμεν κατὰ τοῦ θεοῦ ὅτι ἤγειρεν τὸν Χριστόν, ὃν οὐκ ἤγειρεν εἴπερ ἄρα νεκροὶ οὐκ ἐγείρονται. 16 εἰ γὰρ νεκροὶ οὐκ ἐγείρονται, οὐδὲ Χριστὸς ἐγήγερται· 17 εἰ δὲ Χριστὸς οὐκ ἐγήγερται, ματαία ἡ πίστις ὑμῶν, ἔτι ἐστὲ ἐν ταῖς ἁμαρτίαις ὑμῶν. 18 ἄρα καὶ οἱ κοιμηθέντες ἐν Χριστῷ ἀπώλοντο. 19 εἰ ἐν τῇ ζωῇ ταύτῃ ἐν Χριστῷ ἠλπικότες ἐσμὲν μόνον, ἐλεεινότεροι πάντων ἀνθρώπων ἐσμέν.

---

[1] 10 {C} ἡ σὺν ἐμοί ℵ[c] A D[b] K P Ψ 33 81 88 104 181 326 330 436 451 614 629 630 1241 1877 1881 1962 1984 1985 2127 2492 2495 *Byz Lect* syr[(p),h] cop[sa,bo,fay] arm eth Origen[lat] Basil Chrysostom Jerome Cyril Euthalius Theodoret Ps-Athanasius Antiochus John-Damascus // ἡ εἰς ἐμέ 𝔭[46] syr[hmg] goth Theodoret // σὺν ἐμοί ℵ* B D* G 0243 1739 it[ar,d,dem,e,f,g,t,x,z] vg Origen[gr,lat] Ambrosiaster

[2] 14 {C} ὑμῶν ℵ A D[b,c] G K Γ Ψ 88 104 181 326 436 614 629 630 1877 1962 1984 1985 2127 2495 *Byz Lect* it[d,dem,e,f,g,r1,x,z] vg syr[p,h] cop[samss,bo] arm Marcion Irenaeus[lat] Tertullian Aphraates Ambrosiaster Ephraem Gregory-Elvira Ps-Ignatius Chrysostom Cyril Euthalius Theodoret // ἡμῶν B D[gr*] 0243 33 81 330 451 1241 1739 1881 2492 it[ar] cop[samss,fay] goth Irenaeus[lat] Tertullian Origen Adamantius Cyril-Jerusalem Ps-Ignatius Epiphanius Rufinus Cyril Cosmos Ps-Oecumenius

9 ἐδίωξα...θεοῦ Ac 8.3   10 ἡ χάρις...ἐγενήθη 2 Cor 6.1   περισσότερον...ἐκοπίασα 2 Cor 11.5, 23   15 ἐμαρτυρήσαμεν...νεκροί Ac 1.22; 4.33; 5.32

---

deserve to be called an apostle, because I persecuted God's church. 10 But by God's grace I am what I am, and the grace that he gave me was not without effect. On the contrary, I have worked harder than all the other apostles, although it was not really my own doing, but God's grace working with me. 11 So then, whether it came from me or from them, this is what we all preach, this is what you believe.

Our Resurrection

12 Now, since our message is that Christ has been raised from death, how can some of you say that the dead will not be raised to life? 13 If that is true, it means that Christ was not raised; 14 and if Christ has not been raised from death, then we have nothing to preach, and you have nothing to believe. 15 More than that, we are shown to be lying against God, because we said of him that he raised Christ from death — but he did not raise him, if it is true that the dead are not raised to life. 16 For if the dead are not raised, neither has Christ been raised. 17 And if Christ has not been raised, then your faith is a delusion and you are still lost in your sins. 18 It would also mean that the believers in Christ who have died are lost. 19 If our hope in Christ is good for this life only, and no more,[1] then we deserve more pity than anyone else in all the world.

---

[1] 19 *If our hope in Christ is good for this life only, and no more:* or *If all we have in this life is our hope in Christ*

²⁰ But the truth is that Christ has been raised from death, as the guarantee that those who sleep in death will also be raised. ²¹ For just as death came by means of a man, in the same way the rising from death comes by means of a man. ²² For just as all men die because of their union to Adam, in the same way all will be raised to life because of their union to Christ. ²³ But each one in his proper order: Christ, the first of all; then those who belong to Christ, at the time of his coming. ²⁴ Then the end will come; Christ will overcome all spiritual rulers, authorities, and powers, and hand over the Kingdom to God the Father. ²⁵ For Christ must rule until God defeats all enemies and puts them under his feet. ²⁶ The last enemy to be defeated will be death. ²⁷ For the scripture says, "God put *all* things under his feet." It is clear, of course, that the words "all things" do not include God himself, who puts all things under Christ. ²⁸ But when all things have been placed under Christ's rule, then he himself, the Son, will place himself under God, who placed all under him; and God will rule completely over all.

²⁹ Now, what of those people who are baptized for the dead? What do they hope to accomplish? If it is true, as they claim, that the dead are not raised to life, why are they being baptized for the dead? ³⁰ And as for us — why would we run the risk of danger every hour? ³¹ Brothers, I face death every day! The pride I have in you in our life in Christ Jesus our Lord makes me declare this. ³² If, as it were, I have fought "wild beasts" here in Ephesus, simply from human motives, what have I gained?

20 Νυνὶ δὲ Χριστὸς ἐγήγερται ἐκ νεκρῶν, ἀπαρχὴ τῶν κεκοιμημένων. 21 ἐπειδὴ γὰρ δι᾽ ἀνθρώπου θάνατος, καὶ δι᾽ ἀνθρώπου ἀνάστασις νεκρῶν· 22 ὥσπερ γὰρ ἐν τῷ ᾽Αδὰμ πάντες ἀποθνῄσκουσιν, οὕτως καὶ ἐν τῷ Χριστῷ πάντες ζῳοποιηθήσονται. 23 ἕκαστος δὲ ἐν τῷ ἰδίῳ τάγματι· ἀπαρχὴ Χριστός, ἔπειτα οἱ τοῦ Χριστοῦ ἐν τῇ παρουσίᾳ αὐτοῦ· 24 εἶτα τὸ τέλος, ὅταν παραδιδῷ τὴν βασιλείαν τῷ θεῷ καὶ πατρί, ὅταν καταργήσῃ πᾶσαν ἀρχὴν καὶ πᾶσαν ἐξουσίαν καὶ δύναμιν. 25 δεῖ γὰρ αὐτὸν βασιλεύειν ἄχρι οὗ θῇ πάντας τοὺς ἐχθροὺς ὑπὸ τοὺς πόδας αὐτοῦ. 26 ἔσχατος ἐχθρὸς καταργεῖται ὁ θάνατος·ᵇ 27 **πάντα γὰρ ὑπέταξεν ὑπὸ τοὺς πόδας αὐτοῦ.** ὅταν δὲ εἴπῃ ὅτι πάντα ὑποτέτακται, ᶜ δῆλον ὅτι ἐκτὸς τοῦ ὑποτάξαντος αὐτῷ τὰ πάντα.ᶜ 28 ὅταν δὲ ὑποταγῇ αὐτῷ τὰ πάντα, τότε [καὶ] αὐτὸς ὁ υἱὸς ὑποταγήσεται τῷ ὑποτάξαντι αὐτῷ τὰ πάντα, ἵνα ᾖ ὁ θεὸς [τὰ] πάντα ἐν πᾶσιν.

29 ᾽Επεὶ τί ποιήσουσιν οἱ βαπτιζόμενοι ὑπὲρ τῶν νεκρῶν;ᵈ εἰ ὅλως νεκροὶ οὐκ ἐγείρονται,ᵈ τί καὶ βαπτίζονται ὑπὲρ αὐτῶν; 30 τί καὶ ἡμεῖς κινδυνεύομεν πᾶσαν ὥραν; 31 καθ᾽ ἡμέραν ἀποθνῄσκω, νὴ τὴν ὑμετέραν καύχησιν, [ἀδελφοί,]³ ἣν ἔχω ἐν Χριστῷ ᾽Ιησοῦ τῷ κυρίῳ ἡμῶν. 32 εἰ κατὰ ἄνθρωπον ἐθηριομάχησα ἐν ᾽Εφέσῳ, τί μοι τὸ ὄφελος;ᵉ εἰ νεκροὶ οὐκ ἐγείρονται,ᵉ

---

³ 31 {C} ἀδελφοί, ℵ A B K P 33 81 88 104 181 (326 *transposes*: ἣν ἔχω ἀδελφοί) 330 436 451 1241 1962 2127 itᵃʳ,ʳˡ,ˣ,ᶻ vg syrᵖᵃˡ goth arm Adamantius Augustine Euthalius ∥ ἀδελφοί μου, syrᵖ,ʰ copˢᵃ?ᵇᵒ?ᶠᵃʸ? ∥ ἀδελφοὶ ἡμῶν, eth ∥ *omit* 𝔭⁴⁶ D G Ψ 0243 614 629 630 1739 1877 1881 1984 1985 2492 2495

ᵇ 26 b minor: WH Bov Nes BF² TT Jer ∥ b major: TR AV RV ASV RSV NEB Zür Luth Seg

ᶜ ᶜ 27 c c no parens: TR WH Bov Nes BF² AV RV ASV RSV NEB TT Zür Luth Jer Seg ∥ c parens, c parens: RVᵐᵍ ASVᵐᵍ

ᵈ ᵈ 29 d question, d minor: TR WH Bov Nes BF² RV ASV RSV (NEB) TT Zür Jer Seg ∥ d minor, d question: AV Luth

ᵉ ᵉ 32 e question, e minor: WH Bov Nes BF² RV ASV RSV NEB TT Zür Luth Jer Seg ∥ e minor, e question: TR AV RVᵐᵍ ASVᵐᵍ

---

20 Col 1.18   21 Gn 3.17–19; Ro 5.12, 18   23 1 Th 4.16; Re 20.5   24 παραδιδῷ...πατρί Dn 2.44   25 Ps 110.1; Mt 22.44   26 Re 20.14; 21.4   27 πάντα...αὐτοῦ Ps 8.6   30 Ro 8.36   31 καθ᾽ ἡμέραν ἀποθνῄσκω 2 Cor 4.10–11

Φάγωμεν καὶ πίωμεν,
αὔριον γὰρ ἀποθνήσκομεν.

33 μὴ πλανᾶσθε·

Φθείρουσιν ἤθη χρηστὰ ὁμιλίαι κακαί.

34 ἐκνήψατε δικαίως καὶ μὴ ἁμαρτάνετε, ἀγνωσίαν γὰρ θεοῦ τινες ἔχουσιν· πρὸς ἐντροπὴν ὑμῖν λαλῶ.

The Resurrection Body

35 Ἀλλὰ ἐρεῖ τις, Πῶς ἐγείρονται οἱ νεκροί;^f ποίῳ δὲ σώματι ἔρχονται;^f **36** ἄφρων, σὺ ὃ σπείρεις οὐ ζωοποιεῖται ἐὰν μὴ ἀποθάνῃ· **37** καὶ ὃ σπείρεις, οὐ τὸ σῶμα τὸ γενησόμενον σπείρεις ἀλλὰ γυμνὸν κόκκον εἰ τύχοι σίτου ἤ τινος τῶν λοιπῶν· **38** ὁ δὲ θεὸς δίδωσιν αὐτῷ σῶμα καθὼς ἠθέλησεν, καὶ ἑκάστῳ τῶν σπερμάτων ἴδιον σῶμα. **39** οὐ πᾶσα σὰρξ ἡ αὐτὴ σάρξ, ἀλλὰ ἄλλη μὲν ἀνθρώπων, ἄλλη δὲ σὰρξ κτηνῶν, ἄλλη δὲ σὰρξ πτηνῶν, ἄλλη δὲ ἰχθύων. **40** καὶ σώματα ἐπουράνια, καὶ σώματα ἐπίγεια· ἀλλὰ ἑτέρα μὲν ἡ τῶν ἐπουρανίων δόξα, ἑτέρα δὲ ἡ τῶν ἐπιγείων. **41** ἄλλη δόξα ἡλίου, καὶ ἄλλη δόξα σελήνης, καὶ ἄλλη δόξα ἀστέρων· ἀστὴρ γὰρ ἀστέρος διαφέρει ἐν δόξῃ.

42 Οὕτως καὶ ἡ ἀνάστασις τῶν νεκρῶν. σπείρεται ἐν φθορᾷ, ἐγείρεται ἐν ἀφθαρσίᾳ· **43** σπείρεται ἐν ἀτιμίᾳ, ἐγείρεται ἐν δόξῃ· σπείρεται ἐν ἀσθενείᾳ, ἐγείρεται ἐν δυνάμει· **44** σπείρεται σῶμα ψυχικόν, ἐγείρεται σῶμα πνευματικόν. εἰ ἔστιν σῶμα ψυχικόν, ἔστιν καὶ πνευματικόν. **45** οὕτως καὶ γέγραπται, **Ἐγένετο ὁ πρῶτος ἄνθρωπος Ἀδὰμ εἰς ψυχὴν ζῶσαν·** ὁ ἔσχατος Ἀδὰμ εἰς πνεῦμα ζωοποιοῦν. **46** ἀλλ' οὐ πρῶτον τὸ πνευμα-

---

Byz Lect it^{d,dem,e,f,g} Origen Ambrosiaster Chrysostom Theodoret John-Damascus

ƒ ƒ **35** ƒ question, ƒ question: TR Bov Nes BF² AV RV ASV RSV NEB TT Zür Jer ‖ ƒ minor, ƒ question: WH Luth Seg

32 Φάγωμεν...ἀποθνήσκομεν Is 22.13; 56.12; Lk 12.19—20   **33** Menander, *Thais* (218)
34 ἐκνήψατε δικαίως Ro 13.11; Eph 5.14   ἀγνωσίαν...ἔχουσιν Ac 26.8   πρὸς...λαλῶ
1 Cor 6.5   **36** Jn 12.24   **38** Gn 1.11   **43** Php 3.20-21   **45** Ἐγένετο...ζῶσαν Gn 2.7
ὁ ἔσχατος...ζωοποιοῦν Jn 6.63; 2 Cor 3.6, 17

As the saying goes, "Let us eat and drink, for tomorrow we will die" — if the dead are not raised to life.

33 Do not be fooled: "Bad companions ruin good character." **34** Come back to your right senses and stop your sinful ways. I say this to your shame: some of you do not know God.

The Resurrection Body

35 Someone will ask, "How can the dead be raised to life? What kind of body will they have?" **36** You fool! When you plant a seed in the ground it does not sprout to life unless it dies. **37** And what you plant in the ground is a bare seed, perhaps a grain of wheat, or of some other kind, not the full-bodied plant that will grow up. **38** God provides that seed with the body he wishes; he gives each seed its own proper body.

39 And the flesh of living beings is not all the same kind of flesh: men have one kind of flesh, animals another, birds another, and fish another.

40 And there are heavenly bodies and earthly bodies; there is a beauty that belongs to heavenly bodies, and another kind of beauty that belongs to earthly bodies. **41** The sun has its own beauty, the moon another beauty, and the stars a different beauty; and even among stars there are different kinds of beauty.

42 This is how it will be when the dead are raised to life. When the body is buried it is mortal; when raised, it will be immortal. **43** When buried, it is ugly and weak; when raised, it will be beautiful and strong. **44** When buried, it is a physical body; when raised, it will be a spiritual body. There is, of course, a physical body, so there has to be a spiritual body. **45** For the scripture says: "The first man, Adam, was created a living being"; but the last Adam is the life-giving Spirit. **46** It is not the spiritual that comes first, but the physical, and then the spiritual. ⁴⁷ The first Adam was made of the dust of the earth; the second Adam came from heaven. ⁴⁸ Those who belong to the earth are like the one who was made of earth; those who are of heaven are like the one who came from heaven. ⁴⁹ Just as we wear the likeness of the man made of earth, so we will wear the likeness of the Man from heaven.

⁵⁰ This is what I mean, brothers: what is made of flesh and blood cannot share in God's Kingdom, and what is mortal cannot possess immortality.

⁵¹ Listen to this secret: we shall not all die, but in an instant we shall all be

τικὸν ἀλλὰ τὸ ψυχικόν, ἔπειτα τὸ πνευματικόν. 47 ὁ πρῶτος ἄνθρωπος ἐκ γῆς χοϊκός, ὁ δεύτερος ἄνθρωπος⁴ ἐξ οὐρανοῦ. 48 οἷος ὁ χοϊκός, τοιοῦτοι καὶ οἱ χοϊκοί, καὶ οἷος ὁ ἐπουράνιος, τοιοῦτοι καὶ οἱ ἐπουράνιοι· 49 καὶ καθὼς ἐφορέσαμεν τὴν εἰκόνα τοῦ χοϊκοῦ, φορέσομεν⁵ καὶ τὴν εἰκόνα τοῦ ἐπουρανίου.

50 Τοῦτο δέ φημι, ἀδελφοί, ὅτι σὰρξ καὶ αἷμα βασιλείαν θεοῦ κληρονομῆσαι οὐ δύναται, οὐδὲ ἡ φθορὰ τὴν ἀφθαρσίαν κληρονομεῖ. 51 ἰδοὺ μυστήριον ὑμῖν λέγω· πάντες οὐ κοιμηθησόμεθα, πάντες δὲ ἀλλαγησόμεθα⁶,

⁴ 47 {A} ἄνθρωπος ℵ* B C D* G 0243 33 1739* itar,d,dem,e,f,g,x,z vg copbo eth Tertullian Hippolytus Origengr1/2,lat Cyprian Adamantius Peter-Alexandria Ambrosiaster Hilary Athanasius Priscillian Gregory-Nazianzus acc. to Theodoret Gregory-Elvira Gregory-Nyssa Ambrose Epiphanius Ps-Athanasius ‖ ὁ κύριος 630 (Marcion) ‖ ἄνθρωπος ὁ κύριος ℵc A Dc K P Ψ 81 104 181 326 330 436 451 614 629 1241 1739mg 1877 1881 1962 1984 1985 2127 2492 2495 Byz Lect syrp,h,pal goth arm Origengr1/2 Basil Chrysostom Maximinusacc. to Augustine Cyril Euthalius Theodoret Ps-Athanasius Cosmos John-Damascus ‖ ἄνθρωπος πνευματικός p46 ‖ omit copsa Cyril

⁵ 49 {C} φορέσομεν B I 88 630 1881 Lect copsa eth Irenaeus Origen Aphraates Ephraem Cyril3/5 Theodoret Gennadius-Constantinople Cosmos1/3 Ps-Oecumenius Theophylact ‖ φορέσωμεν p46 ℵ A C D G K P Ψ 0243 33 81 104 181 326 330 436 451 614 629 1241 1739 1877 1962 1984 1985 2127 2492 2495 Byz itar,d,dem,e,f,g,x,z vg copbo goth Marcion Theodotus Irenaeuslat Clement Tertullian Origengr,lat Cyprian (Methodius) Ambrosiaster Hilary Caesarius-Nazianzus Basil Priscillian Gregory-Elvira Gregory-Nyssa Ambrose Macarius Epiphanius Chrysostom Cyril2/5 Euthalius Ps-Athanasius Cosmos2/3 Maximus-Confessor John-Damascus

⁶ 51 {A} οὐ κοιμηθησόμεθα, πάντες δὲ ἀλλαγησόμεθα B Dc K P Ψ 0243evid 81 88 104 181 326 330 436 451 614 629 630 1877 1881 1962 1984 1985 2127 2492 2495 Byz Lect syrp,h copsa,bo goth ethpp Tertullian Origengr1/3,lat Adamantius Greek mssacc. to Acacius Caesarius-Nazianzus Ephraem Titus-Bostraacc. to John-Damascus Apollinaris Diodore Ps-Justin Gregory-Nyssa Greek mssacc. to Didymus Chrysostom Greek mssacc. to Pelagius, Jerome Jerome Greek mssacc. to Maximus-Turin Theodore Cyril Euthalius Theodoret Greek mssacc. to Ps-Jerome Cosmos Andrew John-Damascus ‖ οὐ κοιμηθησόμεθα, οὐ πάντες δὲ ἀλλαγησόμεθα p46 Ac Origen ‖ οὖν κοιμηθησόμεθα, οὐ πάντες

47 ὁ πρῶτος...χοϊκός Gn 2.7   49 ἐφορέσαμεν...χοϊκοῦ Gn 5.3   50 1 Cor 6.13
51–52 πάντες...ἀλλαγησόμεθα 1 Th 4.15–17

52 ἐν ἀτόμῳ, ἐν ῥιπῇ ὀφθαλμοῦ, ἐν τῇ ἐσχάτῃ σάλπιγγι· σαλπίσει γάρ, καὶ οἱ νεκροὶ ἐγερθήσονται ἄφθαρτοι, καὶ ἡμεῖς ἀλλαγησόμεθα. **53** δεῖ γὰρ τὸ φθαρτὸν τοῦτο ἐνδύσασθαι ἀφθαρσίαν καὶ τὸ θνητὸν τοῦτο ἐνδύσασθαι ἀθανασίαν. **54** ὅταν δὲ τὸ φθαρτὸν τοῦτο ἐνδύσηται ἀφθαρσίαν καὶ τὸ θνητὸν τοῦτο ἐνδύσηται ἀθανασίαν[7], τότε γενήσεται ὁ λόγος ὁ γεγραμμένος,

    Κατεπόθη ὁ θάνατος εἰς νῖκος.
55   **ποῦ σου, θάνατε, τὸ νῖκος;**
        ποῦ σου, θάνατε, τὸ κέντρον;[8]

changed, [52] as quickly as the blinking of an eye, when the last trumpet sounds. For when it sounds, the dead will be raised immortal beings, and we shall all be changed. [53] For what is mortal must clothe itself with what is immortal; what will die must clothe itself with what cannot die. [54] So when what is mortal has been clothed with what is immortal, and when what will die has been clothed with what cannot die, then the scripture will come true: "Death is destroyed; victory is complete!"

[55] "Where, O Death, is your victory? Where, O Death, is your power to hurt?"

δὲ ἀλλαγησόμεθα G[gr] ‖ κοιμηθησόμεθα, οὐ πάντες δὲ ἀλλαγησόμεθα ℵ (A* οἱ for οὐ) C 0243* 33 1241 1739 it[g] arm eth Origen[gr2/3,lat] Aphraates Greek mss[acc. to Acacius, Didymus] Didymus[acc. to Jerome] mss[acc. to Pelagius, Jerome, Maximus-Turin, Augustine] Cyril Greek mss[acc. to Ps-Jerome] ‖ ἀναστησόμεθα, οὐ πάντες δὲ ἀλλαγησόμεθα D* it[ar,d,dem,(e),f,x,zvid] vg Marcion Tertullian Jacob-Nisibis Ambrosiaster Hilary Ambrose Gregory-Elvira Latin mss[acc. to Pelagius, Jerome, Augustine] Augustine John-Damascus ‖ omnes inmutabimur it[m]

[7] **54** {C} ὅταν δὲ τὸ φθαρτὸν τοῦτο ἐνδύσηται ἀφθαρσίαν καὶ τὸ θνητὸν τοῦτο ἐνδύσηται ἀθανασίαν (ℵ[c] τὴν ἀθανασίαν) B C[2vid] D K P Ψ (33 τὴν ἀφθαρσίαν...τὴν ἀθανασίαν) 81 88 104 181 330 436 451 614[mg] 629[c] 630 (1241 ἐνδύσεσθαι twice) 1739[mg] 1877[mg] 1881 1962 1984 (1985 οὖν for δέ) (2127 ἀθανασίαν for ἀφθαρσίαν) 2492 2495 Byz l[809m,1441m] it[d,(e)] syr[p,h] Origen Cyprian Chrysostom Jerome Augustine Euthalius Theodoret Cosmos John-Damascus ‖ ὅταν δὲ τὸ θνητὸν τοῦτο ἐνδύσηται τὴν ἀθανασίαν καὶ τὸ φθαρτὸν τοῦτο ἐνδύσηται ἀφθαρσίαν A (326 omit τήν) cop[sams] (arm omit τοῦτο ἐνδύσηται) ‖ ὅταν δὲ τὸ θνητὸν τοῦτο ἐνδύσηται τὴν ἀθανασίαν (𝔭[46] 0121a 0243 1739* omit τήν) ℵ* 088 (629* φθαρτόν for θνητόν and omit τήν) it[ar,dem,x,z] vg cop[sams,bo] goth eth Marcion Irenaeus[gr,lat] (Cyprian) (Adamantius) Ambrosiaster Hilary Athanasius ‖ omit G 614* 1877* it[f,g] cop[boms]

[8] **55** {B} νῖκος; ποῦ σου, θάνατε, τὸ κέντρον; (𝔭[46] B νεῖκος) ℵ* C 088 1739*[vid] 1877 1962 2492 2495 (it[ar] νεῖκος) it[dem,x,z] vg cop[sa,bo] eth[ro] Irenaeus[lat] Tertullian Origen[lat] Eusebius Ambrose ‖ νῖκος; ποῦ σου, ᾅδη, τὸ κέντρον; 0121a 0243 33 81 326 1241 1739[c] (arm) Origen Athanasius Didymus Euthalius ‖ κέντρον; ποῦ σου, θάνατε, τὸ νῖκος; D* (D[c] omit θάνατε) G it[d,e,f,g] Irenaeus Origen[gr,lat] Eusebius Theodoret (Tertullian Cyprian Hilary νεῖκος) ‖ κέντρον; ποῦ σου, ᾅδη, τὸ νῖκος; ℵ[c] A[c] K P Ψ 88 104 181 330 436 451 614 629 630 1881 1984 1985 2127 Byz l[809m,1441m] syr[p,h] goth eth[pp] Origen Athanasius Epiphanius Chrysostom Eutherius Theodoret

---

52 σαλπίσει...ἐγερθήσονται Mt 24.31   **53** 2 Cor 5.4   **54** Κατεπόθη...νῖκος Is 25.8   **55** Ho 13.14

[56] Death gets its power to hurt from sin, and sin gets its power from the Law. [57] But thanks be to God who gives us the victory through our Lord Jesus Christ!

[58] So then, my dear brothers, stand firm and steady. Keep busy always in your work for the Lord, since you know that nothing you do in the Lord's service is ever without value.

The Offering for Fellow Believers

16 Now the matter about the money to be raised to help God's people in Judea: you must do what I told the churches in Galatia to do. [2] On the first day of every week each of you must put aside some money, in proportion to what he has earned, and save it up, so there will be no need to collect money when I come. [3] After I come I shall send the men you have approved, with letters of introduction, to take your gift to Jerusalem. [4] If it seems worth while for me to go, then they will go along with me.

Paul's Plans

[5] I shall come to you after I have gone through Macedonia — for I am going through Macedonia. [6] I shall probably spend some time with you, perhaps the whole winter, and then you can help me to continue my trip, wherever it is I shall go next. [7] For I do not want to see you just briefly in passing. I hope to spend quite a long time with you, if the Lord allows.

[8] But I plan to stay here in Ephesus until the day of Pentecost. [9] There is a real opportunity here for great and worth-while work, even though there are many opponents.

[56] τὸ δὲ κέντρον τοῦ θανάτου ἡ ἁμαρτία, ἡ δὲ δύναμις τῆς ἁμαρτίας ὁ νόμος· [57] τῷ δὲ θεῷ χάρις τῷ διδόντι ἡμῖν τὸ νῖκος διὰ τοῦ κυρίου ἡμῶν Ἰησοῦ Χριστοῦ. [58] Ὥστε, ἀδελφοί μου ἀγαπητοί, ἑδραῖοι γίνεσθε, ἀμετακίνητοι, περισσεύοντες ἐν τῷ ἔργῳ τοῦ κυρίου πάντοτε, εἰδότες ὅτι ὁ κόπος ὑμῶν οὐκ ἔστιν κενὸς ἐν κυρίῳ.

The Contribution for the Saints

16 Περὶ δὲ τῆς λογείας τῆς εἰς τοὺς ἁγίους, ὥσπερ διέταξα ταῖς ἐκκλησίαις τῆς Γαλατίας, οὕτως καὶ ὑμεῖς ποιήσατε. [2] κατὰ μίαν σαββάτου ἕκαστος ὑμῶν παρ' ἑαυτῷ τιθέτω θησαυρίζων ὅ τι ἐὰν εὐοδῶται, ἵνα μὴ ὅταν ἔλθω τότε λογεῖαι γίνωνται. [3] ὅταν δὲ παραγένωμαι, οὓς ἐὰν δοκιμάσητε,[a] δι' ἐπιστολῶν[a] τούτους πέμψω ἀπενεγκεῖν τὴν χάριν ὑμῶν εἰς Ἰερουσαλήμ· [4] ἐὰν δὲ ἄξιον ᾖ τοῦ κἀμὲ πορεύεσθαι, σὺν ἐμοὶ πορεύσονται.

Plans for Travel

[5] Ἐλεύσομαι δὲ πρὸς ὑμᾶς ὅταν Μακεδονίαν διέλθω, Μακεδονίαν γὰρ διέρχομαι· [6] πρὸς ὑμᾶς δὲ τυχὸν παραμενῶ ἢ καὶ παραχειμάσω, ἵνα ὑμεῖς με προπέμψητε οὗ ἐὰν πορεύωμαι. [7] οὐ θέλω γὰρ ὑμᾶς ἄρτι ἐν παρόδῳ ἰδεῖν, ἐλπίζω γὰρ χρόνον τινὰ ἐπιμεῖναι πρὸς ὑμᾶς, ἐὰν ὁ κύριος ἐπιτρέψῃ. [8] ἐπιμενῶ δὲ ἐν Ἐφέσῳ ἕως τῆς πεντηκοστῆς· [9] θύρα γάρ μοι ἀνέῳγεν μεγάλη καὶ ἐνεργής, καὶ ἀντικείμενοι πολλοί.

[a a] **3** a minor, a none: Bov Nes BF[2] RV[mg] ASV (NEB) (TT) (Zür) Luth (Jer) (Seg) ∥ a none, a minor: WH AV RV ASV[mg] (RSV) ∥ a none, a none: TR

56 τὸ δὲ...ἁμαρτία Ro 7.13   ἡ δὲ...νόμος Ro 6.14   **58** ὁ κόπος...κυρίῳ 2 Chr 15.7; Re 14.13

16 1 Περὶ...ἁγίους Ac 11.29; Ro 15.25–26; 2 Cor 8.9; Ga 2.10   **2** κατὰ μίαν σαββάτου Ac 20.7   **5** Μακεδονίαν γὰρ διέρχομαι Ac 19.21   **6** Ro 15.24; Tt 3.12   **7** ἐὰν...ἐπιτρέψῃ Ac 18.21   **8** Ac 19.1, 10   τῆς πεντηκοστῆς Lv 23.15–21; Dt 16.9–11   **9** θύρα...ἐνεργής Ac 19.8–10; 2 Cor 2.12; Col 4.3; Re 3.8

10 Ἐὰν δὲ ἔλθῃ Τιμόθεος, βλέπετε ἵνα ἀφόβως γένηται πρὸς ὑμᾶς, τὸ γὰρ ἔργον κυρίου ἐργάζεται ὡς κἀγώ· 11 μή τις οὖν αὐτὸν ἐξουθενήσῃ. προπέμψατε δὲ αὐτὸν ἐν εἰρήνῃ, ἵνα ἔλθῃ πρός με, ἐκδέχομαι γὰρ αὐτὸν μετὰ τῶν ἀδελφῶν.

12 Περὶ δὲ Ἀπολλῶ τοῦ ἀδελφοῦ, πολλὰ παρεκάλεσα αὐτὸν ἵνα ἔλθῃ πρὸς ὑμᾶς μετὰ τῶν ἀδελφῶν· καὶ πάντως οὐκ ἦν θέλημα ἵνα νῦν ἔλθῃ, ἐλεύσεται δὲ ὅταν εὐκαιρήσῃ.

Final Request and Greetings

13 Γρηγορεῖτε, στήκετε ἐν τῇ πίστει, ἀνδρίζεσθε, κραταιοῦσθε· 14 πάντα ὑμῶν ἐν ἀγάπῃ γινέσθω.

15 Παρακαλῶ δὲ ὑμᾶς, ἀδελφοί· οἴδατε τὴν οἰκίαν Στεφανᾶ, ὅτι ἐστὶν ἀπαρχὴ τῆς Ἀχαΐας καὶ εἰς διακονίαν τοῖς ἁγίοις ἔταξαν ἑαυτούς· 16 ἵνα καὶ ὑμεῖς ὑποτάσσησθε τοῖς τοιούτοις καὶ παντὶ τῷ συνεργοῦντι καὶ κοπιῶντι. 17 χαίρω δὲ ἐπὶ τῇ παρουσίᾳ Στεφανᾶ καὶ Φορτουνάτου καὶ Ἀχαϊκοῦ, ὅτι τὸ ὑμέτερον ὑστέρημα οὗτοι ἀνεπλήρωσαν, 18 ἀνέπαυσαν γὰρ τὸ ἐμὸν πνεῦμα καὶ τὸ ὑμῶν. ἐπιγινώσκετε οὖν τοὺς τοιούτους.

19 Ἀσπάζονται ὑμᾶς αἱ ἐκκλησίαι τῆς Ἀσίας. ἀσπάζεται ὑμᾶς ἐν κυρίῳ πολλὰ Ἀκύλας καὶ Πρίσκα σὺν τῇ κατ᾽ οἶκον αὐτῶν ἐκκλησίᾳ. 20 ἀσπάζονται ὑμᾶς οἱ ἀδελφοὶ πάντες. Ἀσπάσασθε ἀλλήλους ἐν φιλήματι ἁγίῳ.

21 Ὁ ἀσπασμὸς τῇ ἐμῇ χειρὶ Παύλου. 22 εἴ τις οὐ φιλεῖ τὸν κύριον, ἤτω ἀνάθεμα. Μαρανα θα. 23 ἡ χάρις

---

10 Ἐὰν...Τιμόθεος 1 Cor 4.17   τὸ γὰρ...ἐργάζεται Php 2.20   11 μή...ἐξουθενήσῃ 1 Tm 4.12   12 Ἀπολλῶ Ac 18.24; 1 Cor 1.12; 3.5–6   13 ἀνδρίζεσθε, κραταιοῦσθε Ps 31.24; Eph 6.10   15 τὴν οἰκίαν Στεφανᾶ 1 Cor 1.16   ἀπαρχὴ τῆς Ἀχαΐας Ro 16.5   18 ἐπιγινώσκετε...τοιούτους Php 2.29; 1 Th 5.12   19 Ἀκύλας καὶ Πρίσκα Ac 18.2, 18, 26; Ro 16.3   τῇ κατ᾽...ἐκκλησίᾳ Ro 16.5   20 Ἀσπάσασθε...ἁγίῳ Ro 16.16; 2 Cor 13.12; 1 Pe 5.14   21 Col 4.18; 2 Th 3.17   22 εἴ...ἀνάθεμα Ga 1.8, 9

10 If Timothy comes your way, however, be sure to make him feel welcome among you, for he is working for the Lord, just as I am. 11 No one is to look down on him, but you must help him continue his trip in peace, so that he will come back to me; for I am expecting him back with the brothers.

12 Now, about brother Apollos: I have often encouraged him to visit you with the other brothers, but he is not completely convinced that he should go right now. When he gets the chance, however, he will go.

Final Words

13 Be alert, stand firm in the faith, be brave, be strong. 14 Do all your work in love.

15 You know about Stephanas and his family; they are the first Christian converts in Greece, and have given themselves to the service of God's people. I beg you, my brothers, 16 to follow the leadership of such people as these, and of anyone else who works and serves with them.

17 I am happy over the coming of Stephanas, Fortunatus, and Achaicus; they have made up for your absence, 18 and have cheered me up, just as they cheered you up. Such men as these deserve notice.

19 The churches in the province of Asia send you their greetings; Aquila and Priscilla and the church that meets in their house send warm Christian greetings. 20 All the brothers here send greetings.

Greet one another with a brotherly kiss.

21 With my own hand I write this: *Greetings from Paul.*

22 Whoever does not love the Lord — a curse on him!

Marana tha — Our Lord, come!

23 The grace of the Lord Jesus be with you.

²⁴ My love be with you all in Christ Jesus.

τοῦ κυρίου ᾿Ιησοῦ μεθ᾿ ὑμῶν. 24 ἡ ἀγάπη μου μετὰ πάντων ὑμῶν ἐν Χριστῷ ᾿Ιησοῦ.[1]

---

[1] **24** {C} ᾿Ιησοῦ. B 0121a 0243 33 630 1739* 1881 it[f.g.rl] syr[p] cop[sa] Ambrosiaster Euthalius ‖ ᾿Ιησοῦ. ἀμήν. ℵ A C D K P Ψ 88 104 181 326 330 436 451 614 1739[c] 1877 1962 1984 1985 2127 2492 2495 *Byz Lect* it[ar,d,dem,e,gig,x,z] vg syr[h,(pal)] cop[bo] goth arm eth Chrysostom Theodoret John-Damascus ‖ ᾿Ιησοῦ τῷ κυρίῳ ἡμῶν· ἀμήν. 629 ‖ ᾿Ιησοῦ γενεθήτω γενεθήτω. G[gr] ‖ ἀμήν *but omit* ἐν Χριστῷ ᾿Ιησοῦ 81 1241

ΠΡΟΣ ΚΟΡΙΝΘΙΟΥΣ Β

Salutation

1 Παῦλος ἀπόστολος Χριστοῦ Ἰησοῦ διὰ θελήματος θεοῦ, καὶ Τιμόθεος ὁ ἀδελφός, τῇ ἐκκλησίᾳ τοῦ θεοῦ τῇ οὔσῃ ἐν Κορίνθῳ, σὺν τοῖς ἁγίοις πᾶσιν τοῖς οὖσιν ἐν ὅλῃ τῇ Ἀχαΐᾳ· **2** χάρις ὑμῖν καὶ εἰρήνη ἀπὸ θεοῦ πατρὸς ἡμῶν καὶ κυρίου Ἰησοῦ Χριστοῦ.

Paul's Thanksgiving after Affliction

3 Εὐλογητὸς ὁ θεὸς καὶ πατὴρ τοῦ κυρίου ἡμῶν Ἰησοῦ Χριστοῦ, ὁ πατὴρ τῶν οἰκτιρμῶν καὶ θεὸς πάσης παρακλήσεως, **4** ὁ παρακαλῶν ἡμᾶς ἐπὶ πάσῃ τῇ θλίψει ἡμῶν, εἰς τὸ δύνασθαι ἡμᾶς παρακαλεῖν τοὺς ἐν πάσῃ θλίψει διὰ τῆς παρακλήσεως ἧς παρακαλούμεθα αὐτοὶ ὑπὸ τοῦ θεοῦ· **5** ὅτι καθὼς περισσεύει τὰ παθήματα τοῦ Χριστοῦ εἰς ἡμᾶς, οὕτως διὰ τοῦ Χριστοῦ περισσεύει καὶ ἡ παράκλησις ἡμῶν. **6** εἴτε δὲ θλιβόμεθα, ὑπὲρ τῆς ὑμῶν παρακλήσεως καὶ σωτηρίας· εἴτε παρακαλούμεθα, ὑπὲρ τῆς ὑμῶν παρακλήσεως τῆς ἐνεργουμένης ἐν ὑπομονῇ τῶν αὐτῶν παθημάτων ὧν καὶ ἡμεῖς πάσχομεν.[a] **7**[b] καὶ ἡ ἐλπὶς ἡμῶν βεβαία ὑπὲρ ὑμῶν,[a] [b]εἰδότες[1] ὅτι ὡς κοινωνοί ἐστε τῶν παθημάτων, οὕτως καὶ τῆς παρακλήσεως.

---

[1] **6-7** {B} παρακλήσεως καὶ σωτηρίας· εἴτε παρακαλούμεθα, ὑπὲρ τῆς ὑμῶν παρακλήσεως τῆς ἐνεργουμένης ἐν ὑπομονῇ τῶν αὐτῶν παθημάτων ὧν καὶ ἡμεῖς πάσχομεν. 7 καὶ ἡ ἐλπὶς ἡμῶν βεβαία ὑπὲρ ὑμῶν, εἰδότες (𝔭46 *omit* ὧν...παθημάτων) ℵ A C P Ψ 0121a 0243 (81 104 630 *omit* καὶ σωτηρίας...παρακλήσεως) 436 (629 *add* καὶ σωτηρίας *after second*

[a a] **6-7** a major, a minor: Bov (Nes) BF² RV ASV RSV NEB TT Luth Jer Seg ‖ a minor, a major: WH ‖ a minor, a minor: Zür ‖ different text: TR AV

[b b] **6-7** b number 7, b no number: TRᵉᵈ WH Bov Nes BF² AV RV ASV RSV NEB TT Zür Luth Jer Seg ‖ b no number, b number 7: TRᵉᵈ

---

1 Παῦλος...θεοῦ 1 Cor 1.1   **2** Ro 1.7; 1 Cor 1.3   **3** Εὐλογητὸς...Χριστοῦ Eph 1.3; 1 Pe 1.3 θεὸς πάσης παρακλήσεως Ro 15.5   **5** Ps 34.19; 94.19   **6** 2 Cor 4.15, 17

PAUL'S SECOND LETTER TO THE CORINTHIANS

1 From Paul, apostle of Christ Jesus by God's will, and from our brother Timothy —

To the church of God in Corinth, and to all God's people in all Greece:

[2] May God our Father and the Lord Jesus Christ give you grace and peace.

Paul Gives Thanks to God

[3] Let us give thanks to the God and Father of our Lord Jesus Christ, the merciful Father, the God from whom all help comes! [4] He helps us in all our troubles, so that we are able to help those who have all kinds of troubles, using the same help that we ourselves have received from God. [5] Just as we have a share in Christ's many sufferings, so also through Christ we share in his great help. [6] If we suffer, it is for your help and salvation; if we are helped, then you too are helped and given the strength to endure with patience the same sufferings that we also endure. [7] So our hope in you is never shaken; we know that just as you share in our sufferings, you also share in the help we receive.

identity of apostle w/ Church.
" of Christ & Church

621

⁸ For we want to remind you, brothers, of the trouble we had in the province of Asia. The burdens laid upon us were so great and so heavy, that we gave up all hope of living. ⁹ We felt that the sentence of death had been passed against us. But this happened so that we should rely, not upon ourselves, but only on God, who raises the dead. ¹⁰ From such terrible dangers of death he saved us, and will save us; and we have placed our hope in him that he will save us again, ¹¹ as you help us by means of

8 Οὐ γὰρ θέλομεν ὑμᾶς ἀγνοεῖν, ἀδελφοί, ὑπὲρ τῆς θλίψεως ἡμῶν τῆς γενομένης ἐν τῇ ᾿Ασίᾳ, ὅτι καθ᾿ ὑπερβολὴν ὑπὲρ δύναμιν ἐβαρήθημεν, ὥστε ἐξαπορηθῆναι ἡμᾶς καὶ τοῦ ζῆν· 9 ἀλλὰ αὐτοὶ ἐν ἑαυτοῖς τὸ ἀπόκριμα τοῦ θανάτου ἐσχήκαμεν, ἵνα μὴ πεποιθότες ὦμεν ἐφ᾿ ἑαυτοῖς ἀλλ᾿ ἐπὶ τῷ θεῷ τῷ ἐγείροντι τοὺς νεκρούς· 10 ὃς ἐκ τηλικούτων θανάτων² ἐρρύσατο ἡμᾶς καὶ ῥύσεται³, εἰς ὃν ἠλπίκαμεν καὶ ἔτι⁴ ῥύσεται, 11 συννυπουρ-

---

παρακλήσεως *and read* ὑπὲρ ἡμῶν) 1739 1877 1881 (1962 εἴτε δέ) (2127 *omit* ὦν...παθημάτων) it(dem),rl,(x),z vg(cl),ww syrᵖ copsa,bo (arm *add* καὶ σωτηρίας *after second* παρακλήσεως) eth Ambrosiaster Ephraem Jerome Antiochus ‖ παρακλήσεως τῆς ἐνεργουμένης ἐν ὑπομονῇ τῶν αὐτῶν παθημάτων ὧν καὶ ἡμεῖς πάσχομεν καὶ ἡ ἐλπὶς ὑμῶν βεβαία ὑπὲρ ὑμῶν εἴτε παρακαλούμεθα ὑπὲρ τῆς ὑμῶν παρακλήσεως καὶ σωτηρίας, εἰδότες Β (33 ἐλπὶς ἡμῶν...εἴτε οὖν...ἡμῶν παρακλήσεως) 1241 ‖ παρακλήσεως καὶ σωτηρίας, τῆς ἐνεργουμένης ἐν ὑπομονῇ τῶν αὐτῶν παθημάτων ὧν καὶ ἡμεῖς πάσχομεν καὶ ἡ ἐλπὶς ἡμῶν βεβαία ὑπὲρ ὑμῶν εἴτε παρακαλούμεθα ὑπὲρ τῆς ὑμῶν παρακλήσεως καὶ σωτηρίας, εἰδότες D (G ὡς *for* ὧν *and* βλιβαία *for* βεβαία) (K *omit* αὐτῶν) 0209 (88 τοῦ αὐτοῦ *for* τῶν αὐτῶν *and read* ὑπὲρ ἡμῶν) (181 ἐλπὶς ὑμῶν) 326 (330 451 ἐν αὐτῷ *for* τῶν αὐτῶν *and read* ὑπὲρ ἡμῶν *and* ὑπὲρ τῆς ἡμῶν) (614 ὑπὲρ τῆς ἡμῶν) 1984 (1985 τῇ ὑπομονῇ...καὶ ὑμεῖς) 2492 2495 *Byz Lect* itar,d,e,f,g (syrʰ) goth Chrysostom Theodoret John-Damascus

² 10 {D} τηλικούτων θανάτων 𝔭⁴⁶ 81 630 1739ᶜ itd,e syrᵖ,ʰ goth Origengr,lat Ambrosiaster Ephraem (Chrysostom) Jerome Theodoret ‖ τηλικούτου θανάτου ℵ A B C Dgr Ggr K P Ψ 0121a 0209vid 0243 33 88 104 181 326 330 436 451 614 1241 1739* 1877 1881 1962 1984 1985 2127 2492 2495 *Byz Lect* copsa,bo arm Clement ‖ τηλικούτου κινδύνου 629 ‖ *tantis periculis* itar,c,dem,f,x,z vg ‖ *tanta vel periculo mortis* itg

³ 10 {C} καὶ ῥύσεται 𝔭⁴⁶ ℵ B C P 0209vid 33 81 (88) (1962) 2127 itg vgww copsa,bo goth? arm (Athanasius) Euthalius John-Damascus ‖ καὶ ῥύεται Dᶜ Ggr K 0121a 0243 104 181 326 330 436 451 614 629 630 1241 1739 1877 1881 1984 1985 2492 2495 *Byz Lect* ite,[dem],f,(x),z vgcl syrʰ goth? Origengr,lat Ambrosiaster Chrysostom Jerome Theodoret Ps-Oecumenius Theophylact ‖ *omit* A D* Ψ itar,d,e syrᵖ ethᵖᵖ Chrysostom Pelagius

⁴ 10 {C} καὶ ἔτι 𝔭⁴⁶ B Dgr* 0121a 0243 1739 1881 (Athanasius) ‖ ὅτι syrᵖ goth eth ‖ καὶ ὅτι G itg Ambrosiaster Chrysostom Pelagius Jerome ‖ ὅτι καὶ Dᵇ 104 630 2495 itar,d,e syrʰ ‖ ὅτι ἔτι arm ‖ ὅτι καὶ ἔτι ℵ A

---

8 τῆς θλίψεως...᾿Ασίᾳ Ac 19.23; 1 Cor 15.32   10 ῥύσεται...ῥύσεται 2 Tm 4.18

γούντων καὶ ὑμῶν ὑπὲρ ἡμῶν τῇ δεήσει, ἵνα ἐκ πολλῶν προσώπων τὸ εἰς ἡμᾶς χάρισμα διὰ πολλῶν εὐχαριστηθῇ ὑπὲρ ἡμῶν[5].

The Postponement of Paul's Visit

12 Ἡ γὰρ καύχησις ἡμῶν αὕτη ἐστίν, τὸ μαρτύριον τῆς συνειδήσεως ἡμῶν,[c] ὅτι ἐν ἁπλότητι[6] καὶ εἰλικρινείᾳ τοῦ θεοῦ, [καὶ] οὐκ ἐν σοφίᾳ σαρκικῇ ἀλλ' ἐν χάριτι θεοῦ, ἀνεστράφημεν ἐν τῷ κόσμῳ, περισσοτέρως δὲ πρὸς ὑμᾶς. 13 οὐ γὰρ ἄλλα γράφομεν ὑμῖν ἀλλ' ἢ ἃ ἀναγινώσκετε ἢ καὶ ἐπιγινώσκετε, ἐλπίζω δὲ ὅτι ἕως τέλους ἐπιγνώσεσθε, 14 καθὼς καὶ ἐπέγνωτε ἡμᾶς ἀπὸ μέρους, ὅτι καύχημα ὑμῶν ἐσμεν καθάπερ καὶ ὑμεῖς ἡμῶν ἐν τῇ ἡμέρᾳ τοῦ κυρίου[7] Ἰησοῦ.

15 Καὶ ταύτῃ τῇ πεποιθήσει ἐβουλόμην πρότερον πρὸς ὑμᾶς ἐλθεῖν, ἵνα δευτέραν χάριν[8] σχῆτε, 16 καὶ δι' ὑμῶν

C D[c] K P Ψ 33 81 181 326 330 436 451 614 629 1241 1877 1984 1985 2127 2492 *Byz Lect* it[dem,f,x,z] vg cop[sa,bo]

[5] **11** {C} ἡμῶν p[46c] ℵ A C D* G Ψ 0121a 0243 33 81 104 181 326 330 436 451 1739 1877 1881 1962 1984 1985 2127 2492 2495 *Byz*[pt] it[ar,d,dem,e,f,g,rl,x,z] vg syr[p,h] cop[sa,bo] goth arm Ambrosiaster Chrysostom Euthalius Theodoret // ὑμῶν p[46*] B D[c] K P 88 614 629 630 1241 *Byz*[pt] *Lect* Chrysostom John-Damascus Photius[acc. to Ps-Oecumenius] Ps-Oecumenius

[6] **12** {D} ἁπλότητι ℵ[c] D G 104 181 326 330 436 451 614 629 1241 1877 1984 1985 2495 *Byz Lect* it[ar,d,dem vid,e,f,g,x,z] vg syr[p,h] goth Ambrosiaster Chrysostom Theodoret // ἁγιότητι p[46] ℵ* A B C K P Ψ 0121a 0243 33 81 630 1739 1881 1962 2127 2492 *l*[1364] it[rl] cop[sa,bo] arm Clement Origen Euthalius John-Damascus // πραότητι 88 // σπλάγχνοις eth

[7] **14** {C} τοῦ κυρίου p[46vid] A C D K Ψ 88 181 614 1241 1984 1985 2495 *Byz Lect* it[d,e] syr[h] goth Ps-Oecumenius // τοῦ κυρίου ἡμῶν ℵ B G P 0121a 0243 33 81 104 326 330 436 451 629 630 1739 1877 1881 1962 2127 2492 it[ar,dem, f,g,rl,x,z] vg syr[p,h with *] cop[sa,bo] arm eth Ambrosiaster Chrysostom Euthalius Theodoret Antiochus John-Damascus Theophylact

[8] **15** {C} χάριν ℵ* A C D G K Ψ 0243 33 181 326 330 451 629 630 1241

[c] **12** *c* minor: WH Bov Nes BF[2] AV RV ASV Seg // *c* none: TR RSV NEB TT (Zür) (Luth) Jer

12 τὸ μαρτύριον...ἡμῶν He 13.18   ἐν ἁπλότητι...θεοῦ 2 Cor 2.17   οὐκ...σαρκικῇ 1 Cor 1.17   **14** καύχημα ὑμῶν ἐσμεν 2 Cor 5.12   ἐν...Ἰησοῦ Php 2.16   **16** Ac 19.21; 1 Cor 16.5, 6

---

your prayers for us. So it will be that the many prayers for us will be answered, and God will bless us; and many will raise their voices to him in thanksgiving for us.

The Change in Paul's Plans

[12] This is the thing we are proud of: our conscience assures us that our lives in this world, and especially our relations with you, have been ruled by God-given frankness[1] and sincerity, by the power of God's grace, and not by human wisdom. [13] For we write to you only what you can read and understand. And I hope you will come to understand completely [14] what you now understand only in part, that in the Day of the Lord Jesus you can be as proud of us as we shall be of you.

[15] I was so sure of all this that I made plans at first to visit you in order that you might be blessed twice. [16] For I planned to visit you on my way to

---

[1] **12** frankness: *some mss. read* holiness

Macedonia and again on my way back, to get help from you for my trip to Judea. ¹⁷ In planning this did I appear fickle? When I make my plans, do I make them from selfish motives, ready to say "Yes, yes" and "No, no" at the same time? ¹⁸ As God is true, my promise to you was not a "Yes" and a "No." ¹⁹ For Jesus Christ, the Son of God, who was preached among you by Silas, Timothy, and myself, is not one who is "Yes" and "No." On the contrary, he is God's "Yes"; ²⁰ for it is he who is the "Yes" to all of God's promises. This is the reason that through Jesus Christ our "Amen" is said, to the glory of God. ²¹ For it is God himself who makes us sure, with you, of our life in Christ; it is God himself who has set us apart, ²² who placed his mark of ownership upon us, and who gave the Holy Spirit in our hearts as the guarantee of all that he has for us.

²³ I call upon God as my witness — he knows my heart! It was in order to spare you that I decided not to go to Corinth. ²⁴ We are not trying to dictate to you what you must believe, for you stand firm in the faith. Instead, we are working with you for your own happiness.

2 So I made up my mind about this: I would not come to you again to make you sad. ² For if I were to make you sad, who would be left to cheer me up? Only the very persons I had saddened! ³ That is why I wrote that letter to you — I did not want to come to you and be made sad by the very people who should make me glad. For I am convinced that when I am happy, then you too are happy. ⁴ I wrote you with a greatly

διελθεῖν εἰς Μακεδονίαν, καὶ πάλιν ἀπὸ Μακεδονίας ἐλθεῖν πρὸς ὑμᾶς καὶ ὑφ' ὑμῶν προπεμφθῆναι εἰς τὴν Ἰουδαίαν. **17** τοῦτο οὖν βουλόμενος μήτι ἄρα τῇ ἐλαφρίᾳ ἐχρησάμην; ἢ ἃ βουλεύομαι κατὰ σάρκα βουλεύομαι, ἵνα ᾖ παρ' ἐμοὶ τὸ Ναὶ ναὶ καὶ τὸ Οὒ οὔ; **18** πιστὸς δὲ ὁ θεὸς ὅτι ὁ λόγος ἡμῶν ὁ πρὸς ὑμᾶς οὐκ ἔστιν Ναὶ καὶ Οὔ. **19** ὁ τοῦ θεοῦ γὰρ υἱὸς Ἰησοῦς Χριστὸς ὁ ἐν ὑμῖν δι' ἡμῶν κηρυχθείς, δι' ἐμοῦ καὶ Σιλουανοῦ καὶ Τιμοθέου, οὐκ ἐγένετο Ναὶ καὶ Οὔ, ἀλλὰ Ναὶ ἐν αὐτῷ γέγονεν. **20** ὅσαι γὰρ ἐπαγγελίαι θεοῦ, ἐν αὐτῷ τὸ Ναί· διὸ καὶ δι' αὐτοῦ τὸ Ἀμὴν τῷ θεῷ πρὸς δόξαν δι' ἡμῶν. **21** ὁ δὲ βεβαιῶν ἡμᾶς σὺν ὑμῖν εἰς Χριστὸν καὶ χρίσας ἡμᾶς θεός, **22** ὁ καὶ σφραγισάμενος ἡμᾶς καὶ δοὺς τὸν ἀρραβῶνα τοῦ πνεύματος ἐν ταῖς καρδίαις ἡμῶν.

23 Ἐγὼ δὲ μάρτυρα τὸν θεὸν ἐπικαλοῦμαι ἐπὶ τὴν ἐμὴν ψυχήν, ὅτι φειδόμενος ὑμῶν οὐκέτι ἦλθον εἰς Κόρινθον. **24** οὐχ ὅτι κυριεύομεν ὑμῶν τῆς πίστεως, ἀλλὰ συνεργοί ἐσμεν τῆς χαρᾶς ὑμῶν, τῇ γὰρ πίστει ἑστήκατε. **2** ἔκρινα γὰρ¹ ἐμαυτῷ τοῦτο, τὸ μὴ πάλιν ἐν λύπῃ πρὸς ὑμᾶς ἐλθεῖν· **2** εἰ γὰρ ἐγὼ λυπῶ ὑμᾶς, καὶ τίς ὁ εὐφραίνων με εἰ μὴ ὁ λυπούμενος ἐξ ἐμοῦ; **3** καὶ ἔγραψα τοῦτο αὐτὸ ἵνα μὴ ἐλθὼν λύπην σχῶ ἀφ' ὧν ἔδει με χαίρειν, πεποιθὼς ἐπὶ πάντας ὑμᾶς ὅτι ἡ ἐμὴ χαρὰ πάντων ὑμῶν ἐστιν. **4** ἐκ γὰρ πολλῆς θλίψεως καὶ συνοχῆς καρδίας ἔγραψα ὑμῖν διὰ πολλῶν δακρύων,

---

1739 1881 1962 1984 1985 2127 2492 2495 *Byz Lect* it^(ar,d,dem,e,f,g,rl,x,z) vg syr^(p,h) cop^(sa) arm ‖ χαράν ℵ^c B P 81 88 104 436 614 cop^(bo) Theodoret Antiochus

¹ **1** {C} γάρ 𝔭^46 B 0223 0243 33 630 1739 1881 1962 2495 it^(rl) syr^(h,pal) cop^(sams,bo) goth? ‖ δέ ℵ A C D^(b,c) G K P Ψ 081 81 88 104 181 326 330 436 451 614 629 1241 1877 1984 1985 2127 2492 *Byz Lect* it^(arvid,d,dem,e,f,g,x,z) vg syr^p goth? arm ‖ τε D^(gr)* (eth) ‖ *omit* cop^(sa,bomss)

---

17 ἅ...βουλεύομαι 2 Cor 5.16   **19** δι' ἐμοῦ...Τιμοθέου Ac 18.5   **20** δι' αὐτοῦ...ἡμῶν Re 3.14   **21** χρίσας ἡμᾶς θεός 1 Jn 2.27   **22** ὁ καὶ σφραγισάμενος ἡμᾶς Eph 1.13; 4.30 δοὺς...ἡμῶν Ro 8.16; 2 Cor 5.5; Eph 1.14   **23** Ἐγὼ...ψυχήν Ro 1.9; 2 Cor 11.31; Php 1.8; 1 Th 2.5, 10   **24** οὐχ...πίστεως 1 Pe 5.3   **2 1** τὸ μὴ...ἐλθεῖν 1 Cor 4.21; 2 Cor 12.21   **4** ἐκ...δακρύων Ac 20.31

Yes ¿ No

Yes is: Jesus Christ is God's Yes
absolute freedom of Χρ because of God's yes in Jesus

οὐχ ἵνα λυπηθῆτε ἀλλὰ τὴν ἀγάπην ἵνα γνῶτε ἣν ἔχω περισσοτέρως εἰς ὑμᾶς.

Forgiveness for the Offender

5 Εἰ δέ τις λελύπηκεν, οὐκ ἐμὲ λελύπηκεν, ἀλλὰ ἀπὸ μέρους,[a] ἵνα μὴ ἐπιβαρῶ,[a] πάντας ὑμᾶς. **6** ἱκανὸν τῷ τοιούτῳ ἡ ἐπιτιμία αὕτη ἡ ὑπὸ τῶν πλειόνων, **7** ὥστε τοὐναντίον μᾶλλον ὑμᾶς[2] χαρίσασθαι καὶ παρακαλέσαι, μή πως τῇ περισσοτέρᾳ λύπῃ καταποθῇ ὁ τοιοῦτος. **8** διὸ παρακαλῶ ὑμᾶς κυρῶσαι εἰς αὐτὸν ἀγάπην· **9** εἰς τοῦτο γὰρ καὶ ἔγραψα ἵνα γνῶ τὴν δοκιμὴν ὑμῶν, εἰ[3] εἰς πάντα ὑπήκοοί ἐστε. **10** ᾧ δέ τι χαρίζεσθε, κἀγώ· καὶ γὰρ ἐγὼ ὃ κεχάρισμαι, εἴ τι κεχάρισμαι, δι᾽ ὑμᾶς ἐν προσώπῳ Χριστοῦ, **11**[b] ἵνα μὴ πλεονεκτηθῶμεν ὑπὸ τοῦ Σατανᾶ, [b]οὐ γὰρ αὐτοῦ τὰ νοήματα ἀγνοοῦμεν.

Paul's Anxiety and Relief

12 Ἐλθὼν δὲ εἰς τὴν Τρῳάδα εἰς τὸ εὐαγγέλιον τοῦ Χριστοῦ, καὶ θύρας μοι ἀνεῳγμένης ἐν κυρίῳ, **13**[c] οὐκ

---

troubled and distressed heart, and with many tears, not to make you sad, but to make you realize how much I love you all.

Forgiveness for the Offender

⁵ Now, if anyone has made somebody sad, he has not done it to me but to you; or to some of you, at least, since I do not want to be too hard on you. ⁶ It is enough for this person that he has been punished in this way by most of you. ⁷ Now, however, you should forgive him and encourage him, to keep him from becoming so sad as to give up completely. ⁸ Let him know, then, I beg you, that you really do love him. ⁹ For this is the reason I wrote you that letter: I wanted to find out how well you had stood the test, and whether you are always ready to obey my instructions. ¹⁰ When you forgive someone for what he has done, I forgive him too. For when I forgive — if, indeed, I have forgiven any wrong — I do it because of you, in Christ's presence, ¹¹ in order to keep Satan from getting the upper hand over us; for we know what his plans are.

Paul's Anxiety in Troas

¹² When I arrived in Troas to preach the Good News about Christ, I found that the Lord had opened the way for the work there. ¹³ But I was deeply

---

2 7 {C} μᾶλλον ὑμᾶς 𝔭⁴⁶ ℵ C K P Ψ 081 0243 81 88 104 181 326 330 436 451 614 629 630 1241 1739 1877 1962 1984 1985 2127 2492 2495 *Byz Lect* it^ar,dem, f,m,rl,x,z vg syr^h,(pal) cop^sa,bo arm Tertullian Ambrosiaster Chrysostom Augustine Euthalius Theodoret John-Damascus ∥ ὑμᾶς μᾶλλον D G 33 it^d,e,g goth Theodoret ∥ ὑμᾶς A B syr^p eth Jerome Augustine ∥ μᾶλλον 1881

3 9 {B} εἰ ℵ C D G K P Ψ 081 0243 81 88 104 181 326 330 451 614 629 630 1241 1739 1877 1881 1962 1984 1985 2127 2492 *Byz Lect* it^ar,d,dem,e,f,g,m,rl,x,z vg syr^p,h,pal cop^bo goth arm ∥ ᾖ A B 33 (Tertullian) ∥ ὡς 460 1836 cop^sa? ∥ *omit* 𝔭⁴⁶ 436 2495

---

a a **5** a minor, a minor: Bov Nes BF² NEB (Seg) ∥ a minor, a none: TR AV ∥ a none, a none: WH ∥ a dash, a dash: RSV Zür Luth ∥ a parens, a parens: RV ASV TT Jer

b b **10–11** b number 11, b no number: TR^ed WH Bov Nes BF² AV RV ASV RSV NEB TT Zür •Luth Jer Seg ∥ b no number, b number 11: TR^ed

c c **12–13** c number 13, c no number: TR^ed WH Bov Nes BF² AV RV ASV RSV NEB TT Zür Luth Jer Seg ∥ c no number, c number 13: TR^ed

---

5 1 Cor 5.1   **9** εἰ…ὑπήκοοί ἐστε 2 Cor 7.15; 10.6   **11** ἵνα…Σατανᾶ Lk 22.31   **12** θύρας …κυρίῳ Ac 14.27; 1 Cor 16.9; Col 4.3; Re 3.8

worried because I could not find our brother Titus. So I said good-bye to the people there, and went on to Macedonia.

Victory through Christ

[14] But thanks be to God! For in union with Christ we are always led by God as prisoners in Christ's victory procession. Like a sweet smell that spreads everywhere, God uses us to make Christ known to all men. [15] For we are like the sweet smell of the incense that Christ burns to God which goes out to those who are being saved and to those who are being lost. [16] For those who are being lost, it is a deadly stench that kills; for those who are being saved, it is a fragrance that brings life. Who, then, is capable for such a task? [17] We are not like so many others, who handle God's message as if it were cheap merchandise; but because God has sent us, we speak with sincerity in his presence, as servants of Christ.

Servants of the New Covenant

3 Does this sound as if we were again boasting about ourselves? Could it be that, like some other people, we need letters of recommendation to you or from you? [2] You yourselves are the letter we have, written on our hearts, for everyone to know and read. [3] It is clear that Christ himself wrote this letter and sent it by us. It is written not with ink on stone tablets, but on human hearts, with the Spirit of the living God.

ἔσχηκα ἄνεσιν τῷ πνεύματί μου τῷ μὴ εὑρεῖν με Τίτον τὸν ἀδελφόν μου, °ἀλλὰ ἀποταξάμενος αὐτοῖς ἐξῆλθον εἰς Μακεδονίαν.

14 Τῷ δὲ θεῷ χάρις τῷ πάντοτε θριαμβεύοντι ἡμᾶς ἐν τῷ Χριστῷ καὶ τὴν ὀσμὴν τῆς γνώσεως αὐτοῦ φανεροῦντι δι᾽ ἡμῶν ἐν παντὶ τόπῳ· **15** ὅτι Χριστοῦ εὐωδία ἐσμὲν τῷ θεῷ ἐν τοῖς σῳζομένοις καὶ ἐν τοῖς ἀπολλυμένοις, **16** οἷς μὲν ὀσμὴ ἐκ θανάτου εἰς θάνατον, οἷς δὲ ὀσμὴ ἐκ ζωῆς εἰς ζωήν. καὶ πρὸς ταῦτα τίς ἱκανός; **17** οὐ γάρ ἐσμεν ὡς οἱ πολλοί[4] καπηλεύοντες τὸν λόγον τοῦ θεοῦ, ἀλλ᾽ ὡς ἐξ εἰλικρινείας, ἀλλ᾽ ὡς ἐκ θεοῦ κατέναντι θεοῦ ἐν Χριστῷ λαλοῦμεν.

Ministers of the New Covenant

3 Ἀρχόμεθα πάλιν ἑαυτοὺς συνιστάνειν; ἢ μὴ χρῄζομεν ὥς τινες συστατικῶν ἐπιστολῶν πρὸς ὑμᾶς ἢ ἐξ ὑμῶν; **2** ἡ ἐπιστολὴ ἡμῶν ὑμεῖς ἐστε, ἐγγεγραμμένη ἐν ταῖς καρδίαις ἡμῶν[1], γινωσκομένη καὶ ἀναγινωσκομένη ὑπὸ πάντων ἀνθρώπων· **3** φανερούμενοι ὅτι ἐστὲ ἐπιστολὴ Χριστοῦ διακονηθεῖσα ὑφ᾽ ἡμῶν, ἐγγεγραμμένη οὐ μέλανι ἀλλὰ πνεύματι θεοῦ ζῶντος, οὐκ ἐν πλαξὶν λιθίναις ἀλλ᾽ ἐν πλαξὶν καρδίαις σαρκίναις.

---

[4] **17** {C} πολλοί ℵ A B C K P Ψ 0243 33 81 88 104 330 436 451 629 1241 1739 1881 1962 1984 1985 2127 2492 *Byz* it^{ar,d,dem,e,f,x,z} vg cop^{sa,bo} (goth) eth Irenaeus^{gr,lat} Ambrosiaster Basil Didymus Euthalius John-Damascus ∥ λοιποί p⁴⁶ D^{gr} G^{gr} 181 326 614 630 1877 2495 *Lect* syr^{p,h} arm Marcion Ephraem Chrysostom Theodoret ∥ *ceteri vel plurimi* it^g

[1] **2** {C} ἡμῶν p⁴⁶ A B C D G K P Ψ 0243 81 104 181 326 330 451 614 629 630 1241 1739 1877 1962 1984 1985 2127 2492 2495^{vid} *Byz Lect* it^{ar,d,dem,e,f,g,x,z} vg syr^{p,h} cop^{sa,bo} goth arm ∥ ὑμῶν ℵ 33 88 436 1881 eth^{ro}

---

13 ἀποταξάμενος...Μακεδονίαν Ac 20.1   **15** τοῖς σῳζομένοις...ἀπολλυμένοις 1 Cor 1.18   **16** οἷς μὲν...ζωήν Lk 2.34   πρὸς...ἱκανός 2 Cor 3.5–6   **17** ἐξ...λαλοῦμεν 2 Cor 1.12; 1 Pe 4.11

3 1 Ἀρχόμεθα...συνιστάνειν 2 Cor 5.12   συστατικῶν...ὑμῶν Ac 18.27; Ro 16.1   **2** 1 Cor 9.2   **3** πλαξὶν λιθίναις Ex 24.12; 31.18; 34.1; Dt 9.10, 11   πλαξὶν καρδίαις σαρκίναις Pr 3.3; 7.3; Jr 31.33; Eze 11.19; 36.26

4 Πεποίθησιν δὲ τοιαύτην ἔχομεν διὰ τοῦ Χριστοῦ πρὸς τὸν θεόν.ᵃ 5 οὐχ ὅτι ἀφ᾽ ἑαυτῶν ἱκανοί ἐσμενᵇ λογίσασθαί τι ὡς ἐξ ἑαυτῶν, ἀλλ᾽ ἡ ἱκανότης ἡμῶν ἐκ τοῦ θεοῦ, 6 ὃς καὶ ἱκάνωσεν ἡμᾶς διακόνους καινῆς διαθήκης, οὐ γράμματος ἀλλὰ πνεύματος· τὸ γὰρ γράμμα ἀποκτέννει, τὸ δὲ πνεῦμα ζῳοποιεῖ.

7 Εἰ δὲ ἡ διακονία τοῦ θανάτου ἐν γράμμασιν ἐντετυπωμένη λίθοις ἐγενήθη ἐν δόξῃ, ὥστε μὴ δύνασθαι ἀτενίσαι τοὺς υἱοὺς Ἰσραὴλ εἰς τὸ πρόσωπον Μωϋσέως διὰ τὴν δόξαν τοῦ προσώπου αὐτοῦ τὴν καταργουμένην, 8 πῶς οὐχὶ μᾶλλον ἡ διακονία τοῦ πνεύματος ἔσται ἐν δόξῃ; 9 εἰ γὰρ ἡ διακονία² τῆς κατακρίσεως δόξα, πολλῷ μᾶλλον περισσεύει ἡ διακονία τῆς δικαιοσύνης δόξῃ. 10 καὶ γὰρ οὐ δεδόξασται τὸ δεδοξασμένον ἐν τούτῳ τῷ μέρει εἵνεκεν τῆς ὑπερβαλλούσης δόξης· 11 εἰ γὰρ τὸ καταργούμενον διὰ δόξης, πολλῷ μᾶλλον τὸ μένον ἐν δόξῃ.

12 Ἔχοντες οὖν τοιαύτην ἐλπίδα πολλῇ παρρησίᾳ χρώμεθα, 13 καὶ οὐ καθάπερ Μωϋσῆς ἐτίθει κάλυμμα ἐπὶ τὸ πρόσωπον αὐτοῦ, πρὸς τὸ μὴ ἀτενίσαι τοὺς υἱοὺς Ἰσραὴλ εἰς τὸ τέλος τοῦ καταργουμένου. 14 ἀλλὰ ἐπωρώθη τὰ νοήματα αὐτῶν. ἄχρι γὰρ τῆς σήμερον ἡμέρας τὸ αὐτὸ κάλυμμα ἐπὶ τῇ ἀναγνώσει τῆς παλαιᾶς διαθήκης μένειᶜ μὴ ἀνακαλυπτόμενον,ᶜ ὅτι ἐν Χριστῷ κα-

---

² 9 {C} ἡ διακονία B Dᵇ·ᶜ K P 88 181 (330 ἡ γὰρ διακονία) 614 629ᶜ 1241 1877 1881 1962 1984 2127 2492ᶜ Byz Lect itᵃʳ·ᶜ·ᵈᵉᵐ·ᶠ·ˣ·ᶻ vg copᵇᵒ gothᵐˢ arm Ephraem Macarius Chrysostom Augustine Theodoret Ps-Jerome Antiochus John-Damascus ‖ τῇ διακονίᾳ p⁴⁶ ℵ A C D* G Ψ 0243 33 104 326 436 630 1730 itᵈ·ᵉ·ᵍ syrᵖ·ʰ copˢᵃ gothᵐˢ eth Origenᵍʳ·ˡᵃᵗ Ambrosiaster Cyril Cassiodorus ‖ διακονια 81 451 629* 1985 2492* 2495 Euthalius

ᵃ 4 a major: WH Bov Nes BF² RSV NEB TT Luth Jer Seg ‖ a minor: TR WHᵐᵍ AV RV ASV Zür
ᵇ 5 b none: TR WH Bov Nes BF² AV RSV Jer Seg ‖ b minor: WHᵐᵍ RV ASV NEB TT Zür? Luth?
ᶜ ᶜ 14 c none, c minor: WH RSV NEB Luth (Jer) (Seg) ‖ c none, c minor and δ τι: AV RV ASVᵐᵍ (TT) (Zür) ‖ c minor, c none: Nes BF² RVᵐᵍ ASV Jerᵐᵍ Segᵐᵍ ‖ c minor, c minor: TR Bov

5 2 Cor 2.16   6 καινῆς διαθήκης Ex 24.8; Jr 31.31; 32.40; 1 Cor 11.25; He 8.8–13   τὸ γὰρ...ζῳοποιεῖ Jn 6.63; Ro 7.6   7 μὴ...καταργουμένην Ex 34.29–30   9 ἡ διακονία τῆς κατακρίσεως Dt 27.26   ἡ διακονία τῆς δικαιοσύνης Ro 1.17; 3.21   10 τὸ δεδοξασμένον Ex 34.29–30   13 Μωϋσῆς...αὐτοῦ Ex 34.33, 35   14 ἐπωρώθη...αὐτῶν Ro 11.25

---

⁴ We say this because we have confidence in God through Christ. ⁵ For there is nothing in us that allows us to claim that we are capable of doing this work. The capacity we have comes from God: ⁶ for it is he who made us capable of serving the new covenant, which consists not of a written law, but of the Spirit. The written law brings death, but the Spirit gives life.

⁷ The Law was carved in letters on stone tablets, and God's glory appeared when it was given. Even though it faded away, the brightness on Moses' face was so strong that the people of Israel could not keep their eyes fixed on him. If the Law, whose service was to bring death, came with such glory, ⁸ how much greater is the glory that belongs to the service of the Spirit! ⁹ The service by which men are condemned was glorious; how much more glorious is the service by which men are declared innocent! ¹⁰ We may say that, because of the far brighter glory now, the glory that was so bright in the past is gone. ¹¹ For if there was glory in that which lasted for a while, how much more glory is there in that which lasts for ever!

¹² Because we have this hope, we are very bold. ¹³ We are not like Moses, who had to put a veil over his face, so that the people of Israel might not see the brightness fade and disappear. ¹⁴ Their minds, indeed, were closed; and to this very day their minds are covered with the same veil, as they read the books of the old covenant. The veil is removed only when a man is joined to Christ.

[15] Even today, whenever they read the Law of Moses, the veil still covers their minds. [16] But it is removed, as the scripture says: "Moses' veil was removed when he turned[1] to the Lord." [17] Now, "the Lord" in this passage is the Spirit; and where the Spirit of the Lord is present, there is freedom. [18] All of us, then, reflect the glory of the Lord with uncovered faces; and that same glory, coming from the Lord who is the Spirit, transforms us into his very likeness, in an ever greater degree of glory.

Spiritual Treasure in Clay Pots

4 God, in his mercy, has given us this service, and so we do not become discouraged. [2] We put aside all secret and shameful deeds; we do not act with deceit, nor do we falsify the word of God. In the full light of truth, we live in God's sight and try to commend ourselves to everyone's good conscience. [3] For if the gospel we preach is hidden, it is hidden only to those who are being lost. [4] They do not believe because their minds have been kept in the dark by the evil god of this world. He keeps them from seeing the light shining on them, the light that comes from the Good News about the glory of Christ, who is the exact likeness of God. [5] For it is not ourselves that we preach: we preach Jesus Christ as Lord, and ourselves as your servants for Jesus' sake. [6] The God who said, "Out of darkness the light shall shine!" is the same God who made his light shine in our hearts, to bring us the light of the knowledge of God's glory, shining in the face of Christ.

---

[1] **16** Moses' veil was removed when he turned: *or* The veil is removed when a man turns

ταργεῖται· **15** ἀλλ' ἕως σήμερον ἡνίκα ἂν ἀναγινώσκηται Μωϋσῆς κάλυμμα ἐπὶ τὴν καρδίαν αὐτῶν κεῖται· **16 ἡνίκα δὲ ἐὰν ἐπιστρέψῃ πρὸς κύριον, περιαιρεῖται τὸ κάλυμμα.** **17** ὁ δὲ κύριος τὸ πνεῦμά ἐστιν· οὗ δὲ τὸ πνεῦμα κυρίου, ἐλευθερία. **18** ἡμεῖς δὲ πάντες ἀνακεκαλυμμένῳ προσώπῳ τὴν δόξαν κυρίου κατοπτριζόμενοι τὴν αὐτὴν εἰκόνα μεταμορφούμεθα ἀπὸ δόξης εἰς δόξαν, καθάπερ ἀπὸ κυρίου πνεύματος.

Treasure in Earthen Vessels

4 Διὰ τοῦτο, ἔχοντες τὴν διακονίαν ταύτην, καθὼς ἠλεήθημεν, οὐκ ἐγκακοῦμεν, **2** ἀλλὰ ἀπειπάμεθα τὰ κρυπτὰ τῆς αἰσχύνης, μὴ περιπατοῦντες ἐν πανουργίᾳ μηδὲ δολοῦντες τὸν λόγον τοῦ θεοῦ, ἀλλὰ τῇ φανερώσει τῆς ἀληθείας συνιστάνοντες ἑαυτοὺς πρὸς πᾶσαν συνείδησιν ἀνθρώπων ἐνώπιον τοῦ θεοῦ. **3** εἰ δὲ καὶ ἔστιν κεκαλυμμένον τὸ εὐαγγέλιον ἡμῶν, ἐν τοῖς ἀπολλυμένοις ἐστὶν κεκαλυμμένον, **4** ἐν οἷς ὁ θεὸς τοῦ αἰῶνος τούτου ἐτύφλωσεν τὰ νοήματα τῶν ἀπίστων εἰς τὸ μὴ αὐγάσαι τὸν φωτισμὸν τοῦ εὐαγγελίου τῆς δόξης τοῦ Χριστοῦ, ὅς ἐστιν εἰκὼν τοῦ θεοῦ. **5** οὐ γὰρ ἑαυτοὺς κηρύσσομεν ἀλλὰ Ἰησοῦν Χριστὸν κύριον, ἑαυτοὺς δὲ δούλους ὑμῶν διὰ Ἰησοῦν[1]. **6** ὅτι ὁ θεὸς ὁ εἰπών, Ἐκ σκότους φῶς λάμψει, ὃς ἔλαμψεν ἐν ταῖς καρδίαις ἡμῶν πρὸς φωτισμὸν τῆς γνώσεως τῆς δόξης τοῦ θεοῦ ἐν προσώπῳ Χριστοῦ.

---

[1] **5** {C} Ἰησοῦν A*vid? B Dgr Ggr H K P Ψ 0209 81 88 104 181 436 614 1881 1962 2127 2495 *Byz Lect* itar vid syrp, h, pal goth eth Ambrosiaster Cyril-Jerusalem Chrysostom Euthalius Theodoret John-Damascus // Ἰησοῦ 𝔭46 ℵ* Aevid? C 0243 33 1739 itd, dem, e, f, g, r1, x, z vg copsa, bo Marcion Augustine // Χριστόν 326 330 451 1241 1984 1985 2492 // Χριστοῦ ℵa itgig copboms // Ἰησοῦ Χριστοῦ 0186vid itt copboms // Ἰησοῦν Χριστόν 629 630 1877

16 Ex 34.34; Ro 11.23, 26   **17** οὖ...ἐλευθερία Jn 7.39; 8.32, 36; Ro 8.2; Ga 5.1, 13   **18** τὴν δόξαν κυρίου Ex 16.7; 24.17
4 1 ἔχοντες...ταύτην 2 Cor 3.6   **2** μὴ...θεοῦ 2 Cor 2.17; 1 Th 2.5   **3** 1 Cor 1.18   **4** ὁ θεὸς...τούτου Eph 2.2   ὅς...θεοῦ Col 1.15; He 1.3   **5** 2 Cor 1.24   **6** Ἐκ...λάμψει Gn 1.3; Is 9.2   ὅς...Χριστοῦ 2 Cor 3.18

7 Ἔχομεν δὲ τὸν θησαυρὸν τοῦτον ἐν ὀστρακίνοις σκεύεσιν, ἵνα ἡ ὑπερβολὴ τῆς δυνάμεως ᾖ τοῦ θεοῦ καὶ μὴ ἐξ ἡμῶν· 8 ἐν παντὶ θλιβόμενοι ἀλλ' οὐ στενοχωρούμενοι, ἀπορούμενοι ἀλλ' οὐκ ἐξαπορούμενοι, 9 διωκόμενοι ἀλλ' οὐκ ἐγκαταλειπόμενοι, καταβαλλόμενοι ἀλλ' οὐκ ἀπολλύμενοι, 10 πάντοτε τὴν νέκρωσιν τοῦ Ἰησοῦ ἐν τῷ σώματι περιφέροντες, ἵνα καὶ ἡ ζωὴ τοῦ Ἰησοῦ ἐν τῷ σώματι ἡμῶν φανερωθῇ. 11 ἀεὶ γὰρ ἡμεῖς οἱ ζῶντες εἰς θάνατον παραδιδόμεθα διὰ Ἰησοῦν, ἵνα καὶ ἡ ζωὴ τοῦ Ἰησοῦ φανερωθῇ ἐν τῇ θνητῇ σαρκὶ ἡμῶν. 12 ὥστε ὁ θάνατος ἐν ἡμῖν ἐνεργεῖται, ἡ δὲ ζωὴ ἐν ὑμῖν. 13 ἔχοντες δὲ τὸ αὐτὸ πνεῦμα τῆς πίστεως, κατὰ τὸ γεγραμμένον, **Ἐπίστευσα, διὸ ἐλάλησα**, καὶ ἡμεῖς πιστεύομεν, διὸ καὶ λαλοῦμεν, 14 εἰδότες ὅτι ὁ ἐγείρας τὸν κύριον Ἰησοῦν[2] καὶ ἡμᾶς σὺν Ἰησοῦ ἐγερεῖ καὶ παραστήσει σὺν ὑμῖν. 15 τὰ γὰρ πάντα δι' ὑμᾶς, ἵνα ἡ χάρις πλεονάσασα διὰ τῶν πλειόνων τὴν εὐχαριστίαν περισσεύσῃ εἰς τὴν δόξαν τοῦ θεοῦ.

Living by Faith

16 Διὸ οὐκ ἐγκακοῦμεν, ἀλλ' εἰ καὶ ὁ ἔξω ἡμῶν ἄνθρωπος διαφθείρεται, ἀλλ' ὁ ἔσω ἡμῶν ἀνακαινοῦται ἡμέρᾳ καὶ ἡμέρᾳ. 17 τὸ γὰρ παραυτίκα ἐλαφρὸν τῆς θλίψεως ἡμῶν καθ' ὑπερβολὴν εἰς ὑπερβολὴν αἰώνιον βάρος δόξης κατεργάζεται ἡμῖν, 18 μὴ σκοπούντων

---

[2] 14 {C} τὸν κύριον Ἰησοῦν ℵ C D G K P Ψ 048? 81 88 104 181 326 330 451 614 1241 1877 1881 (1962 *omit* τόν) 2127 2495 *Byz Lect* it[d,e,f,g] syr[h] cop[bo] goth eth Ambrosiaster Chrysostom Euthalius Theodoret John-Damascus ‖ τὸν Ἰησοῦν 𝔭[46] B (0243 33 630 1739 1984 1985 *omit* τόν) 629 it[c,dem,r1,x,z] vg cop[sa,boms] arm Tertullian Origen (Chrysostom *omit* τόν) ‖ τὸν κύριον ἡμῶν Ἰησοῦν (it[ar] *add* Χριστόν) syr[p,h with *] ‖ τὸν κύριον Ἰησοῦν Χριστόν 436 ‖ τὸν κύριον Ἰησοῦν ἐκ νεκρῶν 2492

---

7 Ἔχομεν...σκεύεσιν 2 Cor 5.1   8 ἐν παντὶ θλιβόμενοι 2 Cor 1.8; 7.5   11 ἀεὶ...Ἰησοῦν Ro 8.36; 1 Cor 15.31   13 Ἐπίστευσα, διὸ ἐλάλησα Ps 116.10   14 Ro 8.11; 1 Cor 6.14; 15.15, 20   15 τὰ γὰρ πάντα δι' ὑμᾶς 2 Cor 1.3–6   16 ὁ ἔσω...ἀνακαινοῦται Eph 3.16   17 Ro 8.17–18   18 μὴ σκοπούντων...τὰ μὴ βλεπόμενα Col 1.16; He 11.1, 3

---

7 Yet we who have this spiritual treasure are like common clay pots, to show that the supreme power belongs to God, not to us. 8 We are often troubled, but not crushed; sometimes in doubt, but never in despair; 9 there are many enemies, but we are never without a friend; and though badly hurt at times, we are not destroyed. 10 At all times we carry in our mortal bodies the death of Jesus, so that his life also may be seen in our bodies. 11 Throughout our lives we are always in danger of death for Jesus' sake, in order that his life may be seen in this mortal body of ours. 12 This means that death is at work in us; but life is at work in you.

13 The scripture says, "I spoke because I believed." In the same spirit of faith, we also speak because we believe. 14 For we know that God, who raised the Lord Jesus to life, will also raise us up with Jesus and bring us, together with you, into his presence. 15 All this is for your sake; and as God's grace reaches more and more people, they will offer more prayers of thanksgiving, to the glory of God.

Living by Faith

16 For this reason we never become discouraged. Even though our physical being is gradually decaying, yet our spiritual being is renewed day after day. 17 And this small and temporary trouble we suffer will bring us a tremendous and eternal glory, much greater than the trouble. 18 For we fix our attention, not on things that are seen, but on things that are unseen. What can be seen lasts

only for a time; but what cannot be seen lasts for ever.

5 For we know that when this tent we live in — our body here on earth — is torn down, God will have a house in heaven for us to live in, a home he himself made, which will last for ever. ² And now we sigh, so great is our desire to have our home which is in heaven put on over us; ³ for by being clothed with it we shall not be found without a body. ⁴ While we live in this earthly tent we groan with a feeling of oppression; it is not that we want to get rid of our earthly body, but that we want to have the heavenly one put on over us, so that what is mortal will be swallowed up by life. ⁵ God is the one who has prepared us for this change, and he gave us his Spirit as the guarantee of all that he has for us.

⁶ So we are always full of courage. We know that as long as we are at home in this body we are away from the Lord's home. ⁷ For our life is a matter of faith, not of sight. ⁸ We are full of courage, and would much prefer to leave our home in this body and be at home with the Lord. ⁹ More than anything else, however, we want to please him, whether in our home here or there. ¹⁰ For all of us must appear before Christ, to be judged by him, so that each one may receive what he deserves, according to what he has done, good or bad, in his bodily life.

Friendship with God through Christ

¹¹ We know what it means to fear the Lord, and so we try to persuade men. God knows us completely, and I hope that in your hearts you know me as well. ¹² We are not trying to recommend ourselves to you again; rather, we are

ἡμῶν τὰ βλεπόμενα ἀλλὰ τὰ μὴ βλεπόμενα· τὰ γὰρ βλεπόμενα πρόσκαιρα, τὰ δὲ μὴ βλεπόμενα αἰώνια.

5 Οἴδαμεν γὰρ ὅτι ἐὰν ἡ ἐπίγειος ἡμῶν οἰκία τοῦ σκήνους καταλυθῇ, οἰκοδομὴν ἐκ θεοῦ ἔχομεν οἰκίαν ἀχειροποίητον αἰώνιον ἐν τοῖς οὐρανοῖς. 2 καὶ γὰρ ἐν τούτῳ στενάζομεν, τὸ οἰκητήριον ἡμῶν τὸ ἐξ οὐρανοῦ ἐπενδύσασθαι ἐπιποθοῦντες, 3 εἴ γε καὶ ἐνδυσάμενοι οὐ γυμνοὶ εὑρεθησόμεθα. 4 καὶ γὰρ οἱ ὄντες ἐν τῷ σκήνει στενάζομεν^a βαρούμενοι,^a ἐφ' ᾧ οὐ θέλομεν ἐκδύσασθαι ἀλλ' ἐπενδύσασθαι, ἵνα καταποθῇ τὸ θνητὸν ὑπὸ τῆς ζωῆς. 5 ὁ δὲ κατεργασάμενος ἡμᾶς εἰς αὐτὸ τοῦτο θεός, ὁ δοὺς ἡμῖν τὸν ἀρραβῶνα τοῦ πνεύματος.

6 Θαρροῦντες οὖν πάντοτε καὶ εἰδότες ὅτι ἐνδημοῦντες ἐν τῷ σώματι ἐκδημοῦμεν ἀπὸ τοῦ κυρίου, 7 διὰ πίστεως γὰρ περιπατοῦμεν οὐ διὰ εἴδους — 8 θαρροῦμεν δὲ καὶ εὐδοκοῦμεν μᾶλλον ἐκδημῆσαι ἐκ τοῦ σώματος καὶ ἐνδημῆσαι πρὸς τὸν κύριον. 9 διὸ καὶ φιλοτιμούμεθα, εἴτε ἐνδημοῦντες εἴτε ἐκδημοῦντες, εὐάρεστοι αὐτῷ εἶναι. 10 τοὺς γὰρ πάντας ἡμᾶς φανερωθῆναι δεῖ ἔμπροσθεν τοῦ βήματος τοῦ Χριστοῦ, ἵνα κομίσηται ἕκαστος τὰ διὰ τοῦ σώματος πρὸς ἃ ἔπραξεν, εἴτε ἀγαθὸν εἴτε φαῦλον.

The Ministry of Reconciliation

11 Εἰδότες οὖν τὸν φόβον τοῦ κυρίου ἀνθρώπους πείθομεν, θεῷ δὲ πεφανερώμεθα· ἐλπίζω δὲ καὶ ἐν ταῖς συνειδήσεσιν ὑμῶν πεφανερῶσθαι. 12 οὐ πάλιν ἑαυτοὺς συνιστάνομεν ὑμῖν, ἀλλὰ ἀφορμὴν διδόντες ὑμῖν καυχήματος ὑπὲρ ἡμῶν, ἵνα ἔχητε πρὸς τοὺς ἐν προσώπῳ

---

^{a a} **4** a none, a minor: TR Bov Nes BF² (AV) (RV) (ASV) RSV Zür Luth Jer ∥ a minor, a none: NEB TT ∥ a minor, a minor: RV^{mg} ASV^{mg} Seg ∥ a none, a none: WH

1 ἡ ἐπίγειος...σκήνους Job 4.19; 2 Cor 4.7 **2** Ro 8.23 **4** ἐπενδύσασθαι...ζωῆς 1 Cor 15.53–54 **5** ὁ δοὺς...πνεύματος Ro 8.16, 23; 2 Cor 1.22; Eph 1.13 **6** ἐνδημοῦντες... κυρίου He 11.13–16 **7** 1 Cor 13.12 **8** εὐδοκοῦμεν...κύριον Php 1.23 **9** Col 1.10; 1 Th 4.1 **10** Ec 12.14; Ac 17.31; Ro 2.16; 14.10 **11** ἐλπίζω...πεφανερῶσθαι 2 Cor 4.2 **12** οὐ... συνιστάνομεν ὑμῖν 2 Cor 3.1 ἀφορμὴν...ἡμῶν 2 Cor 1.14

καυχωμένους καὶ μὴ ἐν καρδίᾳ. **13** εἴτε γὰρ ἐξέστημεν, θεῷ· εἴτε σωφρονοῦμεν, ὑμῖν. **14** ἡ γὰρ ἀγάπη τοῦ Χριστοῦ συνέχει ἡμᾶς, ᵇκρίναντας τοῦτο, ὅτι εἷς ὑπὲρ πάντων ἀπέθανεν· ἄρα οἱ πάντες ἀπέθανον· **15** ᵇ καὶ ὑπὲρ πάντων ἀπέθανεν ἵνα οἱ ζῶντες μηκέτι ἑαυτοῖς ζῶσιν ἀλλὰ τῷ ὑπὲρ αὐτῶν ἀποθανόντι καὶ ἐγερθέντι.

16 Ὥστε ἡμεῖς ἀπὸ τοῦ νῦν οὐδένα οἴδαμεν κατὰ σάρκα· εἰ καὶ ἐγνώκαμεν κατὰ σάρκα Χριστόν, ἀλλὰ νῦν οὐκέτι γινώσκομεν. **17** ὥστε εἴ τις ἐν Χριστῷ, καινὴ κτίσις· τὰ ἀρχαῖα παρῆλθεν, ἰδοὺ γέγονεν καινά¹· **18** τὰ δὲ πάντα ἐκ τοῦ θεοῦ τοῦ καταλλάξαντος ἡμᾶς ἑαυτῷ διὰ Χριστοῦ καὶ δόντος ἡμῖν τὴν διακονίαν τῆς καταλλαγῆς, **19** ὡς ὅτι θεὸς ἦν ἐν Χριστῷ κόσμον καταλλάσσων ἑαυτῷ, μὴ λογιζόμενος αὐτοῖς τὰ παραπτώματα αὐτῶν, καὶ θέμενος ἐν ἡμῖν τὸν λόγον τῆς καταλλαγῆς. **20** ὑπὲρ Χριστοῦ οὖν πρεσβεύομεν ὡς τοῦ θεοῦ παρακαλοῦντος δι᾽ ἡμῶν· δεόμεθα ὑπὲρ Χριστοῦ, καταλλάγητε τῷ θεῷ. **21** τὸν μὴ γνόντα ἁμαρτίαν ὑπὲρ ἡμῶν ἁμαρτίαν ἐποίησεν, ἵνα ἡμεῖς γενώμεθα δικαιοσύνη θεοῦ ἐν αὐτῷ.

---

¹ **17** {B} καινά 𝔓⁴⁶ ℵ B C D* G 048 0243 1739 1962 itᵈ·ᵉ·ᶠ·ᵍ·ʳˡ·ˣ·ᶻᵛⁱᵈ vgʷʷ syr⁽ᵖ⁾·ᵖᵃˡ copˢᵃ·ᵇᵒ arm ethʳᵒ Clement Origen Hilary Athanasius Ambrose Jerome Augustine Cyril de Promissionibus ∥ καινὰ τὰ πάντα Dᶜ K P Ψ 104 326 436 629 1984 Byzᵖᵗ Lect (𝑙⁸⁰⁹ τὰ δέ) syrʰ goth ethᵖᵖ Marcion Tertullian Origen Apostolic Constitutions Didymus Ps-Ignatius Chrysostom Augustine John-Damascus ∥ τὰ πάντα καινά 33 81 88 181 330 451 614 630 1241 1877 1881 1985 2127 2492 2495 Byzᵖᵗ itᵃʳ·⁽ᵈᵉᵐ⁾ vgᶜˡ Origenˡᵃᵗ Adamantius Methodius Ambrosiaster Athanasius Ephraem Priscillian Ambrose Jerome Augustine Cyril Proclus Euthalius Theodoret Cassiodorus ∥ πάντα τὰ καινά 𝑙¹³⁶⁵

ᵇ ᵇ **14–15** b no number, b number 15: TRᵉᵈ WH Bov Nes BF² AV RV ASV RSV NEB TT Zür Luth J er Seg ∥ b number 15, b no number: TRᵉᵈ

15 ὑπὲρ πάντων ἀπέθανεν 1 Tm 2.6   οἱ ζῶντες...ἐγερθέντι Ro 14.7–8   **17** εἴ...κτίσις Ro 8.1, 10; Ga 6.15   τὰ ἀρχαῖα...καινά Is 43.18; Re 21.5   **18** τοῦ θεοῦ...Χριστοῦ Ro 5.10   **19** θεὸς...ἑαυτῷ Ro 3.24–25; Col 1.19–20   **20** ὑπὲρ...πρεσβεύομεν Is 52.7; Eph 6.20   **21** τὸν μὴ γνόντα ἁμαρτίαν Jn 8.46; He 4.15; 1 Pe 2.22   ὑπὲρ...ἐποίησεν Ga 3.13   ἡμεῖς...αὐτῷ 1 Cor 1.30; Php 3.9

---

trying to give you a good reason to be proud of us, so that you will be able to answer those who boast about a man's appearance, and not about his character. **13** Are we really insane? It is for God's sake. Or are we sane? It is for your sake. **14** For we are ruled by Christ's love for us, now that we recognize that one man died for all men, which means that all men take part in his death. **15** He died for all men so that those who live should no longer live for themselves, but only for him who died and was raised to life for their sake.

16 No longer, then, do we judge anyone by human standards. Even if at one time we judged Christ according to human standards, we no longer do so. **17** When anyone is joined to Christ he is a new being: the old is gone, the new has come. **18** All this is done by God, who through Christ changed us from enemies into his friends, and gave us the task of making others his friends also. **19** Our message is that God was making friends of all men through Christ.¹ God did not keep an account of their sins against them, and he has given us the message of how he makes them his friends.

20 Here we are, then, speaking for Christ, as though God himself were appealing to you through us: on Christ's behalf, we beg you, let God change you from enemies into friends! **21** Christ was without sin, but God made him share our sin in order that we, in union with him, might share the righteousness of God.

---

¹ **19** God was making friends of all men through Christ: or God was in Christ making friends of all men

6 In our work together with God, then, we beg of you: you have received God's grace, and you must not let it be wasted. [2] Hear what God says:

"I heard you in the hour of my favor,
I helped you in the day of salvation."

Listen! This is the hour to receive God's favor, today is the day to be saved!

[3] We do not want anyone to find fault with our work, so we try not to put obstacles in anyone's way. [4] Instead, in everything we do we show that we are God's servants, by enduring troubles, hardships, and difficulties with great patience. [5] We have been beaten, jailed, and mobbed; we have been overworked and have gone without sleep or food. [6] By our purity, knowledge, patience, and kindness we have shown ourselves to be God's servants; by the Holy Spirit, by our true love, [7] by our message of truth, and by the power of God. We have righteousness as our weapon, both to attack and to defend ourselves. [8] We are honored and disgraced; we are insulted and praised. We are treated as liars, yet we speak the truth; [9] as unknown, yet we are known by all; as though we were dead, but, as you see, we live on. Although punished, we are not killed; [10] although saddened, we are always glad; we seem poor, but we make many people rich; we seem to have nothing, yet we really possess everything.

[11] Dear friends in Corinth! We have spoken frankly to you, we have opened wide our hearts. [12] We have not closed our hearts to you; it is you who have closed your hearts to us. [13] I speak now as though you were my children: show us the same feelings that we have for you. Open wide your hearts!

Warning against Pagan Influences

[14] Do not try to work together as equals with unbelievers, for it cannot be done. How can right and wrong be partners? How can light and darkness

6 Συνεργοῦντες δὲ καὶ παρακαλοῦμεν μὴ εἰς κενὸν τὴν χάριν τοῦ θεοῦ δέξασθαι ὑμᾶς — 2 λέγει γάρ,

**Καιρῷ δεκτῷ ἐπήκουσά σου
καὶ ἐν ἡμέρᾳ σωτηρίας ἐβοήθησά σοι·**

ἰδοὺ νῦν καιρὸς εὐπρόσδεκτος, ἰδοὺ νῦν ἡμέρα σωτηρίας — 3 μηδεμίαν ἐν μηδενὶ διδόντες προσκοπήν, ἵνα μὴ μωμηθῇ ἡ διακονία, 4 ἀλλ' ἐν παντὶ συνιστάνοντες ἑαυτοὺς ὡς θεοῦ διάκονοι,[a] ἐν ὑπομονῇ πολλῇ,[a] ἐν θλίψεσιν, ἐν ἀνάγκαις, ἐν στενοχωρίαις, 5 ἐν πληγαῖς, ἐν φυλακαῖς, ἐν ἀκαταστασίαις, ἐν κόποις, ἐν ἀγρυπνίαις, ἐν νηστείαις, 6 ἐν ἁγνότητι, ἐν γνώσει, ἐν μακροθυμίᾳ, ἐν χρηστότητι, ἐν πνεύματι ἁγίῳ, ἐν ἀγάπῃ ἀνυποκρίτῳ, 7 ἐν λόγῳ ἀληθείας, ἐν δυνάμει θεοῦ· διὰ τῶν ὅπλων τῆς δικαιοσύνης τῶν δεξιῶν καὶ ἀριστερῶν, 8 διὰ δόξης καὶ ἀτιμίας, διὰ δυσφημίας καὶ εὐφημίας· ὡς πλάνοι καὶ ἀληθεῖς, 9 ὡς ἀγνοούμενοι καὶ ἐπιγινωσκόμενοι, ὡς ἀποθνῄσκοντες καὶ ἰδοὺ ζῶμεν, ὡς παιδευόμενοι καὶ μὴ θανατούμενοι, 10 ὡς λυπούμενοι ἀεὶ δὲ χαίροντες, ὡς πτωχοὶ πολλοὺς δὲ πλουτίζοντες, ὡς μηδὲν ἔχοντες καὶ πάντα κατέχοντες.

11 Τὸ στόμα ἡμῶν ἀνέῳγεν πρὸς ὑμᾶς, Κορίνθιοι, ἡ καρδία ἡμῶν πεπλάτυνται· 12 οὐ στενοχωρεῖσθε ἐν ἡμῖν, στενοχωρεῖσθε δὲ ἐν τοῖς σπλάγχνοις ὑμῶν· 13 τὴν δὲ αὐτὴν ἀντιμισθίαν, ὡς τέκνοις λέγω, πλατύνθητε καὶ ὑμεῖς.

The Temple of the Living God

14 Μὴ γίνεσθε ἑτεροζυγοῦντες ἀπίστοις· τίς γὰρ μετοχὴ δικαιοσύνῃ καὶ ἀνομίᾳ;[b] ἢ τίς κοινωνία φωτὶ πρὸς

---

[a] [a] **4** a minor, a minor: TR Bov Nes BF² AV RV ASV ∥ a none, a none: Zür ∥ a major, a minor: WH RSV TT Luth ∥ a none, a major: NEB ∥ a major, a none: Jer (Seg)

[b] [b] **14** b question, b question: TR AV RV ASV RSV NEB TT Luth Jer Seg ∥ b minor, b question: WH Bov Nes BF² Zür

---

1 παρακαλοῦμεν...ὑμᾶς 2 Cor 5.20   **2** Καιρῷ...σοι Is 49.8   νῦν...σωτηρίας Lk 4.19–21   **4** συνιστάνοντες ἑαυτούς 2 Cor 4.2   **5** 2 Cor 11.23–27   **6** 1 Tm 4.12   **7** ἐν λόγῳ...θεοῦ 1 Cor 2.4   **9** ἀποθνῄσκοντες...ζῶμεν 2 Cor 4.10   παιδευόμενοι...θανατούμενοι Ps 118.18   **10** λυπούμενοι...χαίροντες 2 Cor 7.4; Php 2.17; Col 1.24; 1 Th 1.6   **13** ὡς τέκνοις λέγω 1 Cor 4.14   **14** Μὴ...ἀπίστοις Eph 5.7, 11

σκότος;[b] **15** τίς δὲ συμφώνησις Χριστοῦ πρὸς Βελιάρ,[c] ἢ τίς μερὶς πιστῷ μετὰ ἀπίστου;[c] **16** τίς δὲ συγκατάθεσις ναῷ θεοῦ μετὰ εἰδώλων; ἡμεῖς γὰρ ναὸς θεοῦ ἐσμεν[1] ζῶντος· καθὼς εἶπεν ὁ θεὸς ὅτι

> Ἐνοικήσω ἐν αὐτοῖς καὶ ἐμπεριπατήσω,
> καὶ ἔσομαι αὐτῶν θεός,
> καὶ αὐτοὶ ἔσονταί μου λαός.

17   διὸ ἐξέλθατε ἐκ μέσου αὐτῶν
> καὶ ἀφορίσθητε, λέγει κύριος,
> καὶ ἀκαθάρτου μὴ ἅπτεσθε·
> κἀγὼ εἰσδέξομαι ὑμᾶς,

18   καὶ ἔσομαι ὑμῖν εἰς πατέρα,
> καὶ ὑμεῖς ἔσεσθέ μοι εἰς υἱοὺς καὶ θυγατέρας,
> λέγει κύριος παντοκράτωρ.

7 ταύτας οὖν ἔχοντες τὰς ἐπαγγελίας, ἀγαπητοί, καθαρίσωμεν ἑαυτοὺς ἀπὸ παντὸς μολυσμοῦ σαρκὸς καὶ πνεύματος, ἐπιτελοῦντες ἁγιωσύνην ἐν φόβῳ θεοῦ.

Paul's Joy at the Church's Repentance

2 Χωρήσατε ἡμᾶς· οὐδένα ἠδικήσαμεν, οὐδένα ἐφθείραμεν, οὐδένα ἐπλεονεκτήσαμεν. **3** πρὸς κατάκρισιν οὐ

---

1 16 {C} ἡμεῖς γὰρ ναὸς θεοῦ ἐσμεν B D* P 33 81* (104 ὑμεῖς) 326 436 1881 1962 (2127 ὑμεῖς) it[d, (e)] syr[pal] cop[sa, bo] eth Origen Didymus Philo-Carpasia Augustine ‖ ἡμεῖς γὰρ ναοὶ θεοῦ ἐσμεν א* 0243 1739 Clement Augustine ‖ ὑμεῖς γὰρ ναὸς θεοῦ ἐστε (see 1 Cor 3.16) 𝔭[46] C D[c] G K Ψ 0209 (א[c] 330 451 1241 1877 2492 ἐστε θεοῦ) 81* 88 181 614 (629 *l*[597,1365] ἐστε ναὸς θεοῦ) 630 ·1984 1985 2495 *Byz Lect* it[ar, dem, f, g, t, x, z] vg syr[p, h] goth arm Tertullian Origen[lat] Ambrosiaster Lucifer Athanasius Chrysostom Euthalius Theodoret John-Damascus

---

[c c] **15** c minor, c question: WH Bov Nes BF[2] NEB Zür ‖ c question, c question: TR AV RV ASV RSV TT Luth Jer Seg

---

16 ἡμεῖς...ἐσμεν 1 Cor 3.16; 6.19   Ἐνοικήσω...λαός Lv 26.12; Jr 32.38; Eze 37.27 **17** Is 52.11; Eze 20.34, 41; Re 18.4   **18** 2 Sm 7.8, 14; Is 43.6; Jr 31.9   κύριος παντοκράτωρ Am 3.13 lxx; 4.13 lxx; Re 4.8; 11.17; 15.3; 21.22

7 2 οὐδένα ἐπλεονεκτήσαμεν 2 Cor 12.17

---

live together? **15** How can Christ and the Devil agree? What does a believer have in common with an unbeliever? **16** How can God's temple come to terms with pagan idols? For we are the temple of the living God! As God himself has said:

> "I will make my home with them
> and live among them,
> I will be their God, and they shall
> be my people."

17 And so the Lord says:

> "You must leave them, and separate
> yourselves from them.
> Have nothing to do with what is
> unclean,
> And I will accept you.

18 I will be your father,
> And you shall be my sons and
> daughters,
> Says the Lord Almighty."

7 All these promises are made to us, my dear friends! Let us, therefore, purify ourselves from everything that makes body or soul unclean, and let us seek to be completely holy, by living in the fear of God.

Paul's Joy

2 Make room for us in your hearts. We have done wrong to no one, we have ruined no one, nor tried to take advantage of anyone. **3** I do not say this to condemn you; for, as I have said before, you are so dear to us that we are together always, whether we live or die. ⁴ I am so sure of you, I take such pride in you! In all our troubles I am still full of courage, I am running over with joy.

⁵ Even after we arrived in Macedonia we did not have any rest. There were troubles everywhere, quarrels with others, fears in our hearts. ⁶ But God, who encourages the downhearted, encouraged us with the coming of Titus. ⁷ It was not only his coming, but also his report of how you encouraged him. He told us how much you want to see me, how sorry you are, how ready you are to defend me; and so I am even happier now.

⁸ For even if that letter of mine made you sad, I am not sorry I wrote it. I could have been sorry about it when I saw that the letter made you sad for a while. ⁹ But now I am happy — not because I made you sad, but because your sadness made you change your ways. That sadness was used by God, and so we caused you no harm. ¹⁰ For the sadness that is used by God brings a change of heart that leads to salvation — and there is no regret in that! But worldly sadness causes death. ¹¹ See what God did with this sadness of yours: how earnest it has made you, how eager to prove your innocence! Such indignation, such alarm, such feelings, such devotion, such readiness to punish wrongdoing! You have shown yourselves to be without fault in the whole matter.

¹² So, even though I wrote that letter, I did it, not because of the one who did wrong, or the one who was wronged. Instead, I wrote it to make plain to

λέγω, προείρηκα γὰρ ὅτι ἐν ταῖς καρδίαις ἡμῶν ἐστε εἰς τὸ συναποθανεῖν καὶ συζῆν. 4 πολλή μοι παρρησία πρὸς ὑμᾶς, πολλή μοι καύχησις ὑπὲρ ὑμῶν· πεπλήρωμαι τῇ παρακλήσει, ὑπερπερισσεύομαι τῇ χαρᾷ ἐπὶ πάσῃ τῇ θλίψει ἡμῶν.

5 Καὶ γὰρ ἐλθόντων ἡμῶν εἰς Μακεδονίαν οὐδεμίαν ἔσχηκεν ἄνεσιν ἡ σὰρξ ἡμῶν, ἀλλ' ἐν παντὶ θλιβόμενοι — ἔξωθεν μάχαι, ἔσωθεν φόβοι. 6 ἀλλ' ὁ παρακαλῶν τοὺς ταπεινοὺς παρεκάλεσεν ἡμᾶς ὁ θεὸς ἐν τῇ παρουσίᾳ Τίτου· 7 οὐ μόνον δὲ ἐν τῇ παρουσίᾳ αὐτοῦ ἀλλὰ καὶ ἐν τῇ παρακλήσει ᾗ παρεκλήθη ἐφ' ὑμῖν, ἀναγγέλλων ἡμῖν τὴν ὑμῶν ἐπιπόθησιν, τὸν ὑμῶν ὀδυρμόν, τὸν ὑμῶν ζῆλον ὑπὲρ ἐμοῦ, ὥστε με μᾶλλον χαρῆναι. 8 ὅτι εἰ καὶ ἐλύπησα ὑμᾶς ἐν τῇ ἐπιστολῇ, οὐ μεταμέλομαι·ᵃ εἰ καὶ μετεμελόμην (ᵃ βλέπω¹ ὅτι ἡ ἐπιστολὴ ἐκείνη εἰ καὶ πρὸς ὥραν ἐλύπησεν ὑμᾶς),ᵃ 9 νῦν χαίρω, οὐχ ὅτι ἐλυπήθητε, ἀλλ' ὅτι ἐλυπήθητε εἰς μετάνοιαν· ἐλυπήθητε γὰρ κατὰ θεόν, ἵνα ἐν μηδενὶ ζημιωθῆτε ἐξ ἡμῶν. 10 ἡ γὰρ κατὰ θεὸν λύπη μετάνοιαν εἰς σωτηρίαν ἀμεταμέλητον ἐργάζεται· ἡ δὲ τοῦ κόσμου λύπη θάνατον κατεργάζεται. 11 ἰδοὺ γὰρ αὐτὸ τοῦτο τὸ κατὰ θεὸν λυπηθῆναι πόσην κατειργάσατο ὑμῖν σπουδήν, ἀλλὰ ἀπολογίαν, ἀλλὰ ἀγανάκτησιν, ἀλλὰ φόβον, ἀλλὰ ἐπιπόθησιν, ἀλλὰ ζῆλον, ἀλλὰ ἐκδίκησιν· ἐν παντὶ συνεστήσατε ἑαυτοὺς ἀγνοὺς εἶναι τῷ πράγματι. 12 ἄρα εἰ καὶ ἔγραψα ὑμῖν, οὐχ ἕνεκεν τοῦ ἀδικήσαντος, οὐδὲ ἕνεκεν τοῦ ἀδικη-

¹ 8 {C} βλέπω 𝔭⁴⁶ᶜ B D* itᵃʳ,ᵈ,ᵉ copˢᵃ? Ambrosiaster Pelagius ∥ βλέπων 𝔭⁴⁶* itᶜ,ᵈᵉᵐ,ˣ,ᶻ vg copˢᵃ? Ambrosiaster ∥ βλέπω γάρ ℵ C Dᶜ G K P Ψ 0243 33 81 88 104 181 326 330 436 451 614 629 630 1241 1739 1877 1881 1962 1984 1985 2127 2492 2495 Byz Lect itᶠ,ᵍ syrᵖ,ʰ copᵇᵒ goth arm Chrysostom Euthalius Theodoret John-Damascus ∥ ἰδοὺ βλέπω eth

ᵃ ᵃ ᵃ 8 a major, a parens, a parens and minor: WH ASV ∥ a major, a dash, a dash and minor: Luth Jer (Seg) ∥ a major, a minor, a minor: Bov Nes BF² (TT) Zür ∥ a minor, a major, a major: TR AV RV ∥ a parens, a parens and minor, a major: RSV ∥ different text: NEB

3 ἐν...καρδίαις...ἐστε 2 Cor 6.11–12; Php 1.7   5 ἐλθόντων...Μακεδονίαν Ac 20.1–2; 2 Cor 2.13   6 ὁ παρακαλῶν...θεός Is 49.13; 2 Cor 1.3–4   8 2 Cor 2.4   10 ἡ δὲ...κατεργάζεται Sir 38.18; Mt 27.3–5; He 12.17

θέντος, ἀλλ' ἕνεκεν τοῦ φανερωθῆναι τὴν σπουδὴν ὑμῶν τὴν ὑπὲρ ἡμῶν πρὸς ὑμᾶς ἐνώπιον τοῦ θεοῦ.[b] 13 διὰ τοῦτο παρακεκλήμεθα.[b]

Ἐπὶ δὲ τῇ παρακλήσει ἡμῶν περισσοτέρως μᾶλλον ἐχάρημεν ἐπὶ τῇ χαρᾷ Τίτου, ὅτι ἀναπέπαυται τὸ πνεῦμα αὐτοῦ ἀπὸ πάντων ὑμῶν· 14 ὅτι εἴ τι αὐτῷ ὑπὲρ ὑμῶν κεκαύχημαι οὐ κατῃσχύνθην, ἀλλ' ὡς πάντα ἐν ἀληθείᾳ ἐλαλήσαμεν ὑμῖν, οὕτως καὶ ἡ καύχησις ἡμῶν ἡ ἐπὶ Τίτου ἀλήθεια ἐγενήθη. 15 καὶ τὰ σπλάγχνα αὐτοῦ περισσοτέρως εἰς ὑμᾶς ἐστιν ἀναμιμνησκομένου τὴν πάντων ὑμῶν ὑπακοήν, ὡς μετὰ φόβου καὶ τρόμου ἐδέξασθε αὐτόν. 16 χαίρω ὅτι ἐν παντὶ θαρρῶ ἐν ὑμῖν.

Liberal Giving

8 Γνωρίζομεν δὲ ὑμῖν, ἀδελφοί, τὴν χάριν τοῦ θεοῦ τὴν δεδομένην ἐν ταῖς ἐκκλησίαις τῆς Μακεδονίας, 2 ὅτι ἐν πολλῇ δοκιμῇ θλίψεως ἡ περισσεία τῆς χαρᾶς αὐτῶν καὶ ἡ κατὰ βάθους πτωχεία αὐτῶν ἐπερίσσευσεν εἰς τὸ πλοῦτος τῆς ἁπλότητος αὐτῶν· 3 ὅτι κατὰ δύναμιν, μαρτυρῶ, καὶ παρὰ δύναμιν,[a] αὐθαίρετοι[a] 4 μετὰ πολλῆς παρακλήσεως δεόμενοι ἡμῶν[b] τὴν χάριν καὶ τὴν κοινωνίαν τῆς διακονίας τῆς εἰς τοὺς ἁγίους — 5 καὶ οὐ καθὼς ἠλπίσαμεν ἀλλ' ἑαυτοὺς ἔδωκαν πρῶτον τῷ κυρίῳ καὶ ἡμῖν διὰ θελήματος θεοῦ, 6 εἰς τὸ παρακαλέσαι ἡμᾶς Τίτον ἵνα καθὼς προενήρξατο οὕτως καὶ ἐπιτελέσῃ εἰς ὑμᾶς καὶ τὴν χάριν ταύτην. 7 ἀλλ' ὥσπερ ἐν παντὶ περισσεύετε, πίστει καὶ λόγῳ καὶ γνώσει καὶ πάσῃ

[b b] **12-13** *b* major, *b* paragraph: WH Bov Nes BF² RSV NEB TT Zür Luth Jer ∥ *b* paragraph, *b* none: TR ∥ *b* major, *b* minor: AV RV ASV ∥ *b* major, *b* major: Seg

[a a] **3** *a* minor, *a* none: WH Bov Nes BF² ∥ *a* none, *a* minor: TR AV Zür Seg ∥ *a* minor, *a* minor: RV ASV RSV NEB TT Jer ∥ *a* none, *a* none: Luth

[b] **4** *b* none: TR Bov Nes BF² AV RV ASV RSV NEB TT Zür Jer Seg ∥ *b* minor: WH Luth?

---

15 τὴν πάντων ὑμῶν ὑπακοήν 2 Cor 2.9
8 1-4 Ro 15.26   **4** τῆς διακονίας...ἁγίους Ac 11.29; 2 Cor 9.1   **7** ἐν παντί...γνώσει 1 Cor 1.5

---

you, in God's sight, how deep is your devotion to us. [13] That is why we were encouraged.

Not only were we encouraged; how happy Titus made us with his happiness over the way in which all of you helped to cheer him up. [14] I did boast of you to him, and you have not disappointed me. We have always spoken the truth to you. In the same way, the boast we made to Titus has proved true. [15] And so his love for you grows stronger, as he remembers how all of you were ready to obey, how you welcomed him with fear and trembling. [16] How happy I am that I can depend on you completely!

Christian Giving

8 We want you to know, brothers, what God's grace has done in the churches in Macedonia. [2] They have been severely tested by the troubles they went through; but their joy was so great that they were extremely generous in their giving, even though they were very poor. [3] I assure you, they gave as much as they were able, and even more than that; of their own free will [4] they begged us and insisted on the privilege of having a part in helping God's people in Judea. [5] It was more than we could have hoped for! First they gave themselves to the Lord; and then, by God's will, they gave themselves to us as well. [6] So we urged Titus, who began this work, to continue it and help you complete this special service of love. [7] You are so rich in all you have: in faith, speech, and knowledge, in your eagerness to help, and in your love for us. And so we want you to be generous also in this service of love.

8 I am not laying down any rules. But by showing how eager others are to help, I am trying to find out how real your own love is. 9 For you know the grace of our Lord Jesus Christ: rich as he was, he made himself poor for your sake, in order to make you rich by means of his poverty.

10 This is my opinion on the matter: it is better for you to finish now what you began last year. You were the first, not only to act, but also to be willing to act. 11 On with it, then, and finish the job! Be as eager to finish it as you were to plan it, and do it with what you have. 12 For if you are eager to give, God will accept your gift on the basis of what you have to give, not on what you don't have.

13-14 I am not trying to relieve others by putting a burden on you; but since you have plenty at this time, it is only fair that you should help those who are in need. Then, when you are in need and they have plenty, they will help you. In this way both are treated equally. 15 As the scripture says,

"The man who gathered much
Did not have too much,
And the man who gathered little
Did not have too little."

16 How we thank God for making Titus as eager as we are to help you! 17 Not only did he welcome our request; he was

σπουδῇ καὶ τῇ ἐξ ἡμῶν ἐν ὑμῖν[1] ἀγάπῃ, ἵνα καὶ ἐν ταύτῃ τῇ χάριτι περισσεύητε.

8 Οὐ κατ᾽ ἐπιταγὴν λέγω, ἀλλὰ διὰ τῆς ἑτέρων σπουδῆς καὶ τὸ τῆς ὑμετέρας ἀγάπης γνήσιον δοκιμάζων· 9 γινώσκετε γὰρ τὴν χάριν τοῦ κυρίου ἡμῶν Ἰησοῦ Χριστοῦ, ὅτι δι᾽ ὑμᾶς ἐπτώχευσεν πλούσιος ὤν, ἵνα ὑμεῖς τῇ ἐκείνου πτωχείᾳ πλουτήσητε. 10 καὶ γνώμην ἐν τούτῳ δίδωμι· τοῦτο γὰρ ὑμῖν συμφέρει, οἵτινες οὐ μόνον τὸ ποιῆσαι ἀλλὰ καὶ τὸ θέλειν προενήρξασθε ἀπὸ πέρυσι· 11 νυνὶ δὲ καὶ τὸ ποιῆσαι ἐπιτελέσατε, ὅπως καθάπερ ἡ προθυμία τοῦ θέλειν οὕτως καὶ τὸ ἐπιτελέσαι ἐκ τοῦ ἔχειν. 12 εἰ γὰρ ἡ προθυμία πρόκειται, καθὸ ἐὰν ἔχῃ εὐπρόσδεκτος, οὐ καθὸ οὐκ ἔχει. 13 οὐ γὰρ ἵνα ἄλλοις ἄνεσις, ὑμῖν θλῖψις·[c] [d]ἀλλ᾽ ἐξ ἰσότητος[c] 14[d] ἐν τῷ νῦν καιρῷ τὸ ὑμῶν περίσσευμα εἰς τὸ ἐκείνων ὑστέρημα, [d]ἵνα καὶ τὸ ἐκείνων περίσσευμα γένηται εἰς τὸ ὑμῶν ὑστέρημα, ὅπως γένηται ἰσότης· 15 καθὼς γέγραπται,

ʽΟ τὸ πολὺ οὐκ ἐπλεόνασεν,
καὶ ὁ τὸ ὀλίγον οὐκ ἠλαττόνησεν.

Titus and His Companions

16 Χάρις δὲ τῷ θεῷ τῷ δόντι τὴν αὐτὴν σπουδὴν ὑπὲρ ὑμῶν ἐν τῇ καρδίᾳ Τίτου, 17 ὅτι τὴν μὲν παρά-

---

[1] **7** {D} ἡμῶν ἐν ὑμῖν 𝔭[46] B 0243 104 330 436 451 630 1739 1881 1962 2492 it[rl] syr[p] cop[sa,bo] arm Origen[lat] Ambrosiaster Ephraem ‖ ὑμῶν ἐν ὑμῖν 88 326 629 ‖ ὑμῶν ἐν ἡμῖν ℵ C D G K P Ψ (33 εἰς ἡμᾶς) 81 181 614 1241 1877 1984 2127 2495 *Byz Lect* it[ar,c,d,dem,e,f,g,x,z] vg syr[h] goth eth Ambrosiaster Chrysostom Augustine Euthalius Theodoret ‖ ὑμῶν νῦν 1985

[cc] **13** *c* minor, *c* none: WH Nes BF² (AV) (RV) RSV (TT) ‖ *c* minor, *c* major: WH[mg] Bov ASV NEB Zür Luth Jer Seg ‖ *c* minor, *c* minor: TR

[ddd] **13-14** *d* no number, *d* number 14, *d* no number: TR[ed] WH? Bov Nes BF² TT Zür Luth Jer Seg ‖ *d* number 14, *d* no number, *d* no number: TR[ed] WH? AV RV ASV RSV NEB ‖ *d* no number, *d* no number, *d* number 14: TR[ed]

7 ἐν ταύτῃ...περισσεύητε 1 Cor 16.1-2   **9** γινώσκετε...ὤν Mt 8.20; Php 2.6-7   **12** Pr 3.27-28; Mk 12.43   **14** ἐν...ὑστέρημα 2 Cor 9.12   **15** ʽΟ τὸ...ἠλαττόνησεν Ex 16.18

κλῆσιν ἐδέξατο, σπουδαιότερος δὲ ὑπάρχων αὐθαίρετος ἐξῆλθεν πρὸς ὑμᾶς. 18 συνεπέμψαμεν δὲ μετ' αὐτοῦ τὸν ἀδελφὸν οὗ ὁ ἔπαινος ἐν τῷ εὐαγγελίῳ διὰ πασῶν τῶν ἐκκλησιῶν 19 — οὐ μόνον δὲ ἀλλὰ καὶ χειροτονηθεὶς ὑπὸ τῶν ἐκκλησιῶν συνέκδημος ἡμῶν σὺν² τῇ χάριτι ταύτῃ τῇ διακονουμένῃ ὑφ' ἡμῶν πρὸς τὴν [αὐτοῦ] τοῦ κυρίου δόξαν καὶ προθυμίαν ἡμῶν — 20 στελλόμενοι τοῦτο μή τις ἡμᾶς μωμήσηται ἐν τῇ ἁδρότητι ταύτῃ τῇ διακονουμένῃ ὑφ' ἡμῶν· 21 **προνοοῦμεν** γὰρ **καλὰ** οὐ μόνον **ἐνώπιον κυρίου** ἀλλὰ **καὶ** ἐνώπιον **ἀνθρώπων.** 22 συνεπέμψαμεν δὲ αὐτοῖς τὸν ἀδελφὸν ἡμῶν ὃν ἐδοκιμάσαμεν ἐν πολλοῖς πολλάκις σπουδαῖον ὄντα, νυνὶ δὲ πολὺ σπουδαιότερον πεποιθήσει πολλῇ τῇ εἰς ὑμᾶς. 23 εἴτε ὑπὲρ Τίτου, κοινωνὸς ἐμὸς καὶ εἰς ὑμᾶς συνεργός· εἴτε ἀδελφοὶ ἡμῶν, ἀπόστολοι ἐκκλησιῶν, δόξα Χριστοῦ. 24 τὴν οὖν ἔνδειξιν τῆς ἀγάπης ὑμῶν καὶ ἡμῶν καυχήσεως ὑπὲρ ὑμῶν εἰς αὐτοὺς ἐνδεικνύμενοι εἰς πρόσωπον τῶν ἐκκλησιῶν.

The Offering for the Saints

9 Περὶ μὲν γὰρ τῆς διακονίας τῆς εἰς τοὺς ἁγίους περισσόν μοί ἐστιν τὸ γράφειν ὑμῖν, 2 οἶδα γὰρ τὴν προθυμίαν ὑμῶν ἣν ὑπὲρ ὑμῶν καυχῶμαι Μακεδόσιν ὅτι Ἀχαΐα παρεσκεύασται ἀπὸ πέρυσι, καὶ τὸ ὑμῶν ζῆλος ἠρέθισεν τοὺς πλείονας. 3 ἔπεμψα δὲ τοὺς ἀδελφούς, ἵνα μὴ τὸ καύχημα ἡμῶν τὸ ὑπὲρ ὑμῶν κενωθῇ ἐν τῷ μέρει τούτῳ, ἵνα καθὼς ἔλεγον παρεσκευασμένοι ἦτε, 4 μή πως ἐὰν ἔλθωσιν σὺν ἐμοὶ Μακεδόνες καὶ εὕρωσιν ὑμᾶς ἀπαρασκευάστους καταισχυνθῶμεν ἡμεῖς,

---

² 19 {D} σύν p⁴⁶ ℵ D G K Ψ 181 330 436 451 614 629 1241 1984 1985 2492 2495 *Byz Lect* it^{ar,d,e,g} syr^h goth Clement Augustine Theodoret ‖ ἐν B C P 0225 0243 33 81 88 104 326 630 1739 1877 1881 1962 2127 it^{dem,f,x,z} vg syr^p cop^{sa,bo} arm eth Ambrosiaster Euthalius John Damascus

21 Pr 3.4 LXX   24 ἡμῶν καυχήσεως ὑπὲρ ὑμῶν 2 Cor 7.14
9 1 τῆς διακονίας...ἁγίους 2 Cor 8.4, 20

---

so eager to help that of his own free will he decided to go to you. [18] With him we are sending the brother who is highly respected in all the churches for his work in preaching the gospel. [19] And besides that, he has been chosen and appointed by the churches to travel with us as we carry out this service of love for the Lord's glory, and to show that we want to help.

[20] We are being careful not to stir up any complaints about the way we handle this generous gift. [21] Our purpose is to do what is right, not only in the sight of the Lord, but also in the sight of men.

[22] So we are sending our brother with them; we have tested him many times, and found him always very eager to help. And now that he has so much confidence in you, he is all the more eager to help. [23] As for Titus, he is my partner who works with me to help you; as for the other brothers who are going with him, they represent the churches and bring glory to Christ. [24] Show your love to them, that all the churches will be sure of it and know that we are right in boasting of you.

Help for Fellow Christians

9 There is really no need for me to write you about the help being sent to God's people in Judea. [2] I know that you are willing to help, and I have boasted of you to the people in Macedonia. "The brothers in Greece," I said, "have been ready to help since last year." Your eagerness has stirred up most of them. [3] Now I am sending these brothers, so that our boasting of you in this matter may not turn out to be empty words, but, just as I said, you will be ready with your help. [4] Or else, if the people from Macedonia should come with me and find out that you are not ready, how ashamed we would be — not to speak of your shame — for feeling so sure of you! ⁵ So I thought it necessary to urge these brothers to go to you ahead of me and get ready in advance the gift you promised to make. Then it will be ready when I arrive, and it will show that you give because you want to, not because you have to.

⁶ Remember this: the man who plants few seeds will have a small crop; the one who plants many seeds will have a large crop. ⁷ Each one should give, then, as he has decided, not with regret or out of a sense of duty; for God loves the one who gives gladly. ⁸ And God is able to give you more than you need, so that you will always have all you need for yourselves and more than enough for every good cause. ⁹ As the scripture says,

"He gives generously to the poor,
His kindness lasts for ever."

¹⁰ And God, who supplies seed for the sower and bread to eat, will also supply you with all the seed you need and make it grow, to produce a rich harvest from your generosity. ¹¹ He will always make you rich enough to be generous at all times, so that many will thank God for your gifts through us. ¹² For this service you perform not only meets the needs of God's people, but also produces an outpouring of grateful thanks to God. ¹³ And because of the proof which this service

ἵνα μὴ λέγω¹ ὑμεῖς, ἐν τῇ ὑποστάσει ταύτῃ. 5 ἀναγκαῖον οὖν ἡγησάμην παρακαλέσαι τοὺς ἀδελφοὺς ἵνα προέλθωσιν εἰς ὑμᾶς καὶ προκαταρτίσωσιν τὴν προεπηγγελμένην εὐλογίαν ὑμῶν,ᵃ ταύτηνᵃ ἑτοίμην εἶναι οὕτως ὡς εὐλογίαν καὶ μὴ ὡς πλεονεξίαν.

6 Τοῦτο δέ, ὁ σπείρων φειδομένως φειδομένως καὶ θερίσει, καὶ ὁ σπείρων ἐπ' εὐλογίαις ἐπ' εὐλογίαις καὶ θερίσει. 7 ἕκαστος καθὼς προῄρηται τῇ καρδίᾳ, μὴ ἐκ λύπης ἢ ἐξ ἀνάγκης, **ἱλαρὸν** γὰρ **δότην** ἀγαπᾷ **ὁ θεός.** 8 δυνατεῖ δὲ ὁ θεὸς πᾶσαν χάριν περισσεῦσαι εἰς ὑμᾶς, ἵνα ἐν παντὶ πάντοτε πᾶσαν αὐτάρκειαν ἔχοντες περισσεύητε εἰς πᾶν ἔργον ἀγαθόν, ᵇ9 καθὼς γέγραπται,

Ἐσκόρπισεν, ἔδωκεν τοῖς πένησιν,
ἡ δικαιοσύνη αὐτοῦ μένει εἰς τὸν αἰῶνα.

10 ὁ δὲ ἐπιχορηγῶν σπέρμα τῷ σπείροντι καὶ ἄρτον εἰς βρῶσιν χορηγήσει καὶ πληθυνεῖ τὸν σπόρον ὑμῶν καὶ αὐξήσει τὰ γενήματα τῆς δικαιοσύνης ὑμῶν·ᵇ 11 ἐν παντὶ πλουτιζόμενοι εἰς πᾶσαν ἁπλότητα, ἥτις κατεργάζεται δι' ἡμῶν εὐχαριστίαν τῷ θεῷ — ᶜ 12 ὅτι ἡ διακονία τῆς λειτουργίας ταύτης οὐ μόνον ἐστὶν προσαναπληροῦσα τὰ ὑστερήματα τῶν ἁγίων, ἀλλὰ καὶ περισσεύουσα διὰ πολλῶν εὐχαριστιῶν² τῷ θεῷ — ᶜ 13 διὰ τῆς δοκιμῆς

¹ 4 {C} λέγω 𝔭⁴⁶ C* D G 048 itᵃʳ,ᵈ,ᵉ,ᵍ copˢᵃᵐˢˢ goth Ambrosiaster Augustine ‖ λέγωμεν ℵ B C² P Ψ 0209 0243 33 81 88 181 326 330 436 451 614 629 630 1241 1739 1877 1881 1962 1984 1985 2127 2492 2495 *Byz Lect* itᵈᵉᵐ,ᶠ,ˣ,ᶻ vg syrᵖ,ʰ copˢᵃᵐˢˢ,ᵇᵒ arm (eth) Chrysostom Euthalius Theodoret John-Damascus

² 12 {B} εὐχαριστιῶν ℵ B C D G K P Ψ 048 0209 0243 33 81 88 104 181 326 330 436 451 614 629 630 1241 1739 1877 1881 1962 1984 1985 2127 2492

ᵃ ᵃ 5 a minor, a none: WH Nes BF² AV RV ASV NEB TT Luth Jer Seg ‖ a none, a minor: RSV Zür ‖ a none, a none: TR Bov

ᵇ ᵇ 9–10 b b no parens: TR Bov Nes BF² RV ASV RSV NEB TT Zür Luth Jer Seg ‖ b parens, b parens: WH AV

ᶜ ᶜ 11–12 c dash, c dash: WH ‖ c major, c major: TR Nes TT Luth Jer Seg ‖ c major, c minor: Bov BF² AV RV ASV Zür ‖ c minor, c major: RSV NEB

6 Pr 11.24; 22.9   7 ἱλαρὸν...θεός Pr 22.8 LXX   9 Ἐσκόρπισεν...αἰῶνα Ps 112.9   10 ὁ δὲ...βρῶσιν Is 55.10   τὰ γενήματα...ὑμῶν Ho 10.12 LXX   11 ἥτις...θεῷ 2 Cor 1.11; 4.15   12 ἡ διακονία...ἁγίων 2 Cor 8.14

τῆς διακονίας ταύτης δοξάζοντες τὸν θεὸν ἐπὶ τῇ ὑποταγῇ τῆς ὁμολογίας ὑμῶν εἰς τὸ εὐαγγέλιον τοῦ Χριστοῦ καὶ ἁπλότητι τῆς κοινωνίας εἰς αὐτοὺς καὶ εἰς πάντας, 14 καὶ αὐτῶν δεήσει ὑπὲρ ὑμῶν ἐπιποθούντων ὑμᾶς διὰ τὴν ὑπερβάλλουσαν χάριν τοῦ θεοῦ ἐφ' ὑμῖν. 15 χάρις τῷ θεῷ ἐπὶ τῇ ἀνεκδιηγήτῳ αὐτοῦ δωρεᾷ.

Paul Defends His Ministry

10 Αὐτὸς δὲ ἐγὼ Παῦλος παρακαλῶ ὑμᾶς διὰ τῆς πραΰτητος καὶ ἐπιεικείας τοῦ Χριστοῦ, ὃς κατὰ πρόσωπον μὲν ταπεινὸς ἐν ὑμῖν, ἀπὼν δὲ θαρρῶ εἰς ὑμᾶς· 2 δέομαι δὲ τὸ μὴ παρὼν θαρρῆσαι τῇ πεποιθήσει ᾗ λογίζομαι τολμῆσαι ἐπί τινας τοὺς λογιζομένους ἡμᾶς ὡς κατὰ σάρκα περιπατοῦντας. 3 ἐν σαρκὶ γὰρ περιπατοῦντες οὐ κατὰ σάρκα στρατευόμεθα—[a] 4 τὰ γὰρ ὅπλα τῆς στρατείας ἡμῶν οὐ σαρκικὰ ἀλλὰ δυνατὰ τῷ θεῷ πρὸς καθαίρεσιν ὀχυρωμάτων—[a] [b]λογισμοὺς καθαιροῦντες 5 [b]καὶ πᾶν ὕψωμα ἐπαιρόμενον κατὰ τῆς γνώσεως τοῦ θεοῦ, καὶ αἰχμαλωτίζοντες πᾶν νόημα εἰς τὴν ὑπακοὴν τοῦ Χριστοῦ, 6 καὶ ἐν ἑτοίμῳ ἔχοντες ἐκδικῆσαι πᾶσαν παρακοήν, ὅταν πληρωθῇ ὑμῶν ἡ ὑπακοή.

7 Τὰ κατὰ πρόσωπον βλέπετε.[c] εἴ τις πέποιθεν ἑαυτῷ Χριστοῦ εἶναι, τοῦτο λογιζέσθω πάλιν ἐφ' ἑαυτοῦ ὅτι καθὼς αὐτὸς Χριστοῦ οὕτως καὶ ἡμεῖς. 8 ἐὰν [τε]

2495 Byz Lect it[ar,c,d,dem,e,f,g,r1,t,x,z vid] vg syr[p,h] cop[sa,bo] goth ‖ εὐχαριστίας arm Ambrosiaster ‖ εὐχαριστίαν p[46] (eth) Cyprian Augustine

[a a] **3-4** a dash, a dash: WH ‖ a parens, a parens: TR AV RV ASV ‖ a major, a major: Luth Jer Seg ‖ a minor, a minor: Bov Nes BF[2] ‖ a major, a minor: NEB Zür ‖ a minor, a major: RSV TT

[b b] **4-5** b no number, b number 5: TR[ed] WH? Bov Nes BF[2] NEB? TT Zür Jer Seg[ed] ‖ b number 5, b no number: TR[ed] WH? AV RV ASV RSV NEB? Luth Seg[ed]

[c] **7** c statement or command: WH Bov Nes BF[2] ‖ c statement: RV ASV NEB[mg] TT[mg] Jer[mg] Seg[mg] ‖ c command: RSV NEB TT Zür Luth Jer Seg ‖ c question: TR AV RV[mg] ASV[mg]

1 ὃς...ταπεινὸς...ὑμῖν 1 Cor 2.3   **2** δέομαι...τινας 1 Cor 4.21   **4** τὰ γὰρ...σαρκικά Eph 6.13-17   **6** πληρωθῇ...ὑπακοή 2 Cor 2.9

---

of yours brings, many will give glory to God for your loyalty to the gospel of Christ, which you profess, and for your generosity in sharing with them and all others. 14 And so they will pray for you with great affection for you because of the extraordinary grace God has shown you. 15 Let us thank God for his priceless gift!

Letter mentioned in 2 Cor 2.3

Paul Defends His Ministry

10 I, Paul, make a personal appeal to you — I who am said to be meek and mild when I am with you, but bold toward you when I am away from you. I beg of you, by the gentleness and kindness of Christ: 2 Do not force me to be bold with you when I come; for I am sure I can be bold with those who say that we act from worldly motives. 3 It is true that we live in the world; but we do not fight from worldly motives. 4 The weapons we use in our fight are not the world's weapons, but God's powerful weapons, with which to destroy strongholds. We destroy false arguments; 5 we pull down every proud obstacle that is raised against the knowledge of God; we take every thought captive and make it obey Christ. 6 And after you have proved your complete loyalty, we will be ready to punish any act of disloyalty.

7 You are looking at things as they are on the outside. Is there someone there who reckons himself to be Christ's man? Well, let him think again about himself, for we are Christ's men just as much as he is. 8 For I am not ashamed,

— Paul apostle
— super-apostles — θεῖος ἀνὴρ
— Corinthians

even if I have boasted somewhat too much of the authority that the Lord has given us — authority to build you up, that is, not to tear you down. ⁹ I do not want it to appear that I am trying to frighten you with my letters. ¹⁰ Someone will say, "Paul's letters are severe and strong, but when he is with us in person he is weak, and his words are nothing!" ¹¹ Such a person must understand that there is no difference between what we write in our letters when we are away, and what we will do when we are there with you.

¹² Of course we would not dare classify ourselves or compare ourselves with some of those who rate themselves so highly. How stupid they are! They make up their own standards to measure themselves by, and judge themselves by their own standards! ¹³ As for us, however, our boasting will not go beyond certain limits; it will stay within the limits of the work which God has set for us, which includes our work among you. ¹⁴ And since you are within those limits, we did not go beyond them when we came to you, bringing the Good News about Christ. ¹⁵ So we do not boast of the work that others have done beyond the limits God set for us. Instead, we hope that your faith may grow, and that we may be able to do a much greater work among you, always within the limits that God has set. ¹⁶ Then we can preach the Good News in other countries beyond you, and shall not have to boast of work already done in another man's field.

¹⁷ But as the scripture says, "Whoever wants to boast, must boast of what the Lord has done." ¹⁸ Because <u>a man is really approved when the Lord thinks well of him, not when he thinks well of himself.</u>

γὰρ περισσότερόν τι καυχήσωμαι περὶ τῆς ἐξουσίας ἡμῶν, ἧς ἔδωκεν ὁ κύριος εἰς οἰκοδομὴν καὶ οὐκ εἰς καθαίρεσιν ὑμῶν, οὐκ αἰσχυνθήσομαι, 9 ἵνα μὴ δόξω ὡς ἂν ἐκφοβεῖν ὑμᾶς διὰ τῶν ἐπιστολῶν· 10 ὅτι, Αἱ ἐπιστολαὶ μέν, φησίν, βαρεῖαι καὶ ἰσχυραί, ἡ δὲ παρουσία τοῦ σώματος ἀσθενὴς καὶ ὁ λόγος ἐξουθενημένος. 11 τοῦτο λογιζέσθω ὁ τοιοῦτος, ὅτι οἷοί ἐσμεν τῷ λόγῳ δι' ἐπιστολῶν ἀπόντες, τοιοῦτοι καὶ παρόντες τῷ ἔργῳ.

12 Οὐ γὰρ τολμῶμεν ἐγκρῖναι ἢ συγκρῖναι ἑαυτούς τισιν τῶν ἑαυτοὺς συνιστανόντων· ἀλλὰ αὐτοὶ ἐν ἑαυτοῖς ἑαυτοὺς μετροῦντες καὶ συγκρίνοντες ἑαυτοὺς ἑαυτοῖς οὐ συνιᾶσιν. 13 ἡμεῖς δὲ¹ οὐκ εἰς τὰ ἄμετρα καυχησόμεθα, ἀλλὰ κατὰ τὸ μέτρον τοῦ κανόνος οὗ ἐμέρισεν ἡμῖν ὁ θεὸς μέτρου, ἐφικέσθαι ἄχρι καὶ ὑμῶν.ᵈ 14 οὐ γὰρ ὡς μὴ ἐφικνούμενοι εἰς ὑμᾶς ὑπερεκτείνομεν ἑαυτούς, ἄχρι γὰρ καὶ ὑμῶν ἐφθάσαμεν ἐν τῷ εὐαγγελίῳ τοῦ Χριστοῦ·ᵈ 15 οὐκ εἰς τὰ ἄμετρα καυχώμενοι ἐν ἀλλοτρίοις κόποις, ἐλπίδα δὲ ἔχοντες αὐξανομένης τῆς πίστεως ὑμῶν ἐν ὑμῖν μεγαλυνθῆναι κατὰ τὸν κανόνα ἡμῶν εἰς περισσείαν, 16 εἰς τὰ ὑπερέκεινα ὑμῶν εὐαγγελίσασθαι, οὐκ ἐν ἀλλοτρίῳ κανόνι εἰς τὰ ἕτοιμα καυχήσασθαι. 17 **Ὁ δὲ καυχώμενος ἐν κυρίῳ καυχάσθω·** 18 οὐ γὰρ ὁ ἑαυτὸν συνιστάνων, ἐκεῖνός ἐστιν δόκιμος, ἀλλὰ ὃν ὁ κύριος συνίστησιν.

---

¹ **12–13** {C} οὐ συνιᾶσιν. ἡμεῖς δὲ 𝔭⁴⁶ ℵᵃ B Hᵛⁱᵈ 0243 33 81 104 330 451 1739 1881 Augustine Euthalius Theodoret ‖ οὐ συνιοῦσιν. ἡμεῖς δὲ Dᶜ Κ Ρ Ψ 0209ᵛⁱᵈ 181 326 436 614 629 630 1241 1877 1962 1984 1985 2127 2492 2495 *Byz Lect* Chrysostom Theodoret John-Damascus ‖ οὐ συνιᾶσιν (or οὐ συνιοῦσιν). ἡμεῖς δὲ itʳˡ syrᵖ·ʰ copˢᵃ·ᵇᵒ goth arm eth ‖ οὐ συνίασιν. ἡμεῖς δὲ ℵ* 88 ‖ συνιοῦσιν. ἡμεῖς δὲ *l*⁶⁰³ ‖ ἡμεῖς δὲ 429 itᵈᵉᵐ·ˣ·ᶻ vg Ephraem Pelagius ‖ *omit* D* G itᵃʳ·ᵈ·ᵉ·ᶠ·ᵍ Ambrosiaster Vigilius Sedulius-Scotus

---

ᵈ ᵈ **13–14** d major, d minor: TR Bov Nes BF² AV RV ASV ‖ d major, d major: RSV NEB TT Zür Luth Jer Seg ‖ d dash, d dash: WH

---

8 καυχήσωμαι...ἡμῶν 2 Cor 12.6   τῆς ἐξουσίας...ὑμῶν 2 Cor 13.10   **11** οἷοι...ἔργῳ 2 Cor 13.2, 10   **12** Οὐ...συνιστανόντων 2 Cor 3.1; 5.12   **13** ἡμεῖς...μέτρου Ro 12.3   **15** οὐκ...κόποις Ro 15.20   **16** εἰς...εὐαγγελίσασθαι Ac 19.21   **17** Jr 9.24 (1 Cor 1.31)   **18** 1 Cor 4.4–5

Paul and the False Apostles

11 Ὄφελον ἀνείχεσθέ μου μικρόν τι ἀφροσύνης· ἀλλὰ καὶ ἀνέχεσθέ μου. **2** ζηλῶ γὰρ ὑμᾶς θεοῦ ζήλῳ, ἡρμοσάμην γὰρ ὑμᾶς ἑνὶ ἀνδρὶ παρθένον ἁγνὴν παραστῆσαι τῷ Χριστῷ· **3** φοβοῦμαι δὲ μή πως, ὡς ὁ ὄφις ἐξηπάτησεν Εὕαν ἐν τῇ πανουργίᾳ αὐτοῦ, φθαρῇ τὰ νοήματα ὑμῶν ἀπὸ τῆς ἁπλότητος [καὶ τῆς ἁγνότητος]¹ τῆς εἰς τὸν Χριστόν. **4** εἰ μὲν γὰρ ὁ ἐρχόμενος ἄλλον Ἰησοῦν κηρύσσει ὃν οὐκ ἐκηρύξαμεν, ἢ πνεῦμα ἕτερον λαμβάνετε ὃ οὐκ ἐλάβετε, ἢ εὐαγγέλιον ἕτερον ὃ οὐκ ἐδέξασθε, καλῶς ἀνέχεσθε. **5** λογίζομαι γὰρ μηδὲν ὑστερηκέναι τῶν ὑπερλίαν ἀποστόλων· **6** εἰ δὲ καὶ ἰδιώτης τῷ λόγῳ, ἀλλ᾽ οὐ τῇ γνώσει, ἀλλ᾽ ἐν παντὶ φανερώσαντες ἐν πᾶσιν εἰς ὑμᾶς.

7 Ἢ ἁμαρτίαν ἐποίησα ἐμαυτὸν ταπεινῶν ἵνα ὑμεῖς ὑψωθῆτε, ὅτι δωρεὰν τὸ τοῦ θεοῦ εὐαγγέλιον εὐηγγελισάμην ὑμῖν; **8** ἄλλας ἐκκλησίας ἐσύλησα λαβὼν ὀψώνιον πρὸς τὴν ὑμῶν διακονίαν,ᵃ **9**ᵇ καὶ παρὼν πρὸς ὑμᾶς καὶ ὑστερηθεὶς οὐ κατενάρκησα οὐθενός· ᵇτὸ γὰρ ὑστέρημά μου προσανεπλήρωσαν οἱ ἀδελφοὶ ἐλθόντες ἀπὸ Μακε-

---

¹ **3** {C} ἀπὸ τῆς ἁπλότητος καὶ τῆς ἁγνότητος 𝔭⁴⁶ ℵ* B G 33 81 88 104 (326 ἁπλότητος *for* ἁγνότητος) 330 451 1962 2492 it^{ar,c,g,rl,t} syr^{h with *} cop^{sa,bo} goth eth Archelaus Athanasius Pelagius Augustine John-Damascus ∥ ἀπὸ τῆς ἁγνότητος καὶ τῆς ἁπλότητος D* it^{d,e} Epiphanius ∥ ἀπὸ τῆς ἁπλότητος ℵᶜ Dᶜ H K R P Ψ 0121a 0243 181 436 614 629 630 1241 1739 1877 1881 1984 1985 2127 2495 *Byz Lect* it^{dem,f,x,z} vg syr^{p,h} arm Clement Origen^{gr,lat} Eusebius Ambrosiaster Lucifer Chrysostom Jerome Euthalius Theodoret ∥ ἀπὸ τῆς ἁγνότητος (Ambrosiaster *add* τοῦ θεοῦ) Lucifer Ambrose Augustine Vigilius

ᵃ **8** *a* statement: TR WH Bov Nes BF² AV RV ASV RSV NEB TT Zür Luth Jer Seg ∥ *a* question: NEB^{mg}

ᵇ ᵇ **8-9** *b* number 9, *b* no number: TR^{ed} WH Bov Nes BF² AV RV ASV RSV NEB TT Zür Luth Jer Seg ∥ *b* no number, *b* number 9: TR^{ed}

---

2 ἡρμοσάμην...Χριστῷ Eph 5.26-27; Ga 1.8-9   **5** 1 Cor 15.10; 2 Cor 12.11; Ga 2.6, 9; Eph 3.4   **7** δωρεάν...ὑμῖν 1 Cor 9.12, 18; 2 Cor 12.13   **3** ὁ ὄφις...αὐτοῦ Gn 3.13   **6** εἰ...λόγῳ 1 Cor 1.17; 2.1, 13 οὐ τῇ γνώσει   **8** Php 4.15   **4** εἰ...ἐδέξασθε   **9** οὐ κατενάρκησα οὐθενός

Paul and the False Apostles

11 I wish you would tolerate me, even when I am a bit foolish. Please do! **2** I am jealous for you just as God is; for you are like a pure virgin whom I have promised in marriage to one man only, who is Christ. **3** I am afraid that your minds will be corrupted and that you will abandon your full and pure devotion to Christ — in the same way that Eve was deceived by the snake's clever lies. **4** For you gladly tolerate anyone who comes to you and preaches a different Jesus, not the one we preached; and you accept a spirit and a gospel completely different from the Spirit and the gospel you received from us!

5 I do not think that I am the least bit inferior to those very special "apostles" of yours! **6** Perhaps I am an amateur in speaking, but certainly not in knowledge; we have made this clear to you at all times and in all conditions.

7 I did not charge you a thing when I preached the Good News of God to you; I humbled myself in order to make you great. Was that wrong of me? **8** While I was working among you I was paid by other churches. I was robbing them, so to speak, to help you. **9** And during the time I was with you I did not bother you for help when I needed money; for the brothers who came from Macedonia brought me everything I

[handwritten notes]
Paul is called a poor public speaker, but in Acts, Paul is an excellent speaker.

γνῶσις — sign of true apostle

1. acceptance of money a sign of good preaching to some

needed. As in the past, so in the future: I will never be a burden to you! [10] By Christ's truth in me, I promise that this boast of mine will not be silenced anywhere in all of Greece. [11] Why do I say this? Because I don't love you? God knows I do!

[12] I will go on doing what I am doing now, in order to keep those other "apostles" from having any reason for boasting and saying that they work in the same way that we do. [13] Those men are not true apostles — they are false apostles, who lie about their work and change themselves to look like real apostles of Christ. [14] Well, no wonder! Even Satan can change himself to look like an angel of light! [15] So it is no great thing if his servants change themselves to look like servants of right. In the end they will get exactly what they deserve for the things they do.

Paul's Sufferings as an Apostle

[16] I repeat: no one should think that I am a fool. But if you do, at least accept me as a fool, just so I will have a little to boast of. [17] Of course what I am saying now is not what the Lord would have me say; in this matter of boasting I am really talking like a fool. [18] But since there are so many who boast for merely human reasons, I will do the same. [19] You yourselves are so wise, and so you gladly tolerate fools! [20] You will tolerate anyone who orders you around, or takes advantage of you, or traps you, or looks down on you, or slaps you in the face. [21] I am ashamed to admit it: we were too timid to do that!

But if anyone dares to boast of something — I am talking like a fool — I will be just as daring. [22] Are they Hebrews? So am I. Are they Israelites? So am I. Are they Abraham's descendants? So am I. [23] Are they Christ's servants? I sound like a madman — but I am a better servant than they are! I have worked much harder, I have been in prison more times, I have been whipped much more, and I have been near death

δονίας· καὶ ἐν παντὶ ἀβαρῆ ἐμαυτὸν ὑμῖν ἐτήρησα καὶ τηρήσω. **10** ἔστιν ἀλήθεια Χριστοῦ ἐν ἐμοὶ ὅτι ἡ καύχησις αὕτη οὐ φραγήσεται εἰς ἐμὲ ἐν τοῖς κλίμασιν τῆς Ἀχαΐας. **11** διὰ τί; ὅτι οὐκ ἀγαπῶ ὑμᾶς; ὁ θεὸς οἶδεν.

12 Ὃ δὲ ποιῶ καὶ ποιήσω, ἵνα ἐκκόψω τὴν ἀφορμὴν τῶν θελόντων ἀφορμήν, ἵνα ἐν ᾧ καυχῶνται εὑρεθῶσιν καθὼς καὶ ἡμεῖς. **13** οἱ γὰρ τοιοῦτοι ψευδαπόστολοι, ἐργάται δόλιοι, μετασχηματιζόμενοι εἰς ἀποστόλους Χριστοῦ. **14** καὶ οὐ θαῦμα, αὐτὸς γὰρ ὁ Σατανᾶς μετασχηματίζεται εἰς ἄγγελον φωτός· **15** οὐ μέγα οὖν εἰ καὶ οἱ διάκονοι αὐτοῦ μετασχηματίζονται ὡς διάκονοι δικαιοσύνης, ὧν τὸ τέλος ἔσται κατὰ τὰ ἔργα αὐτῶν.

Paul's Sufferings as an Apostle

16 Πάλιν λέγω, μή τίς με δόξῃ ἄφρονα εἶναι· εἰ δὲ μήγε, κἂν ὡς ἄφρονα δέξασθέ με, ἵνα κἀγὼ μικρόν τι καυχήσωμαι. [c]**17** ὃ λαλῶ οὐ κατὰ κύριον λαλῶ, ἀλλ' ὡς ἐν ἀφροσύνῃ, ἐν ταύτῃ τῇ ὑποστάσει τῆς καυχήσεως. **18** ἐπεὶ πολλοὶ καυχῶνται κατὰ σάρκα, κἀγὼ καυχήσομαι.[c] **19** ἡδέως γὰρ ἀνέχεσθε τῶν ἀφρόνων φρόνιμοι ὄντες· **20** ἀνέχεσθε γὰρ εἴ τις ὑμᾶς καταδουλοῖ, εἴ τις κατεσθίει, εἴ τις λαμβάνει, εἴ τις ἐπαίρεται, εἴ τις εἰς πρόσωπον ὑμᾶς δέρει. **21** κατὰ ἀτιμίαν λέγω, ὡς ὅτι ἡμεῖς ἠσθενήκαμεν·[d] ἐν ᾧ δ' ἄν τις τολμᾷ, ἐν ἀφροσύνῃ λέγω, τολμῶ κἀγώ. **22** Ἑβραῖοί εἰσιν; κἀγώ. Ἰσραηλῖταί εἰσιν; κἀγώ. σπέρμα Ἀβραάμ εἰσιν; κἀγώ. **23** διάκονοι Χριστοῦ εἰσιν; παραφρονῶν λαλῶ, ὑπὲρ ἐγώ· ἐν κόποις περισσοτέρως, ἐν φυλακαῖς περισσοτέρως, ἐν πληγαῖς ὑπερβαλλόντως, ἐν θανάτοις πολλάκις·

[c c] **17–18** *c c* no parens: TR WH Bov Nes BF² AV RV ASV NEB TT Zür Luth Jer Seg ∥ *c* parens, *c* parens: RSV

[d] **21** *d* major: TR WH Bov Nes BF² AV RV ASV TT Zür Seg ∥ *d* paragraph: RSV NEB Luth Jer

10 ἡ καύχησις...φραγήσεται 1 Cor 9.15   **13** ἐργάται δόλιοι Php 3.2   **16** 2 Cor 12.6
22 Php 3.5   **23** διάκονοι...ἐγώ 1 Cor 15.10

[Handwritten notes:] – servant of Christ for Paul exact opposite of Corinthian's view.
– servant boasts of weakness

24 ὑπὸ Ἰουδαίων πεντάκις τεσσαράκοντα παρὰ μίαν ἔλαβον, **25** τρὶς ἐραβδίσθην, ἅπαξ ἐλιθάσθην, τρὶς ἐναυάγησα, νυχθήμερον ἐν τῷ βυθῷ πεποίηκα· **26** ὁδοιπορίαις πολλάκις, κινδύνοις ποταμῶν, κινδύνοις λῃστῶν, κινδύνοις ἐκ γένους, κινδύνοις ἐξ ἐθνῶν, κινδύνοις ἐν πόλει, κινδύνοις ἐν ἐρημίᾳ, κινδύνοις ἐν θαλάσσῃ, κινδύνοις ἐν ψευδαδέλφοις, **27** κόπῳ καὶ μόχθῳ, ἐν ἀγρυπνίαις πολλάκις, ἐν λιμῷ καὶ δίψει, ἐν νηστείαις πολλάκις, ἐν ψύχει καὶ γυμνότητι· **28** χωρὶς τῶν παρεκτὸς ἡ ἐπίστασίς μοι ἡ καθ' ἡμέραν, ἡ μέριμνα πασῶν τῶν ἐκκλησιῶν. **29** τίς ἀσθενεῖ, καὶ οὐκ ἀσθενῶ; τίς σκανδαλίζεται, καὶ οὐκ ἐγὼ πυροῦμαι;

30 Εἰ καυχᾶσθαι δεῖ, τὰ τῆς ἀσθενείας μου καυχήσομαι. **31** ὁ θεὸς καὶ πατὴρ τοῦ κυρίου Ἰησοῦ οἶδεν, ὁ ὢν εὐλογητὸς εἰς τοὺς αἰῶνας, ὅτι οὐ ψεύδομαι. **32** ἐν Δαμασκῷ ὁ ἐθνάρχης Ἀρέτα τοῦ βασιλέως ἐφρούρει τὴν πόλιν Δαμασκηνῶν πιάσαι με², **33** καὶ διὰ θυρίδος ἐν σαργάνῃ ἐχαλάσθην διὰ τοῦ τείχους καὶ ἐξέφυγον τὰς χεῖρας αὐτοῦ.

Visions and Revelations

12 Καυχᾶσθαι δεῖ¹· οὐ συμφέρον μέν², ἐλεύσομαι δὲ εἰς ὀπτασίας καὶ ἀποκαλύψεις κυρίου. **2** οἶδα ἄνθρωπον

² 32 {C} πιάσαι με B D* it^{ar,d,dem,e,f,x,z vid} vg syr^p cop^sa arm Ambrosiaster Ephraem Procopius ∥ θέλων πιάσαι με G it^g syr^h cop^bo eth ∥ θέλων με πιάσαι 629 1739 ∥ πιάσαι με θέλων ℵ D^c H K P Ψ 0121a 0243 33 81 88 104 181 326 330 436 451 614 630 1241 1877 1881 1962 1984 1985 2127 2492 2495 *Byz Lect* goth Chrysostom Euthalius Theodoret John-Damascus

¹ 1 {C} καυχᾶσθαι δεῖ 𝔭⁴⁶ B D^c G P 0243 33 81 88 104 181 330 451 614 629 630 1241 1739 1881 2127 2492* it^{d,e,g} syr^{p,h} cop^boms goth (arm οὖν δεῖ) Euthalius ∥ καυχᾶσθαι δὲ ℵ D^gr* Ψ cop^bo Theophylact ∥ καυχᾶσθαι δή K 0121a 436 1984 1985 2492^c 2495 *Byz Lect* Athanasius Chrysostom Theodoret John-Damascus Ps-Oecumenius ∥ εἰ καυχᾶσθαι δεῖ H 326 1877 1962 *l*⁵³ it^{ar,dem,f} vg cop^sa Ambrosiaster Euthalius

² 1 {C} συμφέρον μέν 𝔭⁴⁶ ℵ B G^gr 0243 33 (330 1962 μοι for μέν) 1739

24 τεσσαράκοντα παρὰ μίαν Dt 25.3   **25** ἐραβδίσθην Ac 16.22   ἅπαξ ἐλιθάσθην Ac 14.19   **26** κινδύνοις ἐκ γένους Ac 9.23   κινδύνοις ἐξ ἐθνῶν Ac 14.5   **27** 2 Cor 6.5   **29** τίς...ἀσθενῶ 1 Cor 9.22   **30** 2 Cor 12.5   **31** 2 Cor 1.23   **32-33** Ac 9.24-25

more often. **24** Five times I was given the thirty-nine lashes by the Jews; **25** three times I was whipped by the Romans, and once I was stoned; I have been in three shipwrecks, and once I spent twenty-four hours in the water. **26** In my many travels I have been in danger from floods and from robbers, in danger from fellow Jews and from Gentiles; there have been dangers in the cities, dangers in the wilds, dangers on the high seas, and dangers from false friends. **27** There has been work and toil; often I have gone without sleep; I have been hungry and thirsty; I have often been without enough food, shelter, or clothing. **28** And, not to mention other things, every day I am under the pressure of my concern for all the churches. **29** When someone is weak, then I feel weak too; when someone falls into sin, I am filled with distress.

30 If I must boast, I will boast of things that show how weak I am. **31** The God and Father of the Lord Jesus — blessed be his name for ever! — knows that I am not lying. **32** When I was in Damascus, the governor under King Aretas placed guards at the city gates to arrest me. **33** But I was let down in a basket, through an opening in the wall, and escaped from him.

Paul's Visions and Revelations

12 I have to boast, even though it doesn't do any good. But I will now talk about visions and revelations given me by the Lord. **2** I know a certain Christian man who fourteen years ago was snatched up to the highest heaven (I do not know whether this actually happened, or whether he had a vision — only God knows). [3] I repeat, I know that this man was snatched to Paradise (again, I do not know whether this actually happened, or whether it was a vision — only God knows), [4] and there he heard things which cannot be put into words, things that human lips may not speak. [5] So I will boast of this man — but I will not boast about myself, except the things that show how weak I am. [6] If I wanted to boast, I would not be a fool, because I would be telling the truth. But I will not boast, because I do not want anyone to have a higher opinion of me than he has from what he has seen me do and heard me say.

[7] But to keep me from being puffed up with pride because of the wonderful things I saw, I was given a painful physical ailment, which acts as Satan's messenger to beat me and keep me from being proud. [8] Three times I prayed to the Lord about this, and asked him to take it away. [9] His answer was, "My grace is all you need; for my power is strongest when you are weak." I am

ἐν Χριστῷ πρὸ ἐτῶν δεκατεσσάρων — εἴτε ἐν σώματι οὐκ οἶδα, εἴτε ἐκτὸς τοῦ σώματος οὐκ οἶδα, ὁ θεὸς οἶδεν — ἁρπαγέντα τὸν τοιοῦτον ἕως τρίτου οὐρανοῦ. 3 καὶ οἶδα τὸν τοιοῦτον ἄνθρωπον — εἴτε ἐν σώματι εἴτε χωρὶς τοῦ σώματος οὐκ οἶδα, ὁ θεὸς οἶδεν — 4 ὅτι ἡρπάγη εἰς τὸν παράδεισον καὶ ἤκουσεν ἄρρητα ῥήματα ἃ οὐκ ἐξὸν ἀνθρώπῳ λαλῆσαι. 5 ὑπὲρ τοῦ τοιούτου καυχήσομαι, ὑπὲρ δὲ ἐμαυτοῦ οὐ καυχήσομαι εἰ μὴ ἐν ταῖς ἀσθενείαις [μου]. 6 ἐὰν γὰρ θελήσω καυχήσασθαι, οὐκ ἔσομαι ἄφρων, ἀλήθειαν γὰρ ἐρῶ· φείδομαι δέ, μή τις εἰς ἐμὲ λογίσηται ὑπὲρ ὃ βλέπει με ἢ ἀκούει [τι] ἐξ ἐμοῦ[a] 7 καὶ τῇ ὑπερβολῇ τῶν ἀποκαλύψεων.[a] διό[3], ἵνα μὴ ὑπεραίρωμαι, ἐδόθη μοι σκόλοψ τῇ σαρκί, ἄγγελος Σατανᾶ, ἵνα με κολαφίζῃ, ἵνα μὴ ὑπεραίρωμαι[4]. 8 ὑπὲρ τούτου τρὶς τὸν κύριον παρεκάλεσα ἵνα ἀποστῇ ἀπ᾽ ἐμοῦ· 9 καὶ εἴρηκέν μοι, Ἀρκεῖ σοι ἡ χάρις μου· ἡ γὰρ δύναμις ἐν ἀσθενείᾳ

(2127 συμφέρομεν) it[dem,f] vg cop[sa,bo] arm? ∥ συμφέρει D[gr*] 81 it[z?] syr[p] eth Euthalius ∥ συμφέρει μοι D[c] H K (P μέν for μοι) Ψ 88 104 181 326 436 451 614 629 630 1241 1877 1881 1984 1985 2492 2495 *Byz Lect* it[ar,d,e] syr[h] (syr[h with *] δὲ συμφέρει) (goth μέν for μοι) (Ambrosiaster) Athanasius Chrysostom Theodoret John-Damascus Sedulius-Scotus Ps-Oecumenius Theophylact ∥ *expedit mihi quidem* it[g,x]

[3] 7 {D} διό ℵ A B G 0243 33 81 1739 2127 it[g] cop[bo] Euthalius ∥ *omit* p[46] D K P Ψ 88 104 181 326 330 436 451 614 629 630 1241 1877 1881 1962 1984 1985 2492 2495 *Byz Lect* it[ar,c,d,dem,e,f,x,z] vg syr[p,h] cop[sa] goth arm Irenaeus[lat] Origen[lat] Ambrosiaster Athanasius Chrysostom Jerome Augustine Theodoret John-Damascus

[4] 7 {C} ἵνα μὴ ὑπεραίρωμαι p[46] ℵ[c] B I[vid] K (P ὑπεραίρομαι) Ψ 0243 81 88 104 181 326 330 436 451 614 629[c] 630 1241 1739 1877 1881 1962 1984 1985 2127 2492 2495 *Byz Lect* it[ar] syr[p,h] cop[sa,bo] goth arm Tertullian Origen Cyprian Ambrosiaster Hilary Ephraem Basil Ambrose Macarius Chrysostom[1/6] Jerome Palladius Euthalius Theodoret (John-Damascus ὑπεραίρομαι) ∥ *omit* ℵ* A D G 33 629* it[d,dem,e,f,g,x,z] vg eth Irenaeus[gr,lat] Chrysostom[5/6] Augustine

---

[a a] 6–7 *a* none, *a* major: (WH) Nes BF[2] (NEB[mg]) (TT) ∥ *a* major, *a* minor: Bov ∥ *a* major, *a* dash: RVASV[mg] ∥ different text: TR AV ASV RSV NEB Zür Luth Jer Seg

---

5 2 Cor 11.30   6 ἐὰν...ἄφρων 2 Cor 10.8; 11.16   7 ἄγγελος...κολαφίζῃ Job 2.6

τελεῖται. ἥδιστα οὖν μᾶλλον καυχήσομαι ἐν ταῖς ἀσθενείαις μου, ἵνα ἐπισκηνώσῃ ἐπ᾿ ἐμὲ ἡ δύναμις τοῦ
Χριστοῦ. 10 διὸ εὐδοκῶ ἐν ἀσθενείαις, ἐν ὕβρεσιν, ἐν
ἀνάγκαις, ἐν διωγμοῖς καὶ[5] στενοχωρίαις, ὑπὲρ Χριστοῦ·
ὅταν γὰρ ἀσθενῶ, τότε δυνατός εἰμι.

Paul's Concern for the Corinthian Church

11 Γέγονα ἄφρων· ὑμεῖς με ἠναγκάσατε· ἐγὼ γὰρ
ὤφειλον ὑφ᾿ ὑμῶν συνίστασθαι. οὐδὲν γὰρ ὑστέρησα τῶν
ὑπερλίαν ἀποστόλων, εἰ καὶ οὐδέν εἰμι· **12** τὰ μὲν
σημεῖα τοῦ ἀποστόλου κατειργάσθη ἐν ὑμῖν ἐν πάσῃ
ὑπομονῇ, σημείοις τε καὶ τέρασιν καὶ δυνάμεσιν. **13** τί
γάρ ἐστιν ὃ ἡσσώθητε ὑπὲρ τὰς λοιπὰς ἐκκλησίας, εἰ
μὴ ὅτι αὐτὸς ἐγὼ οὐ κατενάρκησα ὑμῶν; χαρίσασθέ
μοι τὴν ἀδικίαν ταύτην. **14** Ἰδοὺ τρίτον τοῦτο ἑτοίμως
ἔχω ἐλθεῖν πρὸς ὑμᾶς, καὶ οὐ καταναρκήσω· οὐ γὰρ
ζητῶ τὰ ὑμῶν ἀλλὰ ὑμᾶς, οὐ γὰρ ὀφείλει τὰ τέκνα τοῖς
γονεῦσιν θησαυρίζειν, ἀλλὰ οἱ γονεῖς τοῖς τέκνοις.
15 ἐγὼ δὲ ἥδιστα δαπανήσω καὶ ἐκδαπανηθήσομαι ὑπὲρ
τῶν ψυχῶν ὑμῶν. εἰ[6] περισσοτέρως ὑμᾶς ἀγαπῶ,
ἧσσον ἀγαπῶμαι;[7] **16** ἔστω δέ, ἐγὼ οὐ κατεβάρησα

---

5 10 {C} καὶ 𝔭[46] ℵ* B 104 326 cop[samss,fay] Origen // ἐν ℵ[c] A D G K P Ψ
33 81 88 181 330 436 451 614 629 1241 1877 1962 1984 1985 2127 2492 2495 *Byz
Lect* it[ar,d,dem,e,f,g,x,z] vg syr[p,h] cop[samss,bo] goth Tertullian Origen[gr,lat]
Chrysostom Euthalius Theodoret John-Damascus // καὶ ἐν 0243 630 1739
1881 arm

6 15 {B} εἰ 𝔭[46] ℵ* A B G[gr] 33[vid] cop[sa,bo,fay] // εἰ καὶ ℵ[c] D[c] K P Ψ 0243
81[vid] 88 104 181 326 330 436 451 614 629 630 1241 1739 1877 1881 1962 1984
1985 2127 2492 2495 *Byz Lect* it[dem,f,x,z] vg syr[p,h] goth arm eth Chrysostom //
omit D* it[ar,d,e,g,rl] Ambrosiaster

7 15 {C} ἀγαπῶ, ἧσσον ἀγαπῶμαι; ℵ* A 33 104* 330 451 1241 1877
1985 2492 2495 syr[p,h] cop[sa,bo,fay] (Ephraem) // ἀγαπῶν ἧσσον ἀγαπῶμαι.
𝔭[46] ℵ[c] B D (G ἔλασσον *for* ἧσσον) K P Ψ 0243 81 88 104[c] 181 326 436 614
629 630 1739 1881 1962 1984 2127 *Byz*[pt] (*Byz*[pt] *Lect* ἧττον) (*l*[603] ἀγαπᾶμε [*sic*])
it[ar,d,dem,e,f,g,rl,x,z] vg goth arm Chrysostom Theodoret John-Damascus

---

10 Php 4.11, 13   **11** οὐδὲν...ἀποστόλων 2 Cor 11.5   **12** Ro 15.19   **13** αὐτὸς...
κατενάρκησα ὑμῶν 2 Cor 11.9   **14** τρίτον...ὑμᾶς 2 Cor 13.1   **15** ἐγὼ δὲ ἥδιστα...ὑμῶν
Php 2.17

---

most happy, then, to be proud of my
weaknesses, in order to feel the protection
of Christ's power over me. **10** I am content with weaknesses, insults, hardships,
persecutions, and difficulties for Christ's
sake. For when I am weak, then I am
strong.

Paul's Concern for the Corinthians

sarcasm

11 I am acting like a fool — but you
have made me do it. You are the ones
who ought to show your approval of me.
For even if I am nothing, I am in no
way inferior to those very special "apostles" of yours. **12** The things that prove
that I am an apostle were done with all
patience among you; there were signs
and wonders and miracles. **13** How were
you treated any worse than the other
churches, except that I did not bother
you for help? Please forgive me for being
so unfair!

14 This is now the third time that I
am ready to come to visit you — and I
will not make any demands on you. It
is you I want, not your money. After
all, children should not have to provide
for their parents, but parents should
provide for their children. **15** I will be
glad to spend all I have, and myself as
well, in order to help you. Will you love
me less because I love you so much?

16 You will agree, then, that I was not
a burden to you. But, someone will say,

I was tricky and trapped you with lies.
[17] How? Did I take advantage of you
through any of the messengers I sent?
[18] I begged Titus to go, and I sent the
other Christian brother with him. Would
you say that Titus took advantage of
you? Do not he and I act from the very
same motives and behave in the same
way?

[19] Perhaps you think that all along
we have been trying to defend ourselves
before you. No! We speak as Christ
would have us speak, in the presence of
God, and everything we do, dear friends,
is done to help you. [20] I am afraid that
when I get there I will find you different
from what I would like you to be and
you will find me different from what
you would like me to be. I am afraid
that I will find quarreling and jealousy,
hot tempers and selfishness, insults and
gossip, pride and disorder. [21] I am afraid
that the next time I come my God will
humiliate me in your presence, and I
shall weep over many who sinned in the
past and have not repented of the immoral things they have done, their sexual
sins and lustful deeds.

Final Warnings and Greetings

13 This is now the third time that I
am coming to visit you. "Any accusation
must be upheld by the evidence of two
or three witnesses" — as the scripture
says. [2] I want to tell you who have
sinned in the past, and all the others;
I said it before, during my second visit
to you, but I will say it again now that
I am away: the next time I come nobody
will escape punishment. [3] You will have
all the proof you want that Christ speaks
through me. When he deals with you he
is not weak; instead he shows his power
among you. [4] For even though it was
in weakness that he was put to death
on the cross, it is by God's power that
he lives. In union with him we also are
weak; but in our relations with you, we
shall live with him by God's power.

ὑμᾶς· ἀλλὰ ὑπάρχων πανοῦργος δόλῳ ὑμᾶς ἔλαβον.
17 μή τινα ὧν ἀπέσταλκα πρὸς ὑμᾶς, δι᾽ αὐτοῦ ἐπλεο-
νέκτησα ὑμᾶς; **18** παρεκάλεσα Τίτον καὶ συναπέστειλα
τὸν ἀδελφόν· μήτι ἐπλεονέκτησεν ὑμᾶς Τίτος; οὐ τῷ
αὐτῷ πνεύματι περιεπατήσαμεν; οὐ τοῖς αὐτοῖς ἴχνεσιν;

19 Πάλαι δοκεῖτε ὅτι ὑμῖν ἀπολογούμεθα;[b] κατέναντι
θεοῦ ἐν Χριστῷ λαλοῦμεν· τὰ δὲ πάντα, ἀγαπητοί,
ὑπὲρ τῆς ὑμῶν οἰκοδομῆς. **20** φοβοῦμαι γὰρ μή πως
ἐλθὼν οὐχ οἵους θέλω εὕρω ὑμᾶς, κἀγὼ εὑρεθῶ ὑμῖν
οἷον οὐ θέλετε, μή πως ἔρις, ζῆλος, θυμοί, ἐριθεῖαι, κατα-
λαλιαί, ψιθυρισμοί, φυσιώσεις, ἀκαταστασίαι· **21** μὴ
πάλιν ἐλθόντος μου ταπεινώσῃ με ὁ θεός μου πρὸς ὑμᾶς,
καὶ πενθήσω πολλοὺς τῶν προημαρτηκότων καὶ μὴ
μετανοησάντων ἐπὶ τῇ ἀκαθαρσίᾳ καὶ πορνείᾳ καὶ
ἀσελγείᾳ ᾗ ἔπραξαν.

Final Warnings and Greetings

13 Τρίτον τοῦτο ἔρχομαι πρὸς ὑμᾶς· **ἐπὶ στόματος
δύο μαρτύρων καὶ τριῶν σταθήσεται πᾶν ῥῆμα.** **2** προείρηκα καὶ προλέγω ὡς παρὼν τὸ δεύτερον καὶ ἀπὼν νῦν
τοῖς προημαρτηκόσιν καὶ τοῖς λοιποῖς πᾶσιν, ὅτι ἐὰν
ἔλθω εἰς τὸ πάλιν οὐ φείσομαι, **3** ἐπεὶ δοκιμὴν ζητεῖτε
τοῦ ἐν ἐμοὶ λαλοῦντος Χριστοῦ· ὃς εἰς ὑμᾶς οὐκ ἀσθενεῖ
ἀλλὰ δυνατεῖ ἐν ὑμῖν. **4** καὶ γὰρ ἐσταυρώθη ἐξ ἀσθενείας, ἀλλὰ ζῇ ἐκ δυνάμεως θεοῦ. καὶ γὰρ ἡμεῖς ἀσθε-
νοῦμεν ἐν αὐτῷ[1], ἀλλὰ ζήσομεν σὺν αὐτῷ ἐκ δυνάμεως
θεοῦ εἰς ὑμᾶς.

---

[1] **4** {B} ἐν αὐτῷ B D K P Ψ 0243 33 81 88 104 181 326 330 436 451 614
629 630 1241 1739 1877 1881 1962 1984 1985 2492 *Byz Lect* it†ar, d, dem, e, x, z vg
syr^h cop^sa, fay goth Ambrosiaster Chrysostom Euthalius Theodoret John-

[b] **19** b question: TR WH AV RV^mg ASV^mg RSV ‖ b statement: Bov Nes BF² RV ASV NEB TT
Zür Luth Jer Seg

18 παρεκάλεσα...ἀδελφόν 2 Cor 8.6, 16–18   **20** φοβοῦμαι...ὑμᾶς 2 Cor 2.1–4   **21** τῶν
προημαρτηκότων 2 Cor 13.2
13 1 Τρίτον...ὑμᾶς 2 Cor 12.14   ἐπὶ...ῥῆμα Dt 19.15 (Mt 18.16; 1 Tm 5.19)   **4** ἐσταυρώθη
ἐξ ἀσθενείας Php 2.7–8

5 Ἑαυτοὺς πειράζετε εἰ ἐστὲ ἐν τῇ πίστει, ἑαυτοὺς δοκιμάζετε· ἢ οὐκ ἐπιγινώσκετε ἑαυτοὺς ὅτι Χριστὸς Ἰησοῦς ἐν ὑμῖν;[a] εἰ μήτι ἀδόκιμοί ἐστε.[a] **6** ἐλπίζω δὲ ὅτι γνώσεσθε ὅτι ἡμεῖς οὐκ ἐσμὲν ἀδόκιμοι. **7** εὐχόμεθα δὲ πρὸς τὸν θεὸν μὴ ποιῆσαι ὑμᾶς κακὸν μηδέν, οὐχ ἵνα ἡμεῖς δόκιμοι φανῶμεν, ἀλλ᾽ ἵνα ὑμεῖς τὸ καλὸν ποιῆτε, ἡμεῖς δὲ ὡς ἀδόκιμοι ὦμεν. **8** οὐ γὰρ δυνάμεθά τι κατὰ τῆς ἀληθείας, ἀλλὰ ὑπὲρ τῆς ἀληθείας. **9** χαίρομεν γὰρ ὅταν ἡμεῖς ἀσθενῶμεν, ὑμεῖς δὲ δυνατοὶ ἦτε· τοῦτο καὶ εὐχόμεθα, τὴν ὑμῶν κατάρτισιν. **10** διὰ τοῦτο ταῦτα ἀπὼν γράφω, ἵνα παρὼν μὴ ἀποτόμως χρήσωμαι κατὰ τὴν ἐξουσίαν ἣν ὁ κύριος ἔδωκέν μοι, εἰς οἰκοδομὴν καὶ οὐκ εἰς καθαίρεσιν.

11 Λοιπόν, ἀδελφοί, χαίρετε, καταρτίζεσθε, παρακαλεῖσθε, τὸ αὐτὸ φρονεῖτε, εἰρηνεύετε, καὶ ὁ θεὸς τῆς ἀγάπης καὶ εἰρήνης ἔσται μεθ᾽ ὑμῶν. **12** ἀσπάσασθε ἀλλήλους ἐν ἁγίῳ φιλήματι. [b] ἀσπάζονται ὑμᾶς οἱ ἅγιοι πάντες.

13[b] Ἡ χάρις τοῦ κυρίου Ἰησοῦ Χριστοῦ καὶ ἡ ἀγάπη τοῦ θεοῦ καὶ ἡ κοινωνία τοῦ ἁγίου πνεύματος μετὰ πάντων ὑμῶν.

Damascus ‖ ἐν ἑαυτῷ 2127 ‖ σὺν αὐτῷ ℵ A G 2495 it[f.g.r1] syr[p] cop[bo] ‖ δι᾽ αὐτῶν arm

---

[a a] **5** a question, a major: TR WH Bov Nes BF[2] RV ASV TT Zür Luth Jer Seg ‖ a question and dash, a exclamation: RSV NEB ‖ a minor, a question: AV

[b b] **12–14** b no number, b number 13: TR WH Bov Nes BF[2] TT Zür Luth Jer Seg ‖ b number 13, b number 14: AV RV ASV RSV NEB

---

5 Ἑαυτοὺς...δοκιμάζετε 1 Cor 11.28   **8** 1 Cor 13.6   **10** 2 Cor 2.3; 10.8, 11   **11** Λοιπόν, ἀδελφοί, χαίρετε Php 4.4   ὁ θεὸς...ὑμῶν Ro 15.33   **12** Ro 16.16; 1 Cor 16.20; 1 Pe 5.14

---

5 Put yourselves to the test and judge yourselves, to find out whether you are living in faith. Surely you know that Christ Jesus is in you? — unless you have completely failed. **6** I trust you will know that we are not failures. **7** We pray to God that you will do no wrong — not in order to show that we are a success, but that you may do what is right, even though we may seem to be failures. **8** For we cannot do a thing against God's truth, but only for it. **9** We are glad when we are weak but you are strong. And so we also pray that you will become perfect. **10** That is why I write this while I am away from you; it is so that when I arrive I will not have to deal harshly with you in using the authority that the Lord gave me — authority to build you up, not to tear you down.

11 And now, brothers, good-bye! Strive for perfection; listen to what I say; agree with one another, and live in peace. And the God of love and peace will be with you.

12 Greet one another with a brotherly kiss.

All God's people send you their greetings.

13 The grace of the Lord Jesus Christ, the love of God, and the fellowship of the Holy Spirit be with you all.

PAUL'S LETTER
TO THE GALATIANS

1 From Paul, whose call to be an apostle did not come from man or by means of man, but from Jesus Christ and God the Father, who raised him from death. ² All the brothers who are here join me in sending greetings to the churches of Galatia:

³ May God our Father and the Lord Jesus Christ give you grace and peace.

⁴ In order to set us free from this present evil age, Christ gave himself for our sins, in obedience to the will of our God and Father. ⁵ To God be the glory for ever and ever! Amen.

The One Gospel

⁶ I am surprised at you! In no time at all you are deserting the one who called you by the grace of Christ, and are going to another gospel. ⁷ Actually, there is no "other gospel," but I say it

ΠΡΟΣ ΓΑΛΑΤΑΣ

Salutation

1 Παῦλος ἀπόστολος, οὐκ ἀπ' ἀνθρώπων οὐδὲ δι' ἀνθρώπου ἀλλὰ διὰ Ἰησοῦ Χριστοῦ καὶ θεοῦ πατρὸς τοῦ ἐγείραντος αὐτὸν ἐκ νεκρῶν, 2 καὶ οἱ σὺν ἐμοὶ πάντες ἀδελφοί, ταῖς ἐκκλησίαις τῆς Γαλατίας· 3 χάρις ὑμῖν καὶ εἰρήνη ἀπὸ θεοῦ πατρὸς ἡμῶν καὶ κυρίου[1] Ἰησοῦ Χριστοῦ, 4 τοῦ δόντος ἑαυτὸν ὑπὲρ τῶν ἁμαρτιῶν ἡμῶν ὅπως ἐξέληται ἡμᾶς ἐκ τοῦ αἰῶνος τοῦ ἐνεστῶτος πονηροῦ κατὰ τὸ θέλημα τοῦ θεοῦ καὶ πατρὸς ἡμῶν, 5 ᾧ ἡ δόξα εἰς τοὺς αἰῶνας τῶν αἰώνων· ἀμήν.

There is No Other Gospel

6 Θαυμάζω ὅτι οὕτως ταχέως μετατίθεσθε ἀπὸ τοῦ καλέσαντος ὑμᾶς ἐν χάριτι [Χριστοῦ][2] εἰς ἕτερον εὐαγγέλιον,[a] 7 ὃ οὐκ ἔστιν ἄλλο·[a] εἰ μή τινές εἰσιν οἱ

---

[1] **3** {C} πατρὸς ἡμῶν καὶ κυρίου ℵ A P Ψ 33 81 (181 ὑμῶν) 326 1241 1962 2127 *l*⁵⁹⁸ it^(ar,c,x) Ambrosiaster Ambrose^(1/2) Chrysostom Maximinus^(acc. to Augustine) Augustine Euthalius ∥ πατρὸς καὶ κυρίου ἡμῶν 𝔭^(46,51vid) B D G H K 88 104 330 436 451 614 629 630 1739 1881 1984 1985 2492 2495 *Byz Lect* it^(d,dem,e,f,g,z) vg syr^(p,h,pal) cop^(sa,boms) goth arm Victorinus-Rome Ambrose^(1/2) Jerome Augustine Theodoret ∥ πατρὸς καὶ κυρίου 1877 (Varimadum) Pelagius Chrysostom Augustine Vigilius John-Damascus ∥ πατρὸς ἡμῶν καὶ κυρίου ἡμῶν cop^(bo) eth

[2] **6** {D} Χριστοῦ 𝔭^(51vid) ℵ A B K P Ψ 33 81 88 104 181 330 436 451 614 629 630 1739 1877 1881 1962 1984 1985 2127 2492 2495 *Byz Lect* it^(dem,f,x) vg syr^(p,h,pal) cop^(bo) goth arm Eusebius Basil Euthalius ∥ Ἰησοῦ Χριστοῦ D 326 1241 *l*⁵⁹⁹ it^(d,e) syr^h with * ∥ Χριστοῦ Ἰησοῦ it^z cop^(sa) Jerome ∥ θεοῦ 7 327 336 Origen^(lat) Theodoret ∥ *omit* 𝔭^(46vid) G H^(vid) it^(ar,g) Marcion Tertullian Cyprian Ambrosiaster Victorinus-Rome Lucifer Ephraem Pelagius

---

[a][a] **6-7** *a* minor, *a* major: WH Bov Nes BF² RV ASV Luth ∥ *a* major, *a* minor: TR AV (ASV^mg) NEB TT Seg ∥ *a* minor, *a* minor: Zür ∥ *a* dash, *a* minor: RSV Jer

---

1 ἀπόστολος...Χριστοῦ Ga 1.11–12; Ac 20.24 **3** Ro 1.7; Php 1.2; Phm 3 **4** τοῦ δόντος ...ἁμαρτιῶν ἡμῶν Ga 2.20; 1 Tm 2.6; Tt 2.14 τοῦ αἰῶνος...πονηροῦ 1 Jn 5.19 **7** τινές...ὑμᾶς Ac 15.24

ταράσσοντες ὑμᾶς καὶ θέλοντες μεταστρέψαι τὸ εὐαγγέλιον τοῦ Χριστοῦ. 8 ἀλλὰ καὶ ἐὰν ἡμεῖς ἢ ἄγγελος ἐξ οὐρανοῦ [ὑμῖν] εὐαγγελίζηται³ παρ᾽ ὃ εὐηγγελισάμεθα ὑμῖν, ἀνάθεμα ἔστω. 9 ὡς προειρήκαμεν, καὶ ἄρτι πάλιν λέγω, εἴ τις ὑμᾶς εὐαγγελίζεται παρ᾽ ὃ παρελάβετε, ἀνάθεμα ἔστω.

10 Ἄρτι γὰρ ἀνθρώπους πείθω ἢ τὸν θεόν; ἢ ζητῶ ἀνθρώποις ἀρέσκειν; εἰ ἔτι ἀνθρώποις ἤρεσκον, Χριστοῦ δοῦλος οὐκ ἂν ἤμην.

How Paul Became an Apostle

11 Γνωρίζω δὲ ὑμῖν, ἀδελφοί, τὸ εὐαγγέλιον τὸ εὐαγγελισθὲν ὑπ᾽ ἐμοῦ ὅτι οὐκ ἔστιν κατὰ ἄνθρωπον· 12 οὐδὲ γὰρ ἐγὼ παρὰ ἀνθρώπου παρέλαβον αὐτό, οὔτε ἐδιδάχθην, ἀλλὰ δι᾽ ἀποκαλύψεως Ἰησοῦ Χριστοῦ.

13 Ἠκούσατε γὰρ τὴν ἐμὴν ἀναστροφήν ποτε ἐν τῷ Ἰουδαϊσμῷ, ὅτι καθ᾽ ὑπερβολὴν ἐδίωκον τὴν ἐκκλησίαν τοῦ θεοῦ καὶ ἐπόρθουν αὐτήν, 14 καὶ προέκοπτον ἐν τῷ Ἰουδαϊσμῷ ὑπὲρ πολλοὺς συνηλικιώτας ἐν τῷ γένει μου, περισσοτέρως ζηλωτὴς ὑπάρχων τῶν πατρικῶν μου παραδόσεων. 15 ὅτε δὲ εὐδόκησεν⁴ ὁ ἀφορίσας με ἐκ

---

³ 8 {D} ὑμῖν εὐαγγελίζηται p⁵¹ᵛⁱᵈ B H 104 630 1739 Archelaus ‖ εὐαγγελίζηται ὑμῖν Dᶜ (Dᵍʳ* 330 451 2492 ὑμᾶς) 33 (1962 ἡμῖν) 1984 2127 Byzᵖᵗ l⁶⁰³ itᵈᵉᵐ,ᶠ,ˣ,ᶻ vg syrᵖ?ʰ?ᵖᵃˡ? copˢᵃ?ᵇᵒ? Chrysostom Theodoret ‖ εὐαγγελίζεται ὑμῖν K P 88 (104 εὐαγγελίσεται) 181 436 614 629 1877 1881 1985 2495 Byzᵖᵗ Lect syrᵖ?ʰ?ᵖᵃˡ? copˢᵃ?ᵇᵒ? Theodoret ‖ εὐαγγελίσηται ὑμῖν ℵ A 81 326 (1241 ἡμῖν) itᵈ,ᵉ syrᵖ?ʰ?ᵖᵃˡ? copˢᵃ?ᵇᵒ? arm Tertullian Adamantius Eusebius (Athanasius Cyril-Jerusalem John-Damascus ὑμᾶς) ‖ ἄλλως εὐαγγελίσηται Marcion Cyprian ‖ εὐαγγελίζηται (Gᵍʳ* εὐαγγελιζαηται [sic]) Ψ itᵃʳ Cyprian Eusebius Basil ‖ εὐαγγελίσηται ℵ* itᵍ Tertullian Ambrosiaster Victorinus-Rome Lucifer Cyril

⁴ 15 {B} εὐδόκησεν p⁴⁶ B G 629 2495 itᵃʳ,ᵈᵉᵐ,ᶠ,ᵍ,ˣ,ᶻ vg syrᵖ,ʰ Irenaeusˡᵃᵗ (Origen) Eusebius Ambrosiaster Victorinus-Rome Faustinusᵃᶜᶜ· ᵗᵒ ᴬᵘᵍᵘˢᵗⁱⁿᵉ Epiphanius Gaudentius Chrysostom Jerome Theodoret ‖ εὐδόκησεν (or

---

7 θέλοντες...Χριστοῦ Ac 15.1　8, 9 ἀνάθεμα ἔστω 1 Cor 16.22　10 Ἄρτι...θεόν 1 Th 2.4　12 Ga 1.1　13 ἐδίωκον...αὐτήν Ac 8.3; 22.4–5; 26.9–11　14 Ac 22.3　15 ὁ ἀφορίσας... καλέσας Is 49.1; Jr 1.5; Ro 1.1

---

because there are some people who are upsetting you and trying to change the gospel of Christ. 8 But even if we, or an angel from heaven, should preach to you a gospel that is different from the one we preached to you, may he be condemned to hell! 9 We have said it before, and now I say it again: if anyone preaches to you a gospel that is different from the one you accepted, may he be condemned to hell!

10 Does this sound as if I am trying to win men's approval? No! I want God's approval! Am I trying to be popular with men? If I were still trying to do so, I would not be a servant of Christ.

How Paul Became an Apostle

11 Let me tell you this, brothers: the gospel that I preach was not made by man. 12 I did not receive it from any man, nor did anyone teach it to me. Instead, it was Jesus Christ himself who revealed it to me. 13 You have been told of the way I used to live when I was devoted to the Jewish religion, how I persecuted without mercy the church of God and did my best to destroy it. 14 I was ahead of most fellow Jews of my age in my practice of the Jewish religion. I was much more devoted to the traditions of our ancestors. 15 But God, in his grace, chose me even

before I was born, and called me to serve him. ¹⁶ And when he decided to reveal his Son to me, so that I might preach the Good News about him to the Gentiles, I did not go to any person for advice, ¹⁷ nor did I go to Jerusalem to see those who were apostles before me. Instead, I went at once to Arabia, and then I returned to Damascus. ¹⁸ It was three years later that I went to Jerusalem to get information from Peter, and I stayed with him for two weeks. ¹⁹ I did not see any other apostle except James, the Lord's brother.

²⁰ What I write is true. I am not lying, so help me God!

²¹ Afterward I went to places in Syria and Cilicia. ²² All this time the members of the Christian churches in Judea did not know me personally. ²³ They knew only what others said: "The man who used to persecute us is now preaching the faith that he once tried to destroy!" ²⁴ And so they praised God because of me.

Paul and the Other Apostles

2 Fourteen years later I went back to Jerusalem with Barnabas; I also took Titus along with me. ² I went because God revealed to me that I should go. In a private meeting with the leaders, I explained to them the gospel message

κοιλίας μητρός μου καὶ καλέσας διὰ τῆς χάριτος αὐτοῦ 16 ἀποκαλύψαι τὸν υἱὸν αὐτοῦ ἐν ἐμοὶ ἵνα εὐαγγελίζωμαι αὐτὸν ἐν τοῖς ἔθνεσιν, εὐθέως οὐ προσανεθέμην σαρκὶ καὶ αἵματι, 17 οὐδὲ ἀνῆλθον εἰς Ἱεροσόλυμα πρὸς τοὺς πρὸ ἐμοῦ ἀποστόλους, ἀλλὰ ἀπῆλθον εἰς Ἀραβίαν, καὶ πάλιν ὑπέστρεψα εἰς Δαμασκόν.

18 Ἔπειτα μετὰ τρία ἔτη ἀνῆλθον εἰς Ἱεροσόλυμα ἱστορῆσαι Κηφᾶν, καὶ ἐπέμεινα πρὸς αὐτὸν ἡμέρας δεκαπέντε· 19 ἕτερον δὲ τῶν ἀποστόλων οὐκ εἶδον, εἰ μὴ Ἰάκωβον τὸν ἀδελφὸν τοῦ κυρίου. 20 ἃ δὲ γράφω ὑμῖν, ἰδοὺ ἐνώπιον τοῦ θεοῦ ὅτι οὐ ψεύδομαι. 21 ἔπειτα ἦλθον εἰς τὰ κλίματα τῆς Συρίας καὶ τῆς Κιλικίας. 22 ἤμην δὲ ἀγνοούμενος τῷ προσώπῳ ταῖς ἐκκλησίαις τῆς Ἰουδαίας ταῖς ἐν Χριστῷ, 23 μόνον δὲ ἀκούοντες ἦσαν ὅτι Ὁ διώκων ἡμᾶς ποτε νῦν εὐαγγελίζεται τὴν πίστιν ἥν ποτε ἐπόρθει, 24 καὶ ἐδόξαζον ἐν ἐμοὶ τὸν θεόν.

Paul Accepted by the Other Apostles

2 Ἔπειτα διὰ δεκατεσσάρων ἐτῶν πάλιν ἀνέβην¹ εἰς Ἱεροσόλυμα μετὰ Βαρναβᾶ, συμπαραλαβὼν καὶ Τίτον· 2 ἀνέβην δὲ κατὰ ἀποκάλυψιν· καὶ ἀνεθέμην αὐτοῖς τὸ εὐαγγέλιον ὃ κηρύσσω ἐν τοῖς ἔθνεσιν, κατ' ἰδίαν δὲ

ηὐδόκησεν) ὁ θεός ℵ A D K P Ψ 33 81 88 104 181 326 330 436 451 614 630 1241 1739 1877 1881 1962 1984 1985 2127 2492 *Byz Lect* it^{d,e} syr^{h with *,pal} cop^{sa,bo} arm eth Irenaeus^{lat} Origen^{gr,lat} Adamantius Eusebius Epiphanius Chrysostom Severian Jerome Augustine Cyril Euthalius Theodoret Vigilius Ps-Athanasius John-Damascus

¹ **1** {B} πάλιν ἀνέβην 𝔭⁴⁶ ℵ A B K P Ψ (33* ἀνέβη) 33^c 81 88 104 181 326 330 436 451 614 629 630 1241 1739 1877 1881 1962 1984 1985 2127 2492 2495 *Byz Lect* it^{dem,f,x,z} vg syr^{(p),h} cop^{sa} arm ‖ πάλιν ἀνῆλθον C Paschal Chronicle ‖ ἀνέβην πάλιν D G it^{ar,d,e,g} goth eth Pelagius Jerome ‖ ἀνέβην it^c cop^{bo} Marcion Irenaeus^{lat} Tertullian Ambrosiaster Chrysostom Augustine

16 ἀποκαλύψαι...ἐμοί Ac 9.3–6; 22.6–10; 26.13–18   ἵνα...ἔθνεσιν Ga 2.7   18 Ac 9.26
19 Ἰάκωβον...κυρίου Mt 13.55; Mk 6.3   20 Ac 9.30
2 1 Ac 15.2

τοῖς δοκοῦσιν, μή πως εἰς κενὸν τρέχω ἢ ἔδραμον.
3 ἀλλ' οὐδὲ Τίτος ὁ σὺν ἐμοί, Ἕλλην ὤν, ἠναγκάσθη
περιτμηθῆναι· 4 διὰ δὲ τοὺς παρεισάκτους ψευδαδέλ-
φους, οἵτινες παρεισῆλθον κατασκοπῆσαι τὴν ἐλευθερίαν
ἡμῶν ἣν ἔχομεν ἐν Χριστῷ Ἰησοῦ, ἵνα ἡμᾶς καταδου-
λώσουσιν·ᵃ 5 οἷς οὐδὲ² πρὸς ὥραν εἴξαμεν τῇ ὑποταγῇ,
ἵνα ἡ ἀλήθεια τοῦ εὐαγγελίου διαμείνῃ πρὸς ὑμᾶς.
6 ἀπὸ δὲ τῶν δοκούντων εἶναί τι —ᵇ ὁποῖοί ποτε ἦσαν
οὐδέν μοι διαφέρει· πρόσωπον [ὁ] θεὸς ἀνθρώπου οὐ
λαμβάνει —ᵇ ἐμοὶ γὰρ οἱ δοκοῦντες οὐδὲν προσανέθεντο,
7 ἀλλὰ τοὐναντίον ἰδόντες ὅτι πεπίστευμαι τὸ εὐαγγέλιον
τῆς ἀκροβυστίας καθὼς Πέτρος τῆς περιτομῆς, ᶜ8 ὁ
γὰρ ἐνεργήσας Πέτρῳ εἰς ἀποστολὴν τῆς περιτομῆς
ἐνήργησεν καὶ ἐμοὶ εἰς τὰ ἔθνη,ᶜ 9 καὶ γνόντες τὴν
χάριν τὴν δοθεῖσάν μοι, Ἰάκωβος καὶ Κηφᾶς καὶ Ἰωάννης, οἱ δοκοῦντες στῦλοι εἶναι, δεξιὰς ἔδωκαν ἐμοὶ καὶ
Βαρναβᾷ κοινωνίας, ἵνα ἡμεῖς εἰς τὰ ἔθνη, αὐτοὶ δὲ εἰς
τὴν περιτομήν· 10 μόνον τῶν πτωχῶν ἵνα μνημονεύωμεν,
ὃ καὶ ἐσπούδασα αὐτὸ τοῦτο ποιῆσαι.

---

² 5 {B} οἷς οὐδέ p⁴⁶ ℵ A B C Dᶜ G K P Ψ 33 81 88 104 181 326 330
436 451 614 629 630 1241 1739 1877 1881 1962 1984 1985 2127 2492 2495 *Byz
Lect* itᵃʳ,ᵈᵉᵐ,ᶠ,ᵍ,ˣ,ᶻ vg syrʰ copˢᵃ,ᵇᵒ goth arm (eth) Marcion Greek mssᵃᶜᶜ·
ᵗᵒ ᴬᵐᵇʳᵒˢⁱᵃˢᵗᵉʳ, Victorinus-Rome Basil Ambrose Ps-Ignatius Epiphanius Chrysos-
tom Pelagius Greek mssᵃᶜᶜ· ᵗᵒ ᴶᵉʳᵒᵐᵉ Jerome Theodoreˡᵃᵗ Augustine Euthalius
Theodoret Ps-Jerome Cassiodorus John-Damascus // οὐδέ syrᵖ Marcion
Greek mssᵃᶜᶜ· ᵗᵒ ᴬᵐᵇʳᵒˢⁱᵃˢᵗᵉʳ Ephraem // οἷς mssᵃᶜᶜ· ᵗᵒ ᴾʳⁱᵐᵃˢⁱᵘˢ, ˢᵉᵈᵘˡⁱᵘˢ // *omit*
D* itᵈ,ᵉ Irenaeusˡᵃᵗ Tertullian Ambrosiaster Greek and Latin mssᵃᶜᶜ· ᵗᵒ
ⱽⁱᶜᵗᵒʳⁱⁿᵘˢ-ᴿᵒᵐᵉ Victorinus-Rome Pelagius Latin mssᵃᶜᶜ· ᵗᵒ ᴶᵉʳᵒᵐᵉ Augustine
Primasius Latin mssᵃᶜᶜ· ᵗᵒ ᶜᵃˢˢⁱᵒᵈᵒʳᵘˢ, Claudius

ᵃ 4 *a* minor: TR Bov Nes BF² AV RV ASV NEB Luth Jer // *a* major: TT // *a* dash: WH RSV
Zür // *a* ellipsis: Seg
ᵇ ᵇ 6 *b* dash: WH Bov Nes BF² TT Zür Luth Jer Seg // *b* parens, *b* parens: AV RV ASV
RSV // *b* parens, *b* parens and dash: NEB // *b* minor, *b* major: TR
ᶜ ᶜ 8 *c c* no dashes or parens: TR WH Bov Nes BF² NEB TT // *c* parens, *c* parens: AV RV ASV
RSV // *c* dash, *c* dash: Zür Luth Jer Seg

---

4 διὰ...ψευδαδέλφους Ac 15.1, 24; Ga 1.7   τὴν ἐλευθερίαν...Χριστῷ Ga 5.1, 13
6 πρόσωπον...λαμβάνει Dt 10.17   7 πεπίστευμαι...ἀκροβυστίας Ac 9.15; 22.21
10 Ac 11.29–30

that I preach to the Gentiles. I did not want my work in the past or in the present to go for nothing. ³ My companion Titus, even though he is Greek, was not forced to be circumcised, ⁴ although some men, who had pretended to be brothers and joined the group, wanted to circumcise him. These people had slipped in as spies, to find out about the freedom we have through our union with Christ Jesus. They wanted to make slaves of us. ⁵ We did not give in to them for a minute, in order to keep the truth of the gospel safe for you.

⁶ But those who seemed to be the leaders — I say this because it makes no difference to me what they were; for God does not judge by outward appearances — those leaders, I say, made no new suggestions to me. ⁷ On the contrary, they saw that God had given me the task of preaching the gospel to the Gentiles, just as he had given Peter the task of preaching the gospel to the Jews. ⁸ For by God's power I was made an apostle to the Gentiles, just as Peter was made an apostle to the Jews. ⁹ James, Peter, and John, who seemed to be the leaders, recognized that God had given me this special task; so they shook hands with Barnabas and me. As partners we all agreed that we would work among the Gentiles and they among the Jews. ¹⁰ All they asked was that we should remember the needy in their group, the very thing I had worked hard to do.

Paul Rebukes Peter at Antioch

[11] When Peter came to Antioch, I opposed him in public, because he was clearly wrong. [12] Before some men who had been sent by James arrived there, Peter had been eating with the Gentile brothers. But after these men arrived, he drew back and would not eat with them, because he was afraid of those who were in favor of circumcising the Gentiles. [13] The other Jewish brothers started acting like cowards, along with Peter; and even Barnabas was swept along by their cowardly action. [14] When I saw that they were not walking a straight path in line with the truth of the gospel, I said to Peter, in front of them all: "You are a Jew, yet you have been living like a Gentile, not like a Jew. How, then, can you try to force Gentiles to live like Jews?"

Jews and Gentiles Are Saved by Faith

[15] Indeed, we are Jews by birth, and not Gentile sinners. [16] Yet we know that a man is put right with God only through faith in Jesus Christ, never by doing what the Law requires. We, too, have believed in Christ Jesus in order to be put right with God through our faith in Christ, and not by doing what the Law requires. For no man is put right with God by doing what the Law requires. [17] If, then, as we try to be put right with God by our union with Christ, it is found that we are sinners as much as the Gentiles are — does that mean that Christ has served the interests of sin? By no

Paul Rebukes Peter at Antioch

11 Ὅτε δὲ ἦλθεν Κηφᾶς εἰς Ἀντιόχειαν, κατὰ πρόσωπον αὐτῷ ἀντέστην, ὅτι κατεγνωσμένος ἦν. **12** πρὸ τοῦ γὰρ ἐλθεῖν τινας[3] ἀπὸ Ἰακώβου μετὰ τῶν ἐθνῶν συνήσθιεν· ὅτε δὲ ἦλθον[4], ὑπέστελλεν καὶ ἀφώριζεν ἑαυτόν, φοβούμενος τοὺς ἐκ περιτομῆς. **13** καὶ συνυπεκρίθησαν αὐτῷ [καὶ] οἱ λοιποὶ Ἰουδαῖοι, ὥστε καὶ Βαρναβᾶς συναπήχθη αὐτῶν τῇ ὑποκρίσει. **14** ἀλλ' ὅτε εἶδον ὅτι οὐκ ὀρθοποδοῦσιν πρὸς τὴν ἀλήθειαν τοῦ εὐαγγελίου, εἶπον τῷ Κηφᾷ ἔμπροσθεν πάντων, Εἰ σὺ Ἰουδαῖος ὑπάρχων ἐθνικῶς καὶ οὐχὶ Ἰουδαϊκῶς ζῇς, πῶς τὰ ἔθνη ἀναγκάζεις Ἰουδαΐζειν;

Jews, like Gentiles, are Saved by Faith

15 Ἡμεῖς φύσει Ἰουδαῖοι καὶ οὐκ ἐξ ἐθνῶν ἁμαρτωλοί,[d] **16** εἰδότες [δὲ] ὅτι οὐ δικαιοῦται ἄνθρωπος ἐξ ἔργων νόμου ἐὰν μὴ διὰ πίστεως Ἰησοῦ Χριστοῦ, καὶ ἡμεῖς εἰς Χριστὸν Ἰησοῦν ἐπιστεύσαμεν, ἵνα δικαιωθῶμεν ἐκ πίστεως Χριστοῦ καὶ οὐκ ἐξ ἔργων νόμου, ὅτι ἐξ ἔργων νόμου **οὐ δικαιωθήσεται πᾶσα** σάρξ. **17** εἰ δὲ ζητοῦντες δικαιωθῆναι ἐν Χριστῷ εὑρέθημεν καὶ αὐτοὶ ἁμαρτωλοί, ἆρα Χριστὸς ἁμαρτίας διάκονος; μὴ γένοιτο.

---

[3] **12** {A} τινας ℵ A B C D^gr G H^vid K P Ψ 33 81 88 104 181 326 330 436 451 614 629 630 1241 1739 1877 1881 1962 1984 1985 2127 2492 2495 *Byz Lect* it^ar,dem,f,g,x,z vg syr^p,h cop^sa,bo goth arm Origen Ambrosiaster Victorinus-Rome Chrysostom Pelagius Euthalius John-Damascus // τινα 𝔭^46vid it^d,e,r^l Irenaeus

[4] **12** {B} ἦλθον A C D^c H K P Ψ 81 88 104 181 326 436 614 629 630 1241 1739 1877 1881 1962 1984 1985 2127 2495 *Byz Lect* it^ar,dem,f,r^l c,x,z vg syr^p,h cop^sa,bo goth arm Ambrosiaster Victorinus-Rome Chrysostom Euthalius John-Damascus // ἦλθεν 𝔭^46vid ℵ B D* G 33 330 451 2492 it^d,e,g,r^l* Irenaeus Origen Pelagius

---

[d] **15** *d* minor: TR WH Bov Nes BF² AV RV ASV RSV TT Zür // *d* major: NEB Luth Jer Seg

---

12 μετὰ...συνήσθιεν Ac 11.3   **16** οὐ δικαιοῦται...σάρξ Ac 15.10, 11; Ro 3.20, 28; 4.5; 11.6; Eph 2.8; Ga 3.11   οὐ δικαιωθήσεται πᾶσα σάρξ Ps 143.2

18 εἰ γὰρ ἃ κατέλυσα ταῦτα πάλιν οἰκοδομῶ, παραβάτην ἐμαυτὸν συνιστάνω. **19** ἐγὼ γὰρ διὰ νόμου νόμῳ ἀπέθανον ἵνα θεῷ ζήσω. ᵉΧριστῷ συνεσταύρωμαι· **20**ᵉ ζῶ δὲ ᶠ οὐκέτι ἐγώ, ζῇ δὲ ἐν ἐμοὶ Χριστός· ὃ δὲ νῦν ζῶ ἐν σαρκί, ἐν πίστει ζῶ τῇ τοῦ υἱοῦ τοῦ θεοῦ⁵ τοῦ ἀγαπήσαντός με καὶ παραδόντος ἑαυτὸν ὑπὲρ ἐμοῦ. **21** οὐκ ἀθετῶ τὴν χάριν τοῦ θεοῦ· εἰ γὰρ διὰ νόμου δικαιοσύνη, ἄρα Χριστὸς δωρεὰν ἀπέθανεν.

Law or Faith

3 ᵊΩ ἀνόητοι Γαλάται, τίς ὑμᾶς ἐβάσκανεν, οἷς κατ’ ὀφθαλμοὺς Ἰησοῦς Χριστὸς προεγράφη ἐσταυρωμένος; **2** τοῦτο μόνον θέλω μαθεῖν ἀφ’ ὑμῶν, ἐξ ἔργων νόμου τὸ πνεῦμα ἐλάβετε ἢ ἐξ ἀκοῆς πίστεως; **3** οὕτως ἀνόητοί ἐστε; ἐναρξάμενοι πνεύματι νῦν σαρκὶ ἐπιτελεῖσθε; **4** τοσαῦτα ἐπάθετε εἰκῇ; εἴ γε καὶ εἰκῇ. **5** ὁ οὖν ἐπιχορηγῶν ὑμῖν τὸ πνεῦμα καὶ ἐνεργῶν δυνάμεις ἐν ὑμῖν ἐξ ἔργων νόμου ἢ ἐξ ἀκοῆς πίστεως; **6** καθὼς Ἀβραὰμ **ἐπίστευσεν τῷ θεῷ, καὶ ἐλογίσθη αὐτῷ εἰς δικαιοσύνην.**

7 Γινώσκετε ἄρα ὅτι οἱ ἐκ πίστεως, οὗτοι υἱοί εἰσιν Ἀβραάμ. **8** προϊδοῦσα δὲ ἡ γραφὴ ὅτι ἐκ πίστεως δικαιοῖ τὰ ἔθνη ὁ θεὸς προευηγγελίσατο τῷ Ἀβραὰμ ὅτι **Ἐνευλογηθήσονται ἐν σοὶ πάντα τὰ ἔθνη.** **9** ὥστε

---

⁵ **20** {B} υἱοῦ τοῦ θεοῦ ℵ A C Dᶜ K P Ψ 33 81 88 104 181 326 436 451 614 629 630 1241 1739 1877 1881 1962 1984 2127 2492 2495 *Byz Lect* itᵃʳˑᵈᵉᵐˑ ᶠˑʳˡˑᵗˑˣˑᶻ vg syrᵖˑʰ copˢᵃˑᵇᵒ goth arm eth Clement Adamantius Ambrosiaster Chrysostom Jerome Augustine Cyril Euthalius Theodoret John-Damascus // θεοῦ τοῦ υἱοῦ 1985 // θεοῦ καὶ Χριστοῦ 𝔭⁴⁶ B D* G itᵈˑᵉˑᵍ Victorinus-Rome Pelagius // τοῦ θεοῦ 330

ᵉ ᵉ **19–20** e no number, e number 20: TRᵉᵈ WH? Bov Nes BF² TT Zür Luth Jer Seg // e number 20, e no number: TRᵉᵈ WH? AV RV ASV RSV NEB
ᶠ **20** f none: TR WH Nes BF² RVᵐᵍ ASV RSV NEB TT Seg // f minor: Bov AV RV Zür Luth Jer

---

19 νόμῳ ἀπέθανον Ro 7.6   **20** τοῦ υἱοῦ...με Ju 13.1; 17.23; 1 Ju 3.16   παραδόντος...ἐμοῦ Ga 1.4; 1 Tm 2.6; Tt 2.14
3 6 ἐπίστευσεν...δικαιοσύνην Gn 15.6 (Ro 4.3)   **8** Ἐνευλογηθήσονται...ἔθνη Gn 12.3 (18.18; Sir 44.21; Ac 3.25)   **9** Ro 4.16

---

means! **18** If I start to build up again what I have torn down, it proves that I am breaking the Law. **19** So far as the Law is concerned, however, I am dead — killed by the Law itself — in order that I might live for God. I have been put to death with Christ on his cross, **20** so that it is no longer I who live, but it is Christ who lives in me. This life that I live now, I live by faith in the Son of God, who loved me and gave his life for me. **21** I do not reject the grace of God. If a man is put right with God through the Law, it means that Christ died for nothing!

Law or Faith

3 You foolish Galatians! Who put a spell on you? Right before your eyes you had a plain description of the death of Jesus Christ on the cross! **2** Tell me just this one thing: did you receive God's Spirit by doing what the Law requires, or by hearing and believing the gospel? **3** How can you be so foolish! You began by God's Spirit; do you now want to finish by your own power? **4** Did all your experience mean nothing at all? Surely it meant something! **5** When God gives you the Spirit and works miracles among you, does he do it because you do what the Law requires, or because you hear and believe the gospel?

6 It is just as the scripture says about Abraham: "He believed God, and because of his faith God accepted him as righteous." **7** You should realize, then, that the people who have faith are the real descendants of Abraham. **8** The scripture saw ahead of time that God would put the Gentiles right with himself through faith. Therefore the scripture preached the Good News to Abraham ahead of time: "Through you God will bless all the people on earth." **9** Abraham believed and was blessed; so all who believe are blessed as he was.

10 Those who depend on obeying the Law live under a curse. For the scripture says, "Whoever does not always obey everything that is written in the book of the Law is under the curse!" 11 Now, it is clear that no man is put right with God by means of the Law; because the scripture says, "He who is put right with God through faith shall live."[1] 12 But the Law does not depend on faith. Instead, as the scripture says, "The man who does everything the Law requires will live by it."

13 But Christ, by becoming a curse for us, has set us free from the curse that the Law brings. As the scripture says, "Anyone who is hanged on a tree is under the curse." 14 Christ did so in order that the blessing God promised Abraham might be given to the Gentiles by means of Christ Jesus, that we, through faith, might receive the Spirit promised by God.

The Law and the Promise

15 Brothers, I am going to use an every-day example: when two men agree on a matter and sign a covenant, no one can break that covenant or add anything to it. 16 Now, God made his promises to Abraham and to his descendant. It does not say, "and to his descendants," meaning many people. It says, "and to your descendant," meaning one person only, who is Christ. 17 This is what I mean: God made a covenant and promised to keep it. The Law, which came four hun-

---

[1] 11 put right with God through faith shall live: *or* put right with God shall live through faith

οἱ ἐκ πίστεως εὐλογοῦνται σὺν τῷ πιστῷ Ἀβραάμ. 10 ὅσοι γὰρ ἐξ ἔργων νόμου εἰσὶν ὑπὸ κατάραν εἰσίν· γέγραπται γὰρ ὅτι **Ἐπικατάρατος πᾶς ὃς οὐκ ἐμμένει πᾶσιν τοῖς γεγραμμένοις ἐν τῷ βιβλίῳ τοῦ νόμου τοῦ ποιῆσαι αὐτά.** 11 ὅτι δὲ ἐν νόμῳ οὐδεὶς δικαιοῦται παρὰ τῷ θεῷ δῆλον, ὅτι **Ὁ δίκαιος ἐκ πίστεως ζήσεται·** 12 ὁ δὲ νόμος οὐκ ἔστιν ἐκ πίστεως, ἀλλ' **Ὁ ποιήσας αὐτὰ ζήσεται ἐν αὐτοῖς.** 13 Χριστὸς ἡμᾶς ἐξηγόρασεν ἐκ τῆς κατάρας τοῦ νόμου γενόμενος ὑπὲρ ἡμῶν κατάρα,[a] ὅτι γέγραπται, **Ἐπικατάρατος πᾶς ὁ κρεμάμενος ἐπὶ ξύλου,**[a] 14 ἵνα εἰς τὰ ἔθνη ἡ εὐλογία τοῦ Ἀβραὰμ γένηται ἐν Χριστῷ Ἰησοῦ, ἵνα τὴν ἐπαγγελίαν[1] τοῦ πνεύματος λάβωμεν διὰ τῆς πίστεως.

The Law and the Promise

15 Ἀδελφοί, κατὰ ἄνθρωπον λέγω· ὅμως ἀνθρώπου κεκυρωμένην διαθήκην οὐδεὶς ἀθετεῖ ἢ ἐπιδιατάσσεται. 16 τῷ δὲ Ἀβραὰμ ἐρρέθησαν αἱ ἐπαγγελίαι καὶ τῷ σπέρματι αὐτοῦ. οὐ λέγει, Καὶ τοῖς σπέρμασιν, ὡς ἐπὶ πολλῶν, ἀλλ' ὡς ἐφ' ἑνός, **Καὶ τῷ σπέρματί σου,** ὅς ἐστιν Χριστός. 17 τοῦτο δὲ λέγω· διαθήκην προκεκυρωμένην ὑπὸ τοῦ θεοῦ[2] ὁ μετὰ τετρακόσια καὶ τριάκοντα

---

[1] **14** {B} ἐπαγγελίαν ℵ A B C D[c] K P Ψ 33 81 88[mg] 104 181 330 436 451 614 629 630 1241 1739 1877 1881 1962 1984 2127 2492 2465 *Byz Lect* it[ar,c,dem,f,(r1),x,z] vg syr[p,h,pal] cop[sa,bo] arm Origen Ambrosiaster Jerome Augustine ‖ εὐλογίαν (*see* 3.14a) 𝔭[46] D* G 88* it[d,e,g,t] Marcion Ambrosiaster Ephraem Vigilius

[2] **17** {B} θεοῦ 𝔭[46] ℵ A B C P Ψ 33 81 330 436 451 1241 1739 1881 2492 it[dem,f,r1,x,z] vg cop[sa,bo] eth Aphraates Ephraem Jerome Augustine Cyril Euthalius John-Damascus ‖ θεοῦ εἰς Χριστόν D[gr] G[gr] I[vid] Κ 0176 88 104 181 614 629 630 1877 1962 1984 1985 2127 2495 *Byz Lect* arm Chrysostom Theo-

---

[a a] **13** *a* minor, *a* minor: TR WH Bov Nes BF[2] AV RV ASV Luth Jer ‖ *a* minor, *a* major: NEB TT ‖ *a* dash, *a* dash: RSV Zür Seg

10 Ἐπικατάρατος...αὐτά Dt 27.26   **11** ἐν...θεῷ Ro 3.20; Ga 2.16   Ὁ δίκαιος...ζήσεται Hab 2.4 (Ro 1.17; He 10.38)   **12** Ὁ ποιήσας...αὐτοῖς Lv 18.5 (Ro 10.5)   **13** Χριστὸς... νόμου Ro 8.3; Ga 4.5   γενόμενος...κατάρα 2 Cor 5.21   Ἐπικατάρατος...ξύλου Dt 21.23   **16** Καὶ τῷ σπέρματί σου Gn 12.7; 13.15; 17.7; 24.7   **17** τετρακόσια...ἔτη Ex 12.40

ἔτη γεγονὼς νόμος οὐκ ἀκυροῖ, εἰς τὸ καταργῆσαι τὴν ἐπαγγελίαν. 18 εἰ γὰρ ἐκ νόμου ἡ κληρονομία, οὐκέτι ἐξ ἐπαγγελίας· τῷ δὲ Ἀβραὰμ δι᾽ ἐπαγγελίας κεχάρισται ὁ θεός. 19 Τί οὖν ὁ νόμος; τῶν παραβάσεων χάριν προσετέθη, ἄχρις οὗ ἔλθῃ τὸ σπέρμα ᾧ ἐπήγγελται, διαταγεὶς δι᾽ ἀγγέλων[b] ἐν χειρὶ μεσίτου. 20 ὁ δὲ μεσίτης ἑνὸς οὐκ ἔστιν, ὁ δὲ θεὸς εἷς ἐστιν.

Slaves and Sons

21 Ὁ οὖν νόμος κατὰ τῶν ἐπαγγελιῶν [τοῦ θεοῦ][3]; μὴ γένοιτο· εἰ γὰρ ἐδόθη νόμος ὁ δυνάμενος ζῳοποιῆσαι, ὄντως ἐκ νόμου ἂν ἦν ἡ δικαιοσύνη. 22 ἀλλὰ συνέκλεισεν ἡ γραφὴ τὰ πάντα ὑπὸ ἁμαρτίαν ἵνα ἡ ἐπαγγελία ἐκ πίστεως Ἰησοῦ Χριστοῦ δοθῇ τοῖς πιστεύουσιν.

23 Πρὸ τοῦ δὲ ἐλθεῖν τὴν πίστιν ὑπὸ νόμον ἐφρουρούμεθα συγκλειόμενοι εἰς τὴν μέλλουσαν πίστιν ἀποκαλυφθῆναι. 24 ὥστε ὁ νόμος <u>παιδαγωγὸς</u> ἡμῶν γέγονεν εἰς Χριστόν, ἵνα ἐκ πίστεως δικαιωθῶμεν· 25 ἐλθούσης δὲ τῆς πίστεως οὐκέτι ὑπὸ παιδαγωγόν ἐσμεν.[c]

26 Πάντες γὰρ υἱοὶ θεοῦ ἐστε διὰ τῆς πίστεως ἐν Χριστῷ Ἰησοῦ. 27 ὅσοι γὰρ εἰς Χριστὸν ἐβαπτίσθητε, Χριστὸν ἐνεδύσασθε· 28 οὐκ ἔνι Ἰουδαῖος οὐδὲ Ἕλλην,

---

dore[lat] Theodoret Paschal Chronicle Theophylact ∥ θεοῦ ἐν Χριστῷ it[ar,d,e,g] syr[p,h] Ambrosiaster Pelagius

[3] 21 {C} τοῦ θεοῦ ℵ A C D[gr] (G omit τοῦ) K P Ψ 33 81 88 181 330 436 451 614 629 630 1241 1739 1877 1881 1962 1984 1985 2127 2492 2495 Byz Lect it[ar,dem,f,g,r1,x,z] vg syr[p,h,pal] cop[sa,bo] arm Ambrosiaster Chrysostom Jerome Augustine Cyril Euthalius Theodoret John-Damascus ∥ τοῦ Χριστοῦ 104 ∥ omit p[46] B it[d,e] Ambrosiaster Victorinus-Rome

[b] 19 b none: TR WH AV RV ASV RSV TT Zür Luth ∥ b minor: Bov Nes BF[2] NEB (Jer) Seg

[c] 25–26 c paragraph: WH Bov Nes BF[2] NEB Zür ∥ c major: TR AV RV ASV TT Luth Jer Seg ∥ c minor: RSV

18 cl...ἐξ ἐπαγγελίας Ro 4.14; 11.6   19 Τί...προσετέθη Ro 5.20   διαταγεὶς δι᾽ ἀγγέλων Ac 7.38, 53; He 2.2   21 Ὁ οὖν...γένοιτο Ro 8.2–4   22 συνέκλεισεν...ἁμαρτίαν Ro 3.11–19; 11.32   23 ὑπὸ νόμον ἐφρουρούμεθα Ga 4.3   24 Ro 10.4   26 Jn 1.12 27 εἰς Χριστὸν ἐβαπτίσθητε Ro 6.3   Χριστὸν ἐνεδύσασθε Ro 13.14   28 οὐκ...Ἕλλην Ro 10.12

3.19 Law given by angels — bad argument
3.24 παιδαγωγός = Jewish rabbi, teacher w/ disciples

---

dred and thirty years later, cannot break that covenant and cancel God's promise. 18 For if what God gives depends on the Law, then it no longer depends on his promise. However, God gave it to Abraham because he had promised it to him.

19 <u>Why was the Law given, then? It was added in order to show what wrongdoing is,</u> and was meant to last until the coming of Abraham's descendant, to whom the promise was made. <u>The Law was handed down by angels, with a man acting as a go-between.</u> 20 But a go-between is not needed when there is only one person; and God is one.

The Purpose of the Law

21 Does this mean that the Law is against God's promises? No, not at all! For if a law had been given that could bring life to men, then man could be put right with God through law. 22 But the scripture has said that the whole world is under the power of sin, so that those who believe might receive the promised gift that is given on the basis of faith in Jesus Christ.

23 Before the time for faith came, however, the Law kept us all locked up as prisoners, until this coming faith should be revealed. 24 So <u>the Law was in charge of us, to be our instructor until Christ came, so that we might be put right with God through faith.</u> 25 Now that the time of faith is here, the instructor is no longer in charge of us.

26 For it is through faith that all of you are God's sons in union with Christ Jesus. 27 For you were baptized into union with Christ, and so have taken upon yourselves the qualities of Christ himself. 28 So <u>there is no difference between Jews and Gentiles, between slaves</u>

and free men, between men and women, you are all one in union with Christ Jesus. [29] If you belong to Christ, then you are the descendants of Abraham, and will receive what God has promised.

4 But to continue: the son who will receive his father's property is treated just like a slave while he is young, even though he really owns everything. [2] While he is young, there are men who take care of him and manage his affairs until the time set by his father. [3] In the same way, we too were slaves of the ruling spirits of the universe, before we reached spiritual maturity. [4] But when the right time finally came, God sent his own Son. He came as the son of a human mother, and lived under the Jewish Law, [5] to set free those who were under the Law, so that we might become God's sons.

[6] To show that you are his sons, God sent the Spirit of his Son into our hearts, the Spirit who cries, "Father, my Father." [7] So then, you are no longer a slave, but a son. And since you are his son, God will give you all he has for his sons.

οὐκ ἔνι δοῦλος οὐδὲ ἐλεύθερος, οὐκ ἔνι ἄρσεν καὶ θῆλυ· πάντες γὰρ ὑμεῖς εἷς ἐστε ἐν Χριστῷ Ἰησοῦ. 29 εἰ δὲ ὑμεῖς Χριστοῦ, ἄρα τοῦ Ἀβραὰμ σπέρμα ἐστέ, κατ' ἐπαγγελίαν κληρονόμοι.

4 Λέγω δέ, ἐφ' ὅσον χρόνον ὁ κληρονόμος νήπιός ἐστιν, οὐδὲν διαφέρει δούλου κύριος πάντων ὤν, 2 ἀλλὰ ὑπὸ ἐπιτρόπους ἐστὶν καὶ οἰκονόμους ἄχρι τῆς προθεσμίας τοῦ πατρός. 3 οὕτως καὶ ἡμεῖς, ὅτε ἦμεν νήπιοι, ὑπὸ τὰ στοιχεῖα τοῦ κόσμου ἤμεθα δεδουλωμένοι· 4 ὅτε δὲ ἦλθεν τὸ πλήρωμα τοῦ χρόνου, ἐξαπέστειλεν ὁ θεὸς τὸν υἱὸν αὐτοῦ, γενόμενον ἐκ γυναικός, γενόμενον ὑπὸ νόμον, 5 ἵνα τοὺς ὑπὸ νόμον ἐξαγοράσῃ, ἵνα τὴν υἱοθεσίαν ἀπολάβωμεν. 6 Ὅτι δέ ἐστε υἱοί, ἐξαπέστειλεν ὁ θεὸς τὸ πνεῦμα τοῦ υἱοῦ αὐτοῦ εἰς τὰς καρδίας ἡμῶν[1], κρᾶζον, Αββα ὁ πατήρ. 7 ὥστε οὐκέτι εἶ δοῦλος ἀλλὰ υἱός· εἰ δὲ υἱός, καὶ κληρονόμος διὰ θεοῦ[2].

---

[1] **6** {B} ἡμῶν 𝔭46 ℵ A B C D* G P 104 1241 1739 1881 1962 1984 1985 *l*597,598 it^{ar,d,e,f,g,m,r1,x,z} vg^{ww} syr^{pal} cop^{sa,bomss} arm Marcion Tertullian Origen^{lat} Ambrosiaster Hilary Athanasius Basil Jerome Augustine Cyril Euthalius Ps-Athanasius^{gr,lat} ∥ ὑμῶν D^c K Ψ 33 81 88 181 326 330 436 451 614 629 630 1877 2127 2492 2495 *Byz Lect* it^{dem} vg^{cl} syr^{p,h} cop^{bomss} goth eth Victorinus-Rome Ephraem Didymus Chrysostom Augustine Cyril Theodoret John-Damascus

[2] **7** {B} διὰ θεοῦ 𝔭46 ℵ* A B C*^{vid} 33 it^{dem,f,g,r3,x,z} vg cop^{bo} Clement Ambrosiaster Victorinus-Rome Basil Ambrose Didymus^{2/3} Augustine Cyril Primasius ∥ θεοῦ 1962 arm eth^{ro} ∥ διὰ θεόν G^{gr} 1881 ∥ διὰ Χριστοῦ 81 630 syr^{pal} cop^{sa} Jerome ∥ διὰ Ἰησοῦ Χριστοῦ 1739 *l*55 (cop^{boms}) ∥ θεοῦ διὰ Χριστοῦ ℵ^c C^2 D K P 88 104 181 330 436 451 614* 629 1241 1877 2492 *Byz Lect* it^{ar,d,e} goth Didymus^{1/3} Chrysostom Theodore^{lat} Euthalius Theodoret John-Damascus ∥ θεοῦ διὰ Ἰησοῦ Χριστοῦ 326 614^c 2127 2495 syr^{p,h} eth^{pp} Theodoret ∥ διὰ θεοῦ ἐν Χριστῷ Ἰησοῦ cop^{boms} ∥ μὲν θεοῦ συγκληρονόμος δὲ Χριστοῦ (*see* Ro 8.17) Ψ 1984 1985 Theodoret Theophylact

---

29 τοῦ Ἀβραάμ...κληρονόμοι Ro 4.13
4 3 ὑπὸ...δεδουλωμένοι Ga 3.23; Col 2.20 **4** τὸ πλήρωμα τοῦ χρόνου Eph 1.10 τὸν υἱὸν ...γυναικός Jn 1.14; Ro 1.3 **5** τοὺς...ἐξαγοράσῃ Ga 3.13 τὴν υἱοθεσίαν ἀπολάβωμεν Ro 8.15 **6** Ro 8.15–16 **7** εἰ δὲ...θεοῦ Ro 8.17; Ga 3.29

Paul's Concern for the Galatians

8 Ἀλλὰ τότε μὲν οὐκ εἰδότες θεὸν ἐδουλεύσατε τοῖς φύσει μὴ οὖσιν θεοῖς· 9 νῦν δὲ γνόντες θεόν, μᾶλλον δὲ γνωσθέντες ὑπὸ θεοῦ, πῶς ἐπιστρέφετε πάλιν ἐπὶ τὰ ἀσθενῆ καὶ πτωχὰ στοιχεῖα, οἷς πάλιν ἄνωθεν δουλεύειν θέλετε; 10 ἡμέρας παρατηρεῖσθε καὶ μῆνας καὶ καιροὺς καὶ ἐνιαυτούς.[a] 11 φοβοῦμαι ὑμᾶς μή πως εἰκῇ κεκοπίακα εἰς ὑμᾶς.

12 Γίνεσθε ὡς ἐγώ, ὅτι κἀγὼ ὡς ὑμεῖς, ἀδελφοί, δέομαι ὑμῶν. οὐδέν με ἠδικήσατε· 13 οἴδατε δὲ ὅτι δι' ἀσθένειαν τῆς σαρκὸς εὐηγγελισάμην ὑμῖν τὸ πρότερον, 14 καὶ τὸν πειρασμὸν ὑμῶν[3] ἐν τῇ σαρκί μου οὐκ ἐξουθενήσατε οὐδὲ ἐξεπτύσατε, ἀλλὰ ὡς ἄγγελον θεοῦ ἐδέξασθέ με, ὡς Χριστὸν Ἰησοῦν. 15 ποῦ οὖν ὁ μακαρισμὸς ὑμῶν; μαρτυρῶ γὰρ ὑμῖν ὅτι εἰ δυνατὸν τοὺς ὀφθαλμοὺς ὑμῶν ἐξορύξαντες ἐδώκατέ μοι. 16 ὥστε ἐχθρὸς ὑμῶν γέγονα ἀληθεύων ὑμῖν; 17 ζηλοῦσιν ὑμᾶς οὐ καλῶς, ἀλλὰ ἐκκλεῖσαι ὑμᾶς θέλουσιν, ἵνα αὐτοὺς ζηλοῦτε. 18 καλὸν δὲ ζηλοῦσθαι ἐν καλῷ πάντοτε, καὶ μὴ μόνον ἐν τῷ παρεῖναί με πρὸς ὑμᾶς,[b] 19 τεκνία μου, οὓς πάλιν ὠδίνω μέχρις οὗ μορφωθῇ Χριστὸς ἐν ὑμῖν·[b] 20 ἤθελον δὲ παρεῖναι πρὸς ὑμᾶς ἄρτι, καὶ ἀλλάξαι τὴν φωνήν μου, ὅτι ἀποροῦμαι ἐν ὑμῖν.

---

3 14 {B} τὸν πειρασμὸν ὑμῶν ℵ* A B C²ᵛⁱᵈ D* G 33 itᵈ,ᵈᵉᵐ,ᵉ,ᶠ,ᵍ,ʳ³,ᶻ vg copᵇᵒ Ambrosiaster Victorinus-Rome Jerome Augustine ∥ τὸν πειρασμὸν ὑμῶν τὸν 1739 1881 (Origen) ∥ τὸν πειρασμόν μου 𝔭⁴⁶ itᵃʳ,ˣ ∥ τὸν πειρασμόν μου τὸν C*ᵛⁱᵈ D⁽ᵇ⁾,ᶜ Κ Ρ Ψ 181 330 451 614 629 630 1877 1962 2127 2492 2495 *Byz Lect* syrʰ copˢᵃ,ᵇᵒᵐˢ Chrysostom Cyril Theodoret John-Damascus ∥ τὸν πειρασμὸν τόν ℵᶜ 81 88 104 326 436 1241 1984 1985 syrᵖ goth arm eth Basil Euthalius Theophylact

---

ᵃ 10 *a* statement: TR WH Bov Nes BF² AV RV ASV NEB TT Zür Luth ∥ *a* exclamation: RSV Jer Seg ∥ *a* question

ᵇᵇ 18-19 *b* minor, *b* major: TR WH Bov Nes BF² Zür Jer ∥ *b* minor, *b* exclamation: Luth ∥ *b* major, *b* minor: AV RV Seg ∥ *b* major, *b* major: NEB TT ∥ *b* major, *b* exclamation: RSV ∥ *b* major, *b* dash: ASV

8 τοῖς...θεοῖς 2 Chr 13.9; Is 37.19; Jr 2.11; 1 Cor 8.4-6   13 δι'...ὑμῖν 1 Cor 2.3   16 Am 5.10

4. 8-31 Consequences and difficulties of Sonship
4. 14 The people met Jesus in Paul

Paul's Concern for the Galatians

8 In the past you did not know God, and so you were slaves of beings who are not gods. 9 But now that you know God — or, I should say, now that God knows you — how is it that you want to turn back to those weak and pitiful ruling spirits? Why do you want to become their slaves all over again? 10 You pay special attention to certain days, months, seasons, and years! 11 I am afraid for you! Can it be that all my work for you has been for nothing?

12 I beg you, my brothers, be like me. After all, I am like you. You have not done me any wrong. 13 You remember why I preached the gospel to you the first time; it was because I was sick. 14 But you did not despise or reject me, even though my physical condition was a great trial to you. Instead, you received me as you would God's angel; you received me as you would Christ Jesus! 15 You were so happy! What has happened? I myself can say this about you: you would have taken out your own eyes, if you could, and given them to me! 16 Have I now become your enemy by telling you the truth?

17 Those other people show a great interest in you, but their intentions are not good. All they want is to separate you from me, so that you will feel the same way toward them as they do toward you. 18 Now, it is good to have so great an interest for a good purpose — this is true always, and not only when I am with you. 19 My dear children! Once again, just like a mother in childbirth, I feel the same kind of pain for you, until Christ's nature is formed in you. 20 How I wish I were with you now, so that I could take a different attitude toward you. I am so worried about you!

The Example of Hagar and Sarah

[21] Let me ask those of you who want to be subject to the Law: do you not hear what the Law says? [22] It says that Abraham had two sons, one by a slave woman, the other by a free woman. [23] His son by the slave woman was born in the usual way, but his son by the free woman was born as a result of God's promise. [24] This can be taken as a figure: the two women are two covenants, one of which (Hagar, that is) comes from Mount Sinai, whose children are born slaves. [25] Hagar stands for Mount Sinai[1] in Arabia, and she is a figure of the present city of Jerusalem, a slave along with all its people. [26] But the heavenly Jerusalem is free, and she is our mother. [27] For the scripture says:

"Be happy, woman who never had children!
Shout and cry with joy, you who never felt the pains of childbirth!
For the woman who was deserted will have more children
Than the woman living with the husband."

[28] Now, you, my brothers, are God's children as a result of his promise, just

---

[1] **25** Hagar stands for Mount Sinai: *some mss. read* Sinai is a mountain

The Allegory of Hagar and Sarah

21 Λέγετέ μοι, οἱ ὑπὸ νόμον θέλοντες εἶναι, τὸν νόμον οὐκ ἀκούετε; **22** γέγραπται γὰρ ὅτι Ἀβραὰμ δύο υἱοὺς ἔσχεν, ἕνα ἐκ τῆς παιδίσκης καὶ ἕνα ἐκ τῆς ἐλευθέρας. **23** ἀλλ' ὁ μὲν ἐκ τῆς παιδίσκης κατὰ σάρκα γεγέννηται, ὁ δὲ ἐκ τῆς ἐλευθέρας δι' ἐπαγγελίας. **24** ἅτινά ἐστιν ἀλληγορούμενα· αὗται γάρ εἰσιν δύο διαθῆκαι, μία μὲν ἀπὸ ὄρους Σινᾶ, εἰς δουλείαν γεννῶσα, ἥτις ἐστὶν Ἁγάρ. **25** τὸ δὲ Ἁγὰρ Σινᾶ[4] ὄρος ἐστὶν ἐν τῇ Ἀραβίᾳ, συστοιχεῖ δὲ τῇ νῦν Ἰερουσαλήμ, δουλεύει γὰρ μετὰ τῶν τέκνων αὐτῆς. **26** ἡ δὲ ἄνω Ἰερουσαλὴμ ἐλευθέρα ἐστίν, ἥτις ἐστὶν μήτηρ ἡμῶν[5]· **27** γέγραπται γάρ,

Εὐφράνθητι, στεῖρα ἡ οὐ τίκτουσα·
ῥῆξον καὶ βόησον, ἡ οὐκ ὠδίνουσα·
ὅτι πολλὰ τὰ τέκνα τῆς ἐρήμου μᾶλλον ἢ τῆς ἐχούσης τὸν ἄνδρα.

28 ὑμεῖς[6] δέ, ἀδελφοί, κατὰ Ἰσαὰκ ἐπαγγελίας τέκνα

---

4 25 {D} δὲ Ἁγὰρ Σινᾶ A B D^{gr} 88 330 436 451 1962 2127 2492 *Lect* syr$^{hmg, pal}$ cop^{bo} ‖ γὰρ Ἁγὰρ Σινᾶ K P Ψ 062^{vid} 33 81 104 181 326 614 629 630 1877 1881 1984^c 1985 2495 *Byz* *l*^{1364,1365} syr$^{p, h}$ cop^{bomss} arm Chrysostom Theodore^{lat} Cyril Theodoret Ps-Oecumenius Theophylact ‖ δὲ Σινᾶ 𝔓^{46} it^{t,x,z} cop^{sa} Ambrosiaster ‖ γὰρ Ἁγὰρ it^{d,e} (Ambrosiaster^{comm}) ‖ γὰρ Σινᾶ ℵ C G 1241 1739 1984* it^{ar,f,g,r3} vg eth Origen^{lat} Ambrosiaster^{txt} Victorinus-Rome Epiphanius Jerome Augustine Cyril John-Damascus ‖ Σινᾶ goth Augustine

5 26 {B} ἡμῶν 𝔓^{46} ℵ* B C* D G Ψ 33 88 1241 1739 1881 2495 it$^{d,dem, e,f,g,r3,x,z}$ vg syr^{p,hmg} cop^{sa,bo} goth eth Marcion Irenaeus Tertullian Origen Pamphilus Eusebius Ambrosiaster Hilary Ephraem Gregory-Elvira Chrysostom Jerome Augustine Marcus Isidore Cyril Theodoret ‖ πάντων ἡμῶν ℵ^c A C^2 K P 81 104 181 326 330 436 451 614 629 630 1877 1962 1984 1985 2127 2492 *Byz Lect* it^{ar,t} syr^{h,pal} arm Irenaeus^{lat} Origen^{lat} Eusebius Victorinus-Rome Hilary Cyril-Jerusalem Ambrose Macarius Pelagius Jerome Theodore^{lat} Augustine Euthalius Theodoret Cosmos Cassiodorus John-Damascus

6 28 {B} ὑμεῖς...ἐστέ. 𝔓^{46} B D* G 33 1739 1881 2127 it^{d,e,g,t} syr^{pal} cop^{sa}

---

22 ἕνα ἐκ τῆς παιδίσκης Gn 16.15   ἕνα ἐκ τῆς ἐλευθέρας Gn 21.2   **23** Ro 9.7–9   **24** μία...γεννῶσα Ro 8.15; Ga 5.1   **26** ἡ δὲ ἄνω Ἰερουσαλήμ He 12.22; Re 3.12; 21.2, 10   **27** Εὐφράνθητι...ἄνδρα Is 54.1   **28** κατὰ...ἐστέ Ro 9.7; Ga 3.29

ἐστέ.[6] 29 ἀλλ' ὥσπερ τότε ὁ κατὰ σάρκα γεννηθεὶς ἐδίωκεν τὸν κατὰ πνεῦμα, οὕτως καὶ νῦν. 30 ἀλλὰ τί λέγει ἡ γραφή; **Ἔκβαλε τὴν παιδίσκην καὶ τὸν υἱὸν αὐτῆς, οὐ γὰρ μὴ κληρονομήσει ὁ υἱὸς τῆς παιδίσκης μετὰ τοῦ υἱοῦ** τῆς ἐλευθέρας. 31 διό, ἀδελφοί, οὐκ ἐσμὲν παιδίσκης τέκνα ἀλλὰ τῆς ἐλευθέρας.[c] **5** τῇ ἐλευθερίᾳ ἡμᾶς Χριστὸς ἠλευθέρωσεν· στήκετε οὖν[1] καὶ μὴ πάλιν ζυγῷ δουλείας ἐνέχεσθε.[c]

Christian Freedom

2 Ἴδε ἐγὼ Παῦλος λέγω ὑμῖν ὅτι ἐὰν περιτέμνησθε Χριστὸς ὑμᾶς οὐδὲν ὠφελήσει. 3 μαρτύρομαι δὲ πάλιν παντὶ ἀνθρώπῳ περιτεμνομένῳ ὅτι ὀφειλέτης ἐστὶν ὅλον τὸν νόμον ποιῆσαι. 4 κατηργήθητε ἀπὸ Χριστοῦ οἵτινες

---

 eth[ro] Irenaeus[gr, lat] Origen[acc. to Jerome] Ambrosiaster Victorinus-Rome Tyconius Ambrose ‖ ἡμεῖς...ἐσμέν. ℵ A C D[c] K P Ψ 062 81 88 104 181 326 330 436 451 614 629 630 1241 1877 1962 1984 1985 2492 2495 *Byz Lect* it[ar, dem, f, r3, x, z] vg syr[p, h] cop[bo] goth arm eth[pp] Chrysostom Jerome Augustine Cyril Euthalius Theodoret John-Damascus

[1] **1** {C} τῇ ἐλευθερίᾳ ἡμᾶς Χριστὸς ἠλευθέρωσεν· στήκετε οὖν ℵ* A B (P εἱλευθέρωσεν) 33 (2127 *omit ἡμᾶς and read* στῆτε) syr[pal] cop[sa] (cop[bo] τῇ γάρ) ‖ τῇ ἐλευθερίᾳ Χριστὸς ἡμᾶς ἠλευθέρωσεν· στήκετε οὖν ℵ[c] (C* ἐλευθέρωσεν) (C² *add* οὖν *after* ἐλευθερίᾳ) (H 1962 στῆτε οὖν) Ψ 81 (104 *add* ᾗ *after* ἐλευθερίᾳ) (181[c] *omit* οὖν) 330 451 1241 1739 1881 2492 (*l*[598]) ‖ τῇ ἐλευθερίᾳ ἡμᾶς Χριστὸς ἠλευθέρωσεν· στήκετε D[gr*] (D[b] ᾗ Χριστὸς ἡμᾶς, D[c] ἡμᾶς ᾗ Χριστὸς) (614 *add* οὖν *after* ἐλευθερίᾳ) (it[ar, x]) ‖ τῇ ἐλευθερίᾳ οὖν ᾗ Χριστὸς ἡμᾶς ἠλευθέρωσεν στήκετε, K 88 181* (326 *add* οὖν) (436 ὁ *for* ᾗ) 629 (630 ὑμᾶς) (1984 ὁ Χριστὸς ἠλευθέρωσεν ἡμᾶς) (1985 ἠλευθέρωσεν ἡμᾶς) *Byz Lect* (*l*[603, 809] *omit* ᾗ) ‖ τῇ ἐλευθερίᾳ ᾗ ὁ Χριστὸς ἡμᾶς ἐξηγόρασε, στήκετε 2495 ‖ ᾗ ἐλευθερίᾳ ἡμᾶς Χριστὸς ἠλευθέρωσεν, στήκετε οὖν G (1877 *transposes:* ἐλευθερίᾳ οὖν Χριστὸς ἡμᾶς) it[f, g, r3vid] (syr[p, h]) goth (arm Χριστὸς ἡμᾶς) ‖ ᾗ ἐλευθερίᾳ ἡμᾶς Χριστὸς ἠλευθέρωσεν, στήκετε it[d, e] vg[ww] (it[dem] vg[cl] eth Χριστὸς ἡμᾶς)

---

[c][c] **4.31—5.1** *c* major, *c* paragraph: RV NEB ‖ *c* paragraph, *c* major: TR Zür Luth Jer ‖ *c* paragraph, *c* paragraph: (WH) Bov Nes BF² AV ASV RSV TT Seg

---

29 ὁ κατὰ...πνεῦμα Gn 21.9   **30** Ἔκβαλε...υἱοῦ Gn 21.10; (Jn 8.35)   **31** Ga 3.29
5 1 τῇ...ἠλευθέρωσεν Jn 8.32, 36; Ga 2.4; 5.13   ζυγῷ δουλείας ἐνέχεσθε Ac 15.10

---

as Isaac was. 29 At that time the son who was born in the usual way persecuted the one who was born because of God's Spirit; and it is the same now. 30 But what does the scripture say? It says, "Throw out the slave woman and her son; for the son of the slave woman will not share the father's property with the son of the free woman." 31 So then, my brothers, we are not the children of a slave woman, but of the free woman.

Preserve Your Freedom

5 Freedom is what we have — Christ has set us free! Stand, then, as free men, and do not allow yourselves to become slaves again. 2 Listen! I, Paul, tell you this: if you allow yourselves to be circumcised, it means that Christ is of no use to you at all. 3 I want to emphasize this, and say again to any man who allows himself to be circumcised: he is obliged to obey the whole Law. 4 Those of you who try to be put right with God by obeying the

Law have cut yourselves off from Christ. You are outside God's grace. ⁵ As for us, our hope is that God will put us right with him; and this is what we wait for, by the power of God's Spirit working through our faith. ⁶ For when we are in union with Christ Jesus, neither circumcision nor the lack of it makes any difference at all; what matters is faith that works through love.

⁷ You were doing so well! Who made you stop obeying the truth? How did he persuade you? ⁸ It was not done by God, who calls you. ⁹ "It takes only a little yeast to raise the whole batch of dough," as they say. ¹⁰ But I still feel sure about you. Our union in the Lord makes me confident that you will not take a different view, and that the man who is upsetting you, whoever he may be, will be punished by God.

¹¹ But as for me, brothers, why am I still persecuted if I continue to preach that circumcision is necessary? If that were true, then my preaching about the cross of Christ would cause no trouble. ¹² I wish that the people who are upsetting you would go all the way: let them go on and castrate themselves!

¹³ As for you, my brothers, you were called to be free. But do not let this freedom become an excuse for letting your physical desires rule you. Instead, let love make you serve one another. ¹⁴ For the whole Law is summed up in one commandment: "Love your neighbor as yourself." ¹⁵ But if you act like animals, hurting and harming each other, then watch out, or you will completely destroy one another.

The Spirit and Human Nature

¹⁶ This is what I say: let the Spirit direct your lives, and do not satisfy the desires of the human nature. ¹⁷ For what our human nature wants is opposed to what the Spirit wants, and what the Spirit wants is opposed to what human nature wants: the two are enemies, and this means that you cannot do what you want to do. ¹⁸ If the Spirit leads you, then you are not subject to the Law.

¹⁹ What human nature does is quite plain. It shows itself in immoral, filthy, and indecent actions; ²⁰ in worship of idols and witchcraft. People become enemies, they fight, become jealous, angry, and ambitious. They separate into parties and groups; ²¹ they are envious,

ἐν νόμῳ δικαιοῦσθε, τῆς χάριτος ἐξεπέσατε. 5 ἡμεῖς γὰρ πνεύματι ἐκ πίστεως ἐλπίδα δικαιοσύνης ἀπεκδεχόμεθα. 6 ἐν γὰρ Χριστῷ Ἰησοῦ οὔτε περιτομή τι ἰσχύει οὔτε ἀκροβυστία, ἀλλὰ πίστις δι' ἀγάπης ἐνεργουμένη.

7 Ἐτρέχετε καλῶς· τίς ὑμᾶς ἐνέκοψεν [τῇ] ἀληθείᾳ μὴ πείθεσθαι; 8 ἡ πεισμονὴ οὐκ ἐκ τοῦ καλοῦντος ὑμᾶς. 9 μικρὰ ζύμη ὅλον τὸ φύραμα ζυμοῖ. 10 ἐγὼ πέποιθα εἰς ὑμᾶς ἐν κυρίῳ ὅτι οὐδὲν ἄλλο φρονήσετε· ὁ δὲ ταράσσων ὑμᾶς βαστάσει τὸ κρίμα, ὅστις ἐὰν ᾖ. 11 ἐγὼ δέ, ἀδελφοί, εἰ περιτομὴν ἔτι κηρύσσω, τί ἔτι διώκομαι; ἄρα κατήργηται τὸ σκάνδαλον τοῦ σταυροῦ. 12 ὄφελον καὶ ἀποκόψονται οἱ ἀναστατοῦντες ὑμᾶς.

13 Ὑμεῖς γὰρ ἐπ' ἐλευθερίᾳ ἐκλήθητε, ἀδελφοί· μόνον μὴ τὴν ἐλευθερίαν εἰς ἀφορμὴν τῇ σαρκί, ἀλλὰ διὰ τῆς ἀγάπης δουλεύετε ἀλλήλοις. 14 ὁ γὰρ πᾶς νόμος ἐν ἑνὶ λόγῳ πεπλήρωται, ἐν τῷ **Ἀγαπήσεις τὸν πλησίον σου ὡς σεαυτόν.** 15 εἰ δὲ ἀλλήλους δάκνετε καὶ κατεσθίετε, βλέπετε μὴ ὑπ' ἀλλήλων ἀναλωθῆτε.

The Fruit of the Spirit and the Works of the Flesh

16 Λέγω δέ, πνεύματι περιπατεῖτε καὶ ἐπιθυμίαν σαρκὸς οὐ μὴ τελέσητε. 17 ἡ γὰρ σὰρξ ἐπιθυμεῖ κατὰ τοῦ πνεύματος, τὸ δὲ πνεῦμα κατὰ τῆς σαρκός· ταῦτα γὰρ ἀλλήλοις ἀντίκειται, ἵνα μὴ ἃ ἐὰν θέλητε ταῦτα ποιῆτε. 18 εἰ δὲ πνεύματι ἄγεσθε, οὐκ ἐστὲ ὑπὸ νόμον. 19 φανερὰ δέ ἐστιν τὰ ἔργα τῆς σαρκός, ἅτινά ἐστιν πορνεία, ἀκαθαρσία, ἀσέλγεια, 20 εἰδωλολατρία, φαρμακεία, ἔχθραι, ἔρις, ζῆλος, θυμοί, ἐριθεῖαι, διχοστασίαι, αἱρέσεις, 21 φθόνοι², μέθαι, κῶμοι, καὶ τὰ ὅμοια τού-

---

² 21 {D} φθόνοι 𝔭⁴⁶ ℵ B 33 81 2492 l⁶⁰³,⁸⁰⁹ itᵗ copˢᵃ Marcion Irenaeusˡᵃᵗ Clement Origenˡᵃᵗ Ambrosiaster Chrysostom¹ᐟ² Jerome Augustine Eutha-

---

6 οὔτε περιτομή...ἀκροβυστία 1 Cor 7.19; Ga 6.15   8 τοῦ καλοῦντος ὑμᾶς Ga 1.6
9 1 Cor 5.6   11 τὸ σκάνδαλον τοῦ σταυροῦ 1 Cor 1.23   13 μόνον...σαρκί 1 Pe 2.16
14 Ἀγαπήσεις...σεαυτόν Lv 19.18 (Mt 5.43; 19.19; 22.39; Mk 12.31; Lk 10.27; Ro 13.9; Jas 2.8)
16 πνεύματι περιπατεῖτε Ro 8.4; Ga 5.25   17 Ro 7.15–23   ἡ γὰρ...ἀντίκειται 1 Pe 2.11
18 πνεύματι ἄγεσθε Ro 8.14   οὐκ...νόμον Ro 6.14; 7.4   19–21 1 Cor 6.9–10; Eph 5.5; Re 22.15

τοις, ἃ προλέγω ὑμῖν καθὼς προεῖπον ὅτι οἱ τὰ τοιαῦτα πράσσοντες βασιλείαν θεοῦ οὐ κληρονομήσουσιν.

22 Ὁ δὲ καρπὸς τοῦ πνεύματός ἐστιν ἀγάπη, χαρά, εἰρήνη, μακροθυμία, χρηστότης, ἀγαθωσύνη, πίστις, 23 [a]πραΰτης, ἐγκράτεια· [a]κατὰ τῶν τοιούτων οὐκ ἔστιν νόμος. 24 οἱ δὲ τοῦ Χριστοῦ [Ἰησοῦ] τὴν σάρκα ἐσταύρωσαν σὺν τοῖς παθήμασιν καὶ ταῖς ἐπιθυμίαις. 25 εἰ ζῶμεν πνεύματι, πνεύματι καὶ στοιχῶμεν. 26 μὴ γινώμεθα κενόδοξοι, ἀλλήλους προκαλούμενοι, ἀλλήλοις φθονοῦντες.

Bear One Another's Burdens

6 Ἀδελφοί, ἐὰν καὶ προλημφθῇ ἄνθρωπος ἔν τινι παραπτώματι, ὑμεῖς οἱ πνευματικοὶ καταρτίζετε τὸν τοιοῦτον ἐν πνεύματι πραΰτητος, σκοπῶν σεαυτόν, μὴ καὶ σὺ πειρασθῇς. 2 Ἀλλήλων τὰ βάρη βαστάζετε, καὶ οὕτως ἀναπληρώσετε[1] τὸν νόμον τοῦ Χριστοῦ. 3 εἰ γὰρ δοκεῖ τις εἶναί τι μηδὲν ὤν, φρεναπατᾷ ἑαυτόν· 4 τὸ δὲ ἔργον ἑαυτοῦ δοκιμαζέτω ἕκαστος, καὶ τότε εἰς ἑαυτὸν

lius ‖ φθόνοι φόνοι A C D G K P Ψ 0122 88 104 181 326 330 436 451 (629 *transposes*: φθόνοι αἱρέσεις φόνοι) 630 1241 1739 1877 1881 1962 1985 2127 2495 *Byz Lect* it[ar,c,d,(dem),e,f,g,x,z] vg syr[p,h] cop[bo] goth arm eth (Cyprian) Ambrosiaster Lucifer Ephraem Priscillian Chrysostom[1/2] Latin mss[acc.] [to Jerome] Theodore[lat] Theodoret John-Damascus

1 **2** {C} ἀναπληρώσετε B G 1962 2495 it[ar,d,dem,e,f,g,t,x,z] vg syr[p,pal] cop[sa,bo] goth eth Marcion Tertullian Cyprian Asterius[acc. to Photius] Ambrosiaster Victorinus-Rome Basil[1/2] Orosius Jerome Augustine Marcus Proclus Theodoret ‖ ἀποπληρώσετε 𝔓[46] ‖ ἀναπληρώσατε ℵ A C D[gr] K P Ψ 0122 33 81 88 104 181 326 330 436 451 614 629 630 1241 1739 1877 1881 1985 2127 2402 *Byz Lect* syr[h] arm Clement Ephraem Athanasius Basil[1/2] Didymus Chrysostom Euthalius Theodoret John-Damascus

[a a] **22-23** *a* number 23, *a* no number: TR[ed] WH Bov Nes BF[2] AV RV ASV RSV NEB? TT Zür Jer Seg ‖ *a* no number, *a* number 23: TR[ed] NEB? Luth

22 Ὁ δὲ...πνεύματος Eph 5.9   **23** κατὰ...νόμος 1 Tm 1.9   **24** Ro 6.6; Col 3.5
25 πνεύματι καὶ στοιχῶμεν Ro 8.4; Ga 5.16   **26** μὴ γινώμεθα κενόδοξοι Php 2.3
6 1 ἐὰν...τοιοῦτον Mt 18.15; Jas 5.19   2 Ἀλλήλων...βαστάζετε Ro 15.1   4 τὸ δὲ... ἕκαστος 1 Cor 11.28; 2 Cor 13.5

[handwritten:] νομος — the principle of Christ
6.4 danger of an ego-trip

get drunk, have orgies, and do other things like these. I warn you now as I have before: those who do these things will not receive the Kingdom of God. 22 But the Spirit produces love, joy, peace, patience, kindness, goodness, faithfulness, 23 humility, and self-control. There is no law against such things as these. 24 And those who belong to Christ Jesus have put to death their human nature, with all its passions and desires. 25 The Spirit has given us life; he must also control our lives. 26 We must not be proud, or irritate one another, or be jealous of one another.

Bear One Another's Burdens

6 My brothers, if someone is caught in any kind of wrongdoing, those of you who are spiritual should set him right; but you must do it in a gentle way. And keep an eye on yourself, so that you will not be tempted, too. 2 Help carry one another's burdens, and in this way you will obey the law of Christ. 3 If someone thinks he is something, when he really is nothing, he is only fooling himself. 4 Each one should judge his own conduct for himself. If it is good, then he can be proud of what he himself has done, without having to compare it with what someone else has done. ⁵ For everyone has to carry his own load.

⁶ The man who is being taught the Christian message should share all the good things he has with his teacher.

⁷ Do not deceive yourselves: no one makes a fool of God. A man will reap exactly what he plants. ⁸ If he plants in the field of his natural desires, from it he will gather the harvest of death; if he plants in the field of the Spirit, from the Spirit he will gather the harvest of eternal life. ⁹ So let us not become tired of doing good; for if we do not give up, the time will come when we will reap the harvest. ¹⁰ So then, as often as we have the chance we should do good to everyone, but especially to those who belong to our family in the faith.

Final Warning and Greeting

¹¹ See what big letters I make as I write to you now with my own hand! ¹² Those who want to show off and brag about external matters are the ones who are trying to force you to be circumcised. They do it, however, only that they may not be persecuted for the cross of Christ. ¹³ Even those who practice circumcision do not obey the Law; they want you to be circumcised so they can boast that you submitted to this physical ceremony. ¹⁴ As for me, however, I will boast only of the cross of our Lord Jesus Christ; for by means of his cross the world is dead to me, and I am dead to the world. ¹⁵ It does not matter at all whether or not one is circumcised. What does matter is being a new creature. ¹⁶ As for those who follow this rule in their lives, may peace and mercy be with them — with them and with all God's people!

μόνον τὸ καύχημα ἕξει καὶ οὐκ εἰς τὸν ἕτερον· 5 ἕκαστος γὰρ τὸ ἴδιον φορτίον βαστάσει. 6 Κοινωνείτω δὲ ὁ κατηχούμενος τὸν λόγον τῷ κατηχοῦντι ἐν πᾶσιν ἀγαθοῖς. 7 Μὴ πλανᾶσθε, θεὸς οὐ μυκτηρίζεται· ὃ γὰρ ἐὰν σπείρῃ ἄνθρωπος, τοῦτο καὶ θερίσει· 8 ὅτι ὁ σπείρων εἰς τὴν σάρκα ἑαυτοῦ ἐκ τῆς σαρκὸς θερίσει φθοράν, ὁ δὲ σπείρων εἰς τὸ πνεῦμα ἐκ τοῦ πνεύματος θερίσει ζωὴν αἰώνιον. 9 τὸ δὲ καλὸν ποιοῦντες μὴ ἐγκακῶμεν, καιρῷ γὰρ ἰδίῳ θερίσομεν μὴ ἐκλυόμενοι. 10 ἄρα οὖν ὡς καιρὸν ἔχομεν, ἐργαζώμεθα τὸ ἀγαθὸν πρὸς πάντας, μάλιστα δὲ πρὸς τοὺς οἰκείους τῆς πίστεως.

Final Warning and Benediction

11 Ἴδετε πηλίκοις ὑμῖν γράμμασιν ἔγραψα τῇ ἐμῇ χειρί. 12 ὅσοι θέλουσιν εὐπροσωπῆσαι ἐν σαρκί, οὗτοι ἀναγκάζουσιν ὑμᾶς περιτέμνεσθαι, μόνον ἵνα ᵃ τῷ σταυρῷ τοῦ Χριστοῦᵃ μὴ διώκωνται· 13 οὐδὲ γὰρ οἱ περιτεμνό-μενοι² αὐτοὶ νόμον φυλάσσουσιν, ἀλλὰ θέλουσιν ὑμᾶς περιτέμνεσθαι ἵνα ἐν τῇ ὑμετέρᾳ σαρκὶ καυχήσωνται. 14 ἐμοὶ δὲ μὴ γένοιτο καυχᾶσθαι εἰ μὴ ἐν τῷ σταυρῷ τοῦ κυρίου ἡμῶν Ἰησοῦ Χριστοῦ, δι' οὗ ἐμοὶ κόσμος ἐσταύρωται κἀγὼ κόσμῳ. 15 οὔτε γὰρ περιτομή τί ἐστιν οὔτε ἀκροβυστία, ἀλλὰ καινὴ κτίσις. 16 καὶ ὅσοι τῷ κανόνι τούτῳ στοιχήσουσιν, εἰρήνη ἐπ' αὐτοὺς καὶ ἔλεος, καὶ ἐπὶ τὸν Ἰσραὴλ τοῦ θεοῦ.

---

² 13 {C} περιτεμνόμενοι ℵ A C Dᵍʳ K P 33 81 88 104 181 326 436 629 1241 1739 1877 1962 1984 1985 *Byz* itᵃʳ,ᵈᵉᵐ,ᶠ,ˣ,ᶻ vg syrᵖ,ʰ copˢᵃ arm Marcion Chrysostom Jerome Euthalius Theodoret John-Damascus ‖ περιτετμημένοι 𝔭⁴⁶ B (G περιτεμνημένοι) Ψ 330 451 614 630 2127 2492 2495 *Lect* itᵈ,ᵉ,ᵍ,ʳ³ copᵇᵒ goth eth Ambrosiaster Victorinus-Rome Pelagius Jerome Augustine

---

ᵃ ᵃ 12 *a a* no dashes: TR Bov Nes BF² AV RV ASV RSV NEB TT Luth Jer Seg ‖ *a* none, *a* dash: WH ‖ *a* dash, *a* dash: Zür

---

5 Ro 14.12 **6** 1 Cor 9.11, 14 **8** Jn 3.6; 6.63; Ro 8.13 **9** τὸ δὲ...ἐγκακῶμεν 2 Th 3.13 **12** οὗτοι...διώκωνται Ga 5.11 **14** ἐμοὶ...Χριστοῦ 1 Cor 1.31; 2.2 **15** οὔτε γὰρ... ἀκροβυστία 1 Cor 7.19; Ga 5.6 *καινὴ κτίσις* 2 Cor 5.17 **16** εἰρήνη...Ἰσραήλ Ps 125.5; 128.6

17 Τοῦ λοιποῦ κόπους μοι μηδεὶς παρεχέτω, ἐγὼ γὰρ τὰ στίγματα τοῦ Ἰησοῦ ἐν τῷ σώματί μου βαστάζω.

18 Ἡ χάρις τοῦ κυρίου ἡμῶν Ἰησοῦ Χριστοῦ μετὰ τοῦ πνεύματος ὑμῶν, ἀδελφοί· ἀμήν.

---

17 ἐγὼ...βαστάζω 2 Cor 4.10

[17] To conclude: let no one give me any more trouble; for the scars I have on my body show that I am the slave of Jesus.

[18] May the grace of our Lord Jesus Christ be with you all, my brothers. Amen.

PAUL'S LETTER TO THE EPHESIANS

1 From Paul, who by God's will is an apostle of Christ Jesus —

To God's people who live in Ephesus,[1] those who are faithful in their life in Christ Jesus:

[2] May God our Father and the Lord Jesus Christ give you grace and peace.

Spiritual Blessings in Christ

[3] Let us give thanks to the God and Father of our Lord Jesus Christ! For he has blessed us, in our union with Christ, by giving us every spiritual gift in the heavenly world. [4] Before the world was made, God had already chosen us to be his in Christ, so that we would be holy and without fault before him. Because of his love, [5] God had already decided that through Jesus Christ he would bring us to himself as his sons — this was his pleasure and purpose. [6] Let us praise God for his glorious grace, for the free gift he gave us in his dear Son! [7] For by the death of Christ we are set free, and our sins are forgiven. How great is the grace of God, [8] which he

---

[1] **1** *Some mss. omit* in Ephesus

ΠΡΟΣ ΕΦΕΣΙΟΥΣ

Salutation

1 Παῦλος ἀπόστολος Χριστοῦ ᾿Ιησοῦ διὰ θελήματος θεοῦ τοῖς ἁγίοις τοῖς οὖσιν [ἐν ᾿Εφέσῳ][1] καὶ πιστοῖς ἐν Χριστῷ ᾿Ιησοῦ· **2** χάρις ὑμῖν καὶ εἰρήνη ἀπὸ θεοῦ πατρὸς ἡμῶν καὶ κυρίου ᾿Ιησοῦ Χριστοῦ.

Spiritual Blessings in Christ

3 Εὐλογητὸς ὁ θεὸς καὶ πατὴρ τοῦ κυρίου ἡμῶν ᾿Ιησοῦ Χριστοῦ, ὁ εὐλογήσας ἡμᾶς ἐν πάσῃ εὐλογίᾳ πνευματικῇ ἐν τοῖς ἐπουρανίοις ἐν Χριστῷ, **4** καθὼς ἐξελέξατο ἡμᾶς ἐν αὐτῷ πρὸ καταβολῆς κόσμου, εἶναι ἡμᾶς ἁγίους καὶ ἀμώμους κατενώπιον αὐτοῦ[a] ἐν ἀγάπῃ,[a] **5** προορίσας ἡμᾶς εἰς υἱοθεσίαν διὰ ᾿Ιησοῦ Χριστοῦ εἰς αὐτόν, κατὰ τὴν εὐδοκίαν τοῦ θελήματος αὐτοῦ, **6** εἰς ἔπαινον δόξης τῆς χάριτος αὐτοῦ ἧς ἐχαρίτωσεν ἡμᾶς ἐν τῷ ἠγαπημένῳ, **7** ἐν ᾧ ἔχομεν τὴν ἀπολύτρωσιν διὰ τοῦ αἵματος αὐτοῦ, τὴν ἄφεσιν τῶν παραπτωμάτων, κατὰ τὸ πλοῦτος τῆς χάριτος αὐτοῦ,[b] **8** ἧς ἐπερίσσευσεν

---

[1] **1** {C} ἐν ᾿Εφέσῳ ℵ^c A B³ D G K P Ψ? 33 81 88 104 181 326 330 436 451 614 629 630 1241 1877 1881 1962 1984 1985 2127 2492 2495 *Byz Lect* it^{ar,c,d,dem,e,f,g,r1,x,z} vg syr^{p,h} cop^{sa,bo} goth arm Ambrosiaster (Victorinus-Rome) Chrysostom Pelagius Theodore^{lat} Cyril Theodoret Ps-Jerome Cassiodorus John-Damascus ‖ *omit* 𝔭⁴⁶ ℵ* B* 424^c 1739 (Marcion) (Tertullian) Origen (Ephraem) mss^{acc. to Basil}

[a a] **4** *a* none, *a* minor: TR WH AV RV ASV RSV^{mg} (NEB) (Jer) ‖ *a* minor, *a* none: Nes BF² RV^{mg} ASV^{mg} (RSV) (NEB^{mg}) TT Zür (Luth) (Seg) ‖ *a* none, *a* none: Bov

[b b b] **7-8** *b* minor, *b* none: (WH) Bov Nes BF² ‖ *b* minor, *b* none, *b* minor: TR AV RV ASV ‖ *b* minor, *b* none, *b* major: (NEB) TT Zür Luth (Jer) (Seg) ‖ *b* none, *b* major, *b* none: RSV

---

1 Παῦλος...θεοῦ 1 Cor 1.1; Col 1.1 **3** ὁ εὐλογήσας...Χριστῷ Eph 2.6 **4** ἐξελέξατο ...αὐτῷ Jn 15.16; 17.24; 2 Th 2.13 εἶναι...αὐτοῦ Eph 5.27; Col 1.22 **5** εἰς υἱοθεσίαν...Χριστοῦ Jn 1.12 **6** τῷ ἠγαπημένῳ Mt 3.17; Col 1.13 **7** ἐν...παραπτωμάτων Col 1.14, 20 τὸ πλοῦτος...αὐτοῦ Eph 2.7

εἰς ἡμᾶς[b] ἐν πάσῃ σοφίᾳ καὶ φρονήσει[b] 9 γνωρίσας ἡμῖν τὸ μυστήριον τοῦ θελήματος αὐτοῦ, κατὰ τὴν εὐδοκίαν αὐτοῦ ἣν προέθετο ἐν αὐτῷ 10 εἰς οἰκονομίαν τοῦ πληρώματος τῶν καιρῶν, ἀνακεφαλαιώσασθαι τὰ πάντα ἐν τῷ Χριστῷ, τὰ ἐπὶ τοῖς οὐρανοῖς καὶ τὰ ἐπὶ τῆς γῆς· [c]ἐν αὐτῷ, 11[c] ἐν ᾧ καὶ ἐκληρώθημεν προορισθέντες κατὰ πρόθεσιν τοῦ τὰ πάντα ἐνεργοῦντος κατὰ τὴν βουλὴν τοῦ θελήματος αὐτοῦ, 12 εἰς τὸ εἶναι ἡμᾶς εἰς ἔπαινον δόξης αὐτοῦ τοὺς προηλπικότας ἐν τῷ Χριστῷ· 13 ἐν ᾧ καὶ ὑμεῖς ἀκούσαντες τὸν λόγον τῆς ἀληθείας, τὸ εὐαγγέλιον τῆς σωτηρίας ὑμῶν, ἐν ᾧ καὶ πιστεύσαντες ἐσφραγίσθητε τῷ πνεύματι τῆς ἐπαγγελίας τῷ ἁγίῳ, 14 ὅς[2] ἐστιν ἀρραβὼν τῆς κληρονομίας ἡμῶν,[d] εἰς ἀπολύτρωσιν τῆς περιποιήσεως, εἰς ἔπαινον τῆς δόξης αὐτοῦ.

Paul's Prayer

15 Διὰ τοῦτο κἀγώ, ἀκούσας τὴν καθ' ὑμᾶς πίστιν ἐν τῷ κυρίῳ Ἰησοῦ καὶ τὴν ἀγάπην τὴν εἰς πάντας τοὺς ἁγίους[3], 16 οὐ παύομαι εὐχαριστῶν ὑπὲρ ὑμῶν

---

[2] 14 {C} ὅς ℵ D[gr] K Ψ 33 88 330 436 451 614 629 630 1241 1984 1985 2127 2492 Byz Lect it[ar,c,dem,f,r1,x,z] vg (syr[p,h]) goth Victorinus-Rome Didymus[gr,lat] Chrysostom[comm] Theodoret John-Damascus Photius[acc. to Ps-Oecumenius] Ps-Oecumenius Theophylact ‖ ὅ 𝔭[46] A B G P 81 104 181 326 1739 1877 1881 1962 2495 it[d,e,g] Origen Athanasius[gr,lat] Ephraem Didymus Chrysostom[txt] Cyril

[3] 15 {B} καὶ τὴν ἀγάπην τὴν εἰς πάντας τοὺς ἁγίους (see Col 1.4) ℵ[v] D[v] (D[ϑ] G omit second τὴν) K Ψ 88 330 451 614 629 630 1241 1877 1962 1984 1985 2492 2495 Byz Lect it[ar,c,d,dem,e,f,g,r1,x,z] vg syr[p,h] cop[sa,bomss] goth arm Ambrosiaster Victorinus-Rome Ephraem Chrysostom Theodore[lat] Augustine Theodoret John-Damascus ‖ καὶ τὴν ἀγάπην τῆς κοινωνίας αὐτοῦ

[c,c] 10–11 c no number, c number 11: TR[ed] WH? Nes BF[2] AV RV ASV RSV NEB TT Zür Luth Jer Seg ‖ c number 11, c no number: TR[ed] WH? Bov

[d] 14 d minor: TR WH Nes AV[ed] RV ASV NEB Seg ‖ d none: Bov BF[2] AV[ed] RSV (TT) Zür Luth Jer

9 γνωρίσας...μου ἡμῖν Ro 16.25, Eph 3.3, 9   10 τοῦ πληρώματος τῶν καιρῶν Ga 4.4 ἀνακεφαλαιώσασθαι...Χριστῷ Col 1.16, 20   11 προορισθέντες κατὰ πρόθεσιν Ro 8.28–29 13 τὸν λόγον...εὐαγγέλιον Col 1.5 ἐσφραγίσθητε...ἁγίῳ Eph 4.30   14 ὅς...κληρονομίας ἡμῶν 2 Cor 1.22; 5.5   15 ἀκούσας...ἁγίους Col 1.4   16 εὐχαριστῶν...μου Col 1.3; 1 Th 1.2

---

gave to us in such large measure! In all his wisdom and insight 9 God did what he had purposed, and made known to us the secret plan he had already decided to complete by means of Christ. 10 God's plan, which he will complete when the time is right, is to bring all creation together, everything in heaven and on earth, with Christ as head.

11 For all things are done according to God's plan and decision; and God chose us to be his own people in union with Christ because of his own purpose, based on what he had decided from the very beginning. 12 Let us, then, who were the first to hope in Christ, praise God's glory!

13 And so it was with you also: when you heard the true message, the Good News that brought you salvation, you believed in Christ, and God put his stamp of ownership on you by giving you the Holy Spirit he had promised. 14 The Spirit is the guarantee that we shall receive what God has promised his people, and assures us that God will give complete freedom to those who are his. Let us praise his glory!

Paul's Prayer

15 For this reason, ever since I heard of your faith in the Lord Jesus and your love for all God's people, 16 I have not stopped giving thanks to God for you.

I remember you in my prayers, [17] and ask the God of our Lord Jesus Christ, the glorious Father, to give you the Spirit, who will make you wise and reveal God to you, so that you will know him. [18] I ask that your minds may be opened to see his light, so that you will know what is the hope to which he has called you, how rich are the wonderful blessings he promises his people, [19] and how very great is his power at work in us who believe. This power in us is the same as the mighty strength [20] which he used when he raised Christ from death, and seated him at his right side in the heavenly world. [21] Christ rules there above all heavenly rulers, authorities, powers, and lords; he is above all titles of power in this world and in the next. [22] God put all things under Christ's feet, and gave him to the church as supreme Lord over all things. [23] The church is Christ's body, the completion of him who himself completes all things everywhere.[2]

From Death to Life

2 In the past you were spiritually dead because of your disobedience and sins. [2] At that time you followed the world's evil way; you obeyed the ruler of the spiritual powers in space, the spirit who now controls the people who disobey God. [3] Actually all of us were like them, and lived according to our natural desires, and did whatever suited the wishes

---

[2] **23** who himself completes all things everywhere: *or* who is himself completely filled with God's fulness

μνείαν ποιούμενος ἐπὶ τῶν προσευχῶν μου, **17** ἵνα ὁ θεὸς τοῦ κυρίου ἡμῶν Ἰησοῦ Χριστοῦ, ὁ πατὴρ τῆς δόξης, δώῃ ὑμῖν πνεῦμα σοφίας καὶ ἀποκαλύψεως ἐν ἐπιγνώσει αὐτοῦ, **18** πεφωτισμένους τοὺς ὀφθαλμοὺς τῆς καρδίας [ὑμῶν] εἰς τὸ εἰδέναι ὑμᾶς τίς ἐστιν ἡ ἐλπὶς τῆς κλήσεως αὐτοῦ, τίς ὁ πλοῦτος τῆς δόξης τῆς κληρονομίας αὐτοῦ ἐν τοῖς ἁγίοις, **19** καὶ τί τὸ ὑπερβάλλον μέγεθος τῆς δυνάμεως αὐτοῦ εἰς ἡμᾶς τοὺς πιστεύοντας κατὰ τὴν ἐνέργειαν τοῦ κράτους τῆς ἰσχύος αὐτοῦ **20** ἣν ἐνήργησεν ἐν τῷ Χριστῷ ἐγείρας αὐτὸν ἐκ νεκρῶν, καὶ καθίσας ἐν δεξιᾷ αὐτοῦ ἐν τοῖς ἐπουρανίοις **21** ὑπεράνω πάσης ἀρχῆς καὶ ἐξουσίας καὶ δυνάμεως καὶ κυριότητος καὶ παντὸς ὀνόματος ὀνομαζομένου οὐ μόνον ἐν τῷ αἰῶνι τούτῳ ἀλλὰ καὶ ἐν τῷ μέλλοντι· **22** καὶ **πάντα ὑπέταξεν ὑπὸ τοὺς πόδας αὐτοῦ**, καὶ αὐτὸν ἔδωκεν κεφαλὴν ὑπὲρ πάντα τῇ ἐκκλησίᾳ, **23** ἥτις ἐστὶν τὸ σῶμα αὐτοῦ, τὸ πλήρωμα τοῦ τὰ πάντα ἐν πᾶσιν πληρουμένου.

From Death to Life

2 Καὶ ὑμᾶς ὄντας νεκροὺς τοῖς παραπτώμασιν καὶ ταῖς ἁμαρτίαις ὑμῶν, **2** ἐν αἷς ποτε περιεπατήσατε κατὰ τὸν αἰῶνα τοῦ κόσμου τούτου, κατὰ τὸν ἄρχοντα τῆς ἐξουσίας τοῦ ἀέρος, τοῦ πνεύματος τοῦ νῦν ἐνεργοῦντος ἐν τοῖς υἱοῖς τῆς ἀπειθείας· **3** ἐν οἷς καὶ ἡμεῖς πάντες ἀνεστράφημέν ποτε ἐν ταῖς ἐπιθυμίαις τῆς σαρκὸς ἡμῶν,

---

τὴν εἰς πάντας τοὺς ἁγίους 181 ‖ καὶ τὴν εἰς πάντας τοὺς ἁγίους ἀγάπην 81 104 326 436 2127 eth Cyril Euthalius ‖ καὶ τὴν εἰς πάντας τοὺς ἁγίους 𝔭⁴⁶ ℵ* A B P 33 1739 1881 cop^bo Origen Pelagius Jerome Augustine Cyril

17 Col 1.9–10   πνεῦμα σοφίας Is 11.2; Wsd 7.7   **18** ἡ ἐλπὶς...αὐτοῦ Eph 4.4   τῆς κληρονομίας...ἁγίοις Col 1.12   **19–20** τί...νεκρῶν 2 Cor 13.4; Col 2.12   **20** καθίσας... ἐπουρανίοις Ps 110.1; Mt 22.44; Mk 16.19; Ac 2.34; He 1.3; 8.1; 10.12; 12.2   **21** ὑπεράνω... μέλλοντι Col 1.16; 2.10   **22** πάντα ὑπέταξεν...αὐτοῦ Ps 8.6   αὐτὸν...ἐκκλησία Eph 4.15; Col 1.18   **22–23** τῇ ἐκκλησίᾳ...αὐτοῦ Ro 12.5; 1 Cor 12.27; Col 1.18   **23** τὸ πλήρωμα... πληρουμένου Eph 4.10; Col 1.19

2 1 Eph 2.5; Col 2.13   **2** ἐν αἷς...τούτου Col 3.7; Tt 3.3   κατὰ...ἀέρος Jn 12.31; Eph 6.12 τοῖς...ἀπειθείας Eph 5.6

ποιοῦντες τὰ θελήματα τῆς σαρκὸς καὶ τῶν διανοιῶν, καὶ ἤμεθα τέκνα φύσει ὀργῆς ὡς καὶ οἱ λοιποί· 4 ὁ δὲ θεὸς πλούσιος ὢν ἐν ἐλέει, διὰ τὴν πολλὴν ἀγάπην αὐτοῦ ἣν ἠγάπησεν ἡμᾶς, 5 καὶ ὄντας ἡμᾶς νεκροὺς τοῖς παραπτώμασιν συνεζωοποίησεν τῷ Χριστῷ[1] — χάριτί ἐστε σεσωσμένοι — 6 καὶ συνήγειρεν καὶ συνεκάθισεν ἐν τοῖς ἐπουρανίοις ἐν Χριστῷ Ἰησοῦ, 7 ἵνα ἐνδείξηται ἐν τοῖς αἰῶσιν τοῖς ἐπερχομένοις τὸ ὑπερβάλλον πλοῦτος τῆς χάριτος αὐτοῦ ἐν χρηστότητι ἐφ᾽ ἡμᾶς ἐν Χριστῷ Ἰησοῦ. 8 τῇ γὰρ χάριτί ἐστε σεσωσμένοι διὰ πίστεως· καὶ τοῦτο οὐκ ἐξ ὑμῶν, θεοῦ τὸ δῶρον· 9 οὐκ ἐξ ἔργων, ἵνα μή τις καυχήσηται. 10 αὐτοῦ γάρ ἐσμεν ποίημα, κτισθέντες ἐν Χριστῷ Ἰησοῦ ἐπὶ ἔργοις ἀγαθοῖς οἷς προητοίμασεν ὁ θεὸς ἵνα ἐν αὐτοῖς περιπατήσωμεν.

One in Christ

11 Διὸ μνημονεύετε ὅτι ποτὲ ὑμεῖς τὰ ἔθνη ἐν σαρκί, οἱ λεγόμενοι ἀκροβυστία ὑπὸ τῆς λεγομένης περιτομῆς ἐν σαρκὶ χειροποιήτου, 12 ὅτι ἦτε τῷ καιρῷ ἐκείνῳ χωρὶς Χριστοῦ, ἀπηλλοτριωμένοι τῆς πολιτείας τοῦ Ἰσραὴλ καὶ ξένοι τῶν διαθηκῶν τῆς ἐπαγγελίας, ἐλπίδα μὴ ἔχοντες καὶ ἄθεοι ἐν τῷ κόσμῳ. 13 νυνὶ δὲ ἐν Χριστῷ Ἰησοῦ ὑμεῖς οἵ ποτε ὄντες μακρὰν ἐγενήθητε ἐγγὺς ἐν τῷ αἵματι τοῦ Χριστοῦ.

---

[1] 5 {C} τῷ Χριστῷ ℵ A^vid D G^gr K P Ψ 81 88 104 181 326 330 436 451 614 629^c 630 1241 1739 1877 1881 1962 1984 1985 2127 2492 2495 *Byz Lect* it^(c,d,dem,e,f,r1,w,x,z) vg^ww goth Hilary Pelagius Jerome Theodore^lat Ps-Jerome Cassiodorus ‖ ἐν τῷ Χριστῷ p^46 B 33 l^599 it^(ar,g) vg^cl cop^(sa,bo) arm? Ambrosiaster Victorinus-Rome Ephraem Ambrose Chrysostom John-Damascus ‖ *with Christ* it^g syr^(p,(h),pal) Origen^lat Hilary Jerome

3 ἤμεθα...ὀργῆς Col 3.6   5 ὄντας...παραπτώμασιν Eph 2.1; Col 2.13   ὄντας... Χριστῷ Lk 15.24, 32; Ro 6.13   χάριτί ἐστε σεσωσμένοι Ac 15.11; Eph 2.8   6 συνήγειρεν ...ἐν Χριστῷ Ἰησοῦ Col 2.12   7 τὸ ὑπερβάλλον...αὐτοῦ Eph 1.7   8 τῇ...πίστεως Ac 15.11; Ga 2.16; Eph 2.5   θεοῦ τὸ δῶρον Jn 4.10; He 6.4   9 οὐκ ἐξ ἔργων Ro 3.28; 2 Tm 1.9; Tt 3.5   μή τις καυχήσηται 1 Cor 1.29   10 κτισθέντες...ἀγαθοῖς Tt 2.14   11 ποτέ...σαρκί Eph 5.8 12 ἀπηλλοτριωμένοι...ἐπαγγελίας Ro 9.4; Col 1.21   ἐλπίδα μὴ ἔχοντες 1 Th 4.13 13 ὑμεῖς...ἐγγύς Is 57.19   ἐγενήθητε...Χριστοῦ Col 1.20

---

of our own bodies and minds. Like everyone else, we too were naturally bound to suffer God's wrath.

4 But God's mercy is so abundant, and his love for us is so great, 5 that while we were spiritually dead in our disobedience he brought us to life with Christ; it is by God's grace that you have been saved. 6 In our union with Christ Jesus he raised us up with him to rule with him in the heavenly world. 7 He did this to demonstrate for all time to come the abundant riches of his grace in the love he showed us in Christ Jesus. 8 For it is by God's grace that you have been saved, through faith. It is not your own doing, but God's gift. 9 There is nothing here to boast of, since it is not the result of your own efforts. 10 God is our Maker, and in our union with Christ Jesus he has created us for a life of good works, which he has already prepared for us to do.

One in Christ

11 You Gentiles by birth — who are called the uncircumcised by the Jews, who call themselves the circumcised (which refers to what men themselves do on their bodies) — remember what you were in the past. 12 At that time you were apart from Christ. You were foreigners, and did not belong to God's chosen people. You had no part in the covenants, which were based on God's promises to his people. You lived in this world without hope and without God! 13 But now, in union with Christ Jesus, you who used to be far away have been brought near by the death of Christ.

¹⁴ For Christ himself has brought us peace, by making the Jews and Gentiles one people. With his own body he broke down the wall that separated them and kept them enemies. ¹⁵ He abolished the Jewish Law, with its commandments and rules, in order to create out of the two races a single new people in union with himself, thus making peace. ¹⁶ By his death on the cross Christ destroyed the hatred; by means of the cross he united both races into one single body and brought them back to God. ¹⁷ So Christ came and preached the Good News of peace to all — to you Gentiles, who were far away from God, and to the Jews, who were near to him. ¹⁸ It is through Christ that all of us, Jews and Gentiles, are able to come in the one Spirit into the presence of the Father.

¹⁹ So then, you Gentiles are not foreigners or strangers any longer; you are now fellow-citizens with God's people, and members of the family of God! ²⁰ You, too, are built upon the foundation laid by the apostles and prophets, the cornerstone being Christ Jesus himself. ²¹ He is the one who holds the whole building together and makes it grow into a sacred temple in the Lord. ²² In union with him you too are being built together with all the others into a house where God lives through his Spirit.

Paul's Work for the Gentiles

3 For this reason I, Paul, the prisoner of Christ Jesus for the sake of you Gentiles, pray to God. ² Surely you have

---

14 Αὐτὸς γάρ ἐστιν ἡ εἰρήνη ἡμῶν, ὁ ποιήσας τὰ ἀμφότερα ἓν καὶ τὸ μεσότοιχον τοῦ φραγμοῦ λύσας,ᵃ ᵇτὴν ἔχθραν,ᵃ ἐν τῇ σαρκὶ αὐτοῦ,ᵃ **15**ᵇ τὸν νόμον τῶν ἐντολῶν ἐν δόγμασινᵃ καταργήσας, ἵνα τοὺς δύο κτίσῃ ἐν αὐτῷ εἰς ἕνα καινὸν ἄνθρωπον ποιῶν εἰρήνην, **16** καὶ ἀποκαταλλάξῃ τοὺς ἀμφοτέρους ἐν ἑνὶ σώματι τῷ θεῷ διὰ τοῦ σταυροῦ, ἀποκτείνας τὴν ἔχθραν ἐν αὐτῷ. **17** καὶ ἐλθὼν **εὐηγγελίσατο εἰρήνην** ὑμῖν **τοῖς μακρὰν καὶ εἰρήνην τοῖς ἐγγύς·** **18** ὅτι δι᾽ αὐτοῦ ἔχομεν τὴν προσαγωγὴν οἱ ἀμφότεροι ἐν ἑνὶ πνεύματι πρὸς τὸν πατέρα. **19** ἄρα οὖν οὐκέτι ἐστὲ ξένοι καὶ πάροικοι, ἀλλὰ ἐστὲ συμπολῖται τῶν ἁγίων καὶ οἰκεῖοι τοῦ θεοῦ, **20** ἐποικοδομηθέντες ἐπὶ τῷ θεμελίῳ τῶν ἀποστόλων καὶ προφητῶν, ὄντος ἀκρογωνιαίου αὐτοῦ Χριστοῦ Ἰησοῦ, **21** ἐν ᾧ πᾶσα οἰκοδομὴ² συναρμολογουμένη αὔξει εἰς ναὸν ἅγιον ἐν κυρίῳ, **22** ἐν ᾧ καὶ ὑμεῖς συνοικοδομεῖσθε εἰς κατοικητήριον τοῦ θεοῦ ἐν πνεύματι.

Paul's Ministry to the Gentiles

3 Τούτου χάριν ἐγὼ Παῦλος ὁ δέσμιος τοῦ Χριστοῦ [Ἰησοῦ] ὑπὲρ ὑμῶν τῶν ἐθνῶν — **2** εἴ γε ἠκούσατε τὴν

---

² **21** {B} πᾶσα οἰκοδομή ℵ* B D G K Ψ 33 104 181 330 436 451 614 629 630 1739* 1877 1962 2127 2492 2495 *Byz Lect* goth Clement Origen Basil Ps-Justin Chrysostom Theodoret ∥ πᾶσα ἡ οἰκοδομή ℵᵃ A C P 81 88 326 (1241 πᾶσα ἡ κοδομή) 1739ᶜ 1881 1984 1985 syrᵖ·ʰ copˢᵃ·ᵇᵒ arm eth Origen (Basil ἡ πᾶσα οἰκοδομή) Chrysostom Euthalius Theophylact

---

ᵃ ᵃ ᵃ ᵃ **14-15** *a* minor, *a* minor, *a* minor, *a* none: Bov (NEB) Zür ∥ *a* minor, *a* none, *a* minor, *a* none: TR WH ∥ *a* minor, *a* none, *a* minor, *a* minor: AV RV ASV Jer ∥ *a* minor, *a* minor, *a* none, *a* none: Nes BF² (RSV) TT Luth (Seg)

ᵇ ᵇ **14-15** *b* no number, *b* number 15: TRᵉᵈ WH Bov Nes BF² NEB TT Zür Jer ∥ *b* number 15, *b* no number: TRᵉᵈ AV RV ASV RSV Luth Seg

---

14 Αὐτὸς...ἡμῶν Is 9.6   ὁ ποιήσας...λύσας 1 Cor 12.13; Ga 3.28   **14-15** τὴν ἔχθραν... καταργήσας Col 2.14   **15** κτίσῃ...καινὸν ἄνθρωπον 2 Cor 5.17   **16** ἀποκαταλλάξῃ... σταυροῦ Col 1.20, 22   **17** Is 57.19; 52.7; Zch 9.10   **18** Ro 5.2; Eph 3.12   **19** Eph 3.6; He 12.22-23   **20** ἐποικοδομηθέντες...ἀποστόλων Re 21.14; Mt 16.18   ὄντος...Ἰησοῦ Is 28.16; 1 Pe 2.6   **21** Eph 4.15-16; Col 2.19   ναόν...κυρίῳ 1 Cor 3.16; 2 Cor 6.16   **22** 2 Pe 2.5
3 1 ὁ δέσμιος...Ἰησοῦ Eph 4.1; Php 1.7, 13; Phm 1, 9   **2** τὴν οἰκονομίαν...ὑμᾶς Col 1.25

οἰκονομίαν τῆς χάριτος τοῦ θεοῦ τῆς δοθείσης μοι εἰς ὑμᾶς, **3** [ὅτι] κατὰ ἀποκάλυψιν ἐγνωρίσθη μοι τὸ μυστήριον, καθὼς προέγραψα ἐν ὀλίγῳ, **4** πρὸς ὃ δύνασθε ἀναγινώσκοντες νοῆσαι τὴν σύνεσίν μου ἐν τῷ μυστηρίῳ τοῦ Χριστοῦ, **5** ὃ ἑτέραις γενεαῖς οὐκ ἐγνωρίσθη τοῖς υἱοῖς τῶν ἀνθρώπων ὡς νῦν ἀπεκαλύφθη τοῖς ἁγίοις ἀποστόλοις αὐτοῦ καὶ προφήταις ἐν πνεύματι, **6** εἶναι τὰ ἔθνη συγκληρονόμα καὶ σύσσωμα καὶ συμμέτοχα τῆς ἐπαγγελίας ἐν Χριστῷ Ἰησοῦ διὰ τοῦ εὐαγγελίου, **7** οὗ ἐγενήθην διάκονος κατὰ τὴν δωρεὰν τῆς χάριτος τοῦ θεοῦ τῆς δοθείσης μοι κατὰ τὴν ἐνέργειαν τῆς δυνάμεως αὐτοῦ.[a] **8** ἐμοὶ τῷ ἐλαχιστοτέρῳ πάντων ἁγίων ἐδόθη ἡ χάρις αὕτη,[a] τοῖς ἔθνεσιν εὐαγγελίσασθαι τὸ ἀνεξιχνίαστον πλοῦτος τοῦ Χριστοῦ, **9** καὶ φωτίσαι [πάντας][1] τίς ἡ οἰκονομία τοῦ μυστηρίου τοῦ ἀποκεκρυμμένου ἀπὸ τῶν αἰώνων ἐν τῷ θεῷ τῷ τὰ πάντα κτίσαντι, **10** ἵνα γνωρισθῇ νῦν ταῖς ἀρχαῖς καὶ ταῖς ἐξουσίαις ἐν τοῖς ἐπουρανίοις διὰ τῆς ἐκκλησίας ἡ πολυποίκιλος σοφία τοῦ θεοῦ, **11** κατὰ πρόθεσιν τῶν αἰώνων ἣν ἐποίησεν ἐν τῷ Χριστῷ Ἰησοῦ τῷ κυρίῳ ἡμῶν, **12** ἐν ᾧ ἔχομεν τὴν παρρησίαν καὶ προσαγωγὴν ἐν πεποιθήσει διὰ τῆς πίστεως αὐτοῦ. **13** διὸ αἰτοῦμαι μὴ ἐγκακεῖν ἐν ταῖς θλίψεσίν μου ὑπὲρ ὑμῶν, ἥτις ἐστὶν δόξα ὑμῶν.

---

[1] **9** {D} φωτίσαι πάντας 𝔭[46] ℵ[c] B C D G K P Ψ 33 81 88 104 181 326 330 436 451 614 629 630 1241 1877 1962 1984 1985 2127 2492 2495 *Byz Lect* it[ar,c,d,dem,e,f,g,x,z] vg syr[p,h] cop[sa,bo] goth arm Marcion Tertullian Adamantius Ambrosiaster[1/2] Victorinus-Rome Didymus Chrysostom Cyril[1/2] Euthalius ∥ φωτίσαι ℵ* A 1739 1881 Origen Ambrosiaster[1/2] Hilary Jerome Augustine Cyril[1/2]

[a a] **7–8** *a* major, *a* minor: TR Bov Nes BF[2] AV RV ASV RSV (NEB) TT Zür Luth Jer (Seg) ∥ *a* dash, *a* dash: WH

---

3 Eph 1.9–10; Col 1.26   **6** Eph 2.13, 18–19   **7** οὗ...δοθείσης μοι Col 1.23, 25   **8** ἐμοὶ... χάρις αὕτη 1 Cor 15.9–10   τοῖς ἔθνεσιν εὐαγγελίσασθαι Ga 1.16   τὸ...Χριστοῦ Eph 1.7   **9** τίς...θεῷ Ro 16.25; Col 1.26   **10** γνωρισθῇ...θεοῦ 1 Pe 1.12   ἡ...θεοῦ Ro 11.33   **12** ἐν... πεποιθήσει Ro 5.20; He 4.16; 10.19   **13** ταῖς θλίψεσίν μου ὑπὲρ ὑμῶν Col 1.24

heard that God, in his grace, has given me this work to do for your good. [3] God revealed his secret plan and made it known to me. (I have written briefly about this, [4] and if you will read what I have written you can learn my understanding of the secret of Christ.) [5] In past times men were not told this secret, but God has revealed it now by the Spirit to his holy apostles and prophets. [6] The secret is this: by means of the gospel the Gentiles have a part with the Jews in God's blessings; they are members of the same body, and share in the promise that God made in Christ Jesus.

[7] I was made a servant of the gospel by God's special gift, which he gave me through the working of his power. [8] I am less than the least of all God's people; yet God gave me this privilege of taking to the Gentiles the Good News of the infinite riches of Christ, [9] and to make all men see how God's secret plan is to be put into effect. God, who is the Creator of all things, kept his secret hidden through all the past ages, [10] in order that at the present time, by means of the church, the angelic rulers and powers in the heavenly world might know God's wisdom, in all its different forms. [11] God did this according to his eternal purpose, which he achieved through Christ Jesus our Lord. [12] In union with him, and through our faith in him, we have the freedom to enter into God's presence with all confidence. [13] I beg you, then, do not be discouraged because I am suffering for you; it is all for your benefit.

The Love of Christ

¹⁴ For this reason, then, I fall on my knees before the Father, ¹⁵ from whom every family in heaven and on earth receives its true name. ¹⁶ I ask God, from the wealth of his glory, to give you power through his Spirit to be strong in your inner selves, ¹⁷ and that Christ will make his home in your hearts, through faith. I pray that you may have your roots and foundations in love, ¹⁸ and that you, together with all God's people, may have the power to understand how broad and long and high and deep is Christ's love. ¹⁹ Yes, may you come to know his love — although it can never be fully known — and so be completely filled with the perfect fulness of God.

²⁰ To him who is able to do so much more than we can ever ask for, or even think of, by means of the power working in us: ²¹ to God be the glory in the church and in Christ Jesus, for all time, for ever and ever! Amen.

To Know the Love of Christ

14 Τούτου χάριν κάμπτω τὰ γόνατά μου πρὸς τὸν πατέρα², **15** ἐξ οὗ πᾶσα πατριὰ ἐν οὐρανοῖς καὶ ἐπὶ γῆς ὀνομάζεται, **16** ἵνα δῷ ὑμῖν κατὰ τὸ πλοῦτος τῆς δόξης αὐτοῦ δυνάμει κραταιωθῆναι διὰ τοῦ πνεύματος αὐτοῦ εἰς τὸν ἔσω ἄνθρωπον, **17** κατοικῆσαι τὸν Χριστὸν διὰ τῆς πίστεως ἐν ταῖς καρδίαις ὑμῶν,ᵇ ᶜἐν ἀγάπῃᵇ ἐρριζωμένοι καὶ τεθεμελιωμένοι, **18**ᶜ ἵνα ἐξισχύσητε καταλαβέσθαι σὺν πᾶσιν τοῖς ἁγίοις τί τὸ πλάτος καὶ μῆκος καὶ ὕψος καὶ βάθος, **19** γνῶναί τε τὴν ὑπερβάλλουσαν τῆς γνώσεως ἀγάπην τοῦ Χριστοῦ, ἵνα πληρωθῆτε εἰς πᾶν τὸ πλήρωμα τοῦ θεοῦ³.

20 Τῷ δὲ δυναμένῳ ὑπὲρ πάντα ποιῆσαι ὑπερεκπερισσοῦ ὧν αἰτούμεθα ἢ νοοῦμεν κατὰ τὴν δύναμιν τὴν ἐνεργουμένην ἐν ἡμῖν, **21** αὐτῷ ἡ δόξα ἐν τῇ ἐκκλησίᾳ καὶ ἐν Χριστῷ Ἰησοῦ εἰς πάσας τὰς γενεὰς τοῦ αἰῶνος τῶν αἰώνων· ἀμήν.

---

² **14** {B} πατέρα 𝔭⁴⁶ ℵ* A B C P 33 81 1739 1962 2127 2492 itᵈᵉᵐ syrᵖᵃˡ copˢᵃ,ᵇᵒ eth (Clement) Origen²ᐟ³ Cyril-Jerusalem Epiphanius Jerome Augustine Cyril Euthalius Vigilius ∥ πατέρα τοῦ κυρίου ἡμῶν Ἰησοῦ Χριστοῦ (see 1.3) ℵᶜ D G K Ψ 88 104 181 326 330 436 451 614 629 630 1241 1877 1881 1984 1985 2495 *Byz Lect* itᵃʳ,ᶜ,ᵈ,ᵉ,ᶠ,ᵍ,ᵗ,ˣ,ᶻ vg syrᵖ,ʰ goth arm Origenᵍʳ¹ᐟ³,ˡᵃᵗ Ambrosiaster Victorinus-Rome Ephraem Basil Ps-Justin Chrysostom Latin mssᵃᶜᶜ·ᵗᵒ ᴶᵉʳᵒᵐᵉ Theodore Theodoret John-Damascus Photius

³ **19** {B} πληρωθῆτε εἰς πᾶν τὸ πλήρωμα τοῦ θεοῦ ℵ A C D G K P Ψ (81 πληροφορηθῆτε) 88 104 181 326 330 436 451 614 629 630 1241 1739 1877 1962 1984 1985 2127 2492 2495 *Byz Lect* itᵃʳ,ᶜ,ᵈ,ᵈᵉᵐ,ᵉ,ᶠ,ᵍ,(ˣ),ᶻ vg syrᵖ,ʰ,ᵖᵃˡ copᵇᵒ goth ∥ πληρωθῆτε εἰς πᾶν τὸ πλήρωμα τοῦ Χριστοῦ 1881 ∥ πληρωθῇ πᾶν τὸ πλήρωμα τοῦ θεοῦ 𝔭⁴⁶ B copˢᵃ ∥ πληρωθῇ πᾶν τὸ πλήρωμα τοῦ θεοῦ εἰς ὑμᾶς 33

ᵇ ᵇ **17** *b* minor, *b* none: TR Bov Nes BF² (AV) (RV) (ASV) (RSV) (TT) Zür (Luth) (Jer) (Seg) ∥ *b* none, *b* major: WH NEB

ᶜ ᶜ **17–18** *c* no number, *c* number 18: TRᵉᵈ WH Bov Nes BF² AV RV ASV RSV NEB TT Zür Luth Jer Seg ∥ *c* number 18, *c* no number: TRᵉᵈ

---

16 δῷ...κραταιωθῆναι Col 1.11   **17** κατοικῆσαι...ὑμῶν Jn 14.23   ἐρριζωμένοι καὶ τεθεμελιωμένοι Col 1.23; 2.7   **18** Col 2.2   **19** πληρωθῆτε...θεοῦ Col 2.10   **20** κατὰ τὴν δύναμιν...ἡμῖν Col 1.29

The Unity of the Body

4 Παρακαλῶ οὖν ὑμᾶς ἐγὼ ὁ δέσμιος ἐν κυρίῳ ἀξίως περιπατῆσαι τῆς κλήσεως ἧς ἐκλήθητε, **2** μετὰ πάσης ταπεινοφροσύνης καὶ πραΰτητος, μετὰ μακροθυμίας, ἀνεχόμενοι ἀλλήλων ἐν ἀγάπῃ, **3** σπουδάζοντες τηρεῖν τὴν ἑνότητα τοῦ πνεύματος ἐν τῷ συνδέσμῳ τῆς εἰρήνης· **4** ἐν σῶμα καὶ ἐν πνεῦμα, καθὼς καὶ ἐκλήθητε ἐν μιᾷ ἐλπίδι τῆς κλήσεως ὑμῶν· **5** εἷς κύριος, μία πίστις, ἐν βάπτισμα· **6** εἷς θεὸς καὶ πατὴρ πάντων, ὁ ἐπὶ πάντων καὶ διὰ πάντων καὶ ἐν πᾶσιν.

7 Ἑνὶ δὲ ἑκάστῳ ἡμῶν ἐδόθη ἡ χάρις κατὰ τὸ μέτρον τῆς δωρεᾶς τοῦ Χριστοῦ. **8** διὸ λέγει,

Ἀναβὰς εἰς ὕψος ᾐχμαλώτευσεν αἰχμαλωσίαν,
ἔδωκεν[1] δόματα τοῖς ἀνθρώποις.

(ᵃ**9** τὸ δὲ Ἀνέβη τί ἐστιν εἰ μὴ ὅτι καὶ κατέβη[2] εἰς τὰ κατώτερα [μέρη] τῆς γῆς; **10** ὁ καταβὰς αὐτός ἐστιν καὶ ὁ ἀναβὰς ὑπεράνω πάντων τῶν οὐρανῶν, ἵνα πληρώσῃ

---

[1] **8** {C} ἔδωκεν (see Ps 67.19 LXX) 𝔭⁴⁶ ℵ* A C² D* G 33 88 1241 1962 *l*³⁷ it^ar, c, d, dem, e, f, g, mon, t, x, z vg cop^sa, bo Marcion Justin Irenaeus^lat Tertullian Origen^lat Eusebius Ambrosiaster Hilary Lucifer Jerome ∥ καὶ ἔδωκεν ℵᶜ B C*,³ Dᶜ K P Ψ 81 104 181 326 330 436 451 614 629 630 1739 1877 1881 1984 1985 2127 2492 2495 *Byz Lect* syr^p,h goth arm eth Origen Victorinus-Rome Chrysostom Augustine Cyril Euthalius Theodoret John-Damascus

[2] **9** {B} κατέβη 𝔭⁴⁶ ℵ* A C* D G I^vid 082 33 81 1241 1739 1881 it^ar, d, e, g, mon cop^sams, bo eth Theodotus^acc. to Clement Irenaeus^lat Clement Tertullian Origen^gr, lat Eusebius Victorinus-Rome Hilary Lucifer Ambrose Chrysostom Pelagius Jerome Augustine Cyril Euthalius Theodoret Ps-Jerome Ps-Oecumenius ∥ κατέβη πρῶτον ℵᶜ B Cᶜ K P Ψ 88 104 181 326 330 436 451 614 629 630 1877 1962 1984 1985 2127 2492 2495 *Byz Lect* it^c, dem, f, t, x, z vg syr^p,h cop^sa goth arm Eusebius Ambrosiaster Theodoret Cassiodorus DJohn-amascus

---

ᵃ ᵃ **9-10** *a* parens, *a* parens: AV RV ASV RSV ∥ *a a* no parens: TR WH Bov Nes BF² NEB TT Zür Luth Jer Seg

---

1 ὁ δέσμιος ἐν κυρίῳ Eph 3.1; Php 1.7, 13; Phm 1, 9   ἀξίως...ἐκλήθητε Col 1.10   **2** Col 3.12-13   **3** Col 3.14-15   **4** ἐν σῶμα Ro 12.5; Eph 2.16   ἐν πνεῦμα Eph 2.18   **5** εἷς κύριος Jn 10.16; 1 Cor 8.6   **6** 1 Cor 12.6   **7** Ro 12.3, 6; 1 Cor 12.11   **8** Ἀναβὰς...ἀνθρώποις Ps 68.18 (Col 2.15)   **9** Jn 3.13

The Unity of the Body

4 I urge you, then — I who am a prisoner because I serve the Lord: live a life that measures up to the standard God set when he called you. ² Be humble, gentle, and patient always. Show your love by being helpful to one another. ³ Do your best to preserve the unity which the Spirit gives, by the peace that binds you together. ⁴ There is one body and one Spirit, just as there is one hope to which God has called you. ⁵ There is one Lord, one faith, one baptism; ⁶ there is one God and Father of all men, who is Lord of all, works through all, and is in all.

⁷ Each one of us has been given a special gift, in proportion to what Christ has given. ⁸ As the scripture says,

"When he went up to the very heights
He took many captives with him;
He gave gifts to men."

⁹ Now, what does "he went up" mean? It means that first he came down — that is, down to the lower depths of the earth. ¹⁰ So he who came down is the same one who went up, above and beyond the heavens, to fill the whole uni-

verse with his presence. [11] It was he who "gave gifts to men": he appointed some to be apostles, others to be prophets, others to be evangelists, others to be pastors and teachers. [12] He did this to prepare all God's people for the work of Christian service, to build up the body of Christ. [13] And so we shall all come together to that oneness in our faith and in our knowledge of the Son of God; we shall become mature men, reaching to the very height of Christ's full stature. [14] Then we shall no longer be children, carried by the waves, and blown about by every shifting wind of the teaching of deceitful men, who lead others to error by the tricks they invent. [15] Instead, by speaking the truth in a spirit of love, we must grow up in every way to Christ, who is the head. [16] Under his control all the different parts of the body fit together, and the whole body is held together by every joint with which it is provided. So when each separate part works as it should, the whole body grows and builds itself up through love.

The New Life in Christ

[17] In the Lord's name, then, I say this and insist on it: do not live any longer like the heathen, whose thoughts are worthless, [18] and whose minds are in the dark. They have no part in the life that God gives, because they are completely ignorant and stubborn. [19] They have lost all feeling of shame; they give themselves over to vice, and do all sorts of indecent things without restraint.

[20] That was not what you learned about Christ! [21] You certainly heard about him, and as his followers you were taught the truth which is in Jesus. [22] So get rid of your old self, which made you live as

τὰ πάντα.)ᵃ **11** καὶ αὐτὸς ἔδωκεν τοὺς μὲν ἀποστόλους, τοὺς δὲ προφήτας, τοὺς δὲ εὐαγγελιστάς, τοὺς δὲ ποιμένας καὶ διδασκάλους, **12** πρὸς τὸν καταρτισμὸν τῶν ἁγίωνᵇ εἰς ἔργον διακονίας, εἰς οἰκοδομὴν τοῦ σώματος τοῦ Χριστοῦ, **13** μέχρι καταντήσωμεν οἱ πάντες εἰς τὴν ἑνότητα τῆς πίστεως καὶ τῆς ἐπιγνώσεως τοῦ υἱοῦ τοῦ θεοῦ, εἰς ἄνδρα τέλειον, εἰς μέτρον ἡλικίας τοῦ πληρώματος τοῦ Χριστοῦ, **14** ἵνα μηκέτι ὦμεν νήπιοι, κλυδωνιζόμενοι καὶ περιφερόμενοι παντὶ ἀνέμῳ τῆς διδασκαλίας ἐν τῇ κυβείᾳ τῶν ἀνθρώπων ἐν πανουργίᾳ πρὸς τὴν μεθοδείαν τῆς πλάνης, **15** ἀληθεύοντες δὲ ἐν ἀγάπῃ αὐξήσωμεν εἰς αὐτὸν τὰ πάντα, ὅς ἐστιν ἡ κεφαλή, Χριστός, **16** ἐξ οὗ πᾶν τὸ σῶμα συναρμολογούμενον καὶ συμβιβαζόμενον διὰ πάσης ἁφῆς τῆς ἐπιχορηγίας κατ' ἐνέργειαν ἐν μέτρῳ ἑνὸς ἑκάστου μέρους τὴν αὔξησιν τοῦ σώματος ποιεῖται εἰς οἰκοδομὴν ἑαυτοῦ ἐν ἀγάπῃ.

The Old Life and the New

17 Τοῦτο οὖν λέγω καὶ μαρτύρομαι ἐν κυρίῳ, μηκέτι ὑμᾶς περιπατεῖν καθὼς καὶ τὰ ἔθνη περιπατεῖ ἐν ματαιότητι τοῦ νοὸς αὐτῶν, **18** ἐσκοτωμένοι τῇ διανοίᾳ ὄντες, ἀπηλλοτριωμένοι τῆς ζωῆς τοῦ θεοῦ,ᶜ διὰ τὴν ἄγνοιαν τὴν οὖσαν ἐν αὐτοῖς, διὰ τὴν πώρωσιν τῆς καρδίας αὐτῶν, **19** οἵτινες ἀπηλγηκότες ἑαυτοὺς παρέδωκαν τῇ ἀσελγείᾳ εἰς ἐργασίαν ἀκαθαρσίας πάσης ἐν πλεονεξίᾳ. **20** ὑμεῖς δὲ οὐχ οὕτως ἐμάθετε τὸν Χριστόν, **21** εἴ γε αὐτὸν ἠκούσατε καὶ ἐν αὐτῷ ἐδιδάχθητε, καθώς ἐστιν ἀλήθειαᵈ ἐν τῷ Ἰησοῦ, **22** ἀποθέσθαι ὑμᾶς κατὰ τὴν προτέραν ἀναστροφὴν τὸν παλαιὸν ἄνθρωπον τὸν φθει-

---

ᵇ **12** b none: WH Βον Nes BF² AVᵉᵈ NEB TT Zür Luth Jer ∥ b minor: TR AVᵉᵈ RV ASV RSV (Seg)
ᶜ **18** c minor: TR WH Βον Nes BF² ASV NEB TT Luth? Seg ∥ c none: AV RV RSV Zür Jer
ᵈ **21** d none: TR WH Βον Nes BF² AV RV ASV RSV NEB TT Zür Luth Jer Seg ∥ d minor: WHᵐᵍ

---

11 1 Cor 12.28   **12** πρὸς...διακονίας 2 Tm 3.17   εἰς...Χριστοῦ 1 Pe 2.5   **13** εἰς ἄνδρα τέλειον Col 1.28   **14** μηκέτι ὦμεν νήπιοι 1 Cor 14.20   **15** ὅς...Χριστός Eph 1.22; 5.23; Col 1.18   **16** Col 2.19   **17-18** μηκέτι...ὄντες Ro 1.21   **18** ἀπηλλοτριωμένοι...θεοῦ Eph 2.12; Col 1.21   διὰ τὴν ἄγνοιαν...αὐτοῖς 1 Pe 1.14   **19** Col 3.5   **22** ἀποθέσθαι...ἄνθρωπον Col 3.9   τὸν παλαιὸν...ἀπάτης Ga 6.8

ρόμενον κατὰ τὰς ἐπιθυμίας τῆς ἀπάτης, 23 ἀνανεοῦσθαι δὲ τῷ πνεύματι τοῦ νοὸς ὑμῶν, 24 καὶ ἐνδύσασθαι τὸν καινὸν ἄνθρωπον[e] τὸν κατὰ θεὸν[e] κτισθέντα ἐν δικαιοσύνῃ καὶ ὁσιότητι τῆς ἀληθείας.

Rules for the New Life

25 Διὸ ἀποθέμενοι τὸ ψεῦδος **λαλεῖτε ἀλήθειαν ἕκαστος μετὰ τοῦ πλησίον αὐτοῦ**, ὅτι ἐσμὲν ἀλλήλων μέλη. 26 **ὀργίζεσθε καὶ μὴ ἁμαρτάνετε·** ὁ ἥλιος μὴ ἐπιδυέτω ἐπὶ [τῷ] παροργισμῷ ὑμῶν, 27 μηδὲ δίδοτε τόπον τῷ διαβόλῳ. 28 ὁ κλέπτων μηκέτι κλεπτέτω, μᾶλλον δὲ κοπιάτω ἐργαζόμενος ταῖς ἰδίαις χερσὶν τὸ ἀγαθόν,[3] ἵνα ἔχῃ μεταδιδόναι τῷ χρείαν ἔχοντι. 29 πᾶς λόγος σαπρὸς ἐκ τοῦ στόματος ὑμῶν μὴ ἐκπορευέσθω, ἀλλὰ εἴ τις ἀγαθὸς πρὸς οἰκοδομὴν τῆς χρείας, ἵνα δῷ χάριν τοῖς ἀκούουσιν. 30 καὶ μὴ λυπεῖτε τὸ πνεῦμα τὸ ἅγιον τοῦ θεοῦ, ἐν ᾧ ἐσφραγίσθητε εἰς ἡμέραν ἀπολυτρώσεως. 31 πᾶσα πικρία καὶ θυμὸς καὶ ὀργὴ καὶ κραυγὴ καὶ βλασφημία ἀρθήτω ἀφ' ὑμῶν σὺν πάσῃ κακίᾳ. 32 γίνεσθε εἰς ἀλλήλους χρηστοί, εὔσπλαγχνοι, χαριζόμενοι ἑαυτοῖς

you used to — the old self which was being destroyed by its deceitful desires. [23] Your hearts and minds must be made completely new. [24] You must put on the new self, which is created in God's likeness, and reveals itself in the true life that is upright and holy.

[25] No more lying, then! Everyone must tell the truth to his brother, for we are all members together in the body of Christ. [26] If you become angry, do not let your anger lead you into sin; and do not stay angry all day. [27] Don't give the Devil a chance. [28] The man who used to rob must stop robbing and start working, to earn an honest living for himself, and to be able to help the poor. [29] Do not use harmful words in talking. Use only helpful words, the kind that build up and provide what is needed, so that what you say will do good to those who hear you. [30] And do not make God's Holy Spirit sad; for the Spirit is God's mark of ownership on you, a guarantee that the Day will come when God will set you free. [31] Get rid of all bitterness, passion, and anger. No more shouting or insults! No more hateful feelings of any sort! [32] Instead, be kind and tender-hearted to one another, and forgive one another, as God has forgiven you in Christ.

---

[3] **28** {D} ταῖς ἰδίαις χερσὶν τὸ ἀγαθόν, ℵ* A D G 81 104 330 451 1241 2127 2492 it[c, d, f, (g), mon, t] vg[cl] syr[p] goth arm eth Ambrosiaster Victorinus-Rome Basil Jerome Augustine Euthalius Antiochus John-Damascus ∥ τὸ ἀγαθὸν ταῖς ἰδίαις χερσίν, K 436 1877 1962 2495 syr[h] Theodoret ∥ τὸ ἀγαθὸν ταῖς χερσίν, Ψ 88 326 614 630 1984 1985 Byz Lect Chrysostom John-Damascus Ps-Oecumenius Theophylact ∥ ταῖς χερσὶν τὸ ἀγαθόν, p[46,vid] ℵ[c] B it[ar, e, x, z] vg[ww] cop[sams, bo] Ambrosiaster ∥ ἐν ταῖς χερσὶν αὐτοῦ τὸ ἀγαθόν, (181 τὸ ἀγαθὸν ταῖς χερσὶν αὐτοῦ,) 629 ∥ τὸ ἀγαθόν, P 33 1739 1881 it[m] Clement Origen ∥ ταῖς χερσὶν ἰδίαις, cop[sams] ∥ ταῖς χερσίν, cop[sa] Tertullian

---

[e e] **24** e none, e none: TR WH Bov Nes BF² NEB ∥ e minor, e none: AV RV ASV RSV TT Zür Luth Jer Seg ∥ e none, e minor: RV[mg] ASV[mg]

---

23 Ro 12.2   **24** ἐνδύσασθαι...ἄνθρωπον Col 3.10   ἄνθρωπον...κτισθέντα Gn 1.26 **25** λαλεῖτε...αὐτοῦ Zch 8.16; Col 3.8–9   **26** ὀργίζεσθε...ἁμαρτάνετε Ps 4.4; Jas 1.19–20 **28** ἐργαζόμενος...ἀγαθόν 1 Th 4.11   **29** πᾶς...ἐκπορευέσθω Eph 5.4; Col 3.8   δῷ... ἀκούουσιν Col 4.6   **30** μὴ...θεοῦ Is 63.10; 1 Th 5.19   ἐν...ἀπολυτρώσεως Eph 1.13–14   **31** Col 3.8 **32** Col3.12–13   χαριζόμενοι...ὑμῖν Mt 6.14; 18.22–35

Living in the Light

5 Since you are God's dear children, you must try to be like him. ² Your life must be controlled by love, just as Christ loved us and gave his life for us, as a sweet-smelling offering and sacrifice which pleases God.

³ Since you are God's people, it is not right that any questions of immorality, or indecency, or greed should even be mentioned among you. ⁴ Nor is it fitting for you to use obscene, foolish, or dirty words. Rather you should give thanks to God. ⁵ You may be sure of this: no man who is immoral, indecent, or greedy (for greediness is a form of idol worship) will ever receive a share in the Kingdom of Christ and of God.

⁶ Do not let anyone deceive you with foolish words: it is because of these very things that God's wrath will come upon

καθὼς καὶ ὁ θεὸς ἐν Χριστῷ ἐχαρίσατο ὑμῖν⁴. **5** γίνεσθε οὖν μιμηταὶ τοῦ θεοῦ, ὡς τέκνα ἀγαπητά, **2** καὶ περιπατεῖτε ἐν ἀγάπῃ, καθὼς καὶ ὁ Χριστὸς ἠγάπησεν ἡμᾶς¹ καὶ παρέδωκεν ἑαυτὸν ὑπὲρ ἡμῶν προσφορὰν² καὶ θυσίαν τῷ θεῷ εἰς ὀσμὴν εὐωδίας. **3** πορνεία δὲ καὶ ἀκαθαρσία πᾶσα ἢ πλεονεξία μηδὲ ὀνομαζέσθω ἐν ὑμῖν, καθὼς πρέπει ἁγίοις, **4** καὶ αἰσχρότης καὶ μωρολογία ἢ εὐτραπελία, ἃ οὐκ ἀνῆκεν, ἀλλὰ μᾶλλον εὐχαριστία. **5** τοῦτο γὰρ ἴστε γινώσκοντες ὅτι πᾶς πόρνος ἢ ἀκάθαρτος ἢ πλεονέκτης, ὅ ἐστιν εἰδωλολάτρης, οὐκ ἔχει κληρονομίαν ἐν τῇ βασιλείᾳ τοῦ Χριστοῦ καὶ θεοῦ.

Walk as Children of Light

6 Μηδεὶς ὑμᾶς ἀπατάτω κενοῖς λόγοις, διὰ ταῦτα γὰρ ἔρχεται ἡ ὀργὴ τοῦ θεοῦ ἐπὶ τοὺς υἱοὺς τῆς ἀπειθείας.

---

4 32 {B} ὑμῖν 𝔭⁴⁶ ℵ A G P 81 326 330 614 629 2127 2492 itᵃʳ,ᶜ,ᵈ,ᵈᵉᵐ,ᵉ,ᶠ,ᵍ,ᵐᵒⁿ,ᵗ,ˣ vgᵉˡ copˢᵃ,ᵇᵒ goth eth Clement Tertullian Origenˡᵃᵗ Ambrosiaster Victorinus-Rome Chrysostom²ᐟ³ Pelagius Jerome Euthalius John-Damascus ∥ ὑμῶν 451 ∥ ἡμῖν 𝔭⁴⁹ᵛⁱᵈ B Dᵍʳ K Ψ 33 88 104 181 436 630 1241 1739 1877 1881 1962 1984 1985 2495 *Byz Lect* itᶻ vgʷʷ syrᵖ,ʰ copᵇᵒᵐˢˢ arm Origen Chrysostom¹ᐟ³ Augustine Theodoret Ps-Jerome Cassiodorus John-Damascus Theophylact ∥ ἡμᾶς 1311

1 2 {C} ἡμᾶς 𝔭⁴⁶ ℵᶜ D G K Ψ 33 88 104 181 330 436 451 614 629 630 1739 1877 1881 1962 1984 1985 2127 2492 2495 *Byz Lect* itᶜ,ᵈ,ᵈᵉᵐ,ᵉ,ᵍ,ᵗ,ˣ,ᶻ vg syrᵖ,ʰ goth arm Clement¹ᐟ² Aphraates Ambrosiaster Basil Chrysostom Jerome Theodoret Ps-Jerome John-Damascus ∥ ὑμᾶς ℵ* A B P 0159 81 326 1241 *l*⁵⁹⁷ itᵃʳ,ᶠ,ᵐ,ᵐᵒⁿ copˢᵃ,ᵇᵒ eth Clement¹ᐟ² Victorinus-Rome Pelagius Augustine Euthalius Cassiodorus John-Damascus Theophylact

2 2 {B} ὑπὲρ ἡμῶν προσφοράν 𝔭⁴⁶,⁴⁹ (ℵ *transposes*: ὑπὲρ ἡμῶν θυσίαν καὶ προσφοράν) A (D 1984 1985 *transpose*: προσφορὰν ὑπὲρ ἡμῶν) G K P Ψ 0159 33 81 88 104 181 326 330 436 451 614 629 630 1739 1877 1881 1962 2127 2492 2495 *Byz Lect* itᵃʳ,ᶜ,ᵈ,ᵈᵉᵐ,ᵉ,ᶠ,ᵍ,ᵗ,ˣ,ᶻ vg syrᵖ,ʰ goth arm Clement Origen Aphraates Ambrosiaster Basil Chrysostom Jerome Theodoret John-Damascus ∥ ὑπὲρ ὑμῶν προσφοράν B itᵐ,ᵐᵒⁿ copˢᵃ,ᵇᵒ eth Origen Ambrosiaster Victorinus-Rome Augustine John-Damascus ∥ ὑπὲρ ἡμῶν ἐν φθορᾷ 1241

---

1 Mt 5.48   **2** περιπατεῖτε ἐν ἀγάπῃ Ro 14.15   ὁ Χριστὸς...ἡμῶν Ga 2.20   προσφορὰν ...θεῷ Ps 40.6; He 10.10   εἰς ὀσμὴν εὐωδίας Ex 29.18; Eze 20.41   **3** Col 3.5   **4** αἰσχρότης... ἀνῆκεν Eph 4.29; Col 3.8   **5** πᾶς...θεοῦ 1 Cor 6.9–10; Col 3.5   **6** Μηδεὶς...λόγοις Col 2.4, 8 ἔρχεται...ἀπειθείας Ro 1.18; Col 3.6

7 μὴ οὖν γίνεσθε συμμέτοχοι αὐτῶν· 8 ἦτε γάρ ποτε σκότος, νῦν δὲ φῶς ἐν κυρίῳ· ὡς τέκνα φωτὸς περιπατεῖτε 9 — ὁ γὰρ καρπὸς τοῦ φωτός[3] ἐν πάσῃ ἀγαθωσύνῃ καὶ δικαιοσύνῃ καὶ ἀληθείᾳ — 10 δοκιμάζοντες τί ἐστιν εὐάρεστον τῷ κυρίῳ· 11 καὶ μὴ συγκοινωνεῖτε τοῖς ἔργοις τοῖς ἀκάρποις τοῦ σκότους, μᾶλλον δὲ καὶ ἐλέγχετε, 12 τὰ γὰρ κρυφῇ γινόμενα ὑπ' αὐτῶν αἰσχρόν ἐστιν καὶ λέγειν· 13 τὰ δὲ πάντα ἐλεγχόμενα ὑπὸ τοῦ φωτὸς φανεροῦται, 14[a] πᾶν γὰρ τὸ φανερούμενον φῶς ἐστιν. [a]διὸ λέγει,

Ἔγειρε, ὁ καθεύδων,
καὶ ἀνάστα ἐκ τῶν νεκρῶν,
καὶ ἐπιφαύσει σοι ὁ Χριστός.

15 Βλέπετε οὖν ἀκριβῶς πῶς[4] περιπατεῖτε, μὴ ὡς ἄσοφοι ἀλλ' ὡς σοφοί, 16 ἐξαγοραζόμενοι τὸν καιρόν, ὅτι αἱ ἡμέραι πονηραί εἰσιν. 17 διὰ τοῦτο μὴ γίνεσθε ἄφρονες, ἀλλὰ συνίετε τί τὸ θέλημα τοῦ κυρίου. 18 καὶ μὴ μεθύσκεσθε οἴνῳ, ἐν ᾧ ἐστιν ἀσωτία, ἀλλὰ πληροῦσθε

those who do not obey him. [7] So have nothing at all to do with such people. [8] You yourselves used to be in the darkness, but since you have become the Lord's people you are in the light. So you must live like people who belong to the light. [9] For it is the light that brings a rich harvest of every kind of goodness, righteousness, and truth. [10] Try to learn what pleases the Lord. [11] Have nothing to do with people who do worthless things that belong to the darkness. Instead, bring these out to the light. [12] (It is really too shameful even to talk about the things they do in secret.) [13] And when all things are brought out to the light, then their true nature is clearly revealed, [14] for anything that is clearly revealed becomes light. That is why it is said,

"Wake up, sleeper,
Rise from the dead!
And Christ will shine upon you."

[15] So pay close attention to how you live. Don't live like ignorant men, but like wise men. [16] Make good use of every opportunity you get, because these are bad days. [17] Don't be fools, then, but try to find out what the Lord wants you to do.

[18] Do not get drunk with wine, which will only ruin you; instead, be filled with

---

[3] **9** {B} φωτός 𝔭[49] ℵ A B D* G P 33 81 330 629 1739* 1881 1962 2127 2492 *Lect* it[ar,c,d,dem,e,f,g,mon,x,z] vg syr[p,pal] cop[sa,bo] goth arm eth Origen Gregory-Thaumaturgus Ambrosiaster Victorinus-Rome Lucifer Jerome Augustine Euthalius ∥ πνεύματος (*see* Ga 5.22) 𝔭[46] D[c] K Ψ 88 104 181 326 436 451 614 630 1241 1739[mg] 1877 1984 1985 2495 *Byz* l[809] syr[h] Chrysostom Theodore[lat] Theodoret John-Damascus

[4] **15** {B} οὖν ἀκριβῶς πῶς 𝔭[46] ℵ* B 33 81 104 436 1241 1739 1962 cop[sa] Origen Chrysostom John-Damascus ∥ οὖν πῶς ἀκριβῶς D[gr] G K P Ψ 88 181 326 330 451 614 630 1877 1881 1984 1985 2127 2492 2495 *Byz Lect* it[f,g,mon] syr[p,h,pal] arm Ambrosiaster Victorinus-Rome Lucifer (Chrysostom) Jerome Theodoret John-Damascus ∥ οὖν ἀδελφοὶ πῶς ἀκριβῶς ℵ[c] A 629 it[ar,c,dem,x,z] vg cop[homss] Pelagius ∥ οὖν ἀκριβῶς ἀδελφοὶ πῶς cop[bo] ∥ οὖν πῶς it[d,e] eth

---

[a a] **13–14** *a* number 14, *a* no number: WH? Nes BF[2] NEB? TT Jer ∥ *a* no number, *a* number 14: TR WH? Bov AV RV ASV RSV NEB? Zür Luth Seg

---

8 ἦτε...κυρίῳ Eph 2.11, 13; Col 1.13; 1 Pe 2.9   τέκνα φωτός Lk 16.8; Jn 12.36   **10** Ro 12.2 **11** μὴ...σκότους Ro 16.17; 2 Th 3.6; 2 Jn 10–11   **13** τὰ...φανεροῦται Jn 3.20–21   **14** Ἔγειρε, ὁ καθεύδων Is 26.19; 51.17; 52.1; 60.1; Ro 13.11   ἀνάστα...νεκρῶν Is 26.19   ἐπιφαύσει... Χριστός Is 60.1   **16** ἐξαγοραζόμενοι τὸν καιρόν Col 4.5   ὅτι...πονηραί εἰσιν Am 5.13 **17** συνίετε...κυρίου Ro 12.2; Col 1.9   **18** μὴ μεθύσκεσθε οἴνῳ Pr 23.31 LXX

the Spirit. ¹⁹ Speak to one another in the words of psalms, hymns, and sacred songs; sing hymns and psalms to the Lord, with praise in your hearts. ²⁰ Always give thanks for everything to God the Father, in the name of our Lord Jesus Christ.

Wives and Husbands

²¹ Submit yourselves to one another, because of your reverence for Christ. ²² Wives, submit yourselves to your husbands, as to the Lord. ²³ For a husband has authority over his wife in the same way that Christ has authority over the church; and Christ is himself the Savior of the church, his body. ²⁴ And so wives must submit themselves completely to their husbands, in the same way that the church submits itself to Christ.

²⁵ Husbands, love your wives in the same way that Christ loved the church and gave his life for it. ²⁶ He did this to

ἐν πνεύματι, 19 λαλοῦντες ἑαυτοῖς [ἐν] ψαλμοῖς καὶ ὕμνοις καὶ ᾠδαῖς πνευματικαῖς⁵, ᾄδοντες καὶ ψάλλοντες τῇ καρδίᾳ ὑμῶν τῷ κυρίῳ, 20 εὐχαριστοῦντες πάντοτε ὑπὲρ πάντων ἐν ὀνόματι τοῦ κυρίου ἡμῶν Ἰησοῦ Χριστοῦ τῷ θεῷ καὶ πατρί⁶,ᵇ 21 ὑποτασσόμενοι ἀλλήλοις ἐν φόβῳ Χριστοῦ.

Wives and Husbands

22 Αἱ γυναῖκες τοῖς ἰδίοις ἀνδράσιν ὡς⁷ τῷ κυρίῳ, 23 ὅτι ἀνήρ ἐστιν κεφαλὴ τῆς γυναικὸς ὡς καὶ ὁ Χριστὸς κεφαλὴ τῆς ἐκκλησίας, αὐτὸς σωτὴρ τοῦ σώματος. 24 ἀλλὰ ὡς ἡ ἐκκλησία ὑποτάσσεται τῷ Χριστῷ, οὕτως καὶ αἱ γυναῖκες τοῖς ἀνδράσιν ἐν παντί. 25 Οἱ ἄνδρες, ἀγαπᾶτε τὰς γυναῖκας, καθὼς καὶ ὁ Χριστὸς ἠγάπησεν τὴν ἐκκλησίαν καὶ ἑαυτὸν παρέδωκεν ὑπὲρ αὐτῆς, 26 ἵνα

---

⁵ **19** {C} ᾠδαῖς πνευματικαῖς ℵ Dᵍʳ G K P Ψ 048? 33 81 88 104 (181 πνευματικούς) 326 330 436 451 614 629 630 1241 1739 1877 1881 1962 1984 1985 2127 2492 2495 *Byz Lect* itᵃʳ,ᶜ,ᵈᵉᵐ,f,g,mon,x,z vg syrᵖ,ʰ,ᵖᵃˡ copˢᵃ,ᵇᵒ goth arm ‖ ᾠδαῖς πνευματικαῖς ἐν χάριτι A ‖ ᾠδαῖς 𝔭⁴⁶ B itᵈ,ᵉ Ambrosiaster ‖ *omit* Augustine

⁶ **20** {C} θεῷ καὶ πατρί ℵ A B Dᵇ I K P Ψ 33 81 88 104 181 326 330 436 451 614 629 630 1241 1739 1877 1881 1962 1984 1985 2127 2492 2495 *Byz Lect* itᶜ,ᵈᵉᵐ,f,(x*),z vg syrᵖ,ʰ copˢᵃ,ᵇᵒ ‖ πατρὶ καὶ θεῷ 𝔭⁴⁶ D*,ᶜ G itᵃʳ,ᵈ,ᵉ,ᵍ,ᵐᵒⁿ syrᵖᵃˡ goth arm Victorinus-Rome Vigilius ‖ *omit* Pelagius

⁷ **22** {C} γυναῖκες τοῖς ἰδίοις ἀνδράσιν ὡς 𝔭⁴⁶ B Clement¹ᐟ² Origen Greek mssᵃᶜᶜ· ᵗᵒ ᴶᵉʳᵒᵐᵉ Jerome Theodore ‖ γυναῖκες τοῖς ἰδίοις ἀνδράσιν ὑποτάσσεσθε ὡς K 181 326 614 629 630 1984 *Byz Lect* syrᵖ,ʰ Chrysostom ‖ γυναῖκες ὑποτάσσεσθε τοῖς ἰδίοις ἀνδράσιν ὡς D G 1985 *l*⁵⁵ itᵈ,ᵉ,(ᵍ?) ‖ γυναῖκες ὑποτασσέσθωσαν τοῖς ἰδίοις ἀνδράσιν ὡς Ψ copˢᵃ,ᵇᵒ ‖ γυναῖκες τοῖς ἰδίοις ἀνδράσιν ὑποτασσέσθωσαν ὡς ℵ A I P 33 81 88 104 330 436 451 1241 1739 1877 1881 1962 2127 2492 2495 itᵃʳ,ᶜ,ᵈᵉᵐ,f,(ᵍ?),ᵐᵒⁿ,x,z vg syrᵖᵃˡ goth arm eth Clement¹ᐟ² Origen Ambrosiaster Victorinus-Rome Basil Jerome Euthalius Theodoret John-Damascus

---

ᵇ **20** *b* minor: TR WH Bov Nes BF² AV RV ASV Luth ‖ *b* major: RSV NEB TT Jer Seg ‖ *b* exclamation: Zür

---

19 Col 3.16 ᾄδοντες…κυρίῳ Ps 33.2, 3 **20** Col 3.17 **21** 1 Pe 5.5 **22** Gn 3.16; Col 3.18; 1 Pe 3.1 **23** ἀνήρ…γυναικός 1 Cor 11.3 **24** αἱ γυναῖκες τοῖς ἀνδράσιν Col 3.19; 1 Pe 3.7 **25** ὁ Χριστὸς…ἐκκλησίαν Eph 1.22; Col 1.18 **25–26** ἑαυτὸν…ἁγιάσῃ He 10.10, 14; 13.12

αὐτὴν ἁγιάσῃ καθαρίσας τῷ λουτρῷ τοῦ ὕδατος ἐν ῥήματι, 27 ἵνα παραστήσῃ αὐτὸς ἑαυτῷ ἔνδοξον τὴν ἐκκλησίαν, μὴ ἔχουσαν σπίλον ἢ ῥυτίδα ἤ τι τῶν τοιούτων, ἀλλ' ἵνα ᾖ ἁγία καὶ ἄμωμος. 28 οὕτως ὀφείλουσιν καὶ οἱ ἄνδρες ἀγαπᾶν τὰς ἑαυτῶν γυναῖκας ὡς τὰ ἑαυτῶν σώματα. ὁ ἀγαπῶν τὴν ἑαυτοῦ γυναῖκα ἑαυτὸν ἀγαπᾷ, 29 οὐδεὶς γάρ ποτε τὴν ἑαυτοῦ σάρκα ἐμίσησεν, ἀλλὰ ἐκτρέφει καὶ θάλπει αὐτήν, καθὼς καὶ ὁ Χριστὸς τὴν ἐκκλησίαν, 30 ὅτι μέλη ἐσμὲν τοῦ σώματος αὐτοῦ[8]. 31 **ἀντὶ τούτου καταλείψει ἄνθρωπος τὸν πατέρα καὶ τὴν μητέρα καὶ προσκολληθήσεται πρὸς τὴν γυναῖκα αὐτοῦ, καὶ ἔσονται οἱ δύο εἰς σάρκα μίαν.** 32 τὸ μυστήριον τοῦτο μέγα ἐστίν, ἐγὼ δὲ λέγω εἰς Χριστὸν καὶ εἰς τὴν ἐκκλησίαν. 33 πλὴν καὶ ὑμεῖς οἱ καθ' ἕνα ἕκαστος τὴν ἑαυτοῦ γυναῖκα οὕτως ἀγαπάτω ὡς ἑαυτόν, ἡ δὲ γυνὴ ἵνα φοβῆται τὸν ἄνδρα.

Children and Parents

6 Τὰ τέκνα, ὑπακούετε τοῖς γονεῦσιν ὑμῶν ἐν κυρίῳ[1],[a] τοῦτο γάρ ἐστιν δίκαιον.[a] 2 **τίμα τὸν πατέρα σου καὶ**

[8] 30 {B} αὐτοῦ p46 ℵ* A B 048 33 81 1739* 1881 copsa, bo eth Origenlat Methodius Euthalius Ps-Jerome ‖ αὐτοῦ καὶ ἐκ τῶν ὀστέων αὐτοῦ (see Gn 2.23) 1985 ‖ αὐτοῦ ἐκ τῆς σαρκὸς αὐτοῦ καὶ ἐκ τῶν ὀστέων αὐτοῦ (see Gn 2.23) ℵc D G P Ψ 88 104 181 326 330 436 451 614 (629vid omit τῶν) 630 1241 1739mg 1877 1962 1984 2127 2492 2495 Byz Lect itar,c,d,dem,e,f,g,mon,x,z vg syrp,h arm Irenaeusgr,lat Ambrosiaster Victorinus-Rome Chrysostom Jerome Theodore Theodoret John-Damascus ‖ αὐτοῦ ἐκ τῆς σαρκὸς αὐτοῦ καὶ τῶν στόματος αὐτοῦ (see Gn 2.23) K

[1] 1 {C} ἐν κυρίῳ p46 ℵ A Dc K P Ψ 33 81 88 104 181 326 330 436 451 614 629 630 1241 1739 1877 1881 1962 1984 1985 2127 2492 2495 Byz Lect itar,c,dem, mon,x,z vg syrp,h copsa,bo arm eth Origen Ambrosiaster Basil Chrysostom Jerome Euthalius Theodoret John-Damascus ‖ omit B D* G itd,e,f,g Marcion Clement Tertullian Cyprian Ambrosiaster (Pelagius)

a a 1 a minor, a major: WH Bov Nes BF2 AV RV ASV RSV NEB TT Zür Luth Jer Seg ‖ a major, a minor ‖ a minor, a minor: TR

26 καθαρίσας τῷ λουτρῷ Tt 3.5   27 2 Cor 11.2; Col 1.22   30 Ro 12.5; 1 Cor 6.15; 12.27; Eph 1.22-23; Col 1.18   31 Gn 2.24 (Mt 19.5)   32 Re 19.7
6 1 Col 3.20   2-3 τίμα...μητέρα and ἵνα...γῆς Ex 20.12; Dt 15.16 (Mt 15.4)

dedicate the church to God, by his word, after making it clean by the washing in water, [27] in order to present the church to himself, in all its beauty, pure and faultless, without spot or wrinkle, or any other imperfection. [28] Men ought to love their wives just as they love their own bodies. A man who loves his wife loves himself. [29] (No one ever hates his own body. Instead, he feeds it and takes care of it, just as Christ does the church; [30] for we are members of his body.) [31] As the scripture says, "For this reason, a man will leave his father and mother, and unite with his wife, and the two will become one." [32] There is a great truth revealed in this scripture, and I understand it applies to Christ and the church. [33] But it also applies to you: every husband must love his wife as himself, and every wife must respect her husband.

Children and Parents

6 Children, it is your Christian duty to obey your parents, for this is the right thing to do. [2] "Honor your father and mother" is the first commandment that has a promise added: ³ "so that all may be well with you, and you may live a long time in the land."

⁴ Parents, do not treat your children in such a way as to make them angry. Instead, raise them with Christian discipline and instruction.

Slaves and Masters

⁵ Slaves, obey your human masters, with fear and trembling; and do it with a sincere heart, as though you were serving Christ. ⁶ Do this not only when they are watching you, to gain their approval; but with all your heart do what God wants, as slaves of Christ. ⁷ Do your work as slaves cheerfully, then, as though you served the Lord, and not merely men. ⁸ Remember that the Lord will reward every man, whether slave or free, for the good work he does.

⁹ Masters, behave in the same way toward your slaves; and stop using threats. Remember that you and your slaves belong to the same Master in heaven, who treats everyone alike.

The Whole Armor of God

¹⁰ Finally, build up your strength in union with the Lord, and by means of his mighty power. ¹¹ Put on all the armor that God gives you, so that you will stand up against the Devil's evil tricks. ¹² For we are not fighting against human beings, but against the wicked

τὴν μητέρα,ᵇ ἥτις ἐστὶν ἐντολὴ πρώτηᵇ ἐν ἐπαγγελίᾳ,ᵇ 3 ἵνα εὖ σοι γένηται καὶ ἔσῃ μακροχρόνιος ἐπὶ τῆς γῆς. 4 Καὶ οἱ πατέρες, μὴ παροργίζετε τὰ τέκνα ὑμῶν, ἀλλὰ ἐκτρέφετε αὐτὰ ἐν παιδείᾳ καὶ νουθεσίᾳ κυρίου.

Slaves and Masters

5 Οἱ δοῦλοι, ὑπακούετε τοῖς κατὰ σάρκα κυρίοις μετὰ φόβου καὶ τρόμου ἐν ἁπλότητι τῆς καρδίας ὑμῶν ὡς τῷ Χριστῷ, 6 μὴ κατ' ὀφθαλμοδουλίαν ὡς ἀνθρωπάρεσκοι ἀλλ' ὡς δοῦλοι Χριστοῦ ποιοῦντες τὸ θέλημα τοῦ θεοῦᶜ ἐκ ψυχῆς,ᶜ 7 μετ' εὐνοίας δουλεύοντες, ὡς τῷ κυρίῳ καὶ οὐκ ἀνθρώποις, 8 εἰδότες ὅτι ἕκαστος, ἐάν τι ποιήσῃ ἀγαθόν, τοῦτο κομίσεται παρὰ κυρίου, εἴτε δοῦλος εἴτε ἐλεύθερος. 9 Καὶ οἱ κύριοι, τὰ αὐτὰ ποιεῖτε πρὸς αὐτούς, ἀνιέντες τὴν ἀπειλήν, εἰδότες ὅτι καὶ αὐτῶν καὶ ὑμῶν ὁ κύριός ἐστιν ἐν οὐρανοῖς, καὶ προσωπολημψία οὐκ ἔστιν παρ' αὐτῷ.

The Battle against Evil

10 Τοῦ λοιποῦ ἐνδυναμοῦσθε ἐν κυρίῳ καὶ ἐν τῷ κράτει τῆς ἰσχύος αὐτοῦ. 11 ἐνδύσασθε τὴν πανοπλίαν τοῦ θεοῦ πρὸς τὸ δύνασθαι ὑμᾶς στῆναι πρὸς τὰς μεθοδείας τοῦ διαβόλου· 12 ὅτι οὐκ ἔστιν ἡμῖν² ἡ πάλη πρὸς αἷμα καὶ

---

² 12 {D} ἡμῖν ℵ A Dᶜ I K P 0230 33 88 104 181 326 330 436 451 614 629 630 1241 1739 1877 1881 1962 1984 1985 2127 2492 2495 *Byz Lect* itᵃʳ,ᶜ,ᵈᵉᵐ,ᵍ*,ˣ,ᶻ vg syrʰ copˢᵃᵐˢˢ,ᵇᵒ arm Clement Tertullian Origenᵍʳ,ˡᵃᵗ Cyprian Methodius

---

ᵇ ᵇ ᵇ **2** *b* minor, *b* none, *b* minor: TR WH Bov Nes BF² AVᵉᵈ (NEB) TT Luth Jer ∥ *b* parens, *b* none *b* parens: AVᵉᵈ RV ASV RSV ∥ *b* dash, *b* none, *b* dash: Seg ∥ *b* dash, *b* none, *b* major: Zür ∥ *b* minor *b* minor, *b* none: WHᵐᵍ
ᶜ ᶜ **6** *c* none, *c* minor: TR Bov Nes BF² AV RV ASV RSV (NEB) TT Zür (Luth) (Jer) (Seg) ∥ *c* minor, *c* none: WH

---

4 οἱ πατέρες...ὑμῶν Col 3.21   ἐκτρέφετε...κυρίου Dt 6.7, 20–25; Ps 78.4; Pr 19.18; 22.6 **5–7** Col 3.22–23; Tt 2.9–10   **8** 2 Cor 5.10; Col 3.24–25   **9** οἱ...οὐρανοῖς Col 4.1 προσωπολημψία...αὐτῷ Dt 10.17; 2 Chr 19.17; Ac 10.34; Col 3.25   **11** ἐνδύσασθε...θεοῦ Ro 13.12; 2 Cor 10.4   **12** Jn 14.30; Eph 2.2; 1 Pe 5.8–9

σάρκα, ἀλλὰ πρὸς τὰς ἀρχάς, πρὸς τὰς ἐξουσίας, πρὸς τοὺς κοσμοκράτορας τοῦ σκότους τούτου, πρὸς τὰ πνευματικὰ τῆς πονηρίας ἐν τοῖς ἐπουρανίοις. 13 διὰ τοῦτο ἀναλάβετε τὴν πανοπλίαν τοῦ θεοῦ, ἵνα δυνηθῆτε ἀντιστῆναι ἐν τῇ ἡμέρᾳ τῇ πονηρᾷ καὶ ἅπαντα κατεργασάμενοι στῆναι. 14 στῆτε οὖν **περιζωσάμενοι τὴν ὀσφὺν ὑμῶν ἐν ἀληθείᾳ,** καὶ **ἐνδυσάμενοι τὸν θώρακα τῆς δικαιοσύνης,** 15 καὶ ὑποδησάμενοι **τοὺς πόδας ἐν ἑτοιμασίᾳ τοῦ εὐαγγελίου τῆς εἰρήνης,** 16 ἐν πᾶσιν ἀναλαβόντες τὸν θυρεὸν τῆς πίστεως, ἐν ᾧ δυνήσεσθε πάντα τὰ βέλη τοῦ πονηροῦ [τὰ] πεπυρωμένα σβέσαι· 17 καὶ **τὴν περικεφαλαίαν τοῦ σωτηρίου** δέξασθε, καὶ **τὴν μάχαιραν τοῦ πνεύματος,** ὅ ἐστιν **ῥῆμα θεοῦ,** 18 διὰ πάσης προσευχῆς καὶ δεήσεως[d] προσευχόμενοι ἐν παντὶ καιρῷ ἐν πνεύματι, καὶ εἰς αὐτὸ ἀγρυπνοῦντες ἐν πάσῃ προσκαρτερήσει καὶ δεήσει περὶ πάντων τῶν ἁγίων, 19 καὶ ὑπὲρ ἐμοῦ, ἵνα μοι δοθῇ λόγος ἐν ἀνοίξει τοῦ στόματός μου,[e] ἐν παρρησίᾳ[e] γνωρίσαι τὸ μυστήριον τοῦ εὐαγγελίου[3] 20 ὑπὲρ οὗ πρεσβεύω ἐν ἁλύσει, ἵνα ἐν αὐτῷ παρρησιάσωμαι ὡς δεῖ με λαλῆσαι.

spiritual forces in the heavenly world, the rulers, authorities, and cosmic powers of this dark age. [13] So take up God's armor now! Then when the evil day comes, you will be able to resist the enemy's attacks, and after fighting to the end, you will still hold your ground.

[14] So stand ready: have truth for a belt tight around your waist; put on righteousness for your breastplate, [15] and the readiness to announce the Good News of peace as shoes for your feet. [16] At all times carry faith as a shield; with it you will be able to put out all the burning arrows shot by the Evil One. [17] And accept salvation for a helmet, and the word of God as the sword that the Spirit gives you. [18] Do all this in prayer, asking for God's help. Pray on every occasion, as the Spirit leads. For this reason keep alert and never give up; pray always for all God's people. [19] And pray also for me, that God will give me a message, when I am ready to speak, that I may speak boldly and make known the gospel's secret. [20] For the sake of this gospel I am an ambassador, though now I am in prison. Pray, therefore, that I may be bold in speaking of it, as I should.

Eusebius Athanasius (Ephraem) Ambrose Didymus Ps-Ignatius Antiochus ∥ ὑμῖν 𝔭[46] B D* G Ψ 81 *l*[53,597vid] it[d,e,f,gᶜ,m,mon] syr[p,pal] goth eth Ambrosiaster Lucifer Ephraem Priscillian Pelagius Augustine Cassiodorus ∥ *omit* cop[sa] Origen[lat]

[3] **19** {B} τοῦ εὐαγγελίου ℵ A D I K P Ψ 33 81 88 104 181 326 330 436 451 614 629 630 1241 1739 1877 1881 1962 1984 1985 2127 2492 2495 *Byz Lect* it[ar,c,d,dem,e,f,x,z] vg syr[p,h] cop[sa,bo,fayᵐˢ] goth arm Ambrosiaster[txt] Chrysostom Jerome Euthalius Theodoret John-Damascus ∥ *omit* B G it[g,mon] cop[fayᵐˢ] Tertullian Ambrosiaster[comm] Victorinus-Rome Ephraem

---

[d] **18** *d* none: TR AV RV ASV Zür Luth Seg ∥ *d* minor: WH Bov Nes BF² RSV NEB TT Jer
[e] **19** *e* minor, *e* none: WH Bov Nes BF² RV ASV NEB (TT) Zür (Jer) Seg ∥ *e* none, *e* minor: AV RV[mg] ASV[mg] (RSV) Luth ∥ *e* none, *e* none: TR

---

14 περιζωσάμενοι...ἀληθείᾳ Is 11.5; Lk 12.35; 1 Pe 1.13   ἐνδυσάμενοι...δικαιοσύνης Is 59.17; Wsd 5.18; 1 Th 5.8   **15** ὑποδησάμενοι...εἰρήνης Is 52.7; Na 1.15; Ro 10.15   **16** τὰ βέλη...πεπυρωμένα Ps 7.13   **17** τὴν περικεφαλαίαν τοῦ σωτηρίου Is 59.17; 1 Th 5.8   τὴν μάχαιραν...θεοῦ Is 11.4; 49.2; Ho 6.5; He 4.12   **18** διὰ...καιρῷ Lk 18.1; Col 4.2–3; 1 Th 5.17   **19** Ac 4.29; Col 4.3; 2 Th 3.1   **20** ὑπὲρ οὗ πρεσβεύω 2 Cor 5.20; Phm 9   ἵνα...λαλῆσαι Col 4.4

Final Greetings

21 Tychicus, our dear brother and faithful servant in the Lord's work, will give you all the news about me, so that you may know how I am getting along. 22 That is why I am sending him to you — to tell you how all of us are getting along, and so bring courage to your hearts.
23 May God the Father and the Lord Jesus Christ give peace and love to all the brothers, with faith. 24 May God's grace be with all those who love our Lord Jesus Christ with undying love.

Final Greetings

21 Ἵνα δὲ καὶ ὑμεῖς εἰδῆτε τὰ κατ' ἐμέ, τί πράσσω, πάντα γνωρίσει ὑμῖν Τυχικὸς ὁ ἀγαπητὸς ἀδελφὸς καὶ πιστὸς διάκονος ἐν κυρίῳ, 22 ὃν ἔπεμψα πρὸς ὑμᾶς εἰς αὐτὸ τοῦτο ἵνα γνῶτε τὰ περὶ ἡμῶν καὶ παρακαλέσῃ τὰς καρδίας ὑμῶν.

23 Εἰρήνη τοῖς ἀδελφοῖς καὶ ἀγάπη μετὰ πίστεως ἀπὸ θεοῦ πατρὸς καὶ κυρίου Ἰησοῦ Χριστοῦ. 24 ἡ χάρις μετὰ πάντων τῶν ἀγαπώντων τὸν κύριον ἡμῶν Ἰησοῦν Χριστὸν ἐν ἀφθαρσίᾳ.

21–22 Τυχικὸς...ὑμᾶς Ac 20.4; Col 4.7–8; 2 Tm 4.12   24 πάντων...Χριστόν 1 Pe 1.8

ΠΡΟΣ ΦΙΛΙΠΠΗΣΙΟΥΣ

Salutation

1 Παῦλος καὶ Τιμόθεος δοῦλοι Χριστοῦ Ἰησοῦ πᾶσιν τοῖς ἁγίοις ἐν Χριστῷ Ἰησοῦ τοῖς οὖσιν ἐν Φιλίπποις σὺν ἐπισκόποις καὶ διακόνοις· **2** χάρις ὑμῖν καὶ εἰρήνη ἀπὸ θεοῦ πατρὸς ἡμῶν καὶ κυρίου Ἰησοῦ Χριστοῦ.

Paul's Prayer for the Philippians

3 Εὐχαριστῶ τῷ θεῷ μου ἐπὶ πάσῃ τῇ μνείᾳ ὑμῶν,[a] **4** πάντοτε ἐν πάσῃ δεήσει μου ὑπὲρ πάντων ὑμῶν[a] μετὰ χαρᾶς τὴν δέησιν ποιούμενος,[a] **5** ἐπὶ τῇ κοινωνίᾳ ὑμῶν εἰς τὸ εὐαγγέλιον ἀπὸ τῆς πρώτης ἡμέρας ἄχρι τοῦ νῦν, **6** πεποιθὼς αὐτὸ τοῦτο, ὅτι ὁ ἐναρξάμενος ἐν ὑμῖν ἔργον ἀγαθὸν ἐπιτελέσει ἄχρι ἡμέρας Χριστοῦ Ἰησοῦ· **7** καθώς ἐστιν δίκαιον ἐμοὶ τοῦτο φρονεῖν ὑπὲρ πάντων ὑμῶν, διὰ τὸ ἔχειν με ἐν τῇ καρδίᾳ ὑμᾶς, ἔν τε τοῖς δεσμοῖς μου καὶ ἐν τῇ ἀπολογίᾳ καὶ βεβαιώσει τοῦ εὐαγγελίου συγκοινωνούς μου τῆς χάριτος πάντας ὑμᾶς ὄντας. **8** μάρτυς γάρ μου ὁ θεός, ὡς ἐπιποθῶ πάντας ὑμᾶς ἐν σπλάγχνοις Χριστοῦ Ἰησοῦ. **9** καὶ τοῦτο προσεύχομαι,[b] ἵνα ἡ ἀγάπη ὑμῶν ἔτι μᾶλλον καὶ μᾶλλον περισσεύῃ ἐν ἐπιγνώσει καὶ πάσῃ αἰσθήσει, **10** εἰς τὸ δοκιμάζειν ὑμᾶς τὰ διαφέροντα, ἵνα ἦτε εἰλικρινεῖς καὶ ἀπρόσκοποι εἰς ἡμέραν Χριστοῦ, **11** πεπληρωμένοι καρπὸν δικαιοσύνης τὸν διὰ Ἰησοῦ Χριστοῦ εἰς δόξαν καὶ ἔπαινον θεοῦ[1].

---

[1] **11** {C} καὶ ἔπαινον θεοῦ ℵ A B Dᶜ I K P Ψ 33 81 88 104 181 326 330 436 451 614 620 630 1241 1730 1877 1881 1984 1985 2127 2492 2495 *Byz Lect* it^{ar,c,d,dem,div,e,f,rl,x} vg syr^{p,h} cop^{sa,bo,fay} arm ‖ καὶ ἔπαινον Χριστοῦ Dᵍʳ* 1962 ‖ καὶ ἔπαινόν μοι G itᵍ ‖ θεοῦ καὶ ἔπαινον ἐμοί 𝔭⁴⁶ ‖ καὶ ἔπαινον αὐτοῦ itᶻ ‖ καὶ ἔπαινον 1925

---

^{a a a} **3-4** *a* minor, *a* none, *a* minor: TR Bov Nes BF² AV RV ASV RSV (NEB) TT (Zür) (Jer) (Seg) ‖ *a* none, *a* minor, *a* minor: WH ‖ *a* dash, *a* none, *a* dash: Luth

^b **9** *b* minor: TR Bov Nes BF² AV RV ASV NEB TT Zür Luth Jer Seg ‖ *b* none: WH RSV

---

2 Ro 1.7; Ga 1.3; Phm 3   **3** Ro 1.8; 1 Cor 1.4   **6** ὁ ἐναρξάμενος...ἀγαθόν Php 2.13 ἡμέρας Χριστοῦ Ἰησοῦ 1 Cor 1.8; Php 1.10; 2.16   **8** μάρτυς...θεός Ro 1.9; 2 Cor 1.23; 1 Th 2.5 **10** τὸ...διαφέροντα Ro 2.18; 12.2; He 5.14 ἡμέραν Χριστοῦ 1 Cor 1.8; Php 1.6; 2.16   **11** Jn 15.8

PAUL'S LETTER TO THE PHILIPPIANS

1 From Paul and Timothy, servants of Christ Jesus — To all God's people living in Philippi who believe in Christ Jesus, together with the church leaders and helpers:

² May God our Father and the Lord Jesus Christ give you grace and peace.

Paul's Prayer for His Readers

³ I thank my God for you all every time I think of you; ⁴ and every time I pray for you, I pray with joy, ⁵ because of the way in which you have helped me in the work of the gospel, from the very first day until now. ⁶ And so I am sure of this: that God, who began this good work in you, will carry it on until it is finished in the Day of Christ Jesus. ⁷ You are always in my heart! And so it is only right for me to feel this way about you. For you have all shared with me in this privilege that God has given me, both now that I am in prison and also while I was free to defend and firmly establish the gospel. ⁸ God knows that I tell the truth when I say that my deep feeling for you comes from the heart of Christ Jesus himself.

⁹ This is my prayer for you: I pray that your love will keep on growing more and more, together with true knowledge and perfect judgment, ¹⁰ so that you will be able to choose what is best. Then you will be free from all impurity and blame on the Day of Christ. ¹¹ Your lives will be filled with the truly good qualities which Jesus Christ alone can produce, for the glory and praise of God.

To Live is Christ

[12] I want you to know, my brothers, that the things that have happened to me have really helped the progress of the gospel. [13] As a result, the whole palace guard and all the others here know that I am in prison because I am a servant of Christ. [14] And my being in prison has given most of the brothers more confidence in the Lord, so that they grow bolder all the time in preaching the message without fear.

[15] Of course some of them preach Christ because they are jealous and quarrelsome, but others preach him with all good will. [16] These do so from love, for they know that God has given me the work of defending the gospel. [17] The others do not proclaim Christ sincerely, but from a spirit of selfish ambition; they think that they will make more trouble for me while I am in prison.

[18] It does not matter! I am happy about it — just so Christ is preached in every way possible, whether from wrong or right motives. And I will continue to be happy, [19] for I know that, because of your prayers and the help which comes from the Spirit of Jesus Christ, I shall be set free. [20] For my deep desire and hope is that I shall never fail my duty, but that at all times, and especially right now, I shall be full of courage, so that with my whole self I shall bring honor to Christ, whether I live or die. [21] For what is life? To me, it is Christ!

To Me to Live is Christ

12 Γινώσκειν δὲ ὑμᾶς βούλομαι, ἀδελφοί, ὅτι τὰ κατ' ἐμὲ μᾶλλον εἰς προκοπὴν τοῦ εὐαγγελίου ἐλήλυθεν, **13** ὥστε τοὺς δεσμούς μου φανεροὺς ἐν Χριστῷ γενέσθαι ἐν ὅλῳ τῷ πραιτωρίῳ καὶ τοῖς λοιποῖς πᾶσιν, **14** καὶ τοὺς πλείονας τῶν ἀδελφῶν ἐν κυρίῳ πεποιθότας τοῖς δεσμοῖς μου περισσοτέρως τολμᾶν ἀφόβως τὸν λόγον λαλεῖν[2].

15 Τινὲς μὲν καὶ διὰ φθόνον καὶ ἔριν, τινὲς δὲ καὶ δι' εὐδοκίαν τὸν Χριστὸν κηρύσσουσιν· **16**[c] οἱ μὲν ἐξ ἀγάπης, εἰδότες ὅτι εἰς ἀπολογίαν τοῦ εὐαγγελίου κεῖμαι, **17**[c] οἱ δὲ ἐξ ἐριθείας τὸν Χριστὸν καταγγέλλουσιν, οὐχ ἁγνῶς, οἰόμενοι θλῖψιν ἐγείρειν τοῖς δεσμοῖς μου. **18** τί γάρ; πλὴν ὅτι παντὶ τρόπῳ, εἴτε προφάσει εἴτε ἀληθείᾳ, Χριστὸς καταγγέλλεται, καὶ ἐν τούτῳ χαίρω· ἀλλὰ καὶ χαρήσομαι, **19** οἶδα γὰρ ὅτι τοῦτό μοι ἀποβήσεται εἰς σωτηρίαν διὰ τῆς ὑμῶν δεήσεως καὶ ἐπιχορηγίας τοῦ πνεύματος Ἰησοῦ Χριστοῦ, **20** κατὰ τὴν ἀποκαραδοκίαν καὶ ἐλπίδα μου ὅτι ἐν οὐδενὶ αἰσχυνθήσομαι, ἀλλ' ἐν πάσῃ παρρησίᾳ ὡς πάντοτε καὶ νῦν μεγαλυνθήσεται Χριστὸς ἐν τῷ σώματί μου, εἴτε διὰ ζωῆς εἴτε διὰ θανάτου. **21** ἐμοὶ γὰρ τὸ ζῆν Χριστὸς καὶ τὸ ἀποθανεῖν

---

[2] **14** {D} λόγον λαλεῖν 𝔭[46vid] D[c] K 181 614 630 1739 1881 (1984 *transposes*: λαλεῖν τὸν λόγον) (1985 *transposes*: λαλῶν τὸν λόγον) (2495 λόγον λαβεῖν) *Byz Lect* it[rl] syr[h] Marcion Chrysostom Theodoret John-Damascus ‖ λόγον κυρίου λαλεῖν G it[g] ‖ λόγον τοῦ θεοῦ λαλεῖν ℵ A B P Ψ 33 81 88 104 326 330 436 451 629 1241 1877 1962 2127 2492 it[ar,c,dem,div,f,x,z] vg syr[p,h with *] cop[sa,bo,fay] goth arm eth Clement Ambrosiaster[txt] Chrysostom Euthalius ‖ λόγον λαλεῖν τοῦ θεοῦ D* it[d,e] Ambrosiaster[comm] ‖ τοῦ θεοῦ λόγον λαλεῖν 42 234 483

[c c] **16-17** c verse 16, c verse 17: WH Bov Nes BF[2] RV ASV RSV NEB TT Zür Luth Jer Seg ‖ c verse 17 (numbered 16), c verse 16 (numbered 17): TR AV

---

12 τὰ...ἐλήλυθεν 2 Tm 2.9   **13** τοὺς δεσμούς μου Eph 3.1; 4.1; Phm 1, 9   **19** τοῦτο...σωτηρίαν Job 13.16   διὰ...δεήσεως 2 Cor 1.11   **20** ἐν οὐδενί...Χριστός 1 Pe 4.16   **21** ἐμοὶ ...Χριστός Ga 2.20

κέρδος. **22** εἰ δὲ τὸ ζῆν ἐν σαρκί,[d] τοῦτό μοι καρπὸς ἔργου·[d] καὶ τί αἱρήσομαι[e] οὐ γνωρίζω. **23** συνέχομαι δὲ ἐκ τῶν δύο, τὴν ἐπιθυμίαν ἔχων εἰς τὸ ἀναλῦσαι καὶ σὺν Χριστῷ εἶναι, πολλῷ [γὰρ] μᾶλλον κρεῖσσον· **24** τὸ δὲ ἐπιμένειν [ἐν] τῇ σαρκὶ ἀναγκαιότερον δι' ὑμᾶς. **25** καὶ τοῦτο πεποιθὼς[f] οἶδα[f] ὅτι μενῶ καὶ παραμενῶ πᾶσιν ὑμῖν εἰς τὴν ὑμῶν προκοπὴν καὶ χαρὰν τῆς πίστεως, **26** ἵνα τὸ καύχημα ὑμῶν περισσεύῃ ἐν Χριστῷ Ἰησοῦ ἐν ἐμοὶ διὰ τῆς ἐμῆς παρουσίας πάλιν πρὸς ὑμᾶς.

27 Μόνον ἀξίως τοῦ εὐαγγελίου τοῦ Χριστοῦ πολιτεύεσθε, ἵνα εἴτε ἐλθὼν καὶ ἰδὼν ὑμᾶς εἴτε ἀπὼν ἀκούω τὰ περὶ ὑμῶν, ὅτι στήκετε ἐν ἑνὶ πνεύματι, μιᾷ ψυχῇ συναθλοῦντες τῇ πίστει τοῦ εὐαγγελίου, **28** καὶ μὴ πτυρόμενοι ἐν μηδενὶ ὑπὸ τῶν ἀντικειμένων, [g]ἥτις ἐστὶν αὐτοῖς ἔνδειξις ἀπωλείας, ὑμῶν δὲ σωτηρίας, καὶ τοῦτο ἀπὸ θεοῦ· **29** ὅτι ὑμῖν ἐχαρίσθη τὸ ὑπὲρ Χριστοῦ, οὐ μόνον τὸ εἰς αὐτὸν πιστεύειν ἀλλὰ καὶ τὸ ὑπὲρ αὐτοῦ πάσχειν,[g] **30** τὸν αὐτὸν ἀγῶνα ἔχοντες οἷον εἴδετε ἐν ἐμοὶ καὶ νῦν ἀκούετε ἐν ἐμοί.

Christian Humility and Christ's Humility

2 Εἴ τις οὖν παράκλησις ἐν Χριστῷ, εἴ τι παραμύθιον ἀγάπης, εἴ τις κοινωνία πνεύματος, εἴ τις σπλάγχνα καὶ οἰκτιρμοί, **2** πληρώσατέ μου τὴν χαρὰν ἵνα τὸ αὐτὸ φρονῆτε, τὴν αὐτὴν ἀγάπην ἔχοντες, σύμψυχοι, τὸ ἕν[1]

---

[1] **2** {B} ἕν 𝔭46 ℵ* B D G K P 88 104 181 326 330 436 451 614 629 630 1739

[d][d] **22** d minor, d major: TR Bov AV RVmg ASVmg RSV TT ∥ d none, d minor: Zür (Luth) Jer ∥ d dash, d minor: RV ASV ∥ d minor, d dash: WH ∥ d none, d question: NEB Seg ∥ d minor, d minor: WHmg Nes BF2

[e] **22** e none: TR WH Bov Nes BF2 AV RV ASV RSV TT (Zür) (Luth) Jer ∥ e question: WHmg RVmg ASVmg NEB Seg

[f][f] **25** f none, f none: WH ∥ f none, f minor: TR Bov Nes BF2 NEB (Seg) ∥ f minor, f none: AV RV ASV RSV TT (Zür) (Luth) Jer

[g][g] **28–29** g g no parens: TR Bov Nes BF2 AV RV ASV RSV NEB TT Zür Luth Jer Seg ∥ g parens, g parens: WH

22 τοῦτο...ἔργου Ro 1.13   **23** τὴν ἐπιθυμίαν...κρεῖσσον 2 Cor 5.8   **27** Μόνον... πολιτεύεσθε Eph 4.1; Col 1.10; 1 Th 2.12   συναθλοῦντες...εὐαγγελίου Php 4.3   **30** τὸν... εἴδετε ἐν ἐμοί Ac 16.22   νῦν...ἐμοί Php 1.13

Death, then, will bring something even better. **22** But if by living on I can do more worth-while work, then I am not sure which I should choose. **23** I am caught from both sides: I want very much to leave this life and be with Christ, which is a far better thing; **24** but it is much more important, for your sake, that I remain alive. **25** I am sure of this, and so I know that I will stay. I will stay on with you all, to add to your progress and joy in the faith. **26** So when I am with you again you will have even more reason to be proud of me, in your life in Christ Jesus.

27 Now, the important thing is that your manner of life be as the gospel of Christ requires, so that, whether or not I am able to go to see you, I will hear that you stand firm with one common purpose, and fight together, with only one wish, for the faith of the gospel. **28** Don't be afraid of your enemies; always be courageous, and this will prove to them that they will lose, and that you will win — for it is God who gives you the victory! **29** For you have been given the privilege of serving Christ, not only by believing in him, but also by suffering for him. **30** Now you can take part with me in the fight. It is the same one you saw me fighting in the past and the same one I am still fighting, as you hear.

Christ's Humility and Greatness

2 Does your life in Christ make you strong? Does his love comfort you? Do you have fellowship with the Spirit? Do you feel kindness and compassion for one another? **2** I urge you, then, make me completely happy by having the same thoughts, sharing the same love, and being one in soul and mind.

[3] Don't do anything from selfish ambition, or from a cheap desire to boast; but be humble toward each other, never thinking you are better than others. [4] And look out for each other's interests, not just for your own. [5] The attitude you should have is the one that Christ Jesus had:

[6] He always had the very nature of God,
But he did not think that by force he should try to become[1] equal with God.

[7] Instead, of his own free will he gave it all up,
And took the nature of a servant.
He became like man, he appeared in human likeness;

[8] He was humble and walked the path of obedience to death — his death on the cross.

[9] For this reason God raised him to the highest place above,
And gave him the name that is greater than any other name,

[10] So that, in honor of the name of Jesus,
All beings in heaven, and on the earth, and in the world below
Will fall on their knees,

[11] And all will openly proclaim that Jesus Christ is the Lord,
To the glory of God the Father.

---

[1] 6 to become: *or* to remain

φρονοῦντες, 3 μηδὲν κατ᾽ ἐριθείαν μηδὲ κατὰ κενοδοξίαν, ἀλλὰ τῇ ταπεινοφροσύνῃ ἀλλήλους ἡγούμενοι ὑπερέχοντας. ἑαυτῶν, 4 μὴ τὰ ἑαυτῶν ἕκαστος σκοποῦντες, ἀλλὰ καὶ τὰ ἑτέρων[a] ἕκαστοι[2].[a] 5 τοῦτο[3] φρονεῖτε ἐν ὑμῖν ὃ καὶ ἐν Χριστῷ Ἰησοῦ, 6 ὃς ἐν μορφῇ θεοῦ ὑπάρχων οὐχ ἁρπαγμὸν ἡγήσατο τὸ εἶναι ἴσα θεῷ, 7 ἀλλὰ ἑαυτὸν ἐκένωσεν μορφὴν δούλου λαβών, ἐν ὁμοιώματι ἀνθρώπων γενόμενος· [b]καὶ σχήματι εὑρεθεὶς ὡς ἄνθρωπος 8[b] ἐταπείνωσεν ἑαυτὸν γενόμενος ὑπήκοος μέχρι θανάτου, θανάτου δὲ σταυροῦ. 9 διὸ καὶ ὁ θεὸς αὐτὸν ὑπερύψωσεν καὶ ἐχαρίσατο αὐτῷ τὸ ὄνομα τὸ ὑπὲρ πᾶν ὄνομα, 10 ἵνα ἐν τῷ ὀνόματι Ἰησοῦ πᾶν γόνυ κάμψῃ ἐπουρανίων καὶ ἐπιγείων καὶ καταχθονίων, 11 καὶ πᾶσα γλῶσσα ἐξομολογήσεται ὅτι κύριος Ἰησοῦς Χριστὸς εἰς δόξαν θεοῦ πατρός.

1877 1881 1984 1985 2127 2492 *Byz Lect* it[d,e,g,m] syr[p,h] arm? eth Clement Ambrosiaster Victorinus-Rome Hilary Basil Pelagius Augustine ‖ αὐτό ℵ* A C I Ψ 33 81 1241 1962 2495 it[ar,c,dem,div,f,x,z] vg goth Euthalius

[2] 4 {B} ἕκαστοι 𝔭46 ℵ A B D[gr] P Ψ 33 81[vid] 104 1241 1739 1881 1962 2127 Victorinus-Rome Basil Augustine Cyril Euthalius ‖ ἕκαστος C K 88 181 326 330 436 451 614 629 630 1877 1984 1985 2492 2495 *Byz Lect* it[d,e] syr[p,h] (cop[bo?]) goth arm Chrysostom Theodoret John-Damascus ‖ *omit* G it[ar,c,dem,div,f,g,m,x,z] vg cop[sa] eth Ambrosiaster

[3] 5 {C} τοῦτο ℵ* A B C Ψ 33 81 1241 1985 2495 (*Lect beginning of lection*) it[t] cop[sa,bo] arm eth Origen Euthalius ‖ τοῦτο γάρ 𝔭46 ℵ[c] D G K P 88 104 181 326 436 614 630 1739 1877 1881 1962 1984 2127 *Byz* it[ar,c,d,dem,div,e,f,g,m,x,z] vg syr[h,pal] goth Ambrosiaster Victorinus-Rome Hilary Chrysostom Theodoret John-Damascus ‖ τοῦτο οὖν 330 451 2492 ‖ καὶ τοῦτο syr[p]

[a a] **4–5** *a* none, *a* major: WH Bov Nes BF² AV? RV ASV RSV NEB TT Zür Jer Seg ‖ *a* major, *a* none: WH[mg] Luth ‖ different text: TR AV?

[b b] **7–8** *b* no number, *b* number 8: TR[ed] WH Bov Nes BF² TT Zür Luth Jer ‖ *b* number 8, *b* no number: TR[ed] AV RV ASV RSV NEB Seg

---

3 μηδὲ κατὰ κενοδοξίαν Ga 5.26 ἀλλήλους...ἑαυτῶν Ro 12.10 **4** 1 Cor 10.24, 33 **6** οὐχ...θεῷ Jn 1.1, 2; 17.5 **7** ἑαυτὸν ἐκένωσεν 2 Cor 8.9 ἐν...γενόμενος Jn 1.14; Ro 8.3; He 2.14, 17 **8** ἐταπείνωσεν...θανάτου Jn 10.17; He 5.8; 12.2 **9** ὁ θεὸς αὐτὸν ὑπερύψωσεν Ac 2.33; He 1.3 ἐχαρίσατο...ὄνομα Eph 1.21; He 1.4 **10–11** πᾶν...ἐξομολογήσεται Is 45.23; Ro 14.11

Shining as Lights in the World

12 Ὥστε, ἀγαπητοί μου, καθὼς πάντοτε ὑπηκούσατε, μὴ ὡς[4] ἐν τῇ παρουσίᾳ μου μόνον ἀλλὰ νῦν πολλῷ μᾶλλον ἐν τῇ ἀπουσίᾳ μου, μετὰ φόβου καὶ τρόμου τὴν ἑαυτῶν σωτηρίαν κατεργάζεσθε· **13** θεὸς γάρ ἐστιν ὁ ἐνεργῶν ἐν ὑμῖν καὶ τὸ θέλειν καὶ τὸ ἐνεργεῖν ὑπὲρ τῆς εὐδοκίας. **14** πάντα ποιεῖτε χωρὶς γογγυσμῶν καὶ διαλογισμῶν, **15** ἵνα γένησθε ἄμεμπτοι καὶ ἀκέραιοι, τέκνα θεοῦ ἄμωμα μέσον γενεᾶς σκολιᾶς καὶ διεστραμμένης,[c] ἐν οἷς φαίνεσθε ὡς φωστῆρες ἐν κόσμῳ, **16** λόγον ζωῆς ἐπέχοντες, εἰς καύχημα ἐμοὶ εἰς ἡμέραν Χριστοῦ, ὅτι οὐκ εἰς κενὸν ἔδραμον οὐδὲ εἰς κενὸν ἐκοπίασα. **17** ἀλλὰ εἰ καὶ σπένδομαι ἐπὶ τῇ θυσίᾳ καὶ λειτουργίᾳ τῆς πίστεως ὑμῶν, χαίρω καὶ συγχαίρω πᾶσιν ὑμῖν· **18** τὸ δὲ αὐτὸ καὶ ὑμεῖς χαίρετε καὶ συγχαίρετέ μοι.

Timothy and Epaphroditus

19 Ἐλπίζω δὲ ἐν κυρίῳ Ἰησοῦ Τιμόθεον ταχέως πέμψαι ὑμῖν, ἵνα κἀγὼ εὐψυχῶ γνοὺς τὰ περὶ ὑμῶν. **20** οὐδένα γὰρ ἔχω ἰσόψυχον ὅστις γνησίως τὰ περὶ ὑμῶν μεριμνήσει, **21** οἱ πάντες γὰρ τὰ ἑαυτῶν ζητοῦσιν, οὐ τὰ Ἰησοῦ Χριστοῦ. **22** τὴν δὲ δοκιμὴν αὐτοῦ γινώσκετε, ὅτι ὡς πατρὶ τέκνον σὺν ἐμοὶ ἐδούλευσεν εἰς τὸ εὐαγγέλιον.

---

[4] **12** {B} ὡς p⁴⁶ ℵ A C D G K P Ψ 81 88 104 181 326 330 436 451 614 629 630 1739 1877 1881 1962 1984 1985 2127 2492 2495 *Byz Lect* it^(ar,c,d,dem,div*,e,f,g,x,z*) vg syr^h ∥ *omit* B 33 1241 it^(div^c,z^c) syr^p cop^(sa,bo) arm eth Ambrosiaster Chrysostom Cassiodorus

---

[c] **15** *c minor:* TR WH Bov Nes BF² AV RV ASV RSV NEB TT Zür Luth Jer Seg ∥ *c major:* NEB^mg

---

12 μετὰ...κατεργάζεσθε Ps 2.11; 1 Pe 1.17   **13** θεὸς...ὑμῖν Jn 15.5; 1 Cor 12.6; 15.10; 2 Cor 3.5; 1 Th 2.13   **14** πάντα...γογγυσμῶν 1 Cor 10.10; 1 Pe 4.9   **15** γενεᾶς... διεστραμμένης Dt 32.5; Mt 10.16; Ac 2.40   ἐν...κόσμῳ Dn 12.3; Mt 5.14; Eph 5.8 **16** λόγον...ἐμοί 1 Th 2.19   ἡμέραν Χριστοῦ 1 Cor 1.8; Php 1.6, 10   οὐκ...ἐκοπίασα Is 49.4; 65.23; Ga 2.2   **17** σπένδομαι...ὑμῶν Ro 15.16; 2 Tm 4.6   **18** τὸ...χαίρετε Php 3.1; 4.4 **21** 2 Tm 4.10

Shining as Lights in the World

[12] So then, dear friends, as you always obeyed me when I was with you, it is even more important that you obey me now, while I am away from you. <u>Keep on working, with fear and trembling, to complete your salvation,</u> [13] <u>for God is always at work in you to make you willing and able to obey his own purpose.</u> [14] Do everything without complaining or arguing, [15] that you may be innocent and pure, as God's perfect children who live in a world of crooked and mean people. You must shine among them like stars lighting up the sky, [16] as you offer them the message of life. If you do so, I shall have reason to be proud of you on the Day of Christ; for it will show that all my effort and work have not been wasted. [17] Perhaps my life's blood is to be poured out like an offering on the sacrifice that your faith offers to God. If that is so, I am glad, and share my joy with you all. [18] In the same way, you too must be glad and share your joy with me.

Timothy and Epaphroditus

[19] I trust in the Lord Jesus that I will be able to send Timothy to you soon, so that I may be encouraged by news of you. [20] He is the only one who shares my feelings, and who really cares about you. [21] Everyone else is concerned only about his own affairs, not about the cause of Jesus Christ. [22] And you yourselves know how he has proved his worth, how he and I, like father and son, have worked together for the sake of

the gospel. [23] I hope to send him to you, then, as soon as I know how things are going to turn out for me; [24] and I trust in the Lord that I myself will be able to come to you soon.

[25] I have thought it necessary to send you our brother Epaphroditus, who has worked and fought by my side, and who has served as your messenger in helping me. [26] He is anxious to see you all, and is very upset because you heard that he was sick. [27] Indeed he was sick, and almost died — but God had pity on him; and not only on him but on me, too, and spared me even greater sorrow. [28] I am all the more eager, therefore, to send him to you, so that you will be glad again when you see him, and my own sorrow will disappear. [29] Receive him, then, with all joy, as a brother in the Lord. Show respect to all such men as he, [30] because he risked his life and nearly died, for the sake of the work of Christ, in order to give me the help that you yourselves could not give.

The True Righteousness

3 And in conclusion, my brothers, may the Lord give you much joy. It doesn't bother me to repeat what I have written before, and it will add to your safety.

23 τοῦτον μὲν οὖν ἐλπίζω πέμψαι ὡς ἂν ἀφίδω τὰ περὶ ἐμὲ ἐξαυτῆς· **24** πέποιθα δὲ ἐν κυρίῳ ὅτι καὶ αὐτὸς ταχέως ἐλεύσομαι.

25 Ἀναγκαῖον δὲ ἡγησάμην Ἐπαφρόδιτον τὸν ἀδελφὸν καὶ συνεργὸν καὶ συστρατιώτην μου, ὑμῶν δὲ ἀπόστολον καὶ λειτουργὸν τῆς χρείας μου, πέμψαι πρὸς ὑμᾶς, **26** ἐπειδὴ ἐπιποθῶν ἦν πάντας ὑμᾶς[5], καὶ ἀδημονῶν διότι ἠκούσατε ὅτι ἠσθένησεν. **27** καὶ γὰρ ἠσθένησεν παραπλήσιον θανάτῳ· ἀλλὰ ὁ θεὸς ἠλέησεν αὐτόν, οὐκ αὐτὸν δὲ μόνον ἀλλὰ καὶ ἐμέ, ἵνα μὴ λύπην ἐπὶ λύπην σχῶ. **28** σπουδαιοτέρως οὖν ἔπεμψα αὐτὸν ἵνα ἰδόντες αὐτὸν πάλιν χαρῆτε κἀγὼ ἀλυπότερος ὦ. **29** προσδέχεσθε οὖν αὐτὸν ἐν κυρίῳ μετὰ πάσης χαρᾶς, καὶ τοὺς τοιούτους ἐντίμους ἔχετε, **30** ὅτι διὰ τὸ ἔργον Χριστοῦ[6] μέχρι θανάτου ἤγγισεν, παραβολευσάμενος τῇ ψυχῇ ἵνα ἀναπληρώσῃ τὸ ὑμῶν ὑστέρημα τῆς πρός με λειτουργίας.

The True Righteousness

3 Τὸ λοιπόν, ἀδελφοί μου, χαίρετε ἐν κυρίῳ. τὰ αὐτὰ γράφειν ὑμῖν ἐμοὶ μὲν οὐκ ὀκνηρόν, ὑμῖν δὲ ἀσφαλές.

---

[5] **26** {C} ὑμᾶς p[46] ℵ[c] (B *transposes*: ὑμᾶς πάντας) G K P Ψ 181 614 629 630 1739 1881 *Byz Lect* it[ar,c,dem,div,f,g,x,z] vg cop[sa] goth Ambrosiaster Victorinus-Rome Chrysostom Theodoret Cassiodorus[1/2] ∥ ὑμᾶς ἰδεῖν ℵ* A C D I[vid] 33 81 88 104 326 330 436 451 1241 1877 1962 1984 1985 2127 2492 2495[vid] it[d,e] syr[p,h,pal] cop[bo] arm eth Euthalius Cassiodorus[1/2] John-Damascus Theophylact

[6] **30** {C} Χριστοῦ p[46] B G 88 436 614 629 1739 1881 Origen ∥ τοῦ Χριστοῦ D K 181 326 630 1877 1984 2495 *Byz Lect* Chrysostom[txt] Theodoret John-Damascus ∥ Χριστοῦ *or* τοῦ Χριστοῦ it[ar,c,d,dem,div,e,f,g,x,z] vg syr[p] cop[sa] goth Ambrosiaster Victorinus-Rome ∥ κυρίου ℵ A P Ψ 33 81 104 330 451 1241 1962 2127 2492 syr[h] cop[bo] arm eth Euthalius ∥ τοῦ θεοῦ 1985 Chrysostom ∥ *omit* C

---

25 ὑμῶν δὲ...χρείας μου Php 4.18   **29** 1 Cor 16.16, 18; 1 Tm 5.17
3 1 χαίρετε ἐν κυρίῳ Php 2.18; 4.4

2 Βλέπετε τοὺς κύνας, βλέπετε τοὺς κακοὺς ἐργάτας, βλέπετε τὴν κατατομήν. 3 ἡμεῖς γάρ ἐσμεν ἡ περιτομή, οἱ πνεύματι θεοῦ[1] λατρεύοντες καὶ καυχώμενοι ἐν Χριστῷ Ἰησοῦ καὶ οὐκ ἐν σαρκὶ πεποιθότες, 4 καίπερ ἐγὼ ἔχων πεποίθησιν καὶ ἐν σαρκί. εἴ τις δοκεῖ ἄλλος πεποιθέναι ἐν σαρκί, ἐγὼ μᾶλλον· 5 περιτομῇ ὀκταήμερος, ἐκ γένους Ἰσραήλ, φυλῆς Βενιαμείν, Ἑβραῖος ἐξ Ἑβραίων, κατὰ νόμον Φαρισαῖος, 6 κατὰ ζῆλος διώκων τὴν ἐκκλησίαν, κατὰ δικαιοσύνην τὴν ἐν νόμῳ γενόμενος ἄμεμπτος. 7 [ἀλλὰ] ἅτινα ἦν μοι κέρδη, ταῦτα ἥγημαι διὰ τὸν Χριστὸν ζημίαν. 8 ἀλλὰ μενοῦνγε καὶ ἡγοῦμαι πάντα ζημίαν εἶναι διὰ τὸ ὑπερέχον τῆς γνώσεως Χριστοῦ Ἰησοῦ τοῦ κυρίου μου, δι᾽ ὃν τὰ πάντα ἐζημιώθην, καὶ ἡγοῦμαι σκύβαλα ἵνα Χριστὸν κερδήσω 9 καὶ εὑρεθῶ ἐν αὐτῷ, μὴ ἔχων ἐμὴν δικαιοσύνην τὴν ἐκ νόμου ἀλλὰ τὴν διὰ πίστεως Χριστοῦ, τὴν ἐκ θεοῦ δικαιοσύνην ἐπὶ τῇ πίστει, 10 τοῦ γνῶναι αὐτὸν καὶ τὴν δύναμιν τῆς ἀναστάσεως αὐτοῦ καὶ κοινωνίαν παθημάτων αὐτοῦ, συμμορφιζόμενος τῷ θανάτῳ αὐτοῦ, 11 εἴ πως καταντήσω εἰς τὴν ἐξανάστασιν τὴν ἐκ νεκρῶν.

---

[1] **3** {C} θεοῦ ℵ* A B C Dᶜ G K 33 81 104 181 326 330 451 614 629 630 1241 1739 1877 1881 1985 2492 2495 *Byz Lect* itᵍ syrʰᵐᵍ copˢᵃ, ᵇᵒ arm? Origen Eusebius Athanasius Greek mssᵃᶜᶜ· ᵗᵒ Ambrose Ambrose Didymusˡᵃᵗ Greek and Latin mssᵃᶜᶜ· ᵗᵒ Augustine Augustine Euthalius Theodoret John-Damascus ‖ θεῷ ℵᶜ D* P Ψ 88 436 1962 (1984 θείῳ) 2127 itᵃʳ,ᶜ,ᵈ,ᵈᵉᵐ,ᵈⁱᵛ,ᵉ,ᶠ,ᵐ,ˣ,ᶻ vg syrⁿ·ʰ goth arm? cth Origenᵍʳ·ˡᵃᵗ Ambrosiaster Victorinus Rome Latin mssᵃᶜᶜ· ᵗᵒ Ambrose Chrysostom Theodoreˡᵃᵗ Greek and Latin mssᵃᶜᶜ· ᵗᵒ Augustine Theodoret ‖ *omit* 𝔭⁴⁶

---

2 Βλέπετε τοὺς κύνας Ps 22.16, 20; Re 22.15   3 Ro 2.29   4 ἐγὼ ἔχων...σαρκί 2 Cor 11.18   5 περιτομῇ ὀκταήμερος Lk 1.59; 2.21   ἐκ...Ἑβραίων 2 Cor 11.22   κατὰ νόμον Φαρισαῖος Ac 23.6; 26.5   6 διώκων τὴν ἐκκλησίαν Ac 8.3; 22.4; 26.9–11   7 Mt 13.44, 46; Lk 14.33   9 τὴν διὰ...πίστει Ro 3.21–22   10 τὴν...αὐτοῦ, συμμορφιζόμενος...αὐτοῦ Ro 3.3–5   κοινωνίαν παθημάτων αὐτοῦ Ro 8.17; Ga 6.17   11 καταντήσω...νεκρῶν Ac 4.2; Re 20.5–6

[2] Watch out for those who do evil things, those dogs, men who insist on cutting the body. [3] For we, not they, are the ones who have received the true circumcision, for we worship God by his Spirit, and rejoice in our life in Christ Jesus. We do not put any trust in external ceremonies. [4] I could, of course, put my trust in such things. If anyone thinks he can be safe in external ceremonies, I have even more reason to feel that way. [5] I was circumcised when I was a week old. I am an Israelite by birth, of the tribe of Benjamin, a pure-blooded Hebrew. So far as keeping the Jewish Law is concerned, I was a Pharisee, [6] and I was so zealous that I persecuted the church. So far as a man can be righteous by obeying the commands of the Law, I was without fault. [7] But all those things that I might count as profit I now reckon as loss, for Christ's sake. [8] Not only those things; I reckon everything as complete loss for the sake of what is so much more valuable, the knowledge of Christ Jesus my Lord. For his sake I have thrown everything away; I consider it all as mere garbage, so that I might gain Christ, [9] and be completely united with him. No longer do I have a righteousness of my own, the kind to be gained by obeying the Law. I now have the righteousness that is given through faith in Christ, the righteousness that comes from God, and is based on faith. [10] All I want is to know Christ and experience the power of his resurrection; to share in his sufferings and become like him in his death, [11] in the hope that I myself will be raised from death to life.

Running Toward the Goal

[12] I do not claim that I have already succeeded in this, or have already become perfect. I keep going on to try to possess it, for Christ ·Jesus has already possessed me. [13] Of course, brothers, I really do not think that I have already reached it; the one thing I do, however, is to forget what is behind me and do my best to reach what is ahead. [14] So I run straight toward the goal in order to win the prize, which is God's call through Christ Jesus to the life above.

[15] All of us who are spiritually mature should have this same attitude. If, however, some of you have a different attitude, God will make this clear to you. [16] However that may be, let us go forward according to the same rules we have followed until now.

[17] Keep on imitating me, brothers, all of you. We have set the right example

Pressing toward the Mark

12 Οὐχ ὅτι ἤδη ἔλαβον ἢ ἤδη τετελείωμαι[2], διώκω δὲ εἰ καὶ καταλάβω, ἐφ' ᾧ καὶ κατελήμφθην ὑπὸ Χριστοῦ ['Ιησοῦ]. **13** ἀδελφοί, ἐγὼ ἐμαυτὸν οὐ[3] λογίζομαι κατειληφέναι· [a]ἓν δέ, τὰ μὲν ὀπίσω ἐπιλανθανόμενος τοῖς δὲ ἔμπροσθεν ἐπεκτεινόμενος, **14**[a] κατὰ σκοπὸν διώκω εἰς τὸ βραβεῖον τῆς ἄνω κλήσεως τοῦ θεοῦ ἐν Χριστῷ 'Ιησοῦ. **15** Ὅσοι οὖν τέλειοι, τοῦτο φρονῶμεν· καὶ εἴ τι ἑτέρως φρονεῖτε, καὶ τοῦτο ὁ θεὸς ὑμῖν ἀποκαλύψει· **16** πλὴν εἰς ὃ ἐφθάσαμεν, τῷ αὐτῷ στοιχεῖν[4].

17 Συμμιμηταί μου γίνεσθε, ἀδελφοί, καὶ σκοπεῖτε

---

[2] **12** {B} ἔλαβον ἢ ἤδη τετελείωμαι 𝔭[61vid] ℵ A B D[c] K P Ψ 33 81 88 (104 τέθεαμαι) 181 326 330 436 451 614 629 630 1241 1739 1877 1881 1962 1984 (1985 *omit* ἢ ἤδη) 2127 2492 2495 *Byz* it[c, dem, div, x, z] vg syr[p, h] cop[sa, bo] goth arm Clement Tertullian Origen[lat] Eusebius Victorinus-Rome Hilary ∥ ἔλαβον ἢ ἤδη δεδικαίωμαι ἢ ἤδη τετελείωμαι (*see* 1 Cor 4.4?) (𝔭[46] τελείωμαι) D* G[c] it[ar, d, e, f, (g)] Irenaeus[lat] Ambrosiaster ∥ ἔλαβον ἢ ἤδη τετελείωμαι. δεδικαίομαι ἢ ἤδη τετελείωμαι G[gr] ∥ τετελείωμαι it[t]

[3] **13** {C} οὐ 𝔭[46] B D[c] G K Ψ 88 181 326 630 1739 1877 1881 2495 *Byz* it[c, d, dem, div, e, f, g, x, z] vg syr[p, h] cop[sa] arm Tertullian Origen[lat] Victorinus-Rome Ephraem Chrysostom Jerome[1/2] ∥ οὔπω ℵ A D[gr]* P 33 81 104 330 436 451 614 (629 *transposes*: οὔπω ἐμαυτόν) 1241 1962 1984 1985 2127 2492 it[ar] syr[h with *] cop[bo] goth eth Clement Ambrosiaster Basil Chrysostom Jerome[1/2] Euthalius Theodoret Cosmos Antiochus Paschal Chronicle John-Damascus

[4] **16** {B} τῷ αὐτῷ στοιχεῖν 𝔭[16, 46] ℵ* A B I[vid] 33 1739 cop[sa, bo] eth[ro] Hilary Augustine Theodotus-Ancyra Ferrandus ∥ τὸ αὐτὸ φρονεῖν 1881 ∥ τὸ αὐτὸ φρονεῖν, τῷ αὐτῷ στοιχεῖν (D* τῷ αὐτοι [*sic*]) (G συνστοιχεῖν) it[ar, d, e, g] Ambrosiaster Victorinus-Rome ∥ τὸ αὐτὸ φρονεῖν, τῷ αὐτῷ κανόνι στοιχεῖν (D[c] 436 στοιχεῖν κανόνι) 81 104 330 451 (629 φρονεῖν καὶ τῷ) 1241 2127 2492 it[c, dem, div, f, x, z] vg goth arm Euthalius ∥ τῷ αὐτῷ στοιχεῖν κανόνι, τὸ αὐτὸ φρονεῖν ℵ[c] K P Ψ 88 181 326 614 630 1877 1962 1984 1985 2495 *Byz* syr[p, h] eth[pp] Chrysostom Theodore Theodoret John-Damascus ∥ τῷ αὐτῷ κανόνι στοιχεῖν, τὸ αὐτὸ φρονεῖν 69 1908

[a a] **13-14** *a* no number, *a* number 14: TR[ed] WH Bov Nes BF[2] AV RV ASV RSV NEB TT Zür Luth Jer Seg ∥ *a* number 14, *a* no number: TR[ed]

---

12 διώκω...καταλάβω 1 Tm 6.12, 19　　κατελήμφθην...'Ιησοῦ Ac 9.5-6　　**14** 1 Cor 9.24　　**15** Ὅσοι...φρονῶμεν Mt 5.48; 1 Cor 2.6　　**16** Ga 6.16　　**17** Συμμιμηταί μου γίνεσθε 1 Cor 4.16; 11.1　σκοπεῖτε...ἡμᾶς 1 Th 1.7; 1 Pe 5.3

τοὺς οὕτω περιπατοῦντας καθὼς ἔχετε τύπον ἡμᾶς. 18 πολλοὶ γὰρ περιπατοῦσιν οὓς πολλάκις ἔλεγον ὑμῖν, νῦν δὲ καὶ κλαίων λέγω, τοὺς ἐχθροὺς τοῦ σταυροῦ τοῦ Χριστοῦ, 19 ὧν τὸ τέλος ἀπώλεια, ὧν ὁ θεὸς ἡ κοιλία καὶ ἡ δόξα ἐν τῇ αἰσχύνῃ αὐτῶν, οἱ τὰ ἐπίγεια φρονοῦντες. 20 ἡμῶν γὰρ τὸ πολίτευμα ἐν οὐρανοῖς ὑπάρχει, ἐξ οὗ καὶ σωτῆρα ἀπεκδεχόμεθα κύριον Ἰησοῦν Χριστόν, 21 ὃς μετασχηματίσει τὸ σῶμα τῆς ταπεινώσεως ἡμῶν σύμμορφον τῷ σώματι τῆς δόξης αὐτοῦ κατὰ τὴν ἐνέργειαν τοῦ δύνασθαι αὐτὸν καὶ ὑποτάξαι αὐτῷ[5] τὰ πάντα. 4 Ὥστε, ἀδελφοί μου ἀγαπητοὶ καὶ ἐπιπόθητοι, χαρὰ καὶ στέφανός μου, οὕτως στήκετε ἐν κυρίῳ, ἀγαπητοί.

Exhortations

2 Εὐοδίαν παρακαλῶ καὶ Συντύχην παρακαλῶ τὸ αὐτὸ φρονεῖν ἐν κυρίῳ. 3 ναὶ ἐρωτῶ καὶ σέ, γνήσιε σύζυγε[a], συλλαμβάνου αὐταῖς, αἵτινες ἐν τῷ εὐαγγελίῳ συνήθλησάν μοι μετὰ καὶ Κλήμεντος καὶ τῶν λοιπῶν συνεργῶν μου[1], ὧν τὰ ὀνόματα ἐν βίβλῳ ζωῆς. 4 Χαίρετε ἐν κυρίῳ πάντοτε· πάλιν ἐρῶ, χαίρετε. 5 τὸ ἐπιεικὲς ὑμῶν γνωσθήτω πᾶσιν ἀνθρώποις. ὁ κύριος ἐγγύς.[b]

---

[5] **21** {B} αὐτῷ 81[vid] ‖ αυτω ℵ* A B* D* G P ‖ αὐτῷ B³ K 33 88 330 451 614 629 1739 1877 1881 1962 1984 1985 2127 2492 2495 *Byz*[pt] *Lect* it[d,e,g] syr[p,h] cop[sa?bo?] Eusebius Victorinus-Rome Epiphanius Chrysostom Cyril Euthalius ‖ ἑαυτῷ ℵ[c] D[c] Ψ 104 181 326 436 630 1241 *Byz*[pt] *l*[598,599] it[ar,c,dem, div,f,x,z] vg arm Hilary Ambrose Chrysostom Theodoret John-Damascus

[1] **3** {B} τῶν λοιπῶν συνεργῶν μου 𝔭[46] ℵ[c] A B D G I[vid] K P Ψ 33 81 88 104 181 326 330 436 451 614 629 630 1241 1739 1877 1881 1962 1984 1985 2127 2492 2495 *Byz* *Lect* it[ar,c,d,dem,div,e,f,g,x,z] vg syr[p,h] cop[sa,bo] goth arm Origen Eusebius ‖ τῶν συνεργῶν μου καὶ τῶν λοιπῶν 𝔭[16vid] ℵ*

[a] **3** σύζυγε: TR WH Bov Nes BF² AV RV ASV RSV NEB TT Zür[mg] Luth (Jer) Seg ‖ Σύζυγε: WH[mg] Zür (Jer)

[b] **5** *b* major: TR Bov Nes BF² AV RV ASV RSV TT Zür Luth Jer Seg ‖ *b* minor: WH NEB

18 τοὺς...Χριστοῦ 1 Cor 1.23; Ga 6.12   **19** ὧν ὁ θεὸς ἡ κοιλία Ro 16.18   οἱ τὰ ἐπίγεια φρονοῦντες Ro 8.5-0   **20** ἡμῶν...ὑπάρχει Eph 2.6, 19, He 12.22   **21** ὃς μετασχηματίσει... αὐτόν Ro 8.29; 1 Cor 15.43-53   ὑποτάξαι...πάντα 1 Cor 15.28

4 1 ἀδελφοί...μου 1 Th 2.19-20   **3** βίβλῳ ζωῆς Ex 32.32, 33; Ps 69.28; Dn 12.1; Re 3.5; 13.8 17.8; 20.12, 15; 21.27   **4** Php 3.1   **5** ὁ κύριος ἐγγύς He 10.37; Jas 5.8, 9

for you; so pay attention to those who follow it. [18] I have told you this many times before, and now I repeat it, with tears: there are many whose lives make them enemies of Christ's death on the cross. [19] They are going to end up in hell, for their god is their bodily desires, they are proud of what they should be ashamed of, and they think only of things that belong to this world. [20] We, however, are citizens of heaven, and we eagerly wait for our Savior to come from heaven, the Lord Jesus Christ. [21] He will change our weak mortal bodies and make them like his own glorious body, using that power by which he is able to bring all things under his rule.

Instructions

4 So, then, my brothers — and how dear you are to me, and how I miss you! how happy you make me, and how proud I am of you! — this, dear brothers, is how you should stand firm in your life in the Lord.

[2] Euodia and Syntyche, please, I beg you, try to agree as sisters in the Lord. [3] And you too, my faithful partner, I want you to help these women; for they have worked hard with me to spread the gospel, together with Clement and all my other fellow workers, whose names are in God's book of the living.

[4] May you always be joyful in your life in the Lord. I say it again: rejoice!

[5] Show a gentle attitude toward all.

The Lord is coming soon. ⁶ Don't worry about anything, but in all your prayers ask God for what you need, always asking him with a thankful heart. ⁷ And God's peace, which is far beyond human understanding, will keep your hearts and minds safe, in Christ Jesus.

⁸ In conclusion, my brothers, fill your minds with those things that are good and deserve praise: things that are true, noble, right, pure, lovely, and honorable. ⁹ Put into practice what you learned and received from me, both from my words and from my deeds. And the God who gives us peace will be with you.

Thanks for the Gift

¹⁰ How great is the joy I have in my life in the Lord! After so long a time, you once more had the chance of showing that you care for me. I don't mean that you had quit caring for me — you did not have a chance to show it. ¹¹ And I am not saying this because I feel neglected; for I have learned to be satisfied with what I have. ¹² I know what it is to be in need, and what it is to have more than enough. I have learned this secret, so that anywhere, at any time, I am content, whether I am full or hungry, whether I have too much or too little. ¹³ I have the strength to face all conditions by the power that Christ gives me.

¹⁴ But it was very good of you to help me in my troubles. ¹⁵ You Philippians yourselves know very well that when I left Macedonia, in the early days of preaching the Good News, you were the only church to help me; you were the only ones who shared my profits and losses. ¹⁶ More than once, when I needed help in Thessalonica, you sent it to me. ¹⁷ It is not that I just want to receive

6 μηδὲν μεριμνᾶτε, ἀλλ' ἐν παντὶ τῇ προσευχῇ καὶ τῇ δεήσει μετὰ εὐχαριστίας τὰ αἰτήματα ὑμῶν γνωριζέσθω πρὸς τὸν θεόν.ᶜ 7 καὶ ἡ εἰρήνη τοῦ θεοῦ ἡ ὑπερέχουσα πάντα νοῦν φρουρήσει τὰς καρδίας ὑμῶν καὶ τὰ νοήματα ὑμῶν ἐν Χριστῷ Ἰησοῦ.

8 Τὸ λοιπόν, ἀδελφοί, ὅσα ἐστὶν ἀληθῆ, ὅσα σεμνά, ὅσα δίκαια, ὅσα ἁγνά, ὅσα προσφιλῆ, ὅσα εὔφημα, εἴ τις ἀρετὴ καὶ εἴ τις ἔπαινος, ταῦτα λογίζεσθε· 9 ἃ καὶ ἐμάθετε καὶ παρελάβετε καὶ ἠκούσατε καὶ εἴδετε ἐν ἐμοί, ταῦτα πράσσετε· καὶ ὁ θεὸς τῆς εἰρήνης ἔσται μεθ' ὑμῶν.

Acknowledgment of the Philippians' Gift

10 Ἐχάρην δὲ ἐν κυρίῳ μεγάλως ὅτι ἤδη ποτὲ ἀνεθάλετε τὸ ὑπὲρ ἐμοῦ φρονεῖν, ἐφ' ᾧ καὶ ἐφρονεῖτε ἠκαιρεῖσθε δέ. 11 οὐχ ὅτι καθ' ὑστέρησιν λέγω, ἐγὼ γὰρ ἔμαθον ἐν οἷς εἰμι αὐτάρκης εἶναι. 12 οἶδα καὶ ταπεινοῦσθαι, οἶδα καὶ περισσεύειν· ἐν παντὶ καὶ ἐν πᾶσιν μεμύημαι καὶ χορτάζεσθαι καὶ πεινᾶν, καὶ περισσεύειν καὶ ὑστερεῖσθαι. 13 πάντα ἰσχύω ἐν τῷ ἐνδυναμοῦντί με. 14 πλὴν καλῶς ἐποιήσατε συγκοινωνήσαντές μου τῇ θλίψει.

15 Οἴδατε δὲ καὶ ὑμεῖς, Φιλιππήσιοι, ὅτι ἐν ἀρχῇ τοῦ εὐαγγελίου, ὅτε ἐξῆλθον ἀπὸ Μακεδονίας, οὐδεμία μοι ἐκκλησία ἐκοινώνησεν εἰς λόγον δόσεως καὶ λήμψεως εἰ μὴ ὑμεῖς μόνοι· 16 ὅτι καὶ ἐν Θεσσαλονίκῃ καὶ ἅπαξ καὶ δὶς εἰς τὴν χρείαν μοι² ἐπέμψατε. 17 οὐχ ὅτι ἐπιζητῶ

---

² 16 {C} εἰς τὴν χρείαν μοι ℵ B Gᵍʳ K Ψ 33 88 181 1739 1877 1881 2127 2495 *Byz Lect* itᶜ,ᵈ,ᵈᵉᵐ,ᵈⁱᵛ,ᵉ,ᶠ,ˣ,ᶻᶜ vg ∥ εἰς τὴν χρείαν μου Dᶜ P 614 629 630 1962 1984 1985 it⁽ᵃʳ⁾,ʳ² ∥ τὴν χρείαν μοι 𝔭⁴⁶ A 81 104 326 330 436 451 1241 2492

ᶜ 6 c major: TR Bov Nes BF² AV RV ASV RSV NEB TT Jer Seg ∥ c minor: WH ∥ c exclamation: Zür Luth

6 μηδὲν μεριμνᾶτε Mt 6.25; 1 Pe 5.7   τῇ προσευχῇ...εὐχαριστίας Col 4.2   7 Is 26.3; Jn 14.27; Col 3.15   8 Ro 12.17   9 ὁ θεὸς τῆς εἰρήνης Ro 15.33; 16.20; 1 Cor 14.33; 1 Th 5.23   11 ἐν...εἶναι 1 Tm 6.6   13 2 Cor 12.10; 2 Tm 4.17   15 2 Cor 11.9

τὸ δόμα, ἀλλὰ ἐπιζητῶ τὸν καρπὸν τὸν πλεονάζοντα εἰς
λόγον ὑμῶν. 18 ἀπέχω δὲ πάντα καὶ περισσεύω· πεπλήρωμαι δεξάμενος παρὰ Ἐπαφροδίτου τὰ παρ' ὑμῶν,
ὀσμὴν εὐωδίας, θυσίαν δεκτήν, εὐάρεστον τῷ θεῷ.
19 ὁ δὲ θεός μου πληρώσει πᾶσαν χρείαν ὑμῶν κατὰ
τὸ πλοῦτος αὐτοῦ ἐν δόξῃ ἐν Χριστῷ Ἰησοῦ. 20 τῷ δὲ
θεῷ καὶ πατρὶ ἡμῶν ἡ δόξα εἰς τοὺς αἰῶνας τῶν αἰώνων·
ἀμήν.

Final Greetings

21 Ἀσπάσασθε πάντα ἅγιον ἐν Χριστῷ Ἰησοῦ. ἀσπάζονται ὑμᾶς οἱ σὺν ἐμοὶ ἀδελφοί. 22 ἀσπάζονται ὑμᾶς
πάντες οἱ ἅγιοι, μάλιστα δὲ οἱ ἐκ τῆς Καίσαρος οἰκίας.
23 ἡ χάρις τοῦ κυρίου Ἰησοῦ Χριστοῦ μετὰ τοῦ πνεύματος ὑμῶν.[3]

---

l[261?] syr[h] goth eth ∥ τὴν χρείαν μου D[gr*] arm Ambrosiaster Augustine ∥
μοι εἰς τὴν χρείαν μου (syr[p]) cop[sa,bo] ∥ *in unum mihi* it[z*] ∥ *in necessitatem
meam vel usibus meis* it[g]

3 23 {B} ὑμῶν. B G 1739*[vid] 1881 it[f,g] cop[sa] Victorinus-Rome Chrysostom Euthalius ∥ ὑμῶν. ἀμήν. 𝔭[46] ℵ A D K P Ψ 33 81 88 104 181 326 330
436 451 614 629 630 1241 1739[c vid] 1877 1962 1984 1985 2127 2492 2495 *Byz
Lect* it[ar,c,d,dem,div,e,r²,x,z] vg syr[p,h] cop[bo] arm eth Ambrosiaster Theodoret
John-Damascus

---

17 ἐπιζητῶ τὸν...ὑμῶν 1 Cor 9.11   **18** ὀσμὴν εὐωδίας Gn 8.21; Ex 29.18; Eze 20.41
22 οἱ ἐκ...οἰκίας Phn 1.13

gifts; rather, I want to see profit added
to your account. 18 Here, then, is my
receipt for everything you have given
me — and it has been more than enough!
I have all I need, now that Epaphroditus
has brought me all your gifts. These are
like a sweet-smelling offering to God, a
sacrifice which is acceptable and pleasing
to him. 19 And my God, with all his
abundant wealth in Christ Jesus, will
supply all your needs. 20 To our God and
Father be the glory for ever and ever.
Amen.

Final Greetings

21 Greetings to all God's people who
belong to Christ Jesus. The brothers
here with me send you their greetings.
22 All God's people here send greetings,
especially those who belong to the Emperor's palace.
23 May the grace of the Lord Jesus
Christ be with you all.

PAUL'S LETTER
TO THE COLOSSIANS

1 From Paul, who by God's will is an apostle of Christ Jesus, and from our brother Timothy —

² To God's people in Colossae, those who are our faithful brothers in Christ:

May God our Father give you grace and peace.

Prayer of Thanksgiving

³ We always give thanks to God, the Father of our Lord Jesus Christ, when we pray for you. ⁴ For we have heard of your faith in Christ Jesus, and of your love for all God's people. ⁵ When the true message, the Good News, first came to you, you heard of the hope it offers. So your faith and love are based on what you hope for, which is kept safe for you in heaven. ⁶ The gospel is bring-

ΠΡΟΣ ΚΟΛΟΣΣΑΕΙΣ

Salutation

1 Παῦλος ἀπόστολος Χριστοῦ Ἰησοῦ διὰ θελήματος θεοῦ καὶ Τιμόθεος ὁ ἀδελφός **2** τοῖς ἐν Κολοσσαῖς ἁγίοις καὶ πιστοῖς ἀδελφοῖς ἐν Χριστῷ· χάρις ὑμῖν καὶ εἰρήνη ἀπὸ θεοῦ πατρὸς ἡμῶν[1].

Paul Thanks God for the Colossians

3 Εὐχαριστοῦμεν τῷ θεῷ πατρί[2] τοῦ κυρίου ἡμῶν Ἰησοῦ Χριστοῦ[a] πάντοτε[a] περὶ ὑμῶν προσευχόμενοι, **4** ἀκούσαντες τὴν πίστιν ὑμῶν ἐν Χριστῷ Ἰησοῦ καὶ τὴν ἀγάπην ἣν ἔχετε εἰς πάντας τοὺς ἁγίους **5** διὰ τὴν ἐλπίδα τὴν ἀποκειμένην ὑμῖν ἐν τοῖς οὐρανοῖς, ἣν προηκούσατε ἐν τῷ λόγῳ τῆς ἀληθείας[b] τοῦ εὐαγγελίου[b] **6** τοῦ παρόντος

---

[1] **2** {B} ἡμῶν B D K Ψ 33 81 181 330 451 1739 1881 1984 1985 *l*[1365] it[ar,d,div,e,mon,x,z][mg] vg[ww] syr[p,h] cop[sa] arm eth[ro] Origen[lat] Chrysostom Theodore[lat] ∥ ἡμῶν καὶ κυρίου Ἰησοῦ Χριστοῦ ℵ A C G I 88 104 326 436 614 629 630 (1241 2492 ὑμῶν) 1962 2127 2495 *Byz Lect* it[c,f,g] vg[cl] cop[bo] eth[pp] Ambrosiaster Theodoret John-Damascus ∥ ἡμῶν καὶ κυρίου ἡμῶν Ἰησοῦ Χριστοῦ 1877 ∥ ἡμῶν καὶ Ἰησοῦ Χριστοῦ τοῦ κυρίου ἡμῶν P (it[dem] Χριστοῦ Ἰησοῦ) syr[h with *]

[2] **3** {D} θεῷ πατρί B C* 1739 Augustine ∥ θεῷ τῷ πατρί D* G Chrysostom ∥ θεῷ (or θεῷ τῷ) πατρί it[c,d,g,mon] syr[p,h] cop[sa,bo] eth Pelagius Theodore[lat] Augustine Cassiodorus[1/2] ∥ θεῷ καὶ πατρί ℵ A C² D[c] I K P Ψ 33 81 88 104 181 326 330 436 451 614 629 630 1877 1881 1962 1984 2127 2492 2495 *Byz Lect* it[ar,dem,div,e,f,x,z] vg arm Ambrosiaster Euthalius Theodoret Cassiodorus[1/2] John-Damascus

---

[a a] **3** *a* none, *a* none: WH Bov Nes BF² ∥ *a* none, *a* minor: RSV (NEB) TT (Zür) (Luth) Jer ∥ *a* minor, *a* none: TR AV RV ASV (Seg)

[b b] **5** *b* none, *b* none: TR WH Bov Nes BF² NEB TT ∥ *b* minor, *b* minor: Zür Jer Seg ∥ *b* none, *b* minor: AV RV ASV Luth ∥ *b* minor, *b* none: RSV

---

1 Παῦλος...θεοῦ 1 Cor 1.1; Eph 1.1   **3** Eph 1.16; 1 Th 1.2   **4** Eph 1.15   **5** τὴν ἐλπίδα ...οὐρανοῖς 1 Pe 1.4   τῷ...εὐαγγελίου Eph 1.13

εἰς ὑμᾶς,ᶜ καθὼς καὶ ἐν παντὶ τῷ κόσμῳ ἐστὶν καρποφο-
ρούμενον καὶ αὐξανόμενονᶜ καθὼς καὶ ἐν ὑμῖν,ᶜ ἀφ' ἧς
ἡμέρας ἠκούσατε καὶ ἐπέγνωτε τὴν χάριν τοῦ θεοῦ ἐν
ἀληθείᾳ· 7 καθὼς ἐμάθετε ἀπὸ Ἐπαφρᾶ τοῦ ἀγαπητοῦ
συνδούλου ἡμῶν, ὅς ἐστιν πιστὸς ὑπὲρ ἡμῶν³ διάκονος
τοῦ Χριστοῦ, 8 ὁ καὶ δηλώσας ἡμῖν τὴν ὑμῶν ἀγάπην
ἐν πνεύματι.

The Person and Work of Christ

9 Διὰ τοῦτο καὶ ἡμεῖς, ἀφ' ἧς ἡμέρας ἠκούσαμεν, οὐ
παυόμεθα ὑπὲρ ὑμῶν προσευχόμενοι καὶ αἰτούμενοι ἵνα
πληρωθῆτε τὴν ἐπίγνωσιν τοῦ θελήματος αὐτοῦ ἐν πάσῃ
σοφίᾳ καὶ συνέσει πνευματικῇ, 10 περιπατῆσαι ἀξίως
τοῦ κυρίου εἰς πᾶσαν ἀρεσκείαν,ᵈ ἐν παντὶ ἔργῳ ἀγαθῷᵈ
καρποφοροῦντες καὶ αὐξανόμενοι τῇ ἐπιγνώσει τοῦ θεοῦ,
11 ἐν πάσῃ δυνάμει δυναμούμενοι κατὰ τὸ κράτος τῆς
δόξης αὐτοῦ εἰς πᾶσαν ὑπομονὴν καὶ μακροθυμίαν,ᵉ μετὰ
χαρᾶςᵉ 12 εὐχαριστοῦντες τῷ πατρὶ⁴ τῷ ἱκανώσαντι

---

³ 7 {C} ἡμῶν 𝔭⁴⁶ ℵ* A B Dᵍʳ* G 326* 436 itᵍ,ᵐᵒⁿ* Ambrosiasterᶜᵒᵐᵐ //
ὑμῶν ℵᶜ C Dᶜ K P Ψ 33 81 88 104 181 326ᶜ 330 451 614 629 630 1241 1739
1877 1881 1962 1984 1985 2127 2492 2495 *Byz Lect* itᵃʳ,ᶜ,ᵈ,ᵈᵉᵐ,ᵈⁱᵛ,ᵉ,ᶠ,ˣ,ᶻ vg syrᵖ,ʰ
copˢᵃ,ᵇᵒ goth arm eth Ambrosiasterᵗˣᵗ Ephraem Chrysostom Pelagius
Theodoreˡᵃᵗ Euthalius Theodoret John-Damascus Sedulius-Scotus

⁴ 12 {C} τῷ πατρί 𝔭⁶¹ A C* D K P Ψ 33 81* 181 630 1241 1739* 1962 1984
1985 *Byz l*⁵⁹⁷ itᵈ,ᵉ,ᵐᵒⁿ vgʷʷ syrʰ copˢᵃ,ᵇᵒ goth arm eth Basil¹/² Didymus²/³
Theodoreˡᵃᵗ Augustine Cyril Euthalius Ps-Jerome Cassiodorus John-
Damascus // ἅμα τῷ πατρί 𝔭⁴⁶ B // τῷ πατρὶ τοῦ Χριστοῦ 330 451 2492 // τῷ

ᶜᶜᶜ **6** c minor, c none, c minor: WH Bov Nes BF² (NEB) TT // c major, c minor, c minor: RV
ASV // c major, c major, c none: (Jer) Seg // c minor, c minor, c none: Luth // c minor, c dash, c minor:
RSV // c dash, c none, c dash: Zür // different text: TR AV

ᵈ ᵈ **10** d minor, d none: (TR) Bov Nes BF² AV RV ASV RSV (NEB) Zür (Luth) Jer Seg // d major,
d none: TT // d none, d none: WH // d minor, d minor: RVᵐᵍ ASVᵐᵍ

ᵉ ᵉ **11** e minor, e none: Nes BF² NEBᵐᵍ TT Zür (Luth) Jer Seg // e none, e minor: TR WH
Bov AV RV ASV RSV (NEB) Segᵐᵍ

---

6 καθὼς...κόσμῳ 1 Tm 3.16   ἐστὶν...αὐξανόμενον Ro 1.13   **7** Ἐπαφρᾶ...Χριστοῦ
Col 4.12   **9** προσευχόμενοι...πνευματικῇ Eph 1.15–17; Php 1.9   τὴν...αὐτοῦ Eph 1.9; 5.17
10 περιπατῆσαι...ἀρεσκείαν Eph 4.1; Php 1.27   ἐν...καρποφοροῦντες Eph 2.10   **11** ἐν...
αὐτοῦ Eph 1.19; 3.16

---

ing blessings and spreading through the whole world, just as it has among you ever since the day you first heard of the grace of God and came to know it as it really is. 7 You learned this from Epaphras, our dear fellow servant, who is a faithful worker for Christ on our behalf. 8 He told us of the love that the Spirit has given you.

9 For this reason we always pray for you, ever since we heard about you. We ask God to fill you with the knowledge of his will, with all the wisdom and understanding that his Spirit gives. 10 Then you will be able to live as the Lord wants, and always do what pleases him. Your lives will be fruitful in all kinds of good works, and you will grow in your knowledge of God. 11 May you be made strong with all the strength which comes from his glorious might, that you may be able to endure everything with patience. 12 And give thanks, with joy, to the Father who has made

you fit to have your share of what God has reserved for his people in the kingdom of light. ¹³ For he rescued us from the power of darkness and brought us safe into the kingdom of his dear Son, ¹⁴ by whom we are set free and our sins are forgiven.

The Person and Work of Christ

¹⁵ Christ is the visible likeness of the invisible God. He is the first-born Son, superior to all created things. ¹⁶ For by him God created everything in heaven and on earth, the seen and the unseen things, including spiritual powers, lords, rulers, and authorities. God created the whole universe through him and for him. ¹⁷ He existed before all things, and in union with him all things have their proper place. ¹⁸ He is the head of his body, the church; he is the source of the body's life; he is the first-born Son who was raised from death, in order that he alone might have the first place in all things. ¹⁹ For it was by God's own decision that the Son has in himself the full nature of God. ²⁰ Through the Son, then, God decided to bring the whole universe back to himself. God made peace through his Son's death on the cross, and so brought back to himself all things, both on earth and in heaven.

ὑμᾶς⁵ εἰς τὴν μερίδα τοῦ κλήρου τῶν ἁγίων ἐν τῷ φωτί· 13 ὃς ἐρρύσατο ἡμᾶς ἐκ τῆς ἐξουσίας τοῦ σκότους καὶ μετέστησεν εἰς τὴν βασιλείαν τοῦ υἱοῦ τῆς ἀγάπης αὐτοῦ, 14 ἐν ᾧ ἔχομεν τὴν ἀπολύτρωσιν, τὴν ἄφεσιν τῶν ἁμαρτιῶν· 15 ὅς ἐστιν εἰκὼν τοῦ θεοῦ τοῦ ἀοράτου, πρωτότοκος πάσης κτίσεως, 16 ὅτι ἐν αὐτῷ ἐκτίσθη τὰ πάντα ἐν τοῖς οὐρανοῖς καὶ ἐπὶ τῆς γῆς, τὰ ὁρατὰ καὶ τὰ ἀόρατα, εἴτε θρόνοι εἴτε κυριότητες εἴτε ἀρχαὶ εἴτε ἐξουσίαι· τὰ πάντα δι' αὐτοῦ καὶ εἰς αὐτὸν ἔκτισται, 17 καὶ αὐτός ἐστιν πρὸ πάντων καὶ τὰ πάντα ἐν αὐτῷ συνέστηκεν. 18 καὶ αὐτός ἐστιν ἡ κεφαλὴ τοῦ σώματος, τῆς ἐκκλησίας· ὅς ἐστιν ἀρχή, πρωτότοκος ἐκ τῶν νεκρῶν, ἵνα γένηται ἐν πᾶσιν αὐτὸς πρωτεύων, 19 ὅτι ἐν αὐτῷ εὐδόκησεν πᾶν τὸ πλήρωμα κατοικῆσαι 20 καὶ δι' αὐτοῦ ἀποκαταλλάξαι τὰ πάντα εἰς αὐτόν, εἰρηνοποιήσας διὰ τοῦ αἵματος τοῦ σταυροῦ αὐτοῦ, [δι' αὐτοῦ]⁶ εἴτε τὰ ἐπὶ τῆς γῆς εἴτε τὰ ἐν τοῖς οὐρανοῖς.

πατρὶ καὶ θεῷ 2495 ‖ τῷ θεῷ πατρί ℵ itᶜ,ᶠ,ᵍ,ᵐ,ˣ,ᶻ vgᶜˡ syrᵖ copˢᵃᵐˢ,ᵇᵒᵐˢ Origenˡᵃᵗ Cassiodorus ‖ θεῷ τῷ πατρί Gᵍʳ ‖ τῷ θεῷ καὶ πατρί C³ 81ᶜ 88 104 326 436 614 629 1739ᵐᵍ 1877 2127 *Lect* itᵃʳ,ᵈᵉᵐ,ᵈⁱᵛ syrʰ with * Ambrosiaster Athanasius Basil¹ᐟ² Didymus¹ᐟ³ Pelagius Theodoret Vigilius Ps-Jerome Cassiodorus ‖ *omit* 1881

⁵ **12** {C} ὑμᾶς ℵ B 104 629 1739 1881 1984 1985 2127 2492* syrʰᵐᵍ copˢᵃ goth arm eth Ambrosiaster Ephraem Didymus¹ᐟ³ Pelagius Theodoreˡᵃᵗ Ps-Jerome Theophylact ‖ ἡμᾶς A C D G K P Ψ 33 81ᵛⁱᵈ 88 181 326 330 436 451 614 630 1241 1877 1962 2492ᶜ 2495 *Byz Lect* itᵃʳ,ᶜ,ᵈ,ᵈᵉᵐ,ᵈⁱᵛ,ᵉ,ᶠ,ᵍ,ᵐ,ᵐᵒⁿ,ˣ,ᶻ vg syrᵖ,ʰ copᵇᵒ Origenˡᵃᵗ Ambrosiaster Athanasius Basil Didymus²ᐟ³ Chrysostom Pelagius Augustine Cyril Euthalius Theodoret Vigilius Ps-Jerome Cassiodorus

⁶ **20** {D} δι' αὐτοῦ 𝔭⁴⁶ ℵ A C Dᶜ K P Ψ 048 33 88 181 326 330 451 614 629 630 2492 2495 *Byz*ᵖᵗ *Lect* syrᵖ,ʰ copᵇᵒ goth Chrysostom Theodoret John-Damascus ‖ *omit* B D* G I 81 104 436 1241 1739 1877 1881 1962 1984 1985 2127 *Byz*ᵖᵗ *l*⁸⁰⁹ itᵃʳ,ᶜ,ᵈ,ᵈᵉᵐ,ᵈⁱᵛ,ᵉ,ᶠ,ᵍ,ᵐᵒⁿ,ˣ,ᶻ vg copˢᵃ arm eth Origenᵍʳ,ˡᵃᵗ Ambrosiaster Ephraem Cyril Euthalius Theophylact

---

12 τοῦ κλήρου τῶν ἁγίων Eph 1.18 **13** τῆς ἐξουσίας τοῦ σκότους Lk 22.53; Eph 2.2; 6.12 τοῦ υἱοῦ...αὐτοῦ Mt 3.17; Eph 1.6 **14** Eph 1.7 **15** ὅς...θεοῦ 2 Cor 4.4; He 1.3 τοῦ θεοῦ τοῦ ἀοράτου Jn 1.18; 1 Tm 6.16 **16** Jn 1.3, 10 **17** αὐτός...πάντων Jn 1.1; 8.58 **18** αὐτός ...ἐκκλησίας Eph 1.22–23; 4.15; 5.23 ὅς...νεκρῶν Ac 4.2; 26.23; Re 1.5 **19** Jn 1.16; Eph 1.23; Col 2.9 **20** δι' αὐτοῦ...αὐτόν Eph 1.7; 2.16; 1 Jn 2.2 εἰρηνοποιήσας...αὐτοῦ Ro 5.1; Eph 2.13 δι' αὐτοῦ...οὐρανοῖς Eph 1.10

21 Καὶ ὑμᾶς ποτε ὄντας ἀπηλλοτριωμένους καὶ ἐχθροὺς τῇ διανοίᾳ ἐν τοῖς ἔργοις τοῖς πονηροῖς, ᶠ **22** ᵍ νυνὶ δὲ ἀποκατηλλάγητε⁷ ᵍἐν τῷ σώματι τῆς σαρκὸς αὐτοῦ διὰ τοῦ θανάτου, ᶠ ᵍπαραστῆσαι ὑμᾶς ἁγίους καὶ ἀμώμους καὶ ἀνεγκλήτους κατενώπιον αὐτοῦ, **23** εἴ γε ἐπιμένετε τῇ πίστει τεθεμελιωμένοι καὶ ἑδραῖοι καὶ μὴ μετακινούμενοι ἀπὸ τῆς ἐλπίδος τοῦ εὐαγγελίου οὗ ἠκούσατε, τοῦ κηρυχθέντος ἐν πάσῃ κτίσει τῇ ὑπὸ τὸν οὐρανόν, οὗ ἐγενόμην ἐγὼ Παῦλος διάκονος.

Paul's Ministry to the Church

24 Νῦν χαίρω ἐν τοῖς παθήμασιν ὑπὲρ ὑμῶν, καὶ ἀνταναπληρῶ τὰ ὑστερήματα τῶν θλίψεων τοῦ Χριστοῦ ἐν τῇ σαρκί μου ὑπὲρ τοῦ σώματος αὐτοῦ, ὅ ἐστιν ἡ ἐκκλησία, **25** ἧς ἐγενόμην ἐγὼ διάκονος κατὰ τὴν οἰκονομίαν τοῦ θεοῦ τὴν δοθεῖσάν μοι εἰς ὑμᾶς πληρῶσαι τὸν λόγον τοῦ θεοῦ, **26** τὸ μυστήριον τὸ ἀποκεκρυμμένον ἀπὸ τῶν αἰώνων καὶ ἀπὸ τῶν γενεῶν — νῦν δὲ ἐφανερώθη τοῖς ἁγίοις αὐτοῦ, **27** οἷς ἠθέλησεν ὁ θεὸς γνωρίσαι τί τὸ πλοῦτος τῆς δόξης τοῦ μυστηρίου τούτου

---

⁷ **22** {D} ἀποκατηλλάγητε (𝔭⁴⁶ ἀποκαταλλάγητε) B Hilary Ephraem ‖ ἀποκατηλλάκηται 33 ‖ ἀποκατήλλαξεν ℵ A C Dᶜ K 048 88 (104 ἀπήλλαξεν) 181 326 436 614 629 630 1241 1739 1881 1962 1984 1985 2495 *Byz Lect* itᵃʳ,ᶜ,ᵈᵉᵐ, ᵈⁱᵛ,ᶠ,ᵐᵒⁿ,ˣ,ᶻ vg syrᵖ,ʰ copˢᵃ,ᵇᵒ arm? Chrysostom Cyril Euthalius Theodoret John-Damascus ‖ ἀπεκατήλλαξεν P Ψ 81 330 451 1877 2127 2492 arm? ‖ ἀποκαταλλαγέντες D* C itᵈ,ᵉ,ᵍ,ᵐ goth Irenaeusˡᵃᵗ Ambrosiaster

ᶠ ᶠ **21–22** ᶠ ᶠ no dashes: TR Bov Nes BF² AV RV ASV RSV NEB TT Zür Luth Jer Seg ‖ ᶠ dash; ᶠ dash: WH

ᵍ ᵍ ᵍ **21–22** ᵍ number 22, ᵍ no number, ᵍ no number: TRᵉᵈ WH Bov Nes BF² ASV RSV NEB TT Zür Luth Jer Segᵉᵈ ‖ ᵍ no number, ᵍ number 22, ᵍ no number: TRᵉᵈ AV RV Segᵉᵈ ‖ ᵍ no number, ᵍ no number, ᵍ number 22: Segᵉᵈ

---

21 ὑμᾶς...διανοίᾳ Ro 5.10; Eph 2.12; 4.18   **22** ἀποκατηλλάγητε...θανάτου Eph 2.14, 16   παραστῆσαι...αὐτοῦ Eph 5.27   **23** εἴ...πίστει He 3.14   τῇ...ἑδραῖοι Eph 3.17   τοῦ κηρυχθέντος...οὐρανόν Mk 16.15; 1 Tm 3.16   **24** χαίρω...ὑμῶν Eph 3.13   **25** Eph 3.2, 7–8   **26** Ro 16.25–26; Eph 3.3, 5, 9–10   **27** οἷς...ἔθνεσιν Ro 16.25; Eph 3.9   τὸ πλοῦτος τῆς δόξης Eph 1.18

---

21 At one time you were far away from God and made yourselves his enemies by the evil things you did and thought. **22** But now, by means of the physical death of his Son, God has made you his friends, in order to bring you, holy and pure and innocent, into his presence. **23** You must, of course, continue faithful on a firm and sure foundation, and not allow yourselves to be shaken from the hope you gained when you heard the gospel. It is of this gospel that I, Paul, became a servant — this gospel which has been preached to everybody in the world.

Paul's Ministry to the Church

24 And now I am happy about my sufferings for you. For by means of my physical sufferings I help complete what still remains of Christ's sufferings on behalf of his body, which is the church. **25** And I have been made a servant of the church by God, who gave me this task to perform for your good. It is the task of fully proclaiming his message, **26** which is the secret he hid through all past ages from all mankind, but has now revealed to his people. **27** For this is God's plan: to make known his secret to his people, this rich and glorious secret which he has for all peoples. And the secret is this: Christ is in you, which means that you will share the glory of God. 28 So we preach Christ to all men. We warn and teach everyone, with all possible wisdom, in order to bring each one into God's presence as a mature individual in union with Christ. 29 To get this done I toil and struggle, using the mighty strength that Christ supplies, which is at work in me.

2 Let me tell you how hard I have worked for you, and for the people in Laodicea, and for all those who do not know me personally. 2 I do so that their hearts may be filled with courage and that they may be drawn together in love and have the full wealth of assurance which true understanding brings. And so they will know God's secret, which is Christ himself. 3 He is the key that opens all the hidden treasures of God's wisdom and knowledge.

4 I tell you, then: do not let anyone fool you with false arguments, no matter how good they seem to be. 5 For even though I am absent in body, yet I am with you in spirit, and I am glad as I see the resolute firmness with which you stand together in your faith in Christ.

ἐν τοῖς ἔθνεσιν, ὅ ἐστιν Χριστὸς ἐν ὑμῖν, ἡ ἐλπὶς τῆς δόξης· 28 ὃν ἡμεῖς καταγγέλλομεν νουθετοῦντες πάντα ἄνθρωπον καὶ διδάσκοντες πάντα ἄνθρωπον ἐν πάσῃ σοφίᾳ, ἵνα παραστήσωμεν πάντα ἄνθρωπον τέλειον ἐν Χριστῷ· 29 εἰς ὃ καὶ κοπιῶ ἀγωνιζόμενος κατὰ τὴν ἐνέργειαν αὐτοῦ τὴν ἐνεργουμένην ἐν ἐμοὶ ἐν δυνάμει.

2 Θέλω γὰρ ὑμᾶς εἰδέναι ἡλίκον ἀγῶνα ἔχω ὑπὲρ ὑμῶν καὶ τῶν ἐν Λαοδικείᾳ καὶ ὅσοι οὐχ ἑόρακαν τὸ πρόσωπόν μου ἐν σαρκί, 2 ἵνα παρακληθῶσιν αἱ καρδίαι αὐτῶν, συμβιβασθέντες ἐν ἀγάπῃ καὶ εἰς πᾶν πλοῦτος τῆς πληροφορίας τῆς συνέσεως, εἰς ἐπίγνωσιν τοῦ μυστηρίου τοῦ θεοῦ, Χριστοῦ[1], 3 ἐν ᾧ εἰσιν πάντες οἱ θησαυροὶ τῆς σοφίας καὶ γνώσεως ἀπόκρυφοι. 4 Τοῦτο λέγω ἵνα μηδεὶς ὑμᾶς παραλογίζηται ἐν πιθανολογίᾳ. 5 εἰ γὰρ καὶ τῇ σαρκὶ ἄπειμι, ἀλλὰ τῷ πνεύματι σὺν ὑμῖν εἰμι, χαίρων καὶ βλέπων ὑμῶν τὴν τάξιν καὶ τὸ στερέωμα τῆς εἰς Χριστὸν πίστεως ὑμῶν.

---

[1] 2 {B} τοῦ θεοῦ, Χριστοῦ 𝔭46 B Hilary Pelagius Ps-Jerome ‖ τοῦ θεοῦ D^b H P 436* 1881 cops^ams ‖ τοῦ Χριστοῦ 81 1241 (1739 omit τοῦ) Euthalius ‖ τοῦ θεοῦ καὶ Χριστοῦ l^809* Cyril ‖ τοῦ θεοῦ ὅ ἐστιν Χριστός D* it^ar,d,e,x (eth) (Ephraem) Pelagius Augustine Vigilius ‖ τοῦ θεοῦ τοῦ ἐν Χριστῷ 33 (Clement θεοῦ ἐν) Ambrosiaster ‖ τοῦ θεοῦ πατρὸς ἐν Χριστῷ Ἰησοῦ arm ‖ τοῦ θεοῦ πατρὸς τοῦ Χριστοῦ (ℵ* 048 πατρὸς Χριστοῦ) A C (it^div Ἰησοῦ Χριστοῦ, it^c,f,z vg^ww cops^amss Χριστοῦ Ἰησοῦ) cop^bo Ps-Jerome ‖ τοῦ θεοῦ πατρὸς καὶ τοῦ Χριστοῦ 0208 1908 (it^dem καὶ κυρίου ἡμῶν Χριστοῦ Ἰησοῦ, it^mon κυρίου ἡμῶν Ἰησοῦ Χριστοῦ and omit καὶ) (vg^cl cop^boms add Ἰησοῦ) syr^p Chrysostom (Pelagius) Theodore^lat (Cassiodorus) ‖ τοῦ θεοῦ καὶ πατρὸς τοῦ Χριστοῦ ℵ^b Ψ 1962 1984 1985 2127 l^603,809mg syr^h ‖ τοῦ θεοῦ καὶ πατρὸς καὶ τοῦ Χριστοῦ D^c K (88 καὶ τοῦ πατρός) 104 181 326 330 436^mg 451 614 (629 add Ἰησοῦ) 630 1877 2492 2495 Byz Lect (syr^h second καὶ with *) Theodoret John-Damascus

---

27 Χριστὸς...δόξης 1 Tm 1.1　28 παραστήσωμεν...Χριστῷ Eph 4.13　29 κατὰ... δυνάμει Eph 3.7, 20; Php 4.13
2 2 τοῦ μυστηρίου...Χριστοῦ Eph 3.4; Col 1.26; 4.3　3 Is 45.3; En 46.3; 1 Cor 1.24, 30; Eph 3.19 οἱ...ἀπόκρυφοι Pr 2.3-4　4 Ro 16.18; Eph 5.6; Col 2.8　5 εἰ γὰρ...σὺν ὑμῖν εἰμι 1 Cor 5.3

Fullness of Life in Christ

6 Ὡς οὖν παρελάβετε τὸν Χριστὸν Ἰησοῦν τὸν κύριον, ἐν αὐτῷ περιπατεῖτε, 7 ἐρριζωμένοι καὶ ἐποικοδομούμενοι ἐν αὐτῷ καὶ βεβαιούμενοι [ἐν] τῇ πίστει καθὼς ἐδιδάχθητε, περισσεύοντες ἐν εὐχαριστίᾳ². 8 βλέπετε μή τις ὑμᾶς ἔσται ὁ συλαγωγῶν διὰ τῆς φιλοσοφίας καὶ κενῆς ἀπάτης κατὰ τὴν παράδοσιν τῶν ἀνθρώπων, κατὰ τὰ στοιχεῖα τοῦ κόσμου καὶ οὐ κατὰ Χριστόν· 9 ὅτι ἐν αὐτῷ κατοικεῖ πᾶν τὸ πλήρωμα τῆς θεότητος σωματικῶς, 10 καὶ ἐστὲ ἐν αὐτῷ πεπληρωμένοι, ὅς ἐστιν ἡ κεφαλὴ πάσης ἀρχῆς καὶ ἐξουσίας, 11 ἐν ᾧ καὶ περιετμήθητε περιτομῇ ἀχειροποιήτῳ ἐν τῇ ἀπεκδύσει τοῦ σώματος τῆς σαρκός, ἐν τῇ περιτομῇ τοῦ Χριστοῦ, 12 συνταφέντες αὐτῷ ἐν τῷ βαπτισμῷ³, ἐν ᾧ καὶ συνηγέρθητε διὰ τῆς πίστεως τῆς ἐνεργείας τοῦ θεοῦ τοῦ ἐγείραντος αὐτὸν ἐκ νεκρῶν· 13 καὶ ὑμᾶς νεκροὺς ὄντας τοῖς παραπτώμασιν καὶ τῇ ἀκροβυστίᾳ τῆς σαρκὸς ὑμῶν, συνεζωοποίησεν ὑμᾶς⁴ σὺν αὐτῷ,ᵃ χαρισάμενος ἡμῖν πάντα τὰ παραπτώ-

Fulness of Life in Christ

6 Since you have accepted Christ Jesus as Lord, live in union with him. 7 Keep your roots deep in him, build your lives on him, and become ever stronger in your faith, as you were taught. And be filled with thanksgiving.

8 See to it, then, that no one makes a captive of you with the worthless deceit of human wisdom, which comes from the teachings handed down by men, and from the ruling spirits of the universe, and not from Christ. 9 For the full content of divine nature lives in Christ, in his humanity, 10 and you have been given full life in union with him. He is supreme over every spiritual ruler and authority.

11 In union with him you were circumcised, not with the circumcision that is made by men, but with Christ's own circumcision, which consists of being freed from the power of this sinful body. 12 For when you were baptized, you were buried with Christ, and in baptism you were also raised with Christ through your faith in the active power of God, who raised him from death. 13 You were at one time spiritually dead because of your sins, and because you were Gentiles outside the Law. But God has now brought you to live with Christ! God forgave us

---

² 7 {C} ἐν εὐχαριστίᾳ ℵ* A C Iᵛⁱᵈ 0208ᵛⁱᵈ 33 81 88 1241 1739 1881 1962 itˣ vgʷʷ copˢᵃ eth Archelaus Euthalius Ps-Jerome Cassiodorus ∥ ἐν αὐτῇ P Ψ 048? John-Damascusᵗˣᵗ ∥ ἐν αὐτῇ ἐν εὐχαριστίᾳ B Dᶜ H K 104 181 326 330 436 451 614 629 630 1877 1984 2127 2492 (2495 omit second ἐν) Byz Lect itᵃʳ,ᵐᵒⁿ syrᵖ,ʰ copˢᵃᵐˢ,ᵇᵒ arm Ambrosiaster Ephraem Chrysostom Pelagius Theodoreˡᵃᵗ Augustine Theodoret John-Damascus ∥ ἐν αὐτῷ ἐν εὐχαριστίᾳ ℵᵇ D* itᶜ,ᵈ,ᵈᵉᵐ,ᵈⁱᵛ,ᵉ,f,z vgᶜˡ syrʰᵐᵍ Pelagius Ps-Jerome Cassiodorus

³ 12 {C} βαπτισμῷ p⁴⁶ ℵᶜ B D* G 1739 1881 2127 Tertullian Origenˡᵃᵗ Ambrosiaster Hilary Basil Chrysostom Jerome ∥ βαπτίσματι ℵ* A C Dᶜ K P Ψ 33 81 88 104 181 326 330 436 451 614 629 630 1241 1877 1962 1984 2492 2495 Byz Lect Tertullian Origenˡᵃᵗ Hilary Basil Ambrose Chrysostom Jerome Theodoret Ps-Athanasius John-Damascus ∥ βαπτίσματι or βαπτισμῷ itᵃʳ,ᶜ,ᵈ,ᵈᵉᵐ,ᵈⁱᵛ,ᵉ,f,g,ᵐᵒⁿ,ˣ,z vg syrᵖ,ʰ,ᵖᵃˡ copˢᵃ,ᵇᵒ goth arm ∥ βαπτίσματι εἰς τὸν ᾅδην Ps-Athanasius

⁴ 13 {C} ὑμᾶς ℵ* A C K 81 326 436ᵐᵍ 614 629 630 1739 1877 1881 2495

ᵃ ᵃ ᵃ 13-14 a minor, a minor, a minor: TR Bov ∥ a minor, a major, a minor: Nes BF² AV Luth ∥ a major, a minor, a minor: WH NEB ∥ a minor, a minor, a major: WHᵐᵍ RSV (Zür) ∥ a minor,

---

7 ἐποικοδομούμενοι ἐν αὐτῷ Eph 2.20, 22   8 Ro 16.18; Eph 5.6; Col 2.4   9 Jn 1.14, 16   10 ὅς...ἐξουσίας Eph 1.21-22   11 Ro 2.29   12 Ro 6.4   ἐν ᾧ καὶ συνηγέρθητε Col 3.1   τοῦ θεοῦ...νεκρῶν Eph 1.19-20   13 ὑμᾶς νεκροὺς...αὐτῷ Eph 2.1, 5

all our sins. [14] He canceled the unfavorable record of our debts, with its binding rules, and did away with it completely by nailing it to the cross. [15] And on that cross Christ freed himself from the power of tι.e spiritual rulers and authorities;[1] he made a public spectacle of them by leading them as captives in his victory procession.

[16] So let no one make rules about what you eat or drink, or about the subject of holy days, or the new moon festival, or the Sabbath. [17] All such things are only a shadow of things in the future; the reality is Christ. [18] Do not allow yourselves to be condemned by anyone who claims to be superior because of special visions, and insists on false humility and the worship of angels. Such a person is all puffed up, for no reason at all, by his human way of thinking, [19] and has stopped holding on to Christ, who is the head. Under Christ's control the whole body is nourished and held together by its joints and ligaments, and grows as God wants it to grow.

Dying and Living with Christ

[20] You have died with Christ and are set free from the ruling spirits of the universe. Why, then, do you live as though you belonged to this world? Why do you obey such rules as [21] "Don't handle this," "Don't taste that," "Don't touch the other"? [22] All these things become useless, once they are used. These are only man-made rules and

---

[1] **15** Christ freed himself from the power of the spiritual rulers and authorities: or Christ stripped the spiritual rulers and authorities of their power

---

ματα,[a] 14 ἐξαλείψας τὸ καθ' ἡμῶν χειρόγραφον τοῖς δόγμασιν ὃ ἦν ὑπεναντίον ἡμῖν,[a] καὶ αὐτὸ ἦρκεν ἐκ τοῦ μέσου προσηλώσας αὐτὸ τῷ σταυρῷ· 15 ἀπεκδυσάμενος τὰς ἀρχὰς καὶ τὰς ἐξουσίας ἐδειγμάτισεν[b] ἐν παρρησίᾳ,[b] θριαμβεύσας αὐτοὺς ἐν αὐτῷ.

16 Μὴ οὖν τις ὑμᾶς κρινέτω ἐν βρώσει καὶ ἐν πόσει ἢ ἐν μέρει ἑορτῆς ἢ νεομηνίας ἢ σαββάτων, 17 ἅ ἐστιν σκιὰ τῶν μελλόντων, τὸ δὲ σῶμα τοῦ Χριστοῦ. 18 μηδεὶς ὑμᾶς καταβραβευέτω θέλων ἐν ταπεινοφροσύνῃ καὶ θρησκείᾳ τῶν ἀγγέλων, ἃ[5] ἑόρακεν ἐμβατεύων, εἰκῇ φυσιούμενος ὑπὸ τοῦ νοὸς τῆς σαρκὸς αὐτοῦ, 19 καὶ οὐ κρατῶν τὴν κεφαλήν, ἐξ οὗ πᾶν τὸ σῶμα διὰ τῶν ἀφῶν καὶ συνδέσμων ἐπιχορηγούμενον καὶ συμβιβαζόμενον αὔξει τὴν αὔξησιν τοῦ θεοῦ.

The New Life in Christ

20 Εἰ ἀπεθάνετε σὺν Χριστῷ ἀπὸ τῶν στοιχείων τοῦ κόσμου, τί ὡς ζῶντες ἐν κόσμῳ δογματίζεσθε, 21 Μὴ ἅψῃ μηδὲ γεύσῃ μηδὲ θίγῃς, 22 ἅ ἐστιν πάντα εἰς φθορὰν τῇ ἀποχρήσει, κατὰ τὰ ἐντάλματα καὶ διδασκαλίας

---

it[c] syr[p,h] cop[sa,bo] eth Euthalius Theodoret John-Damascus Ps-Oecumenius // ἡμᾶς p[46] B 33 88 181 Lect it[mon] syr[pal] arm Marcion Ambrose // omit ℵ[c] D G P Ψ 0208 104 330 436* 451 1241 1962 1984 2127 2492 Byz it[ar,d,dem,div,e,f,g,x,z] vg goth Tertullian Ambrosiaster Hilary Chrysostom Theodoret Theophylact

[5] 18 {B} ἃ p[46] ℵ* A B D* I 33 1739 it[d,e,m] cop[sa,bo] eth Marcion Tertullian Origen[gr,lat] Ambrosiaster Lucifer mss[acc. to Jerome, Augustine] Augustine // μή 81 // ἃ μή ℵ[c] C D[c] K P Ψ 88 104 181 326 330 436 451 614 629 630 1241 1877 1881 1962 1984 1985 2127 2492 2495 Byz Lect it[ar,c,dem,div,f,g,mon,x,z] vg syr[p,h] goth arm Origen[gr,lat] Ambrose Chrysostom Pelagius Jerome Theodore[lat] Augustine Theodoret John-Damascus // ἃ οὐκ G

---

a major, a major: RV ASV Seg // a major, a major, a major: TT // a exclamation, a exclamation, a minor: Jer

b b 15 b none, b minor: TR Bov Nes BF² AV RV ASV RSV NEB TT (Zür) (Luth) Jer Seg // b minor, b none // b none, b none: WH

---

14 ἐξαλείψας...μέσου Eph 2.14-15   προσηλώσας...σταυρῷ Eph 2.16; 1 Pe 2.24
16 Ro 14.1-12   17 ἅ...μελλόντων He 8.5; 10.1   19 τὴν κεφαλήν...θεοῦ Eph 2.21; 4.15-16
20 Ga 4.3-5, 9   22 τὰ...ἀνθρώπων Is 29.13; Mt 15.9

τῶν ἀνθρώπων; 23 ἅτινά ἐστιν λόγον μὲν ἔχοντα σοφίας ἐν ἐθελοθρησκίᾳ καὶ ταπεινοφροσύνῃ καὶ[6] ἀφειδίᾳ σώματος, οὐκ ἐν τιμῇ τινι πρὸς πλησμονὴν τῆς σαρκός.

3 Εἰ οὖν συνηγέρθητε τῷ Χριστῷ, τὰ ἄνω ζητεῖτε, οὗ ὁ Χριστός ἐστιν ἐν δεξιᾷ τοῦ θεοῦ καθήμενος· 2 τὰ ἄνω φρονεῖτε, μὴ τὰ ἐπὶ τῆς γῆς· 3 ἀπεθάνετε γάρ, καὶ ἡ ζωὴ ὑμῶν κέκρυπται σὺν τῷ Χριστῷ ἐν τῷ θεῷ. 4 ὅταν ὁ Χριστὸς φανερωθῇ, ἡ ζωὴ ὑμῶν[1], τότε καὶ ὑμεῖς σὺν αὐτῷ φανερωθήσεσθε ἐν δόξῃ.

5 Νεκρώσατε οὖν τὰ μέλη τὰ ἐπὶ τῆς γῆς, πορνείαν, ἀκαθαρσίαν, πάθος, ἐπιθυμίαν κακήν, καὶ τὴν πλεονεξίαν ἥτις ἐστὶν εἰδωλολατρία, 6 δι᾽ ἃ ἔρχεται ἡ ὀργὴ τοῦ θεοῦ [ἐπὶ τοὺς υἱοὺς τῆς ἀπειθείας][2]· 7 ἐν οἷς καὶ ὑμεῖς περιεπατήσατέ ποτε ὅτε ἐζῆτε ἐν τούτοις. 8 νυνὶ δὲ ἀπόθεσθε καὶ ὑμεῖς τὰ πάντα, ὀργήν, θυμόν, κακίαν,

teachings. 23 Of course they appear to have wisdom in their forced worship of angels, and false humility, and severe treatment of the body; but they have no real value in controlling physical passions.

3 You have been raised to life with Christ. Set your hearts, then, on the things that are in heaven, where Christ sits on his throne at the right side of God. 2 Keep your minds fixed on things there, not on things here on earth. 3 For you have died, and your life is hidden with Christ in God. 4 Your real life is Christ, and when he appears, then you too will appear with him and share his glory!

The Old Life and the New

5 You must put to death, then, the earthly desires at work in you, such as immorality, indecency, lust, evil passions, and greed (for greediness is a form of idol worship). 6 Because of such things God's wrath will come upon those who do not obey him.[1] 7 And you yourselves at one time used to live among such men, when your life was dominated by those desires.

8 But now you must get rid of all these things: anger, passion, and hateful feelings. No insults or obscene talk must

---

[6] **23** {D} ταπεινοφροσύνῃ καί ℵ A C D^gr H K P Ψ 33 81 88 104 181 326 330 436 451 614 629 630 1241 1877 1881 1962 1984 1985 2127 2492 2495 *Byz Lect* it^c,dem,div,x,z vg syr^p cop^sa arm Jerome Augustine Euthalius // ταπεινοφροσύνῃ τοῦ νοός καί (see 2.18) G it^ar,d,e,f,g (it^m,mon *omit* καί) syr^h (cop^bo) (goth) (Ambrosiaster) Hilary Pelagius (Augustine) // ταπεινοφροσύνῃ 𝔓^46 B 1739 Origen^lat Ambrosiaster Hilary Ambrose Pelagius Paulinus-Nola // ταπεινοφροσύνης Clement

[1] **4** {C} ὑμῶν 𝔓^46 ℵ C D* G P Ψ 33 81 88 104 1739 1881 1984 2127 *l*^809 it^ar,c,d,dem,div,e,f,g,mon,t,x,z vg cop^bo goth arm eth Origen^gr1/2 Cyprian Eusebius Ambrosiaster Hilary Gregory-Nyssa Didymus Chrysostom Cyril Euthalius Theodoret John-Damascus // ἡμῶν B D^c H K 181 326 330 436 451 614 629 630 1241 1877 1962 1985 2492 2495 *Byz Lect* syr^p,h cop^sa Origen^gr1/2,lat Hilary Ambrose

[2] **6** {D} θεοῦ ἐπὶ τοὺς υἱοὺς τῆς ἀπειθείας (see Eph 5.6) ℵ A C D^vid G H I K P Ψ 33 81 88 104 181 326 330 436 451 614 629 630 (1241 *omit* τοῦ θεοῦ) 1739 1877 1881 1902 1984 1985 2127 2492 2495 *Byz Lect* it^ar,c,d,dem,div,e,f,g,mon,t,x,z vg syr^p,h cop^bo arm eth^pp goth Clement Chrysostom Theodore^lat Augustine Euthalius Theodoret // θεοῦ 𝔓^46 B cop^sa eth^ro Clement Cyprian Macrobius Ambrosiaster Ephraem Jerome

---

23 ἀφειδίᾳ σώματος 1 Tm 4.3 πλησμονὴν τῆς σαρκός Ro 13.14
3 1 Εἰ...Χριστῷ Col 2.12 οὗ...καθήμενος Ps 110.1; Mt 22.44; Mk 16.19; Ac 2.34; Eph 1.20; He 1.3; 8.1; 10.12; 12.2 **2** Mt 6.33 **3** ἀπεθάνετε γάρ Ro 6.2; 2 Cor 5.14 **4** ὁ Χριστός... ὑμῶν Ga 2.20; Php 1.21 ὑμεῖς...δόξῃ 1 Cor 15.43; Php 3.21; 1 Jn 3.2 **5** Ro 6.6, 11; 8.13; Eph 4.19; 5.3, 5 **6** Eph 5.6 **8** Eph 4.25–31; 5.4

---

[1] **6** *Some mss. omit* upon those who do not obey him

ever come from your lips. ⁹ Do not lie to one another, for you have put off the old self with its habits, ¹⁰ and have put on the new self. This is the new man which God, its creator, is constantly renewing in his own image, to bring you to a full knowledge of himself. ¹¹ As a result, there are no Gentiles and Jews, circumcised and uncircumcised, barbarians, savages, slaves, or free men, but Christ is all, Christ is in all!

¹² You are the people of God; he loved you and chose you for his own. Therefore, you must put on compassion, kindness, humility, gentleness, and patience. ¹³ Be helpful to one another, and forgive one another, whenever any of you has a complaint against someone else. You must forgive each other in the same way that the Lord has forgiven you. ¹⁴ And to all these add love, which binds all things together in perfect unity. ¹⁵ The peace that Christ gives is to be the judge in your hearts; for to this peace God has called you together in the one body. And be thankful. ¹⁶ Christ's message, in all its richness, must live in your hearts. Teach and instruct each

βλασφημίαν, αἰσχρολογίαν ἐκ τοῦ στόματος ὑμῶν· 9 μὴ ψεύδεσθε εἰς ἀλλήλους, ἀπεκδυσάμενοι τὸν παλαιὸν ἄνθρωπον σὺν ταῖς πράξεσιν αὐτοῦ, 10 καὶ ἐνδυσάμενοι τὸν νέον τὸν ἀνακαινούμενον εἰς ἐπίγνωσιν κατ' εἰκόνα τοῦ κτίσαντος αὐτόν, 11 ὅπου οὐκ ἔνι Ἕλλην καὶ Ἰουδαῖος, περιτομὴ καὶ ἀκροβυστία, βάρβαρος, Σκύθης, δοῦλος, ἐλεύθερος, ἀλλὰ [τὰ] πάντα καὶ ἐν πᾶσιν Χριστός.

12 Ἐνδύσασθε οὖν ὡς ἐκλεκτοὶ τοῦ θεοῦ, ἅγιοι καὶ ἠγαπημένοι, σπλάγχνα οἰκτιρμοῦ, χρηστότητα, ταπεινοφροσύνην, πραΰτητα, μακροθυμίαν, 13 ἀνεχόμενοι ἀλλήλων καὶ χαριζόμενοι ἑαυτοῖς ἐάν τις πρός τινα ἔχῃ μομφήν· καθὼς καὶ ὁ κύριος³ ἐχαρίσατο ὑμῖν οὕτως καὶ ὑμεῖς· 14 ἐπὶ πᾶσιν δὲ τούτοις τὴν ἀγάπην, ὅ ἐστιν σύνδεσμος τῆς τελειότητος. 15 καὶ ἡ εἰρήνη τοῦ Χριστοῦ βραβευέτω ἐν ταῖς καρδίαις ὑμῶν, εἰς ἣν καὶ ἐκλήθητε ἐν ἑνὶ σώματι· καὶ εὐχάριστοι γίνεσθε. 16 ὁ λόγος τοῦ Χριστοῦ⁴ ἐνοικείτω ἐν ὑμῖν πλουσίως,ᵃ ἐν πάσῃ σοφίᾳᵃ διδάσκοντες καὶ νουθετοῦντες ἑαυτοὺςᵇ ψαλμοῖς, ὕμνοις,

---

³ 13 {C} κύριος 𝔭⁴⁶ A B D* G *l*⁸⁰⁹ it^(c,d,dem,div,e,f,g,m,x,z) vg Pelagius Augustine^(1/2) ‖ Χριστός ℵ^c C D^c K P Ψ 81 88 104 181 326 330 436 451 614 629 630 1241 1739 1877 1881 1962 1984 1985 2127 2492 2495 *Byz Lect* it^(ar,mon) syr^(p,h) cop^(sa,bo) goth eth Clement Ambrosiaster Chrysostom Theodore^lat Euthalius Leo Theodoret Antiochus John-Damascus ‖ θεός ℵ* ‖ θεὸς ἐν Χριστῷ 33 arm Augustine^(1/2)

⁴ 16 {B} Χριστοῦ 𝔭⁴⁶ ℵ^c B C² D G K P Ψ 81 181 326 614 629 630 1739 1877 1881 2492 2495 *Byz Lect* it^(ar,c,d,dem,div,e,f,g,m,mon,x,z) vg syr^((p),h) cop^(sa,bo ms) goth arm Ambrosiaster Chrysostom Euthalius John-Damascus ‖ θεοῦ A C* 33 104 330 436 451 1241 1962 1984 1985 *l*⁵⁹⁹,¹³⁶⁵ eth Augustine Theodoret Theophylact^mg ‖ κυρίου ℵ* I 2127 cop^bo Clement

---

ᵃ ᵃ 16 *a* minor, *a* none: Bov Nes BF² ASV RSV (NEB) TT Zür (Luth) (Jer) Seg ‖ *a* none, *a* minor: TR WH AV RV ASV^mg

ᵇ 16 *b* none: WH AV RV ASV Zür Luth Seg ‖ *b* minor: TR Bov Nes BF² RSV (NEB) TT (Jer)

---

9 μὴ...ἀλλήλους Eph 4.25 ἀπεκδυσάμενοι...αὐτοῦ Eph 4.22 10 Eph 4.24 κατ' εἰκόνα ...αὐτόν Gn 1.26–27 11 Ga 3.28; 1 Cor 12.13; (Ro 10.12) 12 ἐκλεκτοὶ τοῦ θεοῦ 1 Pe 2.9 σπλάγχνα...μακροθυμίαν Eph 4.2, 32 13 χαριζόμενοι ἑαυτοῖς and καθὼς...ὑμεῖς Mt 6.14; Eph 4.32; 5.2 14 Ro 13.8, 10; Eph 4.3 15 ἡ εἰρήνη...ὑμῶν Php 4.7 ἐκλήθητε...σώματι 1 Cor 12.13, 27; Eph 4.4 16 διδάσκοντες...θεῷ Eph 5.19

ᾠδαῖς πνευματικαῖς° ἐν χάριτι° ᾄδοντες ἐν ταῖς καρδίαις ὑμῶν τῷ θεῷ[5]· 17 καὶ πᾶν ὅ τι ἐὰν ποιῆτε ἐν λόγῳ ἢ ἐν ἔργῳ, πάντα ἐν ὀνόματι κυρίου Ἰησοῦ, εὐχαριστοῦντες τῷ θεῷ πατρὶ[6] δι’ αὐτοῦ.

Social Duties of the New Life

18 Αἱ γυναῖκες, ὑποτάσσεσθε τοῖς ἀνδράσιν, ὡς ἀνῆκεν ἐν κυρίῳ. 19 Οἱ ἄνδρες, ἀγαπᾶτε τὰς γυναῖκας καὶ μὴ πικραίνεσθε πρὸς αὐτάς.

20 Τὰ τέκνα, ὑπακούετε τοῖς γονεῦσιν κατὰ πάντα, τοῦτο γὰρ εὐάρεστόν ἐστιν ἐν κυρίῳ. 21 Οἱ πατέρες, μὴ ἐρεθίζετε τὰ τέκνα ὑμῶν, ἵνα μὴ ἀθυμῶσιν.

22 Οἱ δοῦλοι, ὑπακούετε κατὰ πάντα τοῖς κατὰ σάρκα κυρίοις, μὴ ἐν ὀφθαλμοδουλίᾳ ὡς ἀνθρωπάρεσκοι, ἀλλ’ ἐν ἁπλότητι καρδίας,[d] φοβούμενοι τὸν κύριον. 23 ὃ ἐὰν ποιῆτε, ἐκ ψυχῆς ἐργάζεσθε, ὡς τῷ κυρίῳ καὶ οὐκ ἀνθρώποις, 24 εἰδότες ὅτι ἀπὸ κυρίου ἀπολήμψεσθε τὴν ἀνταπόδοσιν τῆς κληρονομίας.[e] τῷ κυρίῳ Χριστῷ δουλεύετε·[e] 25 ὁ γὰρ ἀδικῶν κομίσεται ὃ ἠδίκησεν, καὶ

other with all wisdom. Sing psalms, hymns, and sacred songs; sing to God, with thanksgiving in your hearts. 17 Everything you do or say, then, should be done in the name of the Lord Jesus, as you give thanks through him to God the Father.

Personal Relations in the New Life

18 Wives, be obedient to your husbands, for that is what you should do as Christians.

19 Husbands, love your wives, and do not be harsh with them.

20 Children, it is your Christian duty to obey your parents always, for that is what pleases God.

21 Parents, do not irritate your children, or they might become discouraged.

22 Slaves, obey your human masters in all things, and do it not only when they are watching you, just to gain their approval, but do it with a sincere heart, because of your reverence for the Lord. 23 Whatever you do, work at it with all your heart, as though you were working for the Lord, and not for men. 24 Remember that the Lord will reward you; you will receive what he has kept for his people. For Christ is the real Master you serve. 25 And the wrongdoer, who-

---

[5] 16 {B} τῷ θεῷ 𝔭[46vid] ℵ A B C* D* G Ψ[c] 33 81 1739 1881 (1962 2127 *transpose* τῷ θεῷ *after* ᾄδοντες) it[d,div,e,f,g,m,mon,x,z] vg syr[p,h] cop[sa,bo] arm Clement Ambrosiaster Chrysostom[2/3] Euthalius // τῷ κυρίῳ C[2] D[c] K Ψ* 104 181 326 330 436 451 614 629 630 1241 1877 1984 1985 2492 2495 *Byz Lect* it[ar,c,dem,(gig)] cop[bo mss] goth Ambrosiaster Ephraem Chrysostom[1/3] Pelagius Theodoret John-Damascus

[6] 17 {C} θεῷ πατρί 𝔭[46vid] ℵ A B C 81 1739 1985 it[ar,m,mon] syr[p] cop[sa,bo] goth oth Ambrose // θεῷ καὶ πατρί (800 Eph 5.20) D G K Ψ 33 88 104 181 330 436 451 614 629 630 1241 1877 1881 1962 1984 2127 2492 2495 *Byz Lect* it[c,d,dem,div,e,f,g,x,z] vg syr[h] arm Clement Ambrosiaster Chrysostom Euthalius Theodoret Antiochus John-Damascus // πατρὶ καὶ θεῷ 326

° ° 16 c none, c none: TR Bov Nes BF[2] RSV TT // c none, c minor: WH // c minor, c none: AV RV ASV (NEB) (Zür) (Luth) (Jer) (Seg)

[d] 22 d minor: TR WH AV RV ASV RSV NEB TT Zür (Luth) Jer Seg // d none: Bov Nes BF[2]

[e] [e] 24 e major, e minor: Bov Nes BF[2] TT Jer // e minor, e major: RV ASV RSV // e major, e major: WH NEB Seg // e major, e exclamation: Luth // e exclamation, e exclamation: Zür // different text: TR AV

17 πᾶν...Ἰησοῦ 1 Cor 10.31 εὐχαριστοῦντες...αὐτοῦ Eph 5.20 18 Gn 3.16; Eph 5.22; 1 Pe 3.1 19 Οἱ...γυναῖκας Eph 5.25; 1 Pe 3.7 20 Eph 6.1 21 Οἱ...ὑμῶν Eph 6.4 22–25 Eph 6.5–8

ever he is, will be paid for the wrong things he does; for God treats everyone alike.

4 Masters, be right and fair in the way you treat your slaves. Remember that you too have a Master in heaven.

Instructions

[2] Be persistent in prayer, and keep alert as you pray, with thanks to God. [3] At the same time pray also for us, that God will give us a good opportunity to preach his message, to tell the secret of Christ. For that is why I am now in prison. [4] Pray, then, that I may speak in such a way as to make it clear, as I should.

[5] Be wise in the way you act toward those who are not believers, making good use of every opportunity you have. [6] Your speech should always be pleasant and interesting, and you should know how to give the right answer to every person.

Final Greetings

[7] Our dear brother Tychicus, who is a faithful worker and fellow servant in the Lord's work, will give you all the news about me. [8] That is why I am sending him to you, to cheer you up by telling you how all of us are getting along. [9] With him goes Onesimus, the dear and faithful brother, who belongs to your group. They will tell you everything that is happening here.

[10] Aristarchus, who is in prison with me, sends you greetings, and so does Mark, the cousin of Barnabas. (You

οὐκ ἔστιν προσωπολημψία. **4** Οἱ κύριοι, τὸ δίκαιον καὶ τὴν ἰσότητα τοῖς δούλοις παρέχεσθε, εἰδότες ὅτι καὶ ὑμεῖς ἔχετε κύριον ἐν οὐρανῷ.

Exhortations

2 Τῇ προσευχῇ προσκαρτερεῖτε, γρηγοροῦντες ἐν αὐτῇ ἐν εὐχαριστίᾳ, **3** προσευχόμενοι ἅμα καὶ περὶ ἡμῶν, ἵνα ὁ θεὸς ἀνοίξῃ ἡμῖν θύραν τοῦ λόγου, λαλῆσαι τὸ μυστήριον τοῦ Χριστοῦ, δι' ὃ καὶ δέδεμαι, **4** ἵνα φανερώσω αὐτὸ ὡς δεῖ με λαλῆσαι. **5** Ἐν σοφίᾳ περιπατεῖτε πρὸς τοὺς ἔξω, τὸν καιρὸν ἐξαγοραζόμενοι. **6** ὁ λόγος ὑμῶν πάντοτε ἐν χάριτι, ἅλατι ἠρτυμένος, εἰδέναι πῶς δεῖ ὑμᾶς ἑνὶ ἑκάστῳ ἀποκρίνεσθαι.

Final Greetings

7 Τὰ κατ' ἐμὲ πάντα γνωρίσει ὑμῖν Τυχικὸς ὁ ἀγαπητὸς ἀδελφὸς καὶ πιστὸς διάκονος καὶ σύνδουλος ἐν κυρίῳ, **8** ὃν ἔπεμψα πρὸς ὑμᾶς εἰς αὐτὸ τοῦτο, ἵνα γνῶτε τὰ περὶ ἡμῶν[1] καὶ παρακαλέσῃ τὰς καρδίας ὑμῶν, **9** σὺν Ὀνησίμῳ τῷ πιστῷ καὶ ἀγαπητῷ ἀδελφῷ, ὅς ἐστιν ἐξ ὑμῶν· πάντα ὑμῖν γνωρίσουσιν τὰ ὧδε.

10 Ἀσπάζεται ὑμᾶς Ἀρίσταρχος ὁ συναιχμάλωτός μου, καὶ Μᾶρκος ὁ ἀνεψιὸς Βαρναβᾶ (ᵃπερὶ οὗ ἐλάβετε

[1] **8** {C} γνῶτε τὰ περὶ ἡμῶν A B D* G P 048 33 81 88 1962 2127 2492ᵛⁱᵈ? *l*599 itᵃʳ,ᵈ,ᵉ,ᵍ,ᵐᵒⁿ syrᵖᵃˡ copˢᵃ arm eth Ephraem Jerome²ᐟ³ Theodore Euthalius Theodoret ∥ γνῶτε τὰ περὶ ὑμῶν ℵ* 1241 ∥ γνῷ τὰ περὶ ἡμῶν 330 451 *l*598 ∥ γνῷ τὰ περὶ ὑμῶν 𝔭⁴⁶ ℵᶜ C Dᶜ K Ψ 104 181 326 436 614 629 630 1739 1877 1881 1984 1985 2495 *Byz Lect* itᶜ,ᵈᵉᵐ,ᵈⁱᵛ,f,x,z vg syrᵖ,ʰ (copˢᵃᵐˢˢ γνῷ) copᵇᵒ goth Ambrosiaster Chrysostom Pelagius Jerome¹ᐟ³ John-Damascus

ᵃ ᵃ ᵃ **10** a parens, a minor, a parens: TR WH Bov Nes BF² AV RV ASV NEB TT ∥ a parens, a dash, a parens: RSV ∥ a minor, a dash, a dash: Zür Luth ∥ a minor, a major, a major: Jer Seg

25 οὐκ ἔστιν προσωπολημψία Dt 10.17; 2 Chr 19.17; Ac 10.34; Eph 6.9
4 1 Lv 25.43, 53; Eph 6.9 **2** Τῇ προσευχῇ προσκαρτερεῖτε Eph 6.18; Php 4.6; 1 Th 5.17 **3** προσευχόμενοι...Χριστοῦ Eph 6.19; 2 Th 3.1; Ro 15.30; 1 Cor 16.9 **3-4** δι'...λαλῆσαι Eph 6.20 **5** Eph 5.15–16; 1 Th 4.11–12 **6** ὁ...χάριτι Eph 4.29 ἅλατι ἠρτυμένος Mk 9.50 εἰδέναι...ἀποκρίνεσθαι 1 Pe 3.15 **7-8** Eph 6.21–22 **9** Ὀνησίμῳ...ἀδελφῷ Phm 10–12 **10** Ἀρίσταρχος...μου Ac 19.29; 27.2; Phm 24 Μᾶρκος...Βαρναβᾶ Ac 12.12, 25; 13.13; 15.37–39; Phm 24

ἐντολάς,ᵃ ἐὰν ἔλθῃ πρὸς ὑμᾶς δέξασθε αὐτόν)ᵃ, **11** καὶ Ἰησοῦς ὁ λεγόμενος Ἰοῦστος,ᵇ οἱ ὄντες ἐκ περιτομῆςᵇ οὗτοι μόνοι συνεργοὶ εἰς τὴν βασιλείαν τοῦ θεοῦ, οἵτινες ἐγενήθησάν μοι παρηγορία. **12** ἀσπάζεται ὑμᾶς Ἐπαφρᾶς ὁ ἐξ ὑμῶν, δοῦλος Χριστοῦ [Ἰησοῦ], πάντοτε ἀγωνιζόμενος ὑπὲρ ὑμῶν ἐν ταῖς προσευχαῖς, ἵνα σταθῆτε τέλειοι καὶ πεπληροφορημένοι ἐν παντὶ θελήματι τοῦ θεοῦ. **13** μαρτυρῶ γὰρ αὐτῷ ὅτι ἔχει πολὺν πόνον ὑπὲρ ὑμῶν καὶ τῶν ἐν Λαοδικείᾳ καὶ τῶν ἐν Ἱεραπόλει. **14** ἀσπάζεται ὑμᾶς Λουκᾶς ὁ ἰατρὸς ὁ ἀγαπητὸς καὶ Δημᾶς. **15** Ἀσπάσασθε τοὺς ἐν Λαοδικείᾳ ἀδελφοὺς καὶ Νύμφαν καὶ τὴν κατ' οἶκον αὐτῆς² ἐκκλησίαν. **16** καὶ ὅταν ἀναγνωσθῇ παρ' ὑμῖν ἡ ἐπιστολή, ποιήσατε ἵνα καὶ ἐν τῇ Λαοδικέων ἐκκλησίᾳ ἀναγνωσθῇ, καὶ τὴν ἐκ Λαοδικείας ἵνα καὶ ὑμεῖς ἀναγνῶτε. **17** καὶ εἴπατε Ἀρχίππῳ, Βλέπε τὴν διακονίαν ἣν παρέλαβες ἐν κυρίῳ, ἵνα αὐτὴν πληροῖς.

18 Ὁ ἀσπασμὸς τῇ ἐμῇ χειρὶ Παύλου. μνημονεύετέ μου τῶν δεσμῶν. ἡ χάρις μεθ' ὑμῶν.³

---

² **15** {C} Νύμφαν καὶ τὴν κατ' οἶκον αὐτῆς B 1739 1877 1881 syrʰ·ᵖᵃˡᵐˢ copˢᵃ Origen ‖ Νυμφᾶν καὶ τὴν κατ' οἶκον αὐτοῦ D (G τὴν οἱ κατ' οἶκον) K Ψ 181 (330* 451 Νύμφας) (330ᶜ 1241 Νύμφαν) 436 614 629 630 1984 1985 2495 *Byz Lect* syrᵖ·ʰᵐᵍ goth Chrysostom Theodoreˡᵃᵗ·ᶜᵒᵐᵐ Theodoret John-Damascus ‖ Νύμφαν (or Νυμφᾶν) καὶ τὴν κατ' οἶκον αὐτῆς (or αὐτοῦ) itᵃʳ·ᶜ·ᵈ·ᵈᵉᵐ·ᵈⁱᵛ·ᵉ·ᶠ·ᵍ·ᵐᵒⁿ·ˣ·ᶻ vg arm Pelagius Ambrosiaster Cassiodorus ‖ Νύμφαν (or Νυμφᾶν) καὶ τὴν κατ' οἶκον αὐτῶν ℵ A C P 33 81 (88 104 326 Νυμφᾶν) 1962 (2127 Νήφαν) 2492 syrᵖᵃˡᵐˢ copᵇᵒ Theodoreˡᵃᵗ (Euthalius Νύμφαν)

³ **18** {A} ὑμῶν. ℵ* A B C G 048 33 81 1881 itᶠ·ᵍ syrᵖᵃˡᵐˢ copˢᵃ·ᵇᵒᵐˢˢ arm ethʳᵒ Ambrosiaster Euthalius ‖ ὑμῶν. ἀμήν. ℵᶜ D K P Ψ 88 104 181 326 330 436 451 614 629 630 1241 1739 1877 1962 1984 2127 2492 2495 *Byz Lect* itᵃʳ·ᶜ·ᵈ·ᵈⁱᵛ·ᵉ·ᵐᵒⁿ·ˣ·ᶻ vg syrᵖ·ʰ·ᵖᵃˡᵐˢ copᵇᵒᵐˢˢ goth Chrysostom Cassiodorus ‖ ὑμῶν πάντοτε. ἀμήν. 1985

ᵇ ᵇ **11** *b* minor, *b* none: Bov Nes BF² (RSV) (NEB) (TT) (Luth) (Jer) (Seg) ‖ *b* minor, *b* major: TR AV RV ASV Zür ‖ *b* minor, *b* minor: WH

---

12 Ἐπαφρᾶς…Ἰησοῦ Col 1.7; Phm 23   **14** Λουκᾶς…Δημᾶς 2 Tm 4.10, 11; Phm 24   **17** Ἀρχίππῳ Phm 2   **18** Ὁ…Παύλου 1 Cor 16.21; 2 Th 3.17

have already received instructions about him, to welcome him if he comes your way.) [11] Joshua, called Justus, also sends greetings. These three are the only Jewish converts who work with me for the Kingdom of God, and they have been a great help to me. [12] Greetings from Epaphras, another member of your group, and a servant of Christ Jesus. He always prays fervently for you, asking God to make you stand firm, mature, and fully convinced, in complete obedience to his will. [13] I can personally testify to his hard work for you, and for the people in Laodicea and Hierapolis. [14] Luke, our dear doctor, and Demas send you their greetings.

[15] Give our best wishes to the brothers in Laodicea, and to Nympha and the church that meets in her house. [16] After you read this letter, make sure that it is read also in the church at Laodicea. At the same time, you are to read the letter Laodicea will send you. [17] And tell Archippus: "Be sure to finish the task you were given in the Lord's service."

[18] With my own hand I write this: *Greetings from Paul.* Do not forget my chains!

May God's grace be with you.

PAUL'S FIRST LETTER TO THE THESSALONIANS

1 From Paul, Silas, and Timothy —
To the people of the church in Thessalonica, who belong to God the Father and the Lord Jesus Christ:
May grace and peace be yours.

The Life and Faith of the Thessalonians

² We always thank God for you all, and always mention you in our prayers. ³ For we remember before our God and Father how you put your faith into practice, how your love made you work so hard, and how your hope in our Lord Jesus Christ is firm. ⁴ We know, brothers, that God loves you and has chosen you to be his own. ⁵ For we brought the Good News to you, not with words only, but also with power and the Holy Spirit, and with complete conviction of its truth. You know how we lived when we were with you; it was for your own good.

ΠΡΟΣ ΘΕΣΣΑΛΟΝΙΚΕΙΣ Α

Salutation

1 Παῦλος καὶ Σιλουανὸς καὶ Τιμόθεος τῇ ἐκκλησίᾳ Θεσσαλονικέων ἐν θεῷ πατρὶ καὶ κυρίῳ Ἰησοῦ Χριστῷ· χάρις ὑμῖν καὶ εἰρήνη[1].

The Thessalonians' Faith and Example

2 Εὐχαριστοῦμεν τῷ θεῷ πάντοτε[a] περὶ πάντων ὑμῶν,[a] μνείαν ποιούμενοι ἐπὶ τῶν προσευχῶν ἡμῶν,[b] [c]ἀδιαλείπτως[b] **3**[c] μνημονεύοντες ὑμῶν τοῦ ἔργου τῆς πίστεως καὶ τοῦ κόπου τῆς ἀγάπης καὶ τῆς ὑπομονῆς τῆς ἐλπίδος τοῦ κυρίου ἡμῶν Ἰησοῦ Χριστοῦ ἔμπροσθεν τοῦ θεοῦ καὶ πατρὸς ἡμῶν,[d] **4** εἰδότες, ἀδελφοὶ ἠγαπημένοι ὑπὸ [τοῦ] θεοῦ, τὴν ἐκλογὴν ὑμῶν,[d] **5** ὅτι τὸ εὐαγγέλιον ἡμῶν οὐκ ἐγενήθη εἰς ὑμᾶς ἐν λόγῳ μόνον ἀλλὰ καὶ ἐν δυνάμει καὶ ἐν πνεύματι ἁγίῳ καὶ [ἐν] πληροφορίᾳ πολλῇ, καθὼς οἴδατε οἷοι ἐγενήθημεν [ἐν] ὑμῖν δι'

---

1 1 {B} εἰρήνη B G Ψ 629 1739 1881 1984 1985 it[ar,c,dem,div,f,g,r²,x,z] vg syr[p,palms] cop[sa,fay] arm eth[ro] Origen Ambrosiaster Chrysostom[comm] Theodore[lat] Theophylact ‖ εἰρήνη ἀπὸ θεοῦ καὶ κυρίου Ἰησοῦ Χριστοῦ it[d,e] ‖ εἰρήνη ἀπὸ θεοῦ πατρὸς καὶ κυρίου Ἰησοῦ Χριστοῦ (*see* 2 Th 1.2) D[gr] 2127 it[mon] cop[boms] Chrysostom[txt] Theodoret John-Damascus ‖ εἰρήνη ἀπὸ θεοῦ πατρὸς ἡμῶν καὶ κυρίου Ἰησοῦ Χριστοῦ (*see* 2 Th 1.2 mg) ℵ A I K P 33 81 88 104 (181 ὑμῶν) 326 330 451 614 630 1241 1877 1962 2492 2495 *Byz Lect* syr[h with *,palms] (syr[h] *omit* ἀπὸ θεοῦ πατρός) Euthalius ‖ εἰρήνη ἀπὸ θεοῦ πατρὸς καὶ κυρίου ἡμῶν Ἰησοῦ Χριστοῦ 436 ‖ εἰρήνη ἀπὸ θεοῦ πατρὸς ἡμῶν καὶ κυρίου ἡμῶν Ἰησοῦ Χριστοῦ cop[bo] eth[pp]

[a,a] **2** *a* none, *a* minor: TR Bov Nes BF² AV RV ASV RSV NEB TT (Zür) (Luth) (Jer) Seg ‖ *a* minor, *a* none ‖ *a* none, *a* none: WH

[b,b] **2** *b* minor, *b* none: TR WH Bov Nes BF² AV RV ASV TT Zür Luth Jer Seg ‖ *b* none, *b* minor: RSV NEB

[c,c] **2-3** *c* no number, *c* number 3: TR[ed] WH Bov Nes BF² RSV NEB? TT? Zür ‖ *c* number 3, *c* no number: TR[ed] AV RV ASV NEB? Luth Jer Seg

[d,d] **3-4** *d* minor, *d* minor: WH Bov Nes BF² ‖ *d* major, *d* minor: RV ASV RSV (NEB) TT Luth Seg ‖ *d* minor, *d* major: TR AV Zür ‖ *d* major, *d* major: Jer

1 Παῦλος...Χριστῷ 2 Th 1.1; Ac 17.1 **2** Php 1.3-4; Col 1.3; 2 Th 1.11 **3** ὑμῶν...ἐλπίδος 1 Cor 13.13; Col 1.4-5 **5** τὸ...δυνάμει 1 Cor 2.4-5; 4.20

ὑμᾶς. 6 καὶ ὑμεῖς μιμηταὶ ἡμῶν ἐγενήθητε καὶ τοῦ κυρίου, δεξάμενοι τὸν λόγον ἐν θλίψει πολλῇ μετὰ χαρᾶς πνεύματος ἁγίου, 7 ὥστε γενέσθαι ὑμᾶς τύπον πᾶσιν τοῖς πιστεύουσιν ἐν τῇ Μακεδονίᾳ καὶ ἐν τῇ Ἀχαΐᾳ. 8 ἀφ' ὑμῶν γὰρ ἐξήχηται ὁ λόγος τοῦ κυρίου οὐ μόνον ἐν τῇ Μακεδονίᾳ καὶ [ἐν τῇ] Ἀχαΐᾳ, ἀλλ' ἐν παντὶ τόπῳ ἡ πίστις ὑμῶν ἡ πρὸς τὸν θεὸν ἐξελήλυθεν, ὥστε μὴ χρείαν ἔχειν ἡμᾶς λαλεῖν τι· 9 αὐτοὶ γὰρ περὶ ἡμῶν ἀπαγγέλλουσιν ὁποίαν εἴσοδον ἔσχομεν πρὸς ὑμᾶς, καὶ πῶς ἐπεστρέψατε πρὸς τὸν θεὸν ἀπὸ τῶν εἰδώλων δουλεύειν θεῷ ζῶντι καὶ ἀληθινῷ, 10 καὶ ἀναμένειν τὸν υἱὸν αὐτοῦ ἐκ τῶν οὐρανῶν, ὃν ἤγειρεν ἐκ [τῶν] νεκρῶν, Ἰησοῦν τὸν ῥυόμενον ἡμᾶς ἐκ τῆς ὀργῆς τῆς ἐρχομένης.

Paul's Ministry in Thessalonica

2 Αὐτοὶ γὰρ οἴδατε, ἀδελφοί, τὴν εἴσοδον ἡμῶν τὴν πρὸς ὑμᾶς ὅτι οὐ κενὴ γέγονεν, 2 ἀλλὰ προπαθόντες καὶ ὑβρισθέντες καθὼς οἴδατε ἐν Φιλίπποις ἐπαρρησιασάμεθα ἐν τῷ θεῷ ἡμῶν λαλῆσαι πρὸς ὑμᾶς τὸ εὐαγγέλιον τοῦ θεοῦ ἐν πολλῷ ἀγῶνι. 3 ἡ γὰρ παράκλησις ἡμῶν οὐκ ἐκ πλάνης οὐδὲ ἐξ ἀκαθαρσίας οὐδὲ ἐν δόλῳ, 4 ἀλλὰ καθὼς δεδοκιμάσμεθα ὑπὸ τοῦ θεοῦ πιστευθῆναι τὸ εὐαγγέλιον οὕτως λαλοῦμεν, οὐχ ὡς ἀνθρώποις ἀρέσκοντες ἀλλὰ θεῷ τῷ δοκιμάζοντι τὰς καρδίας ἡμῶν. 5 οὔτε γάρ ποτε ἐν λόγῳ κολακείας ἐγενήθημεν, καθὼς οἴδατε, οὔτε ἐν προφάσει πλεονεξίας, θεὸς μάρτυς, 6 οὔτε ζητοῦντες ἐξ ἀνθρώπων δόξαν, οὔτε ἀφ' ὑμῶν οὔτε ἀπ' ἄλλων, 7ᵃ δυνάμενοι ἐν βάρει εἶναι ὡς Χριστοῦ ἀπό-

---

ᵃ ᵃ **2.6–7** a number 7, a no number: TRᵉᵈ WH Bov Nes BF² TT Zür Luth Jer Segᵉᵈ ∥ a no number, a number 7: TRᵉᵈ AV RV ASV RSV NEB Segᵉᵈ

---

6 ὑμεῖς...ἐγενήθητε 1 Cor 4.16; 2 Th 3.9 δεξάμενοι...πολλῇ Ac 17.5–9 **7** 1 Pe 5.3 **8** ἐν παντὶ...ἐξελήλυθεν Ro 1.8 ἐπεστρέψατε...ἀληθινῷ Ac 14.15 **10** ἀναμένειν... οὐρανῶν Tt 2.13 ὃν...νεκρῶν Ac 17.31 Ἰησοῦν...ἐρχομένης 1 Th 5.9
2 1 1 Th 1.5, 9 **2** προπαθόντες...Φιλίπποις Ac 16.19–24 ἐπαρρησιασάμεθα...ἀγῶνι Ac 17.1–5 **4** δεδοκιμάσμεθα...εὐαγγέλιον 1 Tm 1.11 οὐχ...ἀρέσκοντες Ga 1.10 θεῷ... ἡμῶν Jr 11.20 **5** ἐν λόγῳ...πλεονεξίας Ac 20.33; 2 Pe 2.3 θεὸς μάρτυς 1 Th 2.10
6 ζητοῦντες...ἄλλων Jn 5.41, 44

---

6 You imitated us and the Lord: and even though you suffered much, you received the message with the joy that comes from the Holy Spirit. 7 So you became an example to all believers in Macedonia and Greece. 8 For the message about the Lord went out from you not only to Macedonia and Greece, but the news of your faith in God has gone everywhere. There is nothing, then, that we need to say. 9 All those people speak of how you received us when we visited you, and how you turned away from idols to God, to serve the true and living God 10 and to wait for his Son to come from heaven — his Son Jesus, whom he raised from death, and who rescues us from God's wrath that is to come.

Paul's Work in Thessalonica

2 For you yourselves know, brothers, that our visit to you was not a failure. 2 You know how we had already been mistreated and insulted in Philippi before we came to you in Thessalonica. Yet our God gave us courage to tell you the Good News that comes from him, even though there was much opposition. 3 For the appeal we make to you is not based on error or impure motives, nor do we try to trick anyone. 4 Instead, we always speak as God wants us to, because he approved us and entrusted the Good News to us. We do not try to please men, but to please God, who tests our motives. 5 For you know very well that we did not come to you with flattering talk, nor did we use words to cover up greed — God is our witness! 6 We did not try to get praise from anyone, either from you or from others, 7 even though we could have made demands on you as apostles of Christ. But we were gentle when we were with you, as gentle as a mother taking care of her children. [8] Because of our love for you we were ready to share with you not only the Good News from God but even our own lives. You were so dear to us! [9] Surely you remember, brothers, how we worked and toiled! We worked day and night so we would not be any trouble to you as we preached to you the Good News from God.

[10] You are our witnesses, and so is God: our conduct toward you who believe was pure, and right, and without fault. [11] You know that we treated each one of you just as a father treats his own children. [12] We encouraged you, we comforted you, and we kept urging you to live the kind of life that pleases God, who calls you to share his own Kingdom and glory.

[13] And for this other reason, also, we always give thanks to God. When we brought you God's message, you heard it and accepted it, not as man's message but as God's message, which indeed it is. For God is at work among you who believe. [14] You, my brothers, had the same things happen to you that happened to the churches of God in Judea,

στολοι. [a]ἀλλὰ ἐγενήθημεν ἤπιοι[1] ἐν μέσῳ ὑμῶν, ὡς ἐὰν τροφὸς θάλπῃ τὰ ἑαυτῆς τέκνα· 8 οὕτως ὁμειρόμενοι ὑμῶν εὐδοκοῦμεν μεταδοῦναι ὑμῖν οὐ μόνον τὸ εὐαγγέλιον τοῦ θεοῦ ἀλλὰ καὶ τὰς ἑαυτῶν ψυχάς, διότι ἀγαπητοὶ ἡμῖν ἐγενήθητε. 9 μνημονεύετε γάρ, ἀδελφοί, τὸν κόπον ἡμῶν καὶ τὸν μόχθον· νυκτὸς καὶ ἡμέρας ἐργαζόμενοι πρὸς τὸ μὴ ἐπιβαρῆσαί τινα ὑμῶν ἐκηρύξαμεν εἰς ὑμᾶς τὸ εὐαγγέλιον τοῦ θεοῦ. 10 ὑμεῖς μάρτυρες καὶ ὁ θεός, ὡς ὁσίως καὶ δικαίως καὶ ἀμέμπτως ὑμῖν τοῖς πιστεύουσιν ἐγενήθημεν, 11 καθάπερ οἴδατε ὡς ἕνα ἕκαστον ὑμῶν ὡς πατὴρ τέκνα ἑαυτοῦ 12[b] παρακαλοῦντες ὑμᾶς καὶ παραμυθούμενοι [b]καὶ μαρτυρόμενοι [b]εἰς τὸ περιπατεῖν ὑμᾶς ἀξίως τοῦ θεοῦ τοῦ καλοῦντος[2] ὑμᾶς εἰς τὴν ἑαυτοῦ βασιλείαν καὶ δόξαν.

13 Καὶ διὰ τοῦτο καὶ ἡμεῖς εὐχαριστοῦμεν τῷ θεῷ ἀδιαλείπτως, ὅτι παραλαβόντες λόγον ἀκοῆς παρ' ἡμῶν τοῦ θεοῦ ἐδέξασθε οὐ λόγον ἀνθρώπων ἀλλὰ καθὼς ἐστιν ἀληθῶς λόγον θεοῦ, ὃς καὶ ἐνεργεῖται ἐν ὑμῖν τοῖς πιστεύουσιν. 14 ὑμεῖς γὰρ μιμηταὶ ἐγενήθητε, ἀδελφοί, τῶν ἐκκλησιῶν τοῦ θεοῦ τῶν οὐσῶν ἐν τῇ

---

[1] 7 {C} ἤπιοι A C[2?] D[c] K P Ψ[c] 33 81 88 104[c] 181 326* 330 436 614 629 630 1241 1739 1877 1881 1984 1985 2127 2492 *Byz Lect* syr[p,h] cop[sa,fay] arm Clement Origen[3/4] Basil Chrysostom Theodore[lat] Euthalius Theodoret John-Damascus Theophylact // νήπιοι 𝔭[65] ℵ B C* D* G I Ψ* 104* 326[c] 451 1962 2495 it[ar,c,d,dem,div,e,f,g,mon,x,z] vg cop[sams,bo] eth Clement Origen[grl/4,lat] Ambrosiaster Ephraem Jerome Augustine Cyril

[2] 12 {C} καλοῦντος B D G H K P Ψ 33 81 88 181 330 436 451 614 629 630 1241 1739 1877 1881 1962 1984 1985 2127 2492 2495 *Byz Lect* it[d,e,g,mon] syr[hmg] Ambrosiaster Ephraem Chrysostom[2/3] Pelagius Euthalius John-Damascus // καλέσαντος ℵ A 104 326 it[ar,c,dem,div,f,m,x,z] vg syr[p,h] cop[sa,bo,fay] goth arm Ambrosiaster Chrysostom[1/3] Theodore[lat] Theodoret Vigilius

[b b b] 11–12 *b* number 12, *b* no number, *b* no number: TR[ed] WH Bov Nes BF[2] TT Zür Jer Seg // *b* no number, *b* number 12, *b* no number: TR[ed] Luth // *b* no number, *b* no number, *b* number 12: AV RV ASV RSV NEB

9 νυκτὸς...ὑμῶν Ac 20.34; 1 Cor 4.12   12 τὸ...θεοῦ Eph 4.1; Php 1.27; 2 Th 1.5 τοῦ θεοῦ... δόξαν 1 Pe 5.10   13 ἡμεῖς...ἀδιαλείπτως 1 Th 1.2; 2 Th 2.13   ἐδέξασθε...θεοῦ Ga 1.11–12

Ἰουδαίᾳ ἐν Χριστῷ Ἰησοῦ, ὅτι τὰ αὐτὰ ἐπάθετε καὶ ὑμεῖς ὑπὸ τῶν ἰδίων συμφυλετῶν καθὼς καὶ αὐτοὶ ὑπὸ τῶν Ἰουδαίων, 15 τῶν καὶ τὸν κύριον ἀποκτεινάντων Ἰησοῦν καὶ τοὺς προφήτας[3], καὶ ἡμᾶς ἐκδιωξάντων, καὶ θεῷ μὴ ἀρεσκόντων, καὶ πᾶσιν ἀνθρώποις ἐναντίων, 16 κωλυόντων ἡμᾶς τοῖς ἔθνεσιν λαλῆσαι ἵνα σωθῶσιν, εἰς τὸ ἀναπληρῶσαι αὐτῶν τὰς ἁμαρτίας πάντοτε. ἔφθασεν δὲ ἐπ᾽ αὐτοὺς ἡ ὀργὴ εἰς τέλος.

Paul's Desire to Visit the Church Again

17 Ἡμεῖς δέ, ἀδελφοί, ἀπορφανισθέντες ἀφ᾽ ὑμῶν πρὸς καιρὸν ὥρας, προσώπῳ οὐ καρδίᾳ, περισσοτέρως ἐσπουδάσαμεν τὸ πρόσωπον ὑμῶν ἰδεῖν ἐν πολλῇ ἐπιθυμίᾳ. 18 διότι ἠθελήσαμεν ἐλθεῖν πρὸς ὑμᾶς, ἐγὼ μὲν Παῦλος καὶ ἅπαξ καὶ δίς, καὶ ἐνέκοψεν ἡμᾶς ὁ Σατανᾶς. 19 τίς γὰρ ἡμῶν ἐλπὶς ἢ χαρὰ ἢ στέφανος καυχήσεως —c ἢ οὐχὶ καὶ ὑμεῖς —c ἔμπροσθεν τοῦ κυρίου ἡμῶν Ἰησοῦ ἐν τῇ αὐτοῦ παρουσίᾳ; 20 ὑμεῖς γάρ ἐστε ἡ δόξα ἡμῶν καὶ ἡ χαρά.

3 Διὸ μηκέτι στέγοντες εὐδοκήσαμεν καταλειφθῆναι ἐν Ἀθήναις μόνοι, 2 καὶ ἐπέμψαμεν Τιμόθεον, τὸν ἀδελφὸν ἡμῶν καὶ συνεργὸν τοῦ θεοῦ ἐν τῷ εὐαγγελίῳ τοῦ Χριστοῦ[1], εἰς τὸ στηρίξαι ὑμᾶς καὶ παρακαλέσαι ὑπὲρ

to the people there who belong to Christ Jesus. You suffered the same persecutions from your own countrymen that they suffered from the Jews, [15] who killed the Lord Jesus and the prophets, and persecuted us. How displeasing they are to God! How hostile they are to all men! [16] They even tried to stop us from preaching to the Gentiles the message that would bring them salvation. This is the last full measure of the sins they have always committed. And now God's wrath has at last fallen upon them!

Paul's Desire to Visit Them Again

[17] As for us, brothers, when we were separated from you for a little while — not in our thoughts, of course, but only in body — how we missed you and how hard we tried to see you again! [18] We wanted to go back to you. I, Paul, tried to go back more than once, but Satan would not let us. [19] After all, it is you — you, and no one else! — who are our hope, our joy, and our reason for boasting of our victory in the presence of our Lord Jesus when he comes. [20] Indeed, you are our pride and our joy!

3 Finally, we could not bear it any longer. So we decided to stay on alone in Athens [2] while we sent Timothy, our brother who works with us for God in preaching the Good News about Christ. We sent him to strengthen you and help

---

[3] **15** {A} προφήτας ℵ A B D* G I P 0208[vid] 33 81 88 436 629 1739 1881 1962 2127 it[ar,c,d,dem,div,e,f,g,mon,x,z] vg cop[sa,bo,fay] arm eth Tertullian Origen[gr,lat] Adamantius Ambrosiaster Euthalius ‖ ἰδίους προφήτας D[c] K Ψ 104 181 320 330 451 614 630 1241 1877 1984 1985 2492 2495 Byz Lect syr[p,h] goth Marcion Chrysostom Theodoret John-Damascus

[1] **2** {B} καὶ συνεργὸν τοῦ θεοῦ ἐν τῷ εὐαγγελίῳ τοῦ Χριστοῦ D* 33

---

c c **19** c dash, c dash: WH Bov Nes BF² ‖ c dash, c none: Luth ‖ c question, c none: TR AV (RV) (ASV) Zür (Seg) ‖ c question, c question: (RSV) (TT) ‖ c minor, c minor: NEB Jer

---

14 τὰ...συμφυλετῶν Ac 17.5   **15** τῶν καὶ...προφήτας Ac 2.23; 7.52   **16** τὸ...ἁμαρτίας Gn 15.16; Mt 23.32-33   **17** περισσοτέρως...ἐπιθυμίᾳ 1 Th 3.10   **19** Php 2.16; 4.1; 2 Th 1.4
3 1 εὐδοκήσαμεν...μόνοι Ac 17.15   **2** Τιμόθεον...θεοῦ Ac 16.1-3

your faith, ³ that none of you should turn back because of these persecutions. You yourselves know that such persecutions are part of God's will for us. ⁴ For while we were still with you, we told you ahead of time that we were going to be persecuted; and, as you well know, that is exactly what happened. ⁵ That is why I had to send Timothy. I could not bear it any longer, so I sent him to find out about your faith. Surely it could not be that the Devil had tempted you, and all our work had been for nothing!

⁶ Now Timothy has come back to us from you, and he has brought the welcome news about your faith and love. He has told us that you always think well of us, and that you want to see us just as much as we want to see you. ⁷ So, in all our trouble and suffering we have been encouraged about you, brothers. It was your faith that encouraged us, ⁸ for now we really live if you stand firm in your life in the Lord. ⁹ For now we can give thanks to God for you. We thank him for the joy we have before our God because of you. ¹⁰ Day and night we ask him with all our heart to let us see you personally and supply what is needed in your faith.

τῆς πίστεως ὑμῶν 3 τὸ μηδένα σαίνεσθαι ἐν ταῖς θλίψεσιν ταύταις. αὐτοὶ γὰρ οἴδατε ὅτι εἰς τοῦτο κείμεθα· 4 καὶ γὰρ ὅτε πρὸς ὑμᾶς ἦμεν, προελέγομεν ὑμῖν ὅτι μέλλομεν θλίβεσθαι, καθὼς καὶ ἐγένετο καὶ οἴδατε. 5 διὰ τοῦτο κἀγὼ μηκέτι στέγων ἔπεμψα εἰς τὸ γνῶναι τὴν πίστιν ὑμῶν, μή πως ἐπείρασεν ὑμᾶς ὁ πειράζων καὶ εἰς κενὸν γένηται ὁ κόπος ἡμῶν.

6 Ἄρτι δὲ ἐλθόντος Τιμοθέου πρὸς ἡμᾶς ἀφ' ὑμῶν καὶ εὐαγγελισαμένου ἡμῖν τὴν πίστιν καὶ τὴν ἀγάπην ὑμῶν, καὶ ὅτι ἔχετε μνείαν ἡμῶν ἀγαθὴνᵃ πάντοτε,ᵃ ἐπιποθοῦντες ἡμᾶς ἰδεῖν καθάπερ καὶ ἡμεῖς ὑμᾶς,ᵇ 7 διὰ τοῦτο παρεκλήθημεν, ἀδελφοί, ἐφ' ὑμῖν ἐπὶ πάσῃ τῇ ἀνάγκῃ καὶ θλίψει ἡμῶν διὰ τῆς ὑμῶν πίστεως, 8 ὅτι νῦν ζῶμεν ἐὰν ὑμεῖς στήκετε ἐν κυρίῳ. 9 τίνα γὰρ εὐχαριστίαν δυνάμεθα τῷ θεῷ ἀνταποδοῦναι περὶ ὑμῶν ἐπὶ πάσῃ τῇ χαρᾷ ᾗ χαίρομεν δι' ὑμᾶς ἔμπροσθεν τοῦ θεοῦ ἡμῶν, 10 νυκτὸς καὶ ἡμέρας ὑπερεκπερισσοῦ δεόμενοι εἰς τὸ ἰδεῖν ὑμῶν τὸ πρόσωπον καὶ καταρτίσαι τὰ ὑστερήματα τῆς πίστεως ὑμῶν;

---

itᵈ·ᵉ·ᵐᵒⁿ* Ambrosiaster Pelagius Ps-Jerome ‖ καὶ συνεργὸν ἐν τῷ εὐαγγελίῳ τοῦ Χριστοῦ B 1962 ‖ καὶ διάκονον ἐν τῷ εὐαγγελίῳ τοῦ Χριστοῦ itᶻ* Cassiodorus ‖ καὶ διάκονον τοῦ θεοῦ ἐν τῷ εὐαγγελίῳ τοῦ Χριστοῦ ℵ A P Ψ 81 629* 1241 1739 1881 itᵃʳ·ᶜ·ᵈᵉᵐ·ᵈⁱᵛ·ˣ vg syrʰ copˢᵃ·ᵇᵒ·ᶠᵃʸ goth eth Basil Pelagius Theodoreˡᵃᵗ Euthalius ‖ διάκονον τοῦ συνεργὸν τοῦ θεοῦ ἐν τῷ εὐαγγελίῳ τοῦ Χριστοῦ G itᶠ·ᵍ ‖ καὶ διάκονον τοῦ θεοῦ καὶ συνεργὸν ἡμῶν ἐν τῷ εὐαγγελίῳ τοῦ Χριστοῦ Dᶜ K 88 104 181 326 330 436 451 614 629ᵐᵍ 630 1877 1984 1985 2127 2492 2495 *Byz Lect* syrᵖ·ʰ ʷⁱᵗʰ * Chrysostom (Theodoret) John-Damascus ‖ καὶ συνεργὸν ἡμῶν καὶ διάκονον αὐτοῦ ἐν τῷ εὐαγγελίῳ τοῦ θεοῦ καὶ συνεργὸν τοῦ Χριστοῦ syrᵖᵃˡᵛⁱᵈ ‖ καὶ συνεργὸν τοῦ εὐαγγελίου τοῦ θεοῦ καὶ πατρὸς τοῦ Χριστοῦ arm

---

ᵃ ᵃ **6** a none, a minor: Bov Nes BF² AV RV ASV RSV NEB TT (Zür) (Luth) Jer Seg ‖ a minor, a none ‖ a none, a none: TR WH
ᵇ **6** b minor: TR WH Bov Nes BF² AV RV ASV Zür ‖ b major: NEB TT Luth Jer Seg ‖ b dash: RSV

---

3 τὸ...θλίψεσιν ταύταις Eph 3.13   αὐτοί...κείμεθα 2 Tm 3.12   **4** προελέγομεν... θλίβεσθαι Ac 14.22   **5** εἰς...πίστιν ὑμῶν Php 2.16   **6** ἐλθόντος...ὑμῶν Ac 18.5 **7** 2 Th 1.4

11 Αὐτὸς δὲ ὁ θεὸς καὶ πατὴρ ἡμῶν καὶ ὁ κύριος ἡμῶν Ἰησοῦς κατευθύναι τὴν ὁδὸν ἡμῶν πρὸς ὑμᾶς· **12** ὑμᾶς δὲ ὁ κύριος πλεονάσαι καὶ περισσεύσαι τῇ ἀγάπῃ εἰς ἀλλήλους καὶ εἰς πάντας, καθάπερ καὶ ἡμεῖς εἰς ὑμᾶς, **13** εἰς τὸ στηρίξαι ὑμῶν τὰς καρδίας ἀμέμπτους ἐν ἁγιωσύνῃ ἔμπροσθεν τοῦ θεοῦ καὶ πατρὸς ἡμῶν ἐν τῇ παρουσίᾳ τοῦ κυρίου ἡμῶν Ἰησοῦ μετὰ πάντων τῶν ἁγίων αὐτοῦ.[2]

A Life Pleasing to God

4 Λοιπὸν οὖν, ἀδελφοί, ἐρωτῶμεν ὑμᾶς καὶ παρακαλοῦμεν ἐν κυρίῳ Ἰησοῦ, ἵνα καθὼς παρελάβετε παρ' ἡμῶν τὸ πῶς δεῖ ὑμᾶς περιπατεῖν καὶ ἀρέσκειν θεῷ, καθὼς καὶ περιπατεῖτε, ἵνα περισσεύητε μᾶλλον. **2** οἴδατε γὰρ τίνας παραγγελίας ἐδώκαμεν ὑμῖν διὰ τοῦ κυρίου Ἰησοῦ. **3** τοῦτο γάρ ἐστιν θέλημα τοῦ θεοῦ, ὁ ἁγιασμὸς ὑμῶν, ἀπέχεσθαι ὑμᾶς ἀπὸ τῆς πορνείας, **4** εἰδέναι ἕκαστον ὑμῶν τὸ ἑαυτοῦ σκεῦος κτᾶσθαι ἐν ἁγιασμῷ καὶ τιμῇ, **5** μὴ ἐν πάθει ἐπιθυμίας καθάπερ καὶ τὰ ἔθνη τὰ μὴ εἰδότα τὸν θεόν, **6** τὸ μὴ ὑπερβαίνειν καὶ πλεονεκτεῖν ἐν τῷ πράγματι τὸν ἀδελφὸν αὐτοῦ, διότι ἔκδικος κύριος περὶ πάντων τούτων, καθὼς καὶ προείπαμεν ὑμῖν καὶ διεμαρτυράμεθα. **7** οὐ γὰρ ἐκάλεσεν ἡμᾶς ὁ θεὸς ἐπὶ ἀκαθαρσίᾳ ἀλλ' ἐν ἁγιασμῷ. **8** τοιγαροῦν ὁ ἀθετῶν οὐκ ἄνθρωπον ἀθετεῖ ἀλλὰ τὸν θεὸν τὸν [καὶ] διδόντα τὸ πνεῦμα αὐτοῦ τὸ ἅγιον εἰς ὑμᾶς.

---

[2] **13** {B} αὐτοῦ. אᶜ B Dᶜ C K Ψ 33 88 104 181 326 330 436 451 611 620 1241 1739 1877 1881 1962 1984 1985 2127 2492 2495 *Byz Lect* itᶠ·ᵍ syrᵖ·ʰ·ᵖᵃˡ copˢᵃ·ᵇᵒᵐˢˢ goth arm Tertullian Ambrosiaster Ephraem Chrysostom Pelagius Theodoreˡᵃᵗ Theodoret Ps-Jerome John-Damascus ‖ . ἀμήν. 629 ‖ αὐτοῦ. ἀμήν. א* A D* 81 itᵃʳ·ᶜ·ᵈ·ᵈᵉᵐ·ᵈⁱᵛ·ᵉ·ᵐᵒⁿ·ˣ·ᶻ vg copᵇᵒ eth Euthalius Ps-Jerome Cassiodorus

13 τό...ἁγιωσύνῃ Php 1.10   ἐν τῇ παρουσίᾳ...αὐτοῦ Zch 14.5; 2 Th 1.7, 10
4 1 2 Th 3.6   **3** τοῦτο...ἁγιασμὸς ὑμῶν 1 Th 5.23; He 10.10; 1 Pe 1.16   **4** 1 Cor 6.13, 15
5 τὰ...θεόν Ps 79.6; Jr 10.25   **6** ἔκδικος κύριος Ps 94.1; Sir 5.3   **7** 2 Th 2.13–14; 1 Pe 1.15–16
8 ὁ...θεόν Lk 10.16   τὸν θεόν...ὑμᾶς Eze 36.27; 37.14; Ro 5.5; 2 Cor 1.22; Ga 4.6; 1 Jn 3.24

---

[11] May our God and Father himself, and our Lord Jesus, prepare the way for us to come to you! [12] May the Lord make your love for one another and for all people grow more and more and become as great as our love for you. [13] In this way he will make your hearts strong, and you will be perfect and holy in the presence of our God and Father when our Lord Jesus comes with all who belong to him.

A Life that Pleases God

[4] Finally, brothers, you learned from us how you should live in order to please God. This is, of course, the way you have been living. And now we beg and urge you, in the name of the Lord Jesus, to do even more. [2] For you know the instructions we gave you, by the authority of the Lord Jesus. [3] This is God's will for you: he wants you to be holy and completely free from immorality. [4] Each of you men should know how to take a wife[1] in a holy and honorable way, [5] not with a lustful desire, like the heathen who do not know God. [6] In this matter, then, no man should do wrong to his brother or violate his rights. We have told you this before, we strongly warned you, that the Lord will punish those who do such wrongs. [7] God did not call us to live in immorality, but in holiness. [8] So then, whoever rejects this teaching is not rejecting man, but God, who gives you his Holy Spirit.

---

[1] **4** *how to take a wife: or how to control his own body*

⁹ There is no need to write you about love for your fellow believers. For you yourselves have been taught by God how you should love one another. ¹⁰ And you have behaved in this way toward all the brothers in all of Macedonia. So we beg you, brothers, to do even more. ¹¹ Make it your aim to live a quiet life, to mind your own business, and earn your own living, just as we told you before. ¹² In this way you will win the respect of those who are not believers, and will not have to depend on anyone for what you need.

The Lord's Coming

¹³ Brothers, we want you to know the truth about those who have died, so that you will not be sad, as are those who have no hope. ¹⁴ We believe that Jesus died and rose again; so we believe that God will bring with Jesus those who have died believing in him. ¹⁵ For this is the Lord's teaching we tell you: we who are alive on the day the Lord comes will not go ahead of those who have died. ¹⁶ There will be the shout of command, the archangel's voice, the sound of God's trumpet, and the Lord himself will come down from heaven! Those who have died believing in Christ will be raised to life first; ¹⁷ then we who are living at that time will all be gathered up along with them in the clouds to meet the Lord in the air. And so we will always be with the Lord. ¹⁸ Therefore, cheer each other up with these words.

Be Ready for the Lord's Coming

5 There is no need to write you, brothers, about the times and occasions when these things will happen. ² For you yourselves know very well that the Day

⁹ Περὶ δὲ τῆς φιλαδελφίας οὐ χρείαν ἔχετε γράφειν ὑμῖν, αὐτοὶ γὰρ ὑμεῖς θεοδίδακτοί ἐστε εἰς τὸ ἀγαπᾶν ἀλλήλους· 10 καὶ γὰρ ποιεῖτε αὐτὸ εἰς πάντας τοὺς ἀδελφοὺς [τοὺς] ἐν ὅλῃ τῇ Μακεδονίᾳ. παρακαλοῦμεν δὲ ὑμᾶς, ἀδελφοί, περισσεύειν μᾶλλον, 11 καὶ φιλοτιμεῖσθαι ἡσυχάζειν καὶ πράσσειν τὰ ἴδια καὶ ἐργάζεσθαι ταῖς χερσὶν ὑμῶν, καθὼς ὑμῖν παρηγγείλαμεν, 12 ἵνα περιπατῆτε εὐσχημόνως πρὸς τοὺς ἔξω καὶ μηδενὸς χρείαν ἔχητε.

The Lord's Coming

13 Οὐ θέλομεν δὲ ὑμᾶς ἀγνοεῖν, ἀδελφοί, περὶ τῶν κοιμωμένων, ἵνα μὴ λυπῆσθε καθὼς καὶ οἱ λοιποὶ οἱ μὴ ἔχοντες ἐλπίδα. 14 εἰ γὰρ πιστεύομεν ὅτι Ἰησοῦς ἀπέθανεν καὶ ἀνέστη, οὕτως καὶ ὁ θεὸς τοὺς κοιμηθέντας διὰ τοῦ Ἰησοῦ ἄξει σὺν αὐτῷ.

15 Τοῦτο γὰρ ὑμῖν λέγομεν ἐν λόγῳ κυρίου, ὅτι ἡμεῖς οἱ ζῶντες οἱ περιλειπόμενοι εἰς τὴν παρουσίαν τοῦ κυρίου οὐ μὴ φθάσωμεν τοὺς κοιμηθέντας· 16 ὅτι αὐτὸς ὁ κύριος ἐν κελεύσματι, ἐν φωνῇ ἀρχαγγέλου καὶ ἐν σάλπιγγι θεοῦ, καταβήσεται ἀπ' οὐρανοῦ, καὶ οἱ νεκροὶ ἐν Χριστῷ ἀναστήσονται πρῶτον, 17 ἔπειτα ἡμεῖς οἱ ζῶντες οἱ περιλειπόμενοι ἅμα σὺν αὐτοῖς ἁρπαγησόμεθα ἐν νεφέλαις εἰς ἀπάντησιν τοῦ κυρίου εἰς ἀέρα· καὶ οὕτως πάντοτε σὺν κυρίῳ ἐσόμεθα. 18 Ὥστε παρακαλεῖτε ἀλλήλους ἐν τοῖς λόγοις τούτοις.

5 Περὶ δὲ τῶν χρόνων καὶ τῶν καιρῶν, ἀδελφοί, οὐ χρείαν ἔχετε ὑμῖν γράφεσθαι, 2 αὐτοὶ γὰρ ἀκριβῶς οἴδατε ὅτι ἡμέρα κυρίου ὡς κλέπτης ἐν νυκτὶ οὕτως

---

9 Jn 13.34   ὑμεῖς θεοδίδακτοί ἐστε Jr 31.33–34   **10** ποιεῖτε...Μακεδονίᾳ 2 Th 3.4   **11** πράσσειν...ὑμῶν Eph 4.28; 2 Th 3.8, 12   **12** περιπατῆτε...ἔξω 1 Cor 5.12–13; Col 4.5   **13** οἱ λοιποί...ἐλπίδα Eph 2.12   **14** Ἰησοῦς...ἀνέστη Ro 14.9; 1 Cor 15.3–4, 12   **15** Τοῦτο ...κυρίου 1 Cor 7.10, 25   οἱ ζῶντες...κυρίου 1 Cor 15.51   **16** ὁ κύριος...καταβήσεται ἀπ' οὐρανοῦ 1 Th 1.10; 2 Th 1.7   οἱ νεκροί...πρῶτον 1 Cor 15.52   **17** σὺν κυρίῳ ἐσόμεθα Jn 12.26; 17.24

5 1 Mt 24.36   **2** ἡμέρα...ἔρχεται Mt 24.42–44; Lk 12.39–40; 2 Pe 3.10; Re 3.3; 16.15

ἔρχεται. 3 ὅταν λέγωσιν, Εἰρήνη καὶ ἀσφάλεια, τότε αἰφνίδιος αὐτοῖς ἐφίσταται ὄλεθρος ὥσπερ ἡ ὠδὶν τῇ ἐν γαστρὶ ἐχούσῃ, καὶ οὐ μὴ ἐκφύγωσιν. 4 ὑμεῖς δέ, ἀδελφοί, οὐκ ἐστὲ ἐν σκότει, ἵνα ἡ ἡμέρα ὑμᾶς ὡς κλέπτης[1] καταλάβῃ,[a] 5 πάντες γὰρ ὑμεῖς υἱοὶ φωτός ἐστε καὶ υἱοὶ ἡμέρας.[b] οὐκ ἐσμὲν νυκτὸς οὐδὲ σκότους· [b] 6 ἄρα οὖν μὴ καθεύδωμεν ὡς οἱ λοιποί, ἀλλὰ γρηγορῶμεν καὶ νήφωμεν. 7 οἱ γὰρ καθεύδοντες νυκτὸς καθεύδουσιν, καὶ οἱ μεθυσκόμενοι νυκτὸς μεθύουσιν· 8 ἡμεῖς δὲ ἡμέρας ὄντες νήφωμεν, **ἐνδυσάμενοι θώρακα** πίστεως καὶ ἀγάπης καὶ **περικεφαλαίαν** ἐλπίδα **σωτηρίας**· 9 ὅτι οὐκ ἔθετο ἡμᾶς ὁ θεὸς εἰς ὀργὴν ἀλλὰ εἰς περιποίησιν σωτηρίας διὰ τοῦ κυρίου ἡμῶν Ἰησοῦ Χριστοῦ, 10 τοῦ ἀποθανόντος ὑπὲρ ἡμῶν ἵνα εἴτε γρηγορῶμεν εἴτε καθεύδωμεν ἅμα σὺν αὐτῷ ζήσωμεν. 11 Διὸ παρακαλεῖτε ἀλλήλους καὶ οἰκοδομεῖτε εἷς τὸν ἕνα, καθὼς καὶ ποιεῖτε.

Final Exhortations and Greetings

12 Ἐρωτῶμεν δὲ ὑμᾶς, ἀδελφοί, εἰδέναι τοὺς κοπιῶντας ἐν ὑμῖν καὶ προϊσταμένους ὑμῶν ἐν κυρίῳ καὶ νουθετοῦντας ὑμᾶς, 13 καὶ ἡγεῖσθαι αὐτοὺς ὑπερεκπερισσοῦ ἐν ἀγάπῃ διὰ τὸ ἔργον αὐτῶν. εἰρηνεύετε ἐν ἑαυτοῖς. 14 παρακαλοῦμεν δὲ ὑμᾶς, ἀδελφοί, νουθετεῖτε τοὺς ἀτάκτους, παραμυθεῖσθε τοὺς ὀλιγοψύχους, ἀντέ-

[1] **4** {A} κλέπτης ℵ D G K P Ψ 0226[vid] 33 81 88 104 181 326 330 436 451 614 629 630 1241 1739 1877 1881 1962 1984 1985 2127 2492[vid] 2495 *Byz Lect* it[ar,c,d,dem,div,e,f,g,mon,x,z] vg syr[p,h] cop[sa,bo mss] goth arm eth Eusebius Ambrosiaster Ephraem Chrysostom Theodore[lat] Euthalius Theodoret John-Damascus ∥ κλέπτας A B cop[bo]

[a] **4-5** *a* minor: WH ∥ *a* major: Bov Nes BF[2] RV ASV RSV TT Zür°Luth ∥ different text: TR AV NEB? Jer? Seg?

[b b] **5** *b* major, *b* minor: WH Bov Nes BF[2] RV ASV NEB ∥ *b* minor, *b* major: TR AV RSV Zür ∥ *b* major, *b* major: TT Luth Jer Seg

3 λέγωσιν ἀσφάλεια Jr 6.14; 8.11; Eze 10.10   αἰφνίδιος...ὄλεθρος Mt 24.39; Lk 21.34-35   ὥσπερ...ἐχούσῃ Jn 16.21-22   **5** Ro 13.12; Eph 5.9   **8** ἐνδυσάμενοι...σωτηρίας Is 59.17; Wsd 5.18; Eph 6.14, 17   **9** 1 Th 1.10; 2 Th 2.14   **10** Ro 14.8-9; 1 Th 4.14   **11** οἰκοδομεῖτε... ἕνα Jd 20   **12** 1 Cor 16.18; 1 Tm 5.17   **14** παρακαλοῦμεν...ἀτάκτους 2 Th 3.6, 11, 15

of the Lord will come like a thief comes at night. [3] When people say, "Everything is quiet and safe," then suddenly destruction will hit them! They will not escape — it will be like the pains that come upon a woman who is about to give birth. [4] But you, brothers, are not in the darkness, and the Day should not take you by surprise like a thief. [5] All of you are people who belong to the light, who belong to the day. We are not of the night or of the darkness. [6] So then, we should not be sleeping, like the others; we should be awake and sober. [7] It is at night when people sleep; it is at night when people get drunk. [8] But we belong to the day, and we should be sober. We must wear faith and love as a breastplate, and our hope of salvation as a helmet. [9] God did not choose us to suffer his wrath, but to possess salvation through our Lord Jesus Christ. [10] who died for us in order that we might live together with him, whether we are alive or dead when he comes. [11] For this reason encourage one another, and help one another, just as you are now doing.

Final Instructions and Greetings

[12] We beg you, brothers, to pay proper respect to those who work among you, those whom the Lord has chosen to guide and instruct you. [13] Treat them with the greatest respect and love, because of the work they do. Be at peace among yourselves.

[14] We urge you brothers: warn the idle, encourage the timid, help the weak,

be patient with all. ¹⁵ See that no one pays back wrong for wrong, but at all times make it your aim to do good to one another and to all people.

¹⁶ Be joyful always, ¹⁷ pray at all times, ¹⁸ be thankful in all circumstances. This is what God wants of you, in your life in Christ Jesus.

¹⁹ Do not restrain the Holy Spirit; ²⁰ do not despise inspired messages. ²¹ Put all things to the test: keep what is good, ²² and avoid every kind of evil.

²³ May the God who gives us peace make you completely his, and keep your whole being, spirit, soul, and body, free from all fault, at the coming of our Lord Jesus Christ. ²⁴ He who calls you will do it, for he is faithful!

²⁵ Pray also for us, brothers.

²⁶ Greet all the brothers with a brotherly kiss.

²⁷ I urge you, by the authority of the Lord, to read this letter to all the brothers.

χεσθε τῶν ἀσθενῶν, μακροθυμεῖτε πρὸς πάντας. **15** ὁρᾶτε μή τις κακὸν ἀντὶ κακοῦ τινι ἀποδῷ, ἀλλὰ πάντοτε τὸ ἀγαθὸν διώκετε εἰς ἀλλήλους καὶ εἰς πάντας.

16 Πάντοτε χαίρετε, **17** ἀδιαλείπτως προσεύχεσθε, **18** ἐν παντὶ εὐχαριστεῖτε· τοῦτο γὰρ θέλημα θεοῦ ἐν Χριστῷ Ἰησοῦ εἰς ὑμᾶς. **19** τὸ πνεῦμα μὴ σβέννυτε, **20** προφητείας μὴ ἐξουθενεῖτε·ᶜ **21** πάντα δὲ² δοκιμάζετε,ᶜ τὸ καλὸν κατέχετε, **22** ἀπὸ παντὸς εἴδους πονηροῦ ἀπέχεσθε.

23 Αὐτὸς δὲ ὁ θεὸς τῆς εἰρήνης ἁγιάσαι ὑμᾶς ὁλοτελεῖς, καὶ ὁλόκληρον ὑμῶν τὸ πνεῦμα καὶ ἡ ψυχὴ καὶ τὸ σῶμα ἀμέμπτως ἐν τῇ παρουσίᾳ τοῦ κυρίου ἡμῶν Ἰησοῦ Χριστοῦ τηρηθείη. **24** πιστὸς ὁ καλῶν ὑμᾶς, ὃς καὶ ποιήσει.

25 Ἀδελφοί, προσεύχεσθε καὶ³ περὶ ἡμῶν.

26 Ἀσπάσασθε τοὺς ἀδελφοὺς πάντας ἐν φιλήματι ἁγίῳ. **27** Ἐνορκίζω ὑμᾶς τὸν κύριον ἀναγνωσθῆναι τὴν ἐπιστολὴν πᾶσιν τοῖς ἀδελφοῖς⁴.

---

² **21** {C} δέ ℵᶜ B D G K P Ψ 181 326 436 1241 1739 1877 1881 1984 1985 2492 2495 *Byz*ᵖᵗ *l*¹³⁶⁵ itᵃʳ,ᶜ,ᵈ,ᵈᵉᵐ,ᵈⁱᵛ,ᵉ,ᶠᶜ,ᵍ,ᵐᵒⁿ,ᵗ,ˣ,ᶻ vg syrʰ copˢᵃ,ᵇᵒᵐˢˢ goth eth Clement Ambrosiaster Basil²ᐟ³ Chrysostom¹ᐟ² Pelagius John-Damascus Theophylact ‖ *omit* ℵ* A 33 81 88 104 330 451 614 629 630 1962 2127 *Byz*ᵖᵗ *Lect* itᶠ* syrᵖ,ᵖᵃˡ copᵇᵒ arm Tertullian Origenᵍʳ,ˡᵃᵗ Ambrosiaster Ephraem Basil¹ᐟ³ Chrysostom¹ᐟ² Jerome Augustine Euthalius Theodoret Ps-Jerome Cassiodorus

³ **25** {C} καί 𝔭³⁰ B D* 33 81 104 326 330 436 451 1739 1877 1881 2492 itᵈ,ᵉ syrʰ,ᵖᵃˡ copˢᵃ goth arm Origen Chrysostom Theodore Euthalius ‖ *omit* ℵ A Dᶜ G K P Ψ 88 181 614 629 630 1241 1962 1984 1985 2127 2495 *Byz Lect* itᵃʳ,ᶜ,ᵈᵉᵐ,ᵈⁱᵛ,ᶠ,ᵍ,ᵐᵒⁿ,ˣ,ᶻ vg syrᵖ copᵇᵒ eth Ambrosiaster Theodoret John-Damascus

⁴ **27** {B} ἀδελφοῖς ℵ* B D G 436 itᵈ,ᵉ,ᶠ,ᵍ,ᵐᵒⁿ copˢᵃ ethʳᵒ Ambrosiaster

ᶜ ᶜ **20-21** *c* major, *c* minor: WH Bov Nes BF² Zür Luth ‖ *c* minor, *c* major: RSV (NEB) Jer ‖ *c* major, *c* major: RVᵐᵍ ASVᵐᵍ Seg ‖ different text: TR AV RV ASV NEBᵐᵍ¹ TT

15 Pr 20.22; Ro 12.17; 1 Pe 3.9   **16** Php 4.4   **17** Lk 18.1; Ro 12.12; Col 4.2   **18** ἐν παντὶ εὐχαριστεῖτε Eph 5.20   **19** Eph 4.30   **20** 1 Cor 14.1, 39   **21** πάντα δὲ δοκιμάζετε 1 Jn 4.1 **22** Job 1.1, 8; 2.3   **23** ὁ θεὸς τῆς εἰρήνης Ro 15.33; 2 Th 3.16   **24** πιστὸς ὁ καλῶν ὑμᾶς 1 Cor 1.9; 2 Th 3.3   **25** 2 Th 3.1   **26** Ro 16.16; 1 Cor 16.20

28 ʽΗ χάρις τοῦ κυρίου ἡμῶν ᾽Ιησοῦ Χριστοῦ μεθ᾽ ὑμῶν.[5]

28 The grace of our Lord Jesus Christ be with you.

Ephraem Pelagius Euthalius Cassiodorus ‖ ἀγίοις 1984 1985 Theophylact ‖ ἀγίοις ἀδελφοῖς אᶜ A K P Ψ 33 81 88 104 181 326 330 451 614 629 630 1241 1739 1877 1881 1962 2127 2492 2495 *Byz Lect* it[ar,c,dem,div,x,z] vg syr[p,h,pal] cop[bo] goth arm eth[pp] Chrysostom Euthalius[mss] Theodoret John-Damascus

[5] 28 {B} ὑμῶν. B D* G 33 181 1881 it[d,f,g] syr[pal] cop[sa] arm Ambrosiaster ‖ ὑμῶν. ἀμήν. א A Dᶜ K P Ψ 81 88 104 326 330 436 451 614 629 630 1241 1739 1877 1962 1984 1985 2127 2492 2495 *Byz Lect* it[ar,c,dem,div,e,mon,x,z] vg syr[p,h] cop[bo] goth eth Chrysostom Euthalius

PAUL'S SECOND LETTER TO THE THESSALONIANS

1 From Paul, Silas and Timothy —
To the people of the church in Thessalonica, who belong to God our Father and the Lord Jesus Christ:

[2] May God the Father and the Lord Jesus Christ give you grace and peace.

The Judgment at Christ's Coming

[3] We must thank God at all times for you, brothers! It is right for us to do so, because your faith is growing so much and the love each of you has for the others is becoming greater. [4] That is why we ourselves boast about you in the churches of God. We boast about the way you continue to endure and believe, through all the persecutions and sufferings you are experiencing.

[5] Here is the proof of God's righteous judgment, for as a result of all this you will become worthy of his Kingdom, for which you are suffering. [6] For God will do what is right: he will bring suffering on those who make you suffer, [7] and he will give relief to you who suffer, and to us as well. He will do this when the Lord Jesus appears from heaven with his mighty angels, [8] with a flaming fire, to

714

ΠΡΟΣ ΘΕΣΣΑΛΟΝΙΚΕΙΣ Β

Salutation

1 Παῦλος καὶ Σιλουανὸς καὶ Τιμόθεος τῇ ἐκκλησίᾳ Θεσσαλονικέων ἐν θεῷ πατρὶ ἡμῶν καὶ κυρίῳ Ἰησοῦ Χριστῷ· 2 χάρις ὑμῖν καὶ εἰρήνη ἀπὸ θεοῦ πατρὸς καὶ κυρίου[1] Ἰησοῦ Χριστοῦ.

The Judgment at Christ's Coming

3 Εὐχαριστεῖν ὀφείλομεν τῷ θεῷ πάντοτε περὶ ὑμῶν, ἀδελφοί, καθὼς ἄξιόν ἐστιν, ὅτι ὑπεραυξάνει ἡ πίστις ὑμῶν καὶ πλεονάζει ἡ ἀγάπη ἑνὸς ἑκάστου πάντων ὑμῶν εἰς ἀλλήλους, 4 ὥστε αὐτοὺς ἡμᾶς ἐν ὑμῖν ἐγκαυχᾶσθαι ἐν ταῖς ἐκκλησίαις τοῦ θεοῦ ὑπὲρ τῆς ὑπομονῆς ὑμῶν καὶ πίστεως ἐν πᾶσιν τοῖς διωγμοῖς ὑμῶν καὶ ταῖς θλίψεσιν αἷς ἀνέχεσθε, 5 ἔνδειγμα τῆς δικαίας κρίσεως τοῦ θεοῦ, εἰς τὸ καταξιωθῆναι ὑμᾶς τῆς βασιλείας τοῦ θεοῦ, ὑπὲρ ἧς καὶ πάσχετε, 6 εἴπερ δίκαιον παρὰ θεῷ ἀνταποδοῦναι τοῖς θλίβουσιν ὑμᾶς θλῖψιν 7 καὶ ὑμῖν τοῖς θλιβομένοις ἄνεσιν μεθ' ἡμῶν ἐν τῇ ἀποκαλύψει τοῦ κυρίου Ἰησοῦ ἀπ' οὐρανοῦ μετ' ἀγγέλων δυνάμεως αὐτοῦ[a] 8 **ἐν πυρὶ φλογός,**[a] διδόντος ἐκδίκησιν

---

[1] 2 {C} πατρὸς καὶ κυρίου B D P 0111[vid] 33 1739 1881 1985 it[d,e,mon] Pelagius Theophylact ‖ πατρὸς ἡμῶν καὶ κυρίου ℵ A G I K 81 88 104 181 326 330 436 451 614 629 630 1241 1877 1962 1984 2127 2492 2495 *Byz Lect* it[ar,c,dem,div,f,g,x,z] vg syr[h] cop[sa] goth arm eth Origen[lat] Ambrosiaster Chrysostom Pelagius Euthalius Theodoret ‖ πατρὸς καὶ κυρίου ἡμῶν syr[pal] cop[bomss] ‖ πατρὸς ἡμῶν καὶ κυρίου ἡμῶν syr[p] cop[sams,bo]

---

a a **7-8** *a* none, *a* minor: TR WH Bov Nes BF² RV ASV RSV (NEB) TT Zür Luth ‖ *a* minor *a* none: AV[ed] ‖ *a* minor, *a* minor: AV[ed] Jer Seg

1 1 Th 1.1 **2** Ro 1.7 **3** Εὐχαριστεῖν...ὑμῶν 1 Th 1.2; 2 Th 2.13 **4** αὐτοὺς... ἐγκαυχᾶσθαι 2 Cor 7.4; 1 Th 2.19 ἐν πᾶσιν...ἀνέχεσθε Re 1.9 **5** ἔνδειγμα...θεοῦ Php 1.28 εἰς...θεοῦ Lk 20.35; 1 Th 2.12 **6** Ro 12.19; Re 18.6, 7 **7** ἐν τῇ ἀποκαλύψει...αὐτοῦ Zch 14.5; Mt 25.31; 1 Th 3.13; 4.16 **8** ἐν...θεόν Ps 79.6; Is 66.15; Jr 10.25

τοῖς **μὴ εἰδόσιν θεὸν** καὶ τοῖς μὴ ὑπακούουσιν τῷ
εὐαγγελίῳ τοῦ κυρίου ἡμῶν Ἰησοῦ, 9 οἵτινες δίκην
τίσουσιν ὄλεθρον αἰώνιον **ἀπὸ προσώπου τοῦ κυρίου καὶ
ἀπὸ τῆς δόξης τῆς ἰσχύος αὐτοῦ,** 10 ὅταν ἔλθῃ ἐνδοξασθῆναι ἐν τοῖς ἁγίοις αὐτοῦ καὶ θαυμασθῆναι ἐν πᾶσιν
τοῖς πιστεύσασιν, ὅτι ἐπιστεύθη τὸ μαρτύριον ἡμῶν ἐφ᾽
ὑμᾶς, ἐν τῇ ἡμέρᾳ ἐκείνῃ. 11 εἰς ὃ καὶ προσευχόμεθα
πάντοτε περὶ ὑμῶν, ἵνα ὑμᾶς ἀξιώσῃ τῆς κλήσεως ὁ
θεὸς ἡμῶν καὶ πληρώσῃ πᾶσαν εὐδοκίαν ἀγαθωσύνης
καὶ ἔργον πίστεως ἐν δυνάμει, 12 ὅπως ἐνδοξασθῇ τὸ
ὄνομα τοῦ κυρίου ἡμῶν Ἰησοῦ ἐν ὑμῖν, καὶ ὑμεῖς ἐν
αὐτῷ, κατὰ τὴν χάριν τοῦ θεοῦ ἡμῶν καὶ κυρίου Ἰησοῦ
Χριστοῦ.

The Man of Lawlessness

2 Ἐρωτῶμεν δὲ ὑμᾶς, ἀδελφοί, ὑπὲρ τῆς παρουσίας
τοῦ κυρίου ἡμῶν Ἰησοῦ Χριστοῦ καὶ ἡμῶν ἐπισυναγω-
γῆς ἐπ᾽ αὐτόν, 2 εἰς τὸ μὴ ταχέως σαλευθῆναι ὑμᾶς
ἀπὸ τοῦ νοὸς μηδὲ θροεῖσθαι μήτε διὰ πνεύματος μήτε
διὰ λόγου μήτε δι᾽ ἐπιστολῆς ὡς δι᾽ ἡμῶν, ὡς ὅτι ἐνέ-
στηκεν ἡ ἡμέρα τοῦ κυρίου.[a] 3 μή τις ὑμᾶς ἐξαπατήσῃ
κατὰ μηδένα τρόπον· ὅτι ἐὰν μὴ ἔλθῃ ἡ ἀποστασία
πρῶτον καὶ ἀποκαλυφθῇ ὁ ἄνθρωπος τῆς ἀνομίας[1], ὁ

---

[1] **3** {C} ἀνομίας ℵ B 81 88[mg] 104 326 436 1739 1881 2127 l[1365] (it[mon]) cop[sa,bo]
arm Marcion Tertullian Origen[grl/5] Ambrosiaster Cyril-Jerusalem Ambrose
Jerome Euthalius John-Damascus ∥ ἁμαρτίας A D G K P Ψ 88* 181 330 451
614 629 630 1241 1877 1962 1984 1985 2492 2495 *Byz Lect* it[ar,c,d,dem,div,e,f,g,x,z]
vg syr[p.h] goth eth Irenaeus[lat] Tertullian Hippolytus Origen[gr4/5,lat] Eusebius
Ambrosiaster Ephraem Cyril-Jerusalem Ambrose Chrysostom Pelagius
Jerome Theodore[lat] Augustine Theodoret John-Damascus

---

[a] **2** *a* major: TR WH Bov Nes BF[2] AV RSV NEB TT Zür Luth Jer Seg ∥ *a* dash: WH[mg] ∥
a minor: RV ASV

---

8 τοῖς...Ἰησοῦ Ro 2.8; 1 Pe 4.17   **9** ἀπὸ προσώπου...αὐτοῦ Is 2.10, 19, 21
10 ἐνδοξασθῆναι...αὐτοῦ Ps 88.8 LXX; Is 49.3; Col 3.4; 1 Th 3.13   ἐν τοῖς...θαυμασθῆναι
Ps 67.36 LXX   **11** προσευχόμεθα...ὑμῶν Col 1.9   **12** ἐνδοξασθῇ...ἡμῶν Is 24.15; 66.5; Mal 1.11
2 1 τῆς παρουσίας...ἐπ᾽ αὐτόν 1 Th 4.13–17   **3** ἐὰν...πρῶτον 1 Tm 4.1   ὁ υἱὸς τῆς
ἀπωλείας Jn 17.12

---

punish those who do not know God and
those who do not obey the Good News
about our Lord Jesus. [9] They will suffer
the punishment of eternal destruction,
separated from the presence of the Lord
and from his glorious might, [10] when he
comes on that Day to receive glory from
all his people and honor from all who
believe. You too will be among them,
for you have believed the message that
we told you.

[11] This is why we always pray for you.
We ask our God to make you worthy of
the life he called you to live. May he,
by his power, fulfil all your desire for
goodness and complete your work of
faith. [12] In this way the name of our
Lord Jesus will receive glory from you,
and you from him, by the grace of our
God and the Lord Jesus Christ.

The Wicked One

2 Concerning the coming of our Lord
Jesus Christ and our being gathered
together to be with him: I beg you,
brothers, [2] do not be so easily confused
in your thinking or upset by the claim
that the Day of the Lord has come.
Perhaps this was said by someone prophesying, or by someone preaching. Or it
may have been said that we wrote this
in a letter. [3] Do not let anyone fool you
in any way. For the Day will not come
until the final Rebellion takes place and
the Wicked One appears, who is destined

to hell. ⁴ He will oppose everything which men worship and everything which men consider divine. He will put himself above them all, and even go in and sit down in God's temple and claim to be God!

⁵ Don't you remember? I told you all this while I was with you. ⁶ Yet there is something that keeps this from happening now, and you know what it is. At the proper time, then, the Wicked One will appear. ⁷ The Mysterious Wickedness is already at work, but what is going to happen will not happen until the one who holds it back is taken out of the way. ⁸ Then the Wicked One will appear, and the Lord Jesus will kill him with the breath from his mouth and destroy him with his glorious appearing, when he comes. ⁹ The Wicked One will come with the power of Satan and perform all kinds of miracles and false signs

υἱὸς τῆς ἀπωλείας, 4 ὁ ἀντικείμενος **καὶ ὑπεραιρόμενος ἐπὶ πάντα** λεγόμενον **θεὸν** ἢ σέβασμα, ὥστε αὐτὸν **εἰς τὸν ναὸν τοῦ θεοῦ καθίσαι**², ἀποδεικνύντα ἑαυτὸν ὅτι ἔστιν **θεός.**ᵇ 5 Οὐ μνημονεύετε ὅτι ἔτι ὢν πρὸς ὑμᾶς ταῦτα ἔλεγον ὑμῖν; 6 καὶ νῦν τὸ κατέχον οἴδατε, εἰς τὸ ἀποκαλυφθῆναι αὐτὸν ἐν τῷ ἑαυτοῦ καιρῷ. 7 τὸ γὰρ μυστήριον ἤδη ἐνεργεῖται τῆς ἀνομίας· μόνον ὁ κατέχων ἄρτι ἕως ἐκ μέσου γένηται. 8 καὶ τότε ἀποκαλυφθήσεται **ὁ ἄνομος,** ὃν ὁ κύριος [᾿Ιησοῦς]³ **ἀνελεῖ**⁴ **τῷ πνεύματι τοῦ στόματος αὐτοῦ** καὶ καταργήσει τῇ ἐπιφανείᾳ τῆς παρουσίας αὐτοῦ, 9 οὗ ἐστιν ἡ παρουσία κατ᾽ ἐνέργειαν τοῦ Σατανᾶ ἐν πάσῃ δυνάμει καὶ σημείοις καὶ τέρασιν

---

² **4** {B} καθίσαι ℵ A B D* Ψ (P 2492 καθῆσαι) 33 81 88 104 330 436 451 629 1739 1881 1962 2127 itᵃʳ,ᶜ,ᵈ,ᵈᵉᵐ,ᵈⁱᵛ,ᵉ,f,ᵐᵒⁿ,ˣ,ᶻ vg syrʰ copˢᵃ,ᵇᵒ goth arm eth Marcion Irenaeusˡᵃᵗ Tertullian Hippolytus Origenᵍʳ,ˡᵃᵗ Eusebius Ambrosiaster Cyril-Jerusalem Apollinarisᵃᶜᶜ· ᵗᵒ ᴶᵉʳᵒᵐᵉ Euthalius John-Damascus ∥ ὡς θεὸν καθίσαι Dᶜ (Gᶜ καθεισαι) K (181 καθῆσαι) 326 614 630 1241 1877 2495 *Byz Lect* itᵍᵉ syrᵖ,ʰ ʷⁱᵗʰ * Irenaeus Ephraem Chrysostom Cyril Theodoret ∥ καθίσαι ὡς θεόν 1984 (1985 καθίστισι) Theophylact ∥ ἵνα θεὸν καθίσαι (G* καθέσαι) itᵍ*

³ **8** {C} ᾿Ιησοῦς ℵ A D* G P Ψ 33 81 104 330 436 451 1241 1877 1962 1985 2127 2492 *l*¹³⁶⁵ itᶜ,ᵈ,ᵈᵉᵐ,ᵉ,f,ᵍ,ᵐᵒⁿ,ˣ (itᵈⁱᵛ,ᶻ ᾿Ιησοῦς Χριστός) vg syrᵖ,ʰ copˢᵃ,ᵇᵒ arm eth Irenaeusˡᵃᵗ Tertullian Hippolytus Origenᵍʳ²/³,ˡᵃᵗ Ambrosiaster Hilary Athanasius Basil Apostolic Constitutions Cyril-Jerusalem Chrysostom Augustine Cyril Euthalius Theodoret John-Damascus ∥ *deus Ihesus for* κύριος ᾿Ιησοῦς itᵃʳ ∥ *omit* B Dᶜ K 88 181 326 614 629 630 1739 1881 1984 2495 *Byz Lect* copᵇᵒᵐˢ Origenᵍʳ¹/³ Ephraem Cyril-Jerusalem Macarius Theodoret Vigilius John-Damascus Ps-Oecumenius

⁴ **8** {C} ἀνελεῖ A B P 81 88 104 330 436 451 1877 1962 2127 2492 *l*¹³⁶⁵ copˢᵃ?ᵇᵒ? Hippolytus Origen Athanasius Basil Cyril-Jerusalem Macarius Euthalius Theodoret John-Damascus ∥ ἀνέλοι ℵᵇ (ℵ* ἀναλοῖ) G 33 1739 ∥ ἀναλώσει Dᶜ K Ψ 181 326 614 629 630 1241 1984 2495 *Byz Lect* syrᵖ,ʰ copˢᵃ?ᵇᵒ? Origen Basil Cyril-Jerusalem Chrysostom Theodoret John-Damascus Ps-Oecumenius Theophylact ∥ ἀναιρεῖ Hippolytus ∥ ἀνελεῖ *or* ἀνέλοι *or* ἀναλώσει itᵃʳ,ᶜ,ᵈ,ᵈᵉᵐ,ᵈⁱᵛ,ᵉ,f,ᵍ,ᵐᵒⁿ,ˣ,ᶻ vg Irenaeusˡᵃᵗ Tertullian Origenˡᵃᵗ Hilary

---

ᵇ **3–4** *b* major: TR Nes BF² ∥ *b* dash: WH Bov ∥ different construction: AV RV ASV RSV NEB TT Zür Luth Jer Seg

---

4 ὁ ἀντικείμενος...σέβασμα Dn 11.36   αὐτὸν...θεός Eze 28.2   **8** ὁ ἄνομος...αὐτοῦ Job 4.9; Is 11.4; Re 19.15   **9** Mt 24.24; Re 13.11–13

ψεύδους 10 καὶ ἐν πάσῃ ἀπάτῃ ἀδικίας τοῖς ἀπολλυμένοις, ἀνθ' ὧν τὴν ἀγάπην τῆς ἀληθείας οὐκ ἐδέξαντο
εἰς τὸ σωθῆναι αὐτούς. 11 καὶ διὰ τοῦτο πέμπει αὐτοῖς
ὁ θεὸς ἐνέργειαν πλάνης εἰς τὸ πιστεῦσαι αὐτοὺς τῷ
ψεύδει, 12 ἵνα κριθῶσιν πάντες οἱ μὴ πιστεύσαντες τῇ
ἀληθείᾳ ἀλλὰ εὐδοκήσαντες τῇ ἀδικίᾳ.

Chosen for Salvation

13 Ἡμεῖς δὲ ὀφείλομεν εὐχαριστεῖν τῷ θεῷ πάντοτε
περὶ ὑμῶν, ἀδελφοὶ ἠγαπημένοι ὑπὸ κυρίου, ὅτι εἵλατο
ὑμᾶς ὁ θεὸς ἀπαρχὴν⁵ εἰς σωτηρίαν ἐν ἁγιασμῷ πνεύματος
καὶ πίστει ἀληθείας, 14 εἰς ὃ ἐκάλεσεν ὑμᾶς διὰ τοῦ
εὐαγγελίου ἡμῶν, εἰς περιποίησιν δόξης τοῦ κυρίου ἡμῶν
Ἰησοῦ Χριστοῦ. 15 ἄρα οὖν, ἀδελφοί, στήκετε, καὶ
κρατεῖτε τὰς παραδόσεις ἃς ἐδιδάχθητε εἴτε διὰ λόγου
εἴτε δι' ἐπιστολῆς ἡμῶν. 16 Αὐτὸς δὲ ὁ κύριος ἡμῶν
Ἰησοῦς Χριστὸς καὶ [ὁ] θεὸς ὁ πατὴρ ἡμῶν, ὁ ἀγαπήσας
ἡμᾶς καὶ δοὺς παράκλησιν αἰωνίαν καὶ ἐλπίδα ἀγαθὴν
ἐν χάριτι, 17 παρακαλέσαι ὑμῶν τὰς καρδίας καὶ
στηρίξαι ἐν παντὶ ἔργῳ καὶ λόγῳ ἀγαθῷ.

Pray for Us

3 Τὸ λοιπὸν προσεύχεσθε, ἀδελφοί, περὶ ἡμῶν, ἵνα
ὁ λόγος τοῦ κυρίου τρέχῃ καὶ δοξάζηται καθὼς καὶ
πρὸς ὑμᾶς, 2 καὶ ἵνα ῥυσθῶμεν ἀπὸ τῶν ἀτόπων καὶ

---

⁵ 13 {C} ἀπαρχήν B Gᵍʳ P 33 81 326 1739 1877 (1881 ἀπ' ἀπαρχήν)
itᶜ,ᵈᵉᵐ,ᵈⁱᵛ,ᶠ,ˣ,ᶻ vg syrʰ copᵇᵒ Didymus Ambrose Cyril Euthalius John-
Damascusᶜᵒᵐᵐ ‖ ἀπ' ἀρχῆς ℵ D K Ψ 104 181 330 436 451 614 629 630 1241
1962 1984 1985 2127 2492 2495 Byz Lect itᵃʳ,ᵈ,ᵉ,ᵍ,ᵐᵒⁿ syrᵖ copˢᵃ arm eth
Ambrosiaster Chrysostom Pelagius Theodoreˡᵃᵗ Theodoret Vigilius John-
Damascusᵗˣᵗ ‖ ἑαυτῷ ἀπ' ἀρχῆς 88

11 εἰς...ψεύδει 2 Tm 4.4   13 Ἡμεῖς...περὶ ὑμῶν 1 Th 1.2; 2 Th 1.3   ἠγαπημένοι ὑπὸ
κυρίου Dt 33.12   εἵλατο...ἀπαρχήν Jn 15.16; Eph 1.4   13-14 εἰς σωτηρίαν...ὑμᾶς
1 Th 4.7; 5.9
3 1 προσεύχεσθε...ἡμῶν Col 4.3; 1 Th 5.25

---

and wonders, 10 and use every kind of
wicked deceit on those who will perish.
They will perish because they did not
welcome and love the truth so as to be
saved. 11 For this reason God sends the
power of error to work in them so that
they believe what is false. 12 The result
is that all who have not believed the
truth, but have taken pleasure in sin,
will be condemned.

You Are Chosen for Salvation

13 We must thank God at all times for
you, brothers, you whom the Lord loves.
For God chose you as the first to be
saved by the Spirit's power to make you
God's own people, and by your faith in
the truth. 14 God called you to this
through the Good News we preached to
you; he called you to possess your share
of the glory of our Lord Jesus Christ.
15 So then, brothers, stand firm and hold
on to those truths which we taught you,
both in our preaching and in our letter.
16 May our Lord Jesus Christ himself,
and God our Father, who loved us and
in his grace gave us eternal courage and
a good hope, 17 fill your hearts with
courage and make you strong to do and
say all that is good.

Pray for Us

3 Finally, brothers, pray for us, that
the Lord's message may continue to
spread rapidly and receive glory, just
as it did among you. 2 Pray also that
God will rescue us from wicked and evil

men. For not all people believe the message.

[3] But the Lord is faithful. He will make you strong and keep you safe from the Evil One. [4] And the Lord gives us confidence in you; we are sure that you are doing and will continue to do what we tell you.

[5] May the Lord lead your hearts to the love for God and to the endurance that is given by Christ.

The Obligation to Work

[6] In the name of the Lord Jesus Christ we command you, brothers: keep away from all brothers who are living a lazy life, who do not follow the instructions that we gave them. [7] You yourselves know very well that you should do just what we did. We were not lazy when we were with you. [8] We did not accept anyone's support without paying for it. Instead, we worked and toiled; day and night we kept working so as not to be an expense to any of you. [9] We did this, not because we do not have the right to demand our support; we did it to be an example for you to follow. [10] While we were with you we told you: "Whoever does not want to work is not allowed to eat."

[11] We say this because we hear that there are some people among you who live lazy lives, who do nothing except meddle in other people's business. [12] In the name of the Lord Jesus Christ we

πονηρῶν ἀνθρώπων· οὐ γὰρ πάντων ἡ πίστις. **3** πιστὸς δέ ἐστιν ὁ κύριος, ὃς στηρίξει ὑμᾶς καὶ φυλάξει ἀπὸ τοῦ πονηροῦ. **4** πεποίθαμεν δὲ ἐν κυρίῳ ἐφ᾽ ὑμᾶς, ὅτι ἃ παραγγέλλομεν [καὶ] ποιεῖτε καὶ ποιήσετε. **5** Ὁ δὲ κύριος κατευθύναι ὑμῶν τὰς καρδίας εἰς τὴν ἀγάπην τοῦ θεοῦ καὶ εἰς τὴν ὑπομονὴν τοῦ Χριστοῦ.

Warning against Idleness

6 Παραγγέλλομεν δὲ ὑμῖν, ἀδελφοί, ἐν ὀνόματι τοῦ κυρίου Ἰησοῦ Χριστοῦ,[a] στέλλεσθαι ὑμᾶς ἀπὸ παντὸς ἀδελφοῦ ἀτάκτως περιπατοῦντος καὶ μὴ κατὰ τὴν παράδοσιν ἣν παρελάβοσαν[1] παρ᾽ ἡμῶν. **7** αὐτοὶ γὰρ οἴδατε πῶς δεῖ μιμεῖσθαι ἡμᾶς, ὅτι οὐκ ἠτακτήσαμεν ἐν ὑμῖν **8** οὐδὲ δωρεὰν ἄρτον ἐφάγομεν παρά τινος, ἀλλ᾽ ἐν κόπῳ καὶ μόχθῳ νυκτὸς καὶ ἡμέρας ἐργαζόμενοι πρὸς τὸ μὴ ἐπιβαρῆσαί τινα ὑμῶν· **9** οὐχ ὅτι οὐκ ἔχομεν ἐξουσίαν, ἀλλ᾽ ἵνα ἑαυτοὺς τύπον δῶμεν ὑμῖν εἰς τὸ μιμεῖσθαι ἡμᾶς. **10** καὶ γὰρ ὅτε ἦμεν πρὸς ὑμᾶς, τοῦτο παρηγγέλλομεν ὑμῖν, ὅτι εἴ τις οὐ θέλει ἐργάζεσθαι μηδὲ ἐσθιέτω. **11** ἀκούομεν γάρ τινας περιπατοῦντας ἐν ὑμῖν ἀτάκτως, μηδὲν ἐργαζομένους ἀλλὰ περιεργαζομένους· **12** τοῖς δὲ τοιούτοις παραγγέλλομεν καὶ παρακαλοῦμεν

---

[1] **6** {C} παρελάβοσαν ℵ* A (D* ἐλάβοσαν) 33 88 Basil ‖ παρέλαβον ℵ° Dᶜ K P Ψ 81 104 181 326 330 451 614 629 630 1241 1739 1877 1881 1984 1985 2127 2492 *Byz Lect* Origen Basil Chrysostom Euthalius Theodoret John-Damascus Theophylact ‖ παρελάβοσαν or παρέλαβον itᵃʳ,ᶜ,ᵈ,ᵈᵉᵐ,ᵈⁱᵛ,ᵉ,f,(g?),m,mon,x,z vg syrᵖ copˢᵃᵐˢ Cyprian Lucifer Augustine ‖ παρέλαβεν 1962 Basil Ps-Oecumenius ‖ παρελάβετε B G 436 2495 (itᵍ?) syrʰ copˢᵃ,(ᵇᵒ) goth arm Origen Macrobius Ambrosiaster Basil Theodoret Ps-Jerome

---

[a] **6** *a minor*: TR Bov Nes BF² AV RV ASV RSV NEB TT Zür Luth Jer Seg ‖ *a none*: WH

---

3 πιστὸς...κύριος 1 Cor 1.9; 1 Th 5.24   **4** πεποίθαμεν...ὑμᾶς 2 Cor 7.16; Ga 5.10   ἃ...ποιήσετε 2 Cor 7.15; 1 Th 4.10   **6** Mt 18.17; Ro 16.17   **7** αὐτοὶ...ἡμᾶς Php 3.17; 1 Th 1.6   **8** ἐν...ἐργαζόμενοι 1 Cor 4.12; 1 Th 2.9   **9** οὐχ...ἐξουσίαν Mt 10.10; 1 Cor 9.4, 6   ἑαυτοὺς...ἡμᾶς 1 Cor 4.16; 1 Th 1.6   **10** εἴ...ἐσθιέτω 1 Th 4.11   **11** μηδὲν...περιεργαζομένους 1 Tm 5.13   **12** τοῖς...ἐργαζόμενοι Eph 4.28; 1 Th 4.11

ἐν κυρίῳ Ἰησοῦ Χριστῷ ἵνα μετὰ ἡσυχίας ἐργαζόμενοι τὸν ἑαυτῶν ἄρτον ἐσθίωσιν. **13** Ὑμεῖς δέ, ἀδελφοί, μὴ ἐγκακήσητε καλοποιοῦντες. **14** εἰ δέ τις οὐχ ὑπακούει τῷ λόγῳ ἡμῶν διὰ τῆς ἐπιστολῆς, τοῦτον σημειοῦσθε, μὴ συναναμίγνυσθαι αὐτῷ, ἵνα ἐντραπῇ· **15** καὶ μὴ ὡς ἐχθρὸν ἡγεῖσθε, ἀλλὰ νουθετεῖτε ὡς ἀδελφόν.

Benediction

16 Αὐτὸς δὲ ὁ κύριος τῆς εἰρήνης δῴη ὑμῖν τὴν εἰρήνην διὰ παντὸς ἐν παντὶ τρόπῳ². ὁ κύριος μετὰ πάντων ὑμῶν.

17 Ὁ ἀσπασμὸς τῇ ἐμῇ χειρὶ Παύλου, ὅ ἐστιν σημεῖον ἐν πάσῃ ἐπιστολῇ·ᵇ οὕτως γράφω.ᵇ **18** ἡ χάρις τοῦ κυρίου ἡμῶν Ἰησοῦ Χριστοῦ μετὰ πάντων ὑμῶν.³

---

² **16** {B} τρόπῳ ℵ Aᶜ B Dᶜ K P Ψ 81 88 104 181 326 330 436 451 614 629 630 1241 1739 1877 1881 1962 1984 1985 2127 2492 2495 *Byz Lect* syrᵖˑʰ copˢᵃˑᵇᵒ (arm) (eth) Euthalius Theodoret John-Damascus ∥ τόπῳ A* D* G 33 itᵃʳˑᶜˑᵈˑᵈᵉᵐˑᵈⁱᵛˑᵉˑᶠˑᵍˑᵐᵒⁿˑˣˑᶻ vg goth Ambrosiaster Chrysostom

³ **18** {C} ὑμῶν. ℵ* B 33 1739 itᶻ* copˢᵃˑᵇᵒᵐˢˢ arm Ambrosiaster Athanasius Pelagius ∥ ὑμῶν. ἀμήν. ℵᶜ A D G K P Ψ 81 88 104 181 326 330 436 451 614 629 630 1241 1877 1881 1962 1984 1985 2127 2492 2495 *Byz Lect* itᵃʳˑᶜˑᵈˑᵈᵉᵐˑᵈⁱᵛˑᵉˑᶠˑᵍˑᵐᵒⁿˑˣ vg syrᵖˑʰ copᵇᵒ goth eth Euthalius

---

ᵇ ᵇ **17** *b* minor, *b* major: TR WH Bov Nes BF² AV RV ASV RSV NEB Zür Seg ∥ *b* major, *b* minor: NEBᵐᵍ ∥ *b* major, *b* major: TT Luth Jer

---

13 Ga 6.9   **14** εἰ δέ...συναναμίγνυσθαι αὐτῷ 1 Cor 5.9, 11   **15** νουθετεῖτε ὡς ἀδελφόν 1 Th 5.14   **16** ὁ κύριος τῆς εἰρήνης Ro 15.33; 1 Th 5.23   **17** 1 Cor 16.21

command these people and warn them: they must lead orderly lives and work to earn their own living. ¹³ But you, brothers, must not get tired of doing good. ¹⁴ There may be someone there who will not obey the message we send you in this letter. If so, take note of him and have nothing to do with him, so that he will be ashamed. ¹⁵ But do not treat him as an enemy; instead, warn him as a brother.

Final Words

¹⁶ May the Lord himself, who is our source of peace, give you peace at all times and in every way. The Lord be with you all.

¹⁷ With my own hand I write this: *Greetings from Paul.* This is the way I sign every letter; this is how I write.

¹⁸ May the grace of our Lord Jesus Christ be with you all.

PAUL'S FIRST LETTER TO TIMOTHY

1 From Paul, an apostle of Christ Jesus by order of God our Savior and Christ Jesus our hope —

² To Timothy, my true son in the faith:

May God the Father and Christ Jesus our Lord give you grace, mercy, and peace.

Warnings against False Teaching

³ I want you to stay in Ephesus, just as I urged you when I was on my way to Macedonia. Some people there are teaching false doctrines, and you must order them to stop. ⁴ Tell them to give up those legends and long lists of names of ancestors, for these only produce arguments; they do not serve God's plan, which is known by faith. ⁵ The purpose of this order is to arouse the love that comes from a pure heart, a clear conscience, and a genuine faith. ⁶ Some men have turned away from these and have lost their way in foolish discussions. ⁷ They want to be teachers of God's law, but they do not understand their own words or the matters about which they speak with so much confidence.

⁸ We know that the Law is good, if it is used as it should be used. ⁹ It must be remembered, of course, that laws are made, not for good people, but for lawbreakers and criminals, for the godless and sinful, for those who are not religious or spiritual, for men who kill their fathers or mothers, for murderers, ¹⁰ for the immoral, for sexual perverts, for kidnappers, for those who lie and give false testimony or do anything else contrary to the true teaching. ¹¹ That is the teaching found in the gospel that was entrusted to me to announce, the Good News from the glorious and blessed God.

720

ΠΡΟΣ ΤΙΜΟΘΕΟΝ Α

Salutation

1 Παῦλος ἀπόστολος Χριστοῦ Ἰησοῦ κατ᾽ ἐπιταγὴν θεοῦ σωτῆρος ἡμῶν καὶ Χριστοῦ Ἰησοῦ τῆς ἐλπίδος ἡμῶν **2** Τιμοθέῳ γνησίῳ τέκνῳ ἐν πίστει· χάρις, ἔλεος, εἰρήνη ἀπὸ θεοῦ πατρὸς καὶ Χριστοῦ Ἰησοῦ τοῦ κυρίου ἡμῶν.

Warning against False Doctrine

3 Καθὼς παρεκάλεσά σε προσμεῖναι ἐν Ἐφέσῳ πορευόμενος εἰς Μακεδονίαν, ἵνα παραγγείλῃς τισὶν μὴ ἑτεροδιδασκαλεῖν **4** μηδὲ προσέχειν μύθοις καὶ γενεαλογίαις ἀπεράντοις, αἵτινες ἐκζητήσεις παρέχουσιν μᾶλλον ἢ οἰκονομίαν θεοῦ τὴν ἐν πίστει· **5** τὸ δὲ τέλος τῆς παραγγελίας ἐστὶν ἀγάπη ἐκ καθαρᾶς καρδίας καὶ συνειδήσεως ἀγαθῆς καὶ πίστεως ἀνυποκρίτου, **6** ὧν τινες ἀστοχήσαντες ἐξετράπησαν εἰς ματαιολογίαν, **7** θέλοντες εἶναι νομοδιδάσκαλοι, μὴ νοοῦντες μήτε ἃ λέγουσιν μήτε περὶ τίνων διαβεβαιοῦνται.

8 Οἴδαμεν δὲ ὅτι καλὸς ὁ νόμος ἐάν τις αὐτῷ νομίμως χρῆται, **9** εἰδὼς τοῦτο, ὅτι δικαίῳ νόμος οὐ κεῖται, ἀνόμοις δὲ καὶ ἀνυποτάκτοις, ἀσεβέσι καὶ ἁμαρτωλοῖς, ἀνοσίοις καὶ βεβήλοις, πατρολῴαις καὶ μητρολῴαις, ἀνδροφόνοις, **10** πόρνοις, ἀρσενοκοίταις, ἀνδραποδισταῖς, ψεύσταις, ἐπιόρκοις, καὶ εἴ τι ἕτερον τῇ ὑγιαινούσῃ διδασκαλίᾳ ἀντίκειται, **11** κατὰ τὸ εὐαγγέλιον τῆς δόξης τοῦ μακαρίου θεοῦ, ὃ ἐπιστεύθην ἐγώ.

---

1 Χριστοῦ...ἐλπίδος ἡμῶν Col 1.27 **2** γνησίῳ...πίστει Tt 1.4 **3** Καθὼς... Μακεδονίαν Ac 20.1 **4** μηδὲ προσέχειν μύθοις 1 Tm 4.7; Tt 1.14 **5** τὸ δὲ...καρδίας Ro 13.10 **6** ἐξετράπησαν εἰς ματαιολογίαν 1 Tm 6.4, 20; Tt 1.10 **8** καλὸς ὁ νόμος Ro 7.12, 16 **10** τῇ ὑγιαινούσῃ διδασκαλίᾳ 1 Tm 4.6; 6.3; 2 Tm 4.3; Tt 1.9; 2.1

Thankfulness for Mercy

12 Χάριν ἔχω τῷ ἐνδυναμώσαντί[1] με Χριστῷ Ἰησοῦ τῷ κυρίῳ ἡμῶν, ὅτι πιστόν με ἡγήσατο θέμενος εἰς διακονίαν, **13** τὸ πρότερον ὄντα βλάσφημον καὶ διώκτην καὶ ὑβριστήν· ἀλλὰ ἠλεήθην, ὅτι ἀγνοῶν ἐποίησα ἐν ἀπιστίᾳ, **14** ὑπερεπλεόνασεν δὲ ἡ χάρις τοῦ κυρίου ἡμῶν μετὰ πίστεως καὶ ἀγάπης τῆς ἐν Χριστῷ Ἰησοῦ. **15** πιστὸς[2] ὁ λόγος καὶ πάσης ἀποδοχῆς ἄξιος, ὅτι Χριστὸς Ἰησοῦς ἦλθεν εἰς τὸν κόσμον ἁμαρτωλοὺς σῶσαι· ὧν πρῶτός εἰμι ἐγώ, **16** ἀλλὰ διὰ τοῦτο ἠλεήθην, ἵνα ἐν ἐμοὶ πρώτῳ ἐνδείξηται Χριστὸς Ἰησοῦς τὴν ἅπασαν μακροθυμίαν, πρὸς ὑποτύπωσιν τῶν μελλόντων πιστεύειν ἐπ' αὐτῷ εἰς ζωὴν αἰώνιον. **17** τῷ δὲ βασιλεῖ τῶν αἰώνων, ἀφθάρτῳ, ἀοράτῳ, μόνῳ θεῷ, τιμὴ καὶ δόξα εἰς τοὺς αἰῶνας τῶν αἰώνων· ἀμήν.

18 Ταύτην τὴν παραγγελίαν παρατίθεμαί σοι, τέκνον Τιμόθεε, κατὰ τὰς προαγούσας ἐπὶ σὲ προφητείας, ἵνα στρατεύῃ ἐν αὐταῖς τὴν καλὴν στρατείαν, **19** ἔχων πίστιν καὶ ἀγαθὴν συνείδησιν, ἥν τινες ἀπωσάμενοι περὶ τὴν πίστιν ἐναυάγησαν· **20** ὧν ἐστιν Ὑμέναιος καὶ Ἀλέξανδρος, οὓς παρέδωκα τῷ Σατανᾷ ἵνα παιδευθῶσιν μὴ βλασφημεῖν.

---

[1] **12** {B} ἐνδυναμώσαντι ℵc A D G H I K P Ψ 81 88 104 181 326 436 614 629 630 1241 1739 1877 1881 1962 1984 1985 2127 2492 2495 *Byz Lect* itar,c,(d), dem,div,f,mon,x,z vg syrp,h copbo arm Epiphanius ‖ ἐνδυναμοῦντι (*see* Php 4.13) ℵ* 33 330 451 *l*603 itg copsa Epiphanius Theophylact

[2] **15** {A} πιστός ℵ A D Ggr H K P Ψ 33 81 88 104 181 326 330 436 451 614 629 630 1241 1739 1877 1881 1962 1984 1985 2127 2492 2495 *Byz Lect* itar,c,d,dem,div,f,t,x,z vg syrp,h copsa,bo goth arm Augustine ‖ ἀνθρώπινος (*see* 3.1 mg) itmon,rl Ambrosiaster mssacc. to Jerome Augustine Julian-Eclanum Vigilius ‖ *humanus vel fidelis* itg

---

12 πιστόν...διακονίαν Ac 9.15; Ga 1.15–16   **13** τὸ...ὑβριστήν Ac 8.3; 9.1–2; 1 Cor 15.9; Ga 1.13   **15** Χριστὸς...σῶσαι Lk 15.2; 19.10   **17** μόνῳ θεῷ Ro 16.27   **18** στρατεύῃ... στρατείαν 1 Tm 6.12; 2 Tm 4.7; Jd 3   **20** Ὑμέναιος 2 Tm 2.17   Ἀλέξανδρος 2 Tm 4.14 παρέδωκα τῷ Σατανᾷ 1 Cor 5.5

Gratitude for God's Mercy

[12] I give thanks to Christ Jesus our Lord, who has given me strength for my work. I thank him for considering me worthy, and appointing me to serve him, [13] even though in the past I spoke evil of him, and persecuted and insulted him. But God was merciful to me, because I did not believe and so did not know what I was doing. [14] And our Lord poured out his abundant grace on me and gave me the faith and love which are ours in union with Christ Jesus. [15] This is a true saying, to be completely accepted and believed: Christ Jesus came into the world to save sinners. I am the worst of them, [16] but it was for this very reason that God was merciful to me, in order that Christ Jesus might show his full patience in dealing with me, the worst of sinners, as an example for all those who would later believe in him and receive eternal life. [17] To the eternal King, immortal and invisible, the only God — to him be honor and glory for ever and ever! Amen.

[18] Timothy, my child, I entrust this command to you. It is according to the words of prophecy spoken long ago about you. Let those words be your weapons as you fight the good fight, [19] and keep your faith and clear conscience. Some men have not listened to their conscience, and have made a ruin of their faith. [20] Among them are Hymenaeus and Alexander, whom I have handed over to the power of Satan, so that they will be taught to stop speaking evil of God.

Church Worship

2 First of all, then, I urge that petitions and prayers, requests and thanksgivings be offered to God for all men; [2] for kings and all others who are in authority, that we may live a quiet and peaceful life, in entire godliness and proper conduct. [3] This is good and it pleases God our Savior, [4] who wants all men to be saved and to come to know the truth. [5] For there is one God, and there is one who brings God and men together, the man Christ Jesus, [6] who gave himself to redeem all men. That was the proof, at the right time, that God wants all men to be saved, [7] and this is why I was sent as an apostle and teacher of the Gentiles, to proclaim the message of faith and truth. I am not lying, I am telling the truth!

[8] I want men everywhere to pray, men who are dedicated to God and can lift up their hands in prayer without anger or argument.

[9] I also want women to be modest and sensible about their clothes and to dress properly; not with fancy hair styles, or with gold ornaments or pearls or expensive dresses, [10] but with good deeds, as is proper for women who claim to be religious. [11] Women should learn in silence and all humility. [12] I do not allow women to teach or to have authority over men; they must keep quiet. [13] For Adam was created first, and then Eve. [14] And it was not Adam who was de-

Instructions concerning Prayer

2 Παρακαλῶ οὖν πρῶτον πάντων ποιεῖσθαι δεήσεις, προσευχάς, ἐντεύξεις, εὐχαριστίας, ὑπὲρ πάντων ἀνθρώπων, 2 ὑπὲρ βασιλέων καὶ πάντων τῶν ἐν ὑπεροχῇ ὄντων, ἵνα ἤρεμον καὶ ἡσύχιον βίον διάγωμεν ἐν πάσῃ εὐσεβείᾳ καὶ σεμνότητι. 3 τοῦτο καλὸν καὶ ἀπόδεκτον ἐνώπιον τοῦ σωτῆρος ἡμῶν θεοῦ, 4 ὃς πάντας ἀνθρώπους θέλει σωθῆναι καὶ εἰς ἐπίγνωσιν ἀληθείας ἐλθεῖν. 5 εἷς γὰρ θεός, εἷς καὶ μεσίτης θεοῦ καὶ ἀνθρώπων, ἄνθρωπος Χριστὸς Ἰησοῦς, 6 ὁ δοὺς ἑαυτὸν ἀντίλυτρον ὑπὲρ πάντων, τὸ μαρτύριον καιροῖς ἰδίοις· 7 εἰς ὃ ἐτέθην ἐγὼ κῆρυξ καὶ ἀπόστολος — ἀλήθειαν λέγω[1], οὐ ψεύδομαι — διδάσκαλος ἐθνῶν ἐν πίστει καὶ ἀληθείᾳ.

8 Βούλομαι οὖν προσεύχεσθαι τοὺς ἄνδρας ἐν παντὶ τόπῳ, ἐπαίροντας ὁσίους χεῖρας χωρὶς ὀργῆς καὶ διαλογισμοῦ.[a] 9 ὡσαύτως [καὶ] γυναῖκας ἐν καταστολῇ κοσμίῳ μετὰ αἰδοῦς καὶ σωφροσύνης κοσμεῖν ἑαυτάς, μὴ ἐν πλέγμασιν καὶ χρυσίῳ ἢ μαργαρίταις ἢ ἱματισμῷ πολυτελεῖ, 10 ἀλλ' ὃ πρέπει γυναιξὶν ἐπαγγελλομέναις θεοσέβειαν, δι' ἔργων ἀγαθῶν. 11 γυνὴ ἐν ἡσυχίᾳ μανθανέτω ἐν πάσῃ ὑποταγῇ· 12 διδάσκειν δὲ γυναικὶ οὐκ ἐπιτρέπω, οὐδὲ αὐθεντεῖν ἀνδρός, ἀλλ' εἶναι ἐν ἡσυχίᾳ. 13 Ἀδὰμ γὰρ πρῶτος ἐπλάσθη, εἶτα Εὔα· 14 καὶ Ἀδὰμ

---

[1] **7** {B} λέγω אᶜ A D* G P Ψ 81 104 330 451 629 1739 1881 2492 *Lect* itᶜ,ᵈ,ᵈᵉᵐ,ᵈⁱᵛ,ᶠ,ᵍ,ᵐᵒⁿ,ʳˡ,ˣ,ᶻ vg syrᵖ,ʰ copˢᵃ,ᵇᵒ eth Ambrosiaster Chrysostom Ps-Athanasius John-Damascus ∥ λέγω ἐν Χριστῷ (see Ro 9.1) א* Dᶜ H K 33ᵛⁱᵈ 88 181 326 614 630 1241 1877 2127 (2495 λέγω ἐγώ) *Byz* lᵉ⁵⁹⁸ itᵃʳ goth arm (Pelagius) Euthalius Theodoret ∥ λέγω Χριστός [sic] 436 ∥ omit ἀλήθειαν λέγω 1984 1985

---

[a] **8-9** *a minor:* TR RSV Zür ∥ *a major:* AV RV ASV NEB TT Luth ∥ *a paragraph:* WH Bov Nes BF² Jer Seg

---

1 Παρακαλῶ...εὐχαριστίας Eph 6.18; Php 4.6   **3** τοῦ...θεοῦ 1 Tm 1.1; 4.10   **4** Eze 18.23; 2 Pe 3.9   **5** εἷς γὰρ θεός Ro 3.29–30; 10.12   εἷς...Ἰησοῦς He 12.24   **6** ὁ δοὺς...πάντων Ga 1.4; 2.20; Tt 2.14   **7** Ac 9.15; Ga 2.7–8; 1 Tm 1.11   **9** 1 Pe 3.3–5   **10** 1 Tm 5.10   **11-12** 1 Cor 14.34   **13** Gn 1.27; 2.7, 22; 1 Cor 11.8–9   **14** Gn 3.6, 13; 2 Cor 11.3

οὐκ ἠπατήθη, ἡ δὲ γυνὴ ἐξαπατηθεῖσα ἐν παραβάσει γέγονεν. 15 σωθήσεται δὲ διὰ τῆς τεκνογονίας, ἐὰν μείνωσιν ἐν πίστει καὶ ἀγάπῃ καὶ ἁγιασμῷ μετὰ σωφροσύνης.[a]

Qualifications of Bishops

3 Πιστὸς[1] ὁ λόγος·[a] εἴ τις ἐπισκοπῆς ὀρέγεται, καλοῦ ἔργου ἐπιθυμεῖ. 2 δεῖ οὖν τὸν ἐπίσκοπον ἀνεπίλημπτον εἶναι, μιᾶς γυναικὸς ἄνδρα, νηφάλιον, σώφρονα, κόσμιον, φιλόξενον, διδακτικόν, 3 μὴ πάροινον, μὴ πλήκτην, ἀλλὰ ἐπιεικῆ, ἄμαχον, ἀφιλάργυρον, 4 τοῦ ἰδίου οἴκου καλῶς προϊστάμενον, τέκνα ἔχοντα ἐν ὑποταγῇ μετὰ πάσης σεμνότητος· ([b]5 εἰ δέ τις τοῦ ἰδίου οἴκου προστῆναι οὐκ οἶδεν, πῶς ἐκκλησίας θεοῦ ἐπιμελήσεται;)[b] 6 μὴ νεόφυτον, ἵνα μὴ τυφωθεὶς εἰς κρίμα ἐμπέσῃ τοῦ διαβόλου. 7 δεῖ δὲ καὶ μαρτυρίαν καλὴν ἔχειν ἀπὸ τῶν ἔξωθεν, ἵνα μὴ εἰς ὀνειδισμὸν ἐμπέσῃ καὶ παγίδα τοῦ διαβόλου.

Qualifications of Deacons

8 Διακόνους ὡσαύτως σεμνούς, μὴ διλόγους, μὴ οἴνῳ πολλῷ προσέχοντας, μὴ αἰσχροκερδεῖς, 9 ἔχοντας τὸ μυστήριον τῆς πίστεως ἐν καθαρᾷ συνειδήσει. 10 καὶ οὗτοι δὲ δοκιμαζέσθωσαν πρῶτον, εἶτα διακονείτωσαν ἀνέγκλητοι ὄντες. 11 γυναῖκας ὡσαύτως σεμνάς, μὴ

---

[1] **1** {B} πιστός ℵ A Dᵘ Gᵍʳ K P Ψ 33 81 88 104 181 326 330 436 451 614 629 630 1241 1739 1877 1881 1962 1984 1985 2127 2402 2405 *Byz Lect* itᵃʳ,ᶜ,ᵈᵉᵐ, ᵈⁱᵛ,ᵗ,ᵗ,ˣ,ᶻ vg syrᵖ,ʰ copˢᵃ,ᵇᵒ goth arm ‖ ἀνθρώπινος (see 1.15 mg) D* itᵈ,ᵐ,ᵐᵒⁿ Ambrosiaster mssᵃᶜᶜ· ᵗᵒ ᴶᵉʳᵒᵐᵉ Augustine Sedulius-Scotus ‖ *humanus vel fidelis* itᵍ

ᵃ ᵃ **2.15—3.1** *a* paragraph, *a* minor: TR Bov Nes BF² AV RV ASV RSV (NEB) NEBᵐᵍ¹ TT Zür Luth Jer Seg ‖ *a* major, *a* paragraph: WH RVᵐᵍ ASVᵐᵍ NEBᵐᵍ²

ᵇ ᵇ **5** *b* parens, *b* parens: WH Nes BF² AV RV ASV TT ‖ *b* dash, *b* dash: Bov Zür ‖ *b b* no dashes or parens: TR RSV NEB Luth Jer Seg

---

2-7 Tt 1.6-9   **7** δεῖ...ἔξωθεν 2 Cor 8.21   **11** μὴ διαβόλους Tt 2.3

---

ceived; it was the woman who was deceived and broke God's law. 15 But a woman will be saved through having children, if she perseveres[1] in faith and love and holiness, with modesty.

Leaders in the Church

3 This is a true saying: If a man is eager to be a church leader he desires an excellent work. 2 A church leader must be a man without fault; he must have only one wife,[1] be sober, self-controlled, and orderly; he must welcome strangers in his home; he must be able to teach; 3 he must not be a drunkard or a violent man, but gentle and peaceful; he must not love money; 4 he must be able to manage his own family well, and make his children obey him with all respect. 5 For if a man does not know how to manage his own family, how can he take care of the church of God? 6 He must not be a man who has been recently converted; else he will swell up with pride and be condemned, as the Devil was. 7 He should be a man who is respected by the people outside the church, so that he will not be disgraced and fall into the Devil's trap.

Helpers in the Church

8 Church helpers must also be of a good character and sincere; they must not drink too much wine or be greedy; 9 they should hold to the revealed truth of the faith with a clear conscience. 10 They should be tested first, and then, if they pass the test, they should serve. 11 Their wives also must be of good

---

[1] **15** she perseveres: *or* they persevere

[1] **2** have only one wife: *or* be married only once

character, and not gossip; they must be sober and honest in everything. **12** A church helper must have only one wife,[2] and be able to manage his children and family well. **13** Those who do a good work win for themselves a good standing and are able to speak boldly about the faith that is ours in union with Christ Jesus.

The Great Secret

14 As I write this letter to you, I hope to come and see you soon. **15** But if I delay, this letter will let you know how we should conduct ourselves in God's household, which is the church of the living God, the pillar and support of the truth. **16** No one can deny how great is the secret of our religion!

He appeared in human form,
  Was shown to be right by the Spirit,
  And was seen by angels.
He was preached among the nations,
  Was believed in the world,
  And was taken up to heaven.

False Teachers

4 The Spirit says clearly that some men will abandon the faith in later times; they will obey lying spirits and follow the teachings of demons. **2** These teachings come from the deceit of men who are liars, and whose consciences are dead,

---

[2] **12** have only one wife: *or* be married only once

διαβόλους, νηφαλίους, πιστὰς ἐν πᾶσιν. **12** διάκονοι ἔστωσαν μιᾶς γυναικὸς ἄνδρες, τέκνων καλῶς προϊστάμενοι καὶ τῶν ἰδίων οἴκων· **13** οἱ γὰρ καλῶς διακονήσαντες βαθμὸν ἑαυτοῖς καλὸν περιποιοῦνται καὶ πολλὴν παρρησίαν ἐν πίστει τῇ ἐν Χριστῷ Ἰησοῦ.

The Mystery of Our Religion

14 Ταῦτά σοι γράφω, ἐλπίζων ἐλθεῖν πρὸς σὲ τάχιον· **15** ἐὰν δὲ βραδύνω, ἵνα εἰδῇς πῶς δεῖ ἐν οἴκῳ θεοῦ ἀναστρέφεσθαι, ἥτις ἐστὶν ἐκκλησία θεοῦ ζῶντος, στῦλος καὶ ἑδραίωμα τῆς ἀληθείας. **16** καὶ ὁμολογουμένως μέγα ἐστὶν τὸ τῆς εὐσεβείας μυστήριον·
    Ὃς[2] ἐφανερώθη ἐν σαρκί,
        ἐδικαιώθη ἐν πνεύματι,
        ὤφθη ἀγγέλοις,
    ἐκηρύχθη ἐν ἔθνεσιν,
        ἐπιστεύθη ἐν κόσμῳ,
        ἀνελήμφθη ἐν δόξῃ.

Prediction of Apostasy

4 Τὸ δὲ πνεῦμα ῥητῶς λέγει ὅτι ἐν ὑστέροις καιροῖς ἀποστήσονταί τινες τῆς πίστεως, προσέχοντες πνεύμασιν πλάνοις καὶ διδασκαλίαις δαιμονίων,[a] **2** ἐν ὑποκρίσει ψευδολόγων,[a] κεκαυστηριασμένων τὴν ἰδίαν συνείδησιν,

---

[2] **16** {B} ὅς ℵ* A*[vid] C* G[gr] 33 2127 l[599] syr[hmg,pal] goth eth[pp] Origen[lat] Epiphanius Jerome Theodore Eutherius[acc. to Theodoret] Cyril Cyril[acc. to Ps-Oecumenius] Liberatus ∥ ὅ D* it[ar,c,d,dem,div,f,g,mon,x,z] vg Ambrosiaster Victorinus-Rome Hilary Pelagius Augustine ∥ ω 061 ∥ ὅς *or* ὅ syr[p,h] cop[sa,bo] arm eth[ro] Ephraem? ∥ θεός ℵ[e] A[2] C[2] D[c] K P Ψ 81 104 181 326 330 436 451 614 629 630 1241 1739 1877 1881 1962 1984 1985 2492 2495 *Byz Lect* Gregory-Nyssa Didymus Chrysostom Theodoret Euthalius ∥ ὁ θεός 88

[a a] **1-2** *a minor, a minor:* TR Bov Nes BF[2] AV RV ASV TT ∥ *a none, a mlnor:* WH Zür Luth ∥ *a minor, a none:* RSV NEB Jer Seg

15 ἥτις...ζῶντος Eph 2.19–22   **16** Ὅς...σαρκί Jn 1.14   ἀνελήμφθη ἐν δόξῃ Mk 16.19; Ac 1.9
4 1 ἐν ὑστέροις καιροῖς 2 Tm 3.1; 2 Pe 3.3; 1 Jn 2.18; Jd 18

3 κωλυόντων γαμεῖν, ἀπέχεσθαι βρωμάτων ἃ ὁ θεὸς ἔκτισεν εἰς μετάλημψιν μετὰ εὐχαριστίας τοῖς πιστοῖς καὶ ἐπεγνωκόσι τὴν ἀλήθειαν. 4 ὅτι πᾶν κτίσμα θεοῦ καλόν, καὶ οὐδὲν ἀπόβλητον μετὰ εὐχαριστίας λαμβανόμενον, 5 ἁγιάζεται γὰρ διὰ λόγου θεοῦ καὶ ἐντεύξεως.

A Good Minister of Christ Jesus

6 Ταῦτα ὑποτιθέμενος τοῖς ἀδελφοῖς καλὸς ἔσῃ διάκονος Χριστοῦ Ἰησοῦ, ἐντρεφόμενος τοῖς λόγοις τῆς πίστεως καὶ τῆς καλῆς διδασκαλίας ᾗ παρηκολούθηκας· 7 τοὺς δὲ βεβήλους καὶ γραώδεις μύθους παραιτοῦ. γύμναζε δὲ σεαυτὸν πρὸς εὐσέβειαν· 8 ἡ γὰρ σωματικὴ γυμνασία πρὸς ὀλίγον ἐστὶν ὠφέλιμος, ἡ δὲ εὐσέβεια πρὸς πάντα ὠφέλιμός ἐστιν, ἐπαγγελίαν ἔχουσα ζωῆς τῆς νῦν καὶ τῆς μελλούσης.[b] 9 πιστὸς ὁ λόγος καὶ πάσης ἀποδοχῆς ἄξιος·[b] 10 εἰς τοῦτο γὰρ κοπιῶμεν καὶ ἀγωνιζόμεθα[1], ὅτι ἠλπίκαμεν ἐπὶ θεῷ ζῶντι, ὅς ἐστιν σωτὴρ πάντων ἀνθρώπων, μάλιστα πιστῶν.

11 Παράγγελλε ταῦτα καὶ δίδασκε. 12 μηδείς σου τῆς νεότητος καταφρονείτω, ἀλλὰ τύπος γίνου τῶν πιστῶν ἐν λόγῳ, ἐν ἀναστροφῇ, ἐν ἀγάπῃ, ἐν πίστει, ἐν ἁγνείᾳ. 13 ἕως ἔρχομαι πρόσεχε τῇ ἀναγνώσει, τῇ παρακλήσει, τῇ διδασκαλίᾳ. 14 μὴ ἀμέλει τοῦ ἐν σοὶ χαρίσματος, ὃ ἐδόθη σοι διὰ προφητείας μετὰ ἐπιθέσεως

---

[1] 10 {C} ἀγωνιζόμεθα ℵ* A C G⁽ᵍʳ⁾ K Ψ 33 88 104 326 *l*⁵⁹⁹ Cyril // ὀνειδιζόμεθα ℵᶜ D (P ὀνειδιζώμεθα) 81 181 330 436 451 614 629 630 1241 1739 1877 (1881 1985 ὠνειδιζόμεθα) 1962 1984 2127 2492 2495 *Byz Lect* it⁽ᵃʳ,ᶜ,(ᵈ),ᵈᵉᵐ,ᵈⁱᵛ,f,(g),mon,x,z⁾ vg syr^(p,h) cop^(sa,bo) goth arm eth Origen Ambrosiaster Chrysostom Theodore^(lat) Euthalius Theodoret Antiochus John-Damascus

---

b b 8–9 *b* major, *b* minor: WH Bov Nes BF² NEB TT Seg // *b* minor, *b* major: (TT^mg) // *b* major; major: TR AV RV ASV RSV NEB^mg Zür Luth Jer

---

3 βρωμάτων...μετάλημψιν Gn 9.3 μετάλημψιν μετὰ εὐχαριστίας Ro 14.6; 1 Cor 10.30–31 4 πᾶν...καλόν Gn 1.31; Ac 10.15 7 1 Tm 1.4; 6.20; 2 Tm 2.16; Tt 1.14 8 ἡ δὲ εὐσέβεια...ἐστιν 1 Tm 6.6 9 1 Tm 1.15 10 θεῷ...ἀνθρώπων 1 Tm 2.3-4 12 μηδείς...καταφρονείτω Tt 2.15 14 2 Tm 1.6 μετὰ...πρεσβυτερίου Ac 6.6; 8.17; 1 Tm 5.22

as if burnt with a hot iron. 3 Such men teach that it is wrong to marry, and to eat certain foods. But God created these foods to be eaten, after a prayer of thanks, by those who are believers and have come to know the truth. 4 Everything that God has created is good; nothing is to be rejected, but all is to be received with a prayer of thanks; 5 for the word of God and the prayer make it acceptable to God.

A Good Servant of Christ Jesus

6 If you give these instructions to the brothers you will be a good servant of Christ Jesus, as you feed yourself spiritually on the words of faith and of the true teaching which you have followed. 7 But keep away from those godless legends, which are not worth telling. Keep yourself in training for a godly life. 8 Physical exercise has some value in it, but spiritual exercise is valuable in every way, for it promises life both for now and for the future. 9 This is a true saying, to be completely accepted and believed. 10 That is why we struggle and work hard, for we have placed our hope on the living God, who is Savior of all men, and especially of those who believe.

11 Command and teach these things. 12 Do not let anyone look down on you because you are young, but be an example for the believers, in your speech, your conduct, your love, faith, and purity. 13 Give your time and effort, until I come, to the public reading of the Scriptures, and to preaching and teaching. 14 Do not neglect the spiritual gift that is in you, which was given to you when the prophets spoke and the elders laid

their hands on you. ¹⁵ Practice these things and give yourself to them, in order that your progress may be seen by all. ¹⁶ Watch yourself, and watch your teaching. Keep on doing these things, for if you do you will save both yourself and those who hear you.

Responsibilities toward Believers

5 Do not rebuke an older man, but appeal to him as if he were your father. Treat the younger men as your brothers, ² the older women as mothers, and the younger women as sisters, with all purity.

³ Show respect for widows who really are widows. ⁴ But if a widow has children or grandchildren, they should learn first to carry out their religious duties toward their own family and in this way repay their parents and grandparents, for that is what pleases God. ⁵ The woman who is a true widow, with no one to take care of her, has placed her hope in God and continues to pray and ask him for his help night and day. ⁶ But the widow who gives herself to pleasure has already died, even though she lives. ⁷ Give them this command, so that no one will reproach them. ⁸ But if someone does not take care of his relatives, especially the members of his own family, he has denied the faith and is worse than an unbeliever.

⁹ Do not add any widow to the list of widows unless she is more than sixty years old. In addition, she must have been married only once, ¹⁰ and have a reputation for good deeds: a woman who brought up her children well, received strangers in her home, washed the feet of God's people, helped those in trouble, and gave herself to all kinds of good works.

¹¹ But do not include the younger widows in the list; for when their desires make them want to marry, they turn away from Christ, ¹² and so become guilty of breaking their first promise to him. ¹³ They also learn to waste their time in going around from house to house; but even worse, they learn to be gossips and busybodies, talking of things they should not. ¹⁴ So I would rather that the younger widows get married, have children, and take care of their homes, so as to give our enemies no chance of speaking evil of us. ¹⁵ For some widows have

τῶν χειρῶν τοῦ πρεσβυτερίου. **15** ταῦτα μελέτα, ἐν τούτοις ἴσθι, ἵνα σου ἡ προκοπὴ φανερὰ ᾖ πᾶσιν. **16** ἔπεχε σεαυτῷ καὶ τῇ διδασκαλίᾳ· ἐπίμενε αὐτοῖς· τοῦτο γὰρ ποιῶν καὶ σεαυτὸν σώσεις καὶ τοὺς ἀκούοντάς σου.

Duties toward Others

5 Πρεσβυτέρῳ μὴ ἐπιπλήξῃς, ἀλλὰ παρακάλει ὡς πατέρα, νεωτέρους ὡς ἀδελφούς, **2** πρεσβυτέρας ὡς μητέρας, νεωτέρας ὡς ἀδελφὰς ἐν πάσῃ ἁγνείᾳ.

3 Χήρας τίμα τὰς ὄντως χήρας. **4** εἰ δέ τις χήρα τέκνα ἢ ἔκγονα ἔχει, μανθανέτωσαν πρῶτον τὸν ἴδιον οἶκον εὐσεβεῖν καὶ ἀμοιβὰς ἀποδιδόναι τοῖς προγόνοις, τοῦτο γάρ ἐστιν ἀπόδεκτον ἐνώπιον τοῦ θεοῦ. **5** ἡ δὲ ὄντως χήρα καὶ μεμονωμένη ἤλπικεν ἐπὶ θεὸν καὶ προσμένει ταῖς δεήσεσιν καὶ ταῖς προσευχαῖς νυκτὸς καὶ ἡμέρας· **6** ἡ δὲ σπαταλῶσα ζῶσα τέθνηκεν. **7** καὶ ταῦτα παράγγελλε, ἵνα ἀνεπίλημπτοι ὦσιν. **8** εἰ δέ τις τῶν ἰδίων καὶ μάλιστα οἰκείων οὐ προνοεῖται, τὴν πίστιν ἤρνηται καὶ ἔστιν ἀπίστου χείρων. **9** Χήρα καταλεγέσθω μὴ ἔλαττον ἐτῶν ἑξήκοντα γεγονυῖα, ἑνὸς ἀνδρὸς γυνή, **10** ἐν ἔργοις καλοῖς μαρτυρουμένη, εἰ ἐτεκνοτρόφησεν, εἰ ἐξενοδόχησεν, εἰ ἁγίων πόδας ἔνιψεν, εἰ θλιβομένοις ἐπήρκεσεν, εἰ παντὶ ἔργῳ ἀγαθῷ ἐπηκολούθησεν. **11** νεωτέρας δὲ χήρας παραιτοῦ· ὅταν γὰρ καταστρηνιάσωσιν τοῦ Χριστοῦ, γαμεῖν θέλουσιν, **12** ἔχουσαι κρίμα ὅτι τὴν πρώτην πίστιν ἠθέτησαν· **13** ἅμα δὲ καὶ ἀργαὶ μανθάνουσιν, περιερχόμεναι τὰς οἰκίας, οὐ μόνον δὲ ἀργαὶ ἀλλὰ καὶ φλύαροι καὶ περίεργοι, λαλοῦσαι τὰ μὴ δέοντα. **14** βούλομαι οὖν νεωτέρας γαμεῖν, τεκνογονεῖν, οἰκοδεσποτεῖν, μηδεμίαν ἀφορμὴν διδόναι τῷ ἀντικειμένῳ λοιδορίας χάριν· **15** ἤδη γάρ τινες ἐξετράπησαν ὀπίσω

---

1 Πρεσβυτέρῳ μὴ ἐπιπλήξῃς Lv 19.32   **5** ἡ δὲ…θεόν Jr 49.11   προσμένει…ἡμέρας Lk 2.37; 18.7   **10** εἰ ἐξενοδόχησεν He 13.2 εἰ ἁγίων πόδας ἔνιψεν Jn 13.14   **13** ἀργαὶ… περίεργοι 2 Th 3.11   **14** βούλομαι…γαμεῖν 1 Cor 7.9

τοῦ Σατανᾶ. **16** εἴ τις πιστή[1] ἔχει χήρας, ἐπαρκείτω αὐταῖς, καὶ μὴ βαρείσθω ἡ ἐκκλησία, ἵνα ταῖς ὄντως χήραις ἐπαρκέσῃ.

17 Οἱ καλῶς προεστῶτες πρεσβύτεροι διπλῆς τιμῆς ἀξιούσθωσαν, μάλιστα οἱ κοπιῶντες ἐν λόγῳ καὶ διδασκαλίᾳ· **18** λέγει γὰρ ἡ γραφή, **Βοῦν ἀλοῶντα οὐ φιμώσεις·** καί, Ἄξιος ὁ ἐργάτης τοῦ μισθοῦ αὐτοῦ. **19** κατὰ πρεσβυτέρου κατηγορίαν μὴ παραδέχου, ἐκτὸς εἰ μὴ **ἐπὶ δύο ἢ τριῶν μαρτύρων.** **20** τοὺς ἁμαρτάνοντας ἐνώπιον πάντων ἔλεγχε, ἵνα καὶ οἱ λοιποὶ φόβον ἔχωσιν. **21** Διαμαρτύρομαι ἐνώπιον τοῦ θεοῦ καὶ Χριστοῦ Ἰησοῦ καὶ τῶν ἐκλεκτῶν ἀγγέλων, ἵνα ταῦτα φυλάξῃς χωρὶς προκρίματος, μηδὲν ποιῶν κατὰ πρόσκλισιν. **22** Χεῖρας ταχέως μηδενὶ ἐπιτίθει, μηδὲ κοινώνει ἁμαρτίαις ἀλλοτρίαις· σεαυτὸν ἁγνὸν τήρει. **23** Μηκέτι ὑδροπότει, ἀλλὰ οἴνῳ ὀλίγῳ χρῶ διὰ τὸν στόμαχον καὶ τὰς πυκνάς σου ἀσθενείας.

24 Τινῶν ἀνθρώπων αἱ ἁμαρτίαι πρόδηλοί εἰσιν, προάγουσαι εἰς κρίσιν, τισὶν δὲ καὶ ἐπακολουθοῦσιν· **25** ὡσαύτως καὶ τὰ ἔργα τὰ καλὰ πρόδηλα, καὶ τὰ ἄλλως ἔχοντα κρυβῆναι οὐ δύνανται.

6 Ὅσοι εἰσὶν ὑπὸ ζυγὸν δοῦλοι, τοὺς ἰδίους δεσπότας πάσης τιμῆς ἀξίους ἡγείσθωσαν, ἵνα μὴ τὸ ὄνομα τοῦ θεοῦ καὶ ἡ διδασκαλία βλασφημῆται. **2** οἱ δὲ πιστοὺς ἔχοντες δεσπότας μὴ καταφρονείτωσαν, ὅτι ἀδελφοί εἰσιν·

---

[1] **16** {C} πιστή א A C Gᵍʳ P 048 33 81 1739 1881 itᵐᵒⁿ,ˣ,ᶻ vgʷʷ copˢᵃ,ᵇᵒ ethᵖᵖ Ambrosiaster Athanasius Ambrose Augustine Euthaliusᵐˢ* Ps-Jerome Cassiodorus ∥ πιστός itᵈⁱᵛ,ᶠ,ᵍⁱᵍ vgᶜˡ ethʳᵒ Ambrose Theodoreˡᵃᵗ Augustine ∥ πιστὸς ἢ πιστή D K Ψ 88 104 181 326 330 436 451 614 629 630 1241 1877 1962 1984 1985 2127 2492 2495 *Byz Lect* itᵃʳ,ᶜ,ᵈ syrᵖ,ʰ Ambrosiaster Priscillian Ambrose Chrysostom Pelagius Euthaliusᵐˢᶜ Theodoret John-Damascus ∥ πιστός or πιστή arm ∥ πιστάς itᵈᵉᵐ,ᵍ

---

17 Οἱ...ἀξιούσθωσαν 1 Cor 16.18; Php 2.29   **18** Βοῦν...φιμώσεις Dt 25.4 (1 Cor 9.9) Ἄξιος...αὐτοῦ Mt 10.10; Lk 10.7   **19** κατηγορίαν...μαρτύρων Dt 17.6; 19.15; Mt 18.16; 2 Cor 13.1   **20** τοὺς...ἔλεγχε Ga 2.14; Eph 5.11   **22** Χεῖρας...ἐπιτίθει 1 Tm 4.14
6 1 Eph 6.5; Tt 2.9–10

---

already turned away to follow Satan. [16] But if any woman who is a believer has widows in her family, she must take care of them, and not put the burden on the church, so that it may take care of the widows who are all alone.

[17] The elders who do good work as leaders should be considered worthy of receiving double pay, especially those who work hard at preaching and teaching. [18] For the scripture says, "Do not tie up the mouth of the ox when it is treading out the grain," and, "The worker deserves his wages." [19] Do not listen to an accusation against an elder unless it is brought by two or three witnesses. [20] Rebuke publicly all those who commit sins, so that the rest may be afraid.

[21] In the presence of God, and of Christ Jesus, and of the holy angels, I solemnly call upon you to obey these instructions without showing any prejudice or favor to anyone in anything you do. [22] Be in no hurry to lay hands on anyone for the Lord's service. Take no part in the sins of others; keep yourself pure.

[23] Do not drink water only, but take a little wine to help your digestion, since you are sick so often.

[24] The sins of some men are plain to see, and their sins go ahead of them to judgment; but the sins of others are seen only later. [25] In the same way good deeds are plainly seen, and even those that are not so plain cannot be hidden.

6 All who are slaves must consider their masters worthy of all respect, so that no one will speak evil of the name of God and of our teaching. [2] Slaves belonging to masters who are believers must not despise them because they are their brothers. Instead, they are to serve them even better, because those who benefit from their work are believers whom they love.

False Teaching and True Riches

You must teach and preach these things. [3] Whoever teaches a different doctrine and does not agree with the true words of our Lord Jesus Christ and with the teaching of our religion [4] is swollen with pride and knows nothing. He has an unhealthy desire to argue and quarrel about words, and this brings on jealousy, dissension, insults, evil suspicions, [5] and constant arguments from men whose minds do not function and who no longer have the truth. They think that religion is a way to become rich.

[6] Well, religion does make a man very rich, if he is satisfied with what he has. [7] What did we bring into the world? Nothing! What can we take out of the world? Nothing! [8] So then, if we have food and clothes, that should be enough for us. [9] But those who want to get rich fall into temptation and are caught in the trap of many foolish and harmful

ἀλλὰ μᾶλλον δουλευέτωσαν, ὅτι πιστοί εἰσιν καὶ ἀγαπητοί[a] οἱ τῆς εὐεργεσίας ἀντιλαμβανόμενοι.

False Teaching and True Wealth

Ταῦτα δίδασκε καὶ παρακάλει. 3 εἴ τις ἑτεροδιδασκαλεῖ καὶ μὴ προσέρχεται ὑγιαίνουσιν λόγοις,[b] τοῖς τοῦ κυρίου ἡμῶν Ἰησοῦ Χριστοῦ,[b] καὶ τῇ κατ' εὐσέβειαν διδασκαλίᾳ, 4 τετύφωται, μηδὲν ἐπιστάμενος, ἀλλὰ νοσῶν περὶ ζητήσεις καὶ λογομαχίας, ἐξ ὧν γίνεται φθόνος, ἔρις, βλασφημίαι, ὑπόνοιαι πονηραί, 5 διαπαρατριβαὶ διεφθαρμένων ἀνθρώπων τὸν νοῦν καὶ ἀπεστερημένων τῆς ἀληθείας, νομιζόντων πορισμὸν εἶναι τὴν εὐσέβειαν[1]. 6 ἔστιν δὲ πορισμὸς μέγας ἡ εὐσέβεια μετὰ αὐταρκείας· 7 οὐδὲν γὰρ εἰσηνέγκαμεν εἰς τὸν κόσμον, ὅτι[2] οὐδὲ ἐξενεγκεῖν τι δυνάμεθα· 8 ἔχοντες δὲ διατροφὰς καὶ σκεπάσματα, τούτοις ἀρκεσθησόμεθα. 9 οἱ δὲ βουλόμενοι πλουτεῖν ἐμπίπτουσιν εἰς πειρασμὸν καὶ παγίδα καὶ

[1] 5 {A} εὐσέβειαν ℵ A D* G 048 33 81 88 1739 1881 it[c,d,dem,div,f,g,rl] vg cop[sa,bo] goth[A] eth[ro] Origen Ambrose ∥ εὐσέβειαν· ἀφίστασο ἀπὸ τῶν τοιούτων D[c] K P Ψ 061 104 181 326 330 436 451 614 629 630 1241 1877 1962 1984 1985 2127 2492 2495 Byz Lect it[ar,m,mon] syr[p,h] goth[B] arm eth[pp] Irenaeus Cyprian Ambrosiaster Lucifer Ephraem Chrysostom (Pelagius) Theodore Euthalius Theodoret John-Damascus

[2] 7 {C} ὅτι ℵ* A G 048 061 33 81 1739 1881 it[g,rl] Origen ∥ καὶ cop[sa,bo] arm eth ∥ ἀλλ' (Polycarp) Augustine ∥ δῆλον ὅτι ℵ[c] D[c] K P Ψ (88 δῆλον δέ) 104 181 326 330 436 451 614 629 630 1241 1877 1962 1984 1985 2127 2492 2495 Byz Lect syr[p,h] Marcion Basil Macarius Chrysostom Euthalius Theodoret John-Damascus ∥ ἀληθὲς ὅτι D* it[ar,d,m] (syr[hmg]) goth Cyprian Ambrosiaster Pelagius Theodore[lat] Augustine Paulinus-Nola ∥ δῆλον ὅτι or ἀληθὲς ὅτι it[c,dem,div,f,mon,x,z] vg ∥ omit Ephraem Orsisius Jerome Augustine Cyril

[a] 2 a none: WH Bov Nes BF[2] RV ASV RSV NEB TT Jer Seg ∥ a minor: TR WH[mg] AV Zür? Luth
[b] [b] 3 b minor, b minor: WH Bov AV RV ASV Zür Jer ∥ b none, b minor: Nes BF[2] Seg ∥ b none, b none: TR RSV TT Luth ∥ b dash, b dash: NEB

2 ἀλλὰ...ἀγαπητοί Phm 16   3 εἰ...Χριστοῦ Ga 1.6–9; 2 Tm 1.13   5 διεφθαρμένων... νοῦν 2 Tm 3.8   ἀπεστερημένων τῆς ἀληθείας 2 Tm 4.4; Tt 1.14   6 ἔστιν...εὐσέβεια 1 Tm 4.8 μετὰ αὐταρκείας Php 4.11–12; He 13.5   7 Ec 5.15; Job 1.21   8 Pr 30.8   9 Pr 23.4; 28.22

ἐπιθυμίας πολλὰς ἀνοήτους καὶ βλαβεράς, αἵτινες βυθί-
ζουσιν τοὺς ἀνθρώπους εἰς ὄλεθρον καὶ ἀπώλειαν· **10** ῥίζα
γὰρ πάντων τῶν κακῶν ἐστιν ἡ φιλαργυρία, ἧς τινες
ὀρεγόμενοι ἀπεπλανήθησαν ἀπὸ τῆς πίστεως καὶ ἑαυτοὺς
περιέπειραν ὀδύναις πολλαῖς.

The Good Fight of Faith

11 Σὺ δέ, ὦ ἄνθρωπε θεοῦ, ταῦτα φεῦγε· δίωκε δὲ
δικαιοσύνην, εὐσέβειαν, πίστιν, ἀγάπην, ὑπομονήν, πραϋ-
παθίαν. **12** ἀγωνίζου τὸν καλὸν ἀγῶνα τῆς πίστεως,
ἐπιλαβοῦ τῆς αἰωνίου ζωῆς, εἰς ἣν ἐκλήθης καὶ ὡμολό-
γησας τὴν καλὴν ὁμολογίαν ἐνώπιον πολλῶν μαρτύρων.
13 παραγγέλλω [σοι] ἐνώπιον τοῦ θεοῦ τοῦ ζωογο-
νοῦντος τὰ πάντα καὶ Χριστοῦ Ἰησοῦ τοῦ μαρτυρήσαντος
ἐπὶ Ποντίου Πιλάτου τὴν καλὴν ὁμολογίαν, **14** τηρῆσαί
σε τὴν ἐντολὴν ἄσπιλον ἀνεπίλημπτον μέχρι τῆς ἐπιφανείας τοῦ κυρίου ἡμῶν Ἰησοῦ Χριστοῦ, **15** ἣν καιροῖς
ἰδίοις δείξει ὁ μακάριος καὶ μόνος δυνάστης, ὁ βασιλεὺς
τῶν βασιλευόντων καὶ κύριος τῶν κυριευόντων, **16** ὁ
μόνος ἔχων ἀθανασίαν, φῶς οἰκῶν ἀπρόσιτον, ὃν εἶδεν
οὐδεὶς ἀνθρώπων οὐδὲ ἰδεῖν δύναται· ᾧ τιμὴ καὶ κράτος
αἰώνιον· ἀμήν.

17 Τοῖς πλουσίοις ἐν τῷ νῦν αἰῶνι παράγγελλε μὴ
ὑψηλοφρονεῖν μηδὲ ἠλπικέναι ἐπὶ πλούτου ἀδηλότητι,
ἀλλ' ἐπὶ θεῷ τῷ παρέχοντι ἡμῖν πάντα πλουσίως εἰς
ἀπόλαυσιν, **18** ἀγαθοεργεῖν, πλουτεῖν ἐν ἔργοις καλοῖς,
εὐμεταδότους εἶναι, κοινωνικούς, **19** ἀποθησαυρίζοντας
ἑαυτοῖς θεμέλιον καλὸν εἰς τὸ μέλλον, ἵνα ἐπιλάβωνται
τῆς ὄντως[3] ζωῆς.

---

[3] **19** {B} ὄντως ℵ A D* G Ψ 81 104 330 451 1739 1877 2127 2492 it[ar,c,d,dem,
div,e,f,g,m,mon,x,z] vg syr[p,h] cop[sa,bo] arm eth Ambrosiaster Basil Euthalius //

11 2 Tm 2.22   **12** ἀγωνίζου…πίστεως 1 Cor 9.25–26; 2 Tm 4.7   **13** Χριστοῦ…ὁμολο-
γίαν Jn 18.36 37; 19.11   **15** βασιλεὺς τῶν βασιλευόντων Dt 10.17; 2 Macc 13.4; 3 Macc 5.35;
Re 17.14 κύριος τῶν κυριευόντων Re 17.14   **16** φῶς οἰκῶν ἀπρόσιτον Ps 104.2 ὃν…
δύναται Ex 33.20   **17** παράγγελλε…ἀδηλότητι Ps 62.10; Lk 12.20   **19** ἀποθησαυρίζοντας
…μέλλον Mt 6.20

---

desires, which pull men down to ruin
and destruction. **10** For the love of money
is a source of all kinds of evil. Some have
been so eager to have it that they have
wandered away from the faith and have
broken their hearts with many sorrows.

Personal Instructions

11 But you, man of God, avoid all these
things. Strive for righteousness, godliness,
faith, love, endurance, and gentleness.
12 Run your best in the race of faith,
and win eternal life for yourself; for it
was to this life that God called you when
you made your good profession of faith
before many witnesses. **13** Before God,
who gives life to all things, and before
Christ Jesus, who made the good profession before Pontius Pilate, I command you: **14** Obey the commandment
and keep it pure and faultless, until
the Day our Lord Jesus Christ will
appear. **15** His appearing will be brought
about at the right time by God, the
blessed and only Ruler, the King of
kings and the Lord of lords. **16** He alone
is immortal; he lives in the light that
no one can approach. No one has ever
seen him, no one can ever see him. To
him be honor and eternal might! Amen.

17 Command those who are rich in the
things of this life not to be proud, and
to place their hope, not on such an uncertain thing as riches, but on God,
who generously gives us everything for
us to enjoy. **18** Command them to do
good, to be rich in good works, to be
generous and ready to share with others.
19 In this way they will store up for
themselves a treasure which will be a
solid foundation for the future. And then
they will be able to win the life which
is true life.

[20] Timothy, keep safe what has been turned over to your care. Avoid the godless talk and foolish arguments of "Knowledge," as some people wrongly call it. [21] For some have claimed to possess it, and as a result they have lost the way of faith.

God's grace be with you all.

20 Ὦ Τιμόθεε, τὴν παραθήκην φύλαξον, ἐκτρεπόμενος τὰς βεβήλους κενοφωνίας καὶ ἀντιθέσεις τῆς ψευδωνύμου γνώσεως, **21** ἥν τινες ἐπαγγελλόμενοι περὶ τὴν πίστιν ἠστόχησαν.

Ἡ χάρις μεθ᾽ ὑμῶν.[4]

αἰωνίου Dᶜ K P 88 181 326 436 614 629 630 1241 1881 1962 1984 1985 2495 *Byz Lect* copᵇᵒᵐˢ Chrysostom Theodoreˡᵃᵗ Euthaliusᵐˢ Theodoret Antiochus John-Damascus Ps-Oecumenius Theophylact ∥ ὄντως αἰωνίου 69 296 467 1175

[4] **21** {C} ἡ χάρις μεθ᾽ ὑμῶν. ℵ* A G 33 81 itᵍ copᵇᵒᵐˢˢ ∥ ἡ χάρις μετὰ σοῦ. D* 1881 itᵃʳ·ᵈ arm ∥ ἡ χάρις μεθ᾽ ὑμῶν. ἀμήν. ℵᶜ P copᵇᵒ ∥ ἡ χάρις μετὰ σοῦ. ἀμήν. Dᶜ K Ψ 88 104 181 326 330 436 451 614 629 630 1241 1739 1877 1962 1984 1985 2127 2492 2495 *Byz Lect* itᶜ·ᵈᵉᵐ·ᵈⁱᵛ·ᵉ·ᶠ·ᵐᵒⁿᵛⁱᵈ·ˣ·ᶻ vg syrᵖ·ʰ copᵇᵒᵐˢ eth Theodoret John-Damascus ∥ *omit* itᵐ copˢᵃ Chrysostom Euthaliusᵐˢˢ

---

20 Ὦ...φύλαξον 2 Tm 1.14   ἐκτρεπόμενος...κενοφωνίας 1 Tm 4.7   **21** 1 Tm 1.6; 2 Tm 2.18

ΠΡΟΣ ΤΙΜΟΘΕΟΝ Β

Salutation

1 Παῦλος ἀπόστολος Χριστοῦ Ἰησοῦ διὰ θελήματος
θεοῦ κατ' ἐπαγγελίαν ζωῆς τῆς ἐν Χριστῷ Ἰησοῦ
2 Τιμοθέῳ ἀγαπητῷ τέκνῳ· χάρις, ἔλεος, εἰρήνη ἀπὸ
θεοῦ πατρὸς καὶ Χριστοῦ Ἰησοῦ τοῦ κυρίου ἡμῶν.

Loyalty to the Gospel

3 Χάριν ἔχω τῷ θεῷ, ᾧ λατρεύω ἀπὸ προγόνων ἐν
καθαρᾷ συνειδήσει, ὡς ἀδιάλειπτον ἔχω τὴν περὶ σοῦ
μνείαν ἐν ταῖς δεήσεσίν μου[a] νυκτὸς καὶ ἡμέρας,[a] **4** ἐπιποθῶν σε ἰδεῖν, μεμνημένος σου τῶν δακρύων, ἵνα
χαρᾶς πληρωθῶ,[b] **5** ὑπόμνησιν λαβὼν τῆς ἐν σοὶ ἀνυποκρίτου πίστεως, ἥτις ἐνῴκησεν πρῶτον ἐν τῇ μάμμῃ
σου Λωΐδι καὶ τῇ μητρί σου Εὐνίκῃ, πέπεισμαι δὲ ὅτι
καὶ ἐν σοί. **6** δι' ἣν αἰτίαν ἀναμιμνῄσκω σε ἀναζωπυρεῖν
τὸ χάρισμα τοῦ θεοῦ, ὅ ἐστιν ἐν σοὶ διὰ τῆς ἐπιθέσεως
τῶν χειρῶν μου· **7** οὐ γὰρ ἔδωκεν ἡμῖν ὁ θεὸς πνεῦμα
δειλίας, ἀλλὰ δυνάμεως καὶ ἀγάπης καὶ σωφρονισμοῦ.
8 μὴ οὖν ἐπαισχυνθῇς τὸ μαρτύριον τοῦ κυρίου ἡμῶν
μηδὲ ἐμὲ τὸν δέσμιον αὐτοῦ, ἀλλὰ συγκακοπάθησον τῷ
εὐαγγελίῳ κατὰ δύναμιν θεοῦ, **9** τοῦ σώσαντος ἡμᾶς
καὶ καλέσαντος κλήσει ἁγίᾳ, οὐ κατὰ τὰ ἔργα ἡμῶν
ἀλλὰ κατὰ ἰδίαν πρόθεσιν καὶ χάριν, τὴν δοθεῖσαν ἡμῖν

---

[a] [a] **3** a none, a minor: TR Bov Nes BF² AV (NEB) TT Zür (Luth) (Jer) Seg ∥ a minor, a none: WH RV ASV RSV

[b] **4** b minor: TR Bov Nes BF² AV RV ASV (RSV) (NEB) Zür (Luth) (Jer) (Seg) ∥ b none: WH RVmg ASVmg TT

3 ἀπὸ προγόνων Php 3.5   ἐν καθαρᾷ συνειδήσει Ac 23.1; 24.16   **5** τῇ μητρί σου
Εὐνίκῃ Ac 16.1   **6** ἀναζωπυρεῖν...μου 1 Tm 4.14   **7** οὐ...δειλίας Ro 8.15   **8** τῷ...θεοῦ
Ro 1.16   **9** τοῦ...χάριν Eph 2.8-9; Tt 3.5

PAUL'S SECOND LETTER TO TIMOTHY

1 From Paul, an apostle of Christ Jesus by God's will, sent to proclaim the promised life which we have in union with Christ Jesus —

2 To Timothy, my dear son:

May God the Father and Christ Jesus our Lord give you grace, mercy, and peace.

Thanksgiving and Encouragement

3 I give thanks to God, whom I serve with a clear conscience, as my ancestors did. I thank him as I remember you always in my prayers, night and day. **4** I remember your tears, and I want to see you very much, that I may be filled with joy. **5** I remember the sincere faith you have, the kind of faith that your grandmother Lois and your mother Eunice also had. I am sure that you have it also. **6** For this reason I remind you to keep alive the gift that God gave to you when I laid my hands on you. **7** For the Spirit that God has given us does not make us timid; instead, his Spirit fills us with power and love and self-control.

8 Do not be ashamed, then, of witnessing for our Lord; neither be ashamed of me, his prisoner. Instead, take your part in suffering for the Good News, as God gives you the strength for it. **9** He saved us and called us to be his own people, not because of what we have done, but because of his own purpose and grace. He gave this grace to us in Christ Jesus before the beginning of time, ¹⁰ but now it has been revealed to us through the appearing of our Savior, Christ Jesus. For Christ has ended the power of death, and through the Good News he has revealed immortal life.

¹¹ God has appointed me to proclaim the Good News as an apostle and teacher, ¹² and it is for this reason that I suffer these things. But I am still full of confidence, for I know whom I have trusted, and I am sure that he is able to keep safe until that Day what he has entrusted to me.[1] ¹³ Hold to the true words that I taught you, as the example for you to follow, and stay in the faith and love that are ours in union with Christ Jesus. ¹⁴ Keep the good things that have been entrusted to you, through the power of the Holy Spirit who lives in us.

¹⁵ You know that everyone in the province of Asia deserted me, including Phygelus and Hermogenes. ¹⁶ May the Lord show mercy to the family of Onesiphorus, because he cheered me up many times. He was not ashamed that I am in prison, ¹⁷ but as soon as he arrived in Rome he started looking for me until he found me. ¹⁸ May the Lord grant him to receive mercy from the Lord on that Day! And you know very well how much he did for me in Ephesus.

---

[1] **12** what he has entrusted to me: *or* what I have entrusted to him

ἐν Χριστῷ Ἰησοῦ πρὸ χρόνων αἰωνίων, **10** φανερωθεῖσαν δὲ νῦν διὰ τῆς ἐπιφανείας τοῦ σωτῆρος ἡμῶν Χριστοῦ Ἰησοῦ, καταργήσαντος μὲν τὸν θάνατον φωτίσαντος δὲ ζωὴν καὶ ἀφθαρσίαν διὰ τοῦ εὐαγγελίου, **11** εἰς ὃ ἐτέθην ἐγὼ κῆρυξ καὶ ἀπόστολος καὶ διδάσκαλος¹.ᶜ **12** δι' ἣν αἰτίαν καὶ ταῦτα πάσχω,ᶜ ἀλλ' οὐκ ἐπαισχύνομαι, οἶδα γὰρ ᾧ πεπίστευκα, καὶ πέπεισμαι ὅτι δυνατός ἐστιν τὴν παραθήκην μου φυλάξαι εἰς ἐκείνην τὴν ἡμέραν. **13** ὑποτύπωσιν ἔχε ὑγιαινόντων λόγων ὧν παρ' ἐμοῦ ἤκουσαςᵈ ἐν πίστει καὶ ἀγάπῃ τῇ ἐν Χριστῷ Ἰησοῦ.ᵈ **14** τὴν καλὴν παραθήκην φύλαξον διὰ πνεύματος ἁγίου τοῦ ἐνοικοῦντος ἐν ἡμῖν.

15 Οἶδας τοῦτο, ὅτι ἀπεστράφησάν με πάντες οἱ ἐν τῇ Ἀσίᾳ, ὧν ἐστιν Φύγελος καὶ Ἑρμογένης. **16** δῴη ἔλεος ὁ κύριος τῷ Ὀνησιφόρου οἴκῳ, ὅτι πολλάκις με ἀνέψυξενᵉ καὶ τὴν ἅλυσίν μου οὐκ ἐπαισχύνθη,ᵉ **17** ἀλλὰ γενόμενος ἐν Ῥώμῃ σπουδαίως ἐζήτησέν με καὶ εὗρεν **18** —ᶠ δῴη αὐτῷ ὁ κύριος εὑρεῖν ἔλεος παρὰ κυρίου ἐν ἐκείνῃ τῇ ἡμέρᾳ —ᶠ καὶ ὅσα ἐν Ἐφέσῳ διηκόνησεν, βέλτιον σὺ γινώσκεις.

---

¹ **11** {C} καὶ διδάσκαλος ℵ* A I syrᵖᵃˡ ‖ καὶ διάκονος 33 ‖ διδάσκαλος ἐθνῶν (see 1 Tm 2.7) C P 1984 ‖ καὶ διδάσκαλος ἐθνῶν (see 1 Tm 2.7) ℵᶜ D G K Ψ 81 88 104 181 326 330 436 451 614 629 630 1241 1739 1877 1881 1962 1985 2127 2492 2495 *Byz Lect* itᵃʳ,ᶜ,ᵈ,ᵈᵉᵐ,ᵈⁱᵛ,ᵉ,ᶠ,ᵍ,ᵐᵒⁿᵛⁱᵈ,ˣ,ᶻ vg syrᵖ,ʰ copˢᵃ,ᵇᵒ goth arm eth Ambrosiaster Ephraem Chrysostom Theodoreˡᵃᵗ Euthalius Theodoret John-Damascus

---

ᶜ ᶜ **11-12** c major, c minor: WH Bov Nes BF² AV RV ASV NEB TT Zür Luth Jer Seg ‖ c minor; c major: RSV ‖ c minor, c minor: TR

ᵈ ᵈ **13** d none, d minor: WH Bov Nes BF² ‖ d minor, d major: TR AV RV ASV RSV NEB TT Luth Jer (Seg) ‖ d minor, d exclamation: Zür ‖ d major, d none

ᵉ ᵉ **16** e none, e minor: (WH) Bov Nes BF² (AV) (RV) (ASV) TT Zür Luth (Jer) Seg ‖ e major, e minor: RSV NEB ‖ e minor, e minor: TR

ᶠ ᶠ **17-18** f dash, f dash: WH Bov Nes BF² RSV ‖ f parens, f parens: RV ASV TT ‖ f major, f major: NEB Luth Jer Seg ‖ f minor, f major: TR ‖ f major, f minor: AV ‖ f major, f exclamation: Zür

---

10 τοῦ σωτῆρος...θάνατον 1 Cor 15.15, 57; He 2.14   **11** 1 Tm 2.7   **14** τὴν...φύλαξον 1 Tm 6.20   **15** ἀπεστράφησαν...Ἀσίᾳ 2 Tm 4.16   **18** δῴη...ἡμέρᾳ Jd 21

A Good Soldier of Christ Jesus

2 Σὺ οὖν, τέκνον μου, ἐνδυναμοῦ ἐν τῇ χάριτι τῇ ἐν Χριστῷ Ἰησοῦ, 2 καὶ ἃ ἤκουσας παρ' ἐμοῦ διὰ πολλῶν μαρτύρων, ταῦτα παράθου πιστοῖς ἀνθρώποις, οἵτινες ἱκανοὶ ἔσονται καὶ ἑτέρους διδάξαι. 3 συγκακοπάθησον ὡς καλὸς στρατιώτης Χριστοῦ Ἰησοῦ. 4 οὐδεὶς στρατευόμενος ἐμπλέκεται ταῖς τοῦ βίου πραγματείαις, ἵνα τῷ στρατολογήσαντι ἀρέσῃ· 5 ἐὰν δὲ καὶ ἀθλῇ τις, οὐ στεφανοῦται ἐὰν μὴ νομίμως ἀθλήσῃ. 6 τὸν κοπιῶντα γεωργὸν δεῖ πρῶτον τῶν καρπῶν μεταλαμβάνειν. 7 νόει ὃ λέγω· δώσει γάρ σοι ὁ κύριος σύνεσιν ἐν πᾶσιν.

8 Μνημόνευε Ἰησοῦν Χριστὸν ἐγηγερμένον ἐκ νεκρῶν, ἐκ σπέρματος Δαυίδ, κατὰ τὸ εὐαγγέλιόν μου· 9 ἐν ᾧ κακοπαθῶ μέχρι δεσμῶν ὡς κακοῦργος,[a] ἀλλὰ ὁ λόγος τοῦ θεοῦ οὐ δέδεται.[a] 10 διὰ τοῦτο πάντα ὑπομένω διὰ τοὺς ἐκλεκτούς, ἵνα καὶ αὐτοὶ σωτηρίας τύχωσιν τῆς ἐν Χριστῷ Ἰησοῦ μετὰ δόξης αἰωνίου. 11 πιστὸς ὁ λόγος·

εἰ γὰρ συναπεθάνομεν, καὶ συζήσομεν·
12 εἰ ὑπομένομεν, καὶ συμβασιλεύσομεν·
εἰ ἀρνησόμεθα, κἀκεῖνος ἀρνήσεται ἡμᾶς·
13 εἰ ἀπιστοῦμεν, ἐκεῖνος πιστὸς μένει,
ἀρνήσασθαι γὰρ ἑαυτὸν οὐ δύναται.

An Approved Workman

14 Ταῦτα ὑπομίμνησκε, διαμαρτυρόμενος ἐνώπιον τοῦ θεοῦ[1] [b] μὴ λογομαχεῖν,[b] ἐπ' οὐδὲν χρήσιμον, ἐπὶ κατα-

---

1 14 {C} θεοῦ ℵ C G I 330 436 451 614 629 630 1877 1962 2492 2495 *l*598 it*ar,dem,div,f,g,gig,mon*vid,z*o* syr*hmg* cop*sa,bo* arm eth Ephraem Ambrose

a a 9 *a* minor, *a* major: TR Bov Nes BF² AV RV ASV NEB TT Zür Luth ‖ *a* major, *a* minor: WH ‖ *a* major, *a* major: RSV Jer Seg

b b 14 *b* none, *b* minor: Bov Nes BF² RSV NEB TT Jer ‖ *b* minor, *b* minor: WH RV ASV Zür Luth ‖ *b* none, *b* none: TR AV Seg

6 1 Cor 9.7, 10   8 Ἰησοῦν...νεκρῶν 1 Cor 15.4, 20   ἐκ σπέρματος Δαυίδ Ro 1.3
9 Eph 3.1; Php 1.12–14   10 πάντα...ἐκλεκτούς Col 1.24   12 εἰ ἀρνησόμεθα...ἡμᾶς Mt 10.33;
Lk 12.9   13 εἰ...μένει Ro 3.3–4 ἀρνήσασθαι...δύναται Nu 23.19; Tt 1.2   14 μὴ...χρήσιμον
1 Tm 6.4; Tt 3.9

A Loyal Soldier of Christ Jesus

2 As for you, my son, be strong through the grace that is ours in union with Christ Jesus. ² Take the words that you heard me preach in the presence of many witnesses, and give them into the keeping of men you can trust, men who will be able to teach others also.

³ Take your part in suffering, as a loyal soldier of Christ Jesus. ⁴ A soldier in active service wants to please his commanding officer, and so does not get mixed up in the affairs of civilian life. ⁵ An athlete who runs in a race cannot win the prize unless he obeys the rules. ⁶ The farmer who has done the hard work should have the first share of the harvest. ⁷ Think about what I am saying, for the Lord will enable you to understand all things.

⁸ Remember Jesus Christ, who was raised from death, who was a descendant of David, as told in the Good News I preach. ⁹ Because I preach the Good News I suffer, and I am even chained like a criminal. But the word of God is not in chains, ¹⁰ and for this reason I endure everything for the sake of God's chosen people, in order that they too may obtain the salvation that is in Christ Jesus, together with eternal glory. ¹¹ This is a true saying:

"If we have died with him, we shall also live with him;
¹² If we continue to endure, we shall also rule with him;
If we deny him, he also will deny us;
¹³ If we are not faithful, he remains faithful,
For he cannot be false to himself."

An Approved Worker

¹⁴ Remind your people of this, and give them solemn warning in God's presence

not to fight over words. It does no good,
but only ruins the people who listen.
[15] Do your best to win full approval in
God's sight, as a worker who is not
ashamed of his work, one who correctly
teaches the message of God's truth.
[16] Keep away from godless and foolish
discussions, which only drive people farther away from God. [17] What they teach
will be like an open sore that eats away
the flesh. Two of these teachers are
Hymenaeus and Philetus. [18] They have
left the way of truth and are upsetting
the faith of some believers by saying
that our resurrection has already taken
place. [19] But the solid foundation that
God has laid cannot be shaken; and these
words are written on it: "The Lord
knows those who are his"; and, "Whoever says that he belongs to the Lord
must turn away from wrongdoing."
[20] In a large house there are dishes and
bowls of all kinds: some are made of
silver and gold, others of wood and clay;
some are for special occasions, others for
ordinary use. [21] If anyone makes himself
clean from all these evil things, he will
be used for special purposes, for he is
dedicated and useful to his Master, ready
to be used for every good work. [22] Avoid
the passions of youth, and strive for
righteousness, faith, love, and peace,
along with those who with a pure heart
call for the Lord to help them. [23] But
stay away from foolish and ignorant

στροφῇ τῶν ἀκουόντων. **15** σπούδασον σεαυτὸν δόκιμον
παραστῆσαι τῷ θεῷ, ἐργάτην ἀνεπαίσχυντον, ὀρθοτο-
μοῦντα τὸν λόγον τῆς ἀληθείας. **16** τὰς δὲ βεβήλους
κενοφωνίας περιΐστασο· ἐπὶ πλεῖον γὰρ προκόψουσιν
ἀσεβείας, **17** καὶ ὁ λόγος αὐτῶν ὡς γάγγραινα νομὴν
ἕξει· ὧν ἐστιν Ὑμέναιος καὶ Φίλητος, **18** οἵτινες περὶ
τὴν ἀλήθειαν ἠστόχησαν, λέγοντες [τὴν] ἀνάστασιν[2] ἤδη
γεγονέναι, καὶ ἀνατρέπουσιν τήν τινων πίστιν. **19** ὁ
μέντοι στερεὸς θεμέλιος τοῦ θεοῦ ἕστηκεν, ἔχων τὴν
σφραγῖδα ταύτην· **Ἔγνω κύριος τοὺς ὄντας αὐτοῦ**, καί,
Ἀποστήτω ἀπὸ ἀδικίας πᾶς ὁ ὀνομάζων τὸ ὄνομα
κυρίου. 20 Ἐν μεγάλῃ δὲ οἰκίᾳ οὐκ ἔστιν μόνον σκεύη
χρυσᾶ καὶ ἀργυρᾶ ἀλλὰ καὶ ξύλινα καὶ ὀστράκινα, καὶ
ἃ μὲν εἰς τιμὴν ἃ δὲ εἰς ἀτιμίαν· **21** ἐὰν οὖν τις ἐκκαθάρῃ
ἑαυτὸν ἀπὸ τούτων, ἔσται σκεῦος εἰς τιμήν, ἡγιασμένον,
εὔχρηστον τῷ δεσπότῃ, εἰς πᾶν ἔργον ἀγαθὸν ἡτοιμασμένον. **22** τὰς δὲ νεωτερικὰς ἐπιθυμίας φεῦγε, δίωκε
δὲ δικαιοσύνην, πίστιν, ἀγάπην, εἰρήνην μετὰ τῶν ἐπικαλουμένων[3] τὸν κύριον ἐκ καθαρᾶς καρδίας. **23** τὰς δὲ

Chrysostom[3/5] Pelagius Ps-Jerome Cassiodorus Theophylact[comm] ǁ κυρίου A D
K P Ψ 048 81 88 104 181 326 1241 1739 1881 1984 1985 2127 *Byz Lect* it[c,d,e,x,z*]
vg syr[(p),h] cop[sams,boms] goth Ambrosiaster Chrysostom[2/5] Theodore[lat]
Euthalius Theodoret Ps-Jerome Primasius John-Damascus Theophylact[txt] ǁ
Χριστοῦ 206 429 1758 ǁ *omit* 33

2 18 {C} τὴν ἀνάστασιν A C D K P Ψ 81 88 104 181 326 330 436 451
614 629 630 1241 1739 1877 1881 1962 1984 1985 2127 2492 2495 *Byz Lect* cop[sa,bo]
Chrysostom Euthalius Theodoret John-Damascus ǁ ἀνάστασιν ℵ G 048
33 Cyril

3 22 {C} τῶν ἐπικαλουμένων ℵ D K P Ψ 88 181 614 629 630 1241 1739 1881
1962 1984 2127 2495 *Byz Lect* it[ar,c,d,dem,div,e,f,m,mon,x,z] vg syr[p] cop[boms]
goth arm Ambrosiaster Chrysostom[comm] Euthalius John-Damascus Ps-
Oecumenius Theophylact ǁ τὸν καλούμενον 1985 ǁ πάντων τῶν ἐπικαλουμένων (*see* 1 Cor 1.2) C (G *omit* τῶν) I 048 33 81 104 326 330 436 451 1877
2492 it[g] syr[h] cop[sa,boms] eth Chrysostom[txt] Isidore Theodoret ǁ πάντων τῶν
ἀγαπώντων (*see* Eph 6.24) A

---

15 ἐργάτην ἀνεπαίσχυντον 1 Tm 4.6; Tt 2.7–8　　**16** τὰς...περιΐστασο 1 Tm 4.7
17 Ὑμέναιος 1 Tm 1.20　　**19** Ἔγνω...αὐτοῦ Nu 16.5; Jn 10.14; 1 Cor 8.3　　Ἀποστήτω...
κυρίου Nu 16.26　　**21** εὔχρηστον...ἡτοιμασμένον 2 Tm 3.17　　**22** τὰς...εἰρήνην 1 Tm 6.11
23 τὰς...παραιτοῦ 1 Tm 4.7

μωρὰς καὶ ἀπαιδεύτους ζητήσεις παραιτοῦ, εἰδὼς ὅτι γεννῶσιν μάχας· 24 δοῦλον δὲ κυρίου οὐ δεῖ μάχεσθαι, ἀλλὰ ἤπιον εἶναι πρὸς πάντας, διδακτικόν, ἀνεξίκακον, 25 ἐν πραΰτητι παιδεύοντα τοὺς ἀντιδιατιθεμένους, μήποτε δώῃ αὐτοῖς ὁ θεὸς μετάνοιαν εἰς ἐπίγνωσιν ἀληθείας, 26 καὶ ἀνανήψωσιν ἐκ τῆς τοῦ διαβόλου παγίδος, ἐζωγρημένοι ὑπ᾽ αὐτοῦ εἰς τὸ ἐκείνου θέλημα.

The Character of Men in the Last Days

3 Τοῦτο δὲ γίνωσκε, ὅτι ἐν ἐσχάταις ἡμέραις ἐνστήσονται καιροὶ χαλεποί· 2 ἔσονται γὰρ οἱ ἄνθρωποι φίλαυτοι, φιλάργυροι, ἀλαζόνες, ὑπερήφανοι, βλάσφημοι, γονεῦσιν ἀπειθεῖς, ἀχάριστοι, ἀνόσιοι, 3 ἄστοργοι, ἄσπονδοι, διάβολοι, ἀκρατεῖς, ἀνήμεροι, ἀφιλάγαθοι, 4 προδόται, προπετεῖς, τετυφωμένοι, φιλήδονοι μᾶλλον ἢ φιλόθεοι, 5 ἔχοντες μόρφωσιν εὐσεβείας τὴν δὲ δύναμιν αὐτῆς ἠρνημένοι· καὶ τούτους ἀποτρέπου. 6 ἐκ τούτων γάρ εἰσιν οἱ ἐνδύνοντες εἰς τὰς οἰκίας καὶ αἰχμαλωτίζοντες γυναικάρια σεσωρευμένα ἁμαρτίαις, ἀγόμενα ἐπιθυμίαις ποικίλαις, 7 πάντοτε μανθάνοντα καὶ μηδέποτε εἰς ἐπίγνωσιν ἀληθείας ἐλθεῖν δυνάμενα. 8 ὃν τρόπον δὲ Ἰάννης καὶ Ἰαμβρῆς ἀντέστησαν Μωϋσεῖ, οὕτως καὶ οὗτοι ἀνθίστανται τῇ ἀληθείᾳ, ἄνθρωποι κατεφθαρμένοι τὸν νοῦν, ἀδόκιμοι περὶ τὴν πίστιν· 9 ἀλλ᾽ οὐ προκόψουσιν ἐπὶ πλεῖον, ἡ γὰρ ἄνοια αὐτῶν ἔκδηλος ἔσται πᾶσιν, ὡς καὶ ἡ ἐκείνων ἐγένετο.

Last Charge to Timothy

10 Σὺ δὲ παρηκολούθησάς μου τῇ διδασκαλίᾳ, τῇ ἀγωγῇ, τῇ προθέσει, τῇ πίστει, τῇ μακροθυμίᾳ, τῇ ἀγάπῃ, τῇ ὑπομονῇ, 11 τοῖς διωγμοῖς, τοῖς παθήμασιν,

24 δοῦλον...μάχεσθαι 1 Tm 3.3; Tt 1.7   25 μετάνοιαν...ἀληθείας 1 Tm 2.4
3 1 ἐν ἐσχάταις ἡμέραις 1 Tm 4.1   2-4 Ro 1.29-31   5 ἔχοντες μόρφωσιν εὐσεβείας Mt 7.15, 21; Ro 2.20; Tt 1.16   6 οἱ ἐνδύνοντες...ἁμαρτίαις Tt 1.11   7 εἰς...δυνάμενα 2 Tm 2.25   8 Ἰάννης...Μωϋσεῖ Ex 7.11, 22   ἄνθρωποι...νοῦν 1 Tm 6.5

arguments; you know that they end up in quarrels. 24 The Lord's servant must not quarrel. He must be kind toward all, a good and patient teacher, 25 who is gentle as he corrects his opponents. It may be that God will give them the opportunity to repent and come to know the truth. 26 And then they will return to their senses and escape from the trap of the Devil, who had caught them and made them obey his will.

The Last Days

3 Remember this! There will be difficult times in the last days. 2 For men will be selfish, greedy, boastful, and conceited; they will be insulting, disobedient to their parents, ungrateful, and irreligious; 3 they will be unkind, merciless, slanderers, violent, and fierce; they will hate the good; 4 they will be treacherous, reckless, and swollen with pride; they will love pleasure rather than God; 5 they will hold to the outward form of our religion, but reject its real power. Keep away from these men. 6 Some of them go into homes and get control over weak women who are weighed down by the guilt of their sins and driven by all kinds of desires, 7 women who are always trying to learn but who never can come to know the truth. 8 As Jannes and Jambres were opposed to Moses, so also these men are opposed to the truth — men whose minds do not function and who are failures in the faith. 9 But they will not go very far, because everyone will see how stupid they are, just as it happened to Jannes and Jambres.

Last Instructions

10 But you have followed my teaching, my conduct, and my purpose in life; you have observed my faith, my patience, my love, my endurance, 11 my persecu-

tions, and my sufferings. You know all the things that happened to me in Antioch, Iconium, and Lystra, the terrible persecutions I endured! But the Lord rescued me from them all. ¹² All who want to live a godly life in union with Christ Jesus will be persecuted; ¹³ but evil men and impostors will keep on going from bad to worse, deceiving others and being deceived themselves. ¹⁴ But as for you, continue in the truths that you were taught and firmly believe. For you know who your teachers were, ¹⁵ and you know that ever since you were a child you have known the Holy Scriptures, which are able to give you the wisdom that leads to salvation through faith in Christ Jesus. ¹⁶ For all Scripture is inspired by God and is useful¹ for teaching the truth, rebuking error, correcting faults, and giving instruction for right living, ¹⁷ so that the man who serves God may be fully qualified and equipped to do every kind of good work.

4 I solemnly call upon you in the presence of God and of Christ Jesus, who will judge all men, living and dead: because of his coming and of his Kingdom, I command you ² to preach the message, to insist upon telling it, whether the time is right or not; to convince, reproach, and encourage, teaching with all patience. ³ For the time will come when men will not listen to true teaching, but will follow their own desires, and will collect for themselves more and more teachers who will tell them what they are itching to hear. ⁴ They will turn away from listening to the truth and give their attention to legends. ⁵ But you must keep control of yourself in all circumstances; endure suffering, do the work of a preacher of the Good News, and perform your whole duty as a servant of God.

¹ **16** all Scripture is inspired . . . and is useful: *or* every Scripture inspired . . . is also useful

οἷά μοι ἐγένετο ἐν Ἀντιοχείᾳ, ἐν Ἰκονίῳ, ἐν Λύστροις, οἵους διωγμοὺς ὑπήνεγκα· καὶ ἐκ πάντων με ἐρρύσατο ὁ κύριος. 12 καὶ πάντες δὲ οἱ θέλοντες ζῆν εὐσεβῶς ἐν Χριστῷ Ἰησοῦ διωχθήσονται· 13 πονηροὶ δὲ ἄνθρωποι καὶ γόητες προκόψουσιν ἐπὶ τὸ χεῖρον, πλανῶντες καὶ πλανώμενοι. 14 σὺ δὲ μένε ἐν οἷς ἔμαθες καὶ ἐπιστώθης, εἰδὼς παρὰ τίνων ἔμαθες, 15 καὶ ὅτι ἀπὸ βρέφους [τὰ] ἱερὰ γράμματα οἶδας, τὰ δυνάμενά σε σοφίσαι εἰς σωτηρίαν διὰ πίστεως τῆς ἐν Χριστῷ Ἰησοῦ. 16 πᾶσα γραφὴ θεόπνευστος καὶ ὠφέλιμος πρὸς διδασκαλίαν, πρὸς ἐλεγμόν, πρὸς ἐπανόρθωσιν, πρὸς παιδείαν τὴν ἐν δικαιοσύνῃ, 17 ἵνα ἄρτιος ᾖ ὁ τοῦ θεοῦ ἄνθρωπος, πρὸς πᾶν ἔργον ἀγαθὸν ἐξηρτισμένος.

4 Διαμαρτύρομαι ἐνώπιον τοῦ θεοῦ καὶ Χριστοῦ Ἰησοῦ, τοῦ μέλλοντος κρίνειν ζῶντας καὶ νεκρούς, καὶ τὴν ἐπιφάνειαν¹ αὐτοῦ καὶ τὴν βασιλείαν αὐτοῦ· 2 κήρυξον τὸν λόγον, ἐπίστηθι εὐκαίρως ἀκαίρως, ἔλεγξον, ἐπιτίμησον, παρακάλεσον, ἐν πάσῃ μακροθυμίᾳ καὶ διδαχῇ. 3 ἔσται γὰρ καιρὸς ὅτε τῆς ὑγιαινούσης διδασκαλίας οὐκ ἀνέξονται, ἀλλὰ κατὰ τὰς ἰδίας ἐπιθυμίας ἑαυτοῖς ἐπισωρεύσουσιν διδασκάλους κνηθόμενοι τὴν ἀκοήν, 4 καὶ ἀπὸ μὲν τῆς ἀληθείας τὴν ἀκοὴν ἀποστρέψουσιν, ἐπὶ δὲ τοὺς μύθους ἐκτραπήσονται. 5 σὺ δὲ νῆφε ἐν πᾶσιν, κακοπάθησον, ἔργον ποίησον εὐαγγελιστοῦ, τὴν διακονίαν σου πληροφόρησον.

---

¹ **1** {C} καὶ τὴν ἐπιφάνειαν ℵ* A C D* G 33 1739 2495 itᵃʳ,ᶜ,ᵈ,ᵈⁱᵛ,ᵉ,ᶠ,ᵍ,ᵗ,ˣ,ᶻ vgʷʷ copᵇᵒ Didymus (Chrysostom) Augustine Cyril ∥ κατὰ τὴν ἐπιφάνειαν ℵᶜ Dᶜ K P Ψ 81 88 104 181 326 330 436 451 614 629 630 1241 1877 1881 1962 1984 1985 2127 2492 *Byz Lect* vgᶜˡ syrᵖ·ʰ copˢᵃ goth arm eth (Ambrosiaster) (Chrysostom) Pelagius Theodoreˡᵃᵗ Euthalius Theodoret John-Damascus ∥ καὶ κατὰ τὴν ἐπιφάνειαν itᵈᵉᵐ Augustine Primasius

---

11 ἐν Ἀντιοχείᾳ Ac 13.50 ἐν Ἰκονίῳ Ac 14.5 ἐν Λύστροις Ac 14.19 ἐκ...ὁ κύριος Ps. 34.19 **12** Mt 16.24; Jn 15.20; Ac 14.22 **14** εἰδὼς...ἔμαθες 2 Tm 2.2 **15** τὰ δυνάμενα...Ἰησοῦ Jn 5.39 **16** πᾶσα γραφὴ θεόπνευστος 2 Pe 1.21 ὠφέλιμος πρὸς διδασκαλίαν Ro 15.4 **17** πρὸς...ἐξηρτισμένος 2 Tm 2.21

4 1 Χριστοῦ...νεκρούς Ac 10.42; Ro 14.9-10; 1 Pe 4.5 **2** ἐπίστηθι εὐκαίρως ἀκαίρως Ac 20.20, 31 **3** ἔσται...ἀνέξονται 1 Tm 4.1 **4** ἐπὶ...ἐκτραπήσονται 1 Tm 4.7; Tt 1.14

6 Ἐγὼ γὰρ ἤδη σπένδομαι, καὶ ὁ καιρὸς τῆς ἀναλύσεώς μου ἐφέστηκεν. 7 τὸν καλὸν ἀγῶνα ἠγώνισμαι, τὸν δρόμον τετέλεκα, τὴν πίστιν τετήρηκα· 8 λοιπὸν ἀπόκειταί μοι ὁ τῆς δικαιοσύνης στέφανος, ὃν ἀποδώσει μοι ὁ κύριος ἐν ἐκείνῃ τῇ ἡμέρᾳ, ὁ δίκαιος κριτής, οὐ μόνον δὲ ἐμοὶ ἀλλὰ καὶ πᾶσι[2] τοῖς ἠγαπηκόσι τὴν ἐπιφάνειαν αὐτοῦ.

Personal Instructions

9 Σπούδασον ἐλθεῖν πρός με ταχέως· 10 Δημᾶς γάρ με ἐγκατέλιπεν ἀγαπήσας τὸν νῦν αἰῶνα, καὶ ἐπορεύθη εἰς Θεσσαλονίκην, Κρήσκης εἰς Γαλατίαν[3], Τίτος εἰς Δαλματίαν· 11 Λουκᾶς ἐστιν μόνος μετ᾿ ἐμοῦ. Μᾶρκον ἀναλαβὼν ἄγε μετὰ σεαυτοῦ, ἔστιν γάρ μοι εὔχρηστος εἰς διακονίαν. 12 Τυχικὸν δὲ ἀπέστειλα εἰς Ἔφεσον. 13 τὸν φαιλόνην ὃν ἀπέλιπον ἐν Τρῳάδι παρὰ Κάρπῳ ἐρχόμενος φέρε, καὶ τὰ βιβλία, μάλιστα τὰς μεμβράνας. 14 Ἀλέξανδρος ὁ χαλκεὺς πολλά μοι κακὰ ἐνεδείξατο·[a] ἀποδώσει αὐτῷ ὁ κύριος κατὰ τὰ ἔργα αὐτοῦ·[a] 15 ὃν

---

[2] 8 {C} πᾶσι ℵ A C Dᶜ G I K P Ψ 33 81 88 104 181 326 330 436 451 614 629 630 1241 1739ᵐᵍ 1877 1962 1984 1985 2127 2492 2495 *Byz Lect* itᵍ syrʰ copˢᵃ,ᵇᵒ,ᶠᵃʸ goth arm eth Cyprian Archelaus Adamantius Ephraem Chrysostom Jerome Augustine Euthalius Theodoret John-Damascus // *omit* D* 1739* 1881 itᵃʳ,ᶜ,ᵈ,ᵈᵉᵐ,ᵈⁱᵛ,ᵉ,ᶠ,ᵗ,ˣ,ᶻ vg syrᵖ Ambrosiaster Ambrose Augustine Primasius

[3] 10 {B} Γαλατίαν A D G K P Ψ 33 88 181 330 451 614 629 630 1241 1739 1877 1881 1962 1984 1985 2127 2492 2495 *Byz Lect* itᵃʳ,ᶜ,ᵈ,ᵈᵉᵐ,ᵈⁱᵛ,ᵉ,ᶠ,ᵍ,ˣ,ᶻ vgᶜˡ syrᵖ,ʰ copᵇᵒᵐˢˢ goth ethᵖᵖ Irenaeusˡᵃᵗ Ambrosiaster Ephraem Chrysostom Pelagius Theodoreˡᵃᵗ Euthalius Theodoret Ps-Jerome Primasius Cassiodorus John-Damascus // Γαλλίαν ℵ C 81 104 326 436 vgʷʷ copˢᵃ,ᵇᵒᵐˢˢ ethʳᵒ Eusebius Epiphanius // Γαλιλαίαν copᵇᵒᵐˢˢ arm

ᵃ ᵃ 14 *a a* no dashes: TR Bov Nes BF² AV RV ASV RSV NEB TT Zür Luth Jer Seg // *a* dash, *a* dash: WH

6 Ἐγώ...σπένδομαι Php 2.17   7 τὸν καλόν...ἠγώνισμαι 1 Tm 6.12   8 ἀπόκειται... στέφανος 1 Cor 9.25; Php 3.14; 2 Tm 2.5; Jas 1.12; 1 Pe 5.4; Re 2.10   10 Δημᾶς Col 4.14; Phm 24   Τίτος 2 Cor 8.23; Ga 2.3; Tt 1.4   11 Λουκᾶς Col 4.14; Phm 24   Μᾶρκον Ac 12.12, 25; 13.13; 15.37–39; Col 4.10; Phm 24   12 Τυχικόν Ac 20.4; Eph 6.21–22; Col 4.7–8   13 Τρῳάδι Ac 20.6   14 Ἀλέξανδρος 1 Tm 1.20   ἀποδώσει...αὐτοῦ 2 Sm 3.39; Ps 28.4; 62.12; Pr 24.12; Ro 2.6

---

6 As for me, the hour has come for me to be sacrificed; the time is here for me to leave this life. 7 I have done my best in the race, I have run the full distance, I have kept the faith. 8 And now the prize of victory is waiting for me, the crown of righteousness which the Lord, the righteous Judge, will give me on that Day — and not only to me, but to all those who wait with love for him to appear.

Personal Words

9 Do your best to come to me soon. 10 For Demas fell in love with this present world and has deserted me; he has gone off to Thessalonica. Crescens went to Galatia, and Titus to Dalmatia. 11 Only Luke is with me. Get Mark and bring him with you, for he can help me in the work. 12 I sent Tychicus to Ephesus. 13 When you come, bring my coat that I left in Troas with Carpus; bring the books too, and especially the ones made of parchment.

14 Alexander the metalworker did me great harm; the Lord will reward him according to what he has done. 15 Be

on your guard against him yourself, for he was violently opposed to our message.

¹⁶ No one stood by me the first time I defended myself; all deserted me. May God not count it against them! ¹⁷ But the Lord stayed with me and gave me strength, so that I was able to proclaim the full message for all the Gentiles to hear; and I was rescued from the lion's mouth. ¹⁸ And the Lord will rescue me from all evil, and take me safely into his heavenly Kingdom. To him be the glory for ever and ever! Amen.

Final Greetings

¹⁹ I send greetings to Prisca and Aquila, and to the family of Onesiphorus. ²⁰ Erastus stayed in Corinth, and I left Trophimus in Miletus, because he was sick. ²¹ Do your best to come before winter.

Eubulus, Pudens, Linus, and Claudia send their greetings, and so do all the other brothers.

²² The Lord be with your spirit. God's grace be with you all.

καὶ σὺ φυλάσσου, λίαν γὰρ ἀντέστη τοῖς ἡμετέροις λόγοις.

16 Ἐν τῇ πρώτῃ μου ἀπολογίᾳ οὐδείς μοι παρεγένετο, ἀλλὰ πάντες με ἐγκατέλιπον· ᵇ μὴ αὐτοῖς λογισθείη· ᵇ **17** ὁ δὲ κύριός μοι παρέστη καὶ ἐνεδυνάμωσέν με, ἵνα δι' ἐμοῦ τὸ κήρυγμα πληροφορηθῇ καὶ ἀκούσωσιν πάντα τὰ ἔθνη, καὶ ἐρρύσθην ἐκ στόματος λέοντος. **18** ῥύσεταί με ὁ κύριος ἀπὸ παντὸς ἔργου πονηροῦ καὶ σώσει εἰς τὴν βασιλείαν αὐτοῦ τὴν ἐπουράνιον, ᾧ ἡ δόξα εἰς τοὺς αἰῶνας τῶν αἰώνων· ἀμήν.

Final Greetings

19 Ἄσπασαι Πρίσκαν καὶ Ἀκύλαν καὶ τὸν Ὀνησιφόρου οἶκον. **20** Ἔραστος ἔμεινεν ἐν Κορίνθῳ, Τρόφιμον δὲ ἀπέλιπον ἐν Μιλήτῳ ἀσθενοῦντα. **21** Σπούδασον πρὸ χειμῶνος ἐλθεῖν. Ἀσπάζεταί σε Εὔβουλος καὶ Πούδης καὶ Λίνος καὶ Κλαυδία καὶ οἱ ἀδελφοὶ πάντες. **22** Ὁ κύριος μετὰ τοῦ πνεύματός σου. ἡ χάρις μεθ' ὑμῶν.[4]

---

[4] **22** {B} ἡ χάρις μεθ' ὑμῶν. ℵ* A C G 33 81 1881 it^{f,g} cop^{bomss} eth^{ro} Ambrosiaster ∥ ἡ χάρις μεθ' ἡμῶν. 460 1908 Chrysostom Theodore Theodoret Ps-Oecumenius Theophylact ∥ ἡ χάρις μετὰ σοῦ. arm ∥ ἡ χάρις μεθ' ἡμῶν. ἀμήν. 1984 it^z cop^{boms} ∥ ἡ χάρις μεθ' ὑμῶν. ἀμήν. ℵ^c D^c K P Ψ 88 104 181 326 436 451 614 629 630 1241 1739 1877 1962 1985 2127 2492 2495 *Byz Lect* it^{c,dem,div,x} vg syr^h cop^{bomss} eth^{pp} Ambrosiaster Euthalius Primasius John-Damascus ∥ ἡ χάρις μετὰ σοῦ. ἀμήν. syr^p cop^{boms} ∥ ἔρρωσ' ἐν εἰρήνῃ. ἀμήν. D* it^{ar,d,e} ∥ *omit* 330 cop^{sa} Ambrosiaster Pelagius Ps-Jerome

---

^{b b} **16** *b b* no dashes: TR Bov Nes BF² AV RV ASV RSV NEB Zür Luth Jer Seg ∥ *b* dash , *b* dash: WH ∥ *b* dash, *b* major: TT

---

16 πάντες με ἐγκατέλιπον 2 Tm 1.15   **17** ὁ δὲ...παρέστη Ac 27.23   δι' ἐμοῦ...ἔθνη Ac 23.11   ἐρρύσθην...λέοντος Ps 22.21; Dn 6.21; 1 Macc 2.60   **19** Πρίσκαν καὶ Ἀκύλαν Ac 18.2   τὸν Ὀνησιφόρου οἶκον 2 Tm 1.16–17   **20** Ἔραστος Ac 19.22; Ro 16.23   Τρόφιμον Ac 20.4; 21.29

ΠΡΟΣ ΤΙΤΟΝ

Salutation

1 Παῦλος δοῦλος θεοῦ, ἀπόστολος δὲ Ἰησοῦ Χριστοῦ κατὰ πίστιν ἐκλεκτῶν θεοῦ καὶ ἐπίγνωσιν ἀληθείας τῆς κατ᾽ εὐσέβειαν [a] **2** ἐπ᾽ ἐλπίδι ζωῆς αἰωνίου, ἣν ἐπηγγείλατο ὁ ἀψευδὴς θεὸς πρὸ χρόνων αἰωνίων,[b][a] **3** ἐφανέρωσεν δὲ καιροῖς ἰδίοις[b] τὸν λόγον αὐτοῦ ἐν κηρύγματι ὃ ἐπιστεύθην ἐγὼ κατ᾽ ἐπιταγὴν τοῦ σωτῆρος ἡμῶν θεοῦ,[a] **4** Τίτῳ γνησίῳ τέκνῳ κατὰ κοινὴν πίστιν· χάρις καὶ εἰρήνη[1] ἀπὸ θεοῦ πατρὸς καὶ Χριστοῦ Ἰησοῦ τοῦ σωτῆρος ἡμῶν.

Titus' Work in Crete

5 Τούτου χάριν ἀπέλιπόν σε ἐν Κρήτῃ, ἵνα τὰ λείποντα ἐπιδιορθώσῃ καὶ καταστήσῃς κατὰ πόλιν πρεσβυτέρους, ὡς ἐγώ σοι διεταξάμην, **6** εἴ τίς ἐστιν ἀνέγκλητος, μιᾶς γυναικὸς ἀνήρ, τέκνα ἔχων πιστά, μὴ ἐν κατηγορίᾳ ἀσωτίας ἢ ἀνυπότακτα. **7** δεῖ γὰρ τὸν ἐπίσκοπον ἀνέγκλητον εἶναι ὡς θεοῦ οἰκονόμον, μὴ αὐθάδη, μὴ ὀργίλον, μὴ πάροινον, μὴ πλήκτην, μὴ

---

[1] **4** {B} χάρις καὶ εἰρήνη ℵ C* D G P Ψ 088 629 2127 it[ar,c,d,dem,div,e,f,g,x,z] vg syr[p] cop[bo] goth arm Origen[lat] Ambrosiaster Chrysostom Jerome Theodore[lat] Augustine Cassiodorus John-Damascus ‖ χάρις εἰρήνη 1739 1881 ‖ χάρις ὑμῖν καὶ εἰρήνη 33 (cop[ss] σοι for ὑμῖν) ‖ χάρις, ἔλεος, εἰρήνη A C² K 81 88 104 181 326 330 436 451 614 630 1241 1877 1962 2495 Byz Lect[m] l[1365] cop[boms] Theodoret John-Damascus[txt] Ps-Oecumenius Theophylact ‖ χάρις, ἔλεος, καὶ εἰρήνη 1984 1985 2492 syr[h] ‖ εἰρήνη σοι καὶ χάρις eth[ro] ‖ εἰρήνη σοι καὶ χάρις καὶ ἔλεος eth[pp]

[a,a,a] **1-3** (see footnote b) a a a no dashes or parens: TR WH Bov Nes BF² AV RV ASV RSV NEB Luth Jer ‖ a dash, a no dash or parens, a dash: Seg ‖ a no dash or parens, a parens, a parens: TT ‖ a no dash or parens, a dash, a dash: Zür

[b,b] **2-3** (see footnote a) b minor, b none: TR Bov Nes BF² AV RV ASV NEB (TT) (Zür) Luth Seg ‖ b none, b minor: WH ‖ b none, b none: RSV Jer

3 ἐφανέρωσεν...κηρύγματι Eph 1.9-10   κηρύγματι...θεοῦ 1 Tm 1.1, 11   τοῦ σωτῆρος ἡμῶν θεοῦ Tt 2.10; 3.4   **4** Τίτῳ 2 Cor 8.23; Ga 2.3; 2 Tm 4.10   γνησίῳ...πίστιν 1 Tm 1.2 **6-9** 1 Tm 3.2-7; 2 Tm 2.24-26

PAUL'S LETTER TO TITUS

1 From Paul, a servant of God and an apostle of Jesus Christ.

I was chosen and sent to help the faith of God's chosen people and lead them to the truth taught by our religion, [2] which is based on the hope for eternal life. God, who does not lie, promised us this life before the beginning of time, [3] and at the right time he revealed it in his message. This was entrusted to me, and I proclaim it by order of God our Savior.

[4] I write to Titus, my true son in the faith that we share:

May God the Father and Christ Jesus our Savior give you grace and peace.

Titus' Work in Crete

[5] I left you in Crete for you to put in order the things that still needed doing, and to appoint church elders in every town. Remember my instructions: [6] an elder must be without fault; he must have only one wife,[1] and his children must be believers and not have the reputation of being wild or disobedient. [7] For since he is in charge of God's work, the church leader should be without fault. He must not be arrogant or quick-tempered, or a drunkard, or violent, or

---

[1] **6** have only one wife: or be married only once

greedy. [8] He must be hospitable and love what is good. He must be self-controlled, upright, holy, and disciplined. [9] He must hold firmly to the message, which can be trusted and which agrees with the doctrine. In this way he will be able to encourage others with the true teaching, and also show the error of those who are opposed to it.

[10] For there are many who rebel and deceive others with their nonsense, especially the converts from Judaism. [11] It is necessary to stop their talking, for they are upsetting whole families by teaching what they should not, for the shameful purpose of making money. [12] It was a Cretan himself, one of their own prophets, who said: "Cretans are always liars, and wicked beasts, and lazy gluttons." [13] And what he said is true. For this reason you must rebuke them sharply, that they might have a healthy faith, [14] and no longer hold on to Jewish legends and to human commandments which come from men who have rejected the truth. [15] Everything is pure to those who are themselves pure; but nothing is pure to those who are defiled and unbelieving, for their minds and consciences have been defiled. [16] They claim that they know God, but their actions deny it. They are hateful and disobedient, not fit to do anything good.

Sound Doctrine

2 But you must teach what is required by sound doctrine. [2] Tell the older men to be sober, sensible, and self-controlled; to be sound in their faith, love, and endurance. [3] In the same way tell the

αἰσχροκερδῆ, 8 ἀλλὰ φιλόξενον, φιλάγαθον, σώφρονα, δίκαιον, ὅσιον, ἐγκρατῆ, 9 ἀντεχόμενον τοῦ κατὰ τὴν διδαχὴν πιστοῦ λόγου, ἵνα δυνατὸς ᾖ καὶ παρακαλεῖν ἐν τῇ διδασκαλίᾳ τῇ ὑγιαινούσῃ καὶ τοὺς ἀντιλέγοντας ἐλέγχειν.

10 Εἰσὶν γὰρ πολλοὶ [καὶ][2] ἀνυπότακτοι, ματαιολόγοι καὶ φρεναπάται, μάλιστα οἱ ἐκ τῆς περιτομῆς, 11 οὓς δεῖ ἐπιστομίζειν, οἵτινες ὅλους οἴκους ἀνατρέπουσιν διδάσκοντες ἃ μὴ δεῖ αἰσχροῦ κέρδους χάριν. 12 εἶπέν τις ἐξ αὐτῶν, ἴδιος αὐτῶν προφήτης,

Κρῆτες ἀεὶ ψεῦσται, κακὰ θηρία, γαστέρες ἀργαί.
13 ἡ μαρτυρία αὕτη ἐστὶν ἀληθής. δι᾽ ἣν αἰτίαν ἔλεγχε αὐτοὺς ἀποτόμως, ἵνα ὑγιαίνωσιν ἐν τῇ πίστει, 14 μὴ προσέχοντες Ἰουδαϊκοῖς μύθοις καὶ ἐντολαῖς ἀνθρώπων ἀποστρεφομένων τὴν ἀλήθειαν. 15 πάντα καθαρὰ τοῖς καθαροῖς· τοῖς δὲ μεμιαμμένοις καὶ ἀπίστοις οὐδὲν καθαρόν, ἀλλὰ μεμίανται αὐτῶν καὶ ὁ νοῦς καὶ ἡ συνείδησις. 16 θεὸν ὁμολογοῦσιν εἰδέναι, τοῖς δὲ ἔργοις ἀρνοῦνται, βδελυκτοὶ ὄντες καὶ ἀπειθεῖς καὶ πρὸς πᾶν ἔργον ἀγαθὸν ἀδόκιμοι.

The Teaching of Sound Doctrine

2 Σὺ δὲ λάλει ἃ πρέπει τῇ ὑγιαινούσῃ διδασκαλίᾳ.[a] 2 πρεσβύτας νηφαλίους εἶναι, σεμνούς, σώφρονας, ὑγιαίνοντας τῇ πίστει, τῇ ἀγάπῃ, τῇ ὑπομονῇ. 3 πρεσβύ-

---

[2] **10** {C} πολλοὶ καί D G I K Ψ 181 326 330 451 1241 1739 1881 1985ᶜ 2495 *Byz Lect* it[d,e,f,g,m,zᵛⁱᵈ] vg Hilary Lucifer Chrysostom Jerome Euthalius Theodoret Cassiodorus John-Damascus ∥ πολλοί ℵ A C P 088 33 81 88 104 436 614 629 630 1877 1984 2127 2492 it[ar,c,dem,div,x] syr[p,h] cop[sa,bo] goth arm eth Clement Ambrosiaster Hilary Chrysostom Pelagius Augustine Theodoret Antiochus Ps-Oecumenius Theophylact ∥ omit εἰσὶν...φρεναπάται 1985*

[a] **1** *a* major: WH Bov Nes BF[2] RSV NEB Luth Jer Seg ∥ *a* minor: TR AV RV ASV TT Zür

---

9 τῇ διδασκαλίᾳ τῇ ὑγιαινούσῃ 1 Tm 1.10; 2 Tm 4.3; Tt 2.1　　**11** ὅλους οἴκους ἀνατρέπουσιν 2 Tm 3.6　　αἰσχροῦ κέρδους χάριν Jn 10.12; 1 Pe 5.2　　**12** Κρῆτες...ἀργαί Epimenides, *de Oraculis*　　**13** ἔλεγχε αὐτοὺς ἀποτόμως 2 Tm 4.2　　**14** μὴ...μύθοις 1 Tm 1.4; 4.7　　**15** πάντα...καθαροῖς Mt 15.11; Ro 14.20　　**16** θεὸν...ἀρνοῦνται 1 Jn 1.6; 2.4

2 1 2 Tm 1.13　　τῇ ὑγιαινούσῃ διδασκαλίᾳ 1 Tm 1.10; 2 Tm 4.3; Tt 1.9　　**3** 1 Tm 3.11

τιδας ὡσαύτως ἐν καταστήματι ἱεροπρεπεῖς, μὴ διαβόλους μηδὲ οἴνῳ πολλῷ δεδουλωμένας, καλοδιδασκάλους, 4 ἵνα σωφρονίζωσιν τὰς νέας φιλάνδρους εἶναι, φιλοτέκνους, 5 σώφρονας, ἁγνάς, οἰκουργούς, ἀγαθάς, ὑποτασσομένας τοῖς ἰδίοις ἀνδράσιν, ἵνα μὴ ὁ λόγος τοῦ θεοῦ βλασφημῆται. 6 τοὺς νεωτέρους ὡσαύτως παρακάλει σωφρονεῖν· [b] 7 περὶ πάντα[b] σεαυτὸν παρεχόμενος τύπον καλῶν ἔργων,[c] ἐν τῇ διδασκαλίᾳ[c] ἀφθορίαν,[c] σεμνότητα, 8 λόγον ὑγιῆ ἀκατάγνωστον, ἵνα ὁ ἐξ ἐναντίας ἐντραπῇ μηδὲν ἔχων λέγειν περὶ ἡμῶν φαῦλον. 9 δούλους ἰδίοις δεσπόταις ὑποτάσσεσθαι[d] ἐν πᾶσιν,[d] εὐαρέστους εἶναι, μὴ ἀντιλέγοντας, 10 μὴ νοσφιζομένους, ἀλλὰ πᾶσαν πίστιν ἐνδεικνυμένους ἀγαθήν, ἵνα τὴν διδασκαλίαν τὴν τοῦ σωτῆρος ἡμῶν θεοῦ κοσμῶσιν ἐν πᾶσιν.

11 Ἐπεφάνη γὰρ ἡ χάρις τοῦ θεοῦ σωτήριος πᾶσιν ἀνθρώποις, 12 παιδεύουσα ἡμᾶς ἵνα ἀρνησάμενοι τὴν ἀσέβειαν καὶ τὰς κοσμικὰς ἐπιθυμίας σωφρόνως καὶ δικαίως καὶ εὐσεβῶς ζήσωμεν ἐν τῷ νῦν αἰῶνι, 13 προσδεχόμενοι τὴν μακαρίαν ἐλπίδα καὶ ἐπιφάνειαν τῆς δόξης τοῦ μεγάλου θεοῦ καὶ σωτῆρος ἡμῶν[e] Ἰησοῦ Χριστοῦ,[e] 14 ὃς ἔδωκεν ἑαυτὸν ὑπὲρ ἡμῶν ἵνα λυτρώσηται ἡμᾶς ἀπὸ πάσης ἀνομίας καὶ καθαρίσῃ ἑαυτῷ λαὸν περιούσιον, ζηλωτὴν καλῶν ἔργων. 15 Ταῦτα λάλει καὶ παρακάλει καὶ ἔλεγχε μετὰ πάσης ἐπιταγῆς· μηδείς σου περιφρονείτω.

---

[b][b] **6–7** b minor, b none: TR WH Bov (AV) RV ASV (RSV) Zür (Luth) Jer[mg] ∥ b none, b minor: Nes BF[2] NEB (TT) Jer Seg

[c][c][c] **7** c minor, c none, c minor: WH Bov Nes BF[2] (AV) RV ASV RSV (NEB) (TT) Zür Luth Jer Seg ∥ c minor, c none, c none: (TR) ∥ c none, c minor, c minor: WH[mg]

[d][d] **9** d none, d minor: WH Nes BF[2] NEB TT Luth Jer Seg ∥ d minor, d none: TR Bov AV RV ASV RSV Zür

[e][e] **13** e none, e minor: TR WH Bov Nes BF[2] AV RV ASV RSV NEB TT Zür Luth ∥ e minor, e minor: WH[mg] (Jer) (Seg)

---

5 ὑποτασσομένας...ἀνδράσιν Eph 5.22   **7** σεαυτὸν...ἔργων 1 Tm 4.12; 1 Pe 5.3   **8** ὁ ἐξ...φαῦλον 1 Pe 2.15   **9** δούλους...ὑποτάσσεσθαι Eph 6.5; 1 Tm 6.1; 1 Pe 2.18   **10** τοῦ σωτῆρος ἡμῶν θεοῦ Tt 1.3; 3.4   **12** ἀρνησάμενοι...ἐπιθυμίας 1 Jn 2.16 σωφρόνως...αἰῶνι Eph 1.4   **13** 1 Cor 1.7; Php 3.20   **14** ὃς ἔδωκεν ἑαυτὸν ὑπὲρ ἡμῶν Ga 1.4; 2.20; 1 Tm 2.6 λυτρώσηται...ἀνομίας Ps 130.8 καθαρίσῃ...περιούσιον Ex 19.5; Dt 4.20; 7.6; 14.2; Eze 37.23; 1 Pe 2.9 ζηλωτὴν καλῶν ἔργων Eph 2.10; 1 Pe 3.13   **15** μηδείς σου περιφρονείτω 1 Tm 4.12

older women to behave as women who live a holy life should. They must not be slanderers, or slaves to wine. They must teach what is good [4] in order to train the younger women to love their husbands and children, [5] to be self-controlled and pure, and to be good housewives, who obey their husbands, so that no one will speak evil of the message from God.

[6] In the same way urge the young men to be self-controlled. [7] You yourself, in all things, must be an example in good works. Be sincere and serious in your teaching. [8] Use sound words that cannot be criticized, so that your enemies may be put to shame by not having anything bad to say about us.

[9] Slaves are to obey their masters and please them in all things. They must not talk back to them, [10] or steal from them. Instead, they must show that they are always good and faithful, so as to bring credit to the teaching about God our Savior in all they do.

[11] For God has revealed his grace for the salvation of all men. [12] That grace instructs us to give up ungodly living and worldly passions, and to live self-controlled, upright, and godly lives in this world, [13] as we wait for the blessed Day we hope for, when the glory of our great God and Savior Jesus Christ will appear. [14] He gave himself for us, to rescue us from all wickedness and make us a pure people who belong to him alone and are eager to do good.

[15] Teach these things, and use your full authority as you encourage and rebuke your hearers. Let none of them look down on you.

Christian Conduct

3 Remind your people to submit to rulers and authorities, to obey them, to be ready to do every good thing. ² Tell them not to speak evil of anyone, but to be peaceful and friendly, and always show a gentle attitude toward all men. ³ For we ourselves were once foolish, disobedient, and wrong. We were slaves to passions and pleasures of all kinds. We spent our lives in malice and envy; others hated us and we hated them. ⁴ But when the kindness and love of God our Savior appeared, ⁵ he saved us. It was not because of any good works that we ourselves had done, but because of his own mercy that he saved us through the washing by which the Holy Spirit gives us new birth and new life. ⁶ For God abundantly poured out the Holy Spirit on us, through Jesus Christ our Savior, ⁷ that by his grace we might be put right with God and come into possession of the eternal life we hope for. ⁸ This is a true saying.

I want you to give special emphasis to these matters, so that those who believe in God may be concerned with giving their time to doing good works. These are good and useful for men. ⁹ But avoid stupid arguments, long lists of names of ancestors, quarrels, and fights about the Law. They are useless and worthless. ¹⁰ Give at least two warnings to the man who causes divisions, and then have nothing more to do with him. ¹¹ For you know that such a person is corrupt, and his sins prove that he is wrong.

Maintain Good Deeds

3 Ὑπομίμνησκε αὐτοὺς ἀρχαῖς¹ ἐξουσίαις ὑποτάσσεσθαι, πειθαρχεῖν, πρὸς πᾶν ἔργον ἀγαθὸν ἑτοίμους εἶναι, 2 μηδένα βλασφημεῖν, ἀμάχους εἶναι, ἐπιεικεῖς, πᾶσαν ἐνδεικνυμένους πραΰτητα πρὸς πάντας ἀνθρώπους. 3 Ἦμεν γάρ ποτε καὶ ἡμεῖς ἀνόητοι, ἀπειθεῖς, πλανώμενοι, δουλεύοντες ἐπιθυμίαις καὶ ἡδοναῖς ποικίλαις, ἐν κακίᾳ καὶ φθόνῳ διάγοντες, στυγητοί, μισοῦντες ἀλλήλους. 4 ὅτε δὲ ἡ χρηστότης καὶ ἡ φιλανθρωπία ἐπεφάνη τοῦ σωτῆρος ἡμῶν θεοῦ, 5 οὐκ ἐξ ἔργων τῶν ἐν δικαιοσύνῃ ἃ ἐποιήσαμεν ἡμεῖς ἀλλὰ κατὰ τὸ αὐτοῦ ἔλεος ἔσωσεν ἡμᾶς διὰ λουτροῦ παλιγγενεσίας καὶ ἀνακαινώσεως πνεύματος ἁγίου, 6 οὗ ἐξέχεεν ἐφ᾽ ἡμᾶς πλουσίως διὰ Ἰησοῦ Χριστοῦ τοῦ σωτῆρος ἡμῶν, 7 ἵνα δικαιωθέντες τῇ ἐκείνου χάριτι κληρονόμοι γενηθῶμεν κατ᾽ ἐλπίδα ζωῆς αἰωνίου.ᵃ

8 Πιστὸς ὁ λόγος,ᵃ καὶ περὶ τούτων βούλομαί σε διαβεβαιοῦσθαι, ἵνα φροντίζωσιν καλῶν ἔργων προΐστασθαι οἱ πεπιστευκότες θεῷ. ταῦτά ἐστιν καλὰ καὶ ὠφέλιμα τοῖς ἀνθρώποις· 9 μωρὰς δὲ ζητήσεις καὶ γενεαλογίας καὶ ἔριν καὶ μάχας νομικὰς περιΐστασο, εἰσὶν γὰρ ἀνωφελεῖς καὶ μάταιοι. 10 αἱρετικὸν ἄνθρωπον μετὰ μίαν καὶ δευτέραν νουθεσίαν παραιτοῦ, 11 εἰδὼς ὅτι ἐξέστραπται ὁ τοιοῦτος καὶ ἁμαρτάνει, ὢν αὐτοκατάκριτος.

---

¹ 1 {C} ἀρχαῖς ℵ A C D^{gr}* G Ψ 33 104 1739 1881 it^g ∥ ἀρχαῖς καί D^c K P 81 88 181 326 330 436 451 614 629 630 1241 1877 1984 1985 2127 2492 2495 *Byz* it^{ar,c,d,dem,div,e,f,m,(t),x,z} vg syr^{p,h,pal} cop^{sa,bo} arm eth Ambrosiaster Lucifer Basil Chrysostom Jerome Euthalius Theodoret John-Damascus

ᵃ ᵃ **7–8** *a* paragraph, *a* minor: TR WH Bov Nes BF² (Jer) Seg ∥ *a* major, *a* paragraph: RSV NEB Luth ∥ *a* major, *a* minor: AV RV ASV TT Zür

1 Ὑπομίμνησκε…ὑποτάσσεσθαι Ro 13.1; 1 Pe 2.13   **3** Ἦμεν…ἀνόητοι 1 Cor 6.11; Eph 2.2; 5.8   **4** τοῦ σωτῆρος ἡμῶν θεοῦ Tt 1.3; 2.10   **5** οὐκ…ἡμᾶς Eph 2.8–9; 2 Tm 1.9 διὰ λουτροῦ παλιγγενεσίας Eph 5.26   ἀνακαινώσεως πνεύματος ἁγίου Jn 3.5   **6** Jl 2.28 **7** δικαιωθέντες…χάριτι Ro 3.24   **9** 2 Tm 2.14, 16, 23   **10** Mt 18.15–17   **11** ἐξέστραπται …ἁμαρτάνει 1 Tm 6.4–5

Personal Instructions and Greetings

12 Ὅταν πέμψω Ἀρτεμᾶν πρὸς σὲ ἢ Τυχικόν, σπούδασον ἐλθεῖν πρός με εἰς Νικόπολιν, ἐκεῖ γὰρ κέκρικα
παραχειμάσαι. **13** Ζηνᾶν τὸν νομικὸν καὶ Ἀπολλῶν
σπουδαίως πρόπεμψον, ἵνα μηδὲν αὐτοῖς λείπῃ. **14** μανθανέτωσαν δὲ καὶ οἱ ἡμέτεροι καλῶν ἔργων προΐστασθαι
εἰς τὰς ἀναγκαίας χρείας, ἵνα μὴ ὦσιν ἄκαρποι.

15 Ἀσπάζονταί σε οἱ μετ᾽ ἐμοῦ πάντες. Ἄσπασαι
τοὺς φιλοῦντας ἡμᾶς ἐν πίστει. ἡ χάρις μετὰ πάντων
ὑμῶν.[2]

---

[2] **15** {B} πάντων ὑμῶν. 𝔭[61vid] ℵ* A C D* 048 1739 1881 *l*[809m] it[d] cop[sa, bomss]
arm eth[ro] Ambrosiaster Pelagius Jerome ‖ πάντων ὑμῶν. ἀμήν. ℵ[c] D[c] G
H K P Ψ 88 104 326 330 436 (451 ἡμῶν) 614 629 630 1241 1877 1984 1985 2127
2492 2495 *Byz* *l*[147m,1150a m,1005] lt[ar,c,dem,div,e,f,g,x,z] vg syr[p,h] cop[bo] eth[pp] Chrysostom Euthalius Theodoret John-Damascus ‖ τοῦ πνεύματός σου. (*see* 2 Tm
4.22) 33 ‖ πάντων ὑμῶν καὶ μετὰ τοῦ πνεύματός σου. 81

---

12 Τυχικόν Ac 20.4; Eph 6.21–22; Col 4.7–8; 2 Tm 4.12   **13** Ἀπολλῶν Ac 18.24; 1 Cor 3.5–6;
16.12   **14** μανθανέτωσαν...χρείας Eph 4.28; Tt 2.14

Final Instructions

[12] When I send Artemas or Tychicus
to you, do your best to come to me in
Nicopolis, for I have decided to spend the
winter there. [13] Do your best to help
Zenas the lawyer and Apollos to get
started on their travels, and see to it
that they have everything they need.
[14] Have our people learn to give their
time in doing good works, to provide for
real needs; they should not live useless
lives.

[15] All who are with me send you
greetings. Give our greetings to our
friends in the faith.

God's grace be with you all.

PAUL'S LETTER TO PHILEMON

[1] From Paul, a prisoner for the sake of Christ Jesus, and from our brother Timothy —
To our friend and fellow worker Philemon, [2] and the church that meets in your house, and our sister Apphia, and our fellow soldier Archippus:
[3] May God our Father and the Lord Jesus Christ give you grace and peace.

Philemon's Love and Faith

[4] Every time I pray, brother Philemon, I mention you and give thanks to my God. [5] For I hear of your love for all God's people and the faith you have in the Lord Jesus. [6] My prayer is that our fellowship with you as believers will bring about a deeper understanding of every blessing which we have in our life in Christ. [7] Your love, dear brother, has brought me great joy and much encouragement! For you have cheered the hearts of all God's people.

A Request for Onesimus

[8] For this reason I could be bold enough, as your brother in Christ, to order you to do what should be done. [9] But love compels me to make a request instead. I do this even though I am Paul, the ambassador of Christ Jesus and at present also a prisoner for his sake. [10] So I make a request to you on

744

Salutation

1 Παῦλος δέσμιος Χριστοῦ 'Ιησοῦ καὶ Τιμόθεος ὁ ἀδελφὸς Φιλήμονι τῷ ἀγαπητῷ καὶ συνεργῷ ἡμῶν 2 καὶ 'Απφίᾳ τῇ ἀδελφῇ καὶ 'Αρχίππῳ τῷ συστρατιώτῃ ἡμῶν καὶ τῇ κατ' οἶκόν σου ἐκκλησίᾳ· 3 χάρις ὑμῖν καὶ εἰρήνη ἀπὸ θεοῦ πατρὸς ἡμῶν καὶ κυρίου 'Ιησοῦ Χριστοῦ.

Philemon's Love and Faith

4 Εὐχαριστῶ τῷ θεῷ μου πάντοτε μνείαν σου ποιούμενος ἐπὶ τῶν προσευχῶν μου, 5 ἀκούων σου τὴν ἀγάπην καὶ τὴν πίστιν ἣν ἔχεις πρὸς τὸν κύριον 'Ιησοῦν καὶ εἰς πάντας τοὺς ἁγίους, 6 ὅπως ἡ κοινωνία τῆς πίστεώς σου ἐνεργὴς γένηται ἐν ἐπιγνώσει παντὸς ἀγαθοῦ τοῦ ἐν ἡμῖν[1] εἰς Χριστόν· 7 χαρὰν γὰρ πολλὴν ἔσχον καὶ παράκλησιν ἐπὶ τῇ ἀγάπῃ σου, ὅτι τὰ σπλάγχνα τῶν ἁγίων ἀναπέπαυται διὰ σοῦ, ἀδελφέ.

Paul Pleads for Onesimus

8 Διό, πολλὴν ἐν Χριστῷ παρρησίαν ἔχων ἐπιτάσσειν σοι τὸ ἀνῆκον, 9 διὰ τὴν ἀγάπην μᾶλλον παρακαλῶ,[a] τοιοῦτος ὢν ὡς Παῦλος πρεσβύτης, νυνὶ δὲ καὶ δέσμιος Χριστοῦ 'Ιησοῦ —[a] 10 παρακαλῶ σε περὶ τοῦ ἐμοῦ

[1] 6 {C} ἐν ἡμῖν A C D K Ψ 048? 81 88 326 330 436 614 630 1241 1877[c] 1984*[vid] 1985 2495 Lect[m] it[d,e,z*] syr[hmg] Ambrosiaster Chrysostom[txt] Pelagius[1/2] Euthalius Theodoret John-Damascus Ps-Oecumenius[txt] ‖ ἐν ὑμῖν 𝔭[61] ℵ G P 33 104 451 1739 1877* 1881 1984[cvid] 2492 Byz it[ar,div,f,g,x] vg syr[p,h] cop[sa,bo] arm Chrysostom[comm] Jerome Primasius Cassiodorus Ps-Oecumenius[comm] Theophylact ‖ omit 629 it[c,dem,gig,z*] Pelagius[1/2] Ps-Jerome

[a a] 9 a minor, a dash: WH ‖ a minor, a major: AV RV ASV TT Zür Luth (Jer) ‖ a major, a dash: NEB ‖ a dash, a dash: RSV ‖ a major, a minor: Nes Seg ‖ a minor, a minor: TR Bov BF[2]

1 δέσμιος Χριστοῦ 'Ιησοῦ Eph 3.1; 4.1; Php 1.7, 13; Phm 9   2 'Αρχίππῳ Col 4.17   3 Ro 1.7; Ga 1.3; Php 1.2   4 Ro 1.8–9   6 ἡ κοινωνία...ἐπιγνώσει Php 1.9; Col 1.9   7 χαρὰν ...σου 2 Cor 7.4   9 δέσμιος Χριστοῦ 'Ιησοῦ Eph 3.1; 4.1; Php 1.7, 13; Phm 1   10 τοῦ ἐμοῦ τέκνου 1 Cor 4.15; Ga 4.19

τέκνου, ὃν ἐγέννησα ἐν τοῖς δεσμοῖς Ὀνήσιμον, ᵇ11 τόν ποτέ σοι ἄχρηστον νυνὶ δὲ [καὶ] σοὶ καὶ ἐμοὶ εὔχρηστον,ᵇ 12ᶜ ὃν ἀνέπεμψά σοι, ᶜαὐτόν, τοῦτ' ἔστιν τὰ ἐμὰ σπλάγχνα·² 13 ὃν ἐγὼ ἐβουλόμην πρὸς ἐμαυτὸν κατέχειν, ἵνα ὑπὲρ σοῦ μοι διακονῇ ἐν τοῖς δεσμοῖς τοῦ εὐαγγελίου, 14 χωρὶς δὲ τῆς σῆς γνώμης οὐδὲν ἠθέλησα ποιῆσαι, ἵνα μὴ ὡς κατὰ ἀνάγκην τὸ ἀγαθόν σου ᾖ ἀλλὰ κατὰ ἑκούσιον. 15 τάχα γὰρ διὰ τοῦτο ἐχωρίσθη πρὸς ὥραν ἵνα αἰώνιον αὐτὸν ἀπέχῃς, 16 οὐκέτι ὡς δοῦλον ἀλλὰ ὑπὲρ δοῦλον, ἀδελφὸν ἀγαπητόν, μάλιστα ἐμοί, πόσῳ δὲ μᾶλλον σοὶ καὶ ἐν σαρκὶ καὶ ἐν κυρίῳ.

17 Εἰ οὖν με ἔχεις κοινωνόν, προσλαβοῦ αὐτὸν ὡς ἐμέ. 18 εἰ δέ τι ἠδίκησέν σε ἢ ὀφείλει, τοῦτο ἐμοὶ ἐλλόγα· 19 ἐγὼ Παῦλος ἔγραψα τῇ ἐμῇ χειρί, ἐγὼ ἀποτίσω·ᵈ ἵνα μὴ λέγω σοι ὅτι καὶ σεαυτόν μοι προσ-

behalf of Onesimus, who is my own son in Christ; for while in prison I became his spiritual father. ¹¹ At one time he was of no use to you, but now he is useful both to you and to me.

¹² I am sending him back to you now, and with him goes my heart. ¹³ I would like to keep him here with me, while I am in prison for the gospel's sake, so that he could help me in your place. ¹⁴ However, I do not want to force you to help me; rather, I would like for you to do it of your own free will. So I will not do a thing unless you agree.

¹⁵ It may be that Onesimus was away from you for a short time so that you might have him back for all time. ¹⁶ For now he is not just a slave, but much more than a slave: he is a dear brother in Christ. How much he means to me! And how much more he will mean to you, both as a slave and as a brother in the Lord!

¹⁷ So, if you think of me as your partner, welcome him back just as you would welcome me. ¹⁸ If he has done you any wrong, or owes you anything, charge it to my account. ¹⁹ Here, I will write this with my own hand: *I, Paul, will pay you back.* (I should not have to remind you, of course, that you owe your very life to

---

² 12 {B} ἀνέπεμψά σοι, αὐτόν, τοῦτ' ἔστιν τὰ ἐμὰ σπλάγχνα ℵ* A 33 ‖ ἀνέπεμψα, σὺ δὲ αὐτόν, τοῦτ' ἔστιν τὰ ἐμὰ σπλάγχνα Gᵍʳ ‖ ἀνέπεμψά σοι, τοῦτ' ἔστιν τὰ σπλάγχνα τὰ ἐμὰ προσλαβοῦ· 629 ‖ ἀνέπεμψά σοι αὐτόν, τοῦτ' ἔστιν τὰ ἐμὰ σπλάγχνα προσλαβοῦ C* ‖ ἀνέπεμψα, σὺ δὲ αὐτόν, τοῦτ' ἔστιν τὰ ἐμὰ σπλάγχνα προσλαβοῦ· ℵᶜ (Dᶜ 104 ἔπεμψα) K P (Ψ σοι δέ) 81 326 330* 436 614 630 1241 1739 1881 1984 1985 2495 *Byz Lect*ᵘ¹ itᵈⁱᵛ·ᶠ·ᶻ* vgʷʷ syrʰ goth John-Damascus ‖ ἔπεμψά σοι, σὺ δὲ αὐτόν, τοῦτ' ἔστιν τὰ ἐμὰ σπλάγχνα προσλαβοῦ· (C² ἀνέπεμψα) (D* ἔπεψα) 88 (1877 itᵈᵉᵐ ἀνέπεμψα πρὸς σέ) itᵃʳ·ᶜ·ˣ·ᶻᶜ vgᶜˡ ἀνέπεμψα) syrᵖ (Chrysostom ἔπεμψα πρὸς σέ,) Jerome ‖ ἀνέπεμψα· σὺ δὲ αὐτὸν προσλαβοῦ, τοῦτ' ἔστιν τὰ ἐμὰ σπλάγχνα· 330ᵐᵍ 451 2492 (69 431 462 προσλαβοῦ αὐτόν) syrᵖᵃˡ Theodoret ‖ ἀνέπεμψά σοι, σὺ δὲ αὐτὸν προσλαβοῦ, τοῦτ' ἔστιν τὰ ἐμὰ σπλάγχνα· (048 ἔπεμψα) itᵍ (copˢᵃ·ᵇᵒ προσλαβοῦ αὐτόν) (arm ἔπεμψα) (eth *omit* σὺ δέ)

ᵇ ᵇ 11 *b b* no parens: TR WH Bov Nes BF² AV RV ASV NEB TT Zür Luth Jer Seg ‖ *b* parens, *b* parens: RSV

ᶜ ᶜ 11–12 *c* number 12, *c* no number: TRᵉᵈ WH Bov Nes BF² AV RV ASV RSV NEB? TT Zür Luth Jer Seg ‖ *c* no number, *c* number 12: TRᵉᵈ NEB?

ᵈ 19 *d* major: TR WH Bov Nes BF² AV RV ASV TT Luth (Seg) ‖ *d* dash: RSV NEB Zür ‖ *d* ellipsis: Jer

---

10 Ὀνήσιμον Col 4.9   13 ὑπὲρ...διακονῇ Php 2.30   14 μὴ...ἑκούσιον 2 Cor 9.7; 1 Pe 5.2   16 οὐκέτι...ἀγαπητόν 1 Tm 6.2   19 ἐγὼ...χειρί Ga 6.11; 2 Th 3.17

me.) ²⁰ So, my brother, please do me
this favor, for the Lord's sake; cheer
up my heart, as a brother in Christ!

²¹ I am sure, as I write this, that you
will do what I ask — in fact I know that
you will do even more. ²² At the same
time, get a room ready for me, because
I hope that God will answer the prayers
of all of you and give me back to you.

Final Greetings

²³ Epaphras, who is in prison with me
for the sake of Christ Jesus, sends you
his greetings, ²⁴ and so do my fellow
workers Mark, Aristarchus, Demas, and
Luke.

²⁵ May the grace of the Lord Jesus
Christ be with you all.

ὀφείλεις. **20** ναί, ἀδελφέ, ἐγώ σου ὀναίμην ἐν κυρίῳ·
ἀνάπαυσόν μου τὰ σπλάγχνα ἐν Χριστῷ.

21 Πεποιθὼς τῇ ὑπακοῇ σου ἔγραψά σοι, εἰδὼς ὅτι
καὶ ὑπὲρ ἃ λέγω ποιήσεις. **22** ἅμα δὲ καὶ ἑτοίμαζέ μοι
ξενίαν, ἐλπίζω γὰρ ὅτι διὰ τῶν προσευχῶν ὑμῶν χαρι-
σθήσομαι ὑμῖν.

Final Greetings

23 Ἀσπάζεταί σε Ἐπαφρᾶς ὁ συναιχμάλωτός μου ἐν
Χριστῷ Ἰησοῦ, **24**^e Μᾶρκος, ^e Ἀρίσταρχος, Δημᾶς, Λου-
κᾶς, οἱ συνεργοί μου. **25** Ἡ χάρις τοῦ κυρίου³ Ἰησοῦ
Χριστοῦ μετὰ τοῦ πνεύματος ὑμῶν.⁴

---

³ **25** {C} κυρίου ℵ P 33 81 104 451 1739 1881 2492 syr^{h, pal} arm ∥ κυρίου
ἡμῶν A C D K Ψ 88 326 330 614 629 630 1241 1877 1984^c 2495 *Byz Lect*^m it^{ar,c,d,}
^{dem,div,e,f,x,z} vg syr^p cop^{sa,bo} eth Chrysostom Theodore^{lat} Euthalius

⁴ **25** {B} ὑμῶν. A D* 048 33 81 1881 it^{d,z*} cop^{sa, bo mss} arm Ambrosiaster
Jerome ∥ ὑμῶν. ἀμήν. ℵ C D^c K P Ψ 88 104 326 330 451 614 629 630 1241
1739 1877 1984 2492 2495 *Byz l*^{1153a m,1441 m} it^{ar,c,dem,div,e,f,x,z c} vg syr^{p,h,pal} cop^{bo}
eth Ambrosiaster Chrysostom Theodore^{lat} Euthalius Theodoret Primasius
John-Damascus ∥ σου. ἀμήν. it^{gig}

---

^{e e} **23–24** *e* number 24, *e* no number: TR^{ed} WH? Bov Nes BF² AV RV ASV RSV NEB TT Zür
Luth Jer Seg ∥ *e* no number, *e* number 24: TR^{ed} WH?

---

23 Ἐπαφρᾶς Col 1.7; 4.12   **24** Μᾶρκος Ac 12.12, 25; 13.13; 15.37–39; Col 4.10; 2 Tm 4.11
Ἀρίσταρχος Ac 19.29; 27.2; Col 4.10   Δημᾶς Col 4.14; 2 Tm 4.10   Λουκᾶς Col 4.14; 2 Tm 4.11

ΠΡΟΣ ΕΒΡΑΙΟΥΣ

God Has Spoken by His Son

1 Πολυμερῶς καὶ πολυτρόπως πάλαι ὁ θεὸς λαλήσας τοῖς πατράσιν ἐν τοῖς προφήταις **2** ᵃ ἐπ' ἐσχάτου τῶν ἡμερῶν τούτων ἐλάλησεν ἡμῖν ἐν υἱῷ, ᵃὃν ἔθηκεν κληρονόμον πάντων, δι' οὗ καὶ ἐποίησεν τοὺς αἰῶνας· **3** ὃς ὢν ἀπαύγασμα τῆς δόξης καὶ χαρακτὴρ τῆς ὑποστάσεως αὐτοῦ, φέρων τε τὰ πάντα τῷ ῥήματι τῆς δυνάμεως αὐτοῦ, καθαρισμὸν¹ τῶν ἁμαρτιῶν ποιησάμενος ἐκάθισεν ἐν δεξιᾷ τῆς μεγαλωσύνης ἐν ὑψηλοῖς, **4** τοσούτῳ κρείττων γενόμενος τῶν ἀγγέλων ὅσῳ διαφορώτερον παρ' αὐτοὺς κεκληρονόμηκεν ὄνομα.

The Son Superior to Angels

5 Τίνι γὰρ εἶπέν ποτε τῶν ἀγγέλων,
  Υἱός μου εἶ σύ,
    ἐγὼ σήμερον γεγέννηκά σε; ᵇ
καὶ πάλιν,
  Ἐγὼ ἔσομαι αὐτῷ εἰς πατέρα,
    καὶ αὐτὸς ἔσται μοι εἰς υἱόν; ᵇ

---

¹ **3** {C} καθαρισμόν ℵ A B Dᵇ H* P Ψ 33 81 181* 436 629 1962 2492 itᵉ,ᵈᵉᵐ,ᵈⁱᵛ,f,t,v,x,z vg syrᵖᵃˡ arm Cyril-Jerusalem Didymus Cyril Euthalius Ps-Athanasius Cassiodorus John-Damascusᶜᵒᵐᵐ Sedulius-Scotus ∥ δι' ἑαυτοῦ καθαρισμόν Dᶜ Hᶜ K 0121b 88 104 181ᵐᵍ 326 330 451 614 630 1241 1739 1877 1881 1984 1985 2495 *Byz Lect* itᵃʳ,ᵈ,ᵉ syrᵖ,ʰ copˢᵃ,ᵇᵒ,ᶠᵃʸ (eth) Origen Athanasius Chrysostom Augustine Theodoret Vigilius John-Damascusᵗˣᵗ ∥ δι' αὐτοῦ καθαρισμόν 𝔭⁴⁶ Dᵍʳ* 2127 *l*⁰⁰³ Theodoret

ᵃ ᵃ **1-2** *a* number 2, *a* no number: TRᵉᵈ WH Bov Nes BF² AV RV ASV RSV NEB TT Zür Luth Jer Seg ∥ *a* no number, *a* number 2: TRᵉᵈ
ᵇ ᵇ **5** *b* question, *b* question: TR Bov Nes BF² AV RV ASV RSV TT Zür Luth Seg ∥ *b* minor, *b* question: WH ∥ *b* minor, *b* statement: (NEB) ∥ *b* question, *b* statement: Jer

2 ὃν...πάντων Ps 2.8; Mt 21.38   δι'...αἰῶνας Jn 1.3; Col 1.16   **3** χαρακτήρ...αὐτοῦ 2 Cor 4.4; Col 1.15   ἐκάθισεν...ὑψηλοῖς Ps 110.1; Mt 22.44; Mk 16.19; Ac 2.34; Eph 1.20; He 8.1; 10.12; 12.2   **4** διαφορώτερον...ὄνομα Eph 1.21; Php 2.9   **5** Υἱός...σε Ps 2.7 (Ac 13.33; He 5.5)   Ἐγὼ...υἱόν 2 Sm 7.14; 1 Chr 17.13

THE LETTER
TO THE HEBREWS

God's Word through His Son

1 In the past God spoke to our ancestors many times and in many ways through the prophets, **2** but in these last days he has spoken to us through his Son. He is the one through whom God created the universe, the one whom God has chosen to possess all things at the end. **3** He shines with the brightness of God's glory; he is the exact likeness of God's own being, and sustains the universe with his powerful word. After he had made men clean from their sins, he sat down in heaven at the right side of God, the Supreme Power.

The Son Greater than the Angels

4 The Son was made greater than the angels, just as the name that God gave him is greater than theirs. **5** For God never said to any of his angels,
  "You are my Son;
  Today I have become your Father."
Nor did God say to any angel,
  "I will be his Father,
  And he shall be my Son."

[6] When God was about to send his first-born Son into the world, he also said,
"All of God's angels must worship him."

[7] This is what God said about the angels:
"God makes his angels winds,
And he makes his servants flames of fire."

[8] About the Son, however, God said:
"Your throne, O God, will last for ever and ever!
With justice you rule over your kingdom.

[9] You love the right and hate the wrong,
That is why God, your God, chose you
And gave you the joy of an honor far greater
Than he gave to your companions."

[10] He also said:
"You, Lord, in the beginning created the earth,
And with your own hands you made the heavens.

[11] They will all disappear, but you will remain.
They will all grow old like clothes;

[12] You will fold them up like a coat,
And they will be changed like clothes.
But you are the same, and you will never grow old."

6 ὅταν δὲ πάλιν εἰσαγάγῃ τὸν πρωτότοκον εἰς τὴν οἰκουμένην, λέγει,
   Καὶ προσκυνησάτωσαν αὐτῷ πάντες ἄγγελοι θεοῦ.

7 καὶ πρὸς μὲν τοὺς ἀγγέλους λέγει,
   Ὁ ποιῶν τοὺς ἀγγέλους αὐτοῦ πνεύματα,
      καὶ τοὺς λειτουργοὺς αὐτοῦ πυρὸς φλόγα·

8 πρὸς δὲ τὸν υἱόν,
   Ὁ θρόνος σου, ὁ θεός, εἰς τὸν αἰῶνα τοῦ αἰῶνος,
      καὶ [c] ἡ ῥάβδος τῆς εὐθύτητος ῥάβδος τῆς βασιλείας σου[2].

9 ἠγάπησας δικαιοσύνην καὶ ἐμίσησας ἀνομίαν·
   διὰ τοῦτο ἔχρισέν σε[d] ὁ θεός,[d] ὁ θεός σου,[d]
      ἔλαιον ἀγαλλιάσεως παρὰ τοὺς μετόχους σου·

10 καί,
   Σὺ κατ' ἀρχάς, κύριε, τὴν γῆν ἐθεμελίωσας,
      καὶ ἔργα τῶν χειρῶν σού εἰσιν οἱ οὐρανοί·

11 αὐτοὶ ἀπολοῦνται, σὺ δὲ διαμένεις·
      καὶ πάντες ὡς ἱμάτιον παλαιωθήσονται,

12 καὶ ὡσεὶ περιβόλαιον ἑλίξεις αὐτούς,
      ὡς ἱμάτιον καὶ[3] ἀλλαγήσονται·
   σὺ δὲ ὁ αὐτὸς εἶ
      καὶ τὰ ἔτη σου οὐκ ἐκλείψουσιν.

---

[2] 8 {C} σου (see Ps 45.7) A D K P Ψ 0121b 33 81 88 104 181 326 330 436 451 614 629 630 1241 1739 1877 1881 1962 1984 1985 2127 2492 2495 *Byz Lect* it[ar,c,d,dem,div,e,f,t,v,x,z] vg syr[p,h] cop[sa,bo,fay] arm Chrysostom Cyril Euthalius ∥ αὐτοῦ p[46] ℵ B ∥ *omit* syr[pal]

[3] 12 {C} ὡς ἱμάτιον καί p[46] ℵ A B 1739 arm eth ∥ καὶ ὡς ἱμάτιον D[abs1] it[d,e] ∥ ὡς ἱμάτιον D[gr*] ∥ καί D[c] K P Ψ 0121b 33 81 88 104 181 326 330 436 451 614 629 630 1241 1877 1881 1962 1984 1985 2127 2492 2495 *Byz Lect* it[ar,c,dem,div,f,t,v,x,z] vg syr[p,h,pal] cop[sa,bo,fay] Athanasius Chrysostom Cyril Euthalius Theodoret

---

[c] 8 c none: WH Bov Nes BF[2] RV ASV NEB TT ∥ c minor: Zür Luth Jer Seg ∥ different text: TR AV RSV

[d d d] 9 d none, d minor, d minor: TR WH AV RV ASV RSV (NEB[mg]) ∥ d minor, d minor, d none: Bov Nes BF[2] NEB TT Zür Luth Jer Seg

---

6 Καὶ...θεοῦ Dt 32.43 LXX (Ps 97.7)   7 Ὁ ποιῶν...φλόγα Ps 104.4   8–9 Ὁ θρόνος... μετόχους σου Ps 45.6–7   10–12 Σὺ...ἐκλείψουσιν Ps 102.25–27

13 πρὸς τίνα δὲ τῶν ἀγγέλων εἴρηκέν ποτε,

Κάθου ἐκ δεξιῶν μου

     ἕως ἂν θῶ τοὺς ἐχθρούς σου ὑποπόδιον τῶν
ποδῶν σου;

14 οὐχὶ πάντες εἰσὶν λειτουργικὰ πνεύματα εἰς διακονίαν ἀποστελλόμενα διὰ τοὺς μέλλοντας κληρονομεῖν σωτηρίαν;

The Great Salvation

2 Διὰ τοῦτο δεῖ περισσοτέρως προσέχειν ἡμᾶς τοῖς ἀκουσθεῖσιν, μήποτε παραρυῶμεν. 2 εἰ γὰρ ὁ δι᾽ ἀγγέλων λαληθεὶς λόγος ἐγένετο βέβαιος, καὶ πᾶσα παράβασις καὶ παρακοὴ ἔλαβεν ἔνδικον μισθαποδοσίαν, 3 πῶς ἡμεῖς ἐκφευξόμεθα τηλικαύτης ἀμελήσαντες σωτηρίας;ᵃ ἥτις, ἀρχὴν λαβοῦσα λαλεῖσθαι διὰ τοῦ κυρίου, ὑπὸ τῶν ἀκουσάντων εἰς ἡμᾶς ἐβεβαιώθη,ᵃ 4 συνεπιμαρτυροῦντος τοῦ θεοῦ σημείοις τε καὶ τέρασιν καὶ ποικίλαις δυνάμεσιν καὶ πνεύματος ἁγίου μερισμοῖς κατὰ τὴν αὐτοῦ θέλησιν.ᵃ

The Pioneer of Salvation

5 Οὐ γὰρ ἀγγέλοις ὑπέταξεν τὴν οἰκουμένην τὴν μέλλουσαν, περὶ ἧς λαλοῦμεν. 6 διεμαρτύρατο δέ πού τις λέγων,

Τί ἐστιν ἄνθρωπος ὅτι μιμνήσκῃ αὐτοῦ, ᵇ

    ἢ **υἱὸς ἀνθρώπου** **ὅτι ἐπισκέπτῃ αὐτόν;** ᵇ

ᵃ ᵃ ᵃ **3-4** a question, a minor, a statement: TR Bov Nes BF² RV ASV RSV NEB TT Jer Seg ∥ a minor, a minor, a question: WH AV Zür ∥ a minor, a question, a statement: Luth

ᵇ ᵇ **6** b minor, b question: TR WH RSV NEB Zür Luth Jer Seg ∥ b question, b question: Bov Nes BF² AV RV ASV TT

---

13 Κάθου...ποδῶν σου Ps 110.1   14 εἰς...σωτηρίαν Ps 34.8; 91.11

2 2 ὁ δι᾽...λόγος Ac 7.38, 53; Ga 3.19   3 πῶς...σωτηρίας He 10.29; 12.25   4 πνεύματος ...θέλησιν 1 Cor 12.4, 11   **6-8** Τί...αὐτοῦ Ps 8.5-7 LXX

---

¹³ God never did say to any of his angels:

"Sit here at my right side,

Until I put your enemies

As a footstool under your feet."

¹⁴ What are the angels, then? They are all spirits who serve God and are sent by him to help those who are to receive salvation.

The Great Salvation

2 That is why we must hold on all the more firmly to the truths we have heard, so that we will not be carried away. ² The message given by the angels was shown to be true, and anyone who did not follow it or obey it received the punishment he deserved. ³ How, then, shall we escape if we pay no attention to such a great salvation? The Lord himself first announced this salvation, and those who heard him proved to us that it is true. ⁴ At the same time God added his witness to theirs by doing signs of power, wonders, and many kinds of miracles. He also distributed the gifts of the Holy Spirit according to his will.

The Leader to Salvation

⁵ For God did not make the angels rulers over the world he was about to create — the world of which we speak. ⁶ Instead, as it is said somewhere in the Scriptures:

"What is man, O God, that you should think of him?

What is mere man, that you should care for him?

[7] You made him for a little while
   lower than the angels,
You gave him the glory and honor
   that belong to a king,
[8] And made him ruler over all things."
It says that God made man "ruler over
all things"; this clearly includes everything. But we do not see man ruling
over all things now. [9] But we do see
Jesus! For a little while he was made
lower than the angels, so that through
God's grace he should die for all men.
We see him crowned with glory and
honor now because of the death he
suffered. [10] It was only right for God —
who creates and preserves all things —
to make Jesus perfect through suffering,
in order to bring many sons to share his
glory. For Jesus is the one who leads
them to salvation.

[11] He makes men pure from their sins,
and both he and those who are made
pure all have the same Father. That
is why Jesus is not ashamed to call them
his brothers. [12] As he says,

   "I will speak about you, O God,
      to my brothers,
   I will sing hymns to you before the
      whole gathering."

[13] He also says, "I will put my trust in
God." And he also says, "Here I am with
the children that God has given me."

---

7   ἠλάττωσας αὐτὸν βραχύ τι παρ' ἀγγέλους,
      δόξῃ καὶ τιμῇ ἐστεφάνωσας αὐτόν[1],
8   πάντα ὑπέταξας ὑποκάτω τῶν ποδῶν αὐτοῦ.[c]
ἐν τῷ γὰρ ὑποτάξαι [αὐτῷ] τὰ πάντα οὐδὲν ἀφῆκεν
αὐτῷ ἀνυπότακτον. νῦν δὲ οὔπω ὁρῶμεν αὐτῷ τὰ πάντα
ὑποτεταγμένα· 9 τὸν δὲ **βραχύ τι παρ' ἀγγέλους ἠλατ-
τωμένον** βλέπομεν Ἰησοῦν διὰ τὸ πάθημα τοῦ θανάτου
δόξῃ καὶ τιμῇ ἐστεφανωμένον, ὅπως χάριτι θεοῦ[2] ὑπὲρ
παντὸς γεύσηται θανάτου.

10 Ἔπρεπεν γὰρ αὐτῷ, δι' ὃν τὰ πάντα καὶ δι' οὗ
τὰ πάντα, πολλοὺς υἱοὺς εἰς δόξαν ἀγαγόντα τὸν ἀρχηγὸν
τῆς σωτηρίας αὐτῶν διὰ παθημάτων τελειῶσαι. 11 ὅ τε
γὰρ ἁγιάζων καὶ οἱ ἁγιαζόμενοι ἐξ ἑνὸς πάντες· δι' ἣν
αἰτίαν οὐκ ἐπαισχύνεται ἀδελφοὺς αὐτοὺς καλεῖν, 12 λέγων,

    Ἀπαγγελῶ τὸ ὄνομά σου τοῖς ἀδελφοῖς μου,
    ἐν μέσῳ ἐκκλησίας ὑμνήσω σε·
13 καὶ πάλιν,
    Ἐγὼ ἔσομαι πεποιθὼς ἐπ' αὐτῷ·
καὶ πάλιν,
    Ἰδοὺ ἐγὼ καὶ τὰ παιδία ἅ μοι ἔδωκεν ὁ θεός.

---

[1] **7** {C} αὐτόν 𝔓[46] B D[c] K 326 614 630 1241 1984 2495 *Byz*[pt] *Lect* syr[h]
Chrysostom John-Damascus Ps-Oecumenius Theophylact ∥ αὐτόν, καὶ κα-
τέστησας αὐτὸν ἐπὶ τὰ ἔργα τῶν χειρῶν σου (*see* Ps 8.6 LXX) ℵ A C D*
P Ψ 0121b 33 (81 ἑκατέστησας) 88 104 181 330 436 451 629 1739 1877 1881
1962 1985 2127 2492 *Byz*[pt] *l*[597] it[ar,c,d,dem,div,e,f,v,x,z] vg syr[p,h with *] cop[sa,bo,fay]
arm eth Euthalius Theodoret Sedulius-Scotus

[2] **9** {B} χάριτι θεοῦ 𝔓[46] ℵ A B C D K P Ψ 33 81 88 104 181 326 330 436
451 614 629 630 1241 1877 1881 1962 1984 1985 2127 2492 2495 *Byz Lect* it[ar,c,d,]
[dem,div,e,f,t,v,x,z] vg syr[(p),h,pal] cop[sa,bo,fay] arm eth mss[acc. to Origen] Origen[gr2/6]
Eusebius Athanasius Faustinus Chrysostom Jerome Cyril Euthalius ∥
χωρὶς θεοῦ 0121b 1739* mss[acc. to Origen] Origen[gr4/6,lat] Eusebius Ambrosiaster
Ambrose mss[acc. to Ambrose, Jerome] Theodore Theodoret Vigilius Fulgentius
Anastasius-Abbot Ps-Oecumenius Theophylact

[c] **8** *c major*: TR Bov Nes BF² AV RV ASV RSV NEB TT Zür Luth Jer Seg ∥ *c minor*: WH

---

8 πάντα...ἀνυπότακτον 1 Cor 15.27   **9** τὸν...ἐστεφανωμένον Php 2.8–9   **11** οὐκ...
καλεῖν Mt 25.40; Mk 3.35; Jn 20.17   **12** Ἀπαγγελῶ...σε Ps 22.22   **13** Ἐγὼ...αὐτῷ
Is 8.17 LXX (2 Sm 22.3 LXX; Is 12.2)   Ἰδοὺ...θεός Is 8.18

14 ἐπεὶ οὖν τὰ παιδία κεκοινώνηκεν αἵματος καὶ σαρκός, καὶ αὐτὸς παραπλησίως μετέσχεν τῶν αὐτῶν, ἵνα διὰ τοῦ θανάτου καταργήσῃ τὸν τὸ κράτος ἔχοντα τοῦ θανάτου, τοῦτ' ἔστιν τὸν διάβολον, 15 καὶ ἀπαλλάξῃ τούτους, ὅσοι φόβῳ θανάτου διὰ παντὸς τοῦ ζῆν ἔνοχοι ἦσαν δουλείας. 16 οὐ γὰρ δήπου ἀγγέλων ἐπιλαμβάνεται, ἀλλὰ **σπέρματος Ἀβραὰμ ἐπιλαμβάνεται.** 17 ὅθεν ὤφειλεν κατὰ πάντα τοῖς ἀδελφοῖς ὁμοιωθῆναι, ἵνα ἐλεήμων γένηται καὶ πιστὸς ἀρχιερεὺς τὰ πρὸς τὸν θεόν, εἰς τὸ ἱλάσκεσθαι τὰς ἁμαρτίας τοῦ λαοῦ· 18 ἐν ᾧ γὰρ πέπονθεν αὐτὸς πειρασθείς, δύναται τοῖς πειραζομένοις βοηθῆσαι.

Jesus Superior to Moses

3 Ὅθεν, ἀδελφοὶ ἅγιοι, κλήσεως ἐπουρανίου μέτοχοι, κατανοήσατε τὸν ἀπόστολον καὶ ἀρχιερέα τῆς ὁμολογίας ἡμῶν Ἰησοῦν, 2 πιστὸν ὄντα τῷ ποιήσαντι αὐτὸν ὡς καὶ **Μωϋσῆς ἐν ὅλῳ**[1] τῷ οἴκῳ αὐτοῦ. 3 πλείονος γὰρ οὗτος δόξης παρὰ Μωϋσῆν ἠξίωται καθ' ὅσον πλείονα τιμὴν ἔχει τοῦ οἴκου ὁ κατασκευάσας αὐτόν. [a]4 πᾶς γὰρ οἶκος κατασκευάζεται ὑπό τινος, ὁ δὲ πάντα κατασκευάσας θεός.[a] 5 καὶ **Μωϋσῆς** μὲν **πιστὸς ἐν ὅλῳ τῷ οἴκῳ αὐτοῦ** ὡς **θεράπων** εἰς μαρτύριον τῶν λαληθησομένων, 6 **Χριστὸς** δὲ ὡς **υἱὸς** ἐπὶ τὸν οἶκον αὐτοῦ·

---

[1] 2 {C} ὅλῳ (see 3.5; Nu 12.17 LXX) ℵ A C D K P Ψ 0121b 33 81 88 104 181 326 330 436 451 614 629 630 1241 1739 1877 1881 1962 1984 1985 2127 2492 2495 *Byz Lect* it[ar,c,d,dem,div,e,f,v,x,z] vg syr[p,h] arm eth Chrysostom Cyril Euthalius Theodoret John-Damascus // *omit* p[13,46vid] B cop[sa,bo,fay] Ambrose Cyril

---

[a] [a] 4 a a no parens: TR WH Bov Nes BF² AV RV ASV NEB TT Zür Luth Jer Seg // a parens, a parens: RSV

---

14 καταργήσῃ...διάβολον Jn 12.31; 1 Jn 3.8; Re 12.10   16 σπέρματος Ἀβραὰμ ἐπιλαμβάνεται Is 41.8-9   17 κατὰ...ὁμοιωθῆναι Php 2.7; He 2.14   τὸ...λαοῦ 1 Jn 2.2; 4.10   18 He 4.15
3 1 ἀρχιερέα...Ἰησοῦν He 4.14; 6.20; 7.26; 8.1; 9.11   2, 5 Μωϋσῆς...αὐτοῦ Nu 12.7

---

[14] Since the children, as he calls them, are people of flesh and blood, Jesus himself became like them and shared their human nature. He did so that through his death he might destroy the Devil, who has the power over death, [15] and so set free those who were slaves all their lives because of their fear of death. [16] For it is clear that it is not the angels that he helps. Instead, as the scripture says, "He helps the descendants of Abraham." [17] This means that he had to become like his brothers in every way, in order to be their faithful and merciful high priest in his service to God, so that the people's sins would be forgiven. [18] And now he can help those who are tempted, because he himself was tempted and suffered.

Jesus Greater than Moses

3 My Christian brothers, who also have been called by God! Look at Jesus, whom God sent to be the High Priest of the faith we profess. [2] For he was faithful to God, who chose him to do this work, just as Moses was faithful in his work in God's whole house. [3] A man who builds a house receives more honor than the house itself. In the same way, Jesus is worthy of much more glory than Moses. [4] Every house, of course, is built by someone — and God is the one who has built all things. [5] And Moses was faithful in God's whole house. He was a servant and spoke of the things that God would say in the future. [6] But Christ is faithful as the

Son, in charge of God's house. We are his house, if we keep our courage and our confidence in what we hope for.

A Rest for God's People

7 For, as the Holy Spirit says:
"If you hear God's voice today,
8 Do not be stubborn as you were
    when you rebelled against God,
As you were that day in the desert
    when you put him to the test.
9 There your ancestors tempted and
    tried me, says God,
Even though they saw what I did
    for forty years.
10 For that reason I was angry with
    those people,
And I said, 'They are always wrong
    in what they think,
They have never learned my ways.'
11 I was angry and I made a vow:
    'They shall never come in and rest
    with me!'"
12 My brothers: be careful that no one
among you has a heart so bad and unbelieving that he will turn away from
the living God. 13 Instead, in order that
none of you be deceived by sin and become stubborn, you must help one another every day, as long as the "today"

οὗ² οἶκός ἐσμεν ἡμεῖς, ἐὰν τὴν παρρησίαν καὶ τὸ καύχημα τῆς ἐλπίδος κατάσχωμεν³.

A Rest for the People of God

7 Διό,ᵇ καθὼς λέγει τὸ πνεῦμα τὸ ἅγιον,
    Σήμερον ἐὰν τῆς φωνῆς αὐτοῦ ἀκούσητε,
8   μὴ σκληρύνητε τὰς καρδίας ὑμῶν ὡς ἐν τῷ παρα-
        πικρασμῷ,
    κατὰ τὴν ἡμέραν τοῦ πειρασμοῦ ἐν τῇ ἐρήμῳ,
9   οὗ ἐπείρασαν οἱ πατέρες ὑμῶν ἐν δοκιμασίᾳ
        καὶ εἶδον τὰ ἔργα μου 10ᶜ τεσσαράκοντα ἔτη·
    ᶜδιὸ προσώχθισα τῇ γενεᾷ ταύτῃ
    καὶ εἶπον, Ἀεὶ πλανῶνται τῇ καρδίᾳ·
        αὐτοὶ δὲ οὐκ ἔγνωσαν τὰς ὁδούς μου·ᵇ
11 ὡς ὤμοσα ἐν τῇ ὀργῇ μου,
    Εἰ εἰσελεύσονται εἰς τὴν κατάπαυσίν μου.ᵇ
12 Βλέπετε, ἀδελφοί, μήποτε ἔσται ἔν τινι ὑμῶν καρδία πονηρὰ ἀπιστίας ἐν τῷ ἀποστῆναι ἀπὸ θεοῦ ζῶντος, 13 ἀλλὰ παρακαλεῖτε ἑαυτοὺς καθ' ἑκάστην ἡμέραν, ἄχρις οὗ τὸ Σήμερον καλεῖται, ἵνα μὴ σκλη-

² 6 {B} οὗ 𝔭¹³ᵛⁱᵈ ℵ A B C Dᶜ I K P Ψ 33 81 104 181 326 330 436 (451 1985 2492 οὗ ὁ) 614 629 630 1241 1877 1881 1962 1984 2127 2495 *Byz Lect* itᵛ syrᵖ,ʰ,ᵖᵃˡ copˢᵃ,ᵇᵒ arm Athanasius Didymus Jerome // ὅς 𝔭⁴⁶ D* 0121b 88 1739 itᵃʳ,ᶜ,ᵈ,ᵈᵉᵐ,ᵈⁱᵛ,ᵉ,f,x,z vg Lucifer Ambrose

³ 6 {C} κατάσχωμεν 𝔭¹³,⁴⁶ B Ψ copˢᵃ ethʳᵒ Lucifer Ambrose // μέχρι τέλους βεβαίαν κατάσχωμεν (see 3.14) ℵ A C D K P 0121b 33 81 88 104 181 326 330 436 451 614 629 630 1241 1739 1877 1881 (1962 βεβαίως) 1984 1985 2127 2492 2495 *Byz Lect* itᵃʳ,ᵈ,ᵈᵉᵐ,ᵈⁱᵛ,ᵉ,f,ᵛ,(x),z vg syr⁽ᵖ⁾,ʰ,ᵖᵃˡ copᵇᵒ arm ethᵖᵖ Chrysostom Theodoret Euthalius John-Damascus // μέχρι τέλους κατάσχωμεν βεβαίαν 4 itᶜ

ᵇ ᵇ ᵇ 7, 10–11 *b* minor, *b* major, *b* major: WH AVᵉᵈ RV ASV RSV NEB TT Jer Seg // *b* minor, *b* minor, *b* major: Bov Nes BF² Zür Luth // *b* minor, *b* major, *b* minor: TR // *b* parens, *b* major, *b* parens: AVᵉᵈ

ᶜ ᶜ 9–10 *c* number 10, *c* no number: TRᵉᵈ WH Bov Nes BF² TT Zür Jer Segᵉᵈ // *c* no number, *c* number 10: TRᵉᵈ AV RV ASV RSV NEB Luth Segᵉᵈ

6 ἐὰν...κατάσχωμεν Col 1.23; He 3.14   7-11 Σήμερον...κατάπαυσίν μου Ps 95.7-11
8 Ex 17.7; Nu 20.2–5   11 Nu 14.21–23

ρυνθῇ τις ἐξ ὑμῶν ἀπάτῃ τῆς ἁμαρτίας· **14** μέτοχοι γὰρ τοῦ Χριστοῦ γεγόναμεν, ἐάνπερ τὴν ἀρχὴν τῆς ὑπο- στάσεως μέχρι τέλους βεβαίαν κατάσχωμεν,[d] **15** ἐν τῷ λέγεσθαι,

Σήμερον ἐὰν τῆς φωνῆς αὐτοῦ ἀκούσητε,

Μὴ σκληρύνητε τὰς καρδίας ὑμῶν ὡς ἐν τῷ παρα- πικρασμῷ.[d]

16 τίνες γὰρ ἀκούσαντες παρεπίκραναν; ἀλλ’ οὐ πάντες οἱ ἐξελθόντες ἐξ Αἰγύπτου διὰ Μωϋσέως; **17** τίσιν δὲ **προσώχθισεν τεσσαράκοντα ἔτη**; οὐχὶ τοῖς ἁμαρτή- σασιν, ὧν τὰ κῶλα ἔπεσεν ἐν τῇ ἐρήμῳ; **18** τίσιν δὲ **ὤμοσεν μὴ εἰσελεύσεσθαι εἰς τὴν κατάπαυσιν αὐτοῦ** εἰ μὴ τοῖς ἀπειθήσασιν; **19** καὶ βλέπομεν ὅτι οὐκ ἠδυνήθησαν εἰσελθεῖν δι’ ἀπιστίαν.

4 Φοβηθῶμεν οὖν μήποτε καταλειπομένης ἐπαγγελίας εἰσελθεῖν εἰς τὴν κατάπαυσιν αὐτοῦ δοκῇ τις ἐξ ὑμῶν ὑστερηκέναι· **2** καὶ γὰρ ἐσμεν εὐηγγελισμένοι καθάπερ κἀκεῖνοι, ἀλλ’ οὐκ ὠφέλησεν ὁ λόγος τῆς ἀκοῆς ἐκείνους, μὴ συγκεκερασμένους[1] τῇ πίστει τοῖς ἀκούσασιν. **3** εἰσερ- χόμεθα γὰρ[2] εἰς [τὴν] κατάπαυσιν οἱ πιστεύσαντες, καθὼς εἴρηκεν,

in the scripture applies to us. [14] For we are all partners with Christ, if we hold on firmly to the end the confidence we had at the beginning.

[15] This is what the scripture says:

"If you hear God's voice today,
Do not be stubborn as you were
When you rebelled against God."

[16] Who heard God's voice and rebelled against him? Actually it was all the people who were led out of Egypt by Moses. [17] With whom was God angry for forty years? He was angry with the people who sinned, who fell down dead in the desert. [18] When God made his vow, "They shall never come in and rest with me" — of whom was he speak- ing? He was speaking of those who rebelled. [19] We see, then, that they were not able to go in because they did not believe.

4 Now, God has left us the promise that we may go in and rest with him. Let us fear, then, so that none of you will be found to have failed to go in to that rest. [2] For we have heard the Good News, just as they did. They heard the message but it did them no good, be- cause when they heard it they did not receive it with faith. [3] We who believe, then, do go in and rest with God. It is just as he said,

---

[1] **2** {C} συγκεκερασμένους p[13,46] A B C D[gr]* Ψ 0121b (33 συγκεκερα- σμένους) 81 88 1739 2127 Theodore Euthalius ‖ συγκεκραμένους D[c] K P 181 326 330 436 (451 1962 1984[vid] 1985 2492 2495 συγκεκραμένους) 614 629 630 1241 1877 1881 *Byz Lect* Macarius Chrysostom Cyril[1/2] Theodoret Photius[acc. to Ps-Oecumenius] Ps-Oecumenius Theophylact ‖ συγκεκερασμένους *or* συγκεκραμένους it[ar,f,v,m,(a)] vg[ww] syr[h] cop[sams] arm eth Irenaeus[lat] Augus- tine ‖ συγκεκερασμένος א Ephraem Cyril[1/2] Theodoret ‖ συγκεκραμένος 57 (102) ‖ συγκεκερασμένος *or* συγκεκραμένος it[c,(d),dem,div,(e)] vg[cl] syr[p] cop[sa] Luciter ‖ συνκεκεραμμένοι 104

[2] **3** {B} εἰσερχόμεθα γάρ p[13,46] B D K P Ψ 33 88 181 326 330 451 614 629 630 1241 1877 1962 1984 1985 2492 2495 *Byz Lect* it[d,e] syr[h] cop[sa] eth

---

[d d] **14-15** d minor, d major. TR Bov AV RV ASV RSV TT Seg ‖ d major, d minor: NEB Zür Luth Jer ‖ d major, d major: WH Nes BF[2]

14 ἐάνπερ...κατάσχωμεν He 3.6   **15** Σήμερον...παραπικρασμῷ Ps 95.7-8 (He 3.7-8) **16-18** Nu 14.1-35   **17** ὧν...ἐρήμῳ Nu 14.29; 1 Cor 10.10   **18** ὤμοσεν...αὐτοῦ Nu 14.22-23; Ps 95.11; He 3.11

"I was angry and made a vow:
'They shall never come in and rest
with me!'"
He said this even though his work was
finished from the time he created the
world. 4 For somewhere in the Scriptures this is said about the seventh day,
"God rested on the seventh day from
all his works." 5 This same matter is
spoken of again: "They shall never come
in and rest with me." 6 Those who first
heard the Good News did not go in and
rest with God because they did not
believe. There are, then, others who are
allowed to go in and rest with God.
7 That is shown by the fact that God sets
another day which is called "Today."
He speaks of it many years later by
means of David, in the scripture already
quoted,

"If you hear God's voice today,
Do not be stubborn."

8 For if Joshua had led the people into
God's rest, God would not have spoken
later about another day. 9 As it is,
however, there still remains for God's
people a rest like God's resting on the
seventh day. 10 For anyone who goes
in and rests with God will rest from his
own works, just as God rested from his.
11 Let us, then, do our best to go in and
rest with God. We must not, any of us,
disobey as they did and fail to go in.

12 For the word of God is alive and
active. It is sharper than any double-
edged sword. It cuts all the way through,
to where soul and spirit meet, to where
joints and marrow come together. It
judges the desires and thoughts of men's

'Ως ὤμοσα ἐν τῇ ὀργῇ μου,
   Εἰ εἰσελεύσονται εἰς τὴν κατάπαυσίν μου,[a]
καίτοι τῶν ἔργων ἀπὸ καταβολῆς κόσμου γενηθέντων.[a]
4 εἴρηκεν γάρ που περὶ τῆς ἑβδόμης οὕτως, **Καὶ κατέπαυσεν ὁ θεὸς ἐν τῇ ἡμέρᾳ τῇ ἑβδόμῃ ἀπὸ πάντων
τῶν ἔργων αὐτοῦ·** 5 καὶ ἐν τούτῳ πάλιν, **Εἰ εἰσελεύσονται εἰς τὴν κατάπαυσίν μου.** 6 ἐπεὶ οὖν ἀπολείπεται τινὰς εἰσελθεῖν εἰς αὐτήν, καὶ οἱ πρότερον εὐαγγε-
λισθέντες οὐκ εἰσῆλθον δι' ἀπείθειαν, 7 πάλιν τινὰ ὁρίζει
ἡμέραν, **Σήμερον,** ἐν Δαυὶδ λέγων μετὰ τοσοῦτον χρόνον,
καθὼς προείρηται,

   **Σήμερον ἐὰν τῆς φωνῆς αὐτοῦ ἀκούσητε,
   μὴ σκληρύνητε τὰς καρδίας ὑμῶν.**[b]
8 εἰ γὰρ αὐτοὺς Ἰησοῦς κατέπαυσεν, οὐκ ἂν περὶ ἄλλης
ἐλάλει μετὰ ταῦτα ἡμέρας. 9 ἄρα ἀπολείπεται σαββα-
τισμὸς τῷ λαῷ τοῦ θεοῦ· 10 ὁ γὰρ εἰσελθὼν εἰς τὴν
κατάπαυσιν αὐτοῦ καὶ αὐτὸς κατέπαυσεν ἀπὸ τῶν ἔργων
αὐτοῦ ὥσπερ ἀπὸ τῶν ἰδίων ὁ θεός. 11 σπουδάσωμεν
οὖν εἰσελθεῖν εἰς ἐκείνην τὴν κατάπαυσιν, ἵνα μὴ ἐν τῷ
αὐτῷ τις ὑποδείγματι πέσῃ τῆς ἀπειθείας.

12 Ζῶν γὰρ ὁ λόγος τοῦ θεοῦ καὶ ἐνεργὴς καὶ τομώ-
τερος ὑπὲρ πᾶσαν μάχαιραν δίστομον καὶ διϊκνούμενος
ἄχρι μερισμοῦ ψυχῆς καὶ πνεύματος, ἁρμῶν τε καὶ
μυελῶν, καὶ κριτικὸς ἐνθυμήσεων καὶ ἐννοιῶν καρδίας·

Chrysostom Cyril Euthalius Theodoret John-Damascus ‖ εἰσερχώμεθα γάρ
it[ar,c,dem,div,f,v,x,z] vg Lucifer Primasius ‖ εἰσερχώμεθα οὖν ℵ 0121b 81 104
436 1739 1881 2127 cop[bo] ‖ εἰσερχώμεθα οὖν A C ‖ εἰσερχόμεθα δέ syr[p] arm

---

[a a] 3 a minor, a major: TR Bov Nes BF² AV RV ASV RSV TT Zür ‖ a major, a minor: NEB
Luth Jer Seg ‖ a minor, a minor: WH
[b] 7 b major: TR Bov Nes BF² AV RV ASV RSV NEB TT Zür Luth Seg ‖ b minor: WH ‖
b ellipsis: Jer

---

3 'Ως...μου Ps 95.11 (He 3.11; 4.5)   4 Καὶ...αὐτοῦ Gn 2.2   5 Εἰ...μου Ps 95.11 (He 3.11;
4.1)   7 Σήμερον...ὑμῶν Ps 95.7–8 (He 3.7–8)   8 εἰ...κατέπαυσεν Dt 31.7; Jos 22.4
10 ὥσπερ...θεός Gn 2.2; He 4.4   12 Ζῶν...θεοῦ 1 Pe 1.23   ὁ...δίστομον Is 49.2; Eph 6.17;
Re 19.15   ὁ...θεοῦ and κριτικός Jn 12.48

13 καὶ οὐκ ἔστιν κτίσις ἀφανὴς ἐνώπιον αὐτοῦ, πάντα δὲ γυμνὰ καὶ τετραχηλισμένα τοῖς ὀφθαλμοῖς αὐτοῦ, πρὸς ὃν ἡμῖν ὁ λόγος.

Jesus the Great High Priest

14 Ἔχοντες οὖν ἀρχιερέα μέγαν διεληλυθότα τοὺς οὐρανούς, Ἰησοῦν τὸν υἱὸν τοῦ θεοῦ, κρατῶμεν τῆς ὁμολογίας· 15 οὐ γὰρ ἔχομεν ἀρχιερέα μὴ δυνάμενον συμπαθῆσαι ταῖς ἀσθενείαις ἡμῶν, πεπειρασμένον δὲ κατὰ πάντα καθ’ ὁμοιότητα χωρὶς ἁμαρτίας. 16 προσερχώμεθα οὖν μετὰ παρρησίας τῷ θρόνῳ τῆς χάριτος, ἵνα λάβωμεν ἔλεος καὶ χάριν εὕρωμεν εἰς εὔκαιρον βοήθειαν.

5 Πᾶς γὰρ ἀρχιερεὺς ἐξ ἀνθρώπων λαμβανόμενος ὑπὲρ ἀνθρώπων καθίσταται τὰ πρὸς τὸν θεόν, ἵνα προσφέρῃ δῶρά τε καὶ θυσίας ὑπὲρ ἁμαρτιῶν, 2 μετριοπαθεῖν δυνάμενος τοῖς ἀγνοοῦσιν καὶ πλανωμένοις, ἐπεὶ καὶ αὐτὸς περίκειται ἀσθένειαν, 3 καὶ δι’ αὐτὴν ὀφείλει καθὼς περὶ τοῦ λαοῦ οὕτως καὶ περὶ αὐτοῦ προσφέρειν περὶ ἁμαρτιῶν. 4 καὶ οὐχ ἑαυτῷ τις λαμβάνει τὴν τιμήν, ἀλλὰ καλούμενος ὑπὸ τοῦ θεοῦ, καθώσπερ καὶ Ἀαρών.

5 Οὕτως καὶ ὁ Χριστὸς οὐχ ἑαυτὸν ἐδόξασεν γενηθῆναι ἀρχιερέα, ἀλλ’ ὁ λαλήσας πρὸς αὐτόν,

> Υἱός μου εἶ σύ,
> ἐγὼ σήμερον γεγέννηκά σε·

6 καθὼς καὶ ἐν ἑτέρῳ λέγει,

> Σὺ ἱερεὺς εἰς τὸν αἰῶνα
> κατὰ τὴν τάξιν Μελχισέδεκ.

7 ὃς ἐν ταῖς ἡμέραις τῆς σαρκὸς αὐτοῦ, δεήσεις τε καὶ ἱκετηρίας πρὸς τὸν δυνάμενον σῴζειν αὐτὸν ἐκ θανάτου

14 ἀρχιερέα...Ἰησοῦν He 3.11; 6.20; 7.26; 8.1; 9.11   κρατῶμεν τῆς ὁμολογίας He 10.23   15 He 2.17   16 προσερχώμεθα...χάριτος He 10.19
5 2 He 2.17; 4.15   3 Lv 9.7; 16.6   4 καλούμενος...Ἀαρών Ex 28.1   5 Υἱός...σε Ps 2.7 (Ac 13.33; He 1.5)   6 Σὺ...Μελχισέδεκ Ps 110.4 (He 6.20; 7.17)   7 Mt 26.36–46; Mk 14.32–42; Lk 22.39–46

Jesus the Great High Priest
(duplicate header)

hearts. 13 There is nothing that can be hid from God. Everything in all creation is exposed and lies open before his eyes; and it is to him that we must all give account of ourselves.

14 Let us, then, hold firmly to the faith we profess. For we have a great high priest who has gone into the very presence of God — Jesus, the Son of God. 15 Our high priest is not one who cannot feel sympathy with our weaknesses. On the contrary, we have a high priest who was tempted in every way that we are, but did not sin. 16 Let us be brave, then, and come forward to God's throne, where there is grace. There we will receive mercy and find grace to help us just when we need it.

5 Every high priest is chosen from among the people and appointed to serve God on their behalf. He offers gifts and sacrifices for sins. 2 Since he himself is weak in many ways, he is able to be gentle with those who are ignorant and make mistakes. 3 And because he is himself weak, he must offer sacrifices not only for the sins of the people but also for his own sins. 4 No one chooses for himself the honor of being a high priest. It is only by God's call that a man is made a high priest — just as Aaron was called.

5 In the same way, Christ did not take upon himself the honor of being a high priest. Instead, God said to him,

> "You are my Son;
> Today I have become your Father."

6 He also said in another place,

> "You will be a priest for ever,
> In the priestly order of Melchizedek."

7 In his life on earth Jesus made his prayers and requests with loud cries and tears to God, who could save him from

death. Because he was humble and devoted, God heard him. [8] But even though he was God's Son he learned to be obedient by means of his sufferings. [9] When he was made perfect, he became the source of eternal salvation for all those who obey him, [10] and God declared him to be high priest, in the priestly order of Melchizedek.

Warning against Falling Away

[11] There is much we have to say about this matter, but it is hard to explain to you, because you are so slow to understand. [12] There has been enough time for you to be teachers — yet you still need someone to teach you the first lessons of God's message. Instead of eating solid food, you still have to drink milk. [13] Anyone who has to drink milk is still a child, without any experience in the matter of right and wrong. [14] Solid food, on the other hand, is for adults, who have trained and used their tastes to know the difference between good and evil.

6 Let us go forward, then, to mature teaching and leave behind us the beginning of the Christian message. We should not lay again the foundation of turning away from useless works and believing in God; [2] of the teaching about baptisms and the laying on of hands; of the raising

μετὰ κραυγῆς ἰσχυρᾶς καὶ δακρύων προσενέγκας καὶ εἰσακουσθεὶς ἀπὸ τῆς εὐλαβείας, 8 καίπερ ὢν υἱὸς ἔμαθεν ἀφ' ὧν ἔπαθεν τὴν ὑπακοήν· 9 καὶ τελειωθεὶς ἐγένετο πᾶσιν τοῖς ὑπακούουσιν αὐτῷ αἴτιος σωτηρίας αἰωνίου, 10 προσαγορευθεὶς ὑπὸ τοῦ θεοῦ ἀρχιερεὺς **κατὰ τὴν τάξιν Μελχισέδεκ.**

Warning against Apostasy

11 Περὶ οὗ πολὺς ἡμῖν ὁ λόγος καὶ δυσερμήνευτος λέγειν, ἐπεὶ νωθροὶ γεγόνατε ταῖς ἀκοαῖς. 12 καὶ γὰρ ὀφείλοντες εἶναι διδάσκαλοι διὰ τὸν χρόνον, πάλιν χρείαν ἔχετε τοῦ διδάσκειν ὑμᾶς τινὰ[1] τὰ στοιχεῖα τῆς ἀρχῆς τῶν λογίων τοῦ θεοῦ,[a] καὶ γεγόνατε χρείαν ἔχοντες γάλακτος, [καὶ] οὐ στερεᾶς τροφῆς.[a] 13 πᾶς γὰρ ὁ μετέχων γάλακτος ἄπειρος λόγου δικαιοσύνης, νήπιος γάρ ἐστιν· 14 τελείων δέ ἐστιν ἡ στερεὰ τροφή, τῶν διὰ τὴν ἕξιν τὰ αἰσθητήρια γεγυμνασμένα ἐχόντων πρὸς διάκρισιν καλοῦ τε καὶ κακοῦ.

6 Διὸ ἀφέντες τὸν τῆς ἀρχῆς τοῦ Χριστοῦ λόγον ἐπὶ τὴν τελειότητα φερώμεθα, μὴ πάλιν θεμέλιον καταβαλλόμενοι μετανοίας ἀπὸ νεκρῶν ἔργων,[a] καὶ πίστεως ἐπὶ θεόν, 2 βαπτισμῶν διδαχῆς[1],[a] ἐπιθέσεώς τε χειρῶν,

---

[1] **12** {C} τινά Ψ 81 cop[sams] Euthalius Ps-Oecumenius[comm] ‖ τίνα B[c] D[c] K 0122 88 104 181 326 330 436 451 614 (629 *transposes*: ἔχετε ὑμᾶς τοῦ διδάσκειν τίνα) 630 1241 1877 1962 1984 1985 2127 2492 2495 *Byz Lect* it[ar,c,d,dem,div,e,f,x,z] vg syr[p,h] cop[sa,bo] arm eth Origen[lat] Jerome Augustine ‖ τινα p[46] ℵ A B* C D* P 33 ‖ *omit* 1739 1881

[1] **2** {B} διδαχῆς ℵ A C D[gr] I K P 0122 22 81 88 104 181 326 330 436 451 614 629 630 1241 1739 1877 1881 1962 (1984 τε διδαχῆς) 1985 2127 2492 2495 *Byz Lect* it[ar,c,dem,div,f,x,z] vg syr[p,h] cop[sa,bo,fay] arm ‖ διδαχήν p[46] B it[d,(e)]

[a a] **12** *a* minor, *a* major: TR WH Bov Nes BF[2] AV RV ASV NEB TT Zür (Luth) Jer Seg ‖ *a* major, *a* minor: RSV

[a a a] **1-2** *a* minor, *a* minor, *a* minor: TR Bov Nes BF[2] AV RV ASV (Luth) ‖ *a* none, *a* none, *a* none: Zür Jer ‖ *a* minor, *a* none, *a* none: WH NEB ‖ *a* none, *a* minor, *a* minor: RSV ‖ *a* none, *a* minor, *a* none: TT Seg

9 αἴτιος σωτηρίας αἰωνίου Is 45.17   **10** Ps 110.4; He 5.6   **12-13** γεγόνατε...ἐστιν 1 Cor 3.1–3; 1 Pe 2.2   **14** διάκρισιν...κακοῦ Ro 16.19
    6 1 ἀπὸ...θεόν He 9.14

ἀναστάσεώς τε νεκρῶν,[a] καὶ κρίματος αἰωνίου. 3 καὶ τοῦτο ποιήσομεν[2] ἐάνπερ ἐπιτρέπῃ ὁ θεός. 4 Ἀδύνατον γὰρ τοὺς ἅπαξ φωτισθέντας,[b] γευσαμένους τε τῆς δωρεᾶς τῆς ἐπουρανίου καὶ μετόχους γενηθέντας πνεύματος ἁγίου 5 καὶ καλὸν γευσαμένους θεοῦ ῥῆμα δυνάμεις τε μέλλοντος αἰῶνος, 6 καὶ παραπεσόντας, πάλιν ἀνακαινίζειν εἰς μετάνοιαν, ἀνασταυροῦντας ἑαυτοῖς τὸν υἱὸν τοῦ θεοῦ καὶ παραδειγματίζοντας. 7 γῆ γὰρ ἡ πιοῦσα τὸν ἐπ’ αὐτῆς ἐρχόμενον πολλάκις ὑετόν, καὶ τίκτουσα βοτάνην εὔθετον ἐκείνοις δι’ οὓς καὶ γεωργεῖται, μεταλαμβάνει εὐλογίας ἀπὸ τοῦ θεοῦ· 8 **ἐκφέρουσα** δὲ **ἀκάνθας καὶ τριβόλους** ἀδόκιμος καὶ **κατάρας** ἐγγύς, ἧς τὸ τέλος εἰς καῦσιν.

9 Πεπείσμεθα δὲ περὶ ὑμῶν, ἀγαπητοί, τὰ κρείσσονα καὶ ἐχόμενα σωτηρίας, εἰ καὶ οὕτως λαλοῦμεν· 10 οὐ γὰρ ἄδικος ὁ θεὸς ἐπιλαθέσθαι τοῦ ἔργου ὑμῶν καὶ τῆς ἀγάπης ἧς ἐνεδείξασθε εἰς τὸ ὄνομα αὐτοῦ, διακονήσαντες τοῖς ἁγίοις καὶ διακονοῦντες. 11 ἐπιθυμοῦμεν δὲ ἕκαστον ὑμῶν τὴν αὐτὴν ἐνδείκνυσθαι σπουδὴν πρὸς τὴν πληροφορίαν τῆς ἐλπίδος ἄχρι τέλους, 12 ἵνα μὴ νωθροὶ γένησθε, μιμηταὶ δὲ τῶν διὰ πίστεως καὶ μακροθυμίας κληρονομούντων τὰς ἐπαγγελίας.

God's Sure Promise

13 Τῷ γὰρ Ἀβραὰμ ἐπαγγειλάμενος ὁ θεός, ἐπεὶ κατ’ οὐδενὸς εἶχεν μείζονος ὀμόσαι, **ὤμοσεν καθ’ ἑαυτοῦ,**

---

2 3 {B} ποιήσομεν p[46] ℵ B I[vid] K 0122 33 88 614 629 630 1241 1739 1881 1984 2127 2492 *Byz*[pt] *Lect* it[ar,c,d,dem,e,f,x,z] vg syr[p,h] cop[sa,bo,fay] Ambrose Chrysostom Theodoret[txt] Theophylact ∥ ποιήσωμεν A C D[gr] P Ψ 81 104 181 326[vid] 330 436 451 1877 1962 1985 2495 *Byz*[pt] it[div] arm Chrysostom Euthalius Theodoret[comm] John-Damascus

b 4 *b* minor: TR WH[mg] AV (RV[mg]) (ASV[mg]) RSV NEB TT Jer Seg ∥ *b* none: WH Bov Nes BF[2] RV ASV Zür Luth

4–6 Mt 12.31; He 10.26–27; 1 Jn 5.16 **8** Gn 3.17–18 **10** He 10.32–34 **13** ὤμοσεν καθ’ ἑαυτοῦ Gn 22.16

---

of the dead and the eternal judgment. 3 Let us go forward! And this is what we will do, if God allows.

4 For how can those who fall away be brought back to repent again? They were once in God's light. They tasted heaven's gift and received their share of the Holy Spirit. 5 They knew from experience that God's word is good, and they had felt the powers of the coming age. 6 And then they fell away! It is impossible to bring them back to repent again, because they are nailing the Son of God to the cross once more and exposing him to public shame.

7 God blesses the ground that drinks in the rain that often falls on it and grows plants that are useful to those for whom it is cultivated. 8 But if it grows thorns and weeds it is worth nothing; it is in danger of being cursed by God, and will be destroyed by fire.

9 But even if we speak like this, dear friends, we feel sure about you. We know that you have the better blessings that belong to your salvation. 10 God is not unfair. He will not forget the work you did, nor the love you showed for him in the help you gave and still give your fellow Christians. 11 Our great desire is that each one of you keep up his eagerness to the end, so that the things you hope for will come true. 12 We do not want you to become lazy, but to be like those who believe and are patient, and so receive what God has promised.

God's Sure Promise

13 When God made the promise to Abraham, he made a vow to do what he had promised. Since there was no one greater than himself, he used his

own name when he made his vow. ¹⁴ He said, "I promise you that I will bless you and give you many descendants." ¹⁵ Abraham was patient, and so he received what God had promised. ¹⁶ When a man makes a vow he uses the name of someone greater than himself, and a vow settles all arguments between men. ¹⁷ God wanted to make it very clear to those who were to receive what he promised that he would never change his purpose; so he added his vow to the promise. ¹⁸ There are these two things, then, that cannot change and about which God cannot lie. So we who have found safety with him are greatly encouraged to hold firmly to the hope that is placed before us. ¹⁹ We have this hope as an anchor for our hearts. It is safe and sure, and goes through the curtain of the heavenly temple into the inner sanctuary. ²⁰ Jesus has gone in there before us, on our behalf. He has become a high priest for ever, in the priestly order of Melchizedek.

The Priest Melchizedek

7 This Melchizedek was king of Salem and a priest of the Most High God. As Abraham was coming back from the battle in which he killed the kings, Melchizedek met him and blessed him. ² Abraham gave him one tenth of everything he had. (The first meaning of Melchizedek's name is "King of Righteousness." And because he was king of Salem, his name also means "King of Peace.") ³ There is no record of Melchizedek's father or mother, or of any of his ancestors; no record of his birth or of his death. He is like the Son of God: he remains a priest for ever.

⁴ You see, then, how great he was! Abraham, the patriarch, gave him one tenth of all he got in the battle. ⁵ And those descendants of Levi who are priests are commanded by the Law to collect one tenth from the people of Israel — that is, they collect from their own countrymen, even though they too are descendants of Abraham. ⁶ Melchizedek was not descended from Levi, but he collected one tenth from Abraham and

14 λέγων, **Εἰ μὴν εὐλογῶν εὐλογήσω σε καὶ πληθύνων πληθυνῶ σε**· 15 καὶ οὕτως μακροθυμήσας ἐπέτυχεν τῆς ἐπαγγελίας. 16 ἄνθρωποι γὰρ κατὰ τοῦ μείζονος ὀμνύουσιν, καὶ πάσης αὐτοῖς ἀντιλογίας πέρας εἰς βεβαίωσιν ὁ ὅρκος· 17 ἐν ᾧ περισσότερον βουλόμενος ὁ θεὸς ἐπιδεῖξαι τοῖς κληρονόμοις τῆς ἐπαγγελίας τὸ ἀμετάθετον τῆς βουλῆς αὐτοῦ ἐμεσίτευσεν ὅρκῳ, 18 ἵνα διὰ δύο πραγμάτων ἀμεταθέτων, ἐν οἷς ἀδύνατον ψεύσασθαι [τὸν] θεόν, ἰσχυρὰν παράκλησιν ἔχωμεν οἱ καταφυγόντες κρατῆσαι τῆς προκειμένης ἐλπίδος· 19 ἣν ὡς ἄγκυραν ἔχομεν τῆς ψυχῆς, ἀσφαλῆ τε καὶ βεβαίαν καὶ εἰσερχομένην εἰς τὸ ἐσώτερον τοῦ καταπετάσματος, 20 ὅπου πρόδρομος ὑπὲρ ἡμῶν εἰσῆλθεν Ἰησοῦς, **κατὰ τὴν τάξιν Μελχισέδεκ** ἀρχιερεὺς γενόμενος **εἰς τὸν αἰῶνα.**

The Priestly Order of Melchizedek

7 Οὗτος γὰρ ὁ **Μελχισέδεκ, βασιλεὺς Σαλήμ, ἱερεὺς τοῦ θεοῦ τοῦ ὑψίστου, ὁ συναντήσας Ἀβραὰμ ὑποστρέφοντι ἀπὸ τῆς κοπῆς τῶν βασιλέων καὶ εὐλογήσας αὐτόν,** 2 ᾧ καὶ **δεκάτην ἀπὸ πάντων** ἐμέρισεν **Ἀβραάμ,** πρῶτον μὲν ἑρμηνευόμενος βασιλεὺς δικαιοσύνης ἔπειτα δὲ καὶ **βασιλεὺς Σαλήμ,** ὅ ἐστιν βασιλεὺς εἰρήνης, 3 ἀπάτωρ, ἀμήτωρ, ἀγενεαλόγητος, μήτε ἀρχὴν ἡμερῶν μήτε ζωῆς τέλος ἔχων, ἀφωμοιωμένος δὲ τῷ υἱῷ τοῦ θεοῦ, μένει ἱερεὺς εἰς τὸ διηνεκές.

4 Θεωρεῖτε δὲ πηλίκος οὗτος ᾧ δεκάτην Ἀβραὰμ ἔδωκεν ἐκ τῶν ἀκροθινίων ὁ πατριάρχης. 5 καὶ οἱ μὲν ἐκ τῶν υἱῶν Λευὶ τὴν ἱερατείαν λαμβάνοντες ἐντολὴν ἔχουσιν ἀποδεκατοῦν τὸν λαὸν κατὰ τὸν νόμον, τοῦτ' ἔστιν τοὺς ἀδελφοὺς αὐτῶν, καίπερ ἐξεληλυθότας ἐκ τῆς ὀσφύος Ἀβραάμ· 6 ὁ δὲ μὴ γενεαλογούμενος ἐξ αὐτῶν δεδεκάτωκεν Ἀβραάμ, καὶ τὸν ἔχοντα τὰς ἐπαγ-

---

14 **Εἰ**...πληθυνῶ Gn 22.17 (Sir 44.21)   16 πάσης...ὅρκος Ex 22.11   18 ἀδύνατον...θεόν Nu 23.19; 1 Sm 15.29   19 εἰσερχομένην...καταπετάσματος Lv 16.2-3, 12, 15   20 κατὰ...αἰῶνα Ps 110.4; He 5.6; 7.17

7 **1-2** Gn 14.17-20   3 ἀφωμοιωμένος...διηνεκές Ps 110.4   5 οἱ...νόμον Nu 18.21

γελίας εὐλόγηκεν. 7 χωρὶς δὲ πάσης ἀντιλογίας τὸ ἔλαττον ὑπὸ τοῦ κρείττονος εὐλογεῖται. 8 καὶ ὧδε μὲν δεκάτας ἀποθνῄσκοντες ἄνθρωποι λαμβάνουσιν, ἐκεῖ δὲ μαρτυρούμενος ὅτι ζῇ. 9 καὶ ὡς ἔπος εἰπεῖν, δι' Ἀβραὰμ καὶ Λευὶ ὁ δεκάτας λαμβάνων δεδεκάτωται, 10 ἔτι γὰρ ἐν τῇ ὀσφύϊ τοῦ πατρὸς ἦν ὅτε **συνήντησεν αὐτῷ Μελχισέδεκ.**

11 Εἰ μὲν οὖν τελείωσις διὰ τῆς Λευιτικῆς ἱερωσύνης ἦν, ὁ λαὸς γὰρ ἐπ' αὐτῆς νενομοθέτηται, τίς ἔτι χρεία **κατὰ τὴν τάξιν Μελχισέδεκ** ἕτερον ἀνίστασθαι **ἱερέα** καὶ οὐ **κατὰ τὴν τάξιν** Ἀαρὼν λέγεσθαι; 12 μετατιθεμένης γὰρ τῆς ἱερωσύνης ἐξ ἀνάγκης καὶ νόμου μετάθεσις γίνεται. 13 ἐφ' ὃν γὰρ λέγεται ταῦτα φυλῆς ἑτέρας μετέσχηκεν, ἀφ' ἧς οὐδεὶς προσέσχεν τῷ θυσιαστηρίῳ· 14 πρόδηλον γὰρ ὅτι ἐξ Ἰούδα ἀνατέταλκεν ὁ κύριος ἡμῶν, εἰς ἣν φυλὴν περὶ ἱερέων οὐδὲν Μωϋσῆς ἐλάλησεν. 15 καὶ περισσότερον ἔτι κατάδηλόν ἐστιν, εἰ **κατὰ τὴν ὁμοιότητα Μελχισέδεκ** ἀνίσταται **ἱερεὺς** ἕτερος, 16 ὃς οὐ κατὰ νόμον ἐντολῆς σαρκίνης γέγονεν ἀλλὰ κατὰ δύναμιν ζωῆς ἀκαταλύτου, 17 μαρτυρεῖται γὰρ ὅτι

**Σὺ ἱερεὺς εἰς τὸν αἰῶνα
κατὰ τὴν τάξιν Μελχισέδεκ.**

18 ἀθέτησις μὲν γὰρ γίνεται προαγούσης ἐντολῆς[a] διὰ τὸ αὐτῆς ἀσθενὲς καὶ ἀνωφελές,[a] 19 οὐδὲν γὰρ ἐτελείωσεν ὁ νόμος,[a] ἐπεισαγωγὴ δὲ κρείττονος ἐλπίδος, δι' ἧς ἐγγίζομεν τῷ θεῷ.

20 Καὶ καθ' ὅσον οὐ χωρὶς ὀρκωμοσίας, [b] [c]οἱ μὲν γὰρ χωρὶς ὀρκωμοσίας εἰσὶν ἱερεῖς γεγονότες, 21[c] ὁ δὲ μετὰ ὀρκωμοσίας διὰ τοῦ λέγοντος πρὸς αὐτόν,

---

a a a **18-19** a none, a minor, a minor: TR WH Bov Nes BF² ‖ a none, a minor, a major: NEB ‖ a none, a major, a minor: AV ‖ a none, a parens, a parens: RV ASV RSV TT ‖ a none, a dash, a dash: Zür (Jer) Seg ‖ a dash, a minor, a dash: Luth

b b **20-21** b b no dashes or parens: TR RSV NEB TT Luth Jer Seg ‖ b parens, b parens: WH AV RV ASV ‖ b dash, b dash: Bov Nes BF² Zür

c c **20-21** c no number, c number 21: TR^red WH Bov Nes BF² TT Zür Luth Jer ‖ c number 21, c no number: TR^ed AV RV ASV RSV NEB Seg

14 ἐξ Ἰούδα...ἡμῶν Gn 49.10; Is 11.1; Mt 2.6; Re 5.5 **17** Σύ...Μελχισέδεκ Ps 110.4 (He 5.6; 6.20) **19** οὐδὲν...νόμος He 9.9

---

blessed him who received God's promises. 7 There is no doubt that the one who blesses is greater than the one who is blessed. 8 In the case of the priests, the tenth is collected by men who die; but as for Melchizedek, the tenth was collected by one who lives, as the scripture says. 9 And, so to speak, when Abraham paid the tenth, Levi (whose descendants collect the tenth) also paid it. 10 For Levi had not yet been born, but was, so to speak, in the body of his ancestor Abraham when Melchizedek met him.

11 It was on the basis of the Levitical priesthood that the Law was given to the people of Israel. Now, if the work of the Levitical priests had been perfect, there would have been no need for a different kind of priest to appear, one who is in the priestly order of Melchizedek, not in Aaron's order. 12 For when the priesthood is changed, there also has to be a change of the law. 13 And our Lord, of whom these things are said, belonged to a different tribe; and no member of his tribe ever served as a priest at the altar. 14 It is well known that he was born a member of the tribe of Judah; and Moses did not mention this tribe when he spoke of priests.

Another Priest, like Melchizedek

15 The matter becomes even plainer: a different priest has appeared, who is like Melchizedek. 16 He was not made a priest by human rules and regulations; he became a priest through the power of a life which has no end. 17 For the scripture says, "You will be a priest for ever, in the priestly order of Melchizedek." 18 The old rule, then, is set aside, because it was weak and useless. 19 For the Law of Moses could not make anything perfect. And now a better hope has been brought in, through which we come near to God.

20 In addition, there is also God's vow. There was no such vow when the others were made priests. 21 But Jesus became a priest by means of a vow, when God said to him,

"The Lord has made a vow,
And will not change his mind:
'You will be a priest for ever.' "
[22] This difference, then, makes Jesus the guarantee also of a better covenant.

[23] There is another difference: those other priests were many because they died and could not continue their work. [24] But Jesus lives on for ever, and his work as priest does not pass on to someone else. [25] And so he is able, now and always, to save those who come to God through him, because he lives for ever to plead with God for them.

[26] Jesus, then, is the High Priest that meets our needs! He is holy; he has no fault or sin in him; he has been set apart from sinful men and raised above the heavens. [27] He is not like other high priests; he does not need to offer sacrifices every day, for his own sins first, and then for the sins of the people. He offered one sacrifice, once and for all, when he offered himself. [28] The Law of Moses appoints men who are imperfect to be high priests; but the word of God's vow, which came later than the Law, appoints the Son, who has been made perfect for ever.

Jesus Our High Priest

8 Here is the whole point of what we are saying: we have such a high priest as this, who sits at the right of the throne of the Divine Majesty in heaven. [2] He serves as high priest in the Most Holy Place, that is, in the real tent which was put up by the Lord, not by man. [3] Every high priest is appointed to offer gifts and animal sacrifices to God; and so our high priest must also have something to offer. [4] If he were on earth,

"Ωμοσεν κύριος,
    καὶ οὐ μεταμεληθήσεται,
Σὺ ἱερεὺς εἰς τὸν αἰῶνα, [b]
[22] κατὰ τοσοῦτο καὶ κρείττονος διαθήκης γέγονεν ἔγγυος Ἰησοῦς. [23] καὶ οἱ μὲν πλείονές εἰσιν γεγονότες ἱερεῖς διὰ τὸ θανάτῳ κωλύεσθαι παραμένειν· [24] ὁ δὲ διὰ τὸ μένειν αὐτὸν εἰς τὸν αἰῶνα ἀπαράβατον ἔχει τὴν ἱερωσύνην· [25] ὅθεν καὶ σῴζειν εἰς τὸ παντελὲς δύναται τοὺς προσερχομένους δι' αὐτοῦ τῷ θεῷ, πάντοτε ζῶν εἰς τὸ ἐντυγχάνειν ὑπὲρ αὐτῶν.

[26] Τοιοῦτος γὰρ ἡμῖν καὶ ἔπρεπεν ἀρχιερεύς, ὅσιος, ἄκακος, ἀμίαντος, κεχωρισμένος ἀπὸ τῶν ἁμαρτωλῶν, καὶ ὑψηλότερος τῶν οὐρανῶν γενόμενος· [27] ὃς οὐκ ἔχει καθ' ἡμέραν ἀνάγκην, ὥσπερ οἱ ἀρχιερεῖς, πρότερον ὑπὲρ τῶν ἰδίων ἁμαρτιῶν θυσίας ἀναφέρειν, ἔπειτα τῶν τοῦ λαοῦ· [d]τοῦτο γὰρ ἐποίησεν ἐφάπαξ ἑαυτὸν ἀνενέγκας.[d] [28] ὁ νόμος γὰρ ἀνθρώπους καθίστησιν ἀρχιερεῖς ἔχοντας ἀσθένειαν, ὁ λόγος δὲ τῆς ὁρκωμοσίας τῆς μετὰ τὸν νόμον υἱόν[e] εἰς τὸν αἰῶνα τετελειωμένον.

The High Priest of a New and Better Covenant

8 Κεφάλαιον δὲ ἐπὶ τοῖς λεγομένοις, τοιοῦτον ἔχομεν ἀρχιερέα, ὃς ἐκάθισεν ἐν δεξιᾷ τοῦ θρόνου τῆς μεγαλωσύνης ἐν τοῖς οὐρανοῖς, [2] τῶν ἁγίων λειτουργὸς καὶ τῆς σκηνῆς τῆς ἀληθινῆς, ἣν ἔπηξεν ὁ κύριος, οὐκ ἄνθρωπος. [3] πᾶς γὰρ ἀρχιερεὺς εἰς τὸ προσφέρειν δῶρά τε καὶ θυσίας καθίσταται· ὅθεν ἀναγκαῖον ἔχειν τι καὶ τοῦτον ὃ προσενέγκῃ. [4] εἰ μὲν οὖν ἦν ἐπὶ γῆς,

---

[d] [d] **27** d d no parens: TR Bov Nes BF² AV RV ASV RSV NEB TT Zür Luth Jer Seg ∥ d parens, d parens: WH

[e] **28** e none: TR Bov Nes BF² RSV TT Zür? Luth? Jer Seg ∥ e minor: WH AV RV ASV NEB Zür? Luth?

21 Ὤμοσεν...αἰῶνα Ps 110.4 (He 5.6; 6.20; 7.17)   **22** κρείττονος...Ἰησοῦς He 8.6; 12.24   **25** πάντοτε...αὐτῶν Ro 8.34; 1 Jn 2.1   **26** ἡμῖν...ἀρχιερεύς He 3.1; 4.14; 6.20; 8.1; 9.11   **27** ὥσπερ...λαοῦ Lv 9.7; 16.6, 15   **28** ὁ νόμος...ἀσθένειαν He 5.1-2

8 1 τοιοῦτον ἔχομεν ἀρχιερέα He 3.11; 4.14; 6.20; 7.26; 9.11   ἐκάθισεν...οὐρανοῖς Ps 110.1; Mt 22.44; Mk 16.19; Ac 2.34; Eph 1.20; He 1.3; 10.12; 12.2   **2** τῆς σκηνῆς...κύριος Nu 24.6 LXX

οὐδ' ἂν ἦν ἱερεύς, ὄντων τῶν προσφερόντων κατὰ νόμον τὰ δῶρα· ^a5 οἵτινες ὑποδείγματι καὶ σκιᾷ λατρεύουσιν τῶν ἐπουρανίων, καθὼς κεχρημάτισται Μωϋσῆς μέλλων ἐπιτελεῖν τὴν σκηνήν, **Ὅρα** γάρ, φησίν, **ποιήσεις πάντα κατὰ τὸν τύπον τὸν δειχθέντα σοι ἐν τῷ ὄρει·**^a 6 νυνὶ δὲ διαφορωτέρας τέτυχεν λειτουργίας, ὅσῳ καὶ κρείττονός ἐστιν διαθήκης μεσίτης, ἥτις ἐπὶ κρείττοσιν ἐπαγγελίαις νενομοθέτηται.

7 Εἰ γὰρ ἡ πρώτη ἐκείνη ἦν ἄμεμπτος, οὐκ ἂν δευτέρας ἐζητεῖτο τόπος· 8 μεμφόμενος γὰρ αὐτούς[1] λέγει,

Ἰδοὺ ἡμέραι ἔρχονται, λέγει κύριος,
   καὶ συντελέσω ἐπὶ τὸν οἶκον Ἰσραὴλ
   καὶ ἐπὶ τὸν οἶκον Ἰούδα διαθήκην καινήν,
9   **οὐ κατὰ τὴν διαθήκην ἣν ἐποίησα τοῖς πατράσιν αὐτῶν**
   ἐν ἡμέρᾳ ἐπιλαβομένου μου τῆς χειρὸς αὐτῶν
   ἐξαγαγεῖν αὐτοὺς ἐκ γῆς Αἰγύπτου,
ὅτι αὐτοὶ οὐκ ἐνέμειναν ἐν τῇ διαθήκῃ μου,
κἀγὼ ἠμέλησα αὐτῶν, λέγει κύριος.
10   **ὅτι αὕτη ἡ διαθήκη ἣν διαθήσομαι τῷ οἴκῳ Ἰσραὴλ**
   μετὰ τὰς ἡμέρας ἐκείνας, λέγει κύριος,
   διδοὺς νόμους μου εἰς τὴν διάνοιαν αὐτῶν,
   καὶ ἐπὶ καρδίας αὐτῶν ἐπιγράψω αὐτούς,
   καὶ ἔσομαι αὐτοῖς εἰς θεὸν
   καὶ αὐτοὶ ἔσονταί μοι εἰς λαόν.
11   **καὶ οὐ μὴ διδάξωσιν ἕκαστος τὸν πολίτην[2] αὐτοῦ**

---

[1] 8 {C} αὐτούς ℵ* A D* I K P Ψ 33 81 88 326 436 2127 2495 it^{ar,c,d,dem,} ^{div,e,f,x,z} vg cop^{sa,bo,fay} arm Chrysostom^{1/2} Euthalius Theodoret ‖ αὐτοῖς 𝔭⁴⁶ ℵ^c B D^c 104 181 330 451 614 629 630 1241 1739 1877 1881 1962 1984 1985 2492 *Byz Lect* Origen Chrysostom^{1/2} John-Damascus

[2] 11 {B} πολίτην 𝔭⁴⁶ ℵ A B D K 33 88 181 330 451 614 1241 1739 1877 1881 1962 1984^{vid} 2127 2492 2495 *Byz Lect* it^{d,e} syr^{p,h} cop^{sa,bo,fay} arm

^{a a} 5 *a a* no parens: TR Bov Nes BF² AV RV ASV RSV NEB TT Zür Luth Jer Seg ‖ *a* parens, *a* parens: WH

5 οἵτινες...λατρεύουσιν Col 2.17   Ὅρα...ὄρει Ex 25.40   6 κρείττονος...μεσίτης He 7.22; 9.15; 12.24   8–12 Ἰδού...ἔτι Jr 31.31–34   10 He 10.16

he would not be a priest at all, since there are priests who offer the gifts according to the Jewish Law. 5 The work they do as priests is really only a copy and a shadow of what is in heaven. It is the same as it was with Moses. When he was about to put up the tent, God told him, "Be sure to make everything like the pattern you were shown on the mountain." 6 But, as it is, Jesus has been given priestly work which is much greater than theirs, just as the covenant which he arranged between God and men is a better one, because it is based on promises of better things.

7 If there had been nothing wrong with the first covenant, there would have been no need for a second one. 8 But God finds fault with his people when he says:

   "The days are coming, says the Lord,
   When I will draw up a new covenant
     with the people of Israel,
   And with the tribe of Judah.
9 It will not be like the covenant that
     I made with their ancestors
   On the day I took them by the hand
     to lead them out of the land of
     Egypt.
   They were not faithful to the covenant I made with them,
   And so I paid no attention to them,
     says the Lord.
10 Now, this is the covenant that I will
     draw up with the people of Israel
   After those days, says the Lord:
   I will put my laws in their minds,
   And I will write them on their hearts.
   I will be their God,
   And they shall be my people.
11 None of them will have to teach his
     fellow-citizen,

Nor will anyone have to tell his
fellow-countryman,
'Know the Lord.'
For they will all know me,
From the least to the greatest of
them.
[12] I will have mercy on their trans-
gressions,
And I will no longer remember their
sins.''
[13] By speaking of a new covenant, God
has made the first one old; and anything
that is getting old and worn out will
soon disappear.

Earthly and Heavenly Worship

9 The first covenant had rules for worship and a man-made place for worship
as well. [2] A tent was put up, the outside
one, which was called the Holy Place.
In it were the lamp, the table, and the
bread offered to God. [3] Behind the second
curtain was the tent called the Most
Holy Place. [4] In it were the gold altar
for the burning of incense, and the box
of the covenant, all covered with gold.
The box contained the gold jar with the
manna in it, Aaron's rod that had
sprouted leaves, and the two stone tablets with the words of the covenant
written on them. [5] Above the box were
the glorious creatures representing the
Divine Presence, with their wings spread
over the place where sins were forgiven.
But this is not the time to explain everything in detail.

[6] After these arrangements are made,
the priests go into the outside tent every
day to perform their duties; [7] but only
the High Priest goes into the inside tent,
and he does so only once a year. He takes
blood with him which he offers to God
on behalf of himself and for the sins
which the people have committed without knowing they were sinning. [8] The
Holy Spirit clearly teaches from all these
arrangements that the way into the Most
Holy Place has not yet been opened as
long as the outside tent still stands.

καὶ ἕκαστος τὸν ἀδελφὸν αὐτοῦ, λέγων, Γνῶθι
τὸν κύριον,
ὅτι πάντες εἰδήσουσίν με
ἀπὸ μικροῦ ἕως μεγάλου αὐτῶν.
12 ὅτι ἵλεως ἔσομαι ταῖς ἀδικίαις αὐτῶν,
καὶ τῶν ἁμαρτιῶν αὐτῶν οὐ μὴ μνησθῶ ἔτι.
13 ἐν τῷ λέγειν **Καινὴν** πεπαλαίωκεν τὴν πρώτην· τὸ
δὲ παλαιούμενον καὶ γηράσκον ἐγγὺς ἀφανισμοῦ.

The Earthly and the Heavenly Sanctuaries

9 Εἶχε μὲν οὖν [καὶ] ἡ πρώτη δικαιώματα λατρείας τό
τε ἅγιον κοσμικόν. **2** σκηνὴ γὰρ κατεσκευάσθη ἡ πρώτη
ἐν ᾗ ἥ τε λυχνία καὶ ἡ τράπεζα καὶ ἡ πρόθεσις τῶν
ἄρτων, ἥτις λέγεται Ἅγια· **3** μετὰ δὲ τὸ δεύτερον
καταπέτασμα σκηνὴ ἡ λεγομένη Ἅγια Ἁγίων, **4** χρυσοῦν ἔχουσα θυμιατήριον καὶ τὴν κιβωτὸν τῆς διαθήκης
περικεκαλυμμένην πάντοθεν χρυσίῳ, ἐν ᾗ στάμνος χρυσῆ
ἔχουσα τὸ μάννα καὶ ἡ ῥάβδος Ἀαρὼν ἡ βλαστήσασα
καὶ αἱ πλάκες τῆς διαθήκης, **5** ὑπεράνω δὲ αὐτῆς Χερου-
βεὶν δόξης κατασκιάζοντα τὸ ἱλαστήριον· περὶ ὧν οὐκ
ἔστιν νῦν λέγειν κατὰ μέρος.

6 Τούτων δὲ οὕτως κατεσκευασμένων, εἰς μὲν τὴν
πρώτην σκηνὴν διὰ παντὸς εἰσίασιν οἱ ἱερεῖς τὰς λατρείας
ἐπιτελοῦντες, **7** εἰς δὲ τὴν δευτέραν ἅπαξ τοῦ ἐνιαυτοῦ
μόνος ὁ ἀρχιερεύς, οὐ χωρὶς αἵματος, ὃ προσφέρει ὑπὲρ
ἑαυτοῦ καὶ τῶν τοῦ λαοῦ ἀγνοημάτων, **8** τοῦτο δηλοῦντος
τοῦ πνεύματος τοῦ ἁγίου, μήπω πεφανερῶσθαι τὴν τῶν
ἁγίων ὁδὸν ἔτι τῆς πρώτης σκηνῆς ἐχούσης στάσιν,

Chrysostom Theodoret John-Damascus ‖ πλησίον P 81 104 326 436 629 630
1985 it^ar,c,dem,div,f,z vg syr^hmg eth Chrysostom Cyril Euthalius Theophylact ‖ omit πολίτην αὐτοῦ καὶ ἕκαστος τόν it^x

12 τῶν...ἔτι He 10.17
9 2 σκηνὴ γὰρ κατεσκευάσθη Ex 26.1–30   ἥ τε λυχνία Ex 25.31–40   ἡ τράπεζα...ἄρτων
Ex 25.23–30   **3** Ex 26.31–33   **4** χρυσοῦν ἔχουσα θυμιατήριον Ex 30.1–6   τὴν κιβωτὸν...
χρυσίῳ Ex 25.10–16   στάμνος...μάννα Ex 16.33   ἡ ῥάβδος...βλαστήσασα Nu 17.8–10
αἱ πλάκες τῆς διαθήκης Ex 25.16; Dt 10.3–5   **5** ὑπεράνω...ἱλαστήριον Ex 25.18–22   **6** εἰς
...ἐπιτελοῦντες Nu 18.2–6   **7** Ex 30.10; Lv 16.2, 14, 15

9 ᵃἥτις παραβολὴ εἰς τὸν καιρὸν τὸν ἐνεστηκότα,ᵃ καθ’ ἣν δῶρά τε καὶ θυσίαι προσφέρονται μὴ δυνάμεναι κατὰ συνείδησιν τελειῶσαι τὸν λατρεύοντα, **10** μόνον ἐπὶ βρώμασιν καὶ πόμασιν καὶ διαφόροις βαπτισμοῖς, δικαιώματα¹ σαρκὸς μέχρι καιροῦ διορθώσεως ἐπικείμενα.

11 Χριστὸς δὲ παραγενόμενος ἀρχιερεὺς τῶν γενομένων² ἀγαθῶνᵇ διὰ τῆς μείζονος καὶ τελειοτέρας σκηνῆς οὐ χειροποιήτου, τοῦτ’ ἔστιν οὐ ταύτης τῆς κτίσεως, **12** οὐδὲ δι’ αἵματος τράγων καὶ μόσχων διὰ δὲ τοῦ ἰδίου αἵματος, εἰσῆλθεν ἐφάπαξ εἰς τὰ ἅγια, αἰωνίαν λύτρωσιν εὑράμενος. **13** εἰ γὰρ τὸ αἷμα τράγων καὶ ταύρων καὶ σποδὸς δαμάλεως ῥαντίζουσα τοὺς κεκοινωμένους ἁγιάζει πρὸς τὴν τῆς σαρκὸς καθαρότητα, **14** πόσῳ μᾶλλον τὸ αἷμα τοῦ Χριστοῦ, ὃς διὰ πνεύματος αἰωνίου ἑαυτὸν προσήνεγκεν ἄμωμον τῷ θεῷ, καθαριεῖ τὴν συνείδησιν ἡμῶν³ ἀπὸ νεκρῶν ἔργων εἰς τὸ λατρεύειν θεῷ ζῶντι.ᶜ

[9] This is a figure which refers to the present time. It means that the gifts and animal sacrifices offered to God cannot make the worshiper's heart perfect. [10] They have to do only with food, drink, and various cleansing ceremonies. These are all outward rules, which apply only until the time when God will reform all things.

[11] But Christ has already come as the High Priest of the good things that are already here. The tent in which he serves is greater and more perfect; it is not made by men, that is, it is not a part of this created world. [12] When Christ went through the tent and entered once and for all into the Most Holy Place, he did not take the blood of goats and calves to offer as sacrifice; rather, he took his own blood and obtained eternal salvation for us. [13] The blood of goats and bulls and the ashes of the burnt calf are sprinkled on the people who are ritually unclean, and make them clean by taking away their ritual impurity. [14] Since this is true, how much more is accomplished by the blood of Christ! Through the eternal Spirit he offered himself as a perfect sacrifice to God. His blood will make our consciences clean from useless works, so that we may serve the living God.

---

¹ **10** {B} βαπτισμοῖς, δικαιώματα 𝔭⁴⁶ ℵ* A I P 33 81 104 436 1739 1881 2127 syrᵖ copˢᵃ,ᵇᵒ,ᶠᵃʸᵛⁱᵈ arm Origen Cyril Euthalius ‖ βαπτισμοῖς, δικαίωμα D* itᵈ·ᵉ ‖ βαπτισμοῖς καὶ δικαιώματα ℵᶜ B 451 2492 ‖ βαπτισμοῖς καὶ δικαιώμασιν Dᶜ K 88 181 326 330 614 629 630 1241 1877 1962 1984 1985 2495 *Byz Lect* itᵃʳ,ᶜ,ᵈᵉᵐ,ᵈⁱᵛ,(ᶠ),(ˣ),ᶻ vg syrʰ Chrysostom Theodoret John-Damascus

² **11** {C} γενομένων (𝔭⁴⁶ γεναμένων) B D* 1739 itᵈ·ᵉ syrᵖ,ʰ,ᵖᵃˡ Origen (Aphraates) Cyril-Jerusalem Chrysostomᵍʳ,ˡᵃᵗ ‖ μελλόντων ℵ A Dᶜ Iᵛⁱᵈ K P 33 81 88 104 181 326 330 436 451 614 629 630 1241 1877 1881 1962 1984 1985 2127 2492 2495 *Byz Lect* itᵃʳ,ᶜ,ᵈᵉᵐ,ᵈⁱᵛ,ᶠ,(ᵗ),ˣ,ᶻ vg syrʰᵐᵍ copˢᵃ,ᵇᵒ,ᶠᵃʸ arm eth Eusebius Ephraem Cyril-Jerusalem Chrysostom Cyril Proclus Euthalius Theodoret Ps-Athanasius Cosmos John-Damascus

³ **14** {C} ἡμῶν A D* K P 451 1739* 1877 1984 1985 2492 itᵈ,ᵈᵉᵐ,ᵈⁱᵛ,ᵉ,ᵍⁱᵍ

ᵃ ᵃ **9** *a a* no parens: TR WH Bov Nes BF² AV RV ASV TT Zür Luth Jer Seg ‖ *a* parens, *a* parens: RSV NEB

ᵇ **11** *b* none: TR WH ‖ *b* minor: Bov Nes BF² AV RV ASV RSV (NEB) (TT) Zür Luth Jer Seg

ᶜ **14** *c* statement: WH Bov Nes BF² RSV NEB Zür Jer ‖ *c* question: TR AV RV ASV ‖ *c* exclamation: TT Luth Seg

---

9 δῶρα...λατρεύοντα He 10.1–2 **10** μόνον ἐπὶ βρώμασιν Lv 11.2 διαφόροις βαπτισμοῖς Lv 11.25; 15.18; Nu 19.13 **11** Χριστὸς...ἀρχιερεύς He 3.11; 4.14; 6.20; 7.26; 8.1 τῶν γενομένων ἀγαθῶν He 10.1 **13** εἰ...ταύρων Lv 16.3, 14, 15; He 10.4 σποδὸς δαμάλεως Nu 19.9, 17–19 **14** τὸ αἷμα...ἡμῶν 1 Pe 1.18–19; 1 Jn 1.7 ἀπὸ...ζῶντι He 6.1

[15] For this reason Christ is the one who arranges a new covenant, so that those who have been called by God may receive the eternal blessings that God has promised. This can be done because there has been a death which sets men free from the wrongs they did while they were under the first covenant.

[16] Where there is a will, it has to be proved that the man who made it has died. [17] For a will means nothing while the man who made it is alive; it goes into effect only after his death. [18] That is why even the first covenant was made good only with the use of blood. [19] First, Moses told the people all the commandments, as set forth in the Law. Then he took the blood of calves, together with water, and sprinkled both the book of the Law and all the people with hyssop and scarlet wool. [20] He said, "This is the blood which seals the covenant that God has commanded you to obey." [21] In the same way, Moses also sprinkled the blood on the tent and over all the things used in worship. [22] Indeed, according to the Law, almost everything is made clean by blood; and sins are forgiven only if blood is poured out.

Christ's Sacrifice Takes Away Sins

[23] These things, which are copies of the heavenly originals, had to be made clean in this way. But the heavenly things themselves require much better sacrifices. [24] For Christ did not go into a holy place

[15] Καὶ διὰ τοῦτο διαθήκης καινῆς μεσίτης ἐστίν, ὅπως θανάτου γενομένου εἰς ἀπολύτρωσιν τῶν ἐπὶ τῇ πρώτῃ διαθήκῃ παραβάσεων τὴν ἐπαγγελίαν λάβωσιν οἱ κεκλημένοι τῆς αἰωνίου κληρονομίας. [16] ὅπου γὰρ διαθήκη, θάνατον ἀνάγκη φέρεσθαι τοῦ διαθεμένου· [17] διαθήκη γὰρ ἐπὶ νεκροῖς βεβαία, ἐπεὶ μήποτε ἰσχύει ὅτε ζῇ ὁ διαθέμενος.[d] [18] ὅθεν οὐδὲ ἡ πρώτη χωρὶς αἵματος ἐγκεκαίνισται· [19] λαληθείσης γὰρ πάσης ἐντολῆς κατὰ τὸν νόμον ὑπὸ Μωϋσέως παντὶ τῷ λαῷ, λαβὼν τὸ αἷμα τῶν μόσχων[4] μετὰ ὕδατος καὶ ἐρίου κοκκίνου καὶ ὑσσώπου αὐτό τε τὸ βιβλίον καὶ πάντα τὸν λαὸν ἐράντισεν, [20] λέγων, **Τοῦτο τὸ αἷμα τῆς διαθήκης ἧς ἐνετείλατο πρὸς ὑμᾶς ὁ θεός·** [21] καὶ τὴν σκηνὴν δὲ καὶ πάντα τὰ σκεύη τῆς λειτουργίας τῷ αἵματι ὁμοίως ἐράντισεν. [22] καὶ σχεδὸν ἐν αἵματι πάντα καθαρίζεται κατὰ τὸν νόμον, καὶ χωρὶς αἱματεκχυσίας οὐ γίνεται ἄφεσις.

Sin Put Away by Christ's Sacrifice

[23] Ἀνάγκη οὖν τὰ μὲν ὑποδείγματα τῶν ἐν τοῖς οὐρανοῖς τούτοις καθαρίζεσθαι, αὐτὰ δὲ τὰ ἐπουράνια κρείττοσιν θυσίαις παρὰ ταύτας. [24] οὐ γὰρ εἰς χειρο-

vg[cl] syr[p] cop[bomss] Athanasius Ephraem Ambrose Chrysostom[lat] Cyril Euthalius Theodoret ‖ ὑμῶν ℵ D[c] 33 81 88 104 181 326 330 436 629 630 1241 1739[c] 1881 1962 2127 2495 Byz Lect it[ar,c,f,t,x,z] vg[ww] syr[h,pal] cop[sa,bomss] arm eth Athanasius Didymus Macarius Chrysostom John-Damascus ‖ αὐτῶν cop[fay] ‖ omit 614

[4] **19** {C} μόσχων 𝔭[46] ℵ[c] K Ψ 181 1241 1739 1877 1881 1984 1985 2495 syr[p,h,pal] Origen Chrysostom ‖ μόσχων καὶ τράγων P 33 88 104 330 614 630 1962 2127 Byz Lect cop[bo,fay] Theodoret John-Damascus ‖ μόσχων καὶ τῶν τράγων ℵ* A C 81 326 436 451 629 2492 cop[sa] Euthalius Theodoret ‖ μόσχων καὶ τράγων (or τῶν τράγων) it[ar,c,dem,div,f,x,z] vg arm ‖ τράγων καὶ τῶν μόσχων D it[d,e,(t)]

[d] **17** d statement: TR WH Bov Nes BF² AV RV[mg] ASV RSV NEB TT Zür Luth Jer Seg ‖ d question: WH[mg] RV ASV[mg]

15 διαθήκης...ἐστίν He 7.22; 8.6; 12.24   **19** Ex 24.3, 6–8 ἐρίου...ὑσσώπου Lv 14.4; Nu 19.6 **20** Τοῦτο...θεός Ex 24.8   **21** Lv 8.15, 19   **22** χωρὶς...ἄφεσις Lv 17.11

ποίητα εἰσῆλθεν ἅγια Χριστός, ἀντίτυπα τῶν ἀληθινῶν, ἀλλ᾽ εἰς αὐτὸν τὸν οὐρανόν, νῦν ἐμφανισθῆναι τῷ προσώπῳ τοῦ θεοῦ ὑπὲρ ἡμῶν· 25 οὐδ᾽ ἵνα πολλάκις προσφέρῃ ἑαυτόν, ὥσπερ ὁ ἀρχιερεὺς εἰσέρχεται εἰς τὰ ἅγια κατ᾽ ἐνιαυτὸν ἐν αἵματι ἀλλοτρίῳ, 26 ἐπεὶ ἔδει αὐτὸν πολλάκις παθεῖν ἀπὸ καταβολῆς κόσμου· νυνὶ δὲ ἅπαξ ἐπὶ συντελείᾳ τῶν αἰώνων εἰς ἀθέτησιν [τῆς] ἁμαρτίας διὰ τῆς θυσίας αὐτοῦ πεφανέρωται. 27 καὶ καθ᾽ ὅσον ἀπόκειται τοῖς ἀνθρώποις ἅπαξ ἀποθανεῖν, μετὰ δὲ τοῦτο κρίσις, 28 οὕτως καὶ ὁ Χριστός, ἅπαξ προσενεχθεὶς εἰς τὸ πολλῶν ἀνενεγκεῖν ἁμαρτίας, ἐκ δευτέρου χωρὶς ἁμαρτίας ὀφθήσεται τοῖς αὐτὸν ἀπεκδεχομένοις εἰς σωτηρίαν.

10 Σκιὰν γὰρ ἔχων ὁ νόμος τῶν μελλόντων ἀγαθῶν, οὐκ αὐτὴν[1] τὴν εἰκόνα τῶν πραγμάτων, κατ᾽ ἐνιαυτὸν ταῖς αὐταῖς θυσίαις ἃς προσφέρουσιν εἰς τὸ διηνεκὲς οὐδέποτε δύναται[2] τοὺς προσερχομένους τελειῶσαι· 2 ἐπεὶ οὐκ ἂν ἐπαύσαντο προσφερόμεναι,[a] διὰ τὸ μηδεμίαν ἔχειν ἔτι συνείδησιν ἁμαρτιῶν τοὺς λατρεύοντας ἅπαξ κεκαθαρισμένους;[a] 3 ἀλλ᾽ ἐν αὐταῖς ἀνάμνησις ἁμαρτιῶν κατ᾽ ἐνιαυτόν, 4 ἀδύνατον γὰρ αἷμα ταύρων καὶ τράγων ἀφαιρεῖν ἁμαρτίας.

---

[1] 1 {A} οὐκ αὐτήν ℵ A C D H^vid K P Ψ 33 81 88 104 181 326 330 436 451 614 629 630 1241 1739 1877 1881 1962 1984 2127 2492 2495 *Byz Lect* it^ar,c,(d), dem,div,(e),f,r¹,x,z vg syr^p,h cop^sa,bo,fay ∥ οὐ κατά 69 ∥ οὐκ αὐτῶν 1908 ∥ καί 𝔭⁴⁶ ∥ καὶ οὐκ αὐτήν arm

[2] 1 {C} δύναται 𝔭⁴⁶ D*·c H K Ψ^vid 88 181 326 629 630 1739 1881 1962 *Byz* It^c,d,dem,div,e,f,r¹,x vg Origen Chrysostom Theodoret Ps-Oecumenius ∥ δύνανται ℵ A C D^b P 33 81 104 330 436 451 614 1241 1877 1984 2127 2492 2495 *Lect* it^ar,z* syr^p,h cop^sa,bo,fay arm Origen^lat Ephraem Chrysostom Euthalius John-Damascus Theophylact

a a 2 *a minor, a question*: TR WH Bov Nes BF² RV (TT) Zür Jer (Seg) ∥ *a question, a statement*: AV ASV RSV ∥ *a minor, a statement*: NEB Luth

24 νῦν...ἡμῶν 1 Jn 2.1   27 ἀπόκειται...ἀποθανεῖν Gn 3.19   28 ὁ Χριστός, ἅπαξ προσενεχθείς He 10.10   πολλῶν ἀνενεγκεῖν ἁμαρτίας Is 53.12; 1 Pe 2.24   ἐκ... ἀπεκδεχομένοις Php 3.20; 2 Tm 4.8
10 4 αἷμα ταύρων καὶ τράγων Lv 16.15, 21; He 9.13

made by men, a copy of the real one. He went into heaven itself, where he now appears on our behalf in the presence of God. 25 The Jewish High Priest goes into the Holy Place every year with the blood of an animal. But Christ did not go in to offer himself many times; 26 for then he would have had to suffer many times ever since the creation of the world. Instead, he has now appeared once and for all, when all ages of time are nearing the end, to remove sin through the sacrifice of himself. 27 Everyone must die once, and after that be judged by God. 28 In the same manner, Christ also was offered in sacrifice once to take away the sins of many. He will appear a second time, not to deal with sin, but to save those who are waiting for him.

10 The Jewish Law is not a full and faithful model of the real things. It is only a faint outline of the good things to come. The same sacrifices are offered for ever, year after year. How can the Law, then, by means of these sacrifices make perfect the people who come to God? 2 If the people worshiping God had been made really clean from their sins, they would not feel guilty of sin any more, and all sacrifices would stop. 3 As it is, however, the sacrifices serve to remind people of their sins, year after year. 4 For the blood of bulls and goats can never take sins away.

[5] For this reason, when Christ was about to come into the world, he said to God:

"You do not want the sacrifice and offering of animals,
But you have prepared a body for me.
[6] You are not pleased with the offering of animals burned whole on the altar,
Or with sacrifices to take away sins.
[7] Then I said, 'Here am I, O God,
To do what you want me to —
Just as it is written of me in the book of the Law.' "

[8] First he said: "You neither want nor are you pleased with sacrifices and offerings of animals, or with the offering of animals burned on the altar and the sacrifices to take away sins." He said this even though all these sacrifices are offered according to the Law. [9] Then he said, "Here am I, O God, to do what you want me to do." So God does away with all the old sacrifices and puts the sacrifice of Christ in their place. [10] Because Jesus Christ did what God wanted him to do, we are all made clean from sin by the offering that he made of his own body, once and for all.

[11] Every Jewish priest stands and performs his services every day and offers the same sacrifices many times. But these sacrifices can never take away sins. [12] Christ, however, offered one sacrifice for sins, an offering that is good for ever, and then sat down at the right side of God. [13] There he now waits until God puts his enemies as a footstool under

[5] Διὸ εἰσερχόμενος εἰς τὸν κόσμον λέγει,
   Θυσίαν καὶ προσφορὰν οὐκ ἠθέλησας,
   σῶμα δὲ κατηρτίσω μοι·
[6] **ὁλοκαυτώματα καὶ περὶ ἁμαρτίας**
   οὐκ εὐδόκησας.
[7] **τότε εἶπον,**
   ᾿Ιδοὺ ἥκω,
   ἐν κεφαλίδι βιβλίου γέγραπται περὶ ἐμοῦ,
   τοῦ ποιῆσαι, ὁ θεός, τὸ θέλημά σου.
[8] ἀνώτερον λέγων ὅτι **Θυσίας καὶ προσφορὰς καὶ ὁλοκαυτώματα καὶ περὶ ἁμαρτίας οὐκ ἠθέλησας οὐδὲ εὐδόκησας,**[b] αἵτινες κατὰ νόμον προσφέρονται,[b] [9] τότε
εἴρηκεν, ᾿Ιδοὺ ἥκω τοῦ ποιῆσαι τὸ θέλημά σου.[c] ἀναιρεῖ
τὸ πρῶτον ἵνα τὸ δεύτερον στήσῃ·[c] [10] ἐν ᾧ θελήματι
ἡγιασμένοι ἐσμὲν διὰ τῆς προσφορᾶς τοῦ σώματος
᾿Ιησοῦ Χριστοῦ ἐφάπαξ.

[11] **Καὶ** πᾶς μὲν ἱερεὺς[3] ἕστηκεν καθ᾿ ἡμέραν λει-
τουργῶν καὶ τὰς αὐτὰς πολλάκις προσφέρων θυσίας,
αἵτινες οὐδέποτε δύνανται περιελεῖν ἁμαρτίας. [12] οὗτος
δὲ μίαν ὑπὲρ ἁμαρτιῶν προσενέγκας θυσίαν[d] εἰς τὸ
διηνεκὲς[d] **ἐκάθισεν ἐν δεξιᾷ τοῦ θεοῦ,** [13] τὸ λοιπὸν ἐκδε-
χόμενος **ἕως τεθῶσιν οἱ ἐχθροὶ αὐτοῦ ὑποπόδιον τῶν**

[3] [11] {B} ἱερεύς 𝔭[13,46] ℵ D K Ψ 33 81 326 330 629 1241 1739 1881 1984 2495 *Byz Lect* it[ar,c,d,dem,div,e,f,r1,x,z] vg syr[h] cop[bo] Ephraem Chrysostom Euthalius Theodoret[comm] John-Damascus ‖ ἀρχιερεύς A C P 88 104 181 436 451 614 630 1877 1962 2127 2492 syr[p,h with *] cop[sa,fay] arm eth Cyril Theodoret[txt] Cosmos

[b b] **8** *b* minor, *b* minor: TR WH Bov Nes BF² AV ‖ *b* none, *b* major: (TT) Seg ‖ *b* minor, *b* exclamation: Luth ‖ *b* parens, *b* parens: RV ASV RSV ‖ *b* dash, *b* dash: NEB Zür Jer
[c c] **9** *c* major, *c* minor: TR Nes BF² TT ‖ *c* minor, *c* major: WH ‖ *c* major, *c* major: Bov AV RV ASV RSV NEB Zür Luth Jer Seg
[d d] **12** *d* none, *d* none: TR WH Bov Nes BF² ‖ *d* minor, *d* none: RV[mg] ASV[mg] Zür Luth Jer Seg ‖ *d* none, *d* minor: AV RV ASV RSV NEB (TT) Seg[mg]

5–7 Θυσίαν...σου Ps 40.6–8   **8** Θυσίας καὶ προσφοράς Ps 40.6   ὁλοκαυτώματα... εὐδόκησας Ps 40.6   **9** ᾿Ιδού...σου Ps 40.7   **10** ἡγιασμένοι...ἐφάπαξ He 9.12, 28   **11** πᾶς ...θυσίας Ex 29.38   **12** ἐκάθισεν...θεοῦ Ps 110.1 (Mt 22.44; Mk 16.19; Ac 2.34; Eph 1.20; He 1.3; 8.1; 12.2)   **13** ἕως...αὐτοῦ Ps 110.1

ποδῶν αὐτοῦ· **14** μιᾷ γὰρ προσφορᾷ τετελείωκεν εἰς τὸ διηνεκὲς τοὺς ἁγιαζομένους.

15 Μαρτυρεῖ δὲ ἡμῖν καὶ τὸ πνεῦμα τὸ ἅγιον· μετὰ γὰρ τὸ εἰρηκέναι,

16   Αὕτη ἡ διαθήκη ἣν διαθήσομαι πρὸς αὐτοὺς
     μετὰ τὰς ἡμέρας ἐκείνας, λέγει κύριος,
   διδοὺς νόμους μου ἐπὶ καρδίας αὐτῶν,
     καὶ ἐπὶ τὴν διάνοιαν αὐτῶν ἐπιγράψω αὐτούς, ^e

17   καὶ^e τῶν ἁμαρτιῶν αὐτῶν καὶ τῶν ἀνομιῶν αὐτῶν
     οὐ μὴ μνησθήσομαι ἔτι.

18 ὅπου δὲ ἄφεσις τούτων, οὐκέτι προσφορὰ περὶ ἁμαρτίας.

Exhortation and Warning

19 Ἔχοντες οὖν, ἀδελφοί, παρρησίαν εἰς τὴν εἴσοδον τῶν ἁγίων ἐν τῷ αἵματι Ἰησοῦ, **20** ἣν ἐνεκαίνισεν ἡμῖν ὁδὸν πρόσφατον καὶ ζῶσαν διὰ τοῦ καταπετάσματος, τοῦτ᾿ ἔστιν τῆς σαρκὸς αὐτοῦ, **21** καὶ ἱερέα μέγαν ἐπὶ τὸν οἶκον τοῦ θεοῦ, **22** προσερχώμεθα μετὰ ἀληθινῆς καρδίας ἐν πληροφορίᾳ πίστεως, ῥεραντισμένοι τὰς καρδίας ἀπὸ συνειδήσεως πονηρᾶς ^fκαὶ λελουσμένοι τὸ σῶμα ὕδατι καθαρῷ· **23**^f κατέχωμεν τὴν ὁμολογίαν τῆς ἐλπίδος ἀκλινῆ, πιστὸς γὰρ ὁ ἐπαγγειλάμενος· **24** καὶ κατανοῶμεν ἀλλήλους εἰς παροξυσμὸν ἀγάπης καὶ καλῶν ἔργων, **25** μὴ ἐγκαταλείποντες τὴν ἐπισυναγωγὴν ἑαυτῶν, καθὼς ἔθος τισίν, ἀλλὰ παρακαλοῦντες, καὶ τοσούτῳ μᾶλλον ὅσῳ βλέπετε ἐγγίζουσαν τὴν ἡμέραν.

26 Ἑκουσίως γὰρ ἁμαρτανόντων ἡμῶν μετὰ τὸ λαβεῖν τὴν ἐπίγνωσιν τῆς ἀληθείας, οὐκέτι περὶ ἁμαρτιῶν ἀπολείπεται θυσία, **27** φοβερὰ δέ τις ἐκδοχὴ κρίσεως

16-17 *e* minor, *e* none: TR Bov Nes BF² AV Zür Luth (Jer) ǁ *e* dash, *e* none: WH ǁ different construction: RV ASV RSV NEB TT Seg

22-23 *f* no number, *f* number 23: TR^{ed} WH? Bov Nes BF² AV RV ASV RSV NEB? TT Zür Luth Jer Seg ǁ *f* number 23, *f* no number: TR^{ed} WH? NEB?

---

16 Jr 31.33 (He 8.10)   **17** Jr 31.34 (He 8.12)   **19** Ἔχοντες…ἁγίων He 4.16
22 ῥεραντισμένοι…πονηρᾶς Eze 36.25   λελουσμένοι…καθαρῷ Eph 5.26   **23** κατέχωμεν …ἀκλινῆ He 4.14   **26** He 6.4-8

his feet. **14** With one sacrifice, then, he has made perfect for ever those who are clean from sin.

15 For the Holy Spirit also gives us his witness. First he says:

16 "This is the covenant that I will
     make with them
After those days, says the Lord:
I will put my laws in their hearts,
And I will write them on their
     minds."

17 And then he says, "I will not remember their sins and wicked deeds any longer." **18** So when these have been forgiven, an offering to take away sins is no longer needed.

Let Us Come Near to God

19 We have, then, brothers, complete freedom to go into the Most Holy Place by means of the death of Jesus. **20** He opened for us a new way, a living way, through the curtain — that is, through his own body. **21** We have a great priest in charge of the house of God. **22** Let us come near to God, then, with a sincere heart and a sure faith, with hearts that have been made clean from a guilty conscience, and bodies washed with pure water. **23** Let us hold on firmly to the hope we profess, because we can trust God to keep his promise. **24** Let us be concerned with one another, to help one another to show love and to do good. **25** Let us not give up the habit of meeting together, as some are doing. Instead, let us encourage one another, all the more since you see that the Day of the Lord is coming near.

26 For there is no longer any sacrifice that will take away sins if we purposely go on sinning after the truth has been made known to us. **27** Instead, all that is left is to be afraid of what will happen: the Judgment and the fierce fire which will destroy those who oppose God! [28] Anyone who disobeys the Law of Moses is put to death, without any mercy, when judged guilty from the evidence of two or three witnesses. [29] What, then, of the man who despises the Son of God? who treats as a cheap thing the blood of God's covenant which made him pure? who insults the Spirit of grace? Just think how much worse is the punishment he will deserve! [30] For we know who said, "I will take revenge, I will repay"; and who also said, "The Lord will judge his people." [31] It is a terrible thing to fall into the hands of the living God!

[32] Remember how it was with you in the past. In those days, after God's light had shone on you, you suffered many things, yet were not defeated by the struggle. [33] You were at times publicly insulted and mistreated, and at other times you were ready to join those who were being treated in this way. [34] You shared the sufferings of prisoners, and when all your belongings were seized you endured your loss gladly, because you knew that you still had for yourselves something much better, which would last for ever. [35] Do not lose your courage, then, for it brings with it a great reward. [36] You need to be patient, in order to

καὶ πυρὸς ζῆλος ἐσθίειν μέλλοντος τοὺς ὑπεναντίους. **28** ἀθετήσας τις νόμον Μωϋσέως χωρὶς οἰκτιρμῶν **ἐπὶ δυσὶν ἢ τρισὶν μάρτυσιν ἀποθνῄσκει·** **29** πόσῳ δοκεῖτε χείρονος ἀξιωθήσεται τιμωρίας ὁ τὸν υἱὸν τοῦ θεοῦ καταπατήσας, καὶ τὸ αἷμα τῆς διαθήκης κοινὸν ἡγησάμενος ἐν ᾧ ἡγιάσθη, καὶ τὸ πνεῦμα τῆς χάριτος ἐνυβρίσας;[g] **30** οἴδαμεν γὰρ τὸν εἰπόντα,

    Ἐμοὶ ἐκδίκησις, ἐγὼ ἀνταποδώσω·
καὶ πάλιν,

    Κρινεῖ κύριος τὸν λαὸν αὐτοῦ.
31 φοβερὸν τὸ ἐμπεσεῖν εἰς χεῖρας θεοῦ ζῶντος.

32 Ἀναμιμνῄσκεσθε δὲ τὰς πρότερον ἡμέρας, ἐν αἷς φωτισθέντες πολλὴν ἄθλησιν ὑπεμείνατε παθημάτων, **33** τοῦτο μὲν ὀνειδισμοῖς τε καὶ θλίψεσιν θεατριζόμενοι, τοῦτο δὲ κοινωνοὶ τῶν οὕτως ἀναστρεφομένων γενηθέντες· **34** καὶ γὰρ τοῖς δεσμίοις[4] συνεπαθήσατε, καὶ τὴν ἁρπαγὴν τῶν ὑπαρχόντων ὑμῶν μετὰ χαρᾶς προσεδέξασθε, γινώσκοντες ἔχειν ἑαυτοὺς[5] κρείττονα ὕπαρξιν καὶ μένουσαν. **35** μὴ ἀποβάλητε οὖν τὴν παρρησίαν ὑμῶν, ἥτις ἔχει μεγάλην μισθαποδοσίαν, **36** ὑπομονῆς

---

[4] **34** {B} δεσμίοις A D^gr* H 33 (81 δεσμείοις) 1739 2127 *l*[1357] it^ar,c,dem,div,f,(t),x vg syr^p,h,pal cop^sa,bo arm Ephraem Chrysostom Euthalius Valerian Antiochus John-Damascus^comm ‖ δεσμοῖς 𝔭[46] Ψ 104 Origen ‖ δεσμοῖς μου ℵ D^c K P 88 181 326 330 436 614 629 630 1241 1877 1881 1962 1984 2495 *Byz Lect* eth Clement Origen Euthalius Theodoret^txt John-Damascus^txt Ps-Oecumenius^txt Theophylact^txt ‖ τοὺς δεσμούς μου 451 2492 ‖ δεσμοῖς αὐτῶν it^d,e,(rl),z*

[5] **34** {B} ἑαυτούς 𝔭[13,46] ℵ A H Ψ 33 81 88 436 1739 1962 2127 2495 *l*[1365] it^ar,c,d,dem,div,e,f,rl,t,x,z vg syr^p?h? arm Clement Origen Euthalius Cosmos ‖ ἑαυτοῖς D^gr K 104 181 326 330 451 614 (629 *transposes*: ἑαυτοῖς ἔχειν) 630 1241 1877 1984 2492 *Byz Lect* syr^p?h? Chrysostom Isidore Theodoret John-Damascus ‖ ἐν ἑαυτοῖς 1881 *l*[598] Antiochus ‖ *omit* P cop^sa?bo?

---

[g] **29** *g* question: TR AV RV ASV RSV Zür Luth Jer ‖ *g* statement: WH Bov Nes BF² TT ‖ *g* exclamation: NEB Seg

---

27 πυρὸς...ὑπεναντίους Is 26.11   **28** ἐπὶ...ἀποθνήσκει Dt 17.6; 19.15   **29** τὸ αἷμα τῆς διαθήκης Ex 24.8; He 13.20   **30** Ἐμοὶ...ἀνταποδώσω Dt 32.35 (Ro 12.19)   Κρινεῖ...αὐτοῦ Dt 32.36; Ps 135.14   **33** ὀνειδισμοῖς...θεατριζόμενοι 1 Cor 4.9   **36** Lk 21.19; He 6.12

γὰρ ἔχετε χρείαν ἵνα τὸ θέλημα τοῦ θεοῦ ποιήσαντες κομίσησθε τὴν ἐπαγγελίαν. [h]

37 ἔτι γὰρ μικρὸν ὅσον ὅσον,
  ὁ ἐρχόμενος ἥξει καὶ οὐ χρονίσει·
38 ὁ δὲ δίκαιός μου ἐκ πίστεως[6] ζήσεται,
  καὶ ἐὰν ὑποστείληται,
    οὐκ εὐδοκεῖ ἡ ψυχή μου ἐν αὐτῷ.
39 ἡμεῖς δὲ οὐκ ἐσμὲν ὑποστολῆς εἰς ἀπώλειαν, ἀλλὰ πίστεως εἰς περιποίησιν ψυχῆς.

Faith

11 Ἔστιν δὲ πίστις ἐλπιζομένων ὑπόστασις,[a] πραγμάτων[a] ἔλεγχος οὐ βλεπομένων. 2 ἐν ταύτῃ γὰρ ἐμαρτυρήθησαν οἱ πρεσβύτεροι.

3 Πίστει νοοῦμεν κατηρτίσθαι τοὺς αἰῶνας ῥήματι θεοῦ, εἰς τὸ μὴ ἐκ φαινομένων τὸ βλεπόμενον γεγονέναι.

4 Πίστει πλείονα θυσίαν Ἄβελ παρὰ Κάϊν προσήνεγκεν τῷ θεῷ[1], δι' ἧς ἐμαρτυρήθη εἶναι δίκαιος, μαρτυροῦντος ἐπὶ τοῖς δώροις αὐτοῦ τοῦ θεοῦ[2], καὶ δι' αὐτῆς

do the will of God and receive what he promises. 37 For, as the scripture says:
  "Just a little while longer,
  And he who is coming will come;
  He will not delay.
38 My righteous people, however, will believe and live;
  But if any of them turns back, I will not be pleased with him."
39 We are not people who turn back and are lost. Instead, we have faith and are saved.

Faith

11 To have faith is to be sure of the things we hope for, to be certain of the things we cannot see. 2 It was by their faith that the men of ancient times won God's approval.

3 It is by faith that we understand that the universe was created by God's word, so that what can be seen was made out of what cannot be seen.

4 It was faith that made Abel offer to God a better sacrifice than Cain's. Through his faith he won God's approval as a righteous man, for God himself approved his gifts. By means of his faith Abel still speaks, even though he is dead.

[6] **38** {C} δίκαιός μου ἐκ πίστεως p46 ℵ A H* 33vid 1739 itar,c,dem,div,f,r1,x,z0 vg copsa arm Clement Theodoret Primasius Sedulius-Scotus ∥ δίκαιος ἐκ πίστεώς μου D* itd,e syrp,h Eusebius ∥ δίκαιος ἐκ πίστεως p13 Dc Hc K P Ψ 81 88 104 181 326 330 436 451 614 629 630 1241 1877 1881 1962 1984 2127 2492 2495 Byz Lect itt,z* syrpal copbo eth Chrysostom Euthalius Theodoret John-Damascus

[1] **4** {C} τῷ θεῷ (see footnote 2) ℵ A D K P Ψvid 33 81 88 104 181 326 330 436 (451 omit τῷ) 614 629 630 1241 1739 1877 1881 1962 1984 2127 2492 2495 Byz Lect itar,c,d,dem,div,e,f,r1,x,z vg syrp,h copsa,bo arm ∥ omit p13 Clement

[2] **4** {C} αὐτοῦ τοῦ θεοῦ (see footnote 1) p13*,46 ℵc Dc K P Ψ 81 88 104 181 330 436 451 614 629 630 1241 1739 1877 1881 1962 1984 2127 2492 2495 Byz

[h] **36** h major: TR Bov Nes BF2 AV RV ASV RSV NEB TT Zür Luth Jer Seg ∥ h minor: WH
[a] **1** a minor, a none: TR WH Nes BF2 AV? RV ASV RSV? NEB? TT? Zür Luth? Jer? Seg? ∥ a none, a minor: WHmg Bov

37-38 Hab 2.3-4 lxx **37** μικρὸν ὅσον ὅσον Is 26.20 lxx **38** ὁ δὲ...ζήσεται Ro 1.17; Ga 3.11
11 3 κατηρτίσθαι...γεγονέναι Gn 1.1; Ps 33.6, 9; 2 Pe 3.5 εἰς...γεγονέναι Ro 4.17
4 πλείονα...θεοῦ Gn 4.3-10

[5] It was faith that kept Enoch from dying. Instead, he was taken up to God, and nobody could find him, because God had taken him up. The scripture says that before Enoch was taken up he had pleased God. [6] No man can please God without faith. For he who comes to God must have faith that God exists and rewards those who seek him.

[7] It was faith that made Noah hear God's warnings about things in the future that he could not see. He obeyed God, and built an ark in which he and his family were saved. In this way he condemned the world, and received from God the righteousness that comes by faith.

[8] It was faith that made Abraham obey when God called him, and go out to a country which God had promised to give him. He left his own country without knowing where he was going. [9] By faith he lived in the country that God had promised him, as though he were a foreigner. He lived in tents with Isaac and Jacob, who had received the same promise from God. [10] For Abraham was waiting for the city which God has designed and built, the city with permanent foundations.

[11] It was faith that made Abraham able to become a father even though he was too old and Sarah herself was unable to have children.[1] He trusted God to keep his promise. [12] Though he was practically dead, from this one man there came as many descendants as there are

---

[1] **11** Abraham able to become a father even though he was too old and Sarah herself was unable to have children: *some mss. read* Sarah herself was able to conceive even though she was too old to have children

---

ἀποθανὼν ἔτι λαλεῖ. **5** Πίστει Ἐνὼχ μετετέθη τοῦ μὴ ἰδεῖν θάνατον, καὶ **οὐχ ηὑρίσκετο διότι μετέθηκεν αὐτὸν ὁ θεός·** πρὸ γὰρ τῆς μεταθέσεως μεμαρτύρηται **εὐαρεστηκέναι τῷ θεῷ,**[b] **6** χωρὶς δὲ πίστεως ἀδύνατον εὐαρεστῆσαι,[b] πιστεῦσαι γὰρ δεῖ τὸν προσερχόμενον τῷ θεῷ ὅτι ἔστιν καὶ τοῖς ἐκζητοῦσιν αὐτὸν μισθαποδότης γίνεται. **7** Πίστει χρηματισθεὶς Νῶε περὶ τῶν μηδέπω βλεπομένων εὐλαβηθεὶς κατεσκεύασεν κιβωτὸν εἰς σωτηρίαν τοῦ οἴκου αὐτοῦ, δι' ἧς κατέκρινεν τὸν κόσμον, καὶ τῆς κατὰ πίστιν δικαιοσύνης ἐγένετο κληρονόμος.

8 Πίστει καλούμενος Ἀβραὰμ ὑπήκουσεν ἐξελθεῖν εἰς τόπον ὃν ἤμελλεν λαμβάνειν εἰς κληρονομίαν, καὶ ἐξῆλθεν μὴ ἐπιστάμενος ποῦ ἔρχεται. **9** Πίστει παρῴκησεν εἰς γῆν τῆς ἐπαγγελίας ὡς ἀλλοτρίαν, ἐν σκηναῖς κατοικήσας[c] μετὰ Ἰσαὰκ καὶ Ἰακὼβ τῶν συγκληρονόμων τῆς ἐπαγγελίας τῆς αὐτῆς· **10** ἐξεδέχετο γὰρ τὴν τοὺς θεμελίους ἔχουσαν πόλιν, ἧς τεχνίτης καὶ δημιουργὸς ὁ θεός. **11** Πίστει — καὶ αὐτὴ Σάρρα στεῖρα — δύναμιν[3] εἰς καταβολὴν σπέρματος ἔλαβεν καὶ παρὰ καιρὸν ἡλικίας, ἐπεὶ πιστὸν ἡγήσατο τὸν ἐπαγγειλάμενον· **12** διὸ καὶ

Lect it[ar,c,dem,div,f,rl,x] vg syr[p,h] cop[bo] Origen Chrysostom Euthalius[msc] Theodoret John-Damascus ‖ αὐτοῦ τῷ θεῷ ℵ* A D[gr]* 33 326 arm eth Euthalius[ms]* ‖ αὐτῷ τοῦ θεοῦ p[13c] cop[sa] Clement ‖ τῷ θεῷ it[d,e,z]*

[3] **11** {D} πίστει—καὶ αὐτὴ Σάρρα στεῖρα—δύναμιν p[46] D* Ψ ‖ πίστει καὶ αὐτὴ Σάρρα δύναμιν p[13vid] ℵ A D[c] K 33 181 326 330 451 614 629 630 1877 2492 *Byz Lect* Chrysostom Theodoret John-Damascus ‖ πίστει καὶ αὐτὴ Σάρρα ἡ στεῖρα δύναμιν D[bvid] 81 88 1241 1739 1881 1962 cop[sa,bo] Euthalius ‖ πίστει καὶ αὐτὴ Σάρρα στεῖρα (or ἡ στεῖρα) δύναμιν it[ar,c,d,dem,div,e,f,(x),z] vg syr[p] ‖ πίστει καὶ αὐτὴ Σάρρα στεῖρα οὖσα δύναμιν P 104 436 1984 2127 (2495 Σάρα) syr[h] arm eth Theophylact

---

[b b] **5-6** *b* minor, *b* minor: TR WH Bov Nes BF² RV ‖ *b* major, *b* major: RSV Jer ‖ *b* minor, *b* major: NEB ‖ *b* major, *b* minor: AV ASV TT Zür Luth Seg

[c] **9** *c* none: TR WH AV RSV Zür Luth ‖ *c* minor: Bov Nes BF² RV ASV NEB TT Jer Seg

---

5 Ἐνὼχ...θεός Gn 5.24; Sir 44.16; En 70.1-4; Wsd 4.10   **7** χρηματισθεὶς...αὐτοῦ Gn 6.13-22; 7.1; 1 Pe 3.20   τῆς...δικαιοσύνης Ro 3.22; 4.13; 9.30   **8** Gn 12.1-5; Ac 7.2-4   **9** Gn 23.4; 26.3; 35.12, 27   **11** αὐτὴ...ἡλικίας Gn 17.19; 18.11-14; 21.2

ἀφ' ἑνὸς ἐγεννήθησαν, καὶ ταῦτα νενεκρωμένου, **καθὼς τὰ ἄστρα τοῦ οὐρανοῦ** τῷ πλήθει **καὶ ὡς ἡ ἄμμος ἡ παρὰ τὸ χεῖλος τῆς θαλάσσης ἡ ἀναρίθμητος.**

13 Κατὰ πίστιν ἀπέθανον οὗτοι πάντες, μὴ κομισάμενοι τὰς ἐπαγγελίας, ἀλλὰ πόρρωθεν αὐτὰς ἰδόντες καὶ ἀσπασάμενοι, καὶ ὁμολογήσαντες ὅτι ξένοι καὶ παρεπίδημοί εἰσιν ἐπὶ τῆς γῆς· 14 οἱ γὰρ τοιαῦτα λέγοντες ἐμφανίζουσιν ὅτι πατρίδα ἐπιζητοῦσιν. 15 καὶ εἰ μὲν ἐκείνης μνημονεύουσιν ἀφ' ἧς ἐξέβησαν, εἶχον ἂν καιρὸν ἀνακάμψαι· 16 νῦν δὲ κρείττονος ὀρέγονται, τοῦτ' ἔστιν ἐπουρανίου. διὸ οὐκ ἐπαισχύνεται αὐτοὺς ὁ θεὸς θεὸς ἐπικαλεῖσθαι αὐτῶν, ἡτοίμασεν γὰρ αὐτοῖς πόλιν.

17 Πίστει προσενήνοχεν Ἀβραὰμ τὸν Ἰσαὰκ πειραζόμενος, καὶ τὸν μονογενῆ προσέφερεν ὁ τὰς ἐπαγγελίας ἀναδεξάμενος, 18 πρὸς ὃν ἐλαλήθη ὅτι **Ἐν Ἰσαὰκ κληθήσεταί σοι σπέρμα,** 19 λογισάμενος ὅτι καὶ ἐκ νεκρῶν ἐγείρειν δυνατὸς ὁ θεός· ὅθεν αὐτὸν καὶ ἐν παραβολῇ ἐκομίσατο. 20 Πίστει καὶ περὶ μελλόντων εὐλόγησεν Ἰσαὰκ τὸν Ἰακὼβ καὶ τὸν Ἠσαῦ. 21 Πίστει Ἰακὼβ ἀποθνήσκων ἕκαστον τῶν υἱῶν Ἰωσὴφ εὐλόγησεν, καὶ **προσεκύνησεν ἐπὶ τὸ ἄκρον τῆς ῥάβδου αὐτοῦ.** 22 Πίστει Ἰωσὴφ τελευτῶν περὶ τῆς ἐξόδου τῶν υἱῶν Ἰσραὴλ ἐμνημόνευσεν, καὶ περὶ τῶν ὀστέων αὐτοῦ ἐνετείλατο.

23 Πίστει Μωϋσῆς γεννηθεὶς ἐκρύβη τρίμηνον ὑπὸ τῶν πατέρων αὐτοῦ, διότι εἶδον ἀστεῖον τὸ παιδίον,[d] καὶ οὐκ ἐφοβήθησαν τὸ διάταγμα τοῦ βασιλέως. 24 Πίστει Μωϋσῆς μέγας γενόμενος ἠρνήσατο λέγεσθαι υἱὸς θυγατρὸς Φαραώ, 25 μᾶλλον ἑλόμενος συγκακουχεῖσθαι τῷ λαῷ τοῦ θεοῦ ἢ πρόσκαιρον ἔχειν ἁμαρτίας ἀπόλαυσιν,

[d] **23** d minor: TR Bov Nes BF² AV RV ASV RSV NEB TT Zür Luth Jer ∥ d none: WH Seg

12 ἀφ'...νενεκρωμένου Ro 4.19 καθὼς...ἀναρίθμητος Gn 15.5–6; 22.17; 32.12; Ex 32.13; Dt 1.10; 10.22; Dn 3.36 lxx; Slr 44.21 **13** ξένοι...γῆς Gn 23.4; 47.9; 1 Chr 29.15; Ps 39.12; 1 Pe 2.11 **16** οὐκ...αὐτῶν Ex 3.6, 15; 4.5; Mk 12.26 **17** Gn 22.1–10; Jas 2.21 **18** Ἐν...σπέρμα Gn 21.12 (Ro 9.7) **20** Gn 27.27–29, 39–40 **21** Ἰακὼβ...εὐλόγησεν Gn 48.15–16 προσεκύνησεν...αὐτοῦ Gn 47.31 lxx **22** Gn 50.24–25; Ex 13.19 **23** Μωϋσῆς...αὐτοῦ Ex 2.2 οὐκ...βασιλέως Ex 1.22 **24** Ex 2.10–12

stars in the sky, as many as the numberless grains of sand on the seashore. [13] It was in faith that all these persons died. They did not receive the things God had promised, but from a long way off they saw and welcomed them, and admitted openly that they were foreigners and refugees on earth. [14] Those who say such things make it clear that they are looking for a country of their own. [15] They did not think back to the country they had left; if they had, they would have had the chance to return. [16] Instead, it was a better country they longed for, the heavenly country. And so God is not ashamed to have them call him their God, for he has prepared a city for them. [17] It was faith that made Abraham offer his son Isaac as a sacrifice, when God put Abraham to the test. Abraham was the one to whom God had made the promise, yet he was ready to offer his only son as a sacrifice. [18] God had said to him, "It is through Isaac that you will have descendants." [19] Abraham reckoned that God was able to raise Isaac back from death — and, so to speak, Abraham did receive Isaac back from death.

[20] It was faith that made Isaac promise blessings for the future to Jacob and Esau. [21] It was faith that made Jacob bless each of the sons of Joseph just before he died; he leaned on the top of his walking stick and worshiped God. [22] It was faith that made Joseph, when he was about to die, speak of the departure of the Israelites from Egypt, and leave instructions about what should be done with his body. [23] It was faith that made the parents of Moses hide him for three months after he was born. They saw that he was a beautiful child, and they were not afraid to disobey the king's order. [24] It was faith that made Moses, when he was grown, refuse to be called the son of Pharaoh's daughter. [25] He preferred to suffer with God's people rather than

to enjoy sin for a little while. ²⁶ He reckoned that to suffer scorn for the Messiah was worth far more than all the treasures of Egypt; because he kept his eyes on the future reward.

²⁷ It was faith that made Moses leave Egypt without being afraid of the king's anger; he would not turn back, as though he saw the invisible God. ²⁸ It was faith that made him establish the Passover and order the blood sprinkled on the doors, so the Angel of Death would not kill the first-born sons of the Israelites.

²⁹ It was faith that enabled the Israelites to cross the Red Sea as if on dry land; when the Egyptians tried to do it, the water swallowed them up.

³⁰ It was faith that made the walls of Jericho fall down, after the Israelites had marched around them for seven days. ³¹ It was faith that kept the harlot Rahab from being killed with those who disobeyed God, because she gave the spies a friendly welcome.

³² Should I go on? There isn't enough time for me to speak of Gideon, Barak, Samson, Jephthah, David, Samuel, and the prophets. ³³ Through faith they fought whole countries and won. They did what was right and received what God had promised. They shut the mouths of lions, ³⁴ put out fierce fires, escaped being killed by the sword. They were weak but became strong; they were mighty in battle and defeated the armies of foreigners. ³⁵ Through faith women received their dead raised back to life.

Others, refusing to accept freedom, died under torture in order to be raised to a better life. ³⁶ Some were mocked and whipped, and others were tied up and put in prison. ³⁷ They were stoned, they were sawn in two, they were killed with

26 μείζονα πλοῦτον ἡγησάμενος τῶν Αἰγύπτου θησαυρῶν τὸν ὀνειδισμὸν τοῦ Χριστοῦ, ἀπέβλεπεν γὰρ εἰς τὴν μισθαποδοσίαν. 27 Πίστει κατέλιπεν Αἴγυπτον, μὴ φοβηθεὶς τὸν θυμὸν τοῦ βασιλέως, τὸν γὰρ ἀόρατον ὡς ὁρῶν ἐκαρτέρησεν. 28 Πίστει πεποίηκεν τὸ πάσχα καὶ τὴν πρόσχυσιν τοῦ αἵματος, ἵνα μὴ ὁ ὀλοθρεύων τὰ πρωτότοκα θίγῃ αὐτῶν. 29 Πίστει διέβησαν τὴν Ἐρυθρὰν Θάλασσαν ὡς διὰ ξηρᾶς γῆς, ἧς πεῖραν λαβόντες οἱ Αἰγύπτιοι κατεπόθησαν. 30 Πίστει τὰ τείχη Ἰεριχὼ ἔπεσαν κυκλωθέντα ἐπὶ ἑπτὰ ἡμέρας. 31 Πίστει Ῥαὰβ ἡ πόρνη οὐ συναπώλετο τοῖς ἀπειθήσασιν, δεξαμένη τοὺς κατασκόπους μετ' εἰρήνης.

32 Καὶ τί ἔτι λέγω; ἐπιλείψει με γὰρ διηγούμενον ὁ χρόνος περὶ Γεδεών, Βαράκ, Σαμψών, Ἰεφθάε, Δαυίδ τε καὶ Σαμουὴλ καὶ τῶν προφητῶν,ᵉ 33 οἳ διὰ πίστεως κατηγωνίσαντο βασιλείας, εἰργάσαντο δικαιοσύνην, ἐπέτυχον ἐπαγγελιῶν, ἔφραξαν στόματα λεόντων, 34 ἔσβεσαν δύναμιν πυρός, ἔφυγον στόματα μαχαίρης, ἐδυναμώθησαν ἀπὸ ἀσθενείας, ἐγενήθησαν ἰσχυροὶ ἐν πολέμῳ, παρεμβολὰς ἔκλιναν ἀλλοτρίων· 35 ἔλαβον γυναῖκες ἐξ ἀναστάσεως τοὺς νεκροὺς αὐτῶν· ἄλλοι δὲ ἐτυμπανίσθησαν, οὐ προσδεξάμενοι τὴν ἀπολύτρωσιν, ἵνα κρείττονος ἀναστάσεως τύχωσιν· 36 ἕτεροι δὲ ἐμπαιγμῶν καὶ μαστίγων πεῖραν ἔλαβον, ἔτι δὲ δεσμῶν καὶ φυλακῆς· 37 ἐλιθάσθησαν, ἐπρίσθησαν⁴, ἐν φόνῳ μαχαίρης ἀπέθανον, περι-

---

⁴ 37 {D} ἐπρίσθησαν 𝔭⁴⁶ 1241 1984 𝑙⁴⁴,⁵³ syrᵖ (copˢᵃ *transposes*: ἐπρίσθησαν, ἐλιθάσθησαν) ethʳᵒ,ᵖᵖ Origenᵍʳ²/⁷,ˡᵃᵗ Eusebius Acacius Ephraem Jerome Socrates Ps-Augustine Theophylact ǁ ἐπειράσθησαν vgᵐˢ Clement ǁ ἐπρίσθησαν, ἐπειράσθησαν 𝔭¹³ᵛⁱᵈ A Dᶜ K Ψ 88 104 181 330 436 451 614 629 630 1739 1877 1881 1962 2127 2492 *Byz Lect* itᵃʳ,ᶜ,(ᵈ),ᵈᵉᵐ,ᵈⁱᵛ,(ᵉ),ᶠ,ᵗ,ᶻ vg (syrᵖᵃˡ)

ᵉ 32 *e minor:* TR WH Bov Nes BF² AV RV ASV Zür Luth Jer ǁ *e none:* Seg ǁ *e major:* NEB TT ǁ *e dash:* RSV

---

27 κατέλιπεν Αἴγυπτον Ex 2.15; 12.51　28 Ex 12.21–30　29 Ex 14.21–31　30 Jos 6.12–21 31 Jos 2.11–12; 6.21–25; Jas 2.25　33 ἔφραξαν στόματα λεόντων Jdg 14.6–7; 1 Sm 17.34–36; Dn 6.1–27　34 ἔσβεσαν δύναμιν πυρός Dn 3.23–25　35 ἔλαβον...αὐτῶν 1 Kgs 17.17–24; 2 Kgs 4.25–37　ἄλλοι...τύχωσιν 2 Macc 6.18—7.42　36 1 Kgs 22.26–27; 2 Chr 18.25–26; Jr 20.2; 37.15; 38.6　37 ἐλιθάσθησαν 2 Chr 24.21　ἐπρίσθησαν Ascension of Is 5.11–14

ἦλθον ἐν μηλωταῖς, ἐν αἰγείοις δέρμασιν, ὑστερούμενοι, θλιβόμενοι, κακουχούμενοι,ᶠ 38 ὧν οὐκ ἦν ἄξιος ὁ κόσμος,ᶠ ἐπὶ ἐρημίαις πλανώμενοι καὶ ὄρεσιν καὶ σπηλαίοις καὶ ταῖς ὀπαῖς τῆς γῆς.

39 Καὶ οὗτοι πάντες μαρτυρηθέντες διὰ τῆς πίστεως οὐκ ἐκομίσαντο τὴν ἐπαγγελίαν, 40 τοῦ θεοῦ περὶ ἡμῶν κρεῖττόν τι προβλεψαμένου, ἵνα μὴ χωρὶς ἡμῶν τελειωθῶσιν.

The Discipline of the Lord

12 Τοιγαροῦν καὶ ἡμεῖς, τοσοῦτον ἔχοντες περικείμενον ἡμῖν νέφος μαρτύρων, ὄγκον ἀποθέμενοι πάντα καὶ τὴν εὐπερίστατον¹ ἁμαρτίαν, δι' ὑπομονῆς τρέχωμεν τὸν προκείμενον ἡμῖν ἀγῶνα, 2 ἀφορῶντες εἰς τὸν τῆς πίστεως ἀρχηγὸν καὶ τελειωτὴν Ἰησοῦν, ὃς ἀντὶ τῆς προκειμένης αὐτῷ χαρᾶς ὑπέμεινεν σταυρὸν αἰσχύνης καταφρονήσας, ἐν δεξιᾷ τε τοῦ θρόνου τοῦ θεοῦ κεκάθικεν. 3 ἀναλογίσασθε γὰρ τὸν τοιαύτην ὑπομεμενηκότα ὑπὸ τῶν ἁμαρτωλῶν εἰς ἑαυτὸν² ἀντιλογίαν, ἵνα μὴ κάμητε ταῖς ψυχαῖς ὑμῶν ἐκλυόμενοι.

---

copᵇᵒ arm Origenᵍʳ⁵/⁷·ˡᵃᵗ Ephraem Ambrose Chrysostom Theodoret John-Damascus ‖ ἐπιράσθησαν, ἐπιράσθησαν Dᵍʳ* ‖ ἐπειράσθησαν, ἐπρίσθησαν ℵ P (048 ἐπιράσθησαν) 33 81 326 2495 syrᵖ·ʰ copᵇᵒᵐˢ Euthalius ‖ ἐπρήσθησαν, ἐπειράσθησαν 1923 ‖ omit ethᵐˢ

¹ 1 {B} εὐπερίστατον 𝔭¹³ ℵ A Dᵍʳ K P Ψ 33 81 88 104 181 326 330 436 451 614 629 630 1241 1877 1881 1962 1984 2127 2492 2495 Byz Lect itᵃʳ·ᶜ·ᵈᵉᵐ· ᵈⁱᵛ·ᶠ·(ᵍⁱᵍ)·ᵗ vg syr⁽ᵖ⁾·ʰ copˢᵃ·ᵇᵒ ‖ εὐπερίσπαστον 𝔭⁴⁶ 1739 itᵈ⁷ᵉ²ᶻ?

² 3 {D} εἰς ἑαυτόν A P 104 326 1241 1877 John-Damascus ‖ εἰς αὐτόν Dᶜ K Ψ* 88 181 330 436 614 629 630 1739ᶜ 1881 1962 1984 2495 Byz Lect Chrysostom John-Damascus ‖ εἰς ἑαυτόν (or εἰς αὐτόν) itᵃʳ·ᶜ·ᵈᵉᵐ·ᵈⁱᵛ·ᶠ vgᶜˡ syrʰ ‖ εἰς ἑαυτούς ℵ* Dᵍʳ* (81 εἰς αὐτούς) 2127 syrᵖ Ephraem ‖ εἰς αὐτούς 𝔭¹³·⁴⁶ ℵᵇ Ψᶜ 048

ƒ ƒ 37–38 ƒ minor, ƒ minor: TR (WH) Bov Nes BF² (NEB) (Luth) Jer ‖ ƒ parens, ƒ parens: AV RV ASV TT ‖ ƒ dash, ƒ dash: RSV Zür Seg

1 τρέχωμεν...ἀγῶνα 1 Cor 9.24   2 ἐν...κεκάθικεν Ps 110.1; Mt 22.44; Mk 16.19; Ac 2.34; Eph 1.20; He 1.3; 8.1; 10.12

---

the sword. They went around clothed in skins of sheep or goats, poor, persecuted, and mistreated. 38 The world was not good enough for them! They wandered like refugees in the deserts and hills, living in caves and holes in the ground.
39 What a record these men have won by their faith! Yet they did not receive what God had promised, 40 for God had decided on an even better plan for us. His purpose was that they would be made perfect only with us.

God Our Father

12 As for us, we have this large crowd of witnesses around us. Let us rid ourselves, then, of everything that gets in the way, and the sin which holds on to us so tightly, and let us run with determination the race that lies before us. 2 Let us keep our eyes fixed on Jesus, on whom our faith depends from beginning to end. He did not give up because of the cross! On the contrary, because of the joy that was waiting for him, he thought nothing of the disgrace of dying on the cross, and is now seated at the right side of God's throne.
3 Think of what he went through, how he put up with so much hatred from sinful men! So do not let yourselves

become discouraged and give up. ⁴ For
in your struggle against sin you have
not yet had to fight to the point of being
killed. ⁵ Have you forgotten the en-
couraging words which God speaks to
you as his sons?

> "My son, pay attention when the
> Lord punishes you,
> And do not be discouraged when he
> rebukes you.
> ⁶ For the Lord punishes everyone he
> loves,
> And whips everyone he accepts as a
> son."

⁷ Endure what you suffer as being a
father's punishment; because your suffering shows that God is treating you as
his sons. Was there ever a son who was
not punished by his father? ⁸ If you are
not punished as all his sons are, it means
you are not true sons, but bastards.
⁹ In the case of our human fathers, they
punished us and we respected them.
How much more, then, should we submit
to our spiritual Father and live! ¹⁰ Our
human fathers punished us for a short
time, as it seemed right to them. But
God does it for our own good, so that
we may share his holiness. ¹¹ When we
are punished, it seems to us at the time
something to make us sad, not glad.
Later, however, those who have been
disciplined by such punishment reap the
peaceful reward of a righteous life.

Instructions and Warnings

¹² Lift up your limp hands, then, and
strengthen your weak knees! ¹³ Keep
walking on straight paths, so that the
lame foot may not be disabled, but
instead be healed.

¹⁴ Try to be at peace with all men,
and try to live a holy life, for no one will
see the Lord without it. ¹⁵ Be careful

4 Οὔπω μέχρις αἵματος ἀντικατέστητε πρὸς τὴν ἁμαρτίαν ἀνταγωνιζόμενοι,ᵃ **5** καὶ ἐκλέλησθε τῆς παρακλήσεως, ἥτις ὑμῖν ὡς υἱοῖς διαλέγεται,ᵃ

> Υἱέ μου, μὴ ὀλιγώρει παιδείας κυρίου,
> μηδὲ ἐκλύου ὑπ' αὐτοῦ ἐλεγχόμενος·
> **6** ὃν γὰρ ἀγαπᾷ κύριος παιδεύει,
> μαστιγοῖ δὲ πάντα υἱὸν ὃν παραδέχεται.ᵃ

7 εἰς παιδείαν ὑπομένετε· ὡς υἱοῖς ὑμῖν προσφέρεται ὁ θεός· τίς γὰρ υἱὸς ὃν οὐ παιδεύει πατήρ; **8** εἰ δὲ χωρίς ἐστε παιδείας ἧς μέτοχοι γεγόνασιν πάντες, ἄρα νόθοι καὶ οὐχ υἱοί ἐστε. **9** εἶτα τοὺς μὲν τῆς σαρκὸς ἡμῶν πατέρας εἴχομεν παιδευτὰς καὶ ἐνετρεπόμεθα· οὐ πολὺ [δὲ] μᾶλλον ὑποταγησόμεθα τῷ πατρὶ τῶν πνευμάτων καὶ ζήσομεν; **10** οἱ μὲν γὰρ πρὸς ὀλίγας ἡμέρας κατὰ τὸ δοκοῦν αὐτοῖς ἐπαίδευον, ὁ δὲ ἐπὶ τὸ συμφέρον εἰς τὸ μεταλαβεῖν τῆς ἁγιότητος αὐτοῦ. **11** πᾶσα δὲ παιδεία πρὸς μὲν τὸ παρὸν οὐ δοκεῖ χαρᾶς εἶναι ἀλλὰ λύπης, ὕστερον δὲ καρπὸν εἰρηνικὸν τοῖς δι' αὐτῆς γεγυμνασμένοις ἀποδίδωσιν δικαιοσύνης.

12 Διὸ **τὰς παρειμένας χεῖρας καὶ τὰ παραλελυμένα γόνατα ἀνορθώσατε**, **13** καὶ **τροχιὰς ὀρθὰς ποιεῖτε τοῖς ποσὶν** ὑμῶν, ἵνα μὴ τὸ χωλὸν ἐκτραπῇ, ἰαθῇ δὲ μᾶλλον.

Warning against Rejecting God's Grace

14 Εἰρήνην διώκετε μετὰ πάντων,ᵇ καὶ τὸν ἁγιασμόν,ᵇ οὗ χωρὶς οὐδεὶς ὄψεται τὸν κύριον, **15** ἐπισκοποῦντες μή

---

33 451 1739* 2492 Origen Euthalius Theodoret ∥ εἰς ἑαυτούς (or εἰς αὐτούς) itᶻ vgʷʷ copᵇᵒ ∥ ἐν ὑμῖν itᵈ,ᵉ

ᵃ ᵃ ᵃ **4-6** a minor, a minor, a major: TR WH (Bov) Nes BF² TT (Zür) (Luth) ∥ a major, a minor, a major: AV RV ASV NEB Seg ∥ a major, a question, a major: RSV (Jer) ∥ a minor, a minor, a question

ᵇ ᵇ **14** b minor, b minor: TR WH Bov Nes BF² AV NEB ∥ b minor, b none: RV ASV RSV TT Jer Seg ∥ b none, b minor: Zür Luth

5-6 Υἱέ…παραδέχεται Pr 3.11-12 **6** ὃν γὰρ…παιδεύει Re 3.19 **7** ὡς…πατήρ Dt 8.5; 2 Sm 7.14 **9** τῷ…πνευμάτων Nu 16.22; 27.16 **11** καρπὸν εἰρηνικὸν…δικαιοσύνης Jas 3.17-18 **12** τὰς…ἀνορθώσατε Is 35.3; Sir 25.23 **13** τροχιὰς…ὑμῶν Pr 4.26 LXX **14** Εἰρήνην… πάντων Ps 34.14; Ro 12.18

τις ὑστερῶν ἀπὸ τῆς χάριτος τοῦ θεοῦ, μή τις ῥίζα πικρίας ἄνω φύουσα ἐνοχλῇ καὶ δι' αὐτῆς μιανθῶσιν πολλοί, **16** μή τις πόρνος ἢ βέβηλος ὡς Ἠσαῦ, ὃς ἀντὶ βρώσεως μιᾶς ἀπέδοτο τὰ πρωτοτόκια αὐτοῦ. **17** ἴστε γὰρ ὅτι καὶ μετέπειτα θέλων κληρονομῆσαι τὴν εὐλογίαν ἀπεδοκιμάσθη,ᶜ μετανοίας γὰρ τόπον οὐχ εὗρεν,ᶜ καίπερ μετὰ δακρύων ἐκζητήσας αὐτήν.

18 Οὐ γὰρ προσεληλύθατε ψηλαφωμένῳ [ὄρει]³ καὶ κεκαυμένῳ πυρὶ καὶ γνόφῳ καὶ ζόφῳ καὶ θυέλλῃ **19** καὶ σάλπιγγος ἤχῳ καὶ φωνῇ ῥημάτων, ἧς οἱ ἀκούσαντες παρῃτήσαντο μὴ προστεθῆναι αὐτοῖς λόγον· **20** οὐκ ἔφερον γὰρ τὸ διαστελλόμενον, **Κἂν θηρίον θίγῃ τοῦ ὄρους, λιθοβοληθήσεται·** **21** καί, οὕτω φοβερὸν ἦν τὸ φανταζόμενον, Μωϋσῆς εἶπεν, **Ἔκφοβός εἰμι** καὶ ἔντρομος. **22** ἀλλὰ προσεληλύθατε Σιὼν ὄρει καὶ πόλει θεοῦ ζῶντος, Ἰερουσαλὴμ ἐπουρανίῳ, καὶ μυριάσινᵈ ἀγγέλων,ᵈ ᵉπανηγύρειᵈ **23**ᵉ καὶ ἐκκλησίᾳ πρωτοτόκων ἀπογεγραμμένων ἐν οὐρανοῖς, καὶ κριτῇ θεῷ πάντων, καὶ πνεύμασι δικαίων τετελειωμένων, **24** καὶ διαθήκης νέας μεσίτῃ Ἰησοῦ, καὶ αἵματι ῥαντισμοῦ κρεῖττον λαλοῦντι παρὰ τὸν Ἄβελ.

³ **18** {D} ψηλαφωμένῳ ὄρει Dᵍʳ K (P 181 ψιλαφωμένῳ) Ψ 88 (104 ψηλαφουμένῳ) (326 ὄρη) (330 436 1241 1739 1877 ψηλαφομένῳ, 451 ψηλαφαμένῳ) 614 629 630 1881 1962 1984 2127 2492 2495 *Byz Lect* vgᶜˡ Origenˡᵃᵗ Athanasius Ephraem Theodoret Ps-Athanasius John-Damascus Ps-Oecumenius ∥ ὄρει ψηλαφωμένῳ 69 255 462 syrʰ arm Chrysostom ∥ ψηλαφωμένῳ 𝔭⁴⁶ ℵ A C 048 33 (81 ψηλαφομένῳ) itᵃʳ,ᶜ,(ᵈ),ᵈᵉᵐ,ᵈⁱᵛ,ᶠ,ᵗ,(ᶻ) vgʷʷ syrᵖ copˢᵃ,ᵇᵒ eth Origenˡᵃᵗ Chrysostomᶜᵒᵐᵐ Euthalius Primasius

ᶜ ᶜ **17** c minor, c minor: WH Bov Nes BF² RSV TTᵐᵍ Seg ∥ c parens, c parens: RV ASVᵐᵍ (TT) ∥ c major, c minor: TR AV ASV NEB Zür Luth Jer

ᵈ ᵈ ᵈ **22** d none, d minor, d none: TR WH Bov BF² AVᵉᵈ RV ASV RSVᵐᵍ NEB TT Zür Luth Seg ∥ d none, d minor, d minor: Nes AVᵉᵈ Jer ∥ d none, d none, d minor: WHᵐᵍ RSV ∥ d minor, d none, d minor: RVᵐᵍ ASVᵐᵍ

ᵉ ᵉ **22–23** e no number, e number 23: TRᵉᵈ WH? Bov Nes BF² RSV TT Zür Jer ∥ e number 23, e no number: TRᵉᵈ WH? AV RV ASV NEB Luth Seg

15 μή τις ῥίζα...ἐνοχλῇ Dt 29.17 lxx   **16** Ἠσαῦ...αὐτοῦ Gn 25.33–34   **17** Gn 27.30–40   **18–19** Ex 19.16–22; 20.18 21; Dt 4.11–12; 5.22–27   **20** Κἂν...λιθοβοληθήσεται Ex 19.12–13   **21** Ἔκφοβός εἰμι Dt 9.19   **22** Ἰερουσαλὴμ ἐπουρανίῳ Ga 4.26; Re 21.2   μυριάσιν ἀγγέλων Re 5.11   **23** ἀπογεγραμμένων ἐν οὐρανοῖς Lk 10.20   κριτῇ θεῷ πάντων Gn 18.25; Ps 50.6   **24** διαθήκης...Ἰησοῦ He 7.22; 8.6; 9.15   αἵματι ῥαντισμοῦ 1 Pe 1.2   παρὰ τὸν Ἄβελ Gn 4.10

that no one turns back from the grace of God. Be careful that no one becomes like a bitter plant that grows up and troubles many with its poison. **16** Be careful that no one becomes immoral or unspiritual like Esau, who for a single meal sold his rights as the older son. **17** Afterward, you know, he wanted to receive his father's blessing; but he was turned back, because he could not find a way to change what he had done, even though he looked for it with tears.

18 You have not come, as the people of Israel came, to what you can feel, to Mount Sinai with its blazing fire, the darkness and the gloom, the storm, **19** the noise of a trumpet, and the sound of a voice. When the people heard the voice they begged not to have to hear another word, **20** for they could not bear the order which said, "If even an animal touches the mountain it must be stoned to death." **21** The sight was so terrible that Moses said, "I am trembling and afraid!"

22 Instead, you have come to Mount Zion and to the city of the living God, the heavenly Jerusalem, with its thousands of angels. **23** You have come to the joyful gathering of God's oldest sons, whose names are written in heaven. You have come to God, who is the Judge of all men, and to the spirits of righteous men made perfect. **24** You have come to Jesus, who arranged the new covenant, and to the sprinkled blood that tells of much better things than Abel's blood.

²⁵ Be careful, then, and do not refuse to hear him who speaks. Those who refused to hear him who gave the divine message on earth did not escape. How much less shall we escape, then, if we turn away from him who speaks from heaven! ²⁶ His voice shook the earth at that time, but now he has promised, "I will once more shake not only the earth but heaven as well." ²⁷ The words "once more" plainly show that the created things will be shaken and removed, so that the things that are not shaken will remain.

²⁸ Let us be thankful, then, because we receive a kingdom that cannot be shaken. Let us be grateful and worship God in a way that will please him, with reverence and fear; ²⁹ for our God is indeed a destroying fire.

How to Please God

13 Keep on loving one another as brothers in Christ. ² Remember to welcome strangers in your homes. There were some who did it and welcomed angels without knowing it. ³ Remember those who are in prison, as though you were in prison with them. Remember those who are suffering, as though you were suffering as they are.

⁴ Marriage should be honored by all, and husbands and wives must be faithful to each other. God will judge those who are immoral and those who commit adultery.

⁵ Keep your lives free from the love of money, and be satisfied with what you have. For God has said, "I will never leave you; I will never abandon you." ⁶ Let us be bold, then, and say,

"The Lord is my helper,
I will not be afraid!
What can man do to me?"

⁷ Remember your former leaders, who spoke God's message to you. Think back on how they lived and died, and imitate their faith. ⁸ Jesus Christ is the same

25 Βλέπετε μὴ παραιτήσησθε τὸν λαλοῦντα· εἰ γὰρ ἐκεῖνοι οὐκ ἐξέφυγον ἐπὶ γῆς παραιτησάμενοι τὸν χρηματίζοντα, πολὺ μᾶλλον ἡμεῖς οἱ τὸν ἀπ' οὐρανῶν ἀποστρεφόμενοι· 26 οὗ ἡ φωνὴ τὴν γῆν ἐσάλευσεν τότε, νῦν δὲ ἐπήγγελται λέγων, Ἔτι ἅπαξ ἐγὼ σείσω οὐ μόνον **τὴν γῆν** ἀλλὰ καὶ **τὸν οὐρανόν**. 27 τὸ δέ, Ἔτι **ἅπαξ** δηλοῖ [τὴν] τῶν σαλευομένων μετάθεσιν ὡς πεποιημένων, ἵνα μείνῃ τὰ μὴ σαλευόμενα. 28 Διὸ βασιλείαν ἀσάλευτον παραλαμβάνοντες ἔχωμεν χάριν, δι' ἧς λατρεύωμεν εὐαρέστως τῷ θεῷ μετὰ εὐλαβείας καὶ δέους· 29 καὶ γὰρ **ὁ θεὸς** ἡμῶν **πῦρ καταναλίσκον**.

Service Well-Pleasing to God

13 Ἡ φιλαδελφία μενέτω. 2 τῆς φιλοξενίας μὴ ἐπιλανθάνεσθε, διὰ ταύτης γὰρ ἔλαθόν τινες ξενίσαντες ἀγγέλους. 3 μιμνήσκεσθε τῶν δεσμίων ὡς συνδεδεμένοι, τῶν κακουχουμένων ὡς καὶ αὐτοὶ ὄντες ἐν σώματι. 4 Τίμιος ὁ γάμος ἐν πᾶσιν καὶ ἡ κοίτη ἀμίαντος, πόρνους γὰρ καὶ μοιχοὺς κρινεῖ ὁ θεός. 5 Ἀφιλάργυρος ὁ τρόπος· ἀρκούμενοι τοῖς παροῦσιν· αὐτὸς γὰρ εἴρηκεν, **Οὐ μή σε ἀνῶ οὐδ' οὐ μή σε ἐγκαταλίπω**· 6 ὥστε θαρροῦντας ἡμᾶς λέγειν,

**Κύριος ἐμοὶ βοηθός,
[καὶ] οὐ φοβηθήσομαι·
τί ποιήσει μοι ἄνθρωπος;**

7 Μνημονεύετε τῶν ἡγουμένων ὑμῶν, οἵτινες ἐλάλησαν ὑμῖν τὸν λόγον τοῦ θεοῦ, ὧν ἀναθεωροῦντες τὴν ἔκβασιν τῆς ἀναστροφῆς μιμεῖσθε τὴν πίστιν. 8 Ἰησοῦς Χριστὸς ἐχθὲς καὶ σήμερον[a] ὁ αὐτός,[a] καὶ εἰς τοὺς αἰῶνας.

---

[a] [a] **8** a none, a minor: TR WH RV ASV (Zür) Jer ∥ a minor, a none: (Luth?) ∥ a none, a none: Bov Nes BF² (AV) RSV (NEB) (TT) Seg

25 εἰ...ἀποστρεφόμενοι He 2.1–3; 10.28–29   **26** ἡ φωνή...τότε Ex 19.18; Jdg 5.4; Ps 68.8 Ἔτι...οὐρανόν Hg 2.6   **29** ὁ θεὸς...καταναλίσκον Dt 4.24; 9.3; Is 33.14
13 2 ἔλαθον...ἀγγέλους Gn 18.1–8; 19.1–3   **3** μιμνήσκεσθε τῶν δεσμίων Mt 25.36; He 10.34   **4** πόρνους...θεός Ga 5.19, 21; Eph 5.5   **5** Οὐ...ἐγκαταλίπω Dt 31.6 (Gn 28.15; Dt 31.8; Jos 1.5)   **6** Κύριος...ἄνθρωπος Ps 118.6   **7** μιμεῖσθε τὴν πίστιν 1 Cor 4.16; He 6.12

9 διδαχαῖς ποικίλαις καὶ ξέναις μὴ παραφέρεσθε· καλὸν γὰρ χάριτι βεβαιοῦσθαι τὴν καρδίαν, οὐ βρώμασιν, ἐν οἷς οὐκ ὠφελήθησαν οἱ περιπατοῦντες. 10 ἔχομεν θυσιαστήριον ἐξ οὗ φαγεῖν οὐκ ἔχουσιν ἐξουσίαν οἱ τῇ σκηνῇ λατρεύοντες. 11 ὧν γὰρ εἰσφέρεται ζῴων τὸ αἷμα περὶ ἁμαρτίας εἰς τὰ ἅγια διὰ τοῦ ἀρχιερέως, τούτων τὰ σώματα κατακαίεται ἔξω τῆς παρεμβολῆς. 12 διὸ καὶ Ἰησοῦς, ἵνα ἁγιάσῃ διὰ τοῦ ἰδίου αἵματος τὸν λαόν, ἔξω τῆς πύλης ἔπαθεν. 13 τοίνυν ἐξερχώμεθα πρὸς αὐτὸν ἔξω τῆς παρεμβολῆς, τὸν ὀνειδισμὸν αὐτοῦ φέροντες· 14 οὐ γὰρ ἔχομεν ὧδε μένουσαν πόλιν, ἀλλὰ τὴν μέλλουσαν ἐπιζητοῦμεν. 15 δι᾽ αὐτοῦ οὖν[1] ἀναφέρωμεν θυσίαν αἰνέσεως διὰ παντὸς τῷ θεῷ, τοῦτ᾽ ἔστιν καρπὸν χειλέων ὁμολογούντων τῷ ὀνόματι αὐτοῦ. 16 τῆς δὲ εὐποιΐας καὶ κοινωνίας μὴ ἐπιλανθάνεσθε, τοιαύταις γὰρ θυσίαις εὐαρεστεῖται ὁ θεός.

17 Πείθεσθε τοῖς ἡγουμένοις ὑμῶν καὶ ὑπείκετε, αὐτοὶ γὰρ ἀγρυπνοῦσιν ὑπὲρ τῶν ψυχῶν ὑμῶν ὡς λόγον ἀποδώσοντες, ἵνα μετὰ χαρᾶς τοῦτο ποιῶσιν καὶ μὴ στενάζοντες, ἀλυσιτελὲς γὰρ ὑμῖν τοῦτο.

18 Προσεύχεσθε περὶ ἡμῶν, πειθόμεθα γὰρ ὅτι καλὴν συνείδησιν ἔχομεν, ἐν πᾶσιν καλῶς θέλοντες ἀναστρέφεσθαι. 19 περισσοτέρως δὲ παρακαλῶ τοῦτο ποιῆσαι ἵνα τάχιον ἀποκατασταθῶ ὑμῖν.

Benediction and Final Greetings

20 Ὁ δὲ θεὸς τῆς εἰρήνης, ὁ ἀναγαγὼν ἐκ νεκρῶν τὸν ποιμένα τῶν προβάτων τὸν μέγαν ἐν αἵματι διαθήκης

---

[1] 15 {D} αὐτοῦ οὖν ℵᶜ A C Dᶜ 0121b 81 88 104 181 326 330 436 614 629 630 1241 1739 1877 1881 1962 1984 2127 2495 *Byz Lect* itᵃʳ,ᶜ,ᵈᵉᵐ,ᵈⁱᵛ,ᶠ,ᶻ vg syrʰ copˢᵃ,ᵇᵒ arm eth Chrysostom Euthalius Theodoret John-Damascus Ps-Oecumenius ‖ διὰ τοῦτο οὖν K 451 2492 ‖ αὐτοῦ 𝔭⁴⁶ ℵ* D* P Ψ (itᵈ) syrᵖ

9 διδαχαῖς...παραφέρεσθε Eph 4.14   11 Lv 16.27   13 He 11.26   14 He 11.10, 16; 12.22
15 θυσίαν...αὐτοῦ 2 Chr 29.31; Ps 50.14, 23   καρπὸν χειλέων Ho 14.2   16 τοιαύταις...θεός
Php 4.18   17 αὐτοὶ...ὑμῶν Is 62.6; Eze 3.17   18 καλὴν...ἀναστρέφεσθαι Ac 24.16; 2 Cor 1.12
20 ὁ ἀναγαγὼν...προβάτων Is 63.11   τὸν ποιμένα...μέγαν 1 Pe 2.25   αἵματι διαθήκης
Zch 9.11   διαθήκης αἰωνίου Is 55.3; Jr 32.40; Eze 37.26

---

yesterday, today, and for ever. [9] Do not let different and strange teachings lead you from the right way. It is good for our souls to be made strong by God's grace, not by obeying rules about foods; those who obey these rules have not been helped by them.

[10] The priests who serve in the Jewish tent have no right to eat of the sacrifice on our altar. [11] The Jewish High Priest brings the blood of the animals into the Most Holy Place to offer it as a sacrifice for sins; but the bodies of the animals are burned outside the camp. [12] For this reason Jesus also died outside the city gate, in order to cleanse the people from sin with his own blood. [13] Let us, then, go to him outside the camp and share his shame. [14] For there is no permanent city for us here on earth; we are looking for the city which is to come. [15] Let us, then, always offer praise to God as our sacrifice through Jesus; that is, let us always give thanks to his name with our voices. [16] Do not forget to do good and to help one another, for these are the sacrifices that please God.

[17] Obey your leaders and follow their orders. They watch over your souls without resting, since they must give an account of their service to God. If you obey them, they will do their work gladly; else they will do it with sadness, and that would not be of any help to you.

[18] Keep on praying for us. We are sure we have a clear conscience, for we want to do the right thing at all times. [19] And I beg you all the more to pray that God will send me back to you the sooner.

Prayer

[20] God has raised from the dead our Lord Jesus, who is the Great Shepherd of the sheep because of his death, by

which the eternal covenant is sealed.
21 May the God of peace provide you
with every good thing you need in order
to do his will, and may he, through Jesus
Christ, do in us what pleases him. And
to Christ be the glory for ever and ever!
Amen.

Final Words

22 I beg you, my brothers, to listen
patiently to this message of encouragement; for this letter I have written you
is not very long. 23 I want you to know
that our brother Timothy has been let
out of prison. If he comes soon enough,
I will have him with me when I see you.

24 Give our greetings to all your leaders
and to all God's people. The brothers from
Italy send you their greetings.

25 May God's grace be with you all.

αἰωνίου, τὸν κύριον ἡμῶν Ἰησοῦν, 21 καταρτίσαι ὑμᾶς
ἐν παντὶ ἀγαθῷ[2] εἰς τὸ ποιῆσαι τὸ θέλημα αὐτοῦ, ποιῶν[3]
ἐν ἡμῖν[4] τὸ εὐάρεστον ἐνώπιον αὐτοῦ διὰ Ἰησοῦ Χριστοῦ,
ᾧ ἡ δόξα εἰς τοὺς αἰῶνας [τῶν αἰώνων][5]· ἀμήν.

22 Παρακαλῶ δὲ ὑμᾶς, ἀδελφοί, ἀνέχεσθε τοῦ λόγου
τῆς παρακλήσεως, καὶ γὰρ διὰ βραχέων ἐπέστειλα ὑμῖν.
23 Γινώσκετε τὸν ἀδελφὸν ἡμῶν Τιμόθεον ἀπολελυμένον,
μεθ' οὗ ἐὰν τάχιον ἔρχηται ὄψομαι ὑμᾶς.

24 Ἀσπάσασθε πάντας τοὺς ἡγουμένους ὑμῶν καὶ
πάντας τοὺς ἁγίους. ἀσπάζονται ὑμᾶς οἱ ἀπὸ τῆς
Ἰταλίας. 25 ἡ χάρις μετὰ πάντων ὑμῶν.[6]

---

2 21 {A} παντὶ ἀγαθῷ (p46 τῷ ἀγαθῷ) ℵ D* Ψ itar,c,d,dem,div,f,z vg copbo
Gregory-Nyssa Euthalius Fulgentius Primasius // ἔργῳ ἀγαθῷ arm //
παντὶ ἔργῳ ἀγαθῷ C Dc K P 0121b 33 81 88 104 181 326 330 436 451 614
629 630 1241 1739 1877 1881 1962 1984 2127 2492 2495 Byz Lect syrp,h copsa
eth Ephraem Chrysostom Theodoret John-Damascus // παντὶ ἔργῳ καὶ
λόγῳ ἀγαθῷ (see 2 Th 2.17) A

3 21 {C} ποιῶν ℵc Dgr K P Ψ 0121b 33c 88 104 181 326 330 436 614 629
630 1739* 1877 1881 1962 1984 2127 2495 Byz Lect itar,c,dem,div,f vg syrp,h
copsams,boms arm (eth) Chrysostom Euthalius Theodoret John-Damascus //
αὐτῷ ποιῶν ℵ* A C 33* 81 1241 1739mg copsa // ποιῶν ἑαυτῷ copbo Gregory-
Nyssa // αὐτὸ ποιῶν p46 // αὐτὸς ποιῶν 451 2492 itd,z

4 21 {B} ἡμῖν p46 ℵ A Dgr K 0121b 33 81 104 181 326 330 436 451 614 629 1241
1739 1881 1962 2492 Byzpt syrp copsa,bo arm Theodoret Ps-Oecumenius //
ὑμῖν C P Ψ 88 630 1877 1984 2127 2495 Byzpt Lect itar,c,d,dem,div,f,z vg syrh eth
Chrysostom Euthalius Theodoret John-Damascus Theophylact

5 21 {C} τῶν αἰώνων ℵ A (C* τῶν αἰῶνας) K P 0121b 33 81 88 181 326 330
614 629 630 1739 1881 1962 Byz l597 itar,c,dem,div,f,z vg syrp copsamss,bo eth
Chrysostom Euthalius Theodoret John-Damascus // omit p46 C3 Dgr Ψ
104 436 451 1241 1877 2127 2492 2495 Lect syrh copsamss arm Theodoret //
omit ᾧ ἡ δόξα...ἀμήν. 1984

6 25 {C} πάντων ὑμῶν. p46 ℵ* Ivid 33 copsa arm // πάντων ὑμῶν.
ἀμήν. ℵc A C Dc H K P Ψ 0121b 81 88 104 181 326 330 436 451 614 629 630
1739 1877 1881 1962 1984 2127 2492 2495 Byz Lect itar,c,dem,div,f,z vg syrp,h
copbo eth Chrysostom Euthalius Theodoret John-Damascus // πάντων
ἡμῶν. ἀμήν. 1241 // πάντων τῶν ἁγίων. ἀμήν. Dgr*

ΙΑΚΩΒΟΥ

Salutation

1 Ἰάκωβος θεοῦ καὶ κυρίου Ἰησοῦ Χριστοῦ δοῦλος ταῖς δώδεκα φυλαῖς ταῖς ἐν τῇ διασπορᾷ χαίρειν.

Faith and Wisdom

2 Πᾶσαν χαρὰν ἡγήσασθε, ἀδελφοί μου, ὅταν πειρασμοῖς περιπέσητε ποικίλοις, **3** γινώσκοντες ὅτι τὸ δοκίμιον[1] ὑμῶν τῆς πίστεως κατεργάζεται ὑπομονήν· **4** ἡ δὲ ὑπομονὴ ἔργον τέλειον ἐχέτω, ἵνα ἦτε τέλειοι καὶ ὁλόκληροι, ἐν μηδενὶ λειπόμενοι. **5** Εἰ δέ τις ὑμῶν λείπεται σοφίας, αἰτείτω παρὰ τοῦ διδόντος θεοῦ πᾶσιν ἁπλῶς καὶ μὴ ὀνειδίζοντος, καὶ δοθήσεται αὐτῷ. **6** αἰτείτω δὲ ἐν πίστει, μηδὲν διακρινόμενος, ὁ γὰρ διακρινόμενος ἔοικεν κλύδωνι θαλάσσης ἀνεμιζομένῳ καὶ ῥιπιζομένῳ· **7** μὴ γὰρ οἰέσθω ὁ ἄνθρωπος ἐκεῖνος ὅτι λήμψεταί τι παρὰ τοῦ κυρίου,[a] **8** ἀνὴρ δίψυχος,[a] ἀκατάστατος ἐν πάσαις ταῖς ὁδοῖς αὐτοῦ.

Poverty and Riches

9 Καυχάσθω δὲ ὁ ἀδελφὸς ὁ ταπεινὸς ἐν τῷ ὕψει αὐτοῦ, **10** ὁ δὲ πλούσιος ἐν τῇ ταπεινώσει αὐτοῦ, ὅτι ὡς ἄνθος χόρτου παρελεύσεται. **11** ἀνέτειλεν γὰρ ὁ ἥλιος σὺν τῷ καύσωνι καὶ ἐξήρανεν τὸν χόρτον, καὶ τὸ ἄνθος αὐτοῦ ἐξέπεσεν καὶ ἡ εὐπρέπεια τοῦ προσώπου αὐτοῦ ἀπώλετο· οὕτως καὶ ὁ πλούσιος ἐν ταῖς πορείαις αὐτοῦ μαρανθήσεται.

---

[1] **3** {B} δοκίμιον ℵ A B C K P Ψ 049 056 0142 33 81 88 104 181 326 330 436 451 614 629 630 945 1505 1739 1877 2127 2412 2492 2495 *Byz Lect* it[ar,c,dem,div,ff,p,s,(t),z] vg arm // δόκιμον 𝔭[74] 1241

[a] [a] **7-8** *a* minor, *a* minor: WH[mg] Bov Nes BF[2] RV ASV Zür Jer // *a* none, *a* minor: WH RV[mg] ASV[mg] RSV // *a* major, *a* minor: NEB TT Seg // *a* major, *a* none: TR AV NEB[mg] Luth

1 ταῖς...διασπορᾷ Ac 15.23; 1 Pe 1.1   **2** Ro 5.3-5; 1 Pe 1.6   **3** τὸ...πίστεως 1 Pe 1.7
5 Pr 2.3-6   **6** αἰτείτω...διακρινόμενος Mt 7.7; Mk 11.24   **10-11** ὡς...ἀπώλετο Ps 102.4, 11; Is 40.6-7; 1 Pe 1 24

THE LETTER FROM JAMES

1 From James, a servant of God and of the Lord Jesus Christ:

Greetings to all God's people, scattered over the whole world.

Faith and Wisdom

[2] My brothers! Consider yourselves fortunate when all kinds of trials come your way, [3] for you know that when your faith succeeds in facing such trials, the result is the ability to endure. [4] But be sure that your endurance carries you all the way, without failing, so that you may be perfect and complete, lacking nothing. [5] But if any of you lacks wisdom, he should pray to God, who will give it to him; for God gives generously and graciously to all. [6] But you must believe when you pray, and not doubt at all; for whoever doubts is like a wave in the sea that is driven and blown about by the wind. [7] Any such person must not think that he will receive anything from the Lord, [8] for he is unsure and undecided in every step he takes.

Poverty and Riches

[9] The poor brother must be proud when God lifts him up, [10] and the rich brother when God brings him down. For the rich will pass away like the bloom of a wild plant. [11] The sun rises with its blazing heat and burns the plant; its bloom falls off, and its beauty is destroyed. In the same way the rich man will be destroyed while busy conducting his affairs.

Testing and Tempting

[12] Happy is the man who remains faithful under trials; for when he succeeds in passing the test he will be given life, the prize which God has promised to those who love him. [13] If a man is tempted by such testing, he must not say, "This temptation comes from God." For God cannot be tempted by evil, and he himself tempts no one. [14] But a person is tempted when he is drawn away and trapped by his own evil desire; [15] then his evil desire conceives and gives birth to sin; and sin, when it is full-grown, gives birth to death.

[16] Do not be deceived, my dear brothers! [17] Every good gift and every perfect present comes from heaven; it comes down from God, the Creator of the heavenly lights. He does not change, nor does he cause darkness by turning. [18] By his own will he brought us into being through the word of truth, so that we should occupy first place among all his creatures.

Trial and Temptation

12 Μακάριος ἀνὴρ ὃς ὑπομένει πειρασμόν, ὅτι δόκιμος γενόμενος λήμψεται τὸν στέφανον τῆς ζωῆς, ὃν ἐπηγγείλατο[2] τοῖς ἀγαπῶσιν αὐτόν. **13** μηδεὶς πειραζόμενος λεγέτω ὅτι Ἀπὸ θεοῦ πειράζομαι· ὁ γὰρ θεὸς ἀπείραστός ἐστιν κακῶν, πειράζει δὲ αὐτὸς οὐδένα. **14** ἕκαστος δὲ πειράζεται[b] ὑπὸ τῆς ἰδίας ἐπιθυμίας[b] ἐξελκόμενος καὶ δελεαζόμενος· **15** εἶτα ἡ ἐπιθυμία συλλαβοῦσα τίκτει ἁμαρτίαν, ἡ δὲ ἁμαρτία ἀποτελεσθεῖσα ἀποκύει θάνατον.

16 Μὴ πλανᾶσθε, ἀδελφοί μου ἀγαπητοί. **17** πᾶσα δόσις ἀγαθὴ καὶ πᾶν δώρημα τέλειον ἄνωθέν ἐστιν,[c] καταβαῖνον[c] ἀπὸ τοῦ πατρὸς τῶν φώτων, παρ᾽ ᾧ οὐκ ἔνι παραλλαγὴ ἢ τροπῆς ἀποσκίασμα[3]. **18** βουληθεὶς ἀπεκύησεν ἡμᾶς λόγῳ ἀληθείας, εἰς τὸ εἶναι ἡμᾶς ἀπαρχήν τινα τῶν αὐτοῦ κτισμάτων.

---

[2] **12** {B} ἐπηγγείλατο p[23,74vid] ℵ A B Ψ 81 it[ff] cop[sa,bo] arm ∥ ἐπηγγείλατο ὁ κύριος (C omit ὁ) K P 049 056 0142 0246 88 104 181 326 330 436 451 614 629 630 1505 1877 2127 2412 2495 Byz Lect (l[680] omit ὁ) syr[h] (John-Damascus) Ps-Oecumenius Theophylact ∥ ἐπηγγείλατο ὁ θεός 945 1241 1739 2492 it[ar,c,dem,div,p,s,t] vg syr[p] eth John-Damascus

[3] **17** {C} παραλλαγὴ ἢ τροπῆς ἀποσκίασμα ℵ[c] A C K P (Ψ οὐδέ for ἤ) 049 056 0142 81 88 104 181 326 330 436 451 629 630 945 1241 1739 1877 2127 2492 Byz Lect it[ar,c,dem,div,p,svid,t,z] vg syr[p,h] arm Jerome ∥ παραλλαγὴ ἢ [or ἤ] τροπῆς ἀποσκιάσματος ℵ* B ∥ παραλλαγὴ ἢ τροπὴ ἀποσκιάσματος 614 1505 2412 2495 ∥ παραλλαγῆς ἢ τροπῆς ἀποσκιάσματος p[23] ∥ ἀποσκίασμα ἢ τροπὴ ἢ παραλλαγή cop[sa] ∥ παραλλαγὴ ἢ ῥοπῆς ἀποσκίασμα Augustine ∥ παραλλαγὴ ἢ ῥοπὴ ἀποσκιάσματος it[ff] cop[bo?]

[b,b] **14** b none, b none: WH Bov Nes BF[2] ∥ b minor, b none: TR AV RV ASV (RSV) (NEB) Zür Luth Seg ∥ b none, b minor: RV[mg] ASV[mg] TT (Jer)

[c,c] **17** c minor, c none: TR WH AV RV ASV RSV TT (Jer) ∥ c none, c minor: NEB Zür Luth Seg ∥ c none, c none: Bov Nes BF[2]

---

12 λήμψεται...ζωῆς 1 Cor 9.25; 2 Tm 4.8; 1 Pe 5.4; Re 2.10　　**13** μηδεὶς...πειράζομαι Sir 15.11–13　　**17** πᾶσα...πατρός Mt 7.11　　**18** βουληθεὶς ἀπεκύησεν ἡμᾶς Jn 1.13　ἀπεκύησεν...ἀληθείας 1 Pe 1.23

Hearing and Doing the Word

19 Ἴστε, ἀδελφοί μου ἀγαπητοί. ἔστω δὲ[4] πᾶς ἄνθρωπος ταχὺς εἰς τὸ ἀκοῦσαι, βραδὺς εἰς τὸ λαλῆσαι, βραδὺς εἰς ὀργήν· **20** ὀργὴ γὰρ ἀνδρὸς δικαιοσύνην θεοῦ οὐκ ἐργάζεται. **21** διὸ ἀποθέμενοι πᾶσαν ῥυπαρίαν καὶ περισσείαν κακίας ἐν πραΰτητι δέξασθε τὸν ἔμφυτον λόγον τὸν δυνάμενον σῶσαι τὰς ψυχὰς ὑμῶν.

22 Γίνεσθε δὲ ποιηταὶ λόγου καὶ μὴ ἀκροαταὶ μόνον παραλογιζόμενοι ἑαυτούς. **23** ὅτι εἴ τις ἀκροατὴς λόγου ἐστὶν καὶ οὐ ποιητής, οὗτος ἔοικεν ἀνδρὶ κατανοοῦντι τὸ πρόσωπον τῆς γενέσεως αὐτοῦ ἐν ἐσόπτρῳ· **24** κατενόησεν γὰρ ἑαυτὸν καὶ ἀπελήλυθεν καὶ εὐθέως ἐπελάθετο ὁποῖος ἦν. **25** ὁ δὲ παρακύψας εἰς νόμον τέλειον τὸν τῆς ἐλευθερίας καὶ παραμείνας, οὐκ ἀκροατὴς ἐπιλησμονῆς γενόμενος ἀλλὰ ποιητὴς ἔργου, οὗτος μακάριος ἐν τῇ ποιήσει αὐτοῦ ἔσται.

26 Εἴ τις δοκεῖ θρησκὸς εἶναι, μὴ χαλιναγωγῶν γλῶσσαν αὐτοῦ ἀλλὰ ἀπατῶν καρδίαν αὐτοῦ, τούτου μάταιος ἡ θρησκεία. **27** θρησκεία καθαρὰ καὶ ἀμίαντος παρὰ τῷ θεῷ καὶ πατρὶ αὕτη ἐστίν, ἐπισκέπτεσθαι ὀρφανοὺς καὶ χήρας ἐν τῇ θλίψει αὐτῶν, ἄσπιλον ἑαυτὸν τηρεῖν[5] ἀπὸ τοῦ κόσμου.

---

4 19 {B} ἴστε, ἀδελφοί μου ἀγαπητοί. ἔστω δὲ (א* ἴστω) אᶜ B C (81 καὶ ἔστω) 88 436 945 1739 itᵃʳ,ᵈᵉᵐ,ᵈⁱᵛ,ff,ᵖ,ˢ,ᵗ,ᶻ vg (syrʰᵐᵍ arm *omit* δέ) copᵇᵒ (copᵇᵒᵐˢ ἴσμεν) ‖ ἀδελφοί μου ἀγαπητοὶ ἔστω δέ Lect (l603,680,1364 *omit* δέ) ‖ ἴστε δὲ ἀδελφοί μου ἀγαπητοί. ἔστω δέ p74ᵛⁱᵈ (A* καὶ ἐστώς, Aᵒ καὶ ἔστω) (itᶜ ἴστε γάρ) copˢᵃ ‖ ὥστε, ἀδελφοί μου ἀγαπητοί, ἔστω Κ (P* ἔστω δέ) P² Ψ 049 056 0142 0246ᵛⁱᵈ 104 181 326 330 451 614 630 1241 1505 1877 2127 2412 2492 2495 Byz (l1365 ἀγαπητοί μου ἀδελφοί) syrᵖ,ʰ Ps-Oecumenius Theophylact ‖ καὶ νῦν ἀδελφοὶ ἡμῶν ἔστω ethᵖᵖ (ethʳᵒ ἔστε)

5 27 {B} ἄσπιλον ἑαυτὸν τηρεῖν א (A σεαυτόν) B C K P 049 056 0142 33 81 88 104 181 326 330 (436 τηρεῖν ἑαυτόν) 451 629 630 945 1241 1739 1877 2127 2492 Byz Lect itᵃʳ,ᶜ,ᵈᵉᵐ,ᵈⁱᵛ,ff,ᵐ,ᵖ,ˢ,ᵗ,ᶻ vg syrᵖ,ʰ copˢᵃ,ᵇᵒ arm (eth σεαυτόν) ‖ ἀσπίλους ἑαυτοὺς τηρεῖτε 614 1505 2412 2495 ‖ ὑπερασπίζειν αὐτούς p74

---

19 ἔστω...λαλῆσαι Slr 5.11 βραδὺς εἰς ὀργήν Ec 7.9 **21** ἀποθέμενοι...κακίας Col 3.8; 1 Pe 2.1 **22** Γίνεσθε...μόνον Mt 7.26; Ro 2.13 **25** νόμον...ἐλευθερίας Ro 8.2; Ga 6.2; Jas 2.12; 1 Pe 2.16 οὗτος...ἔσται Jn 13.17 **26** μή...γλῶσσαν αὐτοῦ Ps 34.13; 39.1; 141.3

Hearing and Doing

[19] Remember this, my dear brothers! Everyone must be quick to listen, but slow to speak, and slow to become angry. [20] For man's anger does not help to achieve God's righteous purposes. [21] Rid yourselves, then, of every filthy habit and all wicked conduct. Submit to God and accept the word that he plants in your hearts, which is able to save you.

[22] Do not fool yourselves by just listening to his word. Instead, put it into practice. [23] For whoever listens to the word but does not put it into practice is like a man who looks in a mirror and sees himself as he is. [24] He takes a look at himself and then goes away, and at once forgets what he looks like. [25] But the man who looks closely into the perfect law that sets men free, who keeps on paying attention to it, and does not simply listen and then forget it, but puts it into practice — that man will be blessed by God in what he does.

[26] Does anyone think he is a religious man? If he does not control his tongue his religion is worthless and he deceives himself. [27] This is what God the Father considers to be pure and genuine religion: to take care of orphans and widows in their suffering, and to keep oneself from being corrupted by the world.

Warning against Prejudice

2 My brothers! In your life as believers in our Lord Jesus Christ, the Lord of glory, you must never treat people in different ways because of their outward appearance. ² Suppose a rich man wearing a gold ring and fine clothes comes in to your meeting, and a poor man in ragged clothes also comes in. ³ If you show more respect to the well-dressed man and say to him, "Have this best seat here," but say to the poor man, "Stand, or sit down here on the floor by my seat," ⁴ then you are guilty of creating distinctions among yourselves and making judgments based on evil motives.

⁵ Listen, my dear brothers! God chose the poor people of this world to be rich in faith and to possess the Kingdom which he promised to those who love him. ⁶ But you dishonor the poor! Who oppresses you and drags you before the judges? The rich! ⁷ They are the ones who speak evil of that good name which God has given you.

⁸ You will be doing the right thing if you obey the law of the Kingdom, which is found in the scripture, "Love your neighbor as yourself." ⁹ But if you treat people according to their outward appearance, you are guilty of sin, and the Law condemns you as a lawbreaker. ¹⁰ For whoever breaks only one command of the Law is guilty of breaking them all. ¹¹ For the same one who said, "Do not commit adultery," also said, "Do not kill." Even if you do not commit adultery, you have become a lawbreaker if

Warning against Partiality

2 Ἀδελφοί μου, μὴ ἐν προσωπολημψίαις ἔχετε τὴν πίστιν τοῦ κυρίου ἡμῶν Ἰησοῦ Χριστοῦ[a] τῆς δόξης.[b] 2 ἐὰν γὰρ εἰσέλθῃ εἰς συναγωγὴν ὑμῶν ἀνὴρ χρυσοδακτύλιος ἐν ἐσθῆτι λαμπρᾷ, εἰσέλθῃ δὲ καὶ πτωχὸς ἐν ῥυπαρᾷ ἐσθῆτι, 3 ἐπιβλέψητε δὲ ἐπὶ τὸν φοροῦντα τὴν ἐσθῆτα τὴν λαμπρὰν καὶ εἴπητε, Σὺ κάθου ὧδε καλῶς, καὶ τῷ πτωχῷ εἴπητε, Σὺ στῆθι ἢ κάθου ἐκεῖ[1] ὑπὸ τὸ ὑποπόδιόν μου, 4 οὐ διεκρίθητε ἐν ἑαυτοῖς καὶ ἐγένεσθε κριταὶ διαλογισμῶν πονηρῶν;

5 Ἀκούσατε, ἀδελφοί μου ἀγαπητοί. οὐχ ὁ θεὸς ἐξελέξατο τοὺς πτωχοὺς τῷ κόσμῳ πλουσίους ἐν πίστει καὶ κληρονόμους τῆς βασιλείας ἧς ἐπηγγείλατο τοῖς ἀγαπῶσιν αὐτόν; 6 ὑμεῖς δὲ ἠτιμάσατε τὸν πτωχόν. οὐχ οἱ πλούσιοι καταδυναστεύουσιν ὑμῶν, καὶ αὐτοὶ ἕλκουσιν ὑμᾶς εἰς κριτήρια; 7 οὐκ αὐτοὶ βλασφημοῦσιν τὸ καλὸν ὄνομα τὸ ἐπικληθὲν ἐφ' ὑμᾶς; 8 εἰ μέντοι νόμον τελεῖτε βασιλικὸν κατὰ τὴν γραφήν, **Ἀγαπήσεις τὸν πλησίον σου ὡς σεαυτόν,** καλῶς ποιεῖτε· 9 εἰ δὲ προσωπολημπτεῖτε, ἁμαρτίαν ἐργάζεσθε, ἐλεγχόμενοι ὑπὸ τοῦ νόμου ὡς παραβάται. 10 ὅστις γὰρ ὅλον τὸν νόμον τηρήσῃ, πταίσῃ δὲ ἐν ἑνί, γέγονεν πάντων ἔνοχος. 11 ὁ γὰρ εἰπών, **Μὴ μοιχεύσῃς,** εἶπεν καί, **Μὴ φονεύσῃς·** εἰ δὲ οὐ μοιχεύεις, φονεύεις δέ, γέγονας παραβάτης

---

¹ 3 {C} ἢ κάθου ἐκεῖ B 945 1241 1739 2492 *l*⁸⁰⁹ it^ff ‖ ἢ κάθου ὧδε cop^sa ‖ ἐκεῖ καὶ κάθου C* ‖ ἐκεῖ ἢ κάθου A Ψ 33 81 614 630 1505 2412 2495 it^ar,c,dem,div, p,s,t,z vg syr^h Augustine Cyril Hesychius ‖ ἐκεῖ ἢ κάθου ὧδε p⁷⁴*vid* ℵ C² K P 049 056 0142 88 104 181 326 330 436 451 629 1877 2127 *Byz Lect* syr^p cop^bo eth Ps-Oecumenius Theophylact ‖ ἢ ἔλθε κάθου arm

a 1 *a* none: TR WH Bov Nes BF² TT Jer ‖ *a* minor: WH^mg AV RV ASV RSV NEB Zür Luth Seg
b 1 *b* statement: TR Bov Nes BF² AV RV ASV RSV NEB TT Luth Jer Seg ‖ *b* question: WH RV^mg ASV^mg ‖ *b* exclamation: Zür

1 μὴ...ἔχετε Job 34.19; Ac 10.34; Jas 2.9   5 ὁ...κόσμῳ 1 Cor 1.26–28   8 Ἀγαπήσεις... σεαυτόν Lv 19.18 (Mt 19.19; 22.39; Mk 12.31; Lk 10.27; Ro 13.9; Ga 5.14)   9 ἐλεγχόμενοι... παραβάται Dt 1.17   10 πταίσῃ...ἑνί Mt 5.19   11 Μὴ μοιχεύσῃς Ex 20.14; Dt 5.18 (Mt 5.27; 19.18; Mk 10.19; Lk 18.20; Ro 13.9)   Μὴ φονεύσῃς Ex 20.13; Dt 5.17 (Mt 5.21; Mk 10.19; Lk 18.20; Ro 13.9)

νόμου. **12** οὕτως λαλεῖτε καὶ οὕτως ποιεῖτε ὡς διὰ νόμου ἐλευθερίας μέλλοντες κρίνεσθαι. **13** ἡ γὰρ κρίσις ἀνέλεος τῷ μὴ ποιήσαντι ἔλεος· κατακαυχᾶται ἔλεος κρίσεως.

Faith and Works

14 Τί τὸ ὄφελος, ἀδελφοί μου, ἐὰν πίστιν λέγῃ τις ἔχειν, ἔργα δὲ μὴ ἔχῃ; μὴ δύναται ἡ πίστις σῶσαι αὐτόν; **15** ἐὰν ἀδελφὸς ἢ ἀδελφὴ γυμνοὶ ὑπάρχωσιν καὶ λειπόμενοι τῆς ἐφημέρου τροφῆς, **16** εἴπῃ δέ τις αὐτοῖς ἐξ ὑμῶν, Ὑπάγετε ἐν εἰρήνῃ, θερμαίνεσθε καὶ χορτάζεσθε, μὴ δῶτε δὲ αὐτοῖς τὰ ἐπιτήδεια τοῦ σώματος, τί τὸ ὄφελος; **17** οὕτως καὶ ἡ πίστις, ἐὰν μὴ ἔχῃ ἔργα, νεκρά ἐστιν καθ᾽ ἑαυτήν.

18 Ἀλλ᾽ ἐρεῖ τις, Σὺ πίστιν ἔχεις[c] κἀγὼ ἔργα ἔχω.[c] δεῖξόν μοι τὴν πίστιν σου χωρὶς τῶν ἔργων, κἀγώ σοι δείξω ἐκ τῶν ἔργων μου τὴν πίστιν. **19** σὺ πιστεύεις ὅτι εἷς θεός ἐστιν[2];[d] καλῶς ποιεῖς· καὶ τὰ δαιμόνια πιστεύουσιν καὶ φρίσσουσιν. **20** θέλεις δὲ γνῶναι, ὦ ἄνθρωπε κενέ, ὅτι ἡ πίστις χωρὶς τῶν ἔργων ἀργή[3] ἐστιν; **21** Ἀβραὰμ ὁ πατὴρ ἡμῶν οὐκ ἐξ ἔργων ἐδικαιώθη, ἀνενέγκας Ἰσαὰκ τὸν υἱὸν αὐτοῦ ἐπὶ τὸ θυσια-

---

[2] 19 {C} εἷς θεός ἐστιν B 614 630 1505 2412 2495 Theophylact ∥ εἷς ἐστιν ὁ θεός 𝔭[74] ℵ A (945 1241 1739 *omit* ὁ) it[ar,c,dem,div,p,s,z] vg syr[p] cop[sa,bo] arm eth[pp] Cyril[1/2] ∥ εἷς ὁ θεός ἐστιν C 81 2492 syr[h] ∥ ὁ θεὸς εἷς ἐστιν (K[txt] *omit* εἷς) K[mg] 049 056 0142 88 104 181 326 436 629 1877 (330 451 2127 *omit* ὁ) *Byz Lect* Didymus Ps-Oecumenius ∥ εἷς ὁ θεός it[ff] eth[ro] Cyril[1/2] ∥ ἐστιν θεός Ψ

[3] 20 {B} ἀργή B C* 945 1739 it[ar,c,dem,div,ff,s,z] vg[ww] cop[sa] arm ∥ νεκρά (*see* 2,26) ℵ A C² K P Ψ 049 056 0142 33 81 88 104 181 326 330 436 451 614 629 630 1241 1505 1877 2127 2412 2492 2495 *Byz Lect* it[p] vg[cl] syr[p,h] cop[bo] eth Cyril Ps-Athanasius Ps-Oecumenius ∥ κενή 𝔭[74]

[c,c] **18** c none, c major: WH RSV NEB Zür ∥ c minor, c major: TR Bov Nes BF² AV RV ASV TT Luth Seg ∥ c minor, c question: Jer ∥ c question, c major: WH[mg]

[d] **19** d question: WH Bov Nes BF² TT Luth Jer ∥ d statement: TR AV RV ASV RSV NEB Zür Seg

---

12 νόμου ἐλευθερίας Ro 8.2; Ga 6.2; Jas 1.25; 1 Pe 2.16   **13** ἡ...ἔλεος Mt 5.7; 18.32–35
14 Τί...ἔχῃ Mt 7.21   **17** Jas 2.20, 26   **19** τὰ δαιμόνια πιστεύουσιν Mt 8.29; Mk 1.24; 5.7; Lk 4.34   **21** ἀνενέγκας...θυσιαστήριον Gn 22.9, 12

---

you kill. **12** Speak and act as men who will be judged by the law that sets men free. **13** For God will not show mercy when he judges the man who has not been merciful; but mercy triumphs over judgment.

Faith and Actions

14 My brothers! What good is it for a man to say, "I have faith," if his actions do not prove it? Can that faith save him? **15** Suppose there are brothers or sisters who need clothes and don't have enough to eat. **16** What good is there in your saying to them, "God bless you! Keep warm and eat well!" — if you don't give them the necessities of life? **17** This is how it is with faith: if it is alone and has no actions with it, then it is dead.

18 But someone will say, "You have faith and I have actions." My answer is, "Show me how you can have faith without actions; I will show you my faith by my actions." **19** You believe that there is only one God? Good! The demons also believe — and tremble with fear. **20** Foolish man! Do you want to be shown that faith without actions is useless? **21** How was our ancestor Abraham put right with God? It was through his actions, when he offered his son Isaac on the altar. 22 Can't you see? His faith and his actions worked together; his faith was made perfect through his actions. 23 And the scripture came true that said, "Abraham believed God, and because of his faith God accepted him as righteous." And God called him "My friend Abraham." 24 So you see that a man is put right with God by what he does, and not because of his faith alone.

25 It was the same with the prostitute Rahab. She was put right with God because of her actions, by welcoming the Jewish messengers and helping them leave by a different road. 26 For just as the body without the spirit is dead, so also faith without actions is dead.

The Tongue

3 My brothers! Not many of you should become teachers, for you know that we teachers will be judged with greater strictness than others. 2 All of us often make mistakes. The person who never makes a mistake in what he says is perfect, able also to control his whole being. 3 We put the bit into the mouths of horses to make them obey us, and we are able to make them go where we want. 4 Or think of a ship: big as it is, and driven by such strong winds, it can be steered by a very small rudder, and goes wherever the pilot wants it to go. 5 This is how it is with the tongue: small as it is, it can boast about great things.

Just think how large a forest can be set on fire by a tiny flame! 6 And the tongue is like a fire. It is a world of wrong, occupying its place in our bodies

στήριον; 22 βλέπεις ὅτι ἡ πίστις συνήργει τοῖς ἔργοις αὐτοῦ καὶ ἐκ τῶν ἔργων ἡ πίστις ἐτελειώθη,ᵉ 23 καὶ ἐπληρώθη ἡ γραφὴ ἡ λέγουσα, **Ἐπίστευσεν δὲ Ἀβραὰμ τῷ θεῷ, καὶ ἐλογίσθη αὐτῷ εἰς δικαιοσύνην,** καὶ φίλος θεοῦ ἐκλήθη. 24 ὁρᾶτε ὅτι ἐξ ἔργων δικαιοῦται ἄνθρωπος καὶ οὐκ ἐκ πίστεως μόνον. 25 ὁμοίως δὲ καὶ Ῥαὰβ ἡ πόρνη οὐκ ἐξ ἔργων ἐδικαιώθη, ὑποδεξαμένη τοὺς ἀγγέλους καὶ ἑτέρᾳ ὁδῷ ἐκβαλοῦσα; 26 ὥσπερ γὰρ τὸ σῶμα χωρὶς πνεύματος νεκρόν ἐστιν, οὕτως καὶ ἡ πίστις χωρὶς ἔργων νεκρά ἐστιν.

The Tongue

3 Μὴ πολλοὶ διδάσκαλοι γίνεσθε, ἀδελφοί μου, εἰδότες ὅτι μεῖζον κρίμα λημψόμεθα.ᵃ 2 πολλὰ γὰρ πταίομεν ἅπαντες.ᵃ εἴ τις ἐν λόγῳ οὐ πταίει, οὗτος τέλειος ἀνήρ, δυνατὸς χαλιναγωγῆσαι καὶ ὅλον τὸ σῶμα. 3 εἰ δὲ¹ τῶν ἵππων τοὺς χαλινοὺς εἰς τὰ στόματα βάλλομεν εἰς τὸ πείθεσθαι αὐτοὺς ἡμῖν, καὶ ὅλον τὸ σῶμα αὐτῶν μετάγομεν. 4 ἰδοὺ καὶ τὰ πλοῖα, τηλικαῦτα ὄντα καὶ ὑπὸ ἀνέμων σκληρῶν ἐλαυνόμενα, μετάγεται ὑπὸ ἐλαχίστου πηδαλίου ὅπου ἡ ὁρμὴ τοῦ εὐθύνοντος βούλεται· 5 οὕτως καὶ ἡ γλῶσσα μικρὸν μέλος ἐστὶν καὶ μεγάλα αὐχεῖ.

Ἰδοὺ ἡλίκον πῦρ ἡλίκην ὕλην ἀνάπτει·ᵇ 6 καὶ ἡ γλῶσσα πῦρ,ᵇ ὁ κόσμος τῆς ἀδικίας,ᶜ ἡ γλῶσσαᶜ καθί-

---

¹ **3** {D} εἰ δέ 33 104 181 326 330 436 451 2492 itᵃʳ,ᶜ,ᵈᵉᵐ,ᵈⁱᵛ,ᶠᶠ,ᵖ,ˢ,(ᵗ),ᶻ vg copᵇᵒ John-Damascus Ps-Oecumenius ∥ ιδε [= ἴδε, or by itacism, εἰ δέ] ℵᶜ A B C K P Ψ 049 056 0142 ∥ ἴδε 81 88 614 629 630 945 1241 1505 1739 2127 2412 2495 *Byz Lect* syrʰ copˢᵃ arm Theophylact ∥ ἰδού 1877 ∥ ἴδε γάρ (ℵ* εἴδε) syrᵖ ∥ *quare ergo* itᵐ

ᵉ **22** *e statement:* WH Bov Nes BF² RV ASV RSV NEB TT Zür Luth Jer Seg ∥ *e question:* TR AV RVᵐᵍ ASVᵐᵍ

ᵃ ᵃ **1-2** *a major, a major:* AV RV ASV Zür Luth Seg ∥ *a major, a minor:* Bov Nes BF² RSV NEB TT ∥ *a minor, a major:* TR WH Jer

ᵇ ᵇ **5-6** (*see footnote c*) *b major, b minor:* TR WH Bov Nes BF² Jerᵐᵍ ∥ *b exclamation, b minor:* AV RVᵐᵍ ASVᵐᵍ TT Luth Seg ∥ *b exclamation, b major:* RV ASV RSV NEB Zür ∥ *b minor, b major:* Jer

ᶜ ᶜ **6** (*see footnote b*) *c minor, c none:* Bov Nes BF² Jer ∥ *c major, c none:* RVᵐᵍ¹ ASVᵐᵍ¹ TT Luth

22 ἡ πίστις...αὐτοῦ He 11.17 **23** Ἐπίστευσεν...δικαιοσύνην Gn 15.6 (Ro 4.3, 9, 22; Ga 3.6) φίλος θεοῦ ἐκλήθη 2 Chr 20.7; Is 41.8 **25** Jos 2.4, 15; 6.17; He 11.31 **26** Jas 2.17, 20

σταται ἐν τοῖς μέλεσιν ἡμῶν, ἡ σπιλοῦσα ὅλον τὸ σῶμα καὶ φλογίζουσα τὸν τροχὸν τῆς γενέσεως καὶ φλογιζομένη ὑπὸ τῆς γεέννης. 7 πᾶσα γὰρ φύσις θηρίων τε καὶ πετεινῶν ἑρπετῶν τε καὶ ἐναλίων δαμάζεται καὶ δεδάμασται τῇ φύσει τῇ ἀνθρωπίνῃ· 8 τὴν δὲ γλῶσσαν οὐδεὶς δαμάσαι δύναται ἀνθρώπων· ἀκατάστατον κακόν, μεστὴ ἰοῦ θανατηφόρου. 9 ἐν αὐτῇ εὐλογοῦμεν τὸν κύριον καὶ πατέρα, καὶ ἐν αὐτῇ καταρώμεθα τοὺς ἀνθρώπους τοὺς καθ' ὁμοίωσιν θεοῦ γεγονότας· 10 ἐκ τοῦ αὐτοῦ στόματος ἐξέρχεται εὐλογία καὶ κατάρα. οὐ χρή, ἀδελφοί μου, ταῦτα οὕτως γίνεσθαι. 11 μήτι ἡ πηγὴ ἐκ τῆς αὐτῆς ὀπῆς βρύει τὸ γλυκὺ καὶ τὸ πικρόν; 12 μὴ δύναται, ἀδελφοί μου, συκῆ ἐλαίας ποιῆσαι ἢ ἄμπελος σῦκα; οὔτε ἁλυκὸν[2] γλυκὺ ποιῆσαι ὕδωρ.

The Wisdom from Above

13 Τίς σοφὸς καὶ ἐπιστήμων ἐν ὑμῖν; δειξάτω ἐκ τῆς καλῆς ἀναστροφῆς τὰ ἔργα αὐτοῦ ἐν πραΰτητι σοφίας. 14 εἰ δὲ ζῆλον πικρὸν ἔχετε καὶ ἐριθείαν ἐν τῇ καρδίᾳ ὑμῶν, μὴ κατακαυχᾶσθε καὶ ψεύδεσθε κατὰ τῆς ἀληθείας. 15 οὐκ ἔστιν αὕτη ἡ σοφία ἄνωθεν κατερχομένη, ἀλλὰ ἐπίγειος, ψυχική, δαιμονιώδης· 16 ὅπου γὰρ ζῆλος καὶ ἐριθεία, ἐκεῖ ἀκαταστασία καὶ πᾶν φαῦλον πρᾶγμα. 17 ἡ δὲ ἄνωθεν σοφία πρῶτον μὲν ἁγνή ἐστιν, ἔπειτα εἰρηνική, ἐπιεικής, εὐπειθής, μεστὴ ἐλέους καὶ καρπῶν ἀγαθῶν, ἀδιάκριτος, ἀνυπόκριτος· 18 καρπὸς δὲ δικαιοσύνης ἐν εἰρήνῃ σπείρεται τοῖς ποιοῦσιν εἰρήνην.

---

2 12 {B} οὔτε ἁλυκόν A B C* (88 οὐδέ) 2492[txt] (2492[mg] οὕτως) syr[h] cop[sa] arm (John-Damascus) ∥ οὕτως οὐδὲ ἁλυκόν ℵ C² (Ψ οὔτε for οὐδέ) (33 οὕτως οὐδὲ οὐδέ) 81 (1241 καὶ for οὐδέ) 1739 it[ar,c,dem,div,ff,p,t,z] vg syr[p,h with *] cop[bo] (eth) Cyril ∥ οὕτως οὐδεμία πηγὴ ἁλυκὸν καὶ K (P οὔτε μία) 049

Seg ∥ c minor, c minor: RV[mg2] ASV[mg2] ∥ c none, c none: WH RV ASV RSV NEB Zür ∥ different text: TR AV

---

6 ἡ σπιλοῦσα…γενέσεως Mt 12.36–37; 15.11, 18, 19   8 μεστὴ ἰοῦ θανατηφόρου Ps 140.3; Ro 3.13   9 τοὺς ἀνθρώπους…γεγονότας Gn 1.26, 27; 1 Cor 11.7   15 ἡ…κατερχομένη Jas 1.5, 17   18 καρπὸς…σπείρεται Is 32.17; He 12.11 τοῖς ποιοῦσιν εἰρήνην Mt 5.9

and spreading evil through our whole being! It sets on fire the entire course of our existence with the fire that comes to it from hell itself. [7] Man is able to tame, and has tamed, all other creatures — wild animals and birds, reptiles and fish. [8] But no man has ever been able to tame the tongue. It is evil and uncontrollable, full of deadly poison! [9] We use it to give thanks to our Lord and Father, and also to curse our fellow men, created in the likeness of God! [10] Words of thanksgiving and cursing pour out from the same mouth. My brothers! This should not happen! [11] No spring of water pours out sweet and bitter water from the same opening! [12] A fig tree, my brothers, cannot bear olives; a vine cannot bear figs; nor can salty water produce fresh water.

The Wisdom from Above

[13] Is there a wise and understanding man among you? He is to prove it by his good life, by his good deeds performed with humility and wisdom. [14] But if in your heart you are jealous, bitter, and selfish, then you must not be proud and tell lies against the truth. [15] This kind of wisdom does not come down from heaven; it belongs to the world, it is unspiritual and demonic. [16] For where there is jealousy and selfishness, there is also disorder and every kind of evil. [17] But the wisdom from above is pure, first of all; it is also peaceful, gentle, and friendly; it is full of compassion and produces a harvest of good deeds; it is free from prejudice and hypocrisy. [18] And righteousness is the harvest that is produced from the seeds the peacemakers planted in peace.

Friendship with the World

4 Where do all the fights and quarrels among you come from? They come from your passions, which are constantly fighting within your bodies. [2] You want things, but you cannot have them, so you are ready to kill; you covet things, but you cannot get them, so you quarrel and fight. You do not have what you want because you do not ask God for it. [3] And when you ask you do not receive it, because your motives are bad; you ask for things to use for your own pleasures. [4] Unfaithful people! Don't you know that to be the world's friend means to be God's enemy? Whoever wants to be the world's friend makes himself God's enemy. [5] Do not think that the scripture means nothing that says, "The spirit that God placed in us is filled with fierce desires."[1] [6] But the grace that God gives is even stronger. For the scripture says, "God resists the proud, but gives grace to the humble." [7] Submit yourselves, therefore, to God. Oppose the Devil, and he will flee from you. [8] Come near to God, and he will come near to you. Wash your hands, sinners! Cleanse your

---

[1] **5** The spirit that God placed in us is filled with fierce desires: *or* God yearns jealously over the spirit that he placed in us

Friendship with the World

4 Πόθεν πόλεμοι καὶ πόθεν μάχαι ἐν ὑμῖν; οὐκ ἐντεῦθεν, ἐκ τῶν ἡδονῶν ὑμῶν τῶν στρατευομένων ἐν τοῖς μέλεσιν ὑμῶν; 2 ἐπιθυμεῖτε, καὶ οὐκ ἔχετε·[a] φονεύετε[a] καὶ ζηλοῦτε, καὶ οὐ δύνασθε ἐπιτυχεῖν· μάχεσθε καὶ πολεμεῖτε. οὐκ ἔχετε διὰ τὸ μὴ αἰτεῖσθαι ὑμᾶς· 3 αἰτεῖτε καὶ οὐ λαμβάνετε, διότι κακῶς αἰτεῖσθε, ἵνα ἐν ταῖς ἡδοναῖς ὑμῶν δαπανήσητε.[b] 4 μοιχαλίδες[1],[b] οὐκ οἴδατε ὅτι ἡ φιλία τοῦ κόσμου ἔχθρα τοῦ θεοῦ ἐστιν; ὃς ἐὰν οὖν βουληθῇ φίλος εἶναι τοῦ κόσμου, ἐχθρὸς τοῦ θεοῦ καθίσταται. 5 ἢ δοκεῖτε ὅτι κενῶς ἡ γραφὴ λέγει,[c] Πρὸς φθόνον ἐπιποθεῖ τὸ πνεῦμα ὃ κατῴκισεν[2] ἐν ἡμῖν;[c] 6 μείζονα δὲ δίδωσιν χάριν·[c] διὸ λέγει,

Ὁ θεὸς ὑπερηφάνοις ἀντιτάσσεται,
ταπεινοῖς δὲ δίδωσιν χάριν.

7 ὑποτάγητε οὖν τῷ θεῷ· ἀντίστητε δὲ τῷ διαβόλῳ, καὶ φεύξεται ἀφ᾽ ὑμῶν· 8 ἐγγίσατε τῷ θεῷ, καὶ ἐγγιεῖ ὑμῖν. καθαρίσατε χεῖρας, ἁμαρτωλοί, καὶ ἁγνίσατε

---

056 0142 104 181 326 330 436 451 614 629 630 945 (1505 2495 οὐτεμία) 1877 2127 2412 *Byz Lect* Ps-Oecumenius Theophylact

[1] **4** {A} μοιχαλίδες ℵ* A B 33 81 629* 1241 1739 it^ar,c,dem,div,ff,p,s,t,z vg syr^p cop^sa,bo arm eth ‖ μοιχοὶ καὶ μοιχαλίδες ℵ^c K P Ψ 049 056 0142 88 104 181 326 330 436 451 614 629^c 630 945 1505 1877 2127 2412 2492 2495 *Byz Lect* syr^h Ps-Oecumenius Theophylact

[2] **5** {C} κατῴκισεν 𝔭^74 ℵ A B Ψ 049 104 1241 1739 1877* ‖ κατῴκησεν K P 056 0142 33 88 181 326 330 436 451 614 629 630 945 1505 1877^c 2127 2412 2492 2495 (81 *l*^680 κατῴκεισεν) *Byz Lect* it^ar,c,dem,div,ff,l,p,s,t,z vg syr^p,h cop^sa,bo arm Ps-Oecumenius Theophylact

---

^a a **2** *a* major, *a* none: TR WH Bov Nes BF² (AV) (RV) (ASV) RSV^mg TT Zür Luth Seg ‖ *a* none; *a* major: WH^mg (RSV) (NEB) ‖ *a* question, *a* major: Jer

^b b **3–4** *b* major, *b* minor: TR WH Bov Nes BF² AV RV ASV TT Zür Luth Jer ‖ *b* major, *b* exclamation: RSV NEB Seg ‖ *b* minor, *b* major

^c c c **5–6** *c* minor, *c* question, *c* statement: TR (WH) (Bov) Nes BF² AV RV^mg1 ASV^mg1 RSV (NEB) TT Luth Seg ‖ *c* question, *c* question, *c* statement: WH^mg1 RV ASV ‖ *c* question, *c* statement, *c* statement: WH^mg2 RV^mg2 ASV^mg2 ‖ *c* minor, *c* question, *c* none: Jer ‖ *c* minor, *c* minor, *c* question: Zür ‖ *c* minor, *c* minor, *c* statement: Zür^mg

---

1 Ro 7.23; 1 Pe 2.11   **4** ἡ...καθίσταται Ro 8.7; 1 Jn 2.15   **5** Πρὸς...ἡμῖν Ex 20.5
6 Ὁ...χάριν Pr 3.34 LXX (Mt 23.12; 1 Pe 5.5)   **7** ἀντίστητε...διαβόλῳ Eph 6.12; 1 Pe 5.8–9
8 ἐγγίσατε...ὑμῖν Zch 1.3; Mal 3.7   καθαρίσατε χεῖρας, ἁμαρτωλοί Is 1.16

καρδίας, δίψυχοι. **9** ταλαιπωρήσατε καὶ πενθήσατε καὶ κλαύσατε· ὁ γέλως ὑμῶν εἰς πένθος μετατραπήτω καὶ ἡ χαρὰ εἰς κατήφειαν. **10** ταπεινώθητε ἐνώπιον κυρίου, καὶ ὑψώσει ὑμᾶς.

Judging a Brother

11 Μὴ καταλαλεῖτε ἀλλήλων, ἀδελφοί· ὁ καταλαλῶν ἀδελφοῦ ἢ κρίνων τὸν ἀδελφὸν αὐτοῦ καταλαλεῖ νόμου καὶ κρίνει νόμον· εἰ δὲ νόμον κρίνεις, οὐκ εἶ ποιητὴς νόμου ἀλλὰ κριτής. **12** εἷς ἐστιν νομοθέτης καὶ κριτής, ὁ δυνάμενος σῶσαι καὶ ἀπολέσαι· σὺ δὲ τίς εἶ, ὁ κρίνων τὸν πλησίον;

Warning against Boasting

13 Ἄγε νῦν οἱ λέγοντες, Σήμερον ἢ αὔριον πορευσόμεθα εἰς τήνδε τὴν πόλιν καὶ ποιήσομεν ἐκεῖ ἐνιαυτὸν καὶ ἐμπορευσόμεθα καὶ κερδήσομεν· **14** οἵτινες οὐκ ἐπίστασθε τῆς αὔριον³ ποία⁴ ἡ ζωὴ ὑμῶν. ἀτμὶς γὰρ ἐστε⁵ πρὸς ὀλίγον φαινομένη, ἔπειτα καὶ ἀφανιζομένη· **15** ἀντὶ τοῦ λέγειν ὑμᾶς, Ἐὰν ὁ κύριος θέλῃ,ᵈ καὶ ζήσομενᵈ καὶ ποιήσομεν τοῦτο ἢ ἐκεῖνο. **16** νῦν δὲ καυχᾶσθε

³ **14** {D} τῆς αὔριον B Jerome ‖ τὸ τῆς αὔριον ℵ K Ψ 049 056 0142 104 181 326 330 436 451 629 1877 2127 *Byz Lect* itᵃʳ,ᶜ,ᵈᵉᵐ,ᵈⁱᵛ,ff,l,p,s,z vg syrᵖ arm Ps-Oecumenius Theophylact ‖ τὰ τῆς αὔριον A P 33 81 88 614 630 945 1241 1505 1739 2412 2492 2495 syrʰ

⁴ **14** {C} ποία ℵ* B 614 1505 2412 2495 itˡ syrʰ copᵇᵒᵐˢ arm ethʳᵒ ‖ ποία γάρ p⁷⁴ᵛⁱᵈ ℵᶜ A K P Ψ 049 056 0142 33 81 88 104 181 326 330 436 451 629 630 945 1241 1739 1877 2127 2492 *Byz Lect* itᵃʳ,ᶜ,ᵈᵉᵐ,ᵈⁱᵛ,s,z vg syrᵖ copᵇᵒ Ps-Oecumenius Theophylact ‖ ποία δέ itff ethᵖᵖ

⁵ **14** {C} ἀτμὶς γάρ ἐστε B 945 1739 ‖ ἀτμὶς γάρ ἐστε ἡ 81 104 614 2412 2492 syrʰ (arm? ὡς ἀτμίς) eth? Ps-Oecumenius ‖ ἀτμὶς γὰρ ἔσται ἡ K Ψ 049 (P 88 1241 *omit* ἡ) 181 326 436 1505 2127 2495 *Byz*ᵖᵗ *Lect* (itˡ *add* ὡς) (arm? ὡς ἀτμίς) eth? ‖ ἀτμὶς ἔσται ἡ A itᵃʳ,ᶜ,ᵈᵉᵐ,ᵈⁱᵛ,p,s,z (vg copˢᵃ,ᵇᵒ ἔστιν) ‖ ἀτμὶς γὰρ ἐστιν ἡ L 056 0142 330 451 629 630 1877 *Byz*ᵖᵗ itff? Jerome Bede John-Damascus Theophylact ‖ ἡ ℵ ‖ οὐκ ἐὰν ἀτμὶς ἡ syrᵖ

ᵈ ᵈ **15** d minor, d none: TR WH Bov Nes BF² (AV) (RV) (ASV) RSV NEB TT Jer Seg ‖ d none, d minor. Zür Luth

10 Job 5.11; 1 Pe 5.6   **12** σὺ...πλησίον Ro 2.1; 14.4   **13-14** Ἄγε...ὑμῶν Pr 27.1; Lk 12.18–20   **15** Ἐάν...ἐκεῖνο Ac 18.21

hearts, you hypocrites! **9** Be sorrowful, cry, and weep; exchange your laughter for crying, and your joy for gloom! **10** Humble yourselves before God, and he will lift you up.

Warning against Judging a Brother

11 Do not speak against one another, my brothers. Whoever speaks against his brother, or judges him, speaks against the Law and judges it. If you judge the Law, then you are no longer a man who obeys the Law, but one who judges it. **12** God is the only lawgiver and judge. He alone can both save and destroy. Who do you think you are, to judge your fellow man?

Warning against Boasting

13 Now listen to me, you who say, "Today or tomorrow we will travel to a certain city, where we will spend a year, and go into business and make much money." **14** You do not even know what your life tomorrow will be like! For you are like a thin fog, which appears for a moment and then disappears. **15** This, then, is what you should say: "If the Lord is willing, we will live and do this and that." **16** But now you are proud, and you boast; all such boasting is wrong. ¹⁷ So then, the man who does not do the good he knows he should do is guilty of sin.

Warning to the Rich

5 And now, you rich people, listen to me! Weep and wail over the miseries that are coming upon you! ² Your riches have rotted away, and your clothes have been eaten by moths. ³ Your gold and silver are covered with rust, and this rust will be a witness against you, and eat up your flesh like fire. You have piled up riches in these last days. ⁴ You have not paid the wages to the men who work in your fields. Hear their complaints! And the cries of those who gather in your crops have reached the ears of God, the Lord Almighty! ⁵ Your life here on earth has been full of luxury and pleasure. You have made yourselves fat for the day of slaughter. ⁶ You have condemned and murdered the innocent man, and he does not resist you.

Patience and Prayer

⁷ Be patient, then, my brothers, until the Lord comes. See how the farmer is patient as he waits for his land to produce precious crops. He waits patiently for the autumn and spring rains. ⁸ And you also must be patient! Keep your hopes high, for the day of the Lord's coming is near.

ἐν ταῖς ἀλαζονείαις ὑμῶν· πᾶσα καύχησις τοιαύτη πονηρά ἐστιν. 17 εἰδότι οὖν καλὸν ποιεῖν καὶ μὴ ποιοῦντι, ἁμαρτία αὐτῷ ἐστιν.

Warning to the Rich

5 Ἄγε νῦν οἱ πλούσιοι, κλαύσατε ὀλολύζοντες ἐπὶ ταῖς ταλαιπωρίαις ὑμῶν ταῖς ἐπερχομέναις. 2 ὁ πλοῦτος ὑμῶν σέσηπεν καὶ τὰ ἱμάτια ὑμῶν σητόβρωτα γέγονεν, 3 ὁ χρυσὸς ὑμῶν καὶ ὁ ἄργυρος κατίωται, καὶ ὁ ἰὸς αὐτῶν εἰς μαρτύριον ὑμῖν ἔσται καὶ φάγεται τὰς σάρκας ὑμῶν^a ὡς πῦρ·^a ἐθησαυρίσατε ἐν ἐσχάταις ἡμέραις. 4 ἰδοὺ ὁ μισθὸς τῶν ἐργατῶν τῶν ἀμησάντων τὰς χώρας ὑμῶν ὁ ἀφυστερημένος ἀφ' ὑμῶν κράζει, καὶ αἱ βοαὶ τῶν θερισάντων εἰς τὰ ὦτα κυρίου Σαβαὼθ εἰσελήλυθαν. 5 ἐτρυφήσατε ἐπὶ τῆς γῆς καὶ ἐσπαταλήσατε, ἐθρέψατε τὰς καρδίας ὑμῶν ἐν ἡμέρᾳ σφαγῆς. 6 κατεδικάσατε, ἐφονεύσατε τὸν δίκαιον. οὐκ ἀντιτάσσεται ὑμῖν.^b

Patience and Prayer

7 Μακροθυμήσατε οὖν, ἀδελφοί, ἕως τῆς παρουσίας τοῦ κυρίου. ἰδοὺ ὁ γεωργὸς ἐκδέχεται τὸν τίμιον καρπὸν τῆς γῆς, μακροθυμῶν ἐπ' αὐτῷ ἕως λάβῃ¹ **πρόϊμον καὶ ὄψιμον.** 8 μακροθυμήσατε καὶ ὑμεῖς, στηρίξατε τὰς καρδίας ὑμῶν, ὅτι ἡ παρουσία τοῦ κυρίου ἤγγικεν.

¹ **7** {B} λάβῃ 𝔭⁷⁴ B 048 945 1241 1739 itᵃʳ,ᶜ,ᵈᵉᵐ,ᵈⁱᵛ,ᵖ,(ᶻ) vg copˢᵃ arm ‖ λάβῃ ὑετόν A K P Ψ 049 056 0142 81 88 104 181 326 330 451 614 629 630 1505 1877 2127 2412 2492 2495 *Byz Lect* syrᵖ·ʰ Ps-Oecumenius Theophylact ‖ ὑετὸν λάβῃ 436 ‖ λάβῃ καρπόν (ℵ* καρπὸν τόν) ℵᶜ itᶠᶠ syrʰᵐᵍ (copᵇᵒ) Cassiodorus Antiochus

ᵃ ᵃ **3** *a* none, *a* major: TR WHᵐᵍ Bov Nes BF² AV RV ASV RSV NEB TT Zür Luth Seg ‖ *a* major, *a* none: WH RSVᵐᵍ Jer
ᵇ **6** *b* statement: TR WHᵐᵍ Bov Nes BF² AV RV ASV RSV NEB TT Zür Luth Jer Seg ‖ *b* question: WH

17 Lk 12.47
5 1 Lk 6.24   **2** Mt 6.19   **3** φάγεται...πῦρ Ps 21.9; Jdth 16.17   **4** ὁ μισθὸς...κράζει Lv 19.13; Dt 24.14–15; Mal 3.5   αἱ βοαὶ...εἰσελήλυθαν Gn 4.10; Ps 18.6; Is 5.9   **5** ἡμέρᾳ σφαγῆς Jr 12.3; 25.34   **7** πρόϊμον καὶ ὄψιμον Dt 11.14; Jr 5.24; Jl 2.23   **8** ἡ παρουσία...ἤγγικεν Ro 13.11–12; He 10.25; 1 Pe 4.7

9 μὴ στενάζετε, ἀδελφοί, κατ' ἀλλήλων, ἵνα μὴ κριθῆτε· ἰδοὺ ὁ κριτὴς πρὸ τῶν θυρῶν ἕστηκεν. 10 ὑπόδειγμα λάβετε, ἀδελφοί, τῆς κακοπαθείας καὶ τῆς μακροθυμίας τοὺς προφήτας, οἳ ἐλάλησαν ἐν τῷ ὀνόματι κυρίου. 11 ἰδοὺ μακαρίζομεν τοὺς ὑπομείναντας· τὴν ὑπομονὴν Ἰὼβ ἠκούσατε, καὶ τὸ τέλος κυρίου εἴδετε, ὅτι **πολύσπλαγχνός ἐστιν ὁ κύριος καὶ οἰκτίρμων.**

12 Πρὸ πάντων δέ, ἀδελφοί μου, μὴ ὀμνύετε, μήτε τὸν οὐρανὸν μήτε τὴν γῆν μήτε ἄλλον τινὰ ὅρκον· ἤτω δὲ ὑμῶν τὸ Ναὶ ναὶ καὶ τὸ Οὒ οὔ, ἵνα μὴ ὑπὸ κρίσιν πέσητε.

13 Κακοπαθεῖ τις ἐν ὑμῖν; προσευχέσθω· εὐθυμεῖ τις; ψαλλέτω. 14 ἀσθενεῖ τις ἐν ὑμῖν; προσκαλεσάσθω τοὺς πρεσβυτέρους τῆς ἐκκλησίας, καὶ προσευξάσθωσαν ἐπ' αὐτὸν ἀλείψαντες ἐλαίῳ ἐν τῷ ὀνόματι [τοῦ] κυρίου· 15 καὶ ἡ εὐχὴ τῆς πίστεως σώσει τὸν κάμνοντα, καὶ ἐγερεῖ αὐτὸν ὁ κύριος· κἂν ἁμαρτίας ᾖ πεποιηκώς, ἀφεθήσεται αὐτῷ. 16 ἐξομολογεῖσθε οὖν ἀλλήλοις τὰς ἁμαρτίας καὶ εὔχεσθε ὑπὲρ ἀλλήλων, ὅπως ἰαθῆτε.ᶜ πολὺ ἰσχύει δέησις δικαίου ἐνεργουμένη. 17 Ἠλίας ἄνθρωπος ἦν ὁμοιοπαθὴς ἡμῖν, καὶ προσευχῇ προσηύξατο τοῦ μὴ βρέξαι, καὶ οὐκ ἔβρεξεν ἐπὶ τῆς γῆς ἐνιαυτοὺς τρεῖς καὶ μῆνας ἕξ· 18 καὶ πάλιν προσηύξατο, καὶ ὁ οὐρανὸς ὑετὸν ἔδωκεν καὶ ἡ γῆ ἐβλάστησεν τὸν καρπὸν αὐτῆς.

19 Ἀδελφοί μου, ἐάν τις ἐν ὑμῖν πλανηθῇ ἀπὸ τῆς ἀληθείας καὶ ἐπιστρέψῃ τις αὐτόν, 20 γινώσκετε ὅτι²

---

² **20** {D} γινώσκετε ὅτι B 1505 2495 syrʰ eth ∥ γινωσκέτω ὅτι ℵ A K P 049 056 0142 81 88 104 181 326 330 436 451 614 629 630 945 1241 1739

ᶜ **16** c major: TR WH Bov Nes BF² AV RV ASV RSV NEB TT Zür Luth Seg ∥ c paragraph: Jer ∥ c minor

---

9 ὁ κριτὴς...ἕστηκεν Mt 24.33   **11** μακαρίζομεν τοὺς ὑπομείναντας Dn 12.12   πολύσπλαγχνος...οἰκτίρμων Ex 34.6; Ps 103.8; 111.4   **12** Mt 5.34–37   **14** ἀλείψαντες ἐλαίῳ Mk 6.13   **15** ἡ εὐχή...κάμνοντα Mk 16.18   **17** 1 Kgs 17.1; Lk 4.25   **18** 1 Kgs 18.42–45

---

9 Do not complain against one another, brothers, so that God will not judge you. The Judge is near, ready to come in! 10 Brothers, remember the prophets who spoke in the name of the Lord. Take them as examples of patient endurance under suffering. 11 We call them happy because they endured. You have heard of Job's patience, and you know how the Lord provided for him in the end. For the Lord is full of mercy and compassion.

12 Above all, my brothers, do not use an oath when you make a promise; do not swear by heaven, or by earth, or by anything else. Say only "Yes" when you mean yes, and "No" when you mean no, so that you will not come under God's judgment.

13 Is there any one of you who is in trouble? He should pray. Is any one happy? He should sing praises. 14 Is there any one of you who is sick? He should call the church elders, who will pray for him and pour oil on him in the name of the Lord. 15 This prayer, made in faith, will save the sick man: the Lord will restore him to health, and the sins he has committed will be forgiven. 16 Therefore, confess your sins to one another, and pray for one another, so that you will be healed. The prayer of a righteous man has a powerful effect. 17 Elijah was the same kind of person that we are. He prayed earnestly that there would be no rain, and no rain fell on the land for three and a half years. 18 Once again he prayed, and the sky poured out its rain and the earth produced its crops.

19 My brothers! If one of you wanders away from the truth, and another one brings him back again, 20 remember this:

whoever turns a sinner back from his wrong ways will save that sinner's soul from death, and cause a great number of sins to be forgiven.

ὁ ἐπιστρέψας ἁμαρτωλὸν ἐκ πλάνης ὁδοῦ αὐτοῦ σώσει ψυχὴν [αὐτοῦ] ἐκ θανάτου[3] καὶ καλύψει πλῆθος ἁμαρτιῶν.

1877 2127 2412 2492 *Byz Lect*[m] it[ar,c,dem,div,l,p,s,t,z] vg (syr[p]) cop[bo] arm Didymus ‖ ὅτι Ψ ‖ *omit* 𝔭[74] it[ff] cop[sa]

  [3] **20** {D} αὐτοῦ ἐκ θανάτου ℵ A P 048 33 436 1739 it[ar,c,dem,div,p,s,t,z] vg syr[p,h] cop[bo] arm Origen[lat] Didymus Cyril John-Damascus ‖ ἐκ θανάτου αὐτοῦ 𝔭[74] B 614 2412 it[ff] ‖ ἐκ θανάτου K Ψ 049 056 0142 81 88 104 181 326 330 451 629 630 945 1241 1505 1877 2127 2492 2495 *Byz Lect*[m] cop[sa] Origen[latms] Ps-Oecumenius Theophylact ‖ αὐτοῦ Ambrosiaster

  20 καλύψει πλῆθος ἁμαρτιῶν Pr 10.12; 1 Pe 4.8

ΠΕΤΡΟΥ Α

Salutation

1 Πέτρος ἀπόστολος Ἰησοῦ Χριστοῦ ἐκλεκτοῖς παρεπιδήμοις διασπορᾶς Πόντου, Γαλατίας, Καππαδοκίας, Ἀσίας, καὶ Βιθυνίας, **2** κατὰ πρόγνωσιν θεοῦ πατρός, ἐν ἁγιασμῷ πνεύματος, εἰς ὑπακοὴν καὶ ῥαντισμὸν αἵματος Ἰησοῦ Χριστοῦ· χάρις ὑμῖν καὶ εἰρήνη πληθυνθείη.

A Living Hope

3 Εὐλογητὸς ὁ θεὸς καὶ πατὴρ τοῦ κυρίου ἡμῶν Ἰησοῦ Χριστοῦ, ὁ κατὰ τὸ πολὺ αὐτοῦ ἔλεος ἀναγεννήσας ἡμᾶς εἰς ἐλπίδα ζῶσαν δι᾽ ἀναστάσεως Ἰησοῦ Χριστοῦ ἐκ νεκρῶν, **4** εἰς κληρονομίαν ἄφθαρτον καὶ ἀμίαντον καὶ ἀμάραντον, τετηρημένην ἐν οὐρανοῖς εἰς ὑμᾶς **5** τοὺς ἐν δυνάμει θεοῦ φρουρουμένους διὰ πίστεως εἰς σωτηρίαν ἑτοίμην ἀποκαλυφθῆναι ἐν καιρῷ ἐσχάτῳ. **6** ἐν ᾧ ἀγαλλιᾶσθε, ὀλίγον ἄρτι εἰ δέον [ἐστὶν] λυπηθέντες ἐν ποικίλοις πειρασμοῖς, **7** ἵνα τὸ δοκίμιον[1] ὑμῶν τῆς πίστεως πολυτιμότερον χρυσίου τοῦ ἀπολλυμένου, διὰ πυρὸς δὲ δοκιμαζομένου, εὑρεθῇ εἰς ἔπαινον καὶ δόξαν καὶ τιμὴν ἐν ἀποκαλύψει Ἰησοῦ Χριστοῦ. **8** ὃν οὐκ ἰδόντες[2] ἀγαπᾶτε, εἰς ὃν ἄρτι μὴ ὁρῶντες πιστεύοντες δὲ ἀγαλλιᾶσθε χαρᾷ ἀνεκλαλήτῳ καὶ δεδοξασμένῃ, **9** κομιζόμενοι τὸ τέλος τῆς πίστεως ὑμῶν σωτηρίαν ψυχῶν.

---

[1] **7** {B} δοκίμιον ℵ A B C K P Ψ 048 049 056 0142 33 81 88 104 181 326 330 436 451 614 629 630 945 1241 1505 1739 1877 2127 2412 2492 2495 *Byz Lect* it^ar,c,dem,div,l,p,s vg arm ‖ δόκιμον 𝔓72,74 429 it^z vg^mss

[2] **8** {B} ἰδόντες 𝔓72 ℵ B C 048^vid! 330* 451 630 945 1739 *l*^o it^ar,c,dem,div,p,q,s vg syr^p,h cop^sa arm eth Polycarp Irenaeus^lat ‖ εἰδότες A K P Ψ 049 056 0142 33 81 88 104 181 326 330^c 436 614 629 1241 1505 1877 2127 2412 2492 2495 *Byz Lect* cop^bo Clement Euthalius Augustine Cyril Ps-Oecumenius Theophylact

---

1 παρεπιδήμοις...βιθυνίας Jas 1.1 **2** πρόγνωσιν θεοῦ Ro 8.29 ἁγιασμῷ πνεύματος 2 Th 2.13 ῥαντισμὸν αἵματος He 12.24 **3** Εὐλογητὸς...Χριστοῦ 2 Cor 1.3 **5** τοὺς... φρουρουμένους Jn 10.28; 17.11 **6** λυπηθέντες...πειρασμοῖς Jas 1.2 **7** δοκίμιον...πίστεως Job 23.10; Ps 66.10; Pr 17.3; Jas 1.3 διὰ...δοκιμαζομένου Is 48.10; Zch 13.9; Mal 3.3; 1 Cor 3.13 **8** ὃν οὐκ...πιστεύοντες Jn 20.29; 2 Cor 5.7 **9** Ro 6.22

THE FIRST LETTER FROM PETER

1 From Peter, apostle of Jesus Christ — To God's chosen people who live as refugees scattered throughout the provinces of Pontus, Galatia, Cappadocia, Asia, and Bithynia. [2] You were chosen as a result of God the Father's own purpose, to be made a holy people by his Spirit, and to obey Jesus Christ and be made clean by his blood.

May grace and peace be yours in full measure.

A Living Hope

[3] Let us give thanks to the God and Father of our Lord Jesus Christ! Because of his great mercy, he gave us new life by raising Jesus Christ from the dead. This fills us with a living hope, [4] and so we look forward to possess the rich blessings that God keeps for his people. He keeps them for you in heaven, where they cannot decay or spoil or fade away. [5] They are for you, who through faith are kept safe by God's power, as you wait for the salvation which is ready to be revealed at the end of time.

[6] Be glad about this, even though it may now be necessary for you to be sad for a while because of the many kinds of trials you suffer. [7] Their purpose is to prove that your faith is genuine. Even gold, which can be destroyed, is tested by fire; and so your faith, which is much more precious than gold, must also be tested, that it may endure. Then you will receive praise and glory and honor on the Day when Jesus Christ is revealed. [8] You love him, although you have not seen him; you believe in him, although you do not now see him; and so you rejoice with a great and glorious joy, which words cannot express, [9] because you are receiving the purpose of your faith, the salvation of your souls.

¹⁰ It was concerning this salvation that the prophets made careful search and investigation; and they prophesied about this gift that God would give you. ¹¹ They tried to find out when the time would be and how it would come; for the Spirit of Christ in them pointed to this time in predicting the sufferings that Christ would have to endure, and the glory that would follow. ¹² God revealed to these prophets that their work was not for their own benefit, but for yours, as they spoke about the truths which you have now heard. The messengers of the Good News, who spoke by the power of the Holy Spirit sent from heaven, told you these truths. These are truths which even the angels would like to understand.

A Call to Holy Living

¹³ Have your minds ready for action, then. Keep alert, and set your hope completely on the blessing which will be given you when Jesus Christ is revealed. ¹⁴ Be obedient to God, and do not allow your lives to be shaped by those desires that you had when you were still ignorant. ¹⁵ Instead, be holy in all that you do, just as God who called you is holy. ¹⁶ For the scripture says, "You must be holy, because I am holy."

¹⁷ You call him Father, when you pray to God, who judges all men alike, according to what each one has done; you must, therefore, spend the rest of your lives here on earth in reverence for him. ¹⁸ For you know what was paid to set you free from the worthless manner of life you received from your ancestors. It was not something that loses its value, such as silver or gold; ¹⁹ you were set free by the costly sacrifice of Christ, who was like a lamb without defect or spot. ²⁰ He had been chosen by God

10 Περὶ ἧς σωτηρίας ἐξεζήτησαν καὶ ἐξηραύνησαν προφῆται οἱ περὶ τῆς εἰς ὑμᾶς χάριτος προφητεύσαντες, **11** ἐραυνῶντες εἰς τίνα ἢ ποῖον καιρὸν ἐδήλου τὸ ἐν αὐτοῖς πνεῦμα Χριστοῦ προμαρτυρόμενον τὰ εἰς Χριστὸν παθήματα καὶ τὰς μετὰ ταῦτα δόξας· **12** οἷς ἀπεκαλύφθη ὅτι οὐχ ἑαυτοῖς ὑμῖν δὲ διηκόνουν αὐτά, ἃ νῦν ἀνηγγέλη ὑμῖν διὰ τῶν εὐαγγελισαμένων ὑμᾶς πνεύματι[3] ἁγίῳ ἀποσταλέντι ἀπ' οὐρανοῦ, εἰς ἃ ἐπιθυμοῦσιν ἄγγελοι παρακύψαι.

A Call to Holy Living

13 Διὸ ἀναζωσάμενοι τὰς ὀσφύας τῆς διανοίας ὑμῶν, νήφοντες,[a] τελείως[a] ἐλπίσατε ἐπὶ τὴν φερομένην ὑμῖν χάριν ἐν ἀποκαλύψει Ἰησοῦ Χριστοῦ. **14** ὡς τέκνα ὑπακοῆς, μὴ συσχηματιζόμενοι ταῖς πρότερον ἐν τῇ ἀγνοίᾳ ὑμῶν ἐπιθυμίαις, **15** ἀλλὰ κατὰ τὸν καλέσαντα ὑμᾶς ἅγιον καὶ αὐτοὶ ἅγιοι ἐν πάσῃ ἀναστροφῇ γενήθητε, **16** διότι γέγραπται, "Ἅγιοι ἔσεσθε, ὅτι ἐγὼ ἅγιος.

17 Καὶ εἰ πατέρα ἐπικαλεῖσθε τὸν ἀπροσωπολήμπτως κρίνοντα κατὰ τὸ ἑκάστου ἔργον, ἐν φόβῳ τὸν τῆς παροικίας ὑμῶν χρόνον ἀναστράφητε, **18** εἰδότες ὅτι οὐ φθαρτοῖς, ἀργυρίῳ ἢ χρυσίῳ ἐλυτρώθητε ἐκ τῆς ματαίας ὑμῶν ἀναστροφῆς πατροπαραδότου, **19** ἀλλὰ τιμίῳ αἵματι ὡς ἀμνοῦ ἀμώμου καὶ ἀσπίλου Χριστοῦ, **20** προεγνωσμέ-

---

[3] **12** {C} πνεύματι 𝔓⁷² A B Ψ 33 436 Didymus Cyril ∥ ἐν πνεύματι ℵ C K P 049 056 0142 81 88 104 181 326 330 451 614 629 630 945 1241 1505 1739 1877 1881 2127 2412 2492 2495 *Byz Lect* Vigilius Ps-Oecumenius Theophylact

---

[a a] **13** a minor, a none: TR Bov Nes BF² AV RV ASV RSV TT (Zür) (Luth) Jer (Seg) ∥ a none, a minor: WH NEB

---

10 Mt 13.17; Lk 10.24   **11** προμαρτυρόμενον...παθήματα Ps 22; Is 53; Lk 24.26 **12** οἷς...διηκόνουν En 1.2   εἰς...παρακύψαι Eph 3.10   **13** ἀναζωσάμενοι τὰς ὀσφύας Lk 12.35; Eph 6.14   **14** μὴ...ἐπιθυμίαις Ro 12.2; Eph 2.3; 4.17–18   **16** Ἅγιοι...ἅγιος Lv 11.44, 45; 19.2; 20.7   **17** εἰ πατέρα ἐπικαλεῖσθε Ps 89.26; Is 64.8; Jr 3.19; Mt 6.9; Lk 11.2; Wsd 14.3; Slr 23.4 τὸν ἀπροσωπολήμπτως κρίνοντα 2 Chr 19.7; Ac 10.34; Ro 2.11; Ga 2.6; Eph 6.9; Col 3.25 κατὰ...ἔργον Ps 28.4; 62.12; Pr 24.12; Is 59.18; Jr 17.10; Ro 2.6; 1 Cor 3.8; 2 Cor 11.15; 2 Tm 4.14; Re 2.23; 18.6; 20.13, 14; 22.12   **19** Ac 20.28; He 9.12; 1 Pe 1.2 **20** προεγνωσμένου...κόσμου Ac 2.23; Eph 1.4

νου μὲν πρὸ καταβολῆς κόσμου, φανερωθέντος δὲ ἐπ' ἐσχάτου τῶν χρόνων δι' ὑμᾶς 21 τοὺς δι' αὐτοῦ πιστοὺς εἰς θεὸν τὸν ἐγείραντα αὐτὸν ἐκ νεκρῶν καὶ δόξαν αὐτῷ δόντα, ὥστε τὴν πίστιν ὑμῶν καὶ ἐλπίδα εἶναι εἰς θεόν.

22 Τὰς ψυχὰς ὑμῶν ἡγνικότες ἐν τῇ ὑπακοῇ τῆς ἀληθείας[4] εἰς φιλαδελφίαν ἀνυπόκριτον, ἐκ καρδίας[5] ἀλλήλους ἀγαπήσατε ἐκτενῶς, 23 ἀναγεγεννημένοι οὐκ ἐκ σπορᾶς φθαρτῆς ἀλλὰ ἀφθάρτου, διὰ λόγου ζῶντος θεοῦ καὶ μένοντος· 24 διότι

πᾶσα σὰρξ ὡς χόρτος,
καὶ πᾶσα δόξα αὐτῆς ὡς ἄνθος χόρτου·
ἐξηράνθη ὁ χόρτος,
καὶ τὸ ἄνθος ἐξέπεσεν·

25   τὸ δὲ ῥῆμα κυρίου μένει εἰς τὸν αἰῶνα.
τοῦτο δέ ἐστιν τὸ ῥῆμα τὸ εὐαγγελισθὲν εἰς ὑμᾶς.

The Living Stone and the Holy Nation

2 Ἀποθέμενοι οὖν πᾶσαν κακίαν καὶ πάντα δόλον καὶ ὑποκρίσεις καὶ φθόνους καὶ πάσας καταλαλιάς, 2 ὡς ἀρτιγέννητα βρέφη τὸ λογικὸν ἄδολον γάλα ἐπιποθήσατε, ἵνα ἐν αὐτῷ αὐξηθῆτε εἰς σωτηρίαν, 3 εἰ[1] ἐγεύσασθε

---

before the creation of the world, and was revealed in these last days for your sake. [21] Through him you believe in God, who raised him from death and gave him glory; and so your faith and hope are fixed on God.

[22] Now that you have purified yourselves by obeying the truth, and have a sincere love for your fellow believers, love one another earnestly with all your hearts. [23] For through the living and eternal word of God you have been born again as the children of a parent who is immortal, not mortal. [24] As the scripture says,

"All men are like the wild grass,
And all their glory is like its flower;
The grass dies, and its flower falls off,
[25] But the word of the Lord remains
for ever."
This is the word that the Good News brought to you.

The Living Stone and the Holy Nation

2 Rid yourselves, therefore, of all evil; no more lying, or hypocrisy, or jealousy, or insulting language! [2] Be like newborn babies, always thirsty for the pure spiritual milk, so that by drinking it you may grow up and be saved. [3] For,

---

[4] 22 {C} ἀληθείας p72 ℵ A B C Ψ 33 81 436 629 945 1241 1739 1881 2492 syrp,h copsa,bo Clement ∥ ἀληθείας διὰ πνεύματος K P 049 056 0142 88 104 181 326 330 451 614 630 1505 1877 2127 2412 2495 Byz Lect itl arm Priscillian Vigilius Gildas Ps-Oecumenius Theophylact ∥ *fidei per spiritum* itm ∥ *caritatis* itar,c,dem,div,p,z vg

[5] 22 {C} ἐκ καρδίας A B itar,dem,div,z vg Gildas ∥ ἐκ καθαρᾶς καρδίας p72 ℵ* C K P Ψ 049 056 0142 33 81 88 104 181 326 330 436 451 614 629 630 945 1241 1505 1739 1877 1881 2127 2112 2402 2405 Byz Lect itc,p syrp,h copsa,bo arm Priscillian Anthony Ps-Oecumenius Theophylact ∥ ἐκ καρδίας ἀληθινῆς ℵc (eth)

[1] 3 {C} εἰ p72 ℵ* A B itdiv,t (syrp) copsa?bo? Clement ∥ εἴπερ ℵc C K P Ψ 049 056 0142 (33 εἴσπερ) 81 88 104 181 326 330 436 451 614 629 630 945

---

21 τοὺς...πιστοὺς Jn 14.6; Ro 5.1-2   τοὺς...νεκρῶν Ro 4.24; 10.9   22 ἀλλήλους ἀγαπήσατε ἐκτενῶς Jn 13.34; Ro 12.10   23 ἀναγεγεννημένοι...ἀφθάρτου Jn 1.13   λόγου ζῶντος θεοῦ He 4.12   ζῶντος...μένοντος Dn 6.26   24-25 Is 40.6-8 (Jas 1.10-11)
2 1 Eph 4.22; Jas 1.21   2 ὡς...ἐπιποθήσατε 1 Cor 3.2; He 5.12-13   3 ἐγεύσασθε... κύριος Ps 34.8

as the scripture says, "You have tasted the Lord's kindness."

⁴ Come to the Lord, the living stone rejected as worthless by men, but chosen as valuable by God. ⁵ Come as living stones, and let yourselves be used in building the spiritual temple, where you will serve as holy priests, to offer spiritual and acceptable sacrifices to God through Jesus Christ. ⁶ For the scripture says:

"I chose a valuable stone
Which I now place as the cornerstone
in Zion;
And whoever believes in him will
never be disappointed."

⁷ This stone is of great value for you who believe; but for those who do not believe:

"The stone which the builders rejected as worthless
Turned out to be the most important
stone."

⁸ And another scripture says,

"This is the stone that will make
men stumble,
The rock that will make them fall."

They stumbled because they did not believe in the word; such was God's will for them.

⁹ But you are the chosen race, the King's priests, the holy nation, God's own people, chosen to proclaim the wonderful acts of God, who called you from the darkness into his own marvelous

ὅτι χρηστὸς ὁ κύριος. 4 πρὸς ὃν προσερχόμενοι, λίθον ζῶντα, ὑπὸ ἀνθρώπων μὲν ἀποδεδοκιμασμένον παρὰ δὲ θεῷ ἐκλεκτὸν ἔντιμον, 5 καὶ αὐτοὶ ὡς λίθοι ζῶντες οἰκοδομεῖσθε οἶκος πνευματικός[a] εἰς ἱεράτευμα ἅγιον,[a] ἀνενέγκαι πνευματικὰς θυσίας εὐπροσδέκτους θεῷ διὰ Ἰησοῦ Χριστοῦ. 6 διότι περιέχει ἐν γραφῇ,

> Ἰδοὺ τίθημι ἐν Σιὼν λίθον
> ἐκλεκτὸν ἀκρογωνιαῖον ἔντιμον,
> καὶ ὁ πιστεύων ἐπ' αὐτῷ οὐ μὴ καταισχυνθῇ.

7 ὑμῖν οὖν ἡ τιμὴ τοῖς πιστεύουσιν· ἀπιστοῦσιν δὲ

> λίθος ὃν ἀπεδοκίμασαν οἱ οἰκοδομοῦντες
> οὗτος ἐγενήθη εἰς κεφαλὴν γωνίας

8[b] καὶ

> λίθος προσκόμματος
> καὶ πέτρα σκανδάλου·

[b]οἳ προσκόπτουσιν[c] τῷ λόγῳ ἀπειθοῦντες, εἰς ὃ καὶ ἐτέθησαν.

9 Ὑμεῖς δὲ γένος ἐκλεκτόν, βασίλειον ἱεράτευμα, ἔθνος ἅγιον, λαὸς εἰς περιποίησιν, ὅπως τὰς ἀρετὰς ἐξαγγείλητε τοῦ ἐκ σκότους ὑμᾶς καλέσαντος εἰς τὸ θαυμαστὸν αὐτοῦ φῶς·

1241 1505 1739 1877 1881 2127 2412 2492 2495 *Byz Lect* (l¹⁵⁹⁰ ὅπερ) itar,c,dem,p,(z) vg syrh Cyril Ps-Oecumenius Theophylact

---

[a] [a] **5** *a* none, *a* minor: WH Bov Nes BF² RVmg ASVmg NEBmg Zür ‖ *a* minor, *a* none ‖ *a* minor, *a* minor: RV ASV RSV NEB TT (Luth) Jer ‖ different text: TR AV Seg

[b] [b] **7-8** *b* number 8, *b* no number: TRed WH Bov Nes BF² AV RV ASV RSV NEB TT Zür Luth Jer Seg ‖ *b* no number, *b* number 8: TRed

[c] **8** *c* none: TR WH Bov Nes BF² AV RV ASV ‖ *c* minor: RVmg ASVmg (RSV) (NEB) (TT) Zür Luth (Jer) (Seg)

---

4 λίθον...ἀποδεδοκιμασμένον Ps 118.22; Mt 21.42; Ac 4.11　　παρὰ...ἔντιμον Is 28.16 **5** αὐτοί...πνευματικός Eph 2.21-22　　ἱεράτευμα ἅγιον Ex 19.6; Is 61.6; 1 Pe 2.9; Re 1.6; 5.10; 20.6　　ἀνενέγκαι...θεῷ Ro 12.1; He 13.15　　**6** Ἰδού...καταισχυνθῇ Is 28.16 (Ro 9.33) ἀκρογωνιαῖον ἔντιμον Eph 2.20　　**7** λίθος...γωνίας Ps 118.22 (Mt 21.42; Ac 4.11)　　**8** λίθος ...σκανδάλου Is 8.14 (Ro 9.33)　　**9** γένος ἐκλεκτόν Is 43.20 (Dt 7.6; 10.15)　　βασίλειον ἱεράτευμα Ex 19.6 (23.22 lxx); Is 61.6; 1 Pe 2.5; Re 1.6; 5.10; 20.6　　ἔθνος ἅγιον Ex 19.6 (23.22 lxx)　　λαὸς εἰς περιποίησιν Is 43.21; Ex 19.5 (23.22 lxx); Dt 4.20; 7.6; 14.2; Tt 2.14 τὰς ἀρετὰς ἐξαγγείλητε Is 43.21 (42.12)　　ἐκ...φῶς Is 9.2; Ac 26.18; Eph 5.8; Col 1.13

10   οἵ ποτε **οὐ λαὸς**
       νῦν δὲ **λαὸς θεοῦ**,
   οἱ οὐκ ἠλεημένοι
       νῦν δὲ **ἐλεηθέντες**.

Live as Servants of God

11 Ἀγαπητοί, παρακαλῶ ὡς παροίκους καὶ παρεπιδήμους ἀπέχεσθαι τῶν σαρκικῶν ἐπιθυμιῶν, αἵτινες στρατεύονται κατὰ τῆς ψυχῆς· 12 τὴν ἀναστροφὴν ὑμῶν ἐν τοῖς ἔθνεσιν ἔχοντες καλήν, ἵνα, ἐν ᾧ καταλαλοῦσιν ὑμῶν ὡς κακοποιῶν, ἐκ τῶν καλῶν ἔργων ἐποπτεύοντες δοξάσωσιν τὸν θεὸν ἐν ἡμέρᾳ ἐπισκοπῆς.

13 Ὑποτάγητε πάσῃ ἀνθρωπίνῃ κτίσει διὰ τὸν κύριον· εἴτε βασιλεῖ ὡς ὑπερέχοντι, 14 εἴτε ἡγεμόσιν ὡς δι' αὐτοῦ πεμπομένοις εἰς ἐκδίκησιν κακοποιῶν ἔπαινον δὲ ἀγαθοποιῶν· ᵈ15 ὅτι οὕτως ἐστὶν τὸ θέλημα τοῦ θεοῦ, ἀγαθοποιοῦντας φιμοῦν τὴν τῶν ἀφρόνων ἀνθρώπων ἀγνωσίαν·ᵈ 16 ὡς ἐλεύθεροι, καὶ μὴ ὡς ἐπικάλυμμα ἔχοντες τῆς κακίας τὴν ἐλευθερίαν, ἀλλ' ὡς θεοῦ δοῦλοι. 17 πάντας τιμήσατε, τὴν ἀδελφότητα ἀγαπᾶτε, τὸν θεὸν φοβεῖσθε, τὸν βασιλέα τιμᾶτε.

The Example of Christ's Suffering

18 Οἱ οἰκέται ὑποτασσόμενοι ἐν παντὶ φόβῳ τοῖς δεσπόταις, οὐ μόνον τοῖς ἀγαθοῖς καὶ ἐπιεικέσιν ἀλλὰ καὶ τοῖς σκολιοῖς. 19 τοῦτο γὰρ χάρις εἰ διὰ συνείδησιν θεοῦ ὑποφέρει τις λύπας πάσχων ἀδίκως. 20 ποῖον γὰρ κλέος εἰ ἁμαρτάνοντες καὶ κολαφιζόμενοι ὑπομενεῖτε; ἀλλ' εἰ ἀγαθοποιοῦντες καὶ πάσχοντες ὑπομενεῖτε, τοῦτο χάρις παρὰ θεῷ. 21 εἰς τοῦτο γὰρ ἐκλήθητε, ὅτι καὶ

ᵈ ᵈ **15** d d no parens: TR Bov Nes BF² AV RV ASV RSV NEB TT Zür Luth Jer Seg ∥ d parens, d parens: WH

10 Ho 2.23 (1.6, 9; 2.1)   **11** παροίκους καὶ παρεπιδήμους Ps 39.12   ἀπέχεσθαι... ἐπιθυμιῶν Ga 5.01 στρατεύονται...ψυχῆς Ga 5.17; Jas 4.1   **12** ἐπ...θεόν Mt 5.16 ἡμέρᾳ ἐπισκοπῆς Is 10.3; Lk 19.44   **13–14** Ro 13.1–7; Tt 3.1   **15** ἀγαθοποιοῦντας...ἀγνωσίαν 1 Pe 3.16   **16** μή...ἐλευθερίαν Ga 5.13   **17** πάντας τιμήσατε Ro 12.10 τὸν θεόν...τιμᾶτε Pr 24.21   **18** Οἱ...δεσπόταις Eph 6.5; Tt 2.9   **20** εἰ ἀγαθοποιοῦντες...θεῷ 1 Pe 3.14, 17; 4.14

---

light. 10 At one time you were not God's people, but now you are his people; at one time you did not know God's mercy, but now you have received his mercy.

Slaves of God

11 I appeal to you, my friends, as strangers and refugees in this world! Do not give in to bodily passions, which are always at war against the soul. 12 Your conduct among the heathen should be so good that when they accuse you of being evildoers they will have to recognize your good deeds, and therefore praise God on the Day of his coming. 13 Submit yourselves, for the Lord's sake, to every human authority: to the Emperor, who is the supreme authority, 14 and to the governors, who have been sent by him to punish the evildoers and praise those who do good. 15 For this is God's will: he wants you to silence the ignorant talk of foolish men by the good things you do. 16 Live as free men; do not use your freedom, however, to cover up any evil, but live as God's slaves. 17 Respect all men, love your fellow believers, fear God, and respect the Emperor.

The Example of Christ's Suffering

18 You servants must submit yourselves to your masters and show them complete respect, not only to those who are kind and considerate, but also to those who are harsh. 19 God will bless you for this, if you endure the pain of undeserved suffering because you are conscious of his will. 20 For what credit is there in enduring the beatings you deserve for having done wrong? But if you endure suffering even when you have done right, God will bless you for it. 21 It was to this that God called you;

because Christ himself suffered for you and left you an example, so that you would follow in his steps. ²² He committed no sin; no one ever heard a lie come from his lips. ²³ When he was cursed he did not answer back with a curse; when he suffered he did not threaten, but placed his hopes in God, the righteous Judge. ²⁴ Christ himself carried our sins on his body to the cross, so that we might die to sin and live for righteousness. By his wounds you have been healed. ²⁵ You were like sheep that had lost their way; but now you have been brought back to follow the Shepherd and Keeper of your souls.

Wives and Husbands

3 In the same way you wives must submit yourselves to your husbands, so that if some of them do not believe God's word, they will be won over to believe by your conduct. It will not be necessary for you to say a word, ² for they will see how pure and reverent your conduct is. ³ You should not use outward aids to make yourselves beautiful, as in the way you fix your hair, or in the jewelry you put on, or in the dresses you wear. ⁴ Instead, your beauty should consist of your true inner self, the ageless beauty of a gentle and quiet spirit, which is of great value in God's sight. ⁵ For in this way the devout women of the past, who hoped in God, used to make themselves beautiful; they submitted themselves to

Χριστὸς ἔπαθεν[2] ὑπὲρ ὑμῶν, ὑμῖν[3] ὑπολιμπάνων ὑπογραμμὸν ἵνα ἐπακολουθήσητε τοῖς ἴχνεσιν αὐτοῦ·
22 ὃς ἁμαρτίαν οὐκ ἐποίησεν
        οὐδὲ εὑρέθη δόλος ἐν τῷ στόματι αὐτοῦ·
23 ὃς λοιδορούμενος οὐκ ἀντελοιδόρει, πάσχων οὐκ ἠπείλει, παρεδίδου δὲ τῷ κρίνοντι δικαίως· **24** ὃς **τὰς ἁμαρτίας** ἡμῶν **αὐτὸς ἀνήνεγκεν** ἐν τῷ σώματι αὐτοῦ ἐπὶ τὸ ξύλον, ἵνα ταῖς ἁμαρτίαις ἀπογενόμενοι τῇ δικαιοσύνῃ ζήσωμεν· οὗ **τῷ μώλωπι ἰάθητε.** **25** ἦτε γὰρ ὡς **πρόβατα πλανώμενοι,** ἀλλὰ ἐπεστράφητε νῦν ἐπὶ τὸν ποιμένα καὶ ἐπίσκοπον τῶν ψυχῶν ὑμῶν.

Wives and Husbands

3 Ὁμοίως [αἱ] γυναῖκες ὑποτασσόμεναι τοῖς ἰδίοις ἀνδράσιν, ἵνα καὶ εἴ τινες ἀπειθοῦσιν τῷ λόγῳ διὰ τῆς τῶν γυναικῶν ἀναστροφῆς ἄνευ λόγου κερδηθήσονται **2** ἐποπτεύσαντες τὴν ἐν φόβῳ ἁγνὴν ἀναστροφὴν ὑμῶν. **3** ὧν ἔστω οὐχ ὁ ἔξωθεν ἐμπλοκῆς τριχῶν καὶ περιθέσεως χρυσίων ἢ ἐνδύσεως ἱματίων κόσμος, **4** ἀλλ' ὁ κρυπτὸς τῆς καρδίας ἄνθρωπος ἐν τῷ ἀφθάρτῳ τοῦ πραέως καὶ ἡσυχίου πνεύματος, ὅ ἐστιν ἐνώπιον τοῦ θεοῦ πολυτελές. **5** οὕτως γάρ ποτε καὶ αἱ ἅγιαι γυναῖκες αἱ ἐλπίζουσαι εἰς θεὸν ἐκόσμουν ἑαυτάς, ὑποτασσόμεναι

2 21 {B} ἔπαθεν 𝔭72 A B C*vid* K P 049 056 0142 33 81 88 181 326 436 614 630 945 1241 1505 1739 1881 2412 2492 2495 *Byz Lect* it*ar,c,dem,div,p,q,t,z* vg syr*h* cop*sa,bo,fayvid* eth Tertullian Cyprian John-Damascus ∥ ἀπέθανεν (*see* 3.18) ℵ Ψ 104 (330 451 ἐπέθανεν) 629 1877 2127 *l*1441 syr*p* arm Ambrosiaster Ambrose Cyril Fulgentius John-Damascus

3 21 {B} ὑμῶν, ὑμῖν 𝔭72 ℵ A B C Ψ 81 945 1241 1739 2127 it*ar,c,dem,div,z* vg*ww* syr*h* cop*sa* arm eth Ambrose John-Damascus Ps-Oecumenius ∥ ὑμῶν, ἡμῖν 1877 2492 it*t* ∥ ἡμῶν, ὑμῖν K P 049 056 0142 33 88 104 181 326 330 436 451 630 1881 *Byz Lect* it*p,q* vg*cl* cop*fayvid* Tertullian Cyprian Theophylact ∥ ἡμῶν, ἡμῖν 614 629 1505 2412 2495 syr*p* cop*bo* Augustine John-Damascus

21 Χριστὸς...ὑπογραμμόν Jn 13.15   ἐπακολουθήσητε...αὐτοῦ Mt 16.24   **22** Is 53.9; Jn 8.46; 2 Cor 5.21; 1 Jn 3.5   **23** Is 53.7; 1 Pe 3.9   **24** ὃς...ἀνήνεγκεν Is 53.4, 12; He 9.28   ταῖς ...ζήσωμεν Ro 6.2, 11   οὗ...ἰάθητε Is 53.5   **25** ἦτε...πλανώμενοι Is 53.6; Eze 34.5-6; Mt 9.36
        3 1 αἱ...ἀνδράσιν Eph 5.22; Col 3.18; Tt 2.5   **3** ἔστω...κόσμος 1 Tm 2.9

τοῖς ἰδίοις ἀνδράσιν,[a] **6** ὡς Σάρρα ὑπήκουσεν τῷ
'Ἀβραάμ, κύριον αὐτὸν καλοῦσα·[a] ἧς ἐγενήθητε τέκνα[a]
ἀγαθοποιοῦσαι καὶ μὴ φοβούμεναι μηδεμίαν πτόησιν.

7 Οἱ ἄνδρες ὁμοίως συνοικοῦντες κατὰ γνῶσιν, ὡς
ἀσθενεστέρῳ σκεύει τῷ γυναικείῳ ἀπονέμοντες τιμήν,
ὡς καὶ συγκληρονόμοις[1] χάριτος ζωῆς, εἰς τὸ μὴ ἐγκόπτε-
σθαι τὰς προσευχὰς ὑμῶν.

Suffering for Righteousness' Sake

8 Τὸ δὲ τέλος πάντες ὁμόφρονες, συμπαθεῖς, φιλά-
δελφοι, εὔσπλαγχνοι, ταπεινόφρονες, **9** μὴ ἀποδιδόντες
κακὸν ἀντὶ κακοῦ ἢ λοιδορίαν ἀντὶ λοιδορίας, τοὐναντίον
δὲ εὐλογοῦντες, ὅτι εἰς τοῦτο ἐκλήθητε ἵνα εὐλογίαν
κληρονομήσητε.

10 ὁ γὰρ θέλων ζωὴν ἀγαπᾶν
    καὶ ἰδεῖν ἡμέρας ἀγαθὰς
    παυσάτω τὴν γλῶσσαν ἀπὸ κακοῦ
    καὶ χείλη τοῦ μὴ λαλῆσαι δόλον,
11 ἐκκλινάτω δὲ ἀπὸ κακοῦ καὶ ποιησάτω ἀγαθόν,
    ζητησάτω εἰρήνην καὶ διωξάτω αὐτήν.
12 ὅτι ὀφθαλμοὶ κυρίου ἐπὶ δικαίους
    καὶ ὦτα αὐτοῦ εἰς δέησιν αὐτῶν,
    πρόσωπον δὲ κυρίου ἐπὶ ποιοῦντας κακά.
13 Καὶ τίς ὁ κακώσων ὑμᾶς ἐὰν τοῦ ἀγαθοῦ ζηλωταὶ
γένησθε; **14** ἀλλ' εἰ καὶ πάσχοιτε διὰ δικαιοσύνην,

---

¹ **7** {C} συγκληρονόμοις 𝔭⁷² ℵ° (ℵ* συγκληρονόμους) B° (B* συν-
κληρονόμοις) 33 1241 1739 1881 2492 it^{ar,c,dem,div,(m),p,t,z} vg syr^p (cop^{bovid}) arm
eth Ambrose Augustine Cassiodorus Ps-Oecumenius Theophylact ∥
συγκληρονόμοι A C K P Ψ 049 056 0142 81 88 104 181 326 330 436 451 614
629 630 945 1505 1877 2412 2495 *Byz Lect* syr^h cop^{savid} Jerome ∥ συγκληρονόμος 2127

ᵃ ᵃ ᵃ **5–6** a minor, a major, a none: WH Bov Nes BF² RSV ∥ a minor, a major, a minor: TT Zür
Jer Seg ∥ a minor, a minor, a minor: Luth ∥ a major, a minor, a minor: TR ∥ a major, a major, a minor:
AV RV ASV NEB ∥ a parens, a major, a parens: RV^{mg} ASV^{mg}

6 Σάρρα...καλοῦσα Gn 18.12 **7** Οἱ...γυναικείῳ Eph 5.22; Col 3.19 **9** μὴ...εὐλογοῦντες
Mt 5.44; 1 Th 5.15; 1 Pe 2.23 **10–12** Ps 34.12–16 **14** εἰ...μακάριοι Mt 5.44; 1 Pe 2.20; 4.14

---

their husbands. **6** Sarah was like that;
she obeyed Abraham and called him
"My master." You are now her daughters
if you do good and are not afraid of
anything.

7 You husbands, also, in living with
your wives you must recognize that they
are the weaker sex and so you must
treat them with respect; for they also
will receive, together with you, God's
gift of life. Do this so that nothing will
interfere with your prayers.

Suffering for Doing Right

8 To conclude: you must all have the
same thoughts and the same feelings;
love one another as brothers, and be
kind and humble with one another. **9** Do
not pay back evil with evil, or cursing
with cursing; instead pay back with a
blessing, for a blessing is what God
promised to give you when he called you.
10 As the scripture says:

    "Whoever wants to enjoy life and
        have happy days
    Must no longer speak evil, and must
        stop telling lies.
11 He must turn away from evil and
        do good,
    He must seek peace and pursue it.
12 For the Lord keeps his eyes on the
        righteous
    And always listens to their prayers;
    But he turns against those who do
        evil."
13 Who will harm you if you are eager
to do what is good? **14** But even if you
should suffer for doing what is right,

how happy you are! Do not be afraid of men, and do not worry. [15] But have reverence for Christ in your hearts, and make him your Lord. Be ready at all times to answer anyone who asks you to explain the hope you have in you. [16] But do it with gentleness and respect. Keep your conscience clear, so that when you are insulted, those who speak evil of your good conduct as followers of Christ may be made ashamed of what they say. [17] For it is better to suffer for doing good, if this should be God's will, than for doing wrong. [18] For Christ himself died for you; once and for all he died for sins, a good man for bad men, in order to lead you to God. He was put to death physically, but made alive spiritually;

μακάριοι. τὸν δὲ φόβον αὐτῶν μὴ φοβηθῆτε μηδὲ ταραχθῆτε, 15 κύριον δὲ τὸν Χριστὸν[2] ἁγιάσατε ἐν ταῖς καρδίαις ὑμῶν,[b] ἕτοιμοι ἀεὶ πρὸς ἀπολογίαν παντὶ τῷ αἰτοῦντι ὑμᾶς λόγον περὶ τῆς ἐν ὑμῖν ἐλπίδος, 16[c] ἀλλὰ μετὰ πραΰτητος καὶ φόβου, [c]συνείδησιν ἔχοντες ἀγαθήν, ἵνα ἐν ᾧ καταλαλεῖσθε[3] καταισχυνθῶσιν οἱ ἐπηρεά-ζοντες ὑμῶν τὴν ἀγαθὴν ἐν Χριστῷ ἀναστροφήν. 17 κρεῖτ-τον γὰρ ἀγαθοποιοῦντας, εἰ θέλοι τὸ θέλημα τοῦ θεοῦ, πάσχειν ἢ κακοποιοῦντας. 18 ὅτι καὶ Χριστὸς ἅπαξ περὶ ἁμαρτιῶν [ὑπὲρ ὑμῶν][4] ἀπέθανεν[5], δίκαιος ὑπὲρ ἀδίκων, ἵνα ὑμᾶς[6] προσαγάγῃ τῷ θεῷ, θανατωθεὶς μὲν σαρκὶ

[2] **15** {B} τὸν Χριστόν 𝔭[72] ℵ A B C Ψ 33 326[mg] 614 630 945 1739 1881 2412 it[ar,c,dem,div,p,t,z] vg syr[p,h] cop[sa,bo] arm Clement // τὸν θεόν K P 049 056 0142 81 88 104 181 326[txt] 330 436 451 1241 1505 1877 2127 2492 2495 *Byz Lect* (*l*[1441] τὸν θεὸν ἡμῶν) Ps-Oecumenius Theophylact // *omit* de Promissionibus

[3] **16** {B} καταλαλεῖσθε 𝔭[72] B Ψ 614 630 1241 1505 1739 1881 2412 2495 (syr[h]) cop[sa] Clement // καταλαλεῖσθε ὡς κακοποιῶν syr[h with *] cop[bo?] // καταλαλοῦσιν ὑμῶν it[dem,div,(m)] vg arm // καταλαλοῦσιν ὑμῶν ὡς κα-κοποιῶν (*see* 2.12) ℵ A C K P 049 33 81 330 451 629 945 2492 *Lect* (056 0142 88 104 181 326 436 1877 2127 *Byz l*[1364] καταλαλῶσιν) it[ar,c,p,z] syr[p,hmg] cop[bo?] eth Bede Ps-Oecumenius Theophylact

[4] **18** {D} περὶ ἁμαρτιῶν ὑπὲρ ὑμῶν (*see footnote 5*) 𝔭[72] A 1241 (1505 2495 ὑπὲρ ἁμαρτιῶν ὑπὲρ ὑμῶν) arm // περὶ ἁμαρτιῶν ὑπὲρ ἡμῶν (ℵ* τῶν ἁμαρτιῶν) ℵ[c] C[2vid] 33 81 88 104 436 614 630 945 1739 1881 2412 *l*[6] syr[h] cop[bo] eth Didymus // περὶ ὑμῶν ὑπὲρ ἁμαρτιῶν Ψ // περὶ ἁμαρτιῶν ἡμῶν C*[vid] 629 it[ar,c,dem,div,p,z] vg[cl] syr[p] cop[sa] Clement Cyprian Augustine Bede // περὶ ἁμαρτιῶν B K P 049 056 0142 181 326* 330 451 1877 2127 *Byz Lect* vg[ww] cop[boms] Cyprian Cyril Ps-Oecumenius Theophylact // ὑπὲρ ἡμῶν ἁμαρτιῶν 326[c] // ὑπὲρ ἁμαρτιῶν 2492 // ὑπὲρ ἁμαρτωλῶν Didymus

[5] **18** {C} ἀπέθανεν (*see footnote 4*) 𝔭[72] ℵ A C[vid] Ψ 33 88 326[mg] 436 614 629 630 945 1241 1505 1739 1881 2412 2495 *l*[6] it[ar,c,dem,div,p,z] vg syr[p,h] cop[sa,bo] arm eth Cyprian Didymus Augustine Cyril Severus Theophylact[txt] // ἔπαθεν (*see* 2.21) B K P 049 056 0142 81 104 181 326[txt] 330 451 1877 2127 2492 *Byz Lect* Augustine Ps-Oecumenius Theophylact[comm]

[6] **18** {C} ὑμᾶς 𝔭[72] B P Ψ 049 181 326 330 451 1241 1505 1877 2492 2495

[b] **15** *b minor:* WH Bov Nes BF[2] AV RV ASV Zür Jer // *b major:* TR RSV NEB TT Luth Seg

[c] [c] **15-16** *c number 16, c no number:* TR[ed] Bov Nes BF[2] NEB? TT Zür Luth Jer // *c no number, c number 16:* TR[ed] WH AV RV ASV RSV NEB? Seg

14-15 τὸν δὲ...ὑμῶν Is 8.12-13   **18** Χριστὸς...ἀπέθανεν Ro 6.10; Eph 2.18; He 9.28; 10.10

ζωοποιηθεὶς δὲ πνεύματι· 19 ἐν ᾧ καὶ τοῖς ἐν φυλακῇ πνεύμασιν πορευθεὶς ἐκήρυξεν, 20 ἀπειθήσασίν ποτε ὅτε ἀπεξεδέχετο ἡ τοῦ θεοῦ μακροθυμία ἐν ἡμέραις Νῶε κατασκευαζομένης κιβωτοῦ, εἰς ἣν ὀλίγοι, τοῦτ᾽ ἔστιν ὀκτὼ ψυχαί, διεσώθησαν δι᾽ ὕδατος. 21 ὃ⁷ καὶ ὑμᾶς ἀντίτυπον νῦν σῴζει βάπτισμα, οὐ σαρκὸς ἀπόθεσις ῥύπου ἀλλὰ συνειδήσεως ἀγαθῆς ἐπερώτημα εἰς θεόν, δι᾽ ἀναστάσεως Ἰησοῦ Χριστοῦ, 22 ὅς ἐστιν ἐν δεξιᾷ [τοῦ] θεοῦ, πορευθεὶς εἰς οὐρανόν, ὑποταγέντων αὐτῷ ἀγγέλων καὶ ἐξουσιῶν καὶ δυνάμεων.

Good Stewards of God's Grace

4 Χριστοῦ οὖν παθόντος¹ σαρκὶ καὶ ὑμεῖς τὴν αὐτὴν ἔννοιαν ὁπλίσασθε, ὅτι ὁ παθὼν σαρκὶ πέπαυται ἁμαρτίας²,

---

*Byz*ᵖᵗ *l*⁶ it^z syr^{p,h} arm ‖ ἡμᾶς ℵᶜ A C K 056 0142 33 81 88 104 436 614 629 630 945 1739 1881 2127 2412 *Byz*ᵖᵗ *Lect* it^{ar,c,dem,div,p,t} vg syr^{hmg} cop^{sa,bo} Clement Cyprian Peter-Alexandria Didymus Cyril Ps-Oecumenius Theophylact ‖ *omit* ℵ*

⁷ **21** {C} ὅ ℵᶜ A B C K P Ψ 049 056 0142 33 81 88 104 181 326 330 451 614 (629 ὅς) (630 ᾧ) 945 1241 1505 1739 1877 1881 2127 2412 2492 2495 *Byz Lect* it^{ar,c,dem,div,p,z} vg (syr^{p,h}) arm Cyprian Origen^{lat} Didymus Augustine Cyril John-Damascus Ps-Oecumenius Theophylact ‖ ὡς (629 ὅς) cop^{bovid} Augustine^{vid} ‖ *omit* 𝔭⁷² ℵ* 436 eth

¹ **1** {B} παθόντος 𝔭⁷² B C Ψ 049* 330 451 1739 1881 it^{ar,c,dem,div,p,z} vg cop^{sa} Athanasius^{mss} Ambrose Niceta Augustine Theodoret Fulgentius John-Damascus Ps-Oecumenius^{comm} ‖ παθόντος ὑπὲρ ἡμῶν ℵᶜ A K P 056 0142 33 81 88 104 181 326 436 614 629 (630 945 ὑπὲρ ἡμῶν παθόντος) 1241 1877 2127 2412 2492 *Byz Lect* syr^h (cop^{bo} *transposes*: παθόντος σαρκὶ ὑπὲρ ἡμῶν) arm eth Athanasius Basil Didymus Ps-Athanasius Epiphanius Jerome Augustine Cyril Theodoret ‖ παθόντος ὑπὲρ ὑμῶν (ℵ* ἀποθανόντος) (049ᶜ *transposes*: παθόντος σαρκὶ ὑπὲρ ὑμῶν) 1505 2495 syr^p Ps-Oecumenius^{txt} Theophylact

² **1** {B} ἁμαρτίας 𝔭⁷² ℵ* A C K P 81 88 104 181 326 330 436 451 614 629 630 945 1241 1505 1739 2127 2412 2492 2495 *Byz Lect* cop^{sa,bomss} (Jerome) ‖ ἁμαρτίαις ℵᶜ B Ψ it^{ar,c,dem,div,p,z} vg syr^p eth Bede ‖ ἀπὸ ἁμαρτίας 049 056 0142 (1877 τῆς ἁμαρτίας) 1881 *l*⁶² syr^h cop^{bomss}

---

20 Gn 6.1–7.24   **21** σώζει...θεόν He 10.22   **22** Eph 1.20–21
4 1 ὁ...ἁμαρτίας Ro 6.2, 7

---

¹⁹ and in his spiritual existence he went and preached to the imprisoned spirits. ²⁰ These were the spirits of those who had not obeyed God, when he waited patiently during the days that Noah was building the ark. The few people in the ark — eight in all — were saved by the water. ²¹ This water was a figure pointing to baptism, which now saves you, not by washing off bodily dirt, but by the promise made to God from a good conscience. Baptism saves you through the resurrection of Jesus Christ, ²² who has gone to heaven and is at the right side of God, ruling over all angels and heavenly authorities and powers.

Changed Lives

4 Since Christ suffered physically, you too must strengthen yourselves with the same way of thinking; for whoever suffers physically is no longer involved with sin.

² From now on, then, you must live the rest of your earthly lives controlled by God's will, not by human passions. ³ For you have spent enough time in the past doing what the heathen like to do. Your lives were spent in indecency, lust, drunkenness, orgies, drinking parties, and the disgusting worship of idols. ⁴ And now the heathen are surprised when you do not join them in the same wild and reckless living, and so they insult you. ⁵ But they must give an account of themselves to God, who is ready to judge the living and the dead. ⁶ This is why the Good News was preached also to the dead, to those who had been judged in their physical existence as all men are judged; it was preached to them so that in their spiritual existence they may live as God lives.

Good Managers of God's Gifts

⁷ The end of all things is near. You must be self-controlled and alert, to be able to pray. ⁸ Above everything, love one another earnestly, for love covers over many sins. ⁹ Open your homes to each other, without complaining. ¹⁰ Each one, as a good manager of God's different gifts, must use for the good of others the special gift he has received from God. ¹¹ Whoever preaches, must preach God's words; whoever serves, must serve with the strength that God gives him, so that in all things praise may be given to God through Jesus Christ, to whom belong the glory and the power for ever and ever! Amen.

Suffering as a Christian

¹² My dear friends, do not be surprised at the painful test you are suffering, as though something unusual were happen-

2 εἰς τὸ μηκέτι ἀνθρώπων ἐπιθυμίαις ἀλλὰ θελήματι θεοῦ τὸν ἐπίλοιπον ἐν σαρκὶ βιῶσαι χρόνον. 3 ἀρκετὸς γὰρ³ ὁ παρεληλυθὼς χρόνος τὸ βούλημα τῶν ἐθνῶν κατειργάσθαι, πεπορευμένους ἐν ἀσελγείαις, ἐπιθυμίαις, οἰνοφλυγίαις, κώμοις, πότοις, καὶ ἀθεμίτοις εἰδωλολατρίαις.ᵃ 4 ἐν ᾧ ξενίζονται μὴ συντρεχόντων ὑμῶν εἰς τὴν αὐτὴν τῆς ἀσωτίας ἀνάχυσιν, βλασφημοῦντες· 5 οἳ ἀποδώσουσιν λόγον τῷ ἑτοίμως ἔχοντι κρῖναι ζῶντας καὶ νεκρούς. 6 εἰς τοῦτο γὰρ καὶ νεκροῖς εὐηγγελίσθη ἵνα κριθῶσι μὲν κατὰ ἀνθρώπους σαρκὶ ζῶσι δὲ κατὰ θεὸν πνεύματι.

7 Πάντων δὲ τὸ τέλος ἤγγικεν.ᵇ σωφρονήσατε οὖν καὶ νήψατε εἰς προσευχάς·ᵇ 8 πρὸ πάντων τὴν εἰς ἑαυτοὺς ἀγάπην ἐκτενῆ ἔχοντες, ὅτι ἀγάπη καλύπτει πλῆθος ἁμαρτιῶν· 9 φιλόξενοι εἰς ἀλλήλους ἄνευ γογγυσμοῦ· 10 ἕκαστος καθὼς ἔλαβεν χάρισμα, εἰς ἑαυτοὺς αὐτὸ διακονοῦντες ὡς καλοὶ οἰκονόμοι ποικίλης χάριτος θεοῦ. 11 εἴ τις λαλεῖ, ὡς λόγια θεοῦ· εἴ τις διακονεῖ, ὡς ἐξ ἰσχύος ἧς χορηγεῖ ὁ θεός· ἵνα ἐν πᾶσιν δοξάζηται ὁ θεὸς διὰ Ἰησοῦ Χριστοῦ, ᾧ ἐστιν ἡ δόξα καὶ τὸ κράτος εἰς τοὺς αἰῶνας τῶν αἰώνων· ἀμήν.

Suffering as a Christian

12 Ἀγαπητοί, μὴ ξενίζεσθε τῇ ἐν ὑμῖν πυρώσει πρὸς πειρασμὸν ὑμῖν γινομένῃ ὡς ξένου ὑμῖν συμβαίνοντος,

---

3 3 {B} γάρ 𝔓⁷² ℵᶜ A B Ψ 81 436 614 629* 945 1241 1505 1739 1881 2412 2495 itᵃʳ,ᶜ,ᵈᵉᵐ,ᵈⁱᵛ,ᵖ,ᶻ vg syrᵖ·ʰ copˢᵃ? arm Clement Augustine ∥ γὰρ ἡμῖν C K P 049 056 0142 181 326 1877 2492 Byzᵖᵗ l¹⁴⁷ Jerome Ps-Oecumenius ∥ γὰρ ὑμῖν ℵ* 88 104 330 451 629ᶜ 630 2127 Byzᵖᵗ Lect copᵇᵒ eth Augustine Theophylact

---

ᵃ 3 a major: WH Bov Nes BF² RSV NEB TT Zür Luth Jer Seg ∥ a minor: TR AV RV ASV

ᵇ 7 b major, b minor: TR WH Bov Nes BF² ∥ b minor, b major: AV RSV NEB Seg ∥ b major, b major: RV ASV TT Zür Luth Jer

---

3 Eph 2.2–3; Tt 3.3   5 τῷ...νεκρούς Ac 10.42; 2 Tm 4.1   7 Πάντων...ἤγγικεν Ro 13.11–12; 1 Jn 2.18   8 ἀγάπη...ἁμαρτιῶν Pr 10.12; Jas 5.20   10 ἕκαστος...διακονοῦντες Ro 12.6–8   11 ἐν...θεός 1 Cor 10.31   12 τῇ...συμβαίνοντος 1 Pe 1.7

13 ἀλλὰ καθὸ κοινωνεῖτε τοῖς τοῦ Χριστοῦ παθήμασιν χαίρετε, ἵνα καὶ ἐν τῇ ἀποκαλύψει τῆς δόξης αὐτοῦ χαρῆτε ἀγαλλιώμενοι. 14 εἰ ὀνειδίζεσθε ἐν ὀνόματι Χριστοῦ, μακάριοι, ὅτι τὸ τῆς δόξης καὶ τὸ[4] τοῦ θεοῦ πνεῦμα ἐφ' ὑμᾶς ἀναπαύεται[5]. 15 μὴ γάρ τις ὑμῶν πασχέτω ὡς φονεὺς ἢ κλέπτης ἢ κακοποιὸς ἢ ὡς ἀλλοτριεπίσκοπος· 16 εἰ δὲ ὡς Χριστιανός, μὴ αἰσχυνέσθω, δοξαζέτω δὲ τὸν θεὸν ἐν τῷ ὀνόματι τούτῳ. 17 ὅτι ὁ καιρὸς τοῦ ἄρξασθαι τὸ κρίμα ἀπὸ τοῦ οἴκου τοῦ θεοῦ· εἰ δὲ πρῶτον ἀφ' ἡμῶν, τί τὸ τέλος τῶν ἀπειθούντων τῷ τοῦ θεοῦ εὐαγγελίῳ;

18   καὶ εἰ ὁ δίκαιος μόλις σῴζεται,
      ὁ ἀσεβὴς καὶ ἁμαρτωλὸς ποῦ φανεῖται;

19 ὥστε καὶ οἱ πάσχοντες κατὰ τὸ θέλημα τοῦ θεοῦ πιστῷ κτίστῃ παρατιθέσθωσαν τὰς ψυχὰς αὐτῶν ἐν ἀγαθοποιΐᾳ.

ing to you. [13] Rather be glad that you are sharing Christ's sufferings, so that you may be full of joy when his glory is revealed. [14] Happy are you if you are insulted because you are Christ's followers; for this means that the glorious Spirit, the Spirit of God, has come down on you. [15] None of you should suffer for being a murderer, or a thief, or a criminal, or for trying to manage other people's business. [16] But if you suffer because you are a Christian, don't be ashamed of it, but thank God that you bear Christ's name.

[17] The time has come for the Judgment to begin, and God's own people are the first to be judged. If it starts with us, how will it end with those who do not believe the Good News from God? [18] As the scripture says,

   "If it is difficult for good men to be saved,
   What will become of godless and sinful men?"

[19] So then, those who suffer because this is God's will for them, should by their good deeds trust themselves completely to their Creator, who always keeps his promise.

---

[4] **14** {B} δόξης καὶ τό 𝔭[72] B K Ψ 049 181 326[txt] 330 451 629 1877 2127 2492 *Byz*[pt] *l*[147,1441] Clement Tertullian Ephraem Cyril Fulgentius Ps-Oecumenius Theophylact ‖ δόξης it[ar,div,t] vg[ww] syr[p] ‖ δόξης καὶ δυνάμεως it[q] syr[h] cop[sa] eth Cyprian Didymus ‖ δόξης καὶ δυνάμεως καὶ τό A P 056 0142 33 81 88 104 326[mg] 436 614 630 945 1241 1505 1739 1881 2412 2495 *Byz*[pt] *Lect* it[c,dem,(gig),z] cop[bo] arm Ps-Clement Athanasius Antiochus John-Damascus ‖ δόξης καὶ τῆς δυνάμεως αὐτοῦ ℵ* (ℵ[c] omit αὐτοῦ) ‖ *domini virtus in dei* it[p] ‖ *est honoris, gloriae et virtutis dei* vg[cl]

[5] **14** {A} ἀναπαύεται ℵ* B 056 0142 436 629[*vid] 1739 it[c,dem,div,(gig)] vg[cl] syr[p,h?] cop[bo] arm eth Tertullian Origen ‖ ἐπαναπαύεται Λ 81 614 630 2412 2492 ‖ ἀναπέπαυται 33 945 1241 1881 *l*[680] Ephraem Athanasius Didymus Antiochus John-Damascus ‖ ἐπαναπέπαυται 𝔭[72] ℵ[c] syr[p?h?] ‖ ἀναπέμπεται 049 ‖ ἀναπαύεται κατὰ μὲν αὐτοὺς βλασφημεῖται κατὰ δὲ ὑμᾶς δοξάζεται K P (Ψ 104 326[mgvid] 1505 2495 ἐπαναπαύεται) 181 326[txt] 330 451 629[c] (1877 ἡμᾶς) 2127 (88 *Lect* ἀναπέπαυται) *Byz* *l*[1441] it[ar,p,q,t,z] vg[ww] syr[h with *] cop[sa,(boms)] Cyprian Ps-Oecumenius Theophylact

---

13 καθὸ...χαίρετε Ac 5.41   **14** ὀνειδίζεσθε...Χριστοῦ Ps 89.50–51; Ac 5.41; 1 Pe 2.20   τὸ τοῦ...ἀναπαύεται Is 11.2   **17** τοῦ ἄρξασθαι...θεοῦ Jr 25.29; Eze 9.6   τῶν...εὐαγγελίῳ 2 Th 1.8   **18** Pr 11.31 lxx   **19** πιστῷ...αὐτῶν Ps 31.5

The Flock of God

5 I appeal to the church elders among you, I who am an elder myself. I am a witness of Christ's sufferings, and I will have a share of the glory which will be revealed. I appeal to you: ² be shepherds of the flock God gave you, and look after it willingly, as God wants you to, and not unwillingly. Do your work, not for mere pay, but from a real desire to serve. ³ Do not try to rule over those who have been given into your care, but be examples to the flock. ⁴ And when the Chief Shepherd appears, you will receive the glorious crown which will never lose its brightness.

⁵ In the same way, you younger men must submit yourselves to the older men. And all of you must put on the apron of humility, to serve one another; for the scripture says, "God resists the proud, but gives grace to the humble." ⁶ Humble yourselves, then, under God's mighty hand, so that he will lift you up in his own good time. ⁷ Throw all your worries on him, for he cares for you.

⁸ Be alert, be on watch! For your enemy, the Devil, roams around like a roaring lion, looking for someone to

Tending the Flock of God

5 Πρεσβυτέρους οὖν ἐν ὑμῖν παρακαλῶ ὁ συμπρεσβύτερος καὶ μάρτυς τῶν τοῦ Χριστοῦ παθημάτων, ὁ καὶ τῆς μελλούσης ἀποκαλύπτεσθαι δόξης κοινωνός· ᵃ 2 ποιμάνατε τὸ ἐν ὑμῖν ποίμνιον τοῦ θεοῦ, ἐπισκοποῦντες μὴ ἀναγκαστῶς ἀλλὰ ἑκουσίως κατὰ θεόν¹, μηδὲ αἰσχροκερδῶς ἀλλὰ προθύμως, 3 μηδ' ὡς κατακυριεύοντες τῶν κλήρων ἀλλὰ τύποι γινόμενοι τοῦ ποιμνίου· 4 καὶ φανερωθέντος τοῦ ἀρχιποίμενος κομιεῖσθε τὸν ἀμαράντινον τῆς δόξης στέφανον.

5 Ὁμοίως, νεώτεροι, ὑποτάγητε πρεσβυτέροις.ᵇ πάντες δὲ ἀλλήλοιςᵇ τὴν ταπεινοφροσύνην ἐγκομβώσασθε, ὅτι

Ὁ θεὸς ὑπερηφάνοις ἀντιτάσσεται,
    ταπεινοῖς δὲ δίδωσιν χάριν.

6 Ταπεινώθητε οὖν ὑπὸ τὴν κραταιὰν χεῖρα τοῦ θεοῦ, ἵνα ὑμᾶς ὑψώσῃ ἐν καιρῷ, 7 πᾶσαν τὴν μέριμναν ὑμῶν ἐπιρίψαντες ἐπ' αὐτόν, ὅτι αὐτῷ μέλει περὶ ὑμῶν.

8 Νήψατε, γρηγορήσατε. ὁ ἀντίδικος ὑμῶν διάβολος ὡς λέων ὠρυόμενος περιπατεῖ ζητῶν [τινα] καταπιεῖν²·

---

¹ 2 {C} ἐπισκοποῦντες μὴ ἀναγκαστῶς ἀλλὰ ἑκουσίως κατὰ θεόν 𝔭⁷² ℵᶜ A P Ψ 33 81 104 181 326ᵐᵍ 436 (614 630 2412 2495 ἐπισκοπεύοντες) 945 1241 1505 1739 1881 it⁽ᵃʳ⁾,ᵉ,ᵈᵉᵐ,ᵈⁱᵛ,ʰ,⁽ᵐ⁾,ᵖ,q,ᵗ,z vg syrʰ (syrᵖ ἐπισκοποῦντες πνευματικῶς *and omit* κατὰ θεόν) copᵇᵒ arm eth Antiochus (John-Damascus) Theophylact ‖ ἐπισκοποῦντες μὴ ἀναγκαστῶς ἀλλὰ (*or* ἀλλ') ἑκουσίως K 049 056 0142 88 326ᵗˣᵗ 330 451 629 1877 2127 2492 *Byz Lect* (l¹⁴⁴¹ ἀναγκαστικῶς) ‖ μὴ ἀναγκαστῶς ἀλλὰ ἑκουσίως κατὰ θεόν ℵ* copˢᵃ ‖ μὴ ἀναγκαστῶς ἀλλὰ ἑκουσίως B

² 8 {D} τινα καταπιεῖν (ℵ* καταπῖν) ℵᶜ (P l¹³⁶⁵ᵐ τίνα) (K 049 τινά) 81 181 326 629 1241 1505 1739 1881 2127 2495 copᵇᵒ Origen Cyprian Hilary John-Damascus ‖ τίνα καταπίῃ 𝔭⁷² A 056 436 614 630 945 2412 2492 *Byz*

ᵃ **1** *a* minor: TR WH Bov Nes BF² AV RV ASV TT Zür Luth Seg ‖ *a* major: RSV NEB Jer

ᵇ ᵇ **5** *b* major, *b* none: WH Bov Nes BF² RV ASV RSV NEB (TT) Zür Luth Jer (Seg) ‖ *b* minor, *b* major: RVᵐᵍ ASVᵐᵍ ‖ *different text*: TR AV

---

2 ποιμάνατε...θεοῦ Jn 21.15–17; Ac 20.28   **3** μηδ'...κλήρων 2 Cor 1.24 τύποι...ποιμνίου Php 3.17; Tt 2.7   **4** κομιεῖσθε...στέφανον 1 Cor 9.25   **5** Ὁ...χάριν Pr 3.34 LXX (Mt 23.12; Jas 4.6)   **6** Job 22.29; Mt 23.12; Lk 14.11; 18.14; Jas 4.10   **7** πᾶσαν...αὐτόν Ps 55.22; Mt 6.25–30   **8** Νήψατε, γρηγορήσατε 1 Th 5.6

9 ᾧ ἀντίστητε στερεοὶ τῇ πίστει, εἰδότες τὰ αὐτὰ τῶν παθημάτων τῇ ἐν [τῷ] κόσμῳ ὑμῶν ἀδελφότητι ἐπιτελεῖσθαι. 10 Ὁ δὲ θεὸς πάσης χάριτος, ὁ καλέσας ὑμᾶς εἰς τὴν αἰώνιον αὐτοῦ δόξαν ἐν Χριστῷ[3], ὀλίγον παθόντας αὐτὸς καταρτίσει, στηρίξει, σθενώσει, θεμελιώσει[4]. 11 αὐτῷ τὸ κράτος[5] εἰς τοὺς αἰῶνας[6]· ἀμήν.

Final Greetings

12 Διὰ Σιλουανοῦ ὑμῖν τοῦ πιστοῦ ἀδελφοῦ, ὡς λογίζομαι, δι᾽ ὀλίγων ἔγραψα, παρακαλῶν καὶ ἐπιμαρτυρῶν ταύτην εἶναι ἀληθῆ χάριν τοῦ θεοῦ· εἰς ἣν στῆτε.

devour. 9 Be firm in your faith and resist him, for you know that your fellow believers in all the world are going through the same kind of sufferings. 10 But after you have suffered for a little while, the God of all grace, who calls you to share his eternal glory in union with Christ, will himself perfect you, and give you firmness, strength, and a sure foundation. 11 To him be the power for ever! Amen.

Final Greetings

12 I write you this brief letter with the help of Silvanus, whom I regard as a faithful brother. I want to encourage you and give my testimony that this is the true grace of God. Stand firm in it.

*l*680m,1441m,1590m it^ar,c,dem,div,h,p,q,t,z vg syr^p,h arm eth Origen^gr,lat Eusebius Lucifer Ephraem Cyril Jerusalem Chrysostom Cyril Theodoret John-Damascus ‖ τίνα καταπίει 0142 88 104 330 451 1877 *Lect*^m Marcus Ps-Athanasius Antiochus ‖ καταπιεῖν Β Ψ (0206^vid? καταπεῖν) Origen^lat

3 10 {C} Χριστῷ ℵ 0206^vid 614 630 1505 2412 2495 syr^h ‖ τῷ Χριστῷ Β ‖ Χριστῷ Ἰησοῦ 𝔭^72 Α Κ Ρ Ψ 049 056 0142 33 81 88 104 181 326 330 436 451 629 1241 1739 1877 1881 2127 2492 *Byz Lect*^m it^c,dem,div,h,p,q,t,z vg syr^h with * cop^sa,bo arm eth Didymus Ps-Oecumenius Theophylact ‖ Ἰησοῦ Χριστῷ syr^p ‖ Ἰησοῦ (945 *omit preceding* ἐν) it^ar

4 10 {C} σθενώσει, θεμελιώσει ℵ Κ Ρ 049 056 0142 88 104 181 326 330 436 451 629 945 1241 1739 1877 1881 2127 2492 *Byz Lect*^m syr^(p),h cop^sa,bo arm ‖ σθενώσαι, θεμελιῶσαι 614 630 1505 2412 2495 Ps-Oecumenius Theophylact ‖ σθενώσει Α Β Ψ 0206 *l*1365m it^ar,c,dem,div,h,p,z vg eth ‖ θεμελιώσει 𝔭^72 81 it^q,t

5 11 {C} τὸ κράτος (𝔭^72 0206^vid *omit* τό) Α Β Ψ it^ar vg^ww eth^ro ‖ ἡ δόξα 336 915 1835 it^t ‖ ἡ δόξα κράτος Κ 049 056 0142 330 (436 *omit* ἡ) 451 2127 *Lect*^m ‖ ἡ δόξα καὶ τὸ κράτος (*see* 4.11) ℵ Ρ 88 104 181 326 1877 2492 *Byz* it^c,dem,div,p,z vg^cl cop^sa eth^pp (Ps-Oecumenius *omit* τό) Theophylact ‖ τὸ κράτος καὶ ἡ δόξα 33 81 014 030 945 1241 1505 1739 1881 2412 2405 *l*1365m syr^h cop^bo arm ‖ ἡ δόξα καὶ ἡ βασιλεία 629 ‖ *virtus et potestas* it^h,q ‖ *glory and dominion and honor* syr^p

6 11 {C} αἰῶνας 𝔭^72 Β *l*1365m cop^bo arm ‖ αἰῶνας τῶν αἰώνων (*see* 4.11) ℵ Α Κ Ρ Ψ 049 056 0142 0206 33 81 88 104 181 326 330 436 451 614 629 630 945 1241 1505 1739 1877 1881 2127 2412 2492 2495 *Byz Lect*^m it^ar,c,dem,div,h,p,q,t,z vg syr^p,h cop^sa,bo^ms eth Ps-Oecumenius Theophylact

9 ᾧ ἀντίστητε Eph 6.11–13; Jas 4.7   10 Ὁ δὲ...δόξαν 1 Th 2.12

13 Your sister church in Babylon, also chosen by God, sends you greetings, and so does my son Mark. 14 Greet each other with the kiss of Christian love.

May peace be with all of you who belong to Christ.

13 Ἀσπάζεται ὑμᾶς ἡ ἐν Βαβυλῶνι συνεκλεκτὴ καὶ Μᾶρκος ὁ υἱός μου. **14** ἀσπάσασθε ἀλλήλους ἐν φιλήματι ἀγάπης. εἰρήνη ὑμῖν πᾶσιν τοῖς ἐν Χριστῷ[7].[8]

---

[7] **14** {C} Χριστῷ A B Ψ *l*1365m,1441m itc,dem,(gig),q,z vgww syrp copsa,bomss eth ‖ Χριστῷ Ἰησοῦ ℵ K P 049 056 0142 81 88 104 181 326 330 436 451 614 630 945 1241 1505 1739 1877 1881 2127 2412 2492 2495 *Byz Lect*m itdiv,h,p vgcl syrh copbo arm Ps-Oecumenius Theophylact ‖ κυρίῳ Ἰησοῦ 629

[8] **14** {C} *omit* ἀμήν. A B Ψ 81 629 945 1241 1881 itar,(gig),z copsa,bo eth ‖ *add* ἀμήν. ℵ K P 049 056 0142 88 104 181 326 330 436 451 614 630 1505 1739 1877 2127 2412 2492 2495 *Byz Lect*m itc,dem,div,h,p,q vg syrp,h copbomss arm Ps-Oecumenius Theophylact

ΠΕΤΡΟΥ Β

Salutation

1 Συμεὼν[1] Πέτρος δοῦλος καὶ ἀπόστολος Ἰησοῦ Χριστοῦ τοῖς ἰσότιμον ἡμῖν λαχοῦσιν πίστιν ἐν δικαιοσύνῃ τοῦ θεοῦ ἡμῶν καὶ σωτῆρος Ἰησοῦ Χριστοῦ· **2** χάρις ὑμῖν καὶ εἰρήνη πληθυνθείη ἐν ἐπιγνώσει τοῦ θεοῦ καὶ Ἰησοῦ τοῦ κυρίου ἡμῶν.[a]

The Christian's Call and Election

3 Ὡς πάντα ἡμῖν τῆς θείας δυνάμεως αὐτοῦ τὰ πρὸς ζωὴν καὶ εὐσέβειαν δεδωρημένης διὰ τῆς ἐπιγνώσεως τοῦ καλέσαντος ἡμᾶς ἰδίᾳ δόξῃ καὶ ἀρετῇ[2], **4** δι' ὧν τὰ τίμια καὶ μέγιστα ἡμῖν ἐπαγγέλματα δεδώρηται, ἵνα διὰ τούτων γένησθε θείας κοινωνοὶ φύσεως, ἀποφυγόντες τῆς ἐν τῷ κόσμῳ ἐν ἐπιθυμίᾳ φθορᾶς. **5** καὶ αὐτὸ τοῦτο δὲ σπουδὴν πᾶσαν παρεισενέγκαντες ἐπιχορηγήσατε ἐν τῇ πίστει ὑμῶν τὴν ἀρετήν, ἐν δὲ τῇ ἀρετῇ τὴν γνῶσιν, **6** ἐν δὲ τῇ γνώσει τὴν ἐγκράτειαν, ἐν δὲ τῇ ἐγκρατείᾳ τὴν ὑπομονήν, ἐν δὲ τῇ ὑπομονῇ τὴν εὐσέβειαν, **7** ἐν δὲ τῇ εὐσεβείᾳ τὴν φιλαδελφίαν, ἐν δὲ τῇ φιλαδελφίᾳ τὴν ἀγάπην. **8** ταῦτα γὰρ ὑμῖν ὑπάρ-

---

[1] **1** {C} Συμεών ℵ A K P 049 056 0142 0209 104 436 629 945 1505 1739 1881 2127 2495 *Byz* l[800,1153a,1441,1590*] syr[ph,h] arm mss[acc. to Ps-Oecumenius] Theophylact // Σίμων 𝔭[72] B Ψ 81 88 181 330 451 614 630 1241 1877 2412 2492 l[147,603,680,1364,1590mg] it[ar,c,dem,div,h,p,q,z] vg syr[pal] cop[sa,bo] eth Ps-Oecumenius

[2] **3** {D} ἰδίᾳ δόξῃ καὶ ἀρετῇ ℵ A C P Ψ 33 81 88 104 436 614 629 630 945 1241 1505 1739 1881 2412 2495 it[ar,c,dem,div,h,(m),p,q] vg syr[ph,h,pal] cop[sa,bo] arm Didymus Cassian Bede // διὰ δόξης καὶ ἀρετῆς 𝔭[72] B K 049 056 0142 181 330 451 1877 2127 2492 *Byz Lect* l[598m,1365m] Ps-Oecumenius Theophylact // *per propria gloria et virtute* it[z]

[a] **2-3** *a* paragraph: TR Bov Nes BF² RSV NEB TT Zür Luth Jer Seg // *a* minor: WH AV RV ASV

2 χάρις...πληθυνθείη Jd 2   **3** τοῦ...ἀρετῇ 1 Pe 2.9   **6-7** Ga 5.22–23

THE SECOND LETTER FROM PETER

1 From Simon Peter, a servant and apostle of Jesus Christ —

To those who through the righteousness of our God and Savior Jesus Christ have been given a faith as precious as ours:

2 May grace and peace be yours in full measure, through your knowledge of God and of Jesus our Lord.

God's Call and Choice

3 His divine power has given us everything we need to live a godly life through our knowledge of the one who called us to share his own glory and goodness. **4** In this way he has given us precious and very great promises, in order that by receiving what he has promised you may escape from the destructive passion that exists in the world, and come to share the divine nature. **5** For this very reason, do your best to add goodness to your faith; and to your goodness add knowledge; **6** to your knowledge add self-control; to your self-control add endurance; to your endurance add godliness; **7** to your godliness add brotherly love; and to your brotherly love add love. **8** These are the qualities you need, and if you have them in abundance they will make you active and effective in your knowledge of our Lord Jesus Christ. 9 But whoever does not have them is so shortsighted that he cannot see, and has forgotten that his past sins have been washed away.

10 So then, my brothers, try even harder to make God's call and his choice of you a permanent experience; for if you do so you will never fall away. 11 In this way you will be given the full right to enter the eternal Kingdom of our Lord and Savior Jesus Christ.

12 For this reason I will always remind you of these matters, even though you already know them and have been firmly fixed in the truth you have received. 13 I think it only right for me to stir up your memory of these matters, as long as I am still alive. 14 For I know that I shall soon put off this mortal body, as our Lord Jesus Christ plainly told me. 15 I will do my best, then, to provide a way for you to remember these matters at all times after my death.

Eyewitnesses of Christ's Glory

16 For we have not depended on made-up legends in making known to you the mighty coming of our Lord Jesus Christ. With our own eyes we saw his greatness! 17 We were there when he was given honor and glory by God the Father, when the voice came to him from the Supreme Glory, saying, "This is my own

χοντα καὶ πλεονάζοντα οὐκ ἀργοὺς οὐδὲ ἀκάρπους καθίστησιν εἰς τὴν τοῦ κυρίου ἡμῶν Ἰησοῦ Χριστοῦ ἐπίγνωσιν· 9 ᾧ γὰρ μὴ πάρεστιν ταῦτα, τυφλός ἐστιν μυωπάζων, λήθην λαβὼν τοῦ καθαρισμοῦ τῶν πάλαι αὐτοῦ ἁμαρτιῶν. 10 διὸ μᾶλλον, ἀδελφοί, σπουδάσατε βεβαίαν³ ὑμῶν τὴν κλῆσιν καὶ ἐκλογὴν ποιεῖσθαι³· ταῦτα γὰρ ποιοῦντες οὐ μὴ πταίσητέ ποτε· 11 οὕτως γὰρ πλουσίως ἐπιχορηγηθήσεται ὑμῖν ἡ εἴσοδος εἰς τὴν αἰώνιον βασιλείαν τοῦ κυρίου ἡμῶν καὶ σωτῆρος Ἰησοῦ Χριστοῦ.

12 Διὸ μελλήσω ἀεὶ ὑμᾶς ὑπομιμνῄσκειν περὶ τούτων, καίπερ εἰδότας καὶ ἐστηριγμένους ἐν τῇ παρούσῃ ἀληθείᾳ. 13 δίκαιον δὲ ἡγοῦμαι, ἐφ' ὅσον εἰμὶ ἐν τούτῳ τῷ σκηνώματι, διεγείρειν ὑμᾶς ἐν ὑπομνήσει, 14 εἰδὼς ὅτι ταχινή ἐστιν ἡ ἀπόθεσις τοῦ σκηνώματός μου, καθὼς καὶ ὁ κύριος ἡμῶν Ἰησοῦς Χριστὸς ἐδήλωσέν μοι· 15 σπουδάσω δὲ καὶ ἑκάστοτε ἔχειν ὑμᾶς μετὰ τὴν ἐμὴν ἔξοδον τὴν τούτων μνήμην ποιεῖσθαι.

Christ's Glory and the Prophetic Word

16 Οὐ γὰρ σεσοφισμένοις μύθοις ἐξακολουθήσαντες ἐγνωρίσαμεν ὑμῖν τὴν τοῦ κυρίου ἡμῶν Ἰησοῦ Χριστοῦ δύναμιν καὶ παρουσίαν, ἀλλ' ἐπόπται γενηθέντες τῆς ἐκείνου μεγαλειότητος. 17 λαβὼν γὰρ παρὰ θεοῦ πατρὸς τιμὴν καὶ δόξαν φωνῆς ἐνεχθείσης αὐτῷ τοιᾶσδε ὑπὸ τῆς μεγαλοπρεποῦς δόξης, Ὁ υἱός μου ὁ ἀγαπητός μου

---

³ 10 {B} σπουδάσατε βεβαίαν...ποιεῖσθαι 𝔭⁷² B C K P 049 056 0142 0209 181 330 436 451 614 945 1241 1739 1877 1881 2127 2492 *Byz Lect*ᵐ *l*⁶⁰³,⁶⁸⁰ˢ·ᵐ· ¹³⁶⁵ᵐ ᵖᵗ Ambrose Ps-Oecumenius Theophylact ∥ σπουδάσατε ἵνα διὰ τῶν καλῶν ἔργων βεβαίαν...ποιῆσθε (ℵ ποιεῖσθαι) Ψ 81 88 (629 διὰ καλοῦ ἔργου) 630 1505 2412 2495 (*l*¹³⁶⁵ᵐ ᵖᵗ ποιέσθαι) itᵃʳ,ᶜ,ᵈᵉᵐ,ᵈⁱᵛ,ʰ,ᵖ,(ᵗ),ᶻ vg syrʰ,ᵖᵃˡ copˢᵃ,ᵇᵒ arm ∥ σπουδάσατε ἵνα διὰ τῶν καλῶν ὑμῶν ἔργων βεβαίαν...ποιεῖσθε A (104 ἔργων ὑμῶν) syrᵖʰ eth

---

12 μελλήσω...εἰδότας Jd 5   14 ἡ ἀπόθεσις...μου 2 Cor 5.1   καθὼς...ἐδήλωσέν μοι Jn 21.18-19   17-18 Mt 17.1-5; Mk 9.2-7; Lk 9.28-35

οὗτός ἐστιν⁴, εἰς ὃν ἐγὼ εὐδόκησα — ᵇ 18 καὶ ταύτην τὴν φωνὴν ἡμεῖς ἠκούσαμεν ἐξ οὐρανοῦ ἐνεχθεῖσαν σὺν αὐτῷ ὄντες ἐν τῷ ἁγίῳ ὄρει. 19 καὶ ἔχομεν βεβαιότερον τὸν προφητικὸν λόγον, ᾧ καλῶς ποιεῖτε προσέχοντες ὡς λύχνῳ φαίνοντι ἐν αὐχμηρῷ τόπῳ, ἕως οὗ ἡμέρα διαυγάσῃ καὶ φωσφόρος ἀνατείλῃ ἐν ταῖς καρδίαις ὑμῶν· 20 τοῦτο πρῶτον γινώσκοντες, ὅτι πᾶσα προφητεία γραφῆς ἰδίας ἐπιλύσεως οὐ γίνεται· 21 οὐ γὰρ θελήματι ἀνθρώπου ἠνέχθη προφητεία ποτέ, ἀλλὰ ὑπὸ πνεύματος ἁγίου φερόμενοι ἐλάλησαν ἀπὸ θεοῦ⁵ ἄνθρωποι.

False Prophets and Teachers
(Jude 4-13)

2 Ἐγένοντο δὲ καὶ ψευδοπροφῆται ἐν τῷ λαῷ, ὡς καὶ ἐν ὑμῖν ἔσονται ψευδοδιδάσκαλοι, οἵτινες παρεισάξουσιν αἱρέσεις ἀπωλείας, καὶ τὸν ἀγοράσαντα αὐτοὺς δεσπότην ἀρνούμενοι, ἐπάγοντες ἑαυτοῖς ταχινὴν ἀπώλειαν. 2 καὶ πολλοὶ ἐξακολουθήσουσιν αὐτῶν ταῖς ἀσελγείαις, δι' οὓς ἡ ὁδὸς τῆς ἀληθείας βλασφημηθήσεται· 3 καὶ ἐν πλεονεξίᾳ πλαστοῖς λόγοις ὑμᾶς ἐμπορεύσονται· οἷς τὸ κρίμα ἔκπαλαι οὐκ ἀργεῖ, καὶ ἡ ἀπώλεια αὐτῶν οὐ νυστάζει.

4 Εἰ γὰρ ὁ θεὸς ἀγγέλων ἁμαρτησάντων οὐκ ἐφείσατο,

⁴ 17 {C} ὁ υἱός μου ὁ ἀγαπητός μου οὗτός ἐστιν 𝔭⁷² B copˢᵃ?ᵇᵒ? eth? ‖ οὗτός ἐστιν ὁ υἱός μου ὁ ἀγαπητός (see Mt 3.17; 17.5) א A C K Ψ 049 056 (0142 omit μου) 0209 33 81 88 104 181 326 330 436 451 614 629 630 945 1241 1505 1739 1877 1881 2127 2412 2492 2495 Byz Lectᵐ itᵃʳ·ᶜ·ᵈᵉᵐ·ᵈⁱᵛ·ʰ·ᵖ·ᶻ vg syrᵖʰ·ʰ (copˢᵃ?ᵇᵒ? ἀγαπητός μου) arm eth Ps-Oecumenius Theophylact ‖ οὗτός ἐστιν ὁ υἱός μου ὁ ἀγαπητὸς οὗτός ἐστιν P ‖ οὗτός ἐστιν ὁ 1175

⁵ 21 {B} ἀπὸ θεοῦ 𝔭⁷² B P 614 630 945 1241 1505 1739 1881 2412 2492 2495 itᵈᵉᵐ syrʰ copᵇᵒ arm de Promissionibus Fulgentius ‖ οἱ ἅγιοι 431 copˢᵃ ‖ ἀπὸ θεοῦ ἅγιοι C (81 ἅγιοι ἀπὸ θεοῦ) eth Didymus (Theophylact ὑπό) ‖ ἅγιοι θεοῦ א K Ψ 049 056 0142 (A 1877 τοῦ θεοῦ) 33 88 104 181 326 330 436 451 629 2127 Byz Lect l¹⁴³⁹ᵐ itᵃʳ·ᶜ·ᵈⁱᵛ·ʰ·ᵖ·ᶻ vg syrᵖʰ Fulgentius Bede (Ps-Oecumenius οἱ ἅγιοι) ‖ ἅγιοι οἱ θεοῦ l⁸⁰⁹

ᵇ 17 b dash: WH Bov Nes BF² Zür ‖ b major: TR AV RV ASV NEB TT Luth Jer Seg ‖ b minor: RSV

21 ὑπὸ...ἄνθρωποι 2 Tm 3.16; 1 Pe 1.11
2 1 ἐν ὑμῖν...ψευδοδιδάσκαλοι Mt 24.11   τὸν...ἀρνούμενοι Jd 4   2 δι'... βλασφημηθήσεται Is 52.5   3 ἐν...ἐμπορεύσονται Ro 16.18; 1 Th 2.5   4 Jd 6

dear Son, with whom I am well pleased!" 18 We ourselves heard this voice coming from heaven, when we were with him on the sacred mountain.

19 So we are even more confident of the message proclaimed by the prophets. You will do well to pay attention to it, for it is like a lamp shining in a dark place, until the Day dawns and the light of the morning star shines in your hearts. 20 Above all else, however, remember this: no one can explain, by himself, a prophecy in the Scriptures. 21 For no prophetic message ever came just from the will of man, but men were carried along by the Holy Spirit as they spoke the message that came from God.

False Teachers

2 False prophets appeared in the past among the people, and in the same way false teachers will appear among you. They will bring in destructive, untrue doctrines, and deny the Master who saved them, and so bring upon themselves sudden destruction. 2 Even so, many will follow their immoral ways; and, because of what they do, people will speak evil of the Way of truth. 3 In their greed these false teachers will make a profit out of telling you made-up stories. For a long time now their Judge has been ready, and their Destroyer has been wide awake!

4 For God did not spare the angels who sinned, but threw them into hell,

where they are kept chained in darkness, waiting for the Day of Judgment. ⁵ God did not spare the ancient world, but brought the Flood on the world of wicked men; the only ones he saved were Noah, who preached righteousness, and seven other people. ⁶ God condemned the cities of Sodom and Gomorrah, destroying them with fire, and made an example of them for the wicked, of what will happen to them. ⁷ He rescued Lot, a good man, who was troubled by the immoral conduct of lawless men. ⁸ For that good man, living among them, day after day saw and heard such things that his good heart was tormented by their evil deeds. ⁹ And so the Lord knows how to rescue godly men from their trials, and how to keep the wicked under punishment for the Day of Judgment, ¹⁰ especially those who follow their filthy bodily lusts and despise God's authority.

These false teachers are bold and arrogant, and show no respect for the glorious beings above; instead, they insult them. ¹¹ Even the angels, who are so much stronger and mightier than these false teachers, do not accuse them with insults in the presence of the Lord.

ἀλλὰ σιραῖς¹ ζόφου ταρταρώσας παρέδωκεν εἰς κρίσιν τηρουμένους, 5 καὶ ἀρχαίου κόσμου οὐκ ἐφείσατο, ἀλλὰ ὄγδοον Νῶε δικαιοσύνης κήρυκα ἐφύλαξεν, κατακλυσμὸν κόσμῳ ἀσεβῶν ἐπάξας, 6 καὶ πόλεις Σοδόμων καὶ Γομόρρας τεφρώσας κατέκρινεν², ὑπόδειγμα μελλόντων ἀσεβέσιν³ τεθεικώς, 7 καὶ δίκαιον Λὼτ καταπονούμενον ὑπὸ τῆς τῶν ἀθέσμων ἐν ἀσελγείᾳ ἀναστροφῆς ἐρρύσατο·ᵃ 8 βλέμματι γὰρ καὶ ἀκοῇ ὁ δίκαιος ἐγκατοικῶν ἐν αὐτοῖς ἡμέραν ἐξ ἡμέρας ψυχὴν δικαίαν ἀνόμοις ἔργοις ἐβασάνιζεν·ᵃ 9 οἶδεν κύριος εὐσεβεῖς ἐκ πειρασμοῦ ῥύεσθαι, ἀδίκους δὲ εἰς ἡμέραν κρίσεως κολαζομένους τηρεῖν, 10 μάλιστα δὲ τοὺς ὀπίσω σαρκὸς ἐν ἐπιθυμίᾳ μιασμοῦ πορευομένους καὶ κυριότητος καταφρονοῦντας.

Τολμηταί,ᵇ αὐθάδεις, δόξας οὐ τρέμουσινᶜ βλασφημοῦντες, 11 ὅπου ἄγγελοι ἰσχύϊ καὶ δυνάμει μείζονες ὄντες οὐ φέρουσιν κατ᾽ αὐτῶν παρὰ κυρίῳ⁴ βλάσφημον

¹ 4 {D} σιραῖς 𝔭⁷² K P Ψ 049 056 0142 33 88 104 181 326 330 436 451 614 629 630 945 1241 1505 1739 1877 1881 2127 2412 2492 2495 *Byz Lect* l¹⁴³⁹ᵐ it⁽ᵃʳ⁾,ᶜ,ᵈᵉᵐ,ᵈⁱᵛ,ᶻ vg syrᵖʰ,ʰ copᵇᵒ arm Ephraem Didymus Cyril Procopius John-Damascus Ps-Oecumenius Theophylact ∥ σιροῖς ℵ A B C 81ᵛⁱᵈ (itʰ) copˢᵃ Augustine de Promissionibus ∥ *calinis* itᵖ

² 6 {D} κατέκρινεν 𝔭⁷²ᵗˣᵗ B C* 945 1241 1739 1881 copᵇᵒ ∥ κατέπ[ρ]ησεν 𝔭⁷²ᵐᵍ ∥ κατέστρεψεν P ∥ καταστροφῇ κατέκρινεν ℵ A C² K Ψ 049 056 0142 33 81 88 104 181 326 330 436 451 614 629 630 1505 1877 2127 2412 2492 2495 *Byz Lect* l¹⁴³⁹ᵐ itᵃʳ,ᶜ,ᵈᵉᵐ,ᵈⁱᵛ,ʰ,ᵖ,ᶻ vg syrᵖʰ,ʰ copˢᵃ arm eth Ephraem

³ 6 {C} ἀσεβέσιν 𝔭⁷² B P 614 630 1505 2412 2495 syrᵖʰ,ʰ (copˢᵃ,ᵇᵒ) arm ∥ ἀσεβεῖν ℵ A C K Ψ 049 056 0142 33 81 88 104 181 330ᶜ 436 629 945 1241 1739 1877 1881 2127 2492 *Byz Lect* itᵃʳ,ᶜ,ᵈᵉᵐ,ᵈⁱᵛ,(ʰ),ᵖ,ᶻ vg ∥ ἀσέβει 330* 451 (l¹⁴³⁹ᵐ ἀσέβι) ∥ omit 326

⁴ 11 {C} παρὰ κυρίῳ ℵ B C K P 049 88 104 326 945 1739 (1877 περί) 2127 2492 *Byz Lect* syrᵖʰ? ʰ ʷⁱᵗʰ *? arm Ps-Oecumenius Theophylact ∥ παρὰ κυρίου 𝔭⁷² 056 0142 330 451 1241 itᵖ syrᵖʰ? ʰ ʷⁱᵗʰ *? ∥ κυρίου itᵐ ∥ omit A Ψ 33 81 181 436 614 630 1505 1881 2412 2495 itᵃʳ,ᶜ,ᵈᵉᵐ,ᵈⁱᵛ,ᶻ vg syrʰ copˢᵃ,ᵇᵒ eth Ephraem Bede

ᵃ ᵃ **7–8** *a* major, *a* major: Nes BF² TT Luth ∥ *a* minor, *a* major: NEB ∥ *a* dash, *a* major: Seg ∥ *a* dash, *a* dash: WH Bov Zür Jer ∥ *a* parens, *a* parens: TR AV RV ASV RSV

ᵇ **10** *b* minor: WH AV RV ASV (RSV) (NEB) (TT) Zür (Luth) Jer Seg ∥ *b* none: TR Bov Nes BF²

ᶜ **10** *c* none: TR Bov Nes BF² AV RV ASV RSV NEB TT Zür Luth Jer Seg ∥ *c* minor: WH

5 ὄγδοον...ἐφύλαξεν Gn 8.18   κατακλυσμὸν...ἐπάξας 2 Pe 3.6   **6** πόλεις...κατέκρινεν Gn 19.24; Jd 7   **7** Gn 19.1–16   **9** οἶδεν...ῥύεσθαι 1 Cor 10.13   ἀδίκους...τηρεῖν Jd 6   **10** Jd 7–8   **11** Jd 9

κρίσιν. **12** οὗτοι δέ, ὡς ἄλογα ζῷα γεγεννημένα φυσικὰ εἰς ἅλωσιν καὶ φθοράν, ἐν οἷς ἀγνοοῦσιν βλασφημοῦντες, ἐν τῇ φθορᾷ αὐτῶν καὶ φθαρήσονται, **13** ἀδικούμενοι[5] μισθὸν ἀδικίας· ἡδονὴν ἡγούμενοι τὴν ἐν ἡμέρᾳ τρυφήν, σπίλοι καὶ μῶμοι ἐντρυφῶντες ἐν ταῖς ἀπάταις[6] αὐτῶν συνευωχούμενοι ὑμῖν, **14** ὀφθαλμοὺς ἔχοντες μεστοὺς μοιχαλίδος καὶ ἀκαταπαύστους ἁμαρτίας, δελεάζοντες ψυχὰς ἀστηρίκτους, καρδίαν γεγυμνασμένην πλεονεξίας ἔχοντες, κατάρας τέκνα, **15** καταλείποντες εὐθεῖαν ὁδὸν ἐπλανήθησαν, ἐξακολουθήσαντες τῇ ὁδῷ τοῦ Βαλαὰμ τοῦ Βοσόρ[7], ὃς μισθὸν ἀδικίας ἠγάπησεν **16** ἔλεγξιν δὲ ἔσχεν ἰδίας παρανομίας· ὑποζύγιον ἄφωνον ἐν ἀνθρώπου φωνῇ φθεγξάμενον ἐκώλυσεν τὴν τοῦ προφήτου παραφρονίαν.

17 Οὗτοί εἰσιν πηγαὶ ἄνυδροι καὶ ὁμίχλαι ὑπὸ λαίλαπος ἐλαυνόμεναι, οἷς ὁ ζόφος τοῦ σκότους τετήρηται. **18** ὑπέρογκα γὰρ ματαιότητος φθεγγόμενοι δελεάζουσιν ἐν ἐπιθυμίαις σαρκὸς ἀσελγείαις τοὺς ὀλίγως[8] ἀποφεύγοντας τοὺς ἐν πλάνῃ ἀναστρεφομένους, **19** ἐλευθερίαν

---

[5] **13** {C} ἀδικούμενοι p72 ℵ* B P Ψ syrph arm ‖ κομιούμενοι ℵc A C K 049 056 0142 33 81 88 104 181 326 330 436 451 614 629 630 945 1241 1505 1739 1877 1881 2127 2412 2492 2495 *Byz Lect* itar,c,dem,div,m,p,z vg syrh copsa,bo eth Ephraem Jerome Ps-Oecumenius Theophylact

[6] **13** {D} ἀπάταις p72 ℵ A* C K P 049 056 0142 33 81 88 104 181 326 330 436 451 614 629 630 1505 1877 2127 2412 2492 2495 *Byz Lect* syrh copbo arm Jerome Ps-Oecumenius Theophylact ‖ ἀγάπαις (see Jd 12) Ac B Ψ itar,c,dem,div,m,p,z vg syrph,hmg copsa eth Hilary Ephraem ‖ ἀγνοίαις 945 1241 1739 1881

[7] **15** {B} Βοσόρ p72 ℵc A C K P Ψ 048 049 056 0142 81 88 104 181 326 330 436 451 614 629 630 945 1241 1505 1739 1877 1881 2127 2412 2492 (2495 Βοσύρ) *Byz Lect* itar,c,dem,div,p,z vg syrh copbo eth ‖ Βεώρ (see Nu 22.5) B vgmss syrph copsa arm ‖ Βεωορσόρ ℵ*

[8] **18** {C} ὀλίγως p72 ℵc A B Ψ 33 436 (104 630 1505 2495 ὀλίγον) itar,c,dem,div,p,z vg syrph,h copsa,bo eth Jerome Augustine Bede ‖ ὄντως ℵ* C K P 048 049 056 0142 81 88 326 330 451 614 629 945 1739 1877 2127 2412 2492 *Byz Lect* arm Ps-Oecumenius Theophylact ‖ ὄντας 181 1241 1881

---

12 Jd 10   **13** σπίλοι...ὑμῖν Jd 12   **15** ἐξακολουθήσαντες...ἠγάπησεν Nu 22.7; Jd 11; Re 2.14   **16** Nu 22.28   **17** οἷς...τετήρηται Jd 13

[12] But these men act by instinct, like wild animals born to be captured and killed; they insult things they do not understand. They will be destroyed like wild animals; [13] they will be paid with suffering for the suffering they caused. Pleasure for them is to do anything in broad daylight that will satisfy their bodily appetites; they are a shame and a disgrace as they join you in your meals, all the while enjoying their deceitful ways! [14] They want to look at nothing else but immoral women; their appetite for sin is never satisfied. They lead weak people into a trap. Their hearts are trained to be greedy. They are under God's curse! [15] They have left the straight path and have lost their way, they have followed the path taken by Balaam the son of Bosor, who loved the money he would get for doing wrong, [16] and was rebuked for his transgression. For a dumb ass spoke with a human voice and stopped the prophet's insane action.

[17] These men are like dried-up springs, like clouds blown along by a storm; God has reserved a place for them in the deepest darkness. [18] They make proud and stupid statements, and use immoral bodily lusts to trap those who are just barely escaping from among people who live in error. [19] They promise them

freedom, while they themselves are slaves of destructive habits — for a man is a slave of anything that has defeated him. 20 For if men have escaped from the deadly forces of the world through their knowledge of our Lord and Savior Jesus Christ, and then are again caught by them and defeated, such men are in worse condition at the end than they were at the beginning. 21 It would have been much better for them never to have known the way of righteousness than to have known it and then to turn away from the sacred command that was given them! 22 What happened to them shows that the proverb is true, "A dog goes back to what it has vomited," and, "A pig that has been washed goes back to roll in the mud."

The Promise of the Lord's Coming

3 My dear friends! This is now the second letter I have written you. In both letters I have tried to arouse pure thoughts in your minds by reminding you of these things. 2 I want you to remember the words that were spoken long ago by the holy prophets, and the command from the Lord and Savior which was given you by your apostles. 3 First of all, you must understand that in the last days some men will appear whose lives are controlled by their own

αὐτοῖς ἐπαγγελλόμενοι, αὐτοὶ δοῦλοι ὑπάρχοντες τῆς φθορᾶς· ᾧ γάρ τις ἥττηται, τούτῳ δεδούλωται. 20 εἰ γὰρ ἀποφυγόντες τὰ μιάσματα τοῦ κόσμου ἐν ἐπιγνώσει τοῦ κυρίου ἡμῶν καὶ σωτῆρος Ἰησοῦ Χριστοῦ[9] τούτοις δὲ πάλιν ἐμπλακέντες ἥττῶνται, γέγονεν αὐτοῖς τὰ ἔσχατα χείρονα τῶν πρώτων. 21 κρεῖττον γὰρ ἦν αὐτοῖς μὴ ἐπεγνωκέναι τὴν ὁδὸν τῆς δικαιοσύνης ἢ ἐπιγνοῦσιν ὑποστρέψαι ἐκ[10] τῆς παραδοθείσης αὐτοῖς ἁγίας ἐντολῆς. 22 συμβέβηκεν αὐτοῖς τὸ τῆς ἀληθοῦς παροιμίας,

Κύων ἐπιστρέψας ἐπὶ τὸ ἴδιον ἐξέραμα,

καί,

Ὗς λουσαμένη εἰς κυλισμὸν βορβόρου.

The Promise of the Lord's Coming

3 Ταύτην ἤδη, ἀγαπητοί, δευτέραν ὑμῖν γράφω ἐπιστολήν, ἐν αἷς διεγείρω ὑμῶν ἐν ὑπομνήσει τὴν εἰλικρινῆ διάνοιαν, 2 μνησθῆναι τῶν προειρημένων ῥημάτων ὑπὸ τῶν ἁγίων προφητῶν καὶ τῆς τῶν ἀποστόλων ὑμῶν ἐντολῆς τοῦ κυρίου καὶ σωτῆρος· 3 τοῦτο πρῶτον γινώσκοντες, ὅτι ἐλεύσονται ἐπ᾽ ἐσχάτων τῶν ἡμερῶν

---

[9] **20** {C} κυρίου ἡμῶν καὶ σωτῆρος Ἰησοῦ Χριστοῦ 𝔭72 ℵ A C P Ψ 048 056 0142 81 436 614 630 945 1505 1739 2412 2495 it^(ar,c,dem,div,p) vg syr^h cop^(sa?) arm Augustine John-Damascus Theophylact // κυρίου καὶ σωτῆρος ἡμῶν Ἰησοῦ Χριστοῦ 104 330 451 (1241 ὑμῶν) 2127 *l*^1441 Anthony // κυρίου ἡμῶν Ἰησοῦ Χριστοῦ καὶ σωτῆρος ἡμῶν syr^ph // κυρίου καὶ σωτῆρος Ἰησοῦ Χριστοῦ B K 049 88 181 326 1877 2492 *Byz Lect* it^z Ps-Oecumenius // κυρίου ἡμῶν Ἰησοῦ Χριστοῦ 629 1881 cop^bo eth Ephraem Ps-Chrysostom

[10] **21** {C} ὑποστρέψαι ἐκ 𝔭72 B C P 945 1241 1739 1881 John-Damascus // ἐπιστρέψαι ἐκ K 049 056 0142 88 181 326^txt 330 436 451 629 (630 ἀπό) 1877 2127 2492 *Byz Lect* Maximus Ps-Oecumenius (Theophylact ἀπό) // ἐπιστρέψαι (or ὑποστρέψαι) ἐκ it^m syr^(ph,h) cop^(sa,bo) arm Orsisius // εἰς τὰ ὀπίσω ἀνακάμψαι ἀπό ℵ A Ψ 048 33^vid 81 104 (326^mg ἐκ) (614 1505 ἐπιστρέψαι) 2412 2495 it^(ar,c,dem,div,p,z) vg cop^(sams) Ephraem (Didymus) Jerome Augustine Cyril (de Promissionibus) Salvian Ps-Chrysostom (Anthony ὑποστρέψαι)

---

19 ᾧ...δεδούλωται Jn 8.34   **20** γέγονεν...πρώτων Mt 12.45   **21** Lk 12.47–48 **22** Κύων...ἐξέραμα Pr 26.11

3 2 Jd 17   **3** ἐλεύσονται...αὐτῶν Jd 18

ἐν ἐμπαιγμονῇ ἐμπαῖκται κατὰ τὰς ἰδίας ἐπιθυμίας αὐτῶν πορευόμενοι 4 καὶ λέγοντες, Ποῦ ἐστιν ἡ ἐπαγγελία τῆς παρουσίας αὐτοῦ; ἀφ᾽ ἧς γὰρ οἱ πατέρες ἐκοιμήθησαν, πάντα οὕτως διαμένει ἀπ᾽ ἀρχῆς κτίσεως. 5 λανθάνει γὰρ αὐτοὺς τοῦτο θέλοντας, ὅτι οὐρανοὶ ἦσαν ἔκπαλαι καὶ γῆ ἐξ ὕδατος καὶ δι᾽ ὕδατος συνεστῶσα τῷ τοῦ θεοῦ λόγῳ, 6 δι᾽ ὧν ὁ τότε κόσμος ὕδατι κατακλυσθεὶς ἀπώλετο· 7 οἱ δὲ νῦν οὐρανοὶ καὶ ἡ γῆ τῷ αὐτῷ λόγῳ τεθησαυρισμένοι εἰσὶν[a] πυρί,[a] τηρούμενοι εἰς ἡμέραν κρίσεως καὶ ἀπωλείας τῶν ἀσεβῶν ἀνθρώπων.

8 Ἓν δὲ τοῦτο μὴ λανθανέτω ὑμᾶς, ἀγαπητοί, ὅτι μία ἡμέρα παρὰ κυρίῳ ὡς χίλια ἔτη καὶ χίλια ἔτη ὡς ἡμέρα μία. 9 οὐ βραδύνει κύριος τῆς ἐπαγγελίας, ὥς τινες βραδύτητα ἡγοῦνται, ἀλλὰ μακροθυμεῖ εἰς ὑμᾶς[1], μὴ βουλόμενός τινας ἀπολέσθαι ἀλλὰ πάντας εἰς μετάνοιαν χωρῆσαι. 10 Ἥξει δὲ ἡμέρα κυρίου ὡς κλέπτης, ἐν ᾗ οἱ οὐρανοὶ ῥοιζηδὸν παρελεύσονται, στοιχεῖα δὲ καυσούμενα λυθήσεται, καὶ γῆ καὶ τὰ ἐν αὐτῇ ἔργα εὑρεθήσεται[2]. 11 τούτων οὕτως[3] πάντων λυομένων ποτα-

---

[1] **9** {B} εἰς ὑμᾶς 𝔓72 B C P 048vid 056 0142 0156 81 88 181 326 945 1241 1739 1877 1881 2127 copbo arm // εἰς ἡμᾶς K 049 104 330 451 629 2492 *Byz Lect* l1439m Ps-Oecumenius Theophylact // δι᾽ ὑμᾶς ℵ A Ψ 33 436 614 630 1505 2412 2495 itar,c,dem,div,m,p,t,z vg syrph,h copsa,bomss eth Fastidius Augustine Fulgentius

[2] **10** {D} εὑρεθήσεται ℵ B K P 0156vid? 1241 1739 1881 syrph arm Origen // οὐχ εὑρεθήσεται (syrhmg *with* οὐ *in* [ ]) copsa // κατακαήσεται A 048 049 056 0142 33 88 104 181 326 330 436 451 614 (81 629 630 2492 κατακαήσονται) 945 1505 1877 2127 2412 2495 *Byz Lect* l1439m itar,c,dem,p vgcl syrh copbo eth Augustine Cyril John-Damascus Ps-Oecumenius // εὑρεθήσεται λυόμενα 𝔓72 // ἀφανισθήσονται C // *omit* εὑρεθήσεται τούτων itm // *omit* καὶ γῆ...εὑρεθήσεται Ψ itdiv?z vgww Pelagius Cassiodorus Bede Ps-Oecumeniuscomm Theophylact

[3] **11** {C} τούτων οὕτως 𝔓72 B 614 630 945 1241 1505 1739 1881 2412 2495 syrh // τούτων οὖν ℵ A K Ψ 048 049 33 88 104 181 326 330 436 451 629 1877

[a a] **7** *a* none, *a* minor: RV ASV RSV NEB TT (Zür) // *a* minor, *a* none: TR AV Luth // *a* none, *a* none: WH Bov Nes BF2 (Jer) (Seg)

5 οὐρανοί...λόγῳ Gn 1.6–9 **6** Gn 7.11–21; 2 Pe 2.5 **8** μία...μία Ps 90.4 **9** οὐ... ἡγοῦνται Hab 2.3 μὴ...χωρῆσαι 1 Tm 2.4 **10** Ἥξει...κλέπτης Mt 24.43–44; Lk 12.39–40; 1 Th 5.2, 4; Re 3.3; 16.15

---

passions. They will make fun of you [4] and say: "He promised to come, didn't he? Where is he? Our fathers have already died, but everything is still the same as it was since the creation of the world!" [5] They purposely ignore this fact: long ago God spoke, and the heavens and earth were created. The earth was formed out of water, and by water, [6] and it was by water also, the water of the Flood, that the old world was destroyed. [7] But the heavens and earth that now exist are being preserved, by the same word of God, for destruction by fire. They are being kept for the day when wicked men will be judged and destroyed.

[8] But do not forget this one thing, my dear friends! There is no difference in the Lord's sight between one day and a thousand years; to him the two are the same. [9] The Lord is not slow to do what he has promised, as some think. Instead, he is patient with you, because he does not want anyone to be destroyed, but wants all to turn away from their sins.

[10] But the Day of the Lord will come as a thief. On that Day the heavens will disappear with a shrill noise, the heavenly bodies will burn up and be destroyed, and the earth with everything in it will vanish.[1] [11] Since all these things will be

---

[1] **10** vanish: *some mss. read* be found; *other mss. read* be burned up; *one ms. reads* be found destroyed

destroyed in this way, what kind of people should you be? Your lives should be holy and dedicated to God, 12 as you wait for the Day of God, and do your best to make it come soon — the Day when the heavens will burn up and be destroyed, and the heavenly bodies will be melted by the heat. 13 But God has promised new heavens and a new earth, where righteousness will be at home, and we wait for these.

14 And so, my friends, as you wait for that Day, do your best to be pure and faultless in God's sight and to be at peace with him. 15 Look on our Lord's patience as the opportunity he gives you to be saved, just as our dear brother Paul wrote to you, using the wisdom God gave him. 16 This is what he writes in all his letters when he deals with this subject. There are some difficult things in his letters which ignorant and unstable people explain falsely, as they do with other passages of the Scriptures. Thus they bring on their own destruction.

17 But you, my friends, already know this. Be on your guard, then, so that you will not be led away by the errors of lawless men and fall from your secure position. 18 But continue to grow in the grace and knowledge of our Lord and Savior Jesus Christ. To him be the glory, now and for ever! Amen.

πους δεῖ ὑπάρχειν ὑμᾶς[4] ἐν ἁγίαις ἀναστροφαῖς καὶ εὐσεβείαις,[b] 12 προσδοκῶντας καὶ σπεύδοντας τὴν παρουσίαν τῆς τοῦ θεοῦ ἡμέρας, δι᾽ ἣν οὐρανοὶ πυρούμενοι λυθήσονται καὶ στοιχεῖα καυσούμενα τήκεται.[b] 13 **καινοὺς δὲ οὐρανοὺς καὶ γῆν καινὴν** κατὰ τὸ ἐπάγγελμα αὐτοῦ προσδοκῶμεν, ἐν οἷς δικαιοσύνη κατοικεῖ.

14 Διό, ἀγαπητοί, ταῦτα προσδοκῶντες σπουδάσατε ἄσπιλοι καὶ ἀμώμητοι αὐτῷ εὑρεθῆναι ἐν εἰρήνη, 15 καὶ τὴν τοῦ κυρίου ἡμῶν μακροθυμίαν σωτηρίαν ἡγεῖσθε, καθὼς καὶ ὁ ἀγαπητὸς ἡμῶν ἀδελφὸς Παῦλος κατὰ τὴν δοθεῖσαν αὐτῷ σοφίαν ἔγραψεν ὑμῖν, 16 ὡς καὶ ἐν πάσαις ἐπιστολαῖς λαλῶν ἐν αὐταῖς περὶ τούτων, ἐν αἷς ἐστιν δυσνόητά τινα, ἃ οἱ ἀμαθεῖς καὶ ἀστήρικτοι στρεβλοῦσιν ὡς καὶ τὰς λοιπὰς γραφὰς πρὸς τὴν ἰδίαν αὐτῶν ἀπώλειαν. 17 Ὑμεῖς οὖν, ἀγαπητοί, προγινώσκοντες φυλάσσεσθε ἵνα μὴ τῇ τῶν ἀθέσμων πλάνη συναπαχθέντες ἐκπέσητε τοῦ ἰδίου στηριγμοῦ, 18 αὐξάνετε δὲ ἐν χάριτι καὶ γνώσει τοῦ κυρίου ἡμῶν καὶ σωτῆρος Ἰησοῦ Χριστοῦ. αὐτῷ ἡ δόξα καὶ νῦν καὶ εἰς ἡμέραν αἰῶνος. [ἀμήν.][5]

2127 2492 *Byz Lect* l[1439m] it[ar,c,dem,div,(p),z] vg syr[ph] cop[bo] Pelagius Augustine Ps-Oecumenius Theophylact ‖ τούτων οὖν οὕτως 81 syr[hmg] cop[sa] ‖ τούτων δὲ οὕτως C P 056 0142 arm ‖ *omit* (it[m] *see footnote 2*) (eth)

4 **11** {C} ὑμᾶς 𝔭[72c] ℵ[c] A (C* ὑμᾶς ὑμᾶς) C[c] K P Ψ 048? 049 056 0142 33 81 88 181 326 330 436 451 614 629 945 1241 1505 1739 1877 1881 2127 2412 2492 2495 *Byz* l[147,603,680pt,1441,1590] it[ar,c,dem,div,p,z] vg syr[ph,h] cop[sa] arm Augustine ‖ ἡμᾶς ℵ* 104 630 l[62,680pt,809,1153a,1364,1439m] Pelagius Theophylact ‖ *omit* 𝔭[72*,74vid] B it[m] cop[bo?]

5 **18** {D} ἀμήν. 𝔭[72] ℵ A C K P Ψ 049 056 0142 33 81 88 104 181 326 330 436 451 614 629 630 945 1505 1739[c] 1877 2412 2492 2495 *Byz Lect* (l[1441] εἰς τοὺς αἰῶνας τῶν αἰώνων. ἀμήν.) it[ar,c,dem,div,p] vg syr[ph,h] cop[sa,bo] arm eth ‖ *omit* B 1241 1739* 1881 it[z] Augustine Bede

---

[b b] **11–12** b minor, b major: WH Bov Nes BF[2] Zür Jer ‖ b minor, b question: (TR) AV RV ASV ‖ b minor, b exclamation: RSV (TT) Luth ‖ b exclamation, b major: NEB Seg

---

13 καινοὺς...αὐτοῦ Is 65.17; 66.22; Re 21.1 ἐν...κατοικεῖ Is 60.21; 1 Cor 6.9–10; Re 21.27; 22.15 **15** τὴν τοῦ...ἡγεῖσθε Ro 2.4; 2 Pe 3.9 **17** Ὑμεῖς...συναπαχθέντες Mk 13.5 φυλάσσεσθε...στηριγμοῦ 1 Cor 10.12

ΙΩΑΝΝΟΥ Α

The Word of Life

1 Ὁ ἦν ἀπ᾽ ἀρχῆς, ὃ ἀκηκόαμεν, ὃ ἑωράκαμεν τοῖς ὀφθαλμοῖς ἡμῶν, ὃ ἐθεασάμεθα καὶ αἱ χεῖρες ἡμῶν ἐψηλάφησαν, περὶ τοῦ λόγου τῆς ζωῆς —[a] **2** καὶ ἡ ζωὴ ἐφανερώθη, καὶ ἑωράκαμεν καὶ μαρτυροῦμεν καὶ ἀπαγγέλλομεν ὑμῖν τὴν ζωὴν τὴν αἰώνιον ἥτις ἦν πρὸς τὸν πατέρα καὶ ἐφανερώθη ἡμῖν —[a] **3** ὃ ἑωράκαμεν καὶ ἀκηκόαμεν ἀπαγγέλλομεν καὶ ὑμῖν, ἵνα καὶ ὑμεῖς κοινωνίαν ἔχητε μεθ᾽ ἡμῶν. καὶ ἡ κοινωνία δὲ ἡ ἡμετέρα μετὰ τοῦ πατρὸς καὶ μετὰ τοῦ υἱοῦ αὐτοῦ Ἰησοῦ Χριστοῦ. **4** καὶ ταῦτα γράφομεν ἡμεῖς[1] ἵνα ἡ χαρὰ ἡμῶν[2] ᾖ πεπληρωμένη.

God is Light

5 Καὶ ἔστιν αὕτη ἡ ἀγγελία ἣν ἀκηκόαμεν ἀπ᾽ αὐτοῦ καὶ ἀναγγέλλομεν ὑμῖν, ὅτι ὁ θεὸς φῶς ἐστιν καὶ σκοτία ἐν αὐτῷ οὐκ ἔστιν οὐδεμία. **6** Ἐὰν εἴπωμεν ὅτι κοινωνίαν ἔχομεν μετ᾽ αὐτοῦ καὶ ἐν τῷ σκότει περιπατῶμεν,

[1] **4** {C} ἡμεῖς ℵ A* B P Ψ 33 it[z] cop[sams] ∥ ὑμῖν A[c] C K 049 056 0142 81 88 104 181 326 330 436 451 614 629 630 945 1241 1505 1739 1877 1881 2412 2495 *Byz Lect*[m] it[ar,c,dem,div,p,t] vg syr[p,h,pal] cop[sa,bo] arm eth Augustine Bede Ps-Oecumenius Theophylact

[2] **4** {B} ἡμῶν ℵ B Ψ 049 88 181 326 1241 *Lect*[m] *l*[6,59,62] it[p,tpt,z] vg[ww] cop[sa] Ps-Oecumenius[comm] Theophylact[comm] ∥ ὑμῶν A C[qvid] K P 056 0142 33 81 104 330 451 614 629 945 1505 1739 1877 1881 2412 2495 *Byz l*[598m,1021m] it[ar,c,dem,div,tpt] vg[cl] syr[h,pal] cop[bo] arm eth Ps-Oecumenius[txt] Theophylact[txt] ∥ ἡμῶν ἐν ὑμῖν syr[p]

[a a] **1-2** *a* dash, *a* dash: WH Bov Nes BF² RSV Zür Luth Jer Seg ∥ *a* parens, *a* parens: TR AV RV ASV ∥ *a* major, *a* major: NEB TT

1 Ὁ ἦν ἀπ᾽ ἀρχῆς Jn 1.1, 2; 1 Jn 2.13, 14 τοῦ...ζωῆς Jn 1.1; 4; 14 **2** ἡ...ἑωράκαμεν Jn 1.14 **4** ἡ...πεπληρωμένη Jn 15.11; 16.24 **5** ὁ θεὸς φῶς ἐστιν 1 Tm 6.16; Jas 1.17 **6** 1 Jn 2.4 ἐν...ἀλήθειαν Jn 3.21

THE FIRST LETTER OF JOHN

The Word of Life

1 We write to you about the Word of life, which has existed from the very beginning: we have heard it, and we have seen it with our eyes; yes, we have seen it, and our hands have touched it. [2] When this life became visible, we saw it; so we speak of it and tell you about the eternal life which was with the Father and was made known to us. [3] What we have seen and heard we tell to you also, so that you will join with us in the fellowship that we have with the Father and with his Son Jesus Christ. [4] We write this in order that our joy may be complete.

God Is Light

[5] Now this is the message that we have heard from his Son and announce to you: <u>God is light and there is no darkness at all in him.</u> [6] If, then, we say that we have fellowship with him, yet at the same time live in the darkness, we are lying both in our words and in our actions.

⁷ But if we live in the light — just as he is in the light — then we have fellowship with one another, and the blood of Jesus, his Son, makes us clean from every sin.

⁸ If we say that we have no sin, we deceive ourselves and there is no truth in us. ⁹ But if we confess our sins to God, we can trust him, for he does what is right — he will forgive us our sins and make us clean from all our wrongdoing. ¹⁰ If we say that we have not sinned, we make a liar out of God, and his word is not in us.

Christ Our Helper

2 I write you this, my children, so that you will not sin; but if anyone does sin, we have Jesus Christ, the righteous, who pleads for us with the Father. ² For Christ himself is the means by which our sins are forgiven, and not our sins only, but also the sins of all men.

³ If we obey God's commands, then we are sure that we know him. ⁴ If someone says, "I do know him," but does not obey his commands, such a person is a liar and there is no truth in him. ⁵ But he who obeys his word is the one whose love for God has really been made perfect. This is how we can be sure that we live in God: ⁶ he who says that he lives in God should live just as Jesus Christ did.

The New Command

⁷ My dear friends, this command I write you is not new; it is the old command, the one you have had from the very beginning. The old command is the

2.1 Jesus = Paraclete

ψευδόμεθα καὶ οὐ ποιοῦμεν τὴν ἀλήθειαν· **7** ἐὰν δὲ ἐν τῷ φωτὶ περιπατῶμεν ὡς αὐτός ἐστιν ἐν τῷ φωτί, κοινωνίαν ἔχομεν μετ᾽ ἀλλήλων καὶ τὸ αἷμα Ἰησοῦ τοῦ υἱοῦ αὐτοῦ καθαρίζει ἡμᾶς ἀπὸ πάσης ἁμαρτίας. **8** ἐὰν εἴπωμεν ὅτι ἁμαρτίαν οὐκ ἔχομεν, ἑαυτοὺς πλανῶμεν καὶ ἡ ἀλήθεια οὐκ ἔστιν ἐν ἡμῖν. **9** ἐὰν ὁμολογῶμεν τὰς ἁμαρτίας ἡμῶν, πιστός ἐστιν καὶ δίκαιος ἵνα ἀφῇ ἡμῖν τὰς ἁμαρτίας καὶ καθαρίσῃ ἡμᾶς ἀπὸ πάσης ἀδικίας. **10** ἐὰν εἴπωμεν ὅτι οὐχ ἡμαρτήκαμεν, ψεύστην ποιοῦμεν αὐτὸν καὶ ὁ λόγος αὐτοῦ οὐκ ἔστιν ἐν ἡμῖν.

Christ Our Advocate

2 Τεκνία μου, ταῦτα γράφω ὑμῖν ἵνα μὴ ἁμάρτητε. καὶ ἐάν τις ἁμάρτῃ, παράκλητον ἔχομεν πρὸς τὸν πατέρα, Ἰησοῦν Χριστὸν δίκαιον· **2** καὶ αὐτὸς ἱλασμός ἐστιν περὶ τῶν ἁμαρτιῶν ἡμῶν, οὐ περὶ τῶν ἡμετέρων δὲ μόνον ἀλλὰ καὶ περὶ ὅλου τοῦ κόσμου. **3** Καὶ ἐν τούτῳ γινώσκομεν ὅτι ἐγνώκαμεν αὐτόν, ἐὰν τὰς ἐντολὰς αὐτοῦ τηρῶμεν. **4** ὁ λέγων ὅτι Ἔγνωκα αὐτόν, καὶ τὰς ἐντολὰς αὐτοῦ μὴ τηρῶν, ψεύστης ἐστίν, καὶ ἐν τούτῳ ἡ ἀλήθεια οὐκ ἔστιν· **5** ὃς δ᾽ ἂν τηρῇ αὐτοῦ τὸν λόγον, ἀληθῶς ἐν τούτῳ ἡ ἀγάπη τοῦ θεοῦ τετελείωται.ᵃ ἐν τούτῳ γινώσκομεν ὅτι ἐν αὐτῷ ἐσμεν·ᵃ **6** ὁ λέγων ἐν αὐτῷ μένειν ὀφείλει καθὼς ἐκεῖνος περιεπάτησεν καὶ αὐτὸς περιπατεῖν.

The New Commandment

7 Ἀγαπητοί, οὐκ ἐντολὴν καινὴν γράφω ὑμῖν, ἀλλ᾽ ἐντολὴν παλαιὰν ἣν εἴχετε ἀπ᾽ ἀρχῆς· ἡ ἐντολὴ ἡ παλαιά

ᵃ ᵃ **5** *a* major, *a* minor: WH BF² RV ASV RSV NEB TT Seg ∥ *a* minor, *a* major: AV ∥ *a* major, *a* major: TR Bov Nes Zür Luth Jer

---

7 ἐὰν...φωτί Is 2.5   τὸ...ἁμαρτίας He 9.14; Re 1.5; 7.14   **9** ἐὰν...ἁμαρτίας Ps 32.5; Pr 28.13
2 1 παράκλητον...δίκαιον Ro 8.34; He 7.25; 9.24   **2** Jn 1.29; Col 1.20; 1 Jn 4.10, 14   **4** 1 Jn 1.6   **5** ὃς...τετελείωται Jn 14.21, 23; 1 Jn 5.3 ἐν...τετελείωται 1 Jn 4.12, 17   **6** Jn 13.15; 1 Pe 2.21   **7** 2 Jn 5–6   ἐντολὴν παλαιὰν...ἀρχῆς 1 Jn 2.24; 3.11

ἐστιν ὁ λόγος ὃν ἠκούσατε. 8 πάλιν ἐντολὴν καινὴν γράφω ὑμῖν, ὅ ἐστιν ἀληθὲς ἐν αὐτῷ καὶ ἐν ὑμῖν, ὅτι ἡ σκοτία παράγεται καὶ τὸ φῶς τὸ ἀληθινὸν ἤδη φαίνει. 9 ὁ λέγων ἐν τῷ φωτὶ εἶναι καὶ τὸν ἀδελφὸν αὐτοῦ μισῶν ἐν τῇ σκοτίᾳ ἐστὶν ἕως ἄρτι. 10 ὁ ἀγαπῶν τὸν ἀδελφὸν αὐτοῦ ἐν τῷ φωτὶ μένει, καὶ σκάνδαλον ἐν αὐτῷ οὐκ ἔστιν· 11 ὁ δὲ μισῶν τὸν ἀδελφὸν αὐτοῦ ἐν τῇ σκοτίᾳ ἐστὶν καὶ ἐν τῇ σκοτίᾳ περιπατεῖ, καὶ οὐκ οἶδεν ποῦ ὑπάγει, ὅτι ἡ σκοτία ἐτύφλωσεν τοὺς ὀφθαλμοὺς αὐτοῦ.

12 Γράφω ὑμῖν, τεκνία,
   ὅτι ἀφέωνται ὑμῖν αἱ ἁμαρτίαι διὰ τὸ ὄνομα
      αὐτοῦ.
13 γράφω ὑμῖν, πατέρες,
   ὅτι ἐγνώκατε τὸν ἀπ' ἀρχῆς.
   γράφω ὑμῖν, νεανίσκοι,
   ὅτι νενικήκατε τὸν πονηρόν.
14[b] ἔγραψα ὑμῖν, παιδία,
   ὅτι ἐγνώκατε τὸν πατέρα.
   [b]ἔγραψα ὑμῖν, πατέρες,
   ὅτι ἐγνώκατε τὸν ἀπ' ἀρχῆς.
   ἔγραψα ὑμῖν, νεανίσκοι,
   ὅτι ἰσχυροί ἐστε
   καὶ ὁ λόγος τοῦ θεοῦ ἐν ὑμῖν μένει
   καὶ νενικήκατε τὸν πονηρόν.

15 Μὴ ἀγαπᾶτε τὸν κόσμον μηδὲ τὰ ἐν τῷ κόσμῳ. ἐάν τις ἀγαπᾷ τὸν κόσμον, οὐκ ἔστιν ἡ ἀγάπη τοῦ πατρὸς ἐν αὐτῷ· 16 ὅτι πᾶν τὸ ἐν τῷ κόσμῳ, ἡ ἐπιθυμία τῆς σαρκὸς καὶ ἡ ἐπιθυμία τῶν ὀφθαλμῶν καὶ ἡ ἀλαζονεία

message you have already heard. 8 However, the command I write you is new, and its truth is seen in Christ and also in you. For the darkness is passing away, and the real light is already shining. 9 He who says that he is in the light, yet hates his brother, is in the darkness to this very hour. 10 He who loves his brother stays in the light, and so he has nothing in himself that will cause someone else to sin. 11 But he who hates his brother is in the darkness; he walks in it, and he does not know where he is going, because the darkness has made him blind.

12 I write to you, my children, because your sins are forgiven for the sake of Christ's name. 13 I write to you, fathers, because you know him who has existed from the beginning. I write to you, young men, because you have defeated the Evil One. 14 I write to you children, because you know the Father. I write to you, fathers, because you know him who has existed from the beginning. I write to you, young men, because you are strong; the word of God lives in you and you have defeated the Evil One.

15 Do not love the world or anything that belongs to the world. If you love the world, you do not have the love for the Father in you. 16 Everything that belongs to the world — what the sinful self desires, what people see and want, and everything in this world that people

---

b b **13–14** *b* number 14, *b* no number: TR^ed WH Bov Nes BF² TT Zür Luth Jer ‖ *b* no number *b* number 14: TR^ed AV RV ASV RSV NEB Seg

8 ἐντολὴν...γράφω Jn 13.34   ἡ σκοτία παράγεται Ro 13.12   τὸ φῶς...φαίνει Jn 1.9   **9** 1 Jn 2.11; 3.10, 15; 4.20   **10** σκάνδαλον...ἔστιν Ps 119.165; Ro 14.13   **11** ὁ...περιπατεῖ 1 Jn 2.9 ἐν...ὑπάγει Jn 12.35   **12** ἀφέωνται...αὐτοῦ Ps 25.11; 1 Cor 6.11   **13, 14** τὸν ἀπ' ἀρχῆς Jn 1.1, 2; 1 Jn 1.1   **15** ἐάν τις ἀγαπᾷ...ἐν αὐτῷ Ro 8.7; Jas 4.4   **16** ἡ ἐπιθυμία τῆς σαρκός Ro 13.14; Eph 2.3; 1 Pe 2.11   ἡ ἐπιθυμία τῶν ὀφθαλμῶν Pr 27.20   ἡ ἀλαζονεία τοῦ βίου Jas 4.16

are so proud of — none of this comes from the Father; it all comes from the world. [17] The world and everything in it that men desire is passing away; but he who does what God wants lives for ever.

The Enemy of Christ

[18] My children, the end is near! You were told that the Enemy of Christ would come; and now many enemies of Christ have already appeared, and so we know that the end is near. [19] These people really did not belong to our group, and that is why they left us; if they had belonged to our group, they would have stayed with us. But they left so that it might be clear that none of them really belonged to our group.

[20] But you have had the Holy Spirit poured out on you by Christ, and so all of you know the truth. [21] I write you, then, not because you do not know the truth; instead, it is because you do know it, and also know that no lie ever comes from the truth.

[22] Who, then, is the liar? It is he who says that Jesus is not the Christ. This one is the Enemy of Christ — he rejects both the Father and the Son. [23] For he who rejects the Son also rejects the Father; he who accepts the Son has the Father also.

[24] Be sure, then, to keep in your hearts the message you heard from the beginning. If what you heard from the beginning stays in your hearts, then you will always live in union with the Son and the Father. [25] And this is what Christ himself promised to give us — eternal life.

τοῦ βίου, οὐκ ἔστιν ἐκ τοῦ πατρὸς ἀλλὰ ἐκ τοῦ κόσμου ἐστίν. **17** καὶ ὁ κόσμος παράγεται καὶ ἡ ἐπιθυμία αὐτοῦ[1], ὁ δὲ ποιῶν τὸ θέλημα τοῦ θεοῦ μένει εἰς τὸν αἰῶνα.

The Antichrist

18 Παιδία, ἐσχάτη ὥρα ἐστίν, καὶ καθὼς ἠκούσατε ὅτι ἀντίχριστος ἔρχεται, καὶ νῦν ἀντίχριστοι πολλοὶ γεγόνασιν· ὅθεν γινώσκομεν ὅτι ἐσχάτη ὥρα ἐστίν. **19** ἐξ ἡμῶν ἐξῆλθαν, ἀλλ' οὐκ ἦσαν ἐξ ἡμῶν· εἰ γὰρ ἐξ ἡμῶν ἦσαν, μεμενήκεισαν ἂν μεθ' ἡμῶν· ἀλλ' ἵνα φανερωθῶσιν ὅτι οὐκ εἰσὶν πάντες ἐξ ἡμῶν. **20** καὶ ὑμεῖς χρῖσμα ἔχετε ἀπὸ τοῦ ἁγίου, καὶ οἴδατε πάντες[2]. **21** οὐκ ἔγραψα ὑμῖν ὅτι οὐκ οἴδατε τὴν ἀλήθειαν, ἀλλ' ὅτι οἴδατε αὐτήν, καὶ ὅτι πᾶν ψεῦδος ἐκ τῆς ἀληθείας οὐκ ἔστιν. **22** Τίς ἐστιν ὁ ψεύστης εἰ μὴ ὁ ἀρνούμενος ὅτι Ἰησοῦς οὐκ ἔστιν ὁ Χριστός; οὗτός ἐστιν ὁ ἀντίχριστος, ὁ ἀρνούμενος τὸν πατέρα καὶ τὸν υἱόν. **23** πᾶς ὁ ἀρνούμενος τὸν υἱὸν οὐδὲ τὸν πατέρα ἔχει· ὁ ὁμολογῶν τὸν υἱὸν καὶ τὸν πατέρα ἔχει. **24** ὑμεῖς ὃ ἠκούσατε ἀπ' ἀρχῆς ἐν ὑμῖν μενέτω· ἐὰν ἐν ὑμῖν μείνῃ ὃ ἀπ' ἀρχῆς ἠκούσατε, καὶ ὑμεῖς ἐν τῷ υἱῷ καὶ ἐν τῷ πατρὶ μενεῖτε. **25** καὶ αὕτη ἐστὶν ἡ ἐπαγγελία ἣν αὐτὸς ἐπηγγείλατο ἡμῖν[3], τὴν ζωὴν τὴν αἰώνιον.

---

[1] **17** {B} αὐτοῦ ℵ B C K Ψ 049 056 0142 81 88 104 181 326 330 451 614 629 630 1505 1877 1881 2127 2412 2492 2495 *Byz Lect* l[1439m] it[ar,c,dem,div,p,t,z] vg syr[p,h] cop[sa,bo] arm Cyprian Lucifer Didymus Augustine Antiochus John-Damascus ‖ *omit* A P 33 436 945 1241 1739 it[h] cop[sams] Origen

[2] **20** {D} πάντες ℵ B P Ψ cop[sa] Jerome Hesychius ‖ πάντα A C K 049 056 0142 33 81 88 104 181 326 330 436 451 614 629 630 945 1505 1739 1877 1881 2127 2412 2492 2495 *Byz Lect* it[ar,c,dem,div,h,p,z] vg syr[h] cop[bo] arm eth Didymus Ps-Oecumenius Theophylact ‖ *you know everyone* syr[p] ‖ *omit* it[h]

[3] **25** {B} ἡμῖν ℵ A C K P Ψ 049 056 0142 33 81 88 104 181 326 330 436 614 629 630 945 1505 1739 1877 2412 2492 2495 *Byz Lect* it[ar,dem,div,p,z] vg syr[p,h] cop[sa,bo] arm Augustine ‖ ὑμῖν B 451 1241 1881 2127 it[c*,h]

---

17 ὁ κόσμος παράγεται 1 Cor 7.31　ὁ δὲ...αἰῶνα Mt 7.21; Wsd 5.15　　**18** καθὼς... γεγόνασιν Mt 24.5, 24　**19** ἐξ ἡμῶν...ἡμῶν Ac 20.30　ἵνα φανερωθῶσιν...ἡμῶν 1 Cor 11.19 **20** 1 Jn 2.27　**22** 1 Jn 4.3; 2 Jn 7　**23** Jn 5.23; 15.23; 1 Jn 4.15; 5.1; 2 Jn 9　**25** Jn 3.15; 6.40

26 Ταῦτα ἔγραψα ὑμῖν περὶ τῶν πλανώντων ὑμᾶς. 27 καὶ ὑμεῖς τὸ χρῖσμα ὃ ἐλάβετε ἀπ' αὐτοῦ μένει ἐν ὑμῖν, καὶ οὐ χρείαν ἔχετε ἵνα τις διδάσκῃ ὑμᾶς·[c] ἀλλ' ὡς τὸ αὐτοῦ χρῖσμα διδάσκει ὑμᾶς περὶ πάντων, καὶ ἀληθές ἐστιν καὶ οὐκ ἔστιν ψεῦδος,[c] καὶ καθὼς ἐδίδαξεν ὑμᾶς, μένετε ἐν αὐτῷ.

Children of God

28 Καὶ νῦν, τεκνία, μένετε ἐν αὐτῷ, ἵνα ἐὰν φανερωθῇ σχῶμεν παρρησίαν καὶ μὴ αἰσχυνθῶμεν ἀπ' αὐτοῦ ἐν τῇ παρουσίᾳ αὐτοῦ. 29 ἐὰν εἰδῆτε ὅτι δίκαιός ἐστιν, γινώσκετε ὅτι καὶ πᾶς ὁ ποιῶν τὴν δικαιοσύνην ἐξ αὐτοῦ γεγέννηται. 3 ἴδετε ποταπὴν ἀγάπην δέδωκεν ἡμῖν ὁ πατὴρ ἵνα τέκνα θεοῦ κληθῶμεν· καὶ ἐσμέν[1]. διὰ τοῦτο ὁ κόσμος οὐ γινώσκει ἡμᾶς ὅτι οὐκ ἔγνω αὐτόν. 2 Ἀγαπητοί, νῦν τέκνα θεοῦ ἐσμεν,[a] καὶ οὔπω ἐφανερώθη[a] τί ἐσόμεθα.[a] οἴδαμεν ὅτι ἐὰν φανερωθῇ ὅμοιοι αὐτῷ ἐσόμεθα, ὅτι ὀψόμεθα αὐτὸν καθώς ἐστιν. 3 καὶ πᾶς ὁ ἔχων τὴν ἐλπίδα ταύτην ἐπ' αὐτῷ ἁγνίζει ἑαυτὸν καθὼς ἐκεῖνος ἁγνός ἐστιν.

4 Πᾶς ὁ ποιῶν τὴν ἁμαρτίαν καὶ τὴν ἀνομίαν ποιεῖ, καὶ ἡ ἁμαρτία ἐστὶν ἡ ἀνομία. 5 καὶ οἴδατε ὅτι ἐκεῖνος ἐφανερώθη ἵνα τὰς ἁμαρτίας[2] ἄρῃ, καὶ ἁμαρτία ἐν αὐτῷ

---

[1] 1 {B} καὶ ἐσμέν 𝔭[71vid] ℵ A B C P Ψ 33 81 104 436 614 629 630 945 (1241 *omit* καί) 1505 1739 1881 2412 2495 it[ar,c,dem,div,h,p,z] vg syr[p,h] cop[sa,bo] arm eth Augustine Bede Theophylact ∥ *omit* K 049 056 0142 88 181 326 330 451 1877 2127 2492 *Byz Lect* Ps-Oecumenius

[2] 5 {C} ἁμαρτίας A B P 33 436 945 1241 1739 1881 it[ar,c,dem,div,h,p,z] syr[h] cop[bo] arm eth Tertullian (Augustine) Fulgentius ∥ ἁμαρτίας ἡμῶν ℵ C

[c c] 27 c major, c minor: TR WH Bov Nes BF[2] AV RV ASV RSV TT Luth Jer Seg ∥ c minor, c major: NEB ∥ c major, c major: RV[mg] ASV[mg] ∥ c minor, c minor: Zür

[a a a] 2 a minor, a none, a major: TR WH Bov Nes BF[2] AV RV ASV TT (Zür) (Luth) Jer Seg ∥ a minor, a major, a none: NEB[mg] ∥ a major, a none, a minor: RSV NEB

27 τὸ χρῖσμα...ψεῦδος Jn 14.26; 16.13 οὐ χρείαν...ὑμᾶς Jr 31.34 28 μένετε... παρρησίαν 1 Jn 4.17 29 1 Jn 3.10
3 1 τέκνα θεοῦ Jn 1.12, 13; 1 Jn 3.10 οὐκ ἔγνω αὐτόν Jn 16.3 2 ὅμοιοι αὐτῷ ἐσόμεθα 2 Cor 3.18; Php 3.21 4 ὁ...ἁμαρτίαν Mt 7.23 5 τὰς...ἄρῃ Jn 1.29; 1 Pe 2.24; 1 Jn 2.2; 4.10 ἁμαρτία...ἐστιν Is 53.9; Jn 8.46; 2 Cor 5.21; He 4.15; 7.26; 9.14; 1 Pe 1.19; 2.22; 3.18

---

26 I write you this about those who are trying to deceive you. 27 But as for you, Christ has poured out his Spirit on you. As long as his Spirit remains in you, you do not need anyone to teach you. For the Spirit teaches you about everything, and what he teaches is true, not false. Obey the Spirit's teaching, then, and remain in Christ. 28 Yes, my children, remain in him, so that we may be full of courage when he appears and need not hide in shame from him on the Day he comes. 29 You know that Christ is righteous; you should know, then, that everyone who does what is right is God's child.

Children of God

3 See how much the Father has loved us! His love is so great that we are called God's children — and so, in fact, we are. This is why the world does not know us: it has not known God. 2 My dear friends, we are now God's children, but it is not yet clear what we shall become. But this we know: when Christ appears, we shall become like him, because we shall see him as he really is. 3 Everyone who has this hope in Christ keeps himself pure, just as Christ is pure. 4 Whoever sins is guilty of breaking God's law; for sin is a breaking of the law. 5 You know that Christ appeared in order to take away men's sins, and

that there is no sin in him. 6 So everyone
who lives in Christ does not continue
to sin; but whoever continues to sin has
never seen him, nor has he ever known
him.
7 Let no one deceive you, children!
Whoever does what is right is righteous,
just as Christ is righteous. 8 Whoever
continues to sin belongs to the Devil,
for the Devil has sinned from the very
beginning. The Son of God appeared for
this very reason, to destroy the Devil's
works.
9 Whoever is a child of God does not
continue to sin, because God's very
nature is in him; and because God is
his Father, he is not able to continue
to sin. 10 Here is the clear difference
between God's children and the Devil's
children: anyone who does not do what
is right, or does not love his brother, is
not God's child.

Love One Another

11 For the message you heard from the
very beginning is this: we must love one
another. 12 We must not be like Cain;
he belonged to the Evil One, and murdered his own brother. Why did Cain
murder him? Because the things he did
were wrong, but the things his brother
did were right.
13 So do not be surprised, my brothers,
if the people of the world hate you.
14 We know that we have left death and
come over into life; we know it because

οὐκ ἔστιν. **6** *πᾶς ὁ ἐν αὐτῷ μένων οὐχ ἁμαρτάνει· πᾶς*
ὁ ἁμαρτάνων οὐχ ἑώρακεν αὐτὸν οὐδὲ ἔγνωκεν αὐτόν.
7 *Τεκνία, μηδεὶς πλανάτω ὑμᾶς· ὁ ποιῶν τὴν δικαιο-*
σύνην δίκαιός ἐστιν, καθὼς ἐκεῖνος δίκαιός ἐστιν· **8** *ὁ*
ποιῶν τὴν ἁμαρτίαν ἐκ τοῦ διαβόλου ἐστίν, ὅτι ἀπ'
ἀρχῆς ὁ διάβολος ἁμαρτάνει. εἰς τοῦτο ἐφανερώθη ὁ
υἱὸς τοῦ θεοῦ, ἵνα λύσῃ τὰ ἔργα τοῦ διαβόλου. **9** *Πᾶς*
ὁ γεγεννημένος ἐκ τοῦ θεοῦ ἁμαρτίαν οὐ ποιεῖ,[b] *ὅτι*
σπέρμα αὐτοῦ ἐν αὐτῷ μένει·[b] *καὶ οὐ δύναται ἁμαρτά-*
νειν, ὅτι ἐκ τοῦ θεοῦ γεγέννηται. **10** *ἐν τούτῳ φανερά*
ἐστιν τὰ τέκνα τοῦ θεοῦ καὶ τὰ τέκνα τοῦ διαβόλου·[c]
πᾶς ὁ μὴ ποιῶν δικαιοσύνην οὐκ ἔστιν ἐκ τοῦ θεοῦ,
καὶ ὁ μὴ ἀγαπῶν τὸν ἀδελφὸν αὐτοῦ.

Love One Another

11 *Ὅτι αὕτη ἐστὶν ἡ ἀγγελία ἣν ἠκούσατε ἀπ' ἀρχῆς,*
ἵνα ἀγαπῶμεν ἀλλήλους· **12** *οὐ καθὼς Κάϊν ἐκ τοῦ*
πονηροῦ ἦν καὶ ἔσφαξεν τὸν ἀδελφὸν αὐτοῦ· καὶ χάριν
τίνος ἔσφαξεν αὐτόν; ὅτι τὰ ἔργα αὐτοῦ πονηρὰ ἦν, τὰ
δὲ τοῦ ἀδελφοῦ αὐτοῦ δίκαια.[d] **13** *[καὶ] μὴ*[3] *θαυμάζετε,*
ἀδελφοί, εἰ μισεῖ ὑμᾶς ὁ κόσμος. **14** *ἡμεῖς οἴδαμεν ὅτι*
μεταβεβήκαμεν ἐκ τοῦ θανάτου εἰς τὴν ζωήν, ὅτι ἀγα-

K Ψ 049 056 0142 81 88 104 181 326 330 451 614 630 1505 1877 2127 2412 2492 2495 *Byz Lect* vg syr^{p} cop$^{sa, fay}$ Athanasius Ps-Oecumenius Theophylact // *ἁμαρτίας τοῦ κόσμου* 629

[3] **13** {D} *καὶ μή* ℵ C^{vid} P Ψ 629 945 1241 1739 1881 2492 it$^{ar, q, z}$ syr^{p} arm eth // *μή* A B K 049 056 0142 33 81 88 104 181 326 330 436 451 614 630 1505

[b b] **9** *b* minor, *b* major: Bov Nes BF^{2} AV RV ASV NEB TT Zür Luth Jer Seg^{ed} // *b* major, *b* minor: RSV // *b* minor, *b* minor: TR WH Seg^{ed}

[c] **10** *c* minor: WH Bov Nes BF^{2} AV RV ASV RSV NEB TT Zür Luth Jer // *c* major: TR Seg

[d] **12–13** *d* major: TR Bov Nes BF^{2} AV^{ed} RSV TT Zür Jer Seg // *d* paragraph: WH AV^{ed} RV ASV NEB Luth

---

6 *πᾶς...μένων* Ro 6.2, 14; 1 Jn 3.9 **7** *ὁ...ἐστιν* 1 Jn 2.29 **8** *ὁ ποιῶν...ἁμαρτάνει* Jn 8.44 **9** Πᾶς...*ποιεῖ* 1 Jn 5.18 **10** *τὰ τέκνα τοῦ θεοῦ* Jn 1.12, 13; 1 Jn 3.1 **11** Jn 13.34; 15.12, 17; 2 Jn 5 **12** Κάϊν...*αὐτοῦ* Gn 4.8 **13** *μισεῖ...κόσμος* Jn 15.18, 19; 17.14 **14** *μεταβεβήκαμεν ...ζωήν* Jn 5.24

σφάζω — slaughter

πῶμεν τοὺς ἀδελφούς· ὁ μὴ ἀγαπῶν[4] μένει ἐν τῷ θανάτῳ. 15 πᾶς ὁ μισῶν τὸν ἀδελφὸν αὐτοῦ ἀνθρωποκτόνος ἐστίν, καὶ οἴδατε ὅτι πᾶς ἀνθρωποκτόνος οὐκ ἔχει ζωὴν αἰώνιον ἐν αὐτῷ μένουσαν. 16 ἐν τούτῳ ἐγνώκαμεν τὴν ἀγάπην, ὅτι ἐκεῖνος ὑπὲρ ἡμῶν τὴν ψυχὴν αὐτοῦ ἔθηκεν· καὶ ἡμεῖς ὀφείλομεν ὑπὲρ τῶν ἀδελφῶν τὰς ψυχὰς θεῖναι. 17 ὃς δ' ἂν ἔχῃ τὸν βίον τοῦ κόσμου καὶ θεωρῇ τὸν ἀδελφὸν αὐτοῦ χρείαν ἔχοντα καὶ κλείσῃ τὰ σπλάγχνα αὐτοῦ ἀπ' αὐτοῦ, πῶς ἡ ἀγάπη τοῦ θεοῦ μένει ἐν αὐτῷ; 18 Τεκνία, μὴ ἀγαπῶμεν λόγῳ μηδὲ τῇ γλώσσῃ ἀλλὰ ἐν ἔργῳ καὶ ἀληθείᾳ.

Confidence before God

19 [Καὶ] ἐν τούτῳ[5] γνωσόμεθα ὅτι ἐκ τῆς ἀληθείας ἐσμέν, καὶ ἔμπροσθεν αὐτοῦ πείσομεν τὴν καρδίαν ἡμῶν[e] 20 ὅτι ἐὰν καταγινώσκῃ ἡμῶν ἡ καρδία,[e] ὅτι μείζων ἐστὶν ὁ θεὸς τῆς καρδίας ἡμῶν καὶ γινώσκει πάντα.

we love our brothers. Whoever does not love is still in death. 15 Whoever hates his brother is a murderer; and you know that a murderer does not have eternal life in him. 16 This is how we know what love is: Christ gave his life for us. We too, then, ought to give our lives for our brothers! 17 If a man is rich and sees his brother in need, yet closes his heart against his brother, how can he claim that he has love for God in his heart? 18 My children! Our love should not be just words and talk; it must be true love, which shows itself in action.

Courage before God

19 This, then, is how we will know that we belong to the truth. This is how our hearts will feel sure in God's presence. 20 For if our heart condemns us, we know that God is greater than our heart, and he knows everything.

1877 2127 2412 2495 *Byz Lect* it[c.dem,div,h,p] vg syr[h] cop[sa,bo,fay] Lucifer Didymus Ps-Oecumenius Theophylact

[4] **14** {C} ἀγαπῶν ℵ A B 33 629 945 1241 1739 1881 2127 2492 it[c.dem,div,h,p,q,z] vg cop[bo,fay] arm Lucifer Didymus[lat] Augustine ‖ ἀγαπῶν τὸν ἀδελφόν C K Ψ 049 81 88 104 181 326 330 451 *Byz Lect* Cassiodorus Ps-Oecumenius Theophylact ‖ ἀγαπῶν τὸν ἀδελφὸν αὐτοῦ P 056 0142 436 614 630 1505 1877 2412 2495 it[ar] syr[p.h] cop[sa?] eth

[5] **19** {C} καὶ ἐν τούτῳ ℵ C K P Ψ 049 81 88 104 181 330 451 945 1241 1739 1877 1881 2127 2492 *Byz Lect* it[q] syr[p] cop[sa] arm eth Augustine John-Damascus Ps-Oecumenius Theophylact ‖ ἐν τούτῳ A B 326 436 629 it[ar,c,dem,div,h,p,t] vg cop[bo,fay] Clement ‖ ἐκ τούτου syr[h] ‖ καὶ ἐκ τούτου 614 630 1505 2412 2495 ‖ ἀλλ' ἐκ τούτου 206 429 ‖ καὶ τούτων (*and read* γινώσκομεν *for* γνωσόμεθα) 056 0142

[e e] **19–20** *e* none, *e* minor: WH Nes BF² (RV) (ASV[mg]) RSV NEB TT (Seg) ‖ *e* minor, *e* dash: Zür ‖ *e* major, *e* minor: TR Bov AV ASV ‖ *e* minor, *e* minor: Luth Jer

14 ὁ...θανάτῳ 1 Jn 2.11 **15** πᾶς ὁ μισῶν...ἐστίν Mt 5.21, 22 πᾶς ἀνθρωποκτόνος... μένουσαν Ga 5.20–21; Re 21.8 **16** ἐκεῖνος...ἔθηκεν Jn 13.1; 15.13; Ga 2.20; 1 Tm 2.6; Tt 2.14 ἡμεῖς...θεῖναι Php 2.17; 1 Th 2.8 **17** Dt 15.7–8 **18** Jas 2.15–16

21 And so, my dear friends, <u>if our heart does not condemn us, we have courage in God's presence.</u> 22 We receive from him whatever we ask, because we obey his commands and do what pleases him. 23 This is what he commands: that we <u>believe in the name of his Son Jesus Christ and love one another, just as Christ commanded us.</u> 24 Whoever obeys God's commands lives in God and God lives in him. And <u>this is how we know that God lives in us: we know it because of the Spirit he has given us.</u>

The True and the False Spirit

4 My dear friends: do not believe all who claim to have the Spirit, but <u>test them to find out if the spirit they have comes from God. For many false prophets have gone out everywhere.</u> 2 <u>This is how you will be able to know whether it is God's Spirit: everyone who declares that Jesus Christ became mortal man has the Spirit who comes from God.</u> 3 But anyone who denies this about Jesus

21 Ἀγαπητοί, ἐὰν ἡ καρδία[6] μὴ καταγινώσκῃ ἡμῶν[7], παρρησίαν ἔχομεν πρὸς τὸν θεόν, 22 καὶ ὃ ἐὰν αἰτῶμεν λαμβάνομεν ἀπ' αὐτοῦ, ὅτι τὰς ἐντολὰς αὐτοῦ τηροῦμεν καὶ τὰ ἀρεστὰ ἐνώπιον αὐτοῦ ποιοῦμεν. 23 καὶ αὕτη ἐστὶν ἡ ἐντολὴ αὐτοῦ, ἵνα πιστεύσωμεν τῷ ὀνόματι τοῦ υἱοῦ αὐτοῦ Ἰησοῦ Χριστοῦ καὶ ἀγαπῶμεν ἀλλήλους, καθὼς ἔδωκεν ἐντολὴν ἡμῖν. 24 καὶ ὁ τηρῶν τὰς ἐντολὰς αὐτοῦ ἐν αὐτῷ μένει καὶ αὐτὸς ἐν αὐτῷ· καὶ ἐν τούτῳ γινώσκομεν ὅτι μένει ἐν ἡμῖν, ἐκ τοῦ πνεύματος οὗ ἡμῖν ἔδωκεν.

The Spirit of God and the Spirit of Antichrist

4 Ἀγαπητοί, μὴ παντὶ πνεύματι πιστεύετε, ἀλλὰ δοκιμάζετε τὰ πνεύματα εἰ ἐκ τοῦ θεοῦ ἐστιν, ὅτι πολλοὶ ψευδοπροφῆται ἐξεληλύθασιν εἰς τὸν κόσμον. 2 ἐν τούτῳ γινώσκετε τὸ πνεῦμα τοῦ θεοῦ· πᾶν πνεῦμα ὃ ὁμολογεῖ Ἰησοῦν Χριστὸν ἐν σαρκὶ ἐληλυθότα ἐκ τοῦ θεοῦ ἐστιν, 3 καὶ πᾶν πνεῦμα ὃ μὴ ὁμολογεῖ[1] τὸν Ἰησοῦν[2] ἐκ τοῦ

6 21 {C} καρδία A B Ψ 33 436 945 1241 1739 vg^ms Origen Augustine John-Damascus ∥ καρδία ἡμῶν ℵ C K 049 056 0142 81 88 104 181 326 330 451 614 629 630 1505 1877 1881 (2127 2495 ὑμῶν) 2412 2492 *Byz Lect* it^ar,c,dem,div,p,q vg syr^p,h cop^sa?bo?fay? arm eth Clement Origen^gr,lat Cyprian Didymus Hesychius Ps-Athanasius John-Damascus Ps-Oecumenius Theophylact

7 21 {C} καταγινώσκῃ ἡμῶν (ℵ* καταγινώσκω) ℵ^c (A *l*^680 καταγινώσκει) K Ψ 049 056 0142 33 81 104 181 326 330 436 451 614 629 630 945 1739 1877 1881 2127 2412 2492 *Byz Lect* it^ar,c,dem,div,p,q vg syr^p,h cop^sa,bo,fay arm eth Origen^gr,lat Didymus Ps-Athanasius (John-Damascus καταγινώσκει) ∥ καταγινώσκῃ ὑμῶν 1241 1505 2495 ∥ καταγινώσκῃ (B* καταγεινώσκῃ) B^c C Origen Augustine

1 3 {B} μὴ ὁμολογεῖ ℵ A B K Ψ 049 056 0142 33 81 88 104 181 326 330 436 451 614 629 630 945 1241 1505 1739^txt 1877 1881 2127 2412 2492 2495 *Byz Lect* it^q syr^p,h cop^sa,bo arm Polycarp Tertullian Origen Cyprian Priscillian^2/3 Didymus Augustine Cyril Theodoret Fulgentius Ps-Oecumenius Theophylact ∥ λύει 1739^mg it^ar,c,dem,div,p vg Irenaeus^lat Clement Origen^lat Lucifer Priscillian^1/3 Augustine mss^acc. to Socrates Fulgentius

2 3 {B} τὸν Ἰησοῦν A B 945 1241 1739 (1881 *omit* τόν) it^c,div,p,q vg cop^bo

22 ὃ ἐὰν αἰτῶμεν...αὐτοῦ Mt 21.22; Mk 11.24; Jn 14.13; 15.7; 16.23-24　　**23** αὕτη...Χριστοῦ Jn 6.29　ἀγαπῶμεν...ἡμῖν Jn 13.34; 15.12, 17　**24** ἐν τούτῳ...ἔδωκεν Ro 8.9; 1 Jn 4.13　　**4 1** δοκιμάζετε τὰ πνεύματα 1 Th 5.21　　πολλοί...κόσμον Mt 7.15; 1 Jn 2.18; 2 Jn 7　**2** πᾶν πνεῦμα...ἐστιν 1 Cor 12.3　　**3** πᾶν...ἀντιχρίστου 2 Jn 7

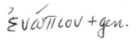

ἐνώπιον + gen.

θεοῦ οὐκ ἔστιν· καὶ τοῦτό ἐστιν τὸ τοῦ ἀντιχρίστου, ὃ
ἀκηκόατε ὅτι ἔρχεται, καὶ νῦν ἐν τῷ κόσμῳ ἐστὶν ἤδη.
4 ὑμεῖς ἐκ τοῦ θεοῦ ἐστε, τεκνία, καὶ νενικήκατε αὐτούς,
ὅτι μείζων ἐστὶν ὁ ἐν ὑμῖν ἢ ὁ ἐν τῷ κόσμῳ. 5 αὐτοὶ
ἐκ τοῦ κόσμου εἰσίν· διὰ τοῦτο ἐκ τοῦ κόσμου λαλοῦσιν
καὶ ὁ κόσμος αὐτῶν ἀκούει. 6 ἡμεῖς ἐκ τοῦ θεοῦ ἐσμεν·
ὁ γινώσκων τὸν θεὸν ἀκούει ἡμῶν, ὃς οὐκ ἔστιν ἐκ τοῦ
θεοῦ οὐκ ἀκούει ἡμῶν. ἐκ τούτου γινώσκομεν τὸ πνεῦμα
τῆς ἀληθείας καὶ τὸ πνεῦμα τῆς πλάνης.

God is Love

7 Ἀγαπητοί, ἀγαπῶμεν ἀλλήλους, ὅτι ἡ ἀγάπη ἐκ
τοῦ θεοῦ ἐστιν, καὶ πᾶς ὁ ἀγαπῶν ἐκ τοῦ θεοῦ γεγέννηται καὶ γινώσκει τὸν θεόν. 8 ὁ μὴ ἀγαπῶν οὐκ ἔγνω
τὸν θεόν, ὅτι ὁ θεὸς ἀγάπη ἐστίν. 9 ἐν τούτῳ ἐφανερώθη ἡ ἀγάπη τοῦ θεοῦ ἐν ἡμῖν, ὅτι τὸν υἱὸν αὐτοῦ τὸν
μονογενῆ ἀπέσταλκεν ὁ θεὸς εἰς τὸν κόσμον ἵνα ζήσωμεν
δι᾽ αὐτοῦ. 10 ἐν τούτῳ ἐστὶν ἡ ἀγάπη, οὐχ ὅτι ἡμεῖς
ἠγαπήκαμεν τὸν θεόν, ἀλλ᾽ ὅτι αὐτὸς ἠγάπησεν ἡμᾶς
καὶ ἀπέστειλεν τὸν υἱὸν αὐτοῦ ἱλασμὸν περὶ τῶν ἁμαρτιῶν ἡμῶν. 11 Ἀγαπητοί, εἰ οὕτως ὁ θεὸς ἠγάπησεν
ἡμᾶς, καὶ ἡμεῖς ὀφείλομεν ἀλλήλους ἀγαπᾶν. 12 θεὸν
οὐδεὶς πώποτε τεθέαται· ἐὰν ἀγαπῶμεν ἀλλήλους, ὁ
θεὸς ἐν ἡμῖν μένει καὶ ἡ ἀγάπη αὐτοῦ τετελειωμένη ἐν
ἡμῖν ἐστιν.

(eth) Irenaeus[lat] Clement Origen[lat] Lucifer Priscillian Didymus[lat] Cyril
mss[acc. to Socrates] ‖ Ἰησοῦν Χριστόν 629* it[ar, dem] (cop[sa, bo]mss τὸν Χριστόν) ‖
τὸν Ἰησοῦν ἐν σαρκὶ ἐληλυθότα Ψ 33 81 436 630 1505 2495 syr[p, h] arm
Theodoret ‖ Ἰησοῦν κύριον ἐν σαρκὶ ἐληλυθότα ℵ ‖ Ἰησοῦν Χριστὸν
ἐν σαρκὶ ἐληλυθότα Κ 056 0142 181 330 (614 2412 τὸν Χριστὸν Ἰησοῦν)
629[c] 1877 2127 2492 (049 88 104 326 451 Byz[pt] Lect τὸν Ἰησοῦν) Byz[pt] l[603,680,
1153a,1364,1590] (Polycarp) (Tertullian) (Cyprian) Augustine Ps-Oecumenius
Theophylact

3 τοῦ ἀντιχρίστου...ἤδη 1 Jn 2.18   4 μείζων...κόσμῳ Mt 12.29   5 Jn 15.19   6 τὸν
θεὸν ἀκούει ἡμῶν Jn 8.47   8 ὁ θεὸς ἀγάπη ἐστίν 1 Jn 4.16   9 Jn 3.16   10 Ro 5.8, 10
ἀπέστειλεν...ἡμῶν 1 Jn 2.2   11 Mt 18.33   12 θεὸν...τεθέαται Jn 1.18   ἡ ἀγάπη...ἐστιν
1 Jn 2.5; 4.17

---

does not have the Spirit from God.
This spirit is from the Enemy of Christ;
you heard that it would come, and now
it is here in the world already.

4 But you belong to God, my children,
and have defeated the false prophets; for
the Spirit who is in you is more powerful
than the spirit in those who belong to
the world. 5 They speak about matters
of the world and the world listens to
them because they belong to the world.
6 But we belong to God. Whoever knows
God listens to us; whoever does not belong to God does not listen to us. This
is the way, then, that we can tell the
difference between the Spirit of truth
and the spirit of error.

God Is Love

7 Dear friends! Let us love one another,
for love comes from God. Whoever loves
is a child of God and knows God. 8 Whoever does not love does not know God,
because God is love. 9 This is how God
showed his love for us: he sent his only
Son into the world that we might have
life through him. 10 This is what love is:
it is not that we have loved God, but
that he loved us and sent his Son to be
the means by which our sins are forgiven.

11 Dear friends, if this is how God
loved us, then we should love one another. 12 No one has ever seen God;
if we love one another, God lives in us
and his love is made perfect within us.

¹³ This is how we are sure that we live in God and he lives in us: he has given us his Spirit. ¹⁴ And we have seen and tell others that the Father sent his Son to be the Savior of the world. ¹⁵ Whoever declares that Jesus is the Son of God, God lives in him, and he lives in God. ¹⁶ And we ourselves know and believe the love which God has for us.

God is love, and whoever lives in love lives in God and God lives in him. ¹⁷ This is the purpose of love being made perfect in us: it is that we may be full of courage on Judgment Day, because our life in this world is the same as Christ's. ¹⁸ There is no fear in love; perfect love drives out all fear. So then, love has not been made perfect in the one who fears, because fear has to do with punishment.

¹⁹ We love because God first loved us. ²⁰ If someone says, "I love God," yet hates his brother, he is a liar. For he cannot love God, whom he has not seen, if he does not love his brother, whom he has seen. ²¹ This, then, is the command that Christ gave us: he who loves God must love his brother also.

13 Ἐν τούτῳ γινώσκομεν ὅτι ἐν αὐτῷ μένομεν καὶ αὐτὸς ἐν ἡμῖν, ὅτι ἐκ τοῦ πνεύματος αὐτοῦ δέδωκεν ἡμῖν. **14** καὶ ἡμεῖς τεθεάμεθα καὶ μαρτυροῦμεν ὅτι ὁ πατὴρ ἀπέσταλκεν τὸν υἱὸν σωτῆρα τοῦ κόσμου. **15** ὃς ἐὰν ὁμολογήσῃ ὅτι Ἰησοῦς ἐστιν ὁ υἱὸς τοῦ θεοῦ, ὁ θεὸς ἐν αὐτῷ μένει καὶ αὐτὸς ἐν τῷ θεῷ. **16** καὶ ἡμεῖς ἐγνώκαμεν καὶ πεπιστεύκαμεν τὴν ἀγάπην ἣν ἔχει ὁ θεὸς ἐν ἡμῖν.

Ὁ θεὸς ἀγάπη ἐστίν, καὶ ὁ μένων ἐν τῇ ἀγάπῃ ἐν τῷ θεῷ μένει καὶ ὁ θεὸς ἐν αὐτῷ μένει. **17** ἐν τούτῳ τετελείωται ἡ ἀγάπη μεθ᾽ ἡμῶν, ἵνα παρρησίαν ἔχωμεν ἐν τῇ ἡμέρᾳ τῆς κρίσεως, ὅτι καθὼς ἐκεῖνός ἐστιν καὶ ἡμεῖς ἐσμεν ἐν τῷ κόσμῳ τούτῳ. **18**ᵃ φόβος οὐκ ἔστιν ἐν τῇ ἀγάπῃ, ᵃἀλλ᾽ ἡ τελεία ἀγάπη ἔξω βάλλει τὸν φόβον, ὅτι ὁ φόβος κόλασιν ἔχει, ὁ δὲ φοβούμενος οὐ τετελείωται ἐν τῇ ἀγάπῃ. **19** ἡμεῖς ἀγαπῶμεν³, ὅτι αὐτὸς πρῶτος ἠγάπησεν ἡμᾶς. **20** ἐάν τις εἴπῃ ὅτι Ἀγαπῶ τὸν θεόν, καὶ τὸν ἀδελφὸν αὐτοῦ μισῇ, ψεύστης ἐστίν· ὁ γὰρ μὴ ἀγαπῶν τὸν ἀδελφὸν αὐτοῦ ὃν ἑώρακεν, τὸν θεὸν ὃν οὐχ ἑώρακεν οὐ δύναται ἀγαπᾶν.⁴ **21** καὶ ταύτην τὴν ἐντολὴν ἔχομεν ἀπ᾽ αὐτοῦ, ἵνα ὁ ἀγαπῶν τὸν θεὸν ἀγαπᾷ καὶ τὸν ἀδελφὸν αὐτοῦ.

---

³ **19** {B} ἀγαπῶμεν A B 945 1241 1739 1881 it^{q vid} vg^{ww} eth^{pp} Pelagius Augustine^{3/4} Bede ∥ *we know* cop^{sa, bo mss} ∥ ἀγαπῶμεν τὸν θεόν ℵ (048^{vid?} οὖν ἀγαπῶμεν) 33 81 326 436 614 629^{vid} 630 1505 2412 2495 *l*^{598m, 599m} it^{c, dem, div, p} vg^{cl} syr^{p, h} cop^{bo} arm (eth^{ro}) Leo ∥ ἀγαπῶμεν αὐτόν K Ψ 049 056 0142 88 104 181 330 451 1877 2127 2492 *Byz Lect*^{m} (*l*^{1356m, 1439m} ἀγαπομεν) Augustine^{1/4} Ps-Oecumenius Theophylact ∥ *delegamus invicem* it^{ar}

⁴ **20** {B} οὐ δύναται ἀγαπᾶν. ℵ B Ψ 630 1505 1739 2495 syr^{h} cop^{sa} Cyprian Lucifer Zeno ∥ πῶς δύναται ἀγαπᾶν; A K 048 049 056 0142 (33 ἀγαπῆσαι) 81 88 104 181 326 330 436 451 614 629 945 1241 1877 1881 2127 2412 2492 *Byz Lect l*^{598m} it^{ar,c,dem,div,p,q} vg syr^{p} cop^{bo} arm eth Cyprian Augustine John-Damascus Ps-Oecumenius Theophylact

---

ᵃ ᵃ **17–18** *a* number 18, *a* no number: TR WH Bov Nes^{ed} BF² AV RV ASV RSV NEB? TT Zür Luth Jer Seg^{ed} ∥ *a* no number, *a* number 18: Nes^{ed} NEB? Seg^{ed}

13 Ro 8.9; 1 Jn 3.24   **14** ὁ...κόσμου Jn 3.17   **15** Ἰησοῦς...θεοῦ 1 Jn 5.5   **16** Ὁ θεὸς ἀγάπη ἐστίν 1 Jn 4.8   **17** ἐν τούτῳ...ἀγάπῃ 1 Jn 2.5; 4.12   **21** Mt 5.44–45; Mk 12.29–31

Faith is Victory over the World

5 Πᾶς ὁ πιστεύων ὅτι Ἰησοῦς ἐστιν ὁ Χριστὸς ἐκ τοῦ θεοῦ γεγέννηται, καὶ πᾶς ὁ ἀγαπῶν τὸν γεννήσαντα ἀγαπᾷ [καὶ]¹ τὸν γεγεννημένον ἐξ αὐτοῦ. **2** ἐν τούτῳ γινώσκομεν ὅτι ἀγαπῶμεν τὰ τέκνα τοῦ θεοῦ, ὅταν τὸν θεὸν ἀγαπῶμεν καὶ τὰς ἐντολὰς αὐτοῦ ποιῶμεν². **3** αὕτη γάρ ἐστιν ἡ ἀγάπη τοῦ θεοῦ, ἵνα τὰς ἐντολὰς αὐτοῦ τηρῶμεν·ᵃ καὶ αἱ ἐντολαὶ αὐτοῦ βαρεῖαι οὐκ εἰσίν,ᵃ **4** ὅτι πᾶν τὸ γεγεννημένον ἐκ τοῦ θεοῦ νικᾷ τὸν κόσμον·ᵃ καὶ αὕτη ἐστὶν ἡ νίκη ἡ νικήσασα τὸν κόσμον, ἡ πίστις ἡμῶν.ᵇ **5** τίς [δέ] ἐστιν ὁ νικῶν τὸν κόσμον εἰ μὴ ὁ πιστεύων ὅτι Ἰησοῦς ἐστιν ὁ υἱὸς τοῦ θεοῦ;

The Witness concerning the Son

6 Οὗτός ἐστιν ὁ ἐλθὼν δι᾽ ὕδατος καὶ αἵματος³, Ἰησοῦς Χριστός· οὐκ ἐν τῷ ὕδατι μόνον ἀλλ᾽ ἐν τῷ ὕδατι καὶ

Our Victory over the World

5 Whoever believes that Jesus is the Messiah is a child of God; and whoever loves a father loves also his child. **2** This is how we know that we love God's children: it is by loving God and obeying his commands. **3** For this is what love for God means: it means that we obey his commands. And his commands are not too hard for us, **4** for every child of God is able to defeat the world. This is how we win the victory over the world: with our faith. **5** Who can defeat the world? Only he who believes that Jesus is the Son of God.

The Witness about Jesus Christ

6 Jesus Christ is the one who came; he came with the water of his baptism and the blood of his death. He came not only with the water, but with both

---

¹ **1** {C} καὶ ℵ A K P 049 056 0142 81 88 104 181 330 436 451 614 629ᵛⁱᵈ 630 945 1241 1505 1739 1877 1881 2127 2412 2492 2495 *Byz Lect* *l*⁵⁹⁸ᵐ itᶜ·ᵖ vgᶜˡ syrᵖ·ʰ copᵇᵒ arm eth Hilary Cyril-Jerusalem Maximinusᵃᶜᶜ· ᵗᵒ ᴬᵘᵍᵘˢᵗⁱⁿᵉ Theodoret Bede Ps-Oecumenius Theophylact ‖ *omit* B Ψ 048 33 326 itᵃʳ·ᵈᵉᵐ·ᵈⁱᵛ·ᵐ· q vgʷʷ copˢᵃ Hilary Augustine

² **2** {C} ποιῶμεν B Ψ 81 326 436 614 1739 2412 2495 *l*¹³¹¹ itᵃʳ·ᶜ·ᵈᵉᵐ·ᵈⁱᵛ·q vg syrᵖ·ʰ copˢᵃ·ᵇᵒ arm eth Lucifer Augustine Theophylact ‖ τηρῶμεν (*see* 5.3) ℵ K P (048ᵛⁱᵈ τηροῦμεν) 049 056 0142 88 104 181 330 451 629 630 945 1241 1505 1877 1881 2127 2492 *Byz Lect* *l*⁵⁹⁸ᵐ itᵖ Ps-Oecumenius

³ **6** {B} αἵματος B K Ψ 049 056 0142 181 330 451 629 1739* 1881 2127 *Byz Lect* itᵃʳ·ᶜ·ᵈᵉᵐ·ᵈⁱᵛ·ᵖ·q vg syrᵖ Tertullian Rebaptism Cyril²ᐟ⁴ Ps-Oecumenius Theophylact ‖ πνεύματος (*see* Jn 3.5) 945 1241 1877* Ambrose Cyril¹ᐟ⁴ ‖ αἵματος καὶ πνεύματος ℵ A 104 436 614 1505 1739ᶜ 1877ᶜ 2412 2495 *l*⁵⁹⁸ᵐ syrʰ copˢᵃ·ᵇᵒ Origen Cyril¹ᐟ⁴ ‖ πνεύματος καὶ αἵματος P 81 88 630 2492 arm eth ‖ αἵματος καὶ πνεύματος ἁγίου 326

ᵃ ᵃ ᵃ **3–4** a major, a minor, a major: Bov Nes BF² NEB Luth Jer Seg ‖ a minor, a minor, a major: WH TT ‖ a major, a major, a minor: RSV ‖ a minor, a major, a minor: AV RV ASV Zür ‖ a major, a minor, a minor: TR

ᵇ **4** b major: TR Bov Nes BF² AV RV ASV RSV TT Zür Luth Jer Seg ‖ b minor: WH NEB

---

1 Πᾶς...γεγέννηται 1 Jn 4.15   πᾶς ὁ ἀγαπῶν...αὐτοῦ 1 Pe 1.22–23   **3** αὕτη...τηρῶμεν Jn 14.15, 23, 24; 2 Jn 6   αἱ...εἰσίν Dt 30.11; Mt 11.30   **5** Ro 8.37; 1 Jn 4.4   **6** Οὗτος...Χριστός Jn 19.34

the water and the blood. And the Spirit himself testifies that this is true; for the Spirit is truth. [7] There are three witnesses, [8] the Spirit, the water, and the blood; and all three agree. [9] We believe the witness that men give; the witness that God gives is much stronger, and this is the witness that God has given about his Son. [10] So whoever believes in the Son of God has this witness in his heart; but whoever does not believe God, has made a liar out of him, for he has not believed what God has said as a

ἐν τῷ αἵματι· καὶ τὸ πνεῦμά ἐστιν τὸ μαρτυροῦν, ὅτι τὸ πνεῦμά ἐστιν ἡ ἀλήθεια. 7 ὅτι τρεῖς εἰσιν οἱ μαρτυροῦντες, 8 τὸ πνεῦμα καὶ τὸ ὕδωρ καὶ τὸ αἷμα[4], καὶ οἱ τρεῖς εἰς τὸ ἕν εἰσιν. 9 εἰ τὴν μαρτυρίαν τῶν ἀνθρώπων λαμβάνομεν, ἡ μαρτυρία τοῦ θεοῦ μείζων ἐστίν, ὅτι αὕτη ἐστὶν ἡ μαρτυρία τοῦ θεοῦ, ὅτι μεμαρτύρηκεν περὶ τοῦ υἱοῦ αὐτοῦ. 10 ὁ πιστεύων εἰς τὸν υἱὸν τοῦ θεοῦ ἔχει τὴν μαρτυρίαν ἐν αὐτῷ[5]· ὁ μὴ πιστεύων τῷ θεῷ[6] ψεύστην πεποίηκεν αὐτόν, ὅτι οὐ πεπίστευκεν εἰς τὴν μαρτυρίαν ἣν μεμαρτύρηκεν ὁ θεὸς περὶ τοῦ υἱοῦ αὐτοῦ.

[4] 7-8 {A} μαρτυροῦντες, 8 τὸ πνεῦμα καὶ τὸ ὕδωρ καὶ τὸ αἷμα ℵ A B K P (Ψ μαρτυροῦσιν) 048 049 056 0142 33 81 88[txt] 104 181 326 330 436 451 614 630 945 1241 1505 1739 1877 1881 2127 2412 2492 2495 *Byz Lect* l[598m] it[ar] vg[ww] syr[p,h] cop[sa,bo] arm eth arab slav Irenaeus Clement Tertullian Hippolytus Origen Cyprian Dionysius Hilary Lucifer Athanasius Basil Faustinus Gregory-Nazianzus Ambrose Didymus Epiphanius Chrysostom Jerome Augustine Cyril ∥ μαρτυροῦντες ἐν τῷ οὐρανῷ, ὁ πατὴρ ὁ λόγος καὶ τὸ ἅγιον πνεῦμα, καὶ οὗτοι οἱ τρεῖς ἕν εἰσι. 8 καὶ τρεῖς εἰσιν οἱ μαρτυροῦντες ἐν τῇ γῇ, τὸ πνεῦμα καὶ τὸ ὕδωρ καὶ τὸ αἷμα (61 ...οὐρανῷ, πατὴρ λόγος καὶ πνεῦμα ἅγιον...τρεῖς εἰς τὸ ἕν...γῇ, πνεῦμα, ὕδωρ καὶ αἷμα) (88[mg] *from Latin* πατὴρ καὶ ὁ λόγος *and omit* καὶ τὸ αἷμα) (629 ...ἐπὶ τοῦ οὐρανοῦ, πατήρ, λόγος καὶ πνεῦμα ἅγιον...τρεῖς εἰς τὸ ἕν...ἐπὶ τῆς γῆς...) 635[mg] (it[m]) vg[cl] ∥ *testificatur dicunt* (or: *dant*) *in terra, spiritus* (or: *spiritus et*) *aqua et sanguis, et hi tres unum sunt in Christo Iesu.* 8 *et tres sunt, qui testimonium dicunt in caelo, pater, verbum et spiritus* (it[c,dem,div] *omit: in Christo Iesu*) it[m,p] (it[q] *omit: et hi tres unum sunt in Christo Iesu*) vg[mss] Varimadum Priscillian Cassian Ps-Vigilius mss[acc. to Victor-Vita] Ps-Athanasius Fulgentius Ansbert

[5] 10 {B} αὐτῷ ∥ αυτω A B P 056 0142 *Lect* ∥ ἑαυτῷ ℵ Ψ 049 88 181 330 451 614 630 945 1505 1739 1877 1881[c] 2412 2492 2495 it[ar,c,dem,div,m,p,q] vg syr[p] cop[sa?] Augustine Cyril Ps-Oecumenius ∥ αὐτῷ K 81 104 326 436 629 1241 1881* 2127 *Byz* l[598m,603] syr[h] cop[bo]

[6] 10 {B} τῷ θεῷ ℵ B K P Ψ 049 056 0142 88 104 181 326 330 451 614 630 945 1505 1739[c] 1877 1881 2127 2412 2492 2495 *Byz Lect* l[598m] it[q] syr[p,h] cop[bomss] Augustine Cyril[3/4] Vigilius Ps-Oecumenius Theophylact ∥ τῷ υἱῷ A 81 436 (629* τὸν υἱόν, 629[c] ἐκ τοῦ υἱοῦ) 1241 1739* it[ar,c,dem,div,p] vg syr[hmg] (eth *add* αὐτοῦ) Cyril[1/4] Bede ∥ τῷ υἱῷ τοῦ θεοῦ 378 cop[sa,bomss] arm ∥ *Iesu Christo* it[m] ∥ *omit* vg[ms*]

7 Jn 15.26   9 τὴν...ἀνθρώπων Jn 5.32-34   ἡ...θεοῦ Jn 5.37; 8.18   10 ὁ πιστεύων... αὐτῷ Ro 8.16; Ga 4.6

11 καὶ αὕτη ἐστὶν ἡ μαρτυρία, ὅτι ζωὴν αἰώνιον ἔδωκεν ἡμῖν ὁ θεός, καὶ αὕτη ἡ ζωὴ ἐν τῷ υἱῷ αὐτοῦ ἐστιν. 12 ὁ ἔχων τὸν υἱὸν ἔχει τὴν ζωήν· ὁ μὴ ἔχων τὸν υἱὸν τοῦ θεοῦ τὴν ζωὴν οὐκ ἔχει.

The Knowledge of Eternal Life

13 Ταῦτα ἔγραψα ὑμῖν ἵνα εἰδῆτε ὅτι ζωὴν ἔχετε αἰώνιον, τοῖς πιστεύουσιν εἰς τὸ ὄνομα τοῦ υἱοῦ τοῦ θεοῦ. 14 καὶ αὕτη ἐστὶν ἡ παρρησία ἣν ἔχομεν πρὸς αὐτόν, ὅτι ἐάν τι αἰτώμεθα κατὰ τὸ θέλημα αὐτοῦ ἀκούει ἡμῶν. 15 καὶ ἐὰν οἴδαμεν ὅτι ἀκούει ἡμῶν ὃ ἐὰν αἰτώμεθα, οἴδαμεν ὅτι ἔχομεν τὰ αἰτήματα ἃ ᾐτήκαμεν ἀπ' αὐτοῦ.

16 Ἐάν τις ἴδῃ τὸν ἀδελφὸν αὐτοῦ ἁμαρτάνοντα ἁμαρτίαν μὴ πρὸς θάνατον, αἰτήσει, καὶ δώσει αὐτῷ ζωήν, τοῖς ἁμαρτάνουσιν μὴ πρὸς θάνατον. ἔστιν ἁμαρτία πρὸς θάνατον· οὐ περὶ ἐκείνης λέγω ἵνα ἐρωτήσῃ. 17 πᾶσα ἀδικία ἁμαρτία ἐστίν, καὶ ἔστιν ἁμαρτία οὐ πρὸς θάνατον.

18 Οἴδαμεν ὅτι πᾶς ὁ γεγεννημένος ἐκ τοῦ θεοῦ οὐχ ἁμαρτάνει, ἀλλ' ὁ γεννηθεὶς ἐκ τοῦ θεοῦ τηρεῖ αὐτόν[7], καὶ ὁ πονηρὸς οὐχ ἅπτεται αὐτοῦ. 19 οἴδαμεν ὅτι ἐκ τοῦ θεοῦ ἐσμεν, καὶ ὁ κόσμος ὅλος ἐν τῷ πονηρῷ κεῖται. 20 οἴδαμεν δὲ ὅτι ὁ υἱὸς τοῦ θεοῦ ἥκει, καὶ δέδωκεν ἡμῖν διάνοιαν ἵνα γινώσκομεν τὸν ἀληθινόν[8]·[c] καὶ ἐσμὲν

witness about his Son. [11] This, then, is the witness: God has given us eternal life, and this life is ours in his Son. [12] Whoever has the Son has this life; whoever does not have the Son of God does not have life.

Eternal Life

[13] I write you this so that you may know that you have eternal life — you who believe in the name of the Son of God. [14] This is why we have courage in God's presence; we are sure that he will hear us if we ask him for anything that is according to his will. [15] He hears us whenever we ask him; since we know this is true, we know also that he gives us what we ask from him.

[16] If anyone sees his brother commit a sin that does not lead to death, he should pray to God, who will give him life. This applies to those whose sins do not lead to death. But there is sin which leads to death, and I do not say that you should pray to God about that. [17] All wrongdoing is sin, but there is sin which does not lead to death.

[18] We know that no child of God keeps on sinning, for the Son of God keeps him safe, and the Evil One cannot harm him.

[19] We know that we belong to God and that the whole world is under the rule of the Evil One.

[20] We know that the Son of God has come and has given us understanding, so that we know the true God. Our

---

7 18 {C} αὐτόν 330 451 614 1505 2412 2495 it[ar,c,dem,div,p,q,t] vg syr[h] cop[bo] Chromatius Jerome ‖ αυτον A* B ‖ ἑαυτόν ℵ A[c] K P Ψ 049 056 0142 33 81 88 181 326 436 629 630 945 1241 1739 1877 1881 2127 2492 *Byz Lect* l[598m] syr[p] cop[sa?] arm Origen Ephraem Ps-Oecumenius Theophylact

8 20 {B} τὸν ἀληθινόν ℵ[c] B K P 049 056 0142 81 88 330 451 1877 2127

---

c 20 *c* major: TR WH Bov Nes BF² RSV NEB TT Zür Luth Jer Seg ‖ *c* minor: WH[mg] AV RV ASV

---

12 Jn 3.36   **13** Jn 20.31   **14** Mt 7.7; Jn 14.13; 15.7, 16; 16.23; 1 Jn 3.21–22   **16** ἔστιν… θάνατον Mt 12.31; He 6.4–6   **18** πᾶς…ἁμαρτάνει 1 Jn 3.9   ὁ γεννηθεὶς…αὐτοῦ Jn 17.15   **20** γινώσκομεν…αἰώνιος Jn 17.3

5.16 Mortal vs. Venial Sin?

lives are in the true God — in his Son
Jesus Christ. This is the true God, and
this is eternal life.

²¹ My children, keep yourselves away
from false gods!

ἐν τῷ ἀληθινῷ, ἐν τῷ υἱῷ αὐτοῦ Ἰησοῦ Χριστῷ. οὗτός
ἐστιν ὁ ἀληθινὸς θεὸς καὶ ζωὴ αἰώνιος. 21 Τεκνία,
φυλάξατε ἑαυτὰ ἀπὸ τῶν εἰδώλων.⁹

2492 *Byz Lect* itᵐ syrᵖ·ʰ copᵇᵒᵐˢˢ arm Hilary Faustinus Cyril¹ᐟ³ Fulgentius ∥
τὸ ἀληθινόν ℵ* itᵃ copˢᵃ·ᵇᵒᵐˢˢ Vigilius Facundus ∥ τὸν ἀληθινὸν θεόν
A Ψ 33 181 326 436 614 630 945 1505 1739 1881 2412 2495 *l*⁵⁹⁸ᵐ itᵃʳ·ᶜ·ᵈᵉᵐ·ᵈⁱᵛ·ᵖ·ᵗ
vg copᵇᵒᵐˢˢ eth Athanasius Basil Didymus Pelagius Augustine Cyril²ᐟ³
Ps-Athanasius ∥ τὸν θεὸν τὸν ἀληθινόν 629 ∥ *patrem* Ambrose

⁹ 21 {A} εἰδώλων. ℵ A B Ψ 33 88 326 436 629 630 1505 1739 1881 2492
2495 itᵃʳ·ᶜ·ᵈᵉᵐ·ᵈⁱᵛ·ᵐ·ᵖ· q vgʷʷ syrᵖ·ʰ copˢᵃ·ᵇᵒ arm eth ∥ εἰδώλων. ἀμήν. K P 049
056 0142 81 181 330 451 614 945 1877 2127 2412 *Byz Lect* vgᶜˡ

---

21 1 Cor 10.14

ΙΩΑΝΝΟΥ Β

Salutation

1 Ὁ πρεσβύτερος ἐκλεκτῇ[a] κυρίᾳ[a] καὶ τοῖς τέκνοις αὐτῆς, οὓς ἐγὼ ἀγαπῶ ἐν ἀληθείᾳ, καὶ οὐκ ἐγὼ μόνος ἀλλὰ καὶ πάντες οἱ ἐγνωκότες τὴν ἀλήθειαν, 2 διὰ τὴν ἀλήθειαν τὴν μένουσαν ἐν ἡμῖν, καὶ μεθ᾽ ἡμῶν ἔσται εἰς τὸν αἰῶνα. 3 ἔσται μεθ᾽ ἡμῶν χάρις ἔλεος εἰρήνη παρὰ θεοῦ πατρός, καὶ παρὰ Ἰησοῦ[1] Χριστοῦ τοῦ υἱοῦ τοῦ πατρός, ἐν ἀληθείᾳ καὶ ἀγάπῃ.

Truth and Love

4 Ἐχάρην λίαν ὅτι εὕρηκα ἐκ τῶν τέκνων σου περιπατοῦντας ἐν ἀληθείᾳ, καθὼς ἐντολὴν ἐλάβομεν παρὰ τοῦ πατρός. 5 καὶ νῦν ἐρωτῶ σε, κυρία[b], οὐχ ὡς ἐντολὴν γράφων σοι καινὴν ἀλλὰ ἣν εἴχομεν ἀπ᾽ ἀρχῆς, ἵνα ἀγαπῶμεν ἀλλήλους. 6 καὶ αὕτη ἐστὶν ἡ ἀγάπη, ἵνα περιπατῶμεν κατὰ τὰς ἐντολὰς αὐτοῦ· αὕτη ἡ ἐντολή ἐστιν, καθὼς ἠκούσατε ἀπ᾽ ἀρχῆς, ἵνα ἐν αὐτῇ περιπατῆτε. 7 ὅτι πολλοὶ πλάνοι ἐξῆλθον εἰς τὸν κόσμον, οἱ μὴ ὁμολογοῦντες Ἰησοῦν Χριστὸν ἐρχόμενον ἐν σαρκί· οὗτός ἐστιν ὁ πλάνος καὶ ὁ ἀντίχριστος. 8 βλέπετε

---

3 {B} Ἰησοῦ Α Β Ψ 048 0232 81 88 326 436 629 1505 1739 2127 it[ar,c,dem, div,p] vg cop[sa] eth ‖ κυρίου Ἰησοῦ ℵ K P 049 056 0142 33 181 330 451 614 630 945 1877 1881 2412 2492 2495 Byz Lect l[1439m] syr[h] cop[bo] arm Ps-Oecumenius Theophylact ‖ κυρίου Ἰησοῦ ἡμῶν syr[ph]

[a a] **1** ἐκλεκτῇ κυρίᾳ: TR[ed] WH Bov Nes BF[2] AV RV ASV RSV Luth? ‖ ἐκλεκτῇ Κυρίᾳ: ASV[mg] NEB TT Zür Luth? Jer Seg ‖ Ἐκλεκτῇ κυρίᾳ: TR[ed] ‖ Ἐκλεκτῇ Κυρίᾳ: WH[mg]

[b] **5** κυρία: TR WH Bov Nes BF[2] AV RV ASV RSV Luth? ‖ Κυρία: ASV[mg] TT Zür Luth? Jer Seg ‖ omit: NEB

---

1 ἐγώ...ἀληθείᾳ 3 Jn 1   **4** Ἐχάρην...ἀληθείᾳ 3 Jn 3   **5** οὐχ...ἀρχῆς 1 Jn 2.7; 2.24; 3.11   ἀγαπῶμεν ἀλλήλους Jn 13.34; 15.12, 17; 1 Jn 3.11   **6** αὕτη...ἐντολὰς αὐτοῦ Jn 14.15, 23, 24; 1 Jn 5.3   **7** πολλοὶ...κόσμον Mt 7.15; 1 Jn 2.18; 4.1   οἱ...ἀντίχριστος 1 Jn 4.3

THE SECOND LETTER OF JOHN

1 From the Elder —
To the dear Lady and to her children, whom I truly love. I am not the only one, but all who know the truth love you, 2 because the truth remains in us and will be with us for ever.
3 May God the Father and Jesus Christ, the Father's Son, give us grace, mercy, and peace; may they be ours in truth and love.

Truth and Love

4 How happy I was to find that some of your children live in the truth, just as the Father commanded us. 5 And so I ask you, dear Lady: let us all love one another. This is no new command I write you; it is the command which we have had from the beginning. 6 This love I speak of means that we must live in obedience to God's commands. The command, as you have heard from the beginning, is this: you must all live in love.
7 Many deceivers have gone out over the world, men who do not declare that Jesus Christ became mortal man. Such a person is a deceiver, he is the Enemy of Christ. 8 Watch yourselves, then, so

that you will not lose what you have worked for, but will receive your reward in full.

⁹ Anyone who does not stay with the teaching of Christ, but goes beyond it, does not have God. Whoever does stay with the teaching has both the Father and the Son. ¹⁰ If anyone comes to you, then, who does not bring this teaching, do not welcome him in your home; do not even say, "Peace be with you." ¹¹ For anyone who wishes him peace becomes his partner in the evil things he does.

Final Words

¹² I have so much to tell you, but I would rather not do it with paper and ink; instead, I hope to visit you and talk

ἑαυτούς, ἵνα μὴ ἀπολέσητε² ἃ εἰργάσασθε³ ἀλλὰ μισθὸν πλήρη ἀπολάβητε². 9 πᾶς ὁ προάγων καὶ μὴ μένων ἐν τῇ διδαχῇ τοῦ Χριστοῦ θεὸν οὐκ ἔχει· ὁ μένων ἐν τῇ διδαχῇ⁴, οὗτος καὶ τὸν πατέρα καὶ τὸν υἱὸν ἔχει. 10 εἴ τις ἔρχεται πρὸς ὑμᾶς καὶ ταύτην τὴν διδαχὴν οὐ φέρει, μὴ λαμβάνετε αὐτὸν εἰς οἰκίαν καὶ χαίρειν αὐτῷ μὴ λέγετε· 11 ὁ λέγων γὰρ αὐτῷ χαίρειν κοινωνεῖ τοῖς ἔργοις αὐτοῦ τοῖς πονηροῖς.

Final Greetings

12 Πολλὰ ἔχων ὑμῖν γράφειν οὐκ ἐβουλήθην διὰ χάρτου καὶ μέλανος, ἀλλὰ ἐλπίζω γενέσθαι πρὸς ὑμᾶς καὶ στόμα πρὸς στόμα λαλῆσαι, ἵνα ἡ χαρὰ ἡμῶν⁵

² 8 {B} ἀπολέσητε...ἀπολάβητε ℵᶜ (ℵ* ἀπολῆσθε) A B Ψ 048? 0232 33 81 88 181 (326* ἀπόλητε, 326ᶜ ἀπολήθειτε) 436 614 630 1241 1505 1739 1881 2412 2492 2495 l¹⁴³⁹ᵐ itᵃʳ,ᶜ,ᵈᵉᵐ,ᵈⁱᵛ,ᵖ vg syrᵖʰ,ʰ copˢᵃ,ᵇᵒ arm eth Irenaeusˡᵃᵗ Lucifer Isidore Ps-Chrysostom John-Damascus Ps-Oecumeniusᶜᵒᵐᵐ Theophylactᶜᵒᵐᵐ ∥ ἀπολέσωμεν...ἀπολάβωμεν K P 049 056 0142 104 330 451 629 945 1877 2127 Byz Lect (l⁶⁰³ ἀπολέσομεν...ἀπολάβομεν) Hilary Lucifer Ps-Oecumeniusᵗˣᵗ Theophylactᵗˣᵗ

³ 8 {C} εἰργάσασθε ℵ A Ψ 0232 33 81 88 326 436 (614 2412 εἰργάσθε) 630 1241 1505 1739 1881 2495 l¹⁴³⁹ itᵃʳ,ᶜ,(ᵈᵉᵐ),ᵈⁱᵛ,(ᵖ) vg syrᵖʰ,ʰ copᵇᵒ arm eth Irenaeusˡᵃᵗ Lucifer Isidore Ps-Chrysostom John-Damascus Ps-Oecumeniusᶜᵒᵐᵐ Theophylactᶜᵒᵐᵐ ∥ εἰργασάμεθα (B* 049*ᵛⁱᵈ 181 ἠργασάμεθα) Bᶜ K P 049ᶜ 056 0142 104 330 451 629 945 1877 2127 (2492 εἰργασόμεθα) Byz Lect (l¹⁴⁷,⁶⁰³ ἐργασώμεθα) syrʰᵐᵍ copˢᵃ Hilary Lucifer Ps-Oecumeniusᵗˣᵗ Theophylactᵗˣᵗ

⁴ 9 {B} διδαχῇ ℵ A B Ψ 33 81 1739 1881 itᶜ vg syrʰ copˢᵃ arm Didymusˡᵃᵗ Fulgentius ∥ διδαχῇ αὐτοῦ itᵈᵉᵐ,ᵈⁱᵛ,ᵖ syrᵖʰ,ʰ with * Lucifer ∥ διδαχῇ τοῦ Χριστοῦ K P 049ᶜ ⁱⁿ ᵐᵍ 056 0142 88 104 181 326 330 436 451 614 629 630 945 1241 1505 1877 2127 2412 2492 2495 Byz Lect l¹⁴³⁹ᵐ itᵃʳ copᵇᵒ eth Ps-Oecumenius Theophylact

⁵ 12 {C} ἡμῶν ℵ K P Ψ 049 056 88 104 181 326 330 451 614 629 630 945 1505 1877 2412 2495 Byz Lect l¹⁴³⁹ᵐ syrᵖʰ,ʰ arm Ps-Oecumenius Theophylact ∥ ὑμῶν A B 0142 33 81 436 1739 1881 2127 2492 itᵃʳ,ᶜ,ᵈᵉᵐ,ᵈⁱᵛ,ᵖ vg copᵇᵒ eth ∥ ἐμοῦ copˢᵃ ∥ omit 309 327 378

9 ὁ μένων...ἔχει 1 Jn 2.23; 4.15   10 εἴ...οἰκίαν Ro 16.17; Eph 5.11; 2 Th 3.6   12 Πολλὰ ...μέλανος 3 Jn 13   στόμα πρὸς...λαλῆσαι Nu 12.8; 3 Jn 14

πεπληρωμένη ᾖ. **13** Ἀσπάζεταί σε τὰ τέκνα τῆς ἀδελφῆς σου τῆς ἐκλεκτῆς.[6]

---

[6] **13** {B} τῆς ἐκλεκτῆς. 𝔭[74vid] ℵ A B P Ψ 33 81 88 104 1739 1881 2127 2492 it[ar,c,dem,div] vg cop[sa,bo] Bede ∥ τῆς ἐκλεκτῆς. ἀμήν. K 049 056 0142 181 326 330 451 614 630 945 1505 1877 2412 2495 *Byz Lect* syr[ph,h] ∥ τῆς ἐκκλησίας. ἀμήν. vg[ms] ∥ *electe ecclesia.* it[p] ∥ τῆς ἐκλεκτῆς τῆς ἐν Ἐφέσῳ. 465[mg] ∥ τῆς ἐκλεκτῆς. ἡ χάρις μεθ' ὑμῶν. ἀμήν. (629 μετὰ σοῦ) syr[h with *] (arm eth[ro] *omit* ἀμήν) eth[pp] Ps-Oecumenius Theophylact ∥ *omit* 436

with you personally, so that we shall be completely happy.

13 The children of your dear Sister send you their greetings.

THE THIRD LETTER
OF JOHN

¹ From the Elder —
To my dear Gaius, whom I truly love.
² My dear friend, I pray that everything may go well with you, and that you may be in good health — as I know you are well in spirit. ³ I was so happy when some brothers arrived and told how faithful you are to the truth — just as you always live in the truth. ⁴ Nothing makes me happier than to hear that my children live in the truth.

Gaius Is Praised

⁵ My dear friend, you are so faithful in the work you do for the brothers, even when they are strangers. ⁶ They have spoken of your love to the church here. Please help them to continue their trip in a way that will please God. ⁷ For they set out on their trip in the service of Christ without accepting any help from unbelievers. ⁸ We Christians, then, must help these men, so that we may share in their work for the truth.

Diotrephes and Demetrius

⁹ I wrote a short letter to the church; but Diotrephes, who loves to be their

ΙΩΑΝΝΟΥ Γ

Salutation

1 Ὁ πρεσβύτερος Γαΐῳ τῷ ἀγαπητῷ, ὃν ἐγὼ ἀγαπῶ ἐν ἀληθείᾳ.
2 Ἀγαπητέ, περὶ πάντων εὔχομαί σε εὐοδοῦσθαι καὶ ὑγιαίνειν, καθὼς εὐοδοῦταί σου ἡ ψυχή. 3 ἐχάρην γὰρ¹ λίαν ἐρχομένων ἀδελφῶν καὶ μαρτυρούντων σου τῇ ἀληθείᾳ, καθὼς σὺ ἐν ἀληθείᾳ περιπατεῖς. 4 μειζοτέραν τούτων οὐκ ἔχω χαράν², ἵνα ἀκούω τὰ ἐμὰ τέκνα ἐν τῇ ἀληθείᾳ περιπατοῦντα.

Cooperation and Opposition

5 Ἀγαπητέ, πιστὸν ποιεῖς ὃ ἐὰν ἐργάσῃ εἰς τοὺς ἀδελφοὺς καὶ τοῦτο ξένους, 6 οἳ ἐμαρτύρησάν σου τῇ ἀγάπῃ ἐνώπιον ἐκκλησίας, οὓς καλῶς ποιήσεις προπέμψας ἀξίως τοῦ θεοῦ· 7 ὑπὲρ γὰρ τοῦ ὀνόματος ἐξῆλθον μηδὲν λαμβάνοντες ἀπὸ τῶν ἐθνικῶν. 8 ἡμεῖς οὖν ὀφείλομεν ὑπολαμβάνειν τοὺς τοιούτους, ἵνα συνεργοὶ γινώμεθα τῇ ἀληθείᾳ.
9 Ἔγραψά τι³ τῇ ἐκκλησίᾳ· ἀλλ' ὁ φιλοπρωτεύων

---

¹ **3** {C} γάρ A B C K P Ψ 048 049 056 0142 88 181 326 330 436 451 614 629 630 945 1505 1739 1877 1881 2412 2492 *Byz Lect* l¹⁴³⁹ᵐ itᵃʳ syrᵖʰ·ʰ copᵇᵒᵐˢˢ Ps-Oecumenius Theophylact ∥ οὖν 1241 ∥ *omit* ℵ 33 81 104 2127 2495 itᶜ·ᵈᵉᵐ·ᵈⁱᵛ·ᵖ vg copˢᵃ·ᵇᵒᵐˢˢ arm eth Cassiodorus

² **4** {B} χαράν ℵ A (C *transposes*: χαρὰν οὐκ ἔχω) K P Ψ 048 049 056 0142 33 81 88 104 181 326 330 436 451 614 629 630 945 1505 1739 1877 1881 2127 2412 2495 *Byz Lect* l¹⁴³⁹ᵐ itᵖ syrᵖʰ·ʰ copˢᵃ arm eth ∥ χάριν B 2492 itᵃʳ·ᶜ·ᵈᵉᵐ·ᵈⁱᵛ vg copᵇᵒ Hilary

³ **9** {C} ἔγραψά τι ℵ* A (B ἔγραψας) 048 1241 1739 (copˢᵃ·ᵇᵒ ἔγραψας) arm ∥ ἔγραψα ἄν ℵᶜ 33 81 181 436 614 630 945 1505 1881 2412 2492 l¹⁴³⁹ᵐ itᵃʳ·ᶜ·ᵈᵉᵐ·ᵈⁱᵛ·ᵖ vg (syrᵖʰ·ʰ) Hilary ∥ ἔγραψα ἄν τι 424ᶜ ∥ ἔγραψα αὐτῇ 326ᶜ ∥ ἔγραψα C K P Ψ 049 056 0142 88 104 326* 330 451 629 1877 2127 2495 *Byz Lect* eth Ps-Oecumenius Theophylact

---

1 ἐγώ...ἀληθείᾳ 2 Jn 1   3 ἐν ἀληθείᾳ περιπατεῖς 2 Jn 4   6 οὓς...θεοῦ Tt 3.13
7 μηδὲν...ἐθνικῶν 1 Cor 9.12, 15

αὐτῶν Διοτρέφης οὐκ ἐπιδέχεται ἡμᾶς. **10** διὰ τοῦτο, ἐὰν ἔλθω, ὑπομνήσω αὐτοῦ τὰ ἔργα ἃ ποιεῖ, λόγοις πονηροῖς φλυαρῶν ἡμᾶς· καὶ μὴ ἀρκούμενος ἐπὶ τούτοις οὔτε αὐτὸς ἐπιδέχεται τοὺς ἀδελφοὺς καὶ τοὺς βουλομένους κωλύει καὶ ἐκ τῆς ἐκκλησίας ἐκβάλλει.

11 Ἀγαπητέ, μὴ μιμοῦ τὸ κακὸν ἀλλὰ τὸ ἀγαθόν. ὁ ἀγαθοποιῶν ἐκ τοῦ θεοῦ ἐστιν· ὁ κακοποιῶν οὐχ ἑώρακεν τὸν θεόν. **12** Δημητρίῳ μεμαρτύρηται ὑπὸ πάντων καὶ ὑπὸ αὐτῆς τῆς ἀληθείας· καὶ ἡμεῖς δὲ μαρτυροῦμεν, καὶ οἶδας ὅτι ἡ μαρτυρία ἡμῶν ἀληθής ἐστιν.

Final Greetings

13 Πολλὰ εἶχον γράψαι σοι, ἀλλ᾽ οὐ θέλω διὰ μέλανος καὶ καλάμου σοι γράφειν· **14** ἐλπίζω δὲ εὐθέως σε ἰδεῖν, καὶ στόμα πρὸς στόμα λαλήσομεν. **15** εἰρήνη σοι. ἀσπάζονταί σε οἱ φίλοι. ἀσπάζου τοὺς φίλους κατ᾽ ὄνομα.

---

11 ὁ ἀγαθοποιῶν...ἐστιν 1 Jn 2.29; 3.6, 9   ὁ κακοποιῶν...θεόν 1 Jn 3.6, 10   **12** ἡ μαρτυρία...ἐστιν Jn 19.35; 21.24   **13** Πολλὰ...γράφειν 2 Jn 12   **14** στόμα...λαλήσομεν Nu 12.8; 2 Jn 12

leader, will not pay any attention to what I say. (10)When I come, then, I will bring up everything he has done: the terrible things he says about us and the lies he tells! But that is not enough for him; he will not receive the brothers when they come, and even stops those who want to receive them and tries to drive them out of the church!

[11] My dear friend, do not imitate what is bad, but imitate what is good. Whoever does good belongs to God; whoever does what is bad has not seen God.

[12] Everyone speaks well of Demetrius; truth itself speaks well of him. And we add our witness, and you know that what we say is true.

Final Greetings

[13] I have so much to tell you, but I do not want to do it with pen and ink. [14] I hope to see you soon, and then we will talk personally.

[15] Peace be with you.

All your friends send greetings. Greet all our friends personally.

THE LETTER
FROM JUDE

[1] From Jude, a servant of Jesus Christ, and the brother of James —

To those who have been called by God, who live in the love of God the Father and the protection of Jesus Christ: [2] May mercy, peace, and love be yours in full measure.

False Teachers

[3] My dear friends! I was doing my best to write to you about the salvation we share in common, when I felt the need of writing you now to encourage you to fight on for the faith which once and for all God has given to his people. [4] For some godless men, who have slipped in unnoticed among us, distort the message about the grace of God to excuse their immoral ways, and reject Jesus Christ, our only Master and Lord. Long ago the Scriptures predicted this condemnation that they have received.

[5] For even though you are fully aware of all this, I want to remind you of how the Lord[1] saved the people of Israel from the land of Egypt, but afterward de-

---

[1] 5 the Lord: *some mss. read* God; *other mss. read* Jesus

ΙΟΥΔΑ

Salutation

1 Ἰούδας Ἰησοῦ Χριστοῦ δοῦλος, ἀδελφὸς δὲ Ἰακώβου, τοῖς ἐν θεῷ πατρὶ ἠγαπημένοις[1] καὶ Ἰησοῦ Χριστῷ τετηρημένοις κλητοῖς· 2 ἔλεος ὑμῖν καὶ εἰρήνη καὶ ἀγάπη πληθυνθείη.

Judgment on False Teachers
(2 Pe. 2.1–17)

3 Ἀγαπητοί, πᾶσαν σπουδὴν ποιούμενος γράφειν ὑμῖν περὶ τῆς κοινῆς ἡμῶν[2] σωτηρίας ἀνάγκην ἔσχον γράψαι ὑμῖν παρακαλῶν ἐπαγωνίζεσθαι τῇ ἅπαξ παραδοθείσῃ τοῖς ἁγίοις πίστει. 4 παρεισέδυσαν γάρ τινες ἄνθρωποι, οἱ πάλαι προγεγραμμένοι εἰς τοῦτο τὸ κρίμα, ἀσεβεῖς, τὴν τοῦ θεοῦ ἡμῶν χάριτα μετατιθέντες εἰς ἀσέλγειαν καὶ τὸν μόνον δεσπότην[a] καὶ κύριον ἡμῶν[a] Ἰησοῦν Χριστὸν ἀρνούμενοι.

5 Ὑπομνῆσαι δὲ ὑμᾶς βούλομαι, εἰδότας ἅπαξ πάντα, ὅτι Ἰησοῦς[3] λαὸν ἐκ γῆς Αἰγύπτου σώσας τὸ δεύτερον

---

[1] 1 {B} ἠγαπημένοις p[72] ℵ A B Ψ 81 88 326[mg] 330 436 451 629 630 1241 1505 1739 (2492 ἠγάπομεν) 2495 *l*[1441] it[ar,c,dem,div,p] vg syr[ph,h] cop[sa,bo] arm eth Origen Lucifer Ephraem Augustine Ps-Athanasius Cassiodorus Ps-Oecumenius Theophylact[comm] ‖ ἡγιασμένοις K P 049 056 0142 104 181 326[txt] 614 945 1877 1881 2127 2412 *Byz Lect l*[6,59,62] Theophylact[txt] ‖ *electis* Hilary

[2] 3 {B} ἡμῶν p[72] ℵ A B Ψ 81 88 326 436 614 630 1739 2412 *l*[6] syr[ph,h] cop[sa] arm Lucifer Cyril Bede Theophylact ‖ ὑμῶν 104 1505 1881 2495 it[ar,c,dem,div,p] vg cop[bo] Hilary Ephraem ‖ *omit* K P 049 056 0142 181 330 451 629 945 1877 2127 2492 *Byz Lect l*[59,62] Cassiodorus Ps-Oecumenius

[3] 5 {D} ἅπαξ πάντα, ὅτι Ἰησοῦς A B 33 81 it[ar,dem,div] vg eth Jerome

---

[a a] 4 *a* none, *a* none: WH Bov Nes BF[2] RSV[mg] Zür Luth Jer Seg ‖ *a* none, *a* minor: RV ASV RSV NEB TT ‖ *a* minor, *a* none: RV[mg] ASV[mg] NEB[mg] ‖ *different text:* TR AV Jer[mg]

---

2 2 Pe 1.2   3 παρακαλῶν ἐπαγωνίζεσθαι 1 Tm 1.18   4 παρεισέδυσαν...ἄνθρωποι Ga 2.4   τὴν...ἀρνούμενοι 2 Pe 2.1   5 Ὑπομνῆσαι...πάντα 2 Pe 1.12   Ἰησοῦς...σώσας Ex 12.51

τοὺς μὴ πιστεύσαντας ἀπώλεσεν, 6 ἀγγέλους τε τοὺς μὴ τηρήσαντας τὴν ἑαυτῶν ἀρχὴν ἀλλὰ ἀπολιπόντας τὸ ἴδιον οἰκητήριον εἰς κρίσιν μεγάλης ἡμέρας δεσμοῖς ἀϊδίοις ὑπὸ ζόφον τετήρηκεν· 7 ὡς Σόδομα καὶ Γόμορρα καὶ αἱ περὶ αὐτὰς πόλεις, τὸν ὅμοιον τρόπον τούτοις ἐκπορνεύσασαι καὶ ἀπελθοῦσαι ὀπίσω σαρκὸς ἑτέρας, πρόκεινται δεῖγμα[b] πυρὸς αἰωνίου[b] δίκην ὑπέχουσαι.

8 Ὁμοίως μέντοι καὶ οὗτοι ἐνυπνιαζόμενοι σάρκα μὲν μιαίνουσιν, κυριότητα δὲ ἀθετοῦσιν, δόξας δὲ βλασφημοῦσιν. 9 ὁ δὲ Μιχαὴλ ὁ ἀρχάγγελος, ὅτε τῷ διαβόλῳ διακρινόμενος διελέγετο περὶ τοῦ Μωϋσέως σώματος, οὐκ ἐτόλμησεν κρίσιν ἐπενεγκεῖν βλασφημίας, ἀλλὰ εἶπεν, Ἐπιτιμήσαι σοι κύριος. 10 οὗτοι δὲ ὅσα μὲν οὐκ οἴδασιν βλασφημοῦσιν, ὅσα δὲ φυσικῶς ὡς τὰ ἄλογα ζῷα ἐπίστανται, ἐν τούτοις φθείρονται. 11 οὐαὶ αὐτοῖς, ὅτι τῇ ὁδῷ τοῦ Κάϊν ἐπορεύθησαν, καὶ τῇ πλάνῃ τοῦ Βαλαὰμ μισθοῦ ἐξεχύθησαν, καὶ τῇ ἀντιλογίᾳ τοῦ Κόρε ἀπώλοντο. 12 οὗτοί εἰσιν οἱ ἐν ταῖς ἀγάπαις ὑμῶν σπιλάδες[c] συνευωχούμενοι[c] ἀφόβως,[c] ἑαυτοὺς ποιμαί-

Cyril ‖ ἅπαξ πάντα, ὅτι κύριος Ephraem ‖ ἅπαξ πάντα, ὅτι ὁ θεός C[2] ‖ ἅπαξ πάντας, ὅτι θεὸς Χριστός 𝔭[72] ‖ ἅπαξ τοῦτο, ὅτι ὁ κύριος (Κ 056 τοῦτο ἅπαξ) 049 (0142 τοῦτο ὑμᾶς) 104 181 326 330 436 451 629 945 1877 2127 Byz Lect l[6,59,62] Ps-Oecumenius Theophylact ‖ πάντα, ὅτι Ἰησοῦς ἅπαξ (88 ὁ Ἰησοῦς) 1241 1739 1881 it[c] cop[(sa),bo] ‖ πάντα, ὅτι κύριος ἅπαξ ℵ Ψ (C* 630 1505 2412 2495 ὁ κύριος) (syr[h] πάντας) ‖ πάντα, ὅτι ὁ θεὸς ἅπαξ 2492 it[p] (syr[ph] πάντας) arm (Lucifer omit ἅπαξ) ‖ see ἅπαξ πάντα, ὅτι κύριος λαόν...σώσας Westcott-Hort[txt] and ἅπαξ πάντα, ὅτι ὁ λαόν... σώσας Westcott-Hort cj

ʰ ʰ 7 b none, b none. TR WII Bov Nes BF⁷ ‖ b minor, b none: AV RV ASV (RSV) (NEB) TT Zür (Luth) Jer Seg ‖ b none, b minor: RV[mg] ASV[mg]

ᶜ ᶜ ᶜ 12 c none, c none, c minor: Bov Nes BF² Luth ‖ c minor, c none: WII (AV) RV ASV ‖ c minor, c none, c minor: TR RSV (NEB) Zür (Jer) ‖ c minor, c none, c none: Seg ‖ c none, c minor, c major: TT

5 τοὺς...ἀπώλεσεν Nu 14.29–30, 35; 1 Cor 10.5   6 2 Pe 2.4, 9   7 Gn 19.4–25; 2 Pe 2.6, 10 8 σάρκα...βλασφημοῦσιν 2 Pe 2.10   9 Assumption of Moses[acc. to Clement,Origen,Didymus] ὁ δὲ...ἀρχάγγελος Dn 10.13, 21; 12.1; Re 12.7 οὐκ...βλασφημίας 2 Pe 2.11 Ἐπιτιμήσαι σοι κύριος Zch 3.2   10 2 Pe 2.12   11 τῇ ὁδῷ τοῦ Κάϊν Gn 4.3–8; 1 Jn 3.12 τῇ πλάνῃ...μισθοῦ Nu 22.7; 31.16; Re 2.14 τῇ ἀντιλογίᾳ...ἀπώλοντο Nu 16.19–35   12 οὗτοι...συνευωχού- μενοι 2 Pe 2.13 ἑαυτοὺς ποιμαίνοντες Eze 34.8

stroyed those who did not believe. 6 Remember the angels who did not stay within the limits of their proper authority, but abandoned their own dwelling-place: God has kept them in the darkness below, bound in eternal chains for that great Day on which they will be condemned. 7 Remember Sodom and Gomorrah, and the nearby towns, whose people acted as the angels did and committed sexual immorality and perversion: they suffer the punishment of eternal fire as a plain warning to all.

8 In the same way also, these men have visions which make them sin against their own bodies; they despise God's authority; they insult the glorious beings above. 9 Not even the chief angel Michael has done this. In his quarrel with the Devil, when they argued about who would have the body of Moses, Michael did not dare condemn the Devil with insulting words, but said, "The Lord rebuke you!" 10 But these men insult things they do not understand; and those things that they know by instinct, like wild animals, are the very things that destroy them. 11 How terrible for them! They have followed the way that Cain took; they have given themselves over to error for the sake of money, as Balaam did; they have been destroyed by rebelling like Korah rebelled. 12 They are like dirty spots in your fellowship meals, with their shameless carousing. They take care of themselves only. They are like clouds carried along by the wind and bringing no rain. They are like trees that bear no

fruit, even in autumn, trees that have been pulled up by the roots and are completely dead. ¹³ They are like wild waves of the sea, with their shameful deeds showing up like foam. They are like wandering stars, for whom God has reserved a place for ever in the deepest darkness.

¹⁴ It was Enoch, the seventh direct descendant from Adam, who long ago prophesied about them: "See! The Lord will come with many thousands of his holy angels, ¹⁵ to bring judgment on all, to condemn all godless sinners for all the godless deeds they have performed, and for all the terrible words those godless men have spoken against God!" ¹⁶ These men are always grumbling and blaming others; they follow their own evil desires; they brag about themselves, and flatter others in order to get their own way.

Warnings and Instructions

¹⁷ But remember, my friends! Remember what you were told in the past by the apostles of our Lord Jesus Christ. ¹⁸ For they said to you, "When the last days come, men will appear who will make fun of you, men who follow their own evil desires." ¹⁹ These are the men who cause divisions, who are controlled only by natural desires, not by the Spirit. ²⁰ But you, my friends, keep on building yourselves up in your most sacred faith. Pray in the power of the Holy Spirit, ²¹ and keep yourselves in the love of God, as you wait for our Lord Jesus Christ in his mercy to give you eternal life.

²² Show mercy toward those who have doubts: ²³ save them, by snatching them

νοντες, νεφέλαι ἄνυδροι ὑπὸ ἀνέμων παραφερόμεναι, δένδρα φθινοπωρινὰ ἄκαρπα δὶς ἀποθανόντα ἐκριζωθέντα, 13 κύματα ἄγρια θαλάσσης ἐπαφρίζοντα τὰς ἑαυτῶν αἰσχύνας, ἀστέρες πλανῆται οἷς ὁ ζόφος τοῦ σκότους εἰς αἰῶνα τετήρηται.

14 Προεφήτευσεν δὲ καὶ τούτοις ἕβδομος ἀπὸ Ἀδὰμ Ἐνὼχ λέγων, Ἰδοὺ ἦλθεν κύριος ἐν ἁγίαις μυριάσιν αὐτοῦ, 15 ποιῆσαι κρίσιν κατὰ πάντων καὶ ἐλέγξαι πάντας τοὺς ἀσεβεῖς περὶ πάντων τῶν ἔργων ἀσεβείας αὐτῶν ὧν ἠσέβησαν καὶ περὶ πάντων τῶν σκληρῶν ὧν ἐλάλησαν κατ' αὐτοῦ ἁμαρτωλοὶ ἀσεβεῖς. 16 Οὗτοί εἰσιν γογγυσταί,ᵈ μεμψίμοιροι,ᵈ κατὰ τὰς ἐπιθυμίας αὐτῶν πορευόμενοι, καὶ τὸ στόμα αὐτῶν λαλεῖ ὑπέρογκα, θαυμάζοντες πρόσωπα ὠφελείας χάριν.

Warnings and Exhortations

17 Ὑμεῖς δέ, ἀγαπητοί, μνήσθητε τῶν ῥημάτων τῶν προειρημένων ὑπὸ τῶν ἀποστόλων τοῦ κυρίου ἡμῶν Ἰησοῦ Χριστοῦ· 18 ὅτι ἔλεγον ὑμῖν, Ἐπ' ἐσχάτου [τοῦ] χρόνου ἔσονται ἐμπαῖκται κατὰ τὰς ἑαυτῶν ἐπιθυμίας πορευόμενοι τῶν ἀσεβειῶν. 19 Οὗτοί εἰσιν οἱ ἀποδιορίζοντες, ψυχικοί, πνεῦμα μὴ ἔχοντες. 20 ὑμεῖς δέ, ἀγαπητοί, ἐποικοδομοῦντες ἑαυτοὺς τῇ ἁγιωτάτῃ ὑμῶν πίστει, ἐν πνεύματι ἁγίῳ προσευχόμενοι, 21 ἑαυτοὺς ἐν ἀγάπῃ θεοῦ τηρήσατε,ᵉ προσδεχόμενοι τὸ ἔλεος τοῦ κυρίου ἡμῶν Ἰησοῦ Χριστοῦ εἰς ζωὴν αἰώνιον. 22 καὶ οὓς μὲν ἐλεᾶτε διακρινομένους⁴, 23 οὓς δὲ σῴζετε ἐκ

---

⁴ **22** {C} ἐλεᾶτε διακρινομένους (*see footnotes 5 and 6*) ℵ B C² Ψ 88 *l*⁶⁸⁰ syrʰ ∥ ἐλέγχετε διακρινομένους A C* 33 81 (181 ἐλέγετε) 326 436 1241 1739

ᵈᵈ **16** *d* minor, *d* minor: TR WH AV RV ASV RSV (NEB) (TT) (Luth) Jer ∥ *d* none, *d* minor: Bov Nes BF² ∥ *d* minor, *d* none: Zür Seg
ᵉ **21** *e* minor: TR Bov Nes BF² AV RV ASV RSV NEB TT (Zür) (Luth) Jer Seg ∥ *e* none: WH

---

12 ὑπὸ ἀνέμων παραφερόμεναι Eph 4.14   **13** κύματα...αἰσχύνας Is 57.20   οἷς... τετήρηται 2 Pe 2.17   **14** ἕβδομος...Ἐνώχ En 60.8   ἦλθεν...αὐτοῦ Dt 33.2; Zch 14.5; Mt 25.31   **14-15** ἦλθεν...ἀσεβεῖς En 1.9   **17** 2 Pe 3.2   **18** Ἐπ'...ἀσεβειῶν 2 Pe 3.3   **20** ἐποικοδομοῦντες...πίστει Col 2.7; 1 Th 5.11   **23** ἐκ πυρὸς ἁρπάζοντες Am 4.11; Zch 3.2

πυρὸς ἁρπάζοντες[5], οὓς δὲ ἐλεᾶτε ἐν φόβῳ[6], μισοῦντες καὶ τὸν ἀπὸ τῆς σαρκὸς ἐσπιλωμένον χιτῶνα.

Benediction

24 Τῷ δὲ δυναμένῳ φυλάξαι ὑμᾶς ἀπταίστους καὶ στῆσαι κατενώπιον τῆς δόξης αὐτοῦ ἀμώμους ἐν ἀγαλλιάσει,[f] **25** μόνῳ[f] θεῷ[g] σωτῆρι ἡμῶν[g] διὰ Ἰησοῦ Χριστοῦ τοῦ κυρίου ἡμῶν δόξα μεγαλωσύνη κράτος καὶ ἐξουσία πρὸ παντὸς τοῦ αἰῶνος καὶ νῦν καὶ εἰς πάντας τοὺς αἰῶνας· ἀμήν.

out of the fire. Show mercy also, mixed with fear, to others as well; but hate their very clothes, stained by their sinful lusts.

Prayer of Praise

Benediction

24 To him who is able to keep you from falling, and present you faultless and joyful before his glory — **25** to the only God our Savior, through Jesus Christ our Lord, be glory, majesty, might, and authority, from all ages past, and now, and for ever and ever! Amen.

1881 it[ar,c,dem,div,p] vg cop[bo] arm Ephraem Cassiodorus Ps-Oecumenius[comm] Theophylact[comm] ∥ ἐλέγχετε διακρινόμενοι 629 (2492 ἐλέγετε) ∥ ἐλεεῖτε διακρινόμενοι K P 049 056 0142 104 330 451 630 945 1877 2127 2412 2495 *Byz Lect* Ps-Oecumenius[txt] Theophylact[txt] ∥ ἐλεεῖτε διακρινομένῳ 1505 ∥ *omit verb and transpose* διακρινομένους (*see footnote 6*) p[72] it[t] syr[ph] cop[sa] Clement[lat] Orsisius Jerome

5 23 {C} οὓς δὲ σῴζετε ἐκ πυρὸς ἁρπάζοντες (*see footnotes 4 and 6*) (ℵ* ἁρπάζετε) ℵ[c] A Ψ 33 81 104 181 326 436 1241 1739 1881 2412 it[ar,c,dem,div,p] vg cop[bo] arm Ephraem ∥ οὓς δὲ σῴζετε ἐκ πυρὸς ἁρπάζοντες ἐν φόβῳ C 630 1505 2495 syr[h] ∥ οὓς δὲ ἐν φόβῳ σῴζετε ἐκ πυρὸς ἁρπάζοντες K P (049 0142 σῴζεται) 056 88 330 451 629 945 1877 2127 2492 *Byz* (*Lect* ἐκ τοῦ πυρός) *l*[147,603m,1439m,1441] Ps-Oecumenius Theophylact ∥ σῴζετε ἐκ πυρὸς ἁρπάζοντες B ∥ ἐκ πυρὸς ἁρπάζετε (p[72] ἁρπάσατε) it[t] syr[ph] cop[sa] Clement[lat] Orsisius Jerome

6 23 {C} οὓς δὲ ἐλεᾶτε ἐν φόβῳ (*see footnotes 4 and 5*) ℵ A B Ψ 33 81 181 326 1739 1881 it[ar,c,dem,div,p*] (it[p°] *add* θεοῦ) vg cop[bo] arm Ephraem ∥ διακρινομένους δὲ ἐλεᾶτε ἐν φόβῳ (p[72] ἐλεεῖτε) it[t] syr[ph] cop[sa] Clement[lat] Orsisius (Jerome *omit* ἐν φόβῳ) ∥ οὓς δὲ ἐλεεῖτε ἐν φόβῳ 436 (629 *add* θεοῦ) 1241 ∥ οὓς δὲ ἐλέγχετε ἐν φόβῳ 88 104 945 (2412 ἐλέγετε) Ps-Oecumenius[comm] Theophylact[comm] ∥ *omit* οὓς δὲ ἐλεᾶτε *and transpose* ἐν φόβῳ (*see footnote 5*) C K P 049 050 0142 330 451 630 1505 1877 2127 2492 2495 *Byz Lect* syr[h] Ps-Oecumenius[txt] Theophylact[txt]

---

f f **24-25** f *minor,* f *none:* TR Bov Nes BF² AV RV ASV RSV NEB TT Zür Luth Jer Seg ∥ f *none,* f *none:* WH ∥ f *none,* f *minor*

g g **25** g *none,* g *none:* WH Bov Nes BF² AV RV ASV RSV Zür Luth Jer Seg ∥ g *none,* g *minor:* RV ASV NEB ∥ g *minor,* g *minor:* TT ∥ *different text:* TR AV

24 Τῷ...ἀμώμους Php 1.10; 1 Th 5.23   **25** μόνῳ...δόξα Ro 16.27

THE REVELATION TO JOHN

1 In this book are written the things that Jesus Christ revealed. These things were given him by God, for him to show God's servants what must happen very soon. Christ made these things known to his servant John by sending his angel to him. [2] John has told all that he has seen. This is his report concerning the message from God and the truth revealed by Jesus Christ. [3] Happy is the one who reads this book, and happy are those who listen to the words of this prophetic message and obey what is written in this book! For the time is near when all this will happen.

Greetings to the Seven Churches

[4] From John to the seven churches in the province of Asia:

Grace and peace be yours from God, who is, who was, and who is to come, and from the seven spirits in front of his throne, [5] and from Jesus Christ, the faithful witness, the first-born Son who was raised from death, who is also the ruler of the kings of the earth.

He loves us, and by his death he has freed us from our sins [6] and made us a kingdom of priests to serve his God and Father. To Jesus Christ be the glory and power for ever and ever! Amen.

836

ΑΠΟΚΑΛΥΨΙΣ ΙΩΑΝΝΟΥ

Introduction and Salutation

1 Ἀποκάλυψις Ἰησοῦ Χριστοῦ, ἣν ἔδωκεν αὐτῷ ὁ θεός,[a] δεῖξαι τοῖς δούλοις αὐτοῦ[a] ἃ δεῖ γενέσθαι ἐν τάχει, καὶ ἐσήμανεν ἀποστείλας διὰ τοῦ ἀγγέλου αὐτοῦ τῷ δούλῳ αὐτοῦ Ἰωάννῃ, **2** ὃς ἐμαρτύρησεν τὸν λόγον τοῦ θεοῦ καὶ τὴν μαρτυρίαν Ἰησοῦ Χριστοῦ, ὅσα εἶδεν. **3** μακάριος ὁ ἀναγινώσκων καὶ οἱ ἀκούοντες τοὺς λόγους τῆς προφητείας καὶ τηροῦντες τὰ ἐν αὐτῇ γεγραμμένα, ὁ γὰρ καιρὸς ἐγγύς.

4 Ἰωάννης ταῖς ἑπτὰ ἐκκλησίαις ταῖς ἐν τῇ Ἀσίᾳ· χάρις ὑμῖν καὶ εἰρήνη ἀπὸ ὁ ὢν καὶ ὁ ἦν καὶ ὁ ἐρχόμενος, καὶ ἀπὸ τῶν ἑπτὰ πνευμάτων ἃ ἐνώπιον τοῦ θρόνου αὐτοῦ, **5** καὶ ἀπὸ Ἰησοῦ Χριστοῦ, ὁ μάρτυς ὁ πιστός, ὁ πρωτότοκος τῶν νεκρῶν καὶ ὁ ἄρχων τῶν βασιλέων τῆς γῆς.

Τῷ ἀγαπῶντι ἡμᾶς καὶ λύσαντι ἡμᾶς ἐκ[1] τῶν ἁμαρτιῶν ἡμῶν ἐν τῷ αἵματι αὐτοῦ —[b] **6** καὶ ἐποίησεν ἡμᾶς βασιλείαν, ἱερεῖς τῷ θεῷ καὶ πατρὶ αὐτοῦ —[b] αὐτῷ ἡ δόξα καὶ τὸ κράτος εἰς τοὺς αἰῶνας [τῶν αἰώνων][2]· ἀμήν.

---

[1] **5** {B} λύσαντι ἡμᾶς ἐκ p[18] ℵ[c] A C 1 2020 2081 it[h?] syr[ph? h?] arm Tyconius Primasius Cassiodorus Andrew[a] ∥ λύσαντι ἐκ ℵ* 1611 2344 it[z] ∥ λύσαντι ὑμᾶς ἀπό 792 eth ∥ λούσαντι ἡμᾶς ἀπό P 046 94 1006 (1828 ἔλουσεν) (1854 2053 ἡμᾶς ἐκ) 1859 2042 2065 2073 2138 2432 (it[ar] *omit ἡμᾶς*) it[c, dem, div, gig, haf, t] vg cop[bo] eth Andrew[bav, p] (Andrew[c] ἔλουσεν) Arethas ∥ καλέσαντι ἡμᾶς ἀπό 2049[mg] (2049[txt] *omit καὶ καλέσαντι ἡμᾶς*)

[2] **6** {C} αἰῶνας τῶν αἰώνων ℵ[c] (ℵ* τὸν αἰῶνα *for* τοὺς αἰῶνας) C 046

[a a] **1** *a* minor, *a* none: TR Bov Nes BF² AV RV[mg] ASV[mg] (NEB) TT Zür? Luth? ∥ *a* none, *a* minor: WH RV ASV ∥ *a* none, *a* minor: RSV Jer Seg

[b b] **5-6** *b* dash, *b* dash: WH ∥ *b* minor, *b* minor: NEB ∥ *b* minor, *b* minor: TR Bov Nes BF² RV ASV TT Seg ∥ *b* none, *b* minor: (AV) RSV Zür Luth (Jer)

---

1 Ἀποκάλυψις...τάχει Dn 2.28, 29, 45; Re 1.19; 22.6   **2** τὸν...Χριστοῦ Re 1.9; 6.9   **3** τηροῦντες...γεγραμμένα Re 22.7   ὁ γὰρ...ἐγγύς Re 22.10   **4** ὁ ὢν Ex 3.14; Re 1.8; 4.8; 11.17; 16.5   ὁ ὢν...ἐρχόμενος Is 41.4; Re 1.8; 4.8   τῶν ἑπτὰ πνευμάτων Re 3.1; 4.5; 5.6   **5** ὁ μάρτυς ὁ πιστός Re 3.14; 19.11   ὁ πρωτότοκος τῶν νεκρῶν Ps 89.27; Col 1.18   ὁ ἄρχων ...γῆς Ps 89.27; Re 19.16   λύσαντι...ἡμῶν Ps 130.8; Is 40.2   **6** ἐποίησεν...θεῷ Ex 19.6; Is 61 6; 1 Pe 2.5, 9; Re 5.10; 20.6

7 Ἰδοὺ ἔρχεται μετὰ τῶν νεφελῶν,
      καὶ ὄψεται αὐτὸν πᾶς ὀφθαλμὸς
   καὶ οἵτινες αὐτὸν ἐξεκέντησαν,
      καὶ κόψονται ἐπ᾽ αὐτὸν πᾶσαι αἱ φυλαὶ τῆς γῆς.
ναί, ἀμήν.
8 Ἐγώ εἰμι τὸ Ἄλφα καὶ τὸ Ὦ³, λέγει κύριος^c ὁ
θεός,^c ὁ ὢν καὶ ὁ ἦν καὶ ὁ ἐρχόμενος, ὁ παντοκράτωρ.

A Vision of Christ

9 Ἐγὼ Ἰωάννης, ὁ ἀδελφὸς ὑμῶν καὶ συγκοινωνὸς ἐν
τῇ θλίψει καὶ βασιλείᾳ καὶ ὑπομονῇ ἐν Ἰησοῦ, ἐγενόμην
ἐν τῇ νήσῳ τῇ καλουμένῃ Πάτμῳ διὰ τὸν λόγον τοῦ θεοῦ
καὶ τὴν μαρτυρίαν Ἰησοῦ. 10 ἐγενόμην ἐν πνεύματι ἐν
τῇ κυριακῇ ἡμέρᾳ, καὶ ἤκουσα ὀπίσω μου φωνὴν μεγάλην
ὡς σάλπιγγος 11 λεγούσης, Ὃ βλέπεις γράψον εἰς
βιβλίον καὶ πέμψον ταῖς ἑπτὰ ἐκκλησίαις, εἰς Ἔφεσον
καὶ εἰς Σμύρναν καὶ εἰς Πέργαμον καὶ εἰς Θυάτιρα καὶ
εἰς Σάρδεις καὶ εἰς Φιλαδέλφειαν καὶ εἰς Λαοδίκειαν.
12 Καὶ ἐπέστρεψα βλέπειν τὴν φωνὴν ἥτις ἐλάλει
μετ᾽ ἐμοῦ· καὶ ἐπιστρέψας εἶδον ἑπτὰ λυχνίας χρυσᾶς,

7 Look, he is coming with the clouds!
Everyone will see him, including those
who pierced him. All peoples of earth
will mourn because of him. Certainly so!
Amen.
8 "I am the Alpha and the Omega,"
says the Lord God Almighty, who is,
who was, and who is to come.

A Vision of Christ

9 I am John, your brother, and in union
with Jesus I share with you in suffering,
and in his Kingdom, and in enduring.
I was put on the island named Patmos
because I had proclaimed God's word and
the truth that Jesus revealed. 10 On the
Lord's day the Spirit took control of me,
and I heard a loud voice, that sounded
like a trumpet, speaking behind me. 11 It
said: "Write down what you see, and
send the book to these seven churches:
in Ephesus, Smyrna, Pergamum, Thyatira, Sardis, Philadelphia, and Laodicea."
12 I turned around to see who was
talking to me. There I saw seven gold

---

7 94 1006 1611 1828 1854 1859 2020 2042 2053 2065 2073 2081 2138 2432 it^{ar,c};
dem,div,gig,h,haf,t,z vg syr^{ph,h} arm eth Andrew^{bav,c,p} Arethas // αἰῶνας 𝔭¹⁸ A
P cop^{bo} Andrew^a // omit εἰς τοὺς αἰῶνας 2344

8 8 {B} Ὦ ℵ^c A C P 046 94 1006 1611 1859 2020 2042 2053 2138 it^h syr^{ph,h}
arm eth Ambrose Diadochus Primasius Arethas // Ὦ ἀρχὴ καὶ τέλος
(see 21.6) ℵ* 1 1828 1854 2065 2073 2081* (2344 τὸ τέλος) 2432 it^{ar,c,dem,div},
gig,haf,t,z vg Origen^{lat} Andrew^{bav,c} // Ὦ ἡ ἀρχὴ καὶ τὸ τέλος (see 21.6)
2081^c Andrew^a cop^{bo?}

---

^{c c} 8 c none, c minor: Bov Nes BF² RV ASV RSV NEB TT Zür Luth Jer Seg // c minor, c none:
RV^{mg} // c minor, c minor: WH // different text: TR AV

---

7 Ἰδού...νεφελῶν Dn 7.13; Mt 24.30; Mk 13.26; Lk 21.27; 1 Th 4.17 ὄψεται...ἐξεκέντησαν
Zch 12.10; Jn 19.34, 37 κόψονται...γῆς Zch 12.10, 12, 14; Mt 24.30   8 Ἐγώ...Ὦ Re 21.6; 22.13
ὁ ὢν Ex 3.14; Re 1.4; 4.8; 11.17; 16.5   ὁ ὢν...ἐρχόμενος Is 41.4; Re 1.4; 4.8   λέγει...
παντοκράτωρ Am 3.13 LXX; 4.13 LXX; Re 4.8; 11.17; 15.3; 16.7, 14; 19.6, 15; 21.22

lamp-stands. [13] Among them stood a being who looked like a man, wearing a robe that reached to his feet, and a gold band around his chest. [14] His hair was white as wool, or as snow, and his eyes blazed like fire; [15] his feet shone like brass melted in the furnace and then polished, and his voice sounded like a mighty waterfall. [16] He held seven stars in his right hand, and a sharp two-edged sword came out of his mouth. His face was as bright as the midday sun. [17] When I saw him I fell down at his feet like a dead man. He placed his right hand on me and said: "Don't be afraid! I am the first and the last. [18] I am the living one! I was dead, but look, I am alive for ever and ever. I have authority over death and the world of the dead. [19] Write, then, the things you see, both the things that are now, and the things that will happen afterward. [20] Here is the secret meaning of the seven stars that you see in my right hand, and of the seven gold lamp-stands: the seven stars are the angels of the seven churches, and the seven lamp-stands are the seven churches."

13 καὶ ἐν μέσῳ τῶν λυχνιῶν ὅμοιον υἱὸν ἀνθρώπου, ἐνδεδυμένον ποδήρη καὶ περιεζωσμένον πρὸς τοῖς μαστοῖς ζώνην χρυσᾶν· 14 ἡ δὲ κεφαλὴ αὐτοῦ καὶ αἱ τρίχες λευκαὶ ὡς ἔριον [d] λευκόν, [d] ὡς χιών, καὶ οἱ ὀφθαλμοὶ αὐτοῦ ὡς φλὸξ πυρός, 15 καὶ οἱ πόδες αὐτοῦ ὅμοιοι χαλκολιβάνῳ ὡς ἐν καμίνῳ πεπυρωμένης[4], καὶ ἡ φωνὴ αὐτοῦ ὡς φωνὴ ὑδάτων πολλῶν, 16 καὶ ἔχων ἐν τῇ δεξιᾷ χειρὶ αὐτοῦ ἀστέρας ἑπτά, καὶ ἐκ τοῦ στόματος αὐτοῦ ῥομφαία δίστομος ὀξεῖα ἐκπορευομένη, καὶ ἡ ὄψις αὐτοῦ ὡς ὁ ἥλιος φαίνει ἐν τῇ δυνάμει αὐτοῦ.

17 Καὶ ὅτε εἶδον αὐτόν, ἔπεσα πρὸς τοὺς πόδας αὐτοῦ ὡς νεκρός· καὶ ἔθηκεν τὴν δεξιὰν αὐτοῦ ἐπ᾽ ἐμὲ λέγων, Μὴ φοβοῦ· ἐγώ εἰμι ὁ πρῶτος καὶ ὁ ἔσχατος, 18 καὶ ὁ ζῶν,[e] καὶ ἐγενόμην νεκρὸς καὶ ἰδοὺ ζῶν εἰμι εἰς τοὺς αἰῶνας τῶν αἰώνων,[e] καὶ ἔχω τὰς κλεῖς τοῦ θανάτου καὶ τοῦ ᾅδου. 19 γράψον οὖν ἃ εἶδες καὶ ἃ εἰσὶν καὶ ἃ μέλλει γενέσθαι μετὰ ταῦτα.[f] 20 τὸ μυστήριον τῶν ἑπτὰ ἀστέρων οὓς εἶδες ἐπὶ τῆς δεξιᾶς μου, καὶ τὰς ἑπτὰ λυχνίας τὰς χρυσᾶς·[f] οἱ ἑπτὰ ἀστέρες ἄγγελοι τῶν ἑπτὰ ἐκκλησιῶν εἰσιν, καὶ αἱ λυχνίαι αἱ ἑπτὰ ἑπτὰ ἐκκλησίαι εἰσίν.

---

[4] **15** {D} πεπυρωμένης A C Primasius ‖ πεπυρωμένῳ א 2053 2432 it[ar,c,dem,div,gig,h?haf,t,z] vg syr[ph,h] cop[sa,bo] eth Irenaeus[lat] Cyprian Victorinus-Pettau Maternus Apringius Primasius Ps-Ambrose Haymo ‖ πεπυρωμένοι P 046 1 94 1006 1611 1828 1854 1859 2020 2042 2065 2073 2081 2138 2344 Tyconius Andrew Arethas

[d d] **14** d none, d minor: TR WH RV ASV (RSV) Zür Luth Jer Seg ‖ d minor, d none: AV ‖ d none, d none: Bov Nes BF² NEB TT

[e e] **18** e minor, e minor: Bov Nes BF² RV ASV RSV NEB Jer ‖ e major, e major: Seg ‖ e dash, e dash: WH ‖ e major, e minor: TT (Zür) (Luth) ‖ different text: TR AV

[f f] **19-20** f major, f minor: WH Bov Nes BF² RSV NEB TT Luth Jer Seg ‖ f minor, f major: TR AV RV ASV Zür

13 ὅμοιον υἱὸν ἀνθρώπου Dn 7.13   ἐνδεδυμένον...χρυσᾶν Eze 9.2, 11 LXX; Dn 10.5   **14** ἡ...χιών Dn 7.9   **14-15** οἱ ὀφθαλμοί...χαλκολιβάνω Dn 10.6; Re 2.18; 19.12   **15** ὡς φωνή...πολλῶν Eze 1.24; 43.2; Re 14.2; 19.6   **16** ἀστέρας ἑπτά Re 1.20; 2.1   ἐκ...ἐκπορευομένη Is 49.2; Re 2.12, 16; 19.15   **17** ἐγώ...ἔσχατος Is 44.6; 48.12; Re 2.8; 22.13   **19** ἃ μέλλει...ταῦτα Is 48.6 LXX; Dn 2.28, 29, 45; Re 1.1; 22.6   **20** ἑπτὰ ἀστέρες Re 1.16; 2.1; 3.1

The Message to Ephesus

2 Τῷ ἀγγέλῳ τῆς ἐν Ἐφέσῳ ἐκκλησίας γράψον·

Τάδε λέγει ὁ κρατῶν τοὺς ἑπτὰ ἀστέρας ἐν τῇ δεξιᾷ αὐτοῦ, ὁ περιπατῶν ἐν μέσῳ τῶν ἑπτὰ λυχνιῶν τῶν χρυσῶν· 2 Οἶδα τὰ ἔργα σου καὶ τὸν κόπον[1] καὶ τὴν ὑπομονήν σου, καὶ ὅτι οὐ δύνῃ βαστάσαι κακούς, καὶ ἐπείρασας τοὺς λέγοντας ἑαυτοὺς ἀποστόλους καὶ οὐκ εἰσίν, καὶ εὗρες αὐτοὺς ψευδεῖς· 3 καὶ ὑπομονὴν ἔχεις, καὶ ἐβάστασας διὰ τὸ ὄνομά μου, καὶ οὐ κεκοπίακες. 4 ἀλλὰ ἔχω κατὰ σοῦ ὅτι τὴν ἀγάπην σου τὴν πρώτην ἀφῆκες. 5 μνημόνευε οὖν πόθεν πέπτωκας, καὶ μετανόησον καὶ τὰ πρῶτα ἔργα ποίησον· εἰ δὲ μή, ἔρχομαί σοι καὶ κινήσω τὴν λυχνίαν σου ἐκ τοῦ τόπου αὐτῆς, ἐὰν μὴ μετανοήσῃς. 6 ἀλλὰ τοῦτο ἔχεις, ὅτι μισεῖς τὰ ἔργα τῶν Νικολαϊτῶν, ἃ κἀγὼ μισῶ. 7 ὁ ἔχων οὖς ἀκουσάτω τί τὸ πνεῦμα λέγει ταῖς ἐκκλησίαις.[a] τῷ νικῶντι δώσω αὐτῷ φαγεῖν ἐκ τοῦ ξύλου τῆς ζωῆς, ὅ ἐστιν ἐν τῷ παραδείσῳ τοῦ θεοῦ.

The Message to Smyrna

8 Καὶ τῷ ἀγγέλῳ τῆς ἐν Σμύρνῃ ἐκκλησίας γράψον·

Τάδε λέγει ὁ πρῶτος καὶ ὁ ἔσχατος, ὃς ἐγένετο νεκρὸς καὶ ἔζησεν· 9 Οἶδά σου τὴν θλῖψιν καὶ τὴν πτωχείαν,

---

[1] 2 {C} κόπον A C P 94 1854 2053 2073 it[ar,c,dem,div,gig,haf,t,z] vg syr[h] Tyconius Jerome Augustine Oecumenius Primasius Andrew[a,bav] ‖ κόπον σου א 046 1 1006 1611 1828 1859 2020 2042 2065 2081 2138 2344 2432 syr[ph] cop[sa,bo] arm eth Andrew[c,p] Arethas ‖ κόπους σου cop[bomss]

[a] 7 a major: WH Bov Nes BF[2] RV ASV RSV TT ‖ a minor: TR AV Zür Jer Seg ‖ a exclamation: NEB Luth

---

1 ἑπτὰ ἀστέρας Re 1.16, 20; 3.1   2 Οἶδα τὰ ἔργα σου Re 3.1, 8, 15   ἐπείρασας... ἀποστόλους 1 Jn 4.1   5 μετανόησον Re 2.16, 22; 3.3, 19   6 μισεῖς...μισῶ Ps 139.21   7 τοῦ ξύλου τῆς ζωῆς Gn 2.9; 3.22, 24; Re 22.2, 14   τῷ παραδείσῳ τοῦ θεοῦ Gn 2.8 lxx; Eze 28.13 lxx; 31.8, 9 lxx   8 ὁ πρῶτος...ἔσχατος Is 44.6; 48.12; Re 1.17; 22.13   9 τὴν πτωχείαν...εἰ Jas 2.5

The Message to Ephesus

2 "To the angel of the church in Ephesus write:

"This is the message from the one who holds the seven stars in his right hand, who walks among the seven gold lampstands. 2 I know what you have done; I know how hard you have worked and how patient you have been. I know that you cannot tolerate evil men, and that you have tested those who say they are apostles but are not, and have found out that they are liars. 3 You are patient, you have suffered troubles for my sake, and you have not given up. 4 But here is what I have against you: you do not love me now as you did at first. 5 Remember how far you have fallen! Turn from your sins and do what you did at first. If you don't turn from your sins, I will come to you and take your lampstand from its place. 6 But here is what you have in your favor: you hate what the Nicolaitans do, as much as I.

7 "If you have ears, then, listen to what the Spirit says to the churches!

"To those who have won the victory I will give the right to eat the fruit of the tree of life that grows in the Garden of God."

The Message to Smyrna

8 "To the angel of the church in Smyrna write:

"This is the message from the one who is the first and the last, who died and lived again. 9 I know your troubles; I know that you are poor — but really you are rich! I know the evil things said against you by those who claim to be Jews, but are not; they are a group that belongs to Satan! [10] Do not be afraid of anything you are about to suffer. Listen! The Devil will put you to the test by having some of you thrown into prison; your troubles will last ten days. Be faithful until death, and I will give you the crown of life.

[11] "If you have ears, then, listen to what the Spirit says to the churches!

"Those who win the victory will not be hurt by the second death."

The Message to Pergamum

[12] "To the angel of the church in Pergamum write:

"This is the message from the one who has the sharp two-edged sword. [13] I know where you live, there where Satan has his throne. You are true to me, and you did not abandon your faith in me even during the time when Antipas, a faithful

ἀλλὰ πλούσιος εἶ, καὶ τὴν βλασφημίαν ἐκ τῶν λεγόντων Ἰουδαίους εἶναι ἑαυτούς, καὶ οὐκ εἰσὶν ἀλλὰ συναγωγὴ τοῦ Σατανᾶ. **10** μηδὲν[2] φοβοῦ ἃ μέλλεις πάσχειν. ἰδοὺ μέλλει βάλλειν ὁ διάβολος ἐξ ὑμῶν εἰς φυλακὴν ἵνα πειρασθῆτε, καὶ ἕξετε[3] θλῖψιν ἡμερῶν δέκα. γίνου πιστὸς ἄχρι θανάτου, καὶ δώσω σοι τὸν στέφανον τῆς ζωῆς. **11** ὁ ἔχων οὖς ἀκουσάτω τί τὸ πνεῦμα λέγει ταῖς ἐκκλησίαις.[b] ὁ νικῶν οὐ μὴ ἀδικηθῇ ἐκ τοῦ θανάτου τοῦ δευτέρου.

The Message to Pergamum

12 Καὶ τῷ ἀγγέλῳ τῆς ἐν Περγάμῳ ἐκκλησίας γράψον·

Τάδε λέγει ὁ ἔχων τὴν ῥομφαίαν τὴν δίστομον τὴν ὀξεῖαν· **13** Οἶδα ποῦ κατοικεῖς, ὅπου ὁ θρόνος τοῦ Σατανᾶ, καὶ κρατεῖς τὸ ὄνομά μου, καὶ οὐκ ἠρνήσω τὴν πίστιν μου καὶ[4] ἐν ταῖς ἡμέραις[5] Ἀντιπᾶς[c] ὁ μάρτυς μου[c]

[2] **10** {C} μηδέν ℵ P 1 94 1006 1611 1828 1854 1859 2042 2053 2065 2073 2081 2138 2344 2432 it[ar,c,dem,div,gig,haf,t,z] vg syr[ph,h] cop[sa] Cyprian Primasius Andrew[a,bav,c] Arethas // μή A C 046 2020 cop[bo] arm eth Andrew[p]

[3] **10** {C} καὶ ἕξετε ℵ 046 94 1006 1611 1828 1859 2020 2042 2138 it[ar,c,dem,div,haf,t,z] vg syr[ph,h] cop[bomss] arm Tyconius Andrew[a,c,p] Haymo Arethas // καὶ ἕξητε 88 110 627 2048 2074 // καὶ ἔχετε C 1 2053 2073 2081 cop[sa] Andrew[mss] // καὶ ἔχητε A P 1854 2065 2344 2432 cop[bo] Primasius Andrew[bav] // omit καὶ ἕξετε θλῖψιν it[gig]

[4] **13** {C} πίστιν μου καί A C 1854 2053 2344 it[ar,c,div,haf,zvid] vg syr[ph] cop[sa,bo] Bede Haymo // πίστιν μου ℵ P 046 1 (94 omit μου) 1006 1611 1828 1859 2020 2042 2065 2073 2081 2138 2432 it[dem,gig,t] syr[h] arm eth Ambrosiaster Primasius Andrew Arethas

[5] **13** {C} ἡμέραις A C 2053 2065 2344 it[ar,c,div,haf,z] vg[(cl),ww] syr[ph] cop[sa,bo] Tyconius Primasius Haymo // ἡμέραις αἷς 046 94 (1006* ἡμέραις αἵ) 1006[c]

[b] **11** b major: WH Bov Nes BF[2] RV ASV RSV TT // b minor: TR AV Zür Jer // b exclamation: NEB Luth Seg

[c] **13** c none, c none: TR Bov Nes BF[2] AV // c minor, c minor: WH // c minor, c none: NEB Zür Luth Jer Seg // c none, c minor: RV ASV RSV (TT)

9 τῶν...Σατανᾶ 2 Cor 11.14, 15; Re 3.9 **10** πειρασθῆτε...δέκα Dn 1.12, 14 τὸν...ζωῆς Jas 1.12 **11** τοῦ θανάτου τοῦ δευτέρου Re 20.14; 21.8 **12** τὴν ῥομφαίαν...ὀξεῖαν Is 49.2; He 4.12; Re 1.16; 2.16; 19.5

ὁ πιστός μου, ὃς ἀπεκτάνθη παρ' ὑμῖν, ὅπου ὁ Σατανᾶς κατοικεῖ. 14 ἀλλ' ἔχω κατὰ σοῦ ὀλίγα, ὅτι ἔχεις ἐκεῖ κρατοῦντας τὴν διδαχὴν Βαλαάμ, ὃς ἐδίδασκεν τῷ Βαλὰκ βαλεῖν σκάνδαλον ἐνώπιον τῶν υἱῶν Ἰσραήλ, φαγεῖν εἰδωλόθυτα καὶ πορνεῦσαι· 15 οὕτως ἔχεις καὶ σὺ κρατοῦντας τὴν διδαχὴν Νικολαϊτῶν ὁμοίως. 16 μετανόησον οὖν· εἰ δὲ μή, ἔρχομαί σοι ταχύ, καὶ πολεμήσω μετ' αὐτῶν ἐν τῇ ῥομφαίᾳ τοῦ στόματός μου. 17 ὁ ἔχων οὖς ἀκουσάτω τί τὸ πνεῦμα λέγει ταῖς ἐκκλησίαις.[d] τῷ νικῶντι δώσω αὐτῷ τοῦ μάννα τοῦ κεκρυμμένου, καὶ δώσω αὐτῷ ψῆφον λευκὴν καὶ ἐπὶ τὴν ψῆφον ὄνομα καινὸν γεγραμμένον ὃ οὐδεὶς οἶδεν εἰ μὴ ὁ λαμβάνων.

The Message to Thyatira

18 Καὶ τῷ ἀγγέλῳ τῆς ἐν Θυατίροις ἐκκλησίας γράψον·

Τάδε λέγει ὁ υἱὸς τοῦ θεοῦ, ὁ ἔχων τοὺς ὀφθαλμοὺς αὐτοῦ ὡς φλόγα πυρός, καὶ οἱ πόδες αὐτοῦ ὅμοιοι χαλκολιβάνῳ· 19 Οἶδά σου τὰ ἔργα καὶ τὴν ἀγάπην καὶ τὴν πίστιν καὶ τὴν διακονίαν καὶ τὴν ὑπομονήν σου, καὶ τὰ ἔργα σου τὰ ἔσχατα πλείονα τῶν πρώτων. 20 ἀλλὰ ἔχω κατὰ σοῦ ὅτι ἀφεῖς τὴν γυναῖκα[b] Ἰεζάβελ, ἡ λέγουσα ἑαυτὴν προφῆτιν, καὶ διδάσκει καὶ πλανᾷ τοὺς ἐμοὺς δούλους πορνεῦσαι καὶ φαγεῖν εἰδωλόθυτα. 21 καὶ ἔδωκα αὐτῇ χρόνον ἵνα μετανοήσῃ, καὶ οὐ θέλει μετανοῆσαι ἐκ

1828 1859 2020 2042 2138 it^{dem} syr^h eth ‖ ἡμέραις ἐν αἷς (א* ταῖς) א^a P 1 1611 1854 2073 2081 2432 it^{gig,(t)} arm Andrew Arethas

[b] 20 {C} γυναῖκα א C P 1 1611 2020 2053 2081 2344 it^{ar,c,dem,div,gig,haf,t,z} vg cop^{sa,bo} arm eth Tertullian Ambrosiaster Tyconius Epiphanius Andrew^{bav} Haymo ‖ γυναῖκά σου (A add τήν) 046 94 1006 1828 1854 1859 2042 2065 2073 2138 2432 syr^{ph,h} Cyprian Primasius Andrew^{a,c,p} Arethas

---

[d] 17 d major: WH Bov Nes BF² RV ASV RSV TT ‖ d minor: TR AV Zür Jer ‖ d exclamation: NEB Luth Seg

---

14 τὴν...πορνεῦσαι Nu 31.16; 25.1–2; Jd 11   16 ἔρχομαί σοι ταχύ Re 3.11; 22.7, 12, 20 τῇ...μου Is 49.2; Re 1.12; 2.16; 19.5   17 τοῦ μάννα τοῦ κεκρυμμένου Ps 78.24 ὄνομα καινόν Is 62.2; 65.15; Re 3.12   18 τούς...χαλκολιβάνῳ Dn 10.6; Re 1.14–15; 19.12   20 Ἰεζάβελ... εἰδωλόθυτα 1 Kgs 16.31; 2 Kgs 9.22   πορνεῦσαι...εἰδωλόθυτα Nu 25.1–2; Re 2.14

---

witness for me, was killed there where Satan lives. 14 But here are a few things I have against you: there with you are some who follow the teaching of Balaam, who taught Balak how to cause the people of Israel to sin by eating food that had been offered to idols, and by committing immorality. 15 In the same way, you also have people among you who follow the teaching of the Nicolaitans. 16 Turn from your sins, then! If not, I will come to you soon and fight against those people with the sword that comes out of my mouth.

17 "If you have ears, then, listen to what the Spirit says to the churches!

"To those who have won the victory I will give some of the hidden manna. I will also give each of them a white stone, on which a new name is written, which no one knows except the one who receives it."

The Message to Thyatira

18 "To the angel of the church in Thyatira write:

"This is the message from the Son of God, whose eyes blaze like fire, whose feet shine like polished brass. 19 I know what you do. I know your love, your faithfulness, your service, and your patience. I know that you are doing more now than you did at first. 20 But here is what I have against you: you tolerate that woman Jezebel, who calls herself a messenger of God. She teaches and misleads my servants into committing immorality and eating food that has been offered to idols. 21 I have given her time to turn from her sins, but she does not wish to turn from her immorality.

²² Therefore I will throw her on a bed where she and those who committed adultery with her will suffer terribly. I will do this now, unless they repent from the wicked things they did with her. ²³ I will also kill her children, and then all the churches will know that I am he who knows men's thoughts and wishes. I will repay each one of you according to what you have done.

²⁴ "But the rest of you in Thyatira have not followed this evil teaching; you have not learned what the others call 'the deep secrets of Satan.' I say to you that I will not put any other burden on you. ²⁵ But you must hold firmly to what you have until I come. ²⁶⁻²⁸ To those who win the victory, who continue to do what I want until the very end, I will give the same authority which I received from my Father: I will give them authority over the nations, to rule them with an iron rod and to break them to pieces like clay pots. I will also give them the morning star.

²⁹ "If you have ears, then, listen to what the Spirit says to the churches!"

τῆς πορνείας αὐτῆς. **22** ἰδοὺ βάλλω αὐτὴν εἰς κλίνην⁷, καὶ τοὺς μοιχεύοντας μετ' αὐτῆς εἰς θλῖψιν μεγάλην, ἐὰν μὴ μετανοήσωσιν ἐκ τῶν ἔργων αὐτῆς⁸·ᵉ **23** καὶ τὰ τέκνα αὐτῆς ἀποκτενῶ ἐν θανάτῳ·ᵉ καὶ γνώσονται πᾶσαι αἱ ἐκκλησίαι ὅτι ἐγώ εἰμι ὁ ἐραυνῶν νεφροὺς καὶ καρδίας, καὶ δώσω ὑμῖν ἑκάστῳ κατὰ τὰ ἔργα ὑμῶν⁹. **24** ὑμῖν δὲ λέγω τοῖς λοιποῖς τοῖς ἐν Θυατίροις, ὅσοι οὐκ ἔχουσιν τὴν διδαχὴν ταύτην, οἵτινες οὐκ ἔγνωσαν τὰ βαθέα τοῦ Σατανᾶ, ὡς λέγουσιν, οὐ βάλλω ἐφ' ὑμᾶς ἄλλο βάρος· **25** πλὴν ὃ ἔχετε κρατήσατε ἄχρις οὗ ἂν ἥξω. **26** καὶ ὁ νικῶν καὶ ὁ τηρῶν ἄχρι τέλους τὰ ἔργα μου,

    δώσω αὐτῷ ἐξουσίαν ἐπὶ **τῶν ἐθνῶν,**

27   καὶ **ποιμανεῖ αὐτοὺς ἐν ῥάβδῳ σιδηρᾷ,**ᶠ

      ὡς τὰ σκεύη τὰ κεραμικὰ συντρίβεται,ᶠ

28ᵍ ὡς κἀγὼ εἴληφα παρὰ τοῦ πατρός μου,ᶠ ᵍκαὶ δώσω αὐτῷ τὸν ἀστέρα τὸν πρωϊνόν. **29** ὁ ἔχων οὖς ἀκουσάτω τί τὸ πνεῦμα λέγει ταῖς ἐκκλησίαις.

---

⁷ **22** {A} κλίνην ℵ C P 046 1 94 1006 1611 1828 1854 1859 2020 2042 2053 2065 2073 2081 2138 2344 2432 itᵃʳ,ᶜ,ᵈᵉᵐ,ᵈⁱᵛ,ᵍⁱᵍ,ʰᵃᶠ,ᵗ,ᶻ vg syrᵖʰ,ʰ copᵇᵒ eth? ‖ φυλακήν A ‖ κλίβανον 2071 arm ‖ ἀσθένειαν 1597 copˢᵃ ‖ luctum mssᵃᶜᶜ· to Primasius

⁸ **22** {B} ἔργων αὐτῆς ℵ C P 046 94 1006 1611 1828 1859 2020 2042 2053 2138 itᵍⁱᵍ,ᶻ vgʷʷ syrʰ copˢᵃ,ᵇᵒ Tertullian Cyprian Primasius Andrewᶜ Haymo Arethas ‖ ἔργων αὐτῶν A 1 1854 2065 2073 2081 2344 itᵃʳ,ᶜ,ᵈᵉᵐ,ᵈⁱᵛ,ʰᵃᶠ,ᵗ vgᶜˡ syrᵖʰ arm eth Primasius Ambrosiaster Andrewᵃ,ᵇᵃᵛ,ᵖ ‖ ἔργου αὐτοῦ 2432 ‖ omit ἐκ τῶν ἔργων αὐτῆς copᵇᵒᵐˢˢ

⁹ **23** {B} ὑμῶν ℵᶜ A C P 1 94 1006 1611 1828 1854 1859 2042 2053 2065 2073 2081 2138 2344 itᶜ,ᵈᵉᵐ,ᵈⁱᵛ,ᵍⁱᵍ,ᵗ,ᶻ vgʷʷ syrᵖʰ,ʰ eth Primasius Andrew Haymo Arethas ‖ ἡμῶν 2432 ‖ αὐτῶν 1626 2058 arm ‖ αὐτοῦ 046 2020 itᵃʳ,ʰᵃᶠ vgᶜˡ copˢᵃ,ᵇᵒ Cyprian Ambrosiaster ‖ omit ℵ*

ᵉ ᵉ **22–23** e minor, e minor: WH Bov Nes BF² ‖ e minor, e major: TR RSV NEB Luth ‖ e major, e minor: AV RV ASV TT Zür Jer Seg

ᶠ ᶠ **27–28** f minor, f minor, f minor: (WH) Bov Nes BF² ‖ f minor, f minor, f major: TR AV RV ASV RSV TT Luth Seg ‖ f major, f minor, f major: RVᵐᵍ ASVᵐᵍ ‖ f none, f exclamation, f major: Jer ‖ f minor, f dash, f dash: (NEB) Zür

ᵍ ᵍ **27–28** g number 28, g no number: TRᵉᵈ WH Bov Nes BF² TT Zür Luth Jer Segᵉᵈ ‖ g no number, g number 28: TRᵉᵈ AV RV ASV RSV NEB Segᵉᵈ

23 ὁ...καρδίας Ps 7.9; Pr 24.12; Jr 11.20; 17.10   δώσω...ὑμῶν Ps 62.12; Pr 24.12; Jr 17.10; Ro 2.6; 2 Tm 4.14; Re 18.6; 20.12, 13   **25** ὃ ἔχετε κρατήσατε Re 3.11   **26–27** δώσω... συντρίβεται Ps 2.8, 9; Ps Sol 17.23–24; Re 12.5   **28** τὸν ἀστέρα τὸν πρωϊνόν Re 22.16

The Message to Sardis

3 Καὶ τῷ ἀγγέλῳ τῆς ἐν Σάρδεσιν ἐκκλησίας γράψον·

Τάδε λέγει ὁ ἔχων τὰ ἑπτὰ πνεύματα τοῦ θεοῦ καὶ τοὺς ἑπτὰ ἀστέρας· Οἶδά σου τὰ ἔργα, ὅτι ὄνομα ἔχεις ὅτι ζῇς, καὶ νεκρὸς εἶ. 2 γίνου γρηγορῶν, καὶ στήρισον τὰ λοιπὰ ἃ ἔμελλον ἀποθανεῖν, οὐ γὰρ εὕρηκά σου [τὰ] ἔργα[1] πεπληρωμένα ἐνώπιον τοῦ θεοῦ μου· 3 μνημόνευε οὖν πῶς εἴληφας καὶ ἤκουσας, καὶ τήρει, καὶ μετανόησον. ἐὰν οὖν μὴ γρηγορήσῃς, ἥξω ὡς κλέπτης, καὶ οὐ μὴ γνῷς ποίαν ὥραν ἥξω ἐπὶ σέ. 4 ἀλλὰ ἔχεις ὀλίγα ὀνόματα ἐν Σάρδεσιν ἃ οὐκ ἐμόλυναν τὰ ἱμάτια αὐτῶν, καὶ περιπατήσουσιν μετ᾽ ἐμοῦ ἐν λευκοῖς, ὅτι ἄξιοί εἰσιν. 5 ὁ νικῶν οὕτως[2] περιβαλεῖται ἐν ἱματίοις λευκοῖς, καὶ οὐ μὴ ἐξαλείψω τὸ ὄνομα αὐτοῦ ἐκ τῆς βίβλου τῆς ζωῆς, καὶ ὁμολογήσω τὸ ὄνομα αὐτοῦ ἐνώπιον τοῦ πατρός μου καὶ ἐνώπιον τῶν ἀγγέλων αὐτοῦ. 6 ὁ ἔχων οὖς ἀκουσάτω τί τὸ πνεῦμα λέγει ταῖς ἐκκλησίαις.

The Message to Philadelphia

7 Καὶ τῷ ἀγγέλῳ τῆς ἐν Φιλαδελφείᾳ ἐκκλησίας γράψον·

Τάδε λέγει ὁ ἅγιος, ὁ ἀληθινός,
  ὁ ἔχων **τὴν κλεῖν Δαυίδ,**
  ὁ ἀνοίγων καὶ οὐδεὶς κλείσει,
  καὶ κλείων καὶ οὐδεὶς ἀνοίγει·

---

1 2 {C} τὰ ἔργα ℵ Γ 040 94 1006 1611 1828 1854 1859 2020 2042 2053 2065 2073 2138 2432 Andrew Arethas ‖ ἔργα A C 1[mg] arm ‖ τὰ ἔργα *or* ἔργα it[ar,c,dem,div,gig,haf,t,z] vg syr[ph,h] cop[sa,bo] ‖ *omit* 2344

2 5 {C} οὕτως ℵ* (A οὕτω) C 94 1006 1859 2065 2138 2344 2432 it[ar,c,dem, div,gig,haf,t,z] vg syr[ph,h] cop[sa,bo] arm eth Primasius ‖ οὗτος ℵ[c] P 046 1 1611 1828 1854 2020 2042 2053 2073 2081 Andrew Arethas

1 τὰ…θεοῦ Re 1.4; 4.5; 5.6   τοὺς ἑπτὰ ἀστέρας Re 1.16, 20; 2.1   Οἶδα…ἔργα Re 2.2; 3.8, 15   **3** μετανόησον Re 2.5, 16, 22; 3.19   ἥξω ὡς κλέπτης…ἐπὶ σέ Mt 24.43–44; Lk 12.39–40; 1 Th 5.2, 4; 2 Pe 3.10; Re 16.15   **4** οὐκ ἐμόλυναν…αὐτῶν Jd 23   **5** ἐν ἱματίοις λευκοῖς Re 3.18; 4.4; 6.11; 7.9, 13; 19.14   οὐ…ζωῆς Ex 32.32, 33; Ps 69.28; Re 17.8; 20.15   τῆς βίβλου τῆς ζωῆς Ex 32.32, 33; Ps 69.28; Dn 12.1; Php 4.3; Re 13.8; 17.8; 20.12, 15; 21.27   ὁμολογήσω…ἀγγέλων αὐτοῦ Mt 10.32; Lk 12.8   **7** ὁ ἔχων…ἀνοίγει Is 22.22; Job 12.14

The Message to Sardis

3 "To the angel of the church in Sardis write:

"This is the message from the one who has the seven spirits of God and the seven stars. I know what you are doing; I know that you have the reputation of being alive, even though you are dead! [2] So wake up, and strengthen what you still have, before it dies completely. For I find that what you have done is not yet perfect in the sight of my God. [3] Remember, then, what you were taught and how you heard it; obey it, and turn from your sins. If you do not wake up, I will come upon you like a thief, and you will not even know the hour when I come. [4] But a few of you there in Sardis have kept your clothes clean. You will walk with me, clothed in white, for you are worthy to do so. [5] Those who win the victory will be clothed like this in white, and I will not remove their names from the book of the living. In the presence of my Father and of his angels I will declare openly that they belong to me.

[6] "If you have ears, then, listen to what the Spirit says to the churches!"

The Message to Philadelphia

[7] "To the angel of the church in Philadelphia write:

"This is the message from the one who is holy and true, who holds the key that belonged to David, who opens so that none can close, who closes so that none can open. ⁸ I know what you do; I know that you have a little power; you have followed my teaching and have been faithful to me. I have opened a door before you, which no one can close. ⁹ Listen! As for that group that belongs to Satan, those liars who claim that they are Jews, but are not, I will make them come before you and fall down and worship you. They will all know that I love you. ¹⁰ Because you have kept my order to be patient, I will also keep you safe from the time of trouble which is coming upon the whole world, to test all the people on earth. ¹¹ I am coming soon. Keep safe what you have, so that no one will rob you of your victory prize. ¹² I will make him who is victorious a pillar in the temple of my God, and he will never again leave it. I will write on him the name of my God, and the name of the city of my God, the new Jerusalem, which will come down out of heaven from my God. I will also write on him my new name.

¹³ "If you have ears, then, listen to what the Spirit says to the churches!"

The Message to Laodicea

¹⁴ "To the angel of the church in Laodicea write:

"This is the message from the Amen, the faithful and true witness, who is the origin of all that God has created. ¹⁵ I know what you have done; I know that you are neither cold nor hot. How I wish you were either one or the other! ¹⁶ But because you are barely warm, neither hot

8 Οἶδά σου τὰ ἔργα —ᵃ ἰδοὺ δέδωκα ἐνώπιόν σου θύραν ἠνεῳγμένην, ἣν οὐδεὶς δύναται κλεῖσαι αὐτήν —ᵃ ὅτι μικρὰν ἔχεις δύναμιν, καὶ ἐτήρησάς μου τὸν λόγον, καὶ οὐκ ἠρνήσω τὸ ὄνομά μου. 9 ἰδοὺ διδῶ ἐκ τῆς συναγωγῆς τοῦ Σατανᾶ, τῶν λεγόντων ἑαυτοὺς Ἰουδαίους εἶναι, καὶ οὐκ εἰσὶν ἀλλὰ ψεύδονται·ᵇ ἰδοὺ ποιήσω αὐτοὺς ἵνα ἥξουσιν καὶ προσκυνήσουσιν ἐνώπιον τῶν ποδῶν σου, καὶ γνῶσιν ὅτι ἐγὼ ἠγάπησά σε. 10 ὅτι ἐτήρησας τὸν λόγον τῆς ὑπομονῆς μου, κἀγώ σε τηρήσω ἐκ τῆς ὥρας τοῦ πειρασμοῦ τῆς μελλούσης ἔρχεσθαι ἐπὶ τῆς οἰκουμένης ὅλης πειράσαι τοὺς κατοικοῦντας ἐπὶ τῆς γῆς. 11 ἔρχομαι ταχύ· κράτει ὃ ἔχεις, ἵνα μηδεὶς λάβῃ τὸν στέφανόν σου. 12 ὁ νικῶν ποιήσω αὐτὸν στῦλον ἐν τῷ ναῷ τοῦ θεοῦ μου, καὶ ἔξω οὐ μὴ ἐξέλθῃ ἔτι, καὶ γράψω ἐπ᾽ αὐτὸν τὸ ὄνομα τοῦ θεοῦ μου καὶ τὸ ὄνομα τῆς πόλεως τοῦ θεοῦ μου, τῆς καινῆς Ἰερουσαλήμ, ἡ καταβαίνουσα ἐκ τοῦ οὐρανοῦ ἀπὸ τοῦ θεοῦ μου, καὶ τὸ ὄνομά μου τὸ καινόν. 13 ὁ ἔχων οὖς ἀκουσάτω τί τὸ πνεῦμα λέγει ταῖς ἐκκλησίαις.

The Message to Laodicea

14 Καὶ τῷ ἀγγέλῳ τῆς ἐν Λαοδικείᾳ ἐκκλησίας γράψον·

Τάδε λέγει ὁ ᾿Αμήν, ὁ μάρτυς ὁ πιστὸς καὶ ἀληθινός, ἡ ἀρχὴ τῆς κτίσεως τοῦ θεοῦ. 15 Οἶδά σου τὰ ἔργα, ὅτι οὔτε ψυχρὸς εἶ οὔτε ζεστός. ὄφελον ψυχρὸς ἦς ἢ ζεστός. 16 οὕτως, ὅτι χλιαρὸς εἶ καὶ οὔτε ζεστὸς οὔτε

ᵃ ᵃ 8 a dash, a dash: WH ∥ a parens, a parens: RV ASV ∥ a major, a major: TR Bov Nes BF² AV TT ∥ a major, a minor: RSV Zür Luth Jer Seg ∥ a minor, a major: NEB
ᵇ 9 b major: TR Bov Nes BF² AV RV ASV (NEB) Luth Seg ∥ b dash: WH RSV TT Zür Jer

8 Οἶδα...ἔργα Re 2.22; 3.1, 15   ἰδού..ἠνεῳγμένην 1 Cor 16.9   9 τῆς συναγωγῆς τοῦ Σατανᾶ 2 Cor 11.14, 15; Re 2.9   ἥξουσιν...σου Is 45.14; 49.23; 60.14   ἐγὼ ἠγάπησά σε Is 43.4   10 Lk 21.19; 2 Tm 2.12; He 10.36   11 ἔρχομαι ταχύ Re 2.16; 22.7, 12, 20   12 γράψω...μου Re 14.1; 22.4   τὸ ὄνομα τῆς πόλεως Eze 48.35   τῆς καινῆς...μου Re 21.2   τὸ ὄνομα...καινόν Is 62.2; 65.15   14 ὁ μάρτυς ὁ πιστός Re 1.5; 19.11   ἡ...θεοῦ Pr 8.22; Jn 1.3; Col 1.15   15 Οἶδα ...ἔργα Re 2.2; 3.1, 8

ψυχρός, μέλλω σε ἐμέσαι ἐκ τοῦ στόματός μου.ᶜ **17** ὅτι λέγεις ὅτι Πλούσιός εἰμι καὶ πεπλούτηκα καὶ οὐδὲν χρείαν ἔχω, καὶ οὐκ οἶδας ὅτι σὺ εἶ ὁ ταλαίπωρος καὶ ἐλεεινὸς καὶ πτωχὸς καὶ τυφλὸς καὶ γυμνός,ᶜ **18** συμβουλεύω σοι ἀγοράσαι παρ' ἐμοῦ χρυσίον πεπυρωμένον ἐκ πυρὸς ἵνα πλουτήσῃς, καὶ ἱμάτια λευκὰ ἵνα περιβάλῃ καὶ μὴ φανερωθῇ ἡ αἰσχύνη τῆς γυμνότητός σου, καὶ κολλούριον ἐγχρῖσαι τοὺς ὀφθαλμούς σου ἵνα βλέπῃς. **19** ἐγὼ ὅσους ἐὰν φιλῶ ἐλέγχω καὶ παιδεύω· ζήλευε οὖν καὶ μετανόησον. **20** ἰδοὺ ἕστηκα ἐπὶ τὴν θύραν καὶ κρούω· ἐάν τις ἀκούσῃ τῆς φωνῆς μου καὶ ἀνοίξῃ τὴν θύραν, εἰσελεύσομαι πρὸς αὐτὸν καὶ δειπνήσω μετ' αὐτοῦ καὶ αὐτὸς μετ' ἐμοῦ. **21** ὁ νικῶν δώσω αὐτῷ καθίσαι μετ' ἐμοῦ ἐν τῷ θρόνῳ μου, ὡς κἀγὼ ἐνίκησα καὶ ἐκάθισα μετὰ τοῦ πατρός μου ἐν τῷ θρόνῳ αὐτοῦ. **22** ὁ ἔχων οὖς ἀκουσάτω τί τὸ πνεῦμα λέγει ταῖς ἐκκλησίαις.

The Heavenly Worship

4 Μετὰ ταῦτα εἶδον, καὶ ἰδοὺ θύρα ἠνεῳγμένη ἐν τῷ οὐρανῷ, καὶ ἡ φωνὴ ἡ πρώτη ἣν ἤκουσα ὡς σάλπιγγος λαλούσης μετ' ἐμοῦ λέγων, Ἀνάβα ὧδε, καὶ δείξω σοι ἃ δεῖ γενέσθαιᵃ μετὰ ταῦτα.ᵃ **2** εὐθέως ἐγενόμην ἐν πνεύματι· καὶ ἰδοὺ θρόνος ἔκειτο ἐν τῷ οὐρανῷ, καὶ ἐπὶ τὸν θρόνον καθήμενος, **3** καὶ ὁ καθήμενος ὅμοιος ὁράσει λίθῳ ἰάσπιδι καὶ σαρδίῳ, καὶ ἶρις κυκλόθεν τοῦ

ᶜ ᶜ **16-17** c major, c minor: WH Bov Nes BF² AV RV ASV TT Zür Seg ‖ c minor, c major: TR ‖ c major, c major: RSV NEB Luth ‖ c major, c exclamation: Jer

ᵃ ᵃ **1-2** a none, a major: TR Bov Nes BF² AV RV ASV RSV NEB TT Zür Luth Jer Seg ‖ a major, a none: WH RVᵐᵍ ASVᵐᵍ

---

17 λέγεις...πεπλούτηκα Ho 12.8   **18** ἱμάτια λευκά Re 3.5; 4.4; 6.11; 7.9, 13; 19.14   ἱμάτια...γυμνότητός σου Re 16.15   **19** ἐγὼ...παιδεύω Pr 3.12; 1 Cor 11.32; He 12.6   μετανόησον Ro 2.5, 16, 22; 3.3   **20** εἰσελεύσομαι πρὸς αὐτόν Jn 14.23

4 1 Ἀνάβα ὧδε Ex 19.20, 24   δείξω...γενέσθαι Dn 2.28, 29, 45; Re 1.1, 19   **2** θρόνος... καθήμενος 1 Kgs 22.19; 2 Chr 18.18; Ps 47.8; Is 6.1; Eze 1.26-27; Sir 1.8; Re 4.9; 5.1, 7, 13; 6.16   7.10, 15; 19.4; 21.5   **3** Eze 1.26-28

---

nor cold, I am about to spit you out of my mouth! **17** 'I am rich and well off,' you say, 'I have all I need.' But you do not know how miserable and pitiful you are! You are poor, naked, and blind. **18** I advise you, then, to buy gold from me, pure gold, in order to be rich. Buy also white clothing to dress yourself and cover up your shameful nakedness. Buy also some medicine to put on your eyes, so that you may see. **19** I reprove and punish all whom I love. Be in earnest, then, and turn from your sins. **20** Listen! I stand at the door and knock; if anyone hears my voice and opens the door, I will come into his house and eat with him, and he will eat with me. **21** To those who win the victory I will give the right to sit by me on my throne, just as I have been victorious, and now sit by my Father on his throne.

22 "If you have ears, then, listen to what the Spirit says to the churches!"

Worship in Heaven

4 At this point I had another vision, and saw an open door in heaven.

And the voice that sounded like a trumpet, which I had heard speaking to me before, said, "Come up here, and I will show you what must happen after this." **2** At once the Spirit took control of me. There in heaven was a throne, with someone sitting on it. **3** His face gleamed like such precious stones as jasper and carnelian; all around the throne there was a rainbow the color of an emerald.

⁴ In a circle around the throne were twenty-four other thrones, on which were seated twenty-four elders dressed in white, and wearing gold crowns. ⁵ From the throne came flashes of lightning, and sounds, and peals of thunder. There were seven lighted torches burning before the throne; these are the seven spirits of God. ⁶ In front of the throne there was what looked like a sea of glass, clear as crystal.

Surrounding the throne, on each of its sides, were four living creatures covered with eyes in front and in back. ⁷ The first living creature looked like a lion; the second looked like a calf; the third had a face like a man's face; and the fourth looked like a flying eagle. ⁸ Each one of the four living creatures had six wings, and they were covered over with eyes, inside and out. They never stop their singing day or night:

"Holy, holy, holy, is the Lord God Almighty,
Who was, who is, and who is to come."

θρόνου ὅμοιος ὁράσει σμαραγδίνῳ. 4 καὶ κυκλόθεν τοῦ θρόνου θρόνους εἴκοσι τέσσαρες, καὶ ἐπὶ τοὺς θρόνους εἴκοσι τέσσαρας πρεσβυτέρους καθημένους περιβεβλημένους ἐν ἱματίοις λευκοῖς, καὶ ἐπὶ τὰς κεφαλὰς αὐτῶν στεφάνους χρυσοῦς. 5 καὶ ἐκ τοῦ θρόνου ἐκπορεύονται ἀστραπαὶ καὶ φωναὶ καὶ βρονταί· καὶ ἑπτὰ λαμπάδες πυρὸς καιόμεναι ἐνώπιον τοῦ θρόνου, ἅ εἰσιν τὰ ἑπτὰ πνεύματα τοῦ θεοῦ, 6 καὶ ἐνώπιον τοῦ θρόνου ὡς θάλασσα ὑαλίνη ὁμοία κρυστάλλῳ.

Καὶ ἐν μέσῳ τοῦ θρόνου καὶ κύκλῳ τοῦ θρόνου τέσσαρα ζῷα γέμοντα ὀφθαλμῶν ἔμπροσθεν καὶ ὄπισθεν· 7 καὶ τὸ ζῷον τὸ πρῶτον ὅμοιον λέοντι, καὶ τὸ δεύτερον ζῷον ὅμοιον μόσχῳ, καὶ τὸ τρίτον ζῷον ἔχων τὸ πρόσωπον ὡς ἀνθρώπου¹, καὶ τὸ τέταρτον ζῷον ὅμοιον ἀετῷ πετομένῳ. 8 καὶ τὰ τέσσαρα ζῷα, ἓν καθ' ἓν αὐτῶν ἔχων ἀνὰ πτέρυγας ἕξ, κυκλόθεν καὶ ἔσωθεν γέμουσιν ὀφθαλμῶν· καὶ ἀνάπαυσιν οὐκ ἔχουσιν ἡμέρας καὶ νυκτὸς λέγοντες,

Ἅγιος ἅγιος ἅγιος
κύριος ᵇ ὁ θεὸς ᵇ ὁ παντοκράτωρ,
ὁ ἦν καὶ ὁ ὢν καὶ ὁ ἐρχόμενος.

---

¹ 7 {C} τὸ πρόσωπον ὡς ἀνθρώπου A (2344 omit τό) itᵃʳ,ᶜ,ᵈᵉᵐ,ᵈⁱᵛ,ʰᵃᶠ,z vg syrᵖʰ copˢᵃᵐˢ? Irenaeusˡᵃᵗ Ps-Ambrose Apringius Primasius Beatus ∥ τὸ πρόσωπον ὡς ἄνθρωπος P 1 (1611* omit τό) 1854 2020 2053 2073 2081 syrʰ Andrewᵃ,ᵇᵃᵛ ∥ πρόσωπον ἀνθρώπου 046 94 1006 1611ᶜ 1828 1859 2042 (2065 2432 τὸ πρόσωπον) 2138 copˢᵃ? arm Irenaeus Andrewᶜ,ᵖ Arethas ∥ ὡς ἀνθρώπου itᵍⁱᵍ,ᵗ ∥ τὸ πρόσωπον ὡς ὅμοιον ἀνθρώπῳ ℵ ∥ πρόσωπον ὡς πρόσωπον υἱοῦ ἀνθρώπου (copᵇᵒ omit first πρόσωπον) eth

ᵇ ᵇ 8 b none, b none: TR Bov Nes BF² AV (RSV) (NEB) ∥ b minor, b minor: WH ∥ b minor, b none: (Zür) Jer ∥ b none, b minor: RV ASV TT Luth Seg

4 ἐπὶ τοὺς...καθημένους Is 24.23 ἱματίοις λευκοῖς Re 3.5, 18; 6.11; 7.9, 13; 19.14   5 ἐκ... βρονταί Ex 19.16; Est 1.1d LXX; Eze 1.13; Re 8.5; 11.19; 16.18   ἑπτὰ λαμπάδες πυρός Eze 1.13; Zch 4.2   ἑπτὰ πνεύματα τοῦ θεοῦ Re 1.4; 5.6   6 ὁμοία κρυστάλλῳ Eze 1.22 6–7 ἐν...πετομένῳ Eze 1.5–10; 10.14   8 τὰ τέσσαρα...πτέρυγας ἕξ Is 6.2   κυκλόθεν... ὀφθαλμῶν Eze 1.18; 10.12   Ἅγιος...κύριος Is 6.3   κύριος...παντοκράτωρ Am 3.13 LXX; 4.13 LXX; Re 1.8; 11.17; 15.3; 16.7, 14; 19.6, 15; 21.22   ὁ ἦν...ἐρχόμενος Is 41.4; Re 1.4, 8 ὁ ὢν Ex 3.14; Re 1.4, 8; 16.5

9 καὶ ὅταν δώσουσιν τὰ ζῷα δόξαν καὶ τιμὴν καὶ εὐχαριστίαν τῷ καθημένῳ ἐπὶ τοῦ θρόνου τῷ ζῶντι εἰς τοὺς αἰῶνας τῶν αἰώνων, **10** πεσοῦνται οἱ εἴκοσι τέσσαρες πρεσβύτεροι ἐνώπιον τοῦ καθημένου ἐπὶ τοῦ θρόνου καὶ προσκυνήσουσιν τῷ ζῶντι εἰς τοὺς αἰῶνας τῶν αἰώνων, καὶ βαλοῦσιν τοὺς στεφάνους αὐτῶν ἐνώπιον τοῦ θρόνου λέγοντες,

11   Ἄξιος εἶ, ὁ κύριος καὶ ὁ θεὸς ἡμῶν,
         λαβεῖν τὴν δόξαν καὶ τὴν τιμὴν καὶ τὴν δύναμιν,
      ὅτι σὺ ἔκτισας τὰ πάντα,
          καὶ διὰ τὸ θέλημά σου ἦσαν καὶ ἐκτίσθησαν.

The Scroll and the Lamb

5 Καὶ εἶδον ἐπὶ τὴν δεξιὰν τοῦ καθημένου ἐπὶ τοῦ θρόνου βιβλίον γεγραμμένον ἔσωθεν[a] καὶ ὄπισθεν[1],[a] κατεσφραγισμένον σφραγῖσιν ἑπτά. **2** καὶ εἶδον ἄγγελον ἰσχυρὸν κηρύσσοντα ἐν φωνῇ μεγάλῃ, Τίς ἄξιος ἀνοῖξαι τὸ βιβλίον καὶ λῦσαι τὰς σφραγῖδας αὐτοῦ; **3** καὶ οὐδεὶς ἐδύνατο ἐν τῷ οὐρανῷ οὐδὲ ἐπὶ τῆς γῆς οὐδὲ ὑποκάτω τῆς γῆς ἀνοῖξαι τὸ βιβλίον οὔτε βλέπειν αὐτό.[b]

---

[1] **1** {B} ἔσωθεν καὶ ὄπισθεν A 1 1828[mg] 2081 syr[h] Origen[1/4] Cyprian Cassiodorus ‖ ἔσωθεν καὶ ἔξωθεν P 046 1006 1611 1828[txt] 1854 1859 2020 2042 2053 2065 2344 2432 it[ar,c,dem,div,gig,haf,z] vg syr[ph] cop[bo] arm eth Hippolytus Origen[1/4] Victorinus-Pettau Aphraates Hilary Oecumenius Primasius Andrew[a,c,p] Ps-Ambrose Beatus Arethas ‖ ἔξωθεν καὶ ἔσωθεν 94 ‖ ἔμπροσθεν καὶ ὄπισθεν ℵ cop[sa] Origen[2/4] ‖ ἔσωθεν καὶ ἔξωθεν καὶ ὄπισθεν Andrew[bav] ‖ ἔσωθεν καὶ ἔξωθεν καὶ ἔμπροσθεν καὶ ὄπισθεν 2073

[a][a] **1** a none, a minor: TR WH Bov Nes BF² AV RV ASV RSV NEB TT Zür Luth Jer Seg ‖ a minor, a none

[b][b] **3-4** b major, b major: TR Bov Nes BF² AV NEB TT Zür Luth Jer Seg ‖ b major, b minor: WH RV ASV ‖ b minor, b major: RSV

9 τῷ καθημένῳ...θρόνου 1 Kgs 22.19; 2 Chr 18.18; Ps 47.8; Is 6.1; Eze 1.26 27; Sir 1.8; Re 4.2; 5.1, 7, 13; 6.16; 7.10, 15; 19.4; 21.5 τῷ ζῶντι...αἰώνων Dn 4.34; 6.26; 12.7   **10** τοῦ καθημένου ...θρόνου 1 Kgs 22.19; 2 Chr 18.18; Ps 47.8; Is 6.1; Eze 1.26–27; Sir 1.8; Re 4.2; 5.1, 7, 13; 6.16; 7.10, 15; 19.4; 21.5

5 1 τοῦ καθημένου...θρόνου 1 Kgs 22.19; 2 Chr 18.18; Ps 47.8; Is 6.1; Eze 1.26–27; Sir 1.8; Re 4.2, 9; 5.7, 13; 6.16; 7.10, 15; 19.4; 21.5   βιβλίον...ὄπισθεν Is 29.11; Eze 2.9–10

9 As often as the four living creatures sing songs of glory and honor and thanks to the one who sits on the throne, who lives for ever and ever, [10] the twenty-four elders fall down before the one who sits on the throne, and worship him who lives for ever and ever. They throw their crowns before the throne, and say:

[11] "Our Lord and God! You are worthy
   To receive glory, and honor, and power.
 For you created all things,
   And by your will they were given existence and life."

The Scroll and the Lamb

5 I saw a scroll in the right hand of the one who sat on the throne; it was covered with writing on both sides, and was sealed with seven seals. [2] And I saw a mighty angel who proclaimed in a loud voice: "Who is worthy to break the seals and open the scroll?" [3] But no one was found in heaven, or on earth, or in the world below, who could open the scroll and look inside it. ⁴ I cried bitterly because no one had been found who was worthy to open the scroll or to look inside it. ⁵ Then one of the elders said to me: "Don't cry. Look! The Lion from Judah's tribe, the great descendant of David, has won the victory and can break the seven seals and open the scroll."

⁶ Then I saw a Lamb standing in the center of the throne, surrounded by the four living creatures and the elders. The Lamb appeared to have been killed. It had seven horns and seven eyes, which are the seven spirits of God which have been sent into all the world. ⁷ The Lamb went and took the scroll from the right hand of the one who sat on the throne. ⁸ As he did so, the four living creatures and the twenty-four elders fell down before the Lamb. Each had a harp, and gold bowls filled with incense, which are the prayers of God's people. ⁹ They sang a new song:

"You are worthy to take the scroll
And to break open its seals.
For you were killed, and by your death
You bought men for God,

4 καὶ² ἔκλαιον πολὺ ὅτι οὐδεὶς ἄξιος εὑρέθη ἀνοῖξαι τὸ βιβλίον οὔτε βλέπειν αὐτό.ᵇ 5 καὶ εἷς ἐκ τῶν πρεσβυτέρων λέγει μοι, Μὴ κλαῖε· ἰδοὺ ἐνίκησεν ὁ λέων ὁ ἐκ τῆς φυλῆς Ἰούδα, ἡ ῥίζα Δαυίδ, ἀνοῖξαι τὸ βιβλίον καὶ τὰς ἑπτὰ σφραγῖδας αὐτοῦ.

6 Καὶ εἶδον ἐν μέσῳ τοῦ θρόνου καὶ τῶν τεσσάρων ζῴων καὶ ἐν μέσῳ τῶν πρεσβυτέρων ἀρνίον ἑστηκὸς ὡς ἐσφαγμένον, ἔχων κέρατα ἑπτὰ καὶ ὀφθαλμοὺς ἑπτά, οἵ εἰσιν τὰ [ἑπτά]³ πνεύματα τοῦ θεοῦ ἀπεσταλμένοι εἰς πᾶσαν τὴν γῆν.ᶜ 7 καὶ ἦλθεν καὶ εἴληφεν ἐκ τῆς δεξιᾶς τοῦ καθημένου ἐπὶ τοῦ θρόνου. 8 καὶ ὅτε ἔλαβεν τὸ βιβλίον, τὰ τέσσαρα ζῷα καὶ οἱ εἴκοσι τέσσαρες πρεσβύτεροι ἔπεσαν ἐνώπιον τοῦ ἀρνίου, ἔχοντες ἕκαστος κιθάραν καὶ φιάλας χρυσᾶς γεμούσας θυμιαμάτων, αἵ εἰσιν αἱ προσευχαὶ τῶν ἁγίων. 9 καὶ ᾄδουσιν ᾠδὴν καινὴν λέγοντες,

Ἄξιος εἶ λαβεῖν τὸ βιβλίον
καὶ ἀνοῖξαι τὰς σφραγῖδας αὐτοῦ,
ὅτι ἐσφάγης καὶ ἠγόρασας τῷ θεῷ⁴ ἐν τῷ αἵματί σου

² 4 {C} καὶ ℵ P 1 1611ᵗˣᵗ 2053 2081 2344 itᵍⁱᵍ syrᵖʰ,ʰ copˢᵃᵐˢˢ,ᵇᵒ eth Origen Hilary Jerome Andrewᵇᵃᵛ // καὶ ἐγώ 046 94 1006 1611ᵐᵍ 1859 2020 2042 2065 2073 2432 itᵃʳ,ᶜ,ᵈᵉᵐ,ᵈⁱᵛ,ʰᵃᶠ,ᶻᵛⁱᵈ vg copˢᵃ arm Tyconius Primasius Andrewᵃ,ᶜ Arethas

³ 6 {C} τὰ ἑπτά 𝔭²⁴ ℵ 046 94 1828 1854 1859 2020 2042 2053 2065 2073 2138 2432 (2344 omit τά) itᶜ,ᵈᵉᵐ,ᵈⁱᵛ,ᵍⁱᵍ,ʰᵃᶠ vgᶜˡ syrᵖʰ,ʰ copˢᵃ,ᵇᵒ arm Hippolytus // τά A Pᵛⁱᵈ 1 1006 1611 2081 itᵃʳ,ᶻ* vgʷʷ eth Irenaeusᵃʳᵐ Apringius Andrewᵇᵃᵛ

⁴ 9 {C} τῷ θεῷ A eth // ἡμᾶς 1 2065* itᶻ* Cyprian Fulgentius // τῷ θεῷ ἡμᾶς ℵ 046 1006 1611 1859 2020 2042 2053 2065ᶜ 2081 2138 2432 copᵇᵒ? Andrewᵃ,ᴾ Arethas // ἡμᾶς τῷ θεῷ 94 1828 2073 2344 itᵃʳ,ᶜ,ᵈᵉᵐ,ᵈⁱᵛ,ᵍⁱᵍ,ʰᵃᶠ vg syrᵖʰ,ʰ copᵇᵒ? arm Hippolytus Cyprian Augustine Primasius Andrewᵇᵃᵛ,ᶜ // ἡμᾶς τῷ θεῷ ἡμῶν copˢᵃ?

ᶜ 6 c major: WH Bov Nes BF² AV RV ASV NEB TT Zür Luth Jer Seg // c minor: TR RSV

5 ὁ λέων...Ἰούδα Gn 49.9–10 ἡ ῥίζα Δαυίδ Is 11.1, 10; Re 22.16 6 ἀρνίον...ἐσφαγμένον Is 53.7; Jn 1.29, 36; Re 5.12; 13.8 ὀφθαλμοὺς ἑπτά Zch 4.10 τὰ ἑπτὰ πνεύματα τοῦ θεοῦ Re 1.4; 4.5 7 τοῦ καθημένου...θρόνου 1 Kgs 22.19; 2 Chr 18.18; Ps 47.8; Is 6.1; Eze 1.26–27; Slr 1.8; Re 4.2, 9; 5.1, 13; 6.16; 7.10, 15; 19.4; 21.5 8 φιάλας...ἁγίων Ps 141.2; Re 8.3, 4 9 ᾠδὴν καινήν Ps 33.3; 40.3; 96.1; 98.1; 144.9; 149.1; Is 42.10; Re 14.3

ἐκ πάσης φυλῆς καὶ γλώσσης καὶ λαοῦ καὶ
ἔθνους,

10 καὶ ἐποίησας αὐτοὺς τῷ θεῷ ἡμῶν βασιλείαν καὶ
ἱερεῖς,
καὶ βασιλεύσουσιν[5] ἐπὶ τῆς γῆς.

11 Καὶ εἶδον, καὶ ἤκουσα φωνὴν ἀγγέλων πολλῶν
κύκλῳ τοῦ θρόνου καὶ τῶν ζῴων καὶ τῶν πρεσβυτέρων,
καὶ ἦν ὁ ἀριθμὸς αὐτῶν μυριάδες μυριάδων καὶ χιλιάδες
χιλιάδων, 12 λέγοντες φωνῇ μεγάλῃ,
Ἄξιός ἐστιν τὸ ἀρνίον τὸ ἐσφαγμένον λαβεῖν
τὴν δύναμιν καὶ πλοῦτον καὶ σοφίαν καὶ ἰσχὺν
καὶ τιμὴν καὶ δόξαν καὶ εὐλογίαν.

13 καὶ πᾶν κτίσμα ὃ ἐν τῷ οὐρανῷ καὶ ἐπὶ τῆς γῆς καὶ
ὑποκάτω τῆς γῆς καὶ ἐπὶ τῆς θαλάσσης, καὶ[6] τὰ ἐν
αὐτοῖς πάντα, ἤκουσα λέγοντας,
Τῷ καθημένῳ ἐπὶ τοῦ θρόνου καὶ τῷ ἀρνίῳ
ἡ εὐλογία καὶ ἡ τιμὴ καὶ ἡ δόξα καὶ τὸ κράτος
εἰς τοὺς αἰῶνας τῶν αἰώνων.

14 καὶ τὰ τέσσαρα ζῷα ἔλεγον, Ἀμήν· καὶ οἱ πρεσβύτεροι ἔπεσαν καὶ προσεκύνησαν.

From every tribe, and language, and
people, and nation.
10 You have made them a kingdom of
priests to serve our God;
And they shall rule on earth."
11 Again I looked, and I heard angels,
thousands and tens of thousands of them!
They stood around the throne, the four
living creatures, and the elders, 12 and
sang in a loud voice:
"The Lamb who was killed
Is worthy to receive power,
Wealth, wisdom, and strength,
Honor, glory, and praise!"
13 And I heard every creature in heaven,
on earth, and in the world below, and
every creature in the sea — all creatures
in the whole universe — and they were
singing:
"To him who sits on the throne, and
to the Lamb,
Be praise and honor, glory and might,
For ever and ever!"
14 The four living creatures answered,
"Amen!" And the elders fell down and
worshiped.

---

[5] 10 {C} βασιλεύσουσιν ℵ P 1 94 1828 1854 2042 2053 2073 2081* 2344
it[c,div,gig,haf,z] vg[ww] syr[ph] cop[sa,bo] arm Hippolytus Cyprian Fulgentius
Andrew[bav,c,p] Arethas[comm] ‖ βασιλεύουσιν A 046 1006 1611 1859 2020 2065
2081[c] 2138 it[ar] syr[h] Andrew[a] ‖ βασιλεύσομεν 2432 it[dem] vg[cl] Maternus
Tyconius Primasius Bede Haymo Arethas[txt]

[6] 13 {C} καὶ ℵ 1611* 2020 2065 2432 it[gig] syr[h] cop[sa,bo] arm eth Primasius
Cassiodorus Andrew[a] ‖ ἐστίν, καὶ A 94 1006 1611[c] 1854 1859 2042 2138 2344
syr[ph?] cop[bomss] Arethas ‖ ἅ ἐστιν, καὶ P 046 1 2073 2081 it[c,dem,div,haf,z] vg
Andrew[bav,p] ‖ ὅσα ἐστίν, καὶ 1828 2053 Andrew[c] ‖ omit it[ar]

---

10 ἐποίησας...ἱερεῖς Ex 19.6; Is 61.6; 1 Pe 2.5, 9; Re 1.6; 20.6   βασιλεύσουσιν...γῆς
Re 20.6; 22.5   11 ἦν...χιλιάδων Dn 7.10; En 14.22; He 12.22   12 τὸ ἀρνίον τὸ ἐσφαγμένον
Is 53.7; Jn 1.29, 36; Re 5.6; 13.8 Ἄξιος...εὐλογίαν 1 Chr 29.11   13 Τῷ καθημένῳ...θρόνου
1 Kgs 22.19; 2 Chr 18.18; Ps 47.8; Is 6.1; Eze 1.26–27; Sir 1.8; Re 4.2, 9; 5.1, 7; 6.16; 7.10, 15; 19.4;
21.5

The Seals

6 Then I saw the Lamb break open the first of the seven seals, and I heard one of the four living creatures say in a voice that sounded like thunder: "Come!" [2] I looked, and there was a white horse. Its rider held a bow, and he was given a crown. He went out as a conqueror to conquer.

[3] Then the Lamb broke open the second seal; and I heard the second living creature say: "Come!" [4] Another horse came out, a red one. Its rider was given the power to bring war on the earth, that men should kill each other; he was given a large sword.

[5] Then the Lamb broke open the third seal; and I heard the third living creature say: "Come!" I looked, and there was a

The Seals

6 Καὶ εἶδον ὅτε ἤνοιξεν τὸ ἀρνίον μίαν ἐκ τῶν ἑπτὰ σφραγίδων, καὶ ἤκουσα ἑνὸς ἐκ τῶν τεσσάρων ζῴων λέγοντος ὡς φωνῇ βροντῆς, Ἔρχου[1]. 2 καὶ εἶδον[2], καὶ ἰδοὺ ἵππος λευκός, καὶ ὁ καθήμενος ἐπ' αὐτὸν ἔχων τόξον, καὶ ἐδόθη αὐτῷ στέφανος, καὶ ἐξῆλθεν νικῶν καὶ ἵνα νικήσῃ.

3 Καὶ ὅτε ἤνοιξεν τὴν σφραγῖδα τὴν δευτέραν, ἤκουσα τοῦ δευτέρου ζῴου λέγοντος, Ἔρχου[3]. 4 καὶ ἐξῆλθεν ἄλλος ἵππος πυρρός, καὶ τῷ καθημένῳ ἐπ' αὐτὸν ἐδόθη αὐτῷ λαβεῖν τὴν εἰρήνην ἐκ τῆς γῆς[4] καὶ ἵνα ἀλλήλους σφάξουσιν, καὶ ἐδόθη αὐτῷ μάχαιρα μεγάλη.

5 Καὶ ὅτε ἤνοιξεν τὴν σφραγῖδα τὴν τρίτην, ἤκουσα τοῦ τρίτου ζῴου λέγοντος, Ἔρχου[5]. καὶ εἶδον[6], καὶ

---

[1] **1** {C} ἔρχου (see footnote 2) A C P 1 94 1006 1611 1854 2020 2053 2065 2073 2081 2432 vg^ww cop^sa,bo Victorinus-Pettau Primasius Andrew^a,bav Arethas ‖ ἔρχου καὶ ἴδε ℵ 046 1828 1859 2042 2138 2344 it^c,dem,div,gig,haf,z vg^cl syr^ph,h eth Primasius Andrew^c,p ‖ ἔρχου καὶ βλέπε 296 2049 ‖ ὅτι ἔρχομαι arm ‖ et veni it^ar

[2] **2** {C} καὶ εἶδον (see footnote 1) ℵ (A C ἴδον) P 1 94 1006 1611 2053 2065 2073 2081 2344 2432 (it^ar et vide) it^c,gig,haf vg syr^h cop^bo arm Andrew^a,p (Andrew^bav ἴδον) ‖ εἶδον cop^sa ‖ καὶ ἤκουσα καὶ εἶδον syr^ph ‖ omit 046 1828 1854 1859 2020 2042 2138 it^dem,div,z Victorinus-Pettau Tyconius Primasius Andrew^c Ps-Ambrose Beatus Haymo Arethas

[3] **3** {C} ἔρχου A C P 046 1 94 1006 1611 1854 1859 2020 2042 2053 2065 2081 2138 2432 vg^ww syr^ph,h cop^sa,bo Andrew^a,bav ‖ ἔρχομαι arm ‖ ἔρχου καὶ ἴδε ℵ 1828 2073 2344 it^ar,c,dem,div,gig,haf,z vg^cl cop^boms eth? Victorinus-Pettau Tyconius Primasius Andrew^c,p ‖ ἔρχου καὶ βλέπε 296 2049 Arethas

[4] **4** {C} ἐκ τῆς γῆς ℵ* C P 046 94 1006 1611 1854 1859 2020 2042 2065 2073 2138 2432 it^ar,c,dem,div,gig,haf,z vg syr^ph?h? cop^sa?bo? arm Primasius Andrew^a,c,p Arethas ‖ ἀπὸ τῆς γῆς 1 1828 2053 syr^ph?h? cop^sa?bo? ‖ ἐπὶ τῆς γῆς 2344 ‖ τῆς γῆς A 2081 Andrew^bav ‖ omit ℵ^c

[5] **5** {C} ἔρχου (see footnote 6) A C P 1 94 1006 1611 1854 2020 2053 2065 2073 2081 2432 it^gig vg^ww syr^ph cop^sa,bo eth Andrew^a,bav ‖ ἔρχου καὶ ἴδε ℵ 046 1828 1859 2042 2138 2344 it^ar,c,dem,div,haf,z vg^cl syr^h Primasius Andrew^c,p Arethas ‖ ἔρχου καὶ βλέπε 296 2049 ‖ ὅτι ἔρχομαι arm

[6] **5** {C} καὶ εἶδον (see footnote 5) ℵ (A ἴδον) C P 1 94 1006 1611

---

2 ἵππος λευκός Zch 1.8; 6.3, 6; Re 19.11   4 ἵππος πυρρός Zch 1.8; 6.2

ἰδοὺ ἵππος μέλας, καὶ ὁ καθήμενος ἐπ᾽ αὐτὸν ἔχων ζυγὸν ἐν τῇ χειρὶ αὐτοῦ. **6** καὶ ἤκουσα ὡς φωνὴν ἐν μέσῳ τῶν τεσσάρων ζῴων λέγουσαν, Χοῖνιξ σίτου δηναρίου, καὶ τρεῖς χοίνικες κριθῶν δηναρίου· καὶ τὸ ἔλαιον καὶ τὸν οἶνον μὴ ἀδικήσῃς.

7 Καὶ ὅτε ἤνοιξεν τὴν σφραγῖδα τὴν τετάρτην, ἤκουσα φωνὴν τοῦ τετάρτου ζῴου λέγοντος, Ἔρχου[7]. **8** καὶ εἶδον[8], καὶ ἰδοὺ ἵππος χλωρός, καὶ ὁ καθήμενος ἐπάνω [αὐτοῦ][9] ὄνομα αὐτῷ [ὁ] Θάνατος, καὶ ὁ ᾅδης ἠκολούθει μετ᾽ αὐτοῦ· καὶ ἐδόθη αὐτοῖς ἐξουσία ἐπὶ τὸ τέταρτον τῆς γῆς, ἀποκτεῖναι ἐν ῥομφαίᾳ καὶ ἐν λιμῷ καὶ ἐν θανάτῳ καὶ ὑπὸ τῶν θηρίων τῆς γῆς.

9 Καὶ ὅτε ἤνοιξεν τὴν πέμπτην σφραγῖδα, εἶδον ὑποκάτω τοῦ θυσιαστηρίου τὰς ψυχὰς τῶν ἐσφαγμένων διὰ τὸν λόγον τοῦ θεοῦ καὶ διὰ τὴν μαρτυρίαν ἣν εἶχον. **10** καὶ ἔκραξαν φωνῇ μεγάλῃ λέγοντες, Ἕως πότε, ὁ δεσπότης ὁ ἅγιος καὶ ἀληθινός, οὐ κρίνεις καὶ ἐκδικεῖς τὸ αἷμα ἡμῶν ἐκ τῶν κατοικούντων ἐπὶ τῆς γῆς; **11** καὶ

black horse. Its rider held a pair of scales in his hand. [6] I heard what sounded like a voice coming from among the four living creatures. It said: "A quart of wheat for a whole day's wages, and three quarts of barley for a whole day's wages. But do not damage the olive oil and the wine!"

[7] Then the Lamb broke open the fourth seal; and I heard the fourth living creature say: "Come!" [8] I looked, and there was a pale-colored horse. Its rider was named Death, and Hades followed close behind. They were given authority over a fourth of the earth, to kill with sword, with famine, with disease, and with the wild animals of earth.

[9] Then the Lamb broke open the fifth seal. I saw underneath the altar the souls of those who had been killed because they had proclaimed God's word and had been faithful in their witnessing. [10] They shouted in a loud voice: "Almighty Lord, holy and true! How long will it be until you will judge the people of earth and punish them for killing us?" [11] Each of them was given a white robe;

2053 2065 2073 2081 2432 vg^ww syr^h cop^bo arm Andrew^p (Andrew^bav ἴδον) ∥ καὶ ἐξῆλθε (omitting καὶ ἰδού) eth Cassiodorus ∥ omit 046 1828 1854 1859 2020 2042 2138 2344 it^ar,c,dem,div,gig,haf,z vg^cl syr^ph cop^sa eth Victorinus-Pettau Primasius Andrew^a,c Ps-Ambrose Beatus Arethas

[7] **7** {C} ἔρχου (see footnote 8) A C P 1 94 1006 1611 1854 2020 2042 2053 2065 2081 2432 vg^ww syr^h cop^sa,bo Andrew^a,bav ∥ ἔρχου καὶ ἴδε ℵ 046 1828 1859 2073 2138 2344 it^ar,c,dem,div,gig,haf,z vg^cl syr^h Primasius Andrew^c,p Beatus Arethas ∥ ἔρχου καὶ βλέπε 296 2049 eth? ∥ ὅτι ἔρχομαι arm

[8] **8** {C} καὶ εἶδον (see footnote 7) (ℵ A C ἴδον) P 1 94 1006 1611 (2053 omit καί) 2065 2073 2081 2432 it^ar vg^ww syr^h cop^sa,bo arm Andrew^a,p (Andrew^bav ἴδον) ∥ καὶ ἐξῆλθον (for καὶ εἶδον καὶ ἰδού) eth ∥ omit 046 1828 1854 1859 2020 2042 2138 2344 it^c,dem,div,gig,haf,z vg^cl syr^ph Victorinus-Pettau Primasius Andrew^c Ps-Ambrose Beatus Arethas

[9] **8** {C} ἐπάνω αὐτοῦ ℵ A 046 94 1006 1828 1859 2020 2042 2073 2138 2344 2432 syr^ph?h? cop^(sa?),bo arm Victorinus-Pettau Primasius Andrew^a,c,p Haymo Arethas ∥ ἐπάνω C P 1 1611 2053 2065 2081 it^c,dem,z vg^ww Oecumenius Andrew^bav Ansbert ∥ ἐπ᾽ αὐτόν 1854 it^ar,div^c,gig?haf vg^cl syr^ph?h?

---

5 ἵππος μέλας Zch 6.2, 6   **8** τὸ...θηρίων τῆς γῆς Jr 14.12; 15.3; Eze 5.12, 17; 14.21; 33.27
10 ἐκδικεῖς...γῆς Dt 32.43; 2 Kgs 9.7; Ps 79.10; Re 19.2

and they were told to rest a little while longer, until the total number was reached of their fellow servants and brothers who were to be killed as they had been.

¹² And I saw the Lamb break open the sixth seal. There was a violent earthquake, and the sun became black, like coarse black cloth, and the moon turned completely red, like blood; ¹³ the stars fell out of the sky to earth, like unripe figs falling from the tree when a strong wind shakes it. ¹⁴ The sky disappeared, like a scroll being rolled up, and every mountain and island was moved from its place. ¹⁵ Then the kings of the earth, the rulers and the military chiefs, the rich and the mighty, and all other men, slave and free, hid themselves in caves and under rocks on the mountains. ¹⁶ They called out to the mountains and to the rocks: "Fall down on us and hide us from the eyes of the one who sits on the throne, and from the wrath of the Lamb! ¹⁷ For the great day of their wrath is here, and who can stand up against it?"

ἐδόθη αὐτοῖς ἑκάστῳ στολὴ λευκή, καὶ ἐρρέθη αὐτοῖς ἵνα ἀναπαύσονται ἔτι χρόνον μικρόν, ἕως πληρωθῶσιν[10] καὶ οἱ σύνδουλοι αὐτῶν καὶ οἱ ἀδελφοὶ αὐτῶν οἱ μέλλοντες ἀποκτέννεσθαι ὡς καὶ αὐτοί.

12 Καὶ εἶδον ὅτε ἤνοιξεν τὴν σφραγῖδα τὴν ἕκτην, καὶ σεισμὸς[11] μέγας ἐγένετο, καὶ ὁ ἥλιος ἐγένετο μέλας ὡς σάκκος τρίχινος, καὶ ἡ σελήνη ὅλη ἐγένετο ὡς αἷμα, **13** καὶ οἱ ἀστέρες τοῦ οὐρανοῦ ἔπεσαν εἰς τὴν γῆν, ὡς συκῆ βάλλει τοὺς ὀλύνθους αὐτῆς ὑπὸ ἀνέμου μεγάλου σειομένη, **14** καὶ ὁ οὐρανὸς ἀπεχωρίσθη ὡς βιβλίον ἑλισσόμενον, καὶ πᾶν ὄρος καὶ νῆσος ἐκ τῶν τόπων αὐτῶν ἐκινήθησαν. **15** καὶ οἱ βασιλεῖς τῆς γῆς καὶ οἱ μεγιστᾶνες καὶ οἱ χιλίαρχοι καὶ οἱ πλούσιοι καὶ οἱ ἰσχυροὶ καὶ πᾶς δοῦλος καὶ ἐλεύθερος ἔκρυψαν ἑαυτοὺς εἰς τὰ σπήλαια καὶ εἰς τὰς πέτρας τῶν ὀρέων· **16 καὶ λέγουσιν τοῖς ὄρεσιν καὶ ταῖς πέτραις, Πέσετε ἐφ' ἡμᾶς καὶ κρύψατε ἡμᾶς** ἀπὸ προσώπου τοῦ καθημένου ἐπὶ τοῦ θρόνου καὶ ἀπὸ τῆς ὀργῆς τοῦ ἀρνίου, **17** ὅτι ἦλθεν ἡ ἡμέρα ἡ μεγάλη τῆς ὀργῆς αὐτῶν[12], καὶ τίς δύναται σταθῆναι;

---

10 11 {C} πληρωθῶσιν A C 2344 it^{ar,c,dem,div,gig,haf,z} vg syr^{ph,h} arm Ps-Ambrose ‖ πληρώσωσιν ℵ P 046 1 94 1006 1828 1854 1859 2020 2042 2053^{txt} 2081 2138 Andrew ‖ πληρώσουσιν 1611 2053^{comm} 2065 2073 2432 ‖ πληρώσονται 296 2049 Arethas

11 12 {B} καὶ σεισμός ℵ C P 046 1 94 1006 1611 1828 1854 1859 2020 2042 2053 2065 2073 2081 2138 2344 2432 it^{ar,div,gig,z} vg^{ww} syr^{ph,h} eth Primasius Andrew^{a,bav,c} Arethas ‖ καὶ ἰδοὺ σεισμός A it^{c,haf} vg^{cl} Primasius ‖ σεισμός it^{dem} cop^{sa,bo} arm Tyconius ‖ omit καὶ σεισμὸς μέγας ἐγένετο cop^{sams}

12 17 {C} αὐτῶν ℵ C 94 1611 1828 1854 2020 2053 2344 it^{ar,c,dem,div,gig,haf,z} vg syr^{ph,h} de Promissionibus Oecumenius Fulgentius Haymo ‖ αὐτοῦ A P 046 1 1006 1859 2042 2065 2073 2081 2138 2432 cop^{sa,bo} arm eth Primasius Andrew Arethas

---

11 στολὴ λευκή Re 3.5, 18; 4.4; 7.9, 13; 19.14   **12** ὁ...αἷμα Jl 2.31; Ac 2.20   **12–13** ὁ... σειομένη Is 13.10; Eze 32.7, 8; Jl 2.10; 3.15; Mt 24.29; Mk 13.24–25; Lk 21.25; Re 8.12 **13–14** οἱ...ἐλισσόμενον Is 34.4   **14** πᾶν...ἐκινήθησαν Re 16.20; 20.11   **15** ἔκρυψαν... ὀρέων Is 2.10, 19, 21; Jr 4.29   **16** λέγουσιν...ἡμᾶς Ho 10.8; Lk 23.30; Re 9.6   τοῦ καθημένου ...θρόνου 1 Kgs 22.19; 2 Chr 18.18; Ps 47.8; Is 6.1; Eze 1.26–27; Sir 1.8; Re 4.2, 9; 5.1, 7, 13; 7.10, 15; 19.4; 21.5   **17** Jl 2.11; Na 1.6; Mal 3.2

The 144,000 of Israel Sealed

7 Μετὰ τοῦτο εἶδον τέσσαρας ἀγγέλους ἑστῶτας ἐπὶ τὰς τέσσαρας γωνίας τῆς γῆς, κρατοῦντας τοὺς τέσσαρας ἀνέμους τῆς γῆς, ἵνα μὴ πνέῃ ἄνεμος ἐπὶ τῆς γῆς μήτε ἐπὶ τῆς θαλάσσης μήτε ἐπὶ πᾶν δένδρον. 2 καὶ εἶδον ἄλλον ἄγγελον ἀναβαίνοντα ἀπὸ ἀνατολῆς ἡλίου, ἔχοντα σφραγῖδα θεοῦ ζῶντος, καὶ ἔκραξεν φωνῇ μεγάλῃ τοῖς τέσσαρσιν ἀγγέλοις οἷς ἐδόθη αὐτοῖς ἀδικῆσαι τὴν γῆν καὶ τὴν θάλασσαν, 3 λέγων, Μὴ ἀδικήσητε τὴν γῆν μήτε τὴν θάλασσαν μήτε τὰ δένδρα ἄχρι σφραγίσωμεν τοὺς δούλους τοῦ θεοῦ ἡμῶν ἐπὶ τῶν μετώπων αὐτῶν. 4 καὶ ἤκουσα τὸν ἀριθμὸν τῶν ἐσφραγισμένων, ἑκατὸν τεσσαράκοντα τέσσαρες χιλιάδες,[a] ἐσφραγισμένοι[a] ἐκ πάσης φυλῆς υἱῶν Ἰσραήλ·

5 ἐκ φυλῆς Ἰούδα δώδεκα χιλιάδες ἐσφραγισμένοι,
ἐκ φυλῆς Ῥουβὴν δώδεκα χιλιάδες,
ἐκ φυλῆς Γὰδ δώδεκα χιλιάδες,
6 ἐκ φυλῆς Ἀσὴρ δώδεκα χιλιάδες,
ἐκ φυλῆς Νεφθαλὶμ δώδεκα χιλιάδες,
ἐκ φυλῆς Μανασσῆ δώδεκα χιλιάδες,
7 ἐκ φυλῆς Συμεὼν δώδεκα χιλιάδες,
ἐκ φυλῆς Λευὶ δώδεκα χιλιάδες,
ἐκ φυλῆς Ἰσσαχὰρ δώδεκα χιλιάδες,
8 ἐκ φυλῆς Ζαβουλὼν δώδεκα χιλιάδες,
ἐκ φυλῆς Ἰωσὴφ δώδεκα χιλιάδες,
ἐκ φυλῆς Βενιαμεὶν δώδεκα χιλιάδες ἐσφραγισμένοι.

The Multitude from Every Nation

9 Μετὰ ταῦτα εἶδον, καὶ ἰδοὺ ὄχλος πολύς, ὃν ἀριθμῆσαι αὐτὸν οὐδεὶς ἐδύνατο, ἐκ παντὸς ἔθνους καὶ φυλῶν

[a] [a] 4 a minor, a none: WH RV ASV TT Luth // a none, a minor: RSV // a none, a none: TR Bov Nes BF² AV NEB? Zür Jer? Seg?

1 τοὺς τέσσαρας ἀνέμους Jr 49.36; Eze 37.9; Dn 7.2; Zch 6.5; Mt 24.31   3 σφραγίσωμεν ...αὐτῶν Eze 9.4; Re 9.4   4 ἑκατὸν...χιλιάδες Re 14.1, 3

The 144,000 People of Israel

7 After this I saw four angels standing at the four corners of the earth, holding back the four winds of the earth, so that no wind should blow on the earth, or on the sea, or on any tree. 2 And I saw another angel coming up from the east with the seal of the living God. He called out in a loud voice to the four angels to whom God had given the power to damage the earth and the sea. 3 The angel said: "Do not harm the earth, or the sea, or the trees, until we mark the servants of our God with a seal on their foreheads." 4 And I was told the number of those who were marked with God's seal on their foreheads: it was a hundred and forty-four thousand, from every tribe of the people of Israel. 5 There were twelve thousand from the tribe of Judah marked with the seal; twelve thousand from the tribe of Reuben; twelve thousand from the tribe of Gad; 6 twelve thousand from the tribe of Asher; twelve thousand from the tribe of Naphtali; twelve thousand from the tribe of Manasseh; 7 twelve thousand from the tribe of Simeon; twelve thousand from the tribe of Levi; twelve thousand from the tribe of Issachar; 8 twelve thousand from the tribe of Zebulun; twelve thousand from the tribe of Joseph; and twelve thousand from the tribe of Benjamin.

The Great Crowd

9 After this I looked, and there was a great crowd — no one could count all the people! They were from every nation,

tribe, people, and language, and they stood in front of the throne and of the Lamb, dressed in white robes, and holding palm branches in their hands. 10 They called out in a loud voice: "Our salvation comes from our God, who sits on the throne, and from the Lamb!" 11 All the angels stood around the throne, the elders, and the four living creatures. Then they fell down on their faces before the throne and worshiped God, 12 saying: "Amen! Praise, and glory, and wisdom, and thanks, and honor, and power, and might, belong to our God for ever and ever! Amen!"

13 One of the elders asked me, "Who are those people dressed in white robes, and where do they come from?" 14 "I don't know, sir. You do," I answered. He said to me: "These are the people who have come safely through the great persecution. They washed their robes and made them white with the blood of the Lamb. 15 That is why they stand before God's throne and serve him day and night in his temple. He who sits on the throne will protect them with his presence. 16 Never again will they hunger or thirst; neither sun nor any scorching

καὶ λαῶν καὶ γλωσσῶν, ἑστῶτες ἐνώπιον τοῦ θρόνου καὶ ἐνώπιον τοῦ ἀρνίου, περιβεβλημένους στολὰς λευκάς, καὶ φοίνικες ἐν ταῖς χερσὶν αὐτῶν· 10 καὶ κράζουσιν φωνῇ μεγάλῃ λέγοντες,

Ἡ σωτηρία τῷ θεῷ ἡμῶν τῷ καθημένῳ ἐπὶ τῷ θρόνῳ καὶ τῷ ἀρνίῳ.

11 καὶ πάντες οἱ ἄγγελοι εἱστήκεισαν κύκλῳ τοῦ θρόνου καὶ τῶν πρεσβυτέρων καὶ τῶν τεσσάρων ζῴων, καὶ ἔπεσαν ἐνώπιον τοῦ θρόνου ἐπὶ τὰ πρόσωπα αὐτῶν καὶ προσεκύνησαν τῷ θεῷ, 12 λέγοντες,

Ἀμήν· ἡ εὐλογία καὶ ἡ δόξα καὶ ἡ σοφία καὶ ἡ εὐχαριστία καὶ ἡ τιμὴ καὶ ἡ δύναμις καὶ ἡ ἰσχὺς τῷ θεῷ ἡμῶν εἰς τοὺς αἰῶνας τῶν αἰώνων· ἀμήν.[1]

13 Καὶ ἀπεκρίθη εἷς ἐκ τῶν πρεσβυτέρων λέγων μοι, Οὗτοι οἱ περιβεβλημένοι τὰς στολὰς τὰς λευκὰς τίνες εἰσὶν καὶ πόθεν ἦλθον; 14 καὶ εἴρηκα αὐτῷ, Κύριέ μου, σὺ οἶδας. καὶ εἶπέν μοι, Οὗτοί εἰσιν οἱ ἐρχόμενοι ἐκ τῆς θλίψεως τῆς μεγάλης, καὶ ἔπλυναν τὰς στολὰς αὐτῶν καὶ ἐλεύκαναν αὐτὰς ἐν τῷ αἵματι τοῦ ἀρνίου.

15 διὰ τοῦτό εἰσιν ἐνώπιον τοῦ θρόνου τοῦ θεοῦ, καὶ λατρεύουσιν αὐτῷ ἡμέρας καὶ νυκτὸς ἐν τῷ ναῷ αὐτοῦ, καὶ ὁ καθήμενος ἐπὶ τοῦ θρόνου σκηνώσει ἐπ᾽ αὐτούς.

16 οὐ πεινάσουσιν ἔτι οὐδὲ διψήσουσιν ἔτι, οὐδὲ μὴ πέσῃ ἐπ᾽ αὐτοὺς ὁ ἥλιος οὐδὲ πᾶν καῦμα,

---

[1] 12 {C} ἀμήν. ℵ A P 046 1 94 1006 1611 (1828 omit τῶν αἰώνων) 1854 1859 2020 2042 2053 2065 2073 2081 2138 2344 2432 it[ar,c,dem,div,gig,haf,t,z] vg syr[ph,h] cop[sa,bo] arm eth Andrew[a,bav,c] Theodore-Studita Haymo Arethas ∥ omit C Fulgentius Primasius Andrew[p]

9 περιβεβλημένους στολὰς λευκάς Re 3.5, 18; 4.4; 6.11; 7.13; 19.14   10 τῷ καθημένῳ... θρόνῳ 1 Kgs 22.19; 2 Chr 18.18; Ps 47.8; Is 6.1; Eze 1.26–27; Sir 1.8; Re 4.2, 9; 5.1, 7, 13; 6.16; 7.15; 19.4; 21.5   13 περιβεβλημένοι...λευκάς Re 3.5, 18; 4.4; 6.11; 7.9; 19.14   14 τῆς θλίψεως τῆς μεγάλης Dn 12.1; Mt 24.21; Mk 13.19   15 ὁ...θρόνου 1 Kgs 22.19; 2 Chr 18.18; Ps 47.8; Is 6.1; Eze 1.26–27; Sir 1.8 Re 4.2, 9; 5.1, 7, 13; 6.16; 7.10; 19.4; 21.5   16 Is 49.10

17 ὅτι τὸ ἀρνίον τὸ ἀνὰ μέσον τοῦ θρόνου **ποιμανεῖ αὐτούς,**
    καὶ ὁδηγήσει αὐτοὺς ἐπὶ ζωῆς πηγὰς ὑδάτων·
    καὶ ἐξαλείψει ὁ θεὸς πᾶν δάκρυον ἐκ τῶν ὀφθαλμῶν αὐτῶν.

The Seventh Seal and the Golden Censer

8 Καὶ ὅταν ἤνοιξεν τὴν σφραγῖδα τὴν ἑβδόμην, ἐγένετο σιγὴ ἐν τῷ οὐρανῷ ὡς ἡμίωρον. 2 καὶ εἶδον τοὺς ἑπτὰ ἀγγέλους οἳ ἐνώπιον τοῦ θεοῦ ἑστήκασιν, καὶ ἐδόθησαν αὐτοῖς ἑπτὰ σάλπιγγες.

3 Καὶ ἄλλος ἄγγελος ἦλθεν καὶ ἐστάθη ἐπὶ τοῦ θυσιαστηρίου ἔχων λιβανωτὸν χρυσοῦν, καὶ ἐδόθη αὐτῷ θυμιάματα πολλὰ ἵνα δώσει ταῖς προσευχαῖς τῶν ἁγίων πάντων ἐπὶ τὸ θυσιαστήριον τὸ χρυσοῦν τὸ ἐνώπιον τοῦ θρόνου. 4 καὶ ἀνέβη ὁ καπνὸς τῶν θυμιαμάτων ταῖς προσευχαῖς τῶν ἁγίων ἐκ χειρὸς τοῦ ἀγγέλου ἐνώπιον τοῦ θεοῦ. 5 καὶ εἴληφεν ὁ ἄγγελος τὸν λιβανωτόν, καὶ ἐγέμισεν αὐτὸν ἐκ τοῦ πυρὸς τοῦ θυσιαστηρίου καὶ ἔβαλεν εἰς τὴν γῆν· καὶ ἐγένοντο βρονταὶ καὶ φωναὶ καὶ ἀστραπαὶ καὶ σεισμός.

The Trumpets

6 Καὶ οἱ ἑπτὰ ἄγγελοι οἱ ἔχοντες τὰς ἑπτὰ σάλπιγγας ἡτοίμασαν αὐτοὺς ἵνα σαλπίσωσιν.

7 Καὶ ὁ πρῶτος ἐσάλπισεν· καὶ ἐγένετο χάλαζα καὶ πῦρ μεμιγμένα ἐν αἵματι, καὶ ἐβλήθη εἰς τὴν γῆν· καὶ τὸ τρίτον τῆς γῆς κατεκάη, καὶ τὸ τρίτον τῶν δένδρων κατεκάη, καὶ πᾶς χόρτος χλωρὸς κατεκάη.

---

17 ποιμανεῖ αὐτούς Ps 23.1; Eze 34.23; Jn 10.11, 14   ὁδηγήσει...ὑδάτων Ps 23.2, Is 49.10, Jr 2.13   ἐξαλείψει...αὐτῶν Is 25.8; Re 21.4
8 3 θυμιάματα...πάντων Ps 141.2; Re 5.8; 8.4   τὸ θυσιαστήριον τὸ χρυσοῦν Ex 30.1-3; Re 9.13   4 τῶν θυμιαμάτων...ἁγίων Ps 141.2; Re 5.8; 8.3   5 τὸν...θυσιαστηρίου Lv 16.12   ἐγένοντο...σεισμός Ex 19.16-19; Est 1.1d LXX; Re 4.5; 11.19; 16.18   7 χάλαζα καὶ πῦρ Ex 9.23-25; Eze 38.22; Wsd 16.22

---

heat will burn them; [17] for the Lamb, who is in the center of the throne, will be their shepherd, and guide them to springs of living water; and God will wipe away every tear from their eyes.''

The Seventh Seal

8 When the Lamb broke open the seventh seal, there was silence in heaven for about half an hour. [2] Then I saw the seven angels who stand before God; they were given seven trumpets.

[3] Another angel, who had a gold incense container, came and stood at the altar. He was given much incense to add to the prayers of all God's people and offer on the altar that stands before the throne. [4] The smoke of the burning incense went up with the prayers of God's people from the hands of the angel standing before God. [5] Then the angel took the incense container, filled it with fire from the altar, and threw it on the earth. There were peals of thunder, sounds, flashes of lightning, and an earthquake.

The Trumpets

[6] Then the seven angels with the seven trumpets prepared to blow them.

[7] The first angel blew his trumpet. Hail and fire, mixed with blood, came pouring down on the earth. A third of the earth was burned up, and a third of the trees were burned up, and every blade of green grass was burned up.

[8] Then the second angel blew his trumpet. Something that looked like a large mountain burning with fire was thrown into the sea. A third of the sea was turned into blood, [9] and a third of all living creatures in the sea died, and a third of all ships were destroyed.

[10] Then the third angel blew his trumpet. A large star, burning like a torch, dropped from the sky and fell on a third of the rivers, and on the springs of water. [11] (The name of the star is Bitterness.) A third of the water turned bitter, and many men died from drinking the water, because it had turned bitter.

[12] Then the fourth angel blew his trumpet. A third of the sun was struck, and a third of the moon, and a third of the stars, so that their light lost a third of its brightness; there was no light during a third of the day and during a third of the night also.

[13] Then I looked, and I heard an eagle that was flying high in the air say in a loud voice: "Oh horror! horror! How horrible it will be for all who live on earth when the sound comes from the trumpets that the other three angels must blow!"

9 Then the fifth angel blew his trumpet. I saw a star which had fallen from the sky to earth; it was given the key to the abyss. [2] The star opened the abyss, and

8 Καὶ ὁ δεύτερος ἄγγελος ἐσάλπισεν· καὶ ὡς ὄρος μέγα πυρὶ[1] καιόμενον ἐβλήθη εἰς τὴν θάλασσαν· καὶ ἐγένετο τὸ τρίτον τῆς θαλάσσης αἷμα, 9 καὶ ἀπέθανεν τὸ τρίτον τῶν κτισμάτων τῶν ἐν τῇ θαλάσσῃ, τὰ ἔχοντα ψυχάς, καὶ τὸ τρίτον τῶν πλοίων διεφθάρησαν.

10 Καὶ ὁ τρίτος ἄγγελος ἐσάλπισεν· καὶ ἔπεσεν ἐκ τοῦ οὐρανοῦ ἀστὴρ μέγας καιόμενος ὡς λαμπάς, καὶ ἔπεσεν ἐπὶ τὸ τρίτον τῶν ποταμῶν καὶ ἐπὶ τὰς πηγὰς τῶν ὑδάτων. 11 καὶ τὸ ὄνομα τοῦ ἀστέρος λέγεται ὁ Ἄψινθος. καὶ ἐγένετο τὸ τρίτον τῶν ὑδάτων εἰς ἄψινθον, καὶ πολλοὶ τῶν ἀνθρώπων ἀπέθανον ἐκ τῶν ὑδάτων, ὅτι ἐπικράνθησαν.

12 Καὶ ὁ τέταρτος ἄγγελος ἐσάλπισεν· καὶ ἐπλήγη τὸ τρίτον τοῦ ἡλίου καὶ τὸ τρίτον τῆς σελήνης καὶ τὸ τρίτον τῶν ἀστέρων,[a] ἵνα σκοτισθῇ τὸ τρίτον αὐτῶν[a] καὶ ἡ ἡμέρα μὴ φάνῃ τὸ τρίτον αὐτῆς, καὶ ἡ νὺξ ὁμοίως.

13 Καὶ εἶδον, καὶ ἤκουσα ἑνὸς ἀετοῦ πετομένου ἐν μεσουρανήματι λέγοντος φωνῇ μεγάλῃ, Οὐαὶ οὐαὶ οὐαὶ τοὺς κατοικοῦντας ἐπὶ τῆς γῆς ἐκ τῶν λοιπῶν φωνῶν τῆς σάλπιγγος τῶν τριῶν ἀγγέλων τῶν μελλόντων σαλπίζειν.

9 Καὶ ὁ πέμπτος ἄγγελος ἐσάλπισεν· καὶ εἶδον ἀστέρα ἐκ τοῦ οὐρανοῦ πεπτωκότα εἰς τὴν γῆν, καὶ ἐδόθη αὐτῷ ἡ κλεὶς τοῦ φρέατος τῆς ἀβύσσου. 2 καὶ ἤνοιξεν τὸ

---

[1] 8 {C} πυρί ℵ A P 052 1 94 1006 1611 1828 1854 2020 2053 2065 2073 2081 2344 2432 it[ar,c,dem,div,gig,(h),haf,z] vg syr[h] cop[sa,bo] arm (eth) Primasius Andrew (Beatus) ‖ *omit* 046 1859 2042 2138 syr[ph] Tyconius Arethas

---

[a] [a] 12 *a* minor, *a* none: WH Bov Nes BF[2] (AV) (RV) (ASV) NEB Zür Luth (Jer) ‖ *a* minor, *a* major: RSV ‖ *a* minor, *a* minor: TR TT Seg

---

8 ἐγένετο...αἷμα Ex 7.20, 21 11 Jr 9.15 12 ἐπλήγη...ὁμοίως Is 13.10; Eze 32.7, 8; Jl 2.10; 3.15; Mt 24.29; Mk 13.24–25; Lk 21.25; Re 6.12–13
9 1 ἡ...ἀβύσσου Re 20.1

φρέαρ τῆς ἀβύσσου, καὶ ἀνέβη καπνὸς ἐκ τοῦ φρέατος ὡς καπνὸς καμίνου μεγάλης, καὶ ἐσκοτώθη ὁ ἥλιος καὶ ὁ ἀὴρ ἐκ τοῦ καπνοῦ τοῦ φρέατος. 3 καὶ ἐκ τοῦ καπνοῦ ἐξῆλθον ἀκρίδες εἰς τὴν γῆν, καὶ ἐδόθη αὐτοῖς ἐξουσία ὡς ἔχουσιν ἐξουσίαν οἱ σκορπίοι τῆς γῆς. 4 καὶ ἐρρέθη αὐτοῖς ἵνα μὴ ἀδικήσουσιν τὸν χόρτον τῆς γῆς οὐδὲ πᾶν χλωρὸν οὐδὲ πᾶν δένδρον, εἰ μὴ τοὺς ἀνθρώπους οἵτινες οὐκ ἔχουσι τὴν σφραγῖδα τοῦ θεοῦ ἐπὶ τῶν μετώπων. 5 καὶ ἐδόθη αὐτοῖς ἵνα μὴ ἀποκτείνωσιν αὐτούς, ἀλλ᾽ ἵνα βασανισθήσονται μῆνας πέντε· καὶ ὁ βασανισμὸς αὐτῶν ὡς βασανισμὸς σκορπίου, ὅταν παίσῃ ἄνθρωπον. 6 καὶ ἐν ταῖς ἡμέραις ἐκείναις ζητήσουσιν οἱ ἄνθρωποι τὸν θάνατον καὶ οὐ μὴ εὑρήσουσιν αὐτόν, καὶ ἐπιθυμήσουσιν ἀποθανεῖν καὶ φεύγει ὁ θάνατος ἀπ᾽ αὐτῶν.

7 Καὶ τὰ ὁμοιώματα τῶν ἀκρίδων ὅμοιοι ἵπποις ἡτοιμασμένοις εἰς πόλεμον, καὶ ἐπὶ τὰς κεφαλὰς αὐτῶν ὡς στέφανοι ὅμοιοι χρυσῷ[1], καὶ τὰ πρόσωπα αὐτῶν ὡς πρόσωπα ἀνθρώπων, 8 καὶ εἶχον τρίχας ὡς τρίχας γυναικῶν, καὶ οἱ ὀδόντες αὐτῶν ὡς λεόντων ἦσαν, 9 καὶ εἶχον θώρακας ὡς θώρακας σιδηροῦς, καὶ ἡ φωνὴ τῶν πτερύγων αὐτῶν ὡς φωνὴ ἁρμάτων ἵππων πολλῶν τρεχόντων εἰς πόλεμον. 10 καὶ ἔχουσιν οὐρὰς ὁμοίας σκορπίοις καὶ κέντρα, καὶ ἐν ταῖς οὐραῖς αὐτῶν ἡ ἐξουσία αὐτῶν ἀδικῆσαι τοὺς ἀνθρώπους μῆνας πέντε. 11 ἔχουσιν ἐπ᾽ αὐτῶν βασιλέα τὸν ἄγγελον τῆς ἀβύσσου· ὄνομα αὐτῷ Ἑβραϊστὶ Ἀβαδδὼν καὶ ἐν τῇ Ἑλληνικῇ ὄνομα ἔχει Ἀπολλύων.

---

[1] 7 {C} ὅμοιοι χρυσῷ ℵ A P 1 1006 1611 1828 (1854 χρυσίῳ) 2053 2065 2073 2081 2344 2432 it[ar,c,dem,div,gig,h][vid],haf,z[vid] vg syr[ph,h] cop[bo][vid] arm eth Primasius Andrew ∥ χρυσοῖ 046 0207 94 1859 2020 2042 2138 cop[sa] Arethas ∥ χρυσοῖ ὅμοιοι χρυσῷ 2351

---

2 καπνὸς...μεγάλης Gn 19.28; Ex 19.18   3 ἐξῆλθον...γῆν Ex 10.12, 15; Wsd 16.9   4 τὴν...μετώπων Eze 9.4; Re 7.3   6 Job 3.21; Jr 8.3; Ho 10.8; Lk 23.30; Re 6.16   7 τὰ...πόλεμον Jl 2.4, 5   8 οἱ...λεόντων Jl 1.6   9 ὡς φωνὴ ἁρμάτων Jl 2.5

smoke poured out of it, like the smoke from a large furnace; the sunlight and the air were made dark by the smoke from the abyss. 3 Locusts came down out of the smoke onto the earth, and they were given power like that of scorpions. 4 They were told not to harm the grass, or the trees, or any other plant; they could harm only the men who do not have the mark of God's seal on their foreheads. 5 The locusts were not allowed to kill these men, but only to torture them for five months. The pain caused by their torture is like the pain a man suffers when stung by a scorpion. 6 During the five months those men will seek death, but will not find it; they will want to die, but death will flee from them.

7 The locusts looked like horses ready for battle; on their heads they had what seemed to be gold crowns, and their faces were like men's faces. 8 Their hair was like women's hair, their teeth were like lions' teeth. 9 Their chests were covered with what looked like iron breastplates, and the sound made by their wings was like the noise of many horse-drawn chariots rushing into battle. 10 They have tails and stings, like those of a scorpion, and it is with their tails that they have the power to hurt men for five months. 11 They have a king ruling over them, who is the angel in charge of the abyss. His name in Hebrew is Abaddon; in Greek the name is Apollyon (meaning "The Destroyer").

¹² The first horror is over; after this there are still two more horrors to come.

¹³ Then the sixth angel blew his trumpet. I heard a voice coming from the corners of the gold altar standing before God. ¹⁴ The voice said to the sixth angel who had the trumpet: "Release the four angels who are bound at the great river Euphrates!" ¹⁵ The four angels were released; they had been prepared for this very hour of this very day of this very month and year, to kill a third of all mankind. ¹⁶ I was told the number of mounted troops: it was two hundred million. ¹⁷ And in my vision I saw the horses and their riders: they had breastplates red as fire, blue as sapphire, and yellow as sulphur. The horses' heads were like lions' heads, and from their mouths came out fire, smoke, and sulphur. ¹⁸ A third of mankind was killed by those three plagues: the fire, the smoke, and the sulphur coming out of the horses' mouths. ¹⁹ For the power of the horses is in their mouths, and also in their tails. Their tails are like snakes, with heads, and they use them to hurt people.

²⁰ The rest of mankind, all those who had not been killed by these plagues,

12 Ἡ οὐαὶ ἡ μία ἀπῆλθεν· ἰδοὺ ἔρχεται ἔτι δύο οὐαὶᵃ μετὰ ταῦτα.ᵃ

13 Καὶ ὁ ἕκτος ἄγγελος ἐσάλπισεν· καὶ ἤκουσα φωνὴν μίαν ἐκ τῶν κεράτων² τοῦ θυσιαστηρίου τοῦ χρυσοῦ τοῦ ἐνώπιον τοῦ θεοῦ, 14 λέγοντα τῷ ἕκτῳ ἀγγέλῳ, ὁ ἔχων τὴν σάλπιγγα, Λῦσον τοὺς τέσσαρας ἀγγέλους τοὺς δεδεμένους ἐπὶ τῷ ποταμῷ τῷ μεγάλῳ Εὐφράτῃ. 15 καὶ ἐλύθησαν οἱ τέσσαρες ἄγγελοι οἱ ἡτοιμασμένοι εἰς τὴν ὥραν καὶ ἡμέραν καὶ μῆνα καὶ ἐνιαυτόν, ἵνα ἀποκτείνωσιν τὸ τρίτον τῶν ἀνθρώπων. 16 καὶ ὁ ἀριθμὸς τῶν στρατευμάτων τοῦ ἱππικοῦ δισμυριάδες μυριάδων· ἤκουσα τὸν ἀριθμὸν αὐτῶν. 17 καὶ οὕτως εἶδον τοὺς ἵππους ἐν τῇ ὁράσειᵇ καὶ τοὺς καθημένους ἐπ' αὐτῶν,ᵇ ἔχοντας θώρακας πυρίνους καὶ ὑακινθίνους καὶ θειώδεις· καὶ αἱ κεφαλαὶ τῶν ἵππων ὡς κεφαλαὶ λεόντων, καὶ ἐκ τῶν στομάτων αὐτῶν ἐκπορεύεται πῦρ καὶ καπνὸς καὶ θεῖον. 18 ἀπὸ τῶν τριῶν πληγῶν τούτων ἀπεκτάνθησαν τὸ τρίτον τῶν ἀνθρώπων, ἐκ τοῦ πυρὸς καὶ τοῦ καπνοῦ καὶ τοῦ θείου τοῦ ἐκπορευομένου ἐκ τῶν στομάτων αὐτῶν. 19 ἡ γὰρ ἐξουσία τῶν ἵππων ἐν τῷ στόματι αὐτῶν ἐστιν καὶ ἐν ταῖς οὐραῖς αὐτῶν· αἱ γὰρ οὐραὶ αὐτῶν ὅμοιαι ὄφεσιν, ἔχουσαι κεφαλάς, καὶ ἐν αὐταῖς ἀδικοῦσιν.

20 Καὶ οἱ λοιποὶ τῶν ἀνθρώπων, οἳ οὐκ ἀπεκτάνθησαν

---

² 13 {C} ἐκ τῶν κεράτων 𝔭⁴⁷ ℵᵃ A 0207 94 1611 2053 2344 itᵃʳ,ᶜ,ᵈⁱᵛ,ᵍⁱᵍ,ʰᵃᶠ,ᶻ vgʷʷ syrʰ copˢᵃᵐˢ,ᵇᵒ eth Oecumenius Bede Ps-Ambrose Haymo ∥ . ἐκ τοῦ κέρατος copˢᵃᵐˢ ∥ ἐκ τῶν τεσσάρων κεράτων P 046 1 1006 1828 1854 1859 2020 2042 2065 2073 2081 2138 2432 itᵈᵉᵐ vgᶜˡ syrᵖʰ Cyprian Primasius Andrew Arethas ∥ omit μίαν ἐκ τῶν κεράτων ℵ* ∥ ἐκ τῶν τεσσάρων ζῴων ἃ ἦν ἐνώπιον τοῦ θυσιαστηρίου τοῦ θεοῦ (for ἐκ...θεοῦ) arm

---

ᵃ ᵃ 12–13 a none, a paragraph: TR WH Bov Nes BF² AV RV ASV RSV NEB TT Zür Luth Seg ∥ a none, a ellipsis and paragraph: Jer ∥ a major, a none

ᵇ ᵇ 17 b none, b minor: WH Bov Nes BF² NEB TT Zür Jer Seg ∥ b minor, b none: TR RSV ∥ b minor, b minor: AV RV ASV ∥ b none, b none: (Luth)

---

13 τοῦ θυσιαστηρίου τοῦ χρυσοῦ Ex 30.1–3; Re 8.3   15 οἱ τέσσαρες...ἀνθρώπων Re 8.7–12

ἐν ταῖς πληγαῖς ταύταις, οὐδὲ[3] μετενόησαν ἐκ τῶν ἔργων τῶν χειρῶν αὐτῶν, ἵνα μὴ προσκυνήσουσιν τὰ δαιμόνια καὶ **τὰ εἴδωλα τὰ χρυσᾶ καὶ τὰ ἀργυρᾶ καὶ τὰ χαλκᾶ καὶ τὰ λίθινα καὶ τὰ ξύλινα, ἃ οὔτε βλέπειν** δύνανται **οὔτε ἀκούειν οὔτε περιπατεῖν,** 21 καὶ οὐ μετενόησαν ἐκ τῶν φόνων αὐτῶν οὔτε ἐκ τῶν φαρμάκων[4] αὐτῶν οὔτε ἐκ τῆς πορνείας αὐτῶν οὔτε ἐκ τῶν κλεμμάτων αὐτῶν.

The Angel and the Little Scroll

10 Καὶ εἶδον ἄλλον ἄγγελον ἰσχυρὸν καταβαίνοντα ἐκ τοῦ οὐρανοῦ, περιβεβλημένον νεφέλην, καὶ ἡ ἶρις ἐπὶ τὴν κεφαλὴν αὐτοῦ, καὶ τὸ πρόσωπον αὐτοῦ ὡς ὁ ἥλιος, καὶ οἱ πόδες αὐτοῦ ὡς στῦλοι πυρός, 2 καὶ ἔχων ἐν τῇ χειρὶ αὐτοῦ βιβλαρίδιον ἠνεῳγμένον. καὶ ἔθηκεν τὸν πόδα αὐτοῦ τὸν δεξιὸν ἐπὶ τῆς θαλάσσης, τὸν δὲ εὐώνυμον ἐπὶ τῆς γῆς, 3 καὶ ἔκραξεν φωνῇ μεγάλῃ ὥσπερ λέων μυκᾶται. καὶ ὅτε ἔκραξεν, ἐλάλησαν αἱ ἑπτὰ βρονταὶ τὰς ἑαυτῶν φωνάς. 4 καὶ ὅτε ἐλάλησαν αἱ ἑπτὰ βρονταί, ἔμελλον γράφειν[1]· καὶ ἤκουσα φωνὴν ἐκ

---

[3] **20** {C} οὐδέ 𝔭[47] ℵ 046 2020 2053[txt] cop[sa,bo] ‖ οὔτε A P 1 1611 2053[comm] 2065 2081 2432 Primasius Andrew[a,bav] ‖ οὐδέ or οὔτε it[ar,c,dem,div,gig,haf,z] vg Cyprian Primasius ‖ οὐ C 94 1006 1828 1854 1859 2042 2073 2138 2344 arm Andrew[c,p] Beatus Arethas ‖ καὶ οὐ 2329 syr[ph,h] Tyconius

[4] **21** {C} φαρμάκων 𝔭[47] ℵ C 1006 1611 1854 1859 2042 2138 cop[bo] Andrew[c] Arethas ‖ φαρμακειῶν (A P 046 1828 2073 2344 φαρμακιῶν) 1 94 2020 2053 2065 2081 2432 syr[ph,h] cop[samss] arm Andrew[a,bavc,p] (Andrew[bav*] φαρμακιῶν) ‖ omit it[ar,z] cop[sams]

[1] **4** {C} ὅτε ἐλάλησαν αἱ ἑπτὰ βρονταί, ἔμελλον γράφειν P 1828 2065 2073 2081 2138 2432 (1 omit αἱ) (A C 046 94 1006 1611 1859 2020 2042 2053[txt] ἤμελλον) it[dem] vg[ww] syr[ph,h] arm eth? Andrew[bav,c,p] Arethas ‖ ὅσα ἐλάλησαν αἱ ἑπτὰ βρονταί, ἔμελλον γράφειν ℵ it[gig] cop[sa] Tyconius Primasius Andrew[a] Beatus ‖ ἤκουσα ὅσα ἐλάλησαν αἱ βρονταὶ καὶ ἤμελλον αὐτὰ γράφειν 𝔭[47] (cop[bo] καὶ ἤκουσα and αἱ ἑπτὰ βρονταί) ‖ ὅτε ἐλάλησαν

---

20 προσκυνήσουσιν...εἴδωλα Dt 32.17; 1 Cor 10.19–20   τὰ εἴδωλα...περιπατεῖν Ps 115.4–7; 135.15–17; Dn 5.23   **20–21** οὐδὲ...κλεμμάτων αὐτῶν Re 16.9, 11, 21

---

did not turn away from what they themselves had made. They did not stop worshiping the demons and the idols of gold, silver, bronze, stone, and wood, which cannot see, or hear, or walk. [21] Nor did those men repent of their murders, their magic, their immorality, or their stealing.

The Angel and the Little Scroll

10 Then I saw another mighty angel coming down out of heaven. He was dressed in a cloud, with a rainbow around his head; his face was like the sun, and his legs were like columns of fire. [2] He had a small scroll open in his hand. He put his right foot on the sea, and his left foot on the land, [3] and called out in a loud voice that sounded like the roar of lions. After he had called out, the seven thunders answered back with a roar. [4] As soon as they spoke, I was about to write. But I heard a voice speak from heaven: "Keep secret what the seven thunders said; do not write it down!''

5 Then the angel that I saw standing on the sea and on the land raised his right hand to heaven 6 and made a vow in the name of God, who lives for ever and ever, who created heaven and all things in it, the earth and all things in it, and the sea and all things in it. The angel said: "There will be no more delay! 7 But when the seventh angel blows his trumpet, then God will accomplish his secret plan, as he announced it to his servants, the prophets.''

8 Then the voice that I had heard speaking from heaven spoke to me again, saying: "Go and take the open scroll

τοῦ οὐρανοῦ λέγουσαν, Σφράγισον ἃ ἐλάλησαν αἱ ἑπτὰ βρονταί, καὶ μὴ αὐτὰ γράψῃς. 5 Καὶ ὁ ἄγγελος ὃν εἶδον ἑστῶτα ἐπὶ τῆς θαλάσσης καὶ ἐπὶ τῆς γῆς

ἦρεν τὴν χεῖρα αὐτοῦ τὴν δεξιὰν εἰς τὸν οὐρανὸν

6 **καὶ ὤμοσεν ἐν τῷ ζῶντι εἰς τοὺς αἰῶνας** τῶν αἰώνων,

ὃς ἔκτισεν τὸν οὐρανὸν καὶ τὰ ἐν αὐτῷ καὶ τὴν γῆν καὶ τὰ ἐν αὐτῇ καὶ τὴν θάλασσαν καὶ τὰ ἐν αὐτῇ[2], ὅτι χρόνος οὐκέτι ἔσται,[a] 7 ἀλλ' ἐν ταῖς ἡμέραις τῆς φωνῆς τοῦ ἑβδόμου ἀγγέλου, ὅταν μέλλῃ σαλπίζειν,[a] καὶ ἐτελέσθη τὸ μυστήριον τοῦ θεοῦ, ὡς εὐηγγέλισεν τοὺς ἑαυτοῦ δούλους τοὺς προφήτας[3].

8 Καὶ ἡ φωνὴ ἣν ἤκουσα ἐκ τοῦ οὐρανοῦ, πάλιν λαλοῦσαν μετ' ἐμοῦ καὶ λέγουσαν, Ὕπαγε λάβε τὸ βιβλίον

αἱ ἑπτὰ βρονταὶ καὶ ἔμελλον γράφειν αὐτά 1854 (2344[vid?] *omit* αὐτά) ∥ ὅτε ἐλάλησαν αἱ ἑπτὰ βρονταὶ τὰς φωνὰς ἑαυτῶν Ps-Ambrose ∥ ὅτε ἐλάλησαν αἱ ἑπτὰ βρονταὶ τὰς φωνὰς ἑαυτῶν, ἔμελλον γράφειν 254 429[c] it[c,div,haf,z°] (it[z*] *scripturas earum* for *scripturus eram*) vg[cl] Haymo ∥ ὅτε ἐλάλησαν αἱ ἑπτὰ βρονταί, ἤμελλον γράφειν τὰ εἰρημένα τοῖς ἑπτὰ πνεύμασι 2053[comm] ∥ ὅτε ἐλάλησαν, ἤμελλον γράφην [=γράφειν] 792 it[ar]

[2] **6** {B} καὶ τὴν θάλασσαν καὶ τὰ ἐν αὐτῇ 𝔭[47] ℵ[c] C P 046 1 94 1006 1828 1854 1859 2053 2065 2073 2081 2138 2432 it[ar,(c),(dem),div,(haf),z] vg (syr[h]) cop[sams,bo] (eth) Andrew Ps-Ambrose Beatus Haymo Arethas ∥ *omit* ℵ* A 1611 2020 2042 2344 it[gig] syr[ph] cop[sa] arm Tyconius Primasius

[3] **7** {C} τοὺς ἑαυτοῦ δούλους τοὺς προφήτας A C P 1611 1854 2020 2053 2065 2073 2081 2432 ∥ τοὺς δούλους αὐτοῦ τοὺς προφήτας 046 1006 1828 1859 2042 2138 syr[ph] ∥ τοῖς ἑαυτοῦ δούλοις τοῖς προφήταις 1 (94 arm δούλοις αὐτοῦ) it[gig] syr[h] ∥ *through his servants, the prophets* it[ar,c,dem,div,haf,z] vg cop[bo] Tyconius (Primasius) Ps-Ambrose ∥ τοὺς ἑαυτοῦ δούλους καὶ τοὺς προφήτας 𝔭[47] ℵ 2344 cop[sa] (eth) ∥ *which his own servants, the prophets, announced* (Beatus)

[a a] **6–7** *a minor, a minor*: TR Bov Nes BF[2] RSV TT Zür Luth Seg ∥ *a major, a minor*: WH AV RV ASV NEB Jer ∥ *a minor, a major*: WH[mg]

4 Σφράγισον...γράψῃς Dn 8.26; 12.4, 9   **5–6** ἦρεν...αἰώνων Dt 32.40; Dn 12.7
6 ὅς...αὐτῇ Gn 14.19, 22; Ex 20.11; Ne 9.6; Ps 146.6   **7** εὐηγγέλισεν...προφήτας Dn 9.6, 10;
Am 3.7; Zch 1.6

τὸ ἠνεωγμένον ἐν τῇ χειρὶ τοῦ ἀγγέλου τοῦ ἑστῶτος ἐπὶ τῆς θαλάσσης καὶ ἐπὶ τῆς γῆς. 9 καὶ ἀπῆλθα πρὸς τὸν ἄγγελον λέγων αὐτῷ δοῦναί μοι τὸ βιβλαρίδιον. καὶ λέγει μοι, Λάβε καὶ κατάφαγε αὐτό, καὶ πικρανεῖ σου τὴν κοιλίαν, ἀλλ' ἐν τῷ στόματί σου ἔσται γλυκὺ ὡς μέλι. 10 καὶ ἔλαβον τὸ βιβλαρίδιον ἐκ τῆς χειρὸς τοῦ ἀγγέλου καὶ κατέφαγον αὐτό, καὶ ἦν ἐν τῷ στόματί μου ὡς μέλι γλυκύ· καὶ ὅτε ἔφαγον αὐτό, ἐπικράνθη ἡ κοιλία μου. 11 καὶ λέγουσίν μοι, Δεῖ σε πάλιν προφητεῦσαι ἐπὶ λαοῖς καὶ ἔθνεσιν καὶ γλώσσαις καὶ βασιλεῦσιν πολλοῖς.

The Two Witnesses

11 Καὶ ἐδόθη μοι κάλαμος ὅμοιος ῥάβδῳ, λέγων, Ἔγειρε καὶ μέτρησον τὸν ναὸν τοῦ θεοῦ καὶ τὸ θυσιαστήριον καὶ τοὺς προσκυνοῦντας ἐν αὐτῷ. 2 καὶ τὴν αὐλὴν τὴν ἔξωθεν[1] τοῦ ναοῦ ἔκβαλε ἔξωθεν καὶ μὴ αὐτὴν μετρήσῃς, ὅτι ἐδόθη τοῖς ἔθνεσιν, καὶ τὴν πόλιν τὴν ἁγίαν πατήσουσιν μῆνας τεσσαράκοντα δύο. 3 καὶ δώσω τοῖς δυσὶν μάρτυσίν μου, καὶ προφητεύσουσιν ἡμέρας χιλίας διακοσίας ἑξήκοντα περιβεβλημένοι σάκκους. 4 οὗτοί εἰσιν αἱ δύο ἐλαῖαι καὶ αἱ δύο λυχνίαι αἱ ἐνώπιον τοῦ κυρίου τῆς γῆς ἑστῶτες. 5 καὶ εἴ τις αὐτοὺς θέλει ἀδικῆσαι, πῦρ ἐκπορεύεται ἐκ τοῦ στόματος αὐτῶν καὶ κατεσθίει τοὺς ἐχθροὺς αὐτῶν· καὶ εἴ τις θελήσει αὐτοὺς ἀδικῆσαι, οὕτως δεῖ αὐτὸν ἀποκτανθῆναι. 6 οὗτοι ἔχουσιν τὴν ἐξουσίαν κλεῖσαι τὸν οὐρανόν, ἵνα μὴ ὑετὸς βρέχῃ

---

[1] **2** {B} ἔξωθεν p47 A P 046 94 1006 1611 1854 1859 2020 2042 2053 2065 2073 2081 2138 2432 itar,c,dem,div,haf,z vg syrh copsa,bo arm eth? Tyconius Primasius Andrewp mssacc. to Ps-Ambrose Arethas ‖ ἔσωθεν ℵ 1 1828 syrph Victorinus-Pettau Andrewa,bav,c mssacc. to Ps-Ambrose

---

9-10 Λάβε...κοιλία μου Eze 2.8; 3.1-3   **11** Δεῖ...πολλοῖς Jr 1.10; 25.30; Dn 3.4; 7.14
11 1 ἐδόθη...μέτρησον Eze 40.3; Zch 2.1-2   **2** τὴν πόλιν...πατήσουσιν Ps 79.1; Is 63.18; Zch 12.3 lxx; Lk 21.24   μῆνας τεσσαράκοντα δύο Re 12.6; 13.5   **4** Zch 4.3, 11-14   **5** 2 Sm 22.9; 2 Kgs 1.10; Ps 97.3; Jr 5.14   **6** οὗτοι...αὐτῶν 1 Kgs 17.1

---

which is in the hand of the angel standing on the sea and on the land." 9 I went to the angel and asked him to give me the little scroll. He said to me, "Take it and eat it; it will turn sour in your stomach, but in your mouth it will be sweet as honey." 10 I took the little scroll from his hand and ate it, and it tasted sweet as honey in my mouth. But after I had swallowed it, it turned sour in my stomach.

11 Then I was told, "Once again you must speak God's message about many peoples and nations, languages and kings."

The Two Witnesses

11 I was then given a measuring stick, like a rod, and told: "Get up and measure the temple of God and the altar, and count those who are worshiping in the temple. 2 But omit the outer courts of the temple. Do not measure them, for they have been given to the heathen, who will trample on the Holy City for forty-two months. 3 I will send my two witnesses, dressed in sackcloth; and they will proclaim God's message during those twelve hundred and sixty days."

4 The two witnesses are the two olive trees and the two lamps that stand before the Lord of the earth. 5 If anyone tries to harm them, fire comes out of their mouths and destroys their enemies; and in this way whoever shall try to harm them will be killed. 6 They have authority to shut up the sky so there will be no rain during the time they speak God's message. They have authority also

over the springs of water, to turn them into blood; they have authority also to strike the earth with every kind of plague as often as they wish.

⁷ When they finish proclaiming their message, the beast that comes up out of the abyss will fight against them. He will defeat them and kill them, ⁸ and their bodies will lie on the street of the great city, where their Lord was nailed to the cross. The symbolic name of that city is Sodom, or Egypt. ⁹ People of all nationalities, from every tribe, language, and nation, will look at their bodies for three and a half days, and will not allow them to be buried. ¹⁰ The people of earth will be happy over the death of these two. They will celebrate, and send presents to one another, because those two prophets brought much suffering upon the people of earth. ¹¹ After three and a half days a life-giving breath came from God and entered them, and they stood up; all who saw them were terribly afraid. ¹² Then the two prophets heard a loud voice say to them from heaven: "Come up here!" As their enemies watched, they went up into heaven in a cloud. ¹³ At that very moment there was a violent earthquake; a tenth of the city was destroyed, and a total of seven thousand people were killed in the earthquake. The rest of the people were terrified and praised the greatness of the God of heaven.

¹⁴ The second horror is over; but look! The third horror will come soon.

The Seventh Trumpet

¹⁵ Then the seventh angel blew his trumpet, and there were loud voices in heaven, saying, "The power to rule over

τὰς ἡμέρας τῆς προφητείας αὐτῶν, καὶ ἐξουσίαν ἔχουσιν ἐπὶ τῶν ὑδάτων στρέφειν αὐτὰ εἰς αἷμα καὶ πατάξαι τὴν γῆν ἐν πάσῃ πληγῇ ὁσάκις ἐὰν θελήσωσιν. 7 καὶ ὅταν τελέσωσιν τὴν μαρτυρίαν αὐτῶν, τὸ θηρίον τὸ ἀναβαῖνον ἐκ τῆς ἀβύσσου ποιήσει μετ' αὐτῶν πόλεμον καὶ νικήσει αὐτοὺς καὶ ἀποκτενεῖ αὐτούς. 8 καὶ τὸ πτῶμα αὐτῶν ἐπὶ τῆς πλατείας τῆς πόλεως τῆς μεγάλης, ἥτις καλεῖται πνευματικῶς Σόδομα καὶ Αἴγυπτος, ὅπου καὶ ὁ κύριος αὐτῶν ἐσταυρώθη. 9 καὶ βλέπουσιν ἐκ τῶν λαῶν καὶ φυλῶν καὶ γλωσσῶν καὶ ἐθνῶν τὸ πτῶμα αὐτῶν ἡμέρας τρεῖς καὶ ἥμισυ, καὶ τὰ πτώματα αὐτῶν οὐκ ἀφίουσιν τεθῆναι εἰς μνῆμα. 10 καὶ οἱ κατοικοῦντες ἐπὶ τῆς γῆς χαίρουσιν ἐπ' αὐτοῖς καὶ εὐφραίνονται, καὶ δῶρα πέμψουσιν ἀλλήλοις, ὅτι οὗτοι οἱ δύο προφῆται ἐβασάνισαν τοὺς κατοικοῦντας ἐπὶ τῆς γῆς. 11 καὶ μετὰ τὰς τρεῖς ἡμέρας καὶ ἥμισυ πνεῦμα ζωῆς ἐκ τοῦ θεοῦ εἰσῆλθεν ἐν αὐτοῖς, καὶ ἔστησαν ἐπὶ τοὺς πόδας αὐτῶν, καὶ φόβος μέγας ἐπέπεσεν ἐπὶ τοὺς θεωροῦντας αὐτούς. 12 καὶ ἤκουσαν φωνῆς μεγάλης ἐκ τοῦ οὐρανοῦ λεγούσης αὐτοῖς, Ἀνάβατε ὧδε· καὶ ἀνέβησαν εἰς τὸν οὐρανὸν ἐν τῇ νεφέλῃ, καὶ ἐθεώρησαν αὐτοὺς οἱ ἐχθροὶ αὐτῶν. 13 Καὶ ἐν ἐκείνῃ τῇ ὥρᾳ ἐγένετο σεισμὸς μέγας, καὶ τὸ δέκατον τῆς πόλεως ἔπεσεν, καὶ ἀπεκτάνθησαν ἐν τῷ σεισμῷ ὀνόματα ἀνθρώπων χιλιάδες ἑπτά, καὶ οἱ λοιποὶ ἔμφοβοι ἐγένοντο καὶ ἔδωκαν δόξαν τῷ θεῷ τοῦ οὐρανοῦ.

14 Ἡ οὐαὶ ἡ δευτέρα ἀπῆλθεν· ἰδοὺ ἡ οὐαὶ ἡ τρίτη ἔρχεται ταχύ.

The Seventh Trumpet

15 Καὶ ὁ ἕβδομος ἄγγελος ἐσάλπισεν· καὶ ἐγένοντο φωναὶ μεγάλαι ἐν τῷ οὐρανῷ λέγοντες,

---

6 ἐξουσίαν ἔχουσιν...αἷμα Ex 7.17, 19–20 πατάξαι...πληγῇ 1 Sm 4.8   7 τὸ θηρίον...ἀβύσσου Dn 7.3; Re 13.1; 17.8 ποιήσει...νικήσει αὐτούς Dn 7.7, 21; Re 12.17; 13.7   8 τῆς πόλεως...ἐσταυρώθη Lk 13.34 καλεῖται...Σόδομα Is 1.10   11 πνεῦμα...αὐτῶν Eze 37.5, 10   12 ἀνέβησαν...οὐρανόν 2 Kgs 2.11   13 Eze 38.19–20

Ἐγένετο ἡ βασιλεία τοῦ κόσμου τοῦ κυρίου ἡμῶν
   καὶ τοῦ Χριστοῦ αὐτοῦ,
καὶ βασιλεύσει εἰς τοὺς αἰῶνας τῶν αἰώνων.
16 καὶ οἱ εἴκοσι τέσσαρες πρεσβύτεροι οἱ ἐνώπιον τοῦ
θεοῦ κάθηνται ἐπὶ τοὺς θρόνους αὐτῶν ἔπεσαν ἐπὶ τὰ
πρόσωπα αὐτῶν καὶ προσεκύνησαν τῷ θεῷ **17** λέγοντες,
   Εὐχαριστοῦμέν σοι, κύριε[a] ὁ θεός[a] ὁ παντοκράτωρ,
      ὁ ὢν καὶ ὁ ἦν,
   ὅτι[2] εἴληφας τὴν δύναμίν σου τὴν μεγάλην
      καὶ ἐβασίλευσας·
18   καὶ τὰ ἔθνη ὠργίσθησαν,
      καὶ ἦλθεν ἡ ὀργή σου
      καὶ ὁ καιρὸς τῶν νεκρῶν κριθῆναι
   καὶ δοῦναι τὸν μισθὸν τοῖς δούλοις σου τοῖς προφήταις
      καὶ τοῖς ἁγίοις καὶ τοῖς φοβουμένοις τὸ ὄνομά
      σου,
         τοὺς μικροὺς καὶ τοὺς μεγάλους,
   καὶ διαφθεῖραι τοὺς διαφθείροντας τὴν γῆν.
19 καὶ ἠνοίγη ὁ ναὸς τοῦ θεοῦ [ὁ] ἐν τῷ οὐρανῷ[3], καὶ
ὤφθη ἡ κιβωτὸς τῆς διαθήκης αὐτοῦ ἐν τῷ ναῷ αὐτοῦ·

the world belongs now to our Lord and his Messiah, and he will rule for ever and ever!'' **16** Then the twenty-four elders who sit on their thrones before God fell down on their faces and worshiped God, **17** saying:

"Lord God Almighty, the one who
   is and who was!
We thank you that you have used
   your great power
And have begun to rule!
18 The heathen were filled with rage,
   For it is the time for your wrath to
      come,
   And for the dead to be judged;
   The time to give the reward to your
      servants the prophets,
   And to all your people, great and
      small,
   To all who fear you.
   It is the time to destroy those who
      destroy the earth!''

19 God's temple in heaven was opened, and the ark holding the covenant was seen in his temple. Then there were

---

2 17 {C} ὅτι ℵ[c] A P 046 1 94 1611 1828 1854 1859 2020 2053 2081 2138 it[gig,h,haf] vg[ww] syr[ph,h] cop[sa] Cyprian Primasius Andrew[bav,c,p] Ps-Ambrose Arethas // qui it[c,dem,div,z] // καὶ ὅτι 𝔓[47] ℵ* C 2344 cop[boms] arm // et qui it[ar] // καὶ ὁ ἐρχόμενος ὅτι 051 1006 2042 2065 2073 2432 vg[cl] (cop[bo]) Tyconius Andrew[a] Beatus

3 19 {C} ὁ ἐν τῷ οὐρανῷ A C 1006 1828 2020 2073 it[gig,h] cop[bo] arm eth Victorinus-Pettau Andrew[c] // ἐν τῷ οὐρανῷ 𝔓[47] ℵ P 046 051 1 94 1611 1854 1859 2042 2053 2065 2081 2138 2344 2432 it[ar,c,dem,div,haf,z] vg syr[ph,h] cop[samss,bomss] Tyconius Andrew[a,bav,p] Arethas // ἐκ τοῦ οὐρανοῦ cop[samss]

[a a] **17** a none, a none: TR Bov Nes BF² AV RSV TT // a minor, a minor: WH // a minor a none: Zür Luth Jer // a none, a minor: RV ASV NEB Seg

---

15 Ἐγένετο...αἰώνων Ex 15.18; Ps 10.16; 22.28; Dn 2.44; 7.14; Ob 21; Zch 14.9 **17** κύριε...παντοκράτωρ Am 3.13 LXX; 4.13 LXX; Re 1.8; 4.8; 15.3; 16.7, 14; 19.6, 15; 21.22 ὁ ὢν Ex 3.14; Re 1.4, 8; 4.8; 16.5 **18** τὰ ἔθνη ὠργίσθησαν Ps 2.1; 46.6 τοῖς δούλοις...προφήταις Dn 9.6, 10; Am 3.7; Zch 1.6 τοῖς φοβουμένοις...μεγάλους Ps 115.13; Re 19.5 **19** ἡ...διαθήκης αὐτοῦ 1 Kgs 8.1, 6; 2 Chr 5.7

flashes of lightning, sounds, peals of thunder, an earthquake, and heavy hail.

The Woman and the Dragon

12 Then a great sign appeared in heaven: there was a woman, whose dress was the sun and who had the moon under her feet, and a crown of twelve stars on her head. ² She was soon to give birth, and the pains and suffering of childbirth made her cry out. ³ Another sign appeared in heaven. There was a huge red dragon with seven heads and ten horns, and a crown on each of his heads. ⁴ With his tail he dragged a third of the stars out of the sky and threw them to earth. He stood in front of the woman who was about to give birth, in order to eat her child as soon as it was born. ⁵ Then the woman gave birth to a son, who will rule over all nations with an iron rod. But the child was snatched away and taken to God and his throne. ⁶ The woman fled to the desert; there God had prepared a place for her, where she will be taken care of for twelve hundred and sixty days. ⁷ Then war broke out in heaven! Michael and his angels fought against the dragon, who fought back with his angels; ⁸ but the dragon was defeated, and he and his angels were not allowed

καὶ ἐγένοντο ἀστραπαὶ καὶ φωναὶ καὶ βρονταὶ καὶ σεισμὸς καὶ χάλαζα μεγάλη.

The Woman and the Dragon

12 Καὶ σημεῖον μέγα ὤφθη ἐν τῷ οὐρανῷ, γυνὴ περιβεβλημένη τὸν ἥλιον, καὶ ἡ σελήνη ὑποκάτω τῶν ποδῶν αὐτῆς, καὶ ἐπὶ τῆς κεφαλῆς αὐτῆς στέφανος ἀστέρων δώδεκα,ᵃ 2 καὶ ἐν γαστρὶ ἔχουσα,ᵃ καὶ κράζει ὠδίνουσα καὶ βασανιζομένη τεκεῖν. 3 καὶ ὤφθη ἄλλο σημεῖον ἐν τῷ οὐρανῷ, καὶ ἰδοὺ δράκων πυρρὸς μέγας, ἔχων κεφαλὰς ἑπτὰ καὶ κέρατα δέκα καὶ ἐπὶ τὰς κεφαλὰς αὐτοῦ ἑπτὰ διαδήματα, 4 καὶ ἡ οὐρὰ αὐτοῦ σύρει τὸ τρίτον τῶν ἀστέρων τοῦ οὐρανοῦ καὶ ἔβαλεν αὐτοὺς εἰς τὴν γῆν. καὶ ὁ δράκων ἕστηκεν ἐνώπιον τῆς γυναικὸς τῆς μελλούσης τεκεῖν, ἵνα ὅταν τέκῃ τὸ τέκνον αὐτῆς καταφάγῃ. 5 καὶ ἔτεκεν υἱόν,ᵇ ἄρσεν, ὃς μέλλει **ποιμαίνειν** πάντα **τὰ ἔθνη ἐν ῥάβδῳ σιδηρᾷ**· καὶ ἡρπάσθη τὸ τέκνον αὐτῆς πρὸς τὸν θεὸν καὶ πρὸς τὸν θρόνον αὐτοῦ.ᶜ 6 καὶ ἡ γυνὴ ἔφυγεν εἰς τὴν ἔρημον, ὅπου ἔχει ἐκεῖ τόπον ἡτοιμασμένον ἀπὸ τοῦ θεοῦ, ἵνα ἐκεῖ τρέφωσιν αὐτὴν ἡμέρας χιλίας διακοσίας ἑξήκοντα.

7 Καὶ ἐγένετο πόλεμος ἐν τῷ οὐρανῷ, ὁ Μιχαὴλ καὶ οἱ ἄγγελοι αὐτοῦ τοῦ πολεμῆσαι μετὰ τοῦ δράκοντος. καὶ ὁ δράκων ἐπολέμησεν καὶ οἱ ἄγγελοι αὐτοῦ, 8 καὶ οὐκ ἴσχυσεν, οὐδὲ τόπος εὑρέθη αὐτῶν ἔτι ἐν τῷ οὐρανῷ.

ᵃ ᵃ **1–2** *a* minor, *a* minor: Bov Nes BF² ASV ∥ *a* major, *a* none: (TR) AV RSV (NEB) (TT) Zür Luth Jer Seg ∥ *a* minor, *a* major: WH RV
ᵇ **5** *b* minor: WH RV ASV (TT) Zür Luth Seg ∥ *b* none: TR Bov Nes BF² AV? RSV? NEB? Jer?
ᶜ **5** *c* major: TR WH Bov Nes BF² AV RV ASV TT Zür Luth Seg ∥ *c* minor: RSV NEB Jer

---

19 ἀστραπαὶ...σεισμός Ex 19.16; Est 1.1d LXX; Eze 1.13; Re 8.5; 16.18   χάλαζα μεγάλη Ex 9.24; Re 16.21
12 2 κράζει...τεκεῖν Is 66.7; Mic 4.10   **3** δράκων...δέκα Dn 7.7   **4** σύρει...γῆν Dn 8.10
5 ἔτεκεν υἱόν Is 7.14; 66.7   μέλλει...σιδηρᾷ Ps 2.9; Re 19.15   **6** ἡμέρας...ἑξήκοντα Re 11.2; 13.5   **7** Μιχαήλ Dn 10.13, 21; 12.1; Jd 9

9 καὶ ἐβλήθη ὁ δράκων ὁ μέγας, ὁ ὄφις ὁ ἀρχαῖος, ὁ καλούμενος Διάβολος καὶ ὁ Σατανᾶς, ὁ πλανῶν τὴν οἰκουμένην ὅλην —ᵈ ἐβλήθη εἰς τὴν γῆν, καὶ οἱ ἄγγελοι αὐτοῦ μετ' αὐτοῦ ἐβλήθησαν. 10 καὶ ἤκουσα φωνὴν μεγάλην ἐν τῷ οὐρανῷ λέγουσαν,

Ἄρτι ἐγένετο ἡ σωτηρία καὶ ἡ δύναμις
    καὶ ἡ βασιλεία τοῦ θεοῦ ἡμῶν
    καὶ ἡ ἐξουσία τοῦ Χριστοῦ αὐτοῦ,
ὅτι ἐβλήθη ὁ κατήγωρ τῶν ἀδελφῶν ἡμῶν,
    ὁ κατηγορῶν αὐτοὺς ἐνώπιον τοῦ θεοῦ ἡμῶν
        ἡμέρας καὶ νυκτός.
11   καὶ αὐτοὶ ἐνίκησαν αὐτὸν διὰ τὸ αἷμα τοῦ ἀρνίου
    καὶ διὰ τὸν λόγον τῆς μαρτυρίας αὐτῶν,
    καὶ οὐκ ἠγάπησαν τὴν ψυχὴν αὐτῶν ἄχρι θανάτου.
12   διὰ τοῦτο εὐφραίνεσθε, οὐρανοὶ
    καὶ οἱ ἐν αὐτοῖς σκηνοῦντες·
οὐαὶ τὴν γῆν καὶ τὴν θάλασσαν,
    ὅτι κατέβη ὁ διάβολος πρὸς ὑμᾶςᵉ
ἔχων θυμὸν μέγαν,
    εἰδὼς ὅτι ὀλίγον καιρὸν ἔχει.

13 Καὶ ὅτε εἶδεν ὁ δράκων ὅτι ἐβλήθη εἰς τὴν γῆν, ἐδίωξεν τὴν γυναῖκα ἥτις ἔτεκεν τὸν ἄρσενα. 14 καὶ ἐδόθησαν τῇ γυναικὶ αἱ δύο πτέρυγες τοῦ ἀετοῦ τοῦ μεγάλου, ἵνα πέτηται εἰς τὴν ἔρημον εἰς τὸν τόπον αὐτῆς, ὅπου τρέφεται ἐκεῖ καιρὸν καὶ καιροὺς καὶ ἥμισυ καιροῦ ἀπὸ προσώπου τοῦ ὄφεως. 15 καὶ ἔβαλεν ὁ ὄφις ἐκ τοῦ στόματος αὐτοῦ ὀπίσω τῆς γυναικὸς ὕδωρ ὡς ποταμόν, ἵνα αὐτὴν ποταμοφόρητον ποιήσῃ. 16 καὶ ἐβοήθησεν ἡ γῆ τῇ γυναικί, καὶ ἤνοιξεν ἡ γῆ τὸ στόμα αὐτῆς καὶ κατέπιεν τὸν ποταμὸν ὃν ἔβαλεν ὁ δράκων ἐκ τοῦ στόματος αὐτοῦ. 17 καὶ ὠργίσθη ὁ δράκων ἐπὶ τῇ γυναικί,

---

ᵈ 9 d dash: WH RSV NEB ∥ d major: AV RV ASV Luth Seg ∥ d minor: TR Bov Nes BF² TT Zür Jer

ᵉ 12 e none: TR Bov Nes BF² RSV NEB TT Luth ∥ e minor: WH AV RV ASV Zür Jer Seg

---

9 ὁ δράκων...Σατανᾶς Re 20.2   ἐβλήθη...γῆν Is 14.12; Lk 10.18; Jn 12.31   10 ὁ κατήγωρ ...νυκτός Job 1.9–11; Zch 3.1   14 καιρὸν...καιροῦ Dn 7.25; 12.7

to stay in heaven any longer. ⁹ The huge dragon was thrown out! He is that old serpent, named the Devil, or Satan, that deceived the whole world. He was thrown down to earth, and all his angels with him.

¹⁰ Then I heard a loud voice in heaven saying: "Now God's salvation has come! Now God has shown his power as King! Now his Messiah has shown his authority! For the accuser of our brothers, who stood before God accusing them day and night, has been thrown out of heaven. ¹¹ Our brothers won the victory over him by the blood of the Lamb, and by the truth which they proclaimed; and they were willing to give up their lives and die. ¹² And so rejoice, you heavens, and all you who live there! But how terrible for the earth and the sea! For the Devil has come down to you, and he is filled with rage, for he knows that he has only a little time left."

¹³ When the dragon realized that he had been thrown down to the earth, he began to pursue the woman who had given birth to the boy. ¹⁴ The woman was given the two wings of a large eagle in order to fly to her place in the desert, where she will be taken care of for three and a half years, safe from the serpent's attack. ¹⁵ Then the serpent made water pour out of his mouth like a river after the woman, so that the flood of water would carry her away. ¹⁶ But the earth helped the woman; it opened its mouth and swallowed the water that had come from the dragon's mouth. ¹⁷ Then the dragon was furious with the woman, and

went off to fight against the rest of her descendants, all those who obey God's commandments and are faithful to the truth revealed by Jesus. [18] And the dragon stood[1] on the seashore.

The Two Beasts

13 Then I saw a beast coming up out of the sea. It had ten horns and seven heads, with a crown on each of its horns, and a wicked name written on its heads. [2] The beast I saw looked like a leopard, with feet like a bear's feet, and a mouth like a lion's mouth. The dragon gave the beast his own power, his throne, and his vast authority. [3] One of the heads of the beast seemed to have been killed, but the fatal wound had healed. The whole earth was amazed and followed after the beast. [4] All people worshiped the dragon because he had given his authority to the beast. They worshiped the beast also, saying: "Who is like the beast? Who can fight against it?"

---

[1] **18** And the dragon stood: *some mss. read* And I stood, *connecting this verse with what follows*

καὶ ἀπῆλθεν ποιῆσαι πόλεμον μετὰ τῶν λοιπῶν τοῦ σπέρματος αὐτῆς, τῶν τηρούντων τὰς ἐντολὰς τοῦ θεοῦ καὶ ἐχόντων τὴν μαρτυρίαν Ἰησοῦ· **18**[f] καὶ ἐστάθη[1] ἐπὶ τὴν ἄμμον τῆς θαλάσσης.

The Two Beasts

13[f] Καὶ εἶδον ἐκ τῆς θαλάσσης θηρίον ἀναβαῖνον, ἔχον κέρατα δέκα καὶ κεφαλὰς ἑπτά, καὶ ἐπὶ τῶν κεράτων αὐτοῦ δέκα διαδήματα, καὶ ἐπὶ τὰς κεφαλὰς αὐτοῦ ὄνομα[1] βλασφημίας. **2** καὶ τὸ θηρίον ὃ εἶδον ἦν ὅμοιον παρδάλει, καὶ οἱ πόδες αὐτοῦ ὡς ἄρκου, καὶ τὸ στόμα αὐτοῦ ὡς στόμα λέοντος. καὶ ἔδωκεν αὐτῷ ὁ δράκων τὴν δύναμιν αὐτοῦ καὶ τὸν θρόνον αὐτοῦ καὶ ἐξουσίαν μεγάλην. **3** καὶ μίαν ἐκ τῶν κεφαλῶν αὐτοῦ ὡς ἐσφαγμένην εἰς θάνατον, καὶ ἡ πληγὴ τοῦ θανάτου αὐτοῦ ἐθεραπεύθη.[a] καὶ ἐθαυμάσθη ὅλη ἡ γῆ ὀπίσω τοῦ θηρίου,[a] **4** καὶ προσεκύνησαν τῷ δράκοντι ὅτι ἔδωκεν τὴν ἐξουσίαν τῷ θηρίῳ, καὶ προσεκύνησαν τῷ θηρίῳ λέγοντες, Τίς ὅμοιος τῷ θηρίῳ, καὶ τίς δύναται πολεμῆσαι μετ' αὐτοῦ;

---

[1] **18** {C} καὶ ἐστάθη p⁴⁷ ℵ A C 1828 1854 2065 2344 2432 it[ar,c,dem,div,gig,haf,z] vg syr[h] arm eth Tyconius Primasius Beatus Haymo ∥ καὶ ἐστάθην P 046 051 1 94 1006 1611 1859 2020 2042 2053 2073 2081 2138 syr[ph] cop[sa,bo] Andrew Arethas

[1] **1** {C} ὄνομα p⁴⁷ ℵ C P 1 1006 2042 2065 2081 it[dem,z*] syr[ph] cop[sa,bo] arm eth Tyconius Primasius Andrew[a,bav,p] Beatus Haymo ∥ ὀνόματα A 046 051 94 1611 1828 1854 1859 2020 2053 2073 2138 2344 2432 it[ar,c,div,gig,haf] vg syr[h] Tyconius Andrew[c] Ps-Ambrose Arethas

---

[f][f] **12.17—13.1** f number 18, f chapter 13.1: TR WH Bov Nes BF² TT Zür Luth Jer Seg ∥ f no number, f chapter 13.1: RSV ∥ f chapter 13.1, f no number: AV RV ASV NEB

[a][a] **3** a major, a minor: WH Bov Nes BF² RV ASV Zür Luth ∥ a minor, a major: TR AV RSV Jer ∥ a major, a major: NEB TT Seg

---

17 ποιῆσαι...Ἰησοῦ Dn 7.7, 21; Re 11.7; 13.7
13 1 ἐκ...ἀναβαῖνον Dn 7.3 θηρίον...βλασφημίας Re 17.3, 7–12 **2** τὸ θηρίον...λέοντος Dn 7.4–6 **3** ἐθαυμάσθη...θηρίου Re 17.8

5 Καὶ ἐδόθη αὐτῷ στόμα λαλοῦν μεγάλα καὶ βλασφημίας, καὶ ἐδόθη αὐτῷ ἐξουσία ποιῆσαι μῆνας τεσσαράκοντα δύο. 6 καὶ ἤνοιξεν τὸ στόμα αὐτοῦ εἰς βλασφημίας πρὸς τὸν θεόν, βλασφημῆσαι τὸ ὄνομα αὐτοῦ καὶ τὴν σκηνὴν αὐτοῦ, τοὺς ἐν τῷ οὐρανῷ σκηνοῦντας[2]. 7 καὶ ἐδόθη αὐτῷ ποιῆσαι πόλεμον μετὰ τῶν ἁγίων καὶ νικῆσαι αὐτούς[3], καὶ ἐδόθη αὐτῷ ἐξουσία ἐπὶ πᾶσαν φυλὴν καὶ λαὸν καὶ γλῶσσαν καὶ ἔθνος. 8 καὶ προσκυνήσουσιν αὐτὸν πάντες οἱ κατοικοῦντες ἐπὶ τῆς γῆς, οὗ οὐ γέγραπται τὸ ὄνομα αὐτοῦ[4] ἐν τῷ βιβλίῳ τῆς ζωῆς τοῦ ἀρνίου τοῦ ἐσφαγμένου[b] ἀπὸ καταβολῆς κόσμου.

5 The beast was allowed to say terribly wicked things, and it was permitted to have authority for forty-two months. 6 It began to curse God, and God's name, and the place where he lives, including all those who live in heaven. 7 It was allowed to fight against God's people and to defeat them, and it was given authority over every tribe and people, every language and nation. 8 All people living on earth will worship it, that is, everyone whose name has not been written, before the world began, in the book of the living that belongs to the Lamb that was killed.

---

[2] 6 {C} τοὺς ἐν τῷ οὐρανῷ σκηνοῦντας (ℵ* σκηνοῦντες) A C 046ᶜ 94 (1006 omit τῷ) 1611 1828 (1854 omit τούς) 1859 2053ᶜᵒᵐᵐ 2138 2344 2432 eth Irenaeus Andrewᶜ ∥ καὶ τοὺς ἐν τῷ οὐρανῷ σκηνοῦντας (ℵᶜ καὶ τοῦ and σκηνοῦντες) P 046* 051 1 2020 2042 2053ᵗˣᵗ (2065 ἐν αὐτῇ [sic] οὐρανῷ) 2073 2081 itᵃʳ,ᶜ,ᵈᵉᵐ,ᵈⁱᵛ,ᵍⁱᵍ,ʰᵃᶠ,ᶻ vg syrʰ copˢᵃ,ᵇᵒ arm Irenaeusˡᵃᵗ Tyconius Primasius Andrewᵃ,ᵇᵃᵛ,ᵖ Arethas ∥ τῶν ἐν τῷ οὐρανῷ σκηνούντων syrᵖʰ ∥ ἐν τῷ οὐρανῷ 𝔭⁴⁷

[3] 7 {B} καὶ ἐδόθη αὐτῷ ποιῆσαι πόλεμον μετὰ τῶν ἁγίων καὶ νικῆσαι αὐτούς ℵ 046 051 94 1006 2073 2138 2344 itᵍⁱᵍ syrᵖʰ copᵇᵒ eth? Tyconius de Promissionibus Andrewᵃ,ᶜ Arethas ∥ καὶ ἐδόθη αὐτῷ πόλεμον ποιῆσαι μετὰ τῶν ἁγίων καὶ νικῆσαι αὐτούς (1ᵐᵍ νικῆσει) 1611 1828 1854 itᵃʳ,ᶜ,ᵈᵉᵐ,ᵈⁱᵛ,ʰᵃᶠ,ᶻ vg eth? Ps-Ambrose ∥ καὶ ἐδόθη αὐτῷ ἐξουσία ποιῆσαι πόλεμον μετὰ τῶν ἁγίων καὶ νικῆσαι αὐτούς 1859 2020 2065 2432 Primasius Beatus ∥ καὶ ἐδόθη αὐτῷ ποιῆσαι πόλεμον καὶ νικῆσαι Tyconius ∥ omit 𝔭⁴⁷ A C P 1ᵗˣᵗ 2042 2053 2081 syrʰ copˢᵃ arm Irenaeusˡᵃᵗ Andrewᵇᵃᵛ,ᵖ

[4] 8 {C} οὗ οὐ γέγραπται τὸ ὄνομα αὐτοῦ (A οὕαι) C 1828 1854 2053 Irenaeusˡᵃᵗ ∥ ὧν οὔτε γέγραπται τὸ ὄνομα 046 1859 2138 ∥ ὧν οὐ γέγραπται τὸ ὄνομα αὐτῶν 1611 syrʰ (syrᵖʰ omit τὸ ὄνομα αὐτῶν) ∥ ὧν οὐ γέγραπται τὸ ὄνομα 94 2020 2081 copˢᵃ,ᵇᵒ Andrewʰᵃᵛ,ᶜ,ᵖ ∥ ὧν οὐ γέγραπται τὰ ὀνόματα αὐτῶν 𝔭⁴⁷ 1006 2065 2432 arm eth Andrewᵃ ∥ ὧν οὐ γέγραπται τὰ ὀνόματα ℵᶜ P 051 1 2042 2073 itᵃʳ,ᶜ,ᵈᵉᵐ,ᵈⁱᵛ,ᵍⁱᵍ,ʰᵃᶠ,ᶻ vg Arethas ∥ ὧν γέγραπται τὰ ὀνόματα αὐτῶν ℵ*

[b] 8 b none: TR WH Bov Nes BF² AV RV ASVᵐᵍ Seg ∥ b minor: RVᵐᵍ ASV RSV NEB TT Zür Luth Jer

5 ἐδόθη...βλασφημίας Dn 7.8, 20, 25; 11.36   μῆνας τεσσαράκοντα δύο Re 11.2; 12.6
7 ποιῆσαι...αὐτούς Dn 7.7, 21; Re 11.7; 12.17   8 τῷ βιβλίῳ τῆς ζωῆς Ex 32.32, 33; Ps 69.28; Dn 12.1; Php 4.3; Re 3.5; 17.8; 20.12, 15; 21.27   τοῦ ἀρνίου τοῦ ἐσφαγμένου Is 53.7; Jn 1.29, 36; Re 5.6, 12

⁹ "Listen, then, if you have ears to hear with! ¹⁰ Whoever is meant to be captured, will surely be captured; whoever is meant to be killed by the sword, will surely be killed by the sword. This calls for endurance and faith on the part of God's people."

¹¹ Then I saw another beast coming up out of the earth. It had two horns like a lamb's horns, and it spoke like a dragon. ¹² It used the vast authority of the first beast in its presence. It forced the earth and all who live on it to worship the first beast, whose fatal wound had been healed. ¹³ This second beast performed great miracles; it made fire come down out of heaven to earth, in the presence of all men. ¹⁴ And it deceived all the people living on earth by means of the miracles which it was allowed to perform in the presence of the first beast. The beast told all the people of the world to build an image in honor of the beast that had been wounded by

9 Εἴ τις ἔχει οὖς ἀκουσάτω.

10 εἴ τις εἰς αἰχμαλωσίαν,
    εἰς αἰχμαλωσίαν ὑπάγει⁵·
εἴ τις ἐν μαχαίρῃ ἀποκτανθῆναι,
    αὐτὸν⁶ ἐν μαχαίρῃ ἀποκτανθῆναι.
ʳὯδέ ἐστιν ἡ ὑπομονὴ καὶ ἡ πίστις τῶν ἁγίων.

11 Καὶ εἶδον ἄλλο θηρίον ἀναβαῖνον ἐκ τῆς γῆς, καὶ εἶχεν κέρατα δύο ὅμοια ἀρνίῳ, καὶ ἐλάλει ὡς δράκων. 12 καὶ τὴν ἐξουσίαν τοῦ πρώτου θηρίου πᾶσαν ποιεῖ ἐνώπιον αὐτοῦ. καὶ ποιεῖ τὴν γῆν καὶ τοὺς ἐν αὐτῇ κατοικοῦντας ἵνα προσκυνήσουσιν τὸ θηρίον τὸ πρῶτον, οὗ ἐθεραπεύθη ἡ πληγὴ τοῦ θανάτου αὐτοῦ. 13 καὶ ποιεῖ σημεῖα μεγάλα, ἵνα καὶ πῦρ ποιῇ ἐκ τοῦ οὐρανοῦ καταβαίνειν εἰς τὴν γῆν ἐνώπιον τῶν ἀνθρώπων. 14 καὶ πλανᾷ τοὺς κατοικοῦντας ἐπὶ τῆς γῆς διὰ τὰ σημεῖα ἃ ἐδόθη αὐτῷ ποιῆσαι ἐνώπιον τοῦ θηρίου, λέγων τοῖς κατοικοῦσιν ἐπὶ τῆς γῆς ποιῆσαι εἰκόνα τῷ θηρίῳ ὃς

---

⁵ 10 {C} εἰς αἰχμαλωσίαν, εἰς αἰχμαλωσίαν ὑπάγει A vgᵂᵂ Ps-Ambrose ‖ εἰς αἰχμαλωσίαν ἀπάγει, εἰς αἰχμαλωσίαν ὑπάγει 1828 it⁽ᵃʳ⁾·ᶜ· ᵈᵉᵐ,ᵈⁱᵛ,ᵍⁱᵍ,ʰᵃᶠ,ᶻ vgᶜˡ syrᵖʰ,ʰ Irenaeusˡᵃᵗ Primasius ‖ αἰχμαλωσίαν συνάγει, εἰς αἰχμαλωσίαν ὑπάγει Arethas ‖ αἰχμαλωτίζει, εἰς αἰχμαλωσίαν ὑπάγει 104 (copˢᵃ) ‖ αἰχμαλωτίζει, αἰχμαλωτισθήσεται 94 ‖ εἰς αἰχμαλωσίαν ὑπάγει 𝔭⁴⁷ ℵ C P 046 1006 1611 (1854 ἀπάγει) 2020 2042 2053 2065 2073ᵐᵍ (2432 omit εἰς) copᵇᵒ (arm) Irenaeusᵃʳᵐ Tyconius Andrewᵇᵃᵛ Beatus ‖ εἰς αἰχμαλωσίαν συνάγει 2081 (1 Andrew omit εἰς) Arethas ‖ ἔχει αἰχμαλωσίαν ὑπάγει 051 1859 2073ᵗˣᵗ 2138 ‖ αἰχμαλωσίαν 1778 ‖ and caused me to be taken captive my thought [sic] eth

⁶ 10 {C} ἀποκτανθῆναι, αὐτόν A ‖ ἀποκτενεῖ αὐτόν 2048 ‖ ἀποκτενεῖ 1828 itᵍⁱᵍ syrᵖʰ copˢᵃˀᵇᵒˀ (arm) ‖ δεῖ αὐτόν 2138 ‖ ἀποκτενεῖ, δεῖ αὐτόν C P (051* ἀποκταινεῖ) 051 1 94 2020 2042 2081 itᵃʳ,ᶜ,ᵈᵉᵐ,ᵈⁱᵛ,ʰᵃᶠ,ᶻ vg copˢᵃˀᵇᵒˀ Irenaeusˡᵃᵗ Primasius Andrewᵃ·ᵖ Arethas ‖ ἀποκτένει [sic], δεῖ αὐτόν 046 1611ᶜ ‖ ἀποκτέννει, δεῖ αὐτόν 1006 1854 2344 2432 Andrewᶜ ‖ ἀποκτείνει, δεῖ αὐτόν ℵ 1611* syrʰ eth Irenaeus ‖ ἀποκτέμνει, δεῖ αὐτόν 2065 ‖ ἀποκτενεῖν δεῖ αὐτόν 2053 ‖ δεῖ αὐτὸν ἀποκτανθῆναι 1859 2073ᵐᵍ (2073ᵗˣᵗ transposes: δεῖ αὐτὸν ἐν μαχαίρᾳ ἀποκτανθῆναι)

---

10 εἴ τις εἰς...ἀποκτανθῆναι Jr 15.2; 43.11   13 ποιεῖ σημεῖα μεγάλα Mt 24.24; 2 Th 2.9 πῦρ...ἀνθρώπων 1 Kgs 18.24–39   14 πλανᾷ...σημεῖα Mt 24.24; 2 Th 2.9–10; Re 19.20 λέγων ...θηρίῳ Dt 13.2–4

ἔχει τὴν πληγὴν τῆς μαχαίρης καὶ ἔζησεν. 15 καὶ ἐδόθη αὐτῷ δοῦναι πνεῦμα τῇ εἰκόνι τοῦ θηρίου, ἵνα καὶ λαλήσῃ ἡ εἰκὼν τοῦ θηρίου καὶ ποιήσῃ ἵνα ὅσοι[7] ἐὰν μὴ προσκυνήσωσιν τῇ εἰκόνι τοῦ θηρίου ἀποκτανθῶσιν. 16 καὶ ποιεῖ πάντας, τοὺς μικροὺς καὶ τοὺς μεγάλους, καὶ τοὺς πλουσίους καὶ τοὺς πτωχούς, καὶ τοὺς ἐλευθέρους καὶ τοὺς δούλους, ἵνα δῶσιν αὐτοῖς χάραγμα ἐπὶ τῆς χειρὸς αὐτῶν τῆς δεξιᾶς ἢ ἐπὶ τὸ μέτωπον αὐτῶν, 17 καὶ[8] ἵνα μή τις δύνηται ἀγοράσαι ἢ πωλῆσαι εἰ μὴ ὁ ἔχων τὸ χάραγμα, τὸ ὄνομα τοῦ θηρίου ἢ τὸν ἀριθμὸν τοῦ ὀνόματος αὐτοῦ. 18 Ὧδε ἡ σοφία ἐστίν· ὁ ἔχων νοῦν ψηφισάτω τὸν ἀριθμὸν τοῦ θηρίου, ἀριθμὸς γὰρ ἀνθρώπου ἐστίν· καὶ ὁ ἀριθμὸς αὐτοῦ ἑξακόσιοι ἑξήκοντα[9] ἕξ.

The Song of the 144,000

14 Καὶ εἶδον, καὶ ἰδοὺ τὸ ἀρνίον ἑστὸς ἐπὶ τὸ ὄρος Σιών, καὶ μετ' αὐτοῦ ἑκατὸν τεσσαράκοντα τέσσαρες χιλιάδες ἔχουσαι τὸ ὄνομα αὐτοῦ καὶ τὸ ὄνομα τοῦ πατρὸς αὐτοῦ γεγραμμένον ἐπὶ τῶν μετώπων αὐτῶν.

the sword, and yet lived. [15] The second beast was allowed to breathe life into the image of the first beast, so that the image could talk and put to death all those who would not worship it. [16] The beast forced all men, small and great, rich and poor, slave and free, to have a mark placed on their right hands and on their foreheads. [17] No one could buy or sell unless he had this mark, that is, the beast's name or the number that stands for the name.

[18] This calls for wisdom. Whoever is intelligent can figure out the meaning of the number of the beast, because the number stands for a man's name. Its number is six hundred and sixty-six.

The Song of the Redeemed

14 Then I looked, and there was the Lamb standing on Mount Zion; with him were a hundred and forty-four thousand people who have his name and his Father's name written on their fore-

---

[7] **15** {C} ποιήσῃ ἵνα ὅσοι A P 1006 2065 2432 it[ar,gig,(z)] vg Hippolytus ‖ ποιήσει ἵνα ὅσοι 1828 it[c,dem,div,haf] syr[ph] cop[sa] Primasius Beatus ‖ *transpose:* ποιήσῃ ὅσοι...ἵνα ἀποκτανθῶσιν 051 1 1854 2073 ‖ ποιήσῃ ὅσοι 046 94 1611 1859 2020 2042 2081 2138 Andrew[a,p] Arethas ‖ ποιήσει ὅσοι ℵ (Irenaeus) Andrew[bav,c] ‖ ἐποίησεν ἵνα πάντες eth ‖ ποιήσει πάντες syr[h] ‖ καὶ ὃς οὐκ arm ‖ ὅσοι cop[bo]

[8] **17** {C} καί p47 ℵc A[vid] P 046 051 1 94 1006 1828 1854 1859 2020 2042 2065 2073 2081 2138 2344 2432 it[ar,c,dem,div,gig,z] vg arm eth Andrew[bav,c,p] Ps-Ambrose Haymo Arethas ‖ *omit* ℵ* C 1611 it[haf] syr[ph,h] cop[sa,bo] Irenaeus Hippolytus Tyconius Primasius Andrew[a] Beatus

[9] **18** {B} ἑξήκοντα p47 ℵ A P 046 051 1 94 1006 1611 1828 1854 1859 2020 2042 2053 2065 2073 2081 2138 2344 2432 it[c,dem,div,gig,haf] vg syr[ph,h] cop[sa,bo] arm eth? Irenaeus Hippolytus Origen Victorinus-Pettau Gregory-Elvira Primasius Andrew Arethas ‖ τεσσαράκοντα (*see* 14.1) it[ar] ‖ δέκα C it[svid?] mss[acc. to Irenaeus] Tyconius[pt]

---

15 ὅσοι...ἀποκτανθῶσιν Dn 3.5-6   **17** χάραγμα...θηρίου Re 14.9, 11; 16.2; 19.20; 20.4
14 1 ἑκατὸν...χιλιάδες Re 7.4; 14.3   ἔχουσαι...αὐτῶν Eze 9.4; Re 3.12; 7.3

heads. ² And I heard a voice from heaven that sounded like the roar of a mighty waterfall, like a loud peal of thunder. The voice I heard sounded like the music made by harpists playing their harps. ³ They stood facing the throne and the four living creatures and the elders, and they sang a new song which no one could learn except the one hundred and forty-four thousand people who have been redeemed from the earth. ⁴ They are the men who have kept themselves pure by not having relations with women; they are unmarried. They follow the Lamb wherever he goes; they have been redeemed from the rest of mankind and are the first ones to be offered to God and to the Lamb. ⁵ They have never been known to lie; they are without fault.

The Three Angels

⁶ Then I saw another angel flying high in the air, with an eternal message of Good News to announce to the peoples of the earth, to every nation and tribe and language and people. ⁷ He said in a loud voice: "Fear God, and praise his

2 καὶ ἤκουσα φωνὴν ἐκ τοῦ οὐρανοῦ ὡς φωνὴν ὑδάτων πολλῶν καὶ ὡς φωνὴν βροντῆς μεγάλης, καὶ ἡ φωνὴ ἣν ἤκουσα ὡς κιθαρῳδῶν κιθαριζόντων ἐν ταῖς κιθάραις αὐτῶν. 3 καὶ ᾄδουσιν [ὡς]¹ ᾠδὴν καινὴν ἐνώπιον τοῦ θρόνου καὶ ἐνώπιον τῶν τεσσάρων ζῴων καὶ τῶν πρεσβυτέρων· καὶ οὐδεὶς ἐδύνατο μαθεῖν τὴν ᾠδὴν εἰ μὴ αἱ ἑκατὸν τεσσαράκοντα τέσσαρες χιλιάδες, οἱ ἠγορασμένοι ἀπὸ τῆς γῆς. 4 οὗτοί εἰσιν οἳ μετὰ γυναικῶν οὐκ ἐμολύνθησαν, παρθένοι γάρ εἰσιν. οὗτοι οἱ ἀκολουθοῦντες τῷ ἀρνίῳ ὅπου ἂν ὑπάγῃ. οὗτοι ἠγοράσθησαν ἀπὸ τῶν ἀνθρώπων ἀπαρχὴ τῷ θεῷ καὶ τῷ ἀρνίῳ, 5 καὶ ἐν τῷ στόματι αὐτῶν οὐχ εὑρέθη ψεῦδος· ἄμωμοί² εἰσιν.

The Messages of the Three Angels

6 Καὶ εἶδον ἄλλον ἄγγελον³ πετόμενον ἐν μεσουρανήματι, ἔχοντα εὐαγγέλιον αἰώνιον εὐαγγελίσαι ἐπὶ τοὺς καθημένους ἐπὶ τῆς γῆς καὶ ἐπὶ πᾶν ἔθνος καὶ φυλὴν καὶ γλῶσσαν καὶ λαόν, 7 λέγων ἐν φωνῇ μεγάλῃ, Φοβή-

---

¹ **3** {C} ὡς A C 051 1 1006 2042 2065 2073 2081 2432 itar,c,dem,div,haf,z vg syrph Andrewa,bav Ps-Ambrose Beatus Haymo // omit p⁴⁷ ℵ P 046 94 1611 1828 1854 1859 2020 2053 2138 (2344 καινὴν ᾠδήν) itgig,t syrh copsa,bo arm eth Methodius Origen Jerome Primasius Andrewc,p Arethas

² **5** {C} ἄμωμοι A C P 1854 2042 2053 2073 2081 itc,div,gig,haf vgww Tyconius Augustine Andrewbav Beatus // ἄμωμοι γάρ p⁴⁷ ℵ 046 1 94 (1006 ἀμωμήτοι) 1611 1828 1859 2020 2065 2138 2344 (2432 ἄμω) itar,dem,t,z vgcl syrph,h copsa,bo arm eth Methodius Origen Augustine Ps-Athanasiuslat Andrewa,c,p Haymo Arethas // ὅτι ἄμωμοι 051

³ **6** {C} ἄλλον ἄγγελον ℵc A C P 051 1006 1611 2053 2065 2073* 2344 2432 itar,c,dem,div,gig,haf,t,z vg syrph,h copbo arm Cyprian Maternus Tyconius Vigilius Primasius Cassiodorus Ps-Ambrose Andrewa,(c) Beatus Haymo // ἄγγελον ἄλλον 1828 // ἦλθεν (omit εἶδον) ἄλλος ἄγγελος eth // ἄγγελον p⁴⁷ ℵ* 046 1 94 1854 1859 2020 2042 2073c 2081 2138 copsa Origen Victorinus-Pettau Ambrose Andrewbav,p Arethas // ἄλλον Tyconius

---

2 ὡς φωνὴν ὑδάτων πολλῶν Eze 1.24; 43.2; Re 1.15; 19.6   **3** ᾄδουσιν ὡς ᾠδὴν καινήν Ps 33.3; 40.3; 96.1; 98.1; 144.9; 149.1; Is 42.10; Re 5.9   ἑκατὸν...χιλιάδες Re 7.4; 14.1   **5** ἐν...ψεῦδος Ps 32.2; Is 53.9; Zph 3.13

θητε τὸν θεὸν καὶ δότε αὐτῷ δόξαν, ὅτι ἦλθεν ἡ ὥρα τῆς κρίσεως αὐτοῦ, καὶ προσκυνήσατε τῷ ποιήσαντι τὸν οὐρανὸν καὶ τὴν γῆν καὶ θάλασσαν καὶ πηγὰς ὑδάτων.

8 Καὶ ἄλλος δεύτερος [ἄγγελος]⁴ ἠκολούθησεν λέγων, Ἔπεσεν, ἔπεσεν Βαβυλὼν ἡ μεγάλη, ἣ ἐκ τοῦ οἴνου τοῦ θυμοῦ τῆς πορνείας αὐτῆς πεπότικεν πάντα τὰ ἔθνη.

9 Καὶ ἄλλος ἄγγελος τρίτος ἠκολούθησεν αὐτοῖς λέγων ἐν φωνῇ μεγάλῃ, Εἴ τις προσκυνεῖ τὸ θηρίον καὶ τὴν εἰκόνα αὐτοῦ, καὶ λαμβάνει χάραγμα ἐπὶ τοῦ μετώπου αὐτοῦ ἢ ἐπὶ τὴν χεῖρα αὐτοῦ, 10 καὶ αὐτὸς πίεται ἐκ τοῦ οἴνου τοῦ θυμοῦ τοῦ θεοῦ τοῦ κεκερασμένου ἀκράτου ἐν τῷ ποτηρίῳ τῆς ὀργῆς αὐτοῦ, καὶ βασανισθήσεται ἐν πυρὶ καὶ θείῳ ἐνώπιον ἀγγέλων ἁγίων καὶ ἐνώπιον τοῦ ἀρνίου. 11 καὶ ὁ καπνὸς τοῦ βασανισμοῦ αὐτῶν εἰς αἰῶνας αἰώνων ἀναβαίνει, καὶ οὐκ ἔχουσιν ἀνάπαυσιν ἡμέρας καὶ νυκτός, οἱ προσκυνοῦντες τὸ θηρίον καὶ τὴν εἰκόνα αὐτοῦ, καὶ εἴ τις λαμβάνει τὸ χάραγμα τοῦ ὀνόματος αὐτοῦ. 12 Ὧδε ἡ ὑπομονὴ τῶν ἁγίων ἐστίν, οἱ τηροῦντες τὰς ἐντολὰς τοῦ θεοῦ καὶ τὴν πίστιν Ἰησοῦ.

13 Καὶ ἤκουσα φωνῆς ἐκ τοῦ οὐρανοῦ λεγούσης, Γράψον· Μακάριοι οἱ νεκροὶ οἱ ἐν κυρίῳ ἀποθνῄσκοντεςᵃ

greatness! For the time has come for him to judge mankind. Bow in worship, then, before God, who made heaven, earth, sea, and the springs of water!''

8 A second angel followed the first one, saying: "She has fallen! The great Babylon has fallen! She gave her wine to all peoples, and made them drink it — the strong wine of her immoral lust!''

9 A third angel followed the first two, saying in a loud voice: "Whoever worships the beast and its image, and receives the mark on his forehead or on his hand, 10 will himself drink God's wine, the wine of his anger, which he has poured at full strength into the cup of his wrath! All who do this will be tormented in fire and sulphur before the holy angels and the Lamb. 11 The smoke of the fire that torments them goes up for ever and ever. There is no relief, day or night, for those who worshiped the beast and its image, for anyone who received the mark of its name.''

12 This calls for endurance on the part of God's people, those who obey God's commandments and are faithful to Jesus.

13 Then I heard a voice from heaven saying: "Write this: Happy are the dead who from now on die in the service of the Lord!'' "Certainly so,'' answers the

---

⁴ 8 {C} δεύτερος ἄγγελος A 046 1 1828 1859 2020 2138 Primasius Cassiodorus Andrewᵃ·ᶜ Arethas ∥ ἄγγελος δεύτερος ℵᶜ (C δεύτερον) P 051 94 1611 2042 2053 2065 2073 2081 2432 itᵍⁱᵍ syrʰ copˢᵃ·ᵇᵒ arm Tyconius Andrewᵇᵃᵛ·ᵖ ∥ δεύτερος pᵃⁱ ℵ* 1006 1854 syrᵖʰ ∥ ἄγγελος 296 2049 itᵃʳ·ˢ·ᵈᵉᵐ· ᵈⁱᵛ·ʰᵃᶠ·ᶻ vg eth Victorinus-Pettau Tyconius Ps-Ambrose

---

ᵃ ᵃ 13 a none, a major: TR WH Bov Nes BF² AVᵉᵈ RV ASV RSV TT (Zür) Luth (Seg) ∥ a major, a minor: RVᵐᵍ ASVᵐᵍ NEB ∥ a major, a dash: Jer ∥ a minor, a minor: AVᵉᵈ

---

7 τῷ...θάλασσαν Ex 20.11; Ps 146.6   8 Ἔπεσεν...μεγάλη Is 21.9; Jr 51.8; Re 18.2 ἐκ... ἔθνη Jr 51.7; Re 17.2; 18.3   9 Εἴ...εἰκόνα αὐτοῦ Re 13.12–17; 14.11; 16.2; 19.20 χάραγμα... αὐτοῦ Re 13.17; 14.11; 16.2; 19.20; 20.4   10 τῷ...αὐτοῦ Ps 75.8; Is 51.17, 22; Jr 25.15; Re 15.7; 16.19 πυρὶ καὶ θείῳ Gn 19.24; Ps 11.6; Eze 38.22; 3 Macc 2.5; Re 19.20; 20.10; 21.8   11 ὁ... ἀναβαίνει Is 34.10; Re 19.3 οἱ...εἰκόνα αὐτοῦ Re 13.12–17; 14.9; 16.2; 19.20 τὸ χάραγμα ...αὐτοῦ Re 13.17; 14.9; 16.2; 20.4

Spirit. "They will enjoy rest from their hard work; for they take with them the results of their service."

The Harvest of the Earth

¹⁴ Then I looked, and there was a white cloud, and sitting on the cloud was a being who looked like a man, with a gold crown on his head and a sharp sickle in his hand. ¹⁵ Then another angel went out from the temple and cried out in a loud voice to the one who was sitting on the cloud: "Use your sickle and reap the harvest, because the right time has come; the earth is ripe for the harvest!" ¹⁶ Then the one who sat on the cloud swung his sickle on the earth, and the earth's harvest was reaped.

¹⁷ Then I saw another angel come out of the temple in heaven, and he also had a sharp sickle.

¹⁸ Then another angel, who is in charge of the fire, came from the altar. He shouted in a loud voice to the angel who had the sharp sickle: "Use your sickle, and cut the grapes from the vineyard of the earth, because the grapes are ripe!" ¹⁹ So the angel swung his sickle on the earth, cut the grapes from the vine, and threw them into the winepress of God's

ἀπ᾽ ἄρτι.ᵃ ναί, λέγει⁵ τὸ πνεῦμα, ἵνα ἀναπαήσονται ἐκ τῶν κόπων αὐτῶν· τὰ γὰρ ἔργα αὐτῶν ἀκολουθεῖ μετ᾽ αὐτῶν.

The Harvest of the Earth

14 Καὶ εἶδον, καὶ ἰδοὺ νεφέλη λευκή, καὶ ἐπὶ τὴν νεφέλην καθήμενον ὅμοιον υἱὸν ἀνθρώπου, ἔχων ἐπὶ τῆς κεφαλῆς αὐτοῦ στέφανον χρυσοῦν καὶ ἐν τῇ χειρὶ αὐτοῦ δρέπανον ὀξύ. **15** καὶ ἄλλος ἄγγελος ἐξῆλθεν ἐκ τοῦ ναοῦ, κράζων ἐν φωνῇ μεγάλῃ τῷ καθημένῳ ἐπὶ τῆς νεφέλης, Πέμψον τὸ δρέπανόν σου καὶ θέρισον, ὅτι ἦλθεν ἡ ὥρα θερίσαι, ὅτι ἐξηράνθη ὁ θερισμὸς τῆς γῆς. **16** καὶ ἔβαλεν ὁ καθήμενος ἐπὶ τῆς νεφέλης τὸ δρέπανον αὐτοῦ ἐπὶ τὴν γῆν, καὶ ἐθερίσθη ἡ γῆ.

17 Καὶ ἄλλος ἄγγελος ἐξῆλθεν ἐκ τοῦ ναοῦ τοῦ ἐν τῷ οὐρανῷ, ἔχων καὶ αὐτὸς δρέπανον ὀξύ. **18** Καὶ ἄλλος ἄγγελος ἐκ τοῦ θυσιαστηρίου⁶, ἔχων ἐξουσίαν ἐπὶ τοῦ πυρός, καὶ ἐφώνησεν φωνῇ μεγάλῃ τῷ ἔχοντι τὸ δρέπανον τὸ ὀξὺ λέγων, Πέμψον σου τὸ δρέπανον τὸ ὀξὺ καὶ τρύγησον τοὺς βότρυας τῆς ἀμπέλου τῆς γῆς, ὅτι ἤκμασαν αἱ σταφυλαὶ αὐτῆς. **19** καὶ ἔβαλεν ὁ ἄγγελος τὸ δρέπανον αὐτοῦ εἰς τὴν γῆν, καὶ ἐτρύγησεν τὴν ἄμπελον τῆς γῆς καὶ ἔβαλεν εἰς τὴν ληνὸν τοῦ θυμοῦ τοῦ

---

⁵ **13** {B} ναί, λέγει ℵᶜ A C P 051 1 1006 1611 1854 2020 2042 2065 2073 2081 2344 2432 itᵃʳ,ᶜ,ᵈᵉᵐ,ᵈⁱᵛ,(ᵍⁱᵍ),ʰᵃᶠ,ᵐ,ᶻ vg syrᵖʰ,ʰ copˢᵃ arm (eth) Tyconius Augustine Primasius Ps-Ambrose Beatus ‖ λέγει ναί 046 94 (1828 λέγοντες) 1859 2138 ‖ καὶ λέγει 2053 ‖ λέγει p⁴⁷ ℵ* copᵇᵒ

⁶ **18** {C} ἄγγελος ἐκ τοῦ θυσιαστηρίου p⁴⁷ A 1611 2053 itᵃʳ,ᶜ,ᵍⁱᵍ vgʷʷ Tyconius Oecumenius Primasius Andrewᵇᵃᵛ ‖ ἄγγελος ἐξῆλθεν ἐκ τοῦ θυσιαστηρίου ℵ C P 046 1 94 1006 1828 1859 2020 2065 2081 2138 2432 itᵈᵉᵐ,ᵈⁱᵛ,ʰ,ʰᵃᶠ vgᶜˡ syrᵖʰ,ʰ copˢᵃ,ᵇᵒ arm (eth) Andrewᵃ,ᶜ,ᵖ Haymo Arethas ‖ ἄγγελος ἐκ τοῦ θυσιαστηρίου ἐξῆλθεν 051 1854 2073 ‖ ἄγγελος ἐξῆλθεν Primasius ‖ ἐκ τοῦ θυσιαστηρίου 2042

---

13 ἀναπαήσονται...κόπων αὐτῶν He 4.10   **14** ἐπὶ...ἀνθρώπου Dn 7.13   **15 ,18** Πέμψον ...γῆς Jl 3.13; Mt 13.39–40   **19** τὴν ληνὸν...μέγαν Re 19.15

θεοῦ τὸν μέγαν[7]. **20** καὶ ἐπατήθη ἡ ληνὸς ἔξωθεν τῆς πόλεως, καὶ ἐξῆλθεν αἷμα ἐκ τῆς ληνοῦ ἄχρι τῶν χαλινῶν τῶν ἵππων ἀπὸ σταδίων χιλίων ἑξακοσίων.

The Angels with the Last Plagues

15 Καὶ εἶδον ἄλλο σημεῖον ἐν τῷ οὐρανῷ μέγα καὶ θαυμαστόν, ἀγγέλους ἑπτὰ ἔχοντας πληγὰς ἑπτὰ τὰς ἐσχάτας, ὅτι ἐν αὐταῖς ἐτελέσθη ὁ θυμὸς τοῦ θεοῦ.

2 Καὶ εἶδον ὡς θάλασσαν ὑαλίνην μεμιγμένην πυρί, καὶ τοὺς νικῶντας ἐκ τοῦ θηρίου καὶ ἐκ τῆς εἰκόνος αὐτοῦ καὶ ἐκ τοῦ ἀριθμοῦ τοῦ ὀνόματος αὐτοῦ ἑστῶτας ἐπὶ τὴν θάλασσαν τὴν ὑαλίνην, ἔχοντας κιθάρας τοῦ θεοῦ. **3** καὶ ᾄδουσιν τὴν ᾠδὴν Μωϋσέως τοῦ δούλου τοῦ θεοῦ καὶ τὴν ᾠδὴν τοῦ ἀρνίου λέγοντες,

Μεγάλα καὶ θαυμαστὰ τὰ ἔργα σου,
  κύριε[a] ὁ θεός[a] ὁ παντοκράτωρ·
δίκαιαι καὶ ἀληθιναὶ αἱ ὁδοί σου,
  ὁ βασιλεὺς τῶν ἐθνῶν[1].

---

[7] **19** {C} τὸν μέγαν C P 046 051 1 1828[mg] 1859 2020 2073 2081[c] 2138 Tyconius Primasius Andrew[bav] Arethas ∥ τὸν μέγα A 94 2081* ∥ τὴν μεγάλην ℵ 1006 1828[txt] 1854 2042 2053 2065 2432 cop[sa, bo] Andrew[a, c, p] ∥ τοῦ μεγάλου 𝔭[47] 1611 ∥ τὸν (or τήν) μέγαν (or μέγα or μεγάλην) it[ar, c, dem, div, gig, h, haf] vg syr[ph, h] arm ∥ omit 181 424 468 eth? Victorinus-Pettau Tyconius

[1] **3** {C} ἐθνῶν ℵ[a] A P 046 051 1 1828 1854 1859 2020 2042 2053 2073[txt] 2081 2138 it[gig] cop[bo] Cyprian Ps-Cyprian Ambrose Andrew Beatus Arethas ∥ πάντων τῶν ἐθνῶν it[h] arm eth Primasius ∥ αἰώνων (see 1 Tm 1.17) 𝔭[47] ℵ[*, c] C 94 1006 1611 2065 2073[mg] 2344[vid] 2432 it[ar, c, dem, div, haf] vg syr[ph, h] cop[sa] Bede Ps-Ambrose Haymo ∥ ἁγίων 296 2049 Victorinus-Pettau Tyconius Apringius Cassiodorus

---

[a a] **3** a none, a none: TR Bov Nes BF[2] AV RSV TT Seg ∥ a minor, a minor: WH ∥ a minor, a none: Zür Luth Jer ∥ a none, a minor: RV ASV NEB

---

20 ἐπατήθη ἡ ληνός Is 63.3; Lm 1.15; Re 19.15
15 1 πληγὰς ἑπτά Lv 26.21; Re 15.6   2 τὴν ᾠδὴν Μωϋσέως Ex 15.1   Μεγάλα... ἔργα σου Ex 15.11; Ps 92.5; 111.2; 139.14   κύριε...παντοκράτωρ Am 3.13 LXX; 4.13 LXX; Re 1.8; 4.8; 11.17; 16.7, 14; 19.6, 15; 21.22   δίκαιαι...σου Dt 32.4; Ps 145.17   ὁ βασιλεὺς τῶν ἐθνῶν Jr 10.10 Theodotion; Tob 13.7, 11; En 9.4; 25.5; 27.3

great anger. **20** The grapes were squeezed out in the winepress outside the city, and blood came out of the winepress in a flood two hundred miles long and about five feet deep.

The Angels with the Last Plagues

15 Then I saw another great and amazing sign in heaven: seven angels with seven plagues. These are the last plagues, for they are the final expression of God's wrath.

2 Then I saw what looked like a sea of glass, mixed with fire; I also saw those who had won the victory over the beast and its image, and over the one whose name is given by a number. They were standing by the sea of glass, holding harps that God had given them. **3** They were singing the song of Moses, the servant of God, and the song of the Lamb:

"Lord, God Almighty,
  How great and wonderful are your
    deeds!
King of all nations,[1]
  How right and true are your ways!

---

[1] **3** all nations: *some mss. read* the ages

4 Who will not fear you, Lord?
Who will refuse to declare your
greatness?
For you alone are holy.
All the nations will come
And worship before you,
For your righteous deeds are seen
by all.''
5 After this I saw the temple in heaven
open, with the tent of God's presence
in it. 6 The seven angels who had the
seven last plagues came out of the
temple; they were dressed in clean white
linen, and had gold bands tied around
their chests. 7 Then one of the four
living creatures gave the seven angels
seven gold bowls full of the wrath of
God, who lives for ever and ever. 8 The
temple was filled with smoke from the
glory and power of God, and no one
could go into the temple until the end
of the seven plagues brought by the
seven angels.

4   τίς οὐ μὴ φοβηθῇ[2], κύριε,
            καὶ δοξάσει τὸ ὄνομά σου;[b]
ὅτι μόνος ὅσιος,[b]
            ὅτι πάντα τὰ ἔθνη ἥξουσιν
            καὶ προσκυνήσουσιν ἐνώπιόν σου,
ὅτι τὰ δικαιώματά σου ἐφανερώθησαν.
5 Καὶ μετὰ ταῦτα εἶδον, καὶ ἠνοίγη ὁ ναὸς τῆς σκηνῆς
τοῦ μαρτυρίου ἐν τῷ οὐρανῷ, 6 καὶ ἐξῆλθον οἱ ἑπτὰ
ἄγγελοι [οἱ] ἔχοντες τὰς ἑπτὰ πληγὰς ἐκ τοῦ ναοῦ,
ἐνδεδυμένοι λίνον[3] καθαρὸν λαμπρὸν καὶ περιεζωσμένοι
περὶ τὰ στήθη ζώνας χρυσᾶς. 7 καὶ ἓν ἐκ τῶν τεσσάρων
ζῴων ἔδωκεν τοῖς ἑπτὰ ἀγγέλοις ἑπτὰ φιάλας χρυσᾶς
γεμούσας τοῦ θυμοῦ τοῦ θεοῦ τοῦ ζῶντος εἰς τοὺς αἰῶνας
τῶν αἰώνων. 8 καὶ ἐγεμίσθη ὁ ναὸς καπνοῦ ἐκ τῆς
δόξης τοῦ θεοῦ καὶ ἐκ τῆς δυνάμεως αὐτοῦ, καὶ οὐδεὶς
ἐδύνατο εἰσελθεῖν εἰς τὸν ναὸν ἄχρι τελεσθῶσιν αἱ ἑπτὰ
πληγαὶ τῶν ἑπτὰ ἀγγέλων.

---

[2] **4** {C} οὐ μὴ φοβηθῇ A C P 046 1 1611 2042 2053 2081 it[c, dem, gig, h] cop[bo]
arm eth Cyprian Ambrose Primasius Andrew[a, bav, p] Beatus ∥ σε οὐ φοβηθῇ
ℵ 1006 (1854 σε μή) 2065 2432 ∥ οὐ μὴ φοβηθῇ σε 051 94 1828 1859 2020 2138
it[ar, div, haf] vg syr[ph, h] cop[sa] Andrew[c] Ps-Ambrose Haymo Arethas ∥ σε οὐ μὴ
φοβηθῇ 𝔭[47] 2073

[3] **6** {B} λίνον P 051 1 1006 1611 1859 2020[txt] 2042 2065 2073[txt] 2081 2138
2432 it[ar, gig, h] vg[cl] syr[ph, h] cop[bo?] arm Tyconius Primasius Andrew Arethas ∥
λίθον (see Eze 28.13) A C 2020[mg] 2053 it[c, dem, div, haf] vg[ww] Oecumenius mss[acc.]
[to Andrew] Bede Ps-Ambrose ∥ λίνουν 𝔭[47] 046 94 1828 ∥ λίνουν ἢ λίθον
2073[comm] ∥ λίνους ℵ ∥ omit cop[sa] eth Cassiodorus

[b b] **4** b question, b minor: TR Bov Nes BF² AV RV ASV (RSV) (NEB) TT Zür (Luth) Jer (Seg) ∥
b minor, b question: WH

---

4 τίς...ὄνομά σου Jr 10.6–7 πάντα...σου Ps 86.9; Mal 1.11   **5** τῆς...μαρτυρίου Ex 38.21;
40.34   **6** ἑπτὰ πληγάς Lv 26.21; Re 15.1   **7** ἑπτὰ φιάλας...θεοῦ Ps 75.8; Is 51.17, 22;
Jr 25.15; Re 14.10; 16.19   **8** ἐγεμίσθη...θεοῦ Ex 40.34; 1 Kgs 8.10–11; 2 Chr 5.13–14; Is 6.4;
Eze 44.4

The Bowls of God's Wrath

16 Καὶ ἤκουσα μεγάλης φωνῆς ἐκ τοῦ ναοῦ λεγούσης τοῖς ἑπτὰ ἀγγέλοις, Ὑπάγετε καὶ ἐκχέετε τὰς ἑπτὰ φιάλας τοῦ θυμοῦ τοῦ θεοῦ εἰς τὴν γῆν.

2 Καὶ ἀπῆλθεν ὁ πρῶτος καὶ ἐξέχεεν τὴν φιάλην αὐτοῦ εἰς τὴν γῆν· καὶ ἐγένετο ἕλκος κακὸν καὶ πονηρὸν ἐπὶ τοὺς ἀνθρώπους τοὺς ἔχοντας τὸ χάραγμα τοῦ θηρίου καὶ τοὺς προσκυνοῦντας τῇ εἰκόνι αὐτοῦ.

3 Καὶ ὁ δεύτερος ἐξέχεεν τὴν φιάλην αὐτοῦ εἰς τὴν θάλασσαν· καὶ ἐγένετο αἷμα ὡς νεκροῦ, καὶ πᾶσα ψυχὴ ζωῆς ἀπέθανεν, τὰ ἐν τῇ θαλάσσῃ.

4 Καὶ ὁ τρίτος ἐξέχεεν τὴν φιάλην αὐτοῦ εἰς τοὺς ποταμοὺς καὶ τὰς πηγὰς τῶν ὑδάτων· καὶ ἐγένετο[1] αἷμα. **5** καὶ ἤκουσα τοῦ ἀγγέλου τῶν ὑδάτων λέγοντος,

Δίκαιος εἶ, ὁ ὢν καὶ ὁ ἦν, ὁ ὅσιος,
  ὅτι ταῦτα ἔκρινας,
6 ὅτι αἷμα ἁγίων καὶ προφητῶν ἐξέχεαν,
  καὶ αἷμα αὐτοῖς δέδωκας πιεῖν·
ἄξιοί εἰσιν.
7 καὶ ἤκουσα τοῦ θυσιαστηρίου λέγοντος,
Ναί, κύριε[a] ὁ θεὸς[a] ὁ παντοκράτωρ,
  ἀληθιναὶ καὶ δίκαιαι αἱ κρίσεις σου.

The Bowls of God's Wrath

16 Then I heard a loud voice speaking from the temple to the seven angels: "Go and pour out the seven bowls of God's wrath on the earth!"

[2] The first angel went and poured out his bowl on the earth. Terrible and painful sores appeared on those who had the mark of the beast, and on those who had worshiped its image.

[3] Then the second angel poured out his bowl on the sea. The water became like the blood of a dead person, and every living creature in the sea died.

[4] Then the third angel poured out his bowl on the rivers and the springs of water, and they turned into blood. [5] I heard the angel in charge of the waters say: "You are righteous in these judgments you have made, O Holy One, who is and who was! [6] They poured out the blood of God's people and of the prophets, and so you have given them blood to drink. They are getting what they deserve!" [7] Then I heard a voice from the altar saying, "Lord, God Almighty! True and righteous indeed are your judgments!"

---

[1] **4** {C} ἐγένετο ℵ C P 046 051 1 94 1828 1859 2020 2065 2073 2081 2138 2432 it^{ar,c,dem,haf} vg arm Tyconius Andrew Ps-Ambrose Beatus Arethas ∥ ἐγένοντο 𝔓^47 A 1006 1611 1854 2042 2053 it^{div,gig,h} syr^{ph,h} cop^{sa,bo} eth Primasius Haymo

[a a] **7** a none, a none: TR Bov Nes BF² AV RSV TT Seg ∥ a minor, a minor: WH ∥ a minor, a none: Zür Luth Jer ∥ a none, a minor: RV ASV NEB

---

1 φωνῆς...ναοῦ Is 66.6; Re 16.17   ἐκχέετε...γῆν Ps 69.24; Jr 10.25; Eze 22.31; Zph 3.8
2 ἐγένετο...ἀνθρώπους Ex 9.10; Dt 28.35   τὸ...θηρίου Re 13.17; 14.9, 11; 19.20; 20.4   τοὺς προσκυνοῦντας...αὐτοῦ Re 13.12–17; 14.9, 11; 19.20   **3** ἐγένετο...θαλάσσῃ Ex 7.17–21
4 τοὺς...αἷμα Ex 7.19–24; Ps 78.44   **5** Δίκαιος εἶ Ps 119.137; 145.17; Dt 32.4   ὁ ὢν Ex 3.14; Re 1.4, 8; 4.8; 11.17   **6** αἷμα...ἐξέχεαν Ps 79.3   αἷμα αὐτοῖς δέδωκας πιεῖν Is 49.26
7 κύριε...παντοκράτωρ Am 3.13 lxx; 4.13 lxx; Re 1.8; 4.8; 11.17; 15.3; 16.14; 19.6, 15; 21.22   ἀληθιναὶ...σου Ps 19.9; 119.137; Re 19.2

⁸ Then the fourth angel poured out his bowl on the sun, and it was allowed to burn men with its fiery heat. ⁹ Men were burned by the fierce heat, and they cursed the name of God, who has authority over these plagues; but they would not turn from their sins and praise his greatness.

¹⁰ Then the fifth angel poured out his bowl on the throne of the beast. Darkness fell over the beast's kingdom, and men bit their tongues because of their pain, ¹¹ and they cursed the God of heaven for their pains and sores. But they did not turn from their evil ways.

¹² Then the sixth angel poured out his bowl on the great river Euphrates. The river dried up, to provide a way for the kings who come from the east. ¹³ Then I saw three unclean spirits, that looked like frogs, coming out of the mouth of the dragon, the mouth of the beast, and the mouth of the false prophet. ¹⁴ They are the spirits of demons that perform miracles. These three spirits go out to the kings over the whole earth, to bring them together for the war on the great day of Almighty God.

¹⁵ "Listen! I am coming like a thief! Happy is he who stays awake and takes care of his clothing, so that he will not walk around naked and be ashamed in public!"

¹⁶ Then the spirits brought the kings together in the place that in Hebrew is called Armageddon.

8 Καὶ ὁ τέταρτος ἐξέχεεν τὴν φιάλην αὐτοῦ ἐπὶ τὸν ἥλιον· καὶ ἐδόθη αὐτῷ καυματίσαι τοὺς ἀνθρώπους ἐν πυρί.ᵇ 9 καὶ ἐκαυματίσθησαν οἱ ἄνθρωποι καῦμα μέγα,ᵇ καὶ ἐβλασφήμησαν τὸ ὄνομα τοῦ θεοῦ τοῦ ἔχοντος τὴν ἐξουσίαν ἐπὶ τὰς πληγὰς ταύτας, καὶ οὐ μετενόησαν δοῦναι αὐτῷ δόξαν.

10 Καὶ ὁ πέμπτος ἐξέχεεν τὴν φιάλην αὐτοῦ ἐπὶ τὸν θρόνον τοῦ θηρίου·ᶜ καὶ ἐγένετο ἡ βασιλεία αὐτοῦ ἐσκοτωμένη,ᶜ καὶ ἐμασῶντο τὰς γλώσσας αὐτῶν ἐκ τοῦ πόνου, 11 καὶ ἐβλασφήμησαν τὸν θεὸν τοῦ οὐρανοῦ ἐκ τῶν πόνων αὐτῶν καὶ ἐκ τῶν ἑλκῶν αὐτῶν, καὶ οὐ μετενόησαν ἐκ τῶν ἔργων αὐτῶν.

12 Καὶ ὁ ἕκτος ἐξέχεεν τὴν φιάλην αὐτοῦ ἐπὶ τὸν ποταμὸν τὸν μέγαν τὸν Εὐφράτην· καὶ ἐξηράνθη τὸ ὕδωρ αὐτοῦ, ἵνα ἑτοιμασθῇ ἡ ὁδὸς τῶν βασιλέων τῶν ἀπὸ ἀνατολῆς ἡλίου. 13 Καὶ εἶδον ἐκ τοῦ στόματος τοῦ δράκοντος καὶ ἐκ τοῦ στόματος τοῦ θηρίου καὶ ἐκ τοῦ στόματος τοῦ ψευδοπροφήτου πνεύματα τρία ἀκάθαρτα ὡς βάτραχοι· 14 εἰσὶν γὰρ πνεύματα δαιμονίων ποιοῦντα σημεῖα, ἃ ἐκπορεύεται ἐπὶ τοὺς βασιλεῖς τῆς οἰκουμένης ὅλης, συναγαγεῖν αὐτοὺς εἰς τὸν πόλεμον τῆς μεγάλης ἡμέρας τοῦ θεοῦ τοῦ παντοκράτορος. 15 Ἰδοὺ ἔρχομαι ὡς κλέπτης. μακάριος ὁ γρηγορῶν καὶ τηρῶν τὰ ἱμάτια αὐτοῦ, ἵνα μὴ γυμνὸς περιπατῇ καὶ βλέπωσιν τὴν ἀσχημοσύνην αὐτοῦ. 16 καὶ συνήγαγεν αὐτοὺς εἰς τὸν τόπον τὸν καλούμενον Ἑβραϊστὶ Ἁρμαγεδών.

ᵇ ᵇ 8–9 b major, b minor: TR Bov Nes BF² AV RV ASV RSV NEB TT Zür (Luth) ∥ b minor, b major: WH Jer Seg

ᶜ ᶜ 10 c major, c minor: WH Bov Nes BF² Zür Luth Jer Seg ∥ c minor, c major: RSV NEB ∥ c minor, c minor: TR AV RV ASV TT

---

9 ἐβλασφήμησαν...δόξαν Re 9.20–21; 16.11, 21   10 ἡ...ἐσκοτωμένη Ex 10.21; Is 8.22   11 Re 9.20–21; 16.9, 21   12 ἐξηράνθη...αὐτοῦ Is 11.15; 44.27; Jr 50.38; 51.36   14 τοὺς... πόλεμον Re 19.19 τοῦ θεοῦ τοῦ παντοκράτορος Am 3.13 LXX; 4.13 LXX; Re 1.8; 4.8; 11.17; 15.3; 16.7; 19.6, 15; 21.22   15 ἔρχομαι ὡς κλέπτης Mt 24.43–44; Lk 12.39–40; 1 Th 5.2, 4; 2 Pe 3.10; Re 3.3   16 τὸν τόπον...Ἁρμαγεδών Jdg 5.19; 2 Kgs 9.27; 23.29; Zch 12.11

17 Καὶ ὁ ἕβδομος ἐξέχεεν τὴν φιάλην αὐτοῦ ἐπὶ τὸν ἀέρα·[d] καὶ ἐξῆλθεν φωνὴ μεγάλη ἐκ τοῦ ναοῦ ἀπὸ τοῦ θρόνου λέγουσα, Γέγονεν.[d] 18 καὶ ἐγένοντο ἀστραπαὶ καὶ φωναὶ καὶ βρονταί, καὶ σεισμὸς ἐγένετο μέγας οἷος οὐκ ἐγένετο ἀφ᾽ οὗ ἄνθρωπος ἐγένετο[2] ἐπὶ τῆς γῆς τηλικοῦτος σεισμὸς οὕτω μέγας. 19 καὶ ἐγένετο ἡ πόλις ἡ μεγάλη εἰς τρία μέρη, καὶ αἱ πόλεις τῶν ἐθνῶν ἔπεσαν. καὶ Βαβυλὼν ἡ μεγάλη ἐμνήσθη ἐνώπιον τοῦ θεοῦ δοῦναι αὐτῇ τὸ ποτήριον τοῦ οἴνου τοῦ θυμοῦ τῆς ὀργῆς αὐτοῦ. 20 καὶ πᾶσα νῆσος ἔφυγεν, καὶ ὄρη οὐχ εὑρέθησαν. 21 καὶ χάλαζα μεγάλη ὡς ταλαντιαία καταβαίνει ἐκ τοῦ οὐρανοῦ ἐπὶ τοὺς ἀνθρώπους· καὶ ἐβλασφήμησαν οἱ ἄνθρωποι τὸν θεὸν ἐκ τῆς πληγῆς τῆς χαλάζης, ὅτι μεγάλη ἐστὶν ἡ πληγὴ αὐτῆς σφόδρα.

The Great Harlot and the Beast

17 Καὶ ἦλθεν εἷς ἐκ τῶν ἑπτὰ ἀγγέλων τῶν ἐχόντων τὰς ἑπτὰ φιάλας, καὶ ἐλάλησεν μετ᾽ ἐμοῦ λέγων, Δεῦρο, δείξω σοι τὸ κρίμα τῆς πόρνης τῆς μεγάλης τῆς καθημένης ἐπὶ ὑδάτων πολλῶν, 2 μεθ᾽ ἧς ἐπόρνευσαν οἱ βασιλεῖς τῆς γῆς, καὶ ἐμεθύσθησαν οἱ κατοικοῦντες τὴν

[2] **18** {C} ἄνθρωπος ἐγένετο (p[47] ἐγένοντο) A cop[sa mss? bo?] ∥ ἐγένετο ἄνθρωπος 2020 cop[sa mss? bo?] arm (eth) ∥ ἄνθρωποι ἐγένοντο ℵ 046 051 1006 1611 1854 2042 2053 2065 2073 2081 2344 2432 it[ar,c,dem,div,gig,haf] vg cop[sa ms? bo mss?] syr[ph,h] (Andrew[ba v]) ∥ οἱ ἄνθρωποι ἐγένοντο 1 94 1828 1859 2138 Andrew[a,e,p] Arethas

[d d] **17** d minor, d major: TR Bov Nes BF² AV RV ASV TT Zür ∥ d dash, d dash: WH ∥ d minor d exclamation: RSV NEB Luth Jer (Seg)

17 ἐξῆλθεν...ναοῦ Is 66.6; Re 16.1   **18** ἐγένοντο...ἐγένετο μέγας Ex 19.16–19; Est 1.1d LXX; Re 4.5; 8.5; 11.19   οἷος...μέγας Dn 12.1   **19** τὸ ποτήριον...ὀργῆς αὐτοῦ Ps 75.8; Is 51.17, 22; Jr 25.15; Re 14.10; 15.7   **20** Re 6.14; 20.11   **21** χάλαζα μεγάλη Ex 9.24; Re 11.19   ἐβλασφήμησαν...πληγῆς Re 16.9, 11   **17** **1** τῆς καθημένης...πολλῶν Jr 51.13; Re 17.15   **2** ἐμεθύσθησαν...αὐτῆς Is 23.17; Jr 51.7; Re 14.8; 18.3

[17] Then the seventh angel poured out his bowl in the air. A loud voice came from the throne in the temple, saying: "It is done!" [18] There were flashes of lightning, sounds, peals of thunder, and a terrible earthquake. There never has been such an earthquake since the creation of man; this was the worst earthquake of all! [19] The great city was split into three parts, and the cities of all countries were destroyed. God remembered great Babylon, and made her drink the wine from his cup — the wine of his furious wrath. [20] All the islands disappeared, all the mountains vanished. [21] Great stones of hail, each weighing as much as a hundred pounds, fell from the sky on men. And men cursed God because of the plague of hail, for it was such a terrible plague.

The Great Prostitute

17 Then one of the seven angels who had the seven bowls came to me and said: "Come, and I will show you how the great prostitute is to be punished, that great city that is built near many rivers. [2] The kings of the earth committed immorality with the great prostitute, and the people of the world became drunk from drinking the wine of her immorality.''

³ The Spirit took control of me, and the angel carried me to a desert. There I saw a woman sitting on a red beast that had wicked names written all over it; the beast had seven heads and ten horns. ⁴ The woman was dressed in purple and scarlet, covered with gold ornaments, precious stones, and pearls. In her hand she held a gold cup full of obscene and filthy things, the result of her immorality. ⁵ On her forehead was written a name that has a secret meaning: "The Great Babylon, mother of all prostitutes and perverts of the world."
⁶ And I saw that the woman was drunk with the blood of God's people, and the blood of those who were killed because they had been loyal to Jesus.

When I saw her I was completely amazed. ⁷ "Why are you amazed?" the angel asked me. "I will tell you the secret meaning of the woman and of the beast that carries her, the beast with seven heads and ten horns. ⁸ The beast you saw was once alive, but lives no longer; it is about to come up from the abyss and will go off to be destroyed. The people living on earth whose names have not been written, before the world began, in the book of the living, will all

γῆν ἐκ τοῦ οἴνου τῆς πορνείας αὐτῆς. 3 καὶ ἀπήνεγκέν με εἰς ἔρημον ἐν πνεύματι. καὶ εἶδον γυναῖκα καθημένην ἐπὶ θηρίον κόκκινον, γέμοντα ὀνόματα βλασφημίας, ἔχων κεφαλὰς ἑπτὰ καὶ κέρατα δέκα. 4 καὶ ἡ γυνὴ ἦν περιβεβλημένη πορφυροῦν καὶ κόκκινον, καὶ κεχρυσωμένη χρυσίῳ καὶ λίθῳ τιμίῳ καὶ μαργαρίταις, ἔχουσα ποτήριον χρυσοῦν ἐν τῇ χειρὶ αὐτῆς γέμον βδελυγμάτων καὶ τὰ ἀκάθαρτα τῆς πορνείας αὐτῆς¹, 5 καὶ ἐπὶ τὸ μέτωπον αὐτῆς ὄνομα γεγραμμένον,ᵃ μυστήριονᵃ,ᵃ Βαβυλὼν ἡ μεγάλη, ἡ μήτηρ τῶν πορνῶν καὶ τῶν βδελυγμάτων τῆς γῆς. 6 καὶ εἶδον τὴν γυναῖκα μεθύουσαν ἐκ τοῦ αἵματος τῶν ἁγίων καὶ ἐκ τοῦ αἵματος τῶν μαρτύρων Ἰησοῦ.

Καὶ ἐθαύμασα ἰδὼν αὐτὴν θαῦμα μέγα. 7 καὶ εἶπέν μοι ὁ ἄγγελος, Διὰ τί ἐθαύμασας; ἐγὼ ἐρῶ σοι τὸ μυστήριον τῆς γυναικὸς καὶ τοῦ θηρίου τοῦ βαστάζοντος αὐτήν, τοῦ ἔχοντος τὰς ἑπτὰ κεφαλὰς καὶ τὰ δέκα κέρατα· 8 τὸ θηρίον ὃ εἶδες ἦν καὶ οὐκ ἔστιν, καὶ μέλλει ἀναβαίνειν ἐκ τῆς ἀβύσσου, καὶ εἰς ἀπώλειαν ὑπάγει²· καὶ θαυμασθήσονται οἱ κατοικοῦντες ἐπὶ τῆς γῆς, ὧν οὐ γέγραπται τὸ ὄνομα ἐπὶ τὸ βιβλίον τῆς ζωῆς ἀπὸ κατα-

---

¹ 4 {C} πορνείας αὐτῆς A 051 1 94 1006 1828 2020 2042 2065 2073 2081 2344 2432 (itᵃʳ καὶ πορνείας) itᶜ,ᵈᵉᵐ,ᵈⁱᵛ,ʰᵃᶠ vg syrᵖʰ eth Tyconius Andrew ∥ πορνείας τῆς γῆς 046 1611 1854 1859 2053 2138 syrʰ Hippolytus (Cyprian) (de Promissionibus) (Primasius) Arethas ∥ πορνείας αὐτῆς καὶ τῆς γῆς ℵ copˢᵃ,ᵇᵒ ∥ πορνείας arm ∥ γῆς itᵍⁱᵍ

² 8 {C} ὑπάγει (see 17.11) A 1611 2053 itᵃʳ,ᶜ,ᵈᵉᵐ,ᵈⁱᵛ,ᵍⁱᵍ,ʰᵃᶠ vg syrᵖʰ copˢᵃ,ᵇᵒ? eth? Irenaeusˡᵃᵗ Hippolytus Primasius Andrewᵃ Ps-Ambrose Arethas ∥ ὑπάγειν ℵ P 046 051 1 94 1006 1828 1854 1859 2020 2042 2065 2073 2081 2138 2432 syrʰ arm Hippolytus Tyconius Andrewᵃ,ᵇᵃᵛ,ᶜ Beatus

---

ᵃ ᵃ ᵃ 5 a minor, a μυστήριον, a minor: WH Bov Nes BF² RVᵐᵍ ASVᵐᵍ Zür Luth Seg ∥ a none, a μυστήριον, a minor: RSV NEB TT ∥ a dash, a μυστήριον, a exclamation and dash: Jer ∥ a minor, a Μυστήριον, a minor: TR AV RV ASV

---

3 γέμοντα...δέκα Re 13.1; 17.7–12   4 κεχρυσωμένη...μαργαρίταις Eze 28.13; Re 18.16 ἔχουσα...χειρὶ αὐτῆς Jr 51.7   6 Re 18.24; 19.2   8 τὸ θηρίον...ἀβύσσου Dn 7.3; Re 11.7; 13.1   τὸ βιβλίον τῆς ζωῆς Ex 32.32, 33; Ps 69.28; Dn 12.1; Php 4.3; Re 3.5; 13.8; 20.12, 15; 21.27

βολῆς κόσμου, βλεπόντων τὸ θηρίον ὅτι ἦν καὶ οὐκ
ἔστιν καὶ παρέσται. 9 ὧδε ὁ νοῦς ὁ ἔχων σοφίαν. αἱ
ἑπτὰ κεφαλαὶ ἑπτὰ ὄρη εἰσίν, ὅπου ἡ γυνὴ κάθηται ἐπ᾽
αὐτῶν.[b] [c]καὶ βασιλεῖς ἑπτά εἰσιν·[b] 10[c] οἱ πέντε ἔπεσαν, ὁ εἷς ἔστιν, ὁ ἄλλος οὔπω ἦλθεν, καὶ ὅταν ἔλθῃ
ὀλίγον αὐτὸν δεῖ μεῖναι.[d] 11 καὶ τὸ θηρίον ὃ ἦν καὶ
οὐκ ἔστιν,[d] καὶ αὐτὸς ὄγδοός ἐστιν καὶ ἐκ τῶν ἑπτά
ἐστιν, καὶ εἰς ἀπώλειαν ὑπάγει. 12 καὶ τὰ δέκα κέρατα
ἃ εἶδες δέκα βασιλεῖς εἰσιν, οἵτινες βασιλείαν οὔπω
ἔλαβον, ἀλλὰ ἐξουσίαν ὡς βασιλεῖς μίαν ὥραν λαμβάνουσιν μετὰ τοῦ θηρίου. 13 οὗτοι μίαν γνώμην ἔχουσιν,
καὶ τὴν δύναμιν καὶ ἐξουσίαν αὐτῶν τῷ θηρίῳ διδόασιν.
14 οὗτοι μετὰ τοῦ ἀρνίου πολεμήσουσιν, καὶ τὸ ἀρνίον
νικήσει αὐτούς, ὅτι κύριος κυρίων ἐστὶν καὶ βασιλεὺς
βασιλέων, καὶ οἱ μετ᾽ αὐτοῦ κλητοὶ καὶ ἐκλεκτοὶ καὶ
πιστοί.

15 Καὶ λέγει μοι, Τὰ ὕδατα ἃ εἶδες, οὗ ἡ πόρνη
κάθηται, λαοὶ καὶ ὄχλοι εἰσὶν καὶ ἔθνη καὶ γλῶσσαι.
16 καὶ τὰ δέκα κέρατα ἃ εἶδες καὶ τὸ θηρίον, οὗτοι
μισήσουσιν τὴν πόρνην, καὶ ἠρημωμένην ποιήσουσιν
αὐτὴν καὶ γυμνήν, καὶ τὰς σάρκας αὐτῆς φάγονται, καὶ
αὐτὴν κατακαύσουσιν ἐν πυρί· 17 ὁ γὰρ θεὸς ἔδωκεν
εἰς τὰς καρδίας αὐτῶν ποιῆσαι τὴν γνώμην αὐτοῦ, καὶ
ποιῆσαι μίαν γνώμην καὶ δοῦναι τὴν βασιλείαν αὐτῶν
τῷ θηρίῳ, ἄχρι τελεσθήσονται οἱ λόγοι τοῦ θεοῦ. 18 καὶ
ἡ γυνὴ ἣν εἶδες ἔστιν ἡ πόλις ἡ μεγάλη ἡ ἔχουσα βασιλείαν ἐπὶ τῶν βασιλέων τῆς γῆς.

be amazed as they look at the beast.
For it was once alive, but lives no longer,
and it will reappear.

9 "This calls for wisdom and understanding. The seven heads are seven
hills, the hills that the woman sits on.
They are also seven kings: 10 five of
them have fallen, one still rules, and
the other one has not yet come; when he
comes he must remain only a little while.
11 And the beast that was once alive, but
lives no longer, is itself an eighth king
who belongs to the first seven and goes
off to be destroyed.

12 "The ten horns you saw are ten
kings who have not yet begun to rule,
but who will be given authority to rule
as kings for one hour with the beast.
13 These ten all have the same purpose,
and give their power and authority to
the beast. 14 They will fight against the
Lamb; but the Lamb, and his called,
chosen, and faithful followers with him,
will defeat them, for he is Lord of lords
and King of kings."

15 The angel also said to me: "The
waters you saw, on which the woman
sits, are peoples and crowds and nations
and languages. 16 The ten horns you
saw, and the beast, will hate the prostitute; they will take away everything she
has and leave her naked; they will eat
her flesh and destroy her with fire. 17 For
God placed in their hearts the desire to
carry out his purpose, by acting with
one accord and giving to the beast their
power to rule, until God's words come
true.

18 "The woman you saw is the great
city that dominates the kings of the
earth."

[b b] **9-10** b major, b minor: WH Bov AV RV ASV RSV NEB Jer Seg ∥ b minor, b major: TR Nes
BF² TT Zür Luth

[c c] **9-10** c no number, c number 10: TR[ed] WH Bov Nes BF² TT Zür Luth Seg[ed] ∥ c number 10,
c no number: TR[ed] AV RV ASV RSV NEB Jer Seg[ed]

[d d] **10-11** d major, d minor: TR WH[mg] Bov Nes BF² AV RV ASV RSV NEB TT Zür Luth Jer
Seg ∥ d minor, d major: WH

---

12 τὰ δέκα κέρατα...εἰσιν Dn 7.24   **14** κύριος...βασιλέων Dt 10.17; Dn 2.47;
2 Macc 13.4; 3 Macc 5.35; En 9.4; 1 Tm 6.15; Re 19.16   **16** αὐτὴν κατακαύσουσιν ἐν πυρί
Lv 21.9; Re 18.8

The Fall of Babylon

18 After this I saw another angel coming down out of heaven. He had great authority, and his splendor brightened the whole earth. [2] He cried out in a loud voice: "She has fallen! The great Babylon has fallen! She is now haunted by demons and unclean spirits; all kinds of filthy and hateful birds live in her. [3] For she gave her wine to all peoples and made them drink it — the strong wine of her immoral lust. The kings of the earth committed immorality with her, and the businessmen of the world grew rich from her unrestrained lust."

[4] Then I heard another voice from heaven, saying:

"Come out, my people! Come out from her!
You must not take part in her sins,
You must not share her punishments!

The Fall of Babylon

18 Μετὰ ταῦτα εἶδον ἄλλον ἄγγελον καταβαίνοντα ἐκ τοῦ οὐρανοῦ, ἔχοντα ἐξουσίαν μεγάλην, καὶ ἡ γῆ ἐφωτίσθη ἐκ τῆς δόξης αὐτοῦ. 2 καὶ ἔκραξεν ἐν ἰσχυρᾷ φωνῇ λέγων,

Ἔπεσεν, ἔπεσεν Βαβυλὼν ἡ μεγάλη,
   καὶ ἐγένετο κατοικητήριον δαιμονίων
καὶ φυλακὴ παντὸς πνεύματος ἀκαθάρτου
   καὶ φυλακὴ παντὸς ὀρνέου ἀκαθάρτου καὶ μεμισημένου,

3   ὅτι ἐκ τοῦ οἴνου τοῦ θυμοῦ τῆς πορνείας[1] αὐτῆς πεπότικεν[2] πάντα τὰ ἔθνη,
   καὶ οἱ βασιλεῖς τῆς γῆς μετ᾽ αὐτῆς ἐπόρνευσαν,
   καὶ οἱ ἔμποροι τῆς γῆς ἐκ τῆς δυνάμεως τοῦ στρήνους αὐτῆς ἐπλούτησαν.

4 Καὶ ἤκουσα ἄλλην φωνὴν ἐκ τοῦ οὐρανοῦ λέγουσαν,
   Ἐξέλθατε, ὁ λαός μου, ἐξ αὐτῆς,
   ἵνα μὴ συγκοινωνήσητε ταῖς ἁμαρτίαις αὐτῆς,
   καὶ ἐκ τῶν πληγῶν αὐτῆς
   ἵνα μὴ λάβητε·

---

[1] **3** {C} τοῦ οἴνου τοῦ θυμοῦ τῆς πορνείας ℵ 046 94 1006 1859 2020 2138 it^dem vg^cl cop^sa, boms Hippolytus Tyconius Andrew^c Arethas ∥ τοῦ θυμοῦ τοῦ οἴνου τῆς πορνείας P 051 1 1828 2042 2065 2073 2081 2432 it^gig cop^bo arm eth^pp Hippolytus Primasius Andrew^a, bav, p ∥ τοῦ οἴνου τοῦ θυμοῦ syr^h Ps-Ambrose ∥ τοῦ θυμοῦ τῆς πορνείας A 1611 2053 it^ar, c, div, haf vg^ww eth^ro Priscillian Ansbert Haymo ∥ τοῦ οἴνου τῆς πορνείας 1854 syr^ph Tyconius Primasius (Andrew^comm) ∥ τῆς πορνείας τοῦ θυμοῦ C

[2] **3** {D} πεπότικεν 94 2042 2065 2432 syr^ph ∥ πεπτώκασιν ℵ (A C πέπτωκαν) 046 1006*vid 1611 cop^sa, bo eth Hippolytus ∥ πέπτωκεν 1854 2053 Oecumenius ∥ πέπωκαν 1828 ∥ πεπώκασιν 1006^cvid 1859 2020 2138 Andrew^c, p Arethas ∥ πέπωκεν P 051 1 2073 2081 Hippolytus Andrew^a, bav ∥ *they drank* it^ar, c, dem, div, gig, haf vg syr^h arm Tyconius Priscillian Beatus Haymo ∥ *omit* πεπότικεν πάντα τὰ ἔθνη Primasius

2 Ἔπεσεν...μεγάλη Is 21.9: Jr 51.8; Re 14.8   ἐγένετο...μεμισημένου Is 13.21; 34.11; Jr 50.39; Bar 4.35   **3** τοῦ οἴνου...ἔθνη Is 23.17; Jr 51.7; Re 14.8; 17.2   **4** Ἐξέλθατε...μου Is 48.20; 52.11; Jr 50.8; 51.6, 9, 45; 2 Cor 6.17

5   ὅτι ἐκολλήθησαν αὐτῆς αἱ ἁμαρτίαι ἄχρι τοῦ οὐρανοῦ,
     καὶ ἐμνημόνευσεν ὁ θεὸς τὰ ἀδικήματα αὐτῆς.

6   ἀπόδοτε αὐτῇ ὡς καὶ αὐτὴ ἀπέδωκεν,
     καὶ διπλώσατε [τὰ] διπλᾶ κατὰ τὰ ἔργα αὐτῆς·
     ἐν τῷ ποτηρίῳ ᾧ ἐκέρασεν κεράσατε αὐτῇ
       διπλοῦν·

7   ὅσα ἐδόξασεν αὐτὴν καὶ ἐστρηνίασεν,
     τοσοῦτον δότε αὐτῇ βασανισμὸν καὶ πένθος.
     ὅτι ἐν τῇ καρδίᾳ αὐτῆς λέγει ὅτι
       Κάθημαι βασίλισσα,
     καὶ χήρα οὐκ εἰμί,
       καὶ πένθος οὐ μὴ ἴδω·

8   διὰ τοῦτο ἐν μιᾷ ἡμέρᾳ ἥξουσιν αἱ πληγαὶ αὐτῆς,
     θάνατος καὶ πένθος καὶ λιμός,
     καὶ ἐν πυρὶ κατακαυθήσεται·
       ὅτι ἰσχυρὸς κύριος ὁ θεός[α] ὁ κρίνας αὐτήν.

9 Καὶ κλαύσουσιν καὶ κόψονται ἐπ' αὐτὴν οἱ βασιλεῖς τῆς γῆς οἱ μετ' αὐτῆς πορνεύσαντες καὶ στρηνιάσαντες, ὅταν βλέπωσιν τὸν καπνὸν τῆς πυρώσεως αὐτῆς, 10 ἀπὸ μακρόθεν ἑστηκότες διὰ τὸν φόβον τοῦ βασανισμοῦ αὐτῆς, λέγοντες,

     Οὐαὶ οὐαί, ἡ πόλις ἡ μεγάλη,
       Βαβυλὼν ἡ πόλις ἡ ἰσχυρά,
     ὅτι μιᾷ ὥρᾳ ἦλθεν ἡ κρίσις σου.

11 Καὶ οἱ ἔμποροι τῆς γῆς κλαίουσιν καὶ πενθοῦσιν ἐπ' αὐτήν[4], ὅτι τὸν γόμον αὐτῶν οὐδεὶς ἀγοράζει οὐκέτι,

---

[α] 8 {C} κύριος ὁ θεός ℵᵘ C P 046 051 1 94 1611 1828 1854 2065 2073 2081 2138 2432 itᵍⁱᵍ,ᵐ syrʰ (copˢᵃ,ᵇᵒ ὁ κύριος) arm Hippolytus Cyprian Tyconius Andrewᵇᵃᵛ,ᶜ,ᵖ Beatus ‖ ὁ θεὸς ὁ κύριος ℵ* ‖ κύριος ὁ θεὸς ὁ παντοκράτωρ 2042 ‖ ὁ θεός A 1006 2053ᶜᵒᵐᵐ itᵃʳ,ᶜ,ᵈᵉᵐ,ᵈⁱᵛ,ʰᵃᶠ vg eth ‖ κύριος 1859 2020 (2053ᵗˣᵗ ὁ κύριος) syrᵖʰ de Promissionibus Apringius Primasius Ps-Ambrose Haymo Arethas

[4] 11 {C} ἐπ' αὐτήν ℵ C P 94 1828 1854 2081ᵐᵍ itᵃʳ,ᶜ,ᵈᵉᵐ,ᵈⁱᵛ,ᵍⁱᵍ,ʰᵃᶠ vg

---

5 ἐκολλήθησαν...οὐρανοῦ Gn 18.20–21; Jr 51.9   6 ἀπόδοτε...ἀπέδωκεν Ps 137.8; Jr 50.15, 29; 2 Th 1.6   7–8 ἐν τῇ καρδίᾳ...πληγαὶ αὐτῆς Is 47.7–9   8 ἐν πυρὶ κατακαυθήσεται Lv 21.9; Re 17.16   ἰσχυρὸς...αὐτήν Jr 50.34   9 Eze 26.16; 27.30–35   10 ἡ πόλις ἡ μεγάλη ...ἰσχυρά Eze 26.17; Dn 4.30   11 Eze 27.36

---

⁵ For her sins are piled up as high as heaven,
And God remembers her wicked ways.
⁶ Treat her exactly as she has treated you,
Pay her back twice as much as she has done.
Fill her cup with a drink twice as strong
As the drink she prepared for you.
⁷ Give her as much suffering and grief
As the glory and luxury she gave herself.
For she keeps telling herself:
'Here I sit, a queen!
I am no widow,
I will never know grief!'
⁸ Because of this her plagues will all strike her in one day:
Disease, grief, and famine;
She will be burned with fire.
For the Lord God, who judges her, is mighty."

⁹ The kings of the earth who shared her immorality and lust will cry and weep for the city when they see the smoke of her burning. ¹⁰ They stand a long way off, because they are afraid of her suffering, and say: "How terrible! How awful! This great and mighty city Babylon! In just one hour you have been punished!"

¹¹ The businessmen of the earth also cry and mourn for her, because no one

buys their goods any longer; [12] no one buys their gold, silver, precious stones, and pearls; their goods of linen, purple cloth, silk, and scarlet; all kinds of rare woods, and all kinds of objects made of ivory and of expensive wood, of bronze, iron, and marble; [13] and cinnamon, spice, incense, myrrh, and frankincense; wine and oil, flour and wheat, cattle and sheep, horses and carriages, slaves and even men's souls. [14] The businessmen say to her: "All the good things you longed to own have disappeared, and all your wealth and glamor are gone, and you will never find them again!" [15] The businessmen, who became rich from doing business in that city, will stand a long way off, because they are afraid of her suffering. They will cry and mourn, [16] and say: "How terrible! How awful for the great city! She used to dress herself in linen and purple and scarlet, and cover herself with gold ornaments, precious stones, and pearls! [17] And in one hour she has lost all this wealth!"

All the ship captains and passengers,

12 γόμον χρυσοῦ καὶ ἀργύρου καὶ λίθου τιμίου καὶ μαργαριτῶν καὶ βυσσίνου καὶ πορφύρας καὶ σιρικοῦ καὶ κοκκίνου, καὶ πᾶν ξύλον θύϊνον καὶ πᾶν σκεῦος ἐλεφάντινον καὶ πᾶν σκεῦος ἐκ ξύλου τιμιωτάτου καὶ χαλκοῦ καὶ σιδήρου καὶ μαρμάρου, **13** καὶ κιννάμωμον καὶ ἄμωμον καὶ θυμιάματα καὶ μύρον καὶ λίβανον καὶ οἶνον καὶ ἔλαιον καὶ σεμίδαλιν καὶ σῖτον καὶ κτήνη καὶ πρόβατα, καὶ ἵππων καὶ ῥεδῶν καὶ σωμάτων, καὶ ψυχὰς ἀνθρώπων.

14   καὶ ἡ ὀπώρα σου τῆς ἐπιθυμίας τῆς ψυχῆς
              ἀπῆλθεν ἀπὸ σοῦ,
        καὶ πάντα τὰ λιπαρὰ καὶ τὰ λαμπρὰ
              ἀπώλετο ἀπὸ σοῦ,
        καὶ οὐκέτι οὐ μὴ αὐτὰ εὑρήσουσιν.

15 οἱ ἔμποροι τούτων, οἱ πλουτήσαντες ἀπ' αὐτῆς, ἀπὸ μακρόθεν στήσονται διὰ τὸν φόβον τοῦ βασανισμοῦ αὐτῆς, κλαίοντες καὶ πενθοῦντες, **16** λέγοντες,
        Οὐαὶ οὐαί, ἡ πόλις ἡ μεγάλη,
            ἡ περιβεβλημένη βύσσινον
                καὶ πορφυροῦν καὶ κόκκινον,
            καὶ κεχρυσωμένη [ἐν] χρυσίῳ
                καὶ λίθῳ τιμίῳ καὶ μαργαρίτῃ,
17ᵃ ὅτι μιᾷ ὥρᾳ ἠρημώθη ὁ τοσοῦτος πλοῦτος.
        ᵃΚαὶ πᾶς κυβερνήτης καὶ πᾶς ὁ ἐπὶ τόπον πλέων[5] καὶ

Hippolytus ∥ ἐπ' αὐτῇ 1006 1611 1859 2020 2053 2065 2073ᵐᵍ 2138 2432 Andrewᶜ Arethas ∥ ἐπ' αὐτήν or ἐπ' αὐτῇ syrᵖʰ·ʰ copˢᵃ·ᵇᵒ arm ∥ ἐν αὐτῇ A ∥ ἐπ' αὐτούς 046 ∥ ἐφ' ἑαυτούς 051 2073ᵗˣᵗ 2081ᵗˣᵗ Andrewᵇᵃᵛ ∥ ἐφ' ἑαυτοῖς 254 2302 Andrewᵃ·ᵖ ∥ ἐν ἑαυτοῖς 1 2042

5 17 {C} ὁ ἐπὶ τόπον πλέων A C 94 1006 1828 1854 1859 2020 2138 itᵃʳ·ᶜ· ᵈᵉᵐ·ᵈⁱᵛ vgʷʷ syrʰ? arm? ∥ ὁ ἐπὶ τὸν τόπον πλέων ℵ 046 0229 (1611 *omit* ὁ) itᵍⁱᵍ·ʰᵃᶠ syrʰ? arm? ∥ ἐπὶ τῶν πλοίων πλέων P 051 2042 2065 2073ᵗˣᵗ 2081 2432

ᵃ ᵃ **16–17** *a* number 17, *a* no number: TRᵉᵈ WH? Bov Nes BF² AV RV ASV RSV NEB TT Zür Luth Jer Seg ∥ *a* no number, *a* number 17: TRᵉᵈ WH?

12–13 Eze 27.12, 13, 22   **15** Eze 27.36   **16** κεχρυσωμένη...μαργαρίτῃ Eze 28.13; Re 17.4 **17** Eze 27.27–29

ναῦται καὶ ὅσοι τὴν θάλασσαν ἐργάζονται ἀπὸ μακρόθεν
ἔστησαν 18 καὶ ἔκραζον βλέποντες τὸν καπνὸν τῆς
πυρώσεως αὐτῆς λέγοντες, Τίς ὁμοία τῇ πόλει τῇ
μεγάλῃ; 19 καὶ ἔβαλον χοῦν ἐπὶ τὰς κεφαλὰς αὐτῶν
καὶ ἔκραζον κλαίοντες καὶ πενθοῦντες, λέγοντες,

Οὐαὶ οὐαί, ἡ πόλις ἡ μεγάλη,

ἐν ᾗ ἐπλούτησαν πάντες οἱ ἔχοντες τὰ πλοῖα
ἐν τῇ θαλάσσῃ ἐκ τῆς τιμιότητος αὐτῆς,
ὅτι μιᾷ ὥρᾳ ἠρημώθη.

20 Εὐφραίνου ἐπ᾽ αὐτῇ, οὐρανέ,

καὶ οἱ ἅγιοι καὶ οἱ ἀπόστολοι καὶ οἱ προφῆται,
ὅτι ἔκρινεν ὁ θεὸς τὸ κρίμα ὑμῶν ἐξ αὐτῆς.

21 Καὶ ἦρεν εἷς ἄγγελος ἰσχυρὸς λίθον ὡς μύλινον
μέγαν καὶ ἔβαλεν εἰς τὴν θάλασσαν λέγων,

Οὕτως ὁρμήματι βληθήσεται

Βαβυλὼν ἡ μεγάλη πόλις,
καὶ οὐ μὴ εὑρεθῇ ἔτι.

22 καὶ φωνὴ κιθαρῳδῶν καὶ μουσικῶν

καὶ αὐλητῶν καὶ σαλπιστῶν
οὐ μὴ ἀκουσθῇ ἐν σοὶ ἔτι,
καὶ πᾶς τεχνίτης πάσης τέχνης[6]
οὐ μὴ εὑρεθῇ ἐν σοὶ ἔτι,

the sailors and all others who earn their living on the sea, stood a long way off, [18] and cried out as they saw the smoke of her burning: "There never has been another city like the great city!" [19] They threw dust on their heads, they cried and mourned: "How terrible! How awful for the great city! She is the city where all who have ships sailing the seas became rich on her wealth! And in one hour she has lost everything!"

[20] Rejoice, because of her destruction, O heaven! Rejoice, God's people, and the apostles and prophets! For God has judged her for what she did to you!

[21] Then a mighty angel picked up a stone the size of a large millstone and threw it into the sea, saying: "This is how the great city Babylon will be thrown down with violence, and will never be seen again. [22] The music of harpists and musicians, of players of the flute and the trumpet, will never be heard in you again! No workman in any trade will ever be found in you again; and the

---

(Hippolytus) Tyconius Andrew Beatus Arethas ‖ ὁ ἐπὶ πόντον πλέων 469 2073[mg] vg[cl] cop[bo] (Primasius *per mare*) ‖ ὁ ἐπὶ τῶν πλοίων ἐπὶ τόπον πλέων syr[ph] ‖ ἐπὶ τῶν πλοίων ὁ ὅμιλος 1 Hippolytus ‖ ὁ ἐπὶ τὸν ποταμὸν πλέων 2053 ‖ *those who sail in the rivers* cop[sa] ‖ *qui a longe navigant* Ps-Ambrose ‖ *qui in longum navigant* Haymo

[6] **22** {C} καὶ πᾶς τεχνίτης πάσης τέχνης C P 046 051 1 94 1006 1611 1828 1854 1859 2020 2042 2065 2073 2081 2344 2432 (it[ar] *omit* πάσης) it[dem.gig] vg syr[h] cop[sa] (eth) Primasius Andrew[bav,c,p] Beatus Arethas ‖ καὶ πᾶς τεχνίτης καὶ πάσης τέχνης 2053 2138 it[c.div.haf] Ps-Ambrose ‖ καὶ πᾶς τεχνίτης ℵ A cop[bo] ‖ *omit* καὶ πᾶς...ἀκουσθῇ ἐν σοὶ ἔτι syr[ph] Hippolytus

---

18 Eze 27.32 **19** Eze 27.30–34 **20** Εὐφραίνου...οὐρανέ Dt 32.43 lxx; Ps 96.11; Is 44.23; 49.13; Jr 51.48 **21** Οὕτως...ἔτι Jr 51.63–64; Eze 26.21 **22** φωνὴ κιθαρῳδῶν...ἔτι Is 24.8; Eze 26.13

sound of the millstone will be heard no more! ²³ Never again will the light of a lamp be seen in you; no more will the voices of bride and groom be heard in you. Your businessmen were the most powerful in all the world, and with your false magic you deceived all the peoples of the world!''

²⁴ Babylon was punished because the blood of prophets and of God's people was found in the city; yes, the blood of all those who have been killed on earth.

19 After this I heard what sounded like the loud voice of a great crowd of people in heaven, saying: "Praise God! Salvation, glory, and power belong to our God! ² True and righteous are his judgments! For he has condemned the great prostitute who was corrupting the earth with her immorality. God has punished her because she killed his servants." ³ Again they shouted: "Praise God! The smoke from the burning of the great city goes up for ever and ever!" ⁴ The twenty-four elders and the four living creatures fell down and worshiped God who was seated on the throne, and said: "Amen! Praise God!"

καὶ φωνὴ μύλου
    οὐ μὴ ἀκουσθῇ ἐν σοὶ ἔτι,
23 καὶ φῶς λύχνου
    οὐ μὴ φάνῃ ἐν σοὶ ἔτι,
καὶ φωνὴ νυμφίου καὶ νύμφης
    οὐ μὴ ἀκουσθῇ ἐν σοὶ ἔτι·
ὅτι οἱ ἔμποροί σου ἦσαν οἱ μεγιστᾶνες τῆς γῆς,
    ὅτι ἐν τῇ φαρμακείᾳ σου ἐπλανήθησαν πάντα
        τὰ ἔθνη,
24 καὶ ἐν αὐτῇ αἷμα προφητῶν καὶ ἁγίων εὑρέθη
    καὶ πάντων τῶν ἐσφαγμένων ἐπὶ τῆς γῆς.

19 Μετὰ ταῦτα ἤκουσα ὡς φωνὴν μεγάλην ὄχλου πολλοῦ ἐν τῷ οὐρανῷ λεγόντων,
    Ἀλληλουϊά·
    ἡ σωτηρία καὶ ἡ δόξα καὶ ἡ δύναμις τοῦ θεοῦ ἡμῶν,
2   ὅτι ἀληθιναὶ καὶ δίκαιαι αἱ κρίσεις αὐτοῦ·
ὅτι ἔκρινεν τὴν πόρνην τὴν μεγάλην
    ἥτις ἔφθειρεν τὴν γῆν ἐν τῇ πορνείᾳ αὐτῆς,
καὶ ἐξεδίκησεν τὸ αἷμα τῶν δούλων αὐτοῦ
    ἐκ χειρὸς αὐτῆς.
3 καὶ δεύτερον εἴρηκαν,
    Ἀλληλουϊά·
    καὶ ὁ καπνὸς αὐτῆς ἀναβαίνει εἰς τοὺς αἰῶνας τῶν
        αἰώνων.
4 καὶ ἔπεσαν οἱ πρεσβύτεροι οἱ εἴκοσι τέσσαρες καὶ τὰ τέσσαρα ζῷα, καὶ προσεκύνησαν τῷ θεῷ τῷ καθημένῳ ἐπὶ τῷ θρόνῳ, λέγοντες,
    Ἀμήν, Ἀλληλουϊά.

Aphraates Tyconius ∥ *omit* καὶ πᾶς...εὑρέθῃ ἐν σοὶ ἔτι 61 69 arm ∥ *omit* καὶ φωνὴ μύλου...ἐν σοὶ ἔτι ℵ syrʰ eth Hippolytusˢˡᵃᵛ

23 φωνή...ἔτι Jr 7.34; 16.9; 25.10   οἱ ἔμποροί...γῆς Is 23.8   ἐν τῇ φαρμακείᾳ σου Is 47.9   **24** ἐν...εὑρέθη Jr 51.49; Eze 24.7; Re 6.10; 17.6; 19.2
19 1 ἤκουσα...Ἀλληλουϊά Tob 13.18   **2** ἀληθιναί...κρίσεις αὐτοῦ Ps 19.9; 119.137; Re 16.7   ἐξεδίκησεν...αὐτοῦ Dt 32.43; 2 Kgs 9.7; Ps 79.10; Re 6.10   **3** ὁ...αἰώνων Is 34.10
4 τῷ καθημένῳ...θρόνῳ 1 Kgs 22.19; 2 Chr 18.18; Ps 47.8; Is 6.1; Eze 1.26-27; Sir 1.8; Re 4.2, 9; 5.1, 7, 13; 6.16; 7.10, 15; 21.5

The Marriage Supper of the Lamb

5 Καὶ φωνὴ ἀπὸ τοῦ θρόνου ἐξῆλθεν λέγουσα,
 Αἰνεῖτε τῷ θεῷ ἡμῶν,
  πάντες οἱ δοῦλοι αὐτοῦ,
 [καὶ] οἱ φοβούμενοι[1] αὐτόν,
  οἱ μικροὶ καὶ οἱ μεγάλοι.
6 καὶ ἤκουσα ὡς φωνὴν ὄχλου πολλοῦ καὶ ὡς φωνὴν
ὑδάτων πολλῶν καὶ ὡς φωνὴν βροντῶν ἰσχυρῶν λεγόντων,
 Ἀλληλουϊά,
 ὅτι ἐβασίλευσεν κύριος[a]
  ὁ θεὸς [ἡμῶν][2] [a] ὁ παντοκράτωρ.
7 χαίρωμεν καὶ ἀγαλλιῶμεν,
  καὶ δώσωμεν[3] τὴν δόξαν αὐτῷ,
 ὅτι ἦλθεν ὁ γάμος τοῦ ἀρνίου,
  καὶ ἡ γυνὴ αὐτοῦ ἡτοίμασεν ἑαυτήν·

The Wedding Feast of the Lamb

5 Then there came from the throne the sound of a voice, saying: "Praise our God, all his servants, and all men, both great and small, who fear him!" 6 Then I heard what sounded like the voice of a great crowd, like the roar of a mighty waterfall, like loud peals of thunder. I heard them say: "Praise God! For the Lord, our Almighty God, is King! 7 Let us rejoice and be glad; let us praise his greatness! For the time has come for the wedding of the Lamb, and his bride

---

[1] 5 {C} καὶ οἱ φοβούμενοι A 046 051 (0229[vid] omit οἱ) 1 94 1006 1611 1854 1859 2020 2042 2053 2065 2073 2081 2138 2344 2432 it[ar,c,dem,div,gig,haf,t] vg syr[ph,h] cop[bo] arm eth Primasius Andrew Arethas ‖ οἱ φοβούμενοι ℵ C P cop[sa,boms]

[2] 6 {C} κύριος ὁ θεὸς ἡμῶν ℵ[a] P 046 94 1611 1854 1859 2020 2042 2053 2065 2073 2138 2344 (it[gig] omit ὁ παντοκράτωρ) it[ar,c,dem,div,haf] vg syr[h] cop[sams] Aphraates Tyconius Andrew Ps-Ambrose Beatus Arethas ‖ κύριος ὁ θεός A 1006 2432 it[t] syr[ph] cop[sa,bo] eth Cyprian ‖ ὁ θεὸς ἡμῶν 051 2081 ‖ ὁ θεὸς ὁ κύριος ἡμῶν ℵ* ‖ ὁ θεός 1 arm eth ‖ κύριος syr[ph*] cop[boms] Primasius

[3] 7 {D} δώσωμεν P 2081 2344 ‖ δώσομεν ℵ[c] A 2042 2053 2065 2432 ‖ δῶμεν ℵ* 046 051 1 94 1006 1611 1854 1859 2020 2073 2138 it[ar,c,dem,div,gig,haf,t] vg syr[ph,h] cop[sa,bo] eth (Cyprian) (Primasius) Andrew[a,c] Ps-Ambrose Arethas

---

[a a] 6 a none, a none: TR Bov Nes BF² AV RSV ‖ a minor, a minor: WH Zür Luth ‖ a minor, a none: Jer ‖ a none, a minor: RV ASV NEB TT Seg

---

5 Αἰνεῖτε...αὐτόν Ps 22.23; 134.1; 135.1   οἱ φοβούμενοι...μεγάλοι Ps 115.13; Re 11.18
6 ὡς φωνὴν ὑδάτων πολλῶν Eze 1.24; 43.2; Re 1.15; 14.2   ἐβασίλευσεν κύριος Ex 15.18; Ps 22.28; 93.1; 97.1; 99.1; Dn 7.14; Zch 14.9; Re 11.15   ὁ θεὸς ἡμῶν ὁ παντοκράτωρ Am 3.13 LXX; 4.13 LXX; Re 1.8; 4.8; 11.17; 15.3; 16.7, 14; 19.15; 21.22

has prepared herself for it. ⁸ She has been permitted to dress herself with clean shining linen.'' (The linen is the righteous deeds of God's people.)

⁹ Then the angel said to me: "Write this: Happy are those who have been invited to the wedding feast of the Lamb.'' And the angel added, "These are the true words of God.'' ¹⁰ I fell down at his feet to worship him, but he said to me: "Don't do it! I am a fellow servant of yours, and of your brothers, all those who hold to the truth that Jesus revealed. Worship God!''

For the truth that Jesus revealed is what inspires the prophets.

The Rider on the White Horse

¹¹ Then I saw heaven open, and there was a white horse. Its rider is called Faithful and True; it is with justice that he judges and fights his battles. ¹² His eyes were like a flame of fire, and he wore many crowns on his head. He had a name written on him, but no one

8   καὶ ἐδόθη αὐτῇ ἵνα περιβάληται
      βύσσινον λαμπρὸν καθαρόν,ᵇ
    τὸ γὰρ βύσσινον τὰ δικαιώματα τῶν ἁγίων ἐστίν.ᵇ
9 Καὶ λέγει μοι, Γράψον· Μακάριοι οἱ εἰς τὸ δεῖπνον τοῦ γάμου τοῦ ἀρνίου κεκλημένοι. καὶ λέγει μοι, Οὗτοι οἱ λόγοι ἀληθινοὶ τοῦ θεοῦ εἰσιν. 10 καὶ ἔπεσα ἔμπροσθεν τῶν ποδῶν αὐτοῦ προσκυνῆσαι αὐτῷ. καὶ λέγει μοι, Ὅρα μή· σύνδουλός σού εἰμι καὶ τῶν ἀδελφῶν σου τῶν ἐχόντων τὴν μαρτυρίαν Ἰησοῦ· τῷ θεῷ προσκύνησον. ἡ γὰρ μαρτυρία Ἰησοῦ ἐστιν τὸ πνεῦμα τῆς προφητείας.

The Rider on the White Horse

11 Καὶ εἶδον τὸν οὐρανὸν ἠνεῳγμένον, καὶ ἰδοὺ ἵππος λευκός, καὶ ὁ καθήμενος ἐπ᾽ αὐτὸν πιστὸς [καλούμενος] καὶ ἀληθινός⁴, καὶ ἐν δικαιοσύνῃ κρίνει καὶ πολεμεῖ. 12 οἱ δὲ ὀφθαλμοὶ αὐτοῦ [ὡς]⁵ φλὸξ πυρός, καὶ ἐπὶ τὴν κεφαλὴν αὐτοῦ διαδήματα πολλά, ἔχων ὄνομα

⁴ 11 {C} πιστὸς καλούμενος καὶ ἀληθινός ℵ ∥ καλούμενος πιστὸς καὶ ἀληθινός 046 94 (1006 καὶ καλούμενος) 1611 1854 1859 2020 2053 2065 2073 2138 2432 itᵈᵉᵐ,ᵈⁱᵛ,(ᵍⁱᵍ),ʰᵃᶠ,ᵗ vgᵉˡ syrᵖʰ,ʰ (copˢᵃ?ᵇᵒ?) (eth?) Irenaeusˡᵃᵗ Origenˡᵃᵗ Cyprian Victorinus-Pettau Tyconius Jerome Apringius Primasius Andrewᶜ Ps-Ambrose Beatus ∥ πιστὸς καὶ ἀληθινὸς καλούμενος 2028 2029 2033 2044 2054 2068 2069 2083 2091 itᵃʳ ∥ vocabatur fidelis, et verax vocatur itᶜ vgʷʷ ∥ πιστὸς καὶ ἀληθινός A P 051 1 2042 2081 arm Hippolytus Andrewᵃ,ᵇᵃᵛ,ᵖ Arethas

⁵ 12 {C} ὡς A 1006 2065 2073 2432 itᵃʳ,ᶜ,ᵈᵉᵐ,ᵈⁱᵛ,ᵍⁱᵍ,ʰᵃᶠ,ᵗ vg syrᵖʰ,ʰ copˢᵃ,(ᵇᵒ) eth Irenaeusˡᵃᵗ Origenˡᵃᵗ Cyprian Tyconius Jerome Primasius Andrewᶜ Beatus Arethas ∥ omit ℵ P 046 051 1 94 1611 1854 1859 2020 2042 2053 2081 2138 arm Hippolytus Andrewᵃ,ᵇᵃᵛ,ᵖ

ᵇ ᵇ 8 b minor, b major: TR WH Bov Nes BF² AV RV ASV ∥ b major, b major: TT Zür Luth Seg ∥ b dash, b major: RSV Jer ∥ b parens, b parens: NEB

8 περιβάληται...ἐστίν Is 61.10   9 Μακάριοι...κεκλημένοι Mt 22.2–3; Lk 14.15   10 Ac 10.25–26; Re 22.8–9   11 τὸν οὐρανὸν ἠνεῳγμένον Eze 1.1; Re 4.1   ἵππος λευκός Zch 1.8; 6.3, 6; Re 6.2   ὁ...ἀληθινός Re 1.5; 3.14   ἐν δικαιοσύνῃ κρίνει Ps 96.13; Is 11.4   12 οἱ...πυρός Dn 10.6; Re 1.15; 2.18   ἔχων ὄνομα...αὐτός Re 2.17

γεγραμμένον ὃ οὐδεὶς οἶδεν εἰ μὴ αὐτός, **13** καὶ περιβεβλημένος ἱμάτιον βεβαμμένον⁶ αἵματι, καὶ κέκληται τὸ ὄνομα αὐτοῦ ὁ λόγος τοῦ θεοῦ. **14** καὶ τὰ στρατεύματα [τὰ] ἐν τῷ οὐρανῷ ἠκολούθει αὐτῷ ἐφ' ἵπποις λευκοῖς, ἐνδεδυμένοι βύσσινον λευκὸν καθαρόν. **15** καὶ ἐκ τοῦ στόματος αὐτοῦ ἐκπορεύεται ῥομφαία ὀξεῖα, ἵνα ἐν αὐτῇ πατάξῃ τὰ ἔθνη, καὶ αὐτὸς **ποιμανεῖ αὐτοὺς ἐν ῥάβδῳ σιδηρᾷ·** καὶ αὐτὸς πατεῖ τὴν ληνὸν τοῦ οἴνου τοῦ θυμοῦ τῆς ὀργῆς τοῦ θεοῦ τοῦ παντοκράτορος. **16** καὶ ἔχει ἐπὶ τὸ ἱμάτιον καὶ ἐπὶ τὸν μηρὸν αὐτοῦ ὄνομα γεγραμμένον· Βασιλεὺς βασιλέων καὶ κύριος κυρίων.

17 Καὶ εἶδον ἕνα ἄγγελον ἑστῶτα ἐν τῷ ἡλίῳ, καὶ ἔκραξεν [ἐν] φωνῇ μεγάλῃ λέγων πᾶσιν τοῖς ὀρνέοις τοῖς πετομένοις ἐν μεσουρανήματι, Δεῦτε συνάχθητε εἰς τὸ δεῖπνον τὸ μέγα τοῦ θεοῦ, **18** ἵνα φάγητε σάρκας βασιλέων καὶ σάρκας χιλιάρχων καὶ σάρκας ἰσχυρῶν καὶ σάρκας ἵππων καὶ τῶν καθημένων ἐπ' αὐτῶν καὶ σάρκας πάντων ἐλευθέρων τε καὶ δούλων καὶ μικρῶν καὶ μεγάλων. **19** Καὶ εἶδον τὸ θηρίον καὶ τοὺς βασιλεῖς τῆς γῆς καὶ τὰ στρατεύματα αὐτῶν συνηγμένα ποιῆσαι τὸν πόλεμον μετὰ τοῦ καθημένου ἐπὶ τοῦ ἵππου καὶ μετὰ τοῦ στρατεύματος αὐτοῦ. **20** καὶ ἐπιάσθη τὸ θηρίον καὶ μετ' αὐτοῦ ὁ ψευδοπροφήτης ὁ ποιήσας τὰ σημεῖα ἐνώπιον αὐτοῦ, ἐν οἷς ἐπλάνησεν τοὺς λαβόντας τὸ

except himself knows what it is. ¹³ The robe he wore was covered with blood. The name by which he is called is "The Word of God." ¹⁴ The armies of heaven followed him, riding on white horses and dressed in clean white linen. ¹⁵ A sharp sword came out of his mouth, with which he will defeat the nations. He will rule over them with a rod of iron, and he will squeeze out the wine in the winepress of the furious wrath of the Almighty God. ¹⁶ On his robe and on his leg was written the name: "King of kings and Lord of lords."

¹⁷ Then I saw an angel standing in the sun. He shouted in a loud voice to all the birds flying in mid-air: "Come, and gather together for God's great feast! ¹⁸ Come and eat the flesh of kings, generals, and soldiers, the flesh of horses and their riders, the flesh of all men, slave and free, great and small!"

¹⁹ Then I saw the beast and the kings of the earth and their armies gathered to fight against the one who rides the horse, and against his army. ²⁰ The beast was taken prisoner, together with the false prophet who had performed miracles in his presence. (It was by those miracles that he had deceived those who had the

---

⁶ **13** {C} βεβαμμένον A 046 051 1 94 1854 1859 2020 2042 2073 2081 2138 syr^ph? cop^sa arm Andrew^a,bav,p Arethas ∥ ἐρραντισμένον 1006 2065 2432 it^ar,c,dem,div,gig,haf,t vg cop^bo eth Irenaeus Hippolytus Origen Cyprian Tyconius Priscillian Jerome Vigilius Apringius Primasius Cassiodorus Andrew^c Bede Ps Ambrose ∥ ῥεραντισμένον P syr^ph? Hippolytus Origen ∥ ἐρραμμένον 2053 vg^mss syr^h Origen ∥ ῥεραμμένον 1611 Origen ∥ περιρεραμμένον ℵ* Irenaeus ∥ περιρεραντισμένον ℵᶜ syr^ph? Cyprian

13 περιβεβλημένος...αἵματι Is 63.1–3   κέκληται...θεοῦ Jn 1.1, 14   **15** ἐκ...ὀξεῖα Is 49.2; Re 1.16; 2.12, 16   αὐτὸς ποιμανεῖ...σιδηρᾷ Ps 2.9; Re 12.5   αὐτὸς πατεῖ τὴν ληνὸν Is 63.3; Lm 1.15; Jl 3.13; Re 14.20   τοῦ θεοῦ τοῦ παντοκράτορος Am 3.13 LXX; 4.13 LXX; Ps 1.6; 1.6; 11.17; 15.3; 16.7, 14; 10.6; 21.22   **16** Βασιλεὺς...κυρίων Dt 10.17; Pm 2.47; 2 Macc 13.4; 3 Macc 5.35; En 9.4; 1 Tm 6.15; Re 17.14   **17–18** ἔκραξεν...μεγάλων Eze 39.17–20   **19** τοὺς βασιλεῖς...αὐτοῦ Ps 2.2   **20** τοὺς λαβόντας...αὐτοῦ Re 13.12–17; 14.9, 11; 16.2   τὸ χάραγμα τοῦ θηρίου Re 13.7; 14.9, 11; 16.2; 20.4

mark of the beast, and those who had worshiped the image of the beast.) The beast and the false prophet were both thrown alive into the lake of fire that burns with sulphur. [21] Their armies were killed by the sword that comes out of the mouth of the one who rides the horse; and all the birds ate all they could of their flesh.

The Thousand Years

20 Then I saw an angel coming down from heaven, holding in his hand the key of the abyss, and a heavy chain. [2] He seized the dragon, that old serpent — that is, the Devil, or Satan — and tied him up for a thousand years. [3] The angel threw him into the abyss, locked it and sealed it, so that he could not deceive the nations any more until the thousand years were over. After that he must be set loose for a little while.

[4] Then I saw thrones, and those who sat on them; they were given the power to judge. I also saw the souls of those who had been executed because they had proclaimed the truth that Jesus revealed and the word of God. They had not worshiped the beast or its image, nor had they received the mark of the beast on their foreheads or hands. They lived and ruled as kings with Christ for a thousand years. [5] (The rest of the dead did not come to life until the thousand years were over.) This is the first raising of the dead. [6] Happy and greatly blessed are those who have a part in this first raising of the dead. The second death has no power over them; they shall be priests of God and of Christ, and they will rule with him for a thousand years.

χάραγμα τοῦ θηρίου καὶ τοὺς προσκυνοῦντας τῇ εἰκόνι αὐτοῦ· ζῶντες ἐβλήθησαν οἱ δύο εἰς τὴν λίμνην τοῦ πυρὸς τῆς καιομένης ἐν θείῳ. **21** καὶ οἱ λοιποὶ ἀπεκτάνθησαν ἐν τῇ ῥομφαίᾳ τοῦ καθημένου ἐπὶ τοῦ ἵππου τῇ ἐξελθούσῃ ἐκ τοῦ στόματος αὐτοῦ, καὶ πάντα τὰ ὄρνεα ἐχορτάσθησαν ἐκ τῶν σαρκῶν αὐτῶν.

The Thousand Years

20 Καὶ εἶδον ἄγγελον καταβαίνοντα ἐκ τοῦ οὐρανοῦ, ἔχοντα τὴν κλεῖν τῆς ἀβύσσου καὶ ἅλυσιν μεγάλην ἐπὶ τὴν χεῖρα αὐτοῦ. **2** καὶ ἐκράτησεν τὸν δράκοντα, ὁ ὄφις ὁ ἀρχαῖος, ὅς ἐστιν Διάβολος καὶ ὁ Σατανᾶς, καὶ ἔδησεν αὐτὸν χίλια ἔτη, **3** καὶ ἔβαλεν αὐτὸν εἰς τὴν ἄβυσσον καὶ ἔκλεισεν καὶ ἐσφράγισεν ἐπάνω αὐτοῦ ἵνα μὴ πλανήσῃ ἔτι τὰ ἔθνη ἄχρι τελεσθῇ τὰ χίλια ἔτη· μετὰ ταῦτα δεῖ λυθῆναι αὐτὸν μικρὸν χρόνον.

4 Καὶ εἶδον θρόνους, καὶ ἐκάθισαν ἐπ' αὐτούς, καὶ κρίμα ἐδόθη αὐτοῖς, καὶ τὰς ψυχὰς τῶν πεπελεκισμένων διὰ τὴν μαρτυρίαν Ἰησοῦ καὶ διὰ τὸν λόγον τοῦ θεοῦ, καὶ οἵτινες οὐ προσεκύνησαν τὸ θηρίον οὐδὲ τὴν εἰκόνα αὐτοῦ καὶ οὐκ ἔλαβον τὸ χάραγμα ἐπὶ τὸ μέτωπον καὶ ἐπὶ τὴν χεῖρα αὐτῶν· καὶ ἔζησαν καὶ ἐβασίλευσαν μετὰ τοῦ Χριστοῦ χίλια ἔτη. **5** οἱ λοιποὶ τῶν νεκρῶν οὐκ ἔζησαν ἄχρι τελεσθῇ τὰ χίλια ἔτη. αὕτη ἡ ἀνάστασις ἡ πρώτη. **6** μακάριος καὶ ἅγιος ὁ ἔχων μέρος ἐν τῇ ἀναστάσει τῇ πρώτῃ· ἐπὶ τούτων ὁ δεύτερος θάνατος οὐκ ἔχει ἐξουσίαν, ἀλλ' ἔσονται ἱερεῖς τοῦ θεοῦ καὶ τοῦ Χριστοῦ, καὶ βασιλεύσουσιν μετ' αὐτοῦ [τὰ][1] χίλια ἔτη.

---

[1] **6** {C} τά ℵ 046 94 1611 1859 2020 2053 2073 cop[sa, bo] ∥ *omit* A 051 1 1006 1854 2042 2065 2081 2138 2432 cop[bo ms] arm Andrew Arethas

20 ζῶντες...θείῳ Is 30.33; Re 20.10, 15   **21** πάντα...αὐτῶν Eze 39.17, 20
20 2 τὸν...Σατανᾶς Re 12.9   **3** ἔβαλεν...ἄβυσσον 2 Pe 2.4; Jd 6   **4** θρόνους...αὐτοῖς Dn 7.9, 22, 27; Lk 22.30; 1 Cor 6.2   τὸ χάραγμα...αὐτῶν Re 13.17; 14.9, 11; 16.2; 19.20
6 ἔσονται...αὐτοῦ Ex 19.6; Is 61.6; 1 Pe 2.5, 9; Re 1.6; 5.10

The Defeat of Satan

7 Καὶ ὅταν τελεσθῇ τὰ χίλια ἔτη, λυθήσεται ὁ Σατανᾶς ἐκ τῆς φυλακῆς αὐτοῦ, **8** καὶ ἐξελεύσεται πλανῆσαι τὰ ἔθνη τὰ ἐν ταῖς τέσσαρσιν γωνίαις τῆς γῆς, τὸν Γὼγ καὶ Μαγώγ, συναγαγεῖν αὐτοὺς εἰς τὸν πόλεμον, ὧν ὁ ἀριθμὸς αὐτῶν ὡς ἡ ἄμμος τῆς θαλάσσης. **9** καὶ ἀνέβησαν ἐπὶ τὸ πλάτος τῆς γῆς καὶ ἐκύκλευσαν τὴν παρεμβολὴν τῶν ἁγίων καὶ τὴν πόλιν τὴν ἠγαπημένην. καὶ κατέβη πῦρ ἐκ τοῦ οὐρανοῦ[2] καὶ κατέφαγεν αὐτούς· **10** καὶ ὁ διάβολος ὁ πλανῶν αὐτοὺς ἐβλήθη εἰς τὴν λίμνην τοῦ πυρὸς καὶ θείου, ὅπου καὶ τὸ θηρίον καὶ ὁ ψευδοπροφήτης, καὶ βασανισθήσονται ἡμέρας καὶ νυκτὸς εἰς τοὺς αἰῶνας τῶν αἰώνων.

The Judgment at the Great White Throne

11 Καὶ εἶδον θρόνον μέγαν λευκὸν καὶ τὸν καθήμενον ἐπ᾽ αὐτόν, οὗ ἀπὸ τοῦ προσώπου ἔφυγεν ἡ γῆ καὶ ὁ οὐρανός, καὶ τόπος οὐχ εὑρέθη αὐτοῖς. **12** καὶ εἶδον τοὺς νεκρούς, τοὺς μεγάλους καὶ τοὺς μικρούς, ἑστῶτας ἐνώπιον τοῦ θρόνου, καὶ βιβλία ἠνοίχθησαν· καὶ ἄλλο βιβλίον ἠνοίχθη, ὅ ἐστιν τῆς ζωῆς· καὶ ἐκρίθησαν οἱ νεκροὶ ἐκ τῶν γεγραμμένων ἐν τοῖς βιβλίοις κατὰ τὰ

---

2 9 {C} ἐκ τοῦ οὐρανοῦ A 2042 2053[comm] cop[bo mss] Tyconius Augustine Primasius Andrew[a] Rupertus ‖ ἀπὸ τοῦ οὐρανοῦ 94 ‖ ἀπὸ τοῦ θεοῦ 1854 it[dem] ‖ ἐκ τοῦ οὐρανοῦ ἀπὸ τοῦ θεοῦ (see 21.2, 10) 046 1859 2020 2138 it[ar,gig] syr[ph] cop[sa,bo] arm (eth) Victorinus-Pettau Tyconius Augustine Andrew[c,p] Ps-Ambrose Arethas ‖ ἀπὸ τοῦ θεοῦ ἐκ τοῦ οὐρανοῦ א[a] P 1006 1611 2053[txt] it[c,div,haf] vg syr[h] Tyconius Jerome Apringius Beatus ‖ ἐκ τοῦ θεοῦ ἀπὸ τοῦ οὐρανοῦ 1 2081 Andrew[bav] ‖ ἐκ θεοῦ ἀπὸ τοῦ οὐρανοῦ 051 2065 2073 2432

---

8 ταῖς...γῆς Eze 7.2   τὸν Γὼγ καὶ Μαγώγ Eze 38.2   **9** κατέβη...αὐτούς 2 Kgs 1.10; Eze 38.22; 39.6   **10** ἐβλήθη...θείου Is 30.33; Re 19.20; 20.15   πυρὸς καὶ θείου Gn 19.24; Ps 11.6; Eze 38.22; 3 Macc 2.5; Re 19.20; 21.8   **11–12** Dn 7.9–10; Mt 25.31–40   **11** ἀπὸ...γῆ Ps 114.3, 7   **12** ἄλλο...ζωῆς Ex 32.32, 33; Ps 69.28; Dn 12.1; Php 4.3; Re 3.5; 13.8; 17.8; 20.15; 21.27   **12–13** κατὰ τὰ ἔργα...αὐτῶν Ps 28.4; 62.12; Pr 24.12; Is 59.18; Jr 17.10; Ro 2.6; 1 Cor 3.8; 2 Cor 11.15; 2 Tm 4.14; 1 Pe 1.17; Re 2.23; 18.6; 22.12

The Defeat of Satan

7 After the thousand years are over, Satan will be set loose from his prison, **8** and he will go out to deceive the nations scattered over all the world, that is, Gog and Magog. Satan will bring them all together for battle, as many as the grains of sand on the seashore. **9** They spread out over the earth and surrounded the camp of God's people and the city that he loves. But fire came down from heaven and destroyed them. **10** Then the Devil, who deceived them, was thrown into the lake of fire and sulphur, where the beast and the false prophet had already been thrown; and they will be tormented day and night, for ever and ever.

The Final Judgment

11 Then I saw a large white throne and the one who sits on it. Earth and heaven fled from his presence, and were seen no more. **12** And I saw the dead, great and small alike, standing before the throne. Books were opened, and then another book was opened, the book of the living. The dead were judged according to what they had done, as was written in the books. [13] Then the sea gave up its dead. Death and the world of the dead also gave up the dead they held. And all were judged according to what they had done. [14] Then death and the world of the dead were thrown into the lake of fire. (This lake of fire is the second death.) [15] Whoever did not have his name written in the book of the living was thrown into the lake of fire.

The New Heaven and the New Earth

21 Then I saw a new heaven and a new earth. The first heaven and the first earth disappeared, and the sea vanished. [2] And I saw the Holy City, the new Jerusalem, coming down out of heaven from God, prepared and ready, like a bride dressed to meet her husband. [3] I heard a loud voice speaking from the throne: "Now God's home is with men! He will live with them, and they shall be his people. God himself will be with them, and he will be their God. [4] He will wipe away all tears from their eyes.

ἔργα αὐτῶν. **13** καὶ ἔδωκεν ἡ θάλασσα τοὺς νεκροὺς τοὺς ἐν αὐτῇ, καὶ ὁ θάνατος καὶ ὁ ᾅδης ἔδωκαν τοὺς νεκροὺς τοὺς ἐν αὐτοῖς, καὶ ἐκρίθησαν ἕκαστος κατὰ τὰ ἔργα αὐτῶν. **14** καὶ ὁ θάνατος καὶ ὁ ᾅδης ἐβλήθησαν εἰς τὴν λίμνην τοῦ πυρός. οὗτος ὁ θάνατος ὁ δεύτερός ἐστιν, ἡ λίμνη τοῦ πυρός. **15** καὶ εἴ τις οὐχ εὑρέθη ἐν τῇ βίβλῳ τῆς ζωῆς γεγραμμένος ἐβλήθη εἰς τὴν λίμνην τοῦ πυρός.

The New Heaven and the New Earth

21 Καὶ εἶδον οὐρανὸν καινὸν καὶ γῆν καινήν· ὁ γὰρ πρῶτος οὐρανὸς καὶ ἡ πρώτη γῆ ἀπῆλθαν, καὶ ἡ θάλασσα οὐκ ἔστιν ἔτι. **2** καὶ τὴν πόλιν τὴν ἁγίαν Ἰερουσαλὴμ καινὴν εἶδον καταβαίνουσαν ἐκ τοῦ οὐρανοῦ ἀπὸ τοῦ θεοῦ, ἡτοιμασμένην ὡς νύμφην κεκοσμημένην τῷ ἀνδρὶ αὐτῆς. **3** καὶ ἤκουσα φωνῆς μεγάλης ἐκ τοῦ θρόνου λεγούσης, **Ἰδοὺ ἡ σκηνὴ** τοῦ θεοῦ μετὰ τῶν ἀνθρώπων, **καὶ σκηνώσει μετ' αὐτῶν, καὶ αὐτοὶ λαοί**[1] **αὐτοῦ ἔσονται, καὶ** αὐτὸς ὁ θεὸς μετ' αὐτῶν ἔσται, [αὐτῶν θεός,][2] **4 καὶ ἐξαλείψει πᾶν δάκρυον ἐκ τῶν**

---

[1] **3** {D} λαοί ℵ A 046 1 94 2042 2053 2081 itᵃʳ Irenaeusˡᵃᵗ Andrewᵃˑᵇᵃᵛ ∥ λαός P 051 1006 1611 1854 1859 2020 2065 2073 2138 2432 itᶜˑᵈᵉᵐˑᵈⁱᵛˑᵍⁱᵍˑʰᵃᶠ vg syrᵖʰˑʰ copˢᵃˑᵇᵒ arm eth Tyconius Ambrose Augustine Primasius Andrewᶜˑᵖ Arethas

[2] **3** {D} μετ' αὐτῶν ἔσται, αὐτῶν θεός, A (1854 2065 2432 itᵃʳ θεὸς αὐτῶν) (2053ᵗˣᵗ ὁ θεός) 2053ᶜᵒᵐᵐ itᶜˑᵈᵉᵐˑᵈⁱᵛˑʰᵃᶠ vg syrᵖʰˑʰ eth Irenaeusˡᵃᵗ Tyconius Ambrose Apringius Ps-Ambrose Beatus ∥ ἔσται μετ' αὐτῶν θεὸς αὐτῶν, P 051 2042 2073 Andrewᵃˑᵇᵃᵛ ∥ μετ' αὐτῶν ἔσται θεός, 1006 1611 (copˢᵃˑᵇᵒᵐˢˢ) ∥ ἔσται μετ' αὐτῶν, ℵ 1 2081 copᵇᵒ eth Ambrose Augustine Primasius Andrewᵇˑᶜ ∥ μετ' αὐτῶν ἔσται, 046 94 1859 2020 2138 itᵍⁱᵍ Irenaeus Haymo Arethas

---

14 ὁ θάνατος...πυρός 1 Cor 15.26, 55   **15** Is 30.33; Mt 25.41; Re 19.20; 20.10; 21.8   τῇ... ζωῆς Ex 32.32, 33; Ps 69.28; Dn 12.1; Php 4.3; Re 3.5; 13.8; 17.8; 20.12; 21.27
21 1 οὐρανὸν...καινήν Is 65.17; 66.22; 2 Pe 3.13   **2** τὴν πόλιν τὴν ἁγίαν Is 52.1 Ἰερουσαλήμ...θεοῦ Re 3.12   ἡτοιμασμένην...αὐτῆς Is 61.10; He 11.10, 16   **3** ἡ σκηνὴ... ἔσται Lv 26.11–12; 2 Chr 6.18; Eze 37.27; Zch 2.10; 2 Cor 6.16   **4** ἐξαλείψει...αὐτῶν Is 25.8; Re 7.17

ὀφθαλμῶν αὐτῶν, καὶ ὁ θάνατος οὐκ ἔσται ἔτι, οὔτε
πένθος οὔτε κραυγὴ οὔτε πόνος οὐκ ἔσται ἔτι· [ὅτι]
τὰ πρῶτα³ ἀπῆλθαν.

5 Καὶ εἶπεν ὁ καθήμενος ἐπὶ τῷ θρόνῳ, Ἰδοὺ καινὰ
ποιῶ πάντα. καὶ λέγει⁴, Γράψον, ὅτιᵃ οὗτοι οἱ λόγοι
πιστοὶ καὶ ἀληθινοί εἰσιν. 6 καὶ εἶπέν μοι, Γέγοναν.
ἐγώ [εἰμι] τὸ Ἄλφα καὶ τὸ Ὦ, ἡ ἀρχὴ καὶ τὸ τέλος.
ἐγὼ τῷ διψῶντι δώσω ἐκ τῆς πηγῆς τοῦ ὕδατος τῆς
ζωῆς δωρεάν. 7 ὁ νικῶν κληρονομήσει ταῦτα, καὶ **ἔσομαι αὐτῷ θεὸς καὶ αὐτὸς ἔσται μοι υἱός.** 8 τοῖς δὲ
δειλοῖς καὶ ἀπίστοις καὶ ἐβδελυγμένοις καὶ φονεῦσιν καὶ
πόρνοις καὶ φαρμάκοις καὶ εἰδωλολάτραις καὶ πᾶσιν τοῖς
ψευδέσιν τὸ μέρος αὐτῶν ἐν τῇ λίμνῃ τῇ καιομένῃ πυρὶ
καὶ θείῳ, ὅ ἐστιν ὁ θάνατος ὁ δεύτερος.

The New Jerusalem

9 Καὶ ἦλθεν εἷς ἐκ τῶν ἑπτὰ ἀγγέλων τῶν ἐχόντων
τὰς ἑπτὰ φιάλας, τῶν γεμόντων τῶν ἑπτὰ πληγῶν τῶν
ἐσχάτων, καὶ ἐλάλησεν μετ' ἐμοῦ λέγων, Δεῦρο, δείξω
σοι τὴν νύμφην τὴν γυναῖκα τοῦ ἀρνίου. 10 καὶ ἀπήνεγκέν με ἐν πνεύματι ἐπὶ ὄρος μέγα καὶ ὑψηλόν, καὶ

³ 4 {C} ὅτι τὰ πρῶτα ℵᵃ 046 1 1854 1859 2020 2081 2138 itᵃʳ·ᵈᵉᵐ vg syrʰ
copˢᵃ·ᵇᵒ arm (eth) Irenaeus Tyconius Augustine Apringius Primasius
Andrewᵃ·ᶜ·ᵖ Arethas ‖ τὰ πρόβατα ℵ* ‖ τὰ πρῶτα A P 051 1006 1611 2053
2065 2073 2432 (itᶜ·ᵈⁱᵛ·ʰᵃᶠ quae prima) Andrewᵇᵃᵛ Beatus ‖ τὰ γὰρ πρῶτα
94 2042 itᵍⁱᵍ ‖ ἐπὶ τὰ πρόσωπα αὐτῆς syrᵖʰ

⁴ 5 {C} λέγει Δ 016 04 1611 1854 2053 2138 itᵈᵉᵐ·ᵍⁱᵍ vgʷʷ syrʰ Irenaeusˡᵃᵗ
Tyconius Apringius Beatus ‖ λέγει μοι ℵ P 051 1 1006 1859 2020 2042 2065
2073 2081 2432 itᵃʳ·ᶜ·ᵈⁱᵛ·ʰᵃᶠ vgᶜˡ syrᵖʰ copˢᵃ·ᵇᵒ arm eth Primasius Andrew
Haymo Arethas

ᵃ 5 a causal: WH Bov Nes BF² AV RV ASV RSV NEB TT Zür Luth Seg ‖
a indirect: TR? ‖ a direct: RVᵐᵍ ASVᵐᵍ Jer

4 οὔτε πένθος...ἔτι Is 35.10; 65.19   5 ὁ θρόνῳ 1 Kgs 22.19; 2 Chr 18.18; Ps 47.8; Is 6.1;
Eze 1.26–27; Sir 1.8; Re 4.2, 9; 5.1, 7, 13; 6.16; 7.10, 15; 19.4   καινὰ ποιῶ πάντα 2 Cor 5.17
6 ἐγώ...Ὦ Re 1.8; 22.13   ἡ...τέλος Is 44.6; 48.12; Re 1.17; 22.13   ἐγώ...δωρεάν Is 55.1;
Jn 7.37; Re 22.17   τῆς πηγῆς...ζωῆς Ps 36.9; Jr 2.13   7 ἔσομαι...υἱός 2 Sm 7.14   8 τῇ
λίμνῃ...θείῳ Is 30.33; Mt 25.41; Re 19.20; 20.10, 15   πυρὶ καὶ θείῳ Gn 19.24; Ps 11.6; Eze 38.22;
3 Macc 2.5; Re 19.20   10 ἀπήνεγκεν...Ἰερουσαλήμ Eze 40.2

There will be no more death, no more
grief, crying, or pain. The old things
have disappeared."
⁵ Then the one who sits on the throne
said, "And now I make all things new!"
He also said to me, "Write this, because
these words are true and can be trusted."
⁶ And he said: "It is done! I am the
Alpha and the Omega, the beginning and
the end. To anyone who is thirsty I will
give a free drink of water from the spring
of the water of life. ⁷ Whoever wins the
victory will receive this from me: I will
be his God, and he will be my son.
⁸ But the cowards, the traitors, and the
perverts, the murderers and the immoral,
those who practice magic and those who
worship idols, and all liars — the place
for them is the lake burning with fire
and sulphur, which is the second death."

The New Jerusalem

⁹ One of the seven angels who had the
seven bowls full of the seven last plagues
came to me and said, "Come, and I will
show you the Bride, the wife of the
Lamb." ¹⁰ The Spirit took control of
me, and the angel carried me to the

top of a very high mountain. He showed me Jerusalem, the Holy City, coming down out of heaven from God, ¹¹ shining with the glory of God. The city shone like a precious stone, like a jasper, clear as crystal. ¹² It had a great, high wall, with twelve gates, and with twelve angels in charge of the gates. On the gates were written the names of the twelve tribes of the people of Israel. ¹³ There were three gates on each side: three on the east, three on the south, three on the north, and three on the west. ¹⁴ The city's wall was built on twelve stones, on which were written the names of the twelve apostles of the Lamb.

¹⁵ The angel who spoke to me had a gold measuring stick, to measure the city, its gates, and its wall. ¹⁶ The city was perfectly square, as long as it was wide. The angel measured the city with his measuring stick: it was fifteen hundred miles long, and was as wide and as high as it was long. ¹⁷ The angel also measured the wall, and it was two hundred and sixteen feet high, according to the normal unit of measure, which he was using. ¹⁸ The wall was made of jasper, and the city itself was made of pure gold, as clear as glass. ¹⁹ The foundation stones of the city wall were adorned with all kinds of precious stones. The first foundation stone was jasper, the second sapphire, the third agate, the fourth emerald, ²⁰ the fifth onyx, the sixth carnelian, the seventh yellow quartz, the eighth beryl, the ninth topaz, the tenth chalcedony, the eleventh turquoise, the twelfth amethyst. ²¹ The twelve gates are twelve pearls; each gate is made from a single pearl. The street of the city is of pure gold, transparent as glass.

ἔδειξέν μοι τὴν πόλιν τὴν ἁγίαν Ἰερουσαλὴμ καταβαίνουσαν ἐκ τοῦ οὐρανοῦ ἀπὸ τοῦ θεοῦ, 11 ἔχουσαν τὴν δόξαν τοῦ θεοῦ· ὁ φωστὴρ αὐτῆς ὅμοιος λίθῳ τιμιωτάτῳ, ὡς λίθῳ ἰάσπιδι κρυσταλλίζοντι· 12 ἔχουσα τεῖχος μέγα καὶ ὑψηλόν, ἔχουσα **πυλῶνας** δώδεκα, καὶ ἐπὶ τοῖς πυλῶσιν ἀγγέλους δώδεκα, καὶ **ὀνόματα** ἐπιγεγραμμένα ἅ ἐστιν **τῶν** δώδεκα **φυλῶν** υἱῶν Ἰσραήλ· **13 ἀπὸ ἀνατολῆς πυλῶνες τρεῖς, καὶ ἀπὸ βορρᾶ πυλῶνες τρεῖς, καὶ ἀπὸ νότου πυλῶνες τρεῖς, καὶ ἀπὸ δυσμῶν πυλῶνες τρεῖς·** 14 καὶ τὸ τεῖχος τῆς πόλεως ἔχων θεμελίους δώδεκα, καὶ ἐπ᾿ αὐτῶν δώδεκα ὀνόματα τῶν δώδεκα ἀποστόλων τοῦ ἀρνίου.

15 Καὶ ὁ λαλῶν μετ᾿ ἐμοῦ εἶχεν μέτρον κάλαμον χρυσοῦν, ἵνα μετρήσῃ τὴν πόλιν καὶ τοὺς πυλῶνας αὐτῆς καὶ τὸ τεῖχος αὐτῆς. 16 καὶ ἡ πόλις τετράγωνος κεῖται, καὶ τὸ μῆκος αὐτῆς ὅσον τὸ πλάτος. καὶ ἐμέτρησεν τὴν πόλιν τῷ καλάμῳ ἐπὶ σταδίων δώδεκα χιλιάδων· τὸ μῆκος καὶ τὸ πλάτος καὶ τὸ ὕψος αὐτῆς ἴσα ἐστίν. 17 καὶ ἐμέτρησεν τὸ τεῖχος αὐτῆς ἑκατὸν τεσσαράκοντα τεσσάρων πηχῶν, μέτρον ἀνθρώπου, ὅ ἐστιν ἀγγέλου. 18 καὶ ἡ ἐνδώμησις τοῦ τείχους αὐτῆς ἴασπις, καὶ ἡ πόλις χρυσίον καθαρὸν ὅμοιον ὑάλῳ καθαρῷ. 19 οἱ θεμέλιοι τοῦ τείχους τῆς πόλεως παντὶ λίθῳ τιμίῳ κεκοσμημένοι· ὁ θεμέλιος ὁ πρῶτος ἴασπις, ὁ δεύτερος σάπφιρος, ὁ τρίτος χαλκηδών, ὁ τέταρτος σμάραγδος, 20 ὁ πέμπτος σαρδόνυξ, ὁ ἕκτος σάρδιον, ὁ ἕβδομος χρυσόλιθος, ὁ ὄγδοος βήρυλλος, ὁ ἔνατος τοπάζιον, ὁ δέκατος χρυσόπρασος, ὁ ἑνδέκατος ὑάκινθος, ὁ δωδέκατος ἀμέθυστος. 21 καὶ οἱ δώδεκα πυλῶνες δώδεκα μαργαρῖται, ἀνὰ εἷς ἕκαστος τῶν πυλώνων ἦν ἐξ ἑνὸς μαργαρίτου. καὶ ἡ πλατεῖα τῆς πόλεως χρυσίον καθαρὸν ὡς ὕαλος διαυγής.

---

11 Is 60.1, 2, 19   **12–13** Ex 28.21; Eze 48.30–35   **15** μέτρον...τεῖχος αὐτῆς Eze 40.3, 5   **16–17** Eze 48.16, 17   **19** οἱ...κεκοσμημένοι Is 54.11–12

22 Καὶ ναὸν οὐκ εἶδον ἐν αὐτῇ, ὁ γὰρ κύριος[b] ὁ θεὸς[b] ὁ παντοκράτωρ[b] ναὸς αὐτῆς ἐστιν, καὶ τὸ ἀρνίον. 23 καὶ ἡ πόλις οὐ χρείαν ἔχει τοῦ ἡλίου οὐδὲ τῆς σελήνης, ἵνα φαίνωσιν αὐτῇ, ἡ γὰρ δόξα τοῦ θεοῦ ἐφώτισεν αὐτήν, καὶ ὁ λύχνος αὐτῆς τὸ ἀρνίον. 24 καὶ περιπατήσουσιν τὰ ἔθνη διὰ τοῦ φωτὸς αὐτῆς· καὶ οἱ βασιλεῖς τῆς γῆς φέρουσιν τὴν δόξαν αὐτῶν εἰς αὐτήν· 25 καὶ οἱ πυλῶνες αὐτῆς οὐ μὴ κλεισθῶσιν ἡμέρας, νὺξ γὰρ οὐκ ἔσται ἐκεῖ· 26 καὶ οἴσουσιν τὴν δόξαν καὶ τὴν τιμὴν τῶν ἐθνῶν εἰς αὐτήν. 27 καὶ οὐ μὴ εἰσέλθῃ εἰς αὐτὴν πᾶν κοινὸν καὶ ποιῶν βδέλυγμα καὶ ψεῦδος, εἰ μὴ οἱ γεγραμμένοι ἐν τῷ βιβλίῳ τῆς ζωῆς τοῦ ἀρνίου.

22 Καὶ ἔδειξέν μοι ποταμὸν ὕδατος ζωῆς λαμπρὸν ὡς κρύσταλλον, ἐκπορευόμενον ἐκ τοῦ θρόνου τοῦ θεοῦ καὶ τοῦ ἀρνίου.[a] 2 ἐν μέσῳ τῆς πλατείας αὐτῆς[a] καὶ τοῦ ποταμοῦ ἐντεῦθεν καὶ ἐκεῖθεν ξύλον ζωῆς ποιοῦν καρποὺς δώδεκα, κατὰ μῆνα ἕκαστον ἀποδιδοῦν τὸν καρπὸν αὐτοῦ, καὶ τὰ φύλλα τοῦ ξύλου εἰς θεραπείαν τῶν ἐθνῶν. 3 καὶ πᾶν κατάθεμα οὐκ ἔσται ἔτι. καὶ ὁ θρόνος τοῦ θεοῦ καὶ τοῦ ἀρνίου ἐν αὐτῇ ἔσται, καὶ οἱ δοῦλοι αὐτοῦ λατρεύσουσιν αὐτῷ, 4 καὶ ὄψονται τὸ πρόσωπον αὐτοῦ, καὶ τὸ ὄνομα αὐτοῦ ἐπὶ τῶν μετώπων αὐτῶν. 5 καὶ νὺξ οὐκ ἔσται ἔτι, καὶ οὐκ ἔχουσιν χρείαν φωτὸς λύχνου καὶ φῶς ἡλίου, ὅτι κύριος ὁ θεὸς φωτίσει ἐπ᾽ αὐτούς, καὶ βασιλεύσουσιν εἰς τοὺς αἰῶνας τῶν αἰώνων.

[b b b] 22 b none, b none, b none. TR Bov Nes BF⁹ AV (RV) (ABV) REV NEB (TT) Seg ∥ b minor, b minor, b minor: WH ∥ b minor, b none, b minor: Zür Luth Jer ∥ b none, b minor, b minor

[a a] 1-2 a major, a none: TR Bov Nes BF² (AV) (RVmg) (ASVmg) TT Zür Luth (Jer) Seg ∥ a none, a major: WH (RV) (ASV) RSV NEB Jermg

---

22 ὁ γὰρ...παντοκράτωρ Am 3.13 LXX; 4.13 LXX; Re 1.8; 4.8; 11.17; 15.3; 16.7, 14; 19.6, 15   23 ἡ πόλις...αὐτήν Is 60.19-20; Re 22.5   24 περιπατήσουσιν...αὐτῆς Is 60.3, 5; Ps Sol 17.34 (31)   25 οἱ πυλῶνες...ἐκεῖ Is 60.11   νὺξ...ἐκεῖ Zch 14.7; Re 22.5   26 οἴσουσιν...αὐτήν Ps 72.10-11; Ps Sol 17.34 (31)   27 οὐ...ψεῦδος Is 52.1; 1 Cor 6.9-10; 2 Pe 3.13; Re 22.15   τῷ...ζωῆς Ex 32.32, 33; Ps 69.28; Dn 12.1; Php 4.3; Re 3.5; 13.8; 17.8; 20.12, 15

22 1 Eze 47.1; Jl 3.18; Zch 14.8   2 τοῦ...ἐθνῶν Gn 2.9; 3.22; Eze 47.12   3 πᾶν...ἔτι Zch 14.11   4 ὄψονται...αὐτοῦ Ps 17.15; 42.2; Mt 5.8   τὸ ὄνομα...αὐτῶν Re 3.12   5 νὺξ...ἔτι Zch 14.7; Re 21.25   οὐκ ἔχουσιν...αὐτούς Is 60.19-20; Re 21.23   βασιλεύσουσιν...αἰώνων Dn 7.18, 27; Re 5.10; 20.6

---

22 I did not see a temple in the city, because its temple is the Lord God, the Almighty, and the Lamb. 23 The city has no need of the sun or the moon to shine on it, for the glory of God shines on it, and the Lamb is its lamp. 24 The peoples of the world will walk by its light, and the kings of the earth will bring their wealth into it. 25 The gates of the city will stand open all day; they will never be closed, because there will be no night there. 26 The greatness and the wealth of the nations will be brought into the city. 27 But nothing that is defiled will enter the city, nor anyone who does shameful things or tells lies. Only those whose names are written in the Lamb's book of the living will enter the city.

22 The angel also showed me the river of the water of life, sparkling like crystal, which comes from the throne of God and of the Lamb, 2 and flows down the middle of the city's street. On each side of the river was the tree of life, which bears fruit twelve times a year, once every month; and its leaves are for the healing of the nations. 3 Nothing that is under God's curse will be found in the city.

The throne of God and of the Lamb will be in the city, and his servants will worship him. 4 They will see his face, and his name will be written on their foreheads. 5 There shall be no more night, and they will not need lamps or sunlight, for the Lord God will be their light, and they will rule as kings for ever and ever.

The Coming of Jesus

[6] Then the angel said to me: "These words are true and can be trusted. And the Lord God, who gives his Spirit to the prophets, sent his angel to show his servants what must happen very soon."

[7] "Listen!" says Jesus. "I am coming soon! Happy are those who obey the prophetic words in this book!"

[8] I, John, have heard and seen all these things. And when I finished hearing and seeing them, I fell down at the feet of the angel who had shown me these things to worship him. [9] But he said to me: "Don't do it! I am a fellow servant of yours, and of your brothers the prophets, and of all those who obey the words in this book. Worship God!" [10] And he said to me: "Do not keep the prophetic words of this book a secret, for the time is near when all this will happen. [11] Whoever is evil must go on doing evil, and whoever is filthy must go on being filthy; whoever is good must go on doing good, and whoever is holy must go on being holy."

[12] "Listen!" says Jesus. "I am coming soon! I will bring my rewards with me to give to each one according to what he has done. [13] I am the Alpha and the Omega, the first and the last, the beginning and the end."

[14] Happy are those who wash their robes clean, and so have the right to eat the fruit from the tree of life, and to go through the gates into the city. [15] But outside the city are the perverts and

The Coming of Christ

6 Καὶ εἶπέν μοι, Οὗτοι οἱ λόγοι πιστοὶ καὶ ἀληθινοί, καὶ ὁ κύριος, ὁ θεὸς τῶν πνευμάτων τῶν προφητῶν, ἀπέστειλεν τὸν ἄγγελον αὐτοῦ δεῖξαι τοῖς δούλοις αὐτοῦ ἃ δεῖ γενέσθαι ἐν τάχει.[b] **7** καὶ ἰδοὺ ἔρχομαι ταχύ.[b] μακάριος ὁ τηρῶν τοὺς λόγους τῆς προφητείας τοῦ βιβλίου τούτου.

8 Κἀγὼ Ἰωάννης ὁ ἀκούων καὶ βλέπων ταῦτα. καὶ ὅτε ἤκουσα καὶ ἔβλεψα, ἔπεσα προσκυνῆσαι ἔμπροσθεν τῶν ποδῶν τοῦ ἀγγέλου τοῦ δεικνύοντός μοι ταῦτα. **9** καὶ λέγει μοι, Ὅρα μή· σύνδουλός σού εἰμι καὶ τῶν ἀδελφῶν σου τῶν προφητῶν καὶ τῶν τηρούντων τοὺς λόγους τοῦ βιβλίου τούτου· τῷ θεῷ προσκύνησον. **10** καὶ λέγει μοι, Μὴ σφραγίσῃς τοὺς λόγους τῆς προφητείας τοῦ βιβλίου τούτου, ὁ καιρὸς γὰρ ἐγγύς ἐστιν. **11** ὁ ἀδικῶν ἀδικησάτω ἔτι, καὶ ὁ ῥυπαρὸς ῥυπανθήτω ἔτι, καὶ ὁ δίκαιος δικαιοσύνην ποιησάτω ἔτι, καὶ ὁ ἅγιος ἁγιασθήτω ἔτι.[c]

12 Ἰδοὺ ἔρχομαι ταχύ, καὶ ὁ μισθός μου μετ' ἐμοῦ, ἀποδοῦναι ἑκάστῳ ὡς τὸ ἔργον ἐστὶν αὐτοῦ. **13** ἐγὼ τὸ Ἄλφα καὶ τὸ Ὦ, ὁ πρῶτος καὶ ὁ ἔσχατος, ἡ ἀρχὴ καὶ τὸ τέλος.[c]

14 Μακάριοι οἱ πλύνοντες τὰς στολὰς αὐτῶν[1], ἵνα ἔσται ἡ ἐξουσία αὐτῶν ἐπὶ τὸ ξύλον τῆς ζωῆς καὶ τοῖς πυλῶσιν εἰσέλθωσιν εἰς τὴν πόλιν. **15** ἔξω οἱ κύνες καὶ

---

[1] **14** {B} πλύνοντες τὰς στολὰς αὐτῶν ℵ A 1006 2020 2053 it[ar,c,dem,div,haf] vg cop[sa] eth Athanasius Fulgentius Apringius (Primasius) Ps-Ambrose Haymo ∥ ποιοῦντες τὰς ἐντολὰς αὐτοῦ 046 1 94 1611 1854 1859 2042 2065

[b b] **6–7** b major, b major: (WH) Bov Nes BF[2] RV ASV TT Zür Luth Seg ∥ b major, b exclamation: Jer ∥ b major, b exclamation and paragraph: NEB ∥ b major, b paragraph: RSV ∥ b paragraph, b major: TR ∥ b major, b minor: AV

[c c] **11–13** c paragraph, c paragraph: TR RSV NEB ∥ c dash with paragraph, c dash with paragraph: WH ∥ c paragraph, c major: Bov Nes BF[2] TT ∥ c major, c major: AV RV ASV Luth Jer ∥ c exclamation, c major: Zür Seg

6 δεῖξαι...τάχει Dn 2.28, 29, 45; Re 1.1, 19   **7** ἔρχομαι ταχύ Re 2.16; 3.11; 22.12, 20   **8–9** ἔπεσα...προσκύνησον Ac 10.25–26; Re 19.10   **10** Μὴ σφραγίσῃς...ἐστιν Dn 12.4 ὁ καιρὸς ...ἐστιν Re 1.3   **12** ἔρχομαι ταχύ Re 2.16; 3.11; 22.7, 20 ὁ μισθός μου μετ' ἐμοῦ Is 40.10; 62.11 ἀποδοῦναι...αὐτοῦ Ps 28.4; 62.12; Pr 24.12; Is 59.18; Jr 17.10; Ro 2.6; 1 Cor 3.8; 2 Cor 11.15; 2 Tm 4.14; 1 Pe 1.17; Re 2.23; 18.6; 20.13, 14   **13** ἐγώ...Ὦ Re 1.8; 21.6 ὁ πρῶτος... ἔσχατος Is 44.6; 48.12; Re 1.17; 2.8 ἡ...τέλος Re 21.6   **14** τὸ ξύλον τῆς ζωῆς Gn 2.9; 3.22; Eze 47.12; Re 22.2, 19   **15** 1 Cor 6.9–10; Re 21.8, 27

οἱ φάρμακοι καὶ οἱ πόρνοι καὶ οἱ φονεῖς καὶ οἱ εἰδωλολάτραι καὶ πᾶς φιλῶν καὶ ποιῶν ψεῦδος.

16 Ἐγὼ Ἰησοῦς ἔπεμψα τὸν ἄγγελόν μου μαρτυρῆσαι ὑμῖν ταῦτα ἐπὶ ταῖς ἐκκλησίαις. ἐγώ εἰμι ἡ ῥίζα
καὶ τὸ γένος Δαυίδ, ὁ ἀστὴρ ὁ λαμπρὸς ὁ πρωϊνός.
17 Καὶ τὸ πνεῦμα καὶ ἡ νύμφη λέγουσιν, Ἔρχου. καὶ
ὁ ἀκούων εἰπάτω, Ἔρχου. καὶ ὁ διψῶν ἐρχέσθω, ὁ
θέλων λαβέτω ὕδωρ ζωῆς δωρεάν.

18 Μαρτυρῶ ἐγὼ παντὶ τῷ ἀκούοντι τοὺς λόγους
τῆς προφητείας τοῦ βιβλίου τούτου· ἐάν τις ἐπιθῇ ἐπ᾿
αὐτά, ἐπιθήσει ἐπ᾿ αὐτὸν ὁ θεὸς τὰς πληγὰς τὰς γεγραμ-
μένας ἐν τῷ βιβλίῳ τούτῳ· **19** καὶ ἐάν τις ἀφέλῃ ἀπὸ τῶν
λόγων τοῦ βιβλίου τῆς προφητείας ταύτης, ἀφελεῖ ὁ θεὸς
τὸ μέρος αὐτοῦ ἀπὸ τοῦ ξύλου τῆς ζωῆς καὶ ἐκ τῆς πόλεως
τῆς ἁγίας, τῶν γεγραμμένων ἐν τῷ βιβλίῳ τούτῳ.

20 Λέγει ὁ μαρτυρῶν ταῦτα, Ναί, ἔρχομαι ταχύ.
Ἀμήν, ἔρχου, κύριε Ἰησοῦ.

21 Ἡ χάρις τοῦ κυρίου Ἰησοῦ[2] μετὰ πάντων[3].[4]

2073 2138 2432 it^gig syr^{ph,h} cop^{bo} (arm τηροῦντες τάς) Tertullian Cyprian
Tyconius Andrew (Beatus) Arethas

[2] 21 {B} κυρίου Ἰησοῦ ℵ A 1611 2053 ∥ κυρίου 1859 ∥ κυρίου Ἰησοῦ
Χριστοῦ 046 051 94 1006 1854 2020 2042 2065 2073 2138 2432 eth Andrew ∥
κυρίου ἡμῶν Ἰησοῦ Χριστοῦ 205 254 2067 it^{ar,c,dem,div,gig,haf} vg syr^{ph,h}
(cop^{sa} omit Χριστοῦ) arm Ps-Ambrose Beatus ∥ omit ἡ χάρις τοῦ κυρίου
Ἰησοῦ 2329 cop^{bo}

[3] 21 {C} μετὰ πάντων A (it^{ar} cum omnibus hominibus) vg^{ww} Tyconius
Beatus ∥ μετὰ πάντων ὑμῶν 296 it^{c,dem,div,haf} vg^{cl} eth Ps-Ambrose ∥ μετὰ
πάντων ἡμῶν 2040 2050 ∥ μετὰ τῶν ἁγίων ℵ it^{gig} ∥ μετὰ τῶν ἁγίων σου
2329 (see footnote 2) ∥ μετὰ πάντων τῶν ἁγίων 046 051 94 1006 1611 1854 1859
2020 2042 2053 2065 2073 2138 2432 syr^h cop^{sa} arm Andrew Arethas ∥
μετὰ πάντων τῶν ἁγίων αὐτοῦ 2030 syr^{ph} ∥ upon all the saints unto age
of the ages cop^{bo} (cop^{boms} age of the age) (see footnote 2)

[4] 21 {C} omit ἀμήν. A 1006 2065^{txt} 2432 it^{ar,gig} Tyconius Andrew^{a,bav}
Beatus Arethas ∥ add ἀμήν. ℵ 046 051 94 1611 1854 1859 2020 2042 2053
2065^{comm} 2073 2138 it^{c,dem,div,haf} vg syr^{ph,h} cop^{sa,bo} arm eth Andrew^{c,p}
Arethas ∥ add ἀμὴν ἀμήν. cop^{boms}

---

16 ἐγώ εἰμι...Δαυίδ Is 11.1, 10; Ro 1.3; Re 5.5 ὁ ἀστήρ...πρωϊνός Nu 24.17; Re 2.28   **17** ὁ
διψῶν...δωρεάν Is 55.1; Jn 7.37; Re 21.6   **18-19** ἐάν τις...προφητείας ταύτης Dt 4.2;
12.32   **19** τοῦ ξύλου τῆς ζωῆς Gn 2.9; 3.22; Eze 47.12; Re 22.2, 14   **20** ἔρχομαι ταχύ
Re 2.16; 3.11; 22.7, 12

---

those who practice magic, the immoral
and the murderers, those who worship
idols, and those who are liars, both in
words and deeds.

[16] "I, Jesus, have sent my angel to
announce these things to you in the
churches. I am the descendant from the
family of David; I am the bright morning
star."

[17] The Spirit and the Bride say,
"Come!"

Everyone who hears this must also
say, "Come!"

Come, whoever is thirsty; accept the
water of life as a gift, whoever wants it.

Conclusion

[18] I, John, solemnly warn everyone who
hears the prophetic words of this book:
if anyone adds anything to them, God
will add to his punishment the plagues
described in this book. [19] And if anyone
takes away anything from the prophetic
words of this book, God will take away
from him his share of the fruit of the
tree of life, and his share of the Holy
City, which are described in this book.

[20] He who gives his testimony to all
this, says, "Certainly so! I am coming
soon!"

So be it. Come, Lord Jesus!

[21] May the grace of the Lord Jesus
be with all.[1]

---

[1] **21** all: *some mss. read* God's people; *others
read* all of God's people

INDEX OF QUOTATIONS

GENESIS

1.1 He 11.3
1.3 2 Cor 4.6
1.6-9 2 Pe 3.5
1.11 1 Cor 15.38
1.26 Eph 4.24
1.26-27 Col 3.10
1.26 27 Jas 3.9
1.27 Mt 19.4
    Mk 10.6
    Ac 17.29
    1 Cor 11.7
    1 Tm 2.13
1.29 Ro 14.2
1.31 1 Tm 4.4
2.2 He 4.4
    4.10
2.7 1 Cor 15.45
    15.47
    1 Tm 2.13
2.8 LXX Re 2.7
2.9 Re 2.7
    22.2
    22.14
    22.19
2.17 Ro 5.12
2.18 1 Cor 11.9
2.21-23 1 Cor 11.8
2.22 1 Tm 2.13
2.24 Mt 19.5
    Mk 10.7-8
    1 Cor 6.16
    Eph 5.31
3.4 Jn 8.44
3.6 Ro 5.12
    1 Tm 2.14
3.13 Ro 7.11
    2 Cor 11.3
    1 Tm 2.14
3.15 Lk 10.19
    Ro 16.20
3.16 1 Cor 11.3
    14.34
    Eph 5.22
    Col 3.18
3.17-18 He 6.8
3.17-19 Ro 8.20
    1 Cor 15.21
3.19 Ro 5.12
    He 9.27
3.22 Re 22.2
    22.14
    22.19

3.22, 24 Re 2.7
4.3-8 Jd 11
4.3-10 He 11.4
4.7 Ro 6.12
4.8 Mt 23.35
    Lk 11.51
    1 Jn 3.12
4.10 He 12.24
    Jas 5.4
4.25—5.32 Lk 3.36-38
5.1 Mt 1.1
    1 Cor 11.7
5.2 Mt 19.4
    Mk 10.6
5.3 1 Cor 15.49
5.24 He 11.5
5.29 Ro 8.20
6.1—7.24 1 Pe 3.20
6.5 Ro 7.18
6.5-12 Lk 17.26
6.9-12 Mt 24.37
6.13-22 He 11.7
6.13—7.24
    Mt 24.38-39
7.1 He 11.7
7.6-23 Lk 17.27
7.11-21 2 Pe 3.6
8.18 2 Pe 2.5
8.21 Ro 7.18
    Php 4.18
9.3 Ro 14.2
    1 Tm 4.3
9.4 Ac 15.20
    15.29
9.6 Mt 26.52
    1 Cor 11.7
11.10-26 Lk 3.34-36
11.31—12.1 Ac 7.2
    7.4
12.1 Ac 7.3
12.1-5 He 11.8
12.3 Ac 3.25
    Ga 3.8
12.5 Ac 7.4
12.7 Ac 7.5
    Ga 3.16
13.15 Ac 7.5
    Ga 3.16
14.17-20 He 7.1-2
14.19 Re 10.6
14.20 Lk 18.12
14.22 Re 10.6
15.5 Ro 4.18
15.5-6 He 11.12

15.6 Ro 4.3
    4.9
    4.22
    Ga 3.6
    Jas 2.23
15.13-14 Ac 7.6-7
15.16 1 Th 2.16
15.18 Ac 7.5
16.1 Ac 7.5
16.11 Lk 1.31
16.15 Ga 4.22
17.5 Ro 4.17
17.7 Lk 1.55
    1.72-73
    Ga 3.16
17.8 Ac 7.5
17.10-11 Ro 4.11
17.10-13 Jn 7.22
17.10-14 Ac 7.8
17.12 Lk 1.59
    2.21
17.17 Ro 4.19
17.19 He 11.11
18.1-8 He 13.2
18.4 Lk 7.44
18.10 Ro 9.9
18.11 Lk 1.18
18.11-14 He 11.11
18.12 1 Pe 3.6
18.14 Mt 19.26
    Mk 10.27
    Lk 1.37
    Ro 9.9
18.18 Ac 3.25
    Ro 4.13
    Ga 3.8
18.20-21 Lk 17.28
18.20, 21 Re 18.5
18.20—19.28 Mt 10.15
18.25 He 12.23
19.1-3 He 13.2
19.1-14 Lk 17.28
19.1-16 2 Pe 2.7
19.4-25 Jd 7
19.15-29 Lk 17.29
19.17 Lk 17.31-32
19.24 2 Pe 2.6
    Re 14.10
    20.10
    21.8
19.24-25 Lk 10.12
19.24-28 Mt 11.23
19.26 Lk 17.31-32
19.28 Re 9.2

21.2 Ga 4.22
    He 11.11
21.3 Mt 1.2
    Lk 3.34
21.4 Ac 7.8
21.9 Ga 4.29
21.10 Ga 4.30
21.12 Mt 1.2
    Ro 9.7
    He 11.18
22.1-10 He 11.17
22.2 Mt 3.17
    Mk 1.11
    12.6
    Lk 3.22
22.9, 12 Jas 2.21
22.16 He 6.13
22.16-17 Lk 1.73-74
22.17 Lk 1.55
    He 6.14
    11.12
22.17-18 Ro 4.13
22.18 Mt 1.1
    Ac 3.25
23.2-20 Ac 7.16
23.4 He 11.9
    11.13
24.7 Ac 7.5
    Ga 3.16
25.21 Ro 9.10
25.22 LXX Lk 1.41
25.23 Ro 9.12
25.26 Mt 1.2
    Lk 3.34
25.33-34 He 12.16
26.3 He 11.9
26.4 Ac 3.25
27.27-29, 39-40 He 11.20
27.30-40 He 12.17
28.12 Jn 1.51
28.15 He 13.5
29.35 Mt 1.2
    Lk 3.33
30.23 Lk 1.25
32.12 He 11.12
33.19 Jn 4.5
    Ac 7.16
35.12, 27 He 11.9
37.11 Ac 7.9
37.28 Ac 7.9
38.8 Mt 22.24
    Mk 12.19
    Lk 20.28

38.29-30 Mt 1.3
39.2, 3, 21, 23 Ac 7.9
41.37-39 Ac 7.10
41.40-44 Ac 7.10
41.54 Ac 7.11
41.55 Jn 2.5
42.1-2 Ac 7.12
42.5 Ac 7.11
45.3-4 Ac 7.13
45.4 Ac 7.9
45.9-11 Ac 7.14
45.16 Ac 7.13
45.18-19 Ac 7.14
46.5-6 Ac 7.15
46.27 LXX Ac 7.14
47.9 He 11.13
47.31 LXX He 11.21
48.4 Ac 7.5
48.15-16 He 11.21
48.22 Jn 4.5
49.9-10 Re 5.5
49.10 He 7.14
49.29-30 Ac 7.16
49.33 Ac 7.15
50.7-13 Ac 7.16
50.24-25 He 11.22

EXODUS

1.5 LXX Ac 7.14
1.6 Ac 7.15
1.7-8 Ac 7.17 18
1.10-11 Ac 7.19
1.22 Ac 7.19
    He 11.23
2.2 Ac 7.20
    He 11.23
2.3-10 Ac 7.21
2.10-12 He 11.24
2.11-12 Ac 7.23-24
2.13-14 Ac 7.26-28
2.14 Lk 12.14
    Ac 7.35
2.15 Ac 7.29
    He 11.27
2.21-22 Ac 7.29
3.2 Mk 12.26
    Lk 20.37
    Ac 7.35
3.2-3 Ac 7.30-31
3.4-10 Ac 7.31-34
3.6 Mt 22.32
    Mk 12.26
    Lk 20.37
    Ac 3.13

EXODUS (cont.)

3.6 He 11.16
3.12 Ac 7.7
3.14 Re 1.4
    1.8
    4.8
    11.17
    16.5
3.15 Mt 22.32
    Mk 12.26
    Ac 3.13
    He 11.16
3.16 Mt 22.32
    Mk 12.26
4.5 He 11.16
4.19 Mt 2.20
4.21 Ro 9.18
4.22 Ro 9.4
6.1, 6 Ac 13.17
7.3 Ac 7.36
    Ro 9.18
7.11 2 Tm 3.8
7.17-21 Re 16.3
7.17, 19-20 Re 11.6
7.19-24 Re 16.4
7.20, 21 Re 8.8
7.22 2 Tm 3.8
8.4 LXX Ac 8.24
8.19 Lk 11.20
8.24 LXX Ac 8.24
9.10 Re 16.2
9.12 Ro 9.18
9.16 Ro 9.17
9.23-25 Re 8.7
9.24 Re 11.19
    16.21
9.28 LXX Ac 8.24
10.12, 15 Re 9.3
10.21 Re 16.10
12.1-27 Mt 26.2
    Lk 22.1
12.3-20 1 Cor 5.8
12.6 Mk 14.12
    Lk 22.7
12.8-11 Lk 22.8
12.11 Lk 12.35
12.14 Lk 22.7
12.14-20 Mt 26.17
12.15 Mk 14.12
    Lk 22.7
12.16 Lk 23.56
12.21 1 Cor 5.7
12.21-30 He 11.28
12.24-27 Lk 2.41
12.40 Ga 3.17
12.46 Jn 19.36
12.51 Ac 13.17

12.51 He 11.27
    Jd 5
13.2 Lk 2.23
13.7 1 Cor 5.7
    5.8
13.9 Mt 23.5
13.12 Lk 2.23
13.15 Lk 2.23
13.19 He 11.22
13.21-22 1 Cor 10.1
14.4, 17 Ro 9.18
14.21 Ac 7.36
14.21-31 He 11.29
14.22-29 1 Cor 10.1
15.1 Re 15.3
15.11 Re 15.3
15.18 Re 11.15
    19.6
16.4 Mt 6.34
    1 Cor 10.3
16.7 2 Cor 3.18
16.15 Jn 6.31
16.18 2 Cor 8.15
16.33 He 9.4
16.35 Ac 13.18
    1 Cor 10.3
17.6 1 Cor 10.4
17.7 He 3.8
18.3-4 Ac 7.29
19.1-6 Ac 7.38
19.5 Tt 2.14
    1 Pe 2.9
19.6 1 Pe 2.5
    2.9
    Re 1.6
    5.10
    20.6
19.12-13 He 12.20
19.16 Re 4.5
    11.19
19.16-19 Re 8.5
    16.18
19.16-22 He 12.18-19
19.18 He 12.26
    Re 9.2
19.20, 24 Re 4.1
20.1-17 Ac 7.38
20.5 Jn 9.2
    Jas 4.5
20.8-10 Mk 2.27
20.9-10 Lk 13.14
20.10 Mt 12.2
    Lk 23.56
20.11 Ac 4.24
    14.15
    Re 10.6
    14.7
20.12 Mt 15.4

20.12 Mk 7.10
    Lk 18.20
    Eph 6.2-3
20.12-16 Mt 19.18-19
    Mk 10.19
20.13 Mt 5.21
    Jas 2.11
20.13-15 Ro 13.9
20.13-16 Lk 18.20
20.14 Mt 5.27
    Jas 2.11
20.17 Ro 7.7
    13.9
20.18-21 He 12.18-19
21.2 Jn 8.35
21.12 Mt 5.21
21.17 Mt 15.4
    Mk 7.10
21.24 Mt 5.38
21.32 Mt 26.15
22.1 Lk 19.8
22.11 He 6.16
22.28 Ac 23.5
23.4-5 Mt 5.44
23.20 Mt 11.10
    Mk 1.2
    Lk 7.27
23.22 LXX 1 Pe 2.9
24.3 He 9.19
24.6-8 1 Cor 11.25
    He 9.19
24.8 Mt 26.28
    Mk 14.24
    Lk 22.20
    1 Cor 11.25
    2 Cor 3.6
    He 9.20
    10.29
24.12 2 Cor 3.3
24.17 2 Cor 3.18
25.9 Ac 7.44
25.10-16 He 9.4
25.16 He 9.4
25.18-22 He 9.5
25.23-30 He 9.2
25.31-40 He 9.2
25.40 Ac 7.44
    He 8.5
26.1-30 He 9.2
26.31-33 Lk 23.45
    He 9.3
26.31-35 Mt 27.51
27.21 Ac 7.44
28.1 He 5.4
28.21 Re 21.12-13
29.18 Eph 5.2
    Php 4.18
29.37 Mt 23.19

29.38 He 10.11
30.1-3 Re 8.3
    9.13
30.1-6 He 9.4
30.7 Lk 1.9
30.10 He 9.7
30.13 Mt 17.24
31.18 Jn 1.17
    2 Cor 3.3
32.1 Ac 7.40
32.4-6 Ac 7.41
32.6 1 Cor 10.7
32.9 Ac 7.51
32.13 He 11.12
32.23 Ac 7.40
32.32 Lk 10.20
    Ro 9.3
32.32, 33 Php 4.3
    Re 3.5
    13.8
    17.8
    20.12
    20.15
    21.27
33.3, 5 Ac 7.51
33.19 Ro 9.15
33.20 Jn 1.18
    1 Tm 6.16
34.1 2 Cor 3.3
34.6 Jas 5.11
34.28 Mt 4.2
    Jn 1.17
34.29-30 2 Cor 3.7
    3.10
34.33 2 Cor 3.13
34.34 2 Cor 3.16
36.35 Lk 23.45
    2 Cor 3.13
38.21 Re 15.5
38.26 Mt 17.24
40.34 Re 15.5
    15.8

LEVITICUS

3.17 Ac 15.20
    15.29
6.16, 26 1 Cor 9.13
7.6, 15 1 Cor 10.18
8.15, 19 He 9.21
9.7 He 5.3
    7.27
11.1-47 Ac 10.14
11.2 He 9.10
11.25 He 9.10
11.44, 45 1 Pe 1.16
12.3 Lk 1.59
    2.21
    Jn 7.22

12.3 Ac 15.1
12.3, 6 Lk 2.22
12.8 Lk 2.24
13.46 Lk 17.12
14.2 Mt 8.4
14.2-3 Lk 17.14
14.2-32 Mk 1.44
    Lk 5.14
14.4 He 9.19
14.4-32 Mt 8.4
15.18 He 9.10
15.25 Mt 9.20
16.2 He 9.7
16.2-3 He 6.19
16.3 He 9.13
16.6 He 5.3
    7.27
16.12 He 6.19
    Re 8.5
16.14 He 9.7
    9.13
16.15 He 6.19
    7.27
    9.7
    9.13
    10.4
16.21 He 10.4
16.27 He 13.11
16.29 Ac 27.9
17.10-14 Ac 15.20
    15.29
17.11 He 9.22
18.5 Mt 19.17
    Lk 10.28
    Ro 7.10
    10.5
    Ga 3.12
18.7-8 1 Cor 5.1
18.16 Mt 14.3-4
    Mk 6.18
18.22 Ro 1.27
19.2 Mt 5.48
    1 Pe 1.16
19.12 Mt 5.33
19.13 Mt 20.8
    Jas 5.4
19.15 Jn 7.24
    Ac 23.3
19.17 Mt 18.15
19.18 Mt 5.43
    19.19
    22.39
    Mk 12.31
    12.33
    Lk 10.27
    Ro 12.19
    13.9
    Ga 5.14

LEVITICUS (cont.)

19.18 Jas 2.8
19.32 1 Tm 5.1
20.7 1 Pe 1.16
20.9 Mt 15.4
     Mk 7.10
20.10 Jn 8.5
20.13 Ro 1.27
20.21 Mt 14.3–4
21.9 Re 17.16
     18.8
23.15–21 Ac 2.1
     1 Cor 16.8
23.29 Ac 3.23
23.34 Jn 7.2
23.36 Jn 7.37
24.5–8 Mt 12.4
24.5–9 Mk 2.26
     Lk 6.4
24.9 Mt 12.4
24.16 Mt 26.65–66
     Mk 14.64
     Jn 10.33
     19.7
24.17 Mt 5.21
24.20 Mt 5.38
25.35–36 Lk 6.35
25.43, 53 Col 4.1
26.11–12 Re 21.3
26.12 2 Cor 6.16
26.21 Re 15.1
     15.6
26.41 Ac 7.51
26.42 Lk 1.72–73
27.30 Mt 23.23
     Lk 11.42

NUMBERS

1.50 Ac 7.44
6.2–5 Ac 21.26
6.3 Lk 1.15
6.5 Ac 21.23–24
6.13–18 Ac 21.23–24
6.13–21 Ac 21.26
6.18 Ac 18.18
6.21 Ac 21.23–24
6.25–26 Ro 1.7
9.12 Jn 19.36
11.4 1 Cor 10.6
11.7–9 Jn 6.31
11.29 1 Cor 14.5
11.34 1 Cor 10.6
12.7 He 3.2, 5
12.8 2 Jn 12
     3 Jn 14
14.1–35 He 3.16–18
14.2 1 Cor 10.10

14.3 Ac 7.39
14.6 Mt 26.65
     Mk 14.63
14.16 1 Cor 10.5
14.21–23 He 3.11
14.22–23 He 3.18
14.23 1 Cor 10.5
14.29 He 3.17
14.29–30 1 Cor 10.5
     Jd 5
14.33 Ac 7.36
14.34 Ac 13.18
14.35 Jd 5
14.36 1 Cor 10.10
15.17–21 Ro 11.16
15.38–39 Mt 23.5
16.5 2 Tm 2.19
16.19–35 Jd 11
16.22 He 12.9
16.26 2 Tm 2.19
16.41–49 1 Cor 10.10
17.8–10 He 9.4
18.2–6 He 9.6
18.8 1 Cor 9.13
18.21 He 7.5
18.31 Mt 10.10
     1 Cor 9.13
19.6 He 9.19
19.9 He 9.13
19.13 He 9.10
19.17–19 He 9.13
20.2–5 He 3.8
20.11 1 Cor 10.4
21.5–6 1 Cor 10.9
21.9 Jn 3.14
22.7 2 Pe 2.15
     Jd 11
22.28 2 Pe 2.16
23.19 Ro 9.6
     2 Tm 2.13
     Hc 6.18
24.6 LXX He 8.2
24.17 Mt 2.2
     Re 22.16
25.1–2 Re 2.14
     2.20
25.1, 9 1 Cor 10.8
27.16 He 12.9
27.17 Mt 9.36
     Mk 6.34
28.9–10 Mt 12.5
30.2 Mt 5.33
31.16 Jd 11
     Re 2.14

DEUTERONOMY

1.10 He 11.12
1.16 Jn 7.51

1.17 Jas 2.9
2.5 - Ac 7.5
4.2 Re 22.18–19
4.7–8 Ro 3.2
4.11–12 He 12.18–19
4.15–19 Ro 1.23
4.20 Tt 2.14
     1 Pe 2.9
4.24 He 12.29
4.35 Mk 12.32
4.35, 39 1 Cor 8.4
5.4–22 Ac 7.38
5.12–14 Mk 2.27
5.13–14 Lk 13.14
5.14 Mt 12.2
     Lk 23.56
5.16 Mt 15.4
     Mk 7.10
     Lk 18.20
5.16–20 Mt 19.18 19
     Mk 10.19
5.17 Mt 5.21
     Jas 2.11
5.17–19 Ro 13.9
5.17–20 Lk 18.20
5.18 Mt 5.27
     Jas 2.11
5.21 Ro 7.7
     13.9
5.22–27 He 12.18–19
6.4 Mk 12.32
     Ro 3.30
     1 Cor 8.4
6.4–5 Mk 12.29–30
6.5 Mt 22.37
     Mk 12.33
     Lk 10.27
6.7 Eph 6.4
6.8 Mt 23.5
6.13 Mt 4.10
6.13–14 Lk 4.8
6.16 Mt 4.7
     Lk 4.12
6.20–25 Eph 6.4
7.1 Ac 13.19
7.6 Ro 9.4
     Tt 2.14
     1 Pe 2.9
7.9 1 Cor 1.9
     10.13
8.3 Mt 4.4
     Lk 4.4
     1 Cor 10.3
8.5 He 12.7
9.3 He 12.29
9.4 Ro 10.6–8
9.10 Ac 7.38
9.10, 11 2 Cor 3.3

9.19 He 12.21
10.3–5 He 9.4
10.12 Lk 10.27
10.15 1 Pe 2.9
10.17 Ac 10.34
     Ro 2.11
     Ga 2.6
     Eph 6.9
     Col 3.25
     1 Tm 6.15
     Re 17.14
     19.16
10.22 Ac 7.14
     He 11.12
11.14 Jas 5.7
11.29 Jn 4.20
12.5–14 Jn 4.20
12.32 Re 22.18–19
13.1–3 Mt 24.24
     Mk 13.22
13.2–4 Re 13.14
13.3 1 Cor 11.19
14.1–2 Ro 9.4
14.2 Tt 2.14
     1 Pe 2.9
15.7–8 1 Jn 3.17
15.11 Mt 26.11
     Mk 14.7
     Jn 12.8
15.12 Jn 8.35
15.16 Eph 6.2–3
16.1–8 Lk 2.41
16.3 1 Cor 5.8
16.9–11 Ac 2.1
     1 Cor 16.8
17.6 Jn 8.17
     1 Tm 5.19
     He 10.28
17.7 Jn 8.7
     1 Cor 5.13
18.1–3 1 Cor 9.13
18.13 Mt 5.48
18.15 Mt 17.5
     Mk 9.7
     Lk 24.27
     Jn 5.46
     7.40
     Ac 7.37
18.15–16 Ac 3.22
18.15, 18 Jn 1.21
     6.14
18.18 Jn 1.45
18.19 Ac 3.23
19.15 Mt 18.16
     Jn 8.17
     2 Cor 13.1
     1 Tm 5.19
     He 10.28

19.19 1 Cor 5.13
19.21 Mt 5.38
21.6–9 Mt 27.24
21.22 Ac 10.39
21.22–23 Mt 27.57–58
     Jn 19.31
21.23 Ga 3.13
22.21 1 Cor 5.13
22.22 Jn 8.5
22.24 1 Cor 5.13
22.30 1 Cor 5.1
23.21 Mt 5.33
23.24–25 Mt 12.1
23.25 Mk 2.23
     Lk 6.1
24.1 Mt 5.31
     19.7
24.1, 3 Mk 10.4
24.7 1 Cor 5.13
24.14 Mk 10.19
24.14–15 Jas 5.4
24.15 Mt 20.8
25.3 2 Cor 11.24
25.4 1 Cor 9.9
     1 Tm 5.18
25.5 Mt 22.24
     Mk 12.19
     Lk 20.28
27.20 1 Cor 5.1
27.26 2 Cor 3.9
     Ga 3.10
28.4 Lk 1.42
28.35 Re 16.2
29.4 Ro 11.8
29.17 LXX He 12.15
29.18 Ac 8.23
30.4 Mt 24.31
     Mk 13.27
30.6 Ro 2.29
30.11 1 Jn 5.3
30.12–14 Ro 10.6–8
31.6 He 13.5
31.7 He 4.8
31.8 He 13.5
31.26–27 Jn 5.45
32.4 Ro 9.14
     Re 15.3
     16.5
32.5 Mt 17.17
     Ac 2.40
     Php 2.15
32.6 Jn 8.41
32.8 Ac 17.26
32.17 1 Cor 10.20
     Re 9.20
32.20 Mt 17.17
32.21 Ro 10.19
     11.11

DEUT. (cont.)

32.21	1 Cor 10.22
32.29	Lk 19.42
32.35	Lk 21.22
	Ro 12.19
	He 10.30
32.36	He 10.30
32.40	Re 10.5–6
32.43	Ro 15.10
	Re 6.10
	19.2
32.43 LXX	He 1.6
	Re 18.20
33.2	Jd 14
33.2 LXX	Mt 25.31
33.3–4	Ac 20.32
	26.18
33.9	Mt 10.37
	Lk 14.26
33.12	2 Th 2.13

JOSHUA

1.5	He 13.5
2.4	Jas 2.25
2.11–12	He 11.31
2.15	Jas 2.25
3.14–17	Ac 7.45
6.12–21	He 11.30
6.17	Jas 2.25
6.21–25	He 11.31
7.19	Jn 9.24
8.33	Jn 4.20
14.1	Ac 13.19
18.1	Ac 7.45
22.4	He 4.8
22.5	Mt 22.37
	Mk 12.29–30
	12.33
	Lk 10.27
23.9	Ac 7.45
24.18	Ac 7.45
24.32	Jn 4.5
	Ac 7.16

JUDGES

2.10	Ac 13.36
2.16	Ac 13.20
5.4	He 12.26
5.19	Re 16.16
5.24	Lk 1.42
13.3	Lk 1.31
13.4	Lk 1.15
13.5, 7	Mt 2.23
14.6–7	He 11.33

RUTH

4.12	Mt 1.3
4.13	Mt 1.4–5
4.17–22	Mt 1.4–5
	Lk 3.31–33
4.17, 22	Mt 1.6
4.18–19	Mt 1.3

1 SAMUEL

1.11	Lk 1.48
1.11 LXX	Lk 1.15
1.17	Mk 5.34
2.1–10	Lk 1.46–55
2.5	Lk 1.53a
2.26	Lk 2.52
3.20	Ac 13.20
4.8	Re 11.6
8.5, 19	Ac 13.21
10.20–21, 24	Ac 13.21
11.15	Ac 13.21
12.3	Ac 20.33
12.22	Ro 11.1, 2
13.14	Ac 13.22
14.45	Mt 10.30
	Lk 21.18
	Ac 27.34
15.22	Mk 12.33
15.29	He 6.18
16.1	Lk 3.31–32
16.7	Jn 8.15
16.12–13	Ac 13.22
16.13	Lk 3.31–32
17.34–36	He 11.33
20.42	Mk 5.34
21.1–6	Mt 12.3–4
	Mk 2.25–26
	Lk 6.3–4

2 SAMUEL

3.39	2 Tm 4.14
5.2	Mt 2.6
5.14	Lk 3.31
7.2–16	Ac 7.45–46
7.8	2 Cor 6.18
7.12	Jn 7.42
	Ac 13.23
7.12–13	Ac 2.30
7.12, 13	Lk 1.32–33
7.14	2 Cor 6.18
	He 1.5
	12.7
	21.7
7.16	Lk 1.32–33
12.24	Mt 1.6

13.19	Mt 26.65
14.11	Ac 27.34
15.9	Mk 5.34
15.35	Mk 2.26
22.3 LXX	He 2.13
22.6	Ac 2.24
22.9	Re 11.5
22.28	Lk 1.51
22.50	Ro 15.9
23.2	Mt 22.43

1 KINGS

2.10	Ac 2.29
	13.36
5.11	Ac 12.20
6.1, 14	Ac 7.47
8.1, 6	Re 11.19
8.10–11	Re 15.8
8.13	Mt 23.21
8.17–18	Ac 7.45–46
8.19–20	Ac 7.47
8.27	Ac 17.24
9.7–8	Mt 23.38
10	Mt 6.29
10.1–10	Mt 12.42
	Lk 11.31
10.4–7	Lk 12.27
16.31	Re 2.20
17.1	Jas 5.17
	Re 11.6
17.1, 7	Lk 4.25
17.9	Lk 4.26
17.9–24	Mt 10.41
17.17	Lk 7.12
17.17–24	He 11.35
17.18	Mt 8.29
	Mk 5.7
17.21	Ac 20.10
17.23	Lk 7.15
18.1	Lk 4.25
18.12	Ac 8.39
18.17	Ac 16.20
18.24–39	Re 13.13
18.42–45	Jas 5.18
18.46	Lk 12.35
19.10, 14	Ro 11.3
19.18	Ro 11.4
19.20	Mt 8.21
	Lk 9.61
22.17	Mt 9.36
	Mk 6.34
22.19	Re 4.2
	4.9
	4.10
	5.1
	5.7
	5.13

22.19	Re 6.16
	7.10
	7.15
	19.4
	21.5
22.26–27	He 11.36

2 KINGS

1.8	Mt 3.4
	Mk 1.6
1.10	Re 11.5
	20.9
1.10, 12	Lk 9.54
2.11	Mk 16.19
	Re 11.12
4.8–37	Mt 10.41
4.25–37	He 11.35
4.29	Lk 10.4
	12.35
4.33	Mt 6.6
4.36	Lk 7.15
4.43–44	Mt 14.20
4.44	Lk 9.17
5.1–14	Lk 4.27
5.10	Jn 9.7
5.19	Mk 5.34
9.1	Lk 12.35
9.7	Re 6.10
	19.2
9.13	Lk 19.36
9.22	Re 2.20
9.27	Re 16.16
12.9	Mk 12.41
23.29	Re 16.16
24.12–16	Mt 1.11

1 CHRONICLES

1.1–4	Lk 3.36–38
1.24–27	Lk 3.34–36
1.28	Lk 3.34
1.34	Mt 1.2
	Lk 3.34
2.1–14	Lk 3.31–33
2.4, 5, 9	Mt 1.3
2.10–12	Mt 1.4–5
2.13–15	Mt 1.6
3.10–14	Mt 1.7–10
3.15–16	Mt 1.11
3.17	Lk 3.27
3.17, 19	Mt 1.12
11.2	Mt 2.6
16.35	Ac 26.17
17.1–14	Ac 7.45–46
17.11	Mt 1.1
17.13	He 1.5
24.10	Lk 1.5

29.11	Re 5.12
29.15	He 11.13

2 CHRONICLES

3.1	Ac 7.47
5.1	Ac 7.47
5.7	Re 11.19
5.13–14	Re 15.8
6.2	Ac 7.47
6.7–8	Ac 7.45–46
6.10	Ac 7.47
6.18	Re 21.3
9	Mt 6.29
9.1–12	Mt 12.42
	Lk 11.31
9.3–6	Lk 12.27
13.9	Ga 4.8
15.6	Mt 24.7
	Mk 13.8
	Lk 21.10
15.7	1 Cor 15.58
18.16	Mt 9.36
	Mk 6.34
18.18	Re 4.2
	4.9
	4.10
	5.1
	5.7
	5.13
	6.16
	7.10
	7.15
	19.4
	21.5
18.25–26	He 11.36
19.7	Ac 10.34
	Ro 2.11
	1 Pe 1.17
19.17	Eph 6.9
	Col 3.25
20.7	Jas 2.23
24.20–21	Mt 23.35
	Lk 11.51
24.21	He 11.37
29.31	He 13.15
30.17	Jn 11.55
36.10	Mt 1.11
36.15–16	Lk 20.10–12
36.16	Mt 5.12
	Lk 6.23
	Ac 7.52

EZRA

3.2	Mt 1.12
	Lk 3.27
4.3	Jn 4.9

EZRA (cont.)

9.1—10.44	Jn 4.9
9.3	Mt 26.65
9.7	Lk 21.24

NEHEMIAH

9.6	Re 10.6
9.15	Jn 6.31
9.36	Jn 8.33
10.37	Ro 11.16
11.1	Mt 4.5

ESTHER

1.1d LXX	Re 4.5
	8.5
	11.19
	16.18
4.1	Mt 11.21
5.3, 6	Mk 6.23
7.2	Mk 6.23

JOB

1.1, 8	1 Th 5.22
1.9–11	Re 12.10
1.20	Mt 26.65
1.21	1 Tm 6.7
2.3	1 Th 5.22
2.6	2 Cor 12.7
2.12	Mt 26.65
3.21	Re 9.6
4.9	2 Th 2.8
4.19	2 Cor 5.1
5.11	Lk 1.52
	Jas 4.10
5.13	1 Cor 3.19
12.7–9	Ro 1.20
12.14	Re 3.7
12.19	Lk 1.52
13.16	Php 1.19
15.8	Ro 11.34
16.9	Ac 7.54
19.26 27 LXX	Jn 19.30
22.29	Mt 23.12
	1 Pe 5.6
23.10	1 Pe 1.7
34.19	Jas 2.1
38.3	Lk 12.35
38.17	Mt 16.18
39.30	Lk 17.37
40.7	Lk 12.35
41.11	Ro 11.35
42.2	Mt 19.26
	Mk 10.27

PSALMS

2.1	Rc 11.18
2.1–2	Ac 4.25–26
2.2	Re 19.19
2.7	Mt 3.17
	17.5
	Mk 1.11
	9.7
	Lk 3.22
	9.35
	Jn 1.49
	Ac 13.33
	He 1.5
	5.5
2.8	He 1.2
2.8, 9	Re 2.26–27
2.9	Re 12.5
	19.15
2.11	Php 2.12
4.4	Eph 4.26
5.9	Ro 3.13
6.3	Jn 12.27
6.8	Mt 7.23
	Lk 13.27
7.9	Re 2.23
7.12	Lk 13.3
	13.5
7.13	Eph 6.16
8.3 LXX	Mt 21.16
8.5–7 LXX	He 2.6–8
8.6	1 Cor 15.27
	Eph 1.22
9.8	Ac 17.31
10.7	Ro 3.14
10.16	Re 11.15
11.6	Re 14.10
	20.10
	21.8
14.1–3	Ro 3.10–12
14.7	Ro 11.26–27
16.8–11	Ac 2.25–28
16.9	Jn 20.9
16.10	Ac 2.31
	1 Cor 15.4
16.10 LXX	Ac 13.35
17.15	Re 22.4
18.2	Lk 1.69
18.4	Ac 2.24
18.6	Jas 5.4
18.49	Ro 15.9
19.1	Ro 1.20
19.4	Ro 10.18
19.9	Re 16.7
	19.2
21.9	Jas 5.3
22	1 Pe 1.11
22.1	Mt 27.46
22.1	Mk 15.34
22.1–18	Mk 9.12
	Lk 24.27
22.5	Ro 5.5
22.7	Mt 27.39
	Mk 15.29
22.7–8	Lk 23.35–36
22.7, 8	Mt 26.24
22.8	Mt 27.43
22.15	Jn 19.28
22.16	Php 3.2
22.16–18	Mt 26.24
22.18	Mt 27.35
	Mk 15.24
	Lk 23.34
	Jn 19.24
22.20	Php 3.2
22.21	2 Tm 4.17
22.22	He 2.12
22.23	Re 19.5
22.28	Re 11.15
	19.6
23.1	Jn 10.11
	Re 7.17
23.2	Re 7.17
23.5	Lk 7.46
24.1	1 Cor 10.26
24.3–4	Mt 5.8
25.11	1 Jn 2.12
25.20	Ro 5.5
25.21	Lk 6.27
26.6	Mt 27.24
26.8	Mt 23.21
28.4	Mt 16.27
	2 Tm 4.14
	1 Pe 1.17
	Re 20.12–13
	22.12
29.3	Ac 7.2
31.5	Lk 23.46
	Ac 7.59
	1 Pe 4.19
31.24	1 Cor 16.13
32.1–2	Ro 4.7–8
32.2	Re 14.5
32.5	1 Jn 1.9
33.2, 3	Eph 5.19
33.3	Re 5.9
	14.3
33.6, 9	He 11.3
34.8	He 1.14
	1 Pe 2.3
34.12–16	1 Pe 3.10–12
34.13	Jas 1.26
34.14	He 12.14
34.15	Jn 9.31
34.19	2 Cor 1.5
	2 Tm 3.11
34.20	Jn 19.36
35.8	Ro 11.9–10
35.13	Ro 12.15
35.16	Ac 7.54
35.19	Jn 15.25
36.1	Ro 3.18
36.9	Re 21.6
37.4	Mt 6.33
37.11	Mt 5.5
37.12	Ac 7.54
38.11	Lk 23.49
39.1	Jas 1.26
39.12	He 11.13
	1 Pe 2.11
40.3	Re 5.9
	14.3
40.6	Eph 5.2
	He 10.8
40.6–8	He 10.5–7
40.7	Lk 7.19
	He 10.9
41.9	Mt 26.23
	Mk 14.18
	Lk 22.21
	Jn 13.18
	17.12
	Ac 1.16
41.13	Lk 1.68
	Ro 9.5
42.2	Re 22.4
42.5, 11	Mt 26.38
	Mk 14.34
	Jn 12.27
43.5	Mt 26.38
	Mk 14.34
44.22	Ro 8.36
45.6–7	He 1.8–9
46.2–3	Lk 21.25
46.6	Re 11.18
47.8	Re 4.2
	4.9
	4.10
	5.1
	5.7
	5.13
	6.16
	7.10
	7.15
	19.4
	21.5
48.2	Mt 5.35
50.6	He 12.23
50.12	Ac 17.25
	1 Cor 10.26
50.14	He 13.15
50.16–21	Ro 2.21
50.23	He 13.15
51.1	Lk 18.13
51.4	Lk 15.18
	Ro 3.4
51.5	Jn 9.34
	Ro 7.14
53.1–3	Ro 3.10–12
55.22	1 Pe 5.7
62.10	Mt 19.22
	1 Tm 6.17
62.12	Mt 16.27
	Ro 2.6
	2 Tm 4.14
	1 Pe 1.17
	Re 2.23
	20.12–13
	22.12
65.7	Lk 21.25
66.10	1 Pe 1.7
66.18	Jn 9.31
67.2	Ac 28.28
67.36 LXX	2 Th 1.10
68.8	He 12.26
68.18	Eph 4.8
69.4	Jn 15.25
69.9	Jn 2.17
	Ro 15.3
69.21	Mt 27.34
	27.48
	Mk 15.23
	15.36
	Lk 23.36
	Jn 19.29
69.22–23	Ro 11.9–10
69.24	Re 16.1
69.25	Ac 1.20
69.28	Php 4.3
	Re 3.5
	13.8
	17.8
	20.12
	20.15
	21.27
72.10–11	Rc 21.26
72.10, 11	Mt 2.11
72.15	Mt 2.11
72.18	Lk 1.68
74.2	Ac 20.28
75.8	Re 14.10
	15.7
	16.19
78.2	Mt 13.35
78.4	Eph 6.4
78.8	Ac 2.40
78.15	1 Cor 10.4
78.24	Jn 6.31
	Re 2.17
78.24–29	1 Cor 10.3
78.31	1 Cor 10.5
78.37	Ac 8.21

PSALMS (cont.)

78.44	Re 16.4
79.1	Lk 21.24
	Re 11.2
79.3	Re 16.6
79.6	1 Th 4.5
	2 Th 1.8
79.10	Re 6.10
	19.2
82.6	Jn 10.34
86.9	Re 15.4
88.8	Lk 23.49
88.8 LXX	2 Th 1.10
89.3–4	Jn 7.42
89.4	Jn 12.34
89.10	Lk 1.51
89.11	1 Cor 10.26
89.20	Ac 13.22
89.26	1 Pe 1.17
89.27	Re 1.5
89.36	Jn 12.34
89.50, 51	1 Pe 4.14
90.4	2 Pe 3.8
91.11	Lk 4.10
	He 1.14
91.11–12	Mt 4.6
91.12	Lk 4.11
91.13	Lk 10.19
92.5	Re 15.3
93.1	Re 19.6
94.1	1 Th 4.6
94.11	1 Cor 3.20
94.14	Ro 11.1, 2
94.19	2 Cor 1.5
95.7–8	He 3.15
	4.7
95.7–11	He 3.7–11
95.11	He 3.18
	4.3
	4.5
96.1	Re 5.9
	14.3
96.11	Re 18.20
96.13	Ac 17.31
	Re 19.11
97.1	Re 19.6
97.3	Re 11.5
97.7	He 1.6
98.1	Re 5.9
	14.3
98.3	Lk 1.54
	Ac 28.28
98.9	Ac 17.31
99.1	Re 19.6
102.4, 11	Jas 1.10–11
102.25–27	He 1.10–12
103.3	Mk 2.7

103.7	Ro 3.2
103.8	Jas 5.11
103.13, 17	Lk 1.50
104.2	1 Tm 6.16
104.4	He 1.7
104.12	Mt 13.32
105.8–9	Lk 1.72–73
105.21	Ac 7.10
105.40	Jn 6.31
106.10	Lk 1.71
106.14	1 Cor 10.6
106.20	Ro 1.23
106.25–27	1 Cor 10.10
106.37	1 Cor 10.20
106.45–46	Lk 1.72
106.48	Lk 1.68
107.3	Mt 8.11
	Lk 13.29
107.9	Lk 1.53
107.20	Ac 10.36
109.4, 5, 7, 8	Jn 17.12
109.8	Ac 1.20
109.25	Mt 27.39
	Mk 15.29
109.28	1 Cor 4.12
110.1	Mt 22.44
	26.64
	Mk 12.36
	14.62
	16.19
	Lk 20.42–43
	22.69
	Ac 2.34–35
	Ro 8.34
	1 Cor 15.25
	Eph 1.20
	Col 3.1
	He 1.3
	1.13
	8.1
	10.12
	10.13
	12.2
110.4	Jn 12.34
	He 5.6
	5.10
	6.20
	7.3
	7.17
	7.21
111.2	Re 15.3
111.4	Jas 5.11
111.9	Lk 1.49
	1.68
112.9	2 Cor 9.9
112.10	Ac 7.54
113—118	Mt 26.30
114.3–7	Re 20.11

115.4–7	Re 9.20
115.13	Re 11.18
	19.5
116.3	Ac 2.24
116.10	2 Cor 4.13
116.11	Ro 3.4
117.1	Ro 15.11
118.6	Ro 8.31
	He 13.6
118.18	2 Cor 6.9
118.20	Jn 10.9
118.22	Lk 20.17
	Ac 4.11
	1 Pe 2.4
	2.7
118.22–23	Mt 21.42
	Mk 12.10–11
118.25–26	Mk 11.9
	Jn 12.13
118.26	Mt 21.9
	23.39
	Lk 13.35
	19.38
119.46	Ro 1.16
119.137	Re 16.5
	16.7
	19.2
119.165	1 Jn 2.10
122.1–5	Jn 4.20
125.5	Ga 6.16
126.5–6	Lk 6.21
128.6	Ga 6.16
130.8	Tt 2.14
	Re 1.5
132.1–5	Ac 7.45–46
132.11	Ac 2.30
134.1	Re 19.5
135.1	Re 19.5
135.14	He 10.30
135.15–17	Re 9.20
137.8	Re 18.6
137.9	Lk 19.44
139.1	Ro 8.27
139.14	Re 15.3
139.21	Re 2.6
140.3	Ro 3.13
	Jas 3.8
141.2	Re 5.8
	8.3
	8.4
141.3	Jas 1.26
143.2	Ro 3.20
	1 Cor 4.4
	Ga 2.16
144.9	Re 5.9
	14.3
145.17	Re 15.3
	16.5

145.18	Ac 17.27
146.6	Ac 4.24
	14.15
	17.24
	Re 10.6
	14.7
147.8	Ac 14.17
147.9	Lk 12.24
147.18	Ac 10.36
147.19–20	Ro 3.2
149.1	Re 5.9
	14.3

PROVERBS

1.16	Ro 3.15–17
2.3–4	Col 2.3
2.3–6	Jas 1.5
2.4	Mt 13.44
3.3	2 Cor 3.3
3.4	Lk 2.52
3.4 LXX	Ro 12.17
	2 Cor 8.21
3.7	Ro 12.16
3.11–12	He 12.5–6
3.12	Re 3.19
3.27–28	2 Cor 8.12
3.34 LXX	Jas 4.6
	1 Pe 5.5
4.26 LXX	He 12.13
7.3	2 Cor 3.3
8.15	Ro 13.1
8.22	Re 3.14
10.9	Ac 13.10
10.12	1 Cor 13.7
	Jas 5.20
	1 Pe 4.8
11.24	2 Cor 9.6
11.31 LXX	1 Pe 4.18
15.29	Jn 9.31
16.33	Ac 1.26
17.3	1 Pe 1.7
18.4	Jn 7.38
19.17	Mt 25.40
19.18	Eph 6.4
20.22	1 Th 5.15
20.27	1 Cor 2.11
22.6	Eph 6.4
22.8 LXX	2 Cor 9.7
22.9	2 Cor 9.6
23.4	1 Tm 6.9
23.31 LXX	Eph 5.18
24.12	Mt 16.27
	Ro 2.6
	2 Tm 4.14
	1 Pe 1.17
	Re 2.23
	20.12–13

24.12	Re 22.12
24.12 LXX	Lk 16.15
24.21	1 Pe 2.17
25.6–7	Lk 14.8–10
25.21	Mt 5.44
25.21–22	Ro 12.20
26.11	2 Pe 2.22
27.1	Jas 4.13–14
27.20	1 Jn 2.16
28.13	1 Jn 1.9
28.22	1 Tm 6.9
29.3	Lk 15.13
29.23	Mt 23.12
30.4	Jn 3.13
30.8	1 Tm 6.8
31.17	Lk 12.35

ECCLESIASTES

1.2	Ro 8.20
5.15	1 Tm 6.7
7.9	Jas 1.19
7.20	Ro 3.10–12
11.5	Jn 3.8
12.14	2 Cor 5.10

ISAIAH

1.9	Ro 9.29
1.10	Re 11.8
1.15	Jn 9.31
1.16	Jas 4.8
2.3	Jn 4.22
2.5	1 Jn 1.7
2.10, 19, 21	2 Th 1.9
	Re 6.15
5.1	Lk 20.9
5.1–2	Mt 21.33
	Mk 12.1
5.9	Jas 5.4
5.21	Ro 12.16
6.1	Jn 12.41
	Re 4.2
	4.9
	4.10
	5.1
	5.7
	5.13
	6.16
	7.10
	7.15
	19.4
	21.5
6.2	Re 4.8
6.3	Re 4.8
6.4	Re 15.8
6.9–10	Mt 13.14–15
	Mk 4.12

Isaiah (cont.)

6.9-10 Lk 8.10
   19.42
   Ac 28.26-27
6.10 Jn 12.40
7.14 Mt 1.23
  Lk 1.31
  Jn 1.45
  Re 12.5
8.8, 10 LXX Mt 1.23
8.12-13 1 Pe 3.14-15
8.14 Lk 2.34
  Ro 9.32
  1 Pe 2.8
8.17 LXX He 2.13
8.18 He 2.13
8.22 Re 16.10
9.1-2 Mt 4.15-16
9.2 Lk 1.78-79
  2 Cor 4.6
  1 Pe 2.9
9.6 Jn 1.45
  Eph 2.14
9.7 Lk 1.32-33
  Jn 12.34
10.3 1 Pe 2.12
10.22-23 Ro 9.27-28
11.1 Mt 2.23
  Ac 13.23
  He 7.14
  Re 5.5
  22.16
11.2 Eph 1.17
  1 Pe 4.14
11.3 Jn 7.24
11.4 Jn 7.24
  Eph 6.17
  2 Th 2.8
  Re 19.11
11.5 Eph 6.14
11.10 Ro 15.12
  Re 5.5
  22.16
11.15 Re 16.12
12.2 He 2.13
13.8 Jn 16.21
13.10 Mt 24.29
  Mk 13.24-25
  Lk 21.25
  Re 6.12-13
  8.12
13.21 Re 18.2
14.12 Lk 10.18
  Re 12.9
14.13, 15 Mt 11.23
  Lk 10.15
19.2 Mt 24.7

19.2 Mk 13.8
  Lk 21.10
19.12 1 Cor 1.20
21.3 Jn 16.21
21.9 Re 14.8
  18.2
22.13 1 Cor 15.32
22.22 Re 3.7
23 Lk 10.13-14
23.1-8 Mt 11.21-22
23.8 Re 18.23
23.17 Re 17.2
  18.3
24.8 Re 18.22
24.15 2 Th 1.12
24.17 Lk 21.35
24.19 LXX Lk 21.25
24.23 Re 4.4
25.8 1 Cor 15.54
  Re 7.17
  21.4
26.3 Php 4.7
26.11 He 10.27
26.17 Jn 16.21
26.19 Eph 5.14
26.20 Mt 6.6
26.20 LXX He 10.37
27.9 Ro 11.27
27.13 Mt 24.31
28.11-12 1 Cor 14.21
28.16 Ro 9.33
  10.11
  1 Cor 3.11
  Eph 2.20
  1 Pe 2.4
  2.6
29.10 Ro 11.8
29.11 Re 5.1
29.13 Col 2.22
29.13 LXX Mt 15.8-9
  Mk 7.6-7
29.14 1 Cor 1.19
29.16 Ro 9.20
30.33 Re 19.20
  20.10
  20.15
  21.8
32.17 Jas 3.18
33.14 He 12.29
33.18 1 Cor 1.20
33.24 Ac 10.43
34.4 Mt 24.29
  Mk 13.24-25
  Re 6.13-14
34.10 Re 14.11
  19.3
34.11 Re 18.2
35.3 He 12.12

35.5 Lk 7.22
  Ac 26.18
35.5-6 Mt 11.5
  Mk 7.37
35.10 Re 21.4
37.19 Ga 4.8
38.10 Mt 16.18
40.1 Lk 2.25
40.2 Re 1.5
40.3 Mt 3.3
  Mk 1.3
  Lk 1.76
  Jn 1.23
40.3-5 Lk 3.4-6
40.5 LXX Lk 2.30-31
  Ac 28.28
40.6-7 Jas 1.10-11
40.6-8 1 Pe 1.24-25
40.10 Re 22.12
40.11 Jn 10.11
40.13 Ro 11.34
  1 Cor 2.16
40.18-20 Ac 17.29
41.4 Re 1.4
  1.8
  4.8
41.8 Lk 1.54
  Jas 2.23
41.8-9 He 2.16
41.10 Ac 18.9-10
42.1 Mt 3.17
  Mk 1.11
  Lk 9.35
42.1-4 Mt 12.18-21
42.5 Ac 17.24
  17.25
42.6 Lk 2.32
  Ac 26.23
42.7 Ac 26.18
42.10 Re 5.9
  14.3
42.12 1 Pe 2.9
42.16 Ac 26.18
42.18 Mt 11.5
43.4 Re 3.9
43.5 Ac 18.9-10
43.6 2 Cor 6.18
43.18 2 Cor 5.17
43.20 1 Pe 2.9
43.21 1 Pe 2.9
43.25 Mk 2.7
  Lk 5.21
44.6 Re 1.17
  2.8
  21.6
  22.13
44.10-17 Ac 17.29
44.23 Re 18.20

44.25 1 Cor 1.20
44.27 Re 16.12
44.28 Ac 13.22
45.3 Col 2.3
45.9 Ro 9.20
45.14 1 Cor 14.25
  Re 3.9
45.15 Ro 11.33
45.17 He 5.9
45.21 Mk 12.32
45.23 Ro 14.11
  Php 2.10-11
46.13 Lk 2.32
47.7-9 Re 18.7-8
47.9 Re 18.23
48.6 LXX Re 1.19
48.10 1 Pe 1.7
48.12 Re 1.17
  2.8
  21.6
  22.13
48.13 Ro 4.17
48.20 Re 18.4
49.1 Ga 1.15
49.2 Eph 6.17
  He 4.12
  Re 1.16
  2.12
  2.16
  19.15
49.3 2 Th 1.10
49.4 Php 2.16
49.6 Lk 2.32
  Jn 8.12
  9.5
  Ac 13.47
  26.23
49.8 2 Cor 6.2
49.10 Re 7.16
  7.17
49.13 Lk 2.25
  2 Cor 7.6
  Re 18.20
49.18 Ro 14.11
49.23 Re 3.9
49.24 Mt 12.29
49.26 Re 16.6
50.6 Mt 26.67
  27.30
50.8 Ro 8.33
51.17 Eph 5.14
51.17, 22 Re 14.10
  15.7
  16.19
52.1 Mt 4.5
  Eph 5.14
  Re 21.2
  21.27

52.5 Ro 2.24
  2 Pe 2.2
52.7 Ac 10.36
  Ro 10.15
  2 Cor 5.20
  Eph 2.17
  6.15
52.9 Lk 2.38
52.10 Lk 2.30-31
52.11 2 Cor 6.17
  Re 18.4
52.13 Ac 3.13
52.15 Ro 15.21
  1 Cor 2.9
53 Lk 24.27
  24.46
  1 Pe 1.11
53.1 Jn 12.38
  Ro 10.16
53.2 Mt 2.23
53.3 Mk 9.12
53.4 Mt 8.17
  1 Pe 2.24
53.4-5 Ro 4.25
53.5 Mt 26.67
  1 Pe 2.24
53.5-6 Ac 10.43
53.6 1 Pe 2.25
53.6-7 Jn 1.29
53.7 Mt 26.63
  27.12
  27.14
  Mk 14.60-61
  15.4-5
  1 Cor 5.7
  1 Pe 2.23
  Re 5.6
  5.12
  13.8
53.7-8 LXX Ac 8.32-33
53.8-9 1 Cor 15.3
53.9 Mt 26.24
  1 Pe 2.22
  1 Jn 3.5
  Re 14.5
53.11 Ro 5.19
53.12 Mt 27.38
  Lk 22.37
  23.33
  23.34
  He 9.28
  1 Pe 2.24
54.1 Ga 4.27
54.11-12 Re 21.19
54.13 Jn 6.45
55.1 Re 21.6
  22.17
55.3 He 13.20

ISAIAH (cont.)

55.3 LXX Ac 13.34
55.6 Ac 17.27
55.8 Ro 11.33
55.10 2 Cor 9.10
56.7 Mt 21.13
    Mk 11.17
    Lk 19.46
56.8 Jn 10.16
56.12 1 Cor 15.32
57.19 Ac 2.39
    Eph 2.13
    2.17
57.20 Jd 13
58.5 Mt 6.16
58.6 Lk 4.18-19
    Ac 8.23
58.7 Mt 25.35-36
58.8 Lk 1.78-79
58.11 Jn 7.38
59.7-8 Ro 3.15-17
59.17 Eph 6.14
    6.17
    1 Th 5.8
59.18 1 Pe 1.17
    Re 20.12-13
    22.12
59.20-21 Ro 11.26-27
60.1 Eph 5.14
60.1-2 Lk 1.78-79
    Jn 1.14
60.1, 2 Re 21.11
60.3, 5 Re 21.24
60.6 Mt 2.11
60.7 Mt 21.13
60.11 Re 21.25
60.14 Re 3.9
60.19 Re 21.11
60.19-20 Re 21.23
    22.5
60.21 2 Pe 3.13
61.1 Mt 11.5
    Lk 7.22
    Ac 4.27
    10.38
61.1 LXX Ac 26.18
61.1-2 Lk 4.18-19
61.2-3 Mt 5.4
61.3 Lk 6.21
61.6 1 Pe 2.5
    2.9
    Re 1.6
    5.10
    20.6
61.10 Re 19.8
    21.2
62.2 Re 2.17

62.2 Re 3.12
62.6 He 13.17
62.11 Mt 21.5
    Re 22.12
63.1-3 Re 19.13
63.3 Re 14.20
    19.15
63.10 Ac 7.51
    Eph 4.30
63.11 He 13.20
63.16 Jn 8.41
63.18 Lk 21.24
    Re 11.2
64.4 1 Cor 2.9
64.8 Jn 8.41
    1 Pe 1.17
65.1 Ro 10.20
65.2 Ro 10.21
65.15 Re 2.17
    3.12
65.17 2 Pe 3.13
    Re 21.1
65.19 Re 21.4
65.23 Php 2.16
66.1 Mt 5.34
    5.35
    23.22
66.1-2 Ac 7.49-50
66.5 2 Th 1.12
66.6 Re 16.1
    16.17
66.7 Re 12.2
    12.5
66.14 Jn 16.22
66.15 2 Th 1.8
66.22 2 Pe 3.13
    Re 21.1
66.24 Mk 9.48

JEREMIAH

1.5 Ga 1.15
1.7 Ac 26.17
1.8 Ac 18.9-10
1.10 Re 10.11
1.17 Lk 12.35
2.11 Ga 4.8
2.13 Re 7.17
    21.6
3.19 1 Pe 1.17
4.4 Ro 2.25
4.29 Re 6.15
5.14 Re 11.5
5.21 Mk 8.18
5.24 Ac 14.17
    Jas 5.7
6.10 Ac 7.51
6.14 1 Th 5.3

6.16 Mt 11.29
7.11 Mt 21.13
    Mk 11.17
    Lk 19.46
7.18 LXX Ac 7.42
7.34 Re 18.23
8.2 Ac 7.42
8.3 Re 9.6
8.11 1 Th 5.3
9.15 Re 8.11
9.24 1 Cor 1.31
    2 Cor 10.17
9.25 Ro 2.25
9.26 Ac 7.51
10.6-7 Re 15.4
10.10 Theodotion
    Re 15.3
10.14 Ro 1.22
10.25 1 Th 4.5
    2 Th 1.8
    Re 16.1
11.20 1 Th 2.4
    Re 2.23
12.3 Jas 5.5
12.7 Mt 23.38
13.25 Ro 1.25
14.12 Re 6.8
14.14 Mt 7.22
15.2 Re 13.10
15.3 Re 6.8
16.9 Re 18.23
16.19 Ro 1.25
17.10 1 Pe 1.17
    Re 2.23
    20.12-13
    22.12
17.21 Jn 5.10
18.6 Ro 9.21
19.13 Ac 7.42
20.2 He 11.36
20.9 1 Cor 9.16
21.7 Lk 21.24
22.5 Mt 23.38
23.1-2 Jn 10.8
23.5-6 1 Cor 1.30
23.18 Ro 11.34
23.23 Ac 17.27
25.10 Re 18.23
25.15 Re 14.10
    15.7
    16.19
25.29 1 Pe 4.17
25.30 Re 10.11
25.34 Jas 5.5
26.11 Ac 6.13
27.15 Mt 7.22
27.20 Mt 1.11
31.9 2 Cor 6.18

31.15 Mt 2.18
31.25 Mt 11.28
    Lk 6.21
31.31 Mt 26.28
    Lk 22.20
    1 Cor 11.25
    2 Cor 3.6
31.31-34 He 8.8-12
31.33 2 Cor 3.3
    He 10.16
31.33-34 Ro 11.27
    1 Th 4.9
    Ac 10.43
    He 10.17
    1 Jn 2.27
32.6-9 Mt 27.9-10
32.38 2 Cor 6.16
32.40 Lk 22.20
    1 Cor 11.25
    2 Cor 3.6
    He 13.20
36.24 Mt 26.65
37.15 He 11.36
38.6 He 11.36
43.11 Re 13.10
46.10 Lk 21.22
49.11 1 Tm 5.5
49.36 Re 7.1
50.6 Mt 10.6
50.8 Re 18.4
50.15 Re 18.6
50.25 Ro 9.22
50.29 Re 18.6
50.34 Re 18.8
50.38 Re 16.12
50.39 Re 18.2
51.6 Re 18.4
51.7 Re 14.8
    17.2
    17.4
    18.3
51.8 Re 14.8
    18.2
51.9 Re 18.4
    18.5
51.13 Re 17.1
51.36 Re 16.12
51.45 Re 18.4
51.48 Re 18.20
51.49 Re 18.24
51.63-64 Re 18.21

LAMENTATIONS

1.15 Re 14.20
    19.15
2.15 Mt 27.39
    Mk 15.29

3.15 LXX Ac 8.23
3.45 1 Cor 4.13

EZEKIEL

1.1 Re 19.11
1.5-10 Re 4.6-7
1.13 Re 4.5
    11.19
1.18 Re 4.8
1.22 Re 4.6
1.24 Re 1.15
    14.2
    19.6
1.26-27 Re 4.2
    4.9
    4.10
    5.1
    5.7
    5.13
    6.16
    7.10
    7.15
    19.4
    21.5
1.26-28 Re 4.3
2.1 Ac 26.16
2.8 Re 10.9-10
2.9-10 Re 5.1
3.1-3 Re 10.9-10
3.17 He 13.17
4.14 Ac 10.14
5.12, 17 Re 6.8
7.2 Re 20.8
9.2 Re 1.13
9.4 Re 7.3
    9.4
    14.1
9.6 1 Pe 4.17
9.11 LXX Re 1.13
10.12 Re 4.8
10.14 Re 4.6-7
11.19 2 Cor 3.3
12.2 Mk 8.18
13.10 1 Th 5.3
13.10-12 Mt 7.27
13.10-15 Ac 23.3
14.21 Re 6.8
16.61, 63 Ro 6.21
17.23 Mt 13.32
    Mk 4.32
    Lk 13.19
18.20 Jn 9.2
18.23 1 Tm 2.4
20.34, 41 2 Cor 6.17
20.41 Eph 5.2
    Php 4.18
21.26 Mt 23.12

EZEKIEL (cont.)

22.27 Mt 7.15
22.31 Re 16.1
24.7 Re 18.24
26—28 Mt 11.21-22
    Lk 10.13-14
26.13 Re 18.22
26.16 Re 18.9
26.17 Re 18.10
26.21 Re 18.21
27.12, 13 Re 18.12-13
27.17 Ac 12.20
27.22 Re 18.12-13
27.27-29 Re 18.17
27.30-34 Re 18.19
27.30-35 Re 18.9
27.32 Re 18.18
27.36 Re 18.11
    18.15
28.2 Ac 12.22
    2 Th 2.4
28.13 Re 17.4
    18.16
28.13 LXX Re 2.7
31.6 Mt 13.32
    Mk 4.32
    Lk 13.19
31.8, 9 LXX Re 2.7
32.7 Mt 24.29
    Lk 21.25
32.7-8 Mk 13.24-25
32.7, 8 Re 6.12-13
    8.12
33.5 Mt 27.25
33.27 Re 6.8
34.2-3 Jn 10.8
34.5 Mt 9.36
34.5-6 1 Pe 2.25
34.8 Mk 6.34
    Jd 12
34.11 Lk 15.4
34.15 Jn 10.11
34.16 Lk 15.4
    19.10
34.17 Mt 25.32
34.23 Jn 1.45
    10.16
    Re 7.17
36.20 Ro 2.24
36.23 Mt 6.9
36.25 He 10.22
36.26 2 Cor 3.3
36.27 1 Th 4.8
    Re 11.11
37.5 Re 7.1
37.9 Re 7.1
37.10 Re 11.11
37.12 Mt 27.52-53

37.14 1 Th 4.8
37.23 Tt 2.14
37.24 Jn 10.16
37.26 He 13.20
37.27 2 Cor 6.16
    Re 21.3
38.2 Re 20.8
38.19-20 Re 11.13
38.22 Re 8.7
    14.10
    20.9
    20.10
    21.8
39.6 Re 20.9
39.17-20 Re 19.17-18
39.17, 20 Re 19.21
40.2 Re 21.10
40.3 Re 11.1
40.3, 5 Re 21.15
43.2 Re 1.15
    14.2
    19.6
44.4 Re 15.8
44.7 Ac 21.28
44.30 Ro 11.16
47.1 Re 22.1
47.12 Re 22.2
    22.14
    22.19
48.16, 17 Re 21.16-17
48.30-35 Re 21.12-13
48.35 Re 3.12

DANIEL

1.12, 14 Re 2.10
2.28 Lk 21.9
2.28, 29 Mt 24.6
    Re 1.1
    1.10
    4.1
    22.6
2.34-35 Mt 21.44
2.44 1 Cor 15.24
    Re 11.15
2.44-45 Mt 21.44
2.45 Theodotion
    Mt 24.6
2.45 Re 1.1
    1.19
    4.1
    22.6
2.47 1 Cor 14.25
    Re 17.14
    19.16
3.4 Re 10.11
3.5-6 Re 13.15
3.5 Mt 4.9

3.6 Mt 13.42
    13.50
3.10 Mt 4.9
3.15 Mt 4.9
3.23-25 He 11.34
3.36 LXX He 11.12
4.2 Jn 4.48
4.12, 21 Mt 13.32
    Mk 4.32
    Lk 13.19
4.30 Re 18.10
4.34 Re 4.9
4.37 Jn 4.48
5.20 Ac 12.23
5.23 Re 9.20
6.1-27 He 11.33
6.21 2 Tm 4.17
6.26 1 Pe 1.23
    Re 4.9
7.2 Re 7.1
7.3 Re 11.7
    13.1
    17.8
7.4-6 Re 13.2
7.7 Re 11.7
    12.3
    12.17
    13.7
7.8 Re 13.5
7.9 Re 1.14
    Re 20.4
7.9-10 Mt 19.28
    Ro 20.11 12
7.10 Re 5.11
7.13 Mt 26.64
    Mk 14.62
    Lk 21.27
    Re 1.7
    1.13
    14.14
7.13-14 Mt 24.30
    Mk 13.26
7.14 Mt 28.18
    Lk 1.33
    Jn 12.34
    Re 10.11
    11.15
    19.6
7.18 Re 22.5
7.20 Re 13.5
7.21 Re 11.7
    12.17
    13.7
7.22 Lk 21.8
    1 Cor 6.2
    Re 20.4
7.24 Re 17.12
7.25 Re 12.14

7.25 Re 13.5
7.27 Re 20.4
    22.5
8.10 Re 12.4
8.16 Lk 1.19
8.26 Re 10.4
9.6, 10 Re 10.7
    11.18
9.21 Lk 1.19
9.24 Ac 10.43
9.26 Lk 21.24
9.27 Mt 24.15
    Mk 13.14
10.5 Re 1.13
10.6 Re 1.14-15
    2.18
    19.12
10.13, 21 Jd 9
    Re 12.7
11.31 Mt 24.15
    Mk 13.14
11.36 2 Th 2.4
    Re 13.5
11.41 Mt 24.10
12.1 Mt 24.21
    Mk 13.19
    Php 4.3
    Jd 9
    Re 3.5
    7.14
    12.7
    13.8
    16.18
    17.8
    20.12
    20.15
    21.27
12.2 Mt 25.46
    Jn 5.29
    11.24
    Ac 24.15
12.3 Mt 13.43
    Eph 2.15
12.4 Re 10.4
    22.10
12.7 Lk 21.24
    Re 4.9
    10.5-6
    12.14
12.9 Re 10.4
12.11 Mt 24.15
    Mk 13.14
12.12 Jas 5.11

HOSEA

1.6, 9 1 Pe 2.10
1.10 Ro 9.26

1.10 Ro 9.27-28
2.1 1 Pe 2.10
2.23 Ro 9.25
    1 Pe 2.10
6.2 Lk 24.46
    1 Cor 15.4
6.5 Eph 6.17
6.6 Mt 9.13
    12.7
    Mk 12.33
9.7 Lk 21.22
10.8 Lk 23.30
    Re 6.16
    9.6
10.12 LXX 2 Cor 9.10
11.1 Mt 2.15
12.8 Re 3.17
13.14 1 Cor 15.55
14.2 He 13.15
14.9 Ac 13.10

JOEL

1.6 Re 9.8
2.2 Mt 24.21
2.4, 5 Re 9.7
2.5 Re 9.9
2.10 Mt 24.29
    Mk 13.24-25
    Re 6.12-13
    8.12
2.11 Re 6.17
2.23 Jas 5.7
2.28 Ac 21.9
    Tt 3.6
2.28-32 Ac 2.17-21
2.30-31 Lk 21.25
2.31 Mt 24.29
    Mk 13.24-25
    Re 6.12
2.32 Ac 2.39
    22.16
    Ro 10.13
3.4-8 Mt 11.21-22
    Lk 10.13-14
3.13 Mk 4.29
    Re 14.15, 18
    19.15
3.15 Mt 24.29
    Mk 13.24-25
    Re 6.12-13
    8.12
3.18 Re 22.1

AMOS

1.9-10 Mt 11.21-22
    Lk 10.13-14

Amos (cont.)

3.7	Re 10.7
	11.18
3.13 LXX	2 Cor 6.18
	Re 1.8
	4.8
	11.17
	15.3
	16.7
	16.14
	19.6
	19.15
	21.22
4.11	Jd 23
4.13 LXX	2 Cor 6.18
	Re 1.8
	4.8
	11.17
	15.3
	16.7
	16.14
	19.6
	19.15
	21.22
5.10	Ga 4.16
5.13	Eph 5.16
5.15	Ro 12.9
5.25–27	Ac 7.42–43
8.9	Mt 27.45
	Mk 15.33
	Lk 23.44–45
9.9	Lk 22.31
9.11–12	Ac 15.16–17

Obadiah

21	Re 11.15

Jonah

1.17	Mt 12.40
	1 Cor 15.4
3.5	Mt 12.41
3.6	Mt 11.21
3.8	Mt 12.41
3.8, 10	Lk 11.32
4.9	Mt 26.38
	Mk 14.34

Micah

4.7	Lk 1.33
4.9	Jn 16.21
4.10	Re 12.2
5.2	Mt 2.6
	Jn 7.42

6.8	Mt 23.23
6.15	Jn 4.37
7.6	Mt 10.21
	10.35–36
	Mk 13.12
	Lk 12.53
7.20	Lk 1.55
	Ro 15.8

Nahum

1.6	Re 6.17
1.15	Ac 10.36
	Ro 10.15
	Eph 6.15

Habakkuk

1.5	Ac 13.41
2.3	2 Pe 3.9
2.3–4 LXX	
	He 10.37–38
2.4	Ro 1.17
	Ga 3.11
2.18–19	1 Cor 12.2
3.17	Lk 13.6

Zephaniah

1.3	Mt 13.41
3.8	Re 16.1
3.13	Re 14.5
3.15	Jn 1.49

Haggai

1.13	Mt 28.20
2.6	He 12.26
2.6, 21	Mt 24.29
	Lk 21.26

Zechariah

1.1	Mt 23.35
1.3	Jas 4.8
1.6	Re 10.7
	11.18
1.8	Re 6.2
	6.4
	19.11
2.1–2	Re 11.1
2.6	Mt 24.31
2.6, 10	Mk 13.27
2.10	Re 21.3
3.1	Re 12.10
3.2	Jd 9

3.2	Jd 23
4.2	Re 4.5
4.3	Re 11.4
4.10	Re 5.6
4.11–14	Re 11.4
6.2	Re 6.4
	6.5
6.3	Re 6.2
	19.11
6.5	Re 7.1
6.6	Re 6.2
	6.5
	19.11
8.6 LXX	Mt 19.26
	Mk 10.27
8.16	Eph 4.25
8.17	1 Cor 13.5
8.23	1 Cor 14.25
9.2–4	Mt 11.21–22
	Lk 10.13–14
9.9	Mt 21.5
	Jn 12.15
9.10	Eph 2.17
9.11	Mt 26.28
	Mk 14.24
	Lk 22.20
	1 Cor 11.25
	He 13.20
10.2	Mt 9.36
	Mk 6.34
11.12	Mt 26.15
11.12–13	Mt 27.9–10
12.3 LXX	Lk 21.24
	Re 11.2
12.10	Mt 24.30
	Jn 19.37
	Re 1.7
12.11	Re 16.16
12.12	Re 1.7
12.14	Mt 24.30
	Re 1.7
13.4	Mk 1.6
13.7	Mt 26.31
	26.56
	Mk 14.27
	14.50
	Jn 16.32
13.9	1 Pe 1.7
14.5	Mt 25.31
	1 Th 3.13
	2 Th 1.7
	Jd 14
14.7	Re 21.25
	22.5
14.8	Re 22.1
14.9	Re 11.15
	19.6
14.11	Re 22.3

Malachi

1.2–3	Ro 9.13
1.6	Lk 6.46
1.7	1 Cor 10.21
1.11	2 Th 1.12
	Re 15.4
1.12	1 Cor 10.21
2.7–8	Mt 23.3
2.10	1 Cor 8.6
3.1	Mt 11.3
	11.10
	Mk 1.2
	Lk 1.17
	1.76
	7.19
	7.27
	Jn 3.28
3.2	Re 6.17
3.3	1 Pe 1.7
3.5	Jas 5.4
3.7	Jas 4.8
4.2	Lk 1.78
4.5	Mt 11.14
4.5–6	Mt 17.10–11
	Mk 9.11–12
	Lk 1.17

Ascension of Isaiah

5.11–14	He 11.37

Assumption of Moses

	Jd 9

Baruch

4.7	1 Cor 10.20
4.35	Re 18.2

Enoch

1.2	1 Pe 1.12
1.9	Jd 14–15
9.4	Re 15.3
	17.14
	19.16
14.22	Re 5.11
25.5	Re 15.3
27.3	Re 15.3
46.3	Col 2.3
51.2	Lk 21.28
60.8	Jd 14
63.10	Lk 16.9
69.27	Jn 5.22
70.1–4	He 11.5

1 Esdras

1.32 LXX	Mt 1.11

Judith

11.19	Mt 9.36
	Mk 6.34
16.17	Jas 5.3

1 Maccabees

1.54	Mt 24.15
	Mk 13.14
2.60	2 Tm 4.17
3.45, 51	Lk 21.24
4.59	Jn 10.22
6.7	Mt 24.15

2 Maccabees

3.26	Lk 24.4
6.18—7.42	He 11.35
13.4	1 Tm 6.15
	Re 17.14
	19.16

3 Maccabees

2.5	Re 14.10
	20.10
	21.8
5.35	1 Tm 6.15
	Re 17.14
	19.16

4 Maccabees

2.5	Ro 7.7
7.19	Mt 22.32

Psalms of Solomon

5.4	Lk 11.21–22
5.9–11 LXX	Mt 6.26
7.6	Jn 1.14
17.23–24	Re 2.26–27
17.34 (31)	Re 21.24
	21.26

Sirach

1.8	Re 4.2
	4.9
	4.10
	5.1
	5.7

SIRACH (cont.)		28.2	Mt 6.12
		28.18	Lk 21.24
1.8	Re 5.13	29.11	Mt 6.20
	6.16		Lk 18.22
	7.10	33.1	Mt 6.13
	7.15	35.19	Mt 16.27
	19.4	37.28	1 Cor 6.12
	21.5	38.18	2 Cor 7.10
1.10	1 Cor 2.9	44.16	He 11.5
5.3	1 Th 4.6	44.21	Ga 3.8
5.11	Jas 1.19		He 6.14
11.19	Lk 12.19–20		11.12
15.11–13	Jas 1.13	48.10	Lk 1.17
16.14	Ro 2.6		
23.1	Mt 6.13	SUSANNA	
23.4	1 Pe 1.17		
25.23	He 12.12	46	Theodotion
27.6	Mt 7.16		Mt 27.24

TOBIT		WISDOM	
4.6 LXX	Jn 3.21	2.11	Ro 9.31
5.15	Mt 20.2	2.18–20	Mt 27.43
7.17	Mt 11.25	2.23	1 Cor 11.7
11.9	Lk 15.20		
13.7, 11	Re 15.3		
13.18	Re 19.1		
14.4	Mt 23.38		
14.5	Lk 21.24		

		16.9	Re 9.3
3.8	1 Cor 6.2	16.13	Mt 16.18
4.10	He 11.5	16.22	Re 8.7
5.5	Ac 20.32	18.1	Ac 9.7
	26.18		22.9
5.15	1 Jn 2.17		
5.18	Eph 6.14		
	1 Th 5.8	OTHER WRITINGS	
5.22	Lk 21.25		
6.18	Jn 14.15	Aratus, *Phaenomena* 5	
7.1	Ac 10.26		Ac 17.28
7.7	Eph 1.17	Cleanthes	
9.1	Jn 1.3		Ac 17.28
9.16	Jn 3.12	Epimenides, *de Oracu-*	
12.12	Ro 9.20	*lis*	Tt 1.12
12.13–14	Ac 5.39	Menander, *Thais* (218)	
14.3	1 Pe 1.17		1 Cor 15.33
15.3	Jn 17.3		
15.7	Ro 9.21		

A

Aaron The brother of Moses, who was chosen by God to be the chief priest in Israel (Exodus 28.1—30.10).

Abyss A very deep hole in the earth where, according to ancient Jewish teaching, the evil spirits are imprisoned until their final punishment.

Achaia A Roman province covering what is now the southern half of Greece (the northern half of modern Greece was known as Macedonia). In this translation "Greece" is used for Achaia and also for *Hellas* (Acts 20.2), which was the native Greek name corresponding to the Roman name Achaia. The capital city of the province was Corinth; other cities in Achaia mentioned in the New Testament are Cenchreae, Athens, and Nicopolis.

Agate A semi-precious stone of varying colors.

Agrippa Herod Agrippa II, great-grandson of Herod the Great, was king of Chalcis, a small country north of Palestine, and ruler of nearby territories. Paul made his defense before him and his sister Bernice (Acts 25.13—26.32).

Alabaster A soft stone, of light creamy color, from which vases and jars were made.

Aloes A sweet-smelling substance, derived from a plant, which the Jews spread on the cloths they wrapped around a body to be buried.

Alpha The first letter of the Greek alphabet. The expression "I am the Alpha and the Omega" (Revelation 1.8; 21.6; 22.13) means "I am the first and the last."

Altar The place where sacrifices were offered to God.

Amen A Hebrew word which means "it is so" or "may it be so." It can also be translated "certainly," "truly," or "surely." In Revelation 3.14 it is used as a title for Christ.

Amethyst A semi-precious stone, usually purple or violet in color.

Ancestor Someone who lived in the past, from whom a person is descended.

Anoint To pour or rub oil on someone in order to honor him, or select him for some special work. The word is also used in a figurative sense. "The Anointed One" is the title of the one whom God chose and appointed to be Savior and Lord. Oil was also used by the Jews on a sick person to make him well; it was also used on a dead body to prepare it for burial.

Apostle One of the group of twelve men whom Jesus chose to be his followers and helpers. The word means "messenger," and is also used in the New Testament of Paul and of other Christian workers.

Areopagus A hill in Athens where the city council met. For this reason the council itself was called Areopagus, even after it no longer met on the hill.

Aretas King of the country of Nabatea, which was to the south and east of Palestine.

Ark (1) The vessel built by Noah in which he, his family, and the animals survived the Flood (Genesis 6.9—8.19). (2) The wooden chest, covered with gold, in which were kept the two stone tablets on which were written the ten commandments. Other sacred objects of the Jews were also kept in the ark, which was placed in the tabernacle (Exodus 25.10–22; Hebrews 9.4–5).

Armageddon The place mentioned in Revelation 16.16; it is not certain whether the name refers to an actual place ("the hill of Megiddo"), or is used as a symbol.

Artemis The Greek name of an ancient goddess of fertility, worshiped especially in Asia Minor.

Asia A Roman province in the western part of what was later known as Asia Minor, and is today part of the country of Turkey. Besides the seven cities of Asia listed in the book of Revelation (1.4, 11; 2.1—3.22), other cities in the province mentioned in the New Testament are Colossae, Hierapolis, and Miletus. The capital of the province was Ephesus.

Atonement, Day of The most important of the Jewish holy days, when the High Priest would offer sacrifice for the sins of the people of Israel (Leviticus 16.29–34). It was held on the 10th day of the month Tishri (around October 1).

Augustus One of the titles of Gaius Octavius, who was Roman Emperor from 27 B.C. to A.D. 14 (Luke 2.1).

B

Baal The name of the god worshiped by the ancient people of Canaan.

Babylon The capital city of the ancient land of Babylonia, east of Palestine, on the rivers Tigris and Euphrates. In the New Testament the name Babylon probably refers to the city of Rome.

Balaam A native of Pethor, near

the Euphrates river, who was asked by Balak, king of Moab, to curse the people of Israel. Instead, Balaam obeyed God's command and blessed Israel (Numbers 22.1—24.25; Deuteronomy 23.3–6; Joshua 13.22).

Balak The king of Moab, a country on the southeast side of the Dead Sea. He led the people of Israel to worship idols (Numbers 22.1—24.25; Revelation 2.14).

Bastard A person born of parents who are not legally married.

Beelzebul The name given to the Devil as the chief of the evil spirits.

Bernice Sister of King Agrippa II (Acts 25.13—26.32).

Beryl A semi-precious stone, usually green or bluish-green in color.

Blasphemy An evil thing said against God.

Breastplate Part of a soldier's armor, made of leather or metal, which covered the breast, and sometimes the back, to protect him from the enemy's attack.

Briar A small plant with thorns on its stem and branches.

C

Caesar The title given to the Roman Emperor.

Carnelian A semi-precious stone, usually red in color.

Census The registration of citizens and their property, to determine how much tax they had to pay.

Chalcedony A semi-precious stone, usually milky or gray in color.

Christ Originally a title, the Greek equivalent of the Hebrew word "Messiah." It means "the Anointed One." Jesus is called the Christ because he is the one whom God chose and sent as Savior and Lord.

Cinnamon The sweet-smelling inner bark of a certain tree, used as a spice on food.

Circumcise To cut off the foreskin of a Jewish baby boy as a sign of God's covenant with the people of Israel (Genesis 17.9–14).

Claudius Roman Emperor A.D. 41–54 (Acts 11.28; 18.2).

Convert A person who is converted, or turned, from one belief or faith to another.

Council The supreme religious court of the Jews, composed of seventy leaders of the Jewish people and presided over by the High Priest.

Covenant The agreement that God made with Abraham (Genesis 17.1–8), and later with the people of Israel (Deuteronomy 29.10–15).

Cummin A small garden plant whose seeds are ground up and used for seasoning foods.

D

Dalmatia The southern half of the province of Illyricum.

Dedication, Feast of The Jewish feast, lasting eight days, which celebrated the restoration and re-dedication of the altar in the Temple by the Jewish patriot Judas Maccabeus, in 165 B.C. The feast began on the 25th day of the month Chislev (around December 10).

Defile To make dirty, or impure. Certain foods and practices were prohibited by the Jewish Law because they were thought to make a person spiritually or ceremonially unclean. In this condition such a person could not take part in the public worship until he had performed certain rituals which would remove the defilement.

Demon An evil spirit with the power to harm people, that was regarded as a messenger and servant of the Devil.

Descendant A person who is related by family line to someone who lived a long time before him.

Dill A small garden plant whose seeds are ground up and used for seasoning foods.

Disciple A person who follows and learns from someone else. The word is used in the New Testament of the followers of John the Baptist and Paul; it is especially used of the followers of Jesus, particularly of the twelve apostles.

Dough Flour mixed with water to be baked into bread.

Dragon An imaginary beast, thought to be like a huge lizard. It is also called a serpent, and appears in the Bible as a figure of the Devil (Revelation 12.3—13.4; 20.2–3).

Drusilla Sister of King Agrippa II and wife of the Roman governor Felix (Acts 24.24).

E

Elders Three different groups in the New Testament are called elders: (1) in the Gospels, the elders are respected Jewish religious leaders, some of whom were members of the supreme Council; (2) in Acts 11—21 and the Epistles, the elders are Christian church officers who had general responsibility for the work of the church; (3) in Revelation, the 24 elders are part of God's court in heaven, perhaps as representatives of God's people.

Elijah The Old Testament prophet who was expected to appear to announce the coming of the Messiah (Malachi 4.5–6; Matthew 17.9–13).

Emerald A very valuable stone, green in color.

Epicureans Those who followed the teaching of Epicurus (died 270 B.C.), who taught that happiness is the highest good in life.

Epileptic A person who suffers from a nervous disease which causes convulsions and fainting.

Eunuch A man who has been made physically incapable of having normal sexual relations.

F

Fast To go without food for a while as a religious duty.

Felix The Roman governor of Judea A.D. 52–60, before whom Paul defended himself (Acts 23.24—24.27).

Festus The Roman governor of Judea A.D. 60–62, before whom Paul defended himself and made his appeal to the Roman Emperor (Acts 25.1—26.32).

Foal The young of an animal of the horse family.

Frankincense A valuable incense, suitable for a gift.

G

Gabriel One of God's chief angels, who was sent to Zechariah, father of John the Baptist (Luke 1.11–20), and to Mary, mother of Jesus (Luke 1.26–38).

Galatia A Roman province in the eastern part of what was later known as Asia Minor, and is today part of the country of Turkey. The cities of Antioch of Pisidia, Iconium, Lystra, and Derbe were in the province of Galatia.

Gall A very bitter liquid made from a certain plant.

Gallio The Roman governor of Greece A.D. 51–52 (Acts 18.12–17).

Gamaliel One of the greatest Jewish teachers, a member of the supreme Council of the Jews (Acts 5.34–40), who had been Paul's teacher (Acts 22.3).

Generation The average period, about 30 years in length, from the time a man becomes an adult to the time his son becomes an adult.

Gennesaret Another name for Lake Galilee (Luke 5.1).

Gentile A person who is not a Jew.

Gomorrah A city near the Dead Sea which God destroyed by fire because of the great wickedness of its people (Genesis 19.24–28).

H

Hades The Greek name, in the New Testament, for the world of the dead; the same as Sheol in the Old Testament.

Hermes The name of a Greek god, who served as messenger of the gods.

Herod (1) Herod the Great (Matthew 2.1–22; Luke 1.5) was king of all the country of the Jews 37–4 B.C. He was responsible for the killing of the baby boys in Bethlehem soon after Jesus was born. (2) Herod (whose full name was Herod Antipas) was ruler of Galilee 4 B.C.–A.D. 39 (Matthew 14.1–10; Mark 6.14–27; Luke 3.1, 19–20; 9.7–9; 13.31; 23.6–12; Acts 4.27; 13.1). He was son of Herod the Great, and although called a king (Mark 6.14), he was not a king as his father had been. He was responsible for the death of John the Baptist. (3) Herod (whose full name was Herod Agrippa I) was ruler of all the

land of the Jews, with the title of king, A.D. 41–44 (Acts 12.1–23). He was grandson of Herod the Great. He put the apostle James to death and arrested Peter.

Herodias The wife of Herod Antipas, ruler of Galilee. Before marrying Herod she had been the wife of his half-brother Philip (Matthew 14.3–12; Mark 6.17–28; Luke 3.19).

Herod's party A political party composed of Jews who favored one of the descendants of Herod the Great to rule over them instead of the Roman governor.

High Priest The priest who occupied the highest office in the Jewish priestly system and was president of the supreme Council of the Jews. Once a year (on the Day of Atonement) he would enter the holiest part of the Temple and offer sacrifice for himself and for the sins of the people of Israel.

Homosexual A man who has sexual relations with another man.

Hyssop A small bushy plant, used in ceremonies of sprinkling.

I

Illyricum A province on the coast of the Adriatic Sea, north of the province of Macedonia, in what is now Yugoslavia.

Incense Material which is burned in order to produce a pleasant smell.

Inn A house where travelers can buy food and lodging.

J

Jasper A semi-precious stone of varying colors. The jasper mentioned in the Bible was probably green.

Jesse The father of King David, one of the ancestors of Jesus (Matthew 1.5–6; Acts 13.22; Romans 15.12).

K

Kingdom of God, Kingdom of heaven The titles used to describe God's ruling over the world as king. There is no difference between the two titles, both of which refer primarily to God's possession and exercise of his power, not to a place or time in history. This Kingdom is spoken of as being already present and also as coming in the future.

L

Law The name the Jews applied to the first five books of the Old Testament, also called the books of Moses. Sometimes the name is also used in a more general sense of the whole Old Testament.

Leper Someone suffering from a disease called leprosy. It is probable that in the Bible the word translated "leprosy" had a wider range of meaning than it does now, and was used as the name of several other skin diseases as well.

Levite A member of the priestly tribe of Levi, who had the duty of helping in the services in the Temple (Numbers 3.1–13).

Locust A grasshopper, a winged insect extremely harmful to plants; locusts fly in huge swarms and eat crops and other plants.

Lot The nephew of Abraham who escaped with his daughters from the city of Sodom when it was destroyed by God. Lot's wife, however, did not escape (Genesis 19.12–29; Luke 17.28–32; 2 Peter 2.6–8).

M

Macedonia A Roman province covering what is now the northern half of Greece. Its capital city was Thessalonica. Other cities in the province mentioned in the New Testament are Neapolis, Philippi, Amphipolis, Apollonia, and Berea.

Magdalene Mary Magdalene, a follower of Jesus, was one of those to whom Jesus appeared after he was raised from death (Mark 15.40–47; Luke 8.2; John 20.1–18). Her name indicates that she was born in Magdala, a town on the west side of Lake Galilee.

Manna The food of the Israelites during their travels in the wilderness. It was small, white, and flaky, and looked like small seeds (Exodus 16.14–21; Numbers 11.7–9).

Messiah The title (meaning "the Anointed One") given to the promised Savior whose coming was promised by the Hebrew prophets; the same as "Christ."

Michael One of God's chief angels (Jude 9; Revelation 12.7).

Mint A small garden plant whose leaves are used for seasoning foods.

Moloch One of the gods of the ancient people of Canaan.

Mustard A large plant which grows from a very small seed. The seeds may be ground into powder and used as spice on food.

Myrrh The hardened sap of a tree, with a pleasant smell, and suitable for a gift (Matthew 2.11; Revelation 18.13). It served also as a medicine (Mark 15.23), and was also used by the Jews in preparing bodies for burial (John 19.39).

N

Nard A plant from which an expensive perfume was made.

Nazarene Someone from the town of Nazareth. The name was used as a title for Jesus, and also as a name for the early Christians (Acts 24.5).

Nicolaitans A group referred to in Revelation 2.6 and 15, whose teachings and actions are condemned. They apparently practiced idolatry, and immorality, but nothing definite is known as to when, where, and by whom the group was started.

Nineveh The ancient capital of Assyria, on the east side of the river Tigris, where the prophet Jonah preached (Jonah 3.1–10; Luke 11.30, 32).

Noah The Old Testament patriarch who built an ark in which he, his family, and the animals were saved from the flood that God sent on the earth (Genesis 6.5—9.28).

O

Omega The last letter of the Greek alphabet. The expression "I am the Alpha and the Omega" (Revelation 1.8; 21.6; 22.13) means "I am the first and the last."

Onyx A semi-precious stone of varying colors.

Outcasts In the Gospels this name, which in many translations appears as "sinners," refers to those Jews who did not obey all the rules laid down by the religious leaders. The Pharisees were especially strict about foods that should not be eaten and about relationships with people who were not Jews. The leaders of the Jews despised these people and condemned Jesus for associating with them (Mark 2.15–17; Luke 7.34; 15.1–2).

P

Parable A story used by Jesus to teach spiritual lessons.

Paradise A name for heaven (Luke 23.43; 2 Corinthians 12.3).

Paralytic Someone who suffers from a disease that prevents him from moving part or all of his body.

Parchment The skin of an animal, usually a sheep or a goat, which was prepared to be written on.

Passover, Feast of The Jewish feast, on the 14th day of the month Nisan (around April 1), which celebrated the deliverance of the ancient Hebrews from their captivity in Egypt. The angel of death killed the first-born in the Egyptian homes but "passed over" the Hebrew homes (Exodus 12.23–27).

Patriarchs The famous ancestors of the Jewish race, such as Abraham, Isaac, and Jacob, with whom God made his covenants.

Pentecost, Day of The Jewish feast of wheat harvest, on the 6th day of the month Sivan (around May 20). The name Pentecost (meaning "fiftieth") comes from the fact that the feast was held 50 days after Passover.

Pervert One who commits unnatural sexual acts.

Pharaoh The title of the kings of ancient Egypt. Two different kings of Egypt are mentioned in the New Testament: the one who ruled during the time of Joseph, the son of Jacob (Acts 7.10–13; Genesis 40.1—50.26), and the one who ruled during the time of

Moses (Acts 7.21; Romans 9.17; Hebrews 11.24; Exodus 1.8—14.31).

Pharisees A Jewish religious party. They were strict in obeying the Law of Moses and other regulations which had been added to it through the centuries.

Pilate Pontius Pilate was the Roman governor of Judea, Samaria, and Idumea, A.D. 26–36 (Mark 15.1–15; Luke 3.1; Acts 3.13; 1 Timothy 6.13).

Potter A man who makes pots and other vessels out of clay.

Preparation, Day of The sixth day of the week, on which the Jews made the required preparations to observe the Sabbath day.

Prophet A man who proclaims God's message to men. (1) The term usually refers to the Old Testament prophets (Matthew 5.12, 17; 13.17), such as Isaiah (Matthew 3.3), Jeremiah (Matthew 2.17), Jonah (Matthew 12.39), Daniel (Matthew 24.15), and Joel (Acts 2.16). (2) The term also refers to prophets in the Church (Acts 13.1; 1 Corinthians 12.28–29; Ephesians 4.11). (3) The term is applied also to John the Baptist (Matthew 11.9; 14.5; Luke 1.76), and to Jesus (Matthew 21.11, 46; Luke 7.16; 24.19; John 9.17). (4) "The Prophet" promised by Moses was expected to appear and announce the coming of the Messiah (Deuteronomy 18.15, 18; John 6.14; 7.40; Acts 3.22–23).

Prune To cut the branches off a fruit tree in order to make it bear more and better fruit.

Q

Quartz A semi-precious stone of varying colors, usually white.

R

Rabbi A Hebrew word which means "my teacher."

Rephan The name of an ancient god that was worshiped as the ruler of the planet Saturn.

Ritual An established form for conducting a religious service.

Rue A small garden plant whose leaves are used for seasoning foods.

S

Sabbath The seventh day of the Jewish week, the holy day on which no work was permitted.

Sadducees A small Jewish religious party, composed largely of priests. They based their beliefs exclusively on the first five books of the Old Testament, and so differed in several matters of belief and practice from the larger party of the Pharisees.

Samaritan A native of Samaria, the province between Judea and Galilee. There was much hatred between the Jews and the Samaritans, because of differences in politics, race, customs, and religion.

Sanctuary A building dedicated to the worship of God. Sometimes the word may refer to the central place of worship, and not to the whole building.

Sapphire A very valuable stone, usually blue in color.

Saul (1) The first king of Israel (1 Samuel 13—31; Acts 13.21); (2) the Hebrew name of the apostle Paul (Acts 7.58; 8.1, 3; 9.1–30; 11.25–30; 12.25; 13.1–9).

Scorpion A small creature, which has eight legs and a long tail with a poisonous sting. It can inflict a very painful, and sometimes fatal, wound.

Scriptures In the New Testament the word refers to the collected body of Jewish sacred writings, known to us as the Old Testament. Various names are used: the Law (or the Law of Moses) and the prophets (Matthew 5.17; 7.12; Luke 2.22; 24.44; Acts 13.15; 28.23); the Holy Scriptures (Romans 1.2; 2 Timothy 3.15); the old covenant (2 Corinthians 3.14). The singular "scripture" refers to a single passage of the Old Testament.

Serpent A name given to the dragon, which appears in the Bible as a figure of the Devil (Revelation 12.3–17; 20.2–3).

Sheepfold An enclosure where sheep were kept, usually at night, to protect them from wild animals and thieves.

Shepherd A man, or boy, who takes care of sheep.

Sickle A tool consisting of a curved metal blade and a wooden handle, used for cutting wheat and other crops.

Sodom A city near the Dead Sea which God destroyed by fire because of the great wickedness of its people (Genesis 19.24–28).

Solomon's Porch A covered court on the east side of the Temple in Jerusalem.

Son of David A title which the Jews used of the expected Messiah as the descendant and successor of King David.

Son of Man The title used by Jesus to refer to himself as the one chosen by God to be the Savior (Mark 10.45). As used by Jesus, this title emphasized both his present lowly condition (Mark 8.31; Luke 9.58) and his future glory (Matthew 25.31; Mark 8.38).

Spice One of several pleasant-smelling vegetable products which were used by the Jews in preparing bodies for burial.

Stoics Those who followed the teachings of the philosopher Zeno (died 265 B.C.), who taught that happiness is to be found in being free from pleasure and pain.

Sulphur A yellow substance which burns with great heat and produces an unpleasant smell.

Synagogue The place where Jews met every Sabbath day for their public worship; it was also used as a social center and as a school for Jewish children during week days.

T

Tabernacle A large tent-like construction, described in detail in Exodus 26, where God had his dwelling among his people.

Tabernacles, Feast of The Jewish feast, lasting eight days, which in New Testament times celebrated the time when the ancient Hebrews lived in tents during their travels through the wilderness. In Old Testament times it was also known as the Feast of Ingathering (Exodus 23.16; Leviticus 23.33–43). The feast began on the 15th day of the month Tishri (around October 6).

Teachers of the Law Men who taught and interpreted the teachings of the Old Testament, especially the first five books.

Tenant A man who raises crops on land owned by someone else, and turns over a large part of the harvest to the owner to pay for the use of his land.

Ten Towns A group of ten Gentile towns, most of which were to the east and southeast of Lake Galilee.

Tiberias Another name of Lake Galilee (John 6.1; 21.1). The town of Tiberias (John 6.23) was on the west side of Lake Galilee.

Tiberius Roman Emperor A.D. 14–37. It was in the 15th year of his rule (about A.D. 29) that John the Baptist began his work (Luke 3.1).

Topaz A semi-precious stone, usually yellow in color.

Turquoise A semi-precious stone, blue or bluish-green in color.

U

Unleavened Bread, Feast of The Jewish feast, lasting seven days after Passover, which also celebrated the deliverance of the ancient Hebrews from Egypt. The name came from the practice of not using leaven (or yeast) in making bread during that week (Exodus 12.14–20). It was held from the 15th to the 22nd day of the month Nisan (around the first week of April).

V

Vow A strong declaration, or promise, usually made while calling upon God to punish the speaker if the statement is not true or the promise is not kept.

W

Winnowing-shovel A tool like a shovel, or large fork, used to separate the wheat from the chaff.

Wreath Flowers or leaves arranged in a circle, to be placed on a person's head. In ancient times a wreath of leaves was the prize given to winners in athletic contests.

Y

Yeast A substance, also called leaven, which is added to flour of wheat or barley to make it rise before being baked into bread.

Yoke A heavy bar of wood which is fitted over the necks of two oxen in order for them to pull a plow or a cart. The word is used figuratively to describe the lessons that a teacher passes on to his pupils.

Z

Zeus The name of the supreme god of the Greeks.

Zion The name of a hill in the city of Jerusalem; the name is often used to mean Jerusalem itself.

INDEX OF SUBJECTS

A

Aaron Ac 7.40; He 5.4; 7.11; 9.4

Abel Mt 23.35; Lk 11.51; He 11.4; 12 24

Abraham Mt 3.9; Lk 16.22–30; Jn 8.33–58; Ro 4.1–22; Ga 3.6–29; He 11.8–11,17; Jas 2.21–23

Adam Ro 5.12–21; 1 Cor 15.22,45–49; 1 Tm 2.13–14

Aeneas Ac 9.33–34

Agabus Ac 11.28; 21.10

Agrippa *See* Herod Agrippa

Ananias
of Damascus Ac 9.10–17; 22.12–16
High Priest Ac 23.2–5; 24.1
Ananias and Sapphira Ac 5.1–11

Andrew Mt 4.18; Mk 13.3; Jn 1.40–42; 6.8; 12.22

Anna Lk 2.36

Annas Lk 3.2; Jn 18.13,24; Ac 4.6

Antioch
of Pisidia Ac 13.13–52
of Syria Ac 11.20–30; 13.1–3; 14.26—15.2; 15.35; Ga 2.11

Apollos Ac 18.24–28; 1 Cor 3.4–6,22; 4.6; 16.12

Apostles Mt 10.2–4; Mk 3.14–19; Lk 6.13–16; Ac 1.13,15–26; Jd 17; Re 21.14

Aquila Ac 18.2–3,18,26; Ro 16.3–5; 1 Cor 16.10; 2 Tm 4.10

Areopagus Ac 17.19–22

Artemis Ac 19.24–28,34–35

Ascension Mk 16.19; Lk 24.50–51; Ac 1.9–11

Athens Ac 17.15—18.1; 1 Th 3.1

Augustus Lk 2.1

B

Babylon 1 Pe 5.13; Re 14.8; 16.19; 17.5; 18.2–24

Baptism
John the Baptist Mt 3.6,11–14; Mk 1.4,5,8; Lk 3.2–20; Jn 1.6–8,19–36; 3.22–30; Ac 13.24–25; 19.3–4
Jesus Mt 3.13–17; Mk 1.9–11; Lk 3.21–22
Christian Mt 28.19; Ac 2.38–41; 8.36–39; 10.48; Ro 6.3–4; 1 Cor 12.13; Ga 3.26–29; Col 2.11–12; 1 Pe 3.21–22
with the Holy Spirit Mt 3.11; Mk 1.8; Lk 3.16; Ac 1.5; 11.16

Barabbas Mt 27.16–26; Mk 15.7–15; Lk 23.18–25; Jn 18.40

Bar-Jesus Ac 13.6–11

Barnabas Ac 4.36–37; 11.22–26; 12.25—15.39; 1 Cor 9.6; Ga 2.1,9,13; Col 4.10

Bartholomew Mt 10.3; Mk 3.18; Lk 6.14; Ac 1.13

Bartimaeus Mk 10.46

Beelzebul Mt 12.22–28; Mk 3.22–26; Lk 11.14–20 (*see* Devil, Satan)

"Benedictus" Lk 1.68–79

Berea Ac 17.10–15

Bernice Ac 25.13–23

Bethany
near Jerusalem Mt 21.17; 26.6–13; Mk 14.3–9; Jn 11.1—12.11
beyond Jordan Jn 1.28

Bethlehem Mt 2.1–21; Lk 2.4–20

Bethphage Mt 21.1; Mk 11.1; Lk 19.29

Bethsaida Mt 11.21; Mk 6.45; 8.22–26; Lk 9.10; Jn 1.44

Bethzatha Jn 5.2

Bread
material Mt 4.3–4; 15.32–38; Mk 6.35–44; Lk 24.30–35; Jn 21.9–13
spiritual Jn 6.25–59
offered to God Mt 12.4; Mk 2.26; Lk 6.4; He 9.2
Lord's Supper Mt 26.26–29; Mk 14.22–25; Lk 22.14–20; 1 Cor 11.23–28

Burial
of Jesus Mt 27.57–61; Mk 15.42–47; Lk 23.50–56; Jn 19.38–42
of others Mt 14.12; Ac 5.6,10; 8.2
spiritual Ro 6.4; Col 2.12

C

Caesar *See* Emperor

Caesarea Ac 8.40; 10.1–8,24–28; 12.19; 21.8–16; 23.3—26.32

Caesarea Philippi Mt 16.13; Mk 8.27

Caiaphas Mt 26.57–66; Lk 3.2; Jn 11.49; 18.13–14,24,28

Cana Jn 2.1–11; 4.46–54

Capernaum Mt 4.13–17; 8.5; 11.23; 17.24; Mk 1.21–28; Jn 2.12; 6.16–59

Cenchreae Ac 18.18; Ro 16.1

Chief Priests Mt 2.4–6; 21.15; 27.1–7; Mk 15.1–11; Lk 20.19–20; Jn 7.32; 19.6–22; Ac 5.24; 9.14,21; 25.2,15

Church Mt 16.18; 18.17; Ac 9.31; 20.28; Ro 16.16; 1 Cor 12.27–31; 14.1–40; Eph 5.23–32; 1 Pe 2.4–10

Cilicia Ac 6.9; 15.23,41; 22.3; Ga 1.21

Circumcision
physical Lk 1.59; 2.21; Jn 7.22–23; Ac 15.1,5; 16.3; Ro 2.25–29; 4.9–12; 1 Cor 7.18–19; Ga 5.2–6; 6.12–16; Php 3.5
spiritual Php 3.3; Col 2.11–12

Cleopas Lk 24.18

Clopas Jn 19.25

Coming of Christ, Final Mt 16.27–28; 24.29–31,36–44; 25.31–46; Mk 13.24–27, 32–37; Lk 12.39–40; 17.22–30; 21.25–28; Jn 14.2–4,18–24; Ac 1.11; Php 3.20–21; 1 Th 4.15—5.11; 2 Th 1.7–10; 2.1–15; He 9.27–28; 2 Pe 3.3–13; 1 Jn 2.28—3.2; Re 22.20

Commandments
of Jewish Law Mt 5.17–48; 19.3–9 16–22; 22.34–40; Mk 12.28–34; Jn 8.5; Ro 7.7–13; 13.8–10; Jas 2.8–13
of God and Christ Mt 5.17–48; Jn 12.49–50; 13.34; 15.10–17; 1 Jn 2.7–8; 3.21–24; 2 Jn 5–6

Conscience Ro 2.15; 9.1; 13.5; 1 Cor 8.7–13; 10.25–30; Tt 1.15; He 9.14; 1 Pe 3.16,21

Corinth Ac 18.1–17; 19.1; 1 Cor 1.1–2; 2 Cor 1.1

Cornelius Ac 10.1–48

Covenant
old Ac 3.25; 7.8; 2 Cor 3.14; Ga 3.17; Eph 2.12; He 9.1–5,15–22; Re 11.19
new Mt 26.27–28; Mk 14.23–24; Lk 22.20; 1 Cor 11.25; 2 Cor 3.6; He 7.22; 8.6–13; 9.15,10–29; 12.24; 13.20

Covetousness Lk 12.15; Ro 7.7–10; Eph 5.3–5; Col 3.5, Jas 4.2

Crete Ac 27.7–21; Tt 1.5,12

Cross
of Christ Mt 27.32–38; Mk 15.21–32; Lk 23.26–43; Jn 19.16–27; 1 Cor 1.23–25; Ga 6.14; Eph 2.16; Col 1.19–20; 2.13–14; He 12.2
of Christ's followers Mt 10.38; 16.24–26; Mk 8.34–35; Lk 9.23–24; 14.27; Ro 6.6; Ga 2.19–20; 6.14

Crown Mt 27.29; Mk 15.17; Jn 19.2,5; 2 Tm 4.8; He 2.9; 1 Pe 5.4; Re 2.10; 6.2; 14.14

Cyprus Ac 4.36; 13.4–12; 15.39

Cyrene Mt 27.32; Mk 15.21; Lk 23.26; Ac 11.20

D

Damascus Ac 9.2–23,27; 22.5–16; 26.12–20; 2 Cor 11.32; Ga 1.17

Darkness
literal Mt 27.45; Mk 15.33; He 12.18
spiritual Mt 4.16; Lk 22.53; Jn 1.5; 3.19–21; 12.35,46; 2 Cor 4.6; Eph 5.8–11; Col 1.13; 1 Jn 1.5–7; 2.8–11

David Mt 22.41–45; Mk 12.35–37; Lk 20.41–44; Ac 2.25–31; 7.45–46; 13.22,34–36; Ro 1.3; 4.6–9; 2 Tm 2.8; Re 3.7; 5.5; 22.16

Day of Judgment Mt 7.22–23; 10.15; 11.22,24; 12.36–37; 25.31–46; Lk 21.34–36; Jn 6.39–40,44; 12.46; Ro 2.16; 1 Th 4.15—5.3; 2 Tm 1.12; 4.8; He 10.25; 2 Pe 3.3–13; 1 Jn 4.17; Re 20.11–15

Death

physical 1 Cor 15.20–26; 1 Th 4.3–16

    Ananias and Sapphira Ac 5.1–10

    Antipas Re 2.13

    Christian martyrs Re 6.9; 17.6; 20.4

    Herod Agrippa I Ac 12.21–23

    James Ac 12.2

    John the Baptist Mt 14.1–12; Mk 6.16–29

    Lazarus Jn 11.1–17

    Old Testament prophets Mt 23.35; Lk 11.50–51; He 11.1–40

    Simon Peter Jn 21.18–19

    Stephen Ac 7.58–60

spiritual Ro 6.1–11; 7.4–6,9–13; Jas 1.14–15; 5.20; 1 Jn 3.14; 5.16–17

of Christ Mt 27.45–50; Mk 15.33–37; Lk 23.44–46; Jn 19.28–30; 1 Cor 15.3; 2 Cor 5.14–15; Php 2.8; Col 1.22; He 2.9,14–15; 1 Pe 3.18

Demas Col 4.14; 2 Tm 4.10; Phm 24

Demons Mt 4.24; 8.16; 9.32–34; 12.22–28; Mk 7.24–30; Lk 11.14–26; Jn 8.48–52; 10.20–21; 1 Cor 10.20–21; 1 Tm 4.1; Re 16.13–14; 18.2 (See Evil Spirits)

Derbe Ac 14.6,20–21; 16.1

Devil Mt 4.1–11; Lk 4.1–13; Jn 13.2; 2 Cor 11.14–15; Eph 6.11; 1 Tm 3.6–7; He 2.14; 1 Pe 5.8; 1 Jn 3.8–10; Jd 9; Re 12.9; 20.1–3,7–10 (See Beelzebul, Satan)

Divorce Mt 5.31–32; 19.3–9; Mk 10.2–12; Lk 16.18; 1 Cor 7.10–16

Dorcas Ac 9.36–41

Dragon Re 12.3—13.4; 16.13; 20.1–3

Drusilla Ac 24.24

E

Egypt, Flight to Mt 2.13–15,19–21

Elders

Jewish Mt 21.23; 26.3,57; 27.1–8,41; 28.12; Ac 4.5–23; 6.12; 24.1

Christian Ac 11.30; 14.23; 15.2,4,6,22; 20.17; Tt 1.5–6; Jas 5.14; 1 Pe 5.1; 2 Jn 1; 3 Jn 1

heavenly Re 4.4,10; 5.8–11; 7.11–14; 11.16–18; 19.4

Elijah Mt 11.10–14; 16.10–13; 27.47–49; Lk 1.17; 4.25–26; Jn 1.21; Ro 11.2–4; Jas 5.17–18

Elizabeth Lk 1.5–61

Emmanuel Mt 1.23

Emmaus Lk 24.13–32

Emperor Mt 22.15–22; Mk 12.13–17; Lk 2.1; 3.1; 20.19–26; Jn 19.12,15; Ac 11.28; 18.2; 25.11–12; 27.24; Php 4.22; 1 Pe 2.13,17

Epaphras Col 1.17; 4.12; Phm 23

Ephesus Ac 18.19–21,24–26; 19.1–41; 20.17–38; 1 Cor 15.32; 16.8; Eph 1.1; 1 Tm 1.3; Re 2.1–7

Ethiopian Ac 8.26–40

Eunice 2 Tm 1.5

Eutychus Ac 20.9–12

Eve 2 Cor 11.3; 1 Tm 2.13

Evil Spirits Mk 1.23–27; 3.11–12; 5.1–20; 9.14–29 (See Demons)

F

Faith

general Mt 9.2; 17.20; 21.21–22; Lk 17.5–6; Ro 1.16–17; 3.27–31; 5.1; 2 Cor 5.7; Ga 3.22–26; He 11.1; Jas 2.14–26

in God Mk 11.22–24; Jn 12.44–45; Ro 4.1–25; Ga 3.1–14; He 11.1–40

in Christ Mt 9.28–29; Mk 2.5; 5.34,36; 9.23–24; Jn 1.12; 3.15–16; 6.28–29; 9.35–38; 11.25–27; 20.27–29,31; Ac 3.16; 16.30–31; Ro 3.22–26; 10.6–17; Ga 2.16–21; 1 Jn 3.23; 5.1–13

False

messiahs Mt 24.24; Mk 13.22

prophets Mt 7.15–20; 24.11; Mk 13.22; 2 Pe 2.1; 1 Jn 4.1; Re 19.20; 20.10

Fasting

Jesus' teaching Mt 6.16–18; 9.14–15; Mk 2.18–20; Lk 5.33–35

Jewish Mk 2.18; Lk 2.37; 18.12

Christian Ac 13.2–3; 14.23

Father (title of God) Mt 6.6–15; 11.25–27; 23.9; Mk 14.36; Lk 2.49; 12.32; 23.34; Jn 5.17–27,36–45; 10.29–38; 14.1–31; 17.1–26; Ro 8.14–17; Ga 4.6–7; He 12.5–9; Jas 1.17; 1 Jn 3.1–2,9–10

Feasts, Religious

Day of Atonement Ac 27.9

Dedication Jn 10.22

New Moon Col 2.16

Passover Mt 26.2,17–25; Mk 14.12–21; Lk 2.41–43; 22.7–13; Jn 2.13–23; 6.4; 11.55–57; 12.12; 13.1; 19.14; Ac 12.4; 1 Cor 5.7–8; He 11.28

Pentecost Ac 2.1; 20.16; 1 Cor 16.8

Tabernacles Jn 7.1–39

Unleavened Bread Mt 26.17; Mk 14.1, 12; Lk 22.1,7; Ac 12.3; 20.6

unspecified Jn 5.1; Col 2.16

Felix Ac 23.23—24.27

Festus Ac 24.27—26.32

Forgiveness Mt 6.12–15; 9.1–8; 12.31–32; 18.21–35; Mk 3.28–30; Lk 7.36–50; 17.3–4; Jn 20.22–23; 2 Cor 2.5–10; Eph 4.32; Col 2.13–14; 1 Jn 1.9

G

Gabriel Lk 1.11–20,26

Galatia Ac 16.6; 18.23; Ga 1.2; 1 Pe 1.1

Galilee

lake Mt 4.13,18; 8.23–27; 9.1; 13.1; 14.22; 15.29; Mk 1.16; 2.13; 3.7; 4.1, 35–41; 6.45–52; Lk 5.1–11; Jn 6.1–24; 21.1–22

province Mt 4.12–17; 19.1; 28.16–20; Mk 1.14–15,35–39; Lk 2.39; 4.14–15; Jn 1.43; 4.43–54; 7.1

Gallio Ac 18.12–17

Gamaliel Ac 5.34–39; 22.3

Genealogy of Jesus Mt 1.2–16; Lk 3.23–38

Gethsemane Mt 26.36–46; Mk 14.32–42

Golgotha Mt 27.33; Mk 15.22; Jn 19.17

Gomorrah Mt 10.15; Ro 9.29; 2 Pe 2.6; Jd 7

Greece Ac 18.12,27; 19.21; 20.2; Ro 15.26; 1 Cor 16.15; 2 Cor 1.1; 9.2; 1 Th 1.7–8

H

Hades Lk 16.23; Re 6.8

Hagar Ga 4.24–25

Hell Mt 5.22,29,30; 10.28; 11.23; 18.8–9; 23.15; Mk 9.43–47; Lk 10.15; 12.5; Jas 3.6; 2 Pe 2.4

Helper Jn 14.16,26; 15.26; 16.7

Herod

the Great Mt 2.1–22; Lk 1.5

Antipas Mt 14.1–10; Mk 6.14–27; 8.15; Lk 3.1,19–20; 9.7–9; 13.31–32; 23.6–12; Ac 4.27; 13.1

Agrippa I Ac 12.1–23

Agrippa II Ac 25.13—26.32

Herodias Mt 14.3–6; Mk 6.17–24; Lk 3.19

High Priest

Jewish Mt 26.3,51,57–67; Mk 14.53–64; Lk 22.50; Jn 11.49–51; 18.12–28; Ac 4.6; 5.17–28; 7.1; 23.1–5; 24.1; He 8.3; 9.7,25; 13.11

Christ He 2.17; 3.1; 4.14—5.10; 7.26—8.7

Holy Spirit

in life and teaching of Jesus Mt 1.18–20; 3.16; 12.28–32; Mk 1.10–12; Lk 1.35; 4.14,18; 10.21; Jn 1.32–34; 3.34; 14.15–17; 15.26–27; 16.7–15; 20.22; Ac 1.2

in early Church Ac 2.1–21; 4.31; 8.14–20; 9.31; 10.44–47; 13.2–4; 19.1–7

in letters of Paul Ro 8.1–27; 1 Cor 12.1–13; Ga 5.16–25

Husbands 1 Cor 7.1–7; Eph 5.25–33; Col 3.19; 1 Pe 3.7

I

Iconium Ac 13.51—14.6; 14.19,21; 16.2; 2 Tm 3.11

Idol Ac 7.41; 17.16; 1 Cor 8.1–13; 10.1–22; 2 Cor 6.16; 1 Th 1.9; 1 Jn 5.21; Re 2.14

Isaac Mt 1.2; 8.11; Ac 7.8; Ro 9.7–10; Ga 4.28; He 11.9,17–20; Jas 2.21

Isaiah Mt 3.3; 4.14; 8.17; 12.17; 13.4; 15.7; Mk 1.2–3; Lk 3.4–6; 4.17–19; Jn 1.23; 12.38–41; Ac 8.28–35; 28.25–27; Ro 9.27–29; 10.16,20–21; 15.12

Israel Mt 10.5–6; 15.24; 27.42; Mk 15.32; Lk 1.80; 2.25,32,34; 24.21; Ac 1.6; 5.31; 13.23–24; Ro 9.1—11.35; He 8.8,10; Re 7.4–8; 21.12

Italy Ac 18.2; 27.1—28.16; He 13.24

J

Jacob Mt 1.2; 8.11; Lk 1.33; Jn 4.5–6,12; 7.12–15; Ro 9.13; He 11.20–21

Jairus Mk 5.21–43; Lk 8.40–56

James

son of Zebedee Mt 4.21; 17.1; Mk 1.19; 5.37; 9.2; 10.35–41; 13.3; 14.33; Lk 5.10; 9.54; Ac 12.2

son of Alphaeus Mt 10.3; Mk 3.18; Lk 6.15; Ac 1.13

son of Mary Mt 27.56; Mk 15.40; 16.1; Lk 24.10

brother of Jesus Mt 13.35; Mk 6.3; Ac 12.17; 15.13–21; 21.17; Ga 1.19; 2.9–10

father of Judas Lk 6.16; Ac 1.13

author of letter Jas 1.1

brother of Jude Jd 1

Jericho Mt 20.29; Mk 10.46; Lk 10.30; 18.35—19.10; He 11.30

Jerusalem

the city Mt 2.1–3; 20.17; 21.1–23; Mk 10.32; 11.1–27; Lk 2.22–38,41–50; 13.31–35; 19.28–44; 21.20–24; Jn 2.13; 5.1; 12.12–19; Ac 1 4; 15.1–29

the heavenly Jerusalem Ga 4.26; He 12.22; Re 3.12; 21.2,10–14

Jesse Mt 1.5–6; Ac 13.22; Ro 15.12

Jesus

name Mt 1.21,25; Lk 1.31; 2.21

genealogy Mt 1.1–17; Lk 3.23–38

birth, infancy, childhood Mt 1.18—2.23; Lk 1.26–38; 2.1–40

baptism and temptation Mt 3.13—4.11; Mk 1.9–13; Lk 3.21–22; 4.1–13

ministry in Galilee Mt 4.12—18.35; Mk 1.14—9.50; Lk 4.14—9.50

Sermon on Mount Mt 5.1—7.29; Lk 6.17–49

confession at Caesarea Philippi Mt 16.13–28; Mk 8.27—9.1; Lk 9.18–27

transfiguration Mt 17.1–13; Mk 9.2–13; Lk 9.28–36

last days in Jerusalem Mt 21.1—27.66; Mk 11.1—15.47; Lk 19.28—23.56; Jn 12.1—19.42

triumphant entry Mt 21.1–11; Mk 11.1–11; Lk 19.29–44; Jn 12.12–19

in the Temple Mt 21.12–17; Mk 12.15–19; Lk 20.45–46

discourse on last things Mt 24.1—25.46; Mk 13.1–37; Lk 21.5–38

last supper Mt 26.17–35; Mk 14.12–31; Lk 22.7–38; Jn 13.1—17.26; 1 Cor 11.23–25

Gethsemane Mt 26.36–46; Mk 14.32–42; Lk 22.39–46

arrest, trial, crucifixion, death, burial Mt 26.47—27.66; Mk 14.32—15.47; Lk 22.47—23.56; Jn 18.1—19.42

resurrection, appearances, ascension Mt 28.1–20; Mk 16.1–20; Lk 24.1–53; Jn 20.1—21.25; Ac 1.1–11

John

the Baptist Mt 3.1–15; 11.2–19; 14.2–12; 21.25–32; Mk 1.4–9; 6.14–29; 11.27–33; Lk 1.5–25,57–80; 3.1–20; 7.18–35; Jn 1.19–36; 3.22–30

son of Zebedee Mk 1.19–20; 5.37; 9.2,38; 10.35–41; 13.3; Lk 9.49,54; 22.8; Ac 3.1—4.23; Ga 2.9

John Mark Ac 12.12,25; 13.5–13; 15.37–39; Col 4.10; 2 Tm 4.11; Phm 24; 1 Pe 5.13

father of Simon Peter Mt 16.17; Jn 1.42; 21.15–17

author of Revelation Re 1.1,4,9; 22.8

member of High Priest's family Ac 4.6

Jonah Mt 12.39–41; 16.4; Lk 11.29–32

Joppa Ac 9.38—10.23

Jordan Mt 3.5–6,13; Mk 1.5,9; 10.1; Lk 3.3; Jn 1.28; 10.40

Joseph

husband of Mary Mt 1.16–25; 2.13–15, 19–23; Lk 2.4–40; 3.23; Jn 1.45; 6.42

brother of Jesus Mt 13.55; *also called* Joses Mk 6.3

brother of the younger James Mt 27.56; *also called* Joses Mk 15.40,47

of Arimathea Mt 27.57–60; Mk 15.43–46; Lk 23.50–53; Jn 19.38–42

one of the patriarchs Jn 4.5; Ac 7.9–14

Barnabas Ac 4.36

Barsabbas Ac 1.23

Judas

Iscariot Mt 26.14–16,47–50; 27.3–8; Mk 14.10–11,43–45; Lk 22.3–6,47–48; Jn 6.70–71; 12.4–6; 13.2,21–30; 18.1–5; Ac 1.16–25

brother of Jesus Mt 13.55; Mk 6.3

apostle Jn 14.22

the Galilean Ac 5.37

of Damascus Ac 9.11

Barsabbas, of Jerusalem Ac 15.22–33

Jude Jd 1

Judea Mt 2.1; 3.1,5; 19.1; 24.16; Lk 1.65; 4.44; Jn 3.22; 7.1–9; 11.7; Ac 21.10; Ro 15.31; Ga 1.22; 1 Th 2.14

Judge

Christ as Judge Jn 5.22–30; 8.15–16; 9.39; 12.47–48; Ac 10.42; 2 Cor 5.10; 2 Tm 4.1; Re 19.11

God as Judge Mt 7.1–2; Lk 6.37; Jn 3.18–19; Ro 2.1–16; 14.10; He 10.30; 12.23; Jas 2.13; 4.12; Re 14.7; 20.11–15

Day of Judgment Mt 10.15; 11.22; 12.36,41–42; Lk 10.14; 11.31–32; Jn 5.24–29; Ac 24.25; 2 Pe 2.9; 3.7; 1 Jn 4.17

K

King

God as King Mt 5.35; 1 Tm 1.17; Re 15.3

Christ as King Mt 25.31–46; Lk 19.38; Jn 12.15; 18.37–38; Re 17.14; 19.16

"King of the Jews" Mt 2.2; 27.11,29,37; Mk 15.2,9–12,18,26; Lk 23.37,38; Jn 18.33,39; 19.19–22

"King of Israel" Mt 27.42; Mk 15.32; Jn 1.49; 12.13

L

Lamb

Feast of Passover Mk 14.12; Lk 22.7

figure or title of Christ Jn 1.29,36; 1 Cor 5.7; 1 Pe 1.19; Re 5.6–14; 7.9–10; 12.11; 17.14; 19.9; 21.22–27

Laodicea Col 2.1; 4.13–16; Re 3.14–22

Lazarus

of parable Lk 16.19–31

from Bethany Jn 11.1–44; 12.1–19

Leper Mt 8.1–4; 26.6; Mk 1.40–45; 14.3; Lk 5.12–16; 17.11–19

Levi (*also called* Matthew) Mk 2.14; Lk 5.27–32

Lord's Prayer Mt 6.9–13; Lk 11.2–4

Lord's Supper Mt 26.17–35; Mk 14.12–31; Lk 22.7–38; 1 Cor 11.23–25

Love
  of God Jn 3.16; 14.23; 16.27; Ro 5.1–11;
    8.39; Eph 1.4–5; 2.4–5; 1 Jn 3.1; 4.7–12
  of Christ Jn 11.3,5; 13.1,34; 15.10–12;
    Ro 8.31–39; 2 Cor 5.14; Ga 2.20;
    Eph 3.19; 5.2; Re 1.5
Luke Col 4.14; 2 Tm 4.11; Phm 24
Lydia Ac 16.14–40
Lysias, Claudius Ac 23.16—24.23
Lystra Ac 14.8–21; 16.1–2; 2 Tm 3.11

M

Macedonia Ac 16.9–12; 19.21–22; 20.1–3;
  1 Cor 16.5; 2 Cor 8.1; Php 4.15; 1 Th
  1.7–8; 1 Tm 1.3
"Magnificat" Lk 1.46–55
Manna Jn 6.31,49; He 9.4; Re 2.17
Mark See John
Martha Lk 10.38–42; Jn 11.1–40; 12.2
Mary
  mother of Jesus Mt 1.18–25; 2.11–15;
    13.55; Mk 6.3; Lk 1.26–56; 2.4–52;
    Jn 2.1–4; 19.25–27; Ac 1.14
  Magdalene Mt 27.56,61; 28.1–10; Mk
    15.40–41,47; 16.1–10; Lk 8.2; 24.10;
    Jn 19.25; 20.1–18
  sister of Martha Lk 10.38–42; Jn
    11.1–45
  mother of John Mark Ac 12.12
  wife of Clopas, mother of James and
    Joses Mt 27.56,61; Mk 15.40,47; 16.1;
    Lk 24.10; Jn 19.25
Matthew Mt 9.9; Mk 3.18; Lk 6.15
  (See Levi)
Matthias Ac 1.23–26
Melchizedek He 5.6,10; 7.1–17
Mercy
  of God Lk 1.50–55,78; 6.36; Ro 9.15–18;
    11.25–32; Eph 2.4–5; Tt 3.5–7; 1 Pe
    1.3–4; 2.10
  of Christ Mt 9.27; 15.22; 17.15; 20.30–31;
    1 Tm 1.13–16; He 2.17; Jd 21
Michael Jd 9; Re 12.7
Miracles and Cures of Jesus
  general references Mt 4.23–24; 8.16;
    9.35; 12.15–16; 14.14; 15.30–31; 19.2;
    21.14; Mk 1.32–34,39; 3.9–12; 6.5,53–56;
    Lk 4.40–41; 5.15; 6.17–19; 7.21; 9.11;
    Jn 2.23; 3.2; 6.2; 12.37; 20.30; Ac 10.38
  driving out demons
    blind and dumb man Mt 12.22
    daughter of woman of Tyre Mt
      15.21–28; Mk 7.24–30
    dumb man Mt 9.32–33; Lk 11.14
    epileptic boy Mt 17.14–20; Mk 9.14–
      29; Lk 9.37–43

  Gerasene men Mt 8.28–34; Mk 5.1–
    20; Lk 8.26–39
  man in Capernaum Mk 1.23–28; Lk
    4.33–37
  Mary Magdalene Mk 16.9; Lk 8.2
  woman in synagogue Lk 13.10–17
other cures
  blind Bartimaeus Mt 20.29–34; Mk
    10.46–52; Lk 18.35–43
  blind man at Bethsaida Mk 8.22–26
  blind beggar in Jerusalem Jn 9.1–7
  two blind men Mt 9.27–31
  deaf and dumb man Mk 7.31–37
  leper Mt 8.1–4; Mk 1.40–45; Lk
    5.12–16
  man with crippled hand Mt 12.9–14;
    Mk 3.1–6; Lk 6.6–11
  man with swollen arms and legs Lk
    14.1–6
  officer's servant Mt 8.5–13; Lk 7.1–10
  paralyzed man in Capernaum Mt
    9.1–8; Mk 2.1–12; Lk 5.17–26
  paralyzed man in Jerusalem Jn 5.1–9
  Peter's mother-in-law Mt 8.14–15;
    Mk 1.29–31; Lk 4.38–39
  slave of High Priest Lk 22.49–51
  son of official Jn 4.46–54
  ten lepers Lk 17.11–19
  woman with severe bleeding Mt
    9.20–22; Mk 5.23–24; Lk 8.43–48
raising of dead
  daughter of Jairus Mt 9.18–19,23–36;
    Mk 5.22–24,35–43; Lk 8.41–42,49–56
  son of widow of Nain Lk 7.11–17
  Lazarus Jn 11.1–44
other miracles
  coin in fish's mouth Mt 17.24–27
  cursing the fig tree Mt 21.18–22;
    Mk 11.12–14
  feeding the five thousand Mt 14.15–
    21; Mk 6.35–44; Lk 9.12–17; Jn
    6.1–14
  feeding the four thousand Mt 15.32–
    38; Mk 8.1–9
  great catch of fish Lk 5.1–11
  another catch of fish Jn 21.1–14
  stilling the storm Mt 8.23–27; Mk
    4.35–41; Lk 8.22–25
  walking on the water Mt 14.23–33;
    Mk 6.47–52; Jn 6.16–21
Miracles and Cures by Others
  the apostles Mt 10.1–8; Mk 6.7–13;
    Lk 9.1–6; Ac 5.12–16
  the seventy-two Lk 10.1–17
  Philip Ac 8.13
  Peter Ac 3.1–11; 9.32–43
  Paul Ac 13.6–12; 14.3; 16.16–18; 19.11–
    12; 2 Cor 12.12

Mount of Olives Mt 21.1; 24.3; 26.30;
  Mk 11.1; 13.3; 14.26; Lk 19.29,37; 21.37;
  22.39; Jn 8.1; Ac 1.12

N

Nain Lk 7.11
Nathanael Jn 1.45–49; 21.2
Nazarene
  title of Jesus Mt 2.23
  name of believers Ac 24.5
Nazareth Mt 2.22–23; 13.53–58; 21.11;
  Mk 1.9; 6.1–6; Lk 1.26; 2.4,39–40,51;
  4.16–30; Jn 1.45–46
Nicodemus Jn 3.1–10; 7.50; 19.39
Nicolaitans Re 2.6,15
Nineveh Mt 12.41; Lk 11.30,32
Noah Mt 24.37–38; Lk 17.26–27; He 11.7;
  1 Pe 3.20; 2 Pe 2.5

O

Obedience
  to God or Christ Mk 1.27; 4.41; Jn
    3.36; Ac 5.29–32; He 5.8–9; 1 Jn 5.2
  to demands of gospel Ro 6.16–17;
    2 Cor 7.15; Php 2.12; 2 Th 1.8; 3.14
  to human authorities Ac 5.37–42; Ro
    13.1–7; Tt 3.1–2; 1 Pe 2.13–17
Onesimus Col 4.9; Phm 10

P

Pamphylia Ac 13.13; 14.24; 15.38; 27.5
Parables
  reason and use Mt 13.10–17,34–35;
    Mk 4.10–12,21–25,33–34; Lk 8.9–10,
    16–18
  told by Jesus
    children sitting Mt 11.16–19; Lk
      7.31–35
    faithful servant Mt 24.45–51; Lk
      12.42–46
    fig tree Mt 24.32–33; Mk 13.28–29;
      Lk 21.29–31
    friend at midnight Lk 11.5–8
    gold coins Lk 19.11–27
    good Samaritan Lk 10.29–37
    great feast Lk 14.15–24
    hidden treasure Mt 13.44
    homeowner Mt 13.51–52
    king going to war Lk 14.31–32
    lamp under a bowl Mt 5.15; Mk
      4.21; Lk 8.16; 11.33
    lost coin Lk 15.8–10
    lost sheep Mt 18.10–14; Lk 15.3–7
    lost son Lk 15.11–32
    mustard seed Mt 13.31–32; Mk 4.30–
      32; Lk 13.18–19
    net Mt 13.47–50

new patch Mt 9.16; Mk 2.21; Lk 5.36

pearl Mt 13.45–46

Pharisee and tax collector Lk 18.9–14

places at wedding feast Lk 14.7–11

rich fool Lk 12.16–21

rich man and Lazarus Lk 16.19–31

seed growing Mk 4.26–29

servant Lk 17.7–10

shrewd manager Lk 16.1–9

sower Mt 13.3–9,18–23; Mk 4.2–9, 13–20; Lk 8.5–8,11–15

ten girls Mt 25.1–13

tenants in the vineyard Mt 21.33–46; Mk 12.1–12; Lk 20.9–19

three servants Mt 25.14–30

tower builder Lk 14.28–30

two debtors Lk 7.40–43

two house builders Mt 7.24–27; Lk 6.47–49

two sons Mt 21.28–32

unforgiving servant Mt 18.23,35

unfruitful fig tree Lk 13.6–9

watchful home owner Mt 24.42–44; Lk 12.39–40

watchful servants Mt 13.33–37; Lk 12.35–38

wedding feast Mt 22.1–14

wedding guests Mt 9.15; Mk 2.19–20; Lk 5.34–35

weeds Mt 13.24–30,36–43

widow and judge Lk 18.1–8

wine and wineskins Mt 9.17; Mk 2.22; Lk 5.37–38

workers in vineyard Mt 20.1–16

yeast Mt 13.33; Lk 13.20–21

Paradise Lk 23.43; 2 Cor 12.3

Passover *See* Feasts

Patmos Re 1.9

Paul

early life

born in Tarsus Ac 22.3

sister Ac 23.16

studied in Jerusalem Ac 22.3

tent maker Ac 18.3

at Stephen's death Ac 7.58; 8.1; 22.20

persecuted Christians Ac 8.3; 22.4–5; 26.10–11; 1 Cor 15.9; Ga 1.13; Php 3.6; 1 Tm 1.13

conversion Ac 9.3–19; 22.6–16; 26.12–18

early ministry

Arabia Ga 1.17

Damascus Ac 9.19–25; 26.20; 2 Cor 11.32–33; Ga 1.17

Jerusalem Ac 9.26–29; 26.20; Ga 1.18–19

Tarsus Ac 9.30

Antioch Ac 11.25–30; 12.25

missionary activity

first tour Ac 13.1—14.28

meeting in Jerusalem Ac 15.1–29; Ga 2.1–10

second tour Ac 15.36—18.23a

third tour Ac 18.23b—20.38

return to Jerusalem Ac 21.1–26

arrest and imprisonment

arrest in Jerusalem Ac 21.27—23.22

prison and trial in Caesarea Ac 23.23—26.32

trip to Rome Ac 27.1—28.16

ministry in Rome Ac 28.17–31

letters

Colossians Col 1.1—4.18

1 Corinthians 1 Cor 1.1—16.24

2 Corinthians 2 Cor 1.1—13.3

Ephesians Eph 1.1—6.24

Galatians Ga 1.1—6.18

Philemon Phm 1–25

Philippians Php 1.1—4.23

Romans Ro 1.1—16.27

1 Thessalonians 1 Th 1.1—5.28

2 Thessalonians 2 Th 1.1—3.18

1 Timothy 1 Tm 1.1—6.21

2 Timothy 2 Tm 1.1—4.22

Titus Tt 1.1—3.15

Peace

from God Lk 2.14; Ro 5.1; 15.33; 2 Cor 13.11; Php 4.7

from Christ Jn 14.27; 16.33; Eph 2.13–18; Col 3.15; 2 Th 3.16

Pentecost *See* Feasts

Pergamum Re 2.12–17

Peter

call to be disciple Mt 4.18–20; Mk 1.16–18; Lk 5.1–11; Jn 1.40–42

declaration about Jesus Mt 16.13–20; Mk 8.27–30; Lk 9.18–21; Jn 6.66–69

on Mount of Transfiguration Mt 17.1–8; Mk 9.2–8; Lk 9.28–36; 2 Pe 1.16–18

in Garden of Gethsemane Mt 26.36–46; Mk 14.32–42; Jn 18.10–11

denies Jesus Mt 26.69–75; Mk 14.66–72; Lk 22.55–62; Jn 18.15–17,25–27

sees risen Lord Lk 24.34; Jn 21.1–23; 1 Cor 15.5

sermon at Pentecost Ac 2.14–42

activity in Jerusalem and elsewhere Ac 3.1—5.16; 18.14–25; 9.32—12.17; 15.6–11

dispute with Paul at Antioch Ga 2.11–14

prediction of his death Jn 21.18–19

letters

1 Peter 1 Pe 1.1—5.14

2 Peter 2 Pe 1.1—3.18

Pharisees Mt 3.7; 9.10–13; 12.1–8,24–28, 38–39; 15.1–9; 16.1–12; 19.3–9; 22.15,34–46; 23.1–36; 27.62–66; 7.36–50; 16.14–15; 18.9–

14; Jn 3.1; 7.32,45–52; Ac 15.5; 23.6–9; 26.5

Philadelphia Re 3.7–13

Philip

apostle Mt 10.3; Jn 1.43–48; 6.5–7; 14.8–10

evangelist Ac 6.5; 8.5–40; 21.8

governor Lk 3.1

first husband of Herodias Mt 14.3; Mk 6.17

Philippi Ac 16.12–40; 20.6; Php 1.1; 1 Th 2.2

Phoebe Ro 16.1

Pilate Mt 27.2–26; Mk 15.1–15; Lk 3.1; 23.1–25; Jn 18.28—19.16; Ac 3.13; 4.27; 13.28; 1 Tm 6.13

Prayer

teaching of Jesus Mt 5.43–45; 6.5–14; Lk 11.1–13; 18.1–8

in life of Jesus Mt 14.23; 26.36–46; Mk 1.35; 6.46; 14.32–42; Lk 3.21; 5.16; 6.12; 9.18,28–29; 11.1; 22.32,39–45; Jn 17.1–26; He 5.7

instructions Ro 8.26; 1 Cor 14.13–15; Eph 6.18; Php 4.6; Col 4.2–4; 1 Th 5.17; 1 Tm 2.1–4,8; Jas 5.13–18; 1 Jn 5.16; Jd 20

Priscilla (Prisca) Ac 18.2,18,26; Ro 16.3; 1 Cor 16.19; 2 Tm 4.19

Prophet

Old Testament Mt 1.22; 2.5,15,17,23; 3.3; 4.7; 11.13; 23.29–33; Lk 13.34; Ac 2.16; 3.17–26; 8.28–35; Ro 1.2; He 1.1; 1 Pe 1.10–12

New Testament Ac 13.1; 1 Cor 12.28–29; Eph 4.11; Re 10.7; 18.20,24; 22.6,9

Agabus Ac 11.27; 21.10

Anna Lk 2.36

Judas and Silas Ac 15.32

John the Baptist Mt 11.9; 14.5; 21.26; Mk 11.32; Lk 1.76; 7.26; 20.6

Jesus Mt 13.57; 21.11,46; Mk 6.4,15; Lk 7.16; 13.33; 24.19; Jn 4.19,44; 9.17

"The Prophet" Jn 1.21,25; 6.14; 7.40; Ac 3.22–23

Q

Quirinius Lk 2.2

R

Resurrection

of Christ Ac 2.22–36; 5.29–32; 10.39–43; 13.29–39; Ro 1.4; 6.4–11; 1 Cor 15.22–28; (*See* Jesus)

of men Jn 5.21–29; 6.39–44; Ac 23.6–8; 1 Cor 15.12–58

daughter of Jairus Mt 9.23–26; Mk 5.35–43; Lk 8.49–56

son of widow of Nain Lk 7.11–17
Lazarus Jn 11.1–44
Dorcas Ac 9.36–42
Rhoda Ac 12.13
Rome Ac 18.2; 19.21; 23.11; 28.14,16; Ro
1.7,15; 2 Tm 1.17

S

Sadducees Mt 3.7; 16.5–12; 22.23–33; Mk
12.18–27; Lk 20.27–39; Ac 4.1; 5.17–18;
23.6–8
Salome Mk 15.40; 16.1
Samaria Lk 17.11; Jn 4.4–43; Ac 1.8;
8.1–25; 15.3
Samaritan
Samaritans who could not receive Jesus
Lk 9.51–56
parable of Good Samaritan Lk 10.29–37
Samaritan leper Lk 17.11–19
Samaritan woman Jn 4.7–30
Sapphira Ac 5.1–11
Sardis Re 3.1–6
Satan Mt 4.10; 12.26; 16.23; Mk 1.13;
3.23–26; 4.15; 8.33; Lk 10.18; 11.18; 13.16;
22.3,31; Jn 13.27; Ac 5.3; Ro 16.20;
1 Cor 5.5; 7.5; 2 Th 2.9; 1 Tm 1.20;
Re 2.9,13,24; 3.9; 12.9; 20.7–8 (*See*
Beelzebul, Devil)
Saul
king of Israel Ac 13.21
apostle Paul Ac 8.1; 9.1–30; 11.25–30;
12.25—13.9
Savior
God Lk 1.47; 1 Tm 1.1; 2.3–4; 4.10;
Tt 3.4–5; Jd 25
Christ Lk 2.11; Jn 4.42; Ac 5.31; 13.23;
Eph 5.23; Php 3.20; 2 Tm 1.10; Tt
2.13–14; 2 Pe 1.11; 2.20; 1 Jn 4.14
Sergius Paulus Ac 13.7–12
Sermon on the Mount Mt 5.1—7.29;
Lk 6.17–49
Sharon Ac 9.35
Sidon Mt 11.21–22; 15.21; Mk 7.31; Lk
4.26; 10.13–14; Ac 12.20; 27.3
Silas Ac 15.22–34; 16.19—17.16; 18.5; 2 Cor
1.19; 1 Th 1.1; 2 Th 1.1; *also called*
Silvanus 1 Pe 5.12
Siloam Lk 13.4; Jn 9.6–11
Simeon Lk 2.25–35
Simon
Peter *See* Peter
the patriot Mt 10.4; Mk 3.19; Lk 6.15;
Ac 1.13
brother of Jesus Mt 13.55; Mk 6.3
the leper of Bethany Mt 26.6; Mk 14.3
of Cyrene Mt 27.32; Mk 15.21; Lk 23.26
the Pharisee Lk 7.36–50
father of Judas Iscariot Jn 6.71; 13.2,26

the magician of Samaria Ac 8.9–24
the leather worker of Joppa Ac 9.43;
10.6,17–23,32
Smyrna Re 2.8–11
Sodom Mt 10.15; 11.23–24; Lk 10.12;
17.29; Ro 9.29; 2 Pe 2.6; Jd 7; Re 11.8
Solomon Mt 6.29; 12.42; Lk 11.31; 12.27;
Ac 7.47
Solomon's Porch Jn 10.23; Ac 3.11; 5.12
Son: titles of Jesus
Son of Man Mt 8.20; 9.6; 10.23; 11.19;
12.8,32; 13.37; 16.13,27–28; 17.9,22; 20.18,
28; 24.29–31,37–44; 25.31; 26.2,24,45,64;
Lk 18.8; Jn 1.51; 3.13–14; 5.27; 6.27,
53,62; 8.28; 9.35; 12.34; 13.31; Ac 7.56
Son of God Mt 4.3,6; 8.29; 14.33; 16.16;
26.63; 27.40,43; Mk 1.1; 15.39; Lk 1.32;
Jn 1.34,49; 3.16–18; 5.19–26; 10.36;
11.27; 19.7; 20.31; Ac 9.20; 13.33; Ro
1.4; 5.10; 8.3,29; 2 Cor 1.19; Ga 2.20;
4.4–6; Eph 4.13; 1 Th 1.10; He 1.2,5;
4.14; 6.6; 10.29; 1 Jn 2.22–24; 3.8;
4.9–10,14–15; 5.9–13
Son of David Mt 9.27; 12.23; 15.22;
20.30–31; 21.9,15
Stephen Ac 6.5—8.2; 22.20
Stoics Ac 17.18
Syria Mt 4.24; Lk 2.2; Ac 15.23,41; 18.18;
20.3; 21.3; Ga 1.21

T

Tabernacle *See* Tent
Tabernacles, Feast of *See* Feasts
Tabitha Ac 9.36–40
Tarsus Ac 9.30; 11.25; 21.39; 22.3
Tax collectors Mt 9.9–13; 11.19; 21.31–32;
Mk 2.14–17; Lk 3.12–13; 5.27–32; 7.29,34;
15.1; 18.9–14; 19.1–10
Taxes Mt 17.24–27; 22.15–22; Mk 12.13–17;
Lk 20.19–26; Ro 13.6–7
Temple
in Jerusalem Mt 4.5; 21.12–17; 24.1–2;
26.55; 27.6,31; Mk 11.15–19; 13.1–2,
15–38; Lk 1.8–23; 2.22–38,41–51; 19.45–
48; 21.5–6; 24.52–53; Jn 2.13–21; 7.14,28;
8.20; 10.23; Ac 2.46; 3.1–11; 5.20–26;
21.26–30
spiritual Jn 2.18–22; 1 Cor 3.16–17;
2 Cor 6.16; Eph 2.21
Tent Ac 7.44; 2 Cor 5.1–5; He 8.1–5;
9.1–22; Re 15.5
Tertius Ro 16.22
Tertullus Ac 24.1–8
Thaddaeus Mt 10.3; Mk 3.18
Thessalonica Ac 17.1–9; Php 4.16; 1 Th
1.1; 2 Th 1.1
Thomas Mt 10.3; Mk 3.18; Lk 6.15;
Jn 11.16; 14.5; 20.24–29; 21.2; Ac 1.13

Thousand Years 2 Pe 3.8; Re 20.1–7
Thyatira Ac 16.14; Re 2.18–28
Tiberias
lake Jn 6.1; 21.1
town Jn 6.23
Tiberius Lk 3.1
Timothy Ac 16.1–3; 17.14–16; 18.5; 19.22;
20.4; Ro 16.21; 1 Cor 4.17; 16.10; 2 Cor
1.1,19; Php 1.1; 2.19–23; Col 1.1; 1 Th 1.1;
3.2,6; 2 Th 1.1; 1 Tm 1.2; 2 Tm 1.2;
Phm 1; He 13.23
Titus 2 Cor 2.13; 7.6–7,13–15; 8.6,16–23;
12.18; Ga 2.1–5; 2 Tm 4.10; Tt 1.4
Troas Ac 16.8–11; 20.6–12; 2 Cor 2.12–13;
2 Tm 4.13
Tychicus Ac 20.4; Eph 6.21–22; Col 4.7–9;
2 Tm 4.12; Tt 3.12
Tyre Mt 11.21–22; 15.21; Mk 3.8; 7.24,31;
Lk 6.17; 10.13–14; Ac 12.20; 21.3–7

U

Unleavened Bread, Feast of *See* Feasts

V

Vine Jn 15.1–11; Re 14.18–20
Vineyard Mt 20.1–16; 21.28–32,33–43; Mk
12.1–12; Lk 20.9–19

W

Widow Mk 12.41–44; Lk 7.12; 18.1–8;
21.1–3; Ac 6.1; 9.39–41; 1 Cor 7.8–9;
1 Tm 5.3–16
Wine
literal Mt 9.17; 27.34; Mk 2.22; 15.23;
Lk 1.15; 5.37–39; 10.34; Jn 2.1–11;
Ro 14.21; Eph 5.18; 1 Tm 3.8; 5.23;
Re 6.6
figurative Re 14.8–10; 17.2; 18.3
Wives 1 Cor 7.1–7; Eph 5.22–24; Col 3.18;
1 Pe 3.1–6
Wrath of God Mt 3.7; Lk 3.7; 21.23;
Jn 3.36; Ro 2.1–11; 5.9; 9.22; 13.4–5;
Eph 2.3; 5.6; Col 3.6; 1 Th 2.16; Re 6.17;
14.10,19; 15.1; 16.1

Y

Yes Mt 5.37; 2 Cor 1.17–20
Yoke Mt 11.29–30

Z

Zacchaeus Lk 19.1–10
Zebedee Mt 4.21; 20.20; 27.56; Mk 1.19–
20; 10.35; Lk 5.10; Jn 21.2
Zechariah Lk 1.5–79
Zion Mt 21.5; Jn 12.15; Ro 9.33; 11.26;
He 12.22; 1 Pe 2.6; Re 14.1

Composition by

MAURICE JACOBS, INC.
1010 ARCH STREET
PHILADELPHIA, PENNSYLVANIA